1993
COLLIER PAMPHLET EDITION
PART 1
BANKRUPTCY CODE

INCLUDING TEXT and LEGISLATIVE HISTORY OF
THE BANKRUPTCY REFORM ACT OF 1978,
AS AMENDED

With accompanying practice aids

Explanatory comments by
ASA S. HERZOG

Bankruptcy Judge, Southern District of New York (Ret.)
Member, National Bankruptcy Conference
Member of the Advisory Committee on Bankruptcy Rules
of the Judicial Conference of the United States (1966–1988)

and

LAWRENCE P. KING

Charles Seligson Professor of Law,
New York University School of Law
Of Counsel, Wachtell, Lipton, Rosen & Katz, N.Y.C.
Member, National Bankruptcy Conference
Former Member of the Advisory Committee on Bankruptcy
Rules of the Judicial Conference of the United States
Co-Author, Duesenberg & King,
Sales and Bulk Transfers Under the U.C.C. (M. Bender)
Co-Author, King & Cook, Creditors' Rights, Debtors'
Protection, and Bankruptcy (M. Bender)

Cover Design: Jill S. Feltham

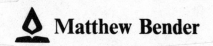 **Matthew Bender**

▼▼ **Times Mirror**
◣ **Books**

Questions About This Publication

For assistance with replacement pages, shipments,
billing or other customer service matters, please
call our Customer Services Department at 1-800-833-9844

Outside the United States and Canada please
call .... (518) 487–3026

Fax number .... (518) 487–3584

To place an order, call 1-800-223-1940
or contact your Matthew Bender representative.

FOR EDITORIAL ASSISTANCE or reprint permission, please call
Katherine Geraci, J.D. at .... **1-800-252-9257 Ext. 8293**
or
Mark Diamond, J.D. at .... **1-800-252-9257 Ext. 8285**

MATTHEW BENDER & CO., INC.
EDITORIAL OFFICES
11 PENN PLAZA, NEW YORK, NY 10001–2006 (212) 967–7707
2101 WEBSTER ST., OAKLAND, CA 94612–3027 (510) 446–7100

(Matthew Bender & Co., Inc.)   (Pub.221)

SYNOPSIS OF CONTENTS

BANKRUPTCY CODE, 11 U.S.C. §§ 101–1330

Additional Statutory Provisions—The Bankruptcy Reform
Act of 1978 (Pub. L. No. 95–598), the Bankruptcy
Amendments and Federal Judgeship Act of 1984 (Pub. L.
No. 98–353), the Bankruptcy Judges, United States
Trustees, and Family Farmer Bankruptcy Act of 1986
(Pub. L. No. 99–554) and amendments through
December 1, 1992

INDEX

TABLE OF CONTENTS
BANKRUPTCY CODE

CHAPTER 1

General Provisions

CHAPTER 3

Case Administration

SUBCHAPTER I

Commencement of a Case

SUBCHAPTER II

Officers

SUBCHAPTER III

Administration

SUBCHAPTER IV

Administrative Powers

CHAPTER 5

Creditors, the Debtor, and the Estate

SUBCHAPTER I

Creditors and Claims

SUBCHAPTER II

Debtor's Duties and Benefits

SUBCHAPTER III

The Estate

CHAPTER 7

Liquidation

SUBCHAPTER I

Officers and Administration

SUBCHAPTER II

Collection, Liquidation, and Distribution of the Estate

SUBCHAPTER III

Stockbroker Liquidation

SUBCHAPTER IV

Commodity Broker Liquidation

CHAPTER 9

Adjustment of Debts of a Municipality

SUBCHAPTER I

General Provisions

SUBCHAPTER II

Administration

SUBCHAPTER III

The Plan

CHAPTER 11

Reorganization

SUBCHAPTER I

Officers and Administration

SUBCHAPTER II

The Plan

SUBCHAPTER III

Postconfirmation Matters

SUBCHAPTER IV

Railroad Reorganization

CHAPTER 12

Adjustment of Debts of a Family Farmer With Regular Annual Income

SUBCHAPTER I

Officers, Administration, and the Estate

SUBCHAPTER II

The Plan

CHAPTER 13

Adjustment of Debts of an Individual With Regular Income

SUBCHAPTER I

Officers, Administration, and the Estate

SUBCHAPTER II

The Plan

ADDITIONAL STATUTORY PROVISIONS

Enacted or Amended by Pub. L. No. 95-598, Pub. L. No. 98-353, and Pub. L. No. 99-554

THE BANKRUPTCY
CODE OF 1978,
AS AMENDED

CHAPTER I

General Provisions

SECTION 101 (11 U.S.C. § 101)

§ 101. **Definitions.** In this title—

(1) "accountant" means accountant authorized under applicable law to practice public accounting, and includes professional accounting association, corporation, or partnership, if so authorized;

(2) "affiliate" means—

(A) entity that directly or indirectly owns, controls, or holds with power to vote, 20 percent or more of the outstanding voting securities of the debtor, other than an entity that holds such securities—

(i) in a fiduciary or agency capacity without sole discretionary power to vote such securities; or

(ii) solely to secure a debt, if such entity has not in fact exercised such power to vote;

(B) corporation 20 percent or more of whose outstanding voting securities are directly or indirectly owned, controlled, or held with power to vote, by the debtor, or by an entity that directly or indirectly owns, controls, or holds with power to vote, 20 percent or more of the outstanding voting securities of the debtor, other than an entity that holds such securities—

(i) in a fiduciary or agency capacity without sole discretionary power to vote such securities; or

(ii) solely to secure a debt, if such entity has not in fact exercised such power to vote;

(C) person whose business is operated under a lease or operating agreement by a debtor, or person substantially all of whose property is operated under an operating agreement with the debtor; or

   (D) entity that operates the business or substantially all of the property of the debtor under a lease or operating agreement;

(3) "Federal depository institutions regulatory agency" means—

   (A) with respect to an insured depository institution (as defined in section 3(c)(2) of the Federal Deposit Insurance Act) for which no conservator or receiver has been appointed, the appropriate Federal banking agency (as defined in section 3(q) of such Act);

   (B) with respect to an insured credit union (including an insured credit union for which the National Credit Union Administration has been appointed conservator or liquidating agent), the National Credit Union Administration;

   (C) with respect to any insured depository institution for which the Resolution Trust Corporation has been appointed conservator or receiver, the Resolution Trust Corporation; and

   (D) with respect to any insured depository institution for which the Federal Deposit Insurance Corporation has been appointed conservator or receiver, the Federal Deposit Insurance Corporation;

(4) "attorney" means attorney, professional law association, corporation, or partnership, authorized under applicable law to practice law;

(5) "claim" means—

   (A) right to payment, whether or not such right is reduced to judgment, liquidated, unliquidated, fixed, contingent, matured, unmatured, disputed, undisputed, legal, equitable, secured, or unsecured; or

   (B) right to an equitable remedy for breach of performance if such breach gives rise to a right to payment, whether or not such right to an equitable remedy is reduced to judgment, fixed, contingent, matured, unmatured, disputed, undisputed, secured, or unsecured;

(6) "commodity broker" means futures commission merchant, foreign futures commission merchant, clearing organization, leverage transaction merchant, or commodity options dealer, as defined in section 761 of this title, with respect to which there is a customer, as defined in section 761(9) of this title;

(7) "community claim" means claim that arose before the commencement of the case concerning the debtor for which property of the kind specified in section 541(a)(2) of this title is liable, whether or not there is any such property at the time of the commencement of the case;

(8) "consumer debt" means debt incurred by an individual primarily for a personal, family, or household purpose;

(9) "corporation"—

    (A) includes—

        (i) association having a power or privilege that a private corporation, but not an individual or a partnership, possesses;

        (ii) partnership association organized under a law that makes only the capital subscribed responsible for the debts of such association;

        (iii) joint-stock company;

        (iv) unincorporated company or association; or

        (v) business trust; but

    (B) does not include limited partnership;

(10) "creditor" means—

    (A) entity that has a claim against the debtor that arose at the time of or before the order for relief concerning the debtor;

    (B) entity that has a claim against the estate of a kind specified in section 348(d), 502(f), 502(g), 502(h) or 502(i) of this title; or

    (C) entity that has a community claim;

(11) "custodian" means—

    (A) receiver or trustee of any of the property of the debtor, appointed in a case or proceeding not under this title;

(B) assignee under a general assignment for the benefit of the debtor's creditors; or

(C) trustee, receiver, or agent under applicable law, or under a contract, that is appointed or authorized to take charge of property of the debtor for the purpose of enforcing a lien against such property, or for the purpose of general administration of such property for the benefit of the debtor's creditors;

(12) "debt" means liability on a claim;

(13) "debtor" means person or municipality concerning which a case under this title has been commenced;

(14) "disinterested person" means person that—

(A) is not a creditor, an equity security holder, or an insider;

(B) is not and was not an investment banker for any outstanding security of the debtor;

(C) has not been, within three years before the date of the filing of the petition, an investment banker for a security of the debtor, or an attorney for such an investment banker in connection with the offer, sale, or issuance of a security of the debtor;

(D) is not and was not, within two years before the date of the filing of the petition a director, officer or employee of the debtor or of an investment banker specified in subparagraph (B) or (C) of this paragraph; and

(E) does not have an interest materially adverse to the interest of the estate or of any class of creditors or equity security holders, by reason of any direct or indirect relationship to, connection with, or interest in, the debtor or an investment banker specified in subparagraph (B) or (C) of this paragraph, or for any other reason;

(15) "entity" includes person, estate, trust, governmental unit, and United States trustee;

(16) "equity security" means—

(A) share in a corporation, whether or not transferable or denominated "stock", or similar security;

(B) interest of a limited partner in a limited partnership; or

(C) warrant or right, other than a right to convert, to purchase, sell, or subscribe to a share, security, or interest of a kind specified in subparagraph (A) or (B) of this paragraph;

(17) "equity security holder" means holder of an equity security of the debtor;

(18) "family farmer" means—

(A) individual or individual and spouse engaged in a farming operation whose aggregate debts do not exceed $1,500,000 and not less than 80 percent of whose aggregate noncontingent, liquidated debts (excluding a debt for the principal residence of such individual or such individual and spouse unless such debt arises out of a farming operation), on the date the case is filed, arise out of a farming operation owned or operated by such individual or such individual and spouse, and such individual or such individual and spouse receive from such farming operation more than 50 percent of such individual's or such individual and spouse's gross income for the taxable year preceding the taxable year in which the case concerning such individual or such individual and spouse was filed; or

(B) corporation or partnership in which more than 50 percent of the outstanding stock or equity is held by one family, or by one family and the relatives of the members of such family, and such family or such relatives conduct the farming operation, and

(i) more than 80 percent of the value of its assets consists of assets related to the farming operation;

(ii) its aggregate debts do not exceed $1,500,000 and not less than 80 percent of its aggregate noncontingent, liquidated debts (excluding a debt for one dwelling which is owned by such corporation or partnership and which a shareholder or partner maintains as a principal residence, unless such debt arises out of a farming operation), on the date the case is filed, arise out of the farming operation owned or operated by such corporation or such partnership; and

    (iii) if such corporation issues stock, such stock is not publicly traded;

(19) "family farmer with regular annual income" means family farmer whose annual income is sufficiently stable and regular to enable such family farmer to make payments under a plan under chapter 12 of this title;

(20) "farmer" means (except when such term appears in the term "family farmer") person that received more than 80 percent of such person's gross income during the taxable year of such person immediately preceding the taxable year of such person during which the case under this title concerning such person was commenced from a farming operation owned or operated by such person;

(21) "farming operation" includes farming, tillage of the soil, dairy farming, ranching, production or raising of crops, poultry, or livestock, and production of poultry or livestock products in an unmanufactured state;

(21A) "farmout agreement" means a written agreement in which—

    (A) the owner of a right to drill, produce, or operate liquid or gaseous hydrocarbons on property agrees or has agreed to transfer or assign all or a part of such right to another entity; and

    (B) such other entity (either directly or through its agents or its assigns), as consideration, agrees to perform drilling, reworking, recompleting, testing, or similar or related operations, to develop or produce liquid or gaseous hydrocarbons on the property;

(22) "financial institution" means a person that is a commercial or savings bank, industrial savings bank, savings and loan association, or trust company and, when any such person is acting as agent or custodian for a customer in connection with a securities contract, as defined in section 741(7) of this title, such customer;

(23) "foreign proceeding" means proceeding, whether judicial or administrative and whether or not under bankruptcy law, in

a foreign country in which the debtor's domicile, residence, principal place of business, or principal assets were located at the commencement of such proceeding, for the purpose of liquidating an estate, adjusting debts by composition, extension, or discharge, or effecting a reorganization;

(24) "foreign representative" means duly selected trustee, administrator, or other representative of an estate in a foreign proceeding;

(25) "forward contract" means a contract (other than a commodity contract) for the purchase, sale, or transfer of a commodity, as defined in section 761(8) of this title, or any similar good, article, service, right, or interest which is presently or in the future becomes the subject of dealing in the forward contract trade, or product or byproduct thereof, with a maturity date more than two days after the date the contract is entered into, including, but not limited to, a repurchase transaction, reverse repurchase transaction, consignment, lease, swap, hedge transaction, deposit, loan, option, allocated transaction, unallocated transaction, or any combination thereof or option thereon;

(26) "forward contract merchant" means a person whose business consists in whole or in part of entering into forward contracts as or with merchants in a commodity, as defined in section 761(8) of this title, or any similar good, article, service, right, or interest which is presently or in the future becomes the subject of dealing in the forward contract trade;

(27) "governmental unit" means United States; State; Commonwealth; District; Territory; municipality; foreign state; department, agency, or instrumentality of the United States (but not a United States trustee while serving as a trustee in a case under this title), a State, a Commonwealth, a District, a Territory, a municipality, or a foreign state; or other foreign or domestic government;

(28) "indenture" means mortgage, deed of trust, or indenture, under which there is outstanding a security, other than a voting-trust certificate, constituting a claim against the debtor, a claim secured by a lien on any of the debtor's property, or an equity security of the debtor;

(29) "indenture trustee" means trustee under an indenture;

(30) "individual with regular income" means individual whose income is sufficiently stable and regular to enable such individual to make payments under a plan under chapter 13 of this title, other than a stockbroker or a commodity broker;

(31) "insider" includes—

(A) if the debtor is an individual—

    (i) relative of the debtor or of a general partner of the debtor;

    (ii) partnership in which the debtor is a general partner;

    (iii) general partner of the debtor; or

    (iv) corporation of which the debtor is a director, officer, or person in control;

(B) if the debtor is a corporation—

    (i) director of the debtor;

    (ii) officer of the debtor;

    (iii) person in control of the debtor;

    (iv) partnership in which the debtor is a general partner;

    (v) general partner of the debtor; or

    (vi) relative of a general partner, director, officer, or person in control of the debtor;

(C) if the debtor is a partnership—

    (i) general partner in the debtor;

    (ii) relative of a general partner in, general partner of, or person in control of the debtor;

    (iii) partnership in which the debtor is a general partner;

    (iv) general partner of the debtor; or

    (v) person in control of the debtor;

(D) if the debtor is a municipality, elected official of the debtor or relative of an elected official of the debtor;

(E) affiliate, or insider of an affiliate as if such affiliate were the debtor; and

(F) managing agent of the debtor;

(32) "insolvent" means—

(A) with reference to an entity other than a partnership and a municipality, financial condition such that the sum of such entity's debts is greater than all of such entity's property, at a fair valuation, exclusive of—

(i) property transferred, concealed, or removed with intent to hinder, delay, or defraud such entity's creditors; and

(ii) property that may be exempted from property of the estate under section 522 of this title;

(B) with reference to a partnership, financial condition such that the sum of such partnership's debts is greater than the aggregate of, at a fair valuation—

(i) all of such partnership's property, exclusive of property of the kind specified in subparagraph (A)(i) of this paragraph; and

(ii) the sum of the excess of the value of each general partner's nonpartnership property, exclusive of property of the kind specified in subparagraph (A) of this paragraph, over such partner's nonpartnership debts; and

(C) with reference to a municipality, financial condition such that the municipality is—

(i) generally not paying its debts as they become due unless such debts are the subject of a bona fide dispute; or

(ii) unable to pay its debts as they become due;

(33) "institution-affiliated party"—

(A) with respect to an insured depository institution (as defined in section 3(c)(2) of the Federal Deposit Insurance Act), has the meaning given it in section 3(u) of the Federal Deposit Insurance Act (12 U.S.C. 1813(u)); and

(B) with respect to an insured credit union, has the meaning given it in section 206(r) of the Federal Credit Union Act (12 U.S.C. 1786(r));

(34) "insured credit union" has the meaning given it in section 101(7) of the Federal Credit Union Act (12 U.S.C. 1752(7));

(35) "insured depository institution"—

(A) has the meaning given it in section 3(c)(2) of the Federal Deposit Insurance Act (12 U.S.C. 1813(c)(2)); and

(B) includes an insured credit union (except in the case of paragraphs (3) and (33)(A) of this subsection);

(36) "judicial lien" means lien obtained by judgment, levy, sequestration, or other legal or equitable process or proceeding;

(37) "lien" means charge against or interest in property to secure payment of a debt or performance of an obligation;

(38) "margin payment" means, for purposes of the forward contract provisions of this title, payment or deposit of cash, a security or other property, that is commonly known in the forward contract trade as original margin, initial margin, maintenance margin, or variation margin, including mark-to-market payments, or variation payments; and [*sic*]

(39) "settlement payment" means, for purposes of the forward contract provisions of this title, a preliminary settlement payment, a partial settlement payment, an interim settlement payment, a settlement payment on account, a final settlement payment, a net settlement payment, or any other similar payment commonly used in the forward contract trade;

(40) "municipality" means political subdivision or public agency or instrumentality of a State;

(41) "person" includes individual, partnership, and corporation, but does not include governmental unit, *Provided, however,* that any governmental unit that acquires an asset from a person as a result of operation of a loan guarantee agreement, or as receiver or liquidating agent of a person, will be considered a person for purposes of section 1102 of this title;

(42) "petition" means petition filed under section 301, 302, 303, or 304 of this title, as the case may be, commencing a case under this title;

(43) "purchaser" means transferee of a voluntary transfer, and includes immediate or mediate transferee of such a transferee;

(44) "railroad" means common carrier by railroad engaged in the transportation of individuals or property, or owner of trackage facilities leased by such a common carrier;

(45) "relative" means individual related by affinity or consanguinity within the third degree as determined by the common law, or individual in a step or adoptive relationship within such third degree;

(46) "repo participant" means an entity that, on any day during the period beginning 90 days before the date of the filing of the petition, has an outstanding repurchase agreement with the debtor;

(47) "repurchase agreement" (which definition also applies to a reverse repurchase agreement) means an agreement, including related terms, which provides for the transfer of certificates of deposit, eligible bankers' acceptances, or securities that are direct obligations of, or that are fully guaranteed as to principal and interest by, the United States or any agency of the United States against the transfer of funds by the transferee of such certificates of deposit, eligible bankers' acceptances, or securities with a simultaneous agreement by such transferee to transfer to the transferor thereof certificates of deposit, eligible bankers' acceptances, or securities as described above, at a date certain not later than one year after such transfers or on demand, against the transfer of funds;

(48) "securities clearing agency" means person that is registered as a clearing agency under section 17A of the Securities Exchange Act of 1934 (15 U.S.C. 78q-1), or whose business is confined to the performance of functions of a clearing agency with respect to exempted securities, as defined in section 3(a)(12) of such Act (15 U.S.C. 78c(12)) for the purposes of such section 17A;

(49) "security"—

    (A) includes—

        (i) note;

        (ii) stock;

        (iii) treasury stock;

        (iv) bond;

        (v) debenture;

        (vi) collateral trust certificate;

        (vii) pre-organization certificate or subscription;

(viii) transferable share;

(ix) voting-trust certificate;

(x) certificate of deposit;

(xi) certificate of deposit for security;

(xii) investment contract or certificate of interest or participation in a profit-sharing agreement or in an oil, gas, or mineral royalty or lease, if such contract or interest is required to be the subject of a registration statement filed with the Securities and Exchange Commission under the provisions of the Securities Act of 1933 (15 U.S.C. 77a et seq.), or is exempt under section 3(b) of such Act (15 U.S.C. 77c(b)) from the requirement to file such a statement;

(xiii) interest of a limited partner in a limited partnership;

(xiv) other claim or interest commonly known as "security"; and

(xv) certificate of interest or participation in, temporary or interim certificate for, receipt for, or warrant or right to subscribe to or purchase or sell, a security; but

(B) does not include—

(i) currency, check, draft, bill of exchange, or bank letter of credit;

(ii) leverage transaction, as defined in section 761(13) of this title;

(iii) commodity futures contract or forward contract;

(iv) option, warrant, or right to subscribe to or purchase or sell a commodity futures contract;

(v) option to purchase or sell a commodity;

(vi) contract or certificate of a kind specified in subparagraph A(xii) of this paragraph that is not required to be the subject of a registration statement filed with the Securities and Exchange Commission and is not exempt under section 3(b) of the Securities Act of 1933 (15 U.S.C. 77c(b)) from the requirement to file such a statement; or

(vii) debt or evidence of indebtedness for goods sold and delivered or services rendered;

(50) "security agreement" means agreement that creates or provides for a security interest;

(51) "security interest" means lien created by an agreement;

(52) "State" includes the District of Columbia and Puerto Rico, except for the purpose of defining who may be a debtor under chapter 9 of this title;

(53) "statutory lien" means lien arising solely by force of a statute on specified circumstances or conditions, or lien of distress for rent, whether or not statutory, but does not include security interest or judicial lien, whether or not such interest or lien is provided by or is dependent on a statute and whether or not such interest or lien is made fully effective by statute;

(54)* "stockbroker" means person—

    (A) with respect to which there is a customer, as defined in section 741(2) of this title; and

    (B) that is engaged in the business of effecting transactions in securities—

        (i) for the account of others; or

        (ii) with members of the general public, from or for such person's own account;

(55)* "swap agreement" means—

    (A) an agreement (including terms and conditions incorporated by reference therein) which is a rate swap agreement, basis swap, forward rate agreement, commodity swap, interest rate option, forward foreign exchange agreement, rate cap agreement, rate floor agreement, rate collar agreement, currency swap agreement, cross-currency rate swap agreement, currency option, any other similar agreement (including any option to enter into any of the foregoing);

    (B) any combination of the foregoing; or

    (C) a master agreement for any of the foregoing together with all supplements;

---

* [*Ed. Note:* Due to a drafting error in the amending legislation, section 101 contains two each of numbered paragraphs (54) through (57). *See* Comment to the 1990 Amendments *infra.*]

(56)* "swap participant" means an entity that, at any time before the filing of the petition, has an outstanding swap agreement with the debtor;

(57)* "timeshare plan" means and shall include that interest purchased in any arrangement, plan, scheme, or similar device, but not including exchange programs, whether by membership, agreement, tenancy in common, sale, lease, deed, rental agreement, license, right to use agreement, or by any other means, whereby a purchaser, in exchange for consideration, receives a right to use accommodations, facilities, or recreational sites, whether improved or unimproved, for a specific period of time less than a full year during any given year, but not necessarily for consecutive years, and which extends for a period of more than three years. A "timeshare interest" is that interest purchased in a timeshare plan which grants the purchaser the right to use and occupy accommodations, facilities, or recreational sites, whether improved or unimproved, pursuant to a timeshare plan;

(54)* "transfer" means every mode, direct or indirect, absolute or conditional, voluntary or involuntary, of disposing of or parting with property or with an interest in property, including retention of title as a security interest and foreclosure of the debtor's equity of redemption;

(55)* "United States," when used in a geographical sense, includes all locations where the judicial jurisdiction of the United States extends, including territories and possessions of the United States;

(56)* "intellectual property" means—

    (A) trade secret;

    (B) invention, process, design, or plant protected under title 35;

    (C) patent application;

    (D) plant variety;

    (E) work of authorship protected under title 17; or

    (F) mask work protected under chapter 9 of title 17;

to the extent protected by applicable nonbankruptcy law; and

(57)* "mask work" has the meaning given it in section 901(a)(2) of title 17.

Legislative History

Paragraph (1) defines "accountant" as an accountant authorized under applicable law to practice accounting. The term includes a professional accounting association, corporation, or partnership if applicable law authorizes such a unit to practice accounting.

[*House Report No. 95–595, 95th Cong., 1st Sess. 308 (1977); Senate Report No. 95–989, 95th Cong., 2d Sess. 21 (1978).*]

Paragraph (2) defines "affiliate." An affiliate is an entity with a close relationship to the debtor. It includes a 20 percent parent or subsidiary of the debtor, whether a corporate, partnership, individual, or estate parent.

The use of "directly or indirectly" in subparagraphs (A) and (B) is intended to cover situations in which there is an opportunity to control, and where the existence of that opportunity operates as indirect control.

The term also includes a person whose business or substantially all of whose property is operated under a lease or operating agreement by the debtor, and any entity that operates the business or substantially all of the property of the debtor under a lease or operating agreement.

"Affiliate" is defined primarily for use in the definition of insider, *infra,* and for use in the chapter 11 reorganization cases.

[*House Report No. 95–595, 95th Cong., 1st Sess. 309 (1977).*]

Paragraph (2) defines "affiliate."

"Affiliate" is defined primarily for use in the definition of insider, *infra,* and for use in the chapter 11 reorganization cases. The definition of "affiliate" does not include an entity acting in a fiduciary or agency capacity if the entity does not have the sole discretionary power to vote 20 percent of the voting securities but hold them solely as security and have not exercised the power to vote [*sic*]. This restriction applies to a corporate affiliate under subparagraph (B) of paragraph (2).

Subsections (C) and (D) of paragraph (2) define affiliate also as those persons and entities whose business or substantially all of whose property is operated under a lease or operating agreement by a debtor and whose business or property is more than 50 percent under the control of the debtor.

[*Senate Report No. 95–989, 95th Cong., 2d Sess. 21 (1978)*]

Section 101(2) defines "affiliate." The House amendment contains a provision that is a compromise between the definition in the

---

* [*Ed. Note:* Due to a drafting error in the amending legislation, section 101 contains two each of numbered paragraphs (54) through (57). *See* Comment to the 1990 Amendments *infra.*]

House-passed version of H.R. 8200 and the Senate amendment in the nature of a substitute to H.R. 8200. Subparagraphs (A) and (B) are derived from the Senate amendment and subparagraph (D) is taken from the House bill, while subparagraph (C) represents a compromise, taking the House position with respect to a person whose business is operated under a lease or an operating agreement by the debtor and with respect to a person substantially all of whose property is operated under an operating agreement by the debtor and the Senate position on leased property. Thus, the definition of "affiliate" excludes persons substantially all of whose property is operated under a lease agreement by a debtor, such as a small company which owns equipment all of which is leased to a larger nonrelated company.

[*124 Cong. Rec. H11,089–90 (Sept. 28, 1978); S17,406 (Oct. 6, 1978).*]

The definition of "attorney" in paragraph (3) [*Ed. Note:* Pub. L. No. 101-647 (1990) redesignated section 101(3) as section 101(4).] is similar to the definition of accountant.

Paragraph (4) [*Ed. Note:* Pub. L. No. 101-647 (1990) redesignated section 101(4) as section 101(5).] defines "claim." The effect of the definition is a significant departure from present law. Under present law, "claim" is not defined in straight bankruptcy. Instead it is simply used, along with the concept of provability in section 63 of the Bankruptcy Act, to limit the kinds of obligations that are payable in a bankruptcy case. The term is defined in the debtor rehabilitation chapters of present law far more broadly. The definition in paragraph (4) adopts an even broader definition of claim that is found in the present debtor rehabilitation chapters. The definition is any right to payment, whether or not reduced to judgment, liquidated, unliquidated, fixed, contingent, matured, unmatured, disputed, undisputed, legal, equitable, secured, or unsecured. The definition also includes as a claim an equitable right to performance that does not give rise to a right to payment. By this broadest possible definition, and by the use of the term throughout the title 11, especially in subchapter I of chapter 5, the bill contemplates that all legal obligations of the debtor, no matter how remote or contingent, will be able to be dealt with in the bankruptcy case. It permits the broadest possible relief in the bankruptcy court.

[*House Report No. 95–595, 95th Cong., 1st Sess. 309 (1977); Senate Report No. 95–989, 95th Cong., 2d Sess. 21. (1978).*]

Section 101(4)(B) [*Ed. Note:* Pub. L. No. 101-647 (1990) redesignated section 101(4) as section 101(5).] represents a modification of the House-passed bill to include the definition of "claim" a right to an equitable remedy for breach of performance if such breach gives rise to a right to payment. This is intended to cause the liquidation or estimation of contingent rights of payment for which there may be an alternative equitable remedy with the result that the equitable remedy will be susceptible to being discharged in bankruptcy. For example, in some States, a judgment for specific performance may be satisfied by an alternative right to payment, in the event performance is refused; in that event, the creditor entitled to specific performance would have a "claim" for purposes of a proceeding under title 11.

On the other hand, rights to an equitable remedy for a breach of performance with respect to which such breach does not give rise to a right to payment are not "claims" and would therefore not be susceptible to discharge in bankruptcy.

In a case under chapter 9 to title II, "claim" does not include a right to payment under an industrial development bond issued by a municipality as a matter of convenience for a third party.

Municipalities are authorized, under section 103(c) of the Internal Revenue Code of 1954, as amended, to issue tax-exempt industrial development revenue bonds to provide for the financing of certain projects for privately owned companies. The bonds are sold on the basis of the credit of the company on whose behalf they are issued, and the principal, interest, and premium, if any, are payable solely from payments made by the company to the trustee under the bond indenture and do not constitute claims on the tax revenues or other funds of the issuing municipalities. The municipality merely acts as the vehicle to enable the bonds to be issued on a tax-exempt basis. Claims that arise by virtue of these bonds are not among the claims defined by this paragraph and amounts owed by private companies to the holders of industrial development revenue bonds are not to be included among the assets of the municipality that would be affected by the plan.

[*124 Cong. Rec. H 11,090 (Sept. 28, 1978) S 17,406 (Oct. 6, 1978).*]

Paragraph (5) [*Ed. Note:* Pub. L. No. 101-647 (1990) redesignated section 101(5) as section 101(6).] defines "commodity broker" by reference to various terms used and defined in subchapter IV of chapter 7, Commodity Broker Liquidation. The terms are described in connection with section 761, *infra.*

Paragraph (6) [*Ed. Note:* Pub. L. No. 101-647 (1990) redesignated section 101(6) as section 101(7).] defines "community claim" for those eight States that have community property laws. The definition is keyed to the liability of the debtor's property for a claim against either the debtor or the debtor's spouse. If the debtor's property is liable for a claim against either, that claim is a community claim.

[*House Report No. 95–595, 95th Cong., 1st Sess. 309 (1977); Senate Report No. 95–989, 95th Cong., 2d Sess. 21 (1978).*]

Section 101(6) [*Ed. Note:* Pub. L. No. 101-647 (1990) redesignated section 101(6) as section 101(7).] defines "community claim" as provided by the Senate amendment in order to indicate that a community claim exists whether or not there is community property in the estate as of the commencement of the case.

[*124 Cong. Rec. II 11,090 (Sept. 28, 1978); S 17,406 (Oct. 6, 1978).*]

Paragraph (7) [*Ed. Note:* Pub. L. No. 101-647 (1990) redesignated section 101(7) as section 101(8).] defines "consumer debt." The definition is adapted from the definition used in various consumer protection laws. It encompasses only a debt incurred by an individual primarily for a personal, family, or household purpose.

[*House Report No. 95–595, 95th Cong., 1st Sess. 309 (1977); Senate Report No. 95–989, 95th Cong., 2d Sess. 22 (1978).*]

Paragraph (7) [*Ed. Note:* Pub. L. No. 101-647 (1990) redesignated section 101(7) as section 101(8).] defines "consumer debt." The definition is adapted from the definition used in various consumer protection laws. It encompasses only a debt incurred by an individual primarily for a personal, family or household purpose.

[*House Report No. 95–595, 95th Cong., 1st Sess. 309 (1977); Senate Report No. 95–989, 95th Cong., 2d Sess. 22 (1978).*]

A consumer debt does not include a debt to any extent the debt is secured by real property.

[*124 Cong. Rec. H 11,090 (Sept. 28, 1978); S 17,406 (Oct. 6, 1978).*]

The definition of "corporation" in paragraph (8) [*Ed. Note:* Pub. L. No. 101-647 (1990) redesignated section 101(8) as section 101(9).] is similar to the definition in current law, section 1(8). The term encompasses any association having the power or privilege that a private corporation, but not an individual or partnership, has; partnership associations organized under a law that makes only the capital subscribed responsible for the debts ofthe partnership; joint-stock company; unincorporated company or association; and business trust. "Unincorporated association" is intended specifically to include a labor union, as well as other bodies that come under that phrase as used under current law. This overrules In the Matter of Freight Drivers Local 600, 3 Banter. [*sic*] Ct. Dec. 528 (E.D. Mo. 1977).

The exclusion of limited partnerships is explicit, and not left to the case law. Neither are general partnerships corporations.

"Creditor" is defined to include only holders of prepetition claims against the debtor. However, it also encompasses certain holders of claims that are deemed to arise before the date of the filing of the petition, such as those injured by the rejection of an executory contract or unexpired lease, certain investment tax credit recapture claim holders, "involuntary gap" creditors, and certain holders of the right of setoff. The term also includes the holder of a prepetition community claim. A guarantor of or surety for a claim against the debtor will also be a creditor, because he will hold a contingent claim against the debtor that will become fixed when he pays the creditor whose claim he has guaranteed or insured.

Paragraph (10) [*Ed. Note:* Pub. L. No. 101-647 (1990) redesignated section 101(10) as section 101(11).] defines "custodian." There is no similar definition in current law. It is defined to facilitate drafting, and means prepetition liquidator of the debtor's property, such as an assignee for the benefit of creditors, a receiver of the debtor's property, or a liquidator or administrator of the debtor's property. The definition of custodian to include a receiver or trustee is descriptive, and not meant to be limited to court officers with those titles. The definition is intended to include other officials of the court if their functions are substantially similar to those of a receiver or trustee.

"Debt" is defined in paragraph (11) [*Ed. Note:* Pub. L. No. 101-647 (1990) redesignated section 101(11) as section 101(12).] as a liability on a claim. The terms are coextensive: a creditor has a "claim" against the debtor; the debtor owes a "debt" to the creditor.

This definition of "debt" and the definition of "claim" on which it is based, proposed 11 U.S.C. § 101(4) [*Ed. Note:* Pub. L. No. 101-647 (1990) redesignated section 101(4) as section 101(5).], does not include a transaction such as a policy loan on an insurance policy. Under that kind of transaction, the debtor is not liable to the insurance company for repayment; the amount owed is merely available to the company for setoff against any benefits that become payable under the policy. As such, the loan is not a claim (it is not a right to payment) that the company can assert against the estate; nor is the debtor's obligation a debt (a liability on a claim) that will be discharged under proposed 11 U.S.C. § 523 or 524.

[*House Report No. 95–595, 95th Cong., 1st Sess. 309–310 (1977); See Senate Report No. 95–989, 95th Cong., 2d Sess. 22–23 (1978).*]

Section 101(11) [*Ed. Note:* Pub. L. No. 101-647 (1990) redesignated section 101(11) as section 101(12).] defines "debt" to mean liability on a claim, as was contained in the House-passed version of H.R. 8200. The Senate amendment contained language indicating that "debt" does not include a policy loan made by a life insurance company to the debtor. That language is deleted in the House amendment as unnecessary since a life insurance company clearly has no right to have a policy loan repaid by the debtor, although such company does have a right of offset with respect to such policy loan. Clearly, then a "debt" does not include a policy loan made by a life insurance company. Inclusion of the language contained in the Senate amendment would have required elaboration of other legal relationships not arising by a liability on a claim. Further the language would have required clarification that interest on a policy loan made by a life insurance company is a debt, and that the insurance company does have right to payment to that interest.

[*124 Cong. Rec. H 11,090 (Sept. 28, 1978); S 17,406 (Oct. 6, 1978).*]

Paragraph (12) [*Ed. Note:* Pub. L. No. 101-647 (1990) redesignated section 101(12) as section 101(13).] defines "debtor." Debtor means person or municipality concerning which a case under the bankruptcy law has been commenced. This is a change in terminology from present law, which calls a person that is proceeding in a straight bankruptcy liquidation case the "bankrupt", and a person or municipality that is proceeding under a debtor rehabilitation chapter (chapters VIII through XIII of the Bankruptcy Act) a "debtor." The general term debtor is used for both kinds of cases in this bill, for ease of reference in chapters 1, 3, and 5 (which apply to straight bankruptcy and reorganization cases), and as a means of reducing the stigma connected with the term bankrupt.

Paragraph (13) [*Ed. Note:* Pub. L. No. 101-647 (1990) redesignated section 101(13) as section 101(14).] defines "disinterested person." The definition is adapted from section 158 of chapter X of current law, though it is expanded and modified in some respects. A person is a disinterested person if the person is not a creditor, equity security holder or insider; is not and was not an investment banker of the debtor for any outstanding security of the debtor (the change from underwriter in current law to investment banker is to make the term more descriptive and to avoid conflict with the definition of underwriter in section 2(11) of the Securities Act of 1933) (15 U.S.C. § 77b(11)); has not been an investment banker for a security of the debtor within three years before the date of the filing of the petition (the change from five years to three years here conforms the definition with the Statute of Limitations in the Securities Act of 1933), or an attorney for such an investment banker; is not an insider of the debtor or of such an investment banker; and does not have an interest materially adverse to the estate.

Representation of a creditor or equity security holder other than in the debtor's bankruptcy case does not necessarily preclude a person from being disinterested. The defined term is used in connection with sections of the proposed bankruptcy code concerning employment of professionals and trustees by the estate or the trustee.

"Entity" is defined, for convenience, in paragraph (14) [*Ed. Note:* Pub. L. No. 101-647 (1990) redesignated section 101(14) as section 101(15).], to include person, estate, trust, and governmental unit. It is the most inclusive of the various defined terms relating to bodies or units.

Paragraph (15) [*Ed. Note:* Pub. L. No. 101-647 (1990) redesignated section 101(15) as section 101(16).] defines "equity security." The term includes shares or stock in a corporation, a limited partner's interest in a limited partnership, and warrants or rights to subscribe in an equity security. The term does not include securities, such as convertible debentures, that are convertible into equity securities, but that have not been converted.

Paragraph (16) [*Ed. Note:* Pub. L. No. 101-647 (1990) redesignated section 101(16) as section 101(17).] defines "equity security holder" for convenience as the holder of an equity securing of the debtor.

The definition of farmer in paragraph (17) [*Ed. Note:* The 1986 Amendments redesignated section 101(17) as section 101(19). Pub. L. No. 101-647 (1990) further redesignated this section as section 101(20).] is derived from the Small Business Act. It encompasses only small farmers, and is not intended to cover agribusiness. The purpose of the definition is for use in the sections of the proposed bankruptcy code prohibiting involuntary cases against farmers. The limits contained in the definition are an 80 percent minimum on income from farming operations in the year before the filing of the petition.

[*House Report No. 95–595, 95th Cong., 1st Sess. 310–311 (1977); Senate Report No. 95–989, 95th Cong., 2d Sess. 23–24 (1978).*]

Section 101(17) [*Ed. Note:* The 1986 Amendments redesignated section 101(17) as section 101(19). Pub. L. No. 101-647 (1990) further redesignated this section as section 101(20).] defines "farmer," as in the Senate amendment with an income limitation percentage of 80 percent instead of 75 percent.

Section 101(18) [*Ed. Note:* The 1986 Amendments redesignated section 101(18) as section 101(20). Pub. L. No. 101-647 (1990) further redesignated this section as section 101(21).] contains a new definition of "farming operation" derived from present law and the definition of "farmer" in the Senate amendment. This definition gives a broad construction to the term "farming operation."

Section 101(20) [*Ed. Note:* Pub. L. No. 98–353 redesignated section 101(20) as section 101(21). The 1986 Amendments further redesignated this section as section 101(23). Pub. L. No. 101-647 (1990) again redesignated this section as section 101(24).] contains a definition of "foreign representative." It clarifies the House bill and Senate amendment by indicating that a foreign representative must be duly selected in a foreign proceeding.

[*124 Cong. Rec. H 11,090 (Sept. 28, 1978); S 17,406–7 (Oct. 6, 1978).*]

"Foreign proceeding" and "foreign representative" are defined in paragraphs . . . [19 and 20]. [*Ed. Note:* Pub. L. No. 98–353 redesignated paragraphs (19) and (20) as paragraphs (20) and (21) respectively. The 1986 Amendments further redesignated these paragraphs as (22) and (23) respectively. Pub. L. No. 101-647 (1990) again redesignated these paragraphs as (23) and (24) respectively.] A foreign proceeding is a proceeding in another country in which the debtor has some substantial connection for the purpose of liquidating the estate of the debtor or the purpose of financial rehabilitation of the debtor. A foreign representative is the representative of the foreign proceeding, such as a trustee or administrator.

Paragraph . . . [21] [*Ed. Note:* Pub. L. No. 98–353 redesignated section 101(21) as section 101(24). The 1986 Amendments further redesignated this section as section 101(26). Pub. L. No. 101-647 (1990) again redesignated this section as section 101(27).] defines "governmental unit" in the broadest sense. The definition encompasses the United States, a State, Commonwealth, District, Territory, municipality or foreign state, and a department, agency, or instrumentality of any of those entities. "Department, agency, or instrumentality" does not include entities that owe their existence to State action such as the granting of a charter or a license but that have no other connection with a State or local government or the Federal Government. The relationship must be an active one in which the department, agency, or instrumentality is actually carrying out some governmental function. The United States trustee, even though an employee of the United States, is not a governmental unit when he is representing an estate in a bankruptcy case.

Paragraph . . . [22] [*Ed. Note:* Pub. L. No. 98–353 redesignated section 101(22) as section 101(25). The 1986 Amendments further redesignated this section as section 101(27). Pub. L. No. 101-647 (1990) again redesignated this section as section 101(28).] defines "indenture." It is similar to the definition of indenture in the Trust Indenture Act of 1939. An indenture is the instrument under which securities, either debt or equity, of the debtor are outstanding.

Paragraph . . . [23] [*Ed. Note:* Pub. L. No. 98–353 redesignated section 101(23) as section 101(26). The 1986 Amendments further redesignated this section as section 101(28). Pub. L. No. 101-647 (1990) again redesignated this section as section 101(29).] defines "indenture trustee" as the trustee under an indenture.

Paragraph (24) [*Ed. Note:* Pub. L. No. 98–353 redesignated section 101(24) as section 101(27). The 1986 Amendments further redesignated this section as section 101(29). Pub. L. No. 101-647 (1990) again redesignated this section as section 101(30).] defines "individual with regular income." The effect of this definition, and its use in section 109(e), is to expand substantially the kinds of individuals that are eligible for relief under chapter 13, Plans for Individuals with Regular Income, which is now available only for wage earners. The definition encompasses all individuals with incomes that are sufficiently stable and regular to enable them to make payments under a chapter 13 plan. Thus, individuals on welfare, social security, fixed pension incomes, or who live on investment incomes, will be able to work out repayment plans with their creditors rather than being forced into straight bankruptcy. Also, self employed individuals will be eligible to use chapter 13 if they have regular income. However, the definition excludes certain stockbrokers and commodity brokers, in order to prohibit them from proceeding under chapter 13 and avoiding the customer protection provisions of chapter 7.

"Insider," defined in paragraph . . . [25] [*Ed. Note:* Pub. L. No. 98–353 redesignated section 101(25) as section 101(28). The 1986 Amendments further redesignated this section as section 101(30). Pub. L. No. 101-647 (1990) again redesignated this section as section 101(31).] is a new term. An insider is one who has a sufficiently close relationship with the debtor that his conduct is made subject to closer scrutiny than those dealing at arms length with the debtor. If the debtor is an individual, then a relative of the debtor, a partnership in which the debtor is a general partner, a general partner of the debtor, and a corporation controlled by the debtor are all insiders. If the debtor is a corporation, then a controlling person, a relative of a controlling person, a partnership in which the debtor is a general partner, and a general partner of the debtor are all insiders. If the debtor is a partnership, then a general partner of or in the debtor, a relative of a general partner in the debtor, and a person in control are all insiders. If the debtor is a municipality, then an elected official of the debtor is an insider. In addition, affiliates of the debtor and managing agents are insiders.

The definition of "insolvent" in paragraph . . . [26] [*Ed. Note:* Pub. L. No. 98–353 redesignated section 101(26) as section 101(29). The 1986 Amendments further redesignated this section as section 101(31). Pub. L. No. 101-647 (1990) again redesignated this section as section 101(32).] is adapted from section 1(19) of current law. An entity is insolvent if its debts are greater than its assets, at a fair valuation, exclusive of property exempted or fraudulently transferred. It is the traditional bankruptcy balance sheet test of insolvency. For a partnership, the definition is modified to account for the liability of a general partner for the partnership's debts. The difference in this definition from that in current law is in the exclusion of exempt property for all purposes in the definition of insolvent.

[*Ed. Note:* The 1988 municipal bankruptcy amendments (Pub. L. No. 100-597) amended the definition of "insolvent."]

Section 1 amends the definition of "insolvent" in section 101(31) of the Bankruptcy Code with respect to municipalities so that an insolvent municipality is one that is either not paying or is unable to pay its debts—except debts that are in good faith disputed—when they come due. The existing definition of insolvent, generally that liabilities exceed non-exempt assets, does not really apply to municipalities. Most of the assets of a municipality are exempt and cannot be used for the repayment of debt. Accordingly, the liabilities of even financially sound municipalities will in most cases exceed their non-exempt assets, and, under existing law, these municipalities would be considered insolvent. The change made by section 1 corrects this, and ensures that financially sound municipalities will not be considered insolvent. What is important to creditors is not the value of a municipality's assets, but rather the ability of the municipality to repay its debts.

[*House Report No. 100-1011, 100th Cong., 2d Sess. 5-6 (1988).*]

Paragraph . . . [27] [*Ed. Note:* Pub. L. No. 98–353 redesignated section 101(27) as section 101(30). The 1986 Amendments further redesignated this section as section 101(32). Pub. L. No. 101-647 (1990) again redesignated this section as section 101(36).] defines "judicial lien." It is one of three [sic] kinds of liens defined in this section. A judicial lien is a lien obtained by judgment, levy, sequestration, or other legal or equitable process or proceeding.

Paragraph . . . [28] [*Ed. Note:* Pub. L. No. 98–353 redesignated section 101(28) as section 101(31). The 1986 Amendments further redesignated this section as section 101(33). Pub. L. No. 101-647 (1990) again redesignated this section as section 101(37).] defines "lien." The definition is new and is very broad. A lien is defined as a charge against or interest in property to secure payment of a debt or performance of an obligation. It includes inchoate liens. In general, the concept of lien is divided into three kinds of liens: judicial liens, security interests, and statutory liens. Those three categories are mutually exclusive and are exhaustive except for certain common law liens.

Paragraph . . . [29] [*Ed. Note:* Pub. L. No. 98–353 redesignated section 101(29) as section 101(32). The 1986 Amendments further redesignated this section as section 101(34). In June, 1990, Congress passed a bill amending title 11 regarding swap agreements and forward contracts. The bill, which became Pub. L. No. 101–311, added several definitions to section 101 and redesignated this section as section 101(36). Pub. L. No. 101-647 (1990) again redesignated this section as section 101(40).] defines "municipality." The definition is adapted from the terms used in the chapter IX (municipal bankruptcy) amendment to the Bankruptcy Act enacted in 1976 (Pub. L. 94–260). That amendment spoke in terms of "political subdivision or public agency or instrumentality of a State." Bankruptcy Act section 84. The term municipality is defined by those three terms for convenience. It does not include the District of Columbia or any territories of the United States.

"Person" is defined in paragraph . . . [30] [*Ed. Note:* Pub. L. No. 98–353 redesignated section 101(30) as section 101(33). The 1986 Amendments further redesignated this section as section 101(35). Pub. L. No. 101–311 redesignated this section as section 101(37). Pub. L. No. 101-647 (1990) again redesignated this section as section 101(41).] The definition is a change in wording, but not in substance, from the definition in section 1(23) of the Bankruptcy Act. The definition is also similar to the one contained in 1 U.S.C. § 1, but is repeated here for convenience and ease of reference. Person includes individual partnership, and corporation. The exclusion of governmental units is made explicit in order to avoid any confusion that may arise if, for example, a municipality is incorporated and thus is legally a corporation as well as governmental unit. The definition does not include an estate or a trust, which are included only in the definition of "entity" in proposed 11 U.S.C. § 101(14).

"Petition" is defined for convenience in paragraph . . . [31]. [*Ed. Note:* Pub. L. No. 98–353 redesignated section 101(31) as section 101(34). The 1986 Amendments further redesignated this section as section 101(36). Pub. L. No. 101–311 redesignated this section as section 101(38). Pub. L. No. 101-647 (1990) again redesignated this section as section 101(42).] Petition is a petition under section 301, 302, 303, or 304 of the bankruptcy code—that is, a petition that commences a case under title 11.

Paragraph . . . [32] [*Ed. Note:* Pub. L. No. 98–353 redesignated section 101(32) as section 101(35). The 1986 Amendments further redesignated this section as section 101(37). Pub. L. No. 101–311 redesignated this section as section 101(39). Pub. L. No. 101-647 (1990) again redesignated this section as section 101(43).] defines "purchaser" as a transferee of a voluntary transfer, such as a sale or gift, and includes an immediate or mediate transferee of purchaser.

The definition of "railroad" in paragraph . . . [33] [*Ed. Note:* Pub. L. No. 98–353 redesignated section 101(33) as section 101(36). The 1986 Amendments further redesignated this section as section 101(38). Pub. L. No. 101–311 redesignated this section as section 101(40). Pub. L. No. 101-647 (1990) again redesignated this section as section 101(44).] is derived from section 77 of the Bankruptcy Act. A railroad is a common carrier by railroad engaged in the transportation of individuals or property, or an owner of trackage facilities leased by such a common carrier. The effect of the definition and the use of the term in section 109(d) is to eliminate the limitation now found in section 77 of the Bankruptcy Act that only railroads engaged in interstate commerce may proceed under the railroad reorganization provisions. The limitation may have been inserted because of a doubt that the commerce power could not reach intrastate railroads. Be that as it may, this bill is enacted under the Bankruptcy Power.

Paragraph . . . [34] [*Ed. Note:* Pub. L. No. 98–353 redesignated section 101(34) as section 101(37). The 1986 Amendments further redesignated this section as section 101(39). Pub. L. No. 101–311 redesignated this section as section 101(41). Pub. L. No. 101-647 (1990) again redesignated this section as section 101(45).] defines "relative" as an individual related by affinity or consanguinity within the third degree as determined by the common law, and includes individuals in a step or adoptive relationship. The definition is similar to current law, but adds the latter phrase. This definition should be applied as of the time when the transaction that it concerns took place. Thus, a former spouse is not a relative, but if, for example, for purposes of the preference section, proposed 11 U.S.C. § 547(b)(4)(B), the transferee was a spouse of the debtor at the time of the transfer sought to be avoided, then the transferee would be relative and subject to the insider rules, even if the transferee was no longer married to the debtor at the time of the commencement of the case or at the time of the commencement of the preference recovery proceeding.

[*House Report No. 95–595, 95th Cong., 1st Sess. 311–14 (1977); see Senate Report No. 95–989, 95th Cong., 2d Sess. 24–26 (1978).*]

Section 1(a) [of Public Law 97–222] provides a definition for "securities clearing agency" and makes conforming redesignations of subsequent definitions.

[*House Report No. 97–420, 97th Cong., 2d Sess. 3 (1982).*]

Paragraph . . . [36] [*Ed. Note:* Public Law 98–353 redesignated section 101(36) as section 101(41). The 1986 Amendments further redesignated this section as section 101(43). Pub. L. No. 101–311 redesignated this section as section 101(45). Pub. L. No. 101-647 (1990) again redesignated this section as section 101(49). This definition was originally designated as section 101(35) by the Bankruptcy Reform Act of 1978, Pub. L. No. 95–598.] defines "security." The definition is new and is modeled on the most recent draft of the American Law Institute's proposed securities code, with some exceptions. The interest of a limited partner in a limited partnership is included in order to make sure that everything that is defined as an equity security is also a "security." Commercial notes are not included in the definition in order to permit payment of debts with such notes under a chapter 11 plan without a valuation of the debtor's business; the exclusion is not intended to require a registration statement if such notes are issued under a chapter 11 plan. The definition, as with the definition of "entity," "insider," and "person," is open ended because the term is not susceptible of precise specification. Thus the courts will be able to use the characterization provided in this definition to treat with new kinds of documents on a flexible basis.

[*House Report No. 95–595, 95th Cong., 1st Sess. 311–14 (1977); See Senate Report No. 95–989, 95th Cong., 2d Sess. 24–26 (1978).*]

Section [101(36)] [*Ed. Note:* Public Law 98–353 redesignated section 101(36) as section 101(41). The 1986 Amendments further redesignated this section as section 101(43). Pub. L. No. 101–311 redesignated this section as section 101(45). Pub. L. No. 101-647 (1990) again redesignated this section as section 101(49). This definition was originally designated as section 101(35) by the Bankruptcy Reform Act of 1978, Pub. L. No. 95–598.] defines "security" as contained in the Senate amendment. H.R. 8200 as adopted by the House excluded certain commercial notes from the definition of "security," and that exclusion is deleted.

[124 Cong. Rec. H 11,090 (Sept, 28, 1978); S 17,407 (Oct. 6, 1978).]

Section 1(b) [of Public Law 97–222] amends section 101(36)(A)(xii) *[Ed. Note:* Pub. L. No. 98–353 redesignated section 101(36)(A)(xii) as 101(41)(A)(xii). The 1986 Amendments further redesignated this section as section 101(43)(A)(xii). In 1990, Pub. L. No. 101–311 redesignated this section as section 101(45)(A)(xii). Pub. L. No. 101-647 (1990) again redesignated this section as section 101(49)(A)(xii). The section was originally designated as 101(35)(A)(xii).] of title 11, as so redesignated, to clarify that an investment contract or certificate of interest or participation is within the scope of the definition of a "security" if it is required to be the subject of a Securities Act registration statement whether or not such a registration statement has been filed.

Section 1(c) conforms the name of a type of contract excluded from the definition of "security" ("forward commodity contract") to the terminology used in other provisions of title 11 ("forward contract") by deleting the word "commodity."

[House Report No. 97–420, 97th Cong., 2d Sess. 3 (1982).]

Paragraphs . . . [37 and 38] *[Ed. Note:* Public Law 98–353 redesignated sections 101(37) and 101(38) as sections 101(42) and 101(43), respectively. The 1986 Amendments further redesignated these sections as sections 101(44) and 101(45). Pub. L. No. 101–311 redesignated these sections as sections 101(46) and 101(47). Pub. L. No. 101-647 (1990) again redesignated these sections as sections 101(50) and 101(51), respectively. These definitions were originally designated as sections 101(36) and (37), respectively, by the Bankruptcy Reform Act of 1978, Pub. L. No. 95–598.] define "security agreement" and "security interest." A security interest is one of the kinds of liens. It is a lien created by an agreement. Security agreement is defined as the agreement creating the security interest. Though these terms are similar to the same terms in the Uniform Commercial Code, article IX, they are broader. For example, the U.C.C. does not cover real property mortgages. Under this definition, such a mortgage is included, as are all other liens created by agreement, even though not covered by the U.C.C. All U.C.C. security interests and security agreements are, however, security interests and security agreements under this definition. Whether a consignment or a lease constitutes a security interest under the bankruptcy code will depend on whether it constitutes a security interest under applicable State or local law.

Paragraph . . . [39] *[Ed. Note:* Public Law 98–353 redesignated section 101(39) as section 101(45). The 1986 Amendments further redesignated this section as section 101(47). Pub. L. No. 101–311 redesignated this section as section 101(49). Pub. L. No. 101-647 (1990) again redesignated this section as section 101(53). This definition was originally designated as section 101(38) by the Bankruptcy Reform Act of 1978, Pub. L. No. 95–598.] defines another kind of lien, "statutory lien." The definition, derived from current law, states that a statutory lien is a lien arising solely by force of statute on specified circumstances or conditions and includes a lien of distress for rent (whether statutory, common law, or otherwise). The definition excludes judicial liens and security interests, whether or not they are provided for or are dependent on a statute, and whether or not they are made fully effective by statute. A statutory lien is only one that arises automatically, and is not based on an agreement to give a lien or on judicial action. Mechanics', materialmen's, and warehousemen's liens are examples. Tax liens are also included in the definition of statutory lien.

"Stockbroker" is defined in paragraph . . . [40] [*Ed. Note:* Public Law 98–353 redesignated section 101(40) as section 101(46). The 1986 Amendments further redesignated this section as section 101(48). Pub. L. No. 101–311 redesignated this section as section 101(50). Pub. L. No. 101-647 (1990) again redesignated this section as section 101(54). Due to a drafting error, section 101 now contains two each of numbered paragraphs (54) through (57). *See* Comment to the 1990 Amendments *infra.* This definition was originally designated as section 101(39) by the Bankruptcy Reform Act of 1978, Pub. L. No. 95–598.] as a person engaged in the business of effecting transactions in securities for the account of others or with members of the general public from or for such person's own account, if the person has a customer, as defined. Thus, the definition, derived from a combination of the definitions of "broker" and "dealer" in the Securities Exchange Act of 1934, encompasses both brokers and dealers. The definition is used in section 109 and in subchapter III of chapter 7, Stockholder Liquidation. The term does not encompass an employee who acts for a principal that "effects" transaction or deals with the public, because such an employee will not have a "customer."

[*Senate Report No. 95–989, 95th Cong., 2d Sess. 26–27 (1978); see House Report No. 95–595, 95th Cong., 1st Sess. 313–14 (1977).*]

Section 1(d) [of Public Law 97–222] clarifies, and makes stylistic changes in, the definition of "stockbroker."

[*House Report No. 97–420, 97th Cong., 2d Sess. 3 (1982).*]

Paragraph [41] [*Ed. Note:* Public Law 98–353 redesignated section 101(41) as section 101(48). The 1986 Amendments further redesignated this section as section 101(50). Pub. L. No. 101–311 redesignated this section as section 101(54). Due to a drafting error, section 101 now contains two each of numbered paragraphs (54) through (57). *See* Comment to the 1990 Amendments *infra.* This definition was originally designated as section 101(40) by the Bankruptcy Reform Act of 1978, Pub. L. No. 95–598.] defines "transfer." It is derived and adapted, with stylistic changes, from section 1(30) of the Bankruptcy Act. A transfer is a disposition of an interest in property. The definition of transfer is as broad as possible. Many of the potentially limiting words in current law are deleted, and the language is simplified. Under this definition, any transfer of an interest in property is a transfer, including a transfer of possession, custody, or control even if there is no transfer of title, because possession, custody, and control are interests in property. A deposit in a bank account or similar account is a transfer.

[Senate Report No. 95–989, 95th Cong., 2d Sess. 26–27 (1978); See House Report No. 95–595, 95th Cong., 1st Sess. 313–14 (1977).]

Section 101[41] [*Ed. Note:* Public Law 98–353 redesignated section 101(41) as section 101(48). The 1986 Amendments further redesignated this section as section 101(50). Pub. L. No. 101–311 redesignated this section as section 101(54). Due to a drafting error, section 101 now contains two each of numbered paragraphs (54) through (57). *See* Comment to the 1990 Amendments *infra.* This definition was originally designated as section 101(40) by the Bankruptcy Reform Act of 1978, Pub. L. No. 95–598.] defines "transfer" as in the Senate amendment. The definition contained in H.R. 8200 as passed by the House included "setoff" in the definition of "transfer." Inclusion of "setoff" is deleted. The effect is that a "setoff" is not subject to being set aside as a preferential "transfer" but will be subject to special rules.

[124 Cong. Rec. H 11,090 (Sept. 28, 1978); S 17,407 (Oct. 6, 1978).]

[*Ed. Note:* Pub. L. No. 100–506 (1988) added paragraphs (52) and (53) to section 101, defining the terms "intellectual property" and "mask work." Pub. L. No. 101–311 redesignated these sections as sections 101(56) and 101(57) respectively. Due to a drafting error, section 101 now contains two each of numbered paragraphs (54) through (57). *See* Comment to the 1990 Amendments *infra.*]

[Section 101(56)] . . . sets forth in some instances both the actual type of property as to which the intellectual property proprietor obtains rights (*e.g.,* invention, process, design, confidential research or development information, work of authorship) and the alternative legal mechanism for protecting that underlying property (*e.g.,* trade secret, patents and copyrights). The amendment broadly defines "intellectual property" to include virtually all types of such rights (other than trademarks and similar rights) whether protected by federal or State law, statutory or common law. The bill in no way defines or alters any substantive intellectual property law, it merely refers to those rights which are already protected by applicable nonbankruptcy law. Proposed Section 101(52) makes clear that the operation of the bill is to cover both the intangible legal right associated with intellectual property and the tangible object or objects, such as books, blueprints and electronic media, in which such intellectual property may be fixed or recorded.

The definition of "intellectual property" is unusual for a federal statute because of its inculsion [*sic*] of trade secret, normally a concept reserved for development by the states. Because bankruptcy processes can alter rights created by state law, this inclusion is appropriate. Also included as a separate category is confidential research or development information. This was done because some states narrowly define trade secret, but accord protection to the developer of confidential technical information falling outside those definitions. The definition is broad and is to be interpreted liberally to carry out the intent of Congress to remove the cloud cast by that recent interpretation of the Bankruptcy Code upon the intellectual property licensing system.

* * *

The second new defined term [section 101(57)] is "mask work," a term included within the definition of "intellectual property." The term is used in recently adopted legislation and is to have the same meaning in title 11 as in section 901(a)(2) of title 17.

[*Senate Report No. 100-505, 100th Cong., 2d Sess. 7-8 (1988).*]

Comment*

Although Section 106(13) of the Bankruptcy Act defined "subsidiary," there was no definition of "affiliate" in the Act. Former Bankruptcy Rule 901(3), however, defined "affiliate" substantially the same as section 101(2). The minimum percentage of ownership or control or holding of outstanding voting securities in section 101(2) is set at 20 percent. An affiliate is also considered an insider. *See* definition of "insider" in section 101(31), *infra.*

There was no definition of "claim" under Chapters I–VII of the former Bankruptcy Act. The rehabilitation chapters of the Act, however, did define "claim." Section 101(5) of the Code is even broader in its definition of "claim" than the rather broad definition of "claim" in Chapter X of the Act.

Concerning section 101(6), there was no comparable definition of "commodity broker" in the Bankruptcy Act. Section 60e related to "stockbroker" liquidations.

Concerning section 101(7), the Bankruptcy Act had no definition of "community claim."

Concerning section 101(8), there was no comparable definition of "consumer debt" in the Bankruptcy Act.

Section 1(8) of the Bankruptcy Act defined "corporation" substantially the same as section 101(9), except that instead of "business trust" as in section 101(8), Section 1(8) of the Act included "any business conducted by a trustee or trustees wherein the beneficial interest or ownership is evidenced by certificate or other written instrument." The Act did not mention "limited partnership."

Concerning section 101(10), Bankruptcy Act Section 1(11) defined creditor to include anyone holding a claim provable in bankruptcy. The Bankruptcy Code abolishes the concept of "provability."

---

* *See* Comments on 1984, 1986, 1988 and 1990 Amendments *infra.*

Concerning section 101(12), Bankruptcy Act Section 1(14) defined debt to include any debt, demand, or claim provable in bankruptcy. The Code abolishes the concept of provability.

Concerning section 101(13), the word "debtor" appeared only in Chapters X, XI and XII of the Act. The term "bankrupt" was eliminated under the Code; the word "debtor" is used in all cases under the Code.

Concerning section 101(14), *see* House Report, *supra,* for changes in definition of "disinterested person" as that term was used in Section 158 of Chapter X and former Bankruptcy Rule 10–202(c)(2).

Concerning section 101(15), there was no comparable definition of "entity" in the Act. *See* definition of "person" in section 101(41), *infra.*

Concerning sections 101(16) and 101(17), there were no comparable definitions of "equity security" and "equity security holders" in the Act.

Section 101(18) defining "family farmer" and section 101(19) defining "family farmer with regular annual income" were added by the 1986 Amendments to delineate who may avail themselves of new chapter 12 entitled "Adjustment of Debts of a Family Farmer With Regular Annual Income."

Concerning section 101(20), "farmer" was defined in the Act to be an individual engaged in farming or tillage of the soil. The Code does not limit the definition to an individual; partnerships and corporations are included. *See* the definition of "person" in section 101(37), *infra.*

Concerning section 101(27), there was no comparable definition of "governmental unit" in the Act. The 1986 Amendments excluded from the definition of "governmental unit" a United States trustee while serving in a case under the Code.

Concerning section 101(31), there was no comparable definition of "insider" in the Bankruptcy Act.

Section 1(19) of the Act defined insolvency substantially the same as section 101(32) of the Code, except that the latter excludes exempt property for all purposes. Also, section 101(32) defines insolvency separately for a partnership taking into account the general partners' liability for partnership debts.

Concerning section 101(36), Section 67 of the Act avoided liens obtained by attachment, judgment, levy, or other legal or equitable process or proceeding within four months of the filing of the petition if the debtor was insolvent when the lien was obtained or if the lien was sought and permitted in fraud of provisions of the Act. This section is not carried over in the Code, but section 547, preferences, would be applicable to judicial liens.

"Lien" is defined in section 101(37), "security interest" is defined in section 101(51) and "statutory lien" is defined in section 101(53), *infra.* "Judicial lien" is defined in section 101(36), *supra.*

Pub. L. No. 101–311 (1990) added new paragraphs (38) defining "margin payment" and (39) defining "settlement payment."

Concerning section 101(40), *see* Chapter IX of the Act, Sections 81(8) and 84 as amended in 1976 (Pub. L. 94-260).

Concerning section 101(41), Section 1(23) of the Act defined "persons" to include corporations (except where otherwise specified), officers, partnerships, and women and where used with reference to acts of bankruptcy (Section 4) included persons who were participants in the forbidden acts of bankruptcy, and agents, officers and board directors or trustees or other similar controlling bodies of corporations.

Concerning section 101(42), that section is not unlike Section 1(23) of the Act which defined "petition" to mean the document filed in a court of bankruptcy or with the clerk thereof, initiating a proceeding under the Act.

Concerning section 101(43), the Act did not define "purchaser" but defined "transfer."

Concerning section 101(44), Section 77 of the Act was entitled "Reorganization of Railroad Engaged in Interstate Commerce." *See* Bankruptcy Rule 8–701(15) and Section 77(m) of the Act for definition of a railroad.

Public Law 97–222 (1982) added a new paragraph defining "securities clearing agency." This definition is now designated as section 101(48).

Concerning section 101(45), "relative" was defined in Section 1(27) of the Act to mean persons related by affinity or consanguinity within the third degree as determined by common law and included a spouse. Bankruptcy Rule 5002, as amended in 1991, prohibits approval of the appointment as trustee or examiner, or employment as an attorney, accountant, appraiser, auctioneer, or other professional person under section 327, section 1103 or section 1114 if the person is a relative of the judge of the court approving the appointment. This Rule also prohibits the approval of the appointment as trustee or examiner of an individual who is a relative of the United States trustee in the region in which the case is pending. Approval also is barred if the trustee, examiner, or other professional is or has been so connected with such judge or United States trustee as to render the appointment or employment improper. "Improper" as used in this connection includes the appearance of impropriety. "Person" includes the firm of any such person and all members, associates, and professional employees of the firm.

Concerning section 101(49), in light of the definition as enacted, the statement in the House Report, *supra*, with respect to the exclusion of commercial notes, is not accurate. The Senate Report does not contain that statement. The definition of "security" was originally designated as section 101(35) by the Bankruptcy Reform Act of 1978, Pub. L. No. 95–598.

There was no comparable definition of "security" in the Bankruptcy Act, except in Section 77(b).

Cf. section 9–105(1)(1) of Uniform Commercial Code concerning section 101(50), as redesignated by Pub. L. No. 101–647 (1990). The definition of "security agreement" was originally designated as section 101(36) by the Bankruptcy Reform Act of 1978, Pub. L. No. 95–598.

Regarding section 101(50), *see* Legislative History concerning the definition of "security agreement," *supra*. The definition of "security interest" in section 101(51) is an adaptation of the definition of the term in section 1-201(37) of the Uniform Commercial Code but expands the meaning of the term to include real estate security.

Concerning section 101(53), Section 1(29a) of the Act defined a statutory lien as one arising solely by force of statute upon specified circumstances or conditions, but excluding any lien provided for or dependent upon an agreement to give security, whether or not such lien is also provided by or dependent on statute and whether or not made fully effective by statute. Section 101(53) of the Code is substantially the same as Section 1(29a) of the Act, but specifically includes a lien of distress for rent. The definition of "statutory lien" was originally designated as section 101(38) by the Bankruptcy Reform Act of 1978, Pub. L. No. 95–598.

Concerning section 101(54), the definition of "stockbroker," Section 1 of the Act (the definitions section) did not define stockbroker. Section 60e, relating to stockbroker liquidations, used, but did not attempt to define, the term "stockbroker"; therefore, it was given its common accepted meaning.

Pub. L. No. 101–311 added paragraphs defining "swap agreement" and defining "swap participant."

Concerning the definition of "transfer," H.R. 8200 included the words "and setoff" at the end of the definition of transfer. These words, however, were deleted in the final version of the bill. The effect is that a "setoff" is not subject to being set aside as a preferential "transfer" but will be subject to special rules.

Section 1(30) of the former Bankruptcy Act defined transfer as follows:

> (30) "Transfer" shall include the sale and every other and different mode, direct or indirect, of disposing of or of parting with property or with an interest therein or with the possession thereof or of fixing a lien upon property or upon an interest therein, absolutely or conditionally, voluntarily or involuntarily, by or without judicial proceedings, as a conveyance, sale, assignment, payment, pledge, mortgage, lien, encumbrance, gift, security, or otherwise; the retention of a security title to property delivered to a debtor shall be deemed a transfer suffered by such debtor.

By simplifying the definition, section 101(54) of the Code is intended to define transfer as broadly as possible to include any disposition of property or an interest in property.

1984 Amendments: A number of definitions were added to § 101 and others were modified. To accommodate the new definitions, the paragraphs of § 101 were renumbered following paragraph (18) [redesignated by the 1986 Amendments as paragraph (20) and redesignated again by the 1990 Amendments as paragraph (21)].

A proviso was added to the definition of "person" in paragraph (33) [redesignated by the 1986 Amendments as paragraph (35) and, in 1990, redesignated first as paragraph (37) by Pub. L. No. 101–311 and then redesignated again by Pub. L. No. 101-647 (1990) as paragraph (41)] which has application in chapter 9 and 11 cases.

A new paragraph (44) [redesignated by the 1986 Amendments as paragraph (46) and, in 1990, redesignated first as paragraph (48) by Pub. L. No. 101–311 and then redesignated again by Pub. L. No. 101-647 (1990) as paragraph (52)] defined "State" to include Puerto Rico and the District of Columbia.

1986 Amendments: Paragraphs (17) defining "family farmer" and (18) defining "family farmer with regular annual income" [redesignated in 1990 as paragraphs (18) and (19), respectively] were added by the 1986 Act. These definitions are necessary to delineate who may avail themselves of chapter 12 entitled "Adjustment of Debts of a Family Farmer With Regular Annual Income," which was also added by the 1986 Act. All following paragraphs have been renumbered.

The first of these paragraphs has been amended to clarify the distinction between "farmer" and "family farmer."

Paragraph (27) [formerly (24)] excludes from the definition of "governmental unit" a United States trustee while serving in a case under title 11.

This section was amended to reflect the creation of a permanent United States trustee system. Section 302(d) of the 1986 Amendments provided different effective dates for the amendments relating to the United States trustee system; except for the districts in Alabama and North Carolina, all judicial districts have United States trustees. *See* Section 302 of the 1986 Amendments, as amended by Pub. L. No. 101-650 (1990), reprinted herein under "Selected Provisions of the Bankruptcy Judges, United States Trustees, and Family Farmer Bankruptcy Act of 1986," regarding effective dates generally.

1988 Amendments: Subsection "(n)" was added to section 365 concerning the rights of licensors and licensees of intellectual property where a case is commenced under the Bankruptcy Code (Pub. L. No. 100-506, 100th Cong., 2d Sess. 1988). Section 101 was also amended to define the terms "intellectual property" and "mask work." ("Mask work," defined in 17 U.S.C. § 901(a)(2), is a highly technical term relating to semi-conductor chip products.)

Pub. L. No. 100-597 added a new paragraph "(C)" the definition of "insolvent," giving a special definition for municipalities. The existing definition of insolvent, generally that liabilities exceed nonexempt assets, does not really apply to municipalities. Most of the assets of a municipality are exempt and cannot be used for the repayment of debt. Accordingly, the liabilities of even financially sound municipalities will in most cases exceed their nonexempt assets, and under existing law, these municipalities would be considered insolvent. The change made by the amendment corrects this, and ensures that financially sound municipalities will not be considered insolvent.

1990 Amendments: Pub. L. No. 101–311 amended title 11 to clarify the status of swap transactions in the event that a case is commenced under title 11. In section 101, four definitions were added and two others were modified.

Clarifying language was added to the definition of "forward contract" and to the definition of "forward contract merchant."

The four definitions added by Pub. L. No. 101–311 are as follows:

"margin payment;"

"settlement payment;"

"swap agreement;" and

"swap participant."

For other provisions of title 11 which were amended or added by Pub. L. No. 101–311, *see* sections 362(b)(6), 362(b)(14), 546(e), 546(g), 548(d)(2)(B), 548(d)(2)(D), 553(b)(1), 556 and 560.

Pub. L. No. 101-647 (Crime Control Act of 1990) amended section 101 (effective on the date of enactment, November 29, 1990) by redesignating paragraphs (3) through (31) as paragraphs (4) through (32) and adding a definition as paragraph (3) for "federal depository institutions regulatory agency." The Act also redesignated paragraphs (32) through (53) as paragraphs (36) through (57) and added three definitions as paragraphs (33), (34) and (35): paragraph (33), as added, defines "institution-affiliated party," paragraph (34) provides the definition for "insured credit union" and paragraph (35) defines "insured depository institution."

However, with the enactment of Pub. L. No. 101-647, an error exists in the numbering of paragraphs at the end of section 101. Prior to the enactment of Pub. L. No. 101-647, Pub. L. No. 101-311 (An Act to Amend Title 11 of the United States Code Regarding Swap Agreements and Forward Contracts), which was enacted on June 25, 1990, had added four paragraphs to section 101 and redesignated other paragraphs, resulting in the last paragraph of the section being redesignated as paragraph (57). Because the drafters of Pub. L. No. 101-647 did not take into account the redesignation of paragraphs by Pub. L. No. 101-311, section 101 now contains two each of numbered paragraphs (54) through (57):

(54) "stockbroker" . . . ;

(55) "swap agreement" . . . ;

(56) "swap participant" . . . ;

(57) "timeshare plan" . . . ;

(54) "transfer" . . . ;

(55) "United States" . . . ;

(56) "intellectual property" . . . ; and

(57) "mask work" . . . .

1992 Amendments: Paragraph (21A) defining "farmout agreement" was added by Pub. L. No. 102-486 ("Energy Policy Act of 1992"). Pub. L. No. 102-486 also added language at the end of section 541(b), commencing with paragraph (4), which excludes from the estate interests pursuant to farmout agreements when those interests would otherwise be included in the estate only by virtue of sections 365 and 544(a)(3). The amendments take effect on the date of enactment, October 23, 1992, but do not apply to cases commenced under title 11 prior to the date of enactment.

Case Annotations

Although federal law controls the definition of a "transfer," state law provides, in the absence of controlling federal law, the construction of "parting with property or with an interest in property" appearing in the section 101 definition of "transfer." For the purposes of payment by ordinary check, a "transfer" occurs on the date of honor in the determination of whether such transfer falls within the 90 day preference period under section 547(b): when a debtor has directed a drawee bank to honor a check and the bank has done so, the debtor has implemented a "mode, direct or indirect . . . of disposing of or parting with property or an interest in property." Barnhill v. Johnson, 503 U.S. —, 112 S. Ct. 1386, 118 L. Ed. 2d 39, 26 C.B.C.2d 323 (1992).

A mortgage interest that survives the discharge of a debtor's personal liability in an earlier case is a "claim" within the terms of section 101(5) and is subject to inclusion in a confirmed chapter 13 plan. Even after a debtor's personal liability has been discharged, a mortgage holder still retains a "right to payment" stemming from its right to the proceeds from the sale of the debtor's property. Johnson v. Home State Bank, 501 U.S. —, 111 S. Ct. 2150, 115 L. Ed 2d 66, 24 C.B.C.2d 1171 (1991).

Restitution obligations constitute debts within the meaning of section 101 and are therefore dischargeable under chapter 13. Pennsylvania Dept. of Public Welfare v. Davenport, 495 U.S. —, 110 S. Ct. 2126, 109 L. Ed. 2d 588, 22 C.B.C.2d 1067 (1990). [*Ed. Note:* Section 1328(a) was amended in 1990 to render restitution claims arising from criminal judgments nondischargeable in chapter 13 cases. *See* Crime Control Act of 1990, Pub. L. No. 101-647.]

The right to performance of a stipulation to clean up a hazardous waste site that obligates the debtor to pay a sum of money to recompense the State for cleanup efforts initiated on the debtor's behalf constitutes a dischargeable claim within the meaning of the Code. Ohio v. Kovacs, 469 U.S. 274, 105 S. Ct. 705, 83 L. Ed. 2d 649, 11 C.B.C.2d 1067 (1985).

The term "claim" is broad enough to encompass an unliquidated, contingent right to payment under a prepetition indemnification agreement, even though the triggering contingency does not occur until after the filing of a petition under the Bankruptcy Code. Consequently, a creditor seeking eventually to enforce such an agreement is obligated to file a timely proof of claim. *In re* Hemingway Transport, Inc., 954 F.2d 1, 26 C.B.C.2d 372 (1st Cir. 1992).

An environmental cleanup order that achieves the dual objectives of removing accumulated wastes and stopping or ameliorating ongoing pollution emanating from such wastes is a nondischargeable claim. *In re* Chateaugay Corp., 944 F.2d 997, 25 C.B.C.2d 620 (2d Cir. 1991).

The Code does not require that a "debt" be a contractual liability, and the status of the bankruptcy courts as courts of equity gives them the power to look behind the form of a transaction, even to the extent of finding that a restitutionary claim constitutes "debt." *In re* United Energy Corp., 944 F.2d 589, 25 C.B.C.2d 740 (9th Cir. 1991).

The language contained in the section 101 definition of "transfer" is sufficiently broad to encompass a leveraged buyout transaction. Mellon Bank, N.A. v. Metro Communications, Inc. and the Pacific 10 Conference v. The Committee of Unsecured Creditors, 945 F.2d 635, 25 C.B.C.2d 1064 (3d Cir. 1991).

A bankruptcy court does not abuse its discretion when it holds that a trustee in jointly administered cases who fails to make required disclosures and who asserts interdebtor claims is not a disinterested person. *In re* BH&P Inc., 949 F.2d 1300, 26 C.B.C.2d 37 (3d Cir. 1991).

A debtor is considered a family farmer for the purposes of subparagraph (A) of the section 101 definition of "family farmer" when there is evidence of a significant contribution to crop production, even if the farm land is rented. *In re* Edwards, 924 F.2d 798, 24 C.B.C.2d 1194 (8th Cir. 1991).

In determining insider status, both the Bankruptcy Code and applicable case law uphold the proposition that control of a debtor is a sufficient basis for insider status; a formal relationship between the parties is persuasive but not a necessary factor. In the Matter of Fabricators, Inc., 926 F.2d 1548, 24 C.B.C.2d 1489 (5th Cir. 1991).

A chapter 7 trustee has no standing to oppose the motion of a partnership debtor's general partner for dismissal on behalf of any creditor because a partnership interest is not a "claim" within the meaning of subparagraph (A) of the section 101 definition of "claim," so that the partnership is not a creditor and the trustee may not act on its behalf. *In re* Riverside-Linden Inv. Co., 925 F.2d 320, 24 C.B.C.2d 1210 (9th Cir. 1991).

The critical aspect of the definition of stockbroker is the requirement that the securities dealer have customers; absent customers, the securities dealer cannot qualify as a stockbroker. In the Matter of Wider, 907 F.2d 570, 24 C.B.C.2d 104 (5th Cir. 1990).

A stone crabbing operation which is not conducted on debtors' property does not constitute a farming operation. *In re* Watford, 898 F.2d 1525, 22 C.B.C.2d 1286 (11th Cir. 1990).

When a debtor's ex-spouse has been awarded a share of the debtor's pension as her "sole and separate" property under the terms of a state court decree dissolving the parties' marriage, the ex-spouse's claim for postpetition arrearages is not discharged by the bankruptcy, as the payments not due and payable at the time the petition was filed do not represent a debt under the Code. Bush v. Taylor, 912 F.2d 989, 23 C.B.C.2d 1294 (8th Cir. 1990).

Although persons not listed as creditors in the bankruptcy petition may be denied relief as part of the pool of general creditors, they may nevertheless be creditors of the debtor. *In re* C-L Cartage Co., Inc., 899 F.2d 1490, 22 C.B.C.2d 901 (6th Cir. 1990).

In determining whether a transfer is made while the debtor is insolvent under section 547(b), because the value of property varies with time and circumstances, the finder of fact must be free to arrive at the "fair valuation" defined in section 101 by the most appropriate means. Solvency and the valuations by which solvency are determined are not matters proved in only one way. Porter and Jarboe v. Yukon Nat'l Bank, 866 F.2d 355, 20 C.B.C.2d 905 (10th Cir. 1989).

A corporate debtor which leases farmland to a tenant farmer must play an active role in the farming operation to satisfy the conduct requirement of section 101. *In re* Tim Wargo & Sons, Inc., 869 F.2d 1128, 20 C.B.C.2d 1362 (8th Cir. 1989).

A guarantor of a claim against a debtor falls within the definition of a creditor, as the guarantor holds a contingent claim against the debtor which will become fixed when he pays the creditor whose claim he has guaranteed. *In re* Robinson Bros. Drilling, Inc., 892 F.2d 850, 21 C.B.C.2d 1405 (10th Cir. 1989).

Consumer debt may include debt secured by real property. Debt derived from the purchase of a home and the making of improvements thereon is a consumer debt. Zolg v. Kelly (*In re* Kelly), 841 F.2d 908, 18 C.B.C.2d 560 (9th Cir. 1988).

When the government has the requisite knowledge of its right to payment based on a breach of contract by one of its suppliers five months before confirmation of the debtor-supplier's chapter 11 plan, the claim is deemed to have arisen at that time under the Code's broad definition of claim, even though the claim is not deemed to be such by the Contract Disputes Act of 1978 until almost five years after confirmation. The Kilbarr Corp. v. General Services Administration (*In re* Remington Rand Corp.), 836 F.2d 825, 18 C.B.C.2d 367 (3d Cir. 1988).

In the definition of "family farmer" in section 101, the parenthetical exclusion of the debt for principal residence is written in ordinary language and has plain meaning and was not intended to modify the $1.5 million aggregate debt limitation. Reiners v. Federal Land Bank of Jackson (In the Matter of Reiners), 846 F.2d 1012, 19 C.B.C.2d 76 (5th Cir. 1988).

For purposes of the insolvency test under section 101, if there is a contingent asset or contingent liability, that asset or liability must be reduced to its present, or expected, value. In the Matter of Xonics Photochemical, Inc., 841 F.2d 198, 18 C.B.C.2d 711 (7th Cir. 1988).

A state law-based claim for breach of warranty asserted against a debtor is a claim against the estate. Southeastern Sprinkler Co. v. Meyertech Corp. (In re Meyertech Corp.), 831 F.2d 410, 18 C.B.C.2d 34 (3d Cir. 1987).

The existence of a state "certificate of public convenience" designating a railroad-debtor as a "common carrier," without more, is inconclusive of the railroad's status as a common carrier for purposes of applying subchapter IV of chapter 11. Wheeling-Pittsburgh Steel Corp. v. McCune, 836 F.2d 153, 17 C.B.C.2d 1471 (3d Cir. 1987).

"Up front" rental income from farm land belonging to the debtor cannot be counted as income from a farming operation for purposes of determining whether the debtor is a farmer since it is not the product of a risk-laden venture in the nature of farming as Congress contemplated. Armstong v. Corn Belt Bank, 812 F.2d 1024, 16 C.B.C.2d 238 (7th Cir. 1987), cert. denied, 484 U.S. 925, 108 S. Ct. 287, 98 L. Ed. 2d 248 (1987).

With respect to a state bar association's involvement in disciplinary matters, it is an instrumentality of the state supreme court engaged in a governmental function and therefore a "governmental unit." In re Wade, 23 C.B.C.2d 41 (9th Cir., B.A.P., 1990).

In order to be found insolvent for purposes of chapter 9 eligibility, a municipality must prove that it will be unable to pay its debts as they become due in the current fiscal year or, based on an adopted budget, in the next fiscal year. The bankruptcy court should then apply a prospective analysis with respect to the debtor's ability to pay its debts and examine the debtor's cash flow, not the debtor's projected budget deficits. In re The City of Bridgeport, 25 C.B.C.2d 269 (B. Ct., D. Conn. 1991).

In applying the section 101 definition of "transfer" to a tax sale under state law, three distinct "transfers" occur: first, when the tax lien attaches to the debtor's property upon the debtor's failure to pay property taxes; second, when the property is sold at a tax sale and the tax sale purchaser acquires a lien as represented by a Certificate of Purchase; and third, when the tax deed itself is issued to the tax sale purchaser upon perfection of the deed and the expiration of the applicable redemption period. In re McKeever, 25 C.B.C.2d 1260 (B. Ct., N.D. Ill. 1991).

References

2 *Collier on Bankruptcy* ch. 101 (Matthew Bender 15th ed.).

1 *Collier Bankruptcy Manual* ch. 101 (Matthew Bender 3d ed.).

1 *Collier Bankruptcy Practice Guide* ch. 1 (Matthew Bender).

Blinn and Bonds, III, *The Bankruptcy Amendments Act of 1984: Something for Everyone,* 47 Tex. B.J. 1050 (1984).

Chatz and Schumm, III, *1984 Bankruptcy Code Amendments—Fresh from the Anvil,* 89 Com. L.J. 317 (1984).

Comment, *The Second Circuit's Novel Approach to Defining Debt Under the Bankruptcy Code: In re Robinson,* 60 St. John's L. Rev. 344 (1986).

Ferguson, *Does Payment by Check Constitute a Transfer Upon Delivery of Payment?,* 64 Am. Bankr. L.J. 93 (1990).

The Intellectual Property Bankruptcy Protection Act: The Legislative Response to Lubrizol Enterprises, Inc. v. Richmond Metal Finishers, Inc., 756 F.2d 1043, [12 C.B.C.2d 310], 16 Rutgers Computer & Tech. L.J. 603 (1990).

Mabey and Jarvis, *In re Frenville: A Critique by the National Bankruptcy Conference's Committee on Claims and Distributions,* 42 Bus. Law. 697 (1987).

Miller, *The Red and the Black — Determining Insolvency for Avoidance of a Transfer,* 1 F & G Bankr. L. Rev. 56 (1989).

Note, *The 1984 Bankruptcy Amendments—Another Flawed Compromise,* 46 Ohio St. L.J. 1035 (1985).

Snider, Rochkind, Green, Stein and Welford, *The Bankruptcy Amendments and Federal Judgeship Act of 1978,* 63 Mich. B.J. 775 (1984).

Thomson, *The Effective Date of Transfers by Check Under Section 547(c)(4) of the Bankruptcy Code: In Support of the Delivery Rule,* 95 Com. L.J. 217 (1990).

SECTION 102 (11 U.S.C. § 102)

§ 102. **Rules of construction.** In this title—

(1) "after notice and a hearing", or a similar phrase—

(A) means after such notice as is appropriate in the particular circumstances, and such opportunity for a hearing as is appropriate in the particular circumstances; but

(B) authorizes an act without an actual hearing if such notice is given properly and if—

(i) such a hearing is not requested timely by a party in interest; or

(ii) there is insufficient time for a hearing to be commenced before such act must be done, and the court authorizes such act;

(2) "claim against the debtor" includes claim against property of the debtor;

(3) "includes" and "including" are not limiting;

(4) "may not" is prohibitive, and not permissive;

(5) "or" is not exclusive;

(6) "order for relief" means entry of an order for relief;

(7) the singular includes the plural;

(8) a definition, contained in a section of this title that refers to another section of this title, does not, for the purpose of such reference, affect the meaning of a term used in such other section; and

(9) "United States trustee" includes a designee of the United States trustee.

Bankruptcy Rule References: 2002 and 9001

Legislative History

Section 102 provides seven rules of construction. Some are derived from current law; others are derived from 1 U.S.C. § 1; a few are new. They apply generally throughout proposed title 11. These are terms that are not appropriate for definition, but that require an explanation.

Paragraph (1) defines the concept of "after notice and a hearing." The concept is central to the bill and to the separation of the administrative and judicial functions of bankruptcy judges. The phrase means after such notice as is appropriate in the particular circumstances (to be prescribed by either the Rules of Bankruptcy Procedure or by the court in individual circumstances that the Rules do not cover. In many cases, the Rules will provide for combined notice of several proceedings), and such opportunity for a hearing as is appropriate in the particular circumstances. Thus, a hearing will not be necessary in every instance. If there is no objection to the proposed action, the action may go ahead without court action. This is a significant change from present law, which requires the affirmative approval of the bankruptcy judge for almost every action. The change will permit the bankruptcy judge to stay removed from the administration of the bankruptcy or reorganization case, and to become involved only when there is a dispute about a proposed action, that is, only when there is an objection. The phrase "such opportunity for a hearing as is appropriate in the particular circumstances" is designed to permit the Rules and the courts to expedite or dispense with hearings when speed is essential. The language "or similar phrase" is intended to cover the few instances in the bill where "after notice and a hearing" is interrupted by another phrase, such as "after notice to the debtor and a hearing."

[*House Report No. 95–595, 95th Cong., 1st Sess. 315 (1977); Senate Report No. 95–989, 95th Cong., 2d Sess. 27 (1978).*]

Section 102 specifies various rules of construction but is not exclusive. Other rules of construction that are not set out in title 11 are nevertheless intended to be followed in construing the bankruptcy code. For example, the phrase "on request of a party in interest" or a similar phrase, is used in connection with an action that the court may take in various sections of the Code. The phrase is intended to restrict the court from acting sua sponte. Rules of bankruptcy procedure or court decisions will determine who is a party in interest for the particular purposes of the provision in question, but the court will not be permitted to act on its own.

Although "property" is not construed in this section, it is used consistently throughout the code in its broadest sense, including cash, all interests in property, such as liens, and every kind of consideration including promises to act or forbear to act as in section 548(d).

Section 102(1) expands on a rule of construction contained in H.R. 8200 as passed by the House and in the Senate amendment. The phrase "after notice and a hearing", or a similar phrase, is intended to be construed according to the particular proceeding to mean after such notice as is appropriate in the particular circumstances, and such opportunity, if any, for a hearing as is appropriate in the particular circumstances. If a provision of title II [*sic;* should be 11] authorizes an act be taken "after notice and a hearing" this means that if appropriate notice is given and no party to whom such notice is sent timely requests a hearing, then the act sought to be taken may be taken without an actual hearing.

In very limited emergency circumstances, there will be insufficient time for a hearing to be commenced before an action must be taken. The action sought to be taken may be taken if authorized by the court at an ex parte hearing of which a record is made in open court. A full hearing after the fact will be available in such an instance.

In some circumstances, such as under section 1128, the bill requires a hearing and the court may act only after a hearing is held. In those circumstances the judge will receive evidence before ruling. In other circumstances, the court may taken action "after notice and a hearing," if no party in interest requests a hearing. In that event a court order authorizing the action to be taken is not necessary as the ultimate action taken by the court implies such an authorization.

[*124 Cong. Rec. H 11,090 (Sept. 28, 1978); S 17,407 (Oct. 6, 1978).*]

Paragraph (2) specifies that "claim against the debtor" includes claim against property of the debtor. This paragraph is intended to cover nonrecourse loan agreements where the creditor's only rights are against property of the debtor, and not against the debtor personally. Thus, such an agreement would give rise to a claim that would be treated as a claim against the debtor personally, for the purposes of the bankruptcy code. However, it would not entitle the holders of the claim to distribution other than from the property in which the holder had an interest.

Paragraph (3) is a codification of American Surety Co. v. Marotta, 287 U.S. 513 (1933). It specifies that "includes" and "including" are not limiting.

Paragraph (4) specifies that "may not" is prohibitive and not permissive (such as in "might not").

Paragraph (5) specifies that "or" is not exclusive. Thus, if a party "may do (a) or (b)," then the party may do either or both. The party is not limited to a mutually exclusive choice between the two alternatives.

Paragraph (6) makes clear that "order for relief" means entry of an order for relief. If the court orally orders relief, but the order is not entered until a later time, then any time measurements in the bill are from entry, not from the oral order. In a voluntary case, the entry of the order for relief is the filing of the petition commencing the voluntary case.

Paragraph (7) specifies that the singular includes the plural. The plural, however, generally does not include the singular. The bill uses only the singular, even when the item in question most often is found in plural quantities, in order to avoid the confusion possible if both rules of construction applied. When an item is specified in the plural, the plural is intended.

[*House Report No. 95–595, 95th Cong., 1st Sess. 316 (1977); Senate Report No. 95–989, 95th Cong., 2d Sess. 28 (1978).*]

Section 102(8) is new. It contains a rule of construction indicating that a definition contained in a section in title 11 that refers to another section of title 11 does not, for the purposes of such reference, take the meaning of a term used in the other section. For example, section 522(a)(2) defines "value" for the purposes of section 522. Section 548(d)(2) defines "value" for purposes of section 548. When section 548 is incorporated by reference in section 522, this rule of construction makes clear that the definition of "value" in section 548 governs its meaning in section 522 notwithstanding a different definition of "value" in section 522(a)(2).

[*124 Cong. Rec. H 11,090–1 (Sept. 28, 1978); S 17,407 (Oct 6, 1978).*]

Comment

There was no rule in the former Bankruptcy Act construing "after notice and hearing." When notice is to be given pursuant to the Bankruptcy Rules, if not otherwise specified, the time within which, the entities to whom, and the form and manner of notice shall be designated by the court. Rule 9007.

Bankruptcy Rule 2002(a) prescribes the significant events in a bankruptcy case that require 20 days notice; Rule 2002(b) lists events requiring 25 days notice; and Rule 2002(d) prescribes what notices must be given to equity security holders in a chapter 11 case. Subdivision (f) of the Rule provides for other notices to be given without prescribing any specific time period. Subdivision (k) specifies the notice required to be transmitted to the United States trustee. Bankruptcy Rule 2002 was amended by the 1991 Amendments to the Bankruptcy Rules and Official Forms, effective August 1, 1991.

The final sentence of the House Report, *supra,* does not appear in the Senate Report and that sentence is not wholly accurate. As enacted, the Code may permit conversion of a nonrecourse claim to recourse in a rehabilitation case. *See* section 1111(b).

There was no comparable provision construing "claim against the debtor" in the former Bankruptcy Act.

The Bankruptcy Code eliminates the term "adjudication." Under 11 U.S.C. § 301 the commencement of a voluntary case under a chapter of title 11 "constitutes an order for relief under such chapter." Therefore, the "order for relief" under chapter 7, the liquidation chapter is not unlike an "adjudication" under the Bankruptcy Act.

1986 Amendments: Paragraph (9) was added to provide that "United States trustee" includes a designee of the United States trustee. This permits the United States trustees to delegate certain duties as, for example, presiding at a meeting of creditors.

This section was amended to reflect the creation of a permanent United States trustee system. Section 302(d) of the 1986 Amendments provided different effective dates for the amendments relating to the United States trustee system; except for the districts in Alabama and North Carolina, all judicial districts have United States trustees. *See* Section 302 of the 1986 Amendments, as amended by Pub. L. No. 101-650 (1990), reprinted herein under "Selected Provisions of the Bankruptcy Judges, United States Trustees, and Family Farmer Bankruptcy Act of 1986," regarding effective dates generally.

Case Annotations

The rule of construction set forth in section 102(2) establishes that the phrase "claim against the debtor" includes a claim against the property of the debtor; an obligation enforceable only against a debtor's property is a "claim against the debtor" for purposes of the Code. Johnson v. Home State Bank, 501 U.S. —, 111 S. Ct. 2150, 115 L. Ed. 2d 66, 24 C.B.C.2d 1171 (1991).

In an emergency situation, a bankruptcy court order granting a debtor's banks superpriority under section 364(c) may be on short notice to unsecured creditors. Unsecured Creditors' Comm. v. First Nat'l Bank

& Trust Co. of Escanaba (*In re* Ellingsen MacLean Oil Co.), 834 F.2d 599, 17 C.B.C.2d 1402 (6th Cir. 1987), *cert. denied*, 488 U.S. 817, 109 S. Ct. 55, 102 L. Ed. 2d 33 (1988).

A general rule of textual construction is that the expression or inclusion of one thing is the exclusion of others. *In re* Eaton, 25 C.B.C.2d 430 (B. Ct., S.D. Idaho 1991).

Since all parties who objected to the debtor's modification of its plan were present and represented by counsel, the court deemed notice sufficient under the circumstances even though the modification hearing was conducted along with the confirmation hearing. *In re* American Solar King Corp., 20 C.B.C.2d 547 (B. Ct., W.D. Tex. 1988).

The "notice and a hearing" requirements of section 102(1) have not been met in the context of a debtor's effort to obtain credit under section 364 when notice is given to creditors of a pending emergency disbursement of funds, but not of incurring debt to do so, and when notice is not attempted by telephone; even under emergency conditions, notice without a hearing is mandatory. *In re* Monach Circuit Indus., Inc., 11 C.B.C.2d 312 (B. Ct., E.D. Pa. 1984).

References

2 *Collier on Bankruptcy* ch. 102 (Matthew Bender 15th ed.).

1 *Collier Bankruptcy Manual* ch. 102 (Matthew Bender 3d ed.).

1 *Collier Bankruptcy Practice Guide* ch. 1 (Matthew Bender).

SECTION 103 (11 U.S.C. § 103)

§ 103. Applicability of chapters.

(a) Except as provided in section 1161 of this title, chapters 1, 3, and 5 of this title apply in a case under chapter 7, 11, 12, or 13 of this title.

(b) Subchapters I and II of chapter 7 of this title apply only in a case under such chapter.

(c) Subchapter III of chapter 7 of this title applies only in a case under such chapter concerning a stockbroker.

(d) Subchapter IV of chapter 7 of this title applies only in a case under such chapter concerning a commodity broker.

(e) Except as provided in section 901 of this title, only chapters 1 and 9 of this title apply in a case under such chapter 9.

(f) Except as provided in section 901 of this title, subchapters I, II, and III of chapter 11 of this title apply only in a case under such chapter.

(g) Subchapter IV of chapter 11 of this title applies only in a case under such chapter concerning a railroad.

(h) Chapter 13 of this title applies only in a case under such chapter.

(i) Chapter 12 of this title applies only in a case under such chapter.

Legislative History

Section 103 prescribes which chapters of the proposed bankruptcy code apply in various cases. All cases, other than cases ancillary to foreign proceedings, are filed under chapter 7, 9, 11, or 13, the operative chapters of the proposed Bankruptcy Code. The general provisions that apply no matter which chapter a case is filed under are found in chapters 1, 3, and 5. Subsection (a) makes this explicit, with an exception for chapter 9. The other provisions, which are self-explanatory, provide the special rules for Stockbroker Liquidations, Commodity Broker Liquidations, Municipal Debt Adjustments, and Railroad Reorganizations.

[*House Report No. 95–595, 95th Cong., 1st Sess. 316 (1977); Senate Report No. 95–989, 95th Cong., 2d Sess. 28 (1978).*]

Under Section 2 [of Public Law 97–222] the exception contained in section 103(d) of title 11 is deleted since the section to which it refers, section 764(c), is deleted. The original reference in section 103(d) to "Section 746(c)" was a typographical error; the reference should have been to "Section 764(c)."

[*House Report No. 97–420, 97th Cong., 2d Sess. 3 (1982).*]

Comment

The structure of the Code is radically different from the former Bankruptcy Act. Under the Code, cases are filed under one of the five operative chapters: 7, 9, 11, 12, or 13, although there is provision for conversion from one chapter to another. Additionally, chapters 7 and 11 have special subchapters relating to the unique problems of stock and commodity brokers and railroad reorganizations.

Chapter 7, liquidation, applies equally to business and consumer cases. Chapter 11 is primarily designed for business cases but may be used by an individual. Chapter 12, relating to adjustment of debts of a family farmer with regular annual income is limited to a "family farmer" as defined in section 101. A family farmer may be an individual or an individual and spouse, or a corporation or partnership that come within the definition of section 101. Moreover, to be eligible for chapter 12, the family farmer must be one with a regular income as defined in section 101. The debt ceiling in chapter 12 is $1,500,000 which permits a family farmer to obtain relief when that farmer could not under chapter 13 which has a considerably lower debt ceiling. Chapter 13, relating to adjustment of debts of an individual with regular income is limited to individuals but not limited to wage earners. Small proprietorships are also permitted to use this chapter. There is a debt ceiling in chapter 13 cases: only an individual who owes noncontingent, liquidated, unsecured debts of less than $100,000 and noncontingent, secured debts of less than $350,000 may be a chapter 13 debtor. There is a like ceiling when an individual and spouse seek to become chapter 13 debtors jointly.

A distinguishing feature of the Code is that the general provisions of chapters 1, 3, and 5 apply no matter under which chapter a case is filed. The provisions in chapters 1, 3, and 5 are not divided along consumer—business lines. Section 103 sets forth self-explanatory exceptions where certain provisions are applicable only under a particular chapter.

Certain provisions, such as discharge, apply only to individuals and not to partnerships or corporations—a distinction based on the kind of entity, not whether the entity is a consumer or business, because frequently individual cases involve small sole proprietorships. These are really business cases, but the needs of the sole proprietor are often the same as the needs of a typical consumer debtor. *See* House Report No. 95–595, 95th Cong., 1st Sess. (1978) 6.

1986 Amendments: Subsection (i) was added to conform § 103 to chapter 12, which was also added in 1986.

Case Annotations

The bankruptcy court cannot interpret subsequent legislation as repealing or modifying the Bankruptcy Code by implication. United Steelworkers of Am. v. Jones & Lamson Machine Co. (*In re* Jones & Lamson Machine Co.), 17 C.B.C.2d 405 (B. Ct., D. Conn. 1987).

Section 522 does not apply to chapter 13 cases for purposes of lien avoidance. Berry v. Pattison (*In re* Berry), 8 C.B.C.2d 967 (B. Ct., E.D. Mich. 1983).

Although chapters 1, 3 and 5 generally apply in a case under chapter 13, a specific provision of chapter 13 that conflicts with a general provision of chapters 1, 3 or 5 controls and should be interpreted as an exception to the general provision. In the Matter of Aycock, 5 C.B.C.2d 856 (B. Ct., E.D.N.C. 1981).

Section 1325(a)(5) is only applicable in chapter 13 cases and can not be applied to an attempt by the debtor to redeem property under section 722 by making installment payments. *In re* Miller, 2 C.B.C.2d 259 (B. Ct., E.D. Mich. 1980).

References

2 *Collier on Bankruptcy* ch. 103 (Matthew Bender 15th ed.).

1 *Collier Bankruptcy Manual* ch. 103 (Matthew Bender 3d ed.).

1 *Collier Bankruptcy Practice Guide* ch. 1 (Matthew Bender).

SECTION 104 (11 U.S.C. § 104)

§ 104. **Adjustment of dollar amounts.** The Judicial Conference of the United States shall transmit to the Congress and to the President before May 1, 1985, and before May 1 of every sixth year after May 1, 1985, a recommendation for the uniform percentage adjustment of each dollar amount in this title and in section 1930 of title 28.

Legislative History

This section requires the Judicial Conference to report to the Congress every four years after the effective date of the bankruptcy code any changes that have occurred in the cost of living during the preceding four years, and the appropriate adjustments to the dollar amounts in the bill. The dollar amounts are found primarily in the exemption section (11 U.S.C. § 522), the wage priority (11 U.S.C. § 507), and the eligibility for chapter 13 (11 U.S.C. § 109). This section requires that the Conference recommend uniform percentage changes in these amounts based solely on cost of living changes. The dollar amounts in the bill would not change on that recommendation, absent Congressional veto. Instead, Congress is required to take affirmative action, by passing a law amending the appropriate section, if it wishes to accomplish change.

If the Judicial Conference has policy recommendations concerning the appropriate dollar amounts in the bankruptcy code based other than on cost of living considerations there are adequate channels through which it may communicate its views. This section is solely for the housekeeping function of maintaining the dollar amounts in the code at fairly constant real dollar levels.

[*House Report No. 95–595, 95th Cong., 1st Sess. 316 (1977).*]

This section requires that the Director of the Administrative Office of the United States Courts report to Congress and the President before Oct. 1, 1985, and before May 1 every six years thereafter a recommendation for adjustment in dollar amounts found in this title. The Committee feels that regular adjustment of the dollar amounts by the Director will conserve congressional time and yet assure that the relative dollar amounts used in the bill are maintained. Changes in the cost of living should be a significant, but not necessarily the only, factor considered by the Director. The fact that there has been an increase in the cost of living does not necessarily mean that an adjustment of dollar amounts would be needed or warranted.

[*Senate Report No. 95–989, 95th Cong., 2d Sess. 28–9 (1978).*]

Section 104 represents a compromise between the House bill and the Senate amendment with respect to the adjustment of dollar amounts in title 11. The House amendment authorizes the Judicial Conference of the United States to transmit a recommendation for the uniform percentage of adjustment for each dollar amount in title 11 and in 28 U.S.C. § 1930 to the Congress and to the President before May 1, 1985, and before May 1 of every sixth year thereafter. The requirement in the House bill that each such recommendation be based only on any change in the cost-of-living increase during the period immediately preceding the recommendation is deleted.

[*124 Cong. Rec. H 11,091 (Sept. 28, 1978); S 17,407 (Oct. 6, 1978).*]

References

2 *Collier on Bankruptcy* ch. 104 (Matthew Bender 15th ed.).

1 *Collier Bankruptcy Manual* ch. 104 (Matthew Bender 3d ed.).

Aldisert, *The Judicial Conference and the New Bankruptcy Act*, 65 A.D.A.J. 229 (1979).

SECTION 105 (11 U.S.C. § 105)

§ 105. Power of court.

(a) The court may issue any order, process, or judgment that is necessary or appropriate to carry out the provisions of this title. No provision of this title providing for the raising of an issue by a party in interest shall be construed to preclude the court from, sua sponte, taking any action or making any determination necessary or appropriate to enforce or implement court orders or rules, or to prevent an abuse of process.

(b) Notwithstanding subsection (a) of this section, a court may not appoint a receiver in a case under this title.

(c) The ability of any district judge or other officer or employee of a district court to exercise any of the authority or responsibilities conferred upon the court under this title shall be determined by reference to the provisions relating to such judge, officer, or employee set forth in title 28. This subsection shall not be interpreted to exclude bankruptcy judges and other officers or employees appointed pursuant to chapter 6 of title 28 from its operation.

Bankruptcy Rule Reference: 9020

Legislative History

Section 105 is derived from section 2a(15) of present law, with two changes. First, the limitations on the power of a bankruptcy judge (powers that were reserved to the district judge) are removed as inconsistent with the separation of the two courts and the increased powers and jurisdiction of the new court. *But see* H.R. 8200 § 405(a)(1) for limitations during the transition period. Second, the bankruptcy judge is prohibited from appointing a receiver in a case under title 11 under any circumstances. The Bankruptcy Code has ample provision for the appointment of trustees when needed. Any appointment of a receiver would simply circumvent the established procedures.

Section 105 is similar in effect to the All Writs Statute, 28 U.S.C. § 1651 . . . The section is repeated here for the sake of continuity from current law and ease of reference, and to cover any powers traditionally exercised by a bankruptcy court that are not encompassed by the All Writs Statute.

This section is also an authorization, as required under 28 U.S.C. § 2283, for a court of the United States to stay the action of a state court. As such, Toucey v. New York Life Insurance Company, 314 U.S. 118 (1941), is overruled.

[House Report No. 95–595, 95th Cong., 1st Sess. 316 (1977).]

Section 105 is derived from section 2a(15) of present law, with two changes. First, the limitation on the power of a bankruptcy judge (the power to enjoin a court being reserved to the district judge) is removed as inconsistent with the increased powers and jurisdiction of the new bankruptcy court. Second, the bankruptcy judge is prohibited from appointing a receiver in a case under title 11 under any circumstances. The bankruptcy code has ample provision for the appointment of a trustee when needed. Appointment of a receiver would simply circumvent the established procedures.

This section is also an authorization, as required under 28 U.S.C. § 2283, for a court of the United States to stay the action of a state court. As such Toucey v. New York Life Insurance Company, 314 U.S. 118 (1941), is overruled.

[Senate Report No. 95–989, 95th Cong., 2d Sess. 29 (1978).]

Comment

The bill as enacted continues some limitations on the powers of the bankruptcy court; accordingly, the two Reports are not entirely accurate.

1984 Amendments: Section 105 was amended by deletion of the word "bankruptcy" wherever it appeared before the word "court" in subsections (a) and (b), and by adding subsection (c).

By not substituting "district court" for "bankruptcy court," section 105(a) authorizes the bankruptcy court, when a case has been referred, to issue any order, etc., necessary or appropriate to carry out the provisions of the Code. Section 105(a) is regarded by some as the source of the bankruptcy court's contempt power. The Ninth Circuit, however, has ruled that neither section 105 of the Code nor 28 U.S.C. § 157 should be read to authorize implicitly bankruptcy judges to exercise the contempt power absent specific indications of Congressional intent to confer such power. Plastiras v. Idell (*In re* Sequoia Auto Brokers, Ltd.), 827 F.2d 1281, 17 C.B.C.2d 622 (9th Cir. 1987).

There is, however, a split among the courts on the issue. In Burd v. Walters (*In re* Walters), 868 F.2d 665, 669 (4th Cir. 1989), the Court of Appeals for the Fourth Circuit concluded that section 105(a) authorized the bankruptcy judge to utilize civil contempt powers to enforce compliance with its orders. The Tenth Circuit also disagreed with the Ninth Circuit in Mountain American Credit Union v. Skinner (*In re* Skinner), 917 F.2d 444 (10th Cir. 1990). For an excellent discussion of the contempt power of the bankruptcy court under section 105(a), *see* In the Matter of Donnig, 98 B.R. 935 (B. Ct., N.D. Ind. 1989).

1986 Amendments: The addition of the second sentence in section 105(a) effectively abrogates the rule of *In re* Gusam Restaurant, 737 F.2d 274, 10 C.B.C.2d 1203 (2d Cir. 1984), which held that when a Code provision required a request by a party in interest, the bankruptcy court could not act *sua sponte.*

This section was amended to reflect the creation of a permanent nationwide United States trustee system. Section 302(d) of the 1986 Amendments provided different effective dates for the amendments relating to the United States trustee system; except for the districts in Alabama and North Carolina, all judicial districts have United States trustees. *See* Section 302 of the 1986 Amendments, as amended by the Judicial Improvements Act of 1990, Pub. L. No. 101-650 (1990), reprinted herein under "Selected Provisions of the Bankruptcy Judges, United States Trustees, and Family Farmer Bankruptcy Act of 1986," regarding effective dates generally; an amendment made to Section 302 by the Judicial Improvements Act of 1990 provides that the 1986 amendment to section 105(a) "shall become effective as of the date of the enactment of the Federal Courts Study Committee Implementation Act of 1990."

Case Annotations

The bankruptcy court may order the IRS to use a reorganized debtor's tax payments to eliminate trust fund obligations prior to offsetting any nontrust fund obligations when the bankruptcy court has concluded that the action is necessary for the reorganization to be successful. United States v. Energy Resources Co., Inc., 495 U.S. —, 110 S. Ct. 2139, 109 L. Ed. 2d 580, 22 C.B.C.2d 1093 (1990).

There is no express authority for substantive consolidation in the Code, but authority does exist through the bankruptcy court's general equitable powers set forth in section 105. FDIC v. Colonial Realty Co., 966 F.2d 57, 26 C.B.C.2d 1687 (2d Cir. 1992).

There are numerous factors which courts may use in deciding a motion for substantive consolidation, no single one of which is determinative. While not specifically authorized by the Bankruptcy Code, bankruptcy courts have the power to order substantive consolidation by virtue of their general equitable powers. The basic criterion for substantive consolidation is whether the economic prejudice of continued debtor separateness outweighs the economic prejudice of consolidation, *i.e.*, whether consolidation will yield benefits which offset the harm it may inflict. Eastgroup Properties v. Southern Motel Assoc., Ltd., 935 F.2d 245, 25 C.B.C.2d 158 (11th Cir. 1991).

The bankruptcy court has the inherent power to award sanctions for bad faith conduct in a bankruptcy court proceeding, but the inherent power does not reach to conduct which occurs outside the bankruptcy court. The bankruptcy court is without authority to order that sanctions levied against a debtor's attorney are nondischargeable because the court may only determine the dischargeability of debts owed by a debtor who has sought protection under the Bankruptcy Code. Matter of Case, 937 F.2d 1014, 25 C.B.C.2d 368 (5th Cir. 1991).

The bankruptcy court has the inherent power to enforce its own judgments and may set aside unauthorized assignments which are in direct contravention to a previous order of the court. *In re* Unioil, 948 F.2d 678, 25 C.B.C.2d 1493 (10th Cir. 1991).

A bankruptcy court's equitable power includes the authorization of late-filed claims, *i.e.*, the power to extend the bar date implies a corresponding power to permit late claims. This procedure is not otherwise permitted under the guidelines of Fed. R. Civ. P. 15(c). Such an equitable consideration would exist in the fact that the debtor provided for the claim in a proposed chapter 13 plan and had notice of creditor intent. Matter of Unroe, 937 F.2d 346, 25 C.B.C.2d 84 (7th Cir. 1991).

Even though section 105 of the Code was apparently intended to be a statutory exception to the Anti-Injunction Act, it is appropriate to use the principles of that Act to measure the bankruptcy court's power in a relitigation injunction situation. Therefore, when a stipulation executed by two parties to resolve a dispute, is incorporated by reference in a bankruptcy court order dismissing a case, it has the same effect as though the court had actually decided the issue. The bankruptcy court has the power to issue an injunction barring state court proceedings relating to the same issue and between the identical parties. *In re* G.S.F. Corp., 938 F.2d 1467, 25 C.B.C.2d 112 (1st Cir. 1991).

A state criminal proceeding to compel repayment of debts that are also the subject of the debtor's bankruptcy case does not amount to a threatened violation of the debtor's federal rights sufficient to support a federal court injunction of the state criminal proceeding. *In re* Fussell, 928 F.2d 712, 24 C.B.C.2d 1695 (5th Cir. 1991).

There is no authority in the Bankruptcy Code that permits a bankruptcy court to impose an indemnification requirement upon a creditor's attorney with respect to a sale of property of the debtor's estate, nor do the court's equitable powers permit indemnity to be imposed upon a creditor's attorney. *In re* Granger Garage, Inc., 921 F.2d 74, 24 C.B.C.2d 305 (6th Cir. 1990).

Although section 105 authorizes the bankruptcy court to issue orders, processes or judgments necessary to carry out the provisions of the Code, such authorization does not reach the imposition of punitive interest against a trustee for failure to timely refund monies owed the debtor as a residual part of the estate. Grant and Bergwerk v. George Schumann Tire & Battery Co., 908 F.2d 874, 23 C.B.C.2d 708 (11th Cir. 1990).

The bankruptcy court which confirmed a debtor's reorganization plan has jurisdiction to enter an injunction order enjoining a creditor from interfering with the debtor's confirmed reorganization plan, but the terms of the injunction must be sufficiently specific and detailed in order to comply with Rule 65(d) of the Fed. R. Civ. P. U.S.A. Dept. of Air Force v. Carolina Parachute Corp., 907 F.2d 1469, 23 C.B.C.2d 620 (4th Cir. 1990).

Section 105 of the Bankruptcy Code does not authorize the bankruptcy court to change the terms of a labor settlement agreement negotiated by a union on behalf of its members or to require acceptance of terms that do not enhance the success of the reorganization as the price for gaining the bankruptcy court's approval of the bankruptcy portions of the settlement. *In re* Continental Airlines Corp., 905 F.2d 883, 23 C.B.C.2d 821 (5th Cir. 1990).

The statutory language of section 105(a) is clear and unambiguous and empowers a bankruptcy court to impose monetary sanctions for civil contempt when necessary and appropriate to carry out the provisions of the Code. *In re* Skinner, 917 F.2d 444, 23 C.B.C.2d 1559 (10th Cir. 1990).

Pursuant to section 105(a), a bankruptcy court has the power to issue civil contempt orders and Congress' delegation of that authority to a non-Article III court is not unconstitutional. *In re* Walters, 868 F.2d 665, 22 C.B.C.2d 263 (4th Cir. 1989).

Under this provision, a court has the authority to enjoin actions which threaten the integrity of a debtor's estate; this includes the power to issue an injunction enjoining third parties from pursuing actions which are the exclusive property of a debtor's estate and are dismissed pursuant to a settlement agreement. In the Matter of Energy Cooperative, Inc., 886 F.2d 921, 22 C.B.C.2d 1224 (7th Cir. 1989).

Section 105(a) does not empower bankruptcy courts to issue orders that defeat rather than carry out explicit provisions of the Bankruptcy Code such as section 365(d)(4). Sea Harvest v. Riviera Land Co., 868 F.2d 1077, 20 C.B.C.2d 1269 (9th Cir. 1989).

The court has the power to enjoin a grant of relief from stay when the stay has lapsed by reason of the inadvertence of the court only if the debtor has properly applied for injunction pursuant to Bankruptcy Rule 7065. *In re* Wedgewood Realty Group, Ltd., 878 F.2d 693, 21 C.B.C.2d 203 (3d Cir. 1989).

Creation of an emergency treatment fund in a chapter 11 case for certain unsecured claimants before a plan of reorganization has been properly presented and approved, violates the language and intent of the Code and the clear policy of chapter 11 and is not justified as an exercise of the court's equitable powers under section 105(a). Official Comm. of Equity Sec. Holders v. Mabey, 832 F.2d 299, 17 C.B.C.2d 1210 (4th Cir. 1987), *cert. denied,* 485 U.S. 962, 108 S. Ct. 1228, 99 L. Ed. 2d 428 (1988).

With the enactment of the 1984 Bankruptcy Amendments, there is no longer an express statutory basis for bankruptcy judges to exercise the power of civil contempt, and section 105 of the Code and 28 U.S.C. § 157 should not be read to authorize implicitly that power absent indications of congressional intent to confer the contempt power. Plastiras v. Idell (*In re* Sequoia Auto Brokers, Ltd.), 827 F.2d 1281, 17 C.B.C.2d 622 (9th Cir. 1987). *See contra,* Burd v. Walters (*In re* Walters), 868 F.2d 665 (4th Cir. 1989).

A debtor who admittedly failed to comply with the Environmental Protection Agency's action to ensure that federal and state environmental laws were being adhered to is not entitled to an injunction under section 105 because the likelihood of success on the merits is nil. Commonwealth Oil Refining Co. v. United States Environmental Protection Agency (In the Matter of Commonwealth Oil Refining Co.), 805 F.2d 1175, 15 C.B.C.2d 1387 (5th Cir. 1986), *cert. denied,* 483 U.S. 1005, 107 S. Ct. 3228, 97 L. Ed. 2d 734 (1987).

References

2 *Collier on Bankruptcy* ch. 105 (Matthew Bender 15th ed.).

1 *Collier Bankruptcy Manual* ch. 105 (Matthew Bender 3d ed.).

2 *Collier Bankruptcy Practice Guide* ch. 39 (Matthew Bender).

3 *Collier Bankruptcy Practice Guide* ch. 40 (Matthew Bender).

Cohen and Hayes, *Contempt Proceedings: Another Dimension to Consumer Protection,* 44 Suffolk U.L. Rev. 1 (1980).

Contempt Power and the Bankruptcy Courts: The New Trend, 14 U. Dayton L. Rev. 335 (1989).

Conti, *An Analytical Model for Substantive Consolidation of Bankruptcy Cases,* 39 Bus. Law. 855 (1983).

Hendel and Reinhardt, *Inhibiting Post-Petition "Bad Check" Criminal Proceedings Against Debtors: The Need for Flexing More Judicial Muscle,* 89 Com. L.J. 236 (1984).

Kratsch and Young, *Criminal Prosecutions and Manipulative Restitution: The Use of State Criminal Courts for Contravention of Debtor Relief,* 1984 Ann. Surv. Bankr. L. 107.

Leal, *The Power of the Bankruptcy Court: Section 105,* 29 So. Tex. L. Rev. 487 (1988).

Mehler, *Criminal Prosecution and Restitution Under the Bankruptcy Code,* 1983 Ann. Surv. Am. L. 817 (1984).

Preemption's Effect on Younger v. Harris *Abstention: May a Bankruptcy Court Enjoin a State Criminal Prosecution?,* 35 Mercer L. Rev. 1345 (1984).

Tatelbaum, *The Multi-tiered Corporate Bankruptcy and Substantive Consolidation—Do Creditors Lose Rights and Protection?* 89 Com. L.J. 285 (1984).

Tilton and Wild, *Protecting Co-Obligors and Non-Debtor Guarantors,* N.Y.L.J., Nov. 14, 1991.

SECTION 106 (11 U.S.C. § 106)

§ 106.   Waiver of sovereign immunity.

(a) A governmental unit is deemed to have waived sovereign immunity with respect to any claim against such governmental unit that is property of the estate and that arose out of the same transaction or occurrence out of which such governmental unit's claim arose.

(b) There shall be offset against an allowed claim or interest of a governmental unit any claim against such governmental unit that is property of the estate.

(c) Except as provided in subsections (a) and (b) of this section and notwithstanding any assertion of sovereign immunity—

(1) a provision of this title that contains "creditor", "entity", or "governmental unit" applies to governmental units; and

(2) a determination by the court of an issue arising under such a provision binds governmental units.

Legislative History

Section 106 provides for a limited waiver of sovereign immunity in bankruptcy cases. Though Congress has the power to waive sovereign immunity for the Federal government completely in bankruptcy cases, the policy followed here is designed to achieve approximately the same result that would prevail outside of bankruptcy. Congress does not, however, have the power to waive sovereign immunity completely with respect to claims of [a] bankrupt estate against a State, though it may exercise its bankruptcy power through the supremacy clause to prevent or prohibit State action that is contrary to bankruptcy policy.

There is, however, a limited change in the result from the result that would prevail in the absence of bankruptcy; the change is two-fold and is within Congress' power *vis-a-vis* both the Federal Government and the States. First, the filing of a proof of claim against the estate by a governmental unit is a waiver by that governmental unit of sovereign immunity with respect to compulsory counterclaims, as defined in the Federal Rules of Civil Procedure, that is, counterclaims arising out of the same transaction or occurrence. The governmental unit cannot receive distribution from the estate without subjecting itself to any liability it has to the estate within the confines of a compulsory counterclaim rule. Any other result would be one-sided. The counterclaim by the estate against the governmental unit is without limit.

Second, the estate may offset against the allowed claim of a governmental unit, up to the amount of the governmental unit's claim, any claim that the debtor, and thus the estate, has against the governmental unit, without regard to whether the estate's claim arose out of the same transaction or occurrence as the government's claim. Under this provision, the setoff permitted is only to the extent of the governmental unit's claim. No affirmative recovery is permitted. Subsection (a) governs affirmative recovery.

Though this subsection creates a partial waiver of immunity when the governmental unit files a proof of claim, it does not waive immunity if the debtor or trustee, and not the governmental unit, files proof of a governmental unit's claim under proposed 11 U.S.C. § 501(c).

This section does not confer sovereign immunity on any governmental unit that does not already have immunity. It simply recognizes any immunity that exists and prescribes the proper treatment of claims by and against that sovereign.

[*House Report No. 95–595, 95th Cong., 1st Sess. 317 (1977); Senate Report No. 95–989, 95th Cong., 2d Sess. 29–30 (1978).*]

Section 106(c) relating to sovereign immunity is new. The provision indicates that the use of the term "creditor," "entity," or "governmental unit" in title 11 applies to governmental units notwithstanding any assertion of sovereign immunity and that an order of the court binds governmental units. The provision is included to comply with the requirement in case law that an express waiver of sovereign immunity is required in order to be effective. Section 106(c) codifies *In re* Gwilliam, 519 F.2d 407 (9th Cir. 1975), and *In re* Dolard, 519 F.2d 282 (9th Cir. 1975), permitting the bankruptcy court to determine the amount and dischargeability of tax liabilities owing by the debtor or the estate prior to or during a bankruptcy case whether or not the governmental unit to which such taxes are owed files a proof of claim. Except as provided in sections 106(a) and (b), subsection (c) is not limited to those issues, but permits the bankruptcy court to bind governmental units on other matters as well. For example, section 106(c) permits a trustee or debtor in possession to assert avoiding powers under title 11 against a governmental unit; contrary language in the House report to H.R. 8200 is thereby overruled.

[*124 Cong. Rec.* H 11,091 *(Sept. 28, 1978); S 17,407 (Oct. 6, 1978).*]

Comment

The former Bankruptcy Act contained no provisions regarding sovereign immunity of governmental units. *See* American Boiler Works, Inc., 123 F. Supp. 352 (W.D. Pa. 1954), *aff'd,* 220 F.2d 319 (3d Cir. 1955), holding that in the absence of specific provision in section 70e regarding the United States, the trustee could not invoke section 70e to defeat the government's claim to title to property by avoiding the transfer of the property involved effected in a contract between the bankrupt and the government.

Case Annotations

Section 106(c) does not waive the federal government's immunity from a bankruptcy trustee's claims for monetary recovery because it does not unequivocally express an intention to waive sovereign immunity. United States v. Nordic Village, Inc., 503 U.S. —, 112 S. Ct. 1011, 117 L. Ed. 2d 181, 26 C.B.C.2d 9 (1992).

Section 106(c) is indicative of declaratory and injunctive relief and does not authorize monetary recovery from the states; a state that has not filed a proof of claim in a bankruptcy case would be bound by a debtor's discharge of debts, including unpaid taxes, but would not be subjected to monetary recovery. In enacting section 106(c), Congress did not abrogate Eleventh Amendment immunity. Therefore, actions by a trustee under sections 542(b) and 547(b) of the Code against a state that has not filed a proof of claim are barred by the Eleventh Amendment. Hoffman v. Connecticut Dept. of Income Maintenance, 492 U.S. 96, 109 S. Ct. 2818, 106 L. Ed. 2d 76, 20 C.B.C.2d 1204 (1989).

Section 106(a), as a plain expression of Congress' intent, creates a limited waiver scheme and is not an abrogation provision with the result that it renders a state liable to suit only when the state participates in a bankruptcy case by filing a claim. *In re* 995 Fifth Avenue Associates, L.P., 963 F.2d 503, 26 C.B.C.2d 1162 (2d Cir.), *cert. denied,* — U.S. —, — S. Ct. —, — L. Ed. 2d — (1992).

A government unit may waive sovereign immunity under section 106(a) by self-help conduct in extracting postpetition payments from the bankruptcy estate, even when it has not filed a formal claim in bankruptcy court, and may be viewed as having filed an "informal proof of claim" under such circumstances, thus satisfying the requirement of section 106(a) that a claim be asserted by the governmental unit before immunity will be waived. *In re* Town & Country Home Nursing Services, Inc., 963 F.2d 1146, 26 C.B.C.2d 1446 (9th Cir. 1992).

By asserting its claim against the estate, the Federal Deposit Insurance Corporation has waived the protections it might otherwise enjoy, both under the doctrine of sovereign immunity and under the Federal Tort Claims Act because section 106 and the Tort Claims Act are not in conflict. Anderson and Propps v. FDIC, 918 F.2d 1139, 24 C.B.C.2d 151 (4th Cir. 1990).

When the IRS establishes a tax claim against a debtor but the debtor has a valid counterclaim against the IRS, section 106(b) limits the waiver of sovereign immunity to an offset of the governmental unit's claim against the estate. United States v. McPeck, 910 F.2d 509, 23 C.B.C.2d 863 (8th Cir. 1990).

Governmental units are immune from damages actions arising from violations of the automatic stay. In re Pearson, 917 F.2d 1215, 23 C.B.C.2d 1535 (9th Cir. 1990).

Section 106(c) does not authorize the award of punitive damages against a governmental unit because the section applies only to declaratory and injunctive relief and does not waive the government's sovereign immunity with respect to monetary awards. Small Business Admin. v. Rinehart, 887 F.2d 165, 21 C.B.C.2d 917 (8th Cir. 1989).

The right of a debtor to assert a setoff claim against a governmental unit does not entitle a surety either to compel a governmental unit to assert a permissive setoff claim or to compel the debtor to assert a counterclaim for setoff against the governmental unit when the debtor has chosen to relinquish the claim. Merritt Commercial Sav. & Loan, Inc. v. Guinee (In re James R. Corbitt Co.), 766 F.2d 850, 13 C.B.C.2d 174 (4th Cir. 1985).

If the bankruptcy court has jurisdiction to make an avoidance determination in a case where the federal government is a defendant, then it has jurisdiction to order recovery of avoided property as well because the right to make an avoidance determination would be meaningless without the concurrent right to order, if appropriate, the recovery of that which was transferred. In re Ballard, 25 C.B.C.2d 823 (B. Ct., W.D. Wis. 1991).

The filing of a bankruptcy petition constitutes an "occurrence" within the meaning of section 106(a), and a city may waive its sovereign immunity as to all of its departments by filing a proof of claim against the debtor's estate for one of its departments, even though that filing involved a different "transaction" from the one underlying the subject adversary proceeding. In re Cook United, Inc., 24 C.B.C.2d 128 (B. Ct., N.D. Ohio 1990).

A bankruptcy court order may discharge a debt owed a state agency even in the absence of the filing of a proof of claim by the agency as the Eleventh Amendment precludes a debtor's affirmative monetary recovery against a state agency that has not filed a proof of claim. In re Brooks Fashion Stores, Inc., 24 C.B.C.2d 1724 (B. Ct., S.D.N.Y. 1991).

When a governmental unit has filed a proof of claim, it has consented to having its claim fully adjudicated by the bankruptcy court and has waived its sovereign immunity rights. In re Bryant, 23 C.B.C.2d 337 (B. Ct., D. Kan. 1990).

Since a chapter 13 wage order is in the nature of injunctive relief, and not monetary recovery, wage orders against governmental entities do not violate sovereign immunity. *In re* Adams, 23 C.B.C.2d 1602 (B. Ct., D.N.J. 1990).

Because Congress intended the bankruptcy court to decide tax questions related to the filing of a bankruptcy petition pursuant to section 505(a), the United States is considered to have waived its sovereign immunity under section 106(c) in a proceeding to determine whether the chapter 7 debtor had incurred postpetition tax liability due to the invasion of a profit-sharing plan which formerly qualified for tax exemption under the Employee Retirement Income Security Act of 1974, 26 U.S.C. § 401. *In re* Witte, 19 C.B.C.2d 1339 (B. Ct., W.D. Mich. 1988).

References

2 *Collier on Bankruptcy* ch. 106 (Matthew Bender 15th ed.).

1 *Collier Bankruptcy Manual* ch. 106 (Matthew Bender 3d ed.).

6 *Collier Bankruptcy Practice Guide* ch. 93 (Matthew Bender).

Bankruptcy Court Jurisdiction and the Power to Enjoin the IRS, 70 Minn. L. Rev. 1279 (1986).

Keeton, *Bankruptcy and Taxes: The Irresistible Force Meets the Immovable Object,* 9 Louisville Law. 10 (1988).

Richman, *More Equal Than Others: State Sovereign Immunity Under the Bankruptcy Code,* 21 Rutgers L.J. 603 (1990).

SECTION 107 (11 U.S.C. § 107)

§ 107. Public access to papers.

(a) Except as provided in subsection (b) of this section, a paper filed in a case under this title and the dockets of a bankruptcy court are public records and open to examination by an entity at reasonable times without charge.

(b) On request of a party in interest, the bankruptcy court shall, and on the bankruptcy court's own motion, the bankruptcy court may—

(1) protect an entity with respect to a trade secret or confidential research, development, or commercial information; or

(2) protect a person with respect to scandalous or defamatory matter contained in a paper filed in a case under this title.

Bankruptcy Rule References: 5001, 5003 and 9018

Legislative History

Subsection (a) of this section makes all papers filed in a bankruptcy case and the dockets of the bankruptcy court public and open to examination at reasonable times without charge. "Docket" includes the claims docket, the proceedings docket, and all papers filed in a case.

Subsection (b) permits the court, on its own motion, and requires the court, on the request of a party in interest, to protect trade secrets, confidential research, development, or commercial information, and to protect persons against scandalous or defamatory matter.

[*House Report No. 95–595, 95th Cong., 1st Sess. 317–18 (1977); Senate Report 95–989, 95th Cong., 2d Sess. 30 (1978).*]

Comment

Bankruptcy Rule 9018 provides the procedure for invoking the court's power under section 107. On motion or *sua sponte* the court may make any order that justice requires to protect the estate or any entity respecting a trade secret or other confidential research, development, or commercial information, or to protect any entity against scandalous or defamatory matter in any filed paper, or to protect government matters that are made confidential by statute or regulation. Any affected entity without notice of the entry of an order under this Rule may move, on notice and hearing, to vacate or modify the order.

Bankruptcy Rule 5001(c) requires that the clerk's office be open during business hours every day except Saturdays, Sundays, and the legal holidays listed in Rule 9006(a).

Bankruptcy Rule 9006(a), as amended in 1991, governs the computation of time periods prescribed by the Federal Rules of Civil Procedure made applicable by the Bankruptcy Rules as well as those prescribed by the Bankruptcy Rules themselves.

Bankruptcy Rule 5003 requires the clerk to keep a docket in each case and to enter thereon each judgment, order, and activity in that case. The entry of a judgment or order in a docket shall show the date the entry is made.

Case Annotations

Although section 107(b) provides that the court may protect an entity with respect to commercial information, this authorization is directed toward the withholding of information about the debtor's commercial operations in order to prevent competitors from attaining an unfair advantage, and there is nothing in section 107(b)(1) which would warrant the impoundment of the list of the debtor's creditors solely to prevent investors from buying the debtor's debentures from public bondholders at lower market prices. *In re* Itel Corp., 6 C.B.C.2d 4 (9th Cir., B.A.P., 1982).

Expungement of bankruptcy records from the public record in order to clear the credit rating of a debtor who, having paid its prepetition debts in full, seeks to have the true but prejudicial information of the dismissal of his case erased, is neither necessary nor proper because the dissemination of the information is neither scandalous nor defamatory matter. Merely prejudicial information cannot be enjoined. *In re* Whitener, 14 C.B.C.2d 395 (B. Ct., E.D. Va. 1986). *See also* In the Matter of DeLorean Motor Co., 8 C.B.C.2d 1089 (B. Ct., E.D. Mich. 1983).

A creditor may be granted a protective order limiting future access to the debtor's schedule containing the creditor's customer list even though the schedule has been open to public inspection for six months due to the creditor's failure to file a memorandum in support of its motion. *In re* Nunn, 12 C.B.C.2d 1158 (B. Ct., E.D. Va. 1985).

A chapter 11 debtor's pleadings, schedules and statement of affairs may be sealed from public access at the request of the trustees of the debtors' mortgage-backed securities, when to do so will protect against the likely massive withdrawal of funds from banks investing in those securities which would result not only in harm to numerous financial institutions involved but also adversely affect non-financial lenders, innocent depositors and taxpayers, and the public at large. *In re* Epic Associates V, 13 C.B.C.2d 952 (B. Ct., E.D. Va. 1985).

Because there is allowed public access to filed motion papers under section 107, any limitation on the dissemination of those papers would infringe upon the rights of free speech guaranteed by the First Amendment of the United States Constitution. In the Matter of Reliable Investors Corp., 11 C.B.C.2d 1103 (B. Ct., W.D. Wis. 1984).

References

2 *Collier on Bankruptcy* ch. 107 (Matthew Bender 15th ed.).

1 *Collier Bankruptcy Manual* ch. 107 (Matthew Bender 3d ed.).

6 *Collier Bankruptcy Practice Guide* ch. 110 (Matthew Bender).

SECTION 108 (11 U.S.C. § 108)

§ 108. Extension of time.

(a) If applicable nonbankruptcy law, an order entered in a nonbankruptcy proceeding, or an agreement fixes a period within which the debtor may commence an action, and such period has not expired before the date of the filing of the petition, the trustee may commence such action only before the later of—

(1) the end of such period, including any suspension of such period occurring on or after the commencement of the case; or

(2) two years after the order for relief.

(b) Except as provided in subsection (a) of this section, if applicable nonbankruptcy law, an order entered in a nonbankruptcy proceeding, or an agreement fixes a period within which the debtor or an individual protected under section 1201 or 1301 of this title may file any pleading, demand, notice, or proof of claim or loss, cure a default, or perform any other similar act, and such period has not expired before the date of the filing of the petition, the trustee may only file, cure, or perform, as the case may be, before the later of—

(1) the end of such period, including any suspension of such period occurring on or after the commencement of the case; or

(2) 60 days after the order for relief.

(c) Except as provided in section 524 of this title, if applicable nonbankruptcy law, an order entered in a nonbankruptcy proceeding, or an agreement fixes a period for commencing or continuing a civil action in a court other than a bankruptcy court on a claim against the debtor, or against an individual with respect to which such individual is protected under section 1201 or 1301 of this title, and such period has not expired before the date of the filing of the petition, then such period does not expire until the later of—

(1) the end of such period, including any suspension of such period occurring on or after the commencement of the case; or

(2) 30 days after notice of the termination or expiration of the stay under section 362, 722, 1201, or 1301 of this title, as the case may be, with respect to such claim.

Legislative History

Subsections (a) and (b), derived from Bankruptcy Act section 11, permit the trustee, when he steps into the shoes of the debtor, an extension of time for filing an action or doing some other act that is required to preserve the debtor's rights. Subsection (a) extends any statute of limitation for commencing or continuing an action by the debtor for two years after the date of the order for relief, unless it would expire later. Subsection (b) gives the trustee two months to take other actions, not covered under subsection (a), such as filing a pleading, demand, notice, or proof of claim or loss (such as an insurance claim), unless the period for doing the relevant act expires later than two months after the date of the order for relief.

Subsection (c) extends the statute of limitations for creditors. Thus, if a creditor is stayed from commencing or continuing an action against the debtor because of the bankruptcy case, then the creditor is permitted an additional 30 days after notice of the event by which the stay is terminated, whether that event be relief from the automatic stay under proposed 11 U.S.C. § 362 or 1301, the closing of the bankruptcy case (which terminates the stay), or the exception from discharge of the debts on which the creditor claims.

[*House Report No. 95–595, 95th Cong., 1st Sess. 318 (1977).*]

* * *

In the case of Federal tax liabilities, the Internal Revenue Code suspends the statute of limitations on a tax liability of a taxpayer from running while his assets are in the control or custody of a court and for six months thereafter (sec. 6503(b) of the Code). The amendment applies this rule in a title 11 proceeding. Accordingly, the statute of limitations on collection of a nondischargeable Federal tax liability of a debtor will resume running after six months following the end of the period during which the debtor's assets are in the control or custody of the bankruptcy court. This rule will provide the Internal Revenue Service adequate time to collect nondischargeable taxes following the end of the title 11 proceedings.

[*Senate Report No. 95–989, 95th Cong., 2d Sess. 30–31 (1978).*]

The House amendment adopts section 108(c)(1) of the Senate amendment which expressly includes any special suspensions of statutes of limitation periods on collection outside bankruptcy when assets are under the authority of a court. For example, section 6503(b) of the Internal Revenue Code suspends collection of tax liabilities while the debtor's assets are in the control or custody of a court, and for six months thereafter. By adopting the language of the Senate amendment, the House amendment insures not only that the period for collection of the taxes outside bankruptcy will not expire during the title 11 proceedings, but also that such period will not expire until at least six months thereafter, which is the minimum suspension period provided by the Internal Revenue Code.

[*124 Cong. Rec. H 11,109 (Sept. 28, 1978); S 17,426 (Oct. 6, 1978).*]

Comment

The last sentence of the House Report, also contained in the Senate Report, appears inaccurate. An exception from discharge does not terminate a stay; a proceeding for relief from the stay would be necessary. Pursuant to section 362(c)(2)(C), the stay is terminated when the discharge is denied.

Section 11 of the former Bankruptcy Act is the source of subsections (a) and (b) of section 108 of the Code. Section 11e, first sentence, is substantially the same as section 108(a) of the Code. Section 11e, second sentence, is substantially the same as section 108(b) of the Code. Section 11 measured dates from date of adjudication, while section 108 of the Code measures dates from the date of entry of an order for relief.

1984 Amendments: The word "and" at the end of subsections (a)(1), (b)(1) and (c)(1) was changed to "or," correcting a technical error. Additionally, the word "nonbankruptcy" was twice inserted in subdivisions (a), (b) and (c).

1986 Amendments: Subsections (b) and (c) were amended to include section 1201 within the operation of section 108.

Case Annotations

Section 108(c) tolls the ten-year period limiting judgment liens on real property in New York until the termination of the automatic stay under section 362(a). When a lienholder holds a valid lien on a debtor's property at the time of commencement of a bankruptcy case and the limitation period governing that lien has not yet expired, the running of the period will be tolled under section 108(c)(1)–(2). *In re* Morton, 866 F.2d 561, 20 C.B.C.2d 465 (2d Cir. 1989).

When an attempt to enforce a perfected lien against property of a chapter 11 debtor is compelled by a nonbankruptcy statute and stayed by section 362, the enforcement period is tolled by section 108(c). *In re* Hunters Run Ltd. Partnership, 875 F.2d 1425, 21 C.B.C.2d 491 (9th Cir. 1989).

Section 108(b) reinforces the interpretation that section 362(a)(1) and (3) does not toll the running of a judicially decreed redemption period for actions stayed by this section's language are not indefinitely stayed by the more general language of section 362(a). Heikkila v. Carver (*In re* Carver), 828 F.2d 463, 17 C.B.C.2d 771 (8th Cir. 1987).

When a bankruptcy petition is filed just before the expiration of a state statutory redemption period resulting from a judgment of foreclosure section 108(b) extends the redemption period for 60 days from the commencement of the bankruptcy case. Goldberg v. Tynan (In the Matter of Tynan), 773 F.2d 177, 13 C.B.C.2d 655 (7th Cir. 1985).

Section 365, not section 108(b), governs the time for curing defaults in executory contracts, and if the time for cure has not expired when the debtor's petition is filed, the contract will still be executory and may be assumed by the debtor. Moody v. Amoco Oil Co., 734 F.2d 1200, 11 C.B.C.2d 1 (7th Cir.), *cert. denied*, 469 U.S. 982, 105 S. Ct. 386, 83 L. Ed. 2d 321 (1984).

Upon the filing of a petition in bankruptcy by a debtor, the automatic extension of a redemption period provided for under section 108(b) is the only relief available to stay the expiration of a statutory redemption period. Johnson v. First Nat'l Bank, 719 F.2d 270, 9 C.B.C.2d 579 (8th Cir. 1983), *cert denied*, 465 U.S. 1012, 104 S. Ct. 1015, 79 L. Ed. 2d 245 (1984).

When a case has been converted from chapter 11 to chapter 7, the chapter 7 trustee has two years from the time of his appointment to institute an adversary proceeding seeking turnover of property to the estate. *In re* Bingham Systems, Inc., 26 C.B.C.2d 1570 (B. Ct., N.D. Miss. 1991).

A debtor whose real property has been sold pursuant to 26 U.S.C. § 6335 has until the expiration of the 180 day period of 26 U.S.C. § 6337(b) or the sixty day period of 11 U.S.C. § 108(b), whichever is later, to redeem the property. *In re* Cooke, 25 C.B.C.2d 11 (B. Ct., W.D.N.C. 1991).

Section 108(a) is inapplicable in determining whether a fraudulent transfer action, maintained by a debtor in possession under section 544(b), has been timely filed. *In re* Mahoney, Trocki & Associates, Inc., 22 C.B.C.2d 1167 (B. Ct., C.D. Cal. 1990).

A bankruptcy court, in the interest of preserving the intent and effect of the confirmation order, may annul the automatic stay and allow creditors to proceed with state court actions which would otherwise be barred by statutes of limitations. *In re* Pettibone Corp., 22 C.B.C.2d 704 (B. Ct., N.D. Ill. 1990).

References

2 *Collier on Bankruptcy* ch. 108 (Matthew Bender 15th ed.).

1 *Collier Bankruptcy Manual* ch. 108 (Matthew Bender 3d ed.).

1 *Collier Bankruptcy Practice Guide* ch. 2 (Matthew Bender).

SECTION 109 (11 U.S.C. § 109)

§ 109. Who may be a debtor.

(a) Notwithstanding any other provision of this section, only a person that resides or has a domicile, a place of business, or property in the United States, or a municipality, may be a debtor under this title.

(b) A person may be a debtor under chapter 7 of this title only if such person is not—

(1) a railroad;

(2) a domestic insurance company, bank, savings bank, cooperative bank, savings and loan association, building and loan association, homestead association, credit union, or industrial bank or similar institution which is an insured bank as defined in section 3(h) of the Federal Deposit Insurance Act (12 U.S.C. 1813(h)); or

(3) a foreign insurance company, bank, savings bank, cooperative bank, savings and loan association, building and loan association, homestead association, or credit union, engaged in such business in the United States.

(c) An entity may be a debtor under chapter 9 of this title if and only if such entity—

(1) is a municipality;

(2) is generally authorized to be a debtor under such chapter by State law, or by a governmental officer or organization empowered by State law to authorize such entity to be a debtor under such chapter;

(3) is insolvent;

(4) desires to effect a plan to adjust such debts; and

(5)(A) has obtained the agreement of creditors holding at least a majority in amount of the claims of each class that such entity intends to impair under a plan in a case under such chapter;

(B) has negotiated in good faith with creditors and has failed to obtain the agreement of creditors holding at least a majority in amount of the claims of each class that such entity intends to impair under a plan in a case under such chapter;

(C) is unable to negotiate with creditors because such negotiation is impracticable; or

(D) reasonably believes that a creditor may attempt to obtain a transfer that is avoidable under section 547 of this title.

(d) Only a person that may be a debtor under chapter 7 of this title, except a stockbroker or a commodity broker, and a railroad may be a debtor under chapter 11 of this title.

(e) Only an individual with regular income that owes, on the date of the filing of the petition, noncontingent, liquidated, unsecured debts of less than $100,000 and noncontingent, liquidated, secured debts of less than $350,000, or an individual with regular income and such individual's spouse, except a stockbroker or a commodity broker, that owe, on the date of the filing of the petition, noncontingent, liquidated, unsecured debts that aggregate less than $100,000 and non-contingent, liquidated, secured debts of less than $350,000 may be a debtor under chapter 13 of this title.

(f) Only a family farmer with regular annual income may be a debtor under chapter 12 of this title.

(g) Notwithstanding any other provision of this section, no individual or family farmer may be a debtor under this title who has been a debtor in a case pending under this title at any time in the preceding 180 days if—

(1) the case was dismissed by the court for willful failure of the debtor to abide by orders of the court, or to appear before the court in proper prosecution of the case; or

(2) the debtor requested and obtained the voluntary dismissal of the case following the filing of a request for relief from the automatic stay provided by section 362 of this title.

Bankruptcy Rule Reference: 1016

Legislative History

This section specifies eligibility to be a debtor under the bankruptcy laws. The first criterion, found in the current Bankruptcy Act section 2a, requires that the debtor reside or have a domicile, a place of business, or property in the United States.

Subsection (b) defines eligibility for liquidation under chapter 7. All persons are eligible except railroads, insurance companies, and certain banking institutions. All three exclusions are contained in current law. However, the banking institution exception is expanded in light of the change in various banking laws since current law was last amended on this point. A change is also made to clarify that the bankruptcy laws cover foreign banks and insurance companies not engaged in the banking or insurance business in the United States but having assets in the

United States. Banking institutions and insurance companies are excluded from liquidation under the bankruptcy laws because they are bodies for which alternate provision is made for their liquidation under various regulatory laws. Conversely, when a foreign bank or insurance company is not engaged in the banking or insurance business in the United States, then those regulatory laws do not apply and the bankruptcy laws are the only ones available for liquidation of any assets found in the United States.

[House Report 95–595, 95th Cong., 1st Sess. 318–19 (1977); See Senate Report No. 95–989, 95th Cong., 2d Sess. 31 (1978).]

The first clause of subsection (b) provides that a railroad is not a debtor except where the requirements of section 1174 are met.

[Senate Report No. 95–989, 95th Cong., 2d Sess. 31 (1978).]

Subsection (c) defines eligibility for chapter 9. Only a municipality that is unable to pay its debts as they mature, and that is not prohibited by State law from proceeding under chapter 9, is permitted to be a chapter 9 debtor. The subsection is derived from Bankruptcy Act section 84, with two changes. First, section 84 requires that the municipality be "generally authorized to file a petition under this chapter by the legislature, or by a governmental officer or organization empowered by State law to authorize the filing of a petition." The "generally authorized" language is unclear, and has generated a problem for a Colorado Metropolitan District that attempted to use chapter IX in 1976. The "not prohibited" language provides flexibility for both the States and the municipalities involved, while protecting State sovereignty as required by Ashton v. Cameron County Water District No. 1, 298 U.S. 513 (1936) and Bekins v. United States, 304 U.S. 27 (1938).

The second change deletes the four prerequisities to filing found in section 84. The prerequisites require the municipality to have worked out a plan in advance, to have attempted to work out a plan without success, to fear that a creditor will attempt to obtain a preference, or to allege that prior negotiation is impracticable. The loopholes in those prerequisites are larger than the requirement itself. It was a compromise from pre-1976 chapter IX, under which a municipality could file only if it had worked out an adjustment plan in advance. In the meantime, chapter IX protection was unavailable. There was some controversy at the time of the enactment of current chapter IX concerning deletion of the pre-negotiation requirement. It was argued that deletion would lead to a rash of municipal bankruptcies. The prerequisites now contained in section 84 were inserted to assuage that fear. They are largely cosmetic and precatory, however, and do not offer any significant deterrent to use of chapter IX. Instead, other factors, such as a general reluctance on the part of any debtor, especially a municipality, to use the bankruptcy laws, operates as a much more effective deterrent against capricious use.

[House Report No. 95–595, 95th Cong., 1st Sess. 319 (1977).]

Subsection (c) provides that only a person who may be a debtor under chapter 7 and a railroad may also be a debtor under chapter 11, but a stockbroker or commodity broker is eligible for relief only under chapter 7. Subsection (d) establishes dollar limitations on the amount of indebtedness that an individual with regular income can incur and yet file under chapter 13.

[*Senate Report No. 95–989, 95th Cong., 2d Sess. 31 (1978).*]

Subsection (d) permits a person that may proceed under chapter 7 to be a debtor under chapter 11, Reorganization, with two exceptions. Railroads, which are excluded from chapter 7, are permitted to proceed under chapter 11. Stockbrokers and commodity brokers, which are permitted to be debtors under chapter 7, are excluded from chapter 11. The special rules for treatment of customer accounts that are the essence of stockbroker and commodity broker liquidations are available only in chapter 7. Customers would be unprotected under chapter 11. The special protective rules are unavailable in chapter 11 because their complexity would make reorganization very difficult at best, and unintelligible at worst. The variety of options available in reorganization cases make it extremely difficult to reorganize and continue to provide the special customer protection necessary in these cases.

Subsection (e) specifies eligibility for chapter 13, Adjustment of Debts of an Individual with Regular Income. An individual with regular income, or an individual with regular income and the individual's spouse, may proceed under chapter 13. As noted in connection with the definition of the term "individual with regular income," this represents a significant departure from current law. The change might have been too great, however, without some limitation. Thus, the debtor (or the debtor and spouse) must have unsecured debts that aggregate less than $100,000 and secured debts that aggregate less than $500,000. These figures will permit the small sole proprietor, for whom a chapter 11 reorganization is too cumbersome a procedure, to proceed under chapter 13. It does not create a presumption that any sole proprietor within that range is better off in chapter 13 than chapter 11. The conversion rules found in section 1307 will govern the appropriateness of the two chapters for any particular individual. The figures merely set maximum limits.

Whether a small business operated by a husband and wife, the so-called "mom and pop grocery store," will be a partnership and thus excluded from chapter 13, or a business owned by an individual, will have to be determined on the facts of each case. Even if partnership papers have not been filed, for example, the issue will be whether the assets of the grocery store are for the benefit of all creditors of the debtor or only for business creditors, and whether such assets may be the subject of a chapter 13 proceeding. The intent of the section is to follow current law that a partnership by estoppel may be adjudicated in bankruptcy and therefore would not prevent a chapter 13 debtor from subjecting assets in such a partnership to the reach of all creditors in a chapter 13 case. However, if the partnership is found to be a partnership by agreement, even informal agreement, then a separate entity exists and the assets of that entity would be exempt from a case under chapter 13.

[*House Report No. 95–595, 95th Cong., 1st Sess. 318–20 (1977).*]

Section 109(b) of the House amendment adopts a provision contained in H.R. 8200 as passed by the House. Railroad liquidations will occur under chapter 11, not chapter 7.

Section 109(c) contains a provision which tracks the Senate amendment as to when a municipality may be a debtor under chapter 11 of title 11. As under the Bankruptcy Act, State law authorization and prepetition negotiation efforts are required.

Section 109(e) represents a compromise between H.R. 8200 as passed by the House and the Senate amendment relating to the dollar amounts restricting eligibility to be a debtor under chapter 13 of title 11. The House amendment adheres to the limit of $100,000 placed on unsecured debts in H.R. 8200 as passed by the House. It adopts a midpoint of $350,000 as a limit on secured claims, a compromise between the level of $500,000 in H.R. 8200 as passed by the House and $200,000 as contained in the Senate amendment.

[*124 Cong. Rec. H 11,091 (Sept. 28, 1978); S 17,407 (Oct. 6, 1978).*]

Comment

Section 2a(1) of the former Bankruptcy Act empowered the courts of bankruptcy to adjudicate persons bankrupt who had their principal place of business, resided or had their domicile within their territorial jurisdictions for the preceding six months, or for the longer portion of the preceding six months than any other jurisdictions, or if they did not meet those prerequisites, had property within their jurisdiction, or, in any cases transferred to them under the Act. Former Bankruptcy Rule 116 eliminated residence or domicile as a useful basis to determine venue of a corporation or partnership.

Venue is governed by 28 U.S.C. § 1408 which provides that a case under chapter 11 may be commenced in the district court for the district in which the domicile, residence, principal place of business in the United States, or principal assets in the United States, of the person or entity that is the subject of such case have been located for the 180 days immediately preceding such commencement, or for a longer portion of such 180-day period than in any other district; or in the district in which a case under title 11 concerning such person's affiliate, general partner, or partnership is pending.

Bankruptcy Rule 1014, amended in 1991, addresses change of venue, dismissal of cases filed in the improper venue and venue procedures for related cases.

Section 4a of the former Bankruptcy Act enumerated those excluded from being a voluntary bankrupt and section 4b specified who could and who could not be an involuntary bankrupt. As noted in the House and Senate Committee Reports, a foreign insurance company and a foreign bank may be debtors under section 109(b)(3) of the Code if not engaged in the insurance or banking business in the United States.

Section 59 of the former Act specified who could file a voluntary petition ("any qualified person," *i.e.,* as provided in section 4) and who could file an involuntary petition.

1984 Amendments: Subsection (f) [redesignated by the 1986 Amendments as subsection (g)] was added and is aimed at repetitious filings. An individual debtor would not be eligible for relief under the Code until the expiration of 180 days after dismissal of the case for failure to abide by court orders or failure to appear, or if the individual obtained voluntary dismissal of his case after a request had been made for relief from the automatic stay. Except for the 180-day limitation in this subsection, dismissal of a case does not prejudice the filing of a subsequent petition.

The 1984 amendments made several other changes in section 109, all technical and minor.

1986 Amendments: Former subsection (f) was redesignated as subsection (g).

The added subsection (f) limits eligibility to be a chapter 12 debtor to "a family farmer with regular annual income." "Family farmer" and "family farmer with regular annual income" are defined in § 101.

1988 Amendments: The amendments to chapter 9 (Pub. L. No. 100-597) required a change in the definition of insolvent in section 101 with respect to a municipality. For like reason, the requirement of section 109(c)(3) that a chapter 9 debtor must be "insolvent or unable to meet such entity's debts as such debts mature" is changed to require only that the municipality "is insolvent."

Case Annotations

An individual not engaged in business is eligible to be a debtor under chapter 11 pursuant to the plain language of section 109(d). The Bankruptcy Code contains no ongoing business requirement for reorganization under chapter 11, and inference of exclusion of persons not engaged in business is unjustified when Congress has expressly excluded stockbrokers and commodities brokers from chapter 11 relief under section 109(d) while otherwise leaving chapter 11 available to any other entity eligible for protection under chapter 7. Toibb v. Radloff, 501 U.S. —, 111 S. Ct. 2197, 115 L. Ed. 2d 145, 24 C.B.C.2d 1178 (1991).

In determining whether a debtor satisfies the limit on unsecured debt under section 109(e), hypothetical costs of the sale of real property securing debt are not to be deducted from the value of the property when the debtor intends to retain the property. *In re* Balbus, 933 F.2d 246, 24 C.B.C.2d 1841 (4th Cir. 1991).

A court should apply the test of section 506(a) in determining whether an undersecured debt should be treated as secured or unsecured for purposes of chapter 13 eligibility. Thus, a creditor has an allowed secured claim only to the extent of the value of the collateral and is unsecured as to the balance. Miller v. United States, acting through Farmers Home Administration, 907 F.2d 80, 23 C.B.C.2d 358 (8th Cir. 1990).

Whether or not a debtor is eligible under section 109(g) does not raise an issue of subject matter jurisdiction. Promenade National Bank v. Phillips (In the Matter of Phillips), 844 F.2d 230, 18 C.B.C.2d 1105 (5th Cir. 1988).

Currency exchanges are not specifically enumerated in the exhaustive list of section 109(b)(2); there is no reason to implicitly exclude them from becoming chapter 11 debtors. Cash Currency Exchange, Inc. v. Shine (In re Cash Currency Exchange, Inc.), 762 F.2d 542, 12 C.B.C.2d 1499 (7th Cir.), cert. denied, 474 U.S. 904, 106 S. Ct. 233, 88 L. Ed. 2d 232 (1985).

In determining whether a debtor exceeds the $100,000 unsecured, liquidated debt threshold, a court should rely primarily upon the debtor's schedules at the time of filing if the schedules were filed in good faith, even if the debtor's amended statement later lists an unsecured claim for more than $100,000. Comprehensive Accounting Corp. v. Pearson (In the Matter of Pearson), 773 F.2d 751, 13 C.B.C.2d 749 (6th Cir. 1985).

In determining the amount of secured and unsecured debt for purposes of determining chapter 13 eligibility, the valuation test of section 506(a) applies and thus it is the value of collateral securing the debt that represents secured debt and the undersecured amount becomes unsecured debt. In the Matter of Day, 747 F.2d 405, 11 C.B.C.2d 733 (7th Cir. 1984).

A debtor who willingly enters into a stipulation which: (1) provides for a receivership by the SBA; (2) limits the power of the debtor's board of directors; and (3) provides for additional loans by the SBA to the debtor all or which is supervised by a federal court does not possess an absolute right to later file a petition under title 11 but does retain the right to seek the district court's approval for the filing of a petition should such a course be in the best interests of the debtor-company. U.S. v. Royal Bus. Funds Corp., 724 F.2d 12, 9 C.B.C.2d 1045 (2d Cir. 1983).

It is a basic principle that a person in bankruptcy, while not necessarily insolvent, must at least owe debts, and a question of the propriety of a bankruptcy case is accordingly raised when the debtor's debts are incurred through parties who allegedly do not legitimately control the debtor. Connell v. Coastal Cable T.V., Inc. (In re Coastal Cable T.V., Inc.), 709 F.2d 762, 8 C.B.C.2d 1211 (1st Cir. 1983).

The determination as to whether a health maintenance organization (HMO) is a domestic insurance company barred from filing a petition for relief under the Bankruptcy Code is made by using the "state classification test," whereby a court looks to the applicable state law under which the HMO was formed to determine whether it is a type of corporation excluded by the Code and gives particular deference to the state's regulatory interest in the business of insurance at the outset of the section 109 analysis. *In re* Grouphealth Partnership, Inc., 26 C.B.C.2d 1338 (B. Ct., E.D. Pa. 1992).

A chapter 9 debtor seeking to enforce an automatic stay against a section 109(c)(5)(B) good faith objection by a creditor must show that it negotiated with its creditors in good faith regarding the terms of its plan of reorganization. *In re* Cottonwood Water and Sanitation District, 26 C.B.C.2d 1786 (B. Ct., D. Colo. 1992).

When a trust which has the status of a self-funded employee welfare benefit plan, would not be provided with a comprehensive scheme of liquidation under state insurance laws, it may file for relief under the Code because Congressional intent in enacting the statute was to provide entities that do not enjoy such a scheme of liquidation with the means to avail themselves of the liquidation and reorganization provisions of the Bankruptcy Code. *In re* Affiliated Food Stores Inc. Group Benefit Trust, 26 C.B.C.2d 104 (B. Ct., N.D. Tex. 1991).

A claim for criminal restitution which is conditioned upon the debtor's ability to pay is not a contingent claim because the liability has already attached, and must be counted toward the ceiling set forth in section 109(e). *In re* Gordon, 25 C.B.C.2d 5 (B. Ct., E.D. Pa. 1991).

Connecticut General Statute § 7-148(c)(1)(A) provides the authority needed for a municipality to file a chapter 9 petition since it gives cities broad authority to institute any proceeding, and bankruptcy relief is a proceeding within the broad scope of that statute. *In re* City of Bridgeport, 25 C.B.C.2d 140 (B. Ct., D. Conn. 1991).

A disputed debt can be a noncontingent debt within the meaning of section 109(e). *In re* Pennypacker, 24 C.B.C.2d 64 (B. Ct., E.D. Pa. 1990).

Under Missouri law, a change in the relationship of the partners caused by one partner's disassociation from carrying on of the business operates as a dissolution of the partnership, and the remaining partner should be treated as a sole proprietor or individual. *In re* Winheim, 23 C.B.C.2d 323 (B. Ct. E.D. Mo. 1990).

Trusts which have as their principal purpose the preservation of property held for the benefit of beneficiaries are not recognized as business trusts and, therefore, cannot use that statutory category to become eligible as a chapter 11 debtor. *In re* Constitutional Trust #2-562, 23 C.B.C.2d 1577 (B. Ct., D. Minn. 1990).

A bankruptcy court will not issue an injunction to prevent the appointment of a receiver to an insolvent savings and loan association owned by a holding company which is owned by a chapter 11 debtor when the debtor has failed to establish the grounds for issuing such an injunction. *In re* Deltacorp, Inc., 22 C.B.C.2d 803 (B. Ct., S.D.N.Y. 1990).

A loan, guaranteed by a debtor, is not included in the calculation of debt for purposes of chapter 13 eligibility as long as the borrower does not default on the loan. *In re* Fischel, 22 C.B.C.2d 1461 (B. Ct., N.D.N.Y. 1989).

References

2 *Collier on Bankruptcy* ch. 109 (Matthew Bender 15th ed.).

1 *Collier Bankruptcy Manual* ch. 109 (Matthew Bender 3d ed.).

1 *Collier Bankruptcy Practice Guide* Pt. 1 (Matthew Bender).

Comment, *Must Courts Apply Section 109(g)(2) When Debtors Intend No Abuse in an Earlier Dismissal of Their Case?* 7 Bankr. Dev. J. 103 (1990).

Lieb, *Chapter 11 Debtor Eligibility: Is a Land Trust Eligible to File a Bankruptcy Case?* 1983 Ann. Surv. Bankr. L. 83.

CHAPTER 3

Case Administration

SUBCHAPTER I

Commencement of a Case

SECTION 301 (11 U.S.C. § 301)

§ 301. **Voluntary cases.** A voluntary case under a chapter of this title is commenced by the filing with the bankruptcy court of a petition under such chapter by an entity that may be a debtor under such chapter. The commencement of a voluntary case under a chapter of this title constitutes an order for relief under such chapter.

Bankruptcy Rule References: 1002, 1004, 1006, 1008 and 5005

Legislative History

Section 301 specifies the manner in which a voluntary bankruptcy case is commenced. The debtor files a petition under this section under the particular operative chapter of the bankruptcy code under which he wishes to proceed. The filing of the petition constitutes an order for relief in the case under that chapter. The section contains no chance [*sic*] from current law, except for the use of the phrase "order for relief" instead of "adjudication." The term adjudication is replaced by a less perjorative phrase in light of the clear power of Congress to permit voluntary bankruptcy without the necessity for an adjudication, as under the 1898 Act, which was adopted when voluntary bankruptcy was a concept not thoroughly tested.

[*House Report No. 95–595, 95th Cong., 1st Sess. 321 (1977); Senate Report 95–989, 95th Cong., 2d Sess. 31 (1978).*]

Sections 301, 302, 303, and 304, are all modified in the House amendment to adopt an idea contained in sections 301 and 303 of the Senate amendment requiring a petition commencing a case to be filed with the bankruptcy court. The exception contained in section 301 of the Senate bill relating to cases filed under chapter 9 is deleted. Chapter 9 cases will be handled by a bankruptcy court as are other title II [*sic:* should be 11] cases.

[124 Cong. Rec. H 11,091 (Sept. 28, 1978); S 17,407 (Oct. 6, 1978).]

Comment

Section 2a(24) of the former Bankruptcy Act defined a "petition" as the document filed in a court of bankruptcy initiating a proceeding under the Act.

Bankruptcy Rule 1002 requires that a petition commencing a case under the Code be filed with the clerk. The 1987 Amendments to the Bankruptcy Rules deleted all provisions relating to the number of copies of the petition to be filed. The 1987 Advisory Committee Note to Rule 1001 states that the number of copies of a petition that must be filed is a matter for local rule. The 1991 Amendments added subdivision (b) to Rule 1002 which requires the clerk to transmit forthwith to the United States trustee a copy of the bankruptcy petition. However, pursuant to Bankruptcy Rule 5005(b)(3), added in 1991, the United States trustee may relieve the clerk of that duty by requesting that the petition or any other document not be transmitted.

The provisions of Rule 1002 providing for distribution of copies of the petition to agencies of the United States have been deleted. The 1987 Advisory Committee Note states that the Director of the Administrative Office will determine on an ongoing basis which government agencies will be provided a copy of the petition. Rule 1008 requires that the petition be verified or contain an unsworn declaration as provided in 28 U.S.C. § 1746.

Bankruptcy Rule 1005 prescribes that the caption of a petition contain the name of the court, title of the case, and docket number, that it include debtor's Social Security and employer's tax identification numbers, and list all other names used by the debtor within 6 years. In an involuntary case, the petition must include all names used by the debtor which are known to the petitioning creditors.

Bankruptcy Rule 1004(a) provides that if all general partners consent, a voluntary petition may be filed on behalf of a partnership by one or more general partners.

Bankruptcy Rule 2009, as amended in 1991, provides for election or appointment of a single trustee for estates jointly administered, or for a separate trustee for each estate. The trustee(s) must keep separate accounts of the property and distribution of each jointly administered case.

Section 342 requires appropriate notice of an order for relief, and Bankruptcy Rule 2002(f) requires the clerk to give the debtor, all creditors and indenture trustees notice by mail of the order for relief. Rule 2002(k) requires the clerk to transmit to the United States trustee a copy of the order for relief. The notice may be combined with the notice of the meeting of creditors, as in Official Form 9.

1984 Amendments: The 1984 amendments added the following subdivision to Bankruptcy Rule 2002:

"(n) In a voluntary case commenced under the Code by an individual debtor whose debts are primarily consumer debts, the clerk, or some other person as the court may direct, shall give the trustee and all creditors notice by mail of the order for relief not more than 20 days after the entry of such order." [Pub. L. No. 98–353, § 321]. [Rule 2002(n) was redesignated as Rule 2002(o) by the 1991 Amendments to the Bankruptcy Rules, which also added the heading *"Notice of Order for Relief in Consumer Case.*]

The derivation of this provision is unknown and its purpose not entirely clear. The rule places a time limit on the notice required under Rule 2002(f)(1) and section 342 only in a consumer debtor case.

Case Annotations

The director of a company that has been closed under state insolvency laws may not be precluded from commencing a case under the Bankruptcy Code for the company provided that the company is eligible to become a debtor. Central Mortgage & Trust, Inc. v. State of Texas (*In re* Central Mortgage & Trust, Inc.), 13 C.B.C.2d 617 (S.D. Tex. 1985).

Under Connecticut law, when a president of a corporation files a bankruptcy petition without specific authorization from the board of directors, the petition will be dismissed even though, upon dismissal, creditors are likely to file an involuntary petition. *In re* Stavola/Manson Elec. Co., Inc., 21 C.B.C.2d 55 (B. Ct., D. Conn. 1988).

The commencement of a voluntary case under title 11 gives the bankruptcy court jurisdiction to administer the case even if it is later determined that the debtor filed the original petition under the wrong chapter. *In re* Tatsis, 16 C.B.C.2d 1054 (B. Ct., W.D.N.C. 1987).

A corporation which has forfeited its charter under state law retains sufficient corporate identity and power necessary to file a voluntary chapter 7 petition. *In re* Heark Corp., 6 C.B.C.2d 440 (B. Ct., D. Md. 1982).

References

2 *Collier on Bankruptcy* ch. 301 (Matthew Bender 15th ed.).

1 *Collier Bankruptcy Manual* ch. 301 (Matthew Bender 3d ed.).

1 *Collier Bankruptcy Practice Guide* ch. 13 (Matthew Bender).

Ayers, *Commencing a Case Under the Bankruptcy Reform Act of 1978: A Primer,* 51 Miss. L.J. 639 (1981).

Kennedy, *The Commencement of a Case Under the New Bankruptcy Code,* 36 Wash. & Lee L. Rev. 977 (1979).

McCoid, II, *The Origins of Voluntary Bankruptcy,* 5 Bankr. Dev. J. 361 (1988).

Treister, Trost, Forman, Klee and Levin, *Commencing a Case Under the Bankruptcy Code,* 34 Prac. Law. 17 (1988).

SECTION 302 (11 U.S.C. § 302)

§ 302. Joint cases.

(a) A joint case under a chapter of this title is commenced by the filing with the bankruptcy court of a single petition under such chapter by an individual that may be a debtor under such chapter and such individual's spouse. The commencement of a joint case under a chapter of this title constitutes an order for relief under such chapter.

(b) After the commencement of a joint case, the court shall determine the extent, if any, to which the debtors' estates shall be consolidated.

Bankruptcy Rule Reference: 1002

Legislative History

A joint case is a voluntary bankruptcy case concerning a wife and husband. Under current law, there is no explicit provision for joint cases. Very often, however, in the consumer debtor context, a husband and wife are jointly liable on their debts, and jointly hold most of their property. A joint case will facilitate consolidation of their estates, to the benefit of both the debtors and their creditors, because the cost of administration will be reduced, and there will be only one filing fee.

Section 302 specifies that a joint case is commenced by the filing of a petition under an appropriate chapter by an individual and that individual's spouse. Thus, one spouse cannot take the other into bankruptcy without the other's knowledge or consent. The filing of the petition constitutes an order for relief under the chapter selected.

Subsection (b) requires the court to determine the extent, if any, to which the estates of the two debtors will be consolidated; that is, assets and liabilities combined in a single pool to pay creditors. Factors that will be relevant in the court's determination include the extent of jointly held property and the amount of jointly-owed debts. The section, of course, is not license to consolidate in order to avoid other provisions of the title to the detriment of either the debtors or their creditors. It is designed mainly for ease of administration.

[*House Report No. 95-595, 95th Cong., 1st Sess. 321 (1977); Senate Report No. 95-989, 95th Cong., 2d Sess. 32 (1978).*]

Comment

Under the Code a joint petition may be filed under any chapter by an individual who may be a debtor under that chapter and such individual's spouse.

Bankruptcy Rule 1015(a) provides that the court may order consolidation of two or more petitions pending in the same court by or against the same debtor.

Bankruptcy Rule 1015(b) provides for joint administration of cases by or against (1) husband and wife, (2) partnership and one or more general partners, (3) two or more general partners, and (4) a debtor and an affiliate. The rule does not deal with substantive consolidation. Case law has developed in which consolidation was held to be proper in appropriate circumstances. *See* Sampell v. Imperial Paper & Color Corp., 313 U.S. 215 (1941); Chemical Bank N.Y. Trust Co. v. Kheel, 369 F.2d 845 (2d Cir. 1966).

Bankruptcy Rule 2009, as amended in 1991, relates to trustees in cases subject to joint administration. Subdivision (a) provides that if joint administration is ordered, creditors may elect a single trustee of one or more of the debtors for estates jointly administered. [Creditors may elect a trustee only in a chapter 7 case.] Subdivision (b) provides that notwithstanding an order for joint administration, the creditors of any debtor may elect a separate trustee for his estate. Subdivision (c), as amended in 1991 to reflect the United States trustee's responsibilities, authorizes the United States trustee to appoint one or more interim trustees for jointly administered estates under chapter 7 and to appoint one or more trustees for jointly administered estates in cases under chapter 12, chapter 13 and, if the appointment of a trustee is ordered, chapter 11.

Subdivision (d) of the rule, as amended in 1991, provides that on a showing that creditors or equity security holders of the different estates will be prejudiced by conflicts of interest of a common trustee who has been elected or appointed, the court shall order the selection of separate trustees for the jointly administered estates.

Subdivision (e), formerly subdivision (f), requires the trustee(s) of jointly administered estates to keep separate accounts of the property and distribution of each.

Case Annotations

Section 302(b) of the Code contemplates that joint debtor estates which include community property should be consolidated unless to do so would prejudice the creditors or the administration of the estate. Ageton v. Cervenka (*In re* Ageton), 5 C.B.C.2d 463 (9th Cir., B.A.P., 1982).

A valid joint petition must be filed voluntarily and must involve spouses and the fact that a petition is joint in nature does not make it a joint petition as contemplated by the Bankruptcy Code. *In re Western Land Bank, Inc.*, 23 C.B.C.2d 1089 (B. Ct., C.D. Cal. 1990).

The estates of husband and wife should not be consolidated when the creditors of one estate will benefit to the detriment of creditors of the other and when the affairs and assets of the couple are not so intermingled as to prevent the efficient administration of the estates if they are not co-administered. *In re* Birch, 16 C.B.C.2d 849 (B. Ct., D.N.H. 1987).

References

2 *Collier on Bankruptcy* ch. 302 (Matthew Bender 15th ed.).

1 *Collier Bankruptcy Manual* ch. 302 (Matthew Bender 3d ed.).

2 *Collier Bankruptcy Practice Guide* ch. 18 (Matthew Bender).

Levy, *Joint Administration and Consolidation*, 85 Com. L.J. 538 (1980).

SECTION 303 (11 U.S.C. § 303)

§ 303. Involuntary cases.

(a) An involuntary case may be commenced only under chapter 7 or 11 of this title, and only against a person, except a farmer, family farmer, or a corporation that is not a moneyed, business, or commercial corporation, that may be a debtor under the chapter under which such case is commenced.

(b) An involuntary case against a person is commenced by the filing with the bankruptcy court of a petition under chapter 7 or 11 of this title—

> (1) by three or more entities, each of which is either a holder of a claim against such person that is not contingent as to liability or the subject of a bona fide dispute, or an indenture trustee representing such a holder, if such claims aggregate at least $5,000 more than the value of any lien on property of the debtor securing such claims held by the holders of such claims;

> (2) if there are fewer than 12 such holders, excluding any employee or insider of such person and any transferee of a transfer that is voidable under section 544, 545, 547, 548, 549, or 724(a) of this title, by one or more of such holders that hold in the aggregate at least $5,000 of such claims;

> (3) if such person is a partnership—

(A) by fewer than all of the general partners in such partnership; or

(B) if relief has been ordered under this title with respect to all of the general partners in such partnership, by a general partner in such partnership, the trustee of such a general partner, or a holder of a claim against such partnership; or

(4) by a foreign representative of the estate in a foreign proceeding concerning such person.

(c) After the filing of a petition under this section but before the case is dismissed or relief is ordered, a creditor holding an unsecured claim that is not contingent, other than a creditor filing under subsection (b) of this section, may join in the petition with the same effect as if such joining creditor were a petitioning creditor under subsection (b) of this section.

(d) The debtor, or a general partner in a partnership debtor that did not join in the petition, may file an answer to a petition under this section.

(e) After notice and a hearing, and for cause, the court may require the petitioners under this section to file a bond to indemnify the debtor for such amounts as the court may later allow under subsection (i) of this section.

(f) Notwithstanding section 363 of this title, except to the extent that the court orders otherwise, and until an order for relief in the case, any business of the debtor may continue to operate, and the debtor may continue to use, acquire, or dispose of property as if an involuntary case concerning the debtor had not been commenced.

(g) At any time after the commencement of an involuntary case under chapter 7 of this title but before an order for relief in the case, the court, on request of a party in interest, after notice to the debtor and a hearing, and if necessary to preserve the property of the estate or to prevent loss to the estate, may order the United States trustee to appoint an interim trustee under section 701 of this title to take possession of the property of the estate and to operate any business of the debtor. Before an order for relief, the debtor may regain possession of property in the possession of a trustee ordered appointed under this subsection if the debtor files such bond as the court requires, conditioned on the debtor's accounting for and delivering to the trustee, if there is an order for relief in the case, such property, or the value, as of the date the debtor regains possession, of such property.

(h) If the petition is not timely controverted, the court shall order relief against the debtor in an involuntary case under the chapter under which the petition was filed. Otherwise, after trial, the court shall order relief against the debtor in an involuntary case under the chapter under which the petition was filed, only if—

(1) the debtor is generally not paying such debtor's debts as such debts become due unless such debts are the subject of a bona fide dispute; or

(2) within 120 days before the date of the filing of the petition, a custodian, other than a trustee, receiver, or agent appointed or authorized to take charge of less than substantially all of the property of the debtor for the purpose of enforcing a lien against such property, was appointed or took possession.

(i) If the court dismisses a petition under this section other than on consent of all petitioners and the debtor, and if the debtor does not waive the right to judgment under this subsection, the court may grant judgment—

(1) against the petitioners and in favor of the debtor for—

(A) costs; or

(B) a reasonable attorney's fee; or

(2) against any petitioner that filed the petition in bad faith, for—

(A) any damages proximately caused by such filing; or

(B) punitive damages.

(j) Only after notice to all creditors and a hearing may the court dismiss a petition filed under this section—

(1) on the motion of a petitioner;

(2) on consent of all petitioners and the debtor; or

(3) for want of prosecution.

(k) Notwithstanding subsection (a) of this section, an involuntary case may be commenced against a foreign bank that is not engaged in such business in the United States only under chapter 7 of this title and only if a foreign proceeding concerning such bank is pending.

Bankruptcy Rule References: 1002, 1003, 1004, 1006, 1011, 1013, 1018 and 2001

Legislative History

Section 303 governs the commencement of involuntary cases under title 11. An involuntary case may be commenced only under chapter 7, Liquidation, or chapter 11, Reorganization. Involuntary cases are not permitted for municipalities, because to do so may constitute an invasion of State sovereignty contrary to the tenth amendment, and would constitute bad policy, by permitting the fate of a municipality, governed by officials elected by the people of the municipality, to be determined by a small number of creditors of the municipality. Involuntary chapter 13 cases are not permitted either. To do so would constitute bad policy, because chapter 13 only works when there is a willing debtor that wants to repay his creditors. Short of involuntary servitude, it is difficult to keep a debtor working for his creditors when he does not want to pay them back. *See* chapter 3, *supra*.

The exceptions contained in current law that prohibit involuntary cases against farmers [ranchers] and eleemosynary institutions are continued. Farmers [and ranchers] are excepted because of the cyclical nature of their business. One drought year or one year of low prices, as a result of which a farmer is temporarily unable to pay his creditors, should not subject him to involuntary bankruptcy. Eleeymosynary (*sic*) institutions, such as churches, schools and charitable organizations and foundations, likewise are exempt from involuntary bankruptcy.

The provisions for involuntary chapter 11 cases is a slight change from present law, based on the proposed consolidation of the reorganization chapters. Currently, involuntary cases are permitted under chapters X and XII but not under chapter XI. The consolidation requires a single rule for all kinds of reorganization proceedings. Because the assets of an insolvent debtor belong equitably to his creditors, the bill permits involuntary cases in order that creditors may realize on their assets through reorganization as well as through liquidation. [*Ed. Note:* The House and Senate Reports stating that an involuntary case may be filed under chapter XII of the Act are in error. The Senate Report adds the bracketed language.]

Subsection (b) of the section specifies who may file an involuntary petition. As under current law, if the debtor has more than twelve creditors, three creditors must join in the involuntary petition. [*Ed. Note:* If there are 12 or more, three creditors must join in the petition.] The dollar amount limitation is changed from current law to $5,000. The new amount applies both to liquidation and reorganization cases in order that there not be an artificial difference between the two chapters that would provide an incentive for one or the other. Subsection (b)(1) makes explicit the right of an indenture trustee to be one of the three petitioning creditors on behalf of the creditors the trustee represents under the indenture. If all of the general partners in a partnership are in bankruptcy, then the trustee of a single general partner may file an involuntary petition against the partnership. Finally, a foreign representative may file an involuntary case concerning the debtor in the foreign proceeding, in order to administer assets in this country. This subsection is not intended to overrule Bankruptcy Rule 104(d), which places certain restrictions on the transfer of claims for the purpose of commencing an involuntary case. That Rule will be continued under section 405(d) of this bill.

[*House Report No. 95–595, 95th Cong., 1st Sess. 321 (1977); Senate Report No. 95–989, 95th Cong., 2d Sess. 33 (1978).*]

Section 303(b)(1) is modified to make clear that unsecured claims against the debtor must be determined by taking into account liens securing property held by third parties.

Section 303(b)(3) adopts a provision contained in the Senate amendment indicating that an involuntary petition may be commenced against a partnership by fewer than all of the general partners in such partnership. Such action may be taken by fewer than all of the general partners notwithstanding a contrary agreement between the partners or State or local law.

[*124 Cong. Rec. H 11, 091 (Sept. 28, 1978), S 17, 407 (Oct. 6, 1978).*]

The amendments made by section 426(b) [of Pub. L. No. 98–353 to 11 U.S.C. § 303(b)(1) and (h)(1)] shall become effective upon the date of enactment of this Act.

[*130 Cong. Rec. H 7482 (June 29, 1984).*]

Subsection (c) permits creditors other than the original petitioning creditors to join in the petition with the same effect as if the joining creditor had been one of the original petitioning creditors. Thus, if the claim of one of the original petitioning creditors is disallowed, the case will not be dismissed for want of three creditors or want of $5,000 in petitioning claims if the joining creditor suffices to fulfill the statutory requirements.

Subsection (d) permits the debtor to file an answer to an involuntary petition. The subsection also permits a general partner in a partnership debtor to answer an involuntary petition against the partnership if he did not join in the petition. Thus, a partnership petition by less than all of the general partners is treated as an involuntary, not a voluntary, petition.

The court may, under subsection (e), require the petitioners to file a bond to indemnify the debtor for such amounts as the court may later allow under subsection (i). Subsection (i) provides for costs, attorneys

fees, and damages in certain circumstances. The bonding requirement
will discourage frivolous petitions as well as spiteful petitions based on
a desire to embarrass the debtor (who may be a competitor of a
petitioning creditor) or to put the debtor out of business without good
cause. An involuntary petition may put a debtor out of business even
if it is without foundation and is later dismissed.

[*Ed. note:* The House and Senate reports are identical except that in
the House Report instead of a separate sentence, the final sentence in
the above paragraph is in parentheses.]

Subsection (f) is both a clarification and a change from existing law.
It permits the debtor to continue to operate any business of the debtor
and to dispose of property as if the case had not been commenced. The
court is permitted, however, to control the debtor's powers under this
subsection by appropriate orders, such as where there is a fear that the
debtor may attempt to abscond with assets, dispose of them at less than
their fair value, or dismantle his business, all to the detriment of the
debtor's creditors.

The court may also, under subsection (g), appoint an interim trustee
to take possession of the debtor's property and to operate any business
of the debtor, pending trial on the involuntary petition. The court may
make such an order only on the request of a party in interest, and after
notice to the debtor and a hearing. There must be a showing that a
trustee is necessary to preserve the property of the estate or to prevent
loss to the estate. The debtor may regain possession by posting a
sufficient bond.

Subsection (h) provides the standard of an order for relief on an
involuntary petition. If the petition is not timely controverted (the Rules
of Bankruptcy Procedure will fix time limits), the court orders relief
under the appropriate chapter. Otherwise the court orders relief, after
a trial, only if the debtor is generally unable to pay its debts as they
mature, of [*sic*] if a custodian was appointed during the 90-day period
preceding the filing of the petition. The former test is the equity
insolvency test. It represents the most significant departure from
present law concerning the grounds for involuntary bankruptcy, which
requires balance sheet insolvency and an act of bankruptcy. This bill
abolishes the concept of acts of bankruptcy. The only basis for an
involuntary case will be the inability of the debtor to meet its debts.

The equity insolvency test has been in equity jurisprudence for
hundreds of years, and though it is new in the bankruptcy context
(except in chapter X), the bankruptcy courts should have no difficulty
in applying it. The second test, appointment of a custodian within 90
days before the petition, is provided for simplicity. It is not a partial
reenactment of acts of bankruptcy. If a custodian of all or substantially
all of the property of the debtor has been appointed, this paragraph
creates an irrebutable presumption that the debtor is unable to pay its
debts as they mature. Moreover, once a proceeding to liquidate assets
has been commenced, the debtor's creditors have an absolute right to
have the liquidation (or reorganization) proceed in the bankruptcy court
and under the bankruptcy laws with all of the appropriate creditor and

debtor protections that those laws provide. Ninety days gives creditors ample time in which to seek bankruptcy liquidation after the appointment of a custodian. If they wait beyond the ninety day period, they are not precluded from filing an involuntary petition. They are simply required to prove equity insolvency rather than the more easily provable custodian test.

[House Report No. 95–595, 95th Cong., 1st Sess. 324 (1977); See Senate Report No. 95–989, 95th Cong., 2d Sess. 34 (1978).]

Section 303(h)(1) in the House amendment is a compromise of standards found in H.R. 8200 as passed by the House and the Senate amendment pertaining to the standards that must be met in order to obtain an order for relief in an involuntary case under title 11. The language specifies that the court will order such relief only if the debtor is generally not paying debtor's debts as they become due.

Section 303(h)(2) reflects a compromise pertaining to section 543 of title 11 relating to turnover of property by a custodian. It provides an alternative test to support an order for relief in an involuntary case. If a custodian, other than a trustee, receiver, or agent appointed or authorized to take charge of less than substantially all of the property of the debtor for the purpose of enforcing a lien against such property, was appointed or took possession within 120 days before the date of the filing of the petition, then the court may order relief in the involuntary case. The test under section 303(h)(2) differs from section 3a(5) of the Bankruptcy Act, which requires an involuntary case to be commenced before the earlier of time such custodian was appointed or took possession. The test in section 303(h)(2) authorizes an order for relief to be entered in an involuntary case from the later date on which the custodian was appointed or took possession.

[124 Cong. Rec. H 11,091 (Sept. 28, 1978); S 17,407 (Oct. 6 1978).]

Subsection (i) permits the court to award costs, reasonable attorney's fees, or damages if an involuntary petition is dismissed other than by consent of all petitioning creditors and the debtor. The damages that the court may award are those that may be caused by the taking of possession of the debtor's property under subsection (g) or section 1104 of the bankruptcy code. In addition, if a petitioning creditor filed the petition in bad faith, the court may award the debtor any damages proximately caused by the filing of the petition. These damages may include such items as loss of business during and after the pendency of the case, and so on. "Or" is not exclusive in this paragraph. The court may grant any or all of the damages provided for under the provision. Dismissal in the best interests of credits [sic] under section 305(a)(1) would not give rise to a damages claim.

Under subsection (j), the court may dismiss the petition by consent only after giving notice to all creditors. The purpose of the subsection is to prevent collusive settlements among the debtor and the petitioning creditors while other creditors, that wish to see relief ordered with respect to the debtor but that did not participate in the case, are left without sufficient protection.

Subsection (k) governs involuntary cases against foreign banks that are not engaged in business in the United States but that have assets located here. The subsection prevents a foreign bank from being placed into bankruptcy in this country unless a foreign proceeding against the bank is pending. The special protection afforded by this section is needed to prevent creditors from effectively closing down a foreign bank by the commencement of an involuntary bankruptcy case in this country unless that bank is involved in a proceeding under foreign law. An involuntary case commenced under this subsection gives the foreign representative an alternative to commencing a case ancillary to a foreign proceeding under section 304.

[*House Report No. 95–595, 95th Cong., 1st Sess. 324 (1977); Senate Report No. 95–989, 95th Cong., 2d Sess. 35 (1978).*]

Comment

Neither the House Report set out above nor the Senate Report are in harmony with subsection (h) as enacted. The excerpt from the Congressional Record reflects the changes made after the Reports were published.

Section 59b of the former Bankruptcy Act provided for the filing of an involuntary petition in bankruptcy and section 4b provided for the involuntary adjudication of "any natural person, except a wage earner or farmer, and any moneyed, business, or commercial corporation, except a building and loan association, a municipal, railroad, insurance, or banking corporation, owing debts to the amount of $1000 or over. . . ."

The concept of alleging commission of an act of bankruptcy as provided in Section 4 of the Act has been discarded by the Code. The requirement that the aggregate amount due to petitioning creditors has been increased from $500 to $5,000.

Under Section 59b of the former Bankruptcy Act, one or more creditors whose claims exceeded $500 could file an involuntary petition if all creditors totaled less than 12, otherwise 3 petitioning creditors were necessary. The same rule is found in section 303(b)(2) of the Code except that the claims of the filing creditors must aggregate at least $5,000.

With respect to partnerships, Section 5b of the Act and former Rule 105(b) authorized less than all the general partners to file against the partnership if the latter was insolvent. This provision is carried over to section 303(b)(3)(A), except that there is no requirement that the partnership be insolvent. The test is whether the partnership is generally not paying its debts. *See* 11 U.S.C. § 303(h).

Section 103(c) of the Code provides that creditors other than the original petitioners can "at any time" join in the petition.

The Act contained no provision similar to section 303(d) of the Code authorizing operation of the business of the debtor until the entry of an order for relief. Section 303(d) represents a substantial change.

The Act contained no provision for an "interim trustee" to operate any business of the debtor pending trial of the involuntary petition. The concept of a "receiver" as provided in section 2a(3) of the Act was abolished by the Code. The duties of an "interim trustee" are not unlike those of a "receiver" authorized to operate the business.

Under section 303(h), if an involuntary petition for liquidation or chapter 11 relief is controverted, the court, after trial, will order relief only (1) if debtor is "generally unable to pay such debtor's debts" as they become due, or if (2) within 120 days prior to filing of the petition a custodian (as defined) was appointed or took possession. Under the Act, it was necessary to establish insolvency as defined in Section 1(19) (the balance sheet test) and prove the commission of one of the six acts of bankruptcy set forth in Section 3a.

Section 303(j) of the Code finds its counterpart in Section 59g of the Act requiring a hearing on notice to creditors before a case could be dismissed on application of the petitioning creditor(s) or for want of prosecution.

There was no counterpart in the Act to section 303(k) of the Code dealing with involuntary proceedings against a foreign bank. *But see In re* Israel British Bank (London) Ltd., 536 F.2d 509 (2d Cir.), *cert. denied,* 429 U.S. 978 (1976) holding that a foreign bank, not conducting banking business in the United States could qualify for the benefits of the Act as a voluntary bankrupt. *See also* Banque de Financement S.A. v. First National Bank of Boston, 568 F.2d 911 (2d Cir. 1977), holding that such a banking corporation was eligible for relief under former Chapter XI.

Rule 1002, as amended in 1991, provides that a petition commencing a case under the Code shall be filed with the clerk and transmitted by the clerk to the United States trustee. Rule 5005(b)(3), however, relieves the clerk of the duty to transmit to the United States trustee any paper under the Bankruptcy Rules, including the petition, that the United States trustee requests not be transmitted. The rule governs the filing of voluntary and involuntary petitions. The 1987 Amendments to the Bankruptcy Rules deleted all provisions relating to the number of copies of a petition that must be filed. The 1987 Advisory Committee Note to Rule 1002 states that the number of copies of a petition that must be filed is a matter for local rule.

Bankruptcy Rule 1003(b) provides that if an answer to a petition filed by fewer than 3 creditors avers that there are 12 or more creditors, the debtor must file with his answer a list of all creditors, their addresses and a brief statement of the nature and amount of their claims. If it appears that there are 12 or more creditors, the court is to afford a reasonable opportunity for other creditors to join in the petition before a hearing is held on the issue. The court is not required to give notice of the petition; the list of creditors filed by debtor affords petitioner(s) an opportunity to obtain the necessary co-petitioners.

In the case of an involuntary petition against a partnership, Rule 1004(b) requires that a copy of the petition be forthwith served or sent to each non-joining partner by the petitioning partner or other petitioners. Note that this is in addition to the copy of the petition that is served with the summons issued by the clerk.

Bankruptcy Rule 1005 prescribes that the caption of a petition contain the name of the court, title of the case, and docket number, that it include debtor's Social Security and employer's tax identification numbers, and that it list all names used by debtor within 6 years. In an involuntary case, the petition shall include all names used by the debtor which are known to the petitioning creditors.

Bankruptcy Rule 1011(a) provides that in the case of a petition against a partnership, any non-joining general partner, or person alleged to be a general partner but who denies the allegation, may contest the petition.

Bankruptcy Rule 2001, as amended in 1991, provides in subdivision (a) that the appointment of an interim trustee in an involuntary chapter 7 case may be ordered at any time after commencement of the case and before entry of the order for relief. Appointment may be ordered only on written motion of a party in interest setting forth the necessity for the appointment, and after hearing on notice to the debtor, petitioning creditors, the United States trustee, and other parties in interest designated by the court. Note that, pursuant to section 303(g), the court orders the United States trustee to appoint the trustee. To conform the Rule to the statute, the 1991 Amendments revised Rule 2001(a) to reflect the United States trustee's responsibility to appoint the interim trustee. Subdivision (b) of the rule requires the movant to furnish a bond, before the appointment is made, to indemnify the debtor for costs, attorney's fee, expenses, and damages allowable under section 303(i). Under subdivision (c), the order directing the appointment of the interim trustee must state the reason the appointment is necessary and specify the trustee's duties. Subdivision (d) requires the interim trustee to forthwith deliver to a trustee elected under section 702 all records and property of the estate and to file a final report and account within 30 days thereafter.

Bankruptcy Rule 1011(a) provides that the debtor (or, in the case of a partnership, any non-joining partner or a person who is alleged to be a general partner but denies the allegation) may contest the petition. Creditors may not contest the petition. Subdivision (b) of the rule requires defenses and objections prescribed by Fed. R. Civ. P. 12, to be served and filed within 20 days after *service* of the summons. The court may prescribe the time for responsive pleading when service is by publication on a party or partner not residing or found in the state where the court sits. Subdivision (c) provides that service of a motion under Civil Rule 12 extends the time to serve and file a responsive pleading. Subdivision (d) permits a claim against a petitioning creditor only to defeat the petition; an affirmative judgment against a petitioning creditor is not permitted. Subdivision (e) provides that no pleading other than the answer is permitted, but the court may order a reply within a prescribed time.

Bankruptcy Rule 1013 requires determination of the issues relating to an involuntary petition to be made "at the earliest practical time" and that the court forthwith enter an order for relief, dismiss the petition, or enter other appropriate orders. Subdivision (b) of the rule provides that if an answer or motion is not timely filed, the court shall on the next day (or as soon thereafter as is practicable) enter an order for the relief sought. Subdivision (c) requires the order for relief to conform substantially to the appropriate Official Form. Official Form No. 14, the Official Form for the "Order for Relief" was abrogated by the 1991 Amendments and was not replaced.

Bankruptcy Rule 1017, as amended in 1991, complements section 303(j). Subdivision (a) provides that (except as provided in sections 707(b), 1208(b) and 1307(b) under which the debtor has the absolute right to have a chapter 12 and 13 case dismissed) a petition shall not be dismissed on motion of a petitioner or for want of prosecution or other cause, or by consent, before a hearing on notice as provided in Rule 2002 (not less than 20 days notice by mail to the debtor, creditors, and indenture trustees). If a list of creditors and their addresses was not previously filed, the debtor must file such list within the time fixed by the court, and upon the failure to do so, the court may order preparation and filing of the list by the debtor or other entity. Subdivision (b) deals with dismissal for nonpayment of any installment of the filing fee ordered pursuant to Rule 1006(b).

Bankruptcy Rule 1018 provides that certain specified rules in Part VII of the rules (Adversary Proceedings) shall apply in all proceedings relating to a contested involuntary petition, unless otherwise provided in the Part I rules otherwise directed by the court. The court may direct that other of the Part VII rules shall also apply.

Bankruptcy Rule 1008 requires all petitions, lists, schedules, statements, and amendments thereto to be verified or contain an unsworn declaration as provided in 28 U.S.C. § 1746. Only the original need be signed but copies must be conformed to the original.

Bankruptcy Rule 1009 permits the debtor to amend, as a matter of course, any voluntary petition, list, schedule or statement. The debtor must give notice to the trustee or any affected entity. On motion of a party in interest, after notice and a hearing the court may direct such amendment.

Bankruptcy Rule 1012, which provided for discovery in a contested petition, was abrogated by the 1987 Amendments to the Bankruptcy Rules because application of the discovery rules in a contested petition is covered by Rule 1018.

1984 Amendments: Section 303(b)(1) was amended by the addition of the words "or the subject of a bona fide dispute." Those same words were added to subsection (h)(1) to indicate that in the case of an involuntary petition it must be shown, if reliance is placed on nonpayment of debts, that debts subject to a bona fide dispute are not to be counted.

1986 Amendments: Section 303(a) was amended by including "family farmer" among the entities against whom an involuntary petition may not be filed.

Section 303(g) was amended to provide that the United States trustee, on order of the court, shall appoint the interim trustee to serve during the "gap" period.

Section 303(a)(1)(C) which provided for damages on dismissal of an involuntary petition has been deleted. The court may award costs and a reasonable attorney's fee if the involuntary petition is dismissed. However, if a petitioning creditor filed the petition in bad faith, the court may award damages and punitive damages in favor of the debtor and against such petitioning creditor.

This section was amended to reflect the creation of a permanent United States trustee system. Section 302(d) of the 1986 Amendments provided different effective dates for the amendments relating to the United States trustee system; except for the districts in Alabama and North Carolina, all judicial districts have United States trustees. *See* Section 302 of the 1986 Amendments, as amended by Pub. L. No. 101-650 (1990), reprinted herein under "Selected Provisions of the Bankruptcy Judges, United States Trustees, and Family Farmer Bankruptcy Act of 1986," regarding effective dates generally.

Case Annotations

The term "consent" as used in section 303(i) means something more than a passive statement of nonopposition to the creditors' motion to dismiss a petition. *In re* R. Eric Peterson Construction Co., Inc., 951 F.2d 1175, 25 C.B.C.2d 1585 (10th Cir. 1991).

A petitioning creditor must first establish a prima facie case that no *bona fide* dispute exists, whereupon the burden shifts to the debtor to present evidence that a *bona fide* dispute does exit, based upon an objective standard. *In re* Rimell, 946 F.2d 1363, 25 C.B.C.2d 1453 (8th Cir. 1991).

An involuntary petition may not be filed against joint debtors. Benny v. Chicago Title Insurance Co. (*In re* Benny), 842 F.2d 1147, 18 C.B.C.2d 821 (9th Cir. 1988).

Postpetition payment of a debt after filing but before the hearing on an involuntary petition does not alter the creditor's status at the filing and does not affect the issue of whether the debt is subject to a bona fide dispute. If a bankruptcy court finds that the creditors have properly filed an involuntary petition, the court must determine as of the date of filing whether the creditors have shown that the debtor was not paying its debts as they became due. Bartmann v. Maverick Tube Corp., 853 F.2d 1540, 19 C.B.C.2d 940 (10th Cir. 1988).

A fully secured creditor can properly join as a petitioning creditor in an involuntary petition. That an alleged chapter 7 debtor subsequently files a voluntary chapter 11 petition does not conclusively prove that on the date of the filing of the prior involuntary petition, the debtor was not paying its debts as they became due. Paradise Hotel Corp. v. Bank of Nova Scotia, 842 F.2d 47, 18 C.B.C.2d 838 (3d Cir. 1988).

In ·assessing whether there is a *"bona fide* dispute," the court need only determine whether there is an objective basis for either a factual or legal dispute as to the validity of a debt. It need not determine the possible outcome of the dispute. In the Matter of Busick, 831 F.2d 745, 17 C.B.C.2d 788 (7th Cir. 1987).

The changes made to section 303 by the 1984 Amendments do not impose jurisdictional requirements; rather, they go to the merits; petitioning creditors cannot prevail unless they can show that their claims are not subject to bona fide dispute but the bankruptcy court is not without jurisdiction prior to this determination. Rubin v. Belo Broadcasting Corp. (*In re* Rubin), 769 F.2d 611, 13 C.B.C.2d 599 (9th Cir. 1985).

It is not the making of a false statement alone that constitutes bad faith, but the wrongful attempt to commence a chapter 11 case. Basin Elec. Power Coop. v. Midwest Processing Co., 769 F.2d 483, 13 C.B.C.2d 500 (8th Cir.), *cert. denied,* 474 U.S. 1083, 106 S. Ct. 854, 88 L. Ed. 2d 894 (1985).

A bona fide dispute exists when the alleged debtor does not admit liability on any of the creditors' claims and the preliminary evidence produced by the creditors to show that the debtor has commingled personal assets with those of a debtor corporation associated with the debtor is found to be inconclusive. *In re* Reid, 773 F.2d 945, 13 C.B.C.2d 781 (7th Cir. 1985).

For purposes of determining whether the jurisdictional requirements for filing an involuntary petition have been met, the value assigned to property in which the debtor has a survivorship interest will be the amount that creditors would be able to recover in a state action to enforce their liens. In the Matter of Tsunis, 10 C.B.C.2d 1287 (E.D.N.Y. 1983), *aff'd,* 733 F.2d 27 (2d Cir. 1984).

When an involuntary petition is filed in bad faith, the intervention by a good faith creditor does not usually purge the taint of the original bad faith filing and such a petition should be dismissed. *In re* Norriss Brothers Lumber Co., Inc., 25 C.B.C.2d 1571 (B. Ct., N.D. Tex. 1991).

A bankruptcy court does not have subject matter jurisdiction when several separate entities are joined in a single involuntary petition because section 303 does not authorize joint involuntary petitions. *In re* Western Land Bank, Inc., 23 C.B.C.2d 1089 (B. Ct., C.D. Cal. 1990).

The debtor's bank accounts in the United States provide the jurisdictional predicate for a foreign representative to commence a section 303(b)(4) bankruptcy case. *In re* Axona Int'l Credit & Commerce, 19 C.B.C.2d 257 (B. Ct., S.D.N.Y. 1988).

A bankruptcy petition filed by fewer than all of the general partners of a debtor partnership, or without their consent, is, in effect, always an involuntary petition. *In re* Memphis-Friday's Assoc., 18 C.B.C.2d 1360 (B. Ct., W.D. Tenn. 1988).

Limited partners are not claim holders by virtue of their partnership interests and cannot file an involuntary petition against the partnership based on their partnership interests. Broadview Savings Bank v. Royal Gate Assoc., Ltd., (*In re* Royal Gate Associates, Ltd.), 18 C.B.C.2d 664 (B. Ct., M.D. Ga. 1988).

References

2 *Collier on Bankruptcy* ch. 303 (Matthew Bender 15th ed.).

1 *Collier Bankruptcy Manual* ch. 303 (Matthew Bender 3d ed.).

1 *Collier Bankruptcy Practice Guide* ch. 14 (Matthew Bender).

Comment, *Involuntary Bankruptcy: The Generally Not Paying Standard,* 33 Mercer L. Rev. 903 (1982).

Loo, *Involuntary Bankruptcy—Judicial Interpretation of the 1984 Amendments,* 20 Hawaii B.J. 49 (1986).

McCoid, II, *The Occasion for Involuntary Bankruptcy,* 61 Am. Bankr. L.J. 195 (1987).

Rosania, *Involuntary Petitions Under the Bankruptcy Reform Act of 1978,* 13 Colo. Law. 1367 (1984).

Treister, Trost, Forman, Klee and Levin, *Commencing a Case Under the Bankruptcy Code,* 34 Prac. Law. 17 (1988).

SECTION 304 (11 U.S.C. § 304)

§ 304. Cases ancillary to foreign proceedings.

(a) A case ancillary to a foreign proceeding is commenced by the filing with the bankruptcy court of a petition under this section by a foreign representative.

(b) Subject to the provisions of subsection (c) of this section, if a party in interest does not timely controvert the petition, or after trial, the court may—

　　(1) enjoin the commencement or continuation of—

　　　　(A) any action against—

　　　　　　(i) a debtor with respect to property involved in such foreign proceeding; or

　　　　　　(ii) such property; or

　　　　(B) the enforcement of any judgment against the debtor with respect to such property, or any act or the commencement or continuation of any judicial proceeding to create or enforce a lien against the property of such estate;

(2) order turnover of the property of such estate, or the proceeds of such property, to such foreign representative; or

(3) order other appropriate relief.

(c) In determining whether to grant relief under subsection (b) of this section, the court shall be guided by what will best assure an economical and expeditious administration of such estate, consistent with—

(1) just treatment of all holders of claims against or interests in such estate;

(2) protection of claim holders in the United States against prejudice and inconvenience in the processing of claims in such foreign proceeding;

(3) prevention of preferential or fraudulent dispositions of property of such estate;

(4) distribution of proceeds of such estate substantially in accordance with the order prescribed by this title;

(5) comity; and

(6) if appropriate, the provision of an opportunity for a fresh start for the individual that such foreign proceeding concerns.

Bankruptcy Rule References: 1002, 1010, 1011 and 1018

Legislative History

This section governs cases filed in the bankruptcy courts that are ancillary to foreign proceedings. That is, where a foreign bankruptcy case is pending concerning a particular debtor and that debtor has assets in this country, the foreign representative may file a petition under this section, which does not commence a full bankruptcy case, in order to administer assets located in this country, to prevent dismemberment by local creditors of assets located here, or for other appropriate relief. The debtor is given the opportunity to controvert the petition.

Subsection (c) requires the court to consider several factors in determining what relief, if any, to grant. The court is to be guided by what will best assure an economical and expeditious administration of the estate, consistent with just treatment of all creditors and equity security holders; protection of local creditors and equity security holders against prejudice and inconvenience in processing claims and interests in the foreign proceeding; prevention of preferential or fraudulent disposition of property of the estate; distribution of the proceeds of the estate substantially in conformity with the distribution provisions of the bankruptcy code; and, if the debtor is an individual, the provision of an opportunity for a fresh start. These guidelines are designed to give the court the maximum flexibility in handling ancillary cases. Principles of international comity and respect for the judgments and laws of other nations suggest that the court be permitted to make the appropriate orders under all of the circumstances of each case, rather than being provided with inflexible rules.

[*House Report No. 95–595, 95th Cong., 1st Sess. 324–325 (1977); Senate Report No. 95–989, 95th Cong., 2d Sess. 35 (1978).*]

Section 304(b) adopts a provision contained in the Senate amendment with modifications. The provision indicates that if a party in interest does not timely controvert the petition in a case ancillary to a foreign proceeding, or after trial on the merits, the court may take various actions, including enjoining the commencement or continuation of any action against the debtor with respect to property involved in the proceeding, or against the property itself; enjoining the enforcement of any judgment against the debtor or the debtor's property; or the commencement or continuation of any judicial proceeding to create or enforce a lien against the property of the debtor or the estate.

Section 304(c) is modified to indicate that the court shall be guided by considerations of comity in addition to the other factors specified therein.

[*124 Cong. Rec. H 11,091 (Sept. 28, 1978); S 17,408 (Oct. 6, 1978).*]

Comment

There was no comparable provision to section 304 in the former Bankruptcy Act. Section 2a(22) of the Act authorized the court to exercise, withhold or suspend exercise of jurisdiction when a bankrupt had been adjudged bankrupt by a court without the United States.

As amended in 1991, Rule 1002 governs the filing of a petition under any chapter of the Code including voluntary and involuntary petitions and a petition in a case ancillary to a foreign proceeding. Under Rule 1010, as revised in 1987, on the filing of a petition commencing a case ancillary to a foreign proceeding, the clerk is to forthwith issue a summons for service on the parties against whom relief is sought pursuant to § 304(b) of the Code and on such other parties as the court may direct.

The manner of service is governed by Rule 1010. Rule 1011(a), (b), (c) and (e) applies to responsive pleadings and motions. Rule 1018 applies when the petition is contested.

Case Annotations

Where both a domestic and a foreign jurisdiction have connections to assets sought to be turned over, the interests of the competing jurisdictions should be bifurcated in the choice-of-law analysis, and a domestic jurisdiction's interest in defining and protecting the property interests of its citizens and businesses is superior to a foreign jurisdiction's interest in orderly administration of the bankruptcy estate. *In re* Koreag, Controle et Revision S.A., 961 F.2d 341, 26 C.B.C.2d 1200 (2d Cir. 1992).

A bankruptcy court may exercise jurisdiction over a section 304 petition provided that both the debtor qualifies for relief under applicable foreign law and that the foreign proceeding is for estate liquidation, composition or extension debt adjustment or discharge, or for effecting reorganization. Goerg v. Parungo (*In re* Goerg), 844 F.2d 1562, 18 C.B.C.2d 1125 (11th Cir. 1988).

Section 304 allows an action to be enjoined when the objective of the proceeding is to establish judgments under which a creditor can collect by enforcement actions against the assets of a debtor and does not require the presence of the assets within the district in order for the court to exercise its jurisdiction. Matter of Kingscroft Insurance Co., Ltd., 26 C.B.C.2d 1530 (B. Ct., S.D. Fla. 1992).

An ancillary proceeding must be dismissed if the foreign distribution of proceeds is not in accordance with title 11. In the Matter of Papaleras Reunidas, S.A., 20 C.B.C.2d 981 (B. Ct., E.D.N.Y. 1989).

An ancillary proceeding was not intended to be a foreign representative's exclusive remedy if proper and adequate administration of the estate requires a full bankruptcy case. *In re* Axona Int'l Credit & Commerce, 19 C.B.C.2d 257 (B. Ct., S.D.N.Y. 1988).

Provided the fairness factors of section 304(c) are met, the bankruptcy court in which a foreign proceeding is pending may make the determination as to whether a foreign reinsurance company's security trust fund held in a bank in the United States is involved in the foreign proceeding. *In re* Lines and Jordan, 18 C.B.C.2d 108 (B. Ct., S.D.N.Y. 1988).

Congress intended that foreign preference and fraudulent transfer actions seeking to recover property located in the United States afford a sufficient basis on which to ground a section 304 petition, even in the instance in which the foreign debtor is not domiciled in, has no place of business in and has no tangible property in the United States. Metzeler v. Bouchard Transp. Co. (*In re* Metzeler), 17 C.B.C.2d 812 (B. Ct., S.D.N.Y. 1987).

References

2 *Collier on Bankruptcy* ch. 304 (Matthew Bender 15th ed.).

1 *Collier Bankruptcy Manual* ch. 304 (Matthew Bender 3d ed.).

2 *Collier Bankruptcy Practice Guide* ch. 19 (Matthew Bender).

Anton, *Creditors' Rights Under Spanish Law,* 33 Am. J. Comp. L. 259 (1985).

Beardsley, *The New French Bankruptcy Statute,* 19 Int'l Law 973 (1985).

Booth, *Recognition of Foreign Bankruptcies: An Analysis and Critique of the Inconsistent Approaches of United States Courts,* 2 Am. Bankr. L.J. 135 (1992).

Gallagher and Hartje, *The Effectiveness of § 304 in Achieving Efficient and Economic Equity in Transnational Insolvency,* 1983 Ann. Surv. Bankr. L. 1.

Morales and Deutsch, *Bankruptcy Code Section 304 and U.S. Recognition of Foreign Bankruptcies: The Tyranny of Comity,* 39 Bus. Law. 1573 (1984).

Resolving Conflicts Under Section 304 of the Bankruptcy Code: In re Metzeler (78 B.R. 674), 3 Conn. J. Int'l L. 439 (1988).

Riesenfeld, *The Status of Foreign Administrators of Insolvent Estates: A Comparative Survey,* 24 Am. J. Comp. L. 288 (1976).

Section 304 of the Bankruptcy Code is Not an Exclusive Remedy in a Nonbankruptcy Court, 19 Vand. J. Transnat'l L. 911 (1986).

Smart, *Carrying on Business as a Basis of Recognition of Foreign Bankruptcies in English Private International Law,* 9 Oxford J. Legal Stud. 557 (1989).

Trautman, *Foreign Creditors in American Bankruptcy Proceedings,* 29 Harv. Int'l L.J. 49 (1988).

Wolff, *Foreign Insolvency Proceedings and the American Bank: The § 304 Problem,* 100 Banking L.J. 4 (1983).

SECTION 305 (11 U.S.C. § 305)

§ 305. Abstention.

(a) The court, after notice and a hearing, may dismiss a case under this title, or may suspend all proceedings in a case under this title, at any time if—

    (1) the interests of creditors and the debtor would be better served by such dismissal or suspension; or

    (2)(A) there is pending a foreign proceeding; and

        (B) the factors specified in section 304(c) of this title warrant such dismissal or suspension.

(b) A foreign representative may seek dismissal or suspension under subsection (a)(2) of this section.

(c) An order under subsection (a) of this section dismissing a case or suspending all proceedings in a case, or a decision not so to dismiss or suspend, is not reviewable by appeal or otherwise by the court of appeals under section 158(d), 1291, or 1292 of title 28 or by the Supreme Court of the United States under section 1254 of title 28.

Legislative History

A principle of the common law requires a court with jurisdiction over a particular matter to take jurisdiction. This section recognizes that there are cases in which it would be appropriate for the court to decline jurisdiction. Abstention under this section, however, is of jurisdiction over the entire case. Abstention from jurisdiction over a particular proceeding in a case is governed by proposed 28 U.S.C. § 1471(c) . . . [(d)]. Thus, the court is permitted, if the interests of creditors and the debtor would be better served by dismissal of the case or suspension of all proceedings in the case, to so order. The court may dismiss or suspend under the first paragraph, for example, if an arrangement is being worked out by creditors and the debtor out of court, there is no prejudice to the rights of creditors in that arrangement, and an involuntary case has been commenced by a few recalcitrant creditors to provide a basis for future threats to extract full payment. The less expensive out-of-court workout may better serve the interests in the case. Likewise, if there is pending a foreign proceeding concerning the debtor and the factors specified in proposed 11 U.S.C. § 304(c) warrant dismissal or suspension, the court may so act.

Subsection (b) gives a foreign representative authority to appear in the bankruptcy court to request dismissal or suspension. Subsection (c) makes the dismissal or suspension order nonreviewable by appeal or otherwise. The bankruptcy court, based on its experience and discretion is vested with the power of decision.

[*House Report No. 95–595, 95th Cong., 1st Sess. 325 (1977); Senate Report No. 95–989, 95th Cong., 2d Sess. 35 (1978).*]

Comment

There was no comparable provision in the former Bankruptcy Act for dismissal or suspension of proceedings in a case because the interests of the debtor would be better served thereby.

Bankruptcy Rule 1017(c) provides that a case shall not be dismissed or a case suspended pursuant to section 305 until after a hearing on notice as provided in Rule 2002(a). This provision refers only to a dismissal or suspension of all proceedings in a case as provided in section 305. It does not concern abstention in hearing an adversary proceeding pursuant to 28 U.S.C. § 1334(c).

Notice should be served on the United States trustee of any hearing on dismissal or conversion.

Pub. L. No. 101-650 (Judicial Improvements Act of 1990) amended section 305 (effective on the date of enactment, December 1, 1990) by inserting the following language before the period in subsection (c): "by the court of appeals under section 158(d), 1291, or 1292 of this title or by the Supreme Court of the United States under section 1254 of this title". However, an error existed in this amendment; in both places where the language "of this title" appeared, the amendment should have instead provided "of title 28" (since sections 158(d), 1291 and 1292 and section 1254 are contained in title 28 and not in title 11). This error was rectified by the "Act to Make Certain Technical Corrections in the Judicial Improvements Act of 1990" (Pub. L. No. 102-198; effective date, December 9, 1991). Pub. L. No. 102-198 replaced "this title" with "title 28" in both places it appeared.

Case Annotations

Section 305(b), read together with section 304, is designed to control dismissal of a competing bankruptcy case when a foreign proceeding is pending and such dismissal order is nonreviewable. Interpool, Ltd. v. Certain Freights of M/Vs, 878 F.2d 111, 21 C.B.C.2d 222 (3d Cir. 1989).

Once the bankruptcy court determines it has jurisdiction, the decision whether to abstain becomes, without exception, an unreviewable exercise of discretion. Cash Currency Exchange, Inc. v. Shine (*In re* Cash Currency Exchange, Inc.), 762 F.2d 542, 12 C.B.C.2d 1499 (7th Cir.), *cert. denied*, 474 U.S. 904, 106 S. Ct. 233, 88 L. Ed. 2d 232 (1985); *but see* Aaronics Equipment Rentals and Sales, Inc. v. Haynes (*In re* Aaronics Equipment Rentals and Sales, Inc.), 14 C.B.C.2d 332 (B. Ct., M.D. La. 1985) (since an abstention decision under section 305 is not reviewable by appeal or otherwise, that decision cannot be made by a bankruptcy judge whose legitimacy depends upon review of his actions).

Dismissal of a case is not appropriate when it would be in the best interest of only one creditor and when it would be detrimental to the debtor and the other creditors, as, for instance, when property is a debtor's sole significant asset and it appears that it has sufficient value to satisfy all claims. *In re* Sky Group International, Inc., 22 C.B.C.2d 403 (B. Ct., W.D. Pa. 1989).

Under section 304(c), the court will suspend a bankruptcy case in favor of a foreign proceeding under principles of comity when the foreign jurisdiction's bankruptcy laws are inherently fair and not repugnant to U.S. bankruptcy concepts of distribution and liquidation. *In re* Axona Int'l Credit & Commerce, 19 C.B.C.2d 257 (B. Ct., S.D.N.Y. 1988).

Abstention by the court would not be in the best interests of the creditors and the chapter 11 debtor when a debtor partnership's only asset, an apartment complex, would then be sold at a foreclosure sale. *In re* Monterey Equities-Hillside, 16 C.B.C.2d 1214 (B. Ct., N.D. Cal. 1987).

References

2 *Collier on Bankruptcy* ch. 305 (Matthew Bender 15th ed.).

1 *Collier Bankruptcy Manual* ch. 305 (Matthew Bender 3d ed.).

Eckloff, *Abuse of Discretion in Bankruptcy Courts,* 58 Den. L.J. 291 (1981).

Preemption's Effect on Younger v. Harris *Abstention: May a Bankruptcy Court Enjoin a State Criminal Prosecution?,* 35 Mercer L. Rev. 1345 (1984).

SECTION 306 (11 U.S.C. § 306)

§ 306. Limited appearance. An appearance in a bankruptcy court by a foreign representative in connection with a petition or request under section 303, 304, or 305 of this title does not submit such foreign representative to the jurisdiction of any court in the United States for any other purpose, but the bankruptcy court may condition any order under section 303, 304, or 305 of this title on compliance by such foreign representative with the orders of such bankruptcy court.

Legislative History

Section 306 permits a foreign representative that is seeking dismissal or suspension under section 305 of an ancillary case or that is appearing in connection with a petition under section 303 or 304 to appear without subjecting himself to the jurisdiction of any other court in the United States, including State courts. The protection is necessary to allow the foreign representative to present his case and the case of the foreign estate, without waiving the normal jurisdictional rules of the foreign country. That is, creditors in this country will still have to seek redress against the foreign estate according to the host country's jurisdictional rules. Any other result would permit local creditors to obtain unfair advantage by filing an involuntary case, thus requiring the foreign representative to appear, and then obtaining local jurisdiction over the representative in connection with his appearance in this country. That kind of bankruptcy law would legalize an ambush technique that has frequently been rejected by the common law in other contexts.

However, the bankruptcy court is permitted under section 306 to condition any relief under section 303, 304, or 305 on the compliance by the foreign representative with the orders of the bankruptcy court. The last provision is not carte blanche to the bankruptcy court to require the foreign representative to submit to jurisdiction in other courts contrary to the general policy of the section. It is designed to enable the bankruptcy court to enforce its own orders that are necessary to the appropriate relief granted under section 303, 304, or 305.

[*House Report No. 95–595, 95th Cong., 1st Sess. 325–326 (1977); Senate Report No. 95–989, 95th Cong., 2d Sess. 36 (1978).*]

Comment

There was no provision in the Act comparable to section 306 of the Bankruptcy Code.

Case Annotations

When a creditor's jurisdictional objections have been overruled by the bankruptcy court, the court may allow the creditor to file a proof of claim after the time for filing has expired, if equity will be better served thereby. Assoc. Fin. Services Co., v. Ohnstad (*In re* Ohnstad), 1 C.B.C.2d 494 (B. Ct., D.S.D. 1980).

References

2 *Collier on Bankruptcy* ch. 306 (Matthew Bender 15th ed.).

1 *Collier Bankruptcy Manual* ch. 306 (Matthew Bender 3d ed.).

2 *Collier Bankruptcy Practice Guide* ch. 19 (Matthew Bender).

SECTION 307 (11 U.S.C. § 307)

§ 307.   **United States trustee.** The United States trustee may raise and may appear and be heard on any issue in any case or proceeding under this title but may not file a plan pursuant to section 1121(c) of this title.

Comment

This section was added by the 1986 Amendments. The words, "may raise and may appear and be heard on any issue" are identical to those used in section 1109(a) relating to the Securities and Exchange Commission, and section 1109(b) relating to a party in interest. The wording in section 307 applies to any case or proceeding under chapters 7, 9, 11, 12 and 13.

Section 307 was enacted to reflect the creation of a permanent and, with the exception of Alabama and North Carolina, nationwide United States Trustee system.

See 28 U.S.C. § 586 *infra* for duties of a United States trustee.

Prior to the 1986 Act, the United States trustee system was restricted to a limited number of districts commonly referred to as pilot areas or districts. Part X of the Rules related only to United States trustees serving in the pilot areas. Because the 1986 Act made the United States trustee system permanent and nationwide, Part X of the rules was abrogated by the 1991 Amendments to the Bankruptcy Rules and Parts I through IX were revised to include the United States trustee wherever appropriate.

Pub. L. No. 101-650 (Judicial Improvements Act of 1990, signed into law on December 1, 1990) contained a provision regarding the standing of a bankruptcy administrator in a case under the Bankruptcy Code. This provision, which applies in the judicial districts in Alabama and North Carolina, mirrors the language of 11 U.S.C. § 307 and reads as follows:

"(b) Standing.—A bankruptcy administrator may raise and may appear and be heard on any issue in any case under title 11, United States Code, but may not file a plan pursuant to section 1121(c) of such title."

Case Annotations

Section 307 grants the United States trustee the right to raise, appear and be heard on any issue, and there is no limitation on the trustee's right to appeal, either in the statute or in the legislative history. *In re* Revco D.S., Inc., 898 F.2d 498, 22 C.B.C.2d 841 (6th Cir. 1990).

While section 307 appears to give the United States trustee broad authority, it is limited by other sections of the Code which specifically provide when he or she may object to confirmation. *In re* Eaton, 25 C.B.C.2d 430 (B. Ct., S.D. Idaho 1991).

The United States trustee's standing to "raise . . . appear and be heard" is not unlimited in scope, and the language of 11 U.S.C. § 307 is not so broad as to permit the United States trustee the unrestricted right to raise any issue as a litigant without a further showing of the need to appear as a litigant. *In re* Washington Mfg. Co., 24 C.B.C.2d 1162 (B. Ct., M.D. Tenn. 1991).

References

2 *Collier on Bankruptcy* ch. 307 (Matthew Bender 15th ed.).

1 *Collier Bankruptcy Manual* ch. 307 (Matthew Bender 3d ed.).

SUBCHAPTER II

Officers

SECTION 321 (11 U.S.C. § 321)

§ 321. Eligibility to serve as trustee.

(a) A person may serve as trustee in a case under this title only if such person is —

    (1) an individual that is competent to perform the duties of trustee and, in a case under chapter 7, 12, or 13 of this title, resides or has an office in the judicial district within which the case is pending, or in any judicial district adjacent to such district; or

    (2) a corporation authorized by such corporation's charter or bylaws to act as trustee, and, in a case under chapter 7, 12, or 13 of this title, having an office in at least one of such districts.

(b) A person that has served as an examiner in the case may not serve as trustee in the case.

(c) The United States trustee for the judicial district in which the case is pending is eligible to serve as trustee in the case if necessary.

Legislative History

Section 321 is adapted from current Bankruptcy Act section 45 and Bankruptcy Rule 209, Subsection (a) specifies that an individual may serve as trustee in a bankruptcy case only if he is competent to perform the duties of trustee and resides or has an office in the judicial district within which the case is pending, or in an adjacent judicial district. A corporation must be authorized by its charter or by-laws to act as trustee, and, for chapter 7 or 13 cases, must have an office in any of the above mentioned judicial districts. The United States trustee for the district in which the case is pending is always eligible to serve as trustee.

Section 321 indicates that an examiner may not serve as a trustee in the case.

[*House Report No. 95–595, 95th Cong., 1st Sess. 326 (1977); See Senate Report No. 95–989, 95th Cong., 2d Sess. 36–37 (1978).*]

Comment

Section 45 of the former Bankruptcy Act specified qualifications of receivers and trustees: (1) individuals competent to perform their duties and reside or have an office in the district, or (2) a corporation authorized by its charter or by-laws to act in such capacity and have an office in the district.

1986 Amendments: Subsection (c), as added in 1986, empowers the United States trustee to serve as trustee in a case "if necessary." Should the United States trustee be unable to find a person willing to serve as trustee in a case, subsection (c) would permit the United States trustee to serve as trustee. The Joint Explanatory Statement of the Committee of Conference for the 1986 Act had the following to say respecting subsection (c):

> The House and Senate Conferees agree that it is not their expectation or intent that the United States trustee will use the authority to serve as case trustee frequently. The United States trustee is to make a good faith, diligent effort to locate a disinterested and qualified trustee. Conferees agreed that United States trustees in the pilot program appear to be using their current authority to serve as case trustee in an appropriate manner.

This section was amended to reflect the creation of a permanent United States trustee system. Section 302(d) of the 1986 Amendments provided different effective dates for the amendments relating to the United States trustee system; except for the districts in Alabama and North Carolina, all judicial districts have United States trustees. *See* Section 302 of the 1986 Amendments, as amended by Pub. L. No. 101-650 (1990), reprinted herein under "Selected Provisions of the Bankruptcy Judges, United States Trustees, and Family Farmer Bankruptcy Act of 1986," regarding effective dates generally.

References

2 *Collier on Bankruptcy* ch. 321 (Matthew Bender 15th ed.).

1 *Collier Bankruptcy Manual* ch. 321 (Matthew Bender 3d ed.).

2 *Collier Bankruptcy Practice Guide* ch. 25 (Matthew Bender).

SECTION 322 (11 U.S.C. § 322)

§ 322. Qualification of trustee.

(a) Except as provided in subsection (b)(1), a person selected under section 701, 702, 703, 1104, 1163, 1302, or 1202 of this title to serve as trustee in a case under this title qualifies if before five days after such selection, and before beginning official duties, such person has filed with the court a bond in favor of the United States conditioned on the faithful performance of such official duties.

(b) (1) The United States trustee qualifies wherever such trustee serves as trustee in a case under this title.

(2) The United States trustee shall determine—

(A) the amount of a bond required to be filed under subsection (a) of this section; and

(B) the sufficiency of the surety on such bond.

(c) A trustee is not liable personally or on such trustee's bond in favor of the United States for any penalty or forfeiture incurred by the debtor.

(d) A proceeding on a trustee's bond may not be commenced after two years after the date on which such trustee was discharged.

Bankruptcy Rule References: 2008, 2010 and 2011

Legislative History

A trustee qualifies in a case by filing, within five days after selection, a bond in favor of the United States, conditioned on the faithful performance of his official duties. This section is derived from the Bankruptcy Act section 50b. The court is required to determine the amount of the bond and the sufficiency of the surety on the bond. Subsection (c), derived from Bankruptcy Act section 50i, relieves the trustee from personal liability and from liability on his bond for any penalty or forfeiture incurred by the debtor. Subsection (d), derived from section 50m, fixes a two-year statute of limitations on any action on a trustee's bond. Finally, subsection (e) dispenses with the bonding requirement for the United States trustee.

[*House Report No. 95–595, 95th Cong., 1st Sess. 326 (1977); Senate Report No. 95–989, 95th Cong., 2d Sess. 37 (1978).*]

Section 322(a) is modified to include a trustee serving in a railroad reorganization under subchapter IV of chapter 11.

[*124 Cong. Rec. H 11,091 (Sept. 28, 1978); S 17,408 (Oct. 6, 1978).*]

Comment

Section 322(c) of the Code relieves trustees from liability personally or on their bonds, for penalties or forfeitures incurred by the debtor.

Section 322(d) has a two-year statute of limitations. An action on a trustee's bond may not be commenced after two years after the date on which such trustee was discharged.

Bankruptcy Rule 2010(b), formerly Rule 2010(c), provides that a proceeding on a trustee's bond may be brought by any party in interest in the name of the United States for the use of the entity injured by the breach of the condition.

Bankruptcy Rule 2008, as amended in 1991, requires the United States trustee to immediately notify the person selected as trustee how to qualify and, if applicable, the amount of the trustee's bond. A person (other than one who has filed a blanket bond) who has been selected as trustee shall notify the court and the United States trustee in writing of acceptance of the office within 5 days after receipt of the notice of selection or shall be deemed to have rejected the office.

Bankruptcy Rule 2009, as amended in 1991, relates to trustees in cases subject to joint administration.

Bankruptcy Rule 2010(a) provides for blanket bonds to cover a person who qualifies as trustee in a number of cases, and a number of trustees each qualifying in a different case. Rule 2010 was revised by the 1991 Amendments to provide that the United States trustee, rather than the court, authorizes blanket bonds.

Bankruptcy Rule 2010(b), providing that a certified copy of the order approving the trustee's bond constitutes conclusive evidence of qualification, was abrogated by the 1991 Amendments. The 1991 Advisory Committee Note states that an order approving a bond is no longer necessary in view of the 1986 Amendments to section 322 of the Code.

Bankruptcy Rule 2012(b), as amended by the 1991 Amendments, provides that when a trustee dies, resigns, is removed or otherwise ceases to hold office, the successor trustee shall prepare, file and transmit to the United States trustee an accounting of the prior administration of the estate.

Bankruptcy Rule 2013(a), providing that aggregate compensation of trustees and others shall not be disproportionate or excessive, was abrogated by the 1991 Amendments. The 1991 Advisory Committee Note states that the matter is more properly left for regulation by the United States trustee who, when making appointments, should be sensitive to disproportionate or excessive fees received by any person.

1986 Amendments: This section was amended to reflect the creation of a permanent United States trustee system. Subsection (b)(1) has been added to § 322 providing that the very act of serving as trustee in a case "qualifies" the United States trustee. This implements § 321(c) which provides that the United States trustee is eligible to serve as a trustee in a case.

Subsection (b)(2) has been amended to provide that the United States trustee shall determine the amount of a trustee's bond and the sufficiency of the surety on such bond.

Section 302(d) of the 1986 Amendments provided different effective dates for the amendments relating to the United States trustee system;

except for the districts in Alabama and North Carolina, all judicial districts have United States trustees. *See* Section 302 of the 1986 Amendments, as amended by Pub. L. No. 101-650 (1990), reprinted herein under "Selected Provisions of the Bankruptcy Judges, United States Trustees, and Family Farmer Bankruptcy Act of 1986," regarding effective dates generally.

Case Annotations

If a trustee is found to be negligent in the distribution of the assets of an estate, the court is obliged to impose personal liability upon the trustee even when there is apparent court authorization for the trustee's alleged negligent actions. *In re* Sturm, 24 C.B.C.2d 1350 (B. Ct., E.D. Pa. 1990).

When a bond requires faithful performance and the trustee negligently performs his duty to preserve estate assets, the trustee has not "faithfully performed all his official duties," and liability under his bond is activated. Estate of Reich v. Burke (*In re* Reich), 13 C.B.C.2d 988 (B. Ct., E.D. Mich. 1985).

References

2 *Collier on Bankruptcy* ch. 322 (Matthew Bender 15th ed.).

1 *Collier Bankruptcy Manual* ch. 322 (Matthew Bender 3d ed.).

2 *Collier Bankruptcy Practice Guide* ch. 25 (Matthew Bender).

SECTION 323 (11 U.S.C. § 323)

§ 323. Role and capacity of trustee.

(a) The trustee in a case under this title is the representative of the estate.

(b) The trustee in a case under this title has capacity to sue and be sued.

Bankruptcy Rule References: 2012 and 6009

Legislative History

Subsection (a) of this section makes the trustee the representative of the estate. Subsection (b) grants the trustee the capacity to sue and to be sued. If the debtor remains in possession in a chapter 11 case, section 1107 gives the debtor in possession these rights of the trustee: the debtor in possession becomes the representative of the estate, and may sue and be sued. The same applies in a chapter 13 case.

[*House Report No. 95–595, 95th Cong., 1st Sess. 326 (1977); Senate Report 95–989, 95th Cong., 2d Sess. 37 (1978).*]

Comment

The final sentence of the Report appears to be inaccurate.

Bankruptcy Rule 6009 authorizes a trustee or debtor in possession, with or without court approval, to prosecute or appear and defend any pending actions or proceedings by or against the debtor, or commence or prosecute any action or proceeding on behalf of the estate before any tribunal.

Case Annotations

A trustee appointed to liquidate and distribute the debtors' property, which was placed in a trust created in a chapter 11 plan, must file income tax returns and pay income tax for both the corporate and individual debtors pursuant to 26 U.S.C. § 6012(b) because of the trustee's status as an assigneee of the property of the corporate debtors and as a fiduciary of a trust consisting of the property of the individual debtor. Holywell Corp. v. Smith, 503 U.S. —, 112 S. Ct. 1021, 117 L. Ed. 2d 196, 26 C.B.C.2d 1 (1992).

As the trustee plays the role most closely analogous to that of a solvent corporation's management, and given that the debtor's directors retain virtually no management powers, it is the trustee that is empowered to exercise the corporation's attorney-client privilege with respect to prepetition communications; moreover, although no federal interests are impaired by the trustee's control, to allow directors to exercise the privilege would frustrate the Bankruptcy Code's intent that the trustee investigate insider fraud and recover misappropriated assets. Commodity Futures Trading Comm. v. Weintraub, 471 U.S. 343, 105 S. Ct. 1986, 85 L. Ed. 2d 372, 12 C.B.C.2d 651 (1985).

A trustee in bankruptcy is a fiduciary representing the estate and the creditors and can bind lienholders in compromising equitable subordination claims against mortgagees where the identification of interests between the trustee and other parties is such that the trustee was acting virtually as their representative. *In re* Medomak Canning, 922 F.2d 895, 24 C.B.C.2d 600 (1st Cir. 1990).

A trustee's representation of the estate does not render the trustee eligible to receive attorney's fees under the Equal Access to Justice Act (28 U.S.C. § 2412(d)(1)(A)) because the estate and creditors are not an "organization" within the EAJA definition. *In re* Davis, 899 F.2d 1136, 23 C.B.C.2d 555 (11th Cir. 1990).

Despite assignment of investors' claims to the trustee for the purpose of collection for their benefit, the trustee lacks standing to assert general causes of action in an attempt to collect money not owed to the estate. Williams v. California 1st Bank, 859 F.2d 664, 19 C.B.C.2d 922 (9th Cir. 1988).

The trustee becomes the sole representative of the estate when the corporate officers and the board of directors resign from their duties, leaving the trustee with the authority to assert or waive the attorney-client privilege. Weissman v. Hassett (*In re* O.P.M. Leasing Services, Inc.), 670 F.2d 383, 5 C.B.C.2d 1252 (2d Cir. 1982).

The trustee's waiver of a corporate debtor's attorney-client privilege is not a bar to the officers' assertion in other proceedings of their own attorney-client privilege. Citibank, N.A. v. Andros, 666 F.2d 1192, 5 C.B.C.2d 1385 (8th Cir. 1981).

In substance, there is no difference between a foreclosure sale and a negotiated sale, so that when the trustee seeks to transfer property which is already the subject of a sales transaction, *i.e.*, a foreclosure sale, to another party for the sole purpose of having the other party taxed on the sale, such a transfer will not be permitted as such a transfer will seriously impair the effective administration of Congress' tax policies. *In re* A.J. Lane & Co., Inc., 25 C.B.C.2d 1202 (B. Ct., D. Mass. 1991).

A debtor has standing to sue a trustee for his negligence in permitting the destruction of an estate's asset in which the debtor has claimed an exemption. Estate of Reich v. Burke (*In re* Reich), 13 C.B.C.2d 988 (B. Ct., E.D. Mich. 1985).

A debtor's ownership interest in hazardous material is an interest included as property of the estate and the estate, represented by a trustee, may be sued and is liable for the removal of such material under the Comprehensive Environmental, Response, Compensation, and Liability Act of 1980. *In re* T.P. Long Chem., Inc., 11 C.B.C.2d 1246 (B. Ct., N.D. Ohio 1985).

References

2 *Collier on Bankruptcy* ch. 323 (Matthew Bender 15th ed.).

1 *Collier Bankruptcy Manual* ch. 323 (Matthew Bender 3d ed.).

2 *Collier Bankruptcy Practice Guide* ch. 26 (Matthew Bender).

Coleman, *Comfort Orders, Legal Titles and the Constitution—Should Sales by the Trustee Be Judicial Sales?*, 47 Ala. Law. 208 (1986).

Klein and Lichenstein, *Trustee or Debtor: Who May Assert the Attorney-Client Privilege in Bankruptcy Proceedings?*, 57 N.Y.S.B.J. 35 (1985).

Lauter, *When Client Is Bankrupt, Whose Privilege Is It?*, Nat'l L.J., Nov. 12, 1984, at 5, col. 1

Note, *Role of the Trustee in Liquidation Sales*, 8 Colo. Law. 1979 (1981).

Podell, *The Trustee: Ally or Adversary?*, 5 Fam. Advoc. 24 (1983).

Waldschmidt, *Recent Cases Affecting Chapter 7 Trustees*, 6 NABTALK 34 (1990).

Weintraub and Resnick, *Bankruptcy Trustee's Strong-Arm Powers Balked by a Constructive Trust*, 22 U.C.C.L.J. 367 (1990).

SECTION 324 (11 U.S.C. § 324)

§ 324. Removal of trustee or examiner.

(a) The court, after notice and a hearing, may remove a trustee, other than the United States trustee, or an examiner, for cause.

(b) Whenever the court removes a trustee or examiner under subsection (a) in a case under this title, such trustee or examiner shall thereby be removed in all other cases under this title in which such trustee or examiner is then serving unless the court orders otherwise.

Bankruptcy Rule Reference: 2012

Legislative History

This section permits the court, after notice and a hearing, to remove a trustee for cause. An exception is made for the United States trustee. Because he is under the supervision and direction of the Attorney General, and subject to removal by the Attorney General for cause, the court would interfere with the duties of that Executive Branch official if it were empowered to remove a United States trustee. That responsibility lies with the Attorney General.

[*House Report No. 95–595, 95th Cong., 1st Sess. 326 (1977).*]

This section permits the court, after notice and a hearing, to remove a trustee for cause.

[*Senate Report No. 95–989, 95th Cong., 2d Sess. 37 (1978).*]

Comment

The court may not remove the United States trustee. 28 U.S.C. § 581(c). However, the court may remove, for cause, a trustee appointed by the United States trustee. 11 U.S.C. § 324(a).

Bankruptcy Rule 2012(b), as amended in 1991, provides that if a trustee is removed, dies, resigns or otherwise ceases to hold office, the successor is automatically substituted as a party in any pending action, proceeding or matter. The successor is required to file and transmit to the United States trustee an accounting of the prior administration of the estate.

1986 Amendments: Subsection (a) was amended to provide that the court may not remove a United States trustee. Only the Attorney General may appoint or remove a United States trustee.

Subsection (b) was added to provide that a trustee or examiner removed in a case is automatically removed from all cases in which they are then serving unless the court orders otherwise.

This section was amended to reflect the creation of a permanent United States trustee system. Section 302(d) of the 1986 Amendments provided different effective dates for the amendments relating to the United States trustee system; except for the districts in Alabama and North Carolina, all judicial districts have United States trustees. *See* Section 302 of the 1986 Amendments, as amended by Pub. L. No. 101-650 (1990), reprinted herein under "Selected Provisions of the Bankruptcy Judges, United States Trustees, and Family Farmer Bankruptcy Act of 1986," regarding effective dates generally.

Case Annotations

A trustee who requests and obtains a court order directing a creditor to withdraw *lis pendens* notices filed against estate property cannot then prosecute a criminal contempt for violation of the order since the trustee is an interested party and such prosecution would constitute an inherent conflict of interest between the interests of the estate and the public. In the Matter of Hipp, Inc., 895 F.2d 1503, 22 C.B.C.2d 876 (5th Cir. 1990).

In cases involving the liquidation of securities dealers, the disinterestedness of a trustee will be determined by the provisions of the Securities Investors Protection Act, not by that of the Bankruptcy Code. *In re* First State Securities Corp., 10 C.B.C.2d 1037 (B. Ct., S.D. Fla. 1984).

A chapter 11 trustee should not be disqualified from administering both a parent company and its wholly owned subsidiary when there does not exist a present, actual conflict of interest and, to the contrary, there exists a unity of interest and singleness of purpose on the part of the parent and subsidiary estates. Hassett v. McColley (*In re* O.P.M. Leasing Services, Inc.), 5 C.B.C.2d 1503 (B. Ct., S.D.N.Y. 1982).

References

2 *Collier on Bankruptcy* ch. 324 (Matthew Bender 15th ed.).

1 *Collier Bankruptcy Manual* ch. 324 (Matthew Bender 3d ed.).

2 *Collier Bankruptcy Practice Guide* ch. 29 (Matthew Bender).

SECTION 325 (11 U.S.C. § 325)

§ 325. **Effect of vacancy.** A vacancy in the office of trustee during a case does not abate any pending action or proceeding, and the successor trustee shall be substituted as a party in such action or proceeding.

Bankruptcy Rule Reference: 2012

Legislative History

Section 325, derived from Bankruptcy Act section 46, specifies that a vacancy in the office of trustee during a case does not abate any pending action or proceeding. The successor trustee, when selected and qualified, is substituted as a party in any pending action or proceeding.

[*House Report No. 95–595, 95th Cong., 1st Sess. 327 (1977); See Senate Report No. 95–989, 95th Cong., 2d Sess. 37 (1978).*]

Comment

Bankruptcy Rule 2012(b) complements section 325, providing that when a trustee dies, resigns, is removed, or otherwise ceases to hold office, the successor is automatically substituted as a party in any pending action, proceeding or matter.

Subdivision (b) was amended in 1991 to require the successor to file and transmit to the United States trustee an accounting of the prior administration of the case. Because a court order is not required for the appointment of a successor trustee, no time period for the filing of the accounting with the court is mandated. The United States trustee has supervisory powers over trustees and may require the successor trustee to file the accounting within a certain time period. *See* 1991 Advisory Committee Note to Rule 2012.

References

2 *Collier on Bankruptcy* ch. 325 (Matthew Bender 15th ed.).

1 *Collier Bankruptcy Manual* ch. 325 (Matthew Bender 3d ed.).

2 *Collier Bankruptcy Practice Guide* ch. 29 (Matthew Bender).

SECTION 326 (11 U.S.C. § 326)

§ 326. Limitation on compensation of trustee.

(a) In a case under chapter 7 or 11, the court may allow reasonable compensation under section 330 of this title of the trustee for the trustee's services, payable after the trustee renders such services, not to exceed fifteen percent on the first $1,000 or less, six percent on any amount in excess of $1,000 but not in excess of $3,000, and three percent on any amount in excess of $3,000, upon all moneys disbursed or turned over in the case by the trustee to parties in interest, excluding the debtor, but including holders of secured claims.

(b) In a case under chapter 12 or 13 of this title, the court may not allow compensation for services or reimbursement of expenses of the United States trustee or of a standing trustee appointed under section 586(b) of title 28, but may allow reasonable compensation under section 330 of this title of a trustee appointed under section 1202(a) or 1302(a) of this title for the trustee's services, payable after the trustee renders such services, not to exceed five percent upon all payments under the plan.

(c) If more than one person serves as trustee in the case, the aggregate compensation of such persons for such service may not exceed the maximum compensation prescribed for a single trustee by subsection (a) or (b) of this section, as the case may be.

(d) The court may deny allowance of compensation for services or reimbursement of expenses of the trustee if the trustee failed to make diligent inquiry into facts that would permit denial of allowance under section 328(c) of this title or, with knowledge of such facts, employed a professional person under section 327 of this title.

Bankruptcy Rule References: 2013 and 2016

Legislative History

This section is derived in part from section 48c of the Bankruptcy Act. It must be emphasized that this section does not authorize compensation of trustees. This section simply fixes the maximum compensation of a trustee. Proposed 11 U.S.C. § 330 authorizes and fixes the standard of compensation. Under section 48c of current law, the maximum limits have tended to become minimums in many cases. This section is not intended to be so interpreted. The limits in this section, together with the limitations found in section 330, are to be applied as outer limits, and not as grants or entitlements to the maximum fees specified.

[*House Report No. 95–595, 95th Cong., 1st Sess. 327 (1977); Senate Report No. 95–989, 95th Cong., 2d Sess. 37 (1978).*]

The maximum fee schedule is derived from section 48c(1), with three changes. First, the authorization of a fee of $150 (no matter what the size of the estate) is deleted. This provision has too often been used to pay trustees while leaving nothing for the creditors. Often, fees under that provision amount to over 90 percent of the assets of the estate. The second change relates to the bases on which the percentage maxima are computed. The maximum fee schedule is based on decreasing percentages of increasing amounts. The amounts are the amounts of money distributed by the trustee to parties in interest, excluding the debtor, but including secured creditors. These amounts were last amended in 1952. Since then, the cost of living has approximately doubled. Thus, the bases were doubled. The third change is of the percentage allowable on the first base of $1,000. It has been increased from 10 percent to 15 percent, to allow a fee of $150 if the assets in the estate total $1,000.

It should be noted that the base on which the maximum fee is computed includes moneys turned over to secured creditors, to cover the situation where the trustee liquidates property subject to a lien and distributes the proceeds. It does not cover cases in which the trustee simply turns over the property to the secured creditor, nor where the trustee abandons the property and the secured creditor is permitted to foreclose. The provision is also subject to the rights of the secured creditor generally under proposed 11 U.S.[C.] § 506, especially section 506(c).

[*House Report No. 95–595, 95th Cong., 1st Sess. 327 (1977).*]

The maximum fee schedule is derived from section 48c(1) of the present act, but with a change relating to the bases on which the percentage maxima are computed. The maximum fee schedule is based on decreasing percentages of increasing amounts. The amounts are the amounts of money distributed by the trustee to parties in interest, excluding the debtor, but including secured creditors. These amounts were last amended in 1952. Since then the cost of living has approximately doubled. Thus, the bases were doubled.

It should be noted that the bases on which the maximum fee is computed includes moneys turned over to secured creditors, to cover the situation where the trustee liquidates property subject to a lien and distributes the proceeds. It does not cover cases in which the trustee simply turns over the property to the secured creditor, nor where the trustee abandons the property and the secured creditor is permitted to foreclose. The provision is also subject to the rights of the secured creditor generally under proposed section 506, especially 506(c). The $150 discretionary fee provision of current law is retained.

[*Senate Report No. 95–989, 95th Cong., 2d Sess. 37–38 (1978).*]

Section 326(a) of the House amendment modifies a provision as contained in H.R. 8200 as passed by the House. The percentage limitation on the fees of a trustee contained in the House bill is retained, but no additional percentage is specified for cases in which a trustee operates the business of the debtor. Section 326(b) of the Senate amendment, is deleted as an unnecessary restatement of the limitation contained in section 326(a) as modified. The provision contained in section 326(a) of the Senate amendment authorizing a trustee to receive a maximum fee of $150 regardless of the availability of assets in the estate is deleted. It will not be necessary in view of the increase in section 326(a) and the doubling of the minimum fee as provided in section 330(b).

[*124 Cong. Rec. H 11,091 (Sept. 28, 1978); S 17,408 (Oct. 6, 1978).*]

Subsection (d) permits a maximum fee of five percent on all payments to creditors under a chapter 13 plan if there is a private trustee elected in the case under section 1302(a). If the United States trustee serves as trustee in the chapter 13 case, no fee is payable for his services, thus freeing more assets for creditors. If a private standing trustee serves, his fee is fixed by the Attorney General under proposed 28 U.S.C. § 586(e), and it will be payable under proposed 11 U.S.C. § 1326(a)(2).

[*House Report No. 95–595, 95th Cong., 1st Sess. 328 (1977).*]

Ed. Note: The House Report refers to subsection (d) of an earlier version of the bill. The reference should be to subsection (b) of section 326. The same is true of the Senate Report which refers to subsection (c). As enacted, a trustee may be appointed but not elected under section 1302(a). Under that section, as amended in 1986, the United States trustee may appoint a standing trustee to serve in cases under chapter 13, may appoint one disinterested person to serve as trustee in the case, or the United States trustee may serve as trustee in the case.]

Subsection (c) permits a maximum fee of five percent on all payments to creditors under a chapter 13 plan to the trustee appointed in the case.

[*Senate Report No. 95–989, 95th Cong., 2d Sess. 38 (1978).*]

Section 326(b) of the House amendment derives from section 326(c) of H.R. 8200 as passed by the House. It is a conforming amendment to indicate a change with respect to the selection of a trustee in a chapter 13 case under section 1302(a) of title 11.

[*124 Cong. Rec. H 11,091 (Sept. 28, 1978); S 17,408 (Oct. 6, 1978).*]

Subsection (c) provides a limitation not found in current law. Even if more than one trustee serves in the case, the maximum fee payable to all trustees does not change. For example, if an interim trustee is appointed and an elected trustee replaces him, the combined total of the fees payable to the interim trustee and the permanent trustee may not exceed the amount specified in this section. Under current law, very often a receiver receives a full fee and a subsequent trustee also receives a full fee. The resultant "double-dipping," especially in cases in which the receiver and the trustee are the same individual, is detrimental to the interests of creditors, and needlessly increases the cost of administering bankruptcy estates.

Subsection (e) permits the court to deny compensation of a trustee if the trustee has been derelict in this duty by employing non-disinterested counsel.

[*House Report No. 95–595, 95th Cong., 1st Sess. 327–328 (1977); See Senate Report No. 95–989, 95th Cong., 2d Sess. 38 (1978).*]

[*Ed. Note:* The reference to subsection (e) in the House and Senate Report is to an earlier version of the bill. The reference should be to subsection (d).]

Comment

Provisions for compensation and reimbursement for expenses were provided in Sections 48a–c, 52b, 62a(1), and 64a(1) of the former Bankruptcy Act.

The *proviso* permitting the court to allow $150 when commissions were less than that amount is deleted in the Code.

Section 48c(2) of the Act permitted the court to allow compensation not to exceed twice maximum custodial commissions in the case of a trustee conducting the business. The Code has no comparable provision.

Under Section 48d of the Act, a single fee was allowed where more than one receiver or trustee served. Under the Code, no receiver may be appointed, but under section 701 an "interim trustee" is to be appointed. In such case, the fee paid to the interim trustee and the trustee who succeeds him may not exceed, in the aggregate, the fee of a single trustee.

Bankruptcy Rule 2016, as amended in 1991, relates to compensation for services and reimbursement of expenses. *See* **Comment** to section 330.

1984 Amendments: Section 326(a) was amended to provide that a trustee's compensation shall be three percent on any amount in excess of $3000 of moneys disbursed or turned over by the trustee.

Subsection (d) was added to permit the court to deny compensation or reimbursement to a trustee when the trustee has failed to make diligent inquiry into facts which under section 328(c) would bar compensation and reimbursement of expenses to a professional person who is employed by a trustee or a chapter 11 committee and who is not disinterested or who has an interest adverse to the estate.

1986 Amendments: Subsection (b) relating to limit of compensation was amended to include chapter 12 within its scope. Compensation may not be allowed to the United States trustee in a chapter 12 or 13 case, but reasonable compensation may be allowed to a trustee appointed pursuant to section 1202 or 1302.

Section 326 was amended to reflect the creation of a permanent United States trustee system. Section 302(d) of the 1986 Amendments provided different effective dates for the amendments relating to the United States trustee system; except for the districts in Alabama and North Carolina, all judicial districts have United States trustees. *See* Section 302 of the 1986 Amendments, as amended by Pub. L. No. 101-650 (1990), reprinted herein under "Selected Provisions of the Bankruptcy Judges, United States Trustees, and Family Farmer Bankruptcy Act of 1986," regarding effective dates generally.

Case Annotations

The amount of the fee to be awarded to a chapter 11 trustee is separate from and independent of the fee that is to be awarded to a chapter 7 trustee in the same case; however, when the same individual has served in both capacities, the court may exercise its discretion to award less than the statutory maximum of section 326(a). *In re* Financial Corp. of America, 23 C.B.C.2d 1181 (9th Cir., B.A.P., 1990).

In calculating compensation for a chapter 7 trustee, the maximum fee may not be calculated by considering "constructive disbursements," *i.e.,* the value of liens which are not paid by the trustee but which remain attached to the property interest transferred by the estate. *In re* Barnett, 25 C.B.C.2d 1564 (B. Ct., N.D. Idaho 1991).

In determining the compensation of operating trustees, it is appropriate in calculating trustees' fees to interpret section 326(a) to allow disbursements made in actual operation of businesses, that is, administrative expenses, to be included among the "moneys disbursed or turned over in the case by the trustee to parties in interest." *In re* Orient River Investments, Ltd., 25 C.B.C.2d 1702 (B. Ct., E.D. Pa. 1991).

A trustee does not bill the estate on an hourly basis, but rather the trustee is simply to be compensated for the value of the trustee's services, subject to the cap of 11 U.S.C. § 326. *In re* Miguel, 24 C.B.C.2d 1459 (B. Ct., E.D. Cal. 1991).

Disbursements made by a trustee during the operation of a chapter 11 case to trade creditors and suppliers should be counted in determining the section 326(a) statutory maximum available to a trustee subject to the reasonableness requirement of section 332. *In re* McNar, Inc., 24 C.B.C.2d 773 (B. Ct., S.D. Cal. 1990).

A court may award a trustee less than the statutory fee of section 326(a) because section 326(a) sets a ceiling on a trustee's fees but does not create an absolute entitlement to a commission in that amount. *In re* Stoecker, 23 C.B.C.2d 915 (B. Ct., N.D. Ill. 1990).

A trustee will not be allowed costs for clerical work including letter writing, telephone answering, message taking, check writing and bank statement balancing. In the Matter of Rauch, 22 C.B.C.2d 751 (B. Ct., E.D. Cal. 1990).

When a chapter 7 trustee seeks compensation in excess of $500, the fee application must include specific details as to the number of hours spent on estate matters; without these details, a bankruptcy court could not justify allowing compensation in excess of the $500 cap. *In re* Samson Industries, Inc., 22 C.B.C.2d 980 (B. Ct., E.D. Pa. 1989).

Paralegals utilized by the trustee to perform a trustee's services are not separately compensable and compensation to the trustee for their services is limited by sections 326 and 331(a). *In re* Lanier Spa, Inc., 21 C.B.C.2d 75 (B. Ct., N.D. Ga. 1989).

The formula in section 326(a) for computing compensation of a trustee represents the unconditional maximum amount of compensation that a trustee may seek for his services pursuant to 11 U.S.C. § 330(a). *In re* Greenley Energy Holdings of Pa., Inc., 20 C.B.C.2d 1367 (B. Ct., E.D. Pa. 1989).

References

2 *Collier on Bankruptcy* ch. 326 (Matthew Bender 15th ed.).

1 *Collier Bankruptcy Manual* ch. 326 (Matthew Bender 3d ed.).

2 *Collier Bankruptcy Practice Guide* ch. 28 (Matthew Bender).

SECTION 327 (11 U.S.C. § 327)

§ 327. Employment of professional persons.

(a) Except as otherwise provided in this section, the trustee, with the court's approval, may employ one or more attorneys, accountants, appraisers, auctioneers, or other professional persons, that do not hold or represent an interest adverse to the estate, and that are disinterested persons, to represent or assist the trustee in carrying out the trustee's duties under this title.

(b) If the trustee is authorized to operate the business of the debtor under section 721, 1202, or 1108 of this title, and if the debtor has regularly employed attorneys, accountants, or other professional persons on salary, the trustee may retain or replace such professional persons if necessary in the operation of such business.

(c) In a case under chapter 7, 12, or 11 of this title, a person is not disqualified for employment under this section solely because of such person's employment by or representation of a creditor, unless there is objection by another creditor or the United States trustee, in which case the court shall disapprove such employment if there is an actual conflict of interest.

(d) The court may authorize the trustee to act as attorney or accountant for the estate if such authorization is in the best interest of the estate.

(e) The trustee, with the court's approval, may employ, for a specified special purpose, other than to represent the trustee in conducting the case, an attorney that has represented the debtor, if in the best interest of the estate, and if such attorney does not represent or hold any interest adverse to the debtor or to the estate with respect to the matter on which such attorney is to be employed.

(f) The trustee may not employ a person that has served as an examiner in the case.

Bankruptcy Rule References: 2014, 2016 and 5002

Legislative History

This section authorizes the trustee, subject to the court's approval, to employ professional persons, such as attorneys, accountants, appraisers, and auctioneers, to represent or perform services for the estate. The trustee may employ only disinterested persons that do not hold or represent an interest adverse to the estate.

Subsection (b) is an exception, and authorizes the trustee to retain or replace professional persons that the debtor has employed if necessary in the operation of the debtor's business. Subsection (c) is an additional exception. The trustee may employ as his counsel a non-disinterested person if the only reason that the attorney is not disinterested is because of his representation of an unsecured creditor.

Subsection (d) permits the court to authorize the trustee, if qualified, to act as his own counsel.

Subsection (e) permits the trustee, subject to the court's approval, to employ for a specified special purpose an attorney that has represented the debtor, if such employment is in the best interest of the estate and if the attorney does not hold or represent an interest adverse to the debtor or the estate with respect to the matter on which he is to be employed. This subsection does not authorize the employment of the debtor's attorney to represent the estate generally or to represent the trustee in the conduct of the bankruptcy case. The subsection will most likely be used when the debtor is involved in complex litigation, and changing attorneys in the middle of the case after the bankruptcy case has commenced would be detrimental to the progress of that other litigation.

[House Report No. 95–595, 95th Cong., 1st Sess. 328 (1977); See Senate Report No. 95–989, 95th Cong., 2d Sess. 38 (1978).]

Section 327(a) of the House amendment contains a technical amendment indicating that attorneys, and perhaps other officers enumerated therein, represent, rather than assist, the trustee in carrying out the trustee's duties.

Section 327(c) represents a compromise between H.R. 8200 as passed by the House and the Senate amendment. The provision states that former representation of a creditor, whether secured or unsecured, will not automatically disqualify a person from being employed by a trustee, but if such person is employed by the trustee, the person may no longer represent the creditor in connection with the case.

Section 327(f) prevents an examiner from being employed by the trustee.

[124 Cong. Rec. H 11,091 (Sept. 28, 1978); S 17,408 (Oct. 6, 1978).]

Comment

Bankruptcy Rule 2014, relating to the employment of professional persons, was amended by the 1991 Amendments. Subdivision (a) provides that an application or order approving employment of attorneys, accountants, appraisers, auctioneers, agents or other professionals (pursuant to 11 U.S.C. §§ 327, 1103 or 1114) be made only on application of the trustee or committee, filed and, except in a chapter 9 municipality case, transmitted to the United States trustee. The application shall state specific facts as to the necessity for such employment, the name of the person to be employed, the reasons for the selection, the professional services to be rendered, any proposed arrangement for compensation, and, to the best of applicant's knowledge, all of such person's connections with the debtor, creditors, any other party in interest, their attorneys and accountants, the United States trustee or any person employed in the office of the United States trustee. (The persons employed must be "disinterested" as that term is defined in section 101.) The application shall be accompanied by a verified statement of the person to be employed setting forth these connections. Subdivision (b) of the rule provides that if a partnership or corporation is employed as attorney or accountant, or if the attorney or accountant is employed on behalf of any professional corporation or partnership, any member or regular associate of the firm may act as attorney or accountant in the case without further court order.

See section 504 as to sharing of compensation.

Rule 5002(a) was revised by the 1991 Amendments to provide that the appointment of an individual as trustee or examiner pursuant to section 1104 shall not be approved if the individual is a relative of the bankruptcy judge approving the appointment or of the United States trustee in the region in which the case is pending. The appointment of an attorney, accountant or other professional pursuant to sections 327, 1103 or 1114 may not be approved by the court if the individual is a relative of the bankruptcy judge approving the employment. Such appointment may be aproved by the court if the individual is a relative of the United States trustee in the region in which the case is pending, unless the court finds that the relationship renders the employment improper under the circumstances of the case. When an individual may not be approved, the firm of the individual, all members, associates and professional employees of the firm also may not be approved for employment or appointment.

Rule 5002(b) was revised in 1991 to provide that a bankruptcy judge may not approve the appointment of a person as trustee or examiner pursuant to section 1104 or approve the employment of an attorney, accountant, appraiser, auctioneer or other professional person pursuant to sections 327, 1103 or 1114 if such person is or has been so connected with the judge or United States trustee as to render the appointment or employment improper.

Bankruptcy Rule 6005 implements section 327 and provides that the court approving employment of an appraiser or auctioneer shall fix the amount or rate of the compensation. No officer or employee of the Judicial Branch of the United States or the United States Department of Justice shall be eligible to act as appraiser or auctioneer. No residence or licensing requirement shall disqualify an appraiser or auctioneer from employment.

1984 Amendments: Section 327(c) was amended so that a person who represents a creditor is not disqualified from employment unless another creditor objects, in which case the court must disapprove such employment if there is an actual conflict of interest.

1986 Amendments: The amendments included references to section 1202 in subsection (b), and to chapter 12 in subsection (c).

Subsection (c) was amended by providing that the United States trustee as well as a creditor may object to the employment of a person because of such person's employment by or representation of a creditor. The reference to the United States trustee in this connection is operative only in a district in which a United States trustee is serving.

This section was amended to reflect the creation of a permanent United States trustee system. Section 302(d) of the 1986 Amendments provided different effective dates for the amendments relating to the United States trustee system; except for the districts in Alabama and North Carolina, all judicial districts have United States trustees. *See* Section 302 of the 1986 Amendments, as amended by Pub. L. No. 101-650 (1990), reprinted herein under "Selected Provisions of the Bankruptcy Judges, United States Trustees, and Family Farmer Bankruptcy Act of 1986," regarding effective dates generally.

Case Annotations

Applicants for appointment as professional persons have a duty to disclose potential conflicts of interest and a failure to disclose such conflicts will not be overlooked when the failure is due to mere negligence. *In re* BH&P Inc., 949 F.2d 1300, 26 C.B.C.2d 37 (3d Cir. 1991).

When the trustee acts as an attorney for the estate in an action against a federal agency to recover preferential transfers and to have a claim equitably subordinated, that trustee is not eligible to be paid attorney's fees under the Equal Access to Justice Act (28 U.S.C. § 2412(d)(1)(A)) because the estate and creditors are not an "organization" within the EAJA definition. *In re* Davis, 899 F.2d 1136, 23 C.B.C.2d 555 (11th Cir. 1990).

When one attorney represents both limited and general partners in bankruptcy cases, there is always a potential for conflict and disqualification is, therefore, proper. *In re* W.F. Development Corp., 905 F.2d 883, 23 C.B.C.2d 617 (5th Cir. 1990).

A debtor's constitutional right to an attorney has not been violated when the bankruptcy court has approved the withdrawal of that attorney from the bankruptcy case. In the Matter of Wynn, 889 F.2d 644, 22 C.B.C.2d 157 (5th Cir. 1989).

Professional employment may be retroactively approved if the bankruptcy court finds, after a hearing, that (1) the applicant satisfies the disinterestedness requirement of section 327(a) and would therefore have been appointed initially, and (2) the particular circumstances presented are so extraordinary as to warrant retroactive approval. A finding of "extraordinary circumstances" can be established by looking at "whether the applicant or some other person bore responsibility for applying for approval; whether the applicant was under time pressure to begin service without approval; the amount of delay after the applicant learned that initial approval had not been granted; the extent to which compensation to the applicant will prejudice innocent third parties; and other relevant factors." Simon v. Greycas, Inc. (*In re* F/S Airlease II, Inc.), 844 F.2d 99, 18 C.B.C.2d 959 (3d Cir. 1988).

The bankruptcy court must decide, case by case, whether a mortgage granted to a law firm as security for payment of its fee presents a conflict of interest. The court should determine whether: (1) the agreement is negotiated in good faith; (2) the agreement is reasonable; (3) the security is commensurate with the magnitude and the value of foreseeable services in the case; (4) the security is needed to ensure employment of competent counsel; (5) there exists any sign of overreaching; and (6) there exists any appearance of or actual conflict of interest. *In re* Martin, 817 F.2d 175, 16 C.B.C.2d 672 (1st Cir. 1987).

Section 327(c) does not permit an attorney to represent the inherently conflicting interest of an individual both as a creditor and as a debtor in possession, and when such a conflict of interest results, compensation for the attorney's services to the estate will be denied. Hunter Sav. Ass'n v. Baggot Law Offices Co. (*In re* Georgetown of Kettering, Ltd.), 750 F.2d 536, 11 C.B.C.2d 1097 (6th Cir. 1984).

When, as a result of oversight, an attorney neglected to obtain prior approval authorizing his employment, the bankruptcy court as a court of equity, may exercise its discretion to grant such approval *nunc pro tunc,* upon proper showing, and to award compensation for all or part of the services performed by the attorney which substantially benefited the debtor's estate. Fanelli v. Hensley (In the Matter of Triangle Chemicals, Inc.), 697 F.2d 1280, 8 C.B.C.2d 116 (5th Cir. 1983).

An attorney who represented both the debtor and the debtor's general partner may not be approved for employment *nunc pro tunc* by the estate because of the actual conflict of interest. Andrew v. Coopersmith (*In re* Downtown Investment Club III), 19 C.B.C.2d 639 (9th Cir., B.A.P., 1988).

A financial consulting service retained by a debtor in possession that assumes responsibility for the debtor's financial operation, may be granted retroactive approval of an employment application prior to a noticed hearing. Although the court can require the hearing in order to make a more informed decision, a qualified professional proceeding under good faith should not be prejudiced by the delay inherent in that procedure and the debtor should not be deprived of necessary services in the interim. *In re* Crest Mirror and Door Co., Inc., 14 C.B.C.2d 529 (9th Cir., B.A.P., 1986).

An advisor/consultant to a debtor is an insider and not a disinterested person within the meaning of section 327(a) and, therefore, is disqualified from employment by the debtor as a professional with the result that failure to disclose such a relationship empowers the court to deny or reduce requested fees. *In re* Sky Valley, Inc., 26 C.B.C.2d 745 (B. Ct., N.D. Ga. 1992).

A chapter 11 plan, proposed by a debtor's attorneys, which can only succeed, absent creditor support, by the cram down provisions of section 1129(b), does not necessarily create a conflict of interest and justify disqualification of the attorneys under section 327 and disallowance of their fees under section 328 because such a result would be antithetical to the structure of the reorganization chapters of the Code, and would discourage attorneys from representing debtors for fear of not getting paid in the face of creditor opposition. *In re* Office Products of America, Inc., 26 C.B.C.2d 941 (B. Ct., W.D. Tex. 1992).

Payment to professional persons is governed by section 327 and its related compensation provisions, not by section 365, and counsel cannot circumvent these provisions and seek compensation via assumption by the debtor of a prepetition employment contract. *In re* Financial News Network Inc., 26 C.B.C.2d 788 (B. Ct., S.D.N.Y. 1991).

Counsel for a limited partnership, acting on its own initiative, cannot bring an action to replace the management structure of his client since to do so would pit counsel against client, would require decisions not within the scope of attorney-client representation, and might force counsel to reveal client confidences. *In re* Hickory Hill Apartments of Columbus, Ltd., 26 C.B.C.2d 631 (B. Ct., S.D. Ohio 1991).

It is impermissible for a trustee to hire himself as his attorney and then hire a second attorney and for both attorneys to bill the estate for time spent in mutual conferences, and a compensation application which includes such billing must be reduced by that amount. *In re* Smartt Construction Co., 25 C.B.C.2d 1196 (B. Ct., D. Colo. 1990).

When a custodian has been excused from compliance with turnover, the custodian must obtain court approval for employment of professional persons under section 327(a). *In re* Posadas Assocs., 24 C.B.C.2d 1801 (B. Ct., D.N.M. 1991).

A company employed by a chapter 11 debtor which creates and collects postbankruptcy receivables which are significant to the debtor's cash flow thereby provides the debtor with professional services which are designed to assist the debtor in fulfilling its chapter 11 duties and thus qualifies the company as a professional under section 327(a). *In re* Metropolitan Hosp., 24 C.B.C.2d 648 (B. Ct., E.D. Pa. 1990).

An attorney's refusal or failure to file an application for an order approving his employment by the debtor when he was still a debtor in possession as required by section 327(a) constitutes grounds for disgorgement of fees. *In re* Rheuban, 24 C.B.C.2d 1083 (B. Ct., C.D. Cal. 1990).

A *per se* rule invalidating "evergreen" retainers will not achieve its asserted goal—ensuring that the professional persons the debtor employs zealously pursue quick resolution of a case—where the initial prospects for swift confirmation of a reorganization plan are already favorable. *In re* Benjamin's-Arnolds, Inc., 24 C.B.C.2d 1396 (B. Ct., D. Minn. 1990).

The inherent conflict in the representation of both sides in a negotiation for the acquisition of a debtor's assets renders evidence that counsel took an interest adverse to either side unnecessary. *In re* Tidewater Memorial Hospital, Inc., 22 C.B.C.2d 793 (B. Ct., E.D. Va. 1990).

An attorney employed by a debtor under section 327 that has been paid a "retainer" fee must place the fee in a trust account and apply to the court for compensation pursuant to sections 330 and 331. *In re* C & P Transport, Inc., 20 C.B.C.2d 1620 (B. Ct., E.D. Cal. 1988).

References

2 *Collier on Bankruptcy* ch. 327 (Matthew Bender 15th ed.).

1 *Collier Bankruptcy Manual* ch. 327 (Matthew Bender 3d ed.).

2 *Collier Bankruptcy Practice Guide* ch. 27 (Matthew Bender).

Attorneys' Fees in Bankruptcy, 19 Gonz. L. Rev. 333 (1983/1984).

Brothers, *Disagreement Among the Districts: Why Section 327(a) of the Bankruptcy Code Needs Help,* 138 U. Pa. L. Rev. 1733 (1990).

Grensky, *The Problem Presented by Professionals Who Fail to Obtain Prior Court Approval of Their Employment or Nunc Pro Tunc Est Bunc,* 62 Am. Bankr. L.J. 185 (1988).

McCullough, *Attorney's Fees in Bankruptcy: Toward Further Reform,* 95 Com. L.J. 133 (1990).

Yerbich, *More on Bankruptcy Practice,* 14 Alaska B. Rag 10 (1990).

SECTION 328 (11 U.S.C. § 328)

§ 328. Limitation on compensation of professional persons.

(a) The trustee, or a committee appointed under section 1102 of this title, with the court's approval, may employ or authorize the employment of a professional person under section 327 or 1103 of this title, as the case may be, on any reasonable terms and conditions of employment, including on a retainer, on an hourly basis, or on a contingent fee basis. Notwithstanding such terms and conditions, the court may allow compensation different from the compensation provided under such terms and conditions after the conclusion of such employment, if such terms and conditions prove to have been improvident in light of developments not capable of being anticipated at the time of the fixing of such terms and conditions.

(b) If the court has authorized a trustee to serve as an attorney or accountant for the estate under section 327(d) of this title, the court may allow compensation for the trustee's services as such attorney or accountant only to the extent that the trustee performed services as attorney or accountant for the estate and not for performance of any of the trustee's duties that are generally performed by a trustee without the assistance of an attorney or accountant for the estate.

(c) Except as provided in section 327(c), 327(e), or 1107(b) of this title, the court may deny allowance of compensation for services and reimbursement of expenses of a professional person employed under section 327 or 1103 of this title if, at any time during such professional person's employment under section 327 or 1103 of this title, such professional person is not a disinterested person, or represents or holds an interest adverse to the interest of the estate with respect to the matter on which such professional person is employed.

Bankruptcy Rule References: 2014 and 2016

Legislative History

This section, which is parallel to section 326, fixes the maximum compensation allowable to a professional person employed under section 327. It authorizes the trustee, with the court's approval, to employ professional persons on any reasonable terms, including on a retainer, on an hourly, or on a contingent fee basis. Subsection (a) further permits the court to allow compensation different from the compensation provided under the trustee's agreement if the prior agreement proves to have been improvident in light of developments unanticipatable at the time of the agreement. The court's power includes the power to increase as well as decrease the agreed upon compensation. This provision is permissive, not mandatory, and should not be used by the court if to do so would violate the code of ethics of the professional involved, such as an accountant.

Subsection (b) limits a trustee that has been authorized to serve as his own counsel to only one fee for each service. The purpose of permitting the trustee to serve as his own counsel is to reduce costs. It is not included to provide the trustee with a bonus by permitting him to receive two fees for the same service or to avoid the maxima fixed in section 326. Thus, this subsection requires the court to differentiate between the trustee's services as trustee, and his services as trustee's counsel, and to fix compensation accordingly. Services that a trustee normally performs for an estate without assistance of counsel are to be compensated under the limits fixed in section 326. Only services that he performs that are normally performed by trustee's counsel may be compensated under the maxima imposed by this section.

Subsection (c) permits the court to deny compensation for services and reimbursement of expenses if the professional person is not disinterested or if he represents or holds an interest adverse to the estate on the matter on which he is employed. The subsection provides a penalty for conflicts of interest.

[*House Report No. 95–595, 95th Cong., 1st Sess. 328–329 (1977); Senate Report No. 95–989, 95th Cong., 2d Sess. 39 (1978).*]

Section 328(c) adopts a technical amendment contained in the Senate amendment indicating that an attorney for the debtor in possession is not disqualified for compensation for services and reimbursement of expenses simply because of prior representation of the debtor.

[*124 Cong. Rec. H 11,091 (Sept. 28, 1978); S 17,408 (Oct. 6, 1978).*]

Comment

Reference should be made to the following related sections: section 1102—appointment of committees in a chapter 11 case; section 327—employment by trustee of attorneys, accountants, and others; section 1103—employment of attorneys, accountants, and agents by a committee under chapter 11.

Both Bankruptcy Rule 2014, relating to the employment of professional persons, and Bankruptcy Rule 5002, relating to restrictions on approval of appointments, were amended by the 1991 Amendments. *See* Comment to section 327 *supra*.

Bankruptcy Rule 2016 relates to compensation and reimbursement of expense. Subdivision (a) provides that an entity seeking compensation or reimbursement (interim or final) must file an application containing a detailed statement of the services rendered, the time expended and expenses incurred, and the amounts requested. The application must include a statement as to the payments theretofore made or promised to applicant for services rendered or to be rendered in any capacity in connection with the case, the source of such compensation, whether any compensation previously received has been shared, whether an agreement or understanding exists with any other entity for sharing of compensation, and the particulars of any such sharing or agreement or understanding therefor, except as between applicant and a member or regular associate in his firm (accountants or attorneys). This rule applies whether application is made by the attorney or accountant or by a creditor or other entity. As amended in 1991, Rule 2016 requires that a copy of the application be transmitted to the United States trustee, except in a chapter 9 municipality case.

Section 330 of the Code sets forth the bases for allowing compensation of professional persons.

Case Annotations

An attorney less than diligent in fulfilling his obligation to the estate to review retention applications for professionals may have his requested fee reduced. *In re* Sky Valley, Inc., 26 C.B.C.2d 745 (B. Ct., N.D. Ga. 1992).

A retainer fee paid by a debtor to its bankruptcy counsel pursuant to a prepetition retainer agreement, which characterizes the retainer fee as "earned on receipt" is actually property of the estate to be held in trust with the right to payment not fixed until the court determines that the "actual and necessary" services are provided, that the fees are reasonable and that the payments are authorized. *In re* NBI, Inc., 25 C.B.C.2d 43 (B. Ct., D. Colo. 1991).

Attorney's fees, although justified, may be reduced when the attorney fails to reveal to the bankruptcy court the true terms of a settlement agreement. *In re* Trout, 22 C.B.C.2d 1274 (B. Ct., D.N.D. 1989).

The court has the power to approve or disprove a previously selected attorney by the debtor, the amount counsel will be paid and the manner of payment. *In re* Shah Int'l, Inc., 20 C.B.C.2d 607 (B. Ct., E.D. Wis. 1988).

Neither the letter nor the spirit of the Code's compensation scheme recommends that payment of a retainer to counsel for the creditors' committee be involuntarily extracted from the debtor even though permitted by section 328(a). *In re* Structurlite Plastics Corp., 19 C.B.C.2d 1308 (B. Ct., S.D. Ohio 1988).

A law firm may not recover attorney's fees when it receives a deposit from a chapter 11 debtor's chief executive officer and then pays itself sums from the deposit for services rendered almost exclusively in opposing a creditors' committee's application for special counsel to recover property from the officer, as there is a conflict of interest in that the services were not rendered "in aid of administration of the estate" but rather in an officer's defense. Matter of Global Int'l Airways Corp., 18 C.B.C.2d 310 (B. Ct., W.D. Mo. 1988).

The bankruptcy court may deny a law firm interim compensation and reimbursement for all out of pocket expenses in a chapter 11 case when the law firm failed to disclose its status as an insider of the debtor corporations. *In re* Michigan Gen. Corp., 17 C.B.C.2d 367 (B. Ct., N.D. Tex. 1987).

References

2 *Collier on Bankruptcy* ch. 328 (Matthew Bender 15th ed.).

1 *Collier Bankruptcy Manual* ch. 328 (Matthew Bender 3d ed.).

2 *Collier Bankruptcy Practice Guide* ch. 28 (Matthew Bender).

Attorneys' Fees in Bankruptcy, 19 Gonz. L. Rev. 333 (1983/1984).

McCullough, *Attorney's Fees in Bankruptcy: Toward Further Reform,* 95 Com. L.J. 133 (1990).

SECTION 329 (11 U.S.C. § 329)

§ 329. Debtor's transactions with attorneys.

(a) Any attorney representing a debtor in a case under this title, or in connection with such a case, whether or not such attorney applies for compensation under this title, shall file with the court a statement of the compensation paid or agreed to be paid, if such payment or agreement was made after one year before the date of the filing of the petition, for services rendered or to be rendered in contemplation of or in connection with the case by such attorney, and the source of such compensation.

(b) If such compensation exceeds the reasonable value of any such services, the court may cancel any such agreement, or order the return of any such payment, to the extent excessive, to—

(1) the estate, if the property transferred—

(A) would have been property of the estate; or

(B) was to be paid by or on behalf of the debtor under a plan under chapter 11, 12, or 13 of this title; or

(2) the entity that made such payment.

Bankruptcy Rule References: 2016 and 2017

Legislative History

This section, derived in large part from current Bankruptcy Act section 60d, requires the debtor's attorney to file with the court a statement of the compensation paid or agreed to be paid to the attorney for services in contemplation of and in connection with the case, and the source of the compensation. Payments to a debtor's attorney provide serious potential for evasion of creditor protection provisions of the bankruptcy laws, and serious potential for overreaching by the debtor's attorney, and should be subject to careful scrutiny.

Subsection (b) permits the court to deny compensation to the attorney, to cancel an agreement to pay compensation, or to order the return of compensation paid, if the compensation exceeds the reasonable value of the services provided. The return of payments already made are generally to the trustee for the benefit of the estate. However, if the property would not have come into the estate in any event, the court will order it returned to the entity that made the payment.

The Bankruptcy Commission recommended a provision similar to this that would have also permitted an examination of the debtor's transactions with insiders. H.R. 31, 94th Cong., 1st Sess. § 4–311(b) (1975). Its exclusion here is to permit it to be dealt with by the Rules of Bankruptcy Procedure. It is not intended that the provision be deleted entirely, only that the flexibility of the Rules is more appropriate for such evidentiary matters.

[*House Report No. 95–595, 95th Cong., 1st Sess. 329 (1977); Senate Report No. 95–989, 95th Cong., 2d Sess. 39–40 (1978).*]

Comment

Bankruptcy Rule 2016(b), amended in 1991, complements section 329(a) of the Code and requires every attorney for a debtor, regardless of whether such attorney applies for compensation, to file and transmit to the United States trustee within 15 days after the order for relief, or such other time fixed by the court, the statement required by section 329, including whether he has shared or agreed to share compensation with any other entity, and the particulars of any sharing or agreement to share. Details of any agreement to share with a member or regular associate of the attorney's law firm is not required. Additionally, the attorney is required to supplement the section 329 statement if an undisclosed payment is made to the attorney or a new or amended agreement is entered into by the debtor and the attorney.

Bankruptcy Rule 2017, amended in 1991, complements section 329(b) of the Code. Subdivision (a) provides that on motion of any party in interest or *sua sponte,* the court may, after notice and hearing, determine whether any payments or transfers of property by the debtor, made directly or indirectly and in contemplation of the filing of a petition by or against the debtor or before entry of the order for relief in an involuntary case, to an attorney for services rendered or to be rendered, is excessive.

Subdivision (b) provides that on motion by the *debtor* or the United States trustee, or *sua sponte,* the court may, after notice and hearing, determine whether any payment of money or transfer of property, *or any agreement therefor,* by the debtor to an attorney after entry of an order for relief of a case is excessive, whether payment or transfer is made or to be made directly or indirectly, if the payment, transfer or agreement therefor is for services in any way related to the case.

1986 Amendments: Chapter 12 is included within the ambit of § 329(b)(1)(B).

Case Annotations

Deference is given to an award of attorneys' fees granted by a bankruptcy judge who has not only presided over the evidentiary hearing regarding fees, but also has had the opportunity to observe the performance of the attorney during the course of the proceedings. *In re* Red

Carpet Corp. of Panama City Beach, 902 F.2d 883, 23 C.B.C.2d 663 (11th Cir. 1990). *See also* Red Carpet Corp. v. Miller, 708 F.2d 1576, 8 C.B.C.2d 1391 (11th Cir. 1983) (holding that a bankruptcy court may deny an attorney for a debtor in possession his fees on account of his wrongdoing or negligence, but cannot assess against him money damages for losses due to such wrongdoing or negligence).

Attorney's fees for representing a debtor in negotiations and litigation with a creditor are connected to the bankruptcy case and subject to approval by the bankruptcy court. *In re* Walters, 868 F.2d 665, 22 C.B.C.2d 263 (4th Cir. 1989).

The language of section 329 should not be so restrictively interpreted as to exclude from scrutiny the work of those non-attorneys who assist in the preparation of bankruptcy case materials; it is the nature of the services rendered rather than the person providing them that should be considered. Goudie v. Morrow (*In re* Telford), 10 C.B.C.2d 91 (9th Cir., B.A.P., 1984).

Section 329(b) proceedings may be conducted in a summary manner because the special relationship between the attorney and the client 1) is vulnerable to overreaching by the attorney when the client faces financial trouble and is in contemplation of bankruptcy; and 2) may provide an unscrupulous debtor a convenient mechanism for hiding assets from creditors. *In re* Rheuban, 24 C.B.C.2d 1083 (B. Ct., C.D. Cal. 1990).

Fees generated for researching "what if" scenarios are to be closely scrutinized and are not compensable if wholly tangential. *In re* Ginji Corp., 24 C.B.C.2d 216 (B. Ct., D. Neb. 1990).

A typing service that holds itself out as being qualified to provide legal services to individual debtors, selects the chapter under which the debtor will file, and prepares the petition and the plan for the debtor is engaging in the unauthorized practice of law. *In re* Bachmann, 23 C.B.C.2d 86 (B. Ct., S.D. Fla. 1990).

Legislative history suggests that payments to the debtor's attorney are potentially subject to evasion of creditor protection provisions of the bankruptcy laws. Therefore, such payments should be subject to careful scrutiny by the court, which may, upon review, refund, return or cancel the payment. *In re* Senior G&A Operating Co., 20 C.B.C.2d 765 (B. Ct., W.D. La. 1989).

A chapter 13 debtor's attorney is entitled to fees as an administrative expense for work performed successfully defending against a creditor's motion to vacate an order of confirmation or to modify the plan, for if the creditor's motion had been successful, the debtor's plan would have failed and unsecured creditors would have received nothing. *In re* Cleveland, 17 C.B.C.2d 1257 (B. Ct., S.D. Cal. 1987).

References

2 *Collier on Bankruptcy* ch. 329 (Matthew Bender 15th ed.).

1 *Collier Bankruptcy Manual* ch. 329 (Matthew Bender 3d ed.).

2 *Collier Bankruptcy Practice Guide* ch. 28 (Matthew Bender).

SECTION 330 (11 U.S.C. § 330)

§ 330. Compensation of officers.

(a) After notice to any parties in interest and to the United States trustee and a hearing, and subject to sections 326, 328, and 329 of this title, the court may award to a trustee, to an examiner, to a professional person employed under section 327 or 1103 of this title, or to the debtor's attorney—

> (1) reasonable compensation for actual, necessary services rendered by such trustee, examiner, professional person, or attorney, as the case may be, and by any paraprofessional persons employed by such trustee, professional person, or attorney, as the case may be, based on the nature, the extent, and the value of such services, the time spent on such services, and the cost of comparable services other than in a case under this title; and

> (2) reimbursement for actual, necessary expenses.

(b) There shall be paid from the filing fee in a case under chapter 7 of this title $45 to the trustee serving in such case, after such trustee's services are rendered.

(c) Unless the court orders otherwise, in a case under chapter 12 or 13 of this title the compensation paid to the trustee serving in the case shall not be less than $5 per month from any distribution under the plan during the administration of the plan.

(d) In a case in which the United States trustee serves as trustee, the compensation of the trustee under this section shall be paid to the clerk of the bankruptcy court and deposited by the clerk into the United States Trustee System Fund established by section 589a of title 28.

Bankruptcy Rule Reference: 2016 and 5004

Legislative History

Section 330 authorizes compensation for services and reimbursement of expenses of officers of the estate. It also prescribes the standards on which the amount of compensation is to be determined. As noted above, the compensation allowable under this section is subject to the maxima set out in sections 326, 328, and 329. The compensation is to be reasonable, for actual necessary services rendered, based on the time, the nature, the extent, and the value of the services rendered, and on the cost of comparable services other than in a case under the bankruptcy code. The effect of the last provision is to overrule *In re* Beverly Crest Convalescent Hospital, Inc., 548 F. 2d 817 (9th Cir. 1976, as amended 1977), which set an arbitrary limit on fees payable, based on the amount of a district judge's salary, and other, similar cases that require fees to be determined based on notions of conservation of the estate and economy of administration. If that case were allowed to stand, attorneys that could earn much higher incomes in other fields would leave the bankruptcy arena. Bankruptcy specialists, who enable the system to operate smoothly, efficiently, and expeditiously, would be driven elsewhere, and the bankruptcy field would be occupied by those who could not find other work and those who practice bankruptcy law only occasionally almost as a public service. Bankruptcy fees that are lower than fees in other areas of the legal profession may operate properly when the attorneys appearing in bankruptcy cases do so intermittently, because a low fee in a small segment of a practice can be absorbed by other work. Bankruptcy specialists, however, if required to accept fees in all of their cases that are consistently lower than fees they could receive elsewhere, will not remain in the bankruptcy field.

This subsection provides for reimbursement of actual, necessary expenses. It further provides for compensation of paraprofessionals employed by professional persons employed by the estate of the debtor. The provision is included to reduce the cost of administering bankruptcy cases. In nonbankruptcy areas, attorneys are able to charge for a paraprofessional's time on an hourly basis, and not include it in overhead. If a similar practice does not pertain in bankruptcy cases, then the attorney will be less inclined to use paraprofessionals even where the work involved could easily be handled by an attorney's assistant, at much lower cost to the estate. This provision is designed to encourage attorneys to use paraprofessional assistance where possible, and to insure that the estate, not the attorney, will bear the cost, to the benefit of both the estate and the attorneys involved.

Subsection (b) specifies that in a case in which the United States trustee serves as trustee, the compensation to which he is entitled is to be paid into the Treasury. These fees will help defray the cost of the United States trustee system.

[*House Report No. 95–595, 95th Cong., 1st Sess. 329–30 (1977).*]

[*Ed. Note:* This last paragraph is not accurate. The matter to which it refers was contained in section 15330, which was repealed by the 1986 Amendments.]

Subdivision (b) as enacted provides for $20 to be paid the trustee from the filing fee.

Section 330 authorizes the court to award compensation for services and reimbursement of expenses of officers of the estate, and other professionals. The compensation is to be reasonable, for economy in administration is the basic objective. Compensation is to be for actual necessary services, based on the time spent, the nature, the extent and the value of the services rendered, and the cost of comparable services in nonbankruptcy cases. There are the criteria that have been applied by the courts as analytic aids in defining "reasonable" compensation.

The reference to "the cost of comparable services" in a nonbankruptcy case is not intended as a change of existing law. In a bankruptcy case fees are not a matter for private agreement. There is inherent a "public interest" that "must be considered in awarding fees." Massachusetts Mutual Life Insurance Co. v. Brock, 405 F. 2d 429, 432 (C.A. 5, 1968), *cert. denied*, 395 U.S. 906 (1969). An allowance is the result of a balance struck between moderation in the interest of the estate and its security holders and the need to be "generous enough to encourage" lawyers and others to render the necessary and exacting services that bankruptcy cases often require. *In re* Yale Express System, Inc., 366 F. Supp. 1376, 1381 (S.D.N.Y. 1973). *See also In re* Delta Food Processing Corp.,—374 F. Supp. 76 82 (N.D. Miss. 1974). Brock, *supra; In re* Bemporad Carpet Mills, Inc., 434 F. 2d 988, 989–90 (C.A. 5, 1970). The rates for similar kinds of services in private employment is one element, among others, in that balance. Compensation in private employment noted in subsection (a) is a point of reference, not a controlling determinant of what shall be allowed in bankruptcy cases.

One of the major reforms in 1938, especially for reorganization cases, was centralized control over fees in the bankruptcy courts. See Brown v. Gerdes, 321 U.S. 178, 182–184 (1944); Leiman v. Guttman, 336 U.S. 1, 4–9 (1949). It was intended to guard against a recurrence of "the many sordid chapters" in "the history of fees in corporate reorganizations." Dickinson Industrial Site, Inc. v. Cowan, 309 U.S. 382, 388 (1940). In the years since then the bankruptcy bar has flourished and prospered, and persons of merit and quality have not eschewed public service in bankruptcy cases merely because bankruptcy courts, in the interests of economy in administration, have not allowed them compensation that may be earned in the private economy of business or the professions. There is no reason to believe that, in generations to come, their successors will be less persuaded by the need to serve in the public interest because of stronger allures of private gain elsewhere.

Subsection (a) provides for compensation of paraprofessionals in order to reduce the cost of administering bankruptcy cases. Paraprofessionals can be employed to perform duties which do not require the full range of skills of a qualified professional. Some courts have not hesitated to recognize paraprofessional services as compensable under existing law. An explicit provision to that effect is useful and constructive.

The last sentence of subsection (a) provides that in the case of a public company—defined in section 1101(3)—the court shall refer, after a hearing, all applications to the Securities and Exchange Commission for a report, which shall be advisory only. In chapter X cases in which the Commission has appeared, it generally filed reports on fee applications. Usually, courts have accorded the SEC's views substantial weight, as representing the opinion of a disinterested agency skilled and experienced in reorganization affairs. The last sentence intends for the advisory assistance of the Commission to be sought only in case of a public company in reorganization under chapter 11.

Subsection (b) reenacts section 249 of chapter X of the Bankruptcy Act (11 U.S.C. § 649). It is a codification of equitable principles designed to prevent fiduciaries in the case from engaging in the specified transactions since they are in a position to gain inside information or to shape or influence the course of the reorganization. Wolf v. Weinstein, 372 U.S. 633 (1963). The statutory bar of compensation and reimbursement is based on the principle that such transactions involve conflicts of interest. Private gain undoubtedly prompts the purchase or sale of claims or stock interests, while the fiduciary's obligation is to render loyal and disinterested service which his position of trust has imposed upon him. Subsection (b) extends to a trustee, his attorney, committees and their attorneys, or any other persons "acting in the case in a representative or fiduciary capacity." It bars compensation to any of the foregoing, who after assuming to act in such capacity has purchased or sold, directly or indirectly, claims against, or stock in the debtor. The bar is absolute. It makes no difference whether the transaction brought a gain or loss, or neither, and the court is not authorized to approve a purchase or sale, before or after the transaction. The exception is for an acquisition or transfer "otherwise" than by a voluntary purchase or sale, such as an acquisition by bequest. See Otis & Co. v. Insurance Bldg. Corp., 110 F.2d 333, 335 (C.A. 1, 1940).

Subsection (c) is intended for no asset liquidation cases where minimal compensation for trustees is needed. The sum of $20 will be allowed in each case, which is double the amount provided under current law.

[*Senate Report No. 95–989, 95th Cong., 2d Sess. 40–41 (1978).*]

[*Ed. Note:* In the final enactment several of the provisions referred to in the Senate bill were deleted. *See* the excerpt from the Congressional Record, *infra*.]

Section 330(a) contains the standard of compensation adopted in H.R. 8200 as passed by the House rather than the contrary standard contained in the Senate amendment. Attorneys' fees in bankruptcy cases can be quite large and should be closely examined by the court. However bankruptcy legal services are entitled to command the same competency of counsel as other cases. In that light, the policy of this section is to compensate attorneys and other professionals serving in a case under title 11 at the same rate as the attorney or other professional would be compensated for performing comparable services other than in a case under title 11. Contrary language in the Senate report accompanying S. 2266 is rejected, and Massachusetts Mutual Life Insurance Company v. Brock, 405 F.2d 429, 432 (5th Cir 1968) is overruled. Notions of economy of the estate in fixing fees are outdated and have no place in bankruptcy code.

Section 330(a)(2) of the Senate amendment is deleted although the Securities and Exchange Commission retains a right to file an advisory report under section 1109.

Section 330(b) of the Senate amendment is deleted as unnecessary, as the limitations contained therein are covered by section 328(c) of H.R. 8200 as passed by the House and contained in the House amendment.

Section 330(c) of the Senate amendment providing for a trustee to receive a fee of $20 for each estate from the filing fee paid to the clerk is retained as section 330(b) of the House amendment. The section will encourage private trustees to serve in cases under title 11 and in pilot districts will place less of a burden on the U.S. trustee to serve in no-asset cases.

Section 330(b) of H.R. 8200 as passed by the House is retained by the House amendment as section 330(c).

[*124 Cong. Rec. H 11,091–2 (Sept. 28, 1978); S 17,408 (Oct. 6, 1978).*]

Comment

Reference should be made to section 326, limitation on trustee's compensation; section 328, limitation on compensation of professional persons; section 329, examination of a debtor's transactions with attorneys. References should also be made to Bankruptcy Rule 2016 *infra* which implements section 330.

Bankruptcy Rule 2002(a)(7) requires the clerk (or some person directed by the court) to give not less than 20 days notice by mail to the debtor, the trustee, all creditors and indenture trustees of hearings on all applications for compensation or reimbursement of expenses totaling in excess of $500. Notice should also be given to the United States trustee. *See* Rule 2002(i). Pursuant to subdivision (i) of the Rule, notice must also be mailed to the committee appointed pursuant to the Code or to their authorized agents. Subdivision (c)(2) of the rule requires that the notice of hearing on applications for compensation or reimbursement specify the applicant and the amounts requested.

Notwithstanding the provisions of subdivision (a), under subdivision (i), the court *may* order that the notice be transmitted to the United States trustee and be mailed only to the committees or to their authorized agents and to the creditors and equity security holders who file with the court a request that all notices be mailed to them.

Bankruptcy Rule 2016(a) provides that an entity seeking compensation or reimbursement, interim or final, must file an application containing a detailed statement of the services rendered, the time expended and expenses incurred, and the amounts requested. The application must include a statement as to the payments theretofore made or promised to applicant for services rendered or to be rendered in any capacity in connection with the case, the source of such compensation, whether any compensation previously received has been shared, whether an agreement or understanding exists with any other entity for sharing of compensation, and the particulars of any such sharing or agreement or understanding therefor, except as between applicant and a member or regular associate of his firm (attorneys or accountants). The rule applies whether application is made by the attorney, accountant, a creditor or other entity.

The 1991 Amendments added a requirement to Rule 2016(a) that a copy of the application for compensation and reimbursement be transmitted by the applicant to the United States trustee, except in a chapter 9 case.

Subsection (b), also amended in 1991, requires every debtor's attorney, whether or not such attorney applies for compensation, to file and transmit to the United States trustee within 15 days after the order for relief the statement required by section 329, including whether the attorney has shared or agreed to share compensation with any other entity. The statement must include the particulars of any such sharing or agreement to share, unless the sharing is with a member or regular associate of the attorney's law firm. A supplemental statement must be filed and transmitted to the United States trustee within 15 days after any payment or agreement not previously disclosed.

Section 330 prescribes the bases for allowing compensation and section 504 prohibits sharing of compensation.

Bankruptcy Rule 5004(b) provides that a bankruptcy judge shall be disqualified from allowing compensation to a person who is a relative of the bankruptcy judge or with whom the judge is so connected as to render it improper for the judge to authorize such compensation. The Advisory Committee Note states that the bankruptcy judge before whom the matter is pending determines whether disqualification is required.

1984 Amendments: The amendment to subsection (b) of section 330 increased the trustee's fee from $20 to $45. Subsection (c) was added to section 330 which provides for a minimum monthly compensation of $5 for chapter 13 trustees from any distribution under the plan. Other changes were clarifying and minor.

1986 Amendments: Subsection (a) was amended to require notice "to any parties in interest and to the United States trustee" of any hearing concerning the award of compensation. Subsection (b) was amended by making it applicable to a chapter 12 trustee.

Subsection (d) was added and provides that compensation of a United States trustee serving as a trustee in a case is to be paid to the clerk of the bankruptcy court.

This section was amended to reflect the creation of a permanent United States trustee system. Section 302(d) of the 1986 Amendments provided different effective dates for the amendments relating to the United States trustee system; except for the districts in Alabama and North Carolina, all judicial districts have United States trustees. *See* Section 302 of the 1986 Amendments, as amended by Pub. L. No. 101-650 (1990), reprinted herein under "Selected Provisions of the Bankruptcy Judges, United States Trustees, and Family Farmer Bankruptcy Act of 1986," regarding effective dates generally.

Case Annotations

The lodestar approach, which is the number of hours reasonably expended multiplied by a reasonable hourly rate, is an appropriate method to use in calculating reasonable compensation under section 330 because it presumptively reflects the novelty and complexity of the issues, the special skill and experience of counsel, the quality of representation, and the results obtained. *In re* Apex Oil Co., 960 F.2d 728, 26 C.B.C.2d 1187 (8th Cir. 1992).

Under section 330, a bankruptcy court will employ a three-pronged review of an attorney's fee application, determining: 1) whether the services are properly compensable as legal services; 2) whether the services are necessary and performance is documented; and 3) how the services will be valued, *i.e.*, whether the necessary services were performed within a reasonable amount of time and the reasonable value of that time. Unsecured Creditors' Committee v. Puget Sound Plywood, Inc., 924 F.2d 955, 24 C.B.C.2d 1147 (9th Cir. 1991).

A judge must consider the following criteria in an attorney fee award determination: 1) the nature and extent of the services rendered; 2) the value of the services provided; 3) the factors laid out in *Johnson v. Georgia Highway Express, Inc.*, which must be accompanied by an explanation of how those factors affect the award; 4) whether the bankruptcy assets were administered as economically as possible; and 5) whether any of the services rendered were duplicative or nonlegal. Grant and Bergwerk v. George Schumann Tire & Battery Co., 908 F.2d 874, 23 C.B.C.2d 708 (11th Cir. 1990).

The prohibition of bonuses necessary to make compensation awards competitive with fees for comparable nonbankruptcy services does not apply to a request under section 330 for bonus compensation for achievement of exceptional results. Burgess v. Klenske (*In re* Manoa Finance Co.), 853 F.2d 687, 19 C.B.C.2d 574 (9th Cir. 1988).

Attorneys' fees in bankruptcy are not a "money judgment" bearing interest under 28 U.S.C. § 1961, but are a necessary expense on which no interest is allowable. St. Paul Fire & Marine Insurance Co. v. Vaughn (*In re* Vaughn), 779 F.2d 1003, 14 C.B.C.2d 133 (4th Cir. 1985).

Section 330 does not empower the bankruptcy court to make attorney fee awards without reference to any schedule of priorities and on the basis of the court's assessment that if actual and necessary services have been rendered, they should be compensated, *i.e.*, the court cannot override a creditor's superpriority claim under section 364 in order to pay fees to attorneys from the creditor's collateral unless the services underlying those fees benefited the creditor. Gen. Elec. Credit Corp. v. Levin & Weintraub (*In re* Flagstaff Foodservice Corp.), 739 F.2d 73, 10 C.B.C.2d 1309 (2d Cir. 1984).

In granting a compensation award under section 330, the bankruptcy court must consider whether the award is commensurate with fees for professional services in nonbankruptcy cases, thereby providing sufficient economic incentive to practice in the bankruptcy courts. Mann v.

McCombs (*In re* McCombs), 751 F.2d 286, 11 C.B.C.2d 1140 (8th Cir. 1984).

Trustees fees should be set according to section 330 criteria and not according to the amount of moneys disbursed. *In re* Financial Corp. of America, 23 C.B.C.2d 1181 (9th Cir., B.A.P., 1990).

Section 330(a) authorizes reasonable compensation for all actual, necessary services rendered in connection with the preparation and presentation of fee applications but a determination must be made as to whether such services are actual and necessary and whether they are compensable in nonbankruptcy cases. *In re* Riverside-Linden Investment Co., 22 C.B.C.2d 1335 (9th Cir., B.A.P., 1990).

A court may deny attorney fees and costs as part of an award if it determines that such an award would benefit beneficiaries at the expense of other creditors. *In re* Milton Poulos, Inc., 22 C.B.C.2d 101 (9th Cir., B.A.P., 1989).

A bankruptcy court may not grant an attorney's request for approval of employment *nunc pro tunc* when the attorney did not file an application for compensation and could have requested court approval of employment much earlier in the case. Andrew v. Coopersmith (*In re* Downtown Investment Club III), 19 C.B.C.2d 639 (9th Cir., B.A.P., 1988).

An attorney may be compensated for services rendered in a chapter 7 case if such services benefit the estate of the debtor instead of the debtor personally. In the Matter of Ryan, 18 C.B.C.2d 906 (N.D. Ill. 1987).

An award of attorney's fees should be commensurate with prevailing rates, with no extra compensation for the attorney's particular skills and difficulties unless the latter were truly exceptional. *In re* Checkmate Stereo & Elecs., Ltd., 6 C.B.C.2d 982 (E.D.N.Y. 1982).

When a debtor in possession pursues a reorganization plan which cannot pass section 1129 scrutiny, it is no longer discharging its duties as a fiduciary of the estate pursuing a legitimate reorganization so that any services rendered by counsel in pursuing the plan and/or opposing conversion of the case to chapter 7 are not "necessary" and counsel should not expect to be compensated for such services. *In re* Office Products of America, Inc., 26 C.B.C.2d 941 (B. Ct., W.D. Tex. 1992).

In analyzing whether "billing judgment" is compensable, the court may approve compensation only where a partner or other senior professional is analyzing on a cumulative basis whether the services performed were efficient, productive, nonduplicative, and generally fair and the review is a great benefit to the estate. *In re* CF&I Fabricators of Utah, Inc., 25 C.B.C.2d 779 (B. Ct., D. Utah 1991).

Section 330 does not contain any exception for "overhead" as an item of expenses, so that if the chapter 7 trustee's compensation is "reasonable" the expenses are payable, or if an expense is "necessary and proper" the trustee is entitled to reimbursement. *In re* Miguel, 24 C.B.C.2d 1459 (B. Ct., E.D. Cal. 1991).

Although three cases are administered jointly, section 330 requires that attorneys appointed in the cases must keep separate time and expense records and must make separate applications for employment and for compensation. In the Matter of Hutter Construction Co, Inc., 24 C.B.C.2d 1958 (B. Ct., E.D. Wis. 1991).

An attorney who unreasonably prolongs a chapter 11 case by filing a last minute application to extend the time to assume or reject the debtor's executory leases when the debtor was obviously unable to successfully reorganize, has not benefitted the estate within the meaning of section 330(a), and is not entitled to maximum compensation. *In re* Muir Training Technologies, Inc., 24 C.B.C.2d 780 (B. Ct., S.D. Cal. 1990).

When a chapter 11 trustee has been appointed soon after the commencement of a case, fees to the debtor's attorneys, in addition to the trustee's counsel, may be allowed, but only after scrupulous inquiry to ascertain whether services were for the benefit of the estate or for some other interest and not entirely duplicative of the trustee's own efforts. *In re* Ginji Corp., 24 C.B.C.2d 216 (B. Ct., D. Neb. 1990).

An enhancement of the lodestar rate is not justified when the results obtained by attorneys are similar to those that would have been obtained by other attorneys in the community. *In re* Property Co. of America, 22 C.B.C.2d 688 (B. Ct., N.D. Tex. 1990).

Funds advanced to a law firm in exchange for a promise to represent only one party in a bankruptcy case constitute advance fee payments subject to court approval. *In re* Hathaway Ranch Partnership, 23 C.B.C.2d 777 (B. Ct., C.D. Cal. 1990).

When a trustee is appointed, only the trustee can perform the statutory duties that are imposed by the Code, and services provided by other members of the trustee's staff, not appointed as co-trustees or employed as professional persons under section 327, are not properly compensable from the estate. *In re* Stoecker, 23 C.B.C.2d 915 (B. Ct., N.D. Ill. 1990).

When the assets of the estate are extremely limited, counsel for the debtor is under a duty to minimize its services and charges responsively to those limited resources. *In re* Roger J. Au & Son, Inc., 23 C.B.C.2d 1267 (B. Ct., N.D. Ohio 1990).

An unsecured creditor in an involuntary chapter 7 case does not impliedly consent to the payment of reasonable trustee's fees when there are no unemcumbered assets available for distribution. The statutory fee promulgated by section 330(b) is satisfactory compensation. *In re* Coast Packing Material Co., 22 C.B.C.2d 412 (B. Ct., S.D. Cal. 1989).

Trustees may be compensated for actual, necessary services already rendered, not for work which is yet to be performed or completed. Additionally, reasonable photocopy expenses are compensable, but secretarial and clerical expenses and ordinary postage costs are overhead expenses which are to be paid by the trustee, and are not compensable. *In re* Orthopaedic Technology, 20 C.B.C.2d 722 (B. Ct., D. Colo. 1989).

References

2 *Collier on Bankruptcy* ch. 330 (Matthew Bender 15th ed.).

1 *Collier Bankruptcy Manual* ch. 330 (Matthew Bender 3d ed.).

2 *Collier Bankruptcy Practice Guide* ch. 28 (Matthew Bender).

Attorneys' Fees in Bankruptcy, 19 Gonz. L. Rev. 333 (1983/1984).

Comment, *Awarding Fair Compensation to Bankruptcy Trustees,* 27 San Diego L. Rev. 993 (1990).

McCullough, *Attorney's Fees in Bankruptcy: Toward Further Reform,* 95 Com. L.J. 133 (1990).

SECTION 331 (11 U.S.C. § 331)

§ 331. Interim compensation.

A trustee, an examiner, a debtor's attorney, or any professional person employed under section 327 or 1103 of this title may apply to the court not more than once every 120 days after an order for relief in a case under this title, or more often if the court permits, for such compensation for services rendered before the date of such an application or reimbursement for expenses incurred before such date as is provided under section 330 of this title. After notice and a hearing, the court may allow and disburse to such applicant such compensation or reimbursement.

Bankruptcy Rule Reference: 2016

Legislative History

Section 331 permits trustees and professional persons to apply to the court not more than once every 120 days for interim compensation and reimbursement payments. The court may permit more frequent applications if the circumstances warrant, such as in very large cases where the legal work is extensive and merits more frequent payments. The court is authorized to allow and order disbusement to the applicant of compensation and reimbursement that is otherwise allowable under section 330. The only affect of this section is to remove any doubt that officers of the estate may apply for, and the court may approve, compensation and reimbursement during the case, instead of being required to wait until the end of the case, which in some instances, may be years. The practice of interim compensation is followed in some courts today, but has been subject to some question. This section explicitly authorizes it.

This section will apply to professionals such as auctioneers and appraisers only if they are not paid on a per job basis.

[*House Report No. 95–595, 95th Cong., 1st Sess. 330 (1977); Senate Report No. 95–989, 95th Cong., 2d Sess. 41–2 (1978).*]

Comment

There was no provision in the former Bankruptcy Act for interim allowance of compensation or reimbursement for expenses. Nevertheless, under special circumstances the courts permitted interim allowance. *See In re* Imperial "400" Nat'l Inc., 324 F. Supp. 582 (D.N.J. 1971). *See also* cases cited in 6A Collier on Bankruptcy paragraph 13.16 n.6 (14th ed.).

Bankruptcy Rule 2016(a), which relates to applications for compensation for services rendered and reimbursement of expenses, applies to an entity seeking interim as well as final compensation or reimbursement of expenses. *See* **Comment** to Section 330.

Case Annotations

The interlocutory nature of an interim fee award may warrant a redetermination of the trustee's application in order to ascertain whether facts were intentionally or unintentionally falsified. In the Matter of Evangeline Refining Co., 890 F.2d 1312, 21 C.B.C.2d 1491 (5th Cir. 1989).

A court determining the compensation to be paid to attorneys pursuant to section 331 in a massive, complex chapter 11 reorganization need not apply any fixed "percentage rule" or standard for interim allowances, but may deal with each round of interim applications in light of the context and the status of the case at the particular stage involved. *In re* Public Serv. Co. of New Hampshire, 20 C.B.C.2d 330 (B. Ct., D.N.H. 1988).

Counsel for creditors' committee could not compel the debtor to pay a retainer although it had expended a large number of billable hours, when counsel was aware that section 331 requires a 120-day waiting period after an order for relief has been entered before interim compensation may be awarded, and counsel subsequently filed an interim fee application and delay in payment of counsel fees did not appear likely. *In re* Structurlite Plastics Corp., 19 C.B.C.2d 1308 (B. Ct., S.D. Ohio 1988).

When a chapter 11 creditors' committee applies for interim compensation for professional persons employed by the committee, and the application is opposed by a creditor with a claim allegedly secured by all of the debtor's assets, the court should deny the award because unless and until the secured creditor's claim is rebutted, it must be treated as allowed, and consequently there would be no unencumbered assets in the estate with which to pay such interim allowances. In the Matter of Codesco, Inc., 5 C.B.C.2d 738 (B. Ct., S.D.N.Y. 1981).

References

2 *Collier on Bankruptcy* ch. 331 (Matthew Bender 15th ed.).

1 *Collier Bankruptcy Manual* ch. 331 (Matthew Bender 3d ed.).

2 *Collier Bankruptcy Practice Guide* ch. 28 (Matthew Bender).

Berkowitz and Berkowitz, *A Practitioner's Guide to Compensation Under Sections 506(c) and 331 of the Bankruptcy Code,* 92 Com. L.J. 136 (1987).

SUBCHAPTER III

Administration

SECTION 341 (11 U.S.C. § 341)

§ 341. Meetings of creditors and equity security holders.

(a) Within a reasonable time after the order for relief in a case under this title, the United States trustee shall convene and preside at a meeting of creditors.

(b) The United States trustee may convene a meeting of any equity security holders.

(c) The court may not preside at, and may not attend, any meeting under this section including any final meeting of creditors.

Bankruptcy Rule References: 2002 and 2003

Legislative History

Subsection (a) of this section requires that there be a meeting of creditors within a reasonable time after the order for relief in the case. The Bankruptcy Act and the current rules of Bankruptcy Procedure provide for a meeting of creditors, and specify the time and manner of the meeting, and the business to be conducted. This bill leaves those matters to the Rules. Under section 405(d) of the bill, the present Rules will continue to govern until new Rules are promulgated. Thus, the present procedure for the meeting will continue. This section does not specify who is to preside at the meeting of creditors. That, too, is left to the Rules. However, it is contemplated that the bankruptcy judge will not preside. Generally, the interim trustee or the United States trustee will preside. In keeping with the thrust of the bill to remove the bankruptcy judge from administrative matters and not to involve him in situations where he will hear evidence outside of the context of a dispute that he must decide, the bankruptcy judge will not be the presiding officer at the meeting, and will not be authorized to question the debtor as he is today. If there were to be any disputes resolved there, the judge might be present, but will not be present for the examination of the debtor, as this has caused too many problems of the dispute-decider hearing inadmissible evidence.

Subsection (b) authorizes the court to order a meeting of equity security holders in cases where such a meeting would be beneficial or useful, for example, in a chapter 11 reorganization case where it will be necessary for the equity security holders to organize in order to be able to participate in the negotiation of a plan of reorganization.

[*House Report No. 95–595, 95th Cong., 1st Sess. 331 (1977); Cf. Senate Report No. 95–989, 95th Cong., 2d Sess. 42 (1978).*]

Section 341 (c) of the Senate amendment [*Ed. Note:* This provison provided that the bankruptcy judge was to preside at the creditor's meeting.] is deleted and a contrary provision is added indicating that the bankruptcy judge will not preside at or attend the first meeting of creditors or equity security holders but a discharge hearing for all individuals will be held at which the judge will preside.

[*124 Cong. Rec. H 11,092 (Sept. 28, 1978); S 17,408 (Oct. 6, 1978).*]

Comment

Former Bankruptcy Rules 204 and 205 required that the bankruptcy judge preside at the meeting and preside over the examination of the bankrupt at the first meeting. Effecting a radical change, section 341(c) of the Code prohibits the court from presiding at or even attending the meeting of creditors. Disputes that arise during the meeting could be brought before the court for resolution without violating the prohibition.

Pursuant to section 901(a) of the Code, section 341 is inapplicable in chapter 9 cases and, pursuant to section 1161, section 341 also is inapplicable to cases involving a railroad.

Bankruptcy Rule 2003, amended in 1991, relates to meetings of creditors or equity security holders. Subdivision (a) requires the United States trustee to call a meeting of creditors to be held not less than 20 nor more than 40 days after the order for relief. In a chapter 12 case, the meeting must be held not less than 20 nor more than 35 days after the order for relief. A later time may be fixed if there is an appeal from or a motion to vacate the order for relief, or if there is a motion to dismiss the case. The meeting may be held at a regular place for holding court or at any other place designated by the United States trustee within the district and convenient for the parties in interest. If the United States trustee designates a place for the meeting which is not regularly staffed by the United States trustee or an assistant who may preside, the meeting may be held not more than 60 days after the order for relief. Subdivision (b)(1) provides that the United States trustee shall preside at the creditors' meeting. The business of the meeting shall include the examination of the debtor under oath, and in a chapter 7 case, may include the election of a trustee or of a creditors' committee. The presiding officer has authority to administer oaths. Subdivision (b)(2) provides that if the United States trustee convenes a meeting of equity security holders, such trustee shall preside at the meeting.

Subdivision (b)(3), applicable only in a chapter 7 case, provides that a creditor may vote if, at or before the meeting, the creditor filed a proof of claim or writing setting forth facts evidencing a right to vote pursuant to section 702(a), unless objection is made to the claim, or the claim is insufficient on its face. A creditor of a partnership may file a proof of claim or writing evidencing a right to vote for the trustee for the estate of a general partner despite the fact that a trustee for the estate of the partnership has previously qualified. In the event of objection to amount or allowability of a claim for the purpose of voting, unless the court orders otherwise, the United States trustee shall tabulate the votes for each alternative presented by the dispute and, if resolution of such dispute is necessary to determine the result of the election, the tabulations for each alternative shall be reported to the court.

Subdivision (c) provides that any examination under oath at the meeting of creditors held under section 341 of the Code shall be recorded verbatim by the United States trustee using electronic sound recording equipment or other means of recording. The record shall be preserved by the United States trustee and available for public access until two years after the case is closed. Upon request, the United States trustee shall certify and provide a copy of the transcript at the requesting entity's expense.

Subdivision (d) requires the presiding officer to transmit to the court the name and address of any person elected trustee or entity elected a committee member. Such officer must promptly inform the court in writing of any dispute in the election, and pending disposition of the dispute the interim trustee is to continue in office. If no motion to resolve the dispute is made to the court within 10 days after the meeting, the interim trustee is to serve as trustee.

Subdivision (e) provides that the meeting may be continued or adjourned from time to time by oral announcement at the meeting without the necessity for further written notice.

Bankruptcy Rule 2002(a)(1) requires not less than 20 days notice by mail to be given by the clerk, or some other person as the court directs, to the debtor, the trustee, all creditors and indenture trustees, of a meeting of creditors held pursuant to section 341. Pursuant to subdivision (i) of the rule, notice must also be given to all committees elected pursuant to section 705 or appointed pursuant to section 1102 of the Code. The court may order that certain notices required by the Rule be transmitted to the United States trustee and mailed only to the elected or appointed committees. The 1991 Amendments added a requirement that a committee appointed pursuant to section 1114 receive copies of certain notices required by Rule 2002, and also added a new subdivision (k) specifying the notices that must be given to the United State trustee.

If a meeting of equity security holders is convened in a chapter 11 case, under subdivision (d) of the rule, the clerk must give notice of the meeting to all equity security holders in the form and manner as directed by the court.

1986 Amendments: Section 341 was amended to provide that the United States trustee convene and preside at the meeting of creditors. The United States trustee is also empowered to convene a meeting of equity security holders.

This section was amended to reflect the creation of a permanent and, with the exception of Alabama and North Carolina, nationwide United States Trustee system.

Case Annotations

When there is evidence of confusion relating to a creditor's power of attorney and vote in the election of a permanent trustee, the bankruptcy court may reopen the section 341(a) meeting of creditors for the purpose of allowing the creditor to file a new proof of claim and/or power of attorney. Rusch Factor Div., BVA Credit Corp. v. Miller (*In re* Mission Carpet Mills, Inc.), 4 C.B.C.2d 502 (9th Cir., B.A.P., 1981).

The standard to be applied in determining whether a Fifth Amendment privilege has been improperly asserted in response to a question posed at a creditors meeting is whether it is perfectly clear, from a careful consideration of all the circumstances in the case, that the witness is mistaken and that the answer cannot possibly have a tendency to incriminate him. *In re* French, 24 C.B.C.2d 1979 (B. Ct., D. Minn. 1991).

A court may order the trustee to close the creditors meeting under section 341(a) because the actions of the trustee are judicially reviewable to protect against abuse. *In re* Vance, 24 C.B.C.2d 377 (B. Ct., N.D. Okla. 1990).

When a debtor is incarcerated or too ill to attend the section 341 meeting of creditors, the bankruptcy court may permit creditors and the trustee to examine the debtor by means of written interrogatories or by telephone. *In re* Vilt, 14 C.B.C.2d 29 (B. Ct., N.D. Ill. 1986).

When attendance of the section 341 meeting by the debtor would cause severe physical hardship and is not required for the administration of the case and failure to attend is beyond the debtor's control, attendance may be waived. *In re* Stewart, 5 C.B.C.2d 575 (B. Ct., N.D. Ohio 1981).

References

2 *Collier on Bankruptcy* ch. 341 (Matthew Bender 15th ed.).

1 *Collier Bankruptcy Manual* ch. 341 (Matthew Bender 3d ed.).

2 *Collier Bankruptcy Practice Guide* ch. 35 (Matthew Bender).

Lake, *Representing Secured Creditors Under the Bankruptcy Code,* 37 Bus. Law. 1153 (1982).

Russell, *Getting Information About Bankruptcy Debtors —How Trustees and Creditors Can Protect Their Interests,* 13 L.A. Law 14 (1990).

Teofan and O'Neill, *Creditor and Consumer Rights — 1990 Annual Survey of Texas Law,* 44 Sw. L.J. 163 (1990).

SECTION 342 (11 U.S.C. § 342)

§ 342. Notice.

(a) There shall be given such notice as is appropriate, including notice to any holder of a community claim, of an order for relief in a case under this title.

(b) Prior to the commencement of a case under this title by an individual whose debts are primarily consumer debts, the clerk shall give written notice to such individual that indicates each chapter of this title under which such individual may proceed.

Bankruptcy Rule Reference: 2002

Legislative History

Subsection (a) of section 342 requires the clerk of the bankruptcy court to give notice of the order for relief. The Rules will prescribe to whom the notice should be sent, and in what manner notice will be given. The Rules already prescribe such things, and they will continue to govern unless changed. Section 405(d) due process will certainly require notice to all creditors and equity security holders. State and Federal governmental representatives responsible for collecting taxes will also receive notice. In cases where the debtor is subject to regulation, the regulatory agency with jurisdiction will receive notice. In order to insure maximum notice to all parties in interest, the Rules will include notice by publication in appropriate cases and for appropriate issues. Other notices will be given as appropriate.

Subsection (b) [*See* **Comment**, *infra.*] is derived from section 21g of the Bankruptcy Act. It specifies that the trustee may file notice of the commencement of the case in land recording offices in order to give notice of the pendency of the case to potential transferees of the debtor's real property. Such filing is unnecessary in the county in which the bankruptcy case is commenced. If notice is properly filed, a subsequent purchaser of the property will not be a bona fide purchaser. Otherwise, a purchaser, including a purchaser at a judicial sale, that has no knowledge of the case, is not prevented from obtaining the status of a bona fide purchaser by the mere commencement of the case. County is defined in title 1 of the United States Code to include other political subdivisions where counties are not used.

Subsection (c) [*See* **Comment**, *infra.*] requires the clerk of the bankruptcy court to notify in writing an individual debtor of each chapter under which the debtor may proceed. If the debtor is an individual with regular income and is not a stockbroker or commodity broker, the notice will be of chapters 7, 11, and 13. The purpose of the provision is to apprise debtors that wish to repay their debts of the availability of chapter 13 in case they were not apprised of its availability before filing a liquidation case.

[*House Report No. 95–595, 95th Cong., 1st Sess. 331–2 (1977); See Senate Report No. 95–989, 95th Cong., 2d Sess. 42 (1978).*]

Section 342(b) and (c) of the Senate amendment are adopted in principle but moved to section 549(c), in lieu of section 342(b) of H.R. 8200 as passed by the House.

Section 342(c) of H.R. 8200 as passed by the House is deleted as a matter to be left to the Rules of Bankruptcy Procedure.

[*124 Cong. Rec. H 11,092 (Sept. 28, 1978); S 17,408 (Oct. 6, 1978).*]

Comment

The Committee Reports refer to earlier versions of section 342. As enacted, the section is substantially revised. All matters pertaining to the notice are left to the rules. *See* section 549(c) dealing with recordation of the petition and real property transfers.

The "order for relief" is akin to the "adjudication." The first notice creditors received of an adjudication under the former Bankruptcy Act was contained in the notice of first meeting of creditors. Neither the Act nor the former Rules provided for giving notice of commencement of a case or of adjudication.

Bankruptcy Rule 2002(f) requires the clerk or some other person as the court directs to give the debtor, all creditors and indenture trustees notice by mail of the order for relief, without specifying any time within which the notice must be given. The notice may be combined with the notice of the meeting of creditors as in Official Form 9.

Bankruptcy Rule 2002(k), as amended in 1991, requires that the clerk or such other person as the court may direct transmit to the United States trustee the order for relief, except in chapter 9 cases or unless the United States trustee otherwise requests.

1984 Amendments: Section 342(a) was amended to require that notice of an order for relief under the Code include notice to the holder of "a community claim." Subsection (b) is new and pursues a theme running through the 1984 amendments that debtors be apprised of the option of debt repayment under chapter 13. In the case of an individual debtor whose debts are primarily consumer debts (*see* section 101 for definition of "consumer debt"), the clerk is required *prior to the commencement of a case,* to give written notice to such individual indicating each chapter of the Code that is available.

It is difficult to see how the clerk can anticipate who will file a petition and at what time. Some practice will undoubtedly develop whereby the clerk can substantially comply with the directive of subsection (b).

Case Annotations

A bankruptcy court's order limiting service of all papers to certain parties is a discretionary one reversible only for an abuse of discretion. Weissman v. Hassett (*In re* O.P.M. Leasing Services, Inc.), 5 C.B.C.2d 1110 (S.D.N.Y. 1981).

Service of notice upon state and federal taxing authorities is not mandatory unless the local bankruptcy rules so provide. *In re* Brooks Fashion Stores, Inc., 24 C.B.C.2d 1724 (B. Ct., S.D.N.Y. 1991).

A creditor who has denied receiving an improperly addressed formal notice but admits knowledge of the bankruptcy case and has received prompt supplementary notice from debtor's counsel is deemed to have received the requisite notice prescribed by section 342. *In re* Torres, 5 C.B.C.2d 950 (B. Ct., E.D.N.Y. 1981).

References

2 *Collier on Bankruptcy* ch. 342 (Matthew Bender 15th ed.).

1 *Collier Bankruptcy Manual* ch. 342 (Matthew Bender 3d ed.).

SECTION 343 (11 U.S.C. § 343)

§ 343. Examination of the debtor. The debtor shall appear and submit to examination under oath at the meeting of creditors under section 341(a) of this title. Creditors, any indenture trustee, any trustee or examiner in the case, or the United States trustee may examine the debtor. The United States trustee may administer the oath required under this section.

Bankruptcy Rule References: 2003, 2004 and 2005

Legislative History

This section, derived from section 21a of the Bankruptcy Act, requires the debtor to appear at the meeting of creditor and submit to examination under oath. The purpose of the examination is to enable creditors and the trustee to determine if assets have improperly been disposed of or concealed or if there are grounds for objection to discharge. The scope of the examination under this section will be governed by the Rules of Bankruptcy Procedure, as it is today. *See* Rules 205(a), 10–213, 11–26. It is expected that the scope prescribed by these rules, that is "only the debtor's acts, conduct, or property or any matter that may affect the administration of the estate or the debtor's right to a discharge" will remain substantially unchanged. Examination of other persons in connection with the bankruptcy case is left completely to the Rules, just as examination of witnesses in civil cases is governed by the Federal Rules of Civil Procedure.

[*House Report No. 95–595, 95th Cong., 1st Sess. 332 (1977), See Senate Report No. 95-989, 95th Cong., 2d Sess. 43 (1978).*]

Comment

Under section 341(c) the judge may not preside at or attend the meeting of creditors or equity security holders.

See also section 1104, concerning appointment of an examiner in a chapter 11 case.

Bankruptcy Rule 2003(b)(1), as amended in 1991, provides that the United States trustee shall preside at the meeting of creditors. Section 102(9) of the Code provides that "United States trustee" includes a designee of the United States trustee. The business transacted at the meeting of creditors held pursuant to section 341 shall include the examination of the debtor under oath and, in a chapter 7 case, may include the election of a trustee or a creditors' committee. The presiding officer is authorized to administer oaths. Subdivision (c) of the rule provides that any examination under oath be recorded verbatim by electronic sound recording equipment or other means of recording.

Bankruptcy Rule 2004 deals with examinations and in subdivision (a) provides that on motion of any party in interest, the court may order the examination of "any entity."

Subdivision (b) of Rule 2004 relates to the scope of the examination. The examination of any entity under the rule *or of the debtor under section 343* may relate only to the acts, conduct, property liabilities and financial condition of the debtor, to any matter which may affect the administration of the estate, to the debtor's right to a discharge, and in a chapter 11, 12 or 13 case, the operation of any business and desirability of continuing it, the source of funding the plan and the consideration thereof, and any other matter relevant to the case or formulation of a plan.

Subdivision (d) provides that for cause shown and on such terms as it may impose, the court may order the debtor to be examined under subdivision (a) at any time or place it designates, within or without the district wherein the case is pending.

Subdivision (e) provides that an entity other than a debtor shall not be required to attend as a witness unless first tendered mileage and witness fee for one day's attendance. If a debtor resides over 100 miles from the place of examination when required to appear for examination under Rule 2004, the mileage allowed a witness must be tendered for any distance over 100 miles from debtor's residence at the date of filing the first petition commencing a case under the Code *or* his residence at the time he is required to appear, whichever is less.

Bankruptcy Rule 2005 relates to the apprehension and removal of a debtor to compel his attendance for examination. The rule is applicable when it appears from an affidavit of an interested party that the examination of the debtor is necessary for the proper administration of the estate and that there is reasonable cause to believe that the debtor is about to leave or has left his residence or principal place of business to avoid examination, or that the debtor has evaded service of a subpoena or order to attend for examination, or has willfully disobeyed such subpoena or order. The rule prescribes the procedure for causing the examination of the debtor and for his removal.

1986 Amendments: Section 343, as amended, permits the United States trustee, as well as creditors, the trustee and examiners to examine the debtor at the meeting of creditors. The United States trustee is empowered to administer the oath to the debtor at the section 343 meeting.

Case Annotations

A debtor is entitled to the benefit of the attorney-client privilege. *In re* O.P.M. Leasing Services, Inc., 4 C.B.C.2d 1149 (S.D.N.Y. 1981), *aff'd,* 670 F.2d 383, 5 C.B.C.2d 1252 (2d Cir. 1982).

A debtor's attendance at the creditors' meeting is crucial to allow creditors and the trustee the ability to gather information; however, the court may waive a debtor's attendance when the debtor is too ill, is incarcerated, or has other reasons beyond his control. In such instances, the court may permit creditors and the trustee to question the debtor by telephone or interrogatories, or examine a codebtor. *In re* Vilt, 14 C.B.C.2d 29 (B. Ct., N.D. Ill. 1986).

Notwithstanding the provisions of 11 U.S.C. § 343, a debtor's failure to appear and testify at the creditor's meeting will be excused and will not affect his case when the debtor's spouse is able to testify and give all pertinent information, and the reason for the debtor's failure to appear is that he is in military service and stationed overseas. *In re* Edwards, 1 C.B.C.2d 440 (B. Ct., S.D. Fla. 1979).

References

2 *Collier on Bankruptcy* ch. 343 (Matthew Bender 15th ed.).

1 *Collier Bankruptcy Manual* ch. 343 (Matthew Bender 3d ed.).

2 *Collier Bankruptcy Practice Guide* ch. 36 (Matthew Bender).

SECTION 344 (11 U.S.C. § 344)

§ 344. Self-incrimination; immunity. Immunity for persons required to submit to examination, to testify, or to provide information in a case under this title may be granted under part V of title 18.

Legislative History

Part V of title 18 of the United States Code governs the granting of immunity to witnesses before Federal tribunals. The immunity provided under part V is only use immunity, not transactional immunity. Part V applies to all proceedings before Federal courts, before Federal grand juries, before administrative agencies, and before Congressional committees. It requires the Attorney General or the United States attorney to request or to approve any grant of immunity, whether before a court, grand jury, agency, or Congressional committee.

This section carried part V over into bankruptcy cases. Thus, for a witness to be ordered to testify before a bankruptcy court in spite of a claim of privilege, the United States attorney for the district in which the court sits would have to request from the district court for that district the immunity order. The rule would apply to both debtors, creditors, and any other witnesses in a bankruptcy case. If the immunity were granted, the witness would be required to testify. If not, he could claim the privilege against self-incrimination.

Part V is a significant departure from current law. Under section 7a(10) of the Bankruptcy Act, a debtor is required to testify in all circumstances, but any testimony he gives may not be used against him in any criminal proceeding, except testimony given in any hearing on objections to discharge. With that exception, section 7a(10) amounts to a blanket grant of use immunity to all debtors. Immunity for other witnesses in bankruptcy courts today is governed by part V of title 18.

The consequences of a claim of privilege by a debtor under proposed law and under current law differ as well. Under section 14c(6) of current law, any refusal to answer a material question approval by the court will result in the denial of a discharge, even if the refusal is based on the privilege against self-incrimination. Thus, the debtor is confronted with the choice between losing his discharge and opening himself up to possible criminal prosecution.

Under section 727(a)(6) of the proposed title 11, a debtor is only denied a discharge if he refuses to testify after having been granted immunity. If the debtor claims the privilege and the United States attorney does not request immunity from the district courts, then the debtor may refuse to testify and still retain his right to a discharge. It removes the Scylla and Charibdis choice for debtors that exists under the Bankruptcy Act.

[*House Report No. 95–595, 95th Cong., 1st Sess. 332–3 (1977); Senate Report No. 95–989, 95th Cong., 2d Sess. 43–4 (1978).*]

Comment

Section 7 of the former Bankruptcy Act provided in paragraph (a)(10), (which required a debtor to appear for examination at the first meeting) "but no testimony, or any evidence which is directly or indirectly derived from such testimony given by him, shall be offered in any criminal proceeding, except such testimony as may be given by him in the hearing upon objections to his discharge. . . ."

The difference between the use of immunity granted by said Section 7a(10) and immunity under part V of title 18 which governs under the Code, is clearly stated in the House and Senate Reports, as is the difference in the consequences (right to discharge) for refusal to testify where (a) immunity is not granted, and (b) immunity is granted by order of the district court on request of the United States Attorney.

Case Annotations

While the trustee's objection to the debtor's discharge is a separate adversary proceeding under Rule 7001 from a Rule 2004 examination, for the purposes of determining whether the debtor's statements made at previous Rule 2004 examinations constituted a waiver of the Fifth Amendment privilege, the prior testimony will be deemed to have occurred in the "same judicial proceeding" if the subject matter of the adversary proceeding is inextricably interwoven with the main bankruptcy proceeding. As a result, the debtor may not invoke a blanket Fifth Amendment privilege and refuse to answer any further questions on topics previously covered because it would allow the debtor prematurely to close the door which he had freely opened. *In re* Mudd, 20 C.B.C.2d 524 (B. Ct., N.D. Tex. 1989).

References

2 *Collier on Bankruptcy* ch. 344 (Matthew Bender 15th ed.).

1 *Collier Bankruptcy Manual* ch. 344 (Matthew Bender 3d ed.).

2 *Collier Bankruptcy Practice Guide* ch. 36 (Matthew Bender).

Kurland, *A Debtor's Prism: Immunity for Bankrupts Under the Bankruptcy Reform Act of 1978* (Pt. 1) 55 Am. Bankr. L.J. 177 (1981).

Leibowitz, *Self-Incrimination Under the Bankruptcy Act,* 52 Am. Bankr. L.J. 77 (1981).

SECTION 345 (11 U.S.C. § 345)

§ 345. Money of estates.

(a) A trustee in a case under this title may make such deposit or investment of the money of the estate for which such trustee serves as will yield the maximum reasonable net return on such money, taking into account the safety of such deposit or investment.

(b) Except with respect to a deposit or investment that is insured or guaranteed by the United States or by a department, agency, or instrumentality of the United States or backed by the full faith and credit of the United States, the trustee shall require from an entity with which such money is deposited or invested—

(1) a bond—

(A) in favor of the United States;

(B) secured by the undertaking of a corporate surety approved by the United States trustee for the district in which the case is pending; and

(C) conditioned on—

(i) a proper accounting for all money so deposited or invested and for any return on such money;

(ii) prompt repayment of such money and return; and

(iii) faithful performance of duties as a depository; or

(2) the deposit of securities of the kind specified in section 9303 of title 31.

(c) An entity with which such moneys are deposited or invested is authorized to deposit or invest such moneys as may be required under this section.

Legislative History

This section is a significant departure from section 61 of the Bankruptcy Act. It permits a trustee in a bankruptcy case to make such deposit of investment of the money of the estate for which he serves as will yield the maximum reasonable net return on the money, taking into account the safety of such deposit or investment. Under current law, the trustee is permitted to deposit money only with banking institutions. Thus, the trustee is generally unable to secure a high rate of return on money of estates pending distribution, to the detriment of creditors. Under this section, the trustee may make deposits in savings and loans, may purchase government bonds, or make such other deposit or investment as is appropriate. Under proposed 11 U.S.C. § 541(a)(6), and except as provided in subsection (c) of this section, any interest or gain realized on the deposit or investment of funds under this section will become property of the estate, and will thus enhance the recovery of creditors.

In order to protect the creditors, subsection (b) requires certain precautions against loss of the money so deposited or invested. The trustee must require from a person with which he deposits or invests money of an estate a bond in favor of the United States secured by approved corporate surety and conditioned on a proper accounting for all money deposited or invested and for any return on such money.

Alternately, the trustee may require the deposit of securities of the kind specified in section 15 of title 6 of the United States Code, [*See* Comment, *infra*] which governs the posting of security by banks that receive public moneys on deposit. These bonding requirements do not apply to deposits or investments that are insured or guaranteed the United States or a department, agency, or instrumentality of the United States, or that are backed by the full faith and credit of the United States.

Subsection (c) permits the United States trustee to aggregate for deposit or investment money of estates for which he serves as trustee. The aggregation will enable him to obtain a higher return on the money so deposited. The United States trustee is required to maintain records separately identifying the money of each estate included in the aggregation. Any return on the deposits or investments that the United States trustee makes is paid into the Treasury. These funds will further defray the cost of the United States trustee system.

[*Ed. Note:* Subdivision (c) mentioned in the House Report refers to the United States trustee system, which had been moved to chapter 15 as part of a pilot program. Chapter 15 was subsequently repealed by the 1986 Amendments.]

This provision is not exclusive, and thus does not prohibit a private standing chapter 13 trustee from aggregating funds. The Rules of Bankruptcy Procedure will be able to provide for aggregation under appropriate circumstances and adequate safeguards in cases where there is a significant need, such as in districts in which there is a standing chapter 13 trustee. In such a case, the interest or return on the funds would help defray the cost of administering the cases in which the private standing trustee serves.

[*House Report No. 95–595, 95th Cong., 1st Sess. 333–4 (1977); See Senate Report No. 95–989, 95th Cong., 2d Sess. 44 (1978).*]

The House amendment moves section 345(c) of the House bill to chapter 15 as part of the pilot program for the U.S. trustees. The bond required by section 345(b) may be a blanket bond posted by the financial depository sufficient to cover deposits by trustees in several cases, as is done under current law.

[*424 Cong. Rec. H 11,092 (Sept. 28, 1978); S 17,408 (Oct. 6, 1978).*]

Comment

Section 345(b)(2) was amended by Pub. L. No. 97–258 (1982) which substituted "section 9303 of title 31" where "section 15 of title 6" had previously appeared.

Bankruptcy Rule 5008 entitled "Funds of the Estate" was abrogated by the 1991 Amendments. The Advisory Committee Note states: "This rule is abrogated in view of the amendments to section 345(b) of the Code and the role of the United States trustee in approving bonds and supervising trustees."

1984 Amendments: Subsection (c) was added to section 345 by the 1984 amendments.

1986 Amendments: Section 345(b)(1)(B) was amended to provide that the United States trustee approve the bond required from an entity with whom a trustee deposits or invests money of the estate.

This section was amended to reflect the creation of a permanent United States trustee system. Section 302(d) of the 1986 Amendments provided different effective dates for the amendments relating to the United States trustee system; except for the districts in Alabama and North Carolina, all judicial districts have United States trustees. *See* Section 302 of the 1986 Amendments, as amended by Pub. L. No. 101-650 (1990), reprinted herein under "Selected Provisions of the Bankruptcy Judges, United States Trustees, and Family Farmer Bankruptcy Act of 1986," regarding effective dates generally.

Case Annotations

A chapter 11 debtor with deposits in foreign banking institutions is required to comply with the investment guidelines for collateralization provided for in section 345(b). Matter of Interco Inc., 25 C.B.C.2d 137 (B. Ct., E.D. Mo. 1991).

Generally, a law firm representing a debtor in possession has a duty to invest funds held by it in an interest bearing account; the firm will be liable for interest which could have been received but was not because of the firm's failure to invest. Judge v. Pincus, Verlin, Hahn & Reich, P.C. (*In re* J & J Distrib. Corp.), 17 C.B.C.2d 1127 (B. Ct., E.D. Pa. 1987).

The court may waive the requirements for security for monies deposited by an examiner from the debtor's estate when appropriate. Harris v. S.S. Jupiter Seas, Inc. (*In re* S.S. Jupiter Seas, Inc.), 1 C.B.C.2d 770 (B. Ct., S.D. Fla. 1980).

References

2 *Collier on Bankruptcy* ch. 345 (Matthew Bender 15th ed.).

1 *Collier Bankruptcy Manual* ch. 345 (Matthew Bender 3d ed.).

SECTION 346 (11 U.S.C. § 346)

§ 346. Special tax provisions.

(a) Except to the extent otherwise provided in this section, subsections (b), (c), (d), (e), (g), (h), (i), and (j) of this section apply notwithstanding any State or local law imposing a tax, but subject to the Internal Revenue Code of 1954 (26 U.S.C. § 1 *et seq.*)

(b)(1) In a case under chapter 7, 12, or 11 of this title concerning an individual, any income of the estate may be taxed under a State or local law imposing a tax on or measured by income only to the estate, and may not be taxed to such individual. Except as provided in section 728 of this title, if such individual is a partner in a partnership, any gain or loss resulting from a distribution of property from such partnership, or any distributive share of income, gain, loss, deduction, or credit of such individual that is distributed, or considered distributed, from such partnership, after the commencement of the case is gain, loss, income, deduction, or credit, as the case may be, of the estate.

(2) Except as otherwise provided in this section and in section 728 of this title, any income of the estate in such a case, and any State or local tax on or measured by such income, shall be computed in the same manner as the income and the tax of an estate.

(3) The estate in such a case shall use the same accounting method as the debtor used immediately before the commencement of the case.

(c)(1) The commencement of a case under this title concerning a corporation or a partnership does not effect a change in the status of such corporation or partnership for the purposes of any State or local law imposing a tax on or measured by income. Except as otherwise provided in this section and in section 728 of this title, any income of the estate in such case may be taxed only as though such case had not been commenced.

(2) In such a case, except as provided in section 728 of this title, the trustee shall make any tax return otherwise required by State or local law to be filed by or on behalf of such corporation or partnership in the same manner and form as such corporation or partnership, as the case may be, is required to make such return.

(d) In a case under chapter 13 of this title, any income of the estate or the debtor may be taxed under a State or local law imposing a tax on or measured by income only to the debtor, and may not be taxed to the estate.

(e) A claim allowed under section 502(f) or 503 of this title, other than a claim for a tax that is not otherwise deductible or a capital expenditure that is not otherwise deductible, is deductible by the entity to which income of the estate is taxed unless such claim was deducted by another entity, and a deduction for such a claim is deemed to be a deduction attributable to a business.

(f) The trustee shall withhold from any payment of claims for wages, salaries, commissions, dividends, interest, or other payments, or collect, any amount required to be withheld or collected under applicable State or local tax law, and shall pay such withheld or collected amount to the appropriate governmental unit at the time and in the manner required by such tax law, and with the same priority as the claim from which such amount was withheld was paid.

(g)(1) Neither gain nor loss shall be recognized on a transfer—

(A) by operation of law, of property to the estate;

(B) other than a sale, of property from the estate to the debtor; or

(C) in a case under chapter 11 or 12 of this title concerning a corporation, of property from the estate to a corporation that is an affiliate participating in a joint plan with the debtor, or that is a successor to the debtor under the plan, except that gain or loss may be recognized to the same extent that such transfer results in the recognition of gain or loss under section 371 of the Internal Revenue Code of 1954 (26 U.S.C. § 371).

(2) The transferee of a transfer of a kind specified in this subsection shall take the property transferred with the same character, and with the transferor's basis, as adjusted under subsection (j)(5) of this section, and holding period.

(h) Notwithstanding sections 728(a) and 1146(a) of this title, for the purpose of determining the number of taxable periods during which the debtor or the estate may use a loss carryover or a loss carryback, the taxable period of the debtor during which the case is commenced is deemed not to have been terminated by such commencement.

(i)(1) In a case under chapter 7, 12, or 11 of this title concerning an individual, the estate shall succeed to the debtor's tax attributes, including—

(A) any investment credit carryover;

(B) any recovery exclusion;

(C) any loss carryover;

(D) any foreign tax credit carryover;

(E) any capital loss carryover; and

(F) any claim of right.

(2) After such a case is closed or dismissed, the debtor shall succeed to any tax attribute to which the estate succeeded under paragraph (1) of this subsection but that was not utilized by the estate. The debtor may utilize such tax attributes as though any applicable time limitations on such utilization by the debtor were suspended during the time during which the case was pending.

(3) In such a case, the estate may carry back any loss of the estate to a taxable period of the debtor that ended before the order for relief under such chapter the same as the debtor could have carried back such loss had the debtor incurred such loss and the case under this title had not been commenced, but the debtor may not carry back any loss of the debtor from a taxable period that ends after such order to any taxable period of the debtor that ended before such order until after the case is closed.

(j)(1) Except as otherwise provided in this subsection, income is not realized by the estate, the debtor, or a successor to the debtor by reason of forgiveness or discharge of indebtedness in a case under this title.

(2) For the purposes of any State or local law imposing a tax on or measured by income, a deduction with respect to a liability may not be allowed for any taxable period during or after which such liability is forgiven or discharged under this title. In this paragraph, "a deduction with respect to a liability" includes a capital loss incurred on the disposition of a capital asset with respect to a liability that was incurred in connection with the acquisition of such asset.

(3) Except as provided in paragraph (4) of this subsection, for the purpose of any State or local law imposing a tax on or measured by income, any net operating loss of an individual or corporate debtor, including a net operating loss

carryover to such debtor, shall be reduced by the amount of indebtedness forgiven or discharged in a case under this title, except to the extent that such forgiveness or discharge resulted in a disallowance under paragraph (2) of this subsection.

(4) A reduction of a net operating loss or a net operating loss carryover under paragraph (3) of this subsection or of basis under paragraph (5) of this subsection is not required to the extent that the indebtedness of an individual or corporate debtor forgiven or discharged—

(A) consisted of items of a deductible nature that were not deducted by such debtor; or

(B) resulted in an expired net operating loss carryover or other deduction that—

(i) did not offset income for any taxable period; and

(ii) did not contribute to a net operating loss in or a net operating loss carryover to the taxable period during or after which such indebtedness was discharged.

(5) For the purposes of a State or local law imposing a tax on or measured by income, the basis of the debtor's property or of property transferred to an entity required to use the debtor's basis in whole or in part shall be reduced by the lesser of—

(A)(i) the amount by which the indebtedness of the debtor has been forgiven or discharged in a case under this title; minus

(ii) the total amount of adjustments made under paragraphs (2) and (3) of this subsection; and

(B) the amount by which the total basis of the debtor's assets that were property of the estate before such forgiveness or discharge exceeds the debtor's total liabilities that were liabilities both before and after such forgiveness or discharge.

(6) Notwithstanding paragraph (5) of this subsection, basis is not required to be reduced to the extent that the debtor elects to treat as taxable income, of the taxable period in which indebtedness is forgiven or discharged, the amount of

indebtedness forgiven or discharged that otherwise would be applied in reduction of basis under paragraph (5) of this subsection.

(7) For the purposes of this subsection, indebtedness with respect to which an equity security, other than an interest of a limited partner in a limited partnership, is issued to the creditor to whom such indebtedness was owed, or that is forgiven as a contribution to capital by an equity security holder other than a limited partner in the debtor, is not forgiven or discharged in a case under this title—

(A) to any extent that such indebtedness did not consist of items of a deductible nature; or

(B) if the issuance of such equity security has the same consequences under a law imposing a tax on or measured by income to such creditor as a payment in cash to such creditor in an amount equal to the fair market value of such equity security, then to the lesser of—

(i) the extent that such issuance has the same such consequences; and

(ii) the extent of such fair market value.

Legislative History

Subsection (a) indicates that subsections (b), (c), (d), (e), (g), (h), (i), and (j) apply notwithstanding any State or local tax law, but are subject to Federal tax law.

Subsection (b)(1) provides that in a case concerning an individual under chapter 7 or 11 of title 11, income of the estate is taxable only to the estate and not to the debtor. The second sentence of the paragraph provides that if such individual is a partner, the tax attributes of the partnership are distributable to the partner's estate rather than to the partner, except to the extent that section 728 of title 11 provides otherwise.

Subsection (b)(2) states a general rule that the estate of an individual is to be taxed as an estate. The paragraph is made subject to the remainder of section 346 and section 728 of title 11.

Subsection (b)(3) requires the accounting method, but not necessarily the accounting period, of the estate to be the same as the method used by the individual debtor.

Subsection (c)(1) states a general rule that the estate of a partnership or a corporated debtor is not a separate entity for tax purposes. The income of the debtor is to be taxed as if the case were not commenced, except as provided in the remainder of section 346 and section 728.

Subsection (c)(2) requires the trustee, except as provided in section 728 of title 11, to file all tax returns on behalf of the partnership or corporation during the case.

Subsection (d) indicates that the estate in a chapter 13 case is not a separate taxable entity and that all income of the estate is to be taxed to the debtor.

Subsection (e) establishes a business deduction consisting of allowed expenses of administration except for tax or capital expenses that are not otherwise deductible. The deduction may be used by the estate when it is a separate taxable entity or by the entity to which the income of the estate is taxed when it is not.

Subsection (f) imposes a duty on the trustee to comply with any Federal, State, or local tax law requiring withholding or collection of taxes from any payment of wages, salaries, commissions, dividends, interest, or other payments. Any amount withheld is to be paid to the taxing authority at the same time and with the same priority as the claim from which such amount withheld was paid.

Subsection (g)(1)(A) indicates that neither gain nor loss is recognized on the transfer by law of property from the debtor or a creditor to the estate. Subparagraph (B) provides a similar policy if the property of the estate is returned from the estate to the debtor other than by a sale of property to debtor. Subparagraph (C) also provides for nonrecognition of gain or loss in a case under chapter 11 if a corporate debtor transfers property to a successor corporation or to an affiliate under a joint plan. An exception is made to enable a taxing authority to cause recognition of gain or loss to the extent provided in I.R.C. section 371 (as amended by section 109 of this bill).

Subsection (g)(2) provides that any of the three kinds of transferees specified in paragraph (1) take the property with the same character, holding period, and basis in the hands of the transferor at the time of such transfer. The transferor's basis may be adjusted under section 346(j)(5) even if the discharge of indebtedness occurs after the transfer of property. Of course, no adjustment will occur if the transfer is from the debtor to the estate or if the transfer is from an entity that is not discharged.

Subsection (h) provides that the creation of the estate of an individual under chapters 7 or 11 of title 11 as a separate taxable entity does not affect the number of taxable years for purposes of computing loss carryovers or carrybacks. The section applies with respect to carryovers or carrybacks of the debtor transferred into the estate under section 346 (i)(1) of title 11 or back to the debtor under section 346 (i)(2) of title 11.

Subsection (i)(1) states a general rule that an estate that is a separate taxable entity nevertheless succeeds to all tax attributes of the debtor. The six enumerated attributes are illustrative and not exhaustive.

Subsection (i)(2) indicates that attributes passing from the debtor into an estate that is a separate taxable entity will return to the debtor if unused by the estate. The debtor is permitted to use any such attribute as though the case had not been commenced.

Subsection (i)(3) permits an estate that is a separate taxable entity to carryback losses of the estate to a taxable period of the debtor that ended before the case was filed. The estate is treated as if it were the debtor with respect to time limitations and other restrictions. The section makes clear that the debtor may not carryback any loss of his own from a tax year during the pendency of the case to such a period until the case is closed. No tolling of any period of limitation is provided with respect to carrybacks by the debtor of post-petition losses.

Subsection (j) sets forth seven special rules treating with the tax effects of forgiveness or discharge of indebtedness. The terms "forgiveness" and "discharge" are redundant, but are used to clarify that "discharge" in the context of a special tax provision in title 11 includes forgiveness of indebtedness whether or not such indebtedness is "discharged" in the bankruptcy sense.

Paragraph (1) states the general rule that forgiveness of indebtedness is not taxable except as otherwise provided in paragraphs (2)–(7). The paragraph is patterned after sections 268, 395, and 520 of the Bankruptcy Act.

Paragraph (2) disallows deductions for liabilities of a deductible nature in any year during or after the year of cancellation of such liabilities. For the purposes of this paragraph, "a deduction with respect to a liability" includes a capital loss incurred on the disposition of a capital asset with respect to a liability that was incurred in connection with the acquisition of such asset.

Paragraph (3) causes any net operating loss of a debtor that is an individual or corporation to be reduced by any discharge of indebtedness except as provided in paragraphs (2) or (4). If a deduction is disallowed under paragraph (2), then no double counting occurs. Thus, paragraph (3) will reflect the reduction of losses by liabilities that have been forgiven, including deductible liabilities or nondeductible liabilities such as repayment of principal on borrowed funds.

Paragraph (4) specifically excludes two kinds of indebtedness from reduction of net operating losses under paragraph (3) or from reduction of basis under paragraph (5). Subparagraph (A) excludes items of a deductible nature that were not deducted or that could not be deducted such as gambling losses or liabilities for interest owed to a relative of the debtor. Subparagraph (B) excludes indebtedness of a debtor that is an individual or corporation that resulted in deductions which did not offset income and that did not contribute to an unexpired net operating loss or loss carryover. In these situations, the debtor has derived no tax benefit so there is no need to incur an offsetting reduction.

Paragraph (5) provides a two-point test for reduction of basis. The paragraph replaces sections 270, 396, and 522 of the Bankruptcy Act. Subparagraph (A) sets out the maximum amount by which basis may be reduced—the total indebtedness forgiven less adjustments made under paragraphs (2) and (3). This avoids double counting. If a deduction is disallowed under paragraph (2) or a carryover is reduced under paragraph (3) then the tax benefit is neutralized, and there is no need to reduce basis. Subparagraph (B) reduces basis to the extent the debtor's total basis of assets before the discharge exceeds total preexisting liabilities still remaining after discharge of indebtedness. This is a "basis solvency" limitation which differs from the usual test of solvency because it measures against the remaining liabilities the benefit aspect of assets, their basis, rather than their value. Paragraph (5) applies so that any transferee of the debtor's property who is required to use the debtor's basis takes the debtor's basis reduced by the lesser of (A) and (B). Thus, basis will be reduced, but never below a level equal to undischarged liabilities.

Paragraph (6) specifies that basis need not be reduced under paragraph (5) to the extent the debtor treats discharged indebtedness as taxable income. This permits the debtor to elect whether to recognize income, which may be advantageous if the debtor anticipates subsequent net operating losses, rather than to reduce basis.

Paragraph (7) establishes two rules excluding from the category of discharged indebtedness certain indebtedness that is exchanged for an equity security issued under a plan or that is forgiven as a contribution to capital by an equity security holder. Subparagraph (A) creates the first exclusion to the extent indebtedness consisting of items not of a deductible nature is exchanged for an equity security, other than the interests of a limited partner in a limited partnership, issued by the debtor or is forgiven as a contribution to capital by an equity security holder. Subparagraph (B) excludes indebtedness consisting of items of a deductible nature, if the exchange of stock for debts has the same effect as a cash payment equal to the value of the equity security, in the amount of the fair market value of the equity security or, if less, the extent to which such exchange has such effect. The two provisions treat the debtor as if it had originally issued stock instead of debt. Subparagraph (B) rectifies the inequity under current law between a cash basis and accrual basis debtor concerning the issuance of stock in exchange for previous services rendered that were of a greater value than the stock. Subparagraph (B) also changes current law by taxing forgiveness of indebtedness to the extent that stock is exchanged for the accrued interest component of a security, because the recipient of such stock would not be regarded as having received money under the Carman doctrine.

[*House Report No. 95–595, 95th Cong., 1st Sess. 334–7 (1977); Senate Report No. 95–989, 95th Cong., 2d Sess. 44–7 (1978).*]

Section 346 of the House amendment, together with sections 728 and 1146, represents special tax provisions applicable in bankruptcy. The policy contained in those sections reflects the policy that should be applied in Federal, State, and local taxes in the view of the House Committee on the Judiciary. The House Ways and Means Committee and the Senate Finance Committee did not have time to process a bankruptcy tax bill during the 95th Congress. It is anticipated that early in the 96th Congress, and before the effective date of the bankruptcy code, the tax committees of Congress will have an opportunity to consider action with respect to amendments to the Internal Revenue Code and the special provisions in title 11. Since the special tax provisions are likely to be amended during the first part of the 96th Congress, it is anticipated that the bench and bar will also study and comment on these special tax provisions prior to their revision.

[*124 Cong. Rec. H 11,092 (Sept. 28, 1978); S 17,408 (Oct. 6, 1978).*]

Section 346. Special tax provisions: State and local rules. This section provides special tax provisions dealing with the treatment, under State or local, but not Federal, tax law, of the method of taxing bankruptcy estates of individuals, partnerships, and corporations; survival and allocation of tax attributes between the bankruptcy and the estate; return filing requirements; and the tax treatment of income from discharge of indebtedness. The Senate bill removed these rules pending adoption of Federal rules on these issues in the next Congress. The House amendment returns the State and local tax rules to section 346 so that they may be studied by the bankruptcy and tax bars who may wish to submit comments to Congress.

Withholding rules: Both the House bill and Senate amendment provide that the trustee is required to comply with the normal withholding rules applicable to the payment of wages and other payments. The House amendment retains this rule for State and local taxes only. The treatment of withholding of Federal taxes will be considered in the next Congress.

[*124 Cong. Rec. H 11,109 (Sept. 28, 1978); S 17,426 (Oct. 6, 1978).*]

Comment

There was very little in the Bankruptcy Act comparable to the pervasive tax provisions of section 346 of the Code.

Subdivision (i) of section 346 of the Code codifies the law of Segal v. Rochelle, 382 U.S. 375 (1976), on carrybacks.

1986 Amendments: The only changes effected by the 1986 Amendments were the inclusion of chapter 12 within the operation of subsections (b)(1), (g)(1)(C), and (i)(1).

Case Annotations

Although section 346(i) does not apply to corporate debtors, that does not imply that Congress intended to treat net operating loss carryforwards of corporate debtors differently than those of individual debtors. Rather, since a corporate debtor's estate is not a separate entity for tax purposes, there was no need to provide that carryforwards be transferred to the estate and then back to the corporate debtor at the conclusion of the case. *In re* Prudential Lines, Inc., 928 F.2d 565, 24 C.B.C.2d 1503 (2d Cir. 1991).

Pursuant to 26 U.S.C. § 6012(b)(3), a chapter 7 trustee who is liquidating the estate of a corporate debtor is liable for federal income tax upon interest earned on the estate's funds. Rott v. Eggar (In the Matter of Knight's Mill, Inc.), 7 C.B.C.2d 655 (B. Ct., E.D. Mich. 1982).

References

2 *Collier on Bankruptcy* ch. 346 (Matthew Bender 15th ed.).

1 *Collier Bankruptcy Manual* ch. 346 (Matthew Bender 3d ed.).

2 *Collier Bankruptcy Practice Guide* ch. 93 (Matthew Bender).

Ellis, *Marital Tax Indemnification Agreements: Exception to Bankruptcy Discharge,* 19 Colo. Law 639 (1990).

Falk, *Are Trust Fund Tax Payments Beyond the Trustee's Reach?,* 2 G & G Bankr. L. Rev. 10 (1990).

Fitzgerald, *Section 6672 of the Internal Revenue Code and a Chapter 11 Reorganization Under the Bankruptcy Code—A Taxpayer's Potential Discharge of an IRS Penalty?,* 46 J. Mo. B. 551 (1990).

Hippke, *Special Tax Provisions of the Bankruptcy Reform Act of 1978,* 1979 Ann. Survey of Bankr. Law 127 (1979).

Litton, *The Proper Treatment of ERISA Qualified Pension Plans in Bankruptcy: A Tax Perspective,* 11 Va. Tax Rev. 195 (1991).

Onsager, *Assigning Tax Liability Between the Bankruptcy Estate and the Individual Debtor,* 75 J. Tax'n 102 (1991).

Postpetition Interest on Tax Claims in Bankruptcy Proceedings, 36 Tax Law 793 (1983).

Rothman, *Responsible Persons and Irresponsible Doctrine: The Allocation of the Bankrupt's Postpetition Payments on Unpaid Prepetition Federal Taxes,* 95 Com. L.J. 24 (1990).

Sabino, *The Allocation of Payments to Trust Fund Taxes in Bankruptcy Reorganizations: The IRS v. the Bankruptcy Court,* 17 J. Corp. Tax'n 339 (1991).

St. James, *Federal Tax Liens—Making Bankruptcy Attractive to Creditors,* 46 Bus. Law. 157 (1990).

Tax Aspects of Dispositions of Property to Satisfy Indebtedness, 46 Iowa State Bar News Bulletin 11 (1986).

Van Brauman, *The Carryforward of New Operating Losses and Other Tax Attributes After Bankruptcy Reorganizations,* 23 St. Mary's L.J. 461 (1991).

Webster, *Tax Aspects of the Bankruptcy Reform Act of 1978,* 10 Tax Advisor 220 (1979).

SECTION 347 (11 U.S.C. § 347)

§ 347. Unclaimed property.

(a) Ninety days after the final distribution under section 726, 1226, or 1326 of this title in a case under chapter 7, 12, or 13 of this title, as the case may be, the trustee shall stop payment on any check remaining unpaid, and any remaining property of the estate shall be paid into the court and disposed of under chapter 129 of title 28.

(b) Any security, money, or other property remaining unclaimed at the expiration of the time allowed in a case under chapter 9, 11, or 12 of this title for the presentation of a security or the performance of any other act as a condition to participation in the distribution under any plan confirmed under section 943(b), 1129, 1173, or 1225 of this title, as the case may be, becomes the property of the debtor or of the entity acquiring the assets of the debtor under the plan, as the case may be.

Bankruptcy Rule References: 3010 and 3011

Legislative History

Section 347 is derived from Bankruptcy Act section 66. Subsection (a) requires the trustee to stop payment on any distribution check that is unpaid sixty days after the final distribution in a case under chapter 7 or 13. The unclaimed funds, and any other property of the estate are paid into the court and disposed of under chapter 129 of title 28, which requires the clerk of court to hold the funds for their owner for five years, after which they escheat to the Treasury.

Subsection (b) specifies that any property remaining unclaimed at the expiration of the time allowed in a chapter 9 or 11 case for presentation (exchange) of securities or the performance of any other act as a condition to participation in the plan reverts to the debtor or the entity acquiring the assets of the debtor under the plan. Conditions to participation under a plan include such acts as cashing a check, surrendering securities for cancellation, and so on. Similar provisions are found in section 96(d) and 205 of current law.

[*House Report No. 95–595, 95th Cong., 1st Sess. 337 (1977); Senate Report No. 95–989, 95th Cong., 2d Sess. 47–48 (1978).*]

Section 347(a) of the House amendment adopts a comparable provision contained in the Senate amendment instructing the trustee to stop payment on any check remaining unpaid more than 90 days after the final distribution in a case under chapter 7 or 13. Technical changes are made in section 347(b) to cover distributions in a railroad reorganization.

[*124 Cong. Rec. H 11,092 (Sept. 28, 1978); S 17,408 (Oct. 6, 1978).*]

Comment

The 60 day period mentioned in the House Report was changed to 90 days.

Bankruptcy Rule 3011 implements section 347(a) by requiring the trustee to file a list of all known names and addresses of the entities entitled to payment and the amount to which they are entitled from remaining property of the estate that is paid into the court pursuant to section 347(a). The rule does not apply to chapter 9 or 11 cases which are governed by section 347(b).

Bankruptcy Rule 3010 provides that in a chapter 7 case no dividend less than $5 shall be distributed to any creditor unless authorized by local rule or order. Any such dividend not distributed to a creditor is to be treated in the same manner as unclaimed funds as provided in section 347. Subdivision (b) of Rule 3010 provides that in a chapter 12 or 13 case no payment of less than $15 be distributed unless authorized by local rule or court order. Funds not distributed shall be accumulated and be paid whenever the accumulation aggregates $15. Remaining funds are to be distributed with the final payment.

1986 Amendments: The amendments made § 347 applicable to cases under chapter 12.

Case Annotations

Dividends that go unclaimed, for any reason, revert to the debtor in a chapter 11 case. *In re* Federated Department Stores, Inc., 26 C.B.C.2d 829 (B. Ct., S.D. Ohio 1992).

If section 347(b) applied only to situations in which a plan of reorganization fails to address the issue of distribution of remaining property, that section would be robbed of meaning. *In re* Goldblatt Bros., Inc., 25 C.B.C.2d 953 (B. Ct., N.D. Ill. 1991).

References

2 *Collier on Bankruptcy* ch. 347 (Matthew Bender 15th ed.).

1 *Collier Bankruptcy Manual* ch. 347 (Matthew Bender 3d ed.).

SECTION 348 (11 U.S.C. § 348)

§ 348. Effect of conversion.

(a) Conversion of a case from a case under one chapter of this title to a case under another chapter of this title constitutes an order for relief under the chapter to which the case is converted, but, except as provided in subsections (b) and (c) of this section, does not effect a change in the date of the filing of the petition, the commencement of the case, or the order for relief.

(b) Unless the court for cause orders otherwise, in sections 701(a), 727(a)(10), 727(b), 728(a), 728(b), 1102(a), 1110(a)(1), 1121(b), 1121(c), 1141(d)(4), 1146(a), 1146(b), 1301(a), 1305(a), 1201(a), 1221, and 1228(a) of this title, "the order for relief under this chapter" in a chapter to which a case has been converted under section 706, 1112, 1307, or 1208 of this title means the conversion of such case in such chapter.

(c) Sections 342 and 365(d) of this title apply in a case that has been converted under section 706, 1112, 1307, or 1208 of this title, as if the conversion order were the order for relief.

(d) A claim against the estate or the debtor that arises after the order for relief but before conversion in a case that is converted under section 1112, 1307, or 1208 of this title, other than a claim specified in section 503(b) of this title, shall be treated for all purposes as if such claim had arisen immediately before the date of the filing of the petition.

(e) Conversion of a case under section 706, 1112, 1307, or 1208 of this title terminates the service of any trustee or examiner that is serving in the case before such conversion.

Bankruptcy Rule References: 1017 and 1019

Legislative History

This section governs the effect of the conversion of a case from one chapter of the bankruptcy code to another chapter. Subsection (a) specifies that the date of the filing of the petition, the commencement of the case, or the order for relief are unaffected by conversion, with some exceptions specified in subsections (b) and (c).

Subsection (b) lists certain sections in the operative chapters of the bankruptcy code in which there is a reference to "the order for relief under this chapter." In those sections, the reference is to be read as a reference to the conversion order if the case has been converted into the particular chapter. Subsection (c) specifies that notice is to be given of the conversion order the same as notice was given of the order for relief, and that the time the trustee (or debtor in possession) has for assuming or rejecting executory contracts recommences, thus giving an opportunity for a newly appointed trustee to familiarize himself with the case.

Subsection (d) provides for special treatment of claims that arise during chapter 11 or 13 cases before the case is converted to a liquidation case. With the exception of claims specified in proposed 11 U.S.C. 503(b) (administrative expenses), preconversion claims are treated the same as prepetition claims.

[*House Report No. 95-595, 95th Cong., 1st Sess. 337 (1977); Senate Report No. 95-989, 95th Cong., 2d Sess. 48 (1978).*]

Subsection (e) provides that conversion of a case terminates the service of any trustee serving in the case prior to conversion.

[*Senate Report No. 95-989, 95th Cong., 2d Sess. 48 (1978).*]

The House amendment adopts section 348(b) of the Senate amendment with slight modifications, as more accurately reflecting sections to which this particular effect of conversion should apply.

Section 348(e) of the House amendment is a stylistic revision of similar provisions contained in H.R. 8200 as passed by the House and in the Senate amendment. Termination of services is expanded to cover any examiner serving in the case before conversion, as done in H.R. 8200 as passed by the House.

[*124 Cong. Rec. H 11,092 (Sept. 28, 1978), S 17,508 (Oct. 6, 1978).*]

Comment

The sections referred to in section 348(b) contain the words "the order for relief under this chapter," referring to chapter 7 (Liquidation), chapter 11 (Reorganization), chapter 12 (Adjustment of Debts of a Family Farmer with Regular Annual Income), and chapter 13 (Adjustment of Debts of an Individual With a Regular Income).

Section 342(a) referred to in subsection (c) requires that appropriate notice be given of any "order for relief" under the Code.

Section 365(d), referred to in subsection (c), provides that in a chapter 7 case (Liquidation), unless the trustee assumes an executory contract or unexpired lease within 60 days after the order for relief (or within such additional time as the court, for cause, within such 60 day period, fixes) then such contract or lease is deemed rejected.

Sections 706, 1112, 1208, and 1307, referred to in subsections (c) and (d), all relate to conversion of a case from one chapter to another.

Section 503(b), referred to in subsection (d), specifies the kind of administrative expenses that are allowable in a case under the Code.

Bankruptcy Rule 1017(d), amended in 1991, implementing section 348, provides that a proceeding to convert a case to another chapter [except pursuant to §§ 706(a), 707(b), 1112(a), 1208(a) or (b) or 1307(a) or (b)] is governed by Rule 9014, *i.e.*, it is a contested matter initiated by motion.

Bankruptcy Rule 1019, relating to conversion of a chapter 11, 12 or 13 case to chapter 7, was substantially revised by the 1991 Amendments. In the event of a conversion:

(1)(A) lists, inventories, schedules, and statements of financial affairs theretofore filed are deemed filed in the chapter 7 case unless the court otherwise directs. If not previously filed, the debtor must comply with Rule 1007 as if an order for relief was entered on an involuntary petition on the date of entry of the conversion order;

(B) the statement of intention, if required, shall be filed within 30 days following entry of the order of conversion or before the first date set for the meeting of creditors, whichever is earlier. An extension of time may be granted for cause only on motion made before the time has expired. Notice of an extension shall be given to the United States trustee and to any committee, trustee, or other party as the court may direct. [Added by the 1987 Amendments to the Bankruptcy Rules and revised by the 1991 Amendments.]

(2) a new time period for filing claims, a complaint objecting to discharge, or a complaint to obtain a determination of dischargeability of a debt shall commence pursuant to Rules 3002, 4004, or 4007, provided that a new time period shall not commence if a chapter 7 case has been converted to chapter 11, 12 or 13 and thereafter reconverted to chapter 7 and the time for filing claims, etc., or any extension thereof, expired in the original chapter 7 case;

(3) it is unnecessary to file claims that had been actually filed by a creditor in the superseded case;

(4) after the chapter 7 trustee qualifies or assumes his duties, the trustee or debtor in possession previously acting in the chapter 11, 12 or 13 case, unless otherwise ordered, must forthwith turn over to the chapter 7 trustee all records and property of the estate;

(5) Unless the court directs otherwise, each debtor in possession or trustee in the superseded case shall (A) within 15 days after entry of an order of conversion of a chapter 11 case, file a schedule of unpaid debts incurred after commencement of the superseded case including the name and address of each creditor; and (B) within 30 days after entry of an order of conversion of a chapter 11, 12, or 13 case, file and transmit to the United States trustee a final report and account.

Within 15 days following the entry of the conversion order, unless the court directs otherwise, a chapter 12 or chapter 13 debtor shall file a schedule of unpaid debts incurred after commencement of the chapter 12 or 13 case. If the conversion order is entered after confirmation of a plan, the debtor shall file (A) a schedule of property not listed in the final report and account acquired after the filing of the original petition but before entry of the conversion order; (B) a schedule of unpaid debts not listed in the final report and account incurred after confirmation but before entry of the conversion order; and (C) a schedule of executory contracts and unexpired leases entered into or assumed after the filing of the original petition but before entry of the conversion order. The clerk shall forthwith transmit to the United States trustee a copy of every schedule filed pursuant to this paragraph.

(6) On the filing of the schedule of unpaid debts, the clerk or some other person as the court may direct shall give notice to those entities, including the United States, any state, or any subdivision thereof, that their claims may be filed pursuant to Rules 3001(a)–(d) and 3002. Unless a notice of insufficient assets to pay a dividend is mailed pursuant to Rule 2002(e), the court shall fix the time for filing claims arising from the rejection of executory contracts or unexpired leases under sections 348(c) and 365(d) of the Code.

(7) if the court extends the time to file claims against a surplus (Rule 3002(c)(6)), the extension applies to holders of claims who failed to file within the time prescribed or fixed under (6), above, and notice shall be given to the claimant as provided in Rule 2002.

1986 Amendments: The only changes effected in § 348 are the inclusion of references to chapter 12 in subsections (b), (d), and (e).

Case Annotations

The purpose of section 348(d) is to distinguish between chapter 11 administrative priority and nonpriority claims and it does not address the availability of remedies against discharge and dischargeability. Matter of Pavlovich, 952 F.2d 114, 26 C.B.C.2d 542 (5th Cir. 1992).

Pursuant to the plain language of section 348 and other authority, when a debtor's case is converted from chapter 11 to chapter 7, in order to determine whether a trustee may avoid a transfer, a court should calculate the date of the filing of the petition from the date of the original chapter 11 filing, rather than from the date of the conversion. Vogel v. Russell Transfer, Inc., 852 F.2d 797, 19 C.B.C.2d 1203 (4th Cir. 1988).

When a case is converted from chapter 11 to chapter 7, exemptions are determined as of the filing date of the chapter 11 petition. Stinson v. Williamson (In the Matter of Williamson), 804 F.2d 1355, 15 C.B.C.2d 1225 (5th Cir. 1986).

The conversion of a case from chapter 11 to chapter 7 generates a new time period for filing dischargeability complaints, because the conversion constitutes an order for relief that requires a new and distinct meeting of creditors, the date of which keys the beginning of the time period for filing dischargeability complaints. F & M Marquette Nat'l Bank v. Richards, 780 F.2d 24, 13 C.B.C.2d 1305 (8th Cir. 1985).

The provision of section 348(a) that conversion of a case to another chapter of the Code will not effect a change in the date of the filing of the petition cannot be read to prohibit the changing of a homestead exemption at the time of conversion because that reading would conflict with other provisions, particularly Rule 1007. Armstrong v. Lindberg (*In re* Lindberg), 735 F.2d 1087, 10 C.B.C.2d 1255 (8th Cir.), *cert. denied,* 469 U.S. 1023, 105 S. Ct. 566, 83 L. Ed. 2d 507 (1984).

In a case converted from chapter 11, the time that the debtor in possession is in place does not count against the subsequently appointed chapter 7 trustee. *In re* Bingham Systems, Inc., 26 C.B.C.2d 1570 (B. Ct., N.D. Miss. 1991).

Section 348(b) deals only with the treatment of claims upon conversion and not with the dischargeability of claims upon conversion. *In re* Ramaker, 23 C.B.C.2d 936 (B. Ct., N.D. Iowa 1990).

A chapter 7 estate does not include any wages earned between the filing date of the original chapter 13 petition and the date of conversion subsequent to the confirmation of a plan, even if those wages were part of a chapter 13 estate up until conversion. A chapter 13 trustee holds undistributed funds as an agent for creditors under a confirmed plan and must distribute those funds pursuant to the plan even if his status as trustee ceases upon conversion of the case. *In re* Redick, 18 C.B.C.2d 254 (B. Ct., E.D. Mich. 1987).

Adequate assurance of payment can be requested by a utility only once in a bankruptcy case, *i.e.,* after the order for relief, even if the case is later converted from chapter 13 to chapter 7. Allen v. Philadelphia Elec. Co. (*In re* Allen), 16 C.B.C.2d 527 (B. Ct., E.D. Pa. 1987).

Commercial rental expenses arising postconfirmation in a chapter 13 case have priority as administrative expenses once the case is converted to chapter 11 when the debtor uses the rental premises to generate funds to pay creditors under the chapter 13 plan and the estate has been granted rights to these funds. *In re* Martin, 16 C.B.C.2d 1191 (B. Ct., C.D. Cal. 1987).

Section 348(c) cannot be interpreted to supersede the legislative intent behind the later enacted section 365(d)(4). Accordingly, upon conversion to chapter 7, after the original 60-day period has expired, the trustee is not entitled to a new 60-day period to assume or reject a lease. *In re* The Tandem Group, Inc., 15 C.B.C.2d 170 (B. Ct., C.D. Cal. 1986).

Contract proceeds owed to a secured creditor as part of an unsuccessful chapter 11 plan prior to conversion of a chapter 11 case to chapter 7 constitutes property of the debtor's estate upon conversion since the proceeds were generated by the operation of the estate's assets during pendency of the reorganization attempt until the time of confirmation. Any proceeds received thereafter revert to the debtor if the plan provides for the revesting of estate property in the debtor upon conversion. Kepler v. Independence Bank of Madison (In the Matter of Ford), 14 C.B.C.2d 1399 (B. Ct., W.D. Wis. 1986).

References

2 *Collier on Bankruptcy* ch. 348 (Matthew Bender 15th ed.).

1 *Collier Bankruptcy Manual* ch. 348 (Matthew Bender 3d ed.).

2 *Collier Bankruptcy Practice Guide* ch. 37 (Matthew Bender).

SECTION 349 (11 U.S.C. § 349)

§ 349. Effect of dismissal.

(a) Unless the court, for cause, orders otherwise, the dismissal of a case under this title does not bar the discharge, in a later case under this title, of debts that were dischargable in the case dismissed; nor does the dismissal of a case under this title prejudice the debtor with regard to the filing of a subsequent petition under this title, except as provided in section 109(f) of this title.

(b) Unless the court, for cause, orders otherwise, a dismissal of a case other than under section 742 of this title—

(1) reinstates—

(A) any proceeding or custodianship superseded under section 543 of this title;

(B) any transfer avoided under section 522, 544, 545, 547, 548, 549, or 724(a) of this title, or preserved under section 510(c)(2), 522(i)(2), or 551 of this title; and

(C) any lien voided under section 506(d) of this title;

(2) vacates any order, judgment, or transfer ordered, under section 522(i)(1), 542, 550, or 553 of this title; and

(3) revests the property of the estate in the entity in which such property was vested immediately before the commencement of the case under this title.

Bankruptcy Rule Reference: 1017

Legislative History

Subsection (a) specifies that unless the court for cause orders otherwise, the dismissal of a case is without prejudice. The debtor is not barred from receiving a discharge in a later case of debts that were dischargeable in the case dismissed. Of course, this subsection refers only to pre-discharge dismissals. If the debtor has already received a discharge and it is not revoked, then the debtor would be barred under section 727(a) from receiving a discharge in a subsequent liquidation case for six years. Dismissal of an involuntary on the merits will generally not give rise to adequate cause so as to bar the debtor from further relief.

Subsection (b) specifies that the dismissal reinstates proceedings or custodianships that were superseded by the bankruptcy case, reinstates avoided transfers, reinstates voided liens, vacates any order, judgment, or transfer ordered as a result of the avoidance of a transfer, and revests the property of the estate in the entity in which the property was vested at the commencement of the case. The court is permitted to order a different result for cause. The basic purpose of the subsection is to undo the bankruptcy case, as far as practicable, and to restore all property rights to the position in which they were found at the commencement of the case. This does not necessarily encompass undoing sales of property from the estate to a good faith purchaser. Where there is a question over the scope of the subsection, the court will make the appropriate orders to protect rights acquired in reliance on the bankruptcy case.

[*House Report No. 95-595, 95th Cong., 1st Sess. 337-38 (1977); Senate Report No. 95-989, 95th Cong., 2d Sess. 48-9 (1978).*]

Section 349(b)(2) of the House amendment adds a cross reference to section 553 to reflect the new right of recovery of setoffs created under that section. Corresponding changes are made throughout the House amendment.

[*124 Cong. Rec. S 17,408 (Oct. 6, 1978).*]

Comment

Section 742, referred to in subsection (b) of section 349, deals with SIPA cases and provides for dismissal of the case if SIPC completes liquidation of the debtor.

Section 506(d), referred to in subsection (b)(1)(C), provides that to the extent a secured claim is not allowed, its lien is void except under certain specified circumstances. Upon dismissal of the case, the lien is reinstated.

Former Bankruptcy Rule 120(c) provided that unless the order specified to the contrary, a dismissal of a case otherwise than on the merits was without prejudice. There was no comparable provision in the Act. Prior to the rule, dismissal often operated harshly against the debtor. *See, e.g., In re* Frey, 95 F. Supp. 1007 (S.D.N.Y. 1951). This rule has now been incorporated in section 349.

Section 17b of the former Bankruptcy Act provided that failure of a bankrupt or debtor to obtain a discharge in a prior bankruptcy case for certain specified reasons should not bar the release by discharge in a subsequent case under the Act of debts that were dischargeable in the prior case. One of the specified reasons was dismissal of the prior case without prejudice for failure to pay filing fees or to secure costs.

Section 67a of the former Act relating to avoidance of judicial liens had a proviso to the effect that if the bankrupt or debtor was not finally adjudged a bankrupt and if no arrangement or plan was proposed or confirmed, the nullified lien would be deemed reinstated with the same effect as if it had not been nullified and voided.

Bankruptcy Rule 1017, amended in 1991, deals with dismissal, conversion or suspension of a case. Subdivision (a) requires a hearing on notice and provides for the filing of the list of creditors by the debtor. Subdivision (b) relates to dismissal for failure to pay an installment of the filing fee. Subdivision (c) provides that a case shall not be dismissed pursuant to section 305 until after a hearing on notice.

1984 Amendments: The 1984 amendments added to section 349(a) all the language following the semi-colon. The new language should be read together with new section 109(f) [redesignated by the 1986 Amendments as section 109(g)]. When the case of an individual debtor with mainly consumer debts (as defined in section 101) is dismissed under certain specified circumstances, the debtor may not, under that section, file a new petition until after 180 days following the dismissal. The amendment to section 349(a) makes clear that except for the section 109(f) [now section (g)] situation, a dismissal of a case will not prejudice a debtor with regard to a subsequent petition. The latter section refers to an individual debtor, but section 349(a) has no such limitation.

Case Annotations

A bankruptcy court's decision to retain discretionary jurisdiction of an adversary proceeding is entitled to deference and should be upheld absent a clear showing of abuse of discretion. *In re* Morris, 950 F.2d 1531, 26 C.B.C.2d 465 (11th Cir. 1992).

Pursuant to section 349, bankruptcy courts have the discretion to determine whether there is cause to dismiss a case with prejudice but a debtor may only be denied a future discharge of debts dischargeable in a particular case. The court does not have the power to deny a debtor all future access to the bankruptcy court except as provided for by section 109. *In re* Frieouf, 938 F.2d 1099, 25 C.B.C.2d 481 (10th Cir. 1991).

Under section 349(b), the dismissal of a case reinstates a voided lien, unless the court, for cause, finds otherwise; however, "cause" under section 349(b) does not encompass the desire of debtors to convert indirectly to chapter 12 from chapter 13, by dismissing as of right one case and commencing another and have all dates relate back to the original filing date, when direct conversion is prohibited by law. In the Matter of Sadler, 935 F.2d 918, 24 C.B.C.2d 2017 (7th Cir. 1991).

The dismissal of a confirmed chapter 13 plan causes all property of the estate, including funds accumulated by the trustee under a wage deduction order, to revert to the debtor. Nash v. Kester (*In re* Nash), 765 F.2d 1410, 13 C.B.C.2d 209 (9th Cir. 1985).

A case determined to have been filed in bad faith may be dismissed with prejudice. *In re* Huerta, 26 C.B.C.2d 1236 (B. Ct., C.D. Cal. 1992).

Under section 349(b), funds collected postpetition, but prior to confirmation of plan, by a trustee from a debtor's employer under a wage-withholding order for distribution to creditors but never distributed to creditors should be returned to the debtor upon dismissal of the chapter 13 case. *In re* Slaughter, 26 C.B.C.2d 1501 (B. Ct., N.D. Ill. 1992).

Sections 349 and 109, read together, allow a debtor to refile 180 days after a dismissal and discharge debts that were dischargeable in the previous case. *In re* Samora, 23 C.B.C.2d 1085 (B. Ct., D.N.M. 1990).

When defendants conduct a foreclosure sale without the court's permission and without seeking relief from the automatic stay, section 349(b) controls and revests the property in the debtor. *In re* Sports & Science, Indus., Inc., 20 C.B.C.2d 900 (B. Ct., C.D. Cal. 1989).

Funds held by a trustee pursuant to a confirmed but dismissed chapter 12 plan cannot be returned to a debtor but must be distributed in accordance with the plan. *In re* Samford, 21 C.B.C.2d 656 (B. Ct., E.D. Mo. 1989).

Authority exists under both sections 105 and 349(a) for the court to dismiss a chapter 13 petition as an abuse of the bankruptcy system (when the debtors' petition is an illustration of a blatant attempt to circumvent congressional intent and a demonstration of bad faith), and to condition that dismissal on an injunction preventing the debtors from filing another chapter 13 petition for 180 days. *In re* Dyke, 14 C.B.C.2d 625 (B. Ct., N.D. Ill. 1986).

References

2 *Collier on Bankruptcy* ch. 349 (Matthew Bender 15th ed.).

1 *Collier Bankruptcy Manual* ch. 349 (Matthew Bender 3d ed.).

2 *Collier Bankruptcy Practice Guide* ch. 37 (Matthew Bender).

SECTION 350 (11 U.S.C. § 350)

§ 350. Closing and reopening cases.

(a) After an estate is fully administered and the court has discharged the trustee, the court shall close the case.

(b) A case may be reopened in the court in which such case was closed to administer assets, to accord relief to the debtor, or for other cause.

Bankruptcy Rule References: 3022, 5009 and 5010

Legislative History

Subsection (a) requires the court to close a bankruptcy case after the estate is fully administered and the trustee discharged. The Rules of Bankruptcy Procedure will provide the procedure for case closing. Subsection (b) permits reopening of the case to administer assets, to accord relief to the debtor, or for other cause. Though the court may permit reopening of a case so that the trustee may exercise an avoiding power, laches may constitute a bar to an action that has been delayed too long. The case may be reopened in the court in which it was closed. The Rules will prescribe the procedure by which a case is reopened and how it will be conducted after reopening.

[*House Report No. 95–595, 95th Cong., 1st Sess. 338 (1977); Senate Report No. 95–989, 95th Cong., 2d Sess. 49 (1978).*]

Comment

Bankruptcy Rule 5009, completely revised by the 1991 Amendments, provides that if the trustee in a chapter 7, 12 or 13 case has filed a final report and account and has certified that the estate has been fully administered, and if within 30 days no objection has been filed by the United States trustee or a party in interest, there shall be a presumption that the estate has been fully administered. The 1991 Advisory Committee Note suggests that absent timely objection by the United States trustee or a party in interest, the court may discharge the trustee and close the case pursuant to section 351(a) without further ado.

Rule 3022, also rewritten in 1991, governs the closing of chapter 11 cases.

Bankruptcy Rule 5010 provides that a case may be reopened on motion of the debtor or other party in interest pursuant to section 350(b). In a chapter 7, 12 or 13 case a trustee is not to be appointed by the United States trustee unless the court determines that a trustee is necessary to protect the interest of creditors and the debtor or to insure efficient administration of the case.

Bankruptcy Rule 3022, completely revised by the 1991 Amendments, provides that after an estate is fully administered in a chapter 11 case, the court, on its own motion or on motion of a party in interest, shall enter a final decree closing the case. *See* 1991 Advisory Committee Note to Rule 3012 for factors the court should consider in determining whether the estate has been fully administered. (Note that Bankruptcy Rule 9024, which incorporates Fed. R. Civ. P. 60, exempts motions to reopen cases under the Code from the one year limitation of Rule 60(b).)

Case Annotations

A bankruptcy court may reopen a case for cause when it is necessary to determine whether express provisions of a note and the terms of a reorganization plan should be modified. *In re* Case, 937 F.2d 1014, 25 C.B.C.2d 368 (5th Cir. 1991).

A movant seeking to reopen a case in order to challenge a court-confirmed sale of an estate asset must provide evidence, rather than mere allegations, to succeed on its motion. *In re* Irvin, 950 F.2d 1318, 26 C.B.C.2d 152 (7th Cir. 1991).

The principles of *res judicata* and collateral estoppel are not a bar to reopening a case in order to modify the permanent injunction so that a state action may proceed against the debtor for purposes of determining the debtor's liability only with respect to indemnification by a third party such as an insurer. *In re* Shondel, 950 F.2d 1301, 26 C.B.C.2d 193 (7th Cir. 1991).

A decision whether to reopen a bankruptcy case and allow amendment of schedules is committed to the sound discretion of the bankruptcy judge and will not be set aside absent abuse of discretion. Rosinski v. Boyd (*In re* Rosinski), 759 F.2d 539, 12 C.B.C.2d 923 (6th Cir. 1985).

Whether to reopen a case eight months after it has been closed for the purpose of filing a lien avoidance action pursuant to section 522(f) is within the bankruptcy court's discretion. Hawkins v. Landmark Fin. Co. (*In re* Hawkins), 727 F.2d 324, 10 C.B.C.2d 94 (4th Cir. 1984).

In a no-asset bankruptcy case in which notice had been given pursuant to the Bankruptcy Rules, a debtor may reopen the estate to add an omitted creditor when there is no evidence of fraud, intentional design, or harm to the creditor. Stark v. St. Mary's Hosp. (In the Matter of Stark), 717 F.2d 322, 9 C.B.C.2d 319 (7th Cir. 1983).

The words "for other cause" in section 350(b) suggest that there need only be a reason to reopen a case, and that good cause is not required. *In re* Peterson, 24 C.B.C.2d 571 (B. Ct., D.N.M. 1990).

A motion to reopen a case in order to schedule a nondischargeable debt will be denied since it would accord the debtor no relief. *In re* Candelaria, 22 C.B.C.2d 465 (B. Ct., E.D.N.Y. 1990).

In order to encourage reorganization cases, honest debtors who put forth their best efforts in paying creditors should be given the benefit of the doubt, and be allowed further administration of their cases to seek lien avoidance. *In re* Walters, 22 C.B.C.2d 1747 (B. Ct., D.S.D. 1990).

There is cause to reopen a no-asset case to allow a debtor to add an omitted creditor to his schedules if the opposing creditor asserts that the dischargeability of its claim falls under section 523(a)(2), (4) or (6) and is accordingly not discharged by reason of section 523(a)(3)(B). *In re* Padilla, 18 C.B.C.2d 847 (B. Ct., C.D. Colo. 1987).

The stepdaughter of a chapter 13 debtor has sufficient personal interest and standing as the representative of her twelve-year-old daughter to request the reopening of the debtor's case when the daughter is the successor in interest to the most significant asset in what had been the debtor's estate. *In re* Young, 16 C.B.C.2d 1090 (B. Ct., E.D. Pa. 1987).

References

2 *Collier on Bankruptcy* ch. 350 (Matthew Bender 15th ed.).

1 *Collier Bankruptcy Manual* ch. 350 (Matthew Bender 3d ed.).

6 *Collier Bankruptcy Practice Guide* Part XII (Matthew Bender).

SUBCHAPTER IV

Administrative Powers

SECTION 361 (11 U.S.C. § 361)

§ 361. **Adequate protection.** When adequate protection is required under section 362, 363, or 364 of this title of an interest of an entity in property, such adequate protection may be provided by—

(1) requiring the trustee to make a cash payment or periodic cash payments to such entity, to the extent that the stay under section 362 of this title, use, sale, or lease under section 363 of this title, or any grant of a lien under section 364 of this title results in a decrease in the value of such entity's interest in such property;

(2) providing to such entity an additional or replacement lien to the extent that such stay, use, sale, lease, or grant results in a decrease in the value of such entity's interest in such property; or

(3) granting such other relief, other than entitling such entity to compensation allowable under section 503(b)(1) of this title as an administrative expense, as will result in the realization by such entity of the indubitable equivalent of such entity's interest in such property.

Bankruptcy Rule Reference: 4001

Legislative History

Sections 362, 363, and 364 require, in certain circumstances, that the court determine whether the interest of a secured creditor or co-owner of property with the debtor is adequately protected. The interests of which the court may provide protection in the ways described in this section include equitable as well as legal interests. For example, a right to redeem under a pledge or a right to recover property under a consignment are both interests that are entitled to protection. This section specifies the means by which adequate protection may be provided. It does not require the court to provide it. To do so would place the court in an administrative role. Instead, the trustee or debtor in possession will provide or propose a protection method. If the party that is affected by the proposed action objects, the court will determine whether the protection provided is adequate. The purpose of this section is to illustrate means by which it may be provided and to define the contours of the concept.

The concept is derived from the fifth amendment protection of property interests. *See* Wright v. Union Central Life Ins. Co., 311 U.S. 273 (1940); Louisville Joint Stock Land Bank v. Radford, 295 U.S. 555 (1935). It is not intended to be confined strictly to the constitutional protection required, however. The section, and the concept of adequate protection, is based as much on policy grounds as on constitutional grounds. Secured creditors should not be deprived of the benefit of their bargain. There may be situations in bankruptcy where giving a secured creditor an absolute right to his bargain may be impossible or seriously detrimental to the bankruptcy laws. Thus, this section recognizes the availability of alternate means of protecting a secured creditor's interest. Though the creditor might not receive his bargain in kind, the purpose of the section is to insure that the secured creditor receives in value essentially what he bargained for.

[*Ed. Note:* As enacted, section 361 lists three means of providing adequate protection.]

The section specifies four means of providing adequate protection. They are neither exclusive nor exhaustive. They all rely, however, on the value of the protected entity's interest in the property involved. The section does not specify how value is to be determined, nor does it specify when it is to be determined. These matters are left to case-by-case interpretation and development. It is expected that the courts will apply the concept in light of facts of each case and general equitable principles. It is not intended that the courts will develop a hard and fast rule that will apply in every case. The time and method of valuation is not specified precisely, in order to avoid that result. There are an infinite number of variations possible in dealings between debtors and creditors, the law is continually developing, and new ideas are continually being implemented in this field. The flexibility is important to permit the courts to adapt to varying circumstances and changing modes of financing.

Neither is it expected that the courts will construe the term value to mean, in every case, forced liquidation value or full going concern value. There is wide latitude between those two extremes. In any particular case, especially a reorganization case, the determination of which entity should be entitled to the difference between the going concern value and the liquidation value must be based on equitable considerations based on the facts of the case. It will frequently be based on negotiation between the parties. Only if they cannot agree will the court become involved.

The first method of adequate protection specified is periodic cash payments by the estate, to the extent of a decrease in value of the opposing entity's interest in the property involved. This provision is derived from *In re* Yale Express, Inc., 384 F.2d 990 (2d Cir. 1967) (though in that case it is not clear whether the payments required were adequate to compensate the secured creditors for their loss). The use of periodic payments may be appropriate, where, for example, the property in question is depreciating at a relatively fixed rate. The periodic payments would be to compensate for the depreciation.

The second method is the provision of an additional or replacement lien on other property to the extent of the decrease in value of the property involved. The purpose of this method is to provide the protected entity with a means of realizing the value of the original property, if it should decline during the case, by granting an interest in additional property from whose value the entity may realize its loss.

The third method is the granting of an administrative expense priority to the protected entity to the extent of his loss. This method, more than the others, requires a prediction as to whether the unencumbered assets that will remain if the case is converted from reorganization to liquidation will be sufficient to pay the protected entity in full. It is clearly the most risky, from the entity's perspective, and should be used only when there is relative certainty that administrative expenses will be able to be paid in full in the event of liquidation.

[*Ed. Note:* This method has been deleted and replaced by a provision stating that an administrative expense priority is *not* a proper method.]

The fourth method gives the parties and the courts flexibility by allowing such other relief as will result in the realization by the protected entity of the value of its interest in the property involved. [*Ed. Note:* This language was changed to "indubitable equivalent."] Under this provision, the courts will be able to adapt to new methods of financing and to formulate protection that is appropriate to the circumstances of the case if none of the other methods would accomplish the desired result. For example, another form of adequate protection might be the guarantee by a third party outside the judicial process of compensation for any loss incurred in the case. Adequate protection might also, in some circumstances, be provided by permitting a secured creditor to bid in his claim at the sale of the property and to offset the claim against the price bid in.

The paragraph also defines, more clearly than the others, the general concept of adequate protection, by requiring such relief as will result in the realization of value. It is the general category, and as such, is defined by the concept involved rather than any particular method of adequate protection.

[*House Report No. 95–595, 95th Cong., 1st Sess. 338–40 (1977).*]

Section 362, 363, and 364 require, in certain circumstances, that the court determine in noticed hearings whether the interest of a secured creditor or co-owner of property with the debtor is adequately protected in connection with the sale or use of property. The interests of which the court may provide protection in the ways described in this section include equitable as well as legal interests. For example, a right to enforce a pledge and a right to recover property delivered to a debtor under a consignment agreement or an agreement of sale or return are interests that may be entitled to protection. This section specifies means by which adequate protection may be provided but, to avoid placing the court in an administrative role, does not require the court to provide it. Instead, the trustee or debtor in possession or the creditor will provide or propose a protection method. If the party that is affected by the proposed action objects, the court will determine whether the protection provided is adequate. The purpose of this section is to illustrate means by which it may be provided and to define the limits of the concept.

The concept of adequate protection is derived from the fifth amendment protection of property interests as enunciated by the Supreme Court. *See* Wright v. Union Central Life Ins. Co., 311 U.S. 273 (1940); Louisville Joint Stock Land Bank v. Radford, 295 U.S. 555 (1935).

* * *

. . . It is not, however, intended to be confined strictly to the constitutional requirement. This section and the concept of adequate protection are based as much on policy grounds as on constitutional grounds. Secured creditors should not be deprived of the benefit of their bargain. There may be situations in bankruptcy where giving a secured creditor an absolute right to his bargain may be impossible or seriously detrimental to the policy of the bankruptcy laws. Thus, this section recognizes the availability of alternate means of protecting a secured creditor's interest where such steps are a necessary part of the rehabilitative process. Though the creditor might not be able to retain his lien upon the specific collateral held at the time of filing, the purpose of the section is to insure that the secured creditor receives the value for which he bargained.

The section specifies two exclusive [*Ed. Note:* As enacted, three methods are specified. The word "exclusive" appears to be inaccurate.] means of providing adequate protection, both of which may require an approximate determination of the value of the protected entity's interest in the property involved. The section does not specify how value is to be determined, nor does it specify when it is to be determined. These matters are left to case-by-case interpretation and development. In light of the restrictive [*Ed. Note:* As enacted, the section is less restrictive.] approach of the section to the availability of means of providing adequate protection, this flexibility is important to permit the courts to adapt to varying circumstances and changing modes of financing.

Neither is it expected that the courts will construe the term value to mean, in every case, forced sale liquidation value or full going concern value. There is wide latitude between those two extremes although forced sale liquidation value will be a minimum.

In any particular case, especially a reorganization case, the determination of which entity should be entitled to the difference between the going concern value and the liquidation value must be based on equitable considerations arising from the facts of the case. Finally, the determination of value is binding only for the purposes of the specific hearing and is not to have a *res judicata* effect.

The first method of adequate protection outlined is the making of cash payments to compensate for the expected decrease in value of the opposing entity's interest. This provision is derived from *In re* Bermec Corp., 445 F.2d 367 (2d Cir. 1971), though in that case it is not clear whether the payments offered were adequate to compensate the secured creditors for their loss. The use of periodic payments may be appropriate where, for example, the property in question is depreciating at a relatively fixed rate. The periodic payments would be to compensate for the depreciation and might, but need not necessarily, be in the same amount as payments due on the secured obligation.

The second method is the fixing of an additional or replacement lien on other property of the debtor to the extent of the decrease in value or actual consumption of the property involved. The purpose of this method is to provide the protected entity with an alternative means of realizing the value of the original property, if it should decline during the case, by granting an interest in additional property from whose value the entity may realize its loss. This is consistent with the view expressed in Wright v. Union Central Life Ins. Co., 311 U.S. 273 (1940), where the Court suggested that it was the value of the secured creditor's collateral, and not necessarily his rights in specific collateral, that was entitled to protection.

The section makes no provision for the granting of an administrative priority as a method of providing adequate protection to an entity as was suggested in *In re* Yale Express System, Inc., 384 F.2d 990 (2d Cir. 1967), because such protection is too uncertain to be meaningful.

[*Senate Report No. 95–989, 95th Cong., 2nd Sess. 49, 53–54 (1978).*]

Section 361 of the House amendment represents a compromise between H.R. 8200 as passed by the House and the Senate amendment regarding the issue of "adequate protection" of a secured party. The House amendment deletes the provision found in section 361(3) of H.R. 8200 as passed by the House. It would have permitted adequate protection to be provided by giving the secured party an administrative expense regarding any decrease in the value of such party's collateral. In every case there is the uncertainty that the estate will have sufficient property to pay administrative expenses in full.

Section 361(4) of H.R. 8200 as passed by the House is modified in section 361(3) of the House amendment to indicate that the court may grant other forms of adequate protection, other than an administrative expense, which will result in the realization by the secured creditor of the indubitable equivalent of the creditor's interest in property. In the special instance where there is a reserve fund maintained under the security agreement, such as in the typical bond-holder case, indubitable equivalent means that the bondholders would be entitled to be protected as to the reserve fund, in addition to the regular payments needed to service the debt. Adequate protection of an interest of an entity in property is intended to protect a creditor's allowed secured claim. To the extent the protection proves to be inadequate after the fact, the creditor is entitled to a first priority administrative expense under section 507(b).

In the special case of a creditor who has elected application of creditor making an election under section 1111(b)(2), that creditor is entitled to adequate protection of the creditor's interest in property to the extent of the value of the collateral not to the extent of the creditor's allowed secured claim, which is inflated to cover a deficiency as a result of such election.

[*124 Cong. Rec. H 11,092 (Sept. 28, 1978); S 17,408–9 (Oct. 6, 1978).*]

Comment

Reference should be made to sections 362, 363 and 364 (automatic stay, use of collateral, borrowing money) to which section 361 is particularly relevant; section 506—provisions dealing with valuation; section 507(b) priority when protection is found not to have been adequate; 1111(b)—election to be nonrecourse lender.

1984 Amendments: Section 361(1) was amended by including a cash payment as one of the methods of providing adequate protection.

1986 Amendments: Section 1205 provides a separate test for adequate protection in chapter 12 cases. Section 1205 eliminates the "indubitable equivalent" language of section 361(3) and makes it clear that what needs to be protected is the value of property, not the value of the creditor's "interest" in the property. *See* the Joint Explanatory Statement of the Committee of Conference for the 1986 Act with regard to adequate protection in chapter 12 cases.

Case Annotations

The phrase "value of such entity's interest" in paragraphs (1) and (2) of section 361, when applied to secured creditors, means the value of the collateral without taking into account the creditor's right to immediate possession on default. Thus, an undersecured creditor is not entitled to postpetition interest as compensation for the delay caused by the automatic stay in foreclosing on its collateral. The Supreme Court also held that the use of "indubitable equivalent" in section 361(3) does not require reimbursement for the use value of collateral as it does in the context of confirmation of a chapter 11 plan under section 1129. United Sav. Ass'n of Tex. v. Timbers of Inwood Forest Assocs., Ltd., 484 U.S. 365, 108 S. Ct. 626, 98 L. Ed. 2d 740, 17 C.B.C.2d 1368 (1988).

An agreement providing that a creditor was to receive certain periodic payments in exchange for its agreement to permit the debtor to use certain property out of the ordinary course of business is a method of adequate protection authorized by section 361(1). Travelers Ins. Co. v.

American AgCredit Corp. (*In re* Blehm Land & Cattle Co.), 859 F.2d 137, 19 C.B.C.2d 933 (10th Cir. 1988).

The statutory scheme of section 361 indicates that adequate protection is intended to encompass a broad range of creditor interests and does not mandate an interpetation of the creditors' interest as a whole of the economic bargain; it is clearly susceptible to differing applications over a wide range of fact situations and will depend, *inter alia*, on the nature of the collateral and the proposed use of the collateral. Lend Lease v. Briggs Transp. Co. (*In re* Briggs Transp. Co.), 780 F.2d 1339, 13 C.B.C.2d 1289 (8th Cir. 1985).

When there is an "equity cushion" of 20%, there is adequate protection for a secured creditor. Pistole v. Mellor (*In re* Mellor), 734 F.2d 1396, 10 C.B.C.2d 1353 (9th Cir. 1984).

When a court permits the treatment of a fully secured claim outside the chapter 13 plan, adequate protection should be provided to creditors, and the debtor should be required to file a list of creditors with the court so that the creditors' right to look to the court for adequate protection will prevent the debtor from shielding from the court's scrutiny the status and continued existence of the relationship. In the Matter of Foster, 670 F.2d 478, 6 C.B.C.2d 285 (5th Cir. 1982).

For the purposes of section 361, an allowed secured claim must be valued as of the date of the filing of the bankruptcy petition. *In re* Reddington/Sunarrow Ltd. Partnership, 24 C.B.C.2d 663 (B. Ct., D.N.M. 1990).

A trustee may be relieved from making adequate protection payments to a creditor of the estate, pursuant to Fed. R. Civ. P. 60(b)(6), when it has been discovered postpetition that it may be necessary to monitor and assess pollution risks, traceable to the creditor's tenure, to the debtor's property, and the creditor, as part of a sales agreement, had promised to indemnify, defend, and hold the debtor harmless from all claims and causes of action resulting from or arising out of such pollution. *In re* Mid-Atlantic Fuels, Inc., 24 C.B.C.2d 1066 (B. Ct., S.D. W. Va. 1990).

An undersecured creditor will not receive adequate protection payments for property taxes which are assessed after the last prepetition tax status date because such taxes do not decrease the value of the secured claim. *In re* East-West Associates, 22 C.B.C.2d 765 (B. Ct., S.D.N.Y. 1990).

References

2 *Collier on Bankruptcy* ch. 361 (Matthew Bender 15th ed.).

1 *Collier Bankruptcy Manual* ch. 361 (Matthew Bender 3d ed.).

3 *Collier Bankruptcy Practice Guide* ch. 41 (Matthew Bender).

Adequate Protection and Administrative Expense: Toward a Uniform System for Awarding Superpriorities, 88 Mich. L. Rev. 2168 (1990).

Adequate Protection and the Automatic Stay, 4 Bankr. Dev. J. 61 (1987).

Baird and Jackson, *Corporate Reorganizations and the Treatment of Diverse Ownership Interests: A Comment on Adequate Protection of Secured Creditors in Bankruptcy,* 51 U. Chi. L. Rev. 97 (1984).

Cohen, McLaughlin and Zaretsky, *Practice Problem: The Supreme Court Decision in United Saving Association v. Timbers,* 2 Commercial Law Report 97 (1988).

Comment, *Compensation for Time Value as Part of Adequate Protection During the Automatic Stay in Bankruptcy,* 50 U. Chi. L. Rev. 305 (1983).

Flaschen, *Adequate Protection for Oversecured Creditors,* 61 Am. Bankr. L.J. 341 (1987).

Gordanier, *The Indubitable Equivalent of Reclamation: Adequate Protection for Secured Creditors Under the Code,* 54 Am. Bankr. L.J. 299 (1980).

Ryan, *The Changing Standards of Adequate Protection in Farm Bankruptcy Reorganizations,* 37 Drake L. Rev. 323 (1987–88).

Sack, *Adequate Protection,* 2 Bank. Dev. J. 21 (1985).

Stein, *Options for Handling Adequate Protection Payments for Rents,* 3 F & G Bankr. L. Rev. 18 (1991).

Weintraub & Resnick, *From the Bankruptcy Courts: Puncturing the Equity Cushion—Adequate Protection for Secured Creditors in Reorganization Cases,* 14 U.C.C.L.J. 284 (1982).

SECTION 362 (11 U.S.C. § 362)

§ 362.   Automatic stay.

(a) Except as provided in subsection (b) of this section, a petition filed under section 301, 302, or 303 of this title, or an application filed under section 5(a)(3) of the Securities Investor Protection Act of 1970 (15 U.S.C. 78eee(a)(3)), operates as a stay, applicable to all entities, of—

(1) the commencement or continuation, including the issuance or employment of process, of a judicial, administrative, or other action or proceeding against the debtor that was or could have been commenced before the commencement of the case under this title, or to recover a claim against the debtor that arose before the commencement of the case under this title;

(2) the enforcement, against the debtor or against property of the estate, of a judgment obtained before the commencement of the case under this title;

(3) any act to obtain possession of property of the estate or of property from the estate or to exercise control over property of the estate;

(4) any act to create, perfect, or enforce any lien against property of the estate;

(5) any act to create, perfect, or enforce against property of the debtor any lien to the extent that such lien secures a claim that arose before the commencement of the case under this title;

(6) any act to collect, assess, or recover a claim against the debtor that arose before the commencement of the case under this title;

(7) the setoff of any debt owing to the debtor that arose before the commencement of the case under this title against any claim against the debtor; and

(8) the commencement or continuation of a proceeding before the United States Tax Court concerning the debtor.

(b) The filing of a petition under section 301, 302, or 303 of this title, or of an application under section 5(a)(3) of the Securities Investor Protection Act of 1970 (15 U.S.C. 78eee(a)(3)), does not operate as a stay—

(1) under subsection (a) of this section, of the commencement or continuation of a criminal action or proceeding against the debtor;

(2) under subsection (a) of this section, of the collection of alimony, maintenance, or support from property that is not property of the estate;

(3) under subsection (a) of this section, of any act to perfect an interest in property to the extent that the trustee's rights and powers are subject to such perfection under section 546(b) of this title or to the extent that such act is accomplished within the period provided under section 547(e)(2)(A) of this title;

(4) under subsection (a)(1) of this section, of the commencement or continuation of an action or proceeding by a governmental unit to enforce such governmental unit's police or regulatory power;

(5) under subsection (a)(2) of this section, of the enforcement of a judgment, other than a money judgment, obtained in an action or proceeding by a governmental unit to enforce such governmental unit's police or regulatory power;

(6) under subsection (a) of this section, of the setoff by a commodity broker, forward contract merchant, stockbroker, financial institutions, or securities clearing agency of any mutual debt and claim under or in connection with commodity contracts, as defined in section 761(4) of this title, forward contracts, or securities contracts, as defined in section 741(7) of this title, that constitutes the setoff of a claim against the debtor for a margin payment, as defined in section 101(34), 741(5), or 761(15) of this title, or settlement payment, as defined in section 101(35) or 741(8) of this title, arising out of commodity contracts, forward contracts, or securities contracts against cash, securities, or other property held by or due from such commodity broker, forward contract merchant, stockbroker, financial institutions, or securities clearing agency to margin, guarantee, secure, or settle commodity contracts, forward contracts, or securities contracts;

(7) under subsection (a) of this section, of the setoff by a repo participant, of any mutual debt and claim under or in connection with repurchase agreements that constitutes the setoff of a claim against the debtor for a margin payment, as defined in section 741(5) or 761(15) of this title, or settlement payment, as defined in section 741(8) of this title, arising out of repurchase agreements against cash, securities, or other property held by or due from such repo participant to margin, guarantee, secure or settle repurchase agreements;

(8) under subsection (a) of this section, of the commencement of any action by the Secretary of Housing and Urban Development to foreclose a mortgage or deed of trust in any case in which the mortgage or deed of trust held by the

Secretary is insured or was formerly insured under the National Housing Act and covers property, or combinations of property, consisting of five or more living units;

(9) under subsection (a) of this section, of the issuance to the debtor by a governmental unit of a notice of tax deficiency;

(10) under subsection (a) of this section, of any act by a lessor to the debtor under a lease of nonresidential real property that has terminated by the expiration of the stated term of the lease before the commencement of or during a case under this title to obtain possession of such property; or [sic]

(11) under subsection (a) of this section, of the presentment of a negotiable instrument and the giving of notice of and protesting dishonor of such an instrument;

(12)* under subsection (a) of this section, after the date which is 90 days after the filing of such petition, of the commencement or continuation, and conclusion to the entry of final judgment, of an action which involves a debtor subject to reorganization pursuant to chapter 11 of this title and which was brought by the Secretary of Transportation under the Ship Mortgage Act, 1920 (46 App. U.S.C. 911 et seq.) (including distribution of any proceeds of sale) to foreclose a preferred ship or fleet mortgage, or a security interest in or relating to a vessel or vessel under construction, held by the Secretary of Transportation under section 207 or title XI of the Merchant Marine Act, 1936 (46 App. U.S.C. 1117 and 1271 et seq., respectively), or under applicable State law;

* [Ed. Note: Paragraphs (12) and (13) were added to 11 U.S.C. § 362(b) by § 5001 of the Omnibus Budget Reconciliation Act of 1986, Pub. L. No. 99–509 (1986). Section 5001(b) of Pub. L. No. 99–509 provides:

the amendments made by subsection (a) of this section shall apply only to petitions filed under section 362 of this title 11, United States Code, which are made after August 1, 1986.

This is inaccurate. "Petitions" are not made under § 362. The proper reference probably should be to "requests" made pursuant to § 362(d). If "petitions" were intended, then the reference should be to "cases commenced."

Section 5001(a) also provides that its provisions apply only to title 11 cases commenced before December 31, 1989.]

(13)* under subsection (a) of this section, after the date which is 90 days after the filing of such petition, of the commencement or continuation, and conclusion to the entry of final judgment, of an action which involves a debtor subject to reorganization pursuant to chapter 11 of this title and which was brought by the Secretary of Commerce under the Ship Mortgage Act, 1920 (46 App. U.S.C. 911 et seq.) (including distribution of any proceeds of sale) to foreclose a preferred ship or fleet mortgage in a vessel or a mortgage, deed of trust, or other security interest in a fishing facility held by the the Secretary of Commerce under section 207 or title XI of the Merchant Marine Act, 1936 (46 App. U.S.C. 1117 and 1271 et seq. respectively); or

(14) under subsection (a) of this section, of the setoff by a swap participant, of any mutual debt and claim under or in connection with any swap agreement that constitutes the setoff of a claim against the debtor for any payment due from the debtor under or in connection with any swap agreement against any payment due to the debtor from the swap participant under or in connection with any swap agreement or against cash, securities, or other property of the debtor held by or due from such swap participant to guarantee, secure or settle any swap agreement.

(14)** under subsection (a) of this section, of any action by an accrediting agency regarding the accreditation status of the debtor as an educational institution;

(15) under subsection (a) of this section, of any action by a State licensing body regarding the licensure of the debtor as an educational institution; or

---

* [*Ed. Note:* Paragraphs (12) and (13) were added to 11 U.S.C. § 362(b) by § 5001 of the Omnibus Budget Reconciliation Act of 1986, Pub. L. No. 99–509 (1986). Section 5001(b) of Pub. L. No. 99–509 provides:

the amendments made by subsection (a) of this section shall apply only to petitions filed under section 362 of this title 11, United States Code, which are made after August 1, 1986.

This is inaccurate. "Petitions" are not made under § 362. The proper reference probably should be to "requests" made pursuant to § 362(d). If "petitions" were intended, then the reference should be to "cases commenced."

Section 5001(a) also provides that its provisions apply only to title 11 cases commenced before December 31, 1989.]

** [*Ed. Note:* Due to a drafting error, section 362(b) now contains two paragraphs numbered "(14)." *See* Comment to the 1990 Amendments *infra.*]

(16) under subsection (a) of this section, of any action by a guaranty agency, as defined in section 435(j) of the Higher Education Act of 1965 (20 U.S.C. 1001 et seq.) or the Secretary of Education regarding the eligibility of the debtor to participate in programs authorized under such Act.

(c) Except as provided in subsections (d), (e), and (f) of this section—

(1) the stay of an act against property of the estate under subsection (a) of this section continues until such property is no longer property of the estate; and

(2) the stay of any other act under subsection (a) of this section continues until the earliest of—

(A) the time the case is closed;

(B) the time the case is dismissed; or

(C) if the case is a case under chapter 7 of this title concerning an individual or a case under chapter 9, 11, 12, or 13 of this title, the time a discharge is granted or denied.

(d) On request of a party in interest and after notice and a hearing, the court shall grant relief from the stay provided under subsection (a) of this section, such as by terminating, annulling, modifying, or conditioning such stay—

(1) for cause, including the lack of adequate protection of an interest in property of such party in interest; or

(2) with respect to a stay of an act against property under subsection (a) of this section, if—

(A) the debtor does not have an equity in such property; and

(B) such property is not necessary to an effective reorganization.

(e) Thirty days after a request under subsection (d) of this section for relief from the stay of any act against property of the estate under subsection (a) of this section, such stay is terminated with respect to the party in interest making such request, unless the court, after notice and a hearing, orders such stay continued in effect pending the conclusion of, or as a result of, a final hearing and determination under subsection (d) of this section. A hearing under this subsection may be a preliminary hearing, or may be consolidated with the final hearing under subsection (d) of this section. The court shall order such stay continued in effect pending the conclusion of the final hearing under subsection (d) of this section if there is a reasonable likelihood that the party opposing relief from such stay will prevail at the conclusion of such final hearing. If the hearing under this subsection is a preliminary hearing, then such final hearing shall be commenced not later than thirty days after the conclusion of such preliminary hearing.

(f) Upon request of a party in interest, the court, with or without a hearing, shall grant such relief from the stay provided under subsection (a) of this section as is necessary to prevent irreparable damage to the interest of an entity in property, if such interest will suffer such damage before there is an opportunity for notice and a hearing under subsection (d) or (e) of this section.

(g) In any hearing under subsection (d) or (e) of this section concerning relief from the stay of any act under subsection (a) of this section—

  (1) the party requesting such relief has the burden of proof on the issue of the debtor's equity in property; and

  (2) the party opposing such relief has the burden of proof on all other issues.

(h) An individual injured by any willful violation of a stay provided by this section shall recover actual damages, including costs and attorneys' fees, and, in appropriate circumstances, may recover punitive damages.

Bankruptcy Rule Reference: 4001

Legislative History

The automatic stay is one of the fundamental debtor protections provided by the bankruptcy laws. It gives the debtor a breathing spell from his creditors. It stops all collection efforts, all harassment, and all foreclosure actions. It permits the debtor to attempt a repayment or reorganization plan, or simply to be relieved of the financial pressures that drove him into bankruptcy.

The automatic stay also provides creditor protection. Without it, certain creditors would be able to pursue their own remedies against the debtor's property. Those who acted first would obtain payment of the claims in preference to and to the detriment of other creditors. Bankruptcy is designed to provide an orderly liquidation procedure under which all creditors are treated equally. A race of diligence by creditors for the debtor's assets prevents that.

Subsection (a) defines the scope of the automatic stay, by listing the acts that are stayed by the commencement of the case. The commencement or continuation, including the issuance of process, of a judicial, administrative, or other proceeding against the debtor that was or could have been commenced before the commencement of the bankruptcy case is stayed under paragraph (1). The scope of this paragraph is broad. All proceedings are stayed, including arbitration, license revocation, administrative, and judicial proceedings. Proceeding in this sense encompasses civil actions as well, and all proceedings even if they are not before governmental tribunals.

The provision in this first paragraph prohibiting the issuance of process is designed to prevent the issuance of a writ of execution by a judgment creditor of the debtor to obtain property that was property of the debtor before the case, but that was transferred, subject to the judgment lien, before the case. Because the other paragraphs of this subsection refer only to property of the estate or property of the debtor, neither of which apply to this kind of transferred property, they would not prohibit pursuit of the transferred property by issuance of process. Thus, the prohibition in this paragraph is included and the judgment creditor is allowed to proceed by way of foreclosure against the property, but not by a general writ of execution (in the State court, or wherever the creditor obtained the judgment) against the debtor and all of the debtor's property.

The stay is not permanent. There is adequate provision for relief from the stay elsewhere in the section. However, it is important that the trustee have an opportunity to inventory the debtor's position before proceeding with the administration of the case. Undoubtedly the court will lift the stay for proceedings before specialized or nongovernmental tribunals to allow those proceedings to come to a conclusion. Any party desiring to enforce an order in such a proceeding would thereafter have to come before the bankruptcy court to collect assets. Nevertheless, it will often be more appropriate to permit proceedings to continue in their place of origin, when no great prejudice to the bankruptcy estate would result, in order to leave the parties to their chosen forum and to relieve the bankruptcy court from many duties that may be handled elsewhere.

Paragraph (2) stays the enforcement, against the debtor or against property of the estate, of a judgment obtained before the commencement of the bankruptcy case. Thus, execution and levy against the debtors' prepetition property are stayed, and attempts to collect a judgment from the debtor personally are stayed.

Paragraph (3) stays any act to obtain possession of property of the estate (that is, property of the debtor as of the date of the filing of the petition) or property from the estate (property over which the estate has control or possession). The purpose of this provision is to prevent dismemberment of the estate. Liquidation must proceed in an orderly fashion. Any distribution of property must be by the trustee after he has had an opportunity to familiarize himself with the various rights and interests involved and with the property available for distribution.

Paragraph (4) stays lien creation against property of the estate. Thus, taking possession to perfect a lien or obtaining court process is prohibited. To permit lien creation after bankruptcy would give certain creditors preferential treatment by making them secured instead of unsecured.

Paragraph (5) stays any act to create or enforce a lien against property of the debtor, that is, most property that is acquired after the date of the filing of the petition, property that is exempt, or property that does not pass to the estate, to the extent that the lien secures a prepetition claim. Again, to permit postbankruptcy lien creation or enforcement would permit certain creditors to receive preferential treatment. It may also circumvent the debtors' discharge.

Paragraph (6) prevents creditors from attempting in any way to collect a prepetition debt. Creditors in consumer cases occasionally telephone debtors to encourage repayment in spite of bankruptcy. Inexperienced, frightened, or ill-counseled debtors may succumb to suggestions to repay notwithstanding their bankruptcy. This provision prevents evasion of the purpose of the bankruptcy laws by sophisticated creditors.

Paragraph (7) stays setoffs of mutual debts and credits between the debtor and creditors. As with all other paragraphs of subsection (a), this paragraph does not affect the right of creditors. It simply stays its enforcement pending an orderly examination of the debtors' and creditors' rights.

[*House Report No. 95–595, 95th Cong., 1st Sess. 340–2 (1977); Senate Report No. 95–989, 95th Cong., 2d Sess. 49–51 (1978).*]

Section 362(a)(1) of the House amendment adopts the provision contained in the Senate amendment enjoining the commencement or continuation of a judicial, administrative, or other proceeding to recover a claim against the debtor that arose before the commencement of the case. The provision is beneficial and interacts with section 362(a)(6), which also covers assessment, to prevent harassment of the debtor with respect to pre-petition claims.

Section 362(a)(7) contains a provision contained in H.R. 8200 as passed by the House. The differing provision in the Senate amendment was rejected. It is not possible that a debt owing to the debtor may be offset against an interest in the debtor.

Section 362(a)(8) is new. The provision stays the commencement or continuation of any proceeding concerning the debtor before the United States Tax Court.

[*124 Cong. Rec. H 11,092 (Sept. 28, 1978); S 17,409 (Oct. 6, 1978).*]

Section 3(a) [of Public Law 97–222] clarifies that the automatic stay of section 362(a) is applicable upon the filing of an application under the Securities Investor Protection Act of 1970 (15 U.S.C. § 78eee(a)(3)).

[House Report No. 97–420, 97th Cong., 2d Sess. 3 (1982).]

Subsection (b) lists five exceptions to the automatic stay. [*Ed. Note:* As amended, subsection (b) lists fourteen exceptions.] The effect of an exception is not to make the action immune from injunction.

[House Report No. 95–595, 95th Cong., 1st Sess. 342–3 (1977); Senate Report No. 95–989, 95th Cong., 2d Sess. 51–2 (1978).]

Section 3(b) [of Public Law 97–222] clarifies that the exceptions to the automatic stay are applicable upon the filing of an application under the Securities Investor Protection Act of 1970 (15 U.S.C. § 78eee(a)(3)).

[House Report No. 97–420, 97th Cong., 2d Sess. 3 (1982).]

The court has ample other powers to stay actions not covered by the automatic stay. Section 105, of proposed title 11, derived from Bankruptcy Act section 2a(15), grants the power to issue orders necessary or appropriate to carry out the provisions of title 11. The bankruptcy courts are brought within the scope of the All Writs Statute, 28 U.S.C. § 1651 (1970), and are given the powers of a court of law, equity, and admiralty (H.R. 8200 § 243(a), proposed 28 U.S.C. § 1481). Stays or injunctions issued under these other sections will not be automatic upon the commencement of the case, but will be granted or issued under the usual rules for the issuance of injunctions. By excepting an act or action from the automatic stay, the bill simply requires that the trustee move the court into action, rather than requiring the stayed party to request relief from the stay. There are some actions, enumerated in the exceptions, that generally should not be stayed automatically upon the commencement of the case, for reasons of either policy or practicality. Thus, the court will have to determine on a case-by-case basis whether a particular action which may be harming the estate should be stayed.

With respect to stays issued under other powers, or the application of the automatic stay, to governmental actions, this section and the other sections mentioned are intended to be an express waiver of sovereign immunity of the Federal government, and an assertion of the bankruptcy power over State governments under the Supremacy Clause notwithstanding a State's sovereign immunity.

The first exception is of criminal proceedings against the debtor. The bankruptcy laws are not a haven for criminal offenders, but are designed to give relief from financial over-extension. Thus, criminal actions and proceedings may proceed in spite of bankruptcy.

Paragraph (2) excepts from the stay the collection of alimony, maintenance or support from property that is not property of the estate. This will include property acquired after the commencement of the case, exempted property, and property that does not pass to the estate. The automatic stay is one means of protecting the debtor's discharge. Alimony, maintenance and support obligations are excepted from discharge. Staying collection of them, when not to the detriment of other creditors (because the collection effort is against property that is not property of the estate), does not further that goal. Moreover, it could lead to hardship on the part of the protected spouse or children.

Paragraph (3) excepts any act to perfect an interest in property to the extent that the trustee's rights and powers are limited under section 546(a) of the bankruptcy code. That section permits postpetition perfection of certain liens to be effective against the trustee. If the act of perfection, such as filing, were stayed, the section would be nullified.

Paragraph (4) excepts commencement or continuation of actions and proceedings by governmental units to enforce police or regulatory powers. Thus, where a governmental unit is suing a debtor to prevent or stop violation of fraud, environmental protection, consumer protection, safety, or similar police or regulatory laws, or attempting to fix damages for violation of such a law, the action or proceeding is not stayed under the automatic stay. Paragraph (5) makes clear that the exception extends to permit an injunction and enforcement of an injunction, and to permit the entry of a money judgment, but does not extend to permit enforcement of a money judgment. Since the assets of the debtor are in the possession and control of the bankruptcy court, and since they constitute a fund out of which all creditors are entitled to share, enforcement by a governmental unit of a money judgment would give it preferential treatment to the detriment of all other creditors.

[*House Report No. 95–595, 95 Cong., 1st Sess. 342–3 (1977); Senate Report No. 95–989, 95th Cong., 2d Sess. 51–2 (1978).*]

Paragraph (6) excepts the setoff of any mutual debt and claim for commodity transactions.

Paragraph [(8)] [*Ed. Note:* Pub. No. 98–353 redesignated section 362(b)(8) as section 362(b)(9).] excepts actions by the Secretary of Housing and Urban Development to foreclose or take possession in a case of a loan insured under the National Housing Act. A general exception for such loans is found in current sections 263 and 517, the exception allowed by this paragraph is much more limited.

[*Senate Report No. 95–989, 95th Cong., 2d Sess. 52 (1978).*]   ·

Section 362(b)(4) indicates that the stay under section 362(a)(1) does not apply to affect the commencement or continuation of an action or proceeding by a governmental unit to enforce the governmental unit's police or regulatory power. This section is intended to be given a narrow construction in order to permit governmental units to pursue actions to protect the public health and safety and not to apply to actions by a governmental unit to protect a pecuniary interest in property of the debtor or property of the estate.

Section 362(b)(6) of the House amendment adopts a provision contained in the Senate amendment restricting the exception to the automatic stay with respect to setoffs to permit only the setoff of mutual debts and claims. Traditionally, the right of setoff has been limited to mutual debts and claims and the lack of the clarifying term "mutual" in H.R. 8200 as passed by the House created an unintentional ambiguity, Section 362(b)(7) of the House amendment permits the issuance of a notice of tax deficiency. The House amendment rejects section 362(b)(7) in the Senate amendment. It would have permitted a particular governmental unit to obtain a pecuniary advantage without a hearing on the merits contrary to the exceptions contained in sections 362(b)(4) and (5).

[*124 Cong. Rec. H 11,092 (Sept. 28, 1978); S 17,409 (Oct. 6, 1978).*]

* * *

Mr. MATHIAS.

Is it the distinguished Senator's understanding that the provisions of section 362(b)(6) of the bill before us will protect the right of a commodity broker, forward contract merchant, or clearing organization to liquidate or transfer an open commodity contract held or carried for a bankrupt pursuant to existing contractual rights and that such right will not be subject to any stay sought to be imposed under this act, State law or court order?

Mr. DeCONCINI. Yes.

[*124 Cong. Rec. S 17,433 (Oct. 6, 1978).*]

Section 3(c) [of Public Law 97–222] is intended to clarify that, despite the automatic stay of section 362(a), a commodity broker, forward contract merchant, stockbroker, or securities clearing agency may set off a claim for a margin or settlement payment arising out of commodities contracts, forward contracts, or securities contract against cash, securities or other property which it is holding to margin, guarantee, or secure such contracts, notwithstanding the bankruptcy of the party for whose account such cash, securities, or property is held. This section does not permit a setoff which would be unlawful under any applicable law or regulation.

[*House Report No. 97–420, 97th Cong., 2d Sess. 3 (1982).*]

Section 3(c) of H.R. 4935 [Public Law 97–222] would amend section 362(b)(6) of the code to clarify that a commodity broker, forward contract merchant, stockbroker, or securities clearing agency may set off a claim for a margin or settlement payment against cash, securities, or other property which it is holding, notwithstanding the bankruptcy of the party for whose account such cash, securities, or property is held and despite the automatic stay of section 362(a). This means that if a commodity or securities brokerage firm, forward contract merchant, commodity clearing organization, or securities clearing agency has a claim for a margin or settlement payment against the debtor arising, before or after the filing of the petition, out of commodity contracts, forward contracts, or securities contracts—or the liquidation of those contracts—and holds cash, securities, or other property with respect to the same or other commodity contracts, forward contracts, or securities contracts, it would not be stayed from setting off that claim against such cash, securities, or other property, or against any amount with respect to such contracts that it would be required to pay. In the case of forward contracts, the net amount due to or owing from the debtor would be the sum of the net amounts, if any, due or owing with respect to each such contract of the debtor. This section would not permit a setoff that would be unlawful under any applicable law or regulation.

*   *   *

Mr. MATHIAS. Mr. President, I have a question regarding the scope of section 3(c) of H.R. 4935, which basically would amend section 362(b)(6) of the code to exempt from the general stay of actions against a debtor the setoff of a claim against the debtor for a margin or settlement payment arising from a commodity contract, forward contract, or securities contract against cash, securities, or other property held by a commodity broker, forward contract merchant, or stock broker to margin, guarantee or secure other contracts of the debtor.

The language of section 3(c) is more restrictive than that of section 25(b)(3) of S. 863, the parallel provision of Senate bankruptcy technical amendments bill, which would have exempted from the automatic stay the setoff of any mutual debt and claim regarding futures contracts, forward contracts and other specified contracts. I understand that the purpose of the narrower language of section 3(c) is to prevent setoffs for charges such as commissions, or by entities such as banks, which are not necessary to achieve the market protection functions of section 362(b)(6).

I too am concerned about achievement of these market protection functions. Accordingly, my question is whether a settlement payment owed to a customer with respect to a commodity contract, forward contract, or securities contract is property held by a commodity broker, forward contract merchant, or stockbroker to guarantee or secure the customer's other contracts within the meaning of section 3(c), and may therefore be offset against a margin or settlement payment owed by the customer with respect to that or another contract.

Mr. DOLE. Yes.

[*128 Cong. Rec. S 8,132–33 (July 13, 1982).*]

Subsection (c) of section 362 specifies the duration of the automatic stay. Paragraph (1) terminates a stay of an act against property of the estate when the property ceases to be property of the estate, such as by sale, abandonment, or exemption. It does not terminate the stay against property of the debtor if the property leaves the estate and goes to the debtor. Paragraph (2) terminates the stay of any other act on the earliest of the time the case is closed, the time the case is dismissed, or the time a discharge is granted or denied (unless the debtor is a corporation or partnership in a chapter 7 case).

Subsection (c) governs automatic termination of the stay. Subsections (d) through (g) govern termination of the stay by the court on the request of a party in interest. Subsection (d) requires the court, on request of a party in interest, to grant relief from the stay, such as by terminating, annulling, modifying, or conditioning the stay, for cause. The lack of adequate protection of an interest in property of the party requesting relief from the stay is one cause for relief, but is not the only cause. As noted above, a desire to permit an action to proceed to completion in another tribunal may provide another cause. Other causes might include the lack of any connection with or interference with the pending bankruptcy case. For example, a divorce or child custody proceeding involving the debtor may bear no relation to the bankruptcy case. In that case, it should not be stayed. A probate proceeding in which the debtor is the executor or administrator of another's estate usually will not be related to the bankruptcy case, and should not be stayed. Generally, proceedings in which the debtor is a fiduciary, or involving postpetition activities of the debtor, need not be stayed because they bear no relationship to the purpose of the automatic stay, which is debtor protection from his creditors. The facts of each request will determine whether relief is appropriate under the circumstances.

[*House Report No. 95–595, 95th Cong., 1st Sess. 343–4 (1977); cf. Senate Report No. 95–989, 95th Cong., 2d Sess. 52–3 (1978).*]

Section 362(d) of the House amendment represents a compromise between comparable provisions in the House bill and Senate amendment. Under section 362(d)(1) of the House amendment, the court may terminate, annul, modify, or condition the automatic stay for cause, including lack of adequate protection of an interest in property of a secured party. It is anticipated that the Rules of Bankruptcy Procedure will provide that those hearings will receive priority on the calendar. Under section 362(d)(2) the court may alternatively terminate, annul, modify, or condition the automatic stay for cause including inadequate protection for the creditor. The court shall grant relief from the stay if there is no equity and it is not necessary to an effective reorganization of the debtor.

The latter requirement is contained in section 362(d)(2). This section is intended to solve the problem of real property mortgage foreclosures of property where the bankruptcy petition is filed on the eve of foreclosure. The section is not intended to apply if the business of the debtor is managing or leasing real property, such as a hotel operation, even though the debtor has no equity if the property is necessary to an effective reorganization of the debtor. Similarly, if the debtor does have an equity in the property, there is no requirement that the property be sold under section 363 of title 11 as would have been required by the Senate amendment.

[*124 Cong. Rec. H 11,092–3 (Sept. 28, 1978); S 17,409 (Oct. 6, 1978).*]

Subsection (e) provides a protection for secured creditors that is not available under present law. The subsection sets a time certain within which the bankruptcy court must rule on the adequacy of protection provided of the secured creditor's interest. If the court does not rule within 30 days from a request for relief from the stay, the stay is automatically terminated with respect to the property in question. In order to accommodate more complex cases, the subsection permits the court to make a preliminary ruling after a preliminary hearing. After a preliminary hearing, the court may continue the stay only if there is a reasonable likelihood that the party opposing relief from the stay will prevail at the final hearing. Because the stay is essentially an injunction, the three stages of the stay may be analogized to the three stages of an injunction. The filing of the petition which gives rise to the automatic stay is similar to a temporary restraining order. The preliminary hearing is similar to the hearing on a preliminary injunction, and the final hearing and order is similar to a permanent injunction. The main difference lies in which party must bring the issue before the court. While in the injunction setting, the party seeking the injunction must prosecute the action, in proceedings for relief from the automatic stay, the enjoined party must move. The difference does not, however, shift the burden of proof. Subsection (g) leaves that burden on the party opposing relief from the stay (that is, on the party seeking continuance of the injunction) on the issue of adequate protection.

At the expedited hearing under subsection (e), and at all hearings on relief from the stay, the only issue will be the claim of the creditor and the lack of adequate protection or existence of other cause for relief from the stay. This hearing will not be the appropriate time at which to bring in other issues, such as counterclaims against the creditor on largely unrelated matters. Those counterclaims are not to be handled in the summary fashion that the preliminary hearing under this provision will be. Rather, they will be the subject of more complete proceedings by the trustees to recover property of the estate or to object to the allowance of a claim.

[*House Report No. 95–595, 95th Cong., 1st Sess. 344 (1977); cf. Senate Report No. 95–989, 95th Cong., 2d Sess. 53–55 (1978).*]

Section 362(e) of the House amendment represents a modification of provisions in H.R. 8200 as passed by the House and the Senate amendment to make clear that a final hearing must be commenced within 30 days after a preliminary hearing is held to determine whether a creditor will be entitled to relief from the automatic stay. In order to insure that those hearings will in fact occur within such 30-day period, it is anticipated that the rules of bankruptcy procedure provide that such final hearings receive priority on the court calendar.

[*124 Cong. Rec. H 11,093 (Sept. 28, 1978); S 17,409 (Oct. 6, 1978).*]

Subsection (f) permits *ex parte* relief from the stay in situations in which irreparable damage might occur to the stayed party before there is opportunity for notice and a hearing under the usual procedure. The Rules of Bankruptcy Procedure will provide for a hearing soon after the issuance of any *ex parte* order under this subsection.

[*House Report No. 95–595, 95th Cong., 1st Sess. 344 (1977).*]

See House Report under subsection (e).

Section 362(g) places the burden of proof on the issue of the debtor's equity in collateral on the party requesting relief from the automatic stay and the burden on other issues on the debtor.

[*124 Cong. Rec. H 11,093 (Sept. 28, 1978); S 17,409 (Oct. 6, 1978).*]

Comment

With the exception of an automatic stay provided by Section 148 of the former Bankruptcy Act relating to corporate reorganization cases, automatic stays made their first appearance in the former Rules of Bankruptcy Procedure. (Former Rules 401, 601, 10-601, 11-44, 12-23 and 13-401.)

Section 362 of the Code is explicit in subsection (a)(1)–(8) as to precisely what acts are automatically stayed.

The Code suggests expedited hearings in proceedings for relief from the stay, is explicit with respect to the burden of proof, and clarifies the law as to the types of actions not subject to the stay. Section 362 should be read together with sections 363 and 361.

Public Law 97–222 (1982) makes clear that the provisions of the automatic stay and the exceptions thereto are applicable upon the filing of an application under the Securities Investor Protection Act of 1970 (15 U.S.C. § 78eee (a)(3)).

Bankruptcy Rule 4001, as amended in 1991, deals with relief from the section 362 automatic stay and the use of cash collateral. The rule was expanded by the 1991 Amendments to include a request to prohibit or condition the use, sale or lease of property as is necessary to provide adequate protection of a property interest pursuant to section 363(e) of the Code, and was otherwise substantially revised.

Subdivision (a)(1) of Rule 4001 provides that a motion for relief from the automatic stay or a motion to prohibit or condition the use, sale or lease of property pursuant to section 363(e) shall be made in accordance with section 9014 and served on any appointed or elected committee or its authorized agent. In a chapter 9 or 11 case in which no committee of unsecured creditors has been appointed under section 1102, the motion shall be filed on the creditors included in the list filed pursuant to Rule 1007(d). The motion shall also be served on such others as the court directs.

Subdivision (a)(2), "Final Hearing on Stay," has been deleted as unnecessary because of section 362(e) of the Code.

Congress added a fee of $60 for motions seeking relief from the automatic stay under section 362(d) (the legislation erroneously refers to section 362(b)) effective 30 days after the enactment of Pub. L. No. 101-162, which was November 21, 1989.

Subdivision (a)(3), formerly subdivision (a)(3), provides for *ex parte* relief from the stay or a request to prohibit or condition the use, sale or lease of property pursuant to section 363(e) only if it clearly appears from specific facts (affidavit or verified motion) that immediate and irreparable injury, loss, or damage will result to movant before the adverse party or the attorney for the adverse party can be heard in opposition, and if the movant's attorney certifies in writing the efforts, if any, that have been made to give notice and the reasons why notice should not be required. The party obtaining *ex parte* relief must immediately give oral notice thereof to the trustee or debtor in possession and to the debtor, and must forthwith mail or transmit to such adverse party(ies) a copy of the order granting relief. On two days notice, or shorter notice as the court may prescribe, the adverse party may appear and move to reinstate the stay or to reconsider the order prohibiting or conditioning the use, sale or lease of property, and the court is required to expeditiously hear and determine the motion. (This subdivision implements section 362(f).)

Subdivision (b) of Rule 4001 relates to the use of cash collateral. Subdivision (c) relates to the obtaining of credit. Subdivision (d) concerns agreements relating to adequate protection or any of the matters contained in subdivisions (a) through (c) of this Rule. Subdivisions (b)(1), (c)(1) and (d)(1) were amended to require service on committees that are elected in chapter 7 cases. Service on committees of retired employees appointed under section 1114 of the Code is not required. These subdivisions were further amended to clarify that, in the absence of a creditors' committee, service on the creditors included on the list filed pursuant to Rule 1007(d) is required only in chapter 9 or 11 cases.

The 1991 Amendments added subdivision (d)(4) to the Rule. It provides that the court may direct that procedures prescribed in paragraphs (1), (2) and (3) of subdivision (d) shall not apply. Furthermore, the agreement in settlement of the motion may be approved without further notice if the court determines that a motion made pursuant to subdivisions (a), (b), or (c) was sufficient to afford reasonable notice of the material provisions of the agreement and opportunity for a hearing.

1984 Amendments: Pub. L. No. 98–353 (1984) sought to clarify the status of repurchase agreements in bankruptcy. *See* section 101 for a definition of "repo participant" as an entity who holds a "repurchase agreement," and for the definition of "repurchase agreement."

A variety of amendments in this area were intended to help make secure high return short-term investments of revenues. Section 362(b)(7)—as added by Pub. L. No. 98–353—clarifies that repurchase agreements as defined in section 101 are exempt from the automatic stay provisions.

The following sections contain amendments regarding repurchase agreements: 546(f), 548(d)(2)(C), 553(b)(1) and 559 (559 was added by Pub. L. No. 98–353).

Subsection (h) of section 362, added by the 1984 amendments, should dispel any doubts as to the sanctions that may be imposed for willful violation of the automatic stay apart from contempt proceedings. Under subsection (h), an individual injured by willful violation of the stay "shall" recover the actual damages suffered, including costs and counsel fees. Additionally, in appropriate circumstances, the court may, in its discretion, award punitive damages.

Subsection (e), as amended, provides that if the hearing for relief from the automatic stay is a preliminary hearing, the final hearing is to be commenced not later than thirty days after the *conclusion* of the preliminary hearing.

The amendments made a number of clarifying changes in subsections (a)(1), (a)(3), (b)(3), (b)(6), (b)(8), (d)(1), (e) and (f). Three new paragraphs, (7), (9) and (10), were added to subsection (b) [paragraphs (9) and (10) were redesignated by the 1986 Amendments as paragraphs (10) and (11) respectively in order to correct a numbering error.].

1990 Amendments: Pub. L. No. 101–311 added to section 362(b) a new paragraph (14) which excepts from the automatic stay the setoff of certain mutual debts and claims that are under or in connection with swap agreements (*see* section 101 for the definitions of "swap agreement" and "swap participant"). Additionally, section 362(b)(6) was amended to include references to section 101 [definitions of "margin payment" and "settlement payment"].

Section 362 was amended again by Pub. L. No. 101-508 (Omnibus Budget Reconciliation Act of 1990; effective on date of enactment, November 5, 1990; ceases to be effective October 1, 1996), which added three new exceptions to the automatic stay. The three exceptions were added to section 362(b) as new paragraphs (14), (15 and (16).

However, the enactment of Pub. L. No. 101-508 has created a drafting error in section 362(b). Because the drafters of Pub. L. No. 101-508 did not take into account the prior addition of a paragraph (14) by Pub. L. No. 101-311, section 362(b) now contains two paragraphs both of which are numbered as paragraph (14).

Case Annotations

The automatic stay provisions set forth in section 362(a) do not have any application to an ongoing, nonfinal, administrative proceeding. Thus, the district court did not have jurisdiction to enjoin the Board of Governors of the Federal Reserve System from maintaining administrative proceedings against a bank holding company under FISA. Board of Governors of the Federal Reserve System v. MCorp Financial, Inc., 502 U.S. — , 112 S. Ct. 459, 116 L. Ed. 2d 358, 25 C.B.C.2d 849 (1991).

A debtor has the burden of proof of showing that the collateral is "necessary to an effective reorganization" which requires not only a showing that if there is conceivably to be an effective reorganization, this property will be needed for it but also that the property is essential for an effective reorganization that is in prospect, which means that there must be "a reasonable possibility of a successful reorganization within a reasonable time." United Savs. Ass'n of Tex. v. Timbers of Inwood Forest Assocs., Ltd., 484 U.S. 365, 108 S. Ct. 626, 98 L. Ed. 2d 740, 17 C.B.C.2d 1368 (1988).

The automatic stay provisions of section 362 do not apply to temporary cease and desist orders from the Federal Reserve Board in cases involving a bankrupt bank holding company. Office of Thrift Supervision v. Firstcorp, Inc., 967 F.2d 942, 26 C.B.C.2d 1753 (4th Cir. 1992).

Section 362(a) does not preclude either the filing of a motion to dismiss for mootness or action by a court on such a motion because such action does not constitute the "continuation" of a judicial proceeding against the debtor under that section. Independent Union of Flight Attendants v. Pan American World Airways, Inc., 966 F.2d 457, 26 C.B.C.2d 1183 (9th Cir. 1992).

If a union can bring a dispute involving a collective bargaining agreement before the bankruptcy court and the bankruptcy court has jurisdiction to resolve the dispute, the bankruptcy court may enjoin the proceeding pending in a nonbankruptcy forum and hear the merits of the dispute itself. In re Ionosphere Clubs, Inc., 26 C.B.C.2d 1485 (B. Ct., S.D.N.Y. 1992).

In a chapter 13 case, if the debtor fails to make alimony, maintenance or support payments, the appropriate course for dependants to take is to seek relief from the stay in the bankruptcy court under 362(d). Courts should liberally grant such relief in order to avoid entangling the federal court in family law matters best left to state courts. Carver v. Carver, 954 F.2d 1573, 26 C.B.C.2d 865 (11th Cir. 1992).

A creditor whose claim against a bankruptcy estate is significantly oversecured by a lien on the debtor's property, may not enforce its security interest over a section 362 automatic stay so as to "fence off" the entire property in which it has an interest from all other creditors, as its only entitlement under the Code is the adequate protection of its security interest. Matter of James Wilson Associates, 965 F.2d 160, 26 C.B.C.2d 1673 (7th Cir. 1992).

A creditor's standing as a lienholder does not give him standing in a bankruptcy case to challenge acts allegedly in violation of the automatic stay. In re Pecan Groves of Arizona, 951 F.2d 242, 25 C.B.C.2d 1728 (9th Cir. 1991).

The prepetition filing of a supersedeas bond by a judgment debtor does not preclude operation of the automatic stay, regardless of whether the debtor is the appellant or the appellee. Borman v. Raymark Industries, 946 F.2d 1031, 25 C.B.C.2d 1169 (3d Cir. 1991).

The power to stay a state court order must be distinguished from the power to vacate, and under rules of federal-state comity a bankruptcy or district court may vacate a state judgment only when the judgment is void ab initio. In re James, 940 F.2d 46, 25 C.B.C.2d 471 (3d Cir. 1991).

The Arizona State Bar exists by virtue of a rule promulgated by the Arizona Supreme Court, and for the purpose of prosecuting attorney disciplinary proceedings it is a governmental unit and is exempt from the automatic stay provisions of section 362. In re Wade, 948 F.2d 1122, 25 C.B.C.2d 1287 (9th Cir. 1991).

Presentment of a check for payment is equivalent to the presentment of a negotiable instrument under the Uniform Commercial Code and, therefore, is excepted by section 362(b)(11) from the automatic stay. Roete v. Smith, 936 F.2d 963, 25 C.B.C.2d 177 (7th Cir. 1991).

A United States Department of Labor's enforcement action is outside the scope of the automatic stay under section 362(b)(4) when the remedies are not designed to advance the government's pecuniary interest but are another method of enforcing policies under the Service Contract Act. Eddleman v. U.S. Dep't of Labor, 923 F.2d 782, 24 C.B.C.2d 822 (10th Cir. 1991).

Governmental actions under CERCLA to recover costs expended in response to completed environmental violations are not stayed by the filing of a violator's petition. City of New York v. Exxon Corp., 932 F.2d 1020, 24 C.B.C.2d 1737 (2d Cir. 1991).

The bankruptcy court may properly enjoin a parent corporation from taking a worthless stock deduction on its tax return if to do so would eliminate the value to its debtor-subsidiary in using the net operating loss carryforward in its own reorganization. *In re* Prudential Lines, Inc., 928 F.2d 565, 24 C.B.C.2d 1503 (2d Cir. 1991).

Although section 106(c) binds "governmental units" to the Code's provisions, the Supreme Court has decided that section 106(c) does not abrogate a state's Eleventh Amendment immunity from recovery of a money judgment and, therefore, monetary sanctions are not recoverable against a state university for a violation of the automatic stay. *In re* Gustafson, 924 F.2d 216, 24 C.B.C.2d 1937 (9th Cir. 1991).

When a bankruptcy court declines to grant relief from the automatic stay because it finds a creditor's security interest to be of doubtful validity, such a finding is in the nature of a legal conclusion, and review of this conclusion on appeal to the district court is not subject to the "abuse of discretion" standard of review. *In re* FRG, Inc., 919 F.2d 850, 24 C.B.C.2d 40 (3d Cir. 1990).

While a district court has the power to impose sanctions in a bankruptcy appeal based upon either the inherent power of the judiciary or the statutory authority of 28 U.S.C. § 1927, it is an abuse of a district court's discretion to order the payment of attorney's fees when the party's violation of the automatic stay was not willful and that party's attempt to exempt a claim involving property formerly occupied as a homestead was not wholly frivolous. In the Matter of Sherk, 918 F.2d 1170, 24 C.B.C.2d 502 (5th Cir. 1990).

A debtor's possession of a tenancy at sufferance at the time of filing creates a property interest protected by section 362(a)(3), and a property owner's attempts to evict the debtor therefore violate the automatic stay. *In re* Atlantic Business and Community Corp., 901 F.2d 325, 22 C.B.C.2d 1176 (3d Cir. 1990).

A recoupment is not subject to the automatic stay of section 362(a). In the Matter of Holford, 896 F.2d 176, 22 C.B.C.2d 1097 (5th Cir. 1990).

Under section 362(h), any deliberate act taken in violation of a stay which the violator knows to be in existence, justifies an award of actual damages; an additional finding of maliciousness or bad faith warrants the further imposition of punitive damages. *In re* Crysen/Montenay Energy Co., 902 F.2d 1098, 22 C.B.C.2d 1385 (2d Cir. 1990).

Ordinarily, any action taken in violation of the automatic stay is void and without effect, even when there is no actual notice of the existence of the stay but, where the debtor actively litigates a state court action and does not provide notice of a pending chapter 13 case, it would be inequitable for the court to allow the debtor to invoke the protection of section 362(a). *In re* Calder, 907 F.2d 953, 23 C.B.C.2d 677 (10th Cir. 1990).

The automatic stay does not protect property interests that ceased to be in the debtor's estate prior to the commencement of the bankruptcy case nor can it be used to revive such interests. *In re* Mann, 907 F.2d 923, 23 C.B.C.2d 608 (9th Cir. 1990).

The automatic stay ceases to apply subsequent to confirmation because an order confirming a reorganization plan discharges the debtor from any debt that arose before the date of such confirmation, and vests all the property of the estate in the debtor. U.S. Dept. of Air Force v. Carolina Parachute Corp., 907 F.2d 1469, 23 C.B.C.2d 620 (4th Cir. 1990).

The IRS's issuance to a chapter 13 trustee of a notice of levy on funds payable to a taxpayer by a bankruptcy estate with a confirmed plan without does not violate the automatic stay provision of section 362. Laughlin v. IRS, 912 F.2d 197, 23 C.B.C.2d 736 (8th Cir. 1990).

Governmental units are immune from actions for damages arising from their violations of the automatic stay. *In re* Pearson, 917 F.2d 1215, 23 C.B.C.2d 1535 (9th Cir. 1990).

Although there is no precise test, a bankruptcy court is justified in granting relief from the automatic stay for bad faith when it has found that a debtor has filed the petition (1) at an inappropriate time, (2) despite good financial health, (3) strictly to avoid pending litigation, and (4) to reject an unprofitable contract. *In re* Dixie Broadcasting, Inc., 871 F.2d 1023, 20 C.B.C.2d 1521 (11th Cir. 1989).

A tax sale commenced under state law while the estate is in bankruptcy is void from the outset. *In re* Shamblin, 878 F.2d 324, 21 C.B.C.2d 197 (9th Cir. 1989).

When applicable regulations provide for mandatory and automatic withdrawal of landing and takeoff slots and allow for no discretion on the part of the Federal Aviation Administration ("FAA"), withdrawal of the slots for non-use by the debtor does not involve an affirmative act on the part of the FAA and, consequently, does not constitute an administrative action or proceeding against the debtor that is automatically stayed under section 362(a)(1). *In re* Gull Air, Inc., 890 F.2d 1255, 21 C.B.C.2d 1324 (1st Cir. 1989).

A governmental agency that withheld or froze a payment to a debtor exercised control over the payment so that it violated section 362(a)(3) of the automatic stay. Small Business Admin. v. Rinehart, 887 F.2d 165, 21 C.B.C.2d 917 (8th Cir. 1989).

When the Secretary of Labor brings an injunction action against a debtor to prevent the sale of goods produced in violation of the Fair Labor Standards Act, the Secretary seeks to enforce the government's police power regarding the minimum wage and such suit is therefore exempt from the automatic stay. Brock v. Rusco Industries, Inc., 842 F.2d 270, 18 C.B.C.2d 728 (11th Cir.), *cert. denied,* 488 U.S. 889, 109 S. Ct. 221, 102 L. Ed. 2d 212 (1988).

An action by the United States to recover costs expended to clean up the chapter 11 debtor's hazardous waste site under the Comprehensive Environmental Response, Compensation, and Liability Act (CERCLA), 42 U.S.C. § 9604, is an action pursuant to its regulatory powers which Congress intended to be exempt from the automatic stay up to and including the entry of a monetary judgment; however, the lifting of the automatic stay does not extend to enforcement of the judgment. United States v. Nicolet, Inc., 857 F.2d 202, 19 C.B.C.2d 1405 (3d Cir. 1988).

When the termination of a prime lease for nonpayment of rent would cause the destruction of a debtor's sublease, notice of termination of the prime lease is a violation of the automatic stay, even though the prime tenant has not filed a bankruptcy petition; this result is permissible because the nondebtor's interest is intertwined with that of the debtor. 48th St. Steakhouse, Inc. v. Rockefeller Group, Inc. (*In re* 48th St. Steakhouse, Inc.), 835 F.2d 427, 17 C.B.C.2d 1415 (2d Cir. 1987), *cert. denied,* 485 U.S. 1035, 108 S. Ct. 1596, 99 L. Ed. 2d 910 (1988).

The automatic stay under section 362(a)(3) applies to actions to pierce the corporate veil which under state or federal law belong to the debtor only and to a cause of action that seeks to recover property of the estate when the property is held or controlled by a person or entity other than the debtor. S.I. Acquisition, Inc. v. Eastway Delivery Serv., Inc. (In the Matter of S.I. Acquisition, Inc.), 817 F.2d 1142, 17 C.B.C.2d 207 (5th Cir. 1987).

Since it is the debtor's burden to obtain a timely and expedited hearing on a relief from stay motion, when the automatic stay expires before the district court can hold a hearing requested by the debtor before the bankruptcy court, a resulting foreclosure sale will not be set aside. The 30-day time period of section 362(e) does not begin to run anew when the relief from stay proceeding is transferred from one court to another. River Hills Assocs. v. River Hills Apartments Fund (*In re* River Hills Apartments Fund), 813 F.2d 702, 16 C.B.C.2d 1387 (5th Cir. 1987).

A state's refusal to transfer a liquor license under a statute which disallows such transfer until tax payments are made constitutes an act to collect or recover a claim in violation of section 362(a)(6) even though the state's action is correct—the state must first seek relief from the stay. State of California v. Farmers Markets, Inc. (*In re* Farmers Markets, Inc.), 792 F.2d 1400, 15 C.B.C.2d 93 (9th Cir. 1986).

Section 362(a)(3) stays any action, whether it is against the debtor or a third-party, to obtain possession or to exercise control over property of the estate, which can include product liability insurance policies. Accordingly, actions "related to" bankruptcy proceedings against the insurer or against officers or employees of the debtor who may be entitled to indemnification under such policies or who qualify as additional insureds under the policies are to be stayed under section 362(a)(3). A.H. Robins Co. v. Piccinin, 788 F.2d 994, 15 C.B.C.2d 235 (4th Cir.), *cert. denied,* 479 U.S. 876, 107 S. Ct. 251, 93 L. Ed. 2d 177 (1986).

When a debtor's counterclaim incorporates state contract law and a state court trial is pending on the same issues, the district court may terminate the automatic stay to allow the entire case to be determined in one forum; in doing so, the district court satisfies Congress' intent to give state law claimants a right to have claims heard in state court. Piomba Corp. v. Castlerock Properties (*In re* Castlerock Properties), 781 F.2d 159, 15 C.B.C.2d 20 (9th Cir. 1986).

References

2 *Collier on Bankruptcy* ch. 362 (Matthew Bender 15th ed.).

1 *Collier Bankruptcy Manual* ch. 362 (Matthew Bender 3d ed.).

2 *Collier Bankruptcy Practice Guide* ch. 38 (Matthew Bender).

Brown, *Automatic Stay Litigation: A Primer,* 47 Ala. Law. 319 (1987)

Callahan, *The "Police Power" Exception to the Automatic Stay: What Is Its Scope When Applied to Postpetition Governmental Action Against Property of the Estate?* 18 Cal. Bankr. J. 261 (1990).

Emerson, *Governmental Actions Under the Section 362(b)(4) Bankruptcy Exemption of Police Powers and Pecuniary Interests,* 90 Com. L.J. 101 (1985).

Groschadl, *"Freezing" the Debtor's Bank Account: A Violation of the Automatic Stay,* 57 Am. Bankr. L.J. 75 (1983).

Hoffmann, *The Effect of the Bankruptcy Automatic Stay on State Court Litigation,* 19 Colo. Law. 243 (1990).

Lam, *Cancellations of Insurance: Bankruptcy Automatic Stay Implications,* 59 Am. Bankr. L.J. 267 (1985).

Madan, *The Supreme Issue in Stay Litigation: What Constitutes Adequate Protection for the Undersecured Creditor,* 29 So. Tex. L. Rev. 531 (1988).

Murdich, *Arbitration and the Automatic Stay,* 1 F & G Bankr. L. Rev. 58 (1989).

Newborn, *The Precarious Plight of Corporate and Partnership Debtors Under Section 362(h) of the Bankruptcy Code,* Annual Survey of Bankruptcy Law (1992).

Note, *Section 362(h): Applicable to Corporate Debtors?*, 56 Mo. L. Rev. 769 (1991).

Note, *The 1978 Bankruptcy Reform Act's Police or Regulatory Power Exemption to the Automatic Stay: Unnecessary, Unfounded, and Unrestrained*, 29 Wm. & Mary L. Rev. 855 (1988).

Note, *Creditor's Alter Ego Action Against Debtor's Parent Corporation Deemed Property of Debtor's Estate to Which Automatic Stay Applied (In re S.I. Acquisition)*, 19 Texas Tech. L. Rev. 1213 (1987–88).

Petrizzo, *Litigating a Motion for Relief From Stay in Bankruptcy Court*, 50 Tex. B.J. 266 (1987).

Porter, *Burdens of Proof in Bankruptcy Court*, 17 Colo. L. Rev. 251 (1988).

Tilton and Wild, *Protecting Co-Obligors and Non-Debtor Guarantors*, N.Y.L.J., Nov. 14, 1991.

SECTION 363 (11 U.S.C. § 363)

§ 363.   Use, sale, or lease of property.

(a) In this section, "cash collateral" means cash, negotiable instruments, documents of title, securities, deposit accounts, or other cash equivalents whenever acquired in which the estate and an entity other than the estate have an interest and includes the proceeds, products, offspring, rents, or profits of property subject to a security interest as provided in section 552(b) of this title, whether existing before or after the commencement of a case under this title.

(b)(1) The trustee, after notice and a hearing, may use, sell, or lease, other than in the ordinary course of business, property of the estate.

(2) If notification is required under subsection (a) of section 7A of the Clayton Act (15 U.S.C. 18a) in the case of a transaction under this subsection, then—

(A) notwithstanding subsection (a) of such section, such notification shall be given by the trustee; and

(B) notwithstanding subsection (b) of such section, the required waiting period shall end on the tenth day after the date of the receipt of such notification, unless the court, after notice and hearing, orders otherwise.

(c)(1) If the business of the debtor is authorized to be operated under section 721, 1108, 1304, 1203, or 1204 of this title and unless the court orders otherwise, the trustee may enter into transactions, including the sale or lease of property of the estate, in the ordinary course of business, without notice or a hearing, and may use property of the estate in the ordinary course of business without notice or a hearing.

(2) The trustee may not use, sell, or lease cash collateral under paragraph (1) of this subsection unless—

(A) each entity that has an interest in such cash collateral consents; or

(B) the court, after notice and a hearing, authorizes such use, sale, or lease in accordance with the provisions of this section.

(3) Any hearing under paragraph (2)(B) of this subsection may be a preliminary hearing or may be consolidated with a hearing under subsection (c) of this section, but shall be scheduled in accordance with the needs of the debtor. If the hearing under paragraph (2)(B) of this subsection is a preliminary hearing, the court may authorize such use, sale, or lease only if there is a reasonable likelihood that the trustee will prevail at the final hearing under subsection (e) of this section. The court shall act promptly on any request for authorization under paragraph (2)(B) of this subsection.

(4) Except as provided in paragraph (2) of this subsection, the trustee shall segregate and account for any cash collateral in the trustee's possession, custody, or control.

(d) The trustee may use, sell, or lease property under subsection (b) or (c) of this section only to the extent not inconsistent with any relief granted under section 362(c), 362(d), 362(e), or 362(f) of this title.

(e) Notwithstanding any other provision of this section, at any time, on request of an entity that has an interest in property used, sold, or leased, or proposed to be used, sold, or leased, by the trustee, the court, with or without a hearing, shall prohibit or condition such use, sale, or lease as is necessary to provide adequate protection of such interest.

(f) The trustee may sell property under subsection (b) or (c) of this section free and clear of any interest in such property of an entity other than the estate, only if—

(1) applicable nonbankruptcy law permits sale of such property free and clear of such interest;

(2) such entity consents;

(3) such interest is a lien and the price at which such property is to be sold is greater than the aggregate value of all liens on such property;

(4) such interest is in bona fide dispute; or

(5) such entity could be compelled, in a legal or equitable proceeding, to accept a money satisfaction of such interest.

(g) Notwithstanding subsection (f) of this section, the trustee may sell property under subsection (b) or (c) of this section free and clear of any vested or contingent right in the nature of dower or curtesy.

(h) Notwithstanding subsection (f) of this section, the trustee may sell both the estate's interest, under subsection (b) or (c) of this section, and the interest of any co-owner in property in which the debtor had, at the time of the commencement of the case, an undivided interest as a tenant in common, joint tenant, or tenant by the entirety, only if—

(1) partition in kind of such property among the estate and such co-owners is impracticable;

(2) sale of the estate's undivided interest in such property would realize significantly less for the estate than sale of such property free of the interests of such co-owners;

(3) the benefit to the estate of a sale of such property free of the interests of co-owners outweights the detriment, if any, to such co-owners; and

(4) such property is not used in the production, transmission, or distribution, for sale, of electric energy or of natural or synthetic gas for heat, light, or power.

(i) Before the consummation of a sale of property to which subsection (g) or (h) of this section applies, or of property of the estate that was community property of the debtor and the debtor's spouse immediately before the commencement of the case, the debtor's spouse, or a co-owner of such property, as the case may be, may purchase such property at the price at which such sale is to be consummated.

(j) After a sale of property to which subsection (g) or (h) of this section applies, the trustee shall distribute to the debtor's spouse or the co-owners of such property, as the case may be, and to the estate, the proceeds of such sale, less the costs and expenses, not including any compensation of the trustee, of such sale, according to the interests of such spouse or co-owners, and of the estate.

(k) At a sale under subsection (b) of this section of property that is subject to a lien that secures an allowed claim, unless the court for cause orders otherwise the holder of such claim may bid at such sale, and, if the holder of such claim purchases such property, such holder may offset such claim against the purchase price of such property.

(l) Subject to the provisions of section 365, the trustee may use, sell, or lease property under subsection (b) or (c) of this section, or a plan under chapter 11, 12, or 13 of this title may provide for the use, sale, or lease of property, notwithstanding any provision in a contract, a lease, or applicable law that is conditioned on the insolvency or financial condition of the debtor, on the commencement of a case under this title concerning the debtor, or on the appointment of or the taking possession by a trustee in a case under this title or a custodian, and that effects, or gives an option to effect, a forfeiture, modification, or termination of the debtor's interest in such property.

(m) The reversal or modification on appeal of an authorization under subsection (b) or (c) of this section of a sale or lease of property does not affect the validity of a sale or lease under such authorization to an entity that purchased or leased such property in good faith, whether or not such entity knew of the pendency of the appeal, unless such authorization and such sale or lease were stayed pending appeal.

(n) The trustee may avoid a sale under this section if the sale price was controlled by an agreement among potential bidders at such sale, or may recover from a party to such agreement any amount by which the value of the property sold exceeds the price at which such sale was consummated, and may recover any costs, attorneys' fees, or expenses incurred in avoiding such sale or recovering such amount. In addition to any recovery under the preceding sentence, the court may grant judgment for punitive damages in favor of the estate and against any such party that entered into such an agreement in willful disregard of this subsection.

(o) In any hearing under this section—

(1) the trustee has the burden of proof on the issue of adequate protection; and

(2) the entity asserting an interest in property has the burden of proof on the issue of the validity, priority, or extent of such interest.

Bankruptcy Rule References: 4001, 6004 and 7001

Legislative History

This section defines the rights and powers of the trustee with respect to the use, sale, or lease of property and the rights of other parties that have interests in the property involved. It applies in both liquidation and reorganization cases. [*Ed. Note:* Subsections (b), (d)–(f), (l) apply in chapter 13 cases; *see* section 1303.]

[*House Report No. 95–595; 95th Cong., 1st Sess. 344 (1977); Senate Report No. 95–989, 95th Cong., 2d Sess. 55 (1978).*]

Subsection (a) defines "soft collateral" [*Ed. Note:* As enacted the Code adopts the Senate version with respect to cash collateral. The "soft collateral" concept in the House version was deleted.] as inventory, accounts, contract rights, general intangibles, cash, negotiable instruments, documents of title, securities, or chattel paper in which the estate and an entity other than the estate have an interest, such as a lien or a co-ownership interest. The definition is not restricted to property of the estate that is soft collateral on the date of the filing of the petition. Thus, if "hard" collateral is sold, and the proceeds come within the definition of this subsection, then the proceeds would be soft collateral if they remained subject to the original lien on the "hard" collateral under proposed 11 U.S.C. § 552(b).

[*House Report No. 95–595, 95th Cong., 1st Sess. 344–5 (1977).*]

Subsection (a) defines "cash collateral" as cash, negotiable instruments, documents of title, securities, deposit accounts, or other cash equivalents in which the estate and an entity other than the estate have an interest, such as a lien or a co-ownership interest. The definition is not restricted to property of the estate that is cash collateral on the date of the filing of the petition. Thus, if "non-cash" collateral is disposed of and the proceeds come within the definition of "cash collateral" as set forth in this subsection, the proceeds would be cash collateral as long as they remain subject to the original lien on the "non-cash" collateral under section 552(b). To illustrate, rents received from real property before or after the commencement of the case would be cash collateral to the extent that they are subject to a lien.

[*Senate Report No. 95–989, 95th Cong., 2d Sess. 55 (1978).*]

Section 363(a) of the House amendment defines "cash collateral" as defined in the Senate amendment. The broader definition of "soft collateral" contained in H.R. 8200 as passed by the House is deleted to remove limitations that were placed on the use, lease, or sale of inventory, accounts, contract rights, general intangibles, and chattel paper by the trustee or debtor in possession.

[*124 Cong. Rec. H 11,093 (Sept. 28, 1978); S 17,409 (Oct. 6, 1978).*]

Subsection (b) permits the trustee to use, sell, or lease, other than in the ordinary course of business, property of the estate. The trustee must give notice of any use, sale, or lease under this subsection, and provide an opportunity for objections and a hearing if there are any objections.

[*House Report No. 95–595, 95th Cong., 1st Sess. 345 (1977); Senate Report No. 95–989, 95th Cong., 2d Sess. 55 (1978).*]

Subsection (c) governs ordinary course of business use, sale, or lease. If the business of the debtor is authorized to be operated under section 721, 1108, or 1304 of the bankruptcy code, then the trustee may use, sell, or lease property in the ordinary course of business without need for a notice and a hearing, and may enter into ordinary course transactions without notice of a hearing. This power is subject to several limitations. First, the court may restrict the trustee's powers in the order authorizing operation of the business. Second, with respect to soft collateral, the trustee may use, sell, or lease soft collateral only for a period of five days after he notifies the secured party of his intention to use, sell, or lease the collateral. After that period, he may not use, sell, or lease soft collateral without notice and a hearing. The same preliminary hearing procedure in the automatic stay section applies to this hearing. [*Ed. Note:* As enacted, the Code does not treat soft collateral specially or retain the five day period mentioned in the report. The limitation in subsection (c) is as set forth in the Senate Report. *See* section 102(1) for construction of "notice and hearing."]

The trustee is also limited in his use, sale or lease of property by the concept of adequate protection. He may use, sell, or lease property in which an equity other than the estate has an interest only to the extent not inconsistent with any relief from the stay granted to that interest's holder. Further, the court may prohibit or condition the use, sale, or lease as is necessary to provide adequate protection of that interest. Again, the trustee has the burden of proof on the issue of adequate protection.

[*House Report No. 95–595, 95th Cong., 1st Sess. 344 (1978).*]

Subsection (c) governs use, sale, or lease in the ordinary course of business. If the business of the debtor is authorized to be operated under section 721, 1108, or 1304 of the Bankruptcy Code, then the trustee may use, sell, or lease property in the ordinary course of business or enter into ordinary course transactions without need for notice and hearing. This power is subject to several limitations. First, the court may restrict the trustee's powers in the order authorizing operation of the business. Second, with respect to cash collateral, the trustee may not use, sell, or lease cash collateral except upon court authorization after notice and a hearing, or with the consent of each entity that has an interest in such cash collateral. The same preliminary hearing procedure in the automatic stay section applies to a hearing under this subsection. In addition, the trustee is required to segregate and account for any cash collateral in the trustee's possession, custody, or control.

[*Senate Report No. 95–989, 95th Cong., 2d Sess. 55 (1978).*]

Section 363(c)(2) of the House amendment is derived from the Senate amendment. Similarly, sections 363(c)(3) and (4) are derived from comparable provisions in the Senate amendment in lieu of the contrary procedure contained in section 363(c) as passed by the House. The policy of the House amendment will generally require the court to schedule a preliminary hearing in accordance with the needs of the debtor to authorize the trustee or debtor in possession to use, sell, or lease cash collateral. The trustee or debtor in possession may use, sell, or lease cash collateral in the ordinary course of business only "after notice and a hearing."

[*124 Cong. Rec. H 11,093 (Sept. 28, 1978); S 14,409 (Oct. 6, 1978).*]

Under subsections (d) and (e), the use, sale, or lease of property is further limited by the concept of adequate protection. Sale, use, or lease of property in which an entity other than the estate has an interest may be effected only to the extent not inconsistent with any relief from the stay granted to that interest's holder. Moreover, the court may prohibit or condition the use, sale, or lease as is necessary to provide adequate protection of that interest. Again, the trustee has the burden of proof on the issue of adequate protection. Subsection (e) also provides that where a sale of the property is proposed, an entity that has an interest in such property may bid at the sale thereof and set off against the purchase price up to the amount of such entity's claim. No prior valuation under section 506(a) would limit this bidding right, since the bid at the sale would be determinative of value. [*Ed. Note:* As enacted, this provision appears as subsection (k).]

[*Senate Report No. 95–989, 95th Cong., 2d Sess. 55 (1978).*]

Subsection (f) permits sale of property free and clear of any interest in the property of an entity other than the estate. The trustee may sell free and clear if applicable nonbankruptcy law permits it, if the other entity consents, if the interest is a lien and the sale price of the property is greater than the amount secured by the lien, if the interest is in bona fide dispute, or if other entity could be compelled to accept a money satisfaction of the interest in a legal or equitable proceeding. Sale under this subsection is subject to the adequate protection requirement. Most often, adequate protection in connection with a sale free and clear of other interests will be to have those interests attach to the proceeds of the sale.

At a sale free and clear of other interests, any holder of any interest in the property being sold will be permitted to bid. If that holder is the high bidder, he will be permitted to offset the value of his interest against the purchase price of the property. Thus, in the most common situation, a holder of a lien on property being sold may bid at the sale and, if successful, may offset the amount owed to him that is secured by the lien on the property (but may not offset other amounts owed to him) against the purchase price, and be liable to the trustee for the balance of the sale price, if any.

[*House Report No. 95–595, 95th Cong., 1st Sess. 345 (1977); See Senate Report No. 95–989, 95th Cong., 2d Sess. 56 (1978).*]

Section 363(f) of the House amendment adopts an identical provision contained in the House bill, as opposed to an alternative provision contained in the Senate amendment.

[*124 Cong. Rec. H 11,093 (Sept. 28, 1978); S 17,409 (Oct. 5, 1978).*]

Subsection (g) permits the trustee to sell free and clear of any vested or contingent right in the nature of dower or curtesy.

Subsection (h) permits sale of a co-owner's interest in property in which the debtor had an undivided ownership interest such as a joint tenancy, a tenancy in common, or a tenancy by the entirety. Such a sale is permissible only if partition is impracticable, if sale of the estate's interest would realize significantly less for the estate than sale of the property free of the interests of the co-owners, and if the benefit to the estate of such a sale outweighs any detriment to the co-owners.

[*House Report No. 95–595, 95th Cong., 1st Sess. 346 (1977); Senate Report No. 95–989, 95th Cong., 2d Sess. 56–7 (1978).*]

Section 363(h) of the House amendment adopts a new paragraph (4) representing a compromise between the House bill and Senate amendment. The provision adds a limitation indicating that a trustee or debtor in possession sell jointly owned property only if the property is not used in the production, transmission, or distribution for sale, of electric energy or of natural or synthetic gas for heat, light, or power. This limitation is intended to protect public utilities from being deprived of power sources because of the bankruptcy of a joint owner.

[*124 Cong. Rec. H 11,093 (Sept. 28, 1978); S 17,409 (Oct. 6, 1978).*]

Subsection (i) provides protections for co-owners and spouses with dower, curtesy, or community property rights. It gives a right of first refusal to the co-owner or spouse at the price at which the sale is to be consummated. Subsection (j) requires the trustee to distribute to the spouse or co-owner the appropriate portion of the proceeds of the sale, less certain administrative expenses.

[*House Report No. 95–595, 95th Cong., 1st Sess. 346 (1977); Senate Report No. 95–989, 95th Cong., 2d Sess. 57 (1978).*]

Section 363(k) of the House amendment is derived from the third sentence of section 363(e) of the Senate amendment. The provision indicates that a secured creditor may bid in the full amount of the creditor's allowed claim, including the secured portion and any unsecured portion thereof in the event the creditor is undersecured, with respect to property that is subject to a lien that secures the allowed claim of the sale of the property.

[*124 Cong. Rec. H 11,093 (Sept. 28, 1978); S 17,409 (Oct. 6, 1978).*]

Subsection (k) [*Ed. Note:* should be l] permits the trustee to use, sell, or lease property notwithstanding certain bankruptcy or ipso facto clauses that terminate the debtor's interest in the property or that work a forfeiture or modification of that interest. This subsection is not as broad as the anti-ipso facto provision in proposed 11 U.S.C. § 541(c)(1).

Subsection (l) [*Ed. Note:* should be m] protects good faith purchasers of property sold under this section from a reversal on appeal of the sale authorization, unless the authorization for the sale and the sale itself were stayed pending appeal. The purchaser's knowledge of the appeal if irrelevant to the issue of good faith.

Subsection (m) [*Ed. Note:* should be n] is directed at collusive bidding on property sold under this section. It permits the trustee to void a sale if the price of the sale was controlled by an agreement among potential bidders. The trustee may also recover the excess of the value of the property over the purchase price, and may recover any costs, attorney's fees, or expenses incurred in voiding the sale or recovering the difference. In addition, the court is authorized to grant judgment in favor of the estate and against the collusive bidder if the agreement controlling the sale price was entered into in willful disregard of this subsection. The subsection does not specify the precise measure of damages, but simply provides for punitive damages, to be fixed in light of the circumstances.

[*House Report No. 95–959, 95th Cong., 1st Sess. 344 (1978); Senate Report No. 95–989, 95th Cong., 2d Sess. 55 (1978).*]

Comment

The concept of "notice and hearing" is particularly relevant to section 363. *See* section 102(l) for the rule of construction. *See also* sections 361, 362 as they are related to section 363. Trustee as used in section 363 also means debtor in possession. Section 1107.

Provisions for sale of spousal interests and interests of others with rights in a debtor's property as provided in subsections (g), (h), and (i) of section 363 have their genesis in Section 2a(7) of the former Bankruptcy Act.

Section 363(m), dealing with the effect of reversal on appeal of an order of sale, is derived from former Bankruptcy Rule 805 which provided that unless an order approving a sale of property had been stayed pending appeal, the sale to a good faith purchaser could not be affected by the reversal or modification of such order on appeal, whether or not the purchaser knew of the pendency of the appeal.

Bankruptcy Rule 6004 relates to the use, sale or lease of property. Subdivision (a) requires that notice of a proposed use, sale or lease of property, other than cash collateral, not in the ordinary course of business, be given pursuant to Rule 2002(a)(2), (c)(1), (i) and (k) and, if applicable, in accordance with § 363(b)(2). [Rule 2002(a)(2) requires not less than 20 days notice by mail to the debtor, all creditors and indenture trustees. Rule 2002(c) provides that the notice shall include the time and place of public sale, the terms and conditions of any private sale, and the time fixed for filing objections thereto. A general description of the property, including real property, is sufficient. Rule 2002(i) requires notice to be mailed to the creditors' committees under §§ 705 and 1102 or their authorized agents. The Rule also permits the court to direct that notice be transmitted to the United States trustee and mailed only to the section 705 and 1102 committees and to creditors and equity security holders who file requests that they receive all notices. Finally, the Rule requires that certain notices be given to committees appointed pursuant to section 1114. In any event, notice must be sent to all committees appointed under the Code.]

Subdivision (b) of Rule 6004 requires that an objection to a proposed use, sale or lease of property be served and filed not less than 5 days before the date set for the proposed action, or within the time fixed by the court. An objection to the proposed use, sale, or lease is a contested matter governed by Rule 9014.

Subdivision (c) provides that a motion to sell property free and clear of liens or other interests is to be made pursuant to Rule 9014 and served on the parties who have an interest in such property. The notice provided for in subdivision (a) of the rule must include the date of hearing on the motion and the time within which objections may be filed and served on the debtor in possession or trustee. [Subdivision (c) was added by the 1987 Amendments to the Bankruptcy Rules.]

Subdivision (d) provides that when nonexempt property has an aggregate value less than $2500, a *general notice* of intent to sell such property, other than in the ordinary course of business, given to all creditors, indenture trustees, appointed or elected committees, the United States trustee and other persons as the court may direct, shall be sufficient. Objection to such sale must be served and filed within 15 days of the mailing of the notice or within the time fixed by the court. An objection is governed by Rule 9014.

Subdivision (e) provides that if timely objection is made under subdivision (b) or (d), above, the hearing date may be set in the notice required by subdivision (a) of the rule.

Subdivision (f)(1) provides that all sales *not in the ordinary course of business* may be by private sale or public auction. Unless impracticable, upon completion of a sale an itemized statement of property sold, the name of each purchaser, and the price received for each item or lot or for the property as a whole if sold in bulk, must be filed and a copy transmitted to the United States trustee. If sold by an auctioneer, the auctioneer is required to file the statement with a copy to the United States trustee, trustee, debtor in possession, or chapter 13 debtor; if the property is not sold by an auctioneer, the trustee, debtor in possession, or chapter 13 debtor shall file the statement and transmit a copy to the United States trustee. (Approval of a proposed sale by the court is necessary only if objection thereto is made.)

Subdivision (f)(2) provides that after a sale, the debtor, trustee or debtor in possession, as the case may be, shall execute instruments necessary, or ordered by the court, to effectuate transfer to the purchaser.

Bankruptcy Rule 7001(3) provides that a proceeding to obtain approval under section 363(h) for the sale of both the interest of the estate and of a co-debtor in property is an adversary proceeding governed by the Part VII Rules.

Bankruptcy Rule 2002(a) requires not less than 20 days notice of a proposed use, sale or lease of property other than in the ordinary course of business. The court may shorten the time of notice or direct another method of giving notice. The notice gives creditors an opportunity to object. Absent an objection, under section 102(1) there need not be an actual hearing.

1984 Amendments: Section 363(a) was amended by listing property to be included in the definition of "cash collateral."

Subsection (b) was amended by adding paragraph "(2)" relating to notice of use, sale or lease of property when such notice is required under the Clayton Act (15 U.S.C. § 18a).

Subsection (e) was amended by adding the words "with or without a hearing." The substance of the final sentence of this subsection relating to burden of proof was transposed to a new subsection "o."

Subsection (k) was amended to authorize lien claimants to purchase the property at the sale unless the court orders otherwise.

Subsection (n) was amended by making clarifying changes in the last sentence thereof relating to punitive damages.

Subsection (o) was added providing that the trustee has the burden of proof on the issue of adequate protection (transposed from subsection (e)), and providing for the burden of proof on the issue of the validity, priority and extent of an asserted interest in property.

Clarifying changes were made in subsections (f), (h) and (1).

Case Annotations

Neither the doctrine of intergovernmental tax immunity nor federal law bars the imposition of a state sales tax on the trustee's liquidation sale of property of the estate or the imposition of a state use tax on the purchaser's lessees. California State Board of Equalization v. Sierra

Summit, Inc., 490 U.S. 844, 109 S. Ct. 2228, 104 L. Ed. 2d 910, 20 C.B.C.2d 1501 (1989).

A creditor whose claim against a bankruptcy estate is significantly oversecured by a lien on the debtor's property, may not enforce its security interest over a section 362 automatic stay so as to "fence off" the entire property in which it has an interest from all other creditors, as its only entitlement under section 363(e) is the adequate protection of its security interest. Matter of James Wilson Associates, 965 F.2d 160, 26 C.B.C.2d 1673 (7th Cir. 1992).

If the buyer of an estate's assets under section 363 was a good faith purchaser, the sale may not be modified or set aside on appeal unless the sale was stayed pending appeal pursuant to section 363(m). *In re* Ewell, 958 F.2d 276, 26 C.B.C.2d 857 (9th Cir. 1992).

Even if an individual is a principal in both the buyer and the seller of an asset of the debtor, so long as the individual had no involvement in the sale and the transaction was held at arms length, there is no violation of any good faith requirement of the Code. *In re* Qintex Entertainment, Inc., 950 F.2d 1492, 26 C.B.C.2d 143 (9th Cir. 1991).

Even a reversal on appeal of an order confirming a sale of an estate asset will not affect the validity of the sale if the buyer purchased in good faith and the sale was not stayed pending appeal. In the Matter of Irvin, 950 F.2d 1318, 26 C.B.C.2d 152 (7th Cir. 1991).

When property of the estate is sold by a trustee with court approval, the buyer acquires title clear of all claims in bankruptcy pursuant to section 363(f), and the property may not be brought back into the estate in the absence of fraud or collusion in the sale. In the Matter of Lemco Gypsum, Inc., 910 F.2d 784, 23 C.B.C.2d 999 (11th Cir. 1990).

An appeal of a bankruptcy court's ruling on a foreclosure action generally cannot affect the rights of a good faith purchaser of the foreclosed property, unless the debtor stays the foreclosure sale pending an appeal. *In re* Mann, 907 F.2d 923, 23 C.B.C.2d 608 (9th Cir. 1990).

A creditor has standing to compel a section 363(h) sale of entireties property despite a decision by the trustee not to proceed with the sale, and the sale of a the nondebtor spouse's entirety interest is valid when the benefit to the debtor spouse's estate outweighs the detriment to the nondebtor spouse. In the Matter of Persky, 893 F.2d 15, 21 C.B.C.2d 1460 (2d Cir. 1989).

Sections 363(b)(1) and 704 do not conflict with or invalidate bylaw restrictions on the transferability of patronage margin certificates, as these sections are simply enabling statutes that give the trustee the authority to sell or dispose of property if the debtors would have had the same right under state law. Calvert v. Bongard Creameries and Schauer (*In re* Schauer), 835 F.2d 1222, 18 C.B.C.2d 127 (8th Cir. 1987).

Section 363(c)(2) provides that the trustee may not use, sell or lease cash collateral under section 363(c)(1) unless each entity with an interest in the cash collateral consents or the court, after notice and a hearing, authorizes such use, sale or lease in accordance with the provisions of section 363. Thus, unless the creditor consents, a court order is required even if no hearing is held. New Hampshire Business Dev. Corp. v. Cross Baking Co. (*In re* Cross Baking Co.), 834 F.2d 898, 17 C.B.C.2d 236 (1st Cir. 1987).

When the bankruptcy court authorizes a sale of assets pursuant to section 363(b)(1), it is required to make a finding with respect to the good faith of the purchaser. Such a procedure encourages the finality of the court's approval of sales and places prospective appellants on notice of the need to obtain stays pending appeal. It also ensures that section 363(b)(1) will not be used to circumvent the creditor protections of chapter 11. *In re* Abbotts Dairies of Pennsylvania, Inc., 788 F.2d 143, 14 C.B.C.2d 811 (3d Cir. 1986).

Under Code provisions defining cash collateral as cash in which the estate and an entity other than the estate has an interest, the bankruptcy court must look to state law to determine whether and at what time a mortgagee has an interest in rents, because it is only at that time that there is "cash collateral." Wolters Village Ltd. v. Village Properties, Ltd. (In the Matter of Village Properties, Ltd.), 723 F.2d 441, 10 C.B.C.2d 224 (5th Cir.), *cert. denied,* 466 U.S. 974, 104 S. Ct. 2350, 80 L. Ed. 2d 823 (1984).

A sound business reason is required to grant an application under section 363(b) and the special interest of one group of creditors will not suffice; in making its determination, the court should examine, *inter alia:* (1) the proportionate value of the asset to the estate as a whole; (2) the amount of elapsed time since the filing of the petition; (3) likelihood of reorganization; (4) proceeds to be obtained; and (5) whether the value of the asset is decreasing. Committee of Equity Security Holders v. Lionel Corp. (*In re* Lionel Corp.), 722 F.2d 1063, 9 C.B.C.2d 941 (2d Cir. 1983).

In determining whether a sale of property of the estate should be allowed under section 363(f), the bankruptcy court shall examine its authority to order the sale if title documents indicate that the estate possesses no substantial ownership rights to the property and that any bona fide dispute over the property exists only between third parties. Missouri v. United States Bankruptcy Court, 647 F.2d 768, 4 C.B.C.2d 306 (8th Cir. 1981), *cert. denied,* 454 U.S. 1162, 102 S. Ct. 1035, 71 L. Ed. 2d 318 (1982).

References

2 *Collier on Bankruptcy* ch. 363 (Matthew Bender 15th ed.).

1 *Collier Bankruptcy Manual* ch. 363 (Matthew Bender 3d ed.).

3 *Collier Bankruptcy Practice Guide* ch. 43 (Matthew Bender).

Herzberg, *Opportunity Costs in the Fifth Circuit,* 51 Tex. B.J. 132 (1988).

Madan, *The Supreme Issue in Stay Litigation: What Constitutes Adequate Protection for the Undersecured Creditor,* 29 So. Tex. L. Rev. 531 (1988).

McCafferty, *The Assignment of Rents in the Crucible of Bankruptcy,* 94 Com. L.J. 433 (1989).

Ostapski, *Lost Opportunity Costs in Bankruptcy,* 24 Trial 67 (1988).

Porter, *Burdens of Proof in Bankruptcy Court,* 17 Colo. Law. 251 (1988).

Ray, *Inadequate Protection for the Undersecured Creditor—The Aftermath of Timbers,* 24 Tenn. B.J. 19 (1988).

Selling Out Undersecured Creditors: "Value" Under Section 363(f) of the Bankruptcy Code, 8 Cardozo L. Rev. 1251 (1987).

Williams, *Application of the Cash Collateral Paradigm to the Preservation of the Right to Setoff in Bankruptcy,* 7 Bankr. Dev. J. 27 (1990).

Zitron, *Use, Sales or Lease of Property: New Criteria for Disposition of Property Under Section 363(b)(1),* 2 Bank. Dev. J. 37 (1985).

SECTION 364 (11 U.S.C. § 364)

§ 364.   Obtaining credit.

(a) If the trustee is authorized to operate the business of the debtor under section 721, 1108, 1304, 1203, or 1204 of this title, unless the court orders otherwise, the trustee may obtain unsecured credit and incur unsecured debt in the ordinary course of business allowable under section 503(b)(1) of this title as an administrative expense.

(b) The court, after notice and a hearing, may authorize the trustee to obtain unsecured credit or to incur unsecured debt other than under subsection (a) of this section, allowable under section 503(b)(1) of this title as an administrative expense.

(c) If the trustee is unable to obtain unsecured credit allowable under section 503(b)(1) of this title as an administrative expense, the court, after notice and a hearing, may authorize the obtaining of credit or the incurring of debt—

(1) with priority over any or all administrative expenses of the kind specified in section 503(b) or 507(b) of this title;

(2) secured by a lien on property of the estate that is not otherwise subject to a lien; or

> (3) secured by a junior lien on property of the estate that is subject to a lien.

(d)(1) The court, after notice and a hearing, may authorize the obtaining of credit or the incurring of debt secured by a senior or equal lien on property of the estate that is subject to a lien only if—

> (A) the trustee is unable to obtain such credit otherwise; and

> (B) there is adequate protection of the interest of the holder of the lien on the property of the estate on which such senior or equal lien is proposed to be granted.

> (2) In any hearing under this subsection, the trustee has the burden of proof on the issue of adequate protection.

(e) The reversal or modification on appeal of an authorization under this section to obtain credit or incur debt, or of a grant under this section of a priority or a lien, does not affect the validity of any debt so incurred, or any priority or lien so granted, to an entity that extended such credit in good faith, whether or not such entity knew of the pendency of the appeal, unless such authorization and the incurring of such debt, or the granting of such priority or lien, were stayed pending appeal.

(f) Except with respect to an entity that is an underwriter as defined in section 1145(b) of this title, section 5 of the Securities Act of 1933 (15 U.S.C. 77e), the Trust Indenture Act of 1939 (15 U.S.C. 77aaa *et seq.*), and any State or local law requiring registration for offer or sale of a security or registration or licensing of an issuer of, underwriter of, or broker or dealer in, a security does not apply to the offer or sale under this section of a security that is not an equity security.

Bankruptcy Rule Reference: 4001

Legislative History

This section is derived from provisions in current law governing certificates of indebtedness, but is much broader. It governs all obtaining of credit and incurring of debt by the estate.

Subsection (a) authorizes the obtaining of unsecured credit and the incurring of unsecured debt in the ordinary course of business if the business of the debtor is authorized to be operated under section 721,

1108, or 1304. The debts so incurred are allowable as administrative expenses under section 503(b)(1). The court may limit the estate's ability to incur debt under this subsection.

Subsection (b) permits the court to authorize the trustee to obtain unsecured credit and incur unsecured debts other than in the ordinary course of business, such as in order to wind up a liquidation case, or to obtain a substantial loan in an operating case. Debt incurred under this subsection is allowable as an administrative expense under section 503(b)(1).

Subsection (c) is closer to the concept of certificates of indebtedness in current law. It authorizes the obtaining of credit and the incurring of debt with some special priority, if the trustee is unable to obtain unsecured credit under subsection (a) or (b). The various priorities are (1) with priority over any or all administrative expenses; (2) secured by a lien on unencumbered property of the estate; or (3) secured by a junior lien on encumbered property. The priorities granted under this subsection do not interfere with existing property rights.

Subsection (d) grants the court the authority to authorize the obtaining of credit and the incurring of debt with a superpriority, that is a lien on encumbered property that is senior or equal to the existing lien on the property. The court may authorize such a superpriority only if the trustee is otherwise unable to obtain credit, and if there is adequate protection of the original lien holder's interest. Again, the trustee has the burden of proof on the issue of adequate protection.

Subsection (e) provides the same protection for credit extenders pending an appeal of an authorization to incur debt as is provided under section 363 (1) for purchasers: the credit is not affected on appeal by reversal of the authorization unless the authorization and the incurring of the debt were stayed pending appeal. The protection runs to a good faith lender, whether or not he knew of the pendency of the appeal.

A claim arising as a result of lending or borrowing under this section will be a priority claim, as defined in proposed 11 U.S.C. § 507(1), even if the claim is granted a super-priority over administrative expenses and is to be paid in advance of other first priority claims.

[*House Report No. 95–595, 95th Cong., 1st Sess. 346–47 (1977); Senate Report No. 95–989, 95th Cong., 2d Sess. 57–58 (1978).*]

Section 364(f) of the House amendment is new. This provision continues the exemption found in section 3(a)(7) of the Securities Act of 1933 for certificates of indebtedness issued by a trustee in bankruptcy. The exemption applies to any debt security issued under section 364 of title 11. The section does not intend to change present law which exempts such securities from the Trust Indenture Act, 15 U.S.C. § 77 aaa, *et seq.* (1976).

[*124 Cong. Rec. H 11,093 (Sept. 28, 1976); S 17,409 (Oct. 6, 1978).*]

Comment

Section 116(2) of the former Bankruptcy Act provided that a receiver, trustee or debtor in possession in a Chapter X case could be authorized to issue certificates of indebtedness for cash, property or other consideration "upon such terms and conditions and with such security and priority of payment over existing obligations, secured or unsecured, as in the particular case may be equitable."

The provisions of the former Act in Sections 344 and 446, for issuance of certificates of indebtedness in Chapters XI and XII cases were more restrictive than the provision in Chapter X; the certificates could be issued "upon such terms and conditions and with such security and priority over existing obligations as in the particular case may be equitable."

The provisions of section 364 of the Code governing certificates of indebtedness are more detailed than the provisions of the Act, and adopt the former Chapter X approach.

Where the trustee is unable to obtain credit by other means, subsection (d) grants the court power to authorize the obtaining credit and incurring a debt with a super priority that is a lien senior or equal to an existing lien on the property. But in such case, the trustee must establish that there is adequate protection of the original lien-holder's interest. What constitutes "adequate protection" is prescribed in section 361.

Former Rule 805 provided that unless an order approving the issuance of a certificate of indebtedness is stayed pending appeal, the issuance of a certificate to a good faith holder shall not be affected by reversal or modification of such order on appeal, "whether or not the . . . holder knows of the pendency of the appeal." Sections 364(e) and 365(m) are substantially to the same effect.

Sections 363(m) and 364(e) of the Code provide that unless an order approving a sale of property, or authorizing the obtaining of credit or the incurring of debt is stayed pending appeal, the sale of property or a good faith extension of credit, with or without any priority or lien, shall not be affected by the reversal or modification of such order on appeal, whether or not the purchaser or creditor knows of the pendency of the appeal.

Bankruptcy Rule 4001, as amended in 1991, should be considered in connection with section 364 of the Code. Subdivision (c)(l) provides that a motion for authority to obtain credit shall be made in accordance with Rule 9014 (motion practice) and shall be served on any elected or appointed committee or its authorized agent, or, in a chapter 9 or 11 case in which no committee of unsecured creditors has been appointed under section 1102 of the Code, on the creditors included on the list of creditors filed pursuant to Rule 1007(d), and such others as the court directs. The motion must be accompanied by a copy of the credit agreement.

Subdivision (c)(2) requires a final hearing to commence no earlier than 15 days after service of the motion. If the motion requests, the court may conduct an earlier hearing, but may authorize obtaining credit only to the extent necessary to avoid immediate and irreparable harm to the estate pending final hearing.

Subdivision (c)(3) requires notice of the hearing be given to the parties on whom the service of the motion is required by paragraph (1) and to such others as the court directs.

1986 Amendments: The amendment brought chapter 12 cases within the ambit of section 364.

Case Annotations

Section 364(e) will not shield from the effect of reversal on appeal cure payments made impermissibly under section 365 with respect to an unassumable financial accommodation contract. *In re* Sun Runner Marine, Inc., 945 F.2d 1089, 25 C.B.C.2d 1054 (9th Cir. 1991).

An implicit finding by a bankruptcy court of "good faith" in a section 364(e) context is insufficient and "good faith" under the section should not be presumed. *In re* Revco D.S., Inc., 901 F.2d 1359, 22 C.B.C.2d 1263 (6th Cir. 1990).

The principle underlying the section 364(e) requirement that modification of a financing order on appeal "does not affect the validity of any debt so incurred, or any priority or lien so granted, to an entity that extended such credit in good faith," in conjunction with the doctrine of the law of the case requires that the priority granted by one bankruptcy judge's financing order may not be vacated four years later by a second bankruptcy judge without a finding that the creditor has acted in bad faith. *In re* Kham & Nate's Shoes No. 2, Inc., 908 F.2d 1351, 23 C.B.C.2d 1118 (7th Cir. 1990).

In a case in which a debtor's banks are granted superpriority status pursuant to section 364(c) in exchange for their grant of an emergency extension of credit, a bankruptcy court order in which a debtor agrees to settle all controversies regarding the validity of the banks' security interests by waiving any objections it may have with respect thereto is not beyond the scope of section 364(c) and is entitled to section 364(e) protection. Unsecured Creditors' Comm. v. First Nat'l Bank & Trust Co. of Escanaba (*In re* Ellingsen MacLean Oil Co.), 834 F.2d 599, 17 C.B.C.2d 1402 (6th Cir. 1987), *cert. denied,* 488 U.S. 817, 109 S. Ct. 55, 102 L. Ed. 2d 33 (1988).

Section 364(e) protects a lender by preventing reversal of a cross-collateralization clause unless a stay is obtained pending appeal, and a lender does not act in "bad faith" as a matter of law simply by lending with the purpose of securing a prepetition loan. Burchinal v. Cent. Wash. Bank (*In re* Adams Apple, Inc.), 829 F.2d 1484, 17 C.B.C.2d 1132 (9th Cir. 1987).

To the extent that a cash collateral order permits a debtor to foreclose, in effect, a junior secured creditor's security interest, that order violates section 364(d), which requires that a debtor provide adequate protection of a secured creditor's interest. Owens-Corning Fiberglas Corp. v. Center Wholesale, Inc. (*In re* Center Wholesale, Inc.), 759 F.2d 1440, 12 C.B.C.2d 1107 (9th Cir. 1985).

A financing order which gives a creditor superpriority interest in all present and future property of the debtor in possession has priority over a section 330 claim for professional fees and a court may not read another meaning into section 330 in order to arrive at a preferable result. Gen. Elec. Credit Corp. v. Levin & Weintraub (*In re* Flagstaff Foodservice Corp.), 739 F.2d 73, 10 C.B.C.2d 1309 (2d Cir. 1984).

The knowledge of the pendency of an appeal from a bankruptcy court's order granting a lender special priority does not, in itself, forfeit the protections that the Code gives to a lender even though the lender knows that there are objections to the order; however, if the lender knows his priority is improper but proceeds anyway in the hope that a stay will not be sought or if sought will not be granted, the lender is acting in bad faith and upon appeal the priority should not be allowed. In the Matter of EDC Holding Co., 676 F.2d 945, 6 C.B.C.2d 882 (7th Cir. 1982).

To obtain credit a debtor must show that it has made a reasonable effort to seek other sources of credit available under section 364(a) or (b) such as: (1) approaching lending institutions capable of loaning the amount needed to maintain the debtor's operations; (2) making sure that the lending institution can meet the debtor's time demands; and (3) ensuring that the creditor's offer will not harm the estate. *In re* Ames Department Stores, Inc., 22 C.B.C.2d 1500 (B. Ct., S.D.N.Y. 1990).

References

2 *Collier on Bankruptcy* ch. 364 (Matthew Bender 15th ed.).

1 *Collier Bankruptcy Manual* ch. 364 (Matthew Bender 3d ed.).

3 *Collier Bankruptcy Practice Guide* ch. 44 (Matthew Bender).

Comment, *Adequate Protection—The Equitable Yardstick of Chapter 11*, 22 U. Rich. L. Rev. 455 (1988).

Comment, *Obtaining Operating Capital in a Chapter 11 Reorganization Proceeding Under § 363(c) and § 364(d) of the Bankruptcy Code*, 1983 Ann. Surv. Bankr. L. 217.

Dixon, Jr., *Use of Cash Collateral and Its Proceeds in Bankruptcy*, 3 Legal Notes & Viewpoints Q. 75 (1983).

Giraydo, *Revolving and Non-Revolving Credit Arrangements and the New Bankruptcy Code*, 97 The Banking L.J. 806 (1980).

McCullough, *Analysis of Bankruptcy Code Section 364(d): When Will a Court Allow a Trustee to Obtain Post-Petition Financing by Granting a Superpriority Lien*, 93 Com. L.J. 186 (1988).

SECTION 365 (11 U.S.C. § 365)

§ 365. Executory contracts and unexpired leases.

(a) Except as provided in sections 765 and 766 of this title and in subsections (b), (c), and (d) of this section, the trustee, subject to the court's approval, may assume or reject any executory contract or unexpired lease of the debtor.

(b)(1) If there has been a default in an executory contract or unexpired lease of the debtor, the trustee may not assume such contract or lease unless, at the time of assumption of such contract or lease, the trustee—

    (A) cures, or provides adequate assurance that the trustee will promptly cure, such default;

    (B) compensates, or provides adequate assurance that the trustee will promptly compensate, a party other than the debtor to such contract or lease, for any actual pecuniary loss to such party resulting from such default; and

    (C) provides adequate assurance of future performance under such contract or lease.

(2) Paragraph (1) of this subsection does not apply to a default that is a breach of a provision relating to—

    (A) the insolvency or financial condition of the debtor at any time before the closing of the case;

    (B) the commencement of a case under this title; or

    (C) the appointment of or taking possession by a trustee in a case under this title or a custodian before such commencement.

(3) For the purposes of paragraph (1) of this subsection and paragraph (2)(B) of subsection (f), adequate assurance of future performance of a lease of real property in a shopping center includes adequate assurance—

    (A) of the source of rent and other consideration due under such lease, and in the case of an assignment, that the financial condition and operating performance of the proposed assignee and its guarantors, if any, shall be similar to the financial condition and operating performance of the debtor and its guarantors, if any, as of the time the debtor became the lessee under the lease;

(B) that any percentage rent due under such lease will not decline substantially;

(C) that assumption or assignment of such lease is subject to all the provisions thereof, including (but not limited to) provisions such as a radius, location, use, or exclusivity provision, and will not breach any such provision contained in any other lease, financing agreement, or master agreement relating to such shopping center; and

(D) that assumption or assignment of such lease will not disrupt any tenant mix or balance in such shopping center.

(4) Notwithstanding any other provision of this section, if there has been a default in an unexpired lease of the debtor, other than a default of a kind specified in paragraph (2) of this subsection, the trustee may not require a lessor to provide services or supplies incidental to such lease before assumption of such lease unless the lessor is compensated under the terms of such lease for any services and supplies provided under such lease before assumption of such lease.

(c) The trustee may not assume or assign an executory contract or unexpired lease of the debtor, whether or not such contract or lease prohibits or restricts assignment of rights or delegation of duties, if—

(1)(A) applicable law excuses a party, other than the debtor, to such contract or lease from accepting performance from or rendering performance to an entity other than the debtor or the debtor in possession, whether or not such contract or lease prohibits or restricts assignment of rights or delegation of duties; and

(B) such party does not consent to such assumption or assignment; or

(2) such contract is a contract to make a loan, or extend other debt financing or financial accommodations, to or for the benefit of the debtor, or to issue a security of the debtor;

(3) such lease is of nonresidential real property and has been terminated under applicable nonbankruptcy law prior to the order for relief; or

(4) such lease is of nonresidential real property under which the debtor is lessee of an aircraft terminal or aircraft gate at an airport at which the debtor is the lessee under one or more additional nonresidential leases of an aircraft terminal or aircraft gate and the trustee, in connection with such assumption or assignment, does not assume all such leases or does not assume and assign all of such leases to the same person, except that the trustee may assume or assign less than all of such leases with the airport operator's written consent.

(d)(1) In a case under chapter 7 of this title, if the trustee does not assume or reject an executory contract or unexpired lease of residential real property or of personal property of the debtor within 60 days after the order for relief, or within such additional time as the court, for cause, within such 60-day period, fixes, then such contract or lease is deemed rejected.

(2) In a case under chapter 9, 11, 12, or 13 of this title, the trustee may assume or reject an executory contract or unexpired lease of residential real property or of personal property of the debtor at any time before the confirmation of a plan but the court, on request of any party to such contract or lease, may order the trustee to determine within a specified period of time whether to assume or reject such contract or lease.

(3) The trustee shall timely perform all the obligations of the debtor, except those specified in section 365(b)(2), arising from and after the order for relief under any unexpired lease of nonresidential real property, until such lease is assumed or rejected, notwithstanding section 503(b)(1) of this title. The court may extend, for cause, the time for performance of any such obligation that arises within 60 days after the date of the order for relief, but the time for performance shall not be extended beyond such 60-day period. This subsection shall not be deemed to affect the trustee's obligations under the provisions of subsection (b) or (f) of this section. Acceptance of any such performance does not constitute waiver or relinquishment of the lessor's rights under such lease or under this title.

(4) Notwithstanding paragraphs (1) and (2), in a case under any chapter of this title, if the trustee does not assume or reject an unexpired lease of nonresidential real property under which the debtor is the lessee within 60 days after the date of the order for relief, or within such additional time as the court, for cause, within such 60-day period, fixes, then such lease is deemed rejected, and the trustee shall immediately surrender such nonresidential real property to the lessor.

(5) Notwithstanding paragraphs (1) and (4) of this subsection, in a case under any chapter of this title, if the trustee does not assume or reject an unexpired lease of nonresidential real property under which the debtor is an affected air carrier that is the lessee of an aircraft terminal or aircraft gate before the occurrence of a termination event, then (unless the court orders the trustee to assume such unexpired leases within 5 days after the termination event), at the option of the airport operator, such lease is deemed rejected 5 days after the occurrence of a termination event and the trustee shall immediately surrender possession of the premises to the airport operator; except that the lease shall not be deemed to be rejected unless the airport operator first waives the right to damages related to the rejection. In the event that the lease is deemed to be rejected under this paragraph, the airport operator shall provide the affected air carrier adequate opportunity after the surrender of the premises to remove the fixtures and equipment installed by the affected air carrier.

(6) For the purposes of paragraph (5) of this subsection and paragraph (f)(1) of this section, the occurrence of a termination event means, with respect to a debtor which is an affected air carrier that is the lessee of an aircraft terminal or aircraft gate—

(A) the entry under section 301 or 302 of this title of an order for relief under chapter 7 of this title;

(B) the conversion of a case under any chapter of this title to a case under chapter 7 of this title; or

(C) the granting of relief from the stay provided under section 362(a) of this title with respect to aircraft, aircraft engines, propellers, appliances, or spare parts, as defined in section 101 of the Federal Aviation Act of 1958 (49 App. U.S.C. 1301), except for property of the debtor found by the court not to be necessary to an effective reorganization.

(7) Any order entered by the court pursuant to paragraph (4) extending the period within which the trustee of an affected air carrier must assume or reject an unexpired lease of nonresidential real property shall be without prejudice to—

(A) the right of the trustee to seek further extensions within such additional time period granted by the court pursuant to paragraph (4); and

(B) the right of any lessor or any other party in interest to request, at any time, a shortening or termination of the period within which the trustee must assume or reject an unexpired lease of nonresidential real property.

(8) The burden of proof for establishing cause for an extension by an affected air carrier under paragraph (4) or the maintenance of a previously granted extension under paragraph (7)(A) and (B) shall at all times remain with the trustee.

(9) For purposes of determining cause under paragraph (7) with respect to an unexpired lease of nonresidential real property between the debtor that is an affected air carrier and an airport operator under which such debtor is the lessee of an airport terminal or an airport gate, the court shall consider, among other relevant factors, whether substantial harm will result to the airport operator or airline passengers as a result of the extension or the maintenance of a previously granted extension. In making the determination of substantial harm, the court shall consider, among other relevant factors, the level of actual use of the terminals or gates which are the subject of the lease, the public interest in actual use of such terminals or gates, the existence of competing demands for the use of such terminals or gates, the effect of the court's extension or termination of the period of time to assume or reject the lease on such debtor's ability to successfully reorganize under chapter 11 of this title, and whether the trustee of the affected air carrier is capable of continuing

to comply with its obligations under section 365(d)(3) of this title.

(e)(1) Notwithstanding a provision in an executory contract or unexpired lease, or in applicable law, an executory contract or unexpired lease of the debtor may not be terminated or modified, and any right or obligation under such contract or lease may not be terminated or modified, at any time after the commencement of the case solely because of a provision in such contract or lease that is conditioned on—

    (A) the insolvency or financial condition of the debtor at any time before the closing of the case;

    (B) the commencement of a case under this title; or

    (C) the appointment of or taking possession by a trustee in a case under this title or a custodian before such commencement.

(2) Paragraph (1) of this subsection does not apply to an executory contract or unexpired lease of the debtor, whether or not such contract or lease prohibits or restricts assignment of rights or delegation of duties, if—

    (A)(i) applicable law excuses a party, other than the debtor, to such contract or lease from accepting performance from or rendering performance to the trustee or to an assignee of such contract or lease, whether or not such contract or lease prohibits or restricts assignment of rights or delegation of duties; and

    (ii) such party does not consent to such assumption or assignment; or

    (B) such contract is a contract to make a loan, or extend other debt financing or financial accommodations, to or for the benefit of the debtor, or to issue a security of the debtor.

(f)(1) Except as provided in subsection (c) of this section, notwithstanding a provision in an executory contract or unexpired lease of the debtor, or in applicable law, that prohibits, restricts, or conditions the assignment of such contract or lease, the trustee may assign such contract or lease under paragraph (2) of this subsection; except that the trustee may not assign an unexpired lease of nonresidential real property under which the debtor is an affected air carrier that is the lessee of an aircraft terminal or aircraft gate if there has occurred a termination event.

(2) The trustee may assign an executory contract or unexpired lease of the debtor only if—

(A) the trustee assumes such contract or lease in accordance with the provisions of this section; and

(B) adequate assurance of future performance by the assignee of such contract or lease is provided, whether or not there has been a default in such contract or lease.

(3) Notwithstanding a provision in an executory contract or unexpired lease of the debtor, or in applicable law that terminates or modifies, or permits a party other than the debtor to terminate or modify, such contract or lease or a right or obligation under such contract or lease on account of an assignment of such contract or lease, such contract, lease, right, or obligation may not be terminated or modified under such provision because of the assumption or assignment of such contract or lease by the trustee.

(g) Except as provided in subsections (h)(2) and (i)(2) of this section, the rejection of an executory contract or unexpired lease of the debtor constitutes a breach of such contract or lease—

(1) if such contract or lease has not been assumed under this section or under a plan confirmed under chapter 9, 11, 12, or 13 of this title, immediately before the date of the filing of the petition; or

(2) if such contract or lease has been assumed under this section or under a plan confirmed under chapter 9, 11, 12, or 13 of this title—

(A) if before such rejection the case has not been converted under section 1112, 1307, or 1208 of this title, at the time of such rejection; or

(B) if before such rejection the case has been converted under section 1112, 1307, or 1208 of this title—

(i) immediately before the date of such conversion, if such contract or lease was assumed before such conversion; or

(ii) at the time of such rejection, if such contract or lease was assumed after such conversion.

(h)(1) If the trustee rejects an unexpired lease of real property of the debtor under which the debtor is the lessor, or a timeshare interest under a timeshare plan under which the debtor is the timeshare interest seller, the lessee or timeshare interest purchaser under such lease or timeshare plan may treat such lease or timeshare plan as terminated by such rejection, where the disaffirmance by the trustee amounts to such a breach as would entitle the lessee or timeshare interest purchaser to treat such lease or timeshare plan as terminated by virtue of its own terms, applicable nonbankruptcy law, or other agreements the lessee or timeshare interest purchaser has made with other parties; or, in the alternative, the lessee or timeshare interest purchaser may remain in possession of the leasehold or timeshare interest under any lease or timeshare plan the term of which has commenced for the balance of such term and for any renewal or extension of such term that is enforceable by such lessee or timeshare interest purchaser under applicable nonbankruptcy law.

(2) If such lessee or timeshare interest purchaser remains in possession as provided in paragraph (1) of this subsection, such lessee or timeshare interest purchaser may offset against the rent reserved under such lease or moneys due for such timeshare interest for the balance of the term after the date of the rejection of such lease or timeshare interest, and any such renewal or extension thereof, any damages occurring after such date caused by the nonperformance of any obligation of the debtor under such lease or timeshare plan after such date, but such lessee or timeshare interest purchaser does not have any rights against the estate on account of any damages arising after such date from such rejection, other than such offset.

(i)(1) If the trustee rejects an executory contract of the debtor for the sale of real property or for the sale of a timeshare interest under a timeshare plan, under which the purchaser is in possession, such purchaser may treat such contract as terminated, or, in the alternative, may remain in possession of such real property or timeshare interest.

(2) if such purchaser remains in possession—

(A) such purchaser shall continue to make all payments due under such contract, but may, offset against such payments any damages occurring after the date of the rejection of such contract caused by the non-performance of any obligation of the debtor after such date, but such purchaser does not have any rights against the estate on account of any damages arising after such date from such rejection, other than such offset; and

(B) the trustee shall deliver title to such purchaser in accordance with the provisions of such contract, but is relieved of all other obligations to perform under such contract.

(j) A purchaser that treats an executory contract as terminated under subsection (i) of this section, or a party whose executory contract to purchase real property from the debtor is rejected and under which such party is not in possession, has a lien on the interest of the debtor in such property for the recovery of any portion of the purchase price that such purchaser or party has paid.

(k) Assignment by the trustee to an entity of a contract or lease assumed under this section relieves the trustee and the estate from any liability for any breach of such contract or lease occurring after such assignment.

(l) If an unexpired lease under which the debtor is the lessee is assigned pursuant to this section, the lessor of the property may require a deposit or other security for the performance of the debtor's obligations under the lease substantially the same as would have been required by the landlord upon the initial leasing to a similar tenant.

(m) For purposes of this section 365 and sections 541(b)(2) and 362(b)(10), leases of real property shall include any rental agreement to use real property.

(n)(1) If the trustee rejects an executory contract under which the debtor is a licensor of a right to intellectual property, the licensee under such contract may elect—

(A) to treat such contract as terminated by such rejection if such rejection by the trustee amounts to such a breach as would entitle the licensee to treat such contract as terminated by virtue of its own terms, applicable nonbankruptcy law, or an agreement made by the licensee with another entity; or

(B) to retain its rights (including a right to to [*sic*] enforce any exclusivity provision of such contract, but excluding any other right under applicable nonbankruptcy law to specific performance of such contract) under such contract and under any agreement supplementary to such contract, to such intellectual property (including any embodiment of such intellectual property to the extent protected by applicable nonbankruptcy law), as such rights existed immediately before the case commenced, for—

(i) the duration of such contract; and

(ii) any period for which such contract may be extended by the licensee as of right under applicable nonbankruptcy law.

(2) If the licensee elects to retain its rights, as described in paragraph (1)(B) of this subsection, under such contract—

(A) the trustee shall allow the licensee to exercise such rights;

(B) the licensee shall make all royalty payments due under such contract for the duration of such contract and for any period described in paragraph (1)(B) of this subsection for which the licensee extends such contract; and

(C) the licensee shall be deemed to waive—

(i) any right of setoff it may have with respect to such contract under this title or applicable nonbankruptcy law; and

(ii) any claim allowable under section 503(b) of this title arising from the performance of such contract.

(3) If the licensee elects to retain its rights, as described in paragraph (1)(B) of this subsection, then on the written request of the licensee the trustee shall—

(A) to the extent provided in such contract, or any agreement supplementary to such contract, provide to the licensee any intellectual property (including such embodiment) held by the trustee; and

(B) not interfere with the rights of the licensee as provided in such contract, or any agreement supplementary to such contract, to such intellectual property (including such embodiment) including any right to obtain such intellectual property (or such embodiment) from another entity.

(4) Unless and until the trustee rejects such contract, on the written request of the licensee the trustee shall—

(A) to the extent provided in such contract or any agreement supplementary to such contract—

(i) perform such contract; or

(ii) provide to the licensee such intellectual property (including any embodiment of such intellectual property to the extent protected by applicable nonbankruptcy law) held by the trustee; and

(B) not interfere with the rights of the licensee as provided in such contract, or any agreement supplementary to such contract, to such intellectual property (including such embodiment), including any right to obtain such intellectual property (or such embodiment) from another entity.

(o) In a case under chapter 11 of this title, the trustee shall be deemed to have assumed (consistent with the debtor's other obligations under section 507), and shall immediately cure any deficit under, any commitment by the debtor to the Federal Deposit Insurance Corporation, the Resolution Trust Corporation, the Director of the Office of Thrift Supervision, the Comptroller of the Currency, or the Board of Governors of the Federal Reserve System, or its predecessors or successors, to maintain the capital of an insured depository institution, and any claim for a subsequent breach of the obligations thereunder shall be entitled to priority under section 507. This subsection shall not extend any commitment that would otherwise be terminated by any act of such an agency.

(p) In this section, "affected air carrier" means an air carrier as defined in section 101(3) of the Federal Aviation Act of 1958, that holds 65 percent or more in number of the aircraft gates at an airport—

(1) which is a Large Air Traffic Hub as defined by the Federal Aviation Administration in Report FAA-AP 92-1, February 1992; and

(2) all of whose remaining aircraft gates are leased or under contract on the date of enactment of this subsection.

Bankruptcy Rule Reference: 6006

Legislative History

Subsection (a) of this section authorizes the trustee, subject to the court's approval, to assume or reject an executory contract or unexpired lease. Though there is no precise definition of what contracts are executory, it generally includes contracts on which performance remains due to some extent on both sides. A note is not usually an executory contract if the only performance that remains is repayment. Performance on one side of the contract would have been completed and the contract is no longer executory.

Because of the sensitive nature of the commodities markets and the special provisions governing commodity broker liquidations in sub-chapter IV of chapter 7, the provisions governing rejection, liquidation, or termination of open contractual commitments under proposed 11 U.S.C. § 765, and the provisions governing distribution in proposed 11 U.S.C. § 767 (a) and (c) [should be section 766] will govern if any conflict between those provisions and the provisions of this section arise.

[*House Report No. 95–595, 95th Cong., 1st Sess. 347 (1977); See Senate Report No. 95–989, 95th Cong., 2d Sess. 58 (1978).*]

Subsections (b), (c), and (d) provide limitations on the trustee's powers. Subsection (b) requires the trustee to cure any default in the contract or lease and to provide adequate assurance of future performance if there has been a default, before he may assume. [*Ed. Note:* And to compensate for pecuniary loss.] This provision does not apply to default under *ipso facto* or bankruptcy clauses, which is a significant departure from present law.

Subsection (b)(3) permits termination of leases entered into prior to the effective date of this title in liquidation cases if certain other conditions are met [*Ed. Note:* This provision was deleted prior to enactment.]

Subsection (b)(4) [*Ed. Note:* The reference should be to subsection (c).] prohibits the trustee's assumption of an executory contract requiring the other party to make a loan or deliver equipment to or to issue a security of the debtor. The purpose of this subsection is to make it clear that a party to a transaction which is based upon the financial strength of a debtor should not be required to extend new credit to the debtor whether in the form of loans, lease financing, or the purchase or discount of notes.

Section (b)(5) [*Ed. Note:* The reference should be to subsection (b)(3).] provides that in lease situations common to shopping centers, protections must be provided for the lessor if the trustee assumes the lease, including protection against decline in percentage rents, breach of agreements with other tenants, and preservation of the tenant mix. Protection for tenant mix will not be required in the office building situation.

[*Senate Report No. 95–989, 95th Cong., 2d Sess. 58–59 (1978).*]

Section 365(b)(3) represents a compromise between H.R. 8200 as passed by the House and the Senate amendment. The provision adopts standards contained in section 365(b)(5) of the Senate amendment to define adequate assurance of future performance of a lease of real property in a shopping center.

Section 365(b)(4) of the House amendment indicates that after default the trustee may not require a lessor to supply services or materials without assumption unless the lessor is compensated as provided in the lease.

[*124 Cong. Rec. H 11,093 (Sept. 28, 1978); S 17,409 (Oct. 6, 1978).*]

Subsection (c) prohibits the trustee from assuming or assigning a contract or lease if applicable nonbankruptcy law excuses the other party from performance to someone other than the debtor, unless the other party consents. This prohibition applies only in the situation in which applicable law excuses the other party from performance independent of any restrictive language in the contract or lease itself. The purpose of this subsection, at least in part, is to prevent the trustee from requiring new advances of money or other property. The section permits the trustee to continue to use and pay for property already advanced, but is not designed to permit the trustee to demand new loans or additional transfers of property under lease commitments.

Thus, under this provision, contracts such as loan commitments and letters of credit are nonassignable, and may not be assumed by the trustee.

[*House Report No. 95–595, 95th Cong., 1st Sess. 348 (1977); See Senate Report No. 95–989, 95th Cong., 2d Sess. 59 (1978).*]

Section 365(c) (2) and (3) likewise represent a compromise between H.R. 8200 as passed by the House and the Senate amendment. Section 365(c)(2) is derived from section 365(b)(4) of the Senate amendment but does not apply to a contract to deliver equipment as provided in the Senate amendment. As contained in the House amendment, the provision prohibits a trustee or debtor in possession from assuming or assigning an executory contract of the debtor to make a loan, or extend other debt financing or financial accommodation, to or for the benefit of the debtor, or the issuance of a security of the debtor.

[*124 Cong. Rec. H 11,093 (Sept. 28, 1978); S 17,409 (Oct. 6, 1978).*]

Subsection (d) places time limits on assumption and rejection. In a liquidation case, the trustee must assume within 60 days (or within an additional 60 days, if the court, for cause, extends the time). If not assumed, the contract or lease is deemed rejected. In a rehabilitation case, the time limit is not fixed in the bill. However, if the other party to the contract or lease requests the court to fix a time, the court may specify a time within which the trustee must act. This provision will prevent parties in contractual or lease relationships with the debtor from being left in doubt concerning their status vis-a-vis the estate.

Subsection (e) invalidates *ipso factor [sic]* or bankruptcy clauses. These clauses, protected under present law, automatically terminate the contract or lease, or permit the other contracting party to terminate the contract or lease, in the event of bankruptcy. This frequently hampers rehabilitation efforts. If the trustee may assume or assign the contract under the limitations imposed by the remainder of the section, then the contract or lease may be utilized to assist in the debtor's rehabilitation or liquidation.

The unenforceability of *ipso facto* or bankruptcy clauses proposed under this section will require the courts to be sensitive to the rights of the nondebtor party to executory contracts and unexpired leases. If the trustee is to assume a contract or lease, the courts will have to insure that the trustee's performance under the contract or lease gives the other contracting party the full benefit of his bargain. An example of the complexity that may arise in these situations and the need for a determination of all aspects of a particular executory contract or unexpired lease is the shopping center lease under which the debtor is a tenant in a shopping center.

A shopping center is often a carefully planned enterprise, and though it consists of numerous individual tenants, the center is planned as a single unit, often subject to a master lease or financing agreement. Under these agreements, the tenant mix in a shopping center may be as important to the lessor as the actual promised rental payments, because certain mixes will attract higher patronage of the stores in the center, and thus a higher rental for the landlord from those stores that are subject to a percentage of gross receipts rental agreement. Thus, in order to assure a landlord of his bargained for exchange, the court would have to consider such factors as the nature of the business to be conducted by the trustee or his assignee, whether that business complies with the requirements of any master agreement, whether the kind of business proposed will generate gross sales in an amount such that the percentage rent specified in the lease is substantially the same as what would have been provided by the debtor, and whether the business proposed to be conducted would result in a breach of other clauses in master agreements relating, for example, to tenant mix and location. [*Ed. Note:* As enacted, much of this is contained in subsection (b)(3).]

This subsection does not limit the application of an *ipso facto* or bankruptcy clause to a new insolvency or receivership after the bankruptcy case is closed. That is, the clause is not invalidated in toto, but merely made inapplicable during the case for the purpose of disporition [*sic*] of the executory contract or unexpired lease.

[*House Report No. 95–595, 95th Cong., 1st Sess. 348–9 (1977); See Senate Report No. 95–989, 95th Cong., 2d Sess. 59 (1978).*]

Section 365(e) is a refinement of comparable provisions contained in the House bill and Senate amendment. Sections 365(e)(1) and (2)(A) restate section 365(e) of H.R. 8200 as passed by the House. Section 365(e)(2)(B) expands the section to permit termination of an executory contract or unexpired lease of the debtor if such contract is a contract to make a loan, or extend other debt financing accommodations, to or for the benefit of the debtor, or for the issuance of a security of the debtor.

Characterization of contracts to make a loan, or extend other debt financing or financial accommodations, is limited to the extension of cash or a line of credit and is not intended to embrace ordinary leases or contracts to provide goods or services with payments to be made over time.

[*124 Cong. Rec. H 11,093 (Sept. 28, 1978); S 17,409–10 (Oct. 6, 1978).*]

Subsection (f) partially invalidates restrictions on assignment of contracts or leases by the trustee to a third party. The subsection imposed two restrictions on the trustee: he must first assume the contract or lease, subject to all the restrictions on assumption found in the section, and adequate assurance of future performance must be provided to the other contracting party. Paragraph (3) of the subsection invalidates contractual provisions that permit termination or modification in the event of an assignment, as contrary to the policy of this subsection.

[*House Report No. 95–595, 95th Cong., 1st Sess. 349 (1977); Senate Report No. 95–989, 95th Cong., 2d Sess. 59 (1978).*]

Section 365(f) is derived from H.R. 8200 as passed by the House. Deletion of language in section 365(f)(3) of the Senate amendment is done as a matter of style. Restrictions with respect to assignment of an executory contract or unexpired lease are superfluous since the debtor may assign an executory contract or unexpired lease of the debtor only if such contract is first assumed under section 364(f)(2)(A) [should be 365] of the House amendment.

[*124 Cong. Rec. H 11,093 (Sept. 28, 1978); S 17,410 (Oct. 6, 1978).*]

Subsection (g) defines the time as of which a rejection of an executory contract or unexpired lease constitutes a breach of contract or lease. Generally, the breach is as of the date immediately preceding the date of the petition. The purpose is to treat rejection claims as prepetition claims. The remainder of the subsection specifies different times for cases that are converted from one chapter to another. The provisions of this subsection are not a substantive authorization to breach or reject an assumed contract. Rather, they prescribe the rules for the allowance of claims in case an assumed contract is breached, or if a case under chapter 11 in which a contract has been assumed is converted to a case under chapter 7 in which the contract is rejected.

Subsection (h) protects real property lessees of the debtor if the trustee rejects an unexpired lease under which the debtor is the lessor (or sublessor). The subsection permits the lessee to remain in possession of the leased property or to treat the lease as terminated by the rejection. The balance of the term of the lease referred to in paragraph (1) will include any renewal terms that are enforceable by the tenant, but not renewal terms if the landlord had an option to terminate. Thus, the tenant will not be deprived of his estate for the term for which he bargained. If the lessee remains in possession, he may offset the rent reserved under the lease against damages caused by the rejection, but does not have any affirmative rights against the estate for any damages after the rejection that result from the rejection.

[*House Report No. 95–595, 95th Cong., 1st Sess. 349 (1977); Senate Report No. 95–989, 95th Cong., 2d Sess. 60 (1978).*]

Section 363(h) [*sic*] of the House amendment represents a modification of section 365(h) of the Senate amendment. The House amendment makes clear that in the case of a bankrupt lessor, a lessee may remain in possession for the balance of the term of a lease and any renewal or extension of the term only to the extent that such renewal or extension may be obtained by the lessee without the permission of the landlord or some third party under applicable nonbankruptcy law.

[*124 Cong. Rec. H 11,093 (Sept. 28, 1978); S 17,410 (Oct. 6, 1978).*]

Subsection (i) gives a purchaser of real property under a land installment sales contract similar protection. The purchaser, if the contract is rejected, may remain in possession or may treat the contract as terminated. If the purchaser remains in possession, he is required to continue to make the payments due, but may offset damages that occur after rejection. The trustee is required to deliver title, but is relieved of all other obligations to perform.

A purchaser that treats the contract as terminated is granted a lien on the property to the extent of the purchase price paid. A party with a contract to purchase land from the debtor has a lien on the property to secure the price already paid, if the contract is rejected and the purchaser is not yet in possession.

Subsection (k) relieves the trustee and the estate of liability for a breach of an assigned contract or lease that occurs after the assignment.

[*House Report No. 95–595, 95th Cong., 1st Sess. 349–50 (1977); Senate Report No. 95–989, 95th Cong., 2d Sess. 60 (1978).*]

[*Ed. Note:* The 1988 amendments (Pub. L. No. 100-506) added subsection (n) to section 365.]

1. New paragraph (n)(1) of subsection 365(n)

The first paragraph of the new Section provides that, in the event an executory contract under which the debtor is a licensor of rights to intellectual property is rejected in the licensor's bankruptcy, the licensee may elect one of two sets of consequences to attach to that rejection. The licensee may treat the rejection as terminating the license, leaving the licensee with its various rights as a contract creditor under the Code. This course of action would be available to the licensee without this bill.

The second alternative which the bill explicitly makes available to the licensee is to elect to retain its rights under the license, as such rights existed immediately before the case commenced. . . . When a bankruptcy court finds rejection of an intellectual property license to be appropriate, if the licensee so elects, the bill protects the licensee's right to the intellectual property as it existed at the time of the filing. If the licensee elects to retain such rights, he is required to continue making all royalty payments due under the rejected license. . . .

* * *

2. New paragraph (n)(2) of subsection 365(n)

Section 365 (n)(2) modifies the rights that a retaining licensee would ordinarily have as the nondebtor party to a contract rejected under section 365. So long as the trustee and its successors in interest allow the licensee to exercise the retention rights set forth in section 365, the licensee

(1) is to make all royalty payments due under the rejected license and any available extension which the licensee elects to exercise and

(2) waives any right to set off damages which it incurred as a result of the trustee's rejection and any claim which it might otherwise be allowed under Section 503(b) of title 11 arising from its performance of the rejected contract.

* * *

3. New paragraphs (n)(3) and (n)(4) of subsection 365(n)

Prior to rejection by the debtor licensor but upon nonperformance by the trustee ((n)(4)), as well as upon rejection by the debtor licensor combined with the licensee's election to retain rights in intellectual property ((n)(3)), the trustee, upon written request by the licensee, as provided in the parties' agreements, shall turn over to the licensee intellectual property held by the trustee and shall not interfere with the licensee's contractual rights to use the intellectual property or to obtain it from a third party. The intellectual property referred to is only that which is in existance at the time of petition filing and not anything which first comes into being post-petition. New paragraphs (n)(3) and (n)(4) do not compel future affirmative performance by the trustee, as distinguished from providing the licensee with access to the existing intellectual property, including the delivery or turnover of any existing items specifically required by the contract, and not interfering with the licensee's rights thereto. . . .

[*Senate Report No. 100-505, 100th Cong., 2d Sess. 8-11 (1988).*]

Comment

Bankruptcy Rule 1007(b)(1), as amended in 1991, provides that, except in a chapter 9 case and unless the court orders otherwise, the debtor shall file "a schedule of executory contracts and unexpired leases."

Bankruptcy Rule 6006 relates to executory contracts and unexpired leases. Subdivision (a) provides that proceedings to assume, reject or assign an executory contract or unexpired lease, other than as part of a plan, are governed by Rule 9014, *i.e.*, commenced by motion rather than by summons and complaint.

Subdivision (b) provides that Rule 9014 (motion practice) governs a proceeding by a party to an executory contract or unexpired lease in a chapter 9, 11, 12, or 13 case, to require the trustee, debtor in possession, or debtor, to determine whether to assume or reject the contract or lease.

Subdivision (c) provides that when a motion is made under subdivision (a) or (b), above, the court shall set a hearing on notice to the other party to the contract or lease, to such other parties in interest as the court directs and, except in a chapter 9 municipality case, to the United States trustee.

1984 Amendments: Section 365 was variously amended to make more difficult the assumption and assignment of shopping center leases and further protect shopping center lessors. These added protections follow:

Paragraph (4), added to section 365(c), referring specifically to a lease of nonresidential real property, provides that if the trustee, in a case under any chapter, does not assume or reject within 60 days after the order for relief, or such other time as the court fixes, the lease is deemed rejected and the trustee must surrender the property to the lessor.

Subsection (c)(3) of section 365 in the case of nonresidential leases of real property, requires the trustee to pay rent and other charges until the lease is assumed or rejected.

While the Code provided for assurance that such provisions will not be "substantially" disrupted, this provision was not always enforced. Accordingly, the word "substantially" was deleted from section 365(b)(3)(C), and subsection (c)(1) was amended to include language to the effect that any assumption or assignment of the lease is subject to all provisions of the lease including provisions such as radius, location, use, or exclusivity.

Apart from these major changes other minor, conforming and clarifying changes were made including, in subsection (b)(3)(A) provisions for assurance of financial and operating performance of any assignee. Subsection (i)(1) was amended by including the rights accorded a timeshare interest upon rejection by the trustee of an executory contract for the sale of a timeshare interest where the purchaser is in possession.

See section 541(b)(2), which provides that an interest of any debtor in a nonresidential lease which terminated at its stated term before commencement of or during the case, is not property of the estate.

See also section 362(b)(10), providing that the automatic stay does not stay an act by a lessor under a nonresidential lease that has terminated before or during commencement of the case, to obtain posession of the property.

Subsection (l) specifies the rights of the lessor of real property when an unexpired lease is assigned pursuant to section 365.

Pursuant to subsection (m), for the purposes of sections 365, 541(b)(2), and 362(b)(10), leases of real property include any rental agreement "to use real property."

Subsections (h)(1), (h)(2) and (i) were amended to specify the rights of a purchaser of a timeshare interest under a timeshare plan under which the debtor is the timeshare interest seller, upon rejection of the timeshare interest by the trustee. *See* section 101 for a definition of "timeshare plan."

1986 Amendments: The 1986 Act brought chapter 12 cases within the ambit of section 365(d)(2) and section 365(g)(2)(A). The words "or an assignee of such contract or lease" were deleted from subsection (c)(1)(A) following the words "or the debtor in possession."

1988 Amendments: Subsection (n) was added by Pub. Law No. 100-506 (1988). The subsection provides for the treatment in bankruptcy of executory contracts concerning "intellectual property" as that term is now defined in section 101(56). (*See also* section 101(57), which defines "mask work.")

Subsection (n) is designed to keep secure the rights of intellectual property licensors and licensees which come under the protection of the Bankruptcy Code. If a trustee rejects an executory contract under which the debtor is licensor of intellectual property, the licensee may elect to terminate the contact or to retain its rights. Until the trustee rejects the contract, on the written request of the licensee, the trustee is obliged to perform the contract and provide the licensee with the intellectual property held by the trustee. Should the licensee elect to retain the contract, the trustee is required to provide the licensee with any intellectual property in the trustee's possession and allow the licensee to exercise all rights under the contract. The licensee is required to pay to the trustee all royalties due under the contract. The amendment of section 365 does not apply to cases commenced prior to the date of its enactment.

1990 Amendments: Section 365 was amended by Pub. L. No. 101-647 (Crime Control Act of 1990; effective on the date of enactment, November 29, 1990). This amendment added subsection (o), relating to the trustee's assumption of the debtor's commitments to various depository institutions.

1992 Amendments: Pub. L. No. 102-365 ("Rail Safety Enforcement and Review Act") was enacted on September 3, 1992. Section 19 of this legislation added new paragraphs (5) to (9) to section 365(d) providing that if the trustee does not assume or reject "an unexpired lease of nonresidential real property under which the debtor is an affected air carrier that is the lessee of an aircraft terminal or aircraft gate before the occurrence of a termination event" the lease is deemed rejected 5 days after the occurrence of such "termination event." Paragraph (6), as added by the Rail Safety Enforcement and Review Act, contains a definition of the term "termination event." Pub. L. No. 102-365 also added paragraph (4) to section 365(c) regarding the partial assumption or assignment of airport leases. Additionally, it amended section 365(f)(1) by adding language prohibiting assignments of leases of aircraft terminals or aircraft gates after a "termination event." Finally, Pub. L. No. 102-365 added section 365(p) defining the term "affected air carrier." The amendments to section 365 made by the Rail Safety Enforcement and Review Act are effective only for 12 months from the date of enactment and shall apply to all proceedings involving an affected air carrier as defined in section 365(p) that are pending during the 12 month period. Within nine months of the date of enactment, the Administrator of the Federal Aviation Administration shall report to the appropriate Senate and House committees on whether the amendments shall apply to proceedings commenced after the initial 12 month period.

Explaining the amendments to section 365, Congress by way of a preamble to the changes made the following findings:

(1) there are major airports served by an air carrier that has leased a substantial majority of the airport's gates;

(2) the commerce in the region served by such a major airport can be disrupted if the air carrier that leases most of its gates enters bankruptcy and either discontinues or materially reduces service; and

(3) it is important that such airports be empowered to continue service in the event of such a disruption.

Case Annotations

In considering whether a chapter 11 debtor should be granted permission to reject a collective bargaining agreement, the bankruptcy court, cognizant of the favored status that Congress has given labor agreements, should permit rejection "if the debtor can show that the collective bargaining agreement burdens the estate, and that after careful scrutiny, the equities balance in favor of rejecting the labor contract. . . . Since the policy of Chapter 11 is to permit successful rehabilitation of debtors, rejection should not be permitted without a finding that that policy would be served by such action." NLRB v. Bildisco & Bildisco, 465 U.S. 513, 104 S. Ct. 1188, 79 L. Ed. 2d 482, 9 C.B.C.2d 1219 (1984).

A creditor who does not have an interest in a lease does not have standing to raise a section 365(d)(4) contention that the property covered in the lease is not part of the bankruptcy estate. Matter of James Wilson Associates, 965 F.2d 160, 26 C.B.C.2d 1673 (7th Cir. 1992).

Whether material unperformed obligations remain under a contract and whether that contract is severable are issues that must be determined under state law before a contract can be defined as executory for purposes of section 365 of the Code. *In re* Qintex Entertainment, Inc., 950 F.2d 1492, 26 C.B.C.2d 143 (9th Cir. 1991).

A flooring agreement between a debtor and a lender that, in essence, provides the debtor's guarantee of loans made to purchasers of the debtor's products, is a financial accommodation contract and, therefore, is not assumable under section 365 of the Code because although no loans are made directly to the debtor, the contract operates for the benefit of the debtor. *In re* Sun Runner Marine, Inc., 945 F.2d 1089, 25 C.B.C.2d 1054 (9th Cir. 1991).

A 99 year lease which provides for the rent to be prepaid over the initial three years, and that shifts the allocation of responsibilities from landlord to tenant is not subject to section 365(d)(4) because the terms of the lease make the economic substance of the transaction closer to a sale than a lease. The lease cannot be rejected by operation of law, despite the trustee's failure to move within the statutory time limit. *In re* International Trade Admin. and Home & City Savings Bank, 936 F.2d 744, 24 C.B.C.2d 2123 (2d Cir. 1991).

A joint venture contract which is silent as to automatic termination and as to rights to cure a breach, entitles the debtor, pursuant to section 365(b)(1)(A), to cure, or provide adequate assurances that it will promptly cure, a default so that the contract may be assumed. *In re* Sigel & Co., Ltd., 923 F.2d 142, 24 C.B.C.2d 869 (9th Cir. 1991).

The existence of a master lease is not determinative in the analysis of what defines a shopping center within the meaning of section 365(b)(3), nor does a single unit shopping center need to be an enclosed mall as it may be a cluster of three relatively contiguous buildings. *In re* Joshua Slocum Ltd., 922 F.2d 1081, 24 C.B.C.2d 581 (3d Cir. 1990).

In an action by an attorney to recover attorney's fees from the debtor based on a prepetition fee contract that provides for an hourly/ contingent fee split, the bankruptcy court should conduct the following analysis: 1) acknowledgement of the debtor's breach of the fee contract under section 365(g); 2) assessment of damages under applicable state law, which would allow for recovery of both hourly and contingent fees; 3) determination under section 502(b)(4) and attendant federal bankruptcy standards of the reasonableness of the state law damages claim; and 4) reduction of the attorney's claim by whatever extent it is deemed excessive. *In re* Western Real Estate Fund, Inc., 922 F.2d 522, 24 C.B.C.2d 1012 (10th Cir. 1990).

A bankruptcy court may grant multiple extensions of the time within which a lessee must assume or reject its leases of nonresidential real property so long as a motion to extend is brought prior to the expiration of the period previously extended and as long as there is "cause" for granting the extension. In the Matter of American Healthcare Management, Inc., 900 F.2d 827, 22 C.B.C.2d 1740 (5th Cir. 1990).

Any executory contract for personal services of the debtor which is not assumed either in the course of the proceedings or in the reorganization plan approved by the court is automatically rejected. In the Matter of Taylor, 913 F.2d 102, 23 C.B.C.2d 1035 (3d Cir. 1990).

As part of a reorganization plan, a debtor in possession, subject to approval by the court, may assume certain executory contracts but, when a debtor in possession does assume an executory contract, it takes the contract *cum onere*, that is, subject to existing burdens. U.S. Dept. of Air Force v. Carolina Parachute Corp., 907 F.2d 1469, 23 C.B.C.2d 620 (4th Cir. 1990).

A defaulting debtor's signed petition recognizing an ongoing obligation to maintain unexpired leases and to pay all obligations with regard to those leases does not provide the adequate compensation or assurances required by section 365(b)(1). Sea Harvest v. Riviera Land Co., 868 F.2d 1077, 20 C.B.C.2d 1269 (9th Cir. 1989).

A court may grant consecutive extensions of time for a debtor to assume or reject a lease even after the first sixty days of the filing of a chapter 11 petition if cause to do so exists. *In re* Victoria Station Inc., 875 F.2d 1380, 21 C.B.C.2d 483 (9th Cir. 1989).

A land sale contract is executory in nature when some performance remains due by both parties. It is not relevant whether it is the seller or the purchaser who files for bankruptcy. *In re* Terrell, 892 F.2d 469, 21 C.B.C.2d 1452 (6th Cir. 1989).

If the parties to a lease agreement never intended it to create a true landlord/tenant relationship, the provisions of section 365(d) are inapplicable. When the debtor's obligation to pay rent on the property ceased, although the right to use the property until ultimate termination of the lease remained, the financial obligations remaining were *de minimus,* and the failure to meet any of the remaining obligations under the lease would not entitle the landlord to reclaim the property, the lease does not qualify as an executory contract. City of San Francisco Market Corp. v. Walsh (*In re* Moreggia & Sons), 852 F.2d 1179, 19 C.B.C.2d 949 (9th Cir. 1988).

The failure to make payments under subsection 365(d)(3) constitutes simply one element to be considered, along with other relevant factors, in determining whether cause exists under section 365(d)(4) to extend the 60-day period for assumption or rejection. Southwest Aircraft Servs. v. City of Long Beach and Atl. Aviation (*In re* Southwest Aircraft Servs., Inc.), 831 F.2d 848, 17 C.B.C.2d 976 (9th Cir. 1987), *cert. denied,* 487 U.S. 1206, 108 S. Ct. 2848, 101 L. Ed. 2d 885 (1988).

Even if an agreement or contract is of the type that cannot be assumed by a debtor, it can only be terminated pursuant to the terms of the automatic stay provisions of the Code. Computer Communications, Inc. v. Codex Corp. (*In re* Computer Communications, Inc.), 824 F.2d 725, 17 C.B.C.2d 556 (9th Cir. 1987).

A stipulation that allowed withholding to cure a debtor's default under a contract need not be formally labeled an "assumption of contract" for the bankruptcy court's approval to be considered an approval of an assumption of contract when the intent of the parties, based on the complaints and responses filed, is undisputed. Lindsey v. Department of Labor (*In re* Harris Management Co., Inc.), 791 F.2d 1412, 14 C.B.C.2d 1395 (9th Cir. 1986).

A debtor entering into a postpetition stipulation pursuant to section 1110(a) is subject to the normal requirements of section 365 except that it is not liable for the entire executory contract. Gatx Leasing Corp. v. Airlift Int'l, Inc. (*In re* Airlift Int'l, Inc.), 761 F.2d 1503, 12 C.B.C.2d 1266 (11th Cir. 1985).

When a seller stops goods in transit the underlying contract is executory, and the contract is no less executory when the seller chooses not to suspend performance, but tenders performance subsequent to the filing of the bankruptcy petition; upon postpetition performance, whether or not the contract is assumed; the seller is entitled to administrative expense priority for the value of its goods. Collingwood Grain, Inc. v. Coast Trading Co. (*In re* Coast Trading Co.), 744 F.2d 686, 11 C.B.C.2d 790 (9th Cir. 1984).

Section 365(c)(1)(A) by its terms does not limit its operative effects only to personal service contracts but refers generally to contracts that are not assignable under nonbankruptcy law. *In re* Pioneer Ford Sales, Inc., 729 F.2d 27, 10 C.B.C.2d 524 (1st Cir. 1984).

A bankruptcy court order requiring that a debtor's supplier continue to perform is not a court-approved assumption of the supplier's executory contract since it is not an express order mandating the contract's assumption, but is rather directed toward maintaining the status quo. Data-Link Systems, Inc. v. Whitcomb & Keller Mortgage Co. (In the Matter of Whitcomb & Keller Mortgage Co.), 715 F.2d 375, 9 C.B.C.2d 312 (7th Cir. 1983).

Section 365(c) bars the assignment of the debtor's lease of airport terminal space when the lessor (the United States) has reserved the right to use, occupy and lease the space under applicable law. Pension Benefit Guaranty Corp. v. Braniff Airways, Inc. (*In re* Braniff Airways, Inc.), 700 F.2d 935, 8 C.B.C.2d 522 (5th Cir. 1983).

References

2 *Collier on Bankruptcy* ch. 365 (Matthew Bender 15th ed.).

1 *Collier Bankruptcy Manual* ch. 365 (Matthew Bender 3d ed.).

4 *Collier Bankruptcy Practice Guide* ch. 68 (Matthew Bender).

Andrew, *Executory Contracts in Bankruptcy: Understanding "Rejection,"* 59 Colo. L. Rev. 845 (1988).

Assumption of Unexpired Leases Under Section 365(d)(4), 1986 B.Y.U. L. Rev. 1121.

Bloom and Singer, *The Revised Section 365: Lessor's Panacea?,* 63 Am. Bankr. L.J. 199 (1989).

Brown, Hansen and Salerno, *Technology Licenses Under Section 365(n) of the Banktuptcy Code: The Protections Afforded the Technology User,* 95 Com. L.J. 170 (1990).

Buschmann, III, *Benefits and Burdens: Post-Petition Performance of Unassumed Executory Contracts,* 5 Bankr. Dev. J. 341 (1988).

Comment, *The Enforceability of Use Restrictions in Assignments of Non-Shopping Center Nonresidential Leases Under the Bankruptcy Law,* 57 Temp. L.Q. 821 (1984).

Comment, *Section 365 of the Bankruptcy Code: Out of Balance After 1984?,* 1986 Utah L. Rev. 781.

Comment, *Whether to Assume or Reject a Lease — The Section 365 Dilemma,* 7 Bankr. Dev. J. 125 (1990).

Kurtz, Walter and Wells, *Rejection of Collective Bargaining Agreements in Bankruptcy: A Review, Update and Guide for Debtors,* 96 Com. L.J. 31 (1991).

Luna and Dobberteen, *The Assumption or Rejection of Commercial Leases in Bankruptcy Proceedings,* 9 L.A. Law 22 (1987).

Note, *Treatment of Time-Share Interests Under the Bankruptcy Code,* 59 Ind. L.J. 223 (1984).

Pedowitz, *The Effect of Bankruptcy or Insolvency on Real Estate Transactions—An Overview,* 20 Real Prop., Prob. & Tr. J. 25 (1985).

Roswick and McEvily, *Use Clauses in Shopping Center Leases: The Effect of the Tenant's Bankruptcy,* 14 Real. Est. L.J. 3 (Summer 1985).

Taubenfeld and Hale, *The Effect of a Lessee's Bankruptcy on a Real Property Lease,* 6 Prac. Real Est. Law. 13 (1990).

Weg, *The Secured Creditor's Right to Rents From Real Property,* 17 Real Est. L.J. 29 (1988).

Weintraub and Resnick, *From the Bankruptcy Courts: What is an Executory Contract? A Challenge to the Countryman Test,* 15 U.C.C. L.J. 273 (1983).

Westbrook, *A Functional Analysis of Executory Contracts,* 74 Minn. L. Rev. 227 (1989).

Wines, *An Overview of the 1984 Bankruptcy Amendments: Some Modest Protections for Labor Agreements,* 36 Lab. L.J. 911 (1985).

SECTION 366 (11 U.S.C. § 366)

§ 366. Utility service.

(a) Except as provided in subsection (b) of this section, a utility may not alter, refuse, or discontinue service to, or discriminate against, the trustee or the debtor solely on the basis of the commencement of a case under this title or that a debt owed by the debtor to such utility for service rendered before the order for relief was not paid when due.

(b) Such utility may alter, refuse, or discontinue service if neither the trustee nor the debtor, within 20 days after the date of the order for relief, furnishes adequate assurance of payment, in the form of a deposit or other security, for service after such date. On request of a party in interest and after notice and a hearing, the court may order reasonable modification of the amount of the deposit or other security necessary to provide adequate assurance of payment.

Legislative History

This section gives debtors protection from a cut-off of service by a utility because of the filing of a bankruptcy case. This section is intended to cover utilities that have some special position with respect to the debtor, such as an electric company, gas supplier, or telephone company that is a monopoly in the area so that the debtor cannot easily obtain comparable service from another utility. The utility may not alter, refuse, or discontinue service because of the nonpayment of a bill that would be discharged in the bankruptcy case. [*Ed. Note:* The section is not limited to dischargeable debts.] Subsection (b) protects the utility company by requiring the trustee or the debtor to provide, as soon as practicable, not to exceed 30 days, adequate assurance of payment for service provided after the date of the petition. This subsection will prevent a utility from terminating service until there is a court hearing, if there is a dispute over what is adequate assurance. The court is required, however, to hold the hearing as soon as practicable, but in any event within 30 days after the commencement of the case. If an estate is sufficiently liquid, the guarantee of an administrative expense priority may constitute adequate assurance of payment for future services. It will not be necessary to have a deposit in every case.

[*House Report No. 95–595, 95th Cong., 1st Sess. 350 (1977); See Senate Report No. 95–989, 95th Cong., 2d Sess. 60 (1978).*]

Section 366 of the House amendment represents a compromise between comparable provisions contained in H.R. 8200 as passed by the House and the Senate amendment. Subsection (a) is modified so that the applicable date is the date of the order for relief rather than the date of the filing of the petition. Subsection (b) contains a similar change but is otherwise derived from section 366(b) of the Senate amendment, with the exception that a time period for continued service of 20 days rather than 10 days is adopted.

[*124 Cong. Rec. H 11,093 (Sept. 28, 1978); S 17,410 (Oct. 6, 1978).*]

Comment

There was no provision in the Act comparable to section 366. But this area of bankruptcy law has been the subject of considerable case law. It has been said that an officer of the court operating the debtor's business may be required to make a cash deposit or furnish suitable guarantee before receiving electric, gas or telephone service. *See* Matter of Burbank Corp., 48 F. Supp. 172 (S.D. Cal. 1942). But a utility may not require payment of accumulated obligations of the bankrupt for pre-bankruptcy services as a condition to further service.

1984 Amendments: The 1984 amendments merely made a clarifying change in section 366.

Case Annotations

The Code does not expressly require a utility company to seek the protection of a security deposit as a prerequisite to recovering administrative expenses pursuant to section 506(c). In the Matter of Delta Towers, Ltd., 924 F.2d 74, 24 C.B.C.2d 1431 (5th Cir. 1991).

Since section 366(b) does not control the procedure by which utility termination may occur, it does not preempt state and municipal procedural regulations for such terminations. Robinson v. Michigan Consol. Gas Co., Inc., 918 F.2d 579, 24 C.B.C.2d 49 (6th Cir. 1990).

Section 366 expressly authorizes a utility to request a debtor to furnish adequate assurance of payment in the form of a security deposit and allows the utility to discontinue service if such a deposit is not provided within 20 days after the order for relief. *In re* Hanratty, 907 F.2d 1418, 23 C.B.C.2d 1043 (3d Cir. 1990).

In a chapter 7 case, the appropriate course for a utility, upon the nonpayment of postpetition bills, is to seek termination of services, not to seek an increased amount of security under section 366(b). Begley v. Philadelphia Electric Co., 760 F.2d 46, 12 C.B.C.2d 1000 (3d Cir. 1985).

The phrase "adequate assurance of payment" in section 366(b) does not require an absolute guarantee of payment so long as the utility is protected from an unreasonable risk of nonpayment which must be determined from the facts and circumstances of each case. *In re* Keydata Corp., 4 C.B.C.2d 1018 (1st Cir., B.A.P., 1981).

A prepetition utility deposit may not be used as security for postpetition payments when it is already being used as security for prepetition debts. *In re* Utica Floor Maintenance Co., 8 C.B.C.2d 157 (N.D.N.Y. 1982).

A utility sought to force a debtor to assume or reject a utility service contract under section 365(d). The court held that the electric service agreement was a contract governed by both section 366 as well as 365 and the utility could not force the debtor to pay prepetition debts as a condition of assumption, due to the protection afforded by section 366(a). *In re* Monroe Well Services, Inc., 18 C.B.C.2d 607 (B. Ct., E.D. Pa. 1988).

A debtor who has a history of prompt and complete payments or has substantial unencumbered assets, such that payment of all administrative claims is virtually assured, may not have to give the utility company a deposit to meet the adequate assurance requirements of the Code. *In re* Penn Jersey Corp., 16 C.B.C.2d 1543 (B. Ct., E.D. Pa. 1987).

Adequate assurance of payment can be requested by a utility only once in a bankruptcy case, *i.e.*, after the order for relief, even if the case is later converted from chapter 13 to chapter 7. Allen v. Philadelphia Elec. Co. (*In re* Allen), 16 C.B.C.2d 527 (B. Ct., E.D. Pa. 1987).

When a utility supplier acts as the middleman or conduit between the utility provider and the debtor as user of the utility service, its request for a security deposit from the debtor comes within the parameters of section 366; the amount of the deposit should bear a reasonable relationship to expected or anticipated utility consumption by a debtor. *In re* Coastal Dry Dock & Repair Corp., 15 C.B.C.2d 320 (B. Ct., E.D.N.Y. 1986).

References

2 *Collier on Bankruptcy* ch. 366 (Matthew Bender 15th ed.).

1 *Collier Bankruptcy Manual* ch. 366 (Matthew Bender 3d ed.).

2 *Collier Bankruptcy Practice Guide* ch. 39 (Matthew Bender).

Kimmelman, *"Let There Be Light"? The Pitfalls and Possibilities for Utilities Under the Bankruptcy Code,* 57 Am. Bankr. L.J. 155 (1983).

Note, *Bankruptcy Code Section 366: Balancing a Utility's Right to Terminate Against a Debtor's Fresh Start,* 59 Temple L.Q. 1011 (1986).

CHAPTER 5

Creditors, the Debtor, and the Estate

SUBCHAPTER I

Creditors and Claims

SECTION 501 (11 U.S.C. § 501)

§ 501. Filing of proofs of claims or interests.

(a) A creditor or an indenture trustee may file a proof of claim. An equity security holder may file a proof of interest.

(b) If a creditor does not timely file a proof of such creditor's claim, an entity that is liable to such creditor with the debtor, or that has secured such creditor, may file a proof of such claim.

(c) If a creditor does not timely file a proof of such creditor's claim, the debtor or the trustee may file a proof of such claim.

(d) A claim of a kind specified in section 502(e)(2), 502(f), 502(g), 502(h) or 502(i) of this title may be filed under subsection (a), (b), or (c) of this section the same as if such claim were a claim against the debtor and had arisen before the date of the filing of the petition.

Bankruptcy Rule References: 3001, 3002, 3003, 3004, 3005 and 5005

Legislative History

This section governs the means by which creditors and equity security holders present their claims or interests to the court. Subsection (a) permits a creditor to file a proof of claim or interest. An indenture trustee representing creditors may file a proof of claim on behalf of the creditors he represents.

This subsection is permissive only, and does not require filing of a proof of claim by any creditor. It permits filing where some purpose would be served, such as where a claim that appears on a list filed under proposed 11 U.S.C. § 924 or 1111 was incorrectly stated or listed as disputed, contingent, or unliquidated, where a creditor with a lien is undersecured and asserts a claim for the balance of the debt owed him (his unsecured claim, as determined under proposed 11 U.S.C. § 506(a)), or in a liquidation case where there will be a distribution of assets to the holders of allowed claims. In other instances, such as in no-asset liquidation cases, in situations where a secured creditor does not assert any claim against the estate and a determination of his claims is not requested under proposed 11 U.S.C. § 506(d), or in situations where the claim asserted would be subordinated and the creditor would not recover from the estate in any event, filing of a proof of claim may simply not be necessary. The Rules of Bankruptcy Procedure and practice under the law will guide creditors as to when filing is necessary and when it may be dispensed with. In general, however, unless a claim is listed in a chapter 9 or chapter 11 case and allowed as a result of the list, a proof of claim will be a prerequisite to allowance for unsecured claims, [*Ed. Note:* This statement should not be limited to unsecured claims; *see* § 506(d).] including priority claims and the unsecured portion of a claim asserted by the holder of a lien.

The Rules of Bankruptcy Procedure will set the time limits, the form, and the procedure for filing, which will determine, whether claims are timely or tardily filed. The Rules governing time limits for filing proofs of claims will continue to apply under section 405(d) of the bill. These provide a six-month bar date for the filing of tax claims. In light of the difficult administrative burden on taxing authorities, especially the Internal Revenue Service, in dealing with a bankrupt taxpayer and being required to prepare and file a tax claim, it is anticipated that any amendment to the Rules of Bankruptcy Procedure will not deprive taxing authorities of this amount of time to file proofs of claims.

Subsection (b) permits a codebtor, surety, or guarantor to file a proof of claim on behalf of the creditor to which he is liable if the creditor does not timely file a proof of claim.

In liquidation and individual repayment plan cases, the trustee or the debtor may file a proof of claim if the creditor does not timely file. The purpose of this subsection is mainly to protect the debtor if the creditor's claim is nondischargeable. If the creditor does not file, there would be no distribution on the claim, and the debtor would have a greater debt to repay after the case is closed than if the claim were paid in part or in full in the case or under the plan.

Subsection (d) governs the filing of claims of the kinds specified in subsections (f), (g), (h), (i), or (j) of proposed 11 U.S.C. § 502. The separation of this provision from the other claim filing provisions in this section is intended to indicate that claims of the kind of specified, which do not become fixed or do not arise until after the commencement of the case, must be treated differently for filing purposes such as the bar date for filing claims. The Rules will provide for later filing of claims of these kinds.

[*House Report No. 95–595, 95th Cong., 1st Sess. 351 (1977); Senate Report No. 95–989, 95th Cong., 2d Sess. 61 (1978).*]

The House amendment adopts section 501(b) of the Senate amendment leaving the Rules of Bankruptcy Procedure free to determine where a proof of claim must be filed.

Section 501(c) expands language contained in section 501(c) of the House bill and Senate amendment to permit the debtor to file a proof of claim if a creditor does not timely file a proof of the creditor's claim in a case under title 11.

The House amendment deletes section 501(e) of the Senate amendment as a matter to be left to the rules of bankruptcy procedure. It is anticipated that the rules will enable governmental units, like other creditors, to have a reasonable time to file proofs of claim in bankruptcy cases.

For purposes of section 501, a proof of "interest" includes the interest of a general or limited partner in a partnership, the interest of a proprietor in a sole proprietorship, or the interest of a common or preferred stockholder in a corporation.

[*124 Cong. Rec. H 11,093 (Sept. 28, 1978); S 17,410 (Oct. 6, 1978).*]

Comment

Bankruptcy Rule 3001 relates to proofs of claim generally and Rule 3002 deals with the filing of proofs of claim or interest. Both rules were amended by the 1991 Amendments.

Rule 3001(a) provides that a proof of claim is a written statement of the creditor's claim. A proof of claim should conform substantially to Official Form 10.

Subdivision (b) requires a proof to be executed by the creditor or his authorized agent except as provided in Rules 3004 and 3005 (which permit the filing of a claim on behalf of a creditor who has failed to file).

Subdivision (c) provides that when a claim or interest is founded upon a writing, the original or a *duplicate* shall be filed with the claim (unless lost or destroyed, in which case a statement of the circumstances thereof shall be filed with the claim).

Subdivision (d) requires that a claim for a security interest in property be accompanied by evidence of perfection of the security interest.

Subdivision (e), dealing with transferred claims, was substantially revised in 1991. Paragraph (1) deals with the transfer of claims other than for security before proof of the claim has been filed. Paragraph (2) deals with such transfers, other than ones involving claims based on publicly traded notes, bonds or debentures, after proof of the claim has been filed. Paragraph (3) relates to a claim (other than one based on a publicly traded note, bond or debenture) transferred for security *before* the claim has been filed. Paragraph (4) relates to such transfers *after* the proof of claim has been filed. Paragraph (5) requires at least 30 days notice of a hearing on objections or motions made pursuant to this subdivision. The Advisory Committee Note to subdivision (e) states that it is amended to limit the court's role to the adjudication of disputes regarding transfers of claims. The Note further states that it is not intended either to encourage or discourage postpetition transfers of claims or to affect any remedies otherwise available under nonbankruptcy law to a transferor or transferee such as for misrepresentation in connection with the transfer of a claim.

Subdivision (f) provides that a proof of claim executed and filed according to the rules constitutes prima facie evidence of the validity and amount of the claim.

Subdivision (g) provides that a warehouse receipt, scale ticket, or similar document of the type routinely issued as evidence of title by a grain storage facility, as defined in section 557, shall constitute prima facie evidence of the validity and amount of a claim of ownership of a quantity of grain.

Bankruptcy Rule 3002, relating to the filing of claims or interests, provides in subdivision (a) thereof that in order for an unsecured claim or an equity security interest to be allowed, a creditor or equity security holder must file a claim or proof of interest in accordance with the rule. (Rule 3003 contains special provisions for filing proofs of claim or equity security interest in a chapter 9 or 11 case. A secured claim need not be filed or allowed under sections 502 or 506(d) unless a party in interest requests determination and allowance under section 506. Rules 3004 and 3005 authorize the filing of claims by a debtor or trustee and by a codebtor of the debtor.)

Subdivision (b) requires the proof of claim or interest to be filed in accordance with Rule 5005, *i.e.,* with the clerk in the district where the case is pending. The judge may permit the claim to be filed with him in which case he is to note thereon the filing date and forward it to the clerk.

Subdivision (c) provides that a claim in a chapter 7, 12 or 13 case must be filed *within 90 days* after the first date set for the meeting of creditors held pursuant to section 341(a). There are six exceptions to the 90 day requirement: (1) the United States, a state or a subdivision thereof may move before expiration of the 90 day period for an extension; (2) in the interest of justice and if it will not unduly delay the administration of the case, the court may extend the time for filing a claim by an infant or incompetent or the representative of either; (3) an unsecured claim that arises because of a judgment for the recovery of money or property or because of a judgment denying or avoiding rights in property, may be filed within 30 days after such judgment becomes final. If the judgment imposes a liability or a duty which is not satisfied or performed within such period, the claim may not be allowed; (4) a claim arising from the rejection of an executory contract or unexpired lease may be filed within such time as the court directs; (5) when creditors were notified that there would be no dividend and subsequently payment of a dividend appears possible, the clerk is to notify creditors of that fact and that they may file claims within 90 days after the mailing of the notice; and (6) if all allowed claims have been paid in full in a chapter

7 case and a surplus remains, the court may grant a fixed extension of time for nonfiling creditors to file against the surplus.

Bankruptcy Rule 3003 relates *only* to the filing of claims or equity security interests in chapter 9 or 11 cases. (Subdivision (a).)

Subdivision (b)(1) provides that the schedule of liabilities filed pursuant to section 521(1) of the Code constitutes prima facie evidence of the validity and amount of the claims of creditors whose claims are not scheduled as disputed, contingent, or unliquidated. Unless required to do so under subdivision (c)(2), it is not necessary for a creditor or equity security holder to file proof of claim or interest.

Subdivision (b)(2) provides that the list of equity shareholders filed under Rule 1007(a)(3) constitutes prima facie evidence of the validity and amount of the equity security holders' interests and the holders thereof need not file proofs of claim.

Subdivision (c)(1) permits any creditor or indenture trustee to file a proof of claim within the time fixed by the court under subdivision (c)(3).

Subdivision (c)(2) requires a creditor or equity security holder whose claim or interest is not scheduled or is scheduled as disputed, contingent, or unliquidated to file a proof of claim or interest within the time fixed by the court (subdivision (c)(3)) and upon failure to do so, such creditor shall not be treated as a creditor for purposes of voting and distribution.

Subdivision (c)(3) provides that the court shall fix a time within which proofs of claim or interest may be filed and authorizes the court to extend such time. The 1991 Amendments added a provision to this paragraph that notwithstanding the expiration of such time, a proof of claim may be filed to the extent and under the conditions stated in Rule 3002(c)(2), (c)(3), and (c)(4). The amendment permits the late filing of claims by infants or incompetent persons under the same circumstances that permit late filing in cases under chapters 7, 12, and 13.

Subdivision (c)(4) provides that a proof of claim or interest executed and filed in accordance with this subdivision (c) shall supersede any scheduling of that claim or interest under section 521(1).

Subdivision (c)(5) provides that an indenture trustee may file a claim on behalf of all known or unknown securities issued pursuant to the trust instrument.

Subdivision (d) provides that for the purposes of Rules 3017, 3018, and 3021 and for receiving notices, an entity not a record holder of a security may file a statement of facts which entitle him to be treated as the record holder. Any party in interest may file objection to the statement.

Bankruptcy Rule 3004 conforms with section 501(c), and provides that if a creditor fails to file a claim on or before the date of the meeting of creditors, the debtor or trustee may do so in the name of the creditor within 30 days after expiration of the time for filing claims prescribed by Rule 3002(c) or 3003(c). The clerk must forthwith mail notice of the filing to the creditor, the debtor and the trustee. The creditor may thereafter file a proof pursuant to Rule 3002 or 3003, which proof supersedes the proof filed by the debtor or trustee.

Bankruptcy Rule 3005 provides that if a creditor has not filed a proof of claim pursuant to Rule 3002 or 3003(c), an entity that may be liable on a debt of the debtor, including a surety, guarantor, indorser, or other codebtor, may file in the name of the creditor of the debtor.

1984 Amendments: A purely technical change was made in section 501(d).

Case Annotations

There are no administrative remedies which must be satisfied by a debtor in order to obtain an award of attorney's fees against the IRS for filing an unjustified proof of claim. *In re* Brickell Inv. Corp., 922 F.2d 696, 24 C.B.C.2d 731 (11th Cir. 1991).

A class representative may prosecute a class action suit on behalf of anyone similarly situated who has failed to file a claim form in the chapter 7 case. Such actions are not excluded in bankruptcy cases by virtue of the nonexhaustive list of representative filings in section 501. In the Matter of American Reserve Corp., 840 F.2d 487, 18 C.B.C.2d 501 (7th Cir. 1988).

A request for relief from the automatic stay, together with documents clearly evidencing a creditor's intent to hold the debtor's estate liable and detailing the nature and contingent amount of the claim, constitute an amendable informal proof of claim. Pizza of Hawaii, Inc. v. Shakey's, Inc. (In the Matter of Pizza of Hawaii, Inc.), 761 F.2d 1374, 12 C.B.C.2d 1227 (9th Cir. 1985).

For a document to constitute an informal proof of claim, it must state an explicit demand showing the nature and amount of the claim against the estate and evidence an intent to hold the debtor liable; an informal proof of claim need not appear, nor have been intended to appear, on a bankruptcy court's record or files. Sambo's Restaurants, Inc. v. Wheeler (*In re* Sambo's Restaurants, Inc.), 754 F.2d 811, 12 C.B.C.2d 173 (9th Cir. 1985).

Notice by publication of a claims bar order requiring individual proofs of claim to be filed by a certain date is sufficient notice to non-holding purchasers of a debtor's debentures and satisfies the requirements of due process of law. In the Matter of GAC Corp., 681 F.2d 1295, 6 C.B.C.2d 1430 (11th Cir. 1982).

While a state may proceed with the administration of workers' compensation claims brought by the employees of a debtor, a claim must be filed in bankruptcy court for there to be any satisfaction against the debtor's estate. *In re* Mansfield Tire & Rubber Co., 660 F.2d 1108, 5 C.B.C.2d 204 (6th Cir. 1981).

An amended proof of claim filed after a chapter 13 plan is confirmed and after the claims have been allowed does not automatically become an allowed claim as the amending party must either move for reconsideration of the claims under Bankruptcy Rule 3008, or take other appropriate action. Matter of Carr, 26 C.B.C.2d 636 (B. Ct., D. Neb. 1991).

Section 501 and Bankruptcy Rule 3004 in effect empower a debtor to create an actual controversy, thereby giving the bankruptcy court subject matter jurisdiction, by filing a proof of claim on behalf of a creditor and then opposing allowance of the claim that the debtor had filed on behalf of the creditor. *In re* Kilen, 25 C.B.C.2d 326 (B. Ct., N.D. Ill. 1991).

The scheduling of claims within a chapter 7 case does not constitute the filing of claims, formal or informal, pursuant to section 501, otherwise, there would be no claims deadline and the bankruptcy rule requiring the filing of proofs of claims in chapter 7 cases would have no meaning. *In re* Poor, 24 C.B.C.2d 2111 (B. Ct., M.D. La. 1991).

A creditor with a secured claim that devolves into an undersecured or unsecured claim must timely file an amended, or supplemental, proof of claim, or some otherwise legally sufficient notice of same to the trustee in order to be treated as an unsecured creditor of the estate and thereby receive a *pro rata* distribution of the estate proceeds. *In re* Padget, 24 C.B.C.2d 451 (B. Ct., D. Colo. 1990).

A debtor utilizing Bankruptcy Rule 3004 and section 501(c) must file a proof of claim on behalf of the creditor within a reasonable period of time after the expiration of the claims bar date. A delay of more than three years after the claims bar date's expiration exceeds what is reasonable. *In re* Zimmerman, 24 C.B.C.2d 9 (B. Ct., W.D. Pa. 1990).

An indenture trustee is a proper party to file a proof of claim and it is disingenuous for an indenture trustee to raise an objection that it is not a proper party in interest when its filed proof of claim is contested by a debtor. *In re* Chateaugay Corp., 22 C.B.C.2d 530 (B. Ct., S.D.N.Y. 1990), *aff'd,* 130 B.R. 403 (S.D.N.Y. 1991), *aff'd in part, rev'd in part,* No. 91-5098, 1992 U.S. App. LEXIS 6856 (2d Cir. Apr. 10, 1992).

References

3 *Collier on Bankruptcy* ch. 501 (Matthew Bender 15th ed.).

2 *Collier Bankruptcy Manual* ch. 501 (Matthew Bender 3d ed.).

3 *Collier Bankruptcy Practice Guide* ch. 50 (Matthew Bender).

Averch, *The Ability to Assert Claims on Behalf of the Debtor: Does a Creditor Have a Leg to Stand On?,* 96 Com. L.J. 115 (1991).

Bono, *Class Action Proofs of Claim in Bankruptcy,* 96 Com. L.J. 297 (1991).

Kaye, *The Case Against Class Proofs of Claim in Bankruptcy,* 66 N.Y.U. L. Rev. 897 (1991).

Note, *Reasonable Notice From Secured Creditor Assignees,* 54 U. Cin L. Rev. 1395 (1986).

Sabino, *In a Class by Itself: The Class Proof of Claim in Bankruptcy Proceedings,* 40 DePaul L. Rev. 115 (1990).

SECTION 502 (11 U.S.C. § 502)

§ 502. Allowance of claims or interests.

(a) A claim or interest, proof of which is filed under section 501 of this title, is deemed allowed, unless a party in interest, including a creditor of a general partner in a partnership that is a debtor in a case under chapter 7 of this title, objects.

(b) Except as provided in subsections (e)(2), (f), (g), (h) and (i) of this section, if such objection to a claim is made, the court, after notice and a hearing, shall determine the amount of such claim in lawful currency of the United States as of the date of the filing of the petition, and shall allow such claim in such amount, except to the extent that—

    (1) such claim is unenforceable against the debtor and property of the debtor, under any agreement or applicable law for a reason other than because such claim is contingent or unmatured;

    (2) such claim is for unmatured interest;

    (3) if such claim is for a tax assessed against property of the estate, such claim exceeds the value of the interest of the estate in such property;

    (4) if such claim is for services of an insider or attorney of the debtor, such claim exceeds the reasonable value of such services;

    (5) such claim is for a debt that is unmatured on the date of the filing of the petition and that is excepted from discharge under section 523(a)(5) of this title;

    (6) if such claim is the claim of a lessor for damages resulting from the termination of a lease of real property, such claim exceeds—

        (A) the rent reserved by such lease, without acceleration, for the greater of one year, or 15 percent, not to exceed three years, of the remaining term of such lease, following the earlier of—

(i) the date of the filing of the petition; and

(ii) the date on which such lessor repossessed, or the lessee surrendered, the leased property; plus

(B) any unpaid rent due under such lease, without acceleration, on the earlier of such dates;

(7) if such claim is the claim of an employee for damages resulting from the termination of an employment contract, such claim exceeds—

(A) the compensation provided by such contract, without acceleration, for one year following the earlier of—

(i) the date of the filing of the petition; or

(ii) the date on which the employer directed the employee to terminate, or such employee terminated, performance under such contract; plus

(B) any unpaid compensation due under such contract, without acceleration, on the earlier of such dates; or

(8) such claim results from a reduction, due to late payment, in the amount of an otherwise applicable credit available to the debtor in connection with an employment tax on wages, salaries, or commissions earned from the debtor.

(c) There shall be estimated for purpose of allowance under this section—

(1) any contingent or unliquidated claim, the fixing or liquidation of which, as the case may be, would unduly delay the administration of the case; or

(2) any right to payment arising from a right to an equitable remedy for breach of performance.

(d) Notwithstanding subsections (a) and (b) of this section, the court shall disallow any claim of any entity from which property is recoverable under section 542, 543, 550, or 553 of this title or that is a transferee of a transfer avoidable under section 522(f), 522(h), 544, 545, 547, 548, 549, or 724(a) of this title, unless such entity or transferee has paid the amount, or turned over any such property, for which such entity or transferee is liable under section 522(i), 542, 543, 550, or 553 of this title.

(e)(1) Notwithstanding subsections (a), (b), and (c) of this section and paragraph (2) of this subsection, the court shall disallow any claim for reimbursement or contribution of an entity that is liable with the debtor on or has secured the claim of a creditor, to the extent that—

(A) such creditor's claim against the estate is disallowed;

(B) such claim for reimbursement or contribution is contingent as of the time of allowance or disallowance of such claim for reimbursement or contribution; or

(C) such entity asserts a right of subrogation to the rights of such creditor under section 509 of this title.

(2) A claim for reimbursement or contribution of such an entity that becomes fixed after the commencement of the case shall be determined, and shall be allowed under subsection (a), (b), or (c) of this section, or disallowed under subsection (d) of this section, the same as if such claim had become fixed before the date of filing of the petition.

(f) In an involuntary case, a claim arising in the ordinary course of the debtor's business or financial affairs after the commencement of the case but before the earlier of the appointment of a trustee and the order for relief shall be determined as of the date such claim arises, and shall be allowed under subsection (a), (b), or (c) of this section or disallowed under subsection (d) or (e) of this section, the same as if such claim had arisen before the date of the filing of the petition.

(g) A claim arising from the rejection, under section 365 of this title or under a plan under chapter 9, 11, 12, or 13 of this title, of an executory contract or unexpired lease of the debtor that has not been assumed shall be determined, and shall be allowed under subsection (a), (b), or (c) of this section or disallowed under subsection (d) or (e) of this section, the same as if such claim had arisen before the date of the filing of the petition.

(h) A claim arising from the recovery of property under section 522, 550, or 553 of this title shall be determined, and shall be allowed under subsection (a), (b), or (c) of this section, or disallowed under subsection (d) or (e) of this section, the same as if such claim had arisen before the date of the filing of the petition.

(i) A claim that does not arise until after the commencement of the case for a tax entitled to priority under section 507(a)(7) of this title shall be determined, and shall be allowed under subsection (a), (b), or (c) of this section, or disallowed under subsection (d) or (e) of this section, the same as if such claim had arisen before the date of the filing of the petition.

(j) A claim that has been allowed or disallowed may be reconsidered for cause. A reconsidered claim may be allowed or disallowed according to the equities of the case. Reconsideration of a claim under this subsection does not affect the validity of any payment or transfer from the estate made to a holder of an allowed claim on account of such allowed claim that is not reconsidered, but if a reconsidered claim is allowed and is of the same class as such holder's claim, such holder may not receive any additional payment or transfer from the estate on account of such holder's allowed claim until the holder of such reconsidered and allowed claim receives payment on account of such claim proportionate in value to that already received by such other holder. This subsection does not alter or modify the trustee's right to recover from a creditor any excess payment or transfer made to such creditor.

Bankruptcy Rule References: 3001, 3002, 3003, 3004, 3005 and 3007

Legislative History

A proof of claim or interest is prima facia evidence of the claim or interest. Thus, it is allowed under subsection (a) unless a party, in interest objects. The Rules and case law will determine who is a party in interest for purposes of objection to allowance. The case law is well developed on this subject today. As a result of the change in the liability of a general partner's estate for the debts of this partnership, *see* proposed 11 U.S.C. § 723, the category of persons that are parties in interest in the partnership case will be expanded to include a creditor of a partner against whose estate the trustee of the partnership estate may proceed under proposed 11 U.S.C. § 723(c).

[*House Report No. 95–595, 95th Cong., 1st Sess. 352 (1977); Senate Report No. 95–989, 95th Cong., 2d Sess. 62 (1978).*]

The House amendment adopts a compromise position in section 502(a) between H.R. 8200, as passed by the House, and the Senate amendment. Section 502(a) has been modified to make clear that a party in interest includes a creditor of a partner in a partnership that is a debtor under chapter 7. Since the trustee of the partnership is given an absolute claim against the estate of each general partner under section 723(c), creditors of the partner must have standing to object to claims against the partnership at the partnership level because no opportunity will be afforded at the partner's level for such objection.

[*124 Cong. Rec. H 11,093 (Sept. 28, 1978); S 17,410 (Oct, 6, 1978).*]

Subsection (b) prescribes the grounds on which a claim may be disallowed. The court will apply these standards if there is an objection to a proof of claim. The burden of proof on the issue of allowance is left to the Rules of Bankruptcy Procedure. Under the current chapter XIII Rules, a creditor is required to prove that his claim is free from usury, Rule 13–301. It is expected that the Rules will make similar provision for both liquidation and individual repayment plan cases. *See* Bankruptcy Act section 656(b); H.R. 31, 94th Cong., 1st Sess., § 6–104(a) (1975).

Paragraph (1) requires disallowance if the claim is unenforceable against the debtor for any reason (such as usury, unconscionability, or failure of consideration) other than because it is contingent or unmatured. All such contingent or unmatured claims are to be liquidated by the bankruptcy court in order to afford the debtor complete bankruptcy relief; these claims are generally not provable under present law.

Paragraph (2) requires disallowance to the extent that the claim is for unmatured interest as of the date of the petition. Whether interest is matured or unmatured on the date of bankruptcy is to be determined without reference to any *ipso facto* or bankruptcy clause in the agreement creating the claim. Interest disallowed under this paragraph includes postpetition interest that is not yet due and payable, and any portion of prepaid interest that represents an original discounting of the claim, yet that would not have been earned on the date of bankruptcy. For example, a claim on a $1,000 note issued the day before bankruptcy would only be allowed to the extent of the cash actually advanced. If the original discount was 10 percent so that the cash advanced was only $900, then nonwithstanding the face amount of note, only $900 would be allowed. If $900 was advanced under the note some time before bankruptcy, the interest component of the note would have to be prorated and disallowed to the extent it was for interest after the commencement of the case.

Section 502(b) thus contains two principles of present law. First, interest stops accruing at the date of the filing of the petition, because any claim for unmatured interest is disallowed under this paragraph. Second, bankruptcy operates as the acceleration of the principal amount of all claims against the debtor. One unarticulated reason for this is that the discounting factor for claims after the commencement of the case is equivalent to contractual interest rate on the claim. Thus, this paragraph does not cause disallowance of claims that have not been discounted to a present value because of the irrebutable presumption that the discounting rate and the contractual interest rate (even a zero interest rate) are equivalent.

Paragraph (4) [*Ed. Note:* Section 502(b)(4) was redesignated as section 502(b)(3) by Pub. L. No. 98–353.] requires disallowance of a property tax claim to the extent that the tax due exceeds the value of the property. This too follows current law to the extent the property tax is ad valorem.

Paragraph (5) [*Ed. Note:* Section 502(b)(5) was redesignated as section 502(b)(4) by Pub. L. No. 98–353.] prevents overreaching by the debtor's attorneys and concealing of assets by debtors. It permits the court to examine the claim of a debtor's attorney independently of any other provision of this subsection, and to disallow it to the extent that it exceeds the reasonable value of the attorneys' services.

Postpetition alimony, maintenance or support claims are disallowed under paragraph (6). [*Ed. Note:* Section 502(b)(6) was redesignated as section 502(b)(5) by Pub. L. No. 98–353.] They are to be paid from the debtor's postpetition property, because the claims are nondischargeable.

Paragraph (7) [*Ed. Note:* Section 502(b)(7) was redesignated as section 502(b)(6) by Pub. L. No. 98–353.] derived from current law, limits the damages allowable to a landlord of the debtor. The history of this provision is set out at length in Oldden v. Tonto Realty Co., 143 F.2d 916 (2d Cir. 1944). It is designed to compensate the landlord for his loss while not permitting a claim so large (based on a long-term lease) as to prevent other general unsecured creditors from recovering a dividend from the estate. The damages a landlord may assert from termination of a lease are limited to the rent reserved for the greater of one year or ten percent of the remaining lease term, not to exceed three years, after the earlier of the date of the filing of the petition and the date of surrender or repossession. The sliding scale formula is new, is designed to protect the long-term lessor, and is included as a replacement of the dual provisions in current law of a three-year test for reorganization cases and a one-year test for liquidation cases. This subsection does not apply to limit administrative expense claims for use of the leased premises to which the landlord is otherwise entitled.

This paragraph will not overrule *Oldden,* or the proposition for which it has been read to stand: to the extent that a landlord has a security deposit in excess of the amount of his claim allowed under this paragraph, the excess comes into the estate. Moreover, his allowed claim is for his total damages, as limited by this paragraph. By virtue of proposed 11 U.S.C. §§ 506(a) and 506(d), the claim will be divided into a secured portion and an unsecured portion in those cases in which the deposit that the landlord holds is less than his damages. As under *Oldden,* he will not be permitted to offset his actual damages against his security deposit and then claim for the balance under this paragraph. Rather, his security deposit will be applied in satisfaction of the claim that is allowed under this paragraph.

Paragraph (8) [*Ed. Note:* Section 502(b)(8) was redesignated as section 502(b)(7) by Pub. L. No. 98–353.] is new. It tracks the landlord limitation on damages provision in paragraph (7) [now paragraph (6)] for damages resulting from the breach by the debtor of an employment contract, but limits the recovery to the compensation reserved under an employment contract for the year following the earlier of the date of the petition and the termination of employment.

Paragraph (9) [*Ed. Note:* Section 502(b)(9) was redesignated as section 502(b)(8) by Pub. L. No. 98–353.] requires disallowance of certain employment tax claims. These relate to a Federal tax credit for State unemployment insurance taxes which is disallowed if the State tax is paid late. This paragraph disallows the Federal claim for the tax the same as if the credit had been allowed in full on the Federal return.

[*House Report No. 95–595, 95th Cong., 1st Sess. 352–354 (1977); See Senate Report No. 95–989, 95th Cong., 2d Sess. 62–5 (1978).*]

The House amendment contains a provision in section 502(b)(1) that requires disallowance of a claim to the extent that such claim is unenforceable against the debtor and unenforceable against property of the debtor. This is intended to result in the disallowance of any claim for deficiency by an undersecured creditor on a nonrecourse loan or under a State antideficiency law, special provision for which is made in section 1111, since neither the debtor personally, nor the property of the debtor is liable for such a deficiency. Similarly claims for usurious interest or which could be barred by an agreement between the creditor and the debtor would be disallowed.

Section 502(b)(7)(A) [*Ed. Note:* Section 502(b)(7)(A) was redesignated as section 502(b)(6)(A) by Pub. L. No. 98–353.] represents a compromise between the House bill and the Senate amendment. The House amendment takes the provision in H.R. 8200 as passed by the House of Representatives but increases the percentage from 10 to 15 percent.

As used in section 502(b)(7), [*Ed. Note:* Section 502(b)(7) was redesignated as section 502(b)(6) by Pub. L. No. 98–353.] the phrase "lease of real property" applies only to a "true" or "bona fide" lease and does not apply to financing leases of real property or interests therein, or to leases of such property which are intended as security.

Historically, the limitation on allowable claims of lessors of real property was based on two considerations. First, the amount of the lessor's damages on breach of a real estate lease was considered contingent and difficult to prove. Partly for this reason, claims of a lessor of real estate were not provable prior to the 1934 amendments, to the Bankruptcy Act. Second, in a true lease of real property, the lessor retains all risks and benefits as to the value of the real estate at the termination of the lease. Historically, it was, therefore, considered equitable to limit the claims of real estate lessor.

However, these considerations are not present in "lease financing" transactions where, in substance, the "lease" involves a sale of the real estate and the rental payments are in substance the payment of principal and interest on a secured loan or sale. In a financing lease the lessor is essentially a secured or unsecured creditor (depending upon whether his interest is perfected or not) of the debtor, and the lessor's claim should not be subject to the 502(b)(7) [*Ed. Note:* Section 502(b)(7) was redesignated as section 502(b)(6) by Pub. L. No. 98–353.] limitation. Financing "leases" are in substance installment sales or loans. The "lessors" are essentially sellers or lenders and should be treated as such for purposes of the bankruptcy law.

Whether a "lease" is true or bona fide lease or, in the alternative, a financing "lease" or a lease intended as security depends upon the circumstances of each case. The distinction between a true lease and a financing transaction is based upon the economic substance of the transaction and not, for example, upon the locus of title, the form of the transaction or the fact that the transaction is denominated as a "lease." The fact that the lessee, upon a compliance with the terms of the lease, becomes or has the option to become the owner of the leased property for no additional consideration or for nominal consideration indicates that the transaction is a financing lease or lease intended as security. In such cases, the lessor has no substantial interest in the leased property at the expiration of the lease term. In addition, the fact that the lessee assumes and discharges substantially all the risks and obligations ordinarily attributed to the outright ownership of the property is more indicative of a financing transaction than of a true lease. The rental payments in such cases are in substance payments of principal and interest either on a loan secured by the leased real property or on the purchase of the leased real property. *See, e.g.,* Financial Accounting Standards Board Statement No. 13 and SEC Reg. S-X, 17 C.F.R. sec. 210.3–16(q) (1977); *cf.* First National Bank of Chicago v. Irving Trust Co., 74 F. 2d 263 (2d Cir. 1934); and Albenda and Lief, "Net Lease Financing Transactions Under the Proposed Bankruptcy Act of 1973," 30 Business Lawyer, 713 (1975).

[*124 Cong. Rec. H 11,093–94 (Sept. 28, 1978); S 17,410 (Oct 6, 1978).*]

Section 502. Allowance of Claims or Interests. The House amendment adopts section 502(b)(9) [*Ed. Note:* Section 502(b)(9) was redesignated as section 502(b)(8) by Pub. L. No. 98–353.] of the House bill which disallows any tax claim resulting from a reduction of the Federal Unemployment Tax Act (FUTA) credit (sec. 3302 of the Internal Revenue Code) on account of a tardy contribution to a State unemployment fund if the contribution is attributable to ways [*sic*] or other compensation paid by the debtor before bankruptcy. The Senate amendment allowed this reduction, but would have subordinated it to other claims in the distribution of the estate's assets by treating it as a punitive (non-pecuniary loss) penalty. The House amendment would also not bar reduction of the FUTA credit on account of a trustee's late payment of a contribution to a State unemployment fund if the contribution was attributable to a trustee's payment of compensation earned from the estate.

[*124 Cong. Rec. H 11,110 (Sept. 28, 1978); S 17,426 (Oct. 6, 1978).*]

Subsection (c) requires the estimation of any claim liquidation of which would unduly delay the closing of the estate, such as a contingent claim, or any claim for which applicable law provides only an equitable remedy, such as specific performance. [*Ed. Note:* The definition of "claim" in section 101 was changed; see Cong. Rec., *infra,* indicating that the reference in the Report to specific performance is too broad.] This subsection requires that all claims against the debtor be converted into dollar amounts.

[House Report No. 95–595, 95th Cong., 1st Sess. 354 (1977); Senate Report No. 95–989, 95th Cong., 2d Sess 65 (1978).]

Section 502(c) of the House amendment presents a compromise between similar provisions contained in the House bill and the Senate amendment. The compromise language is consistent with an amendment to the definition of "claim" in section 104(4)(B) *[Ed. Note:* Should be section 101(5)(B).] of the House amendment and requires estimation of any right to an equitable remedy for breach of performance if such breach gives rise to a right to payment. To the extent language in the House and Senate reports indicate otherwise, such language is expressly overruled.

[124 Cong. Rec. H 11,094 (Sept. 28, 1978); S 17,410 (Oct. 6, 1978).]

Subsection (d) is derived from present law. It requires disallowance of a claim of a transferee of a voidable transfer in toto if the transferee has not paid the amount or turned over the property received as required under the sections under which the transferee's liability arises.

Subsection (e), also derived from present law, requires disallowance of the claim for reimbursement or contribution of a codebtor, surety or guarantor of an obligation of the debtor, unless the claim of the creditor on such obligation has been paid in full. The provision prevents competition between a creditor and his guarantor for the limited proceeds in the estate.

[House Report No. 95–595, 95th Cong., 1st Sess. 354 (1977); Senate Report No. 95–989, 95th Cong., 2d Sess. 65 (1978).]

Section 502(e) of the House amendment contains language modifying a similar section in the House bill and Senate amendment. Section 502(e)(1) states the general rule requiring the court to disallow any claim for reimbursement or contribution of an entity that is liable with the debtor on, or that has secured, the claim of a creditor to any extent that the creditor's claim against the estate is disallowed. This adopts a policy that a surety's claim for reimbursement or contribution is entitled to no better status than the claim of the creditor assured by such surety. Section 502(e)(1)(B) alternatively disallows any claim for reimbursement or contribution by a surety to the extent such claim is contingent as of the time of allowance. Section 502(e)(2) is clear that to the extent a claim for reimbursement or contribution becomes fixed after the commencement of the case that it is to be considered a prepetition claim for purposes of allowance. The combined effect of sections 502(e)(1)(B) and 502(e)(2) is that a surety or codebtor is generally permitted a claim for reimbursement or contribution to the extent the surety or codebtor has paid the assured party at the time of allowance. Section 502(e)(1)(C) alternatively indicates that a claim for reimbursement or contribution of a surety or codebtor is disallowed to the extent the surety or codebtor requests subrogation under section 509 with respect to the rights of the assured party. Thus, the surety or codebtor has a choice; to the extent a claim for contribution or reimbursement would be advantageous, such as in the case where such a claim is secured, a surety or codebtor may opt for reimbursement or contribution under section 502(e). On the other hand, to the extent the claim for such surety or codebtor by way of subrogation is more advantageous, such as where such claim is secured, the surety may elect subrogation under section 509.

The section changes current law by making the election identical in all other respects. To the extent a creditor's claim is satisfied by a surety or codebtor, other creditors should not benefit by the surety's inability to file a claim against the estate merely because such surety or codebtor has failed to pay such creditor's claim in full. On the other hand, to the extent the creditor's claim against the estate is otherwise disallowed, the surety or codebtor should not be entitled to increased rights by way of reimbursement or contribution, to the detriment of competing claims of other unsecured creditors, than would be realized by way of subrogation.

While the foregoing scheme is equitable with respect to other unsecured creditors of the debtor, it is desirable to preserve present law to the extent that a surety or codebtor is not permitted to compete with the creditor he has assured until the assured party's claim has paid in full. Accordingly, section 509(c) of the House amendment subordinates both a claim by way of subrogation or a claim for reimbursement or contribution of a surety or codebtor to the claim of the assured party until the assured party's claim is paid in full.

[*124 Cong. Rec. H 11,094 (Sept. 28, 1978); S 17,410–11 (Oct. 6, 1978).*]

Subsection (f) specifies that "involuntary gap" creditors receive the same treatment as prepetition creditors. Under the allowance provisions of this subsection, knowledge of the commencement of the case will be irrelevant. The claim is to be allowed "the same as if such claim had arisen before the date of the filing of the petition." Under the authority granted to debtors to operate pending trial on an involuntary petition, proposed 11 U.S.C. § 303(f), creditors must be permitted to deal with the debtor and be assured that their claims will be paid.

Subsection (g) gives entities injured by the rejection of an executory contract or unexpired lease, either under section 365 or under a plan or reorganization, a prepetition claim for any resulting damages, and requires that the injured entity be treated as a prepetition creditor with respect to that claim.

Subsection (h) gives a transferee of a setoff that is recovered by the trustee a prepetition claim for the amount recovered.

[*House Report No. 95–595, 95th Cong., 1st Sess. 354–55 (1977); Senate Report No. 95–989, 95th Cong., 2d Sess. 65 (1978).*]

Section 502(h) of the House amendment expands similar provisions contained in the House bill and the Senate amendment to indicate that any claim arising from the recovery of property under section 522(i), 550, or 553 shall be determined as though it were a prepetition claim.

[*124 Cong. Rec. H 11,094 (Sept. 28, 1978); S 17,411 (Oct. 6, 1978).*]

Subsection (i) treats the recapture of an investment tax credit in connection with the transfer of property in a bankruptcy case as a prepetition claim, even though the recapture may have occurred after the filing of the petition.

[*House Report No. 95–595, 95th Cong., 1st Sess. 355 (1977).*]

Subsection (i) answers the nonrecourse loan problem and gives the creditor an unsecured claim for the difference between the value of the collateral and the debt in response to the decision in Great National Life Ins. Co. v. Pine Gate Associates, Ltd., Bankruptcy Case No. B75–4345A (N.D. Ga. Sept. 16, 1977).

The bill, as reported, deletes a provision in the bill as originally introduced (former section 502(i)) requiring a tax authority to file a proof of claim for recapture of an investment credit where, during title 11 proceedings, the trustee sells or otherwise disposes of property before the title 11 case began. The tax authority should not be required to submit a formal claim for a taxable event (a sale or other disposition of the asset) of whose occurrence the trustee necessarily knows better than the taxing authority. For procedural purposes, the recapture of investment credit is to be treated as an administrative expense, as to which only a request for payment is required.

[*Senate Report No. 95–989, 95th Cong., 2d Sess. 65 (1978).*]

Section 502(i) of the House amendment adopts a provision contained in section 502(j) of H.R. 8200 as passed by the House but that was not contained in the Senate amendment.

Section 502(i) of H.R. 8200 as passed by the House, but was not included in the Senate amendment, is deleted as a matter to be left to the bankruptcy tax bill next year.

The House amendment deletes section 502(i) of the Senate bill but adopts the policy of that section to a limited extent for confirmation of a plan of reorganization in section 1111(b) of the House amendment.

Section 502(j) of the House amendment is new. The provision codifies section 57k of the Bankruptcy Act.

[*124 Cong. Rec. H 11,094 (Sept. 28, 1978); S 17,411 (Oct. 6, 1978).*]

Comment

Offsets were dealt with in Section 68a of the former Bankruptcy Act which provided that in all cases of mutual debts and mutual credits between the estate of a bankrupt and a creditor, the account shall be stated and one debt shall be set off against the other and the balance only shall be allowed or paid. *Compare,* section 502(b)(3) of the Code.

Section 502(b)(6) of the Code dealing with the claim of a lessor for damages from termination of a lease finds its genesis in Sections 63a(9), 202, 353, and 458 of the former Act. Section 63a(9) made a claim for damages from rejection of an executory contract including unexpired leases of personal or real property, a provable claim but contained a limitation on the amount that may be allowed, *i.e.,* generally the rent reserved in the lease for the year next succeeding date of surrender or reentry of the landlord, whichever first occurs. Sections 202, 353 and 458 contained like provisions for Chapters X, XI and XII cases, except that the maximum damages allowed was fixed at three years rent reserved in the lease rather than the one year limitation of straight bankruptcy.

Section 502(e) is derived from section 57i of the Act and former Bankruptcy Rule 304 which authorized a person liable to the bankrupt, or who secured a creditor of the bankrupt, if the creditor failed to file his claim before the first date set for the first meeting of creditors, to file a claim in the name of the creditor. Such claim would be superseded by one filed thereafter by the creditor.

Bankruptcy Rule 3001, dealing with proofs of claim, prescribes the form and content, states who may execute, and governs transfers of claims before and after the proof is filed. The Rule was amended in 1991. Subdivision (f) of the rule provides that a proof of claim executed and filed in accordance with the rules shall constitute prima facie evidence of the validity and amount of the claim. *See* **Comment** to section 501.

Bankruptcy Rule 3002, also amended in 1991, deals with the filing of proofs of claim or interest, the most notable provision of which is found in subdivision (c) which requires (with six specified exceptions) that in a *chapter 7, 12 or 13 case,* a proof of claim must be filed within 90 days after the first date set for the meeting of creditors called pursuant to section 341(a) of the Code. *See* **Comment** to section 501.

Bankruptcy Rule 3003 deals with the filing of proofs of claim or equity security interests in *chapter 9 or 11 cases.* Generally, under this rule, creditors need not file claims unless they were listed in the schedules as disputed, contingent, or unliquidated. Equity security holders need not file proofs of interest if they were included in the list of equity security holders filed pursuant to Rule 1007(a)(3). *See* **Comment** to section 501.

Bankruptcy Rule 3002(c)(3) provides for the disallowance of the claim of an entity that fails to satisfy a judgment for the recovery of money or property or denying or avoiding rights within 30 days after such judgment become final.

Bankruptcy Rule 3007 requires objections to a claim to be in writing and filed. A copy thereof and notice of hearing must be served on the claimant, the debtor in possession and the trustee at least 30 days prior to the hearing. If the objection to a claim is joined with a counterclaim, it becomes an adversary proceeding governed by the Part VII Rules.

Bankruptcy Rule 3004 permits the debtor or trustee to execute and file a proof of claim in the name of a creditor who fails to file a claim on or before the first date set for the meeting of creditors. The claim on behalf of the creditor must be filed within 30 days after the expiration of the time for filing claims prescribed by Rule 3002(c) or 3003(c), whichever is applicable. Thereupon the clerk is required to forthwith mail notice of the filing to the creditor, the debtor and the trustee. The creditor may file a proof of claim under Rule 3002 or 3003(c) which will supersede the proof filed by the debtor or trustee.

Bankruptcy Rule 3005(a) provides that if the creditor has not filed a proof of claim, an entity that is or may be liable with the debtor or has secured that creditor may, within 30 days after the expiration of the time for filing claims under Rule 3002(c) or 3003(c), whichever is applicable, execute and file a proof of claim in the name of the creditor, or if unknown, in the entity's own name. But no distribution may be made on the claim except on satisfactory proof that the original debt will be diminished by the amount so paid. A claim so filed is superseded by a claim filed by the creditor pursuant to Rule 3002(c) or 3003(c).

Bankruptcy Rule 3005(b) provides that an entity that has filed a claim on behalf of a creditor pursuant to subdivision (a), may file an acceptance or rejection of a plan in the name of the creditor, of in unknown, in his own name. But if the creditor timely files a claim or a notice prior to confirmation of the creditor's intention to act in the creditor's own behalf, the creditor is to be substituted for the obligor with respect to that claim.

Bankruptcy Rule 3006 relates to withdrawal of a proof of claim. It permits withdrawal of a claim as of right, except as provided in the rule. If after the claim is filed, an objection is filed thereto or a complaint is filed against the creditor in an adversary proceeding, or the creditor has accepted or rejected the plan or otherwise participated significantly in the case, such creditor may not withdraw except on order after hearing on notice to the trustee or debtor in possession, and any creditors' committee elected under section 705(a) or appointed under section 1102 of the Code.

Bankruptcy Rule 3008 provides that a party in interest may move for reconsideration of an order allowing or disallowing a claim. After hearing on notice the court shall enter an appropriate order. (Disallowance as well as allowance of a claim may be reconsidered under this rule. Moreover, under Rule 3008 a claim may be reconsidered after a case is closed. If a case is reopened as provided in section 350(b), reconsideration of the allowance or disallowance of a claim may be sought and granted in accordance with Rule 3008.)

1984 Amendments: Section 502(b) was amended to require the court to determine "in lawful United States currency" the amount due on a claim that has been objected to.

Subsection (b)(3), referring to offsets under section 553, was deleted, and all subsequent paragraphs of subsection (b) were renumbered.

Subsection (c)(1) was amended to provide that estimation of a claim be made when fixing or liquidating would unduly delay the "administration" rather than the "closing" of the case.

Subsection (j) dealing with reconsideration of allowed claims was deleted and a new subsection (j) was substituted providing for reconsideration of disallowed as well as allowed claims, and treating the subject in more detail.

1986 Amendments: The only change effected by the 1986 Act was to bring chapter 12 cases within the operation of subsection (g).

Case Annotations

The court may approve a settlement of a claim against the bankruptcy estate so long as the court is aware of the factual and legal issues involved in determining that the settlement is reasonable. *In re* New Concept Housing, Inc., 951 F.2d 932, 26 C.B.C.2d 287 (8th Cir. 1991).

While the burden of persuasion is always on a claimant, the burden of proof for claims is a shifting one: a claim is *prima facie* valid if it alleges facts sufficient to support a legal liability to the claimant; if the objector then produces evidence to refute at least one of the allegations essential to the claim's legal sufficiency, the burden of going forward shifts back to the claimant to prove the validity of the claim by a preponderance of the evidence. *In re* Allegheny International, Inc., 954 F.2d 167, 26 C.B.C.2d 663 (3d Cir. 1992).

Although the existence of a claim is controlled by state law, the allowance or disallowance of a claim in bankruptcy is a matter of federal law left to the bankruptcy court's exercise of its equitable powers. *In re* Johnson, 960 F.2d 396, 26 C.B.C.2d 1054 (4th Cir. 1992).

Unamortized original issue discount is "unmatured interest" within the meaning of section 502(b)(2) and should be calculated by the constant interest method. Because unamortized original issue discount (OID) on new debt that results from a face value debt-for-debt exchange consists only of the discount carried over from the old debt at the time of the exchange, it is not subject to section 502(b)(2) for that section affects only the old OID. *In re* Chateaugay Corp., 961 F.2d 378, 26 C.B.C.2d 1174 (2d Cir. 1992).

The term "lease of real property" does not apply to lease financing transactions or to leases intended as security, but, rather applies only to a true lease. *In re* PCH Associates, 949 F.2d 585, 25 C.B.C.2d 1393 (2d Cir. 1991).

A trustee may not recover postconfirmation payments on the basis of 502(j) because that section is not intended to provide a basis to attack the finality of a binding order of confirmation. *In re* Chattanooga Wholesale Antiques, Inc., 930 F.2d 458, 24 C.B.C.2d 1556 (6th Cir. 1991).

Equitable subordination principles never come into play unless a claim is an allowed claim. When a claim is disallowed it means that the estate owes no debt to the holder of such a claim and this moots any issue as to the holder's distributive rights to the assets and, therefore, to subordination. Max Sugarman Funeral Home, Inc., v. A.D.B. Investors, 926 F.2d 1248, 24 C.B.C.2d 1414 (1st Cir. 1991).

A debtor in possession must have the same rights and duties to object to claims and to file motions for reconsideration of claims as a trustee. As an allegation of fraud constitutes sufficient cause to sustain a motion for reconsideration under section 502(j), the debtor is entitled to reconsideration of a bankruptcy court order when its motion sufficiently raises an issue of fraud with respect to a secured claim. *In re* Int'l Yacht and Tennis, Inc., 922 F.2d 699, 24 C.B.C.2d 725 (11th Cir. 1991).

Failure to include a creditor's name on a financing statement that substantially complies with all other requirements for perfecting security interests under state law cannot be considered a "minor error" as the legislature intended that phrase to be understood. *In re* Copper King Inn, Inc., 918 F.2d 1404, 23 C.B.C.2d 1547 (9th Cir. 1990).

Employees whose collective bargaining agreement has been rejected and who would have had a claim for damages for lost future wages and benefits under the agreement are entitled to unsecured claims for those damages accruing from the time of the rejection of the agreement until the employer would have ceased operations.*In re* Continental Airlines Corp., 901 F.2d 1259, 23 C.B.C.2d 795 (5th Cir. 1990).

When an objection is based on the contention that a plan misclassifies the objectionable claim, that objection must be made prior to the confirmation of the plan. *In re* Justice Oaks II, Ltd., 898 F.2d 1544, 22 C.B.C.2d 1304 (11th Cir. 1990).

The legislative history and policy behind section 502(d) illustrates that the section is intended to have the coercive effect of insuring compliance with judicial orders. In the Matter of Davis, 889 F.2d 658, 22 C.B.C.2d 285 (5th Cir. 1989).

Congress intended, through subparagraphs (A) and (B) of section 502(b)(6), to provide lessors with actual damages for past rent and to place a limit on damages for speculative future rent payments in long-term leases so that in section 502(b)(6)(B) the word "due" should be interpreted to mean "owing." *In re* Vause, 886 F.2d 794, 21 C.B.C.2d 1346 (6th Cir. 1989).

In determining whether to enforce postpetition tax interest against a chapter 7 debtor, each case must be viewed on the basis of administrative convenience and fairness to creditors, and collateral estoppel should not apply to prevent actions attempting to enforce such claims. *In re* Hanna, 872 F.2d 829, 20 C.B.C.2d 1453 (8th Cir. 1989).

The application of section 502(e)(1)(B) to exclude claims of contingent CERCLA contributions will not impermissibly contravene or inhibit the policies and goals underlying CERCLA when the cleanup has been completed and the responsibility for the damages should be substantially if not totally apportioned once the cases are concluded. *In re* The Charter Co., 862 F.2d 1500, 20 C.B.C.2d 915 (11th Cir. 1989).

Section 502(b)(7), which limits claims arising out of rejection of executory employment contracts, does not apply to a contract governing the payment of vested retirement benefits. Folsom v. Prospect Hill Resources (*In re* Prospect Hill Resources, Inc.), 837 F.2d 453, 18 C.B.C.2d 324 (11th Cir. 1988).

An order expunging a creditor's claim in an ongoing bankruptcy case is a final order immediately appealable to the district court and need not be preceded by a motion for reconsideration pursuant to section 502(j), as a motion for reconsideration is not a jurisdictional precondition to an appeal. In the Matter of Walsh Trucking Co., Inc. v. Insurance Co. of North America, 838 F.2d 698, 18 C.B.C.2d 183 (3d Cir. 1988).

A discharge clause in an insider's employment agreement which absolves the debtor of liability for future compensation to the employee in the event of the debtor's liquidation is not per se valid; a hearing with appropriate notice is required to determine if the bankruptcy resulted from the debtor's misconduct. Stevenson v. Stevenson Associates (*In re* Stevenson Associates, Inc.), 777 F.2d 415, 14 C.B.C.2d 44 (8th Cir. 1985).

A bankruptcy court has the authority under section 502(c)(1) to fix the estimated value of an unliquidated claim and may fix the value of an "on-call" contract as of the date the bankruptcy petition is filed. Addison v. Langston (In the Matter of Brints Cotton Mktg., Inc.), 737 F.2d 1338, 11 C.B.C.2d 588 (5th Cir. 1984).

In an appeal of a bankruptcy court's estimate of a contingent claim based upon a state court action against the debtor, the clearly erroneous standard of review is applicable to the court's findings of fact regardless of whether such findings were based upon an examination of undisputed or stipulated documentary evidence, rather than upon the oral testimony of witnesses, and the bankruptcy court may value the ultimate merits of that action and assign the contingent claim a zero value pending resolution of the state litigation, rather than base its estimation upon an assessment of probability of the suit's success. Bittner v. Borne Chemical Co., 691 F.2d 134, 7 C.B.C.2d 376 (3d Cir. 1982).

While a retirement system, although unable to sue a member in order to recoup an amount that has been given to that member as an advance against future retirement benefits, may deduct additional sums from that member's paycheck or reduce the amount that is eventually disbursed to that member upon retirement or resignation, the retirement system's claim relating to such advance is unenforceable against the debtor under section 502(b) since it is not a debt which can be discharged in bankruptcy. *In re* Villarie, 648 F.2d 810, 4 C.B.C.2d 494 (2d Cir. 1981).

An allowable claim for lease termination damages under section 502(b)(6) should not be reduced by the amount that a debtor-lessor paid to a landlord for postpetition rent. *In re* Atlantic Container Corp., 26 C.B.C.2d 597 (B. Ct., N.D. Ill. 1991).

Although on its face section 502(b)(6) neither includes nor excludes guarantors from the statutory limit on damages, a literal reading of the section results in the limitation of the allowance of damages that a lessor of real property may recover from a chapter 11 estate for termination of a lease, regardless of the identity of the entity that is the debtor. Matter of Interco, Inc., 26 C.B.C.2d 1087 (B. Ct., E.D. Mo. 1992).

The estimation procedure under section 502(c) is not complete unless a creditor has an unlimited right to reconsideration under section 502(j) for, were it otherwise, the creditor is placed in a prejudicial posture in trying to defend his or her own claims. *In re* MCorp Financial, Inc., 26 C.B.C.2d 1805 (B. Ct., S.D. Tex. 1992).

Although a debtor may bifurcate an undersecured creditor's claim into an allowed secured claim and an unsecured claim, extinguishment of the underlying mortgage lien should be conditioned upon payment of the full amount of the allowed secured claim and discharge of that debt in order to prevent the debtor from encumbering or selling the property and leaving the creditor with no viable option to reestablish its lien. *In re* Kinder, 26 C.B.C.2d 1654 (B. Ct., W.D. Okla. 1992).

A claim cannot be totally expunged if the claimant objects to only a portion of it. *In re* Woodstone Limited Partnership, 25 C.B.C.2d 1638 (B. Ct., E.D.N.Y. 1991).

Section 502(b)(6) sets forth a mechanical method for calculating a landlord's maximum damages and is dependent only upon the terms of the parties' lease so that any postpetition rental payments made by the debtor are irrelevant to this calculation and, therefore, may not be deducted when determining the amount of the landlord's claim. Furthermore, a landlord's claim for rent under section 502 will not be allowed to the extent it is unenforceable by reason of a prior settlement between the landlord and the debtor agreeing to deduct postpetition rental payments from the section 502 damages. *In re* Conston Corp., 25 C.B.C.2d 573 (B. Ct., E.D. Pa. 1991).

A claim for assessed taxes filed in a bankruptcy case by a taxing authority is entitled to the benefit of two presumptions, *i.e.,* that the tax assessment is correct and that a filed proof of claim is deemed allowed unless objected to. As to the tax assessment, the taxpayer bears the burden of establishing that the tax is incorrect, while the ultimate burden of persuasion that a claim in a bankruptcy case is correct rests with the claimant. Thus, if the tax claim is objected to, the taxing authority must provide credible evidence to support the accuracy of its assessment or the claim will not be allowed. *In re* Dakota Industries, Inc., 25 C.B.C.2d 905 (B. Ct., D.S.D. 1991).

An insolvent chapter 7 corporate debtor lacks standing and is without preliminary interest to seek specific allocation of payments of two debts owed to the IRS when it is not the corporate debtor which might suffer actual injury redressable by the court, but rather the debtor corporation's responsible persons who face personal liability for the trust fund tax liability. *In re* F. A. Dellastatious, Inc., 24 C.B.C.2d 907 (B. Ct., E.D. Va. 1990).

References

3 *Collier on Bankruptcy* ch. 502 (Matthew Bender 15th ed.).

2 *Collier Bankruptcy Manual* ch. 502 (Matthew Bender 3d ed.).

3 *Collier Bankruptcy Practice Guide* ch. 51 (Matthew Bender).

Eckoff, *Security Interest in Insurance Proceeds,* 58 Den. L.J. 293 (1981).

Korobkin, *"Killing the Husband": Disallowing Contingent Claims for Contribution or Indemnity in Bankruptcy,* 11 Cardozo L. Rev. 735 (1990).

Note, *Post-Petition Trading in Chapter 11 Claims: A Call for Augmentation of Federal Rules of Bankruptcy Procedure 3001(e)(2),* 58 Fordham L. Rev. 1053 (1990).

Steinmetz, *Judgment Lien Claimants' Rights Against Homestead Exemption Interest: An Equitable Distribution of Mortgage Foreclosure Sale Proceeds,* 4 Wis. L. Rev. 697 (1981).

Weintraub and Rosnick, *Allowance of Claims and Priorities Under the New Bankruptcy Code,* 12 U.C.C.L.J. 291 (1980).

SECTION 503 (11 U.S.C. § 503)

§ 503. Allowance of administrative expenses.

(a) An entity may file a request for payment of an administrative expense.

(b) After notice and a hearing, there shall be allowed administrative expenses, other than claims allowed under section 502(f) of this title, including—

(1)(A) the actual, necessary costs and expenses of preserving the estate, including wages, salaries, or commissions for services rendered after the commencement of the case:

(B) any tax—

(i) incurred by the estate, except a tax of a kind specified in section 507(a)(7) of this title; or

(ii) attributable to an excessive allowance of a tentative carryback adjustment that the estate received, whether the taxable year to which such adjustment relates ended before or after the commencement of the case; and

(C) any fine, penalty, or reduction in credit relating to a tax of a kind specified in subparagraph (B) of this paragraph;

(2) compensation and reimbursement awarded under section 330(a) of this title;

(3) the actual, necessary expenses, other than compensation and reimbursement specified in paragraph (4) of this subsection, incurred by—

(A) a creditor that files a petition under section 303 of this title;

(B) a creditor that recovers, after the court's approval, for the benefit of the estate any property transferred or concealed by the debtor;

(C) a creditor in connection with the prosecution of a criminal offense relating to the case or to the business or property of the debtor;

(D) a creditor, an indenture trustee, an equity security holder, or committee representing creditors or equity security holders other than a committee appointed under section 1102 of this title, in making a substantial contribution in a case under chapter 9 or 11 of this title; or

(E) a custodian superseded under section 543 of this title, and compensation for the services of such custodian;

(4) reasonable compensation for professional services rendered by an attorney or an accountant of an entity whose expense is allowable under paragraph (3) of this subsection, based on the time, the nature, the extent, and the value of such services, and the cost of comparable services other than in a case under this title, and reimbursement for actual, necessary expenses incurred by such attorney or accountant;

(5) reasonable compensation for services rendered by an indenture trustee in making a substantial contribution in a case under chapter 9 or 11 of this title, based on the time, the nature, the extent and the value of such services other than in a case under this title; and

(6) the fees and mileage payable under chapter 119 of title 28.

Legislative History

Subsection (a) of this section permits administrative expense claimants to file with the court a request for payment of an administrative expense. The Rules of Bankruptcy Procedure will specify the time, the form and the method of such a filing.

[*House Report No. 95–595, 95th Cong., 1st Sess. 355 (1977); Senate Report No. 95–989, 95th Cong., 2d Sess. 66 (1978).*]

Section 503(a) of the House amendment represents a compromise between similar provisions in the House bill and the Senate amendment by leaving to the Rules of Bankruptcy Procedure the determination of the location at which a request for payment of an administrative expense may be filed. The preamble to section 503(b) of the House bill makes a similar change with respect to the allowance of administrative expenses.

[*124 Cong. Rec. H 11,094 (Sept. 28, 1978); S 17,411 (Oct. 6 1978).*]

Subsection (b) specifies the kinds of administrative expenses that are allowable in a case under the bankruptcy code. The subsection is derived mainly from section 64a(1) of the Bankruptcy Act, with some changes. The actual, necessary costs and expenses of preserving the estate, including wages, salaries, or commissions for services rendered after the commencement of the case, and any taxes on, measured by, or withheld from such wages, salaries, or commissions, are allowable as administrative expenses. The latter portion relating to taxes codifies in part Otte v. United States, 419 U.S. 43 (1974).

[*House Report No. 95–595, 95th Cong., 1st Sess. 355 (1977); Senate Report No. 95–989, 95th Cong., 2d Sess. 66 (1978).*]

Taxes which the Internal Revenue Service may find due after giving the trustee a so-called "quickie" tax refund and later doing an audit of the refund are also payable as administrative expenses. The tax code permits the trustee of an estate which suffers a net operating loss to carry back the loss against an earlier profit year of the estate or of the debtor and to obtain a tentative refund for the earlier year, subject, however, to a later full audit of the loss which led to the refund. The bill, in effect, requires the Internal Revenue Service to issue a tentative refund to the trustee (whether the refund was applied for by the debtor or by the trustee), but if the refund later proves to have been erroneous in amount, the Service can request that the tax attributable to the erroneous refund be payable by the estate as an administrative expense.

[*Senate Report No. 95–989, 95th Cong., 2d Sess. 66 (1978).*]

Postpetition payments to an individual debtor for services rendered to the estate are administrative expenses, and are not property of the estate when received by the debtor. This situation would most likely arise when the individual was a sole proprietor and was employed by the estate to run the business after the commencement of the case. An individual debtor in possession would be so employed, for example. *See* Local Loan v. Hunt, 292 U.S. 234, 243 (1943).

Compensation and reimbursement awarded officers of the estate under section 330 are allowable as administrative expenses. Actual, necessary expenses, other than compensation of a professional person, incurred by a creditor that files an involuntary petition, by a creditor that recovers property for the benefit of the estate, by a creditor that acts in connection with the prosecution of a criminal offense relating to the case, by a creditor, indenture trustee, equity security holder, or committee of creditors or equity security holders (other than official committees) that makes a substantial contribution to a reorganization or municipal debt adjustment case, or by a superseded custodian, are all allowable administrative expenses. The phrase "substantial contribution in the case" is derived from Bankruptcy Act sections 242 and 243. It does not require a contribution that leads to confirmation of a plan, for in many cases, it will be a substantial contribution if the person involved uncovers facts that would lead to a denial of confirmation, such as fraud in connection with the case.

Paragraph (4) permits reasonable compensation for professional services rendered by an attorney or an accountant of an equity whose expense is compensable under the previous paragraph. Paragraph (5) permits reasonable compensation for an indenture trustee in making a substantial contribution in a reorganization or municipal debt adjustment case. Finally, paragraph (6) permits witness fees and mileage as prescribed under chapter 119 of title 28.

[*House Report No. 95–595, 95th Cong., 1st Sess. 355 (1977); See Senate Report No. 95–989, 95th Cong., 2d Sess. 66–67 (1978).*]

Section 503(b)(1) adopts the approach taken in the House bill as modified by some provisions contained in the Senate amendment. The preamble to section 503(b) makes clear that none of the paragraphs of section 503(b) apply to claims or expenses of the kind specified in section 502(f) that arise in the ordinary course of the debtor's business or financial affairs and that arise during the gap between the commencement of an involuntary case and the appointment of a trustee or the order for relief, whichever first occurs. The remainder of section 503(b) represents a compromise between H.R. 8200 as passed by the House and the Senate amendments. Section 503(b)(3)(E) codifies present law in cases such as Randolph v. Scruggs, 190 U.S. 533, which accords administrative expense status to services rendered by a prepetition custodian or other party to the extent that such services actually benefit the estate. Section 503(b)(4) of the House amendment conforms to the provision contained in H.R. 8200 as passed by the House and deletes language contained in the Senate amendment providing a different standard of compensation under section 330 of that amendment.

[*124 Cong. Rec. H 11,094–95 (Sept. 28, 1978); S 17,411 (Oct, 6 1978).*]

Comment

Bankruptcy Rule 5004 (b) provides that a bankruptcy judge shall be disqualified from allowing compensation to a person who is a relative of the bankruptcy judge or with whom the judge is so connected as to render it improper for the judge to authorize compensation. "Improper" would include the appearance of impropriety.

Case Annotations

An administrative priority will not be given to attorney's fees incurred by a creditor in resisting a trustee's third party action under the Comprehensive Environmental Response, Compensation, and Liability Act (CERCLA) when the action was brought in the ordinary course of the liquidation of the assets of the chapter 7 estate and is rooted in prepetition events. *In re* Hemingway Transport, Inc., 954 F.2d 1, 26 C.B.C.2d 372 (1st Cir. 1992).

Environmental clean-up costs incurred postpetition but related to a prepetition release or threatened release of hazardous waste, are entitled to an administrative priority since such costs are necessary to preserve the estate in the sense that they allow a chapter 11 debtor in possession to continue to operate in compliance with applicable environmental laws. *In re* Chateaugay Corp., 944 F.2d 997, 25 C.B.C.2d 620 (2d Cir. 1991).

It is implied in the overall scheme for chapter 11 reorganization and in the legislative history of the Code and its amendments that Congress intended that the administrative expenses of an official creditors' committee be allowed. *In re* The George Worthington Co., 921 F.2d 626, 24 C.B.C.2d 308 (6th Cir. 1990).

When a debtor follows a chapter 11 reorganization with a second chapter 11 case which involves a liquidation plan, a creditor may not claim an automatic administrative priority in the second chapter 11 case on the basis of guarantees in the original case when the court has determined that the second filing is both proper and distinct from the first; accordingly, the creditor must prove its claims relative to the second filing rather than pointing to the provisions of the original reorganization case. In the Matter of Jartran, Inc., 886 F.2d 859, 21 C.B.C.2d 1141 (7th Cir. 1989).

A court may allow an administrative expense priority for interest accrued on postpetition tax liabilities. *In re* Allied Mechanical Servs., Inc., 885 F.2d 837, 21 C.B.C.2d 821 (11th Cir. 1989).

An administrative expense priority is allowed for postpetition leases that preserve the estate for the benefit of the creditors and the costs are actual and necessary, but will not be granted for hazardous waste cleanup that is a prepetition activity. *In re* Dant & Russell, Inc., 853 F.2d 700, 20 C.B.C.2d 369 (9th Cir. 1988).

When a claim arises from the debtor's postpetition use of leased equipment allegedly in violation of the terms of the prepetition agreement, the appropriate rationale to qualify a claim as an administrative expense under section 503 reflects the actual value conferred on the bankruptcy estate by reason of wrongful acts or breach of agreement. A creditor's claim which arises from prepetition damages to equipment never in the debtor's possession is properly treated as a general unsecured claim rather than as an administrative expense. United Trucking Service v. Trailer Rental Co. (*In re* United Trucking Service), 851 F.2d 159, 19 C.B.C.2d 542 (6th Cir. 1988).

Postpetition expenses relating to prepetition obligations are not entitled to administrative priority when the inducement for a creditor to perform such expenses comes from the prepetition debtor since the resulting consideration is given to that entity and not to the debtor in possession. Employee Transfer Corp. v. Grigsby (*In re* White Motor Corp.), 831 F.2d 106, 17 C.B.C.2d 1077 (6th Cir. 1987).

Since the withdrawal liability of an employer withdrawing from a pension plan under the Multiemployer Pension Plan Amendments Act is based on the employer's contributions to the plan prior to the year before the employer withdraws, the consideration supporting the liability is the work of employees during those earlier years. It therefore cannot qualify as an administrative expense within the meaning of section 503(b)(1)(A) of the Code since it was not incurred for the benefit of the estate's creditors. Trustees of the Amalgamated Insurance Fund v. McFarlin's, Inc., 789 F.2d 98, 14 C.B.C.2d 1075 (2d Cir. 1986).

The term "estate" as used in section 503(b)(1)(B)(i) implies postpetition liabilities, with the result that claims for FICA and income taxes withheld by a debtor in possession from its employees' paychecks but never paid to IRS during an attempted reorganization are entitled to administrative expense priority pursuant to section 501(a)(1) since they are incurred by and are a liability of the estate. Both interest and penalties on taxes are first priorities and are given the same treatment. United States v. Friendship College, Inc. (In re Friendship College, Inc.), 737 F.2d 430, 10 C.B.C.2d 1151 (4th Cir. 1984).

Section 503(b)(1)(A) provides the authority for reimbursement of members of official creditors' committees for expenses incurred while participating in official committee activities, provided that such expenses constitute actual and necessary costs of preserving the estate, and are incurred for the benefit of the estate. These expenses will be allowed only upon application to the court and upon strict scrutiny by the court. In re National Enterprises, Inc., 26 C.B.C.2d 1630 (B. Ct., E.D. Va. 1992).

Pursuant to section 503(b), creditors whose interests are otherwise adequately protected by a committee but who desire a more active role in the course of a chapter 11 case may form an unofficial committee, retain counsel, hire financial advisors and later seek reimbursement of their expenses to the extent they make a substantial contribution to the case. In re Hills Stores Co., 26 C.B.C.2d 1038 (B. Ct., S.D.N.Y. 1992).

When the use of property to store assets of the debtor is an actual cost which is necessary to preserve the assets until they are sold or abandoned, and the estate directly and substantially benefits from the use of the property for storage, the owner of the property is entitled to administrative expense priority under section 503(b)(1)(A). Matter of Great Northern Forest Products, Inc., 26 C.B.C.2d 411 (B. Ct., W.D. Mich. 1991).

Interest accruing on trust fund taxes incurred during the reorganization phase of a case retains its administrative expense status despite the later conversion of the case to chapter 7. So far as administrative tax claims against a chapter 11 estate are concerned, interest ceases to accrue as of the date of a conversion to chapter 7. Matter of Peter Del Grande Corp., 26 C.B.C.2d 1374 (B. Ct., D.N.J. 1992).

When a debtor and insurer have a prepetition insurance contract, the insurer's liability to make payments on postpetition claims for the coverage period arises from the prepetition contract and cannot be transformed into a postpetition administrative expense. In re Firearms Import and Export Corp., 25 C.B.C.2d 1037 (B. Ct., S.D. Fla. 1991).

The estate of a chapter 7 debtor which leases premises as a holdover tenant for the sole purpose of complying with an EPA order to clean up hazardous wastes is subject to an administrative expense claim of the lessor for the period the premises were so occupied. *In re* Bio-Med Laboratories, 25 C.B.C.2d 928 (B. Ct., N.D. Ohio 1991).

Only penalties relating to a tax as described in section 503(b)(1)(B) are covered by section 503(b)(1)(C) so that civil environmental penalties are not covered by the section. *In re* N.P. Mining Co., 24 C.B.C.2d 1603 (B. Ct., N.D. Ala. 1990).

References

3 *Collier on Bankruptcy* ch. 503 (Matthew Bender 15th ed.).

2 *Collier Bankruptcy Manual* ch. 503 (Matthew Bender 3d ed.).

5 *Collier Bankruptcy Practice Guide* ch. 88 *et al.* (Matthew Bender).

Collier on Bankruptcy Taxation (Matthew Bender).

Adequate Protection and Administrative Expense: Toward a Uniform System for Awarding Superpriorities, 88 Mich. L. Rev. 2168 (1990).

Note, *The Administrative Expense Priority in Bankruptcy—A Survey,* 36 Drake L. Rev. 135 (1986–7).

Position Papers on SEC Participation in Chapter 11 Reorganization Cases and Proposed Amendment to Bankruptcy Code Section 503(b), 5 Com. L. Bull. 33 (1990).

Pulliam, Yates and Brewster, *Reimbursement of Creditors' Committee Members' Costs and Expenses Under Section 503(b) of the Bankruptcy Code,* 94 Com. L.J. 93 (1989).

Tilton, *Trade Creditor's Dilemma: Extending Credit to Debtors,* 205:118 N.Y.L.J. 5 (1991).

SECTION 504 (11 U.S.C. § 504)

§ 504.   Sharing of compensation.

(a) Except as provided in subsection (b) of this section, a person receiving compensation or reimbursement under section 503(b)(2) or 503(b)(4) of this title may not share or agree to share—

(1) any such compensation or reimbursement with another person; or

(2) any compensation or reimbursement received by another person under such sections.

(b)(1) A member, partner, or regular associate in a professional association, corporation, or partnership may share compensation or reimbursement received under section 503(b)(2) or 503(b)(4) of this title with another member, partner, or regular associate in such association, corporation, or partnership, and may share in any compensation or remibursement received under such sections by another member, partner, or regular associate in such association, corporation, or partnership.

(2) An attorney for a creditor that files a petition under section 303 of this title may share compensation and reimbursement received under section 503(b)(4) of this title with any other attorney contributing to the services rendered or expenses incurred by such creditor's attorney.

Bankruptcy Rule References: 2014, 2016 and 2017

Legislative History

Section 504 prohibits the sharing of compensation, or fee splitting, among attorneys, other professionals, or trustees. The section provides only two exceptions: partners or associates in the same professional association, partnership, or corporation may share compensation inter se; and attorneys for petitioning creditors that join in a petition commencing an involuntary case may share compensation.

[*House Report No. 95–595, 95th Cong., 1st Sess. 356 (1977); Senate Report No. 95–989, 95th Cong., 2d Sess. 67 (1978).*]

Comment

Section 504 of the Code is considerably more restrictive than former Bankruptcy Rule 219(d) and, in effect, forbids fee splitting.

Bankruptcy Rule 2016(a) provides that the application of an entity seeking compensation for services, or reimbursement of necessary expenses, shall include a statement as to whether any agreement or understanding exists between the applicant and any other entity for the sharing of compensation received or to be received for services rendered in or in connection with the case, and the particulars of any sharing of compensation or agreement or understanding therefor, except that details of any agreement with the applicant for sharing of compensation as a member or regular associate of a firm of lawyers or accountants shall not be required. The 1991 Amendments require the applicant, except in a chapter 9 case, to transmit a copy of the application to the United States trustee.

Case Annotations

No compensation is to be granted an attorney, employed by the debtor while at a firm that he subsequently left, for his postpetition services rendered in his newly formed partnership when those services were unauthorized, were of no benefit to either the administration of the estate or the estate itself and to do so would reduce the estate's excess payout to creditors. *In re* Maller Restaurant Corp., 14 C.B.C.2d 320 (B. Ct., E.D.N.Y. 1985).

References

3 *Collier on Bankruptcy* ch. 504 (Matthew Bender 15th ed.).

2 *Collier Bankruptcy Manual* ch. 504 (Matthew Bender 3d ed.).

2 *Collier Bankruptcy Practice Guide* ch. 28 (Matthew Bender).

Thompson, *Attorney's Fees and Liens,* 85 Comm. L.J. (1980).

SECTION 505 (11 U.S.C. § 505)

§ 505. Determination of tax liability.

(a)(1) Except as provided in paragraph (2) of this subsection, the court may determine the amount or legality of any tax, any fine or penalty relating to a tax, or any addition to tax, whether or not previously assessed, whether or not paid, and whether or not contested before and adjudicated by a judicial or administrative tribunal of competent jurisdiction.

(2) The court may not so determine—

(A) the amount or legality of a tax, fine, penalty, or addition to tax if such amount or legality was contested before and adjudicated by a judicial or administrative tribunal of competent jurisdiction before the commencement of the case under this title; or

(B) any right of the estate to a tax refund, before the earlier of—

(i) 120 days after the trustee properly requests such refund from the governmental unit from which such refund is claimed; or

(ii) a determination by such governmental unit of such request.

(b) A trustee may request a determination of any unpaid liability of the estate for any tax incurred during the administration of the case by submitting a tax return for such tax and a request for such a determination to the governmental unit charged with responsibility for collection or determination of such tax. Unless such return is fraudulent, or contains a material misrepresentation, the trustee, the debtor, and any successor to the debtor are discharged from any liability for such tax—

    (1) upon payment of the tax shown on such return, if—

      (A) such governmental unit does not notify the trustee, within 60 days after such request, that such return has been selected for examination; or

      (B) such governmental unit does not complete such an examination and notify the trustee of any tax due, within 180 days after such request or within such additional time as the court, for cause, permits;

    (2) upon payment of the tax determined by the court, after notice and a hearing, after completion by such governmental unit of such examination; or

    (3) upon payment of the tax determined by such governmental unit to be due.

(c) Notwithstanding section 362 of this title, after determination by the court of a tax under this section, the governmental unit charged with responsibility for collection of such tax may assess such tax against the estate, the debtor, or a successor to the debtor, as the case may be, subject to any otherwise applicable law.

Legislative History

Subsections (a) and (b) are derived, with only stylistic changes, from section 2a(2A) of the Bankruptcy Act, added in 1966. They permit determination by the bankruptcy court of any unpaid tax liability of the debtor that has not been contested before or adjudicated by a judicial or administrative tribunal of competent jurisdiction before the bankruptcy case, and the prosecution by the trustee of an appeal from an order of such a body if the time for review or appeal has not expired before the commencement of the bankruptcy case. As under current Bankruptcy Act section 2a(2A), Arkansas Corporation Commissioner v. Thompson, 313 U.S. 132 (1941), remains good law to permit abstention where uniformity of assessment is of significant importance.

[*House Report No. 95–595, 95th Cong., 1st Sess. 356 (1977); Senate Report No. 95–989, 95th Cong., 2d Sess. 67 (1978).*]

Subsection (c) is new. It codifies in part the referee's decision in *In re* Statmaster Corp., 465 F.2d 987 (5th Cir. 1972). Its purpose is to protect the trustee from personal liability for a tax falling on the estate that is not assessed until after the case is closed. If necessary to permit expeditions [*sic*] closing of the case, the court, on request of the trustee, must order the government unit charged with the responsibility for collection or determination of the tax to audit the trustee's return or be barred from attempting later collection. The court will be required to permit sufficient time to perform an audit, if the taxing authority requests it. The final order of the court and the payment of the tax determined in that order discharges the trustee, the debtor, and any successor to the debtor from any further liability for the tax. *See* Plumb, *The Tax Recommendations of the Commission on the Bankruptcy Laws Tax Procedures,* 88 Harv. L. Rev. 1360, 1423–42 (1975).

[*House Report No. 95–595, 95th Cong., 1st Sess. 356 (1977).*]

Section (c) deals with procedures for obtaining a prompt audit of tax returns filed by the trustee in a liquidation or reorganization case. Under the bill as originally introduced, a trustee who is "in doubt" concerning tax liabilities of the estate incurred during a title 11 proceeding could obtain a discharge from personal liability for himself and the debtor (but not for the debtor or the debtor's successor in a reorganization), provided that certain administrative procedures were followed. The trustee could request a prompt tax audit by the local, State, or Federal governmental unit. The taxing authority would have to notify the trustee and the court within sixty days whether it accepted the return or desired to audit the returns more fully. If an audit were conducted, the tax office would have to notify the trustee of any tax deficiency within four months (subject to an extension of time if the court approved). These procedures would apply only to tax years completed on or before the case was closed and for which the trustee had filed a tax return.

The committee bill eliminates the "in doubt" rule and makes mandatory (rather than optional) the trustee's request for a prompt audit of the estate's tax returns. In many cases, the trustee could not be certain that his returns raised no doubt about possible tax issues. In addition, it is desirable not to create a situation where the taxing authority asserts a tax liability against the debtor (as transferee of surplus assets, if any, returned to him) after the case is over; in any such situation, the debtor would be called on to defend a tax return which he did not prepare. Under the amendment, all disputes concerning these returns are to be resolved by the bankruptcy court, and both the trustee and the debtor himself do not then face potential post-bankruptcy tax liabilities based on these returns. This result would occur as to the debtor, however, only in a liquidation case.

In a reorganization in which the debtor or a successor to the debtor continues in existence, the trustee could obtain a discharge from personal liability through the prompt audit procedure, but the Treasury could still claim a deficiency against the debtor (or his successor) for additional taxes due on returns filed during the title 11 proceedings.

[Senate Report No. 95–989, 95th Cong., 2d Sess. 67–68 (1978).]

Section 505 of the House amendment adopts a compromise position with respect to the determination of tax liability from the position taken in H.R. 8200 as passed by the House and in the Senate amendment.

[124 Cong. Rec. H 11,095 (Sept. 28, 1978); S 17,411 (Oct. 6, 1978).]

Section 505. Determination of tax liability; Authority of bankruptcy court to rule on merits of tax claims—The House amendment authorizes the bankruptcy court to rule on the merits of any tax claim involving an unpaid tax, fine, or penalty relating to a tax, or any addition to a tax, of the debtor or the estate. This authority applies, in general, whether or not the tax, penalty, fine, or addition to tax had been previously assessed or paid. However, the bankruptcy court will not have jurisdiction to rule on the merits of any tax claim which has been previously adjudicated, in a contested proceeding, before a court of competent jurisdiction. For this purpose, a proceeding [*sic*] the United States Tax Court is to be considered "contested" if the debtor filed a petition in the Tax Court by the commencement of the case and the Internal Revenue Service had filed an answer to the petition. Therefore, if a petition and answer were filed in the Tax Court before the title II [*sic:* should be "11"] petition was filed, and if the debtor later defaults in the Tax Court, then, under res judicata principles, the bankruptcy court could not then rule on the debtor's or the estate's liability for the same taxes.

The House amendment adopts the rule of the Senate bill that the bankruptcy court can, under certain conditions, determine the amount of tax refund claim by the trustee. Under the House amendment, if the refund results from an offset or counterclaim to a claim or request for payment by the Internal Revenue Service, or other tax authority, the trustee would not first have to file an administrative claim or refund with the tax authority.

However, if the trustee requests a refund in other situations, he would first have to submit an administrative claim for the refund. Under the House amendment, if the Internal Revenue Service, or other tax authority does not rule on the refund claim within 120 days, then the bankruptcy court may rule on the merits of the refund claim.

Under the Internal Revenue Code, a suit for refund of Federal taxes cannot be filed until six months after a claim for refund is filed with the Internal Revenue Service (sec. 6532(a)). Because of the bankruptcy aim to close the estate as expeditiously as possible, the House amendment shortens to 120 days the period for the Internal Revenue Service to decide the refund claim.

The House amendment also adopts the substance of the Senate bill rule permitting the bankruptcy court to determine the amount of any penalty, whether punitive or pecuniary in nature, relating to taxes over which is has jurisdiction.

Jurisdiction of the tax court in bankruptcy cases: The Senate amendment provided a detailed series of rules concerning the jurisdiction of the United States Tax Court, or similar State or local administrative tribunal to determine personal tax liabilities of an individual debtor. The House amendment deletes these specific rules and relies on procedures to be derived from broad general powers of the bankruptcy court.

Under the House amendment, as under present law, a corporation seeking reorganization under chapter 11 is considered to be personally before the bankruptcy court for purposes of giving that court jurisdiction over the debtor's personal liability for a nondischargeable tax.

The rules are more complex where the debtor is an individual under chapter 7, 11, or 13. An individual debtor or the tax authority can, as under section 17c of the present Bankruptcy Act, file a request that the bankruptcy court determine the debtor's personal liability for the balance of any nondischargeable tax not satisfied from assets of the estate. The House amendment intends to retain these procedures and also adds a rule staying commencement or continuation of any proceeding in the Tax Court after the bankruptcy petition is filed, unless and until that stay is lifted by the bankruptcy judge under section 362(a)(8). The House amendment also stays assessment as well as collection of a prepetition claim against the debtor (sec. 362(a)(6)). A tax authority would not, however, be stayed from issuing a deficiency notice during the bankruptcy case (sec. (b)(7)). The Senate amendment repealed the existing authority of the Internal Revenue Service to make an immediate assessment of taxes upon bankruptcy (sec. 6871(a) of the code). *See* section 321 of the Senate bill. As indicated, the substance of that provision, also affecting State and local taxes, is contained in section 362(a)(6) of the House amendment while the bankruptcy case is pending.

Where no proceeding in the Tax Court is pending at the commencement of the bankruptcy case, the tax authority can, under the House amendment, file a claim against the estate for a prepetition tax liability and may also file a request that the bankruptcy court hear arguments and decided the merits of an individual debtor's personal liability for the balance of any nondischargeable tax liability not satisfied from assets of the estate. Bankruptcy terminology refers to the latter type of request as a creditor's complaint to determine the dischargeability of a debt. Where such a complaint is filed, the bankruptcy court will have personal jurisdiction over an individual debtor, and the debtor himself would have no access to the Tax Court, or to any other court, to determine his personal liability for nondischargeable taxes.

If a tax authority decides not to file a claim for taxes which would typically occur where there are few, if any, assets in the estate, normally the tax authority would also not request the bankruptcy court to rule on the debtor's personal liability for a nondischargeable tax. Under the House amendment, the tax authority would then have to follow normal procedures in order to collect a nondischargeable tax. For example, in the case of nondischargeable Federal income taxes, the Internal Revenue Service would be required to issue a deficiency notice to an individual debtor, and the debtor could then file a petition in the Tax Court—or a refund suit in a district court—as the forum in which to litigate his personal liability for a nondischargeable tax.

Under the House amendment, as under present law, an individual debtor can also file a complaint to determine dischargeability. Consequently, where the tax authority does not file a claim or a request that the bankruptcy court determine dischargeability of a specific tax liability, the debtor could file such a request on his own behalf, so that the bankruptcy court would then determine both the validity of the claim against assets in the estate and also the personal liability of the debtor for any nondischargeable tax.

Where a proceeding is pending in the Tax Court at the commencement of the bankruptcy case, the commencement of the bankruptcy case automatically stays further action in the Tax Court case unless and until the stay is lifted by the bankruptcy court. The Senate amendment repealed a provision of the Internal Revenue case [sic] barring a debtor from filing a petition in the Tax Court after commencement of a bankruptcy case (sec. 6871(b) of the Code). See section 321 of the Senate bill. As indicated earlier, the equivalent of the Code amendment is embodied in section 362(a) (8) of the House amendment, which automatically stays commencement or continuation of any proceeding in the Tax Court until the stay is lifted or the case is terminated. The stay will permit sufficient time for the bankruptcy trustee to determine if he desires to join the Tax Court proceeding on behalf of the estate. Where the trustee chooses to join the Tax Court proceeding, it is expected that he will seek permission to intervene in the Tax Court case and then request that the stay on the Tax Court proceeding be lifted. In such a case, the merits of the tax liability will be determined by the Tax Court, and its decision will bind both the individual debtor as to any taxes which are nondischargeable and the trustee as to the tax claim against the estate.

Where the trustee does not want to intervene in the Tax Court, but an individual debtor wants to have the Tax Court determine the amount of his personal liability for nondischargeable taxes, the debtor can request the bankruptcy court to lift the automatic stay on existing Tax Court proceedings. If the stay is lifted and the Tax Court reaches its decision before the bankruptcy court's decision on the tax claim against the estate, the decision of the Tax Court would bind the bankruptcy court under principles of res judicata because the decision of the Tax Court affected the personal liability of the debtor. If the trustee does not wish to subject the estate to the decision of the Tax Court if the latter court decides the issues before the bankruptcy court rules, the trustee could resist the lifting of the stay on the existing Tax Court proceeding. If the Internal Revenue Service had issued a deficiency notice to the debtor before the bankruptcy case began, but as of the filing of the bankruptcy petition the 90-day period for filing in the Tax Court was still running, the debtor would be automatically stayed from filing a petition in the Tax Court. If either the debtor or the Internal Revenue Service then files a complaint to determine dischargeability in the bankruptcy court, the decision of the bankruptcy court would bind both the debtor and the Internal Revenue Service.

The bankruptcy judge could, however, lift the stay on the debtor to allow him to petition the Tax Court, while reserving the right to rule on the tax authority's claim against assets of the estate. The bankruptcy court could also, upon request by the trustee, authorize the trustee to intervene in the Tax Court for purposes of having the estate also governed by the decision of the Tax Court.

In essence, under the House amendment, the bankruptcy judge will have authority to determine which court will determine the merits of the tax claim both as to claims against the estate and claims against the debtor concerning his personal liability for nondischargeable taxes. Thus, if the Internal Revenue Service, or a State or local tax authority, files a petition to determine dischargeability, the bankruptcy judge can either rule on the merits of the claim and continue the stay on any pending Tax Court proceeding or lift the stay on the Tax Court and hold the dischargeability complaint in abeyance. If he rules on the merits of the complaint before the decision of the Tax Court is reached, the bankruptcy court's decision would bind the debtor as to nondischargeable taxes and the Tax Court would be governed by that decision under principles of of *res judicata*. If the bankruptcy judge does not rule on the merits of the complaint before the decision of the Tax Court is reached, the bankruptcy court will be bound by the decision of the Tax Court as it affects the amount of any claim against the debtor's estate.

If the Internal Revenue Service does not file a complaint to determine dischargeability and the automatic stay on a pending Tax Court proceeding is not lifted, the bankruptcy court could determine the merits of any tax claim against the estate. That decision will not bind the debtor personally because he would not have been personally before the bankruptcy court unless the debtor himself asks the bankruptcy court to rule on his personal liability. In any such situation where no party filed a dischargeability petition, the debtor would have access to the Tax Court to determine his personal liability for a nondischargeable tax debt. While the Tax Court in such a situation could take into account the ruling of the bankruptcy court on claims against the estate in deciding the debtor's personal liability, the bankruptcy court's ruling would not bind the Tax Court under principles of *res judicata,* because the debtor, in that situation, would not have been personally before the bankruptcy court.

If neither the debtor nor the Internal Revenue Service files a claim against the estate or a request to rule on the debtor's personal liability, any pending tax court proceeding would be stayed until the closing of the bankruptcy case, at which time the stay on the tax court would cease and the tax court case could continue for purposes of deciding the merits of the debtor's personal liability for nondischargeable taxes.

Audit of trustee's return: Under both bills, the bankruptcy court could determine the amount of any administrative period taxes. The Senate amendment, however, provided for an expedited audit procedure, which was mandatory in some cases. The House amendment (sec. 505(b)), adopts the provision of the House bill allowing the trustee discretion in all cases whether to ask the Internal Revenue Service, or State or local tax authority for a prompt audit of his returns on behalf of the estate. The House amendment, however, adopts the provision of the Senate bill permitting a prompt audit only on the basis of tax returns filed by the trustee for completed taxable periods. Procedures for a prompt audit set forth in the Senate bill are also adopted in modified form.

Under the procedure, before the case can be closed, the trustee may request a tax audit by the local, State or Federal tax authority of all tax returns filed by the trustee. The taxing authority would have to notify the trustee and the bankruptcy court within 60 days whether it accepts returns or desires to audit the returns more fully. If an audit is conducted, the taxing authority would have to notify the trustee of tax deficiency within 180 days after the original and it [sic] request, subject to extensions of time if the bankruptcy court approves. If the trustee does not agree with the results of the audit, the trustee could ask the bankruptcy court to resolve the dispute. Once the trustee's tax liability for administration period taxes has thus been determined, the legal effect in a case under chapter 7 or 11 would be to discharge the trustee and any predecessor of the trustee, and also the debtor, from any further liability for these taxes.

The prompt audit procedure would not be available with respect to any tax liability as to which any return required to be filed on behalf of the estate is not filed with the proper tax authority. The House amendment also specifies that a discharge of the trustee or the debtor which would otherwise occur will not be granted, or will be void if the return filed on behalf of the estate reflects fraud or material representation [sic] of facts.

For purposes of the above prompt audit procedures, it is intended that the tax authority with which the request for audit is to be filed is, as to Federal taxes, the office of the District Director in the district where the bankruptcy case is pending.

Under the House amendment, if the trustee does not request a prompt audit, the debtor would not be discharged from possible transferee liability if any assets are returned to the debtor.

Assessment after decision: As indicated above, the commencement of a bankruptcy case automatically stays assessment of any tax (sec. 362(a)(6)). However, the House amendment provides (sec. 505(c)) that if the bankruptcy court renders a final judgment with regard to any tax (under the rules discussed above), the tax authority may then make an assessment (if permitted to do so under otherwise applicable tax law) without waiting for termination of the case or confirmation of a reorganization plan.

Trustee's authority to appeal tax cases. The equivalent provision in the House bill (sec. 505(b)) and in the Senate bill (sec. 362(h)) authorizing the trustee to prosecute an appeal or review of a tax case are deleted as unnecessary. Section 541(a) of the House amendment provides that property of the estate is to include all legal or equitable interests of the debtor. These interests include the debtor's causes of action, so that the specific provisions of the House and Senate bills are not needed.

[*124 Cong. Rec. H 11,110–111 (Sept. 28, 1978); S 17,426–28 (Oct. 6, 1978).*]

Comment

Sections 505(a) and (b) are derived from Section 2a(2A) of the former Bankruptcy Act. Subsection (c) codifies in part the bankruptcy judge's decision in *In re* Statmaster Corp., 465 F. 2d 987 (5th Cir. 1972).

Case Annotations

Bankruptcy courts have jurisdiction over disputes involving unemployment compensation tax liability incurred by debtors, but such jurisdiction may include tax disputes concerning others when that dispute affects the debtor and when exercise of that jurisdiction is necessary to rehabilitate the debtor or to administer its estate effectively. *In re* Wolverine Radio Co., 930 F.2d 1132, 24 C.B.C.2d 1702 (6th Cir. 1991).

Although section 505 clarifies the bankruptcy court's jurisdiction over tax claims and does not limit its jurisdiction to debtors, it does not authorize a bankruptcy court to determine the tax liability of nondebtors. Quattrone v. IRS, 895 F.2d 921, 22 C.B.C.2d 427 (3d Cir. 1990).

Payments made to the IRS on prepetition tax liabilities by a chapter 11 debtor are involuntary payments that may not be allocated to pay the debtor's trust fund liabilities first. DuCharmes & Co. v. State of Michigan (*In re* DuCharmes & Co.), 852 F.2d 194, 19 C.B.C.2d 588 (6th Cir. 1988).

Federal tax payments made by a debtor in possession after filing a petition for reorganization under chapter 11, but prior to confirmation of its reorganization plan, are involuntary payments and the bankruptcy court lacks the jurisdiction to order otherwise. United States v. Technical Knockout Graphics, Inc. (*In re* Technical Knockout Graphics, Inc.), 833 F.2d 797, 17 C.B.C.2d 1246 (9th Cir. 1987).

The Bankruptcy Code does not in any way supersede the Anti-Injunction Act, 26 U.S.C. § 7421(a), as there is no indication that this was Congress' intent. LaSalle Rolling Mills, Inc. v. United States (In the Matter of LaSalle Rolling Mills, Inc.), 832 F.2d 390, 17 C.B.C.2d 650 (7th Cir. 1987).

The payments of taxes by a debtor undergoing chapter 11 reorganization are most realistically classified as involuntary for purposes of the debtor's ability to designate to which taxes the payments should be allocated. In the Matter of Ribs-R-Us, Inc., 828 F.2d 199, 17 C.B.C.2d 1098 (3d Cir. 1987).

Whether or not a chapter 11 debtor may allocate the payment of its trust fund tax payments should be determined by weighing the benefits against the detriments to the involved parties, that is, the debtor, its creditors and the Internal Revenue Service. A debtor may allocate its tax payments if it serves the best interests of all parties associated with the transactions. United States v. A & B Heating & Air Conditioning (In the Matter of A & B Heating & Air Conditioning), 823 F.2d 462, 17 C.B.C.2d 409 (11th Cir. 1987), *vacated*, 486 U.S. 1002, 108 S. Ct. 1724, 100 L. Ed. 2d 189 (1988).

The jurisdiction of the bankruptcy court does not extend to enjoin actions by the IRS on the separate tax liabilities imposed upon officers of the debtor corporation pursuant to 26 U.S.C. § 6672 as a result of the corporation's failure to pay taxes even if the penalty would adversely affect the debtor corporation's reorganization. United States v. Huckabee Auto Co., 783 F.2d 1546, 14 C.B.C.2d 483 (11th Cir. 1986).

A bankruptcy court may, in its discretion, refuse to determine the tax liability of a former director of a chapter 11 debtor who is personally responsible for the payment of delinquent trust fund taxes since the liability is that of the director and not the debtor. It may also refuse to determine the tax liability of a former director when the impact upon the debtor is minimal or nonexistent. *In re* American Motor Club, Inc., 26 C.B.C.2d 151 (B. Ct., E.D.N.Y. 1992).

Over the objection of a taxing authority, the bankruptcy court may determine a debtor's liability for trust fund taxes where the authority has not assessed or proposed to assess a tax deficiency, when to do so will involve a determination based on events and conduct that have already occurred, decide a dispute ripe for adjudication, and act to prevent injury to the debtor's fresh start. *In re* Kilen, 25 C.B.C.2d 326 (B. Ct., N.D. Ill. 1991).

References

3 *Collier on Bankruptcy* ch. 505 (Matthew Bender 15th ed.).

2 *Collier Bankruptcy Manual* ch. 505 (Matthew Bender 3d ed.).

6 *Collier Bankruptcy Practice Guide* ch. 93 (Matthew Bender).

Bankruptcy Court Jurisdiction and the Power To Enjoin the IRS, 70 Minn. L. Rev. 1279 (1986).

Collier, *IRS vs. Bankruptcy Court,* 38 La. B.J. 290 (1990).

Comment, *Allocation of Tax Payments Under Chapter 11 Reorganizations — Who Will Decide: IRS or Bankruptcy Courts?* 28 Duq. L. Rev. 677 (1990).

Hippke, *Special Tax Provisions of the Bankruptcy Reform Act of 1978,* 1979 Ann. Survey of Bankruptcy Law 127.

Onsager, *Assigning Tax Liability Between the Bankruptcy Estate and the Individual Debtor* 75 J. Tax'n 102 (1991).

Sabino, *The Allocation of Payments to Trust Fund Taxes in Bankruptcy Reorganizations: The IRS v. the Bankruptcy Court,* 17 J. Corp. Tax'n 160 (1990).

Webster, *Tax Aspects of the Bankruptcy Reform Act of 1978,* 10 Tax Advisor 220 (1979).

SECTION 506 (11 U.S.C. § 506)

§ 506. Determination of secured status.

(a) An allowed claim of a creditor secured by a lien on property in which the estate has an interest, or that is subject to setoff under section 553 of this title, is a secured claim to the extent of the value of such creditor's interest in the estate's interest in such property, or to the extent of the amount subject to setoff, as the case may be, and is an unsecured claim to the extent that the value of such creditor's interest or the amount so subject to setoff is less than the amount of such allowed claim. Such value shall be determined in light of the purpose of the valuation and of the proposed dispostion or use of such property, and in conjunction with any hearing on such disposition or use or on a plan affecting such creditor's interest.

(b) To the extent that an allowed secured claim is secured by property the value of which, after any recovery under subsection (c) of this section, is greater than the amount of such claim, there shall be allowed to the holder of such claim, interest on such claim, and any reasonable fees, costs, or charges provided for under the agreement under which such claim arose.

(c) The trustee may recover from property securing an allowed secured claim the reasonable, necessary costs and expenses of preserving, or disposing of, such property to the extent of any benefit to the holder of such claim.

(d) To the extent that a lien secures a claim against the debtor that is not an allowed secured claim, such lien is void unless—

(1) such claim was disallowed only under section 502(b)(5) or 502(e) of this title; or

(2) such claim is not an allowed secured claim due only to the failure of any entity to file a proof of such claim under section 501 of this title.

Bankruptcy Rule References: 3012 and 7001

Legislative History

Subsection (a) of this section separates an undersecured creditor's claim into two parts: He has a secured claim to the extent of the value of his collateral; and he has an unsecured claim for the balance of his claim. The subsection also provides for the valuation of claims which involve setoffs under section 553. While courts will have to determine value on a case-by-case basis, the subsection makes it clear that valuation is to be determined in light of the purpose of the valuation and the proposed disposition or use of the subject property. This determination shall be made in conjunction with any hearing on such disposition or use of property or on a plan affecting the creditor's interest. To illustrate, a valuation early in the case in a proceeding under sections 361–363 would not be binding upon the debtor or creditor at the time of confirmation of the plan. Throughout the bill, references to secured claims are only to the claim determined to be secured under this subsection, and not to the full amount of the creditor's claim. This provision abolishes the use of the terms "secured creditor" and "unsecured creditor" and substitutes in their places the terms "secured claim" and "unsecured claim."

[*Senate Report No. 95–989, 95th Cong., 2d Sess. 68 (1978); See House Report No. 95–595, 95th Cong., 1st Sess. 356 (1977).*]

Section 506(a) of the House amendment adopts the provision contained in the Senate amendment and rejects a contrary provision as contained in H.R. 8200 as passed by the House. The provision contained in the Senate amendment and adopted by the House amendment recognizes that an amount subject to set-off is sufficient to recognize a secured status in the holder of such right. Additionally a determination of what portion of an allowed claim is secured and what portion is unsecured in binding only for the purpose for which the determination is made. Thus determinations for purposes of adequate protection is not binding for purposes of "cram down" on confirmation in a case under chapter 11.

[*124 Cong Rec. H 11,095 (Sept. 28, 1978); S 17,411 (Oct. 6, 1978).*]

Section 506. Determination of Secured Status: The House amendment deletes section 506(d)(3) of the Senate amendment, which insures that a tax lien securing a nondischargeable tax claim is not voided because a tax authority with notice or knowledge of the bankruptcy case fails to file a claim for the liability (as it may elect not to do, if it is clear there are insufficient assets to pay the liability). Since the House amendment retains section 506(d) of the House bill that a lien is not voided unless a party in interest has requested that the court determine and allow or disallow the claim, provision of the Senate amendment is not necessary.

[*124 Cong. Rec. H 11,111 (Sept. 28, 1978); S 17,428 (Oct. 6, 1978).*]

Subsection (b) codifies current law by entitling a creditor with an oversecured claim to any reasonable fees, costs, or charges provided under the agreement under which the claim arose. These fees, costs, and charges are secured claims to the extent that the value of the collateral exceeds the amount of the underlying claim. [*Ed. Note:* The Senate Report adds the words "(including attorney's fees)," after "reasonable fees".]

[*House Report No. 95–595, 95th Cong., 1st Sess. 356 (1977); Senate Report No. 95–989, 95th Cong., 2d Sess. 68 (1978).*]

Section 506(b) of the House Amendment adopts language contained in the Senate amendment and rejects language contained in H.R. 8200 as passed by the House. If the security agreement between the parties provides for attorneys' fees, it will be enforceable under title 11, notwithstanding contrary law, and is recoverable from the collateral after any recovery under section 506(c).

[*124 Cong. Rec. H 11,095 (Sept. 28, 1978); S 17,411 (Oct. 6, 1978).*]

Subsection (c) also codifies current law by permitting the trustee to recover from property whose value is greater than the sum of the claims secured by a lien on that property that reasonable, necessary costs and expenses of preserving, or disposing of, the property. The recovery is limited to the extent of any benefit to the holder of such claim.

[*House Report No. 95–595, 95th Cong., 1st Sess. 357 (1977); Senate Report No. 95–989, 95th Cong., 2d Sess. 68 (1978).*]

Section 506(c) of the House amendment was contained in H.R. 8200 as passed by the House and adopted, verbatim, in the Senate amendment. Any time the trustee or debtor in possession expends money to provide for the reasonable and necessary cost and expenses of preserving or disposing of a secured creditor's collateral, the trustee or debtor in possession is entitled to recover such expenses from the secured party or from the property securing an allowed secured claim held by such party.

[*124 Cong. Rec. H 11,095 (Sept. 28, 1978); S 17,411 (Oct. 6, 1978).*]

Subsection (d) permits liens to pass through the bankruptcy case unaffected. However, if a party in interest requests the court to determine and allow or disallow the claim secured by the lien under section 502 and the claim is not allowed, then the lien is void to the extent that the claim is not allowed. The voiding provision does not apply to claims disallowed only under section 502(e), which requires disallowance of certain claims against the debtor by a codebtor, surety, or guarantor for contribution or reimbursement.

[*House Report 95–595, 95th Cong., 1st Sess. 357 (1977); cf. Senate Report No. 95–989, 95th Cong., 2d Sess. 68 (1978).*]

Section 506(d) of the House amendment is derived from H.R. 8200 as passed by the House and is adopted in lieu of the alternative test provided in section 506(d) of the Senate amendment. For purposes of section 506(d) of the House amendment, the debtor is a party in interest.

[*124 Cong. Rec. H 11,095 (Sept. 28, 1978); S 17,411 (Oct. 6, 1978).*]

Comment

Subsection (a) of section 506 is derived from former Bankruptcy Rule 306(d):

(d) Secured Claims. If a secured creditor files a proof of claim, the value of the security interest held by him as collateral for his claim shall be determined by the court, and the claim shall be allowed only to the extent it is enforceable for any excess of the claim over such value.

Subsection (b) relates to interest on a secured claim. In this connection, *see In re* Black Ranches, Inc., 362 F. 2d 8 (8th Cir. 1966).

Subsection (c) relates to the expenses of servicing the collateral. In this connection, *see* Textile Banking Co. v. Widener, 265 F. 2d 446 (4th Cir. 1959).

Subsection (d) has no comparable provision in the former Bankruptcy Act.

Bankruptcy Rule 3012 provides that the court may determine the value of a claim secured by a lien on property in which the estate has an interst on motion of any party in interest and after a hearing on notice to the holder of the secured claim and any other entity as the court may direct. (An adversary proceeding is commenced when the validity, priority, or extent of a lien is at issue. Rule 7001. A motion under Rule 3012, however, is a contested matter governed by Rule 9014.)

1984 Amendments: Section 506(d) was amended by rewriting paragraphs (1) and (2). Subsection (d)(2) was renumbered (d)(1) and "502(b)(5) or" inserted. Subsection (d)(1) was renumbered (d)(2), rewritten, and clarified.

Case Annotations

A claim which is both allowed pursuant to section 502 and secured by a lien on real property may not be "stripped down" pursuant to section 506(d). The lien-voiding language of section 506(d) applies only to any real deficiency in the security; any increase in the actual value of the property over the judicially determined value of the property during the pendency of the bankruptcy case should accrue to the creditor. Dewsnup v. Timm, 502 U.S. —, 112 S. Ct. 773, 116 L. Ed. 2d 903, 25 C.B.C.2d 1297 (1992).

Section 506(b) allows postpetition interest on oversecured claims that are secured by either consensual and nonconsensual liens, such as tax liens, based on the plain language of the statute, which makes no distinction between consensual and nonconsensual liens with respect to payment of postpetition interest. This result does not conflict with any other section of the Code, with any significant state or federal interest, or with any legislative history or pre-Code case law. Under section 506(b), recovery of postpetition interest on an oversecured claim is unqualified, while recovery of fees and costs is allowed only if they are reasonable and provided for in the agreement under which the claim arose. United States v. Ron Pair Enterprises, Inc., 489 U.S. 235, 109 S. Ct. 1026, 103 L. Ed. 2d 290, 20 C.B.C.2d 267 (1989).

A creditor's allowed security interest in an automobile should be based on its wholesale price, not the retail price, which represents the debtor's interest, although the debtor's contemplated use of a vehicle in a chapter 13 case may be taken into account in determining its value to a secured creditor. In re Mitchell, 954 F.2d 557, 26 C.B.C.2d 657 (9th Cir. 1992).

While section 1322(b)(2) prohibits modification of a residential mortgage lender's rights, it protects only the secured claim of a lender rather than the lender itself or its entire claim, and whether, and the extent to which, the lender holds a secured claim must first be determined according to section 506(a). Section 506(d), as interpreted in Dewsnup, a chapter 7 case, is not applicable to section 1322(b). In re Bellamy, 962 F.2d 176, 26 C.B.C.2d 1459 (2d Cir. 1992).

Although a deed to land may, on its face, convey absolute ownership to a corporation and superficially indicate that the debtor and the corporation were involved in a joint venture, the deed will be deemed security for funds advanced by the corporation to the debtor, thereby giving the corporation an equitable mortgage if, inter alia, 1) the deed and an accompanying ground lease are properly recorded by the corporation; 2) there is no profit sharing; 3) control rights do not give the corporation the right to control operations or management; 4) the corporation bears no responsibility for losses; and 5) third parties do not believe that the corporation participated in the venture or looked to its creditworthiness as a basis for doing business with the debtor. In re PCH Associates, 949 F.2d 585, 25 C.B.C.2d 1393 (2d Cir. 1991).

The legislative history of section 506(c) extends standing to assert a claim to debtors in possession as well as to trustees. Of course, standing under section 506(c) need not be limited to trustees and debtors in possession. In determining whether a third party has standing to bring a claim under section 506(c), neither prior court approval of an arrangement causing the administrative expense to accrue, nor the prior relationship between the debtor and claimant, nor the claimant's motivation are relevant because the Code only requires that expenditures be "reasonable, necessary costs and expenses of preserving, or disposing of such property" not that the claimant have the best interests of the secured creditors in mind. In re Palomar Truck Corp., 951 F.2d 229, 25 C.B.C.2d 1734 (5th Cir. 1991).

In order to demonstrate whether a proper 506(c) claim has been made, the claimant must show that the expenditure was necessary, the amounts expended were reasonable and the secured creditor benefited from the expenses. If expenditures have enhanced the value of the portion of property which provides the security for the secured creditor's claim, it is clear that those expenditures have benefited the creditor for purposes of section 506(c). In re Parque Forestal, Inc., 949 F.2d 504, 25 C.B.C.2d 1690 (1st Cir. 1991).

The determination of whether a utility company's continued service to a debtor prevented deterioration of the estate or maintained the going concern value is a finding of fact, and the district court is not justified in imposing its own findings of fact unless the bankruptcy court's findings are clearly erroneous. In the Matter of Delta Towers, Ltd., 924 F.2d 74, 24 C.B.C.2d 1431 (5th Cir. 1991).

The intent of the Supreme Court's ruling in *Ron Pair* was not to abolish defenses against claims under section 506(b), but rather to give involuntary liens parity with voluntary ones so far as the applicability of section 506(b) was concerned. In the Matter of Lapiana, 909 F.2d 221, 23 C.B.C.2d 766 (7th Cir. 1990).

When a bankruptcy court disallows a creditor's claim for postpetition interest on loan repayment installments of interest and principal but is silent on the crucial issues as to whether the claim was oversecured and whether the debtor's estate was solvent, the case must be remanded for the bankruptcy court to make these factual findings and appropriate conclusions of law. *In re* Sublett, 895 F.2d 1381, 22 C.B.C.2d 868 (11th Cir. 1990).

Section 506 is a section of general applicability and in a chapter 13 case allows bifurcation of a claim into secured and unsecured portions. Wilson v. Commonwealth Mortgage Corp., 895 F.2d 123, 22 C.B.C.2d 561 (3d Cir. 1990).

A chapter 7 debtor may use section 506(d) to avoid the unsecured portion of a lien on real property in which he does not have equity and which was not administered in the bankruptcy case. Gaglia v. First Federal Savings and Loan Association, 889 F.2d 1304, 22 C.B.C.2d 91 (3d Cir. 1989).

All that a chapter 7 debtor can do through the interaction of sections 506 and 501 is to precipitate foreclosure, possibly for purposes of preventing a creditor from obtaining a deficiency judgment in state court, but the debtor cannot postpone foreclosure or prevent it. Lindsey v. Fed. Land Bank of St. Louis (In the Matter of Lindsey), 823 F.2d 189, 17 C.B.C.2d 363 (7th Cir. 1987).

A secured creditor's consent to the payment of designated expenses is not blanket or implied consent to the deduction of administrative expenses pursuant to section 506(c). Cent. Bank of Mont. v. Cascade Hydraulics and Util. Serv., Inc. (*In re* Cascade Hydraulics and Util. Serv., Inc.), 815 F.2d 546, 16 C.B.C.2d 1509 (9th Cir. 1987).

By its terms, section 506(c) applies only to holders of security interests and not to ownership interests and, consequently, the imposition of the expenses of administering those ownership interests under the auspices of section 506(c) is improper. The equitable authority available to the court through section 105(a) cannot change this result. Bear v. Coben (*In re* Golden Plan of California, Inc.), 812 F.2d 1088, 15 C.B.C.2d 1459 (9th Cir. 1986).

A utility can be awarded payment for unreimbursed postpetition utility fees under section 506(c) when the utility service provided preserved the going concern value of the debtor, thereby benefitting secured creditors. Equitable Gas Co. v. Equibank N.A. (*In re* McKeesport Steel Castings Co.), 799 F.2d 91, 15 C.B.C.2d 563 (3d Cir. 1986).

A superpriority security interest cannot be subordinated to administrative expenses for outstanding payroll taxes as that would discourage creditors from supporting debtors' reorganization efforts; Congress could not have intended that such collateral be used simply to protect management from the consequences of its own wrongful acts. General Electric Credit Corp. v. Peltz (*In re* Flagstaff Foodservice Corp.), 762 F.2d 10, 12 C.B.C.2d 1019 (2d Cir. 1985).

A lien survives a case under the Code although the secured claim that it supports was disallowed as untimely; section 506(d) is limited to situations in which the claim is disallowed for substantive reasons. In the Matter of Tarnow, 749 F.2d 464, 12 C.B.C.2d 3 (7th Cir. 1984).

The trustee may recover from a superpriority creditor's collateral the necessary costs of preserving or disposing of property only to the extent that the creditor will benefit; incidental benefits which accrue from an attempted reorganization are not within section 506(c). Gen. Elec. Credit Corp. v. Levin & Weintraub (*In re* Flagstaff Foodservice Corp.), 739 F.2d 73, 10 C.B.C.2d 1309 (2d Cir. 1984).

Expenditures incurred by the debtor in the usual protection of collateral in possession of his estate do not directly benefit secured creditors and therefore are not recoverable by the debtor. Brookfield Prod. Cred. Assoc. v. Borron, 738 F.2d 951, 10 C.B.C.2d 1314 (8th Cir. 1984).

Section 506(b) does not preclude an oversecured creditor's claim for penalties that had matured postpetition. It also does not preclude an oversecured creditor's claim for tax penalties because the section does not address penalties. It does, however, require disallowance of a claim for postpetition fees and costs when the claim arises by operation of law and not by agreement. *In re* Brentwood Outpatient Ltd., 26 C.B.C.2d 90 (B. Ct., M.D. Tenn. 1991).

To determine whether a secured creditor is entitled to interest on arrearages, the bankruptcy court should follow a three-part analysis which takes the following into account: 1) the nature of the creditor's claim under section 506(b); 2) whether the chapter 13 plan "modifies" or "cures" the mortgage under section 1322(b)(2); and 3) whether the plan otherwise meets all requirements for confirmation under section 1325(a). *In re* Chavez, 26 C.B.C.2d 1192 (B. Ct., D.N.M. 1992).

Both the statutory language and the legislative history of section 506(c) are clear and unambiguous: only the trustee or debtor in possession may surcharge a secured creditor's collateral. Three elements must be present in order to surcharge a secured creditor with administrative expenses pursuant to section 506(c): 1) the expense must be necessary for the preservation or disposal of the collateral; 2) the amount of the expense must be reasonable; and 3) the secured creditor must benefit from the expense. Matter of Great Northern Forest Products, Inc., 26 C.B.C.2d 411 (B. Ct., W.D. Mich. 1991).

Section 506 can be applied to exempt property in a chapter 13 case. *In re* Ward, 25 C.B.C.2d 349 (B. Ct., W.D. Okla. 1991).

Section 506(b) establishes a federal right to reasonable attorney's fees for an oversecured creditor regardless of a state law that awards fees to a prevailing party. Section 506(b) does not preclude an award of attorneys' fees to an oversecured creditor and also an award of attorney's fees to a debtor against that oversecured creditor should the debtor have the right to attorney's fees under state law. *In re* McGaw Property Management, Inc., 25 C.B.C.2d 1517 (B. Ct., C.D. Cal. 1991).

A section 506(c) motion for the levy of a surcharge for administrative expenses against secured property for the reasonable, necessary costs and expenses of preserving that property may be brought by a creditor as well as by the trustee since this is an equitable remedy and an overly narrow reading of the statute could provide a windfall benefit to secured creditors at the expense of creditors who would otherwise be charged with these expenses. *In re* Scopetta-Senra Partnership III, 25 C.B.C.2d 588 (B. Ct., S.D. Fla. 1991).

References

3 *Collier on Bankruptcy* ch. 506 (Matthew Bender 15th ed.).

2 *Collier Bankruptcy Manual* ch. 506 (Matthew Bender 3d ed.).

3 *Collier Bankruptcy Practice Guide* ch. 52 (Matthew Bender).

Aaron, *The Bankruptcy Bench—Reflections on the Secured Creditor in the Bankruptcy Court,* 89 Com. L.J. 357 (1984).

Bacon, *Representation of Secured Creditors in Real Estate Chapter 11 Cases,* 51 Tex. B.J. 622 (1988).

Berkowitz and Berkowitz, *A Practitioner's Guide to Compensation Under Sections 506(c) and 331 of the Bankruptcy Code,* 92 Com. L.J. 136 (1987).

Can a Debtor Void a Real Property Lien That Exceeds the Value of the Collateral? An Interpretation of Section 506(d) of the Bankruptcy Code, 45 Wash. & Lee L. Rev. 1393 (1989).

Cohen, Marwil and Gerard, *Entitlement of Secured Creditors to Default Interest Rates Under Bankruptcy Code Sections 506(b) and 1124,* 45 Bus. Law. 415 (1989).

Comment, *Oversecured Nonconsensual Prepetition Claims Entitled to Postpetition Interest Under 11 U.S.C. Section 506(b) — United States v. Ron Pair Enterprises, Inc.* (109 S. Ct. 1026), 21 Rutgers L.J. 499 (1990).

Comment, *Policing the Borrower: Debtor Misconduct Creates New Duties for Secured Lenders,* 19 Tex. Tech. L. Rev. 1405 (1988).

Heidt, *Interest Under Section 506(b) of the Bankruptcy Code: The Right, the Rate and the Relationship to Bankruptcy Policy,* 1991 Utah L. Rev. 361.

Note, *The Debtor's Right to Restrict Lienholder Recovery to the Value of the Encumbered Property Under Section 506 of the Bankruptcy Code,* 11 J. Corp. L. 433 (1986).

Ziegel, *Presentation on Secured Claims in Bankruptcy: A Comparison of Models,* 1987 Ariz. J. Int'l & Comp. L. 147.

SECTION 507 (11 U.S.C. § 507)

§ 507. Priorities.

(a) The following expenses and claims have priority in the following order:

(1) First, administrative expenses allowed under section 503(b) of this title, and any fees and charges assessed against the estate under chapter 123 of title 28.

(2) Second, unsecured claims allowed under section 502(f) of this title.

(3) Third, allowed unsecured claims for wages, salaries, or commissions, including vacation, severance, and sick leave pay—

(A) earned by an individual within 90 days before the date of the filing of the petition or the date of the cessation of the debtor's business, whichever occurs first; but only

(B) to the extent of $2,000 for each such individual.

(4) Fourth, allowed unsecured claims for contributions to an employee benefit plan—

(A) arising from services rendered within 180 days before the date of the filing of the petition or the date of the cessation of the debtor's business, whichever occurs first; but only

(B) for each such plan, to the extent of—

(i) the number of employees covered by each such plan multiplied by $2,000; less

(ii) the aggregate amount paid to such employees under paragraph (3) of this subsection, plus the aggregate amount paid by the estate on behalf of such employees to any other employee benefit plan.

(5) Fifth, allowed unsecured claims of persons—

(A) engaged in the production or raising of grain, as defined in section 557 (b) (1) of this title, against a debtor who owns or operates a grain storage facility, as defined in section 557 (b) (2) of this title, for grain or the proceeds of grain, or

(B) engaged as a United States fisherman against a debtor who has acquired fish or fish produce from a fisherman through a sale or conversion, and who is engaged in operating a fish produce storage or processing facility

—but only to the extent of $2,000 for each such individual.

(6) Sixth, allowed unsecured claims of individuals, to the extent of $900 for each such individual, arising from the deposit, before the commencement of the case, of money in connection with the purchase, lease, or rental of property, or the purchase of services, for the personal, family, or household use of such individuals, that were not delivered or provided.

(7) Seventh, allowed unsecured claims of governmental units, only to the extent that such claims are for—

(A) a tax on or measured by income or gross receipts—

(i) for a taxable year ending on or before the date of the filing of the petition for which a return, if required, is last due, including extensions, after three years before the date of the filing of the petition;

(ii) assessed within 240 days, plus any time plus 30 days during which an offer in compromise with respect to such tax that was made within 240 days after such assessment was pending, before the date of the filing of the petition; or

(iii) other than a tax of a kind specified in section 523(a)(1)(B) or 523(a)(1)(c) of this title, not assessed before, but assessable, under applicable law or by agreement, after, the commencement of the case;

(B) a property tax assessed before the commencement of the case and last payable without penalty after one year before the date of the filing of the petition;

(C) a tax required to be collected or withheld and for which the debtor is liable in whatever capacity;

(D) an employment tax on a wage, salary, or commission of a kind specified in paragraph (3) of this subsection earned from the debtor before the date of the filing of the petition, whether or not actually paid before such date, for which a return is last due, under applicable law or under any extension, after three years before the date of the filing of the petition;

(E) an excise tax on—

(i) a transaction occurring before the date of the filing of the petition for which a return, if required, is last due, under applicable law or under any extension, after three years before the date of the filing of the petition; or

(ii) if a return is not required, a transaction occurring during the three years immediately preceding the date of the filing of the petition;

(F) a customs duty arising out of the importation of merchandise—

(i) entered for consumption within one year before the date of the filing of the petition;

(ii) covered by an entry liquidated or reliquidated within one year before the date of the filing of the petition; or

(iii) entered for consumption within four years before the date of the filing of the petition but unliquidated on such date, if the Secretary of the Treasury certifies that failure to liquidate such entry was due to an investigation pending on such date into assessment of antidumping or countervailing duties or fraud, or if information needed for the proper appraisement or classification of such merchandise was not available to the appropriate customs officer before such date; or

(G) a penalty related to a claim of a kind specified in this paragraph and in compensation for actual pecuniary loss.

(8) Eighth, allowed unsecured claims based upon any commitment by the debtor to the Federal Deposit Insurance Corporation, the Resolution Trust Corporation, the Director of the Office of Thrift Supervision, the Comptroller of the Currency, or the Board of Governors of the Federal Reserve System, or their predecessors or successors, to maintain the capital of an insured depository institution.

(b) If the trustee, under section 362, 363, or 364 of this title, provides adequate protection of the interest of a holder of a claim secured by a lien on property of the debtor and if, notwithstanding such protection, such creditor has a claim allowable under subsection (a)(1) of this section arising from the stay of action against such property under section 362 of this title, from the use, sale, or lease of such property under section 363 of this title, or from the granting of a lien under section 364(d) of this title, then such creditor's claim under such subsection shall have priority over every other claim under such subsection.

(c) For the purpose of subsection (a) of this section, a claim of a governmental unit arising from an erroneous refund or credit of a tax has the same priority as a claim for the tax to which such refund or credit relates.

(d) An entity that is subrogated to the rights of a holder of a claim of a kind specified in subsection (a)(3), (a)(4), (a)(5),* or (a)(6)* of this section is not subrogated to the right of the holder of such claim to priority under such subsection.

Legislative History

Section 507 specifies the kinds of claims that are entitled to priority in distribution, and the order of the priority. Paragraph (1) grants first priority in distribution, and the order of the priority to allowed administrative expenses and to fees and charge assessed against the estate under chapter 123 of title 28. "Involuntary gap" creditors, granted first priority under current law, are granted second priority by paragraph (2). Paragraph (3) expands and increases the wage priority found in

---

* [*Ed. Note:* The references in section 507(d) to subsections (a)(5) and (a)(6) of that section should have been changed to subsections (a)(6) and (a)(7), respectively, as redesignated by Pub. L. No. 98–353.]

current section 64a(2). The amount entitled to priority is raised from $600 to $2400. The former figure was last adjusted in 1926. Inflation has made it nearly meaningless, and the bill brings it more than up to date. The three-month limit is retained, but is modified to run from the earlier of the date of the filing of the petition or the date of the cessation of the debtor's business. The priority is expanded to cover vacation, severance, and sick leave pay.

Paragraph (4) overrules United States v. Embassy Restaurant, 359 U.S. 29 (1958), which held that fringe benefits were not entitled to wage priority status. The bill recognizes the realities of labor contract negotiations, under which wage demands are often reduced if adequate fringe benefits are substituted. The priority granted is limited to claims for contributions to employee benefit plans such as pension plans, health or life insurance plans, and others, arising from services rendered after the earlier of one year before the bankruptcy case and the date of cessation of the debtor's business. The dollar limit placed on the total of all contributions payable under this paragraph is equal to the difference between the maximum allowable priority under paragraph (3) ($2400 times the number of employees covered by the plan) less the actual distributions under paragraph (3) with respect to those employees.

Paragraph (5) [*Ed. Note:* Section 507(a)(5) was redesignated as section 507(a)(6) by Pub. L. No. 98–353.] is a new priority for consumer creditors—those who have deposited money in connection with the purchase, lease, or rental of property, or the purchase of services, for their personal, family, or household use, that were not delivered or provided.

The sixth priority is for certain taxes. [*Ed. Note:* Section 507(a)(6) was redesignated as section 507(a)(7) by Pub. L. No. 98–353.] Income taxes for which a return is due within three years before the commencement of the case are granted priority. This will include any recapture of an investment credit that is treated as a prepetition claim under proposed 11 U.S.C. § 502(i), and any disallowed refund resulting from a carryback of a loss. Employment and withholding taxes are granted a two-year priority. Property, customs, and excise taxes, as well as taxes for which an extension or installment plan was granted, are given a one-year priority. During the transition period, the phrase "if a case concerning the debtor had been commenced on the date such extension was granted" will be construed as if the bankruptcy code enacted by this bill were in effect on the date the extension was granted, so that the limits specified in the other subparagraphs of this paragraph, rather than in Bankruptcy Act section 17a(1), would be able to be applied to the tax in question.

The priorities established in this section do not require that the claims listed be paid temporaly [*sic*] in the order listed. For example, if it is clear that there are adequate assets in the estate to pay all priority creditors through the fourth or fifth priority, it would be appropriate to pay wage claims as soon as practicable, even before all administrative expenses were determined, because most often the employees that worked for the failing enterprise will need the money they receive in payment of their claims to live on. The same may be true for consumer creditors under the fifth priority.

A tax refund is made in year of refund and not in tax year to which refund pertains. *In re* Able Roofing and Sheet Metal Co., 425 F. 2d 699 (5th Cir. 1970), is *overruled*. Rev. 991, 1031 (1974).

[*House Report No. 95–595, 95th Cong., 1st Sess. 357–8 (1977).*]

Section 507 specifies the kinds of claims that are entitled to priority in distribution, and the order of their priority. Paragraph (1) grants first priority to allowed administrative expenses and to fees and charges assessed against the estate under chapter 123 of title 28. Taxes included as administrative expenses under section 503(b)(1) of the bill generally receive the first priority, but the bill makes certain qualifications: Examples of these specially treated claims are the estate's liability for recapture of an investment tax credit claimed by the debtor before the title 11 case (this liability receives sixth priority) and the estate's employment tax liabilities on wages earned before, but paid after, the petition was filed (this liability generally receives the same priority as the wages).

"Involuntary gap" creditors, granted first priority under current law, are granted second priority by paragraph (2). This priority, covering claims arising in the ordinary course of the debtor's business or financial affairs after a title 11 case has begun but before a trustee is appointed or before the order for relief, includes taxes incurred during the conduct of such activities.

Paragraph (3) expands and increases the wage priority found in current section 64a(2). The amount entitled to priority is raised from $600 to $1800. The former figure was last adjusted in 1926. Inflation has made it nearly meaningless, and the bill brings it more than up to date. The three month limit of current law is retained, but is modified to run from the earlier of the date of the filing of the petition or the date of the cessation of the debtor's business. The priority is expanded to cover vacation, severance, and sick leave pay. The bill adds to the third priority so-called "trust fund" taxes, that is, withheld income taxes and the employees' share of the social security or railroad retirement taxes, but only to the extent that the wages on which taxes are imposed are themselves entitled to third priority.

The employer's share, the employment tax and the employer's share of the social security or railroad retirement tax on third priority compensation, is also included in the third priority category, but only if, and to the extent that the wages and related trust fund taxes have first been paid in full. Because of the claimants urgent need for their wages in the typical cases, the employer's taxes should not be paid before the wage claims entitled to priority, as well as the related trust fund taxes, are fully paid.

Paragraph (4) overrules United States v. Embassy Restaurant, 359 U.S. 29 (1958), which held that fringe benefits were not entitled to wage priority status. The bill recognizes the realities of labor contract negotiations, where fringe benefits may be sustained for wage demands. The priority granted is limited to claims for contributions to employee benefit plans such as pension plans, health or life insurance plans, and others, arising from services rendered within 120 days before the commencement of the case or the date of cessation of the debtor's business, whichever occurs first. The dollar limit placed on the total of all contributions payable under this paragraph is equal to the difference between the maximum allowable priority under paragraph (3), $1,800, times the number of employees covered by the plan less the actual distributions under paragraph (3) with respect to these employees.

Paragraph (5) [*Ed. Note:* Section 507(a)(5) was redesignated as section 507(a)(6) by Pub. L. No. 98–353.] is a new priority for consumer creditors–those who have deposited money in connection with the purchase, lease, or rental of property, or the purchase of services, for their personal, family, or household use, that were not delivered or provided. The priority amount is not to exceed $600. In order to reach only those persons most deserving of this special priority, it is limited to individuals whose adjustable gross income from all sources derived does not exceed $20,000. *See Senate Hearings,* testimony of Prof. Vern Countryman, at pp. 848–849. The income of the husband and wife should be aggregated for the purposes of the $20,000 limit if either or both spouses assert such a priority claim.

The sixth priority [*Ed. Note:* This is the seventh priority; section 507(a)(6) was redesignated as section 507(a)(7) by Pub. L. No. 98–353.] is for certain taxes. Priority is given to income taxes for a taxable year that ended on or before the date of the filing of the petition, if the last due date of the return for such year occurred not more than three years immediately before the date on which the petition was filed [sec. 507(a)(7)(A)(i)]. For the purposes of this rule, the last due date of the return is the last date under any extension of time to file the return which the taxing authority may have granted the debtor.

Employment taxes and transfer taxes (including gift, estate, sales, use and other excise taxes) are also given sixth priority if the transaction or event which gave rise to the tax occurred before the petition date, provided that the required return or report of such tax liabilities was last due within three years before the petition was filed or was last due after the petition date [sec. 507(a)(7)(A)(ii)]. The employment taxes covered under this rule are the employer's share of the social security and railroad retirement taxes and required employer payments toward unemployment insurance.

Priority is given to income taxes and other taxes of a kind described in section 507(a)(6)(A)(i) and (ii) [*Ed. Note:* Section 507(a)(6)(A)(i) and (ii) was redesignated as section 507(a)(7)(A)(i) and (ii) by Pub. L. No. 98–353.] which the Federal, State, or local tax authority had assessed within three years after the last due date of the return, that is, including any extension of time to file the return, if the debtor filed in title 11 within 240 days after the assessment was made [sec. 507(a)(7)(B)(i)]. This rule may bring into the sixth priority the debtor's tax liability for some taxable years which would not qualify for priority under the general three-year rule of section [507(a)(7)(A)].

The sixth priority category [*Ed. Note:* This is now the seventh priority; section 507(a)(6) was redesignated as section 507(a)(7) by Pub. L. No. 98–353.] also includes taxes which the tax authority was barred by law from assessing or collecting at any time during the 300 days before the petition under title 11 was filed [sec. 507(a)(7)(B)(ii)]. In the case of certain Federal taxes, this preserves a priority for tax liabilities for years more than three years before the filing of the petition where the debtor and the Internal Revenue Service were negotiating over an audit of the debtor's returns or were engaged in litigation in the Tax Court. In such situation, the tax law prohibits the service's right to assess a tax deficiency until ninety days after the service sends the taxpayer a deficiency letter or, if the taxpayer files a petition in the Tax Court during the 90-day period, until the outcome of the litigation. A similar priority exists in present law, except that the taxing authority is allowed no time to access and collect the taxes after the restrictions on assessment (discussed above) are lifted. Some taxpayers have exploited this loophole by filing in bankruptcy immediately after the end of the 90-day period or immediately after the close of Tax Court proceedings. The bill remedies this defect by preserving a priority for taxes the assessment of which was barred by law by giving the tax authority 300 days within which to make the assessment after the lifting of the bar and then to collect or file public notice of its tax lien. Thus, if a taxpayer files a title 11 petition at any time during that 300-day period, the tax deficiency will be entitled to priority. If the petition is filed more than 300 days after the restriction on assessment was lifted, the taxing authority will not have priority for the tax deficiency.

Taxes for which an offer in compromise was withdrawn by the debtor, or rejected by a governmental unit, within 240 days before the petition date [sec. 507(a)(7)(B)(iii)] will also receive sixth priority. This rule closes a loophole under present law under which, following an assessment of tax, some taxpayers have submitted a formal offer in compromise, dragged out negotiations with the taxing authority until the tax liability would lose priority under the three-year priority period of present law, and then filed in bankruptcy before the governmental unit could take collection steps.

Also included are certain taxes for which no return or report is required by law [sec. 507(a)(7)(C)], if the taxable transaction occurred within three years before the petition was filed.

Taxes (not covered by the third priority) which the debtor was required by law to withhold or collect from others and for which he is liable in any capacity, regardless of the age of the tax claims [sec. 507(a)(7)(D)] are included. This category covers the so-called "trust fund" taxes, that is, income taxes which an employer is required to withhold from the pay of his employees, the employees' shares of social security and railroad retirement taxes, and also Federal unemployment insurance. This category also includes excise taxes which a seller of goods or services is required to collect from a buyer and pay over to a taxing authority.

This category also covers the liability of a responsible corporate officer under the Internal Revenue Code for income taxes or for the employee's share of employment taxes which, under the tax law, the employer was required to withhold from the wages of employees. This priority will operate where a person found to be a responsible officer has himself filed a petition under title 11, and the priority covers the debtor's liability as an officer under the Internal Revenue Code, regardless of the age of the tax year to which the tax relates.

The priority rules under the bill governing employment taxes can be summarized as follows: In the case of wages earned and actually paid before the petition under title 11 was filed, the liability for the employee's share of the employment taxes, regardless of the prepetition year in which the wages were earned and paid. The employer's share of the employment taxes on all wages earned and paid before the petition receive sixth priority; generally, these taxes will be those for which a return was due within three years before the petition. With respect to wages earned by employees before the petition but actually paid by the trustee after the title 11 case commenced, taxes required to be withheld receives the same priority as the wages themselves. Thus, the employees' share of taxes on third priority wages also receives third priority. Taxes on the balance of such wages receive no priority and are collectible only as general claims because the wages themselves are payable only as general claims and liability for the taxes arises only to the extent the wages are actually paid. The employer's share of employment taxes on third priority wages earned before the petition but paid after the petition was filed receives third priority, but only if the wages in this category have first been paid in full. Assuming there are sufficient funds to pay third priority wages and the related employer taxes in full, the employer's share of taxes on the balance of wage payments becomes a general claim (because the wages themselves are payable as general claims). Both the employees' and the employer's share of employment taxes on wages earned and paid after the petition was filed receive first priority as administrative expenses.

Also covered by this sixth priority [*Ed. Note:* This is the seventh priority since section 507(a)(6) was redesignated as section 507(a)(7) by Pub. L. No. 98–353.] are property taxes required to be assessed within three years before the filing of the petition [sec. 507(a)(7)(E)].

Taxes attributable to a tentative carryback adjustment received by the debtor before the petition was filed, such as a "quickie refund" received under section 6411 of the Internal Revenue Code [sec. 507(a)(7)(F)] are included. However, the tax claim against the debtor will re- [*sic*] in a prepetition loss year for which the tax return was last due, including extensions, within three years before the petition was filed.

Taxes resulting from a recapture, occasioned by a transfer during bankruptcy, of a tax credit or deduction taken during an earlier tax year [sec. 507(a)(7)(G)] are included. A typical example occurs when there is a sale by the trustee of depreciable property during the case and depreciation deductions taken in prepetition years are subject to recapture under section 1250 of the Code.

Taxes owed by the debtor as a transferee of assets from another person who is liable for a tax, if the tax claim against the transferor would have received priority in a chapter 11 case commenced by the transferor within one year before the date of the petition filed by the transferee [sec. 507(a)(7)(H)], are included.

Also included are certain tax payments required to have been made during the 1 year immediately before the petition was filed, where the debtor had previously entered into a deferred payment agreement (including an offer in compromise) to pay an agreed liability in periodic installments but had become delinquent in one or more installments before the petition was filed [sec. 507(a)(7)(I)]. This priority covers all types of deferred or part payment agreements. The priority covers only installments which first became due during the 1 year before the petition but which remained unpaid at the date of the petition. The priority does not come into play, however, if before the case began or during the case, the debtor and the taxing authority agree to a further extension of time to pay the delinquent amounts.

Certain tax-related liabilities which are not true taxes or which are not collected by regular assessment procedures [sec. 507(a)(7)(J)] are included. One type of liability covered in this category is the liability under section 3505 of the Internal Revenue Code of a lender who pays wages directly to employees of another employer or who supplies funds to an employer for the payment of wages. Another is the liability under section 6332 of the Internal Revenue Code, of a person who fails to turn over money or property of the taxpayer in response to a levy. Since the taxing authority must collect such a liability from the third party by suit rather than normal assessment procedures, an extra year is added to the normal three-year priority periods. If a suit was commenced by the taxing authority within the four-year period and before the petition was filed, the priority is also preserved, provided that the suit had not terminated more than one year before the date of the filing of the petition.

Also included are certain unpaid customs duties which have not grown unreasonably "stale" [sec. 507(a)(7)(K)]. These include duties on imports entered for consumption within three years before the filing of the petition if the duties are still unliquidated on the petition date. If an import entry has been liquidated (in general, liquidation is in an administrative determination of the value and tariff rate of the item) or reliquidated, within two years of the filing of the petition the customs liability is given priority. If the Secretary of the Treasury certifies that customs duties were not liquidated because of an investigation into possible assessment of anti-dumping or countervailing duties, or because of fraud penalties, duties not liquidated for this reason during the five years before the importer filed under title 11 also will receive priority.

Subsection (a) of this section also provides specifically that interest on sixth priority tax claims accrued before the filing of the petition is also entitled to sixth priority.

Subsection (b) of this section provides that any fine or penalty which represents compensation for actual pecuniary loss of a governmental unit, and which involves a tax liability entitled to sixth priority, is to receive the same priority.

Subsection (b) also provides that a claim arising from an erroneous refund or credit of tax is to be given the same priority as the tax to which the refund or credit relates.

[*Senate Report No. 95–989, 95th Cong., 2d Sess. 68–73 (1978).*]

Section 507(a)(3) of the House amendment represents a compromise dollar amount and date for the priority between similar provisions contained in H.R. 8200 as passed by the House and the Senate amendments. A similar compromise is contained in section 507(a)(4).

Section 507(a)(5) [*Ed. Note:* Section 507(a)(5) was redesignated as section 507(a)(6) by Pub. L. No. 98–353.] represents a compromise on amount between the priority as contained in H.R. 8200 as passed by the House and the Senate amendment. The Senate provision for limiting the priority to consumers having less than a fixed gross income is deleted.

Section 507(a)(6) [*Ed. Note:* Section 507(a)(6) was redesignated as section 507(a)(7) by Pub. L. No. 98–353.] of the House amendment represents a compromise between similar provisions contained in H.R. 8200 as passed by the House and the Senate amendment.

Section 507(b) of the House amendment is new and is derived from the compromise contained in the House amendment with respect to adequate protection under section 361. Subsection (b) provides that to the extent adequate protection of the interest of a holder of a claim proves to be inadequate, then the creditor's claim is given priority over every other allowable claim entitled to distribution under section 507(a). Section 507(b) of the Senate amendment is deleted.

Section 507(c) of the House amendment is new. Section 507(d) of the House amendment prevents subrogation with respect to priority for certain priority claims. Subrogation with respect to priority is intended to be permitted for administrative claims and claims arising during the gas [*sic*] period.

[*124 Cong. Rec. H 11,095 (Sept. 28, 1978); S 17,411 (Oct. 6, 1978).*]

Section 507. Priorities: Under the House amendment, taxes receive priority as follows:

First. Administrative expenses: The amendment generally follows the Senate amendment in providing expressly that taxes incurred during the administration of the estate share the first priority given to administrative expenses generally. Among the taxes which receives first priority, as defined in section 503, are the employees' and the employer's shares of employment taxes on wages earned and paid after the petition is filed. Section 503(b)(1) also includes in administration expenses a tax liability arising from an excessive allowance by a tax authority of a "quickie refund" to the estate. (In the case of Federal taxes, such refunds are allowed under special rules based on net operating loss carrybacks (sec. 6411 of the Internal Revenue Code)).

An exception is made to first priority treatment for taxes incurred by the estate with regard to the employer's share of employment taxes on wages earned from the debtor before the petition but paid from the estate after the petition has been filed. In this situation, the employer's tax receives either sixth priority or general claim treatment.

The House amendment also adopts the provisions of the Senate amendment which include in the definition of administrative expenses under section 503 any fine, penalty (including "additions to tax" under applicable tax law) or reduction in credit imposed on the estate.

Second. "Involuntary gap" claims: "Involuntary gap" creditors are granted second priority by paragraph (2) of section 507(a). This priority includes tax claims arising in the ordinary course of the debtor's business or financial affairs after he has been placed involuntarily in bankruptcy but before a trustee is appointed or before the order for relief.

Third. Certain taxes on prepetition wages: Wage claims entitled to third priority are for compensation which does not exceed $2,000 and was earned during the 90 days before the filing of the bankruptcy petition or the cessation of the debtor's business. Certain employment taxes receive third priority in payment from the estate along with the payment of wages to which the taxes relate. In the case of wages earned before the filing of the petition, but paid by the trustee (rather than by the debtor) after the filing of the petition, claims for the employees' share of the employment taxes (withheld income taxes and the employees' share of the social security or railroad retirement tax) receive third priority to the extent the wage claims themselves are entitled to this priority.

In the case of wages earned from and paid by the debtor before the filing of the petition, the employer's share of the employment taxes on these wages paid by the debtor receives sixth priority or, if not entitled to that priority, are treated only as general claims. Under the House amendment, the employer's share of employment taxes on wages earned by employees of the debtor, but paid by the trustee after the filing of the bankruptcy petition, will also receive sixth priority to the extent that claims for the wages receive third priority. To the extent the claims for wages do not receive third priority, but instead are treated only as general claims, claims for the employer's share of the employment taxes attributable to those wages will also be treated as general claims. In calculating the amounts payable as general wage claims, the trustee must pay the employer's share of employment taxes on such wages.

Sixth priority.* The House amendment modifies the provisions of both the House bill and Senate amendment in the case of sixth priority taxes. Under the amendment, the following Federal, State and local taxes are included in the sixth priority:

First. Income and gross receipts taxes incurred before the date of the petition for which the last due date of the return, including all

---

* [*Ed. Note:* This is now the seventh priority since section 507(a)(6) was redesignated as section 507(a)(7) by Pub. L. No. 98–353.]

extensions of time granted to file the return, occurred within three years before the date on which the petition was filed, or after the petition date. Under this rule, the due date of the return, rather than the date on which the taxes were assessed, determines the priority.

Second. Income and gross receipts taxes assessed at any time within 240 days before the petition date. Under this rule, the date on which the governmental unit assesses the tax, rather than the due date of the return, determines the priority.

If, following assessment of a tax, the debtor submits an offer in compromise to the governmental unit, the House amendment provides that the 240-day period is to be suspended for the duration of the offer and will resume running after the offer is withdrawn or rejected by the governmental unit, but the tax liability will receive priority if the title 11 petition is filed during the balance of the 240-day period or during a minimum of 30 days after the offer is withdrawn or rejected. This rule modifies a provision of the Senate amendment dealing specifically with offers in compromise. Under the modified rule, if, after the assessment, an offer in compromise is submitted by the debtor and is still pending (without having been accepted or rejected) at the date on which a title 11 petition is filed, the underlying liability will receive sixth priority. However, if an assessment of a tax liability is made but the tax is not collected within 240 days, the tax will not receive priority under [section 507(a)(7)(A)(i)] and the debtor cannot revive a priority for that tax by submitting an offer in compromise.

Third. Income and gross receipts taxes not assessed before the petition date but still permitted, under otherwise applicable tax laws, to be assessed. Thus, for example, a pre-petition tax liability is to receive sixth priority under this rule if, under the applicable statute of limitations, the tax liability can still be assessed by the tax authority. This rule also covers situations referred to in [section 507(a) (7)(B)(ii)] of the Senate amendment where the assessment or collection of a tax was prohibited before the petition pending exhaustion of judicial or administrative remedies, except that the House amendment eliminates the 300-day limitation of the Senate bill. So, for example, if before the petition a debtor was engaged in litigation in the Tax Court, during which the Internal Revenue Code bars the Internal Revenue Service from assessing or collecting the tax, and if the tax court decision is made in favor of the Service before the petition under title 11 is filed, thereby lifting the restrictions on assessment and collection, the tax liability will receive sixth priority even if the tax authority does not make an assessment within 300 days before the petition (provided, of course, that the statute of limitations on assessment has not expired by the petition date).

In light of the above categories of the sixth priority, and tax liability of the debtor (under the Internal Revenue Code or State or local law) as a transferee of property from another person will receive sixth priority without the limitations contained in the Senate amendment so long as the transferee liability had not been assessed by the tax authority by the petition date but could still have been assessed by that date under the applicable tax statute of limitations or, if the transferee liability had been assessed before the petition, the assessment was made no more than 240 days before the petition date.

Also in light of the above categories, the treatment of pre-petition tax liabilities arising from an excessive allowance to the debtor of a tentative carryback adjustment, such as a "quickie refund" under section 6411 of the Internal Revenue Code, is revised as follows: If the tax authority has assessed the additional tax before the petition, the tax liability will receive priority if the date of assessment was within 240 days before the petition date. If the tax authority had not assessed the additional tax by the petition, the tax liability will still receive priority so long as, on the petition date, assessment of the liability is not barred by the statute of limitations.

Fourth. Any property tax assessed before the commencement of the case and last payable without penalty within one year before the petition, or thereafter.

Fifth. Taxes which the debtor was required by law to withhold or collect from others and for which he is liable in any capacity, regardless of the age of the tax claims. This category covers the so-called "trust fund" taxes, that is, income taxes which an employer is required to withhold from the pay of his employees, and the employees' share of social security taxes.

In addition, this category includes the liability of a responsible officer under the Internal Revenue Code (sec. 6672) for income taxes or for the employees' share of social security taxes which that officer was responsible for withholding from the wages of employees and paying to the Treasury, although he was not himself the employer. This priority will operate when a person found to be a responsible officer has himself filed in title 11, and the priority will cover the debtor's responsible officer liability regardless of the age of the tax year to which the tax relates. The U.S. Supreme Court has interpreted present law to require the same result as will be reached under this rule. U.S. v. Sotelo, 436 U.S. — (1978).

This category also includes the liability under section 3505 of the Internal Revenue Code of a taxpayer who loans money for the payment of wages or other compensation.

Sixth. The employer's share of employment taxes on wages paid before the petition and on third-priority wages paid postpetition by the estate. The priority rules under the House amendment governing employment taxes can thus be summarized as follows: Claims for the employees' shares of employment taxes attributable to wages both earned and paid before the filing of the petition are to receive sixth priority. In the case of employee wages earned, but not paid, before the filing of the bankruptcy petition, claims for the employees' share of employment taxes receive third priority to the extent the wages themselves receive third priority. Claims which relate to wages earned before the petition, but not paid before the petition (and which are not entitled to the third priority under the rule set out above), will be paid as general claims. Since the related wages will receive no priority, the related employment taxes would also be paid as nonpriority general claims.

The employer's share of the employment taxes on wages earned and paid before the bankruptcy petition will receive sixth priority to the extent the return for these taxes was last due (including extensions of time) within three years before the filing of the petition or was due after the petition was filed. Older tax claims of this nature will be payable as general claims. In the case of wages earned by employees before the petition, but actually paid by the trustee (as claims against the estate) after the title 11 case commenced, the employer's share of the employment taxes on third priority wage claims will be payable as sixth priority and the employer's taxes on prepetition wages which are treated only as general claims will be payable only as general claims. In calculating the amounts payable as general wage claims, the trustee must pay the employer's share of employment taxes on such wages. The House Amendment thus deletes the provision of the Senate amendment that certain employer taxes receive third priority and are to be paid immediately after payment of third priority wages and the employees' shares of employment taxes on those wages.

In the case of employment taxes relating to wages earned and paid after the petition, both the employees' shares and the employer's share will receive first priority as administration expenses of the estate.

Seventh. Excise taxes on transactions for which a return, if required, is last due, under otherwise applicable law or under any extension of time to file the return, within three years before the petition was filed, or thereafter. If a return is not required with regard to a particular excise tax, priority is given if the transaction or event itself occurred within three years before the date on which the title 11 petition was filed. All Federal, State or local taxes generally considered or expressly treated as excises are covered by this category, including sales taxes, estate and gift taxes, gasoline and special fuel taxes, and wagering and truck taxes.

Eighth. Certain unpaid customs duties. The House amendment covers in this category duties on imports entered for consumption within 1 year before the filing of the petition, but which are still unliquidated on the petition date; duties covered by an entry liquidated or reliquidated within one year before the petition date; and any duty on merchandise entered for consumption within four years before the petition but not liquidated on the petition date, if the Secretary of the Treasury or his delegate certifies that duties were not liquidated because of possible assessment of antidumping or countervailing duties or fraud penalties.

For purposes of the above priority rules, the House amendment adopts the provision of the Senate bill that any tax liability which, under otherwise applicable tax law, is collectible in the form of a "penalty," is to be treated in the same manner as a tax liability. In bankruptcy terminology, such tax liabilities are referred to as pecuniary loss penalties. Thus, any tax liability which under the Internal Revenue Code or State or local tax law is payable as a "penalty," in addition to the liability of a responsible person under section 6672 of the Internal Revenue Code, will be entitled to the priority which the liability would receive if it were expressly labeled as a "tax" under the applicable tax law. However, a tax penalty which is punitive in nature is given subordinated treatment under section 726(a)(4).

The House amendment also adopts the provision of the Senate amendment that a claim arising from an erroneous refund or credit of tax, other than a "quickie refund," is to receive the same priority as the tax to which the refund or credit relates.

The House amendment deletes the express provision of the Senate amendment that tax liability is to receive sixth priority if it satisfies any one of the subparagraphs of section 507(a)(6) [*Ed. Note:* Section 507(a)(6) was redesignated as section 507(a)(7) by Pub. L. No. 98–353.] even if the liability fails to satisfy the terms of one or more other subparagraphs. No change of substance is intended by the deletion, however, in light of section 102(5) of the House amendment, providing a rule of construction that the word "or" is not intended to be exclusive.

The House amendment deletes from the express priority categories of the Senate amendment the priority for a debtor's liability as a third party for failing to surrender property or to pay an obligation in response to a levy for taxes of another, and the priority for amounts provided for under deferred payment agreements between a debtor and the tax authority.

The House amendment also adopts the substance of the definition in section 346(a) the Senate amendment of when taxes are to be considered "incurred" except that the House amendment applies these definitions solely for purposes of determining which category of section 507 tests the priority of a particular tax liability. Thus, for example, the House amendment contains a special rule for the treatment of taxes under the 45-day exception to the preference rules under section 547 and the definitions of when a tax is incurred for priority purposes are not to apply to such preference rules. Under the House amendment, for purposes of the priority rules, a tax on income for a particular period is to be considered "incurred" on the last day of the period. A tax on or measured by some event, such as the payment of wages or a transfer by reason of death or gift, or an excise tax on a sale or other transaction, is to be considered "incurred" on the date of the transaction or event.

[*124 Cong. Rec. H 11,112 (Sept. 28, 1978); S 17,428 (Oct. 6, 1978).*]

Comment

Under Section 64a(4) of the former Bankruptcy Act there was a limitation on wages and commissions not to exceed $600 earned within three months before the date of the commencement of the case. Section 507(a)(3) of the Code retains the 90 day period but increases the amount to $2,000 and includes vacation, severance and sick leave pay. Section 507(a)(4) allows priority for contributions to employee benefit plans arising from services rendered within 180 days before the date of petition and sets forth the formula for determining the amount. Section 507(a)(6) provides for a consumer priority for which there was no comparable provision in the Act. Section 507(a)(7) relating to tax priorities is to be compared with Sections 64a(4) and a(5) of the Act which dealt with the priority to be allowed for tax claims and other debts entitled to priority by reason of the laws of the United States. The priority for other debts owing the United States was deleted.

1984 Amendments: The creation of a new priority in section 507 is one of several amendments relating to grain storage facilities. In this connection subsection (d) was added to section 546, and a new section 557 was added.

The amendments seek to afford a measure of relief to individual farmers and fishermen when grain storage or fish storage facilities file cases under title 11. The amendment to section 507 places such farmers' and fishermen's claims fifth in the order of priorities, but only to the extent of $2000 for each such individual producer. The "Fifth" and "Sixth" priorities were redesignated "Sixth" and "Seventh."

See **Comments** on the 1984 amendments to sections 546(a) and 557.

1990 Amendments: Section 507 was amended by Pub. L. No. 101-647 (Crime Control Act of 1990), effective on the date of enactment, November 29, 1990. This amendment added to subsection (a) a new paragraph (8), thereby establishing an eighth priority.

Case Annotations

Under §§ 6 and 7 of the Fair Labor Standards Act, a secured creditor (and presumably, a bankruptcy trustee) is prevented from selling foreclosed collateral of a company that has failed to pay its employees who produced that collateral during its last weeks of operation—in effect creating a superpriority lien on inventory in favor of the employees—even though the remedy, the payment of the employees unpaid wages, would clearly conflict with the priorities of distribution under the Bankruptcy Code. Citicorp Indus. Credit, Inc. v. Brock, 483 U.S. 27, 107 S. Ct. 2694, 97 L. Ed. 2d 23, 17 C.B.C.2d 875 (1987).

An IRS claim for trust fund taxes retains its seventh priority level claim in the second of serial corporate chapter 11 filings because trust fund tax claims are not intimately tied to a single bankruptcy estate as these tax claims are more akin to a secured lien which is intended to survive the reorganization unaffected. Matter of Official Committee of Unsecured Creditors of White Farm Equipment Co., 943 F.2d 752, 25 C.B.C.2d 612 (7th Cir. 1991).

Unemployment taxes owed on account of wages paid more than ninety days prepetition are entitled to a seventh priority of distribution and are not exempt from discharge pursuant to section 523(a)(1), because Congress intended unemployment taxes to be nondischargeable if the taxes were due within three years of the date of the filing of the debtor's bankruptcy petition. Matter of Pierce, 935 F.2d 709, 25 C.B.C.2d 69 (5th Cir. 1991).

A tax owed to the federal government may be equitably subordinated to other claims only upon a showing of some inequitable conduct on the part of the government. *In re* Mansfield Tire & Rubber Co., 942 F.2d 1055, 25 C.B.C.2d 591 (6th Cir. 1991).

An assignment of a money order cannot be elevated to priority status by inserting language in the assignment which attempts to change the nature of the original transaction because statutory priorities must be strictly enforced in the bankruptcy context. *In re* Northwest Financial Express, Inc., 950 F.2d 561, 25 C.B.C.2d 1594 (8th Cir. 1991).

A purchase money security interest takes priority over any preexisting lien because if the lender has augmented the capital assets of the borrower, previous creditors are not prejudiced. First Interstate Bank of Utah, N.A. v. Internal Revenue Service, 930 F.2d 1521, 24 C.B.C.2d 1765 (10th Cir. 1991).

An uninsured motor vehicle assessment imposed by a state department of motor vehicles against a chapter 7 debtor is an involuntary pecuniary burden levied upon uninsured motorists for a proper governmental purpose and, as such, qualifies as an excise tax for purposes of section 507(a)(7)(E) with the result that it is nondischargeable under section 523(a)(1)(A). Conversely, a fee assessed by a department of motor vehicles against a debtor to cover the cost of serving the debtor with a notice of suspension of driving privileges is an assessment used to defray administrative costs and is not an excise tax, and, therefore, is not excluded from discharge under section 523(a)(7). Williams v. Motley, 925 F.2d 741, 24 C.B.C.2d 1188 (4th Cir. 1991).

Absent a factual determination by the lower court concerning the superpriority status of claims, any expression by an appeals court as to the hierarchy of claims would constitute an advisory opinion and, therefore, be improper. *In re* MacNeil, 907 F.2d 903, 23 C.B.C.2d 513 (9th Cir. 1990).

When the Secretary of Labor brings an injunction action against a debtor to prevent the sale of goods produced in violation of the Fair Labor Standards Act, the Secretary is permitted to enforce the injunction, as Congress intended to keep "hot goods" out of interstate commerce, even though the effect of enforcement will result in employees' wage claims receiving a higher priority than other creditors. Brock v. Rusco Industries, Inc., 842 F.2d 270, 18 C.B.C.2d 728 (11th Cir.), *cert. denied*, 488 U.S. 889, 109 S. Ct. 221, 102 L. Ed. 2d 212 (1988).

Neither the Code nor its legislative history requires court approval of an *ex parte* adequate protection agreement in order to support section 507(b) status. Prior court approval of a memorandum of agreement out of which a disputed expense arose does not *per se* prevent a creditor's entitlement to a superpriority administrative expense. Travelers Ins. Co. v. American AgCredit Corp. (*In re* Blehm Land & Cattle Co.), 859 F.2d 137, 19 C.B.C.2d 933 (10th Cir. 1988).

A state law that classifies what might otherwise be a lesser claim as a proprietary interest reclassifies an interest within the Code's priority scheme, but does not displace the scheme itself and consequently, is not in conflict with the Code. State of California v. Farmers Markets, Inc.

(*In re* Farmers Markets, Inc.), 792 F.2d 1400, 15 C.B.C.2d 93 (9th Cir. 1986).

When a cash collateral order has the effect of foreclosing a junior secured creditor's security interest in the portion of inventory that exceeded in value another creditor's senior lien and the order is, in consequence, void to that extent, the court may grant the junior creditor a superpriority as an equitable remedy, even though section 507(b) itself speaks only to the situation of a creditor whose court sanctioned adequate protection proved inadequate. Owens-Corning Fiberglas Corp. v. Center Wholesale, Inc. (*In re* Center Wholesale, Inc.), 759 F.2d 1440, 12 C.B.C.2d 1107 (9th Cir. 1985).

The term "estate" as used in section 503(b)(1)(B)(i) implies postpetition liabilities, with the result that claims for FICA and income taxes withheld by debtor in possession from its employees' paychecks but never paid to the IRS during an attempted reorganization are entitled to administrative expense priority pursuant to section 507(a)(1) since they are incurred by and are a liability of the estate. United States v. Friendship College, Inc. (*In re* Friendship College, Inc.), 737 F.2d 430, 10 C.B.C.2d 1151 (4th Cir. 1984).

A state law which requires payment to creditors of a liquor establishment before transfer of a liquor license does not establish priorities in contravention of federal bankruptcy law, as it merely establishes a state created lien on the debtor's liquor license in favor of the class of creditors whose claims arose from the use of that asset, and this priority is independent of the debtor's insolvency. Artus v. Alaska Dep't. of Labor (*In re* Anchorage Int'l Inn, Inc.), 718 F.2d 1446, 9 C.B.C.2d 422 (9th Cir. 1983).

Congress did not intend to limit the priority under section 507(a)(4) to claims for unpaid premiums on policies which result from collective bargaining agreements or only to policies that are contributory by a debtor's employees; therefore, an insurance company is entitled to priority payment of premiums under section 507(a)(4) in order to continue a debtor's employee group insurance plans. *In re* Saco Local Dev. Corp., 711 F.2d 441, 8 C.B.C.2d 1093 (1st Cir. 1983).

A claim awarded pursuant to section 507(b) prior to the conversion of a chapter 11 case to a case under chapter 7 does not have priority over chapter 7 administrative expense claims under section 726(b). *In re* Sun Runner Marine, Inc., 26 C.B.C.2d 300 (9th Cir., B.A.P., 1991).

Section 507(a)(4) should be read broadly, entitling insurance companies to priority even if the insurance policies did not result from collective bargaining agreements. Congress intended section 507(a)(4) to extend qualified priority protection to insurance contributions and other fringe benefits in order to protect individuals covered by employee benefit plans maintained by bankrupt employers. *In re* Allegheny International, Inc., 26 C.B.C.2d 1543 (B. Ct., W.D. Pa. 1992).

The four factors of the *Lorber* test, which should be employed to determine whether a claim is a tax for the purposes of section 507(a)(7)(E), are as follows: 1) an involuntary pecuniary burden is laid upon individuals or property; 2) the burden is imposed under authority of the legislature; 3) the burden exists for public purposes, including the purpose of defraying expenses of government; and 4) the burden is imposed under the police or taxing power of the state (this requires a determination as to whether a statutory pecuniary burden placed on an employer is for a public purpose). *In re* Hutchinson, 26 C.B.C.2d 561 (B. Ct., D. Ariz. 1992).

Section 507(b) does not provide superpriority status to a claim of a party whose collateral is diminished in value by the operation of section 724(b), whereas it does provide superpriority status if the value of the collateral is diminished by operation of the automatic stay imposed by section 362(a). *In re* Life Imaging Corp., 25 C.B.C.2d 916 (B. Ct., D. Colo. 1991).

References

3 *Collier on Bankruptcy* ch. 507 (Matthew Bender 15th ed.).

2 *Collier Bankruptcy Manual* ch. 507 (Matthew Bender 3d ed.).

5 *Collier Bankruptcy Practice Guide* ch. 83 *et seq.* (Matthew Bender).

A Debtor Under Reorganization Pursuant to Chapter 11 of the Bankruptcy Code Cannot Designate the Allocation of its Priority Tax Liabilities. In re Ribs-R-Us, Inc. (1987), 33 Vill. L. Rev. 556 (1988).

Adequate Protection and Administrative Expense: Toward a Uniform System for Awarding Superpriorities, 88 Mich. L. Rev. 2168 (1990).

Buckley, *The Bankruptcy Priority Puzzle,* 72 Va. L. Rev. 1393 (1986).

Fuchs, *Bending the Rules — The Necessity Doctrine and Prepetition Debts,* 2 F & G Bankr. L. Rev. 36 (1990).

Hess, *Priority Conflicts Between Security Interests and Washington Statutory Liens for Services or Materials,* 25 Gonz. L. Rev. 453 (1989-90).

Lester and Fleenor, *The Priority Race: Winner Takes the Horse,* 78 Ky. L.J. 615 (1989-90).

Passamano, *Questions of Priority: Secured Lender Versus a Federal Tax Lien,* 93 Com. L.J. 361 (1988).

Schwartzel, *The Priority of Creditors' Claims in Independent Administrations,* 42 Baylor L. Rev. 291 (1990).

White, *Absolute Priority and New Value,* 8 Cooley L. Rev. 1 (1991).

§ 508. Effect of distribution other than under this title.

(a) If a creditor receives, in a foreign proceeding, payment of, or a transfer of property on account of, a claim that is allowed under this title, such creditor may not receive any payment under this title on account of such claim until each of the other holders of claims on account of which such holders are entitled to share equally with such creditor under this title has received payment under this title equal in value to the consideration received by such creditor in such foreign proceeding.

(b) If a creditor of a partnership debtor receives, from a general partner that is not a debtor in a case under chapter 7 of this title, payment of, or a transfer of property on account of, a claim that is allowed under this title and that is not secured by a lien on property of such partner, such creditor may not receive any payment under this title on account of such claim until each of the other holders of claims on account of which such holders are entitled to share equally with such creditor under this title has received payment under this title equal in value to the consideration received by such creditor from such general partner.

Legislative History

This section prohibits a creditor from receiving any distribution in the bankruptcy case if he has received payment of a portion of his claim in a foreign proceeding, until the other creditors in the bankruptcy case in this country that are entitled to share equally with that creditor have received as much as he has in the foreign proceeding.

[*House Report No. 95–595, 95th Cong., 1st Sess. 358 (1977); Senate Report No. 95–989, 95th Cong., 2d Sess. 73 (1978).*]

Section 508(b) of the House amendment is new and provides an identical rule with respect to a creditor of a partnership who receives payment from a partner, to that of a creditor of a debtor who receives a payment in a foreign proceeding involving the debtor.

[*124 Cong. Rec. H 11,095 (Sept. 28, 1978); S 17,411 (Oct. 6, 1978).*]

Comment

There was no comparable provision to section 508 in the former Bankruptcy Act.

References

3 *Collier on Bankruptcy* ch. 508 (Matthew Bender 15th ed.).

2 *Collier Bankruptcy Manual* ch. 508 (Matthew Bender 3d ed.).

6 *Collier Bankruptcy Practice Guide* ch. 92 (Matthew Bender).

SECTION 509 (11 U.S.C. § 509)

§ 509. Claims of codebtors.

(a) Except as provided in subsection (b) or (c) of this section, an entity that is liable with the debtor on, or that has secured, a claim of a creditor against the debtor, and that pays such claim, is subrogated to the rights of such creditor to the extent of such payment.

(b) Such entity is not subrogated to the rights of such creditor to the extent that—

    (1) a claim of such entity for reimbursement or contribution on account of such payment of such creditor's claim is—

        (A) allowed under section 502 of this title;

        (B) disallowed other than under section 502(e) of this title; or

        (C) subordinated under section 510 of this title; or

    (2) as between the debtor and such entity, such entity received the consideration for the claim held by such creditor.

(c) The court shall subordinate to the claim of a creditor and for the benefit of such creditor an allowed claim, by way of subrogration under this section, or for reimbursement or contribution, of an entity that is liable with the debtor on, or that has secured, such creditor's claim, until such creditor's claim is paid in full, either through payments under this title or otherwise.

Bankruptcy Rule References: 3002, 3003 and 3005

Legislative History

Section 509 deals with codebtors generally, and is in addition to the disallowance provision in section 502(e). This section is based on the notion that the only rights available to a surety, guarantor, or comaker are contribution, reimbursement, and subrogation. The right that applies in a particular situation will depend on the agreement between the debtor and the codebtor, and on whether and how payment was made by the codebtor to the creditor. The claim of a surety or codebtor for contribution or reimbursement is discharged even if the claim is never filed, as is any claim for subrogation even if the surety or codebtor chooses to file a claim for contribution or reimbursement instead.

Subsection (a) subrogates the codebtor (whether as a codebtor, surety, or guarantor) to the rights of the creditor, to the extent of any payment made by the codebtor to the creditor. Whether the creditor's claim was filed under section 501(a) or 501(b) is irrelevant. The right of subrogation will exist even if the primary creditor's claim is allowed by virtue of being listed under proposed 11 U.S.C. § 924 or 1111, and not by reason of a proof of claim.

Subsection (b) permits a subrogated codebtor to receive payments in the bankruptcy case only if the creditor has been paid in full, either through payments under the bankruptcy code or otherwise.

[House Report No. 95–595, 95th Cong., 1st Sess. 358–9 (1977); Senate Report No. 95–989, 95th Cong., 2d Sess. 73–4 (1978).]

Section 509 of the House amendment represents a substantial revision of provisions contained in H.R. 8200 as passed by the House and in the Senate amendment. Section 509(a) states a general rule that a surety or co-debtor is subrogated to the rights of a creditor assured by the surety or co-debtor to the extent the surety or co-debtor pays such creditor. Section 509(b) states a general exception indicating that subrogation is not granted to the extent that a claim of a surety or co-debtor for reimbursement or contribution is allowed under section 502 or disallowed other than under section 502(e). Additionally, section 509(b)(1)(C) provides that such claims for subrogation are subordinated to the extent that a claim of the surety or co-debtor for reimbursement or contribution is subordinated under section 510(a)(1) or 510(b). Section 509(b)(2) reiterates the well-known rule that prevents a debtor that is ultimately liable on the debt from recovering from a surety or a co-debtor. Although the language in section 509(b)(2) focuses in terms of receipt of consideration, legislative history appearing elsewhere indicates that an agreement to share liabilities should prevail over an agreement to share profits throughout title 11. This is particularly important in the context of co-debtors who are partners. Section 509(c) subordinates the claim of a surety or co-debtor to the claim of an assured creditor until the creditor's claim is paid in full.

[124 Cong. Rec. H 11,095 (Sept. 28, 1978); S 17,411–12 (Oct 6, 1978).]

Comment

Bankruptcy Rule 3005(a) provides that if a creditor has not filed a proof of claim, an entity that is or may be liable with the debtor, or has secured that creditor may, within 30 days after the expiration of the time for filing claims under Rule 3002(c) or 3003(c), whichever is applicable, execute and file a proof of claim in the name of the creditor, or if unknown, in the entity's own name. But no distribution may be made on the claim except on satisfactory proof that the original debt will be diminished by the amount so paid. A claim so filed is superseded by a claim filed by the creditor pursuant to Rule 3002(c) or 3003(c). This rule makes clear that anyone who may be liable on a debt of the debtor, including a surety, guarantor, indorser, or other codebtor, is authorized to file in the name of the creditor of the debtor.

Subdivision (b) provides that an entity which has filed a claim on behalf of a creditor pursuant to subdivision (a) may file an acceptance or rejection of a plan in the name of the creditor, or if unknown, in the entity's own name. But, if the creditor files a claim within the time permitted by Rule 3003(c), or files a notice prior to confirmation of the creditor's intention to act in the creditor's own behalf, the creditor is to be substituted for the obligor with respect to that claim. (This subdivision applies only in chapter 9 or 11 cases.)

Case Annotations

A cotenant of real property who makes prepetition payments to creditors on behalf of another cotenant, in order to avoid the forfeiture of property which he holds as a tenant in common, is entitled to subrogation under section 509(a), notwithstanding that the payments were made on behalf of his son since his legal obligation to make the payments predominated over any donative intent to benefit the son. In the Matter of Bugos, 760 F.2d 731, 12 C.B.C.2d 711 (7th Cir. 1984).

Section 509(a) and section 502(e)(1)(C) employ the term "subrogated" in a restricted sense referring to sureties, co-debtors or other entities which are liable with the debtor or which have knowingly chosen to secure the claim of a creditor, and absent any showing that the term "subrogation" was intended to be used in a more expansive sense in section 507(d), it is presumed that words used in different parts of an act share the same meaning so that entities which are simply assignees of priority claims should not be denied the priority status of the original claimants. *In re* Missionary Baptist Found. of America, Inc., 667 F.2d 1244, 5 C.B.C.2d 1462 (5th Cir. 1982).

A debtor moving for summary judgment on the basis of section 502(e) must address the effect of related Code section 509 in order for the court to rule on this issue. *In re* Doskocil Companies Inc., 25 C.B.C.2d 557 (B. Ct., D. Kan. 1991).

It is necessary for a party seeking subrogation to have paid a creditor's claim for a postpetition administrative expense, but it is not necessary that the creditor's general unsecured claim arising from rejection be paid as well. A guarantor may use the doctrine of subrogation to benefit from the cure provisions of section 365(b) and from the performance obligations of section 365(d). *In re* Wingspread Corp., 24 C.B.C.2d 244 (B. Ct., S.D.N.Y. 1990).

Claimants who have been required to pay in full, prepetition, upon letters of credit issued by them on account of the debtor in favor of a secured lender, may be subrogated to the rights of the secured lender as to claims filed by them in the bankruptcy case. *In re* Sensor Sys., Inc., 17 C.B.C.2d 1237 (B. Ct., E.D. Pa. 1987).

A partner who pays a partnership obligation arising from a co-partner's wrongful acts done without the innocent partner's knowledge or authorization is entitled to be subrogated to the claims paid by the honest partner, including nondischargeable claims of creditors of the partnership. This is so because the agency relationship and the special relationship of trust that makes partners fiduciaries under state law entitles the wronged partner to seek indemnity from a co-partner. Baxter v. Flick (*In re* Flick), 16 C.B.C.2d 1524 (B. Ct., S.D. Cal. 1987).

References

3 *Collier on Bankruptcy* ch. 509 (Matthew Bender 15th ed.).

2 *Collier Bankruptcy Manual* ch. 509 (Matthew Bender 3d ed.).

3 *Collier Bankruptcy Practice Guide* ch. 54 (Matthew Bender).

Comment, *Reconciling Standby Letters of Credit and the Principles of Subrogation in Section 509,* 7 Bankr. Dev. J. 227 (1990).

SECTION 510 (11 U.S.C. § 510)

§ 510. Subordination.

(a) A subordination agreement is enforceable in a case under this title to the same extent that such agreement is enforceable under applicable nonbankruptcy law.

(b) For the purpose of distribution under this title, a claim arising from rescission of a purchase or sale of a security of the debtor or of an affiliate of the debtor, for damages arising from the purchase or sale of such a security, or for reimbursement or contribution allowed under section 502 on account of such a claim, shall be subordinated to all claims or interests that are senior to or equal the claim or interest represented by such security, except that if such security is common stock, such claim has the same priority as common stock.

(c) Notwithstanding subsections (a) and (b) of this section, after notice and a hearing, the court may—

    (1) under principles of equitable subordination, subordinate for purposes of distribution all or part of an allowed claim to all or part of another allowed claim or all or part of an allowed interest to all or part of another allowed interest; or

(2) order that any lien securing such a subordinated claim be transferred to the estate.

Legislative History

Subsection (a) requires the court to enforce subordination agreements. A subordination agreement will not be enforced, however, in a reorganization case in which the class that is the beneficiary of the agreement has accepted, as specified in proposed 11 U.S.C. § 1126, a plan that waives their rights under the agreement. Otherwise, the agreement would prevent just what chapter 11 contemplates: that seniors may give up rights to juniors in the interest of confirmation of a plan and rehabilitation of the debtor. The subsection also requires the court to subordinate in payment any claim for rescission of a purchase or sale of a security of the debtor or of an affiliate, or for damages arising from the purchase or sale of such a security, to all claims and interests that are senior to the claim or interest represented by the security. Thus, the latter subordination varies with the claim or interest involved. If the security is a debt instrument, the damages or rescission claim will be granted the status of a general unsecured claim. If the security is an equity security, the damages or rescission claim is subordinated to all creditors and treated the same as equity security itself. [*Ed. Note:* The provisions with respect to claims for rescission on purchase of securities have been moved to subsection (b) of section 510.]

[*House Report No. 95–595, 95th Cong., 1st Sess. 359 (1977); Senate Report No. 95–989, 95th Cong., 2d Sess. 74 (1978).*]

Subsection (b) permits the court to subordinate, on equitable grounds, all or any part of an allowed claim or interest to all or any part of another allowed claim or interest, and permits the court to order that any lien securing claim subordinated under this provision be transferred to the estate. This section is intended to codify case law, such as Pepper v. Litton, 308 U.S. 295 (1939), and Taylor v. Standard Gas and Electric Co., 306 U.S. 307 (1938), and is not intended to limit the court's power in any way. The bankruptcy court will remain a court of equity, proposed 28 U.S.C. § 1481; Local Loan v. Hunt, 292 U.S. 234, 240 (1934). Nor does this subsection preclude a bankruptcy court from completely disallowing a claim in appropriate circumstances. *See* Pepper v. Litton, *supra.* The court's power is broader than the general doctrine of equitable subordination, and encompasses subordination on any equitable grounds.

[*House Report No. 95–595, 95th Cong., 1st Sess. 359 (1977).*]

Subsection (b) authorizes the bankruptcy court, in ordering distribution of assets, to subordinate all or any part of any claim to all or any part of another claim, regardless of the priority ranking of either claim. In addition, any lien securing such a subordinated claim may be transferred to the estate. The bill provides, however, that any subordination ordered under this provision must be based on principles of equitable subordination. These principles are defined by case law, and have generally indicated that a claim may normally be subordinated only if its holder is guilty of misconduct. As originally introduced, the bill provided specifically that a tax claim may not be subordinated on equitable grounds. The bill deletes this express exception, but the effect under the amendment should be much the same in most situations since, under the judicial doctrine of equitable subordination, a tax claim would rarely be subordinated. [*Ed. Note:* The provisions with respect to equitable subordination have been moved to subsection (c) of section 510.]

[*Senate Report No. 95–989, 95th Cong., 2d Sess. 74 (1978).*]

Section 510(c)(1) of the House amendment represents a compromise between similar provisions in the House bill and Senate amendment. After notice and a hearing, the court may, under principles of equitable subordination, subordinate for purposes of distribution all or part of an allowed claim to all or part of another allowed claim or all or part of an allowed interest to all or part of another allowed interest. As a matter of equity, it is reasonable that a court subordinate claims to claims and interests to interests. It is intended that the term "principles of equitable subordination" follow existing case law and leave to the courts development of this principle. To date, under existing law, a claim is generally subordinated only if holder of such claim is guilty of inequitable conduct, or the claim itself is of a status susceptible to subordination, such as a penalty or a claim for damages arising from the purchase or sale of a security of the debtor. The fact that such a claim may be secured is of no consequence to the issue of subordination. However, it is inconceivable that the status of a claim as a secured claim could ever be grounds for justifying equitable subordination.

[*124 Cong. Rec. H 11,095 (Sept. 28, 1978); S 17,412 (Oct. 6, 1978).*]

Section 510. Subordination: Since the House amendment authorizes subordination of claims only under principles of equitable subordination, and thus incorporates principles of existing case law, a tax claim would rarely be subordinated under this provision of the bill.

[*124 Cong. Rec. H 11,113 (Sept. 28, 1978); S 17,430 (Oct. 6, 1978).*]

Comment

Pursuant to 28 U.S.C. § 157(b)(2)(B), allowances or disallowances of claims against the estate are "core" proceedings over which the bankruptcy judge has authority to make dispositive judgments and orders. Such authority does not include liquidation or estimation of contingent or unliquidated personal injury tort or wrongful death claims against the estate for purposes of distribution.

The Bankruptcy Act had no provision as to subordination of claims comparable to section 510. But as a court exercising equitable powers, the bankruptcy court frequently subordinated claims for various reasons and enforced consensual subordination agreements. Section 510 codifies such case law as enunciated in Pepper v. Litton, 308 U.S. 295 (1939), and Taylor v. Standard Gas and Electric Co., 306 U.S. 307 (1939). *See*

Herzog & Zweibel, *The Equitable Subordination of Claims in Bankruptcy,* 17 Vand. L. Rev. 83 (1961).

1984 Amendments: Section 510(b) was rewritten. The amendment clarifies the provision regarding subrogation of a claim based on the purchase or sale of common stock.

Case Annotations

To determine that a claim should be equitably subordinated, a court must engage in an inquiry as to whether: 1) the claimant has engaged in some type of inequitable conduct; 2) the misconduct has resulted in injury to creditors or conferred an unfair advantage; and 3) equitable subordination is inconsistent with the provisions of the Code. In reaching a decision as to the necessity of equitable subordination, the court must look at the relationship between the debtor and the claimant; if the claimant is not an insider, evidence of egregious conduct such as fraud, spoliation or overreaching is necessary. However, if the claimant is an insider, the court must closely scrutinize the dealings between the parties. In the Matter of Fabricators, Inc., 926 F.2d 1458, 24 C.B.C.2d 1489 (5th Cir. 1991).

Section 510(c) may not be employed to avoid a transfer or to invalidate the transfer that gave rise to a lien; rather, section 510(c) only empowers the bankruptcy court to "subordinate for purposes of distribution . . . an allowed claim . . . to another allowed claim." Max Sugarman Funeral Home, Inc. v. A.D.B. Investors, 926 F.2d 1248, 24 C.B.C.2d 1414 (1st Cir. 1991).

Marshaling is an equitable remedy addressed to the court's discretion. Marshaling may be invoked only: 1) on behalf of junior secured or lien creditors; 2) where the debtor has two distinct funds; and 3) where the remedy would work no inequity upon the debtor or certain third parties. When a creditor has not established a right to marshal assets under either the common law or a bankruptcy court order, it may not assert a right of equitable subordination to another creditor's liens. *In re* Brazier Forest Products, Inc., 921 F.2d 221, 24 C.B.C.2d 320 (9th Cir. 1990).

Section 510(c) permits bankruptcy courts in chapter 13 cases to subordinate nonpecuniary loss tax penalties, but such subordination is not automatic and can only be imposed after a consideration of the equities of the claims involved. *In re* Burden, 917 F.2d 115, 24 C.B.C.2d 187 (3d Cir. 1990).

When a bank and a debtor have entered into a postpetition financing agreement calling for a maximum of $300,000 to be loaned to the debtor but reserving to the bank the right to cease to make further advances, refusal by the bank to loan more than $75,000 under the agreement is the bank's contractual privilege and does not justify the subordination of its claim. *In re* Kham & Nate's Shoes No. 2, Inc., 908 F.2d 1351, 23 C.B.C.2d 1118 (7th Cir. 1990).

Equitable subordination may only take place if: 1) the claimant has engaged in some type of inequitable conduct; 2) the conduct injured creditors or gave the claimant some unfair advantage; and 3) subordination is not inconsistent with the provisions of the Code, and the claim can only be subordinated to the extent necessary to offset the harm suffered by the debtor and the creditors because of that conduct. In the Matter of Lemco Gypsum, Inc., 911 F.2d 1153, 23 C.B.C.2d 1166 (11th Cir. 1990).

Section 510(c)(1) authorizes courts to equitably subordinate nonpecuniary loss tax penalties to other claims on a case-by-case basis without requiring in every instance inequitable conduct on the part of the creditor claiming parity among other unsecured general creditors. In the Matter of Virtual Network Services Corp., 902 F.2d 1246, 22 C.B.C.2d 1667 (7th Cir. 1990).

A creditor exercising its right to reduce the amount of money advanced to a debtor pursuant to a loan agreement which was executed at arms length and prior to the debtor's insolvency is not acting at the unconscionable level of control necessary to invoke the doctrine of equitable subordination. In re Clark Pipe and Supply Co., Inc., 893 F.2d 693, 22 C.B.C.2d 500 (5th Cir. 1990).

Even under the lesser standard required when the claimants are insiders, the receipt of a preference by an insider, without more, does not constitute the type of inequitable conduct necessary to warrant the subordination of a claim. In re Bellanca Aircraft Corp., 850 F.2d 1275, 20 C.B.C.2d 19 (8th Cir. 1988).

The pursuit of personal gain at the expense of other creditors by a shareholder and insider of the debtor is a breach of fiduciary duty justifying subordination of the shareholder's secured claim to those of unsecured consumer creditors. Estes v. N & D Properties, Inc. (In re N & D Properties, Inc.), 799 F.2d 726, 15 C.B.C.2d 726 (11th Cir. 1986).

Subordination provisions must conform to a rule of explicitness, must be unambiguous, and must provide unequivocal notice to holders of claims regarding payments which may affect their claims, e.g., that amounts otherwise owing from the debtor if the claim had been oversecured must be made up out of the principal claim of the undersecured creditors. The enforcement of a subordination agreement is no longer solely an application of the court's equitable powers but, rather, is mandated by statute and full effect to an agreement enforceable under nonbankruptcy law. In re Ionosphere Clubs, Inc., 26 C.B.C.2d 955 (B. Ct., S.D.N.Y. 1991).

A claimant holding totally worthless common stock in a debtor has no standing to object to a settlement and reorganization which would give the claimant more than the value of its equity interest, would satisfy claims which would otherwise likely be litigated at greater cost to all involved, and would benefit the very parties the objecting claimant contends would be injured by it. In re Drexel Burnham Lambert Group, Inc., 26 C.B.C.2d 1283 (B. Ct., S.D.N.Y. 1992).

There is an emerging view that equitable subordination under section 510(c) does not always require proof of inequitable conduct, since the doctrine does not exist to punish errant creditors but, rather, to adjust the claims of creditors as they stand in equitable relation to each other. The quality of conduct considered to be inequitable under section 510(c) depends on the nature of the legal relationship between the creditor and the debtor. *In re* Aluminum Mills Corp., 25 C.B.C.2d 1120 (B. Ct., N.D. Ill. 1991).

A holder of mandatory redeemable preferred stock is not a subordinated creditor by reason of its claims for fraud in connection with the purchase of its preferred stock so that its claim regarding such purchase will not rise above the level of an equity interest in the stock. *In re* Revco D.S., Inc., 24 C.B.C.2d 91 (B. Ct., N.D. Ohio 1990).

When the senior and junior creditor agree prepetition that the senior creditor would hold a second mortgage lien on the debtor's residence, the senior creditor has rights of subordination. Mihalko & Acceptance Associates of America, Inc. v. Continental Bank and Trust Co. (*In re* Mihalko), 18 C.B.C.2d 1387 (B. Ct., E.D. Pa. 1988).

References

3 *Collier on Bankruptcy* ch. 510 (Matthew Bender 15th ed.).

2 *Collier Bankruptcy Manual* ch. 510 (Matthew Bender 3d ed.).

3 *Collier Bankruptcy Practice Guide* ch. 55 (Matthew Bender).

Cohn, *Subordinated Claims: Their Classification and Voting Under Chapter 11 of the Bankruptcy Code,* 56 Am. Bankr. L.J. 293 (1983).

DeNatale and Abram, *The Doctrine of Equitable Subordination as Applied to Nonmanagement Creditors,* 40 Bus. Law. 417 (1985).

Lopes, *Contractual Subordination and Bankruptcy,* 97 Banking L.J. 204 (1980).

SUBCHAPTER II

Debtor's Duties and Benefits

SECTION 521 (11 U.S.C. § 521)

§ 521. Debtor's duties. The debtor shall—

(1) file a list of creditors, and unless the court orders otherwise, a schedule of assets and liabilities, a schedule of current income and current expenditures, and a statement of the debtor's financial affairs;

(2) if an individual debtor's schedule of assets and liabilities includes consumer debts which are secured by property of the estate—

(A) within thirty days after the date of the filing of a petition under chapter 7 of this title or on or before the date of the meeting of creditors, whichever is earlier, or within such additional time as the court, for cause, within such period fixes, the debtor shall file with the clerk a statement of his intention with respect to the retention or surrender of such property and, if applicable, specifying that such property is claimed as exempt, that the debtor intends to redeem such property, or that the debtor intends to reaffirm debts secured by such property;

(B) within forty-five days after the filing of a notice of intent under this section, or within such additional time as the court, for cause, within such forty-five day period fixes, the debtor shall perform his intention with respect to such property, as specified by subparagraph (A) of this paragraph; and

(C) nothing in subparagraphs (A) and (B) of this paragraph shall alter the debtor's or the trustee's rights with regard to such property under this title;

(3) if a trustee is serving in the case, cooperate with the trustee as necessary to enable the trustee to perform the trustee's duties under this title;

(4) if a trustee is serving in the case, surrender to the trustee all property of the estate and any recorded information, including books, documents, records, and papers, relating to property of the estate, whether or not immunity is granted under section 344 of this title; and

(5) appear at the hearing required under section 524(d) of this title.

Bankruptcy Rule References: 1007, 2015 and 4002

Legislative History

This section lists three duties of the debtor in a bankruptcy case. [*Ed. Note:* As enacted, four duties were specified; Pub. L. No. 98–353 added a fifth.] The Rules of Bankruptcy Procedure will specify the means of carrying out these duties. The first duty is to file with the court a list of creditors, and unless the court orders otherwise, a schedule of assets and liabilities and a statement of his financial affairs. Second, the debtor is required to cooperate with the trustee as necessary to enable the trustee to perform the trustee's duties. Finally, the debtor must surrender to the trustee all property of the estate, and any recorded information, including books, documents, records, and papers, relating to property of the estate. The phrase "recorded information, including books, documents, records, and papers," has been used here and throughout the bill as a more general term, and includes such other form of recorded information as data in computer storage or in other machine readable forms.

The list in this section is not exhaustive of the debtor's duties. Others are listed elsewhere in proposed title 11, such as in section 344, which requires the debtor to submit to examination, or in the Rules of Bankruptcy Procedure, as continued by H.R. 8200 § 405(d) such as the duty to attend any hearing on discharge, Rule 402(2).

[*House Report No. 95–595, 95th Cong., 1st Sess. 359–360 (1977); See Senate Report No. 95–989, 95th Cong., 2d Sess. 75 (1978).*]

Section 521 of the House amendment modifies a comparable provision contained in the House bill and Senate amendment. The Rules of Bankruptcy Procedure should provide where the list of creditors is to be filed. In addition, the debtor is required to attend the hearing on discharge under section 524(d).

[*124 Cong. Rec. H 11,095 (Sept. 28, 1978); S 17,412 (Oct. 6, 1978).*]

Comment

Bankruptcy Rule 4002 prescribes duties of the debtor in addition to other duties prescribed by the Code and the rules including the duty to: (1) attend and submit to examination at the times ordered by the court; (2) attend the hearing on a complaint objecting to discharge and to testify if called as a witness; (3) unless a schedule of property was filed under Rule 1007, inform the trustee immediately in writing of the location of all property in which the debtor has an interest and the name and address of every person holding money or property subject to the debtor's withdrawal or order; (4) cooperate with the trustee in preparing an inventory, the examination of proofs of claim, and the administration of the estate; and (5) file a statement of any change of the debtor's address. [Paragraph (5) was added by the 1987 Amendments to the Bankruptcy Rules.]

Bankruptcy Rule 1007(a)(1), amended in 1991, requires the debtor to file a list containing the name and address of each creditor unless the petition is accompanied by a schedule of liabilities. Subdivision (a)(2) requires the debtor to file such list within 15 days after entry of the order for relief in an involuntary case. Subdivision (a)(3) provides that in a chapter 11 case, unless the court orders otherwise, a list of the debtor's equity security holders of each class showing the number and kind of interests registered in the name of each holder, and the last known address or place of business of each holder, must be filed by the debtor within 15 days after the entry of the order for relief. Subdivision (a)(4) provides that any extension of time to file the lists may be granted only on motion for cause shown and on notice to the United States trustee, any trustee, committee or other party as the court directs.

Subdivision (b)(1) requires the debtor, except in a chapter 9 case and unless the court orders otherwise, to file schedules of assets and liabilities, a schedule of current income and expenditures, a schedule of executory contracts and unexpired leases, and a statement of financial affairs, prepared as prescribed by the appropriate Official Forms (Official Forms 6 and 7, as revised by the 1991 Amendments).

Subdivision (b)(2) of the rule was deleted by the 1991 Amendments.

Subdivision (b)(2), formerly subdivision (b)(3), requires an individual chapter 7 debtor to file the statement of intention as prescribed by section 521(2) (Official Form 8). A copy of the statement must be served on the trustee and the creditors named in the statement on or before the statement is filed. [Subdivision (b)(3) (now subdivision (b)(2)) was added by the 1987 Amendments to the Bankruptcy Rules.]

Subdivision (c) provides that in a voluntary case, schedules and statements must be filed with the petition or, if the petition is accompanied by a list of all creditors and their addresses, within 15 days thereafter; in an involuntary case the schedules and statements other than the statement of intention must be filed within 15 days after entry of the order for relief. The time to file may be extended only on motion for cause shown and on notice to the United States trustee, any elected or appointed committee, trustee, examiner or other party as the court may direct. When a case is converted to chapter 7, the debtor is required to file the schedules and statements within 15 days after entry of the conversion order. Notice of extension must be given to the United States trustee and to any committee, trustee or other party as the court directs.

Subdivision (d) provides that in addition to the list required by subdivision (a), in a chapter 9 case or in a voluntary chapter 11 case, the debtor must file with the petition a list of the 20 largest unsecured creditors, their addresses and the nature of their claims (excluding "insiders" as that term is defined in section 101(25)). (Official Form 4) In an involuntary chapter 11 case, this list must be filed by the debtor within 2 days after entry of the order for relief.

Subdivision (e) applies only to chapter 9 cases.

Subdivision (g) requires the general partners of a debtor partnership to file the schedules and statements.

Subdivision (h) provides that if the debtor acquires or becomes entitled to acquire any interest in property [*See* section 541(a)(5)] the debtor shall within 10 days after the information comes to debtor's knowledge or within such time as the court may allow, file a supplemental schedule in the chapter 7, 11, 12, or 13 case. Any claim to exemptions must be claimed in the supplemental schedule. Such schedule is not required as to property acquired after entry of an order confirming a plan. This duty survives the closing of the case, except as to property acquired after entry of the order confirming a chapter 11, 12 or 13 plan.

See section 524(d) under which the debtor may be required to attend the hearing on discharge.

1984 Amendments: Section 521 was amended by including in paragraph (1) a requirement that the debtor file a schedule of current income and expenditures.

Paragraph (2), (3), and (4) were renumbered (3), (4) and (5) and a new paragraph (2) was inserted. The new paragraph relates to individual debtors whose schedules include consumer debts secured by property of the estate and imposes the additional duties specified in the paragraph.

This amendment, one of more than 30 relating to consumer finance, makes it the duty of a debtor with consumer debts (*see* section 101(7) for definition) secured by property of the estate to take affirmative action as to the collateral before the value thereof is seriously diminished.

Renumbered section 521(4), as amended, requires a debtor to turn over to the trustee all property, recorded information, and documents relating to the property whether or not immunity was granted under section 344. This change, which was made by § 452 of Pub. L. No. 98–353, was stated to be made to section 521(3), as redesignated, but was clearly intended for section 521(4), as redesignated.

Case Annotations

Section 521(2)(A) is a procedural provision requiring a debtor to provide a statement of intent with respect to collateral securing a consumer debt, but it does not require a debtor to choose one of the section's non-exclusive list of options relating to how the debtor plans to treat property. If a consumer debtor decides to redeem collateral by continuing to make monthly payments to a lender under an installment contract, fully complying with 521(2)(A) by providing timely notice of intent, the creditor retains a lien on the property to extent of its value and still has the same rights as any lender under an installment contract without additional vulnerabilities. *In re* Belanger, 962 F.2d 345, 26 C.B.C.2d 1429 (4th Cir. 1992).

As a condition of retaining the property which secures an installment loan, the debtor must either redeem it by making a lump-sum payment or by expressly reaffirming the debt underlying the collateral, but redemption may not be accomplished by means of installment payments. In the Matter of Edwards, 901 F.2d 1383, 23 C.B.C.2d 488 (7th Cir. 1990).

A debtor's duty and ability to cooperate with its chapter 7 trustee is impaired when the debtor's counsel also represents the debtor's sole shareholder and a new corporation formed by that shareholder to engage in a business similar to that of the debtor, and when the shareholder is attempting to purchase estate assets for the new corporation at below value and is the target of preferential transfer avoidance actions; to effectively represent the debtor, counsel must be truly independent. Parker v. Frazier (*In re* Freedom Solar Center, Inc.), 776 F.2d 14, 13 C.B.C.2d 915 (1st Cir. 1985).

When a valid Fifth Amendment claim exists nothing in the Bankruptcy Code or prior case law requires a debtor to turn over personal records to the trustee. Butcher v. Bailey, 753 F.2d 465, 11 C.B.C.2d 1229 (6th Cir.), *cert. dismissed,* 473 U.S. 925, 106 S. Ct. 17, 87 L. Ed. 2d 696 (1985).

Unlike procedure under the 1898 Bankruptcy Act, chapter 11 of the Bankruptcy Code contains no provision authorizing the impoundment of the list of creditors which the debtor in possession or trustee is required to prepare and file pursuant to section 521(1). *In re* Itel Corp., 6 C.B.C.2d 4 (9th Cir., B.A.P., 1982).

The options of surrender, redemption or reaffirmation provided in section 521 are not exclusive and debtors are permitted to remain in possession of mortgaged property absent default on the underlying loan. *In re* Stefano, 26 C.B.C.2d 98 (B. Ct., W.D. Pa. 1991).

When stating his or her intention regarding estate property that secures a debt, a debtor must select from the exclusive list of methods of treatment of that property provided for by section 521(2)(A) and may not simply continue acting under the contract by making monthly payments. Although the Code does require the trustee to make sure that the debtor performs his or her intentions under section 521(2), the court has the power to ensure the debtor's compliance if a trustee is reluctant to do so; a creditor, however, is without standing to do so. *In re* Kennedy, 26 C.B.C.2d 1192 (B. Ct., E.D. Ark. 1992).

The time provisions contained in section 521(2) are merely guidelines and, if a debtor who wishes to redeem property is unable to comply with those time limits because of conflicting time frames established by other sections of the Code or Bankruptcy Rules, the debtor's right to redeem is not impaired and remains in effect until the automatic stay terminates. *In re* Cassar, 26 C.B.C.2d 1637 (B. Ct., D. Colo. 1992).

If an individual debtor desires to retain possession of non-exempt property that secures a consumer debt, section 521(2)(A) permits that debtor only two options, reaffirmation or redemption. To allow the debtor to retain property without choosing one of these options would be tantamount to forcing the creditor into a *de facto* reaffirmation agreement with no recourse against the debtor. Matter of Horne, 25 C.B.C.2d 1471 (B. Ct., N.D. Ga. 1991).

The language of section 521(2)(A) does not limit a debtor who retains personal property subject to a lien but who has not defaulted under the original obligation, to the three options of surrendering the collateral, redeeming it, or reaffirming the underlying debt, *i.e.,* a debtor may retain collateral under the terms of an original contract if that contract is not in default. *In re* Donley, 25 C.B.C.2d 686 (B. Ct., N.D. Fla. 1991).

While a chapter 7 trustee is the proper party to act against a debtor for failure to comply with section 521(2), the Code provides no penalty for the debtor's failure to comply. *In re* Manderson, 24 C.B.C.2d 1155 (B. Ct., N.D. Ala. 1990).

Section 521(4) imposes an affirmative duty upon a debtor to cooperate with the trustee by providing all relevant documents and papers and it is insufficient for the debtor to force the trustee to file an objection to discharge complaint in order to obtain necessary records. *In re* Ridley, 24 C.B.C.2d 163 (B. Ct., D. Mass. 1990).

A nondefaulting chapter 7 debtor has the option to continue installment payments to his creditor as if he, the debtor, had not filed a bankruptcy petition and are not limited to reaffirmation, redemption, or payment of the balance in a lump sum. Century Bank at Broadway v. Peacock (*In re* Peacock), 19 C.B.C.2d 69 (B. Ct., D. Colo. 1988).

References

3 *Collier on Bankruptcy* ch. 521 (Matthew Bender 15th ed.).

2 *Collier Bankruptcy Manual* ch. 521 (Matthew Bender 3d ed.).

Kennedy, *The Commencement of a Case Under the New Bankruptcy Code,* 36 Wash. & Lee L. Rev. 977 (1979).

LoPucki, *The Debtor in Full Control-Systems Failure Under Chapter 11 of the Bankruptcy Code?* (Pt. 2), 57 Am. Bankr. L.J. 247 (1983).

Meyer, *Marketing Farm Products: The Farmer as Debtor and Related Problems of the Buyers of Farm Products,* 4 Agric. L.J. 542 (1983).

Moorer, *The Debtor's Statement of Intention,* 46 J. Mo. B. 375 (1990).

§ 522. Exemptions.

(a) In this section—

(1) "dependent" includes spouse, whether or not actually dependent; and

(2) "value" means fair market value as of the date of the filing of the petition or, with respect to property that becomes property of the estate after such date, as of the date such property becomes property of the estate.

(b) Notwithstanding section 541 of this title, an individual debtor may exempt from property of the estate the property listed in either paragraph (1) or, in the alternative, paragraph (2) of this subsection. In joint cases filed under section 302 of this title and individual cases filed under section 301 or 303 of this title by or against debtors who are husband and wife, and whose estates are ordered to be jointly administered under Rule 1015(b) of the Bankruptcy Rules, one debtor may not elect to exempt property listed in paragraph (1) and the other debtor elect to exempt property listed in paragraph (2) of this subsection. If the parties cannot agree on the alternative to be elected, they shall be deemed to elect paragraph (1), where such election is permitted under the law of the jurisdiction where the case is filed. Such property is—

(1) property that is specified under subsection (d) of this section, unless the State law that is applicable to the debtor under paragraph (2)(A) of this subsection specifically does not so authorize; or, in the alternative,

(2)(A) any property that is exempt under Federal law, other than subsection (d) of this section, or State or local law that is applicable on the date of the filing of the petition at the place in which the debtor's domicile has been located for the 180 days immediately preceding the date of the filing of the petition, or for a longer portion of such 180-day period than in any other place; and

(B) any interest in property in which the debtor had, immediately before the commencement of the case, an interest as a tenant by the entirety or joint tenant to the extent that such interest as a tenant by the entirety or joint tenant is exempt from process under applicable nonbank-ruptcy law.

(c) Unless the case is dismissed, property exempted under this section is not liable during or after the case for any debt of the debtor that arose, or that is determined under section 502 of this title as if such debt had arisen, before the commencement of the case, except—

(1) a debt of a kind specified in section 523(a)(1) or 523(a)(5) of this title;

(2) a debt secured by a lien that is—

(A)(i) not avoided under subsection (f) or (g) of this section or under section 544, 545, 547, 548, 549, or 724(a) of this title; and

(ii) not void under section 506(d) of this title; or

(B) a tax lien, notice of which is properly filed; or

(3) a debt of a kind specified in section 523(a)(4) or 523(a)(6) of this title owed by an institution-affiliated party of an insured depository institution to a Federal depository institutions regulatory agency acting in its capacity as con-servator, receiver, or liquidating agent for such institution.

(d) The following property may be exempted under subsection (b)(1) of this section:

(1) The debtor's aggregate interest, not to exceed $7,500 in value, in real property or personal property that the debtor or a dependent of the debtor uses as a residence, in a cooperative that owns property that the debtor or a depen-dent of the debtor uses as a residence, or in a burial plot for the debtor or a dependent of the debtor.

(2) The debtor's interest, not to exceed $1,200 in value, in one motor vehicle.

(3) The debtor's interest, not to exceed $200 in value in any particular item or $4,000 in aggregate value, in house-hold furnishings, household goods, wearing apparel, appli-ances, books, animals, crops, or musical instruments, that are held primarily for the personal, family, or household use of the debtor or a dependent of the debtor.

(4) The debtor's aggregate interest, not to exceed $500 in value, in jewelry held primarily for the personal, family, or household use of the debtor or a dependent of the debtor.

(5) The debtor's aggregate interest in any property, not to exceed in value $400 plus up to $3,750 of any unused amount of the exemption provided under paragraph (1) of this subsection.

(6) The debtor's aggregate interest, not to exceed $750 in value, in any implements, professional books, or tools, of the trade of the debtor or the trade of a dependent of the debtor.

(7) Any unmatured life insurance contract owned by the debtor, other than a credit life insurance contract.

(8) The debtor's aggregate interest, not to exceed in value $4,000 less any amount of property of the estate transferred in the manner specified in section 542(d) of this title, in any accrued dividend or interest under, or loan value of, any unmatured life insurance contract owned by the debtor under which the insured is the debtor or an individual of whom the debtor is a dependent.

(9) Professionally prescribed health aids for the debtor or a dependent of the debtor.

(10) The debtor's right to receive—

(A) a social security benefit, unemployment compensation, or a local public assistance benefit;

(B) a veterans' benefit;

(C) a disability, illness, or unemployment benefit;

(D) alimony, support, or separate maintenance, to the extent reasonably necessary for the support of the debtor and any dependent of the debtor;

(E) a payment under a stock bonus, pension, profit-sharing, annuity, or similar plan or contract on account of illness, disability, death, age, or length of service, to the extent reasonably necessary for the support of the debtor and any dependent of the debtor, unless—

(i) such plan or contract was established by or under the auspices of an insider that employed the debtor at the time the debtor's rights under such plan or contract arose;

(ii) such payment is on account of age or length of service; and

(iii) such plan or contract does not qualify under section 401(a), 403(a), 403(b), 408, or 409 of the Internal Revenue Code of 1954 (26 U.S.C. § 401(a), 403(b), 408, or 409).

(11) The debtor's right to receive, or property that is traceable to—

(A) an award under a crime victim's reparation law;

(B) a payment on account of the wrongful death of an individual of whom the debtor was a dependent, to the extent reasonably necessary for the support of the debtor and any dependent of the debtor;

(C) a payment under a life insurance contract that insured the life of an individual of whom the debtor was a dependent on the date of such individual's death, to the extent reasonably necessary for the support of the debtor and any dependent of the debtor;

(D) a payment, not to exceed $7,500, on account of personal bodily injury, not including pain and suffering or compensation for actual pecuniary loss, of the debtor or an individual of whom the debtor is a dependent; or

(E) a payment in compensation of loss of future earnings of the debtor or an individual of whom the debtor is or was a dependent, to the extent reasonably necessary for the support of the debtor and any dependent of the debtor.

(e) A waiver of an exemption executed in favor of a creditor that holds an unsecured claim against the debtor is unenforceable in a case under this title with respect to such claim against property that the debtor may exempt under subsection (b) of this section. A waiver by the debtor of a power under subsection (f) or (h) of this section to avoid a transfer, under subsection (g) or (i) of this section to exempt property, or under subsection (i) of this section to recover property or to preserve a transfer, is unenforceable in a case under this title.

(f) Notwithstanding any waiver of exemptions, the debtor may avoid the fixing of a lien on an interest of the debtor in property to the extent that such lien impairs an exemption to which the debtor would have been entitled under subsection (b) of this section, if such lien is—

(1) a judicial lien; or

(2) a nonpossessory, nonpurchase-money security interest in any—

(A) household furnishings, household goods, wearing apparel, appliances, books, animals, crops, musical instruments, or jewelry that are held primarily for the personal, family, or household use of the debtor or a dependent of the debtor;

(B) implements, professional books, or tools, of the trade of the debtor or the trade of a dependent of the debtor; or

(C) professionally prescribed health aids for the debtor or a dependent of the debtor.

(g) Notwithstanding sections 550 and 551 of this title, the debtor may exempt under subsection (b) of this section property that the trustee recovers under section 510(c)(2), 542, 543, 550, 551, or 553 of this title, to the extent that the debtor could have exempted such property under subsection (b) of this section if such property had not been transferred, if—

(1)(A) such transfer was not a voluntary transfer of such property by the debtor; and

(B) the debtor did not conceal such property; or

(2) the debtor could have avoided such transfer under subsection (f)(2) of this section.

(h) The debtor may avoid a transfer of property of the debtor or recover a setoff to the extent that the debtor could have exempted such property under subsection (g)(1) of this section if the trustee had avoided such transfer, if—

(1) such transfer is avoidable by the trustee under section 544, 545, 547, 548, 549, or 724(a) of this title or recoverable by the trustee under section 553 of this title: and

(2) the trustee does not attempt to avoid such transfer.

(i)(1) If the debtor avoids a transfer or recovers a setoff under subsection (f) or (h) of this section, the debtor may recover in the manner prescribed by, and subject to the limitations of section 550 of this title, the same as if the trustee had avoided such transfer, and may exempt any property so recovered under subsection (b) of this section.

(2) Notwithstanding section 551 of this title, a transfer avoided under section 544, 545, 547, 548, 549, or 724(a) of this title, under subsection (f) or (h) of this section, or property recovered under section 553 of this title, may be preserved for the benefit of the debtor to the extent that the debtor may exempt such property under subsection (g) of this section or paragraph (1) of this subsection.

(j) Notwithstanding subsections (g) and (i) of this section, the debtor may exempt a particular kind of property under subsections (g) and (i) of this section only to the extent that the debtor has exempted less property in value of such kind than that to which the debtor is entitled under subsection (b) of this section.

(k) Property that the debtor exempts under this section is not liable for payment of any administrative expense except—

(1) the aliquot share of the costs and expenses of avoiding a transfer of property that the debtor exempts under subsection (g) of this section, or of recovery of such property, that is attributable to the value of the portion of such property exempted in relation to the value of the property recovered; and

(2) any costs and expenses of avoiding a transfer under subsection (f) or (h) of this section, or of recovery of property under subsection (i)(1) of this section, that the debtor has not paid.

(l) The debtor shall file a list of property that the debtor claims as exempt under subsection (b) of this section. If the debtor does not file such a list, a dependent of the debtor may file such a list, or may claim property as exempt from property of the estate on behalf of the debtor. Unless a party in interest objects, the property claimed as exempt on such list is exempt.

(m) Subject to the limitation in subsection (b), this section shall apply separately with respect to each debtor in a joint case.

Bankruptcy Rule Reference: 4003

Legislative History

Subsection (a) of this section defines two terms: "dependent" includes the debtor's spouse, whether or not actually dependent; and "value" means fair market value as of the date of the filing of the petition.

[*House Report No. 95–595, 95th Cong., 1st Sess. 360 (1977); Senate Report No. 95–989, 95th Cong., 2d Sess. 75 (1978).*]

Subsection (b), the operative subsection of this section, is a significant departure from present law. It permits an individual debtor in a bankruptcy case a choice between exemption systems. The debtor may choose the Federal exemptions prescribed in subsection (d), or he may choose the exemptions to which he is entitled under other Federal law and the law of the State of his domicile. If the debtor chooses the latter, some of the items that may be exempted under other Federal laws include:

—Foreign Service Retirement and Disability payments, 22 U.S.C. § 1104; [*Ed. Note:* 22 U.S.C. § 4060 replaced repealed 22 U.S.C. § 1104, which was the applicable statutory provision at the time of the enactment of the Bankruptcy Reform Act of 1978, Pub. L. No. 95–598.]

—Social security payments, 42 U.S.C. § 407;

—Injury or death compensation payments from war risk hazards, 42 U.S.C. § 1717;

—Wages of fishermen, seamen, and apprentices, 46 U.S.C. § 601;

—Civil service retirement benefits, 5 U.S.C. §§ 729, 2265;

—Longshoremen's and Harbor Workers' Compensation Act death and disability benefits, 33 U.S.C. § 916;

—Railroad Retirement Act annuities and pensions, 45 U.S.C. § 228(L);

—Veterans benefits, 45 U.S.C. § 352(E); [*Ed. Note:* Correct citation is 38 U.S.C. §§ 770(g) and 3101.];

—Special pensions paid to winners of the Congressional Medal of Honor, 38 U.S.C. § 3101; and

—Federal homestead lands on debts contracted before issuance of the patent, 43 U.S.C. § 175.

He may also exempt an interest in property in which the debtor had an interest as a tenant by the entirety or joint tenant to the extent that interest would have been exempt from process under applicable nonbankruptcy law. The Rules will provide for the situation where the debtor's choice of exemption, Federal or State, was improvident and should be changed, for example, where the court has ruled against the debtor with respect to a major exemption.

Under proposed 11 U.S.C. § 541, all property of the debtor becomes property of the estate, but the debtor is permitted to exempt certain property from property of the estate under this section. Property may be exempt even if it is subject to a lien, but only the unencumbered portion of the property is to be counted in computing the "value" of the property for the purposes of exemption. Thus, for example, a residence worth $30,000 with a mortgage of $25,000 will be exemptable to the extent of $5,000. This follows current law. The remaining value of the property will be dealt with in the bankruptcy case as is any interest in property that is subject to a lien.

As under current law, the debtor will be permitted to convert nonexempted property into exempt property before filing a bankruptcy petition. *See Hearings*, pt. 3, at 1355–58. The practice is not fraudulent as to creditors, and permits the debtor to make full use of the exemptions to which he is entitled under the law.

[*House Report No. 95–595, 95th Cong., 1st Sess. 360–1 (1977).*]

Subsection (b) tracks current law. It permits a debtor the exemptions to which he is entitled under other Federal law and the law of the State of his domicile . . .

[*Senate Report No. 95–989, 95th Cong., 2d Sess. 75 (1978).*]

Section 522 of the House amendment represents a compromise on the issue of exemptions between the position taken in the House bill, and that taken in the Senate amendment. Dollar amounts specified in section 522(d) of the House bill have been reduced from amounts as contained in H.R. 8200 as passed by the House. The States may, by passing a law, determine whether the Federal exemptions will apply as an alternative to State exemptions in bankruptcy cases.

[*124 Cong. Rec. H 11,095 (Sept. 28, 1978); S 17,412 (Oct. 6, 1978).*]

Subsection (c) insulates exempt property from prepetition claims, except tax and alimony, maintenance, or support claims that are excepted from discharge. The bankruptcy discharge will not prevent enforcement of valid liens. The rule of Long v. Bullard, 117 U.S. 617 (1886), is accepted with respect to the enforcement of valid liens on nonexempt property as well as on exempt property. *Cf.* Louisville Joint Stock Land Bank v. Radford, 295 U.S. 555, 583 (1935).

[*House Report No. 95–595, 95th Cong., 1st Sess. 361 (1977); Senate Report No. 95–989, 95th Cong., 2d Sess. 76 (1978).*]

Section 522(c)(1) tracks the House bill and provides that dischargeable tax claims may not be collected out of exempt property.

[*124 Cong. Rec. H 11,095 (Sept. 28, 1978); S 17,412 (Oct. 6, 1978).*]

Section 522. Exemptions: Section 522(c)(1) of the House amendment adopts a provision contained in the House bill that dischargeable taxes cannot be collected from exempt assets. This changes present law, which allows collection of dischargeable taxes from exempt property, a rule followed in the Senate amendment. Nondischargeable taxes, however, will continue to the [*sic*] collectable out of exempt property. It is anticipated that in the next session Congress will review the exemptions from levy currently contained in the Internal Revenue Code with a view to increasing the exemptions to more realistic levels.

[*124 Cong. Rec. H 11,113 (Sept. 28, 1978); S 17,430 (Oct. 6, 1978).*]

Subsection (d) specifies the Federal exemptions to which the debtor is entitled. They are derived in large part from the Uniform Exemptions Act, promulgated by the Commissioners of Uniform State Laws in August, 1976. Eleven categories of property are exempted. First is a homestead to the extent of $10,000, which may be claimed in real or personal property that the debtor or a dependent of the debtor uses as a residence. Second, the debtor may exempt a motor vehicle to the extent of $1500. Third, the debtor may exempt household goods, furnishings, clothing, and similar household items, held primarily for the personal, family, or household use of the debtor or a dependent of the debtor. "Animals" includes all animals, such as pets, livestock, poultry, and fish, if they are held primarily for personal family or household use. The limitation for third category items is $300 on any particular item. The debtor may also exempt up to $750 of personal jewelry.

Paragraph (5) permits the exemption of $500, plus any unused amount of the homestead exemption, in any property, in order not to discriminate against the nonhomeowner. Paragraph (6) grants the debtor up to $1000 in implements, professional books, or tools, of the trade of the debtor a dependent [*sic*]. Paragraph (7) exempts a life insurance contract, other than a credit life insurance contract, owned by the debtor. This paragraph refers to the life insurance contract itself. It does not encompass any other rights under the contract, such as the right to borrow out the loan value. Because of this provision, the trustee may not surrender a life insurance contract, which remains property of the debtor if he chooses the Federal exemptions. Paragraph (8) permits the debtor to exempt up to $5,000 in loan value in a life insurance policy owned by the debtor under which the debtor or an individual of whom the debtor is a dependent is the insured. The exemption provided by this paragraph and paragraph (7) will also include the debtor's rights in a group insurance certificate under which the insured is an individual of whom the debtor is a dependent (assuming the debtor has rights in the policy that could be exempted) or the debtor. A trustee is authorized to collect the entire loan value on every life insurance policy owned by the debtor as property of the estate. First, however, the debtor will choose which policy or polices under which the loan value will be exempted. The $5,000 figure is reduced by the amount of any automatic premium loan authorized after the date of the filing of the petition under section 542(d). Paragraph (9) exempts professionally prescribed health aids.

Paragraph (10) exempts certain benefits that are akin to future earnings of the debtor. These include social security, unemployment compensation, or public assistance benefits, veteran's benefits, disability, illness, or unemployment benefits, alimony, support or separate maintenance (but only to the extent reasonably necessary for the support of the debtor and any dependents of the debtor) and benefits under a certain stock bonus, pension, profitsharing, annuity or similar plan based on illness, disability, death, age or length of service. Paragraph (11) allows the debtor to exempt certain compensation for losses. These include crime victim's reparation benefits, wrongful death benefits (with a reasonably necessary for support limitation), life insurance proceeds (same limitation), compensation for bodily injury, not including pain and suffering ($10,000 limitation), and loss of furture earnings payments (support limitation). This provision in subparagraph (D)(11) is designed to cover payments in compensation of actual bodily injury, such as the loss of a limb, and is not intended to include the attendant costs that accompany such a loss, such as medical payments, pain and suffering, or loss of earnings. Those items are handled separately by the bill.

[*House Report No. 95–595, 95th Cong., 1st Sess. 361–62 (1977).*]

Subsection (e) protects the debtor's exemptions, either Federal or State, by making unenforceable in a bankruptcy case a waiver of exemptions or a waiver of the debtor's avoiding powers under the following subsections.

Subsection (f) protects the debtor's exemptions, his discharge, and thus his fresh start by permitting him to avoid certain liens on exempt property. The debtor may avoid a judicial lien on any property to the extent that the property could have been exempted in the absence of the lien, and may similarly avoid a nonpurchase-money security interest in certain household and personal goods. The avoiding power is independent of any waiver of exemptions.

[*House Report No. 95–595, 95th Cong., 1st Sess. 362 (1977); Senate Report No. 95–989, 95th Cong., 2d Sess. 76 (1978) (under subsection (e)).*]

Section 522(f)(2) is derived from the Senate amendment restricting the debtor to avoidance of nonpossessory, nonpurchase money security interests.

[*124 Cong. Rec. H 11,095 (Sept. 28, 1978); S 17,412 (Oct. 6, 1978).*]

Subsection (g) gives the debtor the ability to exempt property that the trustee recovers under one of the trustee's avoiding powers if the property was involuntarily transferred away from the debtor (such as by fixing of a judicial lien) and if the debtor did not conceal the property. The debtor is also permitted to exempt property that the trustee recovers as the result of the avoiding of the fixing of certain security interests to the extent that the debtor could otherwise have exempted the property.

If the trustee does not pursue an avoiding power to recover a transfer of property that would be exempt, the debtor may pursue it and exempt the property, if the transfer was involuntary and the debtor did not conceal the property. [*Ed. Note:* As enacted, this provision is found in subsection (h).] If the debtor wishes to preserve his right to pursue an action under this provision, then he must intervene in any action brought by the trustee based on the same cause of action. It is not intended that the debtor be given an additional opportunity to avoid a transfer or that the transferee have to defend the same action twice. Rather, the section is primarily designed to give the debtor the rights the trustee could have pursued if the trustee chooses not to pursue them. The debtor is given no greater rights under this provision than the trustee, and thus, the debtor's avoiding powers under proposed 11 U.S.C. §§ 544, 545, 547, and 548, are subject to proposed 11 U.S.C. § 546, as are the trustee's powers.

These subsections are cumulative. The debtor is not required to choose which he will use to gain an exemption. Instead, he may use more than one in any particular instance, just as the trustee's avoiding powers are cumulative.

[*House Report No. 95–595, 95th Cong., 1st Sess. 360 (1977); See Senate Report No. 95–989, 95th Cong., 2d Sess. 76 (1978) (under subsection (f)).*]

Subsection (g) provides that if the trustee does not exercise an avoiding power to recover a transfer of property that would be exempt, the debtor may exercise it and exempt the property, if the transfer was involuntary and the debtor did not conceal the property. If the debtor wishes to preserve his right to pursue any action under this provision, then he must intervene in any action brought by the trustee based on the same cause of action. It is not intended that the debtor be given an additional opportunity to avoid a transfer or that the transferee should have to defend the same action twice. Rather, the section is primarily designed to give the debtor the rights the trustee could have, but has not, pursued. The debtor is given no greater rights under this provision than the trustee, and thus, the debtor's avoiding powers under proposed sections 544, 545, 547, and 548, are subject to proposed 546, as are the trustee's powers.

These subsections are cumulative. The debtor is not required to choose which he will use to gain an exemption. Instead, he may use more than one in any particular instance, just as the trustee's avoiding powers are cumulative.

[*Senate Report No. 95–989, 95th Cong., 2d Sess. 75 (1978).*]

Subsection (i) permits recovery by the debtor of property transferred in an avoided transfer from either the initial or subsequent transferees. It also permits preserving a transfer for the benefit of the debtor. Under either case, the debtor may exempt the property recovered or preserved.

[*House Report No. 95–595, 95th Cong., 1st Sess. 363 (1977); See Senate Report No. 95–989, 95th Cong., 2d Sess. 77 (1978) (under subsection (h)).*]

Subsection (j) makes clear that the debtor may exempt property under the avoiding subsections (f) and (h) only to the extent he has exempted less property than allowed under subsection (b).

[*Senate Report No. 95–989, 95th Cong., 2d Sess. 75 (1978).*]

Subsection (k) makes clear that the debtor's aliquot share of the costs and expenses recovery of property that the trustee recovers and the debtor later exempts, and any costs and expenses of avoiding a transfer by the debtor that the debtor has not already paid.

Subsection (l) requires the debtor to file a list of property that he claims as exempt from property of the estate. Absent an objection to the list, the property is exempted. A dependent of the debtor may file it and thus be protected if the debtor fails to file the list.

[House Report No. 95–595, 95th Cong., 1st Sess. 363 (1977); Senate Report No. 95–989, 95th Cong., 2d Sess. 77 (1978) (under subsection (j) and (k)).]

Subsection (n) provides the rule for a joint case; each debtor is entitled to the Federal exemptions provided under this section or to the State exemptions, whichever the debtor chooses.

[House Report No. 95–595, 95th Cong., 1st Sess. 363 (1977); (the reference should be to subsection (m)).]

Comment

The exemption provisions of section 522 are far-reaching changes from the exemption provisions of the former Bankruptcy Act.

Section 522 of the Code provides for an election by the debtor between non-bankruptcy State law exemptions and a series of exemptions prescribed by the Code. Some states have liberal exemption laws. The debtor may, under the Code, elect to take the Federal or State exemptions; but the debtor must choose one or the other and may not select parts of each. Where State laws are not as generous as the Code regarding exemptions, the debtor will, of course, opt for the Federal exemption. But unfortunately a state may veto the right to elect the Federal exemption by virtue of subsection (b)(1) which states that that Federal exemption is available "unless the state law . . . specifically does not so authorize." But the state cannot exercise the veto by failure to act; it must affirmatively forbid the choice.

Section 522 does not specify when the election must be made. Bankruptcy Rule 4003 relates to exemptions. Subdivision (a) requires the debtor to list the property claimed as exempt under section 522 on the schedule of assets filed pursuant to Rule 1007. *See* Official Form 6. If the debtor fails to claim exemptions or file schedules within the time fixed by Rule 1007, a dependent of the debtor may file the list within 30 days of the expiration of such time.

Rule 4003(b) requires that an objection to a claimed exemption be filed within 30 days after the conclusion of the meeting of creditors held pursuant to Rule 2003(a), or the filing of any amendment to the list or supplemental schedules unless, within such period, further time is granted by the court. Copies of the objections must be delivered or mailed to the trustee and person filing the list and the attorney for such person.

Subdivision (c) places the burden of proving that exemptions are improperly claimed on the objecting party. The issues presented by objections are to be decided by the court after hearing on notice.

Subdivision (d) provides that a proceeding by a debtor to avoid a lien or other transfer of exempt property under section 522(f) is a contested matter governed by Rule 9014 as distinguished from a proceeding by a trustee to avoid a transfer which is an adversary proceeding.

1984 Amendments: Section 522 was amended in several respects. The amendments will, however, have little practical application since most of the States have opted out of the federal exemption law.

Section 522(b) was amended to require a husband and wife filing a joint petition to elect either to use State or federal exemptions, and not to permit separate election.

Subsection (d)(3) was amended by setting an aggregate dollar ceiling of $4000 on the value of personal property (held primarily for personal, family, or household use of the debtor or a dependent) that a debtor may exempt.

Subsection (d)(5) was amended to set a ceiling of $3,750, on the unused amount of the homestead exemption that the debtor may apply to *any* property the debtor seeks to exempt.

Subsection (m) was amended to conform to the change made in subsection (b).

1990 Amendments: Pub. L. No. 101-647 (Crime Control Act of 1990; effective on the date of enactment, November 29, 1990,) amended section 522 by adding subparagraph (3) to subsection (c). To accommodate this addition, the word "or" was deleted at the end of paragraph (1), and the period at the end of paragraph (2) was replaced with "; or".

Case Annotations

When a trustee fails to make a timely objection to a debtor's claimed exemption within the 30 day period for making objections set forth in Rule 4003(b), the trustee may not contest the validity of the exemption after the expiration of the 30 day period, even if the debtor had no colorable basis for claiming the exemption; the debtor's authority to claim exemptions under section 522(l) is not limited to exemptions claimed in good faith. Taylor v. Freeland & Kronz, 503 U.S. —, 112 S. Ct. 1644, 118 L. Ed. 2d 280, 26 C.B.C.2d 487 (1992).

The fixing of a lien which impairs a debtor's interest in exempt property cannot be avoided under section 522(f) unless the debtor possessed the encumbered property interest prior to the attachment of the lien. Farrey v. Sanderfoot, 501 U.S. —, 111 S. Ct. 1825, 114 L. Ed. 2d 337, 24 C.B.C.2d 841 (1991).

Section 522(f), which permits the avoidance of a lien which impairs an exemption to which the debtor would have been entitled to claim but for the existence of a lien, applies equally to both federal and state created exemptions. Owen v. Owen, 501 U.S. —, 111 S. Ct. 1833, 114 L. Ed. 2d 350, 24 C.B.C.2d 850 (1991).

Section 522(f)(2) of the Code does not apply retroactively to liens established prior to the enactment of the Bankruptcy Reform Act of 1978 since neither the statute nor its legislative history offer any clear expression of Congress' intent that section 522(f)(2) was meant to avoid liens established prior to the enactment date, and on the authority of precedent no bankruptcy law should be construed to eliminate property rights in existence prior to the law's enactment without an explicit command from Congress. United States v. Sec. Indus. Bank, 459 U.S. 70, 103 S. Ct. 407, 74 L. Ed. 2d 235, 7 C.B.C.2d 629 (1982).

For an item to qualify as a "household good" under section 522(f)(2)(A), there must be a functional nexus between the goods and the household; the nexus exists when the goods, found in or around the home, are used to support and facilitate daily life within the home. *In re* McGreevy, 955 F.2d 957, 26 C.B.C.2d 693 (4th Cir. 1992).

Pursuant to Missouri nonbankruptcy law, a creditor can reach tenancy by the entirety property if the spouses acted jointly to burden the property and, therefore, property so held does not qualify as exempt property. *In re* Garner, 952 F.2d 232, 26 C.B.C.2d 274 (8th Cir. 1991).

Abandonment by a trustee is not a prerequisite to a debtor's exemption of a claim based upon a pending lawsuit, nor is it a prerequisite to a debtor's standing to pursue an action which the debtor wishes to claim as exempt. However, a trustee must formally abandon the estate's interest in a cause of action in order for the debtor to have an interest in any recovery above the exemptible amount. Wissman v. Pittsburgh National Bank, 942 F.2d 867, 25 C.B.C.2d 605 (4th Cir. 1991).

In Illinois, the "estate of homestead" exemption entitles a debtor to remain in his home rent free until he receives the full cash value of the exemption, for the interaction of bankruptcy law and the exemption makes the debtor in effect a cotenant, with the trustee, of the debtor's former house. In the Matter of Szekely, 936 F.2d 897, 24 C.B.C.2d 2028 (7th Cir. 1991).

A state exemption statute that is clearly incompatible with a state constitutional provision is unconstitutional and, thus, cannot be utilized to exempt property from the bankruptcy estate. *In re* Holt, 894 F.2d 1005, 22 C.B.C.2d 337 (8th Cir. 1990).

The death of a debtor after filing his bankruptcy petition does not constitute an abandonment of the homestead or cause it to lapse and revert back to the estate. *In re* Peterson, 897 F.2d 935, 22 C.B.C.2d 1147 (8th Cir. 1990).

Imposing a narrow definition of tools of the trade on section 522(f)(2)(B) would defeat the goals of Congress in allowing a state legislature to create a state exemption statute that may be more favorable to a debtor, and in giving a debtor the opportunity to choose the most advantageous system to exempt property from the bankruptcy estate. *In re* Thompson, 867 F.2d 416, 22 C.B.C.2d 1191 (7th Cir. 1989).

Under Kansas law, a debtor does not have the right to exempt from the bankruptcy estate the nonforfeiture value of life insurance policies if the policy was obtained within one year prior to the filing for bankruptcy and was acquired for the purpose of defrauding one's creditors. *In re* Mueller, 867 F.2d 568, 20 C.B.C.2d 1431 (10th Cir. 1989).

Absent extrinsic evidence of fraud, debtors' conversion of nonexempt property into exempt property, even while insolvent shortly before filing for bankruptcy, is not evidence of fraudulent intent as to creditors and will not deprive debtors of exemptions to which they are otherwise entitled. Hanson v. First Nat'l Bank in Brookings, 848 F.2d 866, 19 C.B.C.2d 247 (8th Cir. 1988).

Section 522(d)(7) exempts from property of the estate an unmatured life insurance policy that is both owned and payable to the debtor as of the date of filing; section 541(a)(5) sweeps later-acquired proceeds of such a policy into the estate. Woodson v. Fireman's Fund Insurance Co. (*In re* Woodson), 839 F.2d 610, 18 C.B.C.2d 674 (9th Cir. 1988).

A dairy farmer's cows and tractors are not tools of the trade as they are not the modest implements that Congress sought to protect, but rather are the principal capital assets of a small farm. Therefore a lien on the proceeds of these items at an auction sale is not avoidable pursuant to section 522(f). In the Matter of Patterson, 825 F.2d 1140, 17 C.B.C.2d 339 (7th Cir. 1987).

When a case is converted from chapter 11 to chapter 7, exemptions are determined as of the filing date of the chapter 11 petition. Stinson v. Williamson (In the Matter of Williamson), 804 F.2d 1355, 15 C.B.C.2d 1225 (5th Cir. 1986).

Section 522(e) is unavailable to a debtor who has waived his right to a homestead exemption in a security agreement as section 522(e) applies only to waivers of exemption involving "unsecured claims." Dominion Bank of Cumberlands, N.A. v. Nuckolls, 780 F.2d 408, 13 C.B.C.2d 1249 (4th Cir. 1985).

In Maryland, property held in a tenancy by the entirety is not exempt from process to satisfy joint creditors' claims because it is not immune from process under state law when joint creditors may have the automatic stay lifted to proceed against the property in state court. Sumy v. Schlossberg (*In re* Sumy), 777 F.2d 921, 13 C.B.C.2d 1213 (4th Cir. 1985).

When debtors enter into an agreement with a creditor that avoids their homestead rights by the device of connecting real estate into a nonexempt land trust, a subsequent change in exemption law that extends the exemption to land trusts will not govern retroactively even if it is the controlling law at the time their bankruptcy exemptions are claimed; application of the new exemption at the creditor's expense cannot be permitted. Capitol Bank & Trust v. Fascetta, 771 F.2d 1077, 13 C.B.C.2d 612 (7th Cir. 1985).

"An interest of the debtor in property" under section 552(f) means an interest of the debtor measured by taking into account those interests of other parties which may not be avoidable under section 522(f); thus, when the value of two mortgages exceeds the value of a debtor's residence, the debtor has no interest in the property to which an exemption can attach and section 552(f) cannot be used to avoid judgment liens that come between the mortgages. Simonson v. First Bank (*In re* Simonson), 758 F.2d 103, 12 C.B.C.2d 777 (3d Cir. 1985).

Since a creditor with a judgment on a joint debt may levy upon entireties' property and thus on the interests of both spouses, a debtor's interest in that portion of entireties' property reachable by a joint creditor is not exempt under section 522(b)(2)(B). Liberty State Bank and Trust v. Grosslight (In the Matter of Grosslight), 757 F.2d 773, 12 C.B.C.2d 525 (6th Cir. 1985).

Livestock is not the sort of low value personal goods necessary to the debtor that the Code seeks to protect from creditors' "adhesion contract" security interests, and therefore, a debtor may not avoid a lien on livestock under section 522(f)(2)(A). In the Matter of Thompson, 750 F.2d 628, 11 C.B.C.2d 1024 (8th Cir. 1984).

If the date of conversion to chapter 7 controlled what is property of the estate and the date of the chapter 13 filing controlled what exemptions could be claimed, the debtor would be restricted in his selection of exemptions; he could not exempt any property acquired after the chapter 13 filing and he would lose exemptions if he exchanged property after the filing. Accordingly, section 522 cannot be read with section 348 to prohibit the changing of a homestead exemption at the time of conversion. Armstrong v. Lindberg (*In re* Lindberg), 735 F.2d 1087, 10 C.B.C.2d 1255 (8th Cir.), *cert. denied,* 469 U.S. 1073, 105 S. Ct. 566, 83 L. Ed. 2d 507 (1984).

A chapter 7 debtor who is entitled to exempt from her bankruptcy estate surplus funds generated by the prebankruptcy foreclosure sale of her real property may avoid a judicial lien on those funds to the extent that such a lien would impair the exemption. Brown v. Dellinger (*In re* Brown), 734 F.2d 119, 10 C.B.C.2d 1405 (2d Cir. 1984).

For purposes of section 522(f), the refinancing of a loan by grant of a new loan nullifies the purchase money nature of a creditor's interest in collateral when the new loan is not made to acquire rights in new collateral. Matthews v. Transamerica Fin. Serv. (*In re* Matthews), 724 F.2d 798, 10 C.B.C.2d 245 (9th Cir. 1984).

The very purpose of section 522(f) is to permit a debtor to avoid specific types of liens on otherwise exempt property, and to allow states to simply inhibit the operation of this provision by defining all lien-encumbered property as not exempt would render the statute useless. Hall v. Finance One of Georgia, 752 F.2d 582, 11 C.B.C.2d 1367 (11th Cir. 1985). *See also* Maddox v. Southern Discount Co., 713 F.2d 1526, 9 C.B.C.2d 568 (11th Cir. 1983).

New York exemption law permits joint debtors to aggregate their individual homestead exemptions. John T. Mather Mem. Hosp. v. Pearl, 723 F.2d 193, 9 C.B.C.2d 670 (2d Cir. 1983).

A state which "opts-out" of the federal exemptions has the right to limit the types of property interests which the debtors may exempt and to exclude the debtors from exempting household goods to the extent that they are encumbered by liens. Pine v. Credithrift of America, Inc., 717 F.2d 281, 9 C.B.C.2d 271 (6th Cir. 1983), *cert. denied,* 466 U.S. 928, 104 S. Ct. 1711, 80 L. Ed. 2d 183 (1984).

When determining the effect of lien avoidance on the order of priority of liens, the bankruptcy court must look at the relationship of each interest to each other interest. When a judicial lien is first in priority to a consensual lien, but the consensual lien is first in priority to a debtor's homestead exemption, the proper procedure is to avoid the judicial lien to the extent of the debtor's homestead exemption and grant any surplus first to the judicial lien claimant. Then, because the consensual lien is superior to the debtor's homestead exemption, the court should take back the exemption and give it to the next highest consensual lien claimant whose lien has not been otherwise avoided. *In re* Patterson, 26 C.B.C.2d 1728 (9th Cir., B.A.P., 1992).

The concept of impairment should be construed in a manner consistent with the fresh start policy of the Code, and to require an execution sale before a debtor in bankruptcy is able to use the applicable homestead exemption to protect his or her property from creditors would eviscerate the purpose and function of exemptions and cause absurd results. *In re* Herman, 24 C.B.C.2d 791 (9th Cir., B.A.P., 1990).

If a judicial lien creditor has not foreclosed on its lien on a debtor's personal injury judgment at the time the debtor files a petition, then the debtor necessarily retains a sufficient interest in the personal injury judgment to utilize section 522(f) to avoid the lien. *In re* Smith, 24 C.B.C.2d 355 (B. Ct., E.D. Cal. 1990).

References

3 *Collier on Bankruptcy* ch. 522 (Matthew Bender 15th ed.).

2 *Collier Bankruptcy Manual* ch. 522 (Matthew Bender 3d ed.).

4 *Collier Bankruptcy Practice Guide* ch. 74 (Matthew Bender).

Collier Bankruptcy Exemption Guide (Matthew Bender).

Arno, *Protection of Retirement Benefits in Bankruptcy Proceedings,* 15 Barrister 47 (1988).

Avoidance of Liens on Exempt Property and the "Wild Card" Exemption: Augustine v. U.S., 3 Ann. Surv. Banking L. 339 (1984).

Avoidance of Liens: Section 522(f), 4 Bankr. Dev. J. 95 (1987).

Bogdanoff, *Exemptions Under the Bankruptcy Code: Using California's New Homestead Law As a Medium for Analysis,* 72 Calif. L. Rev. 922 (1984).

Chobot, *Preserving Liens Avoided in Bankruptcy—Limitations and Applications*, 62 Am. Bankr. L.J. 149 (1988).

Comment, *In Rem Lien Avoidance in Chapter 7: Lenders Beware*, 7 Bankr. Dev. J. 155 (1990).

Devaney, *The Constitutional Homestead Protection: Can You Waive It?*, 17 Tex. Tech. L. Rev. 1471 (1986).

Fulford and Yurchak, *Perils of Pre-Bankruptcy Planning: Transfers, Exemptions and Taxes*, 17 Colo. Law. 1513 (1988).

Golden, *What Have We Stepped Into? Qualified Plans in Bankruptcy*, 2 F & G Bankr. L. Rev. 10 (1990).

Kelly, *The Tenancy by the Entirety—No Longer a "Super Exemption" for Married Debtors in Bankruptcy Court*, 34 Rh. Is. B.J. 5 (1986).

Klee, *Upsetting the Chapter 11 Balancing Act—Exemptions Erode Purpose of the Statute*, 4 Tex. Law. 24 (1988).

Klein, *Multi-Jurisdictional Analysis on Plan Exemptions*, 42 J. Mo. B. 477 (1986).

Laurence, *In re Holt and the Re-making of Arkansas Exemption Law: Commentary After the Rout*, 43 Ark. L. Rev. 235 (1990).

Miles, *A Debtor's Right to Avoid Liens Against Exempt Property Under Section 522 of the Bankruptcy Code: Meaningless or Meaningful?*, 65 Am. Bankr. L. J. 117 (1991).

No More Bananas in the Oklahoma Split: Exempting ERISA-Qualified Pension Plans Under Section 522(b)(2)(A) of the Bankruptcy Code, 25 Tulsa L.J. 799 (1990).

Note, *"A Fresh Start With Someone Else's Property:" Lien Avoidance, the Homestead Exemption and Divorce Property Divisions Under Section 522(f)(1) of the Bankruptcy Code*, 59 Fordham L. Rev. 423 (1990).

Note, *Section 522 Exemptions: A Look at the Individual Debtor's Reduction of the Bankruptcy Estate*, 5 Bankr. Dev. J. 131 (1987).

Parkinson, *The Lien Avoidance Section of the Bankruptcy Code: Can It Be Avoided by State Exemption Statutes?*, 11 Ohio No. U.L. Rev. 319 (1984).

The Debtor and Conversion of Nonexempt Assets to Exempt Assets on the Eve of Bankruptcy: Astute Bankruptcy Estate Planning or Fraud?, 18 Cap. U.L. Rev. 567 (1989).

Weber and Horner, *ERISA Preemption of the Michigan Retirement Plan Exemption Statute*, 69 Mich. B.J. 1196 (1990).

SECTION 523 (11 U.S.C. § 523)

§ 523.　Exceptions to discharge.

(a) A discharge under section 727, 1141, 1228(a), 1228(b), or 1328(b) of this title does not discharge an individual debtor from any debt—

(1) for a tax or a customs duty—

(A) of the kind and for the periods specified in section 507(a)(2) or 507(a)(7) of this title, whether or not a claim for such tax was filed or allowed;

(B) with respect to which a return, if required—

(i) was not filed; or

(ii) was filed after the date on which such return was last due, under applicable law or under any extension, and after two years before the date of the filing of the petition; or

(C) with respect to which the debtor made a fraudulent return or willfully attempted in any manner to evade or defeat such tax;

(2) for money, property, services, or an extension, renewal, or refinancing of credit, to the extent obtained by—

(A) false pretenses, a false representation, or actual fraud, other than a statement respecting the debtor's or an insider's financial condition;

(B) use of a statement in writing—

(i) that is materially false;

(ii) respecting the debtor's or an insider's financial condition;

(iii) on which the creditor to whom the debtor is liable for such money, property, services, or credit reasonably relied; and

(iv) that the debtor caused to be made or published with intent to deceive; or

(C) for purposes of subparagraph (A) of this paragraph, consumer debts owed to a single creditor and aggregating more than $500 for "luxury goods or services" incurred by an individual debtor on or within forty days before the order for relief under this title, or cash advances aggregating more than $1,000 that are extensions of consumer credit under an open end credit plan obtained by an individual debtor on or within twenty days before the order for relief under this title, are presumed to be nondischargeable: "luxury goods or services" do not include goods or services reasonably acquired for the support or maintenance of the debtor or a dependent of the debtor; an extension of consumer credit under an open end credit plan is to be defined for purposes of this subparagraph as it is defined in the Consumer Credit Protection Act (15 U.S.C. 1601 *et seq.*);

(3) neither listed nor scheduled under section 521(1) of this title, with the name, if known to the debtor, of the creditor to whom such debt is owed, in time to permit—

(A) if such debt is not of a kind specified in paragraph (2), (4), or (6) of this subsection, timely filing of a proof of claim, unless such creditor had notice or actual knowledge of the case in time for such timely filing; or

(B) if such debt is of a kind specified in paragraph (2), (4), or (6) of this subsection, timely filing of a proof of claim and timely request for a determination of dischargeability of such debt under one of such paragraphs, unless such creditor had notice or actual knowledge of the case in time for such timely filing and request;

(4) for fraud or defalcation while acting in a fiduciary capacity, embezzlement, or larceny;

(5) to a spouse, former spouse, or child of the debtor, for alimony to, maintenance for, or support of such spouse or child, in connection with a separation agreement, divorce decree or other order of a court of record, determination made in accordance with State or territorial law by a governmental unit, or property settlement agreement, but not to the extent that—

(A) such debt is assigned to another entity, voluntarily, by operation of law, or otherwise (other than debts assigned pursuant to section 402(a)(26) of the Social Security

Act, or any such debt which has been assigned to the Federal Government or to a State or any political subdivision of such State); or

(B) such debt includes a liability designated as alimony, maintenance, or support, unless such liability is actually in the nature of alimony, maintenance, or support;

(6) for willful and malicious injury by the debtor to another entity or to the property of another entity;

(7) to the extent such debt is for a fine, penalty, or forfeiture payable to and for the benefit of a governmental unit, and is not compensation for actual pecuniary loss, other than a tax penalty—

(A) relating to a tax of a kind not specified in paragraph (1) of this subsection; or

(B) imposed with respect to a transaction or event that occurred before three years before the date of the filing of the petition;

(8) for an educational benefit overpayment or loan made, insured or guaranteed by a governmental unit, or made under any program funded in whole or in part by a governmental unit or nonprofit institution, or for an obligation to repay funds received as an educational benefit, scholarship or stipend, unless—

(A) such loan, benefit, scholarship, or stipend overpayment first became due more than 7 years (exclusive of any applicable suspension of the repayment period) before the date of the filing of the petition; or

(B) excepting such debt from discharge under this paragraph will impose an undue hardship on the debtor and the debtor's dependents;

(9) for death or personal injury caused by the debtor's operation of a motor vehicle if such operation was unlawful because the debtor was intoxicated from using alcohol, a drug, or another substance;

(10) that was or could have been listed or scheduled by the debtor in a prior case concerning the debtor under this title or under the Bankruptcy Act in which the debtor waived

discharge, or was denied a discharge under section 727(a)(2), (3), (4), (5), (6), or (7) of this title, or under section 14c (1), (2), (3), (4), (6), or (7) of such Act; or

(11) provided in any final judgment, unreviewable order, or consent order or decree entered in any court of the United States or of any State, issued by a Federal depository institutions regulatory agency, or contained in any settlement agreement entered into by the debtor, arising from any act of fraud or defalcation while acting in a fiduciary capacity committed with respect to any depository institution or insured credit union; or

(12) for malicious or reckless failure to fulfill any commitment by the debtor to a Federal depository institutions regulatory agency to maintain the capital of an insured depository institution, except that this paragraph shall not extend any such commitment which would otherwise be terminated due to any act of such agency.

(b) Notwithstanding subsection (a) of this section, a debt that was excepted from discharge under subsection (a)(1), (a)(3), or (a)(8) of this section, under section 17a(1), 17a(3), or 17a(5) of the Bankruptcy Act, under section 439A of the Higher Education Act of 1965 (20 U.S.C. 1087-3), or under section 733(g) of the Public Health Service Act (42 U.S.C. 294f) in a prior case concerning the debtor under this title, or under the Bankruptcy Act, is dischargeable in a case under this title unless, by the terms of subsection (a) of this section, such debt is not dischargeable in the case under this title.

(c)(1) Except as provided in subsection (a)(3)(B) of this section, the debtor shall be discharged from a debt of a kind specified in paragraph (2), (4), or (6) of subsection (a) of this section, unless, on request of the creditor to whom such debt is owed, and after notice and a hearing, the court determines such debt to be excepted from discharge under paragraph (2), (4), or (6), as the case may be, of subsection (a) of this section.

(2) Paragraph (1) shall not apply in the case of a Federal depository institutions regulatory agency seeking, in its capacity as conservator, receiver, or liquidating agent for an insured depository institution, to recover a debt described in subsection (a)(2), (a)(4), (a)(6), or (a)(11) owed to such

institution by an institution-affiliated party unless the receiver, conservator, or liquidating agent was appointed in time to reasonably comply, or for a Federal depository institutions regulatory agency acting in its corporate capacity as a successor to such receiver, conservator, or liquidating agent to reasonably comply, with subsection (a)(3)(B) as a creditor of such institution-affiliated party with respect to such debt.

(d) If a creditor requests a determination of dischargeability of a consumer debt under subsection (a)(2) of this section, and such debt is discharged, the court shall grant judgment in favor of the debtor for the costs of, and a reasonable attorney's fee for, the proceeding if the court finds that the position of the creditor was not substantially justified, except that the court shall not award such costs and fees if special circumstances would make the award unjust.

(e) Any institution-affiliated party of a depository institution or insured credit union shall be considered to be acting in a fiduciary capacity with respect to the purposes of subsection (a)(4) or (11).

Bankruptcy Rule References: 2002, 4004 and 4007

Legislative History

This section specifies which of the debtor's debts are not discharged in a bankruptcy case, and certain procedures for effectuating the section. The provision in Bankruptcy Act section 17c granting the bankruptcy courts jurisdiction to determine dischargeability is deleted as unnecessary, in view of the comprehensive grant of jurisdiction prescribed in proposed 28 U.S.C. § 1471(b), which is adequate to cover the full jurisdiction that the bankruptcy courts have today over dischargeability and related issues under Bankruptcy Act section 17c. The Rules of Bankruptcy Procedure will specify, as they do today, who may request determinations of dischargeability, subject, of course, to proposed 11 U.S.C. § 523(c), and when such a request may be made. Proposed 11 U.S.C. § 350, providing for reopening of cases, provides one possible procedure for a determination of dischargeability and related issues after a case is closed.

Subsection (a) lists eight [ten as amended by Pub. L. No. 98–353] debts excepted from discharge. Taxes that are entitled to priority are excepted from discharge under paragraph (1). In addition, taxes with respect to which the debtor made a fraudulent return or willfully attempted to evade or defeat, or with respect to which a return (if required) was not filed or was not filed after the due date and after one year before the bankruptcy case are excepted from discharge. If the taxing authority's claim has been disallowed, then it would be barred by the more modern rules of collateral estoppel from reasserting that claim against the debtor after the case was closed. *See* Plumb, *The Tax Recommendations of the Commission on the Bankruptcy Laws: Tax Procedures*, 88 Harv. L. Rev. 1360, 1388 (1975).

As under Bankruptcy Act section 17a(2), a debt for obtaining money, property, services, or an extension or renewal of credit by false pretenses, a false representation, or actual fraud or by use of a statement in writing respecting the debtor's financial condition that is materially false, on which the creditor reasonably relied, and that the debtor made or published with intent to deceive, is excepted from discharge. This provision is modified only slightly from current section 17a(2). First, "actual fraud" is added as a grounds for exception from discharge. Second, the creditor must not only have relied on a false statement in writing, the reliance must have been reasonable. This codifies case law construing this provision. Third, the phrase "in any manner whatsoever" that appears in current law after "made or published" is deleted as unnecessary. The word "published" is used in the same sense that it is used in slander actions.

Unscheduled debts are excepted from discharge under paragraph (3). The provision, derived from section 17a(3), follows current law, but clarifies some uncertainties generated by the case law construing 17a(3). The debt is excepted from discharge if it was not scheduled in time to permit timely action by the creditor to protect his right, unless the creditor had notice or actual knowledge of the case.

Paragraph (4) excepts debts for embezzlement or larceny. The deletion of willful and malicious conversion from section 17a(2) of the Bankruptcy Act is not intended to effect a substantive change. The intent is to include in the category of nondischargeable debts a conversion under which the debtor willfully and maliciously intends to borrow property for a short period of time with no intent to inflict injury but on which injury is in fact inflicted.

Paragraph (5) excepts from discharge debts to a spouse, former spouse, or child of the debtor for alimony to, maintenance for, or support of, the spouse or child. This language, in combination with the repeal of section 456(b) of the Social Security Act (43 U.S.C. § 656(b)) by section 327 of the bill, will apply to make nondischargeable only alimony, maintenance, or support owed directly to a spouse or dependent. *See Hearings*, pt. 2, at 942. What constitutes alimony, maintenance, or support, will be determined under the bankruptcy laws, not State law. Thus, cases such as *In re* Waller, 494 F.2d 447 (6th Cir. 1974); *Hearings*, pt. 3, at 1308–10, are overruled, and the result in cases such as Fife v. Fife, 1 Utah 2d 281, 265 P.2d 642 (1952) is followed. This provision will, however, make nondischargeable any debts resulting from an agreement by the debtor to hold the debtor's spouse harmless on joint debts, to the extent that the agreement is in payment of alimony, maintenance, or support of the spouse, as determined under bankruptcy law considerations that are similar to considerations of whether a particular agreement to pay money to a spouse is actually alimony or a property settlement. *See Hearings,* pt. 3, at 1287-1290.

[*House Report No. 95–595, 95th Cong., 1st Sess. 363 (1977).*]

A provision of the Social Security Act, previously in effect, would be reinstated, declaring that a child support obligation assigned to a State as a condition of AFDC eligibility is not discharged in bankruptcy. The provision would be effective upon enactment.

[*House Report No. 97–208, 97th Cong., 1st Sess. 986 (1981).*]

Present law.—A child support obligation assigned to a State as a condition of AFDC eligibility may be released by a discharge in bankruptcy under the Bankruptcy Act.

Committee amendment.—The committee amendment would reverse the effect of an amendment made by section 328 of P.L. 95–598 and reinstate a provision of the Social Security Act, previously in effect, declaring that a child support obligation assigned to a State as a condition of AFDC eligibility is not discharged in bankruptcy. The committee believes that a parent's obligation to support his child is not one that should be allowed to be discharged by filing for bankruptcy, and that a child support obligation assigned to a State as a condition of AFDC eligibility should not be subject to termination in that way.

[*Senate Report No. 97–139, 97th Cong., 1st Sess. 523 (1981).*]

Paragraph (6) excepts debts for willful and malicious injury by the debtor to another person or to the property of another person. Under this paragraph, "willful" means deliberate or intentional. To the extent that Tinker v. Colwell, 139 U.S. 473 (1902), held that a looser standard is intended, and to the extent that other cases have relied on *Tinker* to apply a "reckless disregard" standard, they are overruled.

Paragraph (7) excepts from discharge a debt for a fine, penalty, or forfeiture payable to and for the benefit of a governmental unit, that is not compensation for actual pecuniary loss.

Paragraph (8) excepts from discharge debts that the debtor owed before a previous bankruptcy case concerning the debtor in which the debtor was denied a discharge other than on the basis of the six-year bar.

[*House Report No. 95–595, 95th Cong., 1st Sess. 363 (1977).*]

This section specifies which of the debtor's debts are not discharged in a bankruptcy case, and certain procedures for effectuating the section. The provision in Bankruptcy Act section 17c granting the bankruptcy courts jurisdiction to determine dischargeability is deleted as unnecessary, in view of the comprehensive grant of jurisdiction prescribed in proposed 28 U.S.C. § 1334(b), which is adequate to cover the full jurisdiction that the bankruptcy courts have today over dischargeability and related issues under Bankruptcy Act section 17c. The Rules of Bankruptcy Procedure will specify, as they do today, who may request determinations of dischargeability, subject, of course, to proposed 11

U.S.C. § 523(c), and when such a request may be made. Proposed 11 U.S.C. § 350, providing for reopening of cases, provides one possible procedure for a determination of dischargeability and related issues after a case is closed.

Subsection (a) lists nine kinds of debts excepted from discharge. Taxes that are excepted from discharge are set forth in paragraph (1). These include claims against the debtor which receive priority in the second, third and sixth categories (sec. 507(a)(3)(B) and (C) and (6)). These categories include taxes for which the tax authority failed to file a claim against the estate or filed its claim late. Whether or not the taxing authority's claim is secured will also not affect the claim's nondischargeability if the tax liability in question is otherwise entitled to priority.

Also included in the nondischargeable debts are taxes for which the debtor had not filed a required return as of the petition date, or for which a return had been filed beyond its last permitted due date (sec. 523(a)(1)(B)). For this purpose, the date of the tax year to which the return relates is immaterial. The late return rule applies, however, only to the late returns filed within three years before the petition was filed, and to late returns filed after the petition in title 11 was filed. For this purpose, the taxable year in question need not be one or more of the three years immediately preceding the filing of the petition.

Tax claims with respect to which the debtor filed a fraudulent return, entry or invoice, or fraudulently attempted to evade or defeat any tax (sec. 523(a)(1)(C)) are included. The date of the taxable year with regard to which the fraud occurred is immaterial.

Also included are tax payments due under an agreement for deferred payment of taxes, which a debtor had entered into with the Internal Revenue Service (or State or local tax authority) before the filing of the petition and which relate to a prepetition tax liability sec. 523(a)(1)(D) are also nondischargeable. This classification applies only to tax claims which would have received priority under section 507(a) if the taxpayer had filed a title 11 petition on the date on which the deferred payment agreement was entered into. This rule also applies only to installment payments which become due during and after the commencement of the title 11 case. Payments which had become due within one year before the filing of the petition receive sixth priority, and will be nondischargeable under the general rule of section 523(a)(1)(A).

The above categories of nondischargeability apply to customs duties as well as to taxes.

Paragraph (2) provides that as under Bankruptcy Act section 17a(2), a debt for obtaining money, property, services, or a refinancing extension or renewal of credit by false pretenses, a false representation, or actual fraud, or by use of a statement in writing respecting the debtor's financial condition that is materially false, on which the creditor reasonably relied, and which the debtor made or published with intent to deceive, is excepted from discharge. This provision is modified only slightly from current section 17a(2). First, "actual fraud" is added as a ground for exception from discharge. Second, the creditor must not only have relied on a false statement in writing, but the reliance must have been reasonable. This codifies case law construing present section 17a(2). Third, the phrase "in any manner whatsoever" that appears in current law after "made or published" is deleted as unnecessary, the word "published" is used in the same sense that it is used in defamation cases.

Unscheduled debts are excepted from discharge under paragraph (3). The provision, derived from section 17a(3), follows current law, but clarifies some uncertainties generated by the case law construing 17a(3). The debt is excepted from discharge if it was not scheduled in time to permit timely action by the creditor to protect his rights, unless the creditor had notice or actual knowledge of the case.

Paragraph (4) excepts debts for fraud incurred by the debtor while acting in a fiduciary capacity or for defalcation, embezzlement, or misappropriation.

Paragraph (5) provides that debts for willful and malicious conversion or injury by the debtor to another entity or the property of another entity are nondischargeable. Under this paragraph "willful" means deliberate or intentional. To the extent that Tinker v. Colwell, 139 U.S. 473 (1902), held that a less strict standard is intended, and to the extent that other cases relied on *Tinker* to apply a "reckless disregard" standard, they are overruled.

Paragraph (6) excepts from discharge debts to a spouse, former spouse, or child of the debtor for alimony to, maintenance for, or support of the spouse or child. This language, in combination with the repeal of section 456(b) of the Social Security Act (42 U.S.C. § 656 (b)) by section 326 of the bill, will apply to make nondischargeable only alimony, maintenance, or support owed directly to a spouse or dependent. What constitutes alimony, maintenance, or support, will be determined under the bankruptcy law, not State law. Thus, cases such as *In re* Waller, 494 F.2d 447 (6th Cir. 1974), are overruled, and the result in cases such as Fife v. Fife, 1 Utah 2d 281, 265 P.2d 642 (1952) is followed. The proviso, however, makes nondischargeable any debts resulting from an agreement by the debtor to hold the debtor's spouse harmless on joint debts, to the extent that the agreement is in payment of alimony, maintenance, or support of the spouse, as determined under bankruptcy law considerations as to whether a particular agreement to pay money to a spouse is actually alimony or a property settlement.

Paragraph (7) makes nondischargeable certain liabilities for penalties including tax penalties if the underlying tax with respect to which the penalty was imposed is also nondischargeable (sec. 523(a)(7)). These latter liabilities cover those which, but are penal in nature, as distinct from so-called "pecuniary loss" penalties which, in the case of taxes, involve basically the collection of a tax under the label of a "penalty." This provision differs from the bill as introduced, which did not link the nondischarge of a tax penalty with the treatment of the underlying tax. The amended provision reflects the existing position of the Internal Revenue Service as to tax penalties imposed by the Internal Revenue Code (Rev. Rul. 68-574, 1968-2 C.B. 595).

Paragraph (8) follows generally current law and excepts from discharge student loans until such loans have been due and owing for five years. Such loans include direct student loans as well as insured and guaranteed loans. This provision is intended to be self-executing and the lender or institution is not required to file a complaint to determine the nondischargeability of any student loan.

Paragraph (9) [*Ed. Note:* Section 523(a)(9) should have been redesignated as section 523(a)(10) by Pub. L. No. 98–353, which added a new paragraph (9). The section was subsequently redesignated's by the 1986 Amendments.] excepts from discharge debts that the debtor owed before a previous bankruptcy case concerning the debtor in which the debtor was denied a discharge other than on the basis of the six-year bar.

[*Senate Report No. 95–989, 95th Cong., 2d Sess. 77–79 (1978).*]

Section 523(a)(1) represents a compromise between the position taken in the House bill and the Senate amendment. Section 523(a)(2) likewise represents a compromise between the position taken in the House bill and the Senate amendment with respect to the false financial statement exception to discharge. In order to clarify that a "renewal of credit" includes a "refinancing of credit", explicit reference to a refinancing of credit is made in the preamble to section 523(a)(2). A renewal of credit or refinancing of credit that was obtained by a false financial statement within the terms of section 523(a)(2) is nondischargeable. However, each of the provisions of section 523(a)(2) must be proved. Thus, under section 523(a)(2)(A) a creditor must prove that the debt was obtained by false pretenses, a false representation, or actual fraud, other than a statement respecting the debtor's or an insider's financial condition. Subparagraph (A) is intended to codify current case law *e.g.,* Neal v. Clark, 95 U.S. 704 (1887), which interprets "fraud" to mean actual or positive fraud rather than fraud implied in law. Subparagraph (A) is mutually exclusive from subparagraph (B). Subparagraph (B) pertains to the so-called false financial statement. In order for the debt to be nondischargeable, the creditor must prove that the debt was obtained by the use of a statement in writing (i) that is materially false; (ii) respecting the debtor's or an insider's financial condition; (iii) on which the creditor to whom the debtor is liable for obtaining money, property, services, or credit reasonably relied; (iv) that the debtor caused to be made or published with intent to deceive. Section 523(a)(2)(B)(iv) is not intended to change from present law since my statement that the debtor causes to be made or published with the intent to deceive automatically includes a statement that the debtor actually makes or publishes with an intent to deceive. [sic] Section 523(a)(2)(B) is explained in the House report. Under section 523(a)(2)(B)(i) a discharge is barred only as to that portion of a loan with respect to which a false financial statement is materially false.

In many cases, a creditor is required by state law to refinance existing credit on which there has been no default. If the creditor does not forfeit remedies or otherwise rely to his detriment on a false financial statement with respect to existing credit, then an extension, renewal, or refinancing of such credit is nondischargeable only to the extent of the new money advanced; on the other hand, if an existing loan is in default or the creditor otherwise reasonably relies to his detriment on a false financial statement with regard to an existing loan, then the entire debt is nondischargeable under section 523(a)(2)(B). This codifies the reasoning expressed by the second circuit in *In re* Danns, 558 F.2d 114 (2d Cir. 1977).

Section 523(a)(3) of the House amendment is derived from the Senate amendment. The provision is intended to overrule Birkett v. Columbia Bank, 195 U.S. 345 (1904).

Section 523(a)(4) of the House amendment represents a compromise between the House bill and the Senate amendment.

Section 523(a)(5) is a compromise between the House bill and the Senate amendment. The provision excepts from discharge a debt owed to a spouse, former spouse or child of the debtor, in connection with a separation agreement, divorce decree, or property settlement agreement, for alimony to, maintenance for, or support of such spouse or child but not to the extent that the debt is assigned to another entity. If the debtor has assumed an obligation of the debtor's spouse to a third party in connection with a separation agreement, property settlement agreement, or divorce proceeding, such debt is dischargeable to the extent that payment of the debt by the debtor is not actually in the nature of alimony, maintenance, or support of debtor's spouse, former spouse, or child.

Section 523(a)(6) adopts the position taken in the House bill and rejects the alternative suggested in the Senate amendment. The phrase "willful and malicious injury" covers a willful and malicious conversion.

Section 523(a)(7) of the House amendment adopts the position taken in the Senate amendment and rejects the position taken in the House bill. A penalty relating to a tax cannot be nondischargeable unless the tax itself is nondischargeable.

Section 523(a)(8) represents a compromise between the House bill and the Senate amendment regarding educational loans. This provision is broader than current law which is limited to federally insured loans. Only educational loans owing to a governmental unit or a nonprofit institution of higher education are made nondischargeable under this paragraph.

[*124 Cong. Rec. H 11,095–6 (Sept. 28, 1978); S 17,412–13 (Oct. 6, 1978).*]

Section 523. Nondischargeable debts: The House amendment retains the basic categories of nondischargeable tax liabilities contained in both bills, but restricts the time limits on certain nondischargeable taxes. Under the amendment, nondischargeable taxes cover taxes entitled to priority under section 507(a)(6) of title 11 and, in the case of individual debtors under chapters 7, 11, or 13, tax liabilities with respect to which no required return had been filed or as to which a late return had been filed if the return became last due, including extensions, within 2 years before the date of the petition or became due after the petition, or as to which the debtor made a fraudulent return, entry or invoice or fraudulently attempted to evade or defeat the tax.

In the case of individuals in liquidation under chapter 7 or in reorganization under chapter 11 if title 11, [*sic*] section 1141(d)(2) incorporates by reference the exceptions to discharge continued in section 523. Different rules concerning the discharge of taxes where a partnership or corporation reorganizes under chapter 11, apply under section 1141.

The House amendment also deletes the reduction rule contained in section 523(e) of the Senate amendment. Under that rule, the amount of an otherwise nondischargeable tax liability would be reduced by the amount which a governmental tax authority could have collected from the debtor's estate if it had filed a timely claim against the estate but which it did not collect because no such claim was filed. This provision is deleted in order not to effectively compel a tax authority to file claim against the estate in "no asset" cases, along with a dischargeability petition. In no-asset cases, therefore, if the tax authority is not potentially penalized by failing to file a claim, the debtor in such cases will have a better opportunity to choose the prepayment forum, bankruptcy court or the Tax Court, in which to litigate his personal liability for a nondischargeable tax.

The House amendment also adopts the Senate amendment provision limiting the nondischargeability of punitive tax penalities, that is, penalties other than those which represent collection of a principal amount of tax liability through the form of a "penalty." Under the House amendment, tax penalties which are basically punitive in nature are to be nondischargeable only if the penalty is computed by reference to a related tax liability which is nondischargeable or, if the amount of the penalty is not computed by reference to a tax liability, the transaction or event giving rise to the penalty occurred during the three-year period ending on the date of the petition.

[*124 Cong. Rec. H 11,113–14 (Sept. 28, 1978); S 17,430–1 (Oct. 6, 1978).*]

[Section 523(a)(8) was amended in 1979 to clarify that] any educational loan made, insured or guaranteed by a governmental unit, or made or funded in whole or in part by a governmental unit or a non-profit institution of higher education is nondischargeable in bankruptcy for a period of five years (exclusive of any applicable suspension of the repayment period) unless it would cause an undue hardship on the debtor or dependants of the debtor.

[*Senate Report No. 96–230, 96th Cong., 1st Sess. 3 (1979).*]

Subsection (b) of this section permits discharge in a bankruptcy case of an unscheduled debt from a prior case. This provision is carried over from Bankruptcy Act, section 17b. The result dictated by the subsection would probably not be different if the subsection were not included. It is included nevertheless for clarity.

[*House Report No. 95–595, 95th Cong., 1st Sess. 365 (1977); Senate Report No. 95–989, 95th Cong., 2d Sess. 79–80 (1978).*]

Section 523(b) is new. The section represents a modification of similar provisions contained in the House bill and the Senate amendment.

[*124 Cong. Rec. H 11,096 (Sept. 28, 1978); S 17,413 (Oct. 6, 1978).*]

Subsection (c) requires a creditor who is owed a debt that may be expected [*sic*] from discharge under paragraph (2), (4), or (6) (false statements, embezzlement or larceny, or willful and malicious injury) to initiate proceedings in the bankruptcy court for an exception to discharge. If the creditor does not act, the debt is discharged. This provision does not change current law.

[*House Report No. 95–595, 95th Cong., 1st Sess. 365 (1977); Senate Report No. 95–989, 95th Cong., 2d Sess. 80 (1978).*]

Section 523(c) of the House amendment adopts the position taken in the Senate amendment.

[*124 Cong. Rec. H 11,096 (Sept. 28, 1978); S 17,413 (Oct. 6, 1978).*]

Subsection (d) is new. It provides protection to a consumer debtor that dealt honestly with a creditor who sought to have a debt excepted from discharge on grounds of falsity in the incurring of the debt. The debtor is entitled to costs of and a reasonable attorney's fee for the proceeding to determine the dischargeability of a debt under subsection (a)(2), if the creditor initiated the proceeding and the debt was determined to be dischargeable. The court is permitted to award any actual pecuniary loss that the debtor may have suffered as a result of the proceeding (such as loss of a day's pay). The purpose of the provision is to discourage creditors from initiating false financial statement exception to discharge actions in the hopes of obtaining a settlement from an honest debtor anxious to save attorney's fees. Such practices impair the debtor's fresh start.

[*House Report No. 95–595, 95th Cong., 1st Sess. 365 (1977).*]

Subsection (d) is new. It provides protection to a consumer debtor that dealt honestly with a creditor who sought to have a debt excepted from discharge on the ground of falsity in the incurring of the debt. The debtor may be awarded costs and a reasonable attorney's fee for the proceeding to determine the dischargeability of a debt under subsection (a)(2), if the court finds that the proceeding was frivolous or not brought by its creditor in good faith.

The purpose of the provision is to discourage creditors from initiating proceedings to obtaining a false financial statement exception to discharge in the hope of obtaining a settlement from an honest debtor anxious to save attorney's fees. Such practices impair the debtor's fresh start and are contrary to the spirit of the bankruptcy laws.

[*Senate Report No. 95–989, 95th Cong., 2d Sess. 80 (1978).*]

Section 523(d) represents a compromise between the position taken in the House bill and the Senate amendment on the issue of attorneys' fees in false financial statement complaints to determine dischargeability. The provision contained in the House bill permitting the court to award damages is eliminated. The court must grant the debtor judgment or a reasonable attorneys' fee unless the granting of judgment would be clearly inequitable.

[*124 Cong. Rec. H 11,096 (Sept. 28, 1978); S 17,413 (Oct. 6, 1978).*]

Comment

Section 523 of the Code, enumerating exceptions to discharge, is derived from section 17a of the former Bankruptcy Act.

Section 523 of the Code lists ten kinds of debts excepted from discharge. These are, for the most part, similar to the exceptions listed in section 17a of the Act. Section 17a listed "provable" debts that were excepted from discharge. Under the Code, however, the concept of provability is eliminated.

Because it was thought that section 523(a)(8) as originally enacted had an uneven effect upon student loan programs administered by the Department of Health, Education and Welfare in that only loans owing to governmental units or non-profit institutions of higher education were affected, this section was amended in 1979 to read as it appears above.

Section 523(b) permits discharge of an unscheduled debt from a prior case.

On August 13, 1981, section 523(a)(5)(A) was amended (P.L. 97–35) by adding the words "(other than debts assigned pursuant to section 402(a)(26) of the Social Security Act)." The effect of the amendment is that a debt which is a child support obligation that is assigned to a State under section 402(a)(26) of the Social Security Act is not discharged in bankruptcy.

Bankruptcy Rule 4007 relates to dischargeability of particular debts. Subdivision (a) provides that a debtor or any creditor may file a complaint for determination of dischargeability of any debt. Pursuant to subdivision (e) of this rule, and Rule 7001, the proceeding is an adversary proceeding governed by the Part VII Rules.

Pursuant to 28 U.S.C. § 157(b)(2)(I), determinations as to dischargeability of particular debts are "core proceedings" over which the bankruptcy judge has jurisdiction to enter dispositive orders and judgments.

Subdivision (b) of Rule 4007 provides that the complaint (other than one relating to the kinds of debts specified in section 523(c)) may be filed at any time. A case may be reopened without additional filing fee for the purpose of filing a complaint to obtain a determination under this rule.

Subdivision (c), amended in 1991, requires that a complaint to determine dischargeability of a debt pursuant to section 523(c) must be filed not later than 60 days after the first date set for the meeting of creditors held under Rule 2003(a). (This refers to debts based upon false representations, etc., defalcation by a fiduciary, and willful and malicious injury.) The court is to give creditors at least 30 days notice of the time so fixed in the manner provided in Rule 2002. On motion of a party in interest after hearing on notice, the court may, for cause, and before the time has expired, extend the time to file complaints under this subdivision. The 1991 Advisory Committee Note to subdivision (c) states that the subdivision is amended to apply in chapter 12 cases the same time period that applies in chapter 7 and 11 cases for filing a complaint under section 523(c) of the Code to determine dischargeability of certain debts. Under section 1228(a) of the Code, a chapter 12 discharge does not discharge the debts specified in section 523(a) of the Code.

Subdivision (d) relates to a motion by a debtor for a discharge under section 1328(b) in a chapter 13 case. In such event the court is required to enter an order fixing the time for filing a complaint to determine dischargeability of any debt under section 523(c) and shall give not less than 30 days notice of the time so fixed to all creditors as provided in Rule 2002. On motion of a party in interest made before the time to file has expired, the court may, for cause, after notice and hearing, extend the time so fixed under this subdivision.

Pursuant to Rule 5005, the complaint should be filed with the clerk in the district where the case is pending.

See Official Form 18, "Discharge of Debtor," which takes into account the provisions of section 523 of the Code.

1984 Amendments: Section 523(a)(3) was amended by adding subparagraph (C). For the purpose of the subparagraph (c), two definitions are included: (1) "Luxury goods or services"; and (2) "an extension of consumer credit under an open end credit plan." The subparagraph provides that consumer debts owed to a single creditor aggregating more than $500 for luxury goods or services by an individual debtor on or within 45 days before the order for relief, is presumed to be nondischargeable. Similarly, when an individual debtor obtains cash advances aggregating more than $1000 that are extensions of consumer credit under an open end credit plan on or within 20 days before the order for relief, the debt is presumed to be nondischargeable. A rebuttable presumption of nondischargeability results from such conduct.

Subsection (a)(5)(A) was amended to include as nondischargeable, a child support debt assigned to the Federal Government or to a state or political subdivision thereof, or one resulting from paternity litigation.

A new subsection (a)(9) specifically makes a debt arising from a judgment or consent decree incurred as the result of the debtor's operation of a motor vehicle while legally intoxicated nondischargeable.

Subsection (d) was amended by restricting costs and fees to be awarded in an unsuccessful consumer debtor dischargeability proceeding.

1986 Amendments: Former subsection (a)(9), erroneously not redesignated by the 1984 Amendments, was correctly redesignated by these amendments as subsection (a)(10).

Section 523(a) was amended to bring chapter 12 cases within the scope of the section. Subsection (a)(5) was amended to bring within the exclusion from discharge spousal support determined in accordance with State or territorial law by a governmental unit.

1990 Amendments: Pub. L. No. 101-647 (Crime Control Act of 1990) as signed into law on November 29, 1990. It amended section 523(a)(8) by striking the words "for an educational" through "unless" and inserting new language to include government made, insured or guaranteed educational benefit overpayments and obligations to repay scholarships and stipends, in addition to educational loans, as debts excepted from discharge. It also amended subparagraph (a)(8)(A) to replace "such loan first became due before five years" with "such loan, benefit, scholarship, or stipend overpayment first became due more than 7 years". The amendments to section 523(a)(8) became effective 180 days from the date of enactment of Pub. L. No. 101-647. The 1990 legislation also amended subsection (a) by striking the word "or" at the end of paragraph (9), striking the period at the end of paragraph (10) and inserting a semicolon, to accommodate the addition of new paragraphs (11) and (12). It also added subsection (e), as well as redesignating subsection (c) as subsection (c)(1) and adding a new paragraph (2) to subsection (c). The new exceptions to discharge in paragraphs (11) and (12), as well as the addition of new subsections (c)(2) and (e), pertain to certain transactions of the debtor with Federal depository institutions. All amendments other than those to paragraph (8) became effective on the date of enactment.

Pub. L. No. 101-647 further amended subsection (a)(9) with the Criminal Victims Protection Act of 1990, which was also enacted as a separate piece of legislation, Pub. L. No. 101-581 (Criminal Victims Protection Act of 1990) and signed into law on November 15, 1990. The amendment deletes the requirement for the debt to arise from a judgment or consent decree, and clarifies the type of debt excepted from discharge in this subsection to mean a debt "for death or personal injury" caused by the debtor's unlawful operation of a motor vehicle while intoxicated. The law takes effect as of the date of enactment. The identical language currently exists in both Pub. L. No. 101-647 and Pub. L. No. 101-581 because the text in Pub. L. No. 101-647 was not excised when it was duplicated in the separate legislation enacted as Pub. L. No. 101-581. The portion of Pub. L. No. 101-647 (Crime Control Act of 1990) which amends subsection (a)(9), and Pub. L. No. 101-581 (Criminal Victims Protection Act of 1990) do not apply to bankruptcy cases commenced before their respective enactment dates.

Case Annotations

The standard of proof for the dischargeability exceptions in section 523(a) is the ordinary preponderance of the evidence standard. Grogan v. Garner, 498 U.S. —, 111 S. Ct. 654, 112 L. Ed.2d 755, 24 C.B.C.2d 1 (1991).

Section 523(a)(7), which codifies the judicially created exception to discharge for fines and penalties that existed under the 1898 Act, preserves from discharge any condition, including an order of restitution, a state criminal court imposes as part of a criminal sentence. This is so, although restitution, unlike a traditional fine, is forwarded to the victim and may be calculated by reference to the amount of harm the offender has caused, because any sentence following a criminal conviction necessarily considers the penal and rehabilitative interests of the State and those interests are sufficient to place restitution orders within the meaning of section 523(a)(7). Kelly v. Robinson, 479 U.S. 36, 107 S. Ct. 353, 93 L. Ed. 2d 216, 15 C.B.C.2d 890 (1986).

The right to performance of a stipulation to clean up a hazardous waste site that obligates the debtor to pay a sum of money to recompense the State for cleanup efforts initiated on the debtor's behalf constitutes a dischargeable claim within the meaning of the Code. Ohio v. Kovacs, 469 U.S. 274, 100 S. Ct. 705, 83 L. Ed. 2d 649, 11 C.B.C.2d 1067 (1985).

The rule that a creditor must establish nondischargeability of its claim by a preponderance of the evidence, rather than by the former, more stringent, clear and convincing evidence standard, applies retroactively to cases decided prior to the imposition of the new standard by the *Grogan* case. For the purposes of holding a debt not to be dischargeable, fraud may be imputed to an innocent partner regardless of the partner's knowledge or involvement. The test to determine whether a debt should be excepted from discharge as one for money obtained by false pretenses, false representation or actual fraud is whether a debtor benefited in some way from the property obtained by the deception. Matter of Luce, 960 F.2d 1277, 26 C.B.C.2d 990 (5th Cir. 1992).

A creditor must show that its losses were proximately caused by a debtor's misrepresentations to maintain a section 523(a)(2)(B) nondischargeability action. *In re* Siriani, 967 F.2d 302, 26 C.B.C.2d 1845 (9th Cir. 1992).

The bankruptcy court must evaluate the intent of the parties to a divorce agreement as of the time the agreement was made and the court may not simply declare periodic payments to be nondischargeable because the parties label the payments as alimony. The doctrine of quasi estoppel bars a debtor from claiming that periodic payments made pursuant to a divorce agreement are dischargeable as property settlement payments when his course of conduct indicates that he treated the payments as alimony, and when his former spouse relied on the alimony characterization and paid taxes on the "income" to her detriment. In the Matter of Davidson, 947 F.2d 1294, 25 C.B.C.2d 1501 (5th Cir. 1991).

Under section 523(a)(7)(B), tax penalties imposed on an event which occurred more than three years before the filing of a bankruptcy petition are dischargeable. For the purposes of section 523(a)(1)(B), substitute returns do not constitute filed returns absent the taxpayer's signature. *In re* Bergstrom, 949 F.2d 341, 25 C.B.C.2d 1291 (10th Cir. 1991).

On the issue of dischargeability, some form of notice and hearing is required by both section 523 and Bankruptcy Rule 4007; absent notice and hearing, a bankruptcy court ruling that sanctions are nondischargeable constitutes an abuse of discretion. Matter of Case, 937 F.2d 1014, 25 C.B.C.2d 368 (5th Cir. 1991).

Unemployment taxes owed on account of wages paid more than ninety days prepetition are entitled to a seventh priority of distribution and are not exempt from discharge pursuant to section 523(a)(1). Congress intended unemployment taxes to be nondischargeable if the taxes were due within three years of the date of the filing of the debtor's bankruptcy petition. Matter of Pierce, 935 F.2d 709, 25 C.B.C.2d 69 (5th Cir. 1991).

Under section 523(a)(2), a judgment creditor's award based upon fraud which consists of both compensatory and punitive damages is nondischargeable as to the compensatory damages but is dischargeable as to the punitive damages portion of the award. *In re* Levy, 951 F.2d 196, 25 C.B.C.2d 1685 (9th Cir. 1991).

A creditor may not raise an exception to discharge under section 523(a)(6) for the first time on appeal, when it pleaded, litigated and relied solely on section 523(a)(2) in bankruptcy court, as to do so subverts the purpose of Rule 4007(c) requiring that complaints for dischargeability under section 523(a)(6) be filed within sixty days of the section 341(a) creditors' meeting. In the Matter of Bercier, 934 F.2d 689, 24 C.B.C.2d 2021 (5th Cir. 1991).

When a debtor has validly contracted to assume liability for the fees of the creditor's attorney, such fees attach to the underlying debt and are nondischargeable if the underlying debt is found to be nondischargeable. Transouth Fin. Corp. of Florida v. Johnson, 931 F.2d 1505, 24 C.B.C.2d 1919 (11th Cir. 1991).

When it is clear that a debtor has misappropriated funds entrusted to him in a fiduciary capacity, the Code will not discharge the fraudulent debt created by such misappropriation. To establish entitlement as a trust recipient, the claimant must show: 1) that the trust relationship and its legal source exist; and 2) that it can identify the trust funds if they are commingled. *In re* Goldberg, 932 F.2d 273, 24 C.B.C.2d 1745 (3d Cir. 1991).

A creditor who fails to receive formal notice of the bar date for filing claims, but who receives actual knowledge of a debtor's bankruptcy filing prior to the bar date, cannot invoke section 523(a)(3) to except its claim from discharge. *In re* Walker, 927 F.2d 1138, 24 C.B.C.2d 1517 (10th Cir. 1991).

Although section 523(a) is to be narrowly and strictly construed to help preserve the Bankruptcy Code's basic policy of giving an honest debtor a "fresh start," this does not mean that a bankruptcy court, when reviewing a creditor's section 523 allegation, is obliged to view evidence in a manner slanted in the debtor's favor. Therefore, when a debtor submits a financial statement that omits liabilities, fails to disclose that substantial assets have already been pledged to other creditors, and fails to note that the debtor has executed two guarantees it is materially false for purposes of section 523(a)(2). In the Matter of Jordan, 927 F.2d 221, 24 C.B.C.2d 1469 (5th Cir. 1991).

An uninsured motor vehicle assessment imposed by a state department of motor vehicles against a chapter 7 debtor is an involuntary pecuniary burden levied upon uninsured motorists for a proper governmental purpose and, as such, qualifies as an excise tax for purposes of section 507(a)(7)(E) with the result that it is nondischargeable under section 523(a)(1)(A). Williams v. Motley, 925 F.2d 741, 24 C.B.C.2d 1188 (4th Cir. 1991).

Punitive damages awarded in a state court judgment against a debtor may be found to be nondischargeable under section 523(a)(6). When a state court judgment contains an implicit finding of malice for purposes of section 523(a)(6) a debtor has actually litigated the "willful and malicious" issues of section 523(a)(6) with the result that collateral estoppel will be applied to the state court judgment. In re Miera, 926 F.2d 741, 24 C.B.C.2d 961 (8th Cir. 1991).

Creditors have no obligation to verify all of a debtor's statements in order for the court to find that they have relied reasonably on the debtor's false representations. In re Ashley, 903 F.2d 599, 23 C.B.C.2d 176 (9th Cir. 1990).

An unmarried father's obligation to pay the expenses of the mother's pregnancy is owed to the child as opposed to the mother and, therefore, is nondischargeable. In the Matter of Seibert, 914 F.2d 102, 23 C.B.C.2d 1157 (7th Cir. 1990).

When a debtor's ex-spouse was awarded a share of the debtor's pension as her "sole and separate" property under the terms of a state court decree dissolving the parties' marriage, the ex-spouse's claim for postpetition arrearages is not discharged by the bankruptcy, as the ex-wife's share is held by the debtor in a constructive trust. Bush v. Taylor, 912 F.2d 989, 23 C.B.C.2d 1294 (8th Cir. 1990).

Whether a debt was intended to be in the nature of alimony, maintenance or support depends on three principal indicators: 1) the language and substance of the agreement in the context of the surrounding circumstances, and, if necessary, extrinsic evidence, which may be of limited use since the parties are not likely to have contemplated the impact of a bankruptcy on the agreement, 2) the parties' financial circumstances at the time of the settlement, and 3) whether the function served by the obligation at the time of the settlement was to maintain daily necessities. In re Gianakas, 917 F.2d 759, 23 C.B.C.2d 1510 (3d Cir. 1990).

A tax penalty "imposed with respect to a transaction or event that occurred before three years before the date of the filing of the petition" is dischargeable. *In re* Roberts, 906 F.2d 1440, 23 C.B.C.2d 374 (10th Cir. 1990).

The use of fraud to obtain an extension of a debt originally procured non-fraudulently will render the debt nondischargeable. *In re* Gerlach, 897 F.2d 1048, 22 C.B.C.2d 1101 (10th Cir. 1990).

A debtor who has omitted a creditor's name from the schedules has the burden of proof to show that the creditor had notice or actual knowledge of the debtor's case under section 523(a)(3)(A). United States v. Bridges, 894 F.2d 108, 22 C.B.C.2d 674 (5th Cir. 1990).

When a creditor has the same burden of proof in a state court malicious prosecution action as in a nondischargeability action under section 523(a)(6), collateral estoppel bars reconsideration by a bankruptcy court of whether a debtor's conduct satisfied section 523(a)(6)'s culpability requirement. *In re* Braen, 900 F.2d 621, 22 C.B.C.2d 831 (3d Cir. 1990).

A determination by a bankruptcy court that a debt is nondischargeable because it arose from a judgment for driving while intoxicated does not require a legal determination by a state court that liability arose from use of a motor vehicle while intoxicated. Whitson v. Middleton, 898 F.2d 950, 22 C.B.C.2d 258 (4th Cir. 1989).

A bankruptcy court's finding, in its determination of dischargeability, that a creditor reasonably relied on a false financial statement is not subject to *de novo* review but is subject to a clearly erroneous standard of review. In the Matter of Bonnett, 895 F.2d 1155, 22 C.B.C.2d 657 (7th Cir. 1989).

When a debtor is an individual, section 523(a)(3)(B) requires a creditor, with actual knowledge of a bankruptcy case but no notice from the court, to determine the bar date for filing a proof of claim to protect his rights, but, for the purposes of section 523, a corporate debtor is not an individual debtor, and no similar burden of inquiry is placed on the creditor. *In re* Spring Valley Farms, Inc., 863 F.2d 832, 21 C.B.C.2d 651 (11th Cir. 1989).

Because both false representation and reasonable reliance must be proven, there is no need to weigh these factors against each other, for an extremely strong showing that a debtor has made false representations will not excuse a creditor's failure to demonstrate reasonable reliance on those representations. First Bank of Colorado Springs v. Mullet (*In re* Mullet), 817 F.2d 677, 16 C.B.C.2d 1202 (10th Cir. 1987).

An obligation classified by a state court as non-modifiable alimony is not dischargeable even though at the time the support was ordered the concept of rehabilitative alimony was not recognized under state law. In addition, a bankruptcy court should not examine the changed circumstances of the parties to determine whether the party awarded alimony has or no longer has the need for it and consequently, whether a debt for alimony should be dischargeable. Forsdick v. Turgeon, 812 F.2d 801, 16 C.B.C.2d 452 (2d Cir. 1987).

A libel debt is not necessarily excepted from discharge when a jury verdict does not reflect a finding of whether the debtor acted maliciously or merely recklessly. Wheeler v. Laudani, 783 F.2d 610, 14 C.B.C.2d 1057 (6th Cir. 1986).

A bankruptcy court is not prevented under the doctrine of *res judicata* from examining the underlying merits of a state court action that resulted in a stipulated dismissal with prejudice of fraud claims. In particular, the court may look to related breach of contract claims for which judgment was entered against the debtor. Frank v. Daley (*In re* Daley), 776 F.2d 834, 13 C.B.C.2d 927 (9th Cir. 1985), *cert. denied,* 476 U.S. 1159, 106 S. Ct. 2279, 90 L. Ed. 2d 721 (1986).

A breach of a security agreement is "willful and malicious" when the conduct of the debtor is (1) headstrong and knowing (willful) and (2) targeted at the creditor (malicious) in the sense that the conduct is certain or almost certain to cause financial harm. While intentional harm may be difficult to establish, the likelihood of harm in an objective sense may be considered in evaluating intent. Barclays American/Business Credit, Inc. v. Long (*In re* Long), 774 F.2d 875, 13 C.B.C.2d 1036 (8th Cir. 1985).

Section 523(a)(6) excepts from discharge willful and malicious acts, such as conversion, done intentionally without cause or excuse even absent proof of a specific intent to injure. Impulsora del Territorio Sur, S.A. v. Cecchini (*In re* Cecchini), 772 F.2d 1493, 13 C.B.C.2d 789 (1985), *reh'g denied,* 780 F.2d 1440, 14 C.B.C.2d 91 (9th Cir. 1986).

When a court determines that one of two debts owed to a single creditor is nondischargeable and that the other is dischargeable, the proceeds of a foreclosure sale of a mortgage created on account of the two debts should be allocated according to their proportionate share in the total mortgage. To allocate the proceeds according to normal commercial practice, that is, "first-in, first-out," would penalize the creditor. To allocate them against the dischargeable debt first would defeat protections intended for honest debtors. Jennen v. Hunter (*In re* Hunter), 771 F.2d 1126, 13 C.B.C.2d 412 (8th Cir. 1985).

Both compensatory and punitive damages are subject to findings of nondischargeability pursuant to section 523(a)(6). Moraes v. Adams (*In re* Adams), 761 F.2d 1422, 12 C.B.C.2d 1220 (9th Cir. 1985).

Although amendments to schedules should be liberally granted, it is the debtor's duty to show he did not intentionally or recklessly avoid listing the debt. Rosinski v. Boyd (*In re* Rosinski), 759 F.2d 539, 12 C.B.C.2d 923 (6th Cir. 1985).

The Bankruptcy Code does not authorize the award of attorneys' fees to a prevailing creditor in a dischargeability action. *In re* Itule, 23 C.B.C.2d 1408 (9th Cir., B.A.P, 1990).

Under Arizona law, a defalcation occurs when a debtor, as corporate officer responsible for disbursing funds, fails to pay persons furnishing labor and materials the money which he holds in trust for them. The debt arising from that act is nondischargeable in the debtor's personal bankruptcy case. *In re* Baird, 22 C.B.C.2d 1598 (9th Cir., B.A.P., 1990).

In determining whether a spouse's right to support payments has been assigned by operation of law and is, therefore, a dischargeable obligation under section 523(5)(A), a court may apply facts in existence at the time the debtor files his bankruptcy petition rather than at the time of the dischargeability hearing since general Congressional policy favors the date of filing as "a guidepost in establishing a party's rights in bankruptcy." *In re* Combs, 21 C.B.C.2d 1359 (9th Cir., B.A.P., 1989).

References

3 *Collier on Bankruptcy* ch. 523 (Matthew Bender 15th ed.).

2 *Collier Bankruptcy Manual* ch. 523 (Matthew Bender 3d ed.).

4 *Collier Bankruptcy Practice Guide* ch. 75 (Matthew Bender).

Collier Family Law and the Bankruptcy Code ch. 6 (Matthew Bender).

Bohm, *Barring Discharge of Debts in Bankruptcy Through Collateral Estoppel*, 48 Tex. B.J. 1204 (1985).

Collins, *Forging Middle Ground: Revision of Student Loan Debts in Bankruptcy as an Impetus to Amend Section 523(a)(8)*, 75 Iowa L. Rev. 733 (1990).

Comment, *The Exception to Discharge for Willful and Malicious Injury: The Proper Standard for Malice*, 7 Bankr. Dev. J. 245 (1990).

Comment, *Section 523(a)(6): Willful and Malicious Exception From Discharge: The "Implied Malice" Standard*, 16 U. Dayton L. Rev. 155 (1990).

Dischargeability of Restitutive Conditions of Probation—Criminals Find Refuge in the Provisions of the Bankruptcy Reform Act of 1978, 31 Vill. L. Rev. 591 (1986).

Ellis, *Protect Your Client's Alimony From Discharge in Bankruptcy*, 36 Prac. Law. 55 (1990).

Fibich and Floyd, *Impact of Bankruptcy on Family Law*, 29 So. Tex. L. Rev. 637 (1988).

Fitzgerald, *Section 6672 of the Internal Revenue Code and a Chapter 11 Reorganization Under the Bankruptcy Code — A Taxpayer's Potential Discharge of an IRS Penalty?*, 46 J. Mo. B. 551 (1990).

Gold, *The Dischargeability of Divorce Obligations Under the Bankruptcy Code: Five Faulty Premises in the Application Section of 523(a)(5)*, 39 Case W. Res. L. Rev. 455 (1988–89).

Good Faith and Chapter 13 Discharge: How Much Discretion Is Too Much?, 11 Cardozo L. Rev. 657 (1990).

Hillman, *Contract Excuse and Bankruptcy Discharge*, 43 Stan. L. Rev. 99 (1990).

Hinderks, *Preserving Tort Claims Against a Debtor in Bankruptcy; Tort-Based Exceptions to Discharge,* 53 J. Kan. B.A. 31 (1984).

Kessler, *Exceptions to Discharge: The Supreme Court Adopts a Preponderance of the Evidence Standard of Proof in Section 523 Proceedings,* 15 Nova L. Rev. 1411 (1991).

McCafferty and Bubis, *Criminal Restitution and the Bankruptcy Discharge: Should We Reopen Debtors' Prisons?,* 10 Crim. Just. J. 27 (1987).

Miles, *Interpreting the Nondischargeability of Drunk Driving Debts Under Section 523(a)(9) of the Bankruptcy Code: A Case of Judicial Legislation,* 49 Md. L. Rev. 156 (1990).

Morris, *When Are Student Loans Dischargeable?,* 1 F & G Bankr. L. Rev. 56 (1989).

Murphy, *The Dischargeability in Bankruptcy of Debts for Alimony and Property Settlements Arising From Divorce,* 14 Pepperdine L. Rev. 69 (1986).

Note, *The Fraud Exception to Discharge in Bankruptcy: A Reappraisal,* 38 Stan. L. Rev. 891 (1986).

Note, *Section 523(a)(2)(B): Exceptions to Discharge for Fraudulently Obtained Loans,* 5 Bankr. Dev. J. 151 (1987).

Ozols, *Discharge of Tax Shelter Liability in Bankruptcy,* 17 Colo. Law. 245 (1988).

Recent Decisions, *Bankruptcy — Criminal Law — Sentencing — Restitution — Discharge — Drunk Driving Victims' Protection Act — After the United States Supreme Court Decided That Criminal Restitution Sentences Were Dischargeable Debts Under Chapter 13 of the Bankruptcy Code, Congress Overruled the Court's Decision and Amended the Code Accordingly. Pennsylvania Department of Public Welfare v. Davenport, 110 S. Ct. 2126,* 29 Duq. L. Rev. 399 (1991).

Sleeper, *Discharge: Sections 727, 524 and 523,* 2 Bank. Dev. J. 115 (1985).

Spickelmier, *Discharge and Dischargeability Under the Bankruptcy Code: A Guide for the General Practitioner,* 50 Tex. B.J. 727 (1987).

Stewart, *Finality in Bankruptcy: Is There Life After Discharge?,* 7 U. Bridgeport L. Rev. 257 (1986).

United States v. Whizco, Inc. (841 F.2d 147): *Are SMCRA Obligations Dischargeable Under the Bankruptcy Code?,* 5 J. Min. & Pol'y 171 (1989/90).

United States v. Whizco, Inc. (841 F.2d 147): *A Further Refinement of the Conflict Between Bankruptcy Discharge and Environmental Cleanup Obligations,* 20 Envtl. L. 207 (1990).

SECTION 524 (11 U.S.C. § 524)

§ 524.   Effect of discharge.

(a) A discharge in a case under this title—

(1) voids any judgment at any time obtained, to the extent that such judgment is a determination of the personal liability of the debtor with respect to any debt discharged under section 727, 944, 1141, 1228, or 1328 of this title, whether or not discharge of such debt is waived;

(2) operates as an injunction against the commencement or continuation of an action, the employment of process, or an act, to collect, recover or offset any such debt as a personal liability of the debtor, whether or not discharge of such debt is waived; and

(3) operates as an injunction against the commencement or continuation of an action, the employment of process, or an act, to collect or recover from, or offset against, property of the debtor of the kind specified in section 541(a)(2) of this title that is acquired after the commencement of the case, on account of any allowable community claim, except a community claim that is excepted from discharge under section 523, 1228(a)(1), or 1328(a)(1) of this title, or that would be so excepted, determined in accordance with the provisions of sections 523(c) and 523(d) of this title, in a case concerning the debtor's spouse commenced on the date of the filing of the petition in the case concerning the debtor, whether or not discharge of the debt based on such community claim is waived.

(b) Subsection (a)(3) of this section does not apply if—

(1)(A) the debtor's spouse is a debtor in a case under this title, or a bankrupt or a debtor in a case under the Bankruptcy Act, commenced within six years of the date of the filing of the petition in the case concerning the debtor; and

(B) the court does not grant the debtor's spouse a discharge in such case concerning the debtor's spouse; or

(2)(A) the court would not grant the debtor's spouse a discharge in a case under chapter 7 of this title concerning such spouse commenced on the date of the filing of the petition in the case concerning the debtor; and

(B) a determination that the court would not so grant such discharge is made by the bankruptcy court within the time and in the manner provided for a determination under section 727 of this title of whether a debtor is granted a discharge.

(c) An agreement between a holder of a claim and the debtor, the consideration for which, in whole or in part, is based on a debt that is dischargeable in a case under this title is enforceable only to any extent enforceable under applicable nonbankruptcy law, whether or not discharge of such debt is waived, only if—

(1) such agreement was made before the granting of the discharge under section 727, 1141, 1228, or 1328 of this title;

(2) such agreement contains a clear and conspicuous statement which advises the debtor that the agreement may be rescinded at any time prior to discharge or within sixty days after such agreement is filed with the court, whichever occurs later, by giving notice of rescission to the holder of such claim;

(3) such agreement has been filed with the court and, if applicable, accompanied by a declaration or an affidavit of the attorney that represented the debtor during the course of negotiating an agreement under this subsection, which states that such agreement—

(A) represents a fully informed and voluntary agreement by the debtor; and

(B) does not impose an undue hardship on the debtor or a dependent of the debtor;

(4) the debtor has not rescinded such agreement at any time prior to discharge or within sixty days after such agreement is filed with the court, whichever occurs later, by giving notice of rescission to the holder of such claim;

(5) the provisions of subsection (d) of this section have been complied with; and

(6)(A) in a case concerning an individual who was not represented by an attorney during the course of negotiating an agreement under this subsection, the court approves such agreement as—

> (i) not imposing an undue hardship on the debtor or a dependent of the debtor; and

> (ii) in the best interest of the debtor.

> (B) Subparagraph (A) shall not apply to the extent that such debt is a consumer debt secured by real property.

(d) In a case concerning an individual, when the court has determined whether to grant or not to grant a discharge under section 727, 1141, 1228, or 1328 of this title, the court may hold a hearing at which the debtor shall appear in person. At any such hearing, the court shall inform the debtor that a discharge has been granted or the reason why a discharge has not been granted. If a discharge has been granted and if the debtor desires to make an agreement of the kind specified in subsection (c) of this section, then the court shall hold a hearing at which the debtor shall appear in person and at any such hearing the court shall—

> (1) inform the debtor—

> (A) that such an agreement is not required under this title, under nonbankruptcy law, or under any agreement not made in accordance with the provisions of subsection (c) of this section; and

> (B) of the legal effect and consequences of—

> > (i) an agreement of the kind specified in subsection (c) of this section; and

> > (ii) a default under such an agreement;

> (2) determine whether the agreement that the debtor desires to make complies with the requirements of subsection (c)(6) of this section, if the consideration for such agreement is based in whole or in part on a consumer debt that is not secured by real property of the debtor.

(e) Except as provided in subsection (a)(3) of this section, discharge of a debt of the debtor does not affect the liability of any other entity on, or the property of any other entity for, such debt.

(f) Nothing contained in subsection (c) or (d) of this section prevents a debtor from voluntarily repaying any debt.

Bankruptcy Rule References: 4004 and 4008

Legislative History

Subsection (a) specifies that a discharge in a bankruptcy case voids any judgment to the extent that it is a determination of the personal liability of the debtor with respect to a prepetition debt, and operates as an injunction against the commencement or continuation of an action, the employment of process, or any act, including telephone calls, letters, and personal contacts to collect recover or offset any discharged debt as a personal liability of the debtor, or from property of the debtor, whether or not the debtor has waived discharge of the debt involved. The injunction is to give complete effect to the discharge and to eliminate any doubt concerning the effect of the discharge as a total prohibition on debt collection efforts. This paragraph has been expanded over a comparable provision in Bankruptcy Act section 14f to cover any act to collect, such as dunning by telephone or letter, or indirectly through friends, relatives, or employees, harassment, threats of repossession and the like. The change is consonant with the new policy forbidding binding reaffirmation agreements under proposed 11 U.S.C. § 524(d), and is intended to insure that once a debt is discharged, the debtor will not be pressured in any way to repay it. In effect, the discharge extinguishes the debt, and creditors may not attempt to avoid that. The language "whether or not discharge of such debt is waived" is intended to prevent waiver of discharge of a particular debt from defeating the purposes of this section. It is directed at waiver of discharge of a particular debt, not waiver of discharge in toto as permitted under section 727(a)(9).

Subsection (a) also codifies the split discharge for debtors in community property states. If community property was in the estate and community claims were discharged, the discharge is effective against community creditors of the nondebtor spouse as well as of the debtor spouse.

[*House Report No. 95–595, 95th Cong., 1st Sess. 365–6 (1977); Senate Report No. 95–989, 95th Cong., 2d Sess. 80 (1978).*]

Section 524(a) of the House amendment represents a compromise between the House bill and the Senate amendment. Section 524(b) of the House amendment is new, and represents standards clarifying the operation of section 524(a)(3) with respect to community property.

[*124 Cong. Rec. H 11,096 (Sept. 28, 1978); S 17,412–13 (Oct. 6, 1978).*]

Subsection (b) gives further effect to the discharge. [*Ed. Note:* As enacted, this is provided for in subsections (c) and (d).] It prohibits reaffirmation agreements after the commencement of the case with respect to any dischargeable debt. The prohibition extends to agreements the consideration for which in whole or in part is based on a dischargeable debt, and it applies whether or not discharge of the debt involved in the agreement has been waived. Thus, the prohibition on reaffirmation agreements extends to debts that are based on discharged debts. Thus, "second generation" debts, which included all or a part of a discharged debt could not be included in any new agreement for new money. This subsection will not have any effect on reaffirmations of debts discharged under the Bankruptcy Act. It will only apply to discharges granted if commenced under the new title 11 bankruptcy code.

[*House Report No. 95–595, 95th Cong., 1st Sess. 366 (1977); Senate Report No. 95–989, 95th Cong., 2d Sess. 80–81 (1978).*]

Subsection (c) grants an exception to the anti-reaffirmation provision. It permits reaffirmation in connection with the settlement of a proceeding to determine the dischargeability of the debt being reaffirmed, or in connection with a redemption agreement permitted under section 722. In either case, the reaffirmation agreement must be entered into in good faith and must be approved by the court.

[*Senate Report No. 95–989, 95th Cong., 2d Sess. 80 (1978).*]

[*Ed. Note:* Subsections (c)(3) and (4) were redesignated as subsections (c)(5) and (6) by Pub. L. No. 98–353.]

Sections 524(c) and (d) represent a compromise between the House bill and Senate amendment on the issue of reaffirmation of a debt discharged in bankruptcy. Every reaffirmation to be enforceable must be approved by the court, and any debtor may rescind a reaffirmation for 30 days from the time the reaffirmation becomes enforceable. If the debtor is an individual the court must advise the debtor of various effects of reaffirmation at a hearing. In addition, to any extent the debt is a consumer debt that is not secured by real property of the debtor reaffirmation is permitted only if the court approves the reaffirmation agreement, before granting a discharge under section 727, 1141, or 1328, as not imposing a hardship on the debtor or a dependent of the debtor and in the best interest of the debtor; alternatively, the court may approve an agreement entered into in good faith that is in settlement of litigation of a complaint to determine dischargeability or that is entered into in connection with redemption under section 722. The hearing on discharge under section 524(d) will be held whether or not the debtor desires to reaffirm any debts.

[*124 Cong. Rec. H 11,096 (Sept. 28, 1978); S 17,413 (Oct. 6, 1978).*]

Subsection (d) provides the discharge of the debtor does not affect co-debtors or guarantors.

[*Senate Report No. 95–989, 95th Cong., 2d Sess. 80–1 (1978). (The reference should be to subsection (e).)*]

Comment

Section 524, which provides that discharge has the effect of voiding certain judgments and operates as an injunction against commencing or continuing actions against the debtor is derived from section 14f(1) and (2) of the former Bankruptcy Act.

Section 524 of the Code expands Section 14f of the Act by enjoining such act as dunning by telephone or letter (either to debtor, relatives, or employees) and acts of harassment or threats.

See Official Form 18, "Discharge of Debtor," which contains injunctive provisions and notice of the consequences of the discharge.

Bankruptcy Rule 4008 provides that the court may hold the discharge hearing provided for in section 524(d) no more than 30 days after entry of an order granting or denying a discharge on not less than 10 days notice to the debtor and the trustee. A debtor's motion for approval of a reaffirmation agreement must be filed at or before the hearing. (The rule contemplates that the 30-day period for holding the section 524(d) hearing is not to be extended.)

Rule 4004(c), as revised by the 1991 Amendments, provides that in a chapter 7 case, on expiration of the time to file a complaint objecting to discharge and the time to file a motion to dismiss the case under Rule 1017(e), the court shall forthwith grant discharge unless (1) the debtor is not an individual; (2) a complaint objecting to discharge has been filed; (3) the debtor has filed a waiver of discharge; or (4) a motion to dismiss the case under Rule 1017 is pending. However, the court may defer entry of the discharge order for 30 days and, on motion within such period, may defer entry of the order to a date certain. Section 524(c) authorizes a debtor to enter into an enforceable reaffirmation agreement only before entry of the discharge order. This provision of Rule 4004(c) permits deferring the entry of the order to allow time for the debtor to negotiate and enter into such agreements.

1984 Amendments: The amendments to section 524 remove some of the restrictions and court involvement with respect to reaffirmation agreements; they are made more easily obtainable from consumers by these provisions.

A reaffirmation agreement made prior to the granting of a discharge does not require court approval under the 1984 Amendments provided that (1) the agreement contains language advising the debtor of his right to rescind, (2) the debtor was represented by an attorney during the negotiation of the agreement, and (3) the agreement has been filed with the court together with a declaration or affidavit of such attorney that the agreement represents a fully informed and voluntary agreement and does not impose an undue hardship on the debtor. The debtor may rescind prior to discharge or within 60 days after the agreement has been filed whichever is later.

1986 Amendments: Section 524 was amended to include chapter 12 cases within the scope of the section.

Subsection (d) was amended to clarify changes made by the 1984 Act. The discharge hearing at which the debtor must be present and informed as to the consequences of entering in reaffirmation agreement is made permissive. However, if the debtor desires to enter into a postdischarge reaffirmation agreement, the discharge hearing is mandatory.

Case Annotations

The postdischarge permanent injunction against the commencement or continuation of an action against a debtor operates only with respect to the personal liability of the debtor. It is not a bar to actions against the debtor with respect to indemnification by a third party such as a debtor's insurer. In the Matter of Shondel, 950 F.2d 1301, 26 C.B.C.2d 193 (7th Cir. 1991).

Section 524 enjoins a creditor from starting or continuing an action which would place personal liability upon a debtor, but permits a creditor to pursue an action against a debtor for the purpose of establishing the debtor's liability when the establishment of that liability is necessary for the recovery by the creditors from another entity. *In re* Walker, 927 F.2d 1138, 24 C.B.C.2d 1517 (10th Cir. 1991).

An injunction issued against an attorney who seeks recovery of attorney's fees from a third party in a state law claim is proper only insofar as it temporarily precludes the pursuit of fees subject to indemnification by the debtor during the pendency of the bankruptcy case; a permanent injunction improperly insulates nondebtors in violation of section 524(e) without any countervailing justification of debtor protection. *In re* Western Real Estate Fund, Inc., 922 F.2d 592, 24 C.B.C.2d 1012 (10th Cir. 1990).

If a debtor chooses to retain possession of secured collateral, he or she may choose to reaffirm the debt and enter into a new agreement with the creditor for repayment. In the Matter of Edwards, 901 F.2d 1383, 23 C.B.C.2d 488 (7th Cir. 1990).

A bankruptcy court's order discharging or altering an underlying debt does not operate to release a guarantor from its obligation. However, section 524 does not preclude the discharge of a guarantee under the principle of *res judicata,* when it has been accepted and confirmed as an integral part of a chapter 11 plan. Republic Supply Co. v. Shoaf, 815 F.2d 1046, 16 C.B.C.2d 1305 (5th Cir. 1987).

Generally, discharge of the debtor in bankruptcy will not discharge the liabilities of codebtors or guarantors. This general law of bankruptcy cannot be overridden by creditor consent, as part of a confirmed plan, to the release of the codebtors or guarantors from liability. Underhill v. Royal, 769 F.2d 1426, 13 C.B.C.2d 1198 (9th Cir. 1985).

The permanent statutory injunction of section 524(a) will not prevent the liquidation of contingent disputed tort personal injury and death claims after a chapter 11 plan of reorganization has been confirmed, as the injunction may be modified or temporarily lifted if necessary under the court's broad powers under sections 1141–1143 of the Code to achieve the consummation of a plan. Citibank v. White Motor Corp. (*In re* White Motor Credit), 761 F.2d 270, 12 C.B.C.2d 961 (6th Cir. 1985).

Absent evidence necessary to meet the strict limits for revocation of discharge, a creditor may not initiate a postdischarge effort to reach exempted property. Munoz v. Dembs (In the Matter of Dembs), 757 F.2d 777, 12 C.B.C.2d 591 (6th Cir. 1985).

When a creditor objects to reaffirmation of a retail installment contract, the bankruptcy court may not authorize a chapter 7 debtor to retain possession of his collateral in the absence of default since the redemption provision of section 722 and reaffirmation under section 524(c) are the exclusive methods by which a chapter 7 debtor may retain possession of secured collateral, and the sole method of redemption available to a chapter 7 debtor under section 722 is a lump-sum redemption. General Motors Acceptance Corp. v. Bell (*In re* Bell), 700 F.2d 1053, 8 C.B.C.2d 199 (6th Cir. 1983).

The permanent injunction of section 524(a) is not violated when a state official attempted to enforce its assessment of civil penalties for violation of a state statute by revoking the debtor's contractor's license, because the penalties were not compensation for actual pecuniary loss. Poule v. Registrar (*In re* Poule), 19 C.B.C.2d 1059 (9th Cir., B.A.P., 1988).

A bankruptcy court may enjoin a secured creditor from pursuing a claim against a discharged chapter 7 debtor for special damages incidental to the creditor's state replevin action to recover its collateral from the debtor because a chapter 7 debtor may remain in possession of property subject to a valid lien without reaffirming the debt under section 524(c) or redeeming the collateral under section 722. *In re* McNeil, 25 C.B.C.2d 98 (B. Ct., E.D. Pa. 1991).

A chapter 7 debtor's liability for postpetition condominium common charges, special assessments and late fees accrued subsequent to discharge is not extinguished under section 727(b) and the condominium association's collection attempts do not violate the discharge injunction of section 524(d) because under New York law a debtor's obligation to pay the common charges, assessments and late fees attaches to and runs with the ownership of the condominium unit and the debtor is liable for all charges accrued during the period of ownership, excluding the time that the unit constituted property of the bankruptcy estate. *In re* Raymond, 25 C.B.C.2d 401 (B. Ct., S.D.N.Y. 1991).

Under section 524(a) a discharged chapter 7 debtor may subsequently file a petition under chapter 13 to cure arrearages on a home mortgage even though he no longer has personal liability because of his prior discharge in a chapter 7 case. *In re* Manderson, 24 C.B.C.2d 1155 (B. Ct., N.D. Ala. 1990).

A request for a modification of the injunction provisions of section 524(a) is wholly inappropriate in that there is no statutory provision permitting a court to modify the language. *In re* Peterson, 24 C.B.C.2d 571 (B. Ct., D.N.M. 1990).

Section 524(d) is not intended to be read as a chronological outline to reaffirm a debt after discharge, but rather sets forth two requirements for a hearing, *i.e.*, a discharge must have been granted and the debtor must have expressed a desire to reaffirm a debt. *In re* Saeger, 24 C.B.C.2d 442 (B. Ct., D. Minn. 1990).

Subsequent to the debtor's discharge, a creditor may not attempt to obtain a joint judgment against a debtor and his nonfiling wife to reach property held as tenants by the entirety in order to collect a debt that was not secured by a lien on the property prior to the debtor's discharge. The proper course of action is to request a stay of the debtor's discharge to permit the creditor to obtain a judgment and to perfect the judgment lien. *In re* Paeplow, 24 C.B.C.2d 366 (B. Ct., N.D. Ind. 1990).

References

3 *Collier on Bankruptcy* ch. 524 (Matthew Bender 15th ed.).

2 *Collier Bankruptcy Manual* ch. 524 (Matthew Bender 3d ed.).

4 *Collier Bankruptcy Practice Guide* ch. 76 (Matthew Bender).

Ellis, *Marital Tax Indemnification Agreements: Exception to Bankruptcy Discharge,* 19 Colo. Law. 639 (1990).

Hillman, *Contract Excuse and Bankruptcy Discharge,* Stan. L. Rev. 99 (Nov. 1990).

McCafferty and Bubis, *Criminal Restitution and the Bankruptcy Discharge: Should We Reopen Debtors' Prisons?,* 10 Crim. Just. J. 27 (1987).

Note, *Does Section 524(a)(2) of the Bankruptcy Code Bar Criminal Prosecution Concerning Discharged Debts?,* 29 Wm. & Mary L. Rev. 579 (1988).

Rynard, *Malpractice Exposure for Attorney Approval of Reaffirmation Agreements: Avoiding the Pitfalls of Amended Section 524(c),* 3 Bankr. Dev. J. 545 (1986).

Tabb, *The Scope of Fresh Start in Bankruptcy: Collateral Conversions and the Dischargeability Debate,* 59 Geo. Wash. L. Rev. 56 (1990).

SECTION 525 (11 U.S.C. § 525)

§ 525. Protection against discriminatory treatment.

(a) Except as provided in the Perishable Agricultural Commodities Act, 1930 (7 U.S.C. §§ 499a-499s), the Packers and Stockyards Act, 1921 (7 U.S.C. §§ 181-229), and section 1 of the Act entitled "An Act making appropriations for the Department of Agriculture for the fiscal year ending June 30, 1944, and for other purposes," approved July 12, 1943 (57 Stat. 422; 7 U.S.C. § 204), a governmental unit may not deny, revoke, suspend, or refuse to renew a license, permit, charter, franchise, or other similar grant to, condition such a grant to, discriminate with respect to such a grant against, deny employment to, terminate the employment of, or discriminate with respect to employment against, a person that is or has been a debtor under this title or a bankrupt or a debtor under the Bankruptcy Act, or another person with whom such bankrupt or debtor has been associated, solely because such bankrupt or debtor is or has been a debtor under this title or a bankrupt or debtor under the Bankruptcy Act, has been insolvent before the commencement of the case under this title, or during the case but before the debtor is granted or denied a discharge, or has not paid a debt that is dischargeable in the case under this title or that was discharged under the Bankruptcy Act.

(b) No private employer may terminate the employment of, or discriminate with respect to employment against, an individual who is or has been a debtor under this title, a debtor or bankrupt under the Bankruptcy Act, or an individual associated with such debtor or bankrupt, solely because such debtor or bankrupt—

(1) is or has been a debtor under this title or a debtor or bankrupt under the Bankruptcy Act;

(2) has been insolvent before the commencement of a case under this title or during the case but before the grant or denial of a discharge; or

(3) has not paid a debt that is dischargeable in a case under this title or that was discharged under the Bankruptcy Act.

Legislative History

This section is additional debtor protection. It codifies the result of Perez v. Campbell, 402 U.S. 637 (1971), which held that a State would frustrate the Congressional policy of a fresh start for a debtor if it were permitted to refuse to renew a drivers license because a tort judgment resulting from an automobile accident had been unpaid as an result of a discharge in bankruptcy.

Notwithstanding any other laws, section 525[a] prohibits a governmental unit from denying, revoking, suspending, or refusing to renew a license, permit, charter franchise, or other similar grant to, from conditioning such a grant to, from discrimination with respect to such a grant against, deny employment to, terminate the employment of, or discriminate with respect to employment against, a person that is or has been a debtor or that is or has been associated with a debtor. The prohibition extends only to discrimination or other action based solely on the basis of the bankruptcy, on the basis of insolvency before or during bankruptcy prior to a determination of discharge, or on the basis of nonpayment of a debt discharged in the bankruptcy case (the *Perez* situation). It does not prohibit consideration of other factors, such as future financial responsibility or ability, and does not prohibit imposition of requirements such as net capital rules, if applied nondiscriminatorily.

In addition, the section is not exhaustive. The enumeration of various forms of discrimination against former bankrupts is not intended to permit other forms of discrimination. The courts have been developing the *Perez* rule. This section permits further development to prohibit actions by governmental or quasi-governmental organizations that perform licensing functions, such as a State bar association or a medical society, or by other organizations that can seriously affect the debtors' livelihood or fresh start, such as exclusion from a union on the basis of discharge of a debt to the union's credit union.

The effect of the section, and of further interpretations of the *Perez* rule, is to strengthen the anti-reaffirmation policy found in section 524(b). Discrimination based solely on nonpayment could encourage reaffirmations, contrary to the expressed policy.

The section is not so broad as a comparable section proposed by the Bankruptcy Commission, H.R. 31, 94th Cong., 1st Sess. § 4–508 (1975), which would have extended the prohibition to any discrimination, even by private parties. Nevertheless, it is not limiting either, as noted. The courts will continue to mark the contours of the anti-discrimination provision in pursuit of sound bankruptcy policy.

[*House Report No. 95–595, 95th Cong., 1st Sess. 366–7 (1977); Senate Report No. 95–989, 95th Cong., 2d Sess. 81 (1978).*]

Comment

Section 525(a) has no predecessor in the former Bankruptcy Act. It codifies the result of Perez v. Campbell, 402 U.S. 637 (1971) which distinguished and all but overruled Reitz v. Mealey, 314 U.S. 33 (1941) and Kesler v. Department of Public Safety, 369 U.S. 153 (1962) which upheld discriminatory treatment of discharged bankrupts. Section 525 furthers the "fresh start" concept.

1984 Amendments: The amendment adds a subsection "(b)" that extends the protection from discriminatory treatment to private employers.

Case Annotations

Loans designed to provide emergency payments of mortgages are not licenses, permits, charters, franchises nor grants such that if a government agency denies such loans when a debtor files for bankruptcy it does not constitute discrimination against that debtor. *In re* Watts, 876 F.2d 1090, 21 C.B.C.2d 521 (3d Cir. 1989).

Although section 525(a) prohibits a state from penalizing those who choose the protection bankruptcy offers and the benefits of the "fresh start" policy, it does not require a state to ignore the prior existence of a debtor's debt in all circumstances. *In re* Norton, 867 F.2d 313, 20 C.B.C.2d 710 (6th Cir. 1989).

Section 525(a) is to be construed narrowly. Its application is limited to situations analogous to those enumerated in the statute, or alternatively, to alleged discrimination resulting from nonpayment of a debt actually dischargeable in bankruptcy; there must be proof that discrimination was caused solely by the debtor's status as a debtor, for the statute only precludes differentiation between debtors and nondebtors. *In re* Exquisito Servs., Inc., 823 F.2d. 151, 17 C.B.C.2d 324 (5th Cir. 1987).

Ohio's Motor Vehicle Financial Responsibility Act does not discriminate against debtors in violation of section 525 because it applies to all drivers who fail to satisfy judgments, not just those who file under the Bankruptcy Code, and because the statute does not require that a judgment discharged in bankruptcy be satisfied as a condition for restoration of driving privileges. Duffey v. Dollison, 734 F.2d 265, 10 C.B.C.2d 1394 (6th Cir. 1984).

The Bankruptcy Code's fresh start policy does not preclude a college from withholding a transcript from a debtor whose educational loan debts have not been discharged. Johnson v. Edinboro State College, 728 F.2d 163, 10 C.B.C.2d 231 (3d Cir. 1984).

The policy of a credit union, closely affiliated with the company which employs the credit union member, to freeze accounts and discontinue services solely because of the member's bankruptcy filing is the kind of discrimination prohibited by section 525(b). *In re* Patterson, 24 C.B.C.2d 1671 (B. Ct., N.D. Ala. 1990).

Suspension of a debtor's driver's license solely because of nonpayment or delay in payment of Department of Motor Vehicle surcharges violates section 525(a). *In re* Bill, 19 C.B.C.2d 1046 (B. Ct., D.N.J. 1988).

Although section 365(b) requires debtors to pay any prepetition debts owed to creditors in order to assume an executory contract, the public policy of section 525(a) prohibits the Department of Health and Human Services, a governmental unit, from requiring the chapter 11 debtor hospital to repay its prepetition indebtedness as a condition of assuming a Medicare provider contract which is an executory contract under section 365. Hiser v. Blue Cross of Greater Philadelphia (*In re* St. Mary Hospital), 19 C.B.C.2d 1353 (B. Ct., E.D. Pa. 1988).

The requirement that a debtor in possession pay prepetition license fees and taxes as a condition of renewal of its casino license is precluded by section 525. Elsinore Shore Associates v. Casino Control Commission (*In re* Elsinore Shore Associates), 15 C.B.C.2d 1128 (B. Ct., D.N.J. 1986).

The withholding of a minor student's transcript in order to coerce him or his parents into paying the balance of tuition violates the automatic stay and section 525 when the school board, knowing that the debt is no longer collectible from the debtor's parents, attempts instead to hold the minor liable for the debt. *In re* Dembek, 15 C.B.C.2d 611 (B. Ct., N.D. Ohio 1986).

References

3 *Collier on Bankruptcy* ch. 525 (Matthew Bender 15th ed.).

2 *Collier Bankruptcy Manual* ch. 525 (Matthew Bender 3d ed.).

5 *Collier Bankruptcy Practice Guide* ch. 78 (Matthew Bender).

Balkins, *Withholding Transcripts for Non-Payment of Educational Debts: Before and after Bankruptcy*, 15 Williamette L.J. 563 (1979).

Casenote, *Bankruptcy: Suspension of Driving Privileges After Bankruptcy Discharge for Failure To File Proof of Future Financial Resposibility Act Not Discriminatory under 11 U.S.C. § 525(a) of the Bankruptcy Code—Duffey v. Dollison, 734 F.2d 265 (6th Cir. 1984)*, 10 U. Dayton L. Rev. 379 (1984).

Chobot, *Anti-Discrimination Under the Bankruptcy Laws*, 60 Am. Bankr. L.J. 185 (1986).

Comment, *Protection of the Debtor's "Fresh Start" Under the New Bankruptcy Code*, 29 Cath. U.L. Rev. 843 (1980).

SUBCHAPTER III

The Estate

SECTION 541 (11 U.S.C. § 541)

§ 541. Property of the estate.

(a) The commencement of a case under section 301, 302, or 303 of this title creates an estate. Such estate is comprised of all the following property, wherever located and by whomever held:

(1) Except as provided in subsections (b) and (c)(2) of this section, all legal or equitable interests of the debtor in property as of the commencement of the case.

(2) All interests of the debtor and the debtor's spouse in community property as of the commencement of the case that is—

(A) under the sole, equal, or joint management and control of the debtor; or

(B) liable for an allowable claim against the debtor, or for both an allowable claim against the debtor and an allowable claim against the debtor's spouse, to the extent that such interest is so liable.

(3) Any interest in property that the trustee recovers under section 329(b), 363(n), 543, 550, 553, or 723 of this title.

(4) Any interest in property preserved for the benefit of or ordered transferred to the estate under section 510(c) or 551 of this title.

(5) Any interest in property that would have been property of the estate if such interest had been an interest of the debtor on the date of the filing of the petition, and that the debtor acquires or becomes entitled to acquire within 180 days after such date—

(A) by bequest, device, or inheritance;

(B) as a result of a property settlement agreement with debtor's spouse, or of an interlocutory or final divorce decree; or

(C) as beneficiary of a life insurance policy or of a death benefit plan.

(6) Proceeds, product, offspring, rents, or profits of or from property of the estate, except such as are earnings from services performed by an individual debtor after the commencement of the case.

(7) Any interest in property that the estate acquires after the commencement of the case.

(b) Property of the estate does not include—

(1) any power that the debtor may exercise solely for the benefit of an entity other than the debtor;

(2) any interest of the debtor as a lessee under a lease of nonresidential real property that has terminated at the expiration of the stated term of such lease before the commencement of the case under this title, and ceases to include any interest of the debtor as a lessee under a lease of nonresidential real property that has terminated at the expiration of the stated term of such lease during the case;

(3) any eligibility of the debtor to participate in programs authorized under the Higher Education Act of 1965 (20 U.S.C. 1001 et seq.; 42 U.S.C. 2751 et seq.), or any accreditation status or State licensure of the debtor as an educational institution; or,

(4) any interest of the debtor in liquid or gaseous hydrocarbons to the extent that —

(A) the debtor has transferred or has agreed to transfer such interest pursuant to a farmout agreement or any written agreement directly related to a farmout agreement; and

(B) but for the operation of this paragraph, the estate could include such interest only by virtue of section 365 or 544(a)(3) of this title.

(c)(1) Except as provided in paragraph (2) of this subsection, an interest of the debtor in property becomes property of the estate under subsection (a)(1), (a)(2), or (a)(5) of this section notwithstanding any provision in an agreement, transfer instrument, or applicable nonbankruptcy law—

>   (A) that restricts or conditions transfer of such interest by the debtor; or

>   (B) that is conditioned on the insolvency or financial condition of the debtor, on the commencement of a case under this title, or on the appointment of or taking possession by a trustee in a case under this title or a custodian before such commencement, and that effects or gives an option to effect a forfeiture, modification, or termination of the debtor's interest in property.

(2) A restriction on the transfer of a beneficial interest of the debtor in a trust that is enforceable under applicable nonbankruptcy law is enforceable in a case under this title.

(d) Property in which the debtor holds, as of the commencement of the case, only legal title and not an equitable interest, such as a mortgage secured by real property, or an interest in such a mortgage, sold by the debtor but as to which the debtor retains legal title to service or supervise the servicing of such mortgage or interest, becomes property of the estate under subsection (a)(1) or (2) of this section only to the extent of the debtor's legal title to such property, but not to the extent of any equitable interest in such property that the debtor does not hold.

Bankruptcy Rule References: 1007, 6007 and 6008

Legislative History

   This section defines property of the estate, and specifies what property becomes property of the estate. The commencement of a bankruptcy case creates an estate. Under paragraph (1) of subsection (a), the estate is comprised of all legal or equitable interest of the debtor in property, wherever located, as of the commencement of the case. The scope of this paragraph is broad. It includes all kinds of property, including tangible or intangible property, causes of action (see Bankruptcy Act section 70a(6)), and all other forms of property currently specified in section 70a of the Bankruptcy Act section 70a, [*sic*] as well as property recovered by the trustee under section 542 of proposed title 11, if the property recovered was merely out of the possession of the debtor, yet remained "property of the debtor." The debtor's interest in property also includes "title" to property, which is an interest, just as are a possessory interest, or leasehold interest, for example. The result of Segal v.

Rochelle, 382 U.S. 375 (1966), is followed, and the right to a refund is property of the estate.

Though this paragraph will include choses in action and claims by the debtor against others, it is not intended to expand the debtor's rights against others more than they exist at the commencement of the case. For example, if the debtor has a claim that is barred at the time of the commencement of the case by the statute of limitations, then the trustee would not be able to pursue that claim, because he too would be barred. He could take no greater rights than the debtor himself had. *But see* proposed 11 U.S.C. § 108, which would permit the trustee a tolling of the statute of limitations if it had not run before the date of the filing of the petition.

Paragraph (1) has the effect of overruling Lockwood v. Exchange Bank, 190 U.S. 294 (1903), because it includes as property of the estate all property of the debtor, even that needed for a fresh start. After the property comes into the estate, then the debtor is permitted to exempt it under proposed 11 U.S.C. § 522, and the court will have jurisdiction to determine what property may be exempted and what remains as property of the estate. The broad jurisdictional grant in proposed 28 U.S.C. § 1471(b) would have the effect of overruling Lockwood independently of the change made by this provision.

Paragraph (1) also has the effect of overruling Lines v. Frederick, 400 U.S. 18 (1970).

Situations occasionally arise where property ostensibly belonging to the debtor will actually not be property of the debtor, but will be held in trust for another. For example, if the debtor has incurred medical bills that were covered by insurance, and the insurance company had sent the payment of the bills to the debtor before the debtor had paid the bill for which the payment was reimbursement, the payment would actually be held in a constructive trust for the person to whom the bill was owed. This section and proposed 11 U.S.C. § 545 also will not affect various statutory provisions that give a creditor of the debtor a lien that is valid outside as well as inside bankruptcy, or that creates a trust fund for the benefit of a creditor of the debtor. *See* Packers and Stockyards Act section 206, 7 U.S.C. § 196.

Bankruptcy Act section 8 has been deleted as unnecessary. Once the estate is created, no interests in property of the estate remain in the debtor. Consequently, if the debtor dies during the case, only property exempted from property of the estate or acquired by the debtor after the commencement of the case and not included as property of the estate will be available to the representative of the debtor's probate estate. The bankruptcy proceeding will continue in rem with respect to property of the state [*sic*], and the discharge will apply in personam to relieve the debtor, and thus his probate representative, of liability for dischargeable debts.

The estate also includes the interests of the debtor and the debtor's spouse in community property, subject to certain limitations; property that the trustee recovers under the avoiding powers; property that the debtor acquires by bequest, devise, inheritance, a property settlement agreement with the debtor's spouse, or as the beneficiary of a life insurance policy within 180 days after the petition; and proceeds, product, offspring, rents, and profits of or from property of the estate, except such as are earning [*sic*] from services performed by an individual debtor after the commencement of the case. *See* proposed 11 U.S.C. § 503(b)(1). Proceeds here is not used in a confining sense, as defined in the Uniform Commercial Code, but is intended to be a broad term to encompass all proceeds of property of the estate. The conversion in form of property of the estate does not change its character as property of the estate.

[*House Report No. 95–595, 95th Cong., 1st Sess. 367–8 (1977); Senate Report No. 95–989, 95th Cong., 2d Sess. 82–3 (1978).*]

Section 541(a)(7) is new. The provision clarifies that any interest in property that the estate acquires after the commencement of the case is property of the estate; for example, if the estate enters into a contract, after the commencement of the case, such a contract would be property of the estate. The addition of this provision by the House amendment merely clarifies that section 541(a) is an all-embracing definition which includes charges on property, such as liens held by the debtor on property of a third party, or beneficial rights and interests that the debtor may have in property of another. However, only the debtor's interest in such property becomes property of the estate. If the debtor holds bare legal title or holds property in trust for another, only those rights which the debtor would have otherwise had emanating from such interest pass to the estate under section 541. Neither this section nor section 545 will affect various statutory provisions that give a creditor a lien that is valid both inside and outside bankruptcy against a bona fide purchaser of property from the debtor, or that creates a trust fund for the benefit of creditors meeting similar criteria. *See* Packers and Stockyards Act section 206, 7 U.S.C. § 196 (1976).

[*124 Cong. Rec. H 11,096 (Sept. 28, 1978); S 17,413 (Oct. 6, 1978).*]

Section 541. Property of the estate: The Senate amendment provided that property of the estate does not include amounts held by the debtor as trustee and any taxes withheld or collected from others before the commencement of the case. The House amendment removes these two provisions. As to property held by the debtor as a trustee, the House amendment provides that property of the estate will include whatever interest the debtor held in the property at the commencement of the case. Thus, where the debtor held only legal title to the property and the beneficial interest in that property belongs to another, such as exists in the case of property held in trust, the property of the estate includes the legal title, but not the beneficial interest in the property.

As to withheld taxes, the House amendment deletes the rule in the Senate bill as unnecessary since property of the estate does not include the beneficial interest in property held by the debtor as a trustee. Under the Internal Revenue Code of 1954 (section 7501), the amounts of withheld taxes are held to be a special fund in trust for the United States. Where the Internal Revenue Service can demonstrate that the amounts of taxes withheld are still in the possession of the debtor at the commencement of the case, then if a trust is created, those amounts are not property of the estate. Compare *In re* Shakesteers Coffee Shops, 546 F.2d 821 (9th Cir. 1976) with *In re* Glynn Wholesale Building Materials, Inc. (S.D. Ga. 1978) and *In re* Progress Tech Colleges, Inc., 42 Aftr 2d 78-5573 (S.D. Ohio 1977).

Where it is not possible for the Internal Revenue Service to demonstrate that the amounts of taxes withheld are still in the possession of the debtor at the commencement of the case, present law generally includes amounts of withheld taxes as property of the estate. *See, e.g.,* United States v. Randall, 401 U.S. 513 (1973) and *In re* Tamasha Town and Country Club, 483 F.2d 1377 (9th Cir. 1973). Nontheless, a serious problem exists where "trust fund taxes" withheld from others are held to be property of the estate where the withheld amounts are commingled with other assets of the debtor. The courts should permit the use of reasonable assumptions under which the Internal Revenue Service, and other tax authorities, can demonstrate that amounts of withheld taxes are still in the possession of the debtor at the commencement of the case. For example, where the debtor had commingled that amount of withheld taxes in his general checking account, it might be reasonable to assume that any remaining amounts in that account on the commencement of the case are the withheld taxes. In addition, Congress may consider future amendments to the Internal Revenue Code making clear that amounts of withheld taxes are held by the debtor in a trust relationship and, consequently, that such amounts are not property of the estate.

[*124 Cong. Rec. H 11,114 (Sept. 28, 1978); S 17,430-1 (Oct. 6, 1978).*]

Subsection (b) excludes from property of the estate any power, such as a power of appointment, that the debtor may exercise solely for the benefit of an entity other than the debtor. This changes present law which excludes powers solely benefitting other persons but not other entities.

Subsection (c) invalidates restrictions on the transfer of property of the debtor, in order that all the interests of the debtor in property will become property of the estate. The provisions invalidated are those that restrict or condition transfer of the debtor's interest, and those that are conditioned on the insolvency or financial condition of the debtor, on the commencement of a bankruptcy case, or on the appointment of a custodian of the debtor's property. Paragraph (2) of subsection (c), however, preserves restrictions on transfer of a spendthrift trust to the extent that the restriction is enforceable under applicable nonbankruptcy law.

[*House Report No. 95–595, 95th Cong., 1st Sess. 368 (1977); See Senate Report No. 95–989, 95th Cong., 2d Sess. 83 (1978).*]

Section 541(c)(2) follows the position taken in the House bill and rejects the position taken in the Senate amendment with respect to income limitations on a spend-thrift trust.

[*124 Cong. Rec. H 11,096 (Sept. 28, 1978); S 17,413 (Oct. 6, 1978).*]

Section 541(d) of the House amendment is derived from section 541(e) of the Senate amendment and reiterates the general principle that where the debtor holds bare legal title without any equitable interest, that the estate acquires bare legal title without any equitable interest in the property. Examples of this are mortgages sold for which legal title has been retained for servicing. Similarly, if the debtor holds an equitable interest in property without legal title, the estate would acquire only the equitable interest of the debtor in property and not the legal title. Thus, as section 541(a)(1) clearly states, the estate is comprised of all legal or equitable interests of the debtor in property as of the commencement of the case. To the extent such an interest is limited in the hands of the debtor, it is equally limited in the hands of the estate except to the extent that defenses which are personal against the debtor are not effective against the estate.

[*124 Cong. Rec. H 11,096 (Sept. 28, 1978).*]

Section 541(d) of the House amendment is derived from section 541(e) of the Senate amendment and reiterates the general principle that where the debtor holds bare legal title without any equitable interest, that the estate acquires bare legal title without any equitable interest in the property. The purpose of section 541(d) as applied to the secondary mortgage market is identical to the purpose of section 541(e) of the Senate amendment and section 541(d) will accomplish the same result as would have been accomplished by section 541(e). Even if a mortgage seller retains for purposes of servicing legal title to mortgages or interests in morgages sold in the secondary mortgage market, the trustee would be required by section 541(d) to turn over the mortgages or interests in mortgages to the purchaser of those mortgages.

The seller of mortgages in the secondary mortgage market will often retain the original mortgage notes and related documents and the seller will not endorse the notes to reflect the sale to the purchaser. Similarly, the purchaser will often not record the purchaser's ownership of the mortgages or interests in mortgages under State recording statutes. These facts are irrelevant and the seller's retention of the mortgage documents and the purchaser's decision not to record do not change the trustee's obligation to turn the mortgages or interests in mortgages over to the purchaser. The application of section 541(d) to secondary mortgage market transactions will not be affected by the terms of the servicing agreement between the mortgage servicer and the purchaser of the mortgages. Under section 541(d), the trustee is required to recognize the purchaser's title to the mortgages or interests in mortgages and to turn this property over to the purchaser. It makes no difference whether the servicer and the purchaser characterize their relationship as one of trust, agency, or independent contractor.

The purpose of section 541(d) as applied to the secondary mortgage market is therefore to make certain that secondary mortgage market sales as they are currently structured are not subject to challenge by bankruptcy trustees and that purchasers of mortgages will be able to obtain the mortgages or interests in mortgages which they have purchased from trustees without the trustees asserting that a sale of mortgages is a loan from the purchaser to the seller.

Thus, as section 541(a)(1) clearly states, the estate is comprised of all legal or equitable interests of the debtor in property as of the commencement of the case. To the extent such an interest is limited in the hands of the debtor, it is equally limited in the hands of the estate except to the extent that defenses which are personal against the debtor are not effective against the estate.

[*124 Cong. Rec. S 17,413 (Oct. 6, 1978).*]

Comment

Section 541 is derived from section 70a of the former Bankruptcy Act. Section 541 of the Code is broad in scope including all forms of property specified in section 70 of the Act as well as property recovered by the trustee under section 542 of the Code if the property, although out of debtor's possession remained, nevertheless, "property of the debtor." The debtor's interest includes "title" to property which is an interest. The right to a tax refund is included in "property" of the estate. The trustee, under section 541 takes the right of the debtor at the time the case is instituted, but no more. Thus, if a claim is barred by the statute of limitations, then that defense is available as against the trustee, subject, of course, to tolling such statute as provided in section 108.

Note particularly that Lockwood v. Exchange Bank, 190 U.S. 294 (1903) and Lines v. Frederick, 400 U.S. 18 (1970) are, in effect, overruled. After the property comes into the estate, exemptions claimed by the debtor will be determined by the court.

Bankruptcy Rule 6004 deals with the use, sale or lease of property. Rule 6007 deals with abandonment of property. Rule 6004(d) was amended in 1991 to require notice to the United States trustee of the proposed sale or lease of any property not in the regular course of business. Rule 6007 was similarly amended to require notice to the United States trustee of a motion to abandon property of the estate.

Rule 6008 relates to the redemption of property from lien or sale.

Bankruptcy Rule 4003 deals with exemptions.

Bankruptcy Rule 1007(h) implements the provisions and language of section 541(a)(5), providing that if, as provided in that section, the debtor acquires or becomes entitled to acquire any interest in property, the debtor shall within 10 days after the information comes to the debtor's knowledge, or within such further time as the court may allow, file a supplemental schedule in the chapter 7, 11, 12 or 13 case. The court may allow additional time. Exemptions as to any such property must be claimed in the schedule. The duty to file the supplemental schedule survives the closing of the case, except as to property acquired after entry of the order confirming a chapter 11, 12 or 13 plan.

1984 Amendments: The amendments to section 541 added subsection (b) (2), excluding as property of the estate the debtor's interest as lessee of nonresidential real property where the lease has terminated at the expiration of a stated term before or during a case.

The amendment to subsection (d) establishes that section 541(d) does not abrogate the trustee's power to resort to section 544(a)(3) to defeat unrecorded equitable interests in real property.

The amendments repealed subsection (e) providing that the estate have the benefit of any defense available to the debtor against any entity other than the debtor; this provision was moved to section 558.

1990 Amendments: Pub. L. No. 101-508 (Omnibus Budget Reconciliation Act of 1990) was signed into law on November 5, 1990, effective as of the enactment date. It amended section 541(b) by adding paragraph (3). To accommodate the addition of new paragraph (3), the word "or" was deleted at the end of paragraph (1), and a semicolon and "or" were substituted for a period at the end of paragraph (2). The amendments made by Pub. L. No. 101-508 (Omnibus Budget Reconciliation Act of 1990) shall cease to be effective on October 1, 1996.

1992 Amendments: The Energy Policy Act of 1992, Pub. L. No. 102-486, was signed into law on October 24, 1992, effective as of the enactment date (except with respect to cases commenced before the enactment date). It amended section 541(b) by adding paragraph (4) regarding "farmout agreements."

Case Annotations

The plain language of the Bankruptcy Code entitles a debtor to exclude from property of the estate any interest in a plan or trust that contains a transfer restriction enforceable under any relevant nonbankruptcy law; because nothing in section 541(c)(2) limits the source of the "applicable nonbankruptcy law" to state law, the exclusion applies to plans or trusts containing transfer restrictions enforceable under federal nonbankruptcy law, such as ERISA-qualified plans. Patterson v. Shumate, 504 U.S. —, 112 S. Ct. 2242, 119 L. Ed. 2d 519, 26 C.B.C.2d 1119 (1992).

Section 541 will not apply in those instances where property which ostensibly belongs to the debtor is, in reality, held by the debtor in trust for another, as in the instance of withholding taxes held in trust prepetition by the debtor for the IRS. Begier v. Internal Revenue Service, 495 U.S. 954, 110 S. Ct. 2258, 110 L. Ed. 2d 46, 22 C.B.C.2d 1080 (1990).

Property seized by the Internal Revenue Service immediately prior to the filing of the debtor's chapter 11 petition is property of the estate, since the debtor, and not the IRS, retains an ownership interest in the property. United States v. Whiting Pools, Inc., 462 U.S. 198, 103 S. Ct. 2309, 76 L. Ed. 2d 515, 8 C.B.C.2d 710 (1983).

Personal property held as tenants by the entirety by a debtor and his or her spouse is included as property of a bankruptcy estate even if only one spouse is in bankruptcy, when the property is not otherwise exempt. *In re* Garner, 952 F.2d 232, 26 C.B.C.2d 274 (8th Cir. 1991).

Outstanding contract balances owed by state, municipal and federal agencies to a debtor for labor and materials already provided by subcontractors are not held in trust by the agencies but, once paid to the debtor, are held by it in trust for the benefit of the subcontractors and, therefore, do not become part of the estate and may not be used by the debtor for reorganization or to pay other creditors. Universal Bonding Insurance Co. v. Gittens and Sprinkle Enterprises, Inc., 960 F.2d 366, 26 C.B.C.2d 1073 (3d Cir. 1992).

Other than property exempted or excluded by operation of the Bankruptcy Code itself, virtually all of a debtor's property becomes part of the bankruptcy estate. In order for a pension plan to qualify as a spendthrift trust for purposes of exclusion from property of the bankruptcy estate, the court must consider numerous factors, including the degree of restriction on the beneficiary's access to the plan funds and the trustee's dominion and control over the plan. When an alleged spendthrift trust is self-settled so that the trustee and beneficiary are the same individual, the terms of the pension plan to support spendthrift status must be even more restrictive than usual to merit exclusion from the debtor's estate. Pitrat v. Garlikov, 947 F.2d 419, 26 C.B.C.2d 126 (9th Cir. 1991).

In Wisconsin, a security deposit given to a debtor/landlord by a tenant to cover unpaid rent and damages to leased property which the debtor holds in a separate account does not constitute property of the estate because the debtor/landlord has no property interest in the security deposits until he sustains a compensable loss. It is settled that a trustee in bankruptcy succeeds to no greater interest than that held by a debtor and, therefore, if the debtor landlord has no property interest in security deposits because state law mandates that title to the funds remains with the tenants, the trustee, likewise, has no property interest. Matter of Wayco, Inc., 947 F.2d 1330, 25 C.B.C.2d 1358 (7th Cir. 1991).

A net operating loss carryforward attributable to a corporate debtor belongs to the debtor pursuant to section 541 and it does not, under the law of consolidated tax returns, belong to its parent company. *In re* Prudential Lines, Inc., 928 F.2d 565, 24 C.B.C.2d 1503 (2d Cir. 1991).

A restored express trust is not subject to the same tracing requirement which is necessary when a beneficiary attempts to impress a constructive trust upon commingled property of the debtor. *In re* California Trade Technical Schools, Inc., 923 F.2d 641, 24 C.B.C.2d 813 (9th Cir. 1991).

Under Iowa law, contract theory defines the rights of parties holding bank accounts in a joint tenancy, but extrinsic evidence may be admitted to determine the rights of the parties during their lifetime and accordingly, a court may find that a debtor has no present vested interest in such an account if the extrinsic evidence so shows. Ackley State Bank, 920 F.2d 521, 24 C.B.C.2d 291 (8th Cir. 1990).

Upon a partner's filing of a bankruptcy petition, his interest in a debtor partnership became part of the estate and the bankruptcy court retains jurisdiction to approve the trustee's settlement of a dispute between the debtor partner and a nondebtor partner. *In re* Holywell Corp., 913 F.2d 873, 24 C.B.C.2d 69 (11th Cir. 1990).

A state liquor license constitutes property of the estate for purposes of section 541 of the Bankruptcy Code. *In re* Terwilliger's Catering Plus, Inc., 911 F.2d 1168, 23 C.B.C.2d 694 (6th Cir. 1990).

When a debtor's ex-spouse was awarded a share of the debtor's pension as her "sole and separate" property under the terms of a state court decree dissolving the parties' marriage, the ex-spouse's claim for postpetition arrearages is not discharged by the bankruptcy, as the ex-wife's share is held by the debtor in a constructive trust. Bush v. Taylor, 912 F.2d 989, 23 C.B.C.2d 1294 (8th Cir. 1990).

Income payments from inter vivos spendthrift trusts made during the 180 day postpetition period are not "bequests" that become property of the estate. In the Matter of Newman, 903 F.2d 1150, 23 C.B.C.2d 170 (7th Cir. 1990).

A possessory interest in real property is within the ambit of the bankruptcy estate under section 541 and, thus, within the protection of the automatic stay of section 362. *In re* Atlantic Business and Community Corp., 901 F.2d 325, 22 C.B.C.2d 1176 (3d Cir. 1990).

Whereas federal law determines that a cause of action for missing merchandise *may* constitute property of the debtor's estate, state law determines whether the debtor's interest in the cause of action is sufficient to confer on the estate a property right in the action. *In re* Crysen/Montenay Energy Co., 902 F.2d 1098, 22 C.B.C.2d 1385 (2d Cir. 1990).

The bankruptcy court retains jurisdiction over a debtor's property even if the chapter 7 trustee abandons it because the debtor will have an equitable and possibly a statutory right of redemption in that property. *In re* Saylors, 869 F.2d 1434, 20 C.B.C.2d 1129 (11th Cir. 1989).

Section 541(a)(1), which provides that the estate is comprised of all legal and equitable interests of the debtor including choses in action, acknowledges the right of a debtor to proceed against its alter ego and to claim its equitable interest in assets of the alter ego. Steyr-Daimler-Puch of America Corp. v. Pappas, 852 F.2d 132, 20 C.B.C.2d 13 (4th Cir. 1988).

Under Texas law, in the absence of a legally valid agreement when a court determines that a party has been unjustly enriched and that an equitable interest exists equal to the reasonable value of excess benefits received by that party from the debtor, those equitable interests constitute property of the estate pursuant to section 541(a)(1) and are subject to turnover from the unjustly enriched party to the estate under section 542(a). *In re* NWFX, Inc., 864 F.2d 588, 20 C.B.C.2d 101 (8th Cir. 1988).

Whether a debtor has an interest in property is determined by state law and is within the bankruptcy court's jurisdiction. Dewhirst v.

Citibank (Arizona) (*In re* Contractor's Equipment Supply Co.), 861 F.2d 241, 19 C.B.C.2d 1254 (9th Cir. 1988).

Officers and directors liability insurance policies are property of the estate entitled to the protection of the automatic stay since the policies benefit the debtor by insuring it against indemnity claims made by officers and directors. The Minoco Group of Companies, Ltd. v. First Statement Underwriters Agency of New England Reinsurance Corp. (*In re* The Minoco Group of Companies, Ltd.), 799 F.2d 517, 15 C.B.C.2d 1277 (9th Cir. 1986). *See also* MacArthur Co. v. Johns-Manville Corp., 837 F.2d 89, 18 C.B.C.2d 316 (2d Cir. 1988).

Section 522(d)(7) exempts from property of the estate an unmatured life insurance policy that is both owned and payable to the debtor as of the date of filing; section 541(a)(5) sweeps later-acquired proceeds of such a policy into the estate. Woodson v. Fireman's Fund Insurance Co. (*In re* Woodson), 839 F.2d 610, 18 C.B.C.2d 674 (9th Cir. 1988).

In Illinois and Indiana, the bankruptcy trustee, representing creditors, has standing under state law to bring an alter ego claim in pursuing all funds available as section 541 property of the estate. The fact that a defendant has been sued to recover preferential transfers or might someday be a creditor of the estate is insufficient to confer standing on the defendant to raise an alter ego action against the debtor when the trustee is currently bringing the same action. Koch Refining v. Farmers Union Central Exchange, Inc., 841 F.2d 1339, 18 C.B.C.2d 84 (7th Cir. 1987).

An executory contract is property of the estate despite a nonassignability or a bankruptcy default clause therein. Computer Communications, Inc. v. Codex Corp. (*In re* Computer Communications, Inc.), 824 F.2d 725, 17 C.B.C.2d 556 (9th Cir. 1987).

A typical participation transaction can be distinguished from a loan transaction by the fact that a participant will assume the same risks as the person selling the participation (as well as relying on the trustworthiness of the borrower); when one party assumes all of the risks, the relationship is usually debtor-creditor in nature, and if so, section 541(d) does not act to exclude the underlying notes and mortgages from property of the estate. Fireman's Fund Ins. Cos. v. Grover (*In re* Woodson Co.), 813 F.2d 266, 17 C.B.C.2d 80 (9th Cir. 1987).

A shareholders' derivative suit for the recovery of the diminution in value of the debtor corporation's stock caused by the tortious acts of either an officer or director or third person belongs primarily to the debtor corporation, and therefore is within the jurisdiction of the bankruptcy court. Griggin v. Bonapel (*In re* All Am. of Ashburn, Inc.), 805 F.2d 1515, 16 C.B.C.2d 210 (11th Cir. 1986).

Section 541(c)(1)(A) avoids only those restrictions which prevent transfer of a debtor's property to the estate, rather than all transfer restrictions on property in which the debtor holds an interest. Accordingly, section 541(c)(1)(A) does not invalidate a state law governing the transfer of liquor licenses. State of California v. Farmers Markets, Inc.

(*In re* Farmers Markets, Inc.), 792 F.2d 1400, 15 C.B.C.2d 93 (9th Cir. 1986).

Pursuant to section 541(a)(1), property of the estate includes "all legal or equitable interests of the debtor in property as of the commencement of the case" and includes a cause of action for emotional distress where such an action could not be reached by creditors under state law. That the personal injury claim is not transferable or assignable under state law does not defeat its status as property of the estate under section 541, which should be broadly construed. Sierra Switchboard Co. v. Westinghouse Electric Corp., 789 F.2d 706, 14 C.B.C.2d 1064 (9th Cir. 1986).

Property that a debtor has fraudulently conveyed remains "property of the estate," and, thus, the automatic stay under section 362(a) prevents a creditor from continuing to pursue a cause of action to void a fraudulent conveyance after a petition under the Code has been filed. Carlton v. BAWW, Inc., 751 F.2d 781, 12 C.B.C.2d 457 (5th Cir. 1985).

Postpetition employment termination payments to which a chapter 7 debtor is entitled under a prepetition contract are includable in the debtor's estate when they represent value for services completed prior to bankruptcy. Rau v. Ryerson (*In re* Ryerson), 739 F.2d 1423, 11 C.B.C.2d 121 (9th Cir. 1984).

Surplus funds generated by the prebankruptcy foreclosure sale of a chapter 7 debtor's real property are property of the estate if at the time the estate was created, the debtor had a clear contingent interest in the funds. Brown v. Dellinger (*In re* Brown), 734 F.2d 119, 10 C.B.C.2d 1405 (2d Cir. 1984).

A state court's order in a dissolution of marriage action that a residence be sold and the net proceeds be divided equally did not achieve a prepetition division of community property and debt so that the nondebtor spouse's interest in the residence was property of the estate when the state court's order was not part of the chapter 11 case record and the nondebtor spouse's motion for relief from the automatic stay indicated that a division of community property had not occurred. *In re* McCoy, 22 C.B.C.2d 1343 (9th Cir., B.A.P., 1990).

Property held by a debtor in a PACA statutory trust used to pay off supplier creditors is not part of the bankruptcy estate. *In re* Milton Poulos, Inc., 22 C.B.C.2d 101 (9th Cir, B.A.P., 1989).

References

4 *Collier on Bankruptcy* ch. 541 (Matthew Bender 15th ed.).

2 *Collier Bankruptcy Manual* ch. 541 (Matthew Bender 3d ed.).

Bankruptcy Court Rules City Investments in E.S.M. Are Customer Property, 1 Com. L. Bull. 9 (1986).

Christy & Skeldon, *Shumate and Pension Benefits in Bankruptcy,* 2 J. Bankr. L. & Prac. 719 (Nov./Dec. 1992).

Landis, *ERISA Exemptions in Bankruptcy: A Logical Solution,* 66 Am. Bankr. L.J. 253 (Summer 1992).

Law Notes, *Property Rights in Farm Bankruptcy Treatment of Crops and Livestock Under the Farm Lease,* 2 Compleat Law 41 (1985).

Pitts, *Rights to Future Payment as Property of the Estate in Bankruptcy,* 64 Am. Bankr. L.J. 61 (1990).

Property of the Estate After Confirmation of A Chapter 13 Repayment Plan: Balancing Competing Interests, 65 Wash. L. Rev. 677 (1990).

Property of the Estate: Section 541(a)(1), 4 Bankr. Dev. J. 123 (1987).

Russell, *Administration of the Estate,* 2 Bank Dev. J. 81 (1985).

SECTION 542 (11 U.S.C. § 542)

§ 542. Turnover of property to the estate.

(a) Except as provided in subsection (c) or (d) of this section, an entity, other than a custodian, in possession, custody, or control, during the case, of property that the trustee may use, sell, or lease under section 363 of this title, or that the debtor may exempt under section 522 of this title, shall deliver to the trustee, and account for, such property or the value of such property, unless such property is of inconsequential value or benefit to the estate.

(b) Except as provided in subsection (c) or (d) of this section, an entity that owes a debt that is property of the estate and that is matured, payable on demand, or payable on order, shall pay such debt to, or on the order of, the trustee, except to the extent that such debt may be offset under section 553 of this title against a claim against the debtor.

(c) Except as provided in section 362(a)(7) of this title, an entity that has neither actual notice nor actual knowledge of the commencement of the case concerning the debtor may transfer property of the estate, or pay a debt owing to the debtor, in good faith and other than in the manner specified in subsection (d) of this section, to an entity other than the trustee, with the same effect as to the entity making such transfer or payment as if the case under this title concerning the debtor had not been commenced.

(d) A life insurance company may transfer property of the estate or property of the debtor to such company in good faith, with the same effect with respect to such company as if the case under this title concerning the debtor had not been commenced, if such transfer is to pay a premium or to carry out a nonforfeiture insurance option, and is required to be made automatically, under a life insurance contract with such company that was entered into before the date of the filing of the petition and that is property of the estate.

(e) Subject to any applicable privilege, after notice and a hearing, the court may order an attorney, accountant, or other person that holds recorded information, including books, documents, records, and papers, relating to the debtor's property or financial affairs, to to [*sic*] turn over or disclose such recorded information to the trustee.

Bankruptcy Rule Reference: 7001

Legislative History

Subsection (a) of this section requires anyone holding property of the estate on the date of the filing of the petition, or property that the trustee may use, sell, or lease under section 363, to deliver it to the trustee. The subsection also requires an accounting. The holder of property of the estate is excused from the turnover requirement of this subsection if the property held is of inconsequential value to the estate. However, this provision must be read in conjunction with the remainder of the subsection, so that if the property is of inconsequential monetary value, yet has a significant use value for the estate, the holder of the property would not be excused from turnover.

[*House Report No. 95–595, 95th Cong., 1st Sess. 369 (1977); Senate Report No. 95–989, 95th Cong., 2d Sess. 84 (1978).*]

Section 542(a) of the House amendment modifies similar provisions contained in the House bill and the Senate amendment treating with turnover of property to the estate. The section makes clear that any entity, other than a custodian, is required to deliver property of the estate to the trustee or debtor in possession whenever such property is acquired by the entity during the case, if the trustee or debtor in possession may use, sell, or lease the property under section 363, or if the debtor may exempt the property under section 522, unless the property is of inconsequential value or benefit to the estate. This section is not intended to require an entity to deliver property to the trustee if such entity has obtained an order of the court authorizing the entity to retain possession, custody, or control of the property.

[*124 Cong. Rec. H 11,096–7 (Sept. 28, 1978); S 17,413 (Oct. 6, 1978).*]

Subsection (b) requires [an entity that owes] money to the debtor as of the date of the petition, or that holds money payable on demand or payable on order, to pay the money to the order of the trustee. An exception is made to the extent that the entity has a valid right of setoff, as recognized by section 553.

Subsection (c) provides an exception to subsections (a) and (b). It protects an entity that has neither actual notice nor actual knowledge of the case and that transfers, in good faith, property that is deliverable or payable to the trustee to someone other than to the estate or on order of the estate. This subsection codifies the result of Bank of Marin v. England, 385 U.S. 99 (1966), but does not go so far as to permit bank setoff in violation of the automatic stay, proposed 11 U.S.C. § 362(a)(7), even if the bank offsetting the debtor's balance has no knowledge of the case.

[*House Report No. 95–595, 95th Cong., 1st Sess. 369 (1977); Senate Report No. 95–989, 95th Cong., 2d Sess. 84 (1978).*]

The House amendment adopts section 542(c) of the House bill in preference to a similar provision contained in section 542(c) of the Senate amendment. Protection afforded by section 542(c) applies only to the transferor or payor and not to a transferee or payee receiving a transfer or payment, as the case may be. Such transferee or payee is treated under section 549 and section 550 of title 11.

[*124 Cong. Rec. H 11,097 (Sept. 28, 1978); S 17,413 (Oct. 6, 1978).*]

Subsection (d) protects life insurance companies that are required by contract to make automatic premium loans from property that might otherwise be property of the estate.

Subsection (e) requires an attorney, accountant, or other professional that holds recorded information relating to the debtor's property or financial affairs, to surrender it to the trustee. This duty is subject to any applicable claim of privilege, such as attorney-client privilege. It is a new provision that deprives accounts and attorneys of the leverage that they have today, under State law lien provisions, to receive payment in full ahead of other creditors when the information they hold is necessary to the administration of the estate.

[*House Report No. 95–595, 95th Cong., 1st Sess. 369–70 (1977); Senate Report No. 95–989, 95th Cong., 2d Sess. 84 (1978).*]

The extent to which the attorney client privilege is valid against the trustee is unclear under current law and is left to be determined by the courts on a case by case basis.

[*124 Cong. Rec. H 11,097 (Sept. 28, 1978); S 17,413 (Oct. 6, 1978).*]

Comment

Section 362(a)(7), referred to in section 542(c), makes the automatic stay applicable to a set-off of any debt owing to debtor that arose prior to the commencement of the case.

Section 542 refers to turnover by "any entity, other than a custodian." The next section, 543, refers to turnover by a "custodian." Section 101 defines entity as "any person, estate, trust or governmental unit." The 1986 Act [§ 201] amended § 101 of the Code to include the United States trustee within the definition of "entity." A custodian is defined in section 101 as a receiver or trustee appointed in a nonbankruptcy case or proceeding, an assignee for the benefit of creditors or a receiver or trustee appointed to enforce a lien.

Subsection (c) codifies Bank of Marin v. England, 385 U.S. 99 (1966), but only to a limited extent in that it does not permit a bank set-off in violation of the automatic stay of section 362(a)(7) even if the bank has no knowledge of the case.

Subsection (e) requires attorneys and accountants to surrender to the trustee recorded information relating to the debtor's property or financial affairs, subject to any applicable claim of privilege, *i.e.*, attorney-client privilege. The section clarifies an unclear area under prior law, depriving professionals of the leverage they had under State law lien provisions.

Under Bankruptcy Rule 7001(1), a proceeding to recover money or property of the estate is an adversary proceeding governed by the Part VII rules. A proceeding against a custodian (as that term is defined in section 101) under section 543, is, however, a contested matter governed by Rule 9014. *See* **Comment** to section 543.

Pursuant to 28 U.S.C. § 157(b)(2)(E), orders to turn over property of the estate are "core proceedings" over which the bankruptcy judges have jurisdiction to make and enter dispositive orders, judgments and decrees.

1984 Amendments: Section 542(e) was amended by the addition of the words "to turn over or."

Case Annotations

Section 542(e) was not intended to limit the trustee's ability to obtain debtor-corporate information within the corporation's attorney-client privilege; nor was it intended, as the legislative history of section 542(e) makes clear, to be used to create an attorney-client privilege assertable on behalf of the debtor against the trustee. Commodity Futures Trading Commission v. Weintraub, 471 U.S. 343, 105 S. Ct. 1986, 85 L. Ed. 2d 372, 12 C.B.C.2d 651 (1985).

Section 542 does not require that a debtor have a possessory interest in property in order for the Internal Revenue Service to be compelled to turn over property, seized pursuant to a tax lien, to a chapter 11 reorganization debtor; in effect, section 542(a) grants the estate a possessory interest and the IRS' right of possession is replaced, under the Code, by the right to adequate protection of its secured interest; to find otherwise would be to negate Congress' intent that the chapter 11 estate include property wherever located, essential to the reorganization effort. United States v. Whiting Pools, Inc., 462 U.S. 198, 103 S. Ct. 2309, 76 L. Ed. 2d 515, 8 C.B.C.2d 710 (1983).

A turnover order is appropriate when there is evidence that a debtor fraudulently attempted to hide or dispose of assets even if the trustee is unable to specifically identify each piece of the estate property which is converted from one form to another. Evans v. Robbins, 897 F.2d 966, 22 C.B.C.2d 1140 (8th Cir. 1989).

A debtor's unused overpayment to a creditor is not property of the estate for purposes of turnover, but rather is a debt of the creditor to the debtor, and therefore can be used as the creditor's debt in determining whether mutuality exists under the provisions of section 553. Braniff Airways, Inc. v. Exxon Co., U.S.A., 814 F.2d 1030, 16 C.B.C.2d 1447 (5th Cir. 1987).

The trustee assumes the right to assert or waive the attorney-client privilege of a chapter 11 corporate debtor when there are no longer officers or a board of directors for the corporation in order to turn over legal documents to an interested third party. Weissman v. Hassett (*In re* O.P.M. Leasing Services, Inc.), 670 F.2d 383, 5 C.B.C.2d 1252 (2d Cir. 1982).

A determination of (1) whether a party has a secured interest, and (2) whether that secured interest can be adequately protected if demanded by the creditor is a condition precedent to an order for turnover. World Communications, Inc. v. Direct Mktg. Guar. Trust (*In re* World Communications, Inc.), 17 C.B.C.2d 223 (D. Utah 1987).

When a prepetition levy by the IRS on a debtor's bank account results in the distribution of cash to the IRS postpetition, the cash is subject to turnover under section 542(a) pursuant to the Supreme Court decision in *Whiting Pools,* but the IRS is entitled to adequate protection under section 363(e). *In re* Metro Press, Inc., 26 C.B.C.2d 1634 (B. Ct., D. Mass. 1992).

An action for turnover is a core proceeding since it is a substantive right created under federal bankruptcy law, and can only be brought by a trustee or a debtor under section 542. In order to prevail on a turnover motion, a trustee must prove: 1) the possession, custody or control of the property by an entity; 2) that the trustee can utilize the property in accordance with section 363; and 3) that the property's value or benefit to the estate is more than inconsequential. *In re* Matheney, 26 C.B.C.2d 1768 (B. Ct., S.D. Ohio 1992).

Although prepetition estimated tax payments made by the debtor to the IRS are unquestionably in possession of an entity other than the debtor for purposes of section 542, they are not property of the estate under that section since the debtor retains only a contingent reversionary interest in the funds with the result that such transfer is not voidable under section 542. *In re* Halle, 25 C.B.C.2d 1113 (B. Ct., D. Colo. 1991).

A promissory note pledged to and in the possession of a creditor prior to a default by the debtor is property of the estate subject to the turnover provisions of section 542(a). *In re* Leeling, 25 C.B.C.2d 262 (B. Ct., D. Colo. 1991).

In determining the value to place on an attorney's retaining lien, the court is to examine the circumstances of each case, *i.e.,* when the lawsuit to which the lien relates results in an award to the debtor's estate, it is appropriate to permit the professional to share in the reward, but when there is no benefit to the estate, the retaining lien must give way to competing concerns and interests. *In re* Olmsted Utility, Inc., 25 C.B.C.2d 128 (B. Ct., N.D. Ohio 1991).

An escrow fund is property of the debtor's estate if: 1) the debtors made the deposit into the escrow account; and 2) all the default conditions of the escrow agreement had not occurred prepetition because the debtors have retained legal and possibly some equitable title in the fund. An escrow fund, although property of the estate, will not be turned over to the estate if the sellers have a security interest in the fund, established when the deposit acted as security for the debtor-buyer's performance, for which performance the debtor failed to offer adequate protection. *In re* Shapiro, 24 C.B.C.2d 1590 (B. Ct, E.D. Pa. 1991).

While section 542(b) states that a creditor with a right to setoff need not turn over funds automatically or upon demand by a trustee, it does not authorize a creditor which believes it has a right to setoff to take unilateral affirmative action to prevent the debtor from using those funds nor does the section conflict with section 363(a)(3). *In re* First Connecticut Small Business Investment Co., 23 C.B.C.2d 928 (B. Ct., D. Conn. 1990).

Federal bankruptcy policy in furtherance of prompt estate administration must prevail over a state common law retaining lien and accordingly, a trustee in bankruptcy cannot be denied access to files or records held by a debtor's former attorney pertaining to the administration of the estate regardless of any retaining lien the attorney may have against the debtor. *In re* Jarax International, Inc., 18 C.B.C.2d 193 (B. Ct., S.D. Fla. 1987).

References

4 *Collier on Bankruptcy* ch. 542 (Matthew Bender 15th ed.).

2 *Collier Bankruptcy Manual* ch. 542 (Matthew Bender 3d ed.).

3 *Collier Bankruptcy Practice Guide* ch. 62 (Matthew Bender).

Bankruptcy Jurisdiction: Turnover Requirements in Internal Revenue Service Pre-Petition Levies, 1984 Ann. Surv. Am. L. 599.

Comment, *The Legal Standard for a § 542(a) Turnover,* 1983 Ann. Surv. Bankr. L. 265.

Landley, *United States v. Whiting Pools, 674 F.2d 144 (2d Cir. 1982): An Analysis of a Debtor's Right to Turnover Order Against the IRS,* 57 Am. Bankr. L.J. 141 (1983).

Malpass, *A Bankruptcy Debtor's Right to Turnover of Property Held by Creditors: A Perspective on Section 542 and 543 of the Bankruptcy Code,* 85 Com. L.J. 242 (1983).

Sauder, *Bankruptcy and Turnover Proceedings Against the I.R.S.: A Path Toward Reorganization and Rehabilitation Fraught with Pitfalls,* 4 Whittier L. Rev. 87 (1982).

The Outer Limits of Section 542 of the Bankruptcy Code, 7 Cardozo L. Rev. 935 (1986).

SECTION 543 (11 U.S.C. § 543)

§ 543. Turnover of property by a custodian.

(a) A custodian with knowledge of the commencement of a case under this title concerning the debtor may not make any disbursement from, or take any action in the administration of, property of the debtor, proceeds, product, offspring, rents, or profits of such property, or property of the estate, in the possession, custody, or control of such custodian, except such action as is necessary to preserve such property.

(b) A custodian shall—

(1) deliver to the trustee any property of the debtor held by or transferred to such custodian, or proceeds, product, offspring, rents, or profits of such property, that is in such custodian's possession, custody, or control on the date that such custodian acquires knowledge of the commencement of the case; and

(2) file an accounting of any property of the debtor, or proceeds, product, offspring, rents, or profits of such property that, at any time, came into the possession, custody, or control of such custodian.

(c) The court, after notice and a hearing, shall—

(1) protect all entities to which a custodian has become obligated with respect to such property or proceeds, product, offspring, rents, or profits of such property;

(2) provide for the payment of reasonable compensation for services rendered and costs and expenses incurred by such custodian; and

(3) surcharge such custodian, other than an assignee for the benefit of the debtor's creditors that was appointed or took possession more than 120 days before the date of the filing of the petition, for any improper or excessive disbursement, other than a disbursement that has been made in

accordance with applicable law or that has been approved, after notice and a hearing, by a court of competent jurisdiction before the commencement of the case under this title.

(d) After notice and hearing, the bankruptcy court—

(1) may excuse compliance with subsection (a), (b), or (c) of this section, if the interests of creditors and, if the debtor is not insolvent, of equity security holders would be better served by permitting a custodian to continue in possession, custody, or control of such property, and

(2) shall excuse compliance with subsections (a) and (b)(1) of this section if the custodian is an assignee for the benefit of the debtor's creditors that was appointed or took possession more than 120 days before the date of the filing of the petition, unless compliance with such subsections is necessary to prevent fraud or injustice.

Bankruptcy Rule Reference: 6002

Legislative History

This section requires a custodian appointed before the bankruptcy case to deliver to the trustee and to account for property that has come into his possession, custody, or control as a custodian. "Property of the debtor" in section (a) includes property that was property of the debtor at the time the custodian took the property, but the title to which passed to the custodian. The section requires the court to protect any obligations incurred by the custodian, provide for the payment of reasonable compensation for services rendered and costs and expenses incurred by the custodian, and to surcharge the custodian for any improper or excessive disbursement, unless it has been approved by a court of competent jurisdiction. Subsection (d) reinforces the general abstention policy in section 305 by permitting the bankruptcy court to authorize the custodianship to proceed notwithstanding this section.

[*House Report No. 95–595, 95th Cong., 1st Sess. 370 (1977); Senate Report No. 95–989, 95th Cong., 2d Sess. 84 (1978).*]

Section 543(a) is a modification of similar provisions contained in the House bill and the Senate amendment. The provision clarifies that a custodian may always act as is necessary to preserve property of the debtor. Section 543(c)(3) excepts from surcharge a custodian that is an assignee for the benefit of creditors, who was appointed or took possession before 120 days before the date of the filing of the petition whichever is later. The provision also prevents a custodian from being surcharged in connection with payments made in accordance with applicable law.

[*124 Cong. Rec. H 11,097 (Sept. 28, 1978); S 17,413 (Oct. 6, 1978).*]

Comment

Section 543 refers to a "custodian" while the preceding section, 542, refers to "an entity other than a custodian." "Custodian" is defined in section 101 as a receiver or trustee in a nonbankruptcy case or proceeding, an assignee for the benefit of creditors or a trustee, receiver or agent under applicable law or under a contract, that is appointed or authorized to take charge of debtor's property to enforce a lien thereon, or for the purpose of general administration of such property for the debtor's creditors.

In accordance with the general abstention policy set forth in section 305(a), the court may authorize the custodianship to proceed, after notice and hearing, if the interest of creditors (and equity security holders, if the debtor is not insolvent) would be better served thereby.

Bankruptcy Rule 6002(a) provides that any custodian (as defined in section 101) who is required by section 543 to deliver property in the custodian's possession or control to the trustee, must promptly file and transmit to the United States trustee a report and account respecting the property and the administration thereof.

Subdivision (b) of the rule provides that on the filing and transmittal of the report and account and after examination into the custodian's administration, the court shall determine, after hearing on notice, the propriety of such administration including the reasonableness of all disbursements.

[The examination may be intiated on motion of the custodian for approval of his account, on motion (or objecting to the account) by the trustee or other party in interest, or at the courts' own initiative.]

Pursuant to 28 U.S.C. § 157(b)(2)(E), orders to turn over property of the estate are "core proceedings" over which the bankruptcy judges have jurisdiction to make and enter dispositive orders, judgments and decrees.

1984 Amendments: Section 543 was amended by adding a new paragraph (2) to subsection (d) excusing an assignee for the benefit of creditors who was appointed or who took possession more than 120 days prior to the filing of the petition, from compliance with subsections (a) and (b)(1), unless fraud or injustice would result.

Subsections (a), (b) and (c) were amended to make clear that property of the debtor includes "product, offspring, rents or profits" of such property.

Case Annotations

Although section 543 generally requires a custodian of the debtor's property to turn over such property to the trustee, the Internal Revenue

Service (IRS) is not required to turn over property it had seized pursuant to a tax claim prior to the time the debtor's bankruptcy petition was filed, because in such a situation the IRS is not a custodian. United States v. Whiting Pools, Inc., 462 U.S. 198, 103 S. Ct. 2309, 76 L. Ed. 2d 515, 8 C.B.C.2d 710 (1983).

Under state abandoned property laws, the states are custodians of the creditors and are, therefore, not custodians of the debtors within the meaning of the Code. *In re* Federated Department Stores, Inc., 26 C.B.C.2d 8291 (B. Ct., S.D. Ohio 1992).

A custodian that has been excused from turnover will not be allowed to recover attorney's fees under section 543(c)(2) unless prior court approval of employment of professional persons has been obtained. *In re* Posadas Associates, 24 C.B.C.2d 1801 (B. Ct., D.N.M. 1991).

References

4 *Collier on Bankruptcy* ch. 543 (Matthew Bender 15th ed.).

2 *Collier Bankruptcy Manual* ch. 543 (Matthew Bender 3d ed.).

3 *Collier Bankruptcy Practice Guide* ch. 62 (Matthew Bender).

SECTION 544 (11 U.S.C. § 544)

§ 544. Trustee as lien creditor and as successor to certain creditors and purchasers.

(a) The trustee shall have, as of the commencement of the case, and without regard to any knowledge of the trustee or of any creditor, the rights and powers of, or may avoid any transfer of property of the debtor or any obligation incurred by the debtor that is voidable by—

(1) a creditor that extends credit to the debtor at the time of the commencement of the case, and that obtains, at such time and with respect to such credit, a judicial lien on all property on which a creditor on a simple contract could have obtained such a judicial lien, whether or not such a creditor exists;

(2) a creditor that extends credit to the debtor at the time of the commencement of the case, and obtains, at such time and with respect to such credit, an execution against the debtor that is returned unsatisfied at such time, whether or not such a creditor exists; or

(3) a bona fide purchaser of real property, other than fixtures, from the debtor, against whom applicable law permits such transfer to be perfected, that obtains the status of a bona fide purchaser and has perfected such transfer at the time of the commencement of the case, whether or not such a purchaser exists.

(b) The trustee may avoid any transfer of an interest of the debtor in property or any obligation incurred by the debtor that is voidable under applicable law by a creditor holding an unsecured claim that is allowable under section 502 of this title or that is not allowable only under section 502(e) of this title.

Legislative History

Subsection (a) is the "strong arm clause" of current law, now found in Bankruptcy Act section 70c. It gives the trustee the rights of a creditor on a simple contract with a judicial lien on the property of the debtor as of the date of the petition; of a creditor with a writ of execution against the property of the debtor unsatisfied as of the date of the petition; and a bona fide purchaser of the real property of the debtor as of the date of the petition. "Simple contract" as used here is derived from Bankruptcy Act section 60a(4). The third status, that of a bona fide purchaser of real property, is new.

[*House Report No. 95–595, 95th Cong., 1st Sess. 370 (1977); Senate Report No. 95–989, 95th Cong., 2d Sess. 85 (1978).*]

Section 544(a)(3) modifies similar provisions contained in the House bill and Senate amendment so as not to require a creditor to perform the impossible, in order to perfect his interest. Both the lien creditor test in section 544(a)(1), and the bona fide purchaser test in section 544(a)(3) should not require a transferee to perfect a transfer against an entity with respect which applicable law does not permit perfection. The avoiding powers under section 544(a)(1), (2), and (3) are new. In particular, section 544(a)(1) overrules Pacific Finance Corp. v. Edwards, 309 F.2d 224 (9th Cir. 1962), and *In re* Federals, Inc., 553 F.2d 509 (6th Cir. 1977), insofar as those cases held that the trustee did not have the status of a creditor who extended credit immediately prior to the commencement of the case.

[*124 Cong. Rec. H 11,097 (Sept. 28, 1978); S 17,413 (Oct. 6, 1978).*]

Subsection (b) is derived from current section 70e. It gives the trustee the rights of actual unsecured creditors under applicable law to void transfers. It follows Moore v. Bay, 284 U.S. 4 (1931), and overrules those cases that hold section 70e gives the trustee the rights of secured creditors.

[*House Report No. 95–595, 95th Cong., 1st Sess. 370 (1977); Senate Report No. 95–989, 95th Cong., 2d Sess, 85 (1978).*]

The House amendment deletes section 544(c) of the House bill.

[*124 Cong. Rec. H 11,097 (Sept. 28, 1978); S 17,413 (Oct. 6, 1978).*]

Comment

Section 544(a) is derived from section 70c of the former Bankruptcy Act, the so-called "strong arm clause."

Section 544(b) is derived from Section 70e of the former Bankruptcy Act.

The Congressional Report indicates that the rule of Moore v. Bay, 284 U.S. 4 (1931) is continued, and that cases that hold that Section 70e of the former Bankruptcy Act gave the trustee the rights of secured creditors are overruled.

1984 Amendments: The amendments made technical changes in section 544(a) (1), (2) and (3). Subsection (a)(3) was amended to exclude "fixtures" from the operation of the subsection, and gives the trustee the status of a bona fide purchaser who perfected the transfer at the time the case was commenced.

Case Annotations

A trustee who has been put on constructive or inquiry notice does not become a hypothetical *bona fide* purchaser under section 544(a)(3) and therefore may not avoid an unrecorded transfer of land. *In re* Professional Investment Properties of America, 955 F.2d 673, 26 C.B.C.2d 528 (9th Cir. 1992).

Under the power granted by section 544(a)(1), an Oklahoma trustee in bankruptcy can file an action to enforce a judgment creditor's rights granted by Okla. Stat. Ann. tit. 12, § 841. Zilkha Energy Co. v. Leighton, 920 F.2d 1520, 24 C.B.C.2d 299 (10th Cir. 1990).

A trustee may avoid a transfer under a state intentional fraud statute if the transfer was made in furtherance of a proven Ponzi scheme to transferees who evidenced awareness of the existence of the scheme. *In re* Agricultural Research & Technology Group, Inc., 916 F.2d 528, 23 C.B.C.2d 1517 (9th Cir. 1990).

Under Vermont law, a bankruptcy trustee acting as a bona fide purchaser is deemed to lack notice of a properly recorded but otherwise defective mortgage so that he has priority over assignee of the original mortgage. Stern v. Continental Assurance Co. (*In re* Ryan), 851 F.2d 502, 19 C.B.C.2d 490 (1st Cir. 1988).

Actual or constructive notice of a prior unrecorded transfer removes a subsequent purchaser from the protection of applicable recording statute and clear and open possession of real estate constitutes constructive notice prepetition to the rights of a bona fide purchaser. Probasco v. Eads (*In re* Probasco), 839 F.2d 1352, 18 C.B.C.2d 523 (9th Cir. 1988).

In construing a bankruptcy court's jurisdiction, the crucial consideration is whether the action is or is not a core proceeding; an action by a trustee pursuant to section 544(b) to set aside a fraudulent conveyance under state law is core, and may properly be heard by the bankruptcy court. Duck v. Munn (*In re* Mankin), 823 F.2d 1296, 17 C.B.C.2d 469 (9th Cir. 1987), *cert. denied,* 485 U.S. 1006, 108 S. Ct. 148, 99 L. Ed. 2d 698 (1988).

The trustee has the power to set aside or avoid transfers of or encumbrances on the debtor's property in order to marshal or increase the potential assets of the estate, but the trustee does not have the additional power to bring general causes of action on behalf of the estate's creditors. Mixon v. Anderson (*In re* Ozark Restaurant Equip. Co.), 816 F.2d 1222, 16 C.B.C.2d 1148 (8th Cir.), *cert. denied,* 484 U.S. 925, 108 S. Ct. 147, 98 L. Ed. 2d 102 (1987).

A debtor in possession's knowledge of an improperly recorded mortgage does not prevent it from asserting the strong arm clause of section 544(a)(3) because Congress intended that actual knowledge of the debtor be irrelevant under that section. Sandy Ridge Oil Co., Inc. v. Centerre Bank National Association (*In re* Sandy Ridge Oil Co., Inc.), 807 F.2d 1332, 15 C.B.C.2d 1234 (7th Cir. 1986).

In Alabama, a trustee or debtor in possession is charged with constructive notice of a mutual mistake in the recording of a mortgage, and the law permits a reformation of the mortgage. The strong arm clause does not set aside the trustee's duty, as a hypothetical judicial lien creditor, to examine the record and thereby discover the mutual mistake. United States of America v. Smith (*In re* Hagendorfer), 803 F.2d 647, 15 C.B.C.2d 1243 (11th Cir. 1986).

In Virginia, a defective filing of a financing statement is effective against a debtor if the debtor has actual knowledge of the contents of the defective financing statement. The debtor has actual knowledge when he is a signatory to the statement. Dominion Bank of Cumberlands, N.A. v. Nuckolls, 780 F.2d 408, 13 C.B.C.2d 1249 (4th Cir. 1985).

A trustee or debtor in possession has the power as a judicial lien creditor to block a junior secured creditor's request for a marshaling order. Owens-Corning Fiberglas Corp. v. Center Wholesale, Inc. (*In re* Center Wholesale, Inc.), 759 F.2d 1440, 12 C.B.C.2d 1107 (9th Cir. 1985).

The filing of a petition under the Code by a defendant in a suit to void a fraudulent conveyance does not completely extinguish the right to recover property that the defendant may have fraudulently conveyed; a bankruptcy simply causes that right to vest in the trustee and places the future of the fraudulent conveyance lawsuit within the control of the bankruptcy court. Carlton v. BAWW, Inc., 751 F.2d 781, 12 C.B.C.2d 457 (5th Cir. 1985).

A County Commissioner of Finance, who receives title to surplus funds from a prebankruptcy foreclosure sale of a chapter 7 debtor's real property for the purpose of distribution to creditors, is a custodian and the passing of title to him will not prevent the funds from becoming part of the bankruptcy estate. Brown v. Dellinger (*In re* Brown), 734 F.2d 119, 10 C.B.C.2d 1405 (2d Cir. 1984).

A debtor in possession, having the rights of a hypothetical lien creditor, can require an allocation of proceeds from a sale of real property in the estate only to the extent that a course of conduct has not already established payment allocation. Moxley v. Moxley (*In re* Comer), 716 F.2d 168, 9 C.B.C.2d 359 (3d Cir. 1983).

The right to invalidate a non-complying bulk transfer under section 544(b) may be asserted in tandem with the right to enforce a note given in consideration for the transfer. Verco Indus. v. Spartan Plastics (*In re* Verco Indus.), 704 F.2d 1134, 8 C.B.C.2d 554 (9th Cir. 1983).

The language in section 544(a)(3) permitting the trustee to avoid transfers "without regard to any knowledge" was intended by Congress to mean only that the trustee's status as a hypothetical lien creditor should not be affected by any knowledge which he, personally, or any creditors might have of the debtor's previous transactions with various claimants, and should not be construed to permit the trustee to nullify state law protections for a holder of equitable interests in the debtor's real property. McCannon v. Marston (*In re* Hotel Assoc., Inc.), 679 F.2d 13, 6 C.B.C.2d 875 (3d Cir. 1982).

A chapter 13 trustee has standing to file a motion to avoid a non-possessory, nonpurchase money security interest because there is no language in the Code that prohibits a trustee from doing so, and because 544(a)(1) permits a trustee to assert his or her strong-arm powers against certain liens. *In re* Kennedy, 26 C.B.C.2d 1717 (B. Ct., N.D. Miss. 1992).

When a debtor's right to commissions under an agency contract is subject to satisfaction of his or her liabilities to the company, the trustee's rights are likewise limited despite the trustee's powers under section 544 of the Code. *In re* Tomer, 25 C.B.C.2d 22 (B. Ct., S.D. Ill. 1991).

In order to collaterally attack a tax deed transfer, a trustee must demonstrate fraud; mere failure to notify an interested party of the tax deed proceedings is an insufficient basis for such an attack and, therefore, for avoidance pursuant to section 544(b) of the Code. *In re* McKeever, 25 C.B.C.2d 1260 (B. Ct., N.D. Ill. 1991).

The preference rules of section 547, including the ten day grace period for perfection of transfer under 547(e)(2)(A), are not applicable to transfers of property interests otherwise avoidable under section 544(a). *In re* Planned Protective Services, Inc., 25 C.B.C.2d 441 (B. Ct., C.D. Cal. 1991).

An action brought pursuant to Bankruptcy Rule 7001(9) for a declaratory judgment that a clause in an agreement which limits a debtor's interest in its property upon the filing of a bankruptcy petition is unenforceable, is not a disguised avoidance action under section 544 and, therefore, is not subject to the two year statute of limitations imposed by section 546(a). Matter of Railway Reorganization Estate, Inc., 25 C.B.C.2d 1383 (B. Ct., D. Del. 1991).

A trustee, acting solely as a fiduciary on behalf of a debtor's creditors, does not have standing to assert an alter-ego claim that would pierce the corporate veil of a nondebtor corporation. However, the trustee is entitled to "reverse pierce" the corporate veil of a nondebtor corporation of which an individual debtor is a principal if (i) the piercing remedy is available under state law, (ii) equity principles and public interest dictate that the piercing be done, and (iii) the debtor's estate consists of an equity interest in that corporation. *In re* Schuster, 25 C.B.C.2d 1611 (B. Ct., D. Minn. 1991).

The "strong-arm clause" of section 544(a) does not apply to a nondebtor spouse's beneficial interest in an award from a concurrent state divorce action. *In re* Perry, 25 C.B.C.2d 1020 (B. Ct., D. Mass. 1991).

Although a creditor may have subrogation rights over a secured creditor and other unsecured creditors at the time a petition is filed, the unique position created by the strong arm clause of section 544 places a trustee before any unsecured creditors and a creditor's theory of equitable subrogation must fail. *In re* IDK Logging, Inc., 24 C.B.C.2d 157 (B. Ct., E.D. Wash. 1990).

Under New York law, when an alleged security interest in real property is contained in an unrecorded assignment agreement, the trustee with the status of a *bona fide* purchaser may avoid that alleged security interest. *In re* Lasercad Reprographics, 22 C.B.C.2d 305 (B. Ct., S.D.N.Y. 1989).

References

4 *Collier on Bankruptcy* ch. 544 (Matthew Bender 15th ed.).

2 *Collier Bankruptcy Manual* ch. 544 (Matthew Bender 3d ed.).

3 *Collier Bankruptcy Practice Guide* ch. 63 (Matthew Bender).

Alden, Gross and Borowitz, *Real Property Foreclosure as a Fraudulent Coveyance: Proposals for Solving the Durrett Problem*, 38 Bus. Law. 1605 (1983).

Cohen, *"Value" Judgments: Accounts Receivable Financing and Voidable Preferences Under the New Bankruptcy Code*, 66 Minn. L. Rev. 639 (1982).

Peeples, *Five into Thirteen: Lien Avoidance in Chapter 13*, 61 N.C.L. Rev. 849 (1983).

Weintraub and Resnick, *The Trustee's Avoiding Powers and Conditional Attachment Liens—Can Two People Wear the Same Shoes?*, 22 U.C.C.L.J. 88 (1989).

SECTION 545 (11 U.S.C. § 545)

§ 545. Statutory liens. The trustee may avoid the fixing of a statutory lien on property of the debtor to the extent that such lien—

(1) first becomes effective against the debtor—

(A) when a case under this title concerning the debtor is commenced;

(B) when an insolvency proceeding other than under this title concerning the debtor is commenced;

(C) when a custodian is appointed or authorized to take possession;

(D) when the debtor becomes insolvent;

(E) when the debtor's financial condition fails to meet a specified standard; or

(F) at the time of an execution against property of the debtor levied at the instance of an entity other than the holder of such statutory lien;

(2) is not perfected or enforceable at the time of the commencement of the case against a bona fide purchaser that purchases such property at the time of the commencement of the case, whether or not such a purchaser exists;

(3) is for rent; or

(4) is a lien of distress for rent.

Legislative History

This section permits the trustee to avoid the fixing of certain statutory liens. It is derived from sections 67b and 67c of present law. Liens that first become effective on the bankruptcy or insolvency of the debtor are voidable by the trustee. Liens that are not perfected or enforceable on the date of the petition against a bona fide purchaser are voidable. If a transferee is able to perfect under section 546(a) and that perfection relates back to an earlier date, then in spite of the filing of the bankruptcy petition, the trustee would not be able to defeat the lien, because the lien would be perfected and enforceable against a bona fide purchaser that purchased the property on the date of the filing of the petition. Finally, a lien for rent or of distress for rent is voidable, whether the lien is a statutory or common law lien of distress for rent. *See* 11 U.S.C. § 101(37) [*Ed. Note:* With the 1986 Amendments, the definition of "statutory lien" is set forth at section 101(47).]; Bankruptcy Act section 67c(1)(C). The trustee may avoid a transfer of a lien under this section even if the lien has been enforced by sale before the commencement of the case. To that extent, Bankruptcy Act section 67c(5) is not followed, and cases implying a similar restriction with respect to Bankruptcy Act section 67a are overruled.

[*House Report No. 95–595, 95th Cong., 1st Sess. 371 (1977).*]

This section permits the trustee to avoid the fixing of certain statutory liens. It is derived from subsections 67b and 67c of present law. Liens that first become effective on the bankruptcy or insolvency of the debtor are voidable by the trustee. Liens that are not perfected or enforceable on the date of the petition against a bona fide purchaser are voidable. If a transferee is able to perfect under section 546(a) and that perfection relates back to an earlier date, then in spite of the filing of the bankruptcy petition, the trustee would not be able to defeat the lien, because the lien would be perfected and enforceable against a bona fide purchaser that purchased the property on the date of the filing of the petition. Finally, a lien for rent or of distress for rent is voidable, whether the lien is a statutory lien or a common law lien of distress for rent. *See* proposed 11 U.S.C. § 101 (37) [*Ed. Note:* With the 1986 Amendments, the definition of "statutory lien" is set forth at section 101(47).]; Bankruptcy Act section 67(c)(1)(C). The trustee may avoid a lien under this section even if the lien has been enforced by sale before the commencement of the case. To that extent, Bankruptcy Act § 67c(5) is not followed. [Subsection (b) limits the trustee's power to avoid tax liens under Federal, state, or local law. For example, under section 6323 of the Internal Revenue Code. Once public notice of a tax lien has been filed, the Government is generally entitled to priority over subsequent lienholders. However, certain purchasers who acquire an interest in certain specific kinds of personal property will take free of an existing filed tax lien attaching to such property. Among the specific kinds of personal property which a purchaser can acquire free of an existing tax lien (unless the buyer knows of the existence of the lien) are stocks and securities, motor vehicles, inventory, and certain household goods. Under the present Bankruptcy Act (section 67(c)(1)), the trustee may be viewed as a bona fide purchaser, so that he can take over any such designated items free of tax liens even if the tax authority has perfected its lien. However, the reasons for enabling a bona fide purchaser to take these kinds of assets free of an unfiled tax lien, that is, to encourage free movement of these assets in general commerce, do not apply to a trustee in a title 11 case, who is not in the same position as an ordinary bona fide purchaser as to such property. The bill accordingly adds a new subsection (b) to section 545 providing, in effect, that a trustee in bankruptcy does not have the right under this section to take otherwise specially treated items of personal property free of a tax lien filed before the filing of the petition.]

[*Senate Report No. 95–989, 95th Cong., 2d Sess. 85–86 (1978).*]

[*Ed. Note:* Bracketed portion of the Senate Report relates to a subsection which was deleted from the final bill as being unnecessary, as is explained in the excerpts from the Congressional Record which appear *infra.*]

Section 545 of the House amendment modifies similar provisions contained in the House bill and Senate amendment to make clear that a statutory lien may be avoided under section 545 only to the extent the lien violates the perfection standards of section 545. Thus a Federal tax lien is invalid under section 545(2) with respect to property specified in sections 6323 (b) and (c) of the Internal Revenue Code of 1954. As a result of this modification, section 545(b) of the Senate amendment is deleted as unnecessary.

[*124 Cong. Rec. H 11,097 (Sept. 28, 1978); S 17,413 (Oct. 6, 1978).*]

Section 545. Statutory liens: The House amendment retains the provision of section 545(2) of the House bill giving the trustee in a bankruptcy case the same power which a bona fide purchaser has to take over certain kinds of personal property despite the existence of a tax lien covering that property. The amendment thus retains present law, and deletes section 545(b) of the Senate amendment which would have no longer allowed the trustee to step into the shoes of a bona fide purchaser for this purpose.

[*124 Cong. Rec. H 11,114 (Sept. 28, 1978); S 17,431 (Oct. 6, 1978).*]

Comment

Section 545 is derived from Section 67b and c of the former Bankruptcy Act.

Under section 545 the trustee may avoid a lien even though the lien has been enforced by sale prior to commencement of the case and to that extent section 67c(5) of the Act is not followed. Section 545 should be read together with section 724 which, for purposes of a liquidation case, continues the subordination of tax liens to certain priorities listed in section 507, as did section 67c(3).

1984 Amendments: The amendments made technical changes in section 545(1)(C) and (2).

Case Annotations

An account receivable that arises from a lease agreement does not constitute "money" within the meaning of 26 U.S.C. § 6323(h)(4); therefore, a federal tax lien attaching to the receivable within ninety days prepetition is not subject to avoidance under section 545(2). Christison v. United States, 960 F.2d 613, 26 C.B.C.2d 1732 (7th Cir. 1992).

When state law provides that the right to collect real estate taxes is automatically perfected when a creditor's interest in the property arises, a trustee may not avoid the state's tax lien on the property. Maryland Nat'l Bank v. Mayor and City Council of Baltimore (In the Matter of Maryland Glass Corp.), 723 F.2d 1138, 9 C.B.C.2d 1114 (4th Cir. 1983).

A state law vendor's privilege which operates as a non-consensual lien on the value of movable property for which payment has not been received is a valid statutory lien, and as such constitutes a secured claim exempt from the avoiding powers of a trustee or debtor in possession under section 545, and therefore is entitled to adequate protection. Borg-Warner Acceptance Corp. v. Tape City, U.S.A., Inc. (In the Matter of Tape City, U.S.A., Inc.), 677 F.2d 401, 7 C.B.C.2d 121 (5th Cir. 1982).

A debtor in possession, having the same rights as a trustee in a chapter 11 case, is given the status of a hypothetical bona fide purchaser under section 545(2) and, as such, has the power to avoid federal tax liens on properties enumerated under section 6323(b) of the Internal Revenue Code. *In re* Sierer, 24 C.B.C.2d 1039 (B. Ct., N.D. Fla. 1990).

A county's emergency medical services lien that was nonexistent at the date the debtor filed the petition is inchoate and dischargeable under section 545(2). *In re* Claussen, 24 C.B.C.2d 398 (B. Ct., D.S.D. 1990).

Section 545(1)(D) provides that a lien is voidable and requires action by the trustee before the loss of its viability so that if a debtor does not attempt to avoid such lien, it remains valid. *In re* Jones & Lamson Machine Co., Inc., 24 C.B.C.2d 12 (B. Ct., D. Conn. 1990).

A trustee may avoid a transfer of funds upon which the IRS has levied within the ninety day preference period and which were not being properly held by the debtor in trust for the payment of withholding taxes overdue. *In re* Hearing of Illinois, Inc., 22 C.B.C.2d 1199 (B. Ct., C.D. Ill. 1990).

A debtor lacks standing to invoke the avoiding powers under section 542 as to a properly perfected tax lien. *In re* Williams, 22 C.B.C.2d 1429 (B. Ct., W.D.N.C. 1989).

A lien obtained by seizure pursuant to a writ of execution is a judgment lien, and thus is not subject to avoidance under section 545. In the Matter of Veteran Plate Glass Co., 16 C.B.C.2d 574 (B. Ct., N.D. Ohio 1987).

Avoidance of a landlord's lien and its preservation by a trustee operate to sever the lien from the administrative rent claim; therefore, when a landlord buys the right to assert its lien, its receipt from the trustee in settlement of its administrative expense claim need not be deducted from its claim for rent secured by the landlord's lien. C & C Co. v. Seattle First National Bank (*In re* Coal-X Ltd. "76"), 14 C.B.C.2d 1325 (B. Ct., D. Utah 1986).

References

4 *Collier on Bankruptcy* ch. 545 (Matthew Bender 15th ed.).

2 *Collier Bankruptcy Manual* ch. 545 (Matthew Bender 3d ed.).

3 *Collier Bankruptcy Practice Guide* ch. 63 (Matthew Bender).

Bankruptcy Preference Actions: New Value and Inchoate Statutory Liens — An Examination of the Definitive Case Law Split, 21 U. Wst L.A. L. Rev. 89 (1990).

Epling, *Environmental Liens in Bankruptcy,* 44 Bus. Law. 85 (1988).

Hertz, *Loretto Winery: Undermining Section 545,* 18 Cal. Bankr. J. 205 (1990).

Hyman, *The Impact of Bankruptcy on Contractors' Liens: Potential Rewards for Those Who Hurry,* 16 Vt. B.J. & L. Dig. 8 (1990).

Schneyer, *Statutory Liens Under the New Bankruptcy Code—Some Problems Remain,* 55 Am. Bankr. L.J. 1 (1981).

SECTION 546 (11 U.S.C § 546)

§ 546.   Limitations on avoiding powers.

(a) An action or proceeding under section 544, 545, 547, 548, or 553 of this title may not be commenced after the earlier of—

> (1) two years after the appointment of a trustee under section 702, 1104, 1163, 1302, or 1202 of this title; or

> (2) the time the case is closed or dismissed.

(b) The rights and powers of a trustee under sections 544, 545, and 549 of this title are subject to any generally applicable law that permits perfection of an interest in property to be effective against an entity that acquires rights in such property before the date of such perfection. If such law requires seizure of such property or commencement of an action to accomplish such perfection, and such property has not been seized or such action has not been commenced before the date of the filing of the petition, such interest in such property shall be perfected by notice within the time fixed by such law for such seizure or commencement.

(c) Except as provided in subsection (d) of this section, the rights and powers of a trustee under sections 544(a), 545, 547, and 549 of this title are subject to any statutory or common-law right of a seller of goods that has sold goods to the debtor, in the ordinary course of such seller's business, to reclaim such goods if the debtor has received such goods while insolvent, but—

> (1) such a seller may not reclaim any such goods unless such seller demands in writing reclamation of such goods before ten days after receipt of such goods by the debtor; and

> (2) the court may deny reclamation to a seller with such a right of reclamation that has made such a demand only if the court—

(A) grants the claim of such a seller priority as a claim of a kind specified in section 503(b) of this title; or

(B) secures such claim by a lien.

(d) In the case of a seller who is a producer of grain sold to a grain storage facility, owned or operated by the debtor, in the ordinary course of such seller's business (as such terms are defined in section 557 of this title) or in the case of a United States fisherman who has caught fish sold to a fish processing facility owned or operated by the debtor in the ordinary course of such fisherman's business, the rights and powers of the trustee under sections 544(a), 545, 547, and 549 of this title are subject to any statutory or common law right of such producer or fisherman to reclaim such grain or fish if the debtor has received such grain or fish while insolvent, but—

(1) such producer or fisherman may not reclaim any grain or fish unless such producer or fisherman demands, in writing, reclamation of such grain or fish before ten days after receipt thereof by the debtor; and

(2) the court may deny reclamation to such a producer or fisherman with a right of reclamation that has made such a demand only if the court secures such claim by a lien.

(e) Notwithstanding sections 544, 545, 547, 548(a)(2), and 548(b) of this title, the trustee may not avoid a transfer that is a margin payment, as defined in section 101(34), 741(5), or 761(15) of this title, or settlement payment, as defined in section 101(35) or 741(8) of this title, made by or to a commodity broker, forward contract merchant, stockbroker, financial institution, or securities clearing agency, that is made before the commencement of the case, except under section 548(a)(1) of this title.

(f) Notwithstanding sections 544, 545, 547, 548(a)(2), and 548(b) of this title, the trustee may not avoid a transfer that is a margin payment, as defined in section 741(5) or 761(15) of this title, or settlement payment, as defined in section 741(8) of this title, made by or to a repo participant, in connection with a repurchase agreement and that is made before the commencement of the case, except under section 548(a)(1) of this title.

(g) Notwithstanding sections 544, 545, 547, 548(a)(2) and 548(b) of this title, the trustee may not avoid a transfer under a swap agreement, made by or to a swap participant, in connection with a swap agreement and that is made before the commencement of the case, except under section 548(a)(1) of this title.

Legislative History

Subsection (c) adds a statute of limitations to the use by the trustee of the avoiding powers. [*Ed. Note:* As enacted, this is provided for in subsection (a).] The limitation is two years after his appointment, or the time the case is closed or dismissed, whichever occurs later. [*Ed. Note:* This sentence is correct only as to the Senate bill, after which subsection (c) was amended.]

[*Senate Report No. 95–989, 95th Cong., 2d Sess. 87 (1978).*]

The trustee's rights and powers under certain of the avoiding powers are limited by section 546. First, if an interest holder against whom the trustee would have rights still has, under applicable non-bankruptcy law, and as of the date of the petition, the opportunity to perfect his lien against an intervening interest holder, then he may perfect his interest against the trustee. If applicable law requires seizure for perfection, then perfection is by notice to the trustee instead. The rights granted to a creditor under this subsection prevail over the trustee only if the transferee has perfected the transfer in accordance with applicable law, and that perfection relates back to a date that is before the commencement of the case.

The phrase "generally applicable law" relates to those provisions of applicable law that apply both in bankruptcy cases and outside of bankruptcy cases. For example, many State laws, under the Uniform Commercial Code, permit perfection of a purchase-money security interest to relate back to defeat an earlier perfected non-purchase-money security interest if the former was perfected within ten days. U.C.C. section 9-301(2). Such perfection would then be able to defeat a hypothetical judicial lien creditor on the date of the filing of the petition. The purpose of the subsection is to protect, in spite of the surprise intervention of bankruptcy petition, those whom State law protects by allowing them to perfect their lines or interests as of an effective date that is earlier than the date of perfection. It is not designed to give the States an opportunity to enact disguised priorities in the form of liens that apply only in bankruptcy cases.

Subsection (b) specifies that the trustee's rights and powers under the strong arm clause, the successor to creditors provision, the preference section, and the postpetition transaction section are all subject to any statutory or common-law right of a seller, in the ordinary course of business, of goods to the debtor to reclaim the goods if the debtor received the goods on credit while insolvent. The seller must demand reclamation within ten days after receipt of the goods by the debtor. As under nonbankruptcy law, the right is subject to any superior rights of other creditors. The purpose of the provision is to recognize, in part, the validity of section 2-702 of the Uniform Commercial Code, which has generated much litigation, confusion, and divergent decisions in different circuits. The right is subject, however, to the power of the court to deny reclamation and protect the seller by granting him a priority as an administrative expense for his claim arising out of the sale of the goods. [*Ed. Note:* The provision discussed in this paragraph of the report relates to subsection (c) as enacted.]

[*House Report No. 95–595, 95th Cong., 1st Sess. 371–372 (1977); Senate Report No. 95–989, 95th Cong., 2d Sess. 86–87 (1978).*]

Section 546(a) of the House amendment is derived from section 546(c) of the Senate amendment. Section 546(c) of the House amendment is derived from section 546(b) of the Senate amendment. It applies to receipt of goods on credit as well as by cash sales. The section clarifies that a demand for reclamation must be made in writing anytime before 10 days after receipt of the goods by the debtor. The section also permits the court to grant the reclaiming creditor a lien or an administrative expense in lieu of turning over the property.

[*124 Cong. Rec. H 11,097 (Sept. 28, 1978); S 17,413–17,414 (Oct. 6, 1978).*]

Section 4 [of Public Law 97–222] creates a new Section 546(d). This amendment is made simultaneously with the repeal of section 764(c) of title 11. Section 546(d), together with provisions of section 548, prohibits a trustee from avoiding a transfer that is a margin payment to a commodity broker or forward contract merchant or is a settlement payment made by a clearing organization, except where the transfer was made with intent to hinder, delay, or defraud other creditors and was not taken in good faith.

The new section 546(d) [*Ed. Note:* Subsection (d) was redesignated as subsection (e) by Pub. L. No. 98–353.] reiterates the provisions of current section 764(c). The new section also encompasses both stockbrokers and securities clearing agencies.

[*House Report No. 97–420, 97th Cong., 2d Sess. 3 (1982).*]

Simultaneously with the repeal of section 764(c) of title 11, section 4 of H.R. 4935 [Public Law 97–222] would create a new section 546(d). Section 764(c), together with provisions of section 548, generally prohibits a trustee from avoiding a transfer that is a margin payment or settlement payment, except where the transfer, first, was made with an actual intent to hinder, delay, or defraud other creditors and second, was not taken in good faith by the recipient. These provisions apply to margin or settlement payments made by any debtor, whether or not such debtor is a commodity broker. The new section 546(d) [*Ed. Note:* Section 546(d) was redesignated as section 546(e) by Pub. L. No. 98–353.] reiterates and clarifies the provisions of current section 764(c). The new section also encompasses both stockbrokers and securities clearing agencies. Thus, it has been placed among the general provisions in chapter 5 of title 11, rather than among the commodity broker provisions of subchapter IV of chapter 7.

[*128 Cong. Rec. S8, 132–33 (July 13, 1982).*]

Comment

Section 546(c) is derived from section 2–702 of the Uniform Commercial Code. It resolves conflicting decisions as to whether or not section 2–702 is valid if bankruptcy intervenes. Under subsection (c) reclamation is permitted if a demand is made in writing before ten days after the receipt of the goods by an insolvent debtor. But the court may deny such right of reclamation if (A) the seller is granted a priority as an administration expense, or (B) the claim is secured by a lien. This provision protects a debtor seeking to reorganize by giving the debtor use of the goods and at the same time protects the seller by giving the seller either an administration claim priority or a lien.

Section 764(c), which barred a trustee from avoiding a transfer that is a margin payment or a deposit with a commodity broker or forward contract merchant or is a settlement payment by a clearing organization, has been deleted, and with modifications transferred to a new section 546(e). Because the new section encompasses both stockbrokers and security clearing agencies, it properly belongs in chapter 5 rather than in subchapter IV of chapter 7 which deals with commodity brokers.

1984 Amendments: The amendments to section 546(d), together with the amendments to section 507, and the addition of new section 557, are intended to afford relief to farmers and fishermen when storage facilities holding their product file petitions under the Code.

A new subsection (f) bars a trustee from avoiding margin payments (as defined in section 741(5) or 761(15)), or a settlement payment (defined in section 741(8)) made by or to a repo participant, in connection with a repurchase agreement made before commencement of the case, unless made with actual intent to hinder, delay or defraud as provided in section 548(a).

Changes of a technical nature were made in subsections (a)(1), (b), (c), (c)(2), (c)(2)(A) and (d).

1986 Amendments: The 1986 Amendments brought chapter 12 cases within the scope of § 546(a)(1).

1990 Amendments: Pub. L. No. 101–311 amended subsection (e) to include references to section 101(34) [defining "margin payment"] and section 101(35) [defining "settlement payment"].

Subsection (g) was added to bar a trustee from avoiding a transfer made under a swap agreement, made by or to a swap participant, in connection with a swap agreement and that is made before the commencement of the case, except under section 548(a)(1).

Case Annotations

A creditor's right to reclaim goods is not extinguished because a debtor has secured creditors with perfected security interests in the goods sought to be reclaimed. However, if the debtor's confirmed plan provides that the secured creditors' claims are to be satisfied out of the goods to be reclaimed, a subordinate right of reclamation may become valueless. *In re* Pester Refining Co., 964 F.2d 842, 26 C.B.C.2d 1663 (8th Cir. 1992).

Section 546(e) protects a settlement payment by a stockbroker, financial institution, or clearing agency to equity security holders. The term "settlement payment" should not be interpreted so narrowly as to exclude the exchange of stock for consideration in a leveraged buyout. *In re* Kaiser Steel Corp., 953 F.2d 1230, 26 C.B.C.2d 442 (10th Cir. 1991).

Section 546(a)(1) applies to actions filed by a debtor in possession in the stead of a trustee, and the applicable period of limitations begins to run from the date of the filing of a petition for reorganization under chapter 11. Zilkha Energy Co. v. Leighton, 920 F.2d 1520, 24 C.B.C.2d 299 (10th Cir. 1990).

To qualify for the stockbroker defense of section 546(e), a claimant must show: 1) that the payments he received were settlement payments; and 2) that the payments were made by a stockbroker. In the Matter of Wider, 907 F.2d 570, 24 C.B.C.2d 104 (5th Cir. 1990).

In order for a taxing authority to possess a postpetition lien subject to perfection under section 546(b), and therefore an exception to the automatic stay of section 362(a)(4), it is necessary that the authority possess a prepetition interest in property that is more than its so-called "ever-present interest" in all property within its jurisdiction. Makaroff v. The City of Lockport, 916 F.2d 890, 23 C.B.C.2d 1566 (3d Cir. 1990).

The delivery of securities from a "hold-in-custody" repo agreement is part of the settlement process and, therefore, is a settlement payment pursuant to 11 U.S.C. § 546(f). In the Matter of Bevill, Bresler & Schulman Asset Management Corp., 878 F.2d 742, 21 C.B.C.2d 298 (3d Cir. 1989).

When the failure to issue a written order appointing a trustee initially is only an oversight, the oral appointment has given effective actual notice of the appointment and *nunc pro tunc* language of the later written order makes clear the effective date without undue prejudice. Accordingly, the statute of limitations begins to run from the date of the oral appointment order. MortgageAmerica Corp. v. American Fed. Sav. and Loan (*In re* MortgageAmerica Corp.), 831 F.2d 97, 17 C.B.C.2d 941 (5th Cir. 1987).

If an action to avoid preferential and fraudulent transfers is not commenced within two years after the appointment of the trustee, a bankruptcy court has no jurisdiction to hear the action and Bankruptcy Rule 9006 has no effect on this result. Martin v. First Nat'l Bank of Louisville (*In re* Butcher), 829 F.2d 596, 17 C.B.C.2d 1204 (6th Cir. 1987), *cert. denied,* 484 U.S. 1078, 108 S. Ct. 1058, 98 L. Ed. 2d 1020 (1988).

If a seller is prevented under the U.C.C. from reclaiming grain-goods themselves, it is also prevented from "reclaiming" the proceeds of the resale of the grain. Collingwood Grain, Inc. v. Coast Trading Co. (*In re* Coast Trading Co.), 744 F.2d 686, 11 C.B.C.2d 790 (9th Cir. 1984).

Under section 546(c), notice of demand for reclamation will be deemed to have taken place upon dispatch of notice from the seller. A written demand for reclamation must explicitly state that that right is being asserted and a state court lawsuit does not satisfy the demand requirement of section 546(c). Montello Oil Corp. v. Marin Motor Oil, Inc., (In the Matter of Marin Motor Oil, Inc.), 740 F.2d 220, 11 C.B.C.2d 28 (3d Cir. 1984).

When a mortgagee has an interest under a collateral assignment of rents and does not petition the bankruptcy court for appointment of receiver pursuant to state law to collect rents for its benefit, for an order of sequestration or any other order to impound rents, or fails to take any other affirmative action, that mortgagee has failed to perfect its interest under state law. Wolters Village Ltd. v. Village Properties, Ltd. (In the Matter of Village Properties, Ltd.), 723 F.2d 441, 10 C.B.C.2d 224 (5th Cir.), *cert. denied,* 466 U.S. 974, 104 S. Ct. 2350, 80 L. Ed. 2d 823 (1984).

When state law provides that the right to collect real estate taxes is automatically perfected when a creditor's interest in the property arises, a trustee may not avoid the state's tax lien on the property. Maryland Nat'l Bank v. Mayor and City Council of Baltimore (In the Matter of Maryland Glass Corp.), 723 F.2d 1138, 9 C.B.C.2d 1114 (4th Cir. 1983).

A trustee's avoidance and strong arm powers are subject to the statutory or common law rights of a seller of goods to reclaim goods received by a debtor while insolvent, if the seller demands in writing reclamation before ten days after the receipt of such goods by the debtor. *In re* MGS Marketing, 22 C.B.C.2d 1258 (9th Cir., B.A.P., 1990).

The section 546(a)(1) time limitation is applicable only when a trustee has been appointed. A debtor's preference action, initiated four years after its chapter 11 case was commenced, is timely filed if no trustee has been appointed and the case has not been closed or dismissed. *In re* Pullman Construction Industries, Inc., 25 C.B.C.2d 1177 (B. Ct., N.D. Ill. 1991).

A clause in an agreement which substantively limits a debtor's interest in its property upon the filing of a bankruptcy petition but which, in form, purports to relate back to the execution of the agreement, is outside the scope of the limited exception to postpetition lien perfection provided by section 546(b). An action brought pursuant to Bankruptcy Rule 7001(9) for a declaratory judgment on the enforceability of such a clause is not a disguised avoidance action under section 544 and, therefore, is not subject to the two year statute of limitations imposed by section 546(a). Matter of Railway Reorganization Estate, Inc., 25 C.B.C.2d 1383 (B. Ct., D. Del. 1991).

In a case converted from chapter 11, the time that the debtor in possession is in place does not count against the subsequently appointed chapter 7 trustee. *In re* Bingham Systems, Inc., 26 C.B.C.2d 1570 (B. Ct., N.D. Miss. 1991).

Section 546(a) unambiguously sets the bar date for debtors in possession as the time a case is closed or dismissed, rather than as two years from the date the trustee is appointed. *In re* Century Brass Products, Inc., 24 C.B.C.2d 2109 (B. Ct., D. Conn. 1991).

Section 546(a)(1) applies to a debtor in possession when a trustee has not been appointed, and the time limitation delineated in the section begins to run from the date the debtor in possession files its chapter 11 petition. In the Matter of Coastal Group, Inc., 24 C.B.C.2d 1651 (B. Ct., D. Del. 1991).

The value of a reclamation creditor's lien is presumed to be equal to the invoice price for those goods received in the previous ten days and still in the debtor's possession at the time of the written reclamation demand. *In re* Performance Papers, Inc., 24 C.B.C.2d 576 (B. Ct., D. Mich. 1990).

Under section 546(a), for the purposes of filing an avoidance action, the statute of limitations begins to run when the trustee has been appointed a permanent trustee pursuant to section 702. *In re* Hansen, 23 C.B.C.2d 1339 (B. Ct., N.D. Ohio 1990).

In determining whether an interest in future rents is perfected, the proper focus of section 546(b) is whether the entity invoking the section defeats the rights of a hypothetical entity that earlier acquired rights in the property in dispute. *In re* 1301 Connecticut Avenue Associates, 23 C.B.C.2d 1096 (B. Ct., D.D.C. 1990).

When a state law does not contemplate the possibility of a chapter 11 reorganization, regarding the statute of limitations on fraudulent conveyances, then the state statute of limitations may be tolled by the application of section 546(a) to actions brought under section 544. *In re* Mahoney, Trocki & Assoc., Inc., 22 C.B.C.2d 1167 (B. Ct., C.D. Cal. 1990).

References

4 *Collier on Bankruptcy* ch. 546 (Matthew Bender 15th ed.).

2 *Collier Bankruptcy Manual* ch. 546 (Matthew Bender 3d ed.).

3 *Collier Bankruptcy Practice Guide* ch. 63 (Matthew Bender).

Cohen, McLaughlin and Zaretsky, *Seller's Reclamation of Goods in Bankruptcy,* 2 Commercial Law Report 40 (Matthew Bender).

Colletti, *A Title Insurer Looks at the Avoidance Provisions of the Bankruptcy Reform Act of 1978,* 15 Real Prop. Prob. & Tr. J. 588 (1980).

Comment, *In re Kaiser Steel Corporation: Does Section 546(e) of the Bankruptcy Code Apply to a Fraudulent Conveyance Made in the Form of an LBO Payment?,* 19 Fordham Urb. L.J. 87 (1991).

Goldberg, *Reclamation Under Section 546(c) of the Bankruptcy Code,* 3 Com. L. Bull. 25 (1988).

Newmeyer, *Section 546(b) Lienholders — After Bankruptcy Strikes: Strait Is the Gate and Narrow Is the Way That Leads to Perfection,* 91 Okla. B.J. 1435 (1990).

Note, *Repurchase Agreements and the Bankruptcy Code: The Need for Legislative Action,* 52 Fordham L. Rev. 828 (1984).

Note, *Seller's Right of Reclamation: Section 546(c),* 5 Bankr. Dev. J. 175 (1987).

Note, *The Road to Repose: Limitations on Avoidance Actions in Chapter 11 via 11 U.S.C. § 546(a)(2),* 13 Cardozo L.R. 2097 (1991–92).

Nutovic, *The Bankruptcy Preference Laws: Interpreting Code Sections 547(c)(2), 550(a)(1) and 546(a)(1),* 41 Bus. Law. 175 (1985).

Von Mehren, *Section 546(c): An Enigmatic Resolution to the Problem of the Status in Bankruptcy of the Reclaiming Seller,* 60 Am. Bankr. L.J. 227 (1986).

SECTION 547 (11 U.S.C. § 547)

§ 547.   Preferences.

(a) In this section—

(1) "inventory" means personal property leased or furnished, held for sale or lease, or to be furnished under a contract for service, raw materials, work in process, or materials used or consumed in a business, including farm products such as crops or livestock, held for sale or lease;

(2) "new value" means money or money's worth in goods, services, or new credit, or release by a transferee of property previously transferred to such transferee in a transaction that is neither void nor voidable by the debtor or the trustee under any applicable law, including proceeds of such property, but does not include an obligation substituted for an existing obligation;

(3) "receivable" means right to payment, whether or not such right has been earned by performance; and

(4) a debt for a tax is incurred on the day when such tax is last payable without penalty, including any extension.

(b) Except as provided in subsection (c) of this section, the trustee may avoid any transfer of an interest of the debtor in property—

(1) to or for the benefit of a creditor;

(2) for or on account of an antecedent debt owed by the debtor before such transfer was made;

(3) made while the debtor was insolvent;

(4) made—

(A) on or within 90 days before the date of the filing of the petition; or

(B) between 90 days and one year before the date of the filing of the petition, if such creditor at the time of such transfer was an insider; and

(5) that enables such creditor to receive more than such creditor would receive if—

(A) the case were a case under chapter 7 of this title;

(B) the transfer had not been made; and

(C) such creditor received payment of such debt to the extent provided by the provisions of this title.

(c) The trustee may not avoid under this section a transfer—

(1) to the extent that such transfer was—

(A) intended by the debtor and the creditor to or for whose benefit such transfer was made to be a contemporaneous exchange for new value given to the debtor; and

(B) in fact a substantially contemporaneous exchange;

(2) to the extent that such transfer was—

(A) in payment of a debt incurred by the debtor in the ordinary course of business or financial affairs of the debtor and the transferee;

(B) made in the ordinary course of business or financial affairs of the debtor and the transferee; and

(C) made according to ordinary business terms;

(3) that creates a security interest in property acquired by the debtor—

(A) to the extent such security interest secures new value that was—

(i) given at or after the signing of a security agreement that contains a description of such property as collateral;

(ii) given by or on behalf of the secured party under such agreement;

(iii) given to enable the debtor to acquire such property; and

(iv) in fact used by the debtor to acquire such property; and

(B) that is perfected on or before 10 days after the debtor receives possession of such property;

(4) to or for the benefit of a creditor, to the extent that, after such transfer, such creditor gave new value to or for the benefit of the debtor—

(A) not secured by an otherwise unavoidable security interest; and

(B) on account of which new value the debtor did not make an otherwise unavoidable transfer to or for the benefit of such creditor;

(5) that creates a perfected security interest in inventory or a receivable or the proceeds of either, except to the extent that the aggregate of all such transfers to the transferee caused a reduction, as of the date of the filing of the petition and to the prejudice of other creditors holding unsecured claims, of any amount by which the debt secured by such security interest exceeded the value of all security interests for such debt on the later of—

(A)(i) with respect to a transfer to which subsection (b)(4)(A) of this section applies, 90 days before the date of the filing of the petition; or

(ii) with respect to a transfer to which subsection (b)(4)(B) of this section applies, one year before the date of the filing of the petition; or

(B) the date on which new value was first given under the security agreement creating such security interest;

(6) that is the fixing of a statutory lien that is not avoidable under section 545 of this title; or

(7) if, in a case filed by an individual debtor whose debts are primarily consumer debts, the aggregate value of all property that constitutes or is affected by such transfer is less than $600.

(d) The trustee may avoid a transfer of an interest in property of the debtor transferred to or for the benefit of a surety to secure reimbursement of such a surety that furnished a bond or other obligation to dissolve a judicial lien that would have been avoidable by the trustee under subsection (b) of this section. The liability of such surety under such bond or obligation shall be discharged to the extent of the value of such property recovered by the trustee or the amount paid to the trustee.

(e)(1) For the purposes of this section—

(A) a transfer of real property other than fixtures, but including the interest of a seller or purchaser under a contract for the sale of real property, is perfected when a bona fide purchaser of such property from the debtor against whom applicable law permits such transfer to be perfected cannot acquire an interst that is superior to the interest of the transferee; and

(B) a transfer of a fixture or property other than real property is perfected when a creditor on a simple contract cannot acquire a judicial lien that is superior to the interest of the transferee.

(2) For the purposes of this section, except as provided in paragraph (3) of this subsection, a transfer is made—

(A) at the time such transfer takes effect between the transferor and the transferee, if such transfer is perfected at, or within 10 days after, such time;

(B) at the time such transfer is perfected, if such transfer is perfected after such 10 days; or

(C) immediately before the date of the filing of the petition, if such transfer is not perfected at the later of—

(i) the commencement of the case; or

(ii) 10 days after such transfer takes effect between the transferor and the transferee.

(3) For the purposes of this section, a transfer is not made until the debtor has acquired rights in the property transferred.

(f) For the purposes of this section, the debtor is presumed to have been insolvent on and during the 90 days immediately preceding the date of the filing of the petition.

(g) For the purposes of this section, the trustee has the burden of proving the avoidability of a transfer under subsection (b) of this section, and the creditor or party in interest against whom recovery or avoidance is sought has the burden of proving the nonavoidability of a transfer under subsection (c) of this section.

Bankruptcy Rule Reference: 6010

Legislative History

This section is a substantial modification of present law. It modernizes the preference provisions and brings them more into conformity with commercial practice and the Uniform Commercial Code.

Subsection (a) contains three definitions. Inventory, new value, and receivable are defined in their ordinary senses, but are defined to avoid any confusion or uncertainty surrounding the terms.

Subsection (b) is the operative provision of the section. It authorizes the trustee to avoid a transfer if five conditions are met. These are the five elements of a preference action. First, the transfer must be to or for the benefit of a creditor. Second, the transfer must be for or on account of an antecedent debt owed by the debtor before the transfer was made. Third, the transfer must have been made when the debtor was insolvent. Fourth, the transfer must have been made during the 90 days immediately preceding the commencement of the case. If the transfer was to an insider, the trustee may avoid the transfer if it was during the period that begins one year before the filing of the petition and ends 90 days before the filing, if the insider to whom the transfer was made had reasonable cause to believe the debtor was insolvent at the time the transfer was made.

Finally, the transfer must enable the creditor to or for whose benefit it was made to receive a greater percentage of his claim than he would receive under the distributive provisions of the bankruptcy code. Specifically, the creditor must receive more than he would if the case were a liquidation case, if the transfer had not been made, and if the creditor received payment of the debt to the extent provided by the provisions of the Code.

The phrasing of the final element changes the application of the greater percentage test from that employed under current law. Under this language, the court must focus on the relative distribution between classes as well as the amount that will be received by the members of the class of which the preferee is a member. The language also requires the court to focus on the allowability of the claim for which the preference was made. If the claim would have been entirely disallowed, for example, then the test of paragraph (5) will be met, because the creditor would have received nothing under the distributive provisions of the bankruptcy code.

[*House Report No. 95–595, 95th Cong., 1st Sess. 372 (1977); Senate Report No. 95–989, 95th Cong., 2d Sess. 87 (1978).*]

The trustee may avoid a transfer of a lien under this section even if the lien has been enforced by sale before the commencement of the case. To that extent, Bankruptcy Act section 67c(5) is not followed, and cases implying a similar restriction with respect to Bankruptcy Act section 67a are overruled.

This provision will not apply to permit the trustee to recover estimated tax payments by a debtor, because no tax is due when the payements are made. Therefore, the tax on account of which the payment is made is not an antecedent debt. A payment of withholding taxes constitutes a payment of money held in trust under Internal Revenue Code section 7501(a), and thus will not be a preference because the beneficiary of the trust, the taxing authority, is in a separate class with respect to those taxes, if they have been properly held for payment, as they will have been if the debtor is able to make the payments.

[*House Report No. 95–595, 95th Cong., 1st Sess. 372–373 (1977).*]

The trustee may avoid a transfer of a lien under this section even if the lien has been enforced by sale before the commencement of the case.

Subsection (b)(2) of this section in effect exempts from the preference rules payments by the debtor of tax liabilities, regardless of their priority status.

[*Senate Report No. 95–989, 95th Cong., 2d Sess. 87 (1978).*]

Section 547(b)(2) of the House amendment adopts a provision contained in the House bill and rejects an alternative contained in the Senate amendment relating to the avoidance of preferential transfer that is payment of a tax claim owing to a governmental unit. As provided, section 106(c) of the House amendment overrules contrary language in the House report with the result that the Government is subject to avoidance of preferential transfers.

[*124 Cong. Rec. H 11,097 (Sept. 28, 1978); S 17,414 (Oct. 6, 1978).*]

Section 547. Preferences: The House amendment deletes from the category of transfers on account of antecedent debts which may be avoided under the preference rules, section 547(b)(2), the exception in the Senate amendment for taxes owed to governmental authorities. However, for purposes of the "ordinary course" exception to the preference rules contained in section 547(c)(2), the House amendment specifies that the 45-day period referred to in second 547(c)(2)(B) is to begin running in the case of taxes from the last due date, including extensions, of the return with respect to which the tax payment was made.

[*124 Cong. Rec. H 11,114 (Sept. 28, 1978); S 17,431 (Oct. 6, 1978).*]

Subsection (c) contains exceptions to the trustee's avoiding power. If a creditor can qualify under any one of the exceptions, then he is protected to that extent. If he can qualify under several, he is protected by each to the extent he can qualify under each.

The first exception is for a transfer that was intended by all parties to be a comtemporaneous exchange for new value, and was in fact substantially contemporaneous. Normally, a check is a credit transaction. However, for the purposes of this paragraph, a transfer involving a check is considered to be "intended to be contemporaneous," and if the check is presented for payment in the normal course of affairs, which the Uniform Commercial Code specifies as 30 days, U.C.C. section 3-503(2)(a), that will amount to a transfer that is "in fact substantially contemporaneous."

The second exception protects ordinary course of business (or financial affairs, where a business is not involved) transfers. [*Ed. Note:* Subparagraphs (C) and (D) of section 547(c)(2) were redesignated subparagraphs (B) and (C) by Pub. L. No. 98–353.] For the case of a consumer, the paragraph uses the phrase "financial affairs" to include such nonbusiness activities as payment of monthly utility bills. If the debt on account of which the transfer was made was incurred in the ordinary course of both the debtor and the transferee, if the transfer was made not later than 45 days after the debt was incurred, [*Ed. Note:* Pub. L. No. 98–353 deleted the 45-day time limitation.] if the transfer itself was made in the ordinary course of both the debtor and the transferee, and if the transfer was made according to ordinary business terms, then the transfer is protected. The purpose of this exception is to leave undisturbed normal financial relations, because it does not detract from the general policy of the preference section to discourage unusual action by either the debtor or his creditors during the debtor's slide into bankruptcy.

In the tax context, this exception will mean that a payment of taxes when they are due, either originally or under an extension, or within 45 days thereafter, will not constitute a voidable preference. However, if a payment is made later than the last day on which the tax may be paid without penalty, then the payment may constitute a preference, if the other elements of a preference are present. In that case, the tax debt would be an antecedent debt and would not fall under this exception. However, the trustee would be able to recover only if the taxing authority did not have sovereign immunity or had waived it under proposed 11 U.S.C. § 106.

[*House Report No. 95–595, 95th Cong., 1st Sess. 373–374 (1977).*]

Subsection (c) contains exceptions to the trustee's avoiding power. If a creditor can qualify under any one of the exceptions, then he is protected to that extent. If he can qualify under several, he is protected by each to the extent that he can qualify under each.

The first exception is for a transfer that was intended by all parties to be a contemporaneous exchange for new value, and was in fact substantially contemporaneous. Normally, a check is a credit transaction. However, for the purposes of this paragraph, a transfer involving a check is considered to be "intended to be contemporaneous," and if the check is presented for payment in the normal course of affairs, which the Uniform Commercial Code specifies as 30 days, U.C.C. section 3-503(2)(a), that will amount to a transfer that is "in fact substantially contemporaneous."

The second exception protects transfers in the ordinary course of business (or of financial affairs, where a business is not involved). For the case of a consumer, the paragraph uses the phrase "financial affairs" to include such nonbusiness activities as payment of monthly utility bills. If the debt on account of which the transfer was made was incurred in the ordinary course of both the debtor and the transferee, if the transfer was made not later than 45 days after the debt was incurred, [*Ed. Note:* Pub. L. No. 98–353 deleted the 45-day time limitation.] if the transfer itself was made in the ordinary course of both the debtor and the transferee, and if the transfer was made according to ordinary business terms, then the transfer is protected. The purpose of this exception is to leave undisturbed normal financial relations, because it does not detract from the general policy of the preference section to discourage unusual action by either the debtor or his creditors during the debtor's slide into bankruptcy.

[*Senate Report No. 95–989, 95th Cong., 2d Sess. 88 (1978).*]

No limitation is provided for payments to commodity brokers as in section 766 of the Senate amendment other than the amendment to section 548 of title II. Section 547(c)(2) protects most payments.

* * *

Contrary to language contained in the House report, payment of a debt by means of a check is equivalent to a cash payment, unless the check is dishonored. Payment is considered to be made when the check is delivered for purposes of sections 547(c)(1) and (2).

[*124 Cong. Rec. H 11,1097 (Sept. 28, 1978); S 17,414 (Oct. 6, 1978).*]

The third exception is for enabling loans in connection with which the debtor acquires the property that the loan enabled him to purchase after the loan is actually made.

The fourth exception codifies the net result rule in section 60c of current law. If the creditor and the debtor have more than one exchange during the 90-day period, the exchanges are netted out according to the formula in paragraph (4). Any new value that the creditor advances must be unsecured in order for it to qualify under this exception.

Paragraph (5) codifies the improvement in position test, and thereby overrules such cases as DuBay v. Williams, 417 F.2d 1277 (9th Cir. 1966), and Grain Merchants of Indiana, Inc. v. Union Bank and Savings Co., 408 F.2d 209 (7th Cir. 1969). A creditor with a security interest in a floating mass, such as inventory or accounts receivable, is subject to preference attack to the extent he improves his position during the 90-day period before bankruptcy. The test is a two-point test, and requires determination of the secured creditor's position 90 days before the petition and on the date of the petition. If new value was first given after 90 days before the case, the date on which it was first given substitutes for the 90-day point.

[House Report No. 95–595, 95th Cong., 1st Sess. 373 (1977); Senate Report No. 95–989, 95th Cong., 2d Sess. 88 (1978).]

Paragraph (6) governs prepetition setoff. Setoff, even though preferential, is protected if it occurred more than five days before the case, unless it is a setoff under circumstances which would invalidate it under section 553. If the setoff occurred within the five-day period, then it is avoidable only if the trustee may use, sell, or lease the property so recovered.

Paragraph (7) excepts statutory liens validated under section 545 from preference attack. It also protects transfers in satisfaction of such liens, and the fixing of a lien under section 365(j), which protects a vendee whose contract to purchase real property from the debtor is rejected.

[House Report No. 95–595, 95th Cong., 1st Sess. 374 (1977).]

Paragraph (6) excepts statutory liens validated under section 545 from preference attack. It also protects transfers in satisfaction of such liens, and the fixing of a lien under section 365(j), which protects a vendee whose contract to purchase real property from the debtor is rejected.

[Senate Report No. 95–989, 95th Cong., 2d Sess. 88 (1978).]

Section 547(c)(6) of the House bill is deleted and is treated in a different fashion in section 563 of the House amendment.

Section 547(c)(6) represents a modification of a similar provision contained in the House bill and Senate amendment. The exception relating to satisfaction of a statutory lien is deleted. The exception for a lien created under title 11 is deleted since such a lien is a statutory lien that will not be avoidable in a subsequent bankruptcy.

[124 Cong. Rec. H 11,097 (Sept. 28, 1978); S 17,414 (Oct. 6, 1978).]

Subsection (d), derived from section 67a of the Bankruptcy Act, permits the trustee to avoid a transfer to reimburse a surety that posts a bond to dissolve a judicial lien that would have been avoidable under this section. The second sentence protects the surety from double liability.

[House Report No. 95–595, 95th Cong., 1st Sess. 374 (1977); Senate Report No. 95–989, 95th Cong., 2d Sess. 88–89 (1978).]

Subsection (e) determines when a transfer is made, for the purposes of the preference section. Paragraph (1) defines when a transfer is perfected. For real property, a transfer is perfected when it is valid against a bona fide purchaser. For personal property and fixtures, a transfer is perfected when it is valid against a creditor on a simple contract that obtains a judicial lien after the transfer is perfected. "Simple contract" as used here is derived from Bankruptcy Act section 60a(4). Paragraph (2) specifies that a transfer is made when it takes effect between the transferor and the transferee if it is perfected at or within 10 days after that time. Otherwise, it is made when the transfer is perfected. If it is not perfected before the commencement of the case, it is made immediately before the commencement of the case. Paragraph (3) specifies that a transfer is not made until the debtor has acquired rights in the property transferred. This provision, more than any other in the section, overrules *DuBay* and *Grain Merchants,* and in combination with subsection (b)(2), overrules *In re King-Porter Co.,* 446 F.2d 722 (5th Cir. 1971).

Subsection (e) is designed to reach the different results under the 1962 version of Article 9 of the U.C.C. and under the 1972 version because different actions are required under each version in order to make a security agreement effective between the parties.

[*House Report No. 95–595, 95th Cong., 1st Sess. 374–375 (1977); Senate Report No. 95–989, 95th Cong., 2d Sess. 89 (1978).*]

Section 547(e)(1)(B) is adopted from the House bill and Senate amendment without change. It is intended that the simple contract test used in this section will be applied as under section 544(a)(1) not to require a creditor to perfect against a creditor on a simple contract in the event applicable law makes such perfection impossible. For example, a purchaser from a debtor at an improperly noticed bulk sale may take subject to the rights of a creditor on a simple contract of the debtor for one year after the bulk sale. Since the purchaser cannot perfect against such a creditor on a simple contract, he should not be held responsible for failing to do the impossible. In the event the debtor goes into bankruptcy within a short time after the bulk sale, the trustee should not be able to use the avoiding powers under section 544(a)(1) or 547 merely because State law made some transfers of personal property subject to the rights of a creditor on a simple contract to acquire a judicial lien with no opportunity to perfect against such a creditor.

[*124 Cong. Rec. H 11,097 (Sept. 28, 1978); S 17,414 (Oct. 6, 1978).*]

Subsection (f) creates a presumption of insolvency for the 90 days preceding the bankruptcy case. The presumption is as defined in Rule 301 of the Federal Rules of Evidence, made applicable in bankruptcy cases by sections 253 and 254 [*Ed. Note:* Sections 251 and 252 as enacted.] of the bill. The presumption requires the party against whom the presumption exists to come forward with some evidence to rebut the presumption, but the burden of proof remains on the party in whose favor the presumption exists.

[*House Report No. 95–595, 95th Cong., 1st Sess. 375 (1977); Senate Report No. 95–989, 95th Cong., 2d Sess. 89 (1978).*]

Comment

The genesis of section 547 relating to preferences is Section 60 of the former Bankruptcy Act. In addition to clarifying some of the problems that arose under the Act, section 547 represents a substantial modification of former Section 60.

The four-month provision of Section 60a was changed to 90 days except that as to an "insider" (defined in section 101) the trustee may avoid a transfer that was made within one year before the filing of the petition. The requirement of Section 60b that the transferee have "reasonable cause to believe that the debtor is insolvent" was deleted.

Generally, the five elements of a preference as set forth in section 547(b) are similar to the elements of a preference under the Act. Although the third element under section 547(b) is insolvency when the transfer was made, section 547(f) creates a presumption of insolvency for the 90 days preceding the bankruptcy case. The presumption is as defined in Rule 301 in the Federal Rules of Evidence (made applicable to cases under title 11 Bankruptcy Rule 9017). This presumption requires the adverse party to come forward with some evidence to rebut the presumption. Nevertheless, the "burden of proof" remains with the party in whose favor the presumption exists.

Section 67a of the former Bankruptcy Act invalidating judicial liens obtained within four months preceding a petition while the debtor was insolvent was deleted by the Code. With the changes made in section 547, such a lien is, under the Code, voidable as a preference (reasonable cause to believe insolvency no longer being a necessary element).

Under section 522(f), the debtor may avoid the fixing of certain liens on an interest of the debtor in property to the extent that such lien impairs an exemption to which the debtor would have been entitled. Bankruptcy Rule 4003(d) provides that a proceeding by the debtor to avoid a lien or other transfer of property exempt under section 522(f) shall be by motion in accordance with Rule 9014.

Bankruptcy Rule 6010, amended in 1991, provides that if a lien voidable under section 547 has been dissolved by furnishing a bond or other obligation and the surety thereon has been indemnified by transfer of, or lien upon, nonexempt property of the debtor, the surety shall be joined as a defendant in any proceeding to avoid the lien or transfer. Such proceeding is an adversary proceeding governed by the Part VII rules. The 1991 Advisory Committee Note states that the deletion of the last two sentences from Bankruptcy Rule 6010 is intended to conform to section 550(a) of the Code, which provides that the trustee may recover the property transferred in a voidable transfer. The value of the property may be recovered in lieu of the property itself only if the court so orders.

1984 Amendments: Section 547 was amended by adding paragraph "(7)" to subsection (c), excepting from avoidance in the case of an individual with primarily consumer debts, a transfer of property aggregating less than $600.

An important change made in subsection (b)(4) deletes the requirement that an insider must have reasonable cause to believe that the
debtor was insolvent at the time of the transfer (*See* section 101 for the
definition of "insider.")

The amendments deleted subsection (c)(2)(B). As a result, payment
of a debt need not be within 45 days after the debt was incurred,
provided that the other statutory requirements are met.

Subsection (g) was added, prescribing the burden of proof to be borne
by the trustee and by the one against whom recovery or avoidance is
sought.

Technical changes were made in subsections (a)(2) and (4), (b),
(c)(1)(A), (c)(3)(B), (c)(5) and (d).

Pursuant to 28 U.S.C. § 157(b)(2)(F) and (K), proceedings to determine, avoid, or recover preferences, and determinations of the validity,
extent, or priority of liens, are "core proceedings" over which the
bankruptcy judges have authority to make and enter dispositive orders,
judgments and decrees.

1986 Amendments: The 1986 amendment to § 547 added the conjunction "and" at the end of subsection (b)(4)(B), to make clear that all of
the five elements of subsection (b) are required to establish a voidable
preference.

Case Annotations

For the purposes of payment by ordinary check, a "transfer," as
defined by section 101, occurs on the date of honor in the determination
of whether such transfer falls within the 90 day preference period under
section 547(b). A determination that a transfer occurs on the date of
honor is consistent with section 547(e)(2)(A), which provides that a
transfer occurs "at the time the transfer takes effect between the
transferor and the transferee . . ." when, until the moment of honor,
a debtor retains full control over disposition of an account, the account
remains subject to a variety of actions (such as a lien attachment by
third parties) and the debtor retains the ability to stop payment on a
check until the very last moment. Barnhill v. Johnson, 503 U.S. —, 112
S. Ct. 1386, 118 L. Ed. 2d 39, 26 C.B.C.2d 323 (1992).

The text of section 547(c)(2) makes no distinction between long and
short term debt; rather, it focuses upon whether the debt was incurred,
and payment made, in the "ordinary course of business or financial
affairs" of the debtor and the transferee. Therefore, payments on long
term debt, as well as short term debt, may qualify under section 547(c)(2)
for the ordinary course of business exception to the trustee's power to
avoid preferential transfers. Union Bank v. Wolas, 502 U.S. —, 112 S.
Ct. 527, 116 L. Ed. 2d 514, 25 C.B.C.2d 1011 (1991).

A creditor who files a proof of claim against a bankruptcy estate and
is then sued by the trustee to recover a preferential transfer is not
entitled to a jury trial under the Seventh Amendment. Langenkamp v.

Culp, 498 U.S. —, 111 S. Ct. 330, 112 L. Ed. 2d 343, 23 C.B.C.2d 973 (1990).

A debtor does not hold an equitable interest in property held in trust for another; accordingly, although a debtor may hold legal title to such property, such an interest does not constitute "an interest of the debtor in property" for preference purposes. Begier v. IRS, 495 U.S. 954, 110 S. Ct. 2258, 110 L. Ed. 2d 46, 22 C.B.C.2d 1080 (1990).

A fraudulent conveyance action for recovery of monetary sums plainly seeks relief traditionally provided by law courts and a person who has not submitted a claim against the bankruptcy estate when sued by the trustee to recover an allegedly fraudulent monetary transfer is entitled by the Seventh Amendment to a jury trial, notwithstanding Congress' designation of fraudulent conveyance actions as "core proceedings" in 28 U.S.C. § 157(b)(2)(H). Granfinanciera v. Nordberg, 492 U.S. 33, 109 S. Ct. 2782, 106 L. Ed. 2d 26, 20 C.B.C.2d 1216 (1989).

Although the Bankruptcy Code recognizes the elevated status given to a secured creditor by state commercial codes, a creditor is secured under the Code only to the extent of the value of his interest in property of the estate, and section 547(b)(5) does not add any special protections for the secured creditor. In re Virginia-Carolina Financial Corp., 954 F.2d 193, 26 C.B.C.2d 279 (6th Cir. 1992).

For purposes of determining whether there has been a voidable preferential transfer, an insider of the debtor benefits by the debtor paying the insider's debts to the extent that the transfer exceeded the amount that the insider would have received under a chapter 7 distribution. Matter of T.B. Westex Foods, Inc., 950 F.2d 1187, 26 C.B.C.2d 682 (5th Cir. 1992).

A transfer for preference purposes pursuant to a state order occurs on the date that that court's judgment is filed and docketed. For the purposes of section 547(b), the 90-day avoidance period is determined by counting backwards 90 days from the date of the filing of the petition in bankruptcy. Nelson Co. v. Counsel for the Official Committee of Unsecured Creditors v. Amquip Corp., 959 F.2d 1260, 26 C.B.C.2d 979 (3d Cir. 1992).

The analysis to determine whether a payment is made in the ordinary course of business is similar to the analysis for determining whether reasonably equivalent value is present, i.e., the focus should be on the reality of the course of dealing between the parties, not the formal structure of the relationship. In re Jeffrey Bigelow Design Group, Inc., 956 F.2d 479, 26 C.B.C.2d 967 (4th Cir. 1992).

An exchange involving a dishonored check is outside section 547(c)(1) because that exception does not ordinarily apply to credit transactions, and because the dishonor of a check creates an antecedent debt owed by the debtor so that any subsequent attempts at payment would create a preference. Such an exchange also falls outside of the ordinary course of business exception of section 547(c)(2). In re Barefoot, 952 F.2d 795, 25 C.B.C.2d 1719 (4th Cir. 1991).

A bankruptcy court may not require a creditor to prove that its security interest is not a voidable preference under section 547 in order to establish its secured status. Mellon Bank, N.A. v. Metro Communications, Inc. and the Pacific 10 Conference v. The Committee of Unsecured Creditors, 945 F.2d 635, 25 C.B.C.2d 1064 (3d Cir. 1991).

A payment made as restitution for a dishonored check within ninety days of the filing of the bankruptcy petition is a preference under section 547. Reynolds v. Dixie Nissan (*In re* Car Renovators), 946 F.2d 780, 25 C.B.C.2d 1185 (11th Cir. 1991).

For the purposes of calculating new value under section 547(c)(4), a transfer occurs when a check is delivered. If a payment is made by a third party holding a secured claim against the estate, the use of the new value defense to the transferee is precluded because the third party's secured claim would indirectly deplete the estate. *In re* Kroh Brothers Development Co., 930 F.2d 648, 24 C.B.C.2d 1757 (8th Cir. 1991).

A trustee may recover prepetition payments as avoidable preferences under section 547(b)(5) because if the estate is unable to provide a 100 percent distribution, any unsecured creditor who receives a payment during the preference period is in a position to receive more than it would receive in a chapter 7 liquidation, thus fulfilling the "more than" requirement of the statute. *In re* Chattanooga Wholesale Antiques, Inc., 930 F.2d 458, 24 C.B.C.2d 1556 (6th Cir. 1991).

In defining the term "becomes payable," section 547(a)(4) provides a time period with respect to tax claims solely for the purpose of determining when a prepetition transfer may be recovered by a trustee and it is not intended as a universal statement of when taxes "become payable." *In re* Ripley, 926 F.2d 1440, 24 C.B.C.2d 1478 (5th Cir. 1991).

A transfer to a secured creditor of the amount of his lien during the preference period does not constitute an avoidable preference, for under section 547(e)(3); if a lien has a relation back element, secured status is established at the time the transfer of the lien is made. *In re* Hagen, 922 F.2d 742, 24 C.B.C.2d 1216 (11th Cir. 1991).

Under California law, when a trustee either restores trust funds previously comingled with individual funds to the trust account or manifests an intent to restore the trust account by making subsequent deposits, such funds become part of the trust account upon deposit. These funds restored by the debtor to a trust account as restitution within the ninety day preference period may be recoverable by the trustee as a voidable preference if the money could have been used to satisfy the claims of other creditors, and if the elements of section 547(b) are met. *In re* California Trade Technical Schools, Inc., 923 F.2d 641, 24 C.B.C.2d 813 (9th Cir. 1991).

Modification of the terms of an existing obligation may constitute new value, although a calculation of the specific measure of the new value given in the exchange is required. *In re* Spada, 903 F.2d 971, 23 C.B.C.2d 976 (3d Cir. 1990).

While new funds provided by a new creditor to or for the benefit of a debtor to pay an obligation owed to an old creditor are considered earmarked and not voidable as a preference, to the extent that the debtor transfers a security interest in return for the funds, those funds fall under the security interest exception and are not considered earmarked. *In re* Muncrief, 900 F.2d 1220, 23 C.B.C.2d 427 (8th Cir. 1990).

A creditor's personal guarantee to a bank of a loan to the debtor partnership, which was an essential prerequisite to the bank's willingness to lend the funds to the debtor, constitutes either services or credit to the debtor as a contemporaneous exchange for new value. *In re* Bavishi & Associates, 906 F.2d 942, 23 C.B.C.2d 197 (3d Cir. 1990).

The correct method of calculating the amount by which a preference must be reduced by new value when the debtor maintains an open credit line with the creditor is the variation of the net result rule formulated in the *Garland* case, which calculates the difference between the total preferences in the 90 day period and the total advances, provided that each advance is used to offset only prior preferences. *In re* Meredith Manor, Inc., 902 F.2d 257, 23 C.B.C.2d 629 (4th Cir. 1990).

Section 550(a)(1), together with section 547(b)(1) and (b)(4)(B), permits recovery from an outsider transferee for transfers made during the extended preference period when the beneficiary of the transfers is an insider creditor or an insider guarantor. *In re* C-L Cartage Co., Inc., 899 F.2d 1490, 22 C.B.C.2d 901 (6th Cir. 1990).

A creditor's redemption of thrift and passbook savings certificates in exchange for payments from a debtor financial institution did not constitute "new value" within the meaning of section 547(c)(1)(A). *In re* Republic Trust & Savings Co., 897 F.2d 1041, 22 C.B.C.2d 824 (10th Cir. 1990).

The 10 day grace period of section 547(c)(3)(B), not the 20 day period available under Texas law, is the rule to be applied in determining whether a transfer by way of a security interest in personal property has been perfected within 10 days after a debtor has received possession of property. In the Matter of Hamilton, 892 F.2d 1230, 22 C.B.C.2d 292 (5th Cir. 1990).

If evidence supports the claim that a debtor was in the process of liquidation throughout the 90 day period prior to filing a petition, for the purpose of determining whether a creditor improved its position at the expense of other creditors during that period, the appropriate method of valuing the debtor's collateral is the liquidation method. *In re* Clark Pipe and Supply Co., Inc., 893 F.2d 693, 22 C.B.C.2d 500 (5th Cir. 1990).

Pursuant to section 550(a)(1), when a transfer that is avoidable under section 547(b) was made more than 90 days before the filing of the petition under title 11, a trustee may recover that transfer from a creditor when there has been a benefit to an insider of the debtor, despite the fact that the creditor itself is not an insider; however, payments satisfying pension obligations generally are not for the benefit of insiders unless the pension and welfare trusts received contractual guarantees from the insiders, and payments of tax obligations are never for the benefit of insiders. Levit v. Ingersoll Rand Financial Corp., (*In re* V.N. Deprizio Constr. Co.), 874 F.2d 1186, 22 C.B.C.2d 36 (7th Cir. 1989).

In determining what constitutes an ordinary transaction within the meaning of section 547(c)(2), a court may analyze factors such as timing, amount and manner of payment, and circumstances of transfer. Even if a debtor's business transactions are irregular they may be considered ordinary if such transactions are consistent with the course of dealing between the particular parties and, under certain circumstances, courts may examine industry practices in addition to the parties' prior dealings. *In re* Yurika Foods Corp., 888 F.2d 42, 21 C.B.C.2d 1232 (6th Cir. 1989).

For a transaction to qualify for the earmarking doctrine and thus not be voidable as a preference, three factors must be present: the existence of an agreement between the new lender and the debtor that the new funds will be used to pay a specified antecedent debt, performance of that agreement according to its terms, and the transaction viewed as a whole (including the transfer in of the new funds and the transfer out to the old creditor) does not result in any diminution of the estate. McCuskey v. Nat'l Bank of Waterloo (*In re* Bohlen), 859 F.2d 561, 19 C.B.C.2d 986 (8th Cir. 1988).

A trustee may recover any property transferred in violation of section 547(b) from an initial transferee or from the entity for whose benefit such transfer was made. A creditor thus can receive an indirect benefit in the letter of credit context sufficient to meet the requirement of section 547(b)(1). American Bank of Martin County v. Leasing Service Corp. (*In re* Air Conditioning, Inc. of Stuart), 845 F.2d 293, 18 C.B.C.2d 973 (11th Cir. 1988), *cert. denied,* 488 U.S. 993, 102 L. Ed. 2d 584, 109 S. Ct. 557 (1990).

When a debtor makes payments to a creditor, that creditor releases a letter of credit and, in turn, the bank issuing the letter of credit releases the debtor's collateral underlying the letter of credit, new value has been given the debtor so that payments by the debtor to the creditor are not avoidable preferences; new value received by a debtor need not be provided by the creditor to whom the transfer was made, but may be provided by a fully secured third party as long as the "independence principle," preserving the allocation of risk, is not compromised. Gulf Oil Corp. v. Fuel Oil Supply and Terminaling, Inc. (In the Matter of Fuel Oil Supply & Terminaling, Inc.), 837 F.2d 224, 18 C.B.C.2d 462 (5th Cir. 1988).

References

4 *Collier on Bankruptcy* ch. 547 (Matthew Bender 15th ed.).

2 *Collier Bankruptcy Manual* ch. 547 (Matthew Bender 3d ed.).

4 *Collier Bankruptcy Practice Guide* ch. 64 (Matthew Bender).

Bankruptcy: Enhanced Preference Recovery Period for Outside Creditors With Insider Guarantors, 26 Wilamette L. Rev. 811 (1990).

Brands, *The Interplay Between Section 547(b) and 550 of the Bankruptcy Code,* 89 Columb. L. Rev. 530 (1989).

Broome, *Payments on Long-Term Debt as Voidable Preferences: The Impact of the 1984 Bankruptcy Amendments,* 1987 Duke L.J. 78.

Burks, IV, *Oil and Gas Exchange Contracts Guaranteed by a Letter of Credit in a Section 547 Adversary Proceeding,* 1985 Ann. Surv. Bankr. L. 227.

Chobot, *Purchase Money Security Interests: Preference Pitfalls Under the Bankruptcy Code,* 20 Uniform Commercial Code L.J. 81 (1987).

Cohen, McLaughlin and Zaretsky, *Floating Liens and the "Value" of Collateral,* 1 Commercial Law Report 167 (1987).

Comment, *Insider Preferences and the Problem of Self-Dealing Under the Bankruptcy Code,* 57 U. Chi. L. Rev. 603 (1990).

Comment, *Insider Preferences — The Approach of the Fifth Circuit Court of Appeals to the Issue of Non-Insider Liability for Preferential Transfers Benefiting Insider Guarantors,* 60 Miss. L.J. 387 (1990).

Countryman, *The Concept of a Voidable Preference in Bankruptcy,* 38 Vand. L. Rev. 713 (1985).

Duncan, *Preferential Transfers, the Floating Lien, and Section 547(c)(5) of the Bankruptcy Reform Act of 1978,* 36 Ark. L. Rev. 1 (1983).

Eisler, *Beyond the Grace Period: Security Interests as Preference Exceptions Under Section 547 of the Bankruptcy Code,* 1984 Ann. Surv. Bankr. L. 63.

Flechtner, *Preferences, Post-Petition Transfers, and Transactions Involving a Debtor's Downstream Affiliate,* 5 Bankr. Dev. J. 1 (1987).

Friedman, *Lender Exposure Under Sections 547 and 550: Are Outsiders Really Insiders?,* 44 Sw. L.J. 985 (1990).

Fulford and Yurchak, *Perils of Pre-Bankruptcy Planning: Transfers, Exemptions and Taxes,* 17 Colo. Law. 1513 (1988).

Glenn and Anthony, *Insiders' Guaranties May Expose Lender to an Extended Preference Recovery Period,* 64 Fla. B.J. 39 (1990).

Hall, *Preferences and Setoffs: Sections 547 and 553,* 2 Bank. Dev. J. 49 (1985).

Harbeck, *Ponzi Schemes and Preferences: A Cautionary Tale,* 2 F & G Bankr. L. Rev. 17 (1990).

Herzberg and Von Nessen, *Preferring Guarantors: A Comparison of Australian and United States Provisions Regulating Voidable Preferences,* 6 UCLA Pac. Basin L.J. 1 (1989).

Miller, *Guidelines for Investigating Fraudulent Transfers and Preference Payments,* 2 F & G Bankr. L. Rev. 57 (1990).

Note, *Holdway v. Duvoisin: Garnishment Payments as Preferences Under Section 547,* 43 Ark. L. Rev. 247 (1990).

Note, *Indirect Preferences: Recovery Under Section 547 and 550 of the Bankruptcy Code,* 55 Mo. L. Rev. 327 (1990).

Note, *New Value and Preference Avoidance in Bankruptcy,* 69 Wash. U.L.Q. 875 (1991).

Note, *Recharacterizing Insider Preferences as Fraudulent Conveyances: A Different View of Levit v. Ingersoll Rand,* 77 Va. L. Rev. 149 (1991).

Note, *Who Is an "Insider" After the 1984 Amendments to Section 547(b)(4)(B)?,* 5 Bankr. Dev. J. 195 (1987).

Nutovic, *The Bankruptcy Preference Laws: Interpreting Code Sections 547(c)(2), 550(a)(1) and 546(a)(1),* 41 Bus. Law 175 (1985).

Owens, *The Impossible State of Preference Law Under the Bankruptcy Code: Levit v. Ingersoll Rand Financial Corp. and the Problem of Insider-Guaranteed Debt,* 1990 Wis. L. Rev. 1129.

Porter, *Burdens of Proof in Bankruptcy Court,* 17 Colo. Law. 251 (1988).

Reiley, *Farming Failures and Drafting Failures: The Uncertain Posture of Crop Financing Under Article 9 and § 547 of the Bankruptcy Code,* 1983 Ann. Surv. Bankr. L. 29.

Saunders, *Preference Avoidance and Letter of (edit Supported Debt: The Bank's Reimbursement Risk in its Customer's Jankruptcy,* 102 Banking L.J. 240 (1985).

Weintraub and Resnick, *Preferential Payment of Long-Term Debts in the Ordinary Course of Business—The Effect of the 1984 Amendments,* 17 U.C.C. L.J. 263 (1985).

Williams, Jr. and Bick, *Insider Guarantees: Emerging Theories of Preference Recoveries,* 69 Mich. B.J. 691 (1990).

SECTION 548 (11 U.S.C. § 548)

§ 548. Fraudulent transfers and obligations.

(a) The trustee may avoid any transfer of an interest of the debtor in property, or any obligation incurred by the debtor, that was made or incurred on or within one year before the date of the filing of the petition, if the debtor voluntarily or involuntarily—

(1) made such transfer or incurred such obligation with actual intent to hinder, delay, or defraud any entity to which the debtor was or became, on or after the date that such transfer was made or such obligation was incurred, indebted; or

(2) (A) received less than a reasonably equivalent value in exchange for such transfer or obligation; and

(B)(i) was insolvent on the date that such transfer was made or such obligation was incurred, or became insolvent as a result of such transfer or obligation;

(ii) was engaged in business or a transaction, or was about to engage in business or a transaction, for which any property remaining with the debtor was an unreasonably small capital; or

(iii) intended to incur, or believed that the debtor would incur, debts that would be beyond the debtor's ability to pay as such debts matured.

(b) The trustee of a partnership debtor may avoid any transfer of an interest of the debtor in property, or any obligation incurred by the debtor, that was made or incurred on or within one year before the date of the filing of the petition, to a general partner in the debtor, if the debtor was insolvent on the date such transfer was made or such obligation was incurred, or became insolvent as a result of such transfer or obligation.

(c) Except to the extent that a transfer or obligation voidable under this section is voidable under section 544, 545, or 547 of this title, a transferee or obligee of such a transfer or obligation that takes for value and in good faith has a lien on or may retain any interest transferred or may enforce any obligation incurred, as the case may be, to the extent that such transferee or obligee gave value to the debtor in exchange for such transfer or obligation.

(d)(1) For the purposes of this section, a transfer is made when such transfer is so perfected that a bona fide purchaser from the debtor against whom applicable law permits such transfer to be perfected cannot acquire an interest in the property transferred that is superior to the interest in such property of the transferee, but if such transfer is not so perfected before the commencement

of the case, such transfer is made immediately before the date
of the filing of the petition.

(2) In this section—

(A) "value" means property, or satisfaction or securing
of a present or antecedent debt of the debtor, but does not
include an unperformed promise to furnish support to the
debtor or to a relative of the debtor;

(B) a commodity broker, forward contract merchant,
stockbroker, financial institution, or securities clearing
agency that receives a margin payment, as defined in
section 101(34), 741(5) or 761(15) of this title, or settlement payment, as defined in section 101(35) or 741(8) of
this title, takes for value to the extent of such payment;

(C) a repo participant that receives a margin payment,
as defined in section 741(5) or 761(15) of this title, or
settlement payment, as defined in section 741(8) of this
title, in connection with a repurchase agreement, takes for
value to the extent of such payment; and

(D) a swap participant that receives a transfer in connection with a swap agreement takes for value to the extent
of such transfer.

Legislative History

This section is derived in large part from section 67d of the Bankruptcy Act. It permits the trustee to avoid transfers by the debtor in
fraud of his creditors. Its history dates from the statute of 13 Eliz. c.
5 (1570).

The trustee may avoid fraudulent transfers or obligations if made with
actual intent to hinder, delay, or defraud a past or future creditor.
Transfers made for less than a reasonably equivalent consideration are
also vulnerable if the debtor was or thereby became insolvent, was
engaged in business with an unreasonably small capital, or intended to
incur debts that would be beyond his ability to repay.

The trustee of a partnership debtor may avoid any transfer of partnership property to a partner in the debtor if the debtor was or thereby
became insolvent.

If a transferee's only liability to the trustee is under this section, and
if he takes for value and in good faith, then subsection (c) grants him
a lien on the property transferred, or other similar protection.

Subsection (d) specifies that for the purposes of the fraudulent
transfer section, a transfer is made when it is valid against a subsequent

bona fide purchaser. If not made before the case, it is considered made immediately before the case. Subsection (d) also defines "value" to mean property, or the satisfaction or securing of a present or antecedent debt, but does not include an unperformed promise to furnish support to the debtor or a relative of the debtor.

[*House Report No. 95–595, 95th Cong., 1st Sess. 375 (1977); Senate Report No. 95–989, 95th Cong., 2d Sess. 89–90 (1978).*]

Section 548(d)(2) is modified to reflect general application of a provision contained in section 766 of the Senate amendment with respect to commodity brokers. In particular, section 548(d)(2)(B) of the House amendment makes clear that a commodity broker who receives a margin payment is considered to receive the margin payment in return for "value" for purposes of section 548.

[*124 Cong. Rec. H 11,097 (Sept. 28, 1978); S 17,414 (Oct. 6, 1978).*]

Mr. Mathias. Mr. President, I have four questions regarding subchapter IV of chapter 7 of title I of the bill, which deals with commodity related bankruptcies. I note that the bill now before the Senate deletes section 766(b) and (c) of the bill as originally passed by the Senate, S. 2266. I also note, however, that the distinguished Senator's floor statement indicates that the protections previously sought to be provided under section 766(b) and (c) to commodity brokers, forward contract merchants and clearing organizations are now intended to be covered under section 764(c) and section 548(d)(2) of the bill now before us. Is that correct?

Mr. DeConcini. Yes.

Mr. Mathias. Am I correct in understanding of the Senator's statement that the intent of section 764 and section 548(d)(2) is to provide that margin payments and settlement payments previously made by a bankrupt to a commodity broker, forward contract merchant and by or to a clearing organization are nonvoidable transfers by the bankrupts trustee? And is it also true that margin payments will not be considered voidable preferences because they constitute transfers made as contemporaneous exchanges for new value as used in section 547(c)?

Mr. DeConcini. Yes.

Mr. Mathias. I thank the Senator for his assurance that it is the intention of section 764(c) and section 548(d)(2) to protect all margin payments in the customer-broker-clearinghouse chain. This vital protection substantially reduces the likelihood that the bankruptcy of one customer or broker will lead to the bankruptcy of another broker or clearinghouse.

[*124 Cong. Rec. S 17,433 (Oct. 6, 1978).*]

Section 5 [of Public Law 97–222] amends section 548(d)(2)(B) of title 11 to clarify that all margin payments are taken for value to the full extent of such margin payments.

[*House Report No. 97–420, 97th Cong., 2d Sess. 3 (1982).*]

Section 5 of the bill [Public Law 97–222] would amend section 548(d)(2)(B) of the code to clarify that all margin payments are taken for value to the full extent of such margin payments. In other words, the value received by the debtor who makes a margin payment to a commodity broker, forward contract merchant, stockbroker, or securities clearing agency is equal to the amount of such margin payment. This change, coupled with proposed new section 546(d), makes clear the intent of the code to prohibit a debtor's trustee from setting aside any portion of a margin payment except in the event the transferee of such payment did not take it in good faith.

[*128 Cong. Rec. S8, 133 (July 13, 1982).*]

Comment

Section 548 is derived from section 67d of the former Bankruptcy Act.

As under Section 67d of said Act the trustee may, under section 548 of the Code, avoid transfers if made with actual intent to hinder, delay, or defraud a past or future creditor. The trustee may also avoid transfers made for less than a reasonably equivalent consideration if the debtor was or thereby became insolvent, or was engaged in business with unreasonably small capital, or intended to incur debts beyond the debtor's ability to repay. A transfer to a partner, in a partnership case, may be avoided if the partnership was or thereby became insolvent.

Subsection (d) has no comparable provisions in the former Act. It defines "value" to mean property or the satisfaction or securing of a present or antecedent debt, but not an unperformed promise to furnish support to the debtor or debtor's relative.

Subsection (d)(2)(B) also has no comparable provisions in the Act and makes clear that a commodity broker who receives a margin payment is deemed to have received such payment in return for value.

Section 548 deleted former Section 67d(3), which purportedly codified the Rule in Dean v. Davis, 242 U.S. 438 (1917), because its language went beyond the facts of *Dean v. Davis.* Moreover, because *Dean v. Davis* was decided under the statutory counterpart to section 548(a)(1) of the Code, continued retention of the former Section 67d(3) was unnecessary.

1984 Amendments: Subsection (a) was amended probably with the thought to codify the holding of the *Durrett* case and overturning the *Madrid* case. Subsection (d)(2)(C) relates to a repo participant that receives a margin payment in connection with a repurchase agreement. *See* **Comment** to section 362 regarding "repo participant" and "repurchase agreement."

Technical changes were made in subsections (a)(1), (a)(2)(B)(iii), (C) and (d)(1) and (2).

Pursuant to 28 U.S.C. § 157(b)(2)(H), proceedings to determine, avoid, or recover fraudulent conveyances are "core" proceedings that may be heard and determined by the bankruptcy judges.

1990 Amendments: Pub. L. No. 101–311 amended subsection (d)(2)(B) to include references to section 101(34) [defining "margin payment"] and section 101(35) [defining "settlement payment"]; these references, however, do not reflect the subsequent redesignation of paragraphs in section 101 by Pub. L. No. 101–647 (*See* Comment to section 101 *supra*).

Subparagraph (D) was added to subsection (d)(2) to include as one that "takes for value" a swap participant that receives a transfer in connection with a swap agreement, but only to the extent of such transfer.

Case Annotations

A court should presume the reasonableness of the sale price of property sold at a legitimate foreclosure sale, and absent fraud, collusion, or irregular or unlawful procedures, a trustee seeking to avoid such a sale must prove specific factors which undermine confidence in the reasonableness of the foreclosure price. Among the factors to be considered in evaluating the reasonableness of a foreclosure sale are (i) the bargaining positions of the parties; (ii) the marketability of the property sold; (iii) the normally deflated prices found in most foreclosures compared to other markets, (iv) whether the foreclosing party obtained a fair appraisal of the property before the sale; (v) the extent to which the foreclosure sale was advertised; and (vi) the competitive conditions surrounding the sale. *In re* Grissom, 955 F.2d 1440, 26 C.B.C.2d 1002 (11th Cir. 1992).

A determination of insolvency under section 548(a)(2)(B)(i) must include an estimation of the debtor's contingent liabilities, taking into account the probability that the contingency will occur. Covey v. Commercial National Bank of Peoria, 960 F.2d 657, 26 C.B.C.2d 1046 (7th Cir. 1992).

There is no *per se* rule that a leveraged buyout loan collateralized with the target's own assets renders the target-debtor insolvent and, therefore, vulnerable as a fraudulent transfer. Mellon Bank v. Metro Communications, Inc., 945 F.2d 635, 25 C.B.C.2d 1064 (3d Cir. 1991).

For the purposes of section 548, the term "antecedent debt" was intended by Congress to be broadly construed so that unknowing investors in fraudulent schemes might be deemed to have exchanged reasonably equivalent value when their rights of restitution are proportionately reduced by payments received from the scheme. *In re* United Energy Corp., 944 F.2d 589, 25 C.B.C.2d 740 (9th Cir. 1991).

An action under section 548 is brought for the benefit of the debtor and not for the benefit of the estate when the debtor is not required to pursue the action, the claims of secured creditors have been satisfied and the debtor would procure a windfall surplus from the action. Wellman v. Wellman, 933 F.2d 215, 24 C.B.C.2d 1853 (4th Cir.), *cert. denied,* — U.S. —, 112 S. Ct. 339, 116 L. Ed. 2d 279 (1991).

The legislative goals underlying a bankruptcy trustee's avoidance powers and the danger of a debtor improperly manipulating the tax code require that a trustee have the ability to avoid a debtor's irrevocable election to carry forward net operating losses on his tax returns. Once a trustee has avoided a debtor's election to carry forward net operating losses on his tax returns, the trustee is free to elect as he or she sees fit. *In re* Russell, 927 F.2d 413, 24 C.B.C.2d 1526 (8th Cir. 1991).

If, under state law, a disclaimer of an inheritance has the effect of preventing debtor from ever acquiring an interest in such property, and the disclaimer "relates back," then such disclaimer is not a "transfer of an interest of the debtor in property" subject to avoidance by the trustee. *In re* Atchison, 925 F.2d 209, 24 C.B.C.2d 1428 (7th Cir. 1991).

Since it is often impracticable to demonstrate an actual intent to hinder, delay or defraud creditors, it is permissible to infer fraudulent intent from the circumstances surrounding the transfer, taking note of certain recognized indicia or badges of fraud. The presence of a single badge of fraud may spur mere suspicion; the confluence of several can constitute conclusive evidence of an actual intent to defraud, absent significantly clear evidence of a legitimate supervening purpose. Max Sugarman Funeral Home, Inc. v. A.D.B. Investors, 926 F.2d 1248, 24 C.B.C.2d 1414 (1st Cir. 1991).

The appropriate definition of reasonable equivalence is less rigid than the mathematical formula standard endorsed in Durrett v. Washington Nat'l Ins. Co., 621 F.2d 201 (5th Cir. 1980) and, as set forth in Bundles v. Baker, 856 F.2d 815 (7th Cir. 1988), depends on all the facts of each case, important elements of which are fair market value and whether the sale was an arms' length transaction. *In re* Morris Communications NC, Inc., 914 F.2d 458, 23 C.B.C.2d 1456 (4th Cir. 1990).

Loan proceeds received by a debtor in exchange for the guarantee of another's loan, though far less than the value of the loan, can constitute reasonably equivalent value. *In re* Chase & Sanborn Corp., 904 F.2d 588, 23 C.B.C.2d 5 (11th Cir. 1990).

Transfers unsupported by "reasonably equivalent value" may be avoided under section 548(a)(2)(A) in order to protect creditors against the depletion of a debtor's estate; consequently, the provision does not authorize the avoidance of a transfer which confers an economic benefit upon a debtor, either directly or indirectly. *In re* Rodriguez, 895 F.2d 725, 22 C.B.C.2d 633 (11th Cir. 1990).

A trustee may not avoid a debtor's transfer of its interest in a sales transaction with related entities on the basis of not having received a reasonably equivalent value in exchange when the totality of the circumstances in the marketplace was not fairly considered. Jacoway v. Anderson (*In re* Ozark Restaurant Equip. Co.), 835 F.2d 342, 19 C.B.C.2d 35 (8th Cir. 1988).

The date of the foreclosure sale, not the date the deed is executed and delivered, is the appropriate date for determining whether the conveyance of property was within one year of the filing of the bankruptcy petition, because under applicable law the purchaser at the foreclosure sale obtains a vested equitable ownership of the property which is superior to any type of purchase rights obtained after the foreclosure sale. Butler v. Lomas and Nettleton Co., 862 F.2d 1015, 19 C.B.C.2d 1373 (3d Cir. 1988).

The right to invoke either section 548(a) or 544(b) belongs not to a particular unsecured creditor but to the trustee (or debtor in possession); a derivative suit in the name of the debtor is possible, but the creditor must first demonstrate that the debtor is shirking its statutory responsibilities. In the Matter of Xonics Photochemical, Inc., 841 F.2d 198, 18 C.B.C.2d 711 (7th Cir. 1988).

If a debtor has a right under state law to set aside a foreclosure sale after the sale has taken place, after deeds have been recorded, and after the property had been sold to a third-party, then the debtor has the right to do the same in bankruptcy, since the right is property of the estate. Hence, the debtor's failure to obtain a stay pending appeal does not render the appeal of a foreclosure order moot. Rosner v. Worcester (*In re* Worcester), 811 F.2d 1224, 16 C.B.C.2d 589 (9th Cir. 1987).

The sale price at a regularly conducted foreclosure sale, even absent fraud or collusion, cannot automatically be deemed to be a reasonably equivalent value in exchange for the transfer of a debtor's interest; the reasonably equivalent value can only be determined through an evidentiary hearing. First Fed. Sav. and Loan Ass'n v. Hulm (*In re* Hulm), 738 F.2d 323, 11 C.B.C.2d 152 (8th Cir.), *cert. denied*, 469 U.S. 990, 105 S. Ct. 398, 83 L. Ed. 2d 331 (1984).

A bank may properly lend money to a debtor-corporation knowing that the debtor will use the funds for a speculative venture so long as it gives reasonably equivalent value to the debtor in return for its security interest in the debtor's inventory. Jones v. Nat'l City Bank of Rome (*In re* Greenbrook Carpet Co.), 722 F.2d 659, 10 C.B.C.2d 519 (11th Cir. 1984).

An "intent to defraud" his creditors may be inferred from a debtor's acts of transferring property while retaining use, possession and benefit therefrom and from his creation of dummy corporations in order to conceal assets (despite the fact that these acts were not committed on the "eve of bankruptcy" and the debtor is not a corporation). Salomon v. Kaiser (*In re* Kaiser), 722 F.2d 1574, 9 C.B.C.2d 910 (2d Cir. 1983).

A fraudulent transfer may be inferred from the payment by the debtor corporation of $300,000 in exchange for treasury stock, which is not an asset but merely reduces shareholder equity. Consove v. Cohen (*In re* Roco Corp.), 701 F.2d 978, 8 C.B.C.2d 457 (1st Cir. 1983).

References

4 *Collier on Bankruptcy* ch. 548 (Matthew Bender 15th ed.).

2 *Collier Bankruptcy Manual* ch. 548 (Matthew Bender 3d ed.).

4 *Collier Bankruptcy Practice Guide* ch. 65 (Matthew Bender).

Alces and Dorr, Jr., *A Critical Analysis of the New Uniform Fraudulent Transfer Act,* 1985 Ill. L. Rev. 527.

Alden, Gross and Borowitz, *The* Durrett *Controversy and Foreclosure Sales,* N.Y.L.J., Nov. 14, 1984, p.1, col. 1.

The Avoidance of Transfer: Section 548, 3 Bankr. Dev. J. 389 (1986).

Burns, *The Fraudulent Conveyance Laws and the LBO Lender,* 94 Com. L.J. 268 (1989).

Casenote, *Bankruptcy: Nonjudicial Foreclosures as Fraudulent Transfers Under Section 548 of the Bankruptcy Code—Madrid v. Lawyers Title Insurance Corp., 725 F.2d 1197 (9th Cir.), cert. denied, 105 S. Ct. 125 (1984),* 10 U. Dayton L. Rev. 399 (1984).

Comment, *Avoidance of Foreclosure Sales as Fraudulent Transfers Under Section 548(a) of the Bankruptcy Code: An Impetus to Changing State Foreclosure Procedures,* 66 Nev. L. Rev. 383 (1987).

Comment, *Avoidance of Foreclosure Sales Under Section 548 of the Bankruptcy Code: Can the Illinois Mortgage Foreclosure Law Provide the Answer to "Reasonably Equivalent Value?,"* 14 S. Ill. U.L.J. 601 (1990).

Comment, *Guarantees and Section 548(a)(2) of the Bankruptcy Code,* 52 U. Chi. L. Rev. 194 (1985).

Conant, *Beyond Madrid: Resolving the Conflict Within the Ninth Circuit Regarding § 548(a)(2)(A) and Nonjudicial Foreclosure Sales,* 18 Cal. Bankr. J. 221 (1990).

Davis and Standiford, *Foreclosure Sale as a Fraudulent Transfer Under the Bankruptcy Code: A Reasonable Approach to Reasonably Equivalent Value,* 13 Real Est. L.J. 203 (1985).

Defining Reasonably Equivalent Value Under Section 548(a) of the Bankruptcy Code: Is Ristich the Answer?, 44 Wash. & Lee L. Rev. 237 (1987).

Ehrlich, *Avoidance of Foreclosure Sales as Fraudulent Conveyances: Accommodating State and Federal Objectives,* 71 Va. L. Rev. 933 (1985).

Flechtner, *Preferences, Post-Petition Transfers, and Transactions Involving a Debtor's Downstream Affiliate,* 5 Bankr. Dev. J. 1 (1987).

Fulford and Yurchak, *Perils of Pre-Bankruptcy Planning: Transfers, Exemptions and Taxes,* 17 Colo. Law. 1513 (1988).

Henning, *An Analysis of Durrett and Its Impact on Real and Personal Property Foreclosures: Some Proposed Modifications,* 63 N.C.L. Rev. 257 (1985).

Markell, *Toward True and Plain Dealing: A Theory of Fraudulent Transfers Involving Unreasonably Small Capital,* 21 Ind. L. Rev. 469 (1988).

Note, *The Big Chill: Applicability of Section 548(a)(2) of the Bankruptcy Code to Noncollusive Foreclosure Sales,* 53 Fordham L. Rev. 813 (1985).

Pedlar, *When Transfers Between Husband and Wife are Fraudulent,* 5 Fam. Advoc. 32 (1983).

Rafool, *State Foreclosure Sales Under Fraudulent Conveyance Provisions of the Bankruptcy Code,* 79 Ill. B.J. 84 (1991).

Scott, *Dealing With Durrett: Mortgage Foreclosures as Fraudulent Transfers,* 65 Fla. B.J. 13 (1991).

Selassie, *Valuation Issues in Applying Fraudulent Transfer Law to Leveraged Buyouts,* 32 B.C.L. Rev. 377 (1991).

Shanker, *What Every Lawyer Should Know About the Law of Fraudulent Transfers,* 31 Prac. Law. 43 (1985).

Simpson, *Real Property Foreclosures: The Fallacy of* Durrett, 19 Real Prop., Prob. & Tr. J. 73 (1984).

Weintraub and Resnick, *A Secured Creditor's Right to Funds Received by a Trustee in Settlement of an Action to Avoid a Fraudulent Transfer of Collateral,* 21 U.C.C. L.J. 76 (1988).

Weintraub and Resnick, *Mortgage Foreclosure Sales as Fraudulent Conveyances,* 17 U.C.C. L.J. 376 (1985).

SECTION 549 (11 U.S.C. § 549)

§ 549. Postpetition transactions.

(a) Except as provided in subsections (b) or (c) of this section, the trustee may avoid a transfer of property of the estate—

(1) made after the commencement of the case; and

(2)(A) that is authorized only under section 303(f) or 542(c) of this title; or

(B) that is not authorized under this title or by the court.

(b) In an involuntary case, a transfer made after the commencement of such case but before the order for relief to the extent any value, including services, but not including satisfaction or securing of a debt that arose before the commencement of the case, is given after the commencement of the case in exchange for such transfer, notwithstanding any notice or knowledge of the case that the transferee has.

(c) The trustee may not avoid under subsection (a) of this section a transfer of real property to a good faith purchaser without knowledge of the commencement of the case and for present fair equivalent value unless a copy or notice of the petition was filed, where a transfer of such real property may be recorded to perfect such transfer, before such transfer is so perfected that a bona fide purchaser of such property, against whom applicable law permits such transfer to be perfected, could not acquire an interest that is superior to the interest of such good faith purchaser. A good faith purchaser without knowledge of the commencement of the case and for less than present fair equivalent value has a lien on the property transferred to the extent of any present value given, unless a copy or notice of the petition was so filed before such transfer was so perfected.

(d) An action or proceeding under this section may not be commenced after the earlier of—

(1) two years after the date of the transfer sought to be avoided; or

(2) the time the case is closed or dismissed.

Legislative History

This section modifies section 70d of current law. It permits the trustee to avoid transfers of property that occur after the commencement of the case. The transfer must either have been unauthorized, or authorized under a section that protects only the transferor. Subsection (b) protects "involuntary gap" transferees to the extent of any value (including services, but not including satisfaction of a debt that arose before the commencement of the case), given after commencement in exchange for the transfer. Notice or knowledge of the transferee is irrelevant in determining whether he is protected under this provision.

[*House Report No. 95–595, 95th Cong., 1st Sess. 375 (1977); Senate Report No. 95–989, 95th Cong., 2d Sess. 90 (1978).*]

Section 549 of the House amendment has been redrafted in order to incorporate sections 342(b) and (c) of the Senate amendment. Those sections have been consolidated and redrafted in section 549(c) of the House amendment. Section 549(d) of the House amendment adopts a provision contained in section 549(c) of the Senate amendment.

[*124 Cong. Rec. H 11,097 (Sept. 28, 1978); S 17,414 (Oct. 6, 1978).*]

Comment

Section 549 modifies Section 70d of the former Bankruptcy Act. It permits avoidance of transfers that occur after commencement of the case, if the transfer was either unauthorized or authorized under a section that protects only the transferor.

Subsection (b) is intended to protect "involuntary gap" transferees, that is, those to whom property is transferred between the date of filing an involuntary petition and the date of the order for relief. Such transferees are protected to the extent of value given after commencement of the case in exchange for the transfer. "Value" includes services, but not satisfaction of a prebankruptcy debt. Notice or knowledge of the pendency of the case is irrelevent in determining whether the transferee is protected.

1984 Amendments: The changes in subsection (b), which were made by § 464(a) of Pub. L. No. 98–353, were stated to be made to section 549(a), but were clearly intended for section 549(b). Subsection (c), relating to avoidance of postpetition transfers to good faith purchasers, was revised for clarification.

1986 Amendments: The amendment merely substituted "made" for the words "that occurs" in subsection (b).

Case Annotations

Section 549(c) is a narrow exception that does not override the general rule that violations of the automatic stay are void, not voidable. *In re* Schwartz, 954 F.2d 569, 26 C.B.C.2d 649 (9th Cir. 1992).

A creditor who fails to seek authorization from the bankruptcy court to act on behalf of a trustee or debtor in possession lacks standing to assert a claim under section 549 to avoid postpetition transfers as violative of the automatic stay. Matter of Pointer, 952 F.2d 82, 26 C.B.C.2d 551 (5th Cir. 1992).

A chapter 7 trustee may recover a postpetition, preconfirmation payment as an unauthorized transfer of estate property after commencement of the case if the trustee satisfies the three requirements of section 549(a), *i.e.:* 1) the transfer involved property of the estate, as it occurred before confirmation of the plan revested estate property in the debtor; 2) the transfer occurred after commencement of the case; and 3) the transfer was not authorized by any provision of the Code or by the court. *In re* Chattanooga Wholesale Antiques, Inc., 930 F.2d 458, 24 C.B.C.2d 1556 (6th Cir. 1991).

A tax refund suit under 28 U.S.C. § 1346, although based on a claim of an improper postpetition transfer under section 549, is subject to the time limitation imposed by 26 U.S.C. § 6532 and not to the statute of limitations applicable to a section 549 suit. *In re* Russell, 927 F.2d 413, 24 C.B.C.2d 1526 (8th Cir. 1991).

A trustee may not avoid a postpetition transfer of property which does not constitute property of the estate. *In re* Arnold, 908 F.2d 52, 23 C.B.C.2d 493 (6th Cir. 1990).

For a postpetition foreclosure sale to be excepted from the trustee's power to avoid postpetition transfers, a transferee must have perfected its security interest under applicable state law. *In re* Konowitz, 905 F.2d 55, 23 C.B.C.2d 433 (4th Cir. 1990).

Postpetition leases executed in the ordinary course of business are not avoidable. *In re* Dant & Russell, Inc., 853 F.2d 700, 20 C.B.C.2d 369 (9th Cir. 1988).

When a bankruptcy court authorizes a grant of security interests from a debtor to a creditor after the debtor has proceeded under a confirmed chapter 11 plan and the case is later converted to a chapter 7, section 549 does not grant the trustee power to avoid such postpetition grant of security interests. Vogel v. Russell Transfer, Inc., 852 F.2d 797, 19 C.B.C.2d 1203 (4th Cir. 1988).

For purposes of section 549(c), that a subsequent purchaser would have noted that there was an uncancelled mortgage of record indicating that the debtor's foreclosing mortgagee had filed a lis pendens will not excuse that mortgagee's failure to record the deed of foreclosure; section 549(c) requires only an inquiry into whether the mortgagee has taken the steps necessary under state law to perfect its claim against any hypothetical subsequent *bona fide* purchaser. *In re* Ward, 837 F.2d 124, 18 C.B.C.2d 133 (4th Cir. 1988).

The doctrine of equitable estoppel is applicable to the time limitations in section 549(d). Smith v. Mark Twain National Bank, 805 F.2d 278, 15 C.B.C.2d 1160 (8th Cir. 1986).

When a creditor has a security interest in the debtor's accounts receivable and receives warrants for payment to the debtor issued from the state prior to the debtor's bankruptcy petition, the transfer of the proceeds from the warrants to the creditor is a postpetition transaction voidable by the trustee if the warrants are exchanged for a negotiable instrument and converted to cash after the filing. Wilson v. First National Bank, Lubbock, Texas (In the Matter of Missionary Baptist Foundation of America, Inc.), 796 F.2d 752, 15 C.B.C.2d 476 (5th Cir. 1986).

Funds erroneously paid to a taxing authority instead of to a chapter 7 trustee under 724(b) constitute an unauthorized postpetition transfer avoidable under section 549 and recoverable under section 550. *In re* Forrest Marbury House Assocs. Ltd. Partnership, 26 C.B.C.2d 1270 (B. Ct., D.D.C. 1992).

Although a debtor's prepetition estimated tax payments that are applied postpetition by the IRS to tax liabilities are considered postpetition payments for purposes of section 549, they are not property of the estate since the debtor retains only a contingent reversionary interest in the funds at the time of the filing of the petition with the result that such a transfer is not voidable under 549. *In re* Halle, 25 C.B.C.2d 1113 (B. Ct., D. Colo. 1991).

A corollary to the power to continue the posthumous administration of a bankruptcy case is the power to exercise avoiding powers including those causes of action to reverse an unauthorized postpetition transfer pursuant to section 549 and, therefore, these actions do not abate upon the death of a debtor/defendant. *In re* Eads, 26 C.B.C.2d 457 (B. Ct., E.D. Cal. 1991).

A debtor cannot avoid a foreclosure as an avoidable postpetition transfer when the bankruptcy court approved the postpetition transfer. *In re* Fogarty, 23 C.B.C.2d 443 (B. Ct., S.D. Fla. 1990).

References

4 *Collier on Bankruptcy* ch. 549 (Matthew Bender 15th ed.).

2 *Collier Bankruptcy Manual* ch. 549 (Matthew Bender 3d ed.).

3 *Collier Bankruptcy Practice Guide* ch. 63 (Matthew Bender).

Rochelle, III and Feder, *Unauthorized Sales of a Debtor's Property: The Rights of a Purchaser Under Section 549 of the Bankruptcy Code,* 57 Am. Bankr. L.J. 23 (1983).

SECTION 550 (11 U.S.C. § 550)

§ 550. Liability of transferee of avoided transfer.

(a) Except as otherwise provided in this section, to the extent that a transfer is avoided under section 544, 545, 547, 548, 549, 553(b), or 724(a) of this title, the trustee may recover, for the benefit of the estate, the property transferred, or, if the court so orders, the value of such property, from—

(1) the initial transferee of such transfer or the entity for whose benefit such transfer was made; or

(2) any immediate or mediate transferee of such initial transferee.

(b) The trustee may not recover under subsection (a)(2) of this section from—

(1) a transferee that takes for value, including satisfaction or securing of a present or antecedent debt in good faith, and without knowledge of the voidability of the transfer avoided; or

(2) any immediate or mediate good faith transferee of such transferee.

(c) The trustee is entitled to only a single satisfaction under subsection (a) of this section.

(d)(1) A good faith transferee from whom the trustee may recover under subsection (a) of this section has a lien on the property recovered to secure the lesser of—

(A) the cost, to such transferee, of any improvement made after the transfer, less the amount of any profit realized by or accruing to such transferee from such property; and

(B) any increase in the value of such property as a result of such improvement, of the property transferred.

(2) In this subsection, "improvement" includes—

(A) physical additions or changes to the property transferred;

(B) repairs to such property;

(C) payment of any tax on such property;

(D) payment of any debt secured by a lien on such property that is superior or equal to the rights of the trustee; and

(E) preservation of such property.

(e) An action or proceeding under this section may not be commenced after the earlier of—

(1) one year after the avoidance of the transfer on account of which recovery under this section is sought; or

(2) the time the case is closed or dismissed.

Legislative History

Section 550 prescribes the liability of a transferee of an avoided transfer, and enunciates the separation between the concepts of avoiding a transfer and recovering from the transferee. Subsection (a) permits the trustee to recover from the initial transferee of an avoided transfer or from any immediate or mediate transferee of the initial transferee. The words "to the extent that" in the lead in to this subsection are designed to incorporate the protection of transferees found in proposed 11 U.S.C. §§ 549(b) and 548(c). Subsection (b) limits the liability of an immediate or mediate transferee of the initial transferee if such secondary transferee takes for value, in good faith and without knowledge of the voidability of the transfer. An immediate or mediate good faith transferee of a protected secondary transferee is also shielded from liability. This subsection is limited to the trustee's right to recover from subsequent transferees under subsection (a)(2). It does not limit the trustee's rights against the initial transferee under subsection (a)(1). The phrase "good faith" in this paragraph is intended to prevent a transferee from whom the trustee could recover from transfering the recoverable property to an innocent transferee, and receiving a retransfer from him, that is, "washing" the transaction through an innocent third party. In order for the transferee to be excepted from liability under this paragraph, he himself must be a good faith transferee. Subsection (c) is a further limitation on recovery. It specifies that the trustee is entitled to only one satisfactory, [*sic*] under subsection (a), even if more than one transferee is liable.

[*House Report No. 95-595, 95th Cong., 1st Sess. 375-376 (1977); Senate Report No. 95-989, 95th Cong., 2d Sess. 90 (1978).*]

Section 550(a)(1) of the House amendment has been modified in order to permit recovery from an entity for whose benefit an avoided transfer is made in addition to a recovery from the initial transferee of the transfer. Section 550(c) would still apply, and the trustee is entitled only to a single satisfaction. The liability of a transferee under section 550(a) applies only "to the extent that a transfer is avoided." This means that liability is not imposed on a transferee to the extent that a transferee is protected under a provision such as section 548(c) which grants a good faith transferee for value of a transfer that is avoided only as a fraudulent transfer, a lien on the property transferred to the extent of value given.

Section 550(b) of the House amendment is modified to indicate that value includes satisfaction or securing of a present antecedent debt. This means that the trustee may not recover under subsection (a)(2) from a subsequent transferee that takes for "value," provided the subsequent transferee also takes in good faith and without knowledge of the transfer avoided.

[*124 Cong. Rec. H 11,097 (Sept. 28, 1978); S 17,414 (Oct. 6, 1978).*]

Subsection (d) protects good faith transferees, either initial or subsequent, to the extent of the lesser of the cost of any improvement the transferee makes in the transferred property and the increase in value of the property as a result of the improvement. Paragraph (2) of the subsection defines improvement to include physical additions or changes to the property, repairs, payment of taxes on the property, [*Ed. Note:* This was deleted by Pub. L. No. 98-353.] payment of a debt secured by a lien on the property, discharge of a lien on the property, [*Ed. Note:* This was deleted by Pub. L. No. 98-353.] and preservation of the property.

[*House Report No. 95-595, 95th Cong., 1st Sess. 376 (1977); Senate Report No. 95-989, 95th Cong., 2d Sess. 90 (1978).*]

Subsection (e) establishes a statute of limitations on avoidance by the Trustee. The limitation is one year after the avoidance of the transfer or the time the case is closed or dismissed, whichever is earlier.

[*Senate Report No. 95-989, 95th Cong., 2d Sess. 90 (1978).*]

Section 550(e) of the House amendment is derived from section 550(e) of the Senate amendment.

[*124 Cong. Rec. H 11,097 (Sept 28, 1978); S 17,414 (Oct. 6, 1978).*]

Comment

Section 550 is derived from Sections 60b, 67a(3) and 70d(5) of the former Bankruptcy Act.

1984 Amendments: Subsection (d)(2) of section 550 was changed by eliminating subparagraph (E), the contents of which were substantially transferred to subparagraph (D). Minor technical chages were made in subsections (a) and (d)(1)(A) and (B).

Case Annotations

Although 11 U.S.C. § 106(c) waives sovereign immunity, it fails to establish unambiguously that its waiver extends to a bankruptcy trustee's claims for monetary relief. Therefore, a from the IRS funds of the corporate debtor wrongfully used by an officer of the debtor to discharge a personal tax obligation. United States v. Nordic Village, Inc., 503 U.S. —, 112 S. Ct. 1011, 117 L. Ed. 2d 181, 26 C.B.C.2d 9 (1992).

A creditor that receives funds owed to it by the debtor's president under an independent obligation between it and the president, but not based on the obligation existing between the debtor and its president, is the initial transferee of the transfer. Matter of T.B. Westex Foods, Inc., 950 F.2d 1187, 26 C.B.C.2d 682 (5th Cir. 1992).

Section 547 of the Code specifically separates the identification of avoidable transfers from the section 550 identification of who must pay. *In re* H & S Transportation Co., 939 F.2d 355, 25 C.B.C.2d 62 (6th Cir. 1991).

When an ultimate transferee has actual knowledge of the voidable nature of certain prior transfers, it is not a good faith transferee and is instead a transferee from whom, under Code section 550(a)(1), the trustee in bankruptcy is entitled to recover. Max Sugarman Funeral Home, Inc. v. A.D.B. Investors, 926 F.2d 1248, 24 C.B.C.2d 1414 (1st Cir. 1991).

An entity who receives funds and who purchases stock with the funds but who is contractually obligated to pledge the funds to another entity as security for a loan does not have dominion or control over the funds and is not a mediate or immediate transferee for purposes of section 550(a)(2). *In re* Bullion Reserve of North America, Inc., 922 F.2d 544, 24 C.B.C.2d 698 (9th Cir. 1991).

Funds that were improperly removed from escrow by the debtor to pay debts owed to a good faith creditor and subsequently recovered by the trustee in settlement of a preference action, are recovered for the benefit of the bankruptcy estate. *In re* First Capital Mortgage Loan Corp., 917 F.2d 424, 23 C.B.C.2d 1659 (10th Cir. 1990).

A lender to which the debtor sent payments in satisfaction of another's debt that the debtor had guaranteed is an "initial transferee" for purposes of section 547. *In re* Chase & Sanborn Corp., 904 F.2d 588, 23 C.B.C.2d 5 (11th Cir. 1990).

Section 550(a)(1), together with section 547(b)(1) and (b)(4)(B), permits recovery from an outsider transferee for transfers made during the extended preference period when the beneficiary of the transfers is an insider creditor or an insider guarantor. *In re* C-L Cartage Co., Inc., 899 F.2d 1490, 22 C.B.C.2d 901 (6th Cir. 1990).

Pursuant to section 550(a)(1), when a transfer that is avoidable under section 547(b) was made more than 90 days before the filing of the petition under title 11, a trustee may recover that transfer from a creditor when there has been a benefit to an insider of the debtor, despite the fact that the creditor itself is not an insider; however, payments satisfying pension obligations generally are not for the benefit of insiders unless the pension and welfare trusts received contractual guarantees from the insiders, and payments of tax obligations are never for the benefit of insiders. Levit v. Ingersoll Rand Financial Corp., (*In re* V.N. Deprizio Contr. Co.), 874 F.2d 1186, 22 C.B.C.2d 36 (7th Cir. 1989).

Section 550(a)(1) clearly permits a trustee to recover from the initial transferee of a preferential payment and a literal interpretation of sections 547(b) and 550(a)(1), read in conjunction, allows a trustee to avoid a transfer from a debtor to a non-insider creditor, made outside the 90-day preferential period, when the transfer benefits an insider-guarantor. *In re* Robinson Brothers Drilling, Inc., 892 F.2d 850, 21 C.B.C.2d 1405 (10th Cir. 1989).

The term "value" in section 550(b)(1) is different from and does not mean value to the debtor; a natural reading of this section looks to what the transferee gave up, rather than what the debtor received. Bonded Financial Services, Inc. v. European American Bank, 838 F.2d 890, 18 C.B.C.2d 155 (7th Cir. 1988).

For equitable reasons, an initial recipient of funds from a debtor who functions as a "mere conduit" may not always be an "initial transferee"-within the meaning of section 550(a)(1). Huffman v. Commerce Security Corp. (*In re* Harbour), 845 F.2d 1254, 18 C.B.C.2d 1214 (4th Cir. 1988).

A trustee may recover as preferential a transfer made to the unsecured beneficiary under a letter of credit when that letter of credit was expressly for the payment of an antecedent debt for which no new value was extended and was secured by an increased security interest in the debtor's assets. Kellogg v. Blue Trail Energy, Inc. (In the Matter of Compton Corp.), 831 F.2d 586, 17 C.B.C.2d 987 (5th Cir. 1987).

A trustee's right to recover property is limited by the express provisions of section 550 and not state law, and that section requires that a transferee have "knowledge" and not just "constructive notice" of the voidability of the transfer avoided. Smith v. Mixon (*In re* Mixon), 788 F.2d 229, 14 C.B.C.2d 704 (4th Cir. 1986).

The transferee of a cashier's check that was drawn against the funds of a chapter 7 debtor by its owner to pay the tax debt of another corporation has taken for value, in good faith, and without knowledge of the voidability of the transfer. Ross v. United States (*In re* Auto-Pak, Inc.), 16 C.B.C.2d 1301 (D.D.C. 1987).

Funds erroneously paid to a taxing authority instead of to a chapter 7 trustee under 724(b) constitute an unauthorized postpetition transfer avoidable under section 549 and recoverable under section 550. *In re Forrest Marbury House Assocs. Ltd. Partnership,* 26 C.B.C.2d 1270 (B. Ct., D.D.C. 1992).

A transfer to a non-insider creditor that reduces an insider's exposure on the debt cannot be interpreted to include a second transfer, to the insider, in order to prevent a trustee from recovering the transfer from the non-insider as preferential under section 550(a). *In re* Pine Springs Farm & Casino, Inc., 26 C.B.C.2d 1794 (B. Ct., N.D.N.Y. 1992).

A corollary to the power to continue the posthumous administration of a bankruptcy case is the power to exercise avoiding powers including those causes of action to recover the property or its value pursuant to section 550 and, therefore, these actions do not abate upon the death of a debtor/defendant. *In re* Eads, 26 C.B.C.2d 457 (B. Ct., E.D. Cal. 1991).

When the value of transferred property at the time of the petition date or at trial is substantially less than the value of the property as of the time of the transfer, the trustee will be entitled to recover the value of the property at the time of the transfer. *In re* Brown, 23 C.B.C.2d 885 (B. Ct., N.D. Tex. 1990).

The FDIC as receiver is a transferee within the definition of section 101, but in a Purchase and Assumption Agreement does not give up anything and therefore is not a transferee for value entitled to the protection of section 550(b)(1). *In re* Pernie Bailey Drilling Co., Inc., 22 C.B.C.2d 1537 (B. Ct., W.D. La. 1990).

An avoided transfer may be recovered from an entity, even if it was not in existence at the time of the transfer, if it can be proven that it was an entity for whose benefit the transfer was made. Ohio Corrugating Co. v. Security Pac. Business Credit, Inc. (In the Matter of Ohio Corrugating Co.), 16 C.B.C.2d 821 (B. Ct., N.D. Ohio 1987).

References

4 *Collier on Bankruptcy* ch. 550 (Matthew Bender 15th ed.).

2 *Collier Bankruptcy Manual* ch. 550 (Matthew Bender 3d ed.).

3 *Collier Bankruptcy Practice Guide* ch. 63 (Matthew Bender).

Brands, *The Interplay Between Section 547(b) and 550 of the Bankruptcy Code,* 89 Colum. L. Rev. 530 (1989).

Katzen, *Deprizio (In re Deprizio Construction Co.,* 874 F.2d 1186*) and Bankruptcy Code 550: Extended Preference Exposure via Insider Guarantees, and Other Perils of Initial Transferee Liability,* 45 Bus. Law. 511 (1990).

Note, *Levit v. Ingersoll Rand Financial Corp.: The Demise of Independent Preference Liability Under § 550(a),* J. Marshall L. Rev. 501 (1990).

Nutovic, *The Bankruptcy Preference Laws: Interpreting Code Sections 547(c)(2), 550(a)(1) and 546(a)(1),* 41 Bus. Law. 175 (1985).

Zaremba, *The C-L Cartage and Deprizio Cases: A Clean Break From Prior Law and the Consequences to Lenders,* 5 Ohio Law. 14 (1991).

SECTION 551 (11 U.S.C. § 551)

§ 551. **Automatic preservation of avoided transfer.** Any transfer avoided under section 522, 544, 545, 547, 548, 549, or 724(a) of this title, or any lien void under section 506(d) of this title, is preserved for the benefit of the estate but only with respect to property of the estate.

Legislative History

This section is a change from present law. It specifies that any avoided transfer is automatically preserved for the benefit of the estate. Under current law, the court must determine whether or not the transfer should be preserved. The operation of the section is automatic, unlike current law, even though preservation may not benefit the estate in every instance. A preserved lien may be abandoned by the trustee under proposed 11 U.S.C. § 554 if the preservation does not benefit the estate. [The section also preserves for the benefit of the estate any lien that is void under section 506(d)] The section as a whole prevents junior lienors from improving their position at the expense of the estate when a senior lien is avoided.

[*Ed. Note:* The bracketed sentence is omitted from the Senate Report.]

[*House Report No. 95–595, 95th Cong., 1st Sess. 376 (1977); Senate Report No. 95–989, 95th Cong., 2d Sess. 91 (1978).*]

Section 551 is adopted from the House bill and the alternative in the Senate amendment is rejected. The section is clarified to indicate that a transfer avoided or a lien that is void is preserved for the benefit of the estate, but only with respect to property of the estate. This prevents the trustee from asserting an avoided tax lien against after acquired property of the debtor.

[*124 Cong. Rec. H 11,097 (Sept. 28, 1978); S 17,414 (Oct. 6, 1978).*]

Comment

Section 551 is derived from former Rule 611 which in turn was derived from provisions in sections 60b, 67a(3), 67c(2), 67d(6), and 70e(2) of the former Bankruptcy Act.

Under former Rule 611 the court had to determine in an adversary proceeding whether the transfer should be avoided or preserved for the benefit of the estate. Under section 551, however, preservation for the benefit of the estate is automatic requiring no court action.

Case Annotations

A landlord who buys back from a trustee the right to assert a landlord's lien against a debtor's personal property which the trustee had avoided and preserved for the benefit of the estate may also seek postpetition rent and may be entitled to an administrative expense claim for the same rent. C & C Co. v. Seattle First National Bank (*In re* Coal-X Ltd. "76"), 14 C.B.C.2d 1325 (B. Ct., D. Utah 1986).

When a grantor's trust funds have been entirely depleted by the debtor's improper transfer to a bona fide purchaser prior to the filing of the bankruptcy petition, the proceeds recovered by the trustee in settlement of an action against the bona fide purchaser will be treated as property of the estate not subject to a constructive trust in favor of the grantor. Research-Planning, Inc. v. Segal (*In re* First Capital Mortgage Loan Corp.), 14 C.B.C.2d 1306 (B. Ct., D. Utah 1986).

A trustee who acquires a judgment lien by assignment from a creditor of the debtor in settlement of a section 547 preference action may not preserve an avoided lien against property which is not property of the estate; section 551 preserves the identified liens "only with respect to property of the estate." Waldschmidt v. Edgcomb Metals (*In re* Ward), 11 C.B.C.2d 569 (B. Ct., M.D. Tenn. 1984).

References

4 *Collier on Bankruptcy* ch. 551 (Matthew Bender 15th ed.).

2 *Collier Bankruptcy Manual* ch. 551 (Matthew Bender 3d ed.).

3 *Collier Bankruptcy Practice Guide* ch. 63 (Matthew Bender).

Chobot, *Preserving Liens Avoided in Bankruptcy—Limitations and Applications,* 62 Am. Bankr. L.J. 148 (1988).

SECTION 552 (11 U.S.C. § 552)

§ 552.　Postpetition effect of security interest.

(a) Except as provided in subsection (b) of this section, property acquired by the estate or by the debtor after the commencement of the case is not subject to any lien resulting from any security agreement entered into by the debtor before the commencement of the case.

(b) Except as provided in section 363, 506(c), 522, 544, 545, 547, and 548 of this title, if the debtor and an entity entered into a security agreement before the commencement of the case and if the security interest created by such security agreement extends to property of the debtor acquired before the commencement of the case and to proceeds, product, offspring, rents, or profits of such property, then such security interest extends to such proceeds, product, offspring, rents, or profits acquired by the estate after the commencement of the case to the extent provided by such security agreement and by applicable nonbankruptcy law, except to any extent that the court, after notice and a hearing and based on the equities of the case, orders otherwise.

Legislative History

Under the Uniform Commercial Code, Article 9, creditors may take security interests in after-acquired property. This section governs the effect of such a prepetition security interest in postpetition property. It applies to all security interests as defined in section 101 of the bankruptcy code, not only to U.C.C. security interests.

As a general rule, if a security agreement is entered into before the case, then property that the estate acquires is not subject to the security interest created by the security agreement. Subsection (b) provides the only exception. If the security agreement extends to proceeds, product, offspring, rents, or profits of property that the debtor had before the commencement of the case, then the proceeds, etc., continue to be subject to the security interest, except to the extent that the estate acquired the proceeds to the prejudice of other creditors holding unsecured claims. "Extends to" as used here would include an automatically arising security interest in proceeds, as permitted under the 1972 version of the Uniform Commercial Code, as well as an interest in proceeds specifically designated, as required under the 1962 Code or similar statutes covering property not covered by the Code. "Prejudice" is not intended to be a broad term here, but is designed to cover the situation where the estate expends funds that result in an increase in the value of collateral. The exception is to cover the situation where raw materials, for example, are converted into inventory, or inventory into accounts, at some expense to the estate, thus depleting the fund available for general unsecured creditors. The term "proceeds" is not limited to the technical definition of that term in the U.C.C., but covers any property into which property subject to the security interest is converted.

[*House Report No. 95–595, 95th Cong., 1st Sess. 376–377 (1977); See Senate Report No. 95–989, 95th Cong., 2d Sess. 91 (1978).*]

Section 552(a) is derived from the House bill and the alternative provision in the Senate amendment is rejected. Section 552(b) represents a compromise between the House bill and the Senate amendment. Proceeds coverage, but not after acquired property clauses, are valid under title 11. The provision allows the court to consider the equities in each case. In the course of such consideration the court may evaluate any expenditures by the estate relating to proceeds and any related improvement in position of the secured party. Although this section grants a secured party a security interest in proceeds, product, offspring, rents, or profits, the section is explicitly subject to other sections of title 11. For example, the trustee or debtor in possession may use, sell, or lease proceeds, product, offspring, rents, or profits under section 363.

[*124 Cong. Rec. H 11,097–8 (Sept. 28, 1978); S 17,414 (Oct. 6, 1978).*]

Comment

Section 552 is derived from section 9–204(3) of the Uniform Commercial Code, which provides:

(3) Except as provided in subsection (4) a security agreement may provide that collateral, whenever acquired, shall secure all obligations covered by the security agreement.

(4) No security interest attaches under an after-acquired property clause

(a) to crops which become such more than one year after the security agreement is executed except that a security interest in crops which is given in conjunction with a lease or a land purchase or improvement transaction evidenced by a contract, mortgage or deed of trust may if so agreed attach to crops to be grown on the land concerned during the period of such real estate transaction;

(b) to consumer goods other than accessions (Section 9–314) when given as additional security unless the debtor acquires rights in them within ten days after the secured party gives value.

But under subsection (a) of section 552, with the exceptions therein noted, property acquired by the estate or by the debtor after commencement of a case under the Code is not subject to any lien resulting from a security agreement predating the commencement of the case. However, subsection (b) is consistent with the after–acquired provisions of the U.C.C.

1984 Amendments: Several purely technical amendments were made to section 552.

Case Annotations

The term "proceeds" in section 552(b) is limited to the definition and treatment of the term in the Uniform Commercial Code, *i.e.*, state law, and under Virginia law, section 552(b) covers second generation proceeds traceable to the original collateral, even if they are in the form of inventory. *In re* Bumper Sales, Inc., 907 F.2d 1430, 23 C.B.C.2d 498 (4th Cir. 1990).

The increased cash surrender value of a life insurance policy is not a form of proceeds, product, offspring, rents, or profits within the meaning of section 552(b). *In re* Jones, 908 F.2d 859, 23 C.B.C.2d 763 (7th Cir. 1990).

Cash proceeds generated under a prepetition contract for the supply of coal, which were received postpetition, are subject to a prepetition security interest in the contract and its proceeds. United Virginia Bank v. Slab Fork Coal Co. (*In re* Slab Fork Coal Co.), 784 F.2d 1188, 14 C.B.C.2d 471 (4th Cir.), *cert. denied*, 477 U.S. 905, 106 S. Ct. 3275, 91 L. Ed. 2d 565 (1986).

The assignment of future wages as security for a prepetition loan does not create a continuing lien because no property exists until the wages have actually been earned, and, consequently, such a debt is dischargeable in a chapter 7 case. *In re* Soto, 667 F.2d 235, 5 C.B.C.2d 1277 (1st Cir. 1981).

In Arizona, when a properly secured party has a perfected interest in rents without further action under that state's law, the security interest in rents survives the filing of a bankruptcy petition pursuant to section 552(b), and the rents constitute cash collateral subject to the provisions of section 363. *In re* Tucson Industrial Partners, 25 C.B.C.2d 523 (9th Cir., B.A.P., 1991).

Pursuant to section 552(b) and the New York Uniform Commercial Code, if the financing statements for a ship mortgage cover casualty insurance proceeds and there is a loss of the vessel, the mortgagee's security interest in the insurance proceeds remains intact although the proceeds come into existence after the commencement of the bankruptcy case. *In re* McLean Indus., Inc., 25 C.B.C.2d 1090 (B. Ct., S.D.N.Y. 1991).

In the absence of a motion seeking relief from the automatic stay or an order for adequate protection, nothing in the Bankruptcy Code prevents postpetition rent payments in which a mortgagee has a perfected security interest from being applied to reduce the mortgagee's claim. *In re* Oaks Partners, Ltd., 26 C.B.C.2d 721 (B. Ct., N.D. Ga. 1991).

A prepetition security interest does not extend to a postpetition nonrefundable good faith deposit received from a prospective buyer. *In re* Vermont Knitting Co., Inc., 22 C.B.C.2d 1576 (B. Ct., D. Vt. 1990).

Under the "equities of the case" exception of section 552(b), an entity may not be entitled to gross cash collateral proceeds if the interest should be reduced by the reasonable postpetition expenses validly and demonstrably paid or incurred by debtors in maintaining the entity's collateral. In the Matter of Kain, 18 C.B.C.2d 1236 (B. Ct., W.D. Mich. 1988).

The right to avoid transfers under the trustee's avoiding powers does not constitute proceeds, product, offspring, rents or profits of the subject of a security agreement, with the result that section 552(b) does not extend a creditor's security interest to the right to set aside and recover property based on a trustee's avoiding power. *In re* Figearo, 17 C.B.C.2d 1063 (B. Ct., D. Nev. 1987).

Any interest accruing from the proceeds of a court ordered sale that await distribution is not available to satisfy a trustee's administrative claims, but is the property of the secured creditor to which the proceeds would have gone but for the delay incident to the bankruptcy proceedings. *In re* Sherrill, 17 C.B.C.2d 1033 (B. Ct., W.D. Tex. 1987).

If a chapter 12 debtor can propose a plan which adequately protects the interest of a creditor in its collateral, the debtor may use the proceeds of the sale of collateral even if the collateral is covered by a security interest. In the Matter of Wobig, 16 C.B.C.2d 1222 (B. Ct., D. Neb. 1987).

Postpetition rentals of a debtor's land are not after-acquired property of the debtor, and the debtor is not entitled to the rent proceeds, if they are subject to prepetition liens on rent valid under state law except under the equities of the case exception contained in section 552(b). Under that exception, a court may allow a debtor his expenses and taxes in connection with the production of rental income from the farmland. Oliver v. MBank Dallas, N.A. (*In re* Oliver), 16 C.B.C.2d 1096 (B. Ct., N.D. Tex. 1986).

If a secured creditor has a valid security interest in the crops and proceeds of crops growing on the date of the petition, that security interest extends to the postpetition harvest of the crop, subject to the deduction from the proceeds of the debtor's costs and expenses in growing the crop. The security interest also supersedes one entered, under court order, postpetition that purports to be "secured by the proceeds of the crop grown on the land." In the Matter of Vanasdale, 15 C.B.C.2d 1010 (B. Ct., N.D. Ohio 1986).

References

4 *Collier on Bankruptcy* ch. 552 (Matthew Bender 15th ed.).

2 *Collier Bankruptcy Manual* ch. 552 (Matthew Bender 3d ed.).

3 *Collier Bankruptcy Practice Guide* ch. 53 (Matthew Bender).

Cohen, McLaughlin and Zaretsky, *Practice Problem: The Supreme Court Decision in United Saving Association v. Timbers,* 2 Commercial Law Report 97 (1988).

Justice, *Secured Transactions—What Floats Can Be Sunk,* 24 Villanova L. Rev. 867 (1979).

Note, *Security Interests in Notes & Mortgages: Determining the Applicable Law,* 79 Colum. L. Rev. 1414 (1979).

SECTION 553 (11 U.S.C. § 553)

§ 553.   Setoff.

(a) Except as otherwise provided in this section and in sections 362 and 363 of this title, this title does not affect any right of a creditor to offset a mutual debt owing by such creditor to the debtor that arose before the commencement of the case under this title against a claim of such creditor against the debtor that arose before the commencement of the case, except to the extent that—

(1) the claim of such creditor against the debtor is disallowed other than under section 502(b)(3) of this title:

(2) such claim was transferred, by an entity other than the debtor, to such creditor—

(A) after the commencement of the case; or

(B) (i) after 90 days before the date of the filing of the petition; and

(ii) while the debtor was insolvent; or

(3) the debt owed to the debtor by such creditor was incurred by such creditor—

(A) after 90 days before the date of the filing of the petition:

(B) while the debtor was insolvent: and

(C) for the purpose of obtaining a right of setoff against the debtor.

(b)(1) Except with respect to a setoff of a kind described in sections 362(b)(6), 362(b)(7), 362(b)(14), 365(h)(2) or 365(i)(2), of this title, if a creditor offsets a mutual debt owing to the debtor against a claim against the debtor on or within 90 days before the date of the filing of the petition, then the trustee may recover from such creditor the amount so offset to the extent that any insufficiency on the date of such setoff is less than the insufficiency on the later of—

(A) 90 days before the date of the filing of the petition; and

(B) the first date during the 90 days immediately preceding the date of the filing of the petition on which there is an insufficiency.

(2) In this subsection, "insufficiency" means amount, if any, by which a claim against the debtor exceeds a mutual debt owing to the debtor by the holder of such claim.

(c) For the purposes of this section, the debtor is presumed to have been insolvent on and during the 90 days immediately preceding the date of the filing of the petition.

Legislative History

This section preserves, with some changes, the right of setoff in bankruptcy cases now found in section 68 of the Bankruptcy Act. One exception to the right is the automatic stay, discussed in connection with proposed 11 U.S.C. § 362. Another is the right of the trustee to use property under section 363 that is subject to a right of setoff.

The section states that the right of setoff is unaffected by the bankruptcy code except to the extent that the creditor's claim is disallowed, the creditor acquired (other than from the debtor) the claim during the 90 days preceding the case while the debtor was insolvent, the debt being offset was incurred for the purpose of obtaining a right of setoff, while the debtor was insolvent and during the 90-day prebankruptcy period, or the creditor improved his position in the 90-day period (similar to the improvement in position test found in the preference section, 547(c)(5)). Only the last exception is an addition to current law.

As under section 547(f), the debtor is presumed to have been insolvent during the 90 days before the case.

[*House Report No. 95–595, 95th Cong., 1st Sess. 377 (1977); Senate Report No. 95–989, 95th Cong., 2d Sess. 91–92 (1978).*]

Section 553 of the House amendment is derived from a similar provision contained in the Senate amendment, but is modified to clarify application of a two-point test with respect to set offs.

[*124 Cong. Rec. H 11,098 (Sept. 28, 1978); S 17,414 (Oct. 6, 1978).*]

Comment

Section 553 is derived from and preserves, with some changes, the right of set off as set forth in section 68 of the former Bankruptcy Act.

The two important changes are (1) the automatic stay of setoff provided in section 362 of the Code, and (2) the right of the trustee to use property subject to setoff as provided in section 363 of the Code. Section 553 sets forth certain circumstances wherein the right to setoff will be denied, as for instance, where the debt was incurred for the purpose of obtaining the right to setoff (codifying case law to that effect), or where the claim was acquired (other than from the bankrupt) during the 90 days preceding the case while the debtor was insolvent. The debtor is presumed to have been insolvent during the 90 days before the case.

See also section 506(a) for treatment of the setoff claim where exercise of the right to setoff has been stayed under section 362.

1984 Amendments: A technical amendment to section 553(b)(1), changed the reference therein from section 365(h)(1) to section 365(h)(2), and added a reference to section 365(i)(2).

1990 Amendments: Pub. L. No. 101–311 amended subsection (b)(1) by inserting a reference to section 362(b)(14), thus additionally preventing a trustee from recovering an amount offset of the kind described in section 362(b)(14).

Case Annotations

A creditor's right to setoff under section 553 survives confirmation of a debtor's chapter 11 plan despite the provision in section 1141 for discharge of prepetition debts upon confirmation and despite the general discharge purpose of a chapter 11 confirmation so a debtor may continue in business. *In re* De Laurentiis Entertainment Group, Inc., 963 F.2d 1269, 26 C.B.C.2d 1435 (9th Cir. 1992).

To exercise the right of recoupment, there need not be any express contractual right to withhold payments for the transaction and the amount to be recouped need not be certain. In the Matter of Holford, 896 F.2d 176, 22 C.B.C.2d 1097 (5th Cir. 1990).

The right of setoff depends on the existence of mutual debts and claims between a creditor and a debtor but when principal and interest payments are held by a creditor in trust, with contractual language specifying that such payments are the property of the debtor, there is no mutual debt for purposes of setoff. In the Matter of Bevill, Bresler & Schulman Asset Management Corp., 896 F.2d 54, 22 C.B.C.2d 551 (3d Cir. 1990).

Under the mutuality requirement of section 553(a) each party must own his claim in his own right severally, with the right to collect in his own name and in his own right and severally; this requirement is designed to protect against "triangular" setoffs, *e.g.,* when a creditor attempts to set off its debt to a debtor with the latter's debt to a third party. In the Matter of United Sciences of America, Inc., 893 F.2d 720, 22 C.B.C.2d 638 (5th Cir. 1990).

The right to exercise a setoff is not limited by time constraints nor is it tied to the filing of a proof of claim. Turner v United States (*In re* G.S. Omni Corp.), 835 F.2d 1317, 17 C.B.C.2d 1429 (10th Cir. 1987).

There is no requirement in the elements of section 553 that an amount due be computed prior to the filing of the bankruptcy petition in order for it to be available as a setoff under 553, and the order in which the mutual debts arose does not matter. Braniff Airways, Inc. v. Exxon Co., U.S.A., 814 F.2d 1030, 16 C.B.C.2d 1447 (5th Cir. 1987).

Section 553 does not apply to a valid foreclosure of perfected security interests. Smith v. Mark Twain National Bank, 805 F.2d 278, 15 C.B.C.2d 1160 (8th Cir. 1986).

The Bankruptcy Code does not authorize the extension of self-help remedies on the part of prepetition claimants to reach postpetition assets, so that the prepetition debt of one debtor may not be set off against the postpetition claim of another debtor that is owed the prepetition debt—the debts are not mutual and allowing such a transaction would result in pre- and postpetition claims cancelling each other out to the detriment of equally classified claims. Considerations of equity cannot override this reading of the law, for when one claimant gets treatment that is denied others, they have been treated inequitably because of the unequal application of the legal rules. Boston and Maine Corp. v. Chicago Pacific Corp., 785 F.2d 562, 14 C.B.C.2d 715 (7th Cir. 1986).

Because a surety has an equitable right to compel a creditor to assert its right of setoff against an insolvent debtor to prevent the unjust enrichment of the estate at the surety's expense, the right to benefit from a creditor's setoff right demonstrates a surety's interest in a turnover proceeeding so as to enable the surety to intervene. Merritt Commercial Sav. & Loan, Inc. v. Guinee (*In re* James R. Corbitt Co.), 766 F.2d 850, 13 C.B.C.2d 174 (4th Cir. 1985).

All of the monthly benefits that accrue before the filing of a petition in bankruptcy should be considered obligations of the Social Security Administration to the beneficiary 90 days before the petition is filed for the purposes of the "improvement in position" test, even though the benefits are not yet payable, such that the SSA does not have to return monies deducted prepetition for overpayments. Lee v. Schweiker, 739 F.2d 870, 11 C.B.C.2d 834 (3d Cir. 1984).

A transferee has a right of setoff in an action to enforce a note when the note was consideration for a bulk transfer that did not comply with U.C.C. provisions, notwithstanding the fact that the transferee's conduct provided the grounds for invalidation. Verco Indus. v. Spartan Plastics (*In re* Verco Indus.), 704 F.2d 1134, 8 C.B.C.2d 554 (9th Cir. 1983).

A debtor's assumption of an executory contract has no effect on the creditor's setoff rights under section 553 since assumption does not modify the date at which the obligations arose nor does it modify the mutuality of the promises made. A court should not use its equitable discretion to bar or defer setoff when the requirements of section 553 are otherwise satisfied unless: 1) the creditor committed an inequitable, illegal or fraudulent act; 2) the setoff is against public policy; or 3) setoff would significantly harm the debtor's ability to reorganize. *In re* Allen, 26 C.B.C.2d 767 (B. Ct., N.D. Iowa 1992).

A subcontractor with a direct remedy under state law against the surety of a bond guaranteeing a principal contractor's performance is considered to be a principal in a determination of mutuality of rights when the surety seeks to set off that debt under section 553 against an unrelated debt the subcontractor owes to the surety. *In re* Bay State York Co., Inc., 26 C.B.C.2d 1520 (B. Ct., D. Mass. 1992).

When the IRS authorizes a refund and offsets the refund pursuant to 31 U.S.C. § 3720A(c) and 26 U.S.C. § 6402(d)(1) within ninety days of the filing of the bankruptcy petition, the setoff is subject to the provisions of section 553(b). *In re* Hankerson, 25 C.B.C.2d 1429 (B. Ct., E.D. Pa. 1991).

Debts that are not mutual may not be set off even if they are between the same two parties. *In re* Tomer, 25 C.B.C.2d 22 (B. Ct., S.D. Ill. 1991).

Since a claim for the rejection of a lease is classified and treated as a prepetition claim under sections 365(g)(1) and 502(g) of the Code, the prepetition requirement of section 553 with respect to that claim is satisfied. *In re* Express Freight Lines, Inc., 25 C.B.C.2d 341 (B. Ct., E.D. Wis. 1991).

If a contract entered into prepetition sets forth mutual duties and obligations on both sides, these duties and obligations remain prepetition obligations subject to setoff even if they are actually performed postpetition. *In re* Lund, 26 C.B.C.2d 716 (B. Ct., D.N.D. 1990).

Since setoff is permissive and not mandatory, and based on equitable principles, and since the Code contains an implicit policy of encouraging creditors not to precipitate a debtor's decline by exercising setoff rights prepetition, a court should consider a broad range of factors in deciding whether a postpetition setoff should be allowed, including whether the creditor has improved its position vis-a-vis other creditors by its setoff and whether the creditor has violated the statutory automatic stay. *In re* Rooster, Inc., 24 C.B.C.2d 1940 (B. Ct., E.D. Pa. 1991).

Although section 553(b) recognizes and preserves a bank's right of setoff under state law, that right is subject to the automatic stay of section 362(a)(7). *In re* First Connecticut Small Business Investment Co., 23 C.B.C.2d 928 (B. Ct., D. Conn. 1990).

A setoff will not be valid when the creditor deceptively accepted or obtained a deposit with the intent of applying it to a preexisting claim it has against the debtor. *In re* Kittrell, 23 C.B.C.2d 1478 (B. Ct., M.D.N.C. 1990).

Absent the assertion of a prior lien to funds resulting from prepetition medicare underpayments, setoff of prepetition medicare overpayments to a debtor against prepetition underpayments by the Secretary of Health and Human Services is appropriate. *In re* Metropolitan Hospital, 22 C.B.C.2d 577 (B. Ct., E.D. Pa. 1990).

References

4 *Collier on Bankruptcy* ch. 553 (Matthew Bender 15th ed.).

2 *Collier Bankruptcy Manual* ch. 553 (Matthew Bender 3d ed.).

4 *Collier Bankruptcy Practice Guide* ch. 66 (Matthew Bender).

Fourth Circuit Interprets the Subsequent Advance Rule of Bankruptcy Code Section 547(c)(4) to Allow Setoff Against All Prior Preferential Payments, 43 S.C.L. Rev. 18 (1991).

Freeman, *Setoff Under the New Bankruptcy Code: The Effect on Bankers,* 97 Banking L.J. 484 (1980).

Hall, *Preferences and Setoffs: Sections 547 and 553,* 2 Bank. Dev. J. 49 (1985).

Williams, *Application of the Cash Collateral Paradigm to the Preservation of the Right to Setoff in Bankruptcy*, 7 Bankr. Dev. J. 27 (1990).

Zaretsky, *Setoffs, "Freezes" and the Automatic Stay*, N.Y.L.J., Feb. 24, 1986, at 1.

SECTION 554 (11 U.S.C. § 554)

§ 554.   Abandonment of property of the estate.

(a) After notice and a hearing, the trustee may abandon any property of the estate that is burdensome to the estate or that is of inconsequential value and benefit to the estate.

(b) On request of a party in interest and after notice and a hearing, the court may order the trustee to abandon any property of the estate that is burdensome to the estate or that is of inconsequential value and benefit to the estate.

(c) Unless the court orders otherwise, any property scheduled under section 521(1) of this title not otherwise administered at the time of the closing of a case is abandoned to the debtor and administered for purposes of section 350 of this title.

(d) Unless the court orders otherwise, property of the estate that is not abandoned under this section and that is not administered in the case remains property of the estate.

Bankruptcy Rule References: 6007 and 7001

Legislative History

This section authorizes the court to authorize the trustee to abandon any property of the estate that is burdensome to the estate or that is of inconsequential value to the estate. Abandonment may be to any party with a possessory interest in the property abandoned. In order to aid administration of the case, subsection (b) deems the court to have authorized abandonment of any property that is scheduled under section 521(1) and that is not administered before the case is closed. That property is deemed abandoned to the debtor. Subsection (c) specifies that if property is neither abandoned nor administered it remains property of the estate.

[*House Report No. 95–595, 95th Cong., 1st Sess. 377 (1977); Senate Report No. 95–989, 95th Cong., 2d Sess. 92 (1978).*]

Section 554(b) is new and permits a party in interest to request the court to order the trustee to abandon property of the estate that is burdensome to the estate or that is of inconsequential value to the estate.

[*124 Cong. Rec. H 11,098 (Sept. 28, 1978); S 17,414 (Oct. 6, 1978).*]

Comment

Bankruptcy Rule 6007(a), amended in 1991, requires a trustee or debtor in possession, unless the court directs otherwise, to give notice of a proposed abandonment or disposition of property to the United States trustee, all creditors, indenture trustees and committees elected pursuant to section 705 or appointed pursuant to section 1102 of the Code. The rule is applicable in cases under chapters 7, 11, 12, or 13 but does not apply to section 554(c) pursuant to which property is deemed abandoned if not administered.

Subdivision (b) permits a party in interest to serve and file a motion requiring the trustee or debtor in possession to abandon property of the estate. Rule 7001(1) excepts from the category of adversary proceedings, a motion under section 554(b).

Congress added a fee of $60 for motions to compel abandonment of property of the estate under section 554(b). The fee became effective 30 days after the enactment of Pub. L. No. 101-162, which was November 21, 1989.

Subdivision (c) provides that if timely objection under subdivision (a) of the rule, or if a motion under subdivision (b), is made, the court shall set a hearing on notice to the United States trustee and to entities as directed by the court.

1984 Amendments: Section 554(c) was changed so that property not administered before the case is closed is deemed "administered" as well as abandoned and clarifies that abandonment is to the debtor.

Case Annotations

Section 554 does not preempt all state and local laws and the bankruptcy court does not have the power to authorize an abandonment without formulating conditions that will adequately protect the public's health and safety; the trustee may not abandon property in contravention of a state statute or regulation that is reasonably designed to protect the public health and safety from identified hazards. Midlantic National Bank v. New Jersey Dept. of Environmental Protection, 474 U.S. 494, 106 S. Ct. 755, 88 L. Ed. 2d 859, 13 C.B.C.2d 1355 (1986).

A chapter 7 trustee's active pursuit of settlement of a claim, rather than litigation, is not *per se* abandonment of property of the estate or failure to act in the estate's best interests; the chapter 7 trustee is charged with an informed judgment regarding such matters and is entitled to due deference from the reviewing court. *In re* Thompson, 965 F.2d 1136, 26 C.B.C.2d 1306 (1st Cir. 1992).

When a trustee effectively abandons property of the estate, and title reverts back to the debtor, the debtor cannot, as a matter of law, violate 18 U.S.C. § 152, which, by its terms, makes it a crime to knowingly and fraudulently conceal bankruptcy estate assets from the trustee and creditors. United States v. Grant, 946 F.2d 1, 25 C.B.C.2d 818 (1st Cir. 1991).

Property abandoned under section 554 ceases to be property of the estate and the party which holds a possessory right to the property at the time of filing of the bankruptcy petition reacquires that right upon abandonment. *In re* Dewsnup, 908 F.2d 588, 23 C.B.C.2d 1110 (10th Cir. 1990), *aff'd,* 502 U.S.—, 112 S. Ct. 773, 116 L. Ed. 2d 903, 25 C.B.C.2d 1297 (1992).

A trustee may abandon property of the estate without obtaining a court order authorizing abandonment when there is no objection to the proposed abandonment by an interested party. In the Matter of Trim-x, 695 F.2d 296, 7 C.B.C.2d 955 (7th Cir. 1982).

While a foreclosure sale will generate substantial federal and state income tax liabilities that are "burdensome to the estate," an abandonment of the property that constitutes a transfer or sale is itself a taxable event and, therefore, is equally "burdensome to the estate." *In re* A.J. Lane & Co., Inc., 25 C.B.C.2d 1202 (B. Ct., D. Mass. 1991).

A creditor must be given notice and an opportunity for a hearing before an abandonment can be given effect. *In re* Moore, 22 C.B.C.2d 645 (B. Ct., C.D. Cal. 1990).

Section 554(a) requires notice to creditors and parties in interest before any abandonment of property can be affected; mere inaction by the trustee does not accomplish abandonment. *In re* Prospero, 22 C.B.C.2d 199 (B. Ct., C.D. Cal. 1989).

A bankruptcy court cannot authorize the abandonment of property in contravention of state law *unless* conditions are formulated that will adequately protect the public health and safety. In deciding whether to permit a trustee to abandon estate property containing hazardous waste, the court must consider these factors: the imminence of danger to the public health and safety, the extent of probable harm, the amount and type of hazardous waste, the cost of bringing the property into compliance with environmental laws, and the amount and type of funds available for cleanup. *In re* Franklin Signal Corp., 15 C.B.C.2d 869 (B. Ct., D. Minn. 1986). *See also In re* Oklahoma Refining Co., 15 C.B.C.2d 621 (B. Ct., W.D. Okla. 1986).

References

4 *Collier on Bankruptcy* ch. 554 (Matthew Bender 15th ed.).

2 *Collier Bankruptcy Manual* ch. 554 (Matthew Bender 3d ed.).

Bankrutpcy—Abandonment—Trustee in Bankruptcy May Not Abandon Burdensome Property of Debtor's Estate in Contravention of State and Local Environmental Protection Laws—In re Quanta Resources Corp., 15 Seton Hall L. Rev. 967 (1985).

Comment, *Abandonment of Toxic Wastes Under Section 554 of the Bankruptcy Code,* 71 Marq. L. Rev. 353 (1988).

Comment, *Bankruptcy, Hazardous Waste and Mass Tort: A Top Priority Review,* 23 Hous. L. Rev. 1243 (1986).

Leibowitz, *Right of Trustee To Abandon Polluted Property,* N.Y.L.J., Mar. 21, 1985, at 1, col. 1.

Note, *Abandonment of Hazardous Waste Sites in the Course of Bankruptcy Proceedings,* 28 Nat. Resources J. 189 (1988).

Note, *Hazardous Waste Removal, State Court Injunctions, and the Bankruptcy Code: Ohio v. Kovacs,* 54 Cinn. L. Rev. 1101 (1986).

Note, *Ohio v. Kovacs: Financial Freedom for Bankrupt Polluters,* 34 DePaul Law Rev. 1069 (1985)

Paige, *In re Quanta Resources Corp.: Bankruptcy Policy v. Environmental Interests; A Polluted Judicial Theory,* 59 Am. Bankr. L.J. 357 (1985).

Redmond, *Abandonment Rights Under Section 554(a) of the Bankruptcy Code:* Midlantic National Bank v. New Jersey Department of Environmental Protection, 40 Sw. L.J. 1103 (1986).

Weil, *Effects of Real Property Abandonments in Bankruptcy,* 70 J. Tax'n 358 (1989).

SECTION 555 (U.S.C. § 555)

§ 555.   Contractual right to liquidate a securities contract.

The exercise of a contractual right of a stockbroker, financial institution, or securities clearing agency to cause the liquidation of a securities contract, as defined in section 741(7), because of a condition of the kind specified in section 365(e)(1) of this title shall not be stayed, avoided, or otherwise limited by operation of any provision of this title or by order of a court or administrative agency in any proceeding under this title unless such order is authorized under the provisions of the Securities Investor Protection Act of 1970 (15 U.S.C. 78aaa *et seq.*) or any statute administered by the Securities and Exchange Commission. As used in this section, the term "contractual right" includes a right set forth in a rule or bylaw of a national securities exchange, a national securities association, or a securities clearing agency.

Legislative History

Section 6(a) [of Public Law 97–222] adds a new section 555 to title 11 to provide that the exercise of a contractual right of a stockbroker or securities clearing agency to cause the liquidation of a securities contract, because of a condition of the kind specified in section 365(e)(1) of title 11, shall not be stayed, avoided, or otherwise limited in any proceeding under title 11 by a court or administrative agency, unless such order is authorized under the provisions of the Securities Investor Protection Act or any statute administered by the Securities and Exchange Commission. The prompt liquidation of an insolvent's position is generally desirable to minimize the potentially massive losses and chain reaction of insolvencies that could occur if the market were to move sharply in the wrong direction.

[*House Report No. 97–420, 97th Cong., 2d Sess. 3 (1982).*]

Section 6 of H.R. 4935 [Public Law 97–222] would add a new section 555 to the code to assure that a court or administrative agency cannot stay, avoid, or otherwise limit the right of a stockbroker or securities clearing agency to exercise a contractual right to cause the liquidation of a securities contract because of a condition of the kind specified in subparagraphs (A), (B), or (C) of section 365(e)(1).

A savings clause is included in section 555 at the recommendation of the Securities Investor Protection Corporation and Securities and Exchange Commission with regard to certain orders under the Securities Investor Protection Act of 1970 or any statute administered by the Securities and Exchange Commission. The operation of this savings clause is intended to apply only to an order that (i) is sought by a trustee appointed under the Securities Investor Protection Act of 1970 or by the Securities Investor Protection Corporation pursuant to authority conferred by that act, or (ii) is sought or issued by an administrative agency pursuant to authority conferred by a statute administered by the Securities and Exchange Commission.

It is essential that stockbrokers and securities clearing agencies be protected from the issuance of a court or administrative agency order which would stay the prompt liquidation of an insolvent's positions, because market fluctuations in the securities markets create an inordinate risk that the insolvency of one party could trigger a chain reaction of insolvencies of the others who carry accounts for that party and undermine the integrity of those markets.

[*128 Cong. Rec. S 8,133 (July 13, 1982).*]

Comment

1984 Amendments: Section 555 was amended by insertion of the words "financial institution."

References

4 *Collier on Bankruptcy* ch. 555 (Matthew Bender 15th ed.).

2 *Collier Bankruptcy Manual* ch. 555 (Matthew Bender 3d ed.).

SECTION 556 (U.S.C. § 556)

§ 556. Contractual right to liquidate a commodities contract or forward contract.

The contractual right of a commodity broker or forward contract merchant to cause the liquidation of a commodity contract, as defined in section 761(4), or forward contract because of a condition of the kind specified in section 365(e)(1) of this title, and the right to a variation or maintenance margin payment received from a trustee with respect to open commodity contracts or forward contracts, shall not be stayed, avoided, or otherwise limited by operation of any provision of this title or by the order of a court in any proceeding under this title. As used in this section, the term "contractual right" includes a right set forth in a rule or bylaw of a clearing organization or contract market or in a resolution of the governing board thereof and a right, whether or not evidenced in writing, arising under common law, under law merchant or by reason of normal business practice.

Legislative History

Section 6(a) [of Public Law 97–222] also adds a new section 556 to title 11 to state that the contractual right of a commodity broker or forward contract merchant to cause the liquidation of a commodity contract, because of a condition of the kind specified in section 365(e)(1) of title 11, shall not be stayed, avoided, or otherwise limited by a court in any proceeding under title 11. As used in section 556, the terms "variation" and "maintenance" margin payments should be construed in conformity with their use in the definition of the term "margin payment" in section 761(45). Section 556 does not impose upon a trustee any statutory duty to make variation or maintenance margin payments. As used in this section, the right to liquidate a commodity contract is only the right to close out an open position. For example, the right to liquidate does not constitute the right to transfer cash, securities, or property held with respect to such contracts, except to the extent otherwise provided in this title.

[*House Report No. 97–420, 97th Cong., 2d Sess. 4 (1982).*]

Section 6 of H.R. 4935 [Public Law 97–222] would add a new section 556 to the code to make explicit that the bankruptcy of an entity will not prevent a commodity broker or forward contract merchant from causing the liquidation of a commodity contract or forward contract because of a condition of the kind specified in subparagraphs (A) (B) or (C) of section 365(e)(1). The new section would also make explicit the right of a commodity broker or forward contract merchant to receive and retain variation or maintenance margin with respect to commodity contracts or forward contracts of a customer, when and as due, irrespective of whether the commodity contracts are specifically identifiable.

For purposes of section 556, a court order authorized under the provisions of the Securities Investor Protection Act of 1970, as referred to in new section 555 and issued with respect to an entity that is both a stockbroker and a commodity broker or forward contract merchant, would not affect the rights relating to commodity contracts and forward contracts described in section 556. In addition, as used in section 556, the terms "variation" and "maintenance" margin payments would be construed in conformity with their use in the definition of the term "margin payment" in section 761(15).

Section 556 would not impose upon a trustee any statutory duty to make variation or maintenance margin payments. However, in the event a trustee fails to make such payments, a commodity broker or forward contract merchant may exercise its contractual right to liquidate, if it has not already done so. In addition, as used in section 556, the right to liquidate a commodity contract would only be the right to close out an open position. For example, the right to liquidate would not constitute the right to transfer cash, securities, or property held with respect to such contracts, except to the extent otherwise provided in title 11.

[*128 Cong. Rec. S 8,133 (July 13, 1982).*]

Comment

1990 Amendments: Pub. L. No. 101–311 amended section 556 to expand the definition of "contractual right" as used in this section by adding "a right, whether or not evidenced in writing, arising under common law, under law merchant or by reason of normal business practice."

References

4 *Collier on Bankruptcy* ch. 556 (Matthew Bender 15th ed.).

2 *Collier Bankruptcy Manual* ch. 556 (Matthew Bender 3d ed.).

SECTION 557 (11 U.S.C. § 557)

§ 557. Expedited determination of interests in, and abandonment or other disposition of grain assets.

(a) This section applies only in a case concerning a debtor that owns or operates a grain storage facility and only with respect to grain and the proceeds of grain. This section does not affect the application of any other section of this title to property other than grain and proceeds of grain.

(b) In this section—

(1) "grain" means wheat, corn, flaxseed, grain sorghum, barley, oats, rye, soybeans, other dry edible beans, or rice;

(2) "grain storage facility" means a site or physical structure regularly used to store grain for producers, or to store grain acquired from producers for resale; and

(3) "producer" means an entity which engages in the growing of grain.

(c)(1) Notwithstanding sections 362, 363, 365, and 554 of this title, on the court's own motion the court may, and on the request of the trustee or an entity that claims an interest in grain or the proceeds of grain the court shall, expedite the procedures for the determination of interests in and the disposition of grain and the proceeds of grain, by shortening to the greatest extent feasible such time periods as are otherwise applicable for such procedures and by establishing, by order, a timetable having a duration of not to exceed 120 days for the completion of the applicable procedure specified in subsection (d) of this section. Such time periods and such timetable may be modified by the court, for cause, in accordance with subsection (f) of this section.

(2) The court shall determine the extent to which such time periods shall be shortened, based upon—

(A) any need of an entity claiming an interest in such grain or the proceeds of grain for a prompt determination of such interest;

(B) any need of such entity for a prompt disposition of such grain;

(C) the market for such grain;

(D) the conditions under which such grain is stored;

(E) the costs of continued storage or disposition of such grain;

(F) the orderly administration of the estate;

(G) the appropriate opportunity for an entity to assert an interest in such grain; and

(H) such other considerations as are relevant to the need to expedite such procedures in the case.

(d) The procedures that may be expedited under subsection (c) of this section include—

(1) the filing of and response to—

(A) a claim of ownership;

(B) a proof of claim;

(C) a request for abandonment;

(D) a request for relief from the stay of action against property under section 362(a) of this title;

(E) a request for determination of secured status;

(F) a request for determination of whether such grain or the proceeds of grain—

(i) is property of the estate;

(ii) must be turned over to the estate; or

(iii) may be used, sold, or leased; and

(G) any other request for determination of an interest in such grain or the proceeds of grain;

(2) the disposition of such grain or the proceeds of grain, before or after determination of interests in such grain or the proceeds of grain, by way of—

(A) sale of such grain;

(B) abandonment;

(C) distribution; or

(D) such other method as is equitable in the case;

(3) subject to sections 701, 702, 703, 1104, 1202, and 1302 of this title, the appointment of a trustee or examiner and the retention and compensation of any professional person required to assist with respect to matters relevant to the determination of interests in or disposition of such grain or the proceeds of grain; and

(4) the determination of any dispute concerning a matter specified in paragraph (1), (2), or (3) of this subsection.

(e)(1) Any governmental unit that has regulatory jurisdiction over the operation or liquidation of the debtor or the debtor's business shall be given notice of any request made or order entered under subsection (c) of this section.

(2) Any such governmental unit may raise, and may appear and be heard on, any issue relating to grain or the proceeds of grain in a case in which a request is made, or an order is entered, under subsection (c) of this section.

(3) The trustee shall consult with such governmental unit before taking any action relating to the disposition of grain in the possession, custody, or control of the debtor or the estate.

(f) The court may extend the period for final disposition of grain or the proceeds of grain under this section beyond 120 days if the court finds that—

(1) the interests of justice so require in light of the complexity of the case; and

(2) the interests of those claimants entitled to distribution of grain or the proceeds of grain will not be materially injured by such additional delay.

(g) Unless an order establishing an expedited procedure under subsection (c) of this section, or determining any interest in or approving any disposition of grain or the proceeds of grain, is stayed pending appeal—

(1) the reversal or modification of such order on appeal does not affect the validity of any procedure, determination, or disposition that occurs before such reversal or modification, whether or not any entity knew of the pendency of the appeal; and

(2) neither the court nor the trustee may delay, due to the appeal of such order, any proceeding in the case in which such order is issued.

(h)(1) The trustee may recover from grain and the proceeds of grain the reasonable and necessary costs and expenses allowable under section 503(b) of this title attributable to preserving or disposing of grain or the proceeds of grain, but may not recover from such grain or the proceeds of grain any other costs or expenses.

(2) Notwithstanding section 326(a) of this title, the dollar amounts of money specified in such section include the value, as of the date of disposition, of any grain that the trustee distributes in kind.

(i) In all cases where the quantity of a specific type of grain held by a debtor operating a grain storage facility exceeds ten thousand bushels, such grain shall be sold by the trustee and the assets thereof distributed in accordance with the provisions of this section.

Comment

1984 Amendment: The 1984 amendments created a new section 557 relating to grain elevator facilities. The delays that occur in grain elevator bankruptcy cases while competing claims of ownership are being resolved have created special problems for the family farmer. ("Family farmers" is intended to included bona fide family farmers who might have incorporated, but excludes large corporate farming operations.)

Section 557 requires the bankruptcy court to prevent unnecessary and harmful delay in the disposition of grain and its proceeds. The section first states that it applies only to grain storage facilities and to grain or its proceeds. (It should be noted that section 557 does not apply to fishermen and fish processing facilities as do sections 505(a)(5) and 546(d)).

Subsection (b) defines "grain," "grain storage facility" and "producer." Subsection (c) provides that the court *may* on its own motion, and *shall* on the motion of the trustee or any entity claiming an interest in grain or its proceeds, enter an order to expedite the procedure for the determination of interests in and the disposition of the grain or its proceeds, establishing a timetable not to exceed 120 days to complete the procedures set forth in subdivision (d). The standards for shortening time periods are delineated. Subsection (d) sets forth the types of proceedings that may be expedited.

Subsection (e) relates to governmental units having an interest in the case; subsection (f) specifies standards for extending the 120-day period of subsection (c)(1); subsection (g) relates to actions taken pending determination of an appeal when no stay has been obtained; subsection (h) provides that the trustee may recover from the grain and its proceeds only the costs of preserving or disposing of the grain.

Subsection (i) requires that the trustee sell and distribute the proceeds of a quantity of a "specific type" of grain, the value of which exceeds $10,000.

Pub. L. 98–353 (1984), § 354 amended Bankruptcy Rule 3001 by adding a new subdivision (g) to the effect that a warehouse receipt, scale ticket or similar document constitutes prima facie evidence of the validity and amount of a claim of ownership of a quantity of grain.

1986 Amendments: The 1986 amendment inserted the reference to section 1202 in subsection (d)(3).

Case Annotations

Producers-depositors of grain placed in debtor-storage facilities should not be forced to share their interests with secured creditors; distribution of the stored grain or proceeds is to be made to the depositors before any other claims except for the trustee's costs, thus shifting any loss to debtor's secured creditors as the clear purpose of section 557 is to allow producers-depositors of grain placed in debtor-storage facilities to prove their ownership and receive distribution in advance of other classes of creditors, with a warehouse receipt, scale ticket or similar document acceptable as *prima facie* evidence of the validity and amount of the claim. *In re* Esbon Grain Co., 13 C.B.C.2d 1328 (B. Ct., D. Kan. 1985).

References

4 *Collier on Bankruptcy* ch. 557 (Matthew Bender 15th ed.).

2 *Collier Bankruptcy Manual* ch. 557 (Matthew Bender 3d ed.).

Comment, *Bankruptcy and the Perishable Agricultural Commodities Act Trust,* 7 Bankr. Dev. J. 291 (1990).

Note, *Grain Elevator Insolvencies and Help for the Producer: An Examination of the Bankruptcy Act of 1984,* 64 Neb. L. Rev. 463 (1985).

Papke, *Rhetoric and Retrenchment: Agrarian Ideology and American Bankruptcy Law,* 54 Mo. L. Rev. 871 (1989).

SECTION 558 (11 U.S.C. § 558)

§ 558. Defenses of the estate.

The estate shall have the benefit of any defense available to the debtor as against any entity other than the estate, including statutes of limitation, statutes of frauds, usury, and other personal defenses. A waiver of any such defense by the debtor after the commencement of the case does not bind the estate.

Comment

Section 558 provides that the estate shall enjoy the benefit of any defenses available to the debtor, such as statutes of limitation or frauds, usury and other personal defenses. The 1984 Amendments transposed former section 541(e) to section 558 without change.

Case Annotations

If a junior lienholder is fully aware of a senior lienholder's loan with the debtor at an allegedly usurious rate of interest, an action by the junior lienholder later attacking it as usurious when the trustee and the senior lienholder had previously reached a court approved settlement on the loan in which the junior had participated is barred by the doctrine of *res judicata*. Lawrence v. Steinford Holding, B.V. (*In re* Dominelli), 820 F.2d 313, 17 C.B.C.2d 312 (9th Cir. 1987).

The Bankruptcy Code implicitly recognizes the use of offset by a debtor as a "defense" that the debtor may assert under section 558 (formerly section 541(e)). *In re* Braniff Airways, Inc., 12 C.B.C.2d 610 (B. Ct., N.D. Tex. 1984).

References

4 *Collier on Bankruptcy* ch. 558 (Matthew Bender 15th ed.).

2 *Collier Bankruptcy Manual* ch. 558 (Matthew Bender 3d ed.).

SECTION 559 (11 U.S.C. § 559)

§ 559. Contractual right to liquidate a repurchase agreement.

The exercise of a contractual right of a repo participant to cause the liquidation of a repurchase agreement because of a condition of the kind specified in section 365(e)(1) of this title shall not be stayed, avoided, or otherwise limited by operation of any provision of this title or by order of a court or administrative agency in any proceeding under this title, unless, where the debtor is a stockbroker or securities clearing agency, such order is authorized under the provisions of the Securities Investor Protection Act of 1970 (15 U.S.C. 78aaa et seq.) or any statute administered by the Securities and Exchange Commission. In the event that a repo participant liquidates one or more repurchase agreements with a debtor and under the terms of one or more such agreements has agreed to deliver assets subject to repurchase agreements to the debtor, any excess of the market prices received on liquidation of such assets (or if any such assets are not disposed of on the date of liquidation of such repurchase agreements, at the prices available at the time of liquidation of such repurchase agreements from a generally recognized source or the most recent closing bid quotation from such a source) over the sum of the stated repurchase prices and all expenses in connection with the liquidation of such repurchase agreements shall be deemed property of the estate, subject to the available rights of setoff. As used in this section, the term "contractual right" includes a right set forth in a rule or bylaw, applicable to each party to the repurchase agreement, of a national securities exchange, a national securities association, or a securities clearing agency, and a right, whether or not evidenced in writing, arising under common law, under law merchant or by reason of normal business practice.

Comment

Section 559, added by Pub. L. No. 98-353 (1984), § 396(a), relates to the contractual right to liquidate a repurchase agreement. *See* Comment, *supra*, to section 362 regarding repurchase agreements. *See also* section 101 for the definition of "repurchase agreement."

Case Annotations

The transfer of securities to the purchaser from the dealer in a repo agreement is a valid transfer that is exempt from the Bankruptcy Code's avoidance provisions. In the Matter of Bevill, Bresler & Schulman Asset Management Corp., 878 F.2d 742, 21 C.B.C.2d 298 (3d Cir. 1989).

References

4 *Collier on Bankruptcy* ch. 559 (Matthew Bender 15th ed.).

2 *Collier Bankruptcy Manual* ch. 559 (Matthew Bender 3d ed.).

Note, *Repurchase Agreements and the Bankruptcy Code: The Need for Legislative Action,* 52 Fordham L. Rev. 828 (1984).

SECTION 560 (11 U.S.C. § 560)

§ 560. Contractual right to terminate a swap agreement.

The exercise of any contractual right of any swap participant to cause the termination of a swap agreement because of a condition of the kind specified in section 365(e)(1) of this title or to offset or net out any termination values or payment amounts arising under or in connection with any swap agreement shall not be stayed, avoided, or otherwise limited by operation of any provision of this title or by order of a court or administrative agency in any proceeding under this title. As used in this section, the term "contractual right" includes a right, whether or not evidenced in writing, arising under common law, under law merchant, or by reason of normal business practice.

Comment

1990 Amendments: Section 560 was added to chapter 5 by Pub. L. No. 101–311 and relates to the contractual right to terminate swap agreements. *See* section 101 for the definitions of "swap agreement" and "swap participant."

A technical amendment was made to the table of sections for chapter 5 of title 11, U.S.C., to include section 560.

CHAPTER 7

Liquidation

SUBCHAPTER I

Officers and Administration

SECTION 701 (11 U.S.C. § 701)

§ 701. Interim trustee.

(a)(1) Promptly after the order for relief under this chapter, the United States trustee shall appoint one disinterested person that is a member of the panel of private trustees established under section 586(a)(1) of title 28 or that is serving as trustee in the case immediately before the order for relief under this chapter to serve as interim trustee in the case.

(2) If none of the members of such panel is willing to serve as interim trustee in the case, then the United States trustee may serve as interim trustee in the case.

(b) The service of an interim trustee under this section terminates when a trustee elected or designated under section 702 of this title to serve as trustee in the case qualifies under section 322 of this title.

(c) An interim trustee serving under this section is a trustee in a case under this title.

Bankruptcy Rule References: 2001, 2008, 2009, 2013 and 5002

Legislative History

This section requires the court to appoint an interim trustee. The appointment must be made from the panel of private trustees established and maintained by the Director of the Administrative Office under proposed 28 U.S.C. § 604(e). [*Ed. Note:* Reference should be to 28 U.S.C. § 604(f). 28 U.S.C. § 604(f) was repealed by the 1986 Amendments.]

Subsection (a) requires the appointment of an interim trustee to be made promptly after the order for relief, unless a trustee is already serving in the case, such as before a conversion from a reorganization to a liquidation case.

Subsection (b) specifies that the appointment of an interim trustee expires when the permanent trustee is elected or designated under section 702.

Subsection (c) makes clear that an interim trustee is a trustee in a case under the bankruptcy code.

Subsection (d) provides that in a commodity broker case where speed is essential the interim trustee must be appointed by noon of the business day immediately following the order for relief.

[*Senate Report No. 95-989, 95th Cong., 2d Sess. 92 (1978); See also House Report No. 95-595, 95th Cong., 1st Sess. 378 (1977).*]

The House amendment deletes section 701(d) of the Senate amendment. It is anticipated that the Rules of Bankruptcy Procedure will require the appointment of an interim trustee at the earliest practicable moment in commodity broker bankruptcies, but no later than noon of the day after the date of the filing of the petition, due to the volatility of such cases.

[*124 Cong. Rec. H 11,098. (Sept. 28, 1978); S 17,414 (Oct. 6, 1978).*]

Comment

Section 701 requires the appointment by the United States trustee, from among the panel of private trustees, of an "interim trustee" in every liquidation case. Under former Bankruptcy Rule 201 the court could appoint a receiver when necessary in the interest of the estate. The Code abolished the concept of a receiver and substituted the mandatory appointment of an interim trustee from the panel of private trustees established by the United States trustee pursuant to 28 U.S.C. § 586 (a)(1). The interim trustee's appointment terminates when a trustee is elected under section 702 of the Code. The interim trustee may be elected; if no trustee is elected under section 702, the interim trustee becomes the trustee.

Bankruptcy Rule 2008 requires the United States trustee to notify immediately the person selected as trustee how to qualify and, if applicable, the amount of the trustee's bond. A trustee selected in a chapter 7, 12 or 13 case who has filed a blanket bond and who does not notify the United States trustee in writing of rejection of the office within 5 days after notice of selection, is deemed to have accepted the office. Any other person selected as trustee shall give notice to the court and the United States trustee in writing of acceptance of the office within 5 days after receipt of notice of selection or is deemed to have rejected the office. [As revised by the 1991 Amendments.] Since the appointment of a trustee is the responsibility of the United States trustee, any notices required by Rule 2009 should also be given to the United States trustee.

Complementing section 303(g), Bankruptcy Rule 2001 authorizes the court to order the appointment of an interim trustee at any time after the commencement of an involuntary chapter 7 case and before the entry of the order for relief. *See* **Comment** to section 303.

Bankruptcy Rule 2012(a) (as amended in 1991) provides that if a trustee in a chapter 11 case is appointed or the debtor is removed as debtor in possession in a chapter 12 case, the trustee is substituted automatically for the debtor in possession as a party in any pending action, proceeding or matter. Subdivision (b) (as amended in 1991) provides that when a trustee dies, resigns, is removed, or otherwise ceases to hold office during the pendency of a case, the successor must prepare, file and transmit to the United States trustee an accounting of the prior administration of the estate.

Bankruptcy Rule 2009 was revised by the 1991 Amendments. The amendments were necessary, according to the Advisory Committee Note, because the United States trustee rather than the court, has responsibility for appointing trustees pursuant to sections 701, 1104, 1202 and 1302 of the Code. Basically, the rule provides for appointment or election of a single trustee or separate trustees in jointly administered estates. The United States trustee may in like manner appoint one or more trustees for jointly administered estates.

Bankruptcy Rule 2013(a), providing for the limitation on appointment of trustees and employment of professionals, was deleted by the 1991 Amendments because, according to the Advisory Committee Note, the subject of that subdivision is more properly left to regulation by the United States trustee. Under subdivision (b), the clerk is required to keep a public record of fees awarded by the court to trustees, accountants and other professionals and, under subdivision (d), to prepare for public inspection an annual summary (with a copy to the United States trustee) of the names of the persons and firms and total fees awarded them during the preceding year.

Bankruptcy Rule 5002, dealing with restrictions on approval of appointments, has been substantially revised by the 1991 Amendments. Subdivision (a) provides that the appointment of an individual as a trustee or as an examiner under section 1104 shall not be approved by the court if such person is a relative of the judge approving the appointment or the United States trustee where the case is pending. Employment of an attorney, accountant, appraiser, auctioneer, or other professional shall not be approved if the individual is a relative of the judge approving the employment. Such employment may be approved by the court if the individual is a relative of the United States trustee unless the court finds that such relationship renders the employment improper under the circumstances of the case. Whenever the appointment or employment of an individual may not be approved, the individual's firm, partnership or corporation and all members and associates thereof may not be approved for appointment or employment.

Rule 5002(b) prohibits a bankruptcy judge from approving the appointment of a person as trustee or examiner and the employment of an attorney or other professional if that person is or has been so connected with such judge or the United States trustee as to render the appointment or employment improper. ["Improper" as used in Rule 5002 includes the appearance of impropriety.]

Bankruptcy Rule 6009 authorizes the trustee, with or without court approval, to prosecute or appear and defend any pending actions or proceedings by or against the debtor, or commence and prosecute any action or proceeding in behalf of the estate before any tribunal.

1986 Amendments: Subsection (a)(1) was amended to provide that the United States trustee should appoint the interim trustee. Subsection (a)(2) was added providing that if none of the members of the panel of private trustees is willing to serve in a particular case, the United States trustee may serve as the trustee. This provision fills the void that may occur when, in a very small case, no member of the panel is willing to serve as trustee.

The Joint Explanatory Statement of the Committee of the Conference for the 1986 Act had the following to say concerning the United States trustee acting as trustee in a case:

> The House and Senate Conferees agree that it is not their expectation or intent that the United States trustee will use the authority to serve as case trustee frequently. The United States trustee is to make a good faith, diligent effort to locate a disinterested and qualified trustee. Conferees agreed that United States trustees in the pilot program appear to be using their current authority to serve as case trustee in an appropriate manner.

This section was amended to reflect the creation of a permanent United States trustee system. Section 302(d) of the 1986 Amendments provides different effective dates for the amendments relating to the United States trustee system. *See* Section 302 of the 1986 Amendments, reprinted herein under "Selected Provisions of the Bankruptcy Judges, United States Trustees, and Family Farmer Bankruptcy Act of 1986," regarding effective dates generally.

1990 Amendments: Section 302(d)(3) of the Bankruptcy Judges, United States Trustees, and Family Farmer Bankruptcy Act of 1986 was amended by Pub L. No. 101-650 (Judicial Improvements Act of 1990) to extend the period in which the judicial districts in the states of Alabama and North Carolina may remain outside the United States trustee system and to insert new language pertaining to the effective date of the 1986 amendment to section 105 of title 11.

Case Annotations

Although an interim trustee's appointment is temporary in nature, such a trustee's powers encompass the ability to negotiate settlements. In the Matter of Carla Leather, Inc., 11 C.B.C.2d 622 (B. Ct., S.D.N.Y. 1984), *aff'd,* 50 B.R. 764 (S.D.N.Y. 1985).

References

4 *Collier on Bankruptcy* ch. 701 (Matthew Bender 15th ed.).

2 *Collier Bankruptcy Manual* ch. 701 (Matthew Bender 3d ed.).

2 *Collier Bankruptcy Practice Guide* ch. 25 (Matthew Bender).

Stanton, *The United States Trustee System: A Time for Assessment,* 90 Com. L.J. 90 (1985).

Waldschmidt, *Recent Cases Affecting Chapter 7 Trustees,* 6 NABTALK 34 (1990).

SECTION 702 (11 U.S.C. § 702)

§ 702. Election of trustee.

(a) A creditor may vote for a candidate for trustee only if such creditor—

(1) holds an allowable, undisputed, fixed, liquidated, unsecured claim of a kind entitled to distribution under sections 726(a)(2), 726(a)(3), 726(a)(4), 752(a), 766(h), or 766(i) of this title;

(2) does not have an interest materially adverse, other than an equity interest that is not substantial in relation to such creditor's interest as a creditor, to the interest of creditors entitled to such distribution; and

(3) is not an insider.

(b) At the meeting of creditors held under section 341 of this title, creditors may elect one person to serve as trustee in the case if election of a trustee is requested by creditors that may vote under subsection (a) of this section, and that hold at least 20 percent in amount of the claims specified in subsection (a)(1) of this section that are held by creditors that may vote under subsection (a) of this section.

(c) A candidate for trustee is elected trustee if—

(1) creditors holding at least 20 percent in amount of the claims of a kind specified in subsection (a)(1) of this section that are held by creditors that may vote under subsection (a) of this section vote; and

(2) such candidate receives the votes of creditors holding a majority in amount of claims specified in subsection (a)(1)

of this section that are held by creditors that vote for a trustee.

(d) If a trustee is not elected under this section, then the interim trustee shall serve as trustee in the case.

Bankruptcy Rule References: 2003, 2008, 2009 and 2010

Legislative History

Subsection (a) of this section specifies which creditors may vote for a trustee. Only a creditor that holds an allowable, undisputed, fixed, liquidated, unsecured claim that is not entitled to priority, that does not have an interest materially adverse to the interest of general unsecured creditors, and that is not an insider may vote for a trustee. The phrase "materially adverse" is currently used in the Rules of Bankruptcy Procedure, Rule 207(d). The application of the standard requires a balancing of various factors, such as the nature of the adversity. A creditor with a very small equity position would not be excluded from voting solely because he holds a small equity in the debtor. The Rules of Bankruptcy Procedure also currently provide for temporary allowance of claims, and will continue to do so for the purposes of determining who is eligible to vote under this provision.

[*Senate Report No. 95–989, 95th Cong., 2d Sess. 92–93 (1978); See also House Report No. 95–595, 95th Cong., 1st Sess. 378 (1977).*]

Section 7 [of Public Law 97–222] clarifies that customers of debtors under subchapters III or IV are entitled to participate in the election of the trustee.

[*House Report No. 97–420, 97th Cong., 2d Sess. 4 (1982).*]

The House amendment adopts section 702(a)(2) of the Senate amendment. An insubstantial equity interest does not disqualify a creditor from voting for a candidate for trustee. Section 704(8) of the Senate amendment is deleted in the House amendment. Trustees should give constructive notice of the commencement of the case in the manner specified under section 549(c) of title 11.

[*124 Cong. Rec. H 11,098 (Sept. 28, 1978); S 17,414 (Oct. 6, 1978).*]

Subsection (b) permits creditors at the meeting of creditors to elect one person to serve as trustee in the case. Creditors holding at least 20 percent in amount of the claims specified in the preceding paragraph must request election before creditors may elect a trustee.

[*House Report No. 95–595, 95th Cong., 1st Sess. 378 (1977); Senate Report No. 95–989, 95th Cong., 2d Sess. 93 (1978).*]

Subsection (c) specifies that a candidate for trustee is elected trustee if creditors holding at least 20 percent in amount of those claims actually vote, and if the candidate receives the votes of creditors holding a majority in amount of the votable claims held by creditors that vote.

[*House Report No. 95–595, 95th Cong., 1st Sess. 378-379 (1977).*]

Subsection (c) specifies that a candidate for trustee is elected trustee if creditors holding at least 20 percent in amount of those claims actually vote, and if the candidate receives a majority in amount of votes actually cast.

[*Senate Report No. 95–989, 95th Cong., 2d Sess. 93 (1978).*]

Subsection (d) specifies that if a trustee is not elected, then the interim trustee becomes the trustee, and serves in the case permanently.

[*House Report No. 95–595, 95th Cong., 1st Sess. 379 (1977); Senate Report No. 95–989, 95th Cong., 2d Sess. 93 (1978).*]

Comment

Section 702 of the Code changes the process of electing a trustee.

Under the former Bankruptcy Act and former Rules a trustee was elected by a majority in amount and number (claims of $100.00 or less were computed in amount but not in number) of claims of creditors present and voting in person or by proxy. Secured and priority creditors were barred from voting as were relatives or affiliates of the bankrupt, officers, directors and stockholders of a corporate bankrupt and partners of a bankrupt partnership.

Under section 702 of the Code creditors holding 20 percent in *amount* of *all* allowable, undisputed, fixed, liquidated, and unsecured claims entitled to distribution and who do not have an interest materially adverse (an insubstantial equity interest will not disqualify a creditor), may *request* an election. At least 20 percent in *amount* of such creditors must actually vote at the meeting for a trustee, and the candidate that receives the vote of a *majority* in *amount* of the creditors so voting is elected trustee.

If the trustee is not elected in the manner provided, then the interim trustee who was appointed pursuant to section 701 serves as trustee in the case.

The result of section 702 is that unless a substantial proportion of the creditors are truly interested and take an active part in the election of the trustee, the interim trustee selected by the United States trustee from the panel of qualified trustees will serve as the trustee in the case.

The 1982 amendments (Public Law 97–222) make clear that customers of stockbroker and commodity broker debtors are entitled to participate in the election of a trustee.

Bankruptcy Rule 2003 relates to meetings of creditors and provides in subdivision (b)(1) that the business of the meeting may include, in a chapter 7 case, the election of a trustee. Subdivision (b)(3), applicable only in chapter 7 cases, provides that a creditor may vote if at or before the meeting the creditor filed a proof of claim or writing setting forth facts evidencing a right to vote pursuant to section 702(a), unless objection is made to the claim, or the claim is insufficient on its face. If election of a separate trustee for a general partner's estate is ordered (Rule 2009(c)(1)) creditors of the partnership may file a proof of claim or writing showing his right to vote despite the previous qualification of a trustee for the partnership.

Subdivision (d) of the Rule requires the officer presiding at the meeting of creditors to transmit to the court the name and address of any person or entity elected trustee. Section 341(a) of the Code requires the United States trustee to "convene and preside" at a meeting of creditors. Pursuant to section 102(a), United States trustee includes a designee of such trustee. Whoever presides must promptly inform the court in writing of any dispute in the election, and pending disposition of the dispute the interim trustee is to continue in office. If no motion to resolve the dispute is made to the court within 10 days after the meeting, the interim trustee is to serve as trustee. (Whoever presides at the meeting is not authorized to resolve a disputed election. After the dispute is reported by the United States trustee or the person designated to preside at the meeting, the court will act to resolve it only if an interested party timely moves the court for resolution.)

Note that a trustee is not elected in a chapter 11, 12 or 13 case.

Bankruptcy Rule 2006 is a comprehensive regulation of solicitation and voting of proxies in chapter 7 cases. The rule applies only in chapter 7 cases because no voting occurs, other than on a plan, in a chapter 11 case. A holder of two or more proxies is required to file and transmit to the United States trustee a verified list of the proxies to be voted and a verified statement of the pertinent facts and circumstances in connection with the execution and delivery of each proxy, the details of which are set forth in subdivision (e) of the rule.

1984 Amendments: Only technical changes were made in section 702.

Case Annotations

In a trustee election dispute, where the bankruptcy clerk failed to determine who had eligible claims and the percentage of creditors who requested an election, the court, in an attempt to reconstruct the election, may consider the creditors who voted for the interim trustees as not having requested the election because the interim trustees become permanent trustees if no election is held. The 20 percent requesting requirement of section 702(b) is distinct from and independent of the 20 percent voting requirement of section 702(c). *In re* Oxborrow, 913 F.2d 751, 23 C.B.C.2d 876 (9th Cir. 1990).

An interim trustee has standing to object to the election of a chapter 7 trustee under section 702. Section 702(a) and Bankruptcy Rule 3001 require that in order for a claim to qualify as liquidated so that a creditor may vote the claim in a trustee election, the proof of claim filed by a creditor must disclose an agreement or mathematical formula by which its asserted indebtedness may be readily calculated or ascertained. In the Matter of Lindell Drop Forge Co., 22 C.B.C.2d 1120 (B. Ct., W.D. Mich. 1990).

The election of a trustee under chapter 7 may not be disallowed on the basis that he is a pension recipient of a creditor if his rights are fully vested and the creditor has no discretion in making periodic pension payments. *In re* Metro Shippers, Inc., 15 C.B.C.2d 399 (B. Ct., E.D. Pa. 1986).

A creditor may be a business partner of a debtor and yet not be an "insider" in respect of his eligibility to vote for a trustee, when his interests differ from those of the debtor and he is neither controlled by nor is an alter-ego of the debtor. *In re* Blesi, 11 C.B.C.2d 480 (B. Ct., D. Minn. 1984).

When creditors are unable to elect a permanent trustee, and creditors of more than half the unsecured debt agree on a compromise candidate, that candidate may be appointed by the court without an election first being conducted. *In re* National Sugar Refining Co., 10 C.B.C.2d 869 (B. Ct., S.D.N.Y. 1984).

A spouse of the chief operating officer of a chapter 11 debtor, considered an "insider" under section 101, is not eligible to vote for a trustee in a chapter 11 case or in a subsequent liquidation case even though she may have been appointed to the creditors' committee. *In re* Vermont Real Estate Inv. Trust, 6 C.B.C.2d 862 (B. Ct., D. Vt. 1980).

The debtor need not file its schedules before meetings for the election and certification of a trustee as the petitioning creditors may estimate the other debts so as to provide the United States trustee with some means of verifying compliance with the statutory requirements of section 702. In the Matter of Blanchard Management Corp., 4 C.B.C.2d 91 (B. Ct., S.D.N.Y. 1981).

References

4 *Collier on Bankruptcy* ch. 702 (Matthew Bender 15th ed.).

2 *Collier Bankruptcy Manual* ch. 702 (Matthew Bender 3d ed.).

2 *Collier Bankruptcy Practice Guide* ch. 25 (Matthew Bender).

SECTION 703 (11 U.S.C. § 703)

§ 703. Successor trustee.

(a) If a trustee dies or resigns during a case, fails to qualify under section 322 of this title, or is removed under section 324 of this title, creditors may elect, in the manner specified in section 702 of this title, a person to fill the vacancy in the office of trustee.

(b) Pending election of a trustee under subsection (a) of this section, if necessary to preserve or prevent loss to the estate, the United States trustee may appoint an interim trustee in the manner specified in section 701(a).

(c) If creditors do not elect a successor trustee under subsection (a) of this section or if a trustee is needed in a case reopened under section 350 of this title, then the United States trustee—

> (1) shall appoint one disinterested person that is a member of the panel of private trustees established under section 586(a)(1) of title 28 to serve as trustee in the case; or

> (2) may, if none of the disinterested members of such panel is willing to serve as trustee, serve as trustee in the case.

Bankruptcy Rule References: 2008, 2010 and 2012

Legislative History

If the office of trustee becomes vacant during the case, this section makes provision for the selection of a successor trustee. The office might become vacant through death, resignation, removal, failure to qualify under section 322 by posting bond, or the reopening of a case. If it does, creditors may elect a successor in the same manner as they may elect a trustee under the previous section. Pending the election of a successor, the United States trustee may appoint an interim trustee in the usual manner if necessary to preserve or prevent loss to the estate. If creditors do not elect a successor, or if a trustee is needed in a reopened case, then the United States trustee serves as trustee, or else appoints a disinterested member of the panel of private trustees to serve. [*Ed. Note:* The Senate Report on section 703 is identical with the House Report except that it provides for appointment by the "court" instead of by the United States trustee.]

[*House Report No. 95–595, 95th Cong., 1st Sess. 379 (1977); Senate Report No. 95–989, 95th Cong., 2d Sess. 93 (1978).*]

Comment

Former Bankruptcy Rule 209(b) provided that if "a vacancy occurs in the office of trustee," the court would appoint a trustee. Section 703 changed this by providing that in the event of a vacancy resulting from death, resignation, removal or failure to qualify, creditors are afforded the opportunity to elect a trustee in the same manner as provided in section 702. To fill the role between vacancy and election of a successor, subsection (b) permits the United States trustee to appoint an interim trustee as provided in section 701. Pursuant to subsection (c), if creditors fail to elect a successor trustee, or if a trustee is needed in a reopened case (section 350), then the United States trustee "shall" appoint one disinterested person from the panel of private trustees established pursuant to 28 U.S.C. § 586(a)(1).

Bankruptcy Rule 2012(b) provides that if a trustee dies, resigns, is removed or otherwise ceases to hold office, the successor is automatically substituted as a party in any pending action, proceeding or matter; and within the time fixed by the court, the successor is required to file and transmit to the United States trustee an accounting of the prior administration of the estate.

1984 Amendments: Only a technical change was made in section 703(b).

1986 Amendments: Subsection (b) was amended to provide that when a trustee dies, resigns, etc., pending the election of a trustee, the United States trustee may, if necessary, appoint an interim trustee. Subsection (c)(1) was amended to provide that if in a reopened case creditors fail to elect a successor trustee, the United States trustee shall appoint a trustee from the panel of disinterested trustees. Subsection (c)(2) provides that if no member of the panel is willing to serve, the United States trustee may serve as trustee in the case.

The Joint Explanatory Statement of the Committee of the Conference for the 1986 Act had the following to say concerning the United States trustee acting as trustee in a case:

> The House and Senate Conferees agree that it is not their expectation or intent that the United States trustee will use the authority to serve as case trustee frequently. The United States trustee is to make a good faith, diligent effort to locate a disinterested and qualified trustee. Conferees agreed that United States trustees in the pilot program appear to be using their current authority to serve as case trustee in an appropriate manner.

This section was amended to reflect the creation of a permanent United States trustee system. Section 302(d) of the 1986 Amendments provided different effective dates for the amendments relating to the United States trustee system. *See* Section 302 of the 1986 Amendments, as amended by Pub. L. No. 101–650 (1990), reprinted herein under "Selected Provisions of the Bankruptcy Judges, United States Trustees, and Family Farmer Bankruptcy Act of 1986," regarding effective dates generally.

References

4 *Collier on Bankruptcy* ch. 703 (Matthew Bender 15th ed.).

2 *Collier Bankruptcy Manual* ch. 703 (Matthew Bender 3d ed.).

2 *Collier Bankruptcy Practice Guide* ch. 25 (Matthew Bender).

SECTION 704 (11 U.S.C. § 704)

§ 704. Duties of trustee. The trustee shall—

(1) collect and reduce to money the property of the estate for which such trustee serves, and close such estate as expeditiously as is compatible with the best interests of parties in interest;

(2) be accountable for all property received;

(3) ensure that the debtor shall perform his intention as specified in section 521(2)(B) of this title;

(4) investigate the financial affairs of the debtor;

(5) if a purpose would be served, examine proofs of claims and object to the allowance of any claim that is improper;

(6) if advisable, oppose the discharge of the debtor;

(7) unless the court orders otherwise, furnish such information concerning the estate and the estate's administration as is requested by a party in interest;

(8) if the business of the debtor is authorized to be operated, file with the court, with the United States trustee, and with any governmental unit charged with responsibility for collection or determination of any tax arising out of such operation, periodic reports and summaries of the operation of such business, including a statement of receipts and disbursements, and such other information as the United States trustee or the court requires; and

(9) make a final report and file a final account of the administration of the estate with the court and with the United States trustee.

Bankruptcy Rule References: 1019, 2001, 2015, 3011 and 3022

Legislative History

The essential duties of the trustee are enumerated in this section. Others, or elaborations on these, may be prescribed by the Rules of Bankruptcy Procedure to the extent not inconsistent with those prescribed by this section. The duties are derived from section 47a of the Bankruptcy Act.

The trustee's principal duty is to collect and reduce to money the property of the estate for which he serves, and to close up the estate as expeditiously as is compatible with the best interests of parties in interest. He must be accountable for all property received, and must investigate the financial affairs of the debtor. If a purpose would be served (such as if there are assets that will be distributed), the trustee is required to examine proofs of claims and object to the allowance of any claim that is improper. If advisable, the trustee must oppose the discharge of the debtor, which is for the benefit of general unsecured creditors whom the trustee represents.

[*House Report No. 95–595, 95th Cong., 1st Sess. 379 (1977); Senate Report No. 95–989, 95th Cong., 2d Sess. 93 (1978).*]

The trustee is responsible to furnish such information concerning the estate and its administration as is required by a party in interest. If the business of the debtor is authorized to be operated, then the trustee is required to file with governmental units charged with the responsibility for collection or determination of any tax arising out of the operation of the business periodic reports and summaries of the operation, including a statement of receipts and disbursements, and such other information as the court requires.

Finally, the trustee is required to make a final report and file a final account of the administration of the estate with both the court and with the United States trustee.

[*House Report No. 95–595, 95th Cong., 1st Sess. 379 (1977).*]

The trustee is responsible to furnish such information concerning the estate and its administration as is requested by a party in interest. If the business of the debtor is authorized to be operated, then the trustee is required to file with governmental units charged with the responsibility for collection or determination of any tax arising out of the operation of the business periodic reports and summaries of the operation, including a statement of receipts and disbursements, and such other information as the court requires. He is required to give constructive notice of the commencement of the case in the manner specified under section 342(b).

[*Senate Report No. 95–989, 95th Cong., 2d Sess. 93 (1978).*]

Comment

Section 704, enumerating the duties of a trustee, is derived from section 47a of the former Bankruptcy Act.

The House and Senate Reports suggest that other duties, or elaboration of the duties prescribed by section 704, may be prescribed by Rules of Bankruptcy Procedure to the extent not inconsistent with those prescribed by section 704.

Bankruptcy Rule 2015 (as revised in 1991) relates to the duties of a trustee or debtor in possession to keep records, make reports and give notice of the case. Subdivision (a) requires a trustee or debtor in possession

(1) in a chapter 7 case, and if the court so directs, in a chapter 11 case, to file and transmit to the United States trustee within 30 days after qualifying as trustee or debtor in possession a complete inventory of the debtor's property unless such inventory has already been filed;

(2) to keep a record of receipts and disposition of money and property received;

(3) to file the reports and summaries required by section 704(8) including, if payments are made to employees, a statement of the amounts of deductions for taxes required to be withheld and the place where deposited;

(4) as soon as possible, to give notice of the case to every entity known to be holding money or property subject to withdrawal on order of the debtor, including every bank, savings or building and loan association, public utility company, and landlord with whom the debtor has a deposit, and to every insurance company which has issued a policy having a cash surrender value payable to the debtor, except that notice need not be given any entity who has knowledge of or has previously been notified of the case;

(5) in a chapter 11 case, on or before the last day of the month after each calendar quarter until the plan is confirmed, converted, or dismissed, file and transmit to the United States trustee a statement of disbursements made during such calendar quarter and a statement of the amount of the fee required pursuant to 28 U.S.C. section 1930(a)(6) that has been paid for such calendar quarter.

Subdivision (b), added by the 1991 Amendments, provides that in a chapter 12 case, the debtor in possession shall perform the duties prescribed in paragraphs (1) through (4) of subdivision (a), above. If the debtor is removed as debtor in possession, the trustee shall perform the duties of the debtor in possession prescribed in this paragraph.

Subdivision (c) of Rule 2015 relates to a chapter 13 trustee and debtor. Paragraph (1) of the subdivision deals with a *business* case, and provides that in such case the debtor shall perform the duties prescribed by subdivision (a)(1)–(4) of the rule. Paragraph (2) deals with *nonbusiness* cases, and provides that the trustee shall perform the duties prescribed by clause (2) of subdivision (a) of the rule.

Subdivision (d) provides that in a chapter 11 case, the court may direct that copies or summaries of the annual report or of other reports be mailed to the creditors, equity security holders and indenture trustees, and may also direct publication of summaries of the reports. A copy of every report or summary so mailed or published shall be transmitted to the United States trustee. [Subdivision (a)(5) was deleted because filing notice or a copy of the petition to protect real property against unauthorized postpetition transfers is within the discretion of the trustee. The new subdivision (a)(5) was added to enable the United States trustee and the court to determine the appropriate quarterly fee required in chapter 11 cases. Subdivision (a)(7) was abrogated as unnecessary, and subdivision (a)(6) was abrogated because closing of a chapter 11 case is governed by Rule 3022.]

1984 Amendments: Section 521, prescribing the duties of a debtor, was amended by adding a new paragraph "(3)" requiring an individual with consumer debts (*see* section 101 for definition of "consumer debt") secured by property of the estate, to file a statement of intention with regard to the collateral and to take affirmative action on the stated intention. The amendment to section 704 makes it the duty of a trustee to ensure that the debtor performs the written statement of intention. Paragraphs "(3)" to "(8)" were renumbered "(4)" to "(9)."

1986 Amendments: Paragraph (8) of section 704 was amended by providing that a trustee authorized to operate the business file with the United States trustee as well as with the court the periodic reports required by paragraph (8) and such other information as the United States trustee or the court may require. Paragraph (9) requires the trustee to file a final account with the court and with the United States trustee.

Case Annotations

In fixing compensation courts must distinguish trustees' services from attorneys' services, and attorneys may not be compensated for performing those services that are the statutory duty of the trustee. *In re* J.W. Knapp Co., 930 F.2d 386, 24 C.B.C.2d 1546 (4th Cir. 1991).

The main duty of a chapter 7 trustee is to expeditiously close the estate. It serves no purpose within the meaning of section 704(5) for the trustee to engage in a lengthy investigation of an unsecured creditor's claim when the estate is solvent and none of the debtor's general partners object to the claim. *In re* Riverside-Linden Investment Co., 925 F.2d 320, 24 C.B.C.2d 1210 (9th Cir. 1991).

Sections 363(b)(1) and 704 do not conflict with or invalidate bylaw restrictions on the transferability of patronage margin certificates as these sections are simply enabling statutes that give the trustee the authority to sell or dispose of property if the debtors would have had the same right under state law. Calvert v. Bongard Creameries and Schauer (*In re* Schauer), 835 F.2d 1222, 18 C.B.C.2d 127 (8th Cir. 1987).

A trustee can be found individually liable for actions, if negligent, when those actions are outside the bounds of the trustee's authority. The trustee is liable within his official capacity when his actions are willfully and deliberately in violation of his duties. Yadkin Valley Bank & Trust Co. v. McGee, 819 F.2d 74, 16 C.B.C.2d 1491 (4th Cir. 1987).

The reasonable care and due diligence standard is the one by which the conduct of a trustee should be judged, whether the debtor is an individual or a corporation. United States of America v. Aldrich (*In re* Rigden), 795 F.2d 727, 15 C.B.C.2d 1206 (9th Cir. 1986).

While section 704 does not in terms provide the trustee with any duty to object to a debtor's motion to dismiss, such a duty may be inferred from the trustee's duty to collect and reduce to cash the property of the estate. Gill v. Hall (*In re* Hall), 5 C.B.C.2d 1028 (9th Cir., B.A.P., 1981).

A chapter 7 trustee does not have standing to bring an *alter ego* action against third parties related to the debtor because creditors alone are recognized as the proper parties plaintiff in an *alter ego* proceeding. Mixon v. Anderson (*In re* Ozark Restaurant Equipment Co.), 15 C.B.C.2d 827 (W.D. Ark. 1986), *aff'd,* 816 F.2d 1222, 16 C.B.C.2d 1148 (8th Cir.), *cert. denied,* 484 U.S. 848, 108 S. Ct. 147, 98 L. Ed. 2d 102 (1987).

Although the Code requires the trustee to ensure that the debtor performs his or her intentions under section 521(2), the court has the power to ensure the debtor's compliance if a trustee is reluctant to do so; a creditor, however, is without standing to do so. *In re* Kennedy, 26 C.B.C.2d 1192 (B. Ct., E.D. Ark. 1992).

A trustee's only duty to a secured creditor is to exercise reasonable care in acting as a custodian of estate property that serves as the collateral for the holder of the secured claim. *In re* Hutchinson, 25 C.B.C.2d 1247 (B. Ct., M.D.N.C. 1991).

When a debtor's state employment retirement system funds are property of the state but will not mature until the debtor is no longer employed by the state, what the trustee has succeeded to is a contingent right to the return of the money in the event the debtor's employment by the state was terminated, an interest the trustee may sell for whatever the market will pay for such an asset. *In re* Groves, 24 C.B.C.2d 704 (B. Ct., N.D. Ill. 1990).

It is the trustee's principal duty under section 704(5) to object to unsubstantiated, excessive, or unallowable claims; it is not the trustee's obligation to examine a claim with a purpose and view to increasing the claim or improving a claimant's status over that asserted by other creditors. *In re* Padget, 24 C.B.C.2d 451 (B. Ct., D. Colo. 1990).

Although the business judgment rule allows a trustee discretion in balancing the costs and benefits of administering an asset of the estate, some affirmative action must be taken by the trustee with regard to an offer for an asset so that the estate can be closed. *In re* Moore, 22 C.B.C.2d 645 (B. Ct., C.D. Cal. 1990).

Bankruptcy trustees are immune from personal liability for acts performed as a matter of business judgment and in accordance with statutory or other duty or pursuant to court order. However, personal liability will attach to a bankruptcy trustee when the trustee has negligently failed to discover his agent's negligence, negligently obtained a court order, or negligently or willfully carried out an order that he knew or should have known was wrongly procured. An auctioneer acting as an agent of a bankruptcy trustee will be held to the same standards of liability as the trustee. *In re* Center Teleproductions, Inc., 22 C.B.C.2d 920 (B. Ct., S.D.N.Y. 1990).

As part of the trustee's duties, 28 U.S.C. § 960 commands the trustee to comply with state law which require the liquidating trustee selling realty to pay local conveyance taxes. Hoffman v. R & E Builders (In the Matter of Woodland Builders), 19 C.B.C.2d 372 (B. Ct., D. Conn. 1988).

A chapter 11 trustee appointed to operate a debtor's wholly-owned corporation is acting in a fiduciary capacity for the benefit of the estate and its beneficiaries and can be found to have been negligent in, and thus personally surchargeable for, not seeking approval of the employment of counsel for the corporation, among others, and in providing compensation without notice. *In re* Baker, 16 C.B.C.2d 42 (B. Ct., D. Or. 1986).

The debtor is not the proper party plaintiff when the trustee rather than the debtor is vested with the right to maintain the cause of action. Leird Church Furniture Manufacturing Co. v. Union National Bank (*In re* Leird Church Furniture Manufacturing Co.), 14 C.B.C.2d 1124 (B. Ct., E.D. Ark. 1986).

References

4 *Collier on Bankruptcy* ch. 704 (Matthew Bender 15th ed.).

2 *Collier Bankruptcy Manual* ch. 704 (Matthew Bender 3d ed.).

2 *Collier Bankruptcy Practice Guide* ch. 26 (Matthew Bender).

Comment, *Awarding Fair Compensation to Bankruptcy Trustees,* 27 San Diego L. Rev. 993 (1990).

Note, *Role of the Trustee in Liquidation Sales,* 8 Colo. Law. 1879 (1981).

Ulrich, *Bankruptcy Legislation Would Improve Compensation of Chapter 7 Trustees,* 3 F & G Bankr. L. Rev. 29 (1992).

SECTION 705 (11 U.S.C. § 705)

§ 705. Creditors' committee.

(a) At the meeting under section 341(a) of this title, creditors that may vote for a trustee under section 702(a) of this title may elect a committee of not fewer than three, and not more than 11, creditors, each of whom holds an allowable unsecured claim of a kind entitled to distribution under section 726(a)(2) of this title.

(b) A committee elected under subsection (a) of this section may consult with the trustee or the United States trustee in connection with the administration of the estate, make recommendations to the trustee or the United States trustee respecting the performance of the trustee's duties, and submit to the court or the United States trustee any question affecting the administration of the estate.

Bankruptcy Rule References: 2003 and 2007

Legislative History

This section is derived from section 44b of the Bankruptcy [*sic*] without substantial change. It permits election by general unsecured creditors of a committee of not fewer than three members [*Ed. Note:* The Senate Report adds the words "and not more than eleven members."] to consult with the trustee in connection with the administration of the estate, to make recommendations to the trustee respecting the performance of his duties, and to submit to the court any question affecting the administration of the estate. There is no provision for compensation or reimbursement of its counsel.

[*House Report No. 95–595, 95th Cong., 1st Sess. 379–380 (1977); Senate Report No. 95–989, 95th Cong., 2d Sess. 94 (1978).*]

Section 705(a) of the House amendment adopts a provision contained in the Senate amendment that limits a committee of creditors to not more than 11; the House bill contained no maximum limitation.

[*124 Cong. Rec. H 11,098 (Sept. 28, 1978); S 17,414 (Oct. 6, 1978).*]

Comment

Bankruptcy Rule 2003(b)(1) provides that the business transacted at the meeting of creditors may include, in a chapter 7 case, the election of a creditors' committee. Subdivision (d) requires the officer presiding at the meeting (*i.e.,* the United States trustee or the trustee's designee; *see* sections 102(9) and 307) to transmit to the court the name and address of any person elected a member of a committee, and promptly inform the court in writing of any dispute in the election.

1986 Amendments: Section 705(b) was amended to provide that a chapter 7 committee may consult with the trustee or the United States trustee and may submit to the court or to the United States trustee any question involving the administration of the estate.

This section was amended to reflect the creation of a permanent United States trustee system. Section 302(d) of the 1986 Amendments provides different effective dates for the amendments relating to the United States trustee system. *See* Section 302 of the 1986 Amendments, reprinted herein under "Selected Provisions of the Bankruptcy Judges, United States Trustees, and Family Farmer Bankruptcy Act of 1986," regarding effective dates generally.

1990 Amendments: Section 302(d)(3) of the Bankruptcy Judges, United States Trustees, and Family Farmer Bankruptcy Act of 1986 was amended by Pub. L. No. 101-650 (Judicial Improvements Act of 1990) to extend the period in which the judicial districts in the states of Alabama and North Carolina may remain outside the United States trustee system and to insert new language pertaining to the effective date of the 1986 amendment to section 105 of title 11.

Case Annotations

Absent leave of the court, only the chapter 7 trustee is allowed to interpose objections to proofs of claims, and leave to object is not generally accorded to individual creditors. *In re* Thompson, 965 F.2d 1136, 26 C.B.C.2d 1306 (1st Cir. 1992).

There is nothing in the express language of section 705 that authorizes the bankruptcy court to encumber the debtor's estate in a chapter 7 case with the expense of providing counsel to a creditors' committee, and the legislative history shows that this omission was intentional. Official Creditors' Committee v. Metzger (*In re* Dominelli), 788 F.2d 584, 14 C.B.C.2d 932 (9th Cir. 1986).

References

4 *Collier on Bankruptcy* ch. 705 (Matthew Bender 15th ed.).

2 *Collier Bankruptcy Manual* ch. 705 (Matthew Bender 3d ed.).

2 *Collier Bankruptcy Practice Guide* ch. 35 (Matthew Bender).

De Natale, *The Creditors' Committee Under the Bankruptcy Code—A Primer,* 55 Am. Bankr. L.J. 43 (1981).

DiPietro, Jr., *Creditors' Rights in Bankruptcy,* 55 Conn. B.J. 163 (1981).

SECTION 706 (11 U.S.C. § 706)

§ 706. Conversion.

(a) The debtor may convert a case under this chapter to a case under chapter 11, 12, or 13 of this title at any time, if the case has not been converted under section 1112, 1307, or 1208 of this title. Any waiver of the right to convert a case under this subsection is unenforceable.

(b) On request of a party in interest and after notice and a hearing, the court may convert a case under this chapter to a case under chapter 11 of this title at any time.

(c) The court may not convert a case under this chapter to a case under chapter 12 or 13 of this title unless the debtor requests such conversion.

(d) Notwithstanding any other provision of this section, a case may not be converted to a case under another chapter of this title unless the debtor may be a debtor under such chapter.

Bankruptcy Rule References: 1019, 2002, 4004 and 9034

Legislative History

Subsection (a) of this section gives the debtor one absolute right of conversion of a liquidation case to a reorganization or individual repayment plan case. If the case has already once been converted from chapter 11 or 13 to chapter 7, then the debtor does not have that right. The policy of the provision is that the debtor should always be given the opportunity to repay his debts.

[*House Report No. 95–595, 95th Cong., 1st Sess. 380 (1977).*]

Subsection (a) of this section gives the debtor the one-time absolute right of conversion of a liquidation case to a reorganization or individual repayment plan case. If the case has already once been converted from chapter 11 or 13 to chapter 7, then the debtor does not have that right. The policy of the provision is that the debtor should always be given the opportunity to repay his debts, and a waiver of the right to convert a case is unenforceable.

[*Senate Report No. 95–989, 95th Cong., 2d Sess. 94 (1978).*]

Section 706(a) of the House amendment adopts a provision contained in the Senate amendment indicating that a waiver of the right to convert a case under section 706(a) is unenforceable. The explicit reference in title 11 forbidding the waiver of certain rights is not intended to imply that other rights, such as the right to file a voluntary bankruptcy case under section 301, may be waived.

Section 706 of the House amendment adopts a similar provision contained in H.R. 8200 as passed by the House. Competing proposals contained in section 706(c) and section 706(d) of the Senate amendment are rejected.

[*124 Cong. Rec. H 11,098 (Sept. 28, 1978); S 17,414 (Oct. 6, 1978).*]

Subsection (b) permits the court, on request of a party in interest and after notice and a hearing, to convert the case to chapter 11 at any time. The decision whether to convert is left in the sound discretion of the court, based on what will most inure to the benefit of all parties in interest.

Subsection (c) is part of the prohibition against involuntary chapter 13 cases, and prohibits the court from converting a case to chapter 13 without the debtor's consent.

Subsection (d) reinforces section 109 by prohibiting conversion to a chapter unless the debtor is eligible to be a debtor under that chapter.

[*House Report No. 95–595, 95th Cong., 1st Sess. 380 (1977); Senate Report No. 95–989, 95th Cong., 2d Sess. 94 (1978).*]

Comment

Section 706(a) gives the debtor a one-time absolute right to convert a liquidation case to a reorganization or individual repayment plan. But once converted from chapter 11, 12 or 13 to liquidation under chapter 7, the debtor loses that right. This prevents a debtor whose case has been converted from reorganization to liquidation to repeatedly seek conversion back to chapter 11.

Under the Code, an involuntary reorganization case under chapter 11 may be filed and, accordingly, section 706(b) empowers the court to convert a chapter 7 case to a chapter 11 case at any time on request of a party in interest and after notice and hearing. But a case under chapter 12 or 13 may be instituted only by a debtor and, accordingly, section 706(c) provides that the court may not convert a chapter 7 case to a chapter 12 or 13 case unless the debtor requests the conversion.

Bankruptcy Rule 1019 relates to conversion of a chapter 11, 12 or 13 case to chapter 7.

Paragraph (1)(A) provides that lists, inventories, schedules and statements of financial affairs theretofore filed are deemed filed in the chapter 7 cases unless the court otherwise directs. If not previously filed, the debtor is to comply with Rule 1007 as if an order for relief was entered on an involuntary petition on the date of entry of the conversion order.

Paragraph (1)(B), added by the 1987 Amendments to the Bankruptcy Rules, provides the statement of intention [section 521(2)], if required, must be filed within 30 days after entry of the conversion order or before the first date set for the meeting of creditors, whichever is earlier. An extension of time may be granted for cause only on motion made before the time has expired. Notice of any extension is to be given to the United States trustee and to any committee, trustee or other party as the court directs.

Paragraph (2) provides that a new time period for filing claims, complaints objecting to discharge or to obtain a determination of dischargeability of any debt shall commence pursuant to Rules 3002, 4004 or 4007, provided that a new time period shall not commence if a chapter 7 has been converted to a chapter 11, 12 or 13 case and thereafter recoverted to a chapter 7 case, and the time for filing such claims, complaints or any extensions thereof, expired in the original chapter 7 case. Rules 4004 and 4007 should be consulted to determine whether an extension is possible.

Paragraph (3) makes it unnecessary to file claims that had been actually filed in the chapter 11 or 13 case before conversion to chapter 7.

Paragraph (4) provides that after the chapter 7 trustee qualifies or assumes his duties, the trustee or debtor in possession previously acting in the chapter 11, 12 or 13 case, unless otherwise ordered, shall forthwith turn over to the chapter 7 trustee all records and property of the estate.

Paragraph (6) was renumbered "(5)" and substantially revised by the 1991 Amendments. Unless the court otherwise directs, each debtor in possession or trustee in the superseded case shall (A) within 15 days after entry of the conversion of a chapter 11 case, file a schedule of unpaid debts incurred after commencement of the superseded case including name and address of each creditor; and (B) within 30 days after conversion to a chapter 11, 12 or 13 case, file and transmit to the United States trustee a final report and account. Within 15 days after entry of the order of conversion, unless the court directs otherwise, a chapter 13 debtor shall file a schedule of unpaid debts incurred after commencement of a chapter 13 case, and a chapter 12 debtor in possession or, if the chapter 12 debtor is not in possession, the trustee shall file a schedule of unpaid debts incurred after the commencement of a chapter 12 case. If the conversion order follows confirmation, the debtor shall include (A) a schedule of property not listed in the final report and account that was acquired after the filing of the original petition but before entry of the conversion order, (B) a schedule of unpaid debts not listed in the final report and account incurred after confirmation and before the conversion order, and (C) a schedule of executory contracts and unexpired leases entered into or assumed after the filing of the original petition but before entry of the conversion order. A chapter 12 or 13 debtor must file a schedule of unpaid debts incurred after commencement of the chapter 12 or 13 case. The clerk is required to forthwith transmit to the United States trustee a copy of every schedule filed pursuant to this paragraph.

Paragraph (6) requires that on the filing of the schedule of unpaid debts, the clerk (or some other person as the court directs) shall give notice to those entities, including the United States, any state, or any subdivision thereof, that their claims may be filed unders Rules 3001(a)-(d) and 3002. Unless a notice of insufficient assets to pay a dividend is mailed pursuant to Rule 2002(e), the court shall fix the time for filing claims arising from the rejection of executory contracts or unexpired leases under section 348(c) and 365(d) of the Code.

Paragraph (7) provides that if the court extends the time to file claims against a surplus (Rule 3003(c)(6)), the extension shall apply to holders of claims who failed to timely file within the time prescribed or fixed under paragraph 6, above, and notice shall be given to the claimant pursuant to Rule 2002.

[Paragraph (2) was deleted in 1991 because notice of conversion is required by Rules 1017(d), 2002(f)(2) and 9022. Renumbered paragraph (5) was amended to reduce to 15 days the time to file a schedule of postpetition debts and requires inclusion of the name and address of each postpetition creditor. Renumbered paragraph (6) was amended to conform the time for filing postpetition claims to the time for filing prepetition claims.]

1986 Amendments: The 1986 Amendments made the conversion provisions of section 706 applicable in chapter 12 cases.

Case Annotations

When a debtor is not eligible to proceed under chapter 13, "conversion" to that chapter is void *ab initio,* and accordingly the provisions of section 1306 cannot then be invoked to determine what property comprises the estate. Bobroff v. Continental Bank (*In re* Bobroff), 766 F.2d 797, 12 C.B.C.2d 1491 (3d Cir. 1985).

A conversion from chapter 7 to chapter 13 following an adverse decision in a dischargeability suit does not render the conversion "manipulation of the Bankruptcy Code." Street v. Lawson (*In re* Street), 13 C.B.C.2d 1184 (9th Cir., B.A.P., 1985).

Section 706(a) permits a debtor to convert a case from chapter 7 to chapter 13, upon motion and entry of an order, only if the case has not previously been converted from another chapter and absent extreme circumstances constituting bad faith or other gross inequity. *In re* Spencer, 26 C.B.C.2d 1223 (B. Ct., N.D. Okla. 1992).

The provisions of section 706(a) allowing a chapter 7 debtor to convert to chapter 13 "at any time" must be limited to those situations where the debtor's chapter 7 discharge has not been granted or has been revoked upon motion of the debtor. *In re* Jones, 23 C.B.C.2d 451 (B. Ct., E.D. Tenn. 1990).

A creditor may not force individual debtors to convert their chapter 7 case to one under chapter 11 against their will; Congress intended that section 706(b) be used in the instance of corporate rather than individual debtors. *In re* Brophy, 12 C.B.C.2d 1156 (B. Ct., D. Hawaii 1985).

When an involuntary chapter 7 petition is filed against the debtor, a voluntary petition supporting an order for relief under chapter 11 is not a conversion of the case. *In re* Alpine Lumber & Nursery, 5 C.B.C.2d 141 (B. Ct., S.D. Cal. 1981).

When there are no proper and valid objections, a debtor has a right to convert its chapter 7 case to a case under chapter 13 notwithstanding that there may have been a prior conversion to chapter 7 from chapter 11. *In re* Sensibaugh, 4 C.B.C.2d 23 (B. Ct., S.D. Cal. 1981).

References

4 *Collier on Bankruptcy* ch. 706 (Matthew Bender 15th ed.).

2 *Collier Bankruptcy Manual* ch. 706 (Matthew Bender 3d ed.).

2 *Collier Bankruptcy Practice Guide* ch. 37 (Matthew Bender).

SECTION 707 (11 U.S.C. § 707)

§ 707. **Dismissal.** (a) The court may dismiss a case under this chapter only after notice and a hearing and only for cause, including—

(1) unreasonable delay by the debtor that is prejudicial to creditors;

(2) nonpayment of any fees or charges required under chapter 123 of title 28; and

(3) failure of the debtor in a voluntary case to file, within fifteen days or such additional time as the court may allow after the filing of the petition commencing such case, the information required by paragraph (1) of section 521, but only on a motion by the United States trustee.

(b) After notice and a hearing, the court, on its own motion or on a motion by the United States trustee, but not at the request or suggestion of any party in interest, may dismiss a case filed by an individual debtor under this chapter whose debts are primarily consumer debts if it finds that the granting of relief would be a substantial abuse of the provisions of this chapter. There shall be a presumption in favor of granting the relief requested by the debtor.

Bankruptcy Rule References: 1006, 1017, 2002 and 4004

Legislative History

This section authorizes the court to dismiss a liquidation case only for cause, such as unreasonable delay by the debtor that is prejudicial to creditors or nonpayment of any fees and charges required under chapter 123 of title 28. These causes are not exhaustive, but merely illustrative. The section does not contemplate, however, that the ability of the debtor to repay his debts in whole or in part constitutes adequate cause for dismissal. To permit dismissal on that ground would be to enact a non-uniform mandatory chapter 13, in lieu of the remedy of bankruptcy. The Committee has rejected that alternative in the past, and there has not been presented any convincing reason for its enactment in this bill. [*Ed. Note:* The last sentence is omitted from the Senate Report.]

[*House Report No. 95–595, 95th Cong., 1st Sess. 380 (1977); Senate Report No. 95–989, 95th Cong., 2d Sess. 94 (1978).*]

Section 707 of the House amendment indicates that the court may dismiss a case only after notice and a hearing.

[*124 Cong. Rec. H 11,1098 (Sept. 28, 1978); S 17,414 (Oct. 6, 1978).*]

Comment

Bankruptcy Rule 1017 relates to dismissal of a case. Subdivision (a) provides that (except as provided in sections 707(b), 1208(b) and 1307(b) under which a chapter 12 or 13 debtor has the absolute right to have the case dismissed at any time) a case shall not be dismissed on motion of the petitioner or for want of prosecution or other cause or by consent of the parties before a hearing on notice as provided in Rule 2002. Unless a list of creditors and their addresses was previously filed, the debtor must file such a list within the time fixed by the court, and upon debtor's failure to do so, the court may order the preparation and filing of the list by the debtor or other person.

Bankruptcy Rule 2002(f)(2) requires the clerk or some other person as the court directs to give notice to the debtor, all creditors and indenture trustees of the dismissal of a case. Rule 2002(k) requires that the clerk or such other person transmit the notice to the United States trustee.

Subdivision (b) of Rule 1017 provides:

(1) the court may dismiss the case after hearing on notice to the debtor and the trustee for nonpayment of any installment of the filing fee ordered pursuant to Rule 1006(b);

(2) if the case is dismissed or the case closed without payment in full of the filing fee, the installments collected will be distributed as if the filing fee had been paid in full; and

(3) notice of dismissal for failure to pay the filing fee is to be given within 30 days after dismissal to creditors appearing on the list of creditors and to those who have filed claims, as provided in Rule 2002.

Subdivision (c) of the Rule provides that a case shall not be dismissed pursuant to section 305 until after a hearing on notice as provided in Rule 2002(a).

Subdivision (d) of the Rule prescribes the procedure for dismissal or conversion. [Both subdivisions (a) and (d) were amended to provide procedures for dismissal or conversion of a chapter 12 case and are the same as in a chapter 13 case].

Subsection (e) relates to dismissal of an individual's chapter 7 case for substantial abuse pursuant to section 707(b) of the Code.

The three grounds for dismissal set forth in section 707 are merely illustrative and the court may dismiss the case on other grounds when "cause" is shown to exist.

1984 Amendments: Section 707 was amended to add subsection (b) providing a new ground for dismissal. If the court finds that granting relief under chapter 7 would be a "substantial" abuse of the provisions of chapter 7, the court on its own motion or on motion of the United States trustee, but *not at the request or suggestion of any party in interest,* may after adequate hearing, dismiss a chapter 7 petition filed by an individual whose debts are primarily consumer debts. *See* section 101 for the definition of "consumer debt."

The Bankruptcy Rules are to implement section 707(b) and prescribe the practice and procedure to be followed thereunder. The general rule making power of 28 U.S.C. § 2075 is applicable. Pub. L. No. 98–353, § 320. [*See* Bankruptcy Rule 1017(e).]

1986 Amendments: The amendment added paragraph (3) to section 707(a), providing that if a debtor in a voluntary case fails to file within 15 days (or such additional time as the court may allow) after the filing of the petition commencing the case, the information required by section 521(1), the court may dismiss the chapter 7 case, *but only on motion by the United States trustee.* Section 521(1) requires a debtor to file a list of creditors, schedules and statements.

Section 707(b) originally permitted dismissal of a case filed by an individual debtor if the court found that granting relief would be a substantial abuse of the provisions of chapter 7, but dismissal (after notice and hearing) could be only on the court's own motion. The 1986 Amendment permits the United States trustee to make the motion to dismiss.

The Joint Explanatory Statement of the Committee of Conference for the 1986 Act had this to say about the amendment to section 707(b):

> Section 216 of the House bill amended 11 U.S.C. 707(b) to permit a United States Trustee to move the bankruptcy court to dismiss a case filed under Chapter 7 by an individual consumer debtor, where the court finds that the granting of relief would be a substantial abuse of the Chapter 7 process. The Senate bill contained no amendment to Section 707(b), but included a similar provision in Section 238(a)(3). That section amended 11 U.S.C. 704(10) to impose a duty on the panel trustee to bring to the attention of the court information that might enable the court to carry out its responsibilities under 11 U.S.C. 707 and other sections. The Senate recedes.

> Under current law, the court may dismiss a Chapter 7 case on grounds of substantial abuse only 'on its own motion and not at the request or suggestion of any party in interest.' Some question has arisen as to whether United States Trustees and panel trustees are considered 'parties in interest' for purposes of this section, and are thus precluded from bringing information to the attention of the court on the issue of substantial abuse, and moving for dismissal of a Chapter 7 case on those grounds. See, e.g., *In re* Christian, 51 B.R. 118 (Bankr. D.N.J. 1985). The Conference Report clarifies the ability of the U.S. Trustee under Section 707(b) to bring such information to the attention of the court. The original intent of this subsection was to preclude creditors from exercising this function.

> The conferees anticipate that the panel trustee will work closely in conjunction with the United States Trustee to assist in the discharge of the specific authority granted under Section 707(b). This would include bringing to the United States trustee's attention any information or evidence of fraud or abuse which may provide

the basis for dismissal of a case under Section 707(b). The U.S. Trustee may, in his discretion, bring that information to the attention of the court. The conferees anticipate that panel trustees will frequently appear in court regarding the motions filed by the U.S. Trustee under Section 707(b), as amended. Such appearances will be in their capacity as panel trustee and not as a representative of the U.S. Trustee.

This section was amended to reflect the creation of a permanent United States trustee system. Section 302(d) of the 1986 Amendments provides different effective dates for the amendments relating to the United States trustee system. *See* Section 302 of the 1986 Amendments, reprinted herein under "Selected Provisions of the Bankruptcy Judges, United States Trustees, and Family Farmer Bankruptcy Act of 1986," regarding effective dates generally.

1990 Amendments: Section 302(d)(3) of the Bankruptcy Judges, United States Trustees, and Family Farmer Bankruptcy Act of 1986 was amended by Pub. L. No. 101-650 (Judicial Improvements Act of 1990) to extend the period in which the judicial districts in the states of Alabama and North Carolina may remain outside the United States trustee system and to insert new language pertaining to the effective date of the 1986 amendment to section 105 of title 11.

Case Annotations

The debtor's ability to repay his or her debts is only one factor, albeit a significant one, in determining whether substantial abuse has occurred for purposes of applying section 707(b). For purposes of a dismissal motion under section 707(b), the proper test for determining whether a debtor has substantially abused the bankruptcy process is the "totality of circumstances" test, which employs an evaluation of five factors, including whether the petition was filed because of sudden illness, calamity, disability, or unemployment; whether the debtor incurred cash advances and made consumer purchases far in excess of his ability to repay; whether the debtor's proposed budget is excessive or unreasonable; whether the debtor's schedules and statements accurately and reasonably reflect his true financial condition; and whether the petition was filed in good faith. *In re* Green, 934 F.2d 568, 24 C.B.C.2d 1911 (4th Cir. 1991).

A trustee may file a motion to dismiss for substantial abuse under section 707(b) at the initial suggestion of a creditor. *In re* Clark, 927 F.2d 793, 24 C.B.C.2d 1536 (4th Cir. 1991).

A court may take a debtor's good faith and unique hardships into consideration under section 707(b); while the statute does not mandate a future income test, it does not preclude consideration of future income to give meaning to the "substantial abuse" standard. *In re* Walton, 866 F.2d 981, 20 C.B.C.2d 533 (8th Cir. 1989).

"Primarily consumer debts" in section 707(b) suggests an overall ratio of consumer to nonconsumer debts of over 50%, and the consumer debts should be evaluated not only by amount but by their relative number. The test for determining whether a debt should be classified as a business debt, rather than a debt acquired for personal, family or household purposes, is whether it was incurred with an eye toward profit. In the Matter of Booth, 858 F.2d 1051, 19 C.B.C.2d 1284 (5th Cir. 1988).

The debtor's ability to pay his debts when due, as determined by his ability to fund a chapter 13 plan, is the primary factor to be considered in determining whether granting chapter 7 relief would be a substantial abuse. A finding that a debtor is able to pay his debts, standing alone, supports a conclusion of substantial abuse. Zolog v. Kelly (In re Kelly), 841 F.2d 908, 18 C.B.C.2d 560 (9th Cir. 1988).

A chapter 7 trustee has standing to object to a debtor's motion for voluntary dismissal on behalf of unsecured creditors who have not affirmatively consented to the dismissal. Penick v. Tice (In re Penick), 732 F.2d 1211, 10 C.B.C.2d 828 (4th Cir. 1984).

A bankruptcy court must conduct a separate hearing on notice to all parties in interest prior to refusing to dismiss under section 707(b), even when the court raises the issue *sua sponte*. Central National Bank of Woodway-Hewitt v. Spark, 15 C.B.C.2d 988 (W.D. Tex. 1986).

A chapter 7 case in technical compliance with the Bankruptcy Code may nonetheless be dismissed for cause if the debtor's motivation is to exploit the protections of the bankruptcy process to the unconscionable detriment of creditors. In re Hammonds, 26 C.B.C.2d 1473, (B. Ct., D. Colo. 1992).

While courts are not in agreement on the proof necessary to support a dismissal under section 707, they generally break down the question into two parts: (1) whether the debtor's debts are primarily consumer debts and (2) whether the grant of a discharge of such debts constitutes a substantial abuse of the bankruptcy process. In re Scheinberg, 25 C.B.C.2d 1159 (B. Ct., D. Kan. 1991).

While there is a statutory presumption in favor of granting chapter 7 relief to a debtor, that presumption may be rebutted by the trustee under section 707(b) upon a showing of substantial abuse. Substantial abuse is to be determined on a case by case basis, with the court considering the totality of the circumstances and bearing in mind that the basic purpose of chapter 7 is to provide the debtor with a fresh start. In the Matter of Dubberke, 24 C.B.C.2d 415 (B. Ct., S.D. Iowa 1990).

Under section 707(b), if the debtor's honesty, good faith, or need of chapter 7 relief are at issue, the bankruptcy court, pursuant to the *Krohn* decision, must examine the totality of the circumstances, and such an examination must produce sufficient evidence to disturb the statutory presumption favoring the debtor's entitlement to file for chapter 7 relief. In re Wilkes, 23 C.B.C.2d 869 (B. Ct., W.D. Tenn. 1990).

"Cause" has been shown so that a court may dismiss a chapter 7 case when a debtor has failed to disclose all income and to provide adequate information about assets and expenditures, transferred a substantial interest in property for no consideration, and refused to pay a debt that would be within his financial means to pay. *In re* Maide, 21 C.B.C.2d 663 (B. Ct., W.D. Pa. 1989).

When there is no other evidence of bad faith and the debtor's financial future is uncertain, a bankruptcy court may refuse to dismiss a chapter 7 case for substantial abuse even when there is evidence of an ability to fund some type of plan. *In re* Martin, 21 C.B.C.2d 1026 (B. Ct., D. Ark. 1989).

The language of this section does not define "substantial abuse" in terms of a debtor's ability to pay his debts through a chapter 13 plan and in fact makes no reference to the debtor's ability to fund a chapter 13 plan. Substantial abuse in the context of section 707(b) requires evidence of misconduct, impropriety or lack of good faith on the part of debtors. *In re* Wegner, 19 C.B.C.2d 997 (B. Ct., D. Minn. 1988).

Although the debtors' monthly expenditures, including a religious contribution of $672, may be excessive, there is no abuse of the Code when (1) the debtors have returned their automobile to the secured creditor; (2) upon losing their home, the debtors have obtained a rental unit for less cost; and (3) the debtors seem sincere in their religious beliefs. The court cannot impose its own views of religion and financial responsibility on the debtors. *In re* Gaukler, 15 C.B.C.2d 693 (B. Ct., D.N.D. 1986).

A bankruptcy court may dismiss for "cause" under section 707(a) the petition of a debtor operating a toxic waste site when public health and safety will not be jeopardized by dismissal; neither the court nor the trustee has experience in cleaning up toxic waste; clean-up would be delayed and expenses raised by adding a bankruptcy case to previously filed federal and state court actions; and because of the cost of the clean-up, any possible distribution to creditors would be so inconsequential as to make administration of the case an exercise in futility. State of Ohio v. Commercial Oil Service, Inc. (*In re* Commercial Oil Service, Inc.), 14 C.B.C.2d 577 (B. Ct., N.D. Ohio 1986), *aff'd*, 88 B.R. 126 (N.D. Ohio 1987).

References

4 *Collier on Bankruptcy* ch. 707 (Matthew Bender 15th ed.).

2 *Collier Bankruptcy Manual* ch. 707 (Matthew Bender 3d ed.).

2 *Collier Bankruptcy Practice Guide* ch. 37 (Matthew Bender).

Breitowitz, *New Developments in Consumer Bankruptcies: Chapter 7 Dismissal on the Bases of "Substantial Abuse,"* 5 J.L. & Com. 1 (1984).

Comment, *Consumer Bankruptcy: Substantial Abuse and Section 707 of the Bankruptcy Code,* 55 Mo. L. Rev. 247 (1990).

Comment, *The Debtor Trap: The Ironies of Section 707(a),* 7 Bankr. Dev. J. 175 (1990).

Note, *Section 707(b) of the Bankruptcy Code: A Roadmap With a Proposed Standard for Defining Substantial Abuse,* 19 J.L. Reform 1011 (1986).

Proia, *The Interpretation and Application of Section 707(b) of the Bankruptcy Code,* 93 Com. L.J. 367 (1988).

Weintraub and Resnick, *Eligibility for Chapter 13 as a Requirement for Dismissal of Chapter 7 Case Based on "Substantial Abuse": In re Mastroeni,* 19 U.C.C. L.J. 67 (1986).

Wells and Kurtz, *A Critical Analysis of Bankruptcy Code Section 707(b),* 36 Clev. St. L. Rev. 385 (1988).

Wells, Kurtz and Calhoun, *The Implementation of Bankruptcy Code Section 707(b): The Law and the Reality,* 39 Clev. St. L. Rev. 15 (1991).

SUBCHAPTER II

Collection, Liquidation, and Distribution
of the Estate

SECTION 721 (11 U.S.C. § 721)

§ 721. Authorization to operate business. The court may authorize the trustee to operate the business of the debtor for a limited period, if such operation is in the best interest of the estate and consistent with the orderly liquidation of the estate.

Legislative History

This section is derived from section 2a(5) of the Bankruptcy Act. It permits the court to authorize the operation of any business of the debtor for a limited period, if the operation is in the best interest of the estate and consistent with orderly liquidation of the estate. An example is the operation of a watch company to convert watch movements and cases into completed watches which will bring much higher prices than the component parts would have brought.

[*House Report No. 95–595, 95th Cong., 1st Sess. 380 (1977); Senate Report No. 95–989, 95th Cong., 2d Sess. 94 (1978).*]

Comment

Section 2a(5) of the former Bankruptcy Act empowered the court to authorize the business of bankrupts to be conducted for limited periods by receivers or trustees if necessary in the best interest of the estate. Former Rule 201(a) authorized appointment of a receiver "to conduct the business of the bankrupt" and former Rule 216 provided that the court could authorize a trustee to conduct the business and manage the property of the bankrupt for such time as would be in the best interest of the estate and "consistent with orderly liquidation thereof." Receivers are abolished by the Code, section 105.

Section 704(7) requires a trustee where operation of the business is authorized, to file periodic reports. Bankruptcy Rule 2015(a)(3) requires such trustee to file the reports and summaries required by section 704(8) including, if payments are made to employees, a statement of the amounts of deductions for taxes required to be withheld and the place where deposited. [The 1991 Amendments deleted the requirement that the court fix a time for filing the reports and summaries as unnecessary because the United States trustee may request filing within a specified time.]

References

4 *Collier on Bankruptcy* ch. 721 (Matthew Bender 15th ed.).

2 *Collier Bankruptcy Manual* ch. 721 (Matthew Bender 3d ed.).

SECTION 722 (11 U.S.C. § 722)

§ 722. **Redemption.** An individual debtor may, whether or not the debtor has waived the right to redeem under this section, redeem tangible personal property intended primarily for personal, family, or household use, from a lien securing a dischargeable consumer debt, if such property is exempted under section 522 of this title or has been abandoned under section 554 of this title, by paying the holder of such lien the amount of the allowed secured claim of such holder that is secured by such lien.

Bankruptcy Rule Reference: 6008

Legislative History

This section is new and is broader than rights of redemption under the Uniform Commercial Code. It authorizes an individual debtor to redeem tangible personal property intended primarily for personal, family, or household use, from a lien securing a dischargeable consumer debt. It applies only if the debtor's interest in the property is exempt or has been abandoned. The right to redeem extends to the whole of the property, not just the debtor's exempt interest in it. Thus, for example, if a debtor owned a $2,000 car, subject to a $1,200 lien, the debtor could exempt his $800 interest in the car. The debtor is permitted a $1,500 exemption in a car, proposed 11 U.S.C. § 522(d)(2). This section permits him to pay the holder of the lien $1,200 and redeem the entire car, not just the remaining $700 of his exemption. The redemption is accomplished by paying the holder of the lien the amount of the allowed claim secured by the lien. The provision amounts to a right of first refusal for the debtor in consumer goods that might otherwise be repossessed. The right of redemption under this section is not waivable.

[*House Report No. 95–595, 95th Cong., 1st Sess. 380–381 (1977).*]

This section is new and is broader than rights of redemption under the Uniform Commercial Code. It authorizes an individual debtor to redeem tangible personal property intended primarily for personal, family, or household use, from a lien securing a nonpurchase money dischargeable consumer debt. It applies only if the debtor's interest in the property is exempt or has been abandoned.

This right to redeem is a very substantial change from current law. To prevent abuses such as may occur when the debtor deliberately allows the property to depreciate in value, the debtor will be required to pay the fair market value of the goods or the amount of the claim if the claim is less. The right is personal to the debtor and not assignable.

[*Senate Report No. 95–989, 95th Cong., 2d Sess. 95 (1978).*]

Section 722 of the House amendment adopts the position taken in H.R. 8200 as passed by the House and rejects the alternative contained in section 722 of the Senate amendment.

[*124 Cong. Rec. H 11,098 (Sept. 28, 1978); S 17,144 (Oct. 6, 1978).*]

Comment

Section 722 of the Code has no counterpart in the former Bankruptcy Act. In many cases collateral is essential to the debtor's household and the value to him may be much greater than the price it would obtain at a forced sale. This section enables the debtor to retain the property or to regain possession thereof by paying the amount of the "allowed" secured claim of the holder secured by the lien on the property. *See* section 506(a) for valuation of security interests; section 522 for exempt property; section 554 for abandonment of property by the trustee.

Bankruptcy Rule 6008 provides that on motion of the debtor, trustee or debtor in possession, and after a hearing on notice as directed by the court, the court may authorize redemption of property from a lien or from a sale to enforce a lien in accordance with applicable law. (Under section 722 the debtor may redeem, but there is no provision in the Code as to a trustee's right to redeem. Notice should be given to the secured creditor so that he may have the opportunity to object to the proposed redemption.)

Case Annotations

Since there is no legislative history indicating Congressional intent to allow elimination of undersecured liens on property not subject to the redemption provisions of section 722, section 506(d) cannot be read to provide relief similar to section 722 for property not included within the ambit of section 722. Dewsnup v. Timm, 502 U.S. —, 112 S. Ct. 773, 116 L. Ed. 2d 903, 25 C.B.C.2d 1297 (1992).

Although not listed as an alternative in section 521(2)(A), a debtor is permitted to redeem collateral by continuing regular payments under an installment contract, so long as notice of such intention is timely provided. *In re* Belanger, 962 F.2d 345, 26 C.B.C.2d 1429 (4th Cir. 1992).

A debtor may redeem collateral securing a debt by paying the creditor the amount of the secured claim or the fair market value of the collateral, whichever is less. In the Matter of Edwards, 901 F.2d 1383, 23 C.B.C.2d 488 (7th Cir. 1990).

Section 722 constitutes the only redemption remedy Congress provided chapter 7 debtors and to allow comparable lien avoidance on real property pursuant to section 506(d) would render section 722 superfluous. *In re* Lange, 24 C.B.C.2d 798 (9th Cir., B.A.P., 1990).

Section 722 and other Code provisions, specifically, section 524(c), that pertain to a chapter 7 debtor require that redemption be made in a lump sum, but a reaffirmed debt may be paid in installments. Ford Motor Credit Co. v. Polk (*In re* Polk), 17 C.B.C.2d 864 (9th Cir., B.A.P., 1987).

The court may determine the redemption value as the fair market value of the property, and is not restricted to any artificial value previously agreed to in a repurchase agreement. Terre Haute First Nat'l Bank v. Davis (*In re* Davis), 6 C.B.C.2d 625 (C.D. Ill. 1982).

Redemption must be achieved by a lump sum payment, and to permit a redemption to be made through installment payments frustrates the clear meaning of section 722. *In re* Carroll, 4 C.B.C.2d 1042 (9th Cir., B.A.P., 1981).

The continuation of payments under an obligation that is not in default is not an impermissible redemption by installment. *In re* Donley, 25 C.B.C.2d 686 (B. Ct., N.D. Fla. 1991).

Although section 722 is silent as to the method by which a debtor may redeem secured property, Congressional intent was that it be paid in one lump sum; should the debtor wish to pay in installments, his or her only alternative is to negotiate a reaffirmation with the creditor. Matter of Horne, 25 C.B.C.2d 1471 (B. Ct., N.D. Ga. 1991).

References

4 *Collier on Bankruptcy* ch. 722 (Matthew Bender 15th ed.).

2 *Collier Bankruptcy Manual* ch. 722 (Matthew Bender 3d ed.).

3 *Collier Bankruptcy Practice Guide* ch. 77 (Matthew Bender).

Bernert, *Redemption of Collateral From a Consumer Debt Under the Bankruptcy Act,* 52 Okla. B.J. 453 (1981).

SECTION 723 (11 U.S.C. § 723)

§ 723. Rights of partnership trustee against general partners.

(a) If there is a deficiency of property of the estate to pay in full all claims which are allowed in a case under this chapter concerning a partnership and with respect to which a general partner of the partnership is personally liable, the trustee shall have a claim against such general partner for the full amount of the deficiency.

(b) To the extent practicable, the trustee shall first seek recovery of such deficiency from any general partner in such partnership that is not a debtor in a case under this title. Pending determination of such deficiency, the court may order any such partner to provide the estate with indemnity for, or assurance of payment of, any deficiency recoverable from such partner, or not to dispose of property.

(c) Notwithstanding section 728(c) of this title, the trustee has a claim against the estate of each general partner in such partnership that is a debtor in a case under this title for the full amount of all claims of creditors allowed in the case concerning such partnership. Notwithstanding section 502 of this title, there shall not be allowed in such partner's case a claim against such partner on which both such partner and such partnership are liable, except to any extent that such claim is secured only by property of such partner and not by property of such partnership. The claim of the trustee under this subsection is entitled to distribution in such partner's case under section 726(a) of this title the same as any other claim of a kind specified in such section.

(d) If the aggregate that the trustee recovers from the estates of general partners under subsection (c) of this section is greater than any deficiency not recovered under subsection (b) of this section, the court, after notice and a hearing, shall determine an equitable distribution of the surplus so recovered, and the trustee shall distribute such surplus to the estates of the general partners in such partnership according to such determination.

Bankruptcy Rule References: 1004 and 1007

Legislative History

This section is a significant departure from present law. It repeals the jingle rule, which, for ease of administration, denied partnership creditors their rights against general partners by permitting general partners' individual creditors to share in their estates first to the exclusion of partnership creditors. The result under this section more closely tracks generally applicable partnership law, without a significant administrative burden.

Subsection (a) specifies that each general partner in a partnership debtor is liable to the partnership's trustee for any deficiency of partnership property to pay in full all administrative expenses and all claims against the partnership.

Subsection (b) requires the trustee to seek recovery of the deficiency from any general partner that is not a debtor in a bankruptcy case. The court is empowered to order that partner to indemnify the estate or not to dispose of property pending a determination of the deficiency. The language of the subsection is directed to cases under the bankruptcy code. However, if, during the early stages of the transition period, a partner in a partnership is proceeding under the Bankruptcy Act while the partnership is proceeding under the bankruptcy code, the trustee should not first seek recovery against the Bankruptcy Act partner. Rather, the Bankruptcy Act partner should be deemed for the purposes of this section and the rights of the trustee to be proceeding under title 11.

Subsection (c) requires the partnership trustee to seek recovery of the full amount of the deficiency from the estate of each general partner that is a debtor in a bankruptcy case. The trustee will share equally with the partners' individual creditors in the assets of the partners' estates. Claims of partnership creditors who may have filed against the partner will be disallowed to avoid double counting.

[*House Report No. 95–595, 95th Cong., 1st Sess. 381 (1977); Senate Report No. 95–989, 95th Cong., 2d Sess. 95 (1978).*]

Section 723(c) of the House amendment is a compromise between similar provisions contained in the House bill and Senate amendment. The section makes clear that the trustee of a partnership has a claim against each general partner for the full amount of all claims of creditors allowed in the case concerning the partnership. By restricting the trustee's rights to claims of "creditors," the trustee of the partnership will not have a claim against the general partners for administrative expenses or claims allowed in the case concerning the partnership. As under present law, sections of the Bankruptcy Act applying to codebtors and sureties apply to the relationship of a partner with respect to a partnership debtor. *See* sections 501(b), 502(e), 506(d)(2), 509, 524(d), and 1301 of title 11.

[*124 Cong. Rec. H 11,098 (Sept. 28, 1978); S 17,414–17,415 (Oct. 6, 1978).*]

Subsection (d) provides for the case where the total recovery from all of the bankrupt general partners is greater than the deficiency of which the trustee sought recovery. This case would most likely occur for a partnership with a large number of general partners. If the situation arises, the court is required to determine an equitable redistribution of the surplus to the estate of the general partners. The determination will be based on factors such as the relative liability of each of the general partners under the partnership agreement and the relative rights of each of the general partners in the profits of the enterprise under the partnership agreement. [*Ed. Note:* The last sentence of this excerpt from the House report is inaccurate. For a correct statement of the factors to determine relative liability see page 201 of the House Report.]

[*House Report No. 95–595, 95th Cong., 1st Sess. 381 (1977); See Senate Report No. 95–989, 95th Cong., 2d Sess. 95–96 (1978).*]

Comment

The former Bankruptcy Act dealt with payment of partnership debts in Section 5g as follows:

> g. The net proceeds of the partnership property shall be appropriated to the payment of the partnership debts and the net proceeds of the individual estate of each general partner to the payment of his individual debts. Should any surplus remain of the property of any general partner after paying his individual debts, such surplus shall be added to the partnership assets and be applied to the payment of the partnership debts. Should any surplus of the partnership property remain after paying the partnership debts, such surplus shall be distributed among the individual partners, general or limited, or added to the estates of the general partners, as the case may be, in the proportion of their respective interests in the partnership and in the order of distribution provided by the laws of the State applicable thereto.

Section 723 departs from prior law by repealing the so-called jingle rule which, for ease of administration, denied partnership creditors their rights against general partners by permitting the individual creditors of partners to share in their estates first, to the exclusion of partnership creditors.

Nondebtor general partners are liable to the partnership's trustee for any deficiency in the partnership's estate to pay creditors in full as provided by section 723. Bankruptcy Rule 1007(g), as amended in 1991, authorizes the court to require any general partner to file a statement of personal assets and liabilities to provide the trustee with the relevant information. The general partners are required to prepare and file the schedules of the assets and liabilities, schedule of current income and expenditures, schedule of executory contracts and unexpired leases, and statement of financial affairs of the partnership.

See Rule 1004 as to the filing of a petition by or against a partnership.

1984 Amendments: Technical clarifying changes were made in section 723(a) and (c).

Case Annotations

When a partnership is not a debtor in a case under the Bankruptcy Code, neither section 723 nor the jingle rule purports to prescribe the order of distribution of the proceeds of the debtor-partner's estate. *In re* Safren, 16 C.B.C.2d 315 (B. Ct., C.D. Cal. 1986).

According to section 103(b), section 723 is available to a trustee only in a case under chapter 7 and is not available to a trustee in a chapter 11 case despite the fact that the debtors involved are in a liquidating chapter 11 case. *In re* Monetary Group, 13 C.B.C.2d 1459 (B. Ct., M.D. Fla. 1985).

A judgment holding a partner liable for the debts of a debtor partnership does not deprive individual creditors from pursuing their claims and filing an involuntary petition against the partner. *In re* Lamb, 10 C.B.C.2d 1298 (B. Ct., E.D. Tenn. 1984).

References

4 *Collier on Bankruptcy* ch. 723 (Matthew Bender 15th ed.).

2 *Collier Bankruptcy Manual* ch. 723 (Matthew Bender 3d ed.).

1 *Collier Bankruptcy Practice Guide* ch. 5 (Matthew Bender).

Keen, *Problems of the Individual Arising From Bankruptcy and Insolvency: As Stockholder, Officer, Partner and Individual,* 36 N.Y.U. Inst. on Fed. Tax. 383 (1978).

SECTION 724 (11 U.S.C. § 724)

§ 724. Treatment of certain liens.

(a) The trustee may avoid a lien that secures a claim of a kind specified in section 726(a)(4) of this title.

(b) Property in which the estate has an interest and that is subject to a lien that is not avoidable under this title and that secures an allowed claim for a tax, or proceeds of such property, shall be distributed—

(1) first, to any holder of an allowed claim secured by a lien on such property that is not avoidable under this title and that is senior to such tax lien;

(2) second, to any holder of a claim of a kind specified in sections 507(a)(1), 507(a)(2), 507(a)(3), 507(a)(4), 507(a)(5), or 507(a)(6) of this title, to the extent of the amount of such allowed tax claim that is secured by such tax lien;

(3) third, to the holder of such tax lien, to any extent that such holder's allowed tax claim that is secured by such tax lien exceeds any amount distributed under paragraph (2) of this subsection;

(4) fourth, to any holder of an allowed claim secured by a lien on such property that is not avoidable under this title and that is junior to such tax lien;

(5) fifth, to the holder of such tax lien, to the extent that such holder's allowed claim secured by such tax lien is not paid under paragraph (3) of this subsection; and

(6) sixth, to the estate.

(c) If more than one holder of a claim is entitled to distribution under a particular paragraph of subsection (b) of this section, distribution to such holders under such paragraph shall be in the same order as distribution to such holders would have been other than under this section.

(d) A statutory lien the priority of which is determined in the same manner as the priority of a tax lien under section 6323 of the Internal Revenue Code of 1954 (26 U.S.C. § 6323) shall be treated under subsection (b) of this section the same as if such lien were a tax lien.

Legislative History

Subsection (a) of section 724 permits the trustee to avoid a lien that secures a fine, penalty, forfeiture, or multiple, punitive, or exemplary damages claim to the extent that the claim is not compensation for actual pecuniary loss. The subsection follows the policy found in section 57j of the Bankruptcy Act of protecting unsecured creditors from the debtor's wrongdoing, but expands the protection afforded. The lien is made voidable rather than void in chapter 7, in order to permit the lien to be revived if the case is converted to chapter 11, under which penalty liens are not voidable. To make the lien void would be to permit the filing of a chapter 7, the voiding of the lien, and the conversion to a chapter 11, simply to avoid a penalty lien, which should be valid in a reorganization case.

[*House Report No. 95–595, 95th Cong., 1st Sess. 382 (1977); Senate Report No. 95–989, 95th Cong., 2d Sess. 96 (1978).*]

Subsection (b) governs tax liens. It is derived from section 67c(3) of the Bankruptcy Act, without substantial modification in result. It subordinates tax liens to administrative expense and wage claims, and solves certain circuity of liens problems that arise in connection with the subordination. The order of distribution of property subject to a tax lien is as follows: First, to holders of liens senior to the tax lien; second, to administrative expenses, wage claims, and consumer creditors that are granted priority, but only to the extent of the amount of the allowed tax claim secured by the lien. In other words, the priority claimants step into the shoes of the tax collector. Third, to the tax claimant, to the extent that priority claimants did not use up his entire claim. Fourth, to junior lien holders. Fifth, to the tax collector to the extent that he was not paid under paragraph (3). Finally, any remaining property goes to the estate. The result of these provisions are to leave senior and junior lienors and holders of unsecured claims undisturbed. If there are any liens that are equal in status to the tax lien, they share *pari passu* with the tax lien under the distribution provisions of this subsection.

[House Report No. 95–595, 95th Cong., 1st Sess. 382 (1977).]

Subsection (b) governs tax liens. This provision retains the rule of present bankruptcy law (section 67(c)(3) of the Bankruptcy Act) that a tax lien on personal property, if not avoidable by the trustee, is subordinated in payment to unsecured claims having a higher priority than unsecured tax claims. Those other claims may be satisfied from the amount that would otherwise have been applied to the tax lien, and any excess of the amount of the lien is then applied to the tax. Any personal property (or sale proceeds) remaining is to be used to satisfy claims secured by liens which are junior to the tax lien. Any proceeds remaining are next applied to pay any unpaid balance of the tax lien.

[Senate Report No. 95–989, 95th Cong., 2d Sess. 96 (1978).]

Section 724 of the House amendment adopts the provision taken in the House bill and rejects the provision taken in the Senate amendment. In effect, a tax claim secured by a lien is treated as a claim between the fifth and sixth priority in a case under chapter 7 rather than as a secured claim.

[124 Cong. Rec. H 11,098 (Sept. 28, 1978); S 17,415 (Oct. 6, 1978).]

Section 724. Treatment of certain liens: The House amendment modifies present law by requiring the subordination of tax liens on both real and personal property to the payment of claims having a priority. This means that assets are to be distributed from the debtor's estate to pay higher priority claims before the tax claims are paid, even though the tax claims are properly secured. Under present law and the Senate amendment only tax liens on personal property, but not on real property, are subordinated to the payment of claims having a priority above the priority for tax claims.

[124 Cong. Rec. H 11,114 (Sept. 28, 1978); S 17,431 (Oct. 6, 1978).]

Subsection (d) specifies that any statutory lien whose priority is determined in the same manner as a tax lien is to be treated as a tax lien under this section, even if the lien does not secure a claim for taxes. An example is the ERISA lien.

[House Report No. 95–595, 95th Cong., 1st Sess. 382 (1977); Senate Report No. 95–989, 95th Cong., 2d Sess. 96 (1978).]

Comment

Section 724(a) follows the policy of Section 57j of the former Bankruptcy Act of protecting unsecured creditors from a debtor's wrongdoing, but expands the protection afforded by Section 57j.

Section 724(b) governing tax liens is derived from Section 67c(3) of the Act without substantial modification of result.

Section 724 modifies prior law by subordinating tax liens on both real and personal property to the payment of claims having a priority. Thus, assets are to be distributed to pay higher priority claims before tax claims even though the latter are properly secured. Under prior law this rule applied only to tax liens on personal property.

Bankruptcy Rule 7001(2) provides that a proceeding to determine the validity, priority, or extent of a lien or other interest in property is an adversary proceeding governed by the Part VII rules.

Pursuant to 28 U.S.C. § 157(b)(2)(K), determinations of the validity, extent, or priority of liens are "core proceedings" over which the bankruptcy judges have authority to make and enter dispositive orders, judgments and decrees.

1984 Amendments: Technical changes for clarification were made in subsections (b)(2), (b)(3), (c) and (d) of section 724.

Case Annotations

When there is a priority dispute between federal and state tax liens, priority is determined by the general rule of "first in time, first in right." *In re* Terwilliger's Catering Plus, Inc., 911 F.2d 1168, 23 C.B.C.2d 694 (6th Cir. 1990).

When there are competing federal and state tax liens against the balance of funds in a chapter 7 estate, that balance will not be distributed *pro rata* pursuant to section 726, but rather by reference to the nonbankruptcy "first in time" rule. Section 726 has no application to distribution under section 724 since, by its terms, property distributed under section 724 does not become part of the estate unless or until all secured claims have been satisfied. United States v. Darnell (*In re* Darnell), 834 F.2d 1263, 17 C.B.C.2d 1106 (6th Cir. 1987).

Even if the estate has no equity in certain property, the proceeds of the sale of such property may be administered in accordance with section 724(b) rather than compelled to be abandoned under section 554 when administration promises a benefit in the subordination of a tax lien, that is, charging administrative expenses against a secured tax creditor. Morgan v. K.C. Mach. & Tool Co. (*In re* K.C. Mach. & Tool Co.), 816 F.2d 238, 16 C.B.C.2d 702 (6th Cir. 1987).

Once an involuntary petition in bankruptcy has been filed against an insolvent taxpayer the government's rights as a recorded tax lienholder under the federal insolvency statute, 31 U.S.C. § 3713, cease and those rights are governed by priorities established in the Bankruptcy Code. NLT Computer Services Corp. v. Capital Computer Systems, Inc., 755 F.2d 1253, 12 C.B.C.2d 364 (6th Cir. 1985).

Priority between a federal non tax lien and a state sales tax lien is generally determined by federal law, that is, first in time is first in right, but when state law has already established commercial rules, these rules should be followed, unless there is a demonstrated need for national uniformity. Pearlstein v. Small Bus. Admin., 719 F.2d 1169, 9 C.B.C.2d 1134 (D.C. Cir. 1983).

Funds erroneously paid to a taxing authority instead of to a chapter 7 trustee under section 724(b) constitute an unauthorized postpetition transfer avoidable under section 549 and recoverable under section 550. *In re* Forrest Marbury House Assocs. Ltd. Partnership, 26 C.B.C.2d 1270 (B. Ct., D.D.C. 1992).

A cash collateral agreement will not be enforced if it violates section 724(b) of the Code. *In re* Life Imaging Corp., 25 C.B.C.2d 916 (B. Ct., D. Colo. 1991).

The effect of section 724(b) is to take the tax claimant's lien and give it to the administrative claimants; thus whenever property of the estate is burdened by a tax lien (local, state or federal) the amount of that lien can be used to pay administrative expenses. *In re* Packard Properties, Ltd., 22 C.B.C.2d 1476 (B. Ct., N.D. Tex. 1990).

Although subordination may deprive a municipality of private property for public use without compensation, it is not in violation of the Fifth Amendment because it does not work a "taking" in the constitutional sense; subordination under section 724(b) is also not violative of the Tenth Amendment as the section establishes equal treatment for local and federal interests. Forell v. Kent County Treasurer (*In re* Kamstra), 13 C.B.C.2d 266 (B. Ct., W.D. Mich. 1985).

References

4 *Collier on Bankruptcy* ch. 724 (Matthew Bender 15th ed.).

2 *Collier Bankruptcy Manual* ch. 724 (Matthew Bender 3d ed.).

3 *Collier Bankruptcy Practice Guide* ch. 63 (Matthew Bender).

Barney, *The Secret Federal Tax Lien*, 17 Colo. Law. 1521 (1988).

Burleson, *Tax Aspects of Bankruptcy*, 17 Colo. Law. 619 (1988).

Duncan and Lyons, *Federal Tax Liens and the Secured Party*, 21 U.C.C. L.J. 3 (1988).

Passamano, *Questions of Priority: Secured Lender Versus a Federal Tax Lien*, 93 Com. L.J. 361 (1988).

SECTION 725 (11 U.S.C. § 725)

§ 725. **Disposition of certain property.** After the commencement of a case under this chapter, but before final distribution of property of the estate under section 726 of this title, the trustee, after notice and a hearing, shall dispose of any property in which an entity other than the estate has an interest, such as a lien, and that has not been disposed of under another section of this title.

Bankruptcy Rule References: 6007 and 7001

Legislative History

This section requires the court to determine the appropriate disposition of property in which the estate and an entity other than the estate have an interest. It would apply, for example, to property subject to a lien or property co-owned by the estate and another entity. The court must make the determination with respect to property that is not disposed of under another section of the bankruptcy code, such as by abandonment under section 554, by sale or distribution under 363, or by allowing foreclosure by a secured creditor by lifting the stay under section 362. The purpose of the section is to give the court appropriate authority to ensure that collateral or its proceeds is returned to the proper secured creditor, that consigned or bailed goods are returned to the consignor or bailor, and so on. Current law is curiously silent on this point, though case law has grown to fill the void. The section is in lieu of a section that would direct a certain distribution to secured creditors. It gives the court greater flexibility to meet the circumstances, and it is broader, permitting disposition of property subject to a co-ownership interest.

[*House Report No. 95–595, 95th Cong., 1st Sess. 382–383 (1977); Senate Report No. 95–989, 95th Cong., 2d Sess. 96 (1978).*]

Section 725 of the House amendment adopts the substance contained in both the House bill and Senate amendment but transfers an administrative function to the trustee in accordance with the general thrust of this legislation to separate the administrative and the judicial functions where appropriate.

[*124 Cong. Rec. H 11,098 (Sept. 28, 1978); S 17,415 (Oct. 6, 1978).*]

Comment

The House and Senate Reports refer to a determination by the court of appropriate disposition of property in which the estate and another entity have an interest as, for example, property subject to a lien or co-owned by the estate and another entity. But the section as finally enacted transfers this administrative function to the trustee, thus following the policy of the Code to separate judicial and administrative functions where appropriate. Dispositon of property in which both the estate and another entity have an interest is apparently an administrative act that can be properly performed by the trustee as part of his normal duties.

Bankruptcy Rule 6007 relates to the disposition of property. Subdivision (a) requires the trustee to give notice of a proposed abandonment or other disposition of property to the United States trustee, to all creditors, indenture trustees and appointed or elected committees. A party in interest may serve and file an objection within 15 days of the mailing of the notice, or within the time fixed by the court. Subdivision (b) permits a party in interest to serve and file a motion requiring the trustee to abandon property of the estate. Subdivision (c) provides that if timely objection under subdivision (a) is made, the court shall set a hearing on notice to the United States trustee and such entities as directed by the court.

Bankruptcy Rule 7001(3) provides that a proceeding to obtain approval under section 363(h) for the sale of both the interest of the estate and of a codebtor in property is an adversary proceeding governed by the Part VII rules.

1984 Amendments: Section 725 was clarified by insertion of the words "of property of the estate."

Case Annotations

Trust beneficiaries under the Perishable Agricultural Commodities Act (PACA) are entitled to *pro rata* distribution of trust assets when there are insufficient assets to completely meet the trust obligations. In the Matter of United Fruit and Produce Co., Inc., 23 C.B.C.2d 1314 (B. Ct., D. Conn. 1990).

References

4 *Collier on Bankruptcy* ch. 725 (Matthew Bender 15th ed.).

2 *Collier Bankruptcy Manual* ch. 725 (Matthew Bender 3d ed.).

Michlovitz, *Stay Afloat Without "Straight" Bankruptcy,* 5 Fam. Advoc. 10 (1983).

Riesenfeld, *Who Owns What Under Chapter 7,* 5 Fam. Advoc. 28 (1983).

SECTION 726 (11 U.S.C. § 726)

§ 726. Distribution of property of the estate.

(a) Except as provided in section 510 of this title, property of the estate shall be distributed—

(1) first, in payment of claims of the kind specified in, and in the order specified in, section 507 of this title;

(2) second, in payment of any allowed unsecured claim, other than a claim of a kind specified in paragraph (1), (3), or (4) of this subsection, proof of which is—

(A) timely filed under section 501(a) of this title;

(B) timely filed under section 501(b) or 501(c) of this title; or

(C) tardily filed under section 501(a) of this title, if—

(i) the creditor that holds such claim did not have notice or actual knowledge of the case in time for timely filing of a proof of such claim under section 501(a) of this title; and

(ii) proof of such claim is filed in time to permit payment of such claim;

(3) third, in payment of any allowed unsecured claim proof of which is tardily filed under section 501(a) of this title, other than a claim of the kind specified in paragraph (2)(C) of this subsection;

(4) fourth, in payment of any allowed claim, whether secured or unsecured, for any fine, penalty, or forfeiture, or for multiple, exemplary, or punitive damages, arising before the earlier of the order for relief or the appointment of a trustee, to the extent that such fine, penalty, forfeiture, or damages are not compensation for actual pecuniary loss suffered by the holder of such claim;

(5) fifth, in payment of interest at the legal rate from the date of the filing of the petition, on any claim paid under paragraph (1), (2), (3), or (4) of this subsection; and

(6) sixth, to the debtor.

(b) Payment on claims of a kind specified in paragraph (1), (2), (3), (4), (5), (6) or (7) of section 507(a) of this title, or in paragraph (2), (3), (4), or (5) of subsection (a) of this section, shall be made pro rata among claims of the kind specified in each such particular paragraph, except that in a case that has been converted to this chapter under section 1112[,] [*sic*] 1208, or 1307 of this title, a claim allowed under section 503(b) of this title incurred under this chapter after such conversion has priority over a claim allowed under section 503(b) of this title incurred under any other chapter of this title or under this chapter before such conversion and over any expenses of a custodian superseded under section 543 of this title.

(c) Notwithstanding subsections (a) and (b) of this section, if there is property of the kind specified in section 541(a)(2) of this title, or proceeds of such property, in the estate, such property or proceeds shall be segregated from other property of the estate, and such property or proceeds and other property of the estate shall be distributed as follows:

(1) Claims allowed under section 503 of this title shall be paid either from property of the kind specified in section 541(a)(2) of this title, or from other property of the estate, as the interest of justice requires.

(2) Allowed claims, other than claims allowed under section 503 of this title, shall be paid in the order specified in subsection (a) of this section, and, with respect to claims of a kind specified in a particular paragraph of section 507(a) of this title or subsection (a) of this section, in the following order and manner:

(A) First, community claims against the debtor or the debtor's spouse shall be paid from property of the kind specified in section 541(a)(2) of this title, except to the extent that such property is solely liable for debts of the debtor.

(B) Second, to the extent that community claims against the debtor are not paid under subparagraph (A) of this paragraph, such community claims shall be paid from property of the kind specified in section 541 (a)(2) of this title that is solely liable for debts of the debtor.

(C) Third, to the extent that all claims against the debtor including community claims against the debtor are not paid under subparagraph (A) or (B) of this paragraph such claims shall be paid from property of the estate other than property of the kind specified in section 541(a)(2) of this title.

(D) Fourth, to the extent that community claims against the debtor or the debtor's spouse are not paid under subparagraph (A), (B), or (C) of this paragraph, such claims shall be paid from all remaining property of the estate.

Bankruptcy Rule References: 3001 and 3010

Legislative History

This section is the general distribution section for liquidation cases. It dictates the order in which distribution of property of the estate, which has usually been reduced to money by the trustee under the requirements of section 704(1).

First, property is distributed among priority claimants, as determined by section 507, and in the order prescribed by section 507. Second, distribution is to general unsecured creditors. This class excludes priority creditors and the two classes of subordinated creditors specified below. The provision is written to permit distribution to creditors that tardily file claims if their tardiness was due to lack of notice or knowledge of the case. Though it is in the interest of the estate to encourage timely filing, when tardy filing is not the result of a failure to act by the creditor, the normal subordination penalty should not apply. Third distribution is to general unsecured creditors who tardily file. Fourth distribution is to holders of fine, penalty, forfeiture, or multiple, punitive, or exemplary damage claims. These claims are disallowed entirely under present law. They are simply subordinated here. Paragraph (4), in combination with paragraph (2), will require that claims for fines, penalties, and damages be divided into the portion that is in compensation for actual pecuniary loss and the portion that is not. Distribution under the two paragraphs will be made accordingly. Fifth distribution is in payment of interest at the legal rate from the date of the filing of the petition on claims paid under the previous four paragraphs. Any surplus is paid to the debtor.

[*House Report No. 95–595, 95th Cong., 1st Sess. 383 (1977).*]

This section is the general distribution section for liquidation cases. It dictates the order in which distribution of property of the estate, which has usually been reduced to money by the trustee under the requirements of section 704(1).

First, property is distributed among priority claimants, as determined by section 507, and in the order prescribed by section 507. Second, distribution is to general unsecured creditors. This class excludes priority creditors and the two classes of subordinated creditors specified below. The provision is written to permit distribution to creditors that tardily file claims if their tardiness was due to lack of notice or knowledge of the case. Though it is in the interest of the estate to encourage timely filing, when tardy filing is not the result of a failure to act by the creditor, the normal subordination penalty should not apply. Third distribution is to general unsecured creditors who tardily file. Fourth distribution is to holders of fine, penalty, forfeiture, or multiple, punitive, or exemplary damage claims. More of these claims are disallowed entirely under present law. They are simply subordinated here.

Paragraph (4) provides that punitive penalties, including prepetition tax penalties, are subordinated to the payment of all other classes of claims, except claims for interest accruing during the case. In effect, these penalties are payable out of the estate's assets only if and to the extent that a surplus of assets would otherwise remain at the close of the case for distribution back to the debtor.

Paragraph (5) provides that postpetition interest on prepetition claims is also to be paid to the creditor in a subordinated position. Like prepetition penalties, such interest will be paid from the estate only if and to the extent that a surplus of assets would otherwise remain for return to the debtor at the close of the case.

This section also specifies that interest accrued on all claims (including priority and nonpriority tax claims) which accrued before the date of the filing of the title 11 petition is to be paid in the same order of distribution of the estate's assets as the principal amount of the related claims.

Any surplus is paid to the debtor under paragraph (6).

[*Senate Report No. 95-989, 95th Cong., 2d Sess. 96-97 (1978).*]

Section 726(a)(4) adopts a provision contained in the Senate amendment subordinating prepetition penalties and penalties arising in the involuntary gap period to the extent the penalties are not compensation for actual pecuniary laws.

The House amendment deletes a provision following section 726(a)(6) of the Senate amendment providing that the term "claim" includes interest due owed before the date of the filing of the petition as unnecessary since a right to payment for interest due is a right to payment which is within the definition of "claim" in section 101(4) of the House amendment.

[*124 Cong. Rec. H 11,098 (Sept. 28, 1978); S 17,415 (Oct. 6, 1978).*]

Subsection (b) follows current law. It specifies that claims within a particular class are to be paid *pro rata*. This provision will apply, of course, only when there are inadequate funds to pay the holders of claims of a particular class in full. The exception found in the section, which also follows current law, specifies that liquidation administrative expenses are to be paid ahead of reorganization administrative expenses if the case has been converted from a reorganization case to a liquidation case, or from an individual repayment plan case to a liquidation case.

Subsection (c) governs distributions in cases in which there is community property and other property of the estate. The section requires the two kinds of property to be segregated. The distribution is as follows: First, administrative expenses are to be paid, as the court determines on any reasonable equitable basis, from both kinds of property. The court will divide administrative expenses according to such factors as the amount of each kind of property in the estate, the cost of preservation and liquidation of each kind of property, and whether any particular administrative expenses are attributable to one kind of property or the other. Second, claims are to be paid as provided under subsection (a) (the normal liquidation case distribution rules) in the following order and manner: First, community claims against the debtor or the debtor's spouse are paid from community property, except such as is liable solely for the debts of the debtor.

Second, community claims against the debtor, to the extent not paid under the first provision, are paid from community property that is solely liable for the debts of the debtor. Third, community claims to the extent they remain unpaid, and all other claims against the debtor, are paid from noncommunity property. Fourth, if any community claims against the debtor or the debtor's spouse remain unpaid, they are paid from whatever property remains in the estate. This would occur if community claims against the debtor's spouse are large in amount and most of the estate's property is property solely liable, under nonbankruptcy law, for debts of the debtor.

The marshalling rules in this section apply only to property of the estate. However, they will provide a guide to the courts in the interpretation of proposed 11 U.S.C. § 725, relating to distribution of collateral, in cases in which there is community property. If a secured creditor has a lien on both community and non-community property, the marshalling rules here—by analogy would dictate that the creditor be satisfied first out of community property, and then out of separate property.

[*House Report No. 95–595, 95th Cong., 1st Sess. 383–384 (1977); Senate Report No. 95–989, 95th Cong., 2d Sess. 97–98 (1978).*]

Section 726 of the Senate amendment provides that the rule requiring *pro rata* payment of all expenses within a priority category does not apply to the payment of amounts withheld by a bankruptcy trustee. The purpose of this rule was in [sic] insure that the trustee pay the full amount of the withheld taxes to the appropriate governmental tax authority. The House amendment deletes this rule as unnecessary because the existing practice conforms essentially to that rule. If the trustee fails to pay over in full amounts that he withheld, it is a violation of his trustee's duties which would permit the taxing authority to sue the trustee on his bond.

[*124 Cong. Rec. H 11,109 (Sept. 28, 1978); S 17,426 (Oct. 6, 1978).*]

Comment

Section 64 of the former Bankruptcy Act set forth the debts which had priority in advance of payment of dividends to creditors. Section 507 is the comparable provision in the Code.

Section 726 of the Code dictates the order of distribution of the property of the estate which has been reduced to money. Distribution to general unsecured creditors follows payment to priority creditors as provided in section 507. A tardily filed claim may be allowed when the tardiness was due to lack of notice or knowledge of the case; a departure from prior law under which the six-month filing provision was strictly enforced. A creditor with no knowledge of the bankruptcy had a nondischargeable debt, but lack of knowledge of the pendency of the case was not a ground, under the Act, to permit a late filing.

Another important change from prior law involves claims for a fine, penalty, forfeiture, or multiple, punitive, or exemplary damages. Under prior law such claims were disallowed; under the Code they are simply subordinated.

Subsection (b) of section 726 follows prior law, and specifies that the claims of a particular class are to be paid *pro rata* when there are inadequate funds to pay the class in full.

Section 726(b) also follows the prior law by providing that the administration expenses of a liquidation case have priority over the administration expenses of a superseded chapter 11, 12 or 13 case.

Section 726(c) has no predecessor in the Act or former Bankruptcy Rules.

Bankruptcy Rule 3009 requires dividends in chapter 7 cases to be paid as promptly as possible, in amounts and at times ordered by the court, and checks to be payable and mailed to each creditor whose claim has been allowed. If a power of attorney authorizing payment to another entity has been filed (Rule 9010), checks are to be payable to the creditor *and* the entity holding the power of attorney and *mailed to the latter*. The rule leaves to the discretion of the court the amount and times of dividend payments while recognizing the creditors' right to as prompt payment as practicable.

Bankruptcy Rule 3010(a) provides that in a chapter 7 case no dividend of less than $5.00 shall be distributed to any creditor unless authorized by local rule or court order. Funds not distributed are to be treated as unclaimed funds. *See* section 347.

1984 Amendments: Clarifying changes were made in subsections (b) and (c)(1) and (2) of section 726.

1986 Amendments: The reference in section 726(b) to conversion of cases to chapter 7 was amended to include reference to conversion of a chapter 12 case pursuant to section 1208.

Case Annotations

While section 726(b) subordinates chapter 11 administrative expenses to chapter 7 administrative claims when a case is converted from chapter 11 to chapter 7, that section does not subordinate unpaid quarterly trustee payments due under 28 U.S.C. § 1930(a)(6) and the payments are accorded first priority status along with chapter 7 administrative expenses. *In re* Juhl Enterprises, Inc., 921 F.2d 800, 24 C.B.C.2d 643 (8th Cir. 1990).

When the reason for the late filing of a priority claim is the failure to give that creditor notice, that claim should be treated the same as timely filed priority claims entitled to distribution under section 726(a)(1). United States v. Cardinal Mine Supply, Inc., 916 F.2d 1027, 24 C.B.C.2d 26 (6th Cir. 1990).

While section 726(a)(5) provides for the payment of interest on claims specified in kind, unsecured claims timely filed, unsecured claims untimely filed, and allowed claims for penalty, forfeiture, and other similar claims, it does not include interest for an untimely distributed refund to the debtor. Grant and Bergwerk v. George Schumann Tire & Battery Co., 908 F.2d 874, 23 C.B.C.2d 708 (11th Cir. 1990).

Section 726(a)(4) is not rendered meaningless or void by an interpretation of section 510(c)(1) that holds that noncompensatory tax claims may be equitably subordinated. In the Matter of Virtual Network Services Corp., 902 F.2d 1246, 22 C.B.C.2d 1667 (7th Cir. 1990).

Section 726(a)(5) does not mandate that postpetition interest be paid to unsecured creditors even though the possibility exists that the debtor may retain funds from the settlement of a claim 1½ years after confirmation because the creditors are bound by the terms of the plan. Thompson v. Kentucky Lumber Co. (*In re* Kentucky Lumber Co.), 860 F.2d. 674, 19 C.B.C.2d 1292 (6th Cir. 1988).

When there are competing federal and state tax liens against amounts remaining for distribution of a chapter 7 estate, the amounts will not be distributed *pro rata* pursuant to section 726, but rather by reference to the nonbankruptcy "first in time" rule. Section 726 has no application to distribution under section 724 since, by its terms, property distributed under 724 does not become part of the estate unless or until all secured claims have been satisfied. United States v. Darnell (*In re* Darnell), 834 F.2d 1263, 17 C.B.C.2d 1106 (6th Cir. 1987).

A claim awarded pursuant to section 507(b) prior to the conversion of a chapter 11 case to a case under chapter 7 does not have priority over administrative expense claims under section 726(b). *In re* Sun Runner Marine, Inc., 26 C.B.C.2d 300 (9th Cir., B.A.P., 1991).

Section 726(a)(5) is not limited to payment of interest on prepetition claims, but also authorizes the payment of interest on fees and costs awarded under section 330(a). *In re* Riverside-Linden Investment Co., 22 C.B.C.2d 1335 (9th Cir., B.A.P., 1990).

In a community property state, community property as specified in section 541(a)(2), or proceeds of such property, shall be segregated from other property of the estate and distributed in accordance with the scheme set forth in section 726(c). Ageton v. Cervenka (*In re* Ageton), 5 C.B.C.2d 463 (9th Cir., B.A.P., 1981).

When a claim in bankruptcy is based on a contract which provides for a rate of interest and when the "bankrupt estate is solvent," the "legal rate" under section 726(a)(5) is the applicable prejudgment rate for breach of contract actions under state law. *In re* A & L Properties, 20 C.B.C.2d 426 (C.D. Cal. 1988).

For reasons of equity, in chapter 11 cases in which the debtor is solvent, postpetition interest ought to be paid to unsecured creditors before the proceeds of liquidation are returned to the debtor. Reasons to grant such interest are buttressed when there is evidence that the debtor's motives in filing its petition are questionable. *In re* Shaffer Furniture Co., 15 C.B.C.2d 1412 (E.D. Pa. 1987).

Pursuant to section 726(a)(2)(C), a creditor that did not have notice or knowledge of the case may file a proof of claim at any time before administration of the estate is concluded and participate fully with other creditors in the distribution of the estate. *In re* Kuhr, 25 C.B.C.2d 1155 (B. Ct., E.D. Cal. 1991).

Section 726(a)(5) is an exception to the general rule that creditors cannot recover postpetition interest, since it permits the bankruptcy court to pay interest to creditors on their claims when there is a surplus in the estate beyond that necessary to pay both secured and unsecured creditors. *In re* Godsey, 26 C.B.C.2d 452 (B. Ct., M.D. Tenn. 1991).

As the Code only requires that administrative claimants receive *pro rata* payment of their claims, an "evergreen retainer" will not preclude such a payment because the holder of such a retainer can be compelled to disgorge it. *In re* Benjamin's-Arnolds, Inc., 24 C.B.C.2d 1396 (B. Ct., D. Minn. 1990).

Section 726(a)(2)(C) does not operate to render an omitted debt dischargeable; rather it supplements the relief provided the holder of an omitted claim under section 523(a). *In re* Bosse, 24 C.B.C.2d 1256 (B. Ct., C.D. Cal. 1990).

Although a trustee is granted complete authority and discretion with respect to the prosecution and defense of any litigation of the debtor's estate under section 323 of the Code, the debtor or the debtor's principal may have standing to participate in litigation that will generate or protect a surplus in the estate. *In re* Gulph Woods Corp., 24 C.B.C.2d 206 (B. Ct., E.D. Pa. 1990).

A request for an additional fee award under section 503(b)(4) should be treated as an administrative expense under chapter 11, not chapter 7, when the underlying claim from which it derives occurs prior to the conversion of the case to chapter 7. *In re* Hers Cosmetics Corp., 23 C.B.C.2d 304 (B. Ct., C.D. Cal. 1990).

A chapter 7 discharge may be revoked upon motion of the trustee, a creditor or the United States trustee under the following circumstances: (1) when no creditor affected by the outcome objects and all appear to concur in the entry of an order vacating or revoking the order granting the discharge; and (2) where the factors of relative prejudice to other interested parties and lack of culpability of the debtor in obtaining the discharge weigh heavily in favor of the debtor. *In re* Jones, 23 C.B.C.2d 451 (B. Ct., E.D. Tenn. 1990).

Entireties property which is not exempt is property of the estate and may be used to satisfy all creditor claims, including claims against only one of two joint debtors. *In re* Wenande, 21 C.B.C.2d 1424 (B. Ct., D. Wyo. 1989).

References

4 *Collier on Bankruptcy* ch. 726 (Matthew Bender 15th ed.).

2 *Collier Bankruptcy Manual* ch. 726 (Matthew Bender 3d ed.).

3 *Collier Bankruptcy Practice Guide* ch. 51 (Matthew Bender).

Epling, *Proposal for Equality of Treatment for Claims in Chapter 7 and Claims in a Liquidating Chapter 11 Case,* 4 Bankr. Dev. J. 399 (1987).

Herbert and Pacitti, *Down and Out in Richmond, Virginia: The Distribution of Assets in Chapter 7 Bankruptcy Proceedings Closed During 1984-1987,* 22 U. Rich. L. Rev. 303 (1988).

Schweitzer, *Federal Oil Price Controls in Bankruptcy Cases: Government Claims for Repayment of Illegal Overcharges Should Not Be*

Subordinated as "Penalties" Under 11 U.S.C. § 726(a)(4), 42 Okla. L. Rev. 383 (1989).

SECTION 727 (11 U.S.C. § 727)

§ 727. Discharge.

(a) The court shall grant the debtor a discharge, unless—

(1) the debtor is not an individual;

(2) the debtor, with intent to hinder, delay, or defraud a creditor or an officer of the estate charged with custody of property under this title, has transferred, removed, destroyed, mutilated, or concealed, or has permitted to be transferred, removed, destroyed, mutilated, or concealed—

(A) property of the debtor, within one year before the date of the filing of the petition; or

(B) property of the estate, after the date of the filing of the petition;

(3) the debtor has concealed, destroyed, mutilated, falsified, or failed to keep or preserve any recorded information, including books, documents, records, and papers, from which the debtor's financial condition or business transactions might be ascertained, unless such act or failure to act was justified under all of the circumstances of the case;

(4) the debtor knowingly and fraudulently, in or in connection with the case—

(A) made a false oath or account;

(B) presented or used a false claim;

(C) gave, offered, received, or attempted to obtain money, property, or advantage, or a promise of money, property, or advantage, for acting or forbearing to act; or

(D) withheld from an officer of the estate entitled to possession under this title, any recorded information, including books, documents, records, and papers, relating to the debtor's property or financial affairs;

(5) the debtor has failed to explain satisfactorily, before determination of denial of discharge under this paragraph,

any loss of assets or deficiency of assets to meet the debtor's liabilities;

(6) the debtor has refused, in the case—

(A) to obey any lawful order of the court, other than an order to respond to a material question or to testify;

(B) on the ground of privilege against self-incrimination, to respond to a material question approved by the court or to testify, after the debtor has been granted immunity with respect to the matter concerning which such privilege was invoked; or

(C) on a ground other than the properly invoked privilege against self-incrimination, to respond to a material question approved by the court or to testify;

(7) the debtor has committed any act specified in paragraph (2), (3), (4), (5), or (6) of this subsection, on or within one year before the date of the filing of the petition, or during the case, in connection with another case, under this title or under the Bankruptcy Act, concerning an insider;

(8) the debtor has been granted a discharge under this section, under section 1141 of this title, or under sections 14, 371, or 476 of the Bankruptcy Act, in a case commenced within six years before the date of the filing of the petition;

(9) the debtor has been granted a discharge under sections 1228 or 1328 of this title, or under sections 660 or 661 of the Bankruptcy Act, in a case commenced within six years before the date of the filing of the petition, unless payments under the plan in such case totaled at least—

(A) 100 percent of the allowed unsecured claims in such case; or

(B)(i) 70 percent of such claims; and

(ii) the plan was proposed by the debtor in good faith, and was the debtor's best effort; or

(10) the court approves a written waiver of discharge executed by the debtor after the order for relief under this chapter.

(b) Except as provided in section 523 of this title, a discharge under subsection (a) of this section discharges the debtor from all debts that arose before the date of the order for relief under this chapter, and any liability on a claim that is determined under section 502 of this title as if such claim had arisen before the commencement of the case, whether or not a proof of claim based on any such debt or liability is filed under section 501 of this title, and whether or not a claim based on any such debt or liability is allowed under section 502 of this title.

(c)(1) The trustee, a creditor, or the United States trustee may object to the granting of a discharge under subsection (a) of this section.

(2) On request of a party in interest, the court may order the trustee to examine the acts and conduct of the debtor to determine whether a ground exists for denial of discharge.

(d) On request of the trustee, a creditor, or the United States trustee, and after notice and a hearing, the court shall revoke a discharge granted under subsection (a) of this section if—

(1) such discharge was obtained through the fraud of the debtor, and the requesting party did not know of such fraud until after the granting of such discharge;

(2) the debtor acquired property that is property of the estate, or became entitled to acquire property that would be property of the estate, and knowingly and fraudulently failed to report the acquisition of or entitlement to such property, or to deliver or surrender such property to the trustee; or

(3) the debtor committed an act specified in subsection (a)(6) of this section.

(e) The trustee, a creditor, or the United States trustee may request a revocation of a discharge—

(1) under subsection (d)(1) of this section within one year after such discharge is granted; or

(2) under subsection (d)(2) or (d)(3) of this section before the later of—

(A) one year after the granting of such discharge; and

(B) the date the case is closed.

Bankruptcy Rule References: 1017, 2002, 4004, 4005, 4006, 4008 and 7001

Legislative History

This section is the heart of the fresh start provisions of the bankruptcy law. Subsection (a) requires the court to grant a debtor a discharge unless one of eight conditions is met. [*Ed. Note:* The Senate Report lists "nine" conditions.] The first condition is that the debtor is not an individual. This is a change from present law, under which corporations and partnerships may be discharged in liquidation cases, though they rarely are. The change in policy will avoid trafficking in corporate shells and in bankrupt partnerships. "Individual" includes a deceased individual, so that if the debtor dies during the bankruptcy case, he will nevertheless be released from his debts, and his estate will not be liable for them. Creditors will be entitled to only one satisfaction—from the bankruptcy estate and not from the probate estate.

The next three grounds for denial of discharge center on the debtor's wrongdoing in or in connection with the bankruptcy case. They are derived from Bankruptcy Act section 14c. If the debtor, with intent to hinder, delay, or defraud his creditors or an officer of the estate, has transferred, removed, destroyed, mutilated, or concealed, or has permitted any such action with respect to, property of the debtor within the year preceding the case, or property of the estate after the commencement of the case, then the debtor is denied discharge. The debtor is also denied discharge if he has concealed, destroyed, mutilated, falsified, or failed to keep or preserve any books and records from which his financial condition might be ascertained, unless the act or failure to act was justified under all the circumstances of the case. The fourth ground for denial of discharge is the commission of a bankruptcy crime, though the standard of proof is preponderance of the evidence rather than proof beyond a reasonable doubt. These crimes include the making of a false oath or account, the use or presentation of a false claim, the giving or receiving of money for acting or forbearing to act, and the withholding from an officer of the estate entitled to possession of books and records relating to the debtor's financial affairs.

The fifth ground for denial of discharge is the failure of the debtor to explain satisfactorily any loss of assets or deficiency of assets to meet the debtor's liabilities. The sixth ground concerns refusal to testify. It is a change from present law, under which the debtor may be denied discharge for legitimately exercising his right against self-incrimination. Under this provision, the debtor may be denied discharge if he refuses to obey any lawful order of the court, or if he refuses to testify after having been granted immunity or after improperly invoking the constitutional privilege against self-incrimination.]

The seventh ground of discharge is the commission of an act specified in grounds two through six during the year before the debtor's case in connection with another bankruptcy case concerning an insider.

[*House Report No. 95–595, 95th Cong., 1st Sess. 384 (1977); Senate Report No. 95–989, 95th Cong., 2d Sess. 98 (1978).*]

Finally, if the debtor has been granted a discharge in a case commenced within six years preceding the present bankruptcy case, he is denied discharge. This provision, which is no change from current law with respect to straight bankruptcy, is the six-year bar to discharge. Under present law, but not under this bill, confirmation of a composition wage earner plan under chapter XIII is a basis for invoking the six-year bar.

[*House Report No. 95–595, 95th Cong., 1st Sess. 384–385 (1977).*]

The eighth ground for denial of discharge is derived from section 14c(5) of the Bankruptcy Act. If the debtor has been granted a discharge in a case commenced within six years preceding the present bankruptcy case, he is denied discharge. This provision, which is no change from current law with respect to straight bankruptcy, is the six-year bar to discharge. Discharge under chapter 11 will bar a discharge for six years. As under current law, confirmation of a composition wage earner plan under chapter 13 is a basis for invoking the six-year bar.

The ninth ground is approval by the court of a waiver of discharge.

[*Senate Report No. 95–989, 95th Cong., 2d Sess. 98–99 (1978).*]

Sections 727(a) (8) and (9) of the House amendment represent a compromise between provisions contained in section 727(a)(8) of the House bill and Senate amendment. Section 727(a)(8) of the House amendment adopts section 727(a)(8) of the House bill. However, section 727(a)(9) of the House amendment contains a compromise based on section 727(a)(8) of the Senate amendment with respect to the circumstances under which a plan by way of composition under chapter XIII of the Bankruptcy Act or chapter 13 of title 11 should be a bar to discharge in a subsequent proceeding under title 11. The paragraph provides that a discharge under sections 660 or 661 of the Bankruptcy Act or section 1328 of title 11 in a case commenced within six years before the date of the filing of the petition in a subsequent case, operates as a bar to discharge unless, first, payments under the plan totaled at least 100 percent of the allowed unsecured claims in the case; or second, payments under the plan totaled at least 70 percent of the allowed unsecured claims in the case and the plan was proposed by the debtor in good faith and was the debtor's best effort.

It is expected that the Rules of Bankruptcy Procedure will contain a provision permitting the debtor to request a determination of whether a plan is the debtor's "best effort" prior to confirmation of a plan in a case under chapter 13 of title 11. In determining whether a plan is the debtor's "best effort" the court will evaluate several factors. Different facts and circumstances in cases under chapter 13 operate to make any rule of thumb of limited usefulness. The court should balance the debtor's assets, including family income, health insurance, retirement benefits, and other wealth, a sum which is generally determinable, against the forseeable necessary living expenses of the debtor and the debtor's dependents, which unfortunately is rarely quantifiable. In determining the expenses of the debtor and the debtor's dependents, the court should consider the stability of the debtor's employment, if any, the age of the debtor, the number of the debtor's dependents and their ages, the condition of equipment and tools necessary to the debtor's employment or to the operation of his business, and other foreseeable expenses that the debtor will be required to pay during the period of the plan, other than payments to be made to creditors under the plan.

Section 727(a)(10) of the House amendment clarifies a provision contained in section 727(a)(9) of the House bill and Senate amendment indicating that a discharge may be barred if the court approves a waiver of discharge executed in writing by the debtor after the order for relief under chapter 7.

[*124 Cong. Rec. H 11,098 (Sept. 28, 1978); S 17,415 (Oct. 6, 1978).*]

Subsection (b) specifies that the discharge granted under this section discharges the debtor from all debts that arose before the date of the order for relief. It is irrelevant whether or not a proof of claim was filed with respect to the debt, and whether or not the claim based on the debt was allowed.

[*House Report No. 95–595, 95th Cong., 1st Sess. 385 (1977); Senate Report No. 95–989, 95th Cong., 2d Sess. 99 (1978).*]

Section 727(b) of the House amendment adopts a similar provision contained in the Senate amendment modifying the effect of discharge. The provision makes clear that the debtor is discharged from all debts that arose before the date of the order for relief under chapter 7 in addition to any debt which is determined under section 502 as if it were a prepetition claim. Thus, if a case is converted from chapter 11 or chapter 13 to a case under chapter 7, all debts prior to the time of conversion are discharged, in addition to debts determined after the date of conversion of a kind specified in section 502, that are to be determined as prepetition claims. This modification is particularly important with respect to an individual debtor who files a petition under chapter 11 or chapter 13 of title 11 if the case is converted to chapter 7. The logical result of the House amendment is to equate the result that obtains whether the case is converted from another chapter to chapter 7, or whether the other chapter proceeding is dismissed and a new case is commenced by filing a petition under chapter 7.

[*124 Cong. Rec. H 11,098 (Sept. 28, 1978); S 17,415 (Oct. 6, 1978).*]

Subsection (c) permits the trustee, or a creditor, to object to discharge. It also permits the court, on request of a party in interest, to order the trustee to examine the acts and conduct of the debtor to determine whether a ground for denial of discharge exists.

Subsection (d) requires the court to revoke a discharge already granted in certain circumstances. If the debtor obtained the discharge through fraud, if he acquired and concealed property of the estate, or if he refused to obey a court order or to testify, then the discharge is to be revoked.

Subsection (e) permits the trustee or a creditor to request revocation of a discharge within one year after the discharge is granted, on the grounds of fraud, and within one year of discharge or the date of the closing of the case, whichever is later, on other grounds.

[*Senate Report No. 95–989, 95th Cong., 2d Sess. 99 (1978); See also House Report No. 95–595, 95th Cong., 1st Sess. 385 (1977).*]

Comment

Section 727 is derived from Section 14c of the former Bankruptcy Act.

In general, the grounds to bar discharge under the Code are not unlike the grounds enumerated in Section 14c of the Act.

It should be noted that paragraph (1) of section 727 makes it clear that only an individual may obtain a discharge. Under the Act a partnership or corporation could be discharged, although such entities rarely exercised the privilege.

The second, third, fourth and fifth grounds of section 727(a) to bar discharge are derived directly from Section 14c of the Act. The sixth ground is a change from prior law under which a debtor may have been denied discharge for legitimately exercising his constitutional right to invoke the privilege against self-incrimination. Under the Code, the debtor may be denied a discharge if he refuses to obey a lawful order of the court or refuses to testify after having been granted immunity or after improperly invoking the constitutional privilege against self-incrimination.

The seventh ground in section 727(a) has no comparable provision in the Act. Discharge may be denied to an individual who committed one of the acts that bar discharge specified in grounds two through six during the year before the debtor's cases *in connection with another case involving an insider.*

The eighth ground to bar discharge is a previous discharge within six years before filing the petition in a liquidation case or a reorganization case under the Code or under the former Bankruptcy Act.

The ninth ground would bar discharge of a debtor who obtained a discharge within six years before the filing of the petition, in a chapter 13 case under the Code or in a Chapter XIII case under the Act unless (A) 100 percent of allowed unsecured claims were paid in the previous case, or (B) 70 percent of such claims were paid *and* the plan was proposed by the debtor in good faith and was the debtor's best effort. As suggested in the Congressional Record, the Rules of Bankruptcy will probably provide for the debtor to request a hearing to determine whether the plan was the debtor's best effort. The Congressional Record suggests what factors should enter into the determination of "best effort."

The tenth bar to discharge is a written waiver of discharge, executed *after* the order for relief under chapter 7 and *approved by the court.* Section 14a of the Act provided that the bankrupt could, before the hearing on the application for discharge, waive his discharge by a writing filed with the court. Court approval was not required.

Section 727(b) specifies that the discharge releases the debtor from all debts that arose prior to the order for relief regardless of whether or not a proof of claim was filed with respect to the debt, and whether or not the claim was allowed.

Section 727(c) provides that the trustee or a creditor or the United States trustee may object to discharge.

Subsections (d) and (e) of section 727 relate to revocation of discharge and were derived from Section 15 of the Act.

Bankruptcy Rule 4004 relates to discharge. Subdivision (a) provides that a complaint objecting to the debtor's discharge pursuant to section 727(a) is to be filed, in a chapter 7 case, not later than 60 days after the first date set for the meeting of creditors held under section 341(a). In a chapter 11 case, the complaint must be filed not later than the first date set for the confirmation hearing. Not less than 25 days notice of the time so fixed shall be given to the United States trustee and all creditors as provided in Rule 2002(f) and (k), and to the trustee and the trustee's attorney. [The 1991 Amendments require notice to the United States trustee to conform to section 727(c) of the Code which gives the United States trustee the right to object to discharge.]

Subdivision (b) of the Rule authorizes the court, on motion of a party in interest, after hearing on notice to extend, for cause, the time for filing a complaint objecting to discharge, provided that the time to file has not expired. The motion for an extension must be made within the original time period.

Subdivision (c) of the Rule provides that in a chapter 7 case, on expiration of the time for filing a complaint objecting to discharge and the time fixed for filing a motion to dismiss the case pursuant to Rule 1007(e), the court shall forthwith grant the discharge unless (1) the debtor is not an individual, (2) a complaint has been filed objecting to discharge, (3) the debtor filed a waiver of discharge (section 727(a)(10)), or (4) a motion to dismiss the case under Rule 1017(e) is pending. The court may, however, on motion of the debtor, defer entry of the order of discharge for 30 days, and on motion made within such period, may defer entry of the order to a date certain. [Section 524(c) authorizes a debtor to enter into an enforceable reaffirmation agreement only before entry of the discharge order. Deferring the entry of the order allows time for the debtor to enter into such agreements.]

Subdivision (d) of the Rule makes a proceeding commenced by a complaint objecting to discharge an adversary proceeding governed by Part VII of the rules. See also Rule 7001. (Pursuant to Rule 5005, the complaint should be filed with the clerk in the district in which the case is pending.)

Subdivision (e) of the Rule requires an order of discharge to conform to Official Form No. 18.

Subdivision (f) of the Rule provides that a final order of discharge may be registered in any other district by filing a certified copy of the order with the clerk of that district, and when so registered, the order shall have the same effect as an order of that district.

Subdivision (g) of the Rule requires the clerk to promptly mail a copy of the final order of the discharge to all creditors and to the trustee and trustee's attorney (and to the United States trustee). (Rule 2002 specifies the manner of the notice and persons to whom notice must be given.)

Bankruptcy Rule 4005 places the burden of proving the objection to a discharge upon the plaintiff.

Bankruptcy Rule 4006 provides that after an order denying or revoking discharge becomes final, or if a waiver of discharge is filed, the clerk shall promptly give notice thereof to all creditors and to the United States trustee as provided in Rule 2002.

Bankruptcy Rule 4008 provides that the court must hold the section 524(d) discharge hearing within no more than 30 days after entry of an order granting or denying a discharge on not less than 10 days notice to the debtor and the trustee. A debtor's motion for approval of a reaffirmation agreement must be filed at or before the hearing.

Bankruptcy Rule 7041 adopts Fed. R. Civ. P. 41 relating to dismissal of actions, but provides that a complaint objecting to discharge shall not be dismissed at plaintiff's instance save on notice to the trustee, the United States trustee, and such other persons as the court may direct, and upon order containing terms and conditions deemed appropriate.

Bankruptcy Rule 9024 makes it clear that the time to file a complaint to revoke a discharge pursuant to section 727(e) or to revoke an order confirming a plan unders sections 1144, 1230 and 1330 may not be circumvented by invoking Fed. R. Civ. P 60(b).

1984 Amendments: Paragraph (7) of section 727(a) was amended by adding language indicating that the paragraph applies to a case under the Bankruptcy Act as well as to a case under the Code. Clarifying changes were made in subsections (c)(1) and (e)(2)(A).

1986 Amendments: Section 727(c)(1) was amended to authorize the United States trustee to object to the discharge of a debtor under section 727(a). Subsections (d) and (e) were amended to authorize the United States trustee to move to revoke a discharge.

This section was amended to reflect the creation of a permanent United States trustee system. Section 302(d) of the 1986 Amendments provides different effective dates for the amendments relating to the United States trustee system. *See* Section 302 of the 1986 Amendments, reprinted herein under "Selected Provisions of the Bankruptcy Judges, United States Trustees, and Family Farmer Bankruptcy Act of 1986," regarding effective dates generally.

1990 Amendments: Section 302(d)(3) of the Bankruptcy Judges, United States Trustees, and Family Farmer Bankruptcy Act of 1986 was amended by Pub. L. No. 101-650 (Judicial Improvements Act of 1990) to extend the period in which the judicial districts in the states of Alabama and North Carolina may remain outside the United States

trustee system and to insert new language pertaining to the effective
date of the 1986 amendment to section 105 of title 11.

Case Annotations

As a prerequisite to discharge, section 727(a)(3) requires the debtor
to make and preserve adequate records of his or her affairs in order to
protect creditors; once a creditor makes an initial showing that a
debtor's records are inadequate, the burden is on the debtor to justify
the lack of adequate record keeping. Meridian Bank v. Alten, 958 F.2d
1226, 26 C.B.C.2d 846 (3d Cir. 1992).

A creditor has the right to challenge the debtor's discharge and
dischargeability of debt if: 1) the creditor's debt arose at or after
confirmation; and 2) the debtor committed post-confirmation acts that
support denial of discharge or render the debt nondischargeable. Matter
of Pavlovich, 952 F.2d 114, 26 C.B.C.2d 542 (5th Cir. 1992).

A preponderance of the evidence is the correct evidentiary standard
in reviewing allegations of debtor fraud for purposes of a discharge
under section 727(a) or dischargeability under section 523(a). *In re*
Serafini, 938 F.2d 1156, 25 C.B.C.2d 489 (10th Cir. 1991).

A debtor's omission from his asset schedules of a watch, a set of silver
flatware, two shares of stock, golf clubs and two silver cups constitutes
a false oath under section 727(a)(4)(A). Swicegood v. Ginn, 924 F.2d
230, 24 C.B.C.2d 1245 (11th Cir. 1991).

A debtor who spends $18,000 on travel, converts money market funds
into exempt assets, and who satisfies the homestead mortgage on the
eve of filing his bankruptcy petition, has gone beyond permissible
prebankruptcy planning and has exhibited an intent to hinder and delay
creditors which can result in the denial of his discharge. In the Matter
of Bowyer, 916 F.2d 1056, 24 C.B.C.2d 238 (5th Cir. 1990).

An omission of assets from a statement of affairs or schedule may
constitute a false oath under section 727(a)(4)(A) if the omission relates
to a material matter and is made wilfully with intent to defraud. *In re*
Calder, 907 F.2d 953, 23 C.B.C.2d 677 (10th Cir. 1990).

A bankruptcy court may consider a request for revocation of a
discharge upon expiration of the period for filing objections, at which
time the discharge is deemed to have been entered irrespective of the
absence of a formal order. *In re* Dietz, 914 F.2d 161, 23 C.B.C.2d 1006
(9th Cir. 1990).

The right of discharge is generally left to the sound discretion of the
bankruptcy judge. The court of appeals must defer to the bankruptcy
court's conclusion that the discharge should be denied unless its factual
findings are clearly erroneous or it applies an incorrect legal standard.
In re Cox, 904 F.2d 1399, 22 C.B.C.2d 1754 (9th Cir. 1990).

While individuals may be discharged of their debts under chapter 7,
corporations may not; Congress deliberately excluded corporations from

eligibility for a chapter 7 discharge to avoid trafficking in corporate shells and in bankruptcy partnerships. *In re* Goodman, 873 F.2d 598, 22 C.B.C.2d 1159 (2d Cir. 1989).

The determination of whether a right to payment arises prepetition or postpetition is governed by state law, unless an overriding federal law exists. Lugo v. Paulsen, 886 F.2d 602, 21 C.B.C.2d 1121 (3d Cir. 1989).

The holding of *In re Tveten* which permitted bankruptcy courts to consider the value of property converted into nonexempt assets is not applicable to homestead exemptions. *In re* Johnson, 880 F.2d 78, 21 C.B.C.2d 498 (8th Cir. 1989).

When a debtor offers no sufficient reason for the late filing of an answer to a complaint to bar discharge, the entry of default judgment is appropriate and the setting aside of such a default judgment is an abuse of the court's discretion, for a default judgment may not be set aside unless the debtor's attorney demonstrates a showing of excusable neglect or misconduct by the adverse party leading to the late filing. Gower v. Knight (*In re* Knight), 833 F.2d 1514, 17 C.B.C.2d 1321 (11th Cir. 1987).

Although the debtor's listing of a party as a creditor constitutes *prima facie* evidence of that party's interest in the case, once that party's claim has been conclusively disproved, the party loses creditor status and cannot object to the debtor's discharge. Stanley v. Vahlsing (*In re* Vahlsing), 829 F.2d 565, 17 C.B.C.2d 937 (5th Cir. 1987).

The seven-year concealment of an interest in an asset that continues with the "intent to hinder, delay, or defraud a creditor" into the year before the filing of a bankruptcy petition constitutes a form of concealment that occurs within the year before the bankruptcy filing and such concealment, therefore, is within the reach of section 727(a)(2)(A). Thibodeaux v. Olivier (*In re* Olivier), 819 F.2d 550, 16 C.B.C.2d 1330 (5th Cir. 1987).

If a debtor retransfers to himself property he initially transferred to hinder and delay creditors, reveals his actions to creditors, recovers substantially all of the transferred property before filing his bankruptcy petition and is otherwise qualified for a discharge, he may not be denied a discharge. If an involuntary petition interrupts the debtor's recovery efforts, the debtor may still obtain a discharge when he discloses the transfers to his creditors, has been making a good faith effort to recover them at the time of the filing of the involuntary petition, and actually does recover the property within a reasonable period of time. First Beverly Bank v. Adeeb (*In re* Adeeb), 787 F.2d 1339, 14 C.B.C.2d 740 (9th Cir. 1986).

The conversion of nonexempt property to exempt property may constitute a bar to discharge, but only if there is evidence indicating a fraudulent purpose aside from the mere conversion of exempt property; creation of an exempt tenancy by the entirety one day after a creditor obtains a judgment can constitute the requisite intent to defraud. Ford v. Poston (*In re* Ford), 773 F.2d 52, 13 C.B.C.2d 632 (4th Cir. 1985).

A debtor's omission of all references to his involvement in several corporations during the six years preceding bankruptcy constitutes the making of a false oath which is sufficient to bar his discharge, notwithstanding the fact that such information may not have revealed available assets to creditors. Chalik v. Moorefield (*In re* Chalik), 748 F.2d 616, 11 C.B.C.2d 1159 (11th Cir. 1984).

An overpayment of social security benefits may be discharged under section 727(b) because that statute permits discharge of "all debts" not listed in section 523. Rowan v. Morgan, 747 F.2d 1052, 11 C.B.C.2d 721 (6th Cir. 1984).

Collateral estoppel, or issue preclusion, does not bar a trustee's section 727 suit to block a debtor's discharge if the intentional fraud issue, central to the section 727(a)(2) proceeding, was never decided by the bankruptcy court in the trustee's earlier section 548 suit to set aside property transfers as fraudulent. Lovell v. Mixon, 719 F.2d 1373, 9 C.B.C.2d 1065 (8th Cir. 1983).

The obligation to remove hazardous wastes imposed upon a debtor by a state court judgment is a dischargeable claim in bankruptcy if: (1) it imposes an obligation upon the debtor for breach of performance; and (2) such breach also gives rise to an alternative right of payment. State of Ohio v. Kovacs (*In re* Kovacs), 717 F.2d 984, 9 C.B.C.2d 284 (6th Cir. 1983), *aff'd,* 469 U.S. 274, 105 S. Ct. 705, 83 L. Ed. 2d 649, 11 C.B.C.2d 1067 (1985).

When a discharge is not entered "forthwith" after the expiration of the Rule 4004(a) period and until a discharge is actually entered—even though a complaint objecting to discharge under section 727(a) would be untimely—a party may properly file a complaint under section 727(d) to "revoke" the discharge for (i) conduct occurring prior to the expiration of the Rule 4004(a) period which the party did not discover in time to file a complaint under section 727(a) due to the fraud of the debtor; or (ii) conduct occurring after the expiration of the Rule 4004(a) period. *In re* Stevens, 21 C.B.C.2d 1370 (9th Cir., B.A.P., 1989).

Debts are not dischargeable if they are tainted by a subsequent wrongful act by the debtor, including: 1) acts against the property intended to delay, hinder or defraud creditors; 2) acts against any recorded information regarding the debtor's financial condition; 3) knowingly making false claims; and 4) failing to obey a court order. *In re* Chavez, 26 C.B.C.2d 1598 (B. Ct., W.D. Tex. 1992).

The standard of proof to be applied in suits to bar discharge under section 727(a) is the preponderance of the evidence standard. A debtor's explanations as to missing records must be examined in light of the debtor's education, business sophistication, personal financial structure, the size and complexity of the business, and any special circumstances. *In re* Wolfson, 26 C.B.C.2d 1738 (B. Ct., S.D.N.Y. 1992).

As a chapter 7 debtor's death does not abate the liquidation case, a posthumous discharge can be either granted or denied. *In re* Eads, 26 C.B.C.2d 457 (B. Ct., E.D. Cal. 1991).

Prepetition property cannot be used to pay postpetition debts. *In re Tomer*, 25 C.B.C.2d 22 (B. Ct., S.D. Ill. 1991).

If a debtor properly invokes his Fifth Amendment privilege against self-incrimination in response to a question posed at the meeting of creditors, the debtor cannot be denied discharge for failing to answer the question. *In re French*, 24 C.B.C.2d 1979 (B. Ct., D. Minn. 1991).

If a debtor retains significant beneficial interests in property transferred to a family member outside the one year statutory reachback period, such retention will invoke the doctrine of continuing concealment and bring the transfers within the scope of the one year period set forth in section 727(a)(2)(A). *In re Essres*, 24 C.B.C.2d 1265 (B. Ct., D. Colo. 1990).

The time limitations within which a revocation of discharge proceeding may be commenced are an essential prerequisite to such proceeding, and a complaint is untimely if filed more than one year after either the discharge or the closing of the case, regardless of whether a motion filed within the time limit contained identical allegations. *In re Pankey*, 24 C.B.C.2d 1197 (B. Ct., W.D. Tenn. 1991).

Section 727(b) specifically discharges the debtor from all debts arising before the date of conversion to chapter 7 from chapter 11 and does not except in any way chapter 11 administrative expense claims from its reach unless dischargeability is being challenged pursuant to section 523. *In re Ramaker*, 23 C.B.C.2d 936 (B. Ct., N.D. Iowa 1990).

References

4 *Collier on Bankruptcy* ch. 727 (Matthew Bender 15th ed.).

2 *Collier Bankruptcy Manual* ch. 727 (Matthew Bender 3d ed.).

4 *Collier Bankruptcy Practice Guide* ch. 75 (Matthew Bender).

A Series of Questions and Answers re Discharge of Indebtedness, 46 Iowa Bar News Bull. No. 2, p. 12 (1986).

Comment, *Bankruptcy Estate Planning: Grounds for Denial of Discharge Under Section 727(a)(2)(A),* 7 Bankr. Dev. J. 199 (1990).

Jackson, *The Fresh-Start Policy in Bankruptcy Law,* 98 Harv. L. Rev. 1393 (1985).

Note, *The Fraud Exception to Discharge in Bankruptcy: A Reappraisal,* 38 Stan. L. Rev. 891 (1986).

Ozols, *Discharge of Tax Shelter Liability in Bankruptcy,* 17 Colo. Law. 245 (1988).

Sleeper, *Discharge: Sections 727, 524 and 523,* 2 Bank. Dev. J. 115 (1985).

Sullivan, *Reply: Limiting Access to Bankruptcy Discharge*, 1984 Wis. L. Rev. 1069.

Sullivan, Warren and Westbrook, *Rejoinder: Limiting Access to Bankruptcy Discharge*, 1984 Wis. L. Rev. 1087.

Tabb, *The Scope of the Fresh Start in Bankruptcy: Collateral Conversions and the Dischargeability Debate*, 59 Geo. Wash. L. Rev. 56 (1990).

Zuckerman, *New Interpretation of 11 U.S.C. 727(a)(2)(A) Favors Debtors*, 91 Com. L.J. 481 (1986).

SECTION 728 (11 U.S.C. § 728)

§ 728.　Special tax provisions.

(a) For the purposes of any State or local law imposing a tax on or measured by income, the taxable period of a debtor that is an individual shall terminate on the date of the order for relief under this chapter, unless the case was converted under section 1112 or 1208 of this title.

(b) Notwithstanding any State or local law imposing a tax on or measured by income, the trustee shall make tax returns of income for the estate of an individual debtor in a case under this chapter or for a debtor that is a corporation in a case under this chapter only if such estate or corporation has net taxable income for the entire period after the order for relief under this chapter during which the case is pending. If such entity has such income, or if the debtor is a partnership, then the trustee shall make and file a return of income for each taxable period during which the case was pending after the order for relief under this chapter.

(c) If there are pending a case under this chapter concerning a partnership and a case under this chapter concerning a partner in such partnership, a governmental unit's claim for any unpaid liability of such partner for a State or local tax on or measured by income, to the extent that such liability arose from the inclusion in such partner's taxable income of earnings of such partnership that were not withdrawn by such partner, is a claim only against such partnership.

(d) Notwithstanding section 541 of this title, if there are pending a case under this chapter concerning a partnership and a case under this chapter concerning a partner in such partnership, then any State or local tax refund or reduction of tax of such partner that would have otherwise been property of the estate of such partner under section 541 of this title—

(1) is property of the estate of such partnership to the extent that such tax refund or reduction of tax is fairly apportionable to losses sustained by such partnership and not reimbursed by such partner; and

(2) is otherwise property of the estate of such partner.

Legislative History

Section 728 of title 11 contains four subsections which embody special tax provisions that apply in a case under chapter 7. Subsection (a) terminates the taxable year of an individual debtor on the date of the order for relief under chapter 7 of title 11. The date of termination of the individual's taxable year is the date on which the estate first becomes a separate taxable entity. If the case was originally filed under chapter 11 of title 11, then the estate would have been made a separate taxable entity on the date of the order for relief under that chapter. In the rare case of a multiple conversion, then the date of the order for relief under the first chapter under which the estate was a separate taxable entity is controlling.

Subsection (b) permits the trustee of the estate of an individual debtor or a corporation in a case under chapter 7 of title 11 to make a tax return only if the estate or corporation has net taxable income for the entire case. If the estate or corporation has net taxable income at the close of the case, then the trustee files an income tax return for each tax year during which the case was pending. The trustee of a partnership debtor must always file returns for each such taxable period.

Subsection (c) sets forth a marshalling rule pertaining to tax claims against a partner and a partnership in a case under chapter 7 of title 11. To the extent that the income tax liability arose from the inclusion of undistributed earnings in the partner's taxable income, the court is required to disallow the tax claim against the partner's estate and to allow such claim against the partnership estate. No burden is placed on the taxing authority; the taxing authority should file a complete proof of claim in each case and the court will execute the marshalling. If the partnerships' assets are insufficient to satisfy partnership creditors in full, then section 723(c) of title 11 will apply, notwithstanding this subsection, to allow any unsatisfied tax claims to be asserted by the partnership trustee against the estate of the partner. The marshalling rule under this subsection applies only for purposes of allowance and distribution. Thus the tax claim may be nondischargeable with respect to an individual partner.

Subsection (d) requires the court to apportion any tax refund or reduction of tax between the estate of a partner and the estate of his partnership. The standard of apportionment entitles the partnership estate to receive that part of the tax refund or reduction that is attributable to losses sustained by the partnership that were deducted by the partner but for which the partner never reimbursed the partnership. The partner's estate receives any part not allocated to the partnership estate. The section applies notwithstanding section 541 of title 11, which includes the partner's' right to a tax refund or to reduction of tax as property of the partner's estate.

[*House Report No. 95–595, 95th Cong., 1st Sess. 385–386 (1977); Senate Report No. 95–989, 95th Cong., 2d Sess. 99–100 (1978).*]

Section 728 of the House amendment adopts a provision contained in the House bill that was deleted by the Senate amendment.

[*124 Cong. Rec. H 11,098 (Sept. 28, 1978); S 17,415 (Oct. 6, 1978).*]

Section 728. Special tax provisions: Liquidations: The House bill contained special tax provisions concerning the treatment of liquidations cases for State and local tax laws. These provisions deal with the taxable years of an individual debtor, return-filing requirements, and rules allocating State and local tax liabilities and refunds between a bankrupt partner and the partnership of which he is a member. The Senate amendment deleted these rules pending consideration of the Federal tax treatment of bankruptcy in the next Congress. The House amendment returns these provisions to the bill in order that they may be studied by the bankruptcy and tax bars who may wish to submit comments to Congress in connection with its consideration of these provisions in the next Congress.

[*124 Cong. Rec. H 11,114 (Sept. 28, 1978).*]

Comment

There are no provisions in the former Bankruptcy Act comparable to section 728 of the Code.

Section 728 contains tax provisions applicable only to a liquidation case under chapter 7. Subsection (a) provides that the taxable period of an individual debtor for the purpose of any state or local law terminates on the date of the order for relief under chapter 7. The subsection is inapplicable to a case originally filed under chapter 11 in which the estate would have been made a separate taxable entity on the date of the order for relief under that chapter.

Subsection (b) governs the return to be made by the trustee in a chapter 7 case in which the debtor is an individual or a corporation when the estate or the corporation has net taxable income for the entire case.

Subsection (c) states a marshalling rule relating to tax claims against a partner and partnership in a chapter 7 case. The taxing authority files a complete proof of claim and the court executes the marshalling.

Subsection (d) requires the court to apportion tax refunds or tax reduction between the estates of a partner and a partnership.

The Senate originally deleted the tax provisions of section 728 pending consideration of Federal Tax legislation in bankruptcy cases in the next Congress. The provisions were ultimately retained in order to be studied by all interested persons who wished to submit comments when these provisions were considered at the next Congress.

1984 Amendments: Minor technical changes were made in subsections (c) and (e)(2)(A) of section 728.

1986 Amendments: Section 728(a) was amended by including therein a reference to section 1208.

Case Annotations

Since the Code provides no guidance for tax consequences to a trustee who holds title to and invests assets in the debtor's estate, the trustee must file an income tax return and pay tax on the earned interest income. Bavely v. United States (*In re* NAB Food Services, Inc.), 7 C.B.C.2d 944 (B. Ct., S.D. Ohio 1982).

References

4 *Collier on Bankruptcy* ch. 728 (Matthew Bender 15th ed.).

2 *Collier Bankruptcy Manual* ch. 728 (Matthew Bender 3d ed.).

6 *Collier Bankruptcy Practice Guide* ch. 93 (Matthew Bender).

Ehrman, *Treatment of Tax Liabilities Under the Uniform Insurers Liquidation Act and the Bankruptcy Code,* 95 Com. L.J. 75 (1990).

Hippke, *Special Tax Provisions of the Bankruptcy Reform Act of 1978,* 1979 Ann. Surv. Bankr. L. 127 (1979).

Onsager, *Assigning Tax Liability Between the Bankruptcy Estate and the Individual Debtor,* 75 J. Tax'n 102 (1991).

Webster, *Tax Aspects of the Bankruptcy Reform Act of 1978,* 10 Tax Advisor 220 (1979).

SUBCHAPTER III

Stockbroker Liquidation

SECTION 741 (11 U.S.C. § 741)

§ 741.   Definitions for this subchapter. In this subchapter—

(1) "Commission" means Securities and Exchange Commission;

(2) "customer" includes—

(A) entity with whom a person deals as principal or agent and that has a claim against such person on account of a security received, acquired, or held by such person in the ordinary course of such person's business as a stockbroker, from or for the securities account or accounts of such entity—

(i) for safekeeping;

(ii) with a view to sale;

(iii) to cover a consummated sale;

(iv) pursuant to a purchase;

(v) as collateral under a security agreement; or

(vi) for the purpose of effecting registration of transfer; and

(B) entity that has a claim against a person arising out of—

(i) a sale or conversion of a security received, acquired, or held as specified in subparagraph (A) of this paragraph; or

(ii) a deposit of cash, a security, or other property with such person for the purpose of purchasing or selling a security;

(3) "customer name security" means security—

(A) held for the account of a customer on the date of the filing of the petition by or on behalf of the debtor;

(B) registered in such customer's name on such date or in the process of being so registered under instructions from the debtor; and

(C) not in a form transferable by delivery on such date;

(4) "customer property" means cash, security, or other property, and proceeds of such cash, security, or property, received, acquired, or held by or for the account of the debtor, from or for the securities account of a customer—

(A) including—

(i) property that was unlawfully converted from and that is the lawful property of the estate;

(ii) a security held as property of the debtor to the extent such security is necessary to meet a net equity claim of a customer based on a security of the same class and series of an issuer;

(iii) resources provided through the use or realization of a customer's debit cash balance or a debit item includible in the Formula for Determination of Reserve Requirement for Brokers and Dealers as promulgated by the Commission under the Securities Exchange Act of 1934 (15 U.S.C. 78a *et seq.*); and

(iv) other property of the debtor that any applicable law, rule, or regulation requires to be set aside or held for the benefit of a customer, unless including such property as customer property would not significantly increase customer property; but

(B) not including—

(i) a customer name security delivered to or reclaimed by a customer under section 751 of this title; or

(ii) property to the extent that a customer does not have a claim against the debtor based on such property;

(5) "margin payment" means payment or deposit of cash, a security, or other property, that is commonly known to the securities trade as original margin, initial margin, maintenance margin, or variation margin, or as a mark-to-market payment, or that secures an obligation of a participant in a securities clearing agency;

(6) "net equity" means, with respect to all accounts of a customer that such customer has in the same capacity—

(A)(i) aggregate dollar balance that would remain in such accounts after the liquidation, by sale or purchase, at the time of the filing of the petition, of all securities positions in all such accounts, except any customer name securities of such customer; minus

(ii) any claim of the debtor against such customer in such capacity that would have been owing immediately after such liquidation; plus

(B) any payment by such customer to the trustee, within 60 days after notice under section 342 of this title, of any business related claim of the debtor against such customer in such capacity;

(7) "securities contract" means contract for the purchase, sale, or loan of a security, including an option for the purchase or sale of a security, certificate of deposit, or group or index of securities (including any interest therein or based on the value thereof), or any option entered into on a national securities exchange relating to foreign currencies, or the guarantee of any settlement of cash or securities by or to a securities clearing agency;

(8) "settlement payment" means a preliminary settlement payment, a partial settlement payment, an interim settlement payment, a settlement payment on account, a final settlement payment, or any other similar payment commonly used in the securities trade; and

(9) "SIPC" means Securities Investor Protection Corporation.

Legislative History

Section 741 sets forth definitions for subchapter III of chapter 7.

Paragraph (1) defines "Commission" to mean the Securities and Exchange Commission.

Paragraph (2) defines "customer" to include anybody that interacts with the debtor in a capacity that concerns securities transactions. The term embraces cash or margin customers of a broker or dealer in the broadest sense.

Paragraph (3) defines "customer name security" in a restrictive fashion to include only non-transferrable [sic] securities that are registered, or in the process of being registered in a customer's own name. The securities must not be endorsed by the customer and the stockbroker must not be able to legally transfer the securities by delivery, by a power of attorney, or otherwise.

Paragraph (4) defines "customer property" to include all property of the debtor that has been segregated for customers or property that should have been segregated but was unlawfully converted. Clause (i) refers to customer property not properly segregated by the debtor or customer property converted and then recovered so as to become property of the estate. Unlawfully converted property that has been transferred to a third party is excluded until it is recovered as property of the estate by virtue of the avoiding powers. The concept excludes customer name securities that have been delivered to or reclaimed by a customer and any property properly belonging to the stockbroker, such as money deposited by a customer to pay for securities that the stockholder has distributed to such customer.

[*House Report No. 95–595, 95th Cong., 1st Sess. 386–387 (1977); Senate Report No. 95–989, 95th Cong., 2d Sess. 100–101 (1978).*]

Section 8(2) [of Public Law 97–222] redesignates section 741(5) and 741(6) as sections 741(6) and 741(9), respectively.

Section 8(3) provides a definition of the term "margin payment".

[*House Report No. 97–420, 97th Cong., 2d Sess. 4 (1982).*]

Paragraph (5) [*Ed. Note:* Public Law 97–222 redesignates section 741(5) as section 741(6).] defines "net equity" to establish the extent to which a customer will be entitled to share in the single and separate fund. Accounts of a customer are aggregated and offset only to the extent the accounts are held by the customer in the same capacity. Thus, a personal account is separate from an account held as trustee. In a community property state an account held for the community is distinct from an account held as separate property.

The net equity is computed by liquidating all securities positions in the accounts and crediting the account with any amount due to the customer. Regardless of the actual dates, if any, of liquidation, the customer is only entitled to the liquidation value at the time of the filing of the petition. To avoid double counting, the liquidation value of customer name securities belonging to a customer is excluded from net equity. Thus, clause (ii) includes claims against a customer resulting from the liquidation of a security under clause (i). The value of a security on which trading has been suspended at the time of the filing of the petition will be estimated. Once the net liquidation value is computed, any amount that the customer owes to the stockbroker is subtracted including any amount that would be owing after the hypothetical liquidation, such as brokerage fees. Debts owed by the customer to the debtor, other than in a securities related transaction, will not reduce the net equity of the customer. Finally, net equity is increased by any payment by the customer to the debtor actually paid within 60 days after notice. The principal reason a customer would make such a payment is to reclaim customer name securities under section 751.

[House Report No. 95–595, 95th Cong., 1st Sess. 386–387 (1977); Senate Report No. 95–989, 95th Cong., 2d Sess. 100–101 (1978).]

Section 8(5) [of Public Law 97–222] provides definitions of the terms "securities contract" and "settlement payment".

[House Report No. 97–420, 97th Cong., 2d Sess. 4 (1982).]

Paragraph (6) [*Ed. Note:* See legislative history below concerning deletion of this section.] defines "1934 Act" to mean the Securities Exchange Act of 1934.

Paragraph (7) [*Ed. Note:* Pursuant to Public Law 97–222, this definition now appears in section 741(9).] defines "SIPC" to mean the Securities Investor Protection Corporation.

[House Report No. 95–595, 95th Cong., 1st Sess. 386–387 (1977); Senate Report No. 95–989, 95th Cong., 2d Sess. 100–101 (1978).]

Section 741(6) of the House bill and Senate amendment is deleted by the House amendment since the defined term is used only in section 741(4)(A)(iii). A corresponding change is made in that section.

[124 Cong. Rec. H 11,098 (Sept. 28, 1978); S 17,415 (Oct. 6, 1978).]

Comment

Subchapter III of chapter 7 deals with stockbroker liquidations. The subchapter is derived from Section 60e of the former Bankruptcy Act and the Securities Investor Protection Act [SIPA].

The 1982 amendments (Public Law 97–222) renumbered paragraph 5 to read "7" and added paragraph 5 defining "margin payment." Paragraph 6 was renumbered "9," and two definitions were added: paragraph 7, "securities contract" and paragraph 8, "settlement payment."

1984 Amendments: Paragraph (2) of section 741 was amended by changing the word "debtor" to "person" every place the former appeared. Paragraph (7) was amended to expand the definition of "securities contract." Minor technical changes were made to paragraphs (4)(A)(i), (6)(A)(i) and (8).

Case Annotations

Section 741(2)(B)(ii) provides customer status when the purchaser of securities deposits cash with a debtor stockholder so that the debtor may make the purchases, but when the debtor is not provided with a reservoir of cash from which to purchase securities, a claimant is not entitled to customer status under the section. In the Matter of Wider, 907 F.2d 570, 24 C.B.C.2d 104 (5th Cir. 1990).

Transfers of consideration to a securities broker in exchange for the common stock of the broker's customers pursuant to a leveraged buyout transaction are settlement payments which may not be avoided by the debtor or by a trustee. Kaiser Steel Corp. v. Charles Schwab & Co., Inc., 913 F.2d 846, 23 C.B.C.2d 1403 (10th Cir. 1990).

For purposes of the interpretation of 11 U.S.C. § 546(f), "settlement payment" includes the deposit of cash by the purchaser or the deposit or transfer of securities by the dealer as well as transfers which are normally regarded as part of the settlement process, regardless of the date on which the transactions occur in the settlement process. In the Matter of Bevill, Bresler & Schulman Asset Management Corp., 878 F.2d 742, 21 C.B.C.2d 298 (3d Cir. 1989).

A claimant must entrust either cash or securities with the debtor in connection with a securities transaction to be the debtor's "customer" within the meaning of section 741(2) of the Code. In the Matter of SSIW Corp., 3 C.B.C.2d 502 (B. Ct., S.D.N.Y. 1980).

References

4 *Collier on Bankruptcy* ch. 741 (Matthew Bender 15th ed.).

2 *Collier Bankruptcy Manual* ch. 741 (Matthew Bender 3d ed.).

SECTION 742 (11 U.S.C. § 742)

§ 742. Effect of section 362 of this title in this subchapter. Notwithstanding section 362 of this title, SIPC may file an application for a protective decree under the Securities Investor Protection Act of 1970 (15 U.S.C. 78aaa *et seq.*) The filing of such application stays all proceedings in the case under this title unless and until such application is dismissed. If SIPC completes the liquidation of the debtor, then the court shall dismiss the case.

Legislative History

Section 742 indicates that the automatic stay does not prevent SIPC from filing an application for a protective decree under SIPA. If SIPA does file such an application, then all bankruptcy proceedings are suspended until the SIPC action is completed. If SIPC completes liquidation of the stockbroker then the bankruptcy case is dismissed.

[*House Report No. 95–595, 95th Cong., 1st Sess. 387 (1977); Senate Report No. 95–989, 95th Cong., 2d Sess. 101 (1978).*]

Section 742 of the House amendment deletes a sentence contained in the Senate amendment requiring the trustee in an interstate stockbrokerage liquidation to comply with the provisions of subchapter IV of chapter 7 if the debtor is also a commodity broker. The House amendment expands the requirement to require the SIPC trustee to perform such duties, if the debtor is a commodity broker, under section 7(b) of the Securities Investor Protection Act. The requirement is deleted from section 742 since the trustee of an intrastate stockbroker will be bound by the provisions of subchapter IV of chapter 7 if the debtor is also a commodity broker by reason of section 103 of title 11.

[*124 Cong. Rec. H 11,098–11,099 (Sept. 28, 1978); S 17,415 (Oct. 6, 1978).*]

Section 9 [of Public Law 97–222] clarifies that the filing of an application by the Securities Investor Protection Corporation for a protective decree with respect to the debtor stays all Title 11 proceedings involving the debtor, even if commenced under Chapter 11.

[*House Report No. 97–420, 97th Cong., 2d Sess. 4 (1982).*]

Comment

SIPA at 15 U.S.C. § 78eee(b)(2)(B)(i) provides that upon the filing of an application for relief, the court shall stay any pending bankruptcy, and upon appointment of a trustee, shall continue to stay such bankruptcy or any proceeding to recognize, conserve or liquidate the debtor or its property. The purpose of section 742 of the Code is to make the automatic stay in the bankruptcy case ineffective to bar SIPC from filing an application for a protective decree under SIPA.

The 1982 amendments (Public Law 97–222) make clear that an application for protective relief by the SIPC stays all proceedings whether filed under chapter 7 or under chapter 11 of the Code.

References

4 *Collier on Bankruptcy* ch. 742 (Matthew Bender 15th ed.).

2 *Collier Bankruptcy Manual* ch. 742 (Matthew Bender 3d ed.).

SECTION 743 (11 U.S.C. § 743)

§ 743.* *Notice.* The clerk shall give the notice required by section 342 of this title to SIPC and to the Commission.

Legislative History

Section 743 requires that notice of the order for relief be given to SIPC and to the SEC in every stockbroker case.

[*House Report No. 95–595, 95th Cong., 1st Sess. 387 (1977); Senate Report No. 95–989, 95th Cong., 2d Sess. 102 (1978).*]

---

* [*Ed. Note:* Section 743 originally made reference to § 342(a). Although § 283(t) of the 1986 Act purports to strike a reference to subsection (d) of § 342, the intent appears to strike the reference to subsection (a).]

Comment

Section 743 is intended to give prompt notice to SIPC and the SEC of the entry of an order for relief in every stockbroker case so that a SIPA case may be instituted when appropriate before administration proceeds too far in the bankruptcy case.

References

4 *Collier on Bankruptcy* ch. 743 (Matthew Bender 15th ed.).

2 *Collier Bankruptcy Manual* ch. 743 (Matthew Bender 3d ed.).

SECTION 744 (11 U.S.C. § 744)

§ 744. **Executory contracts.** Notwithstanding section 365(d)(1) of this title, the trustee shall assume or reject, under section 365 of this title, any executory contract of the debtor for the purchase or sale of a security in the ordinary course of the debtor's business, within a reasonable time after the date of the order for relief, but not to exceed 30 days. If the trustee does not assume such a contract within such time, such contract is rejected.

Legislative History

Section 744 instructs the court to give the trustee a reasonable time, not to exceed 30 days, to assume or reject any executory contract of the stockbroker to buy or sell securities. Any contract not assumed within the time fixed by the court is considered to be rejected.

[*House Report No. 95–595, 95th Cong., 1st Sess. 387 (1977); Senate Report No. 95–989, 95th Cong., 2d Sess. 102 (1978).*]

Comment

Under section 365(d)(1) of the Code, failure by a trustee in a liquidation case under chapter 7 to assume or reject an executory contract within 60 days after the order for relief (or within such additional time as the court may fix), results in the contract being deemed rejected. Section 744 makes special provision in a stockbroker case regarding an executory contract of the debtor to purchase or sell a security by requiring the trustee to assume or reject within a "reasonable time" after the order for relief "not to exceed 30 days." Failure to assume within such period results in rejection.

See **Comment** to section 365.

References

4 *Collier on Bankruptcy* ch. 744 (Matthew Bender 15th ed.).

2 *Collier Bankruptcy Manual* ch. 744 (Matthew Bender 3d ed.).

SECTION 745 (11 U.S.C. § 745)

§ 745. Treatment of accounts.

(a) Accounts held by the debtor for a particular customer in separate capacities shall be treated as accounts of separate customers.

(b) If a stockbroker or a bank holds a customer net equity claim against the debtor that arose out of a transaction for a customer of such stockbroker or bank, each such customer of such stockbroker or bank shall be treated as a separate customer of the debtor.

(c) Each trustee's account specified as such on the debtor's books, and supported by a trust deed filed with, and qualified as such by, the Internal Revenue Service, and under the Internal Revenue Code of 1954 (26 U.S.C. 1 *et seq.*), shall be treated as a separate customer account for each beneficiary under such trustee account.

Legislative History

Section 745(a) indicates that each account held by a customer in a separate capacity is to be considered a separate account. This prevents the offset of accounts held in different capacities.

Subsection (b) indicates that a bank or another stockbroker that is a customer of a debtor is considered to hold its customers accounts in separate capacities. Thus a bank or other stockbroker is not treated as a mutual fund for purposes of bulk investment. This protects unrelated customers of a bank or other stockholder from having their accounts offset.

Subsection (c) effects the same result with respect to a trust so that each beneficiary is treated as the customer of the debtor rather than the trust itself. This eliminates any doubt whether a trustee holds a personal account in a separate capacity from his trustee's account.

[*House Report No. 95–595, 95th Cong., 1st Sess. 388 (1977); Senate Report No. 95–989, 95th Cong., 2d Sess. 102 (1978).*]

Comment

Subsection (a) is derived from SIPA, 15 U.S.C. § 78fff–3(a)(2):

 a customer who holds accounts with the debtor in separate capacities shall be deemed to be a different customer in each capacity. . . .

Subsection (b) is derived from SIPA, 15 U.S.C. § 78fff-3(a)(5):

 (D) no such advance shall be made by SIPC to the trustee to pay or otherwise satisfy any net equity claim of any customer who is a broker or dealer or bank, other than to the extent that it shall be established to the satisfaction of the trustee, from the books and records of the debtor or from the books and records of a broker or dealer or bank, or otherwise, that the net equity claim of such broker or dealer or bank against the debtor arose out of transactions for customers of such broker or dealer (which customers are not themselves a broker or dealer or bank or a person described in paragraph (4)), in which event, each such customer of such broker or dealer or bank shall be deemed a separate customer of the debtor.

Subsection (c) effects the same result as subsection (b) within respect to a trust, eliminating any doubt whether a trustee holds a personal account in a separate capacity from his account as trustee.

1984 Amendments: Subsection (a) of section 745 was clarified by insertion of the words "the debtor for."

References

4 *Collier on Bankruptcy* ch. 745 (Matthew Bender 15th ed.).

2 *Collier Bankruptcy Manual* ch. 745 (Matthew Bender 3d ed.).

SECTION 746 (11 U.S.C. § 746)

§ 746.   Extent of customer claims.

 (a) If, after the date of the filing of the petition, an entity enters into a transaction with the debtor, in a manner that would have made such entity a customer had such transaction occurred before the date of the filing of the petition, and such transaction was entered into by such entity in good faith and before the qualification under section 322 of this title of a trustee, such entity shall be deemed a customer, and the date of such transaction shall be deemed to be the date of the filing of the petition for the purpose of determining such entity's net equity.

 (b) An entity does not have a claim as a customer to the extent that such entity transferred to the debtor cash or a security that, by contract, agreement, understanding, or operation of law, is—

(1) part of the capital of the debtor; or

(2) subordinated to the claims of any or all creditors.

Legislative History

Section 746(a) protects entities who deal in good faith with the debtor after the filing of the petition and before a trustee is appointed by deeming such entities to be customers. The principal application of this section will be in an involuntary case before the order for relief, because section 701(b) requires prompt appointment of an interim trustee after the order for relief.

Subsection (b) indicates that an entity who holds securities that are either part of the capital of the debtor or that are subordinated to the claims of any creditor of the debtor is not a customer with respect to those securities. This subsection will apply when the stockbroker has sold securities in itself to the customer or when the customer has otherwise placed such securities in an account with the stockbroker.

[*House Report No. 95–595, 95th Cong., 1st Sess. 388 (1977); Senate Report No. 95–989, 95th Cong., 2d Sess. 102 (1978).*]

Comment

Section 746(a) relates to postpetition transactions. Section 746(b) is derived from SIPA, 15 U.S.C. § 78lll(2), which defines "customers" and provides that a "customer" shall not include any person to: "the extent that such person has a claim for cash or securities which by contract, agreement, or understanding, or by operation of law, is part of the capital of the debtor or is subordinated to the claims of any or all creditors of the debtor."

The 1982 amendments (P.L. 97–222) deleted from section 746 reference to transactions "with respect to cash or security," so that the section now applies to customer claims with respect to "a transaction" that would have made an entity a customer had such transaction occurred before the petition was filed.

References

4 *Collier on Bankruptcy* ch. 746 (Matthew Bender 15th ed.).

2 *Collier Bankruptcy Manual* ch. 746 (Matthew Bender 3d ed.).

SECTION 747 (11 U.S.C. § 747)

§ 747. **Subordination of certain customer claims.** Except as provided in section 510 of this title, unless all other customer net equity claims have been paid in full, the trustee may not pay in full or pay in part, directly or indirectly, any net equity claim of a customer that was, on the date the transaction giving rise to such claim occurred—

(1) an insider;

(2) a beneficial owner of at least five percent of any class of equity securities of the debtor, other than—

(A) nonconvertible stock having fixed preferential dividend and liquidation rights; or

(B) interests of limited partners in a limited partnership;

(3) a limited partner with a participation of at least five percent in the net assets or net profits of the debtor; or

(4) an entity that, directly or indirectly, through agreement or otherwise, exercised or had the power to exercise control over the management or policies of the debtor.

Legislative History

Section 747 subordinates to other customer claims all claims of a customer who is an insider, a five percent owner of the debtor, or otherwise in control of the debtor.

[*House Report No. 95–595, 95th Cong., 1st Sess. 388 (1977); Senate Report No. 95–989, 95th Cong., 2d Sess. 102 (1978).*]

Comment

Section 747 is derived from SIPA, 15 U.S.C. § 78fff–3(a)(4), which provides:

(C) No advance shall be made by SIPC to the trustee to pay or otherwise satisfy, directly or indirectly any net equity claim of a customer who is a general partner, officer, or director of the debtor, a beneficial holder of 5 per centum or more of any class of equity security of the debtor (other than a nonconvertible stock having fixed preferential dividend and liquidation rights) a limited partner with a participation of 5 per centum or more in the net assets or net profits of the debtor, or a person who directly or indirectly and through agreement or otherwise had the power to exercise a controlling influence over the management or policies of the debtor; . . .

Section 747 equitably subordinates claims of an "insider" (see definition, section 101), a five percent owner, or one in control, of the debtor, to other customer claims.

References

4 *Collier on Bankruptcy* ch. 747 (Matthew Bender 15th ed.).

2 *Collier Bankruptcy Manual* ch. 747 (Matthew Bender 3d ed.).

SECTION 748 (11 U.S.C. § 748)

§ 748. Reduction of securities to money. As soon as practicable after the date of the order for relief, the trustee shall reduce to money, consistent with good market practice, all securities held as property of the estate, except for customer name securities delivered or reclaimed under section 751 of this title.

Legislative History

Section 748 requires the trustee to liquidate all securities, except for customer name securities, of the estate in a manner consistent with good market practice. The trustee should refrain from flooding a thin market with a large percentage of shares in any one issue. If the trustee holds restricted securities or securities in which trading has been suspended, then the trustee must arrange to liquidate such securities in accordance with the securities laws. A private placement may be the only exemption available with the customer of the debtor the best prospect for such a placement. The subsection does not permit such a customer to bid in his net equity as part of the purchase price; a contrary result would permit a customer to receive a greater percentage on his net equity claim than other customers.

[*House Report No. 95–595, 95th Cong., 1st Sess. 388 (1977); Senate Report No. 95–989, 95th Cong., 2d Sess. 102–103 (1978).*]

Comment

SIPA, 15 U.S.C. § 78fff–1(b), provides that the trustee has no duty to reduce to money any securities in the single and separate fund or in the general estate of the debtor. Section 748 of the Code, however, mandates the trustee to reduce to money "consistent with good market practice" all security held as property of the estate except customer name securities or securities reclaimed under section 751. The Congressional Reports suggest that "good market practice" would cause the trustee to refrain from "flooding a thin market" with a large percentage of shares in any one issue.

References

4 *Collier on Bankruptcy* ch. 748 (Matthew Bender 15th ed.).

2 *Collier Bankruptcy Manual* ch. 748 (Matthew Bender 3d ed.).

SECTION 749 (11 U.S.C. § 749)

§ 749. Voidable transfers. (a) Except as otherwise provided in this section, any transfer of property that, but for such transfer, would have been customer property, may be avoided by the trustee, and such property shall be treated as customer property, if and to the extent that the trustee avoids such transfer under sections 544, 545, 547, 548, or 549 of this title. For the purpose of such sections, the property so transferred shall be deemed to have been property of the debtor and, if such transfer was made to a customer or for a customer's benefit such customer shall be deemed, for the purposes of this section, to have been a creditor.

(b) Notwithstanding sections 544, 545, 547, 548, and 549 of this title, the trustee may not avoid a transfer made before five days after the order for relief if such transfer is approved by the Commission by rule or order, either before or after such transfer, and if such transfer is—

 (1) a transfer of a securities contract entered into or carried by or through the debtor on behalf of a customer, and of any cash, security, or other property margining or securing such securities contract; or

 (2) the liquidation of a securities contract entered into or carried by or through the debtor on behalf of a customer.

Legislative History

Section 749 indicates that if the trustee avoids a transfer, property recovered is customer property to any extent it would have been customer property but for the transfer. The section clarifies that a customer who receives a transfer of property of the debtor is a creditor and that property in a customer's account is property of a creditor for purposes of the avoiding powers.

[*House Report No. 95–595, 95th Cong., 1st Sess. 388 (1977); Senate Report No. 95–989, 95th Cong., 2d Sess. 103 (1978).*]

Section 14 [of Public Law 97–222] makes stylistic changes, deletes an erroneous cross reference, and adds a provision dealing with a limitation on the trustee's avoiding powers consistent with parallel provisions in section 764 applicable to commodity broker liquidations.

[*House Report No. 97–420, 97th Cong., 2d Sess. 4 (1982).*]

Comment

There is no provision in the former Bankruptcy Act or SIPA, 15 U.S.C. § 78fff–1(a), comparable to section 749 of the Code. Under SIPA, a trustee appointed under SIPA has the same powers and title respecting debtor and his property, and the right to avoid preferences, as a bankrupt trustee and a trustee under former Chapter X.

SIPA, 15 U.S.C. § 78fff–1(a), provides in part:

(a) Trustee Powers. A trustee shall be vested with the same powers and title with respect to the debtor and the property of the debtor, including the right to avoid preferences, as a trustee in a case under title 11 of the United States Code. . . .

The 1982 amendments (P.L. 97–222) added subsection (b) to section 744. Subsection (b) is similar to section 764(b) relating to commodity brokers. It prohibits avoidance of any transaction that occurs within 5 days after the petition if approved by the Commission and concerns an open contractual commitment. This allows the Commission to exercise its discretion to protect the integrity of the market by insuring that a transaction cleared with other brokers will not be undone on a preferential or fraudulent transfer theory.

References

4 *Collier on Bankruptcy* ch. 749 (Matthew Bender 15th ed.).

2 *Collier Bankruptcy Manual* ch. 749 (Matthew Bender 3d ed.).

SECTION 750 (11 U.S.C. § 750)

§ 750. **Distribution of securities.** The trustee may not distribute a security except under section 751 of this title.

Legislative History

Section 750 forbids the trustee from distributing a security other than a customer name security. The term "distribution" refers to a distribution to customers in satisfaction of net equity claims and is not intended to preclude the trustee from liquidating securities under proposed 11 U.S.C. § 748.

[*House Report No. 95–595, 95th Cong., 1st Sess. 389 (1977); Senate Report No. 95–989, 95th Cong., 2d Sess. 103 (1978).*]

Comment

There was no provision in the former Bankruptcy Act and there is none in SIPA comparable to section 750.

References

4 *Collier on Bankruptcy* ch. 750 (Matthew Bender 15th ed.).

2 *Collier Bankruptcy Manual* ch. 750 (Matthew Bender 3d ed.).

SECTION 751 (11 U.S.C. § 751)

§ 751. Customer name securities. The trustee shall deliver any customer name security to or on behalf of the customer entitled to such security, unless such customer has a negative net equity. With the approval of the trustee, a customer may reclaim a customer name security after payment to the trustee, within such period as the trustee allows, of any claim of the debtor against such customer to the extent that such customer will not have a negative net equity after such payment.

Legislative History

Section 751 requires the trustee to deliver a customer name security to the customer entitled to such security unless the customer has a negative net equity. The customer's net equity will be negative when the amount owed by the customer to the stockbroker exceeds the liquidation value of the non-customer name securities in the customer's account. If the customer is a net debtor of the stockbroker, then the trustee may permit the customer to repay debts to the stockbroker so that the customer will no longer be in debt to the stockbroker. If the customer refuses to pay such amount, then the court may order the customer to endorse the security in order that the trustee may liquidate such property.

[*House Report No. 95–595, 95th Cong., 1st Sess. 389 (1977); Senate Report No. 95–989, 95th Cong., 2d Sess. 103 (1978).*]

Comment

Section 751 is not unlike SIPA, 15 U.S.C. § 78fff–2(c)(2), which requires the trustee to deliver customer name securities if the customer is not indebted to the debtor; if he is so indebted, he may reclaim customer name securities on payment of the indebtedness.

SIPA, 15 U.S.C. § 78lll(3), defines customer name securities.

References

4 *Collier on Bankruptcy* ch. 751 (Matthew Bender 15th ed.).

2 *Collier Bankruptcy Manual* ch. 751 (Matthew Bender 3d ed.).

SECTION 752 (11 U.S.C. § 752)

§ 752. Customer property.

(a) The trustee shall distribute customer property ratably to customers on the basis and to the extent of such customers' allowed net equity claims and in priority to all other claims, except claims of the kind specified in section 507(a)(1) of this title that are attributable to the administration of such customer property.

(b)(1) The trustee shall distribute customer property in excess of that distributed under subsection (a) of this section in accordance with section 726 of this title.

    (2) Except as provided in section 510 of this title, if a customer is not paid the full amount of such customer's allowed net equity claim from customer property, the unpaid portion of such claim is a claim entitled to distribution under section 726 of this title.

(c) Any cash or security remaining after the liquidation of a security interest created under a security agreement made by the debtor, excluding property excluded under section 741(4)(B) of this title, shall be apportioned between the general estate and customer property in the same proportion as the general estate of the debtor and customer property were subject to such security interest.

Legislative History

Section 752(a) requires the trustee to distribute customer property to customers based on the amount of their net equity claims. Customer property is to be distributed in priority to all claims except expenses of administration entitled to priority under section 507[a](1). It is anticipated that the court will apportion such administrative claims on an equitable basis between the general estate and the customer property of the debtor.

Subsection (b)(1) indicates that in the event customer property exceeds customer net equity claims and administrative expenses, the excess pours over into the general estate. This event would occur if the value of securities increased dramatically after the order for relief but before liquidation by the trustee. Subsection (b)(2) indicates that the unpaid portion of a customer's net equity claim is entitled to share in the general estate as an unsecured claim unless subordinated by the court under proposed 11 U.S.C. § 501. A net equity claim of a customer that is subordinated under section 747 is entitled to share in distribution under section 726(a)(2) unless subordinated under section 510 independently of the subordination under section 747.

Subsection (c) provides for apportionment between customer property and the general estate of any equity of the debtor in property remaining after a secured creditor liquidates a security interest. This might occur if a stockholder hypothecates securities of his own and of his customers if the value of the hypothecated securities exceeds the debt owed to the secured party. The apportionment is to be made according to the ratio of customer property and general property of the debtor that comprised the collateral. The subsection refers to cash and securities of customers to include any customer property unlawfully converted by the stockbroker in the course of such a transaction. The apportionment is made subject to section 741(4)(B) to insure that property in a customer's account that is owed to the stockbroker will not be considered customer property. This recognizes the right of the stockbroker to withdraw money that has been erroneously placed in a customer's account or that is otherwise owing to the stockbroker.

[*House Report No. 95–595, 95th Cong., 1st Sess. 389 (1977); Senate Report No. 95–989, 95th Cong., 2d Sess. 103 (1978).*]

Comment

SIPA, 15 U.S.C. § 78fff–2(b), governs distribution of property of the estate to creditors in a SIPA proceeding. SIPA, 15 U.S.C. § 78fff–2(c), prescribes the priority of payments.

The 1982 amendments (P.L. 97–222) made stylistic changes in subsection (c) regarding the manner of apportionment.

1984 Amendments: Minor technical changes were made in subsections (a) and (b)(2) of section 752.

References

4 *Collier on Bankruptcy* ch. 752 (Matthew Bender 15th ed.).

2 *Collier Bankruptcy Manual* ch. 752 (Matthew Bender 3d ed.).

SUBCHAPTER IV

Commodity Broker Liquidation

SECTION 761 (11 U.S.C. § 761)

§ 761. Definitions for this subchapter. In this subchapter—

(1) "Act" means Commodity Exchange Act (7 U.S.C. 1 *et seq.*);

(2) "clearing organization" means organization that clears commodity contracts made on, or subject to the rules of, a contract market or board of trade;

(3) "Commission" means Commodity Futures Trading Commission;

(4) "commodity contract" means—

(A) with respect to a futures commission merchant, contract for the purchase or sale of a commodity for future delivery on, or subject to the rules of, a contract market or board of trade;

(B) with respect to a foreign futures commission merchant, foreign future;

(C) with respect to a leverage transaction merchant, leverage transaction;

(D) with respect to a clearing organization, contract for the purchase or sale of a commodity for future delivery on, or subject to the rules of, a contract market or board of trade that is cleared by such clearing organization, or commodity option traded on, or subject to the rules of, a contract market or board of trade that is cleared by such clearing organization; or

(E) with respect to a commodity options dealer, commodity option;

(5) "commodity option" means agreement or transaction subject to regulation under section 4c(b) of the Act (7 U.S.C. 6c(b));

(6) "commodity options dealer" means person that extends credit to, or that accepts cash, a security, or other property from, a customer of such person for the purchase or sale of an interest in a commodity option;

(7) "contract market" means board of trade designated as a contract market by the Commission under the Act;

(8) "contract of sale", "commodity", "future delivery", "board of trade", and "futures commission merchant" have the meanings assigned to those terms in the Act;

(9) "customer" means—

(A) with respect to a futures commission merchant—

(i) entity for or with whom such futures commission merchant deals and that holds a claim against such futures commission merchant on account of a commodity contract made, received, acquired, or held by or through such futures commission merchant in the ordinary course of such futures commission merchant's business as a futures commission merchant from or for the commodity futures account of such entity; or

(ii) entity that holds a claim against such futures commission merchant's arising out of—

(I) the making, liquidation, or change in the value of a commodity contract of a kind specified in clause (i) of this subparagraph;

(II) a deposit or payment of cash, a security, or other property with such futures commission merchant for the purpose of making or margining such a commodity contract; or

(III) the making or taking of delivery on such a commodity contract;

(B) with respect to foreign futures commission merchant—

(i) entity for or with whom such foreign futures commission merchant deals and that holds a claim against such foreign futures commission merchant on account of a commodity contract made, received, acquired, or held by or through such foreign futures commission merchant in the ordinary course of such foreign futures commission merchant's business as a foreign futures commission merchant from or for the foreign futures account of such entity; or

(ii) entity that holds a claim against such foreign futures commission merchant arising out of—

(I) the making, liquidation, or change in value of a commodity contract of a kind specified in clause (i) of this subparagraph;

(II) a deposit or payment of cash, a security, or other property with the debtor for the purpose of making or margining such a commodity contract; or

(III) the making or taking of delivery on such a commodity contract;

(C) with respect to a leverage transaction merchant—

(i) entity for or with whom such leverage transaction merchant deals and that holds a claim against such leverage transaction merchant on account of a commodity contract engaged in by or with such leverage transaction merchant in the ordinary course of such leverage transaction merchant's business as a leverage transaction merchant from or for the leverage account of such entity; or

(ii) entity that holds a claim against such leverage transaction merchant arising out of—

(I) the making, liquidation, or change in value of a commodity contract of a kind specified in clause (i) of this subparagraph;

(II) a deposit or payment of cash, a security, or other property with such foreign futures commission merchant for the purpose of entering into or margining such a commodity contract; or

(III) the making or taking of delivery on such a commodity contract;

(D) with respect to a clearing organization, clearing member of such clearing organization with whom such clearing organization deals and that holds a claim against such clearing organization on account of cash, a security, or other property received by such clearing organization to margin, guarantee, or secure a commodity contract in such clearing member's proprietary account or customers' account; or

(E) with respect to a commodity options dealer—

(i) entity for or with whom such commodity options dealer deals and that holds a claim on account of a commodity contract made, received, acquired, or held by or through such commodity options dealer in the ordinary course of such commodity options dealer's business as a commodity options dealer from or for the commodity options account of such entity; or

(ii) entity that holds a claim against such commodity options dealer arising out of—

(I) the making of, liquidation of, exercise of, or a change in value of, a commodity contract of a kind specified in clause (i) of this subparagraph; or

(II) a deposit or payment of cash, a security, or other property with such commodity options dealer for the purpose of making, exercising, or margining such a commodity contract;

(10) "customer property" means cash, a security, or other property, or proceeds of such cash, security, or property, received, acquired, or held by or for the account of the debtor, from or for the account of a customer—

(A) including—

(i) property received, acquired, or held to margin, guarantee, secure, purchase, or sell a commodity contract;

(ii) profits or contractual or other rights accruing to a customer as a result of a commodity contract;

(iii) an open commodity contract;

(iv) specifically identifiable customer property;

(v) warehouse receipt or other document held by the debtor evidencing ownership of or title to property to be delivered to fulfill a commodity contract from or for the account of a customer;

(vi) cash, a security, or other property received by the debtor as payment for a commodity to be delivered to fulfill a commodity contract from or for the account of a customer;

(vii) a security held as property of the debtor to the extent such security is necessary to meet a net equity claim based on a security of the same class and series of an issuer;

(viii) property that was unlawfully converted from and that is the lawful property of the estate; and

(ix) other property of the debtor that any applicable law, rule, or regulation requires to be set aside or held for the benefit of a customer, unless including such property as customer property would not significantly increase customer property; but

(B) not including property to the extent that a customer does not have a claim against the debtor based on such property;

(11) "foreign future" means contract for the purchase or sale of a commodity for future delivery on, or subject to the rules of, a board of trade outside the United States;

(12) "foreign futures commission merchant" means entity engaged in soliciting or accepting orders for the purchase or sale of a foreign future or that, in connection with such a solicitation or acceptance, accepts cash, a security, or other property, or extends credit to margin, guarantee, or secure any trade or contract that results from such a solicitation or acceptance;

(13) "leverage transaction" means agreement that is subject to regulation under section 19 of the Commodity Exchange Act (7 U.S.C. 23), and that is commonly known to the commodities trade as a margin account, margin contract, leverage account, or leverage contract;

(14) "leverage transaction merchant" means person in the business of engaging in leverage transactions;

(15) "margin payment" means payment or deposit of cash, a security, or other property, that is commonly known to the commodities trade as original margin, initial margin, maintenance margin, or variation margin, including mark-to-market payments, settlement payments, variation payments, daily settlement

payments, and final settlement payments made as adjustments to settlement prices;

(16) "member property" means customer property received, acquired, or held by or for the account of a debtor that is a clearing organization, from or for the proprietary account of a customer that is a clearing member of the debtor; and

(17) "net equity" means, subject to such rules and regulations as the Commission promulgates under the Act, with respect to the aggregate of all of a customer's accounts that such customer has in the same capacity—

 (A) the balance remaining in such customer's accounts immediately after—

  (i) all commodity contracts of such customer have been transferred, liquidated, or become identified for delivery; and

  (ii) all obligations of such customer in such capacity to the debtor have been offset; plus

 (B) the value, as of the date of return under section 766 of this title, of any specifically identifiable customer property actually returned to such customer before the date specified in subparagraph (A) of this paragraph; plus

 (C) the value, as of the date of transfer, of—

  (i) any commodity contract to which such customer is entitled that is transferred to another person under section 766 of this title; and

  (ii) any cash, security, or other property of such customer transferred to such other person under section 766 of this title to margin or secure such transferred commodity contract.

Legislative History

This section contains 15 definitions that apply in commodity broker liquidations.

[*House Report No. 95–595, 95th Cong., 1st Sess. 390 (1977); Senate Report No. 95–989, 95th Cong., 2d Sess. 104 (1978).*]

Section 16 [of Public Law 97–222] makes certain clarifying changes and corrects an erroneous cross reference.

[House Report No. 97–420, 97th Cong., 2d Sess. 5 (1982).]

Paragraph (1) defines "Act" to mean the Commodity Exchange Act.

[House Report No. 95–595, 95th Cong., 1st Sess. 390 (1977); Senate Report No. 95–989, 95th Cong., 2d Sess. 104 (1978).]

Paragraph (2) defines "clearing organization" to mean an organization that clears commodity futures contracts for a contract market.

[House Report No. 95–595, 95th Cong., 1st Sess. 390 (1977).]

Paragraph (2) defines "clearing organization" to mean an organization that clear[s] (*i.e.*, matches purchases and sales) commodity futures contracts made on or subject to the rules of a contract market or commodity options transactions made on or subject to the rules of a commodity option exchange. Although commodity option trading on exchanges is currently prohibited, it is anticipated that CFTC may permit such trading in the future.

[Senate Report No. 95–989, 95th Cong., 2d Sess. 104 (1978).]

Paragraph (3) defines "Commission" to mean the Commodity Futures Trading Commission (CFTC).

[House Report No. 95–595, 95th Cong., 1st Sess. 390 (1977).]

Paragraphs (3) and (4) define terms "Commission" and "commodity futures contract".

[Senate Report No. 95–989, 95th Cong., 2d Sess. 104 (1978).]

Paragraph . . . [4] defines "commodity contract" to mean a commodity futures contract (sec. 761(4)), a commodity option (sec. 761(6)), or a leverage contract (sec. 761(15)).

[Senate Report No. 95–989, 95th Cong., 2d Sess. 104 (1978).]

Paragraph . . . [5] defines "commodity option" in the manner defined in CFTC regulations.

[House Report No. 95–595, 95th Cong., 1st Sess. 390 (1977).]

Paragraph . . . [5] defines "commodity option" by reference to section 4c(b) of the Commodity Exchange Act.

[Senate Report No. 95–989, 95th Cong., 2d Sess. 104 (1978).]

Paragraph . . . [6] defines "commodity options dealer" as a person that deals in commodity options. This definition does not exclude an options dealer that has registered as a futures commission merchant. This is consistent with the interim regulations of the Commodity Future [*sic*] Trading Commission, published November 22, 1976, 41 Fed. Reg. 51808.

[House Report No. 95–595, 95th Cong., 1st Sess. 390 (1977).]

Paragraphs . . . [6], [7] and [9] define "commodity options dealer," "contract market," "contract of sale," "commodity," "future delivery," "board of trade," and "futures commission merchant."

[*Senate Report No. 95–989, 95th Cong., 2nd Sess. 104 (1978).*]

Paragraph . . . [7] defines "contract market" to mean a board of trade designated as contract market by the CFTC.

[*House Report No. 95–595, 95th Cong., 1st Sess. 390 (1977).*]

Paragraph . . . [8] indicates that the definitions of "contract of sale", "commodity", "future delivery", "board of trade", and "futures commission merchant" have the same meanings assigned to those terms in the Act. Although the technical phrase "contract of sale" is not used in subchapter IV, it is intended that "contract for the purchase or sale" be construed to mean a "contract of sale".

[*House Report No. 95–595, 95th Cong., 2d Sess. 390 (1977).*]

Paragraph [9] defines "customer" in a similar style. It is anticipated that a debtor with multifaceted characteristics will have separate estates for each different kind of customer. Thus, a debtor that is a leverage transaction merchant and a commodity options dealer would have separate estates for the leverage transaction customers and for the options customers, and a general estate for other creditors. Customers for each kind of commodity broker, except the clearing organization, arise from either of two relationships. In subparagraphs (A), (B), (C), and (E), clause (i) treats with customers to the extent of contractual commitments with the debtor in either a broker or a dealer relationship. Clause (ii) treats with customers to the extent of proceeds from contractual commitments or deposits for the purpose of making contractual commitments. The customer of the clearing organization is a member with a proprietary or customers' account.

[*House Report No. 95–595, 95th Cong., 1st Sess. 390 (1977).*]

Paragraph . . . [9] defines the term "customer" to mean with respect to a futures commission merchant or a foreign futures commission merchant, the entity for whom the debtor carries a commodity futures contract or foreign future, or with whom such a contract is carried (such as another commodity broker), or from whom the debtor has received, acquired, or holds cash, securities, or other property arising out of or connected with specified transactions involving commodity futures contracts or foreign futures. This section also defines "customer" in the context of leverage transaction merchants, clearing organizations, and commodity options dealers. Persons associated with a commodity broker, such as its employees, officers, or partners, may be customers under this definition.

The definition of "customer" serves to isolate that class of persons entitled to the protection subchapter IV provides to customers. In addition, section 101(5) defines "commodity broker" to mean a futures commission merchant, foreign futures commission merchant, clearing organization, leverage transaction merchant, or commodity options dealer, with respect to which there is a customer. Accordingly, the definition of customer also serves to designate those entities which must utilize chapter 7 and are precluded from reorganizing under chapter 11.

[*Senate Report No. 95–989, 95th Cong., 2d Sess. 104–105 (1978).*]

Paragraph [10] defines "customer property" to include all property in customer accounts and property that should have been in those accounts but was diverted through conversion or mistake. Clause (i) refers to customer property not properly segregated by the debtor or customer property converted and then recovered so as to become property of the estate. Clause (vii) is intended to exclude property that would cost more to recover from a third party than the value of the property itself. Subparagraph (B) excludes property in a customer's account that belongs to the commodity broker, such as a contract placed in the account by error, or cash due the broker for a margin payment that the broker has made.

[*House Report No. 95–595, 95th Cong., 1st Sess. 390–391 (1977).*]

Paragraph . . . [10] defines "customer property" to mean virtually all property or proceeds thereof, received, acquired, or held by or for the account of the debtor for a customer arising [out] of or in connection with a transaction involving a commodity contract.

[*Senate Report No. 95–989, 95th Cong., 2d Sess. 105 (1978).*]

Paragraph [11] defines "foreign future" to mean a contract for the purchase or sale of a commodity on a foreign board of trade.

[*House Report No. 95–595, 95th Cong., 1st Sess. 391 (1977).*]

Paragraphs . . . [11], [12], [13] and [14] define "foreign future," "foreign futures commission merchant," "leverage transaction," and "leverage transaction merchant."

[*Senate Report No. 95–989, 95th Cong., 2d Sess. 105 (1978).*]

Paragraph . . . [13] indicates that a "leverage transaction" refers to transactions in rare metals as defined under section 217 of the CFTC Act of 1974.

Paragraph . . . [14] defines "leverage transaction merchant" as a person engaged in the business of leverage transactions.

[*House Report No. 95–595, 95th Cong., 1st Sess. 391 (1977).*]

Paragraph . . . [15] defines "margin payment" to mean a payment or deposit commonly known to the commodities trade as original margin, initial margin, or variation margin. [*Ed. Note:* This excerpt from the Senate Report included the following footnote: "*See* S. Rep. No. 95–850, 95th Cong., 2d Sess. 130, 138 (1978)."]

[*Senate Report No. 95–989, 95th Cong., 2d Sess. 105 (1978).*]

Paragraph . . . [16] defines "member property" in terms of property held for the proprietary account of a member of a clearing organization.

[*House Report No. 95–595, 95th Cong., 1st Sess. 391 (1977).*]

Paragraph . . . [16] defines "member property."

[Senate Report No. 95–595, 95th Cong., 2d Sess. 105 (1978).]

Paragraph . . . [17] defines "net equity" to include the value of all contractual commitments at the time of liquidation or transfer less any obligations owed by the customer to the debtor, such as brokerage fees. In addition, the term includes the value of any specifically identifiable property as of the date of return to the customer and the value of any customer property transferred to another commodity broker as of the date of transfer. This definition places the risk of market fluctuations on the customer until commitments leave the estate.

[House Report No. 95–595, 95th Cong., 1st Sess. 391 (1977).]

Paragraph . . . [17] defines "net equity" to be the sum of (A) the value of all customer property remaining in a customer's account immediately after all commodity contracts of such customer have been transferred, liquidated, or become identified for delivery and all obligations of such customer to the debtor have been offset (such as margin payments, whether or not called, and brokerage commissions) plus (B) the value of specifically identifiable customer property previously returned to the customer by the trustee, plus (C) if the trustee has transferred any commodity contract to which the customer is entitled or any margin or security for such contract, the value of such contract and margin or security. Net equity, therefore, will be the total amount of customer property to which a customer is entitled as of the date of the filing of the bankruptcy petition, although valued at subsequent dates. The Commission is given authority to promulgate rules and regulations to further refine this definition. [*Ed. Note:* This excerpt from the Senate Report included the following footnote: "The amount remaining in such customers accounts would include any customer property that was unlawfully converted. *See* section 761(11)(A)."]

[Senate Report No. 95–989, 95th Cong., 2d Sess. 105 (1978).]

Subchapter IV of chapter 7 represents a compromise between similar chapters in the House bill and Senate amendment. Section 761(2) of the House amendment defines "clearing organization" to cover an organization that clears commodity contracts on a contract market or a board of trade; the expansion of the definition is intended to include clearing organizations that clear commodity options. Section 761(4) of the House amendment adopts the term "commodity contract" as used in section 761(5) of the Senate amendment but with the more precise substantive definitions contained in section 761(8) of the House bill. The definition is modified to insert "board of trade" to cover commodity options. Section 761(5) of the House amendment adopts the definition contained in section 761(6) of the Senate amendment in preference to the definition contained in section 761(4) of the House bill which erroneously included onions, [*sic*]. Section 761(9) of the House amendment represents a compromise between similar provisions contained in section 761(10) of the Senate amendment and section 761(9) of the House Bill. The compromise adopts the substance contained in the House bill and adopts the terminology of "commodity contract" in lieu of "contractual commitment" as suggested in the Senate amendment. Section 761(10) of the House amendment represents a compromise between similar sections in the House bill and Senate amendment regarding the definition of "customer property." The definition of "distribution share" contained in section 761(12) of the Senate amendment is deleted as unnecessary. Section 761(12) of the House amendment adopts a definition of "foreign futures commission merchant" similar to the definition contained in section 761(14) of the Senate amendment. The definition is modified to cover either an entity engaged in soliciting orders or the purchase or sale of a foreign future, or an entity that accepts cash, a security, or other property for credit in connection with such a solicitation or acceptance. Section 761(13) of the House amendment adopts a definition of "leverage transaction" identical to the definition contained in section 761(15) of the Senate amendment. Section 761(15) of the House amendment adopts the definition of "margin payment" contained in section 761(17) of the Senate amendment. Section 761(17) of the House amendment adopts a definition of "net equity" derived from section 761(15) of the House bill.

[*124 Cong. Rec. H 11,099 (Sept. 28, 1978); S 17,415 (Oct. 6, 1978).*]

Comment

There was no provision in the former Bankruptcy Act or former Rules comparable to section 761.

The 1982 amendments (P.L. 97–222) made numerous changes in section 761, all intended to clarify the definitions contained in that section, and to correct an erroneous cross-reference in paragraph (13).

1984 Amendments: A technical change was made to clarify paragraph (10)(A)(viii) of section 761.

Case Annotations

When a commodity futures merchant commissions a sales agent to sell an advisory program to customers for the commodity merchant, and the merchant subsequently files for relief, the sales agent cannot be considered a customer of the merchant under section 761(9). Prime Fin. Sales v. Freehling (*In re* Bengal Trading Corp.), 5 C.B.C.2d 293 (B. Ct., S.D. Fla. 1981).

References

4 *Collier on Bankruptcy* ch. 761 (Matthew Bender 15th ed.).

2 *Collier Bankruptcy Manual* ch. 761 (Matthew Bender 3d ed.).

Feldman and Sommer, *The Special Commodity Provisions of the New Bankruptcy Code,* 37 Bus. Law. 1487 (1982).

Levy, *Customer's Rights in Stockbroker Insolvencies,* 84 Com. L.J. 173 (1979).

White, *Commodity-Related Provisions of the Bankruptcy Act of 1978*, 34 Rec. 262 (1979).

White, *Rights of Commodities Futures Customers in Commodity Broker Bankruptcies*, 1 Agric. L. Rev. 641 (1980).

SECTION 762 (11 U.S.C. § 762)

§ 762. Notice to the Commission and right to be heard.

(a) The clerk shall give the notice required by section 342 of this title to the Commission.

(b) The Commission may raise and may appear and be heard on any issue in a case under this chapter.

Bankruptcy Rule Reference: 2002

Legislative History

Section 762(a) requires notice of the order for relief to be given to the CFTC in every case concerning a commodity broker. Subsection (b) gives the CFTC standing to intervene as a matter of right.

[*House Report No. 95–595, 95th Cong., 1st Sess. 391 (1977).*]

Section 762 provides that the Commission shall be given such notice as is appropriate of an order for relief in a bankruptcy case and that the Commission may raise and may appear and may be heard on any issue in case [*sic*] involving a commodity broker liquidation.

[*Senate Report No. 95–989, 95th Cong., 2d Sess. 105 (1978).*]

Comment

SIPA, 15 U.S.C. § 78eee(c), provides that the SEC may, on its own motion, file notice of appearance in any SIPA proceeding and may thereafter participate as a party.

There was no provision in the former Bankruptcy Act or former Rules comparable to section 762.

Bankruptcy Rule 2002, relating to notices, provides in subdivision (j)(2) thereof, that notices prescribed in Rule 2002 be given, in a commodity broker case, to the Commodity Futures Trading Commission at Washington, D.C. Subdivision (k), added to Rule 2002 by the 1991 Amendments, requires that the United States trustee receive various notices. However, the Rule specifically provides that the United States trustee need not receive any notice, schedule, report, application or other document in a case under SIPA.

References

4 *Collier on Bankruptcy* ch. 762 (Matthew Bender 15th ed.).

2 *Collier Bankruptcy Manual* ch. 762 (Matthew Bender 3d ed.).

Feldman and Sommer, *The Special Commodity Provisions of the New Bankruptcy Code,* 37 Bus. Law. 1487 (1982).

White, *Commodity–Related Provisions of the Bankruptcy Act of 1978,* 34 Rec. 262 (1979).

White, *Rights of Commodities Futures Customers in Commodity Broker Bankruptcies,* 1 Agric. L. Rev. 641 (1980).

SECTION 763 (11 U.S.C. § 763)

§ 763. Treatment of accounts.

(a) Accounts held by the debtor for a particular customer in separate capacities shall be treated as accounts of separate customers.

(b) A member of a clearing organization shall be deemed to hold such member's proprietary account in a separate capacity from such member's customers' account.

(c) The net equity in a customer's account may not be offset against the net equity in the account of any other customer.

Legislative History

Section 763(a) indicates that accounts of customers held in separate capacities are to be considered separately. Thus, in a community property state, a separate property account may not be offset against a community property account even if both accounts are in the same name. A similar result obtains with respect to a trustee or another commodity broker that holds accounts on behalf of real parties in interest.

[*House Report No. 95–595, 95th Cong., 1st Sess. 391 (1977).*]

Section 763 provides for separate treatment of accounts held in separate capacities. A deficit in one account held for a customer may not be offset against the net equity in another account held by the same customer in a separate capacity or held by another customer.

[*Senate Report No. 95–989, 95th Cong., 2d Sess. 105 (1978).*]

Subsection (b) clarifies that a member in a clearing organization holds his proprietary account in a separate capacity than his customers' account.

Subsection (c) indicates that the account of one customer may not be offset against the account of any other customer.

[*House Report No. 95–595, 95th Cong., 1st Sess. 391 (1977).*]

Comment

There was no provision in the former Bankruptcy Act or former Rules comparable to section 763.

1984 Amendments: Technical changes were made in subsection (a) of section 763. The words "the debtor for" were added, and the words "deemed to be" were changed to read "treated as."

References

4 *Collier on Bankruptcy* ch. 763 (Matthew Bender 15th ed.).

2 *Collier Bankruptcy Manual* ch. 763 (Matthew Bender 3d ed.).

Feldman and Sommer, *The Special Commodity Provisions of the New Bankruptcy Code,* 37 Bus. Law. 1487 (1982).

Levy, *Customer's Rights in Stockbroker Insolvencies,* 84 Com. L.J. 173 (1979).

White, *Commodity-Related Provisions of the Bankruptcy Act of 1978,* 34 Rec. 262 (1979).

White, *Rights of Commodities Futures Customers in Commodity Broker Bankruptcies,* 1 Agric. L. Rev. 641 (1980).

SECTION 764 (11 U.S.C. § 764)

§ 764. Voidable transfers.

(a) Except as otherwise provided in this section, any transfer by the debtor of property that, but for such transfer, would have been customer property, may be avoided by the trustee, and such property shall be treated as customer property, if and to the extent that the trustee avoids such transfer under sections 544, 545, 547, 548, 549, or 724(a) of this title. For the purpose of such sections, the property so transferred shall be deemed to have been property of the debtor, and, if such transfer was made to a customer or for a customer's benefit, such customer shall be deemed, for the purposes of this section, to have been a creditor.

(b) Notwithstanding sections 544, 545, 547, 548, 549, and 724(a) of this title, the trustee may not avoid a transfer made before five days after the order for relief, if such transfer is approved by the Commission by rule or order, either before or after such transfer, and if such transfer is—

(1) a transfer of a commodity contract entered into or carried by or through the debtor on behalf of a customer, and of any cash, securities, or other property margining or securing such commodity contract; or

(2) the liquidation of a commodity contract entered into or carried by or through the debtor on behalf of a customer.

Legislative History

Section 764 indicates the extent to which the avoiding powers may be used by the trustee under subchapter IV of chapter 7. If property recovered would have been customer property if never transferred, then subsection (a) indicates that it will be so treated when recovered.

[*House Report No. 95–595, 95th Cong., 1st Sess. 391 (1977).*]

Section 764 permits the trustee to void any transfer of property that, except for such transfer, would have been customer property, to the extent permitted under sections 544, 545, 547, 548, 549, or 724(a).

[*Senate Report No. 95–989, 95th Cong., 2d Sess. 105 (1978).*]

Subsection (b) prohibits avoiding any transaction that occurs before or within five days after the petition if the transaction is approved by the Commission and concerns an open contractual commitment. This enables the Commission to exercise its discretion to protect the integrity of the market by insuring that transactions cleared with other brokers will not be undone on a preference or a fraudulent transfer theory.

Subsection (c) insulates variation margin payments and other deposits from the avoiding powers except to the extent of actual fraud under section 548(a)(1). This facilitates prepetition transfers and protects the ordinary course of business in the market.

[*House Report No. 95–595, 95th Cong., 1st Sess. 391-392 (1977).*]

Section 764 of the House amendment is derived from the House bill.

[*124 Cong. Rec. H 11,099 (Sept. 28, 1978); S 17,415 (Oct. 6, 1978).*]

MR. MATHIAS. I have one final question of the distinguished Senator. My understanding of section 764(b) which makes nonvoidable certain transfers or liquidations of commodity contracts made within five days of filing is that the Commission will not be engaged in approving transfers in each bankruptcy occurrence. Rather, the transfers will be made by the exchanges or clearing organizations under the existing rules of the Commission requiring that trades which are noncompetitive or expit transfers be so identified to the Commission by the affected exchange or clearing organization. Is this a correct interpretation?

MR. DECONCINI. Yes. The above procedure indicates that an expeditious, inexpensive procedure will be available to permit debtors to extend or compose their debts.

MR. MATHIAS. Mr. President. I have four questions regarding subchapter IV of chapter 7 of title I of the bill, which deals with commodity related bankruptcies. I note that the bill now before the Senate deletes section 766(b) and (c) of the bill as originally passed by the Senate, S. 2266. I also note, however, that the distinguished Senator's floor statement indicates that the protections previously sought to be provided under section 766(b) and (c) to commodity brokers, forward contract merchants and clearing organizations are now intended to be covered under section 764(c) and section 548(d)(2) of the bill now before us. Is that correct?

MR. DECONCINI. Yes.

MR. MATHIAS. Am I correct in my understanding of the Senator's statement that the intent of section 764 and section 548(d)(2) is to provide that margin payments and settlement payments previously made by a bankrupt to a commodity broker, forward contract merchant and by or to a clearing organization are nonvoidable transfers by the bankrupts trustee? And is it also true that margin payments will not be considered voidable preferences because they constitute transfers made as contemporaneous exchanges for new value as used in section 547(c)?

MR. DECONCINI. Yes.

MR. MATHIAS. I thank the Senator for his assurance that it is the intention of section 764(c) and section 548(d)(2) to protect all margin payments in the customer-broker-clearinghouse chain. This vital protection substantially reduces the likelihood that the bankruptcy of one customer or broker will lead to the bankruptcy of another broker or clearinghouse.

[*124 Cong. Rec. S 17,433 (Oct. 6, 1978).*]

Section 17(b) [of Public Law 97–222] amends section 764(o) of title 11 to extend the time within which specified transfers or liquidations may be made in an involuntary case. Under the present section, transfers or liquidations must be made before five days after the filing of the petition in order to be eligible for protection by the Commodity Futures Trading Commission from avoidance by the trustee. As amended, the section will prevent a trustee from avoiding transfers or liquidations made before five days after the order for relief, provided such transfers or liquidations are approved by the Commodity Futures Trading Commission.

Section 17(c) repeals section 764(c) of title 11. As explained above, new Section 546(d) incorporates the provisions of current Section 764(c) and makes certain clarifying changes.

[*House Report No. 97–420, 97th Cong., 2d Sess. 5 (1982).*]

Comment

There was no provision in the former Bankruptcy Act or Rules comparable to section 764.

The 1982 amendments (P.L. 97–222) changed subsection (b) to prohibit avoidance of a transfer made 5 days after the order for relief instead of 5 days after the filing of the petition, thus extending the time within which certain transfers or liquidations may be made in an involuntary case. Subsection (c) was deleted from section 764, its provisions now incorporated in section 546(d). See "Comment" to section 546 *supra*.

1984 Amendment: A clarification amendment to subsection (a) of section 764 makes it clear that the transfer referred to is the transfer "by the debtor."

References

4 *Collier on Bankruptcy* ch. 764 (Matthew Bender 15th ed.).

2 *Collier Bankruptcy Manual* ch. 764 (Matthew Bender 3d ed.).

Feldman and Sommer, *The Special Commodity Provisions of the New Bankruptcy Code,* 37 Bus. Law. 1487 (1982).

Teofan and Creel, *The Trustee's Avoiding Powers under the Bankruptcy Act and the New Code,* 85 Com. L.J. 542 (1980).

White, *Commodity-Related Provisions of the Bankruptcy Act of 1978,* 34 Rec. 262 (1979).

SECTION 765 (11 U.S.C. § 765)

§ 765. Customer instructions.

(a) The notice required by section 342 of this title to customers shall instruct each customer—

> (1) to file a proof of such customer's claim promptly, and to specify in such claim any specifically identifiable security, property, or commodity contract; and

> (2) to instruct the trustee of such customer's desired disposition, including transfer under section 766 of this title or liquidation, of any commodity contract specifically identified to such customer.

(b) The trustee shall comply, to the extent practicable, with any instruction received from a customer regarding such customer's desired disposition of any commodity contract specifically identified to such customer. If the trustee has transferred, under section 766 of this title, such a commodity contract the trustee shall transmit any such instruction to the commodity broker to whom such commodity contract was so transferred.

Legislative History

Section 765(a) indicates that a customer must file a proof of claim, including any claim to specifically identifiable property, within such time as the court fixes.

Subsection (b) gives the customer authority to instruct the trustee to liquidate or transfer any specifically identifiable open contractual commitment if such instructions are made of the trustee within such time as the court fixes.

[*House Report No. 95–595, 95th Cong., 1st Sess. 392 (1977).*]

Section 18 [of Public Law 97–222] makes a conforming change. The substitution of the phrase "commodity contract" for the word "commitment" conforms the language of Section 765(b) to that used in the rest of Title 11.

[*House Report No. 97–420, 97th Cong., 2d Sess. 5 (1982).*]

At approximately the same time, the trustee should notify each customer of the debtor's bankruptcy and instruct each customer immediately to submit a claim including any claim to a specifically identifiable security or other property, and advise the trustee as to the desired disposition of commodity contracts carried by the debtor for the customer.

This requirement is placed upon the trustee to insure that producers who have hedged their production in the commodities market are allowed the opportunity to preserve their positions. The theory of the commodity market is that it exists for producers and buyers of commodities and not for the benefit of the speculators whose transactions now comprise the overwhelming majority of trades. Maintenance of positions by hedges may require them to put up additional margin payments in the hours and days following the commodity broker bankruptcy, which they may be unable or unwilling to do. In such cases, their positions will be quickly liquidated by the trustee, but they must have the opportunity to make those margin payments before they are summarily liquidated out of the market to the detriment of their growing crop. The failure of the customer to advise the trustee as to disposition of the customer's commodity contract will not delay a transfer of a contract pursuant to subsection (b) so long as the contract can otherwise be identified to the customer. Nor will the failure of the customer to submit a claim prevent the customer from recovering the net equity in that customer's account, absent a claim the customer cannot participate in the determination of the net equity in the account.

If the customer submits instructions pursuant to subsection (a) after the customer's commodity contracts are transferred to another commodity broker, the trustee must transmit the instruction to the transferee. If the customer's commodity contracts are not transferred before the customer's instructions are received, the trustee must attempt to comply with the instruction, subject to the provisions of section 767(d). [*Ed. Note:* The derivation of this provision, discussed in the Congressional Record excerpt immediately following, explains the imprecise references in this portion of the Senate Report.]

[*Senate Report No. 95–989, 95th Cong., 2d Sess. 107 (1978).*]

Sections 765 and 766 of the House amendment represent a consolidation and redraft of sections 765, 766, 767, and 768 of the House bill and sections 765, 766, 767, and 768 of the Senate amendment. In particular, section 765(a) of the House amendment is derived from section 765(a) of the House bill and section 767(a) of the Senate amendment. Under section 765(a) of the House amendment customers are notified of the opportunity to immediately file proofs of claim and to identify specifically identifiable securities, property, or commodity contracts. The customer is also afforded an opportunity to instruct the trustee regarding the customer's desires concerning disposition of the customer's commodity contracts. Section 767(b) makes clear that the trustee must comply with instructions received to the extent practicable, but in the event the trustee has transferred commodity contracts to a commodity broker, such instructions shall be forwarded to the broker.

[*124 Cong. Rec. H 11,099 (Sept. 28, 1978); S 17,415–17,416 (Oct. 6, 1978).*]

Comment

There was no provision in the former Bankruptcy Act or former Rules comparable to section 765.

1984 Amendment: A minor technical change was made in subsection (a) of section 765.

References

4 *Collier on Bankruptcy* ch. 765 (Matthew Bender 15th ed.).

2 *Collier Bankruptcy Manual* ch. 765 (Matthew Bender 3d ed.).

Feldman and Sommer, *The Special Commodity Provisions of the New Bankruptcy Code,* 37 Bus. Law. 1487 (1982).

Levy, *Customer's Rights in Stockbroker Insolvencies,* 84 Com. L.J. 173 (1979).

White, *Commodity-Related Provisions of the Bankruptcy Act of 1978,* 34 Rec. 262 (1979).

White, *Rights of Commodities Futures Customers in Commodity Broker Bankruptcies,* 1 Agric. L. Rev. 641 (1980).

SECTION 766 (11 U.S.C. § 766)

§ 766. Treatment of customer property.

(a) The trustee shall answer all margin calls with respect to a specifically identifiable commodity contract of a customer until such time as the trustee returns or transfers such commodity contract, but the trustee may not make a margin payment that has the effect of a distribution to such customer of more than that to which such customer is entitled under subsection (h) or (i) of this section.

(b) The trustee shall prevent any open commodity contract from remaining open after the last day of trading in such commodity contract, or into the first day on which notice of intent to deliver on such commodity contract may be tendered, whichever occurs first. With respect to any commodity contract that has remained open after the last day of trading in such commodity contract or with respect to which delivery must be made or accepted under the rules of the contract market on which such commodity contract was made, the trustee may operate the business of the debtor for the purpose of—

(1) accepting or making tender of notice of intent to deliver the physical commodity underlying such commodity contract;

(2) facilitating delivery of such commodity; or

(3) disposing of such commodity if a party to such commodity contract defaults.

(c) The trustee shall return promptly to a customer any specifically identifiable security, property, or commodity contract to which such customer is entitled, or shall transfer, on such customer's behalf, such security, property, or commodity contract to a commodity broker that is not a debtor under this title, subject to such rules or regulations as the Commission may prescribe, to the extent that the value of such security, property, or commodity contract does not exceed the amount to which such customer would be entitled under subsection (h) or (i) of this section if such security, property, or commodity contract were not returned or transferred under this subsection.

(d) If the value of a specifically identifiable security, property, or commodity contract exceeds the amount to which the customer of the debtor is entitled under subsection (h) or (i) of this section, then such customer to whom such security, property, or commodity contract is specifically identified may deposit cash with the trustee equal to the difference between the value of such security, property, or commodity contract and such amount, and the trustee then shall—

(1) return promptly such security, property, or commodity contract to such customer; or

(2) transfer, on such customer's behalf, such security, property, or commodity contract to a commodity broker that is not a debtor under this title, subject to such rules or regulations as the Commission may prescribe.

(e) Subject to subsection (b) of this section, the trustee shall liquidate any commodity contract that—

(1) is identified to a particular customer and with respect to which such customer has not timely instructed the trustee as to the desired disposition of such commodity contract;

(2) cannot be transferred under subsection (c) of this section; or

(3) cannot be identified to a particular customer.

(f) As soon as practicable after the commencement of the case, the trustee shall reduce to money, consistent with good market practice, all securities and other property, other than commodity contracts, held as property of the estate, except for specifically identifiable securities or property distributable under subsection (h) or (i) of this section.

(g) The trustee may not distribute a security or other property except under subsection (h) or (i) of this section.

(h) Except as provided in subsection (b) of this section, the trustee shall distribute customer property ratably to customers on the basis and to the extent of such customers' allowed net equity claims, and in priority to all other claims, except claims of a kind specified in section 507(a)(1) of this title that are attributable to the administration of customer property. Such distribution shall be in the form of—

(1) cash;

(2) the return or transfer, under subsection (c) or (d) of this section, of specifically identifiable customer securities, property, or commodity contracts; or

(3) payment of margin calls under subsection (a) of this section.

Notwithstanding any other provisions of this subsection, a customer net equity claim based on a proprietary account, as defined by Commission rule, regulation, or order, may not be paid either in whole or in part, directly or indirectly, out of customer property unless all other customer net equity claims have been paid in full.

(i) If the debtor is a clearing organization, the trustee shall distribute—

(1) customer property, other than member property, ratably to customers on the basis and to the extent of such customers' allowed net equity claims based on such customers' accounts other than proprietary accounts, and in priority to all other claims, except claims of a kind specified in section 507(a)(1) of this title that are attributable to the administration of such customer property; and

(2) member property ratably to customers on the basis and to the extent of such customers' allowed net equity claims based on such customers' proprietary accounts, and in priority to all other claims, except claims that are attributable to the administration of member property or customer property.

(j)(1) The trustee shall distribute customer property in excess of that distributed under subsection (h) or (i) of this section in accordance with section 726 of this title.

(2) Except as provided in section 510 of this title, if a customer is not paid the full amount of such customer's allowed net equity claim from customer property, the unpaid portion of such claim is a claim entitled to distribution under section 726 of this title.

Legislative History

[*Ed. Note:* In all reports pertinent to the subsections of section 766, references may be inaccurate due to the fact that the sections were originally arranged differently, as is indicated by the pertinent Congressional Record excerpts.]

Subsection (c) permits the trustee to answer all margin calls, to the extent of the customer's net equity claim, with respect to any specifically identifiable open contractual commitment. It should be noted that any payment under subsections (a) or (c) will be considered a reduction of the net equity claim under section 767(a). Thus the customer's net equity claim is a dynamic amount that varies with distributions of specifically identifiable property or margin payments on such property. This approach differs from the priority given to specifically identifiable property under subchapter III of chapter 7 by limiting the priority effect to a right to receive specific property as part of, rather than in addition to, a ratable share of customer property. This policy is designed to protect the small customer who is unlikely to have property in specifically identifiable form as compared with the professional trader. The CFTC is authorized to make rules defining specifically identifiable property under section 302 of the bill, in title III.

[*House Report No. 95–595, 95th Cong., 1st Sess. 393 (1977).*]

Subsection (f) requires the trustee to answer margin calls on specifically identifiable customer commodity contracts, but only to the extent that the margin payment, together with any other distribution made by the trustee to or on behalf of the customer, does not exceed the customer's distribution share.

[*Senate Report No. 95–989, 95th Cong., 2d Sess. 108 (1978).*]

Section 766(a) of the House amendment is derived from section 768(c) of the House bill and section 767(f) of the Senate amendment.

[*124 Cong. Rec. H 11,099 (Sept. 28, 1978); S 17,416 (Oct. 6, 1978).*]

Subsection (d) indicates an exception to the time limits in the rule by requiring the trustee to liquidate any open contractual commitment before the last day of trading or the first day during which delivery may be demanded, whichever first occurs, if transfer cannot be effectuated.

[*House Report No. 95–595, 95th Cong., 1st Sess. 392 (1977).*]

Subsection (g) requires the trustee to liquidate all commodity futures contracts prior to the close of trading in that contract, or the first day on which notice of intent to deliver on that contract may be tendered, whichever occurs first. If the customer desires that the contract be kept open for delivery, the contract should be transferred to another commodity broker pursuant to subsection (b).

If for some reason the trustee is unable to transfer a contract on which delivery must be made or accepted and is unable to close out such contract, the trustee is authorized to operate the business of the debtor for the purpose of accepting or making tender of notice of intent to deliver the physical commodity underlying the contract, facilitating delivery of the physical commodity, or disposing of the physical commodity in the event of a default. Any property received, not previously held, by the trustee in connnection with its operation of the business of the debtor for these purposes, is not by the terms of this subchapter specifically included in the definition of customer property.

[*Senate Report No. 95–989, 95th Cong., 2d Sess. 108 (1978).*]

Section 766(b) of the House amendment is derived from section 765(d) of the House bill, and section 767(g) of the Senate amendment.

[*124 Cong. Rec. H 11,099 (Sept. 28, 1978); S 17,416 (Oct. 6, 1978).*]

Section 768(a) requires the trustee to return specifically identifiable property to the extent that such distribution will not exceed a customer's net equity claim. Thus, if the customer owes money to a commodity broker, this will be offset under section 761(15)(A)(ii). If the value of the specifically identifiable property exceeds the net equity claim, then the customer may deposit cash with the trustee to make up the difference after which the trustee may return or transfer the customer's property.

[*House Report No. 95–595, 95th Cong., 1st Sess. 393 (1977).*]

Subsection (e) instructs the trustee as to the disposition of any security or other property, not disposed of pursuant to subsection (b) or (d), that is specifically identifiable to a customer and to which the customer is entitled. Such security or other property must be returned to the customer or promptly transferred to another commodity broker for the benefit of the customer. If the value of the security or other property retained or transferred, together with any other distribution made by the trustee to or on behalf of the customer, exceeds the customer's distribution share the customer must deposit cash with the trustee equal to that difference before the return or transfer of the security or other property.

[*Senate Report No. 95–989, 95th Cong., 2d Sess. 108 (1978).*]

Section 766(c) of the House amendment is derived from section 768(a) of the House bill and section 767(e) of the Senate amendment.

[*124 Cong. Rec. H 11,099 (Sept. 28, 1978); S 17,416 (Oct. 6, 1978).*]

Section 766(d) of the House amendment is derived from section 768(b) of the House bill and the second sentence of section 767(e) of the Senate amendment.

[*124 Cong. Rec. H 11,099 (Sept. 28, 1978); S 17,416 (Oct. 6, 1978).*]

Subsection (c) sets forth the general rule requiring the trustee to liquidate contractual commitments that are either not specifically identifiable or with respect to which a customer has not instructed the trustee during the time fixed by the court.

[*House Report No. 95–595, 95th Cong., 1st Sess. 392 (1977).*]

Subsection (c) provides that contemporaneously with the estimate of the distribution share and the transfer of identified customer accounts and property, subsection (c) provides that the trustee should make arrangements for the liquidation of all commodity contracts maintained by the debtor that are not identifiable to specific customers. These contracts would, of course, include all such contracts held in the debtor's proprietory account.

At approximately the same time, the trustee should notify each customer of the debtor's bankruptcy and instruct each customer immediately to submit a claim including any claim to a specifically identifiable security or other property, and advise the trustee as to the desired disposition of commodity contracts carried by the debtor for the customer.

This requirement is placed upon the trustee to insure that producers who have hedged their production in the commodities market are allowed the opportunity to preserve their positions. The theory of the commodity market is that it exists for producers and buyers of commodities and not for the benefit of the speculators whose transactions now comprise the overwhelming majority of trades. Maintenance of positions by hedges may require them to put up additional margin payments in the hours and days following the commodity broker bankruptcy, which they may be unable or unwilling to do. In such cases, their positions will be quickly liquidated by the trustee, but they must have the opportunity to make those margin payments before they are summarily liquidated out of the market to the detriment of their growing crop. The failure of the customer to advise the trustee as to disposition of the customer's commodity contract will not delay a transfer of a contract pursuant to subsection (b) so long as the contract can otherwise be identified to the customer. Nor will the failure of the customer to submit a claim prevent the customer from recovering the net equity in that customer's account, absent a claim the customer cannot participate in the determination of the net equity in the account.

If the customer submits instructions pursuant to subsection (a) after the customer's commodity contracts are transferred to another commodity broker, the trustee must transmit the instruction to the transferee. If the customer's commodity contracts are not transferred before the customer's instructions are received, the trustee must attempt to comply with the instruction, subject to the provisions of section 767(d).

Under subsection (d), the trustee has discretion to liquidate any commodity contract carried by the debtor at any time. This discretion must be exercised with restraint in such cases, consistent with the purposes of this subchapter and good business practices. The committee intends that hedged accounts will be given special consideration before liquidation as discussed in connection with subsection (c).

[*Senate Report No. 95–989, 95th Cong., 2d Sess. 107–108 (1978).*]

Section 766(e) of the House amendment is derived from section 765(c) of the House bill and sections 767(c) and (d) of the Senate amendment. The provision clarifies that the trustee may liquidate a commodity contract only if the commodity contract cannot be transferred to a commodity broker under section 766(c), cannot be identified to a particular customer or has been identified with respect to a particular customer, but with respect to which the customer's instructions have not been received.

[*124 Cong. Rec. H 11,099 (Sept. 28, 1978); S 17,416 (Oct. 6, 1978).*]

Subsection (b) indicates that the trustee shall liquidate all securities and other property that is not specifically identifiable property as soon as practicable after the commencement of the case and in accordance with good market practice. If securities are restricted or trading has been suspended, the trustee will have to make an exempt sale or file a registration statement. In the event of a private placement, a customer is not entitled to "bid in" his net equity claim. To do so would enable him to receive a greater percentage recovery than other customers.

[*House Report No. 95–595, 95th Cong., 1st Sess. 392 (1977).*]

Section 19(b) [of Public Law 97–222] amends section 766(b) of title 11 to make clear the trustee's responsibility to close out, or liquidate, any open commodity contract prior to the last day of trading in such contract, irrespective of whether such contract is "actively traded as of the date of filing of the petition."

[*House Report No. 97–420, 97th Cong., 2d Sess. 5 (1982).*]

Finally, subsection (h) requires the trustee to liquidate the debtor's estate as soon as practicable and consistent with good market practice, except for specifically identifiable securities or other property distributable under subsection (e).

[*Senate Report No. 95–989, 95th Cong., 2d Sess. 108 (1978).*]

Section 766(f) of the House amendment is derived from section 766(b) of the House bill and section 767(h) of other property" is not intended to include a commodity contract [*sic*].

[*124 Cong. Rec. H 11,099 (Sept. 28, 1978); S 17,416 (Oct. 6, 1978).*]

Section 766(a) indicates that the trustee may distribute securities or other property only under section 768. This does not preclude a distribution of cash under section 767(a) or distribution of any excess customer property under section 767(c) to the general estate.

[*House Report No. 95–595, 95th Cong., 1st Sess. 392 (1977).*]

Section 766(g) of the House amendment is derived from section 766(a) of the House bill.

[*124 Cong. Rec. H 11,099 (Sept. 28, 1978); S 17,416 (Oct. 6, 1978).*]

Section 767(a) provides for the trustee to distribute customer property pro rata according to customers' net equity claims. The court will determine an equitable portion of customer property to pay administrative expenses. Paragraphs (2) and (3) indicate that the return of specifically identifiable property constitutes a distribution of net equity.

[*House Report No. 95–595, 95th Cong., 1st Sess. 392–393 (1977).*]

Subsection (a) of this section provides that with respect to liquidation of commodity brokers which are not clearing organizations, the trustee shall distribute customer property to customers on the basis and to the extent of such customers' allowed net equity claims, and in priority to all other claims. This section grants customers' claims first priority in the distribution of the estate. Subsection (b) grants the same priority to member property and other customer property in the liquidation of a clearing organization. A fundamental purpose of these provisions is to ensure that the property entrusted by customers to their brokers will not be subject to the risks of the broker's business and will be available for disbursement to customers if the broker becomes bankrupt.

[*Senate Report No. 95–989, 95th Cong., 2d Sess. 105–106 (1978).*]

Section 766(h) of the House amendment is derived from section 767(a) of the House bill and section 765(a) of the Senate amendment. In order to induce private trustees to undertake the difficult and risky job of liquidating a commodity broker, the House amendment contains a provision insuring that a pro rata share of administrative claims will be paid. The provision represents a compromise between the position taken in the House bill, subordinating customer property to all expenses of administration, and the position taken in the Senate amendment requiring the distribution of customer property in advance of any expenses of administration. The position in the Senate amendment is rejected since customers, in any event, would have to pay a brokerage commission or fee in the ordinary course of business. The compromise provision requires customers to pay only those administrative expenses that are attributable to the administration of customer property.

[*124 Cong. Rec. H 11,099 (Sept. 28, 1978); S 17,416 (Oct. 6, 1978).*]

Section 19(d) [of Public Law 97–222] amends section 766(h) of title 11 to implement the intent of the Bankruptcy Code that a customer net equity claim based on a proprietary account may not be paid unless all customer net equity claims which are not based on proprietary accounts have been paid in full.

[*House Report No. 97–420, 97th Cong., 2d Sess. 5 (1982).*]

Subsection (b) indicates that if the debtor is a clearing organization, customer property is to be segregated into customers' accounts and proprietary accounts and distributed accordingly without offset. This protects a member's customers from having their claims offset against the member's proprietary account. Subsection (c)(1) indicates that any excess customer property will pour over into the general estate. This unlikely event would occur only if customers fail to file proofs of claim. Subsection (c)(2) indicates that to the extent customers are not paid in full, they are entitled to share in the general estate as unsecured creditors, unless subordinated by the court under proposed 11 U.S.C. § 510.

[*House Report No. 95–595, 95th Cong., 1st Sess. 393 (1977).*]

Section 766(i) of the House amendment is derived from section 767(b) of the House bill and contains a similar compromise with respect to expenses of administration as the compromise detailed in connection with section 766(h) of the House amendment.

[*124 Cong. Rec. H 11,099 (Sept. 28, 1978); S 17,416 (Oct. 6, 1978).*]

Section 766(j) of the House amendment is derived from section 767(c) of the House bill. No counterpart is contained in the Senate amendment. The provision takes account of the rare case where the estate has customer property in excess of customer claims and administrative expenses attributable to those claims. The section also specifies that to the extent a customer is not paid in full out of customer property, that the unpaid claim will be treated the same as any other general unsecured creditor.

Section 768 of the Senate amendment was deleted from the House amendment as unwise. The provision in the Senate amendment would have permitted the trustee to distribute customer property based upon an estimate of value of the customer's account, with no provision for recapture of excessive disbursements. Moreover, the section would have exonerated the trustee from any liability for such an excessive disbursement. Furthermore, the section is unclear with respect to the customer's rights in the event the trustee makes a distribution less than the share to which the customer is entitled. The provision is deleted in the House amendment so that this difficult problem may be handled on a case-by-case basis by the courts as the facts and circumstances of each case require.

Section 769 of the Senate amendment is deleted in the House amendment as unnecessary. The provision was intended to codify Board of Trade v. Johnson, 264 U.S. 1 (1924). Board of Trade against Johnson is codified in section 363(f) of the House amendment which indicates the only five circumstances in which property may be sold free and clear of an interest in such property of an entity other than the estate.

Section 770 of the Senate amendment is deleted in the House amendment as unnecessary. That section would have permitted commodify brokers to liquidate commodity contracts, notwithstanding any contrary order of the court. It would require an extraordinary circumstance, such as a threat to the national security, to enjoin a commodity broker from liquidating a commodity contract. However, in those circumstances an injunction must prevail. Failure of the House amendment to incorporate section 770 of the Senate amendment does not imply that the automatic stay prevents liquidation of commodity contracts by commodity brokers. To the contrary, whenever by contract, or otherwise, a commodity broker is entitled to liquidate a position as a result of a condition specified in a contract other than a condition or default of the kind specified in section 365(b)(2) of title II, the commodity broker may engage in such liquidation. To this extent, the commodity broker's contract with his customer is treated no differently than any other contract under section 365 of title II.

[*124 Cong. Rec. H 11,099–11,100 (Sept. 28, 1978); S 17,416 (Oct. 6, 1978).*]

Comment

There was no provision in the former Bankruptcy Act or Rules comparable to section 766.

The 1982 amendments (Public Law 97–222) made changes in subsection (b) of section 766 clarifying the trustee's responsibility to close out or liquidate any open commodity contracts before the last day of the trading in such contract, regardless of whether the contract is "actively traded as of the date of the filing of the petition." Subsection (d) was also amended to implement the intent of the Code that a customer's net equity claim based on a proprietary account may not be paid unless all customer net equity claims not based on proprietary accounts have been paid in full. Other changes in section 766 are merely stylistic.

1984 Amendments: A minor amendment to subsection (j)(2) substituted "726" for "726(a)."

Case Annotations

Section 6(d)2 of the Commodity Exchange Act by itself does not mandate the subordination of unsegregated proprietary account claims and it cannot determine priorities in bankruptcy. Furthermore, the 1982 Amendment to section 766(h) requiring subordination of claims of proprietary accounts cannot be applied retroactively. Notz v. Tate (*In re* Chicago Discount Commodity Brokers, Inc.), 14 C.B.C.2d 521 (B. Ct., N.D. Ill. 1986).

A customer may only claim profits from a completed transaction, even if the failure to complete arose from the debtor's negligence or fraud. *In re* Trending Cycles for Commodities Inc., 8 C.B.C.2d 669 (B. Ct., S.D. Fla. 1982).

When a commodity futures merchant commissions a sales agent to sell an advisory program to customers for the commodity merchant, and the merchant subsequently files for relief, the commission monies which the merchant owes to the sales agent cannot be considered customer property under section 766 and should not be held by the trustee. Prime Fin. Sales v. Freehling (*In re* Bengal Trading Corp.), 5 C.B.C.2d 293 (B. Ct., S.D. Fla. 1981).

References

4 *Collier on Bankruptcy* ch. 766 (Matthew Bender 15th ed.).

2 *Collier Bankruptcy Manual* ch. 766 (Matthew Bender 3d ed.).

Feldman and Sommer, *The Special Commodity Provisions of the New Bankruptcy Code,* 37 Bus. Law. 1487 (1982).

Levy, *Customer's Rights in Stockbroker Insolvencies,* 84 Com. L.J. 173 (1979).

White, *Commodity-Related Provisions of the Bankruptcy Act of 1978,* 34 Rec. 262 (1979).

White, *Rights of Commodities Futures Customers in Commodity Broker Bankruptcies,* 1 Agric. L. Rev. 641 (1980).

COMMODITY EXCHANGE ACT

Section 302 of the Bankruptcy Reform Act of 1978 (in title III) amended the Commodity Exchange Act (7 U.S.C. § 1 *et seq.*) by adding the following section which became effective on enactment of the Bankruptcy Reform Act, November 6, 1978.

Sec. 20. (a) Notwithstanding title 11 of the United States Code, the Commission may provide, with respect to a commodity broker that is a debtor under chapter 7 of title 11 of the United States Code, by rule or regulation—

(1) that certain cash, securities, other property, or commodity contracts are to be included in or excluded from customer property or member property;

(2) that certain cash, securities, other property, or commodity contracts are to be specifically identifiable to a particular customer in a specific capacity;

(3) the method by which the business of such commodity broker is to be conducted or liquidated after the date of the filing of the petition under such chapter, including the payment and allocation of margin with respect to commodity contracts not specifically identifiable to a particular customer pending their orderly liquidation;

(4) any persons to which customer property and commodity contracts may be transferred under section 766 of title 11 of the United States Code; and

(5) how the net equity of a customer is to be determined.

(b) As used in this section, the terms "commodity broker," "commodity contract," "customer," "customer property," "member property," "net equity," and "security" have the meanings assigned such terms for the purposes of subchapter IV of chapter 7 of title 11 of the United States Code.

CHAPTER 9

Adjustment of Debts of a Municipality

SUBCHAPTER I

General Provisions

SECTION 901 (11 U.S.C. § 901)

§ 901. Applicability of other sections of this title.

(a) Sections 301, 344, 347(b), 349, 350(b), 361, 362, 364(c), 364(d), 364(e), 364(f), 365, 366, 501, 502, 503, 504, 506, 507(a)(1), 509, 510, 524(a)(1), 524(a)(2), 544, 545, 546, 547, 548, 549(a), 549(c), 549(d), 550, 551, 552, 553, 557, 1102, 1103, 1109, 1111(b), 1122, 1123(a)(1), 1123(a)(2), 1123(a)(3), 1123(a)(4), 1123(a)(5), 1123(b), 1124, 1125, 1126(a), 1126(b), 1126(c), 1126(e), 1126(f), 1126(g), 1127(d), 1128, 1129(a)(2), 1129(a)(3), 1129(a)(6), 1129(a)(8), 1129(a)(10), 1129(b)(1), 1129(b)(2)(A), 1129(b)(2)(B), 1142(b), 1143, 1144, and 1145 of this title apply in a case under this chapter.

(b) A term used in a section of this title made applicable in a case under this chapter by subsection (a) of this section or section 103(e) of this title has the meaning defined for such term for the purpose of such applicable section, unless such term is otherwise defined in section 902 of this title.

(c) A section made applicable in a case under this chapter by subsection (a) of this section that is operative if the business of the debtor is authorized to be operated is operative in a case under this chapter.

Legislative History

Section 901 makes applicable appropriate provisions of other chapters of proposed title 11. The general rule set out in section 103(e) is that only the provisions of chapters 1 and 9 apply in a chapter 9 case. Section

901 is the exception, and specifies other provisions that do apply. They are as follows:

§ 301. Voluntary cases. Application of this section makes clear, as under current chapter IX, that a municipal case can be commenced only by the municipality itself. There are no involuntary chapter 9 cases.

§ 344. Self-incrimination; immunity. Application of this section is of no substantive effect for the administration of the case, but merely provides that the general rules in part V of title 18 govern immunity.

§ 347(b). Unclaimed property. This provision currently appears in section 96(d) of chapter IX.

§ 349. Effect of dismissal. This section governs the effect of a dismissal of a chapter 9 case. It provides in substance that rights that existed before the case that were disturbed by the commencement of the case are reinstated. This section does not concern grounds for dismissal, which are found in section 926.

§ 361. Adequate protection. Section 361 provides the general standard for the protection of secured creditors whose property is used in a case under title 11. Its importance lies in its application to sections 362 and 364.

§ 362. Automatic stay. The automatic stay provisions of the general portions of the title are incorporated into chapter 9. There is an automatic stay provided in current Bankruptcy Act section 85(e). The thrust of section 362 is the same as that of section 85(e), but, of course, its application in chapter 9 is modernized and drafted to conform with the stay generally applicable under the bankruptcy code. An additional part of the automatic stay applicable only to municipal cases is included in section 922.

§§ 364(c), 364(d), 364(e). Obtaining credit. This section governs the borrowing of money by a municipality in reorganization. It is narrower than a comparable provision in current law, section 82(b)(2). The difference lies mainly in the removal under the bill of the authority of the court to supervise borrowing by the municipality in instances in which none of the special bankruptcy powers are involved. That is, if a municipality could borrow money outside of the bankruptcy court, then it should have the same authority in bankruptcy court, under the doctrine of Ashton v. Cameron Water District No. 1, 298 U.S. 513 (1936) and National League of Cities v. Usery, 426 U.S. 833 (1976). Only when the municipality needs special authority, such as subordination of existing liens, or special priority for the borrowed funds, will the court become involved in the authorization.

§ 365. Executory contracts and unexpired leases. The applicability of section 365 incorporates the general power of a bankruptcy court to authorize the assumption or rejection of executory contracts or unexpired leases found in other chapters of the title. This section is comparable to section 82(b)(1) of current law.

§ 366. Utility service. This section gives a municipality the same authority as any other debtor with respect to continuation of utility

service during the proceeding, provided adequate assurance of future payment is provided. No comparable explicit provision is found in current law, although the case law seems to support the same result.

§ 501. Filing of proofs of claims. This section permits filing of proofs of claims in a chapter 9 case. Note, however, that section 924 permits listing of creditors' claims, as under chapter 11 and under section 85(b) of chapter IX.

§ 502. Allowance of claims. This section applies the general allowance rules to chapter 9 cases. This is no change from current law.

§ 503. Administrative expenses. Administrative expenses as defined in section 503 will be paid in a chapter 9 case, as provided under section 89(1) of current law.

§ 504. Sharing of compensation. There is no comparable provision in current law. However, this provision applies generally throughout the proposed law, and will not affect the progress of the case, only the interrelations between attorneys and other professionals that participate in the case.

§ 506. Determination of secured status. Section 506 specifies that claims secured by a lien should be separated, to the extent provided, into secured and unsecured claims. It applies generally. Current law follows this result, though there is no explicit provision.

§ 507(1). Priorities. Paragraph (1) of section 507 requires that administrative expenses be paid first. This rule will apply in chapter 9 cases. It is presently found in section 89(1). The two other priorities presently found in section 89 have been deleted. The second, for claims arising within three months before the case is commenced, is deleted from the statute, but may be within the court's equitable power to award, under the case of Fosdick v. Schall, 99 U.S. 235 (1878). Leaving the provision to the courts permits greater flexibility, as under railroad cases, than an absolute three-month rule. The third priority under current law, for claims which are entitled to priority under the laws of the United States, is deleted because of the proposed amendment to section 3466 of the Revised Statutes contained in section 321(a) of title III of the bill, which previously has given the United States an absolute first priority in chapter X and section 77 cases. Because the priority rules are regularized and brought together in the bankruptcy laws by this bill, the need for incorporation of priorities elsewhere specified is eliminated.

§ 509. Claims of codebtors. This section provides for the treatment of sureties, guarantors, and codebtors. The general rule of postponement found in the other chapters will apply in chapter 9. This section adopts current law.

§ 510. Subordination of claims. This section permits the court to subordinate, on equitable grounds, any claim, and requires enforcement of contractual subordination agreements, and subordination of securities rescission claims. The section recognizes the inherent equitable power of the court under current law, and the practice followed with respect to contractual provisions.

§ 547. Preferences. Incorporation of section 547 will permit the debtor to recover preferences. This power will be used primarily when those who gave the preferences have been replaced by new municipal officers or when creditors coerced preferential payments. Unlike Bankruptcy Act § 85(h), the section does not permit the appointment of a trustee for the purpose of pursuing preferences. Moreover, this bill does not incorporate the other avoiding powers of a trustee for chapter 9, found in current section 85(h).

§ 550. Liability of transfers. Incorporation of this section is made necessary by the incorporation of the preference section, and permits recovery by the debtor from a transferee of an avoided preference.

§ 551. Automatic preservation of avoided transfer. Application of section 551 requires preservation of any avoided preference for the benefit of the estate.

§ 552. Postpetition effect of security interest. This section will govern the applicability after the commencement of the case of security interests granted by the debtor before the commencement of the case.

§ 553. Setoff. Under current law, certain setoff is stayed. Application of this section preserves that result, though the setoffs that are permitted under section 553 are better defined than under present law. Application of this section is necessary to stay the setoff and to provide the offsetting creditor with the protection to which he is entitled under present law.

§ 1122. Classification of claims. This section is derived from current section 88(b), and is substantially similar.

§ 1123(a)(1)–(4), (b). Contents of plan. The general provisions governing contents of a chapter 11 plan are made applicable here, with two exceptions relating to the rights of stockholders, which are not applicable in chapter 9 cases. This section expands current law by specifying the contents of a plan in some detail. Section 91 of current law speaks only in general terms. The substance of the two sections is substantially the same, however.

§ 1124. Impairment of claims. The confirmation standards adopted in chapter 9 are the same as those of chapter 11. This changes current chapter IX, which requires compliance with the fair and equitable rule. The greater flexibility of proposed chapter 11 is carried over into chapter 9, for there appears to be no reason why the confirmation standards for the two chapters should be different, or why the elimination of the fair and equitable rule from corporate reorganizations should not be followed in municipal debt adjustments. The current chapter IX rule is based on the confirmation rules of current chapter X. The change in the latter suggests a corresponding change in the former. Section 1124 is one part of the new confirmation standard. It defines impairment, for use in section 1129.

§ 1125. Postpetition disclosure and solicitation. The change in the confirmation standard necessitates a corresponding change in the disclosure requirements for solicitation of acceptances of a plan. Under current chapter IX, there is no disclosure requirement. Incorporation

of section 1125 will insure that creditors received adequate information before the year required to vote on a plan.

§ 1126(a), (b), (c), (e), (f), (g). Acceptance of plan. Section 1126 incorporates the current chapter IX acceptance requirement: two-thirds in amount and a majority in number, Bankruptcy Act § 92. Section 1125 permits exclusion of certain acceptances from the computation if the acceptances were obtained in bad faith or, unlike current law, if there is a conflict of interest motivating the acceptance.

§ 1127(d). Modification of plan. This section governs the change of a creditor's vote on the plan after a modification is proposed. It is derived from current section 92(e).

§ 1128. Hearing on confirmation. This section requires a hearing on the confirmation of the plan, and permits parties in interest to object. It is the same as Bankruptcy Act §§ 93 and 94(a), though the provision, comparable to section 206 of current chapter X, permitting a labor organization to appear and be heard on the economic soundness of the plan, has been deleted as more appropriate for the Rules.

§ 1129(a)(2), (3), (8), (b)(1), (2). Confirmation of plan. This section provides the boiler-plate language that the plan be proposed in good faith and that it comply with the provisions of the chapter, and also provides the financial standard for confirmation, which replaces the fair and equitable rule.

§ 1142(b). Execution of plan. Derived from Bankruptcy Act § 96(b), this section permits the court to order execution and delivery of instruments in order to execute the plan.

§ 1143. Distribution. This section is the same in substance as section 96(d), which requires presentment or delivery of securities within five years, and bars creditors that do not act within that time.

§ 1144. Revocation of order of confirmation. This section permits the court to revoke the order of confirmation and the discharge if the confirmation of the plan was procured by fraud. There is no comparable provision in current chapter IX.

[House Report No. 95–595, 95th Cong., 1st Sess. 394–397 (1977).]

Chapter 9 of the House amendment represents a compromise between chapter 9 of the House bill and 9 of the Senate amendment. In most respect this chapter follows current law with respect to the adjustment of debts of a municipality. Stylistic changes and minor substantive revisions have been made in order to conform this chapter with other new chapters of the bankruptcy code. There are few major differences between the House bill and the Senate amendment on this issue. Section 901 indicates the applicability of other sections of title 11 in cases under chapter 9. Included are sections providing for creditors' committees under sections 1102 and 1103.

[124 Cong. Rec. H 11,100 (Sept. 28, 1978); S 17,416 (Oct. 6, 1978).]

[Ed. Note: Section 1129(a)(6) was added to the list of sections made applicable in chapter 9 cases by the 1988 municipal bankruptcy amendments (Pub. L. No. 100-597).]

Section 3 makes section 1129(a)(6) of the Bankruptcy Code, which is applicable in chapter 11 cases, applicable in chapter 9 cases as well. Section 1129(a)(6) requires, as a condition to plan confirmation, that any government regulatory commission with post-confirmation jurisdiction over the rates charged by a debtor approve any rate change provided for in the plan or, alternatively, that any rate change provided for in the plan be conditioned on receiving the regulatory commission's approval. Since municipal utilities are subject to the rate regulation in some states, this requirement of section 1129(a)(6) is incorporated into chapter 9.

[*House Report No. 100-1011, 100th Cong., 2d Sess. 6 (1988).*]

Comment

See also, under Legislative History to section 926 the excerpt from the Senate Report.

Section 901 makes applicable to chapter 9 various other provisions of the Code. The House Report, *supra,* contains cross-references describing the contents of each of the provisions thus made applicable to chapter 9 cases. Note particularly that sections 1102 and 1103, providing for creditors committees, are made applicable in chapter 9 cases.

The application of section 301 in chapter 9 cases makes clear that a chapter 9 case can be commenced only by the debtor. As was the case in Chapter IX of the former Bankruptcy Act there is no provision for an involuntary chapter 9 case under the Code.

By incorporating section 1123 by reference, the provisions of chapter 11 relating to contents of a plan become applicable to a chapter 9 case with two exceptions relating to the rights of stockholders which are not applicable in a chapter 9 case.

For Bankruptcy Rules applicable in chapter 9 case, see **Comment** following the various other sections of the Code made applicable in chapter 9 by section 901.

1984 Amendments: A conforming change added section 557 to the list of sections of the Code applicable in a chapter 9 case. Section 557 provides procedures for the expedited determination of interests in grain stored in a grain storage facility owned by a debtor.

1988 Amendments: Section 1129(a)(6), added by the 1988 municipal bankruptcy amendments (Pub. L. No. 100-597), requires as a condition to confirmation of a plan that governmental regulatory commissions have approved rate changes or that rate changes are conditioned on such approval. Because municipal utilities are subject to rate regulation in some states, this requirement of section 1129(a)(6) is incorporated in chapter 9.

Case Annotations

Section 1109 is made applicable to chapter 9 cases by section 901 of the Code. Thus, although "party in interest" is not defined in section 1109(b) or otherwise in the Code, it has come to mean that an entity has a direct legal interest at issue in the case. *In re* City of Bridgeport, 25 C.B.C.2d 95 (D. Conn. 1991).

When a debtor files a petition for relief under chapter 9, such filing does not constitute an automatic order for relief. A creditors' committee may not be formed until a distinct order for relief has been entered by the court in accordance with section 921(d). *In re* Colorado Centre Metropolitan District, 23 C.B.C.2d 397 (B. Ct., D. Colo. 1990).

Since the bankruptcy court has no right to interfere with governmental or political operations of the debtor or to interfere with its property, except in the confirmation process, any use of the debtor's property by the debtor is authorized under this title. In the Matter of Sanitary & Improvement District No. 7 of Lancaster County, Nebraska, 20 C.B.C.2d 880 (B. Ct., D. Neb. 1989).

Section 1122 of the Code applies to a chapter 9 case by virtue of Code section 901. In the Matter of Sanitary and Improvement District 65 of Sarpy County, Nebraska, 16 C.B.C.2d 1477 (B. Ct., D. Neb. 1986).

References

4 *Collier on Bankruptcy* ch. 901 (Matthew Bender 15th ed.).

Amdursky, *The 1988 Municipal Bankruptcy Amendments: History, Purposes and Effects,* 22 Urb. Law. 1 (1990).

Comment, *In re Blackacre Power and Light, The Bankruptcy of a Public Utility,* 50 Alb. L. Rev. 641 (1987).

Greenberg, *Municipal Bankruptcy: Some Basic Aspects,* 10 Urban Law 266 (1978).

Leibowitz, *Municipal Bankruptcy Under the Bankruptcy Code,* N.Y.L.J. June 17, 1982.

Minkel, *Chapter 9 Bankruptcy: Now More Than a Curiosity for Bondholders,* N.Y.L.J. Sept. 29, 1983 at 21.

SECTION 902 (11 U.S.C. § 902)

§ 902. **Definitions for this chapter.** In this chapter—

(1) "property of the estate", when used in a section that is made applicable in a case under this chapter by section 103(e) or 901 of this title, means property of the debtor;

(2) "special revenues" means—

(A) receipts derived from the ownership, operation, or disposition of projects or systems of the debtor that are primarily used or intended to be used primarily to provide transportation, utility, or other services, including the proceeds of borrowings to finance the projects or systems;

(B) special excise taxes imposed on particular activities or transactions;

(C) incremental tax receipts from the benefited area in the case of tax-increment financing;

(D) other revenues or receipts derived from particular functions of the debtor, whether or not the debtor has other functions; or

(E) taxes specifically levied to finance one or more projects or systems, excluding receipts from general property, sales, or income taxes (other than tax-increment financing) levied to finance the general purposes of the debtor.

(3) "special tax payer" means record owner or holder of legal or equitable title to real property against which a special assessment or special tax has been levied the proceeds of which are the sole source of payment of an obligation issued by the debtor to defray the cost of an improvement relating to such real property;

(4) "special tax payer affected by the plan" means special tax payer with respect to whose real property the plan proposes to increase the proportion of special assessments or special taxes referred to in paragraph (2) of this section assessed against such real property; and

(5) "trustee", when used in a section that is made applicable in a case under this chapter by section 103(e) or 901 of this title, means debtor, except as provided in section 926 of this title.

Legislative History

There are only four definitions for use only in chapter 9. The first specifies that when the term "property of the estate" is used in a section in another chapter made applicable in chapter 9 cases, the term will mean "property of the debtor." Paragraphs (2) and (3) adopt the definition of "special taxpayer affected by the plan" that appears in current sections 81(10) and 81(11). Paragraphs (4) provides for "trustee" the same treatment as provided for "property of the estate," specifying that it means "debtor" when used in conjunction with chapter 9.

[*House Report No. 95-595, 95th Cong., 1st Sess. 397 (1977).*]

There are six definitions for use in chapter 9. Paragraph (1) defines what claims are included in a chapter 9 case and adopts the definition now found in section 81(1). All claims against the petitioner generally will be included, with one significant exception. Municipalities are authorized, under section 103(c) of the Internal Revenue Code of 1954, as amended, to issue tax-exempt industrial development revenue bonds to provide for the financing of certain projects for privately owned companies. The bonds are sold on the basis of the credit of the company on whose behalf they are issued, and the principal, interest, and premium, if any, are payable solely from payments made by the company to the trustee under the bond indenture and do not constitute claims on the tax revenues or other funds of the issuing municipalities. The municipality merely acts as the vehicle to enable the bonds to be issued on a tax-exempt basis. Claims that arise by virtue of these bonds are not among the claims defined by this paragraph and amounts owed by private companies to the holders of industrial development revenue bonds are not to be included among the assets of the municipality that would be affected by the plan. *See* Cong. Record, 94th Cong., 1st Sess. H.R. 12073 (statement by Mr. Don Edwards, floor manager of the bill in the House). Paragraph (2) defines the court which means the federal district court or federal district judge before which the case is pending. Paragraph (3) specifies that when the term "property of the estate" is used in a section in another chapter made applicable in chapter 9 cases, the term means "property of the debtor." Paragraphs (4) and (5) adopt the definition of "special taxpayer affected by the plan" that appears in current sections 81(10) and 81(11) of the Bankruptcy Act. Paragraph (6) provides that "trustee" means "debtor" when used in conjunction with chapter 9.

[*Senate Report No. 95-989, 95th Cong., 2d Sess. 109 (1978).*]

Section 902(2) of the Senate amendment is deleted since the bankruptcy court will have jurisdiction over all cases under chapter 9. The concept of a claim being materially and adversely affected reflected in section 902(1) of the Senate amendment has been deleted and replaced with the new concept of "impairment" set forth in section 1124 of the House amendment and incorporated by reference into chapter 9.

[*124 Cong. Rec. H 11,100 (Sept. 28, 1978); S 17,416 (Oct. 6, 1978).*]

[*Ed. Note:* The 1988 amendments (Pub. L. No. 100-597) added paragraph (2) to section 902 to provide a definition for special revenues in chapter 9.]

Five categories of special revenues are covered by the legislation. The first type, described in new subsection (2)(A), consists of receipts derived from the ownership or operation of a debtor's systems or projects used to provide transportation, utilities, or other services. It would include receipts from the operation of water, sewage, waste, or electric systems.

The second type, described in new subsection (2)(B), covers special excise taxes imposed on particular activities or transactions—such as an excise tax on hotel or motel rooms imposed by some municipalities or an excise tax on the sale of alcoholic beverages. A general sales tax, which is not imposed on particular activities or transactions, would not be a special revenue.

The third type, described in new subsection (2)(C), includes as special revenues incremental tax receipts from the benefited area in the case of tax-increment financing. For example, if a financed public improvement causes the property values around it to go up, the owners of this surrounding property may pay higher property taxes because of it. The amount of the increased property taxes attributable to the rise in property value resulting from the public improvement would be special revenues under subsection (2)(C). Although these types of receipts would be collected as part of the general tax levy, they are considered to be attributable to the financed public improvements, and so are not part of the pre-existing tax base of the community.

Examples of the fourth type of special revenues, described in new subsection (2)(D), those derived from particular functions of the debtor, include regulatory fees and stamp taxes imposed for the recording of deeds.

The fifth type of special revenues, described in new subsection (2)(E), includes taxes levied to finance a particular project. This does not include a general property, sales, or income tax, except as described in new subsection (2)(C). A tax levied to finance the construction of a stadium would be a special revenue under clause (2)(E).

[*House Report No. 100-1011, 100th Cong., 2d Sess. 6-7 (1988); Senate Report No. 100-506, 100th Cong., 2d Sess. 21 (1988).*]

Comment

Section 902 is derived from Section 81 of the former Bankruptcy Act.

The definitions of "property of the estate" and "trustee" in paragraphs (1) and (4) have no comparable definitions in former Chapter IX.

Paragraph (4), defining "trustee," is more a rule of construction than a definition. Whenever a non-chapter 9 section made applicable in chapter 9 uses the word "trustee," paragraph (4) requires substitution of the word "debtor." This definition is necessary because, with but one exception, there is no provision for a trustee in chapter 9.

1984 Amendments: The definition of "special tax payer" in paragraph (2) of section 902 was revised for clarification.

1988 Amendments: One of the purposes of revenue bonds is to ensure that if the asset financed fails, general taxpayer funds will not be used to repay the debt. The effect of section 552, which could result in general funds being used to repay revenue bondholders, would defeat this purpose. The amendments would eliminate the problem by making special revenues still subject to a postpetition lien in a chapter 9 case notwithstanding section 552(a).

Another potential problem in a chapter 9 case is that under section 547 coupled with section 552, payments to a holder of a revenue bond within 90 days prior to filing a chapter 9 petition might be deemed a preference. The amendments make section 547 inapplicable to a revenue bond, thus avoiding the potential preference problem.

A third potential problem involves the operation of section 1111(b) (incorporated into chapter 9 by section 901), which might convert special revenue bonds from bonds that have no recourse against general municipal treasury funds into bonds that do have recourse against the treasury. New section 927 ensures that nonrecourse revenue bonds cannot be converted under section 1111(b) into recourse, or general obligation debt.

References

4 *Collier on Bankruptcy* ch. 902 (Matthew Bender 15th ed.).

Greenberg, *Municipal Bankruptcy: Some Basic Aspects,* 10 Urban Law 266 (1978).

Leibowitz, *Municipal Bankruptcy Under the Bankruptcy Code,* N.Y.L.J. June 17, 1982.

Minkel, *Chapter 9 Bankruptcy: Now More Than a Curiosity for Bondholders,* N.Y.L.J. Sept. 29, 1983 at 21.

Sterling, Ankele and Norton, *Colorado Special Districts and Chapter 9 — Part I,* 20 Colo. Law. 2475 (1991).

SECTION 903 (11 U.S.C. § 903)

§ 903.   Reservation of State power to control municipalities.

This chapter does not limit or impair the power of a State to control, by legislation or otherwise, a municipality of or in such State in the exercise of the political or governmental powers of such municipality, including expenditures for such exercise, but—

> (1) a State law prescribing a method of composition of indebtedness of such municipality may not bind any creditor that does not consent to such composition; and

> (2) a judgment entered under such a law may not bind a creditor that does not consent to such composition.

Legislative History

Section 903 is derived, with stylistic changes, from Section 83 of current Chapter IX. It sets forth the primary authority of a State, through its constitution, laws, and other powers, over its municipalities. The proviso in section 83, prohibiting State composition procedures for municipalities, is deleted. In light of the recent Supreme Court case, National League of Cities v. Usery, 426 U.S. 833 (1976), maximum flexibility for the States in solving the debt problems of their municipalities is advisable. In addition, a general policy of the bill is to encourage work-outs short of bankruptcy court. In view of the potential severe dislocation entailed in a chapter 9 case, and the danger for too much federal court intervention in the affairs of a municipality, the deletion of the proviso recognizes the power of the States to assist municipal work-outs short of bankruptcy court.

[*House Report No. 95–595, 95th Cong., 1st Sess. 397–398 (1977).*]

Section 903 is derived, with stylistic changes, from Section 83 of current Chapter IX. It sets forth the primary authority of a State, through its constitution, laws, and other powers, over its municipalities. The proviso in section 83, prohibiting State composition procedures for municipalities, is retained. Deletion of the provision would "permit all States to enact their own versions of Chapter IX," *Municipal Insolvency,* 50 Am. Bankr. L.J. 55, 65, which would frustrate the constitutional mandate of uniform bankruptcy laws. *Constitution of the United States.* Art. I, Sec. 8.

This section provides that the municipality can consent to the court's orders in regard to use of its income or property. It is contemplated that such consent will be required by the court for the issuance of certificates of indebtedness under section 364(c). Such consent could extend to enforcement of the conditions attached to the certificates or the municipal services to be provided during the proceedings. [*Ed. Note:* The second paragraph of the Senate Report to section 903 refers to the subject matter of section 904 and should be read as a comment to that latter section.]

[*Senate Report No. 95–989, 95th Cong., 2d Sess. 110 (1978).*]

Section 903 of the House amendment represents a stylistic revision of section 903 of the Senate amendment. To the extent section 903 of the House bill would have changed present law, such section is rejected.

[*124 Cong. Rec. H 11,100 (Sept. 28, 1978); S 17,416 (Oct. 6, 1978).*]

Comment

Section 903 is derived from Section 83 of the former Bankruptcy Act.

The effect of section 903 is to remove any inference that the legislation accomplishes anything more than to provide a procedure under which municipalities may adjust their indebtedness. Nothing in chapter 9 indicates Congressional attempt to interfere with a state's control over its municipalities.

References

4 *Collier on Bankruptcy* ch. 903 (Matthew Bender 15th ed.).

Greenberg, *Municipal Bankruptcy: Some Basic Aspects,* 10 Urban Law 266 (1978).

Leibowitz, *Municipal Bankruptcy Under the Bankruptcy Code,* N.Y.L.J. June 17, 1982.

Minkel, *Chapter 9 Bankruptcy: Now More Than a Curiosity for Bondholders,* N.Y.L.J. Sept. 29, 1983 at 21.

Sterling, Ankele and Norton, *Colorado Special Districts and Chapter 9 — Part I,* 20 Colo. Law. 2475 (1991).

SECTION 904 (11 U.S.C. § 904)

§ 904. Limitation on jurisdiction and powers of court. Notwithstanding any power of the court, unless the debtor consents or the plan so provides, the court may not, by any stay, order, or decree, in the case or otherwise, interfere with—

(1) any of the political or governmental powers of the debtor;

(2) any of the property or revenues of the debtor; or

(3) the debtor's use or enjoyment of any income-producing property.

Legislative History

This section adopts the policy of section 82(c) of current law. The *Usery* case underlines the need for this limitation on the court's powers. The only change in this section from section 82(c) is to conform the section to the style and cross-references of H.R. 8200. This section makes clear that the court may not interfere with the choices a municipality makes as to what services and benefits it will provide to its inhabitants. [*Ed. Note:* For the citation of the *Usery* case *see* the excerpt from the House Report to section 903, *supra.*]

[*House Report No. 95–595, 95th Cong., 1st Sess. 398 (1977).*]

This section adopts the policy of section 82(c) of current law. The only change in this section from section 82(c) is to conform the section to the style and cross-references of S. 2266. [*Ed. Note: See* editor's note to Senate Report excerpt on section 903, *supra.*]

[*Senate Report No. 95–989, 95th Cong., 2d Sess. 110 (1978).*]

Comment

The limitation imposed on the court by section 904 is the concomitant of the limitation on the statute contained in section 903. While section 903 states that the statute is not to be construed so as to interfere with a state's control over its municipalities, section 904 limits the court in its interpretation and construction of the statute and in its administration of the municipal debt adjustment case.

Case Annotations

When a petitioner requests that an appellate court issue peremptory writs of mandamus and prohibition against a bankruptcy court ruling on the ground that the bankruptcy court had exceeded its jurisdiction by permitting an independent municipal authority to file for relief under chapter 9 without first obtaining state approval, the request for the writs should be denied if a rational and substantial legal argument can be made in support of the questioned jurisdictional ruling and if the bankruptcy court followed any clear dictate of law in exercising its powers. Pennbank v. Washabaugh, 673 F.2d 1301 (unpublished), 5 C.B.C.2d 869 (3d Cir. 1981).

Section 904(2) does not prohibit a court from allowing administrative expenses in a chapter 9 case. *In re* Castle Pines North Metropolitan District, 25 C.B.C.2d 187 (B. Ct., D. Colo. 1991).

The bankruptcy court may not interfere with political or governmental powers of a chapter 9 debtor, property or revenue of the debtor, or the debtor's use or enjoyment of income-producing property. In the Matter of Sanitary & Improvement District No. 7 of Lancaster County, Nebraska, 20 C.B.C.2d 880 (B. Ct., D. Neb. 1989).

References

4 *Collier on Bankruptcy* ch. 904 (Matthew Bender 15th ed.).

Chobot, *Preserving Liens Avoided in Bankruptcy—Limitations and Applications,* 62 Am. Bankr. L.J. 149 (1988).

Greenberg, *Municipal Bankruptcy: Some Basic Aspects,* 10 Urban Law 266 (1978).

Leibowitz, *Municipal Bankruptcy Under the Bankruptcy Code,* N.Y.L.J. June 17, 1982.

Minkel, *Chapter 9 Bankruptcy: Now More Than a Curiosity for Bondholders,* N.Y.L.J. Sept. 29, 1983 at 21.

Sterling, Ankele and Norton, *Colorado Special Districts and Chapter 9 — Part I,* 20 Colo. Law. 2475 (1991).

[SECTION 905. Designation of Judge.

Provision for the designation of the judge to conduct the case under chapter 9 contained in section 905 of the Senate bill is now found in section 921(b) which provides that the chief judge of the circuit embracing the district in which the case is commenced designates a *bankruptcy judge* to conduct the case in lieu of a district judge as under the former Bankruptcy Act.]

[SECTION 906. Eligibility For Relief.

Provisions relating to eligibility for relief, contained in section 906 of the Senate Bill are now located in section 109(c) of the Code.]

SUBCHAPTER II

Administration

SECTION 921 (11 U.S.C. § 921)

§ 921.   Petition and proceedings relating to petition.

(a) Notwithstanding sections 109(d) and 301 of this title, a case under this chapter concerning an unincorporated tax or special assessment district that does not have such district's own officials is commenced by the filing under section 301 of this title of a petition under this chapter by such district's governing authority or the board or body having authority to levy taxes or assessments to meet the obligations of such district.

(b) The chief judge of the court of appeals for the circuit embracing the district in which the case is commenced shall designate the bankruptcy judge to conduct the case.

(c) After any objection to the petition, the court, after notice and a hearing, may dismiss the petition if the debtor did not file the petition in good faith or if the petition does not meet the requirements of this title.

(d) If the petition is not dismissed under subsection (c) of this section, the court shall order relief under this chapter.

(e) The court may not, on account of an appeal from an order for relief, delay any proceeding under this chapter in the case in which the appeal is being taken; nor shall any court order a stay of such proceeding pending such appeal. The reversal on appeal of a finding of jurisdiction does not affect the validity of any debt incurred that is authorized by the court under section 364(c) or 364(d) of this title.

Legislative History

Subsection (a) is derived from section 85(a), second sentence, of current law. There is no substantive change in the law. The subsection permits a municipality that does not have its own officers to be moved into chapter 9 by the action of the body or board that has authority to levy taxes for the municipality.

[*House Report No. 95–595, 95th Cong., 1st Sess. 398 (1977).*]

Section 905 of the Senate amendment is incorporated as section 921(b) of the House amendment with the difference that the chief judge of the circuit embracing the district in which the case is commenced designates a bankruptcy judge to conduct the case in lieu of a district judge as under present law. It is intended that a municipality may commence a case in any district in which the municipality is located, as under present law.

[*124 Cong. Rec. S 17,416 (Oct. 6, 1978).*]

Subsection (c) permits the court to dismiss a petition not filed in good faith or not filed in compliance with the requirements of the chapter. This provision is the fourth sentence of section 85(a).

Subsection (d) directs the court to order relief on the petition if it did not dismiss the case under subsection (c).

Subsection (e) contains the fifth and sixth sentences of section 85(a).

[*House Report No. 95–595, 95th Cong., 1st Sess. 398 (1977).*]

[*Ed. Note:* As enacted, subsection (d) and (e) referred to in the House Report were inaccurately printed as (e) and (f).]

Comment

Subsection (a) of section 921 is derived from the first two sentences of Section 85 of the former Bankruptcy Act.

Subsection (b) effects a radical change from Section 82(d) of the Act in that the chief judge of the circuit designates a *bankruptcy judge* rather than a district judge to conduct the case.

Subsection (c) is derived in part from Section 85(a) of the Act which provided for the filing of an answer to the petition and that "upon the filing of such an answer the court may dismiss the petition after hearing on notice if the petitioner did not file the petition in good faith, or if the petition does not meet the requirements of this chapter."

Subsection (e) is derived from the fifth and sixth sentences of Section 85(a) of the Act.

Bankruptcy Rule 1002(b)(2) formerly required that an original and 5 copies of a chapter 9 petition be filed. The 1987 Amendments to the Bankruptcy Rules eliminated any reference to number of copies of the petition that are to be filed. The Advisory Committee Note to Rule 1002 states: "The number of copies of a petition that must be filed is a matter for local rule." Local rules, therefore, should be consulted as to the number of copies of the petition to be filed.

Bankruptcy Rule 1005 prescribes the contents of the caption to the petition.

Bankruptcy Rule 1006(a) provides that the petition be accompanied by the prescribed filing fee. Title 28 U.S.C. § 1930(a)(2) provides that the filing fee in a chapter 9 case shall be $300.

As to Bankruptcy Rules governing the filing of lists of creditors, see **Comment** to section 924. Although not required to file a list of creditors with the petition, the chapter 9 debtor is required by Bankruptcy Rule 1007(d) to file with the petition a list containing the name, address and claim of the creditors that hold the 20 largest unsecured claims.

1984 Amendments: Section 921 was variously amended to make stylistic changes and to correct an error in numbering the subsections.

The State of Connecticut and the Bridgeport Financial Review Board objected under section 921 to the filing of the debtor's petition. In determining whether a municipality is insolvent for purposes of chapter 9 eligibility, a court should apply a prospective analysis with respect to the debtor's ability to pay its debts and examine the debtor's cash flow, not the debtor's projected budget deficits. *In re* The City of Bridgeport, 25 C.B.C.2d 269 (D. Conn. 1991). *See also In re* City of Bridgeport, 25 C.B.C.2d 140 (B. Ct., D. Conn. 1991).

References

4 *Collier on Bankruptcy* ch. 921 (Matthew Bender 15th ed.).

Leibowitz, *Municipal Bankruptcy Under the Code,* N.Y.L.J. June 17, 1982.

Minkel, *Chapter 9 Bankruptcy: Now More Than a Curiosity for Bondholders,* N.Y.L.J. Sept. 29, 1983 at 21.

SECTION 922 (11 U.S.C. § 922)

§ 922. Automatic stay of enforcement of claims against the debtor.

(a) A petition filed under this chapter operates as a stay, in addition to the stay provided by section 362 of this title, applicable to all entities, of—

(1) the commencement or continuation, including the issuance or employment of process, of a judicial, administrative, or other action or proceeding against an officer or inhabitant of the debtor that seeks to enforce a claim against the debtor; and

(2) the enforcement of a lien on or arising out of taxes or assessments owed to the debtor.

(b) Subsections (c), (d), (e), (f), and (g) of section 362 of this title apply to a stay under subsection (a) of this section the same as such subsections apply to a stay under section 362(a) of this title.

(c) If the debtor provides, under section 362, 364, or 922 of this title, adequate protection of the interest of the holder of a claim secured by a lien on property of the debtor and if, notwithstanding such protection such creditor has a claim arising from the stay of action against such property under section 362 or 922 of this title or from the granting of a lien under section 364(d) of this title, then such claim shall be allowable as an administrative expense under section 503(b) of this title.

(d) Notwithstanding section 362 of this title and subsection (a) of this section, a petition filed under this chapter does not operate as a stay of application of pledged special revenues in a manner consistent with section 927 of this title to payment of indebtedness secured by such revenues.

Bankruptcy Rule References: 4001 and 7062

Legislative History

The automatic stay provided under section 362 of title 11 is incomplete for a municipality, because there is the possibility of action by a creditor against an officer or inhabitant of the municipality to collect taxes due the municipality. Section 85(e)(1) of current chapter IX stays such actions. Section 922 carries over that protection into the proposed chapter 9.

Subsection (b) applies the provisions for relief from the stay that apply generally in section 362 to the stay under section 922.

[*House Report No. 95–595, 95th Cong., 1st Sess. 398 (1977).*]

New subsection (c) gives administrative claim status to a secured creditor who has been given adequate protection to protect its interest, but who suffers loss anyway because of the application of the stay or the granting of a lien under Bankruptcy Code 364(d). This is justified because the loss to the creditor is not due to the creditor's action, but rather to an attempt to benefit the debtor. . . .

[N]ew subsection (d) to section 922 states that the automatic stay of Bankruptcy Code section 362 does not operate to stay paying pledged revenues, consistent with new section 927 of the Bankruptcy Code, to the revenue bondholders holding liens on such revenues.

[*House Report No. 100-1011, 100th Cong., 2d Sess. 7 (1988)*]

[T]he automatic stay that becomes effective against creditors of a municipality is made inapplicable to the payment of principal and interest on municipal bonds paid from pledged revenues. In this context, "pledged revenues" includes funds in the possession of the bond trustee as well as other pledged revenues.

[*Senate Report No. 100-506, 100th Cong., 2d Sess. 13 (1988).*]

Comment

Section 901(a) makes the automatic stay provisions of section 362 applicable in a chapter 9 case. But the stay of section 362 is incomplete for a municipality and additional protection is required. Section 922 carries over the stay provisions of Section 85(e)(1) of the former Bankruptcy Act.

The additional stay of section 922(a) stays actions directed against entities other than the municipality itself. The stay is of actions against an officer or inhabitant of the debtor or against enforcement of liens on or arising out of taxes or assessments owed to the debtor.

Section 901 makes section 362, which sets forth provisions regarding the automatic stay that arises on the filing of a petition, applicable in a chapter 9 case. Bankruptcy Rule 4001, implementing section 362, deals with relief from the automatic stay. The rule, as well as section 362, is applicable in chapter 9 cases. The proper procedure for obtaining relief from the automatic stay is by motion under Rule 9014. See **Comment** to section 362 for particulars regarding Rule 4001.

1984 Amendments: Stylistic and clarification changes were made in section 922.

1988 Amendments: Subsection (c) gives administrative claim status to a secured creditor who has been given adequate protection to protect its interest, but nevertheless suffers loss. Subsection (d) provides that the automatic stay of section 362 does not operate to stay payment of pledged revenues.

References

4 *Collier on Bankruptcy* ch. 922 (Matthew Bender 15th ed.).

Minkel, *Chapter 9 Bankruptcy: Now More Than a Curiosity for Bondholders,* N.Y.L.J. Sept. 29, 1983 at 21.

SECTION 923 (11 U.S.C. § 923)

§ 923. **Notice.** There shall be given notice of the commencement of a case under this chapter, notice of an order for relief under this chapter, and notice of the dismissal of a case under this chapter. Such notice shall also be published at least once a week for three successive weeks in at least one newspaper of general circulation published within the district in which the case is commenced, and in such other newspaper having a general circulation among bond dealers and bondholders as the court designates.

Bankruptcy Rule Reference: 2002

Legislative History

The notice provisions in section 923 are significantly more sparse than those provided under section 85(d) of chapter IX. The exact contours of the notice to be given under chapter 9 are left to the Rules. Because the Rules deal with notice in a municipal case (Rule 9–14), and because section 405(d) of title IV of the bill continues those Rules in effect to the extent not inconsistent with the bill, the notice provisions of current law and Rules would continue to apply.

[*House Report No. 95–595, 95th Cong., 1st Sess. 398 (1977).*]

Section 923 of the House amendment represents a compromise with respect to the notice provisions contained in comparable provisions of the House bill and Senate amendment. As a general matter, title 11 leaves most procedural issues to be determined by the Rules of Bankruptcy Procedure. Section 923 of the House amendment contains certain important aspects of procedure that have been retained from present law. It is anticipated that the Rules of Bankruptcy Procedure will adopt rules similar to the present rules for chapter IX of the Bankruptcy Act.

[*124 Cong. Rec. H 11,100 (Sept. 28, 1978); S 17,416 (Oct. 6, 1978).*]

Comment

Section 923 of the Code, relating to notice, is considerably more sparse than Section 85(d) of the former Bankruptcy Act, leaving the details to be provided by Rules of Bankruptcy Procedure.

Bankruptcy Rule 2002 deals with notices to creditors, equity security holders and the United States. Subdivision (a) requires 20 days notice by mail of the significant events in a case under the Code. Subdivision (b) requires 25 days notice for certain events in a chapter 9, 11, 12 or 13 case. Generally, Rule 9006 permits reduction of time periods. Since notice by mail is complete on mailing, the requirement as to notice is satisfied if the notices are deposited in the mail at least 20 days before the event.

Subdivision (c) of Rule 2002 prescribes the contents of notices; subdivisions (d) and (e) are inapplicable in a chapter 9 case; subdivision (f) provides for other notices, as to which no specific time period applies, including the order for relief, dismissal or conversion of the case, time allowed for filing claims, and the entry of the order confirming the chapter 9 plan; subdivision (g) directs that notices be mailed to the creditors' addresses as they or their authorized agent direct in a filed request, otherwise to the address shown in the list of creditors; subdivision (h) is inapplicable in a chapter 9 case.

Subdivision (i) permits notices required under clauses (2), (3) and (7) of subdivision (a) to be mailed only to the committee or its authorized agents, and to creditors and equity security holders who file requests that they receive all notices. In any event, all notices required by the rule must be sent to all elected or appointed committees appointed under the Code; subdivision (j) prescribes the method of giving notice when the papers in the case disclose a debt to the United States other than for taxes.

Subdivision (k), relating to notices to the United States trustee, specifies that it is inapplicable in chapter 9 cases.

Subdivision (l) authorizes notices by publication if the court finds that notice by mail is impracticable or that it is desirable to supplement mailed notice.

Subdivision (m) permits the court to enter orders designating the matters in which, the persons to whom and the form and manner in which notice is to be sent except where otherwise provided. Subdivision (n) requires that the caption of every notice given under the rule comply with Rule 1005.

References

4 *Collier on Bankruptcy* ch. 923 (Matthew Bender 15th ed.).

Minkel, *Chapter 9 Bankruptcy: Now More Than a Curiosity for Bondholders,* N.Y.L.J. Sept. 29, 1983 at 21.

SECTION 924 (11 U.S.C. § 924)

§ 924. List of creditors. The debtor shall file a list of creditors.

Bankruptcy Rule References: 1007 and 1009

Legislative History

This section directs the debtor to file a list of creditors with the court. A comparable provision is presently contained in section 85(b) of chapter IX. The Rules, in Rule 9–7, copy the provisions of section 85(b), with additional matter. As noted above, section 405(d) of title IV will continue those Rules in effect. Because the form, time of filing, and nature of the list, are procedural matters that may call for some flexibility, those details have been left to the Rules.

[*House Report No. 95–595, 95th Cong., 1st Sess. 399 (1977).*]

This section adopts the provision presently contained in section 85(b) of Chapter IX. A list of creditors, as complete and accurate as practicable, must be filed with the court.

[Senate Report No. 95–989, 95th Cong., 2d Sess. 111 (1978).]

Section 924 of the House amendment is derived from section 924 of the House bill with the location of the filing of the list of creditors to be determined by the rules of bankruptcy procedure. The detailed requirements of section 724 of the Senate bill are anticipated to be incorporated in the rules of bankruptcy procedure. *[Ed. Note:* The reference to section 724 in the second sentence should be to section 924.]

[124 Cong. Rec. H 11,100 (Sept. 28, 1978); S 17,416 (Oct. 6, 1978).]

Comment

Bankruptcy Rule 1007(a) requires the debtor in a voluntary case to file a list of creditors with the petition unless the petition is accompanied by schedules of liabilities. But subdivision (e) of the rule provides that in a chapter 9 case the list required by subdivision (a) shall be filed by the debtor within such time as the court shall fix. Subdivision (e) also provides that:

> If a proposed plan requires a revision of assessments so that the proportion of special assessments or special taxes to be assessed against some real property will be different from the proportion in effect at the date the petition is filed, the debtor shall also file with the court a list showing the name and address of each known holder of title, legal or equitable, to real property adversely affected. On motion for cause shown, the court may modify the requirements of this subdivision and subdivision (a) of this rule.

Bankruptcy Rule 1007(d) provides that a debtor in a chapter 9 case shall file with the petition a list containing the name, address and claim of the creditors that hold the 20 largest unsecured claims as prescribed by Official Form No. 4. Subdivision (f) which formerly prescribed the number of copies of the list to be filed was abrogated by the 1987 Amendments to the Bankruptcy Rules. The Advisory Committee Note to Rule 1007(f) states: "The number of copies of the documents required by this rule will be determined by local rule."

Bankruptcy Rule 1008 requires the list, schedule and statement to be verified or contain an unsworn declaration as provided in 28 U.S.C. § 1746.

Bankruptcy Rule 1009 provides that the list, schedule and statement may be amended by the debtor as a matter of course at any time before the case is closed.

References

4 *Collier on Bankruptcy* ch. 924 (Matthew Bender 15th ed.).

Minkel, *Chapter 9 Bankruptcy: Now More Than a Curiosity for Bondholders,* N.Y.L.J. Sept. 29, 1983 at 21.

SECTION 925 (11 U.S.C. § 925)

§ 925.　**Effect of list of claims.** A proof of claim is deemed filed
under section 501 of this title for any claim that appears in the
list filed under section 924 of this title, except a claim that is
listed as disputed, contingent, or unliquidated.

Bankruptcy Rule Reference: 3003

Legislative History

Section 925 follows the policy contained in section 88(a), though
certain details are left to the Rules. The language of section 925 is the
same as that of proposed 11 U.S.C. § 1111, which applies in chapter
11 cases. The list of creditors filed under section 924 is given weight
as prima facie evidence of the claims listed (except claims that are listed
as disputed, contingent, or unliquidated), which are deemed filed under
section 501, obviating the need for listed creditors to file proofs of claim.

[*House Report No. 95–595, 95th Cong., 1st Sess. 399 (1977); Senate Report
No. 95–989, 95th Cong., 2d Sess. 111 (1978).*]

Section 925 of the Senate amendment regarding venue and fees has
been deleted.

[*124 Cong. Rec. H 11,100 (Sept. 28, 1978); S 17,416 (Oct. 6, 1978).*]

Comment

Section 925 follows the policy of Section 88(a) of the former Bankruptcy Act but leaves details to the Rules.

Bankruptcy Rule 3003(b) (made applicable to chapter 9 and 11 cases
by subdivision (a) thereof) read together with section 925, provides that
the schedule of liabilities filed by the debtor constitutes prima facie
evidence of the validity and amount of the claims of creditors whose
claims are not scheduled as disputed, contingent, or unliquidated.
Unless required to do so under subdivision (c)(2) of the rule, it is not
necessary for a creditor to file a proof of claim.

Subdivision (c)(1) of the Rule permits any creditor or indenture
trustee to file a proof of claim within the time fixed by the court under
subdivision (c)(3).

Subdivision (c)(2) of the Rule requires a creditor whose claim is not
scheduled or is scheduled as disputed, contingent or unliquidated to file
a proof of claim within the time fixed by the court as provided in
subdivision (c)(3), and upon failure to do so, such creditor shall not be
treated as a creditor for voting and distribution.

Subdivision (c)(3) of the Rule provides that the court shall fix the time
within which proofs of claim may be filed, and authorizes the court to
extend such time. Paragraph (c)(3) was amended in 1991 to permit the

late filing of claims by infants or incompetent persons under the same circumstances that permit late filings in cases under chapters 7, 12 and 13. The amendment also provides sufficient time to file a claim arising from postpetition judgment for the recovery of money or property or the avoidance of a lien, or upon rejection of an executory contract or a claim arising unexpired lease.

Subdivision (c)(4) of the Rule provides that a proof of claim executed and filed in accordance with subdivision (c) shall supersede any scheduling (listing) of that claim.

Subdivision (c)(5) of the Rule provides that an indenture trustee may file a claim on behalf of all known or unknown securities issued pursuant to the trust instrument.

Bankruptcy Rule 3006 permits withdrawal of a claim or the acceptance or rejection of a plan. A claim may be withdrawn as of right. If after the claim is filed, an objection is filed thereto, or a complaint is filed against the creditor in an adversary proceeding, or the creditor has accepted or rejected the plan or otherwise participated significantly in the case, such creditor may not withdraw except on order after hearing on notice to the debtor and any elected or appointed creditors' committee selected under the Code. The order shall contain such terms and conditions as the court deems proper. Unless otherwise ordered, an authorized withdrawal of a claim constitutes withdrawal of any related acceptance or rejection of a plan.

Bankruptcy Rule 3007 relates to objections to claims and Bankruptcy Rule 3008 deals with reconsideration of an order allowing or disallowing a claim.

Bankruptcy Rule 2019 deals with the representation of more than one creditor in chapter 9 cases. Every entity or committee representing more than one creditor must file a verified statement with the clerk setting forth the details regarding the claims as specified in subdivision (a) of the rule. Subdivision (b) of the rule sets forth the consequences of failure to comply with the provisions of subdivision (a).

References

4 *Collier on Bankruptcy* ch. 925 (Matthew Bender 15th ed.).

Minkel, *Chapter 9 Bankruptcy: Now More Than a Curiosity for Bondholders,* N.Y.L.J. Sept. 29, 1983 at 21.

SECTION 926 (11 U.S.C. § 926)

§ 926. Avoiding powers.

(a) If the debtor refuses to pursue a cause of action under section 544, 545, 547, 548, 549(a), or 550 of this title, then on request of a creditor, the court may appoint a trustee to pursue such cause of action.

(b) A transfer of property of the debtor to or for the benefit of any holder of a bond or note, on account of such bond or note, may not be avoided under section 547 of this title.

Legislative History

This section adopts current section 85(h) which provides for a trustee to be appointed for the purpose of pursuing an action under an avoiding power, if the debtor refuses to do so. This section is necessary because a municipality might, by reason of political pressure or desire for future good relations with a particular creditor or class of creditors, make payments to such creditors in the days preceding the petition to the detriment of all other creditors. No change in the elected officials of such a city would automatically occur upon filing of the petition, and it might be very awkward for those same officials to turn around and demand the return of the payments following the filing of the petition. Hence, the need for a trustee for such purpose.

The general avoiding powers are incorporated by reference in section 901 and are broader than under current law. Preferences, fraudulent conveyances, and other kinds of transfers will thus be voidable.

Incorporated by reference also is the power to accept or reject executory contracts and leases (section 365). Within the definition of executory contracts are collective bargaining agreements between the city and its employees. Such contracts may be rejected despite contrary State laws. Courts should readily allow the rejection of such contracts where they are burdensome, the rejection will aid in the municipality's reorganization and in consideration of the equities of each case. On the last point, "[e]quities in favor of the city in chapter 9 will be far more compelling than the equities in favor of the employer in chapter 11. Onerous employment obligations may prevent a city from balancing its budget for some time. The prospect of an unbalanced budget may preclude judicial confirmation of the plan. Unless a city can reject its labor contracts, lack of funds may force cutbacks in police, fire, sanitation, and welfare services, imposing hardships on many citizens. In addition, because cities in the past have often seemed immune to the constraint of "profitability" faced by private businesses, their wage contracts may be relatively more onerous than those in the private sector." *Executory Contracts and Municipal Bankruptcy,* 85 Yale L.J. 957, 965 (1976) (footnote omitted). Rejection of the contracts may require the municipalities to renegotiate such contracts by state collective bargaining laws. It is intended that the power to reject collective bargaining agreements will pre-empt state termination provisions, but not state collective bargaining laws. Thus, a city would not be required to maintain existing employment terms during the renegotiation period. [*Ed. Note:* The Senate Report refers to section 928 of the Senate Bill which is section 926 of the Code.]

[*Senate Report No. 95–989, 95th Cong., 2d Sess. 111 (1978).*]

Section 926 of the House amendment is derived from section 928 of the Senate bill. The provision enables creditors to request the court to appoint a trustee to pursue avoiding powers if the debtor refuses to exercise those powers. Section 901 of the House amendment makes a corresponding change to incorporate avoiding powers included in the Senate amendment, but excluded from the House bill.

[*124 Cong. Rec. H 11,100 (Sept. 28, 1978); S 17,416 (Oct. 6, 1978).*]

[*Ed. Note:* The 1988 municipal bankruptcy amendments (Pub. L. No. 100-597) added subsection (b) to section 926.]

[Subsection (b)] amends Bankruptcy Code section 926 to make the preference provisions of section 547 inapplicable to note payments, bond payments, and defeasances in a chapter 9 bankruptcy.

[*House Report No. 100-1011, 100th Cong., 2d Sess. 7 (1988).*]

In the case of a municipality it is not considered necessary to legislate broadly against preferential treatment of bond and noteholders. There is not likely to be a high incidence of preferential treatment of these creditors and, where there is an actual intent to hinder, delay or defraud other creditors, Section 548 would apply. The existing law, under which section 547 applies to municipal bonds and notes, creates unforeseen problems and uncertainties. For example, most municipal revenue bonds involve a pledge of special revenues but do not include a mortgage or other security interest on any revenue source. The application of Section 547 to them could cause payments of such bonds in the normal course to be treated as preferences since the lien on revenues received during the preference period could be treated as coming into existence during the preference period and not before. In addition, the deposit of money or securities in escrow to "defease" in the lien of a prior bond indenture, which is a common occurrence, could also be treated as a preference notwithstanding the absence of any preferential intent or actual damage to other creditors. This section is intended to allow municipalities and their holders of notes and bonds to have the same rights under state law and constitutional provisions as to transfers and benefits conferred prior to the institution of a Chapter 9 case.

[*Senate Report No. 100-506, 100th Cong., 2d Sess. 22 (1988).*]

Comment

Section 926 is derived from Section 85(h) of the former Bankruptcy Act.

The provision for appointment of a trustee to pursue a cause of action under section 544, 545, 547, 548, 549(a) or 550 if the debtor refuses to pursue such cause of action is the only exception to section 902(4) which provides that there shall be no trustee in a chapter 9 case. The appointment may not be made by the court *sua sponte,* but requires a motion by a creditor. (*But see* section 105(a).) The provision is necessary because a debtor may be reluctant to bring an action against one of its creditors during the course of a chapter 9 case.

Except for the trustee appointed pursuant to section 926, the word "trustee" in any section of the Code that is made applicable to a chapter 9 case by section 901 means the debtor.

Sections 321–326 of the Code relating to eligibility, qualification, role, capacity, removal and limitation of compensation of a trustee are not made applicable in a chapter 9 case by section 901. Nor does section 901 make applicable to chapter 9 cases section 707 relating to appointment of an interim trustee, section 702 relating to election of a trustee, or section 1104 providing for appointment of a chapter 11 trustee.

1988 Amendments: Troubled municipalities which desperately need additional financing may experience the reluctance of the market to purchase their revenue bond securities because of the possibility that under the Bankruptcy Code, a refunding issue or payment of pledged revenues within the 90-day period might be deemed to be a preference under section 547. Subsection (b) addresses this issue.

It is unlikely that a chapter 9 debtor would prefer some bondholders over others. Nevertheless, the ability of municipalities to obtain future financing will be enhanced if bond or note payments made in good faith during the period prior to bankruptcy cannot be avoided postpetition as a preference. A fraudulent transfer to noteholders or bondholders can still be avoided because of the applicability of section 548 to chapter 9 cases.

References

4 *Collier on Bankruptcy* ch. 926 (Matthew Bender 15th ed.).

Gabriel, *Louisiana Chapter Nine (Part Two): Priorities and Proceeds,* 35 Loy. L. Rev. 1087 (1990).

Minkel, *Chapter 9 Bankruptcy: Now More Than a Curiosity for Bondholders,* N.Y.L.J. Sept. 29, 1983 at 21.

SECTION 927 (11 U.S.C. § 927)

§ 927. Limitation on recourse.

The holder of a claim payable solely from special revenues of the debtor under applicable nonbankruptcy law shall not be treated as having recourse against the debtor on account of such claim pursuant to section 1111(b) of this title.

Legislative History

[*Ed. Note:* The 1988 municipal bankruptcy amendments (Pub. L. No. 100-597) redesignated section 927 as section 930, and inserted the following three sections: 927, 928 and 929.]

[N]ew section 927 [was added] to chapter 9 to ensure that nonrecourse revenue bonds cannot be converted, under section 1111(b) of the Bankruptcy Code, into recourse, or general obligation debt.

[*House Report No. 100-1011, 100th Cong., 2d Sess. 7 (1988).*]

Section 1111(b) provides that in some circumstances non-recourse debt may be treated as recourse debt. Many municipal obligations are, by reason of constitutional, statutory or charter provisions, payable solely from special revenues and not the full faith and credit of the municipality. This amendment leaves these legal and contractual limitations intact without otherwise altering the provisions with respect to non-recourse financing. Thus, this section avoids the potential conversion of revenue bonds into General Obligation bonds under Section 1111(b).

[*Senate Report No. 100-506, 100th Cong., 2d Sess. 22 (1988).*]

Comment

1988 Amendments: Permitting a revenue bond to be converted into a general obligation bond, in addition to hindering the prospects for troubled municipalities to obtain future financing because of lender concerns over loss of lien status, may violate some state constitutions and statutes, in states where general obligation bonds can be issued constitutionally only with the approval of the electorate, or in states with statutes setting forth the general debt limit (towards which revenue bonds do not count). Section 927 leaves the legal and contractual limitations of revenue bonds and state law intact without otherwise altering Bankruptcy Code provisions with respect to nonrecourse financing.

References

4 *Collier on Bankruptcy* ch. 927 (Matthew Bender 15th ed.).

SECTION 928 (11 U.S.C. § 928)

§ 928. Post petition effect of security interest.

(a) Notwithstanding section 552(a) of this title and subject to subsection (b) of this section, special revenues acquired by the debtor after the commencement of the case shall remain subject to any lien resulting from any security agreement entered into by the debtor before the commencement of the case.

(b) Any such lien on special revenues, other than municipal betterment assessments, derived from a project or system shall be subject to the necessary operating expenses of such project or system, as the case may be.

Legislative History

[*Ed. Note: The 1988 municipal bankruptcy amendments (Pub. L. No. 100-597) added section 928 to the Bankruptcy Code.*]

New subsection (a) states that a lien on special revenues acquired by the debtor after the commencement of the case cannot be avoided under Bankruptcy Code section 552(a); the lien is still valid post-petition. Without new subsection (a), the risk exists that a lien on special revenues could be avoided under Bankruptcy Code section 552(a), effectively turning the revenue bond into a general obligation bond.. . . By eliminating this risk, [subsection (a)] should make it easier for troubled municipalities to obtain needed financing of public projects.

* * *

Subsection 928(b) sets forth a minimum standard for paying operating expenses ahead of debt service when revenues are pledged. It is not intended to displace any broader standard contained in the terms of the pledge or applicable nonbankruptcy law.

[*House Report No. 100-1011, 100th Cong., 2d Sess. 7-8 (1988).*]

Comment

1988 Amendments: Subsection (a) renders section 552 (a) inapplicable to special revenue bonds. Thus, even though special revenues are received after a chapter 9 petition is filed and is subject to a security interest (the bonds) as after-acquired property, the security interest in the revenues remains valid and enforceable. Subsection (b) ensures that in the case of project financing (such as financing construction of an electric generating plant by debt secured by a lien on revenues generated by sale of power from the plant) or system financing (such as financing improvements to a local electric distribution system by debt secured by a lien on revenues of the entire system), the lien on special revenues will be subordinate to the necessary operating expenses of the project or system. This is important to keep the project or system in condition to generate the necessary revenues and provide residents with the service intended.

References

4 *Collier on Bankruptcy* ch. 928 (Matthew Bender 15th ed.).

SECTION 929 (11 U.S.C. § 929)

§ 929. Municipal leases.

A lease to a municipality shall not be treated as an executory contract or unexpired lease for the purposes of section 365 or 502(b)(6) of this title solely by reason of its being subject to termination in the event the debtor fails to appropriate rent.

Legislative History

[*Ed. Note: The 1988 municipal bankruptcy amendments (Pub. L. No. 100-597) added section 929 to the Bankruptcy Code.*]

[N]ew section 929 bring[s] treatment of municipal leases in bankruptcy into conformity with how such leases are treated and used in the world of municipal finance. New section 929 says that a lease to a municipality shall not be treated as an executory contract or unexpired lease subject to assumption or rejection under section 365, or that could give rise to a damage claim limited by section 502(b)(2)(6), just because it is subject to termination in the event the debtor fails to appropriate rent.

[*House Report 100-1011, 100th Cong., 2d Sess. 8 (1988).*]

Comment

1988 Amendments: For reasons unique to municipalities, many financial leases are required to be subject to appropriation of the rent. They are generally marketed as debt obligations and treated as such for tax purposes. To be consistent, section 929 treats municipal leases as such for bankruptcy purposes.

References

4 *Collier on Bankruptcy* ch. 929 (Matthew Bender 15th ed.).

SECTION 930 (11 U.S.C. § 930)

§ 930. Dismissal.

(a) After notice and a hearing, the court may dismiss a case under this chapter for cause, including—

(1) want of prosecution;

(2) unreasonable delay by the debtor that is prejudicial to creditors;

(3) failure to propose a plan within the time fixed under section 941 of this title;

(4) if a plan is not accepted within any time fixed by the court;

(5) denial of confirmation of a plan under section 943(b) of this title and denial of additional time for filing another plan or a modification of a plan; or

(6) if the court has retained jurisdiction after confirmation of a plan—

(A) material default by the debtor with respect to a term of such plan; or

(B) termination of such plan by reason of the occurrence of a condition specified in such plan.

(b) The court shall dismiss a case under this chapter if confirmation of a plan under this chapter is refused.

Bankruptcy Rule Reference: 1017

Legislative History

Section 926 generally conforms to section 98(a) of current law. Stylistic changes have been made to conform the language with that used in chapter 11, section 1112. The section permits dismissal by the court for unreasonable delay by the debtor that is prejudicial to creditors, failure to propose a plan, failure of confirmation of a plan, or material default by the debtor under a confirmed plan. The only significant change from current law lies in the second ground. Currently, section 98(a)(2) provides for dismissal if a proposed plan is not accepted, and section 98(b) *requires* dismissal if an accepted plan is not confirmed. In order to provide greater flexibility to the court, the debtor, and creditors, the bill allows the court to permit the debtor to propose another plan if the first plan is not confirmed. In that event, the debtor need not, as under current law, commence the case all over again. This could provide savings in time and administrative expenses if a plan is denied confirmation. [*Ed. Note:* The House Report refers to section 927 as enacted. Section 927 was subsequently redesignated section 930 by Pub. L. No. 100-597.]

[*House Report No. 95–595, 95th Cong., 1st Sess. 399 (1977).*]

Section 927 conforms to section 98 of current law. The Section permits dismissal by the court for unreasonable delay by the debtor, failure to propose a plan, failure of acceptance of a plan, or default by the debtor under a conformed plan. Mandatory dismissal is required if confirmation is refused. [*Ed. Note:* Section 927 was redesignated section 930 by Pub. L. No. 100-597.]

[*Senate Report No. 95–989, 95th Cong., 2d Sess. 111 (1978).*]

Section 927(b) of the House amendment is derived from section 927(b) of the Senate bill. The provision requires mandatory dismissal if confirmation of a plan is refused. [*Ed. Note:* Section 927(b) was redesignated section 930(b) by Pub. L. No. 100-597.]

[*124 Cong. Rec. H 11,100 (Sept. 28, 1978).*]

Comment

Section 930 is derived from Section 98(a) of the former Bankruptcy Act.

Section 930(a) provides for permissive dismissal, *i.e.,* it specifies grounds on which the court *may* but is not required to dismiss a chapter 9 case. The general ground is "for cause." The list is not exhaustive. The court retains the general equitable power to dismiss for such cause as it determines, in the sound exercise of its discretion, warrants dismissal.

Bankruptcy Rule 1017 deals with dismissal of a case and provides that a case shall not be dismissed before a hearing on notice as provided in Rule 2002(a). Unless a list of creditors and their addresses was previously filed, the debtor must file such a list within the time fixed by the court, and upon the debtor's failure to do so, the court may order the preparation and filing of the list by the debtor or other person. Subdivisions (b) and (c) of Rule 1017 are not applicable in a chapter 9 case. Subdivision (d) provides that a proceeding to dismiss is governed by Rule 9014, *i.e.,* is a contested matter initiated by motion.

1984 Amendments: Subsection (b) of section 930 was clarified by the insertion of the words "of a plan under this chapter."

1988 Amendments: The 1988 municipal bankruptcy amendments (Pub. L. No. 100-597) redesignated section 927 as section 930, and inserted three new sections: 927, 928 and 929.

References

4 *Collier on Bankruptcy* ch. 930 (Matthew Bender 15th ed.).

Given and Murdich, *Bankruptcy Court Dismisses Bridgeport's Chapter 9 Petition,* 3 F & G Bankr. L. Rev. 55 (1992).

Minkel, *Chapter 9 Bankruptcy: Now More Than a Curiosity for Bondholders,* N.Y.L.J. Sept. 29, 1983 at 21.

Schwartz, *This Way to the Egress: Should Bridgeport's Chapter 9 Filing Have Been Dismissed?,* 2 Am. Bankr. L.J. 103 (1992).

SUBCHAPTER III

The Plan

SECTION 941 (11 U.S.C. § 941)

§ 941. **Filing of plan.** The debtor shall file a plan for the adjustment of the debtor's debts. If such plan is not filed with the petition, the debtor shall file such a plan at such later time as the court fixes.

Bankruptcy Rule Reference: 3016

Legislative History

Section 941 gives the debtor the exclusive right to propose a plan, and directs that the debtor propose one either with the petition or within such time as the court directs. The section follows current law, section 90(a).

[*House Report No. 95–595, 95th Cong., 1st Sess. 399 (1977); Senate Report No. 95–989, 95th Cong., 2d Sess. 112 (1978).*]

Comment

Section 941 is derived from the first two sentences of Section 90(a) of the former Bankruptcy Act.

Bankruptcy Rule 3016 relates to filing of a plan and disclosure statement in a chapter 9 case. Subdivision (a), as amended in 1991, provides that a party in interest, other than the debtor, may not file a plan after entry of an order approving a disclosure statement unless confirmation of the plan relating to the disclosure statement has been denied or the court otherwise directs. In a chapter 11 case the debtor has an exclusive period in which to file a plan after which any party in interest may file a plan. Section 941, however, provides that the chapter 9 debtor has the exclusive right to file a plan. Section 1121 which permits the filing of a plan by one other than the debtor is not made applicable in chapter 9 cases by section 901.

Subdivision (b) of the Rule requires every proposed plan and any modification thereof to be dated.

Subdivision (c) of the Rule provides that in a chapter 9 case, a disclosure statement pursuant to section 1125 or evidence showing compliance with section 1125(b) must be filed with the plan or within a time fixed by the court. (Postpetition solicitation of votes on a plan requires transmittal of a disclosure statement, the contents of which have been approved by the court (section 1125 which is applicable in chapter 9 cases under section 901). Prepetition solicitation must either have conformed with applicable nonbankruptcy law, or, if none, the disclosure must have been of adequate information as set forth in section 1125. (Section 1126). See Rule 3017 for provisions as to the hearing on the disclosure statement.)

Bankruptcy Rule 3017(a) provides that after the disclosure statement is filed, the court must hold a hearing on not less than 25 days notice to the debtor, creditors and other parties in interest to consider the statement and objections or modifications thereto. The plan and statement must be mailed with the notice of hearing only to the debtor, trustee, any committee appointed under the Code, the S.E.C. and any party in interest requesting in writing a copy of the plan or statement. Objections to the statement must be filed and served on the debtor, any committee appointed under the Code, and any other entity designated by the court, at any time prior to approval of the statement or by such earlier date as the court may fix.

Subdivision (b) provides that after the hearing, the court shall determine whether the statement should be approved.

Subdivision (c) requires the court on or before approval of the statement, to fix a time within which holders of claims and interest may accept or reject the plan and *may* fix a date for the hearing on confirmation.

Subdivision (d) provides that the requirements for notice and transmission to all creditors, equity security holders and, in a chapter 11 case, the United States trustee, following approval of the statement. This subdivision was extensively revised by the 1991 Amendments. The Amendments add specific notice requirements for any unimpaired class of equity security holders or creditors to which the court directed that the plan or statement not be sent, and also require the court to consider the procedures for transmitting the necessary documents and information to beneficial holders of stock, bonds, debentures, notes and other securities. *See* Bankruptcy Rule 3017.

Bankruptcy Rule 3018(a), as revised in 1991, provides that a plan may be accepted or rejected in accordance with section 1126 of the Code. An equity security holder or creditor whose claim is based on security of record must be such holder on the date of entry of the order approving the disclosure statement. For cause, and after notice and hearing, the court may permit the change or withdrawal of an acceptance or rejection.

Subdivision (b) provides that an equity security holder or creditor whose claim is based on a security of record who accepted or rejected the plan before the commencement of the case shall not be deemed to have accepted or rejected the plan under section 1126(b) unless such entity was the holder of record of the security on the date specified in the solicitation of such acceptance or rejection for the purposes of such solicitation.

Subdivision (c), relates to the form of an acceptance of rejection (Official Form 14). The creditors or equity security holders may accept or reject any number of plans submitted, and if more than one plan is accepted, the preference(s) may be indicated.

Subdivision (d) provides that a creditor whose claim has been allowed in part as secured and in part as unsecured, may accept or reject a plan in both capacities.

Bankruptcy Rule 2002(b) requires not less than 25 days notice by mail of the time fixed for filing objections and the hearing to consider approval of a disclosure statement and of the time fixed for filing objections and the hearing to consider confirmation of a plan.

References

4 *Collier on Bankruptcy* ch. 941 (Matthew Bender 15th ed.).

Fippinger, *Securities Law Disclosure Requirements for the Political Subdivision Threatened with Bankruptcy,* 10 Fordham Urb. L.J. 541 (1981–1982).

Leibowitz, *Municipal Bankruptcy Under the Bankruptcy Code,* N.Y.L.J. June 17, 1982.

Minkel, *Chapter 9 Bankruptcy: Now More Than a Curiosity for Bondholders,* N.Y.L.J. Sept. 29, 1983 at 21.

Winograd, *San Jose Revisited: A Proposal for Negotiated Modification of Public Sector Bargaining Agreements Rejected Under Chapter 9 of the Bankruptcy Code,* 37 Hastings L.J. 231 (1985).

SECTION 942 (11 U.S.C. § 942)

§ 942. **Modification of plan.** The debtor may modify the plan at any time before confirmation, but may not modify the plan so that the plan as modified fails to meet the requirements of this chapter. After the debtor files a modification, the plan as modified becomes the plan.

Bankruptcy Rule Reference: 3019

Legislative History

Section 942 permits the debtor to modify the plan at any time before confirmation, as does section 90(a) of current law.

[*House Report No. 95–595, 95th Cong., 1st Sess. 399 (1977); Senate Report No. 95–989, 95th Cong., 2d Sess. 113 (1978).*]

The House amendment deletes section 942 of the Senate amendment in favor of incorporating section 1125 by cross-reference. Similarly, the

House amendment does not incorporate sections 944 or 945 of the Senate amendment since incorporation of several sections in chapter 11 in section 901 is sufficient.

[*124 Cong. Rec. H 11,100 (Sept. 28, 1978); S 17,417 (Oct. 6, 1978).*]

Comment

Section 942 is derived from the third sentence of Section 90a of the former Bankruptcy Act.

Senate Report No. 95–989, 95th Cong., 2d Sess. (1978) 112 refers to transmission of the plan or a summary thereof to creditors, as follows:

> Section 942 adopts current section 90(b) and provides that the plan, or a summary thereof, will be transmitted by the petitioner or such other person as the court directs, to each creditor whose claim is affected by the plan, to each special taxpayer affected by the plan and to any party in interest that the court designates.

In view of the incorporation of section 1125 into chapter 9 (*see* section 901), it was unnecessary to make further provision for transmission of the plan to creditors. [*See* Congressional Record excerpt *supra.*] Section 1125 requires that at the time of or before solicitation of an acceptance or rejection of a plan there be transmitted to the holders of claims or interests the plan or a summary of the plan together with the written disclosure prescribed by section 1125.

Bankruptcy Rule 3019 provides that after acceptance and before confirmation the proponent may file a modification. If the court finds after hearing and notice to any committee appointed under the Code and others designated by the court that the modification does not adversely change the treatment of the claim of one who has not accepted the modification in writing, the modification shall be deemed accepted by all creditors who previously accepted the plan.

Section 1127 deals with modification of a plan. The only portion of section 1127 made applicable in a chapter 9 case by section 901 is subdivision (d) which provides that any holder of a claim that has accepted or rejected a plan is deemed to have accepted or rejected, as the case may be, such plan as modified, unless, within the time fixed by the court, such holder changes his previous acceptance or rejection.

References

4 *Collier on Bankruptcy* ch. 942 (Matthew Bender 15th ed.).

Fippinger, *Securities Law Disclosure Requirements for the Political Subdivision Threatened with Bankruptcy,* 10 Fordham Urb. L.J. 541 (1981–1982).

Leibowitz, *Municipal Bankruptcy Under the Bankruptcy Code,* N.Y.L.J. June 17, 1982.

Minkel, *Chapter 9 Bankruptcy: Now More Than a Curiosity for Bondhold-ers,* N.Y.L.J. Sept. 29, 1983 at 21.

SECTION 943 (11 U.S.C. § 943)

§ 943.　Confirmation.

(a) A special tax payer may object to confirmation of a plan.

(b) The court shall confirm the plan if—

(1) the plan complies with the provisions of this title made applicable by sections 103(e) and 901 of this title;

(2) the plan complies with the provisions of this chapter;

(3) all amounts to be paid by the debtor or by any person for services or expenses in the case or incident to the plan have been fully disclosed and are reasonable;

(4) the debtor is not prohibited by law from taking any action necessary to carry out the plan;

(5) except to the extent that the holder of a particular claim has agreed to a different treatment of such claim, the plan provides that on the effective date of the plan each holder of a claim of a kind specified in section 507(a)(1) of this title will receive on account of such claim cash equal to the allowed amount of such claim;

(6) any regulatory or electoral approval necessary under applicable nonbankruptcy law in order to carry out any provision of the plan has been obtained, or such provision is expressly conditioned on such approval; and

(7) the plan is in the best interests of creditors and is feasible.

Bankruptcy Rule Reference: 3020

Legislative History

In addition to the confirmation requirements incorporated from section 1129 by section 901, this section specifies additional require-ments. Paragraph (1) requires compliance with the provisions of the title made applicable in chapter 9 cases. This provision follows section 94(b)(2). Paragraph (2) requires compliance with the provisions of chapter 9, as does section 94(b)(2). Paragraph (3) adopts section 94(b)(4), requiring disclosure and reasonableness of all payments to be made in connection with the plan or the case. Paragraph (4), copied from section 92(b)(6), requires that the debtor not be prohibited by law from taking any action necessary to carry out the plan. Paragraph (5) departs from current law by requiring that administrative expenses be paid in full, but not necessarily in cash. Finally, paragraph (6) requires that the plan be in the best interest of creditors and feasible. The best interest test was deleted in section 94(b)(1) of current chapter IX from previous chapter IX, because it was redundant with the fair and equitable rule. However, this bill proposes a new confirmation standard generally for reorganization, one element of which is the best interest of creditors test; *see* section 1129(a)(7). In that section, the test is phrased in terms of liquidation of the debtor. Because that is not possible in a municipal-case, the test here is phrased in its more traditional form, using the words of art "best interest of creditors." The best interest of creditors test here is in addition to the financial standards imposed on the plan by section 1129(a)(8) and 1129(b), just as those provisions are in addition to the comparable best interest test in chapter 11. 11 U.S.C. § 1129(a)(7). The feasibility requirement, added in the revision of chapter IX last year, is retained.

[*House Report No. 95–595, 95th Cong., 1st Sess. 399–400 (1977).*]

Section 946 is adopted from current section 94. The test for confirmation is whether or not the plan is fair and equitable and feasible. The fair and equitable test tracts [*sic*] current chapter X and is known as the strict priority rule. Creditors must be provided, under the plan, the going concern value of their claims. The going concern value contemplates a "comparison of revenues and expenditures taking into account the taxing power and the extent to which tax increases are both necessary and feasible" *Municipal Insolvency, supra,* at p. 64, and is intended to provide more of a return to creditors than the liquidation value if the city's assets could be liquidated like those of a private corporation.

[*Senate Report No. 95–989, 95th Cong., 2d Sess. 113 (1978).*]

Section 943(a) of the House amendment makes clear that a special taxpayer may object to confirmation of a plan. Section 943(b) of the House amendment is derived from section 943 of the House bill respecting confirmation of a plan under chapter 9. It must be emphasized that these standards of confirmation are in addition to standards in section 1129 that are made applicable to chapter 9 by section 901 of the House amendment. In particular, if the requirements of section 1129(a)(8) are not complied with, then the proponent may request application of section 1129(b). The court will then be required to confirm the plan if it complies with the "fair and equitable" test and is in the best interests of creditors. The best interests of creditors test does not mean liquidation value as under chapter XI of the Bankruptcy Act. In making such a determination, it is expected that the court will be guided by standards set forth in Kelley v. Everglades Drainage District, 319 U.S. 415 (1943) and Fano v. Newport Heights Irrigation Dist., 114 F. 2d 563 (9th Cir. 1940), as under present law, the bankruptcy court should make findings as detailed as possible to support a conclusion that this test has been met. However, it must be emphasized that unlike current law, the fair and equitable test under section 1129(b) will not apply if section 1129(a)(8) has been satisfied in addition to the other confirmation standards specified in section 943 and incorporated by reference in section 901 of the House amendment. To the extent that American United Mutual Life Insurance Co. v. City of Avon Park, 311 U.S. 138 (1940) and other cases are to the contrary, such cases are overruled to that extent.

[*124 Cong. Rec. H 11,100 (Sept. 28, 1978); S 17,417 (Oct. 6, 1978).*]

[*Ed. Note:* The 1988 municipal bankruptcy amendments (Pub. L. 100-597) added paragraph (6) to section 943(b).]

[Section 943(b) deals] with plan confirmation requirements in chapter 9. New subsection [(b)](6) says that if regulatory or electoral approval is necessary under nonbankruptcy law to carry out any provision of the plan, either such approval must be obtained before the court can confirm the chapter 9 plan, or this provision of the plan must be expressly conditioned on getting such approval. Many municipal actions require regulatory or electoral approval under constitutional, statutory or charter provisions. These approvals are not limited to rates, but extend often to such other matters as the acquisition or disposition of property or the incurring of indebtedness.

[*House Report No. 100-1011, 100th Cong., 2d Sess. 8-9 (1988); Senate Report No. 100-506, 100th Cong., 2d Sess. (1988).*]

Comment

Subsection (a) of section 943 makes clear that a "special taxpayer" may object to confirmation. "Special taxpayer" is defined in section 902(2).

Subsection (b) sets forth the conditions for confirmation of a plan. Section 943(b)(1) requires that the plan comply with section 103(e) and section 901. Section 103(e) provides that *only* the provisions of chapter 1 (general provisions) and the provisions of chapter 9 apply to a chapter 9 case. Section 901 makes applicable in a chapter 9 case specified provisions of other chapters of the Code. Incorporation into chapter 9 of section 1129 brings in standards for confirmation of a chapter 9 case in addition to the tests set forth in section 943(b). Particularly, if the requirements of section 1129(a)(8) are not complied with, then the proponent of the plan may request application of section 1129(b). The court will then be required to confirm if the plan complies with the "fair and equitable" rule (section 943(b)(6)).

The "fair and equitable" doctrine will not apply, therefore, if each class has either accepted the plan or is not impaired thereby. The conditions that will meet the "fair and equitable" test are set forth in section 1129(b)(2).

The "best interest of creditors" test, set forth in section 943(b)(6) is not the same test as used in former Chapter XI. The "best interest of creditors" test is in addition to the financial standards imposed on the plan by subsections (a)(8) and (b) of section 1129.

Bankruptcy Rule 3020(a) relates to deposit in a chapter 11 case of the consideration to be distributed under the plan. Deposit in chapter 9 cases is governed by section 944(b) which provides for the deposit to be made with a disbursing agent appointed by the court.

Bankruptcy Rule 3020(b) relates to objections to and the hearing on confirmation. Paragraph (b)(1) requires objections to confirmation to be filed and served on the debtor, the proponent of the plan, a committee appointed under the Code and others designated by the court, within a time fixed by the court. An objection to confirmation is a contested matter governed by Rule 9014. Paragraph (b)(2) requires the court to rule on confirmation after hearing as provided in Rule 2002 (not less than 25 days notice by mail). If no timely objection is filed, the court may determine that the plan has been proposed in good faith and not by any means forbidden by law without receiving evidence on such issues.

Subdivision (c) requires that the order of confirmation conform to Official Form 15 and that notice of entry thereof be promptly mailed by the clerk (or some other person an the court may direct) to the debtor, creditors and other parties in interest.

Subdivision (d) provides that, notwithstanding confirmation, the court may enter all orders as thereafter become necessary in administering the estate.

By reason of its incorporation by reference into chapter 9 (*see* section 901), acceptance of a chapter 9 plan is governed by section 1126 which requires, generally, acceptance by creditors holding at least two-thirds in amount and more than one-half in number of allowed claims of each class held by creditors that have voted to accept or reject the plan.

1984 Amendments: A stylistic change was made in subsection (b)(4) and subsection (b)(5) was revised. To be confirmed the plan must provide that each holder of a claim specified in section 507(a)(1) [claims entitled to priority] will receive *cash* on account of such claim equal to the allowed amount of the claim except to the extent that the claimant has agreed to different treatment.

1988 Amendments: Section 943(b) contains the conditions for confirmation of a chapter 9 plan. If the plan has a provision that requires approval of a regulatory agency or of the electorate, subsection (b)(6) requires either that the provision be approved before confirmation or that the provision be expressly conditioned on such approval. Subsection (b)(2) does not require electoral approval of the plan, just approval for an action to be taken under the plan that would otherwise require electoral approval.

References

4 *Collier on Bankruptcy* ch. 943 (Matthew Bender 15th ed.).

Fippinger, *Securities Law Disclosure Requirements for the Political Subdivision Threatened with Bankruptcy,* 10 Fordham Urb. L.J. 541 (1981–1982).

Leibowitz, *Municipal Bankruptcy Under the Bankruptcy Code,* N.Y.L.J. June 15, 1982.

Minkel, *Chapter 9 Bankruptcy: Now More Than a Curiosity for Bondholders,* N.Y.L.J. Sept. 29, 1983 at 21.

SECTION 944 (11 U.S.C. § 944)

§ 944. Effect of confirmation.

(a) The provisions of a confirmed plan bind the debtor and any creditor, whether or not—

    (1) a proof of such creditor's claim is filed or deemed filed under section 501 of this title;

    (2) such claim is allowed under section 502 of this title; or

    (3) such creditor has accepted the plan.

(b) Except as provided in subsection (c) of this section, the debtor is discharged from all debts as of the time when—

    (1) the plan is confirmed;

    (2) the debtor deposits any consideration to be distributed under the plan with a disbursing agent appointed by the court; and

    (3) the court has determined—

        (A) that any security so deposited will constitute, after distribution, a valid legal obligation of the debtor; and

        (B) that any provision made to pay or secure payment of such obligation is valid.

(c) The debtor is not discharged under subsection (b) of this section from any debt—

    (1) excepted from discharge by the plan or order confirming the plan; or

    (2) owed to an entity that, before confirmation of the plan, had neither notice nor actual knowledge of the case.

Bankruptcy Rule References: 3020 and 4004

Legislative History

Subsection (a) makes the provisions of a confirmed plan binding on the debtor and creditors. It is derived from section 95(a) of chapter IX.

Subsections (b) and (c) contain the discharge for a municipality. The discharge is essentially the same as that granted under section 95(b).

[*House Report No. 95–595, 95th Cong., 1st Sess. 400 (1977); See Senate Report No. 95–989, 95th Cong., 2d Sess. 113 (1978).*]

Comment

Section 944(a), setting forth the binding effect of a confirmed plan is derived from Section 95(a) of the former Bankruptcy Act.

Section 944(b), providing for discharge of the debtor is derived with little change from Section 95(b) of the Act.

Note that section 944(b)(2) provides for appointment by the court of a disbursing agent to distribute the consideration to be distributed under the plan, thus modifying Bankruptcy Rule 3020(a) under which no disbursing agent is to be appointed.

Case Annotations

The discharge section of chapter 9 discharges all debts except those owed to an entity that did not have notice or knowledge of the case before confirmation of the plan and does not require creditors to have a reasonable opportunity to file timely proofs of claim prior to confirmation. Although the creditors may not have received notice of the claims bar date, if they: 1) have notice of the case and the opportunity to read the provisions of various disclosure statements and plans which require claims to be filed in order to participate in distribution; 2) have notice that all claims listed are contingent, unliquidated or disputed; and 3) have notice that only those creditors filing claims could participate in distribution, then the confirmation of the plan is binding and those creditors will not be allowed to file a proof of claim after confirmation. In the Matter of Sanitary & Improvement District No. 7, Lancaster County, 23 C.B.C.2d 891 (B. Ct., D. Neb. 1990).

References

4 *Collier on Bankruptcy* ch. 944 (Matthew Bender 15th ed.).

Fippinger, *Securities Law Disclosure Requirements for the Political Subdivision Threatened with Bankruptcy,* 10 Fordham Urb. L.J. 541 (1981–1982).

Leibowitz, *Municipal Bankruptcy Under the Bankruptcy Code,* N.Y.L.J. June 15, 1982.

Minkel, *Chapter 9 Bankruptcy: Now More Than a Curiosity for Bondholders*, N.Y.L.J. Sept. 29, 1983 at 21.

SECTION 945 (11 U.S.C. § 945)

§ 945. Continuing jurisdiction and closing of the case.

(a) The court may retain jurisdiction over the case for such period of time as is necessary for the successful implementation of the plan.

(b) Except as provided in subsection (a) of this section, the court shall close the case when administration of the case has been completed.

Legislative History

Section 945 permits the court to retain jurisdiction over the debtor to ensure successful execution of the plan. The provision is the same as that found in section 96(e) of the Bankruptcy Act.

[*House Report No. 95–595, 95th Cong., 1st Sess. 400 (1977); See Senate Report No. 95–989, 95th Cong., 2d Sess. 113 (1978).*]

Comment

Section 945, derived from Section 96 of the former Bankruptcy Act, permits continuing jurisdiction for as long as the court deems necessary to insure that the plan will be performed. In the ordinary case, administration will be complete when distribution under the plan is complete and all claims have been determined. At such point the case should be closed, subject always to be reopened under section 350(b).

Bankruptcy Rule 3020(d) provides that notwithstanding confirmation, the court may enter all orders as thereafter become necessary in administering the estate.

1984 Amendments: A stylistic change in section 945(a) substituted "implementation" in lieu of "execution."

Case Annotations

A sanitary district's annexation by a city does not affect the court's jurisdiction to determine matters concerning the implementation of the district's confirmed plan. In the Matter of Sanitary & Improvement District No. 7, Lancaster County, 23 C.B.C.2d 891 (B. Ct., D. Neb. 1990).

References

4 *Collier on Bankruptcy* ch. 945 (Matthew Bender 15th ed.).

Fippinger, *Securities Law Disclosure Requirements for the Political Subdivision Threatened with Bankruptcy,* 10 Fordham Urb. L.J. 541 (1981–1982).

Leibowitz, *Municipal Bankruptcy Under the Bankruptcy Code,* N.Y.L.J. June 15, 1982.

Minkel, *Chapter 9 Bankruptcy: Now More Than a Curiosity for Bondholders,* N.Y.L.J. Sept. 29, 1983 at 21.

SECTION 946 (11 U.S.C. § 946)

§ 946. Effect of exchange of securities before the date of the filing of the petition.

The exchange of a new security under the plan for a claim covered by the plan, whether such exchange occurred before or after the date of the filing of the petition, does not limit or impair the effectiveness of the plan or of any provision of this chapter. The amount and number specified in section 1126(c) of this title include the amount and number of claims formerly held by a creditor that has participated in any such exchange.

Legislative History

This section, which follows section 97 of current law, permits an exchange of a security before the case is filed to constitute an acceptance of the plan if the exchange was under a proposal that later became the plan.

[*House Report No. 95–595, 95th Cong., 1st Sess. 400 (1977); See Senate Report No. 95–989, 95th Cong., 2d Sess. 113 (1978).*]

Comment

Section 946 is derived from Section 97 of the former Bankruptcy Act.

References

4 *Collier on Bankruptcy* ch. 946 (Matthew Bender 15th ed.).

Fippinger, *Securities Law Disclosure Requirements for the Subdivision Threatened with Bankruptcy,* 10 Fordham Urb. L.J. 541 (1981–1982).

Leibowitz, *Municipal Bankruptcy Under the Bankruptcy Code,* N.Y.L.J. June 15, 1982.

Minkel, *Chapter 9 Bankruptcy: Now More Than a Curiosity for Bondholders,* N.Y.L.J. Sept. 29, 1983 at 21.

CHAPTER 11

Reorganization

SUBCHAPTER 1

Officers and Administration

SECTION 1101 (11 U.S.C. § 1101)

§ 1101. Definitions for this chapter. In this chapter—

(1) "debtor in possession" means debtor except when a person that has qualified under section 322 of this title is serving as trustee in the case;

(2) "substantial consummation" means—

(A) transfer of all or substantially all of the property proposed by the plan to be transferred;

(B) assumption by the debtor or by the successor to the debtor under the plan of the business or of the management of all or substantially all of the property dealt with by the plan; and

(C) commencement of distribution under the plan.

Legislative History

This section contains definitions of two terms that are used in chapter 11. Paragraph (1) defines debtor in possession to mean the debtor, except when a trustee who has qualified is serving in the case.

Paragraph (2), derived from section 229a of current law, defines substantial consummation. Substantial consummation of a plan occurs when transfer of all or substantially all of the property proposed by the plan to be transferred is actually transferred; when the debtor (or its successor) has assumed the business of the debtor or the management of all or substantially all of the property dealt with by the plan; and when distribution under the plan has commenced. [*Ed. Note:* The Senate Report on this provision contained additional language describing a "public company," a definition that was deleted in the final version of the bill. For reasons why the definition was deleted, *see* 124 Cong. Rec. H 11,101 (Sept. 28, 1978); S 17,418 (Oct. 6, 1978).]

[*House Report No. 95–595, 95th Cong., 1st Sess. 401 (1977); See Senate Report No. 95–989, 2d Sess. 114 (1978).*]

Comment

A "debtor in possession" under chapter 11 of the Code is a debtor in any case who is left in possession of the debtor's property and business, *i.e.,* when no person has qualified and is serving as a trustee. The norm in Chapters XI and XII cases under the former Bankruptcy Act was to permit the debtor to remain in possession unless cause was shown why a receiver or trustee should be appointed.

Under section 1101(a), unless the court orders the appointment of a trustee under section 1104(a), the debtor in a chapter 11 case will remain in possession of the property during the chapter 11 case. If a trustee is serving in a chapter 7 or 13 case that is converted to chapter 11, such conversion terminates the service of the trustee as provided in section 348(e).

Section 1101(2), defining "substantial confirmation," is derived from former Bankruptcy Rule 10–306(c)(2) which in turn was derived from Section 229a of the Act.

Case Annotations

A plan has not been substantially consummated when the transfer of property among shareholders of the debtor has not yet begun. *In re* Modern Steel Treating Co., 25 C.B.C.2d 292 (B. Ct., N.D. Ill. 1991).

Substantial consummation requires completion of or near completion of transfers of property to or from the debtor at or near the time the plan is confirmed. United States v. Novak, 20 C.B.C.2d 131 (D.S.D. 1988).

To satisfy subparagraph (A), more than half rather than a mere preponderance of the plan must have been completed. Jorgensen v. Fed. Land Bank of Spokane (*In re* Jorgensen), 16 C.B.C.2d 157 (9th Cir., B.A.P., 1986).

"Substantial consummation" of a debtor's confirmed plan under section 1101(2)(A) does not include the distributions to creditors to be made over a period of time since such a reading would give no effect to subparagraph (C) which requires only the commencement of distribution under the plan. *In re* Hayball Trucking, Inc., 15 C.B.C.2d 1201 (B. Ct., E.D. Mich. 1986).

The rights of a debtor in possession to withdraw funds from a bank account are identical to and no greater than the rights which that entity had as a prepetition debtor. Cross Keys Motors, Inc. v. Farmers Bank & Trust (*In re* Cross Keys Motors, Inc.), 6 C.B.C.2d 746 (B. Ct., M.D. Pa. 1982).

References

5 *Collier on Bankruptcy* ch. 1101 (Matthew Bender 15th ed.).

2 *Collier Bankruptcy Manual* ch. 1101 (Matthew Bender 3d ed.).

5 *Collier Bankruptcy Practice Guide* ch. 90 (Matthew Bender).

Ellis, *The Shield as a Sword: How Major American Companies Have Used Chapter 11,* 1 F & G Bankr. L. Rev. 31 (1989).

Epstein and Fuller, *Chapters 11 and 13 of the Bankruptcy Code—Observations on Using Case Authority From One of the Chapters in Proceedings Under the Other,* 38 Vand. L. Rev. 901 (1985).

Fortgang and Mayer, *Developments in Trading Claims and Taking Control of Corporations in Chapter 11,* 13 Cardozo L. Rev. 1 (1991).

Fortgang and Mayer, *Trading Claims and Taking Control of Corporations in Chapter 11,* 12 Cardozo L. Rev. 1 (1990).

Goss, *Chapter 11 of the Bankruptcy Code: An Overview for the General Practitioner (Part II: The Reorganization Process),* 4 Utah B.J. 6 (1991).

Heiman and Riley, *Are Vulture Investors Changing the Face of Chapter 11?* 2 F & G Bankr. L. Rev. 5 (1991).

Hendel, *Practical Prefiling Considerations in Chapter 11 Cases,* 2 Com. L. Bull. 10 (1987).

Key, *The Advent of the Serial Chapter 11 Filing and Its Implications,* 8 Bankr. Dev. J. 245 (1991).

Klausner, Pachulski and Godshall, *Chapter 11—The Bank of Last Resort,* 45 Bus. Law. 261 (1989)

Note, *International Environmental Bankruptcy: An Overview of Environmental Bankruptcy Law, Including a State's Claims Against the Multinational Polluter,* 23 Vand. J. Transnat'l L. 345 (1990).

SECTION 1102 (11 U.S.C. § 1102)

§ 1102.　Creditors' and equity security holders' committees.

(a)(1) As soon as practicable after the order for relief under chapter 11 of this title, the United States trustee shall appoint a committee of creditors holding unsecured claims and may appoint additional committees of creditors or of equity security holders as the United States trustee deems appropriate.

(2) On request of a party in interest, the court may order the appointment of additional committees of creditors or of

equity security holders if necessary to assure adequate representation of creditors or of equity security holders. The United States trustee shall appoint any such committee.

(b)(1) A committee of creditors appointed under subsection (a) of this section shall ordinarily consist of the persons, willing to serve, that hold the seven largest claims against the debtor of the kinds represented on such committee, or of the members of a committee organized by creditors before the commencement of the case under this chapter, if such committee was fairly chosen and is representative of the different kinds of claims to be represented.

(2) A committee of equity security holders appointed under subsection (a)(2) of this section shall ordinarily consist of the persons, willing to serve, that hold the seven largest amounts of equity securities of the debtor of the kinds represented on such committee.

Bankruptcy Rule References: 1007, 2002, 2003, 2007 and 2019

Legislative History

This section provides for the appointment of creditors' and equity security holders' committees, which will be the primary negotiating bodies for the formulation of the plan of reorganization. They will represent the various classes of creditors and equity security holders from which they are selected. They will also provide supervision of the debtor in possession and of the trustee, and will protect their constituents' interests.

Subsection (a) requires the court to appoint at least one committee. That committee is to be composed of creditors holding unsecured claims. That court is authorized to appoint such additional committees as are necessary to assure adequate representation of creditors and equity security holders. The provision will be relied upon in cases in which the debtor proposes to affect several classes of debt or equity holders under the plan, and in which they need representation.

[*House Report No. 95–595, 95th Cong., 1st Sess. 401 (1977).*]

This section provides for the election and appointment of committees. Subsection (c) [repealed by Pub. L. No. 99–554 (1986)] provides that this section does not apply in case of a public company, as to which a trustee, appointed under section 1104(a) will have responsibility to administer the estate and to formulate a plan as provided in section 1106(a).

There is no need for the election or appointment of committees for which the appointment of a trustee is mandatory. In the case of a public company there are likely to be several committees, each representing a different class of security holders and seeking authority to retain accountants, lawyers, and other experts, who will expect to be paid. If in the case of a public company creditors or stockholders wish to organize committees, they may do so, as authorized under section 1109(a). Compensation and reimbursement will be allowed for contributions to the reorganization pursuant to section 503(b) (3) and (4).

[*Senate Report No. 95–989, 95th Cong., 2d Sess. 114 (1978).*]

Section 1102(a) of the House amendment adopts a compromise between the House bill and Senate amendment requiring appointment of a committee of creditors holding unsecured claims by the court; the alternative of creditor committee election is rejected.

[*124 Cong. Rec. H 11,102 (Sept. 28, 1978); S 17,419 (Oct. 6, 1978).*]

Subsection (b) contains precatory language directing the court to appoint the persons holding the seven largest claims against the debtor of the kinds represented on a creditors' committee, or the members of a prepetition committee organized by creditors before the order for relief under chapter 11. The court may continue prepetition committee members only if the committee was fairly chosen and is representative of the different kinds of claims to be represented. The court is restricted to the appointment of persons in order to exclude governmental holders of claims or interests.

Paragraph (2) of subsection (b) requires similar treatment for equity security holders' committees. The seven largest holders are normally to be appointed, but the language is only precatory.

[*House Report No. 95–595, 95th Cong., 1st Sess. 401 (1977).*]

Section 1102(b) of the House amendment represents a compromise between the House bill and the Senate amendment by preventing the appointment of creditors who are unwilling to serve on a creditors committee.

[*124 Cong. Rec. H 11,102 (Sept. 28, 1978); S 17,419 (Oct. 6, 1978).*]

Comment

Section 1102(a)(1) of the Code mandates appointment by the United States trustee of at least one committee consisting of unsecured creditors. Under subsection (a)(2), on "request" of a party in interest the court *may* order the appointment of additional committees of creditors or equity security holders (*see* definitions, section 101), if necessary to assure adequate representation.

The language of subsections (b)(1) and (b)(2) is precatory, providing that the committee "shall ordinarily" consist of the creditors holding the seven largest claims or largest amount of equity securities of the kinds represented on such committee. Members of a pre-bankruptcy committee, if fairly chosen and fairly representative, may continue on the committee.

Bankruptcy Rule 2007 deals with the appointment of a creditor's committee organized before the commencement of the case. Subdivision (a) provides that if a committee appointed by the United States trustee [section 1102(a) of the Code] consists of members of a committee organized by creditors prior to commencement of the case, on motion of a party in interest and after a hearing on notice to the United States trustee and other entities as the court directs, the court may determine whether the appointment of the committee satisfies the requirements of section 1102(a).

Subdivision (b) provides that the court may find that a committee of unsecured creditors organized before the commencement of the case in a chapter 11 case was fairly chosen if—

(1) it was selected by a majority in number and amount of claims of unsecured creditors who may vote under 702(a) and who were present in person or represented at the meeting of which all creditors having claims over $1000, or the 100 largest unsecured creditors had at least 5 days notice in writing, and of which meeting minutes were kept, and are available, reporting names of creditors present or represented and voting and the amounts of their claims;

(2) all proxies voted at the meeting for the elected committee were solicited pursuant to Rule 2006 and the lists and statements required by Rule 2006(e) were transmitted to the United States trustee; and

(3) the organization of the committee was in all other respects fair and proper.

Subdivision (c), added by the 1991 Amendments, provides that if the court finds that the appointment failed to satisfy the requirements of section 1102(b)(1) of the Code, after hearing on notice, the court shall direct the United States trustee to vacate the appointment of the committee and may order other appropriate action. [A finding that a prepetition committee was not fairly chosen, does not prohibit the appointment of some or all of its members to the creditors' committee.]

Under Rule 1007(d) the debtor in a voluntary chapter 11 case is required to file with the petition, a list of the 20 largest unsecured creditors. The purpose of such list is to enable the court to comply with the direction of section 1102(a)(1) that a committee be appointed as soon as practicable after the order for relief. See Official Form 4.

Bankruptcy Rule 2003(b)(1), as amended in 1991, provides that the United States trustee shall preside at the section 341 meeting of creditors. The business of the meeting shall include the examination of the debtor under oath. The oath may be administered by the presiding officer. Section 102(9) provides that "United States trustee" shall include a designee of the United States trustee.

Under Bankruptcy Rule 2002(i), all notices of significant events in the case as prescribed by Rule 2002 must be given to the elected or appointed committee or to its authorized agents.

Subsection (k), added in 1991, provides that unless the United States trustee otherwise requests, the clerk or some other person as directed by the court, shall transmit to said trustee notice of most of the matters described in Rule 2002 and notice of all applications for compensation or reimbursement. Notice shall also be given to the United States trustee of any other matter if requested by said trustee or ordered by the court.

1984 Amendments: Subsection (b)(1) was amended to permit a committee organized *before the commencement of the case* to serve as the official committee.

1986 Amendments: Subsection (c) of section 1102 was repealed by the 1986 Amendments. The 1986 Amendments continue to relieve bankruptcy judges of administrative duties by assigning many such duties to the United States trustees. Thus, section 1102(a)(1) provides for appointment of committees by the United States trustee who is given the further power of appointing additional committees as such trustee deems appropriate. Subsection (a)(2) provides that upon application of a party in interest the court may order the United States trustee to appoint additional committees.

This section was amended to reflect the creation of a permanent United States trustee system. Section 302(d) of the 1986 Amendments provides different effective dates for the amendments relating to the United States trustee system. *See* Section 302 of the 1986 Amendments, reprinted herein under "Selected Provisions of the Bankruptcy Judges, United States Trustees, and Family Farmer Bankruptcy Act of 1986," regarding effective dates generally.

1990 Amendments: Section 302(d)(3) of the Bankruptcy Judges, United States Trustees, and Family Farmer Bankruptcy Act of 1986 was amended by Pub. L. No. 101-650 (Judicial Improvements Act of 1990) to extend the period in which the judicial districts in the states of Alabama and North Carolina may remain outside the United States trustee system and to insert new language pertaining to the effective date of the 1986 amendment to section 105 of title 11.

Case Annotations

Because a union is a creditor within the meaning of the definition set forth in section 101, it is entitled to membership on the unsecured creditors' committee. *In re* Altair Airlines, Inc., 727 F.2d 88, 10 C.B.C.2d 343 (3d Cir. 1984).

The determination as to whether a particular creditor is adequately represented on an unsecured creditors' committee and whether additional committees are necessary is within the bankruptcy court's discretion. The function of the unsecured creditors' committee is to act "as a catalyst for negotiation and compromise between the parties in the reorganization process," so that all that is required by the Code is that conflicting groups of creditors have a voice through adequate representation, not that each group of creditors be able to protect all of its interests and achieve all of its goals. *In re* Hills Stores Co., 26 C.B.C.2d 1038 (B. Ct., S.D.N.Y. 1992).

The bankruptcy court may review a United States trustee's refusal to appoint a creditor to the unsecured creditors' committee under an abuse of discretion standard and may order appropriate relief pursuant to section 105(a). Matter of Columbia Gas Sys., Inc. and Columbia Transmission Corp., 25 C.B.C.2d 1444 (B. Ct., D. Del. 1991).

In the cases of closely related debtors, whether to appoint additional committees must be tempered by consideration of the identities and interests of the parties and by the need to prevent possible crucial delay and heightened administrative expenses in the chapter 11 process. It is not always appropriate nor is it mandatory to appoint additional committees merely on the request of a party in interest, even if that party is the United States trustee. *In re* Orfa Corp. of Philadelphia, 24 C.B.C.2d 1280 (B. Ct. E.D. Pa. 1990).

In the context of reorganization, members of a rural electric cooperative likely hold interests sufficiently similar to the interests of shareholders in a corporation that they would qualify as equity security holders for purposes of section 1102(a)(2) and could be the basis for timely creation of a committee. *In re* Eastern Maine Electric Cooperative, Inc., 24 C.B.C.2d 967 (B. Ct., D. Me. 1990).

As general partners are not equity security holders, section 1102(b) does not contemplate their inclusion as members of an equity holders' committee. *In re* Finley, 22 C.B.C.2d 162 (B. Ct., S.D.N.Y. 1988).

Section 1102 is silent as to the power of the bankruptcy court to alter the structure of a committee following the initial appointment of the committee by the United States trustee, and the bankruptcy court has the inherent power to affect the composition of a committee when an asserted justification requiring a judicial determination is brought before the court during the proceeding. Even if individual debenture holders of a chapter 11 debtor are not adequately represented by the unsecured creditors' committee and would benefit from the appointment of a separate committee, when such a remedy would be disruptive and cause delay a bankruptcy court may order the lesser remedy of expanding the committee to protect the interests of the individual debenture holders. *In re* Public Service Co. of New Hampshire, 20 C.B.C.2d 196 (B. Ct., D.N.H. 1988).

When issues arise regarding the debtor's performance of its obligations under the plan, the court is not subject to an explicit time limit for appointing a committee of secured creditors to oversee the debtor's performance under the plan and a secured creditors' committee may be appointed after confirmation of the plan. *In re* Diversified Capital Corp., 19 C.B.C.2d 610 (B. Ct., C.D. Cal. 1988).

An undersecured bank creditor may be a member of the unsecured creditors' committee even though the undersecured creditor's rights and position are different from those of general trade creditors. *In re* Walat Farms, Inc., 15 C.B.C.2d 1466 (B. Ct., E.D. Mich. 1986).

References

5 *Collier on Bankruptcy* ch. 1102 (Matthew Bender 15th ed.).

2 *Collier Bankruptcy Manual* ch. 1102 (Matthew Bender 3d ed.).

5 *Collier Bankruptcy Practice Guide* ch. 83 (Matthew Bender).

Blain and O'Gawa, *Creditors' Committees Under Chapter 11 of the United States Bankruptcy Code: Creation, Composition, Powers, and Duties,* 73 Marq. L. Rev. 581 (1990).

White and Felderstein, *Governmental Units as Persons for the Purpose of Official Committee Membership: A Call for Reform,* 95 Com. L.J. 1 (1990).

SECTION 1103 (11 U.S.C. § 1103)

§ 1103.   Powers and duties of committees.

(a) At a scheduled meeting of a committee appointed under section 1102 of this title, at which a majority of the members of such committee are present, and with the court's approval, such committee may select and authorize the employment by such committee of one or more attorneys, accountants, or other agents, to represent or perform services for such committee.

(b) An attorney or accountant employed to represent a committee appointed under section 1102 of this title may not, while employed by such committee, represent any other entity having an adverse interest in connection with the case. Representation of one or more creditors of the same class as represented by the committee shall not per se constitute the representation of an adverse interest.

(c) A committee appointed under section 1102 of this title may—

(1) consult with the trustee or debtor in possession concerning the administration of the case;

(2) investigate the acts, conduct, assets, liabilities, and financial condition of the debtor, the operation of the debtor's business and the desirability of the continuance of such business, and any other matter relevant to the case or to the formulation of a plan;

(3) participate in the formulation of a plan, advise those represented by such committee of such committee's

determinations as to any plan formulated, and collect and file with the court acceptances or rejections of a plan;

(4) request the appointment of a trustee or examiner under section 1104 of this title; and

(5) perform such other services as are in the interest of those represented.

(d) As soon as practicable after the appointment of a committee under section 1102 of this title, the trustee shall meet with such committee to transact such business as may be necessary and proper.

Bankruptcy Rule References: 2002, 2014 and 5002

Legislative History

Subsection (a) of this section authorizes a committee appointed under section 1102 to select and authorize the employment of counsel, accountants, or other agents, to represent or perform services for the committee. The committee's selection and authorization is subject to the court's approval, and may only be done at a meeting of the committee at which a majority of its members are present. The subsection provides for the employment of more than one attorney. However, this will be the exception, and not the rule; cause must be shown to depart from the normal standard.

[*House Report No. 95–595, 95th Cong., 1st Sess. 402 (1977).*]

This section defines the powers and duties of a committee elected or appointed under section 1102.

Under subsection (a) the committee may, if authorized by the court, employ one or more attorneys, accountants, or other agents to represent or perform services for the committee. Normally one attorney should suffice; more than one may be authorized for good cause. The same considerations apply to the services of others, if the need for any at all is demonstrated.

[*Senate Report No. 95–989, 95th Cong., 2d Sess. 114 (1978).*]

Subsection (b) requires a committee's counsel to cease representation of any other equity in connection with the case after he begins to represent the committee. This will prevent the potential of severe conflicts of interest.

Subsection (c) lists a committee's functions in a chapter 11 case. The committee may consult with the trustee or debtor in possession concerning the administration of the case, may investigate the acts, conduct, assets, liabilities and financial condition of the debtor, the operation of the debtor's business, and the desirability of the continuance of the business, and any other matter relevant to the case or to the formulation of a plan. The committee may participate in the formulation of a plan, advise those it represents of the committee's recommendation with respect to any plan formulated, and collect and file acceptances. These will be its most important functions. The committee may also determine the need for the appointment of a trustee, if one has not previously been appointed, and perform such other services as are in the interest of those represented.

Subsection (d) requires the trustee and each committee to meet as soon as practicable after their appointments to transact such business as may be necessary and proper.

[*House Report No. 95–595, 95th Cong., 1st Sess. 402 (1977).*]

Under subsections (c) and (d) the committee, like any party in interest, may confer with the trustee or debtor regarding the administration of the estate; may advise the court on the need for a trustee under section 1104(b). The committee may investigate matters specified in paragraph (2) of subsection (c), but only if authorized by the court and if no trustee or examiner is appointed.

[*Senate Report No. 95–989, 95th Cong., 2d Sess. 114 (1978).*]

Comment

Section 1103 is largely derived from former Bankruptcy Rule 11–29 governing the role of a committee in a Chapter XI case.

Under section 1103(a), the employment of professionals must be made at a scheduled meeting of the committee at which a majority of members are present, and their selection is subject to court approval.

Under section 1103(b) any professional employed to represent the committee must cease to represent any other entity in the case, thus avoiding any possible conflict of interest.

Section 1103(c) sets forth the duties of a committee.

Because of the combining of former Chapters X, XI, and XII into a single chapter 11, section 1103(c) modified the functions of the committee as provided in former Rule 11–29(a). For example, paragraph (4) provides that the committee may request appointment of a trustee or examiner. Under the Act, however, an examiner could be appointed only in a Chapter X case where the debtor remained in possession.

Section 1103(d) has no comparable provision in the former Bankrutcy Act. It requires the trustee and each committee to meet "as soon as possible" to transact necessary and proper business.

Bankruptcy Rule 2014 relates to the employment of professional persons. Subdivision (a) provides that the order approving employment of attorneys, accountants, appraisers, auctioneers, agents or other professionals by a committee appointed pursuant to section 1103 or 1114 be made only on application of the trustee or committee. The application shall be filed and a copy transmitted by applicant to the

United States trustee. The application shall state the specific facts as to the necessity for such employment, the name of the person to be employed, the reasons for the selection, the professional service to be rendered, any proposed arrangement for compensation and, to the best of applicant's knowledge, all of such person's connections with the debtor, creditors, any other party in interest, and their attorneys and accountants. The application must be accompanied by a verified statement of the person to be employed setting forth the person's connections with the debtor, creditors or any other party in interest, their respective attorneys and accountants, the United States trustee, or any person employed in the office of such trustee. [This paragraph was added in 1987 and amended in 1991.] (The persons employed must be "disinterested" as that term is defined in section 101.)

Subdivision (b) provides that if a partnership or a corporation is employed as attorney or accountant, or if the attorney or accountant is employed on behalf of a professional partnership or corporation, any member or regular associate of the firm may act as attorney or accountant in the case without further order of the court. (The compensation provisions are found in section 504 of the Code.)

Bankruptcy Rule 2002(a)(7) requires 20 days notice by mail to the trustee, all creditors and indenture trustees of the hearings on all applications for compensation or reimbursement of expenses totalling in excess of $500.

Subdivision (k), added in 1991, provides that unless the United States trustee otherwise requests, the clerk or some other person as the court directs, shall transmit to the United States trustee most of the notices required by Rule 2002 and notice of all applications for compensation or reimbursement. The United States trustee shall also receive notice of any other matter if requested by the trustee or ordered by the court.

Bankruptcy Rule 5002, substantially revised by the 1991 Amendments, provides in subdivision (a) that appointment of an individual as trustee or examiner shall not be approved by the court if the individual is a relative of the bankruptcy judge approving the appointment or the United States trustee in the region. The employment of an individual as an attorney, accountant, appraiser, auctioneer, or other professional shall not be approved by the court if such individual is a relative of the bankruptcy judge approving the employment. Such employment may be approved if the individual is a relative of the United States trustee unless the court finds that such relationship renders the employment improper under the circumstances. If an individual may not be approved for appointment or employment under this subdivision, the individual's firm, partnership, corporation and all members and professional employees thereof also may not be approved for appointment or employment.

Subdivision (b) prohibits approval of appointment of a trustee or examiner or employment of a professional who is so connected with the bankruptcy judge or the United States trustee as to render the appointment or employment improper. ["Improper" includes the appearance of impropriety.]

1984 Amendments: Section 1103(b) was amended by substituting "An attorney or accountant" in lieu of "A person." A further amendment to subsection (b) makes it clear that the subsection is concerned only with representation of an entity "having an adverse interest." A new sentence added to subsection (b) provides that representation of one or more creditors of the same class as represented by the committee shall not per se constitute representation of an adverse interest.

A stylistic change was made in subsection (c)(3), while a change in subsection (c)(4) deleted the requirement that a committee could seek appointment of a trustee or examiner only if one "has not previously been appointed" under chapter 11.

Case Annotations

The right of a shareholders' committee to call a shareholders' meeting can be impaired or enjoined only if the committee is guilty of "clear abuse" and causes irreparable injury. "Clear abuse" is more, however, than mere delay or the committee's professed desire to arrogate more bargaining power for itself in the negotiation of the plan; it is the threat of destruction of the entire reorganization process. And a finding of clear abuse must be supplemented by a separate finding of irreparable injury. Manville v. The Equity Security Holders Committee (*In re* Johns-Manville Corp.), 801 F.2d 60, 15 C.B.C.2d 645 (2d Cir. 1986).

A bankruptcy court should not recognize a state law accountant-client privilege as a matter of comity when to do so would prevent the creditors' committee from exercising its right under the Code to investigate the debtor's financial condition. International Horizons, Inc. v. Committee of Unsecured Creditors (In the Matter of International Horizons, Inc.), 689 F.2d 996, 7 C.B.C.2d 584 (11th Cir. 1982).

A release provision, contained in a reorganization plan negotiated by a committee, which preserves the liability of committee members for willful misconduct but otherwise grants them immunity, is consistent with the important role of committees in the bankruptcy system and strikes the proper balance between their fiduciary duty and their grant of limited immunity, both of which are implicit in section 1103(c). *In re* Drexel Burnham Lambert Group, Inc., 26 C.B.C.2d 1283 (B. Ct., S.D.N.Y. 1992).

The application of an unsecured creditors' committee for an order approving its employment of a law firm should be denied when a substantial relationship exists between the law firm's prior representation of the debtor and the issues present in the debtor's chapter 11 case. Although those members of a law firm who were employed by a creditors' committee were not with the law firm at the time the firm represented the debtor prior to commencement of the chapter 11 case, a Chinese wall would not have been in the best interests of the committee since every member of the firm during its representation of the debtor would have had to be screened off from the attorneys representing the committee at a time when the committee needed to be represented by counsel who had not only bankruptcy expertise but also expertise in numerous other practice specialties. In the Matter of Davenport Communications Limited Partnership, 22 C.B.C.2d 1316 (B. Ct., S.D. Iowa 1990).

Since the sale of substantially all the debtor's assets would have a profound effect on the estate and the creditors' committee's ability to form a reorganization plan, it cannot be considered day-to-day business of the debtor. Therefore, the creditors' committee is entitled to sufficient information to evaluate and take a position on the proposed sale, which includes access to the drafts of proposed sale agreements. *In re* Structurlite Plastics Corp., 19 C.B.C.2d 1308 (B. Ct., S.D. Ohio 1988).

Only upon appointment of a legal representative for a group of claimants can that representative pursue action on behalf of the claimants; when class certification is denied the movants are not able to act in a representative capacity for absent class members. Lazard v. Texaco, Inc. (*In re* Texaco Inc.), 18 C.B.C.2d 243 (B. Ct., S.D.N.Y. 1988).

When a legal representative appointed to represent putative asbestos claimants is not in fact a committee, but has been granted the powers and assigned the responsibilities of section 1103 by a bankruptcy court, the court can alter or amend those powers and responsibilities as circumstances might dictate. *In re* UNR Indus., Inc., 16 C.B.C.2d 774 (B. Ct., N.D. Ill. 1987).

References

5 *Collier on Bankruptcy* ch. 1103 (Matthew Bender 15th ed.).

2 *Collier Bankruptcy Manual* ch. 1103 (Matthew Bender 3d ed.).

5 *Collier Bankruptcy Practice Guide* ch. 83 (Matthew Bender).

Blain and O'Gawa, *Creditors' Committees Under Chapter 11 of the United States Bankruptcy Code: Creation, Composition, Powers, and Duties,* 73 Marq. L. Rev. 581 (1990).

The Chapter 11 Creditors' Committee: Statutory Watchdog?, 2 Bankr. Dev. J. 247 (1985).

Comment, *Creditors' Committees' Right to Be Heard in Chapter Eleven Reorganization Actions,* 37 Mercer L. Rev. 1067 (1986).

The Secured Claimholder's Liability for the Costs and Expenses Incurred in Bankruptcy, 90 Com. L.J. 430 (1985).

Tatelbaum and Wannamaker, III, *Reimbursement of Creditors' Committee Expenses in Chapter 11—A Thing of the Past?,* 89 Com. L.J. 518 (1984).

SECTION 1104 (11 U.S.C. § 1104)

§ 1104. Appointment of trustee or examiner.

(a) At any time after the commencement of the case but before confirmation of a plan, on request of a party in interest or the United States trustee, and after notice and a hearing, the court shall order the appointment of a trustee—

(1) for cause, including fraud, dishonesty, incompetence, or gross mismanagement of the affairs of the debtor by current management, either before or after the commencement of the case, or similar cause, but not including the number of holders of securities of the debtor or the amount of assets or liabilities of the debtor; or

(2) if such appointment is in the interest of creditors, any equity security holders, and other interests of the estate, without regard to the number of holders of securities of the debtor or the amount of assets or liabilities of the debtor.

(b) If the court does not order the appointment of a trustee under this section, then at any time before the confirmation of a plan, on request of a party in interest or the United States trustee, and after notice and a hearing, the court shall order the appointment of an examiner to conduct such an investigation of the debtor as is appropriate, including an investigation of any allegations of fraud, dishonesty, incompetence, misconduct, mismanagement, or irregularity in the management of the affairs of the debtor of or by current or former management of the debtor, if—

(1) such appointment is in the interests of creditors, any equity security holders, and other interests of the estate; or

(2) the debtor's fixed, liquidated, unsecured debts, other than debts for goods, services, or taxes, or owing to an insider, exceed $5,000,000.

(c) If the court orders the appointment of a trustee or examiner, if a trustee or an examiner dies or resigns during the case or is removed under section 324 of this title, or if a trustee fails to qualify under section 322 of this title, then the United States trustee, after consultation with parties in interest shall appoint, subject to the court's approval, one disinterested person other than the United States trustee to serve as trustee or examiner, as the case may be, in the case.

Bankruptcy Rule References: 2008, 2009, 2010, 2012, 2013 and 5002

Legislative History

Subsection (a) of this section governs the appointment of trustees in reorganization cases. The court is permitted to order the appointment of one trustee at any time after the commencement of the case if a party in interest so requests. The court may order appointment only if the protection afforded by a trustee is needed and the costs and expenses of a trustee would not be disproportionately higher than the value of the protection afforded.

The protection afforded by a trustee would be needed, for example, in cases where the current management of the debtor has been fraudulent or dishonest, or has grossly mismanaged the company, or where the debtor's management has abandoned the business. A trustee would not necessarily be needed to investigate misconduct of former management of the debtor, because an examiner appointed under this section might well be able to serve that function adequately without displacing the current management. Generally, a trustee would not be needed in any case where the protection afforded by a trustee could equally be afforded by an examiner. Though the device of examiner appears in current chapter X, it is rarely used because of the nearly absolute presumption in favor of the appointment of a trustee. Its use here will give the courts, debtors, creditors, and equity security holders greater flexibility in handling the affairs of an insolvent debtor, permitting the court to tailor the remedy to the case.

The second test, relating to the costs and expenses of a trustee, is not intended to be a strict cost/benefit analysis. It is included to require the court to have due regard for any additional costs or expenses that the appointment of a trustee would impose on the estate.

[*House Report No. 95–595, 95th Cong., 1st Sess. 402 (1977).*]

Subsection (a) provides for the mandatory appointment of a disinterested trustee in the case of a public company, as defined in section 1101(3), within 10 days of the order for relief, or of a successor, in the event of a vacancy, as soon as practicable.

Section 156 of chapter X (11 U.S.C. § 516) requires the appointment of a disinterested trustee if the debtor's liabilities are $250,000 or over. Section 1104(a) marks a substantial change. The appointment of a trustee is mandatory only for a public company, which under section 1103(3), has $5 million in liabilities, excluding tax and trade obligations, and 1,000 security holders. In view of past experience, cases involving public companies will under normal circumstances probably be relatively few in number but of vast importance in terms of public investor interest. [*Ed. Note:* The provision for mandatory appointment of a trustee in the case of a public company was deleted from the final version of the Bill.]

In case of a nonpublic company, the appointment or election of a trustee is discretionary if the interests of the estate and its security holders would be served thereby. A test based on probate costs and benefits of a trusteeship is not practical. The appointment may be made at any time prior to confirmation of the plan.

[*Senate Report No. 95–989, 95th Cong., 2d Sess. 115 (1978).*]

Subsection (b) permits the court, at any time after the commencement of the case and on request of a party in interest, to order the appointment of an examiner, if the court has not ordered the appointment of a trustee. The examiner would be appointed to conduct such an investigation of the debtor as is appropriate under the particular circumstances of the case, including an investigation of any allegations of fraud, dishonesty, or gross mismanagement of the debtor of or by current or former management of the debtor. The standards for the appointment of an examiner are the same as those for the appointment of a trustee; the protection must be needed, and the costs and expenses must not be disproportionately high.

By virtue of proposed 11 U.S.C. § 1109, an indenture trustee and the Securities and Exchange Commission will be parties in interest for the purpose of requesting the appointment of a trustee or examiner.

Subsection (c) directs that the United States trustee actually select and appoint the trustee or examiner ordered appointed under this section. The United States trustee is required to consult with various parties in interest before selecting and appointing a trustee. He is not bound to select one of the members of the panel of private trustees established under proposed 28 U.S.C. § 586(a)(1) which exists only for the purpose of providing trustees for chapter 7 cases. Neither is he precluded from selecting a panel member if the member is qualified to serve as chapter 11 trustee. Appointment by the United States trustee will remove the court from the often criticized practice of appointing an officer that will appear in litigation before the court against an adverse party.

[*House Report No. 95–595, 95th Cong., 1st Sess. 402 (1977).*]

In case of a nonpublic company, if no trustee is appointed, the court may under subsection (c) appoint an examiner, if the appointment would serve the interests of the estate and security holders. The purpose of his appointment is specified in section 1106(b).

[*Senate Report No. 95–989, 95th Cong., 2d Sess. 115 (1978).*]

Section 1104 of the House amendment represents a compromise between the House bill and the Senate amendment concerning the appointment of a trustee or examiner. The method of appointment rather than election, is derived from the House bill; the two alternative standards of appointment are derived with modifications from the Senate amendment, instead of the standard stated in the House bill. For example, if the current management of the debtor gambled away rental income before the filing of the petition, a trustee should be appointed after the petition, whether or not postpetition mismanagement can be shown. However, under no circumstances will cause include the number of security holders of the debtor, or the amount of assets or liabilities of the debtor. The standard also applies to the appointment of an examiner in those circumstances in which mandatory appointment, as previously detailed, is not required.

[*124 Cong. Rec. H 11,102 (Sept. 28, 1978); S 17,419 (Oct. 6, 1978).*]

Comment

Section 1104 governs appointment of a trustee or examiner in chapter 11 cases. The norm, under section 1104, is to leave the debtor in possession unless a party in interest or the United States trustee requests appointment of a trustee or examiner. Upon such request, after notice and hearing the court shall order the appointment of a trustee if one of two conditions is found to exist: (1) fraud, dishonesty, incompetence or gross mismanagement, or (2) a trustee would be in the best interest of creditors, and equity security holders, and other interests, regardless of number of holders of securities or the amount of assets or liabilities. The court orders the appointment of a trustee, but the appointment is made by the United States trustee. This section allows much more flexibility in the appointment of a trustee in a reorganization case than under Chapter X of the former Bankruptcy Act. In a Chapter X case, a trustee was usually the norm because appointment was mandated when the liabilities were $250,000 or more. In Chapters XI and XII a receiver (Chapter XI) and a trustee (Chapter XII) was appointed only when necessary. Thus, under section 1104 of the Code, even in a large case that under the Act would have required the Chapter X machinery, the debtor may be left in possession, resulting in, *inter alia,* economy in the administration costs. On the other hand, in a smaller case which would ordinarily have been filed under Chapter XI of the Act, and where the norm was for the debtor to remain in possession, this practice is continued and a trustee will be appointed only when circumstances warrant it.

There was no provision in the Act for an examiner in Chapter XI or XII cases. Indeed, an examiner was rarely appointed under Chapter X because practically every case filed thereunder had noncontingent, liquidated liabilities in excess of $250,000 and, therefore, appointment of a trustee was the rule rather than the exception.

Under section 1104, however, an examiner may be appointed in any type of reorganization case, large or small, when the debtor is permitted to remain in possession. Here again, appointment must be requested by a party in interest or the United States trustee, there must be a hearing on notice, and it must appear that either (1) the appointment is in the best interest of creditors, and equity security holders, and other interests of the estate, or (2) that the debtor's fixed, liquidated, unsecured debts (other than for goods, services, taxes or owing an insider) exceed $5 million. As in the case of a trustee, the United States trustee appoints the examiner on order of the court.

Bankruptcy Rule 2008 requires the United States trustee to notify immediately the the person selected as trustee how to qualify and the amount of the bond. Unless such person notifies the court and United States trustee in writing of the acceptance of the office within five days after receipt of notice of selection, such person will be deemed to reject the office. (If the trustee accepts, he must qualify within five days after his selection as provided in section 322(a).)

Bankruptcy Rule 2010(a) permits the United States trustee to authorize a blanket bond to cover a person who qualifies as trustee in a number of cases, and a number of trustees each qualifying in a different case. Subdivision (b) provides that a certified copy of the order approving the trustee's bond shall constitute conclusive evidence of qualification.

Bankruptcy Rule 2009(c)(2) provides that in chapter 11 cases, if appointment of a trustee is ordered, the United States trustee may appoint one or more trustees for jointly administered cases. Subdivision (d) provides that on a showing that creditors or equity security holders of the different estates will be prejudiced by conflicts of interest of a common trustee who has been elected or appointed, the court shall order separate trustees for jointly administered estates. Subdivision (e) requires the trustee(s) of jointly administered estates to keep separate accounts of the property and distribution of each.

Bankruptcy Rule 2012(a), added by the 1987 Amendments to the Bankruptcy Rules, provides that a trustee appointed in a chapter 11 case is substituted automatically for the debtor in possession as a party in any pending action, proceeding or matter. Subdivision (b) provides that if a trustee dies, resigns, is removed or otherwise ceases to hold office, the successor is automatically substituted as a party in any pending action, proceeding or matter. Within the time fixed by the court, the successor must file and transmit to the United States trustee an accounting of the prior administration of the estate.

Bankruptcy Rule 2013(a) was deleted by the 1991 Amendments. Subdivision (b), relettered (a), requires the clerk to maintain a public record of fees awarded to trustees, examiners, attorneys, etc., including the name and docket number of the case. Subdivision (b) requires the clerk to prepare an annual summary to reflect total fees by individual or firm name awarded the previous year. The summary shall be open to public inspection without charge and the clerk shall transmit a copy to the United States trustee.

Bankruptcy Rule 5002(b), as amended in 1991, provides that a bankruptcy judge may not approve the appointment of a person as trustee or examiner (Code section 1104) or approve employment of an attorney, accountant, appraiser, auctioneer, or other professional, if that person is or has been so connected with such judge or the United States trustee as to render the appointment or employment improper. ["Improper" includes the appearance of impropriety.]

1986 Amendments: Section 1104(a) was amended to permit the United States trustee as well as a party in interest to request the appointment of a chapter 11 trustee. Subsection (b) was similarly amended to permit the United States trustee to request the appointment of an examiner. Subsection (c), as amended, provides that if the court orders the appointment of a trustee or examiner, the United States trustee, after consultation with parties in interest, shall appoint, subject to the court's approval, one disinterested person [other than the United States trustee] to serve as trustee. In like manner, if a trustee or examiner dies, resigns, is removed or fails to qualify, the United States trustee shall appoint, subject to court approval, one disinterested person to serve as trustee or examiner, as the case may be.

The amendments carry out the intent of the Code to relieve the Bankruptcy Judge of administrative duties by assigning many such duties to the United States trustee.

This section was amended to reflect the creation of a permanent United States trustee system. Section 302(d) of the 1986 Amendments provides different effective dates for the amendments relating to the United States trustee system. *See* Section 302 of the 1986 Amendments, reprinted herein under "Selected Provisions of the Bankruptcy Judges, United States Trustees, and Family Farmer Bankruptcy Act of 1986," regarding effective dates generally.

1990 Amendments: Section 302(d)(3) of the Bankruptcy Judges, United States Trustees, and Family Farmer Bankruptcy Act of 1986 was amended by Pub. L. No. 101-650 (Judicial Improvements Act of 1990) to extend the period in which the judicial districts in the states of Alabama and North Carolina may remain outside the United States trustee system and to insert new language pertaining to the effective date of the 1986 amendment to section 105 of title 11.

Case Annotations

When the bankruptcy court appoints a trustee *sua sponte* and without a broad-gauged evaluation as to whether the debtors' unauthorized conduct was sufficient to warrant the appointment of a trustee, denial of a stay pending appeal of the appointment by the district court does not amount to such judicial usurpation of power as would require the extraordinary remedy of mandamus. In the Matter of Hester, 899 F.2d 361, 23 C.B.C.2d 567 (5th Cir. 1990).

The plain meaning of the word "shall" in section 1104(b) means that a bankruptcy court must order the appointment of an examiner at the United States trustee's request, if the total fixed, liquidated, unsecured debt exceeds $5 million. *In re* Revco D.S., Inc., 898 F.2d 498, 22 C.B.C.2d 841 (6th Cir. 1990).

A court need not find any of the enumerated wrongs of section 1104(a)(1) to justify the appointment of a trustee; it is sufficient that the appointment be in the interest of the creditors. Oklahoma Refining Co. v. Blaik (*In re* Oklahoma Refining Co.), 838 F.2d 1133, 18 C.B.C.2d 278 (10th Cir. 1988).

The appointment of a trustee to manage a chapter 11 debtor corporation is within the discretion of the court; the court may weigh the interests of all concerned, including the creditors, before concluding that an act of dishonesty by the debtor, in the absence of fraud or mismanagement, rises or does not rise to the level of cause needed under section 1104 to warrant the trustee's appointment. Committee of Dalkon Shield Claimants v. A.H. Robins Co., 828 F.2d 239, 17 C.B.C.2d 591 (4th Cir. 1987).

In a chapter 11 case, the court is not a party to the proceeding and, thus, lacks authority to *sua sponte* order the appointment of a trustee. Cournoyer v. Town of Lincoln, 13 C.B.C.2d 1110 (D.R.I. 1985), *aff'd,* 790 F.2d 971, 14 C.B.C.2d 1085 (1st Cir. 1986).

When a debtor fails to provide an adequate record of the proceedings below and only supplies an unsigned confirmation order of a reorganization plan and an order appointing a chapter 11 trustee, there is no sufficient evidence to support a finding that the bankruptcy court acted *sua sponte* in ordering the appointment of a trustee. *In re* Strowski, 20 C.B.C.2d 1443 (9th Cir., B.A.P., 1989).

A court may not appoint a trustee in a chapter 11 case after the plan has been confirmed. *In re* Modern Steel Treating Co., 25 C.B.C.2d 292 (B. Ct., N.D. Ill. 1991).

Although the Bankruptcy Code clearly favors the continuance of the debtor in possession in chapter 11 cases, section 1104 contemplated that when the evidence strongly suggests that the debtor has wilfully disregarded the bankruptcy process, the appropriate circumstances exist for the termination of debtor control and for the appointment of a trustee. *In re* Cumberland Investment Corp., 23 C.B.C.2d 1433 (B. Ct., D.R.I. 1990).

In considering a motion for the appointment of a trustee, a bankruptcy court is not required to conduct a full evidentiary hearing. The party requesting the appointment has the burden of proof in showing "cause," and the evidence supporting the motion for the appointment must be clear and convincing. However, section 1104(a)(2) creates a flexible standard which allows the appointment of a trustee even when no "cause" exists by looking towards the practical realities and necessities. Among the factors to be considered are (i) the trustworthiness of the debtor; (ii) the debtor in possession's past and present performance and prospects for the debtor's rehabilitation; (iii) the confidence, or lack thereof, of the business community and of creditors in present management; and (iv) the benefits derived by the appointment of a trustee, balanced against the cost of the appointment. *In re* Ionosphere Clubs, Inc., 22 C.B.C.2d 1583 (B. Ct., S.D.N.Y. 1990).

Allegations of misconduct alone do not warrant the appointment of an examiner; accusations must be supported by facts such as a transfer of property to a related company or the failure to file an accurate financial report. *In re* Gilman Serv., Inc., 12 C.B.C.2d 27 (B. Ct., D. Mass. 1985).

The court may initiate a request for the appointment of an examiner when, although appointment is necessary, the parties in interest have failed to initiate such request. *In re* Landscaping Servs., Inc., 10 C.B.C.2d 1051 (B. Ct., E.D.N.C. 1984).

When the management of the debtor fails to keep adequate books and records, commingles its assets with the parent corporation and an admittedly adverse interest between the operator and equity holders exists, a trustee should be appointed. *In re* Philadelphia Athletic Club, Inc., 5 C.B.C.2d 458 (B. Ct., E.D. Pa. 1981).

References

5 *Collier on Bankruptcy* ch. 1104 (Matthew Bender 15th ed.).

2 *Collier Bankruptcy Manual* ch. 1104 (Matthew Bender 3d ed.).

5 *Collier Bankruptcy Practice Guide* ch. 85 (Matthew Bender).

SECTION 1105 (11 U.S.C. § 1105)

§ 1105. Termination of trustee's appointment. At any time before confirmation of a plan, on request of a party in interest or the United States trustee, and after notice and a hearing, the court may terminate the trustee's appointment and restore the debtor to possession and management of the property of the estate and of the operation of the debtor's business.

Legislative History

This section authorizes the court to terminate the trustee's appointment and to restore the debtor to possession and management of the property of the estate and to operation of the debtor's business. This section would permit the court to reverse its decision to order the appointment of a trustee in light of new evidence.

[*House Report No. 95–595, 95th Cong., 1st Sess. 403 (1977).*]

This section authorizes the court to terminate the trustee's appointment and to restore the debtor to possession and management of the property of the estate and operation of the debtor's business. Section 1104(a) provides that this section does not apply in the case of a public company for which the appointment of a trustee is mandatory. [*Ed. Note:* The provision for mandatory appointment of a trustee in the case of a public company was deleted from the final version of the bill.]

[*Senate Report No. 95–989, 95th Cong., 2d Sess. 115 (1978).*]

Comment

Section 1105 is derived from former Rule 10–202(d).

Because the Code does not mandate appointment of a trustee, section 1105 permits the court, on request of a party or the United States trustee and after notice and hearing, to terminate the trustee's appointment and restore the debtor to possession regardless of the amount of the debtor's liabilities. Thus, the court may reverse its decision to appoint a trustee in the light of new evidence that the debtor can safely be left in possession of its business and property.

1984 Amendments: A merely stylistic change was made in section 1105.

1986 Amendments: Section 1105 was amended by providing that the United States trustee, as well as a party in interest, may request termination of a trustee's appointment and restoration of the debtor as a debtor in possession.

This section was amended to reflect the creation of a permanent United States trustee system.

Case Annotations

When no evidence is introduced by a debtor seeking to terminate the appointment of a trustee that the appointment was improvidently granted or that there has been a change in circumstances since the date of the appointment, the trustee should not be terminated. *In re* Curlew Valley Assoc., 5 C.B.C.2d 255 (B. Ct., D. Utah 1981).

References

5 *Collier on Bankruptcy* ch. 1105 (Matthew Bender 15th ed.).

2 *Collier Bankruptcy Manual* ch. 1105 (Matthew Bender 3d ed.).

5 *Collier Bankruptcy Practice Guide* ch. 85 (Matthew Bender).

SECTION 1106 (11 U.S.C. § 1106)

§ 1106. Duties of trustee and examiner.

(a) A trustee shall—

(1) perform the duties of a trustee specified in sections 704(2), 704(5), 704(7), 704(8), and 704(9) of this title;

(2) if the debtor has not done so, file the list, schedule, and statement required under section 521(1) of this title;

(3) except to the extent that the court orders otherwise, investigate the acts, conduct, assets, liabilities, and financial condition of the debtor, the operation of the debtor's business and the desirability of the continuance of such business, and any other matter relevant to the case or to the formulation of a plan;

(4) as soon as practicable—

(A) file a statement of any investigation conducted under paragraph (3) of this subsection, including any fact ascertained pertaining to fraud, dishonesty, incompetence, misconduct, mismanagement, or irregularity in the management of the affairs of the debtor, or to a cause of action available to the estate; and

(B) transmit a copy or a summary of any such statement to any creditors' committee or equity security holders' committee, to any indenture trustee, and to such other entity as the court designates;

(5) as soon as practicable, file a plan under section 1121 of this title, file a report of why the trustee will not file a plan, or recommend conversion of the case to a case under chapter 7, 12, or 13 of this title or dismissal of the case;

(6) for any year for which the debtor has not filed a tax return required by law, furnish, without personal liability, such information as may be required by the governmental unit with which such tax return was to be filed, in light of the condition of the debtor's books and records and the availability of such information; and

(7) after confirmation of a plan, file such reports as are necessary or as the court orders.

(b) An examiner appointed under section 1104(c) of this title shall perform the duties specified in paragraphs (3) and (4) of subsection (a) of this section, and, except to the extent that the court orders otherwise, any other duties of the trustee that the court orders the debtor in possession not to perform.

Bankruptcy Rule Reference: 2015

Legislative History

Subsection (a) of this section prescribes the trustee's duties. He is required to perform the duties of a trustee in a liquidation case specified in sections 704(2), (4), (6), (7), and (8). [*Ed. Note:* Subsections (4), (6), (7) and (8) of section 704 were redesignated as subsections (5), (7), (8) and (9) by Pub. L. No. 98–353 (1984).] These include reporting and informational duties, and accountability for all property received. Paragraph (2) of this subsection requires the trustee to file with the court, if the debtor has not done so, the list of creditors, schedule of assets and liabilities, and statement of affairs required under section 521(1).

Paragraph (3) requires the trustee to investigate the acts, conduct, assets, liabilities, and financial condition of the debtor, the operation of the debtor's business, and the desirability of the continuance of the business, and any other matter relevant to the case or to the formulation of a plan. Paragraph (4) requires the trustee to report the results of his investigation to the court and to creditors' committees, equity security holders' committees, indenture trustees and any other entity the court designates.

Paragraph (5) requires the trustee to file a plan or to report why a plan cannot be formulated, or to recommend conversion to liquidation or to an individual repayment plan case, or dismissal. It is anticipated that the trustee will consult with creditors and other parties in interest in the forumlation of a plan, just as the debtor in possession would. Consultation will be necessary in order to make more likely the obtaining of the requisite number of acceptances of the plan that is eventually formulated.

Paragraph (6) requires final reports by the trustee, as the court or the Rules of Bankruptcy Procedure require.

A provision similar to a [*sic*] Bankruptcy Act sections 186, 187 is not included in this chapter, because proposed 11 U.S.C. § 103 makes clear that the provisions of the first three chapters of the bankruptcy code apply equally in chapter 11 and chapter 7 cases.

Subsection (b) gives the trustee's investigative duties to an examiner, if one is appointed. The court is authorized to give the examiner additional duties as the circumstances warrant.

[*House Report No. 95–595, 95th Cong., 1st Sess. 403–404 (1977); See Senate Report No. 95–989, 95th Cong., 2d Sess. 115–116 (1978).*]

Comment

Sections 704(2), (5), (7), (8) and (9) of the Code specify the duties of a liquidation trustee as follows:

(2) be accountable for all property received; . . .

(5) if a purpose would be served, examine proofs of claims and object to the allowance of any claim that is improper; . . .

(7) unless the court orders otherwise, furnish such information concerning the estate and the estate's administration as is requested by a party in interest;

(8) if the business of the debtor is authorized to be operated, file with the court and with any governmental unit charged with responsibility for collection or determination of any tax arising out of such operation, periodic reports and summaries of the operation of such business, including a statement of receipts and disbursements, and such other information as the court requires; and

(9) make a final report and file a final account of the administration of the estate with the court.

The duties of a trustee in a chapter 11 reorganization, as enumerated in section 1106 of the Code, are derived from former Bankruptcy Rule 10–208.

It will be noted that the changes effected by section 1106 are either stylistic or combine and clarify provisions of former Rule 10–208. The section speaks for itself, but it may be noted that while former Rule 11–208(4) mandated the investigation of the debtor and its affairs, section 1106(3) directs the investigation "except to the extent that the court orders otherwise." Under appropriate circumstances the court may restrict or limit the investigation and thus reduce the cost of an all-out examination and "fishing excursion" that may be unnecessary.

Section 1106(6) requires the trustee to furnish such information available to such trustee as may be required by any governmental unit for any year for which debtor failed to file a tax return required by law.

Bankruptcy Rule 2015 amplifies the various duties of a trustee which are found in sections 704 and 1106. Subdivision (a) requires a trustee:

(1) if the court so directs, to file, within 30 days after qualifying as a trustee or debtor in possession, a complete inventory of the debtor's property unless such inventory has already been filed;

(2) to keep a record of receipts and disposition of money and property received;

(3) to file the reports and summaries required by section 704(8) (periodic reports must be filed if business is authorized to be operated) within the time fixed by the court, including, if payments are made to employees, a statement of the amounts of deductions for taxes required to be withheld and the place where deposited;

(4) as soon as possible, to give notice of the case to every entity known to be holding money or property subject to withdrawal or order to the debtor, including every bank, savings or building and loan association, public utility company, and landlord with whom the debtor has a deposit, and to every insurance company which has issued a policy having a cash surrender value payable to the debtor, except that notice need not be given any entity who has knowledge of or has previously been notified of the case;

(5) On or before the last day of the month after each calendar quarter and until a plan is confirmed or the case converted or dismissed, file and transmit to the United States trustee a statement of disbursements made during such quarter and a statement of the amount of the fee required pursuant to 28 U.S.C. § 1930(a)(6) that has been paid for such calendar quarter. [This paragraph was added in 1991 to enable the United States trustee, other parties in interest, and the court to determine the appropriate quarterly fee required by 28 U.S.C. § 1930(a)(6). Former subparagraphs (5), (6) and (7) were deleted.]

Bankruptcy Rule 2015(d) provides that the court may direct that copies or summaries of the annual reports or other reports be mailed to the creditors, equity security holders and indenture trustees, and may also direct publication of summaries of the reports. A copy of every report or summary mailed or published pursuant to this subdivision shall be transmitted to the United States trustee.

1984 Amendments: Section 1106(a)(1) was amended by changing the reference to subsections of section 704 to conform to the changes in the latter. Subsection (b) was amended by insertion of the phrase "except to the extent that the court orders otherwise."

1986 Amendments: The 1986 amendment merely brought chapter 12 cases within the orbit of subsection (a)(5).

Case Annotations

A trustee appointed to liquidate and distribute property of corporate debtors that has been placed in a liquidating trust pursuant to a chapter 11 plan is an "assignee" of the corporate debtors and, therefore, obligated to file income tax returns for them under 26 U.S.C. § 6012(b)(3), regardless of whether the debtors are dissolving or the assignee manages the debtors' business. Additionally, a trustee who, under the plan, is granted powers consistent with those of a fiduciary over property contained in a liquidating trust, including the property of an individual debtor, is obligated to file returns for the individual debtor pursuant to 26 U.S.C. § 6012(b)(4). Holywell Corp. v. Smith, 503 U.S. —, 112 S. Ct. 1021, 117 L. Ed. 2d 196, 26 C.B.C.2d 1 (1992).

Pursuant to the Bankruptcy Protection Act, a court must analyze the "plan, fund, or program maintained or established" by a debtor in order to determine the trustee's obligation to the debtor's retired former employees. When a wage agreement obligates an employer to pay retiree benefits, but also provides for a trust to pay benefits if the employer is no longer in business, there is obviously no intent that the employer's obligation continue beyond the wage agreement and, therefore, when the employer becomes a debtor it is not obligated to pay retiree health benefits. *In re* Chateaugay Corp., 945 F.2d 1205, 25 C.B.C.2d 802 (2d Cir. 1991).

When the parties in a chapter 11 case have stipulated that the court should appoint an examiner rather than designate a trustee and that the debtor in possession be removed from business management and operations, the power to waive the attorney-client privilege will reside with the examiner if he has been given expanded powers and the powers of the debtor in possession have been specifically limited. Boileau v. Dillaway (*In re* Boileau), 736 F.2d 503, 10 C.B.C.2d 1246 (9th Cir. 1984).

A trustee may terminate a chapter 11 company's operations without giving notice to a union if there is a need for immediate action and the union would not benefit from such short notice. Yorke v. NLRB, 709

F.2d 1138, 8 C.B.C.2d 921 (7th Cir. 1983), *cert. denied,* 465 U.S. 1023, 104 S. Ct. 1276, 79 L. Ed. 2d 680 (1984).

A debtor in possession has the broad duties incidental to his title, possession and powers and may be held liable for violations of his fiduciary duties but only if he acted willfully and deliberately in violation of these duties, and not for mere mistakes in judgment. Ford Motor Credit Co. v. Weaver, 680 F.2d 451, 6 C.B.C.2d 1173 (6th Cir. 1982).

Regardless of whether a debtor corporation is closely or publicly held, to deny a trustee access to confidential information in the possession of the debtor corporation's former counsel by permitting shareholders, officers or directors of the debtor corporation the right to assert the debtor's attorney-client privilege would result in the debtor's privilege being used against its own interests and to obstruct the trustee's statutory duties to investigate and manage the affairs of the debtor. *In re* O.P.M. Leasing Services, Inc., 4 C.B.C.2d 1149 (S.D.N.Y. 1981), *aff'd,* 670 F.2d 383, 5 C.B.C.2d 1252 (2d Cir. 1982).

A trustee should not be subject to personal liability for nonpayment of postpetition trust fund taxes when those taxes are incurred during the administration of the estate by the debtor in possession. *In re* ABA Recovery Service, Inc., 22 C.B.C.2d 651 (B. Ct., S.D. Cal. 1990).

A court may order the United States trustee to designate an examiner to inquire into the relationship between a debtor in possession and its sole shareholder who is the debtor's largest secured creditor when both parties are being represented by the same counsel and there exists a potential for conflicts. *In re* Jartran, Inc., 18 C.B.C.2d 71 (B. Ct., N.D. Ill. 1987).

Although an examiner is authorized to perform the duties of a trustee, the bankruptcy court may give the examiner additional duties such as the power to mediate plan negotiations between a debtor and parties in interest. *In re* UNR Indus., Inc., 16 C.B.C.2d 1269 (B. Ct., N.D. Ill. 1987).

References

5 *Collier on Bankruptcy* ch. 1106 (Matthew Bender 15th ed.).

2 *Collier Bankruptcy Manual* ch. 1106 (Matthew Bender 3d ed.).

5 *Collier Bankruptcy Practice Guide* ch. 86 (Matthew Bender).

McCaffery and Holthus, *Putting a Little "Trust" in the Chapter 11 Trustee,* 91 Com. L.J. 469 (1986).

SECTION 1107 (11 U.S.C. § 1107)

§ 1107. Rights, powers, and duties of debtor in possession.

(a) Subject to any limitations on a trustee serving in a case under this chapter, and to such limitations or conditions as the court prescribes, a debtor in possession shall have all the rights, other than the right to compensation under section 330 of this title, and powers, and shall perform all the functions and duties, except the duties specified in sections 1106(a)(2), (3), and (4) of this title, of a trustee serving in a case under this chapter.

(b) Notwithstanding section 327(a) of this title, a person is not disqualified for employment under section 327 of this title by a debtor in possession solely because of such person's employment by or representation of the debtor before the commencement of the case.

Bankruptcy Rule References: 2015, 6009 and 9001

Legislative History

This section places a debtor in possession in the shoes of a trustee in every way. The debtor is given the rights and powers of a chapter 11 trustee. He is required to perform the functions and duties of a chapter 11 trustee (except the investigative duties). He is also subject to any limitations on a chapter 11 trustee, and to such other limitations and conditions as the court prescribes *cf.* Wolf v. Weinstein, 372 U.S. 633, 649–650 (1963).

[*Senate Report No. 95–989, 95th Cong., 2d Sess. 116 (1978); See also House Report No. 95–595, 95th Cong., 1st Sess. 404 (1977).*]

The House amendment adopts section 1107(b) of the Senate amendment which clarifies a point not covered by the House bill. The House amendment adopts section 1108 of the House bill in preference to the style of an identical substantive provision contained in the Senate amendment. Throughout title 11 references to a "trustee" is read to include other parties under various sections of the bill. For example, section 1107 applies to give the debtor in possession all the rights and powers of a trustee in a case under chapter 11; this includes the power of the trustee to operate the debtor's business under section 1108.

[*124 Cong. Rec. H 11,102 (Sept. 28, 1978); S 17,419 (Oct. 6, 1978).*]

Comment

Under section 1107, the debtor in possession is required to perform all the duties specified for a trustee pursuant to section 1106(a) *except* to (1) file the list, schedule and statement (which the debtor in possession is required to file in any event under section 521(1)); (2) conduct an investigation into its own acts, conduct, etc.; and (3) file a statement of investigation or transmit any such statement to any committee, etc.

The debtor in possession is placed in the shoes of a trustee respecting his rights, duties and title.

With the granting of all the rights and powers of a trustee, the debtor in possession has the power of a trustee to operate the business as provided in section 1108. No specific grant is therefore necessary.

Section 1107(b) makes it possible for the debtor in possession to employ an attorney or accountant to represent the debtor in possession in all proceedings under chapter 11. The professional (or other person) is not disqualified because of such person's employment by the debtor prior to the commencement of the case.

Bankruptcy Rule 9001(10) provides that as used in the Bankruptcy Rules, the word "trustee" includes a debtor in possession in a chapter 11 case.

Bankruptcy Rule 2015 relates to the duties of a trustee *or* of a debtor in possession. *See* Comment to section 1106 for discussion of duties.

Bankruptcy Rule 2011 provides that whenever evidence is required that a debtor is a debtor in possession or that a trustee has qualified, the clerk may so certify and the certificate shall constitute conclusive evidence of that fact.

Bankruptcy Rule 6009 authorizes the trustee or debtor in possession, with or without court approval, to prosecute or appear and defend any pending action or proceeding by or against the debtor, or commence and prosecute any action or proceeding in behalf of the estate before any tribunal.

Bankruptcy Rule 2014 deals with the employment of professional persons by a trustee or committee, and pursuant to Rule 9001(10), the provisions of Rule 2014 are applicable to a debtor in posession. *See* Comment to section 1104.

1984 Amendments: Subsection (a) of section 1107 was amended by insertion of the words "serving in a case."

Case Annotations

"In the context of rejection or assumption of collective bargaining agreements, the debtor in possession is the same "entity" which existed before the filing of the bankruptcy petition, but empowered by virtue of the Bankruptcy Code to deal with its contracts and property in a manner it could not have done absent the bankruptcy filing." NLRB v. Bildisco & Bildisco, 465 U.S. 513, 104 S. Ct. 1188, 79 L. Ed. 2d 482, 9 C.B.C.2d 1219 (1984).

A corporate chapter 11 debtor in possession is a proper party to seek an award of attorney's fees under 26 U.S.C. § 7430. *In re* Brickell Investment Corp., 922 F.2d 696, 24 C.B.C.2d 731 (11th Cir. 1991).

The debtor in possession is considered a trustee and is obligated to perform all the obligations and functions of a trustee. *In re* Dant & Russell, Inc., 853 F.2d 700, 20 C.B.C.2d 369 (9th Cir. 1988).

Section 1107(a), which gives the debtor powers of a trustee and subjects the debtor in possession to the limitations placed on a trustee, does not equate service of the debtor in possession with the appointment of a trustee for purposes of section 546(a). *In re* Pullman Constr. Indus., Inc., 25 C.B.C.2d 1177 (B. Ct., N.D. Ill. 1991).

The disinterestedness requirement of section 1107(b) should not be applied less stringently to the debtor in possession, as opposed to the trustee; this section will not override the more stringent requirements of section 327(a) to permit debtors in possession to employ professionals with prepetition claims. *In re* Watervliet Paper Co., Inc., 20 C.B.C.2d 633 (B. Ct., W.D. Mich. 1989).

A debtor's prepetition attorney should not be automatically disqualified from representing the debtor in possession because he is owed fees for nonbankruptcy work done before the chapter 11 petition was filed. However, the attorney may still be disqualified under section 327(a) if the claim for fees gives him an interest adverse to the bankruptcy estate. *In re* Best W. Heritage Inn Partnership, 17 C.B.C.2d 778 (B. Ct., E.D. Tenn. 1987).

When a law firm is an insider to and a creditor of a debtor corporation, and also represents creditors and equity security holders of debtor entities, it cannot be said that the firm does not hold or represent an interest adverse to the debtor corporation, and thus the law firm cannot continue to represent the chapter 11 debtor. *In re* Michigan General Corp., 17 C.B.C.2d 367 (B. Ct., N.D. Tex.), *reh'g denied,* 17 C.B.C.2d 846 (B. Ct., N.D. Tex. 1987).

If the official creditors' committee has instituted an action on behalf of the debtor in possession to avoid a leveraged buyout, the debtor cannot defend the action by intervening as a defendant. Ohio Corrugating Co. v. Security Pac. Business Credit, Inc. (In the Matter of Ohio Corrugating Co.), 16 C.B.C.2d 821 (B. Ct., N.D. Ohio 1987).

An unsecured creditors' committee may be given authorization *nunc pro tunc* to sue to avoid a preference or fraudulent transfer when fairness mandates that the issues be brought to the attention of the court. *In re* Jones, 10 C.B.C.2d 1016 (B. Ct., N.D. Tex. 1984).

References

5 *Collier on Bankruptcy* ch. 1107 (Matthew Bender 15th ed.).

2 *Collier Bankruptcy Manual* ch. 1107 (Matthew Bender 3d ed.).

5 *Collier Bankruptcy Practice Guide* ch. 84 (Matthew Bender).

Chapter 11 Filings Drop in 1987, But Total Filings Keep Climbing, 3 Comm. L. Bull. 8 (1988).

Chapter 11, Haven for Megacases?, 3 Comm. L. Bull. 12 (1988).

Chobot, *Enforcing the Cash Collateral Obligations of Debtors in Possession,* 96 Com. L.J. 136 (1991).

Littman, *Reasonable Assumptions, Responsible Persons and Invisible Boomerangs: Payments of Trust Fund Liabilities in and Before Bankruptcy,* 42 Fla. L. Rev. 711 (1990).

SECTION 1108 (11 U.S.C. § 1108)

§ 1108. Authorization to operate business. Unless the court, on request of a party in interest and after notice and a hearing, orders otherwise, the trustee may operate the debtor's business.

Bankruptcy Rule Reference: 2015

Legislative History

This section permits the debtor's business to continue to be operated, unless the court orders otherwise. Thus, in a reorganization case, operation of the business will be the rule, and it will not be necessary to go to the court to obtain an order authorizing operation.

[*House Report No. 95–595, 95th Cong., 1st Sess. 404 (1977); Senate Report No. 95–989, 95th Cong., 2d Sess. 116 (1978).*]

This section does not presume that a trustee will be appointed to operate the business of the debtor. Rather, the power granted to trustee under this section is one of the powers that a debtor in possession acquires by virtue of proposed 11 U.S.C. § 1107.

[*House Report No. 95–595, 95th Cong., 1st Sess. 404 (1977).*]

[*Ed. Note:* For additional legislative history, *see* Congressional Record excerpt reprinted after section 1107, *supra.*]

Comment

Under section 1108 of the Code, the trustee or debtor in possession may operate the business as a matter of course unless the court orders otherwise.

If the business of the debtor is being operated, Bankruptcy Rule 2015(a)(3) requires the trustee or debtor in possession to file the reports and summaries required by section 704(8) including, if payments are made to employees, a statement of the amounts of deductions for taxes required to be withheld and the place where deposited.

1984 Amendment: Section 1108, as amended, provides that the court may order the trustee not to operate the business only on request of a party in interest and after notice and a hearing.

The United States trustee should receive notice of any hearing relating to the operation of the business by the trustee or debtor in possession in the light of (i) section 307 which empowers the United States trustee to raise and appear and be heard on any issue in any case or proceeding under the Code, and (ii) the provisions of 28 U.S.C. § 586(a)(3) requiring the United States trustee to supervise the administration of cases and trustees in cases under chapters 7, 11 and 13.

Case Annotations

Although section 1108 authorizes a chapter 11 trustee to operate a debtor's business, the trustee may not use the debtor's postpetition earnings derived from services to the business which are also proceeds of the business itself, because such earnings are not property of the estate pursuant to section 541(a)(6); to conclude otherwise would amount to placing the debtor in involuntary servitude in violation of the Thirteenth Amendment of the United States Constitution. Fitzsimmons v. Walsh & Official Creditors' Comm. (*In re* Fitzsimmons), 6 C.B.C.2d 887 (9th Cir., B.A.P., 1982), *aff'd,* 725 F.2d 1268, 10 C.B.C.2d 73 (9th Cir. 1984).

Since a debtor in possession has all of the rights of a trustee pursuant to section 1107(a), the debtor in possession is also authorized to operate its business unless the court orders otherwise. This authorization includes the right to incur and pay postpetition debts in the ordinary course of business without the prior approval of the bankruptcy court. Funding Sys. Asset Management Corp. v. Key Capital Corp. (*In re* Funding Sys. Asset Management Corp.), 16 C.B.C.2d 1289 (B. Ct., W.D. Pa. 1987).

When a trustee is appointed to conduct the business of a chapter 11 entity, the identity of that business is not eradicated or changed to the extent that he can now ignore the bills due and owing for its prior operations properly incurred by the debtor in possession. Flint Hills Food, Inc. v. Von Der Ahe (In the Matter of Isis Foods, Inc.), 6 C.B.C.2d 620 (B. Ct., W.D. Mo.), *aff'd,* 27 B.R. 156 (W.D. Mo. 1982).

The fact that there is no limiting or conditioning language in section 1108 concerning the review by the court of the operation of the business by a trustee whereas that language appears in section 1107(a) limiting the debtor in possession's discretion, suggests a purpose by Congress to have the courts monitor the latter and to allow a fuller rein for the trustee in the management of the estate. *In re* Curlew Valley Assoc., 5 C.B.C.2d 255 (B. Ct., D. Utah 1981).

References

5 *Collier on Bankruptcy* ch. 1108 (Matthew Bender 15th ed.).

2 *Collier Bankruptcy Manual* ch. 1108 (Matthew Bender 3d ed.).

5 *Collier Bankruptcy Practice Guide* ch. 89 (Matthew Bender).

Garner, *Franchise and Dealer Agreements Under Chapter 11 of the Bankruptcy Code,* 59 Am. Bankr. L.J. 99 (1985).

SECTION 1109 (11 U.S.C. § 1109)

§ 1109.   Right to be heard.

(a) The Securities and Exchange Commission may raise and may appear and be heard on any issue in a case under this chapter, but the Securities and Exchange Commission may not appeal from any judgment, order, or decree entered in the case.

(b) A party in interest, including the debtor, the trustee, a creditors' committee, an equity security holders' committee, a creditor, an equity security holder, or any indenture trustee, may raise and may appear and be heard on any issue in a case under this chapter.

Bankruptcy Rule Reference: 2018

Legislative History

Section 1109 authorizes the Securities and Exchange Commission and any indenture trustee to intervene in the case at any time on any issue. They may raise an issue or may appear and be heard on an issue that is raised by someone else. The section, following current law, denies the right of appeal to the Securities and Exchange Commission. It does not, however, prevent the Commission from joining or participating in an appeal taken by a true party in interest. The Commission is merely prevented from initiating the appeal in any capacity.

[*House Report No. 95–595, 95th Cong., 1st Sess. 116 (1977).*]

Subsection (b) provides that the Securities and Exchange Commission may appear by filing an appearance in a case of a public company and may appear in other cases if authorized or requested by the court. As a party in interest in either case, the Commission may raise and be heard on any issue. The Commission may not appeal from a judgment, order, or decree in a case, but may participate in any appeal by any other party in interest. This is the present law under section 208 of chapter X (11 U.S.C. § 608).

[*Ed. Note:* The Senate Bill prior to final amendment, listed the comments to subsections (a) and (b) in the reverse order of the way they appear in the final version.]

Subsection (a) provides, in unqualified terms, that any creditor, equity security holder, or an indenture trustee shall have the right to be heard as a party in interest under this chapter in person, by an attorney, or by a committee. It is derived from section 206 of chapter X (11 U.S.C. 606).

[*Senate Report No. 95–989, 95th Cong., 2d Sess. 116 (1978).*]

Section 1109 of the House amendment represents a compromise between comparable provisions in the House bill and Senate amendment.

As previously discussed the section gives the Securities and Exchange Commission the right to appear and be heard and to raise any issue in a case under chapter 11; however, the Securities and Exchange Commission is not a party in interest, and the Commission may not appeal from any judgment, order, or decree entered in the case. Under section 1109(b) a party in interest, including the debtor, the trustee, creditors committee, equity securities holders committee, a creditor, an equity security holder, or an indentured trustee may raise and may appear and be heard on any issue in a case under chapter 11. Section 1109(c) of the Senate amendment has been moved to subchapter IV pertaining to Railroad Reorganizations.

[*124 Cong. Rec. H 11,102 (Sept. 28, 1978); S 17,419 (Oct. 6, 1978).*]

Comment

As in the case of Section 206 of the former Bankruptcy Act and Rule 10–210(a)(1), from which it is derived, section 1109(b) of the Code continues the broad concept of the absolute right to be heard in order to insure fair representation in the case and prevent excessive control by insider groups.

Pursuant to subsections (a) and (b) of section 1109, the Securities and Exchange Commission as well as a party in interest, including the debtor, the trustee, a creditors' committee, an equity security holders' committee, a creditor, an equity security holder, or any indenture trustee, may raise and may appear and be heard on any issue in a case under chapter 11.

The Securities and Exchange Commission, however, may not appeal from any judgment, order, or decree entered in the case. Although barred from taking an appeal, the Commission may join or participate in an appeal taken by a party in interest.

Bankruptcy Rule 2018(a) provides that in any case under the Code, the court may, after hearing on such notice as it directs, and for cause shown, permit any interested entity to intervene generally or with respect to any specific matter. (See section 101 for definition of "entity.")

Subdivision (b) of the rule permits a State's Attorney General to appear and be heard on behalf of consumer creditors in a chapter 11 case if the court finds it to be in the public interest. The Attorney General may not, however, appeal from any judgment, order or decree.

Subdivision (d) gives a labor union or any employees' association the right to be heard on the economic soundness of a plan affecting the interest of employees in a chapter 9, 11 or 12 case. The union or association may not, however, appeal any judgment, order, or decree, unless otherwise permitted by law.

Subdivision (e) authorizes the court to enter orders governing service of notice and papers on entities permitted to intervene or be heard.

1986 Amendments: Although section 1109 was not amended by the 1986 Act, it should be noted that pursuant to section 307 of the Code, as added by the 1986 Act, the United States trustee may raise and may appear and be heard on any issue in any case or proceeding, but may not file a chapter 11 plan.

Case Annotations

Section 1109(b) was not intended to waive the Code's limitations on standing, including the requirement that the claimant be within the intended protected class of the section relied upon. Matter of James Wilson Assoc., 965 F.2d 160, 26 C.B.C.2d 1673 (7th Cir. 1992).

A bank has standing when it holds a secured interest in a disputed lease because the Second Circuit's general rule for standing is that a party be "directly and adversely affected pecuniarily" by the challenged order of the bankruptcy court and need not formally intervene to preserve the right to appeal. *In re* International Trade Administration, 936 F.2d 744, 24 C.B.C.2d 2123 (2d Cir. 1991).

A creditors' committee is a party in interest under section 1109(b) which is to be construed broadly to allow all parties affected by a chapter 11 case to be heard. *In re* Bumper Sales, Inc., 907 F.2d 1430, 23 C.B.C.2d 498 (4th Cir. 1990).

A creditors' committee has standing to seek an injunction and the enforcement of a stay to halt the payment of proceeds from directors' and officers' liability insurance policies for the payment of legal expenses without first seeking action from the debtor itself and prior permission of the bankruptcy court when to do so would be a formalistic ritual with obviously foreordained results. Louisiana World Exposition, Inc. v. Federal Ins. Co. (*In re* Louisiana World Exposition, Inc.), 832 F.2d 1391, 17 C.B.C.2d 1291 (5th Cir. 1987).

Because a surety has an equitable right to compel a creditor to assert its right of setoff against an insolvent debtor to prevent the unjust enrichment of the estate at the surety's expense, the right to benefit from a creditor's setoff right demonstrates a surety's interest in a turnover proceeding so as to enable the surety to intervene. Merritt Commercial Sav. & Loan, Inc. v. Guinee (*In re* James R. Corbitt Co.), 766 F.2d 850, 13 C.B.C.2d 174 (4th Cir. 1985).

A creditors' committee does not have an absolute statutory right to intervene in an adversary proceeding arising out of a bankruptcy case, but may intervene as of right, pursuant to Rule 7024(a)(2), when its interest is not adequately represented by existing parties to the adversary proceeding; permissive intervention under Rule 7024(b) is also available. Fuel Oil Supply & Terminaling v. Gulf Oil Corp., 762 F.2d 1283, 12 C.B.C.2d 1381 (5th Cir. 1985).

Future tort claimants in an asbestos-related case—individuals who have been exposed to asbestos but have not yet manifested symptoms of asbestos-related disease—have an interest sufficient to require some representation in the reorganization of an asbestos manufacturer that has filed for protection under the bankruptcy laws. *In re* Amatex Corp., 755 F.2d 1034, 12 C.B.C.2d 147 (3d Cir. 1985).

A chapter 11 creditors' committee has an absolute right to intervene in adversary proceedings instituted by the trustee. Official Unsecured Creditors' Comm. v. Michaels (In the Matter of Marin Motor Oil, Inc.), 689 F.2d 445, 7 C.B.C.2d 470 (3d Cir. 1982), *cert. denied*, 459 U.S. 1206, 103 S. Ct. 1196, 75 L. Ed. 2d 440 (1983).

The Commodity Futures Trading Commission has an interest in ensuring that a debtor trading in futures contracts is precluded from proceeding under chapter 11 and therefore has standing to intervene pursuant to section 1109(b) for the purposes of moving to dismiss the debtor's petition and to appeal from an adverse ruling on the motion. Commodity Futures Trading Comm'n v. Co Petro Mktg. Group, Inc. (*In re* Co Petro Mktg. Group, Inc.), 680 F.2d 566, 7 C.B.C.2d 128 (9th Cir. 1982).

Although "party in interest" is not defined in section 1109(b) or otherwise in the Code, in the Second Circuit it has come to mean an entity that has a direct legal interest at issue in the case rather than an entity that is merely interested in the outcome. *In re* City of Bridgeport, 25 C.B.C.2d 94 (B. Ct., D. Conn. 1991).

A fraudulent conveyance claim asserted by a committee of unsecured creditors will not be defeated on the ground of lack of standing, since a successful fraudulent conveyance claim would benefit the entire estate and, thus, is a general claim as opposed to a personal claim of an individual creditor. *In re* Aluminum Mills Corp., 25 C.B.C.2d 1120 (B. Ct., N.D. Ill. 1991).

Case law expansively interprets "party in interest" under section 1109(b) to insure that all interests that may be significantly impacted by a chapter 11 case have an adequate opportunity for fair representation, and the appropriate test to determine whether an entity is a party in interest is whether the entity has a sufficient stake in the outcome of the proceeding so as to require representation. *In re* Torrez, 25 C.B.C.2d 1325 (B. Ct., E.D. Pa. 1991).

In matters that concern the administration of the entire bankruptcy case, section 1109(b) should be expansively construed to allow any party that can demonstrate an interest in the case to appear and be heard. *In re* Hathaway Ranch Partnership, 23 C.B.C.2d 777 (B. Ct., C.D. Cal. 1990).

Disruption of the confirmation process may be proper when a plaintiff, who was once a primary creditor in a chapter 11 case, claims that fraud on the part of the debtor led to the change of his status. *In re* TM Carlton House Partners, Ltd., 22 C.B.C.2d 972 (B. Ct., E.D. Pa. 1990).

A consumers' rights organization is not to be considered as a real party in interest unless it is either a creditor of the debtor or can assert an equitable claim against the estate. *In re* Ionosphere Clubs, Inc., 21 C.B.C.2d 331 (B. Ct., S.D.N.Y. 1989).

A limited partners' committee may be permitted to sue on behalf of the debtor in possession when its claim has the color of right and the debtor in possession has unjustifiably refused to pursue the action. *In re* E.F. Hutton Southwest Properties II, Ltd., 21 C.B.C.2d 572 (B. Ct., N.D. Tex. 1989).

Section 1109(b) is not a statute which confers upon either a prepetition creditor or an administration creditor an absolute or conditional right to intervene in an adversary proceeding for purposes of subdivision (a)(1) or (b)(1) of Bankruptcy Rule 7024. *In re* Neuman, 21 C.B.C.2d 778 (B. Ct., S.D.N.Y. 1989).

Entities who are neither creditors nor shareholders of a debtor in possession do not have any interest in the issue of whether property of the estate is to be used, sold or leased. Thus, an entity which issued an option to purchase shares of its stock to the debtor in possession cannot prevent such sale because of the lack of notice to creditors of the debtor in possession. *In re* McLean Industries, Inc., 20 C.B.C.2d 829 (B. Ct., S.D.N.Y. 1989).

References

5 *Collier on Bankruptcy* ch. 1109 (Matthew Bender 15th ed.).

2 *Collier Bankruptcy Manual* ch. 1109 (Matthew Bender 3d ed.).

5 *Collier Bankruptcy Practice Guide* ch. 90 (Matthew Bender).

SECTION 1110 (11 U.S.C. § 1110)

§ 1110. Aircraft equipment and vessels.

(a) The right of a secured party with a purchase-money equipment security interest in, or of a lessor or conditional vendor of, whether as trustee or otherwise, aircraft, aircraft engines, propellers, appliances, or spare parts, as defined in section 101 of the Federal Aviation Act of 1958 (49 U.S.C. 1301), or vessels of the United States, as defined in subsection B(4) of the Ship Mortgage Act, 1920 (46 U.S.C. 911(4)), that are subject to a purchase-money equipment security interest granted by, leased to, or conditionally sold to, a debtor that is an air carrier operating under a certificate of convenience and necessity issued by the Civil Aeronautics Board, or a water carrier that holds a certificate of public convenience and necessity or permit issued by the Interstate Commerce Commission, as the case may be, to take possession of such equipment in compliance with the provisions of a purchase-money equipment security agreement, lease, or conditional sale contract, as the case may be, is not affected by section 362 or 363 of this title or by any power of the court to enjoin such taking of possession, unless—

(1) before 60 days after the date of the order for relief under this chapter, the trustee, subject to the court's approval, agrees to perform all obligations of the debtor that become due on or after such date under such security agreement, lease, or conditional sale contract, as the case may be; and

(2) any default, other than a default of a kind specified in section 365(b)(2) of this title, under such security agreement, lease, or conditional sale contract, as the case may be—

(A) that occurred before such date is cured before the expiration of such 60-day period; and

(B) that occurs after such date is cured before the later of—

(i) 30 days after the date of such default; and

(ii) the expiration of such 60-day period.

(b) The trustee and the secured party, lessor, or conditional vendor, as the case may be, whose right to take possession is protected under subsection (a) of this section may agree, subject to the court's approval, to extend the 60-day period specified in subsection (a)(1) of this section.

Legislative History

This section, to a large degree, preserves the protection given lessors and conditional vendors of aircraft to a certified air carrier of vessels to a certificated water carrier under section 116(5) and 116(6) of present chapter X. It is modified to conform with the consolidation of chapters X and XI and with the new chapter 11 generally. It is also modified to give the trustee in a reorganization case an opportunity to continue in possession of the equipment in question by curing defaults and by making the required lease or purchase payments. This removes the absolute veto power over a reorganization that lessors and conditional vendors have under present law, while entitling them to protection of their investment.

The section overrides the automatic stay or any power of the court to enjoin taking of possession of certain leased, conditionally sold, or liened equipment, unless the trustee agrees to perform the debtor's obligations and cures all prior defaults (other than defaults under ipso facto or bankruptcy clauses) within 60 days after the order for relief. The trustee and the equipment financer are permitted to extend the 60-day period by agreement. During the first 60 days, the automatic stay will apply to prevent foreclosure unless the creditor gets relief from the stay.

The effect of this section will be the same if the debtor has granted the security interest to the financer or if the debtor is leasing equipment from a financer that has leveraged the lease and leased the equipment subject to a security interest of a third party.

[House Report No. 95–595, 95th Cong., 1st Sess. 405 (1977); Senate Report No. 95–989, 95th Cong., 2d Sess. 116 (1978).]

Section 1110 of the House amendment adopts an identical provision contained in the House bill without modification contained in the Senate amendment. This section protects a limited class of financiers of aircraft and vessels and is intended to be narrowly construed to prevent secured parties or lessors from gaining the protection of the section unless the interest of such lessor or secured party is explicitly enumerated therein. It should be emphasized that under section 1110(a) a debtor in possession or trustee is given 60 days after the order for relief in a case under chapter 11, to have an opportunity to comply with the provisions of section 1110(a).

During this time the automatic stay will apply and may not be lifted prior to the expiration of the 60-day period. Under section 1110(b), the debtor and secured party or lessors are given an opportunity to extend the 60-day period, but no right to reduce the period is intended. It should additionally be noted that under section 1110(a) the trustee or debtor in possession is not required to assume the executory contract or unexpired lease under section 1110; rather if the trustee or debtor in possession complies with the requirements of section 1110(a), the trustee or debtor in possession is entitled to retain the aircraft or vessels subject to the normal requirements of section 365. The discussion regarding aircraft and vessels likewise applies with respect to railroad rolling stock in a railroad reorganization under section 1168.

[124 Cong. Rec. H 11,102 (Sept. 28, 1978); S 17,419 (Oct. 6, 1978).]

Comment

Special provisions for aircraft and vessels were found in Section 116(5) and (6) of the former Bankruptcy Act as follows:

(5) Notwithstanding any other provisions of chapter X, the title of any owner, whether as trustee or otherwise, to aircraft, aircraft engines, propellers, appliances , and spare parts (as any of such are defined in the Civil Aeronautics Act of 1938, as now in effect or hereafter amended) leased, subleased or conditionally sold to any air carrier which is operating pursuant to a certificate of convenience and necessity issued by the Civil Aeronautics Board, and any right of such owner or of any other lessor to such air carrier to take possession of such property in compliance with the provisions of any such lease or conditional sale contract shall not be affected by the provisions of chapter X if the terms of such lease or conditional sale so provide.

(6) Notwithstanding any other provisions of this chapter, the title of any owner, whether as trustee or otherwise, to vessels (as the term is defined in the Ship Mortgage Act, 1920, as now in effect and

hereafter amended) leased, subleased, or conditionally sold to any water carrier which holds a certificate of public convenience and necessity or permit issued by the Interstate Commerce Commission, and any right of such owner of any other lessor to such water carrier to take possession of such property in compliance with the provisions of any such lease or conditional sale contract shall not be affected by the provisions of this chapter if the terms of such lease or conditional sale so provide.

The House and Senate Reports indicate where section 1110 of the Code modifies Section 116(5) and (6) of the Act. Note particularly that section 1110 overrides the automatic stay. It is intended, however, that section 1110 be narrowly construed to prevent secured parties or lessors from obtaining the protection of this section unless the interest of such party is explicitly enumerated in the section. (*See* Congressional Record, this section, *supra*).

Case Annotations

Although the legislative history of section 1110 and its predecessors manifests a desire to help the affected industries modernize their fleets, there is no clear indication that Congress intended to limit protection to acquisition financing. The legislative history of section 1110 indicates that Congress distinguished between leases and security interests. *In re* Continental Airlines, Inc., 932 F.2d 282, 24 C.B.C.2d 1878 (3d Cir. 1991).

A claim arising from a postpetition stipulation under section 1110(a) for an actual necessary expense that materially benefits the estate is an administrative expense under section 503(b). GATX Leasing Corp. v. Airlift Int'l, Inc. (*In re* Airlift Int'l, Inc.), 761 F.2d 1503, 12 C.B.C.2d 1266 (11th Cir. 1985).

For purposes of applying section 1110, a purchase money security interest in equipment is one to the extent that it is taken by a person who, by making advances or incurring an obligation, gives value to enable the debtor to acquire rights in or the use of the collateral if such value is in fact so used. A transfer of title from an original owner to the debtor will not alter the character of a "purchase money equipment security interest," regardless of whether the transfer was a sale or a refinancing or even if the new security agreement incorporates additional sums not part of the original transaction, so long as the original transaction fulfilled the requirements for this type of security interest. *In re* Express Air, Inc., 26 C.B.C.2d 1104 (B. Ct., W.D. Mass. 1992).

The bankruptcy court has no authority to extend the sixty day period of section 1110 and to require evidentiary hearings before repossession can take place under that section. Section 1110 applies only to transactions involving air carriers properly certified at the time the transaction is entered into. Sale-leaseback agreements are subject to section 1110, regardless of whether new equipment is purchased; lease renewals and extensions are also subject to section 1110. *In re* Pan Am Corp., 24 C.B.C.2d 935 (B. Ct., S.D.N.Y. 1991).

A party who advances funds for the purchase of aircraft which are to be included as part of a larger preexisting floating collateral pool is not entitled to protection under section 1110 when the loan to the debtor is secured by property other than that for which the loan has been advanced, the aircraft securing the loan is taken as collateral securing the antecedent debt owed to other lenders who are not entitled to protection under section 1110, and when there exists other collateral in addition to the aircraft purchased with the loan. *In re* Ionosphere Clubs, Inc., 22 C.B.C.2d 953 (B. Ct., S.D.N.Y. 1990).

Under equitable considerations, the continued use of a mortgaged aircraft under section 1110 entitles the mortgagee to be paid the value of the actual use of its collateral. A & S Sales & Leasing, Inc. v. Belize Airways Ltd. and Seidle (*In re* Belize Airways Ltd.), 3 C.B.C.2d 315 (B. Ct., S.D. Fla. 1980).

References

5 *Collier on Bankruptcy* ch. 1110 (Matthew Bender 15th ed.).

2 *Collier Bankruptcy Manual* ch. 1110 (Matthew Bender 3d ed.).

Gerstell and Hoff-Patrinos, *Aviation Financing Problems Under Section 1110 of the Bankruptcy Code,* 61 Am. Bankr. L.J. 1 (1987).

Goldman, Album and Ward, *Repossessing the Spirit of St. Louis: Expanding the Protection of Sections 1110 and 1168 of the Bankruptcy Code,* 41 Bus. Law. 29 (1985).

Trust, *From Airways to Airplanes: A Practical Synthesis for Chapter 11 Sales Outside the Ordinary Course of Business,* 91 Com. L.J. 267 (1986).

SECTION 1111 (11 U.S.C. § 1111)

§ 1111. Claims and interests.

(a) A proof of claim or interest is deemed filed under section 501 of this title for any claim or interest that appears in the schedules filed under section 521(1) or 1106(a)(2) of this title, except a claim or interest that is scheduled as disputed, contingent, or unliquidated.

(b)(1)(A) A claim secured by a lien on property of the estate shall be allowed or disallowed under section 502 of this title the same as if the holder of such claim had recourse against the debtor on account of such claim, whether or not such holder has such recourse, unless—

(i) the class of which such claim is a part elects, by at least two-thirds in amount and more than half in number of allowed claims of such class, application of paragraph (2) of this subsection; or

(ii) such holder does not have such recourse and such property is sold under section 363 of this title or is to be sold under the plan.

(B) A class of claims may not elect application of paragraph (2) of this subsection if—

(i) the interest on account of such claims in such property is of inconsequential value; or

(ii) the holder of a claim of such class has recourse against the debtor on account of such claim and such property is sold under section 363 of this title or is to be sold under the plan.

(2) If such an election is made, then notwithstanding section 506(a) of this title, such claim is a secured claim to the extent that such claim is allowed.

Bankruptcy Rule References: 3002, 3003, 3004, 3005, 3006, 3007, 3008 and 3014

Legislative History

This section dispenses with the need for every creditor and equity security holder to file a proof of claim or interest in a reorganization case. Usually the debtor's schedules are accurate enough that they will suffice to determine the claims or interests allowable in the case. Thus, the section specifies that any claim or interest included on the debtor's schedules is deemed filed under section 501. This does not apply to claims or interests that are scheduled as disputed, contingent, or unliquidated.

[*House Report No. 95–595, 95th Cong., 1st Sess. 405 (1977); Senate Report No. 95–989, 95th Cong., 2d Sess. 117 (1978).*]

A discussion of section 1111(b) of the House amendment is best considered in the context of confirmation and will, therefore, be discussed in connection with section 1129.

[*124 Cong. Rec. H 11,102 (Sept. 28, 1978); S 17,419 (Oct. 6, 1978).*]

Comment

Section 1111(a) of the Code is derived from former Bankruptcy Rules 10–401 and 12–30 relating to Chapters X and XII of the Act. These rules introduced a new concept dispensing with the need to file a claim to participate in the estate and its distribution. The former Rules permitted the use of the lists filed pursuant to Rule 10–108, or the schedule of debts filed pursuant to Rule 12–11 to determine the claims of creditors and other interests in place of a formal proof of claim. This largely eliminated the need to file proof which, for the most part, had little utility. Under the former Rules, however, if a creditor was listed as disputed, contingent, or unliquidated as to amount, or if the court directed the filing of a claim, then the creditor was required to file a claim. This concept was restricted in the former Rules to cases filed under Chapters X and XII. Straight bankruptcy and Chapters XI and XIII cases still required the filing of proofs of claim.

Section 1111(a) extends the freedom from the need to file claims to all cases because of the consolidation of Chapters X, XI and XII of the Act. Thus, in any type of case under chapter 11, when a claim or interest appears in the schedules filed under sections 521(1) or 1106(a)(2) as undisputed, noncontingent, and liquidated, a proof of claim or interest is "deemed filed under section 501" and the creditor or holder of an interest need take no affirmative action in order to participate in the case. By being deemed filed under section 501, it is deemed allowed pursuant to section 502, unless objection is made.

Subsection (b) of section 1111 sets up a general rule that a secured claim is to be treated as a recourse claim in chapter 11 whether or not the claim is non-recourse by agreement or applicable law. Such preferred status for a non-recourse loan terminates (1) if the property securing the loan is sold under section 363 or is to be sold under section 363 or is to be sold under the plan, or (2) if the class of which the secured claim is a part elects (by two thirds in amount and more than half in number) application of section 1111(b)(2) provided that an allowed claim is secured to the full extent the claim is allowed rather than to the extent of the collateral as under section 506(a). A class may elect application of section 1111(b)(2) only if the security is not of inconsequential value, and if the creditor is a recourse creditor, the collateral is not sold under section 363 or is not to be sold under the plan. Under section 363(k) a secured creditor is permitted to bid in the full amount of his claim at a sale.

Section 1111(b) is to be considered with section 1129(a)(7)(c) and section 1129(b) dealing with confirmation of a plan.

Bankruptcy Rule 3003 relates to the filing of claims or equity security interests in chapter 11 cases. Subdivision (b)(1) provides that the schedule of liabilities filed pursuant to section 521(1) constitutes prima facie evidence of the validity and amount of the claims of creditors whose claims are not scheduled as disputed, contingent, or unliquidated. Unless required to do so under subdivision (c)(2) of the rule, it is not necessary for a creditor or equity security holder to file proof of claim or interest.

Subdivision (b)(2) provides that the list of equity security holders filed under Rule 1007(a)(3) constitutes prima facie evidence of the validity and amount of the equity security holders' interests, and the holders thereof need not file proofs of interest.

Subdivision (c)(1) permits any creditor or indenture trustee to file a proof of claim within the time fixed by the court under subdivision (c)(3) of the rule.

Subdivision (c)(2) requires a creditor or equity security holder whose claim or interest is not scheduled or is scheduled as disputed, contingent, or unliquidated to file a proof of claim or interest within the time fixed by the court (subdivision (c)(3), below) and upon failure to do so, such creditor shall not be treated as a creditor for voting and distribution.

Subdivision (c)(3) requires the court to fix a time within which proofs of claim or interest may be filed, and authorizes the court to extend such time. Notwithstanding the expiration of such time, a proof of claim may be filed to the extent and under the conditions stated in Rule 3002(c)(2), (c)(3), and (c)(4). [The last sentence of subdivision (c) was added in 1991 to permit the late filing of claims by infants or incompetent persons under the same circumstances that permit late filing under chapters 7, 12 and 13.]

Subdivision (c)(4) provides that a proof of claim or interest executed and filed in accordance with subdivision (c) shall supersede any scheduling of that claim or interest made under section 521(1).

Subdivision (c)(5) provides that an indenture trustee may file a claim on behalf of all known or unknown securities issued pursuant to the trust instrument.

Subdivision (d) provides that for the purposes of Rules 3017, 3018, and 3020 and for receiving notices, an entity not a record holder of a security may file a statement of facts which entitle that entity to be treated as the record holder. Any party in interest may file objection to the statement.

Bankruptcy Rule 3004 provides that if a creditor fails to file a proof of claim on or before the first date set for the meeting of creditors, the debtor or trustee may do so in the name of the creditor within 30 days after expiration of the time for filing claims prescribed by Rule 3002(c) or 3003(c), whichever is applicable. Thereupon the clerk is required to forthwith mail notice of the filing to the creditor, the debtor and the trustee. The creditor may file a proof of claim under Rule 3002 or 3003(c), which supersedes the proof filed by the debtor or trustee.

Bankruptcy Rule 3005(a) provides that if the creditor has not filed a proof of claim, an entity who is or may be liable with the debtor to, or has secured that creditor may thereafter within 30 days after the expiration of the time for filing claims under Rule 3002 or 3003(c) execute and file a proof claim in the name of the creditor, or if unknown, in the entity's own name. But no distribution may be made on the claim except on satisfactory proof that the original debt will be diminished by the amount so paid. A proof of claim filed by a creditor pursuant to Rule 3002 or 3003(c) supersedes the claim filed by the entity liable with the debtor.

Subdivision (b) provides that an entity which has filed a claim on behalf of a creditor pursuant to subdivision (a) of the rule may file an acceptance or rejection of the plan in the name of the creditor, or if unknown, in the entity's own name. But if the creditor files a notice prior to confirmation of the creditor's intention to act in the creditor's own behalf, the creditor is to be substituted for the obligor with respect to that claim.

Bankruptcy Rule 3006 permits withdrawal of a proof of claim as of right. But, if after the claim is filed, an objection is filed thereto or a complaint is filed against the creditor in an adversary proceeding, or if the creditor has accepted or rejected the plan or otherwise participated significantly in the case, he may not withdraw except on order after hearing on notice to the trustee or debtor in possession, in any elected or appointed creditors' committee selected under section 1102. The order shall contain such terms and conditions as the court deems proper. Unless otherwise ordered, an authorized withdrawal of a claim constitutes withdrawal of any related acceptance or rejection of a plan.

Bankruptcy Rule 3007 requires objection to a claim to be in writing and filed. A copy thereof and notice of hearing must be mailed or otherwise delivered to the claimant, the debtor in possession and the trustee at least 30 days prior to the hearing. If objection to a claim is joined with a counterclaim, it becomes an adversary proceeding.

Bankruptcy Rule 3008 provides that a party in interest may move for reconsideration of an order allowing or disallowing a claim. After hearing on notice the court shall enter an appropriate order.

Bankruptcy Rule 3014 provides that an election of application of section 1111(b)(2) by a class of secured creditors may be made at any time prior to the conclusion of the hearing on the disclosure statement or within such later time as the court may fix. The election must be in writing and signed unless made at the hearing on the disclosure statement. The election, if made by the majorities required by section 1111(b)(1)(A)(i), shall be binding on all members of the class with respect to the plan.

Case Annotations

When the transaction between the debtor and a third party involving the subject property is not an outright sale, the proposed chapter 11 plan is not confirmable and the undersecured creditor is entitled to recourse status under section 1111(b)(1)(A). John Hancock Mutual Life Ins. Co. v. California Hancock (*In re* California Hancock), 19 C.B.C.2d 550 (9th Cir., B.A.P., 1988).

Creditors who have undisputed claims are not required to file proofs of claims, but those with disputed claims are required to file proofs of claims prior to the bar date. *In re* Federated Dep't Stores, Inc. and Allied Corp., 26 C.B.C.2d 829 (B. Ct., S.D. Ohio 1992).

Even when no value in the property of the chapter 11 estate exists to secure the creditor's nonrecourse lien, a claim may be converted from nonrecourse to recourse under section 1111(b)(1) because it is the existence of the lien on the property, not the existence of its value, which triggers the recourse right so that such claim must be classified and provided for in the plan. *In re* Atlanta West VI, 20 C.B.C.2d 148 (B. Ct., N.D. Ga. 1988).

When a creditor holds a lien with no market value, the claim that the debtor may wish to sell the property in the future and would be forced to bargain with the creditor for relinquishment of the lien is not a value recognized in bankruptcy; election can be denied to the class holding the lien. *In re* Rosage, 18 C.B.C.2d 1175 (B. Ct., W.D. Pa. 1987).

A chapter 11 debtor may not escape the provisions of section 1111(b) by requiring that the sale of all properties secured by a lien be held after confirmation of the plan; the claim must still be treated as if the holder had recourse against the debtor unless the class makes the section 1111(b)(2) election. *In re* Western Real Estate Fund, Inc., 17 C.B.C.2d 577 (B. Ct., W.D. Okla. 1987).

Although the language of section 1111(b)(1)(A)(ii) does not specifically refer to foreclosure or abandonment of the collateral to the secured creditor, Congress intended that such dispositions be equally applicable exceptions to the general rule allowing transformation of nonrecourse debt into recourse debt. In the Matter of DRW Property Co., 82, 14 C.B.C.2d 1032 (B. Ct., N.D. Tex. 1986).

A creditor who has made a section 1111(b) election may not later withdraw its election if the plan remains materially unchanged; however, once there has been a material alteration of the plan, retraction is permitted to allow a reevaluation. *In re* Keller, 12 C.B.C.2d 624 (B. Ct., N.D. Iowa 1985).

An interest claim, filed after the filing deadline, that is simply an amendment to an already scheduled debt can be considered timely filed. *In re* Hertz, 10 C.B.C.2d 316 (B. Ct., S.D.N.Y. 1984).

References

5 *Collier on Bankruptcy* ch. 1111 (Matthew Bender 15th ed.).

2 *Collier Bankruptcy Manual* ch. 1111 (Matthew Bender 3d ed.).

5 *Collier Bankruptcy Practice Guide* ch. 88 (Matthew Bender).

Bono, *Class Action Proofs of Claim in Bankruptcy,* 96 Com. L.J. 297 (1991).

Kaye, *The Case Against Class Proofs of Claim in Bankruptcy,* 66 N.Y.U. L. Rev. 897 (1991).

SECTION 1112 (11 U.S.C. § 1112)

§ 1112. Conversion or dismissal.

(a) The debtor may convert a case under this chapter to a case under chapter 7 of this title unless—

(1) the debtor is not a debtor in possession;

(2) the case originally was commenced as an involuntary case under this chapter; or

(3) the case was converted to a case under this chapter other than on the debtor's request.

(b) Except as provided in subsection (c) of this section, on request of a party in interest or the United States trustee, and after notice and a hearing, the court may convert a case under this chapter to a case under chapter 7 of this title or may dismiss a case under this chapter, whichever is in the best interest of creditors and the estate, for cause, including—

(1) continuing loss to or diminution of the estate and absence of a reasonable likelihood of rehabilitation;

(2) inability to effectuate a plan;

(3) unreasonable delay by the debtor that is prejudicial to creditors;

(4) failure to propose a plan under section 1121 of this title within any time fixed by the court;

(5) denial of confirmation of every proposed plan and denial of a request made for additional time for filing another plan or a modification of a plan;

(6) revocation of an order of confirmation under section 1144 of this title, and denial of confirmation of another plan or a modified plan under section 1129 of this title;

(7) inability to effectuate substantial consummation of a confirmed plan;

(8) material default by the debtor with respect to a confirmed plan;

(9) termination of a plan by reason of the occurrence of a condition specified in the plan; or

(10) nonpayment of any fees or charges required under chapter 123 of title 28.

(c) The court may not convert a case under this chapter to a case under chapter 7 of this title if the debtor is a farmer or a corporation that is not a moneyed, business, or commercial corporation, unless the debtor requests such conversion.

(d) The court may convert a case under this chapter to a case under chapter 12 or 13 of this title only if—

(1) the debtor requests such conversion;

(2) the debtor has not been discharged under section 1141(d) of this title; and

(3) if the debtor requests conversion to chapter 12 of this title, such conversion is equitable.

(e) Except as provided in subsections (c) and (f), the court, on request of the United States trustee, may convert a case under this chapter to a case under chapter 7 of this title or may dismiss a case under this chapter, whichever is in the best interest of creditors and the estate if the debtor in a voluntary case fails to file, within fifteen days after the filing of the petition commencing such case or such additional time as the court may allow, the information required by paragraph (1) of section 521, including a list containing the names and addresses of the holders of the twenty largest unsecured claims (or of all unsecured claims if there are fewer than twenty unsecured claims), and the approximate dollar amounts of each of such claims.

(f) Notwithstanding any other provision of this section, a case may not be converted to a case under another chapter of this title unless the debtor may be a debtor under such chapter.

Bankruptcy Rule References: 1007, 1017, 1019, 2002 and 4004

Legislative History

This section brings together all of the conversion and dismissal rules for chapter 11 cases. Subdivision (a) gives the debtor an absolute right to convert a voluntarily commenced chapter 11 case in which the debtor remains in possession to a liquidation case.

[*House Report No. 95–595, 95th Cong., 1st Sess. 405 (1977); Senate Report No. 95–989, 95th Cong., 2d Sess. 117 (1978).*]

Subsection (b) gives wide discretion to the court to make an appropriate disposition of the case when a party in interest requests. The court is permitted to convert a reorganization case to a liquidation case or to dismiss the case, whichever is in the best interest of creditors and the estate, only for cause. Cause may include the inability to effectuate a plan, unreasonable delay by the debtor that is prejudicial to creditors, failure to file a plan within the appropriate time limits, denial of confirmation and any opportunity to modify or propose a new plan, revocation of confirmation and denial of confirmation of a modified plan, inability to effectuate substantial consummation of a confirmed plan, material default by the debtor under the plan, and termination of the plan by reason of the occurence of a condition specified in the plan. The list is not exhaustive. The court will be able to consider other factors as they arise, and to use its equitable powers to reach an appropriate result in individual cases.

[*House Report No. 95–595, 95th Cong., 1st Sess. 405 (1977).*]

Subsection (b) gives the wide discretion to the court to make an appropriate disposition of the case *sua sponte* or upon motion of a party in interest, or the court is permitted to convert a reorganization case to a liquidation case or to dismiss the case, whichever is in the best interest of creditors and the estate, but only for cause. Cause may include the continuing loss to or dimunition of the estate of an insolvent debtor, the absence of a reasonable likelihood of rehabilitation, the inability to effectuate a plan, unreasonable delay by the debtor that is prejudicial to creditors, failure to file a plan within the appropriate time limits, denial of confirmation and any opportunity to modify or propose a new plan, revocation of confirmation and denial of confirmation of a modified plan, inability to effectuate substantial consummation of a confirmed plan, material default by the debtor under the plan, and termination of the plan by reason of the occurrence of a condition specified in the plan. This list is not exhaustive. The court will be able to consider other factors as they arise, and to use its equitable powers to reach an appropriate result in individual cases. The power of the court to act *sua sponte* should be used sparingly and only in emergency situations.

[*Senate Report No. 95–989, 95th Cong., 2d Sess. 117 (1978).*]

Section 1112 of the House amendment represents a compromise between the House bill and Senate amendment with respect to the factors constituting cause for conversion of a case to chapter 7 or dismissal. The House amendment combines two separate factors contained in section 1112(b)(1) and section 1112(b)(2) of the Senate amendment. Section 1112(b)(1) of the House amendment permits the court to convert a case to a case under chapter 7 or to dismiss the case if there is both a continuing loss to or diminution of the estate and the absence of a reasonable likelihood of rehabilitation; requiring both factors to be present simultaneously represents a compromise from the House bill which eliminated both factors from the list of causes enumerated.

[*124 Cong. Rec. H 11,103 (Sept. 28, 1978); S 17,419 (Oct. 6, 1978).*]

Subsection (c) prohibits the court from converting a case concerning a farmer or an eleemosynary institution to a liquidation case unless the debtor consents.

Subsection (d) prohibits conversion of a reorganization case to a chapter 13 case unless the debtor requests conversion and his discharge has not been granted or has been revoked.

[*House Report No. 95–595, 95th Cong., 1st Sess. 406 (1977); Senate Report No. 95–989, 95th Cong., 2d Sess. 117 (1978).*]

Section 1112(c) and 1112(d) of the House amendment is derived from the House bill which differs from the Senate amendment only as a matter of style.

[*124 Cong. Rec. H 11,103 (Sept. 28, 1978); S 17,419 (Oct. 6, 1978).*]

Subsection (e) [*Ed. Note:* The 1986 Amendments redesignated section 1112(e) as section 1112(f).] reinforces section 109 by prohibiting conversion of a chapter 11 case to a case under another chapter proceedings under which the debtor is not permitted to proceed.

[*Senate Report No. 95–989, 95th Cong., 2d Sess. 117 (1978); see also House Report No. 95–595, 95th Cong., 1st Sess. 406 (1977).*]

Comment

Under section 706(a) of the Code, a debtor has a one-time absolute right to convert a case from chapter 7 (liquidation) to chapter 11, 12 or 13, but once converted from chapter 11, 12 or 13 to liquidation under chapter 7, the debtor loses any further right to convert.

Section 1112 relates to conversion and dismissal in chapter 11 cases. A debtor may convert a reorganization case to a liquidation case *if* it is a debtor in possession. The conversion is not permitted if the case originated as an involuntary chapter 11 case or the case was previously converted to chapter 11 on the request of a party other than the debtor.

On request of a party in interest or the United States trustee, however, under section 1112(b) the court may either convert the chapter 11 to a chapter 7 case (except if the debtor is a farmer or a corporation that is *not* a moneyed business or commercial corporation) unless the debtor requests the conversion (see section 1112(c)) whichever is in the best interest of creditors and the estate, for cause. Cause includes (but is not limited to) nine specified circumstances such as continuing loss to or diminution of the estate and absence of reasonable likelihood of rehabilitation, or inability to propose or effectuate a plan, denial of confirmation, material default, or termination of a confirmed plan, etc.

The grounds for conversion or dismissal in section 1112(b) are considerably broader than the grounds set forth in the former Bankruptcy Rules. "Absence of a reasonable likelihood of rehabilitation" had no counterpart in the former Rules, although dismissal for such a reason can be found in case law under the Act. Particularly it must be noted that the ten grounds set forth in section 1112(b) are not exclusive. Conversion or dismissal may be ordered "for cause, including" the ten stated grounds.

Section 1112(d) prohibits conversion of a chapter 11 case to chapter 12 or 13 unless the debtor requests the conversion because an involuntary chapter 12 or 13 is not permitted. Chapter 12 and 13 cases are, under the Code, voluntary only.

Bankruptcy Rule 1017, dealing with dismissal or conversion of a case, implements section 1112. Subdivision (a) provides that (except as provided in sections 707(b), 1208(b) and 1307(b) of the Code) a case shall not be dismissed on motion of the petitioner or for want of prosecution or other cause or by consent of the parties before a hearing on notice as provided in Rule 2002. Unless a list of creditors and their addresses was previously filed, the debtor must file such a list within the time fixed by the court, and upon the debtor's failure to do so, the court may order the preparation and filing of the list by the debtor or other entity.

Subdivision (c) provides that a case shall not be dismissed or a case suspended pursuant to section 305 until after a hearing on notice as provided in Rule 2002(a). Notice should be given to the United States trustee. Subdivision (d) provides that conversion or dismissal pursuant to section 1112(a) shall be on motion filed and served as required by Rule 9013.

Bankruptcy Rule 1019 relates to conversion or reconversion of a chapter 11 case to chapter 7. In such event:

(1)(A) the lists, inventories, schedules, and statements of financial affairs theretofore filed are deemed filed in the chapter 7 case unless the court otherwise directs. If not previously filed, the debtor is to comply with Rule 1007 as if an order for relief was entered on an involuntary petition on the date of entry of the conversion order;

(B) the statement of intention [*see* section 521(2)], if required, shall be filed within 30 days following entry of the order of conversion or before the first date set for the meeting of creditors, whichever is earlier. An extension of time may be granted for cause only on motion made before the time has expired. Notice of an extension shall be given to the United States trustee and to any committee, trustee, or other party as the court may direct.

[Paragraph (2) was deleted by the 1991 amendments because notice of conversion is required by Rules 1017(d), 2002(f)(2) and 9022.]

(2) a new time period for filing claims and complaints objecting to discharge or to obtain a determination of dischargeability of a debt shall commence pursuant to Rules 3002, 4004, or 4007, but a new time period shall not commence if a chapter 7 case had been converted to chapter 11 and thereafter reconverted to chapter 7, and the time for filing claims and such complaints expired in the original chapter 7 case.

(3) it is unnecessary to file claims that had actually been filed by a creditor in the chapter 11 case before conversion to chapter 7.

(4) after qualification and assumption of duties by the chapter 7 trustee, the trustee or debtor in possession previously acting in

the chapter 11 case, unless otherwise ordered, shall forthwith turn over to the chapter 7 trustee all records and property of the estate.

(5) [as amended in 1991] Unless the court directs otherwise, each debtor in possession or trustee in the superseded case (A) within 15 days after entry of the conversion order in a chapter 11 case, file a schedule of unpaid debts incurred after commencement of the superseded case including the name and address of each creditor; and (B) within 30 days following the entry of the order of conversion of a chapter 11, chapter 12, or chapter 13 case, file and transmit to the United States trustee a final report and account.

If the conversion order follows confirmation, the debtor must include (A) a schedule of property not listed in the final report and account that was acquired after the filing of the original petition but before entry of the conversion order, (B) a schedule of unpaid debts not listed in the final report and account incurred after confirmation and before the conversion order, and (C) a schedule of executory contracts and unexpired leases entered into or assumed after the filing of the original petition but before entry of the conversion order. The clerk is required to forthwith transmit to the United States trustee a copy of every schedule filed pursuant to this paragraph.

(6) On filing of the schedule of unpaid debts, the clerk (or some other person as the court directs) shall give notice to those entities, including the United States, any state, or subdivision thereof, that the claims may be filed pursuant to Rules 3001(a)-(d) and 3002. Unless a notice of insufficient assets for payment of a dividend is mailed pursuant to Rule 2002(e), the court shall fix the time to file claims arising from rejection of executory contracts or unexpired leases under sections 348(c) and 365(d) of the Code.

(7) if the court extends the time to file claims against a surplus (Rule 3003(c)(6)), the extension shall apply to holders of claims who failed to timely file within the time prescribed or fixed under paragraph (6), above, and notice shall be given to the claimant.

Bankruptcy Rule 2002(a)(5) requires that not less than 20 days notice by mail be given to the debtor, the trustee, all creditors and indenture trustees of the hearing on dismissal or conversion of a chapter 11 case to another chapter. Subdivision (k), added by the 1991 amendments, provides that unless the United States trustee otherwise requests, the clerk (or some other person as the court directs) shall transmit to the United States trustee most of the notices required by Rule 2002 and notice of hearings on all applications for compensation or reimbursement. Transmittal of such notices must be within the time prescribed in subdivision (a) or (b). The United States trustee shall also receive notice of any other matter requested by such trustee or ordered by the court. Rule 2002(d) provides that in chapter 11 cases, the clerk, unless otherwise ordered, shall give notice to all equity security holders in the form and manner as directed by the court of the hearing on dismissal or conversion to another chapter.

1984 Amendments: Stylistic changes were made in paragraphs (2), (3), (5) and (8) of section 1112(b).

1986 Amendments: The 1986 Act amended section 1112 in several respects. Subsection (b) was amended to provide that the United States trustee may request conversion or dismissal. Subsection (b) was further amended by adding paragraph (10) providing that failure to pay any required fees or charges constitutes cause for conversion or dismissal.

Subsection (d) was amended by adding paragraph (3) providing that if the debtor requests conversion to chapter 12, such conversion must be equitable.

Subsection (e) of § 1112 of the Code was redesignated subsection (f) and a new subsection (e) was added providing for conversion to chapter 7 or dismissal on request of the United States trustee if the debtor in a voluntary case fails to file, within 15 days after filing the petition commencing the case (or within such additional time the court allows) the information required by section 521(1), including a list of the names and addresses of the 20 largest unsecured claims and the approximate dollar amounts of each. [Section 521(1) requires the debtor to file a list of creditors, a schedule of assets and liabilities, a schedule of current income and expenditures, and a statement of financial affairs.] *Only the United States trustee may move for the relief afforded by subsection (e).*

Section 1112 was amended to reflect the creation of a permanent United States trustee system. Section 302(d) of the 1986 Amendments provides different effective dates for the amendments relating to the United States trustee system. *See* Section 302 of the 1986 Amendments, as amended by Pub. L. No. 101-650 (1990), reprinted herein under "Selected Provisions of the Bankruptcy Judges, United States Trustees, and Family Farmer Bankruptcy Act of 1986," regarding effective dates generally.

Case Annotations

A reviewing court should remand for further proceedings if the lower court determined a motion to dismiss under section 1112(b) on an insufficient evidentiary record. *In re* Brown, 951 F.2d 564, 26 C.B.C.2d 202 (3d Cir. 1991).

It is clear that the provisions of the Code permit a debtor to file a second chapter 11 petition to liquidate rather than to reorganize a debtor. The Code permits serial filings in good faith, as well as liquidating chapter 11 plans, and the fact that the drafters may not have fully realized the results in combination does not mean they cannot be so used.

In the Matter of Jartran, Inc., 886 F.2d 859, 21 C.B.C.2d 1141 (7th Cir. 1989).

A bankruptcy court is not required to give exhaustive reasons for its decision to convert, against the debtor's wishes, a chapter 11 case to one under chapter 7. Cause to convert can be found simply in the debtor's inability to effecuate a plan and unreasonable delay by the debtor that is prejudicial to creditors. Koerner v. Colonial Bank (In the Matter of Koerner), 800 F.2d 1358, 15 C.B.C.2d 711 (5th Cir. 1986).

A dismissal of a chapter 11 petition for lack of good faith is appropriate, particularly when there is no realistic possibility of effective reorganization and it is evident that the debtor seeks merely to delay or frustrate legitimate efforts of secured creditors to enforce their rights. Albany Partners, Ltd. v. Westbrook (*In re* Albany Partners, Ltd.), 749 F.2d 670, 12 C.B.C.2d 244 (11th Cir. 1984).

Once a debtor's plan has been proposed in good faith, it is not necessary to conduct an evidentiary hearing as to whether the debtor initially filed its petition in good faith. In the Matter of Madison Hotel Assocs., 749 F.2d 410, 11 C.B.C.2d 771 (7th Cir. 1984).

In assessing the power to dismiss a pending case due to dormancy, the bankruptcy court must look beyond the debtor's inaction and must consider activity of the others affected by the bankruptcy proceedings before it makes a finding that the case is inactive. Louis J. Herbert, Inc. v. Zwart (In the Matter of Zwart), 722 F.2d 1258, 10 C.B.C.2d 108 (5th Cir. 1984).

For the purposes of section 1112(b), a debtor who is no longer actively in business and who hopes to use available chapter 11 remedies to "jump start" its business, and then only after protracted litigation to recover real property, is likely to have its case dismissed or converted under the "absence of a reasonable likelihood of rehabilitation" standard set forth in the statute. *In re* Minnesota Alpha Foundation, 24 C.B.C.2d 1329 (B. Ct., D. Minn. 1990).

Under section 1112(a), after confirmation of a chapter 11 plan the debtor is no longer a debtor in possession and the estate ceases to exist unless the plan provides otherwise. *In re* T.S.P. Industries, Inc., 24 C.B.C.2d 638 (B. Ct. N.D. Ill. 1990).

Dismissal for cause is inappropriate when the debtor has made a good faith effort to refinance its debt through negotiations with the Department of Housing and Urban Development and with other lenders. *In re* Marion Street Partnership, 22 C.B.C.2d 139 (B. Ct., D. Minn. 1989).

Prior to exercising its discretion in dismissing a case the court must find and a debtor must prove that there is "cause" for such dismissal. When a debtor has proven that it has no assets to pay quarterly United States Trustee fees, it has shown "cause" for dismissal of the case. In the Matter of Markhon Industries, Inc., 21 C.B.C.2d 425 (B. Ct., N.D. Ind. 1989).

When a debtor which has sought but failed to obtain injunctive relief in a state court to prevent a creditor from foreclosing on that debtor's property chooses to file a chapter 11 petition to utilize the "automatic stay" rather than to appeal to the appropriate state court, absent some legitimate reorganization objective, a court may find on the facts that the chapter 11 petition is a forum shopping device which constitutes bad faith use of the bankruptcy process and may dismiss the case under section 1112(b). *In re* Walter, 21 C.B.C.2d 1222 (B. Ct., C.D. Cal. 1989).

In order to dismiss or convert a case for "cause" because of a debtor's failure to comply with the United States trustee's requirements, the requirements must be reasonable, and if so, the debtor's violation may be considered, along with other factors, to determine whether "cause" exist to convert or dismiss. When the chapter 11 debtor's business is so small that he could have filed under chapter 13, strict imposition of the requirements of the United States trustee is unwarranted and unnecessary if it would prevent the debtor's access to the courts and to the relief provisions of chapter 11 which Congress intended for small businesses. In the Matter of Crosby, 20 C.B.C.2d 254 (B. Ct., S.D. Ga. 1988).

References

5 *Collier on Bankruptcy* ch. 1112 (Matthew Bender 15th ed.).

2 *Collier Bankruptcy Manual* ch. 1112 (Matthew Bender 3d ed.).

5 *Collier Bankruptcy Practice Guide* ch. 37 (Matthew Bender).

Key, *The Advent of the Serial Chapter 11 Filing and Its Implications,* 8 Bankr. Dev. J. 575 (1991).

Note, *"Consecutive" Chapter 11 Filings: Use or Abuse?,* 19 Fordham Urb. L.J. 111 (1991).

Ponoroff and Knippenberg, *The Implied Good Faith Filing Requirement: Sentinel of an Evolving Bankruptcy Policy,* 85 NW. U.L. Rev. 919 (1991).

SECTION 1113 (11 U.S.C. § 1113)

§ 1113. Rejection of collective bargaining agreements. *

(a) The debtor in possession, or the trustee if one has been appointed under the provisions of this chapter, other than a trustee in a case covered by subchapter IV of this chapter and by title I of the Railway Labor Act, may assume or reject a collective bargaining agreement only in accordance with the provisions of this section.

---

* [*Ed. Note: See also,* following the aforesaid texts, **Comment** with respect to "The Omnibus Budget Reconciliation Act of 1987, Pub. L. No. 100–203" as amending ERISA with respect to pension plans in cases under the Bankruptcy Code.]

(b)(1) Subsequent to filing a petition and prior to filing an application seeking rejection of a collective bargaining agreement, the debtor in possession or trustee (hereinafter in this section "trustee" shall include a debtor in possession), shall—

(A) make a proposal to the authorized representative of the employees covered by such agreement, based on the most complete and reliable information available at the time of such proposal, which provides for those necessary modifications in the employees benefits and protections that are necessary to permit the reorganization of the debtor and assures that all creditors, the debtor and all of the affected parties are treated fairly and equitably; and

(B) provide, subject to subsection (d)(3), the representative of the employees with such relevant information as is necessary to evaluate the proposal.

(2) During the period beginning on the date of the making of a proposal provided for in paragraph (1) and ending on the date of the hearing provided for in subsection (d) (1), the trustee shall meet, at reasonable times, with the authorized representative to confer in good faith in attempting to reach mutually satisfactory modifications of such agreement.

(c) The court shall approve an application for rejection of a collective bargaining agreement only if the court finds that—

(1) the trustee has, prior to the hearing, made a proposal that fulfills the requirements of subsection (b) (1);

(2) the authorized representative of the employees has refused to accept such proposal without good cause; and

(3) the balance of the equities clearly favors rejection of such agreement.

(d)(1) Upon the filing of an application for rejection the court shall schedule a hearing to be held not later than fourteen days after the date of the filing of such application. All interested parties may appear and be heard at such hearing. Adequate notice shall be provided to such parties at least ten days before the date of such hearing. The court may extend the time for the commencement of such hearing for a period not exceeding seven days where the circumstances of the case, and the interests of justice require such extension, or for additional periods of time to which the trustee and representative agree.

(2) The court shall rule on such application for rejection within thirty days after the date of the commencement of the hearing. In the interests of justice, the court may extend such time for ruling for such additional period as the trustee and the employees' representative may agree to. If the court does not rule on such application within thirty days after the date of the commencement of the hearing, or within such additional time as the trustee and the employees' representative may agree to, the trustee may terminate or alter any provisions of the collective bargaining agreement pending the ruling of the court on such application.

(3) The court may enter such protective orders, consistent with the need of the authorized representative of the employee to evaluate the trustee's proposal and the application for rejection, as may be necessary to prevent disclosure of information provided to such representative where such disclosure could compromise the position of the debtor with respect to its competitors in the industry in which it is engaged.

(e) If during a period when the collective bargaining agreement continues in effect, and if essential to the continuation of the debtor's business, or in order to avoid irreparable damage to the estate, the court, after notice and a hearing, may authorize the trustee to implement interim changes in the terms, conditions, wages, benefits, or work rules provided by a collective bargaining agreement. Any hearing under this paragraph shall be scheduled in accordance with the needs of the trustee. The implementation of such interim changes shall not render the application for rejection moot.

(f) No provision of this title shall be construed to permit a trustee to unilaterally terminate or alter any provisions of a collective bargaining agreement prior to compliance with the provisions of this section.

Comment

1984 Amendments: Enactment of section 1113 was in response to the Supreme Court decision in NLRB v. Bildisco & Bildisco, 465 U.S. 513,

9 C.B.C.2d 1219 (1984). The court ruled unanimously that collective bargaining agreements can be rejected under section 365(c) of the Code, but only if it appears that such contract burdens the estate and that the equities balance in favor of rejection. The Court also stipulated that the bankruptcy court would have to be persuaded that reasonable efforts to negotiate were made and were not likely to produce an early and satisfactory solution.

The Court, however, split 5–4 on the question of whether the debtor committed an unfair practice when it unilaterally rejected or modified the labor contract after filing the chapter 11 petition, but before court approval of the rejection of the contract. The majority ruled that unilateral rejection was not an unfair labor practice, and therefore the debtor did not need to comply with section 8(d) of the NLRA prior to seeking permission of the bankruptcy court to reject.

Section 1113 substantially adopts the first portion of the *Bildisco* decision and overrules the 5–4 portion thereof.

Section 1113 prescribes the procedure for rejection or modification of an existing collective bargaining agreement. Subsequent to filing the petition and prior to moving to reject or modify the agreement, the trustee or debtor in possession must make a proposal to the the the representative of the employees, ordinarily a union, spelling out the need for modification of the agreement in order to effect a reorganization and assure fair and equitable treatment of all creditors, the trustee, the debtor in possession and all affected parties. The trustee or debtor in possession must provide the employees' representative with relevant information necessary to evaluate the debtor's proposal, ordinarily balance sheets, profit and loss statements, and projection of income and expenses. The court may authorize rejection only if it finds that the debtor has fulfilled the provisions of section 1113 and the employees' representative has failed to accept the debtor's proposal without good cause.

The Omnibus Budget Reconciliation Act of 1987, Pub. L. No. 100–203, enacted on December 22, 1987, made numerous amendments to ERISA that concern pension benefits in cases under the Bankruptcy Code. Of interest is a change with respect to the standards for "distress termination" of pension plans in a case under the Bankruptcy Code. The criteria for such termination include, among other things, the filing by or against an employer of a petition seeking liquidation or reorganization under the Code. Under the amendments, distress termination of a pension plan in a chapter 11 case will not be permitted unless the bankruptcy court (or other appropriate court) determines that, unless the plan is terminated, the employer will be unable to pay all of its debts pursuant to a reorganization plan, and will be unable to continue in business outside of chapter 11. A further change provides that a chapter 11 case that has been converted to chapter 7 qualifies as a liquidation case for purposes of determining the permissibility of a distress termination.

Other important amendments affect the lien and priority status of Pension Benefit Guaranty Corporation claims in cases under the Code.

1988 Amendments: The Retiree Benefits Bankruptcy Protection Act of 1988, Pub. L. No. 100–334, added to chapter 11 a new section 1114, "Payment of insurance benefits to retired employees," which provides both the procedures and standards for modifying the payment of retiree benefits in a chapter 11 case, including the use of interim modifications prior to the court's issuance of a final order. [*see infra*]

The Act, in addition to enacting section 1114, added paragraph (13) to section 1129(a) [*see infra*], thereby establishing a new requirement for confirmation.

The Act also repealed Section 2 of "An Act to amend the interest provisions of the Declaration of Taking Act," Pub. L. No. 99–656 (1986). Additionally, the Act made permanent and substantially amended Section 608 of the second title VI of "Joint Resolution making continuing appropriations for the fiscal year 1987, and for other purposes," Pub. L. No. 99–591 (1986). Section 608, as amended, provides that the trustee cannot modify retiree benefits unless the trustee and an authorized representative of the former employees with respect to whom such benefits are payable agree to the modification or the court finds that the modification meets the standards of section 1113(b)(1)(A) and the balance of the equities clearly favors the modification. Pursuant to the amendment made to Section 608 by Section 3(a)(3)(B) of the 1988 Act, a chapter 11 trustee or debtor in possession is required to pay any prepetition claims owing to a health care provider that can prove it has the legal right to recover from the patient any such payments, unless repaid by the debtor-former employer; a prepetition claim is thus turned into an administrative expense priority. Section 608, as amended, applies to chapter 11 cases which were pending on June 16, 1988, the date of enactment of the Act. The complete text of Section 608, as amended, immediately follows section 1114, *infra*.

The Act and its amendments became effective on the date of its enactment, June 16, 1988. However, sections 1114 and 1129(a)(13) do not apply to chapter 11 cases which had been commenced before June 16, 1988. For pre-enactment cases, Section 608, as amended, applies.

Case Annotations

A bankruptcy court has no authority to adjudicate unfair labor practice claims, but may take them into account in determining whether a debtor's modifications satisfy section 1113(b) requirements. *In re* Mile Hi Metal Systems, Inc., 899 F.2d 887, 22 C.B.C.2d 611 (10th Cir. 1990).

A debtor may not immediately appeal to the court of appeals the judgment of a bankruptcy appellate panel with respect to an interim relief order under section 1113(e); to obtain review of such an order, the debtor must wait until the bankruptcy court has rendered its ultimate order on the rejection issue. *In re* Landmark Hotel & Casino, Inc., 872 F.2d 857, 21 C.B.C.2d 60 (9th Cir. 1989).

The protections of section 1113 apply to retirees covered by provisions in a collective bargaining agreement so that the unilateral modification of any provision, including a requirement to pay insurance premiums for retiree benefits, of a collective bargaining agreement by an employer is prohibited. United Steelworkers of America v. Unitmet Corp. (*In re* Unimet Corp.), 842 F.2d 879, 18 C.B.C.2d 694 (6th Cir. 1988).

A debtor is not required to prove in all instances, for purposes of section 1113(b)(1), that non-union employees will have their salaries and benefits cut to the same degree that workers' benefits are to be reduced if those same employees are being asked to assume increased responsibilities without a commensurate increase in pay. Truck Drivers Local 807, Int'l Bhd. of Teamsters v. Carey Transp. Inc., 816 F.2d 82, 16 C.B.C.2d 799 (2d Cir. 1987).

Courts should strictly construe "necessary to permit reorganization" following the Congressional intent to incorporate the *REA Express* standard and to abrogate that adopted by the Supreme Court in *Bildisco*. The absence of a "snap-back" provision (increasing workers' benefits if operating results improved) may be a fatal defect. Wheeling-Pittsburgh Steel Corp. v. United Steelworkers of America, 791 F.2d 1074, 14 C.B.C.2d 955 (3d Cir. 1986).

An imminent threat to the debtor's short-term survival, rather than the long-term viability of a reorganization, is the basis for interim relief from a collective bargaining agreement; interim relief of indefinite duration is proper only when an application for rejection of the collective bargaining agreement is pending. *In re* Ionosphere Clubs, Inc. and Eastern Airlines, Inc., 26 C.B.C.2d 1485 (B. Ct., S.D.N.Y. 1992).

Interim changes to the collective bargaining agreement are authorized when the debtor has proven that the interim relief is essential to either: 1) the continuation of the debtor's business; or 2) avoidance of irreparable damage to the estate. In providing for interim relief to alter a collective bargaining agreement, Congress intended that unions should be afforded due process, but that such due process could be on short notice in order to serve the trustee's needs. *In re* United Press Int'l, Inc., 26 C.B.C.2d 813 (B. Ct., S.D.N.Y. 1991).

When a debtor fails to pay wages and benefits in accordance with a collective bargaining agreement, it has effected a unilateral alteration of the agreement, for purposes of section 1113(f), and has not committed a mere "breach" of that agreement. Section 1113(f) does not render the priorities found in section 507(a) inoperative in determining the priority of employee claims arising from a violation of section 1113(f); that is, no superpriority is created with respect to employee claims arising under section 1113. *In re* Armstrong Store Fixtures Corp., 26 C.B.C.2d 350 (B. Ct., W.D. Pa. 1992). *But see In re* Arlene's Sportswear, Inc., 26 C.B.C.2d 1550 (B. Ct., D. Mass. 1992) (the provisions of section 1113 have controlling authority over all other sections of the Bankruptcy Code in establishing the priority of claims when a chapter 11 debtor is bound under a collective bargaining agreement).

A bankruptcy court may not approve an application to reject a collective bargaining agreement unless a preapplication proposal meets the requirements of section 1113(b)(1)(A), (c)(2) and (c)(3) in that a good faith effort to modify the contract has been made, the union has refused to accept the proposal without good cause, and the balance of the equities clearly favor rejection. If, in proposing modifications to a collective bargaining agreement pursuant to section 1113(b)(1)(A), the employer seeks changes which materially exceed its needs to reorganize, rejection will be prohibited. *In re* Pierce Terminal Warehouse, Inc., 25 C.B.C.2d 1597 (B. Ct., N.D. Iowa 1991).

In examining applications to reject collective bargaining agreements, courts should follow the nine-part test formulated in *In re* American Provision Co., with the burden of proof to be borne by the debtor and applying a preponderance of the evidence standard. If the union does not provide any evidence of its reason for declining to accept the debtor's proposal in the face of evidence provided by the debtor that it is not economically feasible for the debtor to continue operating under the original contract, it may be found that the union has rejected the proposal without good cause. *In re* Blue Diamond Coal Co., 25 C.B.C.2d 867 (B. Ct., E.D. Tenn. 1991).

A bankruptcy court retains authority to act pursuant to 11 U.S.C. § 1113(e) after a collective bargaining agreement has expired when the court has previously entered orders modifying the agreement before its expiration. *In re* D.O. & W. Coal Co., 20 C.B.C.2d 280 (B. Ct., W.D. Va. 1988).

The language of Section 2 of the Declaration of Taking Act (Pub. L. No. 99–656) and Section 608 of Pub. L. No. 99–591 cannot be construed to modify the Bankruptcy Code by implication so as to conflict with section 363 of the Code. Accordingly, a debtor in possession cannot be required to use collateral securing a debt to another creditor to pay the health and retirement benefits of former employees as required by a collective bargaining agreement since such use would have the effect of avoiding that creditor's lien. United Steel Workers of America v. Jones & Lamson Mach. Co. (*In re* Jones & Lamson Mach. Co.), 17 C.B.C.2d 405 (B. Ct., D. Conn. 1987).

References

5 *Collier on Bankruptcy* ch. 1113 (Matthew Bender 15th ed.).

2 *Collier Bankruptcy Manual* ch. 1113 (Matthew Bender 3d ed.).

Comment, *The Rejection of Collective Bargaining Agreements in Chapter 11 Reorganizations: The Need for Informed Judicial Decisions,* 134 U. Pa. L. Rev. 1235 (1986).

Ehrenworth and Lally Green, *The New Bankruptcy Procedures for Rejection of Collective Bargaining Agreements: Is the Pendulum Swinging Back?,* 23 Duq. L. Rev. 939 (1985).

Gibson, *Chapter 11 Is a Two-Edged Sword: Union Options in Corporate Chapter 11 Proceedings,* 35 Lab. L.J. 624 (1984).

Gregory, *Labor Contract Rejection in Bankruptcy: The Supreme Court's Attack on Labor in NLRB v. Bildisco,* 25 B.C.L. Rev. 539 (1984).

Hermann and Neff, *Rush to Judgment: Congressional Response to Judicial Recognition of Rejection of Collective Bargaining Agreements Under Chapter 11 of the Bankruptcy Code,* 27 Ariz. L. Rev. 617 (1985).

Kurtz, Walter and Wells, *Rejection of Collective Bargaining Agreements in Bankruptcy: A Review, Update and Guide for Debtors,* 96 Com. L.J. 31 (1991).

McDonald, Jr., *Bankruptcy Reorganziation: Labor Considerations for the Debtor-Employer,* 11 Empl. Rel. L.J. 7 (Summer 1985).

Miller, *The Rejection of Collective Bargaining Agreements Under the Bankruptcy Code—An Abuse or Proper Exercise of the Congressional Power?,* 52 Fordham L. Rev. 1120 (1984).

Note, *Bankruptcy and the Union's Bargain: Equitable Treatment of Collective Bargaining Agreements,* 39 Stan. L. Rev. 1015 (1987).

Note, *Statutory Protection for Union Contracts in Chapter 11 Reorganization Proceedings:* Wheeling-Pittsburgh Steel Corp. v. United Steelworkers, 19 Conn. L. Rev. 401 (1987).

Rait, *Rejection of Collective Bargaining Agreements under Section 1113 of the Bankruptcy Code: The Second Circuit Enters the Arena,* 63 Am. Bankr. L.J. 355 (1989).

SECTION 1114 (11 U.S.C. § 1114)

§ 1114. Payment of insurance benefits to retired employees.

(a) For purposes of this section, the term "retiree benefits" means payments to any entity or person for the purpose of providing or reimbursing payments for retired employees and their spouses and dependents, for medical, surgical, or hospital care benefits, or benefits in the event of sickness, accident, disability, or death under any plan, fund, or program (through the purchase of insurance or otherwise) maintained or established in whole or in part by the debtor prior to filing a petition commencing a case under this title.

(b)(1) For purposes of this section, the term "authorized representative" means the authorized representative designated pursuant to subsection (c) for persons receiving any retiree benefits covered by a collective bargaining agreement or subsection (d) in the case of persons receiving retiree benefits not covered by such an agreement.

(2) Committees of retired employees appointed by the court pursuant to this section shall have the same rights, powers, and duties as committees appointed under sections 1102 and 1103 of this title for the purpose of carrying out the purposes of sections 1114 and 1129(a)(13) and, as permitted by the court, shall have the power to enforce the rights of persons under this title as they relate to retiree benefits.

(c)(1) A labor organization shall be, for purposes of this section, the authorized representative of those persons receiving any retiree benefits covered by any collective bargaining agreement to which that labor organization is signatory, unless (A) such labor organization elects not to serve as the authorized representative of such persons, or (B) the court, upon a motion by any party in interest, after notice and hearing, determines that different representation of such persons is appropriate.

(2) In cases where the labor organization referred to in paragraph (1) elects not to serve as the authorized representative of those persons receiving any retiree benefits covered by any collective bargaining agreement to which that labor organization is signatory, or in cases where the court, pursuant to paragraph (1) finds different representation of such persons appropriate, the court, upon a motion by any party in interest, and after notice and a hearing, shall appoint a committee of retired employees if the debtor seeks to modify or not pay the retiree benefits or if the court otherwise determines that it is appropriate, from among such persons, to serve as the authorized representative of such persons under this section.

(d) The court, upon a motion by any party in interest, and after notice and a hearing, shall appoint a committee of retired employees if the debtor seeks to modify or not pay the retiree benefits or if the court otherwise determines that it is appropriate, to serve as the authorized representative, under this section, of those persons receiving any retiree benefits not covered by a collective bargaining agreement.

(e)(1) Notwithstanding any other provision of this title, the debtor in possession, or the trustee if one has been appointed under the provisions of this chapter (hereinafter in this section "trustee" shall include a debtor in possession), shall timely pay and shall not modify any retiree benefits, except that—

   (A) the court, on motion of the trustee or authorized representative, and after notice and a hearing, may order modification of such payments, pursuant to the provisions of subsections (g) and (h) of this section; or

   (B) the trustee and the authorized representative of the recipients of those benefits may agree to modification of such payments;

after which such benefits as modified shall continue to be paid by the trustee.

   (2) Any payment for retiree benefits required to be made before a plan confirmed under section 1129 of this title is effective has the status of an allowed administrative expense as provided in section 503 of this title.

   (f)(1) Subsequent to filing a petition and prior to filing an application seeking modification of the retiree benefits, the trustee shall—

   (A) make a proposal to the authorized representative of the retirees, based on the most complete and reliable information available at the time of such proposal, which provides for those necessary modifications in the retiree benefits that are necessary to permit the reorganization of the debtor and assures that all creditors, the debtor and all of the affected parties are treated fairly and equitably; and

   (B) provide, subject to subsection (k)(3), the representative of the retirees with such relevant information as is necessary to evaluate the proposal.

   (2) During the period beginning on the date of the making of a proposal provided for in paragraph (1), and ending on the date of the hearing provided for in subsection (k)(1), the trustee shall meet, at reasonable times, with the authorized representative to confer in good faith in attempting to reach mutually satisfactory modifications of such retiree benefits.

   (g) The court shall enter an order providing for modification in the payment of retiree benefits if the court finds that—

(1) the trustee has, prior to the hearing, made a proposal that fulfills the requirements of subsection (f);

(2) the authorized representative of the retirees has refused to accept such proposal without good cause; and

(3) such modification is necessary to permit the reorganization of the debtor and assures that all creditors, the debtor, and all of the affected parties are treated fairly and equitably, and is clearly favored by the balance of the equities;

except that in no case shall the court enter an order providing for such modification which provides for a modification to a level lower than that proposed by the trustee in the proposal found by the court to have complied with the requirements of this subsection and subsection (f): *Provided, however,* That at any time after an order is entered providing for modification in the payment of retiree benefits, or at any time after an agreement modifying such benefits is made between the trustee and the authorized representative of the recipients of such benefits, the authorized representative may apply to the court for an order increasing those benefits which order shall be granted if the increase in retiree benefits sought is consistent with the standard set forth in paragraph (3); and: *Provided further,* That neither the trustee nor the authorized representative is precluded from making more than one motion for a modification order governed by this subsection.

(h)(1) Prior to a court issuing a final order under subsection (g) of this section, if essential to the continuation of the debtor's business, or in order to avoid irreparable damage to the estate, the court, after notice and a hearing, may authorize the trustee to implement interim modifications in retiree benefits.

(2) Any hearing under this subsection shall be scheduled in accordance with the needs of the trustee.

(3) The implementation of such interim changes does not render the motion for modification moot.

(i) No retiree benefits paid between the filing of the petition and the time a plan confirmed under section 1129 of this title becomes effective shall be deducted or offset from the amounts allowed as claims for any benefits which remain unpaid, or from the amounts to be paid under the plan with respect to such claims for unpaid benefits, whether such claims for unpaid benefits are based upon or arise from a right to future unpaid benefits or from any benefits not paid as a result of modifications allowed pursuant to this section.

(j) No claim for retiree benefits shall be limited by section 502(b)(7) of this title.

(k)(1) Upon the filing of an application for modifying retiree benefits, the court shall schedule a hearing to be held not later than fourteen days after the date of the filing of such application. All interested parties may appear and be heard at such hearing. Adequate notice shall be provided to such parties at least ten days before the date of such hearing. The court may extend the time for the commencement of such hearing for a period not exceeding seven days where the circumstances of the case, and the interests of justice require such extension, or for additional periods of time to which the trustee and the authorized representative agree.

(2) The court shall rule on such application for modification within 90 days after the date of the commencement of the hearing. In the interests of justice, the court may extend such time for ruling for such additional period as the trustee and the authorized representative may agree to. If the court does not rule on such application within 90 days after the date of the commencement of the hearing, or within such additional time as the trustee and the authorized representative may agree to, the trustee may implement the proposed modifications pending the ruling of the court on such application.

(3) The court may enter such protective orders, consistent with the need of the authorized representative of the retirees to evaluate the trustee's proposal and the application for modification, as may be necessary to prevent disclosure of information provided to such representative where such disclosure could compromise the position of the debtor with respect to its competitors in the industry in which it is engaged.

(l) This section shall not apply to any retiree, or the spouse or dependents of such retiree, if such retiree's gross income for the 12 months preceding the filing of the bankruptcy petition equals or exceeds $250,000, unless such retiree can demonstrate to the satisfaction of the court that he is unable to obtain health,

medical, life, and disability coverage for himself, his spouse, and
his dependents who would otherwise be covered by the employer's
insurance plan, comparable to the coverage provided by the
employer on the day before the filing of a petition under this title.

* * *

The Retiree Benefits Bankruptcy Protection Act of 1988, Pub.
L. No. 100–334, made permanent and substantially amended
Section 608 of the second title VI of "Joint Resolution making
continuing appropriations for the fiscal year 1987, and for other
purposes," Pub. L. No. 99–591 (1986). Section 608, as amended,
which is set forth below, applies to chapter 11 cases which were
pending on June 16, 1988, the date of enactment of the Act.

Title VI—General Provisions

Sec. 608. (a)(1) Subject to paragraphs (2), (3), (4), and (5),
and notwithstanding title 11 of the United States Code, the
trustee shall pay benefits to retired former employees under
a plan, fund, or program maintained or established by the
debtor prior to filing a petition (through the purchase of
insurance or otherwise) for the purpose of providing medical,
surgical, or hospital care benefits, or benefits in the event of
sickness, accident, disability or death.

(2) The level of benefits required to be paid by this
subsection may be modified prior to the confirmation of a
plan under section 1129 of such title if—

(A) the trustee and an authorized representative of the
former employees with respect to whom such benefits are
payable agree to the modification of such benefit payments; or

(B) the court finds that a modification proposed by the
trustee meets the standards of section 1113(b)(1)(A) of
such title and the balance of the equities clearly favors
such modification.

If such benefits are covered by a collective bargaining agreement, the authorized representative shall be the labor organization that is signatory to such collective bargaining agreement unless there is a conflict of interest.

(3) The trustee shall pay benefits in accordance with this subsection until—

(A) the dismissal of the case involved; or

(B) the effective date of a plan confirmed under section 1129 of such title which provides for the continued payment after confirmation of the plan of all such benefits at the level established under paragraph (2) of this subsection, at any time prior to the confirmation of the plan, for the duration of the period the debtor (as defined in such title) has obligated itself to provide such benefits.

(4) No such benefits paid between the filing of a petition in a case covered by this section and the time a plan confirmed under section 1129 of such title with respect to such case becomes effective shall be deducted or offset from the amount allowed as claims for any benefits which remain unpaid, or from the amount to be paid under the plan with respect to such claims for unpaid benefits, whether such claims for unpaid benefits are based upon or arise from a right to future benefits or from any benefit not paid as a result of modifications allowed pursuant to this section.

(5) No claim for benefits covered by this section shall be limited by section 502(b)(7) of such title.

(b)(1) Notwithstanding any provision of title 11 of the United States Code, the trustee shall pay an allowable claim of any person for a benefit paid—

(A) before the filing of the petition under title 11 of the United States Code; and

(B) directly or indirectly to a retired former employee under a plan, fund, or program described in subsection (a)(1);

if, as determined by the court, such person is entitled to recover from such employee, or any provider of health care to such employee, directly or indirectly, the amount of such benefit for which such person receives no payment from the debtor.

(2) For purposes of paragraph (1), the term "provider of health care" means a person who—

(A) is the direct provider of health care (including a physician, dentist, nurse, podiatrist, optometrist, physician assistant, or ancillary personnel employed under the supervision of a physician); or

(B) administers a facility or institution (including a hospital, alcohol and drug abuse treatment facility, outpatient facility, or health maintenance organization) in which health care is provided.

(c) This section is effective with respect to cases commenced under chapter 11, of title 11, United States Code, in which a plan for reorganization has not been confirmed by the court and in which any such benefit is still being paid on October 2, 1986, and in cases that become subject to chapter 11, title 11 U.S. Code, after October 2, 1986 and before the date of the enactment of the Retiree Benefits Bankruptcy Protection Act of 1988.

(d) This section shall not apply during any period in which a case is subject to chapter 7, title 11 United States Code.

(House Joint Resolution 738, as amended by Senate Amendment No. 3192, Pub. L. No. 99–591 (1986), and the Retiree Benefits Bankruptcy Protection Act of 1988, Pub. L. No. 100–334 (1988). *See* H.R. Rep. No. 1005, 99th Cong., 2d Sess. 608 (1986). As originally enacted, Section 608(a) instructed the trustee to pay benefits until May 15, 1987. Pub. L. No. 100–41 (1987) changed "May 15, 1987" to "September 15, 1987"; Pub. L. No. 100–99 (1987) changed "September 15, 1987" to "October 15, 1987." The reference to "October 15, 1987" was deleted by the Retiree Benefits Bankruptcy Protection Act of 1988, Pub. L. No. 100–334 (1988).)

Legislative History

Mr. EDWARDS of California.

* * *

Mr. Speaker, H.R. 2969 is legislation designed to protect the health, life, and disability benefits of retirees when companies file [a] chapter 11 bankruptcy. This bill is the same as legislation earlier passed by the House in the 100th Congress, with the addition of a new section 3(b).

* * *

In its application to future cases, H.R. 2969, as amended, is identical to legislation passed by the Senate. Section 2 of this bill ensures that benefits will continue to be paid after bankruptcy. Benefits may be modified only if retirees agree or if the court issues an order after evaluating a proposed modification under strict standards.

In its application to pending cases, this bill differs somewhat in form from the Senate version but provides equivalent protection. Section 3 protects both union and nonunion retirees in pending cases by modifying and making permanent section 608 of Public Law 99–591, the temporary legislation that Congress enacted in 1986.

Section 3(a) modifies Public Law 99–591 so that the same provisions regarding the payment of benefits in future chapter 11 cases apply to pending cases. The debtor must continue to pay retiree benefits after the filing of bankruptcy. Such benefits may be modified if the retirees' representative agrees to a proposed modification. The trustee must first make a proposal to the retirees' representative and meet with the representative at reasonable times to confer in good faith in attempting to reach mutually satisfactory modifications.

If the trustee and the representative do not reach an agreement on the proposed modifications, then the court, after a hearing in which all parties may appear, may order the proposed modifications if it finds that they meet applicable standards. The standards that govern modification of union and nonunion benefits in pending cases are the same as those set forth in existing section 1113 of the Bankruptcy Code and those to be applied to retiree benefits in future cases under new section 1114. The court may order only those modifications "that are necessary to permit the reorganization of the debtor and assure that all creditors, the debtor and all of the affected parties are treated fairly and equitably." In addition, the "balance of the equities" must clearly favor the proposed modifications. In short, modification of retiree benefits is permitted only to the extent necessary to prevent the debtor's liquidation and permit a successful reorganization.

It is the intention of section 3(a) to permit modification more than once during a chapter 11 proceeding, if appropriate. If the debtor's financial condition deteriorates during the case, the standards may support a further reduction in benefits. Conversely, an improvement in the debtor's condition may support an increase in benefits after a reduction has already been made. The retirees' representative may apply to the court for such an upward modification, and the court will order the modification if the applicable standards are satisfied.

Section 3(a) also includes provisions for determining who the retirees' authorized representative will be. If retiree benefits are set forth in a collective bargaining agreement, the labor union that is the signatory to the agreement will usually represent the retirees. In the case of nonunion retirees—or in a case where the union does not represent union retirees—the court, pursuant to existing provisions of the Bankruptcy Code, will appoint a committee to represent retirees. The necessary and reasonable expenses of such committee—but not of a labor union—will be reimbursed by the estate, in accordance with normal practice under the bankruptcy laws.

The fact that some specific language appears in section 2 of the bill but not in section 3(a) does not imply that section 3(a) conveys any lesser protections for retiree benefits than section 2.

For these cases pending on the date of enactment, section 3(b) of the bill protects retirees of self-insured employers in pending bankruptcies. Under a self-insured retiree benefit plan, the employer often hires a third party to administer the payment of benefits. Medical treatment is rendered to retirees by a health care provider—such as a hospital— which bills and collects from the third-party administrator after treatment is provided. The administrator then bills the employer for the cost of the care plus an administrative fee. If the employer fails to pay this amount to the administrator, the administrator in some circumstances may, depending upon the relevant contractual documents, be able to reverse the claim to the health care provider, which may in turn reverse the claim so that the retired worker ultimately gets billed for it. It is our intent that retired workers not get billed for these claims.

Section 3(b) of the bill prevents the undesirable situation where a retired worker would have to pay back an administrator or provider for health care, received prior to the employer's bankruptcy, for which the administrator or provider had not yet been paid as of the date the bankruptcy was filed. This provision is directed only at this type of claim, and does not affect or limit the scope of section 608(a) of Public Law 99–591 with respect to retiree benefits, whether from a self-insured employer or otherwise.

The bill takes no position on whether or not a legal right exists for any administrator or health care provider to reverse charges to the retired worker. Resolution to [sic] this issue should be made by the courts, and depends on the relevant contractual documents.

But under section 3(b), if the administrator can prove to the court that it has the contractual right to reverse a benefit paid on behalf of a particular retiree, then the trustee—often the employer itself in a chapter 11 bankruptcy—must immediately pay the full amount owed to the administrator or health care provider without waiting for confirmation of a plan of reorganization. The court must make such a determination for each such health care claim after evaluating a chain of contractual documents that governed payment of the benefit at the time the retiree received treatment, as well as other relevant evidence. It is anticipated that the court's determination can usually be made as a summary disposition. It is the intent of section 3(b) that there be no recovery under its provisions by either a third party administrator or any other person unless reversal of the claim would otherwise be permitted under contractual documents to which the administrator is a party.

Section 3(b) protects the retiree by directing the debtor to reimburse the administrator from funds in the estate where a legal right to reverse exists. If, however, the administrator does not have this contractual right to reverse payment, the claim will be treated in the bankruptcy plan along with the claims of similar—usually general unsecured—creditors. in [*sic*] neither case can the amount be collected from the retirees.

Section 3(b) does two important things: First, it protects the retirees from being sued for benefits promised them by their former employer; and second, it protects the general unsecured creditors from diminution of a debtor's estate, by granting special treatment to claims only in the United States where claims have been found to be legally reversible.

Because of section 3(b), there is no valid reason for a third party administrator to attempt to reverse any claim. For each claim, all the administrator has to do is prove to the court that it has the contractual right to reverse. Once the court determines this right, the trustee must immediately, without waiting for confirmation of a plan, pay the full amount owed on the claim to the third party administrator.

[*134 Cong. Rec. H 3,486–91 (May 23, 1988).*]

Mr. METZENBAUM. Mr. President, this legislation is a major reform in our bankruptcy laws. It protects retiree health and life insurance benefits when companies go into bankruptcy. This measure sends a strong and powerful message to companies which make promises to their workers—you cannot expect to use the bankruptcy courts as a way of reneging on retiree promises.

Bankruptcies are painful for workers, communities, small business suppliers and others. But the burden of turning a company around should not rest on the backs of retirees. They deserve a fair shake from the companies they build and from the law governing the reorganization process.

* * *

Retirees covered under collective-bargaining agreements also have the protections granted under existing section 1113 of the Bankruptcy Code. Thus, the court's decision in United Steelworkers of America against Unimet (sixth circuit, 1988) makes it clear that retiree benefits promised in a collective-bargaining agreement must be honored. Of course, this measure goes much further. For example, it provides protections as a company reorganizes and comes out of bankruptcy.

Thus, the legislation amends section 1129 of title 11 to require that, in order to be confirmed, a plan of reorganization must provide for continued retiree benefit payments at their full unmodified level, or at the modified benefit levels set by the parties under section 1114(e)(1)(B) or the court under section 1114(g). Similar protections are provided for pending cases. And as I already pointed out, it covers nonunion retirees.

This measure is identical to the Senate bill, S. 548, for cases that have not yet commenced. It differs in some respects for pending cases. However, these differences do not reduce the substantive protections afforded retirees.

The provisions of section 3 apply to union and nonunion retirees. The provision which allows modification by the court is intended to permit only those benefit changes which meet the standards of section 1113(b)(1)(A), and only to the extent that the balance of equities clearly favors the modification.

The reference in section 3 to the "standards of section 1113(b)(1)(A)" refers to "necessary modifications in the employees' benefits and protections that are necessary to permit the reorganization of the debtor and assures that all creditors, the debtor and all affected parties are treated fairly and equitably." The benefits subject to these standards are not required to arise from a collective bargaining agreement.

It is also the intent of section 3 to permit modification of the retiree benefit payments only to the extent necessary to permit reorganization of the debtor, which means necessary to prevent the debtor's liquidation.

It is intended that the words "necessary for the reorganization of the debtor" in sections 2 and 3 should be interpreted as the Third Circuit interpreted them in *In re Wheeling Pittsburgh Steel Corporation,* (791 F.2d 1074 (3d Cir. 1986)). There the court held that a proposal to modify a labor contract is "necessary to permit reorganization" when essential to the "goal of preventing the debtor's liquidation." (791 F.2d 1074, at 1089). The interpretation of the "necessary" standard by the Second Circuit in the case of *In re Carey Transportation,* (816 F.2d 82 (2d Cir. 1987)) would not afford retirees the full protections intended by this measure. Modifications should be ordered by a court only if necessary to avoid liquidation, and the amount of modifications ordered should be only those necessary to avoid liquidation.

The phrase "the court finds" means that the court shall schedule a hearing where all interested parties may appear.

"Proposed by the trustee" as used in section 3 means proposed by the trustee to the representative of the retirees. It is intended that the trustee comply with the requirements of section 1113(b)(2).

Thus, before a court can order a modification the trustee must first make a proposal to the authorized representative of the retirees, and "the trustee shall meet at reasonable times, with the authorized representatives to confer in good faith in attempting to reach mutually satisfactory modifications."

Nothing in section 3 shall prohibit a labor organization from electing not to serve as the authorized representative of the retirees for the purposes of section 3.

The court, under section 3, as under section 2, shall allow authorized representatives other than labor organizations reimbursement from the estate for necessary expenses of representation, such as attorneys' fees. Nothing in this legislation is meant to preclude unions from seeking reimbursement for professional services as allowed by section 503(b)(4) of title 11.

It is expected that the court shall follow the procedures set forth in section 1114(c) in determining who shall represent the nonunion retirees.

The fact that some specific language appears in section 2 but not section 3 shall not imply that section 3 conveys fewer rights or protections to retirees than section 2.

For pending cases, it is intended that representatives of the retirees may petition the court to seek increased retiree benefit payments if such payments have previously been modified. The court shall order an increase if the standards set forth in section 3(a) of the bill are met.

Of course, nothing in this legislation shall preclude negotiation of improved benefits through the normal processes of collective bargaining. In the LTV, Steel case, for example, I understand that the steelworkers will seek such improvements in its next round of bargaining at the company.

Section 3 of this measure covers self-insured health insurance arrangements. Importantly, it protects retirees under such arrangements with respect to pipeline claims. These are claims arising from medical services provided under such arrangements before a company enters bankruptcy, but for which the company has not paid.

For cases already pending, the bill provides that the health plan administrator may go to the bankruptcy court and seek payment from the company of such pipeline claims. To receive payment, the administrator must only prove that it has the right to reverse the charges to the health care providers. Alternatively, if the claims are reversed to the health care providers, they can seek payment in court. the [sic] providers must only prove that they have a right to reverse the claims to retirees.

In either case the company must pay the bills. Thus, retirees will not be at risk. Benefits provided postpetition under a self-insured plan are not pipeline claims and like prepetition and postpetition insured benefits and premiums, must be fully paid by the company.

Under section 1114, all retiree benefits—whether insured, self-insured, prepetition or postpetition—must be fully paid by the company.

* * *

Mr. METZENBAUM. Section 3 is effective with respect to cases commenced under chapter 11 after October 2, 1988, [sic] and before the enactment of this legislation. Section 3 is also effective with respect to cases commenced under chapter 11 prior to October 2, 1986, in which a plan for reorganization has not been confirmed by the court and in which any benefit to retired former employees, as defined in section 608(a), is still being paid on October 2, 1986.

Thus, section 608, with the amendments added by this legislation, applied to cases commenced under chapter 11 where any retiree is being paid such a benefit on October 2, 1986, even if some or most of the retirees had their benefits eliminated by the debtor prior to that date. In such situations, the debtor would be required to reinstate those benefits which had been eliminated prior to October 2, 1986, to reimburse retirees for any benefits lost as a result, and to continue to provide the benefits until section 608 as amended allows otherwise.

[*134 Cong. Rec. S 6,823–27 (May 26, 1988).*]

Comment

The Retiree Benefits Bankruptcy Protection Act of 1988, Pub. L. No. 100–334, added to chapter 11 a new section 1114, "Payment of insurance benefits to retired employees," which provides both the procedures and standards for modifying the payment of retiree benefits in a chapter 11 case, including the use of interim modifications prior to the court's issuance of a final order. For the court to enter an order providing for modification in the payment of retiree benefits, the court must find that—

(1) prior to the hearing, the trustee made a proposal that complied with section 1114(f);

(2) the authorized representative of the retirees refused to accept such proposal without good cause; and

(3) modification is necessary to permit the reorganization of the debtor, assures that all creditors, the debtor and all affected parties are treated fairly and equitably, and is clearly favored by the balance of the equities.

The Act, in addition to enacting section 1114, added paragraph (13) to section 1129(a) [*see infra*], thereby establishing a new requirement for confirmation.

The Act also repealed Section 2 of "An Act to amend the interest provisions of the Declaration of Taking Act," Pub. L. No. 99–656 (1986). Additionally, the Act made permanent and substantially amended Section 608 of the second title VI of "Joint Resolution making continuing appropriations for the fiscal year 1987, and for other purposes," Pub. L. No. 99–591 (1986). Section 608, as amended, provides that the trustee cannot modify retiree benefits unless the trustee and an authorized representative of the former employees with respect to whom such benefits are payable agree to the modification or the court finds that the modification meets the standards of section 1113(b)(1)(A) and the balance of the equities clearly favors the modification. Pursuant to the amendment made to Section 608 by Section 3(a)(3)(B) of the 1988 Act, a chapter 11 trustee or debtor in possession is required to pay any prepetition claims owing to a health care provider that can prove it has the legal right to recover from the patient any such payments, unless repaid by the debtor-former employer; a prepetition claim is thus turned into an administrative expense priority. Section 608, as amended, applies to chapter 11 cases which were pending on June 16, 1988, the date of enactment of the Act.

The Act and its amendments became effective on the date of its enactment, June 16, 1988. However, sections 1114 and 1129(a)(13) do not apply to chapter 11 cases which had been commenced before June 16, 1988. For pre-enactment cases, Section 608, as amended, applies.

Case Annotations

The Pension Benefit Guaranty Corporation has the authority pursuant to provisions of the Employment Retirement Income Security Act of 1974 to restore a chapter 11 debtor's terminated pension plans to their pretermination status with the debtor responsible for administering and funding them when the debtor has subsequent to termination commenced new plans substantially restoring benefits lost in the termination by means of the debtor's contribution of funds over and above the PBGC's contribution. Pension Benefit Guaranty Corp. v. LTV Corp., 496 U.S. —, 110 S. Ct. 2668, 110 L. Ed. 2d 579, 22 C.B.C.2d 1237 (1990).

If a welfare plan explicitly reserves to the employer the right to amend, modify, or terminate future benefits, section 1114 of the Code has no application to prevent such amendment, modification, or termination of future, as opposed to already incurred, welfare benefits. If a debtor has no legal obligation under ERISA to refrain from amending, modifying, or terminating such future benefits, it is unnecessary to appoint a committee under section 1114 to represent affected retirees; however, the court may, in its discretion, appoint a committee if some other need would thereby be fulfilled. *In re* Doskocil Co. Inc., 25 C.B.C.2d 699 (B. Ct., D. Kan. 1991).

Section 1114 is the Code's exclusive provision relating to the modification or termination of retiree benefits and is not applicable once a case has been converted to chapter 7; mandated retiree benefit payments have administrative expense status only while a debtor is operating under chapter 11. Although the placement of section 1114 in chapter 11 does require its application to liquidating chapter 11 cases, when a chapter 11 debtor is completely liquidating its assets in contemplation of a final distribution to creditors, the debtor should not be compelled to continue paying full retiree benefits on a priority basis under section 1114. *In re* Ionosphere Clubs, Inc., 26 C.B.C.2d 797 (B. Ct., S.D.N.Y. 1991). *But see In re* GF Corp., 23 C.B.C.2d 267 (B. Ct., N.D. Ohio 1990) (even absent explicit statutory authority in the Code, a bankruptcy court may grant what is in effect superpriority status to a claim for retiree benefits when a debtor in possession is in a liquidation posture and has few unencumbered assets, and to do so is to give full effect to section 1114(e)(1) and (e)(2)).

When an insurance benefit is modified or terminated under section 1114, a retiree has an unsecured prepetition claim for that portion of his benefit that is not being paid. *In re* Ionosphere Clubs, Inc., 26 C.B.C.2d 797 (B. Ct., S.D.N.Y. 1991).

An interim order terminating retirement benefits under section 1114(h)(1) will not be granted when the debtor is not conducting any business and is incapable of making benefit payments because it has no unencumbered funds. *In re* Garfinckels, Inc., 24 C.B.C.2d 1135 (B. Ct., D.D.C. 1991).

The amended version of Section 608 of Public Law No. 99–591 requires the chapter 11 debtor to pay pension benefits only if it has unencumbered assets with which to make such payments. Amended

Section 608 gives retiree benefits an administrative expense status; it is not an exception to 11 U.S.C. § 506(c) permitting secured collateral to be used to make payments without the consent of and/or benefit to the secured creditor. *In re* Jones & Lamson Machine Co., Inc., 21 C.B.C.2d 259 (B. Ct., D. Conn. 1989).

When the retirees of the chapter 11 debtor are not members of a single union and it is questionable whether they are covered by a collective bargaining agreement, they must have an authorized representative other than the union to bargain on their behalf if they are to receive the same retiree benefits under Section 608 as under section 1114 of the Code. In the Matter of Patrick Cudahy Inc., 19 C.B.C.2d 725 (B. Ct., E.D. Wis. 1988).

The language of Section 2 of the Declaration of Taking Act (Pub. L. No. 99–656) and Section 608 of Pub. L. No. 99–591 cannot be construed to modify the Bankruptcy Code by implication so as to conflict with section 363 of the Code. Accordingly, a debtor in possession cannot be required to use collateral securing a debt to another creditor to pay the health and retirement benefits of former employees as required by a collective bargaining agreement since such use would have the effect of avoiding that creditor's lien. United Steel Workers of America v. Jones & Lamson Mach. Co., Inc. (*In re* Jones & Lamson Mach. Co.), 17 C.B.C.2d 405 (B. Ct., D. Conn. 1987).

References

5 *Collier on Bankruptcy* ch. 1114 (Matthew Bender 15th ed.).

App. Vol. 1 *Collier on Bankruptcy* Pt. 26 (Matthew Bender 15th ed.).

2 *Collier Bankruptcy Manual* ch. 1114 (Matthew Bender 3d ed.).

SUBCHAPTER II

The Plan

SECTION 1121 (11 U.S.C. § 1121)

§ 1121. Who may file a plan.

(a) The debtor may file a plan with a petition commencing a voluntary case, or at any time in a voluntary case or an involuntary case.

(b) Except as otherwise provided in this section, only the debtor may file a plan until after 120 days after the date of the order for relief under this chapter.

(c) Any party in interest, including the debtor, the trustee, a creditors' committee, an equity security holders' committee, a creditor, an equity security holder, or any indenture trustee, may file a plan if and only if—

(1) a trustee has been appointed under this chapter;

(2) the debtor has not filed a plan before 120 days after the date of the order for relief under this chapter; or

(3) the debtor has not filed a plan that has been accepted, before 180 days after the date of the order for relief under this chapter, by each class of claims or interests that is impaired under the plan.

(d) On request of a party in interest made within the respective periods specified in subsections (b) and (c) of this section and after notice and a hearing, the court may for cause reduce or increase the 120-day period or the 180-day period referred to in this section.

Bankruptcy Rule Reference: 3016

Legislative History

Subsection (a) permits the debtor to file a reorganization plan with a petition commencing a voluntary case or at any time during a voluntary or involuntary case.

[*House Report No. 95–595, 95th Cong., 1st Sess. 406 (1977); Senate Report No. 95–989, 95th Cong., 2d Sess. 118 (1978).*]

Subsection (b) gives the debtor the exclusive right to file a plan during the first 120 days of the case. There are exceptions, however, enumerated in subsections (c) and (d). If a trustee has been appointed, if the debtor does not meet the 120-day deadline, or if the debtor does meet that deadline but fails to obtain the required consents within 180 days after the filing of the petition, then any party in interest may propose a plan. This includes the debtor, the trustee, a creditors' committee, an equity security holders' committee, a creditor, an equity security holder, and an indenture trustee. The list is not exhaustive. Finally, subsection (d) permits the court for cause, to increase or reduce the 120-day and 180-day periods specified. Cause might include an unusually large or unusually small case, delay by the debtor, or recalcitrance among creditors.

[*House Report No. 95–595, 95th Cong., 1st Sess. 406 (1977).*]

Subsection (b) gives the debtor the exclusive right to file a plan during the first 120 days of the case. There are exceptions, however, enumerated in subsection (c). If a trustee has been appointed, if the debtor does not meet the 120-day deadline, or if the debtor fails to obtain the required consent within 180 days after the filing of the petition, any party in interest may propose a plan. This includes the debtor, the trustee, a creditors' committee, an equity security holders' committee, a creditor, an equity security holder, and an indenture trustee. This list is not exhaustive. In the case of a public company, a trustee is appointed within 10 days of the petition. In such a case, for all practical purposes, any party in interest may file a plan.

[*Ed. Note:* Provision for mandatory appointment of a trustee in the case of a public company was deleted from section 1104 and the last sentence is inapplicable to to section 1121.]

[*Senate Report No. 95–989, 95th Cong., 2d Sess. 118 (1978).*]

Section 1121 of the House amendment is derived from section 1121 of the House bill; section 1121(c)(1) will be satisfied automatically in a case under subchapter IV of title 11.

[*124 Cong. Rec. H 11,103 (Sept. 28, 1978); S 17,419 (Oct. 6, 1978).*]

Subsection (d) permits the court, for cause, to increase or reduce the 120-day and 180-day periods specified. Since the debtor has an exclusive privilege for 6 months during which others may not file a plan, the granted extension should be based on a showing of some promise of probable success. An extension should not be employed as a tactical device to put pressure on parties in interest to yield to a plan they consider unsatisfactory.

[*Senate Report No. 95–989, 95th Cong., 2d Sess. 118 (1978).*]

Comment

Under section 1121(a) the debtor may file a plan with the petition in a voluntary case, or at any time in a voluntary or involuntary case. It would be the unusual and rare situation where a debtor files a plan with the petition.

Subsections (b) and (c) make provision for the filing of a plan by any party in interest, but *if the debtor remains in possession,* the debtor has the exclusive right to file a plan for 120 days after the date of the entry of the order for relief. If it files a plan within that period, the exclusive right continues to allow acceptance of the plan before 180 days after the date of the order for relief. For illustration, if the debtor files a plan on the 120th day after the order for relief, no other plan may be filed until expiration of the debtor's additional 60 days to gain acceptance of the plan.

In summary, any party in interest, including the debtor, the trustee, a creditors' or equity security holders' committee, or any indenture trustee may file a plan if (1) a trustee has been appointed *or* (2) the debtor fails to file a plan within 120 days and gain acceptance within 180 days.

Subsection (d) allows flexibility in the 120-day and 180-day periods, by empowering the court for cause, on request of a party, and after notice and hearing, to increase or reduce those time periods. The "cause" that may invite alteration of the time periods may include an unusually large or small case, undue delay by a debtor, and the like.

Bankruptcy Rule 3016, as amended in 1991, relates to the filing of a plan and disclosure statement in a chapter 11 case. Subdivision (a) provides that a party in interest, other than the debtor, who is authorized to file a plan under 1121(c) of the Code, may not file a plan after entry of an order approving a disclosure statement unless confirmation of the plan relating to the disclosure statement has been denied or the court otherwise directs. [The Advisory Committee Note states, in part, that subdivision (a) is amended to enlarge the time for filing competing plans. The subdivision does not fix a deadline beyond which a debtor may not file a plan.]

Subdivision (b) requires every proposed chapter 11 plan to be dated and identified with the name of the entity or entities submitting or filing it.

Subdivision (c) provides that a disclosure statement pursuant to section 1125 or evidence showing compliance with section 1126(b) must be filed with the plan or within a time fixed by the court. *See* **Comment** to section 1125.

1984 Amendments: Section 1121(d) was amended to require that requests for reduction or extension of the time periods specified in subsection (c) be made within those time periods.

Stylistic changes were made in subsection (c)(3).

1986 Amendments: The 1986 Act made a minor technical change in section 1121(d).

Case Annotations

In section 1125, the term "solicitation" must be read narrowly so that a creditor is not barred from honestly negotiating with other creditors about its unfiled plan. This interpretation does not offend section 1121(b) which provides only that the debtor has the exclusive right to file a plan during the 120-day period after the date of the order for relief, not that the debtor has a right to have its plan considered exclusively. Century Glove, Inc. v. First American Bank of New York, 860 F.2d 94, 20 C.B.C.2d 742 (3d Cir. 1988).

Creation of an emergency treatment fund, in a chapter 11 case, for certain unsecured claimants before a plan of reorganization has been properly presented and approved, violates the language and intent of the Code and the clear policy of chapter 11 and is not justified as an exercise of the court's equitable powers under section 105(a). Official Comm. of Equity Sec. Holders v. Mabey, 832 F.2d 299, 17 C.B.C.2d 1210 (4th Cir. 1987), *cert. denied,* 485 U.S. 962, 108 S. Ct. 2d 1228, 99 L. Ed. 2d 428 (1988).

If a farmer-debtor fails to propose a reorganization plan within 120 days from the filing of a chapter 11 petition, any party in interest may file a plan, including a liquidation plan, that may be confirmed over the farmer's objection. Button Hook Cattle Co. v. Commercial Nat'l Bank and Trust Co. (In the Matter of Button Hook Cattle Co.), 747 F.2d 483, 11 C.B.C.2d 760 (8th Cir. 1984).

The time limits set forth in section 1121(c) within which a debtor is to file a plan exist to prevent him from initiating chapter 11 proceedings only to block liquidation or debt collection; this is so even as to a farmer who, when his exclusive time to propose a plan has expired, becomes subject to a trustee's plan of liquidation. Jasik v. Conrad (In the Matter of Jasik), 727 F.2d 1379, 10 C.B.C.2d 361, *reh'g denied,* 731 F.2d 888 (5th Cir. 1984).

In the absence of a farmer-debtor's filing of a reorganization plan within the first 120 days, a creditor may file a liquidation plan that may be confirmed over the objections of the debtor. That farmers are not explicitly exempted from the effect of sections 1121(c) and 1123 was not a mere congressional oversight, since farmers are not protected from all the dangers and obligations of proceeding under the Bankruptcy Code. *In re* Huebner, 14 C.B.C.2d 1071 (W.D. Wis. 1986).

Although section 1121(a) refers to "a" plan, under the rules of construction in section 102(7) "a" can be taken to mean "many"; accordingly, a debtor may submit several reorganization plans at the same time as long as claimants are clearly advised of their choices. *In re* Werth, 8 C.B.C.2d 480 (D. Colo. 1983).

Although section 1121(c) enumerates specific categories of parties who are considered to be parties in interest, that list is not exclusive. In determining whether a party is a party in interest, the court must determine on a case by case basis whether, within the specific reorganization process context for which the determination is sought, the party qualifies as a party in interest. *In re* River Bend-Oxford Associates, 23 C.B.C.2d 535 (B. Ct., D. Md. 1990).

A debtor may be given a limited, additional opportunity to propose a plan of reorganization if the debtor is successfully operating its business and paying postpetition obligations as an extension in such a case is in the best interests of the estate and the creditors. *In re* Don & Lin Trucking Co., Inc., 22 C.B.C.2d 1323 (B. Ct., N.D. Ala. 1990).

A chapter 11 debtor may be granted an extension of the 120 day and 180 day exclusive periods during which only a debtor may file a plan of reorganization when the chapter 11 case is unusually large and complex. Note may be taken, though it is not dispositive, that there is pending a legitimate appeal from an adverse judgment of several billion dollars that will have a substantial effect on the outcome of the reorganization. *In re* Texaco, Inc., 17 C.B.C.2d 169 (B. Ct., S.D.N.Y. 1987).

References

5 *Collier on Bankruptcy* ch. 1121 (Matthew Bender 15th ed.).

3 *Collier Bankruptcy Manual* ch. 1121 (Matthew Bender 3d ed.).

5 *Collier Bankruptcy Practice Guide* ch. 90 (Matthew Bender).

Exclusivity Period in Section 1121: How Exclusive Is It?, 11 Cardozo L. Rev. 639 (1990).

Herbert, *Consumer Chapter 11 Proceedings: Abuse or Alternative?*, 91 Com. L.J. 234 (1986).

Lam, *Of Exclusivity and for Cause: 11 U.S.C. Section 1121(d) Re-Examined*, 36 Drake L. Rev. 533 (1986–87).

SECTION 1122 (11 U.S.C. § 1122)

§ 1122. Classification of claims or interests.

(a) Except as provided in subsection (b) of this section, a plan may place a claim or an interest in a particular class only if such claim or interest is substantially similar to the other claims or interests of such class.

(b) A plan may designate a separate class of claims consisting only of every unsecured claim that is less than or reduced to an amount that the court approves as reasonable and necessary for administrative convenience.

Bankruptcy Rule Reference: 3013

Legislative History

This section codifies current case law surrounding the classification of claims and equity securities. It requires classification based on the nature of the claims or interests classified, and permits inclusion of claims or interests in a particular class only if the claim or interest being included is substantially similar to the other claims or interests of the class.

[*Ed. Note:* The Senate Report to section 1122(a) included the following footnote as indicative of current case law:

Payments in cash of small claims in full is common practice in reorganization. Brockett v. Winkle Terra Cotta Co., 81 F. 2d 949, 952 (C.A. 8, 1936); *In re* New Rochelle Coal & Lumber Co., 77 F. 2d 881, 882–83 (C.A. 2, 1935); *In re* Realty Associates Security Corp., 53 F. Supp. 1010, 1011 (E.D.N.Y., 1943).]

Subsection (b), also a codification of existing practice, contains an exception. The plan may designate a separate class of claims consisting only of every unsecured claim that is less than or reduced to an amount that the court approves as reasonable and necessary for administrative convenience.

[*House Report No. 95–595, 95th Cong., 1st Sess. 406 (1977); Senate Report No. 95–989, 95th Cong., 2d Sess. 118 (1978).*]

Comment

In designating classes of claims and interests for purposes of section 1123(a) [section 1123 specifies the contents of a chapter 11 plan], the proponent of a plan must comply with the classification standards of section 1122.

Section 1122 *permits* classification of claims and interests subject to the restriction that a claim or interest may be included in a particular class only if it is "substantially similar" to other claims and interests. But the Code does not require that all claims that are substantially similar be placed in the same class. A claim cannot be classified with an interest. While the Code does not elaborate on the meaning of the phrase "substantially similar," the phrase must be construed to mean similar in legal character to other claims against the debtor's assets or other interests in the debtor. In classifying claims, courts have looked at the nature of the claims (*i.e.,* senior or subordinated), and the relationship of the claim to the property of the debtor. Thus, claims of the same kind and the same rank involving the same property may be included within a single class.

Controversies respecting classification have been more prevalent under the Code than under the Act. Considering that chapter 11 does not require application of the absolute priority rule and permits classes to be left unimpaired, classification takes on considerable consequence under the Code.

Bankruptcy Rule 3013 provides that for the purposes of the plan and its acceptance, the court may, on motion after hearing on notice as the court may direct, establish classes of creditors and equity security holders pursuant to section 1122. (Section 1122 sets the standards for classification but provides that such classification is to be made in the plan. This rule recognizes that it may be important to establish classification before a plan can be formulated. The standards for classification set by the Code are not changed by the rule.)

Case Annotations

Substantially similar claims, *i.e.,* those that share common priority and rights against a debtor's estate, should ordinarily be placed in the same class, although for administrative convenience small unsecured claims may be placed in a class separate from their larger counterparts. A chapter 11 reorganization plan may not, however, classify substantially similar claims differently in order to gerrymander an affirmative vote on a reorganization claim. In the Matter of Greystone III Joint Venture, 948 F.2d 134, 26 C.B.C.2d 220 (5th Cir. 1991).

Section 1122 requires substantial similarity between claims placed in the same class, but does not require all substantially similar claims be placed in the same class, and grants some flexibility in classifying unsecured claims. *In re* Bryson Properties, XVIII, 961 F.2d 496, 26 C.B.C.2d 1290 (4th Cir. 1992).

Because of the overwhelming public policy in favor of providing support for children, the separate classification of child support arrearages previously assigned to a county collection agency in a chapter 13 plan does not unfairly discriminate against other unsecured claims. *In re* Leser, 939 F.2d 669, 25 C.B.C.2d 382 (8th Cir. 1991).

A plan proponent's wide discretion to classify claims is not unlimited; classification together of two claims, one of which is secured by and could be satisfied by an insider's equity interest in the claimant and one of which is an unsecured claim not subject to setoff which has been released under a pending agreement, is improper. *In re* Holywell Corp., 913 F.2d 873, 24 C.B.C.2d 69 (11th Cir. 1990).

A union creditor with a claim resulting from the rejection of a collective bargaining agreement may be classified separately from other creditors with claims arising from the rejection of executory contracts, even though the two types of claims are of a similar legal nature and are against the same property and even though the result is to create a class of assenting and a class of dissenting impaired claims, when the interests of the two groups are substantially dissimilar, especially with respect to their future dealings with the debtor. Teamsters National Freight Industry Negotiating Committee v. U.S. Truck Co., Inc. (*In re* U.S. Truck Co., Inc.), 800 F.2d 581, 15 C.B.C.2d 553 (6th Cir. 1986).

Creditors with claims secured by different properties generally are entitled to separate classification under a plan. Brady v. Andrew (*In re* Commercial W. Fin. Corp.), 761 F.2d 1329, 12 C.B.C.2d 1177 (9th Cir. 1985).

It is not permissible to separately classify a pension fund claim that would be subject to Section 4225(b) of the Multiemployer Pension Plan Amendments Act of 1980 in a chapter 11 liquidation from other unsecured claims in a chapter 11 case; the limitation of liability of Section 4225(b) affects only the allowable amount of a withdrawal claim, not its legal nature as an unsecured claim. Granada Wines, Inc. v. New England Teamsters and Trucking Indus. Pension Fund, 748 F.2d 42, 11 C.B.C.2d 715 (1st Cir. 1984).

A bankruptcy court's order issued during the preplan stages of a bankruptcy proceeding empowering a debtor to pay prepetition debts to some creditors in a class while not others does not violate the "like" treatment requirement called for by section 1122 of a class under a plan in effect. Michigan Bureau of Workers' Disability Compensation v. Chateaugay Corp. (*In re* Chateaugay Corp.), 18 C.B.C.2d 1193 (S.D.N.Y 1987).

A classification process should not substantially disturb a creditor's interest, should not uselessly increase the number of classifications unless differences exist in the nature of the claims, and should not arbitrarily classify or discriminate against creditors. *In re* MCorp Fin., Inc., 26 C.B.C.2d 1805 (B. Ct., S.D. Tex. 1992).

A court may allow the classification of an unsecured claim to be paid in full separate from unsecured claims to be partially paid when the separate classification is for the proper and legitimate purpose of facilitating the chapter 11 debtor's reorganization by providing an infusion of new funds and is not designed for manipulative or abusive purposes. *In re* Atlanta West VI, 20 C.B.C.2d 148 (B. Ct., N.D. Ga. 1988).

A chapter 9 debtor can classify the claims of unsecured general obligation bondholders differently from and as superior to the claims of unsecured warrantholders when state law gives bonds preference over warrants should the latter become due at a time when there are insufficient funds available for payment of all obligations. Sanitary and Improvement District 65 of Sarpy County, Neb. v. First Nat'l Bank of Aurora (In the Matter of Sanitary and Improvement District 65 of Sarpy County, Neb.), 16 C.B.C.2d 1477 (B. Ct., D. Neb. 1986), *aff'd*, 79 B.R. 877 (D. Neb. 1987).

References

5 *Collier on Bankruptcy* ch. 1122 (Matthew Bender 15th ed.).

3 *Collier Bankruptcy Manual* ch. 1122 (Matthew Bender 3d ed.).

5 *Collier Bankruptcy Practice Guide* ch. 90 (Matthew Bender).

Reisenfeld, *Classification of Claims and Interests in Chapter 11 and 13 Cases,* 75 Cal. L. Rev. 391 (1987).

SECTION 1123 (11 U.S.C. § 1123)

§ 1123. Contents of plan.

(a) Notwithstanding any otherwise applicable nonbankruptcy law, a plan shall—

(1) designate, subject to section 1122 of this title, classes of claims, other than claims of a kind specified in section 507(a)(1), 507(a)(2), or 507(a)(7) of this title, and classes of interests;

(2) specify any class of claims or interests that is not impaired under the plan;

(3) specify the treatment of any class of claims or interests that is impaired under the plan;

(4) provide the same treatment for each claim or interest of a particular class, unless the holder of a particular claim or interest agrees to a less favorable treatment of such particular claim or interest;

(5) provide adequate means for the plan's implementation such as—

(A) retention by the debtor of all or any part of the property of the estate;

(B) transfer of all or any part of the property of the estate to one or more entities, whether organized before or after the confirmation of such plan;

(C) merger or consolidation of the debtor with one or more persons;

(D) sale of all or any part of the property of the estate, either subject to or free of any lien, or the distribution of all or any part of the property of the estate among those having an interest in such property of the estate;

(E) satisfaction or modification of any lien;

(F) cancellation or modification of any indenture or similar instrument;

(G) curing or waiving of any default;

(H) extension of a maturity date or a change in an interest rate or other term of outstanding securities;

(I) amendment of the debtor's charter; or

(J) issuance of securities of the debtor, or of any entity referred to in subparagraph (B) or (C) of this paragraph, for cash, for property, for existing securities, or in exchange for claims or interests, or for any other appropriate purpose;

(6) provide for the inclusion in the charter of the debtor, if the debtor is a corporation, or of any corporation referred to in paragraph (5)(B) or (5)(C) of this subsection, of a provision prohibiting the issuance of nonvoting equity securities, and providing, as to the several classes of securities possessing voting power, an appropriate distribution of such power among such classes, including, in the case of any class of equity securities having a preference over another class of equity securities with respect to dividends, adequate provisions for the election of directors representing such preferred class in the event of default in the payment of such dividends; and

(7) contain only provisions that are consistent with the interests of creditors and equity security holders and with public policy with respect to the manner of selection of any officer, director, or trustee under the plan and any successor to such officer, director, or trustee.

(b) Subject to subsection (a) of this section, a plan may—

(1) impair or leave unimpaired any class of claims, secured or unsecured, or of interests;

(2) subject to section 365 of this title, provide for the assumption, rejection, or assignment of any executory contract or unexpired lease of the debtor not previously rejected under such section;

(3) provide for—

(A) the settlement or adjustment of any claim or interest belonging to the debtor or to the estate; or

(B) the retention and enforcement by the debtor, by the trustee, or by a representative of the estate appointed for such purpose, of any such claim or interest;

(4) provide for the sale of all or substantially all of the property of the estate, and the distribution of the proceeds of such sale among holders of claims or interests; and

(5) include any other appropriate provision not inconsistent with the applicable provisions of this title.

(c) In a case concerning an individual, a plan proposed by an entity other than the debtor may not provide for the use, sale, or lease of property exempted under section 522 of this title, unless the debtor consents to such use, sale, or lease.

Legislative History

Subsection (a) specifies the matter that a plan of reorganization must contain. The plan must designate classes of claims and interests, and specify, by class, the claims or interests that are unimpaired under the plan. Priority claims are not required to be classified because they may not have arisen when the plan is filed. The plan must provide the same treatment for each claim or interest of a particular class, unless the holder of a particular claim or interest agrees to a different, but not better, treatment of his claim or interest.

Paragraph . . .[4] applies to claims, not creditors. Thus, if a creditor is undersecured, and thus has a secured claim and an unsecured claim under proposed 11 U.S.C. § 506(a), this paragraph will be applied independently to each of his claims.

Paragraph . . .[5] of subsection (a) is derived from section 216 of current law, with some modifications. It requires the plan to provide adequate means for the plans [*sic*] execution. These means may include retention by the debtor of all or any part of the property of the estate, transfer of all or any part of the property of the estate to one or more entities, whether organized pre- or postconfirmation, merger or consolidation of the debtor with one or more persons, sale and distribution of all or any part of the property of the estate, satisfaction or modification of any lien, cancellation or modification of any indenture or similar instrument, curing or waiving of any default, extention of maturity dates or change in interest rates of securities, amendment of the debtor's charter, and issuance of securities.

Subparagraph (C), as it applies in railroad cases, has the effect of overruling St. Joe Paper Co. v. Atlantic Coast Line R.R., 347 U.S. 298 (1954). It will allow the trustee or creditors to propose a plan of merger with another railroad without the consent of the debtor, and the debtor will be bound under proposed 11 U.S.C. § 1141(a). *See Hearings,* pt. 3, at 1616. "Similar instrument" referred to in subparagraph (F) might include a deposit with an agent for distribution, other than an indenture trustee, such as an agent under an agreement in a railroad conditional sale or lease financing agreement.

Paragraph . . .[6] requires the plan to prohibit the issuance of nonvoting equity securities, and to provide for an appropriate distribution of voting power among the various classes of equity securities.

Paragraph . . .[7] requires that the plan contain only provisions that are consistent with the interests of creditors and equity security holders, and with public policy with respect to the selection of officers, directors, and trustees, and their successors.

Subsection (b) specifies the matters that the plan may propose. The plan may impair or leave unimpaired any claim or interest. The plan may provide for the assumption or rejection of executory contracts or unexpired leases not previously rejected under section 365. The plan may also provide for the treatment of claims by the debtor against other entities that are not settled before the confirmation of the plan. The plan may propose settlement or adjustment of any claim or equity security belonging to the estate, or may propose retention and enforcement of such claim or interest by the debtor or by an agent appointed for that purpose.

The plan may also propose the sale of all or substantially all of the property of the estate, and the distribution of the proceeds of the sale among creditors and equity security holders. This would be a liquidating plan. The subsection permits the plan to include any other appropriate provision not inconsistent with the applicable provisions of the bankruptcy code.

Subsection (c) protects an individual debtor's exempt property by prohibiting its use, sale, or lease under a plan proposed by someone other than the debtor, unless the debtor consents.

[*House Report No. 95-595, 95th Cong., 1st Sess. 406 (1977); See Senate Report No. 95-989, 95th Cong., 2d Sess. 118 (1978).*]

Section 1123 of the House amendment represents a compromise between similar provisions of the House bill and Senate amendment. The section has been clarified to clearly indicate that both secured and unsecured claims, or either of them, may be impaired in a case under title 11. In addition assumption or rejection of an executory contract under a plan must comply with section 365 of title 11. Moreover, section 1123(a)(1) has been substantively modified to permit classification of certain kinds of priority claims. This is important for purposes of confirmation under section 1129(a)(9).

Section 1123(a)(5) of the House amendment is derived from a similar provision in the House bill and Senate amendment but deletes the language pertaining to "fair upset price" as an unnecessary restriction. Section 1123 is also intended to indicate that a plan may provide for any action specified in section 1123 in the case of a corporation without a resolution of the board of directors. If the plan is confirmed, then any action proposed in the plan may be taken notwithstanding any otherwise applicable nonbankruptcy law in accordance with section 1142(a) of title 11.

[*124 Cong. Rec. H 11,103 (Sept. 28, 1978); S 17,419 (Oct. 6, 1978).*]

Comment

Section 1123(a)(1) requires a plan to designate (subject to section 1122) classes of claims, other than claims of a kind specified in subsection (a)(1), (a)(2) or (a)(7) of section 507, and classes of interests.

Section 507(a)(1) gives first priority to administrative expenses allowed under section 503(b) (costs of preserving the estate, taxes, fines and penalties incurred by the estate and compensation); section 507(a)(2) gives second priority to unsecured claims incurred after the filing of an involuntary petition and before the earlier of the appointment of a trustee or the order for relief; section 507(a)(7) gives seventh priority to certain unsecured tax claims of governmental units.

Under the former Bankruptcy Act, the overwhelming number of business rehabilitation petitions were filed under Chapter XI, mainly because management could remain in control unless cause existed to oust it; because the absolute priority rule of Chapter X did not apply and thus stockholders were not affected; and, finally, because the entire machinery of Chapter XI was simple compared to that of Chapter X. The great drawback, however, was that the rights of secured creditors could not be affected in a Chapter XI case. A composition or extension plan could only affect unsecured creditors.

The drastic change effected by section 1123 of the Code is that both secured and unsecured claims, or either of them, may be impaired in a reorganization case under chapter 11, and this applies to the larger, complex cases as well as to those cases which under the Act would normally have been filed under Chapter XI.

Section 216 of the former Bankruptcy Act which related to the provisions of a Chapter X plan provided in paragraph (6) thereof that a plan "shall specify the creditor or stockholders or any class of them not to be affected by the plan and the provisions, if any, with respect to them." Section 1123 of the Code, requires in paragraphs (2) and (3) thereof that the plan specify any class or interest that is not "impaired" under the plan, and the treatment of any class of claims or interest that is "impaired" under the plan. Note the use of the word "impaired" in lieu of "affected." Section 1124 sets forth the test for determining whether a claim or interest is "impaired."

Section 1123(a)(5), derived from Section 216 of the former Bankruptcy Act, which requires a plan to provide adequate means for the plan's execution *suggests* ten methods of doing so.

Section 216 of the Act specified the mandatory and permissive contents of a Chapter X plan. Subsections (a) and (b) of section 1123 of the Code also specify mandatory and permissive provisions of a plan.

1984 Amendments: Subsection (a) of section 1123 was amended to provide that the mandatory provisions of a plan must be included notwithstanding otherwise applicable nonbankruptcy law.

Minor technical and stylistic changes were made in subsections (a) (1), (3), (5), (5)(G) and (b)(2).

Case Annotations

The bankruptcy court may order the IRS to use a reorganized debtor's tax payments to eliminate trust fund obligations prior to offsetting any non-trust fund obligations when the bankruptcy court has concluded that the action is necessary for the reorganization to be successful. United States v. Energy Resources Co., Inc., 495 U.S. —, 110 S. Ct. 2139, 109 L. Ed. 2d 580, 22 C.B.C.2d 1093 (1990).

A representative has been sufficiently appointed to fulfill his obligations including the avoidance powers when a debtor has appointed a representative of the estate to pursue specific claims; the debtor and administrative creditors have agreed to the representative's responsibilities; and the reorganization plan which contains such agreement has been voted on and approved by the parties and confirmed by the court. *In re* Sweetwater, 884 F.2d 1323, 21 C.B.C.2d 1034 (10th Cir. 1989).

The avoiding powers provided in chapter 5 of the Code are not "property of the estate," but statutorily created powers to recover property and because they are not property of the estate, they cannot be assigned to a creditors' group pursuant to section 1123(a)(5)(B). Robison v. First Financial Capital Management Corp. (*In re* Sweetwater), 14 C.B.C.2d 247 (D. Utah 1985).

A proposed plan modification which offers no liquidation analysis and which divests some shareholders of all shares while transferring complete ownership to another shareholder violates the equal treatment provisions of section 1123(a)(4). *In re* Modern Steel Treating Co., 25 C.B.C.2d 292 (B. Ct., N.D. Ill. 1991).

The provisions of section 1123 exist to accommodate financial restructuring and are not intended as blanket authority for a distressed business to liquidate itself as a debtor in possession under the protective umbrella of chapter 11 of the Code. *In re* Lyons Transportation Lines, Inc., 24 C.B.C.2d 1438 (B. Ct., W.D. Pa. 1991).

For purposes of determining whether a person is a representative of the estate within the meaning of section 1123(b)(3) entitled to pursue avoidance actions, the benefit envisioned by section 1123(b)(3)(B) encompasses past benefits to the estate, such as the substantial funding of a settlement agreement, even though prosecution of the actions will result in future recovery not to the estate but rather to the new entity. *In re* Churchfield Management & Investment Corp., 24 C.B.C.2d 1386 (B. Ct., N.D. Ill. 1990).

An assignment of the debtor's litigation claims to a representative other than the trustee is permissible when the resulting proceeds from those claims, if any, will be for the benefit of unsecured creditors and shareholders of the debtor corporation. *In re* Crowthers McCall Pattern, Inc., 24 C.B.C.2d 611 (B. Ct., S.D.N.Y. 1990).

A party who succeeds to a debtor's rights under a plan of reorganization does not qualify as a representative of the estate when there is no provision in such plan that the party's successful prosecution of an avoidance action would be for the benefit of unsecured creditors of the estate. *In re* Mako, Inc., 24 C.B.C.2d 341 (B. Ct., W.D. Okla. 1990).

A secured creditor's claim may be modified by the restructuring of its loan pursuant to a chapter 11 plan, and if the creditor is a savings association the restructuring will not subject the creditor to liability for violating the "loan-to-one-borrower" ("LTOB") limits imposed by the FIRREA regulations. *In re* Buttonwood Partners, Ltd., 22 C.B.C.2d 1107 (B. Ct., S.D.N.Y. 1990).

Congress intended to allow a chapter 11 debtor to modify both the maturity date and rate of interest on a secured claim under section 1123(a)(5) if required for the implementation of a proposed plan of reorganization. *In re* Crane Automotive, 19 C.B.C.2d 307 (B. Ct., W.D. Pa. 1988).

In light of the nature of partnerships and their significance under state law, the bankruptcy court may confirm a proposed reorganization plan replacing the general partner with the debtor's affiliated special limited partner in compliance with the debtor's partnership agreement. *In re* Sovereign Group, 1984-21 Ltd., 18 C.B.C.2d 1450 (B. Ct., D. Colo. 1988).

A plan may provide for the retention and enforcement of any claim or interest belonging to the debtor or to the estate by a representative of the estate appointed for such purpose; however, it may not provide for the sale of such a right. Foster Dev. Corp. v. Morning Treat Coffee Co. (*In re* Morning Treat Coffee Co.), 17 C.B.C.2d 1260 (B. Ct., M.D. La. 1987).

It is the burden of debtors to justify substantive consolidation, even when the question arises in the context of an objection to confirmation; among the factors to be considered are necessity of consolidation due to inter-relationship among debtors, whether the benefits of consolidation outweigh the harm to the creditors, and whether there is prejudice that will result from lack of consolidation. *In re* Silver Falls Petroleum Corp., 13 C.B.C.2d 1350 (B. Ct., S.D. Ohio 1985).

References

5 *Collier on Bankruptcy* ch. 1123 (Matthew Bender 15th ed.).

3 *Collier Bankruptcy Manual* ch. 1123 (Matthew Bender 3d ed.).

5 *Collier Bankruptcy Practice Guide* ch. 90 (Matthew Bender).

Epling, *Proposal for Equality of Treatment for Claims in Chapter 7 and Claims in a Liquidating Chapter 11 Case,* 4 Bankr. Dev. J. 399 (1987).

Zaretsky, *Co-Debtor Stays in Chapter 11 Bankruptcy,* 73 Cornell L. Rev. 213 (1988).

SECTION 1124 (11 U.S.C. § 1124)

§ 1124. Impairment of claims or interests. Except as provided in section 1123(a)(4) of this title, a class of claims or interests is impaired under a plan unless, with respect to each claim or interest of such class, the plan—

(1) leaves unaltered the legal, equitable, and contractual rights to which such claim or interest entitles the holder of such claim or interest;

(2) notwithstanding any contractual provision or applicable law that entitles the holder of such claim or interest to demand or receive accelerated payment of such claim or interest after the occurrence of a default—

(A) cures any such default that occurred before or after the commencement of the case under this title, other than a default of a kind specified in section 365(b)(2) of this title;

(B) reinstates the maturity of such claim or interest as such maturity existed before such default;

(C) compensates the holder of such claim or interest for any damages incurred as a result of any reasonable reliance by such holder on such contractual provision or such applicable law; and

(D) does not otherwise alter the legal, equitable, or contractual rights to which such claim or interest entitles the holder of such claim or interest; or

(3) provides that, on the effective date of the plan, the holder of such claim or interest receives, on account of such claim or interest, cash equal to—

(A) with respect to a claim, the allowed amount of such claim; or

(B) with respect to an interest, if applicable, the greater of—

(i) any fixed liquidation preference to which the terms of any security representing such interest entitle the holder of such interest; or

(ii) any fixed price at which the debtor, under the terms of such security, may redeem such security from such holder.

Legislative History

This section is new. It is designed to indicate when contractual rights of creditors or interest holders are not materially affected. The section specifies three ways in which the plan may leave a claim or interest unimpaired.

First, the plan may propose not to alter the legal, equitable, or contractual rights to which the claim or interest entitled its holder.

Second, the plan is permitted to reinstate a claim or interest and thus leave it unimpaired. Reinstatement consists of curing any default (other than a default under an *ipso facto* or bankruptcy clause) and reinstatement of the maturity of the claim or interest. Further, the plan may not otherwise alter any legal, equitable, or contractual right to which the claim or interest entitles its holder.

Third, the plan may leave a claim or interest unimpaired by paying its amount in full other than in securities of the debtor, an affiliate of the debtor participating in a joint plan, or a successor to the debtor. These securities are excluded because determination of their value would require a valuation of the business being reorganized. Use of them to pay a creditor or equity security holder without his consent may be done only under section 1129(b) and only after a valuation of the debtor. Under this paragraph, the plan must pay the allowed amount of the claim in full, in cash or other property, or, in the case of an equity security, must pay the greatest of any fixed liquidation preference to which the terms of the equity security entitle its holder, any fixed price at which the debtor, under the terms of the equity security may redeem such equity security, and the value, as of the effective date of the plan, of the holder's interest in the debtor. The value of the holder's interest need not be determined precisely by valuing the debtor's business if such value is clearly below redemption or liquidation preference values. If such value would require a full-scale valuation of the business, then such interest should be treated as impaired. But, if the debtor corporation is clearly insolvent, then the value of the common stock holder's interest in the debtor is zero, and offering them nothing under the plan of reorganization will not impair their rights.

"Value, as of the effective date of the plan," as used in paragraph (3) and in proposed 11 U.S.C. § § 1179(a)(7)(B), 1128(a)(9), 1129(b), 1172(2) [*sic*], 1325(a)(4), 1325(a)(5)(B), and 1328(b), indicates that the promised payment under the plan must be discounted to present value as of the effective date of the plan. The discounting should be based only on the unpaid balance of the amount due under the plan, until that amount, including interest, is paid in full.

[*House Report No. 95–595, 95th Cong., 1st Sess. 408 (1977).*]

The basic concept underlying this section is not new. It rests essentially on section 107 of chapter X (11 U.S.C. § 507) which states that creditors or stockholders or any class thereof "shall be deemed to be 'affected' by a plan only if their or its interest shall be materially and adversely affected thereby."

This section is designed to indicate when contractual rights of creditors or interest holders are not materially affected. It specifies three ways in which the plan may leave a claim or interest unimpaired.

First, the plan may propose not to alter the legal, equitable, or contractual rights to which the claim or interest entitled its holder.

Second, a claim or interest is unimpaired by curing the effect of a default and reinstating the original terms of an obligation when maturity was brought on or accelerated by the default. The intervention of bankruptcy and the defaults represent a temporary crisis which the plan of reorganization is intended to clear away. The holder of a claim or interest who under the plan is restored to his original position, when others receive less or get nothing at all, is fortunate indeed and has no cause to complain. Curing of the default and the assumption of the debt in accordance with its terms is an important reorganization technique for dealing with a particular class of claims, especially secured claims.

Third, a claim or interest is unimpaired if the plan provides for their payment in cash. In the case of a debt liability, the cash payment is for the allowed amount of the claim, which does not include a redemption premium. If it is an equity security with a fixed liquidation preference, such as a preferred stock, the allowed amount is such liquidation preference, with no redemption premium. With respect to any other equity security, such as a common stock, cash payment must be equal to the "value of such holder's interest in the debtor."

Section 1124 does not include payment "in property" other than cash. Except for a rare case, claims or interests are not by their terms payable in property, but a plan may so provide and those affected thereby may accept or reject the proposed plan. They may not be forced to accept a plan declaring the holders' claims or interests to be "unimpaired."

[*Senate Report No. 95–989, 95th Cong., 2d Sess. 120 (1978).*]

Section 1124 of the House amendment is derived from a similar provision in the House bill and Senate amendment. The section defines the new concept of "impairment" of claims or interests; the concept differs significantly from the concept of "materially and adversely affected" under the Bankruptcy Act. Section 1124(3) of the House amendment provides that a holder of a claim or interest is not impaired, if the plan provides that the holder will receive the allowed amount of the holder's claim, or in the case of an interest with a fixed liquidation preference or redemption price, the greater of such price. This adopts the position contained in the House bill and rejects the contrary standard contained in the Senate amendment.

Section 1124(3) of the House amendment rejects a provision contained in section 1124(3)(B)(iii) of the House bill which would have considered a class of interest not to be impaired by virtue of the fact that the plan provided cash or property for the value of the holder's interest in the debtor.

The effect of the House amendment is to permit an interest not to be impaired only if the interest has a fixed liquidation preference or redemption price. Therefore, a class of interests such as common stock, must either accept a plan under section 1129(a)(8), or the plan must satisfy the requirements of section 1129(b)(2)(C) in order for a plan to be confirmed.

A compromise reflected in section 1124(2)(C) of the House amendment indicates that a class of claims is not impaired under the circumstances of section 1124(2) if damages are paid to rectify reasonable reliance engaged in by the holder of a claim or interest arising from the prepetition breach of a contractual provision, such as an *IPSO [sic] facto* or bankruptcy clause, or law. Where the rights of third parties are concerned, such as in the case of lease premises which have been rerented to a third party, it is not intended that there will be adequate damages to compensate the third party.

[*124 Cong. Rec. H 11,103 (Sept. 28, 1978); S 17,419 (Oct. 6, 1978).*]

Comment

The House Report states that section 1124 is new. The Senate Report states that the underlying concept of the section as it appeared in the Senate version of the Bill is not new, resting essentially in Section 107 of Chapter X of the Act which stated:

Creditors or stockholders or any class thereof shall be deemed to be "affected" by a plan only if their or its interest shall be materially and adversely affected thereby. . . .

The Congressional Record, set forth *supra,* however, points out that the concept of "impairment" as it now appears in section 1124 differs significantly from the concept of "materially and adversely affected."

The concept of impairment is essential to an understanding of the mechanics of reorganization under chapter 11 and of the flexibility of that chapter as a reorganization tool. Whether a class is impaired determines whether such class is required to vote for a plan of reorganization. Moreover, section 1129(a)(8) requires as a condition of confirmation that each class of claims and interests either accept the plan or be unimpaired.

If a claim is not dealt with by the plan, *i.e.,* the legal rights are left unaltered, the claim is not impaired. If a claim has been accelerated, the default (with certain exceptions) may be cured or the maturity reinstated after the filing of the chapter 11 case regardless of contractual provisions and, again, under section 1124 the claim is unimpaired. If however, the holder of a claim or interest is damaged as a result of "reasonable reliance" on a contractual provision or applicable law, the claim or interest is impaired unless the holder is compensated for damages so incurred.

Section 1124(3) is an application of modified so-called "cramdown." Under paragraph (3)(A) a claim is unimpaired if the holder of the claim receives cash equal to the allowed amount of the claim. Under paragraph (3)(B) an "interest" is deemed unimpaired if the holder receives cash equal to the *greater* of (1) any fixed liquidation preference to which the terms of any security representing such interest entitles the holder; and (2) any fixed price at which the debtor under the terms of such security may redeem the security. (*See* section 506(a) as to determination of secured status.) A provision originally contained in the House Bill would have considered a class or interest not to be impaired if the plan provided cash or property for the value of the holder's interest in the debtor. The property concept was rejected in the final Bill. An interest is deemed not to be impaired only if the interest has a fixed liquidation or redemption price.

If a class is impaired and does not accept the plan, then the plan must meet the requirements of section 1129(b)(2)(C) in order for the plan to be confirmed.

1984 Amendments: Section 1124 was amended by a stylistic change in paragraph (2)(A).

Case Annotations

The bankruptcy court may approve a plan that permits a debtor to pay prepetition interest even if it was contractually obligated to pay a higher post-default rate and there was no acceleration of the debt. *In re* Southeast Co, 868 F.2d 335, 20 C.B.C.2d 1348 (9th Cir. 1989).

A creditor holding an order or final judgment of foreclosure is not impaired under section 1124(2) if the debtor's reorganization plan cures the default of the accelerated loan before the foreclosure sale actually occurs or before the judgment merges into the mortgage under state law. In the Matter of Madison Hotel Assocs., 749 F.2d 410, 11 C.B.C.2d 771 (7th Cir. 1984).

While default may accelerate an entire outstanding loan, debt reinstatement cures the default and deaccelerates the debt, and accordingly, interest payments are due only on those amounts falling due during the period of default. Official Committee of Unsecured Creditors of Manville Forest Products Corp. v. Manville Forest Products Corp. (*In re* Manville Forest Products Corp.), 14 C.B.C.2d 1312 (S.D.N.Y. 1986).

Damages incurred as a result of reliance under section 1124(2)(C) do not comprise contractual penalty interest rates and, at most, include additional interest charges on past-due installments of interest and principal. *In re* Southeast Co., 18 C.B.C.2d 359 (9th Cir., B.A.P., 1987).

A chapter 11 debtor may deaccelerate and reinstate a debt that has merged into a foreclosure judgment. Additionally, a chapter 11 mortgage default cure and reinstatement does not require payment of default interest. *In re* Singer Island Hotel, Ltd., 20 C.B.C.2d 436 (B. Ct., S.D. Fla. 1989).

Section 1124(1) does not require that the proposed plan affirmatively "cure" a securities fraud claim by a security holder of the debtor impaired by reason of section 510(b) in order to render the affected claims unimpaired because this not the type of impairment contemplated by section 1124(1); such requirement to "cure" would force the debtor to exclude the securities fraud claims until the other claims of equal or higher dignity were satisfied in full and thus render section 510(b) meaningless. *In re* American Solar King Corp., 20 C.B.C.2d 547 (B. Ct., W.D. Tex. 1988).

A claim does not become impaired or become entitled to the protections of subsection (a)(7) and (b) of section 1129 on account of the amount of time, if reasonable, between the confirmation of the plan and the effective date of the plan if the plan provides that on the effective date of the plan the holder of a claim receives cash otherwise equal to the allowed amount of its claim. *In re* Wonder Corp. of America, 16 C.B.C.2d 566 (B. Ct., D. Conn. 1987).

The Bankruptcy Code no longer requires that impairment be "material and adverse," so that an unsecured creditor's claim may not be significantly impaired and yet still satisfy section 1124 of the Bankruptcy Code. *In re* Witt, 14 C.B.C.2d 1335 (B. Ct., N.D. Iowa 1986).

A claim is impaired, despite a plan's provision for full payment of it, when full payment is to occur on or before the "consummation date," but that date is not defined. A plan must state when payments are to be made and in what amount. *In re* Holthoff, 14 C.B.C.2d 620 (B. Ct., E.D. Ark. 1985).

Because a purchaser at a prepetition foreclosure sale does not enter into any contract or transaction with the debtor and does not acquire a right to an equitable remedy for breach of performance, it cannot be considered a holder of a claim whose rights are subject to modification under section 1124(2); *i.e.,* the purchaser's claim is not subject to deacceleration and the debtor can only retain the foreclosed property by paying the redemption price, assuming the redemption period has not expired. Young v. United States (*In re* Young), 12 C.B.C.2d 983 (B. Ct., E.D. Mich. 1985).

The failure of a reorganization plan to provide for "lost opportunity costs" will not render a claim impaired under section 1124(2)(C). *In re* Kizzac Management Corp., 11 C.B.C.2d 1106 (B. Ct., S.D.N.Y. 1984).

References

5 *Collier on Bankruptcy* ch. 1124 (Matthew Bender 15th ed.).

3 *Collier Bankruptcy Manual* ch. 1124 (Matthew Bender 3d ed.).

5 *Collier Bankruptcy Practice Guide* ch. 90 (Matthew Bender).

Blum, *Treatment of Interest on Debtor Obligations in Reorganizations Under the Bankruptcy Code,* 50 U. Chi. L. Rev. 430 (1983).

Carr, *When Can the Owners Participate in the Reorganized Debtor?: Cram Down as a "Shield" For Creditors,* 15 Ind. L. Rev. 569 (1982).

Cohen, Marwil and Gerard, *Entitlement of Secured Creditors to Default Interest Rates Under Bankruptcy Code Sections 506(b) and 1124,* 45 Bus. Law. 415 (1989).

Comment, *Impairment,* 3 Bankr. Dev. J. 579 (1986).

Davis, Jr., *Status of Defrauded Security Holders in Corporate Bankruptcy,* 1983 Duke L.J. 1 (1983).

Mallory and Phelan, *To Impair or Not to Impair—That Is the Question in Chapter 11 Reorganization,* 17 St. Mary's L.J. 869 (1986).

Rogers, *The Impairment of Secured Creditors Rights in Reorganization: A Study of the Relationship Between the Fifth Amendment and the Bankruptcy Clause,* 96 Harv. L. Rev. 973 (1983).

Schorer, *The Right of the Undersecured Creditor to Postpetition Interest in Bankrupcty on the Value of its Collateral: Implication of Recent Cases,* 21 U.C.C. L.J. 61 (1988).

SECTION 1125 (11 U.S.C. § 1125)

§ 1125. Postpetition disclosure and solicitation.

(a) In this section—

(1) "adequate information" means information of a kind, and in sufficient detail, as far as is reasonably practicable in light of the nature and history of the debtor and the condition of the debtor's books and records, that would enable a hypothetical reasonable investor typical of holders of claims or interests of the relevant class to make an informed judgment about the plan, but adequate information need not include such information about any other possible or proposed plan; and

(2) "investor typical of holders of claims or interests of the relevant class" means investor having—

(A) a claim or interest of the relevant class;

(B) such a relationship with the debtor as the holders of other claims or interests of such class generally have; and

(C) such ability to obtain such information from sources other than the disclosure required by this section as holders of claims or interests in such class generally have.

(b) An acceptance or rejection of a plan may not be solicited after the commencement of the case under this title from a holder of a claim or interest with respect to such claim or interest unless, at the time of or before such solicitation, there is transmitted to such holder the plan or a summary of the plan, and a written disclosure statement approved, after notice and a hearing, by the court as containing adequate information. The court may approve a disclosure statement without a valuation of the debtor or an appraisal of the debtor's assets.

(c) The same disclosure statement shall be transmitted to each holder of a claim or interest of a particular class, but there may be transmitted different disclosure statements, differing in amount, detail, or kind of information, as between classes.

(d) Whether a disclosure statement required under subsection (b) of this section contains adequate information is not governed by any otherwise applicable non-bankruptcy law, rule, or regulation, but an agency or official whose duty is to administer or enforce such a law, rule, or regulation may be heard on the issue of whether a disclosure statement contains adequate information. Such an agency or official may not appeal from, or otherwise seek review of, an order approving a disclosure statement.

(e) A person that solicits acceptance or rejection of a plan, in good faith and in compliance with the applicable provisions of this title, or that participates, in good faith and in compliance with the applicable provisions of this title, in the offer, issuance, sale, or purchase of a security, offered or sold under the plan, of the debtor, of an affiliate participating in a joint plan with the debtor, or of a newly organized successor to the debtor under the plan, is not liable, on account of such solicitation or participation, for violation of any applicable law, rule, or regulation governing solicitation of acceptance or rejection of a plan or the offer, issuance, sale, or purchase of securities.

Bankruptcy Rule References: 2002, 3016 and 3017

Legislative History

   This section is new. It is the heart of the consolidation of the various reorganization chapters found in current law. It requires disclosure before solicitation of acceptances of a plan of reorganization.

Subsection (a) contains two definitions. First, "adequate information" is defined to mean information of a kind, and insufficient [*sic*] detail, as far as is reasonably practical in light of the nature and history of the debtor and the condition of the debtor's books and records, that would enable a hypothetical reasonable investor typical of holders of claims or interests of the relevant class to make an informed judgment about the plan. Second, "investor typical of holders of claims or interest of the relevant class" is defined to mean an investor having a claim or interest of the relevant class, having such a relationship with the debtor as the holders of other claims or interests of the relevant class have, and having such ability to obtain information from sources other than the disclosure statement as holders of claims or interests of the relevant class have. That is, the hypothethical investor against which the disclosure is measured must not be an insider if other members of the class are not insiders, and so on. In other words, the adequacy of disclosure is measured against the typical investor, not an extraordinary one.

The Supreme Court's rulemaking power will not extend to rulemaking that will prescribe what constitutes adequate information. That standard is a substantive standard. Precisely what constitutes adequate information in any particular instance will develop on a case-by-case basis. Courts will take a practical approach as to what is necessary under the circumstances of each case, such as the cost of preparation of the statements, the need for relative speed in solicitation and confirmation, and, of course, the need for investor protection. There will be a balancing of interests in each case. In reorganization cases, there is frequently great uncertainty. Therefore the need for flexibility is greatest.

[*House Report No. 95–595, 95th Cong., 1st Sess. 408 (1977).*]

This section extends disclosure requirements in connection with solicitations to all cases under chapter 11. Heretofore this subject was dealt with by the Bankruptcy Act mainly in the special contexts of railroad reorganizations and chapter X cases.

Subsection (a) defines (1) the subject matter of disclosure as "adequate information" and relates the standard of adequacy to an (2) "investor typical of holders or [*sic*] claims or interests of the relevant class." "Investor" is used broadly here, for it will almost always include a trade creditor or other creditors who originally had no investment intent or interest. It refers to the investment-type decision by those called upon to accept a plan to modify their claims or interests, which typically will involve acceptance of new securities or of a cash payment in lieu thereof.

Both the kind and form of information are left essentially to the judicial discretion of the court, guided by the specification in subparagraph (a)(1) that it be of a kind and in sufficient detail that a reasonable and typical investor can make an informed judgment about the plan. The information required will necessarily be governed by the circumstances of the case.

Reporting and audit standards devised for solvent and continuing businesses do not necessarily fit a debtor in reorganization. Subsection (a)(1) expressly incorporates consideration of the nature and history of the debtor and the condition of its books and records into the determination of what is reasonably practicable to supply. These factors are particularly pertinent to historical data and to discontinued operations of no future relevance.

A plan is necessarily predicated on knowledge of the assets and liabilities being dealt with with an on factually supported expectations as to the future course of the business sufficient to meet the feasibility standard in section 1130(a)(11) of this title. It may thus be necessary to provide estimates or judgments for that purpose. Yet it remains practicable to describe, in such detail as may be relevant and needed, the basis for the plan and the data on which supporters of the plan rely.

[*Senate Report No. 95–989; 95th Cong., 2d Sess. 120 (1978).*]

Subsection (b) is the operative subsection. It prohibits solicitation of acceptances or rejections of a plan after the commencement of the case unless, at the time of the solicitation or before, there is transmitted to the solicitee the plan or a summary of the plan, and a written disclosure statement approved by the court as containing adequate information. The subsection permits approval of the statement without the necessity of a valuation of the debtor or an appraisal of the debtor's assets. However, in some cases, a valuation or appraisal will be necessary to develop adequate information. The court will be able to determine what is necessary in light of the facts and circumstances of each particular case.

[*House Report No. 95–595, 95th Cong., 1st Sess. 408 (1977).*]

Subsection (b) establishes the jurisdiction of the court over this subject by prohibiting solicitation of acceptance or rejection of a plan after the commencement of the case, unless the person solicited receives, before or at the time of the solicitation, a written disclosure statement approved by the court, after notice and hearing, as containing adequate information. As under present law, determinations of value, by appraisal or otherwise, are not required if not needed to accomplish the purpose specified in subsection (a)(1).

[*Senate Report No. 95–989, 95th Cong., 2d Sess. 120 (1978).*]

Subsection (c) requires that the same disclosure statement go to all members of a particular class, but permits different disclosure to different classes.

[*House Report No. 95–595, 95th Cong., 1st Sess. 408 (1977).*]

Subsection (c) requires that the same disclosure statement be transmitted to each member of a class. It recognizes that the information needed for an informed judgment about the plan may differ among classes. A class whose rights under the plan center on a particular fund or asset would have no use for an extensive description of other matters that could not affect them.

[*Senate Report No. 95–989, 95th Cong., 2d Sess. 120 (1978).*]

Subsection (d) excepts the disclosure statements from the requirements of the securities laws (such as section 14 of the 1934 Act and section 5 of the 1933 Act), and from similar State securities laws (blue sky laws, for example). The subsection permits an agency or official whose duty is to administer or enforce such laws (such as the Securities and Exchange Commission or State Corporation Commissioners) to appear and be heard on the issue of whether a disclosure statement contains adequate information, but the agencies and officials are not granted the right of appeal from an adverse determination in any capacity. They may join in an appeal by a true party in interest, however.

[*House Report No. 95–595, 95th Cong., 1st Sess. 408 (1977).*]

Subsection (d) relieves the court of the need to follow any otherwise applicable Federal or state law in determining the adequacy of the information contained in the disclosure statement submitted for its approval. It authorizes an agency or official, Federal or state, charged with administering cognate laws so preempted to advise the court on the adequacy of proposed disclosure statement. But they are not authorized to appeal the court's decision.

Solicitations with respect to a plan do not involve just mere requests for opinions. Acceptance of the plan vitally affects creditors and shareholders, and most frequently the solicitation involves an offering of securities in exchange for claims or interests. The present bankruptcy statute has exempted such offerings under each of its chapters from the registration and disclosure requirements of the Securities Act of 1933, an exemption also continued by section 1145(a)(2) of this title. The extension of the disclosure requirements to all chapter 11 cases justifies the coordinate extension of these exemptions. By the same token, no valid purpose is served not to exempt from the requirements of similar state laws in a matter under the exclusive jurisdiction of the Federal bankruptcy laws.

[*Senate Report No. 95–989, 95th Cong., 2d Sess. 120, 122 (1978).*]

Subsection (e) is a safe harbor provision, and is necessary to make the exemption provided by subsection (d) effective. Without it, a creditor that solicited an acceptance or rejection in reliance on the court's approval of a disclosure statement would be potentially liable under antifraud sections designed to enforce the very sections of the securities laws from which subsection (d) excuses compliance. The subsection protects only persons that solicit in good faith and in compliance with the applicable provisions of the reorganization chapter. It provides protection from legal liability as well as from equitable liability based on an injunctive action by the S.E.C. or other agency or official.

[*House Report No. 95–595, 95th Cong., 1st Sess. 408 (1977).*]

Subsection (e) exonerates any person who, in good faith and in compliance with this title, solicits or participates in the offer, issuance, sale or purchase, under the plan, of a security from any liability, on account of such solicitation or participation, for violation of any law, rule, or regulation governing the offer, issuance, sale, or purchase of securities. This exoneration is coordinate with the exemption from Federal or State registration or licensing requirements provided by section 1145 of this title.

In the nonpublic case, the court, when approving the disclosure statement, has before it the texts of the plan, a proposed disclosure document, and such other information the plan proponents and other interested parties may present at the hearing. In the final analysis the exoneration which subsection (e) grants must depend on the good faith of the plan proponents and of those who participate in the preparation of the disclosure statement and in the solicitation. Subsection (e) does not affect civil or criminal liability for defects and inadequacies that are beyond the limits of the exoneration that good faith provides.

Section 1125 applies to public companies as well, subject to the qualifications of subsection (f). In case of a public company no solicitations of acceptance is permitted unless authorized by the court upon or after approval of the plan pursuant to section 1128(c). In addition to the documents specified in subsection (b), subsection (f) requires transmission of the opinion and order of the court approving the plan and, if filed, the advisory report of the Securities and Exchange Commission or a summary thereof prepared by the Commission. [*Ed. Note:* The last paragraph of this excerpt from the Senate Report refers to material not contained in the final version of the Bill.]

[*Senate Report No. 95–989, 95th Cong., 2d Sess. 120 (1978).*]

Section 1125 of the House amendment is derived from section 1125 of the House bill and Senate amendment except with respect to section 1125(f) of the Senate amendment. It will not be necessary for the court to consider the report of the examiner prior to approval of a disclosure statement. The investigation of the examiner is to proceed on an independent basis from the procedure of the reorganization under chapter 11. In order to ensure that the examiner's report will be expeditious and fair, the examiner is precluded from serving as a trustee in the case or from representing a trustee if a trustee is appointed, whether the case remains in chapter 11 or is converted to chapter 7 or 13.

[*124 Cong. Rec. H 11,103 (Sept. 28, 1978); S 17,420 (Oct. 6, 1978).*]

Comment

Section 1125 deals with solicitation of acceptances or rejections *after* commencement of the chapter 11 case and, as indicated in the House Report, *supra,* "is the heart of the consolidation" of Chapters X, XI and XII of the former Bankruptcy Act into a single chapter. As to pre-bankruptcy solicitation, *see* section 1126(b), *infra.*

Section 1125 requires that a written "disclosure statement" approved by the court after notice and hearing, be transmitted to holders of claims or interests together with the plan or a summary of the plan. Solicitation of acceptances or rejections of a plan may be made only at the time of, or after transmission of the "disclosure statement."

In essence, the hearing on the adequacy of the "disclosure statement" and approval thereof by the court, is substituted for the hearing on and approval of the plan in cases under Chapter X of the former Act. As was the hearing on the plan under Chapter X, the disclosure hearing under section 1125 is probably the major procedural hearing in the chapter 11 case. Thus, while dispensing with court approval of a plan, the Code requires that holders of claims and interests receive such court approved financial information as would permit them to make their own independent and informed judgment on whether or not to accept or reject the plan. Of course, in considering the adequacy of the proposed disclosure, the court will necessarily have to consider the disclosure statement together with the proposed plan to which it relates.

Section 1125(a)(1) requires that the disclosure statement contain "adequate information" in sufficient detail as far as reasonably practicable in the light of the nature and history of the debtor and the condition of debtor's financial records. It must be such information as would enable a hypothetical reasonable investor (typical of the holders of claims and interests of the relevant class) to make an "informed judgment about the plan."

Section 1125(a)(2) defines the hypothetical investor referred to in subsection (a)(1) as an investor having (1) a claim or interest of the relevant class; (2) such a relationship with the debtor as the holders of other claims or interests of such class generally have; and (3) such ability to obtain such information from sources other than the disclosure required by section 1125 as holders of claims or interests in such class generally.

Precisely what constitutes adequate information will have to be determined on a case-by-case basis. The House Report indicates that the standard is substantive and beyond the Supreme Court's rule-making power. (Report p. 408.)

Subsection (c) of section 1125 recognizes that information necessary for an informed judgment may differ among classes and therefore permits different disclosure statements for different classes, provided that the same statement be transmitted to each member of a particular class.

Under subsection (d), adequacy of the information disclosed need not follow otherwise applicable Federal or State law. An agency such as the S.E.C., however, may be heard on the issue of adequacy of the information but may not appeal from an order approving a disclosure statement.

Subsection (e) exonerates one who in good faith and in compliance with the Code solicits or participates in the offer, issuance, sale or purchase, under the plan, of a security, from any violation of any law or rule governing such offer, issuance, etc.

Bankruptcy Rule 3016(c) provides that the disclosure statement pursuant to section 1125 or evidence showing compliance with section 1126(b) must be filed with the plan or within a time fixed by the court. (Postpetition solicitation of votes on a plan requires transmittal of a disclosure statement, the contents of which have been approved by the court as provided in section 1125. Prepetition solicitation, pursuant to section 1126, must either have conformed with applicable nonbankruptcy law, or, if none, the disclosure must have been of adequate information as set forth in section 1125.)

Bankruptcy Rule 3017 deals with court consideration of disclosure statements. Subdivision (a) provides that after the disclosure statement is filed, the court must hold a hearing on not less than 25 days notice to the debtor, creditors, equity security holders and other parties in interest to consider the statement and objections or modifications thereto. The plan and statement must be mailed with notice of hearing only to the debtor, any trustee or committee appointed under the Code, the S.E.C., and any party in interest requesting in writing a copy of the plan or statement. Objections to the statement must be filed and served on the debtor, trustee, any committee appointed under the Code, and any other entity designated by the court, at any time prior to approval of the statement or by such earlier date as the court may fix. In a chapter 11 case, every notice, plan, disclosure statement, and objection required to be served or mailed pursuant to this subdivision shall be transmitted to the United States trustee within the time provided in this subdivision. (A hearing on the disclosure statement must be held regardless of whether objections thereto have been filed. Under the Code a hearing on and approval of the plan is not provided for; however, a hearing on the disclosure statement is mandatory. While all creditors must receive notice of the hearing on the statement, only those explicitly specified in the rule are to receive notice of the filing of disclosure statement or a copy thereof.)

Subdivision (b) provides that after the hearing, the court shall determine whether the statement should be approved.

Subdivision (c) requires the court, on or before the approval of the statement, to fix a time within which holders of claims and interests may accept or reject the plan and may fix a date for the hearing on confirmation.

Subdivision (d), substantially revised by the 1991 Amendments, provides that on approval of a disclosure statement, unless the court orders otherwise with respect to one or more unimpaired classes of creditors or equity security holders, the debtor in possession, trustee or proponent of the plan, or clerk as ordered by the court shall mail to all creditors and equity security holders, and in a chapter 11 case shall transmit to the United States trustee (1) the plan or a court approved summary thereof; (2) the disclosure statement approved by the court; (3) notice of the time for filing acceptances and rejections; (4) such other information as the court directs including any court opinion approving the disclosure statement or a court approved summary thereof.

Subdivision (e), added in 1991, provides that at the hearing held pursuant to subdivision (a) the court shall consider the procedures for transmitting the documents and information required by subdivision (d) to beneficial holders of stock, bonds, debentures, notes and other securities and determine the adequacy of such procedures and enter such orders deemed appropriate. [Subdivision (e) is designed to ensure that appropriate measures are taken for the plan and other documents required to be transmitted to creditors and equity security holders under this Rule to reach the beneficial holders of securities held in nominee name.]

Bankruptcy Rule 2002(b) requires the clerk or some other person as the court directs to give not less than 25 days notice by mail to the debtor, the trustee, all creditors and indenture trustees of the time fixed for filing objections and the hearing to consider approval of the disclosure statement. [Rule 2002(i) requires the clerk (or some other person as the court directs) to transmit to the United States trustee notice of the hearing to consider approval of a disclosure statement in accordance with subdivision (b).] Notice should also be given to the United States trustee. Subdivision (i) requires that the notice be given to all elected or appointed committees. Subdivision (d) requires the clerk, unless otherwise ordered, to give notice to all equity security holders of the time fixed for filing objections to, and the hearing to consider approval of the disclosure statement. Under subdivision (j), notice must also be given to the S.E.C. if it has filed notice of appearance or filed a written request for notices. Under subdivision (l) the court may order publication of the notice if it finds that notice by mail is impracticable or that it is desirable to supplement mailed notice.

1984 Amendments: Section 1125(a)(1) was amended to provide that the definition of "adequate information" need not include information about any other possible or proposed plan. Stylistic and technical changes were made in subsections (a)(2)(B), (d) and (e).

1986 Amendments: The 1986 Act made no changes in section 1125 but it should be noted that Section 113 of the Act amended section 586(a) of title 28 by imposing on the United States trustees the duty of monitoring plans and disclosure statements filed in chapter 11 cases and filing with the court in connection with hearings under sections 1125 and 1128, comments with respect to such plans and disclosure statements.

Case Annotations

Section 1125(b) does not limit the facts which a creditor may receive but only the time when a creditor may be solicited. Rather than limiting the information available to a creditor, section 1125 seeks to guarantee a minimum amount of information to the creditor asked for its vote. Section 1125 does not on its face empower a bankruptcy court to regulate communications among creditors and a creditor may receive information from sources other than the disclosure statement. Century Glove, Inc. v. First American Bank of New York, 860 F.2d 94, 20 C.B.C.2d 742 (3d Cir. 1988).

Under normal circumstances, to meet the "adequate information" requirement in section 1125(a)(1), a disclosure statement need not comply with the disclosure standards of federal securities laws and a bankruptcy court is under no duty to analogize to the securities laws even in the case of complex, publicly-held debtor corporations; the legislative history of section 1125 does not suggest that any such duty was intended. Kirk v. Texaco Inc., 18 C.B.C.2d 331 (S.D.N.Y. 1988).

A debtor's motion for modification, although it contains all the necessary data for disclosure, cannot be substituted as a valid disclosure statement. Andrew v. Coopersmith (*In re* Downtown Investment Club III), 19 C.B.C.2d 639 (9th Cir., B.A.P., 1988).

It is permissible for a court to pass upon confirmation issues such as whether claims have been properly classified in the context of a disclosure proceeding under section 1125 when it is contended that the proposed plan is so fatally flawed that confirmation is not possible. *In re* Bjolmes Realty Trust, 26 C.B.C.2d 700 (B. Ct., D. Mass. 1991).

The acquisition of claims in a certain class by an entity related to the debtor for the purpose of voting on a plan of reorganization is required to be disclosed because it is a material fact relevant to the voting process. *In re* Applegate Property, Ltd., 25 C.B.C.2d 1672 (B. Ct., W.D. Tex. 1991).

When the debtor provided adequate information prior to confirmation concerning an asset, the debtor would not be judicially estopped from recovering from the defendant sums to which it is entitled. *In re* Rooster, Inc., 24 C.B.C.2d 1940 (B. Ct., E.D. Pa. 1991).

A bankruptcy court's finding that the non-assenting creditors' best interests have been satisfied does not carry with it the presumption that a disclosure statement in a plan of reorganization provides adequate information to allow confirmation of the plan. *In re* Crowthers McCall Pattern, Inc., 24 C.B.C.2d 611 (B. Ct., S.D.N.Y. 1990).

When a chapter 11 debtor's disclosure statement improperly excludes a creditor's claim which was converted from nonrecourse to recourse under section 1111(b)(1), the disclosure statement cannot be approved because it lacks "adequate information" concerning the classification, treatment and disclosure of the claim. *In re* Atlanta West VI, 20 C.B.C.2d 148 (B. Ct., N.D. Ga. 1988).

A disclosure statement does meet the adequate information standard of section 1125 when such statement does not contain simple and clear language delineating the consequences of the proposed plan on the claims of the impaired class of unsecured creditors, whom the court has determined to be "average investors" lacking any sophisticated financial knowledge. *In re* Copy Crafters Quickprint, Inc., 20 C.B.C.2d 441 (B. Ct., N.D.N.Y. 1988).

No disclosure statement is called for under section 1125 if a plan has not been filed. Therefore, an agreement by a creditor not to support any other plans in the future does not amount to the solicitation of a rejection of a plan that must be accompanied by a court approved disclosure statement. Trans World Airlines v. Texaco, Inc. (*In re* Texaco Inc.), 18 C.B.C.2d 166 (B. Ct., S.D.N.Y. 1988).

References

5 *Collier on Bankruptcy* ch. 1125 (Matthew Bender 15th ed.).

3 *Collier Bankruptcy Manual* ch. 1125 (Matthew Bender 3d ed.).

5 *Collier Bankruptcy Practice Guide* ch. 90 (Matthew Bender).

Ellis, *The Key to Drafting Chapter 11 Disclosure Statements,* 52 Tex. B.J. 1206 (1989).

Glassman, *Solicitation of Plan Rejections Under the Bankruptcy Code,* 62 Am. Bankr. L.J. 261 (1988).

Merrick, *The Chapter 11 Disclosure Statement in a Strategic Environment,* 44 Bus. Law. 103 (1988).

Note, *Disclosure in Chapter 11 Reorganizations: The Pursuit of Consistency and Clarity,* 70 Cornell L. Rev. 733 (1985).

Phelan and Cheatham, *Would I Lie to You—Disclosure in Bankruptcy Reorganizations,* 9 Sec. Reg. L.J. 140 (1981).

SECTION 1126 (11 U.S.C. § 1126)

§ 1126.   Acceptance of plan.

(a) The holder of a claim or interest allowed under section 502 of this title may accept or reject a plan. If the United States is a creditor or equity security holder, the Secretary of the Treasury may accept or reject the plan on behalf of the United States.

(b) For the purposes of subsections (c) and (d) of this section, a holder of a claim or interest that has accepted or rejected the plan before the commencement of the case under this title is deemed to have accepted or rejected such plan, as the case may be, if—

(1) the solicitation of such acceptance or rejection was in compliance with any applicable nonbankruptcy law, rule, or regulation governing the adequacy of disclosure in connection with such solicitation; or

(2) if there is not any such law, rule, or regulation, such acceptance or rejection was solicited after disclosure to such holder of adequate information, as defined in section 1125(a) of this title.

(c) A class of claims has accepted a plan if such plan has been accepted by creditors, other than any entity designated under subsection (e) of this section, that hold at least two-thirds in amount and more than one-half in number of the allowed claims of such class held by creditors, other than any entity designated under subsection (e) of this section, that have accepted or rejected such plan.

(d) A class of interests has accepted a plan if such plan has been accepted by holders of such interests, other than any entity designated under subsection (e) of this section, that hold at least two-thirds in amount of the allowed interests of such class held by holders of such interests, other than any entity designated under subsection (e) of this section, that have accepted or rejected such plan.

(e) On request of a party in interest, and after notice and a hearing, the court may designate any entity whose acceptance or rejection of such plan was not in good faith, or was not solicited or procured in good faith or in accordance with the provisions of this title.

(f) Notwithstanding any other provision of this section, a class that is not impaired under a plan, and each holder of a claim or interest of such class, are conclusively presumed to have accepted the plan, and solicitation of acceptances with respect to such class from the holders of claims or interests of such class is not required.

(g) Notwithstanding any other provision of this section, a class is deemed not to have accepted a plan if such plan provides that the claims or interests of such class do not entitle the holders of such claims or interests to receive or retain any property under the plan on acount of such claims or interests.

Bankruptcy Rule References: 3016, 3017 and 3018

Legislative History

Subsection (a) of this section permits the holder of a claim or interest allowed under section 502 to accept or reject a proposed plan of reorganization. The subsection also incorporates a provision now found in section 199 of the Bankruptcy Act that authorizes the Secretary of the Treasury to accept or reject a plan on behalf of the United States when the United States is a creditor or equity security holder. The form and procedure for changing or withdrawing an acceptance or rejection of a plan after modification of the plan is left to the Rules of Bankruptcy Procedure.

[*House Report No. 95–595, 95th Cong., 1st Sess. 410 (1977).*]

Subsection (a) of this section permits the holder of a claim or interest allowed under section 502 to accept or reject a proposed plan of reorganization. The subsection also incorporates a provision now found in section 199 of chapter X that authorizes the Secretary of the Treasury to accept or reject a plan on behalf of the United States when the United States is a creditor or equity security holder.

[*Senate Report No. 95–989, 95th Cong., 2d Sess. 122 (1978).*]

Subsection (b) governs acceptances and rejections of plans obtained before the commencement of a reorganization case. This is a common practice under chapter XI today, and chapter IX presently makes explicit provision for it. Subsection (b) counts a prepetition acceptance or rejection toward the required amounts and numbers of acceptances only if the solicitation of the acceptance or rejection was in compliance with any applicable nonbankruptcy law, rule, or regulation governing the adequacy of disclosure in connection with such solicitation (such as section 14 of the Securities Exchange Act of 1934). If there is not any such applicable law, rule, or regulation, then the acceptance or rejection is counted only if it was solicited after disclosure of adequate information, to the holder, as defined in section 1125(a)(1). This permits the court to ensure that the requirements of section 1125 are not avoided by prepetition solicitation.

[*House Report No. 95–595, 95th Cong., 1st Sess. 410 (1977).*]

Subsection (b) governs acceptances and rejections of plans obtained before commencement of a reorganization for a nonpublic company. Paragraph (3) expressly states that subsection (b) does not apply to a public company.

Prepetition solicitation is a common practice under chapter XI today, and chapter IX current [*sic*] makes explicit provision for it. Section 1126(b) counts a prepetition acceptance or rejection toward the required amounts and number of acceptances only if the solicitation of the acceptance or rejection was in compliance with any applicable nonbankruptcy law, rule, or regulation governing the adequacy of disclosure in connection with such solicitation. If there is not any such applicable law, rule, or regulation, then the acceptance or rejection is counted only if it was solicited after disclosure of adequate information, to the holder, as defined in section 1125(a)(1). This permits the court to ensure that the requirements of section 1125 are not avoided by prepetition solicitation.

[*Senate Report No. 95–989, 95th Cong., 2d Sess. 122 (1978).*]

Subsection (c) specifies the required amount and number of acceptances for a class of creditors. A class of creditors has accepted a plan if at least two-thirds in amount and more than one-half in number of the allowed claims of the class that are voted are cast in favor of the plan. The two-thirds and one-half requirements are computed based on a denominator that equals the amount or number of claims that have actually been voted for or against the plan, rather than the total number and amount of claims in the class, as under current chapter X. In addition, there are to be excluded from both the numerator and the denominator in the calculation of the amount and number any claim held by a creditor designated under subsection (e) or (f), relating to conflict of interest and bad faith.

[*House Report No. 95–595, Cong., 1st Sess. 410 (1977).*]

Subsection (c) specifies the required amount and number of acceptances for a class of creditors. A class of creditors has accepted a plan if at least two-thirds in amount and more than one-half in number of the allowed claims of the class that are voted are cast in favor of the plan. The amount and number are computed on the basis of claims actually voted for or against the plan, not as under chapter X on the basis of the allowed claims in the class. Subsection (f) excludes from all these calculations claims not voted in good faith, and claims procured or solicited not in good faith or not in accordance with the provisions of this title.

[*Senate Report No. 95–989, 95th Cong., 2d Sess. 122 (1978).*]

Subsection (d) provides similar treatment for classes of equity securities, but dispenses with the one-half in number required. A class of equity securities has accepted a plan if at least two-thirds in amount of the outstanding securities actually voted are voted for the plan. The same exclusions apply with respect to subsections (e) and (f).

[*House Report No. 95–595, 95th Cong., 1st Sess. 410 (1977).*]

Under subsection (d), with respect to a class of equity securities, it is sufficient for acceptance of the plan if the amount of securities voting for the plan is at least two-thirds of the total actually voted.

[*Senate Report No. 95–989, 95th Cong., 2d Sess. 122 (1978).*]

Subsection . . .[e] permits the court to designate any person whose acceptance or rejection of the plan was not in good faith or in accordance with the provisions of the bankruptcy code.

[*House Report No. 95–595, 95th Cong., 1st Sess. 410 (1977).*]

Subsection . . .[f] provides that no acceptances are required from any class whose claims or interests are unimpaired under the plan or in the order confirming the plan.

[*Senate Report No. 95–989, 95th Cong., 2d Sess. 122 (1978).*]

Subsection (g) states a categorical rule to avoid conflicts of interest. If a class is denied participation in a reorganized debtor, the class is conclusively deemed to have rejected the plan.

[*House Report No. 95–595, 95th Cong., 1st Sess. 410 (1977).*]

Subsection (g) provides that any class denied participation under the plan is conclusively deemed to have rejected the plan. There is obviously no need to submit a plan for a vote by a class that is to receive nothing. But under subsection (g) the excluded class is like a class that has not accepted, and is a dissenting class for purposes of confirmation under section 1130.

[*Senate Report No. 95–989, 95th Cong., 2d Sess. 122 (1978).*]

Section 1126 of the House amendment deletes section 1126(e) as contained in the House bill. Section 105 of the bill constitutes sufficient power in the court to designate exclusion of a creditor's claim on the basis of a conflict of interest. Section 1126(f) of the House amendment adopts a provision contained in section 1127(f) of the Senate bill indicating that a class that is not impaired under a plan is deemed to have accepted a plan and solicitation of acceptances from such class is not required.

[*124 Cong. Rec. H 11,103 (Sept. 28, 1978); S 17,420 (Oct. 6, 1978).*]

Comment

Section 1126 effects a substantial change in the number and amount of acceptances required for confirmation of a plan under the former Bankruptcy Act.

Under section 1126 of the Code, the requisite majorities for acceptance and confirmation of a plan are at least two-thirds in amount and more than one-half in number of allowed claims of each class. This double count of amount and number is a measure to protect against control by a few large creditors. Under section 1126, the plan must be accepted by holders of at least two-thirds in amount of the allowed interests of each class. Thus, in the case of equity securities, the requirement of one-half in number is not required and only two-thirds in amount is required. Under section 1126(e), the court may (on request of a party and after notice and hearing) designate any entity or class whose acceptance or rejection was not accepted, solicited, or procured in good faith.

Under section 1126(f), a class that is not impaired (see section 1124) is conclusively presumed to have accepted the plan. On the other hand, under subsection (g), any class denied participation in payment or compensation pursuant to the plan, is deemed not to have accepted.

Subsection (a) of section 1126 specifies who may accept or reject; the holder of a claim or interest allowed under section 502. Section 502 provides that a claim or interest, proof of which is filed under section 501 is deemed allowed unless objection thereto is filed. Under section 1111, filing is not required. Section 502 also provides for objection and specifies claims that may not be allowed or allowed in part. Section 1126(a) also provides that if the United States is a creditor or equity security holder, the Secretary of the Treasury may accept or reject the plan, thus incorporating a provision found in Section 199 of the former Bankruptcy Act.

Subsection (b) of section 1126 governs acceptances or rejections obtained prior to the commencement of the proceeding. Such acceptance or rejection may be included in the computation only if the solicitation thereof was in compliance with an applicable nonbankruptcy law, rule, or regulation relating to adequacy of disclosure, as, for instance, section 14 of the Securities Exchange Act of 1934. Absent such law, rule, or regulation, acceptance or rejection will be counted only if solicited after disclosure as defined in section 1125(a)(1), thus avoiding circumvention of section 1125(a)(1) by prebankruptcy solicitation.

A most important change in the voting process is that computation is based upon the total amount of claims or interests actually voting rather than on claims proved and allowed as under Chapter XI of the former Bankruptcy Act.

Bankruptcy Rule 3017(c) requires the court, on or before approval of the disclosure statement, to fix a time within which holders of claims and interests may accept or reject the plan. Subdivision (d) provides for transmittal to all creditors and equity security holders of a ballot (Official Form 14) together with the plan and the court approved disclosure statement. *See* **Comment** to section 1125. The 1987 Amendments to the Bankruptcy Rules added an Advisory Committee Note to Rule 3017(d) to the effect that section 1125(c) requires that the entire disclosure statement as approved by the court be transmitted in connection with the voting. Although the rule does not permit mailing a summary in place of the approved disclosure statement, the court may approve a summary of the disclosure statement to be mailed together with the complete disclosure statement to those voting on the plan.

Bankruptcy Rule 3018 relates to acceptance or rejection of plans. Subdivision (a), as amended in 1991, provides that a plan may be accepted or rejected in accordance with section 1126 of the Code within the time fixed by the court pursuant to Rule 3017. Subject to subdivision (b), an equity security holder or creditor whose claim is based on a security of record shall not be entitled to accept or reject a plan unless such entity is the holder of record of the security on the date of entry of the order approving the disclosure statement.

For cause shown, the court, after notice and hearing, may permit a creditor or equity security holder to change or withdraw acceptance or rejection. Although objected to, the court, after notice and hearing, may temporarily allow a claim or interest in an amount which the court deems proper for the purpose of acceptance or rejection.

Subdivision (b), as amended in 1991, provides that an equity security holder or creditor whose claim is based on a security of record who accepted or rejected the plan prior to commencement of the case shall not be deemed to have accepted or rejected pursuant to Code section 1126(b) unless such entity was the holder of record of the security on the date specified in the solicitation of such acceptance or rejection for the purposes of such solicitation. An acceptance or rejection before commencement of the case will not be deemed an acceptance or rejection if the court finds, after notice and hearing, that the plan was not transmitted to substantially all creditors and equity security holders of the same class, that an unreasonably short time was prescribed for acceptance or rejection, or that the solicitation was not in compliance with section 1126(b).

Subdivision (c) prescribes that an acceptance or rejection be in writing, identify the plan(s) accepted or rejected, be signed by the creditor or equity security holder or an authorized agent, and conform to Official Form 14. If more than one plan is transmitted, any number of plans may be accepted or rejected, indicating a preference or preferences among plans so accepted.

Subdivision (d) provides that a creditor whose claim has been allowed as partially secured and partially unsecured may accept or reject a plan in both capacities.

Bankruptcy Rule 3005(a) and (b), as amended in 1991, provides that if a creditor has not filed a proof of claim, an entity that is or may be liable with the debtor or has secured the debt to creditor, may within 30 days after expiration of the time for filing claims under Rule 3002(c) or 3003(c) execute and file a proof of claim in the name of the creditor, or, if unknown, in the entity's own name. The entity who thus files the claim may file an acceptance or rejection of a plan in the name of the creditor, or if unknown, in such entity's own name. But a proof of claim filed by a creditor pursuant to Rule 3002 or 3003(c) supersedes the proof of claim filed by the entity as aforesaid.

1984 Amendments: Subsection (f) of section 1126 was amended by providing that a class that is not impaired is conclusively presumed to have accepted the plan. Stylistic changes were made in subsections (b)(2), (d) and (g).

Case Annotations

When a debtor expressly assumes a lease, the lessee has no claim against the estate under section 1126(a) of the Code. Rather, the rights created by assumption of the lease constitute a postpetition administrative claim under section 503(b)(1)(A) and the holder of such a claim is not entitled to vote on a plan of reorganization. In the Matter of Greystone III Joint Venture, 948 F.2d 134, 26 C.B.C.2d 220 (5th Cir. 1991).

Section 1126(e) grants a court limited discretion to designate or not to designate a vote but because it does not give a court discretion to impose other remedies, whether a bankruptcy court acted properly in imposing costs does not determine whether it acted properly in designating or not designating certain votes. A bankruptcy court's orders imposing costs and designating a vote are separate decisions each to be reviewed for finality. Century Glove, Inc. v. First American Bank of New York, 860 F.2d 94, 20 C.B.C.2d 742 (3d Cir. 1988).

An insider of the debtor cannot purchase a block of claims within a certain class in order to prevent the purchase of such claims by a competing entity and the confirmation of the entity's competing plan without violating the good faith standard of section 1126(e). In re Applegate Property, Ltd., 25 C.B.C.2d 1672 (B. Ct., W.D. Tex. 1991).

A creditor who originally voted to reject a reorganization plan because of a debtor's misrepresentation may not change its vote when the desire to change materialized shortly after the debtor had paid the creditor $25,000 for a general release and reassignment of the uncollected prepetition accounts receivable. In the Matter of Featherworks Corp., 10 C.B.C.2d 212 (E.D.N.Y. 1984).

When modification of a plan renders an impaired claimant unimpaired, and as a result no other members of that class are impaired, the class itself is deemed unimpaired and deemed to have accepted the plan as modified. Additionally, the votes of other creditors whose claims remain unimpaired may be deemed to have accepted the modified plan by operation of section 1126(f), and other claim holders who accepted the plan prior to modification may be deemed to have accepted the plan as modified by operation of Bankruptcy Rule 3019. *In re* American Solar King Corp., 20 C.B.C.2d 547 (B. Ct., W.D. Tex. 1988).

The standard to be applied under section 1126(e) in determining whether a creditor had cast its vote in "good faith" is whether the creditor had some "ulterior" reason for the action by which it looks to gain some special advantage. *In re* A.D.W. Inc., 20 C.B.C.2d 348 (B. Ct., D.N.J. 1988).

Insider votes of an impaired class cast in favor of a plan may be counted under section 1129(a)(10) for purposes of section 1126(c) when there exists at least one other accepting impaired class that contains no insiders. In the Matter of Grimes Furniture, Inc., 12 C.B.C.2d 193 (B. Ct., W.D. Pa. 1985).

The provision in a chapter 11 plan that all classes are unimpaired does not relieve the debtor of the burden of filing a disclosure statement, as a class is not determined to be unimpaired until the debtor files a written disclosure statement which is approved after notice and a hearing by the court as containing adequate information. *In re* Spenard Ventures, Inc., 6 C.B.C.2d 156 (B. Ct., D. Alaska 1982).

References

5 *Collier on Bankruptcy* ch. 1126 (Matthew Bender 15th ed.).

3 *Collier Bankruptcy Manual* ch. 1126 (Matthew Bender 3d ed.).

5 *Collier Bankruptcy Practice Guide* ch. 90 (Matthew Bender).

Africk, *Trading Claims in Chapter 11: How Much Influence Can Be Purchased In Good Faith Under Section 1126?*, 139 Pa. L. Rev. 1393 (1991).

Fortgang and Mayer, *Developments in Trading Claims and Taking Control of Corporations in Chapter 11*, 13 Cardozo L. Rev. 1 (1991).

Fortgang and Mayer, *Trading Claims and Taking Control of Corporations in Chapter 11*, 12 Cardozo L. Rev. 1 (1990).

Franzese, *Secured Financing's Uneasy Place in Bankruptcy: Claims for Interests in Chapter 11*, 19 Hofstra L. Rev. 1 (1990).

Minkel and Baker, *Claims and Control in Chapter 11 Cases: A Call for Neutrality,* 13 Cardozo L. Rev. 35 (1991).

Prendergast, *Applying Federal Securities Law to the Trading of Bankruptcy Claims,* 3 F & G Bankr. L. Rev. 9 (1991).

SECTION 1127 (11 U.S.C. § 1127)

§ 1127. Modification of plan.

(a) The proponent of a plan may modify such plan at any time before confirmation, but may not modify such plan so that such plan as modified fails to meet the requirements of sections 1122 and 1123 of this title. After the proponent of a plan files a modification of such plan with the court, the plan as modified becomes the plan.

(b) The proponent of a plan or the reorganized debtor may modify such plan at any time after confirmation of such plan and before substantial consummation of such plan, but may not modify such plan so that such plan as modified fails to meet the requirements of sections 1122 and 1123 of this title. Such plan as modified under this subsection becomes the plan only if circumstances warrant such modification and the court, after notice and a hearing, confirms such plan as modified, under section 1129 of this title.

(c) The proponent of a modification shall comply with section 1125 of this title with respect to the plan as modified.

(d) Any holder of a claim or interest that has accepted or rejected a plan is deemed to have accepted or rejected, as the case may be, such plan as modified, unless, within the time fixed by the court, such holder changes such holder's previous acceptance or rejection.

Bankruptcy Rule References: 2002 and 3019

Legislative History

Subsection (a) permits the proponent of a plan to modify it at any time before confirmation, subject, of course, to the requirements of sections 1122 and 1123, governing classification and contents of a plan. After the proponent of a plan files a modification with the court, the plan as modified becomes the plan, and is to be treated the same as an original plan.

[*House Report No. 95–595, 95th Cong., 1st Sess. 411 (1977).*]

Under subsection (a) the proponent may file a proposal to modify a plan prior to confirmation. In the case of a public company the modifying proposal may be filed prior to approval. [*Ed. Note:* The language in the Senate report referring to a public company was deleted from the final version of the Bill.]

[*Senate Report No. 95–989, 95th Cong., 2d Sess. 124 (1978).*]

Section 1127(a) of the House amendment adopts a provision contained in the House bill permitting only the proponent of a plan to modify the plan and rejecting the alternative of open modification contained in the Senate amendment.

[*124 Cong. Rec. H 11,103 (Sept. 28, 1978); S 17,420 (Oct. 6, 1978).*]

Subsection (b) permits modification of a plan after confirmation under certain circumstances. The modification must be proposed before substantial consummation of the plan. The requirements of sections 1122 and 1123 continue to apply. The plan as modified under this subsection becomes the plan only if the court confirms the plan as modified under section 1129 and the circumstances warrant the modification.

[*House Report No. 95–595, 95th Cong., 1st Sess. 411 (1977); see Senate Report No. 95–989, 95th Cong., 2d Sess. 124 (1978).*]

Subsection (c) requires the proponent of a modification to comply with the disclosure provisions of section 1125. Of course, if the modification were sufficiently minor, the court might determine that additional disclosure was not required under the circumstances.

Subsection (d) simplifies modification procedure by deeming any creditor or equity security holder that has already accepted or rejected the plan to have accepted or rejected the modification, unless, within the time fixed by the court, the creditor or equity security holder changes this previous acceptance or rejection.

[*House Report No. 95–595, 95th Cong., 1st Sess. 411 (1977).*]

After a plan has been confirmed, but before its substantial consummation, a plan may be modified by leave of court, which subsection (d) provides shall be granted for good cause. Subsection (e) provides that a proposal to modify a plan is subject to the disclosure requirements of section 1125 and as provided in subsection (f). It provides that a creditor or stockholder who voted for or against a plan is deemed to have accepted or rejected the modifying proposal. But if the modification materially and adversely affects any of their interests, they must be afforded an opportunity to change their vote in accordance with the disclosure and solicitation requirements of section 1125. [*Ed. Note:* Subsection (f) of the Senate Report has been deleted from the Bill.]

[*Senate Report No. 95–989, 95th Cong., 2d Sess. 124 (1978).*]

Comment

Section 1127 permits only the *proponent* of the plan to file a modification at any time prior to confirmation provided the modification meets the requirements as to classification and contents of a plan (sections 1122 and 1123). Subsection (b) permits modification after confirmation but before substantial consummation as defined in section 1101(2). Under subsection (c), unless the modification is minor, the modification must comply with the adequate disclosure provisions of section 1125.

Under subsection (d) one who accepted (or rejected) a plan is deemed to have accepted (or rejected) the modified plan unless within a time fixed by the court, the holder of the claim or interest changes its previous vote.

Bankruptcy Rule 3019 provides that after acceptance and before confirmation, the proponent of a plan may file a modification. If the court finds after hearing and notice to the trustee, any committee appointed under the Code and others designated by the court that the modification does not adversely change the treatment of the claim or interest of one who has not accepted the modification in writing, the modification shall be deemed accepted by all creditors and equity security holders who previously accepted the plan. The rule covers minor modifications that do not adversely affect any rights. A modification may be made after acceptance of a plan, with court approval, without submission to creditors and equity security holders if those interests are not affected or changed from what they were under the plan before modification.

Bankruptcy Rule 2002(a) requires that not less than 20 days notice by mail be given to the debtor, the trustee, all creditors and indenture trustees of the time fixed to accept or reject a proposed modification of a plan. Under subdivision (d) such notice must be given to all equity security holders unless the court otherwise orders. Under subdivision (i) notice must also be given to any committees elected or appointed under the Code and, under subdivision (j), to the S.E.C. if it filed notice of appearance or filed a written request for notices. Subdivision (k) requires that such notice be transmitted to the United States trustee.

1984 Amendments: Minor stylistic changes were made in subsections (a) and (b) of section 1127.

Case Annotations

When assessing challenged orders for procedural regularity, orders that were obviously entered without the important requirements of notice, hearing and formal confirmation must be held at least voidable for procedural irregularity. Goodman v. Phillip R. Curtis Enters., Inc. (*In re* Goodman), 809 F.2d 228, 16 C.B.C.2d 277 (4th Cir. 1987).

A proposed plan modification which offers no liquidation analysis and which divests some shareholders of all shares while transferring complete ownership to another shareholder violates the equal treatment provisions of section 1123(a)(4) and may not be confirmed under section

1129(b)(1). *In re* Modern Steel Treating Co., 25 C.B.C.2d 292 (B. Ct., N.D. Ill. 1991).

Pursuant to section 1127(b), the date that a bankruptcy court order confirms a modified chapter 11 plan is the date from which the 180-day time limit for filing a complaint seeking revocation of confirmation must be filed under section 1144. *In re* TM Carlton House Partners, Ltd., 22 C.B.C.2d 972 (B. Ct., E.D. Pa. 1990).

A modification which will not likely trigger a reconsideration of a claimant's acceptance *de facto* satisfies the section 1125 disclosure requirements. When the dilution of the debtor's stock which would result from the debtor's proposed modification would be less than one percent, the dilution is not material because it so small that no previously assenting creditor would be motivated to reconsider its vote because of it and, thus, the requisites of section 1127(c) are satisfied. *In re* American Solar King Corp., 20 C.B.C.2d 547 (B. Ct., W.D. Tex. 1988).

While secton 1127(b) allows only proponents of a plan to modify the plan after it has been confirmed, it is persuasive evidence that modification is permissible in a broader range of circumstances than is permitted revocation by the restrictions of section 1144. Bill Roderick Distrib., Inc. v. A.J. Mackay Co. (*In re* A.J. Mackay Co.), 13 C.B.C.2d 95 (D. Utah 1985).

An entity whose claim has been disallowed does not have standing to object to the modification of a chapter 11 plan. *In re* Rath Packing Co., 13 C.B.C.2d 1317 (B. Ct., N.D. Iowa 1985).

References

5 *Collier on Bankruptcy* ch. 1127 (Matthew Bender 15th ed.).

3 *Collier Bankruptcy Manual* ch. 1127 (Matthew Bender 3d ed.).

5 *Collier Bankruptcy Practice Guide* ch. 90 (Matthew Bender).

Hooper, II, *Confirmation of a Plan Under Chapter 11 of the Bankruptcy Code and the Effect of Confirmation on Creditors' Rights,* 15 Ind. L. Rev. 547 (1982).

Lander and Warfield, *A Review and Analysis of Selected Post-Confirmation Activities in Chapter 11 Reorganizations,* 62 Am. Bankr. L.J. 203 (1986).

Postconfirmation Modification of the Plan of Reorganization: Section 1127(b), 5 Bankr. Dev. J. 211 (1987).

Rahl, *Modification of a Chapter 11 Plan in the Mass Tort Context,* 92 Colum. L. Rev. 192 (1991).

SECTION 1128 (11 U.S.C. § 1128)

§ 1128. Confirmation hearing.

(a) After notice, the court shall hold a hearing on confirmation of a plan.

(b) A party in interest may object to confirmation of a plan.

Bankruptcy Rule References: 2002, 3017, 3020 and 9014

Legislative History

Subsection (a) requires that there be a hearing in every case on the confirmation of the plan. Notice is required. [*Ed. Note:* The Senate Report describes section 1129 of the Senate Bill which concerned the confirmation hearing prior to final amendment.]

[*House Report No. 95–595, 95th Cong., 1st Sess. 411 (1977); see Senate Report No. 95–989, 95th Cong., 2d Sess. 125 (1978).*]

Subsection (b) permits any party in interest to object to the confirmation of the plan. Under section 1109, the SEC and indenture trustees, even though not true parties in interest, may also object to confirmation.

[*House Report No. 95–595, 95th Cong., 1st Sess. 411 (1977).*]

Subsection (b) permits any party in interest to object to the confirmation of the plan. The Securities and Exchange Commission and indenture trustees, as parties in interest under section 1109, may object to confirmation of the plan. [*Ed. Note:* The Senate Report describes section 1129 which concerned the confirmation hearing prior to final amendment.]

[*Senate Report No. 95–989, 95th Cong., 2d Sess. 125 (1978).*]

Comment

Under section 1128, notice of the hearing on confirmation is required. A party in interest may object to confirmation and under section 1109 the S.E.C. and any indenture trustee, although not true parties in interest, may be heard in objection to confirmation.

The 1986 Act added section 307 to the Code providing that the United States trustee may raise and may appear and be heard on any issue in any case or proceeding under the Code, but may not file a plan of reorganization. Accordingly, the United States trustee may appear and be heard at the hearing on confirmation.

Bankruptcy Rule 2002(b) requires the clerk or some other person as the court directs to give not less than 25 days notice by mail to the debtor, the trustee, all creditors and indenture trustees of the time fixed for filing objections and the hearing to consider confirmation of a plan. Under subdivision (d), like notice is to be given to all equity security holders. Under subdivision (i), notice is to be given to all committees elected or appointed under Code or to their authorized agents, and under subdivision (j), to the S.E.C. if it filed notice of appearance or filed a written request for notices. Subdivision (k) requires that such notice be transmitted to the United States trustee.

Bankruptcy Rule 3017(c) provides that on or before approval of the disclosure statement the court shall fix a time within which holders of claims and interest may accept or reject the plan and *may* fix the date for the hearing on confirmation. Subdivision (d) provides that after approval of the disclosure statement there be mailed to all creditors and equity security holders, and transmitted to the United States trustee, the plan and the approved disclosure statement, etc.

Bankruptcy Rule 3020(b)(1) requires objections to confirmation to be filed and served on the debtor, the trustee the proponent of the plan, a committee appointed under the Code and others designated by the court, within a time fixed by the court. A copy of every objection to confirmation shall be transmitted by the objecting party to the United States trustee within the time fixed for filing of objections.An objection to confirmation is a contested matter governed by Rule 9014. Paragraph (b)(2) requires the court to rule on confirmation after hearing as provided in Rule 2002. If no timely objection is filed, the court may determine that the plan has been proposed in good faith and not by any means forbidden by law without receiving evidence on such issues.

Case Annotations

An equity shareholder maintaining a derivative lawsuit against the debtor is entitled as is any other shareholder of the debtor to object to the debtor's plan of organization. *In re* Texaco, Inc., 18 C.B.C.2d 1099 (B. Ct., S.D.N.Y. 1988).

A creditor has been denied due process of law if it is not notified of the debtor's confirmation hearing and, therefore, had no opportunity to comment at the hearing. A creditor who has mere general knowledge of the debtor's reorganization proceeding is not under a duty to inquire about further court action in the proceeding. Reliable Elec. Co. v. Olson Constr. Co., 726 F.2d 620, 10 C.B.C.2d 759 (10th Cir. 1984).

When a tax creditor has had ample opportunity to seek revision of the debtor's amended reorganization plan prior to confirmation but has not moved to do so until after confirmation, and when such revision would be detrimental to the debtor, the creditor's motion to reform the plan is barred by the doctrines of res judicata and estoppel. Martin Marietta Corp. v. County of Madison, Iowa (*In re* Penn Dixie Indus., Inc.), 8 C.B.C.2d 1360 (B. Ct., S.D.N.Y. 1983).

References

5 *Collier on Bankruptcy* ch. 1128 (Matthew Bender 15th ed.).

3 *Collier Bankruptcy Manual* ch. 1128 (Matthew Bender 3d ed.).

5 *Collier Bankruptcy Practice Guide* ch. 90 (Matthew Bender).

Blum, *The "Fair and Equitable" Standard For Confirming Reorganizations Under the New Bankruptcy Code,* 54 Am. Bankr. L.J. 165 (1980).

Hooper, II, *Confirmation of a Plan Under Chapter 11 of the Bankruptcy Code and the Effect of Confirmation on Creditors' Rights,* 15 Ind. L. Rev. 547 (1982).

SECTION 1129 (11 U.S.C. § 1129)

§ 1129. Confirmation of plan.

(a) The court shall confirm a plan only if all of the following requirements are met:

(1) The plan complies with the applicable provisions of this title.

(2) The proponent of the plan complies with the applicable provisions of this title.

(3) The plan has been proposed in good faith and not by any means forbidden by law.

(4) Any payment made or to be made by the proponent, by the debtor, or by a person issuing securities or acquiring property under the plan, for services or for costs and expenses in or in connection with the case, or in connection with the plan and incident to the case, has been approved by, or is subject to the approval of, the court as reasonable; [*sic*]

(5)(A)(i) The proponent of the plan has disclosed the identity and affiliations of any individual proposed to serve, after confirmation of the plan, as a director, officer, or voting trustee of the debtor, an affiliate of the debtor participating in a joint plan with the debtor, or a successor to the debtor under the plan; and

    (ii) the appointment to, or continuance in, such office of such individual, is consistent with the interests of creditors and equity security holders and with public policy; and

(B) the proponent of the plan has disclosed the identity of any insider that will be employed or retained by the reorganized debtor, and the nature of any compensation for such insider.

(6) Any governmental regulatory commission with jurisdiction, after confirmation of the plan, over the rates of the debtor has approved any rate change provided for in the plan, or such rate change is expressly conditioned on such approval.

(7) With respect to each impaired class of claims or interests—

(A) each holder of a claim or interest of such class—

(i) has accepted the plan; or

(ii) will receive or retain under the plan on account of such claim or interest property of a value, as of the effective date of the plan, that is not less than the amount that such holder would so receive or retain if the debtor were liquidated under chapter 7 of this title on such date; or

(B) if section 1111(b)(2) of this title applies to the claims of such class, each holder of a claim of such class will receive or retain under the plan on account of such claim property of a value, as of the effective date of the plan, that is not less than the value of such holder's interest in the estate's interest in the property that secures such claims.

(8) With respect to each class of claims or interests—

(A) such class has accepted the plan; or

(B) such class is not impaired under the plan.

(9) Except to the extent that the holder of a particular claim has agreed to a different treatment of such claim, the plan provides that—

(A) with respect to a claim of a kind specified in section 507(a)(1) or 507(a)(2) of this title, on the effective date of the plan, the holder of such claim will receive on account of such claim cash equal to the allowed amount of such claim;

(B) with respect to a class of claims of a kind specified in section 507(a)(3), 507(a)(4), 507(a)(5) or 507(a)(6) of this title, each holder of a claim of such class will receive—

(i) if such class has accepted the plan, deferred cash payments of a value, as of the effective date of the plan, equal to the allowed amount of such claim; or

(ii) if such class has not accepted the plan, cash on the effective date of the plan equal to the allowed amount of such claim; and

(C) with respect to a claim of a kind specified in section 507(a)(7) of this title, the holder of such claim will receive on account of such claim deferred cash payments, over a period not exceeding six years after the date of assessment of such claim, of a value, as of the effective date of the plan, equal to the allowed amount of such claim.

(10) If a class of claims is impaired under the plan, at least one class of claims that is impaired under the plan has accepted the plan, determined without including any acceptance of the plan by any insider.

(11) Confirmation of the plan is not likely to be followed by the liquidation, or the need for further financial reorganization, of the debtor or any successor to the debtor under the plan, unless such liquidation or reorganization is proposed in the plan.

(12) All fees payable under section 1930, as determined by the court at the hearing on confirmation of the plan, have been paid or the plan provides for the payment of all such fees on the effective date of the plan.

(13) The plan provides for the continuation after its effective date of payment of all retiree benefits, as that term is defined in section 1114 of this title, at the level established pursuant to subsection (e)(1)(B) or (g) of section 1114 of this title, at any time prior to confirmation of the plan, for the duration of the period the debtor has obligated itself to provide such benefits.

(b)(1) Notwithstanding section 510(a) of this title, if all of the applicable requirements of subsection (a) of this section other than paragraph (8) are met with respect to a plan, the court, on request of the proponent of the plan, shall confirm the plan notwithstanding the requirements of such paragraph if the plan does not discriminate unfairly, and is fair and equitable, with respect to each class of claims or interests that is impaired under, and has not accepted, the plan.

(2) For the purpose of this subsection, the condition that a plan be fair and equitable with respect to a class includes the following requirements:

(A) With respect to a class of secured claims, the plan provides—

(i)(I) that the holders of such claims retain the liens securing such claims, whether the property subject to such liens is retained by the debtor or transferred to another entity, to the extent of the allowed amount of such claims; and

(II) that each holder of a claim of such class receive on account of such claim deferred cash payments totaling at least the allowed amount of such claim, of a value, as of the effective date of the plan, of at least the value of such holder's interest in the estate's interest in such property;

(ii) for the sale, subject to section 363(k) of this title, of any property that is subject to the liens securing such claims, free and clear of such liens, with such liens to attach to the proceeds of such sale, and the treatment of such liens on proceeds under clause (i) or (iii) of this subparagraph; or

(iii) for the realization by such holders of the indubitable equivalent of such claims.

(B) With respect to a class of unsecured claims—

(i) the plan provides that each holder of a claim of such class receive or retain on account of such claim property of a value, as of the effective date of the plan, equal to the allowed amount of such claim; or

(ii) the holder of any claim or interest that is junior to the claims of such class will not receive or retain under the plan on account of such junior claim or interest any property.

(C) With respect to a class of interests—

    (i) the plan provides that each holder of an interest of such class receive or retain on account of such interest property of a value, as of the effective date of the plan, equal to the greatest of the allowed amount of any fixed liquidation preference to which such holder is entitled, any fixed redemption price to which such holder is entitled, or the value of such interest; or

    (ii) the holder of any interest that is junior to the interests of such class will not receive or retain under the plan on account of such junior interest any property.

(c) Notwithstanding subsections (a) and (b) of this section and except as provided in section 1127(b) of this title, the court may confirm only one plan, unless the order of confirmation in the case has been revoked under section 1144 of this title. If the requirements of subsections (a) and (b) of this section are met with respect to more than one plan, the court shall consider the preferences of creditors and equity security holders in determining which plan to confirm.

(d) Notwithstanding any other provision of this section, on request of a party in interest that is a governmental unit, the court may not confirm a plan if the principal purpose of the plan is the avoidance of taxes or the avoidance of the application of section 5 of the Securities Act of 1933 (15 U.S.C. 77e). In any hearing under this subsection, the governmental unit has the burden of proof on the issue of avoidance.

Bankruptcy Rule References: 2002 and 3020

Legislative History

[*Ed. Note:* The Senate Report throughout refers to section 1130 of the Senate Bill which concerned confirmation of a plan prior to final amendment.]

    Subsection (a) enumerates the requirement governing confirmation of a plan. The court is required to confirm a plan if and only if all of the requirements are met.

    Paragraph (1) requires that the plan comply with the applicable provisions of chapter 11, such as section 1122 and 1123, governing classification and contents of plan.

    Paragraph (2) requires that the proponent of the plan comply with the applicable provisions of chapter 11, such as section 1125 regarding disclosure.

Paragraph (3) requires that the proponent have proposed the plan in good faith, and not by any means forbidden by law.

Paragraph (4) is derived from section 221 of present law. It requires that any payment made or promised by the proponent, the debtor, or person issuing securities or acquiring property under the plan, for services or for costs and expenses in, or in connection with, the case, or in connection with the plan and incident to the case, be disclosed to the court. In addition, any payment made before confirmation must have been reasonable, and any payment to be fixed after confirmation must be subject to the approval of the court as reasonable.

Paragraph (5) is also derived from section 221 of the Bankruptcy Act. It requires the proponent of the plan to disclose the identity and affiliations of any individual proposed to serve, after confirmation, as a director, officer, or voting trustee of the reorganized debtor. The appointment to or continuance in one of these offices by the individual must be consistent with the interests of creditors and equity security holders and with public policy. The proponent of the plan must also disclose the identity of any insider that will be employed or retained by the reorganized debtor, and the nature of any compensation to be paid to the insider.

Paragraph (6) permits confirmation only if any regulatory commission that will have jurisdiction over the debtor after confirmation of the plan has approved any rate change provided for in the plan. As an alternative, the rate change may be conditioned on such approval.

[*House Report No. 95–595, 95th Cong., 1st Sess. 412 (1977); Senate Report No. 95–989, 95th Cong., 2d Sess. 126 (1978).*]

Paragraph (7) incorporates the former "best interest of creditors" test found in chapter 11, but spells out precisely what is intended. With respect to each class, the holders of the claims or interests of that class must receive or retain under the plan on account of those claims or interest property of a value, as of the effective date of the plan, that is not less than the amount that they would so receive or retain if the debtor were liquidated under chapter 7 on the effective date of the plan.

In order to determine the hypothetical distribution in a liquidation, the court will have to consider the various subordination provisions of proposed 11 U.S.C. 510, 726(a)(3), 726(a)(4), and the postponement provisions of proposed 11 U.S.C. 724. Also applicable in appropriate cases will be the rules governing partnership distributions under proposed 11 U.S.C. 723, and distributions of community property under proposed 11 U.S.C. 726(c). Under subparagraph (A), a particular holder is permitted to accept less than liquidation value, but his acceptance does not bind the class.

Property under subparagraph (B) may include securities of the debtor. Thus, the provision will apply in cases in which the plan is confirmed under proposed 11 U.S.C. 1129(b).

[*House Report No. 95–595, 95th Cong., 1st Sess. 412 (1977).*]

Paragraph (8) does not apply the fair and equitable standards in two situations. The first occurs if there is unanimous consent of all affected holders of claims and interests. It is also sufficient for purposes of confirmation if each holder of a claim or interest receives or retains consideration of a value, as of the effective date of the plan, that is not less than each would have or receive if the debtor were liquidated under chapter 7 of this title. This standard adapts the test of "best interest of creditors" as interpreted by the courts under chapter XI. It is given broader application in chapter 11 of this title since a plan under chapter 11 may affect not only unsecured claims but secured claims and stock as well.

[*Senate Report No. 95–989, 95th Cong., 2d Sess. 126 (1978).*]

Paragraph (8) is central to the confirmation standards. It requires that each class either have accepted the plan or be unimpaired.

Paragraph (9) augments the requirements of paragraph (8) by requiring payment of each priority claim in full. It permits payments over time and payment other than in cash, but payment in securities is not intended to be permitted without consent of the priority claimant even if the class has consented. It also permits a particular claimant to accept less than full payment.

[*House Report No. 95–595, 95th Cong., 1st Sess. 413 (1977).*]

Paragraph . . .[10] requires that at least one class must accept the plan, but any claims or interests held by insiders are not to be included for purposes of determining the number and amount of acceptances.

[*Senate Report 95–989, 95th Cong., 2d Sess. 128 (1978).*]

Paragraph . . .[11] contains the feasibility standards. It requires that the court find that confirmation of the plan is not likely to be followed by the liquidation or need for further financial reorganization of the debtor or any successor to the debtor, unless the plan so contemplates (such as under a liquidating plan).

[*House Report No. 95–595, 95th Cong., 1st Sess. 413 (1977).*]

Paragraph (11) requires a determination regarding feasibility of the plan. It is a slight elaboration of the law that has developed in the application of the word "feasible" in chapter X of the present Act.

[*Senate Report No. 95–989, 95th Cong., 2d Sess. 128 (1978).*]

Section 1129 of the House amendment relates to confirmation of a plan in a case under chapter 11. Section 1129(a)(3) of the House amendment adopts the position taken in the Senate amendment and section 1129(a)(5) takes the position adopted in the House bill. Section 1129 (a)(7) adopts the position taken in the House bill in order to insure that the dissenting members of an accepting class will receive at least what they would otherwise receive under the best interest of creditors test; it also requires that even the members of a class that has rejected the plan be protected by the best interest of creditors test for those rare cramdown cases where a class of creditors would receive more on liquidation than under reorganization of the debtor. Section 1129(a)(7)(C) is discussed in connection with section 1129(b) and section 1111(b). Section 1129(a)(8) of the House amendment adopts the provision taken in the House bill which permits confirmation of a plan as to a particular class without resort to the fair and equitable test if the class has accepted a plan or is unimpaired under the plan.

Section 1129(a)(9) represents a compromise between a similar provision contained in the House bill and the Senate amendment. Under subparagraph (A) claims entitled to priority under section 507(a)(1) or (2) are entitled to receive cash on the effective date of the plan equal to the amount of the claim. Under subparagraph (B) claims entitled to priority under section 507(a)(3), (4), or (5), [*Ed. Note:* section 507(a)(3), (4), (5) or (6), as amended by Pub. L. No. 99–554 (1986).] are entitled to receive deferred cash payments of a present value as of the effective date of the plan equal to the amount of the claims if the class has accepted the plan or cash payments on the effective date of the plan otherwise. Tax claims entitled to priority under section 507(a)(6) [*Ed. Note:* Section 506(a)(6) was redesignated as section 507(a)(7) by Pub. L. No. 99–554 (1986).] of different governmental units may not be contained in one class although all claims on one such unit may be combined and such unit may be required to take deferred cash payments over a period not to exceed 6 years after the date of assessment of the tax with the present value equal to the amount of the claim.

Section 1129(a)(10) is derived from section 1130(a)(12) of the Senate amendment.

[*124 Cong. Rec. H 11,103 (Sept. 28, 1978); S 17,420 (Oct. 6, 1978).*]

Subsection (b) permits the court to confirm a plan notwithstanding failure of compliance with paragraph (8) of subsection (a). The plan must comply with all other paragraphs of subsection (a), including paragraph (9). This subsection contains the so-called cramdown. It requires simply that the plan meet certain standards of fairness to dissenting creditors or equity security holders. The general principle of the subsection permits confirmation notwithstanding nonacceptance by an impaired class if that class and all below it in priority are treated according to the absolute priority rule. The dissenting class must be paid in full before any junior class may share under the plan. If it is paid in full, then junior classes may share. Treatment of classes of secured creditors is slightly different because they do not fall in the priority ladder, but the principle is the same.

Specifically, the court may confirm a plan over the objection of a class of secured claims if the members of that class are unimpaired or if they are to receive under the plan property of a value equal to the allowed amount of their secured claims, as determined under proposed 11 U.S.C. 506(a). The property is to be valued as of the effective date of the plan, thus recognizing the time-value of money. As used throughout this subsection, "property" includes both tangible and intangible property, such as a security of the debtor or a successor to the debtor under a reorganization plan.

The court may confirm over the dissent of a class of unsecured claims, including priority claims, only if the members of the class are unimpaired, if they will receive under the plan property of a value equal to the allowed amount of their unsecured claims, or if no class junior will share under the plan. That is, if the class is impaired, then they must be paid in full or, if paid less than in full, then no class junior may receive anything under the plan. This codifies the absolute priority rule from the dissenting class on down.

With respect to classes of equity, the court may confirm over a dissent if the members of the class are unimpaired, if they receive their liquidation preference or redemption rights, if any, or if no class junior shares under the plan. This, too, is a codification of the absolute priority rule with respect to equity. If a partnership agreement subordinates limited partners to general partners to any degree, then the general principles of paragraph (3) of this subsection would apply to prevent the general partners from being squeezed out.

One requirement applies generally to all classes before the court may confirm under this subsection. No class may be paid more than in full.

The partial codification of the absolute priority rule here is not intended to deprive senior creditor of compensation for being required to take securities in the reorganized debtor that are of an equal priority with the securities offered to a junior class. Under current law, seniors are entitled to compensation for their loss of priority, and the increased risk put upon them by being required to give up their priority will be reflected in a lower value of the securities given to them than the value of comparable securities given to juniors that have not lost a priority position.

Finally, the proponent must request use of this subsection. The court may not confirm notwithstanding nonacceptance unless the proponent requests and the court may then confirm only if subsection (b) is complied with. The court may not rewrite the plan.

A more detailed explanation follows:

The test to be applied by the court is set forth in the various paragraphs of section 1129(b). The elements of the test are new departing from both the absolute priority rule and the best interests of creditors tests found under the Bankruptcy Act. The court is not permitted to alter the terms of the plan. It must merely decide whether the plan complies with the requirements of section 1129(b). If so, the plan is confirmed, if not the plan is denied confirmation.

The procedure followed is simple. The court examines each class of claims or interests designated under section 1123(a)(1) to see if the requirements of section 1129(b) are met. If the class is a class of secured claims, then paragraph (1) contains two tests that must be complied with in order for confirmation to occur. First, under subparagraph (A), the court must be able to find that the consideration given under the plan on account of the secured claim does not exceed the allowed amount of the claim. This condition is not prescribed as a matter of law under section 1129(a) because if the secured claim is compensated in securities of the debtor, a valuation of the business would be necessary to determine the value of the consideration. While section 1129(a) does not contemplate a valuation of the debtor's business, such a valuation will almost always be required under section 1129(b) in order to determine the value of the consideration to be distributed under the plan. Once the valuation is performed, it becomes a simple matter to impose the criterion that no claim will be paid more than in full.

Application of the test under subparagraph (A) also requires a valuation of the consideration "as of the effective date of the plan." This contemplates a present value analysis that will discount value to be received in the future; of course, if the interest rate paid is equivalent to the discount rate used, the present value and face future value will be identical. On the other hand, if no interest is proposed to be paid, the present value will be less than the face future value. For example, consider an allowed secured claim of $1,000 in a class by itself. One plan could propose to pay $1,000 on account of this claim as of the effective date of the plan. Another plan could propose to give a note with a $1,000 face amount due five years after the effective date of the plan on account of this claim. A third plan could propose to give a note in a face amount of $1,000 due five years from the effective date of the plan plus six percent annual interest commencing on the effective date of the plan on account of this claim. The first plan clearly meets the requirements of subparagraph (A) because the amount received on account of the second claim has an equivalent present value as of the effective date of the plan equal to the allowed amount of such claim.

The second plan also meets the requirements of subparagraph (A) because the present value of the five years note as of the effective date of the plan will never exceed the allowed amount of the secured claim; the higher the discount rate, the less present value the note will have. Whether the third plan complies with subparagraph (A) depends on whether the discount rate is less than six percent. Normally, the interest rate used in the plan will be prima facie evidence of the discount rate because the interest rate will reflect an arms length determination of the risk of the security involved and feasibility considerations will tend to understate interest payments. If the court found the discount rate to be greater than or equal to the interest rate used in the plan, then subparagraph (A) would be complied with because the value of the note as of the effective date of the plan would not exceed the allowed amount of the second claim. If, however, the court found the discount rate to be less than the interest rate proposed under the plan, then the present value of the note would exceed $1,000 and the plan would fail of confirmation. On the other hand, it is important to recognize that the future principal amount of a note in excess of the allowed amount of a secured claim may have a present value less than such allowed amount, if the interest rate under the plan is correspondingly less than the discount rate.

Even if the requirements of subparagraph (A) are complied with, the class of secured claims must satisfy one of the three clauses in paragraph (B) in order to pass muster. It is sufficient for confirmation if the class has accepted the plan, or if the claims of the class are unimpaired, or if each holder of a secured claim in the class will receive property of a value as of the effective date of the plan equal to the allowed amount of such claim (unless he has agreed to accept less). It is important to note that under section 506(a), the allowed amount of the secured claim will not include any extent to which the amount of such claim exceeds the value of the property securing such claim. Thus, instead of focusing on secured creditors or unsecured creditors, the statute focuses on secured claims and unsecured claims.

After the court has applied paragraph (1) to each class of secured claims, it then applies paragraph (2) to each class of unsecured claims. Again two separate components must be tested. Subparagraph (A) is identical with the test under section 1129(b)(1)(A) insofar as the holder of an unsecured claim is not permitted to receive property of a value as of the effective date of the plan on account of such claim that is greater than the allowed amount of such claim. In addition, subparagraph (B) requires compliance with one of four conditions. The conditions in clauses (i)–(iii) mirror the conditions of acceptance unimpairment, or full value found in connection with secured claims in section 1129(b)(1)(B).

The condition contained in section 1129(b)(2)(B)(iv) provides another basis for confirming the plan with respect to a class of unsecured claims. It will be of greatest use when an impaired class that has not accepted the plan is to receive less than full value under the plan. The plan may be confirmed under clause (iv) in those circumstances if the class is not unfairly discriminated against with respect to equal classes and if junior classes will receive nothing under the plan. The second criterion is the easier to understand. It is designed to prevent a senior class from giving up consideration to a junior class unless every intermediate class consents, is paid in full, or is unimpaired. This gives immediate creditors a great deal of leverage in negotiating with senior or secured creditors who wish to have a plan that gives value to equity. One aspect of this test that is not obvious is that whether one class is senior, equal, or junior to another class is relative and not absolute. Thus from the perspective of trade creditors holding unsecured claims, claims of senior and subordinated debentures may be entitled to share on an equal basis with the trade claims. However, from the perspective of the senior unsecured debt, the subordinated debentures are junior.

This point illustrates the lack of precision in the first criterion which demands that a class not be unfairly discriminated against with respect to equal classes. From the perspective of unsecured trade claims, there is no unfair discrimination as long as the total consideration given all other classes of equal rank does not exceed the amount that would result from an exact aliquot distribution. Thus if trade creditors, senior debt, and subordinate debt are each owed $100 and the plan proposes to pay the trade debt $15, the senior debt $30, and the junior debt $0, the plan would not unfairly discriminate against the trade debt nor would any other allocation of consideration under the plan between the senior and junior debt be unfair as to the trade debt as long as the aggregate consideration is less than $30. The senior debt could take $25 and give up $5 to the junior debt and the trade debt would have no cause to complain because as far as it is concerned the junior debt is an equal class.

However, in this latter case the senior debt would have been unfairly discriminated against because the trade debt was being unfairly over-compensated; of course the plan would also fail unless the senior debt was unimpaired, received full value, or accepted the plan, because from its perspective a junior class received property under the plan. Application of the test from the perspective of senior debt is best illustrated by the plan that proposes to pay trade debt $15, senior debt $25, and junior debt $0. Here the senior debt is being unfairly discriminated against with respect to the equal trade debt even though the trade debt receives less than the senior debt. The discrimination arises from the fact that the senior debt is entitled to the rights of the junior debt which in this example entitle the senior debt to share on a 2:1 basis with the trade debt.

Finally, it is necessary to interpret the first criterion from the perspective of subordinated debt. The junior debt is subrogated to the rights of senior debt once the senior debt is paid in full. Thus, while the plan that pays trade debt $15, senior debt $25, and junior debt $0 is not unfairly discriminatory against the junior debt, a plan that proposes to pay trade debt $55, senior debt $100, and junior debt $1, would be unfairly discriminatory. In order to avoid discriminatory treatment against the junior debt, at least $10 would have to be received by such debt under those facts.

The criterion of unfair discrimination is not derived from the fair and equitable rule or from the best interests of creditors test. Rather it preserves just treatment of a dissenting class from the class's own perspective.

If each class of secured claims satisfies the requirements of section 1129(b)(1) and each class of unsecured claims satisfies the requirements of section 1129(b)(2), then the court must still see if each class of interests satisfies section 1129(b)(3) before the plan may be confirmed. Again, two separate criteria must be met. Under subparagraph (A) if the interest entitles the holder thereof to a fixed liquidation preference or if such interest may be redeemed at a fixed price, then the holder of such interest must not receive under the plan on account of such interest property of a value as of the effective date of the plan greater than the greater of these two values of the interest. Preferred stock would be an example of an interest likely to have liquidation preference or redemption price.

If an interest such as most common stock or the interest of a general partnership has neither a fixed liquidation preference nor a fixed redemption price, then the criterion in subparagraph (A) is automatically fulfilled. In addition subparagraph (B) contains five clauses that impose alternative conditions of which at least one must be satisfied in order to warrant confirmation. The first two clauses contain requirements of acceptance or unimpairment similar to the first two clauses in paragraphs (1)(B) and (2)(B). Clause (iii) is similar to the unimpairment test contained in section 1124(3)(B) except that it will apply to cover the issuance securities of the debtor of a value as of the effective date of the plan equal to the greater of any fixed liquidation preference or redemption price. The fourth clause allows confirmation if junior interests are not compensated under the plan and the fifth clause allows confirmation if there are no junior interests. These clauses recognized that as long as senior classes receive no more than full payment, the objection of a junior class will not defeat confirmation unless a class junior to it is receiving value under the plan and the objecting class is impaired. While a determination of impairment may be made under section 1124(3)(B)(iii) without a precise valuation of the business when common stock is clearly under water, once section 1129(b) is used, a more detailed valuation is a necessary byproduct. Thus, if no property is given to a holder of an interest under the plan, the interest should be clearly worthless in order to find unimpairment under section 1124(3)(B)(iii) and section 1129(a)(8); otherwise, since a class of interests receiving no property is deemed to object under section 1126(g), the more precise valuation of section 1129(b) should be used.

If all of the requirements of section 1129(b) are complied with, then the court may confirm the plan subject to other limitations such as those found in section 1129(a) and (d).

[*House Report No. 95–595, 95th Cong., 1st Sess. 413–418 (1977).*]

Under paragraph (9)(A), if a class of claims or interests has not accepted the plan, the court will confirm the plan if, for the dissenting class and any class of equal rank, the negotiated plan provides in value no less than under a plan that is fair and equitable. Such review and determination are not required for any other classes that accepted the plan.

Paragraph 9(A) would permit a senior creditor to adjust his participation for the benefit of stockholders. In such a case, junior creditors, who have not been satisfied in full, may not object if, absent the "give-up," they are receiving all that a fair and equitable plan would give them. To illustrate, suppose the estate is valued at $1.5 million and claims and stock are:

	Claims and stock (millions)	Equity (millions)
(1) Senior debt		$1.2
(2) Junior debt	.5	.3
(3) Stock	(¹)	
Total	$1.7	$1.5

¹No value.

Under the plan, the senior creditor gives up $100,000 in value for the benefit of stockholders as follows:

	Millions
(1) Senior debt	$1.1
(2) Junior debt	.3
(3) Stock	.1
Total	$1.5

If the junior creditors dissent, the court may nevertheless confirm the plan since under the fair and equitable standard they had an equity of only $300,000 and the allocation to equity security holders did not affect them.

Paragraph 9(A) provides a special alternative with respect to secured claims. A plan may be confirmed against a dissenting class of secured claims if the plan or order of confirmation provides for the realization of their security (1) by the retention of the property subject to such security; (2) by a sale of the property and transfer of the claim to the proceeds of sale if the secured creditors were permitted to bid at the sale and set off against the purchase price up to the allowed amount of their claims; or (3) by such other method that will assure them the realization of the indubitable equivalent of the allowed amount of their secured claims. The indubitable equivalent language is intended to follow the strict approach taken by Judge Learned Hand in the *In re* Murel Holding Corp., 75 F.2d 941 (2d Cir. 1935).

Paragraph (9)(B) provides that, if a class of claims or interests is excluded from participation under the plan, the court may nevertheless confirm the plan if it determines that no class on a parity with or junior to such participates under the plan. In the previous illustration, no confirmation would be permitted if the negotiated plan would grant a participation to stockholders but nothing for junior creditors. As noted elsewhere, by reason of section 1126(g), an excluded class is a dissenting class under section 1130.

Paragraph (10) states that, to be confirmed, the plan must provide that each holder of a claim under section 507 will receive property, as therein noted, of a value equal to the allowed amount of the claim. There are two exceptions: (A) The holder thereof may agree to a different settlement in part or in whole; (B) where a debtor's business is reorganized under chapter 11, this provision requires that taxes entitles [*sic*] to priority (including administrative claims or taxes) must be paid in cash not later than 120 days after the plan is confirmed, unless the Secretary of the Treasury agrees to other terms or kinds of payment. The bill, as introduced, required full payment in cash within 60 days after the plan is confirmed.

[*Ed. Note:* The lengthy excerpt, *supra,* from the Senate report concerns paragraphs (9) and (10) of section 1130 to the Senate Bill prior to final amendment, the subject matter of which was generally covered in what became section 1129(b) of the final revised Bill.]

[*Senate Report No. 95–989, 95th Cong., 2d Sess. 127–128 (1978).*]

Section 1129(b) is new. Together with section 1111(b) and section 1129(a)(7)(C), this section provides when a plan may be confirmed, notwithstanding the failure of an impaired class to accept the plan under section 1129(a)(8). Before discussing section 1129(b) an understanding of section 1111(b) is necessary. Section 1111(b)(1) [*sic*] the general rule that a secured claim is to be treated as a recourse claim in chapter 11 whether or not the claim is nonrecourse by agreement or applicable law. This preferred status for a nonrecourse loan terminates if the property securing the loan is sold under section 363 or is to be sold under the plan.

The preferred status also terminates if the class of which the secured claim is a part elects application of section 1111(b)(2). Section 1111(b)(2) provides that an allowed claim is a secured claim to the full extent the claim is allowed rather [*sic*] to the extent of the collateral as under section 506(a). A class may elect application of paragraph (2) only if the security is not of inconsequential value and, if the creditor is a recourse creditor, the collateral is not sold under section 363 or to be sold under the plan. Sale of property under section 363 or under the plan is excluded from treatment under section 1111(b) because of the secured party's right to bid in the full amount of his allowed claim at any sale of collateral under section 363(k) of the House amendment.

As previously noted, section 1129(b) sets forth a standard by which a plan may be confirmed notwithstanding the failure of an impaired class to accept the plan.

Paragraph (1) makes clear that this alternative confirmation standard, referred to as "cram down," will be called into play only on the request of the proponent of the plan. Under this cram down test, the court must confirm the plan if the plan does not discriminate unfairly, and is "fair and equitable," with respect to each class of claims or interests that is impaired under, and has not accepted, the plan. The requirement of the House bill that a plan not "discriminate unfairly" with respect to a class is included for clarity; the language in the House Report interpreting that requirement, in the context of subordinated debentures, applies equally under the requirements of section 1129(b)(1) of the House amendment.

Although many of the factors interpreting "fair and equitable" are specified in paragraph (2), others, which were explicated in the description of section 1129(b) in the House report, were omitted from the House amendment to avoid statutory complexity and because they would undoubtedly be found by a court to be fundamental to "fair and equitable" treatment of a dissenting class. For example, a dissenting class should be assured that no senior class receives more than 100 percent of the amount of its claims. While that requirement was explicitly included in the House bill, the deletion is intended to be one of style and not one of substance.

Paragraph (2) provides guidelines for a court to determine whether a plan is fair and equitable with respect to a dissenting class. It must be emphasized that the fair and equitable requirement applies only with respect to dissenting classes. Therefore, unlike the fair and equitable rule contained in chapter X and section 77 of the Bankruptcy Act under section 1129(b)(2), senior accepting classes are permitted to give up value to junior classes as long as no dissenting intervening class receives less than the amount of its claims in full. If there is no dissenting intervening class and the only dissent is from a class junior to the class to which value have [*sic*] been given up, then the plan may still be fair and equitable with respect to the dissenting class, as long as no class senior to the dissenting class has received more than 100 percent of the amount of its claims.

Paragraph (2) contains three subparagraphs, each of which applies to a particular kind of class of claims or interests that is impaired and has not accepted the plan. Subparagraph (A) applies when a class of secured claims is impaired and has not accepted the plan. The provision applies whether or not section 1111(b) applies. The plan may be crammed down notwithstanding the dissent of a secured class only if the plan complies with clause (i), (ii), or (iii).

Clause (i) permits cram down if the dissenting class of secured claims will retain its lien on the property whether the property is retained by the debtor or transferred. It should be noted that the lien secures the allowed secured claim held by such holder. The meaning of "allowed secured claim" will vary depending on whether section 1111(b)(2) applies to such class.

If section 1111(b)(2) applies then the "electing" class is entitled to have the entire allowed amount of the debt related to such property secured by a lien even if the value of the collateral is less than the amount of the debt. In addition, the plan must provide for the holder to receive, on account of the allowed secured claims, payments, either present or deferred, of a principal face amount equal to the amount of the debt and of a present value equal to the value of the collateral.

For example, if a creditor loaned $15,000,000 to a debtor secured by real property worth $18,000,000 and the value of the real property had dropped to $12,000,000 by the date when the debtor commenced a proceeding under chapter 11, the plan could be confirmed notwithstanding the dissent of the creditor as long as the lien remains on the collateral to secure a $15,000,000 debt, the [sic] face amount of present or extended payments to be made to the creditor under the plan is at least $15,000,000, and the present value of the present or deferred payments is not less than $12,000,000. The House report accompanying the House bill described what is meant by "present value".

Clause (ii) is self explanatory. Clause (iii) requires the court to confirm the plan notwithstanding the dissent of the electing secured class if the plan provides for the realization by the secured class of the indubitable equivalence of the secured claims. The standard of "indubitable equivalence" is taken from *In re* Murel Holding Corp., 75 F.2d 941 (2d Cir. 1935) (Learned Hand. Jr.).

Abandonment of the collateral to the creditor would clearly satisfy indubitable equivalence, as would a lien on similar collateral. However, present cash payments less than the secured claim would not satisfy the standard because the creditor is deprived of an opportunity to gain from a future increase in value of the collateral. Unsecured notes as to the secured claim or equity securities of the debtor would not be the indubitable equivalent. With respect to an oversecured creditor, the secured claim will never exceed the allowed claim.

Although the same language applies, a different result pertains with respect to a class of secured claims to which section 1111(b)(2) does not apply. This will apply to all claims secured by a right of setoff. The court must confirm the plan notwithstanding the dissent of such a class of secured claims if any of three alternative requirements is met. Under clause (i) the plan may be confirmed if the class retains a right of setoff or a lien securing the allowed secured claims of the class and the holders will receive payments of a present value equal to the allowed amount of their secured claims. Contrary to electing classes of secured creditors who retain a lien under subparagraph (A)(i)(I) to the extent of the entire claims secured by such lien, nonelecting creditors retain a lien on collateral only to the extent of their allowed secured claims and not to the extent of any deficiency, and such secured creditors must receive present or deferred payments with a present value equal to the allowed secured claim, which in turn is only the equivalent of the value of the collateral under section 506(a).

Any deficiency claim of a nonelecting class of secured claims is treated as an unsecured claim and is not provided for under subparagraph (A). The plan may be confirmed under clause (ii) if the plan proposes to sell the property free and clear of the secured party's lien as long as the lien will attach to the proceeds and will receive treatment under clause (i) or (iii). Clause (iii) permits confirmation if the plan provides for the realization by the dissenting nonelecting class of secured claims of the indubitable equivalent of the secured claims of such class.

Contrary to an "electing" class to which section 1111(b)(2) applies, the nonelecting class need not be protected with respect to any future appreciation in value of the collateral since the secured claim of such a class is never undersecured by reason of section 506(a). Thus the lien secures only the value of interest of such creditor in the collateral. To the extent deferred payments exceed that amount, they represent interest. In the event of a subsequent default, the portion of the face amount of deferred payment representing unaccrued interest will not be secured by the lien.

Subparagraph (B) applies to a dissenting class of unsecured claims. The court must confirm the plan notwithstanding the dissent of a class of impaired unsecured claims if the plan provides for such claims to receive property with a present value equal to the allowed amount of the claims. Unsecured claims may receive any kind of "property," which is used in its broadest sense, as long as the present value of the property given to the holders of unsecured claims is equal to the allowed amount of the claims. Some kinds of property, such as securities, may require difficult valuations by the court; in such circumstances the court need only determine that there is a reasonable likelihood that the property given the dissenting class of impaired unsecured claims equals the present value of such allowed claims.

Alternatively, under clause (ii), the court must confirm the plan if the plan provides that holders of any claims or interests junior to the interests of the dissenting class of impaired unsecured claims will not receive any property under the plan on account of such junior claims or interests. As long as senior creditors have not been paid more than in full, and classes of equal claims are being treated so that the dissenting class of impaired unsecured claims is not being discriminated against unfairly, the plan may be confirmed if the impaired class of unsecured claims receives less than 100 cents on the dollar (or nothing at all) as long as no class junior to the dissenting class receives anything at all. Such an impaired dissenting class may not prevent confirmation of a plan by objection merely because a senior class has elected to give up value to a junior class that is higher in priority than the impaired dissenting class of unsecured claims as long as the above safeguards are met.

Subparagraph (C) applies to a dissenting class of impaired interests. Such interests may include the interests of general or limited partners in a partnership, the interests of a sole proprietor in a proprietorship, or the interests of common or preferred stockholders in a corporation. If the holders of such interests are entitled to a fixed liquidation preference or fixed redemption price on account of such interests then the plan may be confirmed notwithstanding the dissent of such class of interests as long as it provides the holders property of a present value equal to the greatest of the fixed redemption price, or the value of such interests. In the event there is no fixed liquidation preference or redemption price, then the plan may be confirmed as long as it provides the holders of such interests property of a present value equal to the value of such interests. If the interests are "under water" then they will be valueless and the plan may be confirmed notwithstanding the dissent of that class of interests even if the plan provides that the holders of such interests will not receive any property on account of such interests.

Alternatively, under clause (ii), the court must confirm the plan notwithstanding the dissent of a class of interests if the plan provides that holders of any interests junior to the dissenting class of interests will not receive or retain any property on account of such junior interests. Clearly, if there are no junior interests junior to the class of dissenting interests, then the condition of clause (ii) is satisfied. The safeguards that no claim or interest receive more than 100 percent of the allowed amount of such claim or interest and that no class be discriminated against unfairly will insure that the plan is fair and equitable with respect to the dissenting class of interests.

Except to the extent of the treatment of secured claims under subparagraph (A) of this statement, the House report remains an accurate description of confirmation of section 1129(b). Contrary to the example contained in the Senate report, a senior class will not be able to give up value to a junior class over the dissent of an intervening class unless the intervening class receives the full amount, as opposed to value, of its claims or interests.

One last point deserves explanation with respect to the admittedly complex subject of confirmation. Section 1129(a)(7)(C) in effect exempts secured creditors making an election under section 1111(b)(2) from application of the best interest of creditors test. In the absence of an election the amount such creditors receive in a plan of liquidation would be the value of their collateral plus any amount recovered on the deficiency in the case of a recourse loan. However, under section

1111(b)(2), the creditors are given an allowed secured claim to the full
extent the claim is allowed and have no unsecured deficiency. Since
section 1129(b)(2)(A) makes clear that an electing class need receive
payments of a present value only equal to the value of the collateral,
it is conceivable that under such a "cram down" the electing creditors
would receive nothing with respect to the deficiency. The advantage to
the electing creditors is that they have a lien securing the full amount
of the allowed claim so that if the value of the collateral increases after
the case is closed, the deferred payments will be secured claims. Thus
it is both reasonable and necessary to exempt such electing class from
application of section 1129(a)(7) as a logical consequence of permitting
election under section 1111(b)(2).

[*124 Cong. Rec. H 11,103 (Sept. 28, 1978); S 17,420 (Oct. 6, 1978).*]

Subsection (c) of section 1129 governs confirmation when more than
one plan meets the requirements of the section. The court must consider
the preferences of creditors and equity security holders in determining
which plan to confirm.

[*House Report No. 95–595, 95th Cong., 1st Sess. 418 (1977).*]

Under subsection (c) the court may confirm only one plan, unless the
order of confirmation has been revoked under section 1144. If the
requirements for confirmation are met with respect to more than one
plan, the court shall consider the preferences of creditors and stockholders in deciding which plan to confirm.

[*Senate Report No. 95–989, 95th Cong., 2d Sess. 128 (1978).*]

Subsection (d) requires the court to deny confirmation if the principal
purpose of the plan is the avoidance of taxes (through use of section
346 and 1146, and applicable provisions of State law or the Internal
Revenue Code governing bankruptcy reorganizations) or the avoidance
of section 5 of the Securities Act of 1933 (through use of section 1145).

[*House Report No. 95–595, 95th Cong., 1st Sess. 418 (1977).*]

Subsection (d) provides that the bankruptcy court may not confirm
a plan of reorganization if its principal purpose is the avoidance of taxes
or the avoidance of section 5 of the Securities Act of 1933 (15 U.S.C.
§ 77e). This rule modifies a similar provision of present law (section 269
of the Bankruptcy Act).

[*Senate Report No. 95–989, 95th Cong., 2d Sess. 128 (1978).*]

Comment

Section 1129 relates to confirmation of a plan in a chapter 11
reorganization. Subsection (a) is derived from Section 221 of the former
Bankruptcy Act.

Section 1129 adopts the "best interest" rule, that is, under subsection
(a)(7)(A)(ii), if each holder of a class has not accepted the plan, the
creditors in that class must receive or retain on account of such claim

or interest *as of the effective date of the plan,* not less than such holder would receive or retain if the debtor were liquidated under chapter 7 on such date. Under subsection (a)(8), the "best interest" rule is the confirmation standard if the plan is accepted by the requisite majorities of each impaired class.

The plan may be confirmed under subsection (b)(1) if it does not discriminate unfairly and is *fair and equitable* with respect to each class of claims or interests that is impaired under the plan that has not accepted the plan. Subsection (b)(2) specifies the factors or guidelines interpreting "fair and equitable." The "fair and equitable" rule applies only with respect to a dissenting class, thus representing a marked difference from the application of the rule in Chapter X cases under the former Bankruptcy Act. Under section 1129(b)(2), senior accepting creditors may give up value to junior classes provided no dissenting intervening class receives less than the full amount of its claims. If no such dissenting intervening class exists, and the only dissent is from a class junior to the class which has given up value then the plan may still be fair and equitable with respect to the dissenting class provided no senior class has received more than 100 percent of its claims. Under former Chapter X of the Act, however, a plan was not fair and equitable unless each class in descending order first received full compensation for its claims or interests. Under the Code, generally the fair and equitable rule is applied starting only from the most senior dissenting class, descending to the lowest junior class.

Subsection (b)(2) provides for "cram-down" particularly with respect to secured creditors notwithstanding the dissent of an impaired class if the plan complies with the requirements set forth. The application of the "cram-down" provisions is stated in the Congressional Record, *supra.*

As regards secured creditors and their treatment in section 1129(b)(2)(A), particular reference should be made to section 1111(b).

Bankruptcy Rule 3020(a) provides that prior to entry of the confirmation order, the court may order the deposit, with the trustee or debtor in possession, of the consideration required by the plan to be distributed on confirmation. Money deposited is to be kept in a special account established for the exclusive purpose of distribution. Subdivision (b), amended in 1991, relates to objections and to the hearing on confirmation, and provides that objections to confirmation shall be filed and served on the debtor, the trustee, the proponent of the plan, any committee appointed under the Code and on any other entity designated by the court, within the time fixed by the court. A copy of every objection to confirmation shall be transmitted by the objecting party to the United States trustee within the time fixed for filing of objections. If no timely objection is filed, the court may determine that the plan has been proposed in good faith and not by any means forbidden by law without receiving evidence on such issues.

Subdivision (c) requires the order of confirmation to conform to Official Form 15 and that notice of entry thereof be promptly mailed by the clerk, or some other person as the court directs, to the debtor, the trustee, creditors, equity security holders and other parties in interest. Notice of entry of the confirmation order shall be transmitted to the United States trustee as provided in Rule 2002(k).

Subdivision (d) provides that notwithstanding confirmation, the court may enter all orders as thereafter become necessary in administering the estate.

Bankruptcy Rule 2002(f)(7) provides for notice to the debtor, creditors and indenture trustees of the entry of an order confirming a chapter 11 plan. Under subdivisions (i) and (j), notice of entry of the order must also be given to any committee elected or appointed under the Code and to the S.E.C. if it filed notice of appearance or filed a written request for notices. Subsection (k) requires that notice be transmitted to the United States trustee.

1984 Amendments: Subsection (a)(10) of section 1129 was amended to clarify that a plan must be accepted by at least one class of claims that is impaired under the plan if at least one class is impaired. Prior to the amendment there was a conflict in the cases as to whether the existence of an unimpaired class, which is *deemed* to accept the plan pursuant to section 1126(f), satisfied the requirement of section 1129(a)(10) that at least one class of claims had to accept the plan. The amendment removes the ambiguity and requires the affirmative acceptance of the plan by at least one impaired class of claims unless all classes of claims are left unimpaired.

Subsection (d) was amended by addition of the final sentence placing the burden of proof on a governmental unit when it is contended that the purpose of the plan is tax avoidance or avoidance of the application of the Securities Act of 1933.

A stylistic change combined subparagraphs (A) and (B) of subsection (a) (4) into a single paragraph (4).

Subsection (a)(6) was amended by insertion of the word "governmental."

Subsection (a)(7) was clarified to indicate that the paragraph relates to "impaired" classes or interests.

Technical or stylistic changes were made in paragraphs (1), (2), (6), (7), (7)(B) and (8) of subsection (a) and subsection (b)(2).

1986 Amendments: The 1986 Act added to section 1129(a) a twelfth requirement as a prerequisite to confirmation, *i.e.,* that all fees payable under section 1930 of title 28, as determined by the court at the confirmation hearing, have been paid or the plan provides for payment of all such fees on the effective date of the plan.

This section was amended to reflect the creation of a permanent United States trustee system. Section 302(d) of the 1986 Amendments provides different effective dates for the amendments relating to the United States trustee system. *See* Section 302 of the 1986 Amendments, reprinted herein under "Selected Provisions of the Bankruptcy Judges, United States Trustees, and Family Farmer Bankruptcy Act of 1986," regarding effective dates generally.

1988 Amendments: Paragraph (13) was added to section 1129(a) by the Retiree Benefits Bankruptcy Protection Act of 1988, Pub. L. No. 100–334, to establish another requirement for confirming a chapter 11 plan. Under paragraph (13), the plan must provide for the payment of all retiree benefits, at the level established pursuant to subsection (e)(1)(B) or (g) of section 1114 [also added by the Act], at any time prior to confirmation of the plan, for the duration the debtor has obligated itself to provide such benefits.

The Act, in addition to including paragraph (13) in section 1129(a), added to chapter 11 a new section 1114, "Payment of insurance benefits to retired employees," which provides both the procedures and standards for modifying the payment of retiree benefits in a chapter 11 case, including the use of interim modifications prior to the court's issuance of a final order [*see supra*].

The Act repealed Section 2 of "An Act to amend the interest provisions of the Declaration of Taking Act," Pub. L. No. 99–656 (1986). Additionally, the Act made permanent and substantially amended Section 608 of the second title VI of "Joint Resolution making continuing appropriations for the fiscal year 1987, and for other purposes," Pub. L. No. 99–591 (1986). Section 608, as amended, provides that the trustee cannot modify retiree benefits unless the trustee and an authorized representative of the former employees with respect to whom such benefits are payable agree to the modification or the court finds that the modification meets the standards of section 1113(b)(1)(A) and the balance of the equities clearly favors the modification. Pursuant to the amendment made to Section 608 by Section 3(a)(3)(B) of the 1988 Act, a chapter 11 trustee or debtor in possession is required to pay any prepetition claims owing to a health care provider that can prove it has the legal right to recover from the patient any such payments, unless repaid by the debtor-former employer; a prepetition claim is thus turned into an administrative expense priority. Section 608, as amended, applies to chapter 11 cases which were pending on June 16, 1988, the date of enactment of the Act. The complete text of Section 608, as amended, immediately follows section 1114, *supra.*

The Act and its amendments became effective on the date of its enactment, June 16, 1988. However, sections 1114 and 1129(a)(13) do not apply to chapter 11 cases which had been commenced before June 16, 1988. For pre-enactment cases, Section 608, as amended, applies.

1990 Amendments: Although section 1129 was not amended in 1990, it should be noted that section 1129(a), as currently enacted, does not take into account the addition of an eighth priority by the Crime Control Act of 1990, Pub. L. No. 101-647 (1990) (effective on the date of enactment, November 29, 1990). It is unclear whether the omission of the eighth priority was intentional or an oversight on the part of the drafters. Section 507(a)(8) grants priority status to allowed unsecured claims based upon any commitment made by the debtor to certain federal regulatory agencies to maintain the capital of an insured depository institution. *See* 11 U.S.C. § 507(a)(8).

Case Annotations

Chapter 11 debtors' contribution of labor, experience and expertise does not constitute a contribution of "money or money's worth" for purposes of confirmation of a reorganization plan, when the plan would allow the debtors to retain an equity interest in property despite the fact that unsecured creditors' claims were not satisfied in full; the absolute priority rule applies, and the plan cannot be confirmed over the objections of unsecured creditors. Norwest Bank Worthington v. Ahlers, 485 U.S. 197, 108 S. Ct. 963, 99 L. Ed. 2d 169, 18 C.B.C.2d 262 (1988).

In determining whether to order the Internal Revenue Service (IRS) to apply involuntary payments to trust fund taxes first, a bankruptcy court should consider whether the allocation of payments increases the risk that the IRS may not collect its total tax debt, and whether that risk is nonetheless justified by an offsetting increased likelihood of rehabilitation. *In re* Energy Resources Co., 871 F.2d 223, 20 C.B.C.2d 1552 (1st Cir. 1989), *aff'd*, 495 U.S. —, 110 S. Ct. 2139, 109 L. Ed. 2d 580, 22 C.B.C.2d 1093 (1990).

A chapter 11 plan which separates unsecured claims into three classes and provides for equal treatment of the portion of the claims to be paid, but which also provides for personal guarantees of payment for the claims in two of the classes, cannot be confirmed over the objection of the third class of creditors whose claims are not guaranteed as to payment. Priority tax claimants for whom section 1129(a)(9)(C) gives preferential treatment are not an impaired class that can accept a plan and thereby bind truly impaired creditors to a cramdown. *In re* Bryson Properties, XVIII, 961 F.2d 496, 26 C.B.C.2d 1290 (4th Cir. 1992).

A chapter 11 plan that provides for negative amortization of a creditor's claim should not be rejected by a court on that ground *per se* but should be evaluated on a case by case basis: it is conceivable that negative amortization would provide the creditor with the present value of its claim and meet the "fair and equitable" standard of section 1129(b). Great Western Bank v. Sierra Woods Group, 953 F.2d 1174, 26 C.B.C.2d 342 (9th Cir. 1992).

The principle that liens pass through bankruptcy unaffected is not absolute. A bankruptcy court can compel a secured creditor to forego its liens and accept a chapter 11 plan of reorganization provided that the creditor receives the "indubitable equivalent" of its secured interest. Matter of James Wilson Assoc., 965 F.2d 160, 26 C.B.C.2d 1673 (7th Cir. 1992).

While a plan which does not meet the standards of section 1129(b)(2) cannot be fair and equitable, technical compliance with all requirements of that section does not assure that a plan is "fair and equitable." In making that determination, a court must consider the entire plan in the context of the rights of the creditors under state law and the particular facts and circumstances of the case. In the Matter of D & F Construction, Inc., 865 F.2d 673, 20 C.B.C.2d 716 (5th Cir. 1989).

The market value approach, which is also applicable to chapter 12 reorganizations, sets the discount rate at the yield for treasury bonds with a two percent upward adjustment to account for risk. United States v. Doud, 869 F.2d 1144, 20 C.B.C.2d 1156 (8th Cir. 1989).

An impaired creditor's failure to vote on or object to a plan of reorganization constitutes acceptance of the plan for purposes of section 1129(b). Heins v. Ruti-Sweetwater, Inc. (In re Ruti-Sweetwater, Inc.), 836 F.2d 1263, 17 C.B.C.2d 1459 (10th Cir. 1988). But see In re Townco Realty, Inc., 18 C.B.C.2d 13 (B. Ct., S.D. Fla. 1987) (failure of an impaired class to vote cannot constitute acceptance of a plan under section 1129(a)(8)).

The interest rate on deferred taxes is not set statutorily, but must be based on that rate of interest that the debtor would pay to borrow a similar amount on similar terms in the commercial loan market. For that reason, the section 1129(a)(9) interest rate on a tax claim cannot be based on the interest rate on treasury obligations since that is the government's cost of borrowing and no private borrower can be as creditworthy as the federal government. The 26 U.S.C. § 6621 interest rate is also not an appropriate indicator of the relevant market rate because it does not take into account the risk or security of the borrower. United States v. Camino Real Landscape Maintenance Contractors, Inc. (In re Camino Real Landscape Maintenance Contractors, Inc.), 818 F.2d 1503, 16 C.B.C.2d 1341 (9th Cir. 1987).

A plan that permits an equity security holder to acquire an equity interest in the reorganized debtor does not violate section 1129(b)(2)(B)(ii) when the holder is giving up its prior interest and is making a substantial capital contribution that is both necessary and sufficient to make the plan a success. Teamsters National Freight Industry Negotiating Committee v. U.S. Truck Co., Inc. (In re U.S. Truck Co., Inc.), 800 F.2d 581, 15 C.B.C.2d 553 (6th Cir. 1986).

A debtor paying priority tax claims over a six year period must apply interest to those claims at the rate established under 26 U.S.C. § 6621, since that rate represents Congress' attempt to charge taxpayers the prevailing market rate on delinquent tax liabilities. Before the rate can be applied, however, it must be determined whether the rate reflects the risk of nonpayment, the quality and existence of security and the repayment period and, if it does not, it is to be adjusted accordingly. United States v. Neal Pharmacal Co., 789 F.2d 1283, 14 C.B.C.2d 708 (8th Cir. 1986).

A plan that fails to provide for the possibility of the recovery of a large judgment by a creditor in a pending civil case is not feasible and, therefore, cannot be confirmed. Pizza of Hawaii, Inc. v. Shakey's, Inc. (In the Matter of Pizza of Hawaii, Inc.), 761 F.2d 1374, 12 C.B.C.2d 1227 (9th Cir. 1985).

So long as a plan "provides for" future payment of the present value of senior claims, section 1129(b) requires the bankruptcy court to confirm the reorganization plan notwithstanding the objection of a class of impaired unsecured senior creditors that some payments will go to the debtor before such senior creditors are paid in full. The absolute priority rule does not prohibit payments to a junior class of claimants before a senior class is paid in full. *In re* Johnston, 26 C.B.C.2d 165 (9th Cir., B.A.P., 1992).

For the new value exception to apply and a plan proposing it to be confirmed, the plan must be fair and equitable and the proposed capital contribution must be necessary for an effective reorganization and reasonably equivalent in value to the interest in the reorganized debtor that is to be retained by the contributing equity holder. A chapter 11 plan proposing to use the new value exception to the absolute priority rule is not "fair and equitable" if it shifts most of the risk of loss to an unsecured class. *In re* SLC Ltd. V, 26 C.B.C.2d 1347 (B. Ct., D. Utah 1992).

Acceptance by an impaired class must be determined without including any acceptance by an insider, and must be determined at the time the vote is taken, not at the time the claim arises. A debtor may "cram down" its plan over the objection of a creditor if the dissenting class of creditors receives treatment which allocates value to the class consistent with the treatment afforded to other classes with similar legal claims against the debtor. *In re* MCorp Fin., Inc., 26 C.B.C.2d 1805 (B. Ct., S.D. Tex. 1992).

A reorganization plan fails the absolute priority rule of the "fair and equitable" test for confirmation over the objections of creditors when, upon close scrutiny of the plan, it is determined that insiders of the debtor are not making a substantial new economic commitment to the reorganization of the debtor but, rather, are simply reacquiring their ownership rights in exchange for a small contribution of cash that will be immediately returned to them or will be used to retire obligations for which they are already personally liable. *In re* Creekside Landing, Ltd., 26 C.B.C.2d 1589 (B. Ct., M.D. Tenn. 1992).

Lack of interest payments in a chapter 11 debtor's long term repayment plan is an impairment under section 1129(a)(8) that requires denial of confirmation unless the plan meets the other criteria of section 1129(a) and the "cram down" provisions of 1129(b). *In re* Ribs Auto Sales, Inc., 26 C.B.C.2d 1398 (B. Ct., E.D. Va. 1992).

When determining the cramdown interest rate to be applied to a wrap around mortgage, the court should impose the "time value of money approach" which takes an appropriate risk free rate and adds an upward adjustment to take into account risks associated with the debtor, the security, and the plan. *In re* Oaks Partners, Ltd., 26 C.B.C.2d 721 (B. Ct., N.D. Ga. 1991).

The contribution of adequate new capital in money or money's worth, in return for a future participation in an enterprise which is reasonably equivalent to the contribution, is an independent act and does not violate the absolute priority rule, but, when former equity holders make such contributions, creditors are entitled to the present value of all property of an insolvent debtor existing at confirmation before stockholders may participate. *In re* Woodscape Ltd. Partnership, 26 C.B.C.2d 305 (B. Ct., D. Md. 1991).

While the definition of "fair and equitable" with respect to a debtor's proposed plan is no longer a matter of common law, its codification in section 1129(b) continues to retain the new value exception as well as a "partial" absolute priority rule, both of which were well-known elements of the common law definition, even though the plain language of the statute does not contain this exception. The new value exception may be applied when certain clear conditions are met, as when the value is: (1) new, (2) necessary, (3) reasonably equivalent to the interest being received, (4) substantial, and (5) in money or money's worth. *In re* Triple R Holdings, L.P., 26 C.B.C.2d 356 (B. Ct., N.D. Cal. 1991).

In establishing the appropriate "cramdown" rate of interest to be applied in chapter 11 cases, the primary emphasis should be upon determining the appropriate riskless rate to reach the present value of the deferred stream of payments to the secured creditor, with an additional upward adjustment possible in an appropriate case to take into account any general risk attributable to the closeness of the decision finding the proposed plan to be feasible. *In re* Computer Optics, Inc., 24 C.B.C.2d 1812 (B. Ct., D.N.H. 1991).

If there has not yet been an occasion for a decision defining the scope of a regulatory authority's jurisdiction in the reorganization of an electric cooperative, and the regulatory authority has state law authority over electric utilities, it is appropriate that a court allow the regulatory authority to be heard at hearings to consider disclosure statements and proposed plans of reorganization of the cooperative. *In re* Eastern Maine Electric Cooperative, Inc., 24 C.B.C.2d 967 (B. Ct., D. Me. 1990).

Although appraisal evidence should generally be presented, it is not the *sine qua non* of compliance with the best interests of creditors test codified in section 1129(a)(7)(ii). *In re* Crowthers McCall Pattern, Inc., 24 C.B.C.2d 611 (B. Ct., S.D.N.Y. 1990).

Section 1129(b)(2)(A)(i)(II), which requires deferred cash payments to be valued as of the plan's effective date, is not fulfilled if the plan's effective date lacks certainty. *In re* SIS Corp., 24 C.B.C.2d 473 (B. Ct., N.D. Ohio 1990).

Language in a plan of reorganization that is ambiguous in form will be interpreted against the party who is responsible for creating the ambiguity. *In re* Mako, Inc., 24 C.B.C.2d 341 (B. Ct., W.D. Okla. 1990).

To be consistent with the requirement that in a chapter 11 case a creditor must receive an amount not less than it would receive in a liquidation as of the effective date of the plan, the secured amount of a creditor's claim should be determined by valuing collateral as of the confirmation date. In the Matter of Seip, 24 C.B.C.2d 123 (B. Ct., D. Neb. 1990).

An individual debtor's chapter 11 plan which attempts to restrict the nonbankruptcy law rights of holders of nondischargeable debts and to defer discharge until all such debts have been satisfied will not be confirmed. *In re* Amigoni, 22 C.B.C.2d 468 (B. Ct., N.D. Ill. 1989).

References

5 *Collier on Bankruptcy* ch. 1129 (Matthew Bender 15th ed.).

3 *Collier Bankruptcy Manual* ch. 1129 (Matthew Bender 3d ed.).

5 *Collier Bankruptcy Practice Guide* ch. 90 (Matthew Bender).

Anderson, *The Reorganization Plan, the Collateral, and Third-Party Guarantors,* 1 F & G Bankr. L. Rev. 18 (1989).

Ayer, *Rethinking Absolute Priority After Ahlers,* 87 Mich. L. Rev. 963 (1989).

The Absolute Priority Rule and the Family Farmer—Setting a Debtor's Priorities Straight: Norwest Bank Worthington v. Ahlers, 22 Creighton L. Rev. 139 (1988/89).

Bell, *Making Cramdown Palatable: Postconfirmation Interest on Secured Claims in a Chapter 11 Cramdown,* 23 Willamette L. Rev. 405 (1987).

Carbiener, *Present Value in Bankruptcy: The Search for an Appropriate Cramdown Discount Rate,* 32 S.D.L. Rev. 42 (1987).

Chapter 11 Confirmation: Increasing Judicial Discretion, 4 Bankr. Dev. J. 191 (1987).

Comment, *Postpetition Financing: Is There Life After Debt?,* 8 Bankr. Dev. J. 575 (1991).

Harwood, *Obtaining Credit in Chapter 11,* 32 N.H.B.J. 35 (1991).

Lenders Face New Headaches as Courts Trim Mortgages, Com. L. Bull. 11 (1990).

Leveraged Debtors Opt for New Out: Prepackaged Chapter 11, 5 Com. L. Bull. 8 (1990).

Levin, *Retention of Ownership Interest Over Creditor Objection—How Intangible and Insubstantial May the Substantial Contribution Be?,* 92 Com. L. J. 101 (1987).

Maxwell, *Handling Unpaid Trust Fund Taxes in Chapter 11,* 1 F & G Bankr. L. Rev. 15 (1989).

Miller, *Valuing the Assets in a Chapter 11 Reorganization,* 1 F & G Bankr. L. Rev. 54 (1989).

Note, *The Proper Discount Rate Under the Chapter 11 Cramdown Provision: Should Secured Creditors Retain Their State Law Entitlements?,* 72 Va. L. Rev. 1499 (1986).

Pollard and Brooks, *Deferring Interest and Reducing Plan Payments Through Negative Amortization,* 3 F & G Bankr. L. Rev. 5 (1991).

Schermer and Bartz, *Negative Amortization and Plan Confirmation: Is It Fair and Equitable Under Section 1129(b) of the Bankruptcy Code?,* 8 Bankr. Dev. J. 1 (1991).

White, *Absolute Priority and New Value,* 8 Cooley L. Rev. 1 (1991).

SUBCHAPTER III

Postconfirmation Matters

SECTION 1141 (11 U.S.C. § 1141)

§ 1141. Effect of confirmation.

(a) Except as provided in subsections (d)(2) and (d)(3) of this section, the provisions of a confirmed plan bind the debtor, any entity issuing securities under the plan, any entity acquiring property under the plan, and any creditor, equity security holder, or general partner in the debtor, whether or not the claim or interest of such creditor, equity security holder, or general partner is impaired under the plan and whether or not such creditor, equity security holder, or general partner has accepted the plan.

(b) Except as otherwise provided in the plan or the order confirming the plan, the confirmation of a plan vests all of the property of the estate in the debtor.

(c) Except as provided in subsections (d)(2) and (d)(3) of this section and except as otherwise provided in the plan or in the order confirming the plan, after confirmation of a plan, the property dealt with by the plan is free and clear of all claims and interests of creditors, equity security holders, and of general partners in the debtor.

(d)(1) Except as otherwise provided in this subsection, in the plan, or in the order confirming the plan, the confirmation of a plan—

   (A) discharges the debtor from any debt that arose before the date of such confirmation, and any debt of a kind specified in section 502(g), 502(h) or 502(i) of this title, whether or not—

      (i) a proof of the claim based on such debt is filed or deemed filed under section 501 of this title;

(ii) such claim is allowed under section 502 of this title; or

(iii) the holder of such claim has accepted the plan; and

(B) terminates all rights and interests of equity security holders and general partners provided for by the plan.

(2) The confirmation of a plan does not discharge an individual debtor from any debt excepted from discharge under section 523 of this title.

(3) The confirmation of a plan does not discharge a debtor if—

(A) the plan provides for the liquidation of all or substantially all of the property of the estate;

(B) the debtor does not engage in business after consummation of the plan; and

(C) the debtor would be denied a discharge under section 727(a) of this title if the case were a case under chapter 7 of this title.

(4) The court may approve a written waiver of discharge executed by the debtor after the order for relief under this chapter.

Bankruptcy Rule References: 2002, 3020, 4004, 4005, 4006 and 4008

Legislative History

Subsection (a) of this section makes the provision of a confirmed plan binding on the debtor, an entity issuing securities under the plan, any entity acquiring property under the plan, and any creditor, equity security holder, or general partner in the debtor, whether or not the claim or interest of the creditor, equity security holder, or partner is impaired under the plan and whether or not he has accepted the plan. There are two exceptions, enumerated in paragraph (2) and (3) of subsection (d).

Unless the plan or the order confirming the plan provides otherwise, the confirmation of a plan vests all of the property of the estate in the debtor and releases it from all claims and interests of creditors, equity security holders and general partners.

[*House Report No. 95–595, 95th Cong., 1st Sess. 418 (1977); Senate Report No. 95–989, 95th Cong., 2d Sess. 129 (1978).*]

Subsection (d) contains the discharge for a reorganized debtor. Paragraph (1) specifies that the confirmation of a plan discharges the debtor from any debt that arose before the date of the order for relief unless the plan or the order confirming the plan provides otherwise. The discharge is effective against those claims whether or not proof of the claim is filed (or deemed filed), and whether or not the claim is allowed. The discharge also terminates all rights and interests of equity security holders and general partners provided for by the plan. The paragraph permits the plan or the order confirming the plan to provide otherwise, and excepts certain debts from the discharge as provided in paragraphs (2) and (3).

Paragraph (2) of subsection (d) makes clear what taxes remain nondischargeable in the case of a corporate debtor emerging from a reorganization under chapter 11. Nondischargeable taxes in such a reorganization are the priority taxes (under section 507) and tax payments which come due during and after the proceeding under a deferred or part-payment agreement which the debtor had entered into with the tax authority before the bankruptcy proceedings began. On the other hand, a corporation which is taken over by its creditors through a plan of reorganization will not continue to be liable for nonpriority taxes arising from the corporation's prepetition fraud, failure to file a return, or failure to file a timely return, since the creditors who take over the reorganized company should not bear the burden of acts for which the creditors were not at fault.

Paragraph (3) specifies that the debtor is not discharged by the confirmation of a plan if the plan is a liquidating plan and if the debtor would be denied discharge in a liquidation case under section 727. Specifically, if all or substantially all of the distribution under the plan is of all or substantially all of the property of the estate or the proceeds of it, if the business, if any, of the debtor does not continue, and if the debtor would be denied a discharge under section 727 (such as if the debtor were not an individual or if he had committed an act that would lead to denial of discharge), the chapter 11 discharge is not granted.

Paragraph (4) authorizes the court to approve a waiver of discharge by the debtor.

[Senate Report No. 95–989, 95th Cong., 2d Sess. 129 (1978).]

Section 1141(d) of the House amendment is derived from a comparable provision contained in the Senate amendment. However, section 1141(d)(2) of the House amendment is derived from the House bill as preferable to the Senate amendment. It is necessary for a corporation or partnership undergoing reorganization to be able to present its creditors with a fixed list of liabilities upon which the creditors or third parties can make intelligent decisions. Retaining an exception for discharge with respect to nondischargeable taxes would leave an undesirable uncertainty surrounding reorganizations that is unacceptable. Section 1141(d)(3) is derived from the Senate amendment. Section 1141(d)(4) is likewise derived from the Senate amendment.

[124 Cong. Rec. H 11,105 (Sept. 28, 1978); S 17,422 (Oct. 6, 1978).]

Comment

Section 1141(a), derived from Section 224(a) of the former Bankruptcy Act, states who is bound by the provisions of a confirmed plan.

Section 1141(b), derived from the first clause of Section 216(10) of the former Act, provides for vesting the estate in the debtor except as otherwise provided in the plan or in the order approving the plan.

Section 1141(c), derived from Section 226 of the former Act, provides that with certain exceptions property dealt with by the plan is free and clear of claims and interests of creditors, stockholders and general partners.

Section 1141(d), derived from Section 228 of the former Act, contains the rules applicable to discharge of debts in a chapter 11 case.

Under section 1141(d)(1) confirmation discharges a debtor from claims whether or not proofs are filed, and whether or not the claim is allowed. Such discharge terminates all rights and interests of equity security holders and general partners provided for by the plan, but the plan or the order confirming discharge *may provide otherwise.* Subsections (d)(2) and (d)(3) except certain debts from discharge. Under paragraph (2), an *individual* debtor is not discharged of debts enumerated in section 523(a), and under paragraph (3) a debtor is not discharged by a liquidating plan or if debtor would be denied discharge under section 727(a) were the case under chapter 7. Subsection (d)(4), providing that the court may approve a written waiver of discharge executed by the debtor, had no counterpart in the former Bankruptcy Act.

Bankruptcy Rule 4004(a) provides that a complaint objecting to the debtor's discharge is to be filed, in a chapter 11 case, not later than the first date set for the confirmation hearing. Not less than 25 days notice of the time so fixed shall be given in the manner provided by Rule 2002(f) to the United States trustee and to all creditors, and to the trustee and the trustee's attorney. Subdivision (d) makes a proceeding commenced by a complaint objecting to discharge an adversary proceeding governed by Part VII of the rules.

Bankruptcy Rule 4005 provides that at the trial on a complaint objecting to a discharge, the plaintiff has the burden of providing the objection.

Bankruptcy Rule 4006 provides that if an order is entered denying or revoking a discharge or if a waiver of discharge is filed, the clerk, after the order becomes final or the waiver is filed, shall promptly give notice thereof to all creditors as provided in Rule 2002.

As to debts of an *individual* chapter 11 debtor that are excepted from discharge by sections 1141(d)(1) and 523, *see* Comment to section 523.

As to denial of discharge of a chapter 11 debtor pursuant to sections 1141(d)(2) and 727(a), *see* Comment to section 727.

1984 Amendments: Minor technical changes were made in subsection (a) of section 1141, and subsection (c) was revised for clarification.

Case Annotations

Section 1141(a), which provides that a confirmed plan is binding on all creditors, does not excuse the trustee from the duty to file returns and pay taxes for the debtors when the plan is silent on the issue. Holywell v. Smith, 503 U.S. —, 112 S. Ct. 1021, 117 L. Ed. 2d 196, 26 C.B.C.2d 1 (1992).

A preconfirmation chapter 11 creditor, bound by a chapter 11 confirmation order, may not, upon conversion of the debtor's case to chapter 7, contest the discharge or dischargeability of the debt owed to the creditor on the basis of preconfirmation acts or the preconfirmation debt. A creditor has the right to challenge a debtor's discharge and dischargeability of debt if: 1) the creditor's debt arose at or after confirmation; and 2) the debtor committed postconfirmation acts that support denial of discharge or render the debt nondischargeable. Matter of Pavlovich, 952 F.2d 114, 26 C.B.C.2d 542 (5th Cir. 1992).

A creditor's right to setoff under section 553 survives confirmation of a debtor's chapter 11 plan despite the provision in section 1141 for discharge of prepetition debts upon confirmation and despite the general discharge purpose of a chapter 11 confirmation to enable a debtor to continue in business. In re De Laurentiis Entertainment Group, Inc., 963 F.2d 1269, 26 C.B.C.2d 1435 (9th Cir. 1992).

An IRS claim for trust fund taxes retains its seventh priority level claim in a second of serial corporate chapter 11 filings because the section 523 exception to the discharge of *individual* debtors for tax liability does not support the inference that Congress intended corporate debtors to receive a discharge from all debts that arose prior to confirmation of the reorganization plan. Matter of Official Comm. of Unsecured Creditors of White Farm Equip. Co., 943 F.2d 752, 25 C.B.C.2d 612 (7th Cir. 1991).

A creditor may not be bound by a debtor's confirmed reorganization plan if it did not receive formal notice of the bar date or confirmation hearing because to so bind the creditor would violate its Fifth Amendment due process rights. Although a creditor may have actual knowledge of the pendency of a bankruptcy proceeding, absent formal notice of deadlines, bar dates and hearings, its claims cannot be discharged. In re Unioil, 948 F.2d 678, 25 C.B.C.2d 1493 (10th Cir. 1991). See also In re Spring Valley Farms, Inc., 863 F.2d 832, 21 C.B.C.2d 651 (11th Cir. 1989) (section 1141 will not operate to discharge the debt of a creditor who was known to a debtor but who failed to receive notice of the claims's bar date, even if the creditor had actual knowledge of the existence of the chapter 11 case).

Participants to a chapter 11 plan who are not creditors of the estate are not bound by the plan until they acquire property thereunder or unless they agree to be so bound pursuant to general contract law. Paul v. Monts, 906 F.2d 1468, 23 C.B.C.2d 380 (10th Cir. 1990).

Differences in the treatment of malicious and willful tort claims in individual bankruptcy cases and corporate reorganization cases have a rational basis and as such are constitutional, even if the claims are of involuntary creditors such as the holders of mass tort claims. Beard v. A.H. Robins Co., Inc., 828 F.2d 1029, 17 C.B.C.2d 595 (4th Cir. 1987).

Because assets which are not drawn into a confirmed plan vest in the debtor upon confirmation, matters concerning the disposition of such non-plan assets do not affect the implementation or execution of the plan. This does not mean, however, that the court loses all jurisdiction over those assets, for any modification of the plan might extend to the realization of estate property not included in the original plan. Goodman v. Phillip R. Curtis Enters., Inc. (*In re* Goodman), 809 F.2d 228, 16 C.B.C.2d 277 (4th Cir. 1987).

When a creditor has received mail notice of the proof of claim bar date, has chosen to participate in a chapter 11 case, cannot demonstrate that the trustee had knowledge of alleged prepetition antitrust violations and, in bad faith, tried to prevent the filing of the antitrust claims, the finality of the confirmation of the reorganization plan will be given effect so as to prevent the creditor from pursuing long after the consummation of the plan the antitrust actions, which it alleges were unknown to it during the reorganization case; the creditor has received all the notice due it under the Constitution. *In re* Penn Central Transp. Co., 771 F.2d 762, 13 C.B.C.2d 422 (3d Cir.) (decided under the 1898 Act), *cert. denied sub nom.* Pinney Dock & Transport Co. v. Penn Central Corp., 474 U.S. 1033, 106 S. Ct. 596, 88 L. Ed. 2d 576 (1985).

Challengers to the validity of the assignment of the powers of avoidance of a debtor in possession to a creditor group are not foreclosed from mounting a postconfirmation challenge to the plan containing the assignment if the issue was not directly adjudicated or involved in the confirmation proceedings. Robison v. First Financial Capital Management Corp. (*In re* Sweetwater), 14 C.B.C.2d 247 (D. Utah 1985).

A corporate debtor which is not entitled to a chapter 7 discharge cannot be discharged under a liquidating chapter 11 plan; therefore, a liquidating corporate debtor with a reorganization plan that includes a provision regarding discharge of all its liabilities violates sections 1129(a)(1) and 1141. *In re* MCorp Fin., Inc., 26 C.B.C.2d 1805 (B. Ct., S.D. Tex. 1992). *See also In re* SIS Corp., 24 C.B.C.2d 473 (B. Ct., N.D. Ohio 1990).

The scope of a plan's implementation is delineated by the Supreme Court decision in *U.S. v. Energy Resources Co.,* calling for a broad, flexible approach in bankruptcy and, therefore, section 1141(d)(2) giving a debtor the ability to deal effectively with its nondischargeable debts is consistent with that decision. *In re* Mercado, 24 C.B.C.2d 1895 (B. Ct., C.D. Cal. 1991).

The constitutionality of a discharge following confirmation of a plan may be challenged when creditors who lacked sufficient notice to file a claim are deprived of due process, but claimants that are not known to be creditors are bound by the confirmation even though they did not receive formal notice. *In re* Brooks Fashion Stores, Inc., 24 C.B.C.2d 1724 (B. Ct., S.D.N.Y. 1991).

Given the policies underlying the nondischargeability of individual debts under section 1141(d)(2), a plan which attempts to discharge debts ordered as restitution for criminal acts will not be confirmed. *In re* Amigoni, 22 C.B.C.2d 468 (B. Ct., N.D. Ill. 1989).

If a debtor agrees to a confirmed reorganization plan that contains an extension of the time period for the filing of objections to discharge, the plan's limitations are controlling and not the limitations specified in Bankruptcy Rule 4004(a). *In re* Moussa, 20 C.B.C.2d 1427 (B. Ct., N.D. Tex. 1989).

When a creditor is on notice of a confirmation and discharge injunction and is deemed to be on notice of their effect intentionally proceeds to enforce a debt subject to a chapter 11 discharge, a court may conclude that the creditor knowingly and willfully violated the injunction by commencing litigation and, accordingly, find that creditor in contempt of court. Bowen v. Residential Fin. Corp. (*In re* Bowen), 19 C.B.C.2d 1010 (B. Ct., D. Minn. 1988).

A corporate debtor's reorganization plan may be conditioned upon the payment of all debts that are extinguished or compromised in the plan, but the bankruptcy court may not bar the corporate debtor's discharge of a claim pursuant to section 523. Krueger v. Push & Pull Enterprises, Inc. (*In re* Push & Pull Enterprises, Inc.), 18 C.B.C.2d 1156 (B. Ct., N.D. Ind. 1988).

When the underlying liability has been discharged in the confirmed plan and language in the sale agreement precludes successor liability, successor liability is preempted by the Code and section 1141(c), which specifically frees a debtor's property from creditors' claims, so that the purchaser of a debtor's assets cannot be held liable in a tort action arising from an accident that occurred after the sale but prior to confirmation of the chapter 11 plan. Volvo White Truck Corp. v. Chambersburg Beverage, Inc. (*In re* White Motor Credit Corp.), 17 C.B.C.2d 293 (B. Ct., N.D. Ohio 1987).

References

5 *Collier on Bankruptcy* ch. 1141 (Matthew Bender 15th ed.).

3 *Collier Bankruptcy Manual* ch. 1141 (Matthew Bender 3d ed.).

5 *Collier Bankruptcy Practice Guide* ch. 90 (Matthew Bender).

Comment, *The Night Before Bankruptcy: The Eighth Circuit's Response to Bankruptcy Estate Planning (Norwest Bank Nebraska v. Tveten, 848 F.2d 871, and Panuska v. Johnson, 80 B.R. 953)*, 15 Wm. Mitchell L. Rev. 643 (1989).

SECTION 1142 (11 U.S.C. § 1142)

§ 1142. Implementation of plan.

(a) Notwithstanding any otherwise applicable nonbankruptcy law, rule, or regulation relating to financial condition, the debtor and any entity organized or to be organized for the purpose of carrying out the plan shall carry out the plan and shall comply with any orders of the court.

(b) The court may direct the debtor and any other necessary party to execute or deliver or to join in the execution or delivery of any instrument required to effect a transfer of property dealt with by a confirmed plan, and to perform any other act, including the satisfaction of any lien, that is necessary for the consummation of the plan.

Bankruptcy Rule Reference: 3020

Comment

Section 1142 of the Code is derived from Sections 224(2) and 227 of the former Bankruptcy Act.

There is no House or Senate Report discussing the provisions relating to the execution of the plan as provided in section 1142.

Bankruptcy Rule 3020(d) provides that notwithstanding confirmation, the court may enter all orders as thereafter become necessary in administering the estate.

Bankruptcy Rule 3022, as amended in 1991, provides that after an estate is fully administered in a chapter 11 case, the court on its own motion or on motion of a party in interest, shall enter a final decree closing the case. [The Advisory Committee Note to this rule states that entry of a final decree closing a chapter 11 case should not be delayed solely because the payments required by the plan have not been completed. The Note lists factors the court should consider in determining whether the estate has been fully administered.]

1984 Amendments: The heading for section 1142 was changed from "Execution of plan" to "Implementation of plan" and minor technical changes were made in subsections (a) and (b).

Case Annotations

Federal tax payments made by a debtor in possession after filing a petition for reorganization under chapter 11, but prior to confirmation of its reorganization plan, are involuntary payments and the bankruptcy court lacks the jurisdiction to order otherwise. United States v. Technical Knockout Graphics, Inc. (*In re* Technical Knockout Graphics, Inc.), 833 F.2d 797, 17 C.B.C.2d 1246 (9th Cir. 1987).

Although the bankruptcy court is granted postconfirmation authority, this authority limits the court to matters concerning the implementation or execution of a confirmed plan. Goodman v. Phillip R. Curtis Enters., Inc. (*In re* Goodman), 809 F.2d 228, 16 C.B.C.2d 277 (4th Cir. 1987).

The bankruptcy court may direct a recalcitrant debtor or other party to perform any act necessary to consummate an approved plan, including the transfer of property under the control of a nondebtor party. Harlow v. Palouse Producers, Inc. (*In re* Harlow Properties, Inc.), 13 C.B.C.2d 1438 (9th Cir., B.A.P., 1985).

A bankruptcy court cannot compel execution of a document if there is no agreement among the parties to the document on the terms of the document. *In re* Modern Steel Treating Co., 25 C.B.C.2d 292 (B. Ct., N.D. Ill. 1991).

The bankruptcy court has discretion, under section 1142(b) of the Code, to fix a reasonable time for distribution of dividends pursuant to a plan. *In re* Goldblatt Bros., Inc., 25 C.B.C.2d 953 (B. Ct., N.D. Ill. 1991).

In confirming a chapter 11 plan which contains provisions relating to retained jurisdiction, a bankruptcy court may retain jurisdiction over postconfirmation litigation only to the point of substantial consummation of the plan as defined in section 1101(2) of the Code. A bankruptcy court should require the relevant jurisdictional provisions to be narrowly written in order to limit the retained jurisdiction to postconfirmation matters appropriately within the bankruptcy court's purview, rather than to broadly confer on it additional jurisdiction that might prove to be broader than appropriate. *In re* Bankeast Corp., 25 C.B.C.2d 1164 (B. Ct., D.N.H. 1991).

When an unexpired lease between a debtor-lessor and a lessee provides for a default in the event that the lessee deserts the premises and ceases to operate a discount store as the lease requires, the lessee has breached the lease as a matter of law if it ceases to operate a discount store and removes its inventory. *In re* Oklahoma Plaza Investors, Ltd., 24 C.B.C.2d 1572 (B. Ct., N.D. Okla. 1991).

A court may order a debtor to implement the terms of a confirmed plan that requires investors to make loan commitments to protect the value of a creditor's collateral, notwithstanding the fact that the order of confirmation is on appeal and an adverse determination might injure the investors. *In re* Century Investment Fund Limited Partnership, 23 C.B.C.2d 1172 (B. Ct., E.D. Wis. 1990).

Resolution of issues involving the disposition of property pursuant to alleged oral agreements between nondebtor third parties after that property has left the estate is not necessary for the administration of the estate or the implementation of the plan and is without the postconfirmation jurisdiction of the bankruptcy court. *In re* Greenley Energy Holdings of Pennsylvania, Inc., 22 C.B.C.2d 853 (B. Ct., E.D. Pa. 1990).

A forum selection clause contained in the postpetition service agreement entered into by the debtor which refers only to the district and state court, with no mention of the bankruptcy court as a potential forum for dispute resolution, will be binding upon the bankruptcy court and will not be overruled unless procured by fraud or overreaching, when enforcement would violate strong public policy of the forum or when enforcement would so seriously inconvenience a party as to be unreasonable. Approval by the bankruptcy court of a postpetition service agreement does not alone confer jurisdiction upon the bankruptcy court to resolve all subsequent disputes regardless of their connection to the bankruptcy case. *In re* Almarc Corp., 20 C.B.C.2d 616 (B. Ct., E.D. Pa. 1988).

References

5 *Collier on Bankruptcy* ch. 1142 (Matthew Bender 15th ed.).

3 *Collier Bankruptcy Manual* ch. 1142 (Matthew Bender 3d ed.).

5 *Collier Bankruptcy Practice Guide* ch. 90 (Matthew Bender).

SECTION 1143 (11 U.S.C. § 1143)

§ 1143.   Distribution. If a plan requires presentment or surrender of a security or the performance of any other act as a condition to participation in distribution under the plan, such action shall be taken not later than five years after the date of the entry of the order of confirmation. Any entity that has not within such time presented or surrendered such entity's security or taken any such other action that the plan requires may not participate in distribution under the plan.

Bankruptcy Rule References: 3021 and 3022

Legislative History

Section 1143 fixes a five year limitation on presentment or surrender of securities or the performance of any other act that is a condition to participation in distribution under the plan. The five years runs from the date of the entry of the order of confirmation. Any entity that does not take the appropriate action with [*sic*] the five-year period is barred from participation in the distribution under the plan.

[*House Report No. 95–595, 95th Cong., 1st Sess. 419 (1977); Senate Report No. 95–989, 95th Cong., 2d Sess. 130 (1978).*]

Comment

Section 1143 is derived from former Bankruptcy Rule 10–405(b) derived in turn from Section 204 of the former Bankruptcy Act.

When a plan requires presentment or surrender of a security or performance of an act as a condition to participate in distribution, section 1143 is mandatory in requiring performance not later than 5 years after confirmation. Former Bankruptcy Rule 10–405(b) was similarly mandatory, while Section 204 of the Act was permissive in this respect.

Bankruptcy Rule 3021 requires distribution, after confirmation, in accordance with the provisions of the plan to holders of stock, bonds, debentures, notes, and other securities of record at the time of the commencement of distribution, whose claims or equity security interests have not been disallowed, and to other creditors whose claims have been allowed, and to indenture trustees who have filed claims under Rule 3003(c)(5) and which are allowed.

Bankruptcy Rule 3022, as amended in 1991, provides that after an estate is fully administered in a chapter 11 case, the court, on its own motion or on motion of a party in interest, shall enter a final order closing the case. [The Advisory Committee Note to this Rule states that entry of a final decree closing a chapter 11 case should not be delayed solely because the payments required by the plan have not been completed.]

Case Annotations

A pledge that does not cover indebtedness owed to a pledgor by the debtor cannot be interpreted to cover new common stock issued by the debtor under a plan of reorganization in cancellation of that indebtedness. In the Matter of Majestic Energy Corp., 835 F.2d 87, 18 C.B.C.2d 78 (5th Cir. 1987).

While section 1143 provides a five year time limit for distribution, it only applies to creditors who must perform an "act" as a condition to participating in the distribution under a plan. *In re* Goldblatt Bros., Inc., 25 C.B.C.2d 953 (B. Ct., N.D. Ill. 1991).

References

5 *Collier on Bankruptcy* ch. 1143 (Matthew Bender 15th ed.).

3 *Collier Bankruptcy Manual* ch. 1143 (Matthew Bender 3d ed.).

6 *Collier Bankruptcy Practice Guide* ch. 92 (Matthew Bender).

SECTION 1144 (11 U.S.C. § 1144)

§ 1144. **Revocation of an order of confirmation.** On request of a party in interest at any time before 180 days after the date of the entry of the order of confirmation, and after notice and a hearing, the court may revoke such order if and only if such order was procured by fraud. An order under this section revoking an order of confirmation shall—

(1) contain such provisions as are necessary to protect any entity acquiring rights in good faith reliance on the order of confirmation; and

(2) revoke the discharge of the debtor.

Bankruptcy Rule References: 7001 and 9024

Legislative History

If an order of confirmation was procured by fraud, then the court may revoke the order on request of a party in interest if the request is made before 180 days after the date of the entry of the order of confirmation. The order revoking the order of confirmation must revoke the discharge of the debtor, and contain such provisions as are necessary to protect any entity acquiring rights in good faith reliance on the order of confirmation.

[*House Report No. 95–595, 95th Cong., 1st Sess. 419 (1977); Senate Report No. 95–989, 95th Cong., 2d Sess. 130 (1978).*]

Comment

Section 1144, providing for revocation of an order of confirmation is derived from Chapter XI, Section 386 of the former Bankruptcy Act.

The ground for revocation of confirmation in section 1144 of the Code is the same as under the former Bankruptcy Act—that confirmation was procured by fraud. Under the Code "request" for revocation must be made within 180 days after entry of the order of confirmation, while under the Act an "application" to revoke must have been made within a like period, measured by months (six months).

The order of revocation, under the Code, requires revocation of debtor's discharge but provides protection of those who acquired rights in "good faith reliance" on the order of confirmation.

Bankruptcy Rule 7001(5) provides that a proceeding in the bankruptcy court to revoke an order of confirmation of a chapter 11 plan is an adversary proceeding commenced by service of a summons and complaint and governed by the Part VII rules.

Bankruptcy Rule 9024 makes it clear that the time to file a complaint to revoke an order confirming a plan under section 1144 may not be circumvented by invoking Fed. R. Civ. P 60(b).

1984 Amendments: Section 1144 was amended to emphasize that an order of confirmation may be revoked "if and only" if procured by fraud.

Case Annotations

A court cannot revoke an order of confirmation when the motion to revoke is made more than 180 days after confirmation. *In re* Modern Steel Treating Co., 25 C.B.C.2d 292 (B. Ct., N.D. Ill. 1991).

Pursuant to section 1127(b), the date that a bankruptcy court order confirms a modified chapter 11 plan is the date from which the 180-day time limit for filing a complaint seeking revocation of confirmation must be filed under section 1144. *In re* TM Carlton House Partners, Ltd., 22 C.B.C.2d 972 (B. Ct., E.D. Pa. 1990).

The showing of fraud as the only basis for revocation of a plan does not supersede the court's power under F.R. Civ. P. 60(b)(4) to vacate a plan due to lack of notice. *In re* Rideout, 18 C.B.C.2d 1165 (B. Ct., N.D. Ohio 1988).

A debtor's statements with regard to the value of his property may be the basis of a proceeding under section 1144 even if those statements constitute "opinions," provided that the remaining elements of section 1144 are met. Reliance by a creditor or third party is not a necessary element of fraud under section 1144; it is sufficient that a showing is made that the court relied on the debtor's misrepresentations as to the value of property and that a creditor or third party was damaged thereby. United States v. Kostoglou (*In re* Kostoglou), 17 C.B.C.2d 69 (B. Ct., N.D. Ohio 1987).

Once a chapter 11 plan is confirmed, the debtors' subsequent inability to consummate the plan will not permit conversion of the case so as to receive a chapter 7 discharge. *In re* Metrocraft Publishing Servs., Inc., 10 C.B.C.2d 1182 (B. Ct., N.D. Ga. 1984).

There must be clear, concrete proof of actual fraud to revoke confirmation of a reorganization plan under section 1144. *In re* Hertz, 10 C.B.C.2d 316 (B. Ct., S.D.N.Y. 1984).

References

5 *Collier on Bankruptcy* ch. 1144 (Matthew Bender 15th ed.).

3 *Collier Bankruptcy Manual* ch. 1144 (Matthew Bender 3d ed.).

5 *Collier Bankruptcy Practice Guide* ch. 90 (Matthew Bender).

SECTION 1145 (11 U.S.C. § 1145)

§ 1145. Exemption from securities laws.

(a) Except with respect to an entity that is an underwriter as defined in subsection (b) of this section, section 5 of the Securities Act of 1933 (15 U.S.C. 77e) and any State or local law requiring registration for offer or sale of a security or registration or licensing of an issuer of, underwriter of, or broker or dealer in, a security does not apply to—

(1) the offer or sale under a plan of a security of the debtor, of an affiliate participating in a joint plan with the debtor, or of a successor to the debtor under the plan—

(A) in exchange for a claim against, an interest in, or a claim for an administrative expense in the case concerning, the debtor or such affiliate; or

(B) principally in such exchange and partly for cash or property;

(2) the offer of a security through any warrant, option, right to subscribe, or conversion privilege that was sold in the manner specified in paragraph (1) of this subsection, or the sale of a security upon the exercise of such a warrant, option, right, or privilege;

(3) the offer or sale, other than under a plan, of a security of an issuer other than the debtor or an affiliate, if—

(A) such security was owned by the debtor on the date of the filing of the petition;

(B) the issuer of such security is—

(i) required to file reports under section 13 or 15(d) of the Securities Exchange Act of 1934 (15 U.S.C. 78m or 78o(d)); and

(ii) in compliance with the disclosure and reporting provision of such applicable section; and

(C) such offer or sale is of securities that do not exceed—

(i) during the two-year period immediately following the date of the filing of the petition, four percent of the securities of such class outstanding on such date; and

(ii) during any 180-day period following such two-year period, one percent of the securities outstanding at the beginning of such 180-day period; or

(4) a transaction by a stockbroker in a security that is executed after a transaction of a kind specified in paragraph (1) or (2) of this subsection in such security and before the expiration of 40 days after the first date on which such

security was bona fide offered to the public by the issuer or by or through an underwriter, if such stockbroker provides, at the time of or before such transaction by such stockbroker, a disclosure statement approved under section 1125 of this title, and, if the court orders, information supplementing such disclosure statement.

(b)(1) Except as provided in paragraph (2) of this subsection and except with respect to ordinary trading transactions of an entity that is not an issuer, an entity is an underwriter under section 2(11) of the Securities Act of 1933 (15 U.S.C. 77b(11)), if such entity—

(A) purchases a claim against, interest in, or claim for an administrative expense in the case concerning, the debtor, if such purchase is with a view to distribution of any security received or to be received in exchange for such a claim or interest;

(B) offers to sell securities offered or sold under the plan for the holders of such securities;

(C) offers to buy securities offered or sold under the plan from the holders of such securities, if such offer to buy is—

(i) with a view to distribution of such securities; and

(ii) under an agreement made in connection with the plan, with the consummation of the plan, or with the offer or sale of securities under the plan; or

(D) is an issuer, as used in such section 2(11), with respect to such securities.

(2) An entity is not an underwriter under section 2(11) of the Securities Act of 1933 or under paragraph (1) of this subsection with respect to an agreement that provides only for—

(A)(i) the matching or combining of fractional interests in securities offered or sold under the plan into whole interests; or

(ii) the purchase or sale of such fractional interests from or to entities receiving such fractional interests under the plan; or

(B) the purchase or sale for such entities of such fractional or whole interests as are necessary to adjust for any remaining fractional interests after such matching.

(3) An entity other than an entity of the kind specified in paragraph (1) of this subsection is not an underwriter under section 2(11) of the Securities Act of 1933 with respect to any securities offered or sold to such entity in the manner specified in subsection (a)(1) of this section.

(c) An offer or sale of securities of the kind and in the manner specified under subsection (a)(1) of this section is deemed to be a public offering.

(d) The Trust Indenture Act of 1939 (15 U.S.C. 77aaa et seq.) does not apply to a note issued under the plan that matures not later than one year after the effective date of the plan.

Legislative History

This section, derived from similar provisions found in sections 264, 393, and 518 of the Bankruptcy Act, provides a limited exemption from the securities laws for securities issued under a plan of reorganization and for certain other securities. Subsection (a) exempts from the requirements of section 5 of the Securities Act of 1933 and from any State or local law requiring registration or licensing of an issuer of, underwriter of, or broker or dealer in, a security, the offer or sale of certain securities.

Paragraph (1) of subsection (a) exempts the offer or sale under section 364 of any security that is not an equity security or convertible into an equity security. This paragraph is designed to facilitate the issuance of certificates of indebtedness, and should be read in light of the amendment made in section 306 of Title III to section 3(a)(7) of the 1933 Act.

Paragraph (2) of subsection (a) exempts the offer or sale of any security of the debtor, a successor to the debtor, or an affiliate in a joint plan, distributed under a plan if such security is exchanged in principal part for securities of the debtor or for allowed claims or administrative expenses. This exemption is carried over from present law, except as to administrative claims, but is limited to prevent distribution of securities to other than claim holders or equity security holders of the debtor or the estate.

[*House Report No. 95–595, 95th Cong., 1st Sess. 419 (1977); Senate Report No. 95–989, 95th Cong., 2d Sess. 130 (1978).*]

Paragraph (3) of subsection (a) exempts the offer or sale of any security that arises from the exercise of a subscription right or from the exercise of a conversion privilege when such subscription right or conversion privilege was issued under a plan. This exemption is necessary in order to enhance the marketability of subscription rights or conversion privileges, including warrants, offered or sold under a plan. This is present law.

[*House Report No. 95–595, 95th Cong., 1st Sess. 419 (1977).*]

Paragraph (4) of subsection (a) exempts sales of portfolio securities, excluding securities of the debtor or its affiliate, owned by the debtor on the date of the filing of the petition. The purpose of this exemption is to allow the debtor or trustee to sell or distribute, without allowing manipulation schemes, restricted portfolio securities held or acquired by the debtor. Subparagraph (B) of § 1145(a)(4) limits the exemption to securities of a company that is required to file reports under section 13 of the Securities Act and that is in compliance with all requirements for the continuance of trading those securities. This limitation effectively prevents selling into the market "cats and dogs" of a nonreporting company. Subparagraph (C) places a limitation on the amount of restricted securities that may be distributed. During the case, the trustee may sell up to four percent of each class of restricted securities at any time during the first two years and one percent during any 180-day period thereafter. This relaxation of the resale rules for debtors in holding restricted securities is similar to but less extensive than the relaxation in SEC Rule 114(c)(3)(v) for the estates of deceased holders of securities.

Paragraph (5) contains an exemption for brokers and dealers (stockbrokers, as defined in title 11) akin to the exemption provided by section 4(3)(A) of the Securities Act of 1933. Instead of being required to supply a prospectus, however, the stockbroker is required to supply the approved disclosure statement, and if the court orders, information supplementing the disclosure statement. Under present law, the stockbroker is not required to supply anything. [*Ed. Note:* Paragraph (5) referred to in the House and Senate Reports was deleted from the Bill.]

Subsection (b) is new. The subsection should be read in light of the amendment in section 306 of title III to the 1933 Act. It specifies the standards under which a creditor, equity security holder, or other entity acquiring securities under the plan may resell them. The Securities Act places limitations on sales by underwriters. This subsection defines who is an underwriter, and thus restricted, and who is free to resell. Paragraph (1) enumerates real underwriters that participate in a classical underwriting. A person is an underwriter if he purchases a claim against, interest in, or claim for an administrative expense in the case concerning, the debtor, with a view to distribution of any security received or to be received in exchange for the claim or interest. This provision covers the purchase of a certificate of indebtedness issued under proposed 11 U.S.C. § 364 and purchased from the debtor, if the purchase of the certificate was with a view to distribution.

A person is also an underwriter if he offers to sell securities offered or sold under the plan for the holders of such securities, or offers to buy securities offered or sold under the plan from the holders of such securities, if the offer to buy is with a view to distribution of the securities and under an agreement made in connection with the plan, with the consummation of the plan or with the offer or sale of securities under the plan. Finally, a person is an underwriter if he is an issuer, as used in section 2(11) of the Securities Act of 1933.

Paragraph (2) of subsection (b) exempts from the definition of underwriter any entity to the extent that any agreement that would bring the entity under the definition in paragraph (1) provides only for the matching combination of fractional interests in the covered securities or the purchase or sale of fractional interests. This paragraph and paragraph (1) are modeled after former Rule 133 of the Securities and Exchange Commission.

Paragraph (3) specifies that if an entity is not an underwriter under the provisions of paragraph (1), as limited by paragraph (2), then the entity is not an underwriter for the purposes of the Securities Act of 1933 with respect to the covered securities, that is, those offered or sold in an exempt transaction specified in subsection (a)(2). This makes clear that the current definition of underwriter in section 2(11) of the Securities Act of 1933 does not apply to such a creditor. The definition in that section technically applies to any person that purchases securities with "a view to distribution." If literally applied, it would prevent any creditor in a bankruptcy case from selling securities received without filing a registration statement or finding another exemption.

Subsection (b) is a first run transaction exemption and does not exempt a creditor that, for example, some years later becomes an underwriter by reacquiring securities originally issued under a plan.

Subsection (c) makes an offer or sale of securities under the plan in exempt transaction (as specified in subsection (a)(2)) a public offering, in order to prevent characterization of the distribution as a "private placement" which would result in restrictions, under Rule 144 of the S.E.C., on the resale of the securities.

[*House Report No. 95–595, 95th Cong., 1st Sess. 420–421 (1977); Senate Report No. 95–989, 95th Cong., 2d Sess. 132 (1978).*]

Section 1145 of the House amendment deletes a provision contained in section 1145(a)(1) of the House bill in favor of a more adequate provision contained in section 364(f) of the House amendment. In addition, section 1145(d) has been added to indicate that the Trust Indenture Act does not apply to a commercial note issued under a plan, if the note matures not later than 1 year after the effective date of the plan. Some commercial notes receive such an exemption under 304(a)(4) of the Trust Indenture Act of 1939 (15 U.S.C. § 77ddd(a)(4)) and others may receive protection by incorporation by reference into the Trust Indenture Act of securities exempt under section 3a(3), (7), (9), or (10) of the Securities Act of 1933.

In light of the amendments made to the Securities Act of 1933 in title III of the House amendment to H.R. 8200, a specific exemption from the Trust Indenture Act is required in order to create certainty regarding plans of reorganization. Section 1145(d) is not intended to imply that commercial notes issued under a plan that matures more than 1 year after the effective date of the plan are automatically covered by the Trust Indenture Act of 1939 since such notes may fall within another exemption thereto.

One other point with respect to section 1145 deserves comment. Section 1145(a)(3) grants a debtor in possession or trustee in chapter 11 an extremely narrow portfolio security exemption from section 5 of the Securities Act of 1933 or any comparable State law. The provision was considered by Congress and adopted after much study. The exemption is reasonable and is more restrictive than comparable provisions under the Securities Act relating to the estate of decedents. Subsequent to passage of H.R. 8200 by the House of Representatives, the Securities and Exchange Commission promulgated Rule 148 to treat with this problem under existing law. Members of Congress received opinions from attorneys indicating dissatisfaction with the Commission's rule [*sic*] although the rule has been amended, the ultimate limitation of 1 percent promulgated by the Commission is wholly unacceptable.

The Commission rule would permit a trustee or debtor in possession to distribute securities at the rate of 1 percent every 6 months. Section 1145(a)(3) permits the trustee to distribute 4 percent of the securities during the 2-year period immediately following the date of the filing of the petition. In addition, the security must be of a reporting company under section 13 of the Securities and Exchange Act of 1934, and must be in compliance with all applicable requirements for the continuing of trading in the security on the date that the trustee offers or sells the security.

With these safeguards the trustee or debtor in possession should be able to distribute 4 percent of the securities of a class at any time during the 2-year period immediately following the date of the filing of the petition in the interests of expediting bankruptcy administration. The same rationale that applies in expeditiously terminating decedents' estates applies no less to an estate under title 11.

[*124 Cong. Rec. H 11,105 (Sept. 28, 1978); S 17,422 (Oct. 6, 1978).*]

Comment

Section 1145 is derived from provisions found in Sections 264, 393 and 515 of the former Bankruptcy Act which related to cases under Chapters X, XI and XII respectively.

Section 1145 of the Code deals with the issuance or distribution of security that may be required under the plan or in the liquidation of portfolio securities. The House Report gives a detailed analysis of each subsection of section 1145.

Exempted Securities

Section 306 of the Bankruptcy Reform Act of 1978 (in title III) amended section 3(a)(7), (9), (10) of the Securities Act of 1933 (15 U.S.C. § 77c(a)(7), (9), (10)), effective October 1, 1979 (*see* section 402(a) of the Act) as follows:

SEC. 3. (a) Except as hereinafter expressly provided, the provisions of this title shall not apply to any of the following classes of securities:

(1) . . .

* * *

(7) Certificates issued by a receiver or by a trustee or debtor in possession in a case under title 11 of the United States Code, with the approval of the court;

* * *

(9) Except with respect to a security exchanged in a case under title 11 of the United States Code, any security exchanged by the issuer with its existing security holders exclusively where no commission or other remuneration is paid or given directly or indirectly for soliciting such exchange;

(10) Except with respect to a security exchanged in a case under title 11 of the United States Code, any security which is issued in exchange for one or more bona fide outstanding securities, claims or property interests, or partly in such exchange and partly for cash, where the terms and conditions of such issuance and exchange are approved, after a hearing upon the fairness of such terms and conditions at which all persons to whom it is proposed to issue securities in such exchange shall have the right to appear, by any court, or by any official or agency of the United States, or by any State or Territorial banking or insurance commission or other governmental authority expressly authorized by law to grant such approval; . . . .

1984 Amendments: Subsection (a)(3)(B)(i) was amended by insertion of "or 15(d)" and "or 78o(d)." Subsection (a)(3)(B)(ii) was revised, and technical changes were made in subsections (b)(1), (b)(1)(C), (b)(2)(A) and (d).

Case Annotations

Section 1145(b)(1)(D) is intended to include in its definition of "issuer" only the "control person" language of Section 2(11) of the 1933 Securities Act, with the result that a chapter 11 debtor attempting to issue notes pursuant to section 364(b) and (f) is not an underwriter within the meaning of section 1145. Matter of Standard Oil & Exploration of Delaware, Inc., 26 C.B.C.2d 923 (B. Ct., W.D. Mich. 1992).

When a wholly-owned subsidiary of the parent company joins with another of the parent company's subsidiaries, which is a debtor, as a proponent of the proposed chapter 11 plan, then the nondebtor subsidiary is an "affiliate" of the debtor subsidiary within the meaning of section 101(2) and is qualified for exemption from the 1933 Securities Act under section 1145(a)(1) as an "affiliate participating in a joint venture with the debtor." *In re* Frontier Airlines, Inc., 20 C.B.C.2d 486 (B. Ct., D. Colo. 1988).

When an entity will assume the goodwill, property rights and major assets of the chapter 11 debtor, and will also undertake to be burdened with the debtor's liabilities and obligations, the entity is a "successor" to the debtor for the purposes of the exemption provided by section 1145. *In re* Stanley Hotel, Inc., 5 C.B.C.2d 64 (B. Ct., D. Colo. 1981).

References

5 *Collier on Bankruptcy* ch. 1145 (Matthew Bender 15th ed.).

3 *Collier Bankruptcy Manual* ch. 1145 (Matthew Bender 3d ed.).

5 *Collier Bankruptcy Practice Guide* ch. 89 (Matthew Bender).

SECTION 1146 (11 U.S.C. § 1146)

§ 1146. Special tax provisions.

(a) For the purpose of any State or local law imposing a tax on or measured by income, the taxable period of a debtor that is an individual shall terminate on the date of the order for relief under this chapter, unless the case was converted under section 706 of this title.

(b) The trustee shall make a State or local tax return of income for the estate of an individual debtor in a case under this chapter for each taxable period after the order for relief under this chapter during which the case is pending.

(c) The issuance, transfer, or exchange of a security, or the making or delivery of an instrument of transfer under a plan confirmed under section 1129 of this title, may not be taxed under any law imposing a stamp tax or similar tax.

(d) The court may authorize the proponent of a plan to request a determination, limited to questions of law, by a State or local governmental unit charged with responsibility for collection or determination of a tax on or measured by income, of the tax effects, under section 346 of this title and under the law imposing such tax, of the plan. In the event of an actual controversy, the court may declare such effects after the earlier of—

(1) the date on which such governmental unit responds to the request under this subsection; or

(2) 270 days after such request.

Legislative History

Section 1146 of title 11 specifies five subsections which embody special tax provisions that apply in a case under chapter 11 of title 11. Subsection (a) indicates that the tax year of an individual debtor terminates on the date of the order for relief under chapter 11. Termination of the taxable year of the debtor commences the tax period of the estate. If the case was converted from chapter 7 of title 11 then the estate is created as a separate taxable entity dating from the order for relief under chapter 7. If multiple conversion of the case occurs, then the estate is treated as a separate taxable entity on the date of the order for relief under the first chapter under which the estate is a separate taxable entity.

[*House Report No. 95–595, 95th Cong., 1st Sess. 421 (1977).*]

Section 1146 provides special tax rules applicable to title 11 reorganizations. Subsection (a) provides that the taxable period of an individual debtor terminates on the date of the order for relief, unless the case has been converted into a reorganization from a liquidation proceeding.

[*Senate Report No. 95–989, 95th Cong., 2d Sess. 132 (1978).*]

Subsection (b) requires the trustee of an estate of an individual debtor to file an income tax return for each taxable period during which the case is pending.

[*House Report No. 95–595, 95th Cong., 1st Sess. 421 (1977).*]

Subsection (b) requires the trustee of the estate of an individual debtor in a reorganization to file a tax return for each taxable period while the case is pending after the order for relief. For corporations in chapter 11, the trustee is required to file the tax returns due while the case is pending (sec. 346(c)(2)).

[*Senate Report No. 95–989, 95th Cong., 2d Sess. 132 (1978).*]

Subsection (c) exempts from stamp taxes the issuance, transfer, or exchange of a security, or the making or delivery of an instrument of transfer under a plan. The subsection is derived from section 267 of the Bankruptcy Act.

[*House Report No. 95–595, 95th Cong., 1st Sess. 421 (1977).*]

Subsection (c) exempts from Federal, State, or local stamp taxes the issuance, transfer, or exchange of a security, or the making or delivery of an instrument of transfer under a plan. This subsection is derived from section 267 of the present Bankruptcy Act.

[*Senate Report No. 95–989, 95th Cong., 2d Sess. 132 (1978).*]

Subsection (d) permits the court to authorize the proponent of a plan to request a taxing authority to declare the tax effects of such plan. In the event of an actual controversy, the court may declare the tax effects of the plan of reorganization at any time after the earlier of action by such taxing authority or 270 days after the request. Such a declaration, unless appealed, becomes a final judgment and binds any tax authority that was requested by the proponent to determine the tax effects of the plan.

[*House Report No. 95–595, 95th Cong., 1st Sess. 421 (1977).*]

Subsection (d) permits the court to authorize the proponent of a reorganization plan to request from the Internal Revenue Service (or State or local tax authority) an advance ruling on the tax effects of the proposed plan. If a ruling is not obtained within 270 days after the request was made, or if a ruling is obtained but the proponent of the plan disagrees with the ruling, the bankruptcy court may resolve the dispute and determine the tax effects of the proposed plan.

[*Senate Report No. 95–989, 95th Cong., 2d Sess. 133 (1978).*]

Section 1146 of the House amendment represents a compromise between the House bill and Senate amendment.

[*124 Cong. Rec. H 11,105 (Sept. 28, 1978); S 17,422 (Oct. 6, 1978).*]

Section 1146. Special tax provisions: reorganization: The House bill provided rules on the effect of bankruptcy on the taxable year of the debtor and on tax return filing requirements for State and local taxes only. The House bill also exempted from State or local stamp taxes the issuance, transfer, or exchange of a security, or the making or delivery of an instrument of transfer under a plan. The House bill also authorized the bankruptcy court to declare the tax effects of a reorganization plan after the proponent of the plan had requested a ruling from State or local tax authority and either had received an unfavorable ruling or the tax authority had not issued a ruling within 270 days.

The Senate amendment deleted the rules concerning the taxable years of the debtors and tax return filing requirements since the Federal rules were to be considered in the next Congress. It broadened the rule exempting transfers of securities to include Federal stamp or similar taxes, if any. In addition, the Senate amendment deleted the provision which permitted the bankruptcy court to determine the tax effects of a plan.

The House amendment retains the State and local rules in the House bill with one modification. Under the House amendment, the power of the bankruptcy court to declare the tax effects of the plan is limited to issues of law and not to questions of fact such as the allowance of specific deductions. Thus, the bankruptcy court could declare whether the reorganization qualified for taxfree status under State or local tax rules, but it could not declare the dollar amount of any tax attributes that survive the reorganization.

[*124 Cong. Rec. H 11,115 (Sept. 28, 1978); S 17,432 (Oct. 6, 1978).*]

Comment

Section 1146(a) and (b) had no counterpart in the former Bankruptcy Act. Subsection (c) relating to State or local stamp tax or similar tax is derived from Section 267 of the Act.

Section 1146 contains four subsections embodying special tax provisions applying to a chapter 11 case. Subsection (a) deals with the tax year of an individual debtor (for purposes of state or local tax laws) unless that case was originally a liquidation case under chapter 7 that has been converted to a chapter 11 case; subsection (b) requires the trustee to make the state or local tax return for an individual debtor for each taxable year *after* entry of the order for relief; subsection (c) is an exemption from state or local stamp tax laws; and subdivision (d) enables the debtor to obtain a speedy determination (270 days maximum) of the tax effect of a plan. The determination is limited to "questions of law." Thus, the court could declare whether the reorganization qualified for tax free status under state or local law, but could not fix the dollar amounts of any tax attributes that survive the reorganization.

1984 Amendments: Minor technical changes were made in section 1146.

Case Annotations

For a tax to come within the purview of section 1146(c) as a stamp tax, it should possess the following attributes: 1) it is imposed only at the time of transfer or sale of the property at issue; 2) the amount due is determined by the consideration for, the par value of, or the value of the property being transferred; 3) the tax rate is relatively low—one percent or less; 4) it is imposed irrespective of whether the transferor enjoyed a gain or suffered a loss on the underlying transaction; and 5) it is a prerequisite to recording. New York Tax Law § 1441, a gains tax on real estate sales, is not a stamp tax or similar tax, especially since it is based on the profitability of the underlying transaction, and, therefore, is not within the meaning and reach of section 1146(c). *In re* 995 Fifth Avenue Assoc., L.P., 963 F.2d 503, 26 C.B.C.2d 1162 (2d Cir.), *cert denied,* — U.S. —, — S. Ct. —, — L. Ed. 2d — (1992).

A real estate transfer tax is substantially similar to a stamp tax and accordingly is not allowable under the provisions of section 1146(c). However, a capital gains tax cannot be considered to be related to a stamp tax under section 1146(c) because the tax derives from the financial gain the debtor attains rather than from the entire consideration it receives or from the nature of the transaction itself. *In re* Jacoby-Bender, Inc., 10 C.B.C.2d 626 (E.D.N.Y. 1984), *aff'd,* 758 F.2d 840 (2d Cir. 1985).

For the exemption from tax liability to apply, a three pronged test must be fufilled: (1) the tax must be a stamp or similar tax; (2) imposed upon the making or delivery of an instrument transferring an interest in real property; and (3) in connection with a confirmed bankruptcy plan.

In re 995 Fifth Avenue Assocs., L.P., 23 C.B.C.2d 400 (B. Ct., S.D.N.Y. 1990).

A postpetition, preconfirmation sale of a debtor's real property is considered to be "under a plan" and exempt from local taxes when it appears that a chapter 11 plan will not be confirmed absent the sale of real property. *In re* Permar Provisions, Inc., 17 C.B.C.2d 1022 (B. Ct., E.D.N.Y. 1987).

A real estate transfer tax may not be applied to a real estate transaction under a reorganization plan even when the tax is applied against the purchaser rather than the debtor as it might affect the price, an effect the Code seeks to counter. *In re* Cantrup, 13 C.B.C.2d 682 (B. Ct., D. Colo. 1985).

References

5 *Collier on Bankruptcy* ch. 1146 (Matthew Bender 15th ed.).

3 *Collier Bankruptcy Manual* ch. 1146 (Matthew Bender 3d ed.).

6 *Collier Bankruptcy Practice Guide* ch. 93 (Matthew Bender).

Berguist & Groff, *Reorganizing the Financially Troubled Corporation After the Bankruptcy Tax Act of 1980,* 36 Tax L. Rev. 517 (1981).

Comment, *Allocation of Tax Payments Under Chapter 11 Reorganizations-Who Will Decide: IRS or Bankruptcy Courts?,* 28 Duq. L. Rev. 677 (1990).

Falk, *Are Trust Fund Tax Payments Beyond the Trustee's Reach?,* 2 F & G Bankr. L. Rev. 10 (1990).

Fitzgerald, *Section 6672 of the Internal Revenue Code and a Chapter 11 Reorganization Under the Bankruptcy Code—A Taxpayer's Potential Discharge of an IRS Penalty?,* 46 J. Mo. B. 551 (1990).

Gelfeld and Lobl, *Tax Planning Opportunities for Debtor Corporations in Title 11 Proceedings,* 91 Com. L.J. 417 (1986).

Goldring, *The Supreme Court and the Transfer Tax Exemption for Sales in Chapter 11,* 1 F & G Bankr. L. Rev. 49 (1990).

Hoke, *The Tax Consequences of Restructuring Troubled Corporations' Debt,* 3 F & G Bankr. L. Rev. 31 (1991).

Medlin, *Maximize NOL Through Basis Reduction,* 22 Tax Advisor 437 (1991).

Miller, *How to Get Relief From Filing Federal Income Tax Returns,* 2 F & G Bankr. L. Rev. 41 (1990).

Sabino, *The Allocation of Payments to Trust Fund Taxes in Bankruptcy Reorganizations: The IRS v. the Bankruptcy Court,* 17 J. Corp. Tax'n 339 (1991).

Sheinfeld and Caldwell, *Taxes: An Analysis of the Tax Provisions of the Bankruptcy Tax Act of 1980,* 55 Am. Bankr. L.J. 97 (1981).

Van Brauman, *The Carryforward of Net Operating Losses and Other Tax Attributes After Bankruptcy Reorganizations,* 23 St. Mary's L.J. 461 (1991).

Wood, *IRS Proposes Regulations on NOLs and Bankruptcy,* 3 F & G Bankr. L. Rev. 35 (1992).

Yerbich, *Life with the Federal Tax Lien (or "FTL"),* 15 Alaska B. Reg. 14 (1991).

SUBCHAPTER IV

Railroad Reorganization

SECTION 1161 (11 U.S.C. § 1161)

§ 1161. **Inapplicability of other sections.** Sections 341, 343, 1102(a)(1), 1104, 1105, 1107, 1129(a)(7), and 1129(c) of this title do not apply in a case concerning a railroad.

Bankruptcy Rule References: 1002, 1007, 3016 and 3017

Legislative History

This section makes certain other sections of the bankruptcy code inapplicable in railroad reorganizations. The excluded sections are 341 (Meetings of creditors and equity security holders), 343 (Examination of debtor), 1104 (Appointment of trustee or examiner), 1129(7) (relating to the best interest of creditors test), and 1144 (Revocation of confirmation).

[House Report No. 95–595, 95th Cong., 1st Sess. 422 (1977).]

This section makes inapplicable sections of the bill which are either inappropriate in railroad reorganizations, or relate to matters which are otherwise dealt with in subchapter IV.

[Senate Report No. 95–989, 95th Cong., 2d Sess. 133 (1978).]

Comment

Section 1161 makes inapplicable to railroad reorganizations, certain sections of the Code that are inappropriate in that type of reorganization:

Section 341: Meetings of creditors and equity security holders.

Section 343: Examination of the debtor.

Section 1102(a)(1): Appointment of unsecured creditors' committee.

Section 1104: Appointment of trustee or examiner.

Section 1105: Termination of trustee's appointment.

Section 1107: Rights, powers, and duties of a debtor in possession.

Section 1129(a)(7): Best interest of creditors test.

Section 1129(c): Only one plan may be confirmed; court to consider preferences of creditors and equity security holders in determining which of several plans to confirm.

The provisions for a railroad reorganization were not incorporated into a separate chapter but constitute Subchapter IV of chapter 11. Accordingly, except for the provisions made inapplicable by section 1161, all the provisions applicable to any reorganization under chapter 11 are applicable in a railroad reorganization. Thus, there is no provision in subchapter IV of chapter 11 as to eligibility for relief. Eligibility is found in section 109(d) of chapter 1: "Only a person that may be a debtor under chapter 7 . . . and a railroad may be a debtor under chapter 11 of this title." The Senate Report on S.2266 with respect to the now deleted section on eligibility follows:

Section 1163. Debtors eligible for relief

Debtors eligible for relief under subchapter IV include any common carrier by railroad engaged in either freight or passenger service in either interstate or foreign commerce, as well as any owner of trackage facilities leased by a carrier. The exclusion in present section 77(m) of street or suburban electric railways is omitted as unnecessary.

[*Senate Report No. 95–989, 95th Cong., 2d Sess. 133 (1978).*]

As enacted the Code does not require that the railroad be engaged in interstate commerce.

The 1987 Amendments to the Bankruptcy Rules deleted the provisions of Rule 1002 regarding the number of copies of petition that must be filed. The Advisory Committee Note to the rule states: "The number of copies of a petition that must be filed is a matter for local rule."

Title 28 U.S.C. § 1930(a)(4), as amended in 1986, provides for a filing fee of $1,000 for a case commenced under chapter 11 of title 11 concerning a railroad.

Bankruptcy Rule 1007 relating to the filing of a list of creditors and equity security holders is applicable in a railroad reorganization.

The provisions of Rule 1007(d) requiring the debtor to file with its petition a list of the 20 largest unsecured creditors is applicable in a chapter 11 railroad reorganization case. The avowed purpose of the rule is to aid the court in appointing a creditors' committee. While section 1102(a)(1) (mandatory appointment of a committee) is made inapplicable by section 1161, the court may, under section 1102(a)(2), at the request of a party in interest, appoint committees of creditors and equity security holders.

References

5 *Collier on Bankruptcy* ch. 1161 (Matthew Bender 15th ed.).

Graybeal, *Reflection on the Golden Spike: A Look at the Bankruptcy Reform Act and Railroad Reorganization,* 6 Hastings Const. L.Q. 1107 (1979).

SECTION 1162 (11 U.S.C. § 1162)

§ 1162. **Definition.** In this subchapter, "Commission" means Interstate Commerce Commission.

Legislative History

Two definitions are provided: That Commission means the Interstate Commerce Commission, and that "person" includes a governmental unit for purposes of the subchapter. The latter definition is made necessary because governmental unit is excluded from the definition of person in section 101(30). [*Ed. Note:* Amendments made to section 101 have changed the numbering of paragraphs in that section; accordingly, the definition of "person" is now found in section 101(41).]

[*Senate Report No. 95–989, 95th Cong., 2d Sess. 133 (1978).*]

Section 1162 of the House amendment is derived from section 1162(1) of the Senate bill.

[*124 Cong. Rec. H 11,105 (Sept. 28, 1978); S 17,422 (Oct. 6, 1978).*]

References

5 *Collier on Bankruptcy* ch. 1162 (Matthew Bender 15th ed.).

Graybeal, *Reflection on the Golden Spike: A Look at the Bankruptcy Reform Act and Railroad Reorganization,* 6 Hastings Const. L.Q. 1107 (1979).

SECTION 1163 (11 U.S.C. § 1163)

§ 1163. **Appointment of trustee.** As soon as practicable after the order for relief the Secretary of Transportation shall submit a list of five disinterested persons that are qualified and willing to serve as trustees in the case. The United States trustee shall appoint one of such persons to serve as trustee in the case.

Legislative History

This section requires the appointment of an independent trustee in a railroad reorganization case. The court may appoint one or more disinterested persons to serve as trustee in the case.

[*House Report No. 95–595, 95th Cong., 1st Sess. 422 (1977).*]

Requires the court to appoint a trustee in every case [*sic*]. Since the trustee may employ whatever help he needs, multiple trusteeships are unnecessary and add to the cost of administration.

[*Senate Report No. 95–989, 95th Cong., 2d Sess. 133 (1978).*]

Section 1163 of the House amendment represents a compromise between the House bill and Senate amendment with respect to the appointment of a trustee in a railroad reorganization. As soon as practicable after the order for relief, the Secretary of Transportation is required to submit a list of five disinterested persons who are qualified to serve as trustee and the court will then appoint one trustee from the list to serve as trustee in the case.

The House amendment deletes section 1163 of the Senate amendment in order to cover intrastate railroads in a case under subchapter IV of chapter 11. The bill does not confer jurisdiction on the Interstate Commerce Commission with respect to intrastate railroads.

[*124 Cong. Rec. H 11,105 (Sept. 28, 1978); S 17,422 (Oct. 6, 1978).*]

Comment

Former Bankruptcy Rule 8–202(a) provided for the appointment by the court of "one or more trustees" and former Rule 8–202(c) required that a trustee be "disinterested" and competent to perform his duties.

Section 1163 of the Code introduced a new factor: the Secretary of Transportation is required to file a list of five disinterested persons who are "qualified" and willing to serve and the United States trustee is mandated to appoint *one* of the five named persons to serve as trustee. *See* section 101 of the Code for definition of "disinterested person."

Section 1163 of S. 2266 made only railroads engaged in interstate transportation eligible for relief in a railroad reorganization. Deletion of this section from the final version of the Code makes subchapter IV of chapter 11 applicable to intrastate railroads. *See* Congressional Record, *supra*.

Bankruptcy Rule 2008 requires the United States trustee to notify immediately the person selected as trustee how to qualify and, if applicable, the amount of the trustee's bond. The person selected as trustee must notify the court and the United States trustee in writing of the acceptance of the office within five days after receipt of notice of selection, or shall be deemed to have rejected the office.

Bankruptcy Rule 2015 requires a trustee in a chapter 11 case within 30 days after qualifying as a trustee to file and transmit to the United States trustee a complete inventory of the debtors' property unless such inventory has already been filed and to keep a record of receipts and disposition of money and property received. The trustee is also required to give notice of the case to specified entities known to be holding money or property subject to withdrawal or order of the debtor. The 1991 amendments deleted Rule 2002(a)(5) because the filing of a notice of or copy of the petition to protect real property against unauthorized postpetition transfers in a particular case is within the discretion of the trustee. Subdivision (a)(5), added by the 1991 Amendments to the Bankruptcy Rules and Official Forms, provides that in a chapter 11 case, on or before the last day of the month after each calendar quarter until a plan is confirmed or the case converted or closed, the debtor in possession shall file and transmit to the United States trustee a statement of disbursements made during such calendar quarter and statement of the amount of the fee required pursuant to 28 U.S.C. § 1930(a)(6). Subdivision (d) of the rule provides that the court may direct that copies of annual reports or of other reports be mailed to the creditors, equity security holders and indenture trustees, and may also direct publication of summaries of the reports. A copy of every report or summary mailed or published pursuant to this subdivision shall be transmitted to the United States trustee. The provisions of this rule amplify the duties of a trustee set forth in section 1106 which is applicable in railroad reorganization cases.

1986 Amendments: The 1986 Act made a minor technical change in section 1163 and provided that after submission by the Secretary of Transportation of a list of 5 names of persons qualified and willing to serve as trustee in the case, the United States trustee shall appoint one of such persons to serve as trustee in the case.

This section was amended to reflect the creation of a permanent United States trustee system. Section 302(d) of the 1986 Amendments provides different effective dates for the amendments relating to the United States trustee system. *See* Section 302 of the 1986 Amendments, reprinted herein under "Selected Provisions of the Bankruptcy Judges, United States Trustees, and Family Farmer Bankruptcy Act of 1986," regarding effective dates generally.

References

5 *Collier on Bankruptcy* ch. 1163 (Matthew Bender 15th ed.).

Graybeal, *Reflection on the Golden Spike: A Look at the Bankruptcy Reform Act and Railroad Reorganization,* 6 Hasting Const. L.Q. 1107 (1979).

SECTION 1164 (11 U.S.C. § 1164)

§ 1164. Right to be heard. The Commission, the Department of Transportation, and any State or local commission having regulatory jurisdiction over the debtor may raise and may appear and be heard on any issue in a case under this chapter, but may not appeal from any judgment, order, or decree entered in the case.

Bankruptcy Rule Reference: 2018

Legislative History

This section gives the same right to raise, and appear and be heard on, any issue in a railroad reorganization case to the Interstate Commerce Commission, the Department of Transportation, and any State or local commission having regulatory jurisdiction over the debtor as is given to the S.E.C. and indenture trustees under section 1109 in ordinary reorganization cases. The right of appeal is denied the I.C.C., the Department of Transportation, and State and local regulatory agencies, the same as it is denied the S.E.C.

[*House Report No. 95–595, 95th Cong., 1st Sess. 422 (1977).*]

Section 1164 of the Senate amendment is deleted as a matter to be left to the Rules of Bankruptcy Procedure. It is anticipated that the rules will require a petition in a railroad reorganization to be filed with the Interstate Commerce Commission and the Secretary of Transportation in a case concerning an interstate railroad. [*Ed. Note:* Section 1164 of the Senate amendment concerned notice to the Interstate Commerce Commission.]

Section 1164 of the House amendment is derived from section 1163 of the House bill. The section makes clear that the Interstate Commerce Commission, the Department of Transportation, and any State or local commission having regulatory jurisdiction over the debtor may raise and appear and be heard on any issue in a case under subchapter IV of chapter 11, but may not appeal from any judgment, order, or decree in the case. As under section 1109 of title 11, such intervening parties are not parties in interest.

[*124 Cong. Rec. H 11,106 (Sept. 28, 1978); S 17,422 (Oct. 6, 1978).*]

Comment

Section 1161 does not make section 1109 dealing with the right to be heard in a chapter 11 case inapplicable in a railroad reorganization case, and therefore sections 1109 and 1164 must be read together.

Bankruptcy Rule 2018 relates to intervention and the right to be heard. Subdivision (a) provides that in a case under the Code, the court may, after hearing on such notice as it directs, and for cause shown, permit any interested entity to intervene generally or with respect to any specific matter.

Subdivision (b) permits a State's Attorney General to appear and be heard on behalf of consumer creditors in a chapter 11 case if the court finds it to be in the public interest. Such Attorney General, however, may not appeal from any judgment, order or decree.

Subdivision (d) gives a labor union or an employees' association the right to be heard on the economic soundness of a plan affecting the interest of employees in a chapter 11 case. The 1987 Amendment of Rule 2018(d) provides that a labor union or employees' association which exercises its right to be heard pursuant to subdivision (d) shall not be entitled to appeal any judgment, order, or decree relating to the plan, unless otherwise permitted by law. The 1987 Advisory Committee Note states that the amendment makes it clear that the prohibition against appeals by labor unions is limited only to their participation in connection with the hearing on the plan as provided in subdivision (d). If a labor union would otherwise have the right to file an appeal or to be a party to an appeal, subdivision (d) does not preclude the labor union from exercising that right.

Subdivision (e) authorizes the court to enter orders governing service of notice and papers on entities permitted to intervene or be heard.

The 1986 Act added section 307 to the Bankruptcy Code. It provides that the United States trustee may raise and appear and be heard on any issue in any case or proceeding under the Code. The United States trustee, however, may not file a plan pursuant to section 1121(c).

References

5 *Collier on Bankruptcy* ch. 1164 (Matthew Bender 15th ed.).

Graybeal, *Reflection on the Golden Spike: A Look at the Bankruptcy Reform Act and Railroad Reorganization,* 6 Hastings Const. L.Q. 1107 (1979).

SECTION 1165 (11 U.S.C. § 1165)

§ 1165. **Protection of the public interest.** In applying sections 1166, 1167, 1169, 1170, 1171, 1172, 1173, and 1174 of this title, the court and the trustee shall consider the public interest in addition to the interests of the debtor, creditors, and equity security holders.

Legislative History

Section 1165 requires the court, in consideration of the relief to be granted upon the filing of an involuntary petition, to take into account the "public interest" in the preservation of the debtor's rail service. This is an important factor in railroad reorganization, which distinguishes them from other business reorganizations. Hence, this section modifies the provisions in sections 303 and 305 that govern generally when the business of a debtor may continue to operate, when relief under the Act sought should be granted, and when the petition should be dismissed.

Section 1167 imposes on the trustee the obligations, in addition to his other duties and responsibilities, to take into account the "public interest" in the preservation of the debtor's rail service.

[*Senate Report No. 95–989, 95th Cong., 2d Sess. 133 (1978).*]

Section 1165 of the House amendment represents a modification of sections 1165 and 1167 of the Senate amendment requiring the court and the trustee to consider the broad, general public interest in addition to the interests of the debtor, creditors, and equity security holders in applying specific sections of the subchapter.

[*124 Cong. Rec. H 11,106 (Sept. 28, 1978); S 17,422 (Oct. 6, 1978).*]

Comment

See the following sections:

Section 1166: Effect of Interstate Commerce Act and of Federal, State, or local regulations.

Section 1167: Collective bargaining agreements.

Section 1169: Effect of rejection of lease of railroad line.

Section 1170: Abandonment of railroad line.

Section 1171: Priority claims.

Section 1172: Contents of plan.

Section 1173: Confirmation of plan.

Section 1174: Liquidation.

Case Annotations

The public interest involved is one factor to be considered by a court when determining in a railroad reorganization case whether to enjoin a creditor from depriving the estate of the use of property in which that creditor may have an interest. *In re* Auto-Train Corp., 3 C.B.C.2d 239 (B. Ct., D.D.C. 1980).

References

5 *Collier on Bankruptcy* ch. 1165 (Matthew Bender 15th ed.).

SECTION 1166 (11 U.S.C. § 1166)

§ 1166. **Effect of Interstate Commerce Act and of Federal, State, or local regulations.** Except with respect to abandonment under section 1170 of this title, or merger, modification of the financial structure of the debtor, or issuance or sale of securities under a plan, the trustee and the debtor are subject to the provisions of subtitle IV of title 49 that are applicable to railroads, and the trustee is subject to orders of any Federal, State, or local regulatory body to the same extent as the debtor would be if a petition commencing the case under this chapter had not been filed, but—

> (1) any such order that would require the expenditure, or the incurring of an obligation for the expenditure, of money from the estate is not effective unless approved by the court; and

(2) the provisions of this chapter are subject to section 601(b) of the Regional Rail Reorganization Act of 1973 (45 U.S.C. 791(b)).

Legislative History

The same rules apply with respect to Federal, State, or local regulations. The trustee is subject to the orders of a Federal, State, or local regulatory body to the same extent as the debtor would be if the case had not been commenced. However, any order that would require the expenditure, or the incurring of an obligation for the expenditure, of money is not effective under [*sic*] approved by the court.

Section 1164 makes the debtor railroad subject to the provisions of the Interstate Commerce Act that are applicable to railroads, and the trustee subject to the orders of the Interstate Commerce Commission to the same extent as the debtor would have been if the case had not been commenced. There are several exceptions. The section does not apply with respect to abandonment of rail lines, which is provided for under section 1169, or with respect to merger under a plan, modification of the financial structure of the debtor by reason of the plan, or the issuance or sale of securities under a plan. Further, the orders of the I.C.C. are not effective if the order would require the expenditure or the incurring of an obligation for the expenditure of money from the estate, unless approved by the court, and the provisions of this chapter are subject to section 601(b) of the Regional Rail Reorganization Act of 1973.

[House Report No. 95–595, 95th Cong., 1st Sess. 422 (1977).]

Section 1168 makes the trustee subject to the Interstate Commerce Act and to lawful orders of the Interstate Commerce Commission, the United States Department of Transportation, and State and regulatory bodies. The approval of the court is required, however, if the order requires the expenditure of money or the incurring of an expenditure other than the payment of certain interline accounts. The limitation of "lawful orders" of State commissions to those involving "safety, location of tracks, and terminal facilities," which is contained in present section 77(c)(2), is eliminated.

Subsection (1) further provides that the debtor must pay in cash all amounts owed other carriers for current balances owed for interline freight, passenger and per deim, including incentive per diem, for periods both prior and subsequent to the filing of the petition, without the necessity of court approval.

Subsection (2) makes the provisions of the chapter subject to section 601(b) of the Regional Rail Reorganization Act, which excludes the Interstate Commerce Commission from any participation in the reorganization of certain northeast railroads that have transferred their rail properties to Consolidated Rail Corporation (Conrail). [*Ed. Note:* Section 1166 is derived in part from 1168 of S. 2266.]

[*Senate Report No. 95–989, 95th Cong., 2d Sess. 134 (1978).*]

Section 1166 of the House amendment is derived from sections 1164 and 1165 of the House bill. An alternative proposal contained in section 1168(1) of the Senate bill is rejected as violative of the principle or [*sic*] equal treatment of all creditors under title 11.

[*124 Cong. Rec. H 11,106 (Sept. 28, 1978); S 17,422 (Oct. 6, 1978).*]

Comment

Section 1166 makes clear that in operating the business of the railroad the trustee is subject, with several specified exceptions, to the orders of the Interstate Commerce Commission as the debtor would be if the case had not been commenced. Unless there is a specific exemption in the Code, all chapter 11 debtors are subject to applicable government regulations. When required, a chapter 11 debtor must obtain governmental approval or authorization.

1984 Amendments: A minor technical change was made in section 1166.

References

5 *Collier on Bankruptcy* ch. 1166 (Matthew Bender 15th ed.).

SECTION 1167 (11 U.S.C. § 1167)

§ 1167. Collective bargaining agreements. Notwithstanding section 365 of this title, neither the court nor the trustee may change the wages or working conditions of employees of the debtor established by a collective bargaining agreement that is subject to the Railway Labor Act except in accordance with section 6 of such Act (45 U.S.C. 156).

Legislative History

Section 1167 is derived from present section 77(n). It provides that notwithstanding the general section governing the rejection of executory contracts (section 365), neither the court nor the trustee may change the wages or working conditions of employees of the debtor established by a collective bargaining agreement that is subject to the Railway Labor Act, except in accordance with section 6 of that Act. The subject of railway labor is too delicate and has too long a history for this code to upset established relationships. The balance has been struck over the years. This provision continues that balance unchanged.

[*House Report No. 95–595, 95th Cong., 1st Sess. 423 (1977).*]

Section 1176 is derived from present section 77(n). It provides that notwithstanding the general section governing the rejection of executory contracts (section 365), neither the court nor the trustee may change the wages or working conditions of employees of the debtor established by a collective bargaining agreement that is subject to the Railway Labor Act, except in accordance with section 6 of that Act. As reported by the subcommittee this section provided that wages and salaries of rail employees could not be affected by the trustee, but that work rules could be rejected by the trustee. The reorganization court was given the authority to review the trustee's decisions and to settle any disputes arising from the rejection. This provision was withdrawn by the full committee, and hearings will be conducted next year by the Human Resources Committee in the area of rail labor contracts and the trustee's ability to reject them in a bankruptcy situation. [*Ed. Note:* The Senate Report refers to section 1176 of the Senate Bill now incorporated in section 1167 of the Code.]

[*Senate Report No. 95–989, 95th Cong., 2d Sess. 137 (1978).*]

Comment

Section 1167 is derived from Section 77(n) of the former Bankruptcy Act which provided, in part:

"No judge or trustee acting under this Act shall change the wages or working conditions of railroad employees except in the manner prescribed in the Railway Labor Act, as amended June 21, 1934, or as it may be hereafter amended."

Case Annotatons

The provisions of section 1167 of the Bankruptcy Code are restricted to railroad reorganization and do not apply to other types of transportation companies, even if those companies' collective bargaining agreements are subject to the Railway Labor Act. Air Florida Pilots Ass'n v. Air Florida, Inc. (*In re* Air Florida Sys., Inc.), 12 C.B.C.2d 661 (B. Ct., S.D. Fla. 1985).

References

5 *Collier on Bankruptcy* ch. 1167 (Matthew Bender 15th ed.).

SECTION 1168 (11 U.S.C. § 1168)

§ 1168. Rolling stock equipment.

(a) The right of a secured party with a purchase-money equip- ment security interest in, or of a lessor or conditional vendor of, whether as trustee or otherwise, rolling stock equipment or accessories used on such equipment, including superstructures and racks, that are subject to a purchase-money equipment security interest granted by, leased to, or conditionally sold to, the debtor to take possession of such equipment in compliance with the provisions of a purchase-money equipment security agreement, lease, or conditional sale contract, as the case may be, is not affected by section 362 or 363 of this title or by any power of the court to enjoin such taking of possession, unless—

(1) before 60 days after the date of the commencement of a case under this chapter, the trustee, subject to the court's approval, agrees to perform all obligations of the debtor under such security agreement, lease, or conditional sale contract, as the case may be; and

(2) any default, other than a default of a kind specified in section 365(b)(2) of this title, under such security agreement, lease, or conditional sale contract, as the case may be—

(A) that occurred before such date and is an event of default therewith is cured before the expiration of such 60-day period; and

(B) that occurs or becomes an event of default after such date is cured before the later of—

(i) 30 days after the date of such default or event of default; and

(ii) the expiration of such 60-day period.

(b) The trustee and the secured party, lessor, or conditional vendor, as the case may be, whose right to take possession is protected under subsection (a) of this section, may agree, subject to the court's approval, to extend the 60-day period specified in subsection (a)(1) of this section.

Legislative History

This section, derived with changes from the last sentence of present section 77(j), protects the interests of rolling stock equipment financers, while providing the trustee with some opportunity to cure defaults, agree to make payments, and retain and use the equipment. The provision is parallel to section 1110, concerning aircraft equipment and vessels.

[*House Report No. 95–595, 95th Cong., 1st Sess. 423 (1977).*]

Section 1175 continues the protection accorded in present section 77(j) to the rights of holders of purchase-money equipment security, and of lessors or conditional vendors of railroad rolling stock, but accords to the trustee a limited period within which to assume the debtor's obligation and to cure any defaults. The rights of such lenders are not affected by the automatic stay and related provisions of sections 362 and 363, or by any power of the court, unless (1) within 60 days after the commencement of the case (or such longer period as may be agreed to by the secured party, lessor or conditional vendor) the trustees, with the approval of the court, agrees to perform all of the debtor's obligations under the security agreement, lease or conditional sale contract, and (2) all defaults are cured within the 60-day period. Defaults described in section 365(b)(2)—defaults which are breaches of provisions relating to the insolvency or financial condition of the debtor, or the commencement of a case under this title, or the appointment of a trustee—are, for obvious reasons, excepted. [*Ed. Note:* The Senate Report refers to section 1175, and the House Report refers to section 1166, both of which sections related to rolling stock equipment now treated in section 1168 of the Code.]

[*Senate Report No. 95–989, 95th Cong., 2d Sess. 136 (1978).*]

Section 1168 of the House amendment incorporates a provision contained in section 1166 of the House bill instead of the provision contained in section 1175 of the Senate amendment for the reasons stated in connection with the discussion of section 1110 of the House amendment.

[*124 Cong. Rec. H 11,106 (Sept. 28, 1978); S 17,422 (Oct. 6, 1978).*]

Comment

Section 1168, as in its counterpart in section 1110 relating to aircraft equipment and vessels, sets forth what is in effect a special use of collateral rule that differs substantially in procedure and, to some extent, in substance, from the provisions generally governing the use of collateral. Lessors, conditional sellers and secured equipment purchase money lenders are stayed by the section 362 automatic stay from repossessing their collateral; however, if the collateral is railroad rolling stock or equipment, section 1168 limits the stay to 60 days from the commencement of the case. Within that time, the trustee may agree, subject to the court's approval, to perform the debtor's obligation under the lease, contract or security agreement. *See also* section 1110 with respect to aircraft equipment and vessels.

Case Annotations

If a debtor leases railroad cars to its subsidiaries but is not a railroad as defined by section 101(33) [redesignated as section 101(36) by the Bankruptcy Amendments and Federal Judgeship Act of 1984, Pub. L. No. 98–353, and section 101(38) by the Bankruptcy Judges, United States Trustees, and Family Farmer Bankruptcy Act of 1986, Pub. L. No. 99–554], it is not subject to the provisions of section 1165. *In re* Funding Systems Railcars, Inc., 5 C.B.C.2d 834 (B. Ct., N.D. Ill. 1981).

References

5 *Collier on Bankruptcy* ch. 1168 (Matthew Bender 15th ed.).

Goldman, Album and Ward, *Repossessing the Spirit of St. Louis: Expanding the Protection of Sections 1110 and 1168 of the Bankruptcy Code,* 41 Bus. Lawyer 29 (1985).

SECTION 1169 (11 U.S.C. § 1169)

§ 1169. Effect of rejection of lease of railroad line.

(a) Except as provided in subsection (b) of this section, if a lease of a line of railroad under which the debtor is the lessee is rejected under section 365 of this title, and if the trustee, within such time as the court fixes, and with the court's approval, elects not to operate the leased line, the lessor under such lease, after such approval, shall operate the line.

(b) If operation of such line by such lessor is impracticable or contrary to the public interest, the court, on request of such lessor, and after notice and a hearing, shall order the trustee to continue operation of such line for the account of such lessor until abandonment is ordered under section 1170 of this title, or until such operation is otherwise lawfully terminated, whichever occurs first.

(c) During any such operation, such lessor is deemed a carrier subject to the provisions of subtitle IV of title 49 that are applicable to railroads.

Bankruptcy Rule Reference: 6006

Legislative History

This section governs the effect of the rejection by the trustee of an unexpired lease of railroad line under which the debtor is the lessee. If the trustee rejects such a lease, and if the trustee, within such time as the court allows, and with the approval of the court, elects not to operate the leased line, then the lessor under the lease must operate the line.

[*House Report No. 95–595, 95th Cong., 1st Sess. 423 (1977).*]

Section 1177 continues, essentially without change, the provisions relating to the rejection by the trustee of a lease of a line of railroad now contained in section 77(c)(6). Subsection (a) requires the lessor of a line of railroad to operate it if the lease is rejected by the trustee and the trustee, with the approval of the court, elects not to operate the leased line. [*Ed. Note:* The Senate Report refers to section 1177 of the Senate Bill, now incorporated in section 1169 of the Code.]

[*Senate Report No. 95–989, 95th Cong., 2d Sess. 137 (1978).*]

Subsection (b) excuses the lessor from the requirement to operate the line under certain circumstances. If operation of the line by the lessor is impracticable or contrary to the public interest, the court, on request of the lessor, must order the trustee to continue operation of the line for the account of the lessor until abandonment is ordered under section 1169, governing abandonments generally, or until the operation is otherwise lawfully terminated, such as by an order of the I.C.C.

[*House Report No. 95–595, 95th Cong., 1st Sess. 423 (1977).*]

Subsection (b), however, further provides that if operation by the lessor is impractical or contrary to the public interest, the court shall require the trustee to operate the line for the account of the lessor until the operation is lawfully terminated.

[*Senate Report No. 95–989, 95th Cong., 2d Sess. 137 (1978).*]

Subsection (c) deems the lessor a carrier subject to the provisions of the Interstate Commerce Act during the operation of the line before abandonment.

[*House Report No. 95–595, 95th Cong., 1st Sess. 423 (1977).*]

Subsection (c) provides that during such operation, the lessor is a carrier subject to the Interstate Commerce Act.

[*Senate Report No. 95–989, 95th Cong., 2d Sess. 137 (1978).*]

Comment

Section 1169, which conforms substantially to Section 77(c)(6) of the former Bankruptcy Act, is designed to protect the public interest by providing a mechanism which insures the continuation of rail service after a debtor who is operating over leased lines rejects a railroad lease. If the trustee, with court approval, elects not to continue operations, then the lessor must resume operation of the line. The lessor may seek to have the court instruct the debtor to operate the line and the court must make that direction if operation by the lessor is impracticable or contrary to public interest. In such event, the debtor-lessee operates the property for the lessor's account until the line is abandoned or terminated.

Section 365 of the Code, dealing with the rejections of executory contracts and unexpired leases, is applicable in railroad reorganization cases. *See* section 1161.

Bankruptcy Rule 6006 provides in subdivision (a) thereof, that Rule 9014 (motion practice) governs proceedings to assume, reject or assign an executory contract or unexpired lease other than as part of a plan.

Subdivision (b) provides that Rule 9014 governs a proceeding by a party to an executory contract or unexpired lease to require the trustee to determine whether to assume or reject the contract or lease.

Subdivision (c) provides that when a motion is made under subdivision (a) or (b), the court shall set a hearing on notice to the other party to the contract, to the United States trustee and to such other parties in interest as the court directs.

1984 Amendments: A minor technical change was made in section 1169.

References

5 *Collier on Bankruptcy* ch. 1169 (Matthew Bender 15th ed.).

SECTION 1170 (11 U.S.C. § 1170)

§ 1170.   Abandonment of railroad line.

(a) The court, after notice and a hearing, may authorize the abandonment of all or a portion of a railroad line if such abandonment is—

(1)(A) in the best interest of the estate; or

(B) essential to the formulation of a plan; and

(2) consistent with the public interest.

(b) If, except for the pendency of the case under this chapter, such abandonment would require approval by the Commission under a law of the United States, the trustee shall initiate an appropriate application for such abandonment with the Commission. The court may fix a time within which the Commission shall report to the court on such application.

(c) After the court receives the report of the Commission, or the expiration of the time fixed under subsection (b) of this section, whichever occurs first, the court may authorize such abandonment, after notice to the Commission, the Secretary of Transportation, the trustee, any party in interest that has requested notice, any affected shipper or community, and any other entity prescribed by the court, and a hearing.

(d)(1) Enforcement of an order authorizing such abandonment shall be stayed until the time for taking an appeal has expired, or, if an appeal is timely taken, until such order has become final.

(2) If an order authorizing such abandonment is appealed, the court, on request of a party in interest, may authorize suspension of service on a line or a portion of a line pending the determination of such appeal, after notice to the Commission, the Secretary of Transportation, the trustee, any party

in interest that has requested notice, any affected shipper or community, and any other entity prescribed by the court, and a hearing. An appellant may not obtain a stay of the enforcement of an order authorizing such suspension by the giving of a supersedeas bond or otherwise, during the pendency of such appeal.

(e)(1) In authorizing any abandonment of a railroad line under this section, the court shall require the rail carrier to provide a fair arrangement at least as protective of the interests of employees as that established under section 11347 of title 49.

(2) Nothing in this subsection shall be deemed to affect the priorities or timing of payment of employee protection which might have existed in the absence of this subsection.

Bankruptcy Rule Reference: 6007

Legislative History

Subsection (a) permits the court to authorize the abandonment of a railroad line if the abandonment is consistent with the public interest and either in the best interest of the estate or essential to the formulation of a plan. This avoids the normal abandonment requirements of generally applicable railroad regulatory law. The authority to abandon or not to abandon lines of railroad is, of course, subject to the fifth amendment of the Constitution, which may in particular cases require abandonment in order not to erode a secured creditor's interest in the debtor's property even though the public interest dictates otherwise. [*Ed. Note:* The Senate Report on subsection (a) ends after the second sentence.]

Subsection (b) permits some participation by the Interstate Commerce Commission in the abandonment process. The ICC's role, however, is only advisory. The ICC will represent the public interest, while the trustee and various creditors and equity security holders will represent the interests of those who have invested money in the enterprise. The court will balance the various interests and make an appropriate decision. The subsection specifies that if, except for the pendency of the railroad reorganization case, the proposed abandonment would require ICC approval, then the trustee, with the approval of the court, must initiate an application for the abandonment with the ICC The court may then fix a time within which the ICC must report to the court on the application. [*Ed. Note:* The Senate Report uses the word "Commission" where the House Report uses "ICC."]

Subsection (c) permits the court to act after it has received the report of the ICC or the time fixed under subsection (b) has expired, whichever occurs first. The court may then authorize the abandonment after notice and a hearing. The notice must go to the ICC, the Secretary of Transportation, the trustee, and party in interest that has requested notice, any affected shipper or community, and any other entity that the court specifies.

Subsection (d) stays the enforcement of an abandonment until the time for taking an appeal has expired, or if an appeal has been taken, until the order has become final. However, the court may, and after notice and a hearing, on request of a party in interest authorize termination of service on the line or a portion of the line pending the determination of the appeal. The notice required is the same as that required under subsection (c). If the court authorizes termination of service pending determination of the appeal, an appellant may not obtain a stay of the enforcement of the order authorizing termination, either by the giving of a supersedeas bond or otherwise, during the pendency of the appeal.

[*House Report No. 95–595, 95th Cong., 1st Sess. 423 (1977); Senate Report No. 95–989, 95th Cong., 2d Sess. 137 (1978).*]

Comment

Section 1170 represents a major change from Section 77 of the former Bankruptcy Act. Power to authorize abandonments, *i.e.,* permanent discontinuance of the railroad services and removal of track, is shifted from the Interstate Commerce Commission to the reorganization court. The court, however, may not exercise that power until the Commission is given the opportunity to consider the proposed abandonment and to render a report to the court. The court is given authority to fix a time within which the Commission is to file its report. Although a purpose of section 1170 is a faster resolution of abandonment cases, it is clear that Congress wanted the court to have the benefit of the Commission's informed opinion. Obviously there should be cooperation between the court and the Commission, but if the Commission's report is not filed within the time fixed by the court, the Code is clear that abandonment may proceed without the report being filed.

Section 554 of the Code, dealing with abandonment of the property of the estate is applicable in railroad reorganization cases. *See* section 1161.

Bankruptcy Rule 6007(a) requires a trustee, unless the court directs otherwise, to give notice of a proposed abandonment or disposition of property to the United States trustee and to all creditors, indenture trustees and appointed or elected committees. A party in interest may serve and file an objection within 15 days of the mailing of the notice, or within the time fixed by the court.

Subdivision (b) permits a party in interest to serve and file a motion requiring the trustee to abandon property of the estate.

Subdivision (c) provides that if timely objection under subdivision (a), or a motion under subdivision (b), is made, the court shall set a hearing on notice to the United States trustee and to the entities as directed by the court.

Staggers Rail Act of 1980: The Staggers Rail Act of 1980, Pub. L. No. 96–448, added subsection (e) to section 1170.

The provision puts employees of rail carriers which entered bankruptcy after the effective date of the Bankruptcy Act of 1978 in the same position as employees of rail carriers that entered bankruptcy prior to the Bankruptcy Act of 1978 with respect to employee protection.

1984 Amendments: Subsection (a) of section 1170 added language that makes the abandonment provisions applicable to abandonment of "all or a portion" of a railroad line. Subsection (d)(2) was amended by changing "termination" of service, to "suspension" of service.

Case Annotations

A creditor's motion for relief from the automatic stay in order to repossess the very ties and track of a railroad is actually a motion to abandon the railroad. Abandonment of a railroad line may not be authorized unless the railroad's financial situation is hopeless and insolvable, it is in the best interest of the estate and it would not adversely affect the public interest. *In re* Eureka S. R.R., Inc., 16 C.B.C.2d 1101 (B. Ct., N.D. Cal. 1987).

When there was a cessation of operation of the railroad debtor authorized by the bankruptcy court because of the debtor's undisputed lack of cash, there was no abandonment and the mechanism of section 1170 was not required. *In re* Auto-Train Corp., 4 C.B.C.2d 853 (B. Ct., D.D.C. 1981).

References

5 *Collier on Bankruptcy* ch. 1170 (Matthew Bender 15th ed.).

Graybeal, *Reflection on the Golden Spike: A Look at the Bankruptcy Reform Act and Railroad Reorganization,* 6 Hastings Const. L.Q. 1107 (1979).

SECTION 1171 (11 U.S.C. § 1171)

§ 1171. Priority claims.

(a) There shall be paid as an administrative expense any claim of an individual or of the personal representative of a deceased individual against the debtor or the estate, for personal injury to or death of such individual arising out of the operation of the debtor or the estate, whether such claim arose before or after the commencement of the case.

(b) Any unsecured claim against the debtor that would have been entitled to priority if a receiver in equity of the property of the debtor had been appointed by a Federal court on the date of the order for relief under this title shall be entitled to the same priority in the case under this chapter.

Legislative History

This section is derived from current law, Subsection (a) grants an administrative expense priority to the claim of any individual (or of the personal representative of a deceased individual) against the debtor or the estate for personal injury to or death of the individual arising out of the operation of the debtor railroad or the estate, whether the claim arose before or after commencement of the case. The priority under current law, found in section 77(n), applies only to employees of the debtor. This subsection expands the protection provided.

Subsection (b) follows present section 77(b) of the Bankruptcy Act by giving priority to any unsecured claims that would be entitled to priority if a receiver in equity of the property of the debtor had been appointed by a Federal court on the date of the order for relief under the bankruptcy laws. As under current law, the courts will determine the precise contours of the priority recognized by this subsection in each case.

[*House Report No. 95–595, 95th Cong., 1st Sess. 424 (1977).*]

Section 1171 of the House amendment is derived from section 1170 of the House bill in lieu of section 1173(a)(9) of the Senate amendment.

[*124 Cong. Rec. H 11,106 (Sept. 28, 1978); S 17,422 (Oct. 6, 1978).*]

Comment

Under Section 77(n) of the former Bankruptcy Act, personal injury claims of employees which arose either before or after the filing of a Section 77 reorganization petition were treated as operating expenses. Section 1171(a) eliminates the discrimination against non-employee tort claimants by requiring that all tort claims resulting in personal injury or death arising from operation of the railroad be paid as expenses of administration.

Section 1171(b) continues the policy of Section 77(b) of making the six-months creditors priority rule of equity receiverships applicable to railroad reorganizations. The precise definition of the six-months rule has been the subject of litigation. *See* Southern Ry. v. Flourny, 301 F.2d 847 (4th Cir. 1962) and *In re* Penn Central Transp. Co., 458 Supp. 1234 (E.D. Pa. 1978). The six-months rule will probably be the subject of litigation until the Supreme Court has occasion to clarify the law.

1984 Amendments: Subsection (b) of section 1171 was amended by changing "such" priority to "the same" priority.

Case Annotations

Congress has deliberately limited the application of the Six Month Rule, which allowed a receiver to pay certain prepetition debts from postpetition proceeds, to the area of railroad reorganization. In the Matter of B & W Enters., Inc., 713 F.2d 534, 9 C.B.C.2d 302 (9th Cir. 1983).

Although a chapter 11 debtor may be engaged in the transportation business, the Six Month Rule applies only to railroad reorganization cases. In enacting the Bankruptcy Code, Congress expressly rejected a proposal that a debtor railroad be required to pay interline balances, stating that to do so would distort the central bankruptcy principle of equality of treatment of unsecured creditors. In re McLean Industries, Inc., 21 C.B.C.2d 1022 (B. Ct., S.D.N.Y. 1989).

The granting of priority to a claim requires that the claim be for services rendered that were necessary for the operation of the debtor, such as legal fees, and that the services were rendered in the expectation that they would be paid for out of current revenues, as was clearly the expectation when in the prepetition period the railroad had no general credit upon which claimants could have relied. However, there is no requirement that the claimant establish either a diverted fund or necessity of payment. In re Michigan Interstate Railway Co., Inc., 19 C.B.C.2d 21 (B. Ct., E.D. Mich. 1988).

References

5 Collier on Bankruptcy ch. 1171 (Matthew Bender 15th ed.).

Graybeal, Reflection on the Golden Spike: A Look at the Bankruptcy Reform Act and Railroad Reorganization, 6 Hastings Const. L.Q. 1107 (1979).

SECTION 1172 (11 U.S.C. § 1172)

§ 1172. Contents of plan.

(a) In addition to the provisions required or permitted under section 1123 of this title, a plan—

(1) shall specify the extent to and the means by which the debtor's rail service is proposed to be continued, and the extent to which any of the debtor's rail service is proposed to be terminated; and

(2) may include a provision for—

(A) the transfer of any or all of the operating railroad lines of the debtor to another operating railroad; or

(B) abandonment of any railroad line in accordance with section 1170 of this title.

(b) If, except for the pendency of the case under this chapter, transfer of, or operation of or over, any of the debtor's rail lines by an entity other than the debtor or a successor to the debtor under the plan would require approval by the Commission under a law of the United States, then a plan may not propose such a transfer or such operation unless the proponent of the plan initiates an appropriate application for such a transfer or such operation with the Commission and, within such time as the court may fix, not exceeding 180 days, the Commission, with or without a hearing, as the Commission may determine, and with or without modification or condition, approves such application, or does not act on such application. Any action or order of the Commission approving, modifying, conditioning, or disapproving such application is subject to review by the court only under sections 706(2)(A), 706(2)(B), 706(2)(C), and 706(2)(D) of title 5.

(c)(1) In approving an application under subsection (b) of this section, the Commission shall require the rail carrier to provide a fair arrangement at least as protective of the interests of employees as that established under section 11347 of title 49.

(2) Nothing in this subsection shall be deemed to affect the priorities or timing of payment of employee protection which might have existed in the absence of this subsection.

Legislative History

A plan is [*sic*] a railroad reorganization case may include provisions in addition to those required and permitted under an ordinary reorganization plan. It may provide for the transfer of any or all of the operating railroad lines of the debtor to another operating railroad.

Paragraph (1) contemplates a liquidating plan for the debtor's rail lines, much as occurred in the Penn Central case by transfer of operating lines to ConRail. Such a liquidating plan is not per se contrary to the public interest, and the court will have to determine on a case-by-case basis, with the guidance of the Interstate Commerce Commission and of other parties in interest, whether the particular plan proposed is in the public interest, as required under proposed 11 U.S.C. § 1172(3).

The plan may also provide for abandonment in accordance with section 1169, governing abandonment generally. Neither of these provisions in a plan, transfer or abandonment of lines, requires ICC approval. Confirmation of the plan by the court authorizes the debtor to comply with the plan in accordance with section 1142(a) notwithstanding any bankruptcy law to the contrary.

[*House Report No. 95–595, 95th Cong., 1st Sess. 424 (1977).*]

Section 1172 of the House amendment is derived from section 1171 of the House bill in preference to section 1170 of the Senate amendment with the exception that section 1170(4) of the Senate amendment is incorporated into section 1172(a)(1) of the House amendment.

Section 1172(b) of the House amendment is derived from section 1171(c) of the Senate amendment. The section gives the Interstate Commerce Commission the exclusive power to approve or disapprove the transfer of, or operation of or over, any of the debtor's rail lines over which the Commission has jurisdiction, subject to review under the Administrative Procedures Act. The section does not apply to a transfer of railroad lines to a successor of the debtor under a plan of reorganization by merger or otherwise.

The House amendment deletes section 1171(a) of the Senate amendment as a matter to be determined by the Rules of Bankruptcy Procedure. It is anticipated that the rules will specify the period of time, such as 18 months, within which a trustee must file with the court a proposed plan of reorganization for the debtor or a report why a plan cannot be formulated. Incorporation by reference of section 1121 in section 1161 of title 11 means that a party in interest will also have a right to file a plan of reorganization. This differs from the position taken in the Senate amendment which would have permitted the Interstate Commerce Commission to file a plan of reorganization.

[*124 Cong. Rec. H 11,106 (Sept. 28, 1978); S 17,422 (Oct. 6, 1978).*]

Comment

By incorporating railroad reorganizations as a subchapter of chapter 11, all the provisions of chapter 11 (except those inappropriate sections enumerated in section 1161) are applicable in a railroad reorganization under subchapter IV of chapter 11. Thus, section 1123 which sets forth the contents of a plan of reorganization, is applicable to a railroad reorganization under subchapter IV. The purpose of section 1172 is to provide additional provisions required or permitted in addition to the mandatory and permissive provisions set forth in section 1123.

Bankruptcy Rule 3016(a), as amended in 1991, provides that the debtor may file a plan at any time. A party in interest, other than the debtor, authorized by section 1121(c) to file a plan, may not file a plan after entry of an order approving a disclosure statement unless confirmation of the plan relating to the disclosure statement has been denied or the court otherwise directs. (Section 1125 dealing with a disclosure statement is applicable in a railroad reorganization case. See section 1161.)

Subdivision (b) requires every proposed plan and any modification thereof to be dated and identified with the name of the entity or entities filing it.

Subdivision (c) provides that a disclosure statement pursuant to section 1125 or evidence showing compliance with section 1126(b) must be filed with the plan or within a time fixed by the court. *See* Comment to section 1125. [The Advisory Committee Note states with respect to the 1991 amendment to Rule 3016(a) that its purpose is to enlarge the time for filing competing plans. A party in interest may not file a plan without leave of court only if an order approving a disclosure statement relating to another plan has been entered and a decision on confirmation of the plan has not been entered. This subdivision does not fix a deadline beyond which a debtor may not file a plan.]

Staggers Rail Act of 1980: The Staggers Rail Act of 1980, Pub. L. No. 96–448, added subsection (c) to section 1172.

The provision puts employees of rail carriers which entered bankruptcy after the effective date of the Bankruptcy Act of 1978 in the same position as employees of rail carriers that entered bankruptcy prior to the Bankruptcy Act of 1978 with respect to employee protection.

Case Annotations

A railroad debtor need not pay postpetition interest or postpetition taxes if private creditors' shares would be reduced, operating expenses could not be met and the public interest would be better served. *In re* Boston and Maine Corp., 719 F.2d 493, 9 C.B.C.2d 1377 (1st Cir. 1983) (decided under the former Act).

References

5 *Collier on Bankruptcy* ch. 1172 (Matthew Bender 15th ed.).

Graybeal, *Reflection on the Golden Spike: A Look at the Bankruptcy Reform Act and Railroad Reorganization,* 6 Hastings Const. L.Q. 1107 (1979).

SECTION 1173 (11 U.S.C. § 1173)

§ 1173. Confirmation of plan.

(a) The court shall confirm a plan if—

(1) the applicable requirements of section 1129 of this title have been met;

(2) each creditor or equity security holder will receive or retain under the plan property of a value, as of the effective date of the plan, that is not less than the value of property that each such creditor or equity security holder would so receive or retain if all of the operating railroad lines of the debtor were sold, and the proceeds of such sale, and the other

property of the estate, were distributed under chapter 7 of this title on such date;

(3) in light of the debtor's past earnings and the probable prospective earnings of the reorganized debtor, there will be adequate coverage by such prospective earnings of any fixed charges, such as interest on debt, amortization of funded debt, and rent for leased railroads, provided for by the plan; and

(4) the plan is consistent with the public interest.

(b) If the requirements of subsection (a) of this section are met with respect to more than one plan, the court shall confirm the plan that is most likely to maintain adequate rail service in the public interest.

Legislative History

This section requires the court to confirm a plan if the applicable requirements of section 1129 (relating to confirmation of reorganization plans generally) are met, if the best interest test is met, and if the plan is compatible with the public interest.

The test in this paragraph is similar to the test prescribed for ordinary corporate reorganizations. However, since a railroad cannot liquidate its assets and sell them for scrap to satisfy its creditors, the test focuses on the value of the railroad as a going concern. That is, the test is based on what the assets, sold as operating rail lines, would bring.

The public interest requirement, found in current law, will now be decided by the court, with the ICC representing the public interest before the court, rather than in the first instance by the ICC. Liquidation of the debtor is not, *per se,* contrary to the public interest.

[*House Report No. 95–595, 95th Cong., 1st Sess. 425 (1977).*]

Section 1173 adapts the provisions dealing with reorganization plans generally contained in section 1130 to the particular requirements of railroad reorganization plans, as set out in present section 77(e). Subsection (a) specifies the findings which the court must make before approving a plan: (1) The plan complies with the applicable provisions of the chapter; (2) the proponent of the plan complies with the applicable provisions of the chapter; (3) the plan has been proposed in good faith; (4) any payments for services or for costs or expenses in connection with the case or the plan are disclosed to the court and are reasonable, or, if to be paid later, are subject to the approval of the court as reasonable; (5) the proponent of the plan has disclosed the identity and affiliations of the individuals who will serve as directors, officers, or voting trustees, such appointments or continuations in office are consistent with the interests of creditors, equity security holders, and the proponent [*sic*] the public, and has disclosed the identity and compensation of any insider who will be employed or retained under the plan; (6) that rate changes proposed in the plan have been approved by the appropriate regulatory commission, or that the plan is contingent on such approval; (7) that confirmation of the plan is not likely to be followed by further reorganization or liquidation, unless it is contemplated by the plan; (8) that the plan, if there is more than one, is the one most likely to maintain adequate rail service; and (9) that the plan provides the priority traditionally accorded by section 77(b) to claims by rail creditors for necessary services rendered during the 6 months preceding the filing of the petition in bankruptcy.

[*Senate Report No. 95–989, 95th Cong., 2d Sess. 135 (1978).*]

Section 1173 of the House amendment concerns confirmation of a plan of railroad reorganization and is derived from section 1172 of the House bill as modified In particular, section 1173(a)(3) of the House amendment is derived from section 1170(3) of the Senate amendment. Section 1173(b) is derived from section 1173(a)(8) of the Senate amendment.

[*124 Cong. Rec. H 11,106 (Sept. 28, 1978); S 17,423 (Oct. 6, 1978).*]

Comment

The incorporation of railroad reorganizations as an integral part of chapter 11 makes all the provisions of chapter 11 (with the exception of certain inappropriate sections enumerated in section 1161) applicable in railroad reorganizations. Thus, the general requirements for confirmation prescribed by section 1129 are applicable to railroad reorganization cases [except section 1129(a)(7) and section 1129(c) which are made inapplicable by section 1161]. Section 1173 prescribes certain requirements for a railroad reorganization in addition to the relevant requirement of section 1129.

See **Comment** to section 1129 for applicable Bankruptcy Rules.

1984 Amendments: Subdivision (a)(4) of section 1173 was amended by providing that a plan be "consistent" with the public interest instead of "compatible" with such interest.

References

5 *Collier on Bankruptcy* ch. 1173 (Matthew Bender 15th ed.).

Graybeal, *Reflection in the Golden Spike: A Look at the Bankruptcy Reform Act and Railroad Reorganization,* 6 Hastings Const. L.Q. 1107 (1979).

SECTION 1174 (11 U.S.C. § 1174)

§ 1174. **Liquidation.** On request of a party in interest and after notice and a hearing, the court may, or, if a plan has not been confirmed under section 1173 of this title before five years after the date of the order for relief, the court shall order the trustee to cease the debtor's operation and to collect and reduce to money all of the property of the estate in the same manner as if the case were a case under chapter 7 of this title.

Legislative History

Section 1174 permits the court to convert the case to a liquidation under chapter 7 if the court finds that the debtor cannot be reorganized, or if various time limits specified in the subchapter are not met. Section 77 does not authorize a liquidation of a railroad under the Bankruptcy Act. If the railroad is not reorganizable, the only action open to the court is to dismiss the petition, which would in all likelihood be followed by a State court receivership, with all of its attendant disadvantages. If reorganization is impossible, the debtor should be liquidated under the Bankruptcy Act.

[*Senate Report No. 95–989, 95th Cong., 2d Sess. 136 (1978).*]

Section 1174 of the House amendment represents a compromise between the House bill and Senate amendment on the issue of liquidation of a railroad. The provision permits a party in interest at any time to request liquidation. In addition, if a plan has not been confirmed under section 1173 of the House amendment before 5 years after the date of order for relief, the court must order the trustee to cease the debtor's operation and to collect and reduce to money all of the property of the estate in the same manner as if the case were a case under chapter 7 of title 11. The approach differs from the conversion to chapter 7 under section 1174 of the Senate bill in order to make special provisions contained in subchapter IV of chapter 11 applicable to liquidation. However, maintaining liquidation in the context of chapter 11 is not intended to delay liquidation of the railroad to a different extent than if the case were converted to chapter 7.

[*124 Cong. Rec. H 11,106 (Sept. 28, 1978); S 17,423 (Oct. 6, 1978).*]

Comment

There was no comparable provision in Section 77 of the former Bankruptcy Act relating to railroad reorganizations that provided for liquidation if a plan could not be confirmed. Under the Act, dismissal of the case was the only alternative to confirmation. Section 1174 of the Code does not provide for a liquidation by conversion to chapter 7, but requires the trustee to collect and reduce to money all of the property "in the same manner as if the case were a case under chapter 7." Presumably, this approach is intended to expedite liquidation.

References

5 *Collier on Bankruptcy* ch. 1174 (Matthew Bender 15th ed.).

Graybeal, *Reflection on the Golden Spike: A Look at the Bankruptcy Reform Act and Railroad Reorganization,* 6 Hastings Const. L.Q. 1107 (1979).

CHAPTER 12

Adjustment of Debts of a Family Farmer With Regular Annual Income

SUBCHAPTER I

Officers, Administration, and the Estate

SECTION 1201 (11 U.S.C. § 1201)

§ 1201. Stay of action against codebtor.

(a) Except as provided in subsections (b) and (c) of this section, after the order for relief under this chapter, a creditor may not act, or commence or continue any civil action, to collect all or any part of a consumer debt of the debtor from any individual that is liable on such debt with the debtor, or that secured such debt, unless—

(1) such individual became liable on or secured such debt in the ordinary course of such individual's business; or

(2) the case is closed, dismissed, or converted to a case under chapter 7 of this title.

(b) A creditor may present a negotiable instrument, and may give notice of dishonor of such an instrument.

(c) On request of a party in interest and after notice and a hearing, the court shall grant relief from the stay provided by subsection (a) of this section with respect to a creditor, to the extent that—

(1) as between the debtor and the individual protected under subsection (a) of this section, such individual received the consideration for the claim held by such creditor;

(2) the plan filed by the debtor proposes not to pay such claim; or

(3) such creditor's interest would be irreparably harmed by continuation of such stay.

(d) Twenty days after the filing of a request under subsection (c)(2) of this section for relief from the stay provided by subsection (a) of this section, such stay is terminated with respect to the party in interest making such request, unless the debtor or any individual that is liable on such debt with the debtor files and serves upon such party in interest a written objection to the taking of the proposed action.

Bankruptcy Rule Reference: 4001

Comment

Section 1201 is the counterpart of section 1301. It is designed to protect a debtor in a chapter 12 case from pressure on the part of creditors who might pursue friends or relatives who have cosigned an obligation of a debtor. The section operates to stay automatically an act or civil action to collect a consumer debt of the debtor from a codebtor, unless the codebtor became liable on, or secured the debt in the ordinary course of the codebtor's business, or the case is closed, dismissed, or converted to a chapter 7 case.

Bankruptcy Rule 4001 prescribes the procedure for relief from an automatic stay provided by the Code. Subdivision (a) provides that the motion for relief shall be served on any elected or appointed committee and if no committee has been appointed pursuant to section 1102, on the creditors included on the list filed pursuant to Rule 1007(d) and on such other entities as the court directs.

The creditor may, nevertheless, present a negotiable instrument and give notice of dishonor in order to protect substantive rights against the debtor.

Finally, the stay is applicable only if the codebtor is really a codebtor. To the extent that the codebtor actually received consideration for the creditor's claim, the creditor is entitled to have the stay lifted.

The eligibility to be a chapter 12 debtor is prescribed in section 109(f) and, therefore, chapter 12 does not provide "who may be a debtor."

Case Annotations

When the primary beneficiaries of corporate borrowing are the shareholders of a farming corporation, they cannot be classified as innocent co-obligors extending family or personal obligations, and therefore cannot fall under the protection of section 1201. *In re* SFW, Inc., 18 C.B.C.2d 584 (B. Ct., S.D. Cal. 1988).

In a chapter 12 case, a creditor may obtain relief from the automatic stay against codebtors to pursue its claim when it appears that the creditor will almost certainly receive no material payment of its unsecured claim through the proposed *pro rata* payments of the plan. *In re* Binstock, 17 C.B.C.2d 905 (B. Ct., D.N.D. 1987).

References

5 *Collier on Bankruptcy* ch. 1201 (Matthew Bender 15th ed.).

3 *Collier on Bankruptcy* ch. 1201 (Matthew Bender 3d ed.).

Collier Farm Bankruptcy Guide ch. 4 (Matthew Bender 1st ed.).

Comment, *American Savings Bank v. Waschkat: Iowa Continues to Frustrate the Rights of Codebtors,* 75 Iowa L. Rev. 259 (1989).

Papke, *Rhetoric and Retrenchment: Agrarian Ideology and American Bankruptcy Law,* 54 Mo. L. Rev. 871 (1989).

SECTION 1202 (11 U.S.C. § 1202)

§ 1202. Trustee.

(a) If the United States trustee has appointed an individual under section 586(b) of title 28 to serve as standing trustee in cases under this chapter and if such individual qualifies as a trustee under section 322 of this title, then such individual shall serve as trustee in any case filed under this chapter. Otherwise, the United States trustee shall appoint one disinterested person to serve as trustee in the case or the United States trustee may serve as trustee in the case if necessary.

(b) The trustee shall—

(1) Perform the duties specified in sections 704(2), 704(3), 704(5), 704(6), 704(7), and 704(9) of this title;

(2) perform the duties specfied [*sic*] in section 1106(a)(3) and 1106(a)(4) of this title if the court, for cause and on request of a party in interest, the trustee, or the United States trustee, so orders;

(3) appear and be heard at any hearing that concerns—

(A) the value of property subject to a lien;

(B) confirmation of a plan;

(C) modification of the plan after confirmation; or

(D) the sale of property of the estate;

(4) ensure that the debtor commences making timely payments required by a confirmed plan; and

(5) if the debtor ceases to be a debtor in possession, perform the duties specified in sections 704(8), 1106(a)(1), 1106(a)(2), 1106(a)(6), 1106(a)(7), and 1203.

Bankruptcy Rule References: 2012, 2015 and 5002

Comment

Section 1202(a) is the counterpart of section 1302(a), as the latter was amended by the 1986 Act. It provides administrative flexibility by permitting the United States trustee to appoint an individual from the panel of disinterested trustees.

Subsection (b)(1) specifies the duties of the trustee, tracking section 1302(b)(1). Subsection (b)(2) has no counterpart in section 1302. On request of a party in interest, the trustee or the United States trustee, the court may, for cause, order the trustee to perform the duties specified in section 1106(a)(3) and (a)(4), thus borrowing from chapter 11 as well as from chapter 13.

Subsection (b)(3) tracks section 1302(b)(2) but adds the duty of the trustee to appear and be heard at any hearing regarding the sale of property of the estate.

Subsection (b)(5) varies from section 1302(c), providing that if the debtor ceases to be a debtor in possession, the trustee is to perform the duties specified in sections 704(8), 1106(a)(1), (2), (6), and (7), and 1203.

Bankruptcy Rule 2012(a) provides that if a debtor is removed as a debtor in possession in a chapter 12 case, the trustee is substituted automatically for the debtor in possession as a party in interest in any pending action, proceeding, or matter. Subdivision (b) provides that when a trustee dies, resigns, is removed, or otherwise ceases hold office, the successor is automatically substituted as party in any pending action, proceeding or matter and shall file an accounting of the prior administration of the estate.

Bankruptcy Rule 5002, as amended in 1991, provides that a bankruptcy judge may not approve the appointment of a person as a trustee or approve employments of an attorney, accountant, appraiser, auctioneer or other professional, if that person is or has been so connected with the judge or the United States trustee as to render the appointment or employment improper. ["Improper" includes the appearance of impropriety.]

Bankruptcy Rule 2015(a) relates to the duties of a trustee or debtor in possession and specifies these duties, the first four of which are:

(1) file and transmit to the United States trustee a complete inventory of the property of the debtor within 30 days after qualifying as a trustee or a debtor in possession.

(2) keep records of receipts and disposition of money and property received;

(3) file reports and summaries required by section 704(8) if the business is authorized to be operated including a statement of deductions for taxes withheld from employees;

(4) give notice of the case to every entity holding money or property subject to withdrawal or order of the debtor;

Subdivision (b), added by the 1991 amendments, provides that in a chapter 12 case, the debtor in possession shall perform the duties prescribed in clauses (1)-(4) of subdivision (a). If the debtor is removed as debtor in possession, the trustee shall perform the duties of the debtor in possession prescribed in this paragraph.

When Section 255 of the Bankruptcy Judges, United States Trustees, and Family Farmer Bankruptcy Act of 1986, Pub. L. No. 99–554, enacted section 1202 as part of chapter 12, section 1202 consisted of subsections (a), (b), (c) and (d). Subsections (c) and (d), however, were deleted by Section 227 of Subtitle A of Title II of the 1986 Act. Because the deletion of subsections (c) and (d) was part of the Subtitle A amendments regarding United States trustees, the effective date of the repeal of subsections (c) and (d) of section 1202, pursuant to Section 302(d) of Title III of the 1986 Act, corresponded with the date on which the United States trustee system became effective. On that date, which varied among the judicial districts, 28 U.S.C. § 586 became the operative statute instead of subsections (c) and (d) of section 1202. *See* 28 U.S.C. § 586, reprinted in the section on United States trustees in **Additional Statutory Provisions**, *infra,* following the Bankruptcy Code. *See also* Section 302 of the 1986 Amendments, as amended by Pub. L. No. 101-650 (1990), reprinted herein under "Selected Provisions of the Bankruptcy Judges, United States Trustees, and Family Farmer Bankruptcy Act of 1986," regarding effective dates generally. Pub. L. No. 101-650 (Judicial Improvements Act of 1990) (signed into law December 1, 1990) amended Section 302(d)(3) of the Bankruptcy Judges, United States Trustees, and Family Farmer Bankruptcy Act of 1986 by extending the period in which the judicial districts in the states of Alabama and North Carolina may remain outide the United States trustee system.

Case Annotations

Because the trustee has a general duty to monitor payments under a chapter 12 reorganization plan, and because administrative expense claims warrant special attention, attorney's fees must be paid by the trustee, rather than directly by the debtor. *In re* Beard, 25 C.B.C.2d 1746 (B. Ct., S.D. Ohio 1991).

A chapter 12 trustee may not investigate a debtor's business unless specifically ordered to do so by the court. The issuance of such order is within the authority of the bankruptcy court; once given, a positive duty is placed upon the trustee to investigate. Under section 1202(b)(2), a significant quantum of evidence is required to allow a postconfirmation

Bankruptcy Rule 2004 examination of debtors. The threshold test is more than mere suspicion, yet less than that entitling one to a judgment that fraud took place. *In re* Gross, 24 C.B.C.2d 1297 (B. Ct., D.S.D. 1990).

Comparison of the duties set forth in section 1202(b) with those of section 1302(b) suggests that Congress intended the role of the chapter 12 trustee to be broader than that of the chapter 13 trustee. In the Matter of Logemann, 19 C.B.C.2d 926 (B. Ct., S.D. Iowa 1988).

References

5 *Collier on Bankruptcy* ch. 1202 (Matthew Bender 15th ed.).

3 *Collier Bankruptcy Manual* ch. 1202 (Matthew Bender 3d ed.).

Collier Farm Bankruptcy Guide ch. 4 (Matthew Bender 1st ed.).

SECTION 1203 (11 U.S.C. § 1203)

§ 1203. **Rights and powers of debtor.** Subject to such limitations as the court may prescribe, a debtor in possession shall have all the rights, other than the right to compensation under section 330, and powers, and shall perform all the functions and duties, except the duties specified in paragraphs (3) and (4) of section 1106(a), of a trustee serving in a case under chapter 11, including operating the debtor's farm.

Comment

Section 1203 specifies the rights and powers of a chapter 12 debtor. It differs from the provisions in section 1303 relating to the rights and powers of a chapter 13 debtor. The chapter 12 debtor has all the rights [other than the right to compensation under section 330] and all the powers, functions and duties of a chapter 11 trustee, including operating the debtor's farm. Excepted are the duties prescribed in section 1106(a)(3) and (4) which relate to investigation by a chapter 11 trustee of the acts, conduct, etc., of the chapter 11 debtor.

References

5 *Collier on Bankruptcy* ch. 1203 (Matthew Bender 15th ed.).

3 *Collier Bankruptcy Manual* ch. 1203 (Matthew Bender 3d ed.).

Collier Farm Bankruptcy Guide ch. 4 (Matthew Bender 1st ed.).

Papke, *Rhetoric and Retrenchment: Agrarian Ideology and American Bankruptcy Law,* 54 Mo. L. Rev. 871 (1989).

SECTION 1204 (11 U.S.C. § 1204)

§ 1204.   Removal of debtor as debtor in possession.

(a) On request of a party in interest, and after notice and a hearing, the court shall order that the debtor shall not be a debtor in possession for cause, including fraud, dishonesty, incompetence, or gross mismanagement of the affairs of the debtor, either before or after the commencement of the case.

(b) On request of a party in interest, and after notice and a hearing, the court may reinstate the debtor in possession.

Comment

Section 1204(a) provides for removing the debtor from possession for cause, including fraud, dishonesty, incompetence, or gross mismanagement. The cause for such action may have occurred before or after the commencement of the case. This section is patterned, in part, after section 1104(a) which provides for appointment of a chapter 11 trustee for very much the same reasons as set forth in section 1204(a). In order to remove a debtor as debtor in possession, there must be a request (motion) by a "party in interest." The wording of this section is not unlike that of section 1104(a)(1) dealing with appointment of a trustee in a chapter 11 case. In considering a motion for appointment of a trustee pursuant to section 1104(a)(1), the court is not required to conduct a full evidentiary hearing. The party requesting appointment of a trustee has the burden of proof. The evidence supporting appointment of a trustee must be clear and convincing.

Subsection (b), providing for reinstating the debtor in possession, is patterned after a like provision in section 1105 regarding a chapter 11 debtor in possession.

The Joint Explanatory Statement of the Committee of Conference for the 1986 Act, with respect to § 1204, reads as follows:

> In the event the Chapter 12 debtor is dispossessed and a trustee is substituted for the debtor in possession, the Conference contemplates that the trustee, or the trustee's designee, will be responsible for operating the farm. This transfer of duties is modeled after provisions in Chapter 11. However, it is important to note that the Conferees do not authorize the Chapter 12 trustee to file a plan of reorganization, as is the case of Chapter 11.

References

5 *Collier on Bankruptcy* ch. 1204 (Matthew Bender 15th ed.).

3 *Collier Bankruptcy Manual* ch. 1204 (Matthew Bender 3d ed.).

Collier Farm Bankruptcy Guide ch. 4 (Matthew Bender 1st ed.).

SECTION 1205 (11 U.S.C. § 1205)

§ 1205.   Adequate protection.

(a) Section 361 does not apply in a case under this chapter.

(b) In a case under this chapter, when adequate protection is required under section 362, 363, or 364 of this title of an interest of an entity in property, such adequate protection may be provided by—

> (1) requiring the trustee to make a cash payment or periodic cash payments to such entity, to the extent that the stay under section 362 of this title, use, sale, or lease under section 363 of this title, or any grant of a lien under section 364 of this title results in a decrease in the value of property securing a claim or of an entity's ownership interest in property;

> (2) providing to such entity an additional or replacement lien to the extent that such stay, use, sale, lease, or grant results in a decrease in the value of property securing a claim or of an entity's ownership interest in property;

> (3) paying to such entity for the use of farmland the reasonable rent customary in the community where the property is located, based upon the rental value, net income, and earning capacity of the property; or

> (4) granting such other relief, other than entitling such entity to compensation allowable under section 503(b)(1) of this title as an administrative expense, as will adequately protect the value of property securing a claim or of such entity's ownership interest in property.

Comment

Section 1205 provides a special test for adequate protection in chapter 12 cases. The reason for the chapter 12 version of adequate protection is clearly stated in the Joint Explanatory Statement of the Committee of Conference for the 1986 Act as follows:

> "Under current law, the filing of a bankruptcy petition operates as an automatic stay against any act to create, perfect, or enforce a lien against property of the estate. The secured creditor must file a motion

to have the stay lifted in order to proceed with foreclosure. The primary basis for lifting the stay is a lack of adequate protection. This term is not defined in the Bankruptcy Code, but examples of adequate protection are set out in 11 U.S.C. 361.

"The Fourth and Ninth Circuits have held that adequate protection requires the debtor to compensate the secured creditor for so-called 'lost opportunity costs' in those cases where the value of the collateral is less than the amount of debt secured by the collateral. *In re American Mariner Industries, Inc.*, 734 F.2d 426 (9th Cir. 1984); *Grundy National Bank v. Tandem Mining Corp.*, 754 F.2d 1436 (4th Cir. 1985). The payment of lost opportunity costs requires the periodic payment of a sum of cash equal to the interest that the undercollateralized secured creditor might earn on an amount of money equal to the value of the collateral securing the debt.

"Lost opportunity costs payments present serious barriers to farm reorganizations, because farmland values have dropped so dramatically in many sections of the country—making for many undercollateralized secured lenders. Family farmers are usually unable to pay lost opportunity costs. Thus, family farm reorganizations are often throttled in their infancy upon motion to lift the automatic stay.

"Accordingly, section 1205 of the conference report provides a separate test for adequate protection in Chapter 12 cases. It eliminates the need of the family farmer to pay lost opportunity costs, and adds another means for providing adequate protection for farmland—paying reasonable market rent. Section 1205 eliminates the 'indubitable equivalent' language of 11 U.S.C. 361(3) and makes it clear that what needs to be protected is the value of property, not the value of the creditor's 'interest' in property.

"It is expected that this provision will reduce unnecessary litigation during the term of the automatic stay, and will allow the family farmer to devote proper attention to plan preparation."

Case Annotations

A secured creditor is not entitled to adequate protection for the mere use of the collateral especially when the value of the collateral is not declining. In the Matter of Bluridg Farms, Inc., 19 C.B.C.2d 1081 (B. Ct., S.D. Iowa 1988).

When a creditor's claim is secured by farmland, the payment by the debtor of a fair rental value constitutes adequate protection so that the chapter 12 debtor will in no event provide the creditor with more than the fair rental value of the land, *i.e.*, the reasonable rent customary in the community where the collateral is located. *In re* Kocher, 18 C.B.C.2d 544 (B. Ct., S.D. Ohio 1987).

A chapter 12 debtor is not required to pay lost opportunity costs in the form of interest payments or otherwise for the retention of secured equipment to adequately protect a secured creditor. *In re* Rennich, 16 C.B.C.2d 202 (B. Ct., D.S.D. 1987).

References

5 *Collier on Bankruptcy* ch. 1205 (Matthew Bender 15th ed.).

3 *Collier Bankruptcy Manual* ch. 1205 (Matthew Bender 3d ed.).

Collier Farm Bankruptcy Guide ch. 4 (Matthew Bender 1st ed.).

Lallier, *Feds Spring New Farm Bankruptcy Rules—Can They Save the Family Farm?*, 2 Minn. Law 20 (1986).

Matson, *Understanding the New Family Farmer Bankruptcy Act*, 21 U. Rich. L. Rev. 521 (1987).

Ryan, *The Changing Standards of Adequate Protection in Farm Bankruptcy Reorganizations*, 37 Drake L. Rev. 323 (1987–88).

SECTION 1206 (11 U.S.C. § 1206)

§ 1206.　Sales free of interests.　After notice and a hearing, in addition to the authorization contained in section 363(f), the trustee in a case under this chapter may sell property under section 363(b) and (c) free and clear of any interest in such property of an entity other than the estate if the property is farmland or farm equipment, except that the proceeds of such sale shall be subject to such interest.

Bankruptcy Rule Reference: 6004

Comment

Section 1206 is intended to assist the process of reorganization by permitting chapter 12 debtors to scale down their operations by the sale of farmland and farm equipment free and clear of any interests. The proceeds of sale will be subject to such interests.

In connection with § 1206, the Conference Report states:

"Most family farm reorganizations, to be successful, will involve the sale of unnecessary property. This section of the Conference Report allows Chapter 12 debtors to scale down the size of their farming operations by selling unnecessary property.

"This section modifies 11 U.S.C. 363(f) to allow family farmers to sell assets not needed for the reorganization prior to confirmation without the consent of the secured creditor, subject to approval of the court.

"This section also explicitly makes clear that the creditor's interest (which includes a lien) would attach to the proceeds of the sale. Of course, the holders of secured claims would have the right to bid at the sale to the extent permitted under 11 U.S.C. 363(k)."

[Joint Explanatory Statement of the Committee of Conference, for the 1986 Act.]

Section 1206 adds the sale of farmland or farm equipment to the situations which section 363(d) lists as free and clear of any interest other than that of the estate. The section makes clear that the creditor's interest would attach to the proceeds of the sale of farmland or farm equipment.

Bankruptcy Rule 6004 relates to the sale of property of the estate. Subdivision (a) provides for notice; subdivision (b) provides for objections; subdivision (c) deals with sales "free and clear"; subdivision (d) deals with sales of property under $2500; subdivision (e) provides for hearing; and subdivision (f) relates to the conduct of sales not in the ordinary course of business.

References

5 *Collier on Bankruptcy* ch. 1206 (Matthew Bender 15th ed.).

3 *Collier Bankruptcy Manual* ch. 1206 (Matthew Bender 3d ed.).

Collier Farm Bankruptcy Guide ch. 4 (Matthew Bender 1st ed.).

Bromley, *The Chapter 12 Family Farmer Bankruptcy Law—Changing the Rules,* 60 Wis. B. Bull. 18 (1987).

SECTION 1207 (11 U.S.C. § 1207)

§ 1207. Property of the estate.

(a) Property of the estate includes, in addition to the property specified in section 541 of this title—

(1) all property of the kind specified in such section that the debtor acquires after the commencement of the case but before the case is closed, dismissed or converted to a case under chapter 7 of this title, whichever occurs first; and

(2) earnings from services performed by the debtor after the commencement of the case but before the case is closed, dismissed, or converted to a case under chapter 7 of this title, whichever occurs first.

(b) Except as provided in section 1204, a confirmed plan, or an order confirming a plan, the debtor shall remain in possession of all property of the estate.

Comment

Section 1207 finds its counterpart in section 1306 of chapter 13. Section 541 describes and specifies what constitutes property of the estate and this includes the estate in a chapter 12 case. Section 1207 specifies "property of the estate" in a chapter 12 case in addition to the property set forth in section 541, as amended by Pub. L. No. 101-508 (Omnibus Budget Reconciliation Act of 1990) (effective on date of enactment, November 5, 1990).

Section 1207(a) provides that property of the kind enumerated in section 541 acquired after the filing of the petition but before the case is closed, dismissed, or converted, whichever first occurs, is included in "property of the estate." Section 1207(a)(2) similarly provides that earnings from debtor's services after commencement of the case but before the case is closed, dismissed, or converted, whichever first occurs, is included in "property of the estate."

Section 1207(b) provides that the debtor remain in possession of all property of the estate except under specified circumstances. The debtor shall not remain in possession if under section 1204(a) the court, for cause, orders the removal of the debtor as debtor in possession. Also, the debtor shall not remain in possession of the property of the estate to the extent provided in a confirmed plan or in an order confirming the plan.

Case Annotations

Postconfirmation funds held by a chapter 12 trustee but unpaid to creditors at the time the chapter 12 case is converted to a chapter 7 liquidation, revest in the debtor at the time of the conversion and become subject to his claim of exemption. *In re* Plata, 958 F.2d 918, 26 C.B.C.2d 914 (9th Cir. 1992).

A chapter 12 plan does not violate the Fifth Amendment when a secured creditor receives equal value pursuant to 11 U.S.C. § 1225(a)(5). Additionally, Congress intended that chapter 12 should apply retroactively to obligations acquired prior to its enactment. Travelers Insurance Co. v. Bullington, 878 F.2d 354, 21 C.B.C.2d 765 (11th Cir. 1989).

Proceeds of an insurance policy which were collateral for a secured claim but which were omitted from the confirmed chapter 12 plan and subsequently revested in the debtor are property of the bankruptcy estate. *In re* Martin, 25 C.B.C.2d 932 (B. Ct., N.D. Iowa 1991).

References

5 *Collier on Bankruptcy* ch. 1207 (Matthew Bender 15th ed.).

3 *Collier Bankruptcy Manual* ch. 1207 (Matthew Bender 3d ed.).

Collier Farm Bankruptcy Guide ch. 4 (Matthew Bender 1st ed.).

SECTION 1208 (11 U.S.C. § 1208)

§ 1208.   Conversion or dismissal.

(a) The debtor may convert a case under this chapter to a case under chapter 7 of this title at any time. Any waiver of the right to convert under this subsection is unenforceable.

(b) On request of the debtor at any time, if the case has not been converted under section 706 or 1112 of this title, the court shall dismiss a case under this chapter. Any waiver of the right to dismiss under this subsection is unenforceable.

(c) On request of a party in interest, and after notice and a hearing, the court may dismiss a case under this chapter for cause, including—

    (1) unreasonable delay, or gross mismanagement, by the debtor that is prejudicial to creditors;

    (2) nonpayment of any fees and charges required under chapter 123 of title 28;

    (3) failure to file a plan timely under section 1221 of this title;

    (4) failure to commence making timely payments required by a confirmed plan;

    (5) denial of confirmation of a plan under section 1225 of this title and denial of a request made for additional time for filing another plan or a modification of a plan;

    (6) material default by the debtor with respect to a term of a confirmed plan;

    (7) revocation of the order of confirmation under section 1230 of this title, and denial of confirmation of a modified plan under section 1229 of this title;

    (8) termination of a confirmed plan by reason of the occurrence of a condition specified in the plan; or

    (9) continuing loss to or diminution of the estate and absence of a reasonable likelihood of rehabilitation.

(d) On request of a party in interest, and after notice and a hearing, the court may dismiss a case under this chapter or convert a case under this chapter to a case under chapter 7 of this title upon a showing that the debtor has committed fraud in connection with the case.

(e) Notwithstanding any other provision of this section, a case may not be converted to a case under another chapter of this title unless the debtor may be a debtor under such chapter.

Bankruptcy Rule References: 1017 and 1019

Comment

Section 1208 is patterned after section 1307 of chapter 13 with several changes necessitated by the different objects of chapter 12 and 13.

Subsection (a) gives the chapter 12 debtor the absolute right to convert the case to chapter 7 and this right may not be waived.

Subsection (b) mandates the court to dismiss a chapter 12 case on request of the debtor provided that the case has not been converted under section 706 or 1112 and, again, this right may not be waived.

Subsection (c) provides that on request of a party in interest, and after notice and a hearing, the court may dismiss the chapter 12 case for cause including the reasons specified in subsection (c). The first ground for dismissal under section 1307 of chapter 13 is unreasonable delay by the debtor. The first ground enumerated in section 1208 is unreasonable delay *or gross mismanagement* by the debtor. Paragraphs (9) and (10) of section 1307(c) are not carried over into section 1208 as inappropriate for chapter 12 cases. A reason for dismissal not found in section 1307(c) is paragraph (9) of section 1208(c): "continuing loss to or diminution of the estate and absence of a reasonable likelihood of rehabilitation." Under subsection (c) the court may only dismiss the case. The court may not convert the case to another chapter.

Subsection (d) provides that on request of a party in interest (after notice and a hearing) the court may dismiss the chapter 12 case. The court may also convert the case to a case under chapter 7, but only "upon a showing that the debtor has committed fraud" in connection with the case.

Bankruptcy Rule 1017 deals with dismissal or conversion. Except as provided in section 1208(b) [pursuant to which the debtor has an absolute right to have the chapter 12 case dismissed] a case shall not be dismissed on motion of the petitioner or for want of prosecution or other cause or by consent of the parties before a hearing on notice as provided in Rule 2002. For such notice the debtor must file a list of all creditors and their addresses within the time fixed by the court unless the list was previously filed.

Bankruptcy Rule 1019 relates to conversion of a case to chapter 7. *See* Comment to section 1307 for discussion of Rule 1019, which by its very terms is made applicable to chapter 12 cases.

Bankruptcy Rule 2002(f) requires the clerk, or some other person as the court may direct, to give notice by mail to the debtor and all creditors of dismissal of the case. Subdivision (k) requires that notice of dismissal be transmitted to the United States trustee.

Case Annotations

Once fraud has become an issue in a case, the court may delay action on a section 1208(b) motion for dismissal long enough to allow an investigation of the alleged fraud. The broad purpose of the Bankruptcy Code is best served by interpreting section 1208(d) to allow a court to convert a case to chapter 7 upon a showing of fraud even though the debtor has moved for dismissal of his case under section 1208(b); such an interpretation presents no conflict with the express language of section 1208(b) as nothing in the section requires that a court act immediately upon a debtor's request for voluntary dismissal. *In re* Graven, 936 F.2d 378, 24 C.B.C.2d 2006 (8th Cir. 1991).

Based on the plain language of Section 302 of the 1986 Act and the lack of any expression to the contrary from Congress, conversion of a chapter 11 case pending prior to the enactment of chapter 12 into a chapter 12 case is prohibited, even though the debtor would qualify for protection under chapter 12 as a family farmer in economic crisis. United States v. Erickson Partnership, 856 F.2d 1068, 19 C.B.C.2d 841 (8th Cir. 1988).

A party in interest is free to move for dismissal or relief from stay at any time and may pursue such remedies even within the 90-day filing period. *In re* Fenske, 20 C.B.C.2d 1054 (B. Ct., D.N.D. 1988).

A chapter 12 case is available only to the honest debtor and evidence of fraud will allow the court to dismiss the case or convert it to a chapter 7 case. *In re* Zurface, 20 C.B.C.2d 1298 (B. Ct., S.D. Ohio 1989).

Section 1208(a) grants an absolute nonwaivable right to have a chapter 12 case converted to chapter 7 and does not prohibit the conversion of a chapter 12 case to chapter 11. In the Matter of Bird, 18 C.B.C.2d 229 (B. Ct., W.D. Mich. 1987).

The legislative history of chapter 12 indicates that Congress intentionally opted to deny a chapter 12 debtor the ability to convert a chapter 12 case to chapter 11. *In re* Christy, 17 C.B.C.2d 1187 (B. Ct., E.D. Va. 1987). *But see In re* Orr, 16 C.B.C.2d 640 (B. Ct., E.D.N.C. 1987).

In order to determine if an extension of time in which to file a new chapter 12 plan should be granted, the court should consider how soon after the order for relief the original chapter 12 plan was filed, how comprehensive and complete the first plan was, the reasons for denial of confirmation of the first plan, the likelihood of successful confirmation of a new plan, how long an extension is requested, whether the debtor's initial plan is proposed in good faith and not to delay, and whether the debtor's cash flow projections show that reorganization is possible. *In re* Bentson, 16 C.B.C.2d 1411 (B. Ct., D. Minn. 1987).

References

5 *Collier on Bankruptcy* ch. 1208 (Matthew Bender 15th ed.).

3 *Collier Bankruptcy Manual* ch. 1208 (Matthew Bender 3d ed.).

Collier Farm Bankruptcy Guide ch. 4 (Matthew Bender 1st ed.).

SUBCHAPTER II

The Plan

SECTION 1221 (11 U.S.C. § 1221)

§ 1221. Filing of plan. The debtor shall file a plan not later than 90 days after the order for relief under this chapter, except that the court may extend such period if an extension is substantially justified.

Bankruptcy Rule Reference: 3015

Comment

Section 1221 provides that the chapter 12 debtor is the sole party with authority to file a plan. The section also requires that the plan be filed not later than 90 days after the order for relief, *i.e.,* the date the chapter 12 petition was filed, unless the court grants an extension of time if such extension is "substantially justified." "Substantially justified" is a new term under the Code. If the debtor fails to file timely a plan, a party may move to dismiss the case, but may move for conversion to chapter 7 *only* on a showing that the debtor has committed fraud in connection with the case.

28 U.S.C. § 586(a)(3)(C) requires the United States trustee to monitor plans filed under chapter 12 and to file with the court in connection with hearings under sections 1224 and 1229 comments with respect to such plan. Accordingly, a copy of the plan should be transmitted to the United States trustee.

Bankruptcy Rule 3015(b), added by the 1991 amendments, provides that the debtor may file a chapter 12 plan with the petition. If a plan is not filed with the petition, it shall be filed within the time prescribed by section 1221 of the Code. Subdivision (c) requires every proposed plan and any modification thereof to be dated. Subdivision (d) requires the plan (or a summary thereof) to be included with each notice of the hearing on confirmation. The court may require the debtor to furnish sufficient copies of the plan to enable the clerk to include a copy with each notice of the hearing. Subdivision (e) requires the clerk to forthwith transmit a copy of the plan and any modification thereof to the United States trustee.

Case Annotations

Chapter 12 debtors may withdraw their first plan to file a second plan, if the original 90 days after an order for relief, pursuant to section 1221, have not expired. *In re* Ryan, 16 C.B.C.2d 488 (B. Ct., M.D. Fla. 1987).

References

5 *Collier on Bankruptcy* ch. 1221 (Matthew Bender 15th ed.).

3 *Collier Bankruptcy Manual* ch. 1221 (Matthew Bender 3d ed.).

Collier Farm Bankruptcy Guide ch. 4 (Matthew Bender 1st ed.).

Brody, *Chapter 12 Bankruptcy for the Family Farmer,* 9 Louisville Law. 16 (1988).

Chapter 12: Relief for the Family Farmer, 5 Bankr. Dev. J. 229 (1987).

Chatz, Cohen, Feinstein and Morgan, *Farm Bankruptcy and Chapter 12,* 3 Comm. L. Bull. 25 (1988).

Papke, *Rhetoric and Retrenchment: Agrarian Ideology and American Bankruptcy Law,* 54 Mo. L. Rev. 871 (1989).

Ventura, *Chapter 12—Adjustment of Debts of a Family Farmer With Regular Annual Income—An Overview,* 51 Tex. B.J. 342 (1988).

SECTION 1222 (11 U.S.C. § 1222)

§ 1222. Contents of plan.

(a) The plan shall—

(1) provide for the submission of all or such portion of future earnings or other future income of the debtor to the supervision and control of the trustee as is necessary for the execution of the plan;

(2) provide for the full payment, in deferred cash payments, of all claims entitled to priority under section 507 of this title, unless the holder of a particular claim agrees to a different treatment of such claim; and

(3) if the plan classifies claims and interests, provide the same treatment for each claim or interest within a particular class unless the holder of a particular claim or interest agrees to less favorable treatment.

(b) Subject to subsections (a) and (c) of this section, the plan may—

(1) designate a class or classes of unsecured claims, as provided in section 1122 of this title, but may not discriminate unfairly against any class so designated; however, such plan may treat claims for a consumer debt of the debtor if an individual is liable on such consumer debt with the debtor differently than other unsecured claims;

(2) modify the rights of holders of secured claims, or of holders of unsecured claims, or leave unaffected the rights of holders of any class of claims;

(3) provide for the curing or waiving of any default;

(4) provide for payments on any unsecured claim to be made concurrently with payments on any secured claim or any other unsecured claim;

(5) provide for the curing of any default within a reasonable time and maintenance of payments while the case is pending on any unsecured claim or secured claim on which the last payment is due after the date on which the final payment under the plan is due;

(6) subject to section 365 of this title, provide for the assumption, rejection, or assignment of any executory contract or unexpired lease of the debtor not previously rejected under such section;

(7) provide for the payment of all or part of a claim against the debtor from property of the estate or property of the debtor;

(8) provide for the sale of all or any part of the property of the estate or the distribution of all or any part of the property of the estate among those having an interest in such property;

(9) provide for payment of allowed secured claims consistent with section 1225(a)(5) of this title, over a period exceeding the period permitted under section 1222(c);

(10) provide for the vesting of property of the estate, on confirmation of the plan or at a later time, in the debtor or in any other entity; and

(11) include any other appropriate provision not inconsistent with this title.

(c) Except as provided in subsections (b)(5) and (b)(9), the plan may not provide for payments over a period that is longer than three years unless the court for cause approves a longer period, but the court may not approve a period that is longer than five years.

Comment

Section 1222 is patterned after section 1322 of chapter 13. Subsection (a) sets forth the mandatory provisions of a chapter 12 plan.

Subsection (a)(1) requires inclusion of a provision for submission of future earnings, but only as necessary to fund the plan. Subsection (a)(2) requires provision for payment in full in deferred cash payments to priority claims [section 507] unless a particular creditor agrees to different treatment. Subsection (a)(3) requires that the plan provide equal treatment for each claim or interest within a particular class unless the holder of a particular claim or interest agrees to less favorable treatment.

Subsection (b) lists the permissive provisions of a plan. Section 1222(b)(2) permits the plan to modify the rights of all holders of claims, secured and unsecured, including those of a residential mortgagee. Thus, a debtor could reschedule the payment terms of a claim secured by an interest in the residence and farmland, a type of modification specifically forbidden to chapter 13 debtors by section 1322(b)(2). Under section 1222(b)(4), a chapter 12 plan may provide for concurrent payment of unsecured claims with secured and unsecured priority claims. Thus, neither priority nor secured claims are entitled as a matter of right to payment in advance of unsecured claims.

Case Annotations

A 30 year mortgage is an allowable exception to the 11 U.S.C. § 1222(c) five year limit if it is consistent with 11 U.S.C. § 1225(a)(5). Travelers Insurance Co. v. Bullington, 878 F.2d 354, 21 C.B.C.2d 765 (11th Cir. 1989).

Under South Dakota law, a debtor may not cure a default after a foreclosure sale. The state's statutory right of redemption cannot be modified under section 1222, because application of section 1222 would override the automatic extension provided by section 108(b). Justice v. Valley Nat'l Bank, 849 F.2d 1078, 19 C.B.C.2d 172 (8th Cir. 1988).

When a chapter 12 reorganization plan provides for payment of delinquent taxes, the payments shall be made through the trustee, rather than directly by the debtor, especially when the creditor has not expressly consented to such direct payment. *In re* Beard, 25 C.B.C.2d 1746 (B. Ct., S.D. Ohio 1991).

A chapter 12 plan may provide for repayment to extend the five year limit provided that it is consistent with section 1225(a)(5). In the Matter of LLL Farms, 22 C.B.C.2d 1182 (B. Ct., M.D. Ga. 1990).

The right to modify a secured claim or cure any default in a contract under sections 1222(b)(2) or (b)(3) does not cease until a foreclosure sale has taken place. *In re* Kratz, 20 C.B.C.2d 929 (B. Ct., S.D. Ohio 1988).

The chapter 12 debtor is permitted to make direct payments to secured creditors. *In re* Cannon, 20 C.B.C.2d 593 (B. Ct., N.D. Fla. 1988).

In a modified chapter 12 plan, there is no statutory limit on the length of time over which secured claims may be paid. *In re* Hart, 19 C.B.C.2d 777 (B. Ct., E.D.N.C. 1988).

A debtor has the right to surrender collateral to a secured creditor. In the Matter of Arthur, 18 C.B.C.2d 943 (B. Ct., W.D. Mich. 1988).

Pursuant to chapter 12, a reorganization plan may extend repayment terms for secured claims for periods of time that the court finds to be reasonable, including a period of 30 years when the claim is secured by real property. *In re* Bullington, 17 C.B.C.2d 1438 (B. Ct., M.D. Ga. 1987).

When issues such as preferences, lien avoidance and fraudulent transfer will require the commencement of adversary proceedings, the debtor's proposed chapter 12 plan should contain alternative treatments for creditors based on the possible outcomes of later determination of these issues. *In re* Bentson, 16 C.B.C.2d 1411 (B. Ct., D. Minn. 1987).

A chapter 12 debtor's ability to surrender land bank and production credit association stock to satisfy or reduce secured claims should not be frustrated by the Farm Credit Act of 1971 (12 U.S.C. § 2001, *et seq.*), since the surrender of property securing a claim is specifically recognized as permissible in chapter 12. *In re* Massengill, 16 C.B.C.2d 1375 (B. Ct., E.D.N.C. 1987).

References

5 *Collier on Bankruptcy* ch. 1222 (Matthew Bender 15th ed.).

3 *Collier Bankruptcy Manual* ch. 1222 (Matthew Bender 3d ed.).

Collier Farm Bankruptcy Guide ch. 4 (Matthew Bender 1st ed.).

Cramdown Under the New Chapter 12 of the Bankruptcy Code: A Boom to the Farmer, A Bust to the Lender?, 23 Land & Water L. Rev. 227 (1988).

Comment, *Bankruptcy and the Perishable Agricultural Commodities Act Trust*, 7 Bankr. Dev. J. 291 (1990).

Comment, *The Power to Cure Default Under Chapter 12*, 7 Bankr. Dev. J. 261 (1990).

Comment, *The New Chapter 12 of the Bankruptcy Code: A More Efficient Approach for Family Farmer Reorganizations*, 57 Miss. L.J. 85 (1987).

Depperschmidt and Kratzke, *The Search for the Proper Interest Rate Under Chapter 12 (Family Farmer Bankruptcy Act)*, 67 N.D.L. Rev. 455 (1991).

Dunn, *Chapter 12 of the U.S. Bankruptcy Code: Recent Issues and Cases*, 76 Ill. B.J. 376 (1988).

Flaccus, *One Year + of Experience with Chapter 12 Bankruptcies: The Litigated Issues*, 1988 Ark. L. Notes 1.

Frasier, *The New Bankruptcy Code Chapter 12: Friend of the Family Farmer?*, 41 Wash. St. B. News 29 (1987).

Hostetler, *Farm Reorganization Under Chapter 12 of the Bankruptcy Code*, 31 Res Gestae 210 (1987).

Jensen, *Obtaining Operating Capital in a Chapter 12 Farm Reorganization*, 54 Mo. L. Rev. 75 (1989).

King, *Chapter 12: Adjustment of Debts of a Family Farmer With Regular Income*, 29 So. Tex. L. Rev. 615 (1988).

Martin, *Chapter 12 After Almost One Year in the Bankruptcy Courts*, 37 Drake L. Rev. 211 (1987–88).

Papke, *Rhetoric and Retrenchment: Agrarian Ideology and American Bankruptcy Law*, 54 Mo. L. Rev. 871 (1989).

The Absolute Priority Rule and the Family Farmer—Setting a Farm Debtor's Priorities Straight: Norwest Bank Worthington v. Ahlers [108 S. Ct. 963], 22 Creighton L. Rev. 139 (1988/89).

SECTION 1223 (11 U.S.C. § 1223)

§ 1223. Modification of plan before confirmation.

(a) The debtor may modify the plan at any time before confirmation, but may not modify the plan so that the plan as modified fails to meet the requirements of section 1222 of this title.

(b) After the debtor files a modification under this section, the plan as modified becomes the plan.

(c) Any holder of a secured claim that has accepted or rejected the plan is deemed to have accepted or rejected, as the case may be, the plan as modified, unless the modification provides for a change in the rights of such holder from what such rights were under the plan before modification, and such holder changes such holder's previous acceptance or rejection.

Bankruptcy Rule Reference: 3019

Comment

Subsection (a) permits the debtor to modify the plan at any time before confirmation.

The debtor may modify the plan before confirmation without court approval so long as the modified plan, which becomes the plan on filing, complies with section 1222.

Subsection (c) refers only to holders of secured claims.

Section 1223 deals with modification of a plan *before* confirmations. Modification of a plan *after* confirmation is dealt with in section 1229, *infra.*

Bankruptcy Rule 3019 provides that after acceptance and before confirmation, the proponent of a plan may file a modification. After hearing and notice to the trustee, any committee appointed under the Code and others designated by the court, if the court finds that the modification does not adversely change the treatment of the claim of one who has not accepted the modification in writing, the modification shall be deemed accepted by all creditors who previously accepted the plan.

References

5 *Collier on Bankruptcy* ch. 1223 (Matthew Bender 15th ed.).

3 *Collier Bankruptcy Manual* ch. 1223 (Matthew Bender 3d ed.).

Collier Farm Bankruptcy Guide ch. 4 (Matthew Bender 1st ed.).

SECTION 1224 (11 U.S.C. § 1224)

§ 1224. **Confirmation hearing.** After expedited notice, the court shall hold a hearing on confirmation of the plan. A party in interest, the trustee, or the United States trustee may object to the confirmation of the plan. Except for cause, the hearing shall be concluded not later than 45 days after the filing of the plan.

Bankruptcy Rule Reference: 3020

Comment

Section 1224 is patterned after section 1324 of chapter 13 with two important changes: the confirmation hearing is held after "expedited notice," and, except for cause, the hearing must be concluded not later than 45 days after the filing of the plan. The Joint Explanatory Statement of the Committee of Conference for the 1986 Act had the following to say concerning section 1224:

"Section 1224 requires that Chapter 12 confirmation hearings be concluded within forty-five days after the filing of the plan. The Conferees are aware that this imposes a burden on the bankruptcy courts. Therefore, an exception for cause is provided. While a backlog of cases is sufficient cause for an extension of the forty-five day requirement, the Conferees expect this exception to be used sparingly in order to facilitate the proper operation of Chapter 12—which proper operation depends on prompt action."

Rule 2002(b) requires the clerk or some other person as the court directs to give not less than 25 days notice by mail to the debtor, the trustee and all creditors of the time fixed for filing objections to, and the hearing to consider confirmation of the plan. 28 U.S.C. § 586(a)(3)(C) requires the United States trustee to monitor plans filed under chapter 12 and to file with the court in connection with hearings under sections 1224 and 1229 comments with respect to such plan. Accordingly, subdivision (k) of Rule 2002 provides that the clerk or some other person designated by the court shall transmit to the trustee notice of the time for filing objections and the hearing to consider confirmation of a chapter 12 plan.

Bankruptcy Rule 3020(b)(1) requires objection to confirmation to be filed and served on the debtor, the trustee, the proponent of the plan, any committee appointed under the Code and others designated by the court, within a time fixed by the court. A copy of every objection to confirmation shall be transmitted by the objecting party to the United States trustee within the time fixed for the filing of objections. An objection to confirmation is a contested matter governed by Rule 9014. Subdivision (b)(2) requires the court to rule on confirmation after the hearing provided in Rule 2002. If no timely objection is filed, the court may determine that the plan has been proposed in good faith and not by any means forbidden by law without receiving evidence on such issues.

Case Annotations

The use of the exception for cause under section 1224 is limited to providing aid for the courts when it is not possible to conclude the confirmation hearing within 45 days after the plan is filed. Accordingly, chapter 12 debtors who seek an extension of time in order to work out problems with certain creditors and to file a second amended plan have failed to establish cause for an extension of the 45-day requirement of section 1224. *In re* Ryan, 16 C.B.C.2d 488 (B. Ct., M.D. Fla. 1987).

References

5 *Collier on Bankruptcy* ch. 1224 (Matthew Bender 15th ed.).

3 *Collier Bankruptcy Manual* ch. 1224 (Matthew Bender 3d ed.).

Collier Farm Bankruptcy Guide ch. 4 (Matthew Bender 1st ed.).

SECTION 1225 (11 U.S.C. § 1225)

§ 1225. Confirmation of plan.

(a) Except as provided in subsection (b), the court shall confirm a plan if—

(1) the plan complies with the provisions of this chapter and with the other applicable provisions of this title;

(2) any fee, charge, or amount required under chapter 123 of title 28, or by the plan, to be paid before confirmation, has been paid;

(3) the plan has been proposed in good faith and not by any means forbidden by law;

(4) the value, as of the effective date of the plan, of property to be distributed under the plan on account of each allowed unsecured claim is not less than the amount that would be paid on such claim if the estate of the debtor were liquidated under chapter 7 of this title on such date;

(5) with respect to each allowed secured claim provided for by the plan—

(A) the holder of such claim has accepted the plan;

(B)(i) the plan provides that the holder of such claim retain the lien securing such claim; and

(ii) the value, as of the effective date of the plan, of property to be distributed by the trustee or the debtor under the plan on account of such claim is not less than the allowed amount of such claim; or

(C) the debtor surrenders the property securing such claim to such holder; and

(6) the debtor will be able to make all payments under the plan and to comply with the plan.

(b)(1) If the trustee or the holder of an allowed unsecured claim objects to the confirmation of the plan, then the court may not approve the plan unless, as of the effective date of the plan—

(A) the value of the property to be distributed under the plan on account of such claim is not less than the amount of such claim; or

(B) the plan provides that all of the debtor's projected disposable income to be received in the three-year period, or such longer period as the court may approve under section 1222(c), beginning on the date that the first payment is due under the plan will be applied to make payments under the plan.

(2) For purposes of this subsection, "disposable income" means income which is received by the debtor and which is not reasonably necessary to be expended—

(A) for the maintenance or support of the debtor or a dependent of the debtor; or

(B) for the payment of expenditures necessary for the continuation, preservation, and operation of the debtor's business.

(c) After confirmation of a plan, the court may order any entity from whom the debtor receives income to pay all or any part of such income to the trustee.

Bankruptcy Rule Reference: 3020

Comment

Section 1225 is patterned after section 1325 of chapter 13. As is the case under chapter 13, section 1225 does not require acceptance by unsecured creditors. Instead, the "best interest of creditors" rule is applied as a condition to confirmation.

Paragraphs (1), (2) and (3) of section 1225(a) require that a plan comply with chapter 12 and with other applicable provisions of title 11, that fees to be paid prior to confirmation have been paid, and that the plan is proposed in good faith and not by any means forbidden by law.

While paragraph (4) addresses the treatment of unsecured claimants, paragraph (5) deals with secured claims. Two alternative methods are provided for treating a secured creditor who has not accepted the plan: (1) the plan provide that such creditor retain his lien *and* the value (as of the effective date of the plan) of property to be distributed under the plan is not less than the allowed amount of the claim, or (2) the plan provide for surrender to the secured creditor of the property securing the claim. Abandonment of the collateral is important when read in the light of section 506(a), which limits the secured creditor to the value of the security.

Bankruptcy Rule 3020(b)(2) requires the court to rule on confirmation after hearing as provided in Rule 2002. If no timely objection is filed, the court may determine that the plan has been proposed in good faith and not by any means forbidden by law without receiving evidence on such issues.

Rule 3020(c) provides that the order of confirmation shall conform to Official Form 15 and notice of entry thereof be mailed promptly to the debtor, the trustee, creditors, equity security holders and other parties in interest. Notice of entry of the order of confirmation shall be transmitted to the United States trustee as provided in Rule 2002(k).

The Joint Explanatory Statement of the Committee of Conference for the 1986 Act had the following to say regarding section 1225(b):

> Section 1225 defines "disposable income" as income which is not reasonably necessary to be expended for the maintenance or support of the debtor or a dependent of the debtor or for the payment of expenditures necessary for the continuation, preservation, and operation of the debtor's business.

> The Conferees recognize that family farmers who are eligible for Chapter 12 may be involved in *minor* businesses not directly related to the farming operation. The Conferees intend that the term "debtor's business" in section 1225 include such businesses.

Case Annotations

A chapter 12 plan that proposes not to contest the validity of a creditor's claim while at the same time reserving the right to pursue a state court tort claim for damages against that creditor can be a plan filed in good faith. So long as a chapter 12 plan treats a creditor's claim in accordance with section 1225(a)(5)(B), a debtor may pursue a state court tort claim for damages that would not affect the approved plan of reorganization. *In re* Mann Farms, Inc., 917 F.2d 1210, 24 C.B.C.2d 20 (9th Cir. 1990).

While the determination of what factors to apply in determining the cramdown interest rate is reviewed by an appeals court *de novo,* the application of these factors to a certain case is a question of fact and therefore should be overturned only when clearly erroneous. *In re* Fowler, 903 F.2d 694, 22 C.B.C.2d 1659 (9th Cir. 1990).

Absent special circumstances, a bankruptcy court should use the current market rate of interest used for similar loans in the region when determining the appropriate rate of interest fixed in a chapter 12 plan. The current market rate of interest is the appropriate method for determining the interest rate under a chapter 12 plan because: (1) bankruptcy court, counsel, lenders and borrowers are familiar with current rates on like-type loans; (2) chapter 12 is predicated upon the theory that the lender is making a new loan to the debtor and thus the most appropriate rate is the current market rate; and (3) the market approach ensures fairness for both the debtor and the lender. *In re* Hardzog, 901 F.2d 858, 22 C.B.C.2d 1253 (10th Cir. 1990).

Section 1225(a)(5)(B) is identical to section 1325(a)(5)(B) and should be similarly construed. When a "cramdown" occurs and a creditor is forced to write-down a portion of its note, a creditor is entitled to receive the current market rate on the "new loan." United States v. Arnold, 878 F.2d 925, 21 C.B.C.2d 266 (6th Cir. 1989).

Computer projections of future farm yields based on some of the farmer's data and other data collected by a government agency was found to prove the feasibility of a chapter 12 plan when there was no evidence that the plan was not feasible. Travelers Insurance Co. v. Bullington, 878 F.2d 354, 21 C.B.C.2d 765 (11th Cir. 1989).

The court will confirm a plan if the secured creditor will receive value as well as retain a lien on the property, with the going rate to be determined at the confirmation hearing pursuant to 11 U.S.C. § 1129(b). United States v. Doud, 865 F.2d 1144, 20 C.B.C.2d 1156 (8th Cir. 1989).

Section 1225(a)(5)(C) permits a debtor to surrender to an oversecured creditor part of the property securing the debt sufficient to satisfy the allowed claim and, when read in harmony with sections 506 and 1222(b)(7) and (8) of the Code, does not require either surrender of all of the collateral or an additional lien on unsurrendered property. *In re* Kerwin-White, 25 C.B.C.2d 237 (B. Ct., D. Vt. 1991).

The "fair repayment" of a secured claim in the context of confirmation of a chapter 12 reorganization plan consists of proving that the proposed repayment duration comports with customary lending practices or current market standards rather than with mathematical present value. *In re* Koch, 25 C.B.C.2d 666 (B. Ct., N.D. Iowa 1991).

While the prevailing view with respect to 28 U.S.C. § 586 is that the trustee may only assess his ten percent commission on payments made under the plan of reorganization and not on disbursements made outside the plan by the debtors themselves, nothing in sections 1225 and 1226 of the Bankruptcy Code requires that payments made under the plan flow through the trustee. *In re* Beard, 25 C.B.C.2d 1746 (B. Ct., S.D. Ohio 1991).

The proceeds from a postpetition harvest of crops planted prepetition are part of the debtor's section 541 estate and must be included in the liquidation test of section 1225(a)(4). A debtor's exclusion from the liquidation test of his as yet unharvested crops planted postpetition is proper as the proceeds from this harvest will clearly be postpetition assets that do not fall within the section 541 definition of property of the estate. *In re* Foos, 24 C.B.C.2d 899 (B. Ct., S.D. Ohio 1990).

Section 1225(b)(1) is an independent requirement for the confirmation of a chapter 12 plan when invoked by an appropriate objection by an unsecured creditor or the trustee and is not satisfied simply because the debtor has satisfied the "best interest of the creditors" test of section 1225(a)(4). Because neither the Code nor the Bankruptcy Rules specifically burdens the trustee with the duty to calculate disposable income and since the debtor has all of the necessary financial information to do the task, a debtor has both the duty and the ultimate burden of persuasion to show that he is fulfilling the disposable income requirement of section 1225(b)(1). *In re* Kuhlman, 24 C.B.C.2d 481 (B. Ct., D.S.D. 1990).

Under the totality of the circumstances, a chapter 12 plan is not proposed in good faith when: (1) property is conveyed solely to keep it in the family, and (2) it is filed in close proximity to the filing of a chapter 7 petition by the conveyors of that property. *In re* Marshall, 22 C.B.C.2d 168 (B. Ct., C.D. Ill. 1989).

When a debtor has sufficient assets to prevent a loss to its secured claim holder, then its agreement to pay interest based on the current yield of a fifteen-year term Treasury Bond plus two percent constitutes payment of present value. In the Matter of LLL Farms, 22 C.B.C.2d 1182 (B. Ct., M.D. Ga. 1990).

When a debtor voluntarily ceases to operate by turning away business, fails to collect nearly a half million in accounts receivable when revenue is desperately needed, and then files a chapter 12 plan that projects new income from operations never before conducted by the debtor, the plan is not feasible and should not be confirmed. *In re* Cluck, 21 C.B.C.2d 318 (B. Ct., E.D. Okla. 1989).

The bankruptcy court shall confirm a chapter 12 plan if it is proposed in good faith and not forbidden by law. The requirements for such a confirmation are substantially similar to those of chapter 13. Some common badges of fraud and indicia of bad faith which may lead a court to deny confirmation of a plan include: litigation pending or anticipated at the time of conveyance, transfer of all assets of the debtor for inadequate consideration, failure to record the instrument of conveyance, sale on credit to an unworthy purchaser or on flimsy credit terms, parties to the transfer are related by blood or marriage, reservation of the benefit to the transferor or his family, transfer of all or a part of property by the transferor by gift when there is no provision for payment of the debts, and the retention of control and domination of the corporation to which assets are transferred. *In re* Zurface, 20 C.B.C.2d 1298 (B. Ct., S.D. Ohio 1989).

A debtor should not be allowed to modify his confirmed reorganization plan when he would reduce the yearly amounts he has agreed to pay his unsecured creditors, when there has been no change in the value of his unencumbered assets since confirmed and, through his own fault, the original estimate of value in the liquidation analysis of his confirmed plan was not accurate. *In re* Cooper, 20 C.B.C.2d 313 (B. Ct., S.D. Ill. 1989).

Although the current market rate may be the appropriate interest rate to be applied to determine the present value of a vendors' allowed secured claim, the rate proposed may not appropriately reflect the current market rate of interest for long term loans secured by a mortgage against real property. *In re* Kratz, 20 C.B.C.2d 929 (B. Ct., S.D. Ohio 1988).

The debtor is authorized to act as a disbursing agent to enter into and complete ordinary farm purchases or pay ordinary farm expenses; however, there is no legislative history or other evidence that Congress intended to authorize a debtors' direct payment of impaired claims. In the Matter of Finkbine, 20 C.B.C.2d 598 (B. Ct., S.D. Ohio 1988).

To be confirmable, a chapter 12 plan must demonstrably preserve the interests of secured creditors by distributing to each creditor property having a value as of the effective date of the plan not less than an allowed amount of the claim pursuant to section 1225(a)(5)(B)(ii). *In re* Fenske, 20 C.B.C.2d 1054 (B. Ct., D.N.D. 1988).

When modifying a chapter 12 plan, if a debtor can prove that retaining property which was scheduled to be sold in his original plan would improve his overall profitability, the debtor will have fulfilled the feasibility requirement of section 1225(a)(6). *In re* Hart, 19 C.B.C.2d 777 (B. Ct., E.D.N.C. 1988).

When the creditor does not accept the plan and the plan does not provide for the surrender of the collateral, the court will utilize the discount rate in determining the sufficiency of the plan. Use or sale of collateral is permissible provided that the creditor is given adequate protection in the event of default, and present security interests attach to any newly purchased collateral. In the Matter of Underwood, 19 C.B.C.2d 78 (B. Ct., D. Neb. 1988). *See also In re* Hansen, 18 C.B.C.2d 235 (B. Ct., D.N.D. 1987).

The court may use approaches outside the market approach or comparable sales approach to determine the fair market value of property in a secured claim for "cramdown" purposes under section 1225(a)(5) when the debtor's plan is one of reorganization and not of liquidation. The court may determine the amount of a secured claim using the income approach to farmland based on net income or net rental per acre. *In re* Snider Farms, Inc., 18 C.B.C.2d 980 (B. Ct., N.D. Ind. 1987).

References

5 *Collier on Bankruptcy* ch. 1225 (Matthew Bender 15th ed.).

3 *Collier Bankruptcy Manual* ch. 1225 (Matthew Bender 3d ed.).

Collier Farm Bankruptcy Guide ch. 4 (Matthew Bender 1st ed.).

Comment, *Bankruptcy and the Perishable Agricultural Commodities Act Trust,* 7 Bankr. Dev. J. 291 (1990).

Comment, *The Power to Cure Default Under Chapter 12,* 7 Bankr. Dev. J. 261 (1990).

Flaccus and Dixon, *The New Bankruptcy Chapter 12: A Computer Analysis of If and When a Farmer Can Successfully Reorganize,* 41 Ark. L. Rev. 263 (1988).

Hamilton, *Securing Creditor Interests in Federal Farm Program Payments,* 33 So. Dak. L. Rev. 1 (1988).

Papke, *Rhetoric and Retrenchment: Agrarian Ideology and American Bankruptcy Law,* 54 Mo. L. Rev. 871 (1989).

Sanders, *Plan Confirmation Under Section 1225 of the Bankruptcy Code: Sowing the Seeds of Inconsistency,* 8 Bankr. Dev. J. 291 (1991).

Tremper, *The Montana Family Farmer Under Chapter 12 Bankruptcy,* 49 Mont. L. Rev. 40 (1988).

Willcock, *Cooperatives and the Bankrupt Farmer,* 9 Louisville Law. 18 (1988).

SECTION 1226 (11 U.S.C. § 1226)

§ 1226. Payments.

(a) Payments and funds received by the trustee shall be retained by the trustee until confirmation or denial of confirmation of a plan. If a plan is confirmed, the trustee shall distribute any such payment in accordance with the plan. If a plan is not confirmed, the trustee shall return any such payments to the debtor, after deducting—

(1) any unpaid claim allowed under section 503(b) of this title; and

(2) if a standing trustee is serving in the case, the percentage fee fixed for such standing trustee.

(b) Before or at the time of each payment to creditors under the plan, there shall be paid—

(1) any unpaid claim of the kind specified in section 507(a)(1) of this title; and

(2) if a standing trustee appointed under section 1202(d) of this title is serving in the case, the percentage fee fixed for such standing trustee under section 1202(e) of this title.

(c) Except as otherwise provided in the plan or in the order confirming the plan, the trustee shall make payments to creditors under the plan.

Bankruptcy Rule References: 3010 and 3011

Comment

Section 1226(a) requires the trustee to retain payments and funds received until confirmation or denial of the plan. This differs from chapter 13 wherein, pursuant to section 1326, the debtor is required to begin making payments within 30 days of filing a plan.

Upon confirmation of the chapter 12 plan, the trustee is to distribute the payments the trustee retained in accordance with provisions of the plan. If the plan is not confirmed the trustee must return the payments to the debtor after making certain specified deductions.

Subsection (c) of section 1226 provides that the chapter 12 trustee act as the disbursing agent for the plan. However, the plan or the order confirming the plan may provide otherwise.

Bankruptcy Rule 3010(b) provides that in chapter 12 cases, no payment less than $15 shall be distributed to any creditor unless authorized by local rule. Funds not so distributed are to be accumulated and paid whenever the accumulation equals $15. Remaining funds are to be distributed with the final payment.

Case Annotations

A bankruptcy court may in its discretion require a chapter 12 debtor to make payments to a trustee prior to plan confirmation. Stahn v. Haeckel, 920 F.2d 555, 24 C.B.C.2d 296 (8th Cir. 1990), *cert. denied,* — U.S. —, 111 S. Ct. 2258, 114 L. Ed. 2d 711 (1991).

Congress intended to use the term "under the plan" of section 1226(c) to mean those payments that result from the operation of chapter 12 bankruptcy law; those payments, which typically involve impaired claims under the protections of chapter 12, should be made by the trustee, and the trustee's fee should be assessed against the funds received from the debtor for that purpose. The statutory chapter 12 trustee's fee should be assessed against all payments made by the trustee, and the trustee should disburse all payments on impaired claims in the absence of a contrary plan provision. Such a provision, however, is committed to the discretion of the bankruptcy court, which is to consider, *inter alia,* the impact of the trustee's fees on the ability of the debtor to reorganize and the adequacy of the trustee's compensation. *In re* Fulkrod, 24 C.B.C.2d 1807 (9th Cir., B.A.P., 1991).

While the prevailing view with respect to 28 U.S.C. § 586 is that the trustee may only assess his ten percent commission on payments made under the plan of reorganization and not on disbursements made outside the plan by the debtors themselves, nothing in sections 1225 and 1226 of the Bankruptcy Code requires that payments made under the plan flow through the trustee. *In re* Beard, 25 C.B.C.2d 1746 (B. Ct., S.D. Ohio 1991).

Proceeds of an insurance policy which were omitted from a confirmed chapter 12 plan and which have revested in the debtor are disposable income subject to distribution to unsecured creditors. *In re* Martin, 25 C.B.C.2d 932 (B. Ct., N.D. Iowa 1991).

Payments made under a confirmed plan remains the fiduciary and statutory duty of the chapter 12 trustee for disbursement even if the case has been converted to chapter 7. *In re* Leach, 21 C.B.C.2d 314 (B. Ct., E.D. Okla. 1989).

Direct payments by the debtor on unimpaired claims can be made and such payments are not assessable for trustee fees. In the Matter of Finkbine, 20 C.B.C.2d 598 (B. Ct., S.D. Ohio 1988).

Given the language of sections 1225(a)(5)(B) and 1226(c), and the cases construing them, it is clear that direct payments are permissible in chapter 12 to secured creditors whose rights are or are not modified. *In re* Land, 18 C.B.C.2d 348 (B. Ct., D. Colo. 1988).

Under a chapter 12 plan, a debtor may make direct payments to secured creditors holding modified claims. *In re* Crum, 18 C.B.C.2d 1090 (B. Ct., N.D. Fla. 1988).

A chapter 12 debtor may be permitted to pay directly secured creditors and administrative attorneys' fees pursuant to a chapter 12 plan. When direct payments are authorized by the court such payments will not be subject to the trustee's statutory percentage fee established by 28 U.S.C. § 586(e). In the Matter of Pianowski, 19 C.B.C.2d 1102 (B. Ct., W.D. Mich. 1988).

But see In the Matter of Logemann, 19 C.B.C.2d 926 (B. Ct., S.D. Iowa 1988) (11 U.S.C. § 1226(c) is not persuasive authority for direct payments on impaired claims).

References

5 *Collier on Bankruptcy* ch. 1226 (Matthew Bender 15th ed.).

3 *Collier Bankruptcy Manual* ch. 1226 (Matthew Bender 3d ed.).

Collier Farm Bankruptcy Guide ch. 4 (Matthew Bender 1st ed.).

SECTION 1227 (11 U.S.C. § 1227)

§ 1227. Effect of confirmation.

(a) Except as provided in section 1228(a) of this title, the provisions of a confirmed plan bind the debtor, each creditor, each equity security holder, and each general partner in the debtor, whether or not the claim of such creditor, such equity security holder, or such general partner in the debtor is provided for by the plan, and whether or not such creditor, such equity security holder, or such general partner in the debtor has objected to, has accepted, or has rejected the plan.

(b) Except as otherwise provided in the plan or the order confirming the plan, the confirmation of a plan vests all of the property of the estate in the debtor.

(c) Except as provided in section 1228(a) of this title and except as otherwise provided in the plan or in the order confirming the plan, the property vesting in the debtor under subsection (b) of this section is free and clear of any claim or interest of any creditor provided for by the plan.

Comment

Section 1227 is patterned after section 1327 of chapter 13 but makes the section applicable to equity security holders and general partners in the debtor as well as to creditors. The provisions of a confirmed plan are binding on the debtor, creditors, equity security holders and the debtor's general partners, if any. Under section 1227(a), the binding effect is operative whether or not the creditor, equity security holder or partner is provided for by the plan and whether or not any of such persons objects to, accepts or rejects the plan. Moreover, the order of confirmation is *res judicata* and not subject to collateral attack.

While section 1227(b) vests all property of the estate in the debtor at confirmation, unless otherwise provided, section 1227(c) deems that all such property will vest in the debtor "free and clear of any claim or interest," except as otherwise provided by the plan or confirmation order.

The Joint Explanatory Statement of the Committee of Conference for the 1986 Act had this to say with regard to section 1227:

"The Conferees are concerned that farmers be able to obtain post confirmation credit. The Conferees are in agreement that current law allows Chapter 13 debtors to do so. Because section 1227 is modeled after section 1327, family farmers may provide in their plans for post-confirmation financing secured by assets that have revested in the debtor. The debtor may also use revested property to the extent it is not encumbered by the plan or order of confirmation to secure post-confirmation credit."

Bankruptcy Rule 3019 provides that after a plan has been accepted and before confirmation, the proponent may file a modification of the plan. If, after hearing on notice to the trustee and any committee appointed under the Code, the court finds that the proposed modification does not adversely change the treatment of the claim of any creditor or interest of any equity security holder who has not in writing accepted the modification, it shall be deemed accepted by all creditors and equity security holders who have previously accepted the plan.

Case Annotations

Confirmation of a chapter 12 plan has the following immediate effects: it binds the debtor and the creditors regardless of whether each creditor is provided for by the plan and whether such creditors have accepted or rejected the plan; it obligates the trustee to make distributions to creditors according to the plan; and it vests in the debtor all rights in property acquired postpetition. *In re* Plata, 958 F.2d 918, 26 C.B.C.2d 914 (9th Cir. 1992).

When a creditor's allowed secured claim is less than the full amount of all of its claims, a portion of the creditor's collateral is omitted from the allowed secured claim and nothing has been done to avoid the lien, the creditor is bound by the terms of a confirmed chapter 12 plan and may not recover proceeds pursuant to the lien after the plan has been confirmed. *In re* Martin, 25 C.B.C.2d 932 (B. Ct., N.D. Iowa 1991).

Once property has been surrendered to a secured creditor, neither the debtor nor the estate has any interest in it. *In re* Kerwin-White, 25 C.B.C.2d 237 (B. Ct., D. Vt. 1991).

References

5 *Collier on Bankruptcy* ch. 1227 (Matthew Bender 15th ed.).

3 *Collier Bankruptcy Manual* ch. 1227 (Matthew Bender 3d ed.).

Collier Farm Bankruptcy Guide ch. 4 (Matthew Bender 1st ed.).

SECTION 1228 (11 U.S.C. § 1228)

§ 1228.   Discharge.

(a) As soon as practicable after completion by the debtor of all payments under the plan, other than payments to holders of allowed claims provided for under section 1222(b)(5) or 1222(b)(10) of this title, unless the court approves a written waiver of discharge executed by the debtor after the order for relief under this chapter, the court shall grant the debtor a discharge of all debts provided for by the plan allowed under section 503 of this title or disallowed under section 502 of this title, except any debt—

(1) provided for under section 1222(b)(5) or 1222(b)(10) of this title; or

(2) of the kind specified in section 523(a) of this title.

(b) At any time after the confirmation of the plan and after notice and a hearing, the court may grant a discharge to a debtor that has not completed payments under the plan only if—

(1) the debtor's failure to complete such payments is due to circumstances for which the debtor should not justly be held accountable;

(2) the value, as of the effective date of the plan, of property actually distributed under the plan on account of each allowed unsecured claim is not less than the amount that would

have been paid on such claim if the estate of the debtor had been liquidated under chapter 7 of this title on such date; and

(3) modification of the plan under section 1229 of this title is not practicable.

(c) A discharge granted under subsection (b) of this section discharges the debtor from all unsecured debts provided for by the plan or disallowed under section 502 of this title, except any debt—

(1) provided for under section 1222(b)(5) or 1222(b)(10) of this title; or

(2) of a kind specified in section 523(a) of this title.

(d) On request of a party in interest before one year after a discharge under this section is granted, and after notice and a hearing, the court may revoke such discharge only if—

(1) such discharge was obtained by the debtor through fraud; and

(2) the requesting party did not know of such fraud until after such discharge was granted.

(e) After the debtor is granted a discharge, the court shall terminate the services of any trustee serving in the case.

Bankruptcy Rule References: 4004, 4006 and 4007

Comment

The discharge provision of section 1228 should be read in conjunction with section 524 which governs discharge generally in bankruptcy cases. Section 1228 provides more specifically what types of debts are dischargeable in chapter 12 cases and under what conditions.

Section 1228(a) provides that as soon as practicable after the debtor completes all payments under the plan (excluding payments of long-term debts and payment to claimants who are to receive property of the estate) the court shall grant the debtor a discharge of all allowed debts and of all disallowed debts provided for by the plan. The debtor may waive discharge but only after the petition is filed. Such waiver must be in writing and approved by the court.

Under section 1228(b), even though a debtor has not completed payments under the plan, the debtor may still obtain a "hardship discharge" on three conditions: (1) the failure to complete payments is due to circumstances for which the debtor should not justly be held accountable, (2) the value, as of the effective date of the plan, of property already distributed under the plan is not less than the amount that would have been paid on those claims had the estate been liquidated under chapter 7, and (3) modification of the plan in accordance with section 1229 is not practicable. Section 523 debts are not included within the scope of a hardship discharge and also are excepted from a subsection (a) discharge.

It should be noted that section 523 was amended by Pub. L. No. 101-647 (1990) (effective November 29, 1990; the amendment to section 523(a)(8) takes effect 180 days after the effective date, and the amendment to section 523(a)(9) applies to cases filed on or after the date of enactment) and Pub. L. No. 101-581 (1990) (effective November 15, 1990 in cases filed on or after that date). The legislation added new language to subsections (a)(8) and (a)(9), added two exceptions to discharge (subsections (a)(11) and (a)(12)) and added sections 523(c)(2) and 523(e). *See* 11 U.S.C. § 523 *supra*.

Bankruptcy Rule 4004(g) requires the clerk to promptly mail a copy of the final order of discharge to the United States trustee and to all creditors and to the trustee and the trustee's attorney.

Bankruptcy Rule 4006 provides that if an order is entered denying or revoking a discharge or if a waiver of discharge is filed, the clerk, after the order becomes final or the waiver is filed, shall promptly give notice thereof to all creditors in the manner provided in Rule 2002. Rule 2002(k) requires that notice of denial or revocation of discharge be transmitted to the United States trustee.

Bankruptcy Rule 4007 relates to the filing of a complaint by the debtor or any creditor to obtain a determination of the dischargeability of any debt. Subdivision (c) of the rule, as amended in 1991, is made applicable to chapter 12 cases. It provides that a complaint to determine dischargeability of any debt pursuant to Code section 523(c) shall be filed not later than 60 days following the first date set for the meeting of the section 341(a) meeting of creditors. All creditors must receive not less than 20 days notice of the time so fixed as provided in Rule 2002. On motion of any party in interest, made before such time has expired, and after hearing on notice, the court may for cause extend the time fixed under this subdivision. [The amendment brings the time periods in chapter 12 in accord with cases under chapter 7 and 11 for filing a complaint under Code section 523(a). Under section 1228(a) of the Code a chapter 12 discharge does not discharge the debts specified in section 523(a).] In 1990, section 523 was amended by Pub. L. No. 101-647 (1990) and Pub. L. No. 101-581 (1990) to, among other changes (see above), add subsection (c)(2), which renders subsection (c)(1) inapplicable, with some exceptions, to certain Federal regulatory agencies which seek to recover the kind of debt described in section 523(a)(2), (a)(4), (a)(6), or (a)(11) owed to an insured depository institution by an institution-affiliated party, as defined in section 101.

Case Annotations

Fraud must be pled with particularity and a trustee's allegation that subsequent to confirmation the debtor transferred some property not on the debtor's schedules is conclusory and insufficient to qualify as fraud. *In re* Gross, 24 C.B.C.2d 1297 (B. Ct., D.S.D. 1990).

References

5 *Collier on Bankruptcy* ch. 1228 (Matthew Bender 15th ed.).

3 *Collier Bankruptcy Manual* ch. 1228 (Matthew Bender 3d ed.).

Collier Farm Bankruptcy Guide ch. 4 (Matthew Bender 1st ed.).

Garelis, *Problems Remain in Handling Discharge of Farm Debt by Solvent Farmers,* 67 J. Tax'n 230 (1987).

Note, *Treatment of Farmers' Discharge of Indebtedness Income Under the Tax Reform Act of 1986,* 72 Iowa L. Rev. 747 (1987).

SECTION 1229 (11 U.S.C. § 1229)

§ 1229. Modification of plan after confirmation.

(a) At any time after confirmation of the plan but before the completion of payments under such plan, the plan may be modified, on request of the debtor, the trustee, or the holder of an allowed unsecured claim, to—

(1) increase or reduce the amount of payments on claims of a particular class provided for by the plan;

(2) extend or reduce the time for such payments; or

(3) alter the amount of the distribution to a creditor whose claim is provided for by the plan to the extent necessary to take account of any payment of such claim other than under the plan.

(b)(1) Sections 1222(a), 1222(b), and 1223(c) of this title and the requirements of section 1225(a) of this title apply to any modification under subsection (a) of this section.

(2) The plan as modified becomes the plan unless, after notice and a hearing, such modification is disapproved.

(c) A plan modified under this section may not provide for payments over a period that expires after three years after the time that the first payment under the original confirmed plan was due, unless the court, for cause, approves a longer period, but the court may not approve a period that expires after five years after such time.

Comment

Under section 1229(a), the court may, after confirmation, modify the plan to increase or reduce payments and extend or reduce time of payments. The plan may be modified to alter the amount of distribution to a creditor provided for in the plan, to the extent necessary to take account of any payment of the creditor's claim other than under the plan. For example, if a third party pays a portion of a creditor's claim, then the amount of distribution to that creditor under the plan may be reduced accordingly.

The modified plan must comply with the normal provisions governing the plan and preconfirmation modification.

The postconfirmation modified plan may not provide for payments beyond three years after the first payment under the originally confirmed plan was due. The court, for cause, however, may extend this period provided that the total period does not exceed five years from the date the first payment under the original plan was due.

Bankruptcy Rule 2002(a)(6) requires not less than 20 days notice to creditor by mail or the time fixed to accept or reject a proposed modification of a plan. Rule 2002(k) provides that the clerk or some other person as the court directs, shall transmit to the United States trustee the notice of the time fixed to accept or reject the proposed modification of a plan.

Bankruptcy Rule 3020 relates to confirmation of a plan. Subdivision (b)(1) requires objections to confirmation to be filed and served on the debtor, the trustee, the proponent of the plan, any committee appointed under the Code and any other entity designated by the court. A copy of every objection to confirmation must be transmitted by the objecting party to the United States trustee within the time fixed for filing objections. An objection to confirmation is contested matter governed by Rule 9014. Subdivision (b)(2) requires the court to rule on confirmation after notice and hearing as provided in Rule 2002. If no objection is filed the court may determine that the plan has been proposed in good faith and not by any means forbidden by law without receiving evidence.

Subdivision (c) requires the order of confirmation to conform to Official Form 15; and notice of entry must be served on the debtor, creditors, equity security holders and other interested parties, and shall be transmitted to the United States trustee.

Subdivision (d) provides that the court may retain jurisdiction to enter all orders necessary to administer the estate.

Bankruptcy Rule 9024 makes it clear the time to file a complaint to revoke a discharge or to revoke an order confirming a plan may not be circumvented by invoking Fed. R. Civ. P. 60(b).

Case Annotations

A debtor should not be allowed to modify his confirmed reorganization plan by which he would reduce the yearly amounts he has agreed to pay his unsecured creditors when there has been no change in the value of his unencumbered assets after confirmation and, through his own fault, the original estimate of value in the liquidation analysis of his confirmed plan was not accurate. *In re* Cooper, 20 C.B.C.2d 313 (B. Ct., S.D. Ill. 1989).

Congress did not intend for a chapter 12 debtor to be restricted to making payments to a secured claim holder within a three to five year period, because such a restriction would make a chapter 12 debtor's right to modify substantially inferior to the modification rights of a chapter 11 debtor. *In re* Hart, 19 C.B.C.2d 777 (B. Ct., E.D.N.C. 1988).

References

5 *Collier on Bankruptcy* ch. 1229 (Matthew Bender 15th ed.).

3 *Collier Bankruptcy Manual* ch. 1229 (Matthew Bender 3d ed.).

Collier Farm Bankruptcy Guide ch. 4 (Matthew Bender 1st ed.).

SECTION 1230 (11 U.S.C. § 1230)

§ 1230. Revocation of an order of confirmation.

(a) On request of a party in interest at any time within 180 days after the date of the entry of an order of confirmation under section 1225 of this title, and after notice and a hearing, the court may revoke such order if such order was procured by fraud.

(b) If the court revokes an order of confirmation under subsection (a) of this section, the court shall dispose of the case under section 1207 of this title, unless, within the time fixed by the court, the debtor proposes and the court confirms a modification of the plan under section 1229 of this title.

Bankruptcy Rule Reference: 7001

Comment

Under section 1230, a court has the discretionary authority to revoke confirmation, after notice and a hearing, if the order of confirmation was obtained by fraud. The power to revoke is made discretionary because the debtor may not have been the source of, or involved in, the fraud. Under such circumstances the court may find it unnecessary or inequitable to revoke the order of confirmation.

If the order of confirmation is revoked, section 1230(b) takes effect. The court can then either dismiss or convert the case or permit the debtor to submit a modified plan.

After revocation, the court may fix a time within which the debtor is to propose a modification of the plan. The court may then, in its discretion, confirm the modification. If there is no modification, the court may dismiss or convert to chapter 7 upon the debtor's request.

Bankruptcy Rule 7001(5) makes a proceeding to revoke the confirmation of a plan an adversary proceeding instituted by service of a summons and complaint and governed by the Part VII Rules.

Case Annotations

Fraud must be pled with particularity and a trustee's allegation that subsequent to confirmation the debtor transferred some property not on the debtor's schedules is conclusory and insufficient to qualify as fraud. Even if the trustee can prove fraud in obtaining confirmation of a chapter 12 plan, the plan may not be revoked or become subject to an unlimited modification under section 1230 if more than 180 days have elapsed since confirmation. *In re* Gross, 24 C.B.C.2d 1297 (B. Ct., D.S.D. 1990).

References

5 *Collier on Bankruptcy* ch. 1230 (Matthew Bender 15th ed.).

3 *Collier Bankruptcy Manual* ch. 1230 (Matthew Bender 3d ed.).

Collier Farm Bankruptcy Guide ch. 4 (Matthew Bender 1st ed.).

SECTION 1231 (11 U.S.C. § 1231)

§ 1231. Special tax provisions.

(a) For the purpose of any State or local law imposing a tax on or measured by income, the taxable period of a debtor that is an individual shall terminate on the date of the order for relief under this chapter, unless the case was converted under section 706 of this title.

(b) The trustee shall make a State or local tax return of income for the estate of an individual debtor in a case under this chapter for each taxable period after the order for relief under this chapter during which the case is pending.

(c) The issuance, transfer, or exchange of a security, or the making or delivery of an instrument of transfer under a plan confirmed under section 1225 of this title, may not be taxed under any law imposing a stamp tax or similar tax.

(d) The court may authorize the proponent of a plan to request a determination, limited to questions of law, by a State or local governmental unit charged with responsibility for collection or determination of a tax on or measured by income, of the tax effects, under section 346 of this title and under the law imposing such tax, of the plan. In the event of an actual controversy, the court may declare such effects after the earlier of—

(1) the date on which such governmental unit responds to the request under this subsection; or

(2) 270 days after such request.

Comment

Section 1231 provides a tax treatment consistent with that available to chapter 11 debtors under section 1146 and is concerned with state and local taxes on or measured by income only.

Subsection (a) specifies when the tax year of an individual debtor ends and when the tax year for chapter 12 begins.

Subsection (b) provides the chapter 12 trustee make and file tax returns on income for the estate of an individual, but not a corporate or partnership, family farmer.

Subsection (d) empowers the court to authorize the proponent of a plan to request a determination, limited to questions of law, by a state, local or governmental unit of questions concerning the tax effects under section 346 of the Code and under the law imposing the tax, of the chapter 12 plan. If there is a controversy, the court in its discretion may declare those effects after 270 days after the request for the tax determination or the date on which the governmental unit responds, whichever occurs first.

References

5 *Collier on Bankruptcy* ch. 1231 (Matthew Bender 15th ed.).

3 *Collier Bankruptcy Manual* ch. 1231 (Matthew Bender 3d ed.).

Collier Farm Bankruptcy Guide ch. 4 (Matthew Bender 1st ed.).

Flaccus, *Taxes, Farmers, and Bankruptcy and the 1986 Tax Changes: Much Has Changed, But Much Remains the Same,* 66 Neb. L. Rev. 459 (1987).

Note, *Treatment of Farmers' Discharge of Indebtedness Income Under the Tax Reform Act of 1986,* 72 Iowa L. Rev. 747 (1987).

CHAPTER 13

Adjustment of Debts of an Individual With Regular Income

SUBCHAPTER I

Officers, Administration, and the Estate

SECTION 1301 (11 U.S.C. § 1301)

§ 1301. Stay of action against codebtor.

(a) Except as provided in subsections (b) and (c) of this section, after the order for relief under this chapter, a creditor may not act, or commence or continue any civil action, to collect all or any part of a consumer debt of the debtor from any individual that is liable on such debt with the debtor, or that secured such debt, unless—

(1) such individual became liable on or secured such debt in the ordinary course of such individual's business; or

(2) the case is closed, dismissed, or converted to a case under chapter 7 or 11 of this title.

(b) A creditor may present a negotiable instrument, and may give notice of dishonor of such an instrument.

(c) On request of a party in interest and after notice and a hearing, the court shall grant relief from the stay provided by subsection (a) of this section with respect to a creditor, to the extent that—

(1) as between the debtor and the individual protected under subsection (a) of this section, such individual received the consideration for the claim held by such creditor;

(2) the plan filed by the debtor proposes not to pay such claim; or

(3) such creditor's interest would be irreparably harmed by continuation of such stay.

(d) Twenty days after the filing of a request under subsection (c)(2) of this section for relief from the stay provided by subsection (a) of this section, such stay is terminated with respect to the party in interest making such request, unless the debtor or any individual that is liable on such debt with the debtor files and serves upon such party in interest a written objection to the taking of the proposed action.

Bankruptcy Rule Reference: 4001

Legislative History

This section is new. It is designed to protect a debtor operating under a chpater 13 individual repayment plan case by insulating him from indirect pressures from his creditors exerted through friends or relatives that may have cosigned an obligation of the debtor. The protection is limited, however, to ensure that the creditor involved does not lose the benefit of the bargain he made for a cosigner. He is entitled to full compensation, including any interest, fees, and costs provided for by the agreement under which the debtor obtained his loan. The creditor is simply required to share with other creditors to the extent that the debtor will repay him under the chapter 13 plan. The creditor is delayed, but his substantive rights are not affected.

Subsection (a) is the operative subsection. It stays action by a creditor after an order for relief under chapter 13. The creditor may not act, or commence or continue any civil action, to collect all or any part of a consumer debt of the debtor from any individual that is liable on such debt with the debtor, or that has secured the debt, unless the individual became liable or secured the debt in the ordinary course of his business, or the case is closed, dismissed, or converted to chapter 7 or 11.

[House Report No. 95–595, 95th Cong., 1st Sess. 426 (1977).]

Subsection (a) automatically stays the holder of a claim based on a consumer debt of the chapter 13 debtor from acting or proceeding in any way, except as authorized pursuant to subsections (b) and (c), against an individual or the property of an individual liable with the chapter 13 debtor, unless such codebtor became liable in the ordinary course of his business, or unless the case is closed, dismissed, or converted to another chapter.

Under the terms of the agreement with the codebtor who is not in bankruptcy, the creditor has a right to collect all payments to the extent they are not made by the debtor at the time they are due. To the extent to which a chapter 13 plan does not propose to pay a creditor his claims, the creditor may obtain relief from the court from the automatic stay and collect such claims from the codebtor. Conversely, a codebtor obtains the benefit of any payments made to the creditor under the plan.

If a debtor defaults on scheduled payments under the plan, then the codebtor would be liable for the remaining deficiency; otherwise, payments not made under the plan may never be made by the codebtor. The obligation of the codebtor to make the creditor whole at the time payments are due remains.

The automatic stay under this section pertains only to the collection of a consumer debt, defined by section 101(7) of this title to mean a debt incurred by an individual primarily for a personal, family, or household purpose. Therefore, not all debts owed by a chapter 13 debtor will be subject to the stay of the codebtor, particularly those business debts incurred by an individual with regular income, as defined by section 101(24) of this title, engaged in business, that is permitted by virtue of section 109(b) and section 1304 to obtain chapter 13 relief.

[Senate Report No. 95–989, 95th Cong., 2d Sess. 138 (1978).]

Subsection (b) permits the creditor, notwithstanding the stay, to present a negotiable instrument and to give notice of dishonor of the instrument, in order to preserve his substantive rights against the codebtor as required by applicable nonbankruptcy law.

[House Report No. 95–595, 95th Cong., 1st Sess. 426 (1977).]

Subsection (b) excepts the giving of notice of dishonor of a negotiable instrument from the reach of the codebtor stay.

[Senate Report No. 95–989, 95th Cong., 2d Sess. 139 (1978).]

Subsection (c) requires the court to grant relief from the stay in certain circumstances. The court must grant relief to the extent that the debtor does not propose to pay, under the plan, the amount owed to the creditor. The court must also grant relief to the extent that the debtor was really the codebtor in the transaction, that is, to the extent that the nondebtor party actually received the consideration for the claim held by the creditor. Finally, the court must grant relief to the extent that the creditor's interest would be irreparably harmed by the stay, for example, where the codebtor filed bankruptcy himself, or threatened to leave the locale, or lost his job.

[House Report No. 95–595, 95th Cong., 1st Sess. 426 (1977).]

Under subsection (c), if the codebtor has property out of which the creditor's claim can be satisfied, the court can grant relief from the stay absent the transfer of a security interest in that property by the codebtor to the creditor. Correspondingly, if there is reasonable cause to believe that property is about to be disposed of by the codebtor which could be used to satisfy his obligation to the creditor, the court should lift the stay to allow the creditor to perfect his rights against such property. Likewise, if property is subject to rapid depreciation or decrease in value the stay should be lifted to allow the creditor to protect his rights to reach such property. Otherwise, the creditor's interest would be irreparably harmed by such stay. Property which could be used to satisfy the claim could be disposed of or encumbered and placed beyond the reach of the creditor. The creditor should be allowed to protect his rights to reach property which could satisfy his claim and prevent its erosion in value, disposal, or encumbrance.

[*Senate Report No. 95–989, 95th Cong., 2d Sess. 139 (1978).*]

Section 1301 of the House amendment is identical with the provision contained in section 1301 of the House bill and adopted by the Senate amendment. Section 1301(c)(1) indicates that a basis for lifting the stay is that the debtor did not receive consideration for the claim by the creditor, or in other words, the debtor is really the "co-debtor." As with other sections in title 11, the standard of receiving consideration is a general rule, but where two co-debtors have agreed to share liabilities in a different manner than profits it is the individual who does not ultimately bear the liability that is protected by the stay under section 1301.

[*124 Cong. Rec. H 11,106 (Sept. 28, 1978); S 17,423 (Oct. 6, 1978).*]

Comment

Section 1301 is designed to protect a debtor in a chapter 13 case from pressure on the part of creditors who might pursue friends or relatives who have cosigned an obligation of a debtor. The section operates to automatically stay an act or civil action to collect a consumer debt of the debtor from a codebtor, unless the codebtor became liable on, or secured, the debt in the ordinary course of his business, or the case is closed, dismissed, or converted to a chapter 7 case.

The creditor may, nevertheless, present a negotiable instrument and give notice of dishonor in order to protect his substantive rights against the codebtor.

Finally, the stay is applicable only if the codebtor is really a codebtor. To the extent that the codebtor actually received consideration for the creditor's claim, the creditor is entitled to have the stay lifted.

Note that eligibility to be a chapter 13 debtor is prescribed in section 109(e) and therefore chapter 13 does not provide "who may be a debtor."

1984 Amendments: The amendment added new subsection (d) which provides for termination of the stay within 20 days after a request for relief from the stay unless the debtor or codebtor serves and files a written objection to the proposed termination.

The words "continuation of" were inserted in subsection (c)(2).

Case Annotations

A creditor is not entitled to relief from the automatic stay to pursue collection efforts against a co-obligor if the debtor's plan proposes to pay the creditor's claim in full and the creditor's fear of the co-obligor's potential insolvency or unavailability is not sufficient irreparable harm to lift the stay. Harris v. Fort Oglethorpe State Bank, 721 F.2d 1052, 9 C.B.C.2d 1016 (6th Cir. 1983).

When a chapter 13 plan does not provide for the payment of legal interest charges, the section 1301(c) stay of action against codebtors may be lifted only as the interest becomes due as the Code discourages the accelerated payment of unaccrued legal interest. Friendly Fin. Discount Corp. v. Bradley (In the Matter of Bradley), 705 F.2d 1409, 8 C.B.C.2d 826 (5th Cir. 1983).

Personal income taxes, although personally owed, do not constitute a consumer debt within the meaning of the Bankruptcy Code, and are not covered by the automatic stay of action against codebtors. *In re* Reiter, 24 C.B.C.2d 1780 (B. Ct., W.D. Tex. 1991).

The automatic stay granted to nonbankrupt codebtors liable on consumer debts in chapter 13 cases does not apply to chapter 11 cases and cannot be read to imply the existence of a comparable stay in chapter 11 cases. Bill Roderick Distrib., Inc. v. A.J. Mackay Co. (*In re* A.J. Mackay Co.), 13 C.B.C.2d 95 (D. Utah 1985).

If a debtor's chapter 13 plan proposes only partial payment of an unsecured creditor's claim, regardless of whether the debtor's plan also proposes not to discharge the creditor's claim, that creditor may obtain relief from the codebtor automatic stay under section 1301(c)(2) to recover the remainder of the claim because this subsection is independent of the other grounds for relief found in section 1301(c). *In re* Fink, 23 C.B.C.2d 1188 (B. Ct., S.D. Ohio 1990).

A creditor may be granted relief from the stay in order to collect a bona fide claim for postpetition interest on an unsecured debt from a contractually liable co-signer when the debtor is absolved from paying accrued postpetition interest pursuant to section 502(b)(2) because postpetition interest would not have been paid had the debtor filed under chapter 7. In the Matter of Hansberry, 6 C.B.C.2d 1101 (B. Ct., S.D. Ohio 1982).

References

5 *Collier on Bankruptcy* ch. 1301 (Matthew Bender 15th ed.).

3 *Collier Bankruptcy Manual* ch. 1301 (Matthew Bender 3d ed.).

6 *Collier Bankruptcy Practice Guide* ch. 101 (Matthew Bender).

Comment, *American Savings Bank v. Waschkat: Iowa Continues to Frustrate the Rights of Codebtors,* 75 Iowa L. Rev. 259 (1989).

Epstein and Fuller, *Chapters 11 and 13 of the Bankruptcy Code— Observations on Using Case Authority From One of the Chapters in Proceedings Under the Other,* 38 Vand. L. Rev. 901 (1985).

Fields, *Taking Interest in a Cure: Compensation for Time Value of Chapter 13 Residential Mortgage Arrears,* Cardozo L.R. Vol. 13, No. 6 (April 1992).

Fries, *Recent Amendments to the Bankruptcy Code—A Politically Motivated Less Fresh Start?,* 56 Mo. L. Rev. 617 (1991).

Kennedy, *Chapter 13 Under the Bankruptcy Code*, 19 Mem. St. U.L. Rev. 137 (1989).

Morris, *Keeping Chapter 13 Debtors Inside the Debt Limits*, 2 F & G Bankr. L. Rev. 48 (1990).

Morris, *The Undersecured Home Mortgage Lender in Chapter 13*, 2 F & G Bankr. L. Rev. 52 (1990).

Note, *The Chapter 13 Provisions: A Doctrine in Need of a Cure*, 74 Minn. L. Rev. 921 (1990).

Roszkowski, *Good Faith and Chapter 13 Plans Providing for Debts Nondischargeable Under Chaper 7 of the Bankruptcy Code: A Proposal to Assure Rehabilitation, Not Liquidation*, 46 Bus. Law. 67 (1990).

Whitford, *Has the Time Come to Repeal Chapter 13?*, 1 F & G Bankr. L. Rev. 44 (1989).

Zaretsky, *Mortgagees' Rights in Chapter 13*, 203 N.Y.L.J. 3 (1990).

SECTION 1302 (11 U.S.C. § 1302)

§ 1302. Trustee.

(a) If the United States trustee appoints an individual under section 586(b) of title 28 to serve as standing trustee in cases under this chapter and if such individual qualifies under section 322 of this title, then such individual shall serve as trustee in the case. Otherwise, the United States trustee shall appoint one disinterested person to serve as trustee in the case or the United States trustee may serve as a trustee in the case.

(b) The trustee shall—

(1) perform the duties specified in sections 704(2), 704(3), 704(4), 704(5), 704(6), 704(7) and 704(9) of this title;

(2) appear and be heard at any hearing that concerns—

(A) the value of property subject to a lien;

(B) confirmation of a plan; or

(C) modification of the plan after confirmation;

(3) dispose of, under regulations issued by the Director of the Administrative Office of the United States Courts, moneys received or to be received in a case under chapter XIII of the Bankruptcy Act; and [*sic*]

(4) advise, other than on legal matters, and assist the debtor in performance under the plan; and

(5) ensure that the debtor commences making timely payments under section 1326 of this title.

(c) If the debtor is engaged in business, then in addition to the duties specified in subsection (b) of this section, the trustee shall perform the duties specified in sections 1106(a)(3) and 1106(a)(4) of this title.

Bankruptcy Rule References: 2008, 2009, 2012, 2015, 5002 and 6009

Legislative History

Subsection (a) permits the debtor's creditors to elect a trustee, subject to the same provisions as are found in sections 702(a), (b), and (c). If the creditors do not elect a trustee, then if a private standing chapter 13 trustee has been appointed for the district in which the case is commenced, he will serve as trustee. Otherwise, the United States trustee serves as trustee in the chapter 13 case. [*Ed. Note:* The provision in H.R. 8200 for election of a trustee by creditors was deleted in favor of appointment by the court. The provision for appointment by a United States trustee was also deleted.]

[*House Report No. 95–595, 95th Cong., 1st Sess. 426 (1977).*]

The principal administrator in a chapter 13 case is the chapter 13 trustee. Experience under chapter XIII of the Bankruptcy Act has shown that the more efficient and effective wage earner programs have been conducted by standing chapter XIII trustees who exercise a broad range of responsibilities in both the design and the effectuation of debtor plans.

Subsection (a) provides administrative flexibility by permitting the bankruptcy judge to appoint an individual from the panel of trustees established pursuant to 28 U.S.C. § 604(f) [*Ed. Note:* 28 U.S.C. § 604(f) was repealed by Pub. L. No. 99-554 (1986).] and qualified under section 322 of title 11, either to serve as a standing trustee in all chapter 13 cases filed in the district or a portion thereof, or to serve in a single case.

[*Senate Report No. 95–989, 95th Cong., 2d Sess. 139 (1978).*]

Subsection (b) specifies the trustee's duties. He is required to perform the duties of a trustee in a liquidation case specified in sections 704(2), (3), (4), (5), (6), and (8), [*Ed. Note:* Pub. L. No. 98–353 added a reference to new section 704(7) and redesignated section 704(8) as section 704(9).] relating to information, investigation, objection to claims, and objection to discharge. In addition, the trustee must appear and be heard at any hearing that concerns the value of property subject to a lien, the feasibility of the plan, or the modification of the plan after confirmation.

[House Report No. 95–595, 95th Cong., 1st Sess. 427 (1977).]

Subsection (b)(1) makes it clear that the chapter 13 trustee is no mere disbursing agent of the monies paid to him by the debtor under the plan [section 1322(a)(1)], by imposing upon him certain relevant duties of a liquidation trustee prescribed by section 704 of this title.

Subsection (b)(2) requires the chapter 13 trustee to appear before and be heard by the bankruptcy court whenever the value of property secured by a lien or the confirmation or modification of a plan after confirmation as provided by sections 1323-1325 is considered by the court.

Subsection (b)(3) *[Ed. Note:* Pub. L. No. 98–353 redesignated section 1302(b)(3) as section 1302(b)(4).] requires the chapter 13 trustee to advise and counsel the debtor while under chapter 13, except on matters more appropriately left to the attorney for the debtor. The chapter 13 trustee must also assist the debtor in performance under the plan by attempting to tailor the requirements of the plan to the changing needs and circumstances of the debtor during the extension period.

[Senate Report No. 95–989, 95th Cong., 2d Sess. 139 (1978).]

Subsection (c) requires that if a private standing chapter 13 trustee is serving in the case, then the trustee must advise, other than on legal matters, and assist the debtor in performance under the plan. Preparation of a chapter 13 plan is not usually a legal matter, but is a financial matter. The trustee is not prohibited from assisting the debtor in preparation of a plan or proposed modifications to a plan to the extent that the preparation consists of financial counseling rather than legal counseling, though such assistance will often be performed by the debtor's attorney.

If a private trustee is not serving in the case, that is, if an elected trustee is serving or if the United States trustee is serving in the case, then the United States trustee must so advise and assist the debtor. If an elected trustee is serving, he will be acting as a representative of the creditors that elected him. It would be highly inappropriate for such a trustee to be advising and assisting the debtor.

[House Report No. 95–595, 95th Cong., 1st Sess. 427 (1977).]

Subsection (c) imposes on the trustee in a chapter 13 case filed by a debtor engaged in business the investigative and reporting duties normally required of a chapter 11 debtor or trustee as prescribed by section 1106(a)(3) and (4).

[Senate Report No. 95–989, 95th Cong., 2d Sess. 139 (1978).]

Subsection . . .[c] gives the trustee an additional duty if the debtor is engaged in business, as defined in section 1304. The trustee must perform the duties specified in sections 1106(a)(3) and 1106(a)(4), relating to investigation of the debtor.

[House Report No. 95–595, 95th Cong., 1st Sess. 427 (1977).]

Section 1302 of the House amendment adopts a provision contained in the Senate amendment instead of the position taken in the House bill.

Sections 1302(d) and (e) [repealed by Pub. L. No. 99–554] are modeled on the standing trustee system contained in the House bill with the court assuming supervisory functions in districts not under the pilot program.

[*124 Cong. Rec. H 11,106 (Sept. 28, 1978); S 17,423 (Oct. 6, 1978).*]

Comment

H.R. 8200 originally provided for election of a chapter 13 trustee by creditors. This provision was deleted in favor of appointment of a trustee by the United States trustee unless the United States trustee has appointed a standing trustee.

Section 1302(b)(1) requires the trustee to perform the duties specified in sections 704(2), (3), (4), (5), (6), (7), and (9) of chapter 7.

If a debtor is engaged in business, subsection (c) requires the trustee to perform in addition to the duties specified in subsection (b) the duties specified in section 1106(a)(3) and (a)(4).

Bankruptcy Rule 2015(a), amended in 1991, relates to the duties of a trustee or debtor in possession and specifies these duties:

(1) in a chapter 7 case and, if the court directs, in a chapter 11 case, file and transmit to the United States trustee a complete inventory of the property of the debtor within 30 days after qualifying as a trustee or a debtor in possession. (Subdivision (b), below, makes this the duty of a chapter 13 debtor in a business case.)

(2) to keep records of receipts and disposition of money and property received;

(3) to file reports and summaries required by section 704(8) if the business is authorized to be operated within the times fixed by the court, including a statement of deductions for taxes withheld from employees;

(4) to give notice of the case to every entity holding money or property subject to withdrawal or order of the debtor;

Subdivision (b), added by the 1991 Amendments, provides that in a chapter 13 case, the debtor in possession shall perform the duties prescribed in clauses (1)–(4) of subdivision (a). If the debtor is removed as debtor in possession, the trustee shall perform the duties of the debtor in possession prescribed in this paragraph.

Subdivision (c) relates to a chapter 13 trustee and debtor. Paragraph (1) deals with a business case, and provides that in such case the *debtor* shall perform the duties prescribed in subdivision (a)(1)–(4). Paragraph (2) deals with non-business cases and requires the trustee to perform the duties prescribed by subdivision (a)(2).

Bankruptcy Rule 2008 requires the United States trustee to immediately notify the person selected as trustee how to qualify and, if applicable, the amount of the trustee's bond. A person selected as trustee (other than a trustee who filed a blanket bond) must notify the court and United States trustee in writing of acceptance of the office within 5 days after receipt of notice of selection, or shall be deemed to have rejected the office.

Bankruptcy Rule 2010(a) permits the United States trustee to authorize a blanket faithful performance bond to cover a person who qualifies as trustee in a number of cases, and a number of trustees each qualifying in a different case.

Bankruptcy Rule 2012(b) provides that if a trustee dies, resigns, is removed or otherwise ceases to hold office, his successor is automatically substituted in any pending action, proceeding, or matter and shall file and transmit to the United States trustee an accounting of the prior administration.

Bankruptcy Rule 2013 requires the clerk to maintain a public record of fees awarded by the court to trustee, accountants, appraisers, auctioneers and other professionals, and to examiners. The record is to include the name and address of recipients of fees, shall be kept current, and open to public inspection without charge. "Trustee" as used in this rule does not include debtor in possession. (This rule is not applicable in the case of standing trustees.)

Bankruptcy Rule 2009(c)(4) relates to trustees in cases of joint administration and provides in subdivision (c) that in a chapter 13 case, one or more trustees may be appointed by the United States trustee for the jointly administered estates.

Bankruptcy Rule 5002, as amended in 1991, provides that a bankruptcy judge may not approve the appointment of a person as a trustee or approve employment of an attorney, accountant, appraiser, auctioneer or other professional, if that person is or has been so connected with the judge or the United States trustee as to render the appointment or employment improper. ["Improper" includes the appearance of impropriety.]

1984 Amendments: Subsection (b)(3) of section 1302 was redesignated (b)(4) and new subsections (b)(3) and (b)(5) were added. Subsection (b)(3) deals with disposition of monies by a chapter 13 trustee. Subsection (b)(5) requires the trustee to ensure that the debtor timely makes the payments required by section 1325. Minor technical changes were made in subsections (e)(1), (e)(1)(A) and (B), and (e)(2)(A).

1986 Amendments: Section 1302(a) was amended to provide that if the United States trustee appoints a standing trustee, and if such individual qualifies, then such individual shall serve as trustee in the case. If no standing trustee has been appointed, the United States trustee is to appoint one disinterested person to serve as trustee or the United States trustee may serve as trustee in the case.

Subsections (d) and (e) dealing with the appointment of standing trustees have been deleted from section 1302. The provisions for appointment of standing trustees have been transferred to 28 U.S.C. § 586(b).

The Joint Explanatory Statement of the Committee of Conference for the 1986 Act, had this to say about the United States trustee serving as trustee in a case:

"The House and Senate Conferees agree that it is not their expectation or intent that the United States trustee will use the authority to serve as case trustee frequently. The United States trustee is to make a good faith, diligent effort to locate a disinterested and qualified trustee. Conferees agreed that United States trustees in the pilot program appear to be using their current authority to serve as case trustee in an appropriate manner."

This section was amended to reflect the creation of a permanent United States trustee system. Section 302(d) of the 1986 Amendments provides different effective dates for the amendments relating to the United States trustee system. *See* Section 302 of the 1986 Amendments, as amended by Pub. L. No. 101-650 (1990), reprinted herein under "Selected Provisions of the Bankruptcy Judges, United States Trustees, and Family Farmer Bankruptcy Act of 1986," regarding effective dates generally. Pub. L. No. 101-650 (Judicial Improvements Act of 1990) (signed into law December 1, 1990) amended Section 302(d)(3) of the Bankruptcy Judges, United States Trustees, and Family Farmer Bankruptcy Act of 1986 by extending the period in which the judicial districts in the states of Alabama and North Carolina may remain outide the United States trustee system.

Case Annotations

No provision expressly requires the trustee to insure that the debtor makes the payments required by a Chapter XIII plan; however, the bankruptcy rules do contemplate active participation by a trustee in effectuating a debtor's plan and inherent in the trustee's fiduciary obligations is the duty to oversee the debtor's compliance with the plan, including the duty to take appropriate action when the debtor does not make the required payments; failure to do so will result in the trustee being held personally liable for breach of his fiduciary duties and a surcharge for the benefit of creditors may be imposed. *In re* Gorski, 766 F.2d 723, 13 C.B.C.2d 244 (2d Cir. 1985) (decided under the 1898 Act).

Although payments on mortgage claims pursuant to section 1322(b)(5) are subject to the standing trustee's percentage fee, the bankruptcy court should exercise its discretion with respect to the computation of the fee, using the ten percent reference in section 1302(e)(1)(B) as a maximum, and taking into consideration the diminished responsibilities of the trustee when the debtor acts as disbursing agent with respect to such payments. In the Matter of Foster, 670 F.2d 478, 6 C.B.C.2d 285 (5th Cir. 1982).

The bankruptcy court may review the fee request of a standing chapter 13 trustee on objection in appropriate instances when the attorney general has no appropriate dispute resolution mechanism under the provisions of 28 U.S.C. § 586(e). *In re* Melita, 19 C.B.C.2d 791 (B. Ct., E.D. Pa. 1988).

A bankruptcy trustee is not authorized to run and operate a chapter 13 debtor's business. *In re* Dodd, 16 C.B.C.2d 1337 (B. Ct., E.D. Cal. 1987).

References

5 *Collier on Bankruptcy* ch. 1302 (Matthew Bender 15th ed.).

3 *Collier Bankruptcy Manual* ch. 1302 (Matthew Bender 3d ed.).

6 *Collier Bankruptcy Practice Guide* ch. 101 (Matthew Bender).

Stille, *Bankruptcy Law's Detectives,* Nat'l L.J., Nov. 19, 1984, p.1., col.1.

Weintraub and Resnick, *Bankruptcy Trustee's Strong-Arm Powers Balked by a Constructive Trust,* 22 U.C.C.L.J. 367 (1990).

SECTION 1303 (11 U.S.C. § 1303)

§ 1303. Rights and powers of debtor. Subject to any limitations on a trustee under this chapter, the debtor shall have, exclusive of the trustee, the rights and powers of a trustee under sections 363(b), 363(d), 363(e), 363(f), and 363(l), of this title.

Legislative History

This section gives the debtor the same rights and powers of a trustee under sections 363 (b), (d), (e), and (f), relating to use, sale, or lease of property other than in the ordinary course of business. These rights and powers are given exclusively to the debtor, and may not be exercised by the chapter 13 trustee.

[*House Report No. 95–595, 95th Cong., 1st Sess. 427 (1977).*]

A chapter 13 debtor is vested with the identical rights and powers, and is subject to the same limitations in regard to their exercise, as those given a liquidation trustee by virtue of section 363(b), (d), (e), (f), and (h) of title 11, relating to the sale, use or lease of property.

[*Senate Report No. 95–989, 95th Cong., 2d Sess. 140 (1978).*]

Section 1303 of the House amendment specifies rights and powers that the debtor has exclusive of the trustees. The section does not imply that the debtor does not also possess other powers concurrently with the trustee. For example, although section 1323 is not specified in section 1303, certainly it is intended that the debtor has the power to sue and be sued.

[*124 Cong. Rec. H 11,106 (Sept. 28, 1978); S 17,423 (Oct. 6, 1978).*]

Comment

Section 363 treats with use, sale or lease of property.

Subsection (b) permits trustee (after notice and hearing) to use, sell, or lease, other than in ordinary course of the business, property of the estate.

Subsection (d) permits such use, sale, or lease of property only to the extent not inconsistent with the stay provisions of section 362(c), (d), (e), or (f).

Subsection (e) provides that at the request of the entity that has an interest in the property, the court shall prohibit or condition such use, sale, or lease as is necessary to provide adequate protection of such interest.

Subsection (f) makes provision for a "free and clear" sale under certain prescribed conditions.

Subsection (1) permits use, sale, or lease of property notwithstanding contractual provisions that become effective upon insolvency or financial condition of debtor or commencement of a bankruptcy case against the debtor, that effect a forfeiture, modification, or termination of debtor's interests in the property involved.

There was no provision in the former Act or Rules comparable to section 1303 of the Code. Under Section 636 of the Act the rights, privileges, and duties of the debtor were the same as if he had been adjudicated a bankrupt. The purpose of section 1303 is to give the debtor (exclusive of the rights of the trustee appointed pursuant to section 1302) the identical power to use, sell, or lease his property in the same manner, and subject to the same limitations, as a liquidation trustee has pursuant to section 363(b), (d), (e), (f), and (l). Thus, as the Congressional Record, *supra,* indicates, the debtor's power to use, sell, or lease his property other than in the ordinary course of business is concurrent with the trustee's power to do the same. The grant of this power is not intended to indicate that the debtor does not also have other powers concurrently with the trustee as, for example, the right to sue and be sued.

Bankruptcy Rule 6004 relates to the use, sale or lease of property. Subdivision (a) deals with notice; subdivision (b) deals with objections to a proposed use, sale or lease of property and provides that an objection to a proposed use, sale, or lease of property is a contested matter governed by Rule 9014. Subdivision (c) requires that a motion for leave to sell free and clear be served on the parties who have liens or other interests in the property. Notice of the proposed sale must include the date of the hearing on the motion and the time within which objections may be filed and served on the debtor or debtor in possession. Subdivision (d) relates to a general notice to all creditors, indenture trustees, committees appointed or elected pursuant to the Code, the United Sates trustee, and other persons as the court directs of the sale of nonexempt property with an aggregate value less than $2500; subdivision (e) provides for inclusion in the notice under subdivision (a) of a hearing on a timely filed objection. Subdivision (f)(1) provides for sale by private sale or by public auction. An itemized statement of the details of the sale must be filed and a copy transmitted to the United States trustee. Subdivision (f)(2) provides that the debtor or trustee shall execute the instruments necessary to effectuate transfer to the purchaser. The United States trustee should receive notice of any proceeding or proposed action relating to the use, sale or lease of property.

Case Annotations

The joint real estate interests of a chapter 13 debtor's spouse are not subject to sale by the debtor under section 363(h) of the Code. *In re* Perry, 25 C.B.C.2d 1019 (B. Ct., D. Mass. 1991).

Section 1303 does not confer standing on the debtor to pursue an avoidance action under section 544(a). *In re* Houston, 20 C.B.C.2d 755 (B. Ct., W.D. Tex. 1989).

Section 1303 grants a chapter 13 debtor only a limited power to utilize a trustee's avoiding powers, including the power to avoid a statutory tax lien, and that limited power is governed by section 522 of the Code. In the Matter of Driscoll, 14 C.B.C.2d 146 (B. Ct., W.D. Wis. 1986).

The express grant of powers provided to a chapter 13 debtor by section 1303 does not restrict the debtor from possessing other powers concurrently with the trustee, so that a chapter 13 debtor also has standing to utilize the trustee's avoiding powers under section 544. *In re* Boyette, 9 C.B.C.2d 349 (B. Ct., N.D. Tex. 1983).

A chapter 13 debtor is not vested with the trustee's exclusive power to avoid liens and transfers, and such avoidance power is not implicit in any of the rights and powers which are vested in the Chapter 13 debtor, including the right to deal with his property and to sue and be sued. *In re* Walls, 5 C.B.C.2d 1490 (B. Ct., S.D. W. Va. 1982).

References

5 *Collier on Bankruptcy* ch. 1303 (Matthew Bender 15th ed.).

3 *Collier Bankruptcy Manual* ch. 1303 (Matthew Bender 3d ed.).

6 *Collier Bankruptcy Practice Guide* ch. 101 (Matthew Bender).

SECTION 1304 (11 U.S.C. § 1304)

§ 1304. Debtor engaged in business.

(a) A debtor that is self-employed and incurs trade credit in the production of income from such employment is engaged in business.

(b) Unless the court orders otherwise, a debtor engaged in business may operate the business of the debtor and, subject to

any limitations on a trustee under sections 363(c) and 364 of this
title and to such limitations or conditions as the court prescribes,
shall have, exclusive of the trustee, the rights and powers of the
trustee under such sections.

(c) A debtor engaged in business shall perform the duties of
the trustee specified in section 704(8) of this title.

Bankruptcy Rule Reference: 2015

Legislative History

Subsection (a) defines, for the purposes of chapter 13, a debtor that
is engaged in business. A debtor is engaged in business if he is self-
employed and incurs trade credit in the production of income from that
employment.

[*House Report No. 95-595, 95th Cong., 1st Sess. 427 (1977).*]

Increased access to the simpler, speedier, and less expensive debtor
relief provisions of chapter 13 is accomplished by permitting debtors
engaged in business to proceed under chapter 13, provided their income
is sufficiently stable and regular to permit compliance with a chapter
13 plan [section 101] and that the debtor (or the debtor and spouse)
do not owe liquidated, noncontingent unsecured debts of $50,000, or
liquidated, noncontingent secured debts of $200,000 (section 109(d)).
[*Ed. Note:* The amounts in section 109(e) are $100,000 unsecured and
$350,000 secured.]

Section 1304(a) states that a self-employed individual who incurs
trade credit in the production of income is a debtor engaged in business.

If the debtor is engaged in business, unless the court orders otherwise,
he may operate his business, and is given the rights and powers of a
trustee under sections 363(c) (relating to ordinary course of business
use, sale, or lease of property) and 364 (relating to obtaining credit).

[*House Report No. 95-595, 95th Cong., 1st Sess. 427 (1977).*]

Subsection (b) empowers a chapter 13 debtor engaged in business to
operate his business, subject to the rights, powers and limitations that
pertain to a trustee under section 363(c) and 364 of title 11, and subject
to such further limitations and conditions as the court may prescribe.

[*Senate Report No. 95-989, 95th Cong., 2d Sess. 140 (1978).*]

Section 1304(b) of the House amendment adopts the approach taken
in the comparable section of the Senate amendment as preferable to the
position taken in the House bill.

[*124 Cong. Rec. H 11,106 (Sept. 28, 1978); S 17,423 (Oct. 6, 1978).*]

Subsection (c) requires a debtor engaged in business to perform the
duties of the trustee specified in section 704(7), [*Ed. Note:* Pub. L. No.

98–353 redesignated section 704(7) as section 704(8).] relating to reporting to tax collecting agencies.

[*House Report No. 95–595, 95th Cong., 1st Sess. 427 (1977).*]

Subsection (c) required a chapter 13 debtor engaged in business to file with the court certain financial statements relating to the operation of the business.

[*Senate Report No. 95–989, 95th Cong., 2d Sess. 140 (1978).*]

Comment

Section 109(e) prescribes who may be a chapter 13 debtor, as follows:

(e) Only an individual with regular income that owes, on the date of the filing of the petition, noncontingent, liquidated, unsecured debts of less than $100,000 and noncontingent, liquidated, secured debts of less than $350,000, or an individual with regular income and such individual's spouse, except a stock-broker or a commodity broker, that owe, on the date of the filing of the petition, noncontingent, liquidated, unsecured debts that aggregate less than $100,000 and noncontingent, liquidated, secured debts of less than $350,000 may be a debtor under chapter 13 of this title.

Under the former Bankruptcy Act, Section 606(3) defined a Chapter XIII debtor to mean a "wage earner," and Section 606(8) defined "wage earner" to mean an individual whose principal income is derived from wages as salary.

The Code does not limit chapter 13 to a "wage earner," but in lieu thereof makes the chapter available to "an individual with a regular income," the only limitation being that his unsecured debts are less than $100,000 and his secured debts are less than $350,000. This opens the door to chapter 13 for the individual who owns a small business, *i.e.,* the typical "mom and pop" grocery store. But the debtor must be an "individual." A partnership and a corporation may not file under chapter 13.

With chapter 13 now available to the small businessperson, it is logical to permit such person to continue to operate the business despite the fact that a trustee is appointed. That is the purpose of section 1304.

Subsection (a) defines one "engaged in business" to mean a debtor who incurs trade credit in order to produce income from such debtor's self-employment.

Subsection (b) authorizes the "debtor engaged in business" to continue to operate the business subject to any limitations on a trustee under section 363(c) (use, sale, or lease of property) and section 364 (obtaining credit) and such further limitations and conditions as the court may impose.

Subsection (c) authorizes a "debtor engaged in business" to perform the duties of a trustee specified in section 704(8), which provides:

(8) if the business of the debtor is authorized to be operated, file with the court and with any governmental unit charged with responsibility for collection or determination of any tax arising out of such operation, periodic reports and summaries of the operation of such business, including a statement of receipts and disbursements, and such other information as the court requires.

Bankruptcy Rule 2015(a) sets forth five duties to be performed by a trustee or debtor in possession. Subdivision (c)(1) of the rule relates specifically to a chapter 13 trustee and debtor, and provides that in a business case the debtor shall perform the duties set forth in clauses (1) to (4) of subdivision (a) including the filing of reports and summaries required by section 704(8) of the Code. Subdivision (c)(2) provides that in a chapter 13 case, when the debtor is not engaged in business, the trustee shall perform the duties prescribed by subdivision (a)(2). *See* **Comment** to section 1302.

1984 Amendments: Section 1304(c) was amended by changing the reference to section 704(7) to read 704(8).

Case Annotations

Since, under section 1304, it is the chapter 13 debtor, rather than the trustee, who is to operate the business, it is also the debtor who must decide the question of assumption or rejection of a nonresidential lease of real property. *In re* Dodd, 16 C.B.C.2d 1337 (B. Ct., E.D. Cal. 1987).

A bankruptcy court should not exercise its jurisdiction to determine the administrative priority of debts for unsecured credit obtained in the ordinary course of business following a confirmed chapter 13 plan if the creditor's lawsuit would not catastrophically affect the debtor's plan, and, as an alternative, the creditor should seek leave to pursue his remedies in a state court forum. *In re* Lewis, 9 C.B.C.2d 512 (B. Ct., W.D.N.Y. 1983).

The assets of a farming partnership by estoppel cannot be administered in the partners' individual chapter 13 cases if the debtors are not self-employed in the farming operations as required by section 1304. Miami Valley Prod. Credit Ass'n v. Tegtmeyer (In the Matter of Tegtmeyer), 8 C.B.C.2d 1372 (B. Ct., S.D. Ohio 1983).

References

5 *Collier on Bankruptcy* ch. 1304 (Matthew Bender 15th ed.).

3 *Collier Bankruptcy Manual* ch. 1304 (Matthew Bender 3d ed.).

6 *Collier Bankruptcy Practice Guide* ch. 101 (Matthew Bender).

SECTION 1305 (11 U.S.C. § 1305)

§ 1305. Filing and allowance of postpetition claims.

(a) A proof of claim may be filed by any entity that holds a claim against the debtor—

(1) for taxes that become payable to a governmental unit while the case is pending; or

(2) that is a consumer debt, that arises after the date of the order for relief under this chapter, and that is for property or services necessary for the debtor's performance under the plan.

(b) Except as provided in subsection (c) of this section, a claim filed under subsection (a) of this section shall be allowed or disallowed under section 502 of this title, but shall be determined as of the date such claim arises, and shall be allowed under section 502(a), 502(b), or 502(c) of this title, or disallowed under section 502(d) or 502(e) of this title, the same as if such claim had arisen before the date of the filing of the petition.

(c) A claim filed under subsection (a)(2) of this section shall be disallowed if the holder of such claim knew or should have known that prior approval by the trustee of the debtor's incurring the obligation was practicable and was not obtained.

Legislative History

Subsection (a) permits the filing of a proof of a claim against the debtor that is for taxes that become payable to a governmental unit while the case is pending, or that arises after the date of the filing of the petition for property or services that are necessary for the debtor's performance under the plan, such as auto repairs in order that the debtor will be able to get to work, or medical bills. The effect of the latter provision, in paragraph (2), is to treat postpetition credit extended to a chapter 13 debtor the same as a prepetition claim for purposes of allowance, distribution, and so on.

[House Report No. 95-595, 95th Cong., 1st Sess. 427-428 (1977).]

Section 1305, exclusively applicable in chapter 13 cases, supplements the provisions of sections 501-511 of title 11, dealing with the filing and allowance of claims. Sections 501-511 apply in chapter 13 cases by virtue of section 103(a) of this title. Section 1305(a) provides for the filing of a proof of claim for taxes and other obligations incurred after the filing of the chapter 13 case.

[*Senate Report No. 95–989, 95th Cong., 2d Sess. 140 (1978).*]

Section 1305(a)(2) of the House amendment modifies similar provisions contained in the House and Senate bills by restricting application of the paragraph to a consumer debt. Debts of the debtor that are not consumer debts should not be subjected to section 1305(c) or section 1328(d) of the House amendment.

[*124 Cong. Rec. H 11,106 (Sept. 28, 1978); S 17,423 (Oct. 6, 1978).*]

Subsection (b) requires that such claims be allowed or disallowed under section 502 as are all other claims, but specifies that they are to be determined as of the date of allowance, rather than as of the date of the petition.

[*House Report No. 95–595, 95th Cong., 1st Sess. 428 (1977).*]

Subsection (b) prescribes that section 502 of title 11 governs the allowance of section 1305(a) claims, except that its standards shall be applied as of the date of allowance of the claim, rather than the date of filing of the petition.

[*Senate Report No. 95–989, 95th Cong., 2d Sess. 140 (1978).*]

Section 1305(b) of the House amendment represents a technical modification of similar provisions contained in the House bill and Senate amendment.

[*124 Cong. Rec. H 11,106 (Sept. 28, 1978); S 17,423 (Oct. 6, 1978).*]

Subsection (c) specifies that a postpetition claim may not be allowed if the holder of the claim knew or should have known of [*sic*] that prior approval by the trustee of the debtor's incurring of the obligation was practicable and was not obtained.

[*House Report No. 95–595, 95th Cong., 1st Sess. 428 (1977).*]

Subsection (c) requires the disallowance of a postpetition claim for property or services necessary for the debtor's performance under the plan, if the holder of the claim knew or should have known that prior approval by the trustee of the debtor's incurring of the obligation was practicable and was not obtained.

[*Senate Report No. 95–989, 95th Cong., 2d Sess. 140 (1978).*]

The House amendment deletes section 1305(d) of the Senate amendment as unnecessary. Section 502(b)(1) is sufficient to disallow any claim to the extent the claim represents the usurious interest or any other charge forbidden by applicable law. It is anticipated that the Rules of Bankruptcy Procedure may require a creditor filing a proof of claim in a case under chapter 13 to include an affirmative statement as contemplated by section 1305(d) of the Senate amendment.

[*124 Cong. Rec. H 11,106 (Sept. 28, 1978); S 17,423 (Oct. 6, 1978).*]

Comment

Section 1305 is derived from former Bankruptcy Rule 13–305 (Post-Petition Claims), the first two paragraphs of which are in turn derived from Section 680 of the Act.

Section 1305 permits certain postpetition claims to be treated the same as prepetition claims. There is no requirement that the holder file a postpetition claim under section 1305. Such creditor may refrain from filing a claim, thus waiving the right to distribution under the plan, in the hope of recovering against the debtor after the case is closed.

Section 1305(a)(1) permits the filing of a postpetition claim for taxes that become payable to a governmental unit while the case is pending.

Section 1305(a)(2) provides that claims for "consumer debts" arising after the order for relief for property or services necessary for debtor's performance under the plan, may be filed.

Section 1305(b) requires that claims filed under section 1305 be allowed or disallowed just as other claims are allowed under section 502, but with this change: such claims are to be determined as of the date of allowance of the claim, rather than the date of filing the petition.

It is important to the success of a chapter 13 plan that the debtor not be allowed to incur unnecessary credit that may prejudice consummation of the plan. The chapter 13 trustee is best situated to evaluate such matters. Therefore, section 1305(c) provides that a postpetition consumer debt claim is to be disallowed if its holder knew or should have known that it was practicable to obtain the approval of the chapter 13 trustee before the consumer debt was incurred and such approval was not obtained.

Case Annotations

For purposes of section 1305(a), social security and income taxes of self-employed debtors become payable at the time the debtors' tax return is due, not at the time that the quarterly installments are due. *In re* Ripley, 926 F.2d 1440, 24 C.B.C.2d 1478 (5th Cir. 1991).

A debtor may not force a postpetition creditor to file a proof of claim nor may the debtor file a proof of claim on behalf of a postpetition creditor. *In re* Goodman, 26 C.B.C.2d 1034 (B. Ct., W.D. Tenn. 1992).

The Internal Revenue Service's need to investigate the prepetition facts of a debtor's financial affairs before it decides to assess a tax or a penalty does not convert a contingent, disputed or unliquidated claim for prepetition taxes into a claim for postpetition taxes, and does not excuse the IRS from ignoring the deadline for filing a proof of claim or obtaining an extension of time within which to file a proof of claim. In the Matter of Workman, 22 C.B.C.2d 117 (B. Ct., N.D. Ga. 1989).

Section 1305(a)(1) does not apply to a prepetition tax deficiency that does not become assessed until after the filing of the petition. Furthermore, the debtor cannot compel the government to accept payment under the plan for taxes incurred after the filing of a chapter 13 petition. The government can choose to collect from the debtor after discharge. *In re* Ryan, 17 C.B.C.2d 827 (B. Ct., E.D. Tenn. 1987).

Section 1305(a)(1) refers specifically to taxes that become payable during the period when the case is pending and does not apply to any interest that accrues upon taxes during that period. *In re* Venable, 12 C.B.C.2d 968 (B. Ct., S.D.N.Y. 1985).

When the allowance of a postpetition medical claim would require a decrease in the amount paid to other participating creditors or an extension of the plan beyond three years, the chapter 13 debtor must apply for a modification of his plan. In the Matter of Nelson, 8 C.B.C.2d 250 (B. Ct., M.D. Ga. 1983).

When a claim for prepetition taxes has been fixed and the debtor's chapter 13 plan confirmed, the IRS may not amend its claim based upon a postpetition assessment of the debtor's liability since the mere fact that the IRS had not assessed the taxes until after the filing of the debtor's petition does not make these postpetition taxes. *In re* Sapienza, 8 C.B.C.2d 227 (B. Ct., W.D.N.Y. 1983).

References

5 *Collier on Bankruptcy* ch. 1305 (Matthew Bender 15th ed.).

3 *Collier Bankruptcy Manual* ch. 1305 (Matthew Bender 3d ed.).

6 *Collier Bankruptcy Practice Guide* ch. 101 (Matthew Bender).

SECTION 1306 (11 U.S.C. § 1306)

§ 1306. Property of the estate.

(a) Property of the estate includes, in addition to the property specified in section 541 of this title—

(1) all property of the kind specified in such section that the debtor acquires after the commencement of the case but before the case is closed, dismissed, or converted to a case under chapter 7, 11, or 12 of this title whichever occurs first; and

(2) earnings from services performed by the debtor after the commencement of the case but before the case is closed, dismissed, or converted to a case under chapter 7, 11, or 12 of this title, whichever occurs first.

(b) Except as provided in a confirmed plan or order confirming a plan, the debtor shall remain in possession of all property of the estate.

Legislative History

A slightly different rule governing property of the estate applies in a chapter 13 case. All property of the estate, as provided in section 541, is property of the estate in a chapter 13 case. In addition, however, property of the kind specified in section 541 that the debtor acquires after the commencement of the case but before conversion, dismissal, or closing of the case is also property of the estate.

[*House Report No. 95–595, 95th Cong., 1st Sess. 428 (1977).*]

Section 541 is expressly made applicable to chapter 13 cases by section 103(a). Section 1306 broadens the definition of property of the estate for chapter 13 purposes to include all property acquired and all earnings from services performed by the debtor after the commencement of the case.

[*Senate Report No. 95–989, 95th Cong., 2d Sess. 140-141 (1978).*]

Section 1306(a)(2) adopts a provision contained in the Senate amendment in preference to a similar provision contained in the House bill.

[*124 Cong. Rec. H 11,106 (Sept. 28, 1978); S 17,423 (Oct. 6, 1978).*]

Subsection (b) specifies that unless the plan or the order confirming the plan provides otherwise, the debtor remains in possession of all property of the estate.

[*House Report No. 95–595, 95th Cong., 1st Sess. 428 (1977).*]

Subsection (b) nullifies the effect of section 521(3), otherwise applicable, by providing that a chapter 13 debtor need not surrender possession of property of the estate, unless required by the plan or order of confirmation.

[*Senate Report No. 95–989, 95th Cong., 2d Sess. 141 (1978).*]

Comment

Section 541 describes and specifies what constitutes property of the estate and this includes the estate in a chapter 13 case. Section 1306 specifies "property of the estate" in a chapter 13 case in addition to the property set forth in section 541.

Section 1306(a)(1) provides that property of the kind enumerated in section 541 acquired after the filing of the petition but before the case is closed, dismissed, or converted, whichever first occurs, is included in "property of the estate." Section 1306(a)(2) similarly provides that earnings from debtor's services after commencement of the case but before the case is closed, dismissed, or converted, whichever first occurs, is included in "property of the estate."

Section 1306(b) provides that the debtor remains in possession of all property of the estate except that the debtor shall not remain in possession of such property to the extent provided in a confirmed plan or in an order confirming the plan.

See **Comment** to section 541.

1986 Amendments: The only change effected by the 1986 Act was the inclusion of chapter 12 cases in subsection (a)(1) and (2).

Case Annotations

Pursuant to section 1306(a), property of the chapter 13 estate includes property acquired more than 180 days postpetition, notwithstanding section 541(a)(5). Educational Assistance Corp. v. Zellner, 827 F.2d 1222, 17 C.B.C.2d 867 (8th Cir. 1987).

Funds received by a trustee under a wage deduction order after the dismissal of a chapter 13 petition never become property of the chapter 13 estate. Nash v. Kester (*In re* Nash), 765 F.2d 1410, 13 C.B.C.2d 209 (9th Cir. 1985).

A pensioner's interest in a trust fund established pursuant to ERISA that is subject to an enforceable transfer restriction valid under state law becomes estate property in a chapter 13 plan upon payment to the debtor under the terms of the trust; only then can the estate property become subject to a payment order under section 1325(b). McLean v. Central States, Southeast and Southwest Areeas Pension Fund (*In re* McLean), 762 F.2d 1204, 12 C.B.C.2d 1431 (4th Cir. 1985).

Because Congress clearly intended that Social Security benefits become part of the chapter 13 debtor's estate under section 1306, the Social Security Act's general anti-assignment provisions are inconsistent with and implicitly repealed by the later enacted Bankruptcy Code; this is so because the anti-assignment provisions were designed solely to insure that a recipient have the resources to meet his basic needs and a debtor's ability to care for himself is not compromised under the scheme of chapter 13. United States v. Devall, 704 F.2d 1513, 8 C.B.C.2d 663 (11th Cir.), *reh'g denied,* 714 F. 2d 1068 (11th Cir. 1983).

Only that portion of postconfirmation income and acquired property needed to fund the plan becomes property of the estate, protected by the automatic stay, and the balance of any postconfirmation income or property is the debtor's individual property not protected by the stay. *In re* Ziegler, 26 C.B.C.2d 900 (B. Ct., N.D. Ill. 1992).

Pursuant to section 1306(a)(1), in community property states a nondebtor spouse's postpetition income is property of the estate to the extent that it covers liability for an allowed claim as property acquired by the chapter 13 debtor. *In re* Reiter, 24 C.B.C.2d 1780 (B. Ct., W.D. Tex. 1991).

As assignee of a vendee, a debtor acquires the same right to receive title on a condominium which the vendee holds at the time of the assignment. *In re* Clifton, 23 C.B.C.2d 1555 (B. Ct., E.D. Mo. 1990).

As section 1306(b) gives a debtor possession of property of the estate, section 1327(b) would be devoid of meaning were it not found to vest both title and ownership in the debtor upon confirmation. *In re* Petruccelli, 22 C.B.C.2d 1519 (B. Ct., S.D. Cal. 1990).

Section 1306 is inapplicable to the definition of property of the estate once a chapter 13 case is converted to another chapter, since under section 103(h), chapter 13 provisions are applicable only in a case under such chapter. Upon conversion, section 541 becomes the sole provision for defining what constitutes the chapter 7 estate. *In re* Lepper, 14 C.B.C.2d 1040 (B. Ct., D. Md. 1986).

References

5 *Collier on Bankruptcy* ch. 1306 (Matthew Bender 15th ed.).

3 *Collier Bankruptcy Manual* ch. 1306 (Matthew Bender 3d ed.).

6 *Collier Bankruptcy Practice Guide* ch. 101 (Matthew Bender).

Cohn, *Deferring Vesting of Property in a Chapter 13 Plan and the Court's Duty to Protect the Interests of Creditors,* 88 Com. L.J. 386 (1983).

Peeples, *Five Into Thirteen: Lien Avoidance in Chapter 13,* 61 N.C.L. Rev. 849 (1983).

Property of the Estate After Confirmation of a Chapter 13 Repayment Plan: Balancing Competing Interests, 65 Wash. L. Rev. 677 (1990).

SECTION 1307 (11 U.S.C. § 1307)

§ 1307.　Conversion or dismissal.

(a) The debtor may convert a case under this chapter to a case under chapter 7 of this title at any time. Any waiver of the right to convert under this subsection is unenforceable.

(b) On request of the debtor at any time, if the case has not been converted under section 706, 1112, or 1208 of this title, the court shall dismiss a case under this chapter. Any waiver of the right to dismiss under this subsection is unenforceable.

(c) Except as provided in subsection (e) of this section, on request of a party in interest or the United States trustee and after notice and a hearing, the court may convert a case under this chapter to a case under chapter 7 of this title, or may dismiss a case under this chapter, whichever is in the best interests of creditors and the estate, for cause, including—

(1) unreasonable delay by the debtor that is prejudicial to creditors;

(2) nonpayment of any fees and charges required under chapter 123 of title 28;

(3) failure to file a plan timely under section 1321 of this title;

(4) failure to commence making timely payments under section 1326 of this title;

(5) denial of confirmation of a plan under section 1325 of this title and denial of a request made for additional time for filing another plan or a modification of a plan;

(6) material default by the debtor with respect to a term of a confirmed plan;

(7) revocation of the order of confirmation under section 1330 of this title, and denial of confirmation of a modified plan under section 1329 of this title;

(8) termination of a confirmed plan by reason of the occurrence of a condition specified in the plan other than completion of payments under the plan;

(9) only on request of the United States trustee, failure of the debtor to file, within fifteen days, or such additional time as the court may allow, after the filing of the petition commencing such case, the information required by paragraph (1) of section 521; or

(10) only on request of the United States trustee, failure to timely file the information required by paragraph (2) of section 521.

(d) Except as provided in subsection (e) of this section, at any time before the confirmation of a plan under section 1325 of this title, on request of a party in interest or the United States trustee and after notice and a hearing, the court may convert a case under this chapter to a case under chapter 11 or 12 of this title.

(e) The court may not convert a case under this chapter to a case under chapter 7, 11, or 12 of this title if the debtor is a farmer, unless the debtor requests such conversion.

(f) Notwithstanding any other provision of this section, a case may not be converted to a case under another chapter of this title unless the debtor may be a debtor under such chapter.

Bankruptcy Rule References: 1017 and 1019

Legislative History

Subsection (a) of section 1307 gives the debtor an absolute right of conversion to a liquidation case at any time.

[*House Report No. 95–595, 95th Cong., 1st Sess. 428 (1977).*]

Subsections (a) and (b) confirm, without qualification, the rights of a chapter 13 debtor to convert the case to a liquidating bankruptcy case under chapter 7 of title 11, at any time, or to have the chapter 13 case dismissed. Waiver of any such right is unenforceable.

[*Senate Report No. 95–989, 95th Cong., 2d Sess. 141 (1978).*]

Section 1307(a) is derived from the Senate amendment in preference to a comparable provision contained in the House bill.

[*124 Cong. Rec. H 11,106 (Sept. 28, 1978); S 17,423 (Oct. 6, 1978).*]

Subsection (b) requires the court, on request of the debtor, to dismiss the case if the case has not already been converted from chapter 7 or 11.

Subsection (c) permits the court to convert the case to chapter 7 or 11, or to dismiss the case, whichever is in the best interests of creditors and the estate, for cause. Cause may include unreasonable delay by the debtor that is prejudicial to creditors, nonpayment of any fees and charges required under chapter 123 of title 28, failure to propose a plan timely under section 1321, denial of confirmation, material default under the plan, revocation of the confirmation order and denial of confirmation of a modified plan, or termination of a confirmed plan by reason of the occurrence of a condition specified in the plan.

[*House Report No. 95–595, 95th Cong., 1st Sess. 428 (1977).*]

Subsection (c) specifies various conditions for the exercise of the power of the court to convert a chapter 13 case to one under chapter 7 or to dismiss the case.

[*Senate Report No. 95–989, 95th Cong., 2d Sess. 141 (1978).*]

Subsection (d) permits preconfirmation conversion to chapter 11 at any time on request of a party in interest. The court will exercise its sound discretion in determining whether to grant the request, based on the nature of the debtor's business and other similar factors.

[*House Report No. 95–595, 95th Cong., 1st Sess. 428 (1977).*]

Subsection (d) deals with the conversion of a chapter 13 case to one under chapter 11.

[*Senate Report No. 95–989, 95th Cong., 2d Sess. 141 (1978).*]

Subsection (e) reinforces section 303 by prohibiting conversion to a liquidation case if the debtor is a farmer and does not consent.

[*House Report No. 95–595, 95th Cong., 1st Sess. 428 (1977).*]

Subsection (e) prohibits conversion of the chapter 13 case filed by a farmer to chapter 7 or 11 except at the request of the debtor.

[*Senate Report No. 95–989, 95th Cong., 2d Sess. 141 (1978).*]

Subsection (f) reinforces section 109 by prohibiting conversion to a chapter under which the debtor is not eligible to proceed.

[*House Report No. 95–595, 95th Cong., 1st Sess. 428 (1977).*]

No case is to be converted from chapter 13 to any other chapter, unless the debtor is an eligible debtor under the new chapter.

[*Senate Report No. 95–989, 95th Cong., 2d Sess. 141 (1978).*]

Comment

Section 1307(a) gives the debtor the absolute right to convert the chapter 13 case to a case under chapter 7, and this right may not be waived.

Subsection (b) mandates the court to dismiss a chapter 13 case on request of the debtor provided that the case has not been converted under section 706 or under section 1112. Any waiver by the debtor of his right to request such dismissal is unenforceable.

In a drastic change from the provisions of the former Bankruptcy Act, section 1307(c) provides that on request of a party in interest or the United States trustee, and after notice and hearing, the court may dismiss or convert the case to *chapter 7* (liquidation), whichever is in the best interest of the estate and creditors, for cause, including (but not limited to), unreasonable delay by debtor that is prejudicial to creditors, failure to pay filing fees, failure to timely file a plan, denial of confirmation (and denial of time to file another or modified plan), material default of a term of a confirmed plan, revocation of the order of confirmation, or termination of the plan by reason of the occurrence of a condition specified therein. But under subsection (e), where debtor is a farmer, conversion to chapter 7 or 11 requires a "request" by debtor. And, of course, a case may not be converted to another chapter unless the debtor is eligible to be a debtor under that chapter. Under the 1986 Amendments the court may also convert the case to chapter 7 or dismiss, but only on request of the United States trustee, if the debtor fails to file within 15 days (or such additional time as the trustee may allow) the information required by section 521(1), *i.e.,* list of creditors, schedules of assets and liabilities, schedule of current income and expenditures, and a statement of the debtor's financial affairs. Also only on request of the United States trustee, the court may convert or dismiss if the debtor fails to timely file the information required by section 521(2), *i.e.,* statement of intention with respect to consumer debts secured by real property.

Under subsection (d), except in the case of a farmer, on request of a party in interest or the United States trustee, and before confirmation, the court may (after notice and hearing) convert the chapter 13 case to a case under chapter 11. This subsection, and subsection (c) permitting conversion to chapter 7 under specified conditions, marks a great departure from prior law. Under subsection (d), the case of a businessman who files under chapter 13, but whose business should properly be reorganized under chapter 11 or 12, may be converted to chapter 11 or 12.

Bankruptcy Rule 1019, as amended in 1991, relates to conversion of a chapter 13 case to chapter 7. Paragraph (1)(A) provides that lists, inventories, schedules, and statements of financial affairs theretofore filed are deemed failed in the chapter 7 case unless the court otherwise directs. If not previously filed, the debtor is to comply with Rule 1007 as if an order for relief was entered on an involuntary petition on the date of entry of the conversion order.

Paragraph (1)(B) requires that the statement of intention [section 521(2)], if required, be filed within 30 days after entry of the conversion order or before the first date set for the meeting of creditors, whichever is earlier. The time may be extended for cause on motion made before the time to file has expired. Notice of any extension must be given to the United States trustee and any committee, trustee, or other party as the court directs.

Paragraph (2) provides that a new time period for filing claims, complaints objecting to discharge or for determination of dischargeability of any debt shall commence pursuant to Rules 3002, 4004, or 4007, provided that a new time period shall not commence if a chapter 7 case has been converted to chapter 11, 12 or 13 and thereafter reconverted to chapter 7 and the time for filing such claims and complaints or any extension thereof has expired in the original chapter 7 case.

Paragraph (3) makes it unnecessary to file claims that had been actually filed in the chapter 13 case before conversion to chapter 7.

Paragraph (4) provides that after the chapter 7 trustee qualifies or assumes his duties, the trustee or debtor in possession acting in the chapter 13 case (unless otherwise ordered) shall forthwith turn over to the chapter 7 trustee all records and property of the estate.

Paragraph (5) [as amended in 1991]: Unless the court directs otherwise, each debtor in possession or trustee in the superseded case (A) within 15 days after entry of the conversion order in a chapter 11 case, file a schedule of unpaid debts incurred after commencement of superseded case including the name and address of each creditor; and (B) within 30 days after entry of a conversion order in a chapter 11, 12 or 13 case, file and transmit to the United States trustee a final report and account. Within 15 days after a conversion order, a chapter 13 debtor shall file a schedule of unpaid debts incurred after commencement of the chapter 13 case. If conversion is after confirmation, the debtor must file (A) a schedule of property not listed in the final report and acquired after filing the original report but before confirmation, (B) schedule of unpaid debts incurred after confirmation but before conversion, and (C) schedule of executory contracts and unexpired leases entered in to or assumed after filing the petition and before conversion. The clerk shall forthwith transmit a copy of every such schedule to the United States trustee.

Paragraph (6) requires that on the filing of the schedule of unpaid debts, the clerk or some person designated by the court shall give notice to those entities (including the United States, any state, or an subdivision thereof) that their claims may be filed under Rule 3001(a)–(d) and 3002. Unless notice of insufficient assets to pay dividend is mailed pursuant to Rule 2002(e), the court shall fix a time for filing claims arising from rejection of executory contracts or unexpired leases under Code sections 348(c) and 365(d).

Paragraph (7) provides that if the court extends the time to file claims against a surplus (Rule 3002(c)(6)), the extension shall apply to holders of claims who failed to timely file within the time prescribed under paragraph (6), above, and notice shall be given to the claimant (Rule 2002).

Bankruptcy Rule 1017 deals with dismissal. Subdivision (a) provides that except as provided in sections 707(b), 1208(b), and 1307 (pursuant to which the debtor has an absolute right to have his chapter 13 case dismissed) a case shall not be dismissed on motion of the petitioner or for want of prosecution or other cause or by consent of the parties before a hearing on notice as provided in Rule 2002. For such notice the debtor shall file a list of all creditors with their addresses within the time fixed by the court unless the list was previously filed. Upon debtor's failure to do so, the court may order the preparation and filing of the list by the debtor or other entity. Subdivision (b) deals with dismissal for nonpayment of any installment of the filing fee, and subdivision (c) provides that a case shall not be dismissed or suspended pursuant to section 305 until after a hearing on notice as provided in Rule 2002(a). Subdivision (d) provides, *inter alia,* that a proceeding to dismiss or convert a case under § 1307(a) or (b) is a contested matter governed by Rule 9014. Conversion or dismissal is obtainable by motion filed and served as provided in Rule 9013. A chapter 13 case shall be converted without court order on the filing by the debtor of a notice of conversion pursuant to § 1307(a) and the date of the filing of the notice shall be deemed the date of the conversion order for the purpose of applying Code section 348(c). The clerk shall forthwith transmit to the United States trustee a copy of such notice.

Bankruptcy Rule 2002(f) requires the clerk to give the debtor and all creditors notice by mail of dismissal of the case and of the entry of an order directing that the case be converted to a case under a different chapter. Rule 2002(k) requires the clerk to transmit to the United States trustee notice of dismissal or conversion of a case to another chapter.

1984 Amendments: Section 1307(c)(4) is new and provides that the debtor's failure to commence timely payments under section 1326 constitutes a ground for conversion to chapter 7 or dismissal. The remaining paragraphs of subsection (c) were renumbered. Subsection (c)(8) [as renumbered] was amended by the addition of the words "other than completion of payments under the plan."

1986 Amendments: The 1986 Act amended section 1307 in several respects. Subsection (c) was amended by authorizing the United States trustee (as well as a party in interest) to request conversion to chapter 7 or dismissal for cause including the reasons set forth in the subsection.

Subsection (c) was further amended by adding paragraphs (9) and (10). Under paragraph (9), only on request of the United States trustee, the court may convert or dismiss if the debtor fails to file within 15 days, or such additional time as the court allows, after the filing of the chapter 13 petition, the information required by section 521(1), *i.e.,* list of creditors, schedules of assests and liabilities, schedule of current income and expenditures, and a statement of debtor's financial affairs. Under paragraph (10), only on request of the United States trustee, the court may convert or dismiss if the debtor fails to timely file the information required by section 521(2), *i.e.,* the statement of debtor's intention with regard to consumer debts secured by property of the estate.

Section 1307(d) was amended by including the United States trustee as a party who may request conversion of a chapter 13 case to a case under chapter 11 or 12.

This section was amended to reflect the creation of a permanent United States trustee system. Section 302(d) of the 1986 Amendments provides different effective dates for the amendments relating to the United States trustee system. *See* Section 302 of the 1986 Amendments, as amended by Pub. L. No. 101-650 (1990), reprinted herein under "Selected Provisions of the Bankruptcy Judges, United States Trustees, and Family Farmer Bankruptcy Act of 1986," regarding effective dates generally. Pub. L. No. 101-650 (Judicial Improvements Act of 1990) (signed into law December 1, 1990) amended Section 302(d)(3) of the Bankruptcy Judges, United States Trustees, and Family Farmer Bankruptcy Act of 1986 by extending the period in which the judicial districts in the states of Alabama and North Carolina may remain outside the United States trustee system.

Case Annotations

A section 1307(c) inquiry into the debtor's good faith in filing a chapter 13 petition requires a bankruptcy court to look at the totality of the circumstances in making the good faith determination, doing so on a case by case basis. There is a substantive overlap in the section 1307 and section 1325 good faith inquiries, and the focus of the good faith inquiry under both sections often is whether the filing is fundamentally fair in a manner that complies with the spirit of the Code. Matter of Love, 957 F.2d 1350, 26 C.B.C.2d 875 (7th Cir. 1992).

A court, in its discretion, may dismiss a case under section 1307(c) for failure to meet a filing deadline, even if the filing delay is relatively short, when the debtors neglect to take advantage of prior opportunities to avoid dismissal. Failure to meet a mandatory deadline cannot be cured by the simple expedient of filing required papers before the court's show cause hearing. A debtor's complete lack of an excuse for missing a mandatory deadline and failure to offer assurances that it will meet future deadlines mandates dismissal of the case, although if the filing delay is relatively short and causes no harm, the case may dismissed without prejudice. *In re* Greene, 24 C.B.C.2d 2001 (B. Ct., N.D. Ohio 1991).

The presence of the word "shall" in section 1307(b) is dispositive in conferring an absolute right upon the debtor to dismiss his chapter 13 case at any time, notwithstanding the presence of competing motions. *In re* Rebeor, 20 C.B.C.2d 206 (B. Ct., N.D.N.Y. 1988). *But see In re* Tatsis, 16 C.B.C.2d 1054 (B. Ct., W.D.N.C. 1987) (a debtor's right to an automatic dismissal of a chapter 13 case is limited when there is already pending a motion to convert the case).

A bankruptcy court may not allow a secured creditor to proceed with a foreclosure owing to a postconfirmation default by a chapter 13 debtor, with or without first obtaining relief from the automatic stay, as the only postconfirmation remedy available to a creditor, secured or unsecured, is to seek dismissal of the case for substantial default under section 1307(c)(6). Mellon Financial Services Corp. No. 9 v. Broman (*In re* Broman), 18 C.B.C.2d 307 (B. Ct., D. Colo. 1988).

Grounds that are insufficient by themselves to justify dismissal cannot be considered cumulatively to constitute lack of "good faith" as to justify dismissal. *In re* Ford, 17 C.B.C.2d 1149 (B. Ct., E.D. Pa. 1987).

Cause does not exist to dismiss a chapter 13 plan, in the instance in which a debtor had missed several plan payments, when it is taken into consideration that the plan is only a few months short of completion and will pay all unsecured claims a 100 percent dividend. *In re* Black, 17 C.B.C.2d 602 (B. Ct., W.D. Va. 1987).

Although the literal language of section 1307(b) grants the debtor an absolute right to dismiss his chapter 13 case, he may not utilize this right when the case was filed for an improper purpose, in bad faith, or to abuse or misuse the bankruptcy process. *In re* Powers, 12 C.B.C.2d 760 (B. Ct., M.D. La. 1985).

As a deceased debtor is not an individual with regular income and as a probate estate is unable to make payments under a chapter 13 plan, the debtor is no longer eligible for chapter 13 relief and the court will dismiss the chapter 13 case pursuant to 1307(c). In the Matter of Jarrett, 6 C.B.C.2d 496 (B. Ct., M.D.N.C. 1982).

References

5 *Collier on Bankruptcy* ch. 1307 (Matthew Bender 15th ed.).

3 *Collier Bankruptcy Manual* ch. 1307 (Matthew Bender 3d ed.).

2 *Collier Bankruptcy Practice Guide* ch. 37 (Matthew Bender).

Flint, *Bankruptcy Policy: Towards a Moral Justification for Financial Rehabilitation of the Consumer Debtor,* 48 Wash. & Lee L. Rev. 515 (1991).

SUBCHAPTER II

The Plan

SECTION 1321 (11 U.S.C. § 1321)

§ 1321. **Filing of plan.** The debtor shall file a plan.

Bankruptcy Rule Reference: 3015

Legislative History

This section requires the debtor to file a repayment plan. The debtor has the exclusive right to propose and file a plan either with the petition or within such time as the Rules prescribe. Creditors may [*sic*] file a plan under any circumstances. [*Ed. Note:* The word "not" appears to have been omitted inadvertently from the last sentence of the excerpt from the House Report. See, *e.g.*, page 123 of that report.]

[*House Report No. 95–595, 95th Cong., 1st Sess. 428 (1977).*]

Chapter 13 contemplates the filing of a plan only by the debtor.

[*Senate Report No. 95–989, 95th Cong., 2d Sess. 141 (1978).*]

Comment

Section 1321 provides that the chapter 13 debtor has the exclusive right to file a plan. This conforms to the concept of chapter 13 being a voluntary act on the part of the debtor. Moreover, in a consumer case, the debtor is the logical one to formulate a workable plan according to his income and expenses.

Bankruptcy Rule 3015(b) provides that a chapter 13 debtor may file a plan with the petition or within 15 days thereafter, and such time may not be extended further except for cause shown and on notice as directed by the court. Subdivision (c) requires every plan and any modification thereof to be dated. Subdivision (d) requires that the plan or a summary thereof be included with notice of hearing on confirmation. If the court so requires, debtor must furnish sufficient copies to enable the clerk to include a copy of the plan with the notice of hearing. Subdivision (e) requires the clerk to forthwith transmit to the United States trustee a copy of the plan or any modification thereof.

Case Annotations

In identifying policy considerations that will allow a creditor to discriminate in favor of one class in a chapter 13 plan, a court should not use a personal view of what class of creditors are to be specially protected but should look to other manifestations of public policy to determine whether or not a class of creditors deserves to be treated specially in the plan. Since ample support in state and federal legislation exists to illustrate that public policy treats child support claimants specially, a court cannot find classification by a debtor discriminating in favor of child support support unfair. *In re* Storberg, 20 C.B.C.2d 579 (B. Ct., D. Minn. 1988).

A local rule prescribing the only acceptable form for a chapter 13 plan does not violate a debtor's exclusive right to file a plan if the rule only dictates the form to be used and not the plan's contents. *In re* Walat, 18 C.B.C.2d 1353 (B. Ct., E.D. Va. 1988).

A proposal in chapter 13 which does not provide for some payment to creditors is not a "plan" and it leaves its proponent deficient in meeting the simple requirement of section 1321 that "The debtor shall file a plan," since a plan which does not propose full payment of the prescribed percentage to creditors within five years of confirmation, violates section 1322(c). In the Matter of Cook, 1 C.B.C.2d 780 (B. Ct., S.D. W. Va. 1980).

References

5 *Collier on Bankruptcy* ch. 1321 (Matthew Bender 15th ed.).

3 *Collier Bankruptcy Manual* ch. 1321 (Matthew Bender 3d ed.).

6 *Collier Bankruptcy Practice Guide* ch. 101 (Matthew Bender).

SECTION 1322 (11 U.S.C. § 1322)

§ 1322. Contents of plan.

(a) The plan shall—

(1) provide for the submission of all or such portion of future earnings or other future income of the debtor to the supervision and control of the trustee as is necessary for the execution of the plan;

(2) provide for the full payment, in deferred cash payments, of all claims entitled to priority under section 507 of this title, unless the holder of a particular claim agrees to a different treatment of such claim; and

(3) if the plan classifies claims, provide the same treatment for each claim within a particular class.

(b) Subject to subsections (a) and (c) of this section, the plan may—

(1) designate a class or classes of unsecured claims, as provided in section 1122 of this title, but may not discriminate unfairly against any class so designated, however, such plan may treat claims for a consumer debt of the debtor if an individual is liable on such consumer debt with the debtor differently than other unsecured claims;

(2) modify the rights of holders of secured claims, other than a claim secured only by a security interest in real property that is the debtor's principal residence, or of holders of unsecured claims, or leave unaffected the rights of holders of any class of claims;

(3) provide for the curing or waiving of any default;

(4) provide for payments on any unsecured claim to be made concurrently with payments on any secured claim or any other unsecured claim;

(5) notwithstanding paragraph (2) of this subsection, provide for the curing of any default within a reasonable time and maintenance of payments while the case is pending on any unsecured claim or secured claim on which the last payment is due after the date on which the final payment under the plan is due;

(6) provide for the payment of all or any part of any claim allowed under section 1305 of this title;

(7) subject to section 365 of this title, provide for the assumption, rejection, or assignment of any executory contract or unexpired lease of the debtor not previously rejected under such section;

(8) provide for the payment of all or part of a claim against the debtor from property of the estate or property of the debtor;

(9) provide for the vesting of property of the estate, on confirmation of the plan or at a later time, in the debtor or in any other entity; and

(10) include any other appropriate provision not inconsistent with this title.

(c) The plan may not provide for payments over a period that is longer than three years, unless the court, for cause, approves a longer period, but the court may not approve a period that is longer than five years.

Bankruptcy Rule References: 3013 and 6006

Legislative History

The plan must provide for the submission of all or such portion of the debtor's future earning or other future income to the supervision and control of the trustee as is necessary for the execution of the plan. The plan must also provide for the full payment of all priority claims, and, if the plan classifies claims, provide the same treatment for each claim within a particular class.

[*House Report No. 95–595, 95th Cong., 1st Sess. 429 (1977).*]

Chapter 13 is designed to serve as a flexible vehicle for the repayment of part or all of the allowed claims of the debtor. Section 1322 emphasizes that purpose by fixing a minimum of mandatory plan provisions.

Subsection (a) requires that the plan submit whatever portion of the future income of the debtor is necessary to implement the plan to the control of the trustee, mandates payment in full of all section 507 priority claims, and requires identical treatment for all claims of a particular class.

[*Senate Report No. 95–989, 95th Cong., 2d Sess. 141 (1978).*]

Section 1322. Tax payments in wage earner plans: The House bill provided that a wage earner plan had to provide that all priority claims would be paid in full. The Senate amendment contained a special rule in section 1325(c) requiring that Federal tax claims must be paid in cash, but that such tax claims can be paid in deferred cash installments under the general rules applicable to the payment of debts in a wage earner plan, unless the Internal Revenue Service negotiates with the debtor for some different medium or time for payment of the tax liability.

The House bill adopts the substance of the Senate amendment rule under section 1322(a)(2) of the House amendment. A wage earner plan must provide for full payment in deferred cash payments, of all priority claims, unless the holder of a particular claim agrees with a different treatment of such claim.

[*124 Cong. Rec. H 11,115 (Sept. 28, 1978); S 17,432 (Oct. 6, 1978).*]

Subsection (b) lists the provisions the plan is permitted to contain. The plan may designate a class or classes of unsecured claims, other than priority claims, subject to the provisions of section 1122, relating to classification of claims. The plan may modify the rights of holders of secured claims or of holders of unsecured claims. It may provide for the curing or waiving of any default. The plan may provide for payments on unsecured claims to be made concurrently with payments on secured claims or priority claims (which are unsecured claims).

Paragraph (5) concerns long-term debt, such as mortgage debt. It permits the plan to provide for the curing [*sic*] any default within a reasonable time, and maintenance of payments while the case is pending on any unsecured claim or secured claim on which the last payment is due after the date on which the final payment under the plan is due. Paragraph (6) permits payment of postpetition claims, as allowed under section 1305. Paragraph (7) permits the plan to provide for the assumption or rejection of any executory contract or unexpired lease not previously rejected under section 365. Paragraph (8) is new. It permits the plan to provide for payment of claims from property of the estate or from property of the debtor, such as exempt property. Paragraph (9) permits the plan to provide for the vesting of property of the estate, on confirmation of the plan or at a later time, in the debtor or in any other entity. Finally, the plan may include any other provisions not inconsistent with the bankruptcy code.

[*House Report No. 95–595, 95th Cong., 1st Sess. 429 (1977).*]

Subsection (b) permits a chapter 13 plan to (1) divide unsecured claims not entitled to priority under section 507 into classes in the manner authorized for chapter 11 claims; (2) modify the rights of holders of secured and unsecured claims, except claims wholly secured by real estate mortgages; (3) cure or waive any default; (4) propose payments on unsecured claims concurrently with payments on any secured claim or any other class of unsecured claims; (5) provide for curing any default on any secured or unsecured claim on which the final payment is due after the proposed final payment under the plan; (6) provide for payment of any allowed postpetition claim; (7) assume or reject any previously unrejected executory contract or unexpired lease of the debtor; (8) propose the payment of all or any part of any claim from property of the estate or of the debtor; (9) provide for the vesting of property of the estate; and (10) include any other provision not inconsistent with other provisions of title 11.

[*Senate Report No. 95–989, 95th Cong., 2d Sess. 141 (1978).*]

Section 1322(b)(2) of the House amendment represents a compromise agreement between similar provisions in the House bill and Senate amendment. Under the House amendment, the plan may modify the rights of holders of secured claims other than a claim secured by a security interest in real property that is the debtor's principal residence. It is intended that a claim secured by the debtor's principal residence may be treated with under section 1322(b)(5) of the House amendment.

[*124 Cong. Rec. H 11,106 (Sept. 28, 1978); S 17,423 (Oct. 6, 1978).*]

Subsection (c) is new. It requires that the plan be limited to a three-year repayment period, unless the court, for cause, permits a longer period. The court may not, however, permit a repayment period that is longer than five years.

[*House Report No. 95–595, 95th Cong., 1st Sess. 429 (1977).*]

Subsection (c) limits the payment period under the plan to 3 years, except that a four-year payment period may be permitted by the court.

[*Ed. Note:* Subsection (c), as enacted, extends the total period allowed to five years.]

[*Senate Report No. 95–989, 95th Cong., 2d Sess. 141 (1978).*]

Section 1322(c) adopts a five-year period derived from the House bill in preference to a four-year period contained in the Senate amendment. A conforming change is made in section 1329(c) adopting the provision in the House bill in preference to a comparable provision in the Senate amendment.

[*124 Cong. Rec. H 11,106 (Sept. 28, 1978); S 17,423 (Oct. 6, 1978).*]

Comment

Section 1322(a) of the Code sets forth the mandatory provisions, and subsection (b) sets forth the permissive provisions of a chapter 13 plan.

Subsection (a)(1) requires inclusion of a provision for submission of future earnings necessary to execution of the plan to the supervision and control of the *trustee,* whereas Section 646(4) of the Act subjected future earnings to the supervision and control of the *court.* Subsection (a)(2) requires provision for payment in full in deferred cash payments to priority claims [section 507] unless a particular creditor agrees to different treatment. Subdivision (a)(3) requires that the plan provide equal treatment for each claim in a particular class.

Subsection (b)(2) departs from prior law by permitting a plan to modify debts secured by real property other than a claim secured only by a secured interest in real property that is the debtor's principal residence. Another departure from prior law is subsection (b)(8) which permits debtor to pay all or part of a claim from property of the debtor. Under prior law payments were made from debtor's future wages or earnings. While this may have been the legislative intent, the Act did not forbid the debtor's proposal to make payments from sources other than wages and earnings.

Under subsection (b)(4) the plan may provide for payments on unsecured claims to be made concurrently with payments on secured claims or unsecured priority claims.

Another departure from the Act is the requirement in subsection (c) that a plan may not provide for payments over a period longer than three years unless the court, for cause, approves a further period not longer than five years. The House Report clearly indicates that subsection (c) does not mean that the court may extend the payment period for an additional five years, but that the total repayment period may not exceed five years. Although the Act did not limit the payment period to three years, many courts declined to confirm a plan in which the pay-out period exceeded three years.

Although not specifically relevant to section 1322, it should be noted that in a significant departure from prior law, acceptance of a plan by creditors is not required. Under section 1325(a)(4), *infra,* all that is required for confirmation is that the plan give unsecured creditors at least what they would receive in a liquidation under chapter 7, *i.e.*, the "best interest" test.

Section 1322(b)(1) provides that the plan may designate a class or classes of unsecured claims, as provided in section 1122 of the Code. Bankruptcy Rule 3013 provides that for the purpose of the plan and its acceptance, the court may, on motion, and after hearing on notice as the court direct, establish classes of creditors pursuant to § 1322(b)(1)

1984 Amendments: Subsection (b)(1) of section 1322 was amended to permit debts guaranteed by an individual to be treated differently in a plan from other unsecured debts. Subsection (b)(2) was amended by adding a phrase providing that the plan may leave unaffected the rights of holders of any class of claims. Technical changes were made in subsection (b)(7).

Case Annotations

A mortgage interest that survives the discharge of a debtor's personal liability in an earlier chapter 7 case is a "claim" within the terms of section 101(5) and is subject to inclusion in a confirmed chapter 13 plan. Even after a debtor's personal liability has been discharged, a mortgage holder still retains a "right to payment" stemming from its right to the proceeds from the sale of the debtor's property. Johnson v. Home State Bank, 501 U.S. —, 111 S. Ct. 2150, 115 L. Ed. 2d 66, 24 C.B.C.2d 1171 (1991).

While section 1322(b)(2) prohibits modification of a residential mortgage lender's rights, it protects only the secured claim of a lender rather than the lender itself or its entire claim, and whether, and the extent to which, the lender holds a secured claim must first be determined according to section 506(a). *In re* Bellamy, 962 F.2d 176, 26 C.B.C.2d 1459 (2d Cir. 1992).

In a chapter 13 plan in which the debtor proposes to resume mortgage payments on long term debt for which the final payment falls due outside the life of the plan, an oversecured creditor is not entitled to postpetition interest on prepetition arrearages if the underlying agreement does not provide for it, because the debtor's repayment of the arrearages constitutes a cure of the default and not, as in a cramdown procedure, the modification of the underlying agreement. *In re* Laguna, 944 F.2d 542, 25 C.B.C.2d 727 (9th Cir. 1991).

In a cure under section 1322(b) of a default in the payment of mortgage installments, the bankruptcy court may confirm a plan if the plan provides for the payment, without interest, of all missed installment payments due as of the filing date unless the agreement and/or applicable nonbankruptcy law requires otherwise. Landmark Financial Services v. Hall, 918 F.2d 1150, 24 C.B.C.2d 232 (4th Cir. 1990).

A debtor that files a petition after entry of a foreclosure judgment but before the foreclosure sale may utilize the cure provisions of section

1322(b) in order to cure the default from which the foreclosure arose. *In re* Thompson, 894 F.2d 1227, 22 C.B.C.2d 250 (10th Cir. 1990). *But see* In the Matter of Roach, 824 F. 2d 1370, 17 C.B.C.2d 493 (3d Cir. 1987).

Section 1322(b)(2) does not preclude the modification of an unsecured portion of an undersecured claim. Wilson v. Commonwealth Mortgage Corp., 895 F.2d 123, 22 C.B.C.2d 561 (3d Cir. 1990).

A debtor's chapter 13 plan does not fall within section 1322(b)(5) when the plan does not provide for a curing of a default on a student loan, but instead provides for a percentage repayment and a partial discharge, and the debt is not precluded from discharge under section 1328(a)(1). Education Assistance Corp. v. Zellner, 827 F.2d 1222, 17 C.B.C.2d 867 (8th Cir. 1987).

Congress intended that in order for debtors to benefit under the Bankruptcy Code, the Code should take precedence over state law allowing a creditor to accelerate and foreclose on the property securing its interest. Downey Sav. and Loan Ass'n v. Metz (In the Matter of Metz), 820 F.2d 1495, 17 C.B.C.2d 63 (9th Cir. 1987).

A plan providing for a six percent payout on an education loan meets the threshold requirements of chapter 13, particularly when the bankruptcy court has included two additional requirements that the debtor: (1) file an amended budget with the court at specific intervals; and (2) provide the trustee with copies of his tax return. Wisconsin Higher Education Corp. v. Bear (In the Matter of Bear), 789 F.2d 577, 14 C.B.C.2d 1054 (7th Cir. 1986).

A postconfirmation default on a debt secured by the debtor's residence, not provided for in a confirmed chapter 13 plan, modifies the creditor's rights in contravention of section 1322(b)(2) and, accordingly, relief from the automatic stay is necessary to afford the creditor the opportunity to enforce its rights. Since the creditor was not provided for by the plan, it is not bound by the plan's provisions under section 1327(a). Western Equities, Inc. v. Harlan (*In re* Harlan), 783 F.2d 839, 14 C.B.C.2d 415 (9th Cir. 1985).

There is no default to cure after a judgment of foreclosure has been entered and sale has been completed. Goldberg v. Tynan (In the Matter of Tynan), 773 F.2d 177, 13 C.B.C.2d 655 (7th Cir. 1985). *But see In re* Kohler, 21 C.B.C.2d 1009 (B. Ct., S.D. Ill. 1989).

An order that interest be paid on mortgage arrearages does not modify the rights of a secured claim holder. Instead, the interest is merely incidental to the "cure" which is excepted from the rule of section 1322(b)(2). Cardinal Fed. Sav. & Loan Ass'n v. Colegrove (*In re* Colegrove), 771 F.2d 119, 13 C.B.C.2d 575 (6th Cir. 1985).

A reading of subsections (b)(2) and (b)(5) of section 1322 together leads to a conclusion that a residential mortgage that would otherwise permit a creditor to declare the entire debt presently due may be modified by a chapter 13 plan to cure a default and reinstate regular installment payments. Foster Mortgage Corp. v. Terry (*In re* Terry), 764 F.2d 1558, 13 C.B.C.2d 121 (11th Cir. 1985).

For pragmatic reasons the cut-off date of the statutory right to cure defaults on a debtor's principal residence is the foreclosure sale of the mortgaged premises. Federal Land Bank v. Glenn (*In re* Glenn), 760 F.2d 1428, 12 C.B.C.2d 1303 (6th Cir.), *cert. denied sub nom.* Miller v. First Federal of Michigan, 474 U.S. 849, 106 S. Ct. 144, 88 L. Ed. 2d 119 (1985).

The "cure" provisions of section 1322(b)(3) and (b)(5) are inapplicable when a debt has reached its maturity date without acceleration, prior to the filing of the chapter 13 petition. Seidel v. Larson (*In re* Seidel), 752 F.2d 1382, 12 C.B.C.2d 106 (9th Cir. 1985).

When state law provides that the mere entry of a foreclosure judgment does not pass title to property, a chapter 13 debtor who proposes to cure prior defaults and to restore mortgage payments on residential property subject to a foreclosure judgment does not thereby modify the rights of a residential mortgagee in contravention of section 1322(b)(2). In the Matter of Clark, 738 F.2d 869, 10 C.B.C.2d 1280 (7th Cir. 1984).

If foreclosure proceedings have not been completed, a chapter 13 debtor may cure a prepetition acceleration into maturity of the unpaid installments due upon his home mortgage and may propose to pay all past due or matured amounts secured by his home mortgage during the term of his plan as neither is a prohibited "modification" of the home mortgage indebtedness. Grubbs v. Houston First American Savings Assoc., 730 F.2d 236, 10 C.B.C.2d 549 (5th Cir. 1984).

Under section 1322(b)(1) unsecured creditors who co-signed notes of the debtor may be designated as members of a separate class from other unsecured creditors, and may therefore be treated differently from other unsecured creditors in a chapter 13 plan. Pub. Fin. Corp. v. Freeman, 712 F.2d 219, 9 C.B.C.2d 156 (5th Cir. 1983).

The Code does not require that each creditor receive either a copy of the debtor's plan or an explicit statement of the plan's proposal regarding the creditor's claim in order to satisfy constitutional due process standards. Lawrence Tractor Co. v. Gregory (In the Matter of Gregory), 705 F.2d 1118, 8 C.B.C.2d 605 (9th Cir. 1983).

Fully secured claims may in some instances be dealt with outside a chapter 13 plan, because such claims must ordinarily be classified separately as each involves a different claim to property of the debtor, and therefore the restrictions under section 1322(b)(1) that a plan may not discriminate unfairly against any class, and under section 1322(a)(3) that if a plan classifies claims it must provide the same treatment for each claim within a particular class, do not come into play. Foster v. Heitkamp (In the Matter of Foster), 670 F.2d 478, 6 C.B.C.2d 285 (5th Cir. 1982).

Determination of the secured claim under 506(a) is irrelevant to the evaluation of the claim for purposes of deciding whether it must be protected by section 1322(b)(2) from modification by the debtor. *In re* Hussman, 26 C.B.C.2d 32 (B. Ct., D. Minn. 1991).

A tax deed claimant under the Michigan Tax Act does not hold a security interest as defined by the Bankruptcy Code, since this interest is not consensual and, therefore, the anti-modification provision of section 1322(b)(2) does not apply. Matter of Sabec, 26 C.B.C.2d 1359 (B. Ct., W.D. Mich. 1992).

The only construction of the Bankruptcy Code that is consistent with both the plain language of section 1322(b)(2), its legislative history, and with the structure and purpose of chapter 13 as a whole, is to preclude the modification of a mortgage on a chapter 13 debtor's principal residence when it constitutes a mortgagee's only security. *In re* Strober, 26 C.B.C.2d 1383 (B. Ct., E.D.N.Y. 1992).

In a chapter 13 plan, it is strictly prohibited to discriminate in favor of a nondischargeable student loan obligation over other unsecured creditors. *In re* Taylor, 26 C.B.C.2d 1110 (B. Ct., W.D. Okla. 1992); *but see* Matter of Tucker, 25 C.B.C.2d 436 (B. Ct., S.D. Iowa 1991) (a debtor has the burden to show that a plan's favorable discriminatory treatment of a student student loan debt has a reasonable basis beyond the fact that student loan obligations are dischargeable to the extent allowed by section 523(a)(8)).

An interest in rents and profits, because it is inextricably bound to realty, is covered by the protection of section 1322(b)(2). *In re* Wright, 25 C.B.C.2d 447 (B. Ct., N.D. Ga. 1991).

A debtor's attempt to accelerate the payment of a specially classified unsecured claim, to the considerable disadvantage of the other unsecured creditors, is indicative of abuse and manipulation of the chapter 13 system and, therefore, violates sections 1322(b)(1) and 1325(a)(1). *In re* Whitelock, 24 C.B.C.2d 1337 (B. Ct., C.D. Utah 1990).

The five year maximum time period in section 1322(c) runs from the date that payments are to begin, *i.e.*, within 45 days of the filing of the case, rather than upon confirmation of the debtor's plan. *In re* Cobb, 24 C.B.C.2d 1272 (B. Ct., E.D. Pa. 1990).

Inclusion of a plan modification provision curing postpetition defaults in payments secured only by a debtor's principal residence does not constitute a modification of a creditor's rights in contravention of section 1322(b)(2) when the debtor's modification does not alter the original trust deed as to payment of future installments. *In re* Gadlen, 22 C.B.C.2d 524 (B. Ct., W.D. Tenn. 1990).

The special protection of section 1322(b)(2) does not permit a debtor to modify monthly payments, change the rate of interest or make any other changes in the agreement, with respect to a creditor whose claim is secured only by a security interest in real property that is the debtor's principal residence. *In re* Hayes, 22 C.B.C.2d 1484 (B. Ct., D. Or. 1990).

References

5 *Collier on Bankruptcy* ch. 1322 (Matthew Bender 15th ed.).

3 *Collier Bankruptcy Manual* ch. 1322 (Matthew Bender 3d ed.).

6 *Collier Bankruptcy Practice Guide* ch. 101 (Matthew Bender).

Cataldo, Murphy & Szabo, *Residential Mortgage Bifurcation Under Chapter 13 of the Bankruptcy Code,* 96 Com. L.J. 225 (1991).

Chapter 13: "Cause" for Extension Under Section 1322(c), 5 Bankr. Dev. J. 249 (1987).

Comment, *Resolving the Conflict Between Chapter 13 of the Bankruptcy Code and the Free Exercise Clause—In re Green: A Step in the Wrong Direction,* 57 Miss. L.J. 163 (1987).

Kennedy, *Chapter 13 Under the Bankruptcy Code,* 19 Mem. St. U.L. Rev. 137 (1989).

Morris, *Keeping Chapter 13 Debtors Inside the Debt Limits,* 2 F & G Bankr. L. Rev. 48 (1990).

Morris, *The Undersecured Home Mortgage Lender in Chapter 13,* 2 F & G Bankr. L. Rev. 52(1990).

Note, *The Chapter 13 Provisions: A Doctrine in Need of a Cure,* 74 Minn. L. Rev. 921 (1990).

Novellino, *A Serious Case of Metaphysics: When In re Brown Was Roach'd,* 95 Com. L.J. 97 (1990).

Polk, *The Chapter 13 Cramdown: New Nightmare for the Lender,* 19 Real Est. L.J. 279 (1991).

Reisenfeld, *Classification of Claims and Interests in Chapter 11 and 13 Cases,* 75 Cal. L. Rev. 391 (1987).

Vukowich, *A Reply to Professor Warren,* 72 Geo. L.J. 1359 (1984).

Warren, *Reducing Bankruptcy Protection for Consumers: A Response,* 72 Geo. L.J. 1333 (1984).

Whitford, *Has the Time Come to Repeal Chapter 13?,* 1 F & G Bankr. L. Rev. 44 (1989).

Williams, *Non-Business Liquidation Under Chapter 13 of the Bankruptcy Code: A Tool To Prevent the Loss of Homeowner Equity,* 59 Am. Bankr. L.J. 283 (1985).

Zaretsky, *Mortgagees' Rights in Chapter 13,* 203 N.Y.L.J. 3 (1990).

SECTION 1323 (11 U.S.C. § 1323)

§ 1323. Modification of plan before confirmation.

(a) The debtor may modify the plan at any time before confirmation, but may not modify the plan so that the plan as modified fails to meet the requirements of section 1322 of this title.

(b) After the debtor files a modification under this section, the plan as modified becomes the plan.

(c) Any holder of a secured claim that has accepted or rejected the plan is deemed to have accepted or rejected, as the case may be, the plan as modified, unless the modification provides for a change in the rights of such holder from what such rights were under the plan before modification, and such holder changes such holder's previous acceptance or rejection.

Bankruptcy Rule Reference: 3019

Legislative History

Subsection (a) permits the debtor to modify the plan at any time before confirmation, but requires that the modified plan conform to section 1322. After the debtor files the modification with the court, the plan as modified becomes the plan.

The debtor is permitted to modify the plan before confirmation without court approval so long as the modified plan, which becomes the plan on filing, complies with the requirements of section 1322.

The original acceptance or rejection of a plan by the holder of a secured claim remains binding unless the modified plan changes the rights of the holder and the holder withdraws or alters its earlier acceptance or rejection.

[*Senate Report No. 95–989, 95th Cong., 2d Sess. 142 (1978).*]

A holder of a secured claim that accepted or rejected a plan is deemed to have accepted or rejected, as the case may be, the plan as modified, unless the modification provides for a change in the rights of the holder of the secured claim that is different from any change proposed under the original plan. The holder of the claim may then change his acceptance or rejection.

[*House Report No. 95–595, 95th Cong., 1st Sess. 429 (1977).*]

Comment

Section 1323(a) permits the debtor to modify the plan at any time prior to confirmation provided the modification complies with section 1322 which sets forth the mandatory and permissive provisions of a plan. Under section 1323(b) upon the filing of a modification, the plan as modified becomes "the plan."

Subsection (c) refers only to holders of secured claims: a holder who has accepted or rejected the plan, is deemed to have accepted or rejected (as the case may be) the modified plan unless the modification provides for a change in the rights of such holder. If rights are changed, then such holder may change his previous acceptance or rejection of the plan.

Section 1323 deals with modifications of a plan *before* confirmation. Modification of the plan *after* confirmation is dealt with in section 1329, *infra*.

Rule 3019 provides that after acceptance and before confirmation, the proponent of a plan may file a modification. After hearing and notice to the trustee, any committee appointed under the Code and any entity designated by the court, if the court finds that the modification does not adversely change the treatment of the claim of one who has not accepted the modification in writing, the modification shall be deemed accepted by all creditors who previously accepted the plan.

Case Annotations

Debtors who experience additional financial difficulties during their chapter 13 case should seek a modification of their plan rather than default on plan payments, incur a dismissal, and then refile. *In re* Huerta, 26 C.B.C.2d 1236 (B. Ct., C.D. Cal. 1992).

References

5 *Collier on Bankruptcy* ch. 1323 (Matthew Bender 15th ed.).

3 *Collier Bankruptcy Manual* ch. 1323 (Matthew Bender 3d ed.).

6 *Collier Bankruptcy Practice Guide* ch. 101 (Matthew Bender).

SECTION 1324 (11 U.S.C. § 1324)

§ 1324. **Confirmation hearing.** After notice, the court shall hold a hearing on confirmation of the plan. A party in interest may object to confirmation of the plan.

Bankruptcy Rule Reference: 3020

Legislative History

This section requires the court to hold a hearing on the confirmation of the plan, after notice to all parties in interest. Any party in interest is permitted to object to confirmation.

[*House Report No. 95–595, 95th Cong., 1st Sess. 429 (1977).*]

Any party in interest may object to the confirmation of a plan, as distinguished from merely rejecting a plan. An objection to confirmation is predicated on failure of the plan or the procedures employed prior to confirmation to conform with the requirements of chapter 13. The bankruptcy judge is required to provide notice and an opportunity for hearing any such objection to confirmation.

[*Senate Report No. 95–989, 95th Cong., 2d Sess. 142 (1978).*]

Comment

Section 1324 requires a hearing "after notice" and the House Report, *supra,* indicates that notice be given "to all parties in interest." Any party in interest may object to confirmation (as distinguished from rejecting the plan) and, as indicated in the Senate Report, *supra,* parties are to be afforded an opportunity for a hearing on any such objections. Objections to confirmation are predicated on failure of the plan (or of the procedures prior to confirmation) to conform with the requirements of chapter 13, as for example, failure to include in the plan one of the mandatory provisions required by section 1322(a).

Bankruptcy Rule 2002(b) requires the clerk or some other person as the court directs to give not less than 25 days notice by mail to the debtor, the trustee and all creditors of the time fixed for filing objections and the hearing to consider confirmation of a plan. Rule 2002(k) requires the clerk (or some other person as the court may direct) to forthwith transmit to the United States trustee the notice of the time fixed for filing objections to confirmation.

Bankruptcy Rule 3020(b)(1) requires objections to confirmation to be filed with the court and served on the debtor, the trustee, the proponent of the plan, any committee appointed under the Code and on any other entity designated by the court, within a time fixed by the court. A copy of every objection to confirmation shall be transmitted by the objecting party to the United States trustee within the time fixed for the filing of objections. [Added by the 1991 Amendments.] An objection to confirmation is a contested matter governed by Rule 9014. Subdivision (b)(2) requires the court to rule on confirmation after hearing as provided in Rule 2002. If no timely objection is filed, the court may determine that the plan has been proposed in good faith and not by any means forbidden by law without receiving any evidence on such issues.

Case Annotations

The United States Attorney is within its rights as a party in interest in participating in the development of the plan and later objecting to the debtor's status. The United States government may not be estopped without a showing of affirmative misconduct. Miller v. United States of America, through Farmers Home Administration, 907 F.2d 80, 23 C.B.C.2d 358 (8th Cir. 1990).

In order to be a "party in interest" under section 1324, one must be the holder of an allowed unsecured claim. *In re* Stewart, 12 C.B.C.2d 86 (B. Ct., D. Or. 1985).

Issues concerning adequate protection must be resolved at the confirmation hearing and, therefore, are *res judicata* as to subsequent proceedings once the chapter 13 plan is confirmed. Majors v. Capitol Chevrolet Co. (*In re* Majors), 6 C.B.C.2d 545 (B. Ct., M.D. Tenn. 1982).

If an objecting creditor fails to appear at a confirmation hearing, a bankruptcy court is under no duty to consider and rule on the objections and may properly overrule the objections for failure to prosecute. *In re* Powell, 5 C.B.C.2d 775 (B. Ct., N.D. Ga. 1981).

A chapter 13 debtor's presence at the confirmation hearing is not a prerequisite to confirmation of the debtor's plan. *In re* Perskin, 4 C.B.C.2d 294 (B. Ct., N.D. Tex. 1981).

References

5 *Collier on Bankruptcy* ch. 1324 (Matthew Bender 15th ed.).

3 *Collier Bankruptcy Manual* ch. 1324 (Matthew Bender 3d ed.).

6 *Collier Bankruptcy Practice Guide* ch. 101 (Matthew Bender).

SECTION 1325 (11 U.S.C. § 1325)

§ 1325. Confirmation of plan.

(a) Except as provided in subsection (b), the court shall confirm a plan if—

(1) the plan complies with the provisions of this chapter and with the other applicable provisions of this title;

(2) any fee, charge, or amount required under chapter 123 of title 28, or by the plan, to be paid before confirmation, has been paid;

(3) the plan has been proposed in good faith and not by any means forbidden by law;

(4) the value, as of the effective date of the plan, of property to be distributed under the plan on account of each allowed unsecured claim is not less than the amount that would be paid on such claim if the estate of the debtor were liquidated under chapter 7 of this title on such date;

(5) with respect to each allowed secured claim provided for by the plan—

(A) the holder of such claim has accepted the plan;

(B)(i) the plan provides that the holder of such claim retain the lien securing such claim; and

(ii) the value, as of the effective date of the plan, of property to be distributed under the plan on account of such claim is not less than the allowed amount of such claim; or

(C) the debtor surrenders the property securing such claim to such holder; and

(6) the debtor will be able to make all payments under the plan and to comply with the plan.

(b)(1) If the trustee or the holder of an allowed unsecured claim objects to the confirmation of the plan, then the court may not approve the plan unless, as of the effective date of the plan—

(A) the value of the property to be distributed under the plan on account of such claim is not less than the amount of such claim; or

(B) the plan provides that all of the debtor's projected disposable income to be received in the three-year period beginning on the date that the first payment is due under the plan will be applied to make payments under the plan.

(2) For purposes of this subsection, "disposable income" means income which is received by the debtor and which is not reasonably necessary to be expended—

(A) for the maintenance or support of the debtor or a dependent of the debtor; and

(B) if the debtor is engaged in business, for the payment of expenditures necessary for the continuation, preservation, and operation of such business.

(c) After confirmation of a plan, the court may order any entity from whom the debtor receives income to pay all or any part of such income to the trustee.

Bankruptcy Rule Reference: 3020

Legislative History

The court is required to confirm the plan if six requirements are met. The plan must comply with the provisions of chapter 13 and with other applicable provisions of the bankruptcy code. Fees and charges required under chapter 123 of title 28 to be paid before confirmation must have been paid. The plan must have been proposed in good faith, and not by any means forbidden by law. The plan must meet the best interest of creditors test with respect to unsecured claims—the value, as of the effective date of the plan, of property to be distributed under the plan on account of each unsecured claim must be not less than the amount that would have been paid on that claim if the estate of the debtor were liquidated under chapter 7 of the effective date of the plan. With respect

to secured claims provided for by the plan, the holder of the claim must
have accepted the plan, or the debtor must either distribute under the
plan the value, as of the effective date of the plan, to the holder of the
claim, property of a value that is not less than the allowed amount of
the secured claim, as determined under proposed 11 U.S.C. § 506(a),
or the debtor must surrender the property securing the claim to the
holder of the claim. Finally, the debtor must be able to make all payment
under the plan and to comply with it.

After confirmation of a plan, the court may order any entity from
whom the debtor receives income to pay it, or a part of it, to the trustee,
who will serve as the disbursing agent under section 1326.

[*House Report No. 95–595, 95th Cong., 1st Sess. 430 (1977).*]

The bankruptcy court must confirm a plan if (1) the plan satisfies the
provisions of chapter 13 and other applicable provisions of title 11; (2)
it is proposed in good faith; (3) it is in the best interests of creditors,
and defined by subsection (a)(4) of section 1325; (4) it has been accepted
by the holder of each allowed secured claim provided for the plan or
where the holder of any such secured claim is to receive value under
the plan not less than the amount of the allowed secured claim, or where
the debtor surrenders to the holder the collateral securing any such
allowed secured claim; (5) the plan is feasible; and (6) the requisite fees
and charges have been paid.

Subsection (b) [*Ed. Note:* Pub. L. No. 98–353 redesignated section
1325(b) as section 1325(c).] authorizes the court to order an entity, as
defined by Section 101(15), to pay any income of the debtor to the
trustee. Any governmental unit is an entity subject to such an order.

[*Senate Report No. 95–989, 95th Cong., 2d Sess. 142 (1978).*]

Section 1325(a)(5)(B) of the House amendment modifies the House
bill and Senate amendment to significantly protect secured creditors in
chapter 13. Unless the secured creditor accepts the plan, the plan must
provide that the secured creditor retain the lien securing the creditor's
allowed secured claim in addition to receiving value, as of the effective
date of the plan of property to be distributed under the plan on account
of the claim not less than the allowed amount of the claim. To this extent,
a secured creditor in a case under chapter 13 is treated identically with
a recourse creditor under section 1111(b)(1) of the House amendment
except that the secured creditor in a case under chapter 13 may receive
any property of a value as of the effective date of the plan equal to the
allowed amount of the creditor's secured claim rather than being
restricted to receiving deferred cash payments. Of course, the secured
creditors' lien only secures the value of the collateral and to the extent
property is distributed of a present value equal to the allowed amount
of the creditor's secured claim the creditor's lien will have been satisfied
in full. Thus the lien created under section 1325(a)(5)(B)(i) is effective
only to secure deferred payments to the extent of the amount of the
allowed secured claim. To the extent the deferred payments exceed the
value of the allowed amount of the secured claim and the debtor
subsequently defaults, the lien will not secure unaccrued interest
represented in such deferred payments.

[*124 Cong. Rec. H 11,107 (Sept. 28, 1978); S 17,423 (Oct. 6, 1978).*]

Comment

Section 651 of the former Bankruptcy Act provided for confirmation where the plan had been accepted by *all* creditors affected thereby, and Section 652 provided for confirmation where the plan had not been accepted by all, but by the required majorities of unsecured creditors affected by the plan and by the secured creditors whose claims were dealt with by the plan.

The drastic change effected by section 1325 is that *acceptance of the plan by unsecured creditors is not required.* Instead, the "best interests of creditors" rule is applied as a condition to confirmation, *i.e.*, the value (as of the effective date of the plan) of property distributed to unsecured creditors is not less than they would receive if the debtor were liquidated under chapter 7, [section 1325(a)(4)].

Paragraphs (6)(1), (2) and (3) of subsection (a) requires that the plan comply with chapter 13, that fees to be paid prior to confirmation have been paid, and that the plan is proposed in good faith and not by any means forbidden by law.

Subsection (a)(5) represents a major change from the former Bankruptcy Act in that it removes the absolute veto power of a secured creditor by providing two alternative methods of treating a secured creditor who has not accepted the plan: (1) the plan provides that such creditor retain his lien *and* the value (as of the effective date of the plan) of property to be distributed under the plan is not less than the allowed amount of the claim, or (2) the plan provide for surrender to the secured creditor of the property securing the claim. Abandonment of the collateral is important when read in the light of section 506(a) which limits the secured creditor to the value of the security.

Subsection (c) empowers the court to order any entity from whom debtor receives income to pay all or any part of such income to the trustee.

See Comment to section 1324 as to notice of time to file objections to confirmation and of the confirmation hearing, and of time and manner of filing objections.

Bankruptcy Rule 3020(b)(2) requires the court to rule on confirmation after hearing as provided in Rule 2002. If no timely objection is filed, the court determine that the plan has been proposed in good faith and not by any means forbidden by law without receiving any evidence on such issues.

Bankruptcy Rule 3020(c) provides that the order of confirmation shall conform to Official Form 15. Notice of entry thereof shall be mailed promptly to the debtor, the trustee, creditors, equity security holders and other parties in interest. Notice of entry of the confirmation order shall be transmitted to the United States trustee as provided in Rule 2002(k). [As amended in 1991.]

1984 Amendments: Section 1325(a) was amended by the addition of the words "Except as provided in subsection (b)." Subsection (b) was redesignated "(c)" and a new subsection (b) was inserted. The new subsection defines "disposable income" and provides that if the trustee or an unsecured claimant objects to confimation, the court may not approve the plan unless the value of the property to be distributed under the plan on account of such claim is not less than the amount of such claim *or* all of debtor's "projected" disposable income to be received in the 3 year period beginning on the date of first payment under the plan will be applied to payment under the plan.

1986 Amendments: The 1986 Act merely substituted "and" for "or" at the end of § 1325(b)(2)(A).

Case Annotations

The full range of Code provisions designed to protect chapter 13 creditors, and the intent of Congress that "claim" be construed broadly, makes it unlikely that Congress intended bankruptcy courts to police chapter 13 abuses through a limitation of the Code's definition of "claim." Johnson v. Home State Bank, 501 U.S. —, 111 S. Ct. 2150, 115 L. Ed. 2d 66, 24 C.B.C.2d 1171 (1991).

A section 1325(a) inquiry into the debtor's good faith in filing his chapter 13 plan requires a bankruptcy court to look at the totality of the circumstances in making the good faith determination, doing so on a case by case basis. When the inquiries into good faith and the confirmation of a plan both focus on fundamental fairness, and the debtor often files the petition and plan simultaneously, there is a substantive overlap in the section 1307 and section 1325 good faith inquiries. Such inquiry often is whether the filing is fundamentally fair in a manner that complies with the spirit of the Code. Matter of Love, 957 F.2d 1350, 26 C.B.C.2d 875 (7th Cir. 1992).

Income derived from overtime wages is not required to be included in projections of the income available to repay creditors in a chapter 13 plan if the overtime income is not definite and if the debtor's health might become impaired from such work. In the Matter of Killough, 900 F.2d 61, 23 C.B.C.2d 472 (5th Cir. 1990).

For the purpose of reviewing a bankruptcy court's factual findings regarding a debtor's good faith in proposing a chapter 13 plan, an appellate court must use the clearly erroneous standard. *In re* LeMaire, 898 F.2d 1346, 22 C.B.C.2d 1008 (8th Cir. 1990).

The fact that a debtor attempts to discharge a debt in a chapter 13 case that is not dischargeable in a chapter 7 case is not conclusive as to bad faith unless it is combined with other factors that reveal an overall effort to avoid paying his creditors. *In re* Caldwell, 895 F.2d 1123, 22 C.B.C.2d 379 (6th Cir. 1990).

Questionable or dishonest prepetition conduct does not *per se* require full repayment of debt obligations; the analysis of a debtor's good faith must take into account all the circumstances surrounding the proposed plan to determine the sincerity and honesty of the debtor. *See In re* Caldwell *supra. See also* Metro Employees Credit Union v. Okoreeh-Baah (*In re* Okoreeh-Baah), 836 F. 2d 1030, 17 C.B.C.2d 1466 (6th Cir. 1988).

The filing of a chapter 13 petition prior to the closing of a preceding chapter 7 case is not dispositive on the issue of bad faith since the receipt of a discharge in that chapter 7 case allows the debtor to file a chapter 13 petition even if the chapter 7 case is not closed. *In re* Saylors, 869 F.2d 1434, 20 C.B.C.2d 1140 (11th Cir. 1989).

The provisions of section 1325(a) are not mandatory and a bankruptcy court may confirm a plan which meets the requirements of section 1322 but not those of section 1325(a)(5)(B). *In re* Szostek, 886 F.2d 1405, 21 C.B.C.2d 889 (3d Cir. 1989).

Although successive filings do not constitute *per se* bad faith, when a debtor has filed a chapter 7 case to discharge all unsecured debts and the court in that case has determined that a secured debt is nondischargeable, the subsequent filing of a chapter 13 case to discharge that debt constitutes bad faith. *In re* Rasmussen, 888 F.2d 703, 21 C.B.C.2d 1060 (10th Cir. 1989). *But see* In the Matter of Chaffin, 836 F.2d 215, 18 C.B.C.2d 477 (5th Cir. 1988) (the fact that a debt was held nondischargeable in a chapter 7 case because it was incurred through fraud is not sufficient as a matter of law to show the debtor acted in bad faith by invoking chapter 13 to obtain a discharge of that debt).

The present value provision of section 1325(a)(5)(B)(ii) does not apply when a debtor cures a default on his home mortgage under section 1322(b)(5) pursuant to a mortgage contract that has no provision for interest on arrearages and there has been no modification of the contract, as home mortgagees were not the intended beneficiaries of section 1325(a)(5)(B)(ii) and the nature of cure assumes a regime under which debtors reinstate defaulted debt contracts in accordance with the conditions of their contracts. *In re* Capps, 836 F.2d 773, 17 C.B.C.2d 1420 (3d Cir. 1987).

The most equitable interest rate to establish when there is an arrearage on secured loans is the prevailing market rate of interest on similar types of secured loans at the time of allowance of the creditor's claim and the confirmation of the plan in bankruptcy with a maximum limitation on such rate to be the underlying contract rate of interest. Cardinal Fed. Sav. & Loan Ass'n v. Colegrove (*In re* Colegrove), 771 F.2d 119, 13 C.B.C.2d 575 (6th Cir. 1985).

Oversecured mortgage creditors cannot receive an additional amount for the time value of money under section 1325(a)(5)(B) as that section is inapplicable to residential mortgages because of the prohibition against modification of mortgage contracts found in section 1322(b)(2). Foster Mortgage Corp. v. Terry (*In re* Terry), 764 F.2d 1558, 13 C.B.C.2d 121 (11th Cir. 1985).

There is no irreconcilable conflict between the antiassignment provisions of ERISA and the Internal Revenue Code and later-enacted section 1325(b) that would render the former implicitly repealed; accordingly an ERISA qualified pension plan trustee cannot be ordered to turn over directly to the chapter 13 trustee pension plan payments owed the debtor. McLean v. Central States, Southeast and Southwest Areas Pension Fund (*In re* McLean), 762 F.2d 1204, 12 C.B.C.2d 1431 (4th Cir. 1985).

It is the debtor's obligation when seeking the court's confirmation of his plan to specify as accurately as possible the amounts which he intends to pay creditors and any ambiguity in the debtor's plan will be interpreted against the debtor since the debtor is the party who drafted the document. Fawcett v. United States (*In re* Fawcett), 758 F.2d 588, 12 C.B.C.2d 1011 (11th Cir. 1985).

The express wording of section 1325(a)(4) and its legislative history clearly indicate that property to be distributed under a chapter 13 plan must be discounted to present value as of the effective date of the plan. Hardy v. Cinco Fed. Credit Union (*In re* Hardy), 755 F.2d 75, 12 C.B.C.2d 127 (6th Cir. 1985).

A court's refusal to provide for an increase in payments into a chapter 13 plan after payments of a fully secured loan outside of the plan are scheduled to cease does not constitute an abuse of discretion, if while the fully secured loan payments are to be made, the debtor is left with only enough income for necessities; such a payment scheme is not, under the circumstances, in bad faith. Friendly Fin. Discount Corp. v. Bradley (In the Matter of Bradley), 705 F.2d 1409, 8 C.B.C.2d 826 (5th Cir. 1983).

Regardless of a state law prohibition on the assignment of state pension fund benefits, a bankruptcy court may issue income deduction orders to a state retirement system in order to fund a debtor's confirmed chapter 13 plan. Regan v. Ross, 691 F.2d 81, 7 C.B.C.2d 485 (2d Cir. 1982).

A fully secured creditor of a chapter 13 debtor is entitled to interest on a mortgage arrearage; thus the bankruptcy court should follow a three part analysis to determine such entitlement: 1) determine the nature of the creditor's claim under section 506(b); 2) determine whether the chapter 13 plan "modifies" or "cures" the mortgage under section 1322(b)(2); and 3) determine whether the plan otherwise meets all requirements for confirmation under section 1325(a). *In re* Chavez, 26 C.B.C.2d 1192 (B. Ct., D.N.M. 1992).

A debtor's chapter 13 plan could only be proposed in good faith if it made a serious, prudent and reasonably effective effort to restore normal financial relations with creditors. *In re* Spencer, 26 C.B.C.2d 1223 (B. Ct., N.D. Okla. 1992).

Although "good faith" is not defined in section 1325(a)(3), cases indicate that the totality of the circumstances should be considered. A number of nonexclusive factors are also relevant to determining whether a debtor has filed his petition and is proceeding in good faith, including, *inter alia,* whether the debtor has misrepresented facts in his plan, unfairly manipulated the Code or otherwise abused the spirit and purposes of chapter 13. While serial or successive chapter 13 filings are not *per se* bad faith filings, the debtor's past history of filings and dismissals is relevant to the determination of whether the new plan has been proposed in good faith. *In re* Huerta, 26 C.B.C.2d 1236 (B. Ct., C.D. Cal. 1992).

If a debtor is otherwise current in plan payments, the fact that the debtor receives outside financial help at unspecified intervals and in unspecified amounts to meet his obligations is, without more, insufficient to hold the plan not feasible. *In re* Ward, 25 C.B.C.2d 349 (B. Ct., W.D. Okla. 1991).

A debtor is not barred from filing a chapter 13 petition in the period between the chapter 7 discharge and the filing of the final report by the chapter 7 trustee. *In re* Manderson, 24 C.B.C.2d 1155 (B. Ct., N.D. Ala. 1990).

The good faith test of § 1325(a)(3) is met upon a finding that a debtor has not manipulated the Code and is funding the chapter 13 plan to the best of his ability; the fact that the plan results in unfair treatment to creditors because they will receive substantially less under chapter 13 than they would have had the the debtor filed under chapter 7 is not indicative of bad faith. *In re* Farley, 23 C.B.C.2d 600 (B. Ct., S.D. Cal. 1990).

An objection to confirmation premised on the length of the proposed chapter 13 plan is without merit; the fact that a plan's projected duration is less than the statutory maximum of 60 months is not necessarily indicative of bad faith. *In re* Carver, 22 C.B.C.2d 810 (B. Ct., S.D. Ohio 1990).

Absent some affirmative action on the part of the housemate, such as legally obligating himself to dedicate a portion of his income for the life of the plan, a housemate's contribution will not be part of the debtor's regular salary in a chapter 13 plan. *In re* Fischel, 22 C.B.C.2d 1461 (B. Ct., N.D.N.Y. 1989).

A bankruptcy court has authority to order a chapter 13 debtor's employer to withhold funds from the debtor's pay and to forward those funds to the chapter 13 trustee to implement the plan. *In re* Worrell, 22 C.B.C.2d 778 (B. Ct., E.D. Va. 1990).

References

5 *Collier on Bankruptcy* ch. 1325 (Matthew Bender 15th ed.).

3 *Collier Bankruptcy Manual* ch. 1325 (Matthew Bender 3d ed.).

6 *Collier Bankruptcy Practice Guide* ch. 101 (Matthew Bender).

Ballam, *The "Good Faith" Requirement for Chapter 13 Bankruptcy Proceeding,* 25 Am. Bus. L.J. 603 (1988).

Comment, *Good Faith Inquiries Under the Bankruptcy Code: Treating the Symptom, Not the Cause,* 61 U. Chi. L. Rev. 795 (1985).

Comment, *Section 1325(b) and Zero Payment Plans in Chapter 13,* 4 Bankr. Dev. J. 449 (1987).

Morris, *Keeping Chapter 13 Debtors Inside the Debt Limits,* 2 F & G Bankr. L. Rev. 48 (1990).

Roszkowski, *Good Faith and Chapter 13 Plans Providing for Debts Nondischargeable Under Chapter 7 of the Bankruptcy Code: A Proposal to Assure Rehabilitation, Not Liquidation,* 46 Bus. Law. 67 (1990).

The Effect of the Disposable Income Test of Section 1325(a)(3), 5 Bankr. Dev. J. 267 (1987).

Winters, *Good Faith Under 1325(a)(3): Debtor's Choice or the Court's Dilemma?,* 92 Com. L.J. 95 (1987).

SECTION 1326 (11 U.S.C. § 1326)

§ 1326. Payments.

(a)(1) Unless the court orders otherwise, the debtor shall commence making the payments proposed by a plan within 30 days after the plan is filed.

(2) A payment made under this subsection shall be retained by the trustee until confirmation or denial of confirmation of a plan. If a plan is confirmed, the trustee shall distribute any such payment in accordance with the plan. If a plan is not confirmed, the trustee shall return any such payment to the debtor, after deducting any unpaid claim allowed under section 503(b) of this title.

(b) Before or at the time of each payment to creditors under the plan, there shall be paid—

(1) any unpaid claim of the kind specified in section 507(a)(1) of this title; and

(2) if a standing trustee appointed under section 586(b) of title 28 is serving in the case, the percentage fee fixed for such standing trustee under section 586(e)(1)(B) of title 28.

(c) Except as otherwise provided in the plan or in the order confirming the plan, the trustee shall make payments to creditors under the plan.

Bankruptcy Rule Reference: 3010

Legislative History

Subsection (a) [*Ed. Note:* Pub. L. No. 98–353 redesignated section 1326(a) as section 1326(b).] requires that before or at the time of each payment any outstanding administrative expenses [*sic*] any percentage fee due for a private standing chapter 13 trustee be paid in full.

[*House Report No. 95–595, 95th Cong., 1st Sess. 430 (1977).*]

Section 1326 supplements the priorities provisions of section 507. Subsection (a) [*Ed. Note:* Pub. L. No. 98–353 redesignated section 1326(a) as section 1326(b).] requires accrued costs of administration and filing fees, as well as fees due the chapter 13 trustee, to be disbursed before payments to creditors under the plan.

[*Senate Report No. 95–989, 95th Cong., 2d Sess. 142 (1978).*]

Section 1326(a)(2) [*Ed. Note:* Pub. L. No. 98–353 redesignated section 1326(a)(2) as section 1326(b)(2).] of the House amendment adopts a comparable provision contained in the House bill providing for standing trustees.

[*124 Cong. Rec. H 11,107 (Sept. 28, 1978); S 17,423 (Oct. 6, 1978).*]

Subsection (b) [*Ed. Note:* Pub. L. No. 98–353 redesignated section 1326(b) as section 1326(c).] designates the trustee as the disbursing agent, unless the plan or the order confirming the plan provides otherwise.

[*House Report No. 95–595, 95th Cong., 1st Sess. 430 (1977).*]

Subsection (b) [*Ed. Note:* Pub. L. No. 98–353 redesignated section 1326(b) as section 1326(c).] makes it clear that the chapter 13 trustee is normally to make distribution to creditors of the payments made under the plan by the debtor.

[*Senate Report No. 95–989, 95th Cong., 2d Sess. 142 (1978).*]

Comment

Section 1326 supplements the priorities provision of section 507(a)(1) which prescribes the first priority:

(1) First, administration expenses allowed under § 503(b) of this title, and any fees and charges assessed against the estate under chapter 123 of title 28.

See section 503(b).

Subsection (c) makes it clear that the chapter 13 trustee (standing trustee or appointed trustee) makes distribution to creditors pursuant to the plan.

Bankruptcy Rule 3010(b) provides that in chapter 13 cases, no payment less than $15 shall be distributed to any creditor unless authorized by local rule or court order. Funds not so distributed are to be accumulated and paid whenever the accumulation equals $15. Remaining funds are to be distributed with the final payment.

1984 Amendments: The amendments inserted a new subsection "(a)" and redesignated subsections "(a)" and "(b)" as "(b)" and "(c)." The new subsection requires the debtor to commence payments proposed under the plan within 30 days after it is filed, unless the court orders otherwise.

1986 Amendments: Prior to the 1986 Act, provisions for appointment of a standing trustee and provisions regarding the percentage fee fixed for such standing trustee were contained in section 1302(d) of the Code. The 1986 Act transferred these provisions to 28 U.S.C. § 586(b) and (e)(1)(B), respectively. Section 1326(b)(2) was amended accordingly.

This section was amended to reflect the creation of a permanent United States trustee system. Section 302(d) of the 1986 Amendments provides different effective dates for the amendments relating to the United States trustee system. *See* Section 302 of the 1986 Amendments, as amended by Pub. L. No. 101-650 (1990), reprinted herein under "Selected Provisions of the Bankruptcy Judges, United States Trustees, and Family Farmer Bankruptcy Act of 1986," regarding effective dates generally. Pub. L. No. 101-650 (Judicial Improvements Act of 1990) (signed into law December 1, 1990) amended Section 302(d)(3) of the Bankruptcy Judges, United States Trustees, and Family Farmer Bankruptcy Act of 1986 by extending the period in which the judicial districts in the states of Alabama and North Carolina may remain outside the United States trustee system.

Case Annotations

Although chapter 13 may allow some fully secured claims to be treated outside the terms of a proposed plan, a plan may not provide for current payments on a mortgage claim to be made outside the plan while the curing of the arrearage on that claim is under the plan pursuant to section 1322(b)(5), although in such cases a debtor may, under the plan, be permitted to act as disbursing agent to make the current mortgage payments directly to creditors. Foster v. Heitkamp (In the Matter of Foster), 670 F.2d 478, 6 C.B.C.2d 285 (5th Cir. 1982).

Attorney's fees must be paid in advance of or concurrently with payments to other creditors unless the attorney waives the right to be paid in that manner. *In re* Shorb, 21 C.B.C.2d 274 (9th Cir., B.A.P., 1989).

When a chapter 13 case is converted to chapter 7, the undistributed payments remain property of the estate, and the chapter 13 trustee is obligated to turn over to the chapter 7 trustee the debtor's postpetition, pre-conversion payments made while under chapter 13. In the Matter of Schmeltz, 23 C.B.C.2d 527 (B. Ct., N.D. Ind. 1990). *See also In re* Lennon, 15 C.B.C.2d 756 (B. Ct., N.D. Ga. 1986).

When the factors of a case allow, a debtor may pay proceeds from the sale of his real estate directly to secured creditors and may directly pay for costs of the sale. *In re* Bettger, 21 C.B.C.2d 1104 (B. Ct., D. Or. 1989).

A chapter 13 plan that provides that the payments required in advance of confirmation be made to the debtor's attorney who would apply those payments against his allowed fees and then turn over any excess to the trustee upon confirmation frustrates a major purpose of section 1326(a) because the court would have no control over the amount of fees the debtor's attorney would be allowed to take in the event of a failed chapter 13 case; it does not further the purpose of bankruptcy, which is to relieve the debtor's financial woes, not the attorney's. *In re* Barbee, 18 C.B.C.2d 340 (B. Ct., N.D. Ill. 1988).

A chapter 13 trustee holds undistributed funds as an agent for creditors under a confirmed plan and must distribute those funds pursuant to the plan even if his status as an official chapter 13 trustee ceases upon conversion of the case to chapter 7. *In re* Redick, 18 C.B.C.2d 254 (B. Ct., E.D. Mich. 1987).

A farmer with regular, though fluctuating, annual income is a person with regular income and may propose a plan funded with annual as opposed to monthly payments, particularly when the majority of the creditors have contracted to receive annual payments from the debtor. *In re* Fiegi, 15 C.B.C.2d 99 (B. Ct., D. Or. 1986).

If a plan designates a debtor as disbursing agent with respect to current mortgage payments to be made under the plan, at the confirmation hearing the debtor will have the burden of showing the ability to make direct payments, as well as the ability to comply with the other terms of the plan. *In re* Tartaglia, 14 C.B.C.2d 1314 (B. Ct., D.R.I. 1986).

In a chapter 13 plan, the trustee cannot make any payment on the claims of creditors unless administrative expenses and fees or charges imposed by title 13 have already been paid at the same time. *In re* Parker, 5 C.B.C.2d 913 (B. Ct., E.D. Tenn. 1981), *aff'd*, 6 C.B.C.2d 1040 (E.D. Tenn. 1982).

References

5 *Collier on Bankruptcy* ch. 1326 (Matthew Bender 15th ed.).

3 *Collier Bankruptcy Manual* ch. 1326 (Matthew Bender 3d ed.).

6 *Collier Bankruptcy Practice Guide* ch. 101 (Matthew Bender).

Youngblood, *Chapter 13 Bankruptcy: "Inside" or "Outside" Plans and Payments,* 51 Tex. B.J. 384 (1988).

SECTION 1327 (11 U.S.C. § 1327)

§ 1327. Effect of confirmation.

(a) The provisions of a confirmed plan bind the debtor and each creditor, whether or not the claim of such creditor is provided for by the plan, and whether or not such creditor has objected to, has accepted, or has rejected the plan.

(b) Except as otherwise provided in the plan or the order confirming the plan, the confirmation of a plan vests all of the property of the estate in the debtor.

(c) Except as otherwise provided in the plan or in the order confirming the plan, the property vesting in the debtor under subsection (b) of this section is free and clear of any claim or interest of any creditor provided for by the plan.

Bankruptcy Rule Reference: 3020

Legislative History

Under this section, the provisions of a confirmed plan are binding on the debtor and each creditor, whether or not the claim of the creditor is dealt with by the plan, and whether or not the creditor has objected to, accepted, or rejected the plan.

Unless the plan or the order confirming the plan provides otherwise, the order of confirmation vests all of the property of the estate in the debtor, and makes that property free and clear of any claim or interest of any creditor.

[*House Report No. 95–595, 95th Cong., 1st Sess. 430 (1977).*]

Subsection (a) binds the debtor and each creditor to the provisions of a confirmed plan, whether or not the claim of the creditor is provided for by the plan and whether or not the creditor has accepted, rejected, or objected to the plan. Unless the plan itself or the order confirming the plan otherwise provides, confirmation is deemed to vest all property of the estate in the debtor, free and clear of any claim or interest of any creditor provided for by the plan.

[*Senate Report No. 95–989, 95th Cong., 2d Sess. 142 (1978).*]

Comment

Section 1327 makes the confirmed plan binding on the debtor and each creditor, whether or not the creditor is dealt with in the plan, and whether or not the creditor has objected to, accepted or rejected the plan. Moreover, the order of confirmation is *res judicata* and not subject to collateral attack. Unless the plan or confirmation order provides otherwise, confirmation vests all of the property of the estate in the debtor *free and clear* of any claim or interest of any creditor.

Case Annotations

A confirmed chapter 13 plan becomes final under section 1327 and absent a showing of fraud under section 1330(a) cannot be challenged under section 1325(a)(5)(B)(ii) for failure to pay a creditor the present value of that creditor's claim. *In re* Szostek, 886 F.2d 1405, 21 C.B.C.2d 889 (3d Cir. 1989).

The full payment of a tax liability provision of a confirmed chapter 13 plan binds the Internal Revenue Service and prohibits its retention of a debtor's tax refund as additional security for the payments to be made under the plan. I.R.S. v. Norton, 717 F.2d 767, 9 C.B.C.2d 336 (3d Cir. 1983).

An unsecured judgment creditor who fails to object to the confirmation of a debtor's chapter 13 plan on the ground of lack of good faith until after the order has become final is precluded from raising that objection in a subsequent dischargeability proceeding. Lawrence Tractor Co. v. Gregory (In the Matter of Gregory), 705 F.2d 1118, 8 C.B.C.2d 605 (9th Cir. 1983).

A chapter 13 debtor has standing to challenge IRS debt collection actions against the debtor's nondebtor spouse when such actions jeopardize the debtor's chapter 13 plan. Pressimone v. Internal Revenue Serv. (*In re* Pressimone), 11 C.B.C.2d 1059 (N.D.N.Y. 1984).

Unless a debtor has defaulted in payments under a chapter 13 plan, confirmation prevents a creditor from obtaining relief from the automatic stay on account of the debtor's lack of equity in real property since an order confirming a chapter 13 plan is *res judicata* as to all issues that would have been decided at the confirmation hearing, with the result that all creditors are bound by the terms of the plan. Anaheim Sav. & Loan Ass'n v. Evans (*In re* Evans), 9 C.B.C.2d 123 (9th Cir., B.A.P., 1983).

Property acquired by the debtor after confirmation (including earnings from services performed by debtor postconfirmation) needed to fund the plan, survives confirmation and becomes property of the estate when it comes into being, notwithstanding section 1327(b). *In re* Ziegler, 26 C.B.C.2d 899 (B. Ct., N.D. Ill. 1992).

Upon confirmation, property of the estate vests in the debtor and ceases to be property of the estate, unless the plan or order of confirmation specifies otherwise. *In re* Petruccelli, 22 C.B.C.2d 1519 (B. Ct., S.D. Cal. 1990). *See also In re* Walker, 18 C.B.C.2d 950 (B. Ct., D.D.C. 1988).

Even if plan payments have been completed, a debtor's property remains property of the estate until the chapter 13 trustee submits the discharge order to the court. *In re* Elmore, 20 C.B.C.2d 1589 (B. Ct., C.D. Cal. 1988).

A nonrecourse debt that is a discharge of a personal liability is not a claim to be affirmed by confirmation of a chapter 13 plan. *In re* Russo, 20 C.B.C.2d 119 (B. Ct., N.D. Ill. 1988).

A secured creditor that fails to file a proof of claim is bound by the terms of the debtor's confirmed chapter 13 plan. Thomas v. Southtrust Bank of Alabama (*In re* Thomas), 19 C.B.C.2d 219 (B. Ct., N.D. Ala. 1988).

When a chapter 13 plan does not provide for the lien on the debtor's property held by another party, confirmation does not vest the property in the debtor free of the lien. Work v. The County of Douglas, in the State of Oregon (*In re* Work), 14 C.B.C.2d 935 (B. Ct., D. Or. 1986).

References

5 *Collier on Bankruptcy* ch. 1327 (Matthew Bender 15th ed.).

3 *Collier Bankruptcy Manual* ch. 1327 (Matthew Bender 3d ed.).

6 *Collier Bankruptcy Practice Guide* ch. 101 (Matthew Bender).

Gupton, *Confirmation of the Chapter 13 Repayment Plan: The Emerging Law,* 17 Ga. St. B.J. 178 (1982).

Zaretsky, *Mortgagees' Rights in Chapter 13,* 203 N.Y.L.J. 3 (1990).

SECTION 1328 (11 U.S.C. § 1328)

§ 1328. Discharge.

(a) As soon as practicable after completion by the debtor of all payments under the plan, unless the court approves a written waiver of discharge executed by the debtor after the order for relief under this chapter, the court shall grant the debtor a discharge of all debts provided for by the plan or disallowed under section 502 of this title, except any debt—

(1) provided for under section 1322(b)(5) of this title;

(2) of the kind specified in paragraph (5) or (8) of section 523(a) or 523(a)(9) of this title; or

(3) for restitution included in a sentence on the debtor's conviction of a crime.

(b) At any time after the confirmation of the plan and after notice and a hearing, the court may grant a discharge to a debtor that has not completed payments under the plan only if—

(1) the debtor's failure to complete such payments is due to circumstances for which the debtor should not justly be held accountable;

(2) the value, as of the effective date of the plan, of property actually distributed under the plan on account of each allowed unsecured claim is not less than the amount that would have been paid on such claim if the estate of the debtor had been liquidated under chapter 7 of this title on such date; and

(3) modification of the plan under section 1329 of this title is not practicable.

(c) A discharge granted under subsection (b) of this section discharges the debtor from all unsecured debts provided for by the plan or disallowed under section 502 of this title, except any debt—

(1) provided for under section 1322(b)(5) of this title; or

(2) of a kind specified in section 523(a) of this title.

(d) Notwithstanding any other provision of this section, a discharge granted under this section does not discharge the debtor from any debt based on an allowed claim filed under section 1305(a)(2) of this title if prior approval by the trustee of the debtor's incurring such debt was practicable and was not obtained.

(e) On request of a party in interest before one year after a discharge under this section is granted, and after notice and a hearing, the court may revoke such discharge only if—

(1) such discharge was obtained by the debtor through fraud; and

(2) the requesting party did not know of such fraud until after such discharge was granted.

Bankruptcy Rule Reference: 4007

Legislative History

Subsection (a) requires the court to grant the debtor a discharge as soon as practicable after the completion of all payment [*sic*] under the plan. The discharge is of all debts except alimony, maintenance, or support, and certain long-term obligations specially provided for under the plan.

[*Ed. Note:* Pub. L. No. 101-647 (1990) and Pub. L. No. 101-581 (1990) amended section 1328(a) to additionally except from discharge under a chapter 13 plan debts which are nondischargeable under section 523(a)(9) and by adding section 1328(a)(3), which excepts from discharge any debt "for restitution included in a sentence on the debtor's conviction of a crime." Pub. L. No. 101-508 (1990) amended section 1328(a)(2) by excepting debts which are nondischargeable under section 523(a)(8) from discharge in a chapter 13 case.]

[*House Report No. 95–595, 95th Cong., 1st Sess. 430 (1977).*]

The court is to enter a discharge, unless waived, as soon as practicable after completion of payments under the plan. The debtor is to be discharged of all debts provided for by the plan or disallowed under section 502, except a debt provided for under the plan the last payment on which was not due until after the completion of the plan, or a debt incurred for willful and malicious conversion of or injury to the property or person of another.

[*Senate Report No. 95–989, 95th Cong., 2d Sess. 142–143 (1978).*]

Section 1328(a) adopts a provision contained in the Senate amendment permitting the court to approve a waiver of discharge by the debtor. It is anticipated that such a waiver must be in writing executed after the order for relief in a case under chapter 13.

[*124 Cong. Rec. H 11,107 (Sept. 28, 1978); S 17,423 (Oct. 6, 1978).*]

Subsection (b) provides for the so-called "hardship" discharge. If the debtor has not completed payments under the plan, the court may grant a discharge anyway, but only if the debtor's failure to complete payments was due to circumstances for which the debtor should not justly be held accountable, the debtor has paid at least liquidation value, as of the effective date of the plan, and modification of the plan under section 1330 is impracticable. This section changes current law by permitting the hardship discharge before three years from the date of confirmation.

[*House Report No. 95–595, 95th Cong., 1st Sess. 430–431 (1977).*]

Subsection (b) is the successor to Bankruptcy Act Section 661. This subsection permits the bankruptcy judge to grant the debtor a discharge at any time after confirmation of a plan, if the court determines, after notice and hearing, that the failure to complete payments under the plan is due to circumstances for which the debtor should not justly be held accountable, the distributions made to each creditor under the plan equal in value the amount that would have been paid to the creditor had the estate been liquidated under chapter 7 of title 11 at the date of the hearing under this subsection, and that modification of the plan is impracticable. [*Ed. Note:* The second full sentence of the Senate Report is misleading. The test is what creditors would have received if the debtor had been liquidated on the effective date of the plan, not the date of the hearing on discharge.]

[*Senate Report No. 95–989, 95th Cong., 2d Sess. 143 (1978).*]

Subsection (c) limits the effect of a hardship discharge. It expects [*sic*] long-term obligations specially provided for under the plan, and all debts that would be expected [*sic*] from discharge under section 523(a) in a liquidation or reorganization case.

[*House Report No. 95–595, 95th Cong., 1st Sess. 431 (1977).*]

The discharge granted under subsection (b) relieves the debtor from all unsecured debts provided for by the plan or disallowed under section 502, except nondischargeable debts described in section 523(a) of title 11 or debts of the type covered by section 1322(b)(5).

[*Senate Report No. 95–989, 95th Cong., 2d Sess. 143 (1978).*]

Subsection (d) excepts from discharge, either ordinary or hardship, a postpetition debt of the kind specified in section 1305(a)(2) if prior approval by the trustee of the debtor's incurring the debt was practicable and was not obtained.

[*House Report No. 95–595, 95th Cong., 1st Sess. 431 (1977).*]

Subsection (d) excepts from any chapter 13 discharge a debt based on an allowed section 1305(a)(2) postpetition claim, if prior trustee approval of the incurring of the debt was practicable but was not obtained.

[*Senate Report No. 95–989, 95th Cong., 2d Sess. 143 (1978).*]

Subsection (e) permits a party in interest to request revocation of discharge before one year after the discharge is granted. The court may revoke the discharge only if the discharge was obtained through fraud, and knowledge of the fraud came to the requesting party after the discharge was granted.

[*House Report No. 95–595, 95th Cong., 1st Sess. 431 (1977).*]

A chapter 13 discharge obtained through fraud and before the moving party gained knowledge of the fraud may be revoked by the court under subsection (e), after notice and hearing, at the request of any party in interest made within 1 year after the discharge was granted.

[*Senate Report No. 95–989, 95th Cong., 2d Sess. 143 (1978).*]

[Pub. L. No. 101-581] will have the effect of overruling the Supreme Court's recent decision in Pennsylvania Department of Public Welfare v. Davenport, 110 S. Ct. 2126 (1990), which held that criminal restitution obligations are dischargeable debts under chapter 13.

[*136 Cong. Rec. S 9663 (July 12, 1990).*]

[Pub. L. No. 101-581] makes the exception to discharge in section 523(a)(9) applicable to chapter 13 debtors.

[*Senate Report No. 101-434, 101st Cong., 2d Sess. (1990).*]

Comment

Under section 1328(a) [unless the court approves a written waiver of discharge executed after the order for relief in the chapter 13 case] upon completion of all payments under the plan a discharge is granted of all debts except any debt provided in section 1322(b)(5), debts of the kind specified in section 523(a)(5), (a)(8) and (a)(9), and debts "for restitution included in a sentence on the debtor's conviction of a crime." Section 1322(b)(5) refers to certain extended long-term debts in which the last payment is due after the date on which the final payment under the plan is due. Section 523(a)(5) refers to any debt due to a spouse, former spouse, or child of the debtor, for alimony to, maintenance for, or support of such spouse or child in connection with a separation agreement, divorce decree, or property settlement agreement. Section 523(a)(8) refers to debts for certain educational benefit overpayments and student loans, while section 523(a)(9) includes those debts for death or personal injury caused by the debtor's operation of a motor vehicle while intoxicated. Pub. L. No. 101-508 (1990) added the exception from discharge for student loans arising under section 523(a)(8). Pub. L. No. 101-647 (1990) and Pub. L. No. 101-581 (1990) added the section 523(a)(9) exception, as well as excepting those debts for restitution included in a sentence on the debtor's conviction of a crime. *See* **1990 Amendments** infra.

Section 1328(b) provides for a "hardship" discharge that is available only if (1) a modification of the plan is not practicable and (2) the creditors have received under the plan payments of at least what they would have received in a liquidation case under chapter 7. This provision is a departure from the practice under the Act where pursuant to section 661 a hardship discharge was not available until the expiration of three years after confirmation. Under the Code, the hardship discharge is available at any time after confirmation where justified by the circumstances.

Section 1328(c) provides that a "hardship" discharge has the same effect as a discharge under subsection (a) with this difference: excepted from the discharge are extended long term debts and *all* the debts specified in section 523(a). In a discharge under subsection (a), only alimony and child support [section 523(a)(5)] are excepted, while in a discharge under subsection (b) all the debts specified in section 523(a) are excepted from discharge.

Subsection (d) excepts from discharge (including a hardship discharge) any debt arising after the date of the order for relief [allowable under section 1305(a)(2)] if prior approval to incurring such debt was practicable and was not obtained.

Subsection (e) relates to the revocation of discharge. It requires the "request" for revocation to be made within one year after discharge is granted; the ground for revocation is fraud in obtaining the discharge; and knowledge of the fraud must have come to the party requesting revocation after the discharge was granted. *See also* section 727(a)(9).

Bankruptcy Rule 4004(g) requires the clerk to promptly mail a copy of the final order of discharge to the United States trustee, to all creditors and to the trustee and the trustee's attorney.

Bankruptcy Rule 4006 provides that after an order denying or revoking discharge is denied, becomes final, or if a waiver of discharge is filed, the clerk shall promptly give notice thereof to all creditors as provided in Rule 2002. (Rule 2002(k) requires that notice of denial or revocation of discharge be transmitted to the United States trustee. Notice of denial or revocation of discharge is important because under section 108(c) suspension of statute of limitations affecting a debt terminates within 30 days after discharge is denied or waived.)

Bankruptcy Rule 4007(d) relates to a motion by a debtor for a discharge under section 1328(b). In such event the court is required, to enter an order fixing the time for filing a complaint to determine the dischargeability of any debt under section 523(c) and shall give not less than 30 days notice of the time so fixed to all creditors as provided in Rule 2002. On motion of a party in interest made before the time to file has expired, the court may, for cause, after notice and hearing, extend the time so fixed under this subdivision. Subdivision (e) provides that a proceeding commenced by a complaint filed under this Rule is an adversary proceeding governed by the Part VII Rules. Pursuant to Rule 5005, the complaint should be filed in the court where the case is pending.

1984 Amendments: Subsection (e)(1) was amended to clarify that it is the fraud of the debtor that may lead to revocation of discharge. Subsection (e)(2) was revised for clarification.

1990 Amendments: Section 1328(a) was amended by Pub. L. No. 101-647 (Crime Control Act of 1990) (effective on the date of enactment, November 29, 1990). Pub. L. No. 101-647 amended section 1328(a)(2) by excepting debts under section 523(a)(9) (debts for death or personal injury caused by the debtor's operation of a motor vehicle while intoxicated) from discharge under a chapter 13 plan. Pub. L. No. 101-647 also added section 1328(a)(3), which excepts from discharge any debt "for restitution included in a sentence on the debtor's conviction of a crime." These amendments do not apply to cases filed before the date of enactment of Pub. L. No. 101-647. This portion of the legislation, entitled the Criminal Victims Protection Act of 1990, was also enacted as a separate piece of legislation, Pub. L. No. 101-581 (Criminal Victims Protection Act of 1990) (effective on the date of enactment, November 15, 1990; does not apply to cases filed before the date of enactment). The identical language currently exists in both Pub. L. No. 101-647 as well as Pub. L. No. 101-581 because the text in Pub. L. No. 101-647 was not excised when it was duplicated in the separate legislation enacted as Pub. L. No. 101-581.

Section 1328(a) was also amended by Pub. L. No. 101-508 (Omnibus Budget Reconciliation Act of 1990) (effective as of the enactment date,

November 5, 1990; does not apply to cases filed before the date of enactment. Pub. L. No. 101-508 ceases to be effective on October 1, 1996). Pub. L. No. 101-508 amended section 1328(a)(2) by excepting debts arising under section 523(a)(8) (debts for certain educational benefit overpayments or student loans) from discharge under a chapter 13 plan.

Case Annotations

Restitution obligations constitute debts within the meaning of section 101 and are therefore dischargeable under chapter 13. Pennsylvania Dept. of Public Welfare v. Davenport, 495 U.S. —, 110 S. Ct. 2126, 109 L. Ed. 2d 588, 22 C.B.C.2d 1067 (1990). [*Ed. Note:* Section 1328(a) was amended in 1990 to render restitution claims arising from criminal judgments nondischargeable in chapter 13 cases. *See* Crime Control Act of 1990, Pub. L. No. 101-647.]

The public policies promoted by not discharging a debt resulting from willful or malicious injury in a chapter 7 case may also be implicated in a chapter 13 case, and a refusal to discharge such a debt in a chapter 13 case is consistent with the policies the Code seeks to advance. *In re* LeMaire, 898 F.2d 1346, 22 C.B.C.2d 1008 (8th Cir. 1990).

In certain circumstances the bankruptcy's "fresh start" goal may not be thwarted by increasing monthly payments in response to a substantial increase in income. Debtors receive their "fresh start" after the discharge in bankruptcy, which does not occur until all payments under the confirmed chapter 13 plan have been made. *In re* Arnold, 869 F.2d 240, 20 C.B.C.2d 1168 (4th Cir. 1989).

The issue of dischargeability is not ripe for resolution unless the court knows whether or not the debtors have successfully completed payments under the plan. *In re* Heincy, 858 F.2d 548, 20 C.B.C.2d 5 (9th Cir. 1988).

Although both section 1328(a) and 42 U.S.C. § 294f(g) deal with the discharge of debts, the provisions of section 294f(g) prevail in the event of a conflict since it is both the more specific and later of the two statutes. Accordingly, when a debtor is seeking to discharge a HEAL loan, he or she must meet the requirements specified in section 295f(g). In the Matter of Johnson, 787 F.2d 1179, 14 C.B.C.2d 1223 (7th Cir. 1986).

Under section 1328(a), a debtor who obtains credit through fraud or dishonesty may still be discharged under chapter 13. Memphis Bank & Trust Co. v. Whitman, 692 F.2d 427, 7 C.B.C.2d 727 (6th Cir. 1982).

A Health Education Assistance Loan should be treated as any other unsecured debt and receive the same pro rata payment under a chapter 13 plan as other unsecured creditors until the passing of the statutory five-year period at which time the bankruptcy court can determine under 42 U.S.C. § 294f(g) whether nondischarge of the debt would be unconscionable. United States v. Cleveland (*In re* Cleveland), 19 C.B.C.2d 654 (9th Cir., B.A.P., 1988).

When a creditor with a debt that is potentially nondischargeable under chapter 7 objects to confirmation of a minimal repayment plan, thereby seeking to prevent discharge of his debt under 11 U.S.C. § 1328(a), the court must conduct or permit a hearing on the issue of good faith. Fidelity & Casualty Co. of N.Y. v. Warren (*In re* Warren), 19 C.B.C.2d 765 (9th Cir., B.A.P., 1988).

If practicable, a debtor must obtain prior approval from the chapter 13 trustee before incurring postpetition consumer debt; otherwise the debt may not be dischargeable. *In re* Goodman, 26 C.B.C.2d 1034 (B. Ct., W.D. Tenn. 1992).

A chapter 13 debtor may not exit bankruptcy free of student loan liability at the expense of other unsecured creditors because such treatment is unreasonable and, therefore, may not be a basis for discriminatory treatment in a chapter 13 plan. *In re* Saulter, 25 C.B.C.2d 1448 (B. Ct., W.D. Mo. 1991).

Congress provided for the dischargeability of certain debts in chapter 13 and not others and therefore, the canons of statutory construction require that debts not listed in 1328(a), although nondischargeable under chapter 7, are dischargeable under chapter 13. *In re* Farley, 23 C.B.C.2d 600 (B. Ct., S.D. Cal. 1990).

When a debtor makes provisions in a chapter 13 plan for a priority tax claim and the Internal Revenue Service fails to timely file its proof of claim, the IRS is barred from participating in the plan and its tax claim is discharged upon completion by the debtor of all payments required under the plan. In the Matter of Workman, 22 C.B.C.2d 117 (B. Ct., N.D. Ga. 1989).

The dischargeability of Health Education Assistance Loans which are determined under 42 U.S.C. § 294f(g) are treated, on a procedural basis, the same as debts in the nature of alimony, maintenance and child support. When all three requirements of 42 U.S.C. § 294f(g) are not fulfilled, a complaint to determine dischargeability of a Health Education Assistance Loan is premature and should be dismissed. *In re* Williams, 21 C.B.C.2d 44 (B. Ct., N.D. Ill. 1989).

Since a debt is only an exception to discharge under section 1328(a)(1) if the debtor's plan voluntarily cures any default, a Merit Rating Plan surcharge will not fall within the meaning of section 1328(a)(1) unless the debtor so chooses, and thus the surcharge will be dischargeable. *In re* Bill, 19 C.B.C.2d 1046 (B. Ct., D.N.J. 1988).

Unassessed prepetition tax debts are treated like other unfixed prepetition debts. A tax creditor with notice of the case has to file a proof of claim in order to be paid under the plan or the debt will be discharged without payment. *In re* Ryan, 17 C.B.C.2d 827 (B. Ct., E.D. Tenn. 1987).

A postpetition tax claim is not discharged by the mere inclusion of it in the debtors' plan, but must be provided for and paid under the plan even if the creditor does not file a proof of claim. Hester v. Powell (*In re* Hester), 15 C.B.C.2d 1082 (B. Ct., E.D. Tenn. 1986).

References

5 *Collier on Bankruptcy* ch. 1328 (Matthew Bender 15th ed.).

3 *Collier Bankruptcy Manual* ch. 1328 (Matthew Bender 3d ed.).

6 *Collier Bankruptcy Practice Guide* ch. 101 (Matthew Bender).

Aiello and Behrens, *Student Loans, Chapter 13 of the Bankruptcy Code and the 1984 Bankruptcy Amendments,* 13 J.C. & U.L. 1 (1986).

Comment, *Dischargeability of Debts Arising From Willful and Malicious Injuries: The Eighth Circuit Assaults Bankruptcy Creditors (In re Hartley,* 874 F.2d 1254 *and In re Le Maire,* 898 F.2d 1346), 16 Wm. Mitchell L. Rev. 797 (1990).

Comment, *The Exception to Discharge for Willful and Malicious Injury: The Proper Standard for Malice,* 7 Bankr. Dev. J. 245 (1990).

Corish & Herbert, *The Debtor's Dilemma: Disposable Income as the Cost of Chapter 13 Discharge in Consumer Bankruptcy,* 47 La. L. Rev. 47 (1986).

Ellis, *Marital Tax Indemnification Agreements: Exception to Bankruptcy Discharge,* 19 Colo. Law. 639 (1990).

Good Faith and Chapter 13 Discharge: How Much Discretion Is Too Much?, 11 Cardozo L. Rev. 657 (1990).

Roszkowski, *Good Faith and Chapter 13 Plans Providing for Debts Nondischargeable Under Chapter 7 of the Bankruptcy Code: A Proposal to Assure Rehabilitation, Not Liquidation,* 46 Bus. Law. 67 (1990).

SECTION 1329 (11 U.S.C. § 1329)

§ 1329. Modification of plan after confirmation.

(a) At any time after confirmation of the plan but before the completion of payments under such plan, the plan may be modified, upon request of the debtor, the trustee, or the holder of an allowed unsecured claim, to—

(1) increase or reduce the amount of payments on claims of a particular class provided for by the plan;

(2) extend or reduce the time for such payments; or

(3) alter the amount of the distribution to a creditor whose claim is provided for by the plan to the extent necessary to take account of any payment of such claim other than under the plan.

(b)(1) Sections 1322(a), 1322(b), and 1323(c) of this title and the requirements of section 1325(a) of this title apply to any modification under subsection (a) of this section.

(2) The plan as modified becomes the plan unless, after notice and a hearing, such modification is disapproved.

(c) A plan modified under this section may not provide for payments over a period that expires after three years after the time that the first payment under the original confirmed plan was due, unless the court, for cause, approves a longer period, but the court may not approve a period that expires after five years after such time.

Legislative History

After confirmation but before the completion of payments, the debtor may request a modification of the plan, to increase or reduce payments under the plan for a particular class, to extend or reduce the time for payments, or to alter the amount of distribution to a creditor whose claim is provided for by the plan, to the extent necessary to take account of any payment of his claim other than under the plan. [*House Report No. 95–595, 95th Cong., 1st Sess. 431 (1977).*]

At any time prior to the completion of payments under a confirmed plan, the plan may be modified, after notice and hearing, to change the amount of payments to creditors or a particular class of creditors and to extend or reduce the payment period. A modified plan may not contain any provision which could not be included in an original plan as prescribed by section 1322. A modified plan may not call for payments to be made beyond four years as measured from the date of the commencement of payments under the original plan. [*Ed. Note:* The period has been reduced to three years that may be extended but not to exceed a total of five years after first payment under the plan was due.]

[*Senate Report No. 95–989, 95th Cong., 2d Sess. 143 (1978).*]

Subsection (b) specifies that the normal provisions governing the plan and preconfirmation modification apply to postconfirmation modification.

In applying the standards of proposed 11 U.S.C. § 1325(a)(4) to the confirmation of a modified plan, "the plan" as used in that section will be the plan as modified under this section, by virtue of the incorporation by reference into this section of proposed 11 U.S.C. § 1323(b). Thus, the application of the liquidation value test must be redetermined at the time of the confirmation of the modified plan. The confirmation of a plan modified under this section requires court approval only if a hearing is requested. Otherwise, the general rules governing "after notice and a hearing" will apply.

Subsection (c) places the same three year limit on the period of payments under the modified plan as is imposed on the original plan. The court is permitted, for cause, to approve a longer period, up to five years.

[*House Report No. 95–595, 95th Cong., 1st Sess. 431 (1977).*]

Comment

Under section 1329(a), the court may, after confirmation, modify the plan to increase or reduce payments and extend or reduce time of payments. The plan may be modified to alter the amount of distribution to a creditor provided for in the plan, to the extent necessary to take account of any payment of such creditor's claim other than under the plan. For example, if a third party pays a portion of a creditor's claim, then the amount of distribution to that creditor under the plan may be reduced accordingly.

The modified plan must, however, comply with the normal provisions governing the plan and pre-confirmation modification.

The post-confirmation modified plan may not provide for payments beyond three years after the first payment under the originally confirmed plan was due. The court, for cause, however, may extend this period, provided that the total period does not exceed five years from the date the first payment under the original plan was due.

Bankruptcy Rule 2002(a)(6) requires not less than 20 days notice to creditors by mail of the time fixed to accept or reject a proposed modification of a plan. Bankruptcy Rule 2002(k) does not require transmittal of this notice to the United States trustee.

Bankruptcy Rule 9024 makes it clear that the time to file a complaint to revoke a discharge pursuant to section 727(e) or to revoke an order confirming a plan under sections 1144 and 1330 may not be circumvented by invoking Fed. R. Civ. P. 60(b).

1984 Amendments: Section 1329(a) was amended by adding language to make it clear that a plan may be modified at the request of the debtor, the trustee, or the holder of an allowed unsecured claim. Other minor technical changes were made in subsection (a).

Case Annotations

Res judicata presents no bar to an upward adjustment of monthly payments under a confirmed chapter 13 plan which takes account of unanticipated and substantial improvement in a debtor's financial condition. To determine whether a change is unanticipated a court may apply an objective test to determine whether the debtor's altered financial circumstances could have been reasonably anticipated at the time of the confirmation by the parties seeking modification. *In re* Arnold, 869 F.2d 240, 20 C.B.C.2d 1168 (4th Cir. 1989).

A bankruptcy court may not enjoin a state court restitution order when the chapter 13 debtors have not requested either a modification of the plan to allow for a reduction in payments or an extension of the repayment period. *In re* Heincy, 858 F.2d 548, 20 C.B.C.2d 5 (9th Cir. 1988).

Although section 1329 provides a statutory mechanism for modification of a confirmed plan in the event a debtor's circumstances change, for example, a long term illness or job layoff, section 1329 should not be read to necessarily preclude a second chapter 13 filing when the first petition was dismissed where similar circumstances prevented completion of the confirmed plan. Johnson v. Vanguard Holding Corp. (*In re* Johnson), 708 F.2d 865, 8 C.B.C.2d 756 (2d Cir. 1983).

The court may modify a confirmed plan by ordering a *nunc pro tunc* amendment in order to reflect payments made by the trustee to unsecured creditors in excess of amount provided for in the plan. Lawrence Tractor Co. v. Gregory (*In re* Gregory), 6 C.B.C.2d 518 (9th Cir., B.A.P., 1982), *aff'd,* 705 F.2d 1118, 8 C.B.C.2d 605 (9th Cir. 1983).

It is inappropriate to use the postconfirmation modification provisions of section 1329(a) to force the addition of a postpetition debt. *In re* Goodman, 26 C.B.C.2d 1034 (B. Ct., W.D. Tenn. 1992).

A recent marriage subsequent to the confirmation of a chapter 13 plan is a substantial change in the debtor's financial condition, entitling him to a modification of his plan. *In re* Walker, 23 C.B.C.2d 81 (B. Ct., N.D.N.Y. 1990).

A creditor's payments provided for by a plan in the form of direct payments by a debtor, is subject to modification pursuant to section 1329(a)(1), if a debtor seeks to alter the plan and provide that payment be made by the chapter 13 trustee. *In re* Gadlen, 22 C.B.C.2d 524 (B. Ct., W.D. Tenn. 1990).

Section 1329 creates a narrow exception to the general rule against relitigation when previously litigated issues have been used unfairly against a party affected by modification of a plan. Section 1329(a)(1) should be interpreted to accommodate modification by reason of changed circumstances so long as the proposed modification would have been appropriate had the circumstances existed originally. *In re* Frost, 20 C.B.C.2d 1286 (B. Ct., S.D. Ohio 1989).

A chapter 13 plan can be modified at any time after confirmation, but it cannot be modified after all plan payments have been completed. *In re* Moss, 20 C.B.C.2d 1 (B. Ct., C.D. Cal. 1988).

The completion of payments under a chapter 13 plan occurs at the point the debtor has paid the percentage of the debt proposed to be paid under the plan, and is not determined by the number of payments he has made. *In re* Chancellor, 17 C.B.C.2d 1013 (B. Ct., N.D. Ill. 1987).

References

5 *Collier on Bankruptcy* ch. 1329 (Matthew Bender 15th ed.).

3 *Collier Bankruptcy Manual* ch. 1329 (Matthew Bender 3d ed.).

6 *Collier Bankruptcy Practice Guide* ch. 101 (Matthew Bender).

Gupton, *Confirmation of the Chapter 13 Repayment Plan: The Emerging Law,* 17 Ga. St. B.J. 178 (1982).

Hill, *Chapter 13 of the New Bankruptcy Code,* 90 N.J. Law. 16 (1980).

Kennedy, *Chapter 13 Under the Bankruptcy Code,* 19 Mem. St. U.L. Rev. 137 (1989).

Leibowitz, *Bankruptcy Practice: Chapter 13 Under the Code,* N.Y.L.J., November 15, 1979, at 1, Col. 1.

Morris, *Keeping Chapter 13 Debtors Inside the Debt Limits,* 2 F & G Bankr. L. Rev. 48 (1990).

Sulmeyer, *Chapter 13 of the Bankruptcy Act,* 1 Legal Notes and Viewpoints 93 (1980).

SECTION 1330 (11 U.S.C. § 1330)

§ 1330. Revocation of an order of confirmation.

(a) On request of a party in interest at any time within 180 days after the date of the entry of an order of confirmation under section 1325 of this title, and after notice and a hearing, the court may revoke such order if such order was procured by fraud.

(b) If the court revokes an order of confirmation under subsection (a) of this section, the court shall dispose of the case under section 1307 of this title, unless, within the time fixed by the court, the debtor proposes and the court confirms a modification of the plan under section 1329 of this title.

Bankruptcy Rule Reference: 7001

Legislative History

The court is permitted to revoke the confirmation order on request of a party in interest at any time within 180 days after the entry of the order of confirmation, if the confirmation was procured by fraud. If the court revokes the order of confirmation, then the court must dispose of the case under section 1307 (conversion or dismissal) unless, within the time fixed by the court, the debtor proposes and the court confirms a modification of the plan under section 1329.

[*House Report No. 95–595, 95th Cong., 1st Sess. 431 (1977).*]

The court may revoke an order of confirmation procured by fraud, after notice and hearing, on application of a party in interest filed within 180 days after the entry of the order. Thereafter, unless a modified plan is confirmed, the court is to convert or dismiss the chapter 13 case as provided in section 1307.

[*Senate Report No. 95–989, 95th Cong., 2d Sess. 143 (1978).*]

Comment

Under section 1330, a court has the discretionary authority to revoke confirmation, after notice and a hearing, if the order of confirmation was obtained by fraud. The power to revoke is made discretionary because the debtor may not have been the source of, or involved in, the fraud. Under such circumstances the court may find it unnecessary or inequitable to revoke the order of confirmation.

If the order of confirmation is revoked, section 1330(b) takes effect. The court can then either dismiss or convert the case or permit the debtor to submit a modified plan.

After revocation, the court may fix a time within which the debtor is to propose a modification of the plan. The court may then, in its discretion, confirm the modification. If there is no modification, the court may dismiss or convert to chapter 7 on the debtor's request.

Bankruptcy Rule 7001(5) makes a proceeding to revoke the confirmation of a chapter 13 plan an adversary proceeding governed by the Part VII rules.

Case Annotations

To prove the fraud necessary for revocation under section 1330, a plaintiff must show that (1) the debtor made a materially false representation regarding his section 1325 compliance; (2) the representation was either known by the debtor to be false or made without belief to its truth, or made with reckless disregard for the truth; (3) the representation was made to induce the court to rely on it; (4) the court did rely on it; and (5) as a consequence of such reliance the court entered the confirmation order. *In re* Hicks, 17 C.B.C.2d 1057 (B. Ct., N.D. Ala. 1987).

A chapter 13 plan which does not provide for the full payment of priority and secured claims is not confirmable and confirmation of it, therefore, is subject to revocation. In the Matter of Driscoll, 14 C.B.C.2d 146 (B. Ct., W.D. Wis. 1986).

When there is no claim that confirmation of a chapter 13 plan was procured through fraud, and no explanation why an objection was first preferred after the plan had been confirmed, even if a court of bankruptcy had power to set aside the plan after confirmation, there would be no basis for granting such relief. *In re* Torres, 5 C.B.C.2d 950 (B. Ct., E.D.N.Y. 1981).

When a confirmation order is procured by fraud the order may be revoked by the court only if the request for revocation is made within 180 days of the confirmation order. Mercantile Holdings, Inc. v. Dobkin (*In re* Dobkin), 4 C.B.C.2d 1247 (B. Ct., N.D. Ill. 1981).

References

5 *Collier on Bankruptcy* ch. 1330 (Matthew Bender 15th ed.).

3 *Collier Bankruptcy Manual* ch. 1330 (Matthew Bender 3d ed.).

6 *Collier Bankruptcy Practice Guide* ch. 101 (Matthew Bender).

Gupton, *Confirmation of the Chapter 13 Repayment Plan; The Emerging Law,* 17 Ga. St. B.J. 178 (1982).

Hill, *Chapter 13 of the New Bankruptcy Code,* 90 N.J. Law. 16 (1980).

ADDITIONAL STATUTORY PROVISIONS

THE BANKRUPTCY REFORM ACT OF 1978

(PUB. L. NO. 95–598)

THE BANKRUPTCY AMENDMENTS AND FEDERAL JUDGESHIP

ACT OF 1984

(PUB. L. NO. 98–353)

THE BANKRUPTCY JUDGES, UNITED STATES TRUSTEES, AND

FAMILY FARMER BANKRUPTCY ACT OF 1986

(PUB. L. NO. 99–554)

ADDITIONAL STATUTORY PROVISIONS

Set forth below are additional statutory provisions enacted or amended by the Bankruptcy Reform Act of 1978 (Pub. L. No. 95–598), the Bankruptcy Amendments and Federal Judgeship Act of 1984 (Pub. L. No. 98–353), the Bankruptcy Judges, United States Trustees, and Family Farmer Bankruptcy Act of 1986 (Pub. L. No. 99–554), the Judicial Improvements and Access to Justice Act of 1988 (Pub. L. No. 100–702), the Judicial Improvement Act of 1990 (Pub. L. No. 101–650), the Departments of Commerce, Justice and State, the Judiciary, and Related Agencies Appropriations Act of 1992 (Pub. L. No. 102–140), An Act to Make Certain Technical Corrections in the Judicial Improvements Act of 1990 (Pub. L. No. 102–198), the Bankruptcy Judgeship Act of 1992 (Pub. L. No. 102-361), the Rail Safety Enforcement and Review Act of 1992 (Pub. L. No. 102-365), and The Energy Policy Act of 1992 (Pub. L. No. 102-486). The subjects of the provisions are addressed in the following order:

DISTRICT COURTS; JURISDICTION (CHAPTER 85)

28 U.S.C. § 1334.   Bankruptcy cases and proceedings.

(a) Except as provided in subsection (b) of this section, the district courts shall have original and exclusive jurisdiction of all cases under title 11.

(b) Notwithstanding any Act of Congress that confers exclusive jurisdiction on a court or courts other than the district courts, the district courts shall have original but not exclusive jurisdiction of all civil proceedings arising under title 11, or arising in or related to cases under title 11.

(c)(1) Nothing in this section prevents a district court in the interest of justice, or in the interest of comity with State courts or respect for State law, from abstaining from hearing a particular proceeding arising under title 11 or arising in or related to a case under title 11.

(2) Upon timely motion of a party in a proceeding based upon a State law claim or State law cause of action, related to a case under title 11 but not arising under title 11 or arising in a case under title 11, with respect to which an action could not have been commenced in a court of the United States absent jurisdiction under this section, the district court shall abstain from hearing such proceeding if an action is commenced, and can be timely adjudicated, in a State forum of appropriate jurisdiction. Any decision to abstain or not abstain made under this subsection is not reviewable by appeal or otherwise by the court of appeals under section 158(d), 1291, or 1292 of this title or by the Supreme Court of the United States under section 1254 of this title. This subsection shall not be construed to limit the applicability of the stay provided for by section 362 of title 11, United States Code, as such section applies to an action affecting the property of the estate in bankruptcy.

(d) The district court in which a case under title 11 is commenced or is pending shall have exclusive jurisdiction of all of the property, wherever located, of the debtor as of the commencement of such case, and of property of the estate.

Comment

This section was amended by § 101 of the 1984 Act.

Subsections (a) and (b) grant to the United States district courts original and exclusive jurisdiction over all cases under title 11 U.S.C., and original but not exclusive jurisdiction over all civil proceedings arising under title 11, or arising in or related to a case under title 11. With respect to the reference of such cases and proceedings to the bankruptcy courts, *see* 28 U.S.C. § 157(a) *infra*.

Subsection (c) permits, in paragraph (1), the district court to abstain from hearing a proceeding (as distinguished from a case), on a discretionary basis, if it is in the interest of justice or comity with State courts, or respect for State law. Paragraph (2), however, provides for mandatory abstention if

(i) a timely motion is made;

(ii) the proceeding is based on a State law claim or cause of action;

(iii) the claim or cause of action is related to a title 11 case but does not arise under title 11 or such case;

(iv) action on the claim or cause of action could not have been brought in federal court absent the title 11 case;

(v) the action is commenced in the State court; and

(vi) the action can be timely adjudicated.

Personal injury or wrongful death tort claims, although otherwise within this section, are excluded from the mandatory abstention provisions by 28 U.S.C. § 157(b)(4) *infra*.

A decision to abstain or not to abstain is not reviewable by appeal or otherwise by the court of appeals or the Supreme Court. The automatic stay of 11 U.S.C. § 362 is expressly stated to be not affected with respect to action concerning property of the estate.

Paragraph (2) does not apply to cases or proceedings in cases pending on the date of enactment, July, 10, 1984. Pub. L. No. 98–353, § 122(b).

Subsection (d) carries over the former provision giving the court, in this instance the district court, exclusive jurisdiction over all the property of the debtor, wherever located.

Bankruptcy Rule 5011 relates to withdrawal and abstention from hearing a proceeding. Subdivision (b) provides that a motion for abstention under 28 U.S.C. § 1334(c) shall be governed by Rule 9014 and served on the parties to the proceeding.

Subdivision (c) of the Rule provides that a motion for withdrawal or abstention shall not stay administration of the case or any proceeding before the bankruptcy judge, except that such judge may stay, on terms and conditions as are proper, proceeding pending disposition of the motion. A motion for a stay ordinarily must be presented first to the bankruptcy judge. If filed in the district court, the motion must state why it was not presented to or obtained from the bankruptcy judge. Relief granted by the district judge shall be on such terms and conditions as the judge deems proper.

1990 Amendments: The Judicial Improvements Act of 1990 (Pub. L. No. 101-650) amended section 1334(c)(2) (effective on the date of enactment, December 1, 1990) by adding the words "or not abstain" after the words "to abstain" and by adding, before the period, the phrase "by the court of appeals under section 158(d), 1291, or 1292 of this title or by the Supreme Court of the United States under section 1254 of this title."

Case Annotations

The grant to district courts in 28 U.S.C. § 1334(d) of exclusive jurisdiction of all property of the debtor, wherever located, as of the commencement of case, and of property of the estate, does not empower a bankruptcy court to compel the return of such property from the United States or a State; the fact that Congress has granted jurisdiction to hear claims does not mean Congress has abrogated all defenses to them. Section 1334(d) cannot be read as a waiver of the government's sovereign immunity. United States v. Nordic Village, 503 U.S. —, 112 S. Ct. 1011, 117 L. Ed. 2d 181, 26 C.B.C.2d 9 (1992).

28 U.S.C. § 1334(b), which authorizes district courts to exercise concurrent jurisdiction over certain bankruptcy-related civil proceedings that would otherwise be subject to the exclusive jurisdiction of "another" court, does not provide jurisdiction when the Board of Governors of the Federal Reserve System bringing the action is not another "court," and when the prosecution of the Board's proceedings, prior to entry of a final order and the commencement of any enforcement action, seems unlikely to impair the bankruptcy court's exclusive jurisdiction over property of the estate protected by 28 U.S.C. § 1334(d). Board of Governors of the Federal Reserve System of the United States v. MCorp Financial, Inc., 502 U.S. —, 112 S. Ct. 459, 116 L. Ed. 2d 358, 25 C.B.C.2d 849 (1991).

A district court's decision to abstain under 28 U.S.C. § 1334(c)(1) is appealable because the finality requirement is less rigidly applied in bankruptcy than in ordinary civil litigation, despite the seemingly mandatory "shall order" language of 28 U.S.C. § 157(b)(5). Cases recognize a district court's discretion to leave personal injury suits where they are pending and, therefore, a motion under this section requires an abstention analysis. *In re* Pan American Corp., 950 F.2d 839, 26 C.B.C.2d 20 (2d Cir. 1991).

When a bankruptcy or district court is asked to impose sanctions for violation of the automatic stay in circumstances where actions underlying the violation involve alimony, maintenance or support, the court should abstain from hearing such request unless the purposes of the stay provision would clearly be served by affording a remedy for its violation and the court would not be required to delve too deeply into family law. Carver v. Carver, 954 F.2d 1573, 26 C.B.C.2d 865 (11th Cir. 1992).

A debtor need not first exhaust administrative remedies under the Medicare Act and the Federal Tort Claims Act in order to sue a federal governmental unit in a bankruptcy case on state law and tort claims. This is because 28 U.S.C. § 1334(b) contains an independent basis for the bankruptcy court's jurisdiction over civil proceedings "related" to bankruptcy. *In re* Town & Country Home Nursing Serv., Inc., 963 F.2d 1146, 26 C.B.C.2d 1446 (9th Cir. 1992).

A tenants' state court action brought against a bankruptcy trustee in his official capacity seeking recovery from the estate is an action "related to" a bankruptcy case because it conceivably could affect the size of the estate and, therefore, is subject to removal pursuant to 28 U.S.C. § 1452. When a party to a state court action against the trustee could have commenced that action in federal court on the basis of 28 U.S.C. § 959(a), the court is not required to abstain from that action when the action has been removed from the state court. Robinson v. Michigan Consol. Gas Co., Inc., 918 F.2d 579, 24 C.B.C.2d 49 (6th Cir. 1990).

In the instance in which the Federal Deposit Insurance Corporation (FDIC) has filed a claim against the debtor's estate for a deficiency judgment, a trustee's complaint for avoidance of fraudulent transfers, equitable subordination, and conversion is a civil proceeding related to a title 11 case. Anderson and Propps v. FDIC, 918 F.2d 1139, 24 C.B.C.2d 151 (4th Cir. 1990).

The test for determining whether a civil proceeding is related to a bankruptcy case is whether the outcome of that proceeding could conceivably have any effect on the estate being administered in bankruptcy. Subject matter jurisdiction may exist when a debtor does not agree under its reorganization plan to indemnify a third-party purchaser who then seeks to assert the indemnification, which could "conceivably" affect the debtor. *In re* Wolverine Radio Co., 930 F.2d 1132, 24 C.B.C.2d 1702 (6th Cir. 1991).

When a district court goes further than mere withdrawal of the reference to the bankruptcy court, the withdrawal order merges into the final judgment and becomes reviewable by appeal. If the court of appeals holds an adversary proceeding to be core, permissive abstention is all the district court may exercise pursuant to 28 U.S.C. § 1334(c)(1) and nothing prevents appellate review of a permissive abstention order. *In re* Ben Cooper, Inc., 924 F.2d 36, 24 C.B.C.2d 861 (2d Cir.), *cert. denied,* — U.S. —, 111 S. Ct. 2041, 114 L. Ed. 2d 126 (1991).

28 U.S.C. § 1334(b) confers jurisdiction upon the court in a "related case," but for subject matter jurisdiction to exist there must be some nexus between the related civil proceeding and a title 11 case. In the Matter of Lemco Gypsum, Inc., 910 F.2d 784, 23 C.B.C.2d 999 (11th Cir. 1990).

A debtor's lawsuit for legal malpractice and breach of fiduciary duty against former attorneys for services rendered prior to the debtor's petition does not satisfy the test for determining whether a suit is a core proceeding arising under title 11 because it does not invoke a substantive right under title 11, nor is it a proceeding that could arise only in the context of a bankruptcy case. Diamond Mortgage Corp. of Illinois v. Sugar, 913 F.2d 1233, 23 C.B.C.2d 1275 (7th Cir. 1990).

Although a related proceeding need not be against the debtor or his property, a proceeding is related to the bankruptcy case if the outcome could alter the debtor's rights, liabilities, options, or freedom of action in any way, thereby impacting on the handling and administration of the bankruptcy estate. *In re* Gardner, 913 F.2d 1515, 23 C.B.C.2d 1304 (10th Cir. 1990).

The district court has original jurisdiction over a proceeding for review of a bankruptcy court's order requiring a debtor's former administrative assistant to turn over a rare coin to the trustee and thus can reshape a trustee's relief and award damages. *In re* Moody, 899 F.2d 383, 22 C.B.C.2d 1331 (5th Cir. 1990).

A bankruptcy court does not have "related to" jurisdiction over a case between a nondebtor responsible person and the Internal Revenue Service. Quattrone v. IRS, 895 F.2d 921, 22 C.B.C.2d 427 (3d Cir. 1990).

The bankruptcy court may abstain from a related proceeding concerning third-party liability policies indemnifying the debtor for all losses it might incur as a result of claims arising from the performance of certain plants that it sold when there are no competing claimants under the policy, the debtor is not attempting to reorganize, the proceeding sounds in state law, and it relates only peripherally and contingently to the debtor's estate. National Union Fire Insurance Co. of Pittsburgh, Pa. v. Titan Energy, Inc. (*In re* Titan Energy, Inc.), 837 F.2d 325, 18 C.B.C.2d 717 (8th Cir. 1988).

Reading 29 U.S.C. § 660(b) of the Occupational Safety and Health Act and 28 U.S.C. § 1334(b) together, the court of appeals has concurrent jurisdiction with the bankruptcy court over a petition to enforce a citation charging the debtor with violations of OSHA. The court of appeals has concurrent jurisdiction with the bankruptcy court to determine the applicability of the automatic stay. Brock v. Morysville Body Works, Inc., 829 F.2d 383, 17 C.B.C.2d 888 (3d Cir. 1987).

Implicit in a motion for abstention in a particular proceeding is a motion for relief from the automatic stay as to that proceeding; the motion for abstention provides notice that a request for relief has been made; a "hearing" is provided by proceedings with respect to the abstention motion. Pursifull v. Eakin, 814 F.2d 1501, 16 C.B.C.2d 881 (10th Cir. 1987).

28 U.S.C. § 157(b)(4) and (5) does not prevent a district court from leaving tort cases in other courts in which they are pending for adjudication; rather, 28 U.S.C. § 1334(c)(1) allows for discretionary abstention and it is only when such abstention does not occur that 28 U.S.C.

§ 157(b)(5) will require that the tort cases be tried in federal district courts. Citibank v. White Motor Corp. (*In re* White Motor Credit), 761 F.2d 270, 12 C.B.C.2d 961 (6th Cir. 1985).

The office of the United States trustee constitutes an agency, and refusal by the United States trustee to conclude a creditors' meeting is final agency action reviewable by the bankruptcy court. An action in the nature of a mandamus petition which arises under title 11 is within the bankruptcy court's subject matter jurisdiction. *In re* Vance, 24 C.B.C.2d 377 (B. Ct., N.D. Okla. 1990).

In California, when a matter would not be within federal jurisdiction absent the bankruptcy petition and can be timely adjudicated in state court, the automatic stay against continuation of the state proceeding should be lifted and, concurrently, a stay of the bankruptcy court adversary proceeding is necessary. While 28 U.S.C. § 1334(c) and Bankruptcy Rule 5011 provide that a district court may abstain from hearing a proceeding after recommendation by a bankruptcy judge to so act, common sense, wise judicial administration, and economy of judicial resources counsel that a bankruptcy judge should consider less cumbersome alternatives and find nonstatutory doctrines to invoke abstention in the appropriate circumstances. Under the *Colorado River* doctrine, a bankruptcy court has the discretion in exceptional circumstances to stay an action for reasons relating to judicial administration. *In re* Bellucci, 24 C.B.C.2d 423 (B. Ct., E.D. Cal. 1990).

References

1 *Collier on Bankruptcy* ch. 3 (Matthew Bender 15th ed.).

1 *Collier Bankruptcy Manual* ch. 3 (Matthew Bender 3d ed.).

Bayles, *Jurisdiction in Bankruptcy to Contest Tax Liability and Arrest Collection Efforts,* 26 Washburn L.J. 423 (1987).

Comment, *The Bankruptcy Amendments and Federal Judgeship Act of 1984: An Unconstitutional Vesting of Subject Matter Jurisdiction,* 23 San Diego L. Rev. 939 (1986).

Countryman, *The Bankruptcy Judges: Jurisdiction by Neglect,* 92 Com. L.J. (1987).

Countryman, *Scrambling to Define Bankruptcy Jurisdiction: The Chief Justice, the Judicial Conference, and the Legislative Process,* 1985 Ann. Surv. Bankr. L. 1.

Ferriell, *The Constitutionality of the Bankruptcy Amendments and Federal Judgeship Act of 1984,* 63 Am. Bankr. L.J. 109 (1989).

Gibson, *Removal of Claims Related to Bankruptcy Cases: What is a "Claim or Cause of Action?",* 34 UCLA L. Rev. 1 (1986).

Hendel and Reinhardt, *Evolution of Bankruptcy Court Jurisdiction after the Bankruptcy Amendments and Federal Judgeship Act of 1984,* 90 Com. L.J. 272 (1985).

King, *Jurisdiction and Procedure Under the Bankruptcy Amendments of 1984*, 38 Vand. L. Rev. 675 (1985).

Schwartzberg, *The Retreat from Pervasive Jurisdiction in Bankruptcy Court*, 7 Bankr. Dev. J. 1 (1990).

DISTRICT COURTS; VENUE; JURY TRIALS
(CHAPTER 87)

28 U.S.C. § 1408.   Venue of cases under title 11.

Except as provided in section 1410 of this title, a case under title 11 may be commenced in the district court for the district—

(1) in which the domicile, residence, principal place of business in the United States, or principal assets in the United States, of the person or entity that is the subject of such case have been located for the one hundred and eighty days immediately preceding such commencement, or for a longer portion of such one-hundred-and-eighty-day period than the domicile, residence, or principal place of business, in the United States, or principal assets in the United States, of such person were located in any other district; or

(2) in which there is pending a case under title 11 concerning such person's affiliate, general partner, or partnership.

Comment

This section provides the proper venue for filing petitions commencing cases under title 11. It differs from the next section, 28 U.S.C. § 1409, which concerns venue of proceedings arising in cases under title 11.

In keeping with the grant of jurisdiction contained in 28 U.S.C. § 1334(a) *supra,* venue is also placed in the district court. Thus, 28 U.S.C. § 1408 provides that the case under title 11 may be commenced in the district court, etc. For the authority of the district court to refer cases and proceedings to the bankruptcy courts, *see* 28 U.S.C. § 157(a) *infra.*

See discussion of Bankruptcy Rule 1014, which deals with venue, in Comment to 28 U.S.C. § 1409 *infra.*

Case Annotations

When a debtor complies with a district court's order transferring its bankruptcy case to another district, the debtor's appeal of that order is moot. Seattle-First National Bank v. Manges, 900 F.2d 795, 23 C.B.C.2d 437 (5th Cir. 1990).

Limited partnerships that indirectly share some common ownership (*i.e*, a general partner of one partnership has a subsidiary that holds an indirect interest in another partnership) are insufficiently related to be "affiliates" within the meaning of 28 U.S.C. § 1408. Even if the limited partnerships share leased office space in a common district, so long as their principal places of business and sole assets are located in different districts, venue is improperly laid in the district where the shared office space is located. Venue is proper only in the districts where their principal places of business and assets are located. *In re* The Sporting Club at Illinois Center, 25 C.B.C.2d 1481 (B. Ct., N.D. Ga. 1991).

Venue is not properly chosen when the debtor resides in one district and the bankruptcy case is filed in another district. *In re* Lazaro, 24 C.B.C.2d 2037 (B. Ct., W.D. Tex. 1991).

A certified writing indicating the location of the debtor's place of business, its filed tax returns and the location of the debtor's books and records are evidence of the debtor's principal place of business. *In re* Standard Tank Cleaning Corp., 24 C.B.C.2d 1409 (B. Ct., E.D.N.Y. 1990).

The venue of a partnership's involuntary bankruptcy petition may lie in the district where the debtor's principal place of business is located or where its principal assets are located. *In re* Monterey Equities-Hillside, 16 C.B.C.2d 1214 (B. Ct., N.D. Cal. 1987).

Venue is proper where the debtor's management, operations, and financial center are located even when the majority of the debtor company's creditors, business locations, and assets are located elsewhere. *In re* Baltimore Food Sys., Inc., 16 C.B.C.2d 578 (B. Ct., D.S.C. 1986).

References

1 *Collier on Bankruptcy* ch. 3 (Matthew Bender 15th ed.).

1 *Collier Bankruptcy Manual* ch. 3 (Matthew Bender 3d ed.).

1 *Collier Bankruptcy Practice Guide* ch. 17 (Matthew Bender).

Chatz and Schumm, III, *1984 Bankruptcy Code Amendments—Fresh from the Anvil,* 89 Com. L.J. 317 (1984).

LoPucki and Whitford, *Venue Choice and Forum Shopping in the Bankruptcy Reorganization of Large, Publicly Held Companies,* 1991 Wis. L. Rev. 11.

Whelan, *Practice Under the 1984 Amendments,* 55 Pa. B.A.Q. 206 (1984).

28 U.S.C. § 1409.   Venue of proceedings arising under title 11 or arising in or related to cases under title 11.

(a) Except as otherwise provided in subsections (b) and (d), a proceeding arising under title 11 or arising in or related to a case under title 11 may be commenced in the district court in which such case is pending.

(b) Except as provided in subsection (d) of this section, a trustee in a case under title 11 may commence a proceeding arising in or related to such case to recover a money judgment of or property worth less than $1,000 or a consumer debt of less than $5,000 only in the district court for the district in which the defendant resides.

(c) Except as provided in subsection (b) of this section, a trustee in a case under title 11 may commence a proceeding arising in or related to such case as statutory successor to the debtor or creditors under section 541 or 544(b) of title 11 in the district court for the district where the State or Federal court sits in which, under applicable nonbankruptcy venue provisions, the debtor or creditors, as the case may be, may have commenced an action on which such proceeding is based if the case under title 11 had not been commenced.

(d) A trustee may commence a proceeding arising under title 11 or arising in or related to a case under title 11 based on a claim arising after the commencement of such case from the operation of the business of the debtor only in the district court for the district where a State or Federal court sits in which, under applicable nonbankruptcy venue provisions, an action on such claim may have been brought.

(e) A proceeding arising under title 11 or arising in or related to a case under title 11, based on a claim arising after the commencement of such case from the operation of the business of the debtor, may be commenced against the representative of the estate in such case in the district court for the district where the State or Federal court sits in which the party commencing such proceeding may, under applicable nonbankruptcy venue provisions, have brought an action on such claim, or in the district court in which such case is pending.

Comment

This section provides the proper venue for proceedings arising in or related to cases under title 11, as distinguished from the title 11 case itself. Venue for the title 11 case is provided for in 28 U.S.C. § 1408 *supra.*

Venue for proceedings is laid in the proper United States district court pursuant to the grant of jurisdiction contained in 28 U.S.C. § 1334(b) *supra.* Nevertheless, the district courts may refer such proceedings to the bankruptcy courts pursuant to 28 U.S.C. § 157(a) *infra.*

Bankruptcy Rule 1014 relates to venue. Subdivision (a)(1) provides that if a petition is filed in a proper district, the court may, on motion and after hearing on notice to the petitioners, the United States trustee and other entities as directed by the court, transfer the case to any other district the court finds to be in the interest of justice or for the convenience of the parties.

Subdivision (a)(2) provides that if a petition is filed in an improper district, the court may, on motion and after hearing on notice to the petitioners, the United States trustee and other entities as directed by the court, dismiss or transfer the case to any other district the court finds to be in the interest of justice or for the convenience of the parties.

Case Annotations

In determining the venue of a turnover proceeding the court must focus on the nature of the claim the creditor asserts against the seized equipment and the basis of the trustee's claim that it should be turned over to the estate. If the creditor's seizure of and the trustee's claim to the equipment arose from the debtor's business operations, venue may be transferred to the state in which action on such claim may have been brought. Thus, 28 U.S.C. § 1409(d) applies to claims whose facts and legal bases originate from the business operations of the debtor; it does not apply to the collection of assets for use in the debtor's business. Appel v. Gable (*In re* B & L Oil Co.), 834 F.2d 156, 17 C.B.C.2d 900 (10th Cir. 1987).

A chapter 7 trustee seeking to recover on postpetition claims must demonstrate that venue in a particular district is proper under applicable nonbankruptcy venue law. *In re* Olympia Holding Corp., 26 C.B.C.2d 1567 (B. Ct., M.D. Fla. 1992).

When a trustee seeks recovery from a creditor of a preferential payment of less than $1,000, the only venue available is the district court for the district in which the creditor resides. Armstrong v. Seattle First Nat'l Bank (*In re* Greiner), 12 C.B.C.2d 363 (B. Ct., D.N.D. 1985).

References

1 *Collier on Bankruptcy* ch. 3 (Matthew Bender 15th ed.).

1 *Collier Bankruptcy Manual* ch. 3 (Matthew Bender 3d ed.).

1 *Collier Bankruptcy Practice Guide* ch. 17 (Matthew Bender).

Langan, *Procedural Fundamentals of Bankruptcy Practice*, 56 Hennepin Law 14 (Mn. 1987).

LoPucki and Whitford, *Venue Choice and Forum Shopping in the Bankruptcy Reorganization of Large, Publicly Held Companies*, 1991 Wis. L. Rev. 11.

Whelan, *Practice Under the 1984 Amendments*, 55 Pa. B.A.Q. 206 (1984).

28 U.S.C. § 1410. Venue of cases ancillary to foreign proceedings.

(a) A case under section 304 of title 11 to enjoin the commencement or continuation of an action or proceeding in a State or Federal court, or the enforcement of a judgment, may be commenced only in the district court for the district where the State or Federal court sits in which is pending the action or proceeding against which the injunction is sought.

(b) A case under section 304 of title 11 to enjoin the enforcement of a lien against a property, or to require the turnover of property of an estate, may be commenced only in the district court for the district in which such property is found.

(c) A case under section 304 of title 11, other than a case specified in subsection (a) or (b) of this section, may be commenced only in the district court for the district in which is located the principal place of business in the United States, or the principal assets in the United States, of the estate that is the subject of such case.

Comment

Section 1410 is a special venue provision for cases commenced under section 304 of the Bankruptcy Code which are denoted as being ancillary to foreign proceedings. Venue is placed in the proper United States district court but reference may be made to the bankruptcy court pursuant to 28 U.S.C. § 157(a), *infra*.

Bankruptcy Rule 1010 deals with service of an involuntary petition and summons and with a petition commencing a case ancillary to a foreign proceeding.

References

1 *Collier on Bankruptcy* ch. 3 (Matthew Bender 15th ed.).

1 *Collier Bankruptcy Manual* ch. 3 (Matthew Bender 3d ed.).

1 *Collier Bankruptcy Practice Guide* ch. 17 (Matthew Bender).

2 *Collier Bankruptcy Practice Guide* ch. 19 (Matthew Bender).

Chatz and Schumm, III, *1984 Bankruptcy Code Amendments—Fresh From the Anvil,* 89 Com. L.J. 317 (1984).

Whelan, *Practice Under the 1984 Amendments,* 55 Pa. B.A.Q. 206 (1984).

28 U.S.C. § 1411.   Jury trials.

(a) Except as provided in subsection (b) of this section, this chapter and title 11 do not affect any right to trial by jury that an individual has under applicable nonbankruptcy law with regard to a personal injury or wrongful death tort claim.

(b) The district court may order the issues arising under section 303 of title 11 to be tried without a jury.

Comment

Subsection (a) is a limitation of what was formerly contained in 28 U.S.C. § 1480. The former provision, added in 1978, retained the right to jury trial as it existed under any statute in effect on September 30, 1979; accordingly, the type of cause of action was not a material consideration. Pursuant to 28 U.S.C. § 1411, however, the only right to jury trial that is retained is that of

(i) an individual;

(ii) existing under applicable nonbankruptcy law;

(iii) concerning a personal injury or wrongful death tort claim.

This subsection does not apply to cases or proceedings arising in or related to such cases that are pending on the date of enactment, July 10, 1984. Pub. L. No. 98–353, § 122(b).

Subsection (b) continues the discretion of the court to permit that issues arising on a contested involuntary petition be tried by jury.

This subsection applies to cases pending on the date of enactment, July 10, 1984. Pub. L. No. 98–353, § 122(a).

Bankruptcy Rule 9015 dealing with trial by jury was abrogated in 1987. As indicated in the 1987 Advisory Committee Note, Rule 9015 was abrogated in order to conform to changes respecting the right to trial by jury made by the Bankruptcy Amendments and Federal Judge-ship Act of 1984.

Case Annotations

A creditor who filed a proof of claim against a bankruptcy estate and is then sued by the trustee to recover a preferential transfer is not entitled to a jury trial under the Seventh Amendment. Langenkamp v. C.A. Culp, 498 U.S. —, 111 S. Ct. 330, 112 L. Ed. 2d 343, 23 C.B.C.2d 973 (1990).

Congress cannot eliminate a party's Seventh Amendment right to a jury trial merely by relabeling the cause of action to which it attaches and placing exclusive jurisdiction in an administrative agency or a specialized court of equity. When defendant in a fraudulent conveyance action brought by a trustee under section 548 has not filed a claim in the bankruptcy case, it has a Seventh Amendment right to a jury trial even though Congress may have denoted the action a core proceeding. Granfinanciera, S.A. v. Nordberg, 492 U.S. 33, 109 S. Ct. 2782, 106 L. Ed. 2d 26, 20 C.B.C.2d 1216 (1989).

Bankruptcy courts are not authorized to conduct jury trials because neither the Bankruptcy Code nor the Bankruptcy Rules reveal any Congressional intent to grant to bankruptcy courts the power to conduct such a trial. *In re* Baker & Getty Fin. Serv., Inc., 954 F.2d 1169, 26 C.B.C.2d 536 (6th Cir. 1992).

By filing a bankruptcy petition, a debtor does not subject its prepetition claims to the bankruptcy court's equitable power and, thereby, lose its Seventh Amendment right to a jury trial on those claims. *In re* Jensen, 946 F.2d 369, 25 C.B.C.2d 1351 (5th Cir. 1991).

The interests served by an order setting a claims filing date are so important that its observance may be required even if it alters the method of fact-finding on the merits of a claim by limiting the availability of a jury trial. The creditor is not entitled to enlargement of the bar date to preserve its demand for jury trial in a preference action. *In re* Hooker Inv., Inc., 937 F.2d 833, 25 C.B.C.2d 75 (2d Cir. 1991).

A request for a jury trial must be in writing. Since bankruptcy courts may not conduct jury trials, to avoid waiver of the right to a jury trial, parties seeking a jury trial must combine their request for a jury trial with a request for transfer of the proceeding to the district court. *In re* Latimer, 918 F.2d 136, 24 C.B.C.2d 230 (10th Cir. 1990).

In a case where the Seventh Amendment requires a jury trial to be held in a bankruptcy proceeding, that trial must take place in the district court, sitting in its original jurisdiction in bankruptcy, because bankruptcy judges lack the power to conduct jury trials. *In re* Kaiser Steel Corp., 911 F.2d 380, 23 C.B.C.2d 745 (10th Cir. 1990).

Under *Granfinanciera* analysis, a chapter 7 trustee's action for a money judgment against a lessee of the debtor which is founded on allegations that the lessee owes rent and is using space not covered by the leases is a traditional common law suit for a legal remedy that is clearly a matter of private, as opposed to public right, so the lessee is entitled under the Seventh Amendment to a jury trial. Beard v. Braunstein, 914 F.2d 434, 23 C.B.C.2d 1247 (3d Cir. 1990).

A bankruptcy court has authority to conduct jury trials when the issues underlying the proceeding are core and legal in nature. Ben Cooper, Inc. v. The Insurance Co. of the State of Pennsylvania, 896 F.2d 1394, 22 C.B.C.2d 729 (2d Cir.), *cert. granted,* — U.S. —, 110 S. Ct. 3269, 111 L. Ed. 2d 779, *vacated and remanded,* — U.S. —, 111 S. Ct. 425, 112 L. Ed. 2d 408 (1990), *opinion reinstated on remand,* 924 F.2d 36, 24 C.B.C.2d 841 (2d Cir. 1991), *cert. denied,* — U.S. —, 111 S. Ct. 2041, 114 L. Ed. 2d 126 (1991).

28 U.S.C. § 157 does not contain any specific or express language granting to a bankruptcy judge the authority to conduct jury trials; the broad grant of authority to bankruptcy judges in section 157 does not imply that the authority to conduct jury trials is an indispensible power necessary to carry out the authority actually conferred by the section. *In re* United Missouri Bank of Kansas City, 901 F.2d 1449, 22 C.B.C.2d 1400 (8th Cir. 1990).

A debtor's right to a trial by jury has not been violated when the debtor has participated in the determination of the issues without a jury and asserted the right for the first time on appeal. In the Matter of Wynn, 889 F.2d 644, 22 C.B.C.2d 157 (5th Cir. 1989).

A plaintiff's removed state court complaint for environmental damages is tantamount to the filing of a proof of claim in the bankruptcy court and the debtor's answer to the complaint in state court is analogous to an objection to a claim in bankruptcy court, so that the proceeding, having been transmuted into a claim resolution proceeding, is one that is integral to the restructuring of the debtor-creditor relationship, involves public rights and, therefore, carries no Seventh Amendment right to a jury trial. *In re* Marshland Dev., Inc., 25 C.B.C.2d 360 (B. Ct., N.D. Cal. 1991).

Once a creditor has filed a proof of claim (in the form of a non-compulsory counterclaim) and has submitted itself to bankruptcy court jurisdiction, the creditor has irrevocably waived a right to a jury trial as to any issue that might arise in that case. The filing of a proof of claim in such circumstances clearly constitutes a knowing, voluntary, and intelligent waiver of the creditor's rights to a jury trial. By choosing the equitably-based bankruptcy forum as the situs to resolve its disputes with another party that is not the debtor, a creditor waives any claim to a jury trial as to its claims against all parties. *In re* Glen Eagle Square, Inc., 25 C.B.C.2d 675 (B. Ct., E.D. Pa. 1991).

Section 1411(a) of title 28 does not afford to a party with a pending state court personal injury suit against the debtor the right to a jury trial on a complaint to determine dischargeability. *In re* Frederick, 25 C.B.C.2d 1739 (B. Ct., S.D. Ind. 1991).

A right to a jury trial does not attach to an action against a trustee regarding his administration of a debtor's estate which is an equitable matter and does not require a jury trial. *In re* EZ Feed Cube Co., Ltd., 23 C.B.C.2d 189 (B. Ct., D. Or. 1990).

A party does not waive the right to a jury trial by filing a permissive counterclaim. *In re* Lee Way Holding Co., 23 C.B.C.2d 806 (B. Ct., S.D. Ohio 1990).

A party's right to a jury trial is dependent upon whether the cause of action is historically legal or equitable in nature. *In re* Clairmont Transfer Co., 23 C.B.C.2d 881 (B. Ct., W.D. Mich. 1990).

A chapter 7 trustee seeking to recover monetary damages for torts and contract violations allegedly committed by the defendant postpetition has a right to a jury trial in an adversary proceeding commenced by the trustee in state court but later removed to the bankruptcy court. In the Matter of O'Sullivan's Fuel Oil Co., 21 C.B.C.2d 646 (B. Ct., D. Conn. 1989).

A mere allegation of fraud as the basis for rescission of a contract is not sufficient to characterize an action as legal in nature so that no right to a jury trial exists on this basis. A right to a jury trial does not attach when a litigant is seeking recovery of a deposit on a land contract because such relief is in the nature of restitution, not money damages. *In re* Friedberg, 21 C.B.C.2d 986 (B. Ct., S.D.N.Y. 1989).

References

1 *Collier on Bankruptcy* ch. 3 (Matthew Bender 15th ed.).

1 *Collier Bankruptcy Manual* ch. 3 (Matthew Bender 3d ed.).

6 *Collier Bankruptcy Practice Guide* ch. 111 (Matthew Bender).

Baird, *Jury Trials After Granfinanciera,* 65 Am. Bankr. L.J. 1 (1991).

Hall, *Granfinanciera, Northern Pipeline, and "Public Rights": May a Bankruptcy Judge Preside Over a Jury Trial?,* 80 Ky. L.J. 499 (1991-92).

Matthews, *The Right to Jury Trial in Bankruptcy Courts: Constitutional Implications in the Wake of Granfinanciera, S.A. v. Nordberg,* 65 Am. Bankr. L.J. 43 (1991).

Sabino, *The Proof of Claim or the Jury Trial?,* 3 F & G Bankr. L. Rev. 18 (1992).

Sear, *New Bankruptcy Rules—Consensus and Change,* 34 La. B.J. 276 (1987).

Skelton and Harris, *Bankruptcy Jurisdiction and Jury Trials: The Constitutional Nightmare Continues,* 8 Bankr. Dev. J. 469 (1991).

28 U.S.C. § 1412. Change of venue.

A district court may transfer a case or proceeding under title 11 to a district court for another district, in the interest of justice or for the convenience of the parties.

Comment

The district court may effect a transfer of a case or proceeding pursuant to this section.

Bankruptcy Rule 1014 relates to change of venue of cases filed in the proper or improper venue. *See* comment to 28 U.S.C. § 1409 *supra*.

Case Annotations

Transfer of venue motions in bankruptcy cases and adversary proceedings should be heard initially by the bankruptcy court which will then file with the district court a report and recommendation outlining proposed findings of fact and a recommendation for disposition of the motion. If there are objections to the motion, they are to be filed with the district court, which will make a *de novo* review of all matters relating to the transfer of venue motion. *In re* Retirement Inn at Forest Lane, Ltd., 18 C.B.C.2d 796 (D. Utah 1988).

So long as an objection to venue has been timely filed, the filing of motions and participation in discovery do not amount to a waiver of that objection to venue. *In re* Sporting Club at Illinois Center, 25 C.B.C.2d 1481 (B. Ct., N.D. Ga. 1991).

Retention rather than dismissal of improperly venued cases is a legitimate alternative for the court when it declines to transfer venue to another district. *In re* Lazaro, 24 C.B.C.2d 2037 (B. Ct., W.D. Tex. 1991).

The bankruptcy court may grant a change of venue if it is in the best interests of the creditors when the majority of the creditors reside in another state and another case is pending before that state's tribunal against the debtor. *In re* Standard Tank Cleaning Corp., 24 C.B.C.2d 1409 (B. Ct., E.D.N.Y. 1990).

When all creditors are centered in the district in which the debtor chose to file and where venue is proper, the court will not transfer venue. *In re* Canavos, 23 C.B.C.2d 104 (B. Ct., E.D. Pa. 1990).

In a change of venue proceeding in which the court must weigh the interests of the state in having local controversies decided within its borders by those familiar with its law against the estate's interest in the most economical administration, the estate's interest is decisive, even though the unpaid claims were incurred with the knowledge that there was a risk of litigation in another venue. *In re* Southwinds Associates Ltd., 23 C.B.C.2d 991 (B. Ct., W.D. Pa. 1990).

The burden created for the United States trustee's office by having to separately administer cases involving debtors owned and operated by a single individual whose business affairs were intertwined should be as significant as any criteria involved in a motion for a change of venue that were developed prior to the creation of the United States trustee's office. *In re* Portjeff Development Corp., 23 C.B.C.2d 1358 (B. Ct., E.D.N.Y. 1990).

In a bankruptcy case in which venue is not proper, the court has the option of transferring the case to the district where venue is proper, or retaining the case despite the improper venue. Dismissal of the case is not a proper remedy. *In re* Monterey Equities-Hillside, 16 C.B.C.2d 1214 (B. Ct., N.D. Cal. 1987).

A bankruptcy court may transfer a removed action to the venue where the underlying bankruptcy case is pending in the interest of justice or for the convenience of parties. Paul v. Chemical Bank (*In re* 666 Associates), 14 C.B.C.2d 15 (B. Ct., S.D.N.Y. 1985).

A bankruptcy court may properly make the final disposition on a motion to transfer venue of a bankruptcy case. McLemore v. Thomasson (*In re* Thomasson), 14 C.B.C.2d 1155 (B. Ct., M.D. Tenn. 1986).

The bankruptcy court no longer has the authority under the 1984 Bankruptcy Amendments to retain a case venued in an improper division of a district of proper venue even if it is in the interest of justice and for the convenience of the parties to do so; there is no provision in the 1984 Amendments akin to repealed 28 U.S.C. § 1477(b) that would permit such a retention. *In re* Romzek, 13 C.B.C.2d 924 (B. Ct., E.D. Mich. 1985).

Because under the 1984 Amendments there is no provision akin to 28 U.S.C. § 1477(b) of the 1978 Reform Act that would permit a bankruptcy court to retain jurisdiction over an improperly venued proceeding even in the absence of objection, the bankruptcy court must dismiss such a proceeding; only the district court may transfer an improperly venued case. Armstrong v. Seattle First Nat'l Bank (*In re* Greiner), 12 C.B.C.2d 363 (B. Ct., D.N.D. 1985).

References

1 *Collier on Bankruptcy* ch. 3 (Matthew Bender 15th ed.).

1 *Collier Bankruptcy Manual* ch. 3 (Matthew Bender 3d ed.).

1 *Collier Bankruptcy Practice Guide* ch. 17 (Matthew Bender).

Comment, *The 1984 Bankruptcy Amendments: What Congress Intended by Changing Section 1475 to Section 1412,* 8 Bankr. Dev. J. 553 (1991).

LoPucki and Whitford, *Venue Choice and Forum Shopping in the Bankruptcy Reorganization of Large, Publicly Held Companies,* 1991 Wis. L. Rev. 11.

Whelan, *Practice Under the 1984 Amendments,* 55 Pa. B.A.Q. 206 (1984).

DISTRICT COURTS; REMOVAL OF CASES FROM STATE COURTS (CHAPTER 89)

Sec.
1452. Removal of claims related to bankruptcy cases.

28 U.S.C. § 1452. Removal of claims related to bankruptcy cases.

(a) A party may remove any claim or cause of action in a civil action other than a proceeding before the United States Tax Court or a civil action by a governmental unit to enforce such governmental unit's police or regulatory power, to the district court for the district where such civil action is pending, if such district court has jurisdiction of such claim or cause of action under section 1334 of this title.

(b) The court to which such claim or cause of action is removed may remand such claim or cause of action on any equitable ground. An order entered under this subsection remanding a claim or cause of action, or a decision to not remand, is not reviewable by appeal or otherwise by the court of appeals under section 158(d), 1291, or 1292 of this title or by the Supreme Court of the United States under section 1254 of this title.

Comment

Removal is permitted to the district court if that court would otherwise have jurisdiction under 28 U.S.C. § 1334, *supra*. Bankruptcy Rule 9027 prescribes the procedure to be followed with respect to removing a claim or cause of action. The rule, as amended by the 1987 and 1991 Amendments to the Bankruptcy Rules, is now in accord with 28 U.S.C. § 1452, which limits removal to the district court. The notice of removal is to be filed with the clerk for the district within which is located the state or federal court where the civil action is pending. The notice must be signed and contain a short, plain statement of the facts that entitle the party to remove. The notice must state that upon removal of the claim or cause of action the proceeding is core or noncore, and if noncore, the party filing the notice does or does not consent to entry of final orders or judgment by the bankruptcy judge. A copy of all process and pleading must be included.

1990 Amendments: The Judicial Improvements Act of 1990 (Pub. L. No. 101-650) amended section 1452(b) of title 28 (effective on the date of enactment, December 1, 1990) by adding, before the period in the second sentence, the phrase "by the court of appeals under section 158(d), 1291, or 1292 of this title or by the Supreme Court of the United States under section 1254 of this title." Accordingly, appeal may be taken to the district court, but not beyond.

Case Annotations

The district court has the power to remand litigation to state court, even though the state action was previously removed to bankruptcy court. Adams v. Sidney Schafer & Assocs., Inc. (*In re* Adams), 809 F.2d 1187, 16 C.B.C.2d 509 (5th Cir. 1987).

So long as one defendant in a multi-defendant proceeding meets the 30-day requirement of Rule 9027, a bankruptcy removal petition will be timely. Creasy v. Coleman Furniture Corp., 736 F.2d 656, 12 C.B.C.2d 1238 (4th Cir. 1985).

The bankruptcy court may issue an order remanding a case to state court if the issues involved arise purely under state law matters, and it is not so imperative that the case be heard by the bankruptcy court. *In re* Ramada Inn-Paragould General Partnership, 26 C.B.C.2d 1853 (B. Ct., E.D. Alaska 1992).

If the final disposition of a cause of action does not rest on the determination of disputed facts, *i.e.,* it is amenable to summary adjudication under Federal Rule of Civil Procedure 12(b)(6) or 56, the Seventh Amendment right to jury trial is not implicated and a motion for remand to state court based on this right is moot. *In re* Fulda Independent Co-op, 25 C.B.C.2d 889 (B. Ct., D. Minn. 1991).

A bankruptcy court does not obtain jurisdiction over a proceeding filed in a district court through removal. To obtain jurisdiction, the case must be referred to the bankruptcy court by the district court. Thomas Steel Corp. v. Bethlehem Rebar Industries, Inc., 21 C.B.C.2d 386 (B. Ct., N.D. Ill. 1989).

A proceeding may be remanded for any equitable reason, and this includes mandatory abstention under 28 U.S.C. § 1334(c)(2). Chiodo v. NBC Bank - Brooks Field (*In re* Chiodo), 19 C.B.C.2d 197 (B. Ct., W.D. Tex. 1988).

An entire state court proceeding may be removed to bankruptcy court when, in light of the federal district court removal statute 28 U.S.C. § 1441(c), a creditor seeks to recover repayment on its loan both from the debtor and the loan guarantor. Foreston Coal International, Inc. v. Red Ash Coal & Coke Corp. (*In re* Red Ash Coal & Coke Corp.), 18 C.B.C.2d 1414 (B. Ct., W.D. Va. 1988).

The party who seeks to remove a state court action to bankruptcy court must determine whether part or all of the action is to be removed, and the state court has no jurisdiction to act on what has been removed, even if the removal was improper, until the bankruptcy court remands those parts over which it lacks original jurisdiction to the state court. The failure to file copies of all of the required state court pleadings with the bankruptcy court does not invalidate a removal petition. Princess Louise Corp. v. Pacific Lighting Leasing Co. (*In re* Princess Louise Corp.), 17 C.B.C.2d 663 (B. Ct., C.D. Cal. 1987).

As 28 U.S.C. § 1452(b) gives only "any equitable ground" as the basis for remand, 28 U.S.C. § 1334(c) does not govern or determine whether a court should abstain from and remand a removed proceeding. General American Corp. v. Merrill Lynch Commodities, Inc. (*In re* Ross), 15 C.B.C.2d 698 (B. Ct., S.D.N.Y. 1986).

References

1 *Collier on Bankruptcy* ch. 3 (Matthew Bender 15th ed.).

1 *Collier Bankruptcy Manual* ch. 3 (Matthew Bender 3d ed.).

28 U.S.C. § 151. Designation of bankruptcy courts.

In each judicial district, the bankruptcy judges in regular active service shall constitute a unit of the district court to be known as the bankruptcy court for that district. Each bankruptcy judge, as a judicial officer of the district court, may exercise the authority conferred under this chapter with respect to any action, suit, or proceeding and may preside alone and hold a regular or special session of the court, except as otherwise provided by law or by rule or order of the district court.

Comment

Pursuant to this provision, the bankruptcy judges in a district constitute a unit of the district court and the unit is to be known as the bankruptcy court. It would appear therefore, that the district judges do not constitute the bankruptcy court although they may have the powers of the bankruptcy judges.

References

1 *Collier on Bankruptcy* ch. 2 (Matthew Bender 15th·ed.).

1 *Collier Bankruptcy Manual* ch. 2 (Matthew Bender 3d ed.).

28 U.S.C. § 152. Appointment of bankruptcy judges.

(a)(1) The United States court of appeals for the circuit shall appoint bankruptcy judges for the judicial districts established in paragraph (2) in such numbers as are established in such paragraph. Such appointments shall be made after considering the recommendations of the Judicial Conference submitted pursuant to subsection (b). Each bankruptcy judge shall be appointed for a term of fourteen years, subject to the provisions of subsection (e). However, upon the expiration of the term, a bankruptcy judge may, with the approval of the judicial council of the circuit, continue to perform the duties of the office until the earlier of the date which is 180 days after the expiration of the term or the date of the appointment of a successor. Bankruptcy judges shall serve as judicial officers of the United States district court established under Article III of the Constitution.

(2) The bankruptcy judges appointed pursuant to this section shall be appointed for the several judicial districts as follows:

* * *

[The list of bankruptcy judges has been omitted.]

* * *

(3) Whenever a majority of the judges of any court of appeals cannot agree upon the appointment of a bankruptcy judge, the chief judge of such court shall make such appointment.

(4) The judges of the district courts for the territories shall serve as the bankruptcy judges for such courts. The United States court of appeals for the circuit within which such a territorial district court is located may appoint bankruptcy judges under this chapter for such district if authorized to do so by the Congress of the United States under this section.

(b)(1) The Judicial Conference of the United States shall, from time to time, and after considering the recommendations submitted by the Director of the Administrative Office of the United States Courts after such Director has consulted with the judicial council of the circuit involved, determine the official duty stations of bankruptcy judges and places of holding court.

(2) The Judicial Conference shall, from time to time, submit recommendations to the Congress regarding the

number of bankruptcy judges needed and the districts in which such judges are needed.

(3) Not later than December 31, 1994, and not later than the end of each 2-year period thereafter, the Judicial Conference of the United States shall conduct a comprehensive review of all judicial districts to assess the continuing need for the bankruptcy judges authorized by this section, and shall report to the Congress its findings and any recommendations for the elimination of any authorized position which can be eliminated when a vacancy exists by reason of resignation, retirement, removal, or death.

(c) Each bankruptcy judge may hold court at such places within the judicial district, in addition to the official duty station of such judge, as the business of the court may require.

(d) With the approval of the Judicial Conference and of each of the judicial councils involved, a bankruptcy judge may be designated to serve in any district adjacent to or near the district for which such bankruptcy judge was appointed.

(e) A bankruptcy judge may be removed during the term for which such bankruptcy judge is appointed, only for incompetence, misconduct, neglect of duty, or physical or mental disability and only by the judicial council of the circuit in which the judge's official duty station is located. Removal may not occur unless a majority of all of the judges of such council concur in the order of removal. Before any order of removal may be entered, a full specification of charges shall be furnished to such bankruptcy judge who shall be accorded an opportunity to be heard on such charges.

Comment

Bankruptcy judges are appointed by the United States Court of Appeals for each circuit for a term of 14 years. This section also prescribes the number of bankruptcy judges that shall be appointed in the various judicial districts. The numbers are subject to change on recommendation of the Judicial Conference of the United States by the Congress. The appointments need not be exclusive to the district. Subsection (d) allows the judicial councils with the approval of the Judicial Conference to designate a bankruptcy judge to serve in an adjacent district or one near to the one for which the judge was appointed.

1986 Amendments: Section 152(a) of title 28 was amended to make provision for the appointment of additional bankruptcy judges.

1988 Amendments: Section 152(a) of title 28 was amended (Pub. L. No. 100-587) to authorize the appointment of seven new bankruptcy judges, with one additional judge in each of the following judicial districts: District of Alaska, District of Arizona, District of Colorado, District of Kansas, Eastern District of Kentucky, Eastern District of Texas, and Western District of Texas.

1990 Amendments: The Judicial Improvements Act of 1990 (Pub. L. No. 101-650) amended section 152 of title 28 (effective on the date of enactment, December 1, 1990) by inserting the following language after the third sentence of subsection (a)(1): "However, upon the expiration of the term, a bankruptcy judge may, with the approval of the judicial council of the circuit, continue to perform the duties of the office until the earlier of the date which is 180 days after the expiration of the term or the date of the appointment of a successor."

1992 Amendments: Pub. L. No. 102-361 ("Bankruptcy Judgeship Act of 1992") was enacted on August 26, 1992. The Act provided for an increase in the number of bankruptcy judges for 17 judicial districts. In addition, Pub. L. No. 102-361 created temporary judgeships in 10 judicial districts. These bankruptcy judges are to be appointed "in the manner prescribed in section 152(a)(1) of title 28, United States Code." The first vacancy in each of these temporary judgeships will not be filled if such vacancy results from the death, retirement, resignation, or removal of a bankruptcy judge and it occurs 5 years or more after enactment. "In the case of a vacancy resulting from the expiration of the term of a bankruptcy judge not described in the preceding sentence, that judge shall be eligible for reappointment as a bankruptcy judge in that district."

The Bankruptcy Judgeship Act of 1992 also added paragraph (3) to section 152(b) of title 28. Paragraph (3) created a means to review and reduce the number of bankruptcy judgeships created by this Act when a vacancy exists by reason of resignation, retirement, removal or death.

Case Annotations

Only courts whose judges enjoy the characteristics of tenure "during good behavior" and irreducible salary provided by Article III of the Constitution have jurisdiction to award fees under the Equal Access to Justice Act ("EAJA") (28 U.S.C. § 2412(d)(1)(A)), although a bankruptcy court could obtain jurisdiction over a noncore EAJA fee application by following the procedure set forth at 28 U.S.C. § 157(c)(1) whereby a final order is to be entered by the district court, or by obtaining the express consent from the parties for entry of a final order by the bankruptcy court. *In re* Davis, 899 F.2d 1136, 23 C.B.C.2d 555 (11th Cir. 1990).

References

1 *Collier on Bankruptcy* ch. 2 (Matthew Bender 15th ed.).

1 *Collier Bankruptcy Manual* ch. 2 (Matthew Bender 3d ed.).

28 U.S.C. § 153.   Salaries; Character of service.

(a) Each bankruptcy judge shall serve on a full-time basis and shall receive as full compensation for his services a salary at an annual rate that is equal to 92 percent of the salary of a judge of the district court of the United States as determined pursuant to section 135, to be paid at such times as the Judicial Conference of the United States determines.

(b) A bankruptcy judge may not engage in the practice of law and may not engage in any other practice, business, occupation, or employment inconsistent with the expeditious, proper, and impartial performance of such bankruptcy judge's duties as a judicial officer. The Conference may promulgate appropriate rules and regulations to implement this subsection.

(c) Each individual appointed under this chapter shall take the oath or affirmation prescribed by section 453 of this title before performing the duties of the office of bankruptcy judge.

(d) A bankruptcy judge appointed under this chapter shall be exempt from the provisions of subchapter I of chapter 63 of title 5, United States Code.

Comment

1987 Amendments: Subsection (a) was amended by Pub. L. No. 100-202 to adjust a bankruptcy judge's annual salary to a rate equal to 92 percent of the salary of a district court judge as determined pursuant to section 135 of title 28.

1988 Amendments: Sections 153 and 156 of title 28 were amended (Pub. L. No. 100-702) to exempt bankruptcy judges and law clerks from the provisions of the Federal Leave Act (5 U.S.C. §§ 6301–6323).

References

1 *Collier on Bankruptcy* ch. 2 (Matthew Bender 15th ed.).

1 *Collier Bankruptcy Manual* ch. 2 (Matthew Bender 3d ed.).

28 U.S.C. § 154. Division of businesses; chief judge.

(a) Each bankruptcy court for a district having more than one bankruptcy judge shall by majority vote promulgate rules for the division of business among the bankruptcy judges to the extent that the division of business is not otherwise provided for by the rules of the district court.

(b) In each district court having more than one bankruptcy judge the district court shall designate one judge to serve as chief judge of such bankruptcy court. Whenever a majority of the judges of such district court cannot agree upon the designation as chief judge, the chief judge of such district court shall make such designation. The chief judge of the bankruptcy court shall ensure that the rules of the bankruptcy court and of the district court are observed and that the business of the bankruptcy court is handled effectively and expeditiously.

References

1 *Collier on Bankruptcy* ch. 2 (Matthew Bender 15th ed.).

1 *Collier Bankruptcy Manual* ch. 2 (Matthew Bender 3d ed.).

28 U.S.C. § 155. Temporary transfer of bankruptcy judges.

(a) A bankruptcy judge may be transferred to serve temporarily as a bankruptcy judge in any judicial district other than the judicial district for which such bankruptcy judge was appointed upon the approval of the judicial council of each of the circuits involved.

(b) A bankruptcy judge who has retired may, upon consent, be recalled to serve as a bankruptcy judge in any judicial district by the judicial council of the circuit within which such district is located. Upon recall, a bankruptcy judge may receive a salary for such service in accordance with regulations promulgated by the Judicial Conference of the United States, subject to the restrictions on the payment of an annuity in subchapter III of chapter 83, and chapter 84, of title 5.

Comment

Since the passage of the Bankruptcy Reform Act of 1978, Pub. L. No. 95-598, 28 U.S.C § 155 has been amended by the Criminal Justice Act Revision of 1986, Pub. L. No. 99-651.

References

1 *Collier on Bankruptcy* ch. 2 (Matthew Bender 15th ed.).

1 *Collier Bankruptcy Manual* ch. 2 (Matthew Bender 3d ed.).

28 U.S.C. § 156. Staff; expenses.

(a) Each bankruptcy judge may appoint a secretary, a law clerk, and such additional assistants as the Director of the Administrative Office of the United States Courts determines to be necessary. A law clerk appointed under this section shall be exempt from the provisions of subchapter I of chapter 63 of title 5, United States Code, unless specifically included by the appointing judge or by local rule of court.

(b) Upon certification to the judicial council of the circuit involved and to the Director of the Administrative Office of the United States Courts that the number of cases and proceedings pending within the jurisdiction under section 1334 of this title within a judicial district so warrants, the bankruptcy judges for such district may appoint an individual to serve as clerk of such bankruptcy court. The clerk may appoint, with the approval of such bankruptcy judges, and in such number as may be approved by the Director, necessary deputies, and may remove such deputies with the approval of such bankruptcy judges.

(c) Any court may utilize facilities or services, either on or off the court's premises, which pertain to the provision of notices, dockets, calendars, and other administrative information to parties in cases filed under the provisions of title 11, United States Code, where the costs of such facilities or services are paid for out of the assets of the estate and are not charged to the United States. The utilization of such facilities or services shall be subject to such conditions and limitations as the pertinent circuit council may prescribe.

(d) No office of the bankruptcy clerk of court may be consolidated with the district clerk of court office without the prior approval of the Judicial Conference and the Congress.

(e) In a judicial district where a bankruptcy clerk has been appointed pursuant to subsection (b), the bankruptcy clerk shall be the official custodian of the records and dockets of the bankruptcy court.

(f) For purposes of financial accountability in a district where a bankruptcy clerk has been certified, such clerk shall be accountable for and pay into the Treasury all fees, costs, and other monies collected by such clerk except uncollected fees not required by an Act of Congress to be prepaid. Such clerk shall make returns thereof to the Director of the Administrative Office of the United States Courts and the Director of the Executive Office For United States Trustees, under regulations prescribed by such Directors.

Comment

1986 Amendments: Subsections (d), (e) and (f) were added to 28 U.S.C. § 156 by the 1986 Amendments.

1988 Amendments: Sections 153 and 156 of title 28 were amended (Pub. L. No. 100-702) to exempt bankruptcy judges and law clerks from the provisions of the Federal Leave Act (5 U.S.C. §§ 6301–6323).

References

1 *Collier on Bankruptcy* ch. 2 (Matthew Bender 15th ed.).

1 *Collier Bankruptcy Manual* ch. 2 (Matthew Bender 3d ed.).

28 U.S.C. § 157.   Procedures.

(a) Each district court may provide that any or all cases under title 11 and any or all proceedings arising under title 11 or arising in or related to a case under title 11 shall be referred to the bankruptcy judges for the district.

(b)(1) Bankruptcy judges may hear and determine all cases under title 11 and all core proceedings arising under title 11, or arising in a case under title 11, referred under subsection (a) of this section, and may enter appropriate orders and judgments, subject to review under section 158 of this title.

(2) Core proceedings include, but are not limited to—

(A) matters concerning the administration of the estate;

(B) allowance or disallowance of claims against the estate or exemptions from property of the estate, and estimation of claims or interests for the purposes of confirming a plan under chapter 11, 12, or 13 of title 11 but not the liquidation or estimation of contingent or unliquidated personal injury tort or wrongful death claims against the estate for purposes of distribution in a case under title 11;

(C) counterclaims by the estate against persons filing claims against the estate;

(D) orders in respect to obtaining credit;

(E) orders to turn over property of the estate;

(F) proceedings to determine, avoid, or recover preferences;

(G) motions to terminate, annul, or modify the automatic stay;

(H) proceedings to determine, avoid, or recover fraudulent conveyances;

(I) determinations as to the dischargeability of particular debts;

(J) objections to discharges;

(K) determinations of the validity, extent, or priority of liens;

(L) confirmations of plans;

(M) orders approving the use or lease of property, including the use of cash collateral;

(N) orders approving the sale of property other than property resulting from claims brought by the estate against persons who have not filed claims against the estate; and

(O) other proceedings affecting the liquidation of the assets of the estate or the adjustment of the debtor-creditor or the equity security holder relationship, except personal injury tort or wrongful death claims.

(3) The bankruptcy judge shall determine, on the judge's own motion or on timely motion of a party, whether a proceeding is a core proceeding under this subsection or is a proceeding that is otherwise related to a case under title 11. A determination that a proceeding is not a core proceeding shall not be made solely on the basis that its resolution may be affected by State law.

(4) Non-core proceedings under section 157(b)(2)(B) of title 28, United States Code, shall not be subject to the mandatory abstention provisions of section 1334(c)(2).

(5) The district court shall order that personal injury tort and wrongful death claims shall be tried in the district court in which the bankruptcy case is pending, or in the district court in the district in which the claim arose, as determined by the district court in which the bankruptcy case is pending.

(c)(1) A bankruptcy judge may hear a proceeding that is not a core proceeding but that is otherwise related to a case under title 11. In such proceeding, the bankruptcy judge shall submit proposed findings of fact and conclusions of law to the district court, and any final order or judgment shall be entered by the district judge after considering the bankruptcy judge's proposed findings and conclusions and after reviewing de novo those matters to which any party has timely and specifically objected.

(2) Notwithstanding the provisions of paragraph (1) of this subsection, the district court, with the consent of all the parties to the proceeding, may refer a proceeding related to a case under title 11 to a bankruptcy judge to hear and determine and to enter appropriate orders and judgments, subject to review under section 158 of this title.

(d) The district court may withdraw, in whole or in part, any case or proceeding referred under this section, on its own motion or on timely motion of any party, for cause shown. The district court shall, on timely motion of a party, so withdraw a proceeding if the court determines that resolution of the proceeding requires consideration of both title 11 and other laws of the United States regulating organizations or activities affecting interstate commerce.

Comment

Subsection (a). All cases and proceedings may be referred by the district court to the bankruptcy court; accordingly, referral is discretionary with the district courts. Presumably, the general referral will be accomplished by local rule of the district court or an order of the district court.

Subsection (b). Bankruptcy courts have jurisdiction to enter final orders in cases and in core proceedings. Core proceedings are set forth in paragraph (2) with catch-all phrases at the beginning and ending of the list. Pursuant to paragraph (3) the determination of whether a proceeding is a core proceeding should not be made solely on its involvement with State law. One exception pertains to the determination of personal injury tort or wrongful death claims. As to these, (1) the mandatory abstention provisions of 28 U.S.C. § 1334(c)(2), *supra,* do not apply and (2) they are to be heard by the district court where the title 11 case is pending or the district court where the claim arose as decided by the district court where the case is pending.

Subsection (c). In non-core proceedings, the bankruptcy court may enter proposed findings of fact and conclusions of law; final determination is to be made by the district court. On objection of a party, the district court is to review de novo those objected to matters. The parties may consent to entry of a final order by the bankruptcy court.

Subsection (d). In its discretion, the district court may withdraw a proceeding from the bankruptcy judge. It shall do so if timely motion is made and resolution requires consideration of title 11 and other federal laws regulating organizations or activities affecting interstate commerce.

Bankruptcy Rule 7008 provides that in an adversary proceeding before a bankruptcy judge, the complaint, counterclaim, cross-claim or third-party complaint shall contain a statement that the proceeding is core or noncore and, if noncore, that the pleader does or does not consent to entry of final orders or judgment by the bankruptcy judge. The Advisory Committee Note states that failure to include consent in the statement does not constitute consent. Only express consent is effective to authorize final judgment or order in a noncore proceeding.

Bankruptcy Rule 7012 requires that the defendant admit or deny the allegation as to whether the proceeding is core or noncore and if noncore, that the party does or does not consent to final orders or judgment of the bankruptcy judge.

Case Annotations

Congress cannot eliminate a party's Seventh Amendment right to a jury trial merely by relabeling the cause of action to which it attaches and placing exclusive jurisdiction in an administrative agency or a specialized court of equity. A person who has not submitted a claim against the bankruptcy estate when sued by the trustee to recover an allegedly fraudulent transfer is entitled by the Seventh Amendment to a jury trial, notwithstanding Congress' designation of fraudulent conveyance actions as "core proceedings" in 28 U.S.C. § 157(b)(2)(H). Granfinanciera, S.A. v. Nordberg, 492 U.S. 33, 109 S. Ct. 2782, 106 L. Ed. 2d 26, 20 C.B.C.2d 1216 (1989).

Use of the word "determine" in 28 U.S.C. § 157(b)(1) only authorizes bankruptcy judges to determine "cases" and "proceedings" and "enter appropriate orders and judgments"; it does not mean that a judge may bind a governmental unit by its determination of issues. Irrespective of section 106 of the Bankruptcy Code, sovereign immunity is not waived in actions against states to recover money judgments. Hoffman v. Connecticut Dept. of Income Maintenance, 492 U.S. —, 109 S. Ct. 2818, 104 L. Ed. 2d 151, 20 C.B.C.2d 1204 (1989).

Because the only proper forum for determining whether assets held by a debtor are held in constructive trust is the bankruptcy court, such proceedings must be considered core and since a determination of the proper beneficiaries of that trust is inextricably tied to the finding that a constructive trust exists and is intimately tied to the traditional bankruptcy functions and estate, that, too, must be considered a core proceeding. *In re* Johnson, 960 F.2d 396, 26 C.B.C.2d 1054 (4th Cir. 1992).

A district court may properly abstain from using its transfer powers under 28 U.S.C. § 157(b)(5) when a case is properly in state court and when the proposed transfer is of questionable validity and thus would engender further delay in disposition of the case. *In re* Pan American Corp., 950 F.2d 839, 26 C.B.C.2d 20 (2d Cir. 1991).

The jurisdiction of a bankruptcy court to render a judgment that was final before the effective date of *Northern Pipeline Construction Co. v. Marathon Pipe Line* must be determined according to the law in effect at the time the judgment was rendered, *i.e.,* a bankruptcy court has jurisdiction over a judgment rendered final pre-*Marathon* even if the judgment concerned a matter that would currently be called a noncore, related proceeding and, therefore, inappropriate for bankruptcy court jurisdiction. *In re* Jogert, Inc., 950 F.2d 1498, 26 C.B.C.2d 181 (7th Cir. 1991).

An action is a core proceeding when the dispute cannot be severed from the remainder of the bankruptcy case and affects the distribution of the debtor's assets. Matter of Case, 937 F.2d 1014, 25 C.B.C.2d 368 (5th Cir. 1991).

Whether federal subject matter jurisdiction exists for a bankruptcy court to decide a state law claim depends upon whether the claim is "related to" the bankruptcy case under 28 U.S.C. § 1334(b), or whether the claim is within the bankruptcy court's core jurisdiction under 28 U.S.C. § 157(b). *In re* Parque Forestal, Inc., 949 F.2d 504, 25 C.B.C.2d 1690 (1st Cir. 1991).

A bankruptcy court does not have jurisdiction to determine whether tort suits filed in violation of the automatic stay are subsequently barred by state statutes of limitations. Pettibone Corp. v. Easley, 935 F.2d 120, 25 C.B.C.2d 1 (7th Cir. 1991).

The court must look to both form and substance of a proceeding to determine the existence of core status, and an action involving issues which arise because of a bankruptcy case and the debtor's assertion of a right under the Code constitutes a core proceeding over which the bankruptcy court has jurisdiction. *In re* Wolverine Radio Co., 930 F.2d 1132, 24 C.B.C.2d 1702 (6th Cir. 1991).

An application for attorney's fees under section 7430 of the Internal Revenue Code is a noncore proceeding. *In re* Brickell Investment Corp., 922 F.2d 696, 24 C.B.C.2d 731 (11th Cir. 1991).

Even proceedings that are core must be withdrawn when they require the bankruptcy court to substantially interpret federal statutes that affect interstate commerce. City of New York v. Exxon Corp., 932 F.2d 1020, 24 C.B.C.2d 1737 (2d Cir. 1991).

A state law claim brought by a noncreditor company against the chief operating officer of a chapter 11 corporate debtor in his individual capacity for breach of a confidentiality agreement is a noncore proceeding when the claim does not fit within one of the enumerated core categories of 28 U.S.C. § 157(b)(2)(B)–(N) and to fit it into a catchall category might cause constitutional problems. Bankruptcy courts cannot conduct jury trials on noncore matters when the parties have not consented because the standard for review of noncore determinations under 28 U.S.C. § 157(c)(1) precludes compliance with the Seventh Amendment; withdrawal of the proceeding to the district court is appropriate, and the district court's denial of withdrawal is an abuse of discretion. *In re* Cinematronics, Inc., 916 F.2d 1444, 24 C.B.C.2d 952 (9th Cir. 1990).

When the district court retains jurisdiction of a proceeding against the Federal Deposit Insurance Corporation after a chapter 7 trustee has been substituted for the plaintiff-debtor, the district court has, in effect, withdrawn the matter from the bankruptcy court to whom it otherwise would have been automatically referred for disposition by a blanket order of reference. Further, the district court in such an instance is the appropriate forum in which to assert a waiver of sovereign immunity pursuant to section 106 of the Code. Anderson and Propps v. FDIC, 918 F.2d 1139, 24 C.B.C.2d 151 (4th Cir. 1990).

Upon a partner's filing of a bankruptcy petition, the partner's interest in a debtor partnership became part of the estate and the bankruptcy court retains jurisdiction to approve the trustee's settlement of a dispute between the debtor partner and a nondebtor partner. *In re* Holywell Corp., 913 F.2d 873, 24 C.B.C.2d 69 (11th Cir. 1990).

Orders granting or denying motions for withdrawal of reference are not final. Allegheny v. Allegheny, 920 F.2d 1127, 24 C.B.C.2d 546 (3d Cir. 1990).

The issue of the priority of distribution pursuant to section 726 of the Code of a Department of Energy claim for restitution for overcharges pursuant to Section 209 of the Economic Stabilization Act, incorporated within Section 5(a)(1) of the Emergency Petroleum Allocation Act, 15 U.S.C. § 754(a)(1) *et seq.,* is an issue of federal bankruptcy law and, therefore, falls within the jurisdiction of a court sitting in bankruptcy and is not within the jurisdiction of the Temporary Emergency Court of Appeals. *In re* Seneca Oil Co., 906 F.2d 1445, 23 C.B.C.2d 361 (10th Cir. 1990).

The bankruptcy court which confirmed a debtor's reorganization plan has jurisdiction to enter an injunction order enjoining a creditor from interfering with the debtor's confirmed reorganization plan but the terms of the injunction must be sufficiently specific and detailed in order to comply with Rule 65(d) of the Fed. R. Civ. P. United States Dept. of the Air Force v. Carolina Parachute Corp., 907 F.2d 1469, 23 C.B.C.2d 620 (4th Cir. 1990).

Equal Access to Justice Act applications may properly be adjudicated by bankruptcy courts only when all parties to the proceeding have expressly consented to such jurisdiction, mere consent to the bankruptcy court's jurisdiction over the underlying bankruptcy case is insufficient. *In re* Davis, 899 F.2d 1136, 23 C.B.C.2d 555 (11th Cir. 1990).

The assertion of a compulsory counterclaim by a defendant who has not filed a proof of claim does not amount to a consent to the bankruptcy court's jurisdiction over a noncore proceeding. Beard v. Braunstein, 914 F.2d 434, 23 C.B.C.2d 1247 (3d Cir. 1990).

A district court judge, sitting in review of a bankruptcy court, who remands the case back to the bankruptcy court for expanded findings of fact may, if a bankruptcy judge is unavailable, carry out his own mandate. *In re* Red Carpet Corp. of Panama City Beach, 902 F.2d 883, 23 C.B.C.2d 663 (11th Cir. 1990).

28 U.S.C. § 157(d) clearly requires that cause be shown before the district court may withdraw a reference *sua sponte. In re* Pruitt, 910 F.2d 1160, 23 C.B.C.2d 721 (3d Cir. 1990).

A bankruptcy court has authority to conduct jury trials when the issues underlying the proceeding are core and legal in nature. Ben Cooper, Inc. v. The Insurance Co. of the State of Pennsylvania, 896 F.2d 1394, 22 C.B.C.2d 729 (2d Cir.), *cert. granted,* — U.S. —, 110 S. Ct. 3269, 111 L. Ed. 2d 779, *vacated and remanded,* — U.S. —, 111 S. Ct. 425, 112 L. Ed. 2d 408 (1990), *opinion reinstated on remand,* 924 F.2d 36, 24 C.B.C.2d 841 (2d Cir. 1991), *cert. denied,* — U.S. —, 111 S. Ct. 2041, 114 L. Ed. 2d 126 (1991).

28 U.S.C. § 157 does not contain any specific or express language granting to a bankruptcy judge the authority to conduct jury trials; the broad grant of authority to bankruptcy judges in section 157 does not imply that the authority to conduct jury trials is an indispensible power necessary to carry out the authority actually conferred by the section. *In re* United Missouri Bank of Kansas City, 901 F.2d 1449, 22 C.B.C.2d 1400 (8th Cir. 1990).

A bankruptcy court has no inherent or statutory power—and none is granted by 11 U.S.C. § 105, 28 U.S.C. § 157, or Bankruptcy Rule

9020—to hear and determine criminal contempts at least as to contempts not committed in or near its presence so that not only must the acquittal or conviction and sentence for such offenses be by the district court, but all critical stages of the trial of such offenses must be before that court. In the Matter of Hipp, Inc., 895 F.2d 1503, 22 C.B.C.2d 876 (5th Cir. 1990).

A claim is not barred by principles of *res judicata* if, in the earlier proceeding, the nonparty's interest was not properly before the court nor adequately represented by a party with standing if the claim is one which would not have presented a core proceeding in the earlier bankruptcy proceedings under *Marathon,* the earlier judgment is not preclusive. Latham v. Wells Fargo Bank, 896 F.2d 979, 22 C.B.C.2d 846 (5th Cir. 1990).

A bankruptcy court does not have jurisdiction to adjudicate a successorship issue under the "collateral issue" exception to the Nation Labor Relations Board's primary jurisdiction when no bankruptcy issue hinges on the successorship determination. *In re* Goodman, 873 F.2d 598, 22 C.B.C.2d 1159 (2d Cir. 1989).

Injunctive orders enjoining those suits against a debtor's insurers that arise out of or relate to the debtor's settled insurance policies do not constitute a de facto discharge in bankruptcy of nondebtor parties and are, therefore, permissible and within the bankruptcy court's authority to enter. MacArthur Co. v. Johns-Manville Corp., 837 F.2d 457, 18 C.B.C.2d 316 (2d Cir. 1988).

An action to determine whether the debtor has misappropriated company stock and as a result has received a disproportionate share of company assets is a noncore, "related to" proceeding. Wood v. Wood (*In re* Wood), 825 F.2d 90, 17 C.B.C.2d 743 (5th Cir. 1987).

A proceeding to prosecute a violation of the automatic stay is a core proceeding. Budget Service Co. v. Better Homes of Virginia, Inc., 804 F.2d 289, 15 C.B.C.2d 1025 (4th Cir. 1986).

Under the plain language of 28 U.S.C. § 157(b)(5), the district court in which the debtor's case was filed has jurisdiction to fix the venue of any tort action against the debtor, irrespective of the district in which such controversy is pending; the district court's power to so act is not preempted by the general venue provisions of 28 U.S.C. § 1412. A.H. Robins Co., Inc. v. Piccinin, 788 F.2d 994, 15 C.B.C.2d 235 (4th Cir.), *cert. denied,* 479 U.S. 876, 107 S. Ct. 251, 93 L. Ed. 2d 177 (1986).

Although the bankruptcy court has jurisdiction to hear and determine a dischargeability action pursuant to 28 U.S.C. § 157(b)(2)(I), the district court also has jurisdiction, under 28 U.S.C. § 1334(b), and may withdraw its reference of a dischargeability action pursuant to 28 U.S.C. § 157(d) upon its own motion; the court may do so when it is called upon to determine a mandatorily withdrawn liability issue, the resolution of which will influence the dischargeability of any resulting judgment, and when the interests of convenience and judicial economy will be advanced. Moraes v. Adams (*In re* Adams), 761 F.2d 1422, 12 C.B.C.2d 1220 (9th Cir. 1985).

References

1 *Collier on Bankruptcy* ch. 3 (Matthew Bender 15th ed.).

1 *Collier Bankruptcy Manual* ch. 3 (Matthew Bender 3d ed.).

Adlerstein and Talvacchia, *Two-Tiered Court: Understanding the U.S. District Court System Whereby Top-Level Federal Judges Review the Decisions of Magistrates and Bankruptcy Judges,* 135 N.J. Law. 26 (1990).

Davidson and Davidson, *Jury Trials: The Bankruptcy Court Dilemma,* 13 L.A. Law. 28 (1990).

Pappone and Orson, *When Can a Bankruptcy Court Conduct a Trial by Jury?,* 1 F & G Bankr. L. Rev. 30 (1989).

Pappone and Welch, *High Court Opens Door to Bankruptcy Trials by Jury,* 1 F & G Bankr. L. Rev. 5 (1989).

28 U.S.C. § 158. Appeals.

(a) The district courts of the United States shall have jurisdiction to hear appeals from final judgments, orders, and decrees, and, with leave of the court, from interlocutory orders and decrees, of bankruptcy judges entered in cases and proceedings referred to the bankruptcy judges under section 157 of this title. An appeal under this subsection shall be taken only to the district court for the judicial district in which the bankruptcy judge is serving.

(b)(1) The judicial council of a circuit may establish a bankruptcy appellate panel, comprised of bankruptcy judges from districts within the circuit, to hear and determine, upon the consent of all the parties, appeals under subsection (a) of this section.

(2) If authorized by the Judicial Conference of the United States, the judicial councils of two or more circuits may establish a joint bankruptcy appellate panel comprised of bankruptcy judges from the districts within the circuits for which such panel is established, to hear and determine, upon the consent of all parties, appeals under subsection (a) of this section.

(3) No appeal may be referred to a panel under this subsection unless the district judges for the district, by

majority vote, authorize such referral of appeals originating within the district.

(4) A panel established under this section shall consist of three bankruptcy judges, provided a bankruptcy judge may not hear an appeal originating within a district for which the judge is appointed or designated under section 152 of this title.

(c) An appeal under subsections (a) and (b) of this section shall be taken in the same manner as appeals in civil proceedings generally are taken to the courts of appeals from the district courts and in the time provided by Rule 8002 of the Bankruptcy Rules.

(d) The courts of appeals shall have jurisdiction of appeals from all final decisions, judgments, orders, and decrees entered under subsections (a) and (b) of this section.

Comment

Subsection (a). Appellate jurisdiction is in the district courts from final orders and, with leave, from interlocutory orders of the bankruptcy court.

Subsection (b). Appellate panels of bankruptcy judges may be authorized by the judicial council of the circuit. Joint bankruptcy appellate panels, composed of bankruptcy judges from the districts within the circuits, may be authorized by the Judicial Conference of the United States. If the district judges by majority vote authorize referral of an appeal to the panel and if the parties to the appeal agree, the appellate panel may hear the appeal.

Subsection (c). The time for appealing is that set out in Bankruptcy Rule 8002 and the procedure is that generally followed for appeals to the court of appeals.

Subsection (d). Courts of appeals have appellate jurisdiction over final decisions rendered by the district court or appellate panels.

Part VIII of the Bankruptcy Rules govern appeals to the District Court or Bankruptcy Appellate Panel.

1990 Amendments: Section 158 was amended by the Judicial Improvements Act of 1990 (Pub. L. No. 101-650, which was effective as of the date of enactment, December 1, 1990). This amendment redesignated paragraphs (2) and (3) of section 158(b) as paragraphs (3) and (4) and added a new paragraph (2) regarding the creation of joint bankruptcy appellate panels governing more than one circuit.

Case Annotations

There is no reason to infer from either Section 1292 or 158(d) of Title 28 that Congress meant to limit appellate review of interlocutory orders in bankruptcy proceedings to orders issued by district courts sitting as trial courts in bankruptcy rather than appellate courts. An interlocutory order issued by a district court sitting as court of appeals in bankruptcy is appealable; Section 158(d) does not preclude courts of appeals, by negative implication contained in its own grant of jurisdiction, from exercising jurisdiction under Section 1291 over district courts sitting in bankruptcy, nor does it preclude jurisdiction under Section 1292. Connecticut Nat'l Bank v. Germain, 503 U.S. —, 112 S. Ct. 1146, 117 L. Ed. 2d 391, 26 C.B.C.2d 17 (1992).

A district court may not make its own independent factual findings when reviewing a decision of the bankruptcy court which failed to make factual findings, but should instead remand to the bankruptcy court so that it may do so. Great Western Bank v. Sierra Woods Group, 953 F.2d 1174, 26 C.B.C.2d 342 (9th Cir. 1992).

For an interlocutory order of a bankruptcy court to be reviewable by the district court, the party seeking appeal must first seek and be granted leave to appeal by the district court. In the Matter of First Fin. Dev. Corp., 960 F.2d 23, 26 C.B.C.2d 1423 (5th Cir. 1992).

An error of nomenclature committed by both the bankruptcy and the district court in labeling the debtor's objection to a claim does not result in a waiver of that ground for objection so long as the debtor's basis for its objection was apparent throughout the proceedings. In re Allegheny Int'l, Inc., 954 F.2d 167, 26 C.B.C.2d 663 (3d Cir. 1992).

An order that finally disposes of a discrete dispute within the larger bankruptcy case is sufficiently final to satisfy 28 U.S.C. § 158(d). In re Drexel Burnham Lambert Group, Inc., 960 F.2d 285, 26 C.B.C.2d 1413 (2d Cir. 1992).

On appeal, a grant of summary judgment is reviewed de novo, and the reviewing court must view the evidence in a light most favorable to the party against whom judgment was had in order to determine whether there are any genuine issues of material fact and whether the lower court correctly applied law. In re De Laurentiis Entertainment Group, Inc., 963 F.2d 1269, 26 C.B.C.2d 1435 (9th Cir. 1992).

If an issue on appeal involves statutory construction, the appellate court will review the opinion of the trial court de novo. In re Bellamy, 962 F.2d 176, 26 C.B.C.2d 1459 (2d Cir. 1992).

For purposes of appellate review, determination of a fraud action requires findings of fact (and is not a mixed question of fact and law), which are subject to a "clearly erroneous" standard of review. In re Jogert, Inc., 950 F.2d 1498, 26 C.B.C.2d 181 (7th Cir. 1991).

An order permitting the filing of a late claim on equitable grounds under the guidelines of Fed. R. Civ. P. 15(c) is a final order for purposes of appeal when claim finality has been established. Matter of Unroe, 937 F.2d 346, 25 C.B.C.2d 84 (7th Cir. 1991).

Although a district court may characterize a bankruptcy court order as interlocutory, if the dispute underlying the order is part of a larger case, the order disposing of the dispute is final in the bankruptcy context. In re G.S.F. Corp., 938 F.2d 1467, 25 C.B.C.2d 113 (1st Cir. 1991).

For the court of appeals to have jurisdiction over a party, the notice of appeal must specifically name each appellant; the use of et al. is insufficient as it fails to provide notice of the identity of the appellants. In re Unioil, 948 F.2d 678, 25 C.B.C.2d 1493 (10th Cir. 1991).

A reviewing court may affirm the judgment of a lower court based on grounds different from those relied upon by the lower court. In re Parque Forestal, Inc., 949 F.2d 504, 25 C.B.C.2d 1690 (1st Cir. 1991).

A chapter 7 trustee has standing to appeal a bankruptcy court's denial of a motion to dismiss a petition for substantial abuse under section 707(b). Although a court of appeals will not ordinarily address matters in the first instance on appeal, it may appropriately do so when the issue has been thoroughly briefed by both parties and can be decided on a record which is complete for the purpose of ruling. In re Clark, 927 F.2d 793, 24 C.B.C.2d 1536 (4th Cir. 1991).

A district court order applying the automatic stay to a governmental action taken to enforce the government's police or regulatory power is an appealable collateral order, and the court of appeals has jurisdiction to hear the appeal. Eddleman v. U.S. Dep't of Labor, 923 F.2d 782, 24 C.B.C.2d 822 (10th Cir. 1991).

The question of what constitutes substantial abuse under Code section 707(b) is, for purposes of appeal, a matter of law to be reviewed de novo by the appellate court which court will overturn the decision below only if clearly erroneous. In re Green, 934 F.2d 568, 24 C.B.C.2d 1911 (4th Cir. 1991).

Under a flexible and pragmatic definition of finality, denial by the bankruptcy court of a demand for a jury trial is not final when resolution of the appeal will not affect the assets of the estate and, more importantly, appellant has a motion pending before the bankruptcy court for judgment on the pleadings, which, if granted, would eliminate any need for a jury trial. Allegheny International, Inc. v. Allegheny Ludlum Steel Corp., 920 F.2d 1127, 24 C.B.C.2d 546 (3d Cir. 1990).

When the bankruptcy and district courts follow the procedure of 28 U.S.C. § 158 whereby a final order is entered by the bankruptcy court and subsequently appealed to the district court, there is no jurisdiction over an application for attorney's fees under the Equal Access to Justice Act. In re Davis, 899 F.2d 1136, 23 C.B.C.2d 555 (11th Cir. 1990).

A court may review an otherwise unappealable order as a request for a writ of mandamus if the order may undermine the purposes and procedures of the bankruptcy laws. In re Pruitt, 910 F.2d 1160, 23 C.B.C.2d 721 (3d Cir. 1990).

For the purposes of 28 U.S.C. § 158(a), a district court has decided an appeal when it has explicitly granted permission to take an interlocutory appeal and when the order contains a review of the bankruptcy court's action for errors, but does not purport to redetermine factual issues *de novo*. *In re* Kaiser Steel Corp., 911 F.2d 380, 23 C.B.C.2d 745 (10th Cir. 1990).

A bankruptcy appellate panel has jurisdiction to hear an appeal from an order denying a temporary restraining order when that order implies a denial of all relief. *In re* Carroll, 903 F.2d 1266, 23 C.B.C.2d 854 (9th Cir. 1990).

Findings of fact by the district court are not jurisdictional in an appellate court, and on appeal, the court of appeals may render a decision when the record sufficiently informs the court of the basis for the trial court's decisions on the material issues or the issues in the appeal do not turn on findings of fact. *In re* Muncrief, 900 F.2d 1220, 23 C.B.C.2d 427 (8th Cir. 1990).

Generally, a final order is one which ends the litigation on the merits and leaves nothing for the court to do but execute the judgment; however, the pendency of certain motions will not preclude review of a district court judge's order when it appears to the court that the only issue left to be resolved is the one before the court on appeal. *In re* Red Carpet Corp. of Panama City Beach, 902 F.2d 883, 23 C.B.C.2d 663 (11th Cir. 1990).

In the bankruptcy context in which finality is accorded a somewhat flexible, pragmatic definition, orders approving the rejection of contracts for a debtor's personal services as a popular musician and refusing to dismiss the debtor's chapter 11 petition are final and appealable. In the Matter of Taylor, 913 F.2d 102, 23 C.B.C.2d 1035 (3d Cir. 1990).

An order confirming a plan of reorganization marks the termination of any distinctive bankruptcy proceeding and is, therefore, appealable, and merely because the debtor may proceed at once to carry out a confirmed plan and because there still exists severable disputes does not preclude finality for purposes of appeal. *In re* Kham & Nate's Shoes No. 2, Inc., 908 F.2d 1351, 23 C.B.C.2d 1118 (7th Cir. 1990).

A district court's order which reverses a bankruptcy court's confirmation of a chapter 12 plan and remands the case for further proceedings which includes the determination of the plan's feasibility is a final appealable order. *In re* Fowler, 903 F.2d 694, 22 C.B.C.2d 1659 (9th Cir. 1990).

Ordinarily, a remand to the bankruptcy court by a district court is not a final, appealable order under 28 U.S.C. § 158(d), unless the remand effectively settles an issue and orders the bankruptcy court to perform merely a ministerial task. *In re* Goodman, 873 F.2d 598, 22 C.B.C.2d 1159 (2d Cir. 1989).

There are five exceptions to the general rule that an appellate court will refuse to consider an issue not presented to the trial court and raised for the first time on appeal: (1) if the refusal would result in a miscarriage of justice; (2) if the appellant had no opportunity to raise the objection; (3) if there is at stake a "substantial interest of justice"; (4) if the proper resolution is beyond any doubt; and (5) if the issue presents significant questions of general impact or great public concern. When a case does not fall within five exceptions and it has been found that a debtor failed to object to a law firm's application for compensation, a debtor's objections to attorneys' fees awarded by a bankruptcy court to special litigation counsel do not present exceptional circumstances precluding application of the rule and may be dismissed. *In re* Daikin Miami Overseas, 868 F.2d 1201, 20 C.B.C.2d 1077 (11th Cir. 1989).

When a district court has previously reversed the holding of a bankruptcy court that a restitution obligation was discharged and a debtor has completed payments under a chapter 13 plan and has received a discharge of his debts under section 1328(a), the issue of whether a restitution obligation is a dischargeable debt is ripe for resolution by a court of appeals. *In re* Johnson-Allen, 871 F.2d 421, 20 C.B.C.2d 966 (3d Cir. 1989), *aff'd sub nom.* Pa. Dept. of Pub. Welfare v. Davenport, 495 U.S. —, 110 S. Ct. 2126, 109 L. Ed. 2d 588, 22 C.B.C.2d 1067 (1989).

The remand of a case by a district court for the determination of fees pursuant to 28 U.S.C. § 1930(a) is a final order. *In re* Prines, 867 F.2d 478, 20 C.B.C.2d 500 (8th Cir. 1989).

While a district court may review a bankruptcy court's denial of a motion to dismiss a petition for bad faith, the court of appeals has no jurisdiction to review the resolution of that appeal because the order is not final for appeal purposes. *In re* Dixie Broadcasting, 871 F.2d 1023, 20 C.B.C.2d 1521 (11th Cir. 1989).

References

1 *Collier on Bankruptcy* ch. 3 (Matthew Bender 15th ed.).

1 *Collier Bankruptcy Manual* ch. 3 (Matthew Bender 3d ed.).

6 *Collier Bankruptcy Practice Guide* ch. 117 (Matthew Bender).

Comment, *Interlocutory Appeals in Bankruptcy Cases: The Conflict Between Judicial Code Section 158 and 1292,* 8 Bankr. Dev. J. 519 (1991).

Comment, *"It Ain't Over Till It's Over:" Interpreting 28 U.S.C. § 158(d) Finality for Bankruptcy Appeals to Circuit Court,* 53 Alb. L. Rev. 889 (1989).

March and Obregon, *Are BAP Decisions Binding on Any Court?,* 18 Cal. Bankr. J. 189 (1990).

Note, *When is an Order Final?: A Result-Oriented Approach to the Finality Requirement for Bankruptcy Appeals to Federal Circuit Courts,* 74 Minn. L. Rev. 1337 (1990).

FILING FEES (CHAPTER 123)

28 U.S.C. § 1930. Bankruptcy fees.

(a) Notwithstanding section 1915 of this title, the parties commencing a case under title 11 shall pay to the clerk of the district court or the clerk of the bankruptcy court, if one has been certified pursuant to section 156(b) of this title, the following filing fees:

> (1) For a case commenced under chapter 7 or 13 of title 11, $120.

> (2) For a case commenced under chapter 9 of title 11, $300.

> (3) For a case commenced under chapter 11 of title 11 that does not concern a railroad, as defined in section 101 of title 11, $600.

> (4) For a case commenced under chapter 11 of title 11 concerning a railroad, as so defined, $1,000.

> (5) For a case commenced under chapter 12 of title 11, $200.

> (6) In addition to the filing fee paid to the clerk, a quarterly fee shall be paid to the United States trustee, for deposit in the Treasury, in each case under chapter 11 of title 11 for each quarter (including any fraction thereof) until a plan is confirmed or the case is converted or dismissed, whichever occurs first. The fee shall be $250 for each quarter in which disbursements total less than $15,000; $500 for each quarter in which disbursements total $15,000 or more but less than $150,000; $1,250 for each quarter in which disbursements total $150,000 or more but less than $300,000; $3,750 for each quarter in which disbursements total $300,000 or more but less than $3,000,000; $5,000 for each quarter in which disbursements total $3,000,000 or more. The fee shall be

payable on the last day of the calendar month following the
calendar quarter for which the fee is owed.

An individual commencing a voluntary case or a joint case
under title 11 may pay such fee in installments. For converting,
on request of the debtor, a case under chapter 7, or 13 of title
11, to a case under chapter 11 of title 11, the debtor shall pay
to the clerk of the court a fee of $400.

(b) The Judicial Conference of the United States may prescribe
additional fees in cases under title 11 of the same kind as the
Judicial Conference prescribes under section 1914(b) of this title.
[*See* Comment under 1989 Amendments *infra*.]

(c) Upon the filing of any separate or joint notice of appeal or
application for appeal or upon the receipt of any order allowing,
or notice of the allowance of, an appeal or a writ of certiorari $5
shall be paid to the clerk of the court, by the appellant or
petitioner.

(d) Whenever any case or proceeding is dismissed in any court
for want of jurisdiction, such court may order the payment of just
costs.

(e) The clerk of the court may collect only the fees prescribed
under this section.

Comment

Bankruptcy Rule 1006(a) provides that every petition be accompanied
by the prescribed filing fee except when the debtor is permitted to pay
the fee in installments.

Subdivision (b)(1) requires the clerk to accept a voluntary petition if
accompanied by an application to pay the filing fee in installments
stating that the debtor is unable to pay the filing fee except in installments, the proposed terms of payment, and that the applicant has not
paid any money or transferred any property to an attorney for services
in connection with the case. Subdivision (b)(2) provides that prior to the
meeting of creditors, the court may order payment to the clerk of the
filing fee in installments and fix the number, amount and dates of
payments. The number of installments may not exceed four, and final
payment must be made no later than 120 days after the filing of the
petition. For cause shown the court may extend the time of an installment provided the final payment is made not later than 180 days after
filing the petition. Subdivision (b)(3) provides that the filing fee must
be paid in full before the debtor may pay an attorney for services in
connection with the case.

[*Ed. Note:* The 1991 Amendments to the Bankruptcy Rules and Official Forms made no changes in Rule 1006.]

1986 Amendments: The 1986 Act added new paragraph (6) to 28 U.S.C. § 1930(a). In a chapter 11 case, in addition to the filing fee of $500, fees scaled to the disbursements made during the previous quarter are to be paid for each quarter to the United States trustee for deposit in the Treasury.

Additionally, the filing fee for a chapter 7 or 13 case was increased from $60 to $90. The filing fee for a case commenced under chapter 11 concerning a railroad was increased from $500 to $1000. For a case commenced under chapter 12, the filing fee is fixed at $200.

This section was amended to reflect the creation of a permanent United States trustee system. Section 302(d) of the 1986 Amendments provides different effective dates for the amendments relating to the United States trustee system. *See* Section 302 of the 1986 Amendments, reprinted herein under "Selected Provisions of the Bankruptcy Judges, United States Trustees, and Family Farmer Bankruptcy Act of 1986," regarding effective dates generally.

1989 Amendments: The Judiciary Appropriations Act of 1990 (Pub. L. No. 101-162), section 406(a) amended 28 U.S.C. § 1930(a)(1) by striking out $90 and inserting in lieu thereof $120.

Section 406(a) also amends 28 U.S.C. § 1930(b) by directing that the Judicial Conference, in addition to other fees fixed by the Conference, prescribe a fee of $60 for motions seeking relief from the automatic stay under section 362(d) (the legislation erroneously refers to section 362(b)) and for a motion to compel abandonment of property under section 554(b).

1990 Amendments: Effective December 21, 1989:

Filing fee to abandon property [Rule 5007]	$60
Filing fee, motion to lift stay [§ 362(d)]	$60
Filing fee, motion to withdraw reference	$60

Effective January 11, 1990:

Deconsolidation fee:	Chapter 7 or 13	$60
	Chapter 11	$250
	Chapter 12	$100
Cross Appeal Docketing fee		$100

1991 Amendments: Pub. L. No. 102-140 (Departments of Commerce, Justice and State, the Judiciary, and Related Agencies Appropriations Act of 1992), signed into law October 28, 1991 and effective 60 days thereafter, amended 28 U.S.C. § 1930(a)(3) by increasing the filing fee for a case commenced under chapter 11 to $600. Pub. L. No. 102-140 also amended § 1930(a)(6) by increasing the quarterly fees paid to the United States trustee.

Miscellaneous Legislation Relating to Determination of Fees for Electronic Access to Information

Section 303 of Pub. L. No. 102-140 (Department of Commerce, Justice and State, the Judiciary, and Related Agencies Appropriations Act), enacted October 28, 1991 and effective 60 days thereafter, provides for the Judicial Conference to prescribe reasonable fees under 28 U.S.C. § 1930 for access to information available through automatic data processing equipment.

1992 Amendments: A miscellaneous fee of $30 per chapter 7 or 13 case has been approved by the Judicial Conference pursuant to 28 U.S.C. § 1930(b), effective December 1, 1992. Although it is not part of the filing fee, the fee will be charged at the commencement of the case and replaces the 50 cents ($.50) per notice fee.

Case Annotations

A bankruptcy court is not considered "a court of the United States" under 28 U.S.C. § 451 and does not have the authority to waive fees imposed under 28 U.S.C. § 1915(a). *In re* Perroton, 958 F.2d 889, 26 C.B.C.2d 890 (9th Cir. 1992).

Under Section 302(e)(3) of the 1986 Act, quarterly fees under 28 U.S.C. § 1930(a)(6) must be assessed for pending cases in pilot program districts from the general effective date of the Act, November 26, 1986, until the plan is confirmed. The assessment of a quarterly fee to fund the United States Trustee Program consistent with the exercise of authority by the trustee over a case satisfies the rational basis test of the equal protection clause of the 14th Amendment. Additionally, the filing date of a debtor's petition does not create a tangible property right such that the imposition of a quarterly fee on pending bankruptcy cases is an unconstitutional taking of property under the 5th Amendment. *In re* Prines, 867 F.2d 478, 20 C.B.C.2d 500 (8th Cir. 1989).

The requirement that a creditor pay a $60 filing fee upon the initiation of an adversary proceeding is not a violation of the Constitution's due process clause and does not unduly burden a creditor's access to the judicial process when the creditor has the ability to pay the fee and is seeking to preserve contractual rather than fundamental rights and the government has a legitimate interest in requiring the filing fee. Otasco, Inc. v. United States (*In re* South), 689 F.2d 162, 7 C.B.C.2d 216 (10th Cir. 1982).

The words "any estate realized" in the Judicial Conference's fee schedule should be read to mean realized from any source, not just recoveries in the underlying adversary proceedings for purposes of payment of filing fees. United States of America v. The Phoenix Group, Inc. (*In re* The Phoenix Group, Inc.), 15 C.B.C.2d 1247 (9th Cir., B.A.P., 1986).

When a creditor, a debtor and a trustee have entered into a stipulation which obviates the commencement of an adversary proceeding, the filing fee to be paid is the fee for filing a stipulation and not the fee that is required to commence an adversary proceeding. *In re* Mullins, 4 C.B.C.2d 460 (9th Cir., B.A.P., 1980).

When a debtor has proven that it has no assets to pay quarterly United States trustee fees, then it has shown "cause" for dismissal of the case. In the Matter of Markhon Indus., Inc., 21 C.B.C.2d 425 (B. Ct., N.D. Ind. 1989).

In forma pauperis relief from filing fees is available in all bankruptcy proceedings with the exception of the filing of the original bankruptcy petition. Palestino v. Palestino (*In re* Palestino), 2 C.B.C.2d 440 (B. Ct., M.D. Fla. 1980).

References

1 *Collier on Bankruptcy* ch. 3 (Matthew Bender 15th ed.).

1 *Collier Bankruptcy Manual* ch. 3 (Matthew Bender 3d ed.).

1 *Collier Bankruptcy Practice Guide* ch. 16 (Matthew Bender).

UNITED STATES TRUSTEES (CHAPTER 39)

Editors' Note: The Bankruptcy Judges, United States Trustees, and Family Farmer Bankruptcy Act of 1986, Pub. L. No. 99–554, established a permanent United States trustee system. Section 302(d) of the 1986 Amendments provides different effective dates for the amendments relating to the United States trustee system. This amendment became effective in a judicial district when that district became part of the nationwide United States trustee system; except for the districts in Alabama and North Carolina, all judicial districts now have United States trustees.

28 U.S.C. § 581.   United States trustees.

(a) The Attorney General shall appoint one United States trustee for each of the following regions composed of Federal judicial districts (without regard to section 451):

(1) The judicial districts established for the States of Maine, Massachusetts, New Hampshire, and Rhode Island.

(2) The judicial districts established for the States of Connecticut, New York, and Vermont.

(3) The judicial districts established for the States of Delaware, New Jersey, and Pennsylvania.

(4) The judicial districts established for the States of Maryland, North Carolina, South Carolina, Virginia, and West Virginia and for the District of Columbia.

(5) The judicial districts established for the States of Louisiana and Mississippi.

(6) The Northern District of Texas and the Eastern District of Texas.

(7) The Southern District of Texas and the Western District of Texas.

(8) The judicial districts established for the States of Kentucky and Tennessee.

(9) The judicial districts established for the States of Michigan and Ohio.

(10) The Central District of Illinois and the Southern District of Illinois; and the judicial districts established for the State of Indiana.

(11) The Northern District of Illinois; and the judicial districts established for the State of Wisconsin.

(12) The judicial districts established for the States of Minnesota, Iowa, North Dakota, and South Dakota.

(13) The judicial districts established for the States of Arkansas, Nebraska, and Missouri.

(14) The District of Arizona.

(15) The Southern District of California; and the judicial districts established for the State of Hawaii, and for Guam and the Commonwealth of the Northern Mariana Islands.

(16) The Central District of California.

(17) The Eastern District of California and the Northern District of California; and the judicial district established for the State of Nevada.

(18) The judicial districts established for the States of Alaska, Idaho (exclusive of Yellowstone National Park), Montana (exclusive of Yellowstone National Park), Oregon, and Washington.

(19) The judicial districts established for the States of Colorado, Utah, and Wyoming (including those portions of Yellowstone National Park situated in the States of Montana and Idaho).

(20) The judicial districts established for the States of Kansas, New Mexico, and Oklahoma.

(21) The judicial districts established for the States of Alabama, Florida, and Georgia and for the Commonwealth of Puerto Rico and the Virgin Islands of the United States.

(b) Each United States trustee shall be appointed for a term of five years. On the expiration of his term, a United States trustee shall continue to perform the duties of his office until his successor is appointed and qualifies.

(c) Each United States trustee is subject to removal by the Attorney General.

Comment

1986 Amendments: The Bankruptcy Judges, United States Trustees, and Family Farmer Act of 1986, Pub. L. No. 99–554, established a permanent and, except for Alabama and North Carolina, nationwide United States trustee system. A number of changes were made in 28 U.S.C. § 581. Under subsection (a), the Attorney General is required to appoint one United States trustee for specified regions each of which is composed of several judicial districts. Under subsection (b), the term of office of the United States trustee is reduced from seven to five years. The words "for cause" were deleted from subsection (c) which provides that each United States trustee is subject to removal by the Attorney General.

Section 102(9) of the Code provides that "United States trustee" includes a designee of the United States trustee.

To conform to the 1986 Amendments, sections of the Bankruptcy Code were amended to require notice to the United States trustee. Additionally, Rule 2002(k) provides that most of the notices required to be given to creditors by Rule 2002(a), all notices required by Rule 2002(b), and most of the notices required by Rule 2002(f) be transmitted to the United States trustee. The United States trustee also receives notice of all applications for compensation and reimbursement for expense. The United States trustee, however, may request that he or she not receive certain notices.

Bankruptcy Rule 9034 provides that (unless the United States trustee requests otherwise) any entity filing a pleading, motion, or objection relating to matters specified in the Rule, shall transmit a copy thereof to the United States trustee within the time required by the Rules for service of the paper.

28 U.S.C. § 582.   Assistant United States trustees.

(a) The Attorney General may appoint one or more assistant United States trustees in any region when the public interest so requires.

(b) Each assistant United States trustee is subject to removal by the Attorney General.

Comment

1986 Amendments: Section 582(a) of title 28 was amended by providing that one or more assistant United States trustees may be appointed by the Attorney General for each *region*. The words "for cause" were deleted from subsection (b) relating to removal of an assistant United States trustee by the Attorney General.

28 U.S.C. § 583.   Oath of office.   Each United States trustee and assistant United States trustee, before taking office, shall take an oath to execute faithfully his duties.

28 U.S.C. § 584.   Official stations.   The Attorney General may determine the official stations of the United States trustees and assistant United States trustees within the regions for which they were appointed.

28 U.S.C. § 585.   Vacancies.

(a) The Attorney General may appoint an acting United States trustee for a region in which the office of the United States trustee is vacant. The individual so appointed may serve until the date on which the vacancy if filled by appointment under section 581 of this title or by designation under subsection (b) of this section.

(b) The Attorney General may designate a United States trustee to serve in not more than two regions for such time as the public interest requires.

Comment

1986 Amendments: Section 585(a) of title 28 was amended to provide that an acting United States trustee appointed to serve in a region in which a vacancy exists, may serve until the vacancy is filled. A new subsection (b) provides that the Attorney General may designate a

United States trustee to serve in not more than two regions "for such time as the public interest requires."

28 U.S.C. § 586.   Duties; supervision by Attorney General.

(a) Each United States trustee, within the region for which such United States trustee is appointed, shall—

(1) establish, maintain, and supervise a panel of private trustees that are eligible and available to serve as trustees in cases under chapter 7 of title 11;

(2) serve as and perform the duties of a trustee in a case under title 11 when required under title 11 to serve as trustee in such a case;

(3) supervise the administration of cases and trustees in cases under chapter 7, 11, or 13 of title 11 by, whenever the United States trustee considers it to be appropriate—

(A) monitoring applications for compensation and reimbursement filed under section 330 of title 11 and, whenever the United States trustee deems it to be appropriate, filing with the court comments with respect to any of such applications;

(B) monitoring plans and disclosure statements filed in cases under chapter 11 of title 11 and filing with the court, in connection with hearings under sections 1125 and 1128 of such title, comments with respect to such plans and disclosure statements;

(C) monitoring plans filed under chapters 12 and 13 of title 11 and filing with the court, in connection with hearings under sections 1224, 1229, 1324, and 1329 of such title, comments with respect to such plans;

(D) taking such action as the United States trustee deems to be appropriate to ensure that all reports, schedules, and fees required to be filed under title 11 and this title by the debtor are properly and timely filed;

(E) monitoring creditors' committees appointed under title 11;

(F) notifying the appropriate United States attorney of matters which relate to the occurrence of any action which may constitute a crime under the laws of the United States and, on the request of the United States attorney, assisting the United States attorney in carrying out prosecutions based on such action;

(G) monitoring the progress of cases under title 11 and taking such actions as the United States trustee deems to be appropriate to prevent undue delay in such progress; and

(H) monitoring applications filed under section 327 of title 11 and, whenever the United States trustee deems it to be appropriate, filing with the court comments with respect to the approval of such applications;

(4) deposit or invest under section 345 of title 11 money received as trustee in cases under title 11;

(5) perform the duties prescribed for the United States trustee under title 11 and this title, and such duties consistent with title 11 and this title as the Attorney General may prescribe; and

(6) make such reports as the Attorney General directs.

(b) If the number of cases under chapter 12 or 13 of title 11 commenced in a particular region so warrants, the United States trustee for such region may, subject to the approval of the Attorney General, appoint one or more individuals to serve as standing trustee, or designate one or more assistant United States trustees to serve in cases under such chapter. The United States trustee for such region shall supervise any such individual appointed as standing trustee in the performance of the duties of standing trustee.

(c) Each United States trustee shall be under the general supervision of the Attorney General, who shall provide general coordination and assistance to the United States trustees.

(d) The Attorney General shall prescribe by rule qualifications for membership on the panels established by United States trustees under paragraph (a)(1) of this section, and qualifications for appointment under subsection (b) of this section to serve as standing trustee in cases under chapter 12 or 13 of title 11. The Attorney General may not require that an individual be an attorney in order to qualify for appointment under subsection (b) of this section to serve as standing trustee in cases under chapter 12 or 13 of title 11.

(e)(1) The Attorney General, after consultation with a United States trustee that has appointed an individual under subsection (b) of this section to serve as standing trustee in cases under chapter 12 or 13 of title 11, shall fix—

(A) a maximum annual compensation for such individual consisting of —

(i) an amount not to exceed the highest annual rate of basic pay in effect for level V of the Executive Schedule; and

(ii) the cash value of employment benefits comparable to the employment benefits provided by the United States to individuals who are employed by the United States at the same rate of basic pay to perform similar services during the same period of time; and

(B) a percentage fee not to exceed—

(i) in the case of a debtor who is not a family farmer, ten percent; or

(ii) in the case of a debtor who is a family farmer, the sum of—

(I) not to exceed ten percent of the payments made under the plan of such debtor, with respect to payments in an aggregate amount not to exceed $450,000; and

(II) three percent of payments made under the plan of such debtor, with respect to payments made after the aggregate amount of payments made under the plan exceeds $450,000;

based on such maximum annual compensation and the actual, neccessary expenses incurred by such individual as standing trustee.

(2) Such individual shall collect such percentage fee from all payments received by such individual under plans in the cases under chapter 12 or 13 of title 11 for which such individual serves as standing trustee. Such individual shall pay to the United States trustee, and the United States

trustee shall deposit in the United States Trustee System Fund—

(A) any amount by which the actual compensation of such individual exceeds 5 per centum upon all payments received under plans in cases under chapter 12 or 13 of title 11 for which such individual serves as standing trustee; and

(B) any amount by which the percentage for all such cases exceeds—

(i) such individual's actual compensation for such cases, as adjusted under subparagraph (A) of paragraph (1); plus

(ii) the actual, necessary expenses incurred by such individual as standing trustee in such cases. Subject to the approval of the Attorney General, any or all of the interest earned from the deposit of payments under plans by such individual may be utilized to pay actual, necessary expenses without regard to the percentage limitation contained in subparagraph (d)(1)(B) of this section.

Comment

1986 Amendments: The 1986 Act amended section 586(a) of title 28 by listing in paragraph (3)(A)–(H) the supervisory powers the United States trustee may exercise whenever such trustee considers it to be appropriate. The United States trustee may monitor compensation applications and plans filed under chapters 11, 12 and 13; take steps to ensure that all reports, schedules and fees are properly and timely filed; notify the United States Attorney of actions that may constitute a crime; monitor the progress of cases under the Code; take action to prevent undue delay; and monitor applications filed under section 327 of the Code. In addition, subsection (a)(5) was amended to provide that the United States trustee perform such duties consistent with the Code as the Attorney General may prescribe.

Subsection (d) was amended to include chapter 12 cases within its scope.

Sections 1302(d) and (e) of the Bankruptcy Code, which dealt with appointment of standing trustees and the compensation of such trustees, has been deleted by the 1986 Act and the subject is covered in 28 U.S.C. § 586 as amended.

This section was amended to reflect the creation of a permanent United States trustee system. Section 302(d) of the 1986 Amendments provides different effective dates for the amendments relating to the United States trustee system. *See* Section 302 of the 1986 Amendments, as amended by Pub. L. No. 101–650 (1990), reprinted herein under "Selected Provisions of the Bankruptcy Judges, United States Trustees, and Family Farmer Bankruptcy Act of 1986," regarding effective dates generally.

To conform to the 1986 Amendments, many sections of the Bankruptcy Code were amended to require notice to the United States trustee. Rule 2002(k) provides that most of the notices required to be given to creditors by Rule 2002(a), all notices required by Rule 2002(b), and most of the notices required by Rule 2002(f) be transmitted to the United States trustee. The United States trustee also receives notice of all applications for compensation and reimbursement for expense. The United States trustee, however, may request that he or she not receive certain notices.

Bankruptcy Rule 9034 provides that (unless the United State trustee requests otherwise) any entity filing a pleading, motion, or objection relating to matters specified in the Rule, shall transmit a copy thereof to the United States trustee within the time required by the Rules for service of the paper.

1990 Amendments: The Treasury, Postal Service and General Government Appropriations Act of 1990, Pub. L. No. 101–509 (effective fiscal year 1991) amended section 586(e)(1)(A) of title 28 regarding the compensation of standing trustees. Pub. L. No. 101–509 provides that this amendment applies to any trustee to whom the provisions of Section 302(d)(3) of the Bankruptcy Judges, United States Trustees, and Family Farmer Bankruptcy Act of 1986 (Pub. L. No. 99–554) are applicable; thus, the amendment applies to all standing trustees, including those serving in the judicial districts in Alabama and North Carolina.

Case Annotations

Granting general standing to the United States trustee to raise issues that were implicitly reserved by section 1325(b) to the trustee and unsecured creditors is not necessary to achieve the purpose of the United States trustee program to accomplish the separation of judicial and administrative functions that formerly were performed by the bankruptcy court. *In re* Eaton, 25 C.B.C.2d 430 (B. Ct., S.D. Iowa 1991).

The bankruptcy court does not have the authority, under the trustee compensation scheme set up by Congress, to review or alter the statutory fees awarded pursuant to 28 U.S.C. § 586(e)(2). *In re* Savage, 16 C.B.C.2d 859 (D.R.I. 1986).

Although a United States trustee is not clearly granted party in interest status in all situations under the Bankruptcy Code, the thrust of the various Code sections and the Congressional intent is that the

United States trustee be accorded party in interest status with respect to administrative responsibilities. *In re* A-1 Trash Pick-Up, Inc., 14 C.B.C.2d 1145 (E.D. Va.), *aff'd*, 802 F.2d 774, 15 C.B.C.2d 1337 (4th Cir. 1986).

While the United States trustee's position is not controlling on the issue of whether additional committees should be appointed, the United States trustee's views are entitled to some degree of deference. *In re* Orfa Corp. of Philadelphia, 24 C.B.C.2d 1280 (B. Ct., E.D. Pa. 1990).

The duties and powers of the United States trustee include the power to supervise the administration of chapter 7 cases by reviewing fee applications, making certain that reports are filed, and taking action to avoid delay in case administration. The United States trustee is not empowered, however, to adjudicate matters of law as the assumption of such a role would be in violation of the Constitutional doctrine of separation of powers. *In re* Johnson, 23 C.B.C.2d 217 (B. Ct., N.D. Cal. 1990).

The United States trustee has the authority to oversee the the administration of the estate and monitor applications for compensation; thus, his objection to an application filed by a panel trustee will not subject him to disqualification. *In re* Southern Tier Energy Products, Inc., 22 C.B.C.2d 1204 (B. Ct., M.D. Pa. 1989).

When a chapter 13 trustee will only receive the net equity, if any, from the proceeds of the sale of property by a debtor the trustee may only be paid a percentage fee on that net equity. *In re* Bettger, 21 C.B.C.2d 1104 (B. Ct., D. Or. 1989).

A chapter 12 debtor may be permitted to pay directly secured creditors and administrative attorneys' fees pursuant to a chapter 12 plan, and when direct payments are authorized by the court such payments will not be subject to the trustee's statutory percentage fee established by 28 U.S.C. § 586(e). In the Matter of Pianowski, 19 C.B.C.2d 1102 (B. Ct., W.D. Mich. 1988).

Payments on all impaired claims are subject to the trustee's percentage fee. In the Matter of Logemann, 19 C.B.C.2d 926 (B. Ct., S.D. Iowa 1988).

Reading chapter 12 and 28 U.S.C. § 586(e), as amended in 1986, together, the issue of whether payments are "under" or "outside" a plan is moot; the critical issue is whether the trustee receives the payment, and if not, no fee can be allowed. *In re* Land, 18 C.B.C.2d 348 (B. Ct., D. Colo. 1988).

A trustee is to be paid commissions only on monies that he actually receives pursuant to the plan. *In re* Wright, 18 C.B.C.2d 413 (B. Ct., W.D. Va. 1988).

Under a chapter 12 plan, a debtor may make direct payments to secured creditors holding modified claims although such would reduce the trustee's commissions. *In re* Crum, 18 C.B.C.2d 1090 (B. Ct., N.D. Fla. 1988).

The standing chapter 12 trustee is entitled to a percentage fee of all payments made under a chapter 12 plan. All payments to impaired claimholders made during the term of the plan, whether disbursed by the debtor or the trustee, are considered to be payments made under the plan and are subject to the trustee's percentage fees. *In re* Rott, 17 C.B.C.2d 381 (B. Ct., D.N.D. 1987).

A chapter 12 trustee in a United States trustee district, like one appointed under chapter 13, is entitled to reasonable compensation as specified by the Attorney General of the United States. Such compensation cannot be amended or abrogated in a chapter 12 plan. *In re* Citrowske, 16 C.B.C.2d 1228 (B. Ct., D. Minn. 1987).

Rather than to apply automatically the statutory percentage fee to current mortgage payments disbursed by a debtor, even though those payments are made "under the plan," the court should allow the trustee's compensation for services in an amount commensurate with the reasonable value of those services. *In re* Tartaglia, 14 C.B.C.2d 1314 (B. Ct., D.R.I. 1986).

An important function of the United States trustee in administering a bankruptcy case is to review the fee arrangement between a debtor and counsel for the debtor. In the Matter of Wilson, 4 C.B.C.2d 1142 (B. Ct., S.D.N.Y. 1981).

References

Brothers, *Disagreement Among the Districts: Why Section 327(a) of the Bankruptcy Code Needs Help,* 138 U. Pa. L. Rev. 1733 (1990).

28 U.S.C. § 587.   Salaries.   Subject to sections 5315 through 5317 of title 5, the Attorney General shall fix the annual salaries of United States trustees and assistant United States trustees at rates of compensation not in excess of the rate of basic compensation provided for Executive Level IV of the Executive Schedule set forth in section 5315 of title 5, United States Code.

Comment

1986 Amendments: Section 587 of title 28 was amended to provide the method of fixing the salaries of United States trustees and assistant United States trustees by the Attorney General.

28 U.S.C. § 588.   Expenses.   Necessary office expenses of the United States trustee shall be allowed when authorized by the Attorney General.

28 U.S.C. § 589.   Staff and other employees.   The United States trustee may employ staff and other employees on approval of the Attorney General.

Comment

The amendments made by section 224 of Pub. L. No. 95–598 took effect on October 1, 1979. See Section 402 under "Transition," *infra*.

References

1 *Collier on Bankruptcy* ch. 6 (Matthew Bender 15th ed.).

1 *Collier Bankruptcy Manual* ch. 6 (Matthew Bender 3d ed.).

Brothers, *Disagreement Among the Districts: Why Section 327(a) of the Bankruptcy Code Needs Help,* 138 U. Pa. L. Rev. 1733 (1990).

Greiman, *An Overview of the United States Trustee Pilot Program,* 1984 Ann. Surv. Bankr. L. 133.

Stanton, *The United States Trustee System: A Time for Assessment,* 90 Com. L.J. 90 (1985).

The U.S. Trustee System: What Practitioners Think, 4 Com. L. Bull. 7 (May/June 1989).

28 U.S.C. § 589a.   United States Trustee System Fund.

(a) There is hereby established in the Treasury of the United States a special fund to be known as the "United States Trustee System Fund" (hereinafter in this section referred to as the "Fund"). Monies in the Fund shall be available to the Attorney General without fiscal year limitation in such amounts as may be specified in appropriations Acts for the following purposes in connection with the operations of United States trustees—

(1) salaries and related employee benefits;

(2) travel and transportation;

(3) rental of space;

(4) communication, utilities, and miscellaneous computer charges;

(5) security investigations and audits;

(6) supplies, books and other materials for legal research;

(7) furniture and equipment;

(8) miscellaneous services, including those obtained by contract; and

(9) printing.

(b) There shall be deposited in the Fund—

(1) one-fourth of the fees collected under section 1930(a)(1) of this title;

(2) 50 per centum of the fees collected under section 1930(a)(3) of this title;

(3) one-half of the fees collected under section 1930(a)(4) of this title;

(4) one-half of the fees collected under section 1930(a)(5);

(5) 60 per centum of the fees collected under section 1930(a)(6) of this title;

(6) three-fourths of the fees collected under the last sentence of section 1930(a) of this title; and

(7) the compensation of trustees received under section 330(d) of title 11 by the clerks of the bankruptcy courts.

(c)(1) Except as provided in paragraph (2), amounts in the Fund which are not currently needed for the purposes specified in subsection (a) shall be kept on deposit or invested in obligations of, or guaranteed by, the United States.

(2) On November 1, 1989, and on November 1 of each year thereafter, the Secretary of the Treasury shall transfer into the general fund of the Treasury the amount, if any, in the Fund that exceeds 110 percent of—

(A) the amount appropriated for the entire current fiscal year for the purposes specified in subsection (a), or

(B) if no appropriation has been made for the entire current fiscal year, the annual equivalent of the aggregate amount appropriated to date for the current fiscal year for the purposes specified in subsection (a).

(d)(1) The Attorney General shall transmit to the Congress, not later than 120 days after the end of each fiscal year, a detailed report on the amounts deposited in the Fund and a description of the expenditures made under this section.

(2) If for each fiscal year in any period of 2 successive fiscal years—

(A) the aggregate amount deposited under subsection (b) in the Fund exceeds 110 percent of expenditures for the purposes specified in subsection (a), or

(B) the costs incurred for the purposes specified in subsection (a) exceed the aggregate amount deposited under subsection (b) in the Fund,

then the Attorney General shall include in such report a recommendation regarding the manner in which the fees payable under section 1930(a) of title 28, United States Code, may be modified to cause the annual amount deposited in the Fund to more closely approximate the annual amount expended from the Fund.

(e) There are authorized to be appropriated to the Fund for any fiscal year such sums as may be necessary to supplement amounts deposited under subsection (b) for the purposes specified in subsection (a).

(f) For the purpose of recovering the cost of services of the United States Trustee System, there shall be deposited as offsetting collections of the appropriation "United States Trustee System Fund," to remain available until expended, the following—

(1) 16.7 per centum of the fees collected under section 1930(a)(3) of this title;

(2) 40 per centum of the fees collected under section 1930(a)(6) of this title.

Comment

1986 Amendments: 28 U.S.C. § 589a, establishing a United States Trustee System Fund, was added to title 28 by the 1986 Amendments.

1989 Amendments: Section 406(c) of the Judiciary Appropriation Act of 1990 (Pub. L. No. 101-162) amended 28 U.S.C. § 589a(b)(1) by striking out "one-third" and inserting in lieu thereof "one-fourth."

1991 Amendments: Pub. L. No. 102-149 (Departments of Commerce, Justice and State, the Judiciary, and Related Appropriations Act), enacted October 28, 1991 and effective 60 days thereafter, amended 28 U.S.C. § 589a by replacing "three-fifths" with "50 per centum" in section 589a(b)(2), by replacing "all" with "60 per centum" in section 589a(b)(5), and by adding a new section 589a(f).

ARBITRATION (CHAPTER 44)

Editors' Note: The Judicial Improvements and Access to Justice Act, Pub. L. No. 100-702, enacted on November 19, 1988, contained a number of provisions recommended by the Judicial Conference for the purpose of improvement of judicial administration. Title IX was designed to provide express statutory authorization for ongoing arbitration programs in ten district courts and to permit the Judicial Conference to expand the program to ten additional districts for pilot arbitration projects on the consent of the parties.

28 U.S.C. § 651. Authorization of arbitration.

(a) Authority of Certain District Courts.—Each United States district court described in section 658 may authorize by local rule the use of arbitration in any civil action, including an adversary proceeding in bankruptcy. A district court described in section 658(1) may refer any such action to arbitration as set forth in section 652(a). A district court described in section 658(2) may refer only such actions to arbitration as are set forth in section 652(a)(1)(A).

(b) Title 9 Not Affected.—This chapter shall not affect title 9.

Comment

Title IX of Pub. L. No. 100-702 established on a five-year experimental basis both consensual and mandatory arbitration in selected federal judicial districts for resolution of certain civil actions including adversary proceedings in bankruptcy. Title IX of the law added Chapter 44 to title 28 United States Code, which is comprised of §§ 651–658.

The district courts in the experimental districts may, by local rule, authorize the use of arbitration in any civil action or adversary proceeding in bankruptcy if the parties consent. 28 U.S.C. §§ 651, 652(a)(1)(A). The consent must be "freely and knowingly obtained, and no party or attorney may be prejudiced for refusing" to consent. 28 U.S.C. § 652(d).

In addition, district courts in the Northern District of California, Middle District of Florida, Western District of Michigan, Western District of Missouri, District of New Jersey, Eastern District of New York, Middle District of North Carolina, Western District of Oklahoma, Eastern District of Pennsylvania, and Western District of Texas may *require* arbitration if only money damages are sought in the amount of $100,000 or less. 28 U.S.C. § 652(a)(1)(B). It has been suggested that this mandatory feature should not apply to adversary proceedings in bankruptcy for the following reason: section 652(a)(1)(B) speaks only to "any civil action"; section 652(a)(1)(A) (arbitration by consent), refers to "any civil action (including any adversary proceeding in bankruptcy)"; and the general provision, section 651(a), which establishes the authority in the relevant district courts, also refers to "any civil action, including an adversary proceeding in bankruptcy." Accordingly, the absence of a reference to adversary proceedings in section 652(a)(1)(B) should mean that Congress meant to and did exclude such proceedings from the possibility of *requiring* arbitration.

In addition to the district courts listed above, the courts in ten other judicial districts may authorize the use of arbitration. These districts are to be approved by the Judicial Conference which shall give notice of such approval to the Federal Judicial Center and the public. 28 U.S.C. § 658(2). These courts may not *require* arbitration.

The other sections cover such areas as trial de novo, payment of arbitrators' fees when trial de novo is unsuccessful, replacement on the calendar when trial de novo is requested, certification of arbitrators, powers of arbitrators, etc. Also included is authority for these district courts to provide by local rule procedures for exemption on motion or sua sponte, any "case" from arbitration "if the objectives of arbitration would not be realized because the case involves complex or novel legal issues," legal issues predominate over issues of fact, or "for other good cause." 28 U.S.C. § 652(c).

GENERAL PROVISIONS APPLICABLE TO COURT OFFICERS AND EMPLOYEES (CHAPTER 57)

28 U.S.C. § 959.   Trustees and receivers suable; management; State laws.

(a) Trustees, receivers or managers of any property, including debtors in possession, may be sued, without leave of the court appointing them, with respect to any of their acts or transactions in carrying on business connected with such property. Such actions shall be subject to the general equity power of such court so far as the same may be necessary to the ends of justice, but this shall not deprive a litigant of his right to trial by jury.

(b) Except as provided in section 1166 of title 11, a trustee, receiver or manager appointed in any cause pending in any court of the United States, including a debtor in possession, shall manage and operate the property in his possession as such trustee, receiver or manager according to the requirements of the valid laws of the State in which such property is situated, in the same manner that the owner or possessor thereof would be bound to do if in possession thereof.

Comment

28 U.S.C. § 959(b) was amended by section 235 of the Bankruptcy Reform Act of 1978, Pub. L. 95–598, to add the except clause at its beginning. Section 1166 is in the railroad reorganization subchapter of chapter 11 of title 11. This amendment took effect on October 1, 1979; *see* section 402(c) of the Act at "Transition."

Case Annotations

Neither the doctrine of intergovernmental tax immunity nor federal law bars the imposition of a state sales tax on the trustee's liquidation sale of property of the estate or the imposition of a state use tax on the purchaser's lessees. California State Board of Equalization v. Sierra

Summit, Inc., 490 U.S. 844, 109 S. Ct. 2228, 104 L. Ed. 2d 910, 20 C.B.C.2d 1501 (1989).

A debtor-landlord may reject leases with residential tenants and be released from the contractual obligations undertaken in those leases but rejection does not exempt the debtor from compliance with obligations imposed on all landlords by a local housing code relating to habitability. Saravia v. 1736 18th Street, N.W., 844 F.2d 823, 18 C.B.C.2d 832 (D.C. Cir. 1988).

A chapter 7 liquidating trustee may not maintain or possess hazardous property of the estate in continuous violation of state environmental laws. Lancaster v. Tenn. (*In re* Wall Tube & Metal Prods. Co.), 831 F.2d 118, 17 C.B.C.2d 736 (6th Cir. 1987).

When state laws forbid the trustee of a bankruptcy case to abandon hazardous waste, the cleanup of the hazardous waste remains the responsibility of the estate. *In re* Stevens, 16 C.B.C.2d 253 (D. Me. 1987).

When, at the time of a trustee's appointment, property belonging to the estate is already environmentally damaged and the trustee lacks funds for a cleanup, a court may find, on the facts, that a proposed settlement agreement among the trustee, New York State, a creditor and a third-party purchaser complies with the goal of the state's environmental statutes when such agreement provides for sale of the property and use of a portion of such proceeds for cleanup and limits the estate's liability to a reasonable portion of the assets which will be made available to it. *In re* Paris Industries Corp., 21 C.B.C.2d 1275 (B. Ct., D. Me. 1989).

A debtor's estate is not immune from the Ohio real estate tax law, which is *in rem* in nature, when the debtor files a petition for relief because the estate's protection during administration is derived from federal authority. In the Matter of Mansfield Tire & Rubber Co., 18 C.B.C.2d 1138 (B. Ct., N.D. Ohio 1987).

A chapter 11 trustee should be given an opportunity at trial to show evidence that an action filed against the estate could unduly impede the administration of the estate before the court decides whether to enjoin that action. Baptist Medical Center of New York v. Singh (*In re* Baptist Medical Center of New York), 18 C.B.C.2d 1 (B. Ct., E.D.N.Y. 1987).

A debtor in possession may not reject its leases with rent-controlled tenants when to do so would bring the debtor into noncompliance with 28 U.S.C. § 959(b) and section 362(b)(4), which stipulate that a debtor may not ignore state laws embodying police and regulatory provisions, despite the debtor's argument that rejection is necessary to an effective reorganization. Any action taken by the debtor must be in accordance with such laws. Friarton Estates Corp. v. The City of New York (*In re* Friarton Estates Corp.), 15 C.B.C.2d 779 (B. Ct., S.D.N.Y. 1986).

A trustee is not compelled to comply with a local Housing Maintenance Code after the rejection of tenant leases pursuant to the business judgment test when that statute conflicts with the express statutory policy codified in section 365(h); as the tenants may file unsecured claims for damages due to rejection, to require the trustee to, nevertheless, provide services, would be to prefer the tenants over other unsecured creditors. *In re* Stable Mews Assocs., Inc., 11 C.B.C.2d 20 (B. Ct., S.D.N.Y. 1984).

References

1 *Collier on Bankruptcy* ch. 3 (Matthew Bender 15th ed.).

1 *Collier Bankruptcy Manual* ch. 3 (Matthew Bender 3d ed.).

Tiller, *Personal Liability of Trustees and Receivers in Bankruptcy,* 53 Am. Bankr. L.J. 75 (1979).

Zabarauskas, *Bankruptcy Law: Toxic Bankruptcy and Life After Kovacs and Midlantic,* 1987 Ann. Sur. Am. L. 749 (1989).

28 U.S.C. § 960.   Tax liability. Any officers and agents conducting any business under authority of a United States court shall be subject to all Federal, State and local taxes applicable to such business to the same extent as if it were conducted by an individual or corporation.

Case Annotations

28 U.S.C. § 960 does not proscribe the imposition of a state sales or use tax on a bankruptcy liquidation sale; nothing in the plain language of this statute, its legislative history, or the structure of the Bankruptcy Code indicates a Congressional intent to the contrary. California State Board of Equalization v. Sierra Summit, Inc., 490 U.S. 844, 109 S. Ct. 2228, 104 L. Ed. 2d 910, 20 C.B.C.2d 1501 (1989).

BANKRUPTCY RULES (CHAPTER 131)

Sec.
2075. Bankruptcy rules.

28 U.S.C. § 2075. Bankruptcy rules. The Supreme Court shall have the power to prescribe by general rules, the forms of process, writs, pleadings, and motions, and the practice and procedure in cases under title 11.

Such rules shall not abridge, enlarge, or modify any substantive right.

Such rules shall not take effect until they have been reported to Congress by the Chief Justice at or after the beginning of a regular session thereof but not later than the first day of May and until the expiration of ninety days after they have been thus reported.

Comment

The rule-making power is retained but as amended by section 247 of the Bankruptcy Reform Act of 1978, 28 U.S.C. § 2075 does not permit the rules to conflict with or supersede any statutory provision. Section 247 of the Act took effect on the enactment date, November 6, 1978; *see* section 402(d) of the Act at "Transition," at p. 602 *infra*.

Bankruptcy Rule 9009 provides that the Official Forms prescribed by the Judicial Conference of the United States shall be observed and used with alterations as may be appropriate. Forms may be combined and their contents rearranged to permit economies in their use. The Director of the Administrative Office of the United States Courts may issue additional forms for use under the Code. The 1991 Amendments added this sentence: "The forms shall be construed to be consistent with these rules and the Code." The Advisory Committee Note states that Rule 9009 is amended to clarify that local court rules may not prohibit or limit the use of the Official Forms.

Acting on that authority, the Director of the Administrative Office of the United States Courts has promulgated forms and instructions in two volumes. Volume I is entitled "Forms and Instructions for the Courts" and Volume II is entitled "Forms and Instructions for the Public."

Bankruptcy Rule 9029 provides that the district court by action of a majority of the judges may make and amend rules governing practice and procedure in all cases and proceedings within the district court's bankruptcy jurisdiction which are not inconsistent with the Bankruptcy Rules and which do not prohibit or limit the use of the Official Forms. A district court may authorize the bankruptcy judges to make rules of practice and procedure not inconsistent with the Rules.

1986 Amendments: Section 305 of the 1986 Act relates to the application of certain Bankruptcy Rules. Subsection (a) deals with rules relating to the United States trustee and the application of Part X of the Bankruptcy Rules. Subsection (b) provides that the Bankruptcy Rules shall apply to cases filed under chapter 12 of the Code, to the extent practicable and not inconsistent with the 1986 Act.

Case Annotations

In Minnesota, a local rule which provided that pursuant to Bankruptcy Rule 4007(c) in individual chapter 11 cases the time for filing a complaint to determine dischargeability of a debt pursuant to section 523(c) was extended to the same final date for filing a complaint objecting to discharge under Rule 4004(a) did not "abridge, enlarge, or modify any substantive right" granted by the Code in extending the time to file a complaint to determine the dischargeability of a particular debt. *In re* Falk, 20 C.B.C.2d 844 (B. Ct., D. Minn. 1989).

Since the Bankruptcy Rules shall not abridge, enlarge or modify any substantive right, the terms of the Bankruptcy Code prevail over conflicting terms in the rules. *In re* Roberts, 16 C.B.C.2d 498 (B. Ct., E.D. Mich. 1987).

The 30-day time limit on removal of cases pending elsewhere to the bankruptcy court does not abridge or modify substantive rights in the manner prohibited by 28 U.S.C. § 2075. James Green Constr. Co. v. Alton Telegraph Printing Co. (*In re* Alton Telegraph Printing Co.), 5 C.B.C.2d 672 (B. Ct., S.D. Ill. 1981).

References

1 *Collier on Bankruptcy* ch. 3 (Matthew Bender 15th ed.).

1 *Collier Bankruptcy Manual* ch. 3 (Matthew Bender 3d ed.).

Campbell and Harwell, *A Survey of the Rules of Bankruptcy Litigation,* 20 Hous Law. 20 (1983).

BANKRUPTCY CRIMES
TITLE 18 UNITED STATES CODE (CHAPTER 9)

18 U.S.C. § 151. Definition.* As used in this chapter, the term "debtor" means a debtor concerning whom a petition has been filed under title 11.

18 U.S.C. § 152. Concealment of assets—False oaths and claims—Bribery. Whoever knowingly and fraudulently conceals from a custodian, trustee, marshal, or other officer of the court charged with the control or custody of property, or from creditors in any case under title 11, any property belonging to the estate of a debtor; or

Whoever knowingly and fraudulently makes a false oath or account in or in relation to any case under title 11; or

Whoever knowingly and fraudulently makes a false declaration, certificate, verification, or statement under penalty of perjury as permitted under section 1746 of title 28, United States Code, in or in relation to any case under title 11; or

Whoever knowingly and fraudulently presents any false claim for proof against the estate of a debtor, or uses such claim in any case under title 11, personally, or by agent, proxy, or attorney, or as agent, proxy, or attorney; or

Whoever knowingly and fraudulently receives any material amount of property from a debtor after the filing of a case under title 11 with intent to defeat the provisions of title 11; or

---

* The following sections of 18 United States Code were amended by section 314 (in title III) of the Bankruptcy Reform Act of 1978, Pub. L. 95–598, effective October 1, 1979 (section 402(a) of the Act at "Transition.")

Whoever knowingly and fraudulently gives, offers, receives or attempts to obtain any money or property, remuneration, compensation, reward, advantage, or promise thereof, for acting or forbearing to act in any case under title 11; or

Whoever, either individually or as an agent or officer of any person or corporation, in contemplation of a case under title 11 by or against him or any other person or corporation, or with intent to defeat the provisions of title 11, knowingly and fraudulently transfers or conceals any of his property or the property of such other person or corporation; or

Whoever, after the filing of a case under title 11 or in contemplation thereof, knowingly and fraudulently conceals, destroys, mutilates, falsifies, or makes a false entry in any document affecting or relating to the property or affairs of a debtor; or

Whoever, after the filing of a case under title 11, knowingly and fraudulently withholds from a custodian, trustee, marshal, or other officer of the court entitled to its possession, any recorded information, including books, documents, records and papers, relating to the property or financial affairs of a debtor.

Shall be fined not more than $5,000 or imprisoned not more than five years, or both.

Comment

Since the passage of the Bankruptcy Reform Act of 1978, Pub. L. No. 95-598, 18 U.S.C. § 152 has been amended by the Anti-Drug Abuse Act of 1988, Pub. L. No. 100-690.

Case Annotations

There can be no violation of section 152 for acts taken with respect to property that is abandoned; upon abandonment of bankruptcy assets, title to those assets reverts back to the original owner as though the bankruptcy estate had never owned them. U.S. v. Grant, 946 F.2d 1, 25 C.B.C.2d 818 (1st Cir. 1991).

18 U.S.C. § 153.   Embezzlement by trustee or officer.

Whoever knowingly and fraudulently appropriates to his own use, embezzles, spends, or transfers any property or secretes or destroys any document belonging to the estate of a debtor, which came into his charge as trustee, custodian, marshal, or other officer of the court, shall be fined not more than $5,000 or imprisoned not more than five years, or both.

18 U.S.C. § 154. Adverse interest and conduct of officers.

Whoever, being a custodian, trustee, marshal, or other officer of the court, knowingly purchases, directly or indirectly, any property of the estate of which he is such officer in a case under title 11; or

Whoever being such officer, knowingly refuses to permit a reasonable opportunity for the inspection of the documents and accounts relating to the affairs of estates in his charge by parties in interest when directed by the court to do so—

Shall be fined not more than $500, and shall forfeit his office, which shall thereupon become vacant.

Case Annotations

An estate's former trustee is not barred, *per se,* from becoming a purchaser of assets of the bankruptcy estate; rather, the court should make a factual inquiry to determine if the former trustee has taken unfair advantage of confidential information he possessed by virtue of his former position as trustee. Gross v. Russo (*In re* Russo), 762 F.2d 239, 12 C.B.C.2d 1359 (2d Cir. 1985) (decided under the 1898 Act).

18 U.S.C. § 155. Fee agreements in cases under title 11 and receiverships. Whoever, being a party in interest, whether as a debtor, creditor, trustee or representative of any of them, or attorney for any such party in interest, in any receivership or case under title 11 in any United States court or under its supervision, knowingly and fraudulently enters into any agreement, express or implied, with another such party in interest or attorney for another such party in interest, for the purpose of fixing the fees or other compensation to be paid to any party in interest or to any attorney for any party in interest for services rendered in connection therewith, from the assets of the estate shall be fined not more than $5,000 or imprisoned not more than one year, or both.

(CHAPTER 96)

Racketeer Influenced And Corrupt Organizations

Sec.

1961. Definitions.

18 U.S.C. § 1961. Definitions. As used in this chapter [18 U.S.C. §§ 1961–1968]—

(1) "racketeering activity" means (A) any act or threat involving murder, kidnaping, gambling, arson, robbery, bribery, extortion, dealing in obscene matter, or dealing in narcotic or other dangerous drugs, which is chargeable under State law and punishable by imprisonment for more than one year; (B) any act which is indictable under any of the following provisions of title 18, United States Code: Section 201 (relating to bribery), section 224 (relating to sports bribery), sections 471, 472, and 473 (relating to counterfeiting), section 659 (relating to theft from interstate shipment) if the act indictable under section 659 is felonious, section 664 (relating to embezzlement from pension and welfare funds), sections 891–894 (relating to extortionate credit transactions), section 1029 (relating to fraud and related activity in connection with access devices), section 1084 (relating to the transmission of gambling information), section 1341 (relating to mail fraud), section 1343 (relating to wire fraud), section 1344 (relating to financial institution fraud), sections 1461–65 (relating to obscene matter), section 1503 (relating to obstruction of justice), section 1510 (relating to obstruction of criminal investigation), section 1511 (relating to the obstruction of State or local law enforcement), section 1512 (relating to tampering with a witness, victim, or an informant), section 1513 (relating to retaliating against a witness, victim, or informant), section 1951 (relating to interference with commerce, robbery, or extortion), section 1952 (relating to racketeering), section 1953 (relating to interstate transportation of wagering paraphernalia), section 1954 (relating to unlawful welfare fund payments), section 1955 (relating to the prohibition of illegal gambling businesses), section 1956 (relating to the laundering of monetary instruments), section 1957 (relating to engaging in monetary transactions in property derived from specified unlawful activity), section 1958 (relating to use of interstate commerce facilities in the commission of

murder-for-hire), sections 2312 and 2313 (relating to interstate transportation of stolen motor vehicles), sections 2314 and 2315 (relating to interstate transportation of stolen property), section 2321 (relating to trafficking in certain motor vehicles or motor vehicle parts), sections 2341–2346 (relating to traffic in contraband cigarettes), sections 2421–24 (relating to white slave traffic), (C) any act which is indictable under title 29, United States Code, section 186 (dealing with restrictions on payments and loans to labor organizations) or section 501(c) (relating to embezzlement from union funds), (D) any offense involving fraud connected with a case under title 11, fraud in the sale of securities, or the felonious manufacture, importation, receiving, concealment, buying, selling, or otherwise dealing in narcotic or other dangerous drugs, punishable under any law of the United States, or (E) any act which is indictable under the Currency and Foreign Transactions Reporting Act.

Comment

Since the passage of the Bankruptcy Reform Act of 1978, Pub. L. No. 95–598, 18 U.S.C. § 1961(1) has been amended by Cigarettes-Distribution-Racketeering, Pub. L. No. 95–575 (1978); Continuing Appropriations, 1985—Comprehensive Crime Control Act of 1984, Pub. L. No. 98–473; the Motor Vehicle Theft Law Enforcement Act of 1984, Pub. L. No. 98–547; the Anti-Drug Abuse Act of 1986, Pub. L. No. 99–570; the Criminal Law and Procedure Technical Amendments Act of 1986, Pub. L. No. 99–646; the Anti-Drug Abuse Act of 1988, Pub. L. No. 100-690; the Financial Institutions Reform, Recovery and Enforcement Act of 1989, Pub. L. No. 101-73; and the Crime Control Act of 1990, Pub. L. No. 101-647.

* * *

(CHAPTER 119)

Wire and Electronic Communications Interception and Interception Of Oral Communications

Sec.

2516. Authorization for interception of wire, oral, or electronic communications.

18 U.S.C. § 2516. Authorization for interception of wire, oral, or electronic communications. (1) The Attorney General, Deputy Attorney General, Associate Attorney General, or any Assistant Attorney General, any acting Assistant Attorney General, or any

Deputy Assistant Attorney General in the Criminal Division specially designated by the Attorney General, may authorize an application to a Federal judge of competent jurisdiction for, and such judge may grant in conformity with section 2518 of this chapter an order authorizing or approving the interception of wire or oral communications by the Federal Bureau of Investigation, or a Federal agency having responsibility for the investigation of the offense as to which the application is made, when such interception may provide or has provided evidence of—

* * *

(e) any offense involving fraud connected with a case under title 11 or the manufacture, importation, receiving, concealment, buying, selling, or otherwise dealing in narcotic drugs, marihuana, or other dangerous drugs, punishable under any law of the United States.

* * *

Comment

Since the passage of the Bankruptcy Reform Act of 1978, Pub. L. No. 95–598, 18 U.S.C. § 2516(1) has been amended by Continuing Appropriations, 1985—Comprehensive Crime Control Act of 1984, Pub. L. No. 98–473; the Electronic Communications Privacy Act of 1986, Pub. L. No. 99–508; the Anti-Drug Abuse Act of 1988, Pub. L. No. 100-690; and the Crime Control Act of 1990, Pub. L. No. 101-647.

* * *

(CHAPTER 203)

Arrest and Commitment

Sec.
3057. Bankruptcy investigation.

18 U.S.C. § 3057.   Bankruptcy investigation.

(a) Any judge, receiver,* or trustee having reasonable grounds for believing that any violation under chapter 9 of this title or

---

* The Code abolishes the office of "receiver." In lieu thereof, an "interim trustee" is appointed at the outset of a chapter 7 case.

other laws of the United States relating to insolvent debtors, receiverships or reorganization plans has been committed, or that an investigation should be had in connection therewith, shall report to the appropriate United States attorney all the facts and circumstances of the case, the names of the witnesses and the offense or offenses believed to have been committed. Where one of such officers has made such report, the others need not do so.

(b) The United States attorney thereupon shall inquire into the facts and report thereon to the judge, and if it appears probable that any such offense has been committed, shall without delay, present the matter to the grand jury, unless upon inquiry and examination he decides that the ends of public justice do not require investigation or prosecution, in which case he shall report the facts to the Attorney General for his direction.

18 U.S.C. § 3613.   Civil Remedies for satisfaction of an unpaid fine.

(a) Lien.—A fine imposed pursuant to the provisions of subchapter C of chapter 227 [18 U.S.C. § 3751] is a lien in favor of the United States upon all property belonging to the person fined. The lien arises at the time of the entry of the judgment and continues until the liability is satisfied, remitted, or set aside, or until it becomes unenforceable pursuant to the provisions of subsection (b).

* * *

(c) Application of other lien provisions.—The provisions of sections 6323, 6331, 6332, 6334 through 6336, 6337(a), 6338 through 6343, 6901, 7402, 7403, 7424 through 7426, 7505(a), 7506, 7701, and 7805 of the Internal Revenue Code of 1954 (26 U.S.C. 6323, 6331, 6332, 6334 through 6336, 6337(a), 6338 through 6343, 6901, 7402, 7303, 7424 through 7426, 7505(a), 7506, 7701 and 7805) and of section 513 of the Act of October 17, 1940, 54 Stat. 1190, apply to a fine and to the lien imposed by subsection (a) as if the liability of the person fined were for an internal revenue tax assessment, except to the extent that the application of such statutes is modified by regulations issued by the Attorney General to accord with differences in the nature of the liabilities. For the purposes of this subsection, references in the preceding sections of the Internal Revenue Code of 1954 to "the Secretary" shall be construed to mean "the Attorney General," and references in those sections to "tax" shall be construed to mean "fine".

* * *

(f) Discharge of debts inapplicable.—No discharge of debts pursuant to a bankruptcy proceeding shall render a lien under this section unenforceable or discharge liability to pay a fine.

[18 U.S.C. § 3571 provides for a sentence of a fine if one is found guilty of an offense and it specifies the maximum amounts of various fines.]

Comment

Since the passage of the Bankruptcy Reform Act of 1978, Pub. L. No. 95-598, 18 U.S.C. § 3613(c) has been amended by the Crime Control Act of 1990, Pub. L. No. 101-647.

(CHAPTER 213)

Limitations

Sec.
3284. Concealment of bankrupt's assets.

18 U.S.C. § 3284. Concealment of bankrupt's assets. The concealment of assets of a debtor in a case under title 11 shall be deemed to be a continuing offense until the debtor shall have been finally discharged or a discharge denied, and the period of limitations shall not begin to run until such final discharge or denial of discharge.

(PART V)

Immunity of Witnesses

Sec.
6001. Definitions.

18 U.S.C. § 6001. Definitions. As used in this part [18 U.S.C. §§ 6001–6005]—

(1) agency of the "United States" means any executive department as defined in section 101 of title 5, United States Code, a

military department as defined in section 102 of title 5, United States Code, the Atomic Energy Commission, the China Trade Act registrar appointed under 53 Stat. 1432 (15 U.S.C. § 143), the Civil Aeronautics Board, the Federal Deposit Insurance Corporation, the Federal Maritime Commission, the Federal Power Commission, the Federal Trade Commission, the Interstate Commerce Commission, the National Labor Relations Board, the National Transportation Safety Board, the Railroad Retirement Board, an arbitration board established under 48 Stat. 1193 (45 U.S.C. § 157), the Securities and Exchange Commission, the Subversive Activities Control Board, or a board established under 49 Stat. 31 (15 U.S.C. § 715d);

(2) "other information" includes any book, paper, document, record, recording, or other material;

(3) "proceeding before an agency of the United States" means any proceeding before such an agency with respect to which it is authorized to issue subpoenas and to take testimony or receive other information from witnesses under oath; and

(4) "court of the United States" means any of the following courts: the Supreme Court of the United States, a United States court of appeals, a United States district court established under chapter 5, title 28, United States Code, a United States bankruptcy court established under chapter 6, title 28, United States Code, the District of Columbia Court of Appeals, the Superior Court of the District of Columbia, the District Court of Guam, the District Court of the Virgin Islands, the United States Claims Court, the Tax Court of the United States, the Court of International Trade, and the Court of Military Appeals.

Comment

Since the passage of the Bankruptcy Reform Act of 1978, Pub. L. No. 95–598, 18 U.S.C. § 6001(4) has been amended by the Customs Courts Act of 1980, Pub. L. No. 96–417, and the Federal Courts Improvement Act of 1982, Pub. L. No. 97–164.

References

1 *Collier on Bankruptcy* ch. 3 (Matthew Bender 15th ed.).

1 *Collier Bankruptcy Manual* ch. 3 (Matthew Bender 3d ed.).

MERCHANT MARINE ACT

Section 334 of the Bankruptcy Reform Act of 1978, Pub. L. 95–598, amended title 9 of the Merchant Marine Act, 1936 (46 U.S.C. § 1241 *et seq.*) by adding section 908 (46 U.S.C. § 1247). This provision was chapter XIV of the Bankruptcy Act. Because it does not govern bankruptcy proceedings it was placed in the Merchant Marine Act rather than the 1978 Bankruptcy Code. Only minor stylistic changes were made.

Merchant Marine Act

Title 9 Miscellaneous Revisions

* * *

§ 908. (a) Notwithstanding any other provision of law, in any proceeding in a bankruptcy, equity, or admiralty court of the United States in which a receiver or trustee may be appointed for any corporation engaged in the operation of one or more vessels of United States registry between the United States and any foreign country, upon which the United States holds mortgages, the court, upon finding that it will inure to the advantage of the estate and the parties in interest and that it will tend to further the purposes of this Act, may constitute and appoint the Secretary of Transportation as sole trustee or receiver, subject to the directions and orders of the court, and in any such proceeding the appointment of any person other than the Secretary as trustee or receiver shall become effective upon the ratification thereof by the Secretary without a hearing, unless the Secretary shall deem a hearing necessary. In no such proceeding shall the Secretary be constituted as trustee or receiver without the Secretary's express consent.

(b) If the court, in any such proceeding, is unwilling to permit the trustee or receiver to operate such vessels in such service pending the termination of such proceeding, without financial aid from the Government, and the Secretary certifies to the court that the continued operation of such vessel is, in the opinion of the Secretary, essential to the foreign commerce of the United States and is reasonably calculated to carry out the purposes and policy of this Act, the court may permit the Secretary to operate the vessels subject to the orders of the court and upon terms decreed by the court sufficient to protect all the parties in interest, for the account of the trustee or receiver, directly or through a managing agent or operator employed by the Secretary, if the Secretary undertakes to pay all operating losses resulting from such operation, and comply with the terms imposed by the court, and such vessel shall be considered to be a vessel of the United States within the meaning of the Suits in Admiralty Act. The Secretary shall have no claim against the corporation, its estate, or its assets for the amount of such payments, but the Secretary may pay such sums for depreciation as it deems reasonable and such other sums as the court may deem just. The payment of such sums, and compliance with other terms duly imposed by the court, together with the payment of the operating losses, shall be in satisfaction of all claims against the Secretary on account of the operation of such vessels.

Comment

Since the passage of the Bankruptcy Reform Act of 1978, Pub. L. No. 95–598, 46 U.S.C. § 1247(a) has been amended by the Maritime Act of 1981, Pub. L. No. 97–31.

References

1 *Collier on Bankruptcy* ch. 5 (Matthew Bender 15th ed.).

1 *Collier Bankruptcy Manual* ch. 5 (Matthew Bender 3d ed.).

SELECTED PROVISIONS OF THE BANKRUPTCY AMENDMENTS AND FEDERAL JUDGESHIP ACT OF 1984

Pub. L. No. 98–353

Set forth below are selected sections of the Bankruptcy Amendments and Federal Judgeship Act of 1984, Pub. L. No. 98–353.

Sec. 113. Section 402(6) of the Act of November 6, 1978 (Public Law 95–598; 92 Stat. 2682), is amended by striking out "shall take effect on June 28, 1984" and inserting in lieu thereof "shall not be effective."

Comment

This section amends § 402(b) of Pub. L. 95–598 (the Bankruptcy Reform Act of 1978) by changing April 1, 1984 to June 28, 1984 and by providing that it shall not take effect. This means that various amendments to the Judicial Code (title 28) which were to take effect on April 1, 1984 are not to take effect at all; the assumption is that they are covered or would be inconsistent with the provisions in the 1984 amendments. *But see* § 121(a), *infra*.

Case Annotations

Although Section 121(a) of the Bankruptcy Amendments of 1984 provides that 28 U.S.C. § 1293(b) was to become effective on July 10, 1984, the passage of Section 121(a) was an oversight, in light of that apparent new appellate scheme adopted in 28 U.S.C. § 158 which was intended to supplant the appellate jurisdiction provisions of the Bankruptcy Reform Act; Section 113 of the Bankruptcy Amendments Act of 1984, which in contradiction to Section 121(a) declared 28 U.S.C. § 1293(b) ineffective, is the valid provision. City Nat'l Bank v. General Coffee Corp. (*In re* General Coffee Corp.), 758 F.2d 1406, 12 C.B.C.2d 863 (11th Cir. 1985).

The apparent inconsistency between Section 113 and Section 121(a) of the Bankruptcy Amendments Act of 1984 should be resolved in favor of Section 113 in order to effectuate the presumably rational statutory scheme enacted by Congress. Precon, Inc. v. JRS Realty Trust (*In re* Brown), 12 C.B.C.2d 427 (D. Me. 1985).

28 U.S.C. § 1293 and all other sections of title 28 of the United States Code which had been made effective by Section 402(b) of the 1978 Reform Act were repealed by Section 113 of the Bankruptcy Amendments of 1984 in line with Congress' intent that 28 U.S.C. § 158 be a comprehensive provision governing all aspects of bankruptcy appellate jurisdiction. Helm v. Helm (*In re* Helm), 12 C.B.C.2d 888 (B. Ct., W.D. Ky. 1985).

Sec. 115. (a) On the date of the enactment of this Act the appropriate district court of the United States shall have jurisdiction of—

(1) cases, and matters and proceedings in cases, under the Bankruptcy Act that are pending immediately before such date in the bankruptcy courts continued by section 404(a) of the Act of November 6, 1978 (Public Law 95–598; 92 Stat. 2687), and

(2) cases under title 11 of the United States Code, and proceedings arising under title 11 of the United States Code or arising in or related to cases under title 11 of the United States Code, that are pending immediately before such date in the bankruptcy courts continued by section 404(a) of the act of November 6, 1978 (Public Law 95–598; 92 Stat. 2687).

(b) On the date of the enactment of this Act, there shall be transferred to the appropriate district court of the United States appeals from final judgments, orders, and decrees of the bankruptcy courts pending immediately before such date in the bankruptcy appellate panels appointed under section 405(c) of the Act of November 6, 1978 (Public Law 95–598; 92 Stat. 2685 [*sic*]).

Case Annotations

Section 115 of the Bankruptcy Amendments of 1984 was intended only to transfer cases from tribunals that would no longer have a separate existence after the enactment of the 1984 Act and therefore cannot be construed as vesting the district courts with jurisdiction over proceedings that were appealed from bankruptcy courts immediately before the enactment of the 1984 Act. Precon, Inc. v. JRS Realty Trust (*In re* Brown), 12 C.B.C.2d 427 (D. Me. 1985).

Sec. 120. (a)(1) Whenever a court of appeals is authorized to fill a vacancy that occurs on a bankruptcy court of the United States, such court of appeals shall appoint to fill that vacancy a person whose character, experience, ability, and impartiality qualify such person to serve in the Federal judiciary.

(2) It is the sense of the Congress that the courts of appeals should consider for appointment under section 152 of title 28, United States Code, to the first vacancy which arises after the date of the enactment of this Act in the office of each bankruptcy judge, the bankruptcy judge who holds such office immediately before such vacancy arises, if such bankruptcy judge requests to be considered for such appointment.

(b) The judicial council of the circuit involved shall assist the court of appeals by evaluating potential nominees and by recommending to such court for consideration for appointment to each vacancy on the bankruptcy court persons who are qualified to be bankruptcy judges under regulations prescribed by the Judicial Conference of the United States. In the case of the first vacancy which arises after the date of the enactment of this Act in the office of each bankruptcy judge, such potential nominees shall include the bankruptcy judge who holds such office immediately before such vacancy arises, if such bankruptcy judge requests to be considered for such appointment and the judicial council determines that such judge is qualified under subsection (c) of this section to continue to serve. Such potential nominees shall receive consideration equal to that given all other potential nominees for such position.

(c) Before transmitting to the court of appeals the names of the persons the judicial council for the circuit deems best qualified to fill any existing vacancy, the judicial council shall have determined that—

(1) public notice of such vacancy has been given and an effort has been made, in the case of each such vacancy, to identify qualified candidates, without regard to race, color, sex, religion, or national origin,

(2) such persons are members in good standing of at least one State bar, the District of Columbia bar, or the bar of the Commonwealth of Puerto Rico, and members in good standing of every other bar of which they are members,

(3) such persons possess, and have a reputation for, integrity and good character,

(4) such persons are of sound physical and mental health,

(5) such persons possess and have demonstrated commitment to equal justice under law,

(6) such persons possess and have demonstrated outstanding legal ability and competence, as evidenced by substantial legal experience, ability to deal with complex legal problems, aptitude for legal scholarship and writing, and familiarity with courts and court processes, and

(7) such persons demeanor, character, and personality indicate that they would exhibit judicial temperament if appointed to the position of United States bankruptcy judge.

Sec. 121. (a) Section 402 of the Act entitled "An Act to establish a uniform Law on the Subject of Bankruptcies" (Public Law 95–598) is amended in subsections (b) and (e) by striking out "June 28, 1984" each place it appears and inserting in lieu thereof "the date of enactment of the Bankruptcy Amendments and Federal Judgeship Act of 1984".

(b) Section 404 of such Act is amended in subsections (a) and (b) by striking out "June 27, 1984" each place it appears and inserting in lieu thereof "the day before the date of enactment of the Bankruptcy Amendments and Federal Judgeship Act of 1984".

(c) Section 406 of such Act is amended by striking out "June 27, 1984" each place it appears and inserting in lieu thereof "the day before the date of enactment of the Bankruptcy Amendments and Federal Judgeship Act of 1984".

(d) Section 409 of such Act is amended by—

(1) striking out "June 28, 1984" each place it appears and inserting in lieu thereof "the day before the date of enactment of the Bankruptcy Amendments and Federal Judgeship Act of 1984"; and

(2) striking out "June 27, 1984" each place it appears and inserting in lieu thereof "the day before the date of enactment of the Bankruptcy Amendments and Federal Judgeship Act of 1984".

(e) The term of office of any bankruptcy judge who was serving on June 27, 1984, is extended to and shall expire at the end of the day of enactment of this Act.

(f) Section 8339 (n) of title 5, United States Code, is amended by striking out "June 28, 1984" and inserting in lieu thereof "the date of enactment of the Bankruptcy Amendments and Federal Judgeship Act of 1984."

(g) Section 8331 (22) of title 5, United States Code, is amended by striking out "June 27, 1984" and inserting in lieu thereof "the day before the date of enactment of the Bankruptcy Amendments and Federal Judgeship Act of 1984".

Comment

Section 121(a) amends § 402 of Pub. L. No. 95–598 (the Bankruptcy Reform Act of 1978) to provide that the effective date of its various provisions is the date of enactment of the 1984 amendments which was July 10, 1984. *But see,* § 113 *supra.*

Case Annotations

In the transition between the 1978 Reform Act and the 1984 Amendments, there was no break in the service of bankruptcy judges because the term of bankruptcy judge serving under Section 404(b) of the Reform Act was to expire on June 27, 1984 "or when his successor takes office." No such successor could have been appointed, however, during the 13-day gap between the expiration of the Act and the enactment of the Amendments, and consequently, Congress could not have violated the Appointments Clause of the Constitution. Section 121(e) is constitutional. Koerner v. Colonial Bank (In the Matter of Koerner), 800 F.2d 1358, 15 C.B.C.2d 711 (5th Cir. 1986).

Even if there were a "gap" between the expiration of the transition period and the effective date of the 1984 Amendments, it was within Congress' authority to extend the terms of previously appointed judges. Robison v. First Financial Capital Management Corp. (*In re* Sweetwater), 14 C.B.C.2d 247 (D. Utah 1985).

Extension of the bankruptcy judges' terms by Congress in the Bankruptcy Amendments of 1984 was within Congress' undoubted authority to create an office, establish and modify its scope and term, and designate officers previously appointed by the judiciary to remain in office. Lombard-Wall Inc. v. New York City Housing Dev. Corp. (*In re* Lombard-Wall Inc.), 13 C.B.C.2d 161 (S.D.N.Y. 1985).

Section 121(e) of the Bankruptcy Amendments and Federal Judgeship Act of 1984 is an appropriate enactment of retroactive legislation, not inconsistent with the Constitution. Moody v. Empire Life Ins. Co. (*In re* Moody), 12 C.B.C.2d 479 (M.D.N.C. 1985).

Sec. 122. (a) Except as otherwise provided in this section, this title and the amendments made by this title shall take effect on the date of the enactment of this Act.

(b) Section 1334(c)(2) of title 28, United States Code, and section 1411(a) of title 28, United States Code, as added by this Act, shall not apply with respect to cases under title 11 of the United States Code that are pending on the date of enactment of this Act, or to proceedings arising in or related to such cases.

(c) Sections 108(b), 113, and 121(e) shall take effect on June 27, 1984.

References

1 *Collier on Bankruptcy* ch. 7 (Matthew Bender 15th ed.).

1 *Collier Bankruptcy Manual* ch. 7 (Matthew Bender 3d ed.).

SELECTED PROVISIONS OF THE BANKRUPTCY JUDGES, UNITED STATES TRUSTEES, AND FAMILY FARMER BANKRUPTCY ACT OF 1986

Pub. L. No. 99-554

Sec. 114.

* * *

(b) Temporary Suspension of Limitation on Appointments.— During the period beginning on the effective date of this Act and ending on October 1, 1989, the provisions of title 5 of the United States Code governing appointments in the competitive service shall not apply with respect to appointments under section 589 of title 28, United States Code.

* * *

TITLE III—TRANSITION AND ADMINISTRATIVE PROVISIONS

SEC. 301. INCUMBENT UNITED STATES TRUSTEES.

(a) Area for Which Appointed.—Notwithstanding any paragraph of section 581(a) of title 28, United States Code, as in effect before the effective date of this Act, a United States trustee serving in such office on the effective date of this Act shall serve the remaining term of such office as United States trustee for the region specified in a paragraph of such section, as amended by this Act, that includes the site at which the primary official station of the United States trustee is located immediately before the effective date of this Act.

(b) Term of Office.—Notwithstanding section 581(b) of title 28, United States Code, as in effect before the effective date of this Act, the term of office of any United States trustee serving in such office on the date of the enactment of this Act shall expire—

(1) 2 years after the expiration date of such term of office under such section, as so in effect, or

(2) 4 years after the date of the enactment of this Act, whichever occurs first.

SEC.302. EFFECTIVE DATES; APPLICATION OF AMENDMENTS.

(a) General Effective Date.—Except as provided in subsections (b), (c), (d), (e) and (f), this Act and the amendments made by this Act shall take effect 30 days after the date of the enactment of this Act.

(b) Amendments Relating to Bankruptcy Judges and Incumbent United States Trustees.—Subtitle A of title I, and sections 301 and 307(a), shall take effect on the date of the enactment of this Act.

(c) Amendments Relating to Family Farmers.—(1) The amendments made by subtitle B of title II shall not apply with respect to cases commenced under title 11 of the United States Code before the effective date of this Act.

(2) Section 1202 of title 11 of the United States Code (as added by the amendment made by section 255 of this Act) shall take effect on the effective date of this Act and before the amendment made by section 227 of this Act.

(3) Until the amendments made by subtitle A of title II of this Act become effective in a district and apply to a case, for purposes of such case—

(A)(i) any reference in section 326(b) of title 11 of the United States Code to chapter 13 of title 11 of the United States Code shall be deemed to be a reference to chapter 12 or chapter 13 of title 11 of the United States Code,

(ii) any reference in such section 326(b) to section 1302(d) of title 11 of the United States Code shall be deemed to be a reference to section 1302(d) of title 11 of the United States [sic] or section 586(b) of title 28 of the United States Code, and

(iii) any reference in such section 326(b) to section 1302(a) of title 11 of the United States Code shall be deemed to be a reference to section 1202(a) or section 1302(a) of title 11 of the United States Code, and

(B)(i) the first two references in section 1202(a) of title 11 of the United States Code (as added by the amendment made by section 255 of this Act) to the United States trustee shall be deemed to be a reference to the court, and

(ii) any reference in such section 1202(a) to section 586(b) of title 28 of the United States Code shall be deemed to be a reference to section 1202(c) of title 11 of the United States Code (as so added).

(d) Application of Amendments to Judicial Districts.—

(1) Certain Regions Not Currently Served by United States Trustees.—(A) The amendments made by subtitle A of title II of this Act, and section 1930(a)(6) of title 28 of the United States Code (as added by section 117(4) of this Act), shall not—

(i) become effective in or with respect to a judicial district specified in subparagraph (B) until, or

(ii) apply to cases while pending in such district before, the expiration of the 270-day period beginning on the effective date of this Act or of the 30-day period beginning on the date the Attorney General certifies under section 303 of this Act the region specified in a paragraph of section 581(a) of title 28, United States Code, as amended by section 111(a) of this Act, that includes such district, whichever occurs first.

(B) Subparagraph (A) applies to the following:

(i) The judicial district established for the Commonwealth of Puerto Rico.

(ii) The District of Connecticut.

(iii) The judicial districts established for the State of New York (other than the Southern District of New York).

(iv) The District of Vermont.

(v) The judicial districts established for the State of Pennsylvania.

(vi) The judicial district established for the Virgin Islands of the United States.

(vii) The District of Maryland.

(viii) The judicial districts established for the State of North Carolina.

(ix) The District of South Carolina.

(x) The judicial districts established for the State of West Virginia.

(xi) The Western District of Virginia.

(xii) The Eastern District of Texas.

(xiii) The judicial districts established for the State of Wisconsin.

(xiv) The judicial districts established for the State of Iowa.

(xv) The judicial districts established for the State of New Mexico.

(xvi) The judicial districts established for the State of Oklahoma.

(xvii) The District of Utah.

(xviii) The District of Wyoming (including those portions of Yellowstone National Park situated in the States of Montana and Idaho).

(xix) The judicial districts established for the State of Alabama.

(xx) The judicial districts established for the State of Florida.

(xxi) The judicial districts established for the State of Georgia.

(2) Certain Remaining Judicial Districts Not Currently Served by United States Trustees.—(A) The amendments made by subtitle A of title II of this Act, and section 1930(a)(6) of title 28 of the United States Code (as added by section 117(4) of this Act), shall not—

(i) become effective in or with respect to a judicial district specified in subparagraph (B) until, or

(ii) apply to cases while pending in such district before,

the expiration of the 2-year period beginning on the effective date of this Act or of the 30-day period beginning on the date the Attorney General certifies under section 303 of this Act the region specified in a paragraph of section 581(a) of title 28, United States Code, as amended by section 111(a) of this Act, that includes such district, whichever occurs first.

(B) Subparagraph (A) applies to the following:

(i) The judicial districts established for the State of Louisiana.

(ii) The judicial districts established for the State of Mississippi.

(iii) The Southern District of Texas and the Western District of Texas.

(iv) The judicial districts established for the State of Kentucky.

(v) The judicial districts established for the State of Tennessee.

(vi) The judicial districts established for the State of Michigan.

(vii) The judicial districts established for the State of Ohio.

(viii) The judicial districts established for the State of Illinois (other than the Northern District of Illinois)

(ix) The judicial districts established for the State of Indiana.

(x) The judicial districts established for the State of Arkansas.

(xi) The judicial districts established for the State of Nebraska.

(xii) The judicial districts established for the State of Missouri.

(xiii) The District of Arizona.

(xiv) The District of Hawaii.

(xv) The judicial district established for Guam.

(xvi) The judicial district established for the Commonwealth of the Northern Mariana Islands.

(xvii) The judicial districts established for the State of California (other than the Central District of California).

(xviii) The District of Nevada.

(xix) The District of Alaska.

(xx) The District of Idaho.

(xxi) The District of Montana.

(xxii) The District of Oregon.

(xxiii) The judicial districts established for the State of Washington.

(3) Judicial Districts for the States of Alabama and North Carolina.—(A) Notwithstanding paragraphs (1) and (2), and any other provision of law, the amendments made by subtitle A of title II of this Act, and section 1930(a)(6) of title 28 of the United States Code (as added by section 117(4) of this Act), shall not—

(i) become effective in or with respect to a judicial district specified in subparagraph (E) until, or

(ii) apply to cases while pending in such district before, [*sic*] such district elects to be included in a bankruptcy region established in section 581(a) of title 28, United States Code, as amended by section 111(a) of this Act, or October 1, 2002, whichever occurs first, except that the amendment to section 105(a) of title 11, United States Code, shall become effective as of the date of the enactment of the Federal Courts Study Committee Implementation Act of 1990.

(B) Any election under subparagraph (A) shall be made upon a majority vote of the chief judge of such district and each bankruptcy judge in such judicial district in favor of such election.

(C) Notice that an election has been made under subparagraph (A) shall be given, not later than 10 days after such election, to the Attorney General and the appropriate Federal Circuit Court of Appeals for such district.

(D) Any election made under subparagraph (A) shall become effective on the date the amendments made by subtitle A of title II of this Act become effective in the region that includes such district or 30 days after the Attorney General receives the notice required under subparagraph (C), whichever occurs later.

(E) Subparagraph (A) applies to the following:

(i) The judicial districts established for the State of Alabama.

(ii) The judicial districts established for the State of North Carolina.

(F)(i) Subject to clause (ii), with respect to cases under chapters 7, 11, 12, and 13 of title 11, United States Code—

(I) commenced before the effective date of this Act, and

(II) pending in a judicial district in the State of Alabama or the State of North Carolina before any election made under subparagraph (A) by such district becomes effective or October 1, 2002, whichever occurs first,

the amendments made by section 113 and subtitle A of title II of this Act, and section 1930(a)(6) of title 28 of the United States Code (as added by section 117(4) of this Act), shall not apply until October 1, 2003, or the expiration of the 1-year period beginning on the date such election becomes effective, whichever occurs first.

(ii) For purposes of clause (i), the amendments made by section 113 and subtitle A of title II of this Act, and section 1930(a)(6) of title 28 of the United States Code (as added by section 117(4) of this Act), shall not apply with respect to a case under chapter 7, 11, 12, or 13 of title 11, United States Code, if—

(I) the trustee in the cases files the final report and account of administration of the estate, required under section 704 of such title, or

(II) a plan is confirmed under section 1129, 1225, or 1325 of such title, before October 1, 2003, or the expiration of the 1-year period beginning on the date such election becomes effective, whichever occurs first.

(G) Notwithstanding section 589a of title 28, United States Code, as added by section 115 of this Act, funds collected as a result of the amendments made by section 117 of this Act in a judicial district in the State of Alabama or the State of North Carolina under section 1930(a) of title 28, United States Code, before the date the amendments made by subtitle A of title II of this Act take effect in such district shall be deposited in the general receipts of the Treasury.

(H) The repeal made by section 231 of this Act shall not apply in or with respect to the Northern District of Alabama until March 1, 1987, or the effective date of any election made under subparagraph (A) by such district, whichever comes first.

(I) In any judicial district in the State of Alabama or the State of North Carolina that has not made the election described in subparagraph (A), any person who is appointed under regulations issued by the Judicial Conference of the United States to administer estates in cases under title 11 of the United States Code may—

(i) establish, maintain, and supervise a panel of private trustees that are eligible and available to serve as trustees in cases under title 11, United States Code, and

(ii) supervise the administration of cases and trustees in cases under chapters 7, 11, 12, and 13 of title 11, United States Code, until the amendments made by subtitle A of title II take effect in such district.

(e) Application of United States Trustee System and Quarterly Fees to Certain Cases.—

(1) In General.—Subject to paragraph (2), with respect to cases under chapters 7, 11, 12, and 13 of title 11, United States Code—

(A) commenced before the effective date of this Act, and

(B) pending in a judicial district referred to in section 581(a) of title 28, United States Code, as amended by section 111(a) of this Act, for which a United States trustee is not authorized before the effective date of this Act to be appointed,

the amendments made by section 113 and subtitle A of title II of this Act, and section 1930(a)(6) of title 28 of the United States Code (as added by section 117(4) of this Act), shall not apply until the expiration of the 3-year period beginning on the effective date of this Act, or of the 1-year period beginning on the date the Attorney General certifies under section 303 of this Act the region specified in a paragraph of such section 581(a), as so amended, that includes such district, whichever occurs first.

(2) Amendments Inapplicable.—For purposes of paragraph (1), the amendments made by section 113 and subtitle A of title II of this Act, and section 1930(a)(6) of title 28 of the United States Code (as added by section 117(4) of this Act), shall not apply with respect to a case under chapter 7, 11, 12, or 13 of title 11, United States Code, if—

(A) the trustee in the case files the final report and account of administration of the estate, required under section 704 of such title, or

(B) a plan is confirmed under section 1129, 1225, or 1325 of such title,

before the expiration of the 3-year period, or the expiration of the 1-year period, specified in paragraph (1), whichever occurs first.

(3) Rule of Construction Regarding Fees for Cases.— This Act and the amendments made by section 117(4) of this Act shall not be construed to require the payment of a fee under paragraph (6) of section 1930(a) of title 28, United States Code, in a case under title 11 of the United States Code for any conduct or period occuring before such paragraph becomes effective in the district in which such case is pending.

(f) Repeal of Chapter 12 of Title 11.—Chapter 12 of title 11 of the United States Code is repealed on October 1, 1993. All cases commenced or pending under chapter 12 of title 11, United States Code, and all matters and proceedings in or relating to such cases, shall be conducted and determined under such chapter as if such chapter had not been repealed. The substantive rights of parties in connection with such cases, matters, and proceedings shall continue to be governed under the laws applicable to such cases, matters, and proceedings as if such chapter had not been repealed.

Comment

Subsection (f), a "sunset" clause will automatically repeal chapter 12 unless its existence is continued by affirmative Congressional action. The chapter would probably not be continued if it was determined that it was not accomplishing the special purpose for which it was created, or if the need for chapter 12 no longer existed.

1990 Amendments: The Judicial Improvements Act of 1990, Pub. L. No. 101-650, (effective on the date of enactment, December 1, 1990) amended Section 302(d)(3) of the Bankruptcy Judges, United States Trustees, and Family Farmer Bankruptcy Act of 1986 (Pub. L. No. 99-554). These amendments extend the period — until October 1, 2002 — in which the judicial districts in the states of Alabama and North Carolina may remain outside the United States trustee system. Pub. L. No. 101-650 further amended section 302(d)(3)(A)(ii) by inserting new language pertaining to the effective date of the 1986 amendment to section 105 of title 11.

Case Annotations

The provisions of chapter 12 were obviously intended to have retroactive effect, since they are meant to deal with the present crisis facing family farmers. *In re* Bullington, 17 C.B.C.2d 1438 (B. Ct., M.D. Ga. 1987).

The Bankruptcy Judges, United States Trustees, and Family Farmer Bankruptcy Act of 1986 does not work to preclude a chapter 12 filing by a debtor whose chapter 13 case filed prior to the Act's effective date was voluntarily or involuntarily dismissed. *In re* Gamble, 17 C.B.C.2d 121 (B. Ct., D. Idaho 1987).

SEC. 303. CERTIFICATION OF JUDICIAL DISTRICTS; NOTICE AND PUBLICATION OF CERTIFICATION.

(a) Certification by Attorney General.—The Attorney General may certify in writing a region specified in a paragraph of section 581(a) of title 28, United States Code (other than paragraph (16)), as amended by section 111(a) of this Act, to the appropriate court of appeals of the United States, for the purpose of informing such court that certain amendments made by this Act will become effective in accordance with section 302 of this Act.

(b) Notice and Publication of Certification.—Whenever the Attorney General transmits a certification under subsection (a), the Attorney General shall simultaneously—

(1) transmit a copy of such certification to the Speaker of the House of Representatives and to the President pro tempore of the Senate, and

(2) publish such certification in the Federal Register.

SEC. 304. ADMINISTRATIVE PROVISIONS.

(a) Cooperative Arrangements.—The Attorney General and the Director of the Administrative Office of the United States Courts may enter into agreements under which United States trustees may—

(1) use—

(A) the services, equipment, personnel, records, reports, and data compilations, in any form, of the courts of the United States, and

(B) the facilities of such courts, and

(2) cooperate in the use by the courts of the United States of—

(A) the services, equipment, personnel, records, reports, and data compilations, in any form, of United States trustees, and

(B) the facilities of such trustees, to prevent duplication during the two-year period beginning on the effective date of this Act.

(b) Information and Documents Relating to Bankruptcy Cases and United States Trustees.—The Director of the Administrative Office of the United States Courts shall make available to United States trustees, at the request of the Attorney General and on a continuing basis, all records, reports, and data compilations relating to—

(1) cases and proceedings under title 11 of the United States Code, and

(2) the duties of United States trustees under titles 11 and 28 of the United States Code.

SEC. 305.   APPLICATION OF CERTAIN BANKRUPTCY RULES.

(a) Rules Relating to the United States Trustee System.—If a United States trustee is not authorized, before the effective date of this Act, to be appointed for a judicial district referred to in section 581(a) of title 28, United States Code, as amended by section 111(a) of this Act, then part X of the Bankruptcy Rules shall not apply to cases in such district until the amendments made by subtitle A of title II of this Act become effective under section 302 of this Act in such district.

(b) Rules Relating to Chapter 12 of Title 11.—The rules prescribed under section 2075 of title 28, United States Code, and in effect on the date of the enactment of this Act shall apply to cases filed under chapter 12 of title 11, United States Code, to the extent practicable and not inconsistent with the amendments made by title II of this Act.

SEC. 306.   SALARY OF INCUMBENT UNITED STATES TRUSTEES.

For service as a United States trustee in the period beginning on the effective date of this Act and ending on the expiration under section 301 of this Act of their respective terms of office, the salary payable to United States trustees serving in such offices on the effective date of this Act shall be fixed in accordance with section 587 of title 28, United States Code, as amended by section 114(a) of this Act.

* * *

SEC. 308.   CONSIDERATION OF CURRENT PRIVATE TRUSTEES FOR APPOINTMENT BY UNITED STATES TRUSTEES.

(a) Trustees in Bankruptcy Cases under Chapter 7.—It is the sense of the Congress that individuals who are serving before the effective date of this Act, as trustees in cases under chapter 7 of title 11, United States Code, should be considered by United States trustees for appointment under section 586(a)(1) of title

28, United States Code, to the panels of private trustees that are established as a result of the amendments made by this Act.

(b) Standing Trustees in Bankruptcy Cases under Chapter 13.—It is the sense of the Congress that individuals who are serving before the effective date of this Act, as standing trustees in cases under chapter 13 of title 11, United States Code, should be considered by the United States trustees for appointment under section 586(b) of title 28, United States Code, as standing trustees who are appointed as a result of the amendments made by this Act.

SEC. 309. APPOINTMENT OF UNITED STATES TRUSTEES BY THE ATTORNEY GENERAL.

It is the sense of the Congress that individuals otherwise qualified who are serving, before the effective date of this Act, as estate administrators under title 11 of the United States Code should be considered by the Attorney General for appointment under sections 581 and 582 of title 28, United States Code, to new positions of United States trustee and assistant United States trustee resulting from the amendments made by this Act.

SEC. 310. ELECTRONIC CASE MANAGEMENT DEMONSTRATION PROJECT.

(a) Establishment of Project.—Not later than 1 year after the effective date of this Act, the Director of the Executive Office for United States Trustees, in consultation with the Director of the Administrative Office of the United States Courts, shall establish an electronic case management demonstration project to be carried out in 3 Federal judicial districts that have a sufficiently large and varied bankruptcy caseload so as to provide a meaningful evaluation of the cost and effectiveness of such system. A contract for such project shall be awarded—

(1) on the basis of competitive bids submitted by qualified nongovernmental entities that are able to design an automated joint information system for use by the United States courts and by United States trustees, and

(2) in accordance with the Federal Property and Administrative Services Act of 1949, the Office of Federal Procurement Policy Act, and title 31 of the United States Code.

(b) Study by General Accounting Office.—Not later than 1 year after the electronic case managment [*sic*] system begins to operate in all of the judicial districts participating in the demonstration project carried out under subsection (a), the General Accounting Office shall conduct a study to compare the cost and effectiveness of such system with the cost and effectiveness of case management systems used in Federal judicial districts that are not participating in such project.

(c) Term of Project.—The demonstration project required by subsection (a) shall be carried out until—

(1) the expiration of the 2-year period beginning on the date the electronic case management system begins to operate in all of the judicial districts participating in such project, or

(2) legislation is enacted to extend, expand, modify, or terminate the operation of such project, whichever occurs first.

(d) Use by Clerks of the Courts.—The electronic case management system demonstrated under the project required by subsection (a) shall provide the clerk of court in each district in which such system is operated, with a means of—

(1) maintaining a complete electronic case file of all relevant information contained in petitions and schedules (and any amendments thereto) relating to debtors in cases under title 11 of the United States Code, including—

(A) a complete list of creditors in each such case, as listed by the debtor,

(B) a complete list of assets scheduled by the debtor, the value of such asset, and any action taken by the trustee or debtor in possession with regard to such asset during the pendency of such case,

(C) a complete list of debts and, with respect to each debt—

(i) any priority of such debt under title 11 of the United States Code,

(ii) whether such debt is secured or unsecured, and

(iii) whether such debt is contingent or noncontingent, and

(D) the debtor's statements of current expenses and income, and

(2) maintaining all calendars and dockets and producing all notices required to be sent in cases under title 11 of the United States Code.

(e) Use by United States Trustees.—The electronic case management system demonstrated under the project required by subsection (a) shall provide, at a minimum, the United States trustee in each district in which such system is operated with—

(1) complete electronic case files which contain, in addition to the information listed in subsection (d), records of case openings, case closings, hearings, and the filing of all motions, trustee appointments, pleadings, and responses, as well as a record of the responses by the United States trustee to those motions, trustee appointments, and pleadings,

(2) a means to generate standardized forms for motions, appointments, pleadings, and responses,

(3) a means to generate standard management reports and letters on an exception basis,

(4) a means to maintain accounting records, reports, and information required to be maintained by debtors in possession and trustees in cases under title 11 of the United States Code,

(5) a means to calculate and record distribution to creditors, final applications and orders for distribution, and final case closing reports, and

(6) a means to monitor the payment of filing and other required fees.

(f) Availability to Certain Governmental Entities.—Unlimited access to information maintained in the electronic case management system demonstrated under the project required by subsection (a) shall be provided at no charge to the following:

(1) The Congress.

(2) The Executive Office for the United States Trustees.

(3) The Administrative Office of the United States Courts.

(4) The clerks of the courts in judicial districts in which such system is operated and persons who review case information, in accordance with section 107(a) of title 11, United States Code, in the offices of the clerks.

(5) The judges on the bankruptcy and district courts in districts in which such system is operated.

(6) Trustees in cases pending in districts in which such system is operated.

(g) Fees for Other Users.—(1) The entity which is awarded a contract to provide the electronic case management system demonstrated under this project may, under guidelines established by the Director of the Executive Office for the United States Trustees in the provisions of such contract, collect reasonable fees from assets of the estate of the debtor in bankruptcy for providing notices and services to the court and trustees under the demonstration project.

(2) Access to information maintained in electronic case files pursuant to the demonstration project may be provided to persons other than those specified in subsection (f), but such access shall be limited to viewing such information only. A reasonable charge for such access may be collected by the entity which is awarded a contract under this section, in accordance with the guidelines established by the Director of the Executive Office for the United States trustees in such contract. A reasonable portion of any charge so collected may be required by the Director to be remitted to the Executive Office for United States Trustees and deposited in the United States Trustee System Fund established in section 589a of title 28, United States Code.

(h) Security.—Access provided under subsection (f) to an entity or an individual shall be subject to such security limitations as may be imposed by the Congress or the head of the affected entity.

SEC. 311. CASES PENDING UNDER THE BANKRUPTCY ACT.

At the end of one calendar year following the date the amendments made by subtitle A of title II of this Act take effect in a district in which any case is still pending under the Bankruptcy

Act, the district court shall withdraw the reference of any such case and, after notice and a hearing, determine the status of the case. Such case shall be remanded to the bankruptcy judge with such instructions as are necessary for the prompt closing of the case and with a requirement that a progress report on the case be provided by the bankruptcy judge after such interval as the district court deems appropriate.

INDEX

INDEX

PUBLISHER'S INDEXING STAFF

Peter Kendrick	Indexing Manager
Jeffrey Schaefer	Indexing Supervisor
John Koser	Indexer

INDEX

[References are to Code Sections, or Comments thereto, of Title 11 U.S. Code (Ex. 101). References to other titles of the U.S. Code pertain to additional statutory material (Ex. 28 U.S.C. 501). Title 28 materials, Transition Sections, Bankruptcy Amendments and Federal Judgeship Act provisions and Bankruptcy Judges, U.S. Trustees, and Family Farmer Act provisions are located following Bankruptcy Code. Consult Bankruptcy Rules Pamphlet for an Index to the Rules.]

A

ABANDONMENT
Court authorization . . . 554
Debtor of excess . . . 554(b)
Property . . . 554(a)
Railroad line (See RAILROADS AND RAIL-
ROAD REORGANIZATION)

ABSTENTION
Dismissal or suspension of proceeding . . .
305
District court . . . 28 U.S.C. 1334(c)
Foreign proceeding . . . 305(a)(2)
Hearing, after . . . 305
Nonappealable . . . 305(c)
Order as to not reviewable . . . 305(c)

ACCEPTANCE OF PLAN
Reorganization (See REORGANIZATION
(CHAPTER 11), subhead: Acceptance of
plan)

ACCOUNTANT
Administrative costs and expenses . . . . . .
503(b)(4)
Definition . . . 101(1)
Employment of . . . 327
Fee splitting
　Exceptions to prohibition . . . 504(b)
　Prohibited . . . 504(a)
Trustee as accountant, compensation . . . .
328(b)
Turnover of books and records . . . 542(e)

ACCOUNTS
Duty to
　Custodian . . . 543(b)(2)
　Trustee . . . 704(2)
S.I.P.C., separate accounts . . . 745(a)

ACTS OF BANKRUPTCY
Concept abolished . . . 303(h) Comment

ADEQUATE PROTECTION
Additional or replacement lien . . . 361(2)

ADEQUATE PROTECTION—Cont.
Administrative expense . . . 361(3)
Chapter 12 . . . 361(3); 1205
Credit, obtaining . . . 364 Comment
Equitable and legal protection . . . 361
Periodic cash payments . . . 361(1)
Priority and . . . 507(b)
Procedures . . . 361
Property, sale or lease of . . . 363(e)
Value, meaning of . . . 361

ADJUDICATION
Order for relief substituted for . . . 301

ADJUSTMENT OF DEBT
Family farmer with regular annual income
　(See FAMILY FARMER BANKRUPTCY
　(CHAPTER 12))
Individual with regular income (See INDIVID-
　UAL'S DEBT ADJUSTMENT (CHAPTER
　13))
Municipalities (See MUNICIPAL DEBT AD-
　JUSTMENT (CHAPTER 9))

ADJUSTMENT OF DOLLAR AMOUNTS
Procedures . . . 104

ADMINISTRATION
Conversion, effect of; termination of services
　. . . 348(c)
Estate, trustee's duties (See TRUSTEE)
Expenses (See ADMINISTRATIVE COSTS
　AND EXPENSES)
Money of estates, precautions against loss
　. . . 345(b)
Special tax provisions under Chapter 13 . .
　346(d)

ADMINISTRATION OF ESTATE
Trustee's duties (See TRUSTEE, subhead:
　Duties)

**ADMINISTRATIVE COSTS AND EX-
PENSES**
Adequate protection . . . 361(3)
After notice and hearing . . . 503(a)

[See page I-1 for explanation of references.]

[See page I-1 for explanation of references.]

[See page I-1 for explanation of references.]

AUTOMATIC STAY—Cont.

Lease, termination of . . . 362(b)(10)

Negotiable instrument, presentment of . . . . 362(b)(11)

Non-automatic stays . . . 362(b)

Petition . . . 362(b)(6)

Property . . . 362(a)

Relief from . . . 363 Comment

Repo participant, setoff of . . . 362(b)(7)

Scope of . . . 361; 362

Securities contract . . . 362(b)(6)

Securities Investor Protection Act of 1970 . . . 362

Setoff . . . 362(a)(7)

S.I.P.C. and . . . 362(a), (b); 742

Tax deficiency notice, governmental unit . . . 362(b)(9)

Violation consequences . . . 362(h)

AUTOMOBILE

Exemption . . . 522(d)(3), (g)(2)

AVOIDED TRANSFER (See TRANSFER)

AVOIDING POWERS OF TRUSTEE

Exemption of debtor . . . 522(h)

Limitations

    Administrative expense alternative . . . 546(b)(2)

    Court grant of lien to reclaiming creditor . . . 546(a)

    Demand for reclamation, receipt of goods . . . 546(c)

    Fish, reclamation of . . . 546(d)

    Generally applicable law and . . . . . 546(b)

    Grain, claims of . . . 546(d)

    Margin payments . . . 546(e), (f)

    Perfection of interest in property and . . . 546(b)

    Purchase money security interest . . . 546(b)

    Right of reclamation . . . 546(c)

    Settlement payments . . . 546(d), (f)

    State laws, effect on . . . 546(b)

    Statute of limitations . . . 546(a)

    Statutory or common law right of seller and . . . 546(c)

Perfection of interests . . . 546(b)

Preferences (See PREFERENCE)

Rights, trustee . . . 546(b)

Statutory liens, fixing of . . . 545

AVOIDING POWERS OF TRUSTEE—Cont.

Transfer of interest of debtor . . . 544(b)

Trustee as lien creditor . . . 544(a)(1)

B

BAD FAITH

Petition filed in, damages . . . 303(i)

BANKRUPTCY AMENDMENTS AND FEDERAL JUDGESHIP ACT

Bankruptcy judges

    Evaluation of potential . . . . 98–353 § 120(b)

    Notice of vacancy . . . . . . 98–353 § 120(c)(1)

    Vacancy, filling of . . . 98–353 § 120

Effective date of provisions . . . . . 98–353 § 121

Effective date of title and amendments . . . 98–353 § 122

Jurisdiction, district court . . . 98–353 § 115

Pending cases under title 11 . . . . 98–353 § 115

BANKRUPTCY CLERK OF COURT

Appointment of . . . 28 U.S.C. 156(b)

Consolidation with office of district clerk of court, restriction against . . . . 28 U.S.C. 156(d)

Custodianship . . . 28 U.S.C. 156(e)

Financial accountability . . . 28 U.S.C. 156(f)

BANKRUPTCY COURT

Automatic stay, power as to . . . 362(b)

Clerk of court (See BANKRUPTCY CLERK OF COURT)

Contempt, power as to . . . 105 Comment

Core or non-core proceedings, authority for final judgment in . . . 28 U.S.C. 157

Designation of . . . 28 U.S.C. 151

District judges, role of . . . 28 U.S.C. 151

Fees . . . 28 U.S.C. 1930, Comment

Judges (See BANKRUPTCY JUDGES)

Petitions, filing of . . . 301; 303

Power of . . . 105(a)

Sessions, holding regular . . . 28 U.S.C. 157

BANKRUPTCY CRIMES (See CRIMINAL ACTIONS)

[See page I-1 for explanation of references.]

BANKRUPTCY JUDGES

Adjacent districts, service in . . . 28 U.S.C. 152(d)

Administrative information . . . . 28 U.S.C. 156(c)

Appointment . . . 28 U.S.C. 152

Authority . . . 28 U.S.C. 151

Bankruptcy Amendments and Federal Judgeship Act provisions (See BANKRUPTCY AMENDMENTS AND FEDERAL JUDGESHIP ACT)

Chapter 11 reorganization
  Professional person, employment of person connected with . . . . . . 1103 Comment
  Trustee or examiner, appointment of person connected with . . . . . 1104 Comment

Chapter 13 trustee, appointment of person connected with . . . 1302 Comment

Chief judges, designation of . . . 28 U.S.C. 154(b)

Clerks appointed by
  Bankruptcy clerk of court (See BANKRUPTCY CLERK OF COURT)
  Law clerks (See LAW CLERKS)

Core procedures defined . . . . . . 28 U.S.C. 157(b)(2)

Court (See BANKRUPTCY COURT)

District judges' powers as . . . 28 U.S.C. 151

Division of business . . . 28 U.S.C. 154(a)

Exemptions . . . 28 U.S.C. 153(d)

Expenses . . . . . 28 U.S.C. 156(c); 28 U.S.C. 156(d); 28 U.S.C. 156(e); 28 U.S.C. 156(f)

Law clerks (See LAW CLERKS)

Non-core proceedings, hearing of . . . . 28 U.S.C. 157(c)(1)

Number in each judicial district . . . . . 28 U.S.C. 152(a)(2)

Oaths and affirmations . . . 28 U.S.C. 153(c)

Personal injury tort proceedings . . . . . 28 U.S.C. 157(b)(5)

Power, exercise of . . . 105(c)

Practice of law by . . . 28 U.S.C. 153(b)

Procedure . . . 28 U.S.C. 157

Professional person, employment of person or firm of person connected with . . . . 327 Comment; 328 Comment

Recall after retirement . . . 28 U.S.C. 155(b)

Removal, criteria for . . . 28 U.S.C. 152(e)

BANKRUPTCY JUDGES—Cont.

Retirement, recall following . . . . 28 U.S.C. 155(b)

Salary, determination of . . 28 U.S.C. 153(a)

Staff appointments . . . 28 U.S.C. 156(a)

Term of . . . 28 U.S.C. 152(a)(1)

Transfers, temporary . . . 28 U.S.C. 155(a)

Wrongful death claims . . . . . . 28 U.S.C. 157(b)(5)

BANKS

(See also CREDIT UNIONS; DEPOSITORY INSTITUTIONS; FINANCIAL INSTITUTIONS)

Chapter 7, ineligibility . . . 109(b)(2), (3)

"Federal depository institutions regulatory agency" defined . . . 101(3)

Foreign, involuntary case . . . 303(k)

BENEFITS

Disability . . . 522(d)(10)(C)

Public assistance . . . 522(d)(10)(A)

Veterans' . . . 522(d)(10)(B)

BEST INTERESTS TEST

Chapter 11 reorganization . . . 1129(a)(4) *et seq.*

Chapter 12 family farmer debt adjustment . . . 1225(a)(4) *et seq.*

Chapter 13 individual debt adjustment . . . . 1325(a)(4) *et seq.*

BONA FIDE PURCHASER

Debtor's realty . . . 544(a)(3)

Postpetition transactions . . . 549(c)

Trustee status as . . . 544 Comment

BOND

Debtor, to protect . . . 303(e)

Investments by trustee . . . 345(b)(1)

Statute of limitations . . . 322(d)

Trustee . . . 322

BOOKS AND RECORDS (See RECORDS AND BOOKS)

BRIBERY

Criminal actions . . . 18 U.S.C. 152

BURDEN OF PROOF

Automatic stay and . . . 362(g)

Chapter 13 postpetition claims; transfer of property . . . 549

Trustee obtaining credit . . . 364(d)

[See page I-1 for explanation of references.]

[See page I-1 for explanation of references.]

[See page I-1 for explanation of references.]

[See page I-1 for explanation of references.]

CONTRACTS—Cont.

Commodities (See COMMODITY CON-
TRACTS)

Executory (See EXECUTORY CONTRACTS)

Forward (See FORWARD CONTRACTS)

Rejection of claim or interest . . . 502(g)

Securities (See SECURITIES CONTRACTS)

Simple contract . . . 544(a)(1); 547(e)

S.I.P.C., executory contract and . . . 744

CONTRACTUAL RIGHT

Defined . . . 555; 556

CONTROLLING PERSON

Subordination of . . . 747(4)

CONVERSION OF CHAPTERS

Chapter 7 or 11 from Chapter 13 . . . . . .
1301(a)(2)

Chapter 7 to Chapter 11 or 13 . . . 706

Chapter 11

    Chapter 7, to . . . 1112(a)

    Chapter 7 or 13, under . . . 348

    Chapter 13, to . . . 706; 1112(d)

    Generally . . . 1112

Chapter 12

    Generally . . . 1208

    Reference to . . . 348 Comment

Claims against estate . . . 348(d)

Condition to . . . 706

Debtor . . . 706(c), (d)

Exception to general rule . . . 348(b)

Generally . . . 348(a); 707; 1330(b)

Limitation; conversion to Chapter 7 . . . . .
1112(c)

Notice; time for rejecting contracts . . . . .
348(d)

Plan, under termination . . . 1112(b)(9)

Power of court . . . 1112(b)

Standard for . . . 1112(f)

Status of pre-conversion claims . . . 348(c)

Termination of appointment of trustee on
conversion . . . 348(e)

Waiver of right . . . 706(a)

CO-OWNERS

Community property, dower, curtesy

    Right of first refusal to . . . 363(i)

Joint tenancy, tenancy in common, tenancy by
the entirety; sale of interest in property
. . . 363(h)

Spouse or co-owner, distribution of appropriate portion of proceeds of sale to . . . . .
363(j)

CO-OWNERS—Cont.

Trustee of interest of, sale of property by
. . . 363(h) - (j)

CORE PROCEEDINGS

Consent of pleader as to entry of judgment by
bankruptcy judge in non-core proceedings
. . . 28 U.S.C. 157

Fraudulent transfers . . . 548 Comment

Liens, determinations of . . . 724 Comment

Non-core proceedings, pleader's consent to
final judgment by bankruptcy judge in
. . . 28 U.S.C. 157

Turnover property of the estate, orders as
. . . 542 Comment; 543 Comment

CORPORATE DEBTOR

Equity security holders, meeting of . . . . .
341(b)

CORPORATION

Defined . . . 101(9)

Involuntary case . . . 303(a)

Person, status as . . . 101(41)

COST OF LIVING

Adjustment for . . . 104

COSTS (See ADMINISTRATIVE COSTS
AND EXPENSES)

COURT OF THE UNITED STATES

Defined . . . 18 U.S.C. 6001

CREDIT

Effect of reversal on appeal . . . 364(e)

Junior secured credit . . . 364(c)

Obtaining business credit . . . 364(a)

Priorities as to . . . 364

Securities Act of 1933, exemptions . . . . .
364(f)

Senior secured credit . . . 364(d)

Status of unsecured credit . . . 364(b)

Superpriority . . . 364 Comment

CREDITOR

Attorney of creditor, administrative expenses
. . . 503(b)(4)

Best interest of (See BEST INTERESTS
TEST)

Committee of (See CREDITORS' COMMIT-
TEE)

Defined . . . 101(10)

Determination of tax liability

    Assessment of tax . . . 505(c)

[See page I-1 for explanation of references.]

[See page I-1 for explanation of references.]

[See page I-1 for explanation of references.]

[See page I-1 for explanation of references.]

DEFINITIONS—Cont.

Foreign proceeding . . . 101(23)
Foreign representative . . . 101(24)
Forward contract . . . 101(25)
Forward contract merchant . . . 101(26)
Future delivery . . . 761(8)
Futures commission merchant . . . 761(8)
Governmental unit . . . 101(27)
Grain . . . 557(b)(1)
Grain storage facility . . . 557(b)(2)
Improvement . . . 550(d)(2)
Indenture . . . 101(28)
Indenture trustee . . . 101(29)
Individual with regular income . . . 101(30)
Insider . . . 101(31)
Insolvent . . . 101(32)
Institution-affiliated party . . . 101(33)
Insured credit union . . . 101(34)
Insured depository institution . . . 101(35)
Intellectual property . . . 101(56)
Inventory . . . 547(a)(1)
Judicial lien . . . 101(36)
Leverage transaction . . . 761(13)
Leverage transaction merchant . . . 761(14)
Lien . . . 101(37)
Margin payment . . 101(38); 741(5); 761(15)
Mask work . . . 101(57)
Member property . . . 761(16)
Municipality . . . 101(40)
Net equity . . . 741(6)
Net equity of . . . 761(17)
New value . . . 547(a)(2)
Person . . . 101(41)
Petition . . . 101(42)
Producer of grain . . . 557(b)(3)
Property of the estate . . . 902(1)
Purchaser . . . 101(43)
Racketeering . . . 18 U.S.C. 1961
Railroad . . . 101(44)
Receivable . . . 547(a)(3)
Relative . . . 101(45)
Repo participant . . . 101(46)
Repurchase agreement . . . 101(47)
Retiree benefits . . . 1114(a)
Securities clearing agency . . . 101(48)
Securities contract . . . 741(7)
Security . . . 101(49)
Security agreement . . . 101(50)
Security interest . . . 101(51)
Settlement payment . . . 101(39); 741(8)
SIPC . . . 741(7)

DEFINITIONS—Cont.

Special revenues; Chapter 9 municipal debt
    adjustment . . . 902(2)
Special taxpayer; Chapter 9 municipal debt
    adjustment
        Affected by the plan . . . 902(4)
        Generally . . . 902(3)
State . . . 101(52)
Statutory lien . . . 101(53)
Stockbroker . . . 101(54)
Substantial consummation . . . 1101(2)
Swap agreement . . . 101(55)
Swap participant . . . 101(56)
Timeshare plan . . . 101(57)
Transfer . . . 101(54)
Trustee; municipal debt adjustment . . . . .
    902(5)
Typical investor . . . 1125(a)(2)
United States . . . 101(55)
Value . . . 522(a)(2); 548(d)(2)

DEPARTMENT OF TRANSPORTATION

Hearing on issue . . . 1164

DEPENDENT

Defined . . . 522(a)(1)

DEPOSIT ACCOUNTS

Meaning of . . . 363(a)

DEPOSITORY INSTITUTIONS

Banks (See BANKS)
Credit unions (See CREDIT UNIONS)
"Federal depository institutions regulatory
    agency" defined . . . 101(3)
Insured depository institutions
    Chapter 11 trustee, obligations assumed
        by . . . 365(o)
    Defined . . . 101(35)
    Exemptions . . . 522(c)(3)

DETERMINATIONS

Secured status, of . . . 506
Tax liability, of . . . 505

DISCHARGE

Approval, prior; not obtained . . . 1328(d)
Chapter 7 . . . 727
Chapter 12 (See FAMILY FARMER BANK-
    RUPTCY (CHAPTER 12))
Chapter 13 (See INDIVIDUAL'S DEBT AD-
    JUSTMENT (CHAPTER 13))
Community claim . . . 524(a)(3)
Contempt in case . . . 727(a)(6)

[See page I-1 for explanation of references.]

[See page I-1 for explanation of references.]

[See page I-1 for explanation of references.]

[See page I-1 for explanation of references.]

[See page I-1 for explanation of references.]

[See page I-1 for explanation of references.]

[See page I-1 for explanation of references.]

FEASIBILITY
Debtor . . . 1325(a)(6)
Feasibility rule; postpetition claims . . . . .
1305(c) Comment

FEDERAL DEPOSITORY INSTITUTIONS REGULATORY AGENCY
Defined . . . 101(3)

FEDERAL STATE ALTERNATIVE
Exemptions . . . 522(b)(1)

FEES
Attorney (See ATTORNEY'S FEES)
Automatic stay, fee for motion seeking relief
from . . . . . 28 U.S.C. 1930 Comment;
362 Comment
Bankruptcy court . . . . . . 28 U.S.C. 1930,
Comment
Confirmation of plan . . . 1325(a)(2)
Electronic access to information, miscella-
neous legislation relating to determination
of . . . . . . 28 U.S.C. 1930, following
1991 Amendments
Filing fees
Electronic access to information . . 28
U.S.C. 1930, following 1991 Amend-
ments
Generally . . . 28 U.S.C. 1930
Miscellaneous fees . . 28 U.S.C. 1930(b)
Quarterly fees . . 28 U.S.C. 1930(a)(6)
United States trustee, compensation paid
to (See COMPENSATION)
Judiciary Appropriations Act of 1990, effect of
. . . 28 U.S.C. 1930 Comment; 363
Comment
Miscellaneous fees . . . 28 U.S.C. 1930(b)
Officers, compensation of . . . 330(a)
Professional persons, compensation of (See
COMPENSATION)
Quarterly fees . . . 28 U.S.C. 1930(a)(6)
Sharing of compensation
Exceptions . . . 504(b)
Prohibition as to . . . 504(a)
United States trustee, compensation paid to
(See COMPENSATION)
United States Trustee System Fund
Amounts deposited in . . . . 28 U.S.C.
589a(b); 28 U.S.C. 589a(f)
Offsetting collections . . . . 28 U.S.C.
589a(f)

FEE SPLITTING
Exceptions . . . 504(b)
Prohibition as to . . . 504(a)

FIDUCIARY CAPACITY
Affiliate defined in terms of . . 101(2)(A)(i)
Exemption to discharge, fraud of fiduciary
. . . 523(a)(11)

FILE RETURN
Tax provisions, duty to file . . . 728(b)

FILING
Case ancillary to foreign case . . . 304(a)
Fees (See FEES)
Involuntary petitions . . . 303(b)
Plan under Chapter 12 . . . 1221

FINAL REPORT
Duty of trustee . . . 704(8)

FINANCIAL CASES, FALSE
Costs in . . . 523(d)

FINANCIAL INSTITUTIONS
Defined . . . 101(22)
Securities contracts, contractual right to
liquidate . . . 555

FINANCIAL STATEMENT
False . . . 523(a)(2)(B)

FINE (See PENALTY, FORFEITURE OR
FINE)

FOREIGN BANKS
Involuntary case . . . 303(k)

FOREIGN FUTURE
Defined . . . 761(11)

**FOREIGN FUTURES COMMISSION MER-
CHANT**
Customer, defined with respect to liquidation
. . . 761(9)(B)
Defined . . . 761(12)

FOREIGN PROCEEDINGS
Abstention . . . 305(a)(2)
Ancillary cases to . . . 304
Defined . . . 101(23)
Dismissal or suspension of a case if pending
. . . 305(2)
Distribution in . . . 508
Foreign bankruptcy case pending . . . 304
Relief granted . . . 304(c)

[See page I-1 for explanation of references.]

FOREIGN PROCEEDINGS—Cont.
Relief granted—Cont.
   Economical and expeditious administra-
     tion of estate . . . 304(c)
   Fresh start, opportunity for . . . 304(c)
Venue of cases ancillary to . . . . 28 U.S.C.
   1410

FOREIGN REPRESENTATIVE
Defined . . . 101(24)
Limited appearance . . . 306
Standing . . . 305(b)

FORFEITURE (See PENALTY, FORFEI-
   TURE OR FINE)

FORMS
Official forms and instructions, promulgation
   of . . . 28 U.S.C. 2075 Comment

FORWARD CONTRACT MERCHANT
Commodities contract or forward contract,
   contractual right to liquidate . . . 556
Defined . . . 101(26)
Transfer
   Avoidance . . . 546(e)
   Fraudulent . . . 548(d)(2)(B)

FORWARD CONTRACTS
Automatic stay . . . 362(b)(6)
Defined . . . 101(25)
Liquidation, contractual right . . . 556
Merchant (See FORWARD CONTRACT
   MERCHANT)
Settlement payments (See SETTLEMENT
   PAYMENTS)

FRAUD
Discharge and . . . 523(a)(2)(A)
Exemption to discharge, fraud of fiduciary
   . . . 523(a)(11)
Revocation of confirmation for . . . 1144
Statute of fraud as defense of estate . . 558
Transfer (See FRAUDULENT TRANSFER)

FRAUDULENT TRANSFER
Actual intent . . . 548(a)(1)
Avoidance of transfer, partnership . . 548(b)
Commodity broker . . . 548(d)(2)(B)
Core proceedings . . . 548 Comment
Good faith, protection of transferee . . . . .
   548(c)
Partnership transfer to partner . . . 548(b)

FRAUDULENT TRANSFER—Cont.
Protection of good faith transferee . . . . . .
   550(b)
Small capital . . . 548(a)(2)(B)
Timing . . . 548(d)(1)

FRESH START CONCEPT
Discriminatory treatment . . . 525 Comment

FRIENDS
Creditor pressure through . . 1301 Comment

FULL PAYMENT
Priority claims of . . . 1322(a)(2)

FUTURE EARNINGS
Loss of, exemptions . . . 522(d)(11)(E)
Submission of plan . . . 1322(a)(1)

FUTURES COMMISSION MERCHANT
Customer defined with respect to liquidation
   . . . 761(9)(A)
Foreign merchant (See FOREIGN FUTURES
   COMMISSION MERCHANT)

G

GOOD FAITH
Reorganization . . . 1126(e)
Transferee liability . . . 548(c); 550(b)

GOVERNMENTAL UNIT
Automatic stay . . . 362(b)(4)
Chapter 9 (See MUNICIPAL DEBT ADJUST-
   MENT (CHAPTER 9))
Defined . . . 101(27)
Discriminatory treatment of debtor . . . 525
Municipal debt readjustment (See MUNICI-
   PAL DEBT ADJUSTMENT (CHAPTER
   9))
Person, status as
   Generally . . . 101(41)
   Pursuit of action on . . . 362(b)(4)
Sovereign immunity
   Offset against . . . 106(b)
   Waiver of . . . 106
Tax liability determination . . . 505
Trustee, duty to file reports . . . 704(7)
Type of . . . 101(27)
Unsecured claims, priority on by governmental
   unit . . . 507(a)(7)

GRAIN
Defined . . . 557(b)(1)

[See page I-1 for explanation of references.]

GRAIN—Cont.
Disposition of
    Costs and expenses, recovery of . . . .
       557(h)(1)
    Extension of period for final . . 557(f)
    Trustee duties to governmental unit
       . . . 557(e)(3)
Interest, determination of
    Procedure, expedition of . . 557(c)(1)
    Profession compensation . . 557(d)(3)
    Stay pending appeal . . . 557(g)
Priority of producers . . . 507(a)(5)(A)
Producer defined . . . 557(b)(3)
Reclamation of . . . 546(d); 546(d)(l)
Storage facility, issuance of title by . . 501
    Comment
Valuation; distribution in kind . . 557(h)(2)

H

HARASSMENT
Discharge, effect of . . . 524 Comment

HARDSHIP
Discharge
    Conditions for . . . 1228 Comment
    Scope of . . . 1328(c)

HEARING
Abstention (See ABSTENTION)
Administrative costs and expenses and . . .
    503(a)
"After notice and hearing"; rules of construc-
    tion . . . 102(1)
Automatic stay, hearing for relief from . . .
    362 Comment
Confirmation . . . 1128(a); 1224
Conversion from Chapter 7 to Chapter 11
    . . . 706
Disclosure statement . . . 1125
Dismissal . . . 707
S.E.C. . . . 762(b)
Use, sale, or lease of property . . 363(c)(3)

HOMESTEAD
Exemption . . . 522(d)(1)

HOUSEHOLD GOODS
Security interest . . . 522(g)(2)

HOUSING AND URBAN DEVELOPMENT
Automatic stay of foreclosure of mortgage by
    . . . 362(b)(8)

I

IMMUNITY
Discharge and . . . 727(a)(6)
Governmental . . . 106
Self-incrimination . . . 344
Sovereign . . . 106

IMPAIRED CLASS
Failure to accept plan . . . 1129(b)

IMPAIRMENT
Concept of . . . 1124 Comment

IMPROVEMENTS
Defined . . . 550(d)(2)

INDEMNITY
Partnership and . . . 723(b)

INDENTURE
Defined . . . 101(28)

INDENTURE TRUSTEE
Administrative expenses . . . 503(b)(3), (5)
Defined . . . 101(29)
Examination of debtor . . . 343
Proof of claim, filing . . . 501(a)
Right to be heard . . . 1109

INDIVIDUAL
Adjustment of debt (See INDIVIDUAL'S
    DEBT ADJUSTMENT (CHAPTER 13))
Discharge only . . . 727(a)(1)
Person, status as . . . 101(41)
Repayment plan . . . 1301 *et seq.*

**INDIVIDUAL'S DEBT ADJUSTMENT
    (CHAPTER 13)**
Abandonment of property . . . 554
Acceptance . . . 1325(a)(5)(A)
Acceptance by creditor not required . . . . .
    1322 Comment
Amount owed, limitations as to . . . 109(e)
Automatic stay
    Exceptions . . . 362(b)
    Generally . . . 362(a)
Best interest test . . . 1325(a)(4) Comment
Business, debtor engaged in . . . 1304
Chapter 7 or 11 from Chapter 13 . . . . . .
    1301(a)(2)
Claim
    Allowance of . . . 502(b)
    Objections . . . 502(a)

[See page I-1 for explanation of references.]

[See page I-1 for explanation of references.]

[See page I-1 for explanation of references.]

[See page I-1 for explanation of references.]

INTEREST
Claims paid fifth, distribution to . . . .
726(a)(5)

INTERESTS, PROOF OF
Claims or interests . . . 501; 704(4)
Filing; equity security holders . . . 501(a)

INTERIM COMPENSATION
Generally . . . 331

INTERIM TRUSTEE
Appointment
Duration of . . . 701(b)
Expiration of . . . 701(c)
Source of disinterested person for . . .
701(a)
United States trustee, role of . . . 701
Comment; 703(b)
Debtor's bond . . . 303(g)
Expiration of appointment . . . 701(c)
Notification of . . . 701 Comment
Termination of . . . 701(b)
Trustee not elected, interim trustee serving in
case where . . . 702(d)

INTERSTATE COMMERCE ACT
Effects of limitation . . . 1166

**INTERSTATE COMMERCE COMMIS-
SION**
Railroad reorganization (See RAILROADS
AND RAILROAD REORGANIZATION)

INTERVENTION AND STANDING
Railroad reorganization . . . 1163
Securities and Exchange Commission . . . .
1109

INVALIDATION
Postpetition security interest . . . 552(a)

INVENTORY
Defined . . . 547(a)(1)
Preferences, exception for . . . 547(c)(5)

INVESTIGATION
Debtor, report on . . . 1106(a)

INVESTMENT
Bond or other security . . . 345(b)
Recapture of investment credit . . . 502(i)
Trustees . . . 345(a)

INVOLUNTARY CASES
Attorney's fees . . . 303(i)(1)(B)

INVOLUNTARY CASES—Cont.
Business, operation of . . . 303(f)
Damages . . . 303(i)
Dismissal . . . 303(j)
Family farmer exclusion . . . 303(a)
Filing, bad faith . . . 303(i)
Petition
Creditor filing . . . 303(c)
Discovery in contested 303
Comment
Dismissal of . . . 303(i)
Eligibility to file . . . 303(b)
Joining after petition filed . . . 303(c)
Names included . . . 301 Comment
Not timely . . . 303(h)
State sovereignty and . . . 303(a) Report
United States trustee's appointment of interim
trustee during "gap" period . . . 303(g)

INVOLUNTARY RELIEF
Debtor subject to . . . 303(a)

**INVOLUNTARY TRANSFER, AVOID-
ING**
Exemption of . . . 522(g)(1)

IPSO FACTO **CLAIMS**
Anti-ipso facto provision . . . 363(k) Report

IPSO FACTO **CLAUSES**
Executory contracts . . . 365(b)(2)

ISSUER
Underwriter as . . . 1145(b)(1)(D)

J

JEWELRY
Exemption . . . 522(d)(4)

JOINT CASES
Consolidation as to . . . 302(b)
Petition under application to all Chapters
. . . 302 Comment
Single petition for . . . 302(a)

JUDGES
Bankruptcy (See BANKRUPTCY JUDGES)
Federal Judgeship Act (See BANKRUTPCY
AMENDMENTS AND FEDERAL JUDGE-
SHIP ACT)

JUDGMENTS
Discharge voids . . . 524(a)

JUDICIAL LIEN
Defined . . . 101(36)

JUDICIAL POWER
Cases ancillary to foreign proceedings, discretion of court . . . 304(c)
Generally . . . 105(a)
Jurisdiction (See JURISDICTION)

JURISDICTION
Appeal, district court jurisdiction to hear . . . 28 U.S.C. 158(a)
Chapter 9 (See MUNICIPAL DEBT ADJUSTMENT (CHAPTER 9))
District court
    Bankruptcy Amendment and Federal Judgeship Act . . . 28 U.S.C. 158(a)
    Cases . . . 28 U.S.C. 1334(a)
    Civil proceedings under title 11 . . 28 U.S.C. 1334(b)
    Property, exclusive jurisdiction of . . . 28 U.S.C. 1334(d)
Municipal debt adjustment (See MUNICIPAL DEBT ADJUSTMENT (CHAPTER 9))

JURY TRIAL
Title 11 effect on right to . . 28 U.S.C. 1411

L

LABOR ORGANIZATIONS
Appeal, right to . . . 1164 Comment
Retired employees, representative for . . . . 1114(c)(1)

LAW CLERKS
Bankruptcy judges, appointed by
    Exemption . . . . . 28 U.S.C. 156(a); 28 U.S.C. 156 Comment
    Generally . . . 28 U.S.C. 156(a)

LEASES
Affiliate relationship based on . . 101(2)(C); 101(2)(D)
Automatic stay of termination . . 362(b)(10)
Claims or interest, *bona fide* . . . . 502(b)(6)(A)
Deposit or security for debtor's obligations under assigned unexpired lease . . 365(l)
Executory contracts (See EXECUTORY CONTRACTS)
Municipal . . . 929
Property of the estate status . . . 541(b)(2)

LEASES—Cont.
Real property, lease of (See REAL PROPERTY, subhead: Lease of)
Rejection of
    Executory contracts (See EXECUTORY CONTRACTS)
    Generally . . . 365(h)(1)
Rental agreement as, status of . . . 365(m)
Unexpired (See UNEXPIRED LEASES)

LESSOR
Claims or interest claim of . . . 502(b)(7)

LEVERAGE TRANSACTION
Defined . . . 761(13)
Merchant
    Customer defined with respect to liquidation . . . 761(9)(C)
    Defined . . . 761(14)

LIABILITIES
Fixed List . . . 1141(d)
Taxes, partner's unpaid . . . 728(c)

LIENS
Avoidance of lien, penalty . . . 724(a)
Core proceedings, determination of liens as . . . 724 Comment
Defined . . . 101(37)
Dismissal of case, reinstatement upon . . . . 349(b)(1)(C); 349 Comment
Distribution
    Equality of . . . 724(c)
    Order of . . . 724(b)
Enforcement period, tolling of . . . . 108(c) Comment
Equivalent to tax liens . . . 724(d)
Fine, penalty, forfeiture, damages
    Avoid . . . 724(a)
    Unpaid fine, lien for satisfaction of . . 18 U.S.C. 3613
    Unsecured creditors, protecting . . . . 724(a)
    Voidable . . . 724
Judicial lien defined . . . 101(36)
Nonbankruptcy statute compelling enforcement, tolling of enforcement period due to . . . 108(c) Comment
Reinstatement upon dismissal of case . . . . 349(b)(1)(C); 349 Comment
Sale free and clear of, Chapter 11 reorganization plan . . . 1123(a)(5)(D)

[See page I-1 for explanation of references.]

[See page I-1 for explanation of references.]

LIQUIDATION (CHAPTER 7)—Cont.
Trustee—Cont.
  Financial affairs investigation . . . . .
    704(4)
  Information concerning estate, duty to
    provide . . . 704(7)
  Intention, assurance of debtor . . . . .
    704(3)
  Interim trustee (See INTERIM TRUSTEE)
  Proof of claims examinations . . . . .
    704(5)
  Resignation . . . 703(a)
  Successor . . . 703
  Tax, filing of . . . 704(8)
Unclaimed property . . . 347(a)

LOAN
Enabling, exception for . . . 547(c)(3)
Premium, automatic . . . 542(d)
Student loans (See STUDENT LOANS)

LONG TERM DEBT
Exception . . . 1328(c)(1)

LUXURY ITEMS
Discharge exception . . . 523(a)(2)(C)

M

MALICIOUS AND WILLFUL INJURY
Discharge, exception to . . . 523(a)(6)

MARGIN PAYMENT
Commodities contracts, contractual right to
  liquidate . . . 556
Defined . . . 101(38); 741(5); 761(15)
Forward contract, contractual right to liquidate
  . . . 556
Settlement payments defined as . . 761(15)
Transfer
  Avoidance . . . 546(e), (f)
  Fraudulent . . . 548(d)(2)(B)
Value . . . 548 Comment

MARSHALLING RULE
Tax . . . 728(c)

MASK WORK
Defined . . . 101(57)

**MEETINGS OF CREDITORS AND EQ-
UITY SECURITY HOLDERS**
Court, exclusion of . . . 341(c)
Equity security holders . . . 341(b)

**MEETINGS OF CREDITORS AND EQ-
UITY SECURITY HOLDERS**—Cont.
Generally . . . 341
Trustee, election of . . . 702
Trustee in liquidation case, election of . . .
  702(b)
United States trustee
  Designees of . . . 1102 Comment
  Role of . . . . . . 341(a); 341(b); 1102
    Comment

MEMBER PROPERTY
Defined . . . 761(6)

MERCHANT MARINE ACT
General application of (Section 908) . . 46
  U.S.C. 1247

MISMANAGEMENT
Duty to investigate . . . 1106(a)(4)

MODIFICATION
Amounts . . . 1329(a)(3)
Confirmation, post . . . 1229
Retired employees benefits payment . . . . .
  1114(f)(1)
Time . . . 1329(a)(2)

MONEY
Estate, of (See MONEY OF ESTATE)
Reduction of securities to . . . 748

MONEY OF ESTATE
Deposit authorization . . . 345(c)
Trustee
  Accounting . . . 345(b)(1)(C)
  Bond
    Generally . . . 345(b)(1)
    United States trustee, approval by
      . . . 345(b)(1)(B)
  Deposit or investment of . . . 345(a)
  Options open to . . . 345
Unclaimed . . . 347(b)

MORTGAGE
Foreclosure by HUD, stay of . . . 362(b)(8)
Indenture . . . 101(28)
Property of estate . . . 541

MOTOR VEHICLES
Discharge of fine incurred for intoxicated
  driving . . . 523(a)(9)

[See page I-1 for explanation of references.]

[See page I-1 for explanation of references.]

NOTICE
Administrative costs and expenses and . . . 503(a)

"After notice and a hearing" (See "AFTER NOTICE AND A HEARING")

Chapter 9 . . . 923

Community claim, holder of . . . 342(a)

Consumer debt cases . . . 342(b)

Dismissal, chapter 7 case . . . 707(b)

Exemption . . . 522(m)

Grain interest, expedition in determination of . . . 557(e)(1)

Municipal debt adjustment . . . 923

Order for relief . . . 342(a)

Professional persons' compensation . . . . . 330(a)

Securities and Exchange Commission 762

S.I.P.C. . . . 743

Tax deficiency, automatic stay of notice of . . . 362(b)(9)

Trustee selected in chapter 7 or 13 case, notification . . . 701 Comment

Use, sale or lease of property . . . 363(b)(2)

O

OBJECTION
Discharge, to . . . 727(c)

OFFICERS
Chapter 13 (See INDIVIDUAL'S DEBT ADJUSTMENT (CHAPTER 13))

Compensation of trustees as officers of estate (See COMPENSATION)

OIL AND GAS
Farmout agreement defined . . . 101(21A)

Property of the estate, interest of debtor in liquid or gaseous hydrocarbons as . . . . 541(b)(4)

OPEN COMMODITY CONTRACTS
Trustee's responsibility in liquidation action . . . 766(b)

OPEN MODIFICATION
Rejection of . . . 1127(a)

OPERATION OF BUSINESS (See BUSINESS, OPERATION OF)

ORAL COMMUNICATIONS
Interception of . . . 18 U.S.C. 2516

ORDER FOR RELIEF (See RELIEF)

P

PARAPROFESSIONAL
Compensation . . . 330(a)

PARTNERSHIPS
Apportionment of carryover . . . 728(d)

Compensation, fee splitting . . . 504

Insider; partnership as debtor . . 101(31)(C)

Insolvency
    Defined . . . 101(32)(B)
    Involuntary cases, as requirement in . . . 303(b)(3)(A) Comment

Involuntary cases
    Answer to petition, filing of . . 303(d)
    Insolvency as requirement in . . . . . . 303(b)(3)(A) Comment
    Petition, filing of . . . 303(b)(3)

Limited partnership, subordination of . . . . 747(3)

Rights of trustee against . . . 723(a)

Special tax provisions . . . 346(b)(1)

Tax claim
    Apportionment . . . 728(d)
    Generally . . . 728(c)

Trustee (See PARTNERSHIP TRUSTEE)

PARTNERSHIP TRUSTEE
Collection, nonbankrupt partners . . 723(b)

General partners
    Claim against estate of . . . 723(c)
    Distribution . . . 723(c)
    First step . . . 723(b)
    Indemnity provided by . . . 723(c)
    Jingle rule . . . 723 Comment
    Not a debtor in case . . . 723(b)
    Recover deficiency . . . 723(b)
    Restriction on disposal of property . . 723(c)
    Rights against . . . 723(a)
    Surplus over deficiency distribution . . . 723(d)

Rights against general partners . . . 723(a)

PARTY IN INTEREST
Automatic stay, relief from . . . 362(d)

Chapter 11 to Chapter 7 . . . 1112(b)

Revocation of order of confirmation 1144

Right to be heard . . . 1109

[See page I-1 for explanation of references.]

PAYMENT
Claims, priority of payment . . . 1129(a)(9)
Custodian . . . 543(c)(2)
Employer to trustee . . . 1325(b)
Full . . . 1325(a)(5)(B)
Priority claims . . . 1326(b)
Retired employees insurance . . . 1114

PAYMENT ON ORDER OF TRUSTEE
Turnover . . . 542(b)

PAYMENTS, ALTER
Modification to . . . 1329(a)(1)

PENALTY, FORFEITURE OR FINE
Automatic stay violations . . . 362(h)
Discharge, exception to . . . 523(a)(7)
Distribution . . . 726(a)(4)
Lien (See LIEN)

PENDING CASES
Debtor, as factor in definition of . . 109(g)

PENSION, PROFIT SHARING, STOCK
Debtors' right to . . . 522(d)(10)(E)
Distress termination of pension plan . . . . .
1113
Pension plan, distress termination of . . . . .
1113

PERSON
Defined . . . 101(41)

PERSONAL INJURY
Bankruptcy judges . . . 28 U.S.C. 157(b)(5)
Railroads . . . 1171

PERSONAL PROPERTY
Redemption . . . 722

PETITION
Answer to; who may file . . . 303(d)
Automatic stay . . . 362(b)(6)
Bankruptcy Court . . . 302; 303; 304
Debtor, filing by . . . 301
Defined . . . 101(42)
Filing of
    Bankruptcy court . . . 301; 303
    Involuntary cases, commencement . . .
    303(b)
Involuntary against partnership . . 303(b)(3)
Involuntary cases (See INVOLUNTARY
  CASES)
Joint . . . 302
Voluntary case, filing of . . . 301

PLANS
Bankruptcy plans (See specific headings, e.g.,
  REORGANIZATION (CHAPTER 11))

POSTCONFIRMATION MODIFICATION
Generally . . . 1127(b)

POSTCONFIRMATION REPORTS
Filing of . . . 1106(a)(6)

POSTPETITION CLAIMS (See CLAIMS
  OR INTERESTS)

POSTPETITION EXPENSES
Necessity of . . . 1305(a)(2)

POSTPETITION PAYMENTS
Administrative costs and expenses . . . 503

POSTPETITION PROPERTY
Chapter 13 . . . 1306(a)(2)

**POSTPETITION SECURITY INTEREST
  EXCEPTION**
Certain after acquired property . . . 552(b)
General invalidation of . . . 552(a)
Municipal debt adjustment . . . 928
Prejudice . . . 552
U.C.C. and . . . 552

POSTPETITION TRANSACTIONS
Claims (See CLAIMS OR INTERESTS)
Good faith purchaser . . . 549(c)
Involuntary case . . . 549(b)
Involuntary gap transfer . . . 549(b)
Protection of good faith transfer . . . 549(c)
Requirements . . . 549(a)(1)
Solicitations . . . 1125(b)
Statute of limitations . . . 549(d)
Transfer, avoidance of postpetition . . . . .
  549(a); 549(a)(2)(B)

POWER OF APPOINTMENT
Exclusion of property of estate . . . 541(b)
Property of estate and . . . 541(b)

PRECONFIRMATION MODIFICATION
Generally . . . 1127(a)

PREFERENCE
Antecedent debt . . . 547(b)
Avoidable . . . 547(b)
Avoiding power
    Burden of proving avoidability of
    transfer . . . 547(g)

[See page I-1 for explanation of references.]

[See page I-1 for explanation of references.]

PROFESSIONAL PERSONS
Administrative costs and expenses . . . . . .
503(b)(2)
Compensation (See COMPENSATION)
Disinterestedness
  Denial of compensation and . . 328(c)
  Generally . . . 327(a)
Employment of
  Bankruptcy judge, employment of person
    or firm of person connected with
    . . . 327 Comment; 328 Comment
  Compensation, limitation on . . . 328
  Generally . . . 327
  United States trustee, objection by . . .
    327(c)
Fee splitting . . . 504
Trustee and creditor, acting for both . . . . .
327(c)
Turnover of books and records . . . 542(e)

PROFIT SHARING, PENSION, STOCK
(See PENSION, PROFIT SHARING,
STOCK)

PROOF OF CLAIMS OR INTERESTS
Chapter 7 liquidation
  Duty to file; customer instruction . . .
    765(a)
  Examination of proof of claim by trustee
    . . . 704(4)-(5)
Chapter 11 reorganization (See REORGANI-
ZATION (CHAPTER 11), subhead: Claims
and interests)
Creditor filing . . . 501
Equity security holders; proof of interest filing
  . . . 501
Filing by creditor, generally . . . 501

PROPERTY
Abandonment . . . 554(a)
Abstention, custodian . . . 543(d)
Adequate protection of interested party . . .
363(e)
Apportionment of . . . 752(c)
Automatic stay and . . . 362(a)
Bankruptcy clause invalidation . . . 363(k)
"Claim against debtor"; rules of construction
  . . . 102(2)
Collusive bidding . . . 363(m)
Community . . . 541(a)(2)
Custodian, duties . . . 543(b)(1)
Customer (See CUSTOMER PROPERTY)

PROPERTY—Cont.
Debt, vesting of . . . 1327(b)
Debtor
  Legal title, without interest . . 541(d)
  Requirement as . . . 109(a)
Disposition of certain property . . . 725
Distribution of proceeds . . . 363(j)
Effect of reversal on appeal . . . 363(l)
Estate property (See PROPERTY OF THE
ESTATE)
Fraudulent use of . . . 18 U.S.C. 152
Free and clear, confirmation . . . 1141(c)
Hearing concerning use, sale , or lease of
  property . . . 363(c)(3)
Inherited, postpetition . . . 541(a)(5)(A)
Intellectual (See INTELLECTUAL PROP-
ERTY)
Lease of . . . 363
Lessee possession, terms of lease . . 363(h)
Managing of property, obtaining credits . . .
  364 Comment
Non-ordinary course use . . . 363(b)
Ordinary course use . . . 363(c)
Other exchanged; debtor's securities . . . . .
  1145(a)(1)(B)
Payment of custodian . . . 543(c)(2)
Postpetition . . . 1306(a)(2)
Preserved . . . 541(a)(4)
Proceeds of . . . 541(a)(6)
Recovered . . . 541(a)(3)
Right of first refusal . . . 363(i)
Sale of (See TRUSTEE, subhead: Sale of
  property)
Securities, debtor's . . . 1145(a)(1)(B)
Soft collateral, defined . . . 363(a)
Surcharge of custodian . . . 543(c)(3)
Transfer or sale of . . . 1123(a)(4)(B)
Trustee and (See TRUSTEE)
Turnover
  Estate property (See PROPERTY OF
    THE ESTATE)
  Generally (See TURNOVER)
Unclaimed . . . 347
Use, sale, or lease of . . . 363
Use not inconsistent with stay . . . 363(d)

PROPERTY OF THE ESTATE
Abandonment of property not administered
  before closing of case . . . 554 Comment
Acquired . . . 541
Chapter 12 . . . 1207
Claims, postpetition . . . 541(a)(5)

[See page I-1 for explanation of references.]

PROPERTY OF THE ESTATE—Cont.

Death, effect of . . . 541

Defined; municipal debt adjustment . . . . . 902(1)

Distribution (See DISTRIBUTION)

Educational institution, rights and status of . . . 541(b)(3)

Exclusion of power of appointment . . . . . 541(b)

Fresh start . . . 541

Ipso facto clauses . . . 541(c)(1)(B)

Kinds of property included . . . 541

Lease, nonresidential real property . . . . . . 541(b)(2)

Oil and gas interests . . . 541(b)(4)

Postpetition inherited property . . . . 541(a)(5)(A)

Postpetition transfers, avoidance . . . 549

Preserved property . . . 541(a)(4)

Restrictions on transfer . . . 541(c)(1)(A)

Sale by trustee (See TRUSTEE, subhead: Sale of property)

Spendthrift trusts . . . 541(c)(2)

Statute of limitation . . . 541

Title to property included . . . 541 Comment

Transfer, invalidation of restrictions . . . . . 541(c)

Turnover

     Action by custodian, prohibition of . . 542(a)

     Automatic premium loans . . . 542(d)

     Bank of Marin . . . 542(c)

     Books and records . . . 542(e)

     Core proceedings, orders as . . . . 542 Comment; 543 Comment

     Debtor responsibility to turnover . . . . 521(4)

     Duty to . . . 543(b)(1)

     Good faith transfer . . . 542(c)

     Privilege claims . . . 542(e)

     Professionals' responsibility to turnover record . . . 542

     Protection, transferee or payee . . . . . 542(c)

     Setoff . . . 542

     Trustee, payment on order of . . . . . 542(b)

Turnover by creditor . . . 542(a)

United States trustee, notice of sale or lease . . . 541 Comment

PROTECTION

Adequate (See ADEQUATE PROTECTION)

Debtor protection; discriminatory treatment . . . 525

Financiers of aircraft . . . 1110

Protective order (See PROTECTIVE ORDER)

Public health . . . 362(b)(4)

Secured creditors . . . 1325(a)(5)(B)

PROTECTIVE ORDER

Defamatory matter . . . 107(b)(2)

Trade secrets . . . 107(b)(1)

PROVABILITY

Abolition of concept . . . 101(10) Comment

PUBLIC INTEREST

Railroad reorganization . . . 1165

PURCHASE

Lien of . . . 365(j)

Purchaser defined . . . 101(43)

Trustee, successor to . . . 544

Q

QUALIFICATION

Trustee . . . 322

R

RACKETEER INFLUENCED AND COR-RUPT ORGANIZATIONS

Racketeering defined . . . 18 U.S.C. 1961

RAILROADS AND RAILROAD REOR-GANIZATION

Abandonment of line

     Appeals . . . 1170d

     Approval by Commission . . . 1170b

     Fair arrangement requirement . . . . . 1170(e)(1)

     Generally . . . 1170

     Notice and hearing . . . 1170c

     Plan, abandonment permissable under . . . 1172(a)(2)

Appointment of trustee . . . 1163

Chapter 7, ineligible . . . 109(b)(1); 109(d)

Chapter 11 sections not applying to . . 1161

Claims, personal injury . . . 1171

Collective bargaining . . . 1167

Committee of creditors, representation . . . 1103(b)

[See page I-1 for explanation of references.]

[See page I-1 for explanation of references.]

REALTY, DEBTOR'S—Cont.
Definition of . . . 547(a)(3)

RECEIVABLES
Preferences, exception for . . . 547(c)(5)

RECEIVER
Appointment by court . . . 105(b)
Suable . . . 28 U.S.C. 959

RECLAMATION
Right to; trustee's powers limited by . . . .
546(c)

RECORDS AND BOOKS
Distribution of, discharge . . . 727(a)(3)
Turnover of . . . 542(e)

REDUCTION TO MONEY
Securities . . . 748

REGULATORY COMMISSION
Rate changes, approval of . . . 1129(a)(6)

REHABILITATION
Conversion or dismissal . . . 1112(b)

REINSTATEMENTS
Dismissal, upon (See DISMISSAL)

REJECTION
Contracts . . . 1322(b)(7)
Disqualification . . . 1126(e)
Executory contracts (See EXECUTORY
CONTRACTS)
Valued out . . . 1126(g)

RELATIVES
Creditor pressure through . . 1301 Comment
Definition . . . 101(45)

RELIEF
Cases ancillary to foreign proceeding . . . .
304(b)
Involuntary cases, basis for granting . . . . .
303(h)
Order for
Conversion and . . . 348(a), (b)
Interim trustee, appointment of . . 701
Involuntary cases, standards for . . . .
303(h)
Notice . . . 342
Rule of construction . . . 102(6)
Standard . . . 303(h)(1)
Transfers affected by . . 749(b); 764(b)

RELIEF—Cont.
Order for—Cont.
United States trustee, transmission to
. . . 342 Comment
Voluntary case, commencement of . .
301
Stay, court's power to enjoin grant of relief
from . . . 105(a) Comment

REMANDED CASES
Removal from state court to district court,
remand following . . . 28 U.S.C. 1452(b)

REMOVAL
Bankruptcy judges . . . 28 U.S.C. 152(e)
Cases, removal of
Governmental unit's police or regulatory
power, proceedings to enforce . . 28
U.S.C. 1452(a)
Remand following . . 28 U.S.C. 1452(b)
State court, removal of case to district
court . . . 28 U.S.C. 1452(b)
United States Tax Court proceedings
. . . 28 U.S.C. 1452(a)
Examiner . . . 324
Trustee . . . 324

RENT
Distress for rent, statutory lien . . . 545(4)
Postpetition security interests . . . 552
Proceeds from . . . 541(a)(6)
Statutory lien . . . 545(3)

REOPENING OF CASE
Generally . . . 350

REORGANIZATION (CHAPTER 11)
Acceptance of plan
Bad faith, designation of parties . . . .
1126(e)
Before commencement . . . 1126(b)
Computing requisite majorities . . . . .
1126(c)
Confirmation of plan, as prerequisite to
. . . 1129(a)(7)(A)
Conflict of interest . . . 1126(e), (g)
Creditor, acceptance or rejection . . . .
1126
Disqualification . . . 1126(e)
Equity security holders, acceptance by
. . . 341(b)
Generally . . . 1126
Participation denied . . . 1126(g)

[See page I-1 for explanation of references.]

[See page I-1 for explanation of references.]

[See page I-1 for explanation of references.]

[See page I-1 for explanation of references.]

[See page I-1 for explanation of references.]

[See page I-1 for explanation of references.]

[See page I-1 for explanation of references.]

SECURITIES—Cont.

Customer

Claims, extent of . . . 746

Customer name securities (See subhead: Customer name securities)

Defined for stock liquidation . . 741(2)

Instructions . . . 765

Margin payments . . . 766(c)

Name securities (See subhead: Customer name securities)

Net equity claims . . . 752(a)

Property . . . 741(4); 752; 766

Stockbroker liquidation . . . 741(2)

Subordination of . . . 747

Treatment of . . . 766

Unsecured claim . . . 752(b)(2)

Customer name securities

Customer property, exclusion from definition of . . . 741(4)(B)(i)

Defined for stockbroker liquidation . . 741(3)

Distribution in stockbroker liquidation . . . 751

Definition of security

Generally . . . 101(49)

Stockbroker liquidation, for . . 741(3)

Distribution

Dividends, minimum amounts for distribution of . . . 347 Comment

Stockholder liquidation . . . 750; 751

Unclaimed property . . . 347(b)

Dividends

Minimum amounts for distribution of . . . 347 Comment

Unclaimed property . . . 347 Comment

Exchange of . . . 946

Exemption from laws under Chapter 11 reorganization . . . 1145

Extent of customer claim

Generally . . . 746

Good faith . . . 746

Interest

Household goods . . . 522(g)(2)

Postpetition (See POSTPETITION SECURITY INTEREST EXCEPTION)

Net equity . . . 741(5)

Notice . . . 762(a)

Portfolio . . . 1145(a)(4)

Property, sale of . . . 363(a)

Reduction of securities to money . . . 748

Reorganization (See REORGANIZATION (CHAPTER 11), subhead: Securities law)

SECURITIES—Cont.

Securities Investor Protection Act (See SECURITIES INVESTOR PROTECTION ACT OF 1970)

Securities Investor Protection Corporation (S.I.P.C.) (See SECURITIES INVESTOR PROTECTION CORPORATION (S.I.P.C.))

Settlement payments defined . . . 741(8)

Treatment of accounts . . . 745(a)

Unclaimed . . . 347(b)

Voidable transfers . . . 749

SECURITIES AND EXCHANGE COMMISSION

Appeal by . . . 1109 Comment

Contractual right to liquidate a securities contract, limitations . . . 555

Defined . . . 741(1)

Intervention by . . . 1109

Notice . . . 743; 762

Transfers, regulation of . . . 749(b)

SECURITIES CLEARING AGENCY

Defined . . . 101(48)

Securities contract (See SECURITIES CONTRACTS)

Transfers

Avoidance . . . 546(b)

Fraudulent . . . 548(d)(2)(B)

SECURITIES CONTRACTS

Automatic stay . . . 362(b)(6)

Chapter 7 liquidation

Apportionment of customer property after . . . 752(c)

Contractual right . . . 555

Financial institutions . . . 555

Securities clearing agency (See SECURITIES CLEARING AGENCY)

Stockbroker (See STOCKBROKER)

Commodities contracts distinguished . . . . 101(49)(B)(iii)-(v)

Defined . . . 741(7)

Transfers, nonavoidable . . . 749(b)

SECURITIES INVESTOR PROTECTION ACT OF 1970

Automatic stay . . . 362

Contractual right to liquidate a securities contract, limitations . . . 555

SECURITIES INVESTOR PROTECTION CORPORATION (S.I.P.C.)

Automatic stay, limitation on . . . 742

SECURITIES INVESTOR PROTECTION CORPORATION (S.I.P.C.)—Cont.
Customers, exclusion from . . . 746(b)
Defined . . . 741(7)
Executory contracts . . . 744
Notice . . . 743
Owner of account, principal of . . . 745(b)
Postpetition transactions . . . 746(a)
Protective decree with respect to debtor . . . 741(9)
Separate accounts . . . 745(a)
Subordination
    Controlling stockholder of . . . 747(2)
    Insider of . . . 747(1)
Trust, account customer of . . . 745(c)

SECURITIES PURCHASING UNDER-WRITERS
Generally . . . 1145(b)(1)(c)

SECURITY AGREEMENT
Defined . . . 101(50)

SECURITY INTEREST
Defined . . . 101(51)

SELF-INCRIMINATION
Generally . . . 344
Privilege against, discharge and . . . . 727(a)(6)

SETOFF
Acquisition of claims . . . 553(a)(2)
Acquisition of debt . . . 553(a)(3)
Allowable claims . . . 553(a)(1)
Automatic stay . . . 362(a)(7)
Claims or interest
    Recovery from avoidance of setoff . . 502(h)
    Reduction for . . . 502(b)(3)
Exception for . . . 547(c)(6)
Exemptions . . . 522(i)(1)
Lessee's right of . . . 365(h)(2)
Mutual debt, claim permitted . . . 362(b)(6)
Presumption of insolvency . . . 553(c)
Repo participant . . . 362(b)(7)
Timeshare interests against rents . . . . 365(h)(2)
Transfer, omission from definition of . . . . 101(54) Comment
Two Point Test . . . 553

SETTLEMENT PAYMENTS
Defined . . . 101(39); 741(8)

SETTLEMENT PAYMENTS—Cont.
Margin payments, defined as . . . 761(15)
Transfers
    Avoidance . . . 546(e), (f)
    Fraudulent . . . 548(d)(2)(B)

SHIPS
Merchant Marine Act, applicability of (Section 908) . . . 46 U.S.C. 1247
Reorganization . . . 1110

SHOPPING CENTER
Leases . . . 365(b)(3)

S.I.P.C. (See SECURITIES INVESTOR PROTECTION CORPORATION (S.I.P.C.))

SMALL BUSINESS
Operation of; Chapter 13 . . 1304 Comment

SOCIAL SECURITY ACT
Discharge of debts, exceptions . . . . 523(a)(5)(A)

SOLICITATION
Acceptances before commencement of case . . . 1125(a)(1); 1126(b)
Acceptances or rejections, prohibition . . . . 1125(b)
Bad faith of . . . 1126(f)
Compliance required of . . . 1127(c)
Postpetition solicitation of acceptances prohibited . . . 1125(b)
Prepetition of . . . 1126(b)
Prohibited, postpetition disclosure . . . . . . 1125(e)

SOVEREIGN IMMUNITY
Waiver . . . 106

SPECIAL TAXPAYER
Defined; municipal debt adjustment . . . . . 902(3), (4)
Municipal debt adjustment; confirmation of plan, objection to . . . 943(a)
Objection to municipal plan . . . 943(a)

SPLIT TAX YEAR
Individual's . . . 1146(a)

SPOUSE
Single petition by . . . 302

STAMP TAX
Exception . . . 1146(c)

[See page I-1 for explanation of references.]

[See page I-1 for explanation of references.]

[See page I-1 for explanation of references.]

[See page I-1 for explanation of references.]

[See page I-1 for explanation of references.]

[See page I-1 for explanation of references.]

[See page I-1 for explanation of references.]

UNMATURED INTEREST
Claims . . . 502(b)(2)

UNSCHEDULED DEBTS
Exceptions to . . . 523(a)(3)

USURY
Defense of estate, as . . . 558

UTILITY SERVICE
Court order as to . . . 366(b)
Discriminate against trustee or debtor 366
Generally . . . 366

V

VACANCY
Effect of . . . 325

VALUE
Defined . . . 548(d)(2)
Meaning of . . . 506(a)
Satisfaction, including . . . 550(b)

VALUE INCLUDES SATISFACTION
Indication of . . . 550(b)

VENUE
Change of . . . 28 U.S.C. 1412
Foreign proceedings, case ancillary to . . 28 U.S.C. 1410
Governing law . . . 109 Comment
Improper venue, cases filed in . . 28 U.S.C. 1412
Petition, filing . . . 28 U.S.C. 1408
Title 11, relationship of case to
    Arising in Title 11 case as distinguished from Title 11 case itself . . . . . 28 U.S.C. 1409
    Commencing cases under Title 11 . . . 28 U.S.C. 1408
    Petition, filing . . . 28 U.S.C. 1408
    Proceedings . . . 28 U.S.C. 1409

VESSELS (See SHIPS)

VESTING
Property in debt . . . 1327(b)

VOLUNTARY CASES
Commencement of . . . 301

VOTING-TRUST CERTIFICATE
Indenture and . . . 101(28)

W

WAGE CLAIM
Priority, unsecured claims . . . 507(a)(3)

WAGE EARNER
Chapter 13 (See INDIVIDUAL'S DEBT ADJUSTMENT (CHAPTER 13))
Consent from unsecured creditors . . . . . . 1325(a)
Conversion or dismissal . . . 1307
Debtor
    Engaged in business . . . 1304
    Who may be . . . 109(e)
Distribution of payments . . . 1326
Individual's debt adjustment (See INDIVIDUAL'S DEBT ADJUSTMENT (CHAPTER 13))
Secured creditors . . . . 506(a); 1322(b)(2); 1325(a)(5)
Who may be a debtor . . . 109(e)

WAGE EARNER PLAN (See INDIVIDUAL'S DEBT ADJUSTMENT (CHAPTER 13))

WAIVER
Discharge of . . . 727(a)(9)
Exemption . . . 522(e)
Sovereign immunity . . . 106

WIFE (See SPOUSE)

WILLFUL AND MALICIOUS INJURY
Discharge, exception to . . . 523(a)(6)

WIRE COMMUNICATIONS
Interception of . . . 18 U.S.C. 2516

WITHDRAWAL OF CASE
District court right for . . . 28 U.S.C. 157(d)

WITHHOLDING TAXES
Wages and salaries, special tax provisions . . . 346(f)
Withholding tax priority . . . 507(a)(7)(C)

WITNESS
Criminal actions, immunity . . . . 18 U.S.C. 6001
Fees; administrative costs and expenses . . . 503(b)(6)
Immunity . . . 344
Self-incrimination . . . 344

[See page I-1 for explanation of references.]

WRONGFUL DEATH ACTIONS
Bankruptcy judges . . . 28 U.S.C. 157(b)(5)

WRONGFUL DEATH ACTIONS—Cont.
Payment, debtor right to receive . . . .
522(d)(11)(B)

THE GRIMMS'

German Folk Tales

Translated by

FRANCIS P. MAGOUN, JR

and

ALEXANDER H. KRAPPE

SOUTHERN ILLINOIS UNIVERSITY PRESS

Carbondale and Edwardsville

FEFFER & SIMONS, INC.

London and Amsterdam

ARCT
URUS
BOOKS ®

Dag Strömbäck

IN FRIENDSHIP AND ESTEEM

FOREWORD

KINDER- UND HAUSMÄRCHEN (*"Folk Tales for Children and the Home"*), as gathered and brought out in its more or less cannonical form by Jacob and Wilhelm Grimm in 1857 and often loosely and inaccurately referred to as "Grimms' Fairy Tales," is a collection of eighteenth-century and earlier German folk tales, in part taken from contemporary oral tradition, in part from older printed sources. As finally presented by the Grimms, these appear in a straightforward, somewhat unadorned though by no means barren style, while a certain matter-of-factness and chattiness colors the whole. Here the translators have assumed the challenging task of trying to reproduce some of these agreeable effects though without hope of more than suggesting Wilhelm Grimm's final achievement of one of the noblest monuments of German prose.

Originally composed by intelligent, keen-witted German peasant folk and told for mutual entertainment by grown-ups for grown-ups, these famous folk tales are, contrary to popular notion, not essentially for younger children, to whom, in fact, only a few are likely to appeal. A limited number, perhaps some twenty or thirty commonly included in almost innumerable select translations especially designed for children, have, to be sure, achieved notable success among children; yet because of its false emphasis, the Grimms subsequently regretted using the word *Kinder* in their title. In favor of the present title, *German Folk Tales,* substituted for the somewhat unwieldy translation of the German original, is that it quite exactly describes the contents, disposes of the misleading emphasis on "children," and leads to no ambiguity since there are no other genuine German folk tales outside of the Grimms' collection. The tales will, as a whole, appeal essentially to grown-ups with a taste for a good story well told. In the diction, style, and development of the various narratives there is nothing childish or juvenile, still less anything mannered or from the point of view of the original teller anything archaic. Consideration of these last points has, it may be re-marked, influenced the translation.

The present work is a complete and entirely new and inde-pendent translation of the two hundred *Kinder- und Haus-märchen,* together with the appended *Kinderlegenden* ("Reli-gious Tales concerning Children"), and aims at as high a degree of fidelity to the original as has seemed compatible with appro-priate and idiomatic English; it is based on the Jubilee-edition (1912) of Reinhold Steig.

This book aims to bring to the general reader a renewed or increased familiarity with the collection as a whole, to the folklorist a trustworthy rendering of the German text, which is often only in appearance easy to translate. Particular pains have been taken to find the correct English equivalents of many words connected with now obsolete occupations and crafts and of objects no longer in common use. In connection with this and for the correct interpretation of certain unusual, dialectal, and today archaic German words and phrases the Translators are grateful to many kind friends, most particularly to Professor Otto Springer, of the University of Pennsylvania.

No attempt has been made at annotation, but the tale numbers will permit ready reference to Johannes Bolte and Georg Polívka's *Anmerkungen zu den Kinder- und Hausmärchen* (5 vols,; Berlin, 1913 ff.). In this classic collection of variants and analogues, the wider affiliations of the tales with one another and with those of other lands is brought out. Alphabetical indexes of the English and German titles of the tales will, it is hoped, prove a useful finding list.

Finally, a special word of appreciation is owing to Mr. Ojars Kratins of the Harvard Graduate School of Arts and Sciences for help with the final check against the German text in June, 1960.

F. P. M., JR., *Harvard University*

CONTENTS

THE FOLK TALES

1 The Frog King, or Iron Henry

Der Froschkönig oder der eiserne Heinrich

IN DAYS OF OLD when wishing still did some good, there lived a king whose daughters were all beautiful; but the youngest was so beautiful that the sun itself, which has, to be sure, seen so many things, was astonished every time it shone in her face. Near the royal manor was a big dark forest, and in that forest under an old linden was a well. Now whenever the day was quite hot, the king's daughter used to go out into the forest and sit down by the cool well. If time hung too heavy on her hands, she would take a golden ball, toss it up in the air, and catch it again; and this was her favorite pastime.

Now it once happened that the golden ball of the king's daughter did not drop into the little hand which she held up but fell to the ground and rolled straight into the water. She followed it with her eyes; but the ball disappeared, and the well was deep, so deep that one couldn't see the bottom. Then she began to weep and wept louder and louder and was unconsolable. And as she was thus lamenting, someone called out to her: "What is the matter, king's daughter? You're crying hard enough to move a stone to pity." She looked about in the direction of the voice and then saw a frog sticking its big ugly head out of the water. "Oh, it's you, old water-splasher," she said. "I'm weeping over my golden ball which fell into the well." "Be quiet and don't weep," answered the frog. "I can certainly help you. But what will you give me if I fetch your plaything up again?" "Anything you wish, dear frog," she said, "my clothes, my pearls and jewels, and even the golden crown I'm wearing." The frog answered, "I don't want your clothes, your pearls and jewels, and your golden crown; but if you'll love me and let me be your companion and playmate, sit beside you at your table, eat from your golden plate, drink out of your cup, and sleep in your bed—if you'll promise me that, I'll go down and bring up your golden ball." "Oh, yes," she said,

3

"I'll promise you everything you want, if you'll only bring back the golden ball." She thought to herself, however, "How foolishly the silly frog's talking; it sits in the water with its kind and croaks and can't be anybody's companion."

On receiving her promise the frog dived in headfirst and in a short time came paddling up again; it had the ball in its mouth and threw it on the grass. The king's daughter was very glad to see her pretty plaything again, picked it up, and ran off with it. "Wait, wait!" cried the frog, "take me with you; I can't run like you." But what good did it do to croak after her, no matter how loud! She didn't listen but hurried home and soon forgot the poor frog, who had to crawl down again into its well.

The next day when she sat down to dinner with the king and all his court and was eating from her golden plate, suddenly, plump, plump, something came crawling up the marble stairs, and when it reached the top, there was a knock at the door and a voice cried, "King's daughter, youngest daughter! Open the door for me." She ran to see who might be outside, and when she opened the door, there was the frog. Then she hurriedly shut the door, sat down again at the table, and was quite frightened. The king saw clearly that her heart was beating furiously and said, "My child, what are you frightened of? There isn't by chance a giant at the door who wants to take you away?" "Oh, no," she answered, "it isn't a giant; it's a nasty frog." "What does the frog want of you?" "Oh, father dear, yesterday as I was sitting in the forest near the well and was playing; my golden ball fell into the water, and because I wept so hard, the frog fetched it up again. And because it insisted, I promised that it should be my companion, though I never thought it could get out of the water. Now it's outside and wants to come in here to me." Meanwhile there was a second knock, and a voice cried:

> "King's daughter, youngest daughter,
> Let me in.
> Don't you know what yesterday
> You told me
> By the cool water of the well?

King's daughter, youngest daughter,
Let me in."

Then the king said: "You must keep your promise. Go now and let it in." She went and opened the door; then the frog hopped in right behind her to her chair. There he sat and cried, "Lift me up." She hesitated, till finally the king commanded her to do so. Once the frog was on the chair, it wanted to get onto the table, and when it was sitting there, it said: "Now push your golden plate nearer me so that we may eat together." She even did this, but it was clear she didn't like doing it. The frog enjoyed its meal, but nearly every morsel stuck in her throat. Finally it said, "Now I have eaten my fill and am tired, so carry me to your room and make ready your silken bed; then we'll lie down to sleep." The king's daughter began to weep and was afraid of the cold frog, which she didn't dare touch and which was now to sleep in her pretty, clean bed. But the king grew angry and said, "You mustn't despise anyone after he has helped you when you were in trouble." Then she took it between her two fingers, carried it up, and put it in a corner; but when she was in her bed, it crawled up and said, "I'm tired and want to sleep as well as you; pick me up or I'll tell your father." Then she got very angry, picked it up, and threw it with all her might against the wall: "Now you can take a rest, you nasty frog!"

But when it fell it wasn't a frog but a king's son, with handsome kindly eyes. Now, as her father wished, he became her dear companion and husband. Then he told her how a wicked witch had laid a spell upon him and how no one could have disenchanted him out of the well except herself, and the next day they'd go together to his kingdom. Then they fell asleep, and the following morning when the sun woke them up, a coach came with a team of eight white horses with white ostrich plumes on their heads and harnessed with golden chains, and behind stood the young king's servant. That was Faithful Henry. Faithful Henry had been so distressed when his lord was transformed into a frog that he'd had three iron bands put around his heart lest it should break from sorrow and sadness. The coach, on the other hand, was to take the young king

to his kingdom. Faithful Henry helped them both into the
coach, once again took up his place behind, and was very happy
about the disenchantment. When they had gone some distance,
the king's son heard a cracking noise behind him as if something had broken. He turned around and said:

> "Henry, the coach is breaking."
> "No, my lord, not the coach;
> It's a band from my heart
> Which suffered sorely
> While you were sitting in the well,
> While you were a frog."

Again and again on the way there was a cracking noise, and
every time the king's son thought that the coach was breaking;
but it was only the bands snapping from Faithful Henry's
heart because his lord was now disenchanted and happy.

2   A Cat and a Mouse in Partnership

Katze und Maus in Gesellschaft

A CAT made the acquaintance of a mouse and talked so much
about its great love and friendship for it that the mouse finally
agreed to share a house and the housekeeping with it. "But
we must make provision for the winter," said the cat, "otherwise we'll suffer from hunger. You, little mouse, can't venture
everywhere, and one of these days you'll fall into a trap." They
acted on this good plan and bought a pot of fat, though they
didn't know where to put it. Finally after long reflection the
cat said, "I know of nowhere it might be kept more safely than
in the church; no one dares take anything away from there;
let's put it under the altar and not touch it till we need it."
Thus the pot of fat was put safely away. It wasn't long, however, before the cat got a craving for it and said to the mouse:
"As I was about to say, mouse, I've been asked by my cousin
to stand sponsor. She's given birth to a son, white with brown

spots, and I'm to stand sponsor for him. Let me go out today, and you look after the house yourself." "Yes, of course," answered the mouse, "for goodness' sake go along and if you eat something good, think of me. I, too, should very much like a drop of the sweet, red christening wine." But all this was quite untrue: the cat had no cousin and had not been asked to stand sponsor. It went straight to the church, sneaked to the pot of fat and began to lick it and licked the top layer off. Then it took a walk over the roofs of the town, enjoyed the view, finally stretched out in the sun, and licked its whiskers every time it thought of the pot of fat. It didn't come home until nightfall. "Well, here you are back again!" said the mouse. "You've no doubt had a splendid day." "It wasn't bad," answered the cat. "What name did they give the child?" asked the mouse. "Top-Layer-Off," said the cat rather dryly. "Top-Layer-Off!" exclaimed the mouse. "That's a strange and very odd name. Is it common in your family?" "What of it?" said the cat. "It's no worse than Crumb-Thief, your godparents' name."

Not long afterward the cat got a fresh craving. It said to the mouse: "You must do me the favor of once more tending the house alone; I've been asked to be sponsor a second time, and since the child has a white ring around its neck, I can't refuse." The good mouse consented, but the cat sneaked behind the town wall to the church and ate up half the pot of fat. "Nothing tastes better," it said, "than what one eats oneself," and was quite content with its day's work. When it came home, the mouse asked, "What name did they give this child?" "Half-Gone," answered the cat. "Half-Gone? Not really! I've never heard that name in all my life. I'll bet it's not in any regular list of names."

The cat's mouth soon watered again for the delicacy. "All good things go by threes," it said to the mouse. "Now I'm again to stand sponsor; the child's all black and only its paws are white; otherwise there's not a white hair on its body. Such a thing occurs only once every few years. You'll surely let me go?" "Top-Layer-Off, Half-Gone," answered the mouse. "These are such curious names and give me such food for thought." "There you sit home in your dark grey woolen coat and your long pigtail," said the cat, "and get notions; that comes from not going out in the day-time." In the cat's absence the mouse tidied the house and set it in order, but the cat with its taste for dainties emptied the pot completely. "Only when it's all gone is one at rest," it said to itself, and, fat and full, didn't come home till after nightfall. The mouse at once asked the name given the third child. "You probably won't like it either," said the cat. "It's All-Gone." "All-Gone!" exclaimed the mouse. "That is a most suspicious name; I've never seen it in print. All-Gone! What can that mean?" It shook its head, rolled itself up in a ball, and lay down to sleep.

From now on the cat was no longer asked to stand sponsor. However, when winter came and nothing to eat was to be found outdoors, the mouse thought of their store of fat and said, "Come, cat, let's go to the pot of fat we've saved up; it'll taste good." "Yes, indeed," answered the cat "you'll relish it as much as if you stuck your tongue out the window." They set out, and when they arrived, there was the pot where they'd left it—only it was empty. "Oho," said the mouse, "now I see what's happened; now it's as clear as day; you really are a true friend to me! You ate everything up while you were standing sponsor: first Top-Layer-Off, then Half-Gone, then . . ." "Will you be still!" cried the cat. "One word more and I'll eat you up." The poor mouse already had "All-Gone" on the tip of its tongue. No sooner had it said it than the cat made a jump at it, seized it and swallowed it up.

See, that's the way the world goes.

3   A Child of Saint Mary

Marienkind

ON THE EDGE of a large forest lived a woodcutter and his wife, and he had only one child, a girl three years old. They were, however, so poor that they no longer had their daily bread and did not know how they could feed her. One morning the woodcutter, bowed down by worry, went out into the forest to work, and as he was chopping wood, suddenly a tall and beautiful woman stood before him with a crown of shining stars upon her head and said "I am the Virgin Mary, mother of the Christ Child; you

are poor and needy; bring me your child, and I shall take her
with me and shall be her mother and care for her." The woodcutter obeyed, fetched his child and gave her over to the Virgin
Mary. She took her with her to Heaven where she fared well,
ate cake and drank sweet milk, and her clothes were of gold,
and the angels played with her. When she was fourteen, the
Virgin once called her and said: "Dear child, I am about to make
a long journey; take charge of the keys to the thirteen doors of
the Kingdom of Heaven. Twelve of these doors you may unlock
and marvel at the glories within, but the thirteenth door, which
this little key opens, is forbidden to you. Be careful not to unlock
it, otherwise misfortune will befall you." The girl promised to
be obedient, and when the Virgin had gone, she began to look
at the dwellings of the Heavenly Kingdom. Every day she unlocked one door until she had opened the twelve. In each dwelling an apostle was sitting in great glory. She delighted in all that
pomp and splendor, and the angels who always accompanied her
rejoiced with her. Now the forbidden door alone was left, and
she felt a great desire to know what was hidden behind it and
said to the angels, "I won't open it wide nor will I go in, but I'll
unlock it so we may get a tiny peek through the crack." "Oh no,"
said the angels, "that would be a sin; the Virgin Mary has
forbidden it, and some misfortune might easily befall you." Then
she kept still, but the desire deep down in her heart did not keep
still but gnawed and gnawed at her and left her no peace. Once
when the angels had all gone out, she thought, "Now I'm quite
alone and might as well look in; no one will know if I do." She
searched out the key and when she had it in her hand, she
couldn't help putting it in the lock, and once she'd put it in,
she couldn't help turning it. Then the door flew open, and she
saw the Holy Trinity sitting in fire and glory. She stopped a
while, viewing everything with amazement; then she touched
the glory a little with her finger, and her finger became all golden.
At once she was seized with a great fear; she slammed the door
and ran away. But her fear didn't leave her, do what she might,
and her heart beat continually and couldn't be quieted. The gold,
too, stayed on her finger, no matter how much she washed it and
rubbed it.

Not long afterward the Virgin Mary returned from her journey. She called the girl to her and asked her to give back the keys

of Heaven. When she handed her the bunch of keys, the Virgin looked into her eyes and said, "Didn't you open the thirteenth door, too?" "No," she replied. Then the Virgin put her hand on the girl's heart, felt it beating violently, and knew very well that she'd transgressed her command and had unlocked that door. Then she said again, "Are you sure you didn't do it?" "No," answered the girl a second time. Then the Virgin looked at the finger which from touching the Heavenly fire had become all golden and saw clearly that the girl had sinned and for a third time said, "Didn't you do it?" "No," said the girl for the third time. Then the Virgin Mary said, "You disobeyed me and, besides, you lied; you are no longer worthy to be in Heaven."

Then the girl sank into a deep sleep, and when she awoke, she was lying down here on Earth in the midst of a wilderness. She wanted to call out but was unable to utter a sound. She jumped up and wanted to run away, but wherever she turned, she was held back by dense thorn hedges which she couldn't break through. In the wasteland in which she found herself there stood an old hollow tree that had to be her dwelling. When night came, she'd crawl into it and sleep there, and when it was stormy and rainy, she'd find shelter in it. But it was a miserable life, and when she thought how fine it had been in Heaven and how the angels had played with her, she wept bitterly. Roots and berries were her only food; she searched for them as far as she could walk. In the autumn she collected the fallen nuts and leaves and carried them into her hollow tree. The nuts were her food for the winter, and when snow and ice came, she'd crawl like a poor little animal into the leaves so as not to freeze. Soon her clothes became torn, and one piece after another dropped off her body. But when the sun shone warm again, she went out and sat down before the tree, and her long hair covered her on all sides like a cloak. Thus she sat year after year, feeling the woe and the misery of the world.

Once upon a time when the trees again were fresh and green, the king of the country was hunting in the forest and was chasing a roe. And because it had fled into the thicket that surrounded that spot in the forest, he dismounted, pulled the bushes apart, and cut a path with his sword. When he finally broke through, he saw a beautiful girl sitting under the tree, and her golden hair covered her to the very tip of her toes. Amazed he stopped and looked at her, then addressed her, saying, "Who are you? Why are you sitting here in the wasteland?" But she made no reply, for she couldn't open her mouth. Then the king continued, "Will you come with me to my palace?" Then she merely nodded a little with her head. But the king took her in his arms, put her on his horse, and rode home with her. When he reached the royal palace, he had fine clothes put on her and gave her everything in plenty, and though she was unable to speak, she was so beautiful and gracious that he began to love her with all his heart, and it wasn't long before he married her.

When about a year had passed, the queen gave birth to a son. Thereupon the next night as she was lying alone in her bed, the Virgin Mary appeared to her and said, "If you will tell the truth and confess that you unlocked the forbidden door, I will unseal your mouth and restore your power of speech; but if you persist in your sin and your stubborn denial, I will take your newborn child away with me." Then the queen was given the power to answer, but she remained obstinate and said, "No, I didn't open the forbidden door," and the Virgin Mary took the newborn child from her arms and disappeared with it. The next morning when the child was not to be found, a rumor spread among the people that the queen was an ogress and had killed her own child. She heard it all yet couldn't deny it. The King, however, was unwilling to believe it because he loved her so.

A year later the queen again gave birth to a son. In the night the Virgin Mary again came to her and said, "If you will confess that you opened the forbidden door, I shall give you back your child and free your tongue, but if you persist in your sin and deny it, I shall take this newborn child with me, too." Then the queen again said, "No, I didn't open the forbidden door." The Virgin took the child out of her arms and carried it with her to Heaven. In the morning when the second child had disappeared, the people said quite openly that the queen had swallowed it, and the king's councilors demanded she be tried. The king, however, loved her so that he didn't want to believe it and ordered his councilors not to mention the subject again on pain of death.

The following year the queen gave birth to a lovely little daughter. Then at night the Virgin Mary appeared to her for the third time and said, "Follow me." She took her by the hand

and led her to Heaven and showed her there her two eldest children: they greeted her with joyous laughter and were playing with the globe of the earth. As the queen was rejoicing in all this, the Virgin said: "Is your heart not yet softened? If you admit that you opened the forbidden door, I shall give you back your two little sons." But for the third time the queen replied, "No, I didn't open the forbidden door." Then the Virgin again let her sink down to Earth and took away her third child, too.

The next morning when this became known, everybody cried out, "The queen is an ogress and must be sentenced," and the king could no longer reject his councilors' advice. Accordingly, she was tried, and because she couldn't reply and couldn't defend herself, she was condemned to die at the stake. The wood was gathered, and when she was tied to a stake and the fire began to burn round about, the hard ice of her pride melted and her heart was moved by repentance, and she thought, "If only before I die I could confess that I opened the door." Then her power of speech was restored, and she cried out in a loud voice, "Yes, Mary, I did do it." Immediately it began to rain, and the rain put out the flames, and a beam of light descended upon her, and the Virgin Mary descended with the two little sons at her side and the newborn daughter in her arms. She spoke kindly to her, "Whoever repents his sin and confesses will be forgiven," and gave her back the three children and freed her tongue and bestowed happiness upon her for the rest of her life.

4 A Tale of a Boy Who
Set Out to Learn Fear

Märchen von einem, der auszog das Fürchten zu lernen

A FATHER had two sons: of these the elder was bright and clever and knew how to get along everywhere, but the younger was dull and couldn't understand or learn anything, and when people saw him, they'd say, "He'll be a burden to his father." Whenever something was to be done, it was always the elder who had to do it. Nevertheless, if his father bade him fetch something late in the evening or even at night and if the way led across a churchyard or some other creepy place, he'd reply, "Oh, no, father, I won't go there, it makes me shudder," for he was afraid. Or, if of an evening stories were told by the fireside that made one shudder, those listening would sometimes say, "Oh, it makes me shudder." The younger son used then to sit in a corner and hear this and couldn't understand what it meant. "They keep saying, 'It makes me shudder, it makes me shudder'; it doesn't make me shudder, there must be some trick I don't understand."

Now his father once happened to say to him, "Listen, you over there in the corner, you're getting big and strong; you've got to learn something to earn your living by. See how hard your brother works while you're just hopeless." "Why, father," he replied, "I very much want to learn something; indeed, if possible, I'd like to learn shuddering; that's something I don't know anything about yet." On hearing that, the elder brother laughed and thought to himself: "Dear God, what a fool my brother is! He'll never get anywhere that way. As the twig is bent, the tree's inclined." The father heaved a sigh and answered, "You'll learn shuddering all right, but you won't earn your living that way."

Soon after that the sexton came to call, and the father told him his tale of woe, how his younger son was so ignorant in everything that he knew nothing and learned nothing. "Just think, when I asked him how he was going to earn his living, he actually asked to learn shuddering." "If that's all," answered the sexton, "he can learn that from me; turn him over to me and I'll plane off the rough edges all right." The father agreed, for he thought, "The boy'll at least be trimmed up a little." So the sexton took him into his home, and he had to ring the church bell. After a few days the sexton roused him at midnight, bade him get up, climb the steeple, and ring the bell. "You'll certainly learn what shuddering is," he thought, and went out secretly. When the boy was up in the steeple and turned around and was about to take hold of the bell rope, he saw a white form standing on the stairs opposite the sound hole. "Who's there?" he cried. But the form made no reply and neither moved nor stirred. "Answer me!" cried the boy, "or else get out; you've no business here at night." But the sexton remained motionless, so that the boy might think it was a specter. The boy called out a second time,

"What do you want here? If you're an honest fellow, speak, or I'll throw you down the stairs." The sexton thought, "His bark's probably worse than his bite," didn't utter a sound, and stood stock-still. Then the boy called to him a third time, and when that did no good, made a dash and pushed the specter down the stairs so that it fell ten steps and lay in a corner. Then he rang the bell, returned home, and without saying a word went to bed and fell asleep. The sexton's wife waited a long time for her husband, but he didn't come back. Finally she got frightened and woke the boy up and asked, "Do you know where my husband has got to? He climbed the steeple ahead of you." "No," answered the boy, "but somebody was standing there on the stairs opposite the sound hole, and because he didn't answer me and wouldn't go away, I took him for a rogue and pushed him downstairs. Just go there and you'll see whether it was he; I'd be sorry if it were." The woman ran off and found her husband lying in a corner; he was groaning and had broken a leg.

She carried him down and then, crying loudly, hurried to the boy's father. "Your boy," she shouted, "caused a serious accident; he threw my husband downstairs so that he broke a leg. Get the good-for-nothing out of our house." The father was frightened, came on the run, and scolded the boy: "What kind of mischief have you been up to? The Evil One must have put you up to it." "Father," he answered, "just listen! I'm quite innocent; he was standing there in the night like someone with evil intentions. I didn't know who it was. Three times I told him to speak up or else go away." "Dear me!" said his father, "you only bring me misfortune. Get out of my sight! I don't want to see you any more." "All right, father, I'll do so quite willingly, only wait till morning; then I'll get out and learn shuddering. Then I'll know at least one craft that I can earn my living by." "Learn whatever you like," said the father; "it's all the same to me. Here's fifty dollars. Take them and go out in the world, and don't tell anyone where you're from or who your father is, for I'm ashamed of you." "Yes, father, as you wish—so long as you ask for nothing more. That much I can easily keep in mind."

When day broke, the boy put the fifty dollars in his pocket, went out on the highway, and kept saying to himself, "If only I could shudder; if only I could shudder." Then a man came along who heard what the boy was saying to himself, and when they had gone a little farther so that one could see the gallows, the man said to him: "You see, there's the tree where seven men were wedded to the ropemaker's daughter and now are learning to fly. Sit down underneath it and wait till night comes; then you'll surely learn shuddering." "If that's all," answered the boy, "it's easy. If I learn shuddering that quickly, you shall have my fifty dollars. Just come back here tomorrow morning." The boy then went to the gallows, sat down underneath, and waited till nightfall. Because he was cold, he made a fire, but about midnight the wind got so cold that even with the fire he couldn't keep warm, and when the wind knocked the bodies of the hanged men against one another and they swung to and fro, he thought, "I'm cold down here by the fire; how frightfully cold and shivering they must be up there!" And because he took pity on them, he set up the ladder, mounted it, untied one after the other, and took all seven down. Then he stirred the fire, blew it up, and placed them around it, that they might get warm. But they sat there and didn't move, and their clothes caught fire. Then he said, "Look out, or I'll hang you up again." But the dead didn't hear, remained silent, and let their poor rags burn away. Then he lost his temper and said, "If you won't look out, I can't help you; I don't want to burn up with you," and hung them up again one after the other. Then he sat down by his fire and fell asleep. The next morning the man came to him, wanted the fifty dollars, and said, "Do you now know what shuddering is?" "No," he replied, "how should I? Those men up there didn't open their mouths and were so stupid that they let the few old rags they had on burn up." Then the man saw that he wouldn't get the fifty dollars that day and went off, saying, "I've never run into anyone like that."

The boy continued on his way and again began saying to himself, "Oh, if only I could shudder! oh, if only I could shudder!" A carter who was walking behind him overheard this and asked, "Who are you?" "I don't know," answered the boy. The carter continued to question him: "Where are you from?" "I don't know." "Who's your father?" "I mustn't tell." "What are you mumbling about all the time?" "Why," replied the boy, "I'd like to shudder, but no one can teach me how." "Stop your silly talk," said the carter; "come along with me and I'll see if I can put you up." The boy went with the carter, and in the evening they reached an inn where they planned to spend the night. On entering the taproom he again said aloud, "If only I could shudder! if only I could shudder!" Hearing that, the innkeeper laughed and said, "If that's what you want, there's a fine chance right here." "Oh, do be still," said the innkeeper's wife. "Many a Paul Pry has already lost his life; it would be a crying shame if his fine eyes should never see the light of day again." But the boy said, "Even if it's as hard as that, I want to learn it; that's why I left home." He gave the innkeeper no peace till the latter told him that not far off was an enchanted castle where one could certainly learn what shuddering was if he'd just stand watch there for three nights. He said that the king had promised his daughter in marriage to anyone who'd venture it, and that she was the most beautiful girl the sun shone upon. Furthermore, there were in the castle huge treasures guarded by evil spirits; this would then become free and would be enough to make a poor man rich. Many had, to be sure, gone in, but as yet no one had ever come out again. The next morning the boy went into the king's presence and said, "If it's allowed, I should very much like to keep watch for three nights in the enchanted castle." The king looked at him, and because he took a fancy to him, said, "You may ask for three things, but they must be inanimate objects; you may take them with you into the castle." Then he answered, "In that case, I ask for a fire, a lathe, and a carpenter's bench and knife."

The king had all this taken into the castle by daylight. As night drew near, the boy went up, kindled a bright fire in one of the rooms, set the carpenter's bench and the knife beside it, and sat down at the lathe. "Oh, if only I could shudder!" he said, "but I shan't learn it here, either." Toward midnight he wanted to stir up the fire, and as he was blowing into it, there came a cry from a corner, "Miaow, miaow, we're so cold!" "You fools," he shouted, "what are you crying for? If you're cold, come here and sit down by the fire and warm yourselves." No sooner had he said that than two big black cats came with a jump, sat down beside him and looked at him quite fiercely with their glowing eyes. After a while when they'd got warm, they said, "Shall we play a round of cards, pal?" "Why not?" he answered. "But first let's see your paws." Then they stretched out their claws. "My!" he said, "what long nails you've got! Wait a minute! I must first clip them for you." Thereupon he seized them by their necks, lifted them up onto the workbench, and made their paws fast in a vice. "I've had a look at your fingers," he said, "and I've lost all desire for cards." Then he killed them and threw them out into the pond. After he'd quieted those two and was about to sit down again by the fire, black cats and black dogs on glowing chains came out of every nook and corner—more and more and more—until he didn't know where to take refuge. They yowled horribly, trampled his fire, pulled it apart, and were about to put it out. He watched them quietly for a while, but when it got too bad, he seized his knife and shouted, "Get out, you scum!" and cut loose at them. Some of them ran away, the others he killed and threw out into the pond. When he came back, he blew up his fire afresh from the coals and warmed himself. As he was sitting thus, he couldn't keep his eyes open any longer and was overcome with a desire to sleep. Just then he looked about him and saw a big bed in a corner. "That's just the thing," he said, and lay down in it. As he was about to shut his eyes, the bed began to move of itself and traveled all through the castle. "Right you are," he said, "only faster!" Then as if drawn by six horses the bed rolled on over thresholds and up and down stairs. All of a sudden, bump, bump, it tipped over and lay upside down on top of him like a mountain. But he flung the covers and pillows into the air and climbed out, saying, "Anyone who wants to may take a ride." He lay down by the fire and slept until daybreak. In the morning the king came and, seeing him lying on the floor, thought that the specters had killed him and that he was dead. So he said, "It's too bad about the fine-looking chap." The boy heard him, got up, and said, "It's not that bad." The king was astonished but very happy and asked him how he'd fared. "Very well," he answered. "One night's over; the other two will pass, also." When he got to the innkeeper's, the latter looked surprised. "I didn't think," he said, "that I'd see you alive again. Now have you learned what shuddering is?" "No," he replied, "it's all no use. If only someone could tell me!"

The second night he again went up into the old castle, sat down by the fire, and again started his old refrain, "If only I could shudder!" As midnight drew near, there was a rumbling, tumbling noise, first soft, then louder and louder; then it grew quiet for a bit. At last half a man came down the chimney with a loud cry and dropped right in front of him. "Hello!" he shouted, "there's still another half; this isn't enough." Then the noise began again: there was a roaring and howling and then the other half dropped down. "Wait a minute," he said; "let me first blow up the fire a little." When he'd done so and was looking about, the two pieces had put themselves together and a horrible man was sitting in his seat. "That's not what we bargained for," said the boy; "it's my bench." The man was about to shove him off, but the boy didn't stand for that; he pushed him off violently and sat down again at his place. Then still more men came tumbling down one after the other. They fetched nine dead men's bones and two dead men's skulls, set them up, and played ninepins. The boy wanted to play, too, and asked, "Listen, may I play, too?" "Yes, if you have money." "Plenty," he answered, "but your bowls aren't quite round." Then he took the dead men's heads, put them in the lathe, and turned them till they were round. "Now they'll roll better," he said; "hurray, now there'll be some fun!" He joined the game and lost a little money, but when the clock struck twelve, everything disappeared before his eyes. He lay down and quietly went to sleep. Next morning the king came and wanted to hear the news. "How did you fare this time?" he asked. "I played ninepins," he answered, "and lost a few farthings." "Didn't you shudder?" "Good heavens, no," he said. "I had a fine time. If only I might know what shuddering is!"

The third night he sat down again on his workbench and quite out of sorts said, "If only I could shudder!" When it got late, six tall men came in carrying a coffin. Then he said, "Ha! ha! That's no doubt my cousin who died only a few days ago." He beckoned with his finger and called out, "Come here, cousin, come here!" They set the coffin on the floor, and he stepped up and opened the lid: there was a dead man inside. He felt the face, but it was as cold as ice. "Just a minute," he said, "I'll warm you up a bit," went to the fire, warmed his hand, and laid it on the face. The dead man, however, remained cold. Then he took him out of the coffin, laid him by the fire, and putting him on his lap, rubbed his arms to get his blood circulating again. When even that did no good, he remembered that "when two people lie together in one bed, they warm each other up," put him in his bed, covered him, and lay down beside him. After a while the dead man got warm and began to move. Then the boy said, "Look here, cousin, suppose I hadn't warmed you?" But the dead man began to shout, "Now I'm going to strangle you." "What!" he said. "Is that the thanks I get? You're going right back into your coffin," picked him up, threw him into the coffin, and closed the lid. Then the six men came and carried it off again. "I simply can't shudder," he said. "I shan't learn it here as long as I live."

Then in came a man who was taller than all the rest and horrible looking; he was old and had a long white beard. "O you scoundrel," he cried, "now you'll soon learn what shuddering is, for you're going to die." "Not so fast!" answered the boy. "If I'm going to die, I must at least be present." "I'll catch you all right," said the monster. "Easy, easy, don't talk so big; I'm as strong as you and, indeed, even stronger." "We'll see," said the old man. "If you're stronger than I, I'll let you go. Come on, let's try." He led him through dark passageways to a smithy fire, took an ax, and with one blow drove one anvil right into the ground. "I can do better than that," said the boy, and stepped up to the other anvil. The old man took up a position close by in order to watch, and his white beard was flowing down. Then the boy seized the ax, split the anvil with one blow, wedging in the old man's beard. "Now I've got you!" said the boy; "now it's your turn to die." Then he seized an iron bar and pitched into the old man until he whimpered and begged him to stop, promising to bestow great riches upon him. The boy pulled out the ax and let him go. The old man led him back into the castle and showed him three chests full of gold in a cellar. "Of this," he said, "one part belongs to the poor, the other to the king, and the third is yours." Thereupon it struck twelve and the specter vanished so that the boy was alone in the darkness. "I'll be able to get out of here just the same," he said, groped about, found the way to his room, and fell asleep by his fire. The next morning the king appeared and said, "Now you must have learned what shuddering is." "No," he answered. "What is it really? My dead cousin was there, and a bearded man came who showed me a lot of money downstairs, but no one told me what shuddering is." Then the king said, "You've disenchanted the castle and are to marry my daughter." "That's all very fine," he replied, "but I still don't know what shuddering is."

The gold was brought upstairs and the wedding celebrated, but the young king, fond as he was of his wife and happy as he was, still kept saying, "If only I could shudder, if only I could shudder." Finally she got tired of it. Her chambermaid said, "I'll manage it so he'll learn what shuddering is." She went to the brook that flowed through the garden and got herself a whole pail of minnows. In the night, as the young king was asleep, his wife pulled off the covers and poured over him the pail of cold water with the minnows so that the little fish wriggled around all over him. Then he woke up and cried out, "Oh, how I'm shuddering, how I'm shuddering, my dear! Yes, now I know what shuddering is."

5   The Wolf and the Seven Young Kids

Der Wolf und die sieben jungen Geisslein

THERE WAS ONCE AN OLD GOAT who had seven little kids, and she loved them as mothers love their children. One day she was going into the forest to fetch food and, calling all seven, said: "Children dear, I'm going out into the forest. Watch out for the wolf; if it gets into the house, it'll eat you all up skin and bones. The rogue often disguises itself, but you'll recognize it at once from its gruff voice and black paws." The kids said, "Mother dear, of course we'll be careful. You may go and needn't worry about us." Then the old goat bleated and set out quite untroubled.

After a while somebody knocked on the front door and called out, "Open the door, children dear. Your mother's here and has brought each of you something." But the kids knew from the gruff voice that it was the wolf. "We shan't open the door," they cried. "You're not our mother; she has a soft sweet voice. Your voice is gruff; you're the wolf." Then the wolf went off to a shop-keeper and bought a big piece of chalk; this it ate and thus made its voice soft. Then it came back, knocked on the front door, and called, "Open the door, children dear. Your mother's here and has brought each of you something." But the wolf had put its black paw in the window. The children saw that and cried: "We shan't open the door. Our mother hasn't got a black paw like you; you're the wolf." Then the wolf went to a baker and said, "I've bumped my foot; put some dough on it for me." When the baker had done so, it went to the miller and said, "Sprinkle some white flour on my paw." The miller thought, "The wolf wants to cheat someone," and refused, but the wolf said, "If you don't, I'll eat you up." Then the miller got scared and whitened its paw. People are like that.

Now for the third time the scoundrel went to the front door, knocked, and said, "Open the door, childen. Your dear mummy's come home and has brought each of you something from the forest." The kids cried out, "First show us your paw so we may know that you're our dear mummy." Then it put its paw in the window, and when they saw it was white, they thought that everything it said was true and opened the door. But what came in was the wolf! They were frightened and tried to hide. One jumped under the table, the second into the bed, the third into the tile stove, the fourth into the kitchen, the fifth into the cupboard, the sixth under the washbasin, and the seventh into the case of the clock on the wall. But the wolf found them all and made short shift of them. It gobbled them up one after the other; the only one it didn't find was the youngest, in the clockcase. When the wolf had satisfied its hunger, it trotted off, lay down outdoors under a tree in the green meadow, and fell asleep.

Not long afterward the old goat came home from the forest. Oh, what a sight met her eyes! The front door was wide open; table, chairs, and benches were overturned; the washbasin lay in pieces; the bedclothes and pillows had been pulled off the bed. She looked for her children, but they were nowhere to be found. She called them one by one by name, but no one answered. Finally, when she came to the youngest, a soft voice cried, "Mother dear, I'm in the clockcase." She took it out, and it told her that the wolf had come and eaten up all the others. Now you can imagine how she wept over her poor children.

At last in her sorrow she went out, and the youngest kid went with her. When she reached the meadow, there was the wolf under the tree, snoring so that the branches shook. She viewed it from all sides and saw something stirring and quivering in its full belly. "Dear God," she thought, "can my poor children that it gobbled up for supper still be alive?" The kid had to run home and fetch scissors, needle, and thread. Then she cut the monster's belly open, and no sooner had she made an incision than one of the kids poked out its head, and as she went on cutting, all six jumped out, one after the other, and were still alive and hadn't suffered any harm at all, for in its greed the monster had swallowed them whole. What a joy that was! They hugged their dear mother and skipped about like a tailor at his own wedding. Then the old goat said, "Now go fetch some ordinary stones and we'll fill the vicious brute's stomach while it's still asleep." In great haste the seven kids fetched the stones and put as many in the wolf's stomach as they could get in. Then the old goat hurriedly sewed it up again so that it noticed nothing and didn't so much as stir.

When the wolf had finally slept itself out, it got on its feet, and because the stones in its stomach made it so very thirsty, it wanted to go to a well and have a drink. But when it began to walk and move about, the stones jostled in its belly and rattled. Then it cried out,

> "What's rumbling and rattling
> About in my stomach?
> I thought it was six kids,
> But it's just plain stones."

And when it got to the well and bent over the water to have a drink, the heavy stones pulled it in, and it drowned miserably. When the seven kids saw that, they came running up and cried aloud, "The wolf's dead! the wolf's dead!" and joyfully danced with their mother around the well.

6   Faithful John

Der treue Johannes

THERE WAS ONCE AN OLD KING. He was ill and thought, "I'm probably on my deathbed." Then he said, "Have Faithful John come to me." Faithful John was his favorite servant and was so named because he'd been faithful to him all his life. When he now came to the bedside, the king said to him: "Most faithful John, I feel that my end is drawing near and I'm worried about nothing but my son. He is still young in years and not always able to look out for himself; unless you promise me to instruct him in everything he ought to know and be his foster father, I shan't be able to shut my eyes in peace." Then Faithful John replied, "I shan't leave him and I'll serve him faithfully, even if it costs me my life." Then the old king said: "Now I will die consoled and in peace," and added, "After my death you're to show him the whole palace, all the chambers, halls, and vaults, and all the treasures that are in them, but you're not to show him the last chamber in the long passageway, in which is hidden the portrait of the daughter of the king of the Golden Roof. If he sees the portrait, he'll fall violently in love with her and will fall down in a faint and because of her will run great dangers. You're to guard him against that." When Faithful John had again given the old king his hand on it, the latter grew quiet, laid his head on his pillow, and died.

When the old king had been carried to his grave, Faithful John told the young king what he had promised his father on his deathbed and said, "I shall certainly keep this promise and be as loyal to you as I was to him, even if it costs me my life." The period of mourning passed; then Faithful John said to him, "Now it's time for you to see your heritage; I'll show you your ancestral palace." Then he led him all about, up and down, and showed him all the treasures and the sumptuous chambers; but there was the one chamber that he didn't open: that is, the one with the dangerous portrait. The picture was placed in such a way that, on opening the door, one looked straight at it, and it was so beautifully done that one might think it was real flesh and blood and alive and that there couldn't be anything lovelier and more beautiful in the whole world. The young king was well aware that Faithful John always passed one particular door by and said, "Why don't you ever open it for me?" "There's something in there," he answered, "that will frighten you." But the king replied, "I've seen the whole palace; now I want to know what's in there." He stepped forward and was about to force the door open when Faithful John held him back, saying, "I promised your father before his death that you shouldn't see what's in that chamber; it might bring you and me great misfortune." "Oh no," answered the young king, "if I don't get in, it'll certainly be my ruin. I shouldn't rest day or night till I'd seen it with my own eyes. I shan't move from the spot till you've unlocked it."

Then Faithful John saw there was nothing further to do about it, and with heavy heart and many sighs picked out the key from the big bunch. When he'd opened the door, he went in first, thinking he'd cover the picture so the king, who was standing behind him, mightn't see it. But what good did that do? The king stood on tiptoe and looked over his shoulder, and when he beheld the portrait of the girl who was so beautiful, sparkling with gold and jewels, he fell down in a faint. Faithful John lifted him up, carried him to his bed, and thought sorrowfully, "The mishap's occurred. Lord God! what will come of it all?" Then he strengthened him with wine until he regained consciousness. The first words he said were, "What beautiful person is that a portrait of?" "It's the daughter of the king of the Golden Roof," Faithful John replied. Then the king went on to say, "My love for her is so great that if all the leaves on the trees were tongues, they couldn't express it. I'll risk my life to win her. You're my most faithful John and must help me."

The faithful servant reflected for a long time on how to accomplish this, for it was difficult as much as to get into the presence of the princess. Finally he hit upon a plan and said to the king, "Everything she has about her is of gold: tables, chairs, dishes, cups, bowls, and all household utensils. There are five tons of gold in your treasury. Have one ton of it wrought by the goldsmiths of your kingdom into all sorts of vessels and utensils, into all kinds of birds, game, and strange animals. She'll like that, and we'll travel to her with these things and try our luck. The king summoned all his goldsmiths. They had to work day and night, till finally the most magnificent things were ready. When everything had been loaded on a ship, Faithful John put on merchant's clothes, and the king had to do the same and disguise himself completely. Then they journeyed overseas and traveled until they came to the city where the daughter of the king of the Golden Roof dwelt.

Faithful John bade the king stay on the ship and wait for him. "Perhaps," he said, "I'll bring the princess with me. Therefore see to it that everything is ready; have the golden vessels put on display and the entire ship decked out." Then he gathered up a number of gold trinkets in his apron, went ashore and straight to the royal palace. When he reached the palace courtyard, a pretty girl was standing by the well; she had two golden pails in her hands and was drawing water, and as she was about to carry away the bright water and had turned around, she saw the stranger and asked who he was. He replied, "I'm a merchant," opened his apron, and let her look in. Then she cried out, "Oh, what beautiful goldware!" set the pails down, and looked at the things one after the other. Then the girl said, "The king's daughter must see this; she's so fond of gold trinkets that she'll buy them all from you." She took him by the hand and led him upstairs, for she was the chambermaid. When the king's daughter saw the goldware, she was most happy and said, "It's so beautifully wrought that I'll buy it all from you." But Faithful John said, "I'm only a rich merchant's servant. What I have here is nothing to what my master has down on board his ship, yes, the most artfully and wonderfully wrought objects ever made of gold." Then she wanted to have everything brought up to her, but he said, "That would take many days, there's so much of it, and it would take so many halls to display it in that there's not enough room in your dwelling." This roused her curiosity and desire more and more, so she finally said, "Take me down to the ship; I'll go there in person and view your master's treasures."

Then Faithful John brought her to the ship and was very happy. On beholding her, the king saw that her beauty was even greater than her portrait had shown, and he thought that his heart would burst with joy. Now she went aboard, and the king escorted her in. But Faithful John stayed behind near the helmsman and ordered the ship to put off: "Set all sail, so that she'll fly like a bird in the air!" Inside the ship, however, the king showed her the gold service, every single piece: dishes, cups, bowls, the birds, game, and strange animals. Many hours passed while she looked at everything, and in her joy she didn't notice that the ship was moving along. After she had looked at the last object, she thanked the merchant and wanted to go home, but when she came to the ship's side, she saw that it was far from land and on the high seas, speeding forward under full sail. "Oh," she cried in fright, "I've been tricked; I'm being abducted and have fallen into the power of a merchant. I'd rather die." But the king took her by the hand and said, "I'm not a merchant; I'm a king and not inferior to you in birth. I've abducted you by guile because of my great, great love for you: the first time I saw your potrait, I fell to the ground in a faint." When the daughter of the king of the Golden Roof heard this, she was consoled, and her heart inclined toward him so that she willingly consented to become his wife.

But it so happened that while they were on the high seas Faithful John, as he was sitting near the bow of the ship and playing some music, saw three ravens flying through the air. Then he stopped playing and listened to what they were saying to one another, for he understood it well. One of them cried, "Well, there he's bringing home the daughter of the king of the Golden Roof." "Yes, indeed," answered the second, "but he hasn't got her yet." Then the third rejoined, "Yes, he has got her; she's sitting beside him in the ship." Then the first spoke again and cried, "What good will that do him? When they reach shore, a horse as red as a fox will come galloping up; he'll want to mount it, and if he does so, it'll run away with him into the air, so that he'll never see the maiden again." Then the second said, "Is there no way of saving him?" "Oh, yes. If someone else quickly mounts the horse, takes out the gun that's surely in the holster, and shoots the horse dead, then the young king will be saved. But who knows that? And if anybody does know it and tells the king, he'll be turned to stone from his toes to his knees." Then the second raven said, "I know still more. Even if the horse is killed, the young king still won't keep his bride. When they enter the palace together, they'll find a perfectly made bridal shirt lying in a bowl, looking as if it were woven of gold and silver, though it's nothing but sulphur and pitch. If he puts it on, it'll burn him to the quick and to the marrow." Then the third said, "Is there absolutely no way of saving him?" "Oh, yes," replied the second. "If someone takes hold of the shirt with gloves on and throws it into the fire so that it burns up, the young king will be saved. But what good's that? Whoever knows this and tells him will turn to stone from his knees to his heart." Then the third said, "I know still more. Even if the bridal shirt is burned up, still the young king won't have his bride. After the wedding, when the ball opens and the young queen dances, she'll suddenly turn pale and fall down as if dead, and unless someone lifts her up and draws three drops of blood from her right breast and spits them out again, she'll die.

But if anybody who knows it tells the secret, his whole body will be turned to stone from top to toe." Having thus spoken, the ravens continued their flight, but Faithful John had understood everything and from that time on was quiet and sad. For if he kept from his master what he'd heard, misfortune would befall the latter, and if he told him, he himself would have to sacrifice his life. Finally, however, he said to himself, "I shall save my master, even if I perish in the attempt."

When they went ashore, it happened as the raven had predicted: a superb horse, red as a fox, came galloping up. "Well," said the king, "it shall carry me to my palace," and was about to mount it. But Faithful John got ahead of him, swung quickly onto it himself, drew the gun from the holster, and shot the horse dead. Then the other servants of the king, who were not very fond of Faithful John, cried, "What a shame to kill the fine animal that was to carry the king to his palace." The king, however, said: "Be still and leave him alone; he's my most faithful John. Who knows to what good purpose he did it!" Now they entered the palace, and there in the hall was a bowl with a perfectly made bridal shirt lying in it, looking as if it were made of gold and silver. The young king stepped up and was about to take hold of it, but Faithful John pushed him aside, seized it with his gloves on, carried it quickly to the fireplace, and let it burn up. The other servants again began to murmur, "Look! Now he's burning even the king's bridal shirt." But the young king said, "Who knows to what good purpose he did it! Leave him alone; he's my most faithful John." Now the wedding was celebrated; the ball began, and the bride, too, entered the hall. Then Faithful John paid close attention and watched her face. Suddenly she turned pale and fell to the ground as if dead. He rushed quickly up, lifted her, and carried her into a chamber; there he laid her down, knelt, and sucked three drops of blood from her right breast and spat them out. At once she began to breathe again and recovered. The young king, however, had been looking on and didn't know why Faithful John had done it. He got angry and shouted, "Throw him into prison!" The next morning Faithful John was condemned to death and led to the gallows. When he stood up there and was about to be executed, he said: "Everyone condemned to die is allowed to say one last word before his end. Am I to have this right, too?" "Yes," answered the king, "it will not be refused you." Then Faithful John said, "I was condemned unjustly and have always been faithful to you," and then told how at sea he'd heard the ravens' conversation and how he'd been forced to do all this to save his master. Then the king cried out, "Oh, my most faithful John, mercy, mercy! Bring him down from the gallows!" But with the last word he uttered, Faithful John had fallen down dead and was a piece of stone.

The king and queen were greatly grieved by this, and the king said, "How ill I rewarded such great loyalty," and had the stone image picked up and placed in his bedchamber next to his bed. Whenever he looked at it he'd weep and say, "If only I could bring you back to life, my most faithful John!" Some time passed, and the queen gave birth to twins, two boys; they grew up and were her joy. Once when the queen was at church and the two children were sitting beside their father and playing, the latter again looked sadly at the stone image and, sighing, said, "Oh, if only I could bring you back to life, my most faithful John!" Then the stone began to speak and said, "Yes, you can bring me back to life if to do so you're willing to sacrifice what you most love." Then the king exclaimed, "I'm willing to sacrifice everything I have in this world for you." Then the stone went on, "If with your own hand you'll cut off the heads of your two children and anoint me with their blood, I'll come back to life." The king was frightened when he heard he'd have to kill his dear children with his own hand, but he thought of Faithful John's great loyalty and how he'd died for him, and drew his sword and with his own hand cut off his children's heads. And when he'd anointed the stone with their blood, it came to life, and Faithful John stood before him hale and hearty. He said to the king, "Your loyalty to me shall not remain unrewarded," took the children's heads, put them in place, and anointed the wounds with their blood. In an instant they were whole again, skipped about, and continued their play as if nothing had happened. Now the king rejoiced greatly, and when he saw the queen coming, hid Faithful John and the two children in a big cupboard. When she came in, he said to her, "Did you pray at church?" "Yes," she answered, "but I was thinking all the time about Faithful John and that he fell into such misfortune on our account." Then he said, "Dear wife, we can bring him back to life, but it will cost us our two children; we'll have to sacrifice them." The queen turned pale and in her heart was frightened, but said, "We owe it to him because of his great loyalty." Then the king was glad that she thought as he'd thought, stepped to the cupboard and, unlocking it, brought out the children and Faithful John, saying, "God be praised! He is disenchanted, and our two children, too, have been given back to us," and told her how it all happened.

Then they lived happily together until their death.

7 The Good Bargain

Der gute Handel

A FARMER drove his cow to market and sold her for seven dollars. On the way home he had to go by a pond and there, when still at a distance, heard the frogs croaking, "Ate, ate!—ate, ate!" "Yes," he said to himself, "They're talking nonsense; I only got seven dollars for it, not eight." As he got near the pond, he called out to them: "Stupid creatures, that's what you are! Don't you know any better? It's seven dollars, not eight." But the frogs stuck to their "Ate, ate!—ate, ate!" "Well, if you won't believe it, I can count it out to you," took the money from his pocket, and counted out seven dollars, twenty-four groats to the dollar. The frogs, however, paid no attention to his figuring and again cried, "Ate, ate!—ate, ate!" "My goodness!" cried the farmer, now quite angry, "if you think you know better than I, count it yourselves," and threw the money down into the water. He stopped and was going to wait till they'd done counting and brought him back his money, but the frogs went on in the same vein and kept croaking, "Ate, ate!—ate, ate!" and didn't so much as toss the money back. He waited quite a while till night came and he had to go home. Then he called the frogs names, shouting: "You water-splashers, you blockheads, you goggle-eyes, you've got big mouths and know how to shout loud enough to make one's ears ache, but you can't count seven dollars. Do you think I'm going to wait till you've finished?" Thereupon he went off, but the frogs still croaked after him, "Ate, ate!—ate, ate!" and he got home quite out of sorts.

Some time later he bought another cow, slaughtered it, and reckoned that if he was lucky in selling the beef, he might get as much as the value of the two cows and have the hide in the bargain. Now when he got to town with the beef, a whole pack of dogs had gathered outside the gate, led by a big deerhound that jumped around the beef, sniffed, and barked, "Want, want!— want, want!" When it wouldn't stop barking, the farmer said to it, "I understand very well that you're saying "Want, want" because you want some of the beef, but I'd certainly be striking a fine bargain if I gave it to you!" The dog merely answered, "Want, want!" "Will you promise not to eat it and to go security for your mates there?" "Want, want!" said the dog. "Well, if you insist, I'll let you have it; I know you all right and also know who you work for. But let me tell you one thing, I must have my money in three days, otherwise it'll fare ill with you. Just bring it out to me." Thereupon he unloaded the beef and turned back home. The dogs fell on the beef, barking loudly, "Want, want!" and the farmer, who heard it from afar, said to himself, "Just listen! now they're all asking for some of it. But the big dog must stand security for them."

Three days later the farmer thought, "Tonight I'll have my money in my pocket," and was quite pleased with himself. But no one came to pay him. "There's no relying on anyone any more," he said, finally lost patience, went into town and to the butcher, and demanded his money. The butcher thought it was a joke, but the farmer said, "No joking! I want my money. Didn't the big dog bring you the whole slaughtered cow three days ago?" Then the butcher got angry, reached for a broomstick, and chased him out. "Just wait," said the farmer, "there's still justice in the world," went into the royal palace, and craved an audience. He was brought into the presence of the king, who was sitting there with his daughter and who asked him what his grievance was. "Oh," he said, "the frogs and the dogs took my property, and the butcher paid me for it with the broomstick," and he told in great detail how it had all happened. On hearing this, the king's daughter burst out laughing, and the king said to him, "I can't give a verdict in your favor here, but you shall have my daughter in marriage. She's never laughed in all her life except just now at you, and I promised her to whoever made her laugh. You may thank the Lord for your good luck. "Oh," replied the farmer, "I don't want her at all; I've got only one wife at home, and she's already too much for me. Every time I come home, I feel as if a wife were standing in every corner." Then the king got angry and said, "You're an ill-mannered boor." "Oh, dear Sir King," answered the farmer, "what can you expect to get from an ox but beef?" "Wait," said the king, "you shall have some other reward. For the present, get out of here, but come back in three days, and I'll have five hundred paid out to you in full measure."

As the farmer was going out the door, the sentry said, "You made the king's daughter laugh; no doubt you got a fitting reward?" "I should say so," answered the farmer, "five hundred are going to be paid out to me." "Listen," said the soldier, "give me some of them. What do you want with all that money?" "Seeing it's you," said the farmer, "you shall have two hundred. Report to the king in three days and have them counted out to you." A Jew who had been standing near by and overheard the conversation ran after the farmer, seized him by his coat and said, "Wonder of wonders, what a lucky fellow you are! I'll change it for you. I'll give you small change. What do you want with the silver dollars?" "Ikey," said the farmer, "you can still have three hundred, but give me the change right now. In three days from today the king'll pay you for it." The Jew rejoiced in the nice little profit and brought the amount in bad groats, three of which are worth two good ones. After three days the farmer, in accordance with the king's command, went into the royal presence. "Take off his coat," said the king, "he's to have his five hundred." "Oh," said the farmer, "they're no longer mine; I gave two hundred to the sentry, and the Jew gave me small change for three hundred. I've no real claim to anything." Meanwhile the soldier and the Jew came in and asked for the shares which they had got away from the farmer, and received the blows in rightful measure. The soldier bore it patiently, for he already knew what a flogging was like, but the Jew whined piteously, "Alack, alas! Are these the silver dollars?" The king had to laugh at the farmer, and since his anger had passed, he said: "Because you lost your reward before you got it,

I'll give you another instead. Go into my treasury and take as much money as you want." The farmer didn't have to be told twice and filled his ample pockets as full as he could; then he went to the inn and counted his money. The Jew had sneaked after him and heard him grumbling to himself, "Now this rascal of a king has really cheated me! Couldn't he have given me the money himself, so I might have known what I had? How am I to know whether what I pocketed so haphazard is the right amount?" "Heaven forbid!" said the Jew to himself; "he's speaking disrespectfully about our lord. I'll run and inform on him, then I'll get a reward and he'll be punished in the bargain." When the king heard about the farmer's remarks, he fell into a rage and bade the Jew go fetch the offender. The Jew ran to the farmer and said, "You're to come to our lord the king right off— just as you are." "I know better what's fitting," answered the farmer. "I'll first have a new coat made for myself. Do you think that a man who's got so much money in his pocket should go to court in rags?" When the Jew saw that the farmer couldn't be budged without another coat, and because he was afraid he'd lose his reward once the king's anger had subsided and that the farmer'd get away unpunished, he said, "Just for friendship's sake I'll lend you a fine coat for a short time. What all one doesn't do for love!" The farmer agreed, put on the Jew's coat, and went off with him. The king reproached the farmer for the bad remarks the Jew had secretly reported against him. "Oh," said the farmer, "what a Jew says is always a lie. They never utter a true word; that fellow there's capable of claiming that I'm wearing his coat." "What do you mean!" cried the Jew. "Isn't that coat mine? Didn't I lend it to you out of friendship, so you could appear before our lord the king?" When the king heard that, he said, "The Jew has surely deceived one of us—me or the farmer," and had a few more silver dollars paid out to the Jew. The farmer went home with the good coat on and the good money in his pocket, saying, "This time I scored."

8 The Queer Minstrel

Der wunderliche Spielmann

THERE WAS ONCE A QUEER MINSTREL. He was walking forlornly through a forest, thinking of this and that, and when he had nothing left to think about, he said to himself, "Time's hanging heavy on my hands here in the forest; I'm going to summon a good companion." Then he took his fiddle from his back and played a tune that rang out through the trees. Soon a wolf came trotting through the thicket. "Oh, here comes a wolf! I don't care for its company," said the minstrel. But the wolf came nearer and said to him, "Well, my dear minstrel, how fine you fiddle! I'd like to learn that, too." "It's easy to learn," answered the minstrel, but you must do everything I tell you." "Oh, minstrel," said the wolf, "I'll mind you as a schoolboy minds his master." The minstrel bade him come along, and when they had gone on together for a bit, they came to an old oak tree that was hollow inside and split down the middle. "Look here," said the minstrel, "if you want to learn to fiddle, you must put your forepaws into this crack." The wolf obeyed, but the minstrel quickly picked up a stone and with one blow wedged its two paws in so tight that the wolf had to stay there a prisoner. "Wait till I come back," said the minstrel and went on his way.

After a while he again said to himself, "Time is hanging heavy on my hands here in the forest; I'm going to summon another companion," took his fiddle and once more fiddled his way through the forest. Not long after, a fox came slinking through the trees. "Oh, here comes a fox!" said the minstrel, "I don't care for its company." The fox approached him and said, "Well, dear minstrel, how fine you fiddle! I'd like to learn that, too." "It's easy to learn," said the minstrel, "only you must do everything I tell you." "Oh, minstrel," answered the fox, "I'll mind you as a schoolboy minds his master." "Follow me," said the minstrel, and when they'd gone on a bit, they came to a footpath with tall bushes on both sides. There the minstrel stopped, bent a hazel sapling down to the ground from one side, holding down the tip with his foot, and then bent down another sapling from the other side, saying, "Very well, fox, if you want to learn something, give me your left forepaw." The fox obeyed, and the minstrel tied its paw to the sapling on the left. "Fox," he said, "now give me your right forepaw," and tied it to the sapling on the right. And when he'd made sure that the knots in the cords were tight enough, he let go, and the saplings sprang up and jerked the fox up, so that it swung to and fro and wriggled in the air. "Wait till I come back," said the minstrel and went on his way.

Again he said to himself, "Time's hanging heavy on my hands here in the forest; I'm going to summon another companion," took his fiddle, and the sound rang out through the forest. Then a hare came hopping along. "Oh, there comes a hare!" said the minstrel, "I didn't want it." "Goodness, dear minstrel," said the hare, "how fine you fiddle! I'd like to learn that, too." "It's easy to learn," said the minstrel, but you must do everything I tell you." "Oh, minstrel," answered the hare, "I'll mind you as a schoolboy minds his master." They went on a bit together till they came to a clearing in the forest where there was an aspen. The minstrel tied a long cord around the hare's neck, attaching one end to the tree. "Lively, hare!" cried the minstrel. "Now hop around the tree twenty times." The hare obeyed, and when it had run around twenty times, the cord had wound twenty times around the trunk, and the hare was caught. No matter how it pulled and tugged, it merely made the cord cut deeper into its soft neck. "Wait till I come back," said the minstrel and went on.

Meanwhile the wolf had pulled and tugged, bitten at the stone, and worked, until at last it had freed its paws and got them out of the crack. Full of anger and rage it ran after the minstrel and wanted to tear him to pieces. When the fox saw the wolf running by, it began to whine and with might and main cried out, "Brother wolf, come and help me; the minstrel's tricked me." The wolf pulled down the saplings, cut the cords with its teeth, and freed the fox, who went along with it and wanted to take vengeance on the minstrel. They found the hare tied up and freed it, too, and then all three went together to look for their common enemy.

Continuing on his way, the minstrel again made his fiddle

resound and this time had better luck. The tune reached the ears of a poor woodcutter who willy-nilly immediately left his work and with his ax under his arm came along to listen to the music. "At last the right companion's coming," said the minstrel. "I was looking for a human being, not for wild animals." He started playing again and played so finely and beautifully that the poor man stood as if in a trance, and his heart rejoiced. As he was standing thus, the wolf, the fox, and the hare came running up, and he saw plainly that they meant no good. Then he raised his shiny ax and got in front of the minstrel as if to say, "Whoever wants to get at him had better look out; for he'll have to deal with me." Then the animals got frightened and ran back into the forest, but the minstrel played one more tune to thank the wood-cutter and then went on.

9   The Twelve Brothers

Die zwölf Brüder

THERE WAS ONCE A KING and a queen who lived happily together and had twelve children, but only boys. Now the king said to his wife, "If the thirteenth child you bear me is a girl, the twelve boys are going to die, so that her estate may be great and the kingdom fall to her alone." He also had twelve coffins made; they were already filled with shavings and in each was a coffin-pillow, and the king had them taken to a locked room. Then he gave the queen the key and commanded her never to say a word about it to anyone.

The mother, however, now used to sit all day long and mourn, so that her youngest son, who was always with her and whom she called Benjamin from the Bible, said to her, "Mother dear, why are you so sad?" "Dearest child," she replied, "I'm not allowed to tell you." But he gave her no peace till she went and unlocked the door of the room and showed him the twelve coffins already filled with shavings. Then she said, "Dearest Benjamin, your father had these coffins made for you and your eleven brothers, for if I give birth to a girl, all of you are to be killed and buried in them." And as she wept while saying this, her son consoled her and said, "Don't weep, mother dear, we'll take care of ourselves and go away." But she said, "Go out into the forest with your eleven brothers and always have one of you in turn sit up in the tallest tree that can be found, keeping watch and looking this way toward the tower of the palace. If I give birth to a son, I'll hoist a white flag, and then you may come back; but if I give birth to a daughter, I'll hoist a red flag. In that case, flee as fast as you can, and may the dear Lord protect you. Every night I'll get up and pray for you: in winter that you may be able to warm yourselves by a fire, in summer that you may not suffer from the heat."

After she had thus given her sons her blessing, they went out into the forest. They took turns keeping watch, one of them always sitting up in the tallest oak and looking toward the tower. When eleven days were up and Benjamin's turn came, he saw a flag being hoisted. It was not the white one, however, but the blood-red flag announcing that they were all to die. When the brothers heard that, they grew angry and said, "To think that we're to suffer death because of a girl! We swear we shall be avenged: wherever we find a girl, we'll shed her red blood."

They went deeper into the forest and in the very middle, where it was darkest, they found a little enchanted cottage, which was unoccupied. Then they said, "Let's stay here, and you, Benjamin, who are the youngest and weakest, shall stay home and keep house, while the rest of us go out and get food." So they went into the forest and shot hares, wild deer, birds and pigeons, and whatever was fit to eat. This they took home to Benjamin, who had to prepare it for them that they might satisfy their hunger. They lived together in the cottage for ten years, and the time passed quickly for them.

The daughter that their mother, the queen, had given birth to was now growing up; she was kindhearted and fair of face and had a golden star on her forehead. Once when there was a lot of washing, she saw twelve men's shirts and asked her mother, "Whose are these twelve shirts? They're much too small for father." Then with a heavy heart her mother answered, "Dear child, they belong to your twelve brothers." "Where are my twelve brothers?" said the girl, "I never heard of them before."

Her mother answered, "God knows where they are! They're wandering about in the world." Then she took the girl and opened a door and showed her the twelve coffins with the shavings and the coffin-pillows. "These coffins," she said, "were meant for your brothers, but they stole away secretly before you were born," and she told her how it had all happened. Then the girl said, "Mother dear, don't weep; I'll go and look for my brothers."

Now she took the twelve shirts and went away straight into the big forest. She walked all day, and in the evening came to the enchanted cottage. There she went in and found a young boy, who asked, "Where do you come from and where are you going?" and was amazed at her beauty, her royal clothes, and the star she had on her forehead. Then she replied, "I'm a king's daughter and am looking for my twelve brothers and shall go as far as the sky is blue, until I find them." She also showed him the twelve shirts which were theirs. Then Benjamin saw that she was his sister and said, "I'm Benjamin, your youngest brother." She began to weep for joy, and so did Benjamin, and they hugged and kissed one another affectionately. Then he said, "Dear sister, there's still one difficulty: we had agreed to kill every girl we met, because we had to leave our kingdom on account of a girl." Then she said, "I'll gladly die if I can thus save my twelve brothers." "No," he answered, "you shan't die. Sit down under this tub and wait until our eleven brothers come home; then I'll fix it up with them." This she did, and at nightfall the others came home from hunting, and dinner was ready, and when they were sitting at table and eating, they asked, "What's the news?" Then Benjamin said, "Haven't you any news?" "No," they answered. Then he went on, "You were in the forest, and I stayed at home, yet I know more than you do." "Well, tell us," they cried. "But will you promise me," he answered, "not to kill the first girl we meet?" "Yes," they all cried, "she shall be spared. Go on and tell us." Then he said, "Our sister's come," and lifted up the tub, and the king's daughter stepped forth in her royal clothes with the golden star on her forehead, and was most beautiful, gentle, and sweet. Then they all rejoiced, fell on her neck and kissed her, and loved her dearly.

Now she stayed home with Benjamin and helped him with the work. The eleven used to go into the forest and catch game, deer, birds and pigeons for their food, and their sister and Benjamin

saw to preparing it. She'd gather firewood and herbs for vegetables and set the pots on the fire, so that the meal was always
ready when the eleven arrived. In other ways, too, she kept the
cottage in order and made up the beds nicely with fresh white
linen, and the brothers were always content and lived with her
most happily.

On one occasion the two had prepared a fine meal, and when
they were all gathered, they sat down, ate and drank, and were
full of good cheer. There was a little garden near the enchanted
cottage, and in it were twelve lilies, the kind also called narcissus.
Now she wanted to please her brothers and picked the twelve
flowers, thinking to give one to each of them after the meal. But
the very moment she picked the flowers, her twelve brothers were
changed into ravens and flew away over the forest, and the house
and the garden had vanished, too. Now the poor girl was alone
in the wild forest, and as she looked about, an old woman was
standing beside her, who said, "My child, what have you done?
Why didn't you leave the twelve white flowers alone? They were
your brothers, who are now changed into ravens forever." Weeping, the girl said, "Is there no way to unspell them?" "No," said
the old woman, "there's only one thing in the whole world, but
that's so hard that you'll not free them that way, for you must
remain silent for seven years, neither speak nor even laugh, and
if you utter a single word only one hour short of the seven years,
all will have been in vain, and your brothers will be killed by that
one word."

Then the girl said in her heart, "I know for certain that I'll
unspell my brothers," and went and chose a tall tree, and sat
down up in it, and spun and neither spoke nor laughed. Now it
so happened that a king was hunting in the forest. He had a big
deerhound that ran up to the tree where the girl was sitting,
jumped around, and yelped and barked up at her. Then the king
came along and saw the beautiful princess with the golden star
on her forehead and was so enchanted by her beauty that he
called out and asked if she were willing to be his wife. She made
no answer, gave, however, a little nod with her head. Then he
climbed the tree himself, carried her down, put her on his horse,
and took her home. The wedding was celebrated with great
pomp and rejoicing, but the bride neither spoke nor laughed.
After they had lived happily together for a few years, the king's

mother, who was a wicked woman, began to slander the young queen and said to the king, "It's a common beggar girl you brought home. Who knows what evil and mischief she's secretly up to? Even if she's dumb and can't talk, at least she might laugh once in a while. Anybody who doesn't laugh has a bad conscience." At first the king was unwilling to believe this, but the old woman kept at it so long and accused her of so many bad things that the king was finally persuaded and condemned her to death.

Now a great fire was kindled in the courtyard, in which she was to be burned, and the king stood upstairs at the window and looked on with tearful eyes, because he still loved her so. When she had already been tied to the stake and the red tongues of fire were licking her clothes, at that moment the last second of the seven years passed. Then a whirring of wings was heard in the air, and the twelve ravens came flying up and lighted there, and as they touched the ground, they were her twelve brothers whom she had saved. They pulled the fire apart, put out the flames, freed their dear sister, and hugged and kissed her. And now that she might open her mouth and speak, she told the king why she'd been dumb and why she'd never laughed. The king rejoiced when he heard she was innocent, and they lived happily together until their death.

But the wicked stepmother was haled into court and put in a barrel filled with boiling oil and poisonous snakes and died an evil death.

10 The Vulgar Crew

Das Lumpengesindel

A COCK said to a hen, "Now's when the nuts are getting ripe; let's go up on the mountain and eat our fill before the squirrel gets them all." "Yes," answered the hen, "let's go and have a good time together." So they both set off for the mountain, and because it was a clear day, they stayed till evening. Now I don't know whether it was because they'd stuffed themselves or because they had got into high spirits, at any rate they didn't want to go home on foot, and the cock had to make a little coach out of nut shells. When it was ready, the hen got in and said to the cock, "Now you hitch yourself up to it." "That's a fine idea!" said the cock. "I'd rather walk home than be hitched up. No, that's not what we bargained for. I'm willing to be coachman and sit on the box, but pull it myself—no!"

While they were thus quarreling, a duck came quacking up: "You robbers! who gave you leave to trespass on my nut mountain? Just wait, you'll catch it," and went for the cock with its bill wide open. The cock wasn't slow, either, and bravely set upon the duck and so belabored it with his spurs that it begged for mercy and as a punishment gladly let itself be hitched to the coach. The cock now mounted the box and was coachman, and then away they went at top speed: "Duck, run as fast as you can." When they had driven some distance, they met two people on foot, a pin and a needle; they called out, "Stop! stop!" and said it'd soon be pitch-dark and that they wouldn't be able to go on a step farther. Besides, the road was muddy, and mightn't they ride along a bit? They'd been at the Tailors' Tavern outside the towngate and had sat too long over their beer. Since they were both thin and didn't take up much room, the cock let them get in, though they had to promise not to step on his or the hen's feet. Late in the evening they arrived at an inn, and because they didn't want to continue their journey at night and because the duck didn't walk very well but lurched from side to side, they determined to stop there. At first the host raised a lot of objections, said that his house was already full up, probably suspecting, indeed, that they weren't a very distinguished company. But at last since they were glib and promised to give him the egg the hen had laid on the journey and said he might keep the duck, who laid an egg every day, he finally said that they might spend the night. So they ordered up hot food and had a high old time.

Early in the morning, at dawn, when everybody was still asleep, the cock woke the hen up, fetched the egg and opened it, and between them they ate it. The shells they threw on the hearth. Then they went to the needle, which was still fast asleep, seized it by the head and stuck it in the cushion of the innkeeper's easy chair, and stuck the pin in his towel. Finally without so much as a word they flew away over the moor. But the duck, who liked to sleep in the open and had stayed out in the innyard, heard them whirring off, roused itself, and found a brook down which it swam. That was quicker than being hitched to the coach.

Not till some hours later did the innkeeper get up; he washed himself and was about to dry himself with the towel when the pin passed across his face, leaving a red mark from ear to ear. Then he went into the kitchen to light his pipe, but as he came to the hearth the eggshells sprang into his eyes. "This morning everything's hitting me on the head," he said and dropped crossly into his easy chair. But he jumped up quick enough, crying, "Ouch!" for the needle had pricked him even worse and not in the head, either. By now he was thoroughly angry and suspected the guests who had come so late the night before. When he went to look for them, they'd gone. Then he vowed never again to take a vulgar crew into his inn—people who consume much, pay nothing, and on top of it all repay one with practical jokes.

11 Brother and Sister

Brüderchen und Schwesterchen

A BROTHER took his sister by the hand and said, "Since mother died, we haven't had a single happy hour. Our stepmother beats us every day, and when we go to her, she kicks us out. Hard left-over crusts of bread are our food, and the dog under the table is better off, for once in a while she throws it some choice morsel. The Lord have mercy, if our mother knew that! Come, let's go out into the world together." All day long they walked over meadows and fields and stones, and when it rained, the girl said, "God and our poor hearts are weeping at the same time."

In the evening they entered a large forest and were so tired from grief and hunger and the long walk that they sat down in a hollow tree and fell asleep.

When they woke up the next morning, the sun was already high in the heavens and was shining nice and warm into the tree. Then the boy said, "Sister, I'm thirsty. If I knew of a spring, I'd go and have a drink; I think I hear the murmur of one." The brother got up, took his sister by the hand, and both went in search of the spring. Their wicked stepmother, however, was a witch, knew all about the two children's departure, had sneaked after them secretly the way witches do, and had bewitched all the springs in the forest. Now when they found a spring that was gushing and sparkling over the rocks, the brother wanted to drink from it. But his sister understood that its murmur meant, "Who drinks of me will be turned into a tiger, who drinks of me will be turned into a tiger," and cried, "Please, brother, don't drink the water, or you'll turn into a wild animal and tear me to pieces." So the brother didn't take a drink, though he was very thirsty, and said, "I'll wait till we come to the next spring." When they got to the second spring, the girl heard it, too, saying, "Who drinks of me will be turned into a wolf, who drinks of me will be turned into a wolf." Then the girl cried, "Brother, please don't drink the water, or you'll turn into a wolf and eat me up." So the brother didn't drink the water and said, "I'll wait till we come to the next spring, but then I must drink, no matter what you say, for I'm far too thirsty." And when they reached the third spring, the girl understood that its murmur meant, "Who drinks of me will be turned into a roe, who drinks of me will be turned into a roe." The girl said, "O Brother, please don't drink the water, or you'll turn into a roe and run away from me." But the boy at once knelt down by the spring, bent over it, and drank the water, and when the first drops touched his lips, he lay there in the form of a fawn.

Now the sister wept over her poor bewitched brother, and the fawn wept, too, and sat sadly beside her. Finally the girl said, "Don't weep, dear little fawn, I'll never leave you." Then she untied her golden garter and put it around the fawn's neck and pulled up rushes and wove them into a soft leash. Thus she tied the little animal to it and led it on, always going deeper and deeper into the forest. And when they had walked a long, long while, they finally came to a cottage, and the girl looked in. And because it was empty, she thought, "Here we can stay and live." Then she gathered leaves and moss to make a soft bed for the fawn, and every morning she'd go out and gather roots, berries, and nuts, and for the fawn she'd bring home tender grass, which it ate out of her hand, was content, and capered around her. In the evening when the sister was tired and had said her prayers, she'd lay her head on the fawn's back; that was her pillow, and on it she'd fall quietly to sleep. If only the brother had had his human shape, it would have been a wonderful life.

For quite a time they were thus alone in the wilderness. Now it happened that the king of the country had a big hunting party in the forest. The woods resounded with the blowing of horns, the baying of hounds, and the merry shouts of the huntsmen. The fawn heard it and would all too well have liked to share in the sport. "Oh," it said to its sister, "let me go out and join the hunt; I can't stand it any longer," and begged so long that she consented. "But," she said to it, "be sure to come back to me in the evening. I'll lock my door against the fierce huntsmen and that I may recognize you, knock on the door and say, "Sister dear, let me in here." Unless you say that, I won't unlock the door." Now the fawn leapt out and felt so fine and gay in the open air. The king and his huntsmen saw the beautiful animal and pursued it but couldn't overtake it; every time they thought they surely had it, it made a leap over the bushes and disappeared. When it grew dark, it ran to the cottage and, knocking, said, "Sister dear, let me in here." The door opened, and it leapt in and rested the whole night on its soft bed. Next morning the hunt began anew, and when the fawn again heard the bugle and the "heigh! heigh!" of the huntsmen, it got restless and said, "Sister, open the door, I've got to go out." The sister opened the door for it and said, "But you must be back again this evening and say your little verse." When the king and his huntsmen again saw the fawn with its golden collar, they all pursued it, but it was too swift and agile for them. This went on all day. Finally by evening, however, the huntsmen had surrounded it, and one of them had wounded it slightly in the leg, so that it limped and made off slowly. Then one of the huntsmen stalked it to the cottage and heard it say, "Sister dear, let me in here," and saw the door opened for it and immediately shut again. The huntsman kept all this well in mind, went to the king, and reported what he had seen and heard. Then the king said, "Tomorrow we'll hunt again."

The sister, however, was greatly frightened on seeing that her fawn had been wounded. She washed off the blood, put herbs on the wound, and said, "Now go to bed, dear fawn, so you'll get well again." The wound, however, was so slight that in the morning the fawn no longer felt it, and when it again heard the merry hunt going on outside, said, "I can't bear it! I must be in it; they won't catch me so easily!" The girl wept and said, "This time they'll kill you, and I'll be all alone here in the forest, forsaken by everyone. I shan't let you out." "Then I'll die here of sheer sadness," replied the fawn; "every time I hear the bugle, I feel I must get going as quickly as possible." Then the girl couldn't but open the door, though with a heavy heart, and the fawn leapt gaily and merrily out into the forest. When the king saw it, he said to his huntsmen, "Now pursue it all day long until nightfall but be careful not to hurt it." No sooner had the sun set than the king said to the huntsmen, "Now come and show me the forest hut," and when he reached the door, he knocked, saying, "Sister dear, let me in here." Then the door opened, and the king stepped in, and there stood a girl more beautiful than any he had ever seen. The girl was frightened when she saw it wasn't her fawn coming in but a man with a golden crown on his head. But the king looked at her in friendly wise, and giving her his hand, said, "Will you come with me to my palace and be my dear wife?" "Oh yes," answered the girl, "only the fawn must come along, too; I shan't abandon it." The king said, "You may keep it as long as you live, and it shall lack nothing." As they were talking, the fawn came leaping in, and the girl tied it up again on the rush leash, which she herself took hold of, and led it out from the forest hut.

The king put the lovely girl on his horse and brought her to his palace, where the wedding was celebrated with great pomp. Now she was queen, and they lived happily together for a long time. The fawn was well taken care of and capered about in the palace garden. However, the wicked stepmother, on whose account the children had gone out into the world, was quite sure that the sister had been torn to pieces by the wild animals in the forest and that the brother in the shape of a fawn had been killed by the huntsmen. But when she heard that they were so happy and well off, her heart swelled with jealousy and envy and gave her no peace, and she could think of nothing but how she might even yet bring misfortune upon the two. Her own daughter, who was as ugly as sin and one-eyed besides, reproached her, saying, "I ought to have had the good luck of being queen." "Just keep still," said the old witch, soothing her, "when the time comes, I'll be on hand." Well, as time passed and the queen gave birth to a handsome boy and the king happened to be out hunting, the old witch assumed the shape of the maid-in-waiting, entered the room where the queen was lying, and said to the sick woman, "Come, your bath's ready; it'll do you good and invigorate you; hurry up before it gets cold." Her daughter was there, too, and they carried the weak queen into the bathroom and put her in the tub. Then they locked the door and made off. In the bathroom, however, they had kindled a terrific fire, so that the beautiful young queen soon suffocated.

When this was done, the old witch took her daughter, put a nightcap on her, and laid her in the queen's bed. She also gave her the shape and looks of the queen, only she couldn't give her back the eye she'd lost. To conceal this from the king, the daughter had to lie on her blind side. When the king came home in the evening and heard that he was the father of a little boy, he was very happy and was about to go to his dear wife's bed and see how she was. But the old witch promptly cried, "My goodness! don't draw back the curtains, the queen mustn't be exposed to light yet and must have quiet." The king went away and didn't know that a substitute queen was in the bed.

At midnight when everybody was asleep, the nurse, who was sitting by the cradle in the nursery and keeping watch alone, saw the door open and the real queen come in. She lifted the child out of the cradle, took it in her arms, and nursed it; then she shook up its little pillow, put the child back, and laid its coverlet over it. Nor did she forget the fawn but went into the corner where it was lying and stroked its back. Then she quietly went out the door again. Next morning the nurse asked the guards whether anybody had entered the palace during the night, but they replied, "No, we didn't see anyone." In this way she came many nights running and never spoke a word, and though the nurse saw her every time, yet she didn't dare breathe a word about it to anyone.

After some time the queen began one night to speak, and said,

> "How's my child? how's my fawn?
> I'll come twice more and then never again."

The nurse didn't answer her, but when the queen again disappeared, she went to the king and told him everything. Then the king said, "Oh God! what can it be? Tonight I'll watch the child myself." In the evening he went to the nursery, and about midnight the queen reappeared and said,

> "How's my child? how's my fawn?
> I'll come once more and then never again."

And as usual she nursed the child before disappearing. The king didn't dare address her but kept watch the following night, too. Again she said,

> "How's my child? how's my fawn?
> I've come this time, but never again."

Then the king could no longer restrain himself, sprang toward her, and said, "You can be none other than my dear wife." Then she replied, "Yes, I am your dear wife," and at that very moment she had, through the grace of God, come back to life again and was hale and hearty. Then she told the king of the crime committed against her by the wicked witch and her daughter. The king had them both haled into court, and their sentence was pronounced. The daughter was led into the forest, where wild animals tore her to pieces, while the witch was tied to a stake and burned to death miserably. And when she'd been burned to ashes, the fawn changed back and got his human form again. The brother and sister lived happily together until their death.

12 Rampion

Rapunzel

THERE WAS ONCE A MAN and his wife; for a long time they'd been longing in vain for a child. Finally the woman expected that God would fulfill her wish. At the back of their house the couple had a little window overlooking a magnificent garden full of the finest flowers and herbs. But it was surrounded by a high wall, and no one dared enter it, because it belonged to a witch who was very powerful and was feared by all. One day the woman was standing by this window and looking down into the garden and saw a bed planted with the finest rampions, looking so fresh and green that her appetite was whetted, and she felt the greatest craving to eat some of them. This craving increased from day to day, and since she knew she couldn't get any, she lost weight and looked pale and wretched. Then her husband got frightened and asked, "What's ailing you, dear wife?" "Oh," she replied, "unless I can eat some of the rampions from the garden behind our house, I'll surely die." Her husband, who loved her, thought, "Rather than let your wife die, you'll fetch her some of the rampions, cost what it may." So at dusk he climbed over the wall into the witch's garden, hurriedly cut a handful of rampions, and brought them to his wife. She at once prepared a salad of them and ate them greedily. But they tasted so good to her, so very good, that the next day her craving grew three times stronger. To pacify her, her husband had once more to scale the garden wall. Thus at dusk he again climbed down, but when he'd got down from the wall, he was terribly frightened, for he saw the witch standing before him. "How do you dare to climb into my garden," she said with an angry look, "and like a thief steal my rampions? You'll pay dear for it." "Oh," he answered, "let justice be tempered with mercy, I did so only from dire necessity: my wife saw your rampions from her window and has such a craving for them that she'd die unless she might eat some." Then the witch's wrath abated and she said to him, "If that's the way it is, I'll let you take as many rampions as you like, but on one condition: you must give me the child your wife will give birth to. The child will be all right, and I'll take care of it like a mother." In his fright the man promised everything, and when his wife was delivered of her child, the witch immediately appeared, christened it Rampion, and took it away with her.

Rampion grew up to be the most beautiful child under the sun. When she was twelve, the witch locked her up in a tower in a forest, and it had neither stairs nor door, only a little window way up at the top. Whenever the witch wanted to get in, she'd stand down below and call,

> "Rampion, Rampion,
> Let down your hair for me."

Rampion had beautiful long hair, as fine as spun gold. Every time she heard the witch's voice, she'd undo her braids and wind them around the casement hinge above; then her hair would drop twenty yards, and the witch would climb up on it.

A few years later the king's son happened to be riding through the forest and passed the tower. Then he heard a song so lovely that he stopped and listened. It was Rampion, who in her solitude whiled away her time singing. The prince wanted to climb up to her and looked for a door in the tower but couldn't find one. He rode home, but the song had so touched his heart that every day he used to go out into the forest and listen. One day when he was standing behind a tree, he saw the witch approach and heard her call out,

> "Rampion, Rampion,
> Let down your hair."

Then Rampion let down her braids, and the witch climbed up on them. "If that's the ladder one gets up there on, I, too, shall try my luck for once." The next day when it began to get dusk, he went to the tower and called out,

> "Rampion, Rampion,
> Let down your hair."

At once the hair came down, and the king's son climbed up.

At first Rampion was greatly frightened to see enter a man such as her eyes had never looked upon before, but the king's son spoke to her kindly and told her how her singing had so moved his heart that it left him no peace and that he had to see her herself. Then Rampion's fear vanished, and when he asked her whether she was willing to accept him as her husband, and she saw that he was young and handsome, she thought to herself, "He'll love me better than old Mrs. Gothel," and said yes, and put her hand in his. "I'll gladly go with you," she said, "but I don't know how I can get down. Every time you come, bring along a skein of silk. I'll braid it into a ladder, and when it's finished, I'll come down on it, and you'll take me on your horse." They agreed that until then he was to come to her every evening, for the old woman came during the day. The old witch didn't notice anything until one day Rampion all of a sudden said to her, "Now tell me, Mrs. Gothel, why it is you're so much heavier for me to pull up than the young king's son? He's up here in a second." "Oh, you wicked child!" cried the witch, "what's this I hear? I thought I'd cut you off from everybody, and now you've deceived me." In her anger she seized Rampion's beautiful hair, wound it a couple of times around her left hand, took a pair of scissors with her right, and slish, slash, cut it off, and the beautiful braids were lying on the floor. And she was so pitiless that she took poor Rampion to a waste land, where she had to live in great misery and wretchedness.

On the evening of the very day on which she had cast Rampion out, the witch fastened the braids she'd cut off to the casement hinge, and when the prince came and called out,

> "Rampion, Rampion,
> Let down your hair."

she let the hair down. The prince climbed up; there, however, he found not his beloved Rampion but the witch, who cast evil and poisonous glances at him. "Ha! ha!" she cried mockingly, "you've come to fetch your sweetheart! But the pretty bird's no longer in its nest and is no longer singing; the cat's got it and will scratch out your eyes, too. Rampion's lost to you, you'll never see her again." The king's son was beside himself with sorrow and in his despair jumped down from the tower. He escaped with his life, but the thorns into which he fell put out his eyes. Then he wandered blindly about in the forest, ate only roots and berries, did nothing but moan and weep over the loss of his beloved wife. Thus for some years he wandered about in misery and finally got into the waste land where Rampion was leading a miserable existence with the twins she had born, a boy and a girl. He heard a voice and it sounded very familiar to him. He went toward it, and as he drew near, Rampion recognized him and fell on his neck and wept. Two of her tears, however, wet his eyes, and they became clear again and he could see with them as well as before. He brought her to his kingdom, where he was received with rejoicing, and they lived happily and contented for a long time.

13 The Three Dwarfs in the Forest

Die drei Männlein im Walde

THERE WAS A MAN whose wife died, and a woman whose husband died, and the man had a daughter, and the woman also had a daughter. The girls knew one another and used to go on walks together and afterward go to the woman's house. Once she said to the man's daughter, "Listen, tell your father I'd like to marry him. Then you'll wash in milk every morning and drink wine, but my daughter will wash in water and drink water." The girl went home and told her father what the woman had said. The man said, "What ought I to do? There's a good and a bad side to marriage." Finally, because he couldn't make up his mind, he took off one of his boots and said, "Take this boot with a hole in the sole. Take it to the loft, hang it up on the big nail there and then pour water into it. If it holds the water, I'll remarry, but if it runs through, I won't." The girl did as she was bid, but the water made the hole close up, and the boot got full to the top. She reported to her father how it turned out. Then he went up himself, and when he saw that she was right, he went to the widow and wooed her, and the wedding took place.

The next morning when the two girls got up, there was milk before the man's daughter to wash in and wine to drink, but before the woman's daughter was water for washing and for drinking. On the second morning there was water for washing and drinking before the man's daughter as well as before the woman's daughter, and on the third morning there was water for washing and drinking before the man's daughter, and milk for washing and wine to drink before the woman's daughter. And that's the way it remained. The woman became her stepdaughter's bitter enemy and thought only of how she might make it worse for her from one day to the next. She was envious, too, because her stepdaughter was pretty and lovely, while her own daughter was ugly and loathsome.

Once upon a time in winter when there'd been a hard frost and hill and dale were covered with snow, the woman made a paper dress and, calling the girl, said, "Put on the dress and go out into the forest and fetch me a basket of strawberries; I've got a craving for some." "Good heavens," said the girl, "strawberries don't grow in winter; the ground is frozen and the snow has covered everything. And why should I go out in a paper dress? It's so cold outdoors that one's breath freezes, the wind will blow right through it, and the thorns will tear it off me." "Do you mean to oppose me?" said the stepmother, "get along out and don't show your face again till you've got the basket of strawberries." Then she gave her a little piece of hard bread and said, "That'll be your food for the day," thinking, "she'll freeze to death out there and starve and never show me her face again."

Now the girl obeyed and, putting on the paper dress, went out with the basket. Far and wide was nothing but snow, and not a green blade was to be seen. When she got into the forest, she saw a cottage with three dwarfs looking out of it. She wished them good day and knocked respectfully at the door. They called out, "Come in," and she entered the room and sat down on the bench by the stove. She wanted to warm herself there and eat her breakfast. Then the dwarfs said, "Give us a little of it, too." "Gladly," she said, broke her piece of bread in two, and gave them half. They asked, "What are you doing here in the forest in winter in your thin dress?" "Alas," she replied, "I'm to fetch a basket of strawberries and mayn't come home without them." When she'd eaten her bread, they gave her a broom, saying, "Sweep away the snow by the back door." But once she was outside, the three dwarfs said to one another, "What shall we give her for being so well-mannered and kindly and for sharing her bread with us?" Then the first said, "I grant her that she shall become prettier every day." The second said, "I grant her that gold pieces shall fall from her mouth every time she utters a word." The third said, "I grant her that a king shall come and marry her."

The girl did as the dwarfs bade. With the broom she swept away the snow behind the cottage, and what do you think she found? A lot of ripe strawberries, peeping out dark red from under the snow! Then joyfully she picked a basketful, thanked the dwarfs, shook hands with each, went home, and was going to bring her stepmother what she'd asked for. As she came in and said, "Good evening," a gold piece at once fell out of her mouth. Then she told what had happened to her in the forest, and with every word she uttered gold pieces fell from her mouth, so that the whole floor was soon covered with them. "Just look at such extravagance!" cried her stepsister, "throwing money about like that!" though secretly she was envious and herself wanted to go out into the forest to look for strawberries. But her mother said, "No, my darling daughter, it's too cold; you might freeze to death." But since she gave her no peace, her mother finally yielded and made her a magnificent fur coat, which she had to put on, and gave her bread and butter and cake to eat on the way.

The girl went into the forest and straight to the cottage. The dwarfs were again on the lookout, but she didn't greet them, and without so much as looking at them or saying how-do-you-do, she stumbled into the room, sat down by the stove, and began to eat her bread and butter and cake. "Give us a little of it," cried the dwarfs, but she replied, "There's not enough for myself; how can I give any to others?" When she'd finished eating, they said, "Here's a broom, sweep it clean for us by the back door." "My goodness! do your own sweeping," she replied, "I'm not your maidservant." When she saw they weren't going to give her anything, she went out the door. Then the dwarfs said to one another, "What shall we give her for being so ill-mannered and having such a wicked and envious heart that begrudges everybody everything?" The first said, "I grant her that she shall become uglier every day." The second said, "I grant her that with every word she utters a toad shall hop out of her mouth." The third said, "I grant her that she shall die a miserable death." The girl looked for strawberries outdoors but when she found none, went home in ill humor. And when she opened her mouth and was about to tell her mother how she'd fared in the forest, with every word a toad hopped out of her mouth, so that everybody was disgusted by her.

Now the stepmother got even more irritated and only thought of how she might inflict all possible suffering on the man's daughter, whose beauty was increasing from day to day. At last she took a kettle, put it on the fire, and boiled some yarn in it. When it was boiled, she hung it on the poor girl's shoulders and gave her an ax. She was to take it to the river that was frozen over, cut a hole in the ice, and ret the yarn. She obeyed and went and cut a hole in the ice. As she was chopping away, a magnificent coach drew near, in which the king was sitting. The coach stopped, and the king asked, "My child, who are you? and what are you doing there?" "I'm a poor girl and I'm retting yarn." Then the king was moved to pity and when he saw how beautiful she was, said, "Do you want to come with me in my coach?" "Oh yes, with all my heart," she answered, for she was glad to get away from her stepmother and stepsister.

So she climbed into the coach and drove off with the king, and when they reached the palace, the wedding was celebrated with great pomp, as the dwarfs had granted it to the girl. A year later the young queen gave birth to a boy, and when her stepmother heard of her great good fortune, she came to the palace with her daughter, as though she wanted to pay a visit. But one day when the king went out and no one else was about, the wicked woman seized the queen by the head while her daughter seized her by the feet, and together they lifted her from her bed and threw her out the window into the river that flowed by. Then her ugly daughter lay down in the bed, and the old woman covered her, head and all. When the king returned and was about to speak to his wife, the old woman cried, "Quiet! quiet! you mustn't do that now. She's perspiring heavily; you must let her rest today." The king was quite unsuspecting and didn't come back till the following morning, and as he talked to his wife and she answered, with every word a toad hopped out of her mouth, where formerly gold pieces had fallen from it. Then he asked what that meant, and the old woman said that it came from the heavy perspiration and would of course go away again.

But in the night the scullery boy saw a duck swim in through the drain. It said,

> "King, what are you doing?
> Are you asleep or are you awake?"

And when the boy didn't answer, it said,

> "What are my guests doing?"

Then the boy replied,

> "They're fast asleep."

The duck asked further,

> "How's my baby?"

He replied,

> "It's sleeping in its cradle."

Then she resumed the shape of the queen, went upstairs, nursed it, fluffed up its crib, covered it, and then swam away again through the drain in the shape of a duck. Thus she appeared two nights running. The third night she said to the scullery boy, "Go tell the king to take his sword and on the threshold to swing it three times over my head." Then the scullery boy went and told the king. He came with his sword and swung it three times over the apparition, and the third time his wife stood before him hale and hearty as before.

Now the king was very happy, but he kept the queen hidden in a chamber till the Sunday, when the child was to be christened. And when it had been christened, he said, "What does a person deserve who takes another from his bed and throws him into the water?" "Nothing less," the old woman answered, "than to be put in a cask studded with nails on the inside and rolled down hill into the water." Then the king said, "You have pronounced your own doom," had such a cask brought and the old woman and her daughter put in it. Then the head was nailed on and the cask rolled down hill and into the river.

14 The Three Spinners

Die drei Spinnerinnen

THERE WAS ONCE A GIRL who was lazy and unwilling to spin, and say what she would, her mother couldn't get her to do it. Finally her mother was carried away with anger and impatience and gave her such a beating that she cried loudly. Now it so happened that just then the queen was driving past, and when she heard the cries, she stopped, came in, and asked the mother why she was beating her daughter so her cries could be heard out in the street. The mother was ashamed to admit her daughter's laziness and said, "I can't stop her spinning; she insists on doing it all the time, and I'm poor and can't get the flax." Then the queen answered, "There's nothing I like to hear more than the sound of spinning and I'm never happier than when I hear the hum of a spinning wheel. Give me your daughter to take with me to my palace; I've got plenty of flax, and she may spin as much as she likes." The mother gladly consented, and the queen took the girl along. When they reached the palace, the queen took her upstairs to three chambers, from floor to ceiling full of the finest flax. "Now spin me this flax," she said, "and when you've finished, you shall marry my eldest son. Though you're poor, it makes no difference; your untiring industry is dowry enough." Deep down in her heart the girl was frightened, for she couldn't spin the flax even if she lived to be three hundred and was at it every day from morning till evening. So when she was all alone, she began to weep and sat thus for three days without lifting her finger. On the third day the queen came and on seeing that nothing had as yet been spun, was surprised, but the girl excused herself by saying she hadn't been able to start work because of her great sorrow over being away from her mother's house. The queen accepted this excuse but on leaving said, "You must start working tomorrow."

When the girl was again alone, she couldn't think of any way out of the difficulty and in her sorrow stepped to the window. Then she saw three women approaching, of whom one had a splayed flat foot, the second a lower lip so large that it hung down over her chin, and the third had a splayed thumb. They stopped in front of the window, looked up, and asked the girl what the trouble was. She complained to them of her difficulty. Then they offered her their help, saying, "If you'll invite us to your wedding and not be ashamed of us and say we're cousins of yours and have us sit at your table, we'll spin your flax in short order." "Gladly," she replied, "just come in and start work right away." Then she let the three queer women in and cleared a place in the first chamber. There they settled down and started spinning. One drew out the thread and treadled, the other wet it, the third twisted it and with her finger rapped on the table, and every time she rapped, a reel of yarn dropped to the floor, most evenly and delicately spun. She concealed the three women from the queen, to whom, every time she came, she showed the amount of yarn spun, so that there was no end to the queen's praise. When the first chamber was empty, they moved on to the second, and finally the third, and that, too, was soon cleared out. Then the three women took their leave, saying to the girl, "Don't forget your promise; it'll be for your benefit."

When the girl showed the queen the empty chambers and the huge pile of yarn, she made arrangements for the wedding, and the bridegroom was glad to get such a skillful and industrious wife and praised her highly. "I've got three relatives," said the girl, "and since they've been very kind to me, I shouldn't like to forget them in my good fortune. Please let me invite them to the wedding and have them sit at my table." The queen and the bridegroom said, "Why shouldn't we let you?" At the beginning of the wedding feast the three women entered in strange garb, and the bride said, "Welcome, dear cousins." "My," said the bridegroom, "how did you strike up a friendship with such repulsive people?" Then he went to the one with the splayed foot and asked, "Where did you get such a splayed foot?" "From treadling," she answered, "from treadling." Then the bridegroom went to the second and said, "How did you get that drooping lower lip?" "From licking thread," she replied, "from licking thread." Then he asked the third, "How did you get your splayed thumb?" "From twisting thread," she answered, "from twisting thread." Then the king's son got frightened and said, "My fair bride shall never again touch a spinning wheel."

Thus she was relieved of the wretched task of spinning flax.

15 Haensel and Gretel

Hänsel und Gretel

NEAR A LARGE FOREST lived a poor woodcutter with his wife and two children. The boy's name was Haensel and the girl's Gretel. The woodcutter had little to eat, and once when a great famine swept the country, he was no longer able to earn even their daily bread. One evening when he was lying in his bed and tossing about and worrying, he sighed and said to his wife, "What's to become of us? How can we feed our poor children when we've nothing left for ourselves?" "Do you know what, husband," answered the wife, "the first thing tomorrow morning we'll take the children out into the densest part of the forest. There we'll kindle them a fire and give each a little piece of bread; then we'll go about our work and leave them there alone; they won't find the way back home, and we'll be rid of them." "No, wife," said the man, "that I won't do. How could I have the heart to leave my children alone in the forest; the wild animals would soon come and tear them to pieces." "O you fool," she said, "then all four of us will starve to death; you might as well start planing the boards for our coffins," and gave him no peace until he agreed. "But all the same I'm sorry for the poor children," said the man.

The two children hadn't been able to get to sleep, either, because they were hungry and heard what their stepmother said to their father. Gretel wept bitter tears and said to Haensel, "Now it's all up with us." "Be quiet, Gretel," said Haensel, "Don't worry, I'll get us out of this, of course." And when the mother and father had fallen asleep, he got up, put on his jacket, opened the lower half of the door, and crept out of the house. The moon was shining bright, and the white pebbles which were in front of the house gleamed like so many new silver coins. Haensel stooped down and put as many of them as he could in his jacket pocket. Then he went back and said to Gretel, "Don't worry, sister dear, and just go to sleep; God won't forsake us." Then he went to bed again.

When day dawned, even before sunrise the mother came and woke the children up, saying, "Get up, you lazybones, we're going into the forest to fetch wood." Then she gave each a piece of bread, saying, "Here's something for your dinner, but don't eat it beforehand; you're not getting anything else." Gretel put the bread in her apron because Haensel had the stones in his pocket. Then they all set out together for the forest. When they'd been walking a little while, Haensel stopped and looked back toward the house and did so again and again. The father said, "Haensel, what are you looking at there, and why are you lagging behind? Watch out or you'll be forgetting your legs." "Oh Father," said Haensel, "I'm looking at my white kitten; it's sitting on top of the roof and wants to say good-bye to me." The woman said, "You fool, that's not your kitten; it's the morning sun shining on the chimney." But Haensel hadn't been looking at the cat but was ever tossing one of the white pebbles from his pocket onto the path.

When they reached the middle of the forest, the father said, "Now gather some wood, children! I'll make a fire for you so you won't get cold." Haensel and Gretel gathered brush, quite a pile of it. The brush was kindled, and when the fire was blazing, the wife said, "Now lie down by the fire, children, and take a rest. We're going into the forest to cut wood; when we're finished, we'll come back and fetch you."

Haensel and Gretel sat by the fire and when it was noon ate their piece of bread. And because they heard the blows of the ax, they thought their father was near by. But it wasn't the ax; it was a branch he'd tied to a dead tree, which the wind was banging back and forth. When they'd been sitting for a long time, their eyes closed from weariness, and they fell fast asleep. When they finally woke up, it was already pitch-dark. Gretel began to weep and said, "How shall we get out of the forest now?" But Haensel consoled her, saying, "Just wait a bit till the moon's up; then we'll easily find our way." When the full moon had risen, Haensel took his sister by the hand and followed the pebbles, which glittered like new silver coins and showed them the way. They kept walking all night and at daybreak were back at their father's house. They knocked at the door, and when the wife opened it and saw Haensel and Gretel, she said, "You naughty children, why did you sleep so long in the forest? We thought you weren't coming back at all." But the father was glad, for he was sorry he'd left them alone in the forest.

Not long after that there was again a famine everywhere, and one night the children heard their mother say in bed to their father, "Everything's been eaten up again; we've only got a half a loaf of bread left and then we'll be at the end of our rope. The children must be sent away. Let's take them deeper into the forest to make sure they won't find the way out again. There's no other salvation for us." With heavy heart the man thought, "It'd be better to share your last morsel with your children," but the woman would listen to nothing he said, scolded him, and reproached him. But one step leads to another, and since he'd given in the first time, he had to the second, also.

The children, however, were still awake and heard the conversation. When the mother and father were asleep, Haensel again got up and was going out to pick up pebbles as before, but the wife had locked the door, and Haensel couldn't get out. Nevertheless, he consoled his sister and said, "Don't weep, Gretel, and just go to sleep; the dear Lord will surely help us."

Early in the morning the wife came and got the children out of bed. They received their piece of bread, but it was even smaller than last time. On their way to the forest Haensel crumbled it up in his pocket and, stopping often, scattered the crumbs on the ground. "Haensel, why are you stopping and looking around?" said his father; "go ahead." "I'm looking at my pigeon; it's sitting on the roof and wants to say good-bye to me," answered Haensel. "You fool!" said the woman, "that's not your pigeon; it's the morning sun shining on the chimney." Nevertheless, Haensel gradually scattered all the bread crumbs along the path.

The woman led the children still deeper into the forest, where they'd never been in all their lives. Then a big fire was again made, and the mother said, "Just sit there, children, and if you feel tired, you can take a little nap. We're going into the forest to cut wood and this evening when we're finished, we'll come and fetch you." When it was noon, Gretel shared her bread with Haensel, who'd scattered his piece along the way. Then they fell asleep, and the evening passed and no one came to get the poor children. They didn't wake up till it was pitch-dark, and Haensel consoled his sister, saying, "Just wait, Gretel, till the moon's up; then we'll see the bread crumbs I scattered. They'll show us the way home." When the moon rose, they set out but didn't find any bread crumbs, for the thousands of birds that fly about in forest and field had pecked them all up. Haensel said to Gretel, "We'll surely find the way," but they didn't find it. They walked all night and still another day from morning till evening but didn't get out of the forest. And they were very hungry, for they had nothing but a few berries that were on the ground, and because they were so tired that their legs wouldn't carry them any farther, they lay down under a tree and fell asleep.

By now it was already the third morning since they'd left their father's house. They began walking again but kept getting deeper and deeper into the forest, and unless help came soon, they were doomed to die of exhaustion. When it was noon, they saw a pretty snow-white bird perched on a branch; it sang so beautifully that they stopped and listened to it. And when it had finished, it flapped its wings and flew ahead of them; they followed it until they came to a cottage. There it lighted on the roof, and when they got quite near, they saw that the cottage was made of bread with a cake roof and that

the windows were of sugar candy. "Let's make for it," said
Haensel, "and have a fine meal. I'll eat a piece of the roof
and, Gretel, you may eat some of the window; that's sweet."
Haensel reached up and broke off a little piece of the roof for
himself to see how it tasted, and Gretel took her place at the
windowpanes and nibbled at them. Then a shrill voice called
out from the living room,

> "Nibble, nibble, nibble!
> Who's nibbling at my cottage?"

The children answered,

> "The wind, the wind,
> The Heavenly Child,"

and went on eating without being put off. Haensel, who quite
liked the taste of the roof, pulled down a large piece, while Gretel
took out a whole round windowpane, sat down, and ate it with
relish. Then suddenly the door opened, and a very old woman
leaning on a crutch came slinking out. Haensel and Gretel
were so frightened that they dropped what they had in their
hands. But the old woman shook her head and said, "Well,
well, you dear children, who brought you here? Come right
in and stay with me; no harm will befall you." She took them
both by the hand and led them into her cottage. They were
served a good meal with milk, pancakes and sugar, apples, and
nuts. Then she made up two pretty beds with white sheets,
and Haensel and Gretel lay down in them and thought they
were in Heaven.

The old woman was, however, only pretending to be kind;
as a matter of fact, she was a wicked witch who lay in wait
for children and who'd built the cottage of bread just to lure
them to her. Once she got a child in her power, she'd kill it,
cook it, and eat it, and that would be a red-letter day for her.
Witches have red eyes and can't see far, but they've a keen sense
of smell, just like animals, and scent the approach of human
beings. As Haensel and Gretel were getting near her, she
laughed wickedly and mockingly said, "I've got them! they
shan't get away from me again!" Early in the morning before
the children were awake, she was already up and, seeing them
both sleeping so sweetly with their full rosy cheeks, muttered

to herself, "That'll be a fine snack." Then with her withered hand she seized Haensel and carried him to a little pen and shut him up behind a grilled door. No matter how hard he cried, it did him no good. Then she went to Gretel, shook her till she woke up, and said, "Get up, you lazybones, fetch some water and cook something good for your brother; he's outside in the pen and must be fattened up. Once he's fat, I'll eat him." Gretel began to weep bitterly, but it was no use: she had to do what the wicked witch ordered her.

Now the best food was cooked for poor Haensel, but Gretel got nothing but crab shells. Every morning the old woman would slink out to the pen and cry, "Haensel! stick out your fingers so I can feel whether you'll be fat soon." But Haensel stuck out a little bone, and the old woman, whose eyesight was poor, couldn't see it and thought it was one of Haensel's fingers and was surprised he didn't get fat. When four weeks had passed and Haensel still stayed thin, she got impatient and wouldn't wait any longer. "Come on, Gretel!" she called out to the girl, "hurry up! bring some water! whether Haensel's fat or lean, I'm going to kill him tomorrow and cook him." Oh, how the poor little sister cried out when she had to carry the water, and how the tears rolled down her cheeks! "Dear Lord, please help us," she cried; "if only the wild animals in the forest had devoured us, then we at least should have died together." "Just stop your whining," said the old woman; "it won't do you any good at all."

Early in the morning Gretel had to go out and hang up the kettle full of water and kindle the fire. "First let's do some baking," said the old woman, "I've already heated up the oven and kneaded the dough." She pushed poor Gretel out to the oven, from which big flames already were leaping. "Crawl in!" said the witch, "and see whether it's properly hot, so we can put the bread in." Once Gretel was in, she intended to shut the oven and roast Gretel in it and then she was going to eat her up, too. But Gretel saw what she was up to and said, "I don't know how to. How do I get in?" "Stupid goose," said the old woman, "the opening's big enough. Why, I could get in myself," waddled up and stuck her head in the oven. Then Gretel gave her a shove so that she slid way in, shut the iron door, and shot the bolt. My! then she began to howl

—something horrible! But Gretel ran away, and the wicked witch burned to death miserably.

Then Gretel went straight to Haensel, opened his pen, and called, "Haensel, we're saved! The old witch is dead!" Then Haensel jumped out like a bird from its cage when the door's opened. How happy they were! They fell on each other's necks, skipped about, and kissed one another, and because they didn't need to be afraid any more, they went into the witch's house, where there were chests of pearls and jewels in every nook and corner. "These are even better than pebbles," said Haensel, filling his pockets as full as he could, while Gretel said, "I want to bring something home, too," and filled her apron. "Now let's be off," said Haensel, "and get out of this enchanted forest." But when they'd been walking for a couple of hours, they reached a big body of water. "We can't get across," said Haensel; "I don't see any plank or bridge." "And there isn't any boat here," answered Gretel, "but there's a white duck. If I ask it, it'll help us across." Then she called out,

> "Duck, duck!
> Here's Haensel and Gretel.
> There's no plank or bridge;
> Take us on your white back."

As a matter of fact, the duck did come up, and Haensel got on it and told his sister to sit down beside him. "No," answered Gretel, "it'll be too heavy for the duck; it had better carry us over one at a time." The good creature did so, and when both were safely across and had gone a short distance, the forest kept getting more and more familiar to them, and finally they spied their father's house from afar. Then they began to run and rushed into the living room and fell on their father's neck. The man hadn't had a single happy hour since he'd left his children alone in the forest. The wife, however, had died. Gretel shook out her apron, and the pearls and jewels bounced about in the room, and Haensel threw one handful after the other from his pocket. Then all their troubles were at an end, and they lived most happily together.

My tale's done. There runs a mouse; whoever catches it may make a great big cap out of its fur.

16   The Snake's Three Leaves

Die drei Schlangenblätter

ONCE UPON A TIME there was a poor man who could no longer provide for his only son. Then the son said to him, "Father dear, things are going so badly for you that I'm becoming a burden. I'd rather go away myself and see if I can earn my living." Then the father gave him his blessing and very sadly took leave of him. At that time the king of a mighty realm was waging war, and the young man enlisted and joined the campaign. When he came face to face with the enemy, a great battle ensued, and it was very dangerous, for there was a perfect hail of bullets, and his comrades were falling all about him. And when the general, too, was killed, the others wanted to seek safety in flight, but the young man stepped forward and encouraged them, crying, "We mustn't let our fatherland go down!" Then the others followed him, and he pressed on and defeated the enemy. When the king heard that he owed his victory to him alone, he promoted him over everybody else, gave him vast treasures, and made him the first citizen of his kingdom.

The king had a daughter who was very beautiful but also very odd. She'd made a vow to marry no one who wouldn't promise, in the event of her dying first, to be buried alive with her. "If he really loves me," she said, "what use will life be to him then?" On the other hand, she was ready to do the same, and should he die first, go down with him into the grave. Thus far this strange vow had frightened away all suitors, but the young man was so taken by her beauty that he paid no attention to anything and asked her father for her hand. "But are you aware," said the king, "of what you must promise?" "If I survive her, I shall have to go down with her into the grave," he replied, "but my love for her is so great that the danger means nothing to me." Then the king consented, and the wedding was celebrated with great pomp.

Now they lived happily and contented for some time. Then it so happened that the young queen fell seriously ill, and no physician was able to save her. When she lay dead, the young king remembered what he'd had to promise and was seized with horror at the thought of being buried alive. But there was no way out: the king had posted sentries at all the gates, and it was impossible to escape that fate. When the day came for the body to be buried in the royal vault, he was led down with it, and the door was bolted and locked.

Beside the coffin stood a table with four candles, four loaves of bread, and four bottles of wine. As soon as these provisions were exhausted, he was bound to die of starvation. Thus he sat there full of sorrow and sadness, each day eating only a tiny bit of bread and drinking only a swallow of wine, and even so, he saw that death was drawing nearer and nearer. While he was thus staring into space, he saw a snake crawl out of a corner of the vault and approach the body, and because he thought it was coming to gnaw at it, he drew his sword and said, "As long as I'm alive, you shan't touch her," and cut it into three pieces. After a while a second snake came crawling out of the corner, but when it saw its companion lying dead and cut to pieces, it went back, returning shortly with three green leaves in its mouth. Then it took the three pieces of the snake, put them properly together, and placed one of the leaves on each of the wounds. Immediately the severed pieces grew together, the snake stirred and came to life again, and both hurried off. The leaves remained on the ground, and the wretched man, who'd witnessed it all, conceived the idea that the wonderful power of the leaves, which had restored the snake to life, might also help a human being. Accordingly, he picked up the leaves and put one on the dead woman's mouth, the other two on her eyes. He'd scarcely done so when the blood stirred in her veins, rose into her pale face, and made it rosy again. Then she drew a breath, opened her eyes, and said, "Oh God, where am I?" "You're with me, dear wife," he answered and told her how it had all happened and how he'd brought her back to life. Then he gave her some wine and bread, and when she'd regained her strength, she got up, and they went to the door and knocked, calling so loud that the guards heard it and reported to the king. The king himself went and opened the door; there he found them both hale and hearty and rejoiced with them over all their trouble now being ended. The young king took along the snake's leaves, gave them to a servant, and said, "Keep them carefully for me and always carry them on you. Who knows under what circumstances they may still be of help to us."

After she'd been brought back to life, a change, however, took place in the woman; it was as if all affection for her husband had vanished from her heart. When some time later he wanted to make a voyage overseas to visit his aged father, and they'd gone aboard ship, she forgot the great love and loyalty he'd showed her and with which he'd saved her from death, and conceived an evil passion for the ship's captain. Once when the young king was lying asleep, she called the captain and took the sleeping man by the head while the captain had to take him by the feet, and thus they threw him overboard into the sea. When the crime had been committed, she said to him, "Now let's go back home and say he died on the voyage. Of course I'll exalt and extol you to my father, so that he'll marry me to you and make you heir to his crown." But the faithful servant, who'd witnessed the whole thing, put off unnoticed in a gig, sat down in it, followed his master, and let the traitors continue their voyage. He fished up the dead man again and with the help of the snake's leaves which he was carrying on him and which he put on his eyes and mouth, succeeded in bringing him back to life.

Night and day they both rowed with might and main, and their little gig made such good time that they got to the old king's court before the others. The king was astonished to see them arrive alone and asked what had befallen them. On learning of his daughter's perfidy he said, "I can't believe she acted so badly, but the truth will soon come out," and had them both go into a secret chamber and conceal themselves from everyone. Soon after, the big ship came in, and with troubled mien the wicked woman appeared before her father. He said, "Why are you returning alone? Where's your husband?" "Oh, father dear," she answered, "I'm returning in great sorrow; my husband fell suddenly ill on the voyage and died, and if the good captain hadn't helped me, I'd have been in a bad way. He was present at his death and can tell you everything." The king said, "I'll bring the dead man back to life," opened the chamber, and had the two come out. On seeing her husband, the wife was thunderstruck, fell on her knees, and begged for mercy. The king said, "There is no mercy; he was willing to die with you and brought you back to life. You, on the other hand, killed him in his sleep, and you shall have your just reward." Then together with her accomplice she was placed in a ship full of holes and put out to sea, where they soon sank beneath the waves.

17 The White Snake

Die weisse Schlange

LONG AGO there lived a king whose wisdom was famed throughout the whole country. He knew everything, and it seemed as though news about the most hidden things was carried to him through the air. He had, however, a strange habit. Every noon when the table had been quite cleared and no one was present, a trusted servant had to bring him one more dish. But it was covered, and the servant himself didn't know what was in it, nor did anyone else, for the king didn't uncover it and didn't eat any of it until he was all alone. This had been going on for quite a long time, when one day the servant, who was removing the dish, was overcome with curiosity and took it into his room. After carefully locking the door, he lifted the cover and saw that a white snake was inside. On seeing it he couldn't restrain his desire to taste it, cut off a small piece, and put it in his mouth. No sooner had it touched his tongue than he heard a strange whispering of small voices outside his window. He went and listened and noticed that it was sparrows that were talking to one another, telling stories about what they'd seen in forest and field. Tasting the snake had given him the power to understand the language of animals.

Now it happened that on that very day the queen lost her finest ring, and suspicion of having stolen it fell on the trusted servant, who had access to everything. The king had him come into his presence and with abusive words threatened to hold him responsible and condemn him unless he could name the guilty party by the next day. There was no use protesting his innocence; he was curtly dismissed. In his anxiety and fear he went down into the courtyard and wondered how he might get out of his difficulty. Some ducks were sitting there peacefully by a running stream, resting and preening themselves and talking confidentially. The servant stopped and listened to what they were saying. They were telling one another how that morning they'd all been waddling about and what good food they'd found. Then one of them said crossly, "Something's sitting heavy on my stomach: in my haste I swallowed a ring that was lying under the queen's window." Then the servant at once seized it by the neck, carried it into the kitchen, and said to the chef, "Just kill this duck; it's good and fat." "Yes," said the chef, weighing it with his hands, "it's not been lazy about feeding itself and has been waiting for a long time now to be roasted." He cut off its neck, and when it was cleaned, the queen's ring was found in its stomach. The servant could now easily prove his innocence to the king, and since the latter was anxious to make amends for his injustice, he granted him a boon and promised him the highest court position he might desire.

The servant declined everything, only asking for a horse and traveling money, for he wanted to see the world and journey about for a time. When his request was granted, he set out and one day passed a pond where he noticed three fish that had been caught in the reeds and were gasping for water. Though people say that fish can't talk, nevertheless he heard them lamenting that they had to perish so miserably. Being kindhearted, he dismounted and put the three captives back into the water. They wriggled with joy, stuck their heads out, and called to him, "We'll remember you for this and repay you for having saved us." He rode on and after a while seemed to hear at his feet a voice in the sand. He listened and heard a king of the ants lamenting, "If only people would keep their clumsy animals off us! That stupid horse there is mercilessly trampling my people to death with its heavy hoofs." He turned the horse onto a side path, and the king of the ants called out to him, "We'll remember you for this and repay you." His way led into a forest, and there he saw a father-raven and a mother-raven standing by their nest and throwing their young out. "Out with you, you good-for-nothings!" they cried; "we can't keep up with your appetites any longer; you're big enough to provide for yourselves." The poor little birds were lying on the ground, fluttering and beating their wings and crying, "We helpless children! We're supposed to provide for ourselves and can't yet fly! What's left for us but to die here of starvation?" Then the goodhearted youth dismounted, killed his horse with his sword, and left it for the young ravens to feed on. They came hopping up, ate their fill, and cried, "We'll remember you for this and repay you."

Now he had to use his own legs, and when he'd walked a long way, he reached a large town. There was a lot of noise and big crowds in the streets, and a man came on horseback and read a proclamation: "The king's daughter is in search of a husband, but whoever wants to woo her will have to carry out a difficult task, and if he fails in this, he will forfeit his life." Many had had a try at it already but had ventured their lives in vain. When the youth saw the king's daughter, he was so dazzled by her great beauty that he forgot all danger, went into the king's presence, and declared himself a suitor.

He was promptly led out to the sea, and a golden ring was thrown in before his eyes. Then the king bade him fetch this ring from the bottom, adding, "If you come up without it, you'll be thrown in again and again, until you perish in the waves." Everybody felt sorry for the handsome youth and then left him alone by the sea. He stood on the shore pondering what to do, when all of a sudden he saw three fishes swimming along, the very ones whose lives he'd saved. The middle one was holding in its mouth a shell, which it laid on the beach at the young man's feet. When the latter picked it up and opened it, there was the golden ring inside. Joyfully he brought it to the king, expecting to be granted the promised reward, but when the king's proud daughter learned that he was her inferior by birth, she scorned him and demanded that he first accomplish a second task. She went down into the garden and herself scattered ten bags of millet in the grass. "He must have it picked up by daybreak tomorrow," she said, "and not one grain may be missing." The youth sat down in the garden and reflected on how he might accomplish this task but could think of nothing and sat there quite sad, expecting to be led to his death at dawn. But when the sun's first rays fell on the garden, he saw the ten bags standing side by side and quite full, and not one grain was missing. During the night the king of ants had come with his thousands and thousands of ants, and the grateful animals had most industriously picked up the millet and gathered it in the bags. The king's daughter herself came down into the garden and saw with amazement that the youth had accomplished the task she had set him. Nevertheless, she still couldn't conquer her proud heart and said, "Though he's accomplished both tasks, still he shan't be my husband until he's brought me an apple from the Tree of Life." The youth didn't know where the Tree of Life was but set out, intending to keep going as long as his legs would carry him, even though he had no hope of finding it. When he'd already passed through three kingdoms and one evening had got into a forest, he sat down under a tree and was about to go to sleep. Then he heard a noise in the branches, and a golden apple fell into his hand. At the same moment three ravens swooped down on him, perched on his knees, and said, "We're the three young ravens you saved from starvation. When we grew up and heard you were looking for the golden apple, we flew across the sea to the end of the world, where the Tree of Life is, and fetched the apple for you." Joyfully the youth set out for home and brought the golden apple to the king's daughter, who now had no further excuse. So they divided the Apple of Life and between them ate it. Then her heart was filled with love for him, and they lived in untroubled happiness to a ripe old age.

18   A Straw, an Ember, and a Bean

Strohhalm, Kohle und Bohne

IN A VILLAGE lived a poor old woman; she'd gathered a mess of beans and was going to cook them. So she kindled a fire on her hearth and to make it burn faster lighted it with a handful of straw. As she was tossing the beans into the pot, one of them got away from her unnoticed and came to rest on the floor beside a straw. Soon after, a glowing ember likewise sprang out of the hearth down beside the other two. Then the straw began to speak and said, "Dear friends, where do you come from?" The ember answered, "I was lucky enough to jump out of the fire. If I hadn't taken violent measures, I'd surely have died; I'd have been burnt to ashes." The bean said, "I just got away with a whole skin, too; for had the old woman got me into the pot, I'd certainly have been cooked to porridge like my comrades and without mercy." "Would my fate have been any better?" said the straw. "The old woman let all my brothers go up in fire and smoke; she seized sixty of them at once and killed them. I fortunately slipped through her fingers." "But what shall we do now?" said the ember. "Since we were lucky enough to escape death, we should, I think," answered the bean, "stick together like good comrades and, to avoid another misfortune here, emigrate together to a foreign country."

This proposal met with the approval of the other two, and they set out together. Soon, however, they came to a little brook, and since there was neither bridge nor plank, they didn't know how to get across. The straw discovered a way out of the difficulty and said, "I'll lay myself across, then you can walk over me like a bridge." The straw then stretched itself from one bank to the other, and the ember, which was of a fiery disposition, tripped in quite lively fashion over the new bridge. But when it reached the middle and heard the water murmuring beneath, it got frightened and stopped and ventured no farther. Then the straw began to burn, broke in two, and fell into the brook; the ember slipped in after it, hissed when it touched the water, and gave up the ghost. The bean, that had prudently remained on the other bank, had to laugh when it saw this and couldn't stop and laughed so hard that it burst. Thus it, too, would have suffered the same fate as the others had it not by sheer good luck been for an itinerant tailor who was resting by the brook. Having a kindly heart, he took out needle and thread and sewed it together again. The bean thanked him kindly, but since he used black thread, all beans ever since have had a black seam.

19   The Fisherman and His Wife

Von dem Fischer un syner Fru

ONCE UPON A TIME there was a fisherman and his wife. They lived together in a chamber pot close by the sea, and every day the fisherman went out and fished. And he fished and fished. And once he was sitting with his hook and line and staring into the bright water. And he sat and sat. Then his hook went deep down to the bottom, and when he pulled it up, he fetched out a big flounder. Then the flounder said to him, "Now listen, fisherman, I pray you let me live; I'm not a real flounder, I'm an enchanted prince. What good will it do you to kill me? I wouldn't taste very good anyhow. Put me back in the water and let me swim away." "Well," said the man, "you don't need to talk so much; a flounder that can talk I'd have let go in any event." Thereupon he put it back in the bright water. The flounder went to the bottom, leaving behind a long streak of blood. Then the fisherman got up and went back to his wife in the chamber pot.

"Husband," said the wife, "didn't you catch anything today?" "No," said the man, "I caught a flounder, but it said it was an enchanted prince; then I let it swim away again." "Didn't you make a wish?" said the wife. "No," said the husband, "what should I be wishing for myself?" "Oh dear," said the woman, "it's too wretched to live forever in a chamber pot; it smells and is so disgusting. You might have wished for a little cottage for us. Go back again and call it. Tell it we'd like to have a little cottage and it'll surely do it." "Oh," said the husband, "why should I go back there?" "Well," said the wife, "after all, you did catch it and let it swim away again. It'll surely do it. Go right away!" The man didn't really want to but didn't want to oppose his wife, so he went to the sea.

When he got there, the sea was quite green and yellow and no longer so bright. Then he stood there and said,

> "Manntje, manntje, timpe te,
> Flounder, flounder in the sea!
> My wife Ilsebill
> Doesn't want what I really want."

Then the flounder came swimming up and said, "Well, what does she want?" "Oh dear," said the man, "I caught you, and my wife says I ought to have wished myself something. She doesn't want to live in a chamber pot any longer, she wants a little cottage." "Just go back," said the flounder, "she's got the whole thing."

Then the man went back, and his wife was no longer sitting in a chamber pot, but there was a little cottage, and his wife was sitting outside the door on a bench. Then she took him by the hand and said to him, "Come in, look! Now this is really much better." Then they went in, and in the cottage was a little entryway and a lovely little living room, and a bedroom with their bed in it, and a kitchen and a pantry, everything of the best, with utensils neatly hung up, tinware and brass that goes with a kitchen. And behind the cottage was a little yard with chickens and ducks and a little garden with vegetables and fruit trees. "Look," said the wife, "isn't this nice?" "Yes," said the husband, "let it stay that way; now we'll live quite contented." "That's something to think about," said the wife. Then they had a bite to eat and went to bed.

Everything went well for about a week or a fortnight, then the wife said, "Listen, husband, the cottage is altogether too cramped, and the yard and garden are very small. The flounder could of course have given us a larger house; I'd like to live in a big stone mansion. Go to the flounder; he'll give us a mansion." "Oh, wife," said the husband, "the cottage is good enough. Why should we want to live in a mansion?" "I know," said the wife, "you just go; the flounder can easily do this." "No, wife," said the man, "the flounder's just given us the cottage; I don't want to go back again, it might offend the flounder." "Just the same you go," said the woman; "it can easily do this and will be glad to. Just go!" The man's heart was very heavy and he didn't want to. He said to himself, "It isn't right," but he went nevertheless.

When he got to the sea, the water was quite rough, dark blue and gray and dead-looking and no longer so green and yellow, though it was still fairly calm. Then he stood there and said,

> "Manntje, manntje, timpe te,
> Flounder, flounder in the sea!
> My wife Ilsebill
> Doesn't want what I really want."

"Well, what does she want?" said the flounder. "Oh," said the man somewhat distressed, "she wants to live in a big stone castle." "Just go home; she's standing before the door," said the flounder.

Then the man went back and thought he was going home, but when he got there, there stood a big stone palace, and his wife was standing right on the steps and was about to enter. She took him by the hand and said, "Come on in." Then he went in with her, and in the castle was a big front hall with a marble floor, and there were lots of servants who opened the great doors, and the walls were all shiny and hung with fine tapestries. In the rooms were only golden chairs and tables, silver chandeliers hung from the ceilings, and all the rooms and chambers were carpeted. Food and the very best wine was on the tables, which threatened to break under their load. Behind the house was a big courtyard with stables for horses and cows, the finest coaches, also a beautiful big garden with the loveliest flowers and fine fruit trees, and a park half a mile long with stags and roe and hares there, and everything one might ever wish for. "Well," said the wife, "isn't that nice?" "Yes, of course," said the man; "let it stay that way and let's live in the fine castle and be content." "We'll think about that," said the wife, "and sleep on it." And so they went to bed.

Next morning the wife was the first to wake up. It was just daybreak, and from her bed she saw the wonderful land spread out before her. Her husband was still stretching himself. Then she nudged him with her elbow and said, "Man, get up and take a look out the window. Look now, can't we be king over all this country? Go to the flounder and tell him we'd like to be king." "Oh, wife," said the man, "why do we want to be king? I don't want to be king." "Well," said the woman, "if you don't want to be king, I do. Go to the flounder; I want to be king." "Oh, wife," said the man, "why do you want to be king? I don't want to say that to it." "Why not?" said the wife. "Go straight there! I must be king." Then the man went and was thoroughly distressed that his wife wanted to be king. "It isn't right, it isn't right," he thought. He didn't want to go there, but he went just the same.

When he got to the sea, it was blackish gray and black and dead-looking, and there was a ground swell and the water smelled terribly, too. Then he stood there and said,

> "Manntje, manntje, timpe te,
> Flounder, flounder in the sea!
> My wife Ilsebill
> Doesn't want what I really want."

"Well, what does she want?" said the flounder. "Alas!" said the man, she wants to be king." "Just go back; that's what she is," said the flounder.

Then the man went back, and when he approached the palace, the castle had become much bigger and had a huge keep, splendidly ornamented, with sentries standing in front of the gate, and there were ever so many soldiers with drums and trumpets. When he went inside, everything was of solid gold and marble, and there were velvet coverings with great golden tassels. Then the doors of the great hall opened, and there was the whole court. His wife was sitting on a high throne of gold and diamonds with a golden crown on her head and in her hand a jeweled scepter of solid gold, and she was

flanked by a row of ladies-in-waiting, each a head shorter than
the next. Then he stepped up and said, "Oh, wife, are you king
now?" "Yes," said the woman, "now I'm king." Then he stood
and looked about and after looking for some time, said, "Oh,
wife, how nice that you're king. Now let's not wish for anything more." "Well, husband," said the woman and got quite
restless, "time's hanging heavy on my hands and I can't stand
it any longer. Go to the flounder! I'm king, and now I must become emperor as well." "Oh, wife," said the man, "why do you
want to be emperor?" "Husband," she said, "go to the flounder!
I want to be emperor." "Oh, wife," said the man, "it can't make
emperors; I don't want to say that to the flounder. There's only
one emperor in the empire. The flounder can't make emperors;
it absolutely can't do that." "What!" said the woman, "I'm king
and you're my vassal. Will you go straight off! straight off! If it
can make kings, it can also make emperors. I insist on being
emperor. Go right away!" So he had to go. While on the way
he got quite frightened and thought to himself, "It just isn't
right; 'emperor' is too brazen. In the end the flounder will get
tired of it."

Meanwhile he got to the sea, and the sea was all black and
soupy and began to boil up so that it made bubbles, and such
a gale passed over the surface that it stirred it, and the man was
frightened. But he stepped up and said,

> "Manntje, manntje, timpe te,
> Flounder, flounder in the sea!
> My wife Ilsebill
> Doesn't want what I really want."

"Well, what does she want?" said the flounder. "Alas, flounder,"
he said, "my wife wants to become emperor." "Just go back,"
said the flounder, "she's emperor already."

Then the man went back, and when he got there, the whole
mansion was of polished marble with alabaster figures and
golden ornaments. Soldiers were marching before the door,
blowing trumpets and beating drums and kettledrums, and
within barons and counts and dukes were walking about as
servants and opened the doors for him, and these were of solid
gold. And when he went in, there was his wife sitting on a
throne wrought of a single piece of gold and two miles high,

and she had on a golden crown three yards high and set with brilliants and carbuncles. In one hand she held the scepter and in the other the imperial apple. On both sides she was flanked by satellites standing in two rows, each person shorter than the next, ranging in size from the tallest giant, who was two miles tall, to the tiniest dwarf only as big as my little finger. And before her were standing many princes and dukes. Then the man stepped up and said, "Wife, are you now emperor?" "Yes," she said, "I'm emperor." Then he stopped and took a good look at her and, after looking at her for some time, he said, "Oh, wife, how nice that you're emperor." "Husband," she said, "why are you standing there? Now that I'm emperor, I want to be pope, too. Go to the flounder!" "Oh, wife," said the man, "what on earth don't you want! You can't be pope; there's only one pope in Christendom; the flounder can't make you that." "Husband," she said, "I want to be pope. Go straight away! I must be pope this very day." "No, wife," said the husband, "I don't want to say that to it; it's not right, it's not right; it's too much of a good thing. The flounder can't make you pope." "Husband, what nonsense!" said the wife, "if it can make me emperor, it can make me pope, too. Go right away! I'm emperor and you're my vassal. Will you please go!" Then he got frightened and went but felt quite faint and trembled and shook, and his knees and calves quaked. A strong wind was blowing over the land and there were scudding clouds as night fell. The leaves were falling from the trees, and the water surged and roared as if it were boiling, and it beat against the shore, and at a distance he saw ships maneuvering in distress and dancing and tossing about on the waves. The sky was still a little blue in the middle, but on the horizon it was as coppery as before a heavy thunderstorm Then quite timid and fearful he stepped up and said,

> "Manntje, manntje, timpe te,
> Flounder, flounder in the sea!
> My wife Ilsebill
> Doesn't want what I really want."

"Well, what does she want," said the flounder. "Alas," said the man, "she wants to be pope." "Go right back; she's pope already," said the flounder.

He went back, and when he got there, there was a big church

with nothing but palaces around it. He forced his way through the crowd. Within everything was illuminated with thousands and thousands of candles, and his wife, dressed in solid gold, was sitting on a still higher throne with three big golden crowns on, and around her stood a multitude of ecclesiastics, and on both sides of her were two rows of candles, the biggest as thick through as the highest tower and so on down to the tiniest church candle. And all the emperors and kings were kneeling before her kissing her slipper. "Wife," said the husband, looking straight at her, "are you now pope?" "Yes," she said, "I'm pope." Then he stepped up and looked straight at her, and it was as if he were looking into the bright sun. When he'd looked at her for a while, he said, "Oh, wife, how nice that you're pope." But she sat as stiff as a ramrod and neither stirred nor moved. Then he said, "Wife, now be content since you're pope, for you can't get any higher." "I'll think that over," said the woman. Then they both went to bed. But she wasn't content, and her ambition didn't let her sleep; she kept thinking all the time how she might get still higher.

The man slept soundly and well, for he'd walked a good deal that day, but his wife couldn't get to sleep and all night long tossed about in her bed and kept thinking how she might get higher. And yet she couldn't think of anything more. Meanwhile it was about sunrise, and when she saw the dawn, she sat up in her bed and gazed into it, and when she saw the sun rise, she thought, "Aha! couldn't I, too, make the sun and moon rise?" "Husband," she said and nudged him in the ribs with her elbow, "wake up and go to the flounder. I want to be like God." The man was still practically asleep, but he got so frightened that he fell out of bed. He thought he hadn't heard right and, rubbing his eyes, said, "Oh, wife, what are you saying?" "Husband," she said, "if I can't make the sun and moon rise and if I can only watch them rise, I shan't be able to bear it. I shan't have another hour of peace until I can make them rise myself." Then she gave him such a terrifying look that a shudder ran over him. "Go right away! I want to be like God." "Oh, wife," said the husband, falling on his knees before her, "the flounder can't do that. It can make an emperor and a pope. I pray you, think it over and remain pope." Then she got angry, her hair flew wildly about her head, she tore her bodice, and gave him a kick, screaming, "I simply won't stand it any longer. Will you go!" Then he put on his trousers and ran off like mad.

Outside a storm was raging so that he could scarcely stay on his feet. Houses and trees were falling, the mountains shaking, and great boulders rolling down into the sea. The sky was absolutely pitch-black, there was thunder and lightning, and the sea was throwing up black waves as high as church steeples and mountains, and all with crests of white foam. Then he shouted but couldn't hear his own voice,

> "Manntje, manntje, timpe te,
> Flounder, flounder in the sea!
> My wife Ilsebill
> Doesn't want what I want at all."

"Well, what does she want?" said the flounder. "Oh," he said, "she wants to be like God." "Just go home, she's back in the chamber pot again."

To this day they're still there.

20   The Brave Little Tailor

Das tapfere Schneiderlein

ONE SUMMER MORNING a tailor was sitting on his bench by the window, was in good spirits, and was sewing away for dear life. Then a farmer's wife came down the street, crying, "Jam for sale! jam for sale!" That sounded good to the tailor's ears, and putting his little head out the window, he called, "Come up, madam, you can dispose of your wares here." With her heavy basket the woman climbed the three flights to the tailor's and had to unpack all her jars in front of him. He examined them all, lifted them up, sniffed at them, and finally said, "It seems like good jam to me, just weigh me out two ounces, madam—no matter if it's a quarter of a pound." The woman who'd hoped to make a good sale, gave him what he asked for but went away grumbling and out of sorts. "Well, God bless my jam," cried the tailor, "and may it give me strength and vigor!" He fetched a loaf of bread from the cupboard, cut off a full slice, and spread it with jam. "That won't taste bad," he said, "but I want first to finish the jacket before I start eating." He put the bread down beside him, went on sewing, and out of sheer joy made bigger and bigger stitches. Meanwhile, the smell of the sweet jam reached the wall, where lots of flies were sitting; they were attracted to it and settled on it in swarms. "Well, who invited you?" said the tailor and drove the unbidden guests away. But the flies, who understood no German, didn't let themselves be dismissed and came back in even greater numbers. Finally the tailor lost his temper and fetching a piece of cloth from behind the stove, said, "Just wait, you'll catch it!" and struck at them unmercifully. When he drew back and counted, no less than seven were lying dead before him with their legs in the air. "Are you as brave as all that!" he said to himself and couldn't help marveling at his own valor; "the whole town must know about this!" He hastily cut out a belt, sewed it together, and in big letters embroidered on it 'Seven at one blow.' "Just the town!" he said, "why the whole world shall know about it!" and his heart jumped for joy like a lamb's tail.

The tailor put the belt around his waist and wanted to go out into the world, thinking his workshop was too small for his bravery. Before leaving, he searched about in the house to see if there wasn't something to take along, but he found only an old cheese, which he put in his pocket. Outside the towngate he noticed a bird caught in the bushes; it had to join the cheese in his pocket. Now he bravely put the miles behind him and, being light of weight and nimble, felt no fatigue. His way led him up on a mountain, and when he reached the highest peak, there sat a powerful giant, taking his ease and looking around. The tailor approached him fearlessly and accosted him, saying, "Good morning, comrade! You're sitting there and viewing the wide world, aren't you? I'm just on my way there and want to test myself. Do you want to come along?" The giant looked at the tailor scornfully and said, "You tramp, you miserable fellow!" "Is that so?" replied the tailor, unbuttoned his coat and showed the giant his belt. "You can read for yourself what sort of a man I am." The giant read, "Seven at one blow," thought it was men slain by the tailor, and began somewhat to respect the little fellow. But he wanted to test him first, took a stone in his hand, and squeezed it so that water trickled out. "Now you do the same," said the giant, "if you've got the strength." "Is that all?" said the tailor, "for a man like me that's mere child's play," put his hand in his pocket, took out the soft cheese, and squeezed it so that the liquid came out. "Well," he said, "wasn't that even a little better?" The giant didn't know what to say and couldn't really believe the little chap had done it. Then he picked up a stone and threw it so high that one could hardly see it with the naked eye. "There, you miserable little creature, now do the same." "That was a good throw," said the tailor, "but after all the stone was bound to fall back to earth; I'm going to throw one that won't come back at all," put his hand in his pocket, took out the bird, and threw it up in the air. The bird, glad to be free, rose, flew away, and didn't come back. "How do you like that, my friend?" asked the tailor. "You can throw all right," said the giant, "but now let's see whether you can carry a decent load." He led the tailor to a huge oak which had been felled and was lying on the ground, and said, "If you're strong enough, help me carry this tree out of the forest." "Gladly," answered the little man, "you just take the trunk on your shoulder, and I'll lift the branches and twigs and carry them. That's the heaviest part, of course." The giant took the trunk on his shoulder, but the tailor sat down on a branch while the giant, who couldn't look around, had to carry away the whole tree and the tailor in the bargain. Back there on the branch the tailor was quite merry and in high spirits and whistled the ditty, "Three tailors were riding out of the gate," as if carrying trees was mere child's play. After dragging the heavy load for quite a way, the giant couldn't go on and called out, "Listen, I've got to drop the tree." The tailor jumped lightly down, seized the tree with both arms as if he'd been carrying it and said to the giant, "You're such a big fellow and can't even carry the tree."

They went on their way together, and as they were passing a cherry tree, the giant seized the top of the tree, where the ripest fruit was hanging, bent it down, put it in the tailor's hand, and told him to eat some. But the tailor was much too weak to hold the tree, and when the giant let go, the tree went up, jerking the tailor into the air. When he came down again unharmed, the giant said, "What does this mean? Aren't you strong enough to hold on to that little shoot?" "It isn't that I'm not strong enough," answered the tailor, "do you think that that would be anything for a man who laid out seven at one blow? I jumped over the tree, because huntsmen were shooting down there in the bushes. Jump over it yourself, if you can." The giant tried to but couldn't get over the tree and remained stuck in the branches. So here, too, the tailor had the best of it.

The giant said, "If you're such a brave fellow, come along to our cave and spend the night with us." The tailor was willing and followed him. When they reached the cave, other giants were sitting there by the fire, and each had a roasted sheep in his hand and was eating. The tailor looked around and thought, "It's a good deal roomier here than in my workshop." The giant showed him a bed and told him to lie down and to sleep as late as he wanted. But the bed was too big for the tailor, so he didn't lie down in it but crept into a corner of the cave. At midnight the giant thought the tailor was sound asleep, got up, took a big iron bar, and smashed the bed in two with one blow, thinking he'd finished the grasshopper off. Early in the morning the giants went into the forest and had quite forgotten the tailor, when all at once he came walking along quite merrily and fearlessly. The giants were terrified and, fearing he might kill them all, took to their heels.

The tailor went on his way, always following his pointed nose. After traveling a long while he came to the courtyard of a royal palace and feeling tired, lay down in the grass and fell asleep. While he was lying there, people came up, looked at him from all sides, and read on his belt, 'Seven at one blow.' "My!" they said, "what does this great warrior want here in peacetime? He must be a mighty lord." They went and reported it to the king, thinking that if war were to break out, he'd be an important and useful man whom they shouldn't let go at any price. The king liked the idea and dispatched one of his courtiers to the tailor; he was to propose military service once he waked up. The messenger stayed near the sleeping man, waited till the latter had stretched himself and opened his eyes, and then carried out his mission. "That's just what I've come here for," he replied, "and I'm ready to enter the king's service." Accordingly, he was honorably received and was assigned a special dwelling.

The soldiers, however, were jealous of the tailor and wished he were a thousand miles away. "What would happen," they said to one another, "if we got into a quarrel with him and he struck us? Seven would fall with each blow. The likes of us can't stand up to that!" They drew up a resolution and, going to the king in a body, asked for their discharge. "We aren't cut out," they said, "to hold our own against a man who kills seven at one blow." The king was sorry to lose all his faithful servants on account of one man, wished he'd never laid eyes on the tailor, and would have been glad to be rid of him. Still, he didn't dare dismiss him, fearing he might kill him and all his people and usurp the royal throne. For a long time he deliberated this way and that and finally hit on a solution. He sent word to the tailor, saying since he was so great a warrior that he wanted to make him a proposal. In a forest in his country were two giants who were doing great damage by robbing, murdering, and putting the country to fire and sword. No one might venture near them without risking his life. Should he overcome and kill these two giants, he'd give him his only daughter in marriage and half his kingdom as a dowry. Furthermore, a hundred horsemen were to accompany him and help him. "That would be just the thing for a man like you," thought the tailor, "a beautiful princess and half a kingdom aren't offered every day." "Oh yes," he answered, "I'll tame the giants easily enough, nor do I need the hundred horsemen to help me. A man who lays out seven at one blow doesn't need to be afraid of two."

The tailor set out, and the hundred horsemen went with him. When he got to the edge of the forest, he said to his escorts, "You just stop here. I'll settle things easily enough with the giants by myself." Then he skipped into the forest, looking to right and to left. After a while he saw both giants: they were lying asleep under a tree and snoring so as to make the branches wave up and down. The tailor quickly gathered both pockets full of stones and then climbed the tree. When he was halfway up, he hitched out on a branch until he was exactly over the sleeping giants and then dropped one stone after an-

other on one of the giants' chests. For a long time the giant
didn't notice anything, but finally he woke up, and giving his
companion a poke, said, "What are you hitting me for?" "You're
dreaming," said the other, "I'm not hitting you." So they lay
down to sleep again. Then the tailor dropped a stone on the
other giant. "What's that mean?" cried the latter. "Why are
you throwing things at me?" "I'm not throwing anything at
you," growled the first giant. For a while they quarreled over
the matter, but because they were both tired, they let it go at
that, and their eyes closed again. Then the tailor resumed his
old game, picked out the biggest stone and dropped it with
full force on the first giant's chest. "That's too much!" he exclaimed, jumped up like a madman and bashed his companion
against the tree so that it shook. The other paid him back in
the same coin, and they fell into such a furious rage that they
tore up trees and struck at one another, until finally both fell
dead on the ground at the same time. Now the tailor jumped
down. "It was sheer luck," he said, "that they didn't tear up the
tree I was sitting in; otherwise I'd have had to jump like a
squirrel onto another. Still, a man like me is nimble." He drew
his sword and dealt each a couple of good blows on the chest,
then went out to the horsemen and said, "The job's done. I've
finished off both of them. But it was hard going: in their des-
peration they tore up trees and defended themselves with them,
but nothing does any good when a man like me comes along
who lays out seven at one blow." "Aren't you wounded?" asked
the horsemen. "No, it turned out all right," answered the tailor,
"they didn't ruffle a hair of my head." The horsemen simply
wouldn't believe him and rode into the forest; there they found
the giants swimming in their own blood and round about lay the
torn-up trees.

The tailor now demanded of the king the promised reward,
but the latter regretted his promise and reflected anew as to
how he might disburden himself of the hero. "Before you get
my daughter and half the kingdom," he said to him, "you've
got to perform still another heroic feat. In the forest a unicorn
is at large and is doing a lot of damage: you must first catch
it." "I'm even less afraid of one unicorn than of two giants.
Seven at one blow, that's me!" He took along a rope and an
ax, went out into the forest, and again bade his companions

wait outside. He didn't have to search long. The unicorn soon appeared and rushed straight at the tailor as if it meant to run him through without further ado. "Easy! easy!" he said, "it doesn't go so fast as all that," stopped and waited until the animal was quite near, and then nimbly jumped behind a tree. The unicorn rushed against the tree with all its might and ran its horn so hard into the tree that it wasn't strong enough to pull it out again, and thus it was caught. "Now I've got the bird," said the tailor, came out from behind the tree, first put a rope around the unicorn's neck, and then with his ax chopped the horn free of the tree. When everything was fixed up, he led the animal off and took it to the king.

The king still wouldn't grant him the promised reward and made a third demand. Before his wedding the tailor would have to catch a wild boar that was doing great damage in the forest, and the huntsmen were to help him. "I'll be glad to do it," said the tailor; "it's child's play." He didn't take the huntsmen along into the forest, and they didn't object, for the wild boar had often given them such a warm reception that they had no desire to waylay it. When the boar saw the tailor, it rushed at him, foaming at the mouth and gnashing its tusks, and was going to throw him to the ground. The nimble hero, however, jumped into a near-by chapel and immediately out again up through one of the windows. The boar followed him, but he skipped around outside and shut the door on it, and the enraged animal was caught, since it was far too heavy and too clumsy to jump out the window. Then the little tailor called the huntsmen to see the prisoner with their own eyes. The hero, however, betook himself to the king who now willy-nilly had to keep his promise and surrender to him his daughter and half the kingdom. Had he known that it was no heroic warrior who was standing before him but only a little tailor, it would have pained him even more. The wedding was celebrated with much pomp and little joy, and a king was made out of a tailor.

After some time the young queen one night heard her husband say in a dream, "Boy, fix the jacket and patch the trousers, or I'll give you a rap over the ears with the yardstick." Then she realized in what circles the young lord had been born, on the following morning complained to her father, and begged him to help her get rid of a husband who was a mere tailor.

The king tried to console her, saying, "Leave your bedroom door open tonight. My servants will be standing outside and once he's asleep, they'll go in, tie him up, and carry him aboard a ship that will send him out into the wide wide world." That satisfied the woman, but the king's squire, who had overheard the whole thing and had a liking for the young lord, reported the plot to him. "I'll put a stop to that," said the tailor. That evening he went to bed with his wife at the usual time. When she thought he'd fallen asleep, she got up, opened the door, and lay down again. The little tailor, however, who'd only been pretending to be asleep, began to cry out in a loud voice, "Boy, fix the jacket and patch the trousers, or I'll give you a rap over the ears with the yardstick. I laid out seven at one blow, killed two giants, led off a unicorn, and captured a wild boar, and am supposed to be afraid of the fellows standing outside the bedroom!" When the men heard the tailor talking like that, they became terribly frightened, ran off as if the Wild Host was after them, and not one was willing to venture near him any more. Thus the tailor was a king and remained a king as long as he lived.

21 Ash Girl

Aschenputtel

A RICH MAN'S WIFE fell ill and, feeling that her end was approaching, called her only daughter to her bedside and said, "Dear child, remain devout and good; then dear God will ever be with you, and I'll look down on you from Heaven and be near you." Then she closed her eyes and passed away. Every day the girl used to go out to her mother's grave and weep and remained devout and good. When winter came, the snow laid a white blanket on the grave, and when in the spring the sun had taken it off again, the man married a second wife.

The wife brought two daughters of her own into the home;

they were pretty and fair of face but ugly and black in their hearts. Then evil days began for the poor stepchild. "Is the stupid goose to sit with us in the living room?" they'd say. "Whoever wants to eat bread must earn it—out with the scullery maid!" They took away her fine clothes, dressed her in an old gray smock and wooden shoes. "Just look at the proud princess! See how dressed up she is!" they'd cry and, laughing, lead her into the kitchen. There she had to do heavy work from morning till night, get up before dawn, carry water, light the fire, cook, and wash. On top of it all her sisters played all sorts of mean tricks on her, mocked her, and used to pour peas and lentils into the ashes so that she'd have to sit and pick them out again. In the evening when she was tired from work, there was no bed for her; she just had to lie down in the ashes beside the hearth. And since for this reason she always looked dusty and dirty, they called her Ash Girl.

Now it so happened that her father was once going to a fair and asked his two stepdaughters what to bring them. "Fine clothes," said one. "Pearls and jewels," said the other. "And you, Ash Girl," he said, "what do you want?" "Father, bring me the first twig that brushes against your hat on the way home. Break it off for me." So he bought fine clothes, pearls and jewels for the two stepsisters. As he was riding home through a green thicket, a hazel twig brushed against him and knocked off his hat; then he broke off the twig and brought it along. When he got home, he gave his stepdaughters what they'd asked for and gave Ash Girl the hazel twig. She thanked him, went to her mother's grave, planted the twig, and wept so bitterly that her tears fell on it and watered it. It grew and became a fine tree. Three times a day Ash Girl would go down there, weep and pray, and every time a little white bird would light on the tree, and every time she uttered a wish, the bird would throw down to her what she had wished.

Now, in order that his son might choose a bride, the king proclaimed a festival which was to last three days and to which all the pretty girls in the land were invited. When the two stepdaughters heard that they, too, were to appear, they were in high spirits and, calling Ash Girl, said, "Comb our hair! brush our shoes! and fasten our buckles! We're going to the festival at the king's palace." Ash Girl obeyed them, but she wept, for she would have liked to go along to the ball, and begged her stepmother to let her. "You, Ash Girl!" she said, "you're covered with dust and dirt, and you want to go to the festival? You've got no clothes and no shoes and you want to dance?" But when she kept on begging, the stepmother finally said, "I emptied a dish of lentils in the ashes; if you pick out the lentils within two hours, you may come along." The girl went out the back door into the garden and cried out, "You tame pigeons, you turtledoves, and all you birds under heaven, come and help me pick them out,

> the good lentils into the pot,
> the bad lentils into your crop."

Then two white pigeons came in through the kitchen window and after them the turtledoves, and finally all the birds under heaven whirred and flocked in and settled down around the ashes. And the pigeons bobbed their heads and began "peck, peck" and then the others began "peck, peck" and they pecked all the good lentils into the dish. It was hardly an hour before they were finished and all flew out again. Then the girl joyfully brought the dish to her stepmother and thought that she might now be allowed to go to the festival, but the stepmother said, "No, Ash Girl, you've got no clothes and don't know how to dance; you'll only be laughed at." When she wept, her stepmother said, "If you can pick two dishes of lentils from the ashes in one hour, you may come along," thinking, "she'll never be able to do this." When she'd emptied the two dishes of lentils into the ashes, the girl went out the back door into the garden and cried, "You tame pigions, you turtledoves, all you birds under heaven, come and help me pick them out,

> the good lentils into the pot,
> the bad into your crop."

Then two white pigeons came in through the kitchen window and after them the turtledoves, and finally all the birds under heaven whirred and flocked in and settled down around the ashes. And the pigeons bobbed their heads and began "peck, peck—peck, peck" and then the others began "peck, peck—peck, peck" and they pecked all the good lentils into the dishes.

And it was hardly half an hour before they finished and all flew out again. Then the girl brought the dishes to her step-mother and was glad, because she thought that she might now go along to the festival. But the latter said, "It'll do you no good. You're not coming along, for you've got no clothes and don't know how to dance. We'd only be ashamed of you." Then she turned her back on her and hurried off with her two haughty daughters.

When everyone had gone, Ash Girl went to her mother's grave under the hazel bush and cried,

> "Little tree, jiggle yourself and shake yourself;
> Scatter gold and silver over me."

Then the bird threw her down a gold and silver dress and silk slippers embroidered with silver. She put the dress on in a hurry and went to the festival. Her sisters, however, and her stepmother didn't recognize her and thought she must be some foreign princess, so beautiful did she look in her gold dress. They didn't so much as think of Ash Girl, who they thought was sitting at home in the dirt, picking lentils out of the ashes. The king's son went up to her, took her by the hand, danced with her, and wouldn't dance with anyone else. He never let go her hand, and when anyone else came to ask her to dance, he'd say, "She's my partner."

She danced till evening and then wanted to go home, but the king's son said, "I'll go with you and escort you," for he wanted to see whose daughter the beautiful girl was. She slipped away from him, however, and jumped into the dovecote. The king's son waited till her father came and told him that the foreign girl had jumped into the dovecote. The old man thought, "Can it be Ash Girl?" They had to fetch him an ax and a pick to break down the dovecote, but there was no one inside. And when they got home, there was Ash Girl in her dirty clothes lying in the ashes, and a dim oil lamp was burning in the fire-place. For Ash Girl had jumped down quickly out the back of the dovecote and had run to the hazel bush. There she'd taken off her fine clothes and laid them on the grave, and the bird had taken them away again, and then she'd sat down in her gray smock in the ashes in the kitchen.

Next day when the festival was resumed, and her parents and stepsisters had gone, Ash Girl again went to the hazel bush and said,

> "Little tree, jiggle yourself and shake yourself;
> Scatter gold and silver over me."

Then the bird threw down an even finer dress than the day before, and when she appeared at the festival in this dress, everyone was amazed at her beauty. The king's son had, however, waited for her coming, at once took her by the hand, and danced only with her. When others came and asked her for a dance, he'd say, "She's my partner." When evening came, she wanted to go, and the king's son followed her to see into which house she went, but she ran away from him and into the garden behind the house. A fine big tree stood there, full of the most magnificent pears. She climbed among the branches like a squirrel, and the king's son didn't know where she'd got to. But he waited till her father came and said to him, "The stranger slipped away from me, and I think she climbed the pear tree." The father thought, "Can it be Ash Girl?" He had an ax fetched and cut down the tree, but there was no one in it. And when they got to the kitchen, there was Ash Girl lying in the ashes as usual, for she'd jumped down on the other side of the tree, had returned her fine clothes to the bird in the hazel bush, and put on her gray smock.

On the third day, when her parents and sisters had gone, Ash Girl again went to her mother's grave and said to the tree,

> "Little tree, jiggle yourself and shake yourself;
> Scatter gold and silver over me."

Then the bird threw down a dress more magnificent and more splendid than anybody had ever had, and the slippers were of solid gold. When she arrived at the festival in this dress, no one from amazement knew what to say. The king's son danced only with her, and when anybody else asked her for a dance, he'd say, "She's my partner."

When it was evening, Ash Girl wanted to leave, and the king's son wanted to escort her, but she got away from him so fast that he couldn't follow her. He had, however, resorted to a trick and had coated the stairs with pitch, so when she ran down stairs, the girl's left slipper stuck there. The king's son picked it up, and it was tiny and dainty and of solid gold. The next morning he went with it to the man and said to him, "Nobody else shall be my wife but the girl whose foot this shoe fits." Then the two sisters rejoiced, for they had pretty feet. The eldest took the shoe to her room and was going to try it on, and her mother was standing beside her, but she couldn't get her big toe in, for the shoe was too small for her. Then her mother handed her a knife, saying, "Cut the toe off; once you're queen, you won't have to walk any more." The girl cut off her toe, forced her foot into the shoe, and, suppressing her pain, went out to the king's son. He took her on his horse as his bride and rode off with her. But they had to pass the grave, and there the two pigeons were sitting on the hazel bush and cried out,

> "Look, look!
> There's blood in the shoe!
> The shoe's too small.
> The right bride's still at home."

Then he looked at her foot and saw the blood oozing out. He turned his horse about and brought the false bride home again. He said she wasn't the right bride and that the other sister should try on the shoe. So the latter went into her room and managed to get her toes in, but her heel was too large. Then her mother handed her a knife, saying, "Cut a piece off your heel; once you're queen, you won't have to walk any more." The girl cut off a piece of her heel, forced her foot into the shoe, and, suppressing her pain, went out to the king's son. He took her on his horse as his bride and rode off with her. As they were passing the hazel bush, the two pigeons were sitting there and cried out,

> "Look, look!
> There's blood in the shoe!
> The shoe's too small.
> The right bride's still back home."

He looked down at her foot and saw the blood oozing out of the shoe, dyeing her white stockings red. Then he turned his horse about and brought the false bride back home. "She isn't the right bride, either," he said. "Haven't you any other daughter?" "No," said the man, "there's only a little misshapen Ash

Girl, daughter by my late wife, but she can't possibly be the bride." The king's son told him to send her up, but her mother replied, "Oh no, she's much too dirty and mustn't be seen." But he insisted on it, and Ash Girl had to be called. She first washed her face and hands and then went and made a deep curtsy before the king's son, who handed her the gold shoe. Then she sat down on a stool, drew her foot out of the heavy wooden shoe and put it in the slipper, which fitted her perfectly. When she stood up and the king looked into her face, he recognized her as the beautiful girl with whom he'd danced and cried, "That's the right bride!" The stepmother and the two sisters were frightened and turned pale with vexation, but he took Ash Girl on his horse and rode off with her. As they passed the hazel bush, the two white pigeons cried,

> "Look, look!
> No blood in the shoe!
> The shoe's not too small.
> He's bringing the right bride home."

And when they'd called out thus, they both came flying down and perched on Ash Girl's shoulders, one on the right, the other on the left, and stayed there.

When her wedding with the king's son was to be celebrated, the two false sisters came and wanted to ingratiate themselves and have a share in her good fortune. As the bridal couple was going to church, the elder sister walked on the right, the younger on the left. Then the pigeons pecked out one of each of their eyes. Later, when they came out of the church, the elder was on the left and the younger on the right. Then the pigeons pecked out the other of their two eyes. Thus for their malice and treachery they were punished with blindness for the rest of their lives.

22   The Riddle

Das Rätsel

THERE WAS ONCE A KING'S SON who conceived a desire to roam about in the world and took with him only a faithful servant. One day he got into a large forest, and when evening came, he could find no lodging and didn't know where to spend the night. Then he saw a girl walking toward a cottage and, as he drew nearer, noticed that she was young and pretty. He spoke to her and said, "Dear child, can my servant and myself have a night's lodging in the cottage?" "Ah yes," said the girl sadly, "indeed you may, but I don't advise it. Don't go in." "Why not?" asked the king's son. Sighing the girl said, "My stepmother's given to black arts and is no friend of strangers." Then he saw clearly that he'd come to the house of a witch but, since it was getting dark and he couldn't go on any farther and, moreover, wasn't afraid, he stepped in. The old woman was sitting in an easy chair by the fire and looked at the strangers with her red eyes. "Good evening," she snarled and asssumed a friendly air, "sit down and rest yourselves." She blew up the embers, over which something was cooking in a little pot. The girl warned the two to watch out and not to eat or drink anything, for the old woman was brewing evil potions. They slept peacefully until early the next morning.

When they were getting ready to go, and the king's son was already on his horse, the old woman said, "Wait a moment, let me first offer you a stirrup cup." While she was fetching it, the king's son rode off, and the servant, who had to girth his saddle, was still alone there when the wicked witch came with the drink. "Take this to your master," she said. But at that very moment the glass broke and the poison sprayed on the horse and was so strong that the animal fell down dead on the spot. The servant ran after his master and told him what had happened, yet he didn't want to leave the saddle behind, so went back to fetch it. When he came to the dead horse, a raven was already perched on it and devouring it. "Who knows whether we'll find anything better today?" said the servant, killed the raven, and took it along. Then they went on all day through the forest but couldn't get out of it. At nightfall they found an inn and entered. The servant handed the innkeeper the raven to prepare for their supper. They had, however, got into a murderers' den, and when it was dark, twelve assassins arrived and were going to kill and rob the strangers. But before getting to work they sat down at table, and the innkeeper and the witch joined them, and together they ate a bowl of soup in which was the minced meat of the raven. No sooner had they swallowed a few pieces than they all fell down dead, for the raven had, of course, been infected by the poison from the horsemeat. So there was no one left in the house save the innkeeper's daughter, who was honest and had had no part in the wicked doings. She opened all doors to the stranger and showed him the accumulated treasures. But the king's son said she was welcome to all of it and that he didn't want anything and rode on with his servant.

After they'd roamed about for quite a time, they came to a city where there was a beautiful but haughty king's daughter. She had proclaimed that whoever propounded her a riddle she couldn't solve would be her husband, but if she did solve it, he'd have to let himself be beheaded. She demanded three days to think it over but was so clever that she always solved the riddles propounded her before the time was up. Nine had already perished in this way by the time the king's son arrived, who, dazzled by her great beauty, was willing to risk his life. So he went into her presence and propounded her a riddle. "What is this?" he said: "One slew nobody and yet slew twelve." She didn't know what it was. She thought and thought but couldn't get the answer. She consulted her riddle books, but it wasn't there; in short, she'd reached the limit of her wisdom. Seeing no way out, she ordered her maid to creep into the gentleman's bedroom, where she was to eavesdrop on his dreams, thinking he might perhaps talk in his sleep and reveal the riddle. But the clever servant had lain down in his master's bed, and when the maid came, he tore off the cloak she'd wrapped herself in and chased her out with a stick.

The second night the king's daughter sent her lady-in-waiting; she was to see whether she'd have better luck eavesdropping, but the servant took away her cloak, too, and chased her out with switches. Now the young lord thought he'd be safe for the third night and lay down in his bed. Then the king's daughter herself came, wrapped in a misty gray cloak, and sat down beside him. And when she thought he was asleep and dreaming, she addressed him, hoping he'd answer in his dream, as many people do. But he was awake and understood and heard everything quite clearly. Then she asked, " 'One slew nobody,' what's that?" He answered, "A raven which ate the carcass of a poisoned horse and died of it." Then she asked, " 'And yet slew twelve,' what's that?" "These are the twelve murderers who ate the raven and died as a result." Now that she knew the riddle, she was about to creep away, but he seized her cloak and she had to leave it behind.

The next morning the king's daughter announced that she'd solved the riddle, and had twelve judges come, and solved it in their presence. But the youth asked to be heard and said, "She came creeping in to me during the night and questioned me, for she'd never have solved it herself." The judges said, "Show us a proof." Then the servant brought the three cloaks, and when the judges saw the misty gray cloak which the king's daughter was accustomed to wearing, they said, "Have the cloak embroidered with gold and silver, and it will be your wedding cloak."

23   The Mouse, the Bird, and the Sausage

Von dem Mäuschen, Vögelchen und der Bratwurst

A MOUSE, a bird, and a sausage once met, set up joint housekeeping, and for a long time lived in peace and prosperity and considerably increased their possessions. The bird's work was to fly daily into the forest and fetch wood; the mouse was to carry water, kindle the fire, and set the table, while the sausage was to do the cooking.

People who are well off are always craving new things, so, while flying about the bird one day met another bird, which it told about its splendid luck and boasted of it. But the other bird called it a poor simpleton who had to do the hard work, while the other two had a good time at home. For, once the mouse had kindled its fire and carried the water, all it had to do was retire to its room and rest till asked to set the table. The sausage stayed near the cooking pots, saw to it that the food was properly cooked and, when mealtime came, just wriggled through the porridge or vegetables a couple of times, and then everything was larded, seasoned, and ready. Once the bird got home and laid down its load, they'd sit down to table and after their meal sleep until the next morning—and that was a glorious life!

Next day the bird, egged on by the other bird, wouldn't fly into the forest, saying it had been servant long enough and that it must have seemed a fool to them; they should change around for once and try it another way. Though the mouse and the sausage, too, implored and entreated, the bird had the upper hand, and the new system had to be tried. So they drew lots, and the lot fell to the sausage, which had to carry wood. The mouse became cook, and the bird was to fetch water.

What happens? The sausage set out for the forest, the bird kindled the fire, the mouse put the pot on, and they waited alone for the sausage to come back with the wood for the following day. But the sausage was so slow coming that both feared the worst, and the bird flew out a bit to meet it. Not far off, however, it found a dog by the wayside who had come upon the poor sausage, and considering it fair prey, had seized and killed it. The bird complained bitterly about it to the dog, calling it a clear case of highway robbery, but it did no good. "For," said the dog, "I found forged letters on the sausage and therefore its life was forfeit."

Sadly the bird took the wood on its back, flew home, and told what it had seen and heard. Both were very sad but agreed to do the best they could and remain together. So the bird set the table and the mouse prepared the meal. It was going to dish it up and season it as the sausage had done by wriggling and slipping through the vegetables in the pots, but before it got half-way through, it was stopped and had to pay for it with life and limb.

When the bird came and was going to serve the meal, there was no cook. Stunned, it threw the wood about, called out, searched, but could no longer find its cook. Accidentally the flames got to the wood, so that a big fire started. The bird hurried to fetch water, but the pail slipped away from it into the well, dragging it down with it. It couldn't save itself and drowned miserably.

24 Dame Holda

Frau Holle

A WIDOW had two daughters. One was pretty and industrious, the other ugly and lazy. But she liked the ugly lazy one much more because she was her own daughter, and the other had to do all the hard work and be the ash girl in the house. Every day the poor girl had to sit down by a well on the highway and spin until the blood spurted from her fingers. Now it so happened that one time the bobbin got all bloody. Then she stooped over to rinse it in the well, but it slipped out of her hand and fell in. She ran weeping to her stepmother and told her of her mishap. But the stepmother scolded her harshly and pitilessly, saying, "If you dropped the bobbin in, then get it out again." So the girl went back to the well and didn't know what to do, and in her great distress jumped into the well to get the bobbin. She lost consciousness, and when she awoke and came to her senses, she was in a beautiful meadow on which the sun was shining, and there were thousands of flowers there.

She walked across this meadow and came to an oven filled with bread, but the bread cried out, "Take me out! take me out! or I'll burn; I've long since been baked." Then she stepped up and with the baker's shovel took out all the loaves one after another. Then she went on and came to a tree full of apples, and the tree called out to her, "Oh shake me, shake me! We apples are all ripe." Then she shook the tree, and the apples dropped like rain, and she shook until not one was left on the tree. When she'd gathered them all in a pile, she went on. Finally she came to a cottage, out of which an old woman was looking, but because she had such big teeth, the girl was frightened and was about to run away. The old woman, however, called after her, "Why are you afraid, dear child? Stay with me; if you'll do all the housework properly, you'll be well off. You've just got to see to it that you make my bed right and shake it up thoroughly, so that the feathers fly. Then it snows on Earth. I'm Dame Holda.

At the old woman's kindly word the girl plucked up her courage, agreed to the proposal, and entered her service. She did everything to the old woman's satisfaction and always shook out her bed so hard that the feathers flew about like snowflakes. In return she led a comfortable existence there, was never scolded, and always got good food. After she'd spent some time with Dame Holda, she got sad and at first didn't herself know what the matter was. Finally she realized that it was homesickness. Though a thousand times better off here than at home, still she yearned to go back. At last she said to Dame Holda, "I've got homesick, and though I'm so well off down here, still I can't stay here longer, I must get back to my people." "I'm glad you want to go back home," said Dame Holda, "and because you've served me faithfully, I'm going to take you back up myself." Then she took her by the hand and led her to a big gate. The gate opened, and as the girl was standing right under it, down came a tremendous shower of gold, and all the gold stuck to her, so that she was covered all over with it. "That's for you, because you've been so industrious," said Dame Holda, who also gave her back the bobbin that had dropped into the well. Immediately the gate closed, and the girl found herself back up on Earth, not far from her mother's house. As she stepped into the yard, the cock that was sitting on the well cried out,

> "Cock-a-doodle-do!
> Our golden maiden's back."

Then she went in to her mother and, because she arrived all covered with gold, she was well received by her and her sister.

Then the girl told them everything that thad happened to her, and when her mother heard how she'd come by such great riches, she wanted to procure the same good fortune for the ugly lazy daughter. So she had to sit down by the well and spin, and to make her bobbin bloody, she pricked her fingers, thrusting her hand into the thorn hedge. Then she threw the bobbin down the well and jumped in herself. Like her sister she came to the beautiful meadow and continued by the same path. When she got to the oven, the bread again called out, "Oh, take me out, take me out, or I'll burn; I've long since been baked." But the lazy girl replied, "As if I wanted to get myself dirty!" and walked on. Soon she came to the apple tree, which called out, "Oh, shake me, shake me! We apples are all ripe." But she answered, "What an idea! One of them might fall on my head," and then walked on. When she got to Dame Holda's, she wasn't afraid, since she'd already heard about her big teeth, and came to terms with her at once. The first day she restrained herself, was industrious, and followed Dame Holda's instructions whenever she told her to do anything, for she thought of all the gold she was going to give her. But on the second day she began slacking, on the third even more so; in fact didn't want to get up at all in the morning. Nor did she make Dame Holda's bed as she should and didn't shake it so that the feathers flew. Dame Holda soon tired of this and gave her notice. The lazy girl was quite content with this and thought that now would come the shower of gold. Dame Holda led her to the gate, but as the girl was standing underneath it, instead of gold a big kettle of pitch was emptied out all over her. "That's to reward you for your services," said Dame Holda, shutting the gate. Then the lazy girl came home all covered with pitch, and on seeing her the cock on the well cried out,

> "Cock-a-doodle-doo!
> Our dirty maiden's back."

The pitch stuck to her and didn't come off as long as she lived.

25 The Seven Ravens

Die sieben Raben

A MAN had seven sons and still no daughter, though he wanted one ever so much. Finally his wife again gave him hopes of a child, and when it was born, it really was a girl. There was great joy in the house, but the child was delicate and small and because she was so delicate, had to be baptized at home. So the father quickly sent one of the boys to the well to fetch baptismal water. The other six went along and, quarreling over who was to be the first to draw the water, dropped the pitcher into the well. There they stood, didn't know what to do, and didn't dare go home. When they didn't return, their father got impatient and said, "I'm sure the good-for-nothings forgot all about it over some game." He was afraid lest the little girl die unbaptized and in his anger cried out, "I wish the boys were all turned into ravens." Hardly had he uttered these words when he heard a whirr of wings in the air above his head, looked up, and saw seven coal-black ravens flying up and away.

It was too late for the parents to revoke the curse, and though they were sad at the loss of their seven sons, they consoled themselves to some extent with their dear daughter, who soon grew strong and got prettier every day. For a long time she didn't even know that she'd had brothers, for her parents were careful not to mention them. But one day she by chance overheard people saying of her, "Of course the girl's pretty, but just the same she's to blame for her seven brothers' misfortune." Then she grew quite sad, went to her mother and father, and asked whether she'd ever had brothers and what had become of them. Now the parents could no longer keep the secret from her, said, however, that it was a stroke of fate, and that her birth had merely been the innocent occasion of it. But it weighed daily on the girl's conscience, and she thought she had to unspell her brothers. She had neither rest nor peace until she'd slipped away secretly and gone out into the wide world to track her brothers and unspell them, cost what it might. All she took was a ring in memory of her parents, a loaf of bread to still her hunger, a jug of water to quench her thirst, and a stool to rest on.

She kept going way, way to the World's End. Then she came to the Sun, but it was too hot and terrifying and devoured little children. She ran quickly away from the Sun and ran to the Moon, but it was altogether too cold, and horrible besides, and wicked, and when it noticed the child, it said, "I smell human flesh, human flesh!" Then she hurried off and came to the Stars; they were kind and good to her, and each was sitting on its own stool. The Morning Star, however, got up, handed her a chicken bone, saying, "Unless you have this bone, you can't unlock the Glass Mountain, and your brothers are in the Glass Mountain."

The girl took the bone, wrapped it up carefully in a cloth, and then went on again, on and on, till she came to the Glass Mountain. The gate was locked, and she was about to take out the bone, but when she unfolded the cloth, it was empty. She'd lost the kind Star's gift! What was she to do now? She wanted to save her brothers and had no key to the Glass Mountain. The good sister then took a knife, cut off a little finger, stuck it in the gate and managed to unlock it. When she went in, a dwarf came to meet her, saying, "My child, what are you looking for?" "I'm looking for my brothers, the seven ravens," she replied. The dwarf said, "My masters the ravens aren't home, but if you don't mind waiting here until they get back, come right in." Then the dwarf brought in the ravens' food on seven little plates and in seven little tumblers, and the girl ate a crumb from each plate and drank a drop out of each tumbler, and into the last tumbler she dropped the ring which she had brought along.

All of a sudden she heard a whirring noise in the air and a flutter of wings, and the dwarf said, "Now my masters the ravens are flying home." Then they arrived, wanted to eat and drink, and looked for their plates and tumblers. Then they said one after the other, "Who's been eating from my plate? who's been drinking from my tumbler? It was a human mouth." And when the seventh got to the bottom of its tumbler, the ring came rolling out. It looked at it and recognized it as its father's and mother's, and said, "May God grant that our sister might be here! then we'd be freed from the spell." When the girl, who was standing behind the door listening, heard this wish, she stepped out, and immediately all the ravens regained their human form. Then they hugged and kissed one another and returned happily home.

26   Red Riding-Hood

Rotkäppchen

ONCE UPON A TIME there lived a sweet little girl who was loved by everyone that as much as looked at her, most of all, however, by her grandmother, who didn't know what all to give the child. Once she gave her a red velvet hood, and because she looked so pretty in it and wouldn't wear anything else, she was just called Red Riding-Hood. One day her mother said to her, "Come, Red Riding-Hood, here's a bit of cake and a bottle of wine; take it out to your grandmother. She's ill and weak and will find it strengthening. Start out before it gets hot, and when you get out there, walk along properly and don't stray off the road, otherwise you'll fall down and break the bottle, and then grandmother won't have any. And when you go into the room, remember to say 'Good morning' and don't first go prying into every nook and corner." "Of course I'll do as you say," said Red Riding-Hood to her mother and gave her her hand on it.

Her grandmother lived out in the forest, a half an hour's walk from the village. When Red Riding-Hood reached the forest, she met a wolf but didn't realize what a bad animal it was and wasn't afraid of it. "Good day, Red Riding-Hood," it said. "Thank you, wolf." "Where are you going so early, Red Riding-Hood?" "To my grandmother's." "What are you carrying under your apron?" "Cake and wine. We baked yesterday, and it'll cheer my ill and weak grandmother up and strengthen her." "Red Riding-Hood, where does your grandmother live?" "Under the three tall oak trees a good quarter of an hour on in the forest," said Red Riding-Hood. "Her house is there; the hazel bushes are below it as of course you know." The wolf thought to itself, "That young and tender thing is a plump little morsel and will taste even better than the old woman; you must be canny about it and catch them both." So it walked for a while beside Red Riding-Hood, then said, "Red Riding-Hood, just see the pretty flowers everywhere! Why don't you look about? I don't believe you're even listening to the birds that are singing so beautifully; you're just walking straight on as if you were going to school, and yet it's such fun out here in the forest."

Red Riding-Hood looked up, and when she saw the sun's rays dancing here and there through the trees and the pretty flowers all about, she thought, "If I bring grandmother a fresh bunch of flowers, it'll make her happy; it's so early that I'll get there in time anyway." So she strayed off the road and went into the forest looking for flowers, and every time she picked one, she'd think there was a still lovelier flower farther off and run after it. Thus she got deeper and deeper into the forest. But the wolf went straight to her grandmother's and knocked on the door. "Who's outside?" "Red Riding-Hood, bringing you cake and wine; open the door." "Just press down the latch," the grandmother called out, "I'm too weak to get up." Then the wolf pressed down the latch, the door flew open, and without saying a word it went straight to the grandmother's bed and swallowed her up. Then it put on her clothes and her nightcap, got into her bed, and drew the curtains.

Red Riding-Hood, however, had been running around after the flowers, and when she'd gathered so many that she couldn't carry any more, she thought of her grandmother again and set out for her house. She was surprised that the door was open, and when she stepped into the room, it seemed so queer to her inside that she thought, "My, I feel so uneasy today, and yet I usually so like being at grandmother's." She called out "Good morning" but got no answer. Then she went up to the bed and drew back the curtains: there was her grandmother lying with her nightcap pulled down over her face and looking so queer. "Why grandmother! What big ears you've got!" "So I can hear you better." "Why grandmother, what big eyes you've got!" "So I can see you better." "Why grandmother, what big hands you've got!" "So I can take hold of you better." "Why grandmother, what a horribly big mouth you've got!" "So I can eat you up better." No sooner had the wolf said this than it made a leap out of the bed and swallowed poor Red Riding-Hood.

When the wolf had satisfied its craving, it went to bed again, fell asleep, and began to snore very loud. A huntsman happened to be passing the house and thought, "How loud the old woman's snoring; you'd better see whether anything's the matter with her." So he entered the room and, when he reached the bed, saw the wolf lying there. "So here's where I find you, you old sinner!" he said, "I've been looking for you for a long time." He was about to aim his gun when it occurred to him that the wolf might have swallowed the grandmother and that there was still a chance of saving her. So he didn't shoot but took a pair of scissors and began to cut open the sleeping wolf's belly. After making a couple of cuts, he saw the bright red hood, and after a few more cuts the girl jumped out and exclaimed, "How frightened I was! It was so dark in the wolf's belly!" And then her old grandmother, too, came out still alive and could scarcely breathe. Red Riding-Hood quickly fetched some big stones and filled the wolf's belly with them. When it woke up, it wanted to skip off, but the stones were so heavy that it at once sank to the ground and died.

Then all three were happy. The huntsman skinned the wolf and went home with the pelt, the grandmother ate the cake and drank the wine Red Riding-Hood had brought her and recovered, but Red Riding-Hood thought, "Never again will I stray off the road and run into the forest when my mother's told me not to."

———————

Some people also tell how once when Red Riding-Hood was again bringing some cake to her grandmother, another wolf accosted her, wanting to make her stray off the road. But Red Riding-Hood was on her guard and, going straight on, told her grandmother that she'd met the wolf and that it had wished her "Good day," but had given her a very wicked look. "If it hadn't been on a highway, it would have eaten me up." "Come," said the grandmother, "let's lock the door so it can't get in." Soon after that the wolf knocked on the door and called out, "Open the door, grandmother! I'm Red Riding-Hood and am bringing you some cake." They kept quiet and didn't open the door. Then Gray-Head slunk around the house a couple of times, finally jumped up on the roof, planning to wait until Red Riding-Hood went home in the evening. Then it meant to stalk her and eat her up in the dark. But the grandmother saw what it was up to. Now it so happened that there was a big stone trough in front of the house, so she said to the child, "I was cooking sausages yesterday, Red Riding-Hood; take the pail and carry the water they were boiled in and fill the trough." Red Riding-Hood kept carrying water till the big trough was quite full. Then the odor of sausage rose to the wolf's nose; it sniffed and looked down and finally stretched out its neck so far that it couldn't hold back and began to slip. It slipped down off the roof and right into the big trough and drowned. But Red Riding-Hood went merrily home, and no one bothered her.

27 The Town Musicians of Bremen

Die Bremer Stadtmusikanten

A MAN had a donkey that for many years had patiently carried bags of grain to the mill, but it had now reached the end of its strength and was getting less and less fit for work. Its master thought of getting rid of it, but the donkey saw that the future boded no good, ran away, and set out for Bremen, where it thought it might become a town musician. After it had been going for a while, it met a hunting dog lying on the roadway, panting as if tired from running. "Why are you panting like that, Hold Fast?" asked the donkey. "Alas," said the hound, "because I'm old and getting feebler every day and am no longer of any use for hunting, my master was going to kill me and so I cleared out. But how am I to earn my daily bread?" "Do you know what?" said the donkey, "I'm going to Bremen to become a town musician there. Come along and join the town band; I'll play the lute, and you can beat the kettledrum." The dog agreed, and they went on. A little later they saw a cat sitting on the roadway looking very sad. "Well, what's the matter with you, old Lick-Your-Whiskers?" said the donkey. "Who can be gay when one's life is at stake?" answered the cat. "Because I'm getting old and my teeth are blunt and I'd much rather sit by the fire and purr than hunt mice, my mistress was going to drown me. True enough, I got away, but now I'm at my wits' end. Where shall I go?" "Come along with us to Bremen; you're an expert serenader; you can become a town musician there." The cat thought that a fine idea and went along. Next the three fugitives passed a farmyard where the cock was sitting on the gate, crowing with all its might. "Your crowing goes right through one," said the donkey. "What are you up to?" "I prophesied good weather," said the cock, "because this is Lady Day, when the Blessed Virgin has washed the Christ Child's shirts and wants to dry them. But because tomorrow is Sunday and guests are coming, the farmer's wife is merciless and has told the cook that she wants to eat me in a stew, and so I'm to have my head cut off tonight. Now I'm crowing with all my might while I still can." "What nonsense, Red-Head," said the donkey, "you'd better come along with us, we're going to Bremen. You can find something better than death anywhere. You've got a good voice, and if we make music together, it's bound to be good." The cock accepted the proposal, and accordingly all four of them set forth together.

However, they couldn't reach the city of Bremen in one day and that evening got into a forest, where they were going to spend the night. The donkey and the dog lay down under a big tree, while the cat and the cock got up in the branches; the cock, in fact, flew up to the very top, where it felt safest. Before falling asleep, it looked around in all directions, thought it saw a light twinkling in the distance, and called out to its companions that there must be a house not too far off, for a light was shining. Then the donkey said, "Then we must set out toward it, for these quarters are bad." The dog thought that a few bones with a little meat on them wouldn't come in amiss, so they started out toward the light. Soon it got brighter and brighter, until they reached a robbers' den that was brilliantly lighted up. The donkey, as the biggest, approached the window and looked in. "What do you see, Gray-Shanks," asked the cock. "What do I see?" answered the donkey, "why, a table set with fine food and drink, and robbers are sitting around it and having a good time." "That would be just the thing for us," said the cock. "Yes, indeed, if we were only inside!" said the donkey. Then the animals took counsel as to how to set about chasing the robbers away and in the end hit upon a trick. The donkey was to put its forefeet on the window sill, the dog to jump up on the donkey's back, and the cat to climb up on the dog. Finally the cock flew up and perched on the cat's head. When that was done, at a signal they all started their music: the donkey brayed, the dog barked, the cat miaowed, and the cock crowed. Then they all plunged through the window into the room, so that the panes rattled. At the terrible din the robbers jumped up, thinking that nothing less than a specter had come in and flew in a panic out into the forest. Now the four companions sat down to the table, made shift with what was left, and ate as if they weren't going to get anything more to eat for a month.

When the four minstrels were finished, they put out the light and looked for a place to sleep, each according to its taste and comfort. The donkey lay down on the dungheap, the dog behind the door, the cat by the warm ashes on the hearth, while the cock perched on the rooftree. And since they were tired from their long journey, they soon fell asleep. When it was past midnight, and the robbers saw from afar that no light was burning in the house and everything seemed quiet, the leader said, "We shouldn't have let ourselves be scared off," and bade one of the band go and search the house. The latter found everything quiet and went into the kitchen to light a candle and, because he mistook the glowing fiery eyes of the cat for live coals, he touched a match to them. The cat, however, didn't take it as a joke but sprang into his face, spitting and scratching. Then he was terribly frightened and ran, trying to get out by the back door. But the dog, which was lying there, jumped up and bit him in the leg, and when he ran across the yard and past the dungheap, the donkey gave him a good kick with its hind foot. And the cock, roused from its sleep by the noise and feeling very lively, cried down from the rooftree, "Cock-a-doodle-doo!" Then the robber ran as fast as his legs would carry him to report to his leader, saying, "Alas, there's a horrible witch in the house; she blew on me and scratched my face with her long fingers. Outside the door there's a man with a knife, who stabbed me in the leg. In the yard is a black monster that beat me with a wooden club, and up on the roof is sitting a judge. He called out, 'Bring me the rascal!' Then I took to my heels." After this the robbers didn't venture into the house any more, but the musicians of Bremen liked it so well there that they didn't want to leave it again.

This tale is on everybody's tongue, and the last person to tell it has just this minute finished.

28   The Singing Bone

Der singende Knochen

ONCE UPON A TIME in a certain country there was much complaint about a wild boar that was rooting up the farmers' fields, killing the cattle, and ripping people up with its tusks. The king promised a big reward to anyone who'd deliver the land of this plague, but the animal was so big and strong that no one dared go near the forest where it lived. Finally the king proclaimed that whoever captured the boar or killed it should have his only daughter in marriage.

Now in that country there lived two brothers, sons of a poor man. They presented themselves and were willing to undertake the risky enterprise. The elder, who was shrewd and clever, did it out of pride; the younger, who was innocent and simple-minded, out of goodness of heart. The king said, "To make more certain of finding the animal, you'd better enter the forest from opposite sides." So the elder entered from the west, the younger from the east. When the younger had been walking for a while, he met a dwarf who was holding a black spear in his hand and who said, "I'll give you this spear, because your heart is pure and good; with it you may confidently face the boar. It'll do you no harm." He thanked the dwarf, shouldered the spear, and proceeded fearlessly. Soon after, he saw the animal, which charged him, but he held out his spear toward it, and in its blind fury the boar ran onto it so violently that its heart was cut in two. Then he put the monster on his shoulder, started for home, and was going to take it to the king.

When he came out the other side, there on the edge of the forest stood a house where people were having a good time dancing and drinking wine. His elder brother had gone in there, thinking that the boar wouldn't run away from him in any event and that he'd first drink himself to the proper pitch of courage. When he saw his younger brother come out of the forest laden with his booty, his envious and wicked heart left him no peace. He called out to him, "Come in, dear brother! rest up and refresh yourself with a tumbler of wine." The younger, suspecting nothing, went in and told him about the good dwarf who'd given him a spear with which he'd killed the boar. The elder kept him there till evening, then they set out together. But when in the dark they came to a bridge over a brook, the elder had the younger go ahead and, when he was halfway across the stream, dealt him a blow from behind so that he fell down dead. He buried him under the bridge, then took the boar and brought it to the king, pretending to have killed it. Thereupon he received the king's daughter in marriage. When the younger brother didn't come back, he said, "No doubt the wild boar ripped him open," and everyone believed it.

But since nothing remains hidden from God, this black deed, too, was bound to come to light. After many years a shepherd was once driving his flock across the bridge and, seeing a snow-white bone down in the sand, thought it would make a fine mouthpiece. So he climbed down, picked it up, and carved a mouthpiece for his horn out of it. When he blew in it for the first time, the bone, to the shepherd's great amazement, began to sing of itself,

> "Oh dear shepherd,
> You're blowing on my bone.
> My brother slew me,
> Buried me under the bridge,
> Because of the wild boar,
> To win the king's daughter."

"What a remarkable horn," said the shepherd, "to sing of itself; I must take it to the king." When he came with it into the king's presence, the horn again began its ditty. The king understood it well and had the ground under the bridge dug up. Then the whole skeleton of the murdered man came to light. The wicked brother couldn't deny the deed, was sewed up in a sack, and drowned alive. But the bones of the murdered man were laid to rest in a fine grave in the churchyard.

29   The Devil with the Three Golden Hairs

Der Teufel mit den drei goldenen Haaren

ONCE UPON A TIME there was a poor woman who gave birth to a boy, and because he was born with a caul, it was prophesied of him that he'd marry the king's daughter in his fourteenth year. Soon after that the king happened to come to the village, though no one knew it was the king, and when he inquired among the people what news there was, they answered, "Not long ago a child was born with a caul, and whatever such a person undertakes turns out fortunate for him. It's also prophesied of him that in his fourteenth year he's to marry the king's daughter." The king, who had an evil heart and was vexed over the prophecy, went to the parents and, acting very friendly, said to them, "You poor people, let me have your child; I'll look out for it." At first they hesitated, but when the stranger offered them a lot of gold for the baby, they thought, "The child is fortune's favored; it's bound to turn out well, whatever happens." So they finally agreed and gave him the baby.

The king laid it in a box and rode off with it, until he came to a deep body of water. There he threw the box in the water, thinking, "I've rid my daughter of the unexpected suitor." The box, however, didn't sink but floated like a little boat, and not a drop of water got in. Thus it floated to within two miles of the king's capital, where there was a mill, and stuck on the weir. A miller's assistant, who by good fortune was standing there and noticed it, pulled it ashore with a hook, expecting to find vast treasures. But when he opened it, there lay a handsome baby boy who was quite hale and hearty. He took him to the miller and his wife, and since they had no children of their own, they rejoiced, saying, "It's a gift of God." They took good care of the foundling, and he grew up in all the virtues.

It so happened that the king once came to the mill during a thunderstorm and asked the couple whether the big boy was their son. "No," they answered, "he's a foundling: fourteen years ago he floated against the weir in a box, and my assistant pulled him out of the water." Then the king realized that he was none other than the child favored of fortune, whom he'd thrown into the water, and said, "You good people, can't the boy take a letter to the queen? I'll give him two gold pieces as a reward." "As the Lord King commands," replied the couple and told the boy to be ready to go. Then the king wrote a letter to the queen which said, "As soon as the boy gets there with this letter, he's to be killed and buried, and the whole thing to be done before I get back."

The boy set out with this letter but lost his way and in the evening got into a big forest. In the dark he saw a little light, went toward it, and came to a cottage. When he went in, an old woman was sitting all alone by the fire. When she saw the boy, she was frightened and said, "Where do you come from and where are you going?" "I'm from the mill," he replied, "and I'm going to the queen, to whom I'm to take a letter, but because I've lost my way in the forest, I'd like to spend the night here." "You poor boy," said the woman, "you've got into a robbers' den, and when they come home, they'll kill you." "Let them come," said the boy, "I'm not afraid, but I'm so tired that I can't go on," stretched out on a bench and fell asleep. Soon afterwards the robbers came and asked angrily what strange boy was lying there. "Oh," said the old woman, "he's an innocent child; he lost his way in the forest, and I took him in out of pity. He's to take a letter to the queen." The robbers opened the letter and read it, and it said that the boy on his arrival was to be killed. Then the hard-hearted robbers took pity, and their leader tore up the letter and wrote another, which said that on his arrival the boy was to be married at once to the king's daughter. They let him lie quietly on the bench till the next morning and when he woke up, gave him the letter and showed him the right road. On receiving and reading the letter, the queen did what it said, had a sumptuous wedding banquet arranged, and the king's daughter was married to fortune's favored. And since the youth was handsome and friendly, she lived happily and contentedly with him.

Some time later the king came back to his palace and saw that the prophecy had been fulfilled and the boy favored of fortune had been married to his daughter. "How did this happen?" he said. "In my letter I gave quite different instructions." Then the queen handed him the letter and said that he should see for himself what it said. The king read the letter and saw clearly that it had been substituted for another. He asked the boy what had happened to the letter that had been entrusted to him and why he'd brought another instead. "I don't know anything about it," answered the boy, "it must have been changed during the night when I was sleeping in the forest." "It won't be as easy as all that for you," said the king angrily. "Anybody who wants my daughter must fetch me from Hell three golden hairs from the Devil's head. If you bring me what I ask, you may keep my daughter." In this way the king hoped to get rid of him for good. But fortune's favored replied, "I'll fetch the golden hairs without fail; I'm not afraid of the Devil." Then he took leave and set out on his journey.

His way led him to a big city where the watchman at the gate asked him what his trade was and what he knew. "I know everything," answered fortune's favored. "Then you can do us a favor," said the watchman, "by telling us why the spring in our market place, which used to give wine, has run dry and now doesn't even give water." "You'll find that out," he answered; "just wait till I come back." Then he went on and reached another city. There the watchman at the gate again asked him what his trade was and what he knew. "I know everything," he replied. "Then you can do us a favor and tell us why a certain tree in our city, which formerly bore golden apples, now doesn't even put forth leaves." "You'll find that out," he answered; "just wait till I come back." Then he went on and came to a big river which he had to cross. The ferryman asked him what his trade was and what he knew. "I know everything," he replied. "Then you can do me a favor," said the ferryman, "and tell me why I have to keep ferrying people back and forth and never get relieved." "You'll find that out," he answered; "just wait till I come back."

Once he was across the river, he found the entrance to Hell. It was black and sooty in there. The Devil wasn't at home, but his grandmother was sitting there in a big easy chair. "What do you want?" she said to him, but didn't look at all cross. "I'd like to have three golden hairs from the Devil's head," he answered; "otherwise I can't keep my wife." "That's asking for a great deal," she said; "when the Devil comes home and if he finds you, it'll go hard with you, but I'm sorry for you and I'll see whether I can help you." Then she transformed him into an ant and said, "Crawl into the pleats of my skirt; you'll be safe there." "Yes," he replied, "that's all very true, but there are three things I'd like to know besides: why a spring that used to give wine has run dry and now doesn't even give water; why a tree that used to bear golden apples now doesn't even put forth leaves; and why a ferryman has to keep ferrying people back and forth and doesn't get relieved." "Those are hard questions," she answered, "but keep very still and listen closely to what the Devil says when I pull out his three golden hairs."

At nightfall the Devil came home. He no sooner entered than he noticed that the air wasn't pure. "I smell human flesh, human flesh," he said; "there's something wrong here." Then he peered into every nook and corner and searched about but could find nothing. His grandmother scolded him, saying, "Everything's just been swept and everything put in order, and now you're up-setting everything again. You're always smelling human flesh! Sit down and eat you supper." When he'd finished eating and drinking, he was tired and, laying his head in his grandmother's lap, told her to pick lice off him for a while. It wasn't long before he fell asleep, breathing heavily and snoring. Then the old woman took hold of a golden hair, pulled it out, and laid it be-side her. "Ouch!" cried the Devil. "What are you doing?" "I had a bad dream," answered his grandmother, "and took hold of your hair." "What did you dream?" asked the Devil. "I dreamed that the well in a market place that used to give wine ran dry and now isn't even giving water. What's wrong there?" "My, if they only knew!" answered the Devil. "There's a toad under a stone in the spring. If they kill it, the wine will flow again." His grandmother again loused him till he fell asleep and snored so that the window rattled. Then she pulled out the second hair. "Ouch!" cried the Devil angrily. "What are you doing?" "Excuse me," she replied, "I did it in a dream." "What did you dream this time?" he asked. "I dreamt that in a certain kingdom there was a fruit tree which used to bear golden apples but now doesn't even put forth leaves. What on earth can be the cause of that?" "My, if they only knew!" answered the Devil. "A mouse is gnawing at the root. If they kill it, the tree will certainly bear golden apples again, but if the mouse gnaws much longer, the tree will wither up completely. However, leave me in peace with your dreams; if you disturb me once more in my sleep, I'll box your ears." His grandmother spoke nicely to him and again loused him till he'd fallen asleep and was snoring. Then she took hold of the third golden hair and pulled it out. The Devil started up, cried out, and was going to deal severely with her, but once again she calmed him down, saying, "Who can do anything about bad dreams?" "What did you dream?" he asked and was quite curious. "I dreamt about a ferryman who complained that he had to keep ferrying people back and forth and didn't get relieved. What's the reason for that?" "Ha, the fool!" replied the Devil. "If someone comes and wants to be ferried across, he must hand him the pole. Then the newcomer will have to do the ferrying, and he'll be free." Since the grandmother had now pulled out the three golden hairs and since the three questions had been answered, she let the old Dragon rest in peace, and he slept till daybreak.

When the Devil had set out again, the old woman took the ant out of the pleat in her skirt and gave fortune's favored back his human form. "Here you have the three golden hairs," she said, "and of course you heard what the Devil said to your three questions." "Yes," he answered, "I heard it and I'll remember it all right." "Then you're all fixed up," she said, "and now you can go your way." He thanked the old woman for her help in need, left Hell, and was happy that everything had turned out so fortunately for him. When he came to the ferryman, he was supposed to give him the promised answer. "First ferry me across," said fortune's favored, "then I'll tell you how you may get relieved," and when he got across, he gave him the Devil's advice: "If anybody else wants to be ferried across, just put the pole in his hand." Then he went on and came to the city where the barren tree stood and where the watchman likewise wanted an answer. Then he told him what he'd heard the Devil say: "Kill the mouse that's gnawing at its root, and it will again bear golden apples." Then the watchman thanked him and rewarded him with two donkeys laden with gold, and they had to go along with him. At last he came to the city whose spring had run dry. Then he told the watchman what the Devil had said: "A toad's sitting in the well under a stone; you must find it and kill it, then it will once more give wine aplenty." The watchman thanked him and likewise gave him two donkeys laden with gold.

Finally's fortune's favored got home to his wife, who was very glad to see him again and to hear how well he'd succeeded in everything. He brought the king what he'd demanded, namely, the Devil's three golden hairs, and when the king saw the four donkeys laden with gold, he was quite happy and said, "Now you've fulfilled all conditions and may keep my daughter. But, dear son-in-law, do tell me where all this gold comes from. It's an enormous treasure." "I crossed a river and I picked it up there," he replied; "it's lying there on the bank instead of sand." "Can I get some of it, too?" asked the king greedily. "As much as you want," he replied. "There's a ferryman on the river. Have him ferry you across, and you'll be able to fill your bags on the other side." The greedy king set out in all haste, and when he came to the river, signaled the ferryman to ferry him across. The ferryman came and let him get on the ferry, but when they got to the other side, the ferryman put the pole in the king's hand and ran away. Thenceforth the king had to ferry as a punishment for his sins.

"Is he still ferrying?" "What do you mean? No one's likely to have taken the pole away from him."

30 The Louse and the Flea

Läuschen und Flöhchen

A LOUSE and a flea kept house together and were brewing beer in an eggshell. Then the louse fell in and was scalded to death. Thereupon the flea began to lament aloud. Then the little door of the room said, "Why are you lamenting, Flea?" "Because

Louse got scalded to death." Then the door began to creak. At this the broom in the corner said, "Why are you creaking, Door?" "I've good reason to creak.

> Louse got scalded to death,
> Flea's weeping."

Then the broom began to sweep furiously. Just then a cart passed and said, "Why are you sweeping, Broom?" "I've good reason to sweep.

> Louse got scalded to death,
> Flea's weeping,
> Door's creaking."

Then the cart said, "Then I'll race," and began to race furiously. Then the dungheap which it passed said, "Why are you racing, Cart?" "I've good reason to race.

> Louse got scalded to death,
> Flea's weeping,
> Door's creaking,
> Broom's sweeping."

Then the dungheap said, "Then I'll burn furiously," and began to burst into flames. There was a tree near the dungheap which said, "Dungheap, why are you burning?" "I've good reason to burn.

> Louse got scalded to death,
> Flea's weeping,
> Door's creaking,
> Broom's sweeping,
> Cart's racing."

Then the tree said, "Then I'll shake," and began to shake so hard that all its leaves fell off. A girl who came by with her water jug saw that and said, "Tree, why are you shaking?" "I've good reason to shake.

> Louse got scalded to death,
> Flea's weeping,
> Door's creaking,
> Broom's sweeping,
> Cart's racing,
> Dungheap's burning."

Then the girl said, "Then I'll break my water jug," and broke it. Then the spring from which the water was gushing said, "Girl, why did you break your water jug?" "I've good reason to break my water jug.

> Louse got scalded to death,
> Flea's weeping,
> Door's creaking,
> Broom's sweeping,
> Cart's racing,
> Dungheap's burning,
> Tree's shaking."

"My!" said the spring, "then I'll start flowing," and began to flow furiously, and everybody was drowned in the water: the girl, the tree, the dungheap, the cart, the door, the flea, and the louse—every one of them.

31 The Girl without Hands

Das Mädchen ohne Hände

A MILLER had gradually been getting poorer and had nothing left but his mill and a big apple tree behind it. Once when he'd gone into the forest to fetch wood, an old man whom he'd never seen before came up to him and said, "Why do you slave away at woodcutting; I'll make you rich if you'll promise to give me what's behind your mill." "What else can that be," thought the miller, "but my apple tree?" said "yes," and made it over to the stranger. The latter laughed mockingly and said, "In three years I'll come and fetch what's mine," and went away. When the miller got home, his wife came to meet him, saying, "Tell me, miller, where does the sudden wealth in our house come from? All at once all the chests and boxes are full. Nobody brought it, and I don't know how it happened." "It comes," he answered, "from a stranger whom I met in the forest and who promised me much treasure. In return I made over to him what's behind our

mill; we can well afford to give the big apple tree in exchange."
"Oh, husband," said the woman greatly frightened, "that was
the Devil, and he didn't mean the apple tree but our daughter.
She was behind the mill sweeping the yard."

The miller's daughter was a pretty and devout girl and for
those three years lived in fear of God and without sin. When the
time was up and the day came that the Evil One was going to
fetch her, she washed herself clean and with chalk drew a circle
around herself. The Devil appeared very early in the morning
but couldn't get near her. Angrily he said to the miller, "Take
all water away from her, so that she'll no longer be able to wash
herself, for otherwise I have no power over her." The miller was
frightened and did so. Next morning the Devil came again, but
she'd wept on her hands, and they were quite clean. Again he
couldn't get near her and said to the miller furiously, "Cut off
her hands, otherwise I can't get at her." The miller was horrified
and answered, "How could I cut off my own child's hands!"
Then the Evil One threatened him, saying, "If you don't do it,
you're mine and I'll fetch you yourself." The father got frightened and promised to obey him, went to the girl and said, "My
child, if I don't cut off both your hands, the Devil will carry me
off, and in my fright I promised him to do it. Please help me in
my need and forgive me the wrong I'm doing you." She replied,
"Father dear, do with me what you will; I'm your child." Then
she stretched out both hands and let them be cut off. The Devil
came a third time, but she'd wept so much and so long on the
stumps that even so they were quite clean. Then he had to give
her up and lost all claim to her.

The miller said to her, "I've gained great wealth through you
and I'll keep you in the greatest luxury for the rest of your life,"
but she answered, "I can't stay here; I want to go away. Charitable people will give me whatever I need." Then she had her
mutilated arms tied to her back and at sunrise started out and
walked the whole day till nightfall. Then she came to a royal
garden and in the moonlight saw there three trees laden with
fruit, but she couldn't get in, for there was a stream of water
around it. And since she'd been walking all day and hadn't had a
bite to eat and was tormented by hunger, she thought, "Oh, if I
were only inside, that I might eat a little of the fruit! Otherwise
I'm bound to perish." Then she knelt down, called on the Lord

God, and prayed. Suddenly an angel came and closed one of the locks in the stream, so that the moat got dry and she could walk through it. Now she went into the garden, and the angel went with her. She saw a tree laden with fruit; they were fine pears but they'd all been counted. Then she stepped up and to still her hunger ate one off the tree with her mouth, but only one. The gardener was looking on, but because the angel was standing by her, he was afraid and thought the girl was a ghost, kept quiet and didn't dare call out or address the ghost. When she'd eaten the pear, her hunger was satisfied, and she went and hid in the bushes. But the king who owned the garden came down next morning, counted the fruit, and noticed that one of the pears was missing. He asked the gardener what had become of it: it wasn't lying under the tree and yet was gone. Then the gardener answered, "Last night a ghost came in; it had no hands and ate one pear off the tree with its mouth." "How did the ghost get in across the water," said the king, "and where did it go after eating the pear?" "Someone came from Heaven in a snow-white dress," answered the gardener, "closed the lock and dammed up the water so that the ghost could walk through the moat. And because it must have been an angel, I was afraid, asked no questions, and didn't call out. When the ghost had eaten the pear, it went back again." "If it's as you say," said the king, "I'll mount watch with you tonight."

When it got dark, the king came into the garden and brought along a priest, who was to address the ghost. All three sat down under the tree and watched. At midnight the girl came creeping out of the bushes, stepped up to the tree, and again ate a pear off it with her mouth. The angel dressed in white stood beside her. Then the priest stepped up and said, "Have you come from God or from the World? Are you a ghost or a human being?" "I'm not a ghost," she replied, "but a poor human being, forsaken by all save God." "If you're forsaken by the whole world," said the king, "I shan't forsake you," took her with him to his royal mansion and, since she was so beautiful and devout, he loved her with all his heart, had silver hands made for her, and took her as his wife.

A year later the king had to go on a journey and commended the young queen to his mother, saying, "When she bears a child, take good care of her and write me a letter about it at once." In time she gave birth to a fine boy. Then the queen-mother at once wrote him a letter, telling him the joyful news. On the way, however, the messenger stopped to rest by a brook and, tired from the long walk, fell asleep. Then the Devil, who was still plotting harm against the devout queen, appeared and exchanged the letter for another, in which it said that the queen had given birth to a changeling. On reading the letter the king was frightened and very sad, but in his reply ordered the queen to be well cared for until his arrival. The messenger went back with the letter, rested at the same spot, and again fell asleep. Then the Devil again appeared and put a different letter into his pouch; this said that the queen and her child were to be put to death. The queen-mother was terribly frightened on receiving the letter, couldn't believe it, and wrote the king once more. But she got the same answer, because each time the Devil substituted a false letter. And the last letter added that, as proof, they were to keep the queen's tongue and eyes.

Then the queen-mother wept at the thought that such innocent blood should be shed, had a hind fetched in the night, cut out its tongue and put out its eyes, and kept them. Then she said to the queen, "I can't have you killed as the king commands, but you mustn't stay here any longer. Go out into the world with your child and never come back again." She tied the child to her back, and the poor woman went away with tears in her eyes. She got into a big, wild forest. There she knelt down and prayed to God, and the angel of the Lord appeared to her and led her to a cottage with a little sign saying, "Anyone may lodge here free." A maiden in a snow-white dress stepped out of the cottage and said, "Welcome, Lady Queen," and led her indoors. Then she untied the little boy on her back, nursed him at her breast, and then laid him in a pretty crib that was all ready. The poor woman said, "How do you know that I was a queen?" The maiden in white replied, "I'm an angel sent by God to care for you and your child." She stayed in that house for seven years and was well cared for, and through the grace of God and because of her piety her hands that had been cut off grew again.

The king finally came back from the wars and the first thing he wanted to see was his wife and child. Then his old mother began to weep, saying, "You wicked man, why did you write me to put two innocent souls to death?" She showed him the two letters which the Evil One had forged and went on to say, "I did as you ordered," and displayed the tokens—the tongue and the eyes. Then the king began to weep even more bitterly over his poor wife and his little son, until his mother took pity and said, "Console yourself, she's still alive. I had a hind killed secretly and the tokens taken from it. As for your wife, I tied her child on her back and bade her go out into the world, and she promised never to come back, since you were so angry with her." Then the king said, "I'll go as far as the sky is blue and neither eat nor drink until I've found my dear wife and child again, unless they've perished in the meantime or died of hunger."

Then the king went roaming abroad for some seven years, looking for her on every cliff and in every cave, but didn't find her and thought she'd perished. He neither ate nor drank during this long time, but God sustained him. At last he got into a big forest and there found the cottage with the sign reading, "Anyone may lodge here free." Then the maiden in white came out, took him by the hand, and led him inside, saying, "Welcome, Lord King." She asked him whence he came. He replied, "I've been roaming about nearly seven years, looking for my wife and child, but I can't find them." The angel offered him food and drink, but he didn't accept it and only wanted to rest a bit. Then he lay down to sleep and covered his face with a cloth.

Then the angel went into the chamber where the queen was sitting with her son, whom she usually called Little Woe-Begone and said to her, "Go out with your child; your husband's come." She went to where he was lying, and the cloth fell from his face. Then she said, "Little Woe-Begone, lift up your father's cloth and cover his face again." The child lifted it up and covered his face with it again. The king heard this in his sleep and on purpose dropped the cloth again. Then the little boy lost patience and said, "Mother dear, how can I cover my father's face? You know I have no father in this world. I've learned the prayer, 'Our Father that art in Heaven,' and you told me that my Father is in Heaven and is our good Lord. How am I to acknowledge such a fierce-looking man? He isn't my father." When the king heard this, he sat up and asked her who she was. Then she told him, "I'm your wife, and this is your son Little Woe-Begone." He saw her hands, which were whole, and said, "My wife had silver hands." She replied, "Our gracious Lord let my natural hands

grow again," and the angel went into the other room, fetched
the silver hands and showed them to him. Only then did he feel
perfectly sure that it was his dear wife and his darling child and
kissed them and was happy, saying, "A heavy load has fallen
from my heart." Then the angel of the Lord gave them all one
last meal, and then they went home to his old mother. There was
much rejoicing everywhere, and the king and the queen celebrated a second wedding and lived happily to their dying day.

32   Clever Hans

Der gescheite Hans

HIS MOTHER ASKED, "Where are you going, Hans?" "To Gretel's,"
answered Hans. "Good luck, Hans." "I'll have it all right.
Good-bye, mother." "Good-bye, Hans." Hans got to Gretel's.
"Good day, Gretel." "Good day, Hans. Bring any news?" "Didn't
bring any, gave it away." Gretel gave Hans a pin. Hans said,
"Good-bye, Gretel." "Good-bye, Hans." Hans took the pin, stuck
it in a haycart, and walked home behind the cart. "Good evening,
mother." "Good evening, Hans. Where have you been?" "Been
at Gretel's." "What did you bring her?" "Didn't bring her anything; she gave me something." "What did Gretel give you?"
"Gave me a pin." "What did you do with the pin, Hans?" "Stuck
it in a haycart." "That was foolish, Hans. You ought to have
stuck it in your sleeve." "No matter, I'll do better next time."

"Where are you going, Hans?" "To Gretel's, mother." "Good
luck, Hans." "I'll have it all right. Good-bye, mother." "Good-bye,
Hans." Hans got to Gretel's. "Good day, Gretel." "Good day,
Hans. Bring any news?" "Didn't bring any, gave it away." Gretel
gave Hans a knife. "Good-bye, Gretel." "Good-bye, Hans." Hans
took the knife, stuck it in his sleeve, and went home. "Good evening, mother." "Good evening, Hans. Where have you been?"
"Been at Gretel's." "What did you bring her?" "Didn't bring her
anything; she gave me something." "What did Gretel give you?"

"Gave me a knife." "What did you do with the knife, Hans?" "Stuck it in my sleeve." "That was foolish, Hans. You ought to have put the knife in your pouch." "No matter, I'll do better next time."

"Where are you going, Hans?" "To Gretel's, mother." "Good luck, Hans." "I'll have it all right. Good-bye, mother." "Good-bye, Hans." Hans got to Gretel's. "Good day, Gretel." "Good day, Hans. Bring any news?" "Didn't bring any, gave it away." Gretel gave Hans a young goat. "Good-bye, Gretel." "Good-bye, Hans." Hans took the kid, tied it legs together, and put it in his pouch. When he got home, it had suffocated. "Good evening, mother." "Good evening, Hans. Where have you been?" "Been at Gretel's." "What did you bring her?" "Didn't bring her anything; she gave me something." "What did Gretel give you?" "Gave me a kid." "What did you do with the kid, Hans?" "Put it in my pouch." "That was foolish, Hans. You ought to have tied the kid to a rope." "No matter, I'll do better next time."

"Where are you going, Hans?" "To Gretel's, mother." "Good luck, Hans." "I'll have it all right. Good-bye, mother." "Good-bye, Hans." Hans got to Gretel's. "Good day, Gretel." "Good day, Hans. Bring any news?" "Didn't bring any, gave it away." Gretel gave Hans a side of bacon. "Good-bye, Gretel." "Good-bye, Hans." Hans took the bacon, tied it to a rope, and dragged it along behind him. The dogs came and ate up the bacon. When he got home, he had the rope in his hand and there was nothing tied to it. "Good evening, mother." "Good evening, Hans. Where have you been?" "Been at Gretel's." "What did you bring her?" "Didn't bring her anything; she gave me something." "What did Gretel give you?" "Gave me a side of bacon." "What did you do with the bacon, Hans?" "Tied it to a rope, was bringing it home, dogs made off with it." "That was foolish, Hans. You ought to have carried the bacon on your head." "No matter, I'll do better next time."

"Where are you going, Hans?" "To Gretel's, mother." "Good luck, Hans." "I'll have it all right. Good-bye, mother." "Good-bye, Hans." Hans got to Gretel's. "Good day, Gretel." "Good day, Hans. Bring any news?" "Didn't bring any, gave it away." Gretel gave Hans a calf. "Good-bye, Gretel." "Good-bye, Hans." Hans took the calf, put it on his head, and the calf kicked his face. "Good evening, mother." "Good evening, Hans. Where have you been?" "Been at Gretel's." "What did you bring her?" "Didn't bring her anything; she gave me something." "What did Gretel give you?" "Gave me a calf." "What did you do with the calf, Hans?" "Put it on my head; it kicked my face." "That was foolish, Hans. You ought to have led the calf and put it by the crib." "No matter, I'll do better next time."

"Where are you going, Hans?" "To Gretel's, mother." "Good luck, Hans." "I'll have it all right. Good-bye, mother." "Goodbye, Hans." Hans got to Gretel's. "Good day, Gretel." "Good day, Hans. Bring any news?" "Didn't bring any, gave it away." "I'll come along with you," said Gretel to Hans. Hans took Gretel, tied her to a rope, led her along, took her to the crib, and fastened her up. Then Hans went to his mother. "Good evening, mother." "Good evening, Hans. Where have you been?" "Been at Gretel's." "What did you bring her?" "Didn't bring her anything." "What did Gretel give you?" "Didn't give me anything; came along herself." "Where did you leave Gretel?" "Led her on a rope, fastened her by the crib, and threw some grass in." "That was foolish, Hans. You ought to have cast friendly eyes at her." "No matter, I'll do better next time."

Hans went to the stable, put out the eyes of all the calves and sheep, and cast them in Gretel's face. Then Gretel got angry, jerked herself loose, and ran away and was Hans's bride no more.

33   The Three Languages

Die drei Sprachen

IN SWITZERLAND there once lived an old count who had only one son, but he was stupid and couldn't learn anything. His father said to him, "Listen, my son, I'm not getting anything into your head, no matter what I do. You've got to get out of here. I'm going to turn you over to a famous master who'll have a try at you." So the boy was sent to a strange city and stayed with the master a whole year. At the end of this time he came home again, and his father asked, "Now, my son, what have you learned?"

"Father," he replied, "I've learned what dogs say when they bark." "Mercy on us," cried the father, "is that all you've learned? I'm going to put you with another master in another city." The boy was taken there and stayed with this master for a year, too. When he came back, his father again asked, "My son, what have you learned?" "Father," he answered, "I've learned what birds say." Then his father flew into a rage and said, "O you hopeless person! You've been spending precious time and have learned nothing. Aren't you ashamed to appear before me? I'm going to send you to a third master, but if you don't learn anything this time, either, I'll no longer own you as my son." The son stayed with the third master likewise for a whole year, and when he returned home and his father asked, "My son, what have you learned?" he replied, "Father dear, this year I've learned what frogs say when they croak." Then his father flew into a fearful rage, jumped up, summoned his servants, and said, "This person is no longer my son. I'm throwing him out and order you to take him out into the forest and put him to death." So they took him out, but when it came to killing him, they were seized with pity, couldn't do it, and let him go. They cut out the eyes and the tongue of a roe so as to be able to bring the old man a token.

The lad went on his way and after a time arrived at a castle where he asked for a night's lodging. "All right," said the lord of the castle, "if you're willing to spend the night down in the old keep, then go there. But I warn you that it's perilous, for it's full of savage dogs that keep barking and howling and at set times have to be given a human being, whom they immediately devour." The whole region was plunged in grief and sorrow on account of this, yet no one could do anything about it. The youth, however, was fearless and said, "Just let me go down to the barking dogs and give me something I can throw to them. They won't do anything to me." Since he insisted, they gave him some food for the fierce animals and took him down to the keep. When he went in, the dogs didn't bark at him, walked around him wagging their tails in friendly fashion, ate what he gave them, and didn't ruffle a hair of his head. Next morning to everybody's astonishment he reappeared safe and sound and said to the lord of the castle, "The dogs revealed to me in their language why they're living there and harming the countryside. They're bewitched and have to guard a great treasure that's down there in the keep and they won't quiet down until it's been taken up. And from their talk I've also learned how this must be done." Then all who heard it rejoiced greatly, and the lord of the castle said he'd adopt him as a son if he accomplished it successfully. Again he went down and because he knew what he had to do, he carried out the task successfully and brought up a chest filled with gold. From then on the howling of the savage dogs was no longer heard. They'd disappeared, and the country was rid of the plague.

Some time later he thought he'd go to Rome. On the way he passed a swamp in which frogs were sitting and croaking. He listened and when he understood what they were saying, became quite pensive and sad. At last he got to Rome. The pope had just died, and the cardinals were in grave doubt as to whom they should designate as his successor. They finally agreed to elect pope the person in whom a divine miracle should be revealed and had decided on this at the very moment when the young count entered the church. Suddenly two snow-white doves lighted on his shoulders and remained there. In this the clergy recognized a sign from God and at once asked him if he would become pope. He was undecided, for he didn't know whether he was worthy of this, but the doves persuaded him to accept, and finally he said "yes." Then he was anointed and consecrated, and thus came to pass what he had heard from the frogs on the way and what had so bewildered him: that he was to become pope. Then he had to sing a mass and didn't know a word of it, but the two doves stayed right on his shoulders and whispered it all in his ear.

34   Clever Elsie

Die kluge Else

THERE WAS A MAN who had a daughter; her name was Clever Elsie. When she was grown up, her father said, "Let's marry her off." "Yes," said her mother, "if only someone would turn up who'd have her!" At last someone from far away turned up; his name was John, and he sued for her hand though he stipulated that Clever Elsie had to be really clever. "Oh," said the father, "she knows what's what," and her mother said, "Why, she can see the wind blowing down the street and can hear flies cough." "All right," said John, "but unless she's awfully clever, I won't take her." When they were sitting at table and had finished eating, her mother said, "Elsie, go down cellar and fetch some beer." So Clever Elsie took a jug from the wall, went to the cellar, and on the way rattled the lid in fine style in order to while away the time. When she got down there, she took a stool and put it in front of the keg, so that she wouldn't have to stoop over, or perhaps hurt her back, or suffer any unexpected injury. Then she set the jug in front of her and turned on the spigot. While the beer was running into the jug, she didn't want to let her eyes be idle and looked up on the wall. After much looking about she saw right above her a pickax which the masons had forgotten and had left sticking there. Then Clever Elsie began to weep, saying, "If I get John and we have a child and it grows up and we send it to the cellar to fetch beer, the pickax will drop on its head and kill it."

There she sat and wept and wailed for all she was worth over the impending misfortune. The people upstairs kept waiting for their drink, but Clever Elsie didn't come and didn't come. Then her mother said to the maid, "Just go down cellar and see where Elsie is." The maid went and found her sitting in front of the keg and wailing loudly. "Elsie, why are you weeping?" "Oh," she said, "I've good reason to weep. If I get John and we have a child and it's grown up and has to draw beer down here, perhaps the pickax will drop on its head and kill it." Then the maid said, "What a clever Elsie we've got!" sat down beside her and likewise began to weep over the misfortune. After a while when the maid didn't come back and the people upstairs were thirsty for their drink, the father said to the manservant, "Just go down cellar and find out what's keeping Elsie and the maid." The man went down: there sat Clever Elsie and the maid, both weeping. So he asked, "Why are you weeping?" "Oh," said Elsie, "I've good reason to weep. If I get John and we have a child and it grows up and has to draw beer down here, the pickax will drop on its head and kill it." Then the man said, "What a clever Elsie we've got!" sat down beside her, and likewise began to howl loudly.

Upstairs they kept waiting for the man, and when he didn't come and didn't come, the husband said to his wife, "Just go down cellar and find out what's keeping Elsie." The wife went down and found all three lamenting and asked the reason. Then Elsie told her, too, that her future child would surely be killed by the pickax as soon as it grew up and had to draw beer, and that the pickax would fall down. Then the mother, too, exclaimed, "What a clever Elsie we've got!" likewise sat down and wept with the rest. Her husband waited upstairs a little longer, but when his wife didn't come back and he kept getting thirstier and thirstier, he said, "Well, I must go down cellar myself and find out what's keeping Elsie." But when he got to the cellar and saw them all weeping and heard that the child that Elsie might perhaps some time give birth to was the cause of it and that the child might be killed by the pickax if it were sitting under it drawing beer at the very moment it fell, he cried out, "How clever our Elsie is!" sat down and wept with the others.

The suitor stayed upstairs alone for a long time. Then since no one seemed to be coming back, he thought, "No doubt they're waiting for me to come downstairs; I'd better go, too, and see what they're doing." When he got down there, the five of them were sitting and weeping and wailing most piteously, each one more than the other. "What misfortune has happened?" he asked. "Oh, John dear," said Elsie, "if we get married and have a child, and it's grown up and we happen to send it down here to draw a drink, then if the pickax that's stuck up in the wall should fall, it might smash its head in and lay it out. Isn't this reason for us to weep?" "Well," said John, "I don't need any greater intelligence for my home and, since you're such a clever Elsie, I'll take you." With these words he took her by the hand, led her upstairs, and married her.

When she'd had John for some time, he said, "Wife, I'm going out to look for work and make some money for us. You go into the field and reap the rye so we may have some bread." "Certainly, John dear, I'll do that." When John had gone, she cooked herself some good porridge and took it with her into the field. When she came to the field, she said to herself, "Which shall I do first, reap first or eat first? Well, I'd better eat first." So she ate up her pot full of porridge, and when she'd eaten her fill, she again said, "Which shall I do, reap first or sleep first? Well, I'd better sleep first." So she lay down in the rye and fell asleep. John had been home long since, but Elsie didn't appear, so he said, "What a clever Elsie I've got! she's so industrious that she doesn't even come home to eat." But when she didn't come back and didn't come back, and night came on, John went out to see how much she had reaped. Nothing, however, had been reaped, and she was lying fast asleep in the rye. Then John hurried home, fetched a bird-snare with little bells, and draped it over her. But she kept right on sleeping. Then he went home, locked the front door, sat down in his chair and worked. At long last when it was already quite dark, Clever Elsie woke up, and when she got up, there was a jingling noise around her, and the bells rang with every step she took. Then she got frightened and began to wonder whether she really was Clever Elsie and said, "Is it me or isn't it me?" But she didn't know the answer and for a while stood there unde-cided. Finally she thought, "I'll go home and ask if it's me or if it isn't me; they're bound to know." She ran up to her front door, but it was locked. Then she knocked at the window and called out, "John, is Elsie inside?" "Yes," answered John, "she's inside." Then she got frightened and said, "Oh, God! so I'm not me," and went to the door of another house, but when the people heard the bells ringing, they wouldn't open the door, and she couldn't get in anywhere. Then she ran out of the village and away, and no one saw her again.

35   The Tailor in Heaven

Der Schneider im Himmel

ONE FINE DAY our good Lord happened to want to take a walk in the Heavenly garden and took along all the apostles and saints so that no one but St. Peter was left in Heaven. The Lord had bidden him not to admit anyone in his absence, and Peter was standing at the gate and keeping watch. Then somebody knocked, and Peter asked who he was and what he wanted. "I'm a poor honest tailor," answered a thin voice, "who begs to be admitted." "Hm, honest," said Peter, "as honest as a thief on the gallows. You were light-fingered and pilfered customers' cloth. You won't get into Heaven; the Lord's forbidden me to admit anyone while He's out." "Do take pity on me," cried the tailor. "There's no question of stealing little bits of patching material that drop off the table of themselves; they're not worth mentioning. Look, I'm limping and I've got blisters on my feet from the journey; I can't possibly turn back. Please let me in. I'm willing to do any dirty work. I'll carry babies, wash their diapers, clean and wipe off the benches they've been playing on, and patch their torn clothes." St. Peter let himself be moved to pity and opened the gate of Heaven just enough to let the lame tailor slip his skinny body in. He had to sit in a corner behind the door and stay there lest the Lord on His return should notice him and get angry.

The tailor obeyed, but once when St. Peter stepped out the door, he got up and, full of curiosity, went about in all the nooks and corners of Heaven, looking at the sights. At last he came to a spot where there were many beautiful and sumptuous chairs, and in the middle a solid gold armchair studded with shining jewels; it was also much higher than the other chairs, and there was a gold footstool in front of it. It was the armchair used by our Lord when He was at home and from which He could see everything that went on down on Earth. The tailor stopped and looked at the armchair for quite a while, for he liked it better than all the rest. Finally he couldn't restrain his curiosity, climbed up and sat down in it. Then he saw everything that was going on down on Earth and noticed an ugly old woman who was standing by a brook doing washing and secretly making away with two veils. At the sight of this the tailor got so angry that he seized the gold footstool and hurled it through Heaven down to Earth at the thieving old woman. Since, however, he couldn't get the footstool back, he slipped quietly out of the armchair and resumed his seat behind the door, looking completely innocent.

When the Lord and Master came back with his heavenly retinue, He didn't notice the tailor behind the door, but when He sat down in his armchair, the footstool was missing. He asked St. Peter where the footstool had got to, but the latter didn't know. Then He asked further whether he'd let anybody in. "I don't know of anyone having been here," replied Peter, "except a lame tailor who's still sitting behind the door." Then the Lord summoned the tailor before Him, asked him if he'd taken away the footstool and where he'd put it. "Oh, Lord," answered the tailor joyfully, "in my anger I threw it down to Earth at an old woman whom I saw stealing two veils while she was doing washing." "Oh, you rogue," said the Lord, "were I to sentence as you do, what do you think would have happened to you long since? By this time I shouldn't have had any chairs, benches, armchairs, yes, stove-pokers, for I'd have thrown them all at sinners. Hereafter you can't stay in Heaven but must go outside the gate again. Now watch out where you get to! Here no one but Myself alone, the Lord, is to mete out punishment."

St. Peter had to take the tailor outside Heaven again, and because his shoes were torn and his feet covered with blisters, he took a stick in his hand and went to Wait-a-While, where pious soldiers sit and make merry.

36 Table-Be-Set, the Gold-Donkey, and Cudgel-Come-out-of-the-Bag

Tischchen deck dich, Goldesel und Knüppel aus dem Sack

IN DAYS OF YORE there was a tailor who had three sons and only one goat. But since they all lived on its milk, the goat had to have good fodder and had to be led to pasture every day. This the boys did in turn. Once the eldest son took it to the churchyard, where the finest grass grew, and let it feed there and skip about. In the evening when it was time to go home, he asked, "Goat, have you had enough?" The goat answered,

> "I've had so much,
> I don't want another blade.
> Bleat! bleat!"

"Then come home," said the boy, took it by the rope, and led it into the stable and tied it up. "Well," said the old tailor, "did the goat get what it's supposed to?" "Oh," replied the son, "it's had so much it doesn't want another blade." But the father wanted to make sure, went down into the stable, patted the dear creature, and asked, "Goat, did you really get enough?" The goat answered,

> "What could I have had my fill of?
> I was just gamboling over graves
> And didn't find a single blade.
> Bleat! bleat!"

"What's this I hear!" cried the tailor, ran upstairs, and said to the boy, "Why, you liar! You said the goat had had enough, and you let it starve," and in his anger took the yardstick from the wall and chased him out with blows.

Next day it was the second son's turn. He picked out a place near the garden hedge, where lots of good grass grew, and the goat grazed it clean. In the evening when he was about to go home, he asked, "Goat, have you had enough?" The goat answered,

> "I've had so much,
> I don't want another blade.
> Bleat! bleat!"

"Then come home," said the boy, led it home and tied it up in the stable. "Well," said the old tailor, "did the goat get what it's supposed to?" "Oh," answered the son, "it's had so much it doesn't want another blade." The tailor wasn't willing to rely on this statement, went down into the stable, and asked, "Goat, did you really get enough?" the goat answered,

> "What could I have had my fill of?
> I was just gamboling over graves
> And didn't find a single blade.
> Bleat! bleat!"

"The unprincipled rascal!" cried the tailor, "to let such a good animal starve!" ran upstairs and with the yardstick beat the boy out the front door.

Now it was the third son's turn. He wanted to do a job of it, picked out some bushes with the finest foliage, and let the goat feed on it. In the evening when he was about to go home, he asked, "Goat, did you really get enough?" The goat answered,

> "I've had so much,
> I don't want another blade.
> Bleat! bleat!"

"Come home then," said the boy, led it into the stable, and tied it up. "Well," said the old tailor, "did the goat get what it's supposed to?" "Oh," answered the son, "it's had so much, it doesn't want another leaf." The tailor didn't believe it, went down and asked, "Goat, did you really get enough?" But the malicious creature replied,

> "What could I have had my fill of?
> I was just gamboling over graves
> And didn't find a single blade.
> Bleat! bleat!"

"Oh, you pack of liars!" cried the tailor, "one as base and undutiful as the other! You won't make a fool of me any longer." Quite beside himself with anger he rushed up and with his yardstick gave the poor boy such a terrible tanning on the back that he ran out of the house.

The old tailor was now alone with his goat. Next morning he went down to the stable, petted the goat, and said, "Come, my dear creature, I lead you to pasture myself." He took it by the rope and led it to green hedges and under clusters of scabious and to whatever goats like to eat. "Now you may eat to your heart's content," he said to it, and let it graze till nightfall. Then he said, "Goat, have you had enough?" It answered,

> "I've had so much,
> I don't want another blade.
> Bleat! bleat!"

"Come home then," said the tailor, led it into the stable, and tied it up. Before leaving he turned around once more and said, "At last you've had enough!" but the goat behaved no better toward him and cried out,

> "What could I have had my fill of?
> I was just gamboling over graves
> And didn't find a single blade.
> Bleat! bleat!"

When the tailor heard this, it gave him pause, and he saw that he had driven his sons away without cause. "Wait, you ungrateful creature," he cried, "driving you away is far too little punishment! I'll brand you so you won't be able to show yourself any more among honest tailors." In great haste he rushed up, got his razor, lathered the goat's head, and shaved it as smooth as the palm of his hand. And since the yardstick would have been too good for it, he took a whip and dealt it such blows that it bounded away wildly.

Sitting thus all alone in his house, the tailor was plunged into great sadness; he'd like to have had his sons back, but no one knew where they'd got to.

The eldest had apprenticed himself to a cabinetmaker and learned the trade diligently and perseveringly, and when his time was up and he was to start traveling, his master gave him a little table of no very special appearance and of ordinary wood. But it had one good property: on putting it down and saying, "Table, be set!" it was at once covered with a clean cloth, and there'd be a plate with a knife and fork beside it, and dishes with all sorts of food, as many as there was room for, also a large glass gleaming with red wine which made one's heart jump for joy. The young journeyman thought, "That's enough for the rest of your life," roamed gaily about the world, and didn't worry whether an inn was good or bad, and whether anything was to be had there or not. If he felt like it, he wouldn't turn in anywhere, but be it in field, in forest, or in some meadow, wherever he fancied, he'd take his table off his back, put it down in front of him, and say, "Be set!" Thereupon everything was there that his heart desired. At last the idea occurred to him to return to his father, whose anger would likely have subsided and, what with table-be-set, would probably gladly welcome him again. Now it happened that on the way home he one evening got to an inn which was crowded with guests. They bade him welcome and invited him to come in and join them and eat with them, otherwise he'd have a hard time getting anything so late. "No," the cabinetmaker replied, "I won't deprive you of the few morsels; you'd better be *my* guests." They laughed and thought he was joking them, but he set up his wooden table in the middle of the room, saying, "Table, be set!" Immediately it was covered with food better than anything the host could have served and whose odor rose agreeably to the guests' noses. "Help yourselves, dear friends," said the cabinetmaker, and the guests, when they saw the point, didn't wait to be asked twice but drew up, took out their knives, and went to it valiantly. What amazed them most of all, however, was that as soon as one dish got empty, a full dish at once took its place. The innkeeper stood in a corner and watched the affair. He didn't know what to say but thought, "You could certainly use a chef like that in your business." The cabinetmaker and his companions made merry far into the night; finally they went to sleep, and the journeyman went to bed, too, putting his wishing-table against the wall. But the innkeeper's thoughts left him no peace and he remembered that there was in his lumber-room an old table that looked just like it. He quietly fetched it and substituted it for the wishing-table. Next morning the cabinet-maker paid for his lodging, picked up his table, and, never dreaming he had a false table, went on his way.

At noon he reached his father's house and was received with great rejoicing. "Well, my dear son, what did you learn?" his father said to him. "Father, I've become a cabinetmaker." "A good trade," replied the old man, "but what did you bring back from your travels?" "Father, the best thing I've brought back is this table." The tailor looked at it from all sides and said, "This isn't exactly a masterpiece of yours; it's an old and poor table." "But it's a set-itself table," answered the son. "Whenever I put it up and tell it to set itself, at once the finest dishes appear and a wine, too, that delights the heart. Just invite all our friends and relatives. For once they shall refresh themselves and enjoy themselves, for the table will give them all they can eat." When the company was assembled, he put up his table in the middle of the room and said, "Table, be set!" But the table didn't stir and remained as bare as any other table that didn't understand speech. Then the poor journeyman realized that his table had been changed on him and was mortified at appearing there as a liar. His relatives, however, laughed at him and had to go back home without having had a bite to eat or a drop to drink. His father fetched his cloth and went on tailoring, and the son started work with a master.

The second son had gone to a miller and had apprenticed himself to him. When his term was up, the master said, "Since you've behaved so well, I'm giving you a donkey of a special kind: it doesn't pull a cart or carry sacks." "What good is it?" asked the young journeyman. "It spits gold," answered the miller. "If you put it on a cloth and say 'Brickle-brit,' the good creature will spit out gold pieces for you from in front and behind." "That's a fine thing," said the journeyman, thanked the master, and set out in the world. Whenever he needed money, he had only to say "Brickle-brit" to his donkey, and it rained gold pieces, and he had no further bother than to pick them up off the ground. Wherever he went, only the best was good enough for him, and the dearer the better, for he always had a full purse. After traveling about the world for some time, he thought, "You'd better look up your father. When you arrive with your gold-donkey, he'll forget his anger and give you a hearty welcome." Now it so happened that he got into the very inn where his brother's table had been changed. He was leading his donkey and the host wanted to take the animal from him and tie it up, but the young journeyman said, "Don't bother, I'll lead Gray-Steed into the stable myself and tie it up myself, for I've got to know where it is." This struck the innkeeper as odd and he thought that a man who had to look after his donkey himself wouldn't have much money to spend. But when the stranger reached into his pocket, took out two gold pieces, and told him to lay in nothing that wasn't really good, he opened his eyes, hurried off, and shopped for the best food he could get.

After the meal the stranger asked what he owed. The host didn't mind chalking up double the amount and said he'd have to add a couple of gold pieces. The journeyman reached into his pocket, but his supply of gold had just run out. "Wait a moment, innkeeper," he said, "I'll just go and get some more gold," taking along the tablecloth. The innkeeper didn't know what that might mean, was curious, and crept after him, and since the guest bolted the stable door, he peeked through a knothole. The stranger spread out the cloth under the donkey, called out "Brickle-brit," and straightway the animal began to spit out gold from in front and behind, so that it really rained down on the ground. "The deuce!" said the innkeeper, "that's minting ducats fast! Not a bad kind of purse."

The guest paid his bill and went to sleep. During the night, however, the innkeeper crept into the stable, led the master minter away, and tied another donkey in its place. Early next morning the journeyman went off with his donkey, thinking he had his gold-donkey. He arrived at his father's at noon; the latter was glad to see him again and gave him a hearty welcome. "What have you become, my son?" asked the old man. "A miller, father dear," he answered. "What did you bring back from your travels?" "Nothing but a donkey." "There are plenty of donkeys hereabouts," said the father, "I'd rather have had a good goat." "Yes," replied the son, "but it's no ordinary donkey; it's a gold-donkey. When I say 'Brickle-brit' the good creature spits out a whole cloth full of gold pieces for one. Just have all the relatives in; I'll make them all rich." "I like that all right," said the tailor, "then I shan't have to toil any longer with the needle," hurried off, and called in his relatives. As soon as they were assembled, the miller told them to make way, spread out his cloth, and led the donkey into the room. "Now pay attention," he said and called out "Brickle-brit," but what dropped weren't gold pieces, and it was clear that the animal understood nothing of that art, for not every donkey's so accomplished. Then the poor miller pulled a long face, realized he'd been cheated, and apologized to his relatives, who went home as poor as they'd come. So there was nothing to do but for the old man to take up his needle again and the lad to hire himself out to a miller.

The third brother had become apprentice to a turner, and because this is a skilled trade, his apprenticeship lasted longest. His brothers, however, told him by letter how ill they'd fared and how on the very last night before reaching home the innkeeper had got their fine wishing-objects away from them. When the turner finished his apprenticeship and was to start journeying, his master, to reward him for his good conduct, gave him a bag, saying, "There's a cudgel in it." "I can carry the bag on my back, and it may be very useful to me, but what good is the cudgel in it? It only makes it heavier." "I'll tell you," answered the master, "if anyone harms you in any way, all you have to say is, 'Cudgel, come out of the bag,' and the cudgel will jump out into the crowd and dance about so merrily on their backs that they won't be able to move or stir for a week. And it won't stop till you say, 'Cudgel, get into the bag!'"

The journeyman thanked him, shouldered the bag, and when anybody came too near and was going to attack him, he'd say, "Cudgel, come out of the bag!" and the cudgel would jump out

and beat the dust out of the coats or jackets on their backs, one
after the other, without waiting for them to take them off. And
this happened so quickly that one's turn came before one could
say "Jack Robinson." It was evening when the young turner
reached the inn where his brothers had been cheated. He put
his knapsack in front of him on the table and began to recount
all the remarkable things he'd seen in the world. "Yes," he said,
"of course one finds a table-be-set, a gold-donkey, and the like
—all very fine things, which I don't despise—but all that's nothing to the treasure I've acquired and which I'm carrying with me
in my bag there." The innkeeper pricked up his ears. "What in
the world can it be?" he thought, "the bag's surely full of jewels,
and by rights I should have it, too, for all good things go by
threes." When it was bedtime, the guest stretched out on the
bench and put his bag under his head for a pillow. When the
innkeeper thought the guest was fast asleep, he softly and cautiously tugged at the bag to see if he could pull it out and slip
in another. But the turner had long been waiting for this, and
just as the innkeeper was about to give a good tug, he called out,
"Cudgel, come out of the bag!" At once the cudgel jumped out,
attacked the innkeeper and gave him a good drubbing. The innkeeper cried piteously, but the louder he cried, the harder the
cudgel beat time to it on his back, until he finally fell to the
ground exhausted. Then the turner said, "If you don't give me
back the table-be-set and the gold-donkey, the dance will start up
again." "Oh no," cried the innkeeper, quite subdued, "I'll gladly
hand over everything, only have this cursed hobgoblin creep
back into the bag." Then the journeyman said, "I'll let mercy
prevail over justice, but watch out for yourself." Then he called
out, "Cudgel, get into the bag!" and made it quiet down.

Next morning the turner went home to his father's with the
table-be-set and the gold-donkey. The tailor was glad to see him
again and asked him, too, what he'd learned abroad. "Father
dear," he answered, "I've become a turner." "A skilled trade,"
said the father. "What did you bring home from your travels?"
"A valuable item, father dear," answered the son, "a cudgel in a
bag." "What!" cried the father, "a cudgel! That's worth while!
You can cut that off any old tree!" "But not one like this, father
dear; if I say 'Cudgel come out of the bag!' the cudgel at once
jumps out and starts a vicious dance with anyone who harbors

me ill, and it doesn't stop till he's on the ground and asking for
mercy. You see, with this cudgel I recovered the table-be-set and
the gold-donkey, which the thievish innkeeper took from my
brothers. Now have them both called and invite all the relatives.
I'm going to give them food and drink and fill their pockets with
gold, besides." The old tailor couldn't really believe it, but just
the same he got the relatives together. Then the turner spread out
a cloth in the room, led in the gold-donkey, and said to his
brother, "Now, dear brother, talk to it." The miller said "Brickle-
brit," and at once gold pieces began raining down on the cloth
like a cloudburst, and the donkey didn't stop till all had so much
that they couldn't carry any more. (From the way you look, I see
you'd like to have been there, too.) Then the turner fetched the
table and said, "Dear brother, now you speak to it," and scarcely
had the cabinetmaker said, "Table, be set!" than it was laid with a
cloth and covered with an abundance of the finest dishes. Then
they had a meal such as the good tailor had never had in his
house, and all the relatives stayed on till far into the night and
were all merry and contented. The tailor locked up his needle
and thread, yardstick and goose, in a cupboard and lived with his
sons in joy and splendor.

But what happened to the goat that was to blame for the tailor's
driving his three sons away? I'll tell you. It was so ashamed of
its bald head that it ran into a fox hole and hid there. When the
fox got home, a pair of big eyes were sparkling at it in the dark,
so that it was frightened and ran off again. It met a bear, and
since the fox looked quite upset, the bear said, "What's the matter, brother fox? What kind of a face are you making?" "Alas,"
said Redcoat, "a fierce animal is sitting in my hole and is staring
at me with fiery eyes." "We'll soon drive it out," said the bear,
went along to the hole and looked in. But on beholding the fiery
eyes, it, too, got scared and would have nothing to do with the
fierce animal and cleared out. It met a bee, and when the bee noticed that the bear didn't seem in any too good spirits, it said,
"Bear, you've certainly got a dreadfully sour expression. What's
become of your good humor?" "You may talk!" answered the
bear. "Why, there's a fierce animal with staring eyes that's sitting
in Redcoat's hole, and we can't drive it out." The bee said, "I'm
sorry for you, bear. I'm a poor, weak creature which you two
won't even look at in passing; still, I think I can help you." So it

flew into the fox hole, settled on the goat's smooth-shaven head, and stung it so badly that it jumped up, crying "Bleat, bleat!" and ran like mad out into the world. And to this day nobody knows where it ran to.

37 Tom Thumb

Daumesdick

ONE EVENING a poor farmer was sitting by the hearth and poking the fire while his wife was spinning. Then he said, "How sad that we have no children! It's so quiet in our house, while in other houses there's so much noise and fun." "Yes," answered his wife with a sigh, "if we only had one single child and even if it were very tiny, only as big as a thumb, I'd be really content. And we'd love it with all our hearts." Now it happened that the wife got sickly and after seven months gave birth to a child which was, to be sure, perfect in all its parts but no taller than a thumb. Then they said, "It's as we wished and it shall be our darling child," and from its size they named it Tom Thumb. They gave him plenty to eat, but the child grew no bigger, just stayed as he was the first hour he was born. Nevertheless he had an intelligent look and soon turned out to be a clever and nimble little thing, lucky in everything he undertook.

One day the farmer was getting ready to go to the forest to cut wood and said to himself, "Now I wish there was somebody to come after me with the cart." "Oh, father," cried Tom Thumb, "of course I'll bring it; you can count on it, it'll be in the forest at the time you say." Then the man laughed, saying, "How can it? You're much too small to lead the horse by the bridle." "That doesn't matter, father. If mother will just hitch up the horse, I'll sit in its ear and call out to it how to go." "Well," answered the father, "we'll try it once."

When the time came, the mother hitched up the horse and put Tom Thumb in its ear, and then the little fellow called out to the horse how to go: "Hup! Whoa! Gee! Ree!" Then everything went as smooth as under a master coachman, and the cart took the right way toward the forest. Now it happened, just as the cart was turning a corner and the little chap was calling "Gee! gee!" that two strangers came along. "My!" said one, "what's that? There goes a cart, and a driver's calling to the horse, yet he isn't to be seen." "That's weird," said the other, "let's follow the cart and see where it stops." The cart went clear into the forest and straight to the spot where the wood was being cut. When Tom Thumb saw his father, he called to him, "You see, father, here I am with the cart. Now take me down." The father held the horse with his left hand and with his right took his little son out of the horse's ear. The boy sat down gaily on a straw.

When the two strangers saw Tom Thumb, they didn't know what to say from amazement. Then one took the other aside and said, "Listen, that little fellow might make our fortunes if we exhibited him for money in a big city. Let's buy him." So they approached the farmer, saying, "Sell us the little man; we'll treat him well." "No," answered the father, "he's the apple of my eye and I won't sell him for all the gold in the world." However, when he heard the proposal, Tom Thumb crept up on the pleat of his father's coat, got on his shoulder, and whispered in his ear, "Father, do give me away; I'll come back again all right." Then his father handed him over to the two men in return for a handsome sum of money. "Where do you want to sit?" they said to him. "Oh, just put me on the brim of your hat, then I can walk up and down and view the landscape and not fall off, either." They did as he asked, and when Tom Thumb had taken leave of his father, they set out with him. They went on till it got dusk. Then the little fellow said, "Take me down; you simply must." "Just stay up there," said the man on whose head he was sitting, "I shan't mind it. The birds, too, sometimes drop something on me." "No," said Tom Thumb, "I know what's proper. Just hurry up and lift me down." The man took off his hat and set the little chap in a ploughed field by the roadside. Then he crawled and jumped a little here and there among the clods of earth, hunted out a mouse hole, and suddenly slipped into it. "Good evening, gentlemen," he called out laughing at them, "now go home without me." They came running up and poked in the mouse hole with sticks but in vain. Tom Thumb crawled farther and farther back, and since it soon got quite dark, they had to walk home again full of rage and with an empty purse.

When Tom Thumb saw that they were gone, he crept out again from the underground passage. "It's so dangerous walking in the dark," he said, "how easily one can break one's neck or leg!" Luckily he ran against an empty snail shell. "Thank goodness," he said, "here I can spend the night in safety," and sat down in it. Before long, as he was falling asleep, he heard two men passing; one of them said, "How shall we go about getting the rich parson's money and his silver?" "I could tell you that," Tom Thumb interrupted. "What's that!" said one of the thieves in a fright. "I heard somebody speak." They stopped and listened. Then Tom Thumb spoke again, "Take me along and I'll help you." "Where are you?" "Just search the ground and notice where the voice comes from," he replied. The thieves finally found him and lifted him up. "You little creature, how are you going to help us?" they said. "Look," he answered, "I'll creep between the iron bars into the parson's room and hand you whatever you want." "All right," they said, "we'll see what you can do." When they got to the rectory, Tom Thumb crawled into the room, at the same time immediately shouted with all his might, "Do you want everything that's here?" The thieves were frightened and said, "Please do talk softly, so as not to wake anybody up." But Tom Thumb acted as though he hadn't understood them and again shouted, "What do you want? Do you want everything that's here?" The cook, who was sleeping in the next room, heard that, sat up in bed and listened. In their fright the thieves had, however, retreated a little; finally they plucked up courage again and thought, "The little chap's trying to tease us," so they came back and whispered to him, "Now be serious and hand us out something." Then Tom Thumb once more shouted out as loud as he could. "I'm quite willing to give you everything. Just put your hands in here." The maid, who was listening, heard this most distinctly, jumped out of bed, and stumbled in through the door. The thieves took to their heels and ran as if the Wild Huntsman was after them. When, however, the maid couldn't see anything, she went to light a candle. When she came along with it, Tom Thumb, without being seen, betook himself to the barn while the maid, having searched every nook and corner and finding nothing, went back to bed and thought she'd just been seeing and hearing things in her sleep.

Tom Thumb climbed about in the hay and found a nice place to sleep; he planned to rest up there until daybreak and then go back to his parents. But other experiences were in store for him. Alas, the world is full of sorrow and misery! Already at the first crack of dawn the maid got up to feed the cattle. Her first trip was to the barn, where she picked up an armful of hay and the very hay in which poor Tom Thumb was lying asleep. He was sleeping so soundly, however, that he didn't notice anything and didn't wake up until he was in the mouth of a cow, which had gathered him in with the hay. "Good heavens," he cried, "how did I get into the fulling mill!" but soon saw where he was. He had to watch out not to get between the cow's teeth and be crushed, and anyway in the end he couldn't help slipping down into the stomach along with the hay. "They forgot the windows in this little room," he said, "and the sun doesn't get in, and no one's bringing a light." On the whole he thought the quarters bad, and, worst of all, more new hay kept coming in the door, and the place got more and more cramped. In his fright he finally shouted as loud as he could, "Don't bring me any more fodder! Don't bring me any more fodder!" The maid was just milking the cow, and when she heard talking without seeing anyone and heard the voice that was the same, too, that she'd heard in the night, she got so frightened that she slipped off her stool and spilled the milk. In all haste she ran to her master, crying, "Good heavens, parson, the cow's been talking!" "You're mad," answered the rector, but all the same he went into the stable himself to see what was up. Scarcely had he set foot there than Tom Thumb shouted, "Don't bring me any more fodder! Don't bring me any more fodder!" Then the rector himself got frightened, thought that an evil spirit had entered the cow, and ordered it killed.

It was slaughtered, but the stomach with Tom Thumb inside it was thrown on the dungheap. Tom Thumb had great difficulty in working himself through but managed to clear the way. Nevertheless, as he was about to stick his head out, a new misfortune occurred. A hungry wolf came along and swallowed the whole stomach in one gulp. Tom Thumb didn't lose courage.

"Perhaps," he thought, "the wolf will listen to reason," and from its belly he called out, "Dear wolf, I know of a wonderful meal for you." "Where can I get it?" said the wolf. "In such and such a house: you'll have to crawl in through the drain, but you'll find all the cake, bacon, and sausage you want," and described his father's house to him in detail. The wolf didn't have to be told twice, squeezed through the drain at night, and ate to its heart's content in the pantry. When it had eaten its fill, it wanted to go away again but it had got so fat that it couldn't go back out the same way. Tom Thumb had counted on this and now began to make a tremendous noise inside the wolf, roaring and yelling as loud as he could. "Will you be quiet," said the wolf, "you're waking the people up." "What do I care?" answered the little fellow. "You've eaten your fill; I want to have some fun, too," and began anew to yell with all his might. This finally awakened his father and mother; they ran to the pantry and looked in through a crack. On seeing the wolf in there, they ran away; the man fetched an ax and his wife a scythe. "Stand back," said the man as they went into the pantry. "If I give it a blow and that doesn't kill it at once, you must go for it and cut it to pieces." Then Tom Thumb heard his father's voice and shouted, "Father dear, I'm here inside the wolf." Then his father said joyfully, "Thank God we've found our dear child again," and ordered his wife to lay the scythe aside so as not to hurt Tom Thumb. Then he hauled off and dealt the wolf such a blow on its head that it fell down dead. Then they got a knife and scissors, cut it open, and pulled the little fellow out again. "My," said the father, "how we've been worrying about you!" "Yes, father, I've been about in the world a lot. Thank heaven that I can breathe fresh air again." "Where all have you been?" "Oh, father, I was in a mouse hole, in a cow's stomach, and a wolf's belly, and now I'll stay with you and mother." "And we shan't sell you again for all the riches in the world," said the parents, hugging and kissing their darling Tom Thumb. They gave him food and drink and had new clothes made for him, for his own had been ruined on the journey.

38 Mistress Fox's Wedding

Die Hochzeit der Frau Füchsin

FIRST TALE

THERE WAS ONCE AN OLD FOX who had nine tails; he thought his wife had been unfaithful to him and wanted to test her. He stretched out under a bench, didn't move a muscle, and acted as though he were stone dead. Mrs. Fox went to her room and shut herself up while her maid, Miss Cat, sat on the hearth and did the cooking. Now when it became known that the old fox had died, suitors presented themselves. Then the maid heard some-one standing outside the front door and knocking. She went and opened the door, and there was a young fox who said,

> "What are you doing, Miss Cat?
> Are you asleep or are you awake?"

She answered,

> "I'm not asleep, I'm awake.
> Do you want to know what I'm doing?
> I'm warming the beer, putting butter in it.
> Will the gentleman be my guest tonight?"

"Thank you just the same, Miss," said the fox, "and what is Mrs. Fox doing?" The maid answered,

> "She's sitting in her room
> In sorrow and mourning.
> She's crying her eyes red
> Because old Mr. Fox is dead."

"Tell her anyway, Miss, that a young fox is here who would very much like to court her." "Very well, sir."

> Then the cat went trippity trap,
> Then the door slammed clippity clap.

"Mrs. Fox, are you there?"
"Oh yes, Kitty, yes."
"A suitor's outside."
"What, my child, does he look like?

Has he, too, nine bushy tails as fine as those of the late Mr. Fox?"
"Oh, no," answered the cat, "he's got only one." "Then I won't
have him."

Miss Cat went down and sent the suitor away. Soon after there
was another knock, and another fox was at the door and wanted
to woo Mrs. Fox. He had two tails but fared no better than the
first. After that other foxes came, each with one tail more than
the one before, but they were all rejected, until at last one came
that had nine tails like old Mr. Fox. When the widow heard that,
she joyfully said to the maid,

> "Now open gate and door
> And sweep out old Mr. Fox."

But as the wedding was about to be celebrated, old Mr. Fox stirred
under the bench, gave the whole crowd a thrashing, and along
with Mrs. Fox drove them all out of the house.

SECOND TALE

When old Mr. Fox died, a wolf appeared as a suitor and knocked
at the door. The cat, who was Mrs. Fox's maid, opened it. The
wolf greeted her and said,

> "Good day, Mrs. Cat von Kehrewitz.
> How do you happen to be sitting all alone?
> What good dish are you preparing there?"

The cat answered,

> "I'm crumbling rolls into my milk.
> Will the gentleman be my guest?"

"Thanks just the same, Mrs. Cat," answered the wolf, "is Mrs.
Fox not at home?" The cat said,

> "She's sitting up in her room,
> Lamenting her sorrow,
> Bewailing her great distress
> Because old Mr. Fox is dead."

The wolf answered,

> "If she wants another husband,
> Just have her come downstairs."

> The cat ran up the stairs
> And let her tail whisk around
> Till she came to the long hall.
> She knocked with her five gold rings:
> "Mrs. Fox, are you there?
> If you want another husband,
> You've just got to go downstairs."

Mrs. Fox asked, "Has the gentleman red trousers on and has he a pointed mouth?" "No," answered the cat. "Then he can't be of any use to me."

When the wolf had been dismissed, there came a dog, a stag, a hare, a bear, a lion, and all the animals in the forest, one after the other, but some one of old Mr. Fox's qualities was always lacking, and every time the cat had to send the suitor away. Finally a young fox came. Then Mrs. Fox said, "Has the gentleman red trousers on and has he got a pointed mouth?" "Yes," said the cat, "he has." "Let him come up then," said Mrs. Fox and ordered the maid to prepare the wedding feast.

> "Cat, sweep out the room
> And throw the old fox out the window.
> He brought so many plump, fat mice
> But always ate them himself,
> Never gave me one."

Then the wedding with young Mr. Fox was celebrated, and there was gaiety and dancing, and if they haven't stopped, they're still dancing.

39 The Elves

Die Wichtelmänner

FIRST TALE

THERE WAS A SHOEMAKER who through no fault of his own had become so poor that he finally had nothing left but the leather for a single pair of shoes. So in the evening he cut out the shoes which he intended to work on the following morning. And because he had a clear conscience, he went peacefully to bed, commended himself to the good Lord, and fell asleep. In the morning, after he'd said his prayers and was about to sit down to work, the two shoes were standing all finished on his workbench. He was astonished and didn't know what to say. He took the shoes in his hand to examine them more closely: the workmanship was so fine that there wasn't a wrong stitch anywhere, just as if they were meant to be a masterpiece. Soon after, a customer came in and, because he liked the shoes so much, he paid more than the usual price for them, and with the money the shoemaker was able to buy leather for two pairs of shoes. In the evening he cut them out and next morning was going to start work with renewed courage, but he didn't need to, for when he got up, they were already finished. Nor was there any lack of customers; the latter paid him so much that he was able to buy leather for four pairs of shoes. The four pairs, too, he found ready in the morning. And so it went on: whatever he cut out in the evening was finished in the morning, so that he soon had a nice income again and finally became a well-to-do man.

Now one evening not long before Christmas when the man had again been cutting, it happened that before going to bed he said to his wife, "How would it be if we stayed up tonight and see who's lending us such a helping hand?" The wife agreed and lighted a candle. Then they hid in corners of the room behind the clothes which had been hung up there and watched closely. When it was midnight, two cute little naked elves came, sat down in front of the shoemaker's bench, took over all the work that had been cut out and with their little fingers began to stitch, sew, and hammer so nimbly and quickly that the shoemaker couldn't keep his eyes off them from amazement. They didn't stop till everything was finished and standing on the workbench. Then they hurried away.

Next morning the wife said, "The little men have made us rich, and we should show our gratitude for this. They're running about so without anything on and are bound to freeze. Do you know what? I'm going to sew shirts, coats, jackets, and trousers for them, also knit a pair of stockings for each, and you make each of them a little pair of shoes." The man said, "I'm quite willing to," and in the evening, when everything was ready, they put on the bench the presents instead of the cut-out leather and then hid in order to see how the dwarves would act. At midnight they came scampering in and were about to start work at once, but when they found not cut-out leather but cute clothes, they were at first astonished and then displayed tremendous pleasure. With all speed they dressed themselves, arranged the fine clothes on themselves, and sang,

> "Aren't we sleek, fine boys?
> Why should we be shoemakers any longer?"

Then they skipped and danced and jumped over chairs and benches, finally dancing out the door. From then on they didn't come again, but the shoemaker prospered as long as he lived and was lucky in everything he undertook.

SECOND TALE

There was once a poor servant girl, who was industrious and clean, swept the house every day and dumped the sweepings on a big pile outside the door. One morning as she was about to get to work again, she found a letter on the pile and, because she didn't know how to read, put the broom in a corner and took the letter to her employers. It was an invitation from the elves, who asked the girl to stand sponsor for a child of theirs. The girl didn't know what she should do. At last after much persuasion and because they told her one mustn't decline such a thing, she accepted. Then the three elves came and led her into a hollow mountain where the little folk lived. Everything there was tiny but indescribably elegant and splendid. The mother was lying in a black ebony bed with pearl knobs, the bedclothes were embroidered with gold, the cradle was of ivory, and the bath tub of gold. The girl stood sponsor and was then about to return home, but the elves besought her to stay with them for three days, so she stayed and passed the time in joyous merrymaking, and the little folk did everything to please her. Finally she wanted to start back. They first filled her pockets full of gold and then led her back out of the mountain. When she got home, she was about to start work, took the broom that was still standing in the corner, and began to sweep. Then strangers came out of the house, asked her who she was and what was her business there.

She had not been, as she'd thought, three days in the mountain with the elves but seven years, and her former employers had in the meanwhile died.

THIRD TALE

The elves had stolen a mother's child out of its cradle and put in a changeling with a fat head and staring eyes who would only eat and drink. In her distress she went to her neighbor and asked her advice. The neighbor told her to carry the changeling into the kitchen, put it on the hearth, build a fire, and boil water in two eggshells: this would make the changeling laugh, and once it laughed, its power would be gone. The woman did just as her neighbor said. As she was putting the eggshells full of water on the fire, the blockhead said,

> "Now I'm as old
> As the Westerwald
> And have never seen anybody cooking in eggshells."

and then began to laugh at this. While it was laughing, all of a sudden a crowd of elves came, brought the right child, put it on the hearth, and took the changeling away with them again.

40   The Robber Bridegroom

Der Räuberbräutigam

THERE WAS ONCE A MILLER who had a beautiful daughter, and
when she was grown up, he wanted to see her provided for and
well married. "If a proper suitor comes and woos her," he
thought, "I'll give her to him." Soon after a suitor came who
seemed to be very wealthy, and since the miller could find no
fault with him, he promised him his daughter. The girl, however,
didn't really love him as much as a bride-to-be is supposed to love
her bridegroom and didn't trust him. Every time she looked at
him or thought of him, she shuddered in her heart.

Once he said to her, "You're my bride-to-be and don't even
call on me." The girl replied, "I don't know where your house
is." Then the bridegroom said, "My house is out in the dark
forest." She tried to get out of it and said she couldn't find the
way there. The bridegroom said, "Next Sunday you've got to
come out to my place; I've already invited the guests and, so that
you can find the way through the forest, I'll sprinkle ashes."
When Sunday came and the girl was supposed to set out, she felt
terribly frightened—she didn't really know why—and to mark
the way she filled both her pockets with peas and lentils. At the
entrance of the forest ashes had been sprinkled. She followed
these but at every step she threw a few peas on the ground to
right and to left. She walked almost the whole day, till she
reached the middle of the forest where it was darkest. There
stood a lonely house, which she didn't like, for it looked so dark
and uncanny. She entered, but there was no one there and the
deepest silence prevailed. Suddenly a voice called out,

> "Turn back, turn back, young bride!
> You're in a murderers' den."

The girl looked up and saw that the voice came from a bird in a
cage hanging on the wall. Again it cried,

> "Turn back, turn back, young bride!
> You're in a murderers' den."

Then the fair bride-to-be went on from one room to another and through the whole house, but it was all empty and not a living soul anywhere. Finally she got even into the cellar, where an old, old woman was sitting and nodding her head. "Can't you tell me," said the girl, "whether my bridegroom lives here?" "Alas, you poor child," answered the old woman, "what a place you've got into! You're in a murderer's den. You think you're a bride-to-be and that you'll soon celebrate your wedding, but your wedding will be with Death. Look, there I've put a big kettle of water on the fire. If they get you in their power, they'll chop you to pieces without mercy, boil you, and eat you, for they're cannibals. If I don't take pity on you and save you, you're lost."

The old woman then took her behind a big barrel where she couldn't be seen. "Be as still as a mouse," she said, "don't stir and don't move, otherwise it's all up with you. At night when the robbers are asleep, we'll escape. I've been waiting for a chance for a long time." The girl had hardly hidden herself when the wicked crew came home. They were dragging another girl along, were drunk, and weren't listening to her cries and lamentations. They gave her wine to drink, three glasses: one of white, one of red, and one of yellow wine. This broke her heart. Then they tore off her fine clothes, put her on a table, chopped her beautiful body to pieces, and sprinkled salt on it. The poor bride-to-be behind the barrel was trembling, for she plainly saw what fate the robbers had in store for her. One of them noticed a gold ring on the murdered girl's little finger and when it couldn't be easily pulled off, took a hatchet and chopped off the finger. The finger flew up over the barrel and fell right in the girl's lap. The robber took a candle to look for it but couldn't find it. Then another said, "Did you look behind the big barrel, too?" But the old woman shouted, "Come and eat and leave the looking till tomorrow; the finger won't run away from you."

Then the robbers said, "The old woman's right," stopped looking and sat down to eat. The old woman put sleeping drops in their wine so that they soon lay down in the cellar, sleeping and snoring. When the girl heard that, she came out from behind the barrel and had to step over the sleepers, who were lying on the ground in rows, and was very much afraid she might wake one of them up. But God helped her safely through. The old woman went upstairs with her, opened the door, and they hurried as quickly as possible out of the murderers' den. The wind had blown away the ashes that had been sprinkled about, but the peas and lentils had sprouted and come up and pointed the way in the moonlight. They walked all night, till in the morning they got to the mill. Then the girl told her father everything that had happened.

When the day when the wedding was to be celebrated, the bridegroom appeared, and the miller had invited all his friends and relatives. As they were sitting at table, each one was asked to tell a story. The bride sat still and said nothing. Then the bridegroom said to the bride, "Now, my dear, don't you know anything?" "Well," she answered, "I'll tell a dream. I went all alone through a forest and finally reached a house where there wasn't a living soul, but on the wall there was a bird in a cage, which called out,

'Turn about, turn about, young bride!
You are in a murderers' den,'

and repeated it. My dear, I was only dreaming that. Then I went through all the rooms, and all were empty, and it was so very weird in there. Finally I went down cellar, where an old, old woman was sitting and nodding her head. I asked her, 'Does my bridegroom live in this house?' She answered, 'Alas, you poor child, you've got into a murderers' den. Your bridegroom does live here but he'll chop you to pieces and kill you and then boil you and eat you.' My dear, I was only dreaming that. The old woman hid me behind a big barrel, and I was scarcely hidden there when the robbers came home, dragging along a girl. They gave her three kinds of wine to drink: white, red, and yellow. Then her heart broke. My dear, I was only dreaming that. Then they took off her fine clothes, chopped her beautiful body to pieces on a table and sprinkled it with salt. My dear, I was only dreaming that. And one of the robbers saw that a ring was still on her ring finger, and because it was hard to pull off, he took a hatchet and chopped it off. The finger flew up over the barrel and fell in my lap, and here's the finger with the ring." With these words she took it out and showed it to those present.

The robber, who during the story had turned as white as chalk, jumped up and wanted to flee, but the guests held him fast and turned him over to the courts. Then he and his whole band were condemned for their infamous deeds.

41 Mr. Korbes

Herr Korbes

THERE WAS ONCE A HEN and a cock who wanted to take a trip together. Then the cock built a fine coach with four red wheels and hitched four mice to it. The hen and the cock got in and off they went together. It wasn't long before they met a cat, who said, "Where are you going?" The cock answered,

> "Off and away
> To Mr. Korbes' house."

"Take me along," said the cat. The cock answered, "Gladly. Sit down in the back so you won't fall off in front.

> Watch out
> Not to soil my red wheels.
> Roll on, you wheels!
> Whistle, you mice!
> Off and away
> To Mr. Korbes' house."

Then came a millstone, then an egg, then a duck, then a pin, and finally a needle. They all sat down in the coach and rode along. But when they got to Mr. Korbes' house, Mr. Korbes wasn't in.

The mice pulled the coach into the barn, the hen and the cock flew up on a perch, the cat sat down in the fireplace, the duck chose the well-sweep, the egg wrapped itself up in a face towel, the pin stuck itself in a chair cushion, the needle jumped up on the bed in the middle of the pillow, and the millstone placed itself above the door. Then Mr. Korbes came home and went to the fireplace to make a fire. Then the cat threw ashes right in his face. He ran quickly into the kitchen to wash himself, but the duck spurted water in his face. He was about to dry himself with the towel, but the egg rolled out towards him, broke, and stuck up his eyes. He wanted to take a rest and sat down in the chair; then the pin pricked him. He flew into a rage and threw himself on the bed, but as he laid his head on the pillow, the needle pricked him so that he screamed and in his fury was about to run out into the wide world. But as he got to the front door, the millstone jumped down and killed him.

Mr. Korbes must have been a very wicked man.

42 The Godfather

Der Herr Gevatter

A POOR MAN had so many children that he had already asked everybody on earth to stand sponsor for them and, when he had still another, there wasn't anybody left to ask. He didn't know what to do and in his plight lay down and fell asleep. Then he dreamed that he was to go outside the towngate and ask the first person he met to stand sponsor for his child. When he woke up, he decided to follow out the dream, went outside the towngate, and the first man he met he asked to be sponsor. The stranger made him a gift of a vial of water, saying, "This is miraculous water: with it you can make the sick well. You have only to see where Death is standing: if he is standing at the head of the bed, give the patient some of the water and he'll get well. But if Death is standing at the foot, it's hopeless and he's doomed to die."

From now on, the man could always tell whether a sick person could be saved or not, became famous through his art, and earned a great deal of money. Once he was summoned to the king's child and on entering saw Death standing at the head of the bed and cured the child with the water. And similarly the second time.

The third time, however, Death was standing at the foot, and the child was doomed to die.

Once the man was going to call on the godfather to tell him how he'd fared with the water, but when he entered the house, it was a very queer establishment. On the second floor the shovel and the broom were quarreling and lashing out violently at one another. He asked them, "Where does the godfather live?" The broom answered, "Up one flight." When he got to the third floor, he saw a lot of dead fingers lying about. He asked, "Where does the godfather live?" One of the fingers answered, "Up one flight." On the fourth floor there was a heap of dead heads, who sent him up another flight. On the fifth floor he saw fish on the fire; they were sizzling in the pan and were frying themselves. They, too, said, "Up one flight." And when he'd climbed the sixth flight, he came to a room and peeked through the keyhole. There he saw the godfather, who had a pair of long horns. When he opened the door and stepped in, the godfather quickly lay down on the bed and covered himself up. Then the man said, "Godfather, what a queer establishment you have in your house. When I got to your second floor, the shovel and the broom were quarreling and hitting one another like anything." "How foolish you are," said the godfather, "that was the man-servant and the maid who were talking to one another." "But on the third floor I saw dead fingers lying about." "My, how stupid you are; they were salsify roots." "On the fourth floor lay a heap of dead heads." "Stupid man, they were cabbage heads." "On the fifth floor I saw fish in the pan: they were sizzling and frying themselves." As he said this, the fish came and served themselves. "And when I got up the fifth flight, I peeked through the keyhole of a door and saw you, godfather, and you had long, long horns." "Why, that's not true."

The man got frightened and ran away, and who knows what else the godfather might have done to him.

43   Mistress Trudy

Frau Trude

ONCE UPON A TIME there was a little girl who was stubborn and inquisitive, and whenever her parents told her to do something, she'd never obey. How could she get along well? One day she said to her parents, "I've heard so much about Mistress Trudy; I'll call on her sometime. People say that her house looks queer and that there are many strange things in it. I've become quite curious." The parents strictly forbade her going there and said, "Mistress Trudy is a wicked woman, given to evil things, and if you go there, we'll disown you."

The girl paid no attention, however, to her parents' orders and went to Mistress Trudy's just the same. When she got there, Mistress Trudy asked her, "Why are you so pale?" "Oh," she answered, shaking all over, "I'm so frightened at what I've seen." "What have you seen?" "I saw a black man on your stairs." "That was a charcoal burner." "Then I saw a green man." "That was a huntsman." "Then I saw a blood-red man." "That was a butcher." "Oh, Mistress Trudy, I shuddered: I looked through the window and I didn't see you but I did see the Devil with his fiery head." "Is that so!" she said. "Then you saw the witch in her proper garb. I've been waiting for you for a long time now and have longed for you. Now you shall furnish me with light." Thereupon she transformed the girl into a log and threw it in the fire, and when it was all aglow, she sat down beside it and, warming herself at it, said, "That really does give a bright light."

44 Godfather Death

Der Gevatter Tod

A POOR MAN had twelve children and had to work day and
night just to keep them in bread. When the thirteenth came
into the world, he didn't know what on earth to do and went
out on the great highway intending to ask the first man he met
to be sponsor. The first man he met was the good Lord, who
already knew what was weighing on his mind and said to him,
"Poor man, I'm sorry for you; I'll stand sponsor for your child,
care for it, and make it happy on Earth." "Who are you?" said
the man. "I'm the good Lord." "Then I don't want you as
godfather," said the man, "You give to the rich and let the poor
starve." The man said this because he didn't know how wisely
God distributes wealth and poverty. So he turned away from
the Lord and went on. Then the Devil approached him and said,
"What are you looking for? If you'll have me as sponsor for
your child, I'll give him gold aplenty and all the joys of the
World besides." "Who are you?" asked the man. "I'm the
Devil." "Then I don't want you as a sponsor; you deceive men
and lead them astray," said the man and went on. Then withered Death stepped up to him and said, "Take me as a sponsor." "Who are you?" asked the man. "I'm Death, who makes
all men equal." Then the man said, "You're the right person;
you fetch rich and poor alike without distinction. You shall act
as sponsor for me." "I'll make your child rich and famous," answered Death, "for whoever has me for a friend can't but
prosper." The man said, "The christening's next Sunday. Be
there on time." Death appeared as he'd promised and made a
thoroughly proper godfather.

When the boy grew up, his godfather appeared one day and
bade him come with him. He led him out into the forest and,
showing him an herb growing there, said, "Now you're to
receive your christening present. I'm making you a famous
physician. When you're summoned to a sick person, I'll ap-

pear every time. If I'm standing at the sick man's head, you may speak up boldly and say that you'll cure him. Then give him some of the herb, and he'll get well. But if I'm standing at the sick man's feet, he's mine and you must say that nothing can be done and that no physician in the world can save him. Beware of using the herb against my will or it might fare ill with you."

It wasn't long before the youth was the most famous physician in the whole world. "He has only to look at a patient and he already knows how things stand: whether he'll get well or is doomed to die." Such was his reputation, and people came from far and near, brought him to the sick, and gave him so much money that he was soon a rich man. Now it happened that the king fell ill. The physician was summoned and was supposed to say whether recovery was possible. As he approached the bed, Death was standing at the sick man's feet, and so there was no herb that would cure him. "If I could outwit Death just once!" thought the physician, "of course he'll take it amiss, but since I'm his godchild, he'll surely let it pass. I'll risk it." Accordingly, he took the sick man and turned him the other way about, so that Death was now standing at his head. Then he gave him some of the herb, and the king recovered and got well again. Death, however, came to the physician and with dark and angry looks shook his finger at him, saying, "You tricked me! This time I'll excuse you, because you're my godchild, but if you dare do it again, you'll catch it, and I'll carry you yourself off with me."

Soon after, the king's daughter fell seriously ill; she was his only child. He wept day and night, till his eyes got blind and he had it proclaimed that whoever would save her from death should be her husband and inherit the crown. When the physician came to the sick girl's bed, he saw Death at her feet. He should have remembered his godfather's warning, but the great beauty of the king's daughter and the advantage of becoming her husband so deluded him that he threw all discretion to the winds. He didn't see that Death was looking at him angrily, that he was raising his hand and shaking his withered fist at him. He picked up the sick girl and put her head where her feet had been. Then he administered the herb to her, and forthwith her cheeks got rosy and life stirred anew.

When Death saw himself cheated out of his own for a second time, he strode up to the physician and said, "You're done for, and now it's your turn," seized him with his icy hand so hard that he couldn't resist, and led him into an underground cavern. There he saw thousands upon thousands of candles burning in endless rows, some large, some medium, others small. Every moment some went out and others flared up again, so that the flames seemed to be perpetually hopping about hither and thither. "You see," said Death, "these are the life-candles of men. The big candles belong to children, the medium-sized to married people in the prime of life, the small to the aged. But children and young people, too, often have just a small candle." "Show me my life-candle," said the physician, supposing it would still be quite big. Death pointed to a tiny stub that was just threatening to go out and said, "You see, there it is." "Oh, dear godfather," said the frightened physician, "light a fresh candle for me. Do it as a favor so I may enjoy my life, become king and the husband of the king's beautiful daughter." "I can't," answered Death, "one candle must go out before a new one starts to burn." "Then put the old one on the new one which will go right on burning when the old one is used up," begged the physician. Death pretended he was going to grant him his wish and fetched a big new candle, but because he wanted to revenge himself, he blundered on purpose in putting the fresh candle on and the stub tipped over and went out. At once the physician dropped to the ground and himself had now fallen into the hands of Death.

45 Tom Thumb's Wanderings

Daumerlings Wanderschaft

A TAILOR had a son who turned out to be small and was no larger than a thumb, so he, too, was called Tom Thumb [cp. No. 37]. But he had plenty of courage and said to his father, "Father, I shall and must go out in the world." "Right, my son," said the old man, took a long darning needle and, holding it over a candle, attached a knob of sealing wax. "Now you've got a rapier for your journey." The little tailor wanted to have one more meal with the family and skipped into the kitchen to see what his mother had cooked for a last time. It was just ready and the dish was on the hearth. Then he said, "Mother, what's there to eat today?" "See for yourself," said the mother. Then Tom Thumb jumped onto the hearth and looked into the dish, but because he craned his neck too far, the steam from the food took him and drove him out the chimney. For a while he rode about in the air on the steam, till finally he came down to earth again.

Now the little tailor was out in the wide world, roamed about, also hired himself out to a master but found fault with the food. "Mistress, if you don't give us better food," said Tom Thumb, "I shall go away and tomorrow morning write with chalk on your front door: 'Too much potato, too little meat! Good-bye, Potato King!'" "What do you really want, Grasshopper?" said the master's wife, who got angry, grabbed a rag, and was going to hit at him. The little tailor crawled nimbly under the thimble, looked out from underneath, and stuck out his tongue at the master's wife. She picked up the thimble and was about to take hold of him, but little Tom Thumb hopped into the rags and, while the master's wife was untangling the rags and hunting for him, he got into a crack in the table. "Ha! ha! Mistress," he cried and stuck his head out, and when she was about to strike, he jumped down into the drawer. Finally, however, she caught him and chased him out of the house.

The little tailor wandered on and got into a big forest. There he met up with a lot of robbers who were planning to steal the king's treasure. When they saw the little tailor, they thought: "A little chap like that can creep through a keyhole and serve us as a passkey." "Hello," one of them cried, "you giant Goliath! Do you want to come along with us to the treasury? You can slip in and throw out the money." Tom Thumb thought it over, finally said "yes," and went along to the treasury. Then he surveyed the door from top to bottom to see if there wasn't a crack in it. He soon discovered one wide enough to let him in. He wanted to slip through straight off, but one of the two guards who were standing before the door noticed him and said to the other, "What ugly spider is crawling there? I'm going to step on it and kill it." "Let the poor creature go," said the other; "it hasn't done anything to you." Tom Thumb got safely through the crack and into the treasury, opened the window beneath which the robbers were standing, and threw out to them one dollar after another. When the little tailor was in the midst of his work, he heard the king coming to inspect his treasury and hastily crept into hiding. The king noticed that many good dollars were missing but couldn't understand who might have stolen them, since the locks and bolts were in good order and everything seemed to be well guarded. Then he went away again, saying to the two guards, "Watch out, somebody's after the money."

When Tom Thumb started work again, they heard the money in there moving and tinkling clickety-click, clickety-click. They hurried quickly in, intending to seize the thief, but the little tailor, who heard them coming, was even quicker, jumped into a corner, and covered himself with a dollar so that nothing was to be seen of him. At the same time he teased the guards, crying out, "Here I am!" The guards ran up but when they got there, he'd already skipped under a dollar in another corner and was shouting, "Hello, here I am!" The guards rushed up, but Tom Thumb was long since in a third corner and shouting, "Hello, here I am!" Thus he made fools of them and chased them about in the treasury so long that they got tired and went away. Gradually he threw out all the dollars, tossing the last one with all his might, then nimbly hopping on it himself, flew along with it through the window to the ground. The robbers praised him highly. "You're a mighty hero," they said, "do you want to become our leader?" Tom Thumb thanked them, saying he first wanted to see the world. They now divided the booty, but the little tailor asked only for a farthing, because he couldn't carry any more.

Then he again buckled his rapier around his waist, said goodbye to the robbers, and started out. He took service with several masters but didn't find the work to his taste. Finally he hired out as a servant in an inn. The maids, however, couldn't abide him; for while they couldn't see him, he saw everything that they did on the sly and reported to the proprietors what they took from the plates and fetched for themselves from the cellar.

Then they said, "Wait, we'll pay you back!" and planned to play a mean trick on him. When soon after that one of the maids was mowing grass in the garden and saw Tom Thumb skipping about and climbing up and down on the plants, she quickly mowed him in with the grass, tied the lot in a big cloth, and secretly threw it to the cows. Now among these was a big black cow, who swallowed him without hurting him. Nevertheless, he didn't like it down there, for it was quite dark and no candle was burning either. When the cow was being milked, he shouted,

> "Strip, strap, strull!
> Will the pail soon be full?"

but because of the noise of the milking no one understood him. Then the master came into the stable and said, "Tomorrow that cow over there is to be slaughtered." Tom Thumb got frightened and cried in a clear voice, "Let me out first; I'm in there." The master, of course, heard this but didn't know where the voice came from. "Where are you?" he asked. "In the black one," he replied. But the master didn't understand what that meant and went away.

Next morning the cow was slaughtered. In the course of chopping up and cutting up the carcass Tom Thumb luckily escaped being struck and got under the sausage meat. When the butcher stepped up and started his work, he shouted as loud as he could, "Don't chop too deep, don't chop too deep! I'm down there." Because of the noise of the chopping-knives no one heard him. Now Poor Tomb Thumb was in real trouble, but need lends speed, and he hopped so nimbly among the chopping-knives that not one touched him and he got off with a whole skin. But he couldn't really escape and couldn't help being stuffed down into a black pudding along with the bits of bacon. The quarters there were rather cramped, and, besides, he was hung up in the chimney to be smoked: there time hung very heavy on his hands. Finally in winter he was taken down, because the pudding was to be served to a guest. While the innkeeper's wife was slicing up the pudding, he took care not to stick his head out too far lest perchance his neck might be cut off along with it. Finally he saw his chance, cleared a way for himself, and jumped out.

Now the little tailor didn't want to stay any longer in the house where he'd fared so ill but at once set out again on his wanderings. His freedom, however, was short-lived; out in the country he met a fox who absent-mindedly snapped him up. "I say there, Mr. Fox," cried the little tailor, "it's I who am sticking in your throat. Let me go!" "You're right," answered the fox, "in eating you I get practically nothing. Promise me the chickens in your father's barnyard and I'll let you go." "Gladly," answered Tom Thumb; "you may have all the chickens, I promise you." Then the fox let him go and even carried him home itself. When his father saw his dear little son again, he gladly gave the fox all the chickens he had. "In return I'm bringing you a pretty piece of money," said Tom Thumb and handed him the farthing he'd acquired on his wanderings.

"But why did they give the fox the poor little chickens to eat?" "Why, you fool, your father, too, would of course care more for his child than for the chickens in the barnyard."

46   Fitcher's Bird

Fitchers Vogel

ONCE UPON A TIME there was a wizard who took the form of a poor man, went begging from house to house, and caught the pretty girls. No one knew where he took them, for they never turned up again. One day he appeared before the door of a man who had three pretty daughters. The wizard looked like a poor, decrepit beggar and was carrying a big basket on his back, as if he were collecting alms in it. He begged for a little food, and when the eldest daughter came out and was about to hand him a piece of bread, he merely touched her, and she had to jump into his basket. Thereupon he hurriedly strode away and carried her to a dark forest, in the middle of which stood his house. Inside the house everything was most sumptuous.

He gave her whatever she wanted, saying, "My dear, you'll surely like it here with me; you've got everything your heart desires." This went on for a few days, then he said, "I've got to go on a journey and leave you alone for a short time. Here are the house keys; you may go everywhere and look at everything except one room, which this little key here opens. That I forbid to you on pain of death." He also gave her an egg, saying, "Take good care of this egg for me, and you'd better carry it about with you all the time, for if it were lost, a great misfortune would result." She took the keys and the egg and promised to carry it all out as he said. When he was gone, she went about the house from top to bottom and looked at everything. The rooms were resplendent with silver and gold, and she thought she'd never seen such magnificence. Finally she came to the forbidden door and was going to go past it, but her curiosity gave her no rest. She looked at the key. It looked like any other key. She put it in the keyhole and turned it a little, then the door flew open. But what did she behold as she stepped in! A big, bloody basin stood in the middle of the room, and in it were dead people all chopped up, and beside it stood a chopping block, and a shiny hatchet was lying on it. She was so frightened that the egg which she was holding in her hand plopped in. She took it out again and wiped off the blood, but in vain, for it reappeared instantly. She wiped and she scraped but couldn't get it off.

Not long afterwards the man returned from his journey, and the first thing he demanded to see was the key and the egg. She handed him the egg but trembled as she did so, and from the red stains he at once saw that she'd been in the blood-drenched room. "Since you entered the room against my will," he said, "you shall re-enter it against yours. Your life is forfeit." He threw her down, dragged her along by the hair, struck off her head on the block, and chopped her up, so that her blood flowed off on the floor. Then he threw her into the basin with the others.

"Now I'll fetch me the second," said the wizard, again went to the house in the guise of a poor man and begged for alms. Then the second daughter brought him a piece of bread. He caught her like the first by merely touching her and carried her off. She fared no better than her sister. She let herself be betrayed by her curiosity, opened the blood-drenched room, looked in, and on his return had to pay for it with her life. Then he went and fetched the third. She, however, was clever and wily. When he'd given her the keys and the egg and had gone off, she first carefully put the egg in a safe place, then surveyed the house, and last of all went into the forbidden room. Alas, what did she see! Both her dear sisters were lying there in the basin cruelly murdered and chopped to pieces. But she started and got the members together and put them properly in place; head, trunk, arms, and legs. When nothing further was missing, the members began to stir and grew together, and both girls opened their eyes and came to life again. Rejoicing, they hugged and kissed one another. On his arrival the man at once asked for the key and the egg, and when he could discover no trace of blood on it, he said, "You've stood the test, you shall be my bride." He now had no further power over her and had to do what she demanded.

"All right," she answered, "before we're married, you must take a basket full of gold to my father and mother and carry it there yourself on your back. Meanwhile, I shall give orders for the wedding." Then she ran to her sisters, whom she'd hidden in a little room, and said, "The moment's come when I can save you. The scoundrel shall carry you back home himself, but as soon as you get home, send me help." She put them both in a basket and covered them all up with gold, so that nothing could be seen of them. Then she called in the wizard and said, "Now carry off the basket, but I'll be looking out my window and watching to see that you don't stop on the way to rest."

The wizard put the basket on his back and went off with it, but it weighed so heavily on him that the sweat ran down his face. Then he sat down and was going to rest a bit, but at once one of the girls in the basket called out, "I'm looking out my window and see that you're resting. Will you get along at once!" He thought his bride-to-be was calling this out to him and got under way. Again he wanted to sit down, but a voice at once cried, "I'm looking out my window and see that you're resting. Will you get along at once!" And every time he stopped, a voice would call out and he'd have to go on, until finally, groaning and out of breath, he brought the basket with the gold and the two girls to their parents' house.

Back home the bride was arranging about the wedding feast
and had the wizard's friends invited to it. Then she took a
death's head with grinning teeth, put on it an ornament and
a wreath of flowers, took it up to the attic window, and set it
facing outward. When everything was ready, she got into a
barrel of honey, cut open the feather bed, and rolled about in
it, so that she looked like a queer bird and no one could recognize her. Then she went out of the house and on the way met
some of the wedding guests. They asked,

> "Fitcher's bird, where are you coming from?"
> "I'm coming from Fitze Fitcher's."
> "And what's the young bride doing there?"
> "She's swept the house from top to bottom
> And is looking out the attic window."

Finally she met the bridegroom, who was walking slowly back.
Like the others, he asked,

> "Fitcher's bird, where are you coming from?"
> "I'm coming from Fitze Fitcher's."
> "And what's the young bride doing there?"
> "She's swept the house from top to bottom
> And is looking out the attic window."

The bridegroom looked up and saw the tricked-out death's
head. He thought it was his bride and nodded to her and
greeted her in friendly fashion. When he'd entered the house
along with his guests, the bride's brothers and relatives arrived
who had been sent to save her. They locked all the doors of
the house so that no one could get away, and set it on fire so
that the Wizard and his crew had to burn to death.

47 The Juniper

Von dem Machandelboom

A LONG TIME AGO, probably a good two thousand years, there lived a rich man who had a beautiful and devout wife, and they loved one another very much. They had no children but very much wanted some. Day and night the wife prayed ever so much about it, but they didn't have any and didn't have any. In front of the house was a yard, and in it stood a juniper. Once in winter the wife was standing under it, peeling herself an apple, and as she was peeling the apple, she cut her finger, and the blood dropped in the snow. "Alas," said the wife and heaved a deep sigh. Then she looked at the blood in front of her and grew quite sad. "If only I had a child as red as blood and as white as snow!" As she said this, she became quite joyful of heart: she felt that something would come of it. She went into the house, and a month passed and the snow went away. After two months things got green. After three months the flowers came up. After four months all the trees in the forest burst into leaf and the green boughs were all intertwined and the birds sang so that the whole forest resounded, and the blossoms fell from the trees. The fifth month passed. Then she stood under the juniper, and it was very fragrant. Her heart leapt for joy, and she fell on her knees and was beside herself. When the sixth month had passed, the fruit got full and firm, and she became very quiet. In the seventh month she reached for the juniper berries and ate them most greedily. Then she grew sad and ill. The eighth month passed, and she called her husband and, weeping, said, "If I die, bury me under the juniper." Then she became quite consoled and joyful, until the ninth month passed. Then she had a child as white as snow and as red as blood, and when she saw it, she was so happy that she died.

Her husband buried her under the juniper and began to weep

very hard. After a time he wept somewhat less and after weeping a little more, stopped. Some time after that he again took a wife.

By his second wife he had a daughter. The first wife's child was a little boy, and he was as red as blood and as white as snow. When the wife looked at her daughter, she loved her very dearly, but then she'd look at the little boy, and it pained her dreadfully, and he seemed to be always in the way. She kept thinking how she'd like to divert the whole inheritance to her daughter, and the Evil One inspired her with a grudge against the little boy. She shoved him about from pillar to post and buffeted him here and cuffed him there, so that the poor child was always in a state of fear. When he got out of school, he had no peace or quiet.

Once the wife went to her room, and her little daughter came up and said, "Mother, give me an apple." "Yes, my child," said the wife and gave her a nice apple from a chest. The chest had a big, heavy lid and a big, sharp iron lock. "Mother," said the little daughter, "isn't brother to have one, too?" That astonished the wife, but she said, "Yes, when he gets out of school." When she saw out the window that he was coming, the Evil One really seemed to possess her, and she made a grab and took her daughter's apple away from her, saying, "You shan't have one before your brother." Then she threw the apple into the chest and shut it. The little boy came in the door, and the Evil One suggested that she say to him in a friendly way, "Son, do you want an apple?" and looked at him angrily. "Mother," said the little boy, "how angry you look! Yes, give me an apple." Then she felt she ought to persuade him. "Come along," she said, opening the lid, "take out an apple for yourself," and as the little boy was bending over the chest, the Evil One whispered to her, and crash! she slammed down the lid, so that his head flew off and fell among the red apples. Then she was overcome with terror and thought, "How can I get out of this?" She went up to her room and took a white cloth from the top drawer of a dresser and put the boy's head back on the neck and tied the neckerchief around it so that nothing could be seen. She set him on a chair outside the front door and put the apple in his hand.

Afterward Marlene went to her mother in the kitchen; the

latter was standing by the fire and had a pot of hot water in front of her which she kept stirring. "Mother," said Marlene, "brother's sitting outside the door looking quite pale, and has an apple in his hand. I asked him to give me the apple, but he didn't answer me. Then I got quite frightened." "Go back," said the mother, "and if he won't answer you, box his ears." Then Marlene went back and said, "Brother, give me the apple," but he kept still. Then she boxed his ears, and his head fell off. At that she was frightened and began to weep and howl and, running to her mother, said, "Oh, mother, I've knocked my brother's head off." She kept on weeping and couldn't be comforted. "Marlene," said her mother, "What have you done! However, keep quiet about it, so that nobody will notice it. There's nothing to be done about it in any event. We'll cook him in vinegar." Then the mother took the little boy and chopped him up, put the pieces in a pot, and cooked him in vinegar. But Marlene stood by and wept and wept, and all her tears fell into the pot and they didn't need any salt.

The father came home and, sitting down to table, said, "Where's my son?" Then the mother served up a great big dish of marinated minced boy, and Marlene wept and couldn't stop. Again the father said, "Where's my son?" "Oh," said the mother, "he's gone across country to mother's great-uncle; he wanted to stay there for a while." "What's he doing there? He didn't even say good-bye to me." "Oh, he very much wanted to go and asked me if he might stay for six weeks. He'll be well looked out for there." "Oh," said the man, "I'm very sad. It isn't right; he should have said good-bye to me." Then he began to eat and said, "Marlene, why are you weeping? Of course brother will come back. Oh, wife," he went on to say, "how good the food tastes! Give me some more," and the more he ate, the more he wanted and said, "Give me some more. The rest of you shan't have any of this. I feel as if it were all mine." He went on eating and threw all the bones under the table until he had quite finished it. Then Marlene went to her dresser, took out her best piece of silk from the bottom drawer, collected all the bones, big and small, from under the table, tied them up in the silk cloth, carried them outside the door, and wept bitter tears. She laid them in the green grass under the juniper and, once she'd put them there, she suddenly felt light of heart and stopped weeping. Then the juniper began to stir, and the branches parted and joined again, just as when one rejoices and claps one's hands like that. At the same time a big mist issued from the tree, and right in the mist a fire seemed to burn, and from out of the fire flew such a beautiful bird that sang so magnificently and flew high up in the air. When it had gone, the juniper was as it had been before, but the cloth with the bones had vanished. Marlene was very happy and contented, just as when her brother was still alive. She went quite happily back into the house, sat down at table, and ate.

The bird, however, flew away and, lighting on a goldsmith's house, began to sing,

> "My mother, she killed me,
> My father, he ate me,
> My sister Marlene
> Collected all my bones,
> Tied them up in a silk cloth,
> Laid them under the juniper.
> Tweet, tweet, what a beautiful bird I am!"

The goldsmith was sitting in his workshop making a gold chain. He heard the bird that was perched on his roof and singing and thought it most beautiful. He got up and as he was walking across the threshold, lost a slipper, but he went right on up the middle of the street with only one slipper and one sock on. He had on his apron and was holding the gold chain in one hand and the tongs in the other, and the sun was shining bright on the street. He went and stopped and looked at the bird. "Bird," he said, "how beautifully you can sing. Sing me that piece again." "No," said the bird, "I don't sing twice for nothing. Give me the gold chain, and I'll sing it again for you." "There," said the goldsmith, "you have the gold chain. Now sing it for me again." Then the bird came, took the gold chain in its right claw, and perching in front of the goldsmith, sang,

> "My mother, she killed me,
> My father, he ate me,
> My sister Marlene
> Collected all my bones,
> Tied them up in a silk cloth,
> Laid them under the juniper.
> Tweet, tweet, what a beautiful bird I am!"

Then the bird flew away to a shoemaker and perching on his roof, sang,

> "My mother, she killed me,
> My father, he ate me,
> My sister Marlene
> Collected all my bones,
> Tied them up in a silk cloth,
> Laid them under the juniper.
> Tweet, tweet, what a beautiful bird I am!"

The shoemaker heard it and ran to the door in his shirt sleeves, looked toward the roof, and had to keep his hand before his eyes lest the sun blind him. "Bird," he said, "how beautifully you can sing." Then he called in through the door, "Wife, come out here, there's a bird. Just look at it; it certainly can sing beautifully." Then he called his daughter and her children and the journeyman, apprentice, and maid, and they all came out onto the street and, looking at the bird, saw how beautiful it was, that it had such bright red and green feathers, with something like pure gold around its neck, and that the eyes in its head twinkled like stars. "Bird," said the shoemaker, "now sing me that piece again." "No," said the bird, "I don't sing twice for nothing. You've got to make me a present of something." "Wife," said the husband, "go to the shop. There's a pair of red shoes on the top shelf; fetch them down." The wife went and fetched the shoes. "There, bird," said the man, "now sing me the piece once more." Then the bird came and taking the shoes in its left claw, flew back up on the roof and sang,

> "My mother, she killed me,
> My father, he ate me,
> My sister Marlene
> Collected all my bones,
> Tied them up in a silk cloth,
> Laid them under the juniper.
> Tweet, tweet, what a beautiful bird I am!"

When it finished, it flew away. It had the chain in its right claw and the shoes in its left and flew far away to a mill. The mill was going clickety-clack, clickety-clack, clickety-clack, and in the mill were sitting twenty miller's apprentices. They were holding a stone and cutting it chip-chip, chip-chip, chip-chip, and the mill was still going clickety-clack, clickety-clack, clickety-clack. The bird perched on a linden that stood outside the mill and sang,

> "My mother, she killed me."

Then one of the apprentices stopped.

> "My father, he ate me."

Then two more stopped and heard,

> "My sister Marlene."

Then four more stopped.

> "Collected all my bones,
> Tied them up in a silk cloth."

Now only eight were chipping.

> "Laid them under . . ."

Now only five.

> ". . . the juniper."

Now only one.

> Tweet, tweet, what a beautiful bird I am!"

Then the last one, too, stopped and heard the last words. "Bird," he said, "how beautifully you sing." Let me hear that, too. Sing it for me once more." "No," said the bird, "I don't sing twice for nothing. Give me the millstone, then I'll sing it again." "Yes," he said, "if it belonged just to me, you should have it." "Yes," said the others, "if it sings once more, it'll have it." Then the bird came down, and all twenty millers took levers and raised the stone, "one, two, three, up!" Then the bird stuck its neck through the hole, putting it on like a collar, flew back up in the tree, and sang,

> "My mother, she killed me,
> My father, he ate me,
> My sister Marlene
> Collected all my bones,

Tied them up in a silk cloth,
Laid them under the juniper.
Tweet, tweet, what a beautiful bird I am!"

When it had finished, it spread its wings and in its right claw had the chain, in its left the shoes, and around its neck the millstone, and it flew far away to its father's house.

The father, the mother, and Marlene were sitting in the living room, and the father was saying, "How happy I feel; I'm in really good spirits." "Not I," said the mother, "I feel very frightened, just as if a storm were brewing." Marlene was sitting and weeping. Then the bird flew up, and as it lighted on the roof, the father said, "Oh, I feel so happy, and the sun's shining so bright outdoors. I feel as though I were going to see an old acquaintance again." "Not I," said the wife, "I'm frightened. My teeth are chattering and I feel as if fire were running through my veins." She tore open her bodice even more. Marlene was sitting in a corner weeping and had her handkerchief in front of her eyes and soaked it with her tears. Then the bird perched on the juniper and sang,

"My mother, she killed me."

The mother stopped up ears and shut her eyes and didn't want to see anything or hear anything, but there was a roaring noise in her ears as in the wildest gale, and her eyes smarted and stung like lightning.

"My father, he ate me."

"Oh, mother," said the man, "there's a beautiful bird. It's singing so wonderfully, the sun's shining so warm, and it smells like pure cinnamon."

"My sister Marlene."

Then Marlene put her head on her knees and wept and wept, but the man said, "I'm going outdoors. I want to see the bird from close at hand." "Oh, don't go!" said the wife, "I feel as though the whole house was shaking and was in flames," but the man went out and looked at the bird.

"Collected all my bones,
Tied them up in a silk cloth,

Laid them under the juniper.
Tweet, tweet, what a beautiful bird I am!"

At these words the bird dropped the gold chain, and it fell around the man's neck, so exactly around it that it fitted him perfectly. Then he went in and said, "See what a lovely bird it is! It made me a present of such a beautiful gold chain; it's so wonderful looking." The woman was very frightened and fell full length on the floor of the room, and her cap fell off her head. Then the bird again sang,

"My mother, she killed me."

"Oh that I were a thousand fathoms under the earth not to hear this!"

"My father, he ate me."

Then the wife fell down as if dead.

"My sister Marlene."

"Oh," said Marlene, "I'll go out, too, and see if the bird will give me something." So she went out.

"Collected all my bones,
Tied them up in a silk cloth."

Then it dropped the shoes down to her.

"Laid them under the juniper.
Tweet, tweet, what a beautiful bird I am!"

Then she felt so gay and happy, put on the new red shoes, and danced and skipped into the house. "Oh," she said, "I was so sad when I went out, and now I feel so gay. It's certainly a beautiful bird. It made me a present of a pair of shoes." "Not I," said the wife, jumping up and her hair standing on end like fiery flames, "I feel as if the world's coming to an end. I, too, want to go out and see whether it'll make me feel better." As she went out the door, crash! the bird threw the millstone on her head, so that she was squashed to death. The father and Marlene heard the noise and went out. Then steam and flames and fire rose from the spot, and when it was over, the little brother was standing there. He took his father and Marlene by the hand, and they were all three very happy and went into the house, sat down to table, and ate.

48   Old Sultan

Der alte Sultan

A FARMER had a faithful dog whose name was Sultan. He'd grown old and lost all his teeth so that he could no longer grip anything tight. On one occasion the farmer was standing with his wife at the front door and said, "I'm going to shoot old Sultan tomorrow; he's no longer good for anything." The wife, who felt sorry for the poor animal, answered, "Since he's served us for so many years and stood by us loyally, we can certainly pension him." "Why!" said the man, "you're crazy. He no longer has a tooth in his head, and no thief's afraid of him, and he might as well pass on now. If he served us, he was well fed in return."

The poor dog, which was lying stretched out near by in the sun, heard everything and was sad that tomorrow was to be his last day. He had a good friend in a wolf and in the evening slunk out to the forest and complained to it of his impending fate. "Listen, friend," said the wolf, "cheer up. I'll help you in your need. I've thought of something. Early tomorrow morning you master and his wife are going haying and will be taking their baby with them because no one will be staying at home. While working they usually lay the child in the shade behind the hedge. You lie down beside it as if you were going to guard it. Then I'll come out of the forest and steal the child. You must rush after me as hard as you can as if you wanted to get it away from me. I'll drop it, and you bring it back to the parents; then they'll think you saved it and will be far too grateful to do you any harm. On the contrary, you'll regain full favor, and they'll give you plenty of everything."

The dog liked the idea, and it was carried out as planned. The father screamed when he saw the wolf running through the fields with his child, but when old Sultan brought it back, he was happy, patted him, and said, "Not a hair of your head shall be hurt, and you shall be pensioned as long as you live." To his wife he said, "Go straight home and cook old Sultan some bread sops that he won't need to chew and bring the pillow from my bed. I'm going to give it to him to lie on." From then on old Sultan was as well off as he could possibly wish.

Soon after the wolf called on the dog and was glad that everything had turned out so well. "But friend," it said, "you'll surely look the other way if I happen to steal a fat sheep from your master? It's hard these days to make both ends meet." "Don't count on that," answered the dog, "I'm remaining faithful to my master and can't allow that." The wolf thought he didn't mean it seriously, came slinking along at night, and was about to carry off the sheep, but the farmer, whom faithful Sultan had informed of the wolf's intention, was lying in wait for it and gave it a good thrashing with a flail. The wolf made off but cried out to the dog, "Just wait, you faithless friend! You'll pay for it!"

The next morning the wolf dispatched a boar and had it challenge the dog to come out to the forest and settle matters there. Old Sultan could find no second but a three-legged cat, and as they went out together, the poor cat limped along, at the same time holding up its tail in pain. The wolf and its second were already at the spot, but when they saw their opponent coming along, they thought he was carrying a sabre, for such they believed the cat's erect tail to be, and as the poor creature hopped along on three legs, they simply thought that each time it was picking up a stone to throw at them. Then they both got frightened: the boar slunk off into the bushes, and the wolf jumped up in a tree. When the dog and the cat drew near, they were surprised that no one appeared. The boar, however, had not been able completely to hide in the bushes, and its ears were still sticking out. As the cat was looking cautiously about, the boar twitched its ears, and the cat, thinking a mouse was stirring there, jumped at it and gave it a good hard bite. Then the boar got up, crying out loudly, and ran away shouting, "The guilty party is sitting up there in the tree." The dog and the cat looked up and saw the wolf, who, ashamed of having cut so timid a figure, accepted the dog's offer of peace.

49 The Six Swans

Die sechs Schwäne

A KING was once hunting in a great forest and was chasing a deer with such zeal that not one of his men could keep up with him. When evening came, he stopped and looked about. Then he saw that he was lost. He looked for a way out of the forest but couldn't find one. Then he saw an old woman bobbing her head and walking toward him; she was, however, a witch. "Good woman," he said to her, "could you show me the way through the forest?" "Oh yes, Sir King," she replied. "I can do that, but there's a condition attached. Unless you fulfill it, you'll never get out of the forest and will have to starve to death here." "What sort of a condition?" asked the king. "I have a daughter," said the old woman, "who's as beautiful as any girl you can find in the world and quite worthy of becoming your wife. If you'll make her your queen, I'll show you the way out of the forest." In his distress of heart the king assented, and the old woman led him to her cottage, where her daughter was sitting by the fire. She received the king as if she'd been expecting him, and he saw that she was very beautiful. Just the same he didn't like her and couldn't look at her without secretly shuddering. After he'd lifted the girl up on his horse, the old woman showed him the way, and the king got back to his royal palace, where the wedding was celebrated.

The king had been married once before and by his first wife had had seven children, six boys and one girl, whom he loved above everything else in the world. Since he feared that the stepmother wouldn't treat them well and even that she'd do them some harm, he took them to a lonely castle in the middle of a forest. It was so hidden and the way to it was so hard to find that he wouldn't have found it himself unless a wise woman had made him a present of a ball of yarn of marvelous property: when he threw it in front of him, it unwound itself and showed him the way. The king went out so often to see his dear children that the queen was struck by his absence. She became curious and wanted to know what he did all alone out in the forest. She gave his servants a lot of money, and they disclosed the secret to her, also told her about the ball of yarn which alone could show the way. Now she had no rest till she'd ferreted out where the king kept the ball of yarn. Then she made white silk shirts and since she'd learned witchcraft from her mother, she sewed a spell in them. One day when the king had ridden out to hunt, she took the shirts and went into the forest, and the ball of yarn showed her the way. The children, who from afar saw someone coming, thought that their dear father was coming to see them and joyfully ran out to meet him. Then over each she threw one of the shirts, and as they touched them, they were changed into swans and flew away over the forest. The queen went home quite content, thinking she was rid of her stepchildren. However, the girl had not run out with her brothers to meet her, and the stepmother knew nothing about her. Next day the king went to visit his children but found only the girl. "Where are your brothers?" asked the king. "Oh, father dear," she answered, "they've gone away and left me alone behind," and told him that from her window she'd seen her brothers fly away over the forest in the form of swans and showed him the feathers they'd dropped in the yard and that she'd picked up. The king was sorry but didn't think that the queen had done the evil deed, and fearing lest the girl, too, might be taken from him, wanted to take her away with him. However, she was afraid of her stepmother and begged the king to be allowed to stay in the forest mansion for at least that one night

The poor girl thought, "I can't stay here any longer. I'll go and look for my brothers." When night came, she fled and went straight into the forest. She walked the whole night and all the next day, till from fatigue she could walk no farther.

Then she saw a hunting lodge, went up, and found a room with six little beds. But she didn't dare lie down in any one of them, crept underneath one, lay down on the hard floor, and was going to spend the night there. When the sun was about to set, she heard a whirring noise and saw six swans flying in through the window. They lighted on the floor and blew at one another so that all their feathers blew off, and their swan skins stripped off them like shirts. The girl looked at them and recognized her brothers, rejoiced, and crawled out from under the bed. The brothers were no less glad to see their sister, but their joy was short-lived. "You can't stay here," they said to her; "this is a robbers' den. If they come home and find you, they'll murder you." "Can't you protect me?" asked the sister. "No," they answered, "for we're only allowed to put off our swan skins a quarter of an hour every evening, during which time we have our human form. Then we're turned into swans again." The sister wept and said, "Can't you be unspelled?" "Oh, no," they answered, "the conditions are too hard. You mustn't speak or laugh for six whole years, and during that time you must sew six shirts for us out of asters. If a single word escapes your lips, all your work will have been in vain." When the brothers had said this, the quarter of an hour had passed, and in the form of swans they again flew out through the window.

The girl, however, firmly resolved to unspell her brothers even if it cost her her life. She left the hunting lodge, went straight into the middle of the forest, sat down up in a tree, and spent the night there. Next morning she went out, gathered asters, and began to sew. She might talk to no one and she had no desire to laugh; she sat there, just looking at her work. When she'd already spent a long time there, the king of the country happened to be hunting in the forest, and his huntsmen came to the tree up in which the girl was sitting. They called out to her, saying, "Who are you?" She made no answer. "Come on down," they said, "we shan't hurt you." She just shook her head. When they continued to ply her with questions, she threw her gold necklace down to them, thinking to satisfy them with that. But they didn't stop, and she threw down her belt, and when even this didn't work, her garters, and little by little everything she had on that could be dispensed with. Finally she had nothing but her shift. The huntsmen, however, didn't let themselves be put off by this, climbed the tree, brought the girl down, and took her to the king. The king asked, "Who are you? What are you doing up in the tree?" She didn't answer. He questioned her in every language he knew, but she remained as silent as a stone. Because she was so beautiful the king's heart was moved, and he conceived a great love for her. He put his cloak about her, set her in front of him on his horse, and took her to his palace. There he had her dressed in fine clothes, and being so beautiful, she was as radiant as the day; nevertheless it was impossible to get a word out of her. He placed her beside him at table, and her modest ways and good manners pleased him so that he said, "I want to marry this girl and none other in the world," and after a few days he married her.

Now the king had a wicked mother. She was not pleased with this marriage and spoke ill of the young queen. "Who knows where the wench who can't speak hails from?" she said. "She's not worthy of a king." A year later, when the queen gave birth to her first child, the old woman took it away from her and smeared her mouth with blood as she slept. Then she went to the king and accused her of being a cannibal. The king wouldn't believe it and didn't allow any harm to be done her. All the time she sat sewing on the shirts and paid no attention to anything else. The next time, when she again gave birth to a fine boy, the false mother-in-law carried out the same deception. Still the king couldn't bring himself to believe her charges. "She's too devout and good," he said, "to do such a thing. If she weren't mute and could defend herself, her innocence would come to light." Yet when for the third time the old woman stole the newborn child and accused the queen, who uttered not a word in her own defense, the king couldn't help it and had to turn her over to the court, which condemned her to be burned to death.

The day arrived when the sentence was to be executed. It happened to be the last day of the six years during which she mightn't speak or laugh. She'd freed her dear brothers from the power of the magic spell: the six shirts were finished, except that the left sleeve was still missing on the last shirt. As she was being led to the pyre, she laid the shirts over her arm, and when she was standing up there and the fire was about to be kindled, she looked about. Then the six swans came flying through the air, and she saw that her liberation was approaching, and her heart leapt for joy. The swans came whirring up to her and alighted, so that she was able to throw the shirts over them. As the shirts touched them, their swan skins dropped off, and her bothers stood before her in the flesh and were hale and fair—except that the youngest lacked his left arm and in its place had a swan's wing attached to his back. They hugged and kissed one another, and the queen went to the king, who was quite dumbfounded, and began to speak, saying "Dearest husband, now I may speak and reveal to you that I'm innocent and have been wrongly accused," and told him about the deception on the part of the old woman, who'd taken her three children from her and had hidden them. Then to the king's great joy they were fetched, and as a punishment the wicked mother-in-law was tied to the pyre and burned to ashes.

But the king and the queen and her six brothers lived for many years in peace and happiness.

50   Hawthorn Blossom

Dornröschen

IN DAYS OF YORE there was a king and a queen who every day used to say, "Oh, if we only had a child!" yet they never had one. Once when the queen was bathing, it happened that a frog crawled ashore out of the water and said to her, "Your wish will be fulfilled: before a year's out, you'll give birth to a daughter." What the frog said came to pass, and the queen gave birth to a girl; she was so beautiful that in his joy the king didn't know what to do and arranged a great feast. He invited not only his relatives, friends, and acquaintances, but also the wise women, that they might be gracious and well disposed toward the child. There were thirteen of them in his kingdom, but because he had only twelve gold plates from which they might eat, one of them had to stay home. The feast was celebrated with all splendor, and when it came to an end, the wise women presented the child with their marvelous gifts. One gave it virtue, the second beauty, the third riches, and so on, with everything the heart desires. When eleven had finished bestowing their gifts, suddenly the thirteenth came in. She wanted to revenge herself for not having been invited, and without greeting anyone or so much as looking at anyone, she cried out in a loud voice, "In her fifteenth year the king's daughter will prick herself with a spindle and fall down dead." Without another word she turned about and left the hall. Everybody was frightened. Then the twelfth, who still had her wish left, stepped up and because she couldn't undo the evil gift but merely temper it, said, "It won't be a real death; the princess will fall into a hundred years' deep sleep."

The king wanted to guard his dear child against this misfortune and issued a decree that all spindles throughout the whole kingdom should be burned. The gifts of the wise women were, however, quite fulfilled in the girl, for she was so beautiful, well mannered, friendly, and intelligent that whoever looked at her couldn't help loving her. On the very day she became fifteen the king and the queen happened not to be at home, and the girl was left all alone in the palace. She went all about, looking into rooms and chambers to her heart's content, and finally even got to an old tower. She climbed up the narrow winding stairs and came to a little door. There was a rusty key in the lock, and when she turned it, the door flew open and in the little room was sitting an old woman with a spindle and spinning her flax industriously. "Good day, Granny," said the king's daughter, "what are you doing there?" "I'm spinning," said the old woman, bobbing her head. "What sort of thing is it that's jumping about so gaily?" asked the girl. She took the spindle and wanted to spin too, but no sooner had she touched the spindle than the spell started working and she pricked her finger with it.

The very moment she felt the prick, she fell down on the bed there and lay in a deep sleep. This sleep spread over the whole palace: the king and the queen, who'd just come home and had entered the great hall, fell asleep, and the entire court with them. The horses in the stable also fell asleep, the dogs in the courtyard, the pigeons on the roof, the flies on the wall, even the fire that was flickering on the hearth died down and fell asleep, and the roast stopped sizzling, and the chef who was about to pull the scullery boy's hair because he'd done something wrong let the boy go and fell asleep. The wind died down, and not a leaf stirred on the trees in front of the palace.

Around about the palace a hawthorn hedge began to grow. This grew higher every year and finally surrounded the entire palace and even grew out beyond it, so that nothing more was to be seen of it, not even the flag on the roof. The legend of the beautiful sleeping Hawthorn Blossom—for such was the name of the king's daughter—went about the country, so that from time to time kings' sons came and tried to break through the hedge and reach the palace. They found it impossible, however, for the hawthorn bushes held together as if they had hands, and the young men remained stuck in them, couldn't get free, and died miserable deaths. Once again after many, many years, a king's son came to the country and heard an old man telling about the hawthorn hedge: a palace was said to be behind it, in which a most beautiful king's daughter, named Hawthorn Blossom, had already been sleeping a hundred years, and the king and the queen and the whole court sleeping along with her. From his grandfather the old man also knew that many kings' sons had already come and tried to break through the hawthorn hedge but had remained stuck in it and had died miserable deaths. Then the youth said, "I'm not afraid; I'll go out and see the fair Hawthorn Blossom." No matter how hard the good old man tried to dissuade him, he wouldn't listen to his words.

Now the hundred years were just up, and the day had come on which Hawthorn Blossom was to wake up again. When the king's son approached the hawthorn hedge, there were nothing but beautiful big hawthorn blossoms that moved aside of themselves and let him through unharmed, closing again behind him like a hedge. In the palace courtyard he saw the horses and spotted hunting dogs lying asleep; on the roof were perched the pigeons with their heads under their wings. When he entered the house, the flies were asleep on the walls.

In the kitchen the chef was still holding his hand as if about to take hold of the scullery boy, and the kitchen maid was sitting in front of the black chicken which she was supposed to pluck. Then he went on and in the great hall saw the whole court lying asleep, and up near the throne lay the king and the queen. He went on still farther, and everything was so quiet that one could hear oneself breathe. Finally he got to the tower and opened the door of the small room in which Hawthorn Blossom was sleeping. There she lay and was so beautiful that he couldn't turn his eyes away and stooped down and kissed her. As he touched her with his lips, Hawthorn Blossom opened her eyes, woke up, and looked at him in friendly fashion. Then they went downstairs together, and the king woke up and the queen and the whole court, and they all looked at one another in astonishment. The horses in the courtyard got up and shook themselves; the hounds jumped about, wagging their tails; the pigeons on the roof drew their heads from under their wings, looked about, and flew out into the country. The flies on the walls went on crawling; the fire in the kitchen came up, blazed, and cooked the meal; the roast began to sizzle again; and the chef boxed the scullery boy's ears so that he cried out; and the maid finished plucking the chicken.

Then they celebrated the wedding of the king's son with Hawthorn Blossom in all splendor, and they lived happily until their death.

51 Foundling Bird

Fundevogel

ONCE UPON A TIME there was a gamekeeper who went hunting in the forest, and when he got there, he heard cries like a small child's. He followed the cries and finally came to a tall tree up in which a little child was sitting. The mother and the child had fallen asleep under the tree, and a bird of prey, seeing the child in her lap, had swooped down, carried it away in its beak, and put it up in the tall tree.

The gamekeeper climbed up and, bringing the child down, thought, "You may as well take it home and bring it up with your Nellie." So he took it home, and the two children grew up together. Because it had been found up in a tree and because it had been carried off by a bird, the child was named Foundling Bird. Foundling Bird and Nellie loved each other so much, so very much, that they were unhappy when out of one another's sight.

Now the gamekeeper had an old cook who one evening took two pails and began to carry water, going out to the well not once but many times. Nellie noticed this and said, "Listen, old Susy, why are you carrying so much water?" "If you'll promise not to tell anybody, I'll tell you." Nellie said no, she wouldn't tell anybody about it. Then the cook said, "Early tomorrow morning when the gamekeeper is out hunting, I'm going to bring the water to a boil, and when its boiling in the kettle, I'm going to throw Foundling Bird in and boil the child in it."

Very early the next morning the gamekeeper got up and went hunting, and the children were still in bed when he left. Then Nellie said to Foundling Bird, "If you won't desert me, I won't desert you," and Foundling Bird said, "Never, no never." Then Nellie said, "I might as well tell you: last night old Susy was carrying ever so many pails of water into the house, so I asked her why she was doing it. She said that if I wouldn't tell anybody, she'd tell me, and I said I certainly wouldn't tell anybody. Then she said that early tomorrow when father had gone hunting, she was going to bring the kettle full of water to a boil, throw you in and boil you. Let's get up quickly, dress, and go away together."

So the two children got up, dressed in a hurry, and made off. When the water was boiling in the kettle, the cook went into the bedroom, intending to fetch Foundling Bird and throw the child in, but when she came in and went up to the beds, both the children were gone. She got terribly frightened and said to herself, "What shall I say now when the gamekeeper comes home and sees that the children are gone? Quick, let's go after them and get them back."

The cook sent three servants after them; they were to run and overtake the children. The children were sitting by the edge of the forest, and when from afar they saw the servants coming on the run, Nellie said to Foundling Bird, "If you won't desert me, I won't desert you," and Foundling Bird said, "Never, no never." Then Nellie said, "You change yourself into a rosebush and I'll change myself into the rose on it." When the three servants got to the edge of the forest, there was nothing there but a rosebush with a rose on it, and no sign of the children. Then they said, "There's nothing doing here," went home, and told the cook they'd seen nothing at all but a rosebush with a rose on it. The old cook scolded them, "You simpletons, you should have cut the rosebush in two, picked the rose, and brought it along home. Now hurry up and do so." So they had to go out and look a second time. The children saw them coming from afar, and Nellie said, "Foundling Bird, if you won't desert me, I won't desert you." Foundling Bird said, "Never, no never." Then Nellie said, "Change yourself into a church, and I'll be the chandelier in it." When the three servants got there, there was nothing but a church with a chandelier inside, so they said to one another, "What are we to do here? Let's go home." When they got home, the cook asked whether they'd found anything, and they said no, they'd found nothing but a church with a chandelier inside. "You fools," scolded the cook, "why didn't you destroy the church and bring home the chandelier?" Now the cook started out herself and with the three servants went after the children. From afar the children saw the three servants coming and the cook waddling behind them. Then Nellie said, "Foundling Bird, if you won't desert me, I won't desert you," and Foundling Bird said, "Never, no never." Then Nellie said, "Change yourself into a pond, and I'll be the duck on it." The cook came up, and when she beheld the pond, she lay down over it and was going to drink it up. The duck, however, swam quickly up, seized her by her head with its bill, and dragged her into the water. Then the old witch had to drown.

Then the children went home together and were ever so happy, and if they haven't died, they're still alive.

52   King Thrushbeard

König Drosselbart

A KING had a daughter who was beautiful beyond measure but so proud and overbearing withal that no suitor was good enough for her. She rejected one after the other and made fun of them in the bargain. Once upon a time the king ordered a great feast to be arranged and from far and near invited men who wanted to get married. They were all lined up according to their rank and dignity: first came the kings, then the dukes, princes, counts, and barons, finally the lesser nobility. The king's daughter was conducted through the lines but she found something to criticize in every man. One was too fat for her: "The wine cask," she said. Another was too tall: "Tall and slender with no bearing." The third was too short: "Short and fat with no grace"; the fourth too pale: "Pallid Death." The fifth was too red in the face: "Turkey cock." The sixth didn't stand straight enough: "Green wood dried out behind the stove." In this way she found something to object to in every one of them and made particular fun of a good king who stood right at the head of the line and whose chin was a little crooked. "Well," she cried, laughing, "his chin's like a thrush's bill," and from that time he was called Thrushbeard. When the king saw that his daughter was doing nothing but making fun of the people and scorning all the suitors who were assembled there, he got angry and swore she'd have to take for a husband the first beggar who came to his door.

A few days later a minstrel began to sing beneath the window in order to earn some small alms. When the king heard it, he said, "Have him come up." The minstrel entered, dressed in his dirty, ragged clothes, came in, sang in the presence of the king and his daughter, and when he had finished, begged for alms. The king said, "Your song has pleased me

so much that I'll give you my daughter there in marriage."
The king's daughter was frightened, but the king said, "I
swore an oath to give you to the first beggar, and I'll keep
it." Objecting did her no good, the parson was fetched, and
she had to let herself be married then and there to the minstrel.
When it was over, the king said, "Now as a beggar woman
it's not fitting for you to stay in my palace any longer; you
can just move on with your husband."

The beggar led her by the hand, and she had to go away
with him on foot. When they got into a big forest, she asked,

> "Whose is the beautiful forest?"
> "It belongs to King Thrushbeard.
> Had you accepted him, it would be yours."
> "Poor girl that I am!
> Had I only accepted King Thrushbeard!"

Next they crossed a meadow, and again she asked,

> "Whose is the beautiful green meadow?"
> "It belongs to King Thrushbeard.
> Had you accepted him, it would be yours."
> "Poor girl that I am!
> Had I only accepted King Thrushbeard!"

Then they passed through a big town, and again she asked,

> "Whose is this beautiful big town?"
> "It belongs to King Thrushbeard.
> Had you accepted him, it would be yours."
> "Poor girl that I am!
> Had I only accepted King Thrushbeard!"

"I'm not at all pleased with your always wishing you had
someone else as a husband," said the minstrel. "Am I not
good enough for you?" Finally they came to a very small cottage,
and then she said,

> "Good heavens, how very small the house is!
> Whose can this wretched, tiny cottage be?"

"This is my house and yours, where we'll live together," answered the minstrel. She had to stoop to get through the low
door. "Where are the servants?" said the king's daughter.
"Servants!" answered the beggar, "Whatever you want done

you must do yourself. Make a fire at once and put the water on so you can cook my meal. I'm all tired out." The king's daughter knew nothing about making fires and cooking, and the beggar had to lend a hand himself and then things went at least so-so. When they'd eaten their poor fare, they went to bed, but in the morning he got her up very early because she was supposed to take care of the house.

For a few days they went in thus for plain and honest living and used up their provisions. Then the man said, "Wife, we can't go on like this, eating and earning nothing. You're to weave baskets." He went out, cut willows, and brought them home. She began to weave, but the rough willows pricked her tender hands. "I see that this doesn't work," said her husband; "you'd better spin; perhaps you're better at that." She sat down and tried to spin, but the hard thread soon cut her soft fingers so that the blood ran down them. "You see," said the husband, "you're not good for any work. I got a poor bargain in marrying you. Now I'll have a try at trading in pots and earthenware. You're to sit down in the market place and sell the wares." "Alas," she thought, "if people from my father's kingdom come to the market and see me sitting there selling, how they'll make fun of me!" It did no good, however; she had to obey if they weren't to starve to death. The first time things went all right, for people gladly bought from the woman because she was so beautiful and paid what she asked; indeed, many gave her the money and left her the pots in the bargain.

They lived on the profit as long as it lasted. Then the husband again bought a lot of new earthenware. She sat down with this in a corner of the market place and arranged it about her and offered it for sale. All of a sudden a drunken hussar came racing up and rode his horse right into the earthenware so that it was all smashed to pieces. She began to weep and in her distress didn't know what to do. "Alas, what will happen to me!" she cried; "what will my husband say to this!" She ran home and told him of her misfortune. "Who on earth sits down in the corner of the market place with earthenware!" said the man. "Just stop your weeping. I see quite well that you're no good for any proper work. I've been up in our king's palace and asked whether they couldn't use a kitchen maid, and they promised me to take you on. In return you'll get your food free."

Now the king's daughter became a kitchen maid, had to help the cook and do the nastiest work. She fastened a little pot inside each of two pouches and in them used to take home what was given her of the leftovers, and they lived on that. It happened that the wedding of the king's eldest son was to be celebrated. The poor woman went up there and stood outside the door of the great hall, since she wanted to see it. When the candles were lighted and the people were going in, each more finely dressed than the last, and everything was magnificent and splendid, with sorrowful heart she thought of her fate and cursed her pride and arrogance which had brought her so low and had plunged her into such great poverty. Of the delicious dishes which were being carried in and out and whose savor rose to her nostrils the servants would once in a while throw her a few bits; she put them in her little pot, intending to take them home.

Suddenly the king's son came in dressed in velvet and silk, with gold chains around his neck. When he saw the beautiful woman standing in the doorway, he seized her by the hand and wanted to dance with her, but she refused and was frightened, for she saw that it was King Thrushbeard who had wooed her and whom she'd scornfully rejected. It did her no good to resist, for he dragged her into the great hall. Then the band to which the pouches were tied broke, and the pots fell out, so that the porridge poured out and the bits of food scattered all over the floor. When the people saw that, there was general laughter and joking, and she was so mortified that she'd rather have been a thousand fathoms under the earth. She ran out the door, wanting to escape, but on the stairway a man overtook her and brought her back, and when she looked at him, it was King Thrushbeard again. He spoke to her in kindly fashion, "Don't be afraid, I and the minstrel who's been living with you in the miserable cottage are one and the same person. For love of you I disguised myself, and I was also the hussar who rode his horse into your earthenware and smashed it. All this was done to humble your proud spirit and to punish you for the arrogance with which you made fun of me." Then she wept bitterly, saying, "I did very wrong and am not worthy to be your wife"; but he said, "Console yourself, the evil days are over. Now we'll celebrate our wedding." Then the ladies-in-waiting came and put the most splendid clothes on her, and her father arrived, and the whole court, and they wished her luck on her wedding with King Thrushbeard, and then the real joy began.

I wish that you and I had been there, too.

53   Snow-White

Schneewittchen

ONCE UPON A TIME in the middle of winter when the snowflakes were falling from the sky like feathers, a queen was sitting by a window with a black ebony frame and was sewing. As she was thus sewing and looking at the snow, she stuck the needle in her finger, and three drops of blood fell into the snow. Because the red looked so pretty in the white snow, she thought to herself, "If only I had a child as white as snow, as red as blood, and as black as the wood of the window frame!" Soon thereafter she had a little daughter who was as white as snow, as red as blood, and whose hair was as black as ebony. Therefore she was called Snow-White, and when the child was born, the queen died.

A year later the king married a second wife. She was a beautiful woman but proud and haughty and couldn't bear being second in beauty to anyone. She had a marvelous mirror: when she stepped up to it and looked at herself in it, she'd say,

> "Mirror, mirror on the wall,
> Who is the fairest in all the land?"

The mirror would then reply,

> "Lady Queen, you are the fairest in the land."

Then she'd be content, knowing that the mirror was telling the truth.

But Snow-White grew up and got more and more beautiful and, when she was seven, she was as beautiful as a bright day and fairer than the queen herself. Once when the queen asked her mirror,

> "Mirror, mirror on the wall,
> Who is the fairest in all the land,"

it replied,

> "Lady Queen, you are the fairest here,
> But Snow-White is a thousand times fairer than you."

Then the queen was frightened and got green and yellow with envy. From that hour, whenever she looked at Snow-White, she'd feel a turn, she hated the girl so. Envy and pride grew like a weed in her heart, higher and higher, so that day or night she no longer had any rest. Then she summoned a huntsman and said, "Take the child out into the forest; I don't want to lay eyes on her again. You're to kill her and bring me her lungs and her liver as a token." The huntsman obeyed and took her out, and when he'd drawn his hunting-knife and was about to pierce Snow-White's innocent heart, she began to weep and said, "Alas, dear huntsman, spare me my life. I'm willing to go into the wild forest and never come back home again," and because she was so beautiful, the huntsman took pity on her and said, "Just run away, poor child." "The wild animals will soon devour you," he thought, feeling just the same as if a heavy load had been lifted from his heart because he didn't have to kill her. Since a young boar came running past, he killed it, took out its lungs and liver, and brought them as a token to the queen. The chef had to cook them in brine, and the wicked woman ate them up, thinking she'd eaten Snow-White's lungs and liver.

Now the poor child was all alone in the big forest and got so frightened that she even eyed all the leaves of the trees and didn't know what to do. She started running and ran over the sharp stones and through the thorn bushes, and the wild animals sprang past her but did her no harm. She ran as long as her legs would carry her till nearly nightfall. Then she saw a little cottage and went in to rest. In the cottage everything was tiny but indescribably pretty and neat. There was a little table there laid with a little white cloth with seven little plates, and each plate with its little spoon, furthermore seven little knives and forks, and seven little tumblers. Along the wall stood seven little beds side by side, spread with snow-white sheets. Because she was so hungry and thirsty. Snow-White ate some vegetables and bread off each plate and drank a drop of wine from each tumbler, for she didn't want to take everything away from any one of them. After that, since she was so tired, she lay down in one of the beds, but not one of them fitted her: one was too long, another too short, till finally the seventh was just right. She lay down in it, commended herself to God, and fell asleep.

When it had got quite dark, the masters of the cottage came home; they were the seven dwarfs who with pick and shovel mined for ore in the mountains. They lighted their seven little candles and, when it was light in the cottage, they saw that someone had been in there, for not everything was the way they'd left it. The first said, "Who's been sitting in my chair?" The second, "Who's been eating off my plate?" The third, "Who's been taking some of my roll?" The fourth, "Who's been eating some of my vegetables?" The fifth, "Who's been handling my fork?" The sixth, "Who's been cutting with my knife?" The seventh, "Who's been drinking out of my tumbler?" Then the first looked about and noticing a little wrinkle in his bed, said, "Who got into my bed?" The others came on the run, exclaiming, "Somebody's been lying in my bed, too!" The seventh, when he looked in his bed, saw Snow-White, who was lying there asleep. He called the others. They came running up and crying out in astonishment, fetched their seven candles and let the light shine on Snow-White. "My goodness, my goodness!" they exclaimed, "how beautiful the child is!" and were so happy that they didn't wake her up but let her go on sleeping in the bed. The seventh dwarf, however, slept with his companions, one hour with each till the night had passed.

When it was morning, Snow-White woke up, and seeing the seven dwarfs, was frightened. They were friendly, however, and asked, "What's your name?" "My name is Snow-

White," she answered. "How did you get to our house?" continued the dwarfs. Then she told them that her stepmother had meant to have her slain, but that the huntsman had made her a present of her life, and that she'd walked all day until she finally found their cottage. "If you'll keep house for us," said the dwarfs, "cook, make the beds, wash, sew, and knit, and if you'll keep everything neat and clean, then you may stay with us and you shall lack nothing." "Yes, very gladly," said Snow-White, stayed on with them and kept their house in order. In the morning they'd go into the mountains to look for ore and gold, in the evening they'd come back, and then their food had to be ready. During the day the girl was alone, and the good little dwarfs warned her, saying, "Watch out for your stepmother. She'll soon know that you're here. Let absolutely nobody in."

The queen, after she thought she'd eaten Snow-White's lungs and liver, had no notion but that she was once more the fairest and most beautiful woman. She stepped up to her mirror and said,

> "Mirror, mirror on the wall,
> Who is the fairest in all the land?"

Then the mirror answered,

> "Lady Queen, you are the fairest here,
> But Snow-White over the mountains
> With the seven dwarfs
> Is a thousand times fairer than you."

Then she was frightened, for she knew that the mirror didn't lie and saw that the huntsman had deceived her and that Snow-White was still alive. Again she thought and thought how she might kill her, for so long as she was not the most beautiful woman in the whole land, her envy gave her no rest. When at last she'd thought up something, she stained her face, dressed herself up as an old peddler woman, and was quite unrecognizable. In this guise she crossed the seven mountains to the seven dwarfs, knocked at the door, and called, "Pretty wares for sale! pretty wares for sale!" Snow-White looked out the window and said, "How do you do, good woman, What have you got for sale?" "Good wares, pretty wares," she answered, "bodice laces of every color," and drew one out that was braided of silks of many colors. "I may safely let this good woman in," thought Snow-White. She unbolted the door and bought the pretty lace. "Child," said the old woman, "how you do look! Come, let me lace you up properly for once." Snow-White, suspecting no harm, stood in front of her and let herself be laced up with the new bodice lace. The old woman, however, laced her up so quickly and so tight that Snow-White lost her breath and fell down as if dead. "Well, you used to be the most beautiful!" she said and hurried out.

Not long after, the seven dwarfs came home in the evening, but how frightened they were to see their dear Snow-White lying on the floor, still and motionless as if dead. They lifted her up, and noticing that she was too tightly laced, cut the lace. Then she began to breathe a little and gradually revived. When the dwarfs heard what had happened, they said, "The old peddler woman was none other than the wicked queen. Watch out and don't let any person come in when we're not with you."

When the wicked woman got home she stepped up to the mirror and asked,

> "Mirror, mirror on the wall,
> Who is the fairest in all the land?"

Then as usual the mirror replied,

> "Lady Queen, you are the fairest here,
> But Snow-White beyond the mountains
> With the seven dwarfs
> Is a thousand times fairer than you."

When she heard this, all her blood went to her heart from fright, for she quite realized that Snow-White had come to life again. "But this time," she said, "I'll think up something that will be the death of you," and with witches' arts, in which she was expert, made a poisoned comb. Then disguising herself and assuming the appearance of a different old woman, she went on over the seven mountains to the seven dwarfs, knocked on the door and called, "Pretty wares for sale! pretty wares for sale!" Snow-White looked out and said, "Get right along! I mayn't let anybody in." "But surely you're allowed to look," said the old woman, took out the poisoned comb and

held it up. The child liked it so well that she let herself be
fooled and opened the door. When they'd agreed on the price,
the old woman said, "Now I'll comb your hair properly for
once." Poor Snow-White, suspecting no harm, let the old woman
go ahead, but hardly had she put the comb in her hair than
the poison in it worked, and the girl fell down unconscious.
"You paragon of beauty!" said the wicked woman, "now you're
done for!" and went away. Fortunately it was near evening,
the time the seven dwarfs would be coming home. When they
saw Snow-White lying on the floor as if dead, they at once
suspected the stepmother, searched about, and found the
poisoned comb. No sooner had they taken it out than Snow-
White regained consciousness and told them what had happened. Once more they warned her to be on her guard and
not to open the door for anyone.

At home the queen stood before her mirror and said,

> "Mirror, mirror on the wall,
> Who is the fairest in all the land?"

Then the mirror answered as before,

> "Lady Queen, you are the fairest here,
> But Snow-White beyond the mountains
> With the seven dwarfs
> Is a thousand times fairer than you."

On hearing the mirror talk thus, she trembled and shook with
anger. "Snow-White shall die!" she cried, "even if it costs me
my very life." Thereupon she went into a solitary chamber,
quite hidden away, where no one ever went and there made
a very poisonous apple. Outside it looked beautiful, white
with red cheeks, so that everybody who saw it longed for it,
but whoever ate even a tiny bit of it was doomed to die. When
the apple was ready, she stained her face and disguised herself as a farmer's wife and went thus over the seven mountains
to the seven dwarfs. She knocked at the door, and Snow-
White put her head out the window, saying, "I mustn't let
anybody in; the seven dwarfs have forbidden me to." "Quite
all right," answered the farmer's wife, "but of course I'll get
rid of my apples. There! I'll make you a present of one."
"No," said Snow-White, "I mustn't accept anything." "Are

you afraid of poison?" said the old woman. "Look, I'll cut the apple in half: you eat the red cheek and I'll eat the white." The apple had been so skillfully made that only the red cheek was poisonous. Snow-White looked greedily at the beautiful apple, and when she saw the farmer's wife eating some, she could no longer resist, put out her hand, and took the poisoned half. Scarcely, however, had she got a bite of it in her mouth than she fell dead to the floor. Then the queen gave her an awful look and burst out into loud laughter, saying, "White as snow, red as blood, black as ebony! This time the dwarfs can't wake you up again!" When she consulted the mirror at home,

> "Mirror, mirror on the wall,
> Who is the fairest in all the land?"

it finally replied,

> "Lady Queen, you are the fairest in the land."

Then her envious heart was at rest, at least as much as an envious heart can be.

When the dwarfs got home in the evening, they found Snow-White lying on the floor. No breath was coming out of her mouth, and she was dead. They lifted her up, looked to see if they might find something poisonous, unlaced her bodice, combed her hair, washed her with water and wine, but all to no purpose. The dear child was dead and remained dead. They laid her on a bier, and all seven sat down beside it and wept for three whole days. They were going to bury her, but she still looked as fresh as a living being and her pretty cheeks were still rosy. "We can't lower her into the dark ground," they said and had a transparent glass coffin made so that one could view her from all sides, put her in it, and on it wrote in letters of gold her name and that she was a king's daughter. Then they placed the coffin on the mountain, and one of them always stayed by it and guarded it, and the birds, too, came and wept over Snow-White, first an owl, then a raven, and finally a dove.

Snow-White lay in the coffin for a long, long time and didn't decay but looked rather as if she were asleep, for she was still as white as snow, as red as blood, and her hair was as black as ebony. A king's son happened to get into the forest and came to the dwarfs' cottage to spend the night. He saw the coffin on the mountain and beautiful Snow-White in it and read what was written on it in letters of gold. Then he said to the dwarfs, "Let me have the coffin; I'll give you whatever you want for it;" but the dwarfs answered, "We won't sell it for all the gold in the world." Then he said, "Make me a present of it then, for I can't live without seeing Snow-White. I'll honor her and esteem her as my most dearly beloved." Since he spoke thus, the good dwarfs took pity on him and gave him the coffin. The king's son now had his servants carry it off on their shoulders. Then by chance they stumbled over a shrub, and from the jolt the poisoned piece of apple which Snow-White had bitten off came out of her throat, and before long she opened her eyes, lifted the coffin lid, raised herself up, and was alive again. "Good heavens, where am I?" she cried. Joyfully the king's son said, "You're with me," and relating what had happened, said, "I love you more than everything on earth. Come with me to my father's palace. You shall be my wife." Then Snow-White fell in love with him and went with him, and their wedding was celebrated with great pomp and splendor.

Snow-White's wicked stepmother was also invited to the feast. Once she was all dressed in beautiful clothes, she stepped up to her mirror and said,

> "Mirror, mirror on the wall,
> Who is the fairest in all the land?"

The mirror answered,

> "Lady Queen, you are the fairest here,
> But the young queen is a thousand times fairer than you."

Then the wicked woman cursed and got so very frightened that she didn't know what to do. At first she didn't want to go to the wedding at all, but that gave her no peace; she had to go and see the young queen. When she came in, she recognized Snow-White and stood motionless from terror and fear. However, iron slippers had already been put over a charcoal fire and were now brought in with tongs and placed before her. Then she had to put the red-hot slippers on and dance until she dropped to the ground dead.

54   The Knapsack, the Cap, and the Horn

Der Ranzen, das Hütlein und das Hörnlein

ONCE UPON A TIME there were three brothers. They'd been getting poorer and poorer, and finally their distress was such that they were starving and had nothing left to eat. "It can't go on like this," they said, "we'd better go out in the world and seek our fortune." So they set out and had walked a long distance and had covered a lot of ground but still hadn't found their fortune. One day they got into a large forest in the middle of which was a mountain, and on getting nearer, they saw that the mountain was of solid silver. Then the eldest said, "Now I've found the good fortune I've been seeking and ask for none greater." He took as much of the silver as he could carry, then turned about and went back home. But the other two said, "We expect something more in the way of good fortune than mere silver," didn't touch it, and went on. After walking a few days more they came to a mountain of solid gold. The second brother stopped, reflected and hesitated. "What shall I do?" he said. "Shall I take so much gold that I'll have enough for the rest of my life, or shall I go on farther?" Finally he made up his mind, filled his pockets as full as he could, said goodbye to his brother, and went home. But the third said, "Silver and gold mean nothing to me. I won't forswear my good fortune; perhaps something better is in store for me." He went on and after walking for three days came to a forest still larger than the others and apparently endless, and finding nothing to eat or drink he nearly perished. Then he climbed a high tree to find out whether from there he could see the limits of the forest, but as far as the eye could reach he saw nothing but treetops. He climbed down the tree again, but hunger tormented him and he thought, "If once again I could eat my fill!" On getting down, to his amazement he saw under the tree a table all set with dishes, whose savor rose to his nostrils. "This time," he said, "my wish has been fulfilled in the nick of time," and without asking who'd brought the food and who'd cooked it, he went up to the table and ate to his heart's content till he'd satisfied his hunger. When he'd finished, he thought, "It's really a pity to let the fine tablecloth spoil here in the forest," folded it neatly and put it in his pouch. Then he went on, and in the evening when he got hungry again, he wanted to test his cloth. He spread it out and said, "Now I wish that you were once more covered with fine dishes." Hardly had the wish passed his lips when dishes with the finest food appeared, as many as there was room for. "Now," he said, "I see in what kitchen the cooking is done for me! You'll be dearer to me than the silver and gold mountain!" for he saw clearly that it was a cloth-be-laid [cp. No. 36].

Still, the cloth wasn't enough to make him settle down at home; he preferred rather to keep wandering about in the world and try his fortune further. One evening in a lonely forest he met a charcoal burner all black with charcoal dust; he was burning charcoal there, had potatoes on the fire, and was going to make his meal of them. "Good evening, Blackbird," he said, "how are you getting on in your solitude?" "One day's like another," answered the charcoal burner, "and potatoes every evening. Do you want some, and will you be my guest?" "Thanks a lot," answered the traveler, "I won't deprive you of your meal; you weren't counting on a guest. However, if you'll put up with me, let me invite you." "Who's going to prepare it for you?" said the charcoal burner; "I see that you haven't anything with you, and there's no one within a couple of hours of here who could give you anything." "Just the same," he answered, "it'll be a meal better than any you've ever tasted." Thereupon he took his cloth out of the knapsack and spreading it on the ground, said, "Cloth, be laid!" and at once all sorts of good food was there and was as hot as if it had just come from the kitchen. The charcoal burner looked very astonished but didn't have to be asked twice. He helped himself and kept putting bigger and bigger pieces into his black mouth. When they'd finished eating, the charcoal burner smiled contentedly and said, "Listen, I approve of your cloth; it would be just the thing for me in the forest where there's no one to cook anything good for me. I propose an exchange:

over there in the corner is hanging an army knapsack which, true enough, is old and doesn't look like much, but it has marvelous powers. Since, however, I no longer need it, I'm willing to exchange it with you for the cloth." "I must first know what sort of marvelous powers these are," he replied. "I'll tell you," answered the charcoal burner, "every time you rap on it with your hand, a corporal appears with six men armed from head to foot and they'll carry out your every order." "All right," he said, "if you insist, then let's exchange," gave the charcoal burner his cloth, took the knapsack down from the hook, slung it on his back, and said good-bye.

When he'd gone some distance, he wanted to test the magic powers of his knapsack and rapped on it. Immediately the seven war heroes appeared before him, and the corporal said, "What does my lord and master wish?" "March off on the double to the charcoal burner and demand my wishing cloth back." They made a left turn and in no time brought what he'd asked for, having taken it from the charcoal burner without much ado. He bade them withdraw again and went on, hoping to meet with still better fortune. At sundown he came to another collier who was preparing his evening meal by the fire. "Do you want to eat with me?" said the sooty fellow; "potatoes and salt but no drippings. If so, sit down with me." "No," he answered, "this time you shall be my guest," and spread out his cloth, which was at once covered with the finest dishes. They ate and drank together and were in good spirits. After the meal the collier said, "Up there on the rooftree is an old worn-out cap with strange properties. If one puts it on and turns it around on one's head, culverins go off as if twelve were lined up together and they shoot down everything, so that no one can stand up against them. The cap's no use to me, and I'm quite willing to exchange it for the cloth." "That's a bargain!" he answered, took the cap and, putting it on, left his cloth behind. He'd gone but a short distance before rapping on his knapsack, and his soldiers had to bring him back his cloth. "Nothing succeeds like success," he thought, "and I feel that my good fortune has not yet come to an end." Nor was he wrong in this thought. After walking still another day he came to a third charcoal burner who, like the others, invited him to a meal of potatoes without drippings. However, he asked the collier to eat with him off his wishing cloth, and the food tasted so good to the latter that in the end he offered him in exchange a horn, which had quite other properties than the cap. When one blew it, all walls and fortifications, indeed, all cities and villages collapsed. True enough, he gave the collier the cloth for it but afterward had his men demand it back, so that finally he had the knapsack, the cap, and the horn. "Now," he said, "I'm a made man, and it's time for me to return home and find out how my brothers are getting along."

By the time he got home, his brothers had built a fine house with their silver and gold and were leading a gay life. He went in, but since he arrived in a half-tattered coat with the shabby cap on his head and the old knapsack on his back, they wouldn't acknowledge him as their brother. They made fun of him, saying, "You claim to be our brother who scorned silver and gold and asked better luck for himself. He'll certainly come in all splendor, driving up as a mighty king and not as a beggar," and they chased him out the door. Then he flew into a rage, rapped on his knapsack till a hundred and fifty men stood lined up before him. He ordered them to surround his brothers' house. Two were to take along hazel rods and tan the two insolent fellows' hides till they knew who he was. There was a frightful uproar: the crowd gathered and wanted to help the two in their plight but could do nothing against the soldiers. Finally a report of this reached the king; he became indignant and had a captain march out with his company and chase the troublemaker out of town. But the man with the knapsack soon had a larger crew assembled, which repulsed the captain and his soldiers so that they had to retire with bloody noses. "We'll tame this vagabond," said the king and the following day sent a larger detachment against him, but it was able to accomplish even less, for he opposed still greater numbers and, to end the business even quicker, turned his cap around on his head a couple of times. Then the artillery began to come into play, and the king's men were beaten and put to flight. "Now I shan't make peace," he said, "until the king gives me his daughter in marriage and I'm ruling the whole kingdom in his name." He had the king notified of this, and the latter said to his daughter, "Need will have its way. What can I do but what he demands? If I want to have peace and keep my crown on my head, I must surrender you."

So the wedding was celebrated, but the king's daughter was vexed because her husband was a commoner and wore a shabby cap and had an old knapsack on his back. She'd gladly have been rid of him again and day and night thought how she might bring this about. Then she thought, "Can his magic powers be in the knapsack?" dissembled, and caressed him, and when his heart softened, said, "If only you'd take off the wretched knapsack! It's so unbecoming to you that I can't but be ashamed of you." "Dear child," he answered, "this knapsack is my greatest treasure; as long as I have it, I fear no power in the world," and confided in her the magic powers with which it was endowed. Then she fell on his neck as if to kiss him but deftly removed the knapsack from his shoulder and ran off with it. As soon as she was alone, she rapped on it and ordered the veterans to arrest their former master and to lead him out of the royal palace. They obeyed, and the false woman had still more men follow him and chase him right out of the country. Now he would have been lost if he hadn't had the cap, but no sooner were his hands free than he waved it a couple of times: at once the guns began to thunder, leveling everything, and the king's daughter had to come herself and beg for mercy. Since she begged so movingly and promised to reform, he let himself be persuaded and granted her peace. She feigned friendliness with him, pretended that she loved him dearly, and after some time succeeded in deluding him so that he confided in her that even if one got hold of his knapsack, the person wouldn't be able to accomplish anything against him so long as the old cap was still his. When she learned the secret, she waited till he was asleep, then took away his cap and had him thrown out in the street. However, he still had the horn left and in great anger blew it with all his might. At once everything collapsed: walls, fortifications, cities, and villages, killing the king and his daughter, and if he hadn't put the horn down and had he blown it just a little longer, everything would have collapsed and not one stone would have remained on top of the other.

Then no one opposed him any longer, and he set himself
up as king of the whole realm.

55 Rumpelstilts

Rumpelstilzchen

ONCE UPON A TIME there was a miller who was poor but who
had a pretty daughter. By chance he got an opportunity to
speak with the king and, in order to make an impression, said
to him, "I have a daughter who can spin straw into gold."
"That's a skill I very much like" said the king to the miller.
"If your daughter is as clever as you say, bring her tomorrow
to my palace, and I'll test her." When the girl was brought
to him, he took her into a room full of straw, gave her a spinning wheel and spindle and said, "Now get to work! And if
by tomorrow morning you haven't spun this straw into gold,
you're doomed to die." Then he personally locked the room, and
she was all alone there.

The poor miller's daughter sat there and for the life of her
didn't know what to do. She had no idea how to spin straw
into gold, and her fear increased until she finally began to weep.
Suddenly the door opened, and a little dwarf came in and said,
"Good evening, miller's daughter. Why are you weeping so?"
"Alas," answered the girl, 'I'm supposed to spin straw into gold
and don't know how." "What will you give me," said the
dwarf, "if I spin it for you?" "My necklace," said the girl. The
dwarf took the necklace, sat down at the spinning wheel, and
whir, whir, whir, three pulls and the spool was full. Then he
put on a second and, whir, whir, whir, three pulls and the second was full, too, and so it went till morning. Then all the
straw was spun and all the spools were full of gold. At sunrise
the king appeared and, seeing the gold, was amazed and joyful,
but his heart grew ever greedier for gold. He had the miller's

daughter taken into another still larger room full of straw and ordered her to spin it, too, in one night, if she valued her life. The girl didn't know what to do and wept. Again the door opened, and the dwarf appeared, saying, "What will you give me if I spin the straw into gold?" "The ring from my finger," answered the girl. The dwarf took the ring, again began to make the spinning wheel whir, and by morning had spun all the straw into glittering gold. At the sight of it the king was frightfully happy but still didn't have enough gold and had the miller's daughter taken into an even larger room full of straw, saying, "This room, too, you must spin tonight; if, however, you succeed, you shall be my wife." "Even if she's just a miller's daughter," he thought, "I won't find a richer wife in the whole wide world." When the girl was alone, the dwarf appeared for the third time and said, "What will you give me if I spin the straw into gold this time, too?" "I've nothing left that I can give you," answered the girl. "Promise me then your first child, if you become queen." "Who knows how things will turn out," thought the miller's daughter and in her plight, not knowing what to do, promised the dwarf what he asked. In return the dwarf once again spun the straw into gold. In the morning when the king came and found everything as he had desired, he celebrated his wedding with her, and the pretty miller's daughter became a queen.

After a year she brought a fine baby into the world and no longer gave any thought to the dwarf. Then he suddenly came into her room, saying, "Now give me what you promised." The queen was frightened and offered the dwarf all the riches of the kingdom if he'd leave her the child, but the dwarf said, "No, a living being is dearer to me than all the treasures in the world." Then the queen began so to lament and weep that the dwarf took pity on her. "I'll give you three days," he said; "if in that time you know my name, you may keep your child."

The whole night through the queen thought of all the names she'd ever heard and sent a messenger across country to enquire far and wide of any other names there might be. When the dwarf came the next day, she began with Caspar, Melchior, and Balthasar, and recited in order all the names she knew, but each time the dwarf would say, "That's not my name." The second day she had enquiries made around in the neighborhood about the names of the people there and recited to the dwarf the strangest and most unusual names. "Is your name by chance Skeleton Beast? or Sheep's Tail? or Boot Lace?" Every time he'd answer, "That's not my name." On the third day the messenger came back and said, "I haven't been able to discover a single new name, but on coming around the corner of the forest to a high mountain, where the fox and the hare say goodnight to one another, I saw a little house with a fire burning outside it and a most ridiculous dwarf hopping around the fire on one foot, crying,

> "Today I'm baking, tomorrow I'll brew,
> Day after tomorrow I'll fetch the queen's child;
> Oh, what a fine thing it is that no one knows
> That my name is Rumpelstilts!"

You can imagine the queen's joy on hearing the name, and when the dwarf came in shortly after and asked, "Well, Lady Queen, what's my name?" she asked first, "Is it Conrad?" "No." "Is it Harry?" "No."

> "Is it perhaps Rumpelstilts?"

"The Devil told you! the Devil told you!" screamed the dwarf and in his anger drove his right foot so deep into the ground that he went down to his waist. Then in his rage he seized his left foot with both hands and tore himself right in two.

56 Lover Roland

Der liebste Roland

ONCE UPON A TIME there was a woman who was a real witch. She had two daughters: one ugly and bad, whom she loved because she was her own daughter, and one beautiful and good, whom she hated because she was her stepdaughter. On one occasion the stepdaughter had a pretty apron which so took the other girl's fancy that she grew envious and told her mother that she wanted the apron and had to have it. "Quiet, my child," said the old woman, "you shall have it all right. Your stepsister has long since deserved to die. Tonight when she's asleep, I'll go and cut off her head. Just be careful to lie on the far side of the bed and push her well to the front." The poor girl would have been done for if she hadn't been standing in a corner and overheard everything. She wasn't allowed to go out all that day, and when it was bedtime, the stepsister had to climb into bed first, in order to lie on the far side. But when the stepsister had fallen asleep, she pushed her gently toward the front and took the place on the far side by the wall. In the night the old woman came creeping up: in her right hand she held an ax, with her left first felt around to see if someone really was lying in the front part of the bed. Then she grasped the ax with both hands, swung it, and cut off her own child's head.

When she'd gone away, the girl got up and went to see her lover, whose name was Roland, and knocked at his door, and when he came out, said to him: "Listen, dearest Roland, we must flee in haste; my stepmother intended to kill me but hit her own child. When day breaks and she sees what she's done, we're lost." "Just the same," said Roland, "I advise you first to take away her magic staff, otherwise we shan't be able to save ourselves if she sets after us and pursues us." The girl fetched the magic staff and then took the dead girl's head and let three drops of blood drip on the floor, one by the bed, one in the kitchen, and one on the stairs. Then she hastened off with her lover.

When the old witch got up in the morning, she called her daughter and was going to give her the apron, but she didn't come. Then she called out, "Where are you?" "Why, here on the stairs, sweeping," replied one drop of blood. The old woman went out but saw no one on the stairs and called a second time, "Where are you?" "Why, here in the kitchen, warming myself," cried the second drop of blood. She went into the kitchen but found no one. Then once again she called out, "Where are you?" "Why, here in bed, sleeping," cried the third drop of blood. She went into the room to the bed. What did she see there! Her own child swimming in her blood, whose head she herself had cut off.

The old witch fell into a rage and rushed to the window and since she was able to see far into the world, spied her stepdaughter hurrying away with her lover Roland. "That will do you two no good," she cried; "though you're already far away, even so you won't escape me." She put on her seven-league boots, in which she covered a league with every step, and it wasn't long before she'd overtaken them both. However, on seeing the old woman striding along, the girl with the witch's staff changed her lover Roland into a lake and herself into a duck swimming in the middle of it. The witch took up a position on the shore, threw in bits of bread, and did her best to lure the duck. But the duck wouldn't be lured, and in the evening the old woman had to go back home, having accomplished nothing. Then the girl and her lover Roland resumed their natural forms and went on all night until daybreak. Then the girl changed herself into a beautiful flower blooming in the middle of a hawthorn hedge and her lover Roland into a fiddler. Not long till the witch came striding up and said to the fiddler, "Dear fiddler, may I please pluck the pretty flower?" "Why, yes," he answered, "I'll strike up a tune while you're doing it." As she hurriedly crept into the hedge to pluck the flower—for she well knew who the flower was—he began to play a tune and, willy-nilly, she couldn't help dancing, for it was a magic dance tune [cp. No. 110]. The faster he played, the more violently she had to jump about, and the thorns tore off her clothes, pricked her till she was bloody and wounded, and since he didn't stop, she had to dance till she lay dead.

Once they were freed, Roland said, "Now I'm going to my father and arrange for the wedding." "Then I'll stay here in the meantime and wait for you," said the girl, "and so that no one may recognize me, I'll change myself into a red field stone." Then Roland went off, and the girl lay in the field in the form of a red stone and waited for her lover. But when Roland got home, he fell into the toils of another woman, who made him forget the girl. The poor girl stayed there a long time, but when finally he didn't come back and didn't come back, she grew sad and changed herself into a flower, thinking, "Someone will probably come along and trample me down."

Now a shepherd was by chance tending his sheep in the field and saw the flower and, because it was so beautiful, plucked it, took it with him, and put it in his box. From that time queer things went on in the shepherd's house. On getting up in the morning he'd find that all the work had already been done, the room swept, table and benches dusted, the fire laid on the hearth, and the water drawn, and when he'd come home at noon, the table would be set and a good meal served. He couldn't imagine how that happened, for he never saw a human being in his house, nor could anyone have hidden himself in the little hut. Quite true, he liked this good service, but finally he got frightened and, going to a wise woman, sought her advice. The wise woman said, "There's magic back of this. Just look some morning very early and see whether anything's moving about in the room. If you see anything, no matter what, quickly throw a white cloth over it; then the magic will be checked." The shepherd did as she said, and next morning at daybreak he saw the chest open of itself and the flower come out. He rushed up to it quickly and threw a white cloth over it. At once the transformation was at an end and before him stood a beautiful girl, who confessed that she'd been the flower and up to that moment had been keeping house for him. She told him her fate, and because he liked her, he asked her whether she'd marry him. But she answered no, for she intended to remain faithful to her lover Roland though he had forsaken her. However, she promised not to go away and said she'd continue to keep house for him.

Now the time came when Roland was to celebrate his wedding. Then, according to old custom it was proclaimed throughout the land that all girls should present themselves and sing in honor of the bridal couple. On hearing this the faithful girl grew so sad that she thought her heart would break. She didn't want to go, but the others came and took her along. When it was her turn to sing, she hung back, until she was the only one left, and then there was nothing for her to do but sing. When she began her song and it reached Roland's ears, he jumped up, crying, "I know that voice; that is the right bride; I want no other." Everything he'd forgotten and that had slipped from his mind had suddenly come back to him. Then the faithful girl celebrated her wedding with her lover Roland; her suffering was now at an end and her joy began.

57 The Gold Bird

Der goldene Vogel

IN OLDEN TIMES there was a king who had beautiful grounds behind his palace. In the grounds stood a tree which bore gold
apples. When the apples got ripe, they were counted, but the
very next morning one was missing. This was reported to the
king, and he ordered that watch be kept under the tree every
night. The king had three sons, and as night came on, he sent
the eldest to the garden. When it was midnight he couldn't fight
off sleep, and the following morning another apple was again
missing. The next night the second son had to mount watch but
fared no better. When it struck twelve, he fell asleep, and in
the morning an apple was missing. Now it was the third son's
turn to stand watch. He, too, was quite willing, but the king
didn't have much confidence in him, thinking that he'd accomplish even less than his brothers. Finally, however, he gave
his permission, so the youth lay down under the tree, kept
watch, and didn't let sleep overpower him. When it struck
twelve, something rustled in the air, and in the light of the
moon he saw a bird flying along whose feathers shone with
solid gold. The bird lighted on the tree and had just pecked
off an apple when the youth shot an arrow at it. The bird
flew away, but the arrow had struck its plumage, and one of
its gold feathers dropped down. The youth picked it up, took
it next morning to the king, and told him what he'd seen in
the night. The king assembled his council, and everyone declared that a feather like this was worth more than the whole
kingdom. "If the feather is so precious," said the king, "I shan't
be satisfied with just one but will and must have the whole
bird."

The eldest son set out, trusting to his cleverness, and thought
he'd surely find the gold bird. When he'd gone some distance,

he saw a fox sitting by the edge of the forest and, leveling his gun, took aim at it. "If you don't shoot me," cried the fox, "I'll give you a good piece of advice in return. You're on your way to the gold bird and this evening you'll come to a village where two inns face one another. One will be brightly lighted and fun will be going on there. Don't turn in there but go into the other, even though it's of mean appearance." "How can such a silly creature be giving me sensible advice?" thought the king's son, and pulled the trigger. But he missed the fox, which, straightening out its tail, ran quickly into the forest. Then he continued on his way and in the evening came to the village with the two inns. In one there was singing and dancing, while the other had a poor and sorry appearance. "I'd certainly be a fool," he thought, "if I went into the shabby inn and avoided the fine one." So he entered the gay inn, led a merry life there, and forgot the bird, his father, and all good advice.

When some time had passed and the eldest son didn't come home and didn't come home, the second son set out to look for the gold bird. Like the eldest he met the fox, who gave him the good advice, which he didn't heed. He came to the two inns, at the window of one of which his brother was standing and from which the noise of revelry resounded. His brother called out to him, and he couldn't resist the temptation, went in, and did nothing but gratify his desires.

Again some time passed. Then the king's youngest son wanted to set out and try his luck. But his father wouldn't allow it, saying, "It's useless; he's even less likely to find the gold bird than his brothers, and if he meets with an accident, he won't know what to do. He hasn't got it in him." Finally, however, when the boy left him no peace, he let him set out. Again the fox was sitting outside the forest, begged for its life, and gave the good piece of advice. The youth was goodhearted and said, "Don't worry, little fox, I won't hurt you." "You won't regret it," answered the fox, "and, to get on faster, climb onto my tail." No sooner had he sat down than the fox began to race at full speed, so that the wind whistled through his hair. When they came to the village, the youth got off, acted on the good advice, and without looking about, went into the mean inn, where he quietly spent the night.

Next morning when he came out into the field, the fox was

already sitting there and said, "I'm going to tell you what else you've got to do. Keep going straight on; finally you'll reach a palace before which a whole troop of soldiers will be lying. However, pay no attention to them, for they will all be sleeping and snoring. Walk right through them and straight into the palace. Go through all the rooms, and finally you'll reach a chamber where there's a gold bird in a wooden cage. Beside it is an empty gold cage just there as an ornament, but be careful not to take the bird out of its poor cage and put it in the splendid cage, otherwise you'll come to grief." After these words the fox again straightened out its tail and the king's son sat down on it; then they raced at full speed, so that the wind whistled through his hair. Arriving at the palace, he found everything as the fox had said. The king's son came to the chamber where the gold bird was in the wooden cage while a gold cage stood beside it, and three golden apples were lying about in the room. He thought it would be ridiculous to leave the beautiful bird in the mean and ugly cage, opened the cage door, took hold of it, and put it in the gold cage. At that very moment, however, the bird uttered a piercing cry. The soldiers awoke, rushed in, and took him off to prison. Next morning he was brought to trial and, since he confessed to everything, was sentenced to death. But the king said he'd grant him his life on the condition that he'd fetch him the gold horse which was swifter than the wind; in that case he should receive as a reward the gold bird in addition to his life.

The king's son set out, but he sighed and was sad, for where would he find the gold horse? All of a sudden he saw his old friend the fox sitting by the wayside. "You see," said the fox, "it happened that way because you didn't listen to me. But take heart, I'll champion your cause and tell you how to get to the gold horse. You must go straight ahead and you'll come to a palace where the horse is stabled. The grooms will be lying outside the stable but will be sleeping and snoring, and you may take the gold horse right out. But you must be careful about one thing: put the mean wood and leather saddle on it, not the gold saddle which is hanging near by, otherwise you'll get into trouble." Then the fox straightened out its tail, the king's son sat down on it, and off they raced at full speed, so that the wind whistled through his hair. Everything happened as the fox had said: he went into the stable where the gold horse was standing, but when he was about to put the mean saddle on it, he thought, "A beautiful animal like that will be insulted if I don't put on the fine saddle to which it's entitled." But scarcely had the gold saddle touched the horse than it began to neigh loudly. The grooms woke up, seized the youth, and threw him into prison. Next morning he was sentenced to death by the court, but the king promised to grant him his life and the gold horse in the bargain if he could fetch the beautiful princess from the gold palace.

With heavy heart the youth set out but by good luck soon found the faithful fox. "I should now abandon you to your misfortune," said the fox, "but I'm sorry for you and once more will help you out of your difficulty. Your way leads straight to the gold palace. You'll arrive there in the evening, and at night when all is still, the beautiful princess will go to the bathhouse to take her bath there. When she goes in, rush at her and give her a kiss; then she'll follow you, and you'll be able to take her away with you. But don't think of letting her first take leave of her parents, otherwise you'll get into trouble." Then the fox straightened out its tail, the king's son sat down on it, and off they raced at full speed, so that the wind whistled through his hair. When he got to the gold palace, it was as the fox had said. He waited till about midnight when everybody was fast asleep and the fair damsel went to the bathhouse; then he rushed out and gave her a kiss. She said she'd gladly go with him but implored him with tears in her eyes to permit her first to take leave of her parents. At first he resisted her request, but when she kept on weeping and fell at his feet, he finally gave in. No sooner had the damsel stepped up to her father's bedside than the latter and everybody else in the palace woke up, and the youth was arrested and put in prison.

Next morning the king said to him, "Your life is forfeit, and you'll be pardoned only if you remove the mountain which is before my windows and blocks my view, and that you must accomplish within eight days. If you succeed, you shall have my daughter as a reward." The king's son set to work, dug and shoveled unceasingly, but when after seven days he saw how little he'd accomplished and that all his labor amounted to so much as nothing, he fell into a state of great depression and gave up all hope. In the evening of the seventh day, however, the fox appeared and said, "You don't deserve my championing your cause; all the same, just go over there and go to sleep. I'll do the work for you." Next morning when he woke up and looked out the window, the mountain had disappeared. Joyfully the youth went to the king and reported that his condition had been fulfilled, and whether he would or no, the king had to keep his word and give him his daughter.

The two set out together, and before long the faithful fox joined them. "True enough, you've got the best thing," it said, "but with the damsel from the gold castle goes the gold horse, too." "How am I to get that?" asked the youth, "I'll tell you," answered the fox, "first of all take the fair damsel to the king who sent you to the gold castle. There'll be tremendous rejoicing; they'll gladly give you the gold horse and will lead it out to you. Mount it at once and shake everybody's hand good-bye, last of all the fair damsel's. When you've got hold of her, pull her up in one motion and race away. No one will be able to overtake you, for the horse is swifter than the wind."

Everything was accomplished successfully, and the king's son took the fair damsel away on the gold horse. The fox didn't stay behind but said to the youth, "Now I'll help you get the gold bird, too. When you're close to the palace where the bird is, have the damsel dismount, and I'll take her under my protection. Then ride the gold horse into the palace yard. On seeing this there will be great rejoicing, and they'll bring you out the gold bird. When you have the cage in your hand, race back to us and take the damsel away with you again." When the plan had succeeded and the king's son was about to ride home with his treasures, the fox said, "Now you are to reward me for my help." "What do you demand for that?" said the youth. "When we reach the forest over there, shoot me dead and cut off my head and my paws." "That would be a fine expression of gratitude," said the king's son, "I can't possibly grant you that." "If you won't do it," said the fox, "then I must leave you. But before I go, I'll give you a good piece of advice. Beware of two things: don't ransom anybody from the gallows and don't sit down on the edge of any well." With that it ran into the forest.

The youth thought, "That's a queer animal with strange notions. Who'd ransom a man from the gallows! And I've never had the slightest desire to sit down on the edge of a well." He rode on with the fair damsel, and his way again led him through the village where his two brothers had stayed. There was a great noise and uproar there, and when he asked what the matter was, they said that two people were to be hanged. On coming nearer he saw that they were his two brothers who had been up to all sorts of bad tricks and had squandered all their possessions. He asked if there wasn't some way to ransom them. "If you're willing to pay for them," answered the people, "but why should you want to waste your money on these evil-doers and ransom them?" However, he didn't hesitate, bought them off, and when they'd been released, they continued their journey in company.

They came to a forest where they'd first met the fox, and since it was cool and pleasant there and the sun very hot, the two brothers said, "Let's rest here a bit by the well and eat and drink." He agreed and in the course of the conversation forgot himself and sat down on the edge of the well, suspecting no harm. But the two brothers pushed him backward into the well, took the damsel, the horse, and the bird, and rode home to their father. "Here we're bringing not only the gold bird," they said, "but we've also got the gold horse and the damsel from the gold palace." There was great rejoicing, but the horse didn't eat, the bird didn't sing, and the damsel sat and wept.

The youngest brother had not perished, however. Fortunately the well was dry, and he landed on soft moss without being hurt, though he couldn't get out again. Even in this predicament the faithful fox didn't desert him but jumped down to where he was and scolded him for having forgotten his advice. "Nevertheless, I can't leave it at that," it said, "I'll help you to the light of day again." It told him to take hold of its tail and to hold onto it tight, and then it pulled him out. "Even now you're not altogether out of danger," said the fox. "Your brothers weren't certain of your death and all around the forest have mounted guards who are to kill you if you show yourself." A poor man was sitting by the wayside, with whom the youth changed clothes and thus reached the king's court. No one recognized him, but the bird began to sing, the horse to eat, and the fair damsel stopped weeping. Astonished, the king asked,

"What can that mean?" The damsel said, "I don't know, but I was so sad and now I'm so happy. I feel as though my true bridegoom had come." She told him all that had happened, though the other brothers had threatened her with death should she give anything away. The king ordered all the people in the palace to be brought into his presence, and the youth, too, came in his ragged clothes in the guise of a poor beggar. The damsel, however, recognized him at once and fell on his neck. The wicked brothers were seized and executed, while he was married to the fair damsel and named the king's heir.

But what happened to the poor fox? A long time afterward the king's son once again went into the forest where he met the fox, who said, "Now you have everything you can wish for, but to my misfortune there's no end, and yet it's in your power to unspell me." Once again it implored him to shoot it and to cut off its head and its paws. Accordingly he did so, and no sooner was it done than the fox turned into a man and was none other than the brother of the fair princess, freed at last from the spell under which he'd lain. And now there was no limit to their happiness as long as they lived.

58 The Dog and the Sparrow

Der Hund und der Sperling

THERE WAS A SHEEPDOG whose master was unkind and let it starve. When it could stand it with him no longer, it went away very sad. On the highway it met a sparrow, which said, "Brother dog, why are you so sad?" "I'm hungry," answered the dog, "and have nothing to eat." Then the sparrow said, "Dear brother, come along with me to town, and I'll see that you get enough," so together they went to town. When they were outside a butcher's shop, the sparrow said to the dog, "Stay here and I'll peck a piece of meat down for you," settled on the counter, looked about to see whether anybody was noticing it, and pecked and pulled and tugged so long at a piece of meat lying near the edge that it slid off. Then the dog seized it, ran into a corner, and ate it up. "Now come along with me to another shop," said the sparrow, "and I'll pull down a second piece for you, so that you may have enough." When the dog had eaten the second piece, too, the sparrow asked, "Brother dog, have you all you want?" "Yes, indeed, as far as meat is concerned," it answered, "but I haven't had any bread yet." "You shall have that, too," said the sparrow, "just come along." The sparrow led it to a baker's shop and pecked at a couple of rolls till they rolled down, and when the dog wanted still more, led it to another shop and again got down some bread for it to eat. When that was eaten up, the sparrow said, "Brother dog, have you had all you want?" "Yes," it replied, "now let's take a little walk outside the town."

Then the two walked out on the highway. The weather was warm, and when they had gone on a bit, the dog said, "I'm tired and should very much like to sleep. "All right, just go to sleep," answered the sparrow, "meanwhile I'll perch on a twig." So the dog lay down on the highway and fell fast asleep. As it lay and slept, a carter came along with a cart drawn by three horses and loaded with two casks of wine. The sparrow saw that he wasn't going to turn out but that he was staying in the rut in which the dog was lying, so it cried out, "Carter, don't do that, or I'll make a poor man of you." But the carter grumbled to himself, "You won't make a poor man of me," cracked his whip and drove the cart over the dog, so that it was killed by the wheels. Then the sparrow cried, "You've run over my brother dog and killed it; that will cost you your cart and your nag." "Just fancy! cart and nag!" said the carter, "how could you hurt me?" and went on. The sparrow crept under the tarpaulin and pecked at one of the bungholes till it got the bung loose, and all the wine ran out without the carter noticing it. But once when he looked back, he saw that the cart was dripping, examined the casks, and found one of them empty. "Alas, poor me!" he exclaimed. "Not poor enough yet," said the sparrow and lighting on the head of one of the horses, pecked out its eyes. When the carter saw that, he pulled out his pickax and was about to hit the sparrow, but the sparrow flew up, and the carter hit his horse on the head so that it fell down dead. "Alas, poor me!" he cried out. "Not poor enough yet," said the sparrow and, when the carter went on with the two horses, again crept under the tarpaulin and pecked loose the bung of the second cask, too, so that all the wine slopped out. When he noticed this, the carter again exclaimed, "Alas, poor me!" but the sparrow answered, "Not yet poor enough," lighted on the head of the second horse and pecked its eyes out. The carter ran up and aimed a blow at it with his pickax, but the sparrow flew up, and the blow hit the horse so that it dropped dead. "Alas, poor me!" "Not poor enough yet," said the sparrow and, lighting on the head of the third horse, pecked at its eyes. In his anger the carter, without looking, aimed a blow at the sparrow, missed it, however, and killed his third horse, too. "Alas, poor me!" he cried out. "Not poor enough yet," exclaimed the sparrow, "now I'm going to ruin you at home," and flew away.

The carter had to leave the cart and went home full of rage and anger. "Alas!" he said to his wife, "what terrible luck I've had! The wine ran out, and all three horses are dead." "Alas, husband," she said, "what wretched bird has flown into our house! It's collected all the birds in the world, and they've lighted on our wheat up there and are eating it up." Then he climbed up, and thousands upon thousands of birds were sitting in the loft and had been eating up the wheat, and the sparrow was sitting in their midst. Then the carter cried, "Alas, poor me!" "Not yet poor enough," answered the sparrow, "it'll even cost you your life, carter," and flew out.

Since the carter had lost all his property, he went down into his sitting room, sat down behind the stove, and was in a poisonous mood. The sparrow, however, was sitting outside the window and cried, "Carter, it'll cost you your life." Then the carter seized the pickax and threw it at the sparrow but all he did was to break the windowpanes without hitting the bird. Then the sparrow hopped into the room, lighted on the stove, and cried, "Carter, it'll cost you your life." The latter, beside himself with blind rage, smashed the stove to pieces, and as fast as the sparrow flew from one spot to another, he smashed all his furniture: mirror, benches, table, and finally the walls in his house, but couldn't hit it. Finally, however, he caught it in his hand. Then his wife said, "Shall I kill it?" "No," he cried, "that would be too mild; it shall die a much more cruel death;

I'm going to swallow it," took it and swallowed it in one gulp. But the sparrow began to flutter inside him, fluttered up again into the man's mouth, then sticking out its head cried, "Carter, it'll cost you your life!" The carter handed his wife the pickax and said, "Wife, kill the bird in my mouth." The wife aimed a blow but missed and hit the carter right on the head, so that he dropped dead.

The sparrow, however, flew up and away.

59   Freddy and Katy Lizzy

Der Frieder und das Katherlieschen

THERE WAS ONCE A MAN whose name was Freddy and a woman whose name was Katy Lizzy. They were married and were living together as a young married couple. One day Freddy said, "Now I'm going out to the field, Katy Lizzy; when I get back, there must be something fried on the table to satisfy my hunger, also a cool drink to quench my thirst." "Go right along, Freddy dear," answered Katy Lizzy, "go right along; everything will be fixed up for you, of course." As mealtime drew near, she took a sausage from the chimney, put it in a frying pan, added butter, and set it on the fire. The sausage started frying and sizzling while Katy Lizzy stood there holding the pan handle, plunged in thought. Then she had a bright idea. "While the sausage is cooking, you might go down cellar and draw the drink," so she propped up the handle, took a jug, went down cellar, and drew the beer. The beer ran into the jug and Katy Lizzy looked on. Then she thought, "Look here, the dog upstairs hasn't been shut up; it might get the sausage out of the pan—that's what!" and was up the cellar stairs in a jiffy. But her spitz already had the sausage in its mouth and was dragging it off along the floor. Katy Lizzy, however, slow about nothing, went after it and chased it some distance into the fields. Nevertheless the dog was quicker than she, didn't drop the sausage but skipped off across the fields. "No use crying over spilt milk," said Katy Lizzy, turned about and since she'd got tired running, walked good and slow and cooled herself off. Meanwhile the beer had been running out of the keg, for Katy Lizzy hadn't turned off the spigot, and when the jug was full and there was no more room for it, it ran into the cellar and didn't stop till the whole keg was quite empty. While still on the stairs Katy Lizzy saw the accident. "Oh, bother!" she cried, "what can you do so that Freddy won't notice it?" She thought a while and finally remembered that a sack of fine wheat flour, bought at the last fair, was still up in the loft, and planned to fetch it down and sprinkle it over the beer. "Indeed," she said, "a stitch in time saves nine," went up to the loft, brought down the sack, and threw it right on the jug full of beer, so that it upset and Freddy's drink, too, was swimming about in the cellar. "That's quite all right," said Katy Lizzy, "the two belong together," and sprinkled the flour all over the cellar. When she had done, she was highly pleased with her work and said, "How clean and neat it looks here now."

At noon Freddy came home. "Well, wife, what have you got for me?" "Oh, Freddy," she answered, "I was going to fry a sausage for you, but while I was drawing the beer to go with it, the dog got it out of the pan, and while I was running after the dog, the beer ran out, and as I was about to dry up the beer with the flour, I upset the jug, too. But don't worry, the cellar is quite dry again." "Katy Lizzy, Katy Lizzy!" said Freddy, "you shouldn't have done that—let the sausage be run away with and the beer run out of the keg and on top of it all throw our fine flour away." "Why, Freddy, I didn't know that; you ought to have told me."

The husband thought, "If your wife is like that, you must watch out better." He'd saved up a tidy sum in silver dollars, which he changed into gold and said to Katy Lizzy, "Look here, these are yellow chicks. I'm going to put them in a pot and bury them in the stable under the cow manger. See to it that you keep away from them or you'll get into trouble." "No, Freddy dear," she said, "I certainly won't touch them." When Freddy had gone, some hucksters with earthenware bowls and pots for sale came into the village and enquired at the young woman's whether she hadn't anything to trade. "Alas, good people," said Katy Lizzy, "I haven't any money and can't buy anything, but if you can use some yellow chicks, of course I'll buy something." "Yellow chicks, why not? Let's see them." "Well, go into the stable and dig under the manger, then you'll find the yellow chicks. I mayn't go along with you." The rogues went there, dug, and found just gold, with which they went off, leaving pots and bowls behind in the house. Katy Lizzy thought she ought to make some use of the new kitchenware, but because there was already plenty of that in the kitchen, she knocked the bottom out of every pot and then put them as ornaments on the fence palings around the house. When Freddy came and saw the new ornaments, he said, "Katy Lizzy, what have you been doing?" "I bought it, Freddy dear, with the yellow chicks that were under the manger. I didn't go there myself; the hucksters had to dig them up for themselves." "Oh, wife," said Freddy, "what have you done! Those weren't chicks. It was solid gold and was our whole fortune! You shouldn't have done that." "Yes, Freddy dear," she answered, "but I didn't know that; you ought to have told me beforehand."

Katy Lizzy stood a while thinking, then said, "Listen, Freddy dear, we'll get the gold back all right. We'll run after the thieves." "Come along then," said Freddy, "and let's try it. However, take some butter and cheese so we'll have something to eat on the way." "Yes, Freddy dear, I'll bring some along." They set out, and because Freddy was the faster walker, Katy Lizzy trailed behind him. "That's in my favor," she thought, "when we turn around, I'll have a head start." They came to a hill with deep ruts on both sides of the road. "Just look," said Katy Lizzy, "how they've torn, ground down, and oppressed the poor Earth! It won't recover as long as it lives!" Out of pity of heart she got out the butter and greased the ruts right and left, so that they wouldn't suffer so much from the wheels, and while she was stooping over in her work of charity, a cheese rolled out of her pocket and down hill. "I've climbed up the hill once," said Katy Lizzy, "and I'm not going down again; let another cheese run and fetch it back." So she took another cheese and rolled it down. The cheeses, however, didn't come back, and she let a third roll down, thinking, "Perhaps they're wating for company and don't like to walk alone." When all three failed to come back, she said, "I don't know what that means, but it's possible that the third missed the way and went astray. I'll just dispatch the fourth to call them back." But the fourth fared no better than the third. Then Katy Lizzy lost her temper and threw the fifth and sixth down, too, and they were the last. She stopped for a while, waiting for them to come back, but when they didn't come and didn't come, she said, "Oh, you're just the right messengers to send to fetch Death; you're so slow coming! Do you think I'll wait for you any longer? I'm going along and you may come after me; your legs are younger than mine." Katy Lizzy went on and found Freddy, who'd stopped and was waiting, because he very much wanted something to eat. "Now let's have what you've brought along." So she handed him the dry bread. "Where's the butter and cheese?" asked her husband. "Oh, Freddy," said Katy Lizzy, "I greased the ruts with butter, and the cheeses will be along soon; one of them ran away from me, and then I sent the others after it to call it." "You shouldn't have done that, Katy Lizzy," said Freddy, "greasing the road with butter and rolling the cheeses down hill." "Yes, Freddy dear, but you ought to have told me."

They both ate the dry bread, and Freddy said, "Katy Lizzy, did you lock up the house when you left?" "No, Freddy, you ought to have told me beforehand." "Then go home again and lock up the house before we go any farther. Also bring along something else for us to eat. I'll wait for you here." On her return, Katy Lizzy thought, "Freddy will want to eat something else; he certainly doesn't like butter and cheese, so I'll bring along some dried fruit and a jug of vinegar to drink." Then she bolted the upper half of the door but took the lower half off the hinges and shouldered it, thinking, if she'd put the door in safekeeping, that the house couldn't but be well guarded. Katy Lizzy took her time walking back, thinking, "Freddy will have all the more time to rest up in." When she'd rejoined him, she said, "There, Freddy, here you have the front door! Now you can lock up the house yourself." "Good heavens!" he said, "what a clever wife I've got! She takes the lower half of the door off the hinges so that everybody can walk in, and bolts the upper half! Now it's too late to go home again, but since you brought the door here, you shall carry it the rest of the way yourself." "I'll carry the door, Freddy, but the dried fruit and the jug of vinegar are getting too heavy for me. I'll hang them on the door and the door can carry them."

Now they went into the forest to look for the rogues but didn't find them, and because it was at last getting dark, they climbed a tree and were going to spend the night there. No sooner were they up in it than some fellows came along, the kind who carry off what doesn't want to go along and who find things before they are lost. They settled down right under the very tree in whose branches Freddy and Katy Lizzy were sitting, made themselves a fire, and were about to divide their booty. Freddy climbed down the other side and collected stones, then climbed up again and was going to stone the rogues to death, but the stones missed the mark, and the rogues called out, "It's nearly morning and the wind is shaking down the pine cones." Katy Lizzy still had the door on her shoulder, and since it pressed on her so, she thought that the dried fruit was to blame and said, "Freddy, I've got to throw down the dried fruit." "No, Katy Lizzy, not now," he answered, "it might give us away." "Oh, Freddy, I must! it's far too heavy for me." "Well, do it then in the Devil's name!" Then the dried fruit rolled down through the branches, and the fellows below said, "That's bird droppings." After a while, since the door still pressed on her, Katy Lizzy said, "Oh, Freddy, I've got to pour the vinegar out." "No, Katy Lizzy, you mustn't do that; it might give us away." "Oh, Freddy, I must! it's far too heavy for me." "Well, do it then in the Devil's name!" Then she poured out the vinegar so that it spattered on the fellows, who said to one another, "The dew is already falling." Finally Katy Lizzy thought, "Could it be the door that's so heavy?" and said, "Freddy, I've got to throw the door down." "No, Katy Lizzy, not now, it might give us away." "Oh, Freddy, I must! it's far too heavy for me." "No, Katy Lizzy, hold on tight to it." "Oh, Freddy, I'm dropping it!" "All right," answered Freddy angrily, "then drop it in the Devil's name!" Then it fell down with a crash, and the fellows below cried out, "The Devil is coming down the tree," and took to their heels, leaving everything behind. In the morning when the two climbed down the tree, they found all their gold again and brought it home.

When they were back home, Freddy said, "Katy Lizzy, now you've got to be industrious and work hard." "Yes, Freddy, of course I shall. I'm going into the field and mow the grain." When Katy Lizzy was out in the field, she said to herself, "Shall I eat before reaping or sleep before reaping? Well, I'd rather eat." Then Katy Lizzy ate, and as she ate she grew sleepy and began to mow and half dreaming mowed up all her clothes, apron, skirt, and shirt. When Katy Lizzy woke up again after a long nap, she stood there half naked and said to herself, "Is it me or isn't it me? Alas, it isn't me!" Meanwhile night had come on, and Katy Lizzy went to the village, knocked at her husband's window, and called out, "Freddy." "What's the matter?" "I'd like to know whether Katy Lizzy is in." "Yes," answered Freddy, "probably she's in and asleep." "All right," she said, "then I'm surely at home already," and ran off.

Outside Katy Lizzy ran into some rogues who were out to steal. She joined them, saying, "I want to help you steal." The rogues thought that she must know the lay of the land and liked the idea. Katy Lizzy went up to the houses, calling out, "You people, have you got anything? We want to steal." Then the rogues thought, "That's a fine way to do!" and wishing they were rid of Katy Lizzy, said to her, "There are turnips in the parson's field outside the village. Go there and pull us some." Katy Lizzy went out into the country and began to pull turnips, but she was so lazy that she didn't pick them up. A man passing by saw her and stopped, thinking it was the Devil rooting about like that in the turnips. He ran to the village to the parson and said, "Parson, the Devil is in your beet field pulling up the turnips." "Good gracious!" answered the parson, "I've a lame foot and can't go out and exorcise him." "I'll carry you piggy-back," said the man and carried him out that way. When they got to the field, Katy Lizzy straightened herself up. "Ah, the Devil!" cried the parson, and both hurried off, and in his great fright the parson was able to run faster with his lame foot than the man with sound legs who'd carried him piggy-back.

60   The Two Brothers

Die zwei Brüder

ONCE UPON A TIME there were two brothers, one rich and one poor. The rich brother was a goldsmith and of evil disposition; the poor brother, who earned his living making brooms, was good and honest. The poor brother had two children, twin brothers who were as like as two peas. From time to time the two boys would go to the rich uncle's house and once in a while would get something to eat from the scraps. Now the poor man, when going into the forest to gather faggots, happened to see a bird that was of solid gold and more beautiful than any he'd ever laid eyes on before. He picked up a pebble, threw it at it, and was lucky enough to hit it. However, only one gold feather dropped down, and the bird flew away. The man took the feather and brought it to his brother, who, looking at it, said, "It's solid gold," and gave him a lot of money for it. Next day the man was climbing a birch tree to cut a few branches; then the same bird flew out of it, and after a search the man found a nest with an egg in it, and the egg was of gold. He took the egg home and showed it to his brother, who again said, "It's solid gold," and gave him what it was worth. Finally the goldsmith said, "I'd certainly like to have the bird itself!" The poor man went a third time into the forest and again saw the gold bird sitting in a tree. He picked up a stone, brought the bird down, and took it to his brother, who gave him a whole lot of money for it. "Now I've enough to get along on," thought the poor man and went home content.

The goldsmith was clever and guileful and well knew what kind of bird it was. He called his wife and said, "Roast me the gold bird and see to it that no part of it is lost. I want to eat it all myself." Now this was no ordinary bird but was of such marvelous power that whoever ate its heart and liver would find a gold piece under his pillow every morning. The wife prepared the bird, put it on a spit, and roasted it. While it was on the fire and the woman by chance had to leave the kitchen on account of other work, the poor broommaker's two children came in, stopped before the spit and gave it a couple of turns, and since just then two little pieces dropped out of the bird into the pan, one of them said, "Let's eat the two little pieces. I'm so hungry, and no one will notice it." Then both ate the two pieces. The woman came along, however, and seeing them eating something, said, "What have you been eating?" "A couple of pieces that dropped out of the bird," they answered. "That was the heart and liver," said the woman terribly frightened, and that her husband shouldn't miss them and get angry, she quickly killed a cockerel, took out its heart and liver, and put them in the gold bird. When the bird was done, she served it to the goldsmith, who ate it all himself and left nothing. The following morning, however, when he reached under his pillow expecting to fetch out the gold piece, there was no more there than any other time.

The two children didn't know what their good fortune was. Next morning when they got up, something fell to the ground with a ringing sound, and when they picked it up, there were two gold pieces. They took them to their father, who, astonished, said, "How can this have happened?" When the next morning they again found two gold pieces and every day the same, he went to his brother and told him the strange story. The goldsmith knew at once how this had come about and that the children had eaten the gold bird's heart and liver, and in order to avenge himself and because he was envious and hardhearted, he said to the father, "Your children are in league with the Evil One. Don't take the gold and don't tolerate them any longer in your house, for he has a hold on them and may bring you yourself to damnation." The father was afraid of the Evil One and, hard as it was for him, took the twins out into the forest and sad of heart left them there.

Now the two children ran about in the forest, tried to find the way home but couldn't find it, and went farther and farther astray. Finally they met a huntsman, who asked, "Whose children are you?" "We're the poor broommaker's boys," they answered and told him that their father didn't want to keep them at home any longer because every morning there was a gold piece under their pillows. "Well," said the huntsman, "that isn't really anything terrible as long as you remain honest and don't turn into lazybones." Since he liked the children and had none of his own, the good man took them home with him, saying, "I'm willing to be your father and bring you up." He taught them hunting and, in case they might need them in the future, saved for them the gold piece that each found on getting up in the morning.

When they were grown up, their foster father one day took them along with him into the forest and said, "Today you're to shoot your final test so that I may release you from your apprenticeship and declare you huntsmen." They went along with him to the hunting station and waited a long time, but no game appeared. The huntsman looked up and seeing a flock of snow-geese flying in a triangle, said to one of them, "Bring down one from each corner," and the boy was successful in his final test. Soon after another formation came flying along in the shape of a figure two; then the huntsman had the other boy likewise bring down one bird from each corner, and his final test was successful, too. Then the foster father said, "I release you; you're accomplished huntsmen." Then the two brothers went into the forest together, took counsel, and came to an agreement. When that evening they sat down to supper, they said to their foster father, "We shan't touch the food or eat a morsel until you grant us one request." "What is your request?" he said. "We've now mastered our craft," they answered, "and must try our skill out in the wide world, too; so give us leave to depart and go our way." Joyfully the old man said, "You're speaking like good huntsmen. What you ask is just what I've been wishing. Go forth and you'll get on well." Then they ate and drank happily together.

When the appointed day arrived, the foster father gave them each a good gun and a dog and had each take as much as he wanted of the gold pieces that had been saved up from his share. He went with them for a bit of the way and, when he said good-bye, gave them a bright and shiny knife, saying, "If ever you separate, be sure to drive the knife into a tree at the parting of your ways. Then if one comes back, he'll be able to see how his absent brother has fared, for the side of the blade facing the way either of you goes will rust if he dies but will stay shiny as long as he's alive." The two brothers kept on and on and got into a forest so large that they couldn't possibly get out of it in one day, so they spent the night there, eating what they'd put in the hunting pouches. They went on a second day, too, without getting out. Since they had nothing to eat, one of them said, "We've got to shoot something, otherwise we'll go hungry," loaded his gun and looked about. When an old hare came running by, he raised his gun, but the hare cried out,

> "Dear huntsman, let me live
> And I'll even give you two of my young."

Forthwith it hopped into the bushes and fetched two of its young. However, the little animals played so gaily and were so nice that the huntsmen hadn't the heart to kill them, so they kept them, and the little hares followed at their heels. Soon after a fox slunk by. They were about to shoot it, but the fox called out,

> "Dear huntsman, let me live
> And I'll even give you two of my young."

It, likewise, brought two fox cubs, which the huntsmen didn't want to kill, either, but added them to the hares for company and they followed them. Not long after a wolf came out of the thicket. The huntsmen aimed at it, but the wolf cried,

> "Dear huntsman, let me live
> And I'll even give you two of my young."

The huntsmen added the two wolf cubs to the other animals, and they went along with them. Then came a bear, who very much wanted to trot about alive a while longer and called out,

> "Dear huntsman, let me live
> And I'll even give you two of my young."

The two young bears were added to the others, and now there were already eight of them. Finally, who should come along but a lion shaking its mane, but the huntsmen weren't afraid of it and aimed their guns at it. The lion also said,

> "Dear huntsman, let me live
> And I'll even give you two of my young."

It, too, fetched its cubs, and so the huntsmen had two lions, two bears, two wolves, two foxes, and two hares, which followed them and served them. Meanwhile none of this had satisfied their hunger, and they said to the foxes, "Listen, you skulkers, get us something to eat, for you're artful and crafty." "Not far from here," they answered, "is a village where in the past we've got many a chicken. We'll show you the way there." They went into the village, bought themselves some food, also had their animals fed, and then went on. The foxes knew about the neighborhood, knew where the chicken yards were, and could guide the huntsmen properly everywhere.

They moved about for a time but could find no position where they might stay together, so they said, "There's no other way; we must separate." They divided the animals between them so that each got one lion, one bear, one wolf, one fox, and one hare. Then they said good-bye, vowed brotherly love until death, and drove the knife their foster father had given them into a tree. Thereupon, one went east, the other west.

Together with his animals the youngest reached a city that was all hung with black crepe. He went into an inn and asked the innkeeper if he couldn't put his animals up. The innkeeper gave them a stable with a hole in the wall; then the hare crept through and fetched a head of cabbage for itself while the fox got a hen and, when he had eaten that, the cock to boot. The wolf, the bear, and the lion being too big couldn't get out, so the innkeeper had them taken right to where a cow was lying in the grass that they might eat their fill. When the huntsman had cared for his animals, the first thing he did was to ask the innkeeper why the city was hung with mourning crepe. "Because tomorrow our king's only daughter is going to die," said the innkeeper. "Is she mortally ill?" asked the huntsman. "No," answered the innkeeper, "she's hale and hearty, but she's got to die just the same." "Why so?" asked the huntsman. "Outside the city is a high mountain where a dragon lives which must every year have a pure virgin, otherwise it ravages the whole country. All virgins have now been delivered up, and not one is left but the king's daughter. There's no mercy, however; she must be delivered up to it, and that's to take place tomorrow." "Why don't they kill the dragon?" said the huntsman. "Alas!" answered the innkeeper, "so many knights have tried it, but all have paid for it with their lives. The king has promised to give his daughter in marriage to the man who conquers the dragon, and he's also to inherit the kingdom after his death."

The huntsman said nothing further but next morning took his animals and with them climbed up the dragon mountain. At the top stood a little church, and on the altar were three tumblers, and by them was a piece of paper with the words written on it, "Whoever drains the tumblers will become the strongest man on earth and will wield the sword which lies buried outside the threshold." The huntsman didn't take a drink but went out and looked for the sword in the ground, couldn't budge it, however. Then he went back and drained the tumblers and was now strong enough to draw out the sword, and his hand was able to wield it with great ease. When the hour came for the maiden to be delivered up to the dragon, she was escorted out by the king, the marshal, and the courtiers. From afar she saw the huntsman up on the dragon mountain and thought that the dragon was standing there waiting for her. She didn't want to go, but finally she had to make the painful journey, for otherwise the whole city would have been lost. The king and courtiers returned home greatly grieving, but the king's marshal had to remain and witness everything from a distance.

When the king's daughter got to the top of the mountain, it wasn't the dragon that was there but the young huntsman, who consoled her and said that he was going to save her, led her into the church, and locked her up in it. Shortly after the seven-headed dragon came along with a great roar and on seeing the huntsman was astonished and said, "What are you doing up here on the mountain?" "I want to fight you," answered the huntsman. "So many a knight has lost his life here!" said the dragon, "I'll settle with you, too," and breathed fire from seven mouths. The fire was supposed to light the dry grass and the huntsman was supposed to suffocate in the fire and vapor, but the animals came running up and trampled out the fire. Then the dragon went for the huntsman, but the latter brandished his sword so that it sang in the air and cut off three of its heads. Then the dragon got really furious, rose up in the air, spewed flames over the huntsman and was about to rush upon him. The huntsman, however, once again whipped out his sword and cut off three more of its heads. The monster grew exhausted and sank down, and even so wanted to go for the huntsman again, but with his last ounce of strength the huntsman cut off its tail, and no longer able to fight, summoned his animals, who tore it to pieces. When the fight was over, the huntsman unlocked the church and found the king's daughter lying on the ground, for she had fainted from anxiety and fright while the fight had been going on. He carried her out, and when she again came to and opened her eyes, he showed her the dragon's torn carcass and told her that she was now free. She was glad and said, "Now you will become my dear husband, for my father promised me in marriage to the man who killed the dragon." She took off her coral necklace and divided it among the animals as a reward. The lion was given the gold clasp, and her handkerchief with her name on it she presented to the huntsman. The latter went and cut out the tongues from the dragon's seven heads, wrapped them in the handkerchief, and put them carefully away.

When that was done, and because he was worn out and tired from the fire and the fight, he said to the maiden, "We're both so worn out and tired that we'd better take a little nap." She assented, and they lay down on the ground, and the huntsman said to the lion, "You're to watch out that no one attacks us while we're sleeping," and both fell asleep. The lion lay down beside them to keep watch, but it, too, was tired from the fight, so it called the bear and said, "Lie down beside me. I must get a little sleep, and if anything comes, wake me up." Then the bear lay down beside it, but it, too, was tired, and calling the wolf, said, "Lie down beside me. I've got to get a little sleep, and if anything comes, wake me up." Then the wolf lay down beside it, but it, too, was tired and, calling the fox, said, "Lie down beside me. I've got to get a little sleep, and if anything comes, wake me up." Then the fox lay down beside it, but it, too, was tired and calling the hare, said, "Lie down beside me. I've got to get a little sleep, and if anything comes, wake me up." Then the hare sat down beside it, but the poor hare, too, was tired, had no one on whom it could call to keep watch, and fell asleep. Thus the king's daughter, the huntsman, the lion, the bear, the wolf, the fox, and the hare were sleeping, and all slept soundly.

When, however, the marshal, who was supposed to look on

from afar, didn't see the dragon fly away with the maiden, and when everything up on the mountain became quiet, he took heart and climbed up. There lay the dragon on the ground torn to pieces and not far off the king's daughter and a huntsman with his animals all fast asleep. Because he was a bad and wicked man, he took his sword and cut off the huntsman's head, seized the maiden in his arms, and carried her down the mountain. She woke up and was frightened, but the marshal said, "You're in my power and must say that it is I who killed the dragon." "I can't do that," she replied, "for it was a huntsman and his animals who did it." Then he drew his sword and threatened to kill her if she didn't obey him and thus forced her to promise to do what he said. Then he brought her into the presence of the king, who was beside himself with joy on seeing his dear child alive. He'd thought she'd been torn to pieces by the monster. The marshal said to him, "I've killed the dragon and freed the maiden and the whole realm; accordingly I ask for her hand in marriage as was promised." "Is he telling the truth?" the king asked the maiden. "Alas, yes," she answered, "it must be true, of course. Nevertheless I stipulate that the wedding not be celebrated for a year and a day," for she hoped to hear in the meantime some word from her dear huntsman.

Up on the dragon mountain the animals were still lying asleep beside their dead master. A big bumble-bee came and settled on the hare's nose, but the hare brushed it away with its paw and went on sleeping. The bee came a second time, but the hare again brushed it off and went on sleeping. Then it came a third time and stung it on the nose so that it woke up. As soon as the hare was awake, it woke up the fox, and the fox woke up the wolf, the wolf the bear, and the bear the lion. When the lion woke up and saw that the maiden was gone and that its master was dead, it began to roar terribly, crying out, "Who did that? Bear, why didn't you wake me up?" The bear asked the wolf, "Why didn't *you* wake me up?" and the wolf asked the fox, "Why didn't *you* wake me up?" and the fox asked the hare, "Why didn't *you* wake me up?" The poor hare was the only one who was left with no answer and had to take the blame. They were about to fall upon it, but it begged them, saying, "Don't kill me! I'll bring our master back to life. I know of a mountain where a certain root grows, and whoever takes it in his mouth will be cured of all diseases and healed of all wounds. The mountain is, however, a two-hundred-hours' walk from here." "You must run there and back in twenty-four hours," said the lion, "and bring the root back with you." The hare raced off and in twenty-four hours was back with the root. The lion replaced the huntsman's head, the hare put the root in his mouth, and at once everything grew together again and the heart beat and life returned. Then the huntsman woke up, was frightened on no longer seeing the maiden, and thought, "She probably went away while I was asleep in order to get rid of me." In its great haste the lion had put its master's head on backwards, though the latter didn't notice it, since he was thinking sadly of the king's daughter. It wasn't till noon, when he wanted to eat something, that he saw that his head was on backwards, couldn't understand it, and asked the animals what had happened to him in his sleep. Then the lion told him that they'd all fallen asleep from fatigue and on waking up had found him dead with his head cut off, that the hare had fetched the Root of Life, and that in its haste the lion had held his head the wrong way around but was anxious to correct its mistake. Then it tore off the huntsman's head again, turned it around, and healed him again with the root.

The huntsman, however, was sad, wandered about in the world and had his animals dance before the public. Exactly a year later he chanced to return to the same city where he had freed the king's daughter from the dragon, and this time the city was all hung with scarlet. He said to the innkeeper, "What does this mean? A year ago the city was hung with crepe. What is the point of the scarlet today?" "A year ago," replied the innkeeper, "our king's daughter was to be delivered up to the dragon, but the marshal fought it and killed it, and tomorrow their wedding is to be celebrated. That's why the city at that time was hung with crepe as a sign of mourning and today with scarlet as a sign of rejoicing."

Next day when the wedding was to take place, the huntsman said at noon to the innkeeper, "Innkeeper, do you really believe that today I shall eat bread from the king's table with you here?" "Well," said the innkeeper, "I'd be willing to bet a hundred gold pieces that that isn't so." The huntsman took the bet and staked a purse with the same number of gold pieces against the innkeeper, then called the hare and said, "Go, dear Hopper, and fetch me some of the bread which the king is eating." The hare, being the least of the animals, couldn't put the task off on anybody else but had to go itself. "My!" it thought, "if I hop through the streets all alone like that, the butchers' dogs will be after me." It happened as it thought. The dogs came after it and were on the point of picking a quarrel with it, but it hopped away as you've never seen the like and took refuge in a sentry box without the soldier noticing it. The dogs came and wanted to get it out, but the soldier was having no nonsense and struck them with the butt of his gun so that they ran away crying and howling. When the hare saw that the coast was clear, it hurried into the palace and right to the king's daughter, sat down under her chair, and scratched her foot. "Get away, will you!" she said, thinking it was her dog. The hare scratched her foot a second time, and again she said, "Get away, will you!" thinking it was her dog. But the hare wasn't being put off and scratched a third time. Then she looked down and recognized the hare by its collar, and taking it in her lap, carried it to her room and said, "Dear hare, what do you want?" It replied, "My master, who killed the dragon, is here and sends me to beg for some bread such as the king eats." Then she rejoiced, had the baker come, and ordered him to bring her a loaf of bread such as the king was accustomed to eat. "The baker must also carry it for me," said the hare, "so that the butchers' dogs don't harm me." The baker carried it for the hare as far as the door of the taproom; then the hare got up on its hind legs, took the loaf in its forepaws, and brought it to its master. "See, innkeeper," said the huntsman, "the hundred gold pieces are mine."

The innkeeper was amazed and the huntsman went on to say, "Yes, innkeeper, I've got the bread all right; now I want to eat some of the king's roast, too." The innkeeper said, "I'd like to see that!" but wouldn't bet any more. The huntsman called the fox and said, "Dear fox, go fetch me a roast such as the king eats." The red fox knew the tricks better than the hare; it hugged nooks and corners without a dog noticing it, sat down under the chair of the king's daughter, and scratched her foot. She looked down, recognized it by its collar, took it with her to her room, and said, "Dear fox, what do you want?" It answered, "My master, who killed the dragon, is here and sends me to beg for a roast such as the king eats." Then she sent for the chef, who had to prepare a roast such as the king was accustomed to eat and had to carry it for the fox as far as the inn door. There the fox took the bowl from him, with its tail first whisked off the flies which had settled on the roast, and then brought it to its master. "Look, innkeeper," said the huntsman, "now there's bread and meat, but I also want vegetables such as the king eats."

Then he called the wolf and said, "Dear wolf, go fetch me vegetables such as the king eats." Being afraid of no one, the wolf went straight into the palace and when it entered the room of the king's daughter, tugged at her dress from behind, so that she had to look around. She recognized it by its collar, and taking it to her bed chamber, said, "Dear wolf, what do you want?" It answered, "My master, who killed the dragon, is here. I'm to beg for some vegetables such as the king eats." She sent for the chef, and he had to prepare vegetables such as the king was accustomed to eat and carry them for the wolf as far as the inn door. Then the wolf took the bowl from him and brought it to its master. "See, innkeeper," said the huntsman, "now I've got bread, meat, and vegetables, but I also want to eat some sweets such as the king eats."

He called the bear and said, "Dear bear, of course you're fond of sweets; go fetch me some sweets such as the king eats." The bear trotted to the palace, and everybody got out of its way. When it got to the sentries, they pointed their guns at it and didn't want to let it into the royal palace, but it stood on its hind legs and with its paws gave a few slaps right and left, so that the whole guard broke up. Then it went straight to the king's daughter, got behind her and growled a little. She looked around and, recognizing the bear, had it come along with her to her room and said, "Dear bear, what do you want?" It answered, "My master, who killed the dragon, is here; I'm to beg for sweets such as the king eats." Then she sent for the confectioner, who had to prepare sweets such as the king was accustomed to eat and carry them for the bear as far as the inn door. The bear first licked up such sugar plums as had rolled off, then stood up, took the bowl, and brought it to its master. "Look, innkeeper," said the huntsman, "now I've got bread, meat, vegetables, and sweets, but I also want to drink wine such as the king drinks."

He summoned his lion and said, "Dear lion, you like to drink yourself into your cups. Go fetch me wine such as the king drinks." The lion stalked across the street, and the people ran away from it. When it got to the sentries, they wanted to bar the way, but it roared just once and all ran off. Now the lion went to the royal apartment and knocked on the door with its tail. The king's daughter came out and was almost frightened at the lion but recognized it by the gold clasp from her necklace and had it come along with her to her room, saying, "Dear lion, what do you want?" It answered, "My master, who killed the dragon, is here; I am to beg for wine such as the king drinks." She summoned the cupbearer, who was to give the lion wine such as the king drank. "I'll go along," said the lion, "and see that I get the right wine." It went down with the cupbearer and when they got to the cellar, the cupbearer was about to draw for it some ordinary wine such as the king's servants drank, but the lion said, "Stop, let me first try the wine," drew itself half a measure and downed it in one gulp. "No," it said, "that's not the right wine." The cupbearer looked at it askance but proceeded to draw wine from another cask, which was for the king's marshal. "Stop," said the lion, "let me first try the wine," drew itself half a measure and drank it. "That's better, but still not the right wine." Then the cupbearer got angry and said, "What can such a stupid creature pretend to know about wine?" but the lion gave him a box on the ear so that he fell down hard on the ground. When he'd picked himself up again, without a single word he led the lion into a little private cellar where the king's wine was stored and of which no one ordinarily got a taste. The lion first drew itself half a measure and, trying the wine, said, "This is very likely the right kind," and had the cupbearer fill six bottles. Then they went upstairs, but when the lion got out of the cellar and into the open, it staggered about and was a little drunk, and the cupbearer had to carry the wine for it as far as the inn door. Then the lion took the basket in its mouth and brought it to its master. "Look, innkeeper," said the huntsman, "here I've got bread, meat, vegetables, sweets, and wine such as the king has. Now I'm going to dine with my animals," sat down, ate and drank, and gave the hare, the fox, the wolf, the bear, and the lion their share of it, and was in high spirits, for he saw that the king's daughter still loved him.

When he'd finished his meal, he said, "Innkeeper, I've eaten and drunk as the king eats and drinks; now I'm going to the king's court and marry his daughter." "How can that happen," asked the innkeeper, "since she already has a bridegroom, and the wedding is being celebrated today?" Then the huntsman pulled out the handkerchief which the king's daughter had given him on the dragon mountain and in which the monster's seven tongues were wrapped and said, "What I'm holding in my hand will help me in this matter." The innkeeper looked at the handkerchief and said, "Even if I believe everything else, I won't believe that, and I'm willing to wager my house and home on it." The huntsman took a purse with a thousand gold pieces, laid it on the table, and said, "I'll stake this against your bet."

At the royal board the king said to his daughter, "What did all the wild animals want which came to see you and went in and out of my palace?" "I mustn't tell," she answered, "but send for the animals' master and you'll be doing the right thing." The king dispatched a servant to the inn and invited the stranger. The servant arrived just as the huntsman had made his bet with the innkeeper and was saying, "Look, innkeeper, now the king is sending a servant and inviting me there, but I shan't go just yet," and to the servant he said, "I beg the lord king to send me royal clothes, a coach and six, and servants to wait on me." When the king heard the answer, he said to his daughter, "What shall I do?" She said, "Have him fetched the way he asks to be and you'll be doing the right thing." Then the king sent royal clothes, a coach and six, and servants to wait on him. When the huntsman saw them coming, he said, "See, innkeeper, now I'm being fetched in the manner I asked," put on the royal clothes, took the handkerchief with the dragons' tongues, and drove to the king. On seeing him coming, the king said to his daughter, "How shall I receive him?" "Go to meet him," she answered, "and you'll be doing the right thing." The king went to meet him and led him upstairs, and his animals followed him.

He assigned him a place between himself and his daughter; being the bridegroom, the marshal was sitting on the opposite side but no longer recognized him. At that moment the dragon's seven heads were displayed, and the king said, "The marshal cut off the dragon's seven heads and therefore I'm giving him my daughter in marriage today." Then the huntsman arose, opened the seven mouths, and said, "Where are the dragon's seven tongues?" The marshal got frightened, turned pale, and didn't know what answer to make, and finally in his anxiety said, "Dragons don't have tongues." "Liars oughtn't to have any," said the huntsman, "but the dragon's tongues are the mark of the victor," and undid the handkerchief, in which lay all seven of them. Then he put each tongue back in the mouth it belonged in and they fitted exactly. Thereupon he took the handkerchief, which was embroidered with the name of the king's daughter, and showing it to the maiden, asked her to whom she'd given it. "To the man who killed the dragon," she answered. He called his animals, took the necklace off each and from the lion the gold clasp and, showing it to the maiden, asked to whom it belonged. "The necklace and the gold clasp were mine," she replied; "I divided it among the animals which helped conquer the dragon." Then the huntsman said, "When, worn out from the fight, I was resting and sleeping, the marshal came and cut off my head, then carried off the king's daughter, and pretended it was he who'd killed the dragon. That he's been lying I prove by the tongues, the handkerchief, and the necklace." He then told how the animals had healed him by means of a marvelous root, that he'd wandered about with them for a whole year, and had finally come back here again, where from the innkeeper's story he learned of the marshal's deception. Then the king asked his daughter, "Is it true that this man killed the dragon?" and she answered, "Yes, it's true. Now I may reveal the marshal's infamy since it has come to light through no doing of mine, for he forced a promise of silence from me. That's why I insisted that the wedding was not to be celebrated for a year and a day." Then the king summoned twelve councilors to pass judgment on the marshal, and they sentenced him to be torn apart by four oxen. In this way the marshal was executed. The king gave his daughter to the huntsman and appointed him his lieutenant for the whole realm. The wedding was most joyfully celebrated, and the young king sent for his father and his foster father and heaped treasures upon them. Nor did he forget the innkeeper but had him come and said, "See, innkeeper, I've married the king's daughter, and your house and home are mine." "Yes," said the innkeeper, "that would be only fair," but the young king said, "Mercy shall be shown: you shall keep your house and home, and I'll make you a present of the thousand gold pieces in the bargain."

Now the young king and young queen were in good spirits and lived happily together. He often went out hunting, because he enjoyed it, and the faithful animals had to go along with him. In the vicinity was a forest which people said was haunted and that once in it, it wasn't easy to get out again. The young king, however, felt a strong desire to hunt in it and gave the old king no peace until he let him. He rode out with a big retinue and on getting to the forest saw a snow-white hind there and said to his men, "Stop here till I come back; I want to chase that fine quarry." He rode into the forest after it with only his animals with him. The retainers stopped and waited till evening, but he didn't come back. Then they rode home and told the young queen the story, "The young king pursued a white hind into the haunted forest and hasn't come back." She was greatly worried about him. He had, however, kept riding after the beautiful quarry without being able to overtake it. Every time he thought it within gunshot, he'd all at once see it racing off again at a great distance. Finally it disappeared altogether. Now noticing that he'd got deep into the forest, he took his horn and blew it but received no answer, for his men couldn't hear it. Since night was closing in and realizing that he couldn't get home that day, he dismounted, made a fire by a tree, and planned to spend the night there. As he was sitting by the fire and his animals, too, had lain down beside him, he seemed to hear a human voice, looked about but could see nothing. Soon after he again heard a moaning sound as if up somewhere. He looked up and saw an old woman sitting in the tree; she kept moaning, "Brr! brr! brr! I'm so cold." "Climb down," he said, "and warm yourself if you're cold," but she said, "No, your animals will bite me." "They won't hurt you, granny," he said, "just come down." She was, however, a witch and said, "I'm going to throw down a switch from the tree. If you'll hit them on the back with it, they won't harm me." She threw down a switch, and he hit them with it; at once they lay still and were turned to stone. When the witch was safe from the animals, she jumped down and touched him, too, with the switch and changed him to stone. Then she laughed and dragged him and the animals into a ditch where there were already a number of such stones.

When the young king didn't come back and didn't come back, the queen's worry and anxiety increased. Now it chanced that just at this time the other brother, who, when they separated, had gone east, returned to the kingdom. He'd been looking for employment and found none, had then wandered about here and there and had been having his animals dance in public. It occurred him that he'd like to take a look at the knife they'd driven into the tree trunk in order to find out how his brother was getting along. When he got there, half his brother's side was rusty, half still shiny. He got frightened and thought, "My brother must have met with some great misfortune, but maybe I can still save him, for half the knife is still shiny." He went west with his animals, and when he reached the city gate, the sentries met him and asked whether they were to announce him to his wife, saying that for some days the young queen had been in great anxiety about his absence and was afraid he'd perished in the haunted forest. The sentries were, of course, convinced that he was the young king in person, since he resembled him so and was, furthermore, followed by the wild animals. He realized that they were talking about his brother and thought, "I'd better pass myself off for him; in that way I can the more easily save him." Accordingly, he had the sentries accompany him to the palace, where he was received with great joy. The young queen had no idea but that he was her husband and asked him why he'd stayed away so long. "I lost my way in the forest," he answered, "and couldn't find my way out any sooner." In the evening he was taken to the royal bed, but he laid a double-edged sword between himself and the young queen. She didn't know what that meant yet didn't dare ask.

He stayed there a few days and meanwhile made every enquiry about the haunted forest. Finally he said, "I've got to hunt there again." The king and the young queen tried to dissuade him, but he insisted and set out with a large retinue. When he reached the forest, it happened with him just as with his brother: he saw a white hind and said to his men, "Stay here and wait until I come back. I want to chase that fine quarry," rode into the forest, and his animals ran after him. He was unable, however, to overtake the hind and got so deep in the forest that he had to spend the night there. When he'd made a fire, he heard a moaning sound above him, "Brr! brr! brr! how cold I am!" He looked up, and there sitting in the tree was the same witch. "If you're cold," he said, "then come down, granny, and warm yourself." "No," she answered, "your animals will bite me," but he said, "No, they won't hurt you." Then she cried out, "I'm going to throw down a switch. If you'll hit them with it, they won't harm me." When the huntsman heard this, he didn't trust the old woman and said, "I won't hit my animals. Come straight down or I'll fetch you." Then she cried, "What do you really think you'll do? You can't hurt me." "If you don't come," he answered, "I'll shoot you down." "Shoot away," she said, "I'm not afraid of your bullets." He raised his gun and took a shot at her, but the witch was proof against all lead bullets, uttered a piercing laugh, and cried, "You won't hit me yet!" The huntsman knew what to do, tore three silver buttons off his coat, and loaded his gun with them. Against these her arts were in vain, and when he pulled the trigger, she at once pitched down with a shriek. Then he set his foot upon her and said, "Old witch, if you don't immediately confess where my brother is, I'll seize you with both hands and throw you into the fire." She was very frightened and, begging for mercy, said, "He's lying with his animals in a ditch and has been turned into stone." Then he forced her to go there with him and threatened her, saying, "You old monkey, now you bring my brother and every creature that's lying here back to life, or else you land in the fire." She took a switch and touched the stones. Thereupon his brother and the animals came to life again, also many others—merchants, craftsmen, and herdsmen; they got up, thanked him for their deliverance, and went home. When the twin brothers saw one another again, they kissed each other and rejoiced greatly. Then they seized the witch, bound her, and put her in the fire, and when she was burned up, the forest opened of itself and was bright and light, and the royal palace could be seen three hours away.

The two brothers went home together and on the road related to one another their adventures. When the younger said that he was the king's lieutenant for the whole country, the other said, "I noticed that, for when I got to the city and was taken for you, I was shown every royal honor. The young queen took me for her husband, and I had to eat by her side and sleep in your bed." When the other heard that, he got so jealous and angry that he drew his sword and cut off his brother's head. When the latter lay dead and he saw his red blood flowing, he greatly regretted what he'd done. "My brother freed me," he exclaimed, "and in return I've killed him," and broke out into loud lamentations. Then his hare came and offered to fetch some of the Root of Life, raced off, and brought it just in time, and the dead man was revived and didn't notice his wound.

Then they went on, and the younger said, "You look like me, you're wearing royal clothes like myself, and the animals follow you as they do me. Let's go in through opposite gates and thus reach the old king at the same time from two sides." So they parted, and the sentries came to the old king at the same time from both gates, reporting that the young king with his animals had returned from the hunt. "It isn't possible," said the king; "the gates are an hour's distance apart." Meanwhile the two brothers came into the courtyard from two sides and both mounted the stairs. Then the king said to his daughter, "Tell me which is your husband; each looks like the other, and I can't tell them apart." Then she was in great distress and couldn't tell. Finally she remembered the necklace she'd given the animals, looked, and found her gold clasp on one of the lions. Then she cried joyfully, "The man whom this lion is following is my true husband!" Then the young king laughed and said, "Yes, that's the right one," and they sat down together at table, ate and drank and were merry. In the evening when the young king went to bed, his wife said, "Why did you always put a double-edged sword in our bed these last nights? I thought you were intending to kill me." Then he realized how loyal his brother had been.

61   The Crofter

Das Bürle

THERE WAS A VILLAGE in which lived none but rich farmers;
only one was poor, and they called him the crofter. He didn't
even have a cow, still less the money to buy one, though he
and his wife would so much like to have had one. Once upon
a time he said to her, "Listen, I have a good idea. There's our
friend the cabinetmaker; he must make us a calf out of wood
and paint it brown so as to look like any other calf. In time
it'll surely get good and big and become a cow." The woman
liked the idea, and with his plane friend cabinetmaker fashioned a proper calf, painted it brown, and made it so that it
lowered its head as if eating.

Next morning when the cows were driven to pasture, the
crofter called in the herdsman and said, "Look here, I've got
a calf, but it's still small and still has to be carried." "All right,"
said the herdsman, took it in his arms, carried it out to the
pasture, and set it down in the grass. The calf stayed right
there as if it were grazing, and the herdsman said, "It'll soon
be walking by itself; just see how it's already eating." In the
evening when he was going to drive the herd home again, he
said to the calf, "If you can stand on your legs and eat your
fill, you can perfectly well walk on your four legs, too. I've
no desire to carry you back home in my arms." The crofter
was standing outside his front door and waiting for his calf,
so when the herdsman drove the animals through the village
and the calf was missing, he enquired about it. "It's still standing out there grazing," answered the herdsman; "it wouldn't
stop and wouldn't come along." "My goodness!" said the
crofter, "I've got to have my animal back." Then together they
returned to the pasture, but somebody had stolen the calf and
it was gone. "It's no doubt gone astray," said the herdsman,
but the crofter said, "That's not good enough," and took the

herdsman to the magistrate, who for his negligence sentenced the former to give the crofter a cow for the calf that had got away.

Now the crofter and his wife had their long-wished-for cow. They were as happy as could be but had neither fodder nor anything else to give it, and so it soon had to be slaughtered. They cured the meat in salt, and the crofter went to town, intending to sell the hide there and buy a new calf with the proceeds. On the way he came to a mill where a raven was sitting with broken wings; out of pity he picked it up, wrapping it in the cowhide. Since the weather was getting very bad, with a strong wind and a driving rain, he couldn't go on, turned into the mill, and asked for lodging. The miller's wife was alone at home and said to the crofter, "Well, lie down on the straw," and gave him some bread and cheese. The crofter ate it and lay down with his cowhide beside him, and the woman thought, "He's tired and is asleep." Meanwhile the priest arrived. The miller's wife received him cordially, saying, "My husband's gone out, so let's give ourselves a treat." The crofter was listening, and when he heard talk about a treat, was vexed that he'd had to be satisfied with bread and cheese. Then the woman set the table and served up four things: a roast, salad, cake, and wine.

As they were sitting down and were about to eat, there was a knock at the door. "Good heavens!" said the woman, "that's my husband!" Quickly she hid the roast in the tile stove, put the wine under her pillow, the salad on the bed, the cake under the bed, and the priest in the cupboard in the entryway. Then she opened the door for her husband and said, "Thank God you're home again; this is regular Doomsday weather." The miller saw the crofter lying on the straw and asked, "What's that fellow doing there?" "Alas," said the woman, "the poor wretch came here in the storm and rain and asked for shelter, so I gave him some bread and cheese and a place on the straw." The husband said, "I've no objection to that, but get me something to eat quick." "I've nothing but bread and cheese," said the wife. "I'll be satisfied with anything," answered the husband, "even with bread and cheese," looked at the crofter and cried, "Come have something more to eat with me." The crofter didn't have to be asked twice, got up, and joined him in the meal. Afterward the miller noticed on the floor the hide in which the raven was wrapped and asked, "What have you there?" "I've got a fortune-teller in it," answered the crofter. "Can it tell my fortune, too?" said the miller. "Why not!" answered the crofter, "but it says only four things and keeps the fifth to itself." The miller was curious and said, "Let it go ahead and fortune-tell." Then the crofter squeezed the raven's head so that it croaked and went "caw, caw." "What did it say?" asked the miller. The crofter answered, "The first thing it said was that there's wine under the pillow." "The deuce!" cried the miller, went and found the wine. "Go on," said the miller. The crofter again made the raven croak and said, "The second thing it said was that there's a roast in the tile stove." "The deuce!" cried the miller, went and found the roast. The crofter made the raven go on fortune-telling and said, "The third thing it said was that there's salad on the bed." "The deuce!" cried the miller, went and found the salad. Finally the crofter, squeezing the raven once again so that it made a noise, said, "The fourth thing it said was that there's a cake under the bed." "The deuce!" cried the miller, went and found the cake.

Now the two sat down together at table, but the miller's wife was seized with a deadly fear, went to bed, and took all the keys with her. The miller would like to have known the fifth thing, too, but the crofter said, "Let's first eat the four other things in peace, for the fifth is something bad." So they ate and afterward dickered over what the miller should pay for the fifth prophecy, finally agreeing on three hundred dollars. Then the crofter once more squeezed the raven's head so that it uttered a loud croak. "What did it say?" asked the miller. "It said," answered the crofter, "that the Devil is in the cupboard out in the entryway." "The Devil has got to get out," said the miller and unlocked the front door. The wife was obliged to surrender the key, and the crofter unlocked the cupboard. Then the priest ran out as fast as he could, and the miller said, "I saw the Black Fellow with my own eyes; the raven was quite right." Next morning the crofter cleared out at dawn with his three hundred dollars.

At home, the crofter's situation gradually improved; he built a nice house, and the farmers said, "The crofter has surely been in the land where gold snow falls and where one carries money home by the bushel." Then the crofter was summoned into the presence of the magistrate and was to tell where his wealth came from. "I sold my cowhide in town for three hundred dollars," he answered. When the farmers heard that, they, too, wanted to profit by this, hurried home, killed all their cows and skinned them with a view to selling the hides in town at this big profit. The magistrate said, "My maid must go ahead of me, however." When the latter got to the merchant in town, he gave her only three dollars per hide, and when the others arrived, he didn't give them even that much, saying, "What can I do with all these hides?"

Now the farmers were vexed at having been tricked by the crofter, wanted to take vengeance on him, and lodged a complaint of fraud with the magistrate. By a unanimous verdict the innocent crofter was sentenced to death and was to be put in a cask full of holes and rolled into the water. He was taken out, and a priest was fetched to read a mass for his soul. All the others had to go away, and when the crofter looked at the clergyman, he recognized the priest who had been with the miller's wife and said to him, "I freed you from the cupboard, you free me from the cask." By chance a shepherd was driving a flock of sheep past, and the crofter knew that the latter had long wanted to become magistrate, so he shouted as loud as he could, "No, I won't do it! Even if the whole world wanted me to, I won't do it!" On hearing that, the shepherd came along and asked, "What's up? What is it you won't do?" "They want to make me magistrate if I'll just get into the cask," said the crofter, "but I'm not doing it." "If that's all there is to becoming magistrate," said the shepherd, "I'd get into the cask at once." "If you're willing to get into it," said the crofter, "you'll also be magistrate." The shepherd agreed, got in, and the crofter slammed on the head of the cask; then he took over the shepherd's flock and drove it off. The priest, however, went to his congregation and said that the requiem had been read. Then they came and rolled the cask toward the water. When it started rolling, the shepherd called out, "I'm quite willing to become magistrate." They had no idea but that it was the crofter who was crying out thus and said, "We think so, too, but first you're going to

have a look about down there," and rolled the cask into the
water.

Then the farmers went home, and as they entered the village,
there was the crofter coming along, too, driving in a flock
of sheep quite contentedly. "Crofter," said the astonished farmers, "where are you coming from? from out of the water?"
"Why, of course," answered the crofter. "I sank deep, deep
down, till at last I reached bottom; then I knocked out the
head of the cask and crawled out. There were lovely meadows
there with many lambs grazing on them, and I brought this
flock from there." "Are there still more there?" asked the farmers. "Why, yes," said the crofter, "more than you can use."
Then the farmers agreed that they, too, were going to fetch
themselves sheep, one flock apiece. "I come first!" said the
magistrate. Now they went together to the water just when
there were little woolly clouds in the blue sky that people
call "little lambs" and which were reflected in the water. Then
the farmers cried, "We can already see the sheep down on the
bottom." The magistrate pushed forward, saying, "Now I'll
go down first and take a look about. If everything is all right,
I'll call you." Then he jumped in and the water went "plop,"
and the others fancied that he was calling out "Come" to them,
and the whole crowd plunged after him in a hurry.

Thus the village died out, and as sole heir the crofter became
a wealthy man.

62 The Queen Bee

Die Bienenkönigin

ONCE UPON A TIME two sons of a king set out on adventures,
got into a wild and dissolute way of life, and never came home
again. The youngest son, who was called the Dunce, set out
to look for his brothers, but when he finally found them, they
made fun of him for expecting, simple as he was, to make his

way in the world while the two eldest couldn't succeed and yet were much cleverer. All three set out together and came to an ant hill. The two eldest wanted to kick it open, watch the little ants crawl about in their fright, and see them carrying away their eggs, but the Dunce said, "Leave the creatures in peace; I won't have you disturb them." They went on and reached a lake where a great, great many ducks were swimming. The two elder brothers wanted to catch a few and roast them, but the Dunce wouldn't have it and said, "Leave the creatures in peace; I won't have you kill them." Finally they came to a bees' nest with so much honey in it that it was running down the tree trunk. The two eldest brothers wanted to build a fire at the foot of the tree and smoke the bees out, so that they might remove the honey, but again the Dunce dissuaded them, saying, "Leave the creatures in peace; I won't have you burn them."

Finally the three brothers got to a palace where there were nothing but stone horses in the stables and not a human being to be seen. They went through all the rooms and at the very end reached a door with three padlocks. In the middle of the door, however, there was a peephole through which one could see into the room. There they saw a grey dwarf sitting at a table. They called out to him once, twice, but he didn't hear them. Finally they called a third time. Then he got up, unlocked the padlocks, and came out. He didn't utter a word but led them to a richly set table, and when they'd eaten and drunk, he took each to his own bedroom.

Next morning the grey dwarf came to the eldest, beckoned and led him to a stone tablet on which were inscribed three tasks by which the palace might be disenchanted. The first was as follows: 'Under the moss in the forest lie the pearls of the king's daughter, a thousand in number; these have to be searched out, and if by sundown even a single one is still missing, the seeker will be turned to stone.' The eldest went out and searched all day, but when the day was at an end, he had found only a hundred. It happened as was inscribed on the tablet: he was turned to stone. Next day the second brother undertook the adventure but didn't fare much better than the eldest. He found only two hundred pearls and was turned to stone.

Finally it was the Dunce's turn; he searched in the moss, but it was very hard to find the pearls and it went very slowly. Then he sat down on a stone and wept. As he was sitting thus, the king of ants, whose life he had once saved, came with five thousand ants, and it was no time at all before the tiny creatures had found all the pearls and piled them up in a heap. The second task was to fetch out of the lake the key to the bedroom of the king's daughter. When the Dunce reached the lake, the ducks he'd once saved came swimming up, dived down, and fetched the key from the bottom. The third task, however, was the hardest. From among the king's three sleeping daughters one had to pick the youngest and most beloved, but they looked exactly alike and were distinguished only in that before falling asleep they had eaten different kinds of sweets: the eldest a lump of sugar, the second a little sirup, the youngest a spoonful of honey. Then the queen bee whom the Dunce had saved from burning came flying up and sampled the mouths of all three. Finally she settled on the mouth which had eaten honey, and thus the king's son recognized the right daughter. Then the spell was broken, all three were freed from their sleep, and everybody who had been turned to stone regained his human shape. The Dunce married the youngest and most beloved and after her father's death became king. His two brothers, however, got the two other sisters.

63   The Three Feathers

Die drei Federn

ONCE UPON A TIME there was a king who had three sons. Of these, two were canny and clever, but the third didn't talk much, was simple-minded, and was just called the Dunce. When the king grew old and weak and began to think about his end, he didn't know which of his sons should inherit the kingdom after him. "Go out," he said to them, "and who-

ever brings me the finest carpet shall be king after my death."
To avoid any quarreling among them he led them outside
his palace, blew three feathers into the air, and said, "Where
they blow, there you go." The first feather flew east, the second west, the third, however, flew straight ahead and not far,
but soon dropped to the ground. One brother now went to
the right, and the second to the left, and they laughed at the
Dunce who had to stay where the third feather had dropped.

The Dunce sat down and was sad. He suddenly noticed a
trapdoor beside the feather; he lifted it up, found a stair, and
went down. Then he came to another door, knocked, and
heard a voice inside calling,

> "Maiden green and small,
> Hop-toad,
> Hop-toad's puppy,
> Hop to and fro!
> Let's see quickly who's outside."

The door opened of itself, and he saw a big fat toad sitting
there with a lot of little toads around about it. The big toad asked
what he desired. "I'd like to have the most beautiful and finest
carpet," he answered. Then it called a young toad and said,

> "Maiden young and small,
> Hop-toad,
> Hop-toad's puppy,
> Hop to and fro!
> Bring me the big box."

The young toad fetched the box. The fat toad opened it and
from it gave the Dunce a carpet more beautiful and fine than
anybody up on earth could have woven. He thanked the toad
and went up again.

The two others, however, regarded their youngest brother
as so stupid that they thought he'd find nothing and get nothing. "Why should we go to any great trouble with our search?"
they said, stripped the coarse rags off the first shepherd's wife
they met, and brought them home to the king. At the same
time the Dunce came back with his fine carpet. When the king
saw that, he was astonished and said, "By right the kingdom
belongs to the youngest." However, the two others left their

father no peace, saying that the Dunce, having no understanding of anything, couldn't possibly become king, and begged
him to establish a new condition. Then the father said, "Whoever brings me the finest ring shall inherit the kingdom," took
the three brothers outdoors, and blew into the air the three
feathers which they were to follow. The two eldest again went
east and west, but the Dunce's feather flew straight ahead and
dropped beside the opening in the earth. Again he went down
to the fat toad and told it he needed the finest ring. It had
its big box brought at once and from it gave him a ring sparkling with precious stones and more beautiful than any goldsmith on earth could have fashioned. The two elder brothers
laughed at the Dunce for going to look for a gold ring, took
no pains at all, just knocked the nails out of an old carriage
tire, and brought it to the king. But when the Dunce displayed
his gold ring, the father again said, "The kingdom belongs to
him." The two elder brothers didn't cease plaguing the king
until he established still a third condition and declared that
whoever brought home the fairest woman should have the kingdom. Once again he blew the three feathers into the air, and
they flew as on the previous occasions.

Without further ado the Dunce went down to the fat toad
and said, "I'm supposed to bring home the fairest woman."
"My!" answered the toad, "the fairest woman! She isn't right
on hand, but nevertheless you shall have her." It gave him
a scooped-out yellow turnip to which six mice were harnessed.
Then the Dunce said quite sadly, "What shall I do with that?"
"Just put one of my little toads in it," answered the toad. At
random he seized one out of the group and put it in the yellow
coach. No sooner was it inside than it became a most beautiful damsel, the turnip became a coach, and the six mice turned
into horses. Then he kissed her, raced off with the horses, and
brought her to the king. Later his brothers came; they'd taken
no pains at all to look for a beautiful woman but had brought
along the first peasant women they'd met. When the king saw
her, he said, "The kingdom belongs to the youngest after my
death." Once more the two eldest deafened the king's ears with
their outcries, saying, "We can't agree to the Dunce becoming
king," and demanded that preference be given to the one
whose woman could jump through a hoop that was hanging

in the middle of the hall. They thought, "The peasant women can do that easily; they're strong enough, but the delicate damsel will jump to her death." Once again the old king yielded. Then the two peasant women actually jumped through the hoop but were so clumsy that they fell and broke their big arms and legs. Then the fair damsel whom the Dunce had brought along, jumped, and jumped through as easily as a roe deer, and all opposition had to cease.

Accordingly he received the crown and ruled wisely for a long time.

64 The Gold Goose

Die goldene Gans

THERE WAS A MAN who had three sons; the youngest was called the Dunce and was despised and made fun of and slighted on every occasion. It happened that the eldest brother was going into the forest to chop wood, but before he set out, his mother gave him a nice fine pancake and a bottle of wine as well, lest he suffer from hunger or thirst. When he got to the forest, he met an old grey dwarf who bade him good day, saying, "Give me a piece of cake from your pouch and let me have a drink of your wine; I'm so hungry and thirsty." But the clever son answered, "If I give you my cake and my wine, I shan't have anything for myself. Get along with you!" left the dwarf standing there and went on. When he started chopping a tree, it wasn't long before he missed, and the ax went into his arm so that he had to go home and be bandaged. That, however, happened through the grey dwarf.

Next, the second son went into the forest, and his mother gave him, as she had the eldest, a pancake and a bottle of wine. He, too, met the old grey dwarf, who begged him for a piece of cake and a draught of wine. But the second son also quite sensibly said, "Whatever I give you I'll lack myself. Get along

with you!" left the dwarf standing there, and went on. The
punishment wasn't long coming: after giving the tree a few
blows, he cut his leg and had to be carried home.

Then the Dunce said, "Father, just let me go out and chop
wood." "Your brothers have hurt themselves doing it," answered the father; "keep away from it; you don't understand
the work at all." The Dunce, however, begged so long that
he finally said, "Well, go along, you'll learn by getting hurt."
His mother gave him a cake made with water and baked in
the ashes, also a bottle of sour beer. When he got to the forest,
he, too, met the old grey dwarf who greeted him, saying "Give
me a piece of your cake and a drink out of your bottle; I'm
so hungry and thirsty." "I've only cake baked in the ashes
and sour beer," answered the Dunce; "if you can put up with
that, let's sit down and eat." They sat down, and when the
Dunce took out his cake baked in the ashes, it was a choice
pancake, and the sour beer a good wine. They ate and drank,
and then the dwarf said, "Since you're so kindhearted and
gladly share what you have, I'll make you a present of good
luck. See the old tree there: cut it down and you'll find something among the roots." Then the dwarf said good-bye.

The Dunce went and cut down the tree. When it fell, there
among the roots was a goose with solid gold feathers. He lifted
the goose out, took it with him, and went to an inn where he
intended to spend the night. The innkeeper had three daughters; they saw the goose, were curious to know what kind of
a remarkable bird it was, and would have loved to have one
of its gold feathers. The eldest thought, "I'll surely get a chance
to pull out a feather," and on one occasion when the Dunce
stepped out, she seized the goose by the wing. But her fingers
and hand stuck fast to it. Soon after that the second came
with no other idea than to get a gold feather for herself, but
scarcely had she touched her sister than she stuck. Finally,
the third daughter, too, came with the same intention. Then
the others shouted, "Stay away! For heaven's sake stay away!"
but she didn't understand why she should stay away, and
thinking, "If they're there, I can be there, too," rushed up,
and on touching her sister stuck to her. Thus they had to
pass the night with the goose.

The next morning the Dunce took his goose under his arm, went away, and didn't bother about the three girls who were stuck to it. They had to keep along with him, left and right, as he chanced to go. Out in the country they met the parson, who, on seeing the procession, said, "Shame on you, you ill-bred girls! Why are you following the young fellow across the fields? Is that the thing to do?" So saying, he seized the youngest by the hand, meaning to pull her back, but when he touched her, he, too, stuck and himself had to run along behind. A short time afterward the sexton appeared and saw the parson who was following on the heels of the three girls. He was amazed and called out, "My goodness, parson! Where are you going in such a hurry? Don't forget that we have a christening today," ran up to him, seized him by the sleeve and in his turn was stuck. As the five were thus trotting along one behind the other, two farmers came from the field with their hoes. The parson called out to them, begging them to free him and the sexton, but as soon as they touched the sexton, they were stuck, and now there were seven of them running after the Dunce and his goose.

He next came to a city where there ruled a king who had a daughter so serious that no one could make her laugh. For this reason he issued an edict that whoever could make her laugh should marry her. When the Dunce heard that, he went into the presence of the king's daughter with his goose and its train, and when she saw the seven people trotting along one behind the other, she burst into loud laughter and simply couldn't stop. Then the Dunce asked for her in marriage, but the king didn't like the son-in-law and made all sorts of excuses, saying he'd first have to produce a man able to drink up a cellar full of wine. The Dunce remembered the grey dwarf as one who might well be able to help him, went out into the forest, and where he'd cut down the tree saw a man sitting and making a very wry face. The Dunce asked what he was taking so to heart. "I'm so thirsty," he answered, "and can't quench my thirst. I can't stand cold water. True enough, I've emptied a cask of wine, but what is a drop on a hot stone?" "Then I can help you," said the Dunce; "just come along with me and you'll have your fill." Thereupon he took him into the king's cellar, and the man fell upon the big casks, and drank and drank till his hips ached, and before one day was done had drunk the whole cellar dry.

Again the Dunce demanded his bride, but the king was vexed that a low-born fellow, whom everybody called a dunce, should carry off his daughter, and laid down new conditions: he'd first have to produce a man able to eat up a mountain of bread. The Dunce didn't stop long to think but went at once out into the forest. There on the same spot was sitting a man who was pulling in a belt around his waist; he looked cross and said, "I've eaten an ovenful of hard unleavened bread, but what good is that when one's as hungry as I? My stomach stays empty, and I have to pull in my belt so as not to die of hunger." At that the Dunce rejoiced and said, "Get up and come with me; you shall eat your fill." He took him to the king's court. The king had had all the flour from the whole kingdom collected and had had a monstrous mountain baked of it. Nevertheless, the man from the forest placed himself in front of it and began to eat, and in one day the whole mountain had vanished.

For the third time the Dunce demanded his bride, but the king again resorted to evasion and demanded a ship able to sail on land and on water. "As soon as you come sailing up in it," he said, "you shall have my daughter in marriage." The Dunce went straight into the forest, where the old grey dwarf to whom he'd given his cake was sitting. "I've drunk and I've eaten for you," he said, "I'll also give you the ship; I'm doing all this because you took pity on me." Then he gave him the ship which could sail on land and on sea, and when the king saw it, he could no longer refuse him his daughter. The wedding was celebrated, and after the king's death, the Dunce inherited the kingdom and for a long time lived happily with his wife.

65   All-Kinds-of-Fur

Allerleirauh

ONCE THERE WAS A KING who had a wife with golden hair, and she was so beautiful that the like of her was not to be found on earth. By chance she fell ill, and when she felt that she was nigh unto death, she called the king and said, "If after my death you wish to remarry, take no one who's not just as beautiful as I and who hasn't golden hair like mine. That you must promise me." When the king had given his word, she closed her eyes and died.

For a long time the king was inconsolable and had no thought of taking a second wife. Finally his councilors said, "There's no other way out, the king must remarry so that we may have a queen." Messengers were sent about far and wide to look for a bride who in beauty might be quite the late queen's equal, but such a one was not to be found in the whole world, and even if she had been found, there was no one with such golden hair. So the messengers returned with nothing accomplished.

Now the king had a daughter who was just as beautiful as her deceased mother and also had the same golden hair. Once when she was grown up, the king looked at her and noticed that in every respect she was like his late wife and suddenly fell violently in love with her. Then he said to his councilors, "I wish to marry my daughter, for she is the image of my deceased wife; if I don't marry her, I shan't be able to find a bride who resembles my wife." On hearing this the councilors were aghast and said, "God has forbidden a father to marry his daughter. No good can come from sin, and the realm will be brought to perdition." The daughter was even more frightened when she learned of her father's resolve, hoped, however, still to dissuade him from his plan. "Before complying with your wish," she said to him, "I must first have three dresses, one as golden as the sun, one as silvery as the moon, and one as glittering as the stars. I further demand a cloak made up of a thousand kinds of pelts and furs, and every animal in your realm must contribute a piece of its skin to it." She thought, however, "It's quite impossible to procure that and thus I shall divert my father from his evil thoughts." But the king persisted in his plan, and the most skillful maidens in his kingdom had to weave the three dresses, one as golden as the sun, one as silvery as the moon, and one as glittering as the stars. His huntsmen had to catch all animals in his realm and remove a piece of their pelts; from that was made a cloak of a thousand kinds of fur. Finally, when everything was ready, the king had the cloak fetched, spread it out before her, and said, "The wedding will be tomorrow."

When the king's daughter saw that there was no longer any hope of changing her father's mind, she decided to run away. In the night when everybody was asleep, she got up and from among her jewels took three things, a gold ring, a tiny gold spinning wheel, and a tiny gold reel. The three dresses of the sun, the moon, and the stars she put into a nutshell, donned the cloak of all kinds of fur, and blackened her hands and face with soot. Then she commended herself to God and went off, walking the whole night until she came to a big forest. Since she was tired, she sat down in a hollow tree and fell asleep.

The sun rose, but she slept on and kept on sleeping when it was already broad daylight. By chance the king to whom the forest belonged was hunting in it, and when his dogs came to the tree, they snuffed, ran around and round it, and barked. "Go see what kind of game has hidden itself there," said the king to the huntsmen. The latter obeyed the order and on their return said, "A queer animal is lying in the hollow tree, the like of which we have never seen before: on its skin are a thousand kinds of fur, and it's lying asleep there." "See if you can take it alive," said the king, "then tie it in the cart and bring it along." When the huntsmen took hold of the girl, she woke up very frightened and cried out to them, "I'm a poor child, forsaken by father and mother. Have pity on me and take me with you." Then they said, "All-Kinds-of-Fur, you're fit for the kitchen. Just come with us; you can sweep up the ashes there." So they put her in the cart and drove home to the royal palace. They assigned her a cubbyhole under the stairs where no light of day penetrated and said, "You can live and sleep there, furry creature." Then she was sent to the kitchen where she carried wood and water, poked the fire, plucked the poultry, sorted the vegetables, swept up the ashes, and did all the dirty work.

For a long time All-Kinds-of-Fur lived there quite wretchedly. Alas, fair king's daughter, what you still have to go through! It once happened, however, that a party was being celebrated in the palace; then she said to the chef, "May I go upstairs for a little while and look on? I'll stand outside the door." "All right, go along," answered the chef, "but you must be back here in half an hour and collect the ashes." She took her oil lamp, went to her cubbyhole, took off the fur cloak, and washed the soot from her hands and face, so that her full beauty came to light again. Then she opened the nut and took out the dress that shone like the sun and, when that was done, went upstairs to the party. Everybody made way for her, for no one knew her and they didn't doubt but that she was a king's daughter. Then the king came to meet her, offered her his hand, and danced with her, thinking to himself, "I've never laid eyes on a girl so beautiful as she." When the dance was over, she curtsied and, as the king was looking around, disappeared, and no one knew where. The sentries stationed outside the palace were summoned and questioned, but no one had seen her.

She had, however, run into her cubbyhole, quickly taken off her dress, blackened her hands and face, put on the fur cloak, and once again was All-Kinds-of-Fur. When she went into the kitchen and was about to start work and sweep up the ashes, the chef said, "Don't bother till tomorrow; instead, cook the king's pudding. I, too, want to look on a little upstairs. But don't you let a single hair fall in; if you do, you'll get nothing more to eat in the future." The chef went off, and All-Kinds-of-Fur cooked the pudding for the king, a bread pudding, as best she could. When it was ready, she fetched her gold ring from the cubbyhole and put it in the bowl in which the pudding was served. When the ball was over, the king had the pudding brought and ate it, and it tasted so good to him that he thought he'd never eaten a better. When he reached the bottom, he saw a gold ring lying there and couldn't imagine how it got there. He had the chef summoned. On hearing the order the chef was frightened and said to All-Kinds-of-Fur, "You surely let a hair drop into the pudding; if so, you'll get a beating." When he entered the king's presence, the latter asked who'd cooked the pudding. "I did," answered the chef. "That's not true," said the king, "for it was a different kind and much better cooked than usual." "I must confess," answered the chef, "that I didn't cook it; the furry creature did." "Go and have her come up," said the king.

When All-Kinds-of-Fur came, the king asked, "Who are you?" "I'm a poor child who no longer has either a father or a mother." "Why are you in my palace?" "I'm good for nothing except to have the boots thrown at my head," she answered. He asked further, "Where did you get the ring that was in the pudding?" "I don't know anything about the ring," she answered. So the king could find out nothing and had to send her away again.

Some time later there was another party. As before, All-Kinds-of-Fur begged the chef for leave to look on. "Yes," he answered, "but be sure to come back in half an hour and cook the king the bread pudding he's so fond of." She ran to her cubbyhole, hurriedly washed herself, took out of the nut the dress which was as silvery as the moon, and put it on. Then, looking like a king's daughter, she went upstairs, and the king came to meet her and was glad to see her again, and since the dance was just beginning, they danced together. When the dance was over, she again disappeared so quickly that the king couldn't see where she'd gone. She jumped into her cubbyhole, turned herself into the furry creature again, and went into the kitchen to cook the bread pudding. When the chef was upstairs, she fetched the gold spinning-wheel and put it in the bowl so that the pudding was served on top of it. It was taken to the king, who ate it and liked it as much as the time before and summoned the chef. The latter again had to admit that it was All-Kinds-of-Fur who'd cooked the pudding. Again All-Kinds-of-Fur was brought before the king, but she answered that she was good only to have the boots thrown at her head and that she knew nothing at all about the tiny gold spinning-wheel.

When for the third time the king arranged a party, it went the same as before. To be sure the chef said, "You're a witch, furry creature, and always put something into the pudding to make it so good that the king likes it better than what I cook," but since she begged so hard, he allowed her to go there for the allotted time. Now she put on a dress which was as glittering as the stars and thus clad went into the hall. Again the king danced with the beautiful maiden and thought she'd never before been so beautiful. While he was dancing and without her noticing it, he put a gold ring on her finger and gave orders that the dance should last quite long. When it was at an end, he wanted to hold her hands tight, but she tore herself away and slipped so quickly among the crowd that she disappeared before his eyes. She ran as fast as she could to her cubbyhole under the stairs, but because she'd stayed out too long, indeed more than half an hour, she hadn't time to take off the beautiful dress but merely threw her fur cloak over it. Neither did she in her haste quite cover herself with soot, but one of her fingers remained white. All-Kinds-of-Fur now hurried into the kitchen, cooked the bread pudding for the king and, when the chef was gone, put the gold reel in it. When the king found the reel at the bottom of the bowl, he summoned All-Kinds-of-Fur. Then noticing her white finger and seeing the ring he had put on her during the dance, he seized her by the hand and held her tight, and when she wanted to tear herself away and run off, her fur cloak opened a little and her starry dress gleamed forth. The king seized the cloak and tore it off. Then her golden hair appeared, and she stood there in full splendor and could no longer conceal herself. When she'd wiped the soot and ashes from her face, she was more beautiful than anybody had ever before seen on earth. "You are my dear bride," said the king, "and we shall never part." Then the wedding was celebrated and they lived happily until their death.

66   The Hare's Bride

Häsichenbraut

THERE WAS A WOMAN and her daughter; they had a fine garden with cabbage in it. A hare used to come there and in winter eat all the cabbage. Then the woman said to her daughter, "Go into the garden and chase away the hare." The girl said to the hare, "Shoo! shoo! you hare, you're eating up all the cabbage." "Come, girl," said the hare, "sit down on my tail and come with me to my hutch." The girl wouldn't do it. The next day the hare came back and was eating the cabbage, and the woman said to her daughter, "Go into the garden and chase away the hare." "Shoo! shoo! you hare," said the girl to the hare, "you're eating up all the cabbage." "Come, girl," said the hare, "sit down on my tail and come with me to my hutch." The girl wouldn't do it. On the third day the hare came again and ate the cabbage, and the woman said to her daughter, "Go into the garden and chase away the hare." "Shoo! shoo! you hare," said the girl, "you're eating up all the cabbage." "Come, girl," said the hare, "sit down on my tail and come with me to my hutch." The girl sat down on the hare's tail, and the hare took her far away to its hutch and said, "Now cook green cabbage and millet. I'm going to invite the wedding guests." The wedding guests assembled. (Who were the wedding guests? That I can tell you as somebody else told me: they were all hares, and a crow was there as parson to marry the couple, and a fox as sexton, and the altar was under a rainbow.)

The girl, however, was sad because she was quite alone. The hare came up and said, "Open the door, open the door! The wedding guests are in high spirits." The bride said nothing and wept. The hare went away, then came back and said, "Open the door, open the door! The wedding guests are hungry." Again the bride said nothing and wept. The hare went away, then came and said, "Open the door, open the door! The wedding guests are waiting." The bride said nothing, and the hare went away; she, however, made a dummy of straw, dressed it in her clothes, gave it a big spoon, stood it before the pot of millet, and went home to her mother. Once again the hare came and said, "Open the door, open the door!" and opened it itself and hit the dummy on the head so that its cap fell off.

Then the hare saw that it wasn't its bride and went sadly away.

67 The Twelve Huntsmen

Die zwölf Jäger

THERE WAS ONCE A KING'S SON who was betrothed to a maiden and loved her very dearly. Once as he was sitting beside her and feeling very happy, news came that his father was on his deathbed and asked to see him once before his end. To his beloved he said, "I must now go away and must leave you, so I'm giving you a ring as a keepsake. When I'm king, I'll come back and fetch you." He rode off, and when he got to his father, the latter was mortally ill and nigh unto death. "Dearest son," he said to him, "I wanted to see you once more before my end. Promise me to marry according to my wish," and mentioned to him a certain king's daughter who was to be his wife. The son was so distressed that he didn't stop a moment to think but said, "Yes, father dear, your will shall be done." Then the king closed his eyes and died.

When the son had been proclaimed king and the period of mourning was past, he had to keep the promise he'd made his father and sued for the hand of the king's daughter. And she was promised to him. His first betrothed learned of that and so grieved over his disloyalty that she almost passed away. Her father said to her, "Dearest child, why are you so sad? You shall have whatever you wish for." She thought for a moment, then said, "Father dear, I wish for eleven maidens exactly like myself in face, form, and stature." "If possible," said the king, "your wish will be fulfilled, and had a long search made throughout his kingdom, until eleven maidens were found exactly like his daughter in face, form, and stature.

When they got there, the king's daughter had twelve hunting costumes made, each like the other, and the eleven maidens had to put them on, and she herself put on the twelfth. Then she said good-bye to her father and rode off with them and rode to the court of her former betrothed whom she so very dearly loved. She enquired whether he needed huntsmen and if he wouldn't take them all into his service. The king looked at her and didn't recognize her, but because they were so good-looking, he said yes, he'd be glad to employ them. Thus they became the king's twelve huntsmen.

Now the king had a lion, a remarkable animal that knew everything that was hidden and secret. One evening it chanced to say to the king, "You think you have twelve huntsmen there?" "Yes," said the king, "twelve huntsmen." "You're wrong," continued the lion, "they're twelve girls." "That simply isn't true," answered the king. "How are you going to prove it to me?" "Oh, just have some peas scattered in your antechamber," answered the lion, "and you'll see at once. Men have a firm tread. When they walk on peas, not a pea will move, but girls walk with a tripping, trotting, shuffling gait, and the peas roll about." The king very much liked the suggestion and had the peas strewn.

One of the king's servants was, however, fond of the huntsmen, and when he heard that they were to be tested, he went and repeated everything to them, saying, "The lion wants to make the king believe that you're girls." The king's daughter thanked him and afterward said to her maidens, "Make a great effort and step firmly on the peas." Next morning when the king had the twelve huntsmen called into his presence and they entered the antechamber where the peas were lying, they stepped so firmly and had such a steady, strong gait that not a single pea rolled or moved. Then they went away again and the king said to the lion, "You lied to me; they walk just like men." "They knew that they were going to be tested and made a great effort," answered the lion; "just have twelve spinning wheels brought into the antechamber; they'll come along and take pleasure in them. No man would do that." The king liked the suggestion and had the spinning wheels placed in the antechamber.

The servant, however, who was well-intentioned toward the huntsmen, went and disclosed the scheme to them. Once they were alone, the king's daughter said to her eleven girls, "Make a great effort and don't look around at the spinning wheels." Next morning when the king had his twelve huntsmen summoned, they went through the antechamber and didn't so much as look at the spinning wheels. Then the king said to the lion, "You lied to me; they're men, for they didn't look at the spinning wheels." "They knew they were going to be tested and made a great effort," answered the lion. But the king would no longer believe the lion.

The twelve huntsmen always accompanied the king on the chase, and the longer he had them the better he liked them. Once when they were hunting, it happened that the news came that the king's betrothed was on her way. When the true bride heard that, it grieved her so that her heart almost stopped and she fell to the ground in a faint. The king thought that something had happened to his dear huntsman, came running up to help him, and drew off his glove. Then he saw the ring he'd given his first betrothed, and looking in her face, recognized her. His heart was so moved that he kissed her, and when she opened her eyes, he said, "You are mine and I am yours, and nobody in the world can change that." To the other bride, however, he sent a messenger and requested her to return to her kingdom, for he already had a wife. When one has found his old key, one doesn't need the new one. Then the wedding was celebrated, and the lion returned to favor, for it really had told the truth.

68   The Swindler and His Master

De Gaudeif un sien Meester

JOHN WANTED to have his son learn a trade, so he went to church and asked Our Lord what would be suitable for him. The sexton was standing behind the altar and said, "Swindling, swindling." Then John went back to his son and told him he must learn swindling, for so Our Lord had told him. With his son he went and looked for a man who understood swindling. They went on for quite a time and got to a very big forest, where there was a little cottage and a very old woman inside. "Do you by chance know anybody who understands swindling?" said John. "You may easily learn that here," said the woman; "my son's passed master at it." He spoke with the son and asked if he was really good at swindling. The master swindler said, "I'm willing to teach your son; come back in a year, and if you still recognize him, I won't take any apprentice fee. If, however, you do not recognize him, you can pay me two hundred dollars."

The father returned home, and the son learned to be good at witchcraft and swindling. When the year was up, the father went off by himself and wondered how to go about recognizing his son. As he was thus walking and wondering, he met a little dwarf who said, "Man, what are you wondering about? You're so sad." "Why, yes," said John, "a year ago I bound my son as an apprentice to a master swindler. He told me to come back in a year, and if I didn't recognize my son, I was to give him two hundred dollars. If I did recognize him, I shouldn't have to pay anything. Now I am very frightened lest I don't recognize him, for I don't know where to get the money." Then the dwarf said that he should take along a crust of bread and go and stand under the fireplace. "Up on the crossbeam is a basket and a bird will look out of it, and that's your son."

John went and threw a crust of black bread in front of the

basket; then the bird came out and looked at it. "Hello, son, are you here?" said the father. The son was glad to see his father, but the master said, "The Devil gave you that notion; how else could you recognize your son?" "Father, let's go," said the boy.

The father started home with his son. On the way a coach came driving along, and the son said to his father, "I'm going to turn myself into a big deerhound, and you can earn a lot of money through me." The gentleman called out of the coach, "Man, will you sell the dog?" "Yes," said the father. "How much money do you want for it?" "Thirty dollars." "Well, that's a lot, but because it's such a frightfully good dog, I'll take it." The gentleman took it into his coach, but when the coach had gone on a bit, the dog jumped out of the coach through the glass window. Then he was no longer a deerhound and rejoined his father.

Together they went home. The next day there was a fair in the neighboring town, and the boy said to his father, "Now I'm going to turn myself into a fine horse. Then sell me, but when you sell me, be sure to take off my bridle, otherwise I can't become a human being again." The father went with the horse to the fair, and the master swindler came and bought the horse for a hundred dollars. The father forgot, however, to take off the bridle. The man went home with the horse and put it in a stall. As the maid was walking across the floor of the barn, the horse said, "Take off my bridle, take off my bridle!" The maid stopped and listened, "My! you can talk?" went up to it and took off its bridle. Then the horse became a sparrow and flew out the door. The wizard likewise turned into a sparrow and flew after it. Then they met and bit one another, but the master was worsted, went into the water and was a fish. The boy, too, became a fish, and again they bit one another, and the master was worsted. Then the master turned himself into a cock, and the boy became a fox and bit the master's head off. Then he died and has been dead to the present day.

69   Yorinda and Yoringel

Jorinde und Joringel

THERE WAS ONCE AN OLD CASTLE in the middle of a big dense forest, and in it an old woman lived all alone. She was an arch-enchantress. During the day she'd turn herself into a cat or an owl, but in the evening she'd resume proper human form. She knew how to lure game and birds and then she'd kill them, cook them, and roast them. If anyone came within a hundred paces of the castle, they'd have to stop dead and couldn't move from the spot until she unspelled them. But if a pure virgin entered this magic circle, she'd transform her into a bird, then shut her up in a basket, and carry the basket to a room in the castle. In her castle she had at least seven thousand such baskets with rare birds of this kind.

Once there was a girl named Yorinda, who was fairer than all other girls. She and a very handsome youth named Yoringel had plighted their troth. They were in the period of their court-ship and took the greatest pleasure in each other's company. On one occasion they took a walk in the forest in order to be able to talk privately with one another. "Be careful not to go so near the castle," said Yoringel. It was a lovely afternoon: through the tree trunks the sun was shining bright into the dark green of the forest, and a turtle dove was singing mourn-fully in the old beeches.

Now and again Yorinda would weep, sit down in the sun-light and sigh, and Yoringel would sigh, too. They were as downcast as if doomed to die. They looked about, were con-fused, and didn't know how to get home. The sun was still half above the mountain, half behind it. Yoringel looked through the bushes and saw the old castle wall close by him; he was alarmed and became frightened to death. Yorinda sang,

> "My bird with the red ringlet
> Is singing 'Woe's me! woe's me! woe's me!'

It's singing of its death to the dove,
Singing 'Woe's me, alas, alas.' "

Yoringel looked for Yorinda, but Yorinda had been turned into a nightingale which was singing "Alas, alas!" An owl with glowing eyes flew thrice around them, thrice crying "Hoo-oo, hoo-oo, hoo-oo!" Yoringel couldn't move; he stood there like a stone, unable to weep, speak, or move hand or foot. Now the sun was down. The owl flew into a shrub and immediately thereafter a bent old woman emerged from it, yellow and thin, with great red eyes and a hooked nose the tip of which reached to her chin. She mumbled something, caught the nightingale, and carried it away in her hand. Yoringel could neither say anything nor could he move from the spot. The nightingale was gone. Finally the woman came back and with a muffled voice said, "Greetings, Zachiel! When the moon shines into the basket, unbind, Zachiel, at the right moment!" Then Yoringel was free. He fell to his knees before the woman and begged her please to give him back his Yorinda, but she said he'd never have her back and went away. He cried out, he wept, he lamented, but all to no purpose. "Alas, what's to become of me?"

Yoringel went away and finally reached a strange village where for a long time he tended sheep. Often he'd walk around the castle, though not too close. Finally he one night dreamed that he'd found a blood-red flower with a beautiful big pearl in the center of it. He picked the flower and with it went to the castle: everything he touched with the flower became unspelled. He also dreamed that with the flower he recovered his Yorinda. When he woke up in the morning, he began to search through hill and dale to find such a flower. He searched till the ninth day; then early in the morning he found the blood-red flower. In the center of it was a big dew drop, as big as the finest pearl. He carried this flower day and night till he reached the castle. When he got within a hundred paces of it, he was not, as before, held fast but walked on up to the gate. Yoringel was very happy, touched the gate with the flower, and it sprang open. He went in across the courtyard listening for the many birds; finally he heard them. He went and found the hall: there was the witch feeding the birds in the seven thousand baskets. On seeing Yoringel she got very, very angry, scolded, spewed venom and gall at him, but couldn't come within two paces of him. He paid no attention to her but went and looked at the baskets with the birds. There were, however, many hundreds of nightingales. How was he to find his Yorinda again? While thus looking, he noticed that the old woman was stealthily removing a basket with a bird in it and going with it toward the door. He rushed up quickly, touched the basket with the flower and the old woman, too. Now she could no longer practise witchcraft, and Yorinda was standing there, had put her arms about his neck and was as beautiful as before. He turned all the other birds, too, back into maidens and then went home with his Yorinda, and they lived happily together for a long time.

70   Fortune's Favored Three

Die drei Glückskinder

A MAN once had his three sons come into his presence and gave the first a cock, the second a scythe, and the third a cat. "I'm already old," he said, "and my death is near, so I wanted to provide for you before my end. I've no money and what I'm giving you seems of small value, but it's merely a matter of your using it sensibly. Just look for a country where such objects are still unknown, and your fortune's made."

After their father's death, the eldest set out with his cock, but wherever he went, cocks were already known. In the towns he'd already see from afar a cock on the steeples and turning with the wind; in the villages he'd hear more than one crowing, and no one was going to marvel at the creature. Accordingly it didn't look as if he'd make his fortune with it. At last, however, he came by chance to an island where the people knew nothing of cocks, didn't even know how to measure time. True enough, they knew when it was morning or evening, but at night, if they didn't sleep straight through, no one knew how to reckon the time. "See," he said, "what a proud creature this is! On its head it has a crown as red as a ruby and wears spurs like a knight. It will call you thrice in the night at definite times, and the sun rises shortly after the last call. When it crows in broad daylight, then get ready, for there's certainly going to be a change in the weather." The people were much pleased with this; for a whole night they didn't sleep and listened with great satisfaction to the cock's calling the time with a loud, clear voice at two, four, and six. They asked him if the creature was for sale and how much he wanted for it. "About as much gold as a donkey can carry," he replied. "A mere trifle for such a valuable creature!" they shouted in a chorus and gladly gave him what he asked for.

When he got home with his riches, his brothers were astonished. The second said, "Now I'm going to set out and see whether I can get rid of my scythe as profitably," but it didn't look as if he would, for everywhere he met farmers with as good scythes on their shoulders as his. Finally he, too, was successful, and likewise on an island where the people knew nothing about scythes. There, when the grain was ripe, they'd bring cannon out to the fields and shoot the grain down. Now this was an uncertain method: many a cannon would fire out over it, another would hit the ears instead of the straw and shoot them off; there was much waste in the process and besides the noise was scandalous. Then the man went to work and mowed it down so quietly and so quickly that the people gaped in astonishment. They were willing to give him whatever he asked for it, and he got a horse with all the gold it could carry.

Now the third brother, too, wanted to sell his cat to the right person. He fared like the others. So long as he stayed on the mainland he accomplished nothing: there were cats everywhere and so many that the newborn young were mostly drowned. Finally he had himself ferried to an island, and by good luck not a cat had ever been seen there, and the mice had, of course, so gained the upper hand that they danced on the tables and benches, whether the master of the house was at home or not. The people complained bitterly about this plague, and the king himself was unable to save himself from it in his palace: in every corner the mice were squeaking and gnawed whatever they could get their teeth on. The cat began her hunt and soon had a few rooms cleared. Then the people begged the king to buy the marvelous animal for the realm. The king gladly gave the price asked, namely, a pack mule laden with gold, and the third brother returned home with the greatest treasures of all.

In the royal palace the cat had great sport with the mice and killed so many that one couldn't keep count of them. Finally it got hot and thirsty from the work, stopped, raised its head, and cried "miaow, miaow." On hearing these strange cries the king and all his people were frightened and in their terror ran down out of the palace in a body. Outside, the king held a council as to what would be best to do: it was finally decided to send a herald to the cat, ordering it to leave the palace or else expect the use of force. The councilors said, "We prefer the plague of mice, an evil to which we are accustomed, rather than sacrifice our lives to such a monster." A squire had to go up into the palace and ask the cat if it would leave the palace peacefully. The cat, however, who in the meantime had only got thirstier, merely answered "miaow, miaow." The squire understood it to say, "Not at all, not at all" and transmitted this reply to the king. "Well," said the councilors, "it must yield to force." Cannon were brought up and the palace shot at and set fire to. When the flames reached the room where the cat was, it jumped out the window unharmed. The besiegers, however, didn't cease fire till the entire palace was razed to the ground.

71   Six Make Their Way in the World

Sechse kommen durch die ganze Welt

THERE WAS ONCE A MAN adept in many arts. He'd fought in the war and had conducted himself bravely and well, but when the war was over, he received his discharge and three farthings for traveling expenses. "Just wait!" he said, "I won't put up with that. If I find the right people, the king will yet have to turn over the treasures of the entire country to me."

He went angrily into the forest and saw standing there a man who had pulled up six trees like so many straws of grain. "Will you be my servant and travel with me?" he said to him. "Yes," answered the other, "but first I want to bring the little bundle of brushwood home to my mother," and, taking one of the trees, twisted it around the other five, put the bundle on his shoulder and carried it off. Then he came back and went along with his master, who said, "We two ought surely to make our way anywhere in the world." When they'd gone some distance, they found a huntsman who was kneeling down; he had raised his gun and was taking aim. The master said to him, "Huntsman, what do you want to shoot at?" "Two miles from here," he answered, "a fly is sitting on the branch of an oak tree; I want to shoot out its left eye." "Oh, come with me," said the man; "if we three stay together, we ought to make our way anywhere in the world." The huntsman was willing and went with him. They came to seven windmills whose sails were turning at a great rate, and yet there was no wind from any quarter and not a leaf was stirring. The man said, "I don't know what's driving the windmills; there's not a breath of air stirring," and went on with his servants. When they'd gone on two miles, they saw a man sitting in a tree holding one of his nostrils and blowing out of the other. "Goodness! what are you doing up there?" asked the man. The other answered, "Two miles from here are seven windmills; see, I'm blowing at them and making them go." "Oh, come with me," said the man; "if we four stay together, we ought to make our way anywhere in the world." Then the blower climbed down the tree and went along. After some time they saw a man who was standing on one leg; he had unbuckled the other and laid it beside him. The master said, "You've certainly made yourself comfortable for a rest." "I'm a runner," he answered, "and so as not to run altogether too fast, I've unbuckled one of my legs. When I run on both legs, I'm swifter than a bird in flight." "Oh, come with me. If we five stay together, we ought to make our way anywhere in the world." So he went with them, and it wasn't long before they met a man who was wearing a cap which he had perched entirely on one ear. "Have some manners, have some manners!" said the master, "don't put your cap on one ear. You look like a Tom-Fool." "I mustn't," said the other, "for when I put my cap on straight, there's a terrible frost, and the birds in the air freeze and drop dead to earth." "Oh, come with me," said the master; "if we six stay together, we ought to make our way anywhere in the world."

Now the six came to a city where the king had proclaimed that whoever was willing to race against his daughter and won was to be her husband, but should he lose, he would have to pay for it with his head. The man reported for the competition and said, "I want my servant to run for me." "Then," answered the king, "you must also pledge his life so that both his head and yours will be at stake." When that had been agreed upon and settled, the man buckled on the runner's other leg and said to him, "Now hurry up and do your part so that we may win." Now it had been agreed that whichever was the first to fetch water from a distant well would be the winner. The runner was given a jug and the king's daughter one as well, and they started running at the same time. But in a jiffy, when the king's daughter had gone but a short distance, the spectators could no longer see the runner, and it was as if a gust of wind had blown past. In a short time he reached the well, filled his jug with water, and turned about again. Halfway home, however, he was overcome with weariness, set down the jug, lay down, and fell asleep. In order not to be too comfortable and so as to wake up again soon, he used as a pillow a horse's skull which was lying on the ground. Meanwhile the king's daughter, who was a good runner, too, at least as good as an ordinary human being, had reached the well and was hurrying back with her jug full of water. When she saw the runner lying there asleep, she was glad and said, "The enemy has been delivered into my hands," emptied his jug, and ran on. All would have been lost if by good luck the keen-eyed huntsman hadn't been standing up on the castle and taking everything in. Then he said, "Just the same, the king's daughter isn't going to win out against us," loaded his gun and shot so skillfully that he shot the horse's skull from under the runner's head without hurting him. Then the runner awoke, jumped up, and saw that his jug was empty and that the king's

daughter was way ahead. But he didn't lose heart, ran back
to the well with the jug, filled it again with water, and was
home ten minutes before the king's daughter. "You see," he
said, "this is the first time I've picked up my feet; what I was
doing before wasn't really running at all."

The king, however, was vexed, and his daughter even more
so, that a discharged common soldier like that should carry her
off; they took council together as to how to get rid of him and
his companions. Then the king said to her, "I've found a way;
don't be alarmed; they won't get back home," and said to them,
"Now have a good time eating and drinking," and led them
to a room with an iron floor and whose doors were also of iron
and the windows guarded with iron bars. In the room was
a table set with delicious food. The king said to them, "Just
go in and enjoy yourselves," and when they were inside had
the door locked and bolted. Then he had the chef come and
ordered him to make a fire under the room till the iron got
red hot. The chef did so, and the fire started, and as they were
sitting at table, the six in the room got very warm and thought
it was on account of the food. When, however, it kept getting
hotter and they wanted to get out and found the door and
the windows locked, they saw that the king had evil designs
and meant to suffocate them. "But he won't succeed," said the
man with the cap, "I'll bring on a frost that will put the fire
to shame and make it creep away." Then he set his cap on
straight, and at once such a frost descended that all the heat
disappeared and the food in the dishes began to freeze. When
a few hours had passed, the king supposed they had perished
in the heat. He had the door opened and was going to see
about them himself, but when the door opened, all six of them
were there hale and hearty and said they were glad to be able
to get out and warm themselves, for in the great cold in the
room the food was freezing fast to the plates. The king went
angrily down to the chef, scolded him, and asked why he
hadn't done as he'd been ordered. "There's fire enough there,"
answered the chef, "just see for yourself." The king saw that
an enormous fire was burning under the iron room and realized that he couldn't do anything to the six that way.

The king pondered anew how he might rid himself of the
bad guests, had the master come, and said, "If you're willing

to accept money and surrender your right to my daughter, you shall have as much as you want." "Why, yes, Sir King," he answered, "give me as much as my servant can carry and I won't demand your daughter." The king agreed, and the man went on to say, "I'll come, then, in a fortnight and fetch it." Then he summoned all the tailors in the whole realm; they had to sit for two weeks and sew a sack. When it was finished, the strong man, the one able to pull up trees, had to take the sack on his shoulders and go with it to the king. "What powerful fellow is that who's carrying on his shoulders a bale of canvas as big as a house?" said the king. He was frightened and thought, "What a lot of gold he'll carry off!" He had brought a barrel of gold that took sixteen of the strongest men to carry, but the strong man seized it with one hand and put it in the sack, saying, "Why don't you bring more right away; that hardly covers the bottom." The king gradually had his whole treasure brought, and the strong man stuffed it into the sack, but it didn't half fill it. "Bring along more," he cried, "those few crumbs aren't filling it up!" Then seven thousand more carts of gold from all over the realm had to be driven there, and the strong man stuffed them into his sack along with the oxen that were hitched to them. "I shan't waste much time over inspection," he said, "but will take what comes, just so it will fill the sack." When everything was in the sack, there was still room for a lot more, and he said, "I just want to make an end of the matter; of course one sometimes ties up a sack even if it isn't quite full." Then he hoisted it on his back and went off with his companions.

When the king saw that one man was carrying away the wealth of the entire country, he grew angry and had his cavalry mount and pursue the six, with orders to take the sack away from the strong man. Two regiments soon overtook them and called out to them, "You're prisoners! Lay down the sack of gold or you'll be cut down." "What are you saying?" said the blower, "we're prisoners, are we? You're more likely to go dancing about in the air!" held one nostril and with the other blew at the two regiments. Then they went in every direction, up into the blue and away over hill and dale, one this way, the other that. A sergeant begged for mercy, saying he had nine wounds and was a good fellow who didn't deserve the affront. Then the blower let up a little, so that he came down again unharmed, and said to him, "Now go home to the king and tell him just to send some more cavalry. I'd blow them all into the air." When the king received this message, he said, "Let the fellows go; there's something uncanny about them."

So the six brought their wealth home, divided it among themselves, and lived happily until their death.

72 The Wolf and the Man

Der Wolf und der Mensch

A FOX was once telling a wolf about man's strength: no animal could resist him, and they'd have to use guile to maintain themselves against him. The wolf answered, "If only I could once manage to see a man! I'd surely go straight for him!" "I can easily help you do that," said the fox; "just come to my house early tomorrow morning and I'll show you one."

The wolf came early, and the fox brought him out to the path the huntsman took every day. First there came an old discharged soldier. "Is that a man?" asked the wolf. "No," answered the fox, "it used to be one." Then came a little boy who was going to school. "Is that a man?" "No, it will be one some day." Finally the huntsman came with a double-barreled gun on his shoulder and wearing a case knife at his side. "Look!" said the fox to the wolf, "there comes a man! You must go for him, but I'll get off to my hole." The wolf went straight for the man. On seeing it the huntsman said, "What a pity I didn't load a bullet," took aim and fired shot into the wolf's face. The wolf made an awful face but didn't let itself get frightened and kept going. Then the huntsman gave it a second load. The wolf suppressed its pain and attacked the huntsman. Then the latter drew his shiny case knife and gave it a couple of cuts right and left, so that, streaming with blood, it ran howling back to the fox. "Well, brother wolf," said the fox, "how did you come out with the man?" "Alas," answered the wolf, "I didn't realize man's strength: first he took a stick from his shoulder and blew into it; then something flew into my face that tickled me perfectly frightfully. Then he blew once again into the stick, and something flew about my nose like lightning and hail. When I got quite near, he pulled a shiny rib out of his body and struck out at me so hard that I was almost left lying dead."

"You see," said the fox, "what a braggart you are: you can't carry out your boasts."

73   The Wolf and the Fox

Der Wolf und der Fuchs

A WOLF had a fox living with it, and whatever the wolf wanted, the fox had to do because it was the weaker. The fox would have been glad to be rid of its master. They were both walking through the forest and the wolf said, "Red fox, get me something to eat or I'll eat you up yourself." "I know of a farmyard where there are a couple of young lambs. If you want to, we'll go and get one." The wolf liked the idea; they went there. The fox stole the lamb, brought it to the wolf, and cleared out. The wolf ate it but wasn't yet satisfied, wanted to have the other, too, and went to fetch it. But because it was so clumsy, the lamb's mother saw it and began to cry and bleat most frightfully, so that the farmers came up on the run. They found the wolf and gave it such an unmerciful beating that it got back to the fox limping and howling. "That was a nice trick you played on me!" it said; "I was going to fetch the other lamb, but the farmers caught me and beat me to a pulp." "Why are you such a glutton?" answered the fox.

The next day they again went into the fields, and the greedy wolf again said, "Red fox, get me something to eat or I'll eat you up yourself." "I know of a farm where the wife will be baking pancakes this afternoon," answered the fox; "let's get some of them." They went there, and the fox slunk around the house, looked and snuffed until it found where the bowl was, pulled down six pancakes, and brought them to the wolf. "There's something for you to eat," it said to the wolf and went its way. The wolf swallowed the pancakes in a jiffy and said, "They call for more," went and jerked down the whole plate so that it broke to pieces. Then there was such a great noise that the wife came out and, seeing the wolf, called the farm hands who hurried up and gave it such a sound thrashing that it got back to the fox in the forest with two lame legs and howling loudly. "What a nasty trick you played on me!" it cried; "the farmers got hold of me and tanned my hide." "Why are you such a glutton?" answered the fox.

The third day, when they were out in the open together and the wolf was having a hard time as much as to limp along, it once again said to the fox, "Red fox, get me something to eat or I'll eat you up yourself." "I know of a man who's been slaughtering," answered the fox, "and the salted meat is in a tub in the cellar. Let's get that." "But I want to go with you right off," said the wolf, "so that you can help me if I can't get away." "All right," said the fox, and showed it the tricks and devices by which they finally got into the cellar. There was any amount of meat there, and the wolf started immediately to eat, thinking, "It will be some time before I stop." The fox enjoyed it, too, kept looking all about, often ran to the hole through which they'd come, and tried it to see that its belly was not too full of food to slip through. "My dear fox," said the wolf, "tell me why you're running back and forth like that and jumping in and out of the cellar?" "Why, I've got to see whether anybody's coming," answered the crafty fellow. "Be sure not to eat too much." "I won't go till the tub is empty," said the wolf. Just then the farmer, who'd heard the noise of the fox jumping in and out, came into the cellar. The fox, on seeing him, was out the hole in one jump. The wolf wanted to follow it but had eaten itself so full that it could no longer get through but stuck there. Then the farmer came with a cudgel and beat it to death.

The fox, however, ran into the forest and was glad to be rid of the old glutton.

74 The Wolf and the Godfather

Der Fuchs und die Frau Gevatterin

A WOLF gave birth to a cub and had the fox invited to be god-father. "The fox is a near relative of ours," she said, "is intelli-gent and very clever. He can teach my little son and help him on in the world." The fox really made a very decent appearance and said, "Dear Mrs. Wolf, thank you for the honor you're showing me; I, too, shall act in a way to make you happy about it." At the christening party the fox ate with gusto and was quite merry, afterward saying, "Dear Mrs. Wolf, it's our duty to look out for the child. You must have good food so that it'll grow up to be strong. I know of a sheep-cote where we can easily get a choice morsel." The wolf liked the proposal and accompanied the fox out to the farm. From a distance he showed her the sheep-cote and said, "You'll be able to creep in there without being seen; meanwhile I'm going to take a look about on the other side and see if I can get a young chicken." However, the fox didn't go there but lay down by the edge of the forest, stretched out its legs, and took a rest.

The wolf crept into the sheep-cote; a dog was lying there, and it barked so loud that the farmers came on the run, caught Mrs. Wolf and poured stinging lye over her coat. Neverthe-less, she finally got away and dragged herself out to the forest. There lay the fox: it assumed a most plaintive tone and said, "Alas, dear Mrs. Wolf, what a terrible time I've been having! The farmers fell upon me and beat me to pieces. If you don't want me to lie here and die, you must carry me off." The wolf could do no more than drag herself slowly forward; neverthe-less she was so concerned over the fox that she took him on her back and carried the godfather, who was hale and hearty, slowly to her home. Then he called out to her, "Good-bye, dear Mrs. Wolf, and enjoy the roast!" laughed at her like any-thing, and ran off.

75   The Fox and the Cat

Der Fuchs und die Katze

A CAT happened to meet Mr. Fox in a forest and thinking, "He's clever, experienced, and very influential," spoke to him in friendly fashion. "Good day, dear Mr. Fox, how do you do? How goes it? How are you getting on in these hard times?" The fox looked the cat over from head to foot quite arrogantly and for some time didn't know whether to deign an answer. Finally he said, "Oh, you wretched lick-whiskers, you spotted fool, you starveling and mouse-hunter, what are you thinking of? You venture to ask how I am? What have you learned? How many tricks do you know?" "I know just one single trick," answered the cat modestly. "What trick is that?" asked the fox. "When the dogs are after me, I can jump up in a tree and save myself." "Is that all?" said the fox. "I am master of a hundred tricks and have, besides, a bag full of ruses. I'm sorry for you. Come along with me and I'll teach you how to get away from the dogs." Just then a huntsman came along with four dogs. The cat jumped nimbly up in a tree and sat down in the top, where branches and leaves hid it completely. "Open your bag of tricks, Mr. Fox! open your bag!" the cat called out to it, but the dogs had already seized it and were holding it tight. "My! Mr. Fox," cried the cat, "you with your hundred tricks are stuck. If you'd been able to climb up like me, you wouldn't have lost your life."

76   The Pink

Die Nelke

THERE WAS A QUEEN whose body Our Lord had closed so that she bore no children. Every morning she'd go into the garden and pray to God in Heaven to give her a son or a daughter. Then an angel from Heaven came and said, "Be content, you shall have a son with wish-fulfilling thoughts; whatever in the world he wishes for he will receive." She went to the king and told him of the happy message, and when her term was up, she bore a son and the king's joy was great.

Every morning she used to go with the child into the game-preserve and wash herself there in a clear spring. It once happened when the child was a little older that she fell asleep while it was lying in her lap. Then the old chef came, who knew that the child had wish-fulfilling thoughts and kidnapped it; he took a chicken, tore it to pieces, and let the blood drip on her apron and dress. Then he carried the child off to a hidden place where a wet nurse had to suckle it, and ran to the king, charging the queen with having let her child be stolen by wild beasts. On seeing the blood on the queen's apron the king believed this and flew into such a rage that he had built a tower with a deep dungeon into which neither sun nor moon ever shone and had his wife put in it and walled up. There she was to stay for seven years without food or drink and was to perish, but God sent two angels from Heaven in the form of white doves; twice daily they had to fly to her and bring her food till the seven years were up.

The chef thought to himself, "If the child has wish-fulfilling thoughts and if I stay here, it might easily prove my undoing," so he left the palace and joined the boy, who by this time was big enough to talk. "Wish yourself a fine mansion with a garden and all that goes with it," he said to him. No sooner was the wish out of the boy's mouth than everything he'd wished for was there. After a while the chef said to him, "It's not good for you to be alone like this; wish yourself a beautiful maiden to keep you company." Then the king's son wished her there, and at once she was standing before him and was more beautiful than any artist could have painted. The two used to play together and loved one another with all their hearts. The old chef used to go hunting like a gentleman. Then the thought occurred to him that the king's son might one day wish to be with his father and thus get him into grave difficulties, so he went out, took the girl aside, and said, "Tonight when the boy is asleep, go to his bed, stab him in the heart with the knife and bring me his heart and tongue. If you don't do it, you'll lose your life!" Thereupon he went away and when he returned next day, she hadn't done it and said, "Why should I shed innocent blood which has harmed no one?" Again the chef said, "If you don't do it, it will cost you your life!" When he had gone, she had a little fawn fetched, had it killed, took out its heart and tongue and put them on a plate, and when she saw the old man coming, she said to the boy, "Lie down in the bed and pull the covers over you."

Then the old scoundrel came in and said, "Where are the boy's heart and tongue?" The girl handed him the plate, but the king's son threw off the covers and said, "You old sinner, why did you want to kill me? Now I'm going to pronounce judgment on you: you shall become a black poodle with a gold chain around your neck and you shall eat red-hot coals, so that the flames burst out of your throat." As he uttered these words, the old man was changed into a poodle with a gold chain around its neck, and the chefs had to bring up live coals, which it swallowed, so that the flames burst out of its throat. The king's son remained there a short time longer, thinking of his mother and wondering if she were still alive. Finally he said to the girl, "I want to go home to my native land; if you'll come with me, I'll support you." "Alas," she answered, "it's so far, and what am I to do in a strange land where no one knows me?" So, since she didn't really want to go and since they didn't want to leave one another, he wished her into a beautiful pink and put it in his pocket.

Then he went his way, and the poodle had to run along with him, and he returned to his native land. Then he went to the tower where his mother was, and since the tower was very high, he wished himself a ladder that would reach the top. He climbed up and looked in, calling out, "Dearest, dearest mother, Lady Queen! Are you still alive or are you dead?" "I've just eaten and am not yet hungry," she answered, thinking that the angels were there. "I'm your dear son," he said, "whom the wild beasts are supposed to have stolen from your lap, but I'm still alive and shall soon save you." He climbed down and went to his father, announced himself as a foreign huntsman and asked if he might enter his service. The king answered "yes," provided he was well trained and could get him game. There had, however, never been any game in the region at all! The huntsman promised to get him just as much game as he could use on the royal board, had the hunt assembled, and ordered them all to go with him into the forest. They went along, and out in the forest he had them form a big circle, open at one side, then placed himself in the center and began to wish. Immediately some two hundred odd game animals came running into the circle, and the huntsmen had to shoot them. Then it was all loaded onto sixty farm wagons and driven home to the king; and for once the latter was able to adorn his table with game after having had none for many years.

The king was very happy about this and commanded his entire court to dine with him on the following day and had a great banquet. When they were all assembled, he said to the huntsman, "Since you're so clever, you shall sit next to me." "Sir King," he answered, "begging Your Majesty's pardon, I'm a simple hunter lad," but the king insisted, saying, "You shall sit next to me," until he did so. As he was sitting there, he thought of his dear mother and wished that one of the king's high officials would just start asking how the queen was faring in the tower, whether she was still alive or had perished. Hardly had he wished this than the marshal began to speak, saying, "Royal Majesty, here we are having a good time, but how is the queen faring in the tower? Is she alive, or has she perished?" The king answered, "She let my dear son be torn to pieces by wild beasts. I wish to hear nothing about it." Then the huntsman got up and said, "Most gracious father, she's still alive, and I am her son; he was not stolen by wild beasts but by that scoundrel, the old chef. He took me from her lap while she was asleep and sprinkled her apron with the blood of a chicken." Then he took the dog with the gold anklet and said, "This is the scoundrel," and had glowing coals brought which the dog had to swallow in the sight of all, so that flames burst out of its throat. Then he asked the king whether he wanted to see him in his true shape and wished him back into the chef, and there he at once stood with his white apron and the knife hanging at his side. On seeing him, the king got angry and ordered him thrown into the deepest dungeon. Then the huntsman went on to say, "Father, do you also want to see the girl who brought me up so tenderly and who afterward was supposed to kill me but didn't though her own life was at stake?" "Indeed I should very much like to see her," answered the king. "Most gracious father," said the son, "I'll show her to you in the form of a beautiful flower," reached into his pocket, took the pink and placed it on the royal board. It was finer than any the king had ever seen. Then the son said, "Now I'll show her in her true form, too," and wished her back into a maiden. She stood there and was more beautiful than any artist could have painted.

Then the king sent two ladies-in-waiting and two servants down in the tower to fetch the queen and bring her to the royal board, but when she was brought there, she ate nothing, saying, "Gracious and merciful God Who sustained me in the tower will soon deliver me." She lived three days more and then died happily. When she was buried, the two white doves which had brought her her food in the tower and were angels from Heaven, followed her and lighted on her grave. The old king had the chef quartered, but his sorrow ate at his heart, and he soon died.

His son married the beautiful maiden whom he had brought home in his pocket in the form of a flower, and whether they're still alive, God alone knows.

77 Clever Peggy

Das kluge Gretel

THERE WAS A COOK whose name was Peggy; she wore shoes with red heels, and when she went out in them, she'd mince along, be quite happy, and say, "You really are a pretty girl!" On getting home she'd take a swallow of wine out of pure happiness, and because wine gives one an appetite, she'd taste the best of her own cooking, and tasting until she had her fill, she'd say, "A cook must know how the food tastes."

It once happened that the master said to her, "Peggy, a guest is coming this evening; prepare me two chickens in your best style." "Very good, sir," answered Peggy. She killed the chickens, scalded them, plucked them, put them on the spit, and toward evening placed them over the fire to broil. The chickens began to get brown and done, but the guest hadn't yet come. Then Peggy called out to the master, "If the guest doesn't come, I'll have to take the chickens off the fire, but it will be a frightful shame if they're not eaten soon while they're still at their juiciest." "I'll go myself then," said the master, "and fetch the guest."

When the master had turned his back, Peggy put the spit with the chickens to one side and thought, "Standing so long near the fire makes one sweat and makes one thirsty. Who knows when they'll be coming! Meanwhile I'll skip down cellar and have a swallow." She ran downstairs, raised a jug to her lips, and saying "God bless you, Peggy," took a good drink. "The wine calls for one drink after another and the fewer interruptions the better," she went on to say and took another deep draught. Then she went and put the chickens back on the fire, buttered them, and turned the spit merrily. Because the broilers smelled so good, Peggy thought, "Maybe I've forgotten something; I'd better taste them." She touched them with her finger and licked it, then said, "My! how good the chickens are! It's a perfect shame not to eat them at once," ran to the window to see whether the master and the guest were coming yet, and saw no one. She went back to the chickens, thinking, "One of the wings is getting burnt; I'd better eat it up," so she cut it off and ate it. It tasted good, and when she was finished with that, she thought, "The other's got to come off, too; otherwise the master will notice that something's missing." When the two wings were consumed, she again went and looked for the master and didn't see him. The thought occurred to her, "Who knows! Perhaps they aren't coming at all but have turned in somewhere." Then she said, "Well, Peggy, cheer up! A start's been made on one of them anyhow; just have another drink and eat it all up. When it's all gone, then you'll be at peace. Why should this good gift of God go to waste?" So once more she went down cellar, had a respectable drink, and ate up one chicken quite happily. When one chicken was eaten up and the master still didn't come, Peggy looked at the other and said, "Where the one is, the other must be, too; the two go together; what's right for one is right for the other. I think another drink wouldn't do me any harm." So she took another hearty drink and had the second chicken run to join the first.

As she was thus at the height of her meal, the master arrived and said, "Hurry up, Peggy, the guest will be right along." "Yes, sir, I'll attend to it at once," answered Peggy. Meanwhile the master looked to see if the table was properly set, took the big knife with which he was going to carve the chickens, and sharpened it out in the passage-way. Just then the guest arrived and knocked politely and courteously at the front door. Peggy went to see who it was, and seeing the guest, put her finger to her lips, saying, "S-s-sh! get out as quick as you can. If my master catches you, you'll be in a bad way. True enough, he invited you for supper but only with the idea of cutting off both your ears. Just hear him sharpening the knife!" The guest heard the sound of sharpening and ran back down the steps as fast as he could. Peggy wasted no time but ran screaming to her master, crying, "You certainly invited a fine guest!" "My goodness, Peggy, why so? What do you mean by that?" "Yes, indeed," she said, "he took the two chickens out of the dish just as I was going to serve them and has run off with them." "That's a nice thing to do!" said the master and regretted the loss of the fine chickens. "He might at least have left one, so there'd be something left for me to eat." He shouted to him to stop, but the guest pretended not to hear.

Then he ran after him with the knife still in his hand, crying, "Just one, just one!" meaning that the guest should at least leave him one chicken and not take both. The guest, however, only supposed that he was to give up one of his ears and ran like mad in order to get both his ears home.

78 The Old Grandfather and the Grandson

Der alte Grossvater und der Enkel

THERE WAS ONCE A VERY OLD MAN whose eyes had grown dim, his ears deaf, and whose knees shook. When he sat at table hardly able to hold his spoon, he'd spill soup on the tablecloth, and a little would even run out of his mouth. This disgusted his son and his daughter-in-law, and so finally the old grandfather had to sit in a corner behind the stove. They gave him his food in an earthenware bowl and not even enough at that. He used to look sadly toward the table, and tears would come to his eyes. One day his trembling hands couldn't even hold the bowl, and it fell to the floor and broke to pieces. The young woman scolded, but he said nothing and merely sighed. For a few farthings she then bought him a wooden bowl, and he had to eat out of that. As they were sitting thus, his little four-year-old grandson was fitting some little boards together on the floor. "What are you doing there?" asked his father. "I'm making a trough for father and mother to eat out of when I'm grown up," answered the child.

The husband and wife looked at one another for a while, finally began to weep, and at once brought the old grandfather to the table. From then they always let him eat with them, and they didn't say anything even when he did spill a little.

79 The Nixie

Die Wassernixe

A LITTLE BROTHER AND SISTER were playing by a well, and as they were playing, both plopped in. Down in the well was a nixie who said, "Now I've got you! Now you're to work good and hard for me," and led them away with her. She gave the girl hard, tangled flax to spin, and she had to carry water in a cask with no bottom. The boy was supposed to chop down a tree with a dull ax, and all they got to eat were dumplings as hard as rocks. Finally the children got so impatient that they waited till one Sunday when the nixie was at church and ran away.

When church was out, the nixie saw that the birds had flown and set after them with long strides. However, the children spied her from afar, and the girl threw a brush behind her; this produced a huge mountain of brushes, with thousands and thousands of briars, which the nixie had to climb over with a great deal of trouble, though she finally got across. When the children saw that, the boy threw a comb behind him; this produced a huge mountain of combs, with thousands and thousands of teeth. The nixie, however, knew how to hold onto them and finally got over them. Then the girl threw a mirror behind her, which produced a mountain of mirrors and was so very, very slippery that she couldn't get over it. Then she thought, "I'll hurry home and fetch my ax and cut the mountain of mirrors in two," but by the time she'd got back and had chopped up the glass, the children had long since fled far away, and the nixie had to trudge back to her well.

80   The Death of the Hen

Von dem Tode des Hühnchens

A COCK AND A HEN once went to the nut mountain and agreed that whichever found a nut meat should share it with the other. Now the hen found a great big nut but said nothing about it, intending to eat the meat alone, but the meat was so big that she couldn't swallow it and it stuck in her throat so that she was afraid she'd choke to death. Then the hen cried, "Cock, please run as fast as you can and get me some water or else I'll choke to death." The cock ran as fast as he could to the well and said, "Well, you're to give me water; the hen is lying on the nut mountain, has swallowed a big nut meat, and is on the point of choking to death." The well answered, "First go to the bride and have her give you red silk." The cock went to the bride and said, "Bride, you're to give me red silk; the silk I'll give to the well, the well will give me water, the water I'll bring to the hen; she's lying on the nut mountain, has swallowed a big nut meat, and is on the point of choking on it." The bride answered, "First run and fetch me my wreath that got caught on a willow." The cock ran to the willow, pulled the wreath off the branch, took it to the bride, who gave him red silk for it; this he took to the well, which gave him water for it. Then the cock took the water to the hen, but when he got there, the hen meanwhile had choked to death, lay there dead, and didn't stir.

Then the cock was so sad that he cried aloud, and all the animals came and mourned over the hen, and six mice made a little wagon to drive the hen to her grave in. When the wagon was finished, they harnessed themselves to it, and the cock drove. On the way a fox came along and said, "Where are you going, cock?" "I'm on the way to bury my hen." "May I ride with you?"

> "Yes, but sit down in the back of the wagon;
> In front you're too heavy for my little horses."

The fox sat down in the back, then a wolf, a bear, a stag, a lion, and all the animals of the forest. Thus they proceeded on their journey until they came to a brook. "How are we going to get across?" said the cock. There was a straw lying by the brook which said, "I'll lay myself across, then you can drive over me." However, when the six mice got on the bridge, the straw slipped and fell into the water, and all six mice fell in and drowned. Then there was the same difficulty as before, and an ember came and said, "I'm big enough; I'll lay myself across, and you're to drive over me." The ember in turn laid itself over the water but unfortunately touched it just slightly, then hissed, went out, and was dead. On seeing that, a stone took pity on them, wanted to help the cock, and lay down across the brook. Then the cock pulled the wagon himself, but when he'd got it almost across, was already on land with the dead hen, and was going to pull along the others who were sitting in back, there were too many of them. The wagon rolled back, and everybody fell into the water and drowned.

Then the cock was all alone with the dead hen and dug her a grave and laid her in it and raised a mound over it. He sat down on it and grieved until he, too, died, and then everybody was dead.

81 Merry Andrew

Bruder Lustig

THERE WAS ONCE A GREAT WAR, and when the war came to an end, many soldiers received their discharge. Merry Andrew, too, received his and nothing else but a small loaf of ration bread and four farthings in cash. With that he went his way.

Now St. Peter had sat down by the wayside in the guise of a poor beggar, and when Merry Andrew came along, begged alms of him. The latter replied, "Dear beggar, what can I give you? I've been a soldier and received my discharge and have nothing

else but this small loaf of ration bread and four farthings in cash.
When that's gone, I'll have to beg just like you. Still, I'll give you
something." Then he divided the loaf into four parts, gave one to
the apostle and a farthing, too. St. Peter thanked him, went on,
in a different shape again sat down as a beggar where the soldier
would be coming along, and when the soldier got there, begged
alms of him as before. Merry Andrew gave the same answer as
before and again gave him a quarter of the bread and a farthing.
St. Peter thanked him and went on and for the third time, though
in a different form, sat down by the wayside as a beggar and
accosted Merry Andrew. Merry Andrew also gave him the third
quarter of the loaf and the third farthing. St. Peter thanked him,
and Merry Andrew went on with only one quarter of the loaf
and one farthing. Then he entered an inn, ate the bread, and with
the farthing had himself served a beer with his bread. When he'd
finished, he went on and again met St. Peter in the guise of a discharged soldier. The latter addressed him with "Good day, comrade. Can you give me a piece of bread and a farthing for a
drink?" "Where am I to get it?" answered Merry Andrew. "I
received my discharge and nothing else but a loaf of ration bread
and four farthings in cash. I met three beggars on the road and
gave each a quarter of my loaf and one farthing; the last quarter
of the loaf I ate in the inn and with the farthing bought a drink.
Now I'm cleaned out, and if you haven't anything left either,
we can go begging together." "No," answered St. Peter, "that
won't be quite necessary. I understand a little something about
doctoring and with that I'll surely earn what I need." "Well,"
said Merry Andrew, "I know nothing about that, so I must go
begging by myself." "Well, just come along," said St. Peter; "if I
earn something, you shall have half of it." "I'm quite agreeable
to that," said Merry Andrew, and accordingly they went on together.

They came to a farmhouse where they heard terrific crying and
lamentation. They entered, and within a man was lying mortally ill and on the point of death, and his wife was weeping and
wailing loudly. "Stop your weeping and wailing," said St. Peter;
"I'll make your husband well again," took an ointment from his
pouch and cured the sick man immediately so that he was able
to get up and was quite well. Then the husband and wife said

most joyfully, "How can we reward you? What can we give you?" St. Peter, however, would accept nothing, and the more the farmer and his wife entreated him, the more firmly he refused. Merry Andrew, however, nudged St. Peter, saying, "Do take something; we really need it." Finally the farmer's wife brought a lamb and told St. Peter he'd have to accept that, but he didn't want to. Then Merry Andrew nudged him in the ribs and said, "For goodness sake, accept it, you foolish devil; we really need it." Finally St. Peter said, "All right, I'll accept the lamb, but I won't carry it; if you want it, you'll have to carry it." "That doesn't matter," said Merry Andrew. "I'll carry it, of course," and took it on his shoulder.

Now they went on and got into a forest; by then the lamb had begun to weigh upon Merry Andrew. He, however, was hungry, and said to St. Peter, "Look, there's a nice place; we might cook the lamb there and eat it." "Right you are," answered St. Peter, "but I don't know anything about cooking. If you want to cook, there's a kettle for you; meanwhile I'll walk about a bit till it's done. But you mustn't start eating till I get back; I'll surely be there on time." "Go along then," said Merry Andrew; "I understand about cooking, and I'll do it all right." St. Peter went off and Merry Andrew made a fire, threw the meat into the kettle, and boiled it. The lamb was already done but still the apostle wasn't back. Merry Andrew took it out of the kettle, carved it, and found the heart. "That's supposed to be the best part," he said, tasted it, and finally ate it all up. At last St. Peter returned and said, "You may eat the whole lamb yourself; I just want the heart. Give me that." Then Merry Andrew took knife and fork, pretended to hunt around diligently in the stew but couldn't find the heart. Finally he said right out, "There isn't any heart." "Why, where can it be?" said the apostle. "I don't know," answered Merry Andrew, "but look what fools we both are! looking for the lamb's heart and it hasn't occurred to either of us that a lamb hasn't got a heart." "My goodness," said St. Peter, "that is something new! Of course every animal has a heart; why shouldn't a lamb have one?" "Of course not, brother, a lamb hasn't got a heart. Just think it over and you'll remember that it really hasn't got one." "Well, all right then," said St. Peter, "if there isn't any heart, then I don't want any other part of the lamb; you can eat it all yourself." "What I can't eat up, I'll take along in my knapsack," said Merry Andrew, ate half the lamb and put the rest in his knapsack.

They went on. Then St. Peter made a stream flow across the road and they had to go through it. "You go ahead," said St. Peter. "No," answered Merry Andrew, "you go ahead," thinking "if the water's too deep, I'll hang back." Then St. Peter waded through, and the water came only to his knees. Now Merry Andrew was going to wade across, too, but the stream swelled and rose to his neck. Then he called out, "Help, brother!" St. Peter said, "Will you also confess that you ate the lamb's heart?" "No," he answered, "I didn't eat it." Then the stream got still bigger and rose to his mouth. "Help, brother!" cried the soldier. St. Peter once again said, "Will you also confess that you ate the lamb's heart?" "No," he answered, "I didn't eat it." St. Peter didn't want to let him drown, caused the stream to subside, and helped him over.

They went on and came to a kingdom where they heard that the king's daughter was mortally ill. "What ho, brother!" said the soldier to St. Peter, "there's a chance for us! If we cure her, we're fixed for life." St. Peter didn't walk fast enough for him. "Now pick up your feet, dear friend," he said to him, "so that we may get there before it's too late." St. Peter, however, kept walking slower and slower despite all of Merry Andrew's urgings and proddings, till at last they heard that the king's daughter had died. "Now we've lost our chance," said Merry Andrew. "That comes from your dawdling along." "Do be quiet," answered St. Peter. "I can do more than make the sick well; I can bring the dead to life, too." "Well," said Merry Andrew, "if that's so, I'm satisfied, but if you do that, you've got to earn us at least half the kingdom." Thereupon they went to the royal palace where everybody was in deep mourning. St. Peter, however, said to the king that he'd bring his daughter back to life and was led to her. Then he said, "Bring me a kettle of water," and when it was brought, ordered everybody out, and Merry Andrew alone was allowed to stay with him. He cut off all the dead girl's limbs, threw them into the water, made a fire under the kettle, and let them boil. When all the flesh had dropped off the bones, he took out the fine white bones, placed them on a table, arranging and disposing them in their natural position. When that was done, he went up to the skeleton and said three times, "In the name of the Most Holy Trinity, dead woman, arise!" and the third time the king's daughter stood up alive, well, and beautiful. The king rejoiced greatly at this and said to St. Peter, "Name your reward; I'll give it to you even if it's half my kingdom." But St. Peter answered, "I don't want anything in return." "Oh, you Tom-Fool!" thought Merry Andrew to himself, nudged his comrade in the ribs, and said, "Don't be so stupid! Even if you don't want anything, I need something." St. Peter didn't want anything, but since the king noticed that the other very much wanted something, he had the treasurer fill his knapsack with gold.

They went on their way, and when they got into a forest, St. Peter said to Merry Andrew, "Now let's divide the gold." "All right," he answered, "we'll do that." Then St. Peter divided the gold and apportioned it in three parts. Thought Merry Andrew, "What a mad idea he's got again! making three lots when there are only two of us!" "Now I've divided it quite exactly," said St. Peter, "one share for me, one share for you, and one share for the man who ate the lamb's heart." "Oh, I ate that, you may believe me," answered Merry Andrew, quickly pocketing the gold. "How can that be true?" said St. Peter. "A lamb hasn't got a heart." "My goodness, brother! Where did you get that idea? Of course a lamb has a heart like every animal. Why should it be the only one not to have one?" "Very well, very well," said St. Peter, "keep the gold yourself, but I won't stay with you any longer and shall go my way alone." "As you like, dear friend," answered the soldier, "good-bye."

Then St. Peter took another road, but Merry Andrew thought, "It's just as well he's trotting off, for he's a queer customer." Now, to be sure, he had enough money but didn't know how to handle it, squandered it, gave it away, and after a certain time again had nothing. Then he came to a country where he heard that the king's daughter had died. "Stop!" he thought, "that may prove to be a good thing. I'll bring her back to life and be paid a good reward." So he went to the king and offered to revive the dead girl. The king had heard that a discharged soldier was traveling about and bringing the dead back to life and thought that Merry Andrew was the man; still, since he had no confidence in him, he first asked his councilors. They said he might as well try it, since his daughter was dead in any event. Merry Andrew had a kettle of water brought, ordered everybody out, cut off all the limbs, threw them into the water, and made a fire underneath just as he had seen St. Peter do. The water began to boil, and the flesh dropped off the bones. Then he took out the bones and placed them on a table, but he didn't know how to arrange them and laid the bones every which way. Then he stood before them and said, "In the name of the Most Holy Trinity, dead woman, arise!" and said it three times. Nevertheless the bones didn't stir. Then he said it thrice more but again in vain. "Get up, my treasure," he cried, "get up, or it won't go well for you." As he said that, St. Peter suddenly came in through the window in his former shape of a discharged soldier and said, "You bad fellow, what are you doing there? How can the dead girl arise when you've thrown her bones about any old way?" "Dear friend, I did it as well as I could," he answered. "This time I'll help you out of the difficulty, but I tell you, if you try anything like that again, things will go badly for you. Nor may you make the slightest request of the king for having done this or accept anything for it." Then St. Peter arranged the bones properly, said three times, "In the name of the Most Holy Trinity, dead woman, arise," and the king's daughter stood up and was well and beautiful as before. Then St. Peter again went out through the window. Merry Andrew was glad that it had turned out so well but was vexed at not being able to accept anything for it. "I'd just like to know," he thought, "why he has such mad notions; for what he gives with one hand he takes away with the other. It makes no sense." The king asked Merry Andrew what he wanted, but he mightn't take anything; however, by dint of hints and subterfuge he got the king to order his knapsack filled with gold and with it went on his way. As he went out, St. Peter was standing at the gate and said, "Look what kind of a fellow you are! Didn't I forbid you to accept anything? And now you've got a knapsack full of gold!" "How can I help it," answered Merry Andrew, "when they put it in?" "Now I'm telling you, you're not to try anything like that a second time, or it will fare ill with you." "Why, brother, don't worry; I now have gold. Why should I bother washing bones?" "Yes," said St. Peter, "the gold will last a long time! However, to stop you from going astray again, I'll give your knapsack the power that everything you wish into it shall be in it. Good-bye. You won't see me again." "Good-bye," said

Merry Andrew and thought, "I'm glad you're going away, you
queer chap; I certainly shan't follow you." However, he thought
nothing more of the magic power that had been given his knapsack.

Merry Andrew traveled about with his money and squandered
it and dissipated it as the first time. When he had nothing but four
farthings left, he passed an inn and said, "The money's got to
go," and ordered three farthings' worth of wine and a farthing's
worth of bread. As he was sitting there drinking, the odor of roast
goose mounted to his nostrils; Merry Andrew peered and looked
about and saw that the landlord had two geese in the warming
oven. Then he remembered that his comrade had told him that
anything he might wish into his knapsack would be in it. "What
ho! you've got to try it with the geese." So he went out and outside the door said, "Now I wish the two roast geese out of the
warming oven into my knapsack." Having said that he unbuckled
his knapsack, looked in, and saw both geese inside. "My! that's
fine," he said, "now I'm a made man," went to a meadow and
took out the roast geese. At the height of his meal two traveling
journeymen came along and with hungry eyes saw the goose
which had not yet been touched. "One's enough for me,"
thought Merry Andrew and calling the two journeymen, said,
"Take the goose and eat it to my good health." They thanked
him, went with it to the inn, ordered half a bottle of wine and a
loaf of bread, took out the goose that had been given them, and
started eating. The innkeeper's wife was looking on and said to
her husband, "The two men are eating a goose; just look and see
whether it's not one of ours out of the warming oven." The innkeeper went over and found the oven empty. "What, you thieving
rogues! You expect to eat your goose so cheap? Pay at once or
I'll give you a thrashing with a green hazel rod." "We're no
thieves," said the two, "a discharged soldier out on the meadow
made us a present of the goose." "You won't pull my leg; the
soldier was here but went out the door like an honest fellow. I
kept my eye on him; you're the thieves and have got to pay."
Since they couldn't pay, he took a stick and beat them out the
door.

Merry Andrew went his way and came to where there was a
splendid manor house and not far from it a poor inn. He went to
the inn and asked for a night's lodging, but the landlord refused

him, saying, "There's no room; the house is full up with quality."
"I'm surprised," said Merry Andrew, "that they come to you instead of going to the splendid house." "Indeed," answered the
innkeeper, "it's quite something to spend a night there: people
who've tried it haven't come out again alive." "If others have
tried it," said Merry Andrew, "I'll try it, too." "Give that idea
up," said the innkeeper; "it'll cost you your life." "It really won't
cost me my life," said Merry Andrew. "Just give me the keys
and plenty to eat and drink." The landlord gave him the keys
and food and drink, and with that Merry Andrew went into the
house, had a good meal and, when at last he got sleepy, lay down
on the floor, for there wasn't any bed there. He soon fell asleep
but in the night was awakened by a great noise. On rousing himself he saw nine ugly devils in the room; they'd formed a circle
and were dancing around him. "Just dance as long as you like,"
said Merry Andrew, "but don't come too near me." Nevertheless
the devils kept crowding in on him and almost stepped on his face
with their dirty feet. "Quiet down, you devils," he said, but they
behaved worse and worse. Then Merry Andrew got angry and
cried out, "Stop it! I'll quiet you down soon enough," took hold
of the leg of a chair and hit out at them. However, the nine devils
against one soldier was, after all, too much, and when he'd strike
the one nearest, the others would seize him by the hair from
behind and pull him about cruelly. "You pack of devils!" he
cried, "now that's too much for me. Just wait! into my knapsack,
all nine of you!" In a trice they were inside, and he buckled it up
and tossed it into a corner. It was suddenly quiet, and Merry
Andrew lay down again and slept until broad daylight. Then the
innkeeper and the nobleman who owned the house came to see
how he'd fared. When they saw him hale and hearty, they were
amazed and asked, "Didn't the ghosts do anything to you?" "I
should think so!" answered Merry Andrew. "I have all nine of
them in my knapsack. You may move right back into your
house; from now on no one will haunt it." The nobleman
thanked him, gave him rich presents, and begged him to stay on
in his service, saying he'd take care of him for the rest of his
days. "No," he answered, "I'm used to a roving life and want to
journey farther afield." So Merry Andrew departed, went into a
smithy, put the knapsack with the nine devils in it on the anvil,
and asked the smith and his apprentices to pound on it. They

pounded with their big hammers as hard as they could, so that the devils set up a piteous howl. Afterward when he opened his knapsack, eight were dead, but one, who had been sitting in a crease, was still alive, slipped out, and went back to Hell.

Then Merry Andrew roamed about the world for a long time more, and anybody who knew might tell a good deal about it. Finally, however, he grew old and began to think of his end. Then he went to a hermit who was known as a devout man and said to him, "I'm tired of roving and now want to try to get into the Heavenly Kingdom." "There are two roads," answered the hermit, "one wide and pleasant, leading to Hell; the other narrow and rough, leading to Heaven." "I'd be a fool," thought Merry Andrew, "to go the narrow and rough way," so he started out, going the wide and pleasant way, and finally got to a big black gate: this was the gate of Hell. Merry Andrew knocked, and the porter looked to see who was there, but when he saw Merry Andrew, he was frightened, for he actually was the ninth devil who had been with the others in the knapsack and who got off with a black eye. Therefore he quickly shot the bolt again and ran to the chief of the devils, saying, "There's a fellow outside with a knapsack who wants to get in, but for goodness sake don't let him in or he'll wish the whole of Hell into his knapsack. Once he had me pounded unmercifully in it." So they shouted out to Merry Andrew to go away again and that he wouldn't get in. "If they don't want me there," he thought, "I'll see if I can find a lodging in Heaven, for I've got to stay somewhere," turned about and went on till he got outside the gate of Heaven at which he also knocked. St. Peter was sitting right there as porter. Merry Andrew recognized him at once and thought, "Here's an old friend; things will go better here," but St. Peter said, "Am I right in thinking that you want to get into Heaven?" "Please let me in, brother; I've got to turn in somewhere. If they'd take me in in Hell, I shouldn't have come here." "No," said St. Peter, "you don't get in here." "Well, if you won't let me in, just take back your knapsack, for I don't want to have anything of yours," said Merry Andrew. "Then give it here," said St. Peter. He passed the knapsack through the grating into Heaven, and St. Peter took it and hung it up beside his easy chair. Then Merry Andrew said, "Now I wish myself into my knapsack." In a trice he was inside and was now in Heaven, and St. Peter had to let him stay there.

82 Gambling Jack

De Spielhansl

THERE WAS ONCE A MAN who did nothing but gamble, and therefore people called him Gambling Jack, and because he never stopped gambling, he gambled away his house and all. On the very last day, when his creditors were already about to seize the house, Our Lord and St. Peter came and said that he was to put them up for the night. "You can spend the night all right," said Gambling Jack, "but I can't give you a bed or anything to eat." Then Our Lord said he'd only have to put them up and that they'd buy some food for themselves. Gambling Jack agreed to this. Then St. Peter gave him threepence and told him to go to the baker and get a loaf of bread. Gambling Jack went, but when he got to the house where the other gamblers lived who had won everything from him, they called out to him, crying, "Come on in, Jack." "Oh, yes," he said, "you want to get the threepence from me, too!" However, they kept on urging him. He went in and gambled even the threepence away. St. Peter and Our Lord waited and waited, and when after a long time he didn't come back, they went to meet him. When Gambling Jack finally came, he pretended that the money had dropped into a pool of water and that he'd been poking about in it. All that time Our Lord already knew, however, that he'd lost it gambling. Then St. Peter again gave him threepence. This time, however, he didn't let himself be led astray and brought them the bread. Then Our Lord asked him if he perhaps had any wine, and he answered, "Alas, master, the casks are all empty." Then Our Lord said he was to go down cellar: "The very best wine is now down there." For a long time he wouldn't believe it, but at last he said, "I'll go down, but I know there isn't any"; yet when he broached the cask, the very best wine ran out. He now brought them the wine, and the two stayed there over night. Early the next day Our Lord told Gambling Jack to ask for three favors, thinking he'd ask for

Heaven, but Gambling Jack asked for cards with which he'd win everything and dice with which he'd win everything, also a tree bearing all sorts of fruit, and if one climbed it, that he couldn't get down till he ordered him to. Our Lord gave him everything he'd asked for and again went on His way with St. Peter.

Now Gambling Jack started gambling in earnest and might soon have won half the world. Then St. Peter said to Our Lord, "Master, this won't do: he'll end by winning the whole world; we must send Death after him." So they sent Death after him. When Death arrived, Gambling Jack was sitting at the gaming table. "Jack," said Death, "step outside for a moment," but Gambling Jack said, "Just wait a minute till the game is over, and meanwhile climb up the tree out there and pick a little something for us to nibble on the way." Then Death climbed up, but when he wanted to get down again, he couldn't, and Gambling Jack let him stay up there for seven years. During that time no one died.

Then St. Peter said to Our Lord, "Master, this won't do. No one is dying any more, and we'll have to go ourselves." So they went straight off and said to Death, "Come down," and Death immediately seized Jack and throttled him. They went off together and got to the Otherworld. Then Gambling Jack went to the gate of Heaven and knocked. "Who's out there?" "Gambling Jack." "Oh, we don't want you, go right away." Then he went to the gate of Purgatory and again knocked. "Who's out there?" "Gambling Jack." "Oh, we've got misery and distress aplenty here. We don't want to gamble; go right away again." Then he went to the gate of Hell, and there they did let him in. There was no one at home except Lucifer and the hunchback devils (for the straight ones happened to have business on Earth), and then he at once sat down and began gambling again. Now Lucifer had nothing but hunchback devils, and Gambling Jack won these away from him, because with his cards he was bound to win everything. He went off with the hunchback devils, and together they went to Hohenfurt [Upper Bavaria], pulled out the hop poles, went up to Heaven with them, and began to assail Heaven. And now Heaven was already collapsing. Then St. Peter said, "Master, this won't do. We must let him in or else he'll overthrow our Heaven," so they let him in. But Gambling Jack at once started gambling again and immediately such a noise and clatter arose that one couldn't hear oneself speak. Again St. Peter said, "Master, this won't do. We must throw him out or else he'll turn all Heaven upside down." So they fell upon him and threw him out, and then his soul split up and bits of it went into other gamblers who are still alive.

83 Lucky John

Hans im Glück

FOR SEVEN YEARS John had served his master; then he said to him, "My time is up, sir; now I'd like to go back home to my mother. Give me my wages." The master replied, "You've served me loyally and honestly: like service, like wage," and gave him a lump of gold as big as John's head. John took his kerchief from his pocket, wrapped up the nugget, shouldered it, and started for home. As he was thus walking along, one foot after the other, he caught sight of a horseman who, fresh and gay, was trotting past on a lively horse. "Alas," said John aloud, "what a fine thing riding is! It's like sitting in a chair: you never strike against a stone, you spare your shoes, and you get along like nothing at all!" The horseman, who heard this, stopped and cried out, "My goodness, John, then why are you walking?" "I have to," he answered, "I've got to carry a big nugget home. True enough, it's gold, but just the same I can't hold my head up and it weighs heavily upon my shoulder, too." "Do you know something," said the horseman, "let's exchange: I'll give you my horse, and you give me your nugget." "With all my heart," said John, "but I warn you, it will be a burden to you." The horseman dismounted, took the gold, helped John up, put the reins firmly in his hands, and said, "If you want to go rather fast, you must click your tongue and call out, "giddap! giddap!"

John was frightfully happy to be sitting on his horse and riding along so free. After a while it occurred to him that they ought to be going even faster and began to click his tongue and call out "giddap! giddap!" The horse set out at a smart trot, and before John knew it, he was thrown and was lying in a ditch that separated the fields from the highway. The horse would have run away, too, had it not been stopped by a farmer who happened to come along driving a cow before him. John picked himself up and set off on foot again, but he was cross and said to the farmer, "Riding is a bad joke, particularly when one runs into a mare like this that bucks and throws one in a way to break one's neck. I shall absolutely never get on it again. I'm all for your cow: one can walk along comfortably behind her, and besides, one is sure of one's milk, butter, and cheese every day. What wouldn't I give to have such a cow!" "Well," said the farmer, "if you like it so much, I'll trade the cow for the horse." John agreed most joyfully: the farmer swung onto the horse and rode off in a hurry.

John drove his cow before him in leisurely fashion, thinking of the lucky bargain. "As long as I just have a piece of bread—and that I'm not likely to lack—I can eat it as often as I please with butter and cheese; when I'm thirsty, I'll milk my cow and drink milk. What more can the heart desire?" Arriving at an inn, he stopped, joyfully ate up everything he had with him, his dinner and supper, and with his last few farthings had a half a glass of beer. Then he drove his cow on before him always in the direction of his mother's village. As midday drew near, the heat grew more oppressive, and John found himself on a heath that would take at least another hour to cross. He got so very hot and thirsty that his tongue stuck to the roof of his mouth. "We can do something about that," thought John, "now I'll milk my cow and refresh myself with the milk." He tied her to a dead tree and, having no pail, put his leather cap underneath, but no matter how hard he tried, not a drop of milk came, and because he was clumsy and awkward, the impatient animal finally gave him such a kick on the head with one of her hind legs that he tumbled down and for some time couldn't think where he was. Fortunately at just that moment a butcher came along with a young pig in a barrow. "What's the game?" he cried and helped good old John up. John told him what had happened. The butcher handed him his bottle, saying, "Have a drink and refresh yourself. The cow probably won't give milk because it's an old creature fit at best to serve as a draft animal or to be slaughtered." "My goodness!" said John, stroking back his hair, "who'd have thought that! It's certainly a fine thing to be able to slaughter such an animal at home. What a lot of meat one gets! However, I'm not very fond of cow meat; it isn't juicy enough for me. But to have a young pig like that! That tastes altogether different—and there are the sausages, too!" "Listen, John," said the butcher, "as a favor I'll trade with you and leave you the pig for the cow." "May God reward your kindness," said John, turned the cow over to him, had him release the little pig from the barrow, and hand him the rope to which it was tied.

John went his way, reflecting on how everything happened to order for him: whenever anything unpleasant occurred, it was always immediately set right. Then he met a boy who was carrying a fine white goose under his arm. They said good-day to one another, and John began to tell of his good luck and how every time he'd made so profitable an exchange. The boy told him he was taking the goose to a christening party. "Just heft it and see how heavy it is," he went on, taking it by the wings; "they've been fattening it for eight weeks. Anyone who takes a bite of it once it's roasted will have to wipe the fat from both sides of his mouth." "Yes, indeed," said John, weighing it with one hand, "it certainly weighs something, but my pig is no mean thing." Meanwhile the boy was looking about in every direction with a worried look and shaking his head. "Listen," he went on, "there may be something wrong about your pig. In the village I just passed through a pig had been stolen from the magistrate's sty. I'm very much afraid that you've got it there. They've sent people out, and it would be a bad business if they caught you with the pig: the least that could happen would be for them to put you in the black hole." Our good John got frightened. "Alas," he said, "help me out of this difficulty! You know the way about here better than I; take my pig and leave me your goose." "Of course I must take a certain risk," answered the boy, "but just the same I don't want to be to blame for your getting into trouble." So he took hold of the rope and quickly drove the pig off into a side road while good John, free of his worries, went on home with the goose under his arm. "As I really think it over," he said to himself, "I have the best of the bargain: first the good roast goose, then the large amount of fat that will drip out which will supply me with goose fat for my bread for three months, and finally the fine white feathers that I'll have my pillow stuffed with—and I'll sleep on that without being rocked! How glad my mother will be!"

After he'd passed through the last village, a scissors-grinder was standing there with his cart; his wheel was humming, and he was singing as a burden,

> "I grind the scissors and turn the wheel
> And trim my sails to suit the wind."

John stopped and watched him; finally he addressed him, saying, "You're well off, because you're so merry in your grinding." "Yes," answered the scissors-grinder, "there's a lot of money in the business. A real scissors-grinder is a man who finds money whenever he puts his hand in his pocket. But where did you buy that fine goose?" "I didn't buy it; I traded it for a pig." "And the pig?" "I got that for a cow." "And the cow?" "I got that for a horse." "And the horse?" "For the horse I gave a nugget of gold as big as my head." "And the gold?" "Why, that was my wages for seven years' service." "You certainly knew a way out every time," said the scissors-grinder; "if you can now manage it so that you hear the money jingle in your pocket on getting up in the morning, your fortune is made." "How am I to do that?" said John. "You must become a scissors-grinder like myself: to do that all you really need is a grindstone, the rest takes care of itself. There! I've got one, a little damaged to be sure, but you don't have to give me anything for it except your goose. Do you want to do it?" "How can you really ask!" answered John, "I'll certainly be the luckiest man on earth! If I have money every time I feel in my pocket, what else do I have to worry about?" "Well," said the grinder, picking up an ordinary heavy field stone that happened to be lying beside him, "here you have another good stone in the bargain; one can hit good and hard on it and you can straighten out your old nails. Take it and take good care of it."

John shouldered the stone and went on contentedly, his eyes sparkling with joy. "I must have been born with a caul," he cried; "everything I wish comes to pass like a child born on Sunday." Meanwhile, since he'd been on his feet since daybreak, he began to get tired; also hunger tormented him, since he had eaten all his provisions at one time in his joy over the cow-trade. Finally he was able to keep going only with the greatest effort and had to stop every other minute; furthermore, the stones were weighing on him unmercifully. Then he couldn't help thinking how fine it would be if he didn't have to carry them just at that time. Walking at a snail's pace he came to a well in the fields, where he meant to rest and refresh himself with a cool drink. Not to damage the stones when he sat down, he carefully put them beside him on the edge of the well. Then he sat down and was about to bend over to drink, made a false move, brushed slightly against them, and both stones went plop into the well. When with his own eyes he saw them disappear into the water, John jumped up for joy, then knelt and with tears in his eyes thanked God for having done him this favor, too, and rid him of the heavy stones, his last obstacle, in such a nice way that he had nothing to reproach himself with. "There's no man under the sun as lucky as I!" he cried out.

With light heart and free of every burden he now skipped along until he got home to his mother's.

84   John Gets Married

Hans heiratet

THERE WAS ONCE A YOUNG FARMER whose name was John; his cousin wanted to get him a rich wife. He put John behind the stove and heated it up well. He then fetched a pot of milk and a lot of white bread, placed a shiny new farthing in his hand, and said, "John, hold on tight to the farthing, crumble the white bread in the milk, stay where you are and don't move from the spot till I come back." "All right," said John, "I'll do just as you say." The matchmaker put on a pair of old patched trousers and going to a rich farmer's daughter in the next village, said, "Don't you want to marry my cousin John? You'll get a fine and clever husband whom you'll like." The girl's miserly father asked, "What are his prospects? Has he plenty of bread to break?" "Dear friend," answered the matchmaker, "my cousin is warm, has a pretty penny in hand, and has plenty of bread to break. Nor has he fewer patches (as they also say of parcels of land) than myself," slapping, as he said this, his patched trousers. "If you'll take the trouble to come along with me, I'll show you at once that everything is as I say." The miser didn't want to let this opportunity slip and said, "If he's like that, I have no further objections to the marriage."

The wedding was celebrated on the appointed day, and when the young woman wanted to go out into the country and see her husband's property, John first took off his Sunday suit and put on his patched coat, saying, "I might spoil my good clothes." Then they went out into the country together, and wherever they went and a vineyard was to be seen and wherever there were fields and meadows, John would point with his finger, at the same time slap a big or little patch in his coat and say, "This patch is mine and that, too. Just look at them, dear," meaning that his wife was not to stare out over the countryside but to look at his coat which was his own.

"Were you at the wedding, too?" "Of course I was there, and in full dress. My hair was powdered with snow, but then the sun came out and melted it. My dress was of spider web, but then I walked through thorn bushes and they tore it off me. My slippers were of glass; I hit against a stone, then they went clink and broke in two."

85 The Gold Children

Die Goldkinder

THERE WAS A POOR MAN and a poor woman who had nothing but a little hut and lived by fishing and from hand to mouth. One day by chance when the husband was sitting by the water and casting his net, he pulled out a fish that was of solid gold. As he was gazing at the fish and marveling at it, the fish began to talk and said, "Listen, fisherman, if you throw me back into the water,

I'll transform your little hut into a magnificent mansion." "What good is a mansion to me," answered the fisherman, "if I haven't anything to eat?" "That, too," continued the gold fish, "will be taken care of: there'll be a cupboard in the mansion; whenever you open it, there'll be dishes in it with the very finest food and as much as you wish." "In that case," said the man, "I can of course afford to do you the favor." "All right," said the fish, "but there's a string attached, namely, not to reveal to any human being in the world whomsoever the source of your good fortune. If you say a single word, it'll all be over and done with."

The man threw the marvelous fish back into the water and went home. Where his cottage used to stand there was now a great mansion. Wide-eyed with amazement he went in and saw his wife dressed in fine clothes sitting in a magnificent parlor. She was utterly delighted and said, "Husband, how did this happen so suddenly? I like it very much." "Yes," said the husband, "I like it, too, but I'm also frightfully hungry, so first of all give me something to eat." "I haven't got anything," said the woman, "nor do I know how to find anything in the new house." "That doesn't matter," said the man, "I see a big cupboard over there. Just open it." When she opened the cupboard, there were cakes, meat, fruit, and wine, smiling at one, as it were. "What else can the heart desire?" the wife cried out joyfully, and they sat down and ate and drank together. When they'd eaten their fill, the wife asked, "But, husband, where does all this wealth come from?" "Alas," he answered, "don't ask me about it, I mustn't tell you. If I reveal it to anyone, our good fortune will vanish again." "All right," she said, "if I'm not supposed to know, I don't want to know." She didn't mean what she said, however; the matter gave her no peace day or night, and she plagued and pestered her husband till in his impatience he out and said that it all came from a wonderful gold fish he'd caught and given its freedom again in exchange for this. As he uttered these words, the beautiful mansion and the cupboard immediately disappeared, and again they were sitting in the old fisherman's hut.

The man had to start all over, ply his trade and fish. Good fortune, however, would have it that once more he pulled out the gold fish. "Listen," said the fish, "if you'll again throw me into the water, I'll again give you the mansion with the cupboard full of good food. Only restrain yourself and, whatever you do, don't reveal from whom you got it, otherwise you'll lose it again." "I'll certainly be careful," answered the fisherman and threw the fish back into the water. At home everything had returned to its former splendor, and his wife was most happy over the good fortune. Nevertheless, her curiosity left her no peace, and in a few days she again began to ask how it had come about and how he'd done it. For some time the husband kept silent on the matter, but finally she made him so angry that he burst out and revealed the secret. That very moment the mansion disappeared, and again they were sitting in the old hut. "Now you've done it," said the man; "now we can again suffer starvation." "Alas," said the wife, "I'd rather not have riches when I don't know from whom they come. When I don't know, I just don't have any peace of mind."

Again the man went fishing, and after a while the same thing happened; he pulled out the gold fish for the third time. "Listen," said the fish, "I plainly see that I'm bound to keep falling back into your hands, so take me home and cut me up into six pieces: of these give two to your wife to eat, two to your horse, and bury two in the ground, and you'll profit from it." The man took the fish home and did as it had told him. It so happened that from the two pieces in the ground grew two gold lilies, that the horse had two gold colts, while the fisherman's wife gave birth to two solid gold children.

The children grew up, became tall and fair, and the lilies and horses grew up with them. Then they said, "Father, we want to mount our gold horses and go out into the world," but he answered sadly, "How shall I bear it when you've gone and I don't know how you are?" "The two gold lilies will stay here," they said, "from them you can see how we are: if they don't wither, we're well; if they do wither, we're ill; if they droop over, we're dead." They rode off and came to an inn where there were a lot of people, and when they saw the two gold children, they began to laugh at them and make fun of them. When one of them heard this, he was mortified, didn't want to go out in the world, turned about, and went back to his father. The other, however, rode on and reached a big forest. When he was about to ride into it, the people said, "You mustn't ride through; it's full of robbers who'll treat you badly, and, indeed, when they see you're made of gold and your horse, too, they'll kill you." However, he didn't let himself be frightened and said, "I shall and must ride through." Then he took bearskins and covered himself and his horse with them, so that nothing more could be seen of the gold, and rode confidently into the forest. When he had ridden on a bit, he heard a noise in the bushes and voices talking with one another. From one side a voice cried, "There's one," and from the other, "Let him go; he's a lazybones [lit., bearskin], poor and shabby as a church mouse. What can we do with him?" Thus the gold child rode safely through the forest, and no harm befell him.

One day he reached a village. There he saw a girl so beautiful that he didn't think there could be one more beautiful in the world, and because he felt such great love for her, he went up to her and said, "I love you with all my heart; will you be my wife?" The girl, too, liked him so much that she agreed, saying, "Yes, I'll be your wife and be faithful to you as long as I live." They celebrated their wedding, and right at the height of the festivities the bride's father came home, and seeing his daughter being married, was astonished and said, "Where is the bridegroom?" They pointed out to him the gold child, who still had his bearskins on. Then the father said angrily, "Never shall a lazybones have my daughter," and was about to kill him. The bride begged him as hard as she could and said, "He's truly my husband, and I love him with all my heart," till finally he allowed himself to be pacified. Nevertheless, he couldn't get the thought out of his mind and the next morning rose early to see his son-in-law and find out whether he was a common ragged beggar, but when he looked in there, he saw a splendid gold man in the bed and the bearskins which he'd thrown off lying on the floor. Then he went back, thinking, "What a good thing it is that I restrained my wrath; I should have done a great wrong."

The gold child, however, dreamed that he was going out to hunt a superb stag, and on waking up in the morning, said to his bride, "I want to go hunting." She was frightened and begged him to stay home, saying, "Some great misfortune may easily befall you," but he answered, "I shall and must go." He got up and went out into the forest, and before long a proud stag stopped in front of him just as in his dream. He raised his gun and was about to shoot it, but the stag raced away. Then he chased after it, over ditches and through bushes, and didn't get tired all day; but in the evening the stag vanished before his eyes, and when the gold child looked about, he was standing in front of a little house and in it was sitting a witch. He knocked at the door, and an old woman came out and asked, "What are you looking for in the big forest so late?" "Did you by any chance see a stag," he said. "Yes," she replied, "I know the stag well," and a little dog which had come out of the house with her barked furiously at the man as she was speaking. "Hush, you wretched cur," he said, "or I'll shoot you dead." Then the witch cried angrily, "What! kill my little dog?" and at once transformed him so that he lay there like a stone, and his bride waited for him in vain, thinking, "What frightened me so and weighed so heavily on my heart has surely come to pass."

Back home, however, the other brother was standing near the gold lilies when suddenly one of them drooped over. "Dear God," he said, "a great misfortune has befallen my brother; I must go and see if perhaps I can save him." But the father said, "Stay here. If I lose you, too, what shall I do?" He replied, "I shall and must go," mounted his gold horse, rode off, and came to the big forest where his brother was lying changed into a stone. The old witch came out of her house, called to him, and meant to trap him, too; but he didn't come near and said, "If you don't bring my brother back to life, I'll shoot you down." Much against her will she touched the stone with her finger, and he at once returned to life as a man.

The two gold children rejoiced to see each other again, hugged and kissed one another, and rode off together out of the forest, the one to his bride, the other home to his father. Then the father said, "I knew very well that you'd unspelled your brother, for the gold lily suddenly straightened up again and went on blooming." Now they lived happily and prospered till their end.

86   The Fox and the Geese

Der Fuchs und die Gänse

A FOX once came to a meadow where there was a flock of fine fat geese. Laughing he said to them, "I've come at just the right time; you're sitting nicely together so I can eat one up after the other." In their fright the geese cackled, jumped up, and began to lament and piteously beg for their lives. But the fox would listen to nothing, saying, "No mercy! you've got to die." Finally one of them plucked up courage and said, "If we poor geese must sacrifice our fresh young lives, at least grant us one single favor and let us say one last prayer, so that we may not die in sin. After that we're willing to line up so that you may pick out the fattest every time." "All right," said the fox, "that's fair and is a pious request; I'm willing to wait while you pray." So the first began a very long prayer, always saying "cack-cack," and because it gave no sign of stopping, the second didn't wait for its turn but also began "cack-cack." The third and fourth followed its example, and soon all were cackling in unison.

When they've done praying, the story will go on, but for the moment they're still going on praying.

87   The Poor Man and the Rich Man

Der Arme und der Reiche

IN OLDEN TIMES when the good Lord Himself was still walking on earth among men, it happened that one evening He was tired and night overtook Him before He could get to an inn. Now on the road before Him stood two houses facing each other, one large and beautiful, the other small and of mean appearance. The big one belonged to a rich man, the small one to a poor man. Our Lord thought, "I'll be no burden on the rich man; I'll spend the night with him." When the rich man heard the knock at his door, he opened the window and asked the stranger what he wanted. Our Lord answered, "I beg a night's lodging." The rich man measured the wanderer from head to foot and because the good Lord was wearing simple clothes and didn't look like a man with much money in his pocket, he shook his head, saying, "I can't take you in; my rooms are filled with herbs and seeds, and were I to lodge everyone who knocks at my door, I'd be a beggar myself. Look for lodgings elsewhere." So saying, he slammed the window to and left the good Lord standing there.

The good Lord turned His back on him and went across to the small house. No sooner had He knocked than the poor man unlatched his door and asked the wanderer to come in. "Spend the night here with me," he said; "it's already dark and you won't get on any farther today in any event." That pleased the good Lord, and He went in. The poor man's wife shook hands with Him, bade Him welcome, and invited Him to make Himself at home and accept what they had: they hadn't much, but what there was they'd more than gladly give Him. She put potatoes on the fire, and while they were boiling, she milked her goat, so that they'd have a little milk with the potatoes. When the table was set, the good Lord sat down and ate with them, and the poor fare tasted good to Him, for there were happy faces about Him. When they'd eaten and it was time to go to bed, the wife took her husband aside and said, "Husband dear, listen. Let's make a shake-down of straw for ourselves tonight so that the poor wanderer can lie in our bed and rest up. He's been walking all day, and that tires one." "Most gladly," he answered, "I'll offer him our bed," went to the good Lord and asked Him if it was agreeable to Him to sleep in their bed and rest His limbs properly. The good Lord didn't want to deprive the two old people of their couch, but they kept urging Him till He finally did so and lay down in their bed. For themselves, however, they made a shake-down on the floor.

The next morning they got up before dawn, prepared as good a breakfast for their guest as they could. Then when the sun

shone through the little window and the good Lord had arisen,
He again ate with them and was then about to go His way.
While standing at the door, He turned around and said, "Because you are so merciful and devout, make three wishes, and I'll
fulfill them for you." Then the poor man said, "What else should
I wish for but eternal salvation and for the two of us good health
as long as we live and a little daily bread. As for the third thing—
I don't know what to wish." "Don't you wish a new house for
the old one?" said the good Lord. "Yes, indeed," said the man,
"if I can get that, too, I'd certainly like it." Then the Lord fulfilled their wishes, transformed the old house into a new one,
once more gave them His blessing, and went on.

It was already broad daylight when the rich man got up. He
leaned out the window and saw facing him a new clean house
with a red tiled roof where an old hut had been before. Then
he opened his eyes in surprise, called his wife, and said, "Tell me,
what's happened? Last night the miserable old hut was still standing there and today there's a fine new house there. Run over
and find out how it came about." The wife went and questioned
the poor man. "Last night," he told her, "a wanderer came, looking for a night's lodging, and this morning on taking leave he
granted us three wishes: eternal salvation, health in this life and
our daily bread, and finally, in place of our old hut a fine new
house." The rich man's wife hurried back and told her husband
how it had all come about. "I could beat myself black and blue!"
said the husband. "Had I only known! That stranger came here
first and wanted to spend the night with us, but I turned him
away." "Hurry up," said the wife, "get on your horse; in that
way you can still overtake the man and then you must get three
wishes for yourself, too."

The rich man followed this good advice, raced off on his
horse, and managed to overtake the good Lord. He spoke in a
polite and kindly fashion, praying Him not to take amiss his not
letting Him in at once, he'd been looking for the door key, but
in the meantime He'd gone. If He happened to come back that
way, He'd have to stay with him. "All right," said the dear
Lord, if I come back sometime, I'll do so." Then the rich man
asked whether he, too, like his neighbor might not make three
wishes. Yes, said the good Lord, he might do so, but it wouldn't
turn out well for him and he'd better not wish. The rich man

said he'd certainly be able to pick out something that would turn out to his own advantage, if he just were sure it would be fulfilled. "Ride home," said the good Lord, "and the three wishes you make will be fulfilled."

Now the rich man had what he'd asked for, rode home, and began to ponder over what he ought to wish for himself. As he was thinking this and let the reins drop, the horse began to jump so that his thoughts were constantly disturbed and he couldn't collect them. He patted it on the neck and said, "Quiet, Lizzy!" but the horse started capering anew. Finally he got angry and cried out quite impatiently, "I wish you'd break your neck!" As he uttered these words, plop, he fell to the ground, and the horse lay dead and didn't stir again. Thus his first wish was fulfilled. Because he was by nature a miser, he didn't want to leave the saddle gear there, cut it off, put it on his back and now had to proceed on foot. "You've still got two wishes," he thought and consoled himself with that.

As he was walking slowly along through the sand and the noonday sun was blazing hot, he got very warm and cross. The saddle pressed on his back, and besides, he hadn't yet decided what to wish. "Even if I wish for all the kingdoms and treasures in the world," he said to himself, "I'll think of all sorts of other things afterward, this and that—I'm sure of that. However, I'll arrange it so that there won't be anything left for me to wish for." Then he heaved a sigh and said, "Indeed, if only I were the Bavarian farmer who also was given three wishes. He knew what to do: he wished for himself first, a lot of beer, secondly, as much beer as he could drink, and thirdly, a keg of beer to boot." Once in a while he thought he had it, but on reflection it would seem too little to him. Then the thought occurred to him how comfortable his wife was at that moment, sitting at home in a cool room and enjoying a good meal. That annoyed him considerably and without realizing it, he said to himself, "I wish she were sitting at home on the saddle and not be able to get down, instead of my carrying it on my back." As the last word left his mouth, the saddle had vanished from his back, and he realized that his second wish, too, had been fulfilled. Then he got really hot, began to run, and wanted to sit down in his room all by himself and think up something big for the last wish. When he got there, however, and opened the living-room door, his wife was sitting in the middle of the room on a saddle, unable to get off it and weeping and wailing. "Don't worry," he said, "I'll wish you all the riches in the world, but just stay where you are." But she called him a sheep's head and said, "What good are all the riches in the world to me when I'm sitting on the saddle. You wished me onto it and you've got to help me get down again, too." Willy nilly, he had to make the third wish that she be freed from the saddle and able to get down. The wish was fulfilled at once, and he got nothing from the whole thing but vexation, trouble, a scolding, and a lost horse.

On the other hand, the poor couple lived contentedly, quietly, and devoutly until their end.

88   The Singing, Hopping Lark

Das singende, springende Löweneckerchen

THERE WAS ONCE A MAN who was about to go on a long journey; on saying good-bye he asked his three daughters what he should bring them. The eldest wanted pearls, the second diamonds, but the third said, "Father dear, I want a singing, hopping lark." "All right," said her father, "if I can get one, you shall have it," kissed all three, and set out. When it was time for him to come home, he'd bought pearls and diamonds for the two eldest, but for the singing, hopping lark for the youngest he'd looked everywhere in vain, and he felt sorry about it, for she was his favorite child. His way took him through a forest, in the middle of which was a fine mansion, and near it a tree. And way up at the top of the tree he saw a lark singing and hopping about. "Well, just in the nick of time!" he said, quite pleased, and called to his servant to climb up and catch the little creature. But when the latter approached the tree, a lion jumped out from under it, shook itself, and roared so that the leaves on the trees trembled. "Whoever wants to steal my singing, hopping lark," it cried, "I'll eat up." Then the man said, "I didn't know the bird was yours; I'm willing to make amends for my wrong and ransom myself with hard cash if only you'll grant me my life." "Nothing can save you," said the lion, "unless you promise to give me what you first meet on arriving home. However, if you do that, I'll grant you your life and in the bargain give you the bird for your daughter." But the man refused, saying, "It might be my youngest daughter who loves me more than the others do and always runs to meet me when I come home." The servant, however, was frightened and said, "Has it absolutely got to be your daughter who'll meet you? It might perfectly well be a cat or a dog." Then the man let himself be persuaded, took the singing, hopping lark, and promised to give the lion what he first met on reaching home.

When he got home and went into his house, the first thing he met was none other than his youngest, favorite daughter, who came running to meet him, hugged and kissed him, and when she saw that he'd brought her a singing, hopping lark, was beside herself with joy. But her father was unable to rejoice and began to weep, saying, "My dearest child, I've paid dearly for the little bird; in return for it I had to promise you to a fierce lion, and once it's got you, it will tear you to pieces and eat you up." He told her everything that had happened and begged her not to go there, come what might. She comforted him, however, saying, "Dearest father, your promise must be kept; I'll go there and surely pacify the lion so that I'll come back to you safe and sound." Next morning she had him show her the way, said good-bye, and walked confidently into the forest. Now the lion was the enchanted son of a king: by day he was a lion and all his retainers were lions, but by night they had their natural human forms. On arriving there she was well received and led into the palace. When night came, he was a handsome man, and the wedding was celebrated with splendor. They lived happily together, awake at night and asleep in the daytime.

On one occasion he came and said, "Tomorrow there'll be a feast in your father's house because your eldest sister is getting married, and if you want to go, my lions will escort you there." She said yes, she'd very much like to see her father again and drove there, accompanied by the lions. There was great joy on her arrival, for all had supposed that she'd been torn to pieces by the lion and long since dead. She told them what a handsome husband she had and how well off she was, stayed with them during the wedding festivities, and then went back into the forest.

When the second daughter got married and she was invited to the wedding, she said to the lion, "This time I won't go there alone; you must come with me." The lion said it would be too dangerous for him, for if the ray of a burning candle fell on him there, he'd be changed into a dove and have to fly with the doves for seven years. "Oh," she said, "just come along with me; I'll take care of you all right and protect you from all light." So they set out together and took their little child along, too. Once there they had a stone hall built with walls so strong and thick that no ray of light could penetrate it: he was to sit there when the wedding candles were lighted. But the door was made of green wood, which split and sprang a tiny crack that no one noticed. The wedding was celebrated with splendor, but when the bridal procession came back from church and with its many torches and candles passed by the hall, a ray as fine as a hair fell upon the king's son, and as this ray touched him, he was transformed. When she came to look for him, she didn't see him, but sitting there was a white dove, which said to her, "I shall have to fly about in the world for seven years, but every seven paces I'll let fall a drop of red blood and a white feather to show you the way, and if you follow the trail, you can unspell me."

Then the dove flew out the door, and she followed it, and every seven paces a drop of red blood and a white feather would drop down and show her the way. Thus she went on and on into the wide, wide world, neither looking about nor resting, and the seven years were almost up. Then she was happy and thought they'd soon be free. But far from it! Once as she was thus walking on in this way the feathers stopped dropping and the drops of red blood, too, and when she looked about, the dove had vanished. Because she thought, "Human beings can't help you now," she climbed up to the Sun and said to it, "You shine into every nook and cranny; have you by any chance seen a white dove flying by?" "No," said the Sun, "I haven't seen one, but here, I'll give you a little box; open it when you are in dire need." She thanked the Sun and went on till evening and the Moon was shining. Then she asked it, "You shine all night and on every field and meadow; have you by any chance seen a white dove flying by?" "No," said the Moon, "I haven't seen one, but here, I'll give you an egg;

break it when you are in dire need." She thanked the Moon and went on till the Night Wind started to blow on her. Then she said to it, "You're blowing over every tree and through all the leaves. Have you by any chance seen a white dove flying by?" "No," said the Night Wind, "I haven't seen one, but I'll ask the other three winds, who may perhaps have seen it." The East Wind and the West Wind came and had seen nothing, but the South Wind said, "I saw the white dove: it flew to the Red Sea, where it turned into a lion again, for the seven years are up. The lion is now fighting a dragon there, but the dragon is an enchanted king's daughter." Then the Night Wind said to her, "I'll give you a piece of advice: go to the Red Sea. There on the right shore stand some big saplings; count them, cut down the eleventh, and hit the dragon with it. Then the lion will be able to overcome it, and both will regain their human forms. After that, look about and you'll see a griffin sitting by the Red Sea; swing onto its back with your beloved and the bird will carry you both home across the sea. Here's a nut, too. When you're over the middle of the sea, drop it; it will sprout immediately, and a big nut tree will grow up out of the water for the griffin to rest on, for if it weren't able to rest, it wouldn't be strong enough to carry you both across. If you forget to throw the nut down, the bird will let you both drop into the sea."

Then she went there and found everything as the Night Wind had said. She counted the saplings by the sea, cut down the eleventh, struck the dragon with it, and the lion overcame it, and at once both regained their human forms. But when the king's daughter, who before had been a dragon, was unspelled, she took the youth in her arms, mounted the griffin, and carried him off with her. The poor girl who'd journeyed so far stood there, again forsaken, and sat down and wept. Finally, however, she took heart and said, "I'll go on as far as the wind blows and the cock crows, until I find him." She went on a long, long way, till she finally came to the palace where the two were living together. Then she heard there'd soon be a festival when they celebrated their wedding. "God will help me once more," she said, opening the box the Sun had given her. In it was a gown as brilliant as the Sun itself. She took it out, put it on, and went up to the palace, and all the people and the bride herself looked at her in amazement. The bride liked the gown so much that she thought it might do for her wedding dress and asked her whether it was for sale. "Not for money or treasures," she answered, "but for flesh and blood." The bride asked her what she meant. Then she said, "Let me sleep for one night in the bridegroom's room." The bride didn't want to and yet she very much wanted to have the gown, so she finally agreed. The chamberlain had, however, to give the king's son a sleeping potion. When night came and the young man was asleep, she was led into his room; she sat down by his bed and said, "I followed you for seven years, went to the Sun and the Moon and the four winds to enquire about you; I helped you against the dragon. Now are you going to forget me entirely?" But the king's son slept on so soundly that it just seemed to him that the wind was rustling outside in the firs. When morning came, she was again led out and had to give up her gold dress.

Since that was of no avail, she was sad and went out on a meadow, where she sat down and wept, and, as she was thus sitting there, she again remembered the egg the Moon had given her. She broke it open, and out came a hen with twelve chicks, all gold; they ran about, peeped and then crept back under their mother's wings—one can't imagine anything lovelier in the world. Then she got up and drove them before her over the meadow, until the bride looked out her window, and then she liked the little chicks so much that she at once came down and asked if they were for sale. "Not for money and treasures, but for flesh and blood! Let me sleep one more night in the bridegroom's room." The bride said yes, meaning to trick her as on the previous evening, but when the king's son went to bed, he asked the chamberlain what the murmuring and rustling in the night had been. Then the chamberlain told him everything, that he'd been forced to give him a sleeping potion because a poor girl had secretly slept in his room, and that he was supposed to give him another that night. "Pour the drink out beside the bed," said the prince. When night came, she was again led into the room, and when she began to tell how sadly she'd fared, he at once recognized his dear wife by her voice, jumped up and cried, "Now at last I am fully unspelled! I've been living as in a dream, for the foreign princess bewitched me so that I had to forget you, but God has in good time freed me of the infatuation." Then both left the palace secretly during the night, for they were afraid of the princess' father, who was a wizard. They mounted the griffin, which carried them across the Red Sea, and when they were in the middle, she dropped the nut. At once a tall nut tree sprouted up, on which the bird rested. Then it carried them home. There they found their child, that had grown tall and handsome, and henceforth they lived happily until their end.

89   The Goose-Girl

Die Gänsemagd

THERE WAS ONCE AN OLD QUEEN whose husband had long since been dead and who had a beautiful daughter. As the latter grew up, she was betrothed to a king's son far away. When the time came for them to be married and the girl had to set out for the foreign country, the old queen packed up for her ever so many valuables and ornaments, gold and silver, tumblers and jewels, everything that belonged in a royal dowry, for she loved her child with all her heart. She also gave her a maid-in-waiting who was to ride with her and deliver her into the hands of the bridegroom. Each of them was given a horse for the journey; the princess' horse was named Falada and could talk. When the hour of departure was at hand, the old queen went to her bedroom, took a little knife and cut her fingers with it so that they bled. Then she put a piece of white cloth underneath and let three drops of blood fall upon it and, giving them to her daughter, said, "Dear child, keep them safely; you'll need them on the journey."

Thus they took sad farewell of one another. The king's daughter put the white cloth in her bosom, mounted her horse, and rode off to meet her bridegroom. When they'd been riding for an hour, she felt very thirsty and said to her maid-in-waiting, "Dismount and fill the tumbler you brought along for me with water from the brook; I'd very much like a drink." "If you're thirsty," said the maid-in-waiting, "get off yourself, lie down by the water, and drink. I don't care to be your servant." Then, because she was very thirsty, the king's daughter dismounted, stooped over the brook and drank, and wasn't allowed to drink out of the gold tumbler. As she exclaimed "Dear Lord!" the three drops of blood answered, "If your mother knew this, her heart within her would break." But the royal bride was meek, said nothing, and got on her horse again. Thus they rode on for some miles, but the day was warm, the sun scorching hot, and she soon got thirsty again. When they came to a stream, again she called out to her maid-in-waiting, "Dismount and give me a drink in my gold tumbler," for she'd long since forgotten all the unkind words. But the maid spoke even more haughtily, "If you want a drink, drink by yourself; I don't care to be your servant." Then being very thirsty, the king's daughter again dismounted, lay down by the running water, wept and said, "Dear Lord!" and the drops of blood again answered, "If your mother knew this, her heart within her would break." As she was drinking in this way and leaning way over, the piece of cloth with the three drops of blood fell out of her bosom and floated away with the current, and in her great anguish she didn't notice it. The maid-in-waiting had, however, been watching and rejoiced to gain control over the bride, for in losing the drops of blood she had become weak and helpless. Now when she was once again about to mount her horse, whose name was Falada, the maid said, "My place is on Falada and yours on my nag," and she had to put up with it. Then the maid brusquely ordered her to take off her royal garments and put on her poor clothes, and finally she had to swear most solemnly under the open sky that she'd say nothing about it to anybody at the royal court. Had she not sworn this oath, she'd have been killed on the spot. Falada saw all this and took good notice of it.

The maid now mounted Falada and the true bride got on the nag, and thus they continued until they finally reached the royal seat. There was great rejoicing there over their arrival, and the king's son hastened to meet them, lifted the maid-in-waiting down from her horse, and thought she was his spouse. She was escorted upstairs, while the true king's daughter had to stay downstairs. The old king was looking out the window and saw her stop in the courtyard and noticed how fair she was, and slender and really beautiful; he went at once to the royal apartment and asked the bride about the girl she had with her and who was standing below in the courtyard, and who she was. "I brought her along with me for company; give the girl some work to do so that she won't stand about idle." But the old king had no work for her and could only say, "I've a very little boy who tends the geese; she may help him." The boy's name was Conrad, and the true bride had to help him tend the geese.

Soon, however, the false bride said to the young king, "Dearest spouse, do me a favor, I beg you." "That I'll do gladly," he answered. "Then summon the skinner and have him cut off the neck of the horse I rode coming here, for it annoyed me on the way." As a matter of fact, she was afraid the horse might tell how she'd treated the king's daughter. When the plan was about to be carried out and faithful Falada was to die, word reached the ears of the true king's daughter, and she secretly promised to pay the skinner some money if he'd render her a small service. In the town was a big dark gateway through which morning and evening she had to pass with the geese, and "would he please nail up Falada's head under the dark gateway where she might see it a few times more." The skinner promised to do so, cut off the head, and nailed it fast under the dark gateway.

Early in the morning when she and Conrad were driving the geese out through the gateway, she said as she passed,

> "O Falada, there you hang!"

Then the head answered,

> "O young queen, there you go!
> And if your mother knew it,
> her heart would break."

In silence she went on out of the town, and they drove the geese into the country. When she came to the pasture, she sat down and undid her hair; it was pure gold, and Conrad saw it and liked the way it shone and was about to pull out a few hairs. Then she said,

> "Blow, blow, wind,
> carry off Conrad's cap
> and make him chase after it
> until I've braided it and fixed it
> and put it up again."

Then such a strong wind came up that it blew Conrad's cap far away, and he had to run after it. By the time he got back, she'd finished combing and putting it up, and he couldn't get hold of a single hair. Then Conrad was angry and didn't speak to her, and thus they tended the geese until evening came. Then they went home.

The next morning as they were driving the geese out through the dark gateway, the girl said,

"O Falada, there you hang!"

Falada answered,

"O young queen, there you go!
And if your mother knew it,
her heart would break."

Out in the country she sat down again in the pasture and began to comb out her hair, and Conrad ran up and was about to grab at it. Then she quickly said,

"Blow, blow, wind,
carry off Conrad's cap
and make him chase after it
until I've braided it and fixed it
and put it up again."

Then the wind blew, and it blew the cap off his head and blew it so far that Conrad had to run after it. And when he came back, she'd long since fixed her hair, and he couldn't get hold of a single strand. Thus they tended the geese until evening came.

In the evening, however, after they'd got home, Conrad went before the old king and said, "I don't want to tend geese with the girl any longer." "Why not?" asked the old king. "Oh, my! she aggravates me all day long." Then the old king ordered him to tell how he got on with her. Then Conrad said, "In the morning when we pass out with the flock through the dark gateway, there's a nag's head there on the wall, and she says to it,

'O Falada, there you hang!'

Then the head answers,

'O young queen, there you go!
and if your mother knew it,
her heart would break.'"

Thus Conrad went on and told what happened out in the pasture and how he had to run after his cap in the wind.

The old king ordered him to drive the geese out again the next day, and when it was morning, he himself took up a position behind the dark gateway and there heard her talking to Falada's head. Then he also followed her into the country and hid in some bushes in the pasture. There he soon saw with his own eyes how the goose girl and the goose boy drove the flock and how after a while she sat down and unbraided her hair, which shone brilliantly. Straightway she again said,

> "Blow, blow, wind,
> carry off Conrad's cap
> and make him chase after it
> until I've braided it and fixed it
> and put it up again."

Then a gust of wind came and went off with Conrad's cap, so that he had to run a long way, while the girl kept on quietly combing and braiding her locks.

All this the old king observed. Then he went back without being noticed and in the evening, when the goose girl came home, he called her aside and asked her why she did all that. "That I may not tell you nor may I confide my sorrow to anyone, for I swore this most solemnly under the open sky; otherwise I should have lost my life." He pressed her and gave her no peace but could get nothing out of her. Then he said, "If you won't tell me anything, then confide your grief to the iron stove there," and went away. Then she crept into the iron stove, began to lament and weep, and poured out her heart, saying, "Here I sit abandoned by everyone and yet I'm a king's daughter; a false maid-in-waiting forced me to take off my royal clothes and has taken my place at the side of my betrothed, while as a goose-girl I must do menial work. If my mother knew it, her heart within her would break." The old king was, however, standing outside by the stovepipe, was listening to her, and heard what she said. Then he came back in and bade her come out of the stove. Then royal clothes were put on her, and she was so beautiful that it seemed a miracle.

The old king called his son and revealed to him the fact that he had a false bride who was nothing but a maid-in-waiting, and that the true bride was standing here, the former goose-girl. The young king was exceedingly happy on seeing her beauty and goodness, and a great feast was prepared to which everybody, all their good friends, were bidden. At the head of the table sat the bridegroom, with the king's daughter on one side, the maid-in-waiting on the other. But the maid-in-waiting was as if bedazzled and no longer recognized the former in her glittering jewels. When they had eaten and drunk and were in high spirits, the old king propounded a riddle to the maid-in-waiting: what punishment would a woman deserve who tricked her lord in such and such a way? At the same time he told the whole story and asked, "What verdict does she deserve?" Then the false bride said, "She deserves nothing better than to be stripped stark naked and put in a barrel studded inside with sharp nails; furthermore, two white horses must be hitched to it and drag her through street after street until she is dead." "You're the person," said the old king, "and you've pronounced your own sentence, and that's what will happen to you." When the verdict was carried out, the young king married the true bride, and both ruled their kingdom in peace and bliss.

90   The Young Giant

Der junge Riese

A FARMER had a son who was as big as your thumb and got no bigger, and in the course of some years didn't grow a hair's breadth. Once when the farmer was going to the fields to do some plowing, the little chap said, "Father, I want to come along with you." "You want to come along?" said the father; "You stay here. Out there you aren't any use; you might even get lost." Then Tom Thumb began to weep, and in order to have peace and quiet his father put him in his pocket and took him along. Out there in the country he took him out again and set him down in a new furrow. As he was sitting there, a big giant came walking over the mountain. "Do you see the big bogyman there?" said the father, wishing to frighten the little fellow into being good. "He's coming to get you." The giant had taken but a few steps with his long legs when he reached the furrow. He lifted little Tom Thumb up carefully with two fingers, looked at him, and without saying a word walked off with him. The father stood there speechless with fright and just supposed that his child was lost and that he'd never lay eyes on him again as long as he lived.

The giant carried the child home and let him nurse at his breast, and Tom Thumb grew and got big and strong after the manner of giants. Two years later the old giant went with him into the forest, and wanting to test him, said, "Pull out a rod." The boy was then already so strong that he tore a young tree, roots and all, out of the ground. But the giant thought, "It's got to be better than that," again took him along and suckled him for two years more. When next he tested him, his strength had so increased that he could pull an old tree out of the ground. Still the giant wasn't satisfied, suckled him for two years more, and when he went with him into the forest that time and said, "Now pull up a decent sized rod," the boy tore the biggest oak out of the ground so that it came crashing down. And for him that was the merest child's play. "That will do now," said the giant, "you've learned your trade," and led him back to the field where it had fetched him.

His father was standing there behind the plough. The young giant went up to him and said, "Look here, father, see what a man your son has grown to be!" The farmer was frightened and said, "No, you're not my son; I don't want you. Go away from me!" "Of course I'm your son; let me get to work; I can plough as well as you and better." "No no! you're not my son and you can't plough, either. Go away from me!" But because he was afraid of the big man, he let go of the plough, stepped back, and sat down on the ground near by. Then the boy took the implement and just pressed one hand on it, but the pressure was so tremendous that the plough went deep into the earth. The farmer couldn't sit there and look on, and called to him, "If you're going to plough, you mustn't press down so terribly hard; it makes for a poor job." But the boy unharnessed the horses, and pulling the plough himself, said, "Just go home, father, and have mother cook a big dish full of food; in the meantime I'll plough up the field easily enough." Then the farmer went home and ordered his wife to prepare the food. The boy ploughed the field, two whole acres, all by himself, then harnessing himself to the harrow, harrowed it all with two harrows at once. When he'd finished, he went into the forest, tore up two oak trees, shouldered them, and on them laid one harrow in front and one behind, also one horse in front and one behind, and carried the whole load to his parents' house as if it were a bundle of straw. When he came into the farmyard, his mother didn't recognize him and asked, "Who is that dreadful big man?" The farmer said, "He's our son." "No, that certainly isn't our son," she said; "we didn't have one so big as that; ours was a tiny thing. Go away!" she called to him, "we don't want you."

The boy held his peace, led the horses into the stable, and gave them their oats and hay properly. When he had finished, he went into the living-room, sat down on the bench, and said, "Mother, now I'd like to eat. Is it almost ready?" "Yes," she said, and brought in two great big dishes full of food, enough to have satisfied herself and her husband for a week. The boy ate it all up himself and asked if she couldn't serve him more. "No," she said, "that's all we have." "That was really just a taste; I've got to have more." She didn't dare oppose him, went off and put a big slaughtering kettle full of food on the fire, and when it was ready, she brought it in. "At last a few more crumbs are coming along," he said, and ate it all up by himself. Still, even this wasn't enough to satisfy his hunger. Then he said, "Father, I see plainly that I won't get enough to eat here at home; if you'll get me an iron beam so strong that I can't break it across my knees, I'll go out into the world." The farmer was happy, hitched his two horses to the wagon, and from the blacksmith fetched a beam so big and thick that the two horses could just move it. The boy laid it across his knees, and snap! he broke it right in the middle like a bean pole and threw it away. The father hitched up four horses and fetched as big and thick a beam as the four horses could move. The boy broke this, too, across his knees and threw it away, saying, "Father, this is no good to me, you must hitch up a better team and fetch a stronger beam." Then his father hitched up eight horses and fetched as big and thick a beam as the eight horses could pull. When his son took hold of it, he broke a piece right off the top and said, "Father, I see that you can't get me the kind of beam I need; I'm not going to stay here any longer."

Then he went away and claimed to be journeyman black-smith. He came to a village where a smith lived; he was a miser, begrudged everybody everything, and wanted everything for himself. The boy went into the smithy and asked if he didn't need a journeyman. "Yes," said the smith, looked at him, and thought, "he's an able fellow; he'll be good at leading off with the hammering and earn his keep." "What wages do you want?" he asked. "I don't want any at all," he answered, "only every fortnight when the other journeymen get paid off, I want to give you two blows which you must put up with." The miser was thoroughly satisfied with this, thinking he'd save a lot of money in that way. The next morning the new journeyman was to lead off with the hammering. When, however, the master brought the red-hot beam and the boy dealt the first blow, the iron flew to pieces and the anvil sank so deep into the ground that they simply couldn't get it out again. Then the miser got angry and said, "My goodness! I can't use you; you hammer alto-gether too roughly. What wages do you want for the one blow?" "I want to give you just a very light tap, nothing else," said the boy, raised up his foot and gave him such a kick that he flew off over four ricks of hay. Then he picked out for himself the thickest iron beam that was in the smithy, took it in his hand as a walking-stick, and went his way.

After going on a while, he came to an outlying estate and asked the superintendent if he didn't need a foreman. "Yes," said the superintendent, "I can use one. You look like an able fellow who can really do something. What do you want as a yearly wage?" Again he answered that he wasn't asking for any wages at all, but every year he wanted to deal him three blows which he'd have to put up with. This satisfied the superintendent, for he, too, was a miser. The next morning the farm servants were supposed to drive to the forest; the other servants were already up, but the boy was still in bed. Then one of them called to him, "It's time to get up; we're going to the forest and you've got to come along." "The deuce!" he said quite roughly and defiantly. "Just go along; as it is, I'll be back home before all the rest of you." Then the others went to the superintendent, told him that the foreman was still in bed and wouldn't drive with them to the forest. The superintendent said to wake him up once more and ask him to hitch up the horses. The foreman, however, replied as before: "Just go along; as it is, I'll be back home before all the rest of you." Then he lay there another two hours; finally he got out of his feather bed, but first fetched himself two bushels of peas from the loft, cooked himself a porridge, and ate it in all peace and quiet. Having done that, he went out, hitched up the horses, and drove to the forest. Not far from the forest was a sunken road through which he had to drive; there he first drove the wagon ahead till the horses had to stop; then he went behind the wagon, took some trees and brush and built a big barricade there, so that no horse could get through. Now coming to the edge of the forest, the others were just driving out with their loaded carts and were going home. "Drive right along," he said to them. "As it is, I'll be home ahead of you." He didn't drive very far into the forest, straightway tore two of the very biggest trees out of the ground, threw them on the wagon, and turned about. When he got to the barricade, the others were still standing there, unable to get through. "You see," he said, "if you'd stayed with me, you'd have got home just as quickly and might have slept another hour." He wanted to drive on, but his horses couldn't get through the barricade, so he unhitched them, put them up on the wagon, himself took hold of the shaft, and "swish" pulled the whole thing through and as easily as if it were loaded with feathers. Once on the other side, he said to the others, "You see, I got through quicker than you," drove on, and the others had to stop. In the farmyard he took one of the trees in his hand, and showing it to the superintendent, said, "Isn't that a fine bit of cordwood?" Then the superintendent said to his wife, "The boy's good; even if he does sleep late, he's back home before the others."

He served the superintendent for a year. When it was up and the other servants got their wages, he said it was time for him to get his, too. The superintendent, however, was frightened at the thought of the blow he was due to receive, and begged him and begged him to let him off: he'd rather be foreman himself and let the boy be superintendent. "No," he said, "I don't want to be a superintendent. I'm a foreman and I want to stay a foreman; but I do want to deal out the blows agreed upon." The superintendent was willing to give him whatever he asked for, but it did no good; the foreman just said no to everything. Then the superintendent didn't know what to do and asked him for a fortnight's respite; he wanted to think up something. The foreman said he might have the fortnight. The superintendent summoned all his clerks; they were to think it over and advise him. The clerks meditated for a long time, finally said that nobody's life was safe from the foreman: he could strike a man dead as easily as he could a midge. The superintendent should order him to go down the well and clean it, and when he was down there, they'd roll up one of the millstones that lay there and throw it on his head; then he'd never come to light again. The plan pleased the superintendent, and the foreman was willing to go down the well. When he was standing at the bottom, they rolled down the biggest millstone and thought his head was bashed in, but he called out, "Chase the chickens away from the well! They're scratching up there in the sand and throwing the grains into my eyes so that I can't see." Then the superintendent said "shoo! shoo!" and made believe he was scaring the chickens away. When the foreman had finished his job, he climbed up and said, "Just look! I really have a fine necklace on," meaning the millstone he was wearing around his neck. Now the foreman wanted to receive his wages, but the superintendent again begged for a fortnight to think it over. The clerks assembled and advised him to send the foreman into an enchanted mill to grind rye there during the night; nobody had ever come out of it alive in the morning. The superintendent liked the proposal, summoned the foreman that very evening, and ordered him to drive a hundred and forty bushels of rye to the mill and grind it that very night; they wanted it badly. Then the foreman went up to the loft and put thirty-five bushels in his right pocket, thirty-five in his left, and took seventy in a long sack which hung half over his back, half over his chest. Loaded thus, he went to the enchanted mill.

The miller told him he could grind there quite all right in the daytime but not at night, since the mill was enchanted and whoever had gone in had been found dead there in the morning. "I'll come through, of course," he said; "just go along and have a good sleep." Then he went into the mill and poured the rye into the hopper. Toward eleven o'clock he went into the miller's room and sat down on the bench. After he'd been sitting there a little while, the door suddenly opened and in came a great big banqueting table, and on the table was placed wine and a roast and a lot of good food, all by itself, for there was nobody there to serve it. Afterward the chairs drew themselves up, but no people came, until suddenly he saw fingers busy with the knives and forks and putting food on the plates, though other than that he could see nothing. Since he was hungry and saw the food, he, too, sat down at the table, ate along with the rest, and enjoyed the meal. When he'd had enough and the others had quite cleaned their plates, too, the candles were suddenly all snuffed out, as he clearly heard, and as it was now pitch dark, he got something like a slap in the face. Then he said, "If anything like that happens again, I'll hit back," and since he got slapped a second time, he too, hit back, and so it went on all night. He took nothing without an argument and gave as good as he received, and wasn't slow in hitting out all about him. At daybreak, however, everything stopped.

When the miller got up, he wanted to see how he was and marveled that he was still alive. Then the foreman said, "I ate my fill, got slapped in the face but also slapped back." The miller was glad, said that the mill was now disenchanted, and would gladly have rewarded him with a lot of money. However, the foreman said, "I don't want any money, I have enough as it is." Then he took the flour on his back, went home, and told the superintendent that he'd done the job and now wanted his wages as agreed. Hearing that, the superintendent got really frightened. He was beside himself, walked up and down the room, and drops of sweat ran down his forehead. To get some fresh air he opened the window, but before he could say Jack-Robinson, the foreman had given him such a kick that he flew out the window into the air and on and on, until he was out of sight. Then the foreman said to the superintendent's wife, "If he doesn't come back, you'll have to take the other blow." "No! no!" she cried, "I can't stand it," and opened the other window because drops of sweat were running down her forehead. Then he gave her a kick so that she, too, flew out, and since she was lighter, she flew much higher than her husband. "Come to me," cried her husband, but she cried, "You come to me, I can't get to you," and there they soared in the air, and neither could get to the other, and whether they're still soaring, I don't know. The young giant, however, took his iron beam and went on his way.

91 The Gnome

Dat Erdmänneken

THERE WAS ONCE A RICH KING who had three daughters; every day they took a walk in the palace garden. The king was very fond of all kinds of fine trees, and one he was so fond of that he'd put a curse on anybody who picked an apple from it and wished him a hundred fathoms under ground. When it was autumn, the apples on that tree got as red as blood. Every day the three daughters would go under the tree to see if the wind hadn't blown down an apple, but they never found a single one, and the tree was so full that it was ready to break, and the branches hung down to the ground. Then the youngest got a great craving and said to her sisters, "Our father loves us far too much to put a curse on us; I think he only did that in the case of strangers. Thereupon the girl picked a very plump apple and ran to her sisters, saying, "Oh, just taste it, dear sisters. I've really never tasted anything so fine in my life." Then the two other daughters also took a bite of the apple, and thereupon all three sank deep down into the earth and were completely lost sight of.

When it was midday, the king wanted to call them to table, but they were nowhere to be found. He searched for them in the palace and in the garden but couldn't find them. Then he became very distressed and had the whole country called up and announced that whoever should bring back his daughters should have one of them in marriage. Then ever so many young men went through the country and searched—you wouldn't believe how many!—for everybody had been fond of the three girls because they were so friendly to everyone and so fair of face. Among others, three young huntsmen set out, and when they'd journeyed a good week, they came to a great manor house. In it were very fine apartments, and in one room a table was set and on it were sweet dishes, still so warm that they were steaming. Yet in the whole manor house there wasn't sight or sound of a human being. They waited half a day more, and the food still kept warm and continued to steam, until at last they were so hungry that they sat down to the food and ate it.

They agreed among themselves to stay in the mansion and to draw lots to see which was to stay home while the other two looked for the daughters. This they did, and the lot fell to the eldest. The next day the two youngest searched while the eldest had to stay home. At noon a tiny little dwarf came and asked for a piece of bread; then the huntsman took some of the bread that he found there and cut off a piece around the loaf and was going to give it to him. As he handed it to him, the little dwarf dropped it and asked him please to give him back the piece. He was about to do so and was bending down, when the dwarf took a stick, seized him by the hair, and dealt him some good hard blows. The next day the second brother had to stay home; he fared no better. In the evening when the other two came back, the eldest said, "Well, how did you get along?" "Oh, very badly." They both lamented their plight but told the youngest nothing about it; they couldn't abide him and always referred to him as "stupid John" because he lacked worldly wisdom.

On the third day the youngest stayed home; then the little dwarf came again and asked for a piece of bread. When he'd given it to him, the dwarf again dropped it and said, would he please hand it back to him. Then the boy said to the little dwarf, "What! can't you pick the piece up again yourself? If you won't even take pains about your daily bread, you really don't deserve to eat!" Then the dwarf got very angry and said he must do it. But the boy wasted no time, took our dear little dwarf and gave him a sound thrashing. Then the dwarf screamed loudly and cried, "Stop, stop! let me go, and in return I'll tell you where the king's daughters are." When he heard that, he stopped beating him, and the dwarf told him that he was a gnome and that there were more than a dozen of them. If he'd just come along with him, he'd show him where the king's daughters were. Then he pointed out to him a deep well, but with no water in it. Then the dwarf said he was certain that the boy's companions were not well-intentioned toward him, and if he wanted to free the king's daughters, he'd have to do it alone. The two other brothers likewise would be quite willing to get the king's daughters back but were not ready to go to any trouble or run any risk in so doing.

He must take a very big basket and with his hunting knife and a bell get into it and be lowered into the well. Down there were three rooms: in each was sitting one of the king's daughters with a many-headed dragon to louse; he'd have to cut its heads off. After saying all that, the gnome vanished. When evening came, the other two arrived and asked how he'd fared. "Oh, all right so far," he said, adding that he'd seen nobody until noon, when a tiny little dwarf had come and asked him for a piece of bread. When he'd given it to him, the dwarf had dropped it and said he might pick it up for him again. When he had not been willing to do that, the dwarf had begun to spit like a cat. He'd misunderstood that, however, and had beaten the dwarf, and then the latter had told him where the king's daughters were. Then the two brothers got so vexed that they turned green with envy.

The next morning they went together to the well and drew lots to see who should be the first to get into the basket. Again the lot fell to the eldest; he had to get in and take the bell with him. Then he said, "When I ring, you must pull me up again quickly." When he was a little way down, the bell rang and they pulled him up again. Then the second got in and did the same. Then it was the youngest's turn, but he let himself go all the way down the well. When he got out of the basket, he took his hunting knife and stopped in front of the first door and listened. There he heard the dragon snoring quite loud. He opened the door slowly and there sat one of the king's daughters with nine dragon heads in her lap and was lousing them. He took his hunting knife and hacked away. Then the nine heads came off. The king's daughter jumped up and fell on his neck, hugged and kissed him a lot and taking her breastplate of red gold, hung it on him. Then he went to the second daughter, who had a seven-headed dragon to louse, and freed her, too; likewise the youngest, who had a four-headed dragon to louse, he also attended to her. They all rejoiced greatly and hugged and kissed him unceasingly. Then he rang very loud until those up above heard him. One after the other he put the king's daughters into the basket and had them all three pulled up. When his turn came, he remembered the gnome's words that his companions were not well-intentioned toward him. He took a big stone that was lying there and put it in the basket. When the basket was about halfway up, the false brothers on top cut the rope so that the basket and the stone fell to the bottom. They thought he was now dead and ran away with the three king's daughters, making them promise to tell their father that they were the two who'd freed them. Then they came to the king and asked for them in marriage.

Meanwhile, the youngest huntsman walked very sadly about in the three rooms and thought that he was now probably doomed to die. Then he saw a flute hanging on the wall and said, "What are you hanging there for? Nobody can be merry here." He also looked at the dragons' heads and said, "You can't help me, either." He walked up and down so many times that he wore the ground smooth. At last he got a new idea: he took the flute from the wall and piped a tune. Suddenly a great many gnomes appeared; with every note he played, one more would come. He kept playing the tune until the room was packed full. They all asked what his desire might be, and he said he'd very much like to get back up on Earth and to the light of day. Then they all took hold of him, of every spear of hair on his head, and flew with him thus up to the surface of the Earth. When he got up there, he went at once to the king's palace, where the wedding of one of the king's daughters was about to take place, and went up to the chamber where the king was with his three daughters. When the girls saw him, they fainted. The king got very angry and straightway had him put into prison, thinking he had harmed the girls. But when the king's daughters came to, they begged the king very earnestly to release him. The king asked them why, and they said they mustn't tell. Their father, however, said that they should tell it to the stove. He went out and listened at the door and heard everything. Then he had the two huntsmen hanged on a gallows and gave his youngest daughter to the other in marriage.

Thereupon I put on a pair of glass shoes and stood on a stone, then it went "clink," and they were broken.

92   The King of the Golden Mountain

Der König vom goldenen Berg

THERE WAS A MERCHANT who had two children, a boy and a girl; both were still little and not yet able to walk. Two ships of his, richly laden, were at sea and his whole fortune was in them; just when he was expecting to make a lot of money with them, news came that they had sunk. Now instead of being rich he was a poor man with nothing left but a field outside the town. In order somewhat to banish his troubles from his mind, he went out to the field, and as he was walking back and forth there, a little black dwarf suddenly stood beside him and asked why he was so sad and what he was taking so to heart. "If you could help me," said the merchant, "I'd gladly tell you." "Who knows?" answered the black dwarf. "Perhaps I can help you." Then the merchant related how his whole fortune had gone to the bottom of the sea and that he had nothing left but this field. "Don't worry," said the dwarf; "if you'll promise me to bring twelve years hence to this spot here the first thing that strikes against your leg when you get home, you shall have as much money as you want." "What else can that be," thought the merchant, "but my dog?" didn't think about his little boy, and saying yes, gave the dwarf a signed and sealed document to this effect and went home.

When he got home, his little boy was so happy that, holding onto the benches, he toddled over to him and seized him firmly by the legs. Then the father got frightened, because he remembered the promise and now realized what he had pledged. However, not yet finding any money in his boxes and chests, he thought it might just have been a joke on the part of the dwarf. A month later he went up to the attic to collect some old tin to sell, and there he saw lying a big pile of money. Now he was in good spirits again, stocked up, became a greater merchant than before, and let God manage the rest. Meanwhile, the boy grew big and at the same time keen and intelligent. But the nearer the twelve years were to being up, the more worried the merchant got, and one could see the anxiety in his face. His son once asked him what was troubling him. The father didn't want to tell him, but he persisted so long that finally he did tell him: he had, without realizing what he was promising, pledged him to a black dwarf and had received a lot of money for it. He'd given a signed and sealed document, and now he would have to hand him over once the twelve years were up. Then the son said, "Oh, Father, don't be afraid; it'll turn out all right; the Black Fellow has no power over me."

The son had himself blessed by the priest, and when the hour came, they went together out to the field; the son drew a circle and placed himself and his father inside it. Then the black dwarf came and spoke to the father: "Have you brought along what you promised me?" The father kept silent, but the son asked, "What do you want here?" "I'm talking to your father and not to you," said the black dwarf. The son answered, "You deceived and misled my father; hand over the document!" "No," said the black dwarf, "I'm not surrendering my rights." They went on talking together for some time longer and finally reached an agreement: the son, not belonging either to the archfiend or to his father, was to get into a little boat that was riding on a stream, and the father was to shove it off with his own foot, and then the son was to be left to the mercy of the current. Then he said good-bye to his father, got into the boat, and the father had to shove it off with his own foot. The boat capsized, so that it was bottom up, with the deck in the water. Believing his son lost, the father went home and mourned for him.

However, the little boat didn't sink but just drifted away, and the youth was sitting safe and sound inside, and it drifted for a long time, until at last it grounded on an unknown coast. There he climbed ashore, saw before him a beautiful mansion, and made for it. But as he entered, he noticed it was enchanted. He went through all the rooms, but they were empty; finally he came to the last room: there a snake was lying coiled up. The snake, however, was an enchanted maiden, who rejoiced when she saw him and said, "Are you coming, my redeemer? I've been waiting for you these twelve years. This kingdom is bewitched, and you must free it." "How can I do that?" he asked. "Tonight twelve black men, draped with chains, will be coming; they'll ask you what you're doing here. Keep silent, however, and don't answer them, and let them do with you what they want. They'll torture you, beat you and stab you; endure everything, only don't speak. At midnight they must be off again. Also on the second night twelve others will come, and on the third, twenty-four, who'll cut off your head. At midnight, however, their power will be gone, and if you've held out that long and not uttered a single solitary word, I shall be freed. I'll come to you with the Water of Life in a bottle; I'll rub you with it, and then you'll be alive again and as well as ever." Then he said, "I'll gladly free you." Now it all happened as she had said: The black men couldn't force a word out of him, and on the third night the snake became a beautiful king's daughter, who came with the Water of Life and revived him. Then she fell on his neck and kissed him, and there was joy and jubilation in the whole mansion. Then their wedding was celebrated, and he was King of the Golden Mountain.

Thus they lived happily together, and the queen bore a fair boy. Eight years had already passed when the king thought of his father, and his heart was moved, and he wanted to visit him some time. But the queen didn't want to let him go away and said, "I know well that this will be my undoing." However, he gave her no peace until she agreed. On parting she gave him among other things a wishing ring and said, "Take this ring and put it on your finger; then you'll be immediately transported to wherever you wish to go. Only you must promise me not to use it to wish me away from here to your father's." He promised her that, put the ring on his finger, and wished himself home outside the town where his father lived. In an instant he was actually there and wanted to go into town; but when he reached the gate, the sentries wouldn't let him in because he had on strange, though very rich and splendid clothes. Then he went up on a mountain where a shepherd was tending his flock, changed clothes with the latter, put on the old shepherd's coat, and thus passed unmolested into the town. When he came to his father's, he made himself known; his father, however, didn't believe that he was his son, saying that he, true enough, had had a son, but that he was long since dead. "Yet seeing that you're a poor, needy shepherd, I'm willing to give you a dish of food." Then the shepherd said to his parents, "Truly, I am your son.

Don't you know any mark on my body by which you can recognize me?" "Yes," said his mother, "our son had a raspberry-mark under his right arm." He turned back his shirt, and they saw the raspberry-mark under his right arm and no longer doubted that he was their son. Thereupon, he told them that he was King of the Golden Mountain and that a king's daughter was his spouse and that they had a fine son who was seven years old. Then his father said, "Now that can't possibly be true! It's a fine king in my opinion who goes about in a tattered shepherd's coat!" Then the son grew angry, and without thinking of his promise, gave the ring a twist and wished both his wife and his child there. In the same instant they were there, but the queen lamented and wept and said he'd broken his word and brought misfortune upon her. "I did it inadvertently," he said, "and not from ill will," and talked to her. She pretended to defer to him, but she harbored evil designs in her heart.

Then he took her outside the town to the field and showed her the stream where the little boat had been shoved off, then said, "I'm tired, sit down; I want to sleep for a bit on your lap." He laid his head on her lap, and she loused him a little until he fell asleep. When he'd gone to sleep, she first pulled the ring from his finger, then drew her foot out from under him, leaving only her slipper behind. Thereupon she took her child in her arms and wished herself back in her kingdom. When he awoke, he was lying there quite deserted, and his wife and child were gone, and the ring from his finger, too; only the slipper was still there as a token. "You can't go home again to your parents," he thought, "they'd say you were a wizard. You'd better pack up and keep going till you get to your kingdom."

Accordingly, he went away and at last came to a mountain before which three giants were standing and fighting one another because they didn't know how to divide their father's inheritance. When they saw him going past, they called out to him and said that little humans were smart and that he should apportion the heritage for them. Now the inheritance consisted in a sword: if one took it in his hand and said, "All heads off but mine," all heads would be lying on the ground. Then there was, secondly, a cloak: whoever put it on was invisible. And thirdly, there was a pair of boots: if one had them on and wished himself anywhere, he was there in a second. "Give me the three objects," he said, "so that I can test whether they're still in good condition." Then they gave him the cloak, and when he'd thrown it over his shoulders, he was invisible and was changed into a fly. Then resuming his true shape he said, "The cloak's all right, now give the sword." They said, "No, we won't give you that. If you should say 'All heads off but mine,' then all our heads would be off and you'd be the only one still with yours." Nevertheless, they gave it to him on condition that he try it out on a tree. He did so, and the sword cut the tree trunk like a piece of straw. Now he wanted to have the boots, but they said, "No, we won't give them away. Were you to put them on and wished yourself up there on the mountain, we'd be left standing down here with nothing." "No," he said, "I won't do that." Then they gave him the boots, too. Now that he had all three objects, he thought only of his wife and child and said to himself, "Oh, were I only up on the Golden Mountain!" and immediately he vanished before the giants' eyes, and thus their inheritance was divided indeed!

When he got near the mansion, he heard cries of joy, fiddles and flutes, and the people told him that his spouse was celebrating her wedding with another man. Then he got angry and said, "The faithless woman! she deceived me and forsook me when I was asleep." Throwing his cloak over him, he went invisible into the mansion. When he entered the great hall, there was a large banquet table covered with delicious dishes, and the guests were eating and drinking, laughing and joking. His wife, however, was sitting in the middle in a royal armchair magnificently clad, and she had the crown on her head. He took up a position behind her, and no one saw him. Every time they'd put a piece of meat on her plate, he'd take it away and eat it, and whenever they'd pour her a glass of wine, he'd take it away and drink it. They kept serving her and still she never had anything, for plate and glass would immediately disappear. Then she became disconcerted and mortified, got up and went to her room and wept. He followed her, however. "Has the Devil got control of me?" she said, "or didn't my redeemer ever come?" Then he struck her in the face, saying, "Didn't your redeemer ever come? He has control of you, you deceiver! Did I deserve that of you?" Then he made himself visible, went into the hall, and cried out. "The wedding is off! The true king has come!" The kings, princes, and councilors who were assembled there jeered and laughed at him, but he was short with them and said, "Will you get out or won't you?" They were about to take him prisoner and were crowding in around him, but he drew his sword and said, "All heads off but mine!" Then all heads rolled to the ground, and he alone was master and once again was King of the Golden Mountain.

93 The Raven

Die Rabe

THERE WAS ONCE A QUEEN who had a daughter, still little and a babe in arms. On one occasion the child was naughty and, no matter what the mother said, wouldn't be quiet. Then the mother got impatient and, since ravens were flying about the castle, opened the window and said, "I wish you were a raven and would fly away, then I'd have some peace." No sooner had she spoken these words than the child was changed into a raven and flew out of her arms and out the window. She flew into a dark forest and stayed there a long time, and her parents had no news of her. Some time later a man who was wending his way through this forest heard the raven call and followed the voice. As he drew nearer, the raven said, "By birth I'm a king's daughter and have been enchanted; you, however, can disenchant me." "What shall I do?" he asked. "Go deeper into the forest," she said, "and you'll find a house and an old woman sitting in it. She'll proffer you food and drink, but you must accept nothing. If you eat and drink anything, you'll fall asleep and will not be able to disenchant me. In the garden behind the house is a big pile of tanbark; you're to stand on it and wait for me. Three days running I'll come to you every afternoon at two o'clock driven in a coach, drawn first by four white stallions, then by four bay stallions, at last by four black stallions. If, however, you're not awake but asleep, I shan't be disenchanted." The man promised to do everything she requested, but the raven said, "Oh, I'm quite sure you won't disenchant me; you'll accept something from the woman." Again the man promised that he'd surely touch neither food nor drink.

When he entered the house, however, the old woman stepped up to him and said, "Poor man, how worn out you are! Come and refresh yourself. Have something to eat and drink." "No," said the man, "I'll neither eat nor drink." But she gave him no peace and said, "Well, if you won't eat, then take a drink from the glass. Once doesn't count." Then he let himself be persuaded and took a drink.

About two o'clock in the afternoon, he went out in the garden and onto the pile of tanbark, intending to wait for the raven. As he was standing there, he suddenly got very tired, couldn't overcome his feeling of fatigue, and lay down for a bit. Yet he didn't want to go to sleep. Hardly had he stretched out, however, when his eyes closed of themselves and he fell asleep and slept so soundly that nothing in the world could have waked him. At two o'clock the raven came driving up drawn by four white stallions, but she was already in full mourning and said, "I know he's asleep," and when she went into the garden, there he was lying asleep on the pile of tanbark. She got out of the coach, went up to him, shook him, and called out to him, but he didn't wake up.

At noon the next day the old woman came again and brought him food and drink, but he wouldn't take it. She gave him no peace, however, and talked to him so long that again he took a drink from the glass. Toward two o'clock he went into the garden and onto the pile of tanbark, intending to wait for the raven. Suddenly he felt so very tired that his limbs no longer supported him; he could do nothing about it, had to lie down, and fell into a deep sleep. When the raven drove up, drawn by four brown stallions, she was already in full mourning and said, "I know he's asleep." She went up to him, but he was lying there asleep and couldn't be awakened. The next day the old woman said, "What's the matter? You're not eating or drinking anything; do you want to die?" "I won't and mustn't eat or drink," he answered. Just the same, she put a dish of food and a glass of wine in front of him, and when the fragrance of the wine mounted his nostrils, he couldn't resist it and took a deep draught. When the time came, he went out into the garden and onto the pile of tanbark and waited for the king's daughter. Then he got even wearier than on the preceding days, lay down, and slept like a log. At two o'clock the raven came and had four black stallions, and the coach and everything was black. She was already in full mourning and said, "I know he's asleep and can't disenchant me." When she got to him, he was lying there fast asleep. She shook him and called him but couldn't wake him up. Then she put a loaf of bread beside him, also a piece of meat, and thirdly a bottle of wine; and however much of this he might consume, it wouldn't become less. Afterward she took a gold ring from her finger and put it on his finger, and her name was engraved in it. Finally she laid a letter there which stated what she'd given him and that it would never be used up, and it also said, "I see clearly that you can't disenchant me here. But if you still want to unspell me, come to the Golden Castle of Stromberg; it's within your power, I well know." When she had given him all that, she got into her coach and drove to the Golden Castle of Stromberg.

When the man woke up and saw that he'd been asleep, he was sad of heart and said, "She's surely driven by, and I haven't disenchanted her." Then his eye fell on the objects beside him, and he read the letter which told how things had gone. Accordingly, he got up and went away and wanted to go to the Golden Castle of Stromberg, though he didn't know where it was. After he'd wandered about the world for a long time, he came to a dark forest and walked on there for a fortnight without being able to find his way out. Then evening again came on, and he was so tired that he lay down in a thicket and fell asleep. The next day he continued farther, and in the evening when he was again about to lie down in a thicket, he heard such a howling and wailing that he couldn't get to sleep. When the hour came when people light their candles, he saw one shining, got up and went toward it. He arrived at a house which seemed very small because a big giant was standing before it. Then he thought to himself, "If you go in and the giant spies you, it may easily be the end of you." Finally he risked it and stepped up. On seeing him the giant said, "It is a good thing you've come; it's been a long time since I've had anything to eat; I'm going to swallow you right down for supper." "Better give up that idea," said the man, "I don't fancy being swallowed up. If it's food you want, I have enough to satisfy you." "If that's true," said the giant, "you needn't worry. I merely wanted to eat you up because I haven't anything else."

They went and sat down at the table, and the man produced the inexhaustible supply of bread, wine, and meat. "I'm delighted with this," said the giant and ate to his heart's content. After supper the man said to him, "Can't you tell me where the Golden Castle of Stromberg is?" "I'll look it up on my map," said the giant; "it shows all towns, villages, and homesteads." He fetched the map that he had in the living room and looked for the castle, but it wasn't on it. "No matter," he said, "I've even bigger maps in the cupboard upstairs; we'll look for it on them." But that, too, proved futile. Now the man wanted to continue his journey, but the giant begged him to wait a few days more until his brother, who'd gone to fetch provisions, came home. When the brother got home, they asked him about the Golden Castle of Stromberg. "When I've eaten my fill, I'll look it up on the map." Then he went with them up to his room, and they looked on his map but couldn't find it. Then he fetched still other old maps, and they didn't give up till at last they found the Golden Castle of Stromberg. But it was many thousand miles away. "How am I going to get there?" asked the man. "I've got two hours' free time," said the giant, "I'll carry you to a point near the castle, but then I must go home and suckle our child." Then the giant carried the man to within about a hundred hours' walk of the castle and said, "You can probably walk the rest of the way alone." Then he turned back, and the man walked on day and night until he finally reached the Golden Castle of Stromberg. The castle was up on a glass mountain, and the enchanted maiden was driving around the castle in her coach, after which she went in. He was delighted to catch a glimpse of her and wanted to climb up to her, but whatever way he started, he'd keep slipping down again on the glass. Seeing that he couldn't reach her, he became greatly distressed and said to himself, "I'll stay down here and wait for her." So he built himself a cabin and stayed there a whole year, and every day he'd see the king's daughter driving up there, yet he couldn't get up to her.

Once from his cabin he saw three robbers hitting one another and called out to them, "God be with you!" At the cry they stopped, but not seeing anybody, started hitting one another again, and it was a thoroughly dangerous business. Again he called, "God be with you!" and again they stopped, looked about, but seeing nobody, again resumed their fight. Then he called out a third time, "God be with you!" and thinking, "I'll have to see what the three are up to," went to where they were and asked why they were going for one another. Then one said he'd found a stick: if he struck a door with it, it would fly open; the second said he'd found a cloak: when he put it on, he was invisible; and the third said he'd caught a horse: with it one could ride everywhere, right up the glass mountain. Now they didn't know whether to hold all this jointly, or whether they should part company. Then the man said, "I'll give you something in exchange for the three objects. Quite true, I haven't any money, but I have other things that are more valuable. Still, I must first make a test and see whether you've really told the truth." Then they let him sit on the horse, put the cloak on him, and handed him the stick, and when he had everything, they could no longer see him; then he gave them some good hard blows, crying, "Now, you lazy fellows, there you've got what you deserve! Are you satisfied?"

Then he rode up the glass mountain. When he got up there outside the castle, it was locked; then he struck on the gate with the stick, and it flew open immediately. He entered and went up the stairs to the big hall. There the maiden was sitting, and in front of her she had a gold goblet full of wine, but she couldn't see him because he had the cloak on. As he stepped up to her, he drew from his finger the ring she'd given him and tossed it into the goblet so that it rang out. "That's my ring," she cried, "so the man, too, must be here who will disenchant me." They searched the whole castle and didn't find him, for he'd gone out, mounted the horse, and thrown off the cloak. On reaching the gate, they saw him and shouted for joy. Then he dismounted and took the king's daughter in his arms. She kissed him and said, "Now you've disenchanted me and tomorrow we'll celebrate our wedding."

94 The Clever Peasant Lass

Die kluge Bauerntochter

THERE WAS ONCE A POOR PEASANT who had no land, just a little hut, and an only daughter. "We should ask the king for a bit of newly cleared woodland," said the daughter. When the king heard of their poverty, he even gave them a plot of grassland. She and her father hoed it up and planned to sow a little rye and similar crops on it. When they had the field almost hoed, they found in the ground a solid gold mortar. "Listen," said the father to the girl, "because our lord king was so gracious and made us a present of this field, we must give him the gold mortar in return." The daughter, however, was unwilling to agree to this and said, "Father, if we have the mortar and not the pestle, we'll have to produce the pestle, too; so we'd better keep quiet about it."

But he wouldn't listen to her and took the mortar to the king, saying he'd found it in the moor and wouldn't he accept it as a token of respect. The king took the mortar and asked if he'd not found anything else. "No," answered the peasant. Then the king said that he should also produce the pestle. The peasant said that they hadn't found it, but for all the good it did him, his statement fell on deaf ears. He was put in prison and was to stay there until he produced the pestle. Every day the servants had to bring him bread and water, the sort of fare one gets in prison; there they heard the man continuously crying, "Alack, alas, if I'd listened to my daughter!" Then the servants went to the king and told him how the prisoner kept crying, "Alas, if I'd only listened to my daughter!" and wouldn't eat or drink. The king ordered the servants to bring the prisoner into his presence and then asked him why he kept crying, "Alas, if I'd listened to my daughter!" "What did your daughter say?" "She said I shouldn't bring the mortar, otherwise I should have to produce the pestle, too." "If you have so clever a daughter, just have her come here." Accordingly, she had to appear before the king. He asked her if she

really was so clever and said that he would propound her a riddle; if she could solve that, he'd marry her. Straightway she said
"yes," she'd like to guess it. Then the king said, "Come to me
neither clothed nor naked, neither riding nor driving, neither on
the road nor off the road. If you can do that, I'll marry you." She
went away and undressed herself completely, then she wasn't
clothed. She took a big fishnet, got in it, and wrapped it all
around her; then she wasn't naked. She borrowed a donkey for a
fee and tied the fishnet to the donkey's tail; it had to drag her
along in the net, and that was neither riding nor driving. Furthermore, the donkey had to drag her in a rut, so that she touched
the ground only with her big toe, and that was neither on the
road nor off the road. When she arrived in this fashion, the king
said that she'd solved the riddle and that all the conditions had
been fulfilled. He then released her father from prison, took her
to himself as his wife, and put the whole royal estate in her charge.

When several years had passed and the king was once going
to a review, some farmers happened to stop in front of the palace
with their carts; they'd been selling wood, and some had ox-
teams, some horses. There was one farmer who had three horses,
one of which gave birth to a young foal, which ran away and lay
down right between two oxen hitched to a cart. Now when the
farmers met, they began to quarrel, hit one another and make a
row, and the one who owned the oxen wanted to keep the foal,
saying that the oxen had had it. The other said "no," that his
horses had had it and that it was his. The dispute came before the
king, and he gave the decision that where the foal had lain, there
it should remain. Thus the owner of the oxen got it, though it
didn't belong to him. The other farmer went away and wept and
wailed over the loss of his foal. Now he had heard that the queen
was very gracious because she, too, came of poor peasant stock.
He went to her and asked if she couldn't help him get his foal
back. She said, "Yes, if you'll promise me you won't betray me,
I'll tell you how. Early tomorrow morning when the king is reviewing the watch, take up a position in the middle of the street
where he must pass. Take a big fishnet and make believe you're
fishing. Keep on fishing and empty out the net as if were full,"
and told him, besides, what answer he should make if he were
questioned by the king. Accordingly, the next day the farmer
stood there and fished on a dry spot. When the king passed by

and saw that, he sent his runner who was to ask what the foolish man was up to. "I'm fishing," he answered. The runner asked how he could fish where there was no water. Said the farmer, "I can fish on a dry spot just as well as two oxen can have a foal." The runner went away and brought the reply to the king. The latter had the farmer come before him and told him that he hadn't hit upon that by himself and asked from whom he'd got it; and he was to own up at once. However, the farmer wouldn't do so and kept saying, "God forbid, I hit upon it myself." But they laid him on a bundle of straw and beat him and tortured him until he confessed that he got it from the queen. When the king got home, he said to his wife, "Why did you play me so false? I no longer want you as my wife. Your time's up, go back where you came from to your peasant hut."

He gave her permission, however, to take along one thing, namely, what was dearest and most precious to her, and that was to be her farewell. "Yes, dear husband," she said, "if you so order, I shall do it," and fell on his neck and kissed him and said she wanted to take leave of him. Then she ordered a strong sleeping potion brought for a farewell drink with him. The king took a deep draught, but she drank but a little. Soon he fell into a deep sleep, and when she saw that, she called a servant, and taking a fine white linen cloth, wrapped him up in it. The servants had to carry him out to a carriage in front of the door, and she drove him home to her hut. Then she put him in her little bed, and he slept right through a day and a night. When he woke up, he looked around and said, "Good heavens, where am I?" and called his servant. But no servant was there. Finally his wife came to the bedside and said, "Dear king, you ordered me to take along what was dearest and most precious to me in the palace. Well, I've nothing dearer or more precious than you, and that's why I took you along." Tears came to the king's eyes, and he said, "Dear wife, you shall be mine and I thine," and took her back with him to the royal palace and married her anew. And they're surely still living today.

95 Old Hildebrand

Der alte Hildebrand

THERE WAS ONCE A FARMER and his wife. The village priest looked with favor on the woman and kept wishing he might just once spend a whole day pleasantly alone with her. That would have been quite agreeable to her, too. Well, once he said to her, "Listen, my dear woman, now I have worked out a plan how for once we can spend a whole day pleasantly together. Do you know what: on Wednesday take to your bed, tell your husband you're sick, wail and complain a lot, and keep it up till Sunday when I preach the sermon. Then in my sermon I'll say: if anybody has at home a sick child, a sick husband, a sick wife, a sick father, a sick mother, a sick sister, brother, or whoever else it may be, and makes a pilgrimage to Cuckold's Mountain in Italy, where for a farthing one gets a measure of bay leaves, then the sick child, the sick husband, the sick wife, the sick father, the sick mother, the sick brother, or whoever else it may be, will get well at once."

"I'll do that, of course," replied the woman. Accordingly, on Wednesday the woman took to her bed and wailed and complained like anything, and her husband brought her everything he could think of, but it did no good. Then when Sunday came, the woman said, "I really feel as wretched as if I were going to die straight off, but one more thing I'd like before my end, you know. I'd like to hear the sermon the priest is going to preach today." "Oh, my child," answered the farmer, "don't do that! You might get worse if you got up. Look, I'll go to the sermon and pay close attention and repeat to you everything the priest says." "Well," said the woman, "go then and pay strict attention and tell me everything you hear." Then the farmer went to the sermon, and the priest began to preach, saying, you know, if anybody had at home a sick child, a sick husband, a sick wife, a sick father, a sick mother, a sick sister, brother, or whoever else it might be, and if he'd make a pilgrimage to Cuckold's Mountain in Italy, where a measure of bay leaves costs a farthing, then they all would get well at once. And if anybody wanted to make the journey, he was to come to him after mass and he'd give him a bag for the bay leaves and the farthing. Then no one was happier than the farmer and after mass he went straight to the priest, who gave him the bag and the farthing. Thereupon he went home and while still at the front door cried out, "Hurray, dear wife, you're as good as well! Today the priest preached that if anybody had at home a sick child, a sick husband, a sick wife, a sick father, a sick mother, a sick sister, brother, or whoever else it might be, and makes a pilgrimage to Cuckold's Mountain in Italy, where a measure of bay leaves costs a farthing, then they all would get well at once. Now I've already got the bag for the bay leaves from the priest, and the farthing, too, and shall set out on my journey at once, so that you may get well the sooner." Thereupon he departed. He'd hardly left, however, when his wife was already up, and in no time the priest was there.

Now let us leave the two aside for a while and go with the farmer. All the time he had been walking right along so as to get to Cuckold's Mountain the quicker, and thus as he was walking, he met his bosom friend. The latter was an egg-dealer and had just come from the market where he had sold his eggs. "Praise the Lord!" said the egg-dealer, "Where are you going in such a hurry, friend?" "On and on forever, friend," said the farmer. "My wife fell sick, and I heard our priest preaching today and he said that if anybody has at home a sick child, a sick husband, a sick wife, a sick father, a sick mother, a sick sister, brother, or whoever else it may be, and makes a pilgrimage to Cuckold's Mountain in Italy, where a measure of bay leaves costs a farthing, his sick child, sick husband, sick wife, sick father, sick mother, sick sister, brother, or whoever else it may be, will get well at once. Then I got me the bag for the bay leaves and the farthing from the priest, and now, you see, I'm starting on my journey." "But listen, dear friend," said the egg-dealer to the farmer, "are you so simple that you can believe anything like that? Do you know what's up? The priest would very much like to spend a whole day pleasantly alone with your wife. That's why they told you that yarn—to get you out of the way." "My goodness!" said the farmer, "I'd certainly like to know if that's true." "Well," said his friend, "I'll tell you what, get into my egg basket; then

I'll carry you home, and there you'll see for yourself." They did so, and the friend put the farmer in his egg basket and carried him home.

When they got home, whoop-la! the fun had already started. The farmer's wife had slaughtered almost everything that was in her farmyard and had baked pancakes, and the priest was there and had brought his fiddle along. The friend knocked, and the farmer's wife asked who was out there. "It's me, my friend," said the egg-dealer, "please put me up for the night. I didn't sell my eggs at market and now I've got to carry them back home. They're much too heavy, I can't carry them any farther, and it's already dark." "Yes, my friend," replied the woman, "but you've come at a very inconvenient time. Well, since there's nothing else to do, come in and sit down there on the bench by the stove." So the friend sat down with his packbasket on the bench by the stove. The priest and the woman, however, were in high spirits. Finally the priest began and said, "Listen, my dear woman, you can sing so well. Sing me one song." "Ah," said the woman, "I can no longer sing; of course, in my young days I could sing all right, but now that's a thing of the past." "Why!" replied the priest, "sing just the same, just a little something." Then the woman began to sing,

> "I sent my husband far away
> To Cuckold's Mountain in Italy."

Then the priest sang,

> "I wish he'd stay there a whole year;
> Why should I care about the bag for bay leaves.
> Halleluia!"

Now the farmer's friend back there by the stove began to sing (I must tell you that the farmer's name was Hildebrand) as follows,

> "Oh you, my dear Hildebrand,
> What are you doing on the stove bench?
> Halleluia!"

Now the farmer in the basket sang,

> "Now I can't stand the singing any longer;
> Now I must climb out of my packbasket,"

climbed out of the basket, and with blows drove the priest out of the house.

96 The Three Birds

De drei Vügelkens

A GOOD THOUSAND YEARS AGO and more there were in this region a lot of petty kings. One of these lived on the Köterberg [Westphalia] and was very fond of hunting. Once as he was setting out from his castle with his huntsmen, three girls were tending their cows at the foot of the mountain, and when they saw the king with his large retinue, the eldest, pointing to the king, cried out to the other two, "Hallo! hallo! if I don't get him, I don't want anybody." Then the second answered from the other side of the mountain, pointing to the man who was walking on the king's right, "Hallo! hallo! if I don't get him, I don't want anybody." Then the youngest called out, pointing to the man walking on the king's left, "Hallo! hallo! if I don't get him, I don't want anybody." Now these were the two ministers. The king heard all this, and when he got back from the hunt, had the three girls brought into his presence and asked them what they had said yesterday by the mountain. They didn't want to say, but the king asked the eldest if she would have him as her husband. She said yes, and her two sisters married the two ministers, for all three were beautiful and fair of face, especially the queen, whose hair was like flax.

The two sisters, however, had no children, and once when the king had to go on a journey, he had them come to the queen to cheer her up because at that time she was with child. She gave birth to a little boy with a bright red star. Then the two sisters said, one to the other, that they'd throw the handsome boy into the river. When they'd thrown him in (I think it was the Weser), a bird flew up in the air and sang,

> "Ready for death,
> Till you hear [from me] again,

> Ready for the lily-bouquet:
> Are you ready, good boy?"

When the two heard that they feared for their lives and made off. When the king got home, they told him that the queen had given birth to a dog. Then the king said, "What God does is for the best."

By the river lived a fisherman who fished the little boy out again while he was still alive, and since his wife had no children, they brought him up. A year later when the king again went on a journey and the queen again gave birth to a boy, the two false sisters took him and threw him, too, into the river. Then the bird again flew up into the air and sang,

> "Ready for death,
> Till you hear [from me] again,
> Ready for the lily-bouquet:
> Are you ready, good boy?"

When the king came back they told him that the queen had again given birth to a dog, and again he said, "What God does is for the best." But the fisherman pulled him, too, out of the river and brought him up.

Again the king went on a journey, and the queen gave birth to a little girl whom the false sisters likewise threw into the river. Then the bird again flew up into the air and sang,

> "Ready for death,
> Till you hear [from me] again,
> Ready for the lily-bouquet:
> Are you ready, good girl?"

When the king came home, they told him that the queen had given birth to a cat. Then the king got angry and had his wife thrown into prison, where she remained for many years. [But the fisherman pulled the girl, too, out and brought her up.]

Meanwhile the children grew up. Once the eldest went out fishing with some other boys, but they didn't want to have him around and said, "You foundling, go away!" Then he became very sad and asked the old fisherman whether that was true. The latter told him that he had once been fishing and had pulled him out of the water. Then the boy said he'd set out and look for his father. The fisherman begged him please to stay, but there was no stopping him, and the fisherman at last gave in.

Then he set out and walked for several days on end. Finally he came to a big and mighty river; an old woman was standing there fishing. "Good day, granny," said the boy. "Many thanks." "You'll be fishing a good long time before you catch a fish." "And you'll search a good long time before you find your father. How are you going to get across the river?" said the woman. "Oh, God alone knows." Then the old woman took him on her back and carried him across, and he searched for a long time and couldn't find his father. When all of a year had passed, the second boy set out, intending to look for his brother. He came to the river, and the same thing happened to him as to his brother.

Now only the daughter was still left at home; she grieved so for her brothers that at last she, too, begged the fisherman to let her set out, for she wanted to hunt for her brothers. Then she, too, came to the big river and said to the old woman, "Good day, granny." "Many thanks." "May God help you in your fishing." When the old woman heard that, she became very affable, carried her across the river, and giving her a rod, said to her, "Now just keep going this way, my dear, and when you go by a big black dog, you must do so quietly and boldly and not laugh or look at it. You'll come to a big castle which will be wide open; you must drop the rod on the threshold and go right through and out the other side. There's an old well there, out of which has grown a big tree. On the tree a bird is hanging in a cage. Take it down. Then also take a glass of water from the well and with both objects go back the same way. Pick up the rod again from the threshold and when you go past the dog again, strike it in the face with it and see to it that you don't miss it. Then come back to me." She found everything there just as the woman had said and on the way back found her two brothers who had been searching for one another through half the world. They walked on together to where the black dog was lying in the road; she struck it in the face and it turned into a handsome prince who went along with them to the river. The old woman was still there and rejoiced greatly that they were all there again and carried them all across the river. Then she, too, went away, for she was now disenchanted. The others, however, went to the old fisherman and all were happy to have found one another again. The bird, however, they hung on the wall.

But the second son couldn't stay quietly at home and took a bow and went hunting. Since he was tired, he took his flute and played a tune. But the king, too, was hunting and heard it and went there, and when he came upon the boy, he said, "Who gave you leave to hunt here?" "Oh, no one." "Whom do you belong to?" "I'm the fisherman's son." "But he hasn't any children." "If you won't believe it, come along with me." The king did so and enquired of the fisherman, who told him everything, and the bird on the wall began to sing,

> "The mother is sitting alone
> right in the prison.
> O king, noble blood,
> those are your children.
> The two false sisters,
> they did harm to the children
> down in the depths of the river
> where the fisherman found them."

Then they were all frightened, and the king took the bird, the fisherman and the three children with him to the castle and had the prison opened and took his wife out again. But she had become very sick and wretched. Then the daughter gave her a drink of water from the well, and she was hale and hearty again, but the two false sisters were burned to death, and the daughter married the prince.

97 The Water of Life

Das Wasser des Lebens

THERE WAS ONCE A KING who fell ill, and no one thought that he would survive. His three sons, however, were greatly distressed by this, went down into the palace garden, and wept. There they met an old man who asked what was troubling them. They told him that their father was so ill that he'd probably die, because nothing was doing him any good. "I know one remedy," said the old man, "it's the Water of Life; if he drinks some of it, he'll get well again, but it's hard to find." "I'll surely find it," said the eldest son. He went to the sick king and begged him to let him set out in search of the Water of Life, for it alone could cure him. "No," said the king, "it's too dangerous a task; I'd rather die." But the son begged so long that the king finally assented. In his heart the prince thought, "If I bring the Water, I'll be my father's favorite and inherit the kingdom."

So he set out, and when he'd been riding for a time, there was a dwarf standing by the road who called out to him, saying, "Where are you going in such a hurry?" "Stupid little shrimp," said the prince quite arrogantly, "that's none of your business!" and rode on. The little dwarf had, however, got angry and had made a bad wish. Soon after, the prince got into a mountain gorge and the farther he rode, the more the mountains closed in, and finally the way got so narrow that he couldn't go on another step. It was impossible to turn the horse about or to get out of the saddle, and he sat there as if imprisoned. The sick king waited a long time for him, but he didn't come. Then the second son said, "Father, let me set out and search for the Water," thinking to himself, "If my brother's dead, the kingdom will fall to me." At first the king was unwilling to let him go either but finally gave in. Accordingly, the prince set out on the same route his brother had taken and likewise met the dwarf, who stopped him and asked where he was going in such a hurry. "Little shrimp," said the prince, "that's none of your business!" and without further ado rode on. However, the dwarf put a curse on him, and like his brother, he got into a mountain gorge and could go neither forward nor back. But that's what happens to arrogant people!

When the second son also failed to come back, the youngest offered to set out and fetch the Water, and in the end the king had to let him go. When he met the dwarf and the latter asked where he was going in such a hurry, he stopped, talked to him, and answering his question, said, "I'm looking for the Water of Life, for my father is mortally ill." "Do you happen to know where it's to be found?" "No," said the prince. "Because you've behaved properly, not arrogantly like your brothers, I'll give you the information and tell you how you can get the Water of Life. It gushes from a spring in the courtyard of an enchanted castle, but you won't make your way inside unless I give you an iron rod and two little loaves of bread. Strike three times with the rod on the iron gate of the castle, then it will fly open; inside will be lying two lions with wide open jaws. If, however, you toss a loaf to each, they'll quiet down. Then hurry and fetch some of the Water of Life before it strikes twelve, otherwise the gate will slam to again and you'll be shut in." The prince thanked him, took the rod and the bread, and set out. When he got there, everything was as the dwarf had said. The gate flew open at the third blow of the rod, and when he had pacified the lions with the bread, he entered the castle and came into a large and handsome hall. In this hall were sitting enchanted princes, from whose fingers he drew the rings. A sword and a loaf of bread were also lying there; these he took with him. Then he got into a room where a beautiful maiden was standing. She rejoiced when she saw him, kissed him, and said he'd disenchanted her and that he should have her whole kingdom, and if he'd come back in a year, they would celebrate their wedding. Then she further told him where the spring with the Water of Life was, but he'd have to hurry and draw the Water before it struck twelve. Then he went farther and at last came to a room where there was a beautiful freshly made bed, and because he was tired, he thought he'd first take a little rest. So he lay down and fell asleep. When he awoke, it was striking quarter to twelve. Then quite frightened he jumped up, ran to the spring, drew water from it with a tumbler that was beside it, and hurried out. Just as he was going out the iron gate, it struck twelve and the gate slammed so hard that it even took off a bit of his heel.

He was happy, however, to have got the Water of Life, set out toward home and again passed the dwarf. When the latter saw the sword and the bread, he said, "With these objects you've acquired something very valuable: with the sword you can slay whole armies, while the bread will never be used up." The prince didn't want to go home to his father without his brothers and said, "Dear dwarf, can't you tell me where my two brothers are? They set out for the Water of Life ahead of me and haven't come back." "They're shut in between two mountains," said the dwarf; "I cast a spell on them and set them there because they were so arrogant." Then the prince entreated the dwarf until he released them, but the latter warned him, saying, "Be on your guard against them, they're evil-hearted."

When his brothers arrived, he was happy and told them how he had fared, that he'd found the Water of Life and had brought along a tumbler full and he'd disenchanted a beautiful princess; she was willing to wait a whole year for him, and then their wedding would take place and he'd get the kingdom. After that they rode on together and came to a country where there was famine and war, and the king really believed he was doomed to die, so dire was the distress. Then the prince went to him and gave him the bread with which he fed and satisfied his whole kingdom. Then the prince gave him the sword, too, and with that he defeated the armies of his foes and was at last able to live in peace and quiet. Then the prince took back his bread and sword, and the three brothers rode on. They came to two more countries where famine and war prevailed, and each time the prince gave the king his bread and sword, and by now had saved three kingdoms. After that they boarded a ship and journeyed overseas. On the voyage the two eldest said to one another, "It's the youngest who found the Water of Life, not we; in return for this our father will give him the kingdom that's ours by right, and he'll deprive us of our good fortune." Then they plotted vengeance and between them planned to ruin him. They waited till once when he was fast asleep; then they poured the Water of Life out of the tumbler, took that water for themselves, and poured bitter salt water into his tumbler.

When at last they reached home, the youngest brought the sick king his tumbler so that he might drink and get well, but no sooner had he drunk a little of the bitter salt water than he got sicker than ever. When he complained of this, the two eldest sons came and accused the youngest of wanting to poison him, saying that they'd brought him the true Water of Life and handed it to him. No sooner had he drunk some of it than he felt his illness vanish and he became as strong and well as in the days of his youth. Then the two went to the youngest and mocked him, saying, "To be sure, you found the Water of Life, but you had the trouble and we the reward. You ought to have been smarter and kept your eyes open; we took it from you while you were asleep at sea, and when the year is up, one of us will fetch the beautiful king's daughter for himself. But watch out that you don't betray us. Father won't believe you anyway, and if you breathe a single word, you'll lose your life in the bargain. If, however, you keep quiet, we'll let you live."

The old king was angry at his youngest son and believed that he had designs on his life. Accordingly, he had the court assembled and passed a verdict against him that he should be secretly shot. Once when the prince was out hunting and suspected no harm; the king's huntsman had to accompany him. When they were all alone out there in the forest and the huntsman was looking very sad, the prince said to him, "Dear huntsman, what's the matter with you?" "I can't tell you," said the huntsman, "and yet I ought to." Then the prince said, "Speak up and say what it is; I'll pardon you for it." "Alas!" said the huntsman, "I'm to shoot you; the king ordered me to." Then the prince was frightened and said, "Dear huntsman, let me live. I'll give you my royal clothes, you give me your poor ones in exchange." "I'll do that gladly," said the huntsman, "I couldn't have shot at you anyway." Then they changed clothes, and the huntsman went home. The prince, however, went deeper into the forest.

After a time three carriages came to the old king, laden with gold and jewels for his youngest son. They'd been sent by the three kings who had defeated their foes with the prince's sword and had fed their countries with his bread and now wanted to show their gratitude. Then the old king thought, "Could my son have been innocent?" and said to his retainers, "If only he were still alive! It grieves me so that I had him killed." "He is still alive," said the huntsman, "I didn't have the heart to carry out your command," and told the king how it had gone. Then a great weight fell from the king's heart, and in every kingdom he had it proclaimed that his son might return and that he would be received into favor.

Before her palace the king's daughter had built a driveway that was all gold and glittering and told her people that whoever came riding to her straight up the road would be the right man and that they were to admit him. But whoever rode up off to the side of the road would not be the right man and that they were not to admit him. When the time was nearly up, the eldest son thought he'd hurry and go to the king's daughter and present himself as her redeemer; then he'd get her as his wife and the kingdom as well. Accordingly, he rode off, and when he got near the palace and saw the beautiful gold driveway, he thought, "It would be a crying shame to ride on it," turned off the road to the side on the right. But when he got outside the gate, the people told him he wasn't the right man and to go away again.

Shortly thereafter the second prince set out, and when he came to the gold driveway and the horse had set one foot down on it, he thought, "It would be a crying shame, it might wear some of it away," turned off it and rode to the side on the left. But when he got outside the gate, the people said he wasn't the right man and to go away again.

When the year was quite up, the third prince wanted to ride out of the forest and away to his beloved and forget his grief in her company. Accordingly, he set out and kept thinking of her and wishing he was already with her and didn't notice the gold driveway at all. Then his horse went right up the middle of it, and when he got outside the gate, it was opened, and the king's daughter received him joyfully and said he was her redeemer and lord of the kingdom. And the wedding was celebrated with great happiness. When it was over, she told him that his father had summoned him to him and had pardoned him. Then he rode home and told the old king everything, how his brothers had deceived him and that he had nonetheless kept quiet about it. The old king was going to punish them, but they'd put to sea and sailed away and didn't come back as long as they lived.

98 Dr. Know-It-All

Doktor Allwissend

THERE WAS ONCE A POOR FARMER named Crab who drove two oxen to town with a cord of wood; this he sold to a doctor for two dollars. As the money was being paid out to him, the doctor was just sitting down to table. The farmer saw what fine food and drink the doctor had, and his heart longed for it, and he, too, would have liked to be a doctor. So he stayed on a little longer and finally asked if he, too, couldn't become a doctor. "Oh, yes," said the doctor, "that can easily be arranged." "What must I do?" asked the farmer. "First of all, buy a primer like this with a picture of a rooster on one of the front pages; secondly, turn your cart and oxen into cash and with it get yourself some clothes and whatever else goes with doctoring; thirdly, have a sign painted with the words "Dr. Know-It-All" and nail it up over your front door." The farmer did everything he was told. Now after he'd been doctoring it for a bit, though not very long, a great and wealthy lord was robbed of some money. He was told about Dr. Know-It-All, who lived in such and such a village and who was bound to know where the money had got to. So the lord had his coach hitched up, drove out to the village, and at his house enquired if he was Dr. Know-It-All. "Yes, I am." "Then you're to come with me and retrieve the stolen money." "All right, but my wife Meg must come along, too." The lord agreed to that and had them both sit in the coach, and they drove off together. When they reached the nobleman's court, the table was set, and first of all he was to eat with them. "Yes, but my wife Meg, too," he said and sat down with her at the table.

Now when the first servant came in with a dish of delicious food, the farmer nudged his wife and said, "Meg, that was the first," meaning it was the man who served the first course. The servant, however, thought he meant "that's the first thief," and because that's what he really was, he got frightened and outside said to his companions, "The doctor knows everything, we're in for trouble; he said I was the first." The second servant didn't want to go in at all but had to. Now as he entered with his dish, the farmer nudged his wife, saying, "Meg, that's the second." This servant likewise got frightened and cleared out. The third fared no better; again the farmer said, "That's the third." The fourth had to bring in a covered dish, and the lord told the doctor to display his skill and guess what was under the cover. As a matter of fact it was crabs. The farmer looked at the dish and not knowing what on earth to do, said, "Ah me, poor Crab!" Hearing that the lord cried, "There, he knows! Now he's bound also to know who has the money."

The servant got terribly frightened and winked at the doctor as a sign to step outside. When he got outside, all four confessed to him that they'd stolen the money. They were quite willing to hand it over and to give him a large sum besides if only he wouldn't betray them—otherwise they'd be done for. Furthermore, they took him to where the money was hidden. The doctor was pleased with this, went back in, sat down at the table and said, "My lord, now I'll look up in my book and see where the money's hidden." The fifth servant, however, crept into the stove and wanted to hear whether the doctor knew anything else. The doctor sat and opened his primer, leafed it here and there, and looked for the rooster. Because he couldn't find it straight off, he said, "I know you're in there, and come out you must!" Then the servant in the stove thought that it was he who was meant, jumped out in a great fright, crying, "The man knows it all." Now Dr. Know-It-All showed the lord where the money was but didn't say who'd stolen it. From both parties he received a large sum as a reward and became a famous man.

99   The Spirit in the Glass-Bottle

Der Geist im Glas

THERE WAS ONCE A POOR WOODCUTTER who worked from early morning till late at night. When finally he'd saved up some money, he said to his boy, "You're my only child; I want to use the money I've earned by the bitter sweat of my brow for your education. If you learn some good suitable profession, you'll be able to support me in my old age, when my limbs have become stiff and I have to stay at home." Then the boy went to a university and studied industriously so that his teachers praised him. He stayed there for some time. When he had studied in a few universities but was not yet perfect in everything, the little pittance that his father had earned was gone, and he had to return home. "Alas," said his father in distress, "I can't give you any more and in these hard times can't earn a farthing more than we need for our daily bread." "Father dear," answered the son, "don't give it a thought; if such is God's will, it will work out to my best advantage. I'll adjust to it, of course."

When the father was on the point of going out into the forest to earn something by chopping and piling cordwood, the son said, "I'll go along and help you." "Indeed, my son," said the father, "that will be hard on you; you're not used to heavy work; you won't stand up under it. Besides, I've only one ax and no money left to buy another." "Just go to the neighbor's," answered the son; "he'll lend you his ax until I've earned enough to buy one for myself." The father borrowed an ax from the neighbor, and the next morning at daybreak they went out together into the forest. The son helped his father and was quite cheerful and lively at the task. Now when the sun was overhead, the father said, "Let's rest and eat our noon meal; afterward it'll go twice as fast." The son took his bread in his hand and said, "You just rest, father, I'm not tired; I'm going to walk about for a bit in the forest and look for birds' nests." "You silly fellow," said the father, "why do you want to walk about there? Afterward you'll be tired and won't be able to lift an arm. Stay here and sit down by me."

The son, however, went into the forest, ate his bread, was very happy, and peered into the green branches to see if by chance he might perhaps discover a nest. Thus he went hither and yon until he at last came to a dangerous oak that was certainly already many hundreds of years old and bigger than five men could reach around. He stopped and looked at it, thinking, "Many a bird, indeed, must have built its nest there." Suddenly he seemed to hear a voice. He listened and heard it call in a very muffled tone, "Let me out! let me out!" He looked about but could see nothing, though the voice seemed to come out from underground. Then he cried, "Where are you?" "I'm down here in the roots of the oak," answered the voice; "let me out! let me out!" The student began to clear away at the foot of the tree and to search among the roots until finally he found a glass bottle in a little hollow place. He picked it up and holding it to the light, saw something shaped like a frog jumping up and down inside. "Let me out! let me out!" it cried anew, and the student, suspecting no harm, took the stopper out of the bottle. Immediately a spirit rose up out of the bottle and began to grow, and grew so fast that in a few moments it was standing before the student like a horrible giant, half as big as the tree. In a terrible voice it cried, "Do you know what your reward is going to be for letting me out?" "No," answered the student fearlessly, "how should I know?" "Then I'll tell you," cried the spirit, "I'll have to break your neck for doing it." "You should have told me that sooner," answered the student, "then I'd have let you stay there. But for all of you my head's going to stay right on, since more people will have to be consulted." "More people or not more people," cried the spirit, "you're going to get the reward that's due you. Do you think that I was shut up there for so long by way of a favor? No, I was being punished. I am the great and mighty Mercury and must break the neck of whoever releases me." "Easy!" answered the student; "things don't happen as quick as that. Besides, I must first know that you actually were in the little bottle and that you're the right spirit. If you can really get back in again, then I'll believe it, and then you can do with me as you like." "That's a trifling trick," said the spirit most arrogantly, shrunk itself and made itself as thin and small as it had been at the outset, so that it crept in again through the same opening and through the neck of the bottle. Scarcely was it inside, however, when the student again pushed in the stopper he had drawn and threw the bottle into its old place among the roots of the oak, thus tricking the spirit.

Now the student was about to go back to his father, but the spirit cried most piteously, "Oh, please let me out! please let me out!" "No," answered the student, "not a second time. Once I've shut him in again, I'm not letting anybody out who's had one try at my life." "If you'll free me," cried the spirit, "I'll give you enough to suffice you as long as you live." "No," answered the student, "you'd trick me again as you did the first time." "You're throwing your good luck away," said the spirit, "I won't do anything to you; on the contrary, I'll reward you handsomely." "I'll risk it," thought the student, "perhaps it'll keep its word, and in any event it won't do me any harm." Then he removed the stopper, and as before the spirit rose up out of the bottle, stretched itself out, and became as big as a giant. "Now you shall have your reward," it said, and handing the student a bit of cloth just like a piece of court plaster, continued, "if with one end you rub a wound, the wound will heal, and if with the other end you rub steel or iron, it will turn to silver." "I must try it first," said the student, went to a tree, scratched the bark with his ax and rubbed it with the proper end of the court plaster. The scratch immediately closed again and was healed. "Well, that's quite all right," he said to the spirit, "Now we can part company." The spirit thanked him for setting it free, and the student thanked the spirit for its present and returned to his father.

"Where have you been gadding about?" said the father; "why did you forget our work? Indeed, I told you that you wouldn't get anything done." "Don't worry, father, I'll make it up." "Yes, make it up!" said the father angrily, "that's no way to do." "Watch, father, I'm going to chop that tree there right down so that it'll fall with a crash." Then he took his court plaster, rubbed the ax with it and dealt a powerful blow, but because the iron had been changed to silver, the edge turned. "My, father! Just see what a bad ax you gave me; it's all bent." Then the father was frightened and said, "Oh, what have you done! Now I must pay for the ax and don't know how I can. That's all the good I'm getting out of your work!" "Don't get angry," answered the son, "I'll pay for the ax all right." "Oh, you stupid fellow!" cried the father, "how will you pay for it? You haven't anything but what I give you. Your head's full of student pranks, but you don't understand anything about wood-chopping."

After a while the student said, "Father, I really can't work any longer; let's call it a day." "What!" he answered. "Do you think I'm going to sit with my hands in my lap like you? I've still got to get something done; you can go along home if you like." "Father, this is the first time I've been here in the forest. I don't know the way alone; please come along with me." Because his anger had abated, the father finally let himself be talked into it and went home with him. Then he said to his son, "Now go and sell the damaged ax and watch out what you get for it. I'll have to earn the balance and pay back the neighbor for it." The son took the ax and carried it into town to a goldsmith who assayed it, put it in the scales, and said, "It's worth four hundred dollars; I haven't that much in cash." "Give me what you have," said the student, "and I'll lend you the rest." The goldsmith gave him three hundred dollars and owed him one hundred. Thereupon the student went home and said, "Father, I've got the money. Go ask the neighbor what he wants for the ax." "That I know already," answered the old man, "one dollar and six pennies." "Well, give him two dollars and twelve pennies; that's double and enough. Look, I have money and to spare," and giving his father one hundred dollars, said, "You'll never be in want; live at your ease." "My goodness," said the old man, "how did you come by this fortune?" Then he told him how it had all happened and how, trusting in his luck, he had made such a rich haul. With the rest of the money, however, he went off again to the university and studied further. And because he was able to heal all wounds with his court plaster, he became the most famous doctor in the world.

100 The Devil's Sooty Brother

Des Teufels russiger Bruder

A DISCHARGED SOLDIER had nothing to live on and didn't know what to do. Then he went out into the forest, and after he'd been walking for a while, met a little dwarf, who, as a matter of fact, was the Devil. The dwarf said to him, "What's the matter with you? You're looking so sad." "I'm hungry, but I have no money," said the soldier. "If you'll hire yourself out to me," said the Devil, "and be my servant, you shall have enough as long as you live. You'll have to serve me for seven years; after that you'll be free again. But I'll tell you one thing. You may not wash yourself, comb your hair, trim your beard, cut your nails or your hair, or wipe any water from your eyes." "Up and at it, if that's how it must be," said the soldier and went off with the dwarf, who took him straight into Hell. Then he told him what he was to do: he'd have to stir the fire under the kettles in which the damned were sitting, keep the house clean, carry the rubbish outdoors, and see to it that everything was in order. But if he peeked as much as once into the kettles, it would go hard with him. "Right you are," said the soldier, "I'll attend to it all right."

Then the old Devil went out again on his wanderings, and the soldier entered upon his duties, put fuel on the fire, swept and carried the rubbish outdoors, just as he had been ordered. When the old Devil came back, he looked to see if everything had been done, evinced satisfaction, and went off again a second time. Now the soldier took a good look about: the kettles were standing round about there in Hell and there was a huge fire under them, and the contents were boiling and bubbling. He would gladly have given his life to look in, had the Devil not so strictly forbidden him. Finally he could no longer resist, lifted the lid a tiny bit from the first kettle and peeked in. There he saw his former sergeant sitting. "Aha, old fellow!" he said, "Do I find you here? You once had me under your thumb, now I've got you," dropped the lid quickly, poked the fire, and added fresh fuel. He went on to the second kettle, lifted the lid a little, too, and peeked, and saw his ensign sitting in it: "Aha, old fellow! Do I find you here? You once had me under your thumb, now I've got you," shut the lid again and fetched another log to make it good and hot for him. Now he also wanted to see who was sitting in the third kettle; it was none other than his general: "Aha, old fellow! Do I find you here? You once had me under your thumb, now I've got you," fetched a bellows and made hell-fire blaze up right under him. Thus he performed his duties in Hell for seven years, didn't wash, didn't comb his hair, didn't trim his beard, didn't cut his nails or his hair, and didn't wipe any water from his eyes. And the seven years passed so quickly that it seemed to him it had only been six months.

When the time was quite up, the Devil came and said, "Well, John, what have you been doing?" "I've been stirring the fire under the kettles, I've been sweeping, and I've been carrying the rubbish outdoors." "But you peeked into the kettles, too. It's lucky you put more wood on the fire, otherwise you'd have lost your life. Now your time is up; do you want to go back home?" "Yes," said the soldier, "I'd also very much like to see what my father is doing back home." "In order that you may get the wages you're entitled to," said the Devil, "go fill your knapsack with sweepings and take them home with you. Furthermore, you're to go unwashed and uncombed, with long hair on your head and with your beard long, with uncut nails and bleary eyes, and if you're asked where you came from, you're to say, 'From Hell.' And if you're asked who you are, you're to say 'the Devil's sooty brother and also my king.'" The soldier said nothing and did as the Devil told him, but he wasn't at all satisfied with his wages.

As soon as he was back up in the forest, he took his knapsack off his back and was about to shake it out, but when he opened it, the sweepings had become pure gold. "I shouldn't have suspected that," he said, was greatly pleased, and walked into town. The innkeeper was standing outside the inn and seeing him coming was afraid because John looked such a fright, worse than a scarecrow. He called to him, saying, "Where do you come from?" "From Hell." "Who are you?" "The Devil's sooty brother and also my king." The innkeeper didn't want to admit him, but when he showed him the gold, he went and unlatched the door himself. Then John made him give him the best room and serve him lavishly; he ate and drank his fill but, as the Devil had ordered, didn't wash and didn't comb his hair. Finally he went to bed. The picture of the knapsack full of gold was always before the innkeeper's eyes, and the latter had no peace until he'd crept in there in the night and stolen it. When John got up next morning and was going to pay the innkeeper and go on his way, his knapsack was gone. However, he wasted no words and thinking, "You've been an innocent victim," turned about and went straight back to Hell. There he complained of his plight to the old Devil and asked his help. The Devil said, "Sit down. I'll wash you and comb your hair, trim your beard, cut your hair and nails, and wipe out your eyes." When he had finished with him, he again gave him the knapsack full of sweepings and said, "Go tell the innkeeper he's to give you back your gold or else I'll come and fetch him, and he'll have to stir the fire in your place." John went up and said to the innkeeper, "You stole my gold; if you don't give it back, you'll go to Hell in my place and will look as grizzly as I did." Then the innkeeper gave him the gold and more besides, and begged him to keep quiet about it. Now John was a rich man.

John set out for home to his father's, bought himself a poor linen overall for his body, and went here and there playing music, for he'd learned that from the Devil in Hell. There was an old king in the land, in whose presence he had to play. The king was so delighted with the music that he promised John his eldest daughter in marriage. But when she heard that she was to marry such a common fellow in a white overall, she said, "Before I'd do that, I'd rather jump into the deepest water." Then the king gave him the youngest, who was quite willing to marry him out of love for her father. Thus the Devil's sooty brother got the king's daughter and, when the old king died, the whole kingdom as well.

101   Bearskin

Der Bärenhäuter

THERE WAS ONCE A YOUNG FELLOW who enlisted as a soldier, conducted himself bravely, and was always in the van when it was raining bullets. As long as the war lasted, all went well, but when peace was concluded, he received his discharge, and his captain said he might go where he pleased. His parents were dead, and no longer having any home, he went to his brothers and begged them to support him until the next war. But the brothers were hardhearted and said, "What can we do with you? We can't make any use of you; see how you can get along on your own." The soldier had only his rifle left; this he shouldered and intended to set out into the world. He reached a big moor where nothing but a circle of trees was to be seen. Very sadly he sat down beneath them and meditated his fate. "I haven't any money," he thought, "I've learned nothing but soldiering, and now because peace is concluded, they don't need me any more. I foresee that I'm bound to starve."

Suddenly he heard a roar, and as he was looking about, a stranger stood before him, wearing a green jacket and looking quite stately, but with a nasty hoof of a foot. "I know just what's wrong with you," said the man; "you shall have as much gold and goods as you can possibly squander, but I must first be sure that you're not afraid so that I shan't be spending my money for nothing." "How do soldiers and fear go together?" he answered; "you can try me out." "Come on then," answered the man, "look behind you!" The soldier turned around and saw a big bear trotting toward him and roaring. "O ho!" said the soldier, "I'll tickle your nose so you won't want to roar any more," took aim and shot the bear in the muzzle so that it collapsed and didn't stir again. "I see clearly," said the stranger, "that you don't lack courage, but there's still another condition that you must fulfill." "So long as it doesn't jeopardize the salvation of my soul," answered the soldier, who saw plainly who was confronting him; "in that case I won't commit myself to anything." "That you'll see for yourself," answered Green-Jacket; "for the next seven years you may neither wash, comb your beard or hair, cut your nails, nor once say the Lord's Prayer. Furthermore, I'll give you a jacket and a cloak which you must wear during this time. If you die within these seven years, you're mine; if, however, you remain alive, you'll be free and rich, too, as long as you live." The soldier reflected on his dire distress, and since he had faced death so often, he was willing to risk it this time, too, and agreed. The Devil took off his green jacket and handed it to the soldier, saying, "With this jacket on, if you reach into the pocket, you'll always have a handful of money." Then he skinned the bear and said, "This shall be your cloak and your bed, too, for you must sleep on it and may not get in any other bed. And because of this costume your name's to be Bearskin." Hereupon the Devil vanished.

The soldier put the jacket on, reached at once into the pocket, and found that everything was as it should be. Then he put on the cloak, went out into the world, was in fine spirits, and abstained from nothing that was pleasant for him and hard on the money. The first year things still went pretty well, but by the second he really looked a fright. His hair covered almost his whole face, his beard was like a piece of coarse felt, his fingers had claws, and his face was so covered with filth that had one sown cress there, it would have sprouted. Everybody who saw him ran away; but because everywhere he gave money to the poor for them to pray that he might not die within the seven years, and because he paid well for everything, he was always able to get lodging just the same. In the fourth year he came to a tavern where the innkeeper wouldn't take him in and wouldn't even let him have a place in the stable for fear his horses would shy. Still, when Bearskin reached into his pocket and pulled out a handful of ducats, the innkeeper yielded and gave him a room in an outbuilding. Even so, he had to promise not to show himself lest the inn get a bad name.

As Bearskin was sitting alone one evening, wishing with all his heart that the seven years were up, he heard a loud lamenting in an adjoining room. He had a compassionate heart, opened the door, and saw an old man weeping bitterly and wringing his hands above his head. Bearskin stepped nearer, but the man jumped up and was about to run away. Hearing a human voice he finally gave in, and by his kindly words Bearskin got him to reveal to him the cause of his trouble. Little by little his fortune had vanished, he and his daughters had to suffer want, and he was so poor that he couldn't even pay the innkeeper and was about to be put in jail. "If those are your only worries," said Bearskin, "I've got plenty of money." He summoned the innkeeper, paid him, and put another purse of gold in the unhappy man's pocket.

When the old man saw that he was freed of his worries, he didn't know how to show his gratitude. "Come with me," he said to Bearskin, "my daughters are marvels of beauty; choose one of them as your wife. When she hears what you've done for me, she won't hesitate. It's true that you're a bit odd looking, but she'll soon fix you up again." That pleased Bearskin and he went along. When the eldest looked at him, she was so horrified by his face that she screamed and ran away. The second stopped, to be sure, and surveyed him from head to foot, then said, "How can I take a husband who no longer looks like a human being? I'd rather prefer the shaved bear that was once on show here and claimed to be a man; it at least had on the fur coat and white gloves of a cavalryman. If he were merely ugly, I could get used to him." But the youngest said, "Father dear, he must be a good man to have helped you out of your distress. If you've promised him a bride in return, your word must be kept." It was a shame that Bearskin's face was covered with filth and hair, otherwise one might have seen how his heart rejoiced within him when he heard these words. He took a ring from his finger, broke it in two, gave her one half and kept the other for himself. In her half he wrote his name and in his half her name, and bade her put her piece carefully away. Thereupon he took his leave, saying, "I must keep wandering for three more years; if I don't come back, you'll be free because then I shall be dead. But pray God to preserve my life."

The poor girl clothed herself all in black, and whenever she thought of her bridegroom, tears would come to her eyes. From her sisters she got nothing but scorn and derision. "Watch out for yourself," said the eldest, "if you give him your hand, he'll hit it with his paw." "Be on your guard," said the second; "bears love sweets, and if you please him, he'll eat you up." "You must always do just as he wants," continued the eldest, "otherwise he'll start growling." And the second went on to say, "My! the wedding will be great sport; bears dance well." The girl kept quite still and didn't let herself be turned from her purpose.

Bearskin moved about the world from place to place, did good where he could, and gave generously to the poor so that they would pray for him. Finally, as the last day of the seven years dawned, he again went out to the moor and sat down under the circle of trees. Before long there was a rush of wind and the Devil was standing before him with a look of annoyance. Then he threw Bearskin the old jacket and demanded his green jacket back. "We haven't got that far yet," answered Bearskin. "First you must clean me up." Willy-nilly, the Devil had to fetch water, wash Bearskin off, comb his hair, and cut his nails. Then he looked like a brave warrior and was far handsomer than ever.

When the Devil had happily departed, Bearskin felt light of heart. He went into town, put on a splendid velvet jacket, took his seat in a coach drawn by four white horses, and drove to his bride's house. No one recognized him; the father thought him a distinguished army colonel and led him into the room where his daughters were sitting. He had to seat himself between the two eldest; they poured him wine, placed the finest delicacies before him, and thought they never in the world had seen a handsomer man. But the bride sat opposite him in her black weeds, didn't raise her eyes or speak a word. When finally he asked the father if he would give him one of his daughters in marriage, the two eldest jumped up, ran to their room, and were going to put on splendid clothes, for each fancied to herself that she would be the one chosen. As soon as the stranger was alone with his bride, he took out the half-ring, tossed it into a tumbler of wine, which he handed her across the table. She took it, but when she'd drunk the wine and found the half-ring lying at the bottom, her heart beat fast. She fetched the other half, which she was wearing on a ribbon around her neck and held it against his half: it was clear that the two halves fitted perfectly. Then he said, "I am your affianced bridegroom whom you saw as Bearskin; however, by the grace of God I've regained my human form and have become clean again." He went up to her, embraced her, and gave her a kiss. Meanwhile the two sisters came back in full regalia, and when they saw that the handsome man had got the youngest and heard that it was Bearskin, they ran out, full of rage and anger; one drowned herself in the well, the other hanged herself on a tree.

That evening there was a knock on the door, and when the bridegroom opened it, it was the Devil in his green jacket. "See," he said, "now I've got two souls for your one."

102   The Wren and the Bear

Der Zaunkönig und der Bär

ONCE IN THE SUMMER when a bear and a wolf were taking a walk in the forest, the bear heard a most beautiful bird song and said, "Brother wolf, what kind of a bird is it that sings so beautifully?" "It's the king of birds," said the wolf; "we must bow down before it." But it was a fence-king, a wren.* "If that's so," said the bear, "I'd also very much like to see the royal

* With play on *Zaunkönig*, literally "hedge-king," German word for "wren."

palace; come take me there." "It isn't the way you imagine," said the wolf; "you must wait until the queen comes." Soon thereafter the queen came and had food in her bill, and so had the king, and they were about to feed their young. The bear would now have liked to follow them right in, but the wolf held him by the sleeve, saying, "No, you must wait until the king and queen have left again." So they took note of the hole where the nest was and trotted off again. The bear, however, was restless, wanted to see the royal palace, and after a short while went back to it. By then the king and the queen had really flown away; it looked in and saw five or six young birds lying there. "Is that the royal palace!" cried the bear, "it's a wretched palace. And you're no royal children; you don't come of honest folk!" When the young hedge-kings heard that, they got terribly angry and cried, "Yes, we do! Our parents are honest folk. Bear, we've got to settle with you!" The bear and the wolf got frightened, turned about, and sat down in their dens.

The young wrens kept crying and making a noise, and when next the parents brought them food, they said. "We won't touch a single fly's leg, even if we starve, until you've first settled whether we come of honest folk or not. The bear was here and insulted us." Then the old king said, "Just calm yourselves, we'll settle it." Thereupon, together with the queen he flew to the bear's den and called in, "Old Growly Bear, why did you insult my children? It'll fare ill with you; we're going to settle the affair by a bloody war." Thus war was declared on the bear. Every four-footed animal was called up: ox, donkey, steer, stag, deer, and every other animal that walks upon the earth. The hedge-king, on the other hand, summoned up everything that flies in the air: not only birds, big and small, but also midges, hornets, bees, and flies had to come along, too.

When the time came for the war to begin, the hedge-king sent out scouts to discover who was the enemy's commanding general. The midge was the wiliest of all, skirmished about in the forest where the enemy had assembled, and finally sat down under a leaf on the tree where the password was being given. There stood the bear, who called the fox into its presence and said, "Fox, you're the most artful of all animals, you're to be general and lead us." "Good," said the fox, "but what kind of a signal are we to agree on?" No one knew. Then the fox said, "I have a fine, long, bushy tail; it looks almost like a red plume. When I hold my tail up, things are going all right, and then you must march forward, but if I let it droop, then run as fast as you can." When the midge heard that, it flew away home and told the king everything down to the last detail. When the day dawned on which the battle was to be fought, wow! there came the four-footed animals on the run with a clatter that made the earth shake. The king, too, came flying through the air with his army that buzzed, shrieked, and swarmed—enough to frighten one. They went for each other from both sides. The king sent a hornet down; it was to settle under the fox's tail and sting for all it was worth. Now when the fox got the first sting, it twitched and lifted one leg, but stood it and still kept its tail up. With the second sting it had to lower it for a second. With the third, however, it could stand it no longer, cried out, and put its tail between its legs. When the animals saw that, they thought that all was lost and began to run, each to its lair. The birds had won the battle.

The hedge-king and the queen flew home to their children and cried, "Children, rejoice! Eat and drink to your hearts' content; we've won the war." But the young wrens said, "We won't eat yet; the bear must first come to our nest and beg pardon and say that we come of honest folk." Then the wren flew to the bear's den and called out, "Growly Bear, you're to come to the nest and beg my children's pardon and say that they come of honest folk, otherwise we'll trample your ribs to pieces." Then the bear crawled there very fearfully and begged pardon. Now the young wrens were at last satisfied, sat down together, ate, drank, and made merry till late into the night.

103 The Sweet Porridge

Der süsse Brei

THERE WAS ONCE A POOR, DEVOUT GIRL who lived alone with her mother, and they had nothing left to eat. Then the child went out into the forest and met an old woman who already knew about her misery and made her a present of a pot to which she was to say, "Pot, cook!" Then it would cook a good sweet millet porridge. And when she said, "Pot, stop!" then it would stop cooking. The girl brought the pot home to her mother, and now they were free of poverty and hunger and ate sweet porridge as often as they liked. On one occasion when the girl had gone out, the mother said, "Pot, cook!" Then it cooked, and she ate her fill. Now she wanted the pot to stop but didn't know the right word, so it kept cooking, and the porridge ran out over the edge, and it cooked on and on, filled the kitchen and the whole house and the next house and then the street, as if it wanted to satisfy the whole world. It was a most dire situation, and no one knew what to do about it. Finally, when only one single house was left, the child came home and just said, "Pot, stop!" Then it stopped cooking, and anybody who wanted to come back into the town had to eat his way through.

104 The Clever People

Die klugen Leute

ONE DAY A FARMER fetched his hornbeam stick from the corner and said to his wife, "Katy, now I'm going across country and shan't be back for three days. If a cattle-dealer calls and wants to buy our three cows, you may dispose of them, but only for two hundred dollars—no less, do you hear?" "In God's name, go along," answered his wife, "I'll attend to it all right." "Yes, you would!" said the husband. "As a small child you once fell on your head and the effect on you still lasts. But I tell you, if you do anything stupid, I'll color your back black and blue, and without paint at that! Just with the stick I have here in my hand. And the coat of paint will last a whole year, you may depend upon it." Thereupon the man went on his way.

The cattle-dealer came the next morning, and the woman

didn't have to enter into any long discussion with him. Once he'd looked the cows over and heard the price, he said, "I'll gladly pay that, they're worth all of that among friends. I'll take the animals right along with me." He unfastened their chains and drove them out of the stable. Just as he was going out the farmyard gate, the woman caught him by the sleeve and said, "You must first give me the two hundred dollars or else I can't let you go." "Right," answered the man, "I just forgot to buckle on my purse. But don't worry, you have surety until I pay you. I'll take two cows with me and leave the third with you; in that way you'll have good surety." The woman got the point and let the man go away with the cows, thinking, "How happy John will be when he sees I worked it so cleverly."

As he had said, the farmer arrived home on the third day and at once asked if the cows had been sold. "Certainly, John dear," answered his wife, "and, as you said, for two hundred dollars. They're hardly worth that, but the man took them without discussion." "Where's the money?" asked her husband. "I haven't got the money," answered his wife; "as a matter of fact, he'd forgotten his purse, but he'll bring it soon. He left me a good surety." "What kind of surety?" asked her husband. "One of the three cows; he won't get it until he's paid for the others. I worked it very cleverly; I kept the smallest; it'll eat the least." The man got angry, raised his stick and with it was about to give her the promised coat of black and blue. All of a sudden he let it drop and said, "You're the stupidest goose that's waddling about on God's green earth, but I'm sorry for you. I'm going out on the highway and wait for three days to see whether I find anybody who's simpler than you. If I do, you'll get off, but if I don't, then you'll get the pay you so well deserve, and no deduction."

He went out on the great highway, sat down on a stone and waited for what might turn up. He saw a haycart coming along, with a woman standing up in the middle instead of sitting on the bundle of straw or walking beside the oxen and leading them. "That's probably one of the kind you're looking for," thought the man, jumped up and ran back and forth in front of the cart like someone not quite in his right mind. "What do you want, friend?" the woman said to him. "I don't know you; where do you come from?" "I fell out of Heaven," answered the man, "and don't know how to get back; can't you drive me up?" "No," said the woman, "I don't know the way. But if you come from Heaven, you can surely tell me how my husband is getting along; he's been there three years now. You must have seen him?" "Of course I've seen him, but not everybody can prosper. He's tending sheep, and the dear creatures give him no end of trouble: they jump up onto the mountains and get lost in the wilderness, and he has to chase after them and herd them together again. He's all in tatters, too, and his clothes will soon be dropping off him. There aren't any tailors there; St. Peter won't let any in, as you know from the story" [No. 35]. "Who'd have thought of that!" exclaimed the woman. "Do you know what! I'll get his Sunday-go-to-meeting coat that's still hanging up in the wardrobe at home; he can wear that with distinction there. Please be as good as to take it along." "That really won't do," answered the farmer. "One mustn't bring clothes into Heaven; they're taken from one at the gate." "Listen to me," said the woman, "yesterday I sold my fine wheat and got a pretty sum of money for it; I'll send him that. If you put the purse in your pouch, nobody will notice it." "If there's no other way," replied the farmer, "then I'll gladly do you the favor." "Just stay right there. I'll drive home and get the purse; I'll be right back. I'm not sitting on the bundle of straw but standing up in the cart to make it easier for the animals." She urged on her oxen, and the farmer thought, "She's ready for the madhouse. If she really brings me the money, my wife can say she's lucky, for she won't get a beating." Before long she came on the run, brought the money, and with her own hands put it in his pouch. Before going away she again thanked him a thousand times for his kindness.

When the woman got home, she found her son who had returned from the fields. She told him what an unexpected experience she'd had and then added, "I'm very happy to have got the opportunity of sending my poor husband something. Who would have imagined that he'd have been short of anything in Heaven?" The son was greatly amazed. "Mother," he said, "a person like that doesn't come from Heaven every day. I want to go right out and see if I can still find the man; he must tell me what it looks like there and how work there is coming along." He saddled his horse and rode off in all haste. He found the farmer sitting under a willow and about to count out the money in the purse. "Have you by chance seen the man who came down from Heaven?" the boy called out to him. "Yes," answered the farmer, "he's started on the way back again and has gone up the mountain there, where he has a somewhat shorter route. You can still overtake him if you ride hard." "Oh, dear!" said the boy, "I've been working terribly hard all day, and the ride here has quite worn me out. You know the man. Be so good as to mount my horse and persuade him to come here." "Well, well," thought the farmer, "here's another fellow who isn't quite right in the head," and saying, "Why shouldn't I do you the favor?" mounted and rode off at a good sharp trot. The boy sat there till nightfall, but the farmer didn't return. "The man from Heaven was certainly in a great hurry and didn't want to turn around," he thought, "and the farmer gave him the horse, too, to take to my father." He went home and told his mother what had happened: he'd sent his father the horse, so that he wouldn't always have to walk about. "You did the right thing," she answered, "your legs are still young, and you can go on foot."

On reaching home the farmer put the horse in the barn next to the pledged cow, then went to his wife and said, "Katy, you were lucky: I found two people who were even simpler fools than you. This time you'll get off without a beating; I'll save it up for another occasion." Then he lighted his pipe and, sitting down in his high-backed chair, said, "That was a good trade—for two cows a sleek horse and a purse full of money besides. If stupidity always brought in so much, I'd be glad to hold it in respect."

That's what the farmer thought, but you surely like the simple-minded people better.

105   Tales about Toads

Märchen von der Unke

I

THERE WAS ONCE A LITTLE CHILD whose mother gave it a bowl of bread and milk every afternoon, and the child would sit down with it outside in the yard. When it began to eat, a toad used to creep out of a chink in the wall, put its head down in the milk and eat with the child. The child took pleasure in this, and when it sat there with its bowl and the toad didn't come straightway, it would cry out to it,

> "Toad, toad, come quick,
>   Come here, you tiny creature;
>   You're to have your bread,
>   You're to refresh yourself with the milk."

Then the toad would come running up and enjoyed what it ate. It appeared to be grateful, too, for it brought the child all sorts of fine things from its secret hoard, sparkling gem-stones, pearls, and gold trinkets. But the toad used only to drink milk and left the bread. On one occasion the child took its spoon and tapped the toad gently on the head, saying, "Creature, eat the bread, too." Its mother, who was standing in the kitchen, heard the child talking to someone, and when she saw that it was hitting a toad with its spoon, she ran out with a stick of wood and killed the good creature.

From then on, a change came over the child. As long as the toad had eaten with it, it had grown big and strong, but now it lost its fine rosy cheeks and got thin. It wasn't long till the bird of death began to cry out in the night, and Robin Redbreast gathered twigs and leaves for the funeral wreath, and soon thereafter the child was lying on its bier.

II

An orphan girl was sitting by the town wall spinning when
she saw a toad come out of a chink at the bottom of the wall.
She quickly spread out beside her a blue silk neckerchief which
toads so love and on which alone they will walk. As soon as
the toad spied it, it turned around, came back carrying a tiny
gold crown, put it on the neckerchief, and then went away
again. The girl picked up the crown; it glistened and was made
of delicately spun gold. Not long afterward the toad came back
a second time, but no longer seeing the crown it crept to the
wall and in its sorrow beat its head against it as long as it had
the strength; finally it lay dead.

If the girl had left the crown alone, the toad would probably
have brought still more of its treasures out of the hole.

III

The toad called, "Hoo-hoo, hoo-hoo!" The child said, "Come
out!" The toad came out, and then the child asked after its
little sister, saying, "Have you by chance seen little Red-Socks?"
"No, not I," said the toad, "How about you? Hoo-hoo, hoo-hoo,
hoo-hoo!"

106 The Poor Miller's Servant and the Cat

Der arme Müllerbursch und das Kätzchen

AN OLD MILLER lived in a mill; he had neither wife nor children,
and three mill servants worked for him. When they had been
with him for some years, he one day said to them, "I'm old and
want to take it easy behind the stove. Set out, and whichever
one of you brings me home the best horse, I'll give him the
mill; in return he'll have to take care of me until I die." Now

the third servant, who was the prentice, was regarded by the others as a simpleton, and they begrudged him the mill. Subsequently he didn't even want it. All three set out together, and when they got outside the village, the two said to simple John, "You may just as well stay here, you'll never get a horse as long as you live." But John went along just the same, and when it was night, they came to a cave and lay down in it to sleep.

The two clever fellows waited till John had gone to sleep, then got up and made off, leaving John and thinking they'd done a good job. (Yes, just the same, you won't prosper!) When the sun rose and John woke up, he was lying in a deep cave; he looked all about and cried, "Oh, God, where am I?" Then he got up, scrambled out of the cave, and went into the forest, thinking, "I'm all alone here and deserted; how on earth am I going to get a horse?" As he was walking along and meditating, he met a little spotted cat, which said very kindly, "John, where are you bound?" "Oh, you can't help me in any event." "I well know what you want," said the cat. "You want a fine horse. Come with me and be my faithful servant for seven years, then I'll give you one, finer than any you've ever seen in your life." "Now that's an extraordinary cat," thought John, "but just the same I'll see whether what she says is true."

Then she took him along with her to her enchanted manor house, where her only servants were cats. They ran up and down stairs nimbly, were jolly and in fine spirits. In the evening when they sat down to table, three had to furnish music: one played the double bass, the second the fiddle, while the third took a trumpet and puffed out its cheeks for all it was worth. When they'd eaten, the table was removed, and the cat said, "Now come, John, and dance with me." "No," he answered, "I won't dance with a pussy-cat, I've never done it." "Then take him to bed," she said to the cats. One lighted the way for him to his bedroom, one took off his shoes, one his stockings, and finally one blew the light out. Next morning they came back and helped him get up. One put on his stockings, one tied his garters, one fetched his shoes, one washed him, and one dried his face with its tail. "That feels very soft," said John. However, he, too, had to serve the cat and chop kindling every day. For that task he was given a silver ax and silver wedges and a silver saw, and the mallet was of copper. Well, he chopped the wood there, stayed there in the house, had good food and drink, but saw no one but the spotted cat and her retinue.

Once she said to him, "Go mow my meadow and ted the grass," gave him a silver scythe and a gold whetstone, ordered him, however, to return everything properly. John went and did what he was ordered to do and, after finishing the task, brought home the scythe, whetstone, and hay, and asked if she wouldn't give him his wages now. "No," said the cat, "you must first perform one more task for me. Here is silver lumber, a carpenter's ax, a square, and everything one needs, all of silver; with this first build me a little house." Then John built the little house and said he'd now done everything and still didn't have his horse. Nevertheless, the seven years had passed for him like six months. The cat asked if he wanted to see her horses. "Yes," said John. Then she opened the little house for him, and when she unlocked the door quite nonchalantly, twelve horses were standing there. My! they were very proud and their coats were glossy and shiny, so that his heart rejoiced at the sight. Now she gave him food and drink and said, "Go home. I shan't give you your horse to take along, but in three days I'll come and bring it to you then." So John set out, and she showed him the way to the mill. But she hadn't given him so much as a new garment, and he had to keep on his ragged old overall that he'd brought there with him and which in the course of seven years had got too tight for him everywhere.

When he reached home, the two other servants were also back; indeed, each had brought his horse along, but one's was blind and the other's was lame. "John," they asked, "where's your horse?" "It'll follow in three days." Then they laughed and said, "Well, John, where are you going to get a horse? It'll be something pretty fine!" John went into the living room, but the miller said he wasn't to come to table: he was so tattered and ragged that one couldn't help being ashamed, should anyone drop in. Then they gave him a bit to eat outside, and when they went to bed that evening, the other two wouldn't give him a bed, and he finally had to crawl into the goose-house and lie down on a little hard straw.

In the morning when he awoke, the three days were already up, and a coach drawn by six horses arrived. My! they glistened so that it was a sight to behold, and a servant was leading a seventh horse, and that was for the poor miller's servant. Out of the coach stepped a resplendent king's daughter and went into the mill, and the king's daughter was the little spotted cat, whom poor John had served for seven years. She asked the miller where the poor miller's servant, the apprentice was. "We couldn't take him into the mill," said the miller. "He's terribly tattered and is lying in the goose-house." Then the king's daughter told them to fetch him at once, so they brought him out, and he had to hold his overall together to cover himself. The servant unbuckled a bundle of magnificent clothing and had to wash him and dress him, and when he was fixed up, no king would have looked finer. Then the maiden demanded to see the horses which the other servants had brought: one was blind, the other lame. Then she had her servant bring the seventh horse. On seeing it the miller said that such a horse had never before entered his courtyard. "And it's for the third servant," she said. "Then he must have the mill," said the miller. But the king's daughter said that there was the horse and he should keep his mill, too, and took her faithful John and had him get into the coach and drove off with him. First they went to the little house he'd built with the silver tools, but it had become a great palace, and everything in it was of silver and gold. Then she married him, and he was rich, so rich that he had enough for as long as he lived.

Therefore no one should say that a simpleton may not get to be something.

107 The Two Travelers

Die beiden Wanderer

MOUNTAIN AND VALLEY do not meet, but certainly human beings do, especially good and bad.

Thus once a shoemaker and a tailor met on a journey. The tailor was a short, nice-looking chap and always jolly and in good spirits. He saw the shoemaker coming in his direction, and noticing by his pack what his trade was, he called out a little lampoon at him:

"Sew the seam,
    pull the thread,
    rub it right and left with wax,
    hit the peg good and hard."

The shoemaker, however, couldn't take a joke, made a face as if he'd swallowed vinegar, and looked as if he was going to grab the little tailor by the collar. But the little chap began to laugh, handed him his bottle, and said, "No offense meant! Have a drink and wash down the gall." The shoemaker took a tremendous drink, and the thunder-cloud began to pass from his face. He gave the bottle back to the tailor, saying, "I've addressed it in proper style, as one says of a big drink, though not of a great thirst. Shall we go on our way together?" "It's all right with me," answered the tailor, "as long as you want to go to a big city where there's no lack of work." "That's just where I wanted to go, too," answered the shoemaker. "One can't earn anything in a little hole, and in the country people prefer to go barefoot." Accordingly, they went on together, always one foot in front of the other like weasels in the snow.

Both had plenty of time but little to eat. Arriving in a town they'd walk about and call on the trade, and because the tailor looked so jolly and gay and had such nice rosy cheeks, everybody was glad to give him something, and when luck would have it, the master craftsman's daughter would even give him a kiss on his way out through the front door. On rejoining the shoemaker he always had more in his pack than the latter. The surly shoemaker used to make a wry face and think, "The bigger the rascal, the greater his luck," but the tailor would begin to laugh and sing and shared with his companion everything he got. If only a few pennies were jingling in his purse, he'd order up just the same and from sheer delight strike on the table so that the glasses danced. His motto was "Easy earned, easy spent."

After journeying for a while they came to a big forest through which the way led to the royal capital. Two footpaths went through it, one taking seven days, the other only two, but neither of them knew which was the shorter. The two travelers sat down under an oak and took council how to provide for themselves and for how many days they should take bread. The shoemaker said, "One must think further ahead than one is going: I'll take along bread for seven days." "What!" said the tailor. "Take bread for seven days on your back like a pack animal and not see the sights? I'm trusting in God and not worrying about anything. The money I have in my purse is as good in summer as in winter, but in hot weather the bread will get dry and mouldy, besides. And my coat, too, only reaches to my ankles. Why shouldn't we hit upon the right track? Bread for two days, and that will be all right." Accordingly, each bought his own supply of bread, and then trusting to fortune they walked into the forest.

In the forest it was as still as in a church. Not a breath was stirring, no brook murmured, no bird sang, and not a ray of sunlight pierced the leafy branches. The shoemaker didn't say a word; the bread weighed so heavy on his back that the sweat was pouring down his cross and gloomy face. The tailor, on the contrary, was quite gay, skipped along, whistled in a leaf or sang a little song, thinking, "God in Heaven must be glad that I'm so happy." So it went for two days, but when on the third day the forest showed no sign of coming to an end and the tailor had eaten up his bread, his spirits drooped just a bit. At the same time he didn't lose heart but trusted in God and his good luck. On the evening of the third day he lay down hungry under a tree and got up again hungry the next morning. It was the same on the fourth day, and when the shoemaker was sitting down on a fallen tree and eating his meal, the tailor could only look on. If he asked for a bit of bread, the other would laugh scornfully, saying, "You've always been so jolly! Now for once you can see what it's like to be unhappy. Birds who sing too early in the morning are struck by the hawk in the evening." In short, he was pitiless.

On the fifth morning the poor tailor was no longer able to get up and from exhaustion could scarcely utter a word; his cheeks were pale and his eyes red. Then the shoemaker said to him, "Today I'll give you a piece of bread, but in return I want to put out your right eye." The unhappy tailor, who nonetheless very much wanted to save his life, could do nothing about it; he wept one last time with both eyes, then presented them, and the shoemaker, who had a heart of stone, put out his right eye with a sharp knife. The tailor remembered what his mother once said to him when he'd been pilfering the pantry: "Eat as much as you want, suffer what you must." After consuming the bread so dearly bought, he got to his feet again, forgot his misfortune, and consoled himself with the thought that he could still see well enough with one eye.

On the sixth day starvation again knocked at the door and almost exhausted his courage. In the evening he again collapsed beside a tree and on the seventh morning he was unable to get up for exhaustion. Death was sitting on the back of his neck. Then the shoemaker said, "I'll be charitable and again give you some bread, but you won't get it for nothing; in return I'll put your other eye out." Then the tailor realized the frivolous life he'd been leading, prayed the dear Lord for forgiveness, and said, "Do what you must, I'm willing to suffer what I must. But remember! Our Lord does not pronounce his judgments every minute and the hour will strike when the evil deed you are doing me and which I have not deserved of you will be atoned for. In good times I shared with you what I had. My craft is of a sort where one stitch must back up the other. When I no longer have my eyes and no longer can sew, I'll have to go begging, so when I'm blind, don't leave me alone here, otherwise I'm sure to perish." But the shoemaker, who had thrust God from his heart, took his knife and put out the tailor's left eye, too. Then he gave him a piece of bread to eat, handed him a stick, and led him along behind him.

As the sun was setting, they emerged from the forest, and outside it in the fields stood a gallows. The shoemaker led the blind tailor there, then left him and went on his way. From weariness, pain, and hunger, the unhappy man fell asleep and slept all night. When dawn came, he awoke but didn't know where he was. Two poor sinners were hanging on the gallows, and on the head of each was sitting a crow. Then one of the hanged men began to speak: "Brother, are you awake?" "Yes, I'm awake," answered the other. "Then I'll tell you something," continued the first. "The dew that last night fell down over us from the gallows will restore the sight of anyone who washes himself with it. If the blind knew that, how many who don't believe it possible might have their sight back!" Hearing that, the tailor took his handkerchief, pressed it on the grass and when it was moistened with dew, washed his sockets with it. Immediately the words of the hanged man came true, and a pair of clear and healthy eyes filled his sockets. Before long the tailor saw the sun rise behind the mountains, the great royal city with its splendid gates and hundred towers lay before him on the plain, and the golden domes and the crosses on the steeples began to glow. He was able to distinguish every leaf on the trees, saw the birds that flew past and the midges that were dancing in the air. He took a needle out of his pouch, and when he was able to thread it as well as ever, his heart leapt for joy. Throwing himself on his knees he thanked God for the grace He had shown him and said his morning prayers, nor did he forget to pray for the poor sinners who were hanging there like bell clappers and striking against one another in the wind. Then he put his pack on his back, soon forgot the great pain he had suffered, and went his way singing and whistling.

The first thing he met was a brown foal that was cavorting about in the fields untethered. He took hold of its mane and was about to swing onto its back and ride into the city when the foal begged for its freedom. "I'm still too young," it said. "Even a light tailor like you will break my back in two; let me go until I've grown strong. A time will come perhaps when I can reward you for this." "Get along," said the tailor; "I see that you're really a regular harum-scarum." He gave it a parting stroke across its back with the switch so that it kicked out with its hind legs for joy, jumped over hedges and ditches, and raced out into the fields.

The little tailor had eaten nothing since yesterday. "To be sure," he said, "the sun's filling my eyes, but no bread is filling my mouth. The first thing I run into that's halfway fit to eat will have to bear the brunt." As he was saying this, a stork stalked very gravely toward him across the meadow. "Stop, stop!" cried the tailor, seizing it by the leg, "I don't know whether you're fit to eat; my hunger leaves me no time to be choosy; I must cut off your head and roast you." "Don't do that," answered the stork, "I'm a sacred bird that nobody harms and that brings great benefit to mankind. Grant me my life and I shall be able to repay you another time." "Well, move on, friend Longlegs," said the tailor. The stork started up, dangled its long legs, and flew off in a leisurely fashion.

"What's to come of all this?" said the tailor to himself, "I'm getting hungrier and hungrier, my stomach emptier and emptier. Whatever crosses my path now is done for." As he said this, he saw some ducklings swimming in a pond. "You come as if to order," he said, caught one of them, and was about to wring its neck. Then an old duck that was in the reeds began to squawk loudly, swam up with a gaping bill, and begged and implored him to have pity on her dear children. "Can't you imagine," she said, "how your mother would grieve if someone was about to take you away and finish you off?" "Quiet, quiet," said the good-natured tailor, "you shall keep your children," and put the captive back into the water.

As he turned around, he was standing before an old tree that was half hollow and saw wild bees flying in and out. "There I'll find the reward for my good deed straight off," said the tailor. "The honey will refresh me." But the queen bee came out and threatened him, saying, "If you touch my people and destroy my nest, our stings will go into your skin like ten thousand red-hot needles; but if you leave us in peace and go your way, some other time we'll do you a service for that." The little tailor saw that there was nothing doing here, either. "Three dishes empty," he said, "and nothing on the fourth—that's a poor meal!" So he dragged himself and his famished stomach into the city, and since it was just striking noon, food at the inn was all ready for him, and he was able to sit down to table at once. When he had eaten his fill, he said, "Now I'll get to work," went about in the city, hunted up a master tailor, and soon found good accommodations, too. Since he had learned his trade thoroughly, it wasn't long before he became famous, and everybody wanted to have his new coat made by the little tailor. Every day his reputation grew. "I can't advance further in my craft," he said, "and yet every day things go better." At last the king appointed him his court tailor.

But how queer the world is! That very same day his former comrade, the shoemaker, also became court bootmaker. When the latter caught sight of the tailor and saw that he again had two sound eyes, his conscience plagued him. "Before he takes revenge on me," he thought to himself, "I must dig a pit for him." But whoso diggeth a pit for others shall fall therein himself [Prov. 26 : 27]. That evening when the bootmaker had called it a day and it had grown dusk, he sneaked to the king and said, "Sire, the tailor is a braggart and has been boasting that he'll recover the gold crown that was lost long ago." "I'd like that," said the king, on the following morning had the tailor summoned to him, and ordered him to recover the crown or to leave the city forever. "Oh ho," thought the tailor, "only a fool promises more than he can do. If the surly king demands of me what no man can do, I shan't wait till tomorrow but get out of town again right today." So he laced up his pack. Nevertheless, once outside the gate he regretted deserting his good fortune and turning his back on the city where he had done so well. He came to the pond where he had made the acquaintance of the ducks; there the same old duck, whose children he had spared, was sitting on the bank preening herself with her bill. She recognized him at once and asked why he was hanging his head like that. "You won't be surprised once you hear what has happened to me," answered the tailor and told her what had befallen him. "If that's all there's to it," said the duck, "we can help you. The crown fell into the water and is lying down there on the bottom; we'll recover it for you at once. Meanwhile, just spread out your handkerchief on the bank." With her twelve ducklings she dived down and in five minutes was back up again and sitting in the middle of the crown. It was resting on her wings, and the twelve ducklings were swimming round it with their bills under it and were helping carry it. They swam ashore and laid the crown on the handkerchief. You wouldn't believe how magnificent the crown was when the sun shone on it; it gleamed like a hundred thousand carbuncles. The tailor tied the four corners of his handkerchief together and carried it to the king, who was in a state of joy and put a gold chain around the tailor's neck.

When the bootmaker saw that one trick had failed, he thought up a second, went to the king, and said, "Sire, the tailor has got just as boastful again; he brags that he can make a wax model of the whole royal palace with everything that is in it, movable and immovable, inside and out." The king had the tailor come and ordered him to make a wax model of the whole royal palace, with everything that was in it, movable and immovable, inside and out. And if he didn't accomplish this, or if as much as a nail in a wall was missing, he'd spend the rest of his life underground in prison. "It's getting worse and worse," thought the tailor, "no one will put up with that," slung his pack on his back and set out. When he got to the hollow tree, he sat down and hung his head. The bees came flying out, and the queen bee asked him if he had a stiff neck, because he was holding his head so crooked. "Oh, no," answered the tailor, "something else is weighing upon me," and told what the king had demanded of him. The bees began to hum and buzz among themselves, and the queen said, "Just go back home, but come back this time tomorrow and bring along a big cloth; everything will be all right." Then he turned back. The bees, however, flew to the royal palace, right in the open windows, crawled about in every nook and corner, and inspected everything most minutely. Then they hurried back and made a wax model of the palace so fast that you'd think it was growing before your eyes. That very evening it was all finished, and when the tailor came the next morning, the whole magnificent building was there, and not a nail was missing in a wall nor a tile on the roof, and it was, furthermore, delicately made and snow-white and smelt sweet as honey. The tailor wrapped it up carefully in his cloth and took it to the king. The latter couldn't marvel enough, put it on display in his biggest hall, and in return made the tailor a present of a big stone house.

The bootmaker, however, persisted, went for the third time to the king, and said, "Sire, word has reached the tailor's ears that no water will spout up in the palace courtyard; accordingly, he's boasted that he'll make it rise in the middle of the yard to the height of a man and be as clear as crystal." The king had the tailor fetched and said, "If tomorrow a stream of water isn't spouting up in my courtyard as you promised, my executioner will make your head shorter in the same yard." The poor tailor didn't stop long to think and hurried out the gates, and because this time his life was at stake, tears rolled down his cheeks. As he was thus sorrowfully walking away, the foal, to whom he had formerly given its freedom and which had become a fine brown horse, came galloping up. "Now the hour is at hand when I shall repay you your kind deed," it said to him. "I already know what you need and you'll soon be helped. Just mount me, my back can stand two of the like of you." The tailor plucked up courage again, mounted it with one jump, and the horse raced into the city at full speed and right into the palace courtyard. It tore around like lightning three times, and the third time it fell down heavily. At that moment, however, there was a frightful crash: a clod of earth in the middle of the courtyard shot up into the air like a bullet and flew out over the palace. Immediately afterward there rose a stream of water as high as a man on horseback, and the water was as clear as crystal, and the sunbeams began to dance on it. When the king saw that, he stood up in amazement and in the sight of all went and embraced the little tailor.

But his good fortune didn't last long. The king had daughters enough, each fairer than the other, but no son. Then the malicious bootmaker betook himself to the king for the fourth time and said, "Sire, the tailor persists in his boastfulness. This time he bragged that, if he wishes, he can have Your Majesty brought a son through the air." The king had the tailor summoned and said, "If you have me brought a son within nine days, you shall have my eldest daughter in marriage." "The reward is certainly great," thought the little tailor, "one would make a special effort to get it. But the cherries hang too high for me; if I climb after them, the branch is likely to break and I will fall." He went home, sat down on his workbench with his legs crossed, and thought over what he might do. "It's no go," he finally cried, "I'll clear out; I really can't live in peace here." He laced up his pack and hurried out the gate. On reaching the meadows, he spied his old friend the stork, who was walking philosophically back and forth there; from time to time it would stop, eye a frog closely, and finally swallow it. The stork came up and said how-do-you-do to him. "I see," it began, "that you have your knapsack on your back. Why are you going to leave the city?" The tailor told him what the king had demanded of him and said he couldn't carry it out and lamented his bad luck. "Don't let any grey hairs grow on that account," said the stork; "I'll help you out of your trouble. For a long time now I've been bringing babies in swaddling clothes to the city, so for once I can fetch a little prince out of the well. Go home and contain yourself. In nine days from today go to the palace; I'll come there." The little tailor went home and was at the palace on time. Before long the stork flew up and knocked on the window. The tailor opened it for it, and friend Longlegs stepped carefully in and walked solemnly across the smooth marble floor. In its bill it had a child, lovely as an angel, which stretched out its little hands toward the queen. The stork laid it in her lap, and she hugged and kissed it and was beside herself with joy. Before flying away again the stork took its traveling case from its shoulder and handed it to the queen; in it were paper bags with sugar candies of many colors; they were divided up among the little princesses. The eldest, however, got nothing, but did get the jolly tailor as a husband. "I feel just as if I'd won the first prize in a lottery," said the tailor. "Yes, my mother was right: she always said that whoever trusts in God and has some luck can't go wrong."

The bootmaker had to make the shoes in which the little tailor danced at the wedding party; afterward he was ordered to leave the city forever. The road toward the forest led him to the gallows. Wearied by anger, rage, and the heat of the day, he threw himself on the ground. When he closed his eyes and was going to sleep, with loud cries the two crows dove down from the heads of the hanged men and picked his eyes out. He ran into the forest like a madman and must have perished there, for nobody has seen him since or heard a word about him.

108   John-My-Hedgehog

Hans mein Igel

THERE WAS ONCE A FARMER who had money and property aplenty,
but rich as he was, his happiness was, nevertheless, not quite
complete: he had a wife but no children. Often when he went
to town with the other farmers, they'd make fun of him and
ask him why he had no children. Finally he grew angry and
on getting home said, "I want to have a child, even if it's a
hedgehog." Then his wife had a child; its upper part was a
hedgehog, its lower a boy. When she saw the child, she was
frightened and said, "See, you've bewitched us." Then her husband said, "What's the good saying all that! The boy must
be christened, though we shan't be able to get a sponsor for
it." "And we can't christen him with any other name than
John-My-Hedgehog," said his wife. When he was christened,
the pastor said, "Because of his quills he can't get into any
proper bed." Then a little straw was fixed up behind the stove,
and John-My-Hedgehog laid upon it. Nor could he suckle
his mother, for he would have pricked her with his quills.
Thus he lay there behind the stove for eight years. His father
got tired of him and thought, "If only he'd die," but he didn't
die and just lay there.

Now it happened that there was a fair in town, and the
farmer was going to it and asked his wife what he should
bring her back. "A bit of meat and a few rolls, just what's
needed for the household," she said. Next he asked the maid:
she wanted a pair of slippers and clocked stockings. Finally
he also said, "John-My-Hedgehog, what would you like?"
"Daddy," he said, "please bring me back a bagpipe." When
the farmer got home, he gave his wife what he'd brought her,
meat and rolls, then gave the maid the slippers and the clocked
stockings, and last of all he went behind the stove and gave
John-My-Hedgehog the bagpipe. When John-My-Hedgehog

got the bagpipe, he said, "Daddy, please go to the blacksmith shop and have my rooster shod, then I'll ride away and never, never come back." The father was happy to be getting rid of him and had his rooster shod. When it was ready, John-My-Hedgehog mounted it, rode off, also taking with him pigs and donkeys, which he meant to tend out there in the forest. In the forest the rooster had to fly with him up into a tall tree, where he sat and tended the donkeys and pigs and stayed years and years until the herd was very large. His father had no news of him. As he sat up in the tree, he used to blow his bagpipe and play very beautiful music.

Once a king came driving by; he'd lost his way and heard the music. He marveled at it and sent his servant there to look about and see where the music was coming from. He looked about but only saw a small animal sitting up in the tree; it was like a rooster with a hedgehog sitting on it, and the latter was playing the music. Then the king told the servant to ask why it was sitting there and if it perhaps knew the road that led to his kingdom. Then John-My-Hedgehog climbed down from the tree and said he was willing to show him the way if the king would promise in writing to give him the first thing he encountered in the royal courtyard on getting home. "I can easily do that," thought the king; "John-My-Hedgehog won't understand it anyhow, and I can write what I like." Then the king took pen and ink and wrote something down, and when he'd done so, John-My-Hedgehog showed him the way, and he got home safe and sound. But his daughter, who saw him from afar, was so happy that she ran to meet him and kissed him. Then he thought of John-My-Hedgehog and told her what had happened to him and said that he'd had to assign to a strange animal the first thing he encountered on getting home. The animal had been sitting on a rooster as on a horse and playing beautiful music. He had, however, written down that it was not to have it, because John-My-Hedgehog couldn't read it, anyway. The princess was happy about this and said that it was a good thing, for she would never have gone there in any event.

John-My-Hedgehog tended his donkeys and pigs, was always jolly, sat up in the tree and played his bagpipe. Now it happened that another king came driving along with his servants and couriers; he had lost his way and didn't know how to get home, for the forest was so big. Then he, too, heard the fine music from afar and told his courier just to go and see what it really was. The courier went under the tree and saw the rooster sitting there and John-My-Hedgehog upon the rooster. The courier asked him what he was doing there. "I'm tending my donkeys and pigs. But what is your wish?" The courier said that they'd lost their way and didn't know how to get back to their kingdom, and would he please show them the way. Then John-My-Hedgehog climbed down from the tree and told the old king that he'd show him the way if he'd give him to have and to hold the first thing he met at home in front of the royal palace. The king said yes and in writing pledged himself to John-My-Hedgehog that he should have it. When that was done, he rode ahead on the rooster and showed the king the way, and the king got back to his kingdom safe and sound. When he entered the courtyard, there was great rejoicing. Now he had an only daughter, who was very beautiful; she ran to meet him, fell on his neck, kissed him and rejoiced that her old father had come back. She also asked him where he'd been so long abroad. He told her that he'd lost his way and almost hadn't come back at all, but as he'd been driving through a big forest, someone, half hedgehog, half human, was sitting astride a rooster up in a tall tree and playing beautiful music. He'd helped him along and showed him the way, but in return the king had promised him what he first met at the royal court, and she was that thing, and he was very sorry about it. She, however, promised that she'd gladly go with John-My-Hedgehog, should he come, and would do so to please her father.

Meanwhile, John-My-Hedgehog tended his pigs, and the pigs had more pigs, and there got to be so many of them that the whole forest was full. Then John-My-Hedgehog didn't want to live in the forest any longer and had word sent to his father to clear out all the stables in the village, for he was coming with so big a herd that everybody who happened to want to might slaughter. On hearing this his father was distressed, for he thought that John-My-Hedgehog was long since dead. John-My-Hedgehog mounted his rooster, drove the pigs before him into the village, and had the slaughtering done.

Whew! Such a butchering and chopping there was that you could hear it two hours' walk away. Afterward John-My-Hedgehog said, "Daddy, have the smith shoe my rooster once more, then I'll ride away and not come back as long as I live." The father had the rooster shod and was glad that John-My-Hedgehog would never come back again.

John-My-Hedgehog rode off to the first kingdom. There the king had given orders for them all to shoot at anybody with a bagpipe who came riding on a rooster, to beat him, stab him, and stop him from getting into the palace. Accordingly, when John-My-Hedgehog came riding up, they fell upon him with bayonets; however, he put spur to the rooster, flew up over the gate to the king's window, alighted there, and cried out to him to give him what he'd promised, otherwise he'd take his life and that of his daughter. Then the king begged his daughter please to go out to him in order to save his life and hers. She dressed herself in white, and her father gave her a coach and six horses, also fine servants, money, and treasure. She got in with John-My-Hedgehog and his rooster and bagpipe beside her; then they said good-bye and departed, and the king thought he would never get to see her again. But things went differently from what he had thought, for when they were a little way out of the city, John-My-Hedgehog took off her fine clothes and, pricking her with his hedgehog skin until she was all covered with blood, said, "This is the reward for your duplicity: go away, I don't want you." Thereupon he chased her home, and she was disgraced as long as she lived.

With his bagpipe, John-My-Hedgehog rode on his rooster to the second kingdom, to which he had also showed the king the way. The latter, on the contrary, had given orders, if anybody like John-My-Hedgehog should come, to present arms, lead him in unopposed, shout "Long may he live!" and bring him into the royal palace. When the king's daughter saw him, she was frightened, because he really looked altogether too strange, but she thought that there was nothing else to do, since she'd promised her father to do it. She welcomed John-My-Hedgehog, and he married her and had to go with her to the royal board, where she sat down beside him, and they ate and drank. When evening came and they were going to bed, she was very much afraid of his quills, but he said that she shouldn't be afraid, that no harm would befall her. He told the old king to detail four men to mount guard outside the chamber door and build a big fire: when he went into the bridal chamber and was about to get into bed he'd crawl out of his hedgehog's skin and leave it beside the bed. Then the men were to rush in quickly and throw it into the fire, and stay there, too, until the fire had consumed it. Now when it struck eleven, he went into the chamber, stripped off the hedgehog skin and left it lying beside the bed. Then the men came, picked it up quickly, and threw it into the fire. When the fire had consumed it, he was disenchanted and lay there in bed in a completely human form, though as coal-black as if he'd been burnt. The king sent for his physician, who washed him with good ointments and put perfume on him; then he became white and was a handsome young gentleman. When the king's daughter saw that, she was happy, and the next morning they arose joyfully, ate and drank. Then the marriage was properly celebrated, and John-My-Hedgehog received the kingdom from the old king.

When some years had passed, he and his wife drove to his father and said he was his son, but the father said he had no son; he'd only had one, and he'd been born with quills like a hedgehog and had gone out in the world. Then he made himself known, and his old father rejoiced and went with him to his kingdom.

> "My tale is done
> and it's going to Gussy's house."

109   The Little Shroud

Das Totenhemdchen

A MOTHER had a little boy seven years old. He was so fair and lovable that no one could look at him without being fond of him, and she loved him more than anything in the world. Now it happened that he suddenly became ill and the good Lord took him unto Himself. The mother couldn't console herself over this and wept day and night. Soon after he was buried, however, the child used to appear at night in the places where in life he had formerly sat and played. When his mother wept, he'd weep, too, and when morning came, he had vanished. But when the mother just wouldn't stop weeping, he came one night in his little white shroud in which he had been laid in his coffin and with the wreath on his head and, sitting down on the bed at her feet, said, "Oh mother, please stop weeping, otherwise I can't get to sleep in my coffin, for my shroud won't get dry from your tears that are all falling upon it." His mother was frightened when she heard that and wept no more. The next night the child returned, holding a light in his hand, and said, "See, now my shroud is nearly dry, and I am at peace in my grave." Then the mother commended her grief to the good Lord and bore it quietly and patiently, and the child didn't come back but slept on in his little underground bed.

110   The Jew in the Hawthorn Hedge

Der Jude im Dorn

THERE WAS ONCE A RICH MAN and he had a servant who worked for him industriously and honestly. He was the first out of bed every morning and the last in bed at night, and whenever there was some hard task that no one would tackle, he was always the first to take it in hand. Withal, he didn't complain but was content with everything and was always jolly. When his year was up, the master gave him no wages, thinking, "That's the smartest thing to do; that way I'll save something; he won't leave me but will be a good fellow and stay on in service." The servant, too, said nothing, did his work the second year as the first, and when at the end of that year he again received no wages, accepted that and stayed on still longer. When the third year, too, was up, the master reflected, reached into his pocket but took nothing out. The servant finally spoke up and said, "Master, for three years I've served you honestly, be so good as to give me my due. I should like to be off and should very much like to have more of a look about the world." Then the miser answered, "Yes, my good servant, you've served me diligently and you shall be paid generously for your work," again reached into his pocket, and one by one paid out three farthings to the servant. "Here's a farthing for each year! That's a bigger and handsomer wage than you would have received from many a master." The good servant, who understood little about money, pocketed his capital and thought, "Now that you've got a pocket full of money, why worry and wear yourself out any longer with hard work?"

Then he went his way up hill and down dale, singing and skipping to his heart's content. Now it happened, as he was going by some bushes, that a little dwarf stepped out and called to him, "Whither bound, Merry Andrew? I see that you're not taking your cares heavily." "Why should I be sad?" answered the servant. "I have plenty. Three years' wages are jingling in my pocket." "How much is your treasure?" the dwarf asked him. "How much? Three farthings in cash and counted out right." "Listen," said the dwarf, "I'm a poor and needy man; make me a present of your three farthings. I can't work any more, whereas you're young and can easily earn your living." Because the servant was kindhearted and took pity on the dwarf, he handed his three farthings over to him, saying, "In God's name, I shan't miss them." Then the dwarf said, "Because I see that you're kindhearted, I shall grant you three wishes, one for each farthing, and they'll be fulfilled for you." "Oh ho!" said the servant, "you're one of those people who knows more than the ordinary. All right, if it's going to be that way, I'll wish myself first a blowgun that will hit everything I aim at; secondly, a fiddle which, when I play it, will make everybody dance who hears the sound; and thirdly, if I make a request of anybody, that he may not refuse it." "You shall have all of that," said the dwarf, reaching into the bushes, and—fancy that!—the fiddle and blowgun

lay right there as if ordered. He handed them to the servant and said, "Whatever you request for yourself, nobody
in the world shall refuse you."

"What more do you want, my dear?" said the servant to
himself and went merrily on. Soon after that he met a Jew
with a long goatee; the latter was standing and listening to
the song of a bird that was sitting high up in the top of a
tree. "Miracle of God!" he cried out, "to think that such a small
creature should have such an awfully powerful voice! If only
it were mine! If one could only sprinkle salt on its tail!" "If
that's all there is to it," said the servant, "the bird will soon
be down," took aim and hit it squarely, and the bird fell down
into the hawthorn hedge. "You dirty dog," he said to the Jew,
"go and fetch out your bird!" "Oh, my!" said the Jew. "If
the gentleman will drop the 'dirty,' the 'dog' will come on the
run! I'm willing to pick up the bird, for after all, you hit it."
He lay down on the ground and began to work his way into
the bushes. When he was in the middle of the hawthorns, a
spirit of mischief got the better of the good servant, so that
he took off his fiddle and started to play. Forthwith the Jew
also began to lift up his feet and jump up in the air, and
the more the servant played, the better went the dance. But
the thorns tore his threadbare coat, combed his goatee, and
pricked and tweaked him all over. "Oh, my!" cried the Jew.
"What's the use of fiddling? Will the gentleman please stop.
I have no desire to dance." But the servant didn't stop, thinking, "You've skinned plenty of people; now the hawthorn
hedge won't be any kinder to you," and started fiddling again
so that the Jew had to jump higher and higher and bits of
his coat remained hanging on the thorns. "Alack, alas!" cried
the Jew. "I will really give the gentleman whatever he demands
if he'll only stop the fiddling—a whole purse of gold!" "If
you're so lavish," said the servant, "then of course I'll stop
my music. Still, I must admit that your dancing was quite
something." Thereupon he took the purse and went his way.

The Jew stood still and, looking after him, was quiet until
the servant was far off and quite out of sight. Then he shouted
as loud as he could, "You wretched musician, you tavern
fiddler! Wait till I get you alone. I'll chase the soles right off
your shoes. You rogue, put a penny in your mouth so that

you may be worth four farthings," and kept on calling him all the bad names he could think of. When he had thus somewhat relieved himself and given vent to his feelings, he went into town to the judge. "Alack, alas! Your honor! See how a bad man robbed me on the public highway and maltreated me. A stone on the ground would be moved to pity! My clothes tattered! my body all pricked and scratched! my poor pittance and my purse taken! ducats upon ducats, each gold piece finer than the last! For God's sake, have the man thrown into prison." "Was it a soldier who treated you like this with his saber?" said the judge. "God forbid," said the Jew, "it was no naked sword that he had but a blowgun hanging on his back and a fiddle around his neck. The scoundrel will be easy to recognize." The judge sent his people out after him; they found the good servant who had been walking along very slowly, and they also found the purse of gold on him. In court he said, "I didn't touch the Jew and didn't take his money. He offered it to me of his own free will just so I'd stop fiddling, because he couldn't stand my music." "God forbid," screamed the Jew, "he's telling lies as readily as one catches flies on the wall," and the judge didn't believe the story, either, and said, "That's a poor excuse; no Jew would do that," and condemned the good servant to the gallows for highway robbery.

As he was being led off, the Jew screamed after him, "You lazy lout, you wretched musician! Now you're getting your just reward." The servant very calmly mounted the ladder with the hangman, but on the top rung he turned around and said to the judge, "Grant me one last request before I die." "Yes," said the Judge, "provided you don't ask for your life." "Not for my life," answered the servant; "I beg you to let me play my fiddle one last time." The Jew raised an outcry, "For God's sake, don't allow it, don't allow it!" but the judge said, "Why should I begrudge him that brief pleasure? It's granted and that's that." Besides, he couldn't refuse him because of what the dwarf had granted the servant. "Alack, alas!" cried the Jew; "tie me up, tie me up tight!" Then the good servant took his fiddle from his neck, placed it properly, and with the first stroke of his bow everybody began to wobble and rock, the judge, the clerk, and the court officers, while the cord that was to tie the Jew tight dropped to the ground.

With the second stroke of the bow they all lifted up their legs, and the hangman let go of the good servant and made ready to dance. With the third stroke everybody jumped up and down and began to dance, and the judge and the Jew were to the fore and hopping best of all. Soon everybody joined in the dancing, all the people who out of curiosity had come to the market place, young and old, fat and lean, all dancing together. Even the dogs that had run along got on their hind legs and hopped about with the rest, and the longer he played the higher jumped the dancers until they were bumping each other's heads and beginning to cry piteously. Finally the judge, quite out of breath, cried, "I'll make you a present of your life if you will only stop fiddling!" The good servant gave in, put down his fiddle, slung it around his neck again and climbed down the ladder. Then stepping up to the Jew who was lying on the ground and gasping for breath, he said, "You dirty dog, now confess where you got your money or I'll take my fiddle from my neck and begin to play again." "I stole it, I stole it!" he screamed, "but you earned it honestly." Then the judge had the Jew led to the gallows and hanged as a thief.

111   The Trained Huntsman

Der gelernte Jäger

THERE WAS ONCE A YOUNG FELLOW who had learned the locksmith's trade and told his father that he now wanted to go out in the world and try his luck. "Yes," said the father, "I have nothing against that," and gave him some money for the journey. So he roved about and looked for work. In time he became unsuccessful at locksmithing, and what's more, he no longer liked it; on the other hand, he developed a yearning for huntsmanship. In the course of his journeyings he met a huntsman clad in green who asked him where he came from and where he was going. He was a journeyman locksmith, said the lad, but he no longer liked the trade and had a yearning for huntsmanship and would he take him on as an apprentice. "O yes, if you want to come with me." So the boy went along, bound himself to him for a number of years and learned huntsmanship. Then he wanted to try his luck further, and the only wage the huntsman gave him was a blowgun which had, however, the property that when one fired a shot with it, one never missed.

He went his way and came to a very big forest whose end he couldn't find in one day. When it was evening, he sat down in a high tree to keep out of the way of wild animals. Toward midnight he thought he saw a little light glimmering faintly from afar; he looked through the branches in its direction and took note of where it was coming from. Even so, he first took off his hat and threw it down in the direction of the light so that, once he had climbed down, he might go toward it as toward a beacon. He climbed down, went after his hat, put it on again, and went straight ahead. The farther he went, the bigger grew the light, and when he got near it, he saw that it was a huge fire. Three giants were sitting by it, had an ox on a spit and were roasting it. One said, "I really must take a taste and see if the meat is almost done," tore off a piece and was about to put it in his mouth when the huntsman shot it out of his hand. "Well, well!" said the giant, "there the wind went and blew the piece out of my hand," and took another. As he was just about to take a bite, the huntsman again shot it away; then the giant slapped his companion who was sitting beside him and cried angrily, "Why did you snatch my piece away from me?" "I didn't snatch it away," said the other. "A sharpshooter probably shot it away." The giant took a third piece but couldn't keep hold of it, for the huntsman shot it out of his hand.

Then the giants said, "He must be a good marksman to shoot away the food from in front of one's mouth; we could use someone like that," and called out loud, "Come here, you sharpshooter, sit down with us by the fire and eat your fill; we won't harm you. But if you don't come and we'll fetch you by force; then you're done for." Then the boy stepped up and said he was a trained huntsman and whatever he aimed his gun at he was quite certain to hit. Then they said, if he'd come along with them, he'd fare well. They told him that outside the forest was a big body of water beyond which was a tower, and in the tower was a beautiful king's daughter whom they very much wanted to carry off. "Yes," he said, "I'll have her here directly." "But there's something else there, too," they continued. "There's a little dog there that starts barking as soon as anybody comes near, and as soon as it barks, everybody in the royal court wakes up. That's why we can't get in. Do you dare to shoot the dog?" "Yes," he said, "that's mere child's play for me." Thereupon he got into a boat and rowed across the water. When he was close to shore, the dog came running up and was about to bark, but he got out his blowgun and shot it dead.

When the giants saw that, they were delighted and thought that they as good as had the king's daughter, but the huntsman wanted first to see how the land lay and said that they should stay outside until he called them. Then he went into the castle, and within it was as still as could be, and everybody was asleep. On opening the door of the first room he saw a saber hanging there on the wall: it was of solid silver with a gold star on it and the king's name. Beside it on a table lay a sealed document; this he opened, and it said that whoever had the saber would be able to kill whatever he ran into. He took the saber from the wall, girded it on, and went his way. Then he came to the room where the king's daughter was lying asleep, and she was so beautiful that he stopped and, looking at her, held his breath, thinking to himself, "How can I put an innocent maiden in the power of those savage giants? They bode her no good." He looked about some more, and there, under the bed, was a pair of slippers: on the right slipper was her father's name with a star, and on the left her own name with a star. She was wearing a big silk neckerchief embroidered with gold, on the right side her father's name, on the left her own, all in gold letters. The huntsman took a pair of scissors and cut off the right corner and put it in his knapsack; then he also took the right slipper with the king's name and put it in his knapsack. The maiden just lay there and slept on and was all sewed up in her shift. Then he cut a piece off the shift, too, and put it in with the rest, yet did it all without touching her. Then he went away and left her sleeping undisturbed.

When he got back to the gate, the giants were still standing outside waiting for him, thinking he'd bring the king's daughter. He called to them to come in, saying that the maiden was already in his power; however, he couldn't open the door for them, but there was a hole through which they'd have to crawl. When the first giant approached, the huntsman wrapped the latter's hair around his hand, pulled the head in, cut it off with one stroke of his saber, and then dragged him all the way in. Then he called the second and cut off his head, too, and last of all the third, and was glad to have freed the beautiful maiden from her enemies. He cut out their tongues and put them in his knapsack. Then he thought, "I'll go home to my father and show him what I've done thus far, then I'll travel about the world. The good fortune that God is willing to grant me will surely overtake me."

When the king in the castle awoke, he saw the three giants lying there dead. He went into his daughter's bedchamber, waked her up, and asked who on earth had killed the giants. "Father dear," she said, "I don't know; I've been asleep." When she got up and was about to put on her slippers, the right slipper was gone, and when she looked at her neckerchief, it was cut through and the right corner was missing. And when she looked at her shift, a piece was gone from that. The king had the whole court assembled, soldiers and everybody who was there, and asked who had freed his daughter and killed the giants.

Now he had a captain who had only one eye and was a hideous person; he said he'd done it. Then the old king said, since he'd done it, he should also marry his daughter. The maiden, however, said, "Father dear, rather than marry him, I'll go out in the world as far as my legs will carry me." Then the king said, if she wouldn't marry him, she was to take off her royal clothing and put on peasant garb and go away. She was to go to a potter and and start an earthenware business. She took off her royal clothing and went to a potter and took a stock of earthenware on credit; she also promised him to pay for it if she'd sold it by evening. The king then said that she was to sit on a corner and sell it; then he ordered some farm wagons to drive right through it and smash it to a thousand pieces. When the king's daughter had laid out her stock by the roadside, the carts came along and reduced it to nothing but shards. She began to weep and said, "Oh, God, now how shall I pay the potter?" In doing this the king had wanted to force her to marry the captain; instead, however, she went back to the potter and asked him if he'd extend her loan. He answered no, she'd first have to pay for the previous stock. Then she went to her father, cried and lamented and said that she wanted to go out in the world. "I'll have a cottage built for you out in the forest," he said. "There you're to stay as long as you live and cook for all comers, but you're not to accept any money." When the cottage was ready, a sign was hung outside the door and on it was written, "Today for nothing, tomorrow for money." There she stayed a long time, and word went abroad that there was a maiden there who cooked for nothing and the sign by the door said so. The huntsman, too, heard that and thought, "That would be something for me; I'm really poor and have no money." He took his blowgun and his knapsack in which everything he'd previously taken with him from the castle still was, went into the forest and soon found the cottage with the sign: "Today for nothing, tomorrow for money." He had, however, girded on the saber with which he'd cut off the three giants' heads, and going thus into the cottage, had himself served something to eat. He rejoiced at the sight of the beautiful girl who was really as pretty as a picture. She asked where he came from and where he was going, and he said, "I'm traveling about the world." Then she asked him where he'd got the sword, for her father's name was on it. He asked if she was the king's daughter. "Yes," she answered. "With this sword," he said, "I cut off the heads of three giants," and as a token took their tongues out of the knapsack. He also showed her the slipper, the corner of the neckerchief, and the piece of the shift. Then she rejoiced, saying it was he who had saved her.

Thereupon they both went to the old king and brought him there, and she led him to her room and told him that the huntsman was really the man who had saved her from the giants. When the old king saw all the tokens, he could no longer be in doubt, and said he was glad to know how it had all happened and that the huntsman should have her in marriage. The maiden rejoiced over this with all her heart. Then they dressed him as if he were a foreign lord, and the king had a banquet prepared. When they went to table, the captain happened to be sitting on the daughter's left, the huntsman on her right, and the captain thought he was a foreign lord who had come on a visit. When they had eaten and drunk, the old king said to the captain that he wanted to propound him a riddle which he was to guess: if a person said he'd killed three giants and was asked where the giants' tongues were, and he had to look and there were none in their heads, how did that come about? Then the captain said, "They probably didn't have any." "Not so," said the king, "every animal has a tongue," and asked further what that person deserved to have done to him. "He deserves to be torn to pieces," answered the captain. Then the king said that he had pronounced his own sentence, and the captain was imprisoned and then quartered. But the king's daughter was married to the huntsman. Afterward he brought his father and mother there, and they lived happily with their son, who after the old king's death got the kingdom.

112 The Threshing-Flail from Heaven

Der Dreschflegel vom Himmel

A FARMER once set out to plow with a pair of oxen. When he got to the field, the horns of the two animals began to grow, kept growing, and by the time he was ready to go home, were so big that he couldn't get in the gate. By good luck a butcher was just coming along to whom he turned over the oxen, and they struck a bargain to the effect that he should bring the butcher a measure of turnip seed, while the latter was to pay him one Brabant dollar for each seed. I call that a good bargain.

Now the farmer went home and carried the measure of turnip seed on his back; on the way, however, he lost one seed out of the bag. The butcher paid him properly as was agreed. If the farmer had not lost the seed, he'd have had one more Brabant dollar.

Meanwhile, as he was going back again, a tree that reached

up to Heaven had grown out of the seed. "Since there's a chance," thought the farmer, "you must really see what the angels are doing up there and for once have a look at them." So he climbed up and saw that the angels up there were threshing oats. He watched them doing this and, as he was looking on, noticed that the tree he was standing on began to wobble, looked down and saw that someone was about to cut it down. "If you pitched down there," he thought, "it would be a bad thing," and in the emergency could think of nothing better to do than to take the oat chaff that was lying there in heaps and twist a cord out of it. He also reached for a hoe and a threshing-flail that were lying about there in Heaven and let himself down by the rope. But he came to earth right in a deep, deep hole, and then it was a real piece of luck that he had the hoe, for with it he hacked out steps for himself, climbed up, and brought the flail along as a token, so that no one could ever doubt his story.

113   The Two Kings' Children

De beiden Künigeskinner

THERE WAS ONCE A KING who had a little boy in whose stars it was fated that he would be killed by a stag when he was sixteen years old. When he reached that age, the huntsmen once went hunting with him. In the forest the king's son got away from the others, suddenly saw a big stag that he wanted to shoot, but couldn't hit it. At last the stag ran far ahead of him, right out of the forest; then instead of the stag, a big tall man suddenly was standing before him who said, "It's a good thing I've got you; I've already worn out six pairs of glass skates chasing after you and wasn't able to catch you." He took him along with him and whisked him over a big body of water up to a great royal mansion. Then the king's son had to sit down at table with him and eat something.

When they'd both had something to eat, the king said, "I have three daughters. You must keep watch by the eldest for one night from nine in the evening till six in the morning. Every time the bell strikes, I myself shall come and call out, and then if you don't answer me, you'll be put to death on the morrow. If, however, you answer me every time, you shall have her in marriage." When the young people got up to the bedchamber, a stone figure of St. Christopher was standing there, to which the king's daughter said, "My father will come at nine o'clock and every hour until three strikes; if he asks anything, you answer him instead of the king's son." The stone Christopher nodded its head very fast, then slower and slower, until it finally stopped again.

The next morning the king said to the boy, "You performed your task well, but I can't give you my daughter. You must keep watch for one night by my second daughter; then I'll consider whether you can have my eldest daughter in marriage. I myself shall come every hour, and if I call you, answer me, and if I call you and you don't answer, your blood shall flow." Then the two went up to the bedchamber where there was a still bigger stone Christopher, to which the king's daughter said, "If my father asks a question, you answer." The big stone Christopher again nodded its head very fast, then slower and slower, until it finally stopped again. The king's son lay down on the threshold, put his hand under his head, and went to sleep.

The next morning the king said to him, "You performed your task really well, but I can't give you my daughter. You must also keep watch for one night by the youngest princess; then I'll consider whether you can have my second daughter in marriage. I myself shall come every hour, and if I call you, answer me, and if I call you and you don't answer me, your blood shall flow." Then they both again went to her bedchamber where there was a much bigger and much taller Christopher than in the first two. The king's daughter said to it, "If my father calls, you answer." The big tall stone Christopher nodded its head a good half hour before stopping again, and the king's son lay down on the threshold and went to sleep.

The next morning the king said, "You kept watch really well, but even so I can't give you my daughter. I have a very big forest; if you cut it down for me between six this morning and six this evening, I'll think about it." Then he gave him a glass ax, a glass wedge, and a glass mattock, and it was reduced to so much powered glass. Then he was very sad, thought that he was now doomed to die, and sitting down, wept. Since it was now midday, the king said, "One of you girls must take him something to eat." "No," said the two eldest, "we won't take him anything; the one he last kept watch by can take him something." So the youngest had to take him something.

On reaching the forest, she asked him how things were going. "Oh," he said, "things are going very badly." He should come, she said, and first eat a little something. "No," he said, "I can't. I've got to die anyhow; I shall no longer eat." Then she spoke to him so very kindly, saying he ought to try just the same, that he came and ate something. When he'd eaten something, she said, "First I'll louse you a bit, then you'll feel differently." When she'd loused him, he got very tired and fell asleep. Then she took her kerchief, tied a knot in it, struck the earth three times with it, saying, "Workers, come out!" Then straightway ever so many gnomes appeared and asked what the king's daughter commanded. "In three hours' time the great forest must be cut down," she said, "and the wood stacked in piles." The gnomes went about and summoned up all their kin to help them with the work. They began at once, and when the three hours were up, exerything was finished, and they went back to the king's daughter and told her. Again she took her white kerchief and said, "Workers, go home!" Then they were all gone again. When the king's son awoke, he was very happy, and she said, "When it strikes six, come home." He did so, and the king asked, "Have you removed the forest?" "Yes," said the king's son.

When they were sitting at table, the king said, "I can't give you my daughter in marriage yet; you must first do something more to win her." He asked what that might be. "I have a very big pond," said the king; "you must go there tomorrow morning and clean it up so that it's as bright as a mirror, and there must be all kinds of fish in it." The next morning the king gave him a glass spade and said, "The pond must be finished by six o'clock." Then he went away. On reaching the pond, he stuck the spade in the muck and it broke off. Then he stuck the hoe in the muck, and it, too, broke. Then he was very sad. At noon the youngest daughter brought him something to eat and asked how things were going with him. The king's son said that things were going very badly and he'd surely have to lose his head. "The tools have broken to bits on me again." "Oh," she said, "you should come and eat something first; then you'll feel differently." "No," he said, "I can't eat, I'm too sad." She then spoke to him so kindly that he came and ate something; then she loused him again, and he fell asleep. Again she took a kerchief, tied a knot in it and, striking the earth three times with the knot, said, "Workers, come out!" Straightway ever so many gnomes came and all asked what might be her wish. "In three hours' time you must have the pond all cleaned up, and it must be so bright that one can see one's reflection in it, and all kinds of fish must be in it." The gnomes went off and summoned up their kin to help them, and in two hours it was finished. Then they came back and said, "We've done what you ordered." Then the king's daughter took the kerchief and again struck the earth three times with it, saying, "Workers, go home!" Then they were all gone again. When the king's son awoke, the pond was finished. Then the king's daughter went away, too, saying he should come home when it was six. When he got home, the king asked, "Have you finished the pond?" "Yes," said the king's son. "That's fine."

When they were again sitting at table, the king said, "You've certainly finished the pond, but I can't give you my daughter yet. You must first do one thing more." "What's that?" asked the king's son. "I have a very big mountain with nothing but thornbushes on it; they must all be cut down. Furthermore, you must build a big mansion as splendid as one can imagine and all the appropriate furnishings must be there." When he got up the next morning, the king gave him a glass ax and a glass auger, too, and said, "It must be finished by six o'clock." When he chopped the first thornbush with the ax, it went into tiny pieces that flew all about him; nor could he use the auger. Then he was very sad and waited to see if his beloved mightn't come and help him in his need. When it was noon, she came and brought him something to eat. He went to meet her and told her everything and let her louse him and fell asleep. Again she took the knot and, striking the earth with it, said, "Workers, come out!" Again ever so many gnomes came and asked what might be her wish. "In three hours' time," she said, "you must cut down all the bushes, and furthermore there must be a mansion up on the mountain that must be as splendid as one can imagine and all the furnishings must be in it." They went off and summoned up their kin to help them, and when the time was up, everything was finished. They came to the king's daughter and told her, and she took the kerchief and struck the earth three times with it, saying, "Workers, go home!" Immediately they were all gone again. When the king's son awoke and saw everything, he was as happy as a bird in the air, and when it struck six, they went home together. Then the king said, "Is the mansion finished?" "Yes," said the king's son.

When they were sitting at table, the king said, "I can't give you my youngest daughter before the two eldest are married." Then the king's son and the king's daughter were very sad, and the king's son didn't know what to do. One night he came to the king's daughter and ran away with her. When they'd gone a short distance, the daughter looked around and saw her father behind them. "Alas!" she said, "what shall we do? My father's behind us and will overtake us! I'll turn you right into a hawthorn and myself into a blossom and protect myself right in the middle of the bush." When her father reached the spot, there stood a hawthorn and a blossom on it. When he was about to pluck the blossom, the thorns pricked his fingers so that he had to go home again. His wife asked him why he hadn't brought them along; he said he'd nearly caught up with them but had suddenly lost sight of them, and that there was a hawthorn and a blossom. "If you'd just plucked the blossom," said the queen, "the bush would probably have come along."

Again he went off to fetch the blossom, but meanwhile the two were already far afield, and the king ran after them. Again the king's daughter looked around, saw her father coming, and said, "Oh! what shall we do now? I'll turn you into a church and myself into the parson, then I'll stand in the pulpit and preach." When the king reached the spot, a church was standing there and a parson was in the pulpit preaching. He listened to the sermon and went back home. When the queen asked why he hadn't brought them along, he said, "No, I ran after them for a long time, and when I thought I had nearly overtaken them, there was a church, and a parson was preaching in the pulpit." "You just ought to have brought the parson," said his wife. "The church would surely have come along. It's no good for me to send you; I'll have to go there myself."

After she'd been gone a while and saw the couple from afar, the king's daughter looked around and, seeing her mother coming, said, "Now our luck has run out; my mother herself is coming. I'll turn you right into a pond and myself into a fish." When the mother reached the spot, there was a big pond there and in the middle a fish was jumping about; it was sticking its head out of the water and looking about and was in fine spirits. She very much wanted to get the fish but couldn't catch it, got very angry, and drank the whole pond dry because she wanted to get the fish. However, she got so sick that she had to vomit and vomited the whole pond out again. Then she said, "I clearly see that all this will do me no good; they might just as well come back to me." Then they went back, and the queen gave her daughter three walnuts, saying, "These can help you in your greatest need."

The young people set off again together. When they'd been walking a good ten hours, they came to the manor house the king's son came from, and near it was a village. On reaching the village the king's son said, "Stay here, dearest. I'll go to the manor first and then come with a coach and servants to fetch you." When he got to the manor, everybody was very glad to have him back. He said he had a bride who was now in the village, and would they go there with a coach and fetch her. They harnessed up right away, and a number of servants got into the coach, but when the king's son was about to get in, his mother gave him a kiss, and then he forgot everything that had happened and even what he was about to do. Then his mother ordered them to unharness again, and they all went back into the house. The girl stayed in the village and waited and waited, and thought he'd come for her, but no one came. Then the king's daughter hired herself out at the mill that belonged to the manor and had to sit every afternoon and clean the vessels. Once the queen came out of the manor and took a walk by the water and, seeing the beautiful girl, said, "What a beautiful girl that is! I've taken quite a fancy to her!" Then everybody took a close look at her, but nobody knew her.

A very long time passed, and the girl served the miller honestly and faithfully. Meanwhile the queen had been looking for a wife for her son; this bride was from far, far away. When she arrived, they were both to be married at once. A great crowd gathered to see it all, and the girl asked the miller if he'd give her time off, too. "Go right along," said the miller. As she was leaving, she opened one of the three walnuts, and in it was a beautiful gown. Putting it on, she wore it to church and stood by the altar. Suddenly the bride and groom arrived and sat down before the altar, and as the parson was about to pronounce his benediction upon them, the bride looked to one side and saw the girl standing there. Then she got up again and said that she wouldn't get married until she had as beautiful a gown as the lady. They went back home and enquired of the lady whether she'd sell the dress. No, she wouldn't sell it, but they might perhaps earn it. They asked her what they should do, and she said that she'd give it to them if she might sleep outside the door of the king's son that night. They said yes, she might do that. Then the servants had to administer the king's son a sleeping-draught.

She lay down on the threshold and whimpered all night: she had had the forest cut down for him, she'd had the pond cleaned out for him, she'd had the manor house built for him, she'd turned him into a hawthorn, then into a church, and finally into a pond, and he'd forgotten her so quickly. The king's son heard none of this, but it had waked up the servants and they had listened and didn't know what it was all about. When they arose the next morning, the bride put on the gown and set out to church with the bridegroom. Meanwhile the beautiful girl opened the second walnut, and in it was an even finer gown; she put it on and, wearing it to church, stood by the altar. Then things went just as the time before. Again the girl lay down for the night outside the threshold that led into the room of the king's son. Again the servants were to administer him a sleeping-draught, but instead, they came and gave him something to keep him awake; thereupon he went to bed. The miller's maid again whimpered before the threshold as much as before and said what she had done. The king's son heard all this, was very sad, and remembered everything that had happened. Then he wanted to go to her, but his mother had locked the door. The next morning, however, he went at once to his beloved and told her everything that had happened and asked her not to be angry with him for having forgotten her so long. Then the king's daughter opened the third walnut, and in it was an even more beautiful dress. She put it on and drove to the church with her bridegroom. Then ever so many children came and gave them flowers and held colored ribbons in front of their feet, and they had the benediction pronounced on them and had a gay wedding. The false mother and the false bride, however, had to go away.

Whoever last told this story has just this instant finished.

114 The Clever Little Tailor

Vom klugen Schneiderlein

THERE WAS ONCE A PRINCESS who was tremendously proud. Whenever a wooer turned up, she'd give him something to guess, and if he couldn't guess it, he was sent away with ridicule. She also let it be known that whoever solved her riddle was to marry her, and anybody might come who wanted to.

Three tailors at last met up. The two eldest thought that they had sewed so many a fine stitch, and hit it right, that they couldn't miss—they'd be bound to hit it in this case, too. The third was a little good-for-nothing harum-scarum who had no understanding of his trade but thought he was bound to be lucky here, for where else would he be? The other two said to him, "You just stay home. With your meager intelligence you won't get very far." But the little tailor didn't let himself be put off and said he'd bet his head on it, was quite sure he'd manage it, and went along as if he owned the whole world.

All three reported to the princess, said that she should propound them her riddles and that the three proper parties had arrived whose intelligence was so fine that one could easily thread it through a needle. Then the princess said, "I have two kinds of hair on my head. What are the colors?" "If that's all there's to it," said the first, "it's probably black and white like the cloth they call 'pepper and salt.'" "Wrong guess!" said the princess. "Let the second answer." Then the second said, "If it isn't black and white, then it's red and brown like my father's frock coat." "Wrong guess!" said the princess. "Let the third answer, who, I see, surely knows." The little tailor stepped boldly up and said, "The princess has one silver and one gold hair on her head, and those are the two kinds of colors." On hearing that the princess turned pale and almost fell down from fright, for the little tailor had hit upon it, and she had firmly believed that no one in the world would get it. When she recovered herself, she said, "At that you haven't won me yet; you must still do one other thing: down in the stable there's a bear with which you're to spend the night. If you're still alive when I get up in the morning, you shall marry me." She thought she'd get rid of the little tailor that way, for thus far the bear had left nobody alive that it had got its paws on. The little tailor didn't let himself be frightened off, was quite content, and said, "Boldly ventured is half won."

When evening came our little tailor was taken down to the bear. The bear straightway wanted to go for the little fellow and give him a hearty welcome with its paw. "Easy, easy!" said the little tailor, "I'll quiet you down quick enough." Then, as if he hadn't a care in the world, he casually took Italian nuts out of his pocket, bit them open and ate the kernels. Seeing that, the bear, too, wanted some nuts. The tailor reached into his pocket and gave it a handful. But these weren't nuts at all, just plain stones. The bear put them in its mouth but couldn't get any open, bite as hard as it would. "My!" it thought, "what a clumsy fool you are! Can't even bite the nuts open," and said to the tailor, "My word! bite the nuts open for me." "There, you see what kind of a fellow you are," said the little tailor. "You have such a big mouth and can't open the little nut!" Then he took the stones, made a quick move, put a nut in his mouth instead, and crack! it was broken. "I must try the thing once again," said the bear; "as I see it, I should think I ought to be able to, too." The tailor again gave it ordinary stones, and the bear worked at them and bit into them with all its might. But don't imagine for a moment that it opened them. When that was over, the tailor took a violin from under his coat and played a piece on it. When the bear heard the music, it couldn't help beginning to dance, and after it had been dancing a little while, the whole business delighted it so that it said to the tailor, "Listen, is fiddling hard?" "Child's play! Just look, I put down the fingers of my left hand and bow away with my right, and there's a high old time—whoop-la! whoop-la!" "To fiddle like that," said the bear, "that's what I'd like to be able to do, too, so that I might dance whenever I wanted to. What do you think about it? Will you give me lessons in it?" "Gladly, indeed," said the little tailor, "provided you've got the knack for it. But put out your paws, they're terribly long. I must cut your nails a little." Then he fetched a vice, and the bear laid its paws in it. The tailor, however, screwed it up tight and said, "Now wait till I come with the scissors," let the bear growl as much as it liked, lay down in the corner on a heap of straw and went to sleep.

That evening when the princess heard the bear growling so terribly, she merely supposed that it was growling for joy and had made an end of the tailor. In the morning she got up quite unconcerned and pleased, but when she looked toward the stable, the little tailor was standing serenely outside it and was as hale and hearty as a fish in water. Then she couldn't say another word against the arrangement, for she had made her promise public. The king ordered a coach, and she had to drive in it to church with the little tailor and was to be married. When they got into the coach, the other two tailors, who were false-hearted and begrudged him his luck, went into the stable and released the bear from the vice. In a great rage the bear ran after the coach. The princess heard it snorting and growling, was frightened, and cried, "Oh! the bear is following us and wants to get you." The little tailor was quick, stood on his head, stuck his legs out the window, and cried, "Do you see the vice? If you don't go away, you'll be in it again." Seeing that, the bear turned about and ran away. Our little tailor then drove calmly to the church, and the princess was married to him, and he lived with her as happy as a lark.

Anybody who doesn't believe it pays a dollar.

115   The Bright Sun Will Bring It to Light

Die klare Sonne bringt's an den Tag

A JOURNEYMAN TAILOR was traveling about in the world and practising his trade, and on one occasion could find no work. His poverty was so great that he hadn't a farthing for food and board. At that time he met a Jew on the way and, thinking the latter probably had a lot of money on him, thrust God from his heart and going straight up to him, said, "Give me your money, or I'll strike you dead." "Grant me my life!" said the Jew. "I have no money, indeed, only eight farthings," but the tailor said, "Of course you have money, and what's more, it's going to come out," used violence and beat him till he was nearly dead. Now when the Jew was on the point of death, he uttered his last words, "The bright sun will bring it to light," and thereupon died. The journeyman tailor reached into his pocket and searched for money but found, as the Jew had said, only eight farthings. Picking the Jew up, he carried him behind a bush and pursued his trade further. When he'd been traveling for a long time, he got work in a town with a master who had a pretty daughter; he fell in love with her, married her, and had a good and happy married life.

After a time, when they already had two children, the father-in-law and the mother-in-law died, and the young people were keeping house alone. One morning as the husband was sitting on the workbench by the window, his wife brought him his coffee, and when he poured it into the saucer and was about to drink it, the sun shone on it, and the reflection flickered here and there on the wall and made circles there. Then the tailor looked up and said, "Yes, it very much wants to bring it to light and can't." "Good gracious, dear husband," said his wife, "what's that? What do you mean by that?" "I mustn't tell you," he answered, but she said, "If you love me, you must tell me," talked to him in the very nicest way, saying that no one would hear of it again, and gave him no peace. Then he told how years ago, when traveling, he'd been all ragged, had had no money, and had killed a Jew, and that in his death throes the Jew had said, "The bright sun will bring it to light." Now the sun had surely just been trying to bring it to light, had flickered on the wall and made circles, but hadn't been able to. Afterward he asked her most particularly not to tell anybody, otherwise he'd lose his life. She promised not to, but when he'd sat down to work, she went to her best friend and confided the story to her and said that she shouldn't repeat it to anybody. Before three days had passed, the whole town knew it, and the tailor was brought to trial and convicted.

The bright sun certainly did bring it to light.

116 The Blue Lantern

Das blaue Licht

THERE WAS ONCE A SOLDIER who had served his king faithfully for many years, but when the war was over and the soldier could no longer serve because of the many wounds he'd received, the king said to him, "You may go home; I don't need you any longer. You won't get any more money, for nobody receives pay unless he renders me services for it." The soldier didn't know how he'd earn his living, went away sorrowfully, and walked all day until in the afternoon he got into a forest. When night fell, he saw a light; he approached it and came to a house where a witch lived. "Please give me a night's lodging and a little food and drink," he said to her, "otherwise I shall perish." "O ho!" she answered, "who gives a runaway soldier anything? Still, I'll be charitable and take you in if you'll do what I require." "What do you require?" asked the soldier. "That you spade up my garden tomorrow morning." The soldier agreed and the next day worked as hard as he could, yet wasn't able to finish it before evening. "I plainly see," said the witch, "that you can't continue your journey today. However, I'll keep you another night, and for that you're to split and chop up a cord of wood for me tomorrow." The soldier needed the whole day for that, and in the evening the witch proposed that he stay another night. "Tomorrow you're to do just a small job for me. Behind my house is an old dry well; my lantern has fallen into it; it burns with a blue light and doesn't go out. You're to bring it back up to me." The next day the old woman led him to the well and let him down in a basket. He found the blue lantern and gave her a signal to pull him up again. She pulled him up, but when he was near the edge, she reached down with her hand and wanted to take the blue lantern away from him. "No," he said, noticing her evil intentions, "I shan't give you the lantern until I have both feet on the ground." Then the witch flew into a rage, dropped him back down into the well, and went away.

The poor soldier fell onto the damp bottom without suffering any harm, and the blue lantern kept burning. But what good could that do him? He saw plainly that he couldn't escape death. For a time he sat very sadly, then by chance he reached into his pocket and found his pipe that was still half filled. "This shall be your last treat," he thought, took it out, lighted it from the blue lantern, and began to smoke. When the smoke had drifted about in the hole, a little black dwarf suddenly stood before him and asked, "Master, what do you command?" "What have I to command you?" replied the soldier much astonished. "I must do everything you command," said the dwarf. "Good," said the soldier. "Then first help me out of the well." The dwarf took him by the hand led him through an underground passage and didn't, however, forget to bring along the blue lantern. On the way the dwarf showed him the treasures which the witch had collected and hidden there, and the soldier took as much gold as he could carry. When he was up on earth, he said to the dwarf, "Now go and tie up the old witch and take her into court." Before long she came riding by on a wild tomcat, as swift as the wind and yelling frightfully, nor was it long before the dwarf was back again. "It's all fixed up," he said, "and the witch is already hanging on the gallows. What more do you command, master?" asked the little fellow. "For the moment, nothing," answered the soldier. "You may go home, but be right on hand if I call you." "You need only light your pipe from the blue lantern," said the dwarf, "and I'll be in your presence immediately." Thereupon he vanished before his eyes.

The soldier turned back to the city he'd come from. He entered the best inn and had fine clothes made for himself, then ordered the innkeeper to furnish a room for him as magnificently as possible. When it was ready and the soldier had moved in, he called the black dwarf and said, "I served the king faithfully, but he dismissed me and let me starve; now I want to take revenge for that." "What am I to do?" asked the little fellow. "Late at night, when the king's daughter is in bed, bring her here in her sleep. She shall perform maid's service for me." "That's easy for me but a dangerous business for you," said the dwarf. "If word of it gets out, it'll go hard for you." When it struck twelve, the door flew open and the dwarf carried in the king's daughter. "Aha! Are you there?" cried the soldier. "Quick on the job! Go get the broom and sweep the room!" When she had finished, he ordered her to come to his easy chair and, sticking out his feet toward her, said, "Pull off my boots," then threw them in her face. She had to pick them up, clean them and polish them. However, she did everything he ordered without resisting, silently and with half-closed eyes. At the first cockcrow the dwarf carried her back to the royal palace and put her back in her bed.

The next morning when the king's daughter got up, she went to her father and told him that she had had a strange dream. "I was carried through the streets like a flash of lightning and taken to a soldier's room; I had to serve him and wait on him like a maid, do all the dirty work, sweep the room, and polish his boots. It was just a dream, and still I'm as tired as if I'd really done it all." "The dream might have been true," said the king. "I'll give you a piece of advice: fill your pocket with peas and make a little hole in the pocket. If you're carried off again, they'll fall out and leave a trail in the street." While the king was speaking thus, the dwarf was standing by invisible and heard everything. At night he again carried the king's sleeping daughter through the streets. To be sure, a certain number of peas fell out of her pocket but they couldn't make a trail, for the cunning dwarf had beforehand strewn peas in all the streets. Again the king's daughter had to perform maid's service till cockcrow.

The next morning the king sent his people out to look for the trail, but it was hopeless, for in every street poor children were sitting and picking up peas and saying, "It rained peas last night." "We must think up something else," said the king. "Keep on your shoes when you go to bed, and before you come back from there, hide one of them. I'll find it all right." The black dwarf heard the plan, and when the soldier asked him to carry the king's daughter there again, he advised against it, saying that he knew of nothing to counter this trick, and if the shoe was found in his room, it might go hard with him. "Do what I tell you," replied the soldier, and the king's daughter had to work like a maidservant the third night, too. But before she was carried back, she hid one shoe under the bed.

The next morning the king had the whole city searched for his daughter's shoe. It was found at the soldier's, and the soldier himself, who at the little fellow's request had cleared out of town, was soon overtaken and thrown into prison. In his flight he'd forgotten the best thing he had, namely, the blue lantern and the gold, and had only one ducat left in his pocket. As he was standing by the window of his prison, now weighed down by chains, he saw one of his comrades walking by. He rapped on the pane, and when the other came up, he said, "Be so good as to bring me the little parcel that I left in the inn; I'll give you a ducat for it." His comrade ran there and brought him what he wanted. As soon as the soldier was alone again, he lighted his pipe and summoned the black dwarf. "Don't be afraid," said the latter to his master. "Go where they lead you and let everything take its course. Only be sure to take the blue lantern along." The next day the soldier was tried in court, and though he'd done nothing bad, the judge condemned him to death just the same. As he was being led out, he begged one last favor of the king. "What kind of a favor?" asked the king. "That I may smoke one more pipeful on the way." "You may smoke three," answered the king, "only don't imagine that I shall make you a present of your life." Then the soldier pulled out his pipe and lighted it from the blue lantern. By the time a few smoke rings had ascended, the dwarf was already standing there, had a little cudgel in his hand, and said, "What does my master command?" "Strike down the false justices there and their bailiffs, and don't spare the king, either, who treated me so shabbily." Then the dwarf zigzagged hither and thither like lightning, and whoever he as much as touched with his cudgel fell right to the ground and didn't dare stir again. The king got frightened, asked for mercy, and just to save his life, gave the soldier his kingdom and his daughter in marriage.

117 The Wayward Child

Das eigensinnige Kind

THERE WAS ONCE A WAYWARD CHILD who didn't do what its mother wanted. For that reason the dear Lord did not look with favor upon it and let it fall ill; no doctor could do anything for it, and it soon lay on its deathbed. Now when it was lowered into the grave and covered over with earth, suddenly its little arm appeared again on the surface and reached up in the air. When they put it down and threw fresh earth over it, that did no good, and the arm kept coming out again. Then the mother herself had to go to the grave and strike the arm with a switch, and when she'd done that, it drew itself in. Now for the first time the child had peace under the earth.

118 The Three Army Surgeons

Die drei Feldscherer

THREE ARMY SURGEONS were traveling abroad in the world, considered that they'd mastered their profession, and came to an inn where they planned to spend the night. The innkeeper asked

where they came from and where they were going. "We're practising our profession about in the world." "Well, give me a demonstration of what you can do," said the innkeeper. Then the first
said that he would cut his own hand off and put it back on whole
the first thing in the morning. The second said he'd tear his heart
out and put it back in whole the first thing in the morning. The
third said he'd put his eyes out and have them back in whole the
first thing in the morning. "If you can do that," said the innkeeper, "then you are accomplished in your profession." They
had a salve and whatever they rubbed it on healed up, and they
always carried with them the little phial it was in. As they had
said, each cut from his body his hand, his heart, and his eyes, laid
them all on a plate, and gave it to the innkeeper. He handed it
to a maid to put away carefully in a cupboard.

The maid, however, had a secret lover, a soldier. When the
innkeeper, the three surgeons, and everybody in the house were
asleep, the soldier came and wanted something to eat. The girl
opened the cupboard and got him something, but being so deeply
in love she forgot to shut the cupboard door, sat down at the table
with her sweetheart, and they gossiped together. While she was
sitting there contentedly, not thinking any mishap, the cat
sneaked in, found the cupboard open, seized the hand, the heart,
and the eyes of the three surgeons, and ran out with them. When
the soldier had eaten and the girl was about to put the things
away again and shut the cupboard, she noticed, of course, that the
plate which the innkeeper had given her was bare. Frightened,
she then said to her lover, "Oh, dear! what on earth shall I do?
The hand's gone, and the heart and eyes, too. How I'll catch it in
the morning!" "Don't worry," he said, "I'll help you out of your
difficulty. There's a thief hanging on the gallows outside; I'll cut
off his hand. Which hand was it?" "The right." The girl gave
him a sharp knife, and he went and, cutting off the poor sinner's
right hand, brought it in. Then he caught a cat and put its eyes
out. Now only the heart was still missing. "Haven't you been
slaughtering? And isn't the pig's carcass in the cellar?" "Yes,"
said the girl. "Well, that's fine," said the soldier, went down and
got a pig's heart. The girl put them all together on the plate and
placed it in the cupboard, and when her sweetheart had said
good-bye, went peacefully to bed.

In the morning when the surgeons got up, they told the maid

to bring them the plate with the hand, the heart, and the eyes. She fetched it out of the cupboard, and the first surgeon attached the thief's hand to himself, rubbed it with his salve, and then and there it had grown on. The second took the cat's eyes and put them back in whole. The third made fast the pig's heart. The innkeeper stood there, admired their skill, and said he'd never seen the like before and that he'd praise them and recommend them to everybody. Thereupon, they paid their bill and continued on their travels.

As they were thus walking along, the one with the pig's heart didn't stay at all with his companions but ran into every nook and corner and snuffed about there the way pigs do. The others wanted to hold him by his coattails, but that did no good; he'd break loose and run to wherever the refuse was most plentiful. The second acted curiously, too, rubbed his eyes, and said to the other, "Friend, what's the matter? These aren't my eyes, I really can't see anything. Will one of you please lead me so that I shan't fall." They walked on with difficulty till evening, when they reached another tavern. As they entered the inn parlor together, a wealthy gentleman was sitting at the table in a corner, counting money. The one with the thief's hand walked around him; his arm twitched a couple of times, and when the gentleman turned around, he reached into the pile and took out a handful of gold. One of the other surgeons saw it and said, "Friend, what are you doing? You mustn't steal. Shame on you!" "Oh, dear," he said, "what can I do about it? My hand twitches, and I have to snatch willy-nilly." Afterward they lay down to sleep, and where they were lying, it was so dark that one couldn't see one's hand before one's face. Suddenly the one with the cat's eyes awoke, roused the others, and said, "Just look, brothers! Do you see the little white mice running about there?" The other two sat up in bed but could see nothing. Then he said, "There's something wrong with us—we didn't get our own parts back. We must return to the innkeeper—he cheated us." Accordingly, the next morning they went there and told the innkeeper that they hadn't got their right parts back: one had a thief's hand, the other cat's eyes, and the third a pig's heart. The innkeeper said that it must be the maid's fault and was about to call her. However, when she'd seen the three coming, she'd run out the back gate and didn't come back. Then the three said he must give them a lot of money, other-

wise they'd burn the inn down over his head. Then he gave them
what he had and could possibly raise, and the three went off with
it. It was enough for them as long as they lived. Just the same,
they'd rather have had their right parts.

119   The Seven Swabians

Die sieben Schwaben

SEVEN SWABIANS once met up. The first was Mr. Schulz, the second
Jim, the third Marty, the fourth Georgie, the fifth Michael, the
sixth Jack, the seventh Guy. All seven had decided to travel
through the world in search of adventure and to perform great
deeds. In order to proceed suitably armed and secure, they
thought it a good idea to have made for themselves a single,
though very strong and long spear. This spear all seven took hold
of together. The boldest and manliest went in front, and that
could only be Mr. Schulz; the others followed in order, Guy
being the last.

One July day it happened, when they had gone a long way and
were still some distance from the village where they had planned
to spend the night, that in the dusk a big beetle or a hornet flew
by, not far from them behind a bush in a meadow, buzzing in a
hostile manner. Mr. Schulz got so frightened that he almost
dropped the spear, and from fright sweat broke out all over him.
"Listen, listen!" he cried to his companions. "My gracious! I
hear a drum." Jim, who had hold of the spear behind Mr. Schulz
and who smelt goodness knows what, said, "No doubt there's
something there, for I smell the powder and the fuse." At these
words Mr. Schulz took flight and in a flash jumped over a
fence. But because he jumped right on the teeth of a rake left
there from the haying, the handle went into his face and dealt
him a dirty blow. "Ouch, ouch!" cried Mr. Schulz. "Take me
prisoner! I surrender, I surrender!" The other six came skipping

up, all of them one after the other crying, "If you're surrendering, I'll surrender, too." Finally, since no enemy was there to tie
them up and lead them off, they saw that they had been deceived,
and to keep the story from getting around and themselves from
being made fools of and mocked, they swore among themselves
to keep quiet about it until someone should unexpectedly blurt
it out. Thereupon they moved on.

The second peril they encountered can't really be compared
to the first. Some days later their way took them over fallow
land. A hare was sitting there asleep in the sun with ears pricked
and its big glassy eyes staring wide open. At the sight of the
fierce and wild animal they all got frightened and took council as
to what would be the least dangerous thing to do. For, should
they flee, there was the risk that the monster might go after them
and swallow them all, skin and bones. So they said, "We'll have
to fight a great and perilous battle. Boldly ventured is half won!"
All seven took hold of the spear, Mr. Schulz at the front, Guy in
the rear. Mr. Schulz still wanted to hold back with the spear, but
Guy in the rear had got quite bold, wanted to cut loose, and
shouted,

> "In the name of all Swabians, thrust away!
> else I wish you'd get lame."

But Jack knew how to cap him and said,

> "By Jove, you've chattered well;
> you're always the last in the dragon hunt."

Mike cried out:

> "It's a near thing
> To being the Devil, indeed."

Now it was Georgie's turn; he said,

> "If it's not the Devil, then it's his mother,
> or the Devil's stepbrother."

Then Marty had a good idea and said to Guy,

> "Go, Guy, you go ahead;
> I'll stand in front of you behind."

Guy, however, didn't listen to that, and Jim said,

> "Schulz, indeed, must be the first,
> to him alone the honor's due."

Then Mr. Schulz took heart and said solemnly,

> "Advance then boldly into battle;
> here one will see which one is brave."

Then they all went for the dragon. Mr. Schulz crossed himself and called on God for aid, but when all that did no good and he got nearer and nearer the enemy, in great dread he cried out, "Smite well! smite well!" The hare was awakened by the noise, got frightened, and hopped quickly away. When Mr. Schulz saw it deserting like that, he cried out joyfully,

> "Good gracious, Guy! look! look! what's that?
> The monster is a hare."

The Swabian League, however, sought further adventures and came to the Mosel, a mucky, quiet, deep river. There aren't many bridges across it, and at a number of points one must be ferried over in boats. Uninformed on this matter, the seven Swabians called out to a man working on the other side of the river and asked how on earth one could get across. Because of the distance and because of their accent the man didn't understand what they wanted and in his Trier dialect asked, "What? what?" Mr. Schulz thought he was just saying, "Wade! Wade through the water!" and because he was in the lead, he got under way and started into the Mosel. Before long he sank into the mud and under the deep onrushing waves; the wind, however, blew his hat over to the other bank, and a frog sat down by it and croaked, "Wat! wat! wat!" The other six heard that and said, "Our comrade, Mr. Schulz, is calling us. If he can wade across, why can't we, too?" Accordingly, they all jumped quickly into the river and drowned.

Thus one frog was the death of the six of them, and no member of the Swabian League got back home.

120   The Three Journeymen

Die drei Handwerksburschen

THERE WERE THREE JOURNEYMEN who'd agreed to stay together on their travels and always to work in the very same town. On one occasion, however, they got no more wages from their masters, so that finally they were quite in rags and had nothing to live on. Then one of them said, "What shall we do? We can't stay here any longer. Let's get under way again, and if we find no work in the town we come to, we'll arrange with the innkeeper to write him where we're stopping, so that one can get news of the other. Then let's split up." That seemed best to the others, too.

They set out and on the way met a handsomely dressed man who asked who they were. "We're journeymen and are looking for work. Up to now we've stayed together, but if we don't find any work, we'll split up." "There's no need for that," said the man. "If you'll do what I tell you, you'll lack neither money nor work. Indeed, you'll become fine gentlemen and ride in coaches." One of them said, "If it doesn't jeopardize our souls, we'll do it, of course." "No," answered the man, "I have no share in you." One of the others had, however, looked at his feet, and when he saw one horse's hoof and one human foot, he didn't want to get involved with him. But the Devil said, "Don't worry, I have no designs on you, rather on the soul of another person who's half mine already and whose cup has merely to be filled to overflowing." Now being safe, they agreed, and the Devil told them what he required. In answer to every question the first was to say, "All three of us"; the second, "For the money"; and the third, "And that was right." They were always to say this one after the other and beyond this must not say a single word. If they violated this order, then all the money would instantly vanish, but as long as they carried this out, their pockets would always be full. Furthermore, at the outset he also gave them straight off as much money as they could carry and ordered them to go into such and such a tavern in the town. They entered, and the host came to meet them, asking, "Do you wish something to eat?" The first answered, "All three of us." "Yes," said the host, "I assume so." The second said, "For the money." "That's a matter of course," said the host. The third said, "And that was right." "Of course it was right," said the host.

Now they were brought good food and drink and were well served. After the meal the matter of paying was bound to come up. When the host handed one of them the bill, the latter said, "All three of us"; the second, "For the money"; the third, "And that was right." "Of course it's right," said the host. "All three pay; I can't give you anything without money." They paid even more than he had asked. The guests watched this and said, "Those people must be mad." "Yes, they certainly are," said the host. "They are a little off." Thus for a time they stayed at the tavern and said nothing but "All three of us—for the money—and that was right." But they saw everything and knew everything that went on there.

It so happened that a great merchant arrived with a lot of money; he said, "Innkeeper, put my money away for me. There are the three mad journeymen here; they might steal it from me." The host did so. As he was carrying the merchant's portmanteau to his room, he felt that it was heavy with gold. Thereupon he gave the three journeymen quarters downstairs, putting the merchant upstairs in a special room. When it was midnight and the innkeeper thought that everybody was asleep, he and his wife went with an ax and beat the rich merchant to death. After committing the murder they went back to bed. When it was day, there was a great hue and cry: the merchant was lying dead in his bed and swimming in his own blood. All the guests assembled in a hurry, and the innkeeper said, "The three mad journeymen did it." The guests confirmed this, saying, "It can't have been anybody else." The host had them summoned and said, "Did you kill the merchant?" "All three of us," said the first; "For the money," said the second; "And that was right," said the third. "Now, there you hear it," said the innkeeper. "They admit it themselves." So they were put into prison and were to be tried.

When they saw that things were taking so serious a turn, they got really frightened, but in the night the Devil came and said,

"Just hold out one day more and don't throw your good luck away. It won't hurt a hair of your heads." The next morning they were brought into court. "Are you the murderers?" said the judge. "All three of us." "Why did you kill the merchant?" "For the money." "You scoundrels!" said the judge, "weren't you in dread because of your sin?" "And that was right." "They've confessed and are stubborn, to boot!" said the judge. "Lead them to death at once." So they were led out, and the innkeeper had to join the circle.

Now as the executioner's assistants took hold of them and they were being led up onto the scaffolding, where the executioner was standing with a naked sword, all at once there came a coach, drawn by bright bay horses and going so fast that sparks flew from the pavement—and out of the window someone was waving a white cloth. "Pardon is coming," said the executioner, and at the same moment out of the coach came a cry, "Pardon, pardon!" Then the Devil in the guise of a distinguished gentleman, splendidly dressed, stepped out and said, "You three are innocent. Now you may talk; speak up and say what you've seen and heard." Then the eldest said, "'We didn't kill the merchant; the murderer is standing there in the circle," and pointed to the innkeeper. "And to prove our statement go into his cellar where many more people are hanging whom he has killed." The judge sent the executioner's assistants there, who found it as had been stated, and when they reported this to the judge, he had the innkeeper led up and his head struck off.

Then the Devil said to the three, "Now I have the soul I was after, but you are free and have money for as long as you live."

121 The King's Son Who is Afraid of Nothing

Der Königssohn, der sich vor nichts fürchtet

THERE WAS ONCE A KING'S SON who got tired of it at home in his father's house and, being afraid of nothing, thought, "I'll go out into the wide world where time will pass quickly for me and I'll see plenty of remarkable things." So he took leave of his parents and set out, going on and on from morning till evening, and it was all one to him where his way led him. By chance he came to the house of a giant and, because he was tired, he sat down outside the door and rested.

As he let his eyes wander here and there, he saw a game lying in the giant's courtyard: it was a set of huge bowls, with ninepins as big as a man. After a while he got a longing to play and set up the pins; he rolled the bowls at them, cried and shouted when the pins fell, and was in high spirits. The giant heard the noise, put his head out the window, and spied a human who was no bigger than other humans, yet was playing with his ninepins. "You little worm," he cried, "why are you bowling with my ninepins? Who gave you the strength to do it?" The king's son looked up and, seeing the giant, said, "O you clumsy lout! So you think you're the only one with strong arms. I can do whatever I like." The giant came down, in great amazement watched the bowling, and said, "Man alive! If you're that good, go get me an apple from the Tree of Life." "What do you want with it?" said the king's son. "I don't want the apple for myself," answered the giant, "but I have a bride-to-be who is asking for it. I've traveled far and wide in the world and can't find the tree." "I'll find it all right," said the king's son, "and I don't know what will stop me from fetching down the apple." "Then you think it's so easy?" said the giant. "The garden the tree is in is surrounded by an iron paling and outside the paling and lying side by side are wild animals that keep watch and let nobody in." "They'll let me in all right," said the king's son. "Yes, but even if you get into the garden and see the apple hanging on the tree, it still isn't yours. Before it hangs a ring through which one must put one's hand if one wants to get at the apple and pick it, and thus far no one has succeeded." "I'll succeed all right," said the king's son.

Then he took leave of the giant, went away over hill and dale, through forest and field, till at last he found the wonderful garden. The animals were lying around about, but they had their heads down, were asleep, and didn't even wake up when he approached. He stepped over them, climbed the paling, and got into the garden safe and sound. There in the middle stood the Tree of Life, and the red apples gleamed on the branches. He climbed up the trunk and, as he was about to reach for an apple, he saw a ring hanging in front of it. Nevertheless, he put his hand through it without difficulty and picked the apple. The ring closed tight on his arm, and he felt as if a tremendous strength were suddenly streaming through his veins. After climbing back down the tree he didn't want to climb over the paling but seized the great gate and had to shake it only once before it burst open with a loud noise. He went out, and the lion that had been lying outside the gate waked up and hurried after him, though not furiously and fiercely; on the contrary, it followed him humbly as its master.

The king's son brought the giant the promised apple and said, "See, I fetched it without difficulty." The giant was delighted his wish had been fulfilled so quickly, hurried to his bride-to-be and gave her the apple she'd asked for. She was a beautiful and clever maiden and, not seeing the ring on his arm, said, "I shan't believe that you fetched the apple until I see the ring on your arm." "All I have to do is go home and get it," said the giant, thinking it would be easy to take by force whatever the weak human wouldn't give up voluntarily. So he demanded the ring of him, but the king's son refused. "Wherever the apple is, the ring must also be," said the giant. "If you don't surrender it voluntarily, you'll have to fight with me for it." They wrestled together a long time, but the giant couldn't get the better of the king's son, who was strengthened by the magic power of the ring. Then the giant thought of a trick and said, "I've got hot fighting, and so have you. Let's bathe in the river and cool off before we begin again." The king's son, who understood nothing of treachery, went with him to the river, stripped off his clothes, also the ring from his arm, and jumped in. The giant immediately grabbed for the ring and ran off with it. The lion, however, who had observed the theft, went for the giant, tore the ring from his hand, and brought it back to its master. Then the giant took up a position behind an oak tree, and when the king's son was busy putting on his clothes again, he attacked him and put out both his eyes.

Now the poor king's son stood there, blind and not knowing what to do. Again the giant came along, took him by the hand like someone who was going to lead him, and led him to the top of a high cliff. He left him standing there, thinking, "Just a few steps farther and he'll pitch to his death, and I can take the ring off him." But the faithful lion had not abandoned its master, held onto his clothes and gradually drew him back. When the giant came to rob the dead man, he saw that his trick had failed. "Is there no way of killing one of those weak human beings?" he said angrily to himself, took hold of the king's son and by another road led him again to the precipice. But the lion, noticing the evil intent, here, too, helped its master out of danger. When they got near the edge, the giant let go of the blind man's hand, intending to leave him alone there, but the lion gave the giant a push so that he pitched down and in falling was smashed at the bottom. Again the faithful animal drew its master back from the precipice and led him to a tree by which ran a clear brook. There the king's son sat down, but the lion lay down and with its paw splashed water into his face. No sooner had a few drops wet the sockets of his eyes than the king's son was again able to see a little and noticed a bird flying just past him and then hit a tree trunk. Thereupon it went down into the water, bathed in it, and then flew up in the air, speeding away through the trees without hitting them as if it had regained its sight. The king's son realized that this was a hint from God, bent over the water, and washed and bathed his face in it. When he got up, his eyes were again as clear as ever. The king's son thanked God for His great mercy and with his lion went on his way through the world.

Now by chance he came to an enchanted castle. A maiden, beautiful of form and fair of face, was standing in the gateway, but she was quite black. She addressed him and said, "Alas! could you free me from the evil spell that has been cast upon me?" "What am I to do?" said the king's son. The maiden answered, "You must spend three nights in the great hall of the enchanted castle, but no fear must enter your heart. If they torture you in the worst way and you endure it without uttering a sound, I shall be disenchanted. They won't be allowed to take your life." "I'm not afraid and with God's help I'll try to do it," said the king's son. He went gaily into the castle and when it got quite dark, sat down in the great hall and waited. Until midnight it was still, then suddenly a great noise started, and little devils appeared from every nook and corner. They acted as if they didn't see him, sat down in the middle of the room, made a fire, and began to gamble. When one would lose, he'd say, "Things aren't right.

Someone is here who is not one of us; it's his fault that I'm losing." "Just wait, you over there behind the stove, I'll get you yet," another would say. The shrieking got louder and louder, so that no one could have listened to it without feeling frightened. The king's son just sat there very quietly and felt no fear. Finally, however, the devils jumped up from the floor and attacked him and there were so many that he couldn't defend himself against them. They pulled him about on the floor, tweaked him, stabbed him, beat him, and tortured him, but he didn't utter a sound. Toward morning they disappeared, and he was so exhausted that he could scarcely move his limbs. When day broke, the black maiden came in to him. In her hand she was carrying a little phial and in it the Water of Life with which she washed him. Straightway he felt all his aches and pains disappear, and fresh strength streamed into his veins. "You've survived one night luckily," she said, "but two more are ahead of you." Again she went away, and as she was leaving, he noticed that her feet had become white. The following night the devils came and began their game anew: they fell upon the king's son and beat him much harder than the night before, so that his body was covered with wounds. Nevertheless, since he stood it all in silence, they had to release him, and when day broke, the maiden came and healed him with the Water of Life. As she was leaving, to his joy he saw that she had already got white to the tips of her fingers. Now he had only to endure one more night, but that was the worst. The devils' frolic resumed. "Are you still there?" they cried. "You're going to be tortured till you stop breathing." They stabbed him and beat him, threw him hither and thither, and pulled his arms and legs as if to tear him to pieces. He endured it all, however, and didn't utter a sound. Finally the devils vanished, but he lay there unconscious and motionless; he couldn't even raise his eyes to see the maiden who came in and sprinkled him with the Water of Life and poured it on him. Yet suddenly he was free of all pain and felt as fresh and well as if he'd waked up from a sleep.

On opening his eyes he saw the maiden standing beside him; she was as white as snow and as beautiful as the day. "Get up," she said, "and brandish your sword three times over the stairs. Then everything will be disenchanted." When he had done so, the whole castle was free of the spell, and the maiden turned out to be a wealthy king's daughter. The servants came and said that the table was already set in the great hall and the food served. Then they sat down, ate and drank together, and in the evening the wedding was celebrated amid great rejoicing.

122   The Lettuce-Donkey

Der Krautesel

THERE WAS ONCE A YOUNG HUNTSMAN who went shooting in the forest. He was gay and merry-hearted, and as he was walking along and whistling in a leaf, there came an ugly old granny who addressed him and said, "Good day, dear huntsman. You're certainly jolly and gay, but I'm suffering from hunger and thirst. Please give me alms." The huntsman took pity on the poor woman, reached into his pocket, and according to his means gave her something. He was about to continue on his way, but the old woman stopped him and said, "Dear huntsman, listen to what I tell you: for your kindness of heart I'm going to give you a present. Just keep going, and in a little while you'll come to a tree in which nine birds are sitting; they'll have a cloak in their claws and will be tussling over it. Aim your gun and shoot into the middle of them: they'll surely drop the cloak down on you, and one of the birds, too, will be hit and drop down dead. Take the cloak along with you. It's a wishing cloak: if you throw it over your shoulders, you need only wish yourself somewhere and in an instant you'll be there. Take the heart out of the dead bird and swallow it whole: then each and every morning you'll find a gold piece under your pillow when you get up."

The huntsman thanked the wise woman and thought to himself, "Those are fair promises she'd made me—if only it would all come true!" However, when he'd gone about a hundred paces, he heard such a noise and a twittering in the branches above him that he looked up. There he saw a lot of birds tugging at a piece of cloth with their bills and claws, uttering cries, tussling and scuffling with one another as if each wanted it for itself. "Well," said the huntsman, "this is extraordinary! It's happening just as granny said." Taking his gun from his shoulder, he aimed it and sent his shot right into their midst, so that the feathers flew about. With loud cries the creatures at once took flight, but one dropped down dead, and the cloak, too, floated down. Then the huntsman did as the old woman had ordered, cut the bird open, looked for the heart, swallowed it, and brought the cloak home with him. The next morning on awakening he remembered the promise and wanted to see whether it had really come true. When he lifted up his pillow, there was the gold piece gleaming before his eyes. The following morning he again found one, and so on every time he got up. He collected a pile of gold and at last thought, "What good does all my gold do me if I stay here at home? I'll set out and have a look about the world."

He took leave of his parents, shouldered his knapsack and gun, and went out in the world. One day he happened to be going through a dense forest, and when it came to an end, there stood an imposing manor house on the plain before him. In one of the windows an old woman and a marvelously beautiful maiden were standing looking down. Now the old woman was a witch and said to the girl, "There comes someone from the forest with a wonderful treasure inside him. We must trick him out of it, my darling daughter; it's more fitting for us than for him. He has a bird's heart with him and that's why there's a gold piece under his pillow every morning." She told her the details and what her game was to be to get hold of it. Finally she threatened her, saying with anger in her eyes, "And if you don't mind me, you'll be sorry." Now when the huntsman got nearer, he saw the girl and said to himself, "I've been going about for such a long time that for once I'll take a rest and turn into this fine mansion. Money I have aplenty." The real reason, however, was that he had his eye on the beautiful girl.

He stepped into the house, was received in friendly fashion and was courteously entertained. Before long he was so in love with the witch-girl that he no longer thought of anything else, did nothing but look into her eyes, and gladly did whatever she asked. Then the old woman said, "Now we must have the bird's heart; he won't notice anything if it's missing." She brewed a drink, and when it was ready, put it in a tumbler and gave it to

the girl who had to offer it to the huntsman. "Now, my beloved," she said, "drink to me." He took the tumbler and after
drinking the potion vomited out the bird's heart. The girl had to
remove it secretly and then swallow it herself, for that was the
old woman's wish. From now on he found no more gold under
his pillow; instead, it was under the girl's pillow, whence the
old woman removed it every morning. But he was so in love
and so infatuated that his only thought was to spend his time with
the girl.

Then the old witch said, "We've got the bird's heart, but we
must also take the wishing-cloak from him." The girl answered,
"Let's leave him that; after all he's lost his fortune." Then the
old woman got angry and said, "A cloak like that is a wonderful
object rarely found here on earth. I shall and must have it."
She suggested ways and means to the girl and said if she didn't
mind her, that it would go hard for her. Then she did as the
old woman bade. On one occasion she took up a position by the
window and looked into the distance as if she were very sad.
"Why are you standing there so sad," asked the huntsman. "Oh,
my dear," she answered, "over yonder is the Jewel Mountain
where precious stones grow. I have such a great longing for
them that, whenever I think of them, I'm quite sad. But who can
fetch them? Only the birds, who have wings, get there, never a
human being!" "If that's all you have to complain about," said
the huntsman, "I'll soon remove that trouble from your heart."
Thereupon he took her under his cloak and wished himself over
to the Jewel Mountain, and the same instant they were both sitting on top of it. Jewels were gleaming on all sides and it was a
joy to look at them; the most beautiful and most valuable they
gathered up. Now through her witch's art the old woman had
so contrived it that the huntsman's eyes grew heavy, and he said
to the girl, "Let's sit down for a bit and rest. I'm so tired that I
can't stay on my feet any longer." They sat down, and he laid his
head in her lap and went to sleep. When he'd gone to sleep, she
undid his cloak from his shoulders, draped it around herself,
picked up the jewels and precious stones, and wished herself
home with them.

When the huntsman had had his sleep and waked up, he saw
that his beloved had deceived him and left him alone on the wild
mountain. "Oh," he said, "how much treachery there is in the

world!", sat there sorrowful and sad of heart, and didn't know what to do. The mountain belonged to fierce and monstrous giants who had their abode up there and were up to their tricks. He'd not been sitting there long before he saw three of them striding toward him. He lay down as if plunged in a deep sleep. The giants came up, and the first gave him a kick and said, "What kind of an earthworm is lying there and inwardly contemplating itself?" The second said, "Stamp it to death!" But the third said scornfully, "That wouldn't be worth doing! Just let it live. It can't stay here, and if it climbs higher up onto the peak, the clouds will get it and carry it away." Talking thus they walked by, but the huntsman heard what they had said and, as soon as they were gone, got up and climbed the peak. After he'd been sitting there a while, a cloud drifted up, seized him, carried him off, and for a long time floated about in the sky. Then it came lower and settled down on a big walled vegetable garden, so that he landed gently among cabbages and other vegetables.

The huntsman looked about and said, "If I only had something to eat! I'm so hungry, and it's going to be hard to proceed farther. Yet here I see not an apple or a pear or any kind of fruit—everywhere just vegetables!" Finally he thought, "In an emergency I can eat some of the lettuce; it doesn't taste especially good but it will refresh me." Accordingly, he picked out a nice head and ate some. Scarcely had he swallowed a few mouthfuls when he had an extraordinary sensation and felt quite changed: he grew four legs, a fat head, and two long ears. To his horror he saw that he was changed into a donkey, but because he still at the same time felt very hungry and the succulent lettuce appealed to his present nature, he kept eating it greedily. At last he got to another kind of lettuce. No sooner had he swallowed some of this than he again felt a transformation and returned to his human form.

Now the huntsman lay down and slept off his weariness. When he awoke the following morning, he picked one head of the bad and one of the good lettuce, thinking, "This ought to help me get back my beloved and punish her treachery." Then he put the heads of lettuce in his bag, climbed over the wall, and went in search of his sweetheart's mansion. After roaming about for a few days, he fortunately found it again. Then he quickly dyed his face brown, so that his own mother wouldn't have known him, entered the mansion, and asked for lodgings. "I'm very tired," he said, "and can go no farther." "Fellow-countryman, who are you and what is your business?" asked the witch. He answered, "I'm the king's messenger and was dispatched in search of the most delicious lettuce that grows under the sun. I've also been lucky enough to find it and am carrying it on me. The sun, however, is far too hot, so that the delicate lettuce threatens to wilt, and I don't know whether I'll get it any farther." When the old woman heard about the delicious lettuce, she greatly longed for some and said, "Dear fellow-countryman, please let me try the wonderful lettuce." "Why not?" he answered. "I brought two heads along and will give you one," opened his bag and handed her the bad head. The witch suspected no harm, and her mouth watered so for the novel dish that she went into the kitchen herself and prepared it. When it was ready, she couldn't wait for it to be on the table but straightway took a couple of leaves and put them in her mouth. No sooner, however, had she swallowed them than she, too, lost her human form and in the shape of a donkey ran down into the courtyard. The servant girl came into the kitchen, saw the lettuce all prepared there, and was going to serve it, but on the way the desire to try things got the better of her—an old habit of hers—and she ate a couple of the leaves. Forthwith the magic power manifested itself, and she, too, was turned into a donkey and ran out to join the old woman. The bowl of lettuce fell to the floor. Meanwhile, the messenger was sitting with the beautiful maiden, and when no one came with the lettuce and she, too, really very much longed for some, she said, "I can't imagine what's become of the lettuce." Then the huntsman thought, "The lettuce has probably already worked," and said, "I'll go to the kitchen and find out." When he got down there, he saw two donkeys running about in the yard and the lettuce lying on the floor. "Quite right," he said. "The two have had their share." He picked up the rest of the leaves, put them in the bowl, and taking them to the girl said, "I'm bringing you the delicious food myself, so you won't have to wait any longer." She ate some and as quickly as the others was robbed of her human shape and ran into the courtyard in the form of a donkey.

When the huntsman had washed his face so that the transformed women could recognize him, he went down into the yard and said, "Now you're to receive the reward for your treachery." He tied all three to a rope and drove them on till he came to a mill. He rapped on the window and the miller put his head out and asked what he wanted. "I have three bad animals," he answered, "that I don't want to keep any longer. If you're willing to take them, give them fodder and a stall, and treat them as I tell you, I'll pay you what you want." "Why not?" said the miller. "But how am I to treat them?" Then the huntsman said that the old donkey—that was the witch—should get three beatings a day and one feeding; the younger—that was the servant—one beating and three feedings, and the youngest—that was the girl—no beatings and three feedings, for he really didn't have the heart to have the girl beaten. Thereupon he went back to the mansion and found there everything he needed.

A few days later the miller came and said he had to report that the old donkey, who'd got so many beatings and only one feeding a day, had died. "The other two," he went on to say, "haven't, to be sure, died and get, furthermore, three feedings a day; still, they're so downcast that they can't last long." Then the huntsman was moved to pity, let his anger pass, and told the miller to drive them back. When they arrived, he gave them some of the good lettuce to eat so that they became human again. Then the beautiful girl fell on her knees before him and said, "Oh, my beloved, forgive me for any evil I've done you! My mother forced me to do it. It happened against my will, for I love you dearly. Your wishing-cloak is hanging in a wardrobe, and I'll take an emetic to get up the bird's heart." Then he felt quite differently and said, "Just keep it. It really makes no difference, because I want to take you as my faithful wife." Then the wedding was celebrated, and they lived happily together until they died.

123 The Old Woman in the Forest

Die Alte im Wald

A POOR SERVANT GIRL and the gentry she worked for were once driving through a great forest, and when they were in the middle of it, robbers came out of a thicket and murdered whoever they found. All perished except the girl, who in her fright had jumped out of the carriage and hidden behind a tree. When the robbers had gone off with their booty, she went to the carriage and saw the terrible misfortune. She began to weep bitterly and said, "What shall I, poor girl, do now? I don't know how to find my way out of the forest; there's not a soul living in it, so I'm surely bound to starve to death." She walked about looking for a path but couldn't find one. When it was evening, she sat down under a tree and commended herself to God, planning to stay there and not go away, come what might. When she'd been sitting there a while, a white dove came flying to her with a little gold key in its bill. It put the key in her hand and said, "Do you see the big tree there? On it is a little lock which the key opens, and there you will find plenty of food and will no longer suffer from hunger." She went to the tree and opened it and found milk in a little bowl and beside it white bread to crumble into it, so that she was able to eat her fill. When she'd had enough, she said, "Now is the time when at home the chickens go to roost; I'm so tired that I, too, should like to lie down in my bed." Then the dove came flying back and brought another gold key in its bill and said, "Open the tree over there, and you'll find a bed." She opened it and found a lovely soft bed; she prayed our dear Lord to keep her during the night, lay down, and went to sleep. In the morning the dove came a third time, again brought a little key and said, "Open the tree over there and you'll find clothes," and when she opened it, she found clothes embroidered with gold and jewels, more splendid than any king's daughter's. Thus she lived for a time, and the dove came every day and looked out for all her wants, and that was a quiet and good life.

On one occasion the dove came and said, "Will you do me a favor?" "Gladly, indeed," said the girl. Then the dove said, "I shall lead you to a little cottage, then you go in; in it by the hearth an old woman will be sitting and will say 'Good day.' However, under no circumstances answer her, no matter what she does, but go on past her on the right. There is a door there; open it, and you'll come into a room where a lot of rings of every sort and description are lying on the table. Among these are magnificent rings with glittering stones, but leave them alone and pick out a simple ring that must also be among them and bring it here to me as quick as you can." The girl went to the cottage and stepped in the door. An old woman was sitting there, who showed great surprise on seeing the girl and said, "Good day, my child." The girl didn't answer her and went to the door. "Where are you going?" she cried, seizing her by the skirt and intending to hold her. "This is my house and no one may come in if I don't want them to." But the girl kept still, got away from her, and went straight into the living room. There on the table lay a huge number of rings that glistened and gleamed before her eyes. She turned them over and looked for the simple ring but couldn't find it. As she was looking for it, she saw the old woman sneaking along with a bird cage in her hand and about to make off with it. The girl went up to her and took the cage out of her hand, and when she lifted it up and looked in, there was sitting a bird with the simple ring in its bill. She took the ring and very joyously ran out of the house with it, thinking that the white dove would come and get the ring. But it didn't come.

Then she leaned against a tree and was going to wait for the dove, and as she was standing thus, the tree seemed to become soft and pliable and lowered its branches. All at once the branches wrapped themselves about her and were two arms, and when she looked around, the tree was a handsome man who embraced her and kissed her affectionately, saying, "You've disenchanted me and freed me from the power of the old woman, who is a wicked witch. She changed me into a tree, and for a few hours every day I was a white dove. As long as she possessed the ring, I couldn't resume my human form." Then all his servants and horses, whom she had likewise turned into trees, were also freed of the spell and stood beside him. Then they drove off to his kingdom, for he was a king's son, and they got married and lived happily.

124   The Three Brothers

Die drei Brüder

THERE WAS A MAN who had three sons and nothing in the way of property beyond the house he lived in. Now each of the sons would very much have liked their father's house after his death, but the father was as fond of one as of the other. He didn't know how to avoid hurting any of their feelings nor did he want to sell the house, for it had been his forebears'. Otherwise he'd have sold it and divided the money among them. Finally he hit on a plan and said to his sons, "Go out in the world and test yourselves. Let each learn a trade, and then when you come back, the one who puts on the best performance shall have the house."

The sons were satisfied with that. The eldest wanted to become a farrier, the second a barber, and the third a fencing-master. They fixed on a time to meet back home and went their ways. It happened that each found an excellent master from whom he learned something good and useful. The smith had to shoe the king's horses and thought, "Now you can't fail to get the house." The barber shaved only elegant gentlemen and likewise thought that the house was already his. The fencing-master received many a stroke, yet gritted his teeth and didn't let himself get discouraged, for he thought to himself, "If you're afraid of a blow, you'll never get the house." When the appointed time came round, they met again at their father's, but they didn't know how to get the best opportunity to display their skill, sat down together and took council. As they were sitting thus, a hare suddenly came running across the field. "My!" said the barber, "it comes at just the right moment," took his basin and soap, worked up a lather until the hare got near, then lathered it on the run and on the run shaved a turned-up moustache on it. While doing this he didn't cut it and didn't hurt one of its hairs. "I like that," said the father. "Unless the others go after it awfully hard, the house is yours." Before long a gentleman in a carriage came racing by at top speed.

"Now, father, you'll see what I can do," said the farrier, rushed after the carriage, ripped the shoes off the horse that was tearing along, and also on the tear put four new shoes on it. "You're an accomplished chap," said the father. "You do your job as well as your brother does his. I don't know whom I ought to give the house to." Then the third said, "Father, just give me a chance, too," and because it was beginning to rain, he drew his sword and made cross-cuts over his head so that not a drop fell on him. And as it began to rain harder and finally was pouring cats and dogs, he brandished his sword faster and faster and thus kept as dry as if he were sitting under cover. When the father saw that, he was astonished and said, "You've put up the best performance; the house is yours."

The two other brothers accepted the decision, as they had previously promised, and because they were very fond of one another, all three stayed together in the house and practised their trades. And since they were so well trained and so skillful, they earned a great deal of money. Thus they lived happily together to a ripe old age, and when one fell sick and died, the other two grieved so much over it that they, too, fell sick and soon died. Then, because they had been so skillful and so fond of each other, all three were laid together in one grave.

125 The Devil and His Grandmother

Der Teufel und seine Grossmutter

A GREAT WAR WAS ON, and the king had many soldiers but gave them such small pay that they couldn't live on it. Then three soldiers got together and planned to desert. One said to the other, "If we're caught, they'll hang us on the gallows. How shall we manage it?" The other said, "See the big rye field over there. If we hide in it, nobody in the world will find us. The army mayn't enter it and must move on tomorrow." They crept into the rye; the army, however, didn't move on but stayed encamped round about it. For two days and two nights they sat in the rye and got so hungry that they almost died. Yet if they went out into the open, it was sure death for them. So they said, "Of what good is our deserting? We'll have to die here miserably." As they were speaking, a fiery dragon came flying through the air; it came down where they were and asked why they'd hidden there. They answered, "We're three soldiers and have deserted because our pay was small. If we stay here, we're bound to die, to dangle on the gallows if we leave the field." "If you'll serve me seven years," said the dragon, "I'll take you right through the army so that no one will catch you." "We have no choice and must accept your offer," they answered. Then the dragon took them in its claws, carried them off through the air over the army and set them down again on the ground far away.

The dragon, however, was none other than the Devil. He gave them a little whip and said, "If you snap and crack it, as much money as you want will dance about before you. Then you can live like great lords, keep horses, and drive in carriages; but when seven years are up, you'll be mine." Then he held out a book to them, in which all three had to sign their names. "However," he said, "before the time is up I shall in addition propound you a riddle; if you can guess it, you'll be free and released from my power." Then the dragon flew away, and they journeyed on with their little whip, had plenty of money, had themselves made gentlemen's clothes, and moved about in the world. Wherever they were, they lived in joy and splendor, drove with horses and carriages, ate and drank, but did no evil. Time passed quickly for them.

When the seven years were drawing to an end, two of them got very anxious and frightened, but the third took it lightly, saying, "Brothers, don't worry. There's nothing the matter with my head; I'll guess the riddle." They went out into the country, sat down there, and the two pulled long faces. Then an old woman came along who asked why they were so sad. "Oh, what business is it of yours? You can't help us anyhow." "Who knows?" she answered. "Just confide your trouble in me." Then they told her they'd been the Devil's servants for almost seven years. He'd provided them with money like nothing at all, but they'd signed themselves over to him and would become his if after the seven years they couldn't solve the riddle. "If you're to be helped," said the old woman, "one of you must go into the forest, where he'll come to the caved-in side of a cliff that looks like a hut. He must go in and then he'll find help." The two gloomy fellows thought, "That won't save us either," and remained seated, but the third, the jolly chap, got up and went into the forest until he found the cliff-hut.

In the hut was sitting a very old woman: she was the Devil's grandmother and she asked him where he came from and what he wanted there. He told her everything that had happened, and because she took a great liking to him, she took pity and said she'd help him. She lifted up a big stone that lay over a cellar and said, "Hide there and you'll be able to hear everything that's said here. Just sit still and don't stir. When the dragon comes, I'll ask him about the riddle. He tells me everything. Then pay attention to what he answers." At twelve midnight the dragon came flying in and asked for his meal. His grandmother set the table and served him food and drink to his heart's content, and they ate and drank together. In the course of the conversation she then asked him how it had gone today and how many souls he'd got. "Things didn't go very well for me today," he answered. "However, I've bagged three soldiers; they're mine for certain." "O yes, three soldiers," she said. "They're cleverer than ordinary people; they may still get away from you." "They're mine," said the Devil scornfully. "I'm going to propound them a riddle which they'll never be able to guess." "What kind of a riddle?" she said. "I'll tell you: in the big North Sea is a dead monkey, that shall be their roast; a whale's rib shall be their silver spoon; and an old hollow horse-hoof shall be their wine glass." When the Devil had gone to bed, the old grandmother lifted up the stone and let the soldier out. "Did you pay close attention to everything?" "Yes," he said. "I know enough and shall manage quite all right." Thereupon he had to go out a different way—secretly through the window—and return with all speed to his companions.

He told them how the Devil had been tricked by his old grandmother and how he had heard from him the solution of the riddle. All were happy and in high spirits, took the whip, and whipped themselves up so much money that it danced about on the ground. When the seven years were quite up, the Devil came with the book, showed them their signatures, and said, "I'm going to take you with me to Hell, where you're to have a meal.

If you can guess what kind of a roast you're going to get, you'll be free and may also keep the little whip." Then the first soldier began, "In the big North Sea is a dead monkey; that will probably be our roast." The Devil was annoyed, went hm! hm! hm! and asked the second, "What's your spoon going to be?" "A whale's rib—that shall be our silver spoon." The Devil made a face, again growled hm! hm! hm! three times, and said to the third, "Do you, too, know what your wine glass is to be?" "An old horse-hoof." Then with a loud howl the Devil flew away and had no further power over them.

But the three soldiers kept the whip, whipped up as much money as they wanted, and lived happily until their end.

126   Loyal Ferdinand and Disloyal Ferdinand

Ferenand getrü und Ferenand ungetrü

THERE WAS ONCE A MAN and a woman who, as long as they were rich, had no children, but when they got poor, had a little boy. When they couldn't get a godfather for him, the husband said he'd go to the next town and see if he could get one there. As he was walking along, he met a poor man who asked him where he was going. He said he was going to see about getting a godfather: he was poor, and nobody was willing to stand sponsor for his child. "Oh," said the poor man, "you're poor and I'm poor. I'll stand sponsor, but I'm so poor that I can't give the child anything. Go tell the midwife just to come to the church with the child." When they all reached the church, the beggar was already there; he gave the child the name Loyal Ferdinand.

As he was leaving the church, the beggar said, "Now just go home; I can't give you anything, and you're not to give me anything, either." Nevertheless, he gave the midwife a key and told her to give it to the father when she got home, and that he should keep it until the child was fourteen years old. Then the child should go out on the heath; there'd be a royal mansion there which the key would fit, and what was in it would belong to him. When the child was seven and had grown big and strong, he once went to play with some other boys; each had received more from his godfather than the next. The child, however, couldn't say anything, wept and went home and said to his father, "Didn't I get anything at all from my godfather?" "O yes," said the father. "You got a key. If there's a royal mansion out on the heath, just go and open it." He went there, but there was no sign of a mansion. Again seven years later, when he was fourteen, he went there a second time and on the heath stood a mansion. When he had opened it, there was nothing in it but a horse, a white horse. The boy was so happy to have the horse that he mounted it and raced to his father. "Now I've got a white horse, too," he said, "and now I, too, am going to travel about."

Then he set out and as he was riding along, there lay a quill on the road. First he was going to pick it up, but then bethought himself, "Oh, you'd better leave it. If you need to write, you'll certainly find a quill where you're going." As he was going on, a voice called out behind him, "Loyal Ferdinand, take it with you." He looked around but saw no one, then went back and picked it up. After riding on again for a while, he passed a body of water. A fish was lying on the bank gasping and panting for air; then he said, "Just a minute, my dear fish! I'll help you get into the water," picked it up by the tail and threw it into the water. Then the fish stuck its head out and said, "Because you helped me out of the muck, I'll give you a flute, and if at any time you drop something into the water, just play it and I'll hand it out to you." Now he rode away. Then a man came toward him who asked him where he was going. "Oh, to the next village." "What's your name?" "Loyal Ferdinand." "Why, we have almost the same name! Mine's Disloyal Ferdinand." They both went to the next village and into the tavern.

Now the bad thing was that Disloyal Ferdinand knew everything that anybody had thought and was going to do; he knew this through all kinds of evil arts. In the tavern there was a very fine girl who had an open countenance and such pleasant manners. She fell in love with Loyal Ferdinand because he was a handsome man and asked him where he was going. "Oh, I'm just traveling about." Then she said he really ought to stay right there: there was a king in that country who very much wanted to engage a servant or an outrider and he ought to enter his service. He answered that he couldn't very well go to a person and offer his services. Then the girl said, "Oh, I'll do that, of course." Accordingly, she went straight to the king and told him that she knew of a fine servant for him. The king was delighted at that and had him come to him and wanted to make him a servant. Loyal Ferdinand preferred, however, to be an outrider, because where his horse was he had to be, too. So the king made him an outrider. When Disloyal Ferdinand learned of this, he said to the girl, "Just a minute! Are you going to help him along and not me?" "Oh," said the girl, "I'll help you along, too," thinking, "You must keep him as a friend, for he's not to be trusted." So she went before the king and offered him as a servant. The king was pleased with that.

Now in the morning when Disloyal Ferdinand used to dress his master, the latter would keep complaining, "Oh, if I only had my beloved with me!" Disloyal Ferdinand, however, always had a grudge against Loyal Ferdinand, and so once when the king was again complaining, he said, "Well, you've got your outrider. Send him there. He'll have to fetch her, and if he doesn't he'll have to be beheaded." Then the king had Loyal Ferdinand come to him and told him that in such and such a place he had a beloved; he was to fetch her for him, and if he didn't do it, he'd have to die. Loyal Ferdinand went into the stable to his white horse and wept and wailed, "Oh, what an unlucky person I am!" Then a voice called out behind him, "Loyal Ferdinand, why are you weeping?" He looked around but saw no one and kept on wailing, "Oh, my dear white horse, now I must leave you! Now I must die!" Then the voice again called, "Loyal Ferdinand, why are you weeping?" Then for the first time he noticed that it was his horse that was asking the question. "Are you doing that, horse? Can you talk?" and repeated, "I've got to go to such and such a place and fetch the bride. Do you perhaps know how I'm to do it?" Then the horse answered, "Go to the king and say, if he'll give you what you must have, then you'll get her for him: if he'll give you a shipload of meat and a shipload of bread, it will work. There will be big giants on the water: if you don't bring meat along for them, they'll tear you to pieces. And there will be big birds: they'd peck the eyes out of your head if you didn't have any bread for them."

Then the king had all the butchers in the land slaughter and all the bakers bake, so that the ships were filled. When they were full, the horse said to Loyal Ferdinand, "Now just mount me and go aboard with me. When the giants come, say;

> 'Easy, easy! my dear giants,
> I've made good provision for you,
> I've brought along something for you.'

And when the birds come, repeat,

> 'Easy, easy! my dear giants,
> I've made good provision for you,
> I've brought along something for you.'

Then they won't do anything to you, and when you come to the royal mansion, the giants will help you. Go up to the mansion and take a few giants with you. The princess will be lying there asleep, but you mustn't wake her up. Rather, the giants must pick her up along with the bed and carry her aboard."

Everything happened as the horse had said, and Loyal Ferdinand gave the giants and the birds what he had brought along for them. In return the giants were obliging and carried the princess in her bed to the king. On entering the king's presence, she said she couldn't love him; she'd have to have her papers that were still left in her mansion. Then at Disloyal Ferdinand's suggestion Loyal Ferdinand was summoned and the king commanded him on pain of death to fetch the papers from the royal mansion. Again he went to the stable and wept and said, "Oh, my dear white horse, now once more I must go away! How shall we do it?" Then the white horse said that they should again load the ship full, and it went as before, and the giants and the birds had their fill of meat and were appeased. When they reached the mansion, the horse told him to go into the princess' bedchamber and that the papers would be lying on the table. Loyal Ferdinand went and got them. When they were at sea, he dropped his quill in the water; then the horse said, "Now I can't help you." Then he remembered the flute and began to play it; then the fish came with the quill in its mouth and brought it to him. He brought the papers to the palace where the wedding was to be held.

The queen, however, couldn't love the king because he had no nose, but she could love Loyal Ferdinand very much. So once when all the gentlemen of the court were assembled, the queen said that she, too, could do tricks, that she could cut off a person's head and put it back on, and that someone really ought to try it. Nobody wanted to be the first, so Loyal Ferdinand, again at Disloyal Ferdinand's suggestion, had to be the one. She cut off his head and put it back on him; it healed up immediately, so that it looked as if he had a red thread around his neck. Then the king said to her, "My dear, where did you learn that?" "Oh," she said, "I understand the trick. Shall I try it once on you, too?" "Yes, indeed," he said. Then she cut off his head and didn't put it back on, pretended she couldn't get it on and that it wouldn't stay put. Then the king was buried and she married Loyal Ferdinand.

But he always rode his white horse. Once when he was sitting on it, it told him to go to another heath which it would show him and then to race it around it three times. When he'd done that, the white horse stood up on its hind legs and changed into a king's son.

127 The Iron Stove

Der Eisenofen

IN THE DAYS when wishing still did some good, a king's son was enchanted by an old witch, so that he had to sit in a big iron stove in the forest. He spent many years there, and no one was able to disenchant him. Once a king's daughter came into the forest: she'd got lost and couldn't find the way back to her father's kingdom. She'd been wandering about like that for nine days and finally was standing in front of the iron box. Then a voice came out of it, asking her, "Where do you come from and where are you going?" "I've lost the way to my father's kingdom," she answered, "and can't get back home." Then the voice spoke from out of the iron stove, "I'll help you get back home, and in short order at that, if you'll agree in writing to do what I ask. I am the son of a greater king than he whose daughter you are, and I want to marry you." She got frightened and thought, "Dear Lord, what shall I do with the iron stove!" But because she was so eager to get back home to her father, she agreed in writing to do what it demanded. Then he said, "You're to come back here, bring a knife with you, and scrape a hole in the iron." He gave her someone as an escort who walked beside her and didn't speak, and brought her home in two hours.

Now there was great rejoicing in the palace when the king's daughter returned, and the old king fell on her neck and kissed her. She was, however, very downcast and said, "Father dear, what a time I had! I shouldn't have got back home from out of the big wild forest if I hadn't walked past an iron stove. In return I had to agree in writing to come back to it, disenchant it and marry it." Then the old king was so frightened that he almost fell in a faint, for he had only the one daughter. Accordingly, they took council and planned to send in her place the miller's daughter who was considered to be beautiful. They brought her out there, gave her a knife, and told her to scrape away at the iron stove. She actually scraped for twenty-four hours but couldn't get the least bit of iron off. At daybreak, the voice in the iron stove called, "It seems to me it's day outside." Then she answered, "It seems so to me, too; I think I hear my father's mill clattering." "So you're a miller's daughter! Then get out of the forest at once and have the king's daughter come." She went away and told the old king that the thing out there didn't want her, that it wanted his daughter.

Then the old king was frightened, and the daughter wept. However, they still had a swineherd's daughter who was even more beautiful than the miller's daughter. They were willing to give her a good deal of money if she'd go to the iron stove in place of the king's daughter. So she was brought out there and she, too, had to scrape for twenty-four hours; but she didn't get any iron off. At daybreak, a voice in the stove cried, "It seems to me it's day outside." Then she answered, "It seems so to me, too; I seem to hear my father's horn blowing." "So you're a swineherd's daughter. Go away at once and have the king's daughter come. And tell her that what I promised her will happen to her: if she doesn't come, everything in the whole realm will fall to pieces and collapse, and not one stone will remain on top of another."

When the king's daughter heard that, she began to weep, but now there was nothing else to do, so she had to keep her promise. She said good-bye to her father, put a knife in her bag, and went to the iron stove out in the forest. When she got there, she began to scrape, and the iron yielded, and in two hours she'd already scraped a little hole. Then she peeked in and saw such a fine-looking young man—my! he was glistening with gold and jewels —that she fell straight in love with him. Now she kept on scraping and made the hole big enough for him to get out. Then he said, "You're mine and I'm thine. You're my bride and have disenchanted me."

He wanted to take her with him to his kingdom, but she begged to be allowed to go once again to her father. The king's son granted her this, but she wasn't to say more than three words to her father and then was to come back. So she went home, but she spoke more than three words. Then the iron stove forthwith disappeared and was moved far away over glass mountains and sharp swords; the king's son, however, was disenchanted and was no longer shut up in it. Then she said good-bye to her father and took some money with her, though not much, and went back into the big forest and looked for the iron stove. But it was not to be found. She searched for nine days, then she got so hungry that she didn't know what to do because she had nothing more to live on. When it was evening, she sat down up in a little tree, planning to spend the night there, because she was afraid of the wild animals. When midnight came, she saw from afar a little light and thought, "Oh, I'd surely be saved there," climbed down the tree, and walked toward the light. On the way she said her prayers.

She came to a little old cottage; a lot of grass had grown up around it, and there was a little pile of wood outside. "Alas!" she thought, "where have you got to?" looked in through the window and saw only fat little toads; but there was also a table prettily laid with wine and a roast, and the plates and tumblers were of silver. Then she plucked up courage and knocked. Immediately the fat toad cried,

"Maiden green and small,
Hop-toad,
Hop-toad's puppy!

Hop back and forth,
Look quick and see who's outside."

Then a little toad came along and opened the door for her. When she stepped in, all bade her welcome, and she had to take a seat. They asked, "Where do you come from? Where are you going?" Then she told everything that had happened to her and said, because she had disobeyed the command to say not more than three words, the stove had gone and the king's son as well. Now she was going to wander over hill and dale and search until she found him. Then the old fat toad said,

"Maiden green and small,
Hop-toad,
Hop-toad's puppy!
Hop back and forth,
Bring me the big box."

The little toad went and brought along the box. Afterward they gave her food and drink and took her to a nicely made bed that was like silk and velvet. She lay down in it and slept the sleep of the just. When day came, she got up, and the old toad gave her three pins from the big box. She was to take them along with her; she'd need them, because she had to pass over a high glass mountain and over three sharp swords, and across a large body of water. If she contrived that, she'd recover her beloved. In addition the toad gave her three objects which she was to guard well, namely, three big pins, a plough-wheel, and three nuts.

Thereupon she set out and, on reaching the glass mountain which was very slippery, stuck the three pins first behind her feet and then in front, and in that way got over it. When she was across, she put them in a place which she noted carefully. Next she came to the three sharp swords; there she got on her plough-wheel and coasted across. Finally she came to a large body of water and when she'd crossed that, found herself in a beautiful big mansion. She entered and applied for a job: she was a poor girl and very much wanted to hire out. (But she knew that the king's son was there, whom she had freed from the iron stove in the big forest.) She was engaged at a low wage as a kitchen maid.

Now the king's son already had another girl in mind whom he wanted to marry, for he thought that his former bride had long since died. In the evening after she'd finished washing up and was through work, she felt in her pocket and found the three nuts the old toad had given her. She bit one open and was going to eat the kernel—and lo and behold! there was a magnificent royal gown in it. When the bride heard about this, she begged for the gown and wanted to buy it, saying, "This is no dress for a servant girl." But the latter said no, she wouldn't sell it, but that she might have it if she'd let her do one thing, namely, sleep for one night in her bridegroom's chamber. The bride let her do this, for the gown was very beautiful, and she had none to compare with it. When it was evening, she said to her bridegroom, "The foolish maid wants to sleep in your room." "If you don't mind, I don't either," he said. Nevertheless, she gave the man a glass of wine in which she put a sleeping potion. Thus they both went to sleep in the chamber, and he slept so soundly that she couldn't wake him up. She wept all night and cried out, "I released you from the wild forest and an iron stove, I searched for you and went over a glass mountain, over three sharp swords, and across a big body of water before I found you, and even so you won't listen to me." The servants were sitting outside the chamber door and heard her weeping all night and in the morning told their master.

The next evening after finishing washing up, she bit the second nut open, and there was another and far more beautiful gown in it. When the bride saw that, she wanted to buy it, too, but the girl didn't want money and stipulated that she be allowed to sleep once more in the bridegroom's chamber. But the bride gave him a sleeping potion, and he slept so soundly that he couldn't hear anything. The kitchen maid, however, wept the whole night, crying out, "I released you from a forest and an iron stove, I searched for you and went over a glass mountain, over three sharp swords, and across a big body of water before I found you, and even so you won't listen to me." The servants were sitting outside the chamber door and heard her weeping all night and in the morning told their master.

On the third evening after finishing washing up, she bit the third nut open, and there was an even more beautiful dress in it, covered with pure gold. When the bride saw that, she wanted to have it, but the girl only surrendered it on the condition that she might sleep a third time in the bridegroom's chamber. The king's son was now on his guard and passed up the drink. When she began to weep and cry out, "Dearest love, I freed you from the cruel wild forest and from an iron stove," the king's son jumped up and said, "You are the true bride; you're mine and I'm thine." Thereupon that very night he got into a carriage with her, and they took the false bride's clothes away, so that she couldn't get up. When they came to the great body of water, they ferried across and when they reached the three sharp swords, they got on the plough-wheel, and at the glass mountain they stuck the three pins in. Thus they finally reached the little old cottage. But when they went in, it was a great mansion: the toads were all disenchanted and were all king's children and were very happy. Then the wedding was celebrated, and they stayed on in the mansion, which was much bigger than her father's. But because the old king complained of having to live alone, they went and brought him to their place and had two kingdoms and led a happy married life.

> Then a mouse came,
> And the tale was finished.

128 The Lazy Spinning Woman

Die faule Spinnerin

IN A VILLAGE lived a man and his wife, and the wife was so lazy that she never wanted to do any work. Whatever her husband gave her to spin, she failed to finish, and whatever she did spin, she didn't reel off but left it wound up on the bobbin. When her husband scolded her, she always had a ready answer and would say, "My goodness, how can I reel when I haven't got a reel. You go first into the forest and get me one." "If that's what's the matter," said her husband, "I'll go into the forest and get some wood for one." Then the wife was afraid that if he had the wood, he'd make a reel and that she'd have to reel off the yarn and then start spinning afresh.

She reflected a bit, then a happy thought struck her and she followed her husband secretly into the forest. When he'd climbed a tree to select the wood and cut it, she crept into the bushes below where he could not see her and called up,

> "Whoever cuts wood for a reel will die;
> Whoever reels yarn on it will come to grief."

The man listened, laid down his ax for a moment and reflected on what that might possibly mean. "O well," he said finally, "what can it have been? You were just hearing things. Don't let yourself be needlessly frightened." Accordingly he took up his ax again and was about to start chopping when the voice again called up from below,

> "Whoever cuts wood for a reel will die;
> Whoever reels yarn on it will come to grief."

He stopped, got frightened and scared and thought about the matter. However, after a few minutes he plucked up courage again, reached for the ax for the third time, and was about to start chopping. But for the third time a voice called out and said loudly,

> "Whoever cuts wood for a reel will die;
> Whoever reels yarn on it will come to grief."

Then he'd had enough of it and lost all enthusiasm and hurriedly climbed down the tree and set out for home. His wife ran as fast as she could through the bypaths in order to get home first. When he stepped into the living room, she was all innocence—as if nothing had happened—and said, "Well, have you brought a good stick for a reel?" "No," he said, "it's clear to me we must give up the idea of your reeling," told her what had happened to him in the forest, and from then on left her in peace about it.

Soon after, however, the husband again began to get annoyed at the mess in the house. "Woman," he said, "it's a perfect disgrace to leave your spun yarn there on the bobbin. "Do you know what?" she said. "Since we haven't managed to contrive a reel, you get up in the loft and I'll stand down below. Then I'll throw the bobbin up to you and you throw it down and that way there'll be a skein just the same." "Yes, that will be all right," said her husband. So they did this. When they had finished, he said, "Now the yarn is skeined; now it must be scoured as well." Again the wife got alarmed and said, "Yes, we'll scour it the first thing to-morrow morning." Nevertheless, she thought up a new trick. Early in the morning she got up, made a fire, and put the kettle on, but instead of yarn she put in a lump of tow and let it boil. Then she went to her husband who was still in bed and said to him, "I've got to go out for a bit. While I'm out, you get up and look to the yarn that's in the kettle on the fire. But you must do it in time—now pay attention!—for if the cock crows and you haven't attended to it, the yarn will turn into tow." Not wanting to leave anything undone the husband was prompt, got up as quick as he could and went into the kitchen. But when he reached the kettle and looked in, to his alarm he saw only a lump of tow. Then the poor husband kept as still as a mouse, thought that he'd blundered and was to blame in the matter, and in the future said nothing about yarn or spinning.

But you yourself must admit that she was a horrid woman.

129 The Four Skillful Brothers

Die vier kunstreichen Brüder

THERE WAS ONCE A POOR MAN who had four sons. When they grew up, he said to them, "Dear children, now you must go out in the world. I have nothing to give you. Set out and go abroad, learn a trade and see how you fare." Then the four brothers got ready for their journey, said good-bye to their father, and went out the gate together. When they'd been traveling for some time, they came to a crossroads which led in four different directions. "Here we must part," said the eldest, "but four years from today let's meet again at this spot and in the meanwhile try our luck."

Each went his way, and the eldest met a man who asked him where he was going and what he intended to do. "I want to learn a trade," he answered. Then the man said, "Come with me and become a thief." "No," he answered, "that's no longer considered a reputable trade, and the end of the story is that one swings for it." "Oh," said the man, "you needn't be afraid of the gallows: I'll simply teach you how to fetch what nobody else can get, and where no one will get on your track." He let himself be persuaded, under the man's schooling became an expert thief, and acquired such skill that once he really wanted it, nothing was safe from him. The second brother met a man who put the same question to him: what did he want to learn abroad. "I don't know yet," he answered. "Well, come with me and become an astronomer. There's nothing better than that; nothing stays hidden from one." He accepted the proposal and became so skilled an astronomer that when he was through studying and was going to move on, his master gave him a telescope and said to him, "With this you can see what goes on on earth and in the heavens, and nothing can stay hidden from you." The third brother was taken as an apprentice by a huntsman who gave him such good instruction in everything that had to do with huntsmanship that he became an expert huntsman. On parting, the master made him a present of a gun, saying, "It doesn't miss. Whatever you train the bead on, you're sure to hit." The youngest brother, likewise, met a man who spoke to him and asked him his plans. "Don't you want to become a tailor?" "I don't know," said the boy. "Sitting cross-legged from morning to night, sweeping back and forth with the needle, and using the goose doesn't appeal to me." "My goodness!" answered the man, "you talk according to your lights. You'll learn a very different kind of tailoring from me, one that's respectable and proper, in a way quite reputable." He let himself be persuaded, went along with him, and learned the man's trade from the bottom up. On parting, the latter gave him a needle, saying, "With this you can sew up whatever you're faced with, be it soft as an egg or hard as steel. It will become all one piece and not a stitch will show."

When the four years agreed upon were up, the four brothers met at the same time at the crossroad, embraced and kissed one another, and returned home to their father. "Well," said the latter, "what wind blew you all back here to me at once?" They told him how they'd fared and that each had learned his trade. One afternoon they were sitting outside the house under a big tree, when their father said, "Now I'm going to test you and see what you can do." Looking up, he said to the second son, "Up there in the top of this tree between two branches is a chaffinch's nest. Tell me how many eggs are in it." The astronomer took his glass, looked up, and said, "Five." To the eldest the father said, "Fetch down the eggs without disturbing the broody bird that's sitting on them." The skillful thief climbed up and took the five eggs from under the bird, which noticed nothing and remained quietly sitting there, and brought them down to his father. His father took them, placed one at each corner of the table and the fifth in the middle, and said to the huntsman, "Shoot the five eggs in two in the middle with one shot." The huntsman aimed his gun and shot the eggs as his father requested—all five, and actually with one shot. (He must certainly have had some of that gunpowder that shoots around a corner.) "Now it's your turn," said the father to the fourth son. "You sew the eggs together again, also the young birds that are in them, and in just such a way that the shot will have done them no harm." The tailor got his needle and sewed as his father had requested. When he'd finished, the thief had to carry the eggs back up the tree into the nest and put them under the bird again without its noticing anything. The little creature sat her full time, and a few days later the chicks crept out of the eggs and where the tailor had sewed them together had a red line around their necks. "Yes," said the father to his sons, "I can't but praise you to the skies. You've improved your time and learned something useful and good. I can't say which of you deserves the palm. If you only get a chance soon to apply your skill, it will become apparent enough."

Not long after there was a great commotion in the country: the king's daughter had been carried off by a dragon. The king grieved over this night and day and announced that whoever brought her back should have her in marriage. Amongst themselves the four brothers said, "That would be a chance to show off our skills," and wanted to set out together and free the king's daughter. "I'll soon find out where she is," said the astronomer, who, looking through his telescope, said, "I already see her; she's sitting far away from here on a rock in the sea, and beside her is the dragon who is guarding her." Then he went to the king and begged for a ship for himself and his brothers, and with them journeyed across the sea until they came to the rock.

The king's daughter was sitting there, but the dragon was lying asleep in her lap. "I mustn't shoot," said the huntsman. "I'd kill the beautiful maiden at the same time." "Then I'll try my luck," said the thief, crept up and stole her from under the dragon but so quietly and deftly that the monster noticed nothing and just snored on. Joyfully they hurried with her aboard the ship and headed for the open sea. The dragon, however, who on waking up missed the king's daughter, came after them, snorting furiously through the air. When it was hovering right over the ship and was about to pounce upon it, the huntsman aimed his gun and shot it through the heart. The monster dropped dead but it was so terribly big that in its fall it smashed the whole ship to bits. Luckily they got hold of a few planks and swam about in the open sea. Thus they were again in dire straits, but the tailor, never slow on the job, took his marvelous needle, hastily basted the planks together with a few big stitches, got on them and gathered up all the pieces of the ship. These, too, he sewed together so skillfully that in short order the ship was again ready to sail, and they were able to travel home safely.

When the king saw his daughter again, there was great rejoicing. He said to the four brothers, "One of you shall have her in marriage, but settle among yourselves which it's to be." Then a violent argument arose among them, for each advanced his claims. The astronomer said, "If I hadn't seen the king's daughter, all your arts would have been in vain: therefore she's mine." The thief said, "What good would seeing her have done if I hadn't got her out from under the dragon? Therefore she's mine." The huntsman said, "You and the king's daughter would have been torn to pieces by the monster if my bullet hadn't hit it: therefore she's mine." The tailor said, "And if I hadn't patched up the ship for you with my skill, you would all have drowned miserably: therefore she's mine." Then the king made the award: "Each of you has an equal claim, and because you can't all have the maiden, none of you shall have her. However, as a reward I shall give each one half a kingdom." This decision pleased the brothers, and they said, "It's better so than that we should fall at odds." Then each received half a kingdom, and they lived very happily with their father as long as it pleased God.

130 One-Eye, Two-Eyes, and Three-Eyes

Einäuglein, Zweiäuglein und Dreiäuglein

THERE WAS A WOMAN who had three daughters. The eldest was called One-Eye because she only had a single eye in the middle of her forehead, the middle daughter was called Two-Eyes because she had two eyes like other human beings, and the youngest was called Three-Eyes because she had three eyes; in her case, too, the third eye was right in the middle of her forehead. But because Two-Eyes didn't look any different from other people, her sisters and her mother couldn't abide her. "You with your two eyes!" they'd say to her. "You're no better than the common run of people. You don't belong to us." They pushed her about, threw her poor cast-off clothes, only gave her their left-overs to eat, and hurt her in every way they could.

Once Two-Eyes had to go out in the fields and tend the goat, but she was still very hungry because her sisters had given her so little to eat. She sat down on a balk and began to weep and wept so hard that two little brooks flowed from her eyes. When once in her distress she looked up, a woman was standing beside her, who asked, "Two-Eyes, why are you weeping?" Two-Eyes answered, "I have good reason to weep. Because I have two eyes like other people, my sisters and my mother can't abide me, push me from corner to corner, throw me old cast-off clothes, and only give me their left-overs to eat. Today they gave me so little that I'm still very hungry." The wise woman said, "Two-Eyes, dry your face. I'll tell you something so you won't be hungry any more. Just say to your goat,

'Goat, bleat!
Table, be set.'

Then a nicely set table will be standing before you with the finest food upon it, so that you can eat to your heart's content.

When you've eaten your fill and don't need the table any longer, just say,

'Goat, bleat!'
Table, be gone!'

Then it will disappear again before your eyes." Thereupon the wise woman went away. Now Two-Eyes thought, "I must try at once and see if what she said is true, for I'm far too hungry," and said,

"Goat, bleat!
Table, be set!"

Scarcely had she uttered the words when a table was standing there, covered with a white cloth, on it a plate and knife and fork and silver spoon. On it were the finest dishes, steaming and still warm, as if they'd just come from the kitchen. Then Two-Eyes repeated the shortest grace she knew, "Lord God, be our guest at all times. Amen," helped herself and enjoyed it greatly. And when she'd had her fill, she said, as the wise woman had taught her,

"Goat, bleat!
Table, be gone!"

Immediately the table and everything on it vanished again. "That's a fine way to keep house," thought Two-Eyes and was very happy and in good spirits. In the evening when she came home with the goat, she found an earthenware bowl with food that her sisters had put out for her. She didn't touch it, however. The next day she again went out with her goat and left untouched the few scraps that had been offered her. The first time and the second time the sisters didn't notice it at all, but when it happened every time, they did take notice and said, "Things aren't right with Two-Eyes. She leaves the food untouched every time, and yet she used to eat up everything that was offered her. She must have found other ways and means."

To get at the truth of the matter, when Two-Eyes drove the goat to pasture, One-Eye was to go along and see what she did out there, and whether anyone brought her any food or drink. Now when Two-Eyes set out again, One-Eye went to her and said, "I'm going along into the fields to see that the goat is properly tended and driven to where the grass is good." Two-Eyes saw, however, what One-Eye had in mind and, driving the goat out to the tall grass, said, "Come, One-Eye, let's sit down. I'll sing you something." One-Eye sat down and was tired from the unaccustomed walk and the heat of the sun, and Two-Eyes kept singing,

> "One-Eye, are you awake?
> One-Eye, are you asleep?"

Then One-Eye shut her one eye and fell asleep. When Two-Eyes saw that One-Eye was fast asleep and couldn't reveal anything, she said,

> "Goat, bleat!
> Table, be set!"

sat down at her table, and ate and drank her fill. Then again she called out,

> "Goat, bleat!
> Table, be gone!"

and everything at once vanished. Two-Eyes now woke One-Eye up and said, "One-Eye, you want to tend the goat and fall asleep doing it! Come, let's go home." They went home, and Two-Eyes again left her bowl untouched, and One-Eye was unable to reveal to her mother why she wouldn't eat, saying by way of excuse, "I fell asleep out there."

The next day the mother said to Three-Eyes, "This time you're to go and find out whether Two-Eyes eats out there, and if anybody brings her food and drink, because she must be eating and drinking on the sly." Then Three-Eyes went to Two-Eyes and said, "I'm going along to see whether the goat's properly tended and driven to where the grass is good." But Two-Eyes saw what Three-Eyes had in mind and, driving the goat out to the tall grass, said, "Let's sit down here, Three-Eyes. I'll sing you something." Three-Eyes sat down and was tired from the walk and the heat of the sun, and Two-Eyes again began the song she'd sung before and sang,

> "Three-Eyes, are you awake?"

but instead of now singing, as she should have done,

> "Three-Eyes, are you asleep?"

she inadvertently sang,

> "*Two*-Eyes, are you asleep?

and kept singing,

> "Three-Eyes, are you awake?
> *Two*-Eyes, are you asleep?"

Then two of Three-Eyes' eyes closed and went to sleep, but the third eye, because it wasn't addressed by the little rhyme, didn't go to sleep. To be sure, Three-Eyes closed it, but only as a trick, just as if it had gone to sleep with the others. Nevertheless, it blinked and could see everything very well indeed. When Two-Eyes thought that Three-Eyes was fast asleep, she said her little rhyme,

> "Goat, bleat!
> Table, be set!"

ate and drank to her heart's content and then bade the table be gone again, saying,

> "Goat, bleat!
> Table, be gone!"

Three-Eyes had seen everything. Then Two-Eyes went to her, woke her up and said, "My, Three-Eyes! Did you fall asleep? You're a good goatherd! Come, let's go home." When they got home, again Two-Eyes ate nothing, and Three-Eyes said to her mother, "Now I know why the proud creature doesn't eat. When she says to the goat out there,

> 'Goat, bleat!
> Table, be set!'

then a table stands before her set with the best food, much better than what we have here. And when she's eaten her fill, she says,

> 'Goat, bleat!
> Table, begone!'

and everything vanishes. I saw it all quite clearly. She put two of my eyes to sleep with a little rhyme, but the one in my forehead luckily stayed awake." Then the envious mother cried, "Do you think you're going to live better than we? You'll lose your taste for that!" fetched a butcher's knife and stuck it into the goat's heart so that it dropped dead.

When Two-Eyes saw that, she went sadly out, sat down on a balk in the field, and wept bitter tears. Suddenly the wise woman was again standing beside her and said, "Two-Eyes, why are you weeping?" "I have good reason to weep," she answered. "My mother stabbed to death the goat which set my table so beautifully every day when I recited your little rhyme. Now I'll have to suffer from hunger and sorrow again." "Two-Eyes," said the wise woman, "I'll give you a good piece of advice: ask your sisters to give you the entrails of the slaughtered goat and bury them in the earth outside the front door. It will bring you luck." She disappeared, and Two-Eyes went home and said to her sisters, "Dear sisters, please give me some part of my goat. I don't ask for anything that's any good; just give me the entrails." Then they laughed and said, "You may have them if that's all you want." Two-Eyes took the entrails and in the evening, according to the wise woman's instructions, buried them secretly outside the front door.

The next morning when they were all awake and stepped outside the front door, there stood a wonderful and splendid tree with leaves of silver, and hanging among them fruit of gold more beautiful and more delicious than anything in the whole wide world. They didn't know how the tree had got there in the night, but Two-Eyes saw that it had grown out of the goat's entrails, for it was standing on the exact spot where she'd buried them in the earth. Then the mother said to One-Eye, "Climb up, my child, and pick the fruit for us." One-Eye climbed up, but as she was about to take hold of one of the gold apples, the branch flew out of her hands. That happened every time, so that she wasn't able to pick a single apple, no matter how she stood. Then the mother said, "Three-Eyes, you climb up. With your three eyes you can look about better than One-Eye." One-Eye slid down and Three-Eyes climbed up, but she was no more skillful, and watch as sharp as she might, the gold apples always drew away. Finally the mother grew impatient and herself climbed up but could get hold of the fruit no better than One-Eye and Three-Eyes and just kept reaching into space. Then Two-Eyes said, "I'll go up. Perhaps I'll be more successful." "You with your two eyes!" cried the sisters. "What do you think you can do?" Nevertheless, Two-Eyes climbed up, and the gold apples didn't draw away from her but of their own accord lowered themselves into her hand so that she was able to pick one after another, and brought down a whole apron full. Her mother took them away from her, and instead of treating poor Two-Eyes any better on this account, as they should have done, her mother and One-Eye and Three-Eyes were merely jealous that she alone was able to get the fruit and were only the harsher with her.

Once when they were standing together by the tree, a young knight happened to come by. "Quick, Two-Eyes! creep under there, so we won't have to be ashamed of you," and in all haste tipped an empty cask that was right by the tree over poor Two-Eyes and also shoved under it the gold apples which she had picked. When the knight got nearer, he turned out to be a handsome gentleman who stopped, admired the splendid gold and silver tree, and said to the two sisters, "Who does this beautiful tree belong to? Whoever will give me a branch from it may in return ask for what they want." Then One-Eye and Three-Eyes answered that the tree was theirs and that, of course, they'd break off a branch for him. They both worked hard at it but couldn't do it, for every time the branches and fruit drew away from them. Then the knight said, "It's certainly strange that the tree belongs to you and yet you haven't got the power to break anything off it." They insisted that the tree was theirs. While they were talking thus, Two-Eyes pushed a few gold apples out from under the cask so that they rolled to the feet of the knight, for Two-Eyes was angry that One-Eye and Three-Eyes weren't telling the truth. When the knight saw the apples, he was astonished and asked where they came from. One-Eye and Three-Eyes answered that they had another sister who wasn't, however, allowed to appear because she had only two eyes like other ordinary people. But the knight demanded to see her and cried, "Two-Eyes, come out!" Then Two-Eyes came quite happily out from under the cask, and the knight marveled at her great beauty and said,

"You, Two-Eyes, can surely break off a branch of the tree for me." "Yes," answered Two-Eyes, "of course I can do that, for the tree belongs to me." She climbed up and with next to no trouble broke off a branch with fine silver leaves and gold fruit and handed it to the knight. Then the knight said, "Two-Eyes, what shall I give you in return?" "Alas," answered Two-Eyes, "from early morning till late at night I suffer from hunger and thirst, trouble and distress. If you'll take me with you and free me, I'd be happy." Then the knight lifted her onto his horse and took her to his father's mansion. There he gave her fine clothes, food and drink to her heart's content, and because he loved her so, he had the marriage benediction said over them, and the wedding was celebrated amid great rejoicing.

When Two-Eyes was carried off this way by the handsome knight, the two sisters at first very much envied her her luck. "However, the wonderful tree remains in our hands," they thought. "Even if we can't pick any fruit from it, just the same everybody will stop in front of it, come to us, and praise it. Who knows where our luck may yet lie!" But the next morning the tree had vanished and with it their hopes, and when Two-Eyes looked out of her chamber, there to her great joy it was standing outside and thus had followed her.

Two-Eyes lived happily for a long time. Once two poor women came to her at the mansion and begged for alms. Two-Eyes looked at them closely and recognized her sisters One-Eye and Three-Eyes, who had got so poor that they were wandering about and had to beg for bread from door to door. Two-Eyes bade them welcome, however, was kind to them and looked after them, so that both regretted deeply the wrong they had done to their sister in their youth.

131   Pretty Katy and Pif-Paf-Poltrie

Die schöne Katrinelje und Pif Paf Poltrie

"GOOD DAY, Father Elder-Tea." "Thanks so much, Pif-Paf-Poltrie." "Might I possibly marry your daughter?" "O yes, you may if Mother Milch-Cow, Brother Haughty-Proud, Sister Cheese-Dear, and pretty Katy are willing."

"Where is Mother Milch-Cow?"
"She's in the barn milking the cow."

"Good day, Mother Milch-Cow." "Thanks so much, Pif-Paf-Poltrie." "Might I possibly marry your daughter?" "O yes, you may if Father Elder-Tea, Brother Haughty-Proud, Sister Cheese-Dear, and pretty Katy are willing."

"Where is Brother Haughty-Proud?"
"He's in the shed chopping wood."

"Good day, Brother Haughty-Proud." "Thanks so much, Pif-Paf-Poltrie." "Might I possibly marry your sister?" "O yes, you may if Father Elder-Tea, Mother Milch-Cow, Sister Cheese-Dear, and pretty Katy are willing."

"Where is Sister Cheese-Dear?"
"She's in the garden cutting herbs."

"Good day, Sister Cheese-Dear." "Thanks so much, Pif-Paf-Poltrie." "Might I possibly marry your sister?" "O yes, you may if Father Elder-Tea, Mother Milch-Cow, Brother Haughty-Proud, and pretty Katy are willing."

"Where is pretty Katy?"
"She's in her room counting her pennies."

"Good day, pretty Katy." "Thanks so much, Pif-Paf-Poltrie." "Will you be my sweetheart?" "O yes, I will if Father Elder-Tea, Mother Milch-Cow, Brother Haughty-Proud, and Sister

Cheese-Dear are willing." "Pretty Katy, how much dowry have you got?" "Fourteen pennies in cash, two and a half farthings due me, half a pound of dried fruit, a handful of pretzels, a handful of roots.

And so it was:
Isn't that a good dowry?"

"Pif-Paf-Poltrie, what trade do you know? Are you a tailor?" "Much better than that." "A shoemaker?" "Much better than that." "A plowman?" "Much better than that." "A joiner?" "Much better than that." "A smith?" "Much better than that." "A miller?" "Much better than that." "A broommaker, perhaps?" "Yes, that's what I am. Isn't that a fine trade?"

132 The Fox and the Horse

Der Fuchs und das Pferd

A FARMER had a faithful horse that had grown old and could no longer do its work. Its master didn't want to feed it any more and said, "I certainly can't use you any longer. Just the same, I have your interest at heart: show that you're still strong enough to bring me a lion, and I'll keep you, but for the present get out of my stable." Thereupon he chased it out into the fields.

The horse was sad and went to the forest to seek a little shelter from the weather. There he met a fox who said, "Why are you hanging your head and walking about in so solitary a fashion?" "Alas," answered the horse, "greed and loyalty do not live together in one dwelling. My master has forgotten the services I rendered him for so many years, and because I really can't plow any more, he will no longer feed me and has chased me away." "Without a word of consolation?" asked the fox. "The consolation was cold: he said if I was still strong enough to bring him a lion, he'd keep me, but he knows well enough that I can't do that." "I'll help you out of this," said the fox. "Just lie down, stretch out, and don't move—as if you were dead." The horse did what the fox ordered.

The fox, however, went to a lion whose den was not far off and said, "There's a dead horse out there. Just come with me and you can have a big meal." The lion went with the fox, and as they were standing by the horse, the fox said, "It really isn't very convenient for you here. Do you know what? I'll tie it to you by its tail so that you can drag it into your den and consume it in perfect peace and quiet." The lion liked the idea, took up its position, and kept very quiet so the fox could tie the horse to it. But the fox tied the lion's legs together with the horse's tail and twisted and laced it all so thoroughly and firmly that it couldn't possibly be pulled apart by force. When the fox had finished its work, it tapped the horse on the shoulder and said, "Pull, horse, pull!" Then the horse gave a sudden jump and dragged the lion away with it. The lion began to roar so loud that all the birds in the forest flew up in the air in terror, but the horse let it roar, pulled and dragged it over the fields to its master's door. When the master saw that, he thought better of himself and said to the horse, "You're to stay with me and live comfortably," and gave it all it wanted to eat until it died.

133   The Worn-Out Dancing-Slippers

Die zertanzten Schuhe

THERE WAS ONCE A KING who had twelve daughters, each more beautiful than the other. They slept together in a big room where their beds stood side by side, and at night when they were in bed, the king would shut the door and bolt it. But when he'd open the door in the morning, he'd see that their slippers were worn out from dancing, and no one could discover how that had happened. Then the king had it proclaimed that whoever could find out where they danced during the night might choose one of them as his bride and be king after him. If, however, anybody presented himself and didn't find out after three days and three nights, his life would be forfeit.

It wasn't long before a king's son presented himself and offered to undertake the venture. He was well received and at night was conducted to a room adjoining the maidens' bedchamber. His bed was set up there, and he was to watch out and see where they went and danced. In order that they might do nothing secretly or go out anywhere else, the chamber door, too, was left open. Nevertheless, the eyes of the king's son got as heavy as lead, and he fell asleep. When he woke up in the morning, all twelve had been to the dance, for their slippers were there and had holes in the soles. It went no differently the second and the third night, and then his head was struck off without mercy. Many more came after that and presented themselves for the venture, but all were fated to lose their lives.

Now it happened that a poor soldier, who was suffering from a wound and could no longer do military service, found himself on the way to the city where the king dwelt. There he met an old woman who asked him where he was going. "I really don't know myself," he said and added jokingly, "I'd like to find out where the king's daughters wear out their slippers dancing, and thus become king." "That's not so hard," said the old woman. "You mustn't drink the wine that will be brought you at night, and you must pretend to have gone fast asleep." Thereupon she gave him a little cloak and said, "When you put that on, you'll be invisible and can then stalk the twelve maidens."

When the soldier got this good advice, he took the matter seriously, plucked up courage, went before the king and presented himself as a suitor. He was received as well as the others had been and was dressed in royal clothes. That evening at bedtime he was led to the anteroom and when he was going to bed, the eldest daughter came and brought him a tumbler of wine. He had, however, tied a sponge under his chin, let the wine run into it, and didn't drink a drop. Then he lay down and after lying there a while, began to snore as if he were sleeping very soundly. The king's twelve daughters heard it and laughed, and the eldest said, "He, too, might have saved his life." Then they got up, opened wardrobes, chests, and boxes, and got out splendid clothes. They decked themselves out before the mirrors, skipped about, and looked forward joyfully to the dance. But the youngest said, "I don't know. You're happy, but I have a strange feeling: a misfortune is surely going to befall us." "You're a perfect goose," said the eldest, "always scared! Have you forgotten how many kings' sons have already been here in vain? I really needn't have given the soldier a potion; the lout wouldn't have waked up anyway."

When they were all ready, they first took a look at the soldier, but he had his eyes shut, neither moved nor stirred, and they believed that they were now quite safe. Then the eldest went to her bed and knocked on it. Immediately it sank into the floor, and they climbed down through the opening, one after the other, the eldest leading the way. The soldier, who had seen the whole thing, didn't hesitate long, threw on his cloak, and climbed down with them, following the youngest. Halfway down the stairs he stepped slightly on her dress. Then she got frightened and cried, "What's that? Who's holding my dress?" "Don't be so silly," said the eldest. "You caught on a hook." They went all the way down and when they were at the bottom, found themselves in a most splendid avenue of trees; all the leaves were of silver and glistened and shone. "You'd better take a token along with you," thought the soldier and broke off a branch. Then a tremendous crackling noise issued from the tree, and again the youngest cried, "Things aren't right! Did you hear the report?" But the eldest said, "Those are shots of joyful celebration because we shall soon have freed our princes." Next they came to an avenue of trees where all the leaves were of gold, and finally to a third where they were of clear diamonds. From both these he broke off a branch, and each time there was a report, so that the youngest started in terror. The eldest, however, maintained that they were shots of joyful celebration. They went on and came to a big body of water; on it were twelve skiffs and in each skiff was sitting a handsome prince. They had been waiting for the twelve maidens, and each took one to himself, while the soldier got in with the youngest. Then the prince said, "I don't know! The boat's much heavier today, and I have to row as hard as I can to make any headway." "What can be the cause of that but the warm weather?" said the youngest. "I feel quite warm, too." On the other side of the water stood a beautiful mansion, brightly lighted, from which came a jolly sound of drums and trumpets. They rowed across, went in, and each prince danced with his beloved, and the soldier danced along invisibly. Whenever one of the maidens was holding a tumbler of wine, he'd drain it dry by the time she got it to her mouth. The youngest was worried about that, too, but the eldest kept silencing her. They danced there till three the next morning; then all the slippers were worn through from dancing, and they had to stop. The princes brought them back across the water, and this time the soldier sat up front by the eldest. On the shore they took leave of their princes and promised to come back the following night. When they got to the stairs, the soldier ran ahead and lay down in his bed, and when the twelve came tripping slowly and wearily in, he was already again snoring so loud that they could all hear it. "We're safe as far as he's concerned," they said. Then they took off their fine clothes, put them away, placed the worn-out dancing slippers under their beds and lay down.

The next morning the soldier decided not to say anything but rather to observe the strange business some more, and went again on the second and third nights. It was all like the first time, and each time they danced until their slippers were in shreds. The third time he took along a tumbler as a token.

When the hour arrived when he was to answer up, he took the three branches and the tumbler and went before the king while the twelve maidens stood behind the door and listened to what he might say. When the king put the question, "Where did my daughters wear out their dancing slippers during the night?" he answered, "With twelve princes in an underground mansion," reported how it happened and took out the tokens. Then the king had his daughters come and asked them if the soldier had told the truth. When they saw that they were betrayed and that there was no use denying it, they had to confess everything. Then the king asked him which one he wanted to marry. "I'm no longer young," he answered, "so give me the eldest." The wedding was celebrated that very same day, and the kingdom was promised him after the king's death.

The princes were again enchanted for as many days as the number of nights they had danced with the twelve maidens.

134   The Six Servants

Die sechs Diener

LONG, LONG AGO there lived an old queen. She was an enchantress, and her daughter was the most beautiful maiden under the sun. But the old woman thought only of how she might lure people to their destruction, and whenever a suitor turned up, she said that whoever wanted to marry her daughter would first have to perform a certain task or die. Many were dazzled by the maiden's beauty and indeed took the risk, but they couldn't carry out the task the old woman assigned them. Then no favor was shown: they had to kneel down, and their heads were struck off.

There was a king's son who also had heard of the maiden's great beauty and said to his father, "Let me go there. I want to sue for her hand." "Never in the world," answered the king. "If you go, it will be your death." Then the son took to his bed and became mortally ill and lay there for seven years, and no doctor could help him. When the father saw that there was no more hope, sad of heart he said to him, "Go and try your luck. I know of no other way to help you." When the son heard this, he rose from his bed, got well, and set out joyfully.

As he was riding across a heath, it happened that he saw from afar something like a big hay pile on the ground, and as he got nearer, he was able to make out that it was the belly of a man who had stretched out there. The belly, however, looked like a small mountain. When the fat man saw the traveler, he straightened up and said, "If you need someone, take me in your service." The king's son answered, "What can I do with such an unwieldy man?" "Oh," said the fat man, "that's just nothing. When I really stretch myself out, I'm three thousand times as fat." "If that's the way it is," said the king's son, "I can use you. Come along with me."

Then the fat man walked along behind the king's son, and

after a while they found another man, lying on the ground with his ear to the grass. "What are you doing there?" asked the king's son. "I'm listening," answered the man. "What are you listening to so attentively?" "I'm listening to what's going on in the world right now, for nothing escapes my ear. I even hear the grass grow." The king's son asked, "Tell me, what do you hear at the court of the old queen who has the beautiful daughter?" "I hear the swish of the sword that's striking off a suitor's head," he answered. "I can use you," said the king's son. "Come along with me."

They went on and by and by saw a pair of feet lying there, also part of the legs, but they couldn't see where they ended. After going on quite a way, they came to the body and finally reached the head, too. "My!" said the king's son, "what a long string-bean you are!" "Oh," answered the tall man, "that's nothing. When I stretch my limbs out properly, I'm three thousand times as long and taller than the highest mountain in the world. I'll gladly serve you if you will take me on." "Come along," said the king's son. "I can use you."

They went on and found a man sitting by the wayside with his eyes blindfolded. The king's son said to him, "Are your eyes so weak that you can't look into the light?" "No," answered the man. "I mustn't take off the bandage, because my look is so powerful that whatever I look at with my eyes bursts to pieces. If that can be of any use to you, I'll gladly serve you." "Come along," answered the king's son. "I can use you."

They went on and found a man lying in the hot sun, and his whole body was freezing cold and shaking so that not a limb was still. "How can you be freezing in this warm sunshine?" said the king's son. "Oh," answered the man, "my nature is of quite a different sort: the hotter it is, the more I freeze, and the frost pierces my very marrow. And the colder it is, the hotter I get; in the midst of ice I can't stand it for the heat, nor in the midst of fire for the cold." "You're a strange fellow," said the king's son, "but if you're willing to serve me, then come along."

Now they went on and saw a man stretching his neck way out, looking about and out over all the mountains. "What are you looking at so eagerly?" said the king's son. The man answered, "My eyes are so keen that I can see over all forests and fields, valleys and mountains, and throughout the whole world." "If you want to," said the king's son, "then come with me, for I'm still one short."

With his six servants the king's son now went into the city where the old queen lived. He didn't tell who he was but said, "If you will give me your beautiful daughter in marriage, I'll carry out whatever task you set me." The enchantress was delighted that such a handsome young man had again fallen into her snares and said, "I'll set you three tasks; if you accomplish all three, you will become my daughter's lord and master."

"What may the first be?" he asked. "That you fetch me a ring that I dropped into the Red Sea." Then the king's son went back to his servants and said, "The first task isn't easy: a ring has to be fetched out of the Red Sea. Now for some advice!" Then the man with the keen eyes said, "I'll see where it is," looked down into the sea and said, "It's caught there on a pointed rock." The tall man carried them there and said, "I'd easily get it out if only I could see it." "Is that all there's to it!" cried the fat man, lay down, and put his mouth to the water. Then the waves flowed into it as into an abyss and he drank up the whole sea so that it got as dry as a meadow. The tall man bent over a little and took the ring out with his hand. Now when he had the ring, the king's son was happy and brought it to the old queen. She was astonished and said, "Yes, that's the right ring.

"You've accomplished the first task successfully, but now comes the second. You see the meadow over there in front of my palace? Three hundred fat oxen are grazing on it: you must consume them hide and hair, bones and horns. And down in the cellar are three hundred casks of wine that you must also drink up. If one hair is left from the oxen or one single drop of wine, your life will be forfeited to me." "Can't I invite any guests? A meal without company has no taste." The old woman laughed maliciously and answered, "You may invite one person to keep you company, but not another one." Then going to his servants the king's son said to the fat man, "Today you shall be my guest and for once in your life eat your fill." Then the fat man extended himself and ate the three hundred oxen so that not a hair was left and asked if there wasn't going to be anything but breakfast. He drank the wine right out of the casks without needing a glass, and swallowed down the last drop.

When the meal was over, the king's son went to the old woman and told her that the second task was accomplished. She marveled, saying, "Up to now nobody has got that far, but there's still one task left," thinking, "You won't escape me and won't keep your head on." "This evening," she said, "I shall bring my daughter to you in your room, and you're to put your arms about her, and while you're sitting there together, watch out not to fall asleep. I shall come at the stroke of twelve, and if then she's no longer in your arms, you've lost out." "That task is easy," thought the king's son. "Of course I'll keep my eyes open." Nevertheless, he called his servants, related to them what the old woman had told him, and said, "Who knows what trick lies behind this! Caution is advisable: you keep watch and see to it that the maiden doesn't get out of my room again." When evening came, the old woman brought her daughter and put her in the arms of the king's son. Then the tall man coiled himself around the two of them, while the fat man took up a position outside the door so that not a living soul could get in. There they both sat, and the maiden didn't say a word, but the moon shone through the window on her face so that he could see her marvelous beauty. He did nothing but look at her, was filled with joy and love, and no weariness fell upon his eyes. That lasted till eleven, then the old woman cast a spell over them all so that they fell asleep, and at that moment, too, the maiden was spirited away. They slept soundly till a quarter to twelve, then the magic lost its power and they all woke up again. "Oh, alack, alas!" cried the king's son. "Now I am lost!" The faithful servants, too, began to lament, but the Listener said, "Be still! I'm going to listen," listened a minute then said, "She's sitting in a rocky crag three hundred hours' walk from here and is lamenting her fate. Tall Man, you alone can help us. If you stand up at full length, you'll be there in a couple of strides." "Yes," answered the tall man, "but the man with the keen eyes has got to come along with me so that we can get the crag out of the way." Then the tall man took the blindfolded man on his back, and in no time at all they were in front of the enchanted crag. As soon as the tall man took the bandage off the other's eyes and the latter looked about, the crag burst into a thousand pieces. Then the tall man took the maiden in his arms, carried her back in a trice, fetched his companion just as quickly, and before it struck twelve, they were all seated again as before and were merry and in high spirits. When twelve struck, the old enchantress came creeping up, made a mocking face as if to say, "Now he's mine," and thought that her daughter was sitting in the crag three hundred hours away. But when she saw her daughter in the arms of the king's son, she was terrified and said, "There is one who is mightier than I." However, she could raise no objection and had to concede the maiden to him.

Then she whispered in the maiden's ear, "Disgraceful you have to obey common people and are not allowed to pick a husband to your liking!" Then the maiden's proud heart was filled with anger and she plotted revenge. The next morning she had three hundred cords of wood brought, said to the king's son that the three tasks had been accomplished, but that she wouldn't become his wife until someone was willing to sit in the middle of the pile of wood and endure the fire. She didn't suppose that any of his servants would burn themselves up for him, and that for love of her he himself would sit down in it, and that then she'd be free. But the servants said, "We've all done something except the frosty man. Now he, too, must do something." They put him in the middle of the pile of wood and lighted it. The fire began to burn and burned for three days until all the wood was consumed, and when the flames died down, the frosty man was standing in the middle of the ashes, shaking like an aspen leaf and saying, "I've never endured such a frost in my life, and if it had lasted any longer, I'd have been frozen stiff."

Now there was no escaping it, and the beautiful maiden had to marry the unknown youth. But as they were driving to church, the old woman said, "I can't stand the disgrace!" and dispatched her soldiers after them: they were to lay everything low that came in their path and bring her back her daughter. The Listener, however, had pricked up his ears and heard the old woman's secret words. "What shall we do?" he said to the fat man. The latter had a plan and once or twice spit out behind the carriage part of the Red Sea water that he'd drunk. Then a big lake was formed, through which the soldiers couldn't advance and in which they drowned. When the enchantress learned of this, she sent her mailed riders, but the Listener heard the rattle of their mail and unbandaged the other man's eyes. The latter looked a bit hard at the enemy, and then they burst to pieces like so much glass.

Now they drove on undisturbed. When the couple received the blessing in the church, the six servants took their leave, saying to their master, "Your wishes are fulfilled, you no longer need us, so we shall go along and seek our fortune."

A half an hour's walk from the royal residence was a village, outside of which a swineherd was tending his pigs. On arriving there the king's son said to his wife, "Do you really know who I am? I'm not a king's son but a swineherd, and the man over there with the herd is my father. You and I must get to work, too, and help him tend the pigs." They put up at the inn, and he secretly told the inn-people to take away her royal clothes during the night. When she woke up in the morning, she had nothing to put on, and the inn-keeper's wife gave her an old skirt and a pair of old woolen stockings, at the same time acting as if it were a great present and saying, "If it wasn't for your husband, I shouldn't have given you the things at all." Then she believed he really was a swineherd, tended the herd with him, and thought, "I've deserved it on account of my arrogance and pride." That lasted for a week, then she could stand it no longer for her feet had got sore. Then some people came and asked if she knew who her husband was. "Yes," she answered, "he's a swineherd and has just gone out to do a little business with ribbons and laces." "Well, come along with us," they said. "We're going to take you to him," and brought her up to the royal mansion. When she entered the great hall, there stood her husband in royal clothes. She didn't recognize him, however, until he fell on her neck and kissed her, saying, "I suffered so much for you. It was right that you, too, should suffer for me."

Only now was the wedding celebrated, and the person who told the story wished he'd been there, too.

135 The White and the Black Bride

Die weisse und die schwarze Braut

A WOMAN was walking across the fields with her daughter and stepdaughter to cut fodder. Then the dear Lord came toward them in the guise of a poor man and asked, "Which is the way to the village?" "If you want to know," said the mother, "look for it yourself," and her daughter added, "If you're worried about not finding it, take along a signpost." But the stepdaughter said, "Poor man, I'll take you. Come with me." Then the dear Lord got angry at the mother and daughter, turned His back on them and enchanted them so that they turned black as night and as ugly as sin. But the Lord was gracious to the poor stepdaughter and went with her, and when they were near the village, He uttered a blessing over her and said, "Choose three things for yourself; I'll grant them to you." Then the girl said, "I'd very much like to become as beautiful and pure as the sun," and forthwith she was white and beautiful like the day. "Then I'd like to have a purse that would never get empty." The dear Lord gave her that, too, but said, "Don't forget the best thing." "As the third thing," she said, "I wish for myself the Eternal Kingdom of Heaven after my death." That, too, was granted her, and thus the dear Lord parted from her.

When the stepmother and her daughter got home and saw that they were both coal-black and ugly, while the stepdaughter was white and beautiful, the stepmother's malice rose even higher in her heart and she thought of nothing but how she might in some way harm the girl. Now the stepdaughter had a brother named Reginer, whom she loved very much, and she told him everything that had happened. On one occasion Reginer said to her, "Dear sister, I want to paint a picture of you so that I can always see you before my eyes, for my love for you is so great that I should like to look at you always." Then she answered, "But please don't let anybody see the picture." He made a painting of his sister and hung the picture in his room; he lived in the king's palace because he served the latter as coachman. Every day he used to go and stand before the picture and thanked God for his dear sister's good fortune.

Now the wife of the king whom he served had just died, and she had been so beautiful that it wasn't possible to find her equal, and the king grieved deeply over this. The court servants noticed, however, that the coachman used to stand every day before the beautiful picture, begrudged him it, and reported the matter to the king. Then the latter had the picture brought to him, and when he saw that it was in every particular like his deceased wife, though even more beautiful, he fell violently in love with it. He had the coachman come before him and asked whose picture it was. The coachman said it was his sister. Then the king decided to marry no other woman than her, gave him a carriage and horses and splendid gold-adorned clothes and dispatched him to fetch his chosen bride. When Reginer arrived with the message, his sister rejoiced, but the black girl was envious of this good fortune, was vexed beyond measure, and said to her mother, "What's the use of all your arts if you can't contrive similar good luck for me?" "Be still!" said the woman. "I'll turn it your way, of course." By her witch's craft she bleared the coachman's eyes so that he was half blind and stopped up the white girl's ears so that she was half deaf. Then they got into the carriage, first the bride in the splendid royal clothes, then the stepmother and her daughter, while Reginer sat on the box and drove. When they'd been going a while, the coachman cried,

> "Cover yourself, sister dear,
> so the rain won't wet you,
> the wind not make you dusty,
> so you'll reach the king in fine style."

"What is my dear brother saying?" asked the bride-to-be. "Oh," said the old woman, "he said you were to take off your gold dress and give it to your stepsister." She took it off and put it on the black sister, who gave her a wretched grey smock in its place. Thus they drove on farther. After a little while her brother again cried out,

> "Cover yourself, sister dear,
> so the rain won't wet you,

> the wind not make you dusty,
> so you'll reach the king in fine style."

"What is my dear brother saying?" asked the bride. "Oh," said the old woman, "he said you were to take off your gold head-dress and give it to your sister." She took off her headdress and put it on the black sister and sat with nothing on her hair. Thus they drove on farther. After a little while her brother again cried,

> "Cover yourself, sister dear,
> so the rain won't wet you,
> the wind not make you dusty,
> so you'll reach the king in fine style."

"What is my dear brother saying?" asked the bride. "Oh," said the old woman, "he said you should just take a look out of the carriage." At that very moment they were driving across a bridge over a deep stream. Now as the bride stood up and leaned out of the carriage, they both pushed her out, so that she pitched right into the water. The very instant she sank out of sight, a snow-white duck rose on the surface of the water and swam downstream. The brother hadn't noticed any of this and drove the carriage on till they reached the court. There he brought the black girl to the king as his sister and thought she really was his sister, because he was blear-eyed and yet saw the gold clothes gleaming. When the king saw the complete hideousness of his intended bride, he got very angry and ordered the coachman thrown into a pit full of adders and snakes. Nevertheless, the old witch knew how to captivate the king and by her arts blear his eyes so that he kept her and her daughter, indeed, so that she seemed quite tolerable to him and he really married her.

One evening when the black bride was sitting on the king's lap, a white duck came swimming into the kitchen through the drain and said to the scullery boy,

> "Little boy, kindle a fire
> so that I may warm my feathers."

The scullery boy did so and made a fire for it on the hearth. Then the duck came and sat down by it, shook itself, and preened its feathers with its bill. As it was thus sitting and making itself comfortable, it asked,

"What's my brother Reginer doing?"

The scullery boy answered,

> "He's prisoner in the pit
> among adders and snakes."

It enquired further,

> "What's the black witch doing in the house?"

The scullery boy answered,

> "She's sitting nice and cozy
> in the king's arms."

Said the duck,

> "God have mercy!"

and swam out the drain.

The next evening it came again and put the same questions, and again the third evening. Then the scullery boy could bear it no longer, went to the king, and revealed all to him. The king wanted to see it for himself, went there the next evening, and when the duck stuck its head in through the drain, took his sword and cut its neck through. Then it suddenly turned into a most beautiful girl just like the picture her brother had made of her. The king rejoiced, and because she was standing there all wet, had splendid clothes brought and put on her. Then she told him how she'd been tricked by guile and duplicity and finally thrown into the river. Her first request was that her brother be taken out of the snake-pit. After the king had fulfilled this request, he went into the room where the old witch was sitting and asked, "What does a woman deserve who does thus and so?" and related what had happened. She was so beguiled that she didn't notice anything and said, "She deserves to be stripped naked and put in a barrel studded with nails, and that a horse be hitched to the barrel and turned loose." All that happened to her and to her black daughter. But the king married the white and beautiful bride and rewarded the loyal brother by making him a wealthy and distinguished man.

136 Iron John

Der Eisenhans

THERE WAS ONCE A KING by whose castle was a big forest in which roamed all kinds of game. On one occasion he sent out a huntsman to shoot a roedeer, but he didn't come back. "Perhaps he's met with an accident," said the king and on the following day sent out two other huntsmen to look for him. But they, too, remained away. On the third day he summoned all his huntsmen and said, "Range through the whole forest and don't stop until you've found all three." But not one of these came home, either, nor was there a sign of a single one of the pack of hounds they'd taken with them. From then on no one was any longer willing to venture into the forest, and it lay there in deep silence and solitude, and only from time to time did one see an eagle or a hawk flying over it. That went on for many years.

Then a foreign huntsman presented himself to the king, sought a position, and offered to go into the perilous forest. The king, however, was unwilling to give his consent, saying, "The forest is haunted. I'm afraid you'll fare no better than the others and won't get out of it again." "Sir," replied the huntsman, "I'm willing to do it at my own risk; I don't know the meaning of fear." So with his dog the huntsman betook himself into the forest. Before long the dog got on the trail of a deer and was going to chase it, but scarcely had it run a few paces when it was standing before a deep pool and could go no farther. Then a naked arm reached out of the water, seized it, and dragged it down. When the huntsman saw that, he went back and fetched three men who had to come with pails and ladle out the water. When they could see bottom, a wild man was lying there whose body was as brown as rusty iron and whose hair hung down over his face and reached to his knees. They bound him with cords and led him away to the palace. Everybody marveled greatly at the wild man, and the king had him put in an iron cage in his courtyard and on pain of death forbade the door of the cage to be opened. The queen herself had to take charge of the key. From now on everybody could again go safely into the forest.

The king had an eight-year-old son. Once he was playing in the courtyard, and while at play his gold ball fell into the cage. The boy ran up and said, "Hand me out my ball." "Not till you've opened the door for me," answered the man. "No, I won't do that; the king's forbidden it," said the boy and ran off. The next day he came back and demanded his ball. The wild man said, "Open my door," but the boy wouldn't. On the third day when the king had gone hunting, the boy came again and said, "Even if I was willing to, I couldn't open the door. I haven't the key." Then the wild man said, "It's under your mother's pillow; you can get it there." The boy, who wanted to have his ball back, threw all scruples to the winds and brought the key. The door opened hard, and the boy jammed his finger. When it was open, the wild man stepped out, gave him the gold ball, and hurried away. The boy got frightened, shouted and called after him, "Oh, wild man, don't go away. If you do, I'll get a beating." The wild man turned around, picked him up, put him on his shoulders, and with swift strides went into the forest. On returning home the king noticed the empty cage and asked the queen how that had happened. She knew nothing about it, looked for the key, but it was gone. She called the boy, but no one answered. The king sent out people to look for him in the fields, but they didn't find him. Then he had no trouble guessing what had taken place, and great grief reigned at the royal court.

When the wild man reached the dark forest again, he set the boy down from his shoulders and said to him, "You'll not see your father and mother again, but I'll keep you with me because you freed me and I'm sorry for you. If you do everything I tell, you'll get along all right. I have plenty of treasures and gold, more, indeed, than anybody in the world." He made the boy a bed of moss on which he went to sleep. The next morning the man led him to a well and said, "Look, the gold well is bright and clear as crystal. You're to sit there and see that nothing falls in; otherwise it will be defiled. Every evening I'll come and see if you've obeyed my command." The boy sat down on the edge of the well, saw how sometimes a gold fish, sometimes a gold snake appeared there, and watched out that nothing fell in. As he was sitting thus, his finger once hurt him so that he involuntarily stuck it in the water. He drew it out again quickly but saw that it was completely gilded over, and no matter how hard he tried to wipe the gold off again, it was all in vain. In the evening Iron John came back, looked at the boy and said, "What happened to the well?" "Nothing, nothing," he answered and kept his finger behind his back so that Iron John shouldn't see it. But the man said, "You dipped your finger in the water. This time we'll let it go, but watch out that you don't let anything fall in again." At the crack of dawn the boy was already sitting by the well and guarding it. Again his finger hurt him and he rubbed it on his head; then unluckily a hair fell into the well. He took it quickly out, but it was already completely gilded. Iron John arrived and already knew what had happened. "You let a hair drop into the well," he said. "I'll overlook it in you once more, but if it happens a third time, the well will be dishonored, and you can no longer stay with me." On the third day the boy was sitting by the well and didn't move his finger, however much it still hurt him. Time passed slowly for him, and he looked at the reflection of his face in the water, and as at the same time he kept leaning farther and farther over and wanted to look himself straight in the eye, his long hair fell down from his shoulders into the water. He straightened up quickly, but his whole shock of hair was already gilded and shone like the sun. You can imagine how frightened the poor boy was. He took his handkerchief and tied it around his head so that the man shouldn't see it. When Iron John arrived, he already knew everything and said, "Untie the handkerchief!" Then the gold hair welled out, and however much the boy apologized, it did no good. "You've not stood the test and you can't say here any longer. Go out in the world where you'll find out what poverty is like. But because at heart you are not bad and I have only good intentions toward you, I'll grant you one thing: if you get into trouble, go to the forest and call 'Iron

John.' Then I'll come and help you. My power is great, greater than you imagine, and I have gold and silver to spare."

Then the king's son left the forest and kept following beaten and unbeaten trails until he finally came to a big city. There he looked for work but couldn't find any and had, besides, learned nothing to earn his living by. Finally he went to the palace and asked if they would keep him. The court people didn't know what they could use him for, but they took a fancy to him and bade him stay. Finally the chef took him in service and said he might carry wood and water and sweep up the ashes. Once when no one else was on hand, the chef ordered him to carry the dishes to the royal board, but since he didn't want to let his gold hair be seen, he kept his cap on. Nothing like that had ever happened to the king before, and he said, "When you come to royal board, you must take off your hat." "Alas, sir," he answered, "I can't. I have a bad scab on my head." Then the king had the chef summoned, scolded him and asked how he could have engaged such a boy: he was to dismiss him at once. The chef felt sorry for him, however, and exchanged him for the gardener's boy.

Now the boy had to plant and water the garden, hoe and dig, and put up with wind and bad weather. Once in the summer when he was working alone in the garden, the day was so hot that he took off his cap to let the breeze cool him off. When the sun shone on his hair, it gleamed and sparkled so that the rays fell in the bedchamber of the king's daughter and she jumped up to see what it was. She spied the boy and called to him, "Boy, bring me a bunch of flowers." In all haste he put on his cap, picked wild flowers and tied them together. As he was going up the stairs with them, he met the gardener, who said, "How can you be bringing the king's daughter a bunch of poor flowers? Hurry up and get others and pick out the fairest and rarest." "O no," answered the boy, "the wild flowers smell stronger and will please her better." When he entered her room, the king's daughter said, "Take off your cap; it's not proper for you to keep it on in my presence." Again he answered, "I mustn't; my head's scabby." But she grabbed for the cap and pulled it off. Then his gold

hair rolled down on his shoulders and was a magnificent
sight. He was about to run away, but she held him by the
arm and gave him a handful of ducats. He went off with
them, thought nothing, however, of the gold, but brought it
to the gardener, saying, "I'm making your children a present
of it; they can play with it." The next day the king's daughter
again called to him to bring her a bunch of wild flowers, and
as he came in with it, she immediately grabbed for his cap
and was going to take it away from him. But he held it tight
with both hands. Again she gave him a handful of ducats,
but he wouldn't keep them and gave them to the gardener
as playthings for his children. The third day was no different:
she couldn't get his cap away from him, and he didn't want
her gold.

Not long after, a war swept over the land. The king assembled his forces and didn't know whether he'd be able to
resist the enemy, who was superior in power and had a big
army. Then the gardener's boy said, "I'm grown up and
want to go along to the war; just give me a horse." The others
laughed and said, "When we're gone, look for one for yourself. We'll leave you one in the stable." When they'd gone,
he went into the stable and took out the horse; it was lame
in one foot and hobbled along plunk-plunk. Nevertheless,
he mounted it and rode off into the dark forest. On reaching the edge of the forest he called out "Iron John!" three
times so loud that it rang through the trees. The wild man
appeared immediately and said, "What do you demand?" "I
demand a strong steed, because I want to go to the war." "You
shall have that and even more than you demand." The wild
man went back into the forest, and before long a groom came
out of the forest leading a steed that snorted through its
nostrils and could hardly be held in check. And behind followed a great warrior band, all in iron armor and their
swords gleaming in the sun. The boy turned his three-legged
horse over to the groom, mounted the other and rode at the
head of the troop. As he drew near the battle field, a large
part of the king's people had already fallen and the others
were on the point of having to give way. Then the youth raced
up with his iron troop, overrode the enemy like a storm,
and struck down everybody who resisted him. They wanted to

flee, but the youth had the upper hand and didn't stop until not a single man was left. However, instead of returning to the king, he led his troop by roundabout ways back to the forest and summoned Iron John. "What do you demand?" the wild man asked. "Take back your steed and your troop and give me my three-legged horse again." Everything he demanded was done, and he rode home on his three-legged horse. When the king returned to his palace, his daughter went to meet him and congratulated him on his victory. "It's not I who gained the victory," he said, "but a foreign knight who came to my aid with his troop." The daughter wanted to know who the foreign knight might be, but the king didn't know and said, "He pursued the enemy, and I haven't seen him since." She enquired of the gardener for his boy, but the former laughed and said, "He's just come home on his three-legged horse. The others have been making fun of him and calling out, 'Here comes our Plunk-Plunk again back.' They also asked, 'Behind which hedge have you been lying asleep all the while?' But he said, 'I did the best thing and without me things would have gone badly.' Then they laughed at him more than ever."

The king said to his daughter, "I'm going to have a great festival announced: it's to last three days, and you are to throw a gold apple. Perhaps the unknown man will come along." When the festival was announced, the youth went out to the forest and called Iron John. "What do you demand?" he asked. "To catch the princess' gold apple." "You've as good as caught it already," said Iron John. "In addition you shall also have a red outfit and ride on a fine bay." When the day arrived, the boy galloped up, took his place among the knights and was recognized by no one. The king's daughter stepped forward and threw a gold apple to the knights, but he alone caught it. However, as soon as he had it, he raced away. For the second day Iron John had him fitted out as a white knight and given a white horse. Again he alone caught the apple, didn't stop a minute, however, but raced away with it. The king grew angry and said, "That mustn't be! He must appear before me and give his name." He ordered, if the knight who caught the apple again made off, that they should set out after him and, if he didn't turn back of his own accord, to hit him and stab at him. On the third day he received a black outfit from Iron John and a black horse, and he also again caught the apple. When he raced away with it, the king's people pursued him, and one got so near him that he wounded his leg with the point of his sword. Nevertheless, he escaped, but his horse jumped so violently that his helmet fell off his head, and they could see that he had gold hair. They rode back and reported everything to the king.

The following day the king's daughter asked the gardener about his boy. "He's working in the garden. The queer chap was at the festival, too, and didn't get back till yesterday evening. He also showed my children three gold apples he'd won." The king ordered him into his presence. He appeared and again had his cap on his head, but the king's daughter went up to him and took it off him. Then his gold hair fell over his shoulders, and he was so handsome that everybody was astonished. "Are you the knight who came to the festival every day, always in a different color, and who caught the three apples?" asked the king. "Yes," he answered, "and there are the apples," took them out of his pocket and handed them to the king. "If you want further proof, you can see the wound that your people inflicted on me when they pursued me. And I am also the knight who helped you to victory over your enemies." "If you can perform such deeds, you're no gardener's boy. Tell me, who is your father?" "My father is a mighty king, and I have gold aplenty and as much as I simply ask for." "I plainly see," said the king, "that I owe you a debt of gratitude. Can I do you any favor?" "Yes," he answered, "indeed you can. Give me your daughter in marriage." Then the maiden laughed and said, "He doesn't stand on ceremony! But I've already seen from his gold hair that he's no gardener's boy." Then she went up and kissed him. His mother and father came to the wedding and were very happy, for they had already given up hope of seeing their dear son again. When they sat down at the wedding table, the music suddenly stopped, the doors opened, and a proud king stepped in with a great retinue. He went up to the boy and embraced him, saying, "I am Iron John and was turned into a wild man by witchcraft, but you have disenchanted me. All the treasures I possess shall be your property."

137 The Three Black Princesses

De drei schwatten Prinzessinnen

THE TOWN OF EAST INDIA was under siege by an enemy who wouldn't leave it before receiving six hundred dollars. Then they had it publicly announced that whoever could raise the amount should become mayor. There was a poor fisherman who with his son was fishing on the sea. The enemy came and captured the son and gave his father six hundred dollars compensation. Then the father went and gave it to the lords of the city. The enemy withdrew and the fisherman became mayor. Then it was proclaimed that whoever failed to address the mayor with "Your Honor" should be executed on the gallows.

The son got out of the hands of the enemy again and came to a great forest on a high mountain. The mountain opened, and he went into a big enchanted mansion where chairs, tables, and benches were all draped in black. Then came three princesses clad entirely in black and with only a little white in their faces. They told him not to be frightened, that they wouldn't do anything to him, and that he could free them. He said he'd gladly do that if he only knew how. Then they said that for a whole year he wasn't to speak to them nor should he look at them. Anything he very much wanted he should just mention; if they were permitted to give an answer, they'd do so.

After he'd been there for a time, he said he'd like to go to his father's. Then they said he should do as follows: take along this purse of money, put on these clothes, and that he'd have to be back there in a week. Then he was picked up and was at once in East India. He could no longer find his father in the fishing hut and asked the people where the poor fisherman was. They told him he mustn't say that or he'd find himself on the gallows. He got to his father and said, "Fisherman, where have you risen to?" Then his father said,

"You mustn't say that. If the lords of the city hear it, you'll find yourself on the gallows." But he simply wouldn't stop and was taken to the gallows. When he got there, he said, "Oh, my lords, please grant me leave to go once again to the old fishing hut." Then he put on his old smock and, coming back to the lords, said, "Now just look carefully! Am I not a poor fisherman's son? In this garb I earned my mother's and father's daily bread." Then they recognized him and begged his forgiveness and took him along to his house. He told them everything as it had happened to him: how he'd gone into the forest on a high mountain, then the mountain had opened, then he'd entered an enchanted mansion where everything was black, and three princesses had come there who were black except for a little white in their faces. They had told him not to be frightened and that he could free them. Then his mother said it mightn't be safe, that he should take a consecrated taper along and let some hot wax drip in their faces.

He went back and felt very shivery and dripped some wax in their faces while they were asleep, and they were already half white. Then all three princesses jumped up and said, "The cursed dog! Our blood will cry out for revenge. Now there is no man born on earth, or will be born, who can free us. We still have three brothers who are bound in seven chains; they'll tear you to pieces." Then there was a screeching noise in the whole mansion, and he managed to jump out the window and broke his leg.

The mansion sank back into the earth, the mountain was closed again, and no one knows where it used to be.

138   Knoest and His Three Sons

Knoist un sine dre Sühne

BETWEEN WERREL AND SOEST [in Westphalia] there lived a man called Knoest. He had three sons: one was blind, the other lame, and the third stark naked. Once they were walking across the fields and saw a hare. The blind son shot it, the lame son caught it, and the naked son put it in his pocket. Then they came to a great tremendous body of water on which were three boats: one was leaky, the other sank, and the third had no bottom. They all went aboard the boat with no bottom. Then they came to a great tremendous forest in which was a great tremendous tree. In the tree was a tremendously big chapel; in the chapel was a hornbeam sexton and a boxwood parson, who sprinkled the holy water with cudgels.

> "Lucky is the man
> Who can dodge the holy water."

139　The Girl from Brakel

Dat Mäken von Brakel

A GIRL FROM BRAKEL [near Paderborn] once went to the chapel of St. Anne below Hindenburg, and because she very much wanted a husband and thought that there was no one else in the chapel, she sang:

> "O holy Saint Anne,
> Help me get a husband quick!
> You know him, of course;
> He lives outside the Suttmer Gate,
> Has yellow hair.
> You know him, of course."

But the sexton was standing behind the altar and heard that and cried in a squeaky voice, "You won't get him, you won't get him." The girl thought that the little Mary, who was beside Mother Anne, had called out that. Then she got angry and cried, "Nonsense, stupid brat! Keep your mouth shut and let your mother talk."

140   The Domestic Servants

Das Hausgesinde

"WHERE ARE YOU GOING?" "To Woelpe [near Nienburg on the Weser]." "I'm going to Woelpe, you're going to Woelpe; then let's go together."

"Have you a husband, too? What's your husband's name?" "Cham." "My husband is Cham, yours is Cham; I'm going to Woelpe, you're going to Woelpe; then let's go together."

"Have you a child, too? What's your child's name?" "Scab." "Mine is Scab, yours is Scab; my husband is Cham, yours is Cham; I'm going to Woelpe, you're going to Woelpe; then let's go together."

"Have you a cradle, too? What's your cradle's name?" "Hippodeige." "My cradle is Hippodeige, your cradle is Hippodeige; my child is Scab, your child is Scab; my husband is Cham, your husband is Cham; I'm going to Woelpe, you're going to Woelpe; then let's go together."

"Have you a servant? What's your servant's name?" "Fix-It-Up." "My servant is Fix-It-Up, your servant is Fix-It-Up; my cradle is Hippodeige, your cradle is Hippodeige; my child is Scab, your child is Scab; my husband is Cham, your husband is Cham; I'm going to Woelpe, you're going to Woelpe; then let's go together."

141 The Lamb and the Fish

Das Lämmchen und Fischchen

THERE WAS ONCE A BROTHER and a sister. They loved each other dearly, but their real mother was dead and they had a stepmother who wasn't kind to them and secretly hurt them in every way. It happened that the two were playing with other children on a meadow before the house, and in the meadow was a pond which came up to one side of the house. The children were running around it, catching each other, and playing a counting-out game:

> "Eenie, meenie, let me live
> And I'll give you my bird;
> Bird will get me straw,
> Straw I'll give the cow;
> Cow will give me milk,
> Milk I'll give the baker;
> Baker will bake me a cake,
> Cake I'll give the cat;
> Cat will catch me mice,
> Mice I'll hang up and smoke
> and cut them up."

While doing this they'd stand in a circle and on whomever the word "up" fell, he had to run off and the others would chase him and catch him. As they were thus happily skipping about, the stepmother watched from the window and was vexed. Since she understood witchcraft, she transformed them both, the brother into a fish, the sister into a lamb. Then the fish swam about in the pond and was sad, and the lamb walked about in the meadow and was sad, ate nothing and didn't touch so much as a blade of grass. Thus a long time passed, and then strangers came as guests to the mansion. The false-hearted stepmother thought, "Now is the right moment," called the chef, and said to him, "Go get the lamb from the meadow and slaughter it; we have nothing else for the guests." Then the chef went and got the lamb and led it into the kitchen and tied its feet; it bore it all patiently. When the chef had got out his knife and was sharpening it on the sill in order to kill the lamb, it saw a fish swimming back and forth in the water outside the kitchen drain and looking up at it. That was the brother; for, when the fish had seen the chef leading the lamb away, it had swum along in the pond up to the house. Then the lamb called down,

> "O brother in the deep lake,
> How, indeed, my heart does ache!
> The chef is sharpening his knife
> To pierce me through the heart."

The fish answered,

> "O little sister way up there,
> How, indeed, my heart does ache
> In this deep lake!"

When the chef heard that the lamb could talk and was calling such sad words down to the fish, he got frightened and thought it couldn't be any ordinary lamb but that it must have been bewitched by the evil mistress of the house. Then he said, "Don't worry! I shan't slaughter you," took another animal and prepared it for the guests and, taking the lamb to a good farmer's wife, told her everything he'd seen and heard. Now the farmer's wife happened to have been the little sister's nurse, and guessing at once who it probably was, went with the lamb to a wise woman. Then the wise woman said a blessing over the lamb and the fish, by which means they recovered their human forms. Afterward she took them both to a little hut in a big forest, where they lived in solitude but were happy and content.

142   Mount Seseli

Simeliberg

THERE WERE TWO BROTHERS, one rich, the other poor. But the rich brother gave the poor brother nothing, and he had to eke out a wretched living dealing in grain. Things often went so badly for him that he had no bread for his wife and children. Once he was going through a forest with his wheelbarrow and noticed to one side a big bald mountain, and because he had never seen it before, he stopped and looked at it with amazement. As he was standing thus, he saw twelve big wild men arrive and, supposing that they were robbers, he pushed his wheelbarrow into the bushes, climbed a tree, and waited to see what would happen. Then the twelve walked up to the mountain and called out, "Mount Sesame, Mount Sesame, open up!" Forthwith the bald mountain opened in the middle and the twelve went in; once they were inside, it shut. After a short time, however, it opened again, and the men came out carrying heavy sacks on their backs. When they were all out again in the daylight, they said, "Mount Sesame, Mount Sesame, close up!" Then the mountain closed and the entrance was no longer visible and the twelve went away.

When they were quite out of sight, the poor man climbed down the tree and was curious to know what secret things were really hidden in the mountain. So he walked up to it and said, "Mount Sesame, Mount Sesame, open up!" and the mountain opened before him, too. Then he stepped inside and the whole mountain was a cavern filled with gold and silver and in back were great piles of pearls and sparkling gems heaped up like so much grain. The poor man had no idea what to do and whether he might take any of the treasure for himself. Finally, he filled his pockets with gold, leaving the pearls and precious stones. On coming out again he likewise said, "Mount Sesame, Mount Sesame, close up!" Then the mountain closed, and he went back home with his wheelbarrow.

Now he had no further need to worry and with his gold could buy bread and wine, too, for his wife and child; he lived happily and decently, gave to the poor, and was kind to everyone. But when the gold was used up, he went to his brother, borrowed a bushel measure, and got some more. Just the same, he touched no part of the really great treasures.

When for the third time he wanted to get some gold, he again borrowed the measure from his brother. But the rich brother had long been envious of his wealth and of the fine establishment which he had set up for himself and couldn't imagine where the wealth came from and what his brother was up to with the measure. Then he thought of a trick and coated the bottom of the measure with pitch, and when he got it back, a gold piece was sticking there. He at once went to his brother and asked, "What have you been measuring with the measure?" "Rye and barley," said the other. Then he showed him the gold piece and threatened to hale him into court unless he told the truth. Then the latter told him everything that had happened.

Immediately the rich man had a wagon hitched up, drove out to the mountain with the idea of making better use of the occasion and of bringing back quite other treasures. When he got outside the mountain, he cried, "Mount Sesame, Mount Sesame, open up!" The mountain opened, and he went in. There lay all the riches before him, and for a long time he couldn't make up his mind what to take first, finally loading up as many precious stones as he could carry. He wanted to get his load out, but because his heart and mind were full of the treasure, he had forgotten the name of the mountain and cried, "Mount Seseli, Mount Seseli, open up!" But that wasn't the right name, and the mountain didn't stir and remained shut. Then he got frightened, but the longer he reflected, the more confused grew his thoughts, and none of the treasure helped him at all. That evening the mountain opened and the twelve robbers came in. When they saw him, they laughed and cried out, "Now at last we have you, my fine bird! Do you think we hadn't noticed that you'd got in here twice before? But we weren't able to catch you. You won't get out again the third time." Then he cried, "It wasn't me, it was my brother!" But beg for his life as he would and say what he might, they struck off his head.

143 Going Traveling

Up Reisen gohn

THERE WAS ONCE A POOR WOMAN who had a son who very much wanted to travel. "How can you go on a journey," said his mother. "We have no money at all for you to take with you." Then the son said, "I'll get along all right; I'll keep saying, 'Not much, not much, not much.'"

He walked on for quite a while and kept saying, "Not much, not much, not much." Then he came to a crowd of fishermen and said, "God help you! Not much, not much, not much." "What are you saying, rascal? Not much?" And really when they cast their nets, they didn't catch much fish and fell on the boy with a stick saying, "Haven't you seen me thresh?" "But what *shall* I say?" said the boy. "You should say 'Catch a lot, catch a lot.'"

Again he walked on for quite a while, saying, "Catch a lot, catch a lot," until he came to a gallows where they had a poor sinner whom they were about to hang. Then he said, "Good morning, catch a lot, catch a lot." "Why are you saying 'Catch a lot,' fellow? Should there be even more wicked people in the world? Isn't this enough?" Again he caught it across his shoulders. "But what *shall* I say?" "You should say 'God comfort the poor soul.'"

Again the boy walked on for quite a while, saying. "God comfort the poor soul." Then he came to a ditch where a skinner stood skinning a horse. "Good morning," said the boy; "God comfort the poor soul." "What are you saying, you wretched fellow?" said the skinner and struck him about the ears with his skinner's hook so that he couldn't see out of his eyes. "But what *shall* I say?" "You should say, 'Lie there in the ditch, you carcass.'"

Then he walked on and kept saying. "Lie there in the ditch, you carcass! lie there in the ditch, you carcass!" Then he passed a stagecoach full of people and said, "Good morning, may you lie in the ditch, you carcass!" Then the coach tipped over in the ditch, and the driver took his whip and gave the boy such a crack that he had to go crawling back to his mother. And he never went traveling again as long as he lived.

144   The Donkey

Das Eselein

THERE ONCE LIVED A KING and a queen who were rich and had everything they wanted except children. This the queen lamented day and night, saying, "I am like a field in which nothing grows." Finally God fulfilled her wishes, but when the child came into the world, it didn't look like a human child but was a young donkey. When the mother saw it, she began really to lament, crying out that she would rather have had no child at all than a donkey, and said that it should be thrown into the water so the fish might eat it up. The king, however, said, "No, God has given him to us and so he shall be my son and heir and after my death sit on the royal throne and wear the royal crown." Accordingly, the donkey was reared. It grew big and its ears grew quite long and straight. In other respects it was of a happy disposition, capered about, played, and was especially fond of music. So he went to a famous minstrel and said, "Teach me your art so that I can play the lute as well as you." "Alas, my dear young lord," answered the minstrel, "that's likely to be hard for you; your fingers certainly aren't made for it and are altogether too big. I'm afraid the strings won't stand it." No pretext availed: the donkey wanted to and was bound to play the lute, was persevering and diligent, and in the end learned to play as well as the master himself.

Once the young lord was walking along reflectively and, coming to a spring, looked in it and saw his donkey form mirrored in the water. He was so distressed about it that he went abroad, taking only one trusted companion with him. They went here and there, finally coming to a kingdom ruled by an old king who had only one daughter, though she was wondrously fair. "Let's stop here," said the donkey, knocked at the gate and cried, "There's a guest outside; open the gate so that he may enter." When the gate wasn't opened, he sat down, took his lute and with his two forefeet played it most beautifully. Then the porter opened his eyes wide and, running to the king, said, "A young donkey is sitting outside the gate; it plays the lute as well as a trained expert." "Then let the musician come in," said the king. However, when the donkey entered, everybody began to laugh at the lute-player.

Now the donkey was to be seated and fed at the lower end of the table with the servants, but it got indignant and said, "I'm no common barnyard donkey, I'm a high-born donkey." Then they said, "If that's what you are, sit down with the warriors." "No," it said, "I'll sit by the king." The king laughed and said good-humoredly, "Yes, it will be as you insist, donkey; come here by me," afterward asking, "Donkey, how do you like my daughter?" The donkey turned its head toward her, looked at her, nodded and said, "Exceptionally well. She's more beautiful than any woman I've yet seen." "Well, then you shall sit by her, too," said the king. "That's just what I'd like," said the donkey and sat down beside her, ate and drank, and knew how to behave itself properly and mannerly.

When the noble animal had been at the king's court for quite a time, it thought, "What's the good of all this? You've got to go back home," dropped its head sadly, went to the king and asked to take its leave. The king, however, had grown fond of it and said, "Donkey, what's the matter with you? You look as sour as a vinegar-cruet. Stay on with me and I'll give you what you ask. Do you want gold?" "No," said the donkey, shaking its head. "Do you want valuables and finery?" "No." "Do you want half my kingdom?" "Oh, no!"

Then the king said, "If I only knew what might satisfy you! Do you want to marry my beautiful daughter?" "Oh, yes," said the donkey, "I'd love to marry her," and all at once was quite cheerful and in good spirits, for that was exactly what it had wanted.

Accordingly, a great and splendid wedding was celebrated. In the evening when the bride and bridegroom were escorted to their bedchamber, the king wanted to find out whether the donkey would conduct itself in a mannerly and polite fashion and ordered a servant to hide in the room. Now once they were both in there, the bridegroom shot the bolt in the door, looked around and, thinking that they were quite alone, suddenly cast off his donkey hide and stood there a handsome royal youth. "Now you see," he said, "who I am, and you see, too, that I was not unworthy of you." Then the bride became happy, kissed him, and loved him dearly. But when morning came, he jumped up, pulled on his donkey hide again, and no human being would have suspected what kind of a person was inside it. Soon the old king came along. "My!" he cried, "the donkey's already awake!" To his daughter he said, "You are surely sad that you didn't marry a regular human being?" "Oh, no, father dear, I love him as if he were the very handsomest man, and I want to keep him as long as I live."

The king was surprised, but the servant who had hidden himself came and revealed all to him. "That can't possibly be true!" said the king. "Well, keep watch yourself tonight; you'll see it with your own eyes, and, do you know what, Sir King, if you take the hide away from him and throw it in the fire, he'll certainly have to show himself in his true form." "That's good advice of yours," said the king, and that night, when they were asleep, he crept in and as he got to the bed, saw a fine youth lying there in the moonlight with the hide which he had stripped off lying on the floor. Then he took it away and had a huge fire built outdoors and the hide thrown in while he himself stood by until it was entirely burned to ashes. But because he wanted to see how the victim of the robbery would act, he stayed awake all night and listened. When the youth had slept himself out, at the first crack of dawn he got up and wanted to put on the donkey hide. But it was not to be found. Then he got frightened and, full of

grief and dread, said, "Now I must see about getting away."
As he stepped out of the room, the king, however, was
standing there and said, "My son, where are you going in
such a hurry? What have you in mind? Stay on here; you're
such a handsome man that you mustn't leave me again. I'll
give you half my kingdom now and after my death you'll get
all of it." "I hope then," said the youth, "that this good beginning may also have a good end. I'll stay on with you."
Then the old king gave him half his kingdom, and when the
king died a year later, he had all of it, and after his father's
death still another kingdom, and he lived in great splendor.

145 The Ungrateful Son

Der undankbare Sohn

ONCE A MAN AND HIS WIFE were sitting outside the front door
with a roast chicken before them which they were going to
eat between them. Then the man saw his old father coming
along and quickly took the chicken and hid it, for he begrudged him any of it. The old man came, had a drink, and
went away. Now the son was about to put the roast chicken
back on the table, but when he reached for it, it had turned
into a big toad that jumped in his face and stayed there and
didn't go away again. And if anybody tried to take it away,
it would give them a poisonous look, as if about to jump in
their faces, so that no one dared touch it. And the ungrateful son had to feed the toad every day, otherwise it would eat
part of his face. And thus he went ceaselessly hither and yon
about in the world.

146 The Turnip

Die Rübe

ONCE THERE WERE TWO BROTHERS, both serving as soldiers, and one was rich, the other poor. Then the poor brother wanted to get out of his difficulties, doffed his soldier's tunic and became a farmer. In this way he dug and hoed his bit of land and planted turnip seed. The seed sprouted, and a turnip grew there that got big and strong and noticeably fatter and just wouldn't stop growing, so that one might call it a queen of all turnips, for never had such a one been seen nor ever will be seen again. At last he thought, "If you sell it, what will you really get for it? And if you want to eat it yourself, the small turnips will be just as good. The best thing is to take it to the king as an act of homage." So he loaded it on the cart, hitched up two oxen, brought it to court, and presented it to the king. "What sort of a rarity is that?" said the king. "I've seen many strange things but never before such a monstrosity. From what kind of seed can it have grown? Or is it unique with you and you are fortune's favored?" "Alas, no!" said the farmer. "I'm no fortune's favored. I'm a poor soldier who, because he could no longer support himself, hung up my uniform and tilled the soil. But I have a brother who is rich and well known to you, Sir, too. I, however, who have nothing, am forgotten by everybody." Then the king took pity on him and said, "You shall be relieved of your poverty, and I shall give you such fine presents that you will be your rich brother's equal." Then he gave him a lot of gold, fields, meadows, and herds, and made him so frightfully rich that the other brother's wealth was simply not to be compared with it.

When the latter heard what his brother had acquired with a single turnip, he envied him and pondered this way and that how he, too, could turn such good luck in his direction. He planned, moreover, to do it much more cleverly, took gold and horses, and brought them to the king, imagining, of course, that the latter would give him a far bigger present in return; for, if his brother received so much for a turnip, what all wouldn't he get for such fine things! The king accepted the gift and said he couldn't think of anything to give him in return that would be rarer and better than the big turnip. So the rich man had to put his brother's turnip on a cart and have it driven home.

Once back home he didn't know on whom to vent his rage and vexation, until evil thoughts entered his mind and he decided to kill his brother. He got hold of some assassins who were to take up a position in an ambush; then he went to his brother and said, "Dear brother, I know of a secret treasure; let's dig it up and divide it between us." The other took to the idea and unsuspectingly went along. But when they got out there, the assassins fell upon him, tied him up, and were about to hang him on a tree. Just as they were doing that, singing and hoofbeats sounded in the distance so that they got frightened, and putting their prisoner head over heels into a sack, hoisted it up onto a branch and took flight. But up there he worked away until he had made a hole in the sack big enough to put his head through.

The person who came along, however, was only a wandering student, a young chap riding along the road through the forest and singing merrily. Now when the man up in the tree noticed that somebody was going by beneath him, he cried out, "Bless me! just in the nick of time!" The student looked all around, didn't know where the voice came from, and finally said, "Who's calling me?" Then an answer came from the treetop, "Raise your eyes. I'm up here in the Sack of Wisdom; in a short while I have learned great things, compared to which all schools offer nothing. In no time at all I shall have mastered everything, will come down, and shall be wiser than everybody. I understand the constellations and the signs of the zodiac, the blowing of all winds, the sand in the sea, the curing of illness, the power of herbs, birds, and stones. Once you were in it, you'd feel what glory flows from the Sack of Wisdom!" When the student heard all that, he marveled and said, "Blessed be the hour in which I have found you! Couldn't I, too, get into the sack for a bit?" The man up in the tree answered as if he didn't very much like the idea. "I'll let you get in for a short while for pay and kind words, but you've got to wait another hour because there's one more thing I must learn first."

When the student had waited a bit, time passed too slowly for him, and he begged, might he please be let in, saying that his thirst for wisdom was far too great. Then the man up there finally pretended to accede and said, "In order that I may get out of the House of Wisdom, you must lower the sack on the cord; then you may get in." So the student let it down, untied the sack, and released him. Then he in turn cried out, "Now pull me up as quick as you can!" and was about to step into the sack feet first. "Stop!" said the other, "that's not the way," seized him by the head, stuck him into the sack headfirst, tied it up, and pulled the disciple of wisdom up the tree on the cord, then swung him to and fro in the air, saying, "How goes it, my dear fellow? See, you already feel wisdom flowing into you and are having a fine experience! Just keep good and still until you get wiser." Then he mounted the student's horse and rode away. An hour later, however, he sent someone to let the student down again.

147   The Little Old Man Made Young by Fire

Das jungeglühte Männlein

WHEN OUR LORD was still walking on earth, He and St. Peter turned one evening into a blacksmith's and readily obtained lodgings. Now a poor beggar, weighed down with old age and illness, happened to enter the same house and asked the smith for alms. Peter took pity on him and said, "Lord and Master, if You will, please cure his illness so that he may earn his own living." Our Lord said meekly to the smith, "Smith, lend me your forge and put in coals for me; I want to make the sick old man young again right now." The smith was quite willing, and St. Peter pumped the bellows, and when the fire was blazing up big and high and sending out sparks, Our Lord took the little old man, pushed him into the forge right in the middle of the glowing fire, so that in there he got as red as a rose bush and praised God in a loud voice. Afterward Our Lord stepped to the tank, put the red-hot little man into it, so that the water closed over him, and when he was properly cooled off, He gave him His blessing. Lo! the little man jumped right out, slender, straight, hale, and hearty, and like a twenty-year-old. The smith, who had been paying very careful attention, invited them all to the evening meal.

Now he had an old, half-blind, hunchbacked mother-in-law who went up to the lad and earnestly enquired whether the fire had burned him badly. He'd never felt better, answered the latter; he'd sat there in the glow of the fire as in cool dew. What the boy said rang all night in the old woman's ears, and when early in the morning Our Lord had gone His way and had, of course, thanked the smith, the latter thought he could make his old mother-in-law young, too, since he had watched everything very carefully, and the business, further-more, properly belonged to his trade. Accordingly, he called out and asked her if she'd like to go skipping along like an eighteen-year-old girl. Because it had been so easy for the lad, she said, "From the bottom of my heart." So the smith made a big fire and pushed the old woman in; she writhed around and let out terrible cries of "murder!" "Sit still! Why are you crying out and jumping around? Let me first blow the fire up good and strong." Then he pumped the bellows anew until all her tatters and rags were burning. The old woman shrieked unceasingly, and the smith thought, "The thing isn't working right," took her out and threw her into the tank. Then she screamed so terribly loud that the smith's wife and daughter-in-law heard it upstairs. Both came running down and saw the old woman howling and taking on and all curled up in the tank, with her face puckered and wrinkled and shapeless.

The two women, both being with child, were so horrified by this that they gave birth to two boys that very night. These were shaped not like human beings but like monkeys and ran into the forest. From them comes the race of monkeys.

148   Creatures of the Lord and of the Devil

Des Herrn und des Teufels Getier

THE LORD GOD had created all animals and had chosen the wolves to be His dogs; goats alone He'd forgotten. Then the Devil got ready and also wanted to create, and made goats with fine long tails. Now when they went out to graze, they usually caught their tails in the thorn hedges. Then the Devil had to go in and take a lot of trouble freeing them. That finally annoyed him and, beside himself, he bit the tail off every goat, as is still to be seen from the stumps to this very day.

Then, to be sure, he let them graze quite untended, but the Lord God happened to see them now gnawing at a fruit tree, now damaging the fine grape vines, now spoiling other tender plants. That moved God to pity, so that out of grace and goodness of heart He set on His wolves who soon tore to pieces the goats that were there. When the Devil heard that, he went before the Lord and said, "Your creation has torn mine to pieces." "Why did you create something to do harm?" answered the Lord. "I had to," said the Devil. "Just as my own thoughts run to harm, what I created could have no other nature, and You must pay me heavy damages." "I'll pay you! As soon as the leaves fall from the oaks, come to me and your money is as good as paid." When the leaves had fallen from the oaks, the Devil came and demanded his due, but the Lord said, "In the church in Constantinople there is a tall oak that still has all its leaves." Raging and cursing, the Devil vanished and set out to look for the oak, wandered about in the desert for six months before finding it, and when he got back, all the other oaks were in the meanwhile in full leaf again.

Then he had to let his debt go, but in his rage he put out the eyes of all the remaining goats and put his own in their place. For this reason all goats have the Devil's eyes and bitten-off tails, and the Devil likes to assume their form.

149 The Cock's Beam

Der Hahnenbalken

THERE WAS ONCE A MAGICIAN who was standing in the midst of a great crowd of people and performing his wonderful tricks. Among other things, he had a cock walk in which picked up a heavy beam and carried it as though it were as light as a feather. Now there was a girl, however, who had just found a four-leaf clover and had thus become so gifted that no deception could work in her presence. She saw that the beam was nothing but a straw. Then she cried out, "Don't you people see that what the cock is carrying there is just a straw and not a beam at all?" The magic delusion immediately vanished, and the people saw what it was and with jeers chased the wizard away ignominiously. However, full of suppressed rage he said, "I'll avenge myself all right!"

After a time the girl was getting married, was all dressed up and walking in a big procession across country to the village where the church was. Suddenly they came to a brook that was very swollen, and there was no bridge, big or small, to walk across on. Then the bride quickly lifted up her skirts and was about to wade through the brook. As she was thus standing right in the water, a man—and it was the magician —mockingly called out beside her, "My! where are your eyes that you think that that's a brook?" Then her eyes opened and she saw that she was standing with her skirts up in the middle of a flax field abloom with blue flowers. Then all the people saw it, too, and chased her away with jeers and laughter.

150   The Old Beggar-Woman

Die alte Bettelfrau

THERE WAS ONCE AN OLD WOMAN. Of course you've seen an old woman begging before now? This woman, too, was begging, and whenever she got anything, she would say, "God reward you!" The beggar-woman came to a door where a waggish boy was warming himself by the fire. To the poor old woman who was standing thus at the door and shivering the boy said in friendly fashion, "Come, granny, warm yourself." She came up but went too near the fire so that her old rags began to burn without her becoming aware of it. The boy was standing there and saw it. He ought to have put it out. Oughtn't he to have put it out? And if he didn't happen to have any water, then he should have wept all the water in his body out through his eyes. That would have provided two nice little brooks to put the fire out with.

151   The Three Lazy Sons

Die drei Faulen

A KING had three sons. They were all equally dear to him, and he didn't know which to name as king after his death. When the time came for him to die, he called them to his bedside and said, "Dear children, I have thought out something that I want to tell you: whichever of you is the laziest shall become king after me." The eldest said, "Father, then the kingdom belongs to me, for I'm so lazy that when I lie down and want to sleep and a drop of rain falls in my eyes, I won't shut them in order to go to sleep." The second said, "Father, the kingdom belongs to me, for I'm so lazy that when I sit warming myself by the fire, I'd rather let my heels burn than draw back my legs." The third said, "Father, the kingdom is mine, for I'm so lazy that were I to be hanged and already had the rope about my neck and if someone put a sharp knife in my hand to cut the rope with, I'd let myself be hanged sooner than lift my hand to the rope." On hearing that the father said, "You've topped it and shall be king."

151 ª The Twelve Lazy Servants

Die zwölf faulen Knechte

TWELVE SERVANTS who had done nothing all day didn't want to exert themselves even by evening but lay down in the grass and boasted about their laziness.

The first said, "What concern of mine is your laziness? I am busy with my own. My chief preoccupation is looking out for my bodily needs. I eat quite a bit and drink even more. When I've had four meals, I fast for a short time till I feel hungry again—that agrees with me best. I'm nothing for early rising; when it gets toward noon, I look for some place to rest, of course. If the master calls, I pretend I didn't hear, and if he calls a second time, I still wait a while before getting up and even then walk very slowly. That way life is bearable."

The second said, "I have a horse to look after but I leave the bit in its mouth, and if I don't want to, I don't feed it and say that it has already eaten. Instead, I lie down in the oatbin and sleep four hours. Afterward I stick out one foot and run it a few times over the horse's body; that's how it's curried and groomed. Who'd take much trouble over such business? Even so the job's too burdensome for me."

The third said, "Why be bothered with work? There's

nothing in it. Once I lay down in the sun and fell asleep. It began to drizzle, but why get up? I let it go on raining, and the deuce with it. Finally it came down cats and dogs and rained so hard that it tore the hair off my head and washed it away and I got a hole in my skull. I put a piece of court plaster on it and so it was fixed up. I've suffered other like injuries, to be sure."

The fourth said, "If I have to attack a piece of work, I first loaf around for an hour to save my strength. Then I take it very easy at the start and ask if there mightn't be others there who could help me. I let them do most of the work and really just look on. But even that's too much for me."

The fifth said, "What does all that amount to! Think of it! I'm supposed to take the manure out of the stable and load it on a cart. I let the work drag out, and when I have a little manure on the fork, I lift it only halfway up and then rest a quarter of an hour before tossing it all the way up. It's more than enough if I move out more than a cart-load a day. I have no desire to work myself to death."

The sixth said, "Shame on you! I'm not afraid of any work, but I lie down for three weeks at a time without once taking off my clothes. What's the use of buckles on one's shoes? For all I care the shoes may drop off my feet—that's no harm. If I want to go upstairs, I drag one foot slowly after the other onto the first step; then I count the remaining steps to see where I'll have to stop and rest."

The seventh said, "In my case that won't do: my master oversees my work, only he's away all day. Still I leave nothing undone; I run as fast as one can if one creeps. If I had to go on, it would take the strength of four sturdy men to push me along. I once came to where six men were lying side by side on a plank and sleeping; I lay down by them and slept, too. I couldn't be waked up again, and when they wanted to get me back home, they had to carry me off."

The eighth said, "I plainly see that I am the only one who is a wide-awake chap: if a stone is in my way, I don't bother to pick up my feet and step over it; I lie down on the ground. And if I get wet, muddy, and dirty, I stay there till the sun has dried me out again. At most I turn so it can shine on me."

The ninth said, "That's a lot! Today the bread was right in

front of me, but I was too lazy to reach for it and almost died of hunger. There was a pitcher there, too, but it was so big and heavy that I didn't want to lift it up and preferred to go thirsty. Just turning around was too much for me; I lay all day like a log."

The tenth said, "I once came to grief through my laziness, got a broken leg and a swollen calf. Three of us were lying in a cart track, and I had my legs stretched out. Then someone came along with a cart, and the wheels went over me. Of course, I might have drawn back my legs, but I didn't hear the cart coming: the midges were buzzing in my ears, crawling into my nose and out again through my mouth. Who'd take the trouble to chase the vermin away!"

The eleventh said, "I gave notice yesterday. I had no desire any longer to fetch heavy books for my master and take them away again. There was no end to it all day long. But to tell the truth, *he* dismissed *me* and didn't want to keep me any longer because his clothes that I had left lying in the dust were eaten up by moths—and quite right!"

The twelfth said, "I had to go across country today with the cart; I made a straw bed for myself in it and went properly to sleep. The reins slipped out of my hand, and when I woke up, the horse had almost got free: the harness was gone, crupper, collar, bridle, and bit. Besides, the cart had got into a slough and was stuck. I let it stay there and stretched out again on the straw. Finally my master himself came and pushed the cart out, and if he hadn't come, I shouldn't be lying here but out there sleeping in peace and quiet."

152   The Little Herdsboy

Das Hirtenbüblein

THERE WAS ONCE A HERDSBOY who, because of the wise answers which he gave to all questions was famed far and wide. The king of the country also heard about it, didn't believe it and had the boy summoned. Then he said to him, "If you can answer three questions which I shall put to you, I shall look upon you as my own child and you shall dwell with me in the royal palace." The boy said, "What are the three questions?"

The king spoke, "The first is: how many drops of water are there in the Great Ocean?" The herdsboy answered: "Sir King, have all the rivers of the world dammed up so that not a single little drop more flows out of them into the Ocean without my first counting it, and then I'll tell you how many drops there are in the Ocean."

The king spoke, "The second question is: how many stars are there in the heavens?" The herdsboy said, "Give me a big sheet of white paper." Then with a pen he made so many tiny dots on it that one could hardly see them and they were scarcely to be counted, and when one looked at them, one's vision blurred. Then he said, "There are as many stars in the heavens as there are dots on the paper here. Just count them!" But no one could do it.

The king spoke, "The third question is: how many seconds has eternity?" Then the herdsboy said, "In Farther Pomerania is the Diamond Mountain; it is four miles high, and at the base four miles through. Every hundred years a little bird comes and sharpens its bill on it, and when the whole mountain has thus been worn away, then the first second of eternity has passed."

"You have solved the three questions like a sage," said the king, "and henceforth you shall dwell with me in my royal palace, and I shall look upon you as my own child."

153 The Star Dollars

Die Sterntaler

THERE WAS ONCE A LITTLE GIRL whose mother and father had died. She was so poor that she no longer had a room to live in nor bed to sleep in and finally had nothing but the clothes on her back and in her hand a piece of bread that some kind soul had given her. But she was devout and good, and because she was so forsaken by the whole world, she went out into the country, trusting in the good Lord. There she met a poor man who said, "Oh, give me something to eat, I'm so hungry." She handed him the whole piece of bread, saying, "God bless you," and went on. Then came a child who cried and said, "My head is so cold, give me something to cover it with." Then she took off her hood and gave it to the child. When she had been walking a little while more, a second child came who had no bodice and was freezing; then she gave it hers. Still farther on a third child begged for a skirt and this she also gave up. At last she got into a forest, and it had already grown dark. Then came still a fourth child and begged for a shirt, and the devout little girl thought, "The night is dark and no one will see you; of course you can give away your shirt," and taking it off she gave even that to the child. As she was standing thus and had nothing at all more left, suddenly the stars fell from the sky and were just solid bright dollars, and although she had given her shirt away, she then had a new one on, and it was of the very finest linen. Then she gathered up the dollars and was rich as long as she lived.

154 The Stolen Farthing

Der gestohlene Heller

ONCE A FATHER was sitting at table at noon with his wife and children and a good friend who had come on a visit and was dining with them. As they were sitting thus and it struck twelve, the visitor saw the door open and a little child come in, clad in snow-white dress and very pale. It neither looked about nor said anything but went straight into the next room. Soon afterward it came back and just as quietly went out the door again. On the second and third day it came in just the same way. Finally the visitor asked the father whose was the lovely child that went into the room every day at noon. "I haven't seen it," he answered, "and in any event I wouldn't know whose child it might be." When it came back the next day, the visitor pointed it out to the father, but the latter didn't see it, nor did the mother and the children see anything. Now the visitor got up, went to the door of the room, opened it a little, and looked in. There he saw the child sitting on the floor, busily picking and digging with its fingers in the cracks in the floor boards; on noticing the visitor, however, it vanished. Now he related what he had seen and described the child exactly. Then the mother recognized it and said, "Alas! it's my dear child that died four weeks ago."

They pulled up the flooring and found two farthings. The child had once got them from its mother to give to a poor man but had thought, "You can buy yourself a rusk with that," had kept the farthings and hidden them in the cracks in the floor. And then it had not rested in its grave and had come every day at noon to look for the farthings. Thereupon the parents at once gave the money to a poor man, and since then the child has not been seen again.

155 Choosing a Bride

Die Brautschau

THERE WAS A YOUNG HERDSBOY who very much wanted to get married and knew three sisters, each as fair as the other, so that it was hard for him to choose among them, and he couldn't decide which he preferred. Then he asked his mother for advice. "Invite all three here," she said, "and put some cheese before them and watch how they cut it." The boy did so. The first sister gobbled up the cheese along with the rind; the second cut the rind off the cheese hurriedly, doing it so hastily that she left a lot of the good part, which she threw away with the rind; the third pared the rind properly, neither too much nor too little. The herdsboy told his mother the whole story. Then she said, "Marry the third." He did so and lived with her happily and contentedly.

156 The Cast-Off Remnants

Die Schickerlinge

THERE WAS ONCE A GIRL who was beautiful, though lazy and careless. When she was asked to spin, it so vexed her that if there was a tiny knot in the flax, she'd at once tear out a whole bunch along with the knot and discard it on the floor beside her. Now she had a maid who was industrious, gathered up the flax which she had thrown away, cleaned it, spun it fine, and had a pretty dress woven out of it.

A young man had been wooing the lazy girl, and the wedding was about to take place. The night before the wedding while the industrious maidservant was dancing merrily around in her pretty dress, the bride said,

> "My! how the girl can hop around
> In my discarded remnants!"

The bridegroom heard this and asked the bride what she meant by it. Then she told him that the maid was wearing a dress made from the flax she had thrown away. When the bridegroom heard that and noticed her laziness and the industry of the poor servant girl, he left her where she was, went to the other, and chose her as his wife.

157   The Sparrow and Its Four Children

Der Sperling und seine vier Kinder

A SPARROW had four little ones in a swallow's nest. Now when they were fledged, bad boys smashed up the nest, though all escaped in a gust of wind. Now, because his sons were out in the world, the old bird sorry that he hadn't first warned them against all kinds of dangers and given them some good advice.

In the autumn lots of sparrows forgathered in a wheat-field, and there the old bird met his four boys, whom he joy-fully took home with him. "Oh, my dear sons, how you've worried me during the summer by taking to the air without instruction from me. Listen to my words and follow your father and watch out carefully. Great are the dangers that young birds have to undergo!" Thereupon, he asked the eldest where he had stayed during the summer and how he had fed himself. "I stayed in gardens and looked for caterpillars and worms till the cherries were ripe." "Oh, my son," said the father, "those aren't bad delicacies, but there is great danger connected with them; therefore always be on the lookout and especially when people walk about a garden carrying long green poles that are hollow inside and have a little hole in the top." "Yes, father," said the son, "but supposing a green leaf were pasted over the hole with wax?" "Where did you see that?" "In a merchant's garden," said the son. "Oh, my son," said the father, "merchants! smart people! If you've been among worldlings, you've learned the ways of the world aplenty! See that you make good use of it and don't be over-confident."

Then he asked the second, "Where did you keep yourself?" "At court," says the son. "Sparrows and simple birds don't serve there where there's much gold, velvet, silks, weapons, equipment, sparrow hawks, owls, and lanner falcons. Stick to a horse stable, where oats are winnowed and where there's threshing; there's where fortune can favor you with peace and quiet and your daily bit of grain." "Yes, father," said the second son, "but supposing the grooms make bird traps and lay their nets and snares in the straw; then many a bird gets caught and strangled." "Where did you see that?" said the old bird. "At court among the grooms." "Oh, my son, the court pages! bad boys! If you've been at court and round the gentry and have got away with your feathers, you've learned quite a bit and surely know how to get on in the world. Just the same, be cautious and watch out. Wolves often eat up smart little puppies, too."

The father had the third one up before him, too. "Where did you seek your fortune?" "I cast my line and bucket on the highways and byways and now and then caught a grain of rye or barley there." "That is certainly fine feed," said the father, "but at the same time be on the lookout against danger and watch out very carefully, especially if anybody bends down and is about to pick up a stone. Then it's no time to linger about." "That's right," said the son, "but supposing someone were carrying a stone or a rock in his bosom or in his pocket?" "Where did you see that?" "Among the miners, father dear. When they go to work, they generally take stones with them." "Miners! workmen! clever people! If you've been around miner boys, you've seen something and learned something.

Be off and look out all the same for your affairs;
Miner lads have killed many a sparrow with a piece of cobalt."

Finally the father came to the youngest son. "You, my dear little chatterbox, always were the stupidest and weakest. Stay with me. There are many coarse and bad birds in the world with crooked bills and long claws that are just lying in wait to gobble up poor little birds. Keep to your own kind and pick up spiders and caterpillars from trees or houses; in that way you will be happy for a long time." "Father dear, whoever supports himself without harming other people gets a long way, and no sparrow hawk, hawk, eagle, or kite will hurt him, especially if every evening and every morning he faithfully commends himself and his honestly earned daily bread to God, Creator and Preserver of all birds of forest or town, to God Who even hearkens to the cry and prayer of young ravens. No sparrow or wren falls to the ground against His will." "Where did you learn this?" "When the big gust of wind tore me away from you," answered the son, "I got to a church where during the summer I garnered flies and spiders from the windows and heard this doctrine preached. There the Father of all sparrows fed me throughout the summer and guarded me from every misfortune and from fierce birds." "In truth, dear son, if you fly into churches and help clear away spiders and buzzing flies and chirp to God like the young ravens and commend yourself to the Eternal Creator, you will be all right, even if the whole world were full of fierce and wily birds,

For whoever commends his case to the Lord,
Is silent, patient, waits, prays, and is discreet and calm,
Keeps faith and keeps his conscience clear,
God will be a Protector and Helper."

158   A Tale of The Land of Cockaigne

Das Märchen vom Schlauraffenland

IN THE DAYS of the Land of Cockaigne I went and saw Rome and the Lateran hanging by a little silk thread and a footless man overtaking a fast horse and a keen-edged sword cutting through a bridge. I saw a young donkey with a silver nose chasing after two fast hares and a spreading linden that hot cakes were growing on. I saw an old dried-up goat carrying a good two hundred cartloads of lard and sixty of salt. Isn't that a big enough lie?

I saw a plough turning furrows without horse or ox, and a year-old child was throwing four millstones from Regensburg to Treves and from Treves into Strasbourg. And a hawk swam across the Rhine, as it had every right to. I heard fish start arguing so loud with one another that it sounded to high heaven, while sweet honey flowed like water from a deep valley onto a high mountain. Strange tales these!

Two crows were mowing a meadow, and I saw two midges busily building a bridge, and two doves were picking a wolf to pieces and two children brought forth two kids, while two frogs were threshing grain. I saw two mice consecrating a bishop, two cats scratching out a bear's tongue. Then a snail came on the run and killed two wild lions. There was a barber there shaving off a woman's beard and two suckling babes were telling their mother to keep quiet. Then I saw two deerhounds carrying a mill out of the water, and an old nag was standing by, saying it was quite all right. And four horses were standing in the courtyard threshing grain as hard as they could, and two goats were heating up an oven and a red cow was sliding the bread into it. Then a cock crowed cock-a-doodle-do. That's the end of the tale: cock-a-doodle-do!

159   A Tall Tale from Ditmarsh

Das Dietmarsische Lügenmärchen

I WANT to tell you something. I saw two roast chickens flying: they flew fast and had their bellies turned toward Heaven, their backs toward Hell. And an anvil and a millstone swam very slowly and quietly across the Rhine, while at Whitsun a frog sat and ate up a ploughshare on the ice. There were three lads there who wanted to catch a hare: one was deaf, the second blind, the third dumb, while a fourth couldn't stir a foot. Would you like to know how it turned out? The blind lad was the first to see the hare trotting across the field, the dumb boy called to the lame chap, and the lame fellow seized it by the collar. Some people wanted to go sailing on land and set their sail in the wind and sailed away over the broad fields. Then they sailed over a high mountain, where they drowned miserably. A crab put a hare to flight, and way up on the roof lay a cow that had climbed up there. In that region flies are as big as goats are here. Open the window and let the lies out!

160 A Riddling Tale

Rätselmärchen

THREE WOMEN were changed into flowers and were in a field. One of them, however, was allowed to be home nights. On one occasion as day was approaching and she had to get back to her playmates in the field and become a flower, she said to her husband, "If you come this forenoon and pluck me, I'll be freed from the spell and from then on may stay with you." So it was done.

Now the question is: How did her husband recognize her, since the flowers were all alike, with no difference among them? Answer: Since during the night she had been at home and not out in the field, no dew had fallen upon her as on the other two. That is how her husband recognized her.

161 Snow-White and Rose-Red

Schneeweischen und Rosenrot

A POOR WIDOW lived alone in a cottage, and before the cottage was a garden in which were two rose bushes: one of them bore white roses, the other red. And she had two children who were like the two rose bushes: one was called Snow-White, the other Rose-Red, and they were as devout and good, as industrious and unspoiled, as ever two children in the world. Snow-White was, however, quieter and gentler than Rose-Red. Rose-Red liked rather to run about in the meadows and fields, look for flowers and catch butterflies, while Snow-White stayed home with her mother, helped her with the housework or read aloud to her when there was nothing else to do. The two children loved each other so, that whenever they went out together, they always walked hand in hand. And when Snow-White would say, "We'll never desert one another," Rose-Red would answer, "Not as long as we live," and their mother would add, "What one has, she must share with the other." Often they would run about alone in the forest and gather berries, but no animal did them any harm. On the contrary, they would come up in friendly fashion: hares would eat a cabbage leaf out of their hands, roes graze at their side, stags jump merrily past, and birds would stay perched on the branches and sing for all they were worth. No misfortune befell them: when they stayed out too late in the forest and night overtook them, they would lie down side by side on the moss and sleep until morning, and their mother knew that and didn't worry about them.

Once when they had spent the night in the forest and the dawn awakened them, they saw a lovely child in a shining white dress sitting beside their resting-place. It got up and looked at them in most kindly fashion, said nothing, however, and walked off into the forest. And when they looked about, there they had been sleeping right beside a precipice and would certainly have fallen over had they gone a few steps more in the dark. Their mother told them that it must have been the angel that watches over good children.

Snow-White and Rose-Red kept their mother's cottage so clean that it was a pleasure to look into it. In summer Rose-Red took care of the house and every morning would put by her mother's bed before she woke up a bunch of flowers with a rose from each bush. In winter Snow-White would light the fire and hang the kettle on the hook; the kettle was of brass but shone like gold because it was scoured so clean. Evenings, when the flakes were falling, the mother would say, "Snow-White, go bolt the door," and then they would sit down by the hearth and their mother would take her glasses and read aloud from a big book and the two girls would listen, sitting and spinning. On the floor beside them lay a lamb, and behind them on a perch sat a white dove with its head tucked under its wing.

One evening when they were thus cosily sitting together, someone knocked on the door as if to be let in. Then their mother said, "Quick, Rose-Red, open the door; it's probably a traveler seeking shelter." Rose-Red went and drew the bolt and thought it might be some poor man; but it wasn't, it was a bear, which stuck its big black head in the door. Rose-Red uttered a loud cry and jumped back: the lamb bleated, the dove fluttered up in the air, and Snow-White hid behind her mother's bed. However, the bear began to talk, saying, "Don't be afraid, I'll do you no harm. I'm half frozen and only want to warm myself a bit in your cottage." "You poor bear," said the mother, "lie down by the fire and just watch out that your fur doesn't catch fire." Then she called, "Snow-White! Rose-Red! come on out. The bear will do you no harm; it means well." Then they both drew near, and gradually the lamb and the dove approached, too, and weren't afraid of it. "Children," said the bear, "beat the snow a little out of my fur," and they fetched a broom and swept its coat clean while the bear stretched out by the fire and growled most contentedly and comfortably. Before long they got on the most friendly terms and had fun with the ungainly guest. They tugged at its coat with their hands, put their feet on its back and rolled it about. Or they would take a hazel-rod and beat away at it and laugh when it growled. The bear took it all in good part, though if they went too far, it would call out, "Spare my life, children.

> Snow-White and Rose-Red
> You're beating your suitor to death!"

When it was time to go to sleep and the others were going to bed, the mother said to the bear, "Of course you may stay there by the hearth; in that way you'll be sheltered from the cold and bad weather." In the first grey light to the dawn the two children let it out, and off it trotted over the snow into the forest. From now on the bear came every evening at the regular time, would lie down by the hearth and let the children play with it as much as they liked. And they were so used to it that they didn't bolt the door till their black friend had come.

When spring came and outdoors everything was green, the bear said one morning to Snow-White, "Now I must go away and may not come back all summer." "Where are you going, dear bear?" asked Snow-White. "I've got to go into the forest and guard my treasures from the wicked dwarfs. In winter when the ground is frozen hard, of course they have to stay underground and can't work their way through, but now that the sun has thawed and warmed the earth, they can break through, climb up, and search and steal. Once anything gets into their hands and is in their caves, it's not discovered again so easily!" Snow-White was very sad to say good-bye, and when she had unbolted the door for it and the bear was squeezing its way out, it caught on the door hook and tore a piece of its skin. Then Snow-White thought she saw something like gold shining through, though she wasn't sure of it. The bear hurried off and soon disappeared behind the trees.

Some time later their mother sent the children into the forest to gather brushwood. Out there they found a big tree that was lying fallen to the ground, and beside the trunk something was jumping up and down in the grass, though they couldn't make out what it was. On coming nearer, they saw a dwarf with an old withered face and a snow-white beard over two feet long. The tip of the beard was caught in a cleft in the trunk and the little fellow was jumping about like a puppy on a leash and was quite helpless. He stared at the girls with his fiery red eyes and screamed, "Why are you standing there! Can't you come here and help me?" "What have you been up to, little dwarf?" asked Rose-Red. "Stupid, inquisitive goose!" answered the dwarf. "I was going to split the trunk to get some small kindling for the kitchen; with big chunks of wood the little food that one of us needs burns right up. We don't gobble down as much as you coarse greedy people. I had already driven the wedge in all right, and everything would have gone finely, but the cursed wood was too slippery so that the wedge unexpectedly flew out and the trunk snapped together so quickly that I no longer could pull my lovely white beard out. Now it's stuck in there and

I can't get away. There those flat stupid pasty faces are laughing! Shame on you! How disgusting you are!" The children worked as hard as they could but were unable to pull the beard out—it was in too tight. "I'll run and get help," said Rose-Red. "Crazy blockheads!" snarled the dwarf. "Think of calling for help straight off! Two of you are too many for me as it is. Can't you think of anything better?" "Don't be so impatient," said Snow-White. "I'll manage, of course," fetched her scissors from her bag and cut off the tip of the beard. As soon as the drawf felt himself free, he seized the sack that was hidden among the roots of the tree and was filled with gold, lifted it out, growling to himself, "Crude people! Think of cutting off a piece of my fine beard! The deuce with you!" With those words he swung his sack onto his back and went off without another look at the children.

Some time later Snow-White and Rose-Red were going to catch a mess of fish. When they got near the brook, they saw something like a big grasshopper hopping toward the water as if it were going to jump in. They ran up and recognized the dwarf. "Where are you going?" said Rose-Red. "You surely don't want to get into the water." "I'm no such fool," screamed the dwarf. "Don't you see that the cursed fish is about to pull me in?" The little fellow had been sitting there fishing and unfortunately the wind had tangled his beard in the line. When immediately afterward a big fish had bitten, the weak creature lacked the strength to land it. The fish kept the upper hand and was dragging the dwarf toward itself. Of course he was holding onto every stalk and rush, but that wasn't doing much good; he had to follow the movements of the fish and was in imminent danger of being drawn into the water. The girls arrived in the nick of time, held him tight, and tried to get the beard free of the line, but in vain, for beard and line were tangled fast together. There was nothing to do but fetch the scissors and cut off some beard, as a result of which a little of it was lost. When the dwarf saw that, he screamed at them, "Is that good manners, you toads, to spoil a man's face? It wasn't enough to dock the tip of my beard! Now you go and cut off the best part of it! Why I can't show myself among my own people! May you be forced to run without soles on your shoes!" Then he fetched a sack of pearls that was lying in the reeds and without another word dragged it away and vanished behind a rock.

Soon after it happened that the mother sent the two girls into town to buy thread, needles, bodice laces, and ribbons. The way took them across a heath on which big boulders lay scattered here and there and where they saw a big bird soaring in the air. It circled slowly above them, kept coming lower and lower, and finally pounced down by a boulder not far off. Immediately afterward they heard a piercing, piteous cry. They ran up and to their consternation saw that the eagle had seized their old acquaintance the dwarf and was about to carry him off. The compassionate children held the dwarf fast and tussled about with the eagle so long that it finally let go its prey. When the dwarf had got over his first fright, he screamed out at them with his shrill voice, "Couldn't you have handled me more decently? You tugged at my thin little coat so that it's all in tatters and full of holes. Clumsy, awkward rowdies, that's what you are!" Then he took his sack of gems and again slipped under the boulder into his cave. By now the girls were used to his ingratitude and went about their business in town. When they got back onto the heath on their way home, they took the dwarf by surprise: he had emptied out his sack of precious stones on a clear spot, not thinking that anybody would be coming along so late. The afternoon sun was shining on the sparkling gems and they glistened and gleamed so magnificently in every color that the children stopped and looked at them. "Why are you standing there gaping?" cried the dwarf, his ashen face growing purple with rage. He was about to go on with his abuse when a loud growl was heard and a black bear trotted out of the forest. The dwarf jumped up in terror but couldn't reach his hiding place, for the bear was already close upon him. Then in anguish of heart he called, "Dear Mister Bear, spare me! I'll give you all my treasures. See the beautiful jewels that are lying there! Grant me my life. What have you got against me, weak little fellow that I am? You wouldn't notice me between your teeth. There! take the two bad girls; they'll be a tender morsel for you—fat as young quail. You're welcome to eat them up." The bear took no notice of what he was saying, struck the malicious creature a single blow with its paw, and he stirred no more.

The girls had run off, but the bear called after them, "Snow-White and Rose-Red, don't be afraid. Wait and I'll come with you." Then they recognized its voice and stopped. When the bear had caught up with them, its bear's skin suddenly dropped off and there he stood, a handsome man clad all in gold. "I am a king's son," he said, "and was enchanted by the wicked dwarf, who had stolen my treasures, so that I had to go about in the forest as a wild bear until I was freed from the spell by his death. Now he has received his well deserved punishment."

Snow-White married him, and Rose-Red his brother, and they shared the great treasures which the dwarf had collected in his cave. Their old mother lived quietly and happily with her children many years more. But she brought the two rose bushes along, and they stood outside her window and every year bore the most beautiful roses, white and red.

162   The Clever Servant

Der kluge Knecht

HOW LUCKY is the master and how well things go with his household when he has a clever servant who, to be sure, listens to his words but doesn't act accordingly and who prefers to follow his own counsel!

That kind of smart Johnny was once dispatched by his master to look for a lost cow. He stayed out a long time, and the master thought, "Faithful John, he spares no pains in his work." But when he didn't come back and didn't come back, his master was afraid that something might have happened to him, got ready to go himself and set out to look for him. He had to look for a long time; finally he spied the servant running up and down a big field. "Now, dear John," said the master, once he had caught up with him, "did you find the cow I sent you out after?" "No, sir," he answered, "I didn't find the cow, but then I didn't look for it." "What did you look for, John?" "Something better, and I was lucky enough to find it." "What is it, John?" "Three blackbirds," answered the servant. "And where are they?" asked the master. "I see one, I hear the second, and I'm after the third," answered the clever servant.

Take example from this, pay no attention to your master and his orders. Do, rather, what occurs to you and do what you want; then you'll be acting just as wisely as clever John.

163   The Glass Coffin

Der gläserne Sarg

ONE SHOULD NEVER say that a poor tailor can't get ahead and attain high honors; all he has to do is to get on the right track and above all have good luck.

This kind of a good and smart tailor boy was once on his travels, came to a big forest and, not knowing the way, got lost. Night fell, and he could only look for a resting place in this scary solitude. He would, to be sure, have found a comfortable bed on the soft moss, but fear of wild animals gave him no rest, and finally he perforce decided to spend the night in a tree. He sought out a tall oak, climbed up to the top, and thanked God that he had kept his tailor's goose, for otherwise the wind that was sweeping through the treetops would have carried him away.

After he had spent some hours in the dark and not without fear and trembling, he spied a short way off the gleam of a light, and thinking it might be a human habitation where he would be better off than in the branches of a tree, he cautiously climbed down and went toward the light. It led him to a little wattled cottage of reeds and rushes. He knocked boldly, the door opened, and by the light that streamed out he saw an old grey-haired dwarf who was wearing a garment made of patches of many colors. "Who are you and what do you want?" he asked in a snarling voice. "I am a poor tailor," he answered, "overtaken by night here in the wilderness, and I implore you to take me into your hut till morning." "Go away," replied the old man in a surly tone. "I'll have nothing to do with tramps. Look for shelter for yourself elsewhere." After these words he was about to slip back into his house, but the tailor held fast to his coattail and begged him so insistently that the old man, who was not as bad as he made himself out to be, finally gave in and took him into his cottage, where he gave him food and then assigned him a very good resting place in a corner.

The weary tailor didn't need to be rocked to sleep but slept peacefully till morning and even then would not have thought of getting up had he not been startled by a loud noise. A violent shrieking and roaring penetrated the thin walls of the house. The tailor, overcome by unexpected bravery, jumped up, put on his clothes in a hurry, and hastened out. There near the house he saw a big black bull and a beautiful stag engaged in the most violent combat. They were going for one another so furiously that the ground shook from the tramp of their hoofs and the air resounded with their cries. For a long time it was uncertain which of the two would carry off the victory. Finally the stag pierced its opponent with its antlers, whereupon the bull sank to the earth with a horrible roar and was finished off by a few blows from the stag.

The tailor, who had viewed the fight with amazement, was still standing there motionless when the stag rushed at him at full gallop and, before he could escape, forked him right up in his antlers. It took him a long time to collect his thoughts, for they went at great speed over sticks and stones, hill and dale, forest and field. He held on to the points of the antlers with both his hands and surrendered himself to his fate. All he realized was that he was flying away. Finally the stag stopped in front of the side of a cliff and let the tailor gently down. The latter, more dead than alive, needed quite some time to collect his thoughts. When he had more or less recovered, the stag, who had stayed beside him, thrust its antlers so violently against a door that was in the cliff that it sprang open. Fiery flames shot out, then a great cloud of steam removed the stag from his view. The tailor didn't know what to do or where to turn in order to get out of this waste land and back among men. While he was thus standing undecided, a voice sounded from out of the cliff calling to him, "Have no fear and step in; no harm will befall you." He hesitated, to be sure, but, impelled by some occult power, he obeyed the voice and through the iron door got into a large and spacious hall whose ceilings, walls, and floors were made of polished, shining flags of square-cut stone, in each of which were cut designs unfamiliar to him. Marveling, he viewed it all and was just on the point of going out again when once more he heard the voice saying to him, "Step onto the stone that is in the middle of the hall and great good fortune awaits you."

His courage had now grown so that he followed the order. The stone began to give way under his feet and sank slowly down. When it had once again come solidly to rest and the tailor looked about, he found himself in a hall that in extent was like the other, though here there was more to look at and admire. In the wall were cut recesses in which stood vessels of clear glass filled with colored alcohol or a bluish smoke. On the floor of the hall stood facing one another two big glass cases which at once excited his curiosity. On stepping up to one of them he saw in it a beautiful building like a manor house, surrounded by outbuildings, stables, and barns, and a number of other pretty objects. Everything was small and extremely carefully and nicely wrought and seemed to have been cut out with the greatest precision by a skillful hand.

He wouldn't yet have turned his eyes from viewing these curiosities had not the voice again let itself be heard. It ordered him to turn around and look at the glass case opposite. How his admiration rose when in it he saw a maiden of surpassing beauty! She lay as if asleep and was wrapped in long blond hair as in a costly cloak. Her eyes were closed tight, but her fresh complexion and a ribbon that her breathing moved up and down left no doubt as to her being alive. With beating heart the tailor was looking at the beautiful girl, when suddenly she opened her eyes and, on seeing him, started with pleasurable fright. "Merciful heavens!" she cried, "the hour of my deliverance is drawing near. Quick! quick! Help me out of my prison. If you slip the bolt on the glass coffin, I shall be disenchanted." Without hesitation the tailor obeyed. At once she raised the glass lid, climbed out and hurried to a corner of the hall where she wrapped herself in an ample cloak. Then she sat down on a stone, bade the young man come up and, after pressing a friendly kiss on his mouth, said, "My long longed-for deliverer, kind Heaven has led you to me and set a limit to my sufferings. On the very day they come to an end, your good fortune will begin. You are the spouse appointed by Heaven, and, loved by me and overwhelmed with all earthly good, you shall spend your life in untroubled joy. Sit down and hear the story of my fate."

"I am the daughter of a wealthy count. My parents died when I was still of tender age and in their last will and testament commended me to my elder brother, who brought me up. We loved one another so tenderly and accorded so in our way of thinking and our tastes that we both decided never to marry but to remain together to the end of our lives. In our home there was no lack of society: neighbors and friends visited us often and to everybody we extended hospitality in full measure. So, too, it happened one evening that a stranger came riding up to our manor and, on pretext of not being able to reach the next town, asked for a night's lodging. We granted his request with complete courtesy, and during the evening meal he entertained us most charmingly with his conversation, which he interspersed with stories. My brother took such a fancy to him that he asked him to spend a few days with us, to which invitation he agreed after some slight hesitation. We didn't leave the table until late in the evening; the stranger was shown a room, while I, being tired, made haste to repose my limbs in my soft feather bed. Scarcely had I dozed off a bit when the sounds of tender and lovely music awakened me. Since I couldn't imagine where the music came from, I was about to call my chambermaid, who slept in the adjoining room, but to my astonishment I found myself deprived of the power of speech by some unknown force that weighed on my breast like an incubus and discovered that I was unable to utter the slightest sound. At the same time, by the gleam of my night light, I saw the stranger step into my room, which was shut off by two tightly locked doors. He drew near me and said that by magic powers at his command he had caused the lovely music to be played in order to wake me up and that he was now forcing his way through all locks to offer me his heart and hand. My abhorrence of his magic arts was, however, so great that I deigned him no answer. For quite a while he stood motionless, probably with a view to waiting for a favorable answer, but since I continued my silence, he said angrily that he would avenge himself and find a way to punish my pride. Whereupon he left the room. I spent a most restless night and fell asleep only toward morning. When I was awakened, I hurried to my brother to inform him of what had happened. But I didn't find him in his room, and the servant told me that he had gone hunting with the stranger at break of day.

"I at once felt that this boded no good. I got dressed quickly, had my favorite palfrey saddled and, accompanied by only one servant, rode at full speed toward the forest. The servant and his horse fell, and since the horse had broken its leg, he could not go on with me. I continued on my way without stopping and in a few minutes saw the stranger coming toward me, leading a fine stag by a rope. I asked him where he had left my brother and how he had got the stag, from whose great eyes I saw tears flowing. Instead of answering me he began to laugh aloud. At that I became exceedingly angry, drew a pistol, and fired at the monster; the bullet, however, rebounded from his chest and went into my horse's head. I fell to the ground and the stranger murmured some words that robbed me of consciousness.

"When I came to my senses again, I found myself in a glass coffin in this underground crypt. The sorcerer appeared once again and said that he had transformed my brother into a stag, reduced the size of my palace and its appurtenances, had enclosed it in the other glass case, imprisoned my followers in glass bottles, and changed them into smoke. Were I willing to accede now to his wish, it would be an easy matter for him to restore everything to its former state; he needed only to open the receptacles and everything would return to its natural form. I answered him no more than the first time. He vanished, leaving me lying in my prison, where a deep sleep fell upon me. Among the visions that passed through my mind was the consoling picture of a young man coming and freeing me, and, as I open my eyes today, I see you and see my dream fulfilled. Help me carry out the rest of what happened in that vision. The first thing is for us to lift the glass case in which my palace is onto yonder broad stone."

As soon as the weight was put on the stone, it raised itself up together with the maiden and young man and rose through an opening in the ceiling into the upper hall, where they could then easily get out into the open. At this point the girl opened the lid, and it was extraordinary to see how palace, out-buildings, and farmsteads expanded and with the greatest speed grew to their natural size. Then they went back into the underground crypt and had the stone bring up the bottles. Scarcely had the maiden opened these when the blue smoke poured out and turned into living people in whom she recognized her servants and retainers. Her joy was further increased when her brother, who had killed the sorcerer when in the form of a bull, came out of the forest in human form. And on the very same day the maiden, in accordance with her promise, gave the lucky tailor her hand at the altar.

164 Lazy Harry

Der faule Heinz

HARRY WAS LAZY, and though he had nothing else to do but drive his goat to pasture every day, on coming home after a full day's work, he would sigh. "It's truly a heavy burden and a tiresome business," he would say, "to drive a goat to pasture year in and year out like that until late in the autumn. If one could at least lie down, when one is about it, and sleep! But no, out there one must keep one's eyes open so that it won't hurt the young trees, force its way through a hedge into a garden, or even run away. How is one to manage to get any rest and enjoy life!" He sat down, collected his thoughts and reflected on how to get this burden off his shoulders. For a long time all meditation was in vain; suddenly the scales seemed to fall from his eyes. "I know what I'll do," he cried out. "I'll marry Fat Katy; she has a goat, too, and can drive mine to pasture along with hers; then I shan't have to torment myself any longer."

So Harry got up, set his weary limbs in motion, went diagonally across the street—for the distance was no greater than that—to where Katy's parents lived, and sued for the hand of their industrious and virtuous daughter. The parents didn't take long to make up their minds. "Birds of a feather flock gladly together," they thought and agreed to the arrangement. Now Fat Katy became Harry's wife and drove both goats to pasture. Those were happy days for Harry, and he didn't have to rest up from any other work but his own laziness. Only once in a while would he go to pasture with her, saying, "It's just so I can enjoy the rest afterward better; otherwise one loses all appreciation of it."

But Fat Katy was no less lazy. "Harry dear," she said one day, "why should we make our lives unnecessarily miserable and burden the best years of our youth? Wouldn't it be better to give our neighbor the two goats that disturb the best part of one's sleep every morning with their bleating, and let him give us the beehive for them? We'll set the hive up in a sunny spot behind the house and bother no further with it. The bees don't need to be tended and driven out to pasture: they'll fly off, find their own way home, and gather honey without giving us the least trouble." "Spoken like an intelligent woman!" answered Harry. "We'll carry out your suggestion without delay. Besides, honey tastes better and is more nourishing than goat's milk and can be kept longer, too." The neighbor was glad to give them a hive of bees for the two goats. The bees flew indefatigably in and out from morning to night and filled the hive with the finest honey, so that in the autumn Harry was able to take out a whole jug full. They set the jug on a shelf that was fastened up on the wall of their bedroom. And because they were afraid that it might be stolen or that mice might come upon it, Katy fetched a stout hazel rod and laid it beside her bed so that she could reach it with her hand without getting up unnecessarily and from bed could drive the uninvited guests away.

Lazy Harry didn't like to get out of bed before noon. "An early riser," he would say, "consumes his substance." One morning as he was still lying in bed in broad daylight and resting up from a long sleep, he said to his wife, "Women love sweets, and you nibble away at the honey on the sly; it would be better, before you've eaten it all up, for us to trade it for a goose and a young gosling." "But not till we have a child to tend them," replied Katy. "Why should I torment myself with the young geese and exert myself unnecessarily over them?" "Do you think our boy will tend the geese? Now-a-days children no longer obey. They do what they want, for they think that they're cleverer than their parents, just like the farmhand who was supposed to look for a cow and chased after three blackbirds." [No. 162] "Oh," answered Katy, "it will go hard with him if he doesn't do what I say. I'll take a stick and tan his hide without counting the blows. Look, Harry!" she cried in her zeal, seizing the stick with which she was going to drive away the mice, "Look! this is how I'll beat him up." She raised her arm but unluckily hit the jug of honey above the bed. The jug bounced against the wall and fell in smithereens, and the fine honey ran onto the floor. "Well, there lie the goose and the young gosling," said Harry, "and don't need to be tended. But it's a blessing the jug didn't fall on my head. We have every reason to be pleased with our fate." And noticing that there was still some honey on one of the shards, he reached for it and said contentedly, "Wife, let's enjoy the bit that's left and then take a little rest after the fright we've had. What difference does it make if we do get up a little later than usual? The day's long enough as it is." "Yes," answered Katy, "one always gets there on time somehow. You know, a snail was once invited to a wedding, set out, and arrived for the christening. In front of the house it tumbled over the fence and said, 'There's no good hurrying.'"

165 The Griffin Bird

Der Vogel Greif

ONCE UPON A TIME there was a king. I have no idea where he ruled or what his name was. He had no son, just an only daughter; she was always ill and no doctor could cure her. It was prophesied to the king that his daughter would eat herself well on apples. Then he had proclaimed throughout the length and breadth of his land that whoever should bring his daughter apples that she could eat herself well on might marry her and become king.

A farmer who had three sons heard of this, too. To the eldest he said, "Go to the storehouse, take a basket full of those fine apples with red cheeks and carry them to court; perhaps the king's daughter can eat herself well on them and you may marry her and will become king." The lad did so and set out. When he had been walking for some time, he met a little grey-haired dwarf who asked him what he had in the basket. Then Ulrich—for that was his name—said, "Tadpoles." Thereupon the dwarf said, "Let it be so and remain so," and went on. At last Ulrich got to the palace and had them announce that he had apples that would make the princess well if she ate some. That greatly pleased the king and he had Ulrich come in to his presence, but oh dear! when he took off the cover, instead of apples he had in the basket tadpoles that were still wriggling. At that the king got angry and had him chased out of the house.

When he got home, he told his father how it had fared with him. Then the father dispatched the second son, whose name was Sam, but it fared with him just as with Ulrich. He, too, met the same little grey-haired dwarf, who asked him what he had there in the basket. "Pigs' bristles," said Sam and the dwarf said, "Let it be so and remain so." When he got to the royal palace and said that he had apples on which the king's daughter could eat herself well, they didn't want to let him in and said that one person had already been there and made fools of them. Sam, however, insisted that he really had apples and that they should let him in. Finally they believed him and brought him before the king. Yet when he uncovered the basket, he had only pigs' bristles. That angered the king frightfully and he had Sam driven out with a whip.

When he got home, he told how it had fared with him. Then came the youngest boy, whom they called Stupid John, and asked his father whether he, too, might go with some apples. "Yes," said his father, "you'd be the right fellow for that! If the clever boys didn't manage it, what do you expect to accomplish?" But the boy didn't give up and said, "Well, father, I want to go too." "Get away from me, you stupid fellow; you must wait till you're smarter," replied his father, turning his back on him. John, however, gave a tug at his father's smock from behind. "Well, father, I want to go, too." "Well, go for all of me! You'll surely come back again," answered the father sullenly. The boy was, however, terribly pleased and jumped for joy. "Yes, go act the fool; you're getting stupider every day," repeated the father. But that made no difference to John, who didn't let his happiness be spoiled. Yet because it was already night, he thought he'd wait till morning; he couldn't get to court that day, anyhow. That night in bed he couldn't sleep and even when he dozed off a bit, he dreamed of fair maidens, palaces, gold and silver, and all sorts of such like things.

Early the next morning he set out and straightway met the tiny little grey-haired dwarf in a grey coat, who asked him what he had there in the basket. John answered that he had apples on which the king's daughter was to eat herself well. "Well," said the dwarf, "let them be such and remain such." At the court, however, they didn't want to let John in at all, for two had already been there saying they were bringing apples, and then one had tadpoles and the other pigs' bristles. John, however, was frightfully insistent that he really didn't have tadpoles but the finest apples that grew in the whole kingdom. Since he talked so sensibly, the porters thought he couldn't be lying and let him in. And they were right, too, in so doing; for when John uncovered the basket in the king's presence, there appeared golden yellow apples. The king rejoiced and at once had some brought to his daughter and now waited in anxious expectation until they brought him a report on the effect they had had. Before long somebody did bring him a report, and who do you think it was? It was his daughter herself! As soon as she had eaten some of the apples, she jumped out of bed cured. The king's happiness cannot be described.

But now he didn't want to give his daughter in marriage to John and said he must first build him a boat that would go faster on dry land than on water. John accepted the condition and went home and related how it had fared with him. Then the father sent Ulrich to the woods to build such a boat. He worked industriously, whistling while he worked. At noon when the sun was at its highest the little grey-haired dwarf came and asked what he was making there. "Wooden dishes," answered Ulrich. The grey-haired dwarf said, "Let it be so and remain so." By evening Ulrich thought he had now built a boat, but when he was about to get into it, it was just wooden dishes.

The next day Sam went into the woods, but it fared exactly the same with him as with Ulrich.

On the third day Stupid John went. He worked very industriously, so that the whole forest resounded with his powerful blows; he sang and whistled very merrily while at work. Then again the little dwarf came at noon when it was hottest and asked what he was making there. "A boat that's to go faster on dry land than on water, and when I've finished it, I'll marry the king's daughter." "Well," said the dwarf, "so it shall be and so it shall remain." In the evening when the sun turned to gold, John had finished his boat and ship and fittings. He got into it and rowed to the royal residence, and the boat went as fast as the wind.

The king saw it from afar, did not yet want to give John his daughter, and said that he must first tend a hundred hares from early morning till late in the evening, and if one of them got away, he would not get his daughter. John was satisfied with that and right off the next day went to pasture with his flock of hares and kept such sharp watch that not one got away from him. Not many hours passed when a maid came from the palace and told John that he was to give her a hare at once, saying that company had come. But John saw clearly what was up and said that he wouldn't give her a hare, that the king could serve his company jugged hare the following day. The maid, however, kept insisting and in the end started an argument. Then John said that if the king's daughter came herself, he would give her a hare. The maid reported this in the palace, and the daughter went herself. Meanwhile the little dwarf again came to John and asked him what he was doing. "Whew! I have to tend a hundred hares so that not one of them gets away, and then I may marry the king's daughter and be king." "Good!" said the dwarf, "then here's a whistle, and if one of them runs away, just whistle and it will come back." When the daughter arrived, John gave her a hare wrapped in a neckerchief, but when she was some hundred yards away, John whistled and the hare jumped out of her basket and in a second was back in the flock. When it was evening, the hare-herd whistled once again, looked to see if they were all there, and then drove them to the palace.

The king marveled at how on earth John had been able to tend a hundred hares without one of them running away, but still he wouldn't give him his daughter anyway, saying that in addition he must bring him a feather from the tail of the griffin bird. John set out at once and marched right straight ahead. In the evening he came to a manor and asked for a night's lodging, for at that time there weren't any inns. The lord of the manor took him in with great pleasure and asked him where he was going. "To the griffin bird," replied John. "Oh, to the griffin bird! They tell me it knows everything. I've lost the key to an iron money-box; you might be so kind as to ask where it is." "Yes, certainly," said John. "I'll do that, of course." Early next morning he continued his journey and on the way arrived at another manor, where he again spent the night. When the people heard that he was going to the griffin bird they said there was a sick daughter in the house, that they had already tried everything, and that nothing worked and would he be so kind as to ask the griffin bird what might make the daughter well again. John said that he'd gladly do this, and went on. Then he came to a river, and instead of a ferry there was a great big man there who had to carry everybody across. The man asked John where his journey was taking him. "To the griffin bird," said John. "Well, when you get to it," said the man then, "ask it why I have to carry everybody across the river." John said, "Yes, certainly, of course I'll do it." Then the man took him on his shoulders and carried him over.

At last John got to the griffin bird's house, but only its wife was at home, not the griffin bird itself. The wife asked him what he wanted, and John told her everything: that he was to get a feather from the griffin bird's tail, and that in one manor house they had lost the key to a money box and he was to ask the griffin bird where the key was; and in another manor house a daughter was ill and he was to find out what might make the daughter well again; then not far from there was a river and a man there, who had to carry people across, and that he, too, would very much like to know why he had to carry all the people across. Then the wife said, "Yes, look here, my good friend, no Christian can talk to the griffin bird; he eats them all up. If you wish, however, you may lie down under its bed and at night when it is quite fast asleep, you could reach up and pluck a feather out of its tail. And as for the matters you are to find out about, I'll ask it myself."

John was quite satisfied with all that and slipped under the bed. In the evening the griffin bird came home and on entering the living room said, "Wife, I smell a Christian." "Yes," said the wife, "one was here today but went away again," and with that the griffin bird said nothing more. In the middle of the night when the griffin bird was snoring loud, John reached up and plucked a feather from its tail. Then the griffin bird suddenly twitched and said, "Wife, I smell a Christian, and it seems to me that something pulled my tail." "You surely dreamed it," said the wife, "and I told you once today already that a Christian was here but that he went away again. He told me all sorts of things. In a manor house they lost a key to a money box and can't find it again." "Oh, the fools!" said the griffin bird. "The key is in the woodshed under the woodpile behind the door." "And then he also said that in a manor house a daughter was sick and they didn't know any way of curing her." "Oh, the fools!" said the griffin bird. "A toad has made a nest of her hair under the cellar stairs, and when she gets her hair back, she'll get well." "And then besides that, he also said that somewhere there is a river and a man there who has to carry everybody across." "Oh, the fool!"

said the griffin bird. "If he would once set one person down in the middle of the river, he wouldn't have to carry any more across."

Early in the morning the griffin bird got up and departed. Then John came out from under the bed and had a fine feather and had heard, too, what the griffin bird had said about the key and the daughter and the man. Then the griffin bird's wife told it to him all over again so he shouldn't forget, and then he went back home.

First he came to the man by the river who at once asked him what the griffin bird had said. Then John said that he should first carry him across and then he would tell him over there. Then the man carried him across. Once over, John told him he should just set one person down once in the middle of the river, then he wouldn't have to carry any more people across. The man was frightfully happy and told John that as an expression of gratitude he would willingly carry him back and forth once more. John said no, he'd spare him the trouble, that he was quite satisfied as it was, and went his way. Then he came to the manor where the daughter was ill. Because she couldn't walk, he took her on his shoulders and carried her down the cellar stairs and, taking the toad's nest out from under the bottom step, put it in the daughter's hand. She jumped down from his shoulders and ran upstairs ahead of him and was quite well. Now the mother and father were frightfully happy and made John presents of gold and silver and gave him whatever else he wanted. When John got to the other manor house, he went at once to the woodshed and, sure enough, found the key under the woodpile behind the door and then took it to the lord of the manor. He, too, rejoiced no little and as a reward gave John much of the gold that was in the box and all sorts of things besides that, such as cows and sheep and goats.

When John got to the king with all the things, with the money and the gold and the silver and the cows, sheep, and goats, the king asked him where on earth he had got it all. Then John said that the griffin bird would give one as much as one wanted. Then the king thought that he could do with that, too, and set out for the griffin bird, but when he came to the river, he happened to be the first to come since John,

and the man set him down in the middle and went away and
the king drowned. John then married his daughter and became
king.

166   Strong John

Der starke Hans

THERE WAS ONCE A MAN and his wife who had only one child
and lived quite alone in a remote valley. It once happened that
the woman was going to the forest to gather fir faggots and
took along little John, who was just two. Since it was right in
the springtime and the child liked gay flowers, she went farther
and farther into the forest with him. Suddenly two robbers
jumped out of the bushes, seized the mother and child, and led
them into the depths of the black forest, where year in and
year out no one ever came. The poor woman besought the
robbers to let her and the child go, but their hearts were of
stone: they heeded neither her requests nor supplications, and
forced her to go on with them. After they had been obliged
to struggle some two hours through underbrush and thorns,
they came to a cliff with a door, on which the robbers knocked
and which opened at once. They had to pass through a long
dark passageway and finally entered a large cave lighted by
a fire that was burning on the hearth. On the wall hung
swords, sabers, and other murderous weapons that gleamed in
the light, and in the middle stood a black table at which
four other robbers were sitting gambling, while at the head
of the table sat the leader. On seeing the woman the latter
came up, addressed her, telling her to keep calm and not
worry, and said they'd do her no harm, but she'd have to
attend to the housekeeping. If she kept everything tidy, she
would suffer nothing at their hands. Then they gave her
something to eat and showed her a bed where she and the
child might sleep.

The woman remained with the robbers for many years, and John grew big and strong. His mother used to tell him stories and taught him to read an old book of chivalry that she found in the cave. When John was nine, he made a stout club from the branch of a fir tree and hid it behind the bed. Then he went to his mother and said, "Mother dear, now tell me who my father is. I want to know and must know." His mother kept silent and didn't want to tell him lest he get homesick. She knew, furthermore, that the wicked robbers wouldn't let John go in any event, yet it would have almost broken her heart for John not to go to his father. That night when the robbers came home from their marauding, John got out his club and standing before the leader, said, "Now I want to know who my father is, and if you don't tell me straight off, I shall knock you down." Then the leader laughed and gave John such a box on the ear that he rolled under the table. John picked himself up again, said nothing, and thought, "I'll wait another year and then try it again. Perhaps it will work better." When the year was up, he again fetched his club, wiped off the dust, looked at it and said, "It's a good stout club." That night the robbers came home, drank one jug of wine after another, and began to nod. Then John brought along his club, again stood before the leader, and asked him who his father was. Again the leader gave him such a hard box on the ear that John rolled under the table. It was not long, however, before he was up again and with the club beat the leader and the robbers so that they could no longer move either arms or legs. His mother stood in a corner and was full of admiration for his bravery and strength. When John had finished his work, he went to his mother and said, "This time I was serious about it and now I must know also who my father is." "Come, John dear," answered his mother, "we shall go and look for him until we find him."

She took the keys to the entrance from the leader, and John got a big flour bag, stowed away gold, silver, and any other fine things he found until it was full, and then put it on his back. They left the cave, and how John's eyes opened when he came out of the darkness into the light of day and saw the green forest, flowers and birds, and the morning sun in the sky! He stood there and marveled at everything as though he weren't quite right in his mind. His mother looked for the way home, and after walking a few hours they were lucky enough to come into their lonely valley and reach their cottage. The father was sitting in the doorway and wept for joy when he recognized his wife and heard that John was his son, both of whom he had long since thought dead. But John, though just twelve, was a head taller than his father. Together they went into the living room, but no sooner had John set his bag on the bench by the stove than the whole house began to creak, the bench collapsed, and then the floor, and the heavy bag dropped down into the cellar. "God preserve us!" cried the father. "What's that? Now you've smashed our cottage to pieces!" "Don't let any grey hairs grow on that account, father dear," answered John, "for there's more in the bag than we need for a new house." John and his father at once began to build a new house, acquire cattle and buy land, and manage their farm. John tilled the fields, and when he walked behind the plough and pushed it into the ground, the steers scarcely had to pull at all.

The following spring John said, "Father, keep all the money and have a hundred-pound walking stick made for me so that I can go abroad." When the stick he wanted was finished, he left his father's house, set out and came to a deep and dark forest. There he heard something crackling and creaking, and looking around, saw a fir tree that was being twisted from top to bottom like a piece of rope, and on raising his eyes, he saw a big chap who had seized hold of the tree and was twisting it like a willow shoot. "Whew!" cried John. "What are you doing up there?" The fellow answered, "Yesterday I gathered faggots and want to twist myself a rope for them." "That's what I like," thought John, "he's strong," and called out to him, "Let it go at that and come along with me." The fellow climbed down and was a whole head taller than John, and the latter wasn't short, you know. "Now your name is Fir-Twister," John said to him. Then they went on and heard something knocking and hammering so hard that the earth trembled with every blow. Soon after they came to a mighty rock before which a giant was standing and knocking off great pieces with his fist. When John asked him what he was up to, he answered, "When I want to sleep nights, bears, wolves, and other vermin of that sort come and sniff and snuff around me and won't let me sleep, so I'm going to build myself a house and lie down in it in order to get some rest." "Yes, indeed," thought John, "you can use him, too," and said to him, "Let the house-building go and come along with me. Your name will be Rock-Breaker." The latter agreed, and all three took their way through the forest, and wherever they came, the wild animals were frightened and ran away from them.

In the evening they arrived at an old abandoned manor house, went up in it, and lay down to sleep in the great hall. Next morning John went down into the garden that had grown wild with neglect and was full of thorns and brush. As he was thus walking about, a boar rushed at him, but he gave it a blow with his stick so that then and there it fell to the ground. Then he shouldered it and brought it up to the house, where they stuck it on a spit, prepared themselves a roast, and were in fine spirits. Now they agreed that every day by turn two should go hunting and one stay home and cook—nine pounds of meat for each. The first day Fir-Twister stayed home while John and Rock-Breaker went hunting. As Fir-Twister was busy cooking, a little old shriveled-up dwarf came to the house and demanded meat of him. "Away with you, you sneak!" he answered. "You don't need any meat." But imagine how astonished Fir-Twister was when the insignificant little dwarf jumped up on him and struck him so hard with his fists that he was unable to defend himself, fell to the ground and gasped for breath. The dwarf didn't go away until he had fully vented his rage on him. When the other two came home from the hunt, Fir-Twister told them nothing of the old dwarf and of the blows he had received, thinking, "When they stay home, then they may try it out once, too, with the little cross-patch," and the mere thought really delighted him.

The next day Stone-Breaker stayed home and fared the same as Fir-Twister: because he wouldn't give him any meat, he received rough treatment at the hands of the dwarf. When the others got home that evening, Fir-Twister saw well enough what Rock-Breaker had been through, but both kept quiet and thought, "John, too, must have a taste of the soup."

John, who had to stay home the following day, was doing what he had to do in the kitchen, and when he was there and skimming the kettle, the dwarf came and without further ado demanded a piece of meat. Then John thought, "He's a poor creature. I'll give him some of my share so that the others won't come off too short," and handed him a piece of meat. When the dwarf had consumed it, he again asked for meat, and good-hearted John gave it to him, saying that that was another nice piece and that he should be satisfied with that. But the dwarf made his demand a third time. "You're impudent," said John and didn't give him any. Then the malicious dwarf was about to jump up on him and treat him as he had Fir-Twister and Rock-Breaker, but he ran into the wrong man. Without any effort John gave him a few blows so that he ran downstairs. John was going to run after him, but, being so tall, fell down over him. When he had got up again, the dwarf was ahead of him. John hurried after him into the forest and saw him slip into a cavern in a rock. Now John turned back home after taking due note of the spot. When the other two got home, they were surprised that John was in such good shape. He told them what had happened, and then they no longer kept silent about how they had fared. John laughed and said, "It serves you right. Why were you so stingy with your meat? Just the same, it's a disgrace that such big and strong men let yourselves be beaten up by the dwarf."

Thereupon they took a basket and rope and all three went to the cavern into which the dwarf had slipped. They let John with his stick down in a basket. When John reached the bottom, he found a door, and when he opened it, there sat a girl, pretty as a picture, indeed, indescribably beautiful, and beside her sat the dwarf grinning at John like a monkey. But the girl was bound in chains and looked at John so sorrowfully that he took great pity on her and thought, "You must get her out of the power of the wicked dwarf," and gave him a blow with his stick so that he dropped dead. Immediately the chains fell off the girl, and John was enraptured by her beauty. She told him she was a king's daughter whom a fierce count had abducted from her home and had shut up here in the rock because she would have nothing to do with him.

The count had appointed the dwarf as watchman, and the latter had caused her plenty of sorrow and distress. Thereupon, John put the girl in the basket and had her pulled up. The basket came down again, but John didn't trust his companions, thinking, "They have showed themselves faithless once in telling you nothing about the dwarf. Who knows what they may be plotting against you?" Then he put his stick in the basket, and there he was lucky, for when the basket was halfway up, they let it drop, and had John really been in it, it would have been the death of him. Now, however, he didn't know how he was going to make his way out of the abyss, and nothing he thought of was any help to him. "It's really too bad," he said, "for you to perish down here." As he was thus walking up and down, he came again to the little room where the girl had been sitting and saw that the dwarf had on his finger a ring that sparkled and shone. Then he took it off and put it on his own finger, and when he turned it around, he suddenly heard something rustling above his head. He looked up and saw aerial spirits hovering there. They said that he was their master and asked what his desire might be. At first John was struck quite dumb but then said they should carry him up. They obeyed instantly, and it was just as if he were flying up. When he got up there, however, there was no longer a soul to be seen, and when he went into the manor, he didn't find anybody there, either. Fir-Twister and Rock-Breaker had hurried off and taken the beautiful girl with them. But John turned the ring, and then the spirits came and told him that the two were at sea. John ran on and on until he reached the shore. Then far, far out at sea he spied a little boat in which his faithless companions were sitting. In a violent rage he jumped without thinking into the sea with his stick and began to swim. But the hundred-pound stick dragged him down so deep that he almost drowned. Then just in time he gave the ring a turn. Immediately the spirits came and carried him like lightning to the little boat. Then he swung his stick and gave his evil companions the reward they deserved and threw them down into the water. Then with the beautiful girl, who had been terribly frightened and whom he had freed for the second time, he rowed home to her father and mother and married her, and all were tremendously happy.

167 The Farmer in Heaven

Das Bürle im Himmel

ONCE UPON A TIME a poor devout farmer died and came to the gate of Heaven. A very rich gentleman was there, too, at the same time, who also wanted to get into Heaven. Then St. Peter came with his key and opened the gate and let the gentleman in. But apparently he didn't notice the farmer and once again shut the gate. Then from outside, the farmer heard the gentleman being joyously received in Heaven and heard them playing and singing inside. Finally, it got quiet again, and St. Peter came, opened the gate, and let the farmer in, too. The farmer supposed that there would be playing and singing, too, when he came, but everything was still. He was, to be sure, received in most kindly fashion, and the angels came to meet him, but no one sang. Then the farmer asked St. Peter why they didn't sing for him as in the case of the rich gentleman. "Things seem to me to be as partial in Heaven as on Earth." Then St. Peter said, "By no means! You are as dear to us as everybody else and are to share all the joys of Heaven like the rich gentleman, only look here! Poor farmers like you come to Heaven every day, but such a rich gentleman comes in only once every hundred years."

168 Lean Lizzy

Die hagere Liese

QUITE DIFFERENT from Lazy Harry and Fat Katy [No. 164] who let nothing interfere with their rest was Lean Lizzy. She slaved away from morning till night and loaded so much work on Tall Larry, her husband, that what he had to carry was heavier than three bags would be for a donkey. But it was all to no purpose: they had nothing and got nowhere.

One night she was lying in bed and was so tired that she couldn't move a limb, yet her thoughts wouldn't let her go to sleep. She poked her husband in the side with her elbow and said, "Larry, are you listening to what I have thought of? If I were to find a gold piece and somebody gave me another, I'd borrow still a third, and you would have to give me one, too. Then as soon as I had the four collected, I'd buy a heifer." Her husband liked the idea. "I really don't know," he said, "where I'll get the gold piece that you want me to give you. However, if you can collect the money and can buy a cow with it, then you'll be doing a good thing if you can carry out your plan. I'll be glad," he added, "if the cow has a calf. Then I'll sometimes get a refreshing drink of milk." "The milk won't be for you," said his wife. "We'll let the calf suckle, so that it will get big and fat, and we'll be able to sell it for a good profit." "Of course," answered her husband, "but even so, we'll take a little milk. That won't do any harm." "Who taught you how to handle cows?" said his wife. "Harm or no harm, I won't have it. You'll not get a single drop of milk, even if you stand on your head! You, Tall Larry, because you're never full, you think you'll consume what I earn by hard work." "Wife," said the man, "be still or I'll put a muzzle on you." "What!" she cried. "You threaten me? You glutton, you gallow's bird, you lazy lout!" She was about to go for him, but Tall Larry straightened himself up, with one hand held Lean Lizzy's skinny arms together and with the other pressed her head in the pillow, let her scold, and held her until she fell asleep from extreme exhaustion.

Whether she went on quarreling the next morning or whether she set out in search of the gold piece she wanted to find, I don't know.

169 The Forest Hut

Das Waldhaus

A POOR WOODCUTTER lived with his wife and three daughters in a little hut on the edge of a lonely forest. One morning when he was going to work as usual, he said to his wife, "Have the eldest girl bring my lunch out into the forest, otherwise I shan't get my work done. And so that she won't lose her way," he added, "I'll take along a bag of millet and scatter the grains as I go." Now when the sun was high over the forest, the girl set out with a pot full of stew. But the sparrows of forest and field, the larks and the finches, blackbirds and siskins had long since pecked up the millet, and the girl couldn't find the track. Then, trusting to luck, she kept on walking until the sun had set and night came on. The trees murmured in the darkness, the owls screeched, and she began to get frightened. Then in the distance she saw a light twinkling among the trees. "There are surely people there who will keep me over night," she thought and walked toward the light. Before long she came to a house whose windows were brightly lighted. She knocked, and a rough voice from within cried, "Come in." The girl stepped into the dark entryway and rapped on the living-room door. "Just come in," called the voice, and when she opened the door, there at the table was sitting a grey-haired old man, his face propped in both hands and his white beard flowing across the table almost down to the floor. And by the stove were lying three animals: a hen, a cock, and a brindled cow. The girl told the old man of her plight and asked for a night's lodging. The man said,

> "Pretty hen,
> Pretty cock,
> And you, pretty spotted cow,
> What do you say to it?"

"Nux!" answered the animals, and that must, of course, have meant "That suits us," for the old man went on to say. "There's an abundance of everything here. Go out to the hearth and cook supper for us." In the kitchen the girl found plenty of everything and cooked up a good dish, but took no thought of the animals. She brought a bowl full of food to the table, sat down with the grey-haired man, ate and satisfied her hunger. When she had had enough, she said, "I'm tired. Where is a bed I can lie down in and sleep?" The animals answered,

> "You ate with him,
>   You drank with him,
>   Of us you took no thought.
>   Now see, too, where you're spending the night!"

Then the old man said, "Just go upstairs and you'll find a room with two feather beds. Shake them and make them up with white linen. Then I'll come, too, and go to bed there." The girl went up, and when she'd shaken the feather beds and made them up fresh, she lay down in one without waiting any longer for the old man. After a time, however, the grey-haired man came, turned his light on the girl, and shook his head. When he saw that she was fast asleep, he opened a trapdoor and lowered her into the cellar.

The woodcutter came home late in the evening and reproached his wife for letting him go hungry all day. "It's not my fault," she answered. "The girl went out with your lunch; she must have lost her way. She'll be back tomorrow, of course." But the woodcutter got up before daybreak, was going to the forest, and demanded that this time the second daughter bring him his meal. "I'll take a bag of lentils along," he said. "The grains are bigger than millet; the girl will see them more easily and can't miss the way." At noon the second girl, too, carried the food out to the forest, but the lentils had vanished. As on the preceding day, the forest birds had pecked them up and not left a single one. The girl wandered about in the forest until it was night; then she, too, came to the old man's hut, was told to come in, and asked for food and a night's lodging. The man with the white beard again asked the animals,

> "Pretty hen,
>   Pretty cock,
>   And you pretty spotted cow,
>   What do you say to it?"

The animals again answered "Nux!" and everything happened as on the day before. The girl cooked up a good dish, ate and drank with the old man and didn't bother about the animals. And when she inquired about her quarters for the night, they answered,

> "You ate with him,
> You drank with him,
> Of us you took no thought.
> Now see, too, where you're spending the night!"

When she had gone to sleep, the old man came, looked at her, shook his head, and lowered her into the cellar.

On the third morning the woodcutter said to his wife, "Today send our youngest child out with my meal. She has always been good and obedient, she'll keep on the right track and not go star-gazing about like those other wild harum-scarums, her sisters." The mother didn't want to do this and said, "Am I to lose my dearest child, too?" "Don't worry!" he answered. "The girl won't lose her way, she is too smart and sensible. I shall take more than enough peas along and scatter them about. They are even bigger than lentils and will show her the way." But when the girl went out with her basket on her arm, the wood pigeons already had the peas in their crops, and she didn't know which way to turn. She was greatly worried and kept thinking how hungry her poor father would be and how her good mother would grieve if she stayed out. Finally, when it got dark, she spied the little light and came to the forest hut. In very friendly fashion she asked if she might stop over night, and the man with the white beard again asked his animals,

> "Pretty hen,
> Pretty cock,
> And you pretty spotted cow,
> What do you say to it?"

"Nux!" they said. Then the girl went to the stove where the animals were lying and patted the hen and the cock, passing her hand over their smooth feathers, and scratched the brindled cow between the horns. And when at the old man's order she had prepared a good stew and the bowl was on the table, she said, "Am I to have my fill and the good animals nothing?

There's more than enough out there; I'll look out for them first." Then she went and fetched barley and scattered it before the hen and cock and brought the cow a whole armful of fragrant hay. "Enjoy yourselves, you dear animals," she said, "and if you're thirsty, you're to have a drink of fresh water, too." Then she brought in a pail of water, and the hen and the cock jumped up on the edge, put their bills in and held their heads up the way birds do when they drink. And the brindled cow took a good big drink, too. When the animals had been fed, the girl sat down with the old man and ate what was left over for her. Before long the hen and the cock began to tuck their heads under their wings and the brindled cow blinked its eyes. Then the girl said, "Shan't we take ourselves to bed?"

> "Pretty hen,
> Pretty cock,
> And you, pretty spotted cow,
> What do you say to that?"

The animals answered, "Nux!

> "You ate with us,
> You drank with us,
> Of us you thought, as is right;
> We wish you a good night."

Then the girl went upstairs, shook up the feather beds and made them up with fresh linen. When it was done, the old man came and lay down in one bed and his white beard reached to his feet. The girl lay down in the other, said her prayers and went to sleep.

She slept peacefully until midnight. Then it got so noisy in the house that the girl woke up. It began to rattle and crackle in the corners and the doors sprang open and banged against the wall, the beams creaked as if being ripped apart, the stairs seemed to be falling down, and finally there was a crash as if the whole roof were collapsing. Then it got still again, and no harm befell the girl, so she lay there quietly and went to sleep again. But when she woke up in the morning, what did her eyes behold? She was lying in a big hall and around about everything shone in regal splendor. On the walls gold flowers were growing upward on a green silk background, the bed was of ivory, and the bedclothes of red velvet, while on a chair beside the bed was a pair of slippers embroidered with pearls. The girl thought it must be a dream, but three richly clad servants came in and asked what her orders were. "Just go away," answered the girl. "I'll get up directly and cook the old man some porridge and then feed the pretty hen, the pretty cock, and the pretty brindled cow." She supposed that the old man had already got up, and looked around at his bed. But it was not he who was lying in it; it was a strange man. And as she was looking at him and saw that he was young and handsome, he awoke, raised himself up and said, "I am a king's son and was enchanted by a wicked witch and had to live in the forest as a grey-haired old man. Nobody might be with me but my three servants in the form of a hen, a cock, and a brindled cow. And the enchantment was not to end until a girl came to us who was so kindhearted that she behaved affectionately not only toward the humans but also toward the animals. And you are that girl, and last night at midnight we were disenchanted by you, and the old forest hut has been changed back into my royal palace." And when they got up, the king's son told the three servants to go and bring the girl's father and mother to the wedding festival. "But where are my two sisters?" asked the girl. "I locked them up in the cellar, and tomorrow morning they will be taken out into the forest and are to serve a charcoal-burner as maids until they have reformed and don't let even poor animals go hungry."

170 Sharing Joy and Sorrow

Lieb und Leid teilen

THERE WAS ONCE A TAILOR who was a quarrelsome person; his wife, who was good, industrious, and devout, could never suit him. Whatever she did, he was dissatisfied, grumbled, scolded, pulled her hair, and beat her. When the authorities finally heard about it, they had him summoned and put into prison to reform.

He lived on bread and water for a time, then he was set free again but had to promise not to beat his wife any more but to live with her in peace and to share joy and sorrow as married people should.

Things went well for a time; then, however, he resumed his old ways, was sulky and quarrelsome, and because he might not beat her, was about to grab her hair and pull it. The wife got away from him and jumped out into the courtyard, but he ran after her with his yardstick and shears, chased her about, and threw at her the yardstick and shears and whatever else was at hand. When he hit her, he would laugh, and when he missed her, he would rage and storm. He carried this on so long that the neighbors came to the woman's aid. Again the tailor was summoned before the authorities and reminded of his promise. "Dear sirs," he answered, "I have kept my promise; I have not beaten her but have shared joy and sorrow with her." The judge said, "How can that be, inasmuch as she is again bringing such serious charges against you?" "I didn't beat her, I just wanted to comb her hair with my hand because she looked so queer, but she got away from me and willfully deserted me. Then I hurried after her and, as a well-intentioned reminder to return to her duties, I threw at her whatever was at hand. I have shared both joy and sorrow with her, for every time I hit her, it was a joy to me and a sorrow to her, while it was a joy to her but a sorrow to me when I missed her." The judges, however, were not satisfied with this answer and had him pay up as he deserved.

171   The Hedge-King, or Wren

Der Zaunkönig

IN DAYS OF OLD, every sound still had sense and meaning. When the smith's hammer rang out, it was crying, "Forge me! forge me!" When the cabinetmaker's plane snarled, it was saying, "There you have it! there you have it!" When the wheels of a mill began to rattle, they were saying, "Help, Lord God! help, Lord God!" And if the miller who started the mill going was a cheat, they would speak in very choice language, first asking slowly, "Who is there? who is there?" and then answering quickly, "The miller, the miller," and finally very fast, "is stealing barefaced, is stealing barefaced—three quarts from every bushel." At that time the birds, too, had their own language which everybody understood. Now it just sounds like twittering, squeaking, and whistling, and in the case of some birds, like music without words.

The birds got the notion that they no longer wanted to be without an overlord and decided to choose one of their number as king. Only one of them, the lapwing, was against it: free it had lived and free it would die, and flying anxiously hither and thither it cried, "Where am I to live? where am I to live?" It retired into lonely and unvisited swamps and didn't show itself among its own kind. The birds now wanted to talk the matter over, and one fine May morning they all assembled from forest and field, eagle and chaffinch, owl and crow, lark and sparrow—why should I name them all?—even the cuckoo came and the hoopoe, its verger, so-called because it always lets itself be heard a few days earlier in the season. Even a tiny little bird that as yet had no name mingled with the throng. The hen, that by chance had heard nothing of the whole matter, marveled at the great assembly. "What, what, what's doing there?" she cackled, but the cock calmed his beloved hen, saying, "Just rich people." He also told her what they were up to. They decided that the bird who could fly highest should be king. On hearing that, the tree toad who was in the bushes cried out as a warning, "No, no, no! no, no, no!" because it thought that many tears would be shed if that were done. But the crow said "Nonsense" and that everything would pass off smoothly.

Then it was decided that they should make their ascent right this fine morning so that nobody could say afterward, "I'd have flown much higher; only evening came on and then I couldn't go any farther." On a given signal the whole flock mounted in the air. The dust rose from the plain, there was a mighty rushing and roaring and beating of wings, and it looked as if a black cloud were moving off. Soon the smaller birds were left behind, couldn't go any farther, and dropped back to earth. The larger birds held out longer, but not one of them could match the eagle, who mounted so high that it might have dug out the sun's eyes. When it realized that the others couldn't get up to it, it thought, "Why should you fly any higher; you're the king as it is," and began to descend again. The birds below it all cried out to it an once, "You must be our king; no one has flown higher than you." "Except me," cried the little nameless fellow who had crept into the eagle's breast feathers. And since it wasn't tired, it mounted up and went up so high that it could see God sitting on His throne. But when it got that far, it folded its wings, descended, and called down with its piercing voice, "I am king, I am king!"

"You our king?" screamed the birds angrily. "You got there by trickery and guile." They made a new condition: the bird that could go deepest into the earth should be their king. How the goose with its broad breast plopped down on the ground again! How fast the cock scratched a hole! The duck came off worst: jumping into a ditch, it sprained its legs and waddled off to the near-by pond, crying, "Dirty work, dirty work!" The nameless little bird, however, looked for a mouse hole, slipped down into it and called out in its shrill voice, "I am king, I am king!"

"You our king?" cried the birds even more angrily. "Do you think your tricks are going to count?" They decided to keep it prisoner in the hole and starve it to death. The owl was put in front of the hole as watchman: if it loved its life, it was not to let the rascal out. But when it got to be evening and the birds felt very exhausted from the exertion of flying, they went to bed with their wives and children. Only the owl remained by the mouse hole, staring in with its big eyes. Meanwhile, it, too, got tired and thought, "You can certainly shut one eye and then keep watch with the other, and the little wretch won't get out of its hole." So it shut one eye and looked fixedly at the mouse hole with the other. The little chap poked out its head and was about to swish away, but the owl at once stepped in front of it, and it drew back its head. Then the owl again opened one eye and shut the other and was planning to alternate that way all night, but when it next shut the one eye, it forgot to open the other, and as soon as both eyes were closed, it fell asleep. The little bird soon noticed that and slipped away.

Since then the owl may not show itself any more by day, otherwise the other birds will be after it and tear its skin. It only flies by night and hates and goes after mice, because they make such horrid holes. Nor does the little bird like to show itself, for it is afraid that it might cost it its life, were it caught. It slips in and out of hedges, and when it is quite safe, it sometimes cries, to be sure, "I am king." Therefore the other birds make fun of it by calling it Hedge-King, or wren.

No one, however, was happier not having to obey the wren than the lark. As soon as the sun rises, it mounts in the air and calls, "Oh, how lovely it is! it's lovely! lovely! lovely! oh, how lovely it is!"

172 The Plaice

Die Scholle

THE FISH had long been dissatisfied that no order prevailed in their domain. No one paid any attention to the other, swam right and left as it fancied, and went between fish that wanted to stay together or else blocked their way. A stronger fish would give a weaker a blow with its tail so that it would go flying off or it would swallow it down without more ado. "How fine it would be if we had a king who would administer law and justice among us," they said, and agreed to choose as their lord the fish that could speed fastest through the waves and bring aid to a weak one. So they drew up in a line by the shore, and the pike gave a signal with its tail, whereupon they all set off together. The pike shot away like an arrow and with it the herring, the minnow, the bass, the carp, and what all. The plaice, too, swam along, hoping to reach the goal.

Suddenly the cry resounded, "The herring is ahead! the herring is ahead!" "Who's ahead?" cried out in vexation the flat, jealous plaice that was far behind, "Who's ahead?" "The her-

ring, the herring" was the answer. "The wretched herring?"
cried the envious fish, "the wretched herring?" Since that time
the plaice has had as a punishment a crooked mouth.

173   Bittern and Hoopoe

Rohrdrommel und Weidehopf

"WHERE DO YOU best like to graze your herds?" someone asked
an old cowherd. "Here, sir, where the grass is not too rich and
not too scant; otherwise it's not right." "Why not?" asked the
gentleman. "Do you hear that dull call coming from the swamp
over there?" answered the cowherd. "That's the bittern; formerly it was a herder, and the hoopoe was, too. I'll tell you the
story."

"A bittern tended its herds on the lush green meadows where
there was no end of flowers; from that its cows got restive and
unruly. The hoopoe, on the other hand, drove its cattle onto
high, dry mountains where the wind plays with the sand, and
its cows got thin and didn't get strong. When it was evening
and the herdsmen were driving their herds home, the bittern
couldn't round up its cows; they were headstrong and ran away
from it. 'Brindled cow, turn about!' it cried, but in vain; they
didn't listen to its call. The hoopoe, on the other hand, couldn't
get its cattle to their feet, so worn out and weak had they become. 'Up, up, up!' it cried, but it was no good; they just lay
there on the sand."

"So it goes if one doesn't use moderation. Even today, though
they no longer tend herds, the bittern cries, 'Brindled cow, turn
about!' and the hoopoe, 'Up, up, up!'"

174 The Owl

Die Eule

A FEW HUNDRED YEARS AGO when people weren't nearly so smart and artful as they are nowadays, a strange episode took place in a small town.

One night one of those big owls that they call eagle owls [Germ. *Schuhu*] got by chance from the neighboring forest into a townsman's barn and, when day broke, didn't dare come out again from its hiding place for fear of the other birds who, if an owl shows itself, raise a frightful uproar. Now when in the morning the house servant went to the barn to fetch straw, he was so terribly frightened by the sight of the owl sitting in a corner that he ran off and informed his master that a monster, the like of which he had not seen as long as he lived, was sitting in the barn, was turning its eyes around and around in its head, and could swallow one up without any trouble. "To be sure," said the master, "I have known you to chase a blackbird about in the fields [No. 162]; you have courage enough for that, yet when you see a dead chicken, you first get a stick before going near it. Well, I must just take a look myself and see what kind of a monster it is," added the master, went quite boldly into the barn and looked about. However, when he saw the strange and monstrous animal with his own eyes, he was no less terrified than the servant. He was out in a couple of jumps, ran to his neighbors and implored them to help him out against an unknown and dangerous animal. Besides, the whole town might be imperiled should it break out of the barn where it was.

A great hue and cry arose in every street. The townsmen came armed with pikes, pitchforks, scythes, and axes as if about to set out against an enemy. Finally the town councilors appeared with the mayor at their head. After forming ranks in the market place, they advanced on the barn, surrounding it on all sides. Then one of the boldest stepped forward and entered with pike lowered, but deadly pale he immediately came running out again with a cry, unable to utter a word. Two more ventured in but fared no better. Finally, one man came forward, a big strong man, famed for his martial deeds, who said, "You're not going to drive the monster away just by looking at it; this is a serious matter. I see, however, that you have all turned into women and that not one of you is willing to beard the lion." He had his armor, sword, and pike brought, and arrayed himself. All acclaimed his courage, though many were concerned about his life. The two barn doors were opened, and one could see the owl that meanwhile had perched in the middle of the barn on a big cross beam. He had a ladder brought, and when he had raised it and got ready to mount, they all called out to him to act manfully and commended him to St. George the dragon-killer. As soon as he was up the ladder, the owl saw that he was going to attack it. Confused by the crowd and the shouting, it didn't know how to get away, rolled its eyes, ruffled its feathers, spread its wings, snapped its beak, and sounded its rough "Shoo-hoo, shoo-hoo." "Thrust, thrust!" cried the crowd outside to the brave hero. "If anybody was standing where I am standing," he answered, "he wouldn't cry 'thrust, thrust!'" To be sure, he put his foot a rung higher but then began to tremble and backed down half unconscious.

Now there was no one left who was willing to face the danger. "Just by its snapping and puffing," they said, "the monster has poisoned and mortally wounded the strongest man to be found among us. Shall the rest of us risk our lives, too?" They took council as to what to do if the whole town was not to be destroyed. For a long time every plan seemed futile until finally the mayor hit on a solution. "In my opinion," he said, "we should at public expense pay the owner for the barn and everything in it: grain, straw, hay, and indemnify him. Then, however, we should burn down the whole structure and the frightful animal along with it. In that way no one need risk his life. This is no moment for economy, and niggardliness would be ill applied." All agreed with him, so the barn was fired at the four corners and the poor owl burned up along with it.

If anyone won't believe this, let him go and ask for himself.

175 The Moon

Der Mond

IN DAYS OF OLD there was a land where the night was ever dark and the sky was spread over it like a black cloth; for there the moon never rose and not a star twinkled in the darkness. At the time of the creation of the world earth light had sufficed.

Once four young men left this land on a journey and came to another realm where at night, when the sun disappeared behind the mountains, there was a luminous globe on an oak tree that shed a soft light far and wide. By this light one could easily see and distinguish everything, even though it wasn't so brilliant as the sun. The travelers stopped and asked a farmer who was passing with his cart what kind of a light that was. "That's the moon," answered the latter. "Our magistrate bought it for three dollars and fastened it on the oak tree. Every day he has to pour oil on it and keep it clean so that it will always burn bright; for this he gets a dollar a week from us."

When the farmer had driven off, one of the lads said, "We could use this lamp; we have an oak tree at home that is just as big, and we can hang it on it. What a pleasure it would be if we didn't have to grope about nights in the dark!" "Do you know something?" said the second. "Let's fetch a cart and horses and take the moon away. Here they can buy themselves another." "I'm good at climbing," said the third, "I will fetch it down." The fourth got a cart and horses while the third climbed the tree, bored a hole in the moon, passed a rope through it, and lowered it. When the shining globe lay in the cart, they covered it with a cloth so that nobody would notice the theft. They brought it safely to their country and set it up on a tall oak. Old and young rejoiced when the new lamp shone over the whole countryside and filled their living rooms and bedrooms with light. The dwarfs came out of their caves in the rocks and the tiny little folk danced on the meadows in their little red jackets.

The four lads kept the moon supplied with oil, snuffed the wick, and every week received their dollar. But they got to be old men, and when one foresaw his death, he arranged for a quarter of the moon to be buried with him in his grave as his property. When he died, the magistrate climbed up the tree and with hedge shears cut off a quarter, and this was laid in the grave. The light of the moon diminished, but not noticeably. When the second died, the second quarter was laid away with him, and the light diminished. It got still weaker with the death of the third, who, likewise, took his portion. And when the fourth was laid in his grave, the former darkness set in again. When the people went out evenings without a lantern, they bumped their heads together.

But when the quarters of the moon united again in the Underworld, then there, where darkness had ever prevailed, the dead got restless and awoke from their sleep. They were astonished at being able to see again. The moonlight sufficed them, for their eyes had got so weak that they would not have been able to stand the brightness of the sun. They got up, became merry and resumed their old ways of life. One group started playing and dancing, others ran to taverns, where they ordered wine, got drunk, rioted and quarreled, and finally raised their cudgels and clubbed one another. The noise got worse and worse and finally penetrated Heaven.

St. Peter, who guards the gate of Heaven, thought that the Underworld had started a rebellion and summoned the Heavenly Hosts to repel the evil enemy should they storm the Abode of the Blessed. But when they didn't come, he got on his horse and rode through the gate of Heaven down to the Underworld. There he pacified the dead, ordered them to lie down again in their graves, took the moon away with him, and hung it up in Heaven.

176   The Span of Life

Die Lebenszeit

WHEN GOD had created the world and was about to determine the span of life of all creatures, the donkey came and asked, "Lord, how long am I to live?" "Thirty years," answered God. "Does that suit you?" "Oh, Lord," replied the donkey, "that is a long time. Think of my laborious existence: carrying heavy loads from morning till night, dragging bags of grain to the mill so that others may eat bread, and encouraged and refreshed by nothing but blows and kicks. Exempt me from a part of that long time." Then God took pity and remitted eighteen years.

The donkey went away consoled, and the dog appeared. To it God said, "How long do you want to live? Thirty years are too many for the donkey, but you'll be satisfied with that." "Lord," said the dog, "is that Thy will? Think how much I have to run; my feet won't last that long. And once I've lost my voice for barking and my teeth for biting, what have I left but to go growling from one corner to the other?" God saw that the dog was right and remitted twelve years.

Then came the monkey. "You surely want to live thirty years," said the Lord to it. "You don't have to work like the donkey and the dog and are always in high spirits." "Oh, Lord," it answered, "it looks that way, but it's different. Even if it rains millet porridge, I have no spoon. I am always supposed to play funny tricks, make faces so that people will laugh, and if they hand me an apple and I take a bite of it, it's sour. How often sadness lurks behind a jest! Thirty years—I can't stand it." God was gracious and remitted ten years.

Finally man appeared, was happy, healthy, and vigorous, and asked God to name his life span. "You are to live thirty years," said the Lord. "Is that enough for you?" "What a short time!" cried man. "When I have built my house and kindled the fire

on my own hearth, when I have planted trees which bloom and
bear fruit, and think that I am going to be happy in my own
life, then I shall have to die. Oh, Lord, extend my time." "I'll
add on the donkey's eighteen years," said God. "That isn't
enough," replied man. "You are also to have the dog's twelve
years." "Still too little." "All right," said God, "I'll give you the
monkey's ten years in the bargain, but you won't get any more."
Man went away but wasn't satisfied.

Thus man lives seventy years. The first thirty are his human
years: they pass quickly. Then he is healthy, merry, works with
zest, and rejoices in his existence. Then follow the donkey's
eighteen years, when one burden after another is put upon him.
He has to carry grain to feed others, and blows and kicks are
the reward of his faithful service. Then come the dog's twelve
years, when he lies in corners and growls and no longer has any
teeth to eat with. And when this period has passed, the monkey's ten years make up the end. Then man is weak-witted and
foolish, does silly things, and becomes the butt of children.

177   The Messengers of Death

Die Boten des Todes

IN OLDEN TIMES a giant was once traveling along the great highway. Then a stranger suddenly jumped at him, crying, "Halt!
not a step farther!" "What!" said the giant, "you little creature
that I can squeeze to death between my fingers, do you mean to
block my way? Who are you to speak so boldly?" "I am Death,"
replied the other. "No one opposes me, and even you must obey
my command." But the giant rebelled and started to wrestle
with Death. It was a long hard struggle; finally the giant gained
the upper hand and struck Death down with his fist so that he
collapsed by a stone. The giant went his way, and Death lay
there conquered and was so impotent that he couldn't get

up again. "What is to happen," he said, "if I lie here in the corner? No one will die in the world any more, and it will get so full of people that they will no longer have any room to stand beside one another."

As he was saying this, a young man came along, vigorous and healthy, singing a song and glancing here and there. When he spied the half-unconscious man, he went sympathetically to him, lifted him up, gave him a fortifying drink from his bottle, and waited until the latter had regained his strength. Raising himself, the stranger asked, "But do you know who I am, and whom you have helped to his feet again?" "No," answered the youth, "I don't know you." "I am Death," he said; "I spare no one nor can I make an exception in your case. But that you may see that I am grateful, I promise not to assail you unawares but shall first send my messengers before I come to fetch you." "All right," said the youth. "It's at least something to know when you're coming and to be safe from you that long." Then he went on, was merry and in good spirits, and lived a happy-go-lucky life.

But youth and health did not last long. Soon came illnesses and pains that tormented him by day and gave him no rest by night. "I shan't die," he said to himself, "for Death will first send his messengers; I only wish that the evil days of illness were over." As soon as he felt well, he began again to live merrily. Then one day someone tapped him on the shoulder. He looked around and Death was standing behind him and said, "Follow me! Your hour of departure from the World has come." "What! are you going to break your word?" answered the man. "Didn't you promise to send your messengers to me before you yourself came? I haven't seen any." "Quiet!" replied Death. "Didn't I send you one messenger after another? Didn't Fever come, attack you, shake you and overthrow you? Didn't Giddiness stupefy your brain? Didn't Gout give you twinges in every limb? Didn't your ears buzz? Didn't Toothache wrack your jaws? Didn't it go black before your eyes? Over and above all that, didn't Sleep, my own brother, remind you of me every night? Didn't you lie at night as if you were already dead?" The man had no answer, yielded to his fate, and went away with Death.

178   Master Awl

Meister Pfriem

MASTER AWL WAS a skinny little man but lively and never at rest one single minute. His face, in which only his snub nose was prominent, was pockmarked and as pale as a corpse, his hair was grey and disheveled, his eyes were small but always in motion, twinkling right and left. He noticed everything, found fault with everything, knew everything better than anybody else, and was always right. When he walked down the street, he swung both arms violently and once he knocked the pail a girl was carrying water in so high in the air that he himself was drenched by it. "Stupid goose!" he cried out at her, shaking himself. "Couldn't you see I was coming along behind you?" By trade he was a shoemaker and when he worked, he pulled his thread through so hard that he would hit with his fist anybody who didn't stand far enough off. No apprentice stayed with him longer than a month because he always had some fault to find with the best work. Either the stitches weren't even or one shoe was longer than the other or one heel higher than the other or the leather wasn't enough. "Wait a minute," he would say to the apprentice, "I'll show you quick enough how to beat hide soft," would fetch a strap, and give him a few blows across the back.

He called them all lazy-bones, yet he didn't accomplish a great deal himself, for he never sat still for a quarter of an hour. If his wife had got up early and lighted the fire, he would jump out of bed and run barefoot into the kitchen. "Do you want to set the house afire?" he'd cry. "That's a fire you could roast an ox with!" or "Maybe wood doesn't cost anything?" If the maids were standing by the washtub laughing and telling each other the news, he would scold them, "There the geese stand cackling and forget their work. And why new soap? Infamous waste and, besides, a shameful indolence! They want to save their hands and not rub the clothes properly." Rushing up, he knocked over a pail of lye so that the whole kitchen was flooded. If anybody was putting up a new house, he would run to the window and look. "They're using that red sandstone again for the wall," he'd cry. "It never dries out; nobody will keep well in that house. And just see how badly the apprentices are laying the stones. The mortar is no good, either; there ought to be gravel in it, not sand. I'll live to see the day when the house collapses over the people's heads." He'd sit down and take a few stitches, then jump up again, undo his leather apron and cry, "I'm just going out a minute and remind the people of their duty." He ran into the carpenters. "What's that!" he cried. "You certainly aren't hewing to the line. Do you think the beams will stand straight? One fine day the whole thing will come unjoined." He grabbed the ax from a carpenter's hand and was about to show him how he ought to hew. However, since a cart loaded with loam came along, he threw the ax aside and went for the farmer who was walking alongside. "You're out of your mind!" he cried. "Who hitches young horses to a heavily loaded cart? The poor animals will drop dead on you on the spot." The farmer didn't answer him, and Awl out of vexation ran back to his workshop.

When about to sit down to work again, the apprentice handed him a shoe. "Is it the same old trouble again?" he cried out at him. "Didn't I tell you not to cut the shoes so broad? Who'd buy a shoe like that?—hardly anything but sole! I insist that my orders be carried out absolutely." "Master," answered the apprentice, "you may well be right in saying that the shoe is no good, but it's the very one you cut out and started to work on yourself. When you jumped up a minute ago, you threw it off the bench and I merely picked it up. An angel from Heaven couldn't please you."

One night Master Awl dreamed he had died and was on the way to Heaven. When he got there, he knocked violently at the gate. "I'm surprised," he said, "that they haven't a knocker on the gate; one might hurt one's knuckles knocking." The Apostle Peter opened the gate and wanted to see who was demanding entry so violently. "Oh, it's you, Master Awl," he said. "To be sure, I'll let you in, but I warn you to drop your old ways and not find fault with anything you see in Heaven. It might fare ill with you." "You might have saved your admonition," Awl replied. "Of course, I know what's right, and here, thank God, everything is perfect and there's nothing to find fault with as on Earth." So he stepped in and walked up and down the great chambers of Heaven. He looked about right and left, though he sometimes shook his head and growled something to himself.

As he was doing this, he saw two angels carrying off a beam. It was the beam that one man had had in his eye while looking for the mote in other people's. But they were carrying the beam crosswise, not lengthwise. "Did you ever see anything so stupid?" thought Master Awl, but he kept quiet and pretended not to mind. "Fundamentally it is all the same how one carries a beam, lengthwise or crosswise, as long as one gets it through, and I see, to be sure, that they're not bumping against anything." Shortly after that he spied two angels drawing water from a well into a vat; at the same time he noticed the vat was pierced with holes and that the water was running out in all directions. They were drenching the Earth with rain. "Great goodness!" he burst out, but luckily remembered himself and thought, "Perhaps it's a mere pastime. If one finds it amusing, one can do silly things like that, especially here in Heaven, where, as I have already noticed, they just idle about." He walked on and and saw a cart that was stuck in a deep hole. "No wonder," he said to the man who was standing beside it. "Who loaded it so stupidly? What have you got there?" "Pious wishes," answered the man. "I couldn't keep on the road with it, but luckily I have pushed the cart up this far and they won't leave me stuck here." As a matter of fact an angel came and hitched on two horses. "All very well," thought Awl, "but two horses won't get the cart out; there must be at least four." Another angel came leading two more horses, didn't hitch them on in front, however, but behind. That was too much for Master Awl. "Blockhead!" he broke out, "what are you doing there? As long as this World has been, has anybody ever pulled a cart out of a hole that way? Here, however, in their proud conceit they think they know everything better." He was about to go on talking, but one of the dwellers in Heaven had seized him by the collar and with irresistible force thrust him out. In the gateway the master turned his head once more toward the cart and saw it being lifted up in the air by four winged horses.

At this moment Master Awl woke up. "Things certainly go differently in Heaven than on Earth," he said to himself, "and much is excused there. But who can look on in patience while horses are being hitched up in front and behind? They had wings, to be sure, but who can know that? Besides, it's awfully stupid to attach a pair of wings to horses when they have got four legs to walk with. But I've got to get up, otherwise they'll be doing everything wrong in the house. It's just lucky I didn't really die."

179 The Goosegirl by the Spring

Die Gänsehirtin am Brunnen

THERE WAS ONCE an old, old woman who lived with her flock of geese in a waste land in the mountains and had a little house there. The waste land was bounded by a great forest, and every morning the old woman took her crutch and waddled into the forest. There she was very busy, more so than one would have believed possible of her advanced age. She gathered grass for her geese, picked the wild fruit as high as her hands could reach, and carried it all home on her back. One might have thought that the heavy burden would have weighed her down to the ground, but she always got it home all right. When she met anybody, she would greet them in most friendly fashion with "How do you do, fellow-countryman! It's fine weather today. Yes, you're surprised I'm lugging the grass, but everybody must take his burden on his back." Just the same, people didn't like to meet her and preferred to make a detour to avoid her. And if a father passed her with his boy, he would say softly to him, "Watch out for the old woman; she's a sly one and a witch."

One morning a handsome young man was walking through the forest. The sun was shining bright, the birds were singing, a cool breeze was blowing through the leaves, and he was joyful and gay. As yet he had met nobody, when suddenly he spied the old witch who was kneeling on the ground, cutting grass with a sickle. She had already piled a whole load on her cloth carrier, and beside it were two baskets filled with wild pears and apples. "But granny," he said, "how can you carry all that away?" "I have got to carry it, dear sir," she answered. "Rich people's children don't need to, but as the farmer says,

> 'Don't look around,
> Your back is bent.'

Will you help me?" she said as he stopped beside her. "You still have a straight back and young legs; it will be easy for you. Besides, my house isn't so far from here; it's out on the heath there behind the mountain. How fast you'll run up there!" The young man took pity on the old woman. "To be sure," he answered, "my father is not a farmer but a rich count; still, that you may see that farmers aren't the only people who can carry something, I'll take on your load." "If you want to try it," she said, "I should be much obliged. You will certainly have to walk for an hour, but what difference is that to you? You must carry those apples and pears there, too." Just the same, the young count had a few misgivings when he heard about the hour's walk, but the old woman didn't let go of him, put the carrier on his back, and hung both baskets on his arm. "See, it's quite light," she said. "No, it isn't light," answered the count and assumed a pained expression. "The load presses on me as heavily as if there were nothing but stones in it, and the apples and pears weigh as if they were of lead. I can hardly breathe." He wanted to put the whole thing down again, but the old woman didn't permit it. "Just look," she said mockingly, "the young gentleman isn't willing to carry what I, an old woman, have so often lugged off. They're ready with pretty speeches, but when it's the real thing, then they want to clear out. Why do you stand there hesitating?" she continued. "Pick up your feet. No one is going to take the pack off you again."

As long as he was walking on the level he was able to hold out, but when they reached the mountain and had to climb and the stones rolled out from under his feet as if they were alive, then it was too much for him. Beads of sweat stood out on his forehead and ran now hot, now cold, down his back. "Granny," he said, "I can't go on. I'm going to rest a bit." "Not at all," answered the old woman. "Once we get there, you may rest, but now you must keep going. Who knows what advantage you may derive from it!" "Old woman, you're impudent," said the count and wanted to throw off the pack, but he struggled in vain; it was stuck on his back as firmly as if it had grown there. He twisted and turned but couldn't get rid of it. The old woman laughed at that and hopped about gaily on her crutch. "Don't get angry, dear sir," she said. "You're getting as red in the face as a turkey cock. Carry your pack patiently. When we reach the house, I'll give you a good tip, of course." What could he do? He had to adjust himself to his fate and crawl along patiently behind the old woman. She seemed to get livelier and livelier and his load heavier and heavier. All at once she took a jump, leapt up on the carrier, and sat down on it. No matter how thin she was, she weighed more than the fattest peasant girl. The young man's knees shook, but every time he stopped going forward, the old woman beat his legs with a rod and with nettles.

Groaning all the way, he climbed the mountain and finally, just as he was about to collapse, reached the old woman's house. When the geese saw her, they lifted their wings and stretching out their necks, ran to meet her, crying "Cackle, cackle." Behind the flock with rod in hand walked an aged slattern, big and strong but ugly as night. "Mother," she said to the old woman, "did something happen to you? You stayed away so long." "Far from it, daughter," she replied. "Nothing happened to me; on the contrary, the kind gentleman there carried my load for me, and just think, when I got tired, he carried me, too, on his back. The trip didn't seem long to us; we made merry and were joking with one another the whole time." At last the old woman slid down, took the pack off the young man's back and the baskets from his arm and looking at him in the friendliest way, said, "Now sit down on the bench outside the door and rest up. You've certainly earned your pay and you'll get it all right." Then to the goosegirl she said, "Go into the house, my daughter; it isn't proper for you to be alone with the young gentleman. One mustn't pour oil on the flames—he might fall in love with you."

The count didn't know whether to laugh or to cry. "Such a darling!" he thought. "And even if she were thirty years younger, she couldn't stir my heart."

Meanwhile, the old woman petted and patted the geese like children and then went with her daughter into the house. The youth stretched himself out on the bench under a wild apple tree. The air was soft and mild. Around about extended a green meadow strewn with primroses, wild thyme, and a thousand other flowers. Through the middle murmured a clear brook on which the sun sparkled, and the white geese promenaded up and down or bathed and preened themselves in the water. "It's really lovely here," he said, "but I'm so tired that I can't keep my eyes open; I'll sleep for a bit. If only a gust of wind doesn't come and blow my legs off my body, for they're as soft as touchwood!"

When he had slept a while, the old woman came and shook him awake. "Get up," she said, "you can't stay here. I made it hard enough for you, to be sure, but it didn't cost you your life. Now I'm going to give you your pay. You don't need money and property; here is something quite different." Thereupon she put in his hand a little box cut from a single emerald. "Keep it carefully," she added. "It will bring you luck." The count jumped up, and then feeling quite refreshed and strong again, thanked the old woman for her present and took himself off without so much as looking around at the beautiful daughter. Even when quite a distance away he still heard the merry cry of the geese from afar.

The count was obliged to wander about in the wilderness for three days before he could find his way out. Then he came into a big city and because no one knew him, he was taken to the royal palace where the king and queen were sitting on their thrones. The count knelt, drew the emerald receptacle from his pocket, and laid it at the queen's feet. She bade him rise, and he had to hand her the little box. But scarcely had she opened it and looked in when she fell to earth as if dead. The count was seized by the king's servants and was to be taken to prison; then the queen opened her eyes and cried out that they were to release him, that everybody was to go out, and that she wanted to speak with him in private.

When the queen was alone, she began to weep bitterly and said, "What good is the splendor and honor that surrounds me?

Every morning I awaken in sorrow and distress. I had three daughters, of whom the youngest was so beautiful that everybody regarded her as a marvel. She was as white as snow, as red as apple blossoms, and her hair was as bright as the sunbeams. When she wept, it wasn't tears that fell from her eyes but just pearls and jewels. When she was fifteen, the king had all three sisters come before his throne. Then you should have seen how the people opened their eyes in amazement when the youngest entered: it was like the sunrise. The king said, 'My daughters, I don't know when my last day will come. Today I am going to decree what each of you shall receive after my death. You all love me, but the one of you who loves me most shall have the best share.' Each said she loved him most. 'Can't you express to me how much you love me?' replied the king. 'In that way I see what you mean.' The eldest said, 'I love my father as much as the sweetest sugar.' The second, 'I love my father as much as my most beautiful gown.' But the youngest was silent. Then her father said, 'And you, my dearest child, how much do you love me?' 'I don't know,' she answered, 'and can't compare my love to anything.' But her father insisted on her naming something. Then at last she said, 'Without salt the best food doesn't taste good to me; accordingly, I love my father like salt.' When the king heard that, he fell into a rage and said, 'If you love me like salt, then your love shall also be repaid in salt.' Then he divided the realm between the two eldest, but on the back of the youngest he had a bag of salt tied, and two servants had to take her out into the wild forest. We all implored and prayed for her," said the queen, "but the king's wrath was not to be appeased. How she wept when she had to leave us! The whole way was strewn with pearls that flowed from her eyes. Soon after that the king regretted his great severity and had the whole forest searched for the poor child. But no one could find her. When I think that the wild animals may have devoured her, I don't know how to contain myself for grief. Sometimes I console myself with the hope that she may still be alive and have hidden herself in a cave or found shelter with charitable people."

"But imagine! When I opened your emerald box, there lay in it a pearl of exactly the sort that used to flow from my daughter's eyes, and thus you can imagine how the sight moved my heart. You must tell me how you came by the pearl." The count told

her that he had received it in the forest from the old woman who
hadn't seemed quite right to him and who was surely a witch. Of
her child, however, he had neither heard nor seen anything. The
king and the queen decided to hunt the old woman up, thinking,
where the pearl had been, there they might get news of their
daughter, too.

Out in the waste land the old woman was sitting with her spinning wheel and spinning. It had already grown dark and a splint
of wood burning down on the hearth gave a feeble light. Suddenly there was a noise outside: the geese were coming home
from pasture and were sounding their hoarse cries. Shortly afterward the daughter entered, but the old woman barely thanked
her, just nodded her head slightly. Her daughter sat down beside
her, took her spinning wheel, and turned the thread as agilely
as a young girl. Thus both sat for two hours without saying a
word to one another. Finally, something rattled at the window
and two fiery eyes stared in. It was an old night owl which thrice
cried "Oo-hoo." The old woman merely raised her eyes slightly,
then said, "Now, daughter, it's time for you to go out and do
your work."

She got up and went out. Where did she go? Across the meadows farther and farther into the valley. Finally she came to a
spring by which stood three old oaks. The moon had meantime
risen big and round over the mountain, and it was so bright that
one could have found a pin. She stripped off a skin that covered
her face, then leaned down over the spring and began to wash
herself. When she had finished, she plunged the skin, too, into
the water and then laid it on the grass to bleach it and dry it again
in the moonlight. But how changed was the girl! You never saw
anything like it! When the mop of grey hair dropped off, golden
hair welled out like rays of the sun and spread like a cloak over
her whole body. And her eyes gleamed as bright as stars in
Heaven and her cheeks glowed a soft red like apple blossoms.
But the beautiful girl was sad. She sat down and wept bitterly.
One tear after another forced its way out of her eyes and rolled
to the ground through her long hair. Thus she sat there and
would have stayed a long time had there not been a crackling and
a rustling in the branches of the near-by tree. She sprang up like
a roe that hears the shot of the huntsman. Just at that moment
the moon was covered by a black cloud and in an instant the girl

had again slipped into her old skin and vanished like a light blown out by the wind. Trembling like an aspen leaf she ran back to the house.

The old woman was standing by the door, and the girl was about to tell her what had happened. But the old woman laughed in kindly fashion and said, "I already know everything." She led her into the living room and lighted a fresh splint; she didn't sit down again at the spinning wheel but fetched a broom and began to sweep and scrub the floor. "Everything must be nice and clean," she said to the girl. "But mother," said the girl, "why are you starting to work at such a late hour? What have you in mind?" "Do you know what time it is?" asked the old woman. "Not yet midnight," answered the girl, "but it is already past eleven." "Don't you remember," continued the old woman, "that you came to me three years ago today? Your time is up, we can no longer remain together." The girl was frightened and said, "Oh, mother dear, are you going to put me out? Where am I to go? I have no friends and no home I can turn to. I've done everything you asked, and you've always been satisfied with me. Don't send me away!" The old woman didn't want to tell the girl what lay ahead of her. "I shan't be staying here any longer," she said to her, "but when I go away, the house and living room must be clean; therefore, don't stop me in my work. As far as you are concerned, don't worry. You'll find a roof to live under, and you'll be satisfied, too, with the wages I shall give you." "But tell me what is going to happen," asked the girl. "Again I tell you, don't interrupt me in my work. Don't say another word. Go into your room, take the skin off your face, and put on the silk gown you were wearing when you came to me. Then wait in your room till I call you."

But I must go back to the king and queen who had set out with the count and were going to search for the old woman in the waste land. During the night the count got separated from them in the forest and had to go on alone. The next day it seemed to him that he was on the right track. He kept on until darkness fell, and he climbed a tree and was going to spend the night there, for he was afraid that he might lose his way. When the moon lighted up the region, he saw a figure wandering down the mountain. She had no staff in her hand, but he could see that it was the goosegirl whom he had seen previously in the old woman's house. "Aha!" he cried, "here she comes. If I get the one witch, the other won't escape me, either." Imagine his surprise when she went to the spring, took off her skin and washed herself, when her golden hair fell down over her, and she was more beautiful than anybody in the world had ever seen. Scarcely daring to breathe he stuck his head out among the leaves just as far as he could and looked hard at her. Whether he leaned over too far, or whatever the trouble was, suddenly the branch crackled, and at the same instant the girl slipped into her skin, sprang away like a roe and, since at the same moment the moon became covered, was lost to his sight.

Hardly had she disappeared when the count climbed down the tree and hurried after her with rapid strides. He had not gone far when in the gloom he saw two figures walking across the meadow. It was the king and the queen who from afar had spied the light in the old woman's cottage and had been walking toward it. The count told them the wonders he had seen at the spring, and they had no doubt but that it was their long-lost daughter. They went on joyfully and soon came to the cottage: the geese were sitting about on the ground, had their heads tucked under their wings and were asleep, and not one stirred. They looked in at the window: there the old woman was quietly sitting and spinning, nodding her head and not looking around. The living room was just as clean as if the little fog dwarfs lived there who track no dust on their feet. But they didn't see their daughter. They looked at all this for a long time, finally plucked up their courage, and tapped lightly on the window. The old woman seemed to have been expecting them, got up and in most friendly fashion called out, "Come right in! Of course, I know you." When they entered the living room, the old woman said, "You might have spared yourselves this long journey if three years ago you had not unjustly cast out your child who is so sweet and good. It has done her no harm to have had to tend geese for three years. She has learned nothing bad from that; on the contrary, she has kept her heart pure. However, you've been amply punished by the grief you have suffered." Then she went to the bedroom and called, "Come out, daughter." Then the door opened, and the king's daughter stepped out in her silk gown with her golden hair and her shining eyes, and it was as if an angel from Heaven were coming.

She went up to her mother and father, fell on their necks and kissed them. They couldn't all help weeping for joy. The young count was standing beside them, and when she saw him, she got as red in the face as a moss rose—she herself didn't know why. "Dear child," said the king, "I have given my kingdom away. What am I to give you?" "She doesn't need anything," said the old woman. "I am making her a present of the tears that she has shed for you. They are fine pearls, fairer than those found in the sea and worth more than your whole realm. And in payment for her services I am giving her my cottage." As the old woman said that, she vanished before their eyes. There was a slight rattling in the walls, and as they looked around, the cottage was transformed into a magnificent palace, and a royal board was set, and the servants were running hither and thither.

There is more to the story, but my grandmother's memory had got weak when she told it to me: she had forgotten the rest. Just the same, I think that the beautiful king's daughter married the count and that they remained in the palace and lived very happily there as long as God granted them to. Whether the snow-white geese which were tended beside the cottage were just girls (no one need take that amiss) whom the old woman had taken under her care, and whether they now regained their human forms and stayed with the young queen as servants, I really don't know, but I suppose so. This much is certain: the old woman was not a witch, as people thought, but a well-meaning wise woman. It was probably she who at birth gave the king's daughter the gift of weeping pearls instead of tears. That doesn't happen any more nowadays, otherwise the poor would soon get rich.

180 Eve's Unequal Children

Die ungleichen Kinder Evas

WHEN ADAM AND EVE were expelled from Paradise, they had to build a house for themselves on barren soil and eat their bread in the sweat of their brows. Adam hoed the fields and Eve spun wool. Every year Eve gave birth to a child, but the children were unequal: some were good-looking, others ill-favored.

After a considerable time had passed, God sent an angel to the couple to notify them that He was coming to inspect their household. Eve, happy that the Lord was so gracious, busily cleaned her house, decked it out with flowers, and strewed rushes on the floor. Then she fetched the children, but only those that were good-looking. She washed and bathed them, combed their hair, put clean shirts on them, and admonished them to be nice and polite in the presence of the Lord. They were to make Him a proper bow, offer their hands, and answer His questions modestly and sensibly. But the ill-favored children were not to show themselves. One she hid under the hay, another under the roof, the third in the straw, the fourth in the stove, the fifth in the cellar, the sixth under a tub, the seventh under the winevat, the eighth under her old fur, the ninth and tenth under the cloth out of which Eve made their clothes, and the eleventh and twelfth under the leather out of which she cut their shoes.

No sooner was she ready than there was a knock on the front door. Adam looked through a crack and saw that it was the Lord. He opened the door respectfully and the Heavenly Father stepped in. There stood the good-looking children in a row, bowed, offered Him their hands, and knelt down. The Lord began to bless them, laid His hands on the first and said to it, "You shall become a mighty king"; likewise to the second, "You a prince"; to the third, "You a count"; to the fourth, "You a knight"; to the fifth, "You a nobleman"; to the sixth, "You a burgher"; to the seventh, "You a merchant"; to the eighth, "You a scholar." In this wise He distributed His rich blessings on all of them.

Seeing that the Lord was so gentle and gracious, Eve thought, "I'll fetch my misshapen children; perhaps He will give them His blessing, too." So she ran and got them out of the hay, straw, stove, and wherever she had hidden them. Then the whole coarse, dirty, scabby, sooty troop arrived. The Lord smiled, looked at them all, and said, "I shall bless these, too." He laid His hands on the first and said to it, "You shall become a farmer"; to the second, "You a fisherman"; to the third, "You a smith"; to the fourth, "You a tanner"; to the fifth, "You a weaver"; to the sixth, "You a shoemaker"; to the seventh, "You a tailor"; to the eighth, "You a potter"; to the ninth, "You a carter"; to the tenth, "You a boatman"; to the eleventh, "You a messenger"; to the twelfth, "You a domestic servant as long as you live."

When Eve heard all this, she said, "Lord, why do You distribute Your blessings so unequally? All of them are really my children, whom I bore. Your grace should extend over all of them equally." But God replied, "Eve, you don't understand it. It is proper and necessary for me through your children to provide for the whole earth. Were they all princes and lords, who would cultivate grain, thresh, grind, and bake? Who would forge, weave, hew, build, dig, cut, and sew? Everybody must have his place, so that one may support the other and all, like the parts of a body, be nourished." Then Eve answered, "Oh, Lord, forgive me! I was too hasty in arguing with You. May Your divine will be done even on my children."

181 The Nixie in the Pond

Die Nixe im Teich

THERE WAS ONCE a miller who with his wife lived happy and contented. They had money and property and grew more prosperous from year to year. But misfortune can come over night: just as their fortune had grown, so year by year it vanished again, and finally the miller could scarcely call even the mill he lived in his own. He was greatly distressed, and when he lay down at the end of a day's work, he got no rest but in his anxiety tossed about in his bed.

One morning he got up well before daybreak and went out into the country, thinking that this might lighten his heart. As he was walking across the mill dam, the first ray of the sun was just appearing, and he heard something roaring in the pond. He turned around and saw a beautiful woman rising slowly out of the water. Her long hair, that she had held over her shoulders with her slender hands, billowed down on both sides and covered her white body. He saw plainly that it was the nixie of the pond and in his fright didn't know whether to go away or stay there. But the nixie spoke with her gentle voice, called him by name, and asked why he was so sad. At first the miller was dumbfounded, but hearing her speak in so friendly a fashion, he took heart and told her that he had formerly been lucky and wealthy but now was so poor that he didn't know what to do. "Don't worry," answered the nixie; "I'll make you richer and luckier than you ever were, only you must promise to give me what has just been born in your house." "What else can that be," thought the miller, "but a puppy or a kitten?" and promised her what she demanded. The nixie went back down into the water while, consoled and in good spirits, the miller hurried to his mill.

He had not yet reached it when the maid stepped out the front door and called to him to rejoice: his wife had just borne him a little boy. The miller stood thunderstruck; he saw clearly that the crafty nixie had known this and had tricked him. With head bowed he went to his wife's bedside, and when she asked him, "Why don't you rejoice over the lovely boy?" he told her what had befallen him and the promise he had made the nixie. "What good does luck and wealth do me," he added, "if I am to lose my child? But what can I do?" Even the relatives who had come to congratulate them knew no way out.

Meanwhile, good fortune returned to the miller's home. Whatever he undertook prospered; it was as if the chests and boxes filled themselves, and the money in the cupboard increased over night. Before long his fortune was greater than ever before. Yet he could not take untroubled pleasure in it: the promise he had made the nixie tormented his heart. Every time he passed the pond he was afraid she might emerge and remind him of his debt. The boy himself he didn't allow near the water. "Watch out!" he would say. "If you touch the water, a hand will come out, seize you, and pull you under." Nevertheless, as year after year went by and the nixie didn't show herself again, the miller began to feel easier.

The boy grew into a young man and was apprenticed to a huntsman. When he had mastered his craft and become a competent huntsman, the lord of the village took him into his service. In the village lived a beautiful and loyal girl whom the huntsman liked, and when his master noticed that, he made him a present of a little cottage. The couple got married, lived tranquilly and happily, and loved each other very dearly.

On one occasion the huntsman was after a roe. As the animal turned out of the forest into the open country, he pursued it and finally brought it down with one shot. He didn't notice that he was in the vicinity of the dangerous pond and after cleaning the animal, went to the water to wash his blood-stained hands. No sooner had he dipped them in than the nixie rose up, embraced him laughingly with her wet arms, and drew him down so fast that the waves closed over him.

When it was evening and the huntsman didn't come home, his wife got worried. She went out in search of him, and since he had so often told her that he must be on his guard against the nixie's snares and not dare go near the pond, she suspected, of course, what had happened. She hurried to the pond and on finding his game bag lying on the bank, could no longer be in doubt about the accident. Wailing and wringing her hands, she called her beloved by name, but in vain. She hurried over to the other side of the pond and called him again. She chided the nixie with harsh words, but no answer came. The surface of the water remained unruffled, and only the face of the half-moon looked down motionless upon her. The poor woman didn't leave the pond. With rapid strides, without rest or pause, she kept going around it again and again, now in silence, now uttering loud cries, now softly whimpering. At last she reached the end of her strength, sank to the ground, and fell into a deep sleep. Soon she had a dream.

Full of anxiety she was climbing up among great boulders; her feet kept getting caught in thorns and creepers, the rain was beating on her face, and the wind was tossing her long hair. When she got to the top, an altogether different scene presented itself. The sky was blue, the air balmy, the ground sloped gently downward, and on a green meadow, dotted with flowers of many colors, stood a neat cottage. She went up to it and opened the door. There sat a white-haired old woman who beckoned to her in a friendly fashion.

At that moment the poor woman woke up. Day had already

dawned, and she decided at once to follow up the dream. Painfully she climbed the mountain, and everything was exactly as she had seen it in the night. The old woman received her in a friendly manner and showed her a chair to sit down in. "You must have suffered a misfortune," she said, "to have sought out my lonely cottage." Weeping, the woman told her what had befallen her. "Console yourself," said the old woman; "I shall help you. Here is a gold comb. Wait till the moon has risen full, then go to the pond, sit down on the edge, and comb your long black hair with this comb. When you have finished, however, lay it down on the bank, and you will see what will happen." The woman went home, but the time till the full moon passed slowly for her. At last the gleaming disk appeared in the sky; then she went out to the pond, sat down, and combed her long black hair with the gold comb. When she had finished, she laid it down by the water's edge. Soon there was a roaring deep down, a wave rose up, rolled to the bank and swept the comb away. It was no longer than it took the comb to sink to the bottom when the surface broke and the huntsman's head rose up. He didn't speak but looked at his wife with sorrowful mien. At the same moment a second wave came rushing on and covered the man's head. Everything vanished, the pond was as still as before, and only the face of the full moon shone upon it.

The woman went home disconsolate, but her dream directed her to the old woman's hut. Again she set out next morning and lamented her sorrow to the wise woman. The old woman gave her a gold flute, saying, "Wait till the moon is full again, then take this flute, sit down on the bank, play a pretty air on it, and when you are done, lay it on the sand. You'll see what will happen." The wife did as the old woman said. No sooner was the flute on the sand than a roaring noise came from out of the depths, a wave rose up, moved forward, and carried the flute away. Soon afterward the surface broke, and not merely the head emerged, but the upper part of the man's body as well. Full of longing he stretched out his arms to her, but a second wave rushed on, covered him, and dragged him down again. "Alas!" said the unhappy woman. "What good does it do me to behold my beloved only to lose him again?"

Grief filled her heart anew, but for the third time the dream led her to the old woman's house. She set out, and the wise woman gave her a gold spinning wheel and consoled her, saying, "All is not yet fulfilled. Wait till the moon is full, then take the spinning wheel, sit down on the bank and spin the bobbin full. And when you have finished, place the spinning wheel near the water and you will see what will happen." The wife carried all this out to the letter. As soon as the full moon appeared, she took the gold spinning wheel to the water's edge and spun industriously until the flax was used up and the bobbin wound quite full of thread. Hardly, however, was the spinning wheel on the bank when there was an even greater roar than usual in the depths of the water: a mighty wave rushed up and carried the wheel away. Soon the head and the man's whole body rose up in a jet of water. He jumped quickly ashore and seizing his wife by the hand, fled. They had gone but a short way, however, when the whole pond rose up with a terrible roar and with torrential violence streamed into the open fields. The fugitives saw death already staring them in the face. Then in her anguish the wife cried to the old woman for help, and at that instant they were transformed, she into a toad, he into a frog. The flood that reached them was unable to kill them, but it tore them apart and carried them far away. When the water had subsided and both touched dry land again, their human forms returned, but neither knew where the other had got to. They found themselves among strange people who were unacquainted with their homeland. High mountains and deep valleys lay between them. To earn their living both had to tend sheep. For many a long year they drove their flocks through forest and field and were filled with sorrow and longing.

Once when the spring again broke forth from the earth, the two were one day driving out their flocks and chance would have it that they met. He spied a flock on a distant slope and drove his sheep in that direction. They met in a valley but didn't recognize one another, yet they were happy not to be so lonely any more. From now on they drove their flocks every day side by side; they didn't talk much yet felt consoled. One evening when the full moon was shining in the sky and the sheep were already at rest, the shepherd fetched out the flute from his pouch and played a beautiful but sad tune. When he had finished, he noticed that the shepherdess was weeping bitterly. "Why are you weeping?" he asked. "Alas!" she answered. "The full moon was shining like that, too, when I played that air on the flute for the last time and when the head of my beloved came up out of the water." He looked at her, and it was as if a film had fallen from his eyes: he recognized his very dear wife. And when she looked at him and the moon shone on his face, she recognized him, too. They embraced and kissed one another, and no one need ask if they were blissfully happy.

182 The Gifts of the Wee Folk

Die Geschenke des kleinen Volkes

A TAILOR AND A GOLDSMITH were journeying together, and one evening, after the sun had gone down behind the mountains, they heard the sound of distant music that kept getting clearer and clearer. The sounds were unusual but so charming that they forgot their weariness and strode on rapidly. The moon had already risen as they reached a hill on which they saw a crowd of little men and women holding one another by the hand and twirling around in the gayest and merriest dance. As they danced, they sang the loveliest songs, and that was the music the travelers had heard. In their midst sat an old man; he was a little bigger than the rest, wore a coat of many colors, and his iron-grey beard hung down over his chest. In great amazement the two men stopped and watched the dance. The old man beckoned them to come in, and the wee folk willingly opened their circle. The goldsmith, who had a hump and, like all hunchbacks, was quite forward, stepped up. The tailor at first felt somewhat shy and held back, but when he saw what fun was going on, he plucked up courage and joined them. At once the circle closed again, and the wee folk went on singing and dancing in the wildest fashion.

The old man, however, took a broad-bladed knife that hung

from his belt, whet it, and when it was properly sharp, looked around at the strangers. They became frightened but hadn't much time for reflection: the old man seized the goldsmith and with the greatest speed shaved his hair and beard off clean. Then the same thing happened to the tailor. But their fears vanished when the old man, having finished the job, clapped them on the shoulder in a friendly manner as if to say that they had done well to let all this happen voluntarily and without resistance. He pointed his finger at a heap of coals that lay to one side and indicated to them by gestures that they might fill their pockets. The two obeyed, though they didn't know what good the coals might do them. Then they went on their way to seek a night's lodging. When they got into the valley, the bell of a near-by monastery was striking twelve. All at once the singing ceased, everything had vanished, and the hill lay lonely in the moonlight.

The two travelers found a lodging and covered themselves with their coats on a bed of straw; being so very sleepy, however, they forgot to take out the coals first. A heavy pressure on their bodies waked them up earlier than usual. They put their hands in their pockets and couldn't believe their eyes when they saw that they were filled not with coals but with pure gold. Furthermore, their hair and beards were fortunately full-grown again. Now they had become rich men; the goldsmith, who in accord with his greedy nature had filled his pockets fuller, had, however, twice as much as the tailor.

When a greedy person has a lot, he demands still more. So the goldsmith proposed to the tailor that they stop over another day and go out again in the evening to get even greater treasures from the old man on the mountain. The tailor didn't want to and said, "I have plenty and am satisfied; now I shall become a master tailor, marry the charming object of my affections (as he called his beloved) and be a happy man." Still, as a favor to the goldsmith he was willing to stop over that day. In the evening the goldsmith slung a couple of extra pouches over his shoulder so as to be able to put lots into them and set out for the hill. As on the previous evening he found the wee folk singing and dancing. Again the old man shaved him clean and indicated that he was to take some coals. He didn't hesitate to pocket as much as his pouches would hold, returned home most happy, and covered himself with his coat. "Even if the gold does press on me," he said, "I'll stand it all right," and finally fell asleep in pleasant anticipation of waking up in the morning a very rich man.

When he opened his eyes, he got up quickly in order to explore his pockets, but imagine his surprise when he took out nothing but black coals, feel around as much as he would. "Anyway, I still have the gold I got night before last," he thought and fetched it. But imagine his fright on seeing that it, too, had turned back into coal. He struck his forehead with his hand that was black with coal dust and felt that his whole head was bald and smooth, and his beard gone, too. His misfortune was not at an end, however. Now for the first time he noticed in addition to the hump on his back that a second, quite as big, had grown on his chest. Then he recognized the punishment for his greed and began to weep aloud. The kind tailor, awakened by this, consoled the unhappy man as much as he could, saying, "You have been my companion on the journey, you are to stay with me and use part of my treasure." He kept his word, but as long as the poor goldsmith lived, he had to carry both humps and cover his bald head with a cap.

183   The Giant and the Tailor

Der Riese und der Schneider

A TAILOR WHO was a great braggart but slow at paying up got the notion of going out for a bit of a walk and taking a look about in the forest. Just as soon as he could, he left his workshop,

> went his way
> over bridges big and small,
> now here, now there,
> ever on and on.

Once out there, he saw in the blue distance a steep mountain and behind it, reaching to heaven, a tower that rose up prominently from a wild and dark forest. "Thunderation!" cried the tailor, "what is that?" And because his curiosity piqued him so, he walked off quickly toward it. But how he gaped and stared when he got near, for the tower had legs, leapt over the steep mountain in one jump, and stood before the tailor in the form of a huge and mighty giant. "What do you want here, you little shrimp?" cried the latter with a voice that sounded as if it were thundering all about. "I'm going to look about and see if I can earn my bit of daily bread in the forest," whispered the tailor. "If that is so," said the giant, "you may, of course, enter my service." "If it must be that way, why not? But what will my wages be?" "You shall hear what your wages will be," said the giant. "Three hundred and sixty-five days every year and leap year a day extra. Is that agreeable to you?" "Well, all right," answered the tailor, thinking to himself, "One must cut one's coat to one's cloth. I'll try to get away again soon."

Thereupon the giant said to him, "Go, you little rascal, and fetch me a jug of water." "Why not rather then the well and the spring along with it?" asked the braggart and went with the jug to the well. "What! the well and the spring, too?" growled the giant, who was a little doltish and simple and who began to get frightened. "The fellow is something more than human; he has a helpful spirit in him. Watch out, John old chap, he's no servant for you!"

When the tailor had fetched the water, the giant ordered him to cut a few logs of wood in the forest and carry them home. "Why not rather the whole forest at once,

> the whole forest
> with trees young and old,
> with everything it has,
> gnarled and smooth?"

asked the tailor and went to cut the wood. "What!

> the whole forest
> with trees young and old,
> with everything it has,
> gnarled and smooth?

and the well along with the spring?" growled the credulous giant to himself and got even more frightened. "The fellow is something more than human; he has a helpful spirit in him. Watch out, John old chap; he's no servant for you!"

When the tailor had brought the wood, the giant ordered him to shoot two or three wild boars for supper. "Why not rather then a thousand at one shot and bring them all here?" asked the conceited tailor. "What!" cried the timid rabbit of a giant and was terribly frightened. "Just let it go for today and lie down and sleep."

The giant was so terrifically frightened that he couldn't sleep a wink all night and thought of this way and that how he should set about ridding himself of the cursed wizard of a servant—the sooner the better. But time takes care of everything. The next morning the giant and the tailor went to a swamp around which were a lot of willows. Then the giant said, "Listen here, tailor! Sit down on one of the willow shoots; I'd give anything to see if you are capable of bending it down." Like a flash the tailor was up there, held his breath and made himself heavy, so heavy in fact that the shoot bent down. But when he had to take breath again, then, because unluckily he had not put a goose in his pocket, to the giant's great delight it hurtled him so high in the air that one could no longer see him at all.

If he hasn't fallen down again, he is surely still soaring about in the air.

184   The Horseshoe Nail

Der Nagel

A MERCHANT had done good business at the fair, sold all his wares, and larded his purse with gold and silver. Now he was about to ride home and wanted to get there before nightfall. So he packed the money in his portmanteau, put it on his horse, and rode off. At noon he stopped in a town to rest. When about to go on, the servant brought him his horse, but said, "Sir, a nail is missing in the left hind shoe." "Let it be missing," replied the merchant. "The shoe will hold for the six hours I still have to go. I'm in a hurry." That afternoon when he again dismounted and had the horse fed some oats, the groom came into the living room and said, "Sir, a shoe is missing from your horse's left hind hoof. Shall I take it to the blacksmith?" "Let it be missing," replied the gentleman. "The horse will easily stand it for the couple of hours that are left. I'm in a hurry." He rode on, but before long the horse began to limp. It didn't limp long before beginning to stumble, and it didn't stumble long before it fell down and broke a leg. The merchant had to leave the horse lying there, unbuckle the portmanteau, take it on his shoulder, and walk home on foot. He didn't get there until late at night. "The damned nail," he said to his wife, "is to blame for the whole misfortune."

Make haste slowly.

185 The Poor Boy in the Grave

Der arme Junge im Grab

THERE WAS ONCE A POOR HERDSBOY whose father and mother had died, and he was put by the authorities in the home of a wealthy man who was to support him and bring him up. But the man and his wife were bad-hearted people, greedy, and grudging, rich though they were, and were annoyed if anybody tasted as much as a piece of their bread. Do what he might, the poor boy got little to eat, though, to make up for it, all the more blows.

One day he was supposed to tend the hen and her chickens, but she ran off with the chicks through a hedgerow. Forthwith a hawk swooped down and carried her off. "Thief, thief! scoundrel!" cried the boy with all his might, but what good did that do? The hawk didn't bring back its prey. The man heard the noise, came running up, and on learning that his hen was gone, flew into a rage and gave the boy such a thrashing that for a couple of days he couldn't move. Then he had to tend the chicks without the hen. But now matters were even more difficult and trying, for one chick would run this way, the other that. Then he thought that he would be doing the clever thing to tie them all together on a string, for then the hawk wouldn't be able to steal a single one from him. But such was far from the case. A few days later when, wearied from running about and from hunger, he fell asleep, the bird of prey came and seized one of the chicks, and since the others were fastened to it, it carried them all off, perched on a tree and ate them up. The farmer was just coming home and when he saw the accident, grew angry and beat the boy so unmercifully that he had to stay in bed for several days.

When he was back on his feet again, the farmer said to him, "You're too stupid for me; I can't use you as a herdsboy. You're to work as an errand boy." Then he sent him to a judge to whom he was to bring a basket full of grapes, and he also gave him a letter to take along. On the way the poor boy was so dreadfully tormented by hunger and thirst that he ate two of the grapes. He brought the judge the basket, but after the latter had read the letter and counted the grapes, he said, "Two are missing." The boy confessed quite honestly that, driven by hunger and thirst, he had eaten the missing grapes. The judge wrote the farmer a letter and demanded the same number of grapes again. These, too, with a letter, the boy had to take to the judge. When again he got so fearfully hungry and thirsty, again he couldn't help eating two grapes. But before eating them he took the letter out of the basket, put it under a stone, and sat down on it, so that the letter might not look on and betray him. Just the same the judge called him to account for the missing grapes. "O dear!" said the boy, "how did you find out? The letter couldn't have known because I first put it under a stone." The judge couldn't but laugh at his simplicity and sent the man a letter urging him to provide better for the poor boy and not to let him lack food and drink. Also he should teach him the difference between right and wrong.

"I'll certainly teach you the difference," said the hard-hearted man. "If, however, you want to eat, you must also work, and if you do anything wrong, you'll be properly instructed by blows." The next day he assigned him a hard task: he was to chop up a few bundles of straw as feed for the horses. At the same time the man uttered this threat: "In five hours," he said, "I shall be back. If the straw hasn't been cut up into chaff, I'll beat you till you can no longer move a limb." The farmer and his wife, the servant and the maid, went to the yearly fair and left behind for the boy nothing but a little piece of bread. The boy took his place at the chaff-cutter and began to work for all he was worth. Since he got hot working, he took off his jacket and threw it on the straw. Anxious lest he shouldn't finish, he kept chopping away and in his zeal inadvertently chopped up his jacket along with the straw. He noticed the accident too late to do anything about it. "Alas!" he cried, "now it's all up with me. The bad man didn't threaten me for nothing. When he comes back and sees what I've done, he'll beat me to death. I'd rather take my own life."

The boy had once heard the farmer's wife say, "I have a pot of poison under my bed." She had only said it, however, to restrain people with a sweet tooth, for there was honey in it. The boy crawled under the bed, fetched out the pot, and ate it all up. "I don't know," he said, "people say that death is bitter; to me it tastes sweet. No wonder the farmer's wife so often wishes she was dead." He sat down on a stool and was reconciled to dying, but instead of getting weaker, he felt himself strengthened by the nourishing food. "It can't have been poison," he said. "However, the farmer once said that there was a bottle of fly-poison in his clothes chest; it's surely real poison and will kill me." But it wasn't fly-poison, just Hungarian wine. The boy got out the bottle and drank it down. "This death, too, tastes sweet," he said, but when soon afterward the wine began to go to his head and stupefy him, he thought his end was approaching. "I feel that I must be dying," he said. "I'll go out to the churchyard and look for a grave." He staggered out, reached the churchyard, and lay down in a freshly dug grave. He began to lose consciousness. Near by was an inn where a wedding was being celebrated. When he heard the music, he thought he was already in Paradise, until in the end he became completely unconscious. The poor boy didn't come to again; the glow of the hot wine and the cold night dew killed him, and he stayed in the grave in which he had laid himself.

When the farmer received news of the boy's death, he got

frightened and was afraid of being haled into court. Indeed, such a fright seized him that he fell to the ground in a faint. His wife, who was standing by the stove with a pan full of drippings, ran to help him, but the pan caught fire and the flames spread to the whole house, and in a few hours it was in ashes. The years that were left to them they spent in poverty and misery, tormented by pangs of conscience.

186 The True Bride

Die wahre Braut

THERE WAS ONCE A GIRL who was young and beautiful, but her mother had died early, and her stepmother imposed every sort of smarting affliction upon her. When she assigned her a task, no matter how difficult, the girl set to it patiently and did her very best. Yet, even so, she couldn't move the evil woman's heart; the latter was always dissatisfied; nothing was ever enough. The more industriously the girl worked, the more she was given to do, and her stepmother's only thought was how she might impose a still greater burden upon her and make her life quite miserable.

One day she said to her, "Here are twelve pounds of feathers. You're to strip them, and if you haven't finished by this evening, you may expect a good thrashing. Do you think you can idle about all day?" The poor girl sat down to her work, but as she worked, the tears flowed down her cheeks, for she saw clearly that it was impossible to finish the task in one day. Every time she'd get a little pile of feathers in front of her and sigh or in her distress clap her hands, the feathers would blow about and she'd have to gather them up again and begin anew. Once she propped her elbows on the table, put her face in her hands and cried, "Is there no one on God's earth who will take pity on me?" As she said this, she heard a soft voice saying, "Console yourself, my child, I have come to help you." The girl looked up, and an old woman was standing beside her. She took the girl by the hand in friendly fashion and said, "Just confide in me what is depressing you." Since she spoke so kindly, the girl told her of her unhappy life: that one burden after another was imposed upon her and that she no longer was able to finish the tasks assigned her. "If I've not done with these feathers this evening, my stepmother will beat me. She has threatened me with it, and I know how she keeps her word." Her tears began to flow again, but the kind old woman said, "Don't worry, my child; take a rest, and in the meanwhile I'll perform your task." The girl lay down on her bed and at once fell asleep. The old woman seated herself at the table with the feathers. My! how the barbs flew off the shafts, though she scarcely touched them with her withered hands! She was soon finished with the twelve pounds. When the girl woke up, great snow-white piles lay heaped up, and everything in the room was properly cleared away. The old woman, however, had vanished. The girl thanked God and sat still until evening came. Then her stepmother entered and was astonished that the task was completed. "Do you see, wench," she said, "what one accomplishes when one is industrious? Couldn't you have started on something else? But there you are, sitting with your hands in your lap!" As she went out, she said, "The creature is something more than human. I must impose harder work upon her."

The next morning she called the girl and said, "Here's a spoon! With it ladle out the big pond by the garden. And if you aren't done by evening, you know what is in store for you." The girl took the spoon and saw that it was perforated, and even if it hadn't been, she would never have ladled out the pond with it. She set right to work, knelt by the water, into which her tears fell, and ladled. But again the kind old woman appeared and, on learning the cause of her distress, said, "Console yourself, my child; go into the bushes and lie down to sleep. I'll do your work, of course." When the old woman was alone, she merely touched the pond: the water rose up like a mist and mingled with the clouds. Gradually the pond got empty, and when the girl awoke before sundown and came near, all she saw left were the fishes wriggling in the mud. She went to her stepmother and reported that the task was completed. "You should have finished long ago," she said and grew pale with vexation. Nevertheless, she thought up something new.

On the third morning she said to the girl, "You must build me a beautiful palace over there on the plain, and it must be ready by evening." The girl was frightened and said, "How can I perform so great a task?" "I won't stand any back-talk," screamed her stepmother. "If you can ladle out the pond with a perforated spoon, you can also build a palace. I want to move in this very day, and if anything is lacking, be it the least little thing in the kitchen or cellar, you know what is in store for you." She chased the girl away, and when the latter reached the valley, there lay rocks piled up on one another. Despite every effort she couldn't so much as move the smallest of them. She sat down and wept, yet she hoped for aid from the kind old woman. The latter didn't make her wait long, came and consoled her, saying, "Just lie down in the shade and sleep. I'll build the palace for you, of course. If you like, you may live in it yourself." When the girl had gone away, the old woman touched the grey rocks. Immediately they stirred, drew together, and stood there as if giants had built the walls. Thereupon, the structure erected itself, and it was as if countless hands were working invisibly, laying stone upon stone. The earth groaned, great pillars rose on high of their own accord and aligned themselves. On the roof the tiles disposed themselves properly, and by noon the big weather vane, in the form of a gold maiden with flowing garments, was turning on the top of the tower. The interior of the palace was completed by evening. How the old woman managed it I don't know, but the walls of the rooms were hung with silk and velvet, there were chairs embroidered in many colors, while richly ornamented armchairs stood by marble tables; crystal chandeliers hung from the ceiling, and their light was reflected in the polished floor. Green parrots sat in gold cages, also exotic birds which sang beautifully. Everywhere a splendor prevailed as if a king was to take occupancy.

The sun was about to set when the girl awoke, and the gleam of a thousand lights met her gaze. She approached with swift steps and entered the palace through the open gate. The stairs were carpeted with red, and flowering shrubs were set on the gold balustrade. On seeing the magnificence of the rooms, she stopped as if paralyzed. Who knows how long she would have stood thus had she not remembered her stepmother. "Alas!" she said to herself, "if only she were at last satisfied and no longer wanted to make life a torment for me!" The girl went and pointed out to her that the palace was finished. "I'll move in at once," she said and got up from her seat. As she entered the palace, she couldn't help putting her hand to her eyes, the brilliance dazzled her so. "Just see," she said to the girl, "how easy it was for you! I should have given you something harder to do." She went through all the rooms and peeked into every corner to see if anything was lacking or was defective, but she could find nothing. "Now let's go downstairs," she said, giving the girl a malicious look. "Kitchen and cellar have still to be looked into, and if you've forgotten anything, you won't escape your punishment." But the fire was burning on the hearth, the food cooking in the pots, fire tongs and shovel were in place, and the shiny brass utensils were ranged on the walls. Nothing was lacking, not even the coal scuttle and water pail. "Where's the entrance to the cellar?" she cried. "If it's not richly stocked with casks of wine, it will go hard with you." She herself raised the trap door and went down the stairs, but scarcely had she taken two steps when the heavy trap, which had only been tilted up, crashed down. The girl heard a cry and quickly lifted up the door to go to her aid, but she had pitched down, and the girl found her lying dead on the cellar floor.

Now the magnificent palace belonged just to the girl alone. At first she couldn't fully realize her good fortune: beautiful gowns hung in the wardrobes, the chests were full of silver and gold or pearls and jewels, and she hadn't a single wish that she couldn't satisfy. Soon the fame of the girl's beauty and wealth spread throughout the whole world. Every day suitors presented themselves, but none was to her liking. Finally a king's son came who was able to move her heart, and she became engaged to him. In the palace garden stood a green linden. One day as they were sitting together under it and chatting, he said to her, "I'm going home to get my father's permission for our marriage. I beg you to wait for me here under this linden; I'll be back again in a few hours." The girl kissed him on his left cheek and said, "Remain true to me and don't let any other girl kiss you on this cheek. I'll wait here under the linden until you return."

The girl remained sitting under the linden until sundown, but he didn't come back. For three days from morning till evening she sat waiting for him, but in vain. When on the fourth day he still wasn't there, she said, "Surely some accident has befallen him; I'll go out in search of him and not return until I have found him." She packed up three of her handsomest gowns, one embroidered with shining stars, the second with silver moons, the third with golden suns, tied up a handful of jewels in her kerchief, and set out. She asked everywhere after her bridegroom, but no one had seen him, no one knew anything about him. She wandered far and wide through the world but didn't find him. At last she hired out as a herdswoman to a farmer and buried her gowns and jewels under a stone. Now she lived as a herdswoman and tended her herd, was sad and full of longing for her beloved. She had a calf that she had tamed and that she used to feed from her hand, and when she'd say,

> "Calf, little calf, kneel down;
>   Don't forget your herdswoman
>   As the king's son did his bride
>   Who was sitting under the green linden,"

the calf would kneel down and be stroked by her.

After she had lived a few years in solitude and sorrow, a report spread through the country that the king's daughter was going to celebrate her marriage. The way to the city led past the village where the girl lived, and it happened, as she was once driving her herd out, that the bridegroom went by. He was sitting proudly on his horse and didn't look at her, but when she looked at him, she recognized her beloved. She felt as if a sharp knife were piercing her heart. "Alas!" she said, "I thought he had remained true to me, but he has forgotten me." The next day he came that way again. When he got near her, she said to the calf,

"Calf, little calf, kneel down;
Don't forget your herdswoman
As the king's son did his bride
Who was sitting under the green linden."

When he heard her voice, he looked down and halted his horse. He looked the herdswoman in the face, then put his hand to his eyes as if trying to recall something but, riding quickly on, soon disappeared. "Alas!" she said, "he no longer recognizes me," and her grief grew greater and greater.

Soon after that a great festival was to be celebrated for three days at the king's court, and the whole country was invited. "Now I'll make one last try," thought the girl, and when evening came, she went to the stone under which she had buried her valuables. She got out the gown with the gold suns, put it on, and bedecked herself with the jewels. Her hair, which she had hidden under a kerchief, she undid, and it fell over her in long curls. In this way she went to the city, and in the darkness nobody noticed her. When she entered the brightly lighted hall, everybody was full of admiration and made way for her, but no one knew who she was. The king's son, though he didn't recognize her, went to meet her. He took her to the dance and was so enchanted by her beauty that he no longer thought of his other bride. When the party was over, she disappeared in the crowd and hurried before daybreak to the village, where she again put on her herdswoman's dress.

The second evening she took out the gown with the silver moons and put a half-moon of jewels in her hair. When she appeared at the party, all eyes turned toward her, and the king's son hastened to her and, quite in love with her, danced with her alone and no longer looked at any other woman. Before she left, she had to promise him to come again to the festival on the last evening.

When she appeared for the third time, she had the star-gown on; it twinkled with every step, and her fillet and belt were of jeweled stars. The king's son had been waiting for her for a long time and pressed his way up to her. "Please tell me," he said, "who you are. I have the feeling that I have already known you for a long time." "Don't you know," she answered, "what I did when you left me?" Then she stepped up to him and kissed him on the left cheek. At that instant it was as if scales had fallen from his eyes, and he recognized the true bride. "Come," he said to her, "I can't stay here any longer," gave her his hand and led her down to the coach.

The horses sped to the miraculous palace as if the wind were harnessed to the coach. Already from afar the brightly lighted windows were gleaming. As they drove past the linden, myriads of glow-worms were swarming in it. It shook its branches and sent down its fragrance. The flowers were blooming on the terrace; from out of the room sounded the song of exotic birds; and in the main hall the entire court was assembled, and the priest was waiting to marry the bridegroom to the true bride.

187   The Hare and the Hedgehog

Der Hase und der Igel

THIS STORY isn't true, boys, but it's true just the same, for my grandfather from whom I have it, when telling it to me with great satisfaction, used always at the same time to say, "Still, it must be true, son; otherwise, of course, one couldn't tell it." Anyway, the story went like this.

It was a Sunday morning at harvest time, just when the buckwheat was in bloom. The sun had risen bright in the sky, the morning breeze was blowing warm over the stubble, up in the air the larks were singing, the bees were buzzing in the buckwheat, the people were going to church in their Sunday best, and all creatures were content, even the hedgehog.

The hedgehog was standing outside its door with arms crossed, was looking out in the morning breeze, and was humming itself a little song, no better and no worse than a hedgehog is in the habit of singing of a fine Sunday morning. As it was still singing to itself in an undertone, it suddenly occurred to it that while its wife was washing and dressing the children, it might as well take a little walk out in the fields and see how its big yellow turnips were. Now, the turnips were nearest its house, and it and its family used to eat them; therefore, it viewed them as its own. No sooner said than done. The hedgehog shut the front door behind it and took its way to the fields. It was not yet very far from the house and was about to go around the blackthorn that was on the edge of the field and turn up toward the turnip patch, when it met the hare that had come out on a similar errand, namely, to take a look at its cabbages. When the hedgehog caught sight of the hare, it bade it a friendly good morning. The hare, however, who in its way was a high-born gentleman and frightfully arrogant besides, didn't acknowledge the hedgehog's greeting but instead said to it, at the same time putting on a very sneering expression, "How do *you* happen to be running about here in the country so early in the morning?" "I'm taking a walk," said the hedgehog. "Taking a walk?" laughed the hare. "I should think you could surely put your legs to better use." This answer annoyed the hedgehog extremely, for it could stand anything, but allowed nothing to be said about its legs for the simple reason that they were bandy by nature. "You're pretty conceited," the hedgehog said to the hare. "Do you think that you can accomplish more with your legs?" "I think so," said the hare. "That's a matter of experiment," remarked the hedgehog. "I bet if we run a race, I'll pass you." "That is ridiculous, what with your bandy legs!" said the hare. "As far as I'm concerned, however, all right, if you're so very, very anxious to. What will the bet be?" "A louis d'or and a bottle of brandy," said the hedgehog. "Done!" said the hare. "Shake on it and then we can start at once." "No, I'm in no such great hurry," remarked the hedgehog. "I'm still quite empty. I'll go home first and have a bite of breakfast and be back here on the spot in half an hour."

Thereupon, since the hare agreed to this, the hedgehog departed. On the way the hedgehog thought to itself, "The hare is counting on its long legs, but I'll get the better of it all right. To be sure it's a high-born gentleman, but just the same it's a fool and will certainly be the one to pay." When the hedgehog got home, it said to its wife, "Wife, get dressed quickly. You have got to go out to the field with me." "What's up?" said the wife. "I've bet the hare a louis d'or and a bottle of brandy. I'm going to race it, and you must be present." "Good heavens, husband!" the hedgehog's wife began to cry, "aren't you mad? Have you lost your mind?" "Shut up, wife!" said the hedgehog. "That's my business. Don't argue in man's affairs. Hurry up and get dressed and then come along." What could the hedgehog's wife do? Of course she had to go along, willy-nilly.

When they were both on the way, the hedgehog said to its wife, "Now pay attention to what I am going to say. Look, we're going to run our race on the long field there. The hare will run in one furrow and I in another, and we'll start at the upper end. All you have to do is to take your place at the lower end of the furrow, and when the hare comes along on the other side, you call out to him, 'I'm already here.'" By that time they had reached the field. The hedgehog showed its wife her place and went to the upper end of the field. When it got up there, the hare was there already. "Can we start?" said the hare. "Certainly," said the hedgehog. "Then off we go!" Thereupon each took its place in its furrow. The hare counted, "On your mark, get set, go!" and away it went down the field like a whirlwind. The hedgehog, however, ran about three steps then ducked down in a furrow and just sat there. Now when the hare, going at full speed, reached the lower end of the field, the hedgehog's wife called out to it, "I'm already here." The hare stopped short and was no little surprised. It had no idea that it wasn't the hedgehog itself who was calling out to it; for, as everybody knows, a hedgehog's wife looks just like her husband. Still, the hare thought, "Something's wrong there." "Let's race back again," it called out and away it went like a whirlwind, so that its ears stood out from its head. But the hedgehog's wife just stayed in her place. Now when the hare got to the top of the field, the hedgehog called out to it, "I'm already here." However, the hare, quite beside itself with vexation, screamed, "Let's race back again!" "I don't mind," answered the hedgehog. "As far as I am concerned, as often as you like." So the hare raced seventy-three times more, and each time the hedgehog stood the test against it. Every time that the hare reached the bottom of the field or the top, either the hedgehog or its wife would say, "I'm already here." On the seventy-fourth time, however, the hare didn't finish. It fell to the ground in the middle of the field, blood gushed from its mouth, and it lay there dead. But the hedgehog took the louis d'or and the bottle of brandy it had won, called its wife from her furrow, and both went home together content. And if they are not dead, they are still alive.

Thus it happened that the hedgehog ran the hare to death on the Heath of Buxtehude [Hanover], and since then no hare has let itself in for a race against a Buxtehude hedgehog.

The moral of this story is, however: first, that no one, no matter how high-born he thinks he is, should venture to make fun of a humble man, even if the latter is only a low-born hedgehog. And secondly, that it's advisable, when one goes a-wooing, to choose a wife from one's own class and who looks just like oneself. If one is a hedgehog, one must see to it that his wife is a hedgehog, too, and so forth.

188 Spindle, Shuttle, and Needle

Spindel, Weberschiffchen und Nadel

THERE WAS ONCE A GIRL whose mother and father died when she was still a small child. Her godmother lived all alone in a cottage on the outskirts of the village and supported herself by spinning, weaving, and sewing. The old woman took the forlorn child in, kept her at her work, and brought her up in all godliness. When the girl was fifteen, the old woman fell ill and, calling the child to her bedside, said, "Dear daughter, I feel that my end is drawing near; I am leaving you the cottage, where you will be sheltered from wind and weather, also a spindle, shuttle, and needle with which you can earn your living." She also laid her hands on her head, blessed her, and said, "Just keep God in your heart, and you'll be all right." Thereupon, she closed her eyes, and when she was laid away in the earth, the girl followed the coffin weeping bitterly and paid her her last respects. The girl now lived all alone in the little house, was industrious, spun, wove, and sewed, and the kind old woman's blessing descended upon everything she did. The flax in the storeroom seemed to increase of itself, and when she had woven a piece of cloth or a carpet, or made a shirt, she would straight away find a buyer who would pay handsomely for it. Thus she suffered no want and was even able to share some of her things with others.

About this time the king's son was traveling about the country looking for a bride. He wasn't to choose a poor girl, and he didn't want a rich girl. Then he said, "She shall be my bride who is both the richest and the poorest." When he came to the village where the girl lived, he asked, as he did everywhere, which girl in the village was the richest and which the poorest. First they named the richest; the poorest, they said, was the girl who lived in the cottage right on the outskirts. The rich girl was sitting all dressed up outside her front door, and when the king's son drew near, she got up, went to meet him, and curtsied to him. He looked at her, didn't say a word, and rode on. When he came to the poor girl's house, she wasn't at the door but was sitting in her little living room. He halted his horse and through the window, through which the bright sun was shining, saw the girl sitting at her spinning wheel and spinning industriously. She looked up and, noticing that the king's son was looking in, blushed again and again, lowered her eyes and kept on spinning. Whether by now the thread was spun quite even I don't know, but she went on spinning until the king's son rode away again. Then she stepped to the window, opened it, and said, "It's so warm in the room," but she looked after him as long as she could see the white plumes on his hat.

The girl sat down again to work in her room and kept on spinning. Then she thought of a saying that the old woman had sometimes repeated while sitting and working, and sang it to herself:

> "Spindle, spindle, do go out
> And bring the suitor to my house."

What happened? The spindle immediately jumped out of her hand and out the door, and when in amazement she stood up and followed it with her eyes, she saw it dancing merrily across the fields and drawing behind it a bright gold thread. Before long it disappeared from her view. Since the girl no longer had her spindle, she took the shuttle, seated herself at the loom, and began to weave.

But the spindle went dancing on and on, and just as the thread was at an end, it caught up with the king's son. "What do I see?" he cried. "The spindle surely wants to show me the way," turned his horse and rode back, following the gold thread. But the girl was sitting at her work and singing,

> "Shuttle, shuttle, weave it fine,
> Bring the suitor to my house."

Immediately the shuttle sprang out of her hand and jumped out the door. Outside the sill, however, it began to weave a carpet more beautiful than anybody has ever seen. On both borders bloomed roses and lilies, and down the center on a gold field green tendrils were climbing up, in which hares and rabbits were hopping, stags and roes stretching out their heads, and up in the branches birds of many colors perched, perfect in every respect except that they were not singing. The shuttle jumped hither and thither, and the whole thing seemed to be growing of itself.

Because the shuttle had run away, the girl sat down to sew. She held the needle in her hand and sang,

> "Needle, needle, sharp and fine,
> Clean the house for the suitor."

Then the needle jumped out of her fingers and flew here and there about the room as quick as lightning. It was just as if invisible spirits were at work. Forthwith the table and benches were upholstered with green cloth, the chairs with velvet, and silk curtains hung down by the windows. Hardly had the needle sewed the last stitch when through the window the girl saw the white plumes of the prince's hat: the spindle had led him along the gold thread. He dismounted, walked into the house along the carpet, and when he entered the living room, the girl was standing there in her poor dress. She was aglow, however, like a rose on the bush. "You're the poorest and also the richest," he said to her. "Come with me; you shall be my bride."

She said nothing but gave him her hand. Then he gave her a kiss, led her out, lifted her onto his horse, and brought her to the royal palace, where the wedding was celebrated with great joy.

The spindle, shuttle, and needle were kept in the Treasure House and held in high esteem.

189   The Farmer and the Devil

Der Bauer und der Teufel

THERE WAS ONCE A CLEVER and artful farmer of whose pranks much could be told. The best story, however, is how he once got hold of the Devil and made a fool of him.

One day the farmer had been tilling his field and was getting ready to go home, since twilight had already set in. Then in the middle of his field he saw a pile of fiery coals, and as he approached it full of wonderment, a little black devil was sitting on the top of the glow. "I suppose you're sitting on a treasure," said the farmer. "Quite so," answered the Devil, "on a treasure containing more gold and silver than you've seen in your life." "The treasure is in my field and belongs to me," said the farmer. "It's yours," answered the Devil, "if for two years you give me half of what your field yields. I have plenty of money, but I have a craving for the fruits of the earth."

The farmer accepted the bargain. "So that there will be no argument about the division," said the farmer, "you are to have what is above ground and I what is below ground." The Devil agreed to that, but the clever farmer had sown turnips. When harvest time came, the Devil appeared and was about to take his produce but found only wilted yellow leaves; the farmer, quite satisfied, dug his turnips. "For once you got ahead of me," said the Devil, "but next time that isn't going to work. Your share will be what grows above ground, mine what's below ground." "That, too, suits me," answered the farmer.

But when sowing time came, the farmer didn't sow turnips again but sowed wheat. The crop ripened, the farmer went to the field and cut the full stalks right down to the ground. When the Devil came, he found nothing but stubble and in a fury went down in a cleft in a rock.

"That's the way one must fool foxes," said the farmer and went and collected his treasure.

190 The Crumbs on the Table

Die Brosamen auf dem Tisch

A COCK once said to his hens, "Just come right into the living room and peck up the crumbs on the table. Our mistress has gone out to pay a call." Then the hens said, "No, no, we're not going to. You know the mistress will skin us alive for it." Then the cock said, "She'll know nothing about it. Come right along. Besides, she never gives us anything good anyhow." Then the hens again said, "No, no, nothing doing! we won't go up there." But the cock gave them no peace until they finally went and jumped up on the table and pecked up the crumbs, making a thorough job of it. At that very moment their mistress arrived and quickly took a stick and beat them and dealt severely with them. When they had been chased out of the house, the hens said to the cock, "Don't, don't, don't, don't you see?" Then the cock laughed and said, "Did-did-didn't I know?" And that's what they had to go home with.

191   The Monkey

Das Meerhäschen

THERE WAS ONCE A PRINCESS in whose castle, high up under the battlements, was a big room with twelve windows facing all points of the compass. Accordingly, when she went up and looked around, she could survey her whole kingdom. Out of the first window she could see far more keenly than other people, out of the second still better, out of the third even more clearly, and so on to the twelfth, where she could see everything above and below ground, and nothing could remain hidden from her. But because she was haughty, unwilling to subject herself to anyone, and wanted to exercise sole mastery, she had it announced that nobody should become her husband who couldn't so hide himself from her that it would be impossible for her to find him. If anyone tried it, however, and she discovered him, his head would be struck off and put on a stake.

There were already ninety-seven stakes outside the castle with dead men's heads on them, and over a long period of time no one came. The princess was delighted and thought, "Now I shall remain free as long as I live." Then three brothers appeared in her presence and declared that they wanted to try their luck. The eldest thought he would be safe if he crept into a lime pit, but of course she spied him out of the first window, had him pulled out and his head struck off. The second crept into the cellar of the castle, but him, too, she spied out of the first window, and it was all over with him: his head went on the ninety-ninth stake. Then the youngest came into her presence and begged her to let him have a day for reflection, also to be so gracious as to give him three chances to be detected. If he failed the third time, he would give no further thought to his life. Because he was so handsome and begged so earnestly, she said, "Yes, I'll grant you this, but it will do you no good."

The next day he reflected for a long time how to hide himself, but in vain. Then he took his gun and went hunting. He saw a raven and drew a bead on it. He was about to fire when the raven cried, "Don't shoot, I'll reward you for it." He lowered his gun, went on, and came to a lake where he surprised a big fish that had come up from the depths to the surface of the water. When he had taken aim, the fish cried, "Don't shoot, I'll reward you for it." He let it dive under, went on, and met a fox that was limping. He fired and missed it; then the fox cried, "Rather than shoot, come here and pull the thorn out of my foot." He did so indeed but then was going to kill the fox and skin it. "Don't do it," said the fox. "I'll reward you for it." The youth let it go and, since it was evening, went back home.

The next day he was supposed to crawl into hiding, but however much he wracked his brains, he couldn't think where to go. He went to the forest to the raven and said, "I spared your life. Now tell me where to creep so that the king's daughter won't see me." The raven bowed its head and thought for a long time. Finally it croaked, "I have it!" fetched an egg from its nest, broke it in two, and enclosed the youth in it, then put it together again and sat on it. When the princess went to the first window, she couldn't discover him, nor at the next ones, and began to get frightened. But she saw him out of the eleventh. She had the raven shot, the egg fetched and broken open, and the youth had to come out. "You've been given one chance," she said. "If you don't do better, you're lost."

The next day he went to the lake, summoned the fish, and said, "I let you live; now tell me where to hide so that the princess won't see me." The fish reflected and finally cried, "I have it! I'll shut you up in my belly." It swallowed him and went down to the bottom of the lake. The princess looked out of her windows. Even through the eleventh she didn't see him and was dumbfounded, though she finally discovered him out of the twelfth. She had the fish caught and killed, and the youth appeared. Anybody can imagine what his feelings were. "You've been given two chances," she said, "but your head will surely go on the hundredth stake."

On the last day he went with heavy heart into the country and met the fox. "You know how to find all the good hiding-places," he said. "I let you live; now advise me where to hide so that the princess won't find me." "A difficult task," answered the fox and assumed a serious expression. Finally it cried, "I have it!" It went with him to a spring, plunged in, and came out a merchant dealing in pet animals. The youth likewise had to plunge into the water and was transformed into a little monkey. The merchant arrived in town and showed the nice little animal. A lot of people gathered to look at it. At last even the princess came, and because she took a great fancy to it, she bought it and gave the merchant a lot of money for it. Before handing it over to her, he said to it, "When the princess goes to the window, crawl quickly under her braid." Now the time came for her to look for him. She went from window to window, from the first to the eleventh, and didn't see him. When even through the twelfth she didn't see him, she was filled with fear and rage and slammed it to so hard that the glass in all the windows broke into a thousand pieces, and the whole castle shook.

She drew back and felt the monkey under her braid. She seized it and threw it onto the floor, crying, "Out of my sight!" It ran to the merchant, and both hurried to the spring, where they plunged in and regained their true forms. The youth thanked the fox, saying, "The raven and the fish are terribly stupid compared to you; you certainly know the right tricks."

The youth went straight into the castle. The princess was already waiting for him and had reconciled herself to her fate. The wedding was celebrated, and now he was king and lord of the whole realm. He never told her where he hid himself the third time and who had helped him, and thus she believed that he had done it all through his own skill and respected him, for she thought to herself, "After all, he is cleverer than you are."

192   The Master Thief

Der Meisterdieb

ONE DAY an old man and his wife were sitting outside their rather poor house wishing to rest a bit from their labors. All at once a magnificent coach and four black horses drove up and a richly dressed gentleman stepped out. The farmer got up, went to the gentleman, and asked what his desire might be and how he might serve him. The stranger gave the old man his hand and said, "I desire nothing but for once to enjoy a country dish. Prepare me potatoes as you usually eat them, then I'll sit down at your table and consume them with pleasure." The farmer smiled and said, "You are a count or a prince or even a duke; high-born gentlemen sometimes have cravings of that sort. However, your wish will be fulfilled." His wife went into the kitchen and began to wash and grate the potatoes, planning to make dumplings of them farmer style.

While she was at work, the farmer said to the stranger, "Come with me for a bit into my garden, where I still have something to do." He had been digging holes in the garden and was now going to set out trees in them. "Have you no children who could help you with the work?" asked the stranger. "No," answered the farmer. "I had, to be sure, a son," and added "but he went out in the world long ago. He was a wild boy, clever and artful, but he wouldn't learn anything and was up to nothing but bad pranks. Finally he ran away, and since then I have seen nothing of him." The old man took a sapling, set it in a hole, and stuck a stake in beside it. When he had shoveled in the earth and stamped it down hard, he tied the trunk firmly to the stake at the bottom, top and middle with a wisp of straw. "But tell me," said the gentleman, "why don't you tie that crooked, gnarled tree that is bent almost to the ground over there in the corner to a stake, too, as you are tying this one, so that it will grow straight?" "Sir," said the old man and smiled, "you speak as you see it; it's plain that you haven't had much to do with gardening. The tree over there is old and gnarled; no one can make it straight now. One must train trees when they're still young." "It's as with your son," said the stranger. "If you had trained him while he was still young, he wouldn't have run away. Now he has probably become old and gnarled, too." "It's certainly a long time since he ran away," answered the old man. "He has surely changed." "Would you still recognize him if he appeared before you?" asked the stranger. "Hardly by his face," answered the farmer, "but he has a mark on him, a mole on his shoulder that looks like a bean." As he said that, the stranger took off his coat, bared his shoulder, and showed the farmer the mole. "Good Lord!" cried the old man, "you are really my son," and love for his child stirred his heart. "But," he added, "how can you be my son? You've become a great lord and live in wealth and abundance. How did you attain this?" "Alas, father," replied the son, "the young tree wasn't tied to a stake and grew crooked. Now it's too old; it won't get straight again. How have I acquired all this? I have become a thief. But don't get frightened, I'm a master thief; for me neither lock nor bolt exists; whatever I crave is mine. Don't imagine that I steal like a common thief; I take only from the surplus of the rich. Poor people are safe; I give to them rather than take anything from them. Similarly, whatever I can have without trouble, craft, or skill, I don't touch." "Alas, my son," said the father, "just the same I don't like it. A thief's a thief. I tell you, it leads to no good end." He took him to his mother, and when she heard that he was her son, she wept for joy. But when he told her that he had become a master thief, then two streams flowed down her face. Finally she said, "Even if he has become a thief, still he's my son, and my eyes have beheld him once again."

They sat down to table, and once again he ate with his parents the mean fare that he had not eaten for a long time. "If our lord, the count up there in the manor, learns who you are and what you are doing," said his father, "he won't take you in his arms and rock you in them the way he used to when he stood sponsor for you; rather he will let you swing on the gallows." "Don't worry, father, he won't do anything to me, for I understand my business. I'll go and see him myself this very day." As evening drew near, the master thief got into his coach and drove to the manor. The count received him courteously because he thought he was a high-born gentleman, but when the stranger made himself known, he turned pale and was silent for quite a time. Finally he said, "You are my godson, therefore I shall temper justice with mercy and deal with you considerately. Because you boast of being a master thief, I shall put your skill to the test. If, however, you fail to pass it, you will have to celebrate a marriage with the roper's daughter, and your wedding music will be the cawing of ravens." "Count," answered the master, "think up three things as hard as you want and if I don't carry out your task, do with me as you like." The count thought for some minutes, then said, "All right. First you're to steal my favorite mount from the stable; secondly, without our noticing it, you're to steal my wife's sheet and mine from under us while we're asleep, also my wife's wedding ring from her finger; as the third and last task, you're to abduct my rector and my verger from the church. Take careful note of all this, for your neck is at stake."

The master betook himself to the nearest town, where he bought the clothes of an old farmer's wife and put them on. Then he stained his face brown and even painted in wrinkles, so that no human being would have recognized him. Finally he filled a small keg with old Hungarian wine in which a strong sleeping-potion was mixed. He put the keg in a sling which he took on his back and with slow, faltering steps went to the count's manor.

It was already dark when he got there. He sat down in the courtyard on a stone, began to cough like a consumptive old woman, and rubbed his hands as though he were freezing. Outside the stable door soldiers were lying around a fire. One of them noticed the old woman and called to her, "Come nearer, granny, and warm yourself here with us. You surely have no regular night's lodging and take it where you find it." The old woman tottered up, asked them to take the sling from her back, and sat down with them by the fire. "What have you got there in your keg, granny," asked one. "A good swallow of wine," she answered. "I support myself by this trade; for money and kind words I'll gladly give you a glass." "Just pass it here," said the soldier, and when he had tasted it, cried, "When the wine's good, I prefer to drink a second glass," had another poured out for him, while the others followed his example.

"I say, comrades," cried one to those who were sitting in the stable, "there's an old woman here who has wine that's as old as herself. Have a swallow, too; it'll warm your stomachs better than our fire." The old woman carried her keg into the stable. One man had seated himself on the count's favorite mount that had its saddle on, another was holding the bridle in his hand, a third had hold of the tail. She poured out drinks, as many as were called for, until the source dried up. Before long the bridle fell from the hand of the man who was holding it: he dropped to the ground and began to snore. The second let go of the tail, lay down, and snored even louder. The man who was sitting in the saddle remained seated, to be sure, but bent his head almost to the horse's neck, fell asleep and breathed out of his mouth like a smith's bellows. The soldiers outside had long since fallen asleep and were lying on the ground as motionless as if made of stone.

When the master-thief saw that he had succeeded, he put a rope in the man's hand instead of the bridle, and in the hand of the other, who had been holding the tail, a wisp of straw instead of the tail. What was he to do with the man who was sitting on the horse's back? He didn't want to throw him off: he might have awakened and raise a hue and cry. But he had a good plan. He unbuckled the surcingle, tied fast to the saddle a couple of ropes that were hanging in rings on the wall, and pulled the sleeping rider, saddle and all, up in the air. Then he wound the ropes around the post and made them fast. He had already unchained the horse, but had he ridden over the stone pavement of the stable yard, the noise would have been heard in the manor. So he first wrapped its hoofs in old rags, then led it cautiously out, swung up on it, and made off. When day had broken, the master galloped up to the manor on the stolen horse. The count had just got up and was looking out the window. "Good morning, count," he called to him, "here's the horse I was lucky enough to get out of the stable. Just see how nicely your soldiers are lying there asleep, and if you care to go into the stable, you will see how comfortable your watchmen have made themselves." The count couldn't help laughing, then said, "You've succeeded once, but you won't be so lucky the second time. And I warn you, if I meet you as a thief, I'll treat you as a thief, too."

That evening when the countess went to bed, she closed tight the hand on which she wore her wedding ring, and the count said, "All doors are locked and bolted. I shall stay awake and wait for the thief, and if he climbs in the window, I'll shoot him down." But the master-thief went out in the dark to the gallows, cut from the noose a poor sinner who was hanging there, and carried him on his back to the palace. There he set a ladder up against the bedroom, put the dead man on his shoulder, and began to mount. When he got high enough so that the dead man's head appeared in the window, the count, who was on the watch in his bed, fired a pistol at him. Immediately the master let the poor sinner drop, himself jumped down from the ladder, and hid in a corner.

The moon that night was so bright that the master could distinctly see the count climb out the window onto the ladder, come down, and carry the dead man into the garden. There he began to dig a hole in which he was going to bury him. "Now," thought the thief, "the lucky moment has come," crept nimbly out of his hiding-place and climbed up the ladder right into the countess' bedroom. "Dear wife," he began in the count's voice, "the thief is dead but, nevertheless, he is my godson and was more a rascal than a miscreant. I don't want to expose him to public disgrace; besides I am sorry for his parents. I shall bury him myself in the garden before daybreak, so that the affair will not become notorious. Give me the sheet, too; I want to wrap him in it and not bury him like a dog." The countess gave him the sheet. "Do you know what?" continued the thief, "I am having a fit of magnanimity. Give me your ring, too; the unhappy man risked his life for it, so let him take it with him to the grave." She was loath to oppose the count, and though she didn't want to do so, nevertheless she drew it from her finger and handed it to him. The thief made off with both objects and got safely home before the count had finished his grave-digging in the garden.

What a long face the count pulled when next morning the master came bringing him the sheet and the ring. "Are you a wizard?" he said to him. "Who fetched you out of the grave in which I myself laid you? and who brought you back to life again?" "It was not I whom you buried," said the thief, "but the poor sinner on the gallows," and related in detail what had happened. The count had to admit that he was a skillful and clever thief. "But you're not through yet," he added. "You have still the third problem to solve, and if you don't succeed in that, nothing will help you." The master smiled and made no answer.

When night fell, he went to the village church with a long sack on his back, a bundle under his arm, and a lantern in his hand. In the sack he had crawfish and in the bundle short wax tapers. He sat down in the graveyard, took out a crawfish, and stuck a taper on its back. Then he lighted it, set the crawfish on the ground, and let it crawl. He took a second out of the sack, did the same with it, and kept on until the last crawfish was out of the sack. Then he put on a long black garment that looked like a monk's cowl and stuck a grey beard on his chin. When at last he was quite unrecognizable, he took the sack the crawfish had been in, went into the church, and mounted the chancel. The belfry clock was just striking twelve. When the last stroke had died away, he called out in a loud, ringing voice, "Harken, ye sinners! The end of all things has come. Doomsday is near. Harken, harken! Whoever wants to come with me to Heaven, let him crawl into the sack. I am Peter who opens and closes the gates of Heaven. Behold! out in the graveyard the dead are stirring and are assembling their members. Come, come, crawl into the sack! The world is coming to an end!"

The cry echoed through the whole village. The rector and the verger, who lived nearest the church, were the first to hear it, and when they spied the lights moving about in the graveyard, realized that something unusual was up and went into the church. They listened to the sermon for a while, then the verger nudged the rector and said, "It wouldn't be a bad thing if we seized the opportunity and both got to Heaven an easy way before the dawn of Doomsday." "Certainly," replied the rector, "those were my thoughts, too. If you want, let's get going." "Yes," answered the verger, "but you, rector, have precedence. I'll follow after you." So the rector stepped forward and mounted the chancel where the master opened the sack. The rector crawled in first, then the verger. Straightway the master tied the sack tight, gathered it up by the mouth, and dragged it down the chancel steps. Every time the two fools' heads hit the steps, he would cry, "Now, of course, we're going over the mountains." Then in the same way he dragged them through the village, and when they went through puddles, he would cry, "Now, of course, we're going through the moist clouds." And when at last he was dragging them up the palace steps, he cried, "Now we're on the steps of Heaven and shall soon be in the vestibule." But on getting upstairs he shoved the sack into the pigeon-loft, and when the pigeons fluttered, he said, "Hear how the angels are rejoicing and beating their wings." Then he shot the bolt and went away.

The next morning he betook himself to the count and told him that he had solved the third task, too, and had abducted the rector and the verger from the church. "Where did you leave them?" asked the lord. "They are in a sack up in the pigeon-loft and imagine they are in Heaven." The count climbed up himself and convinced himself that the thief had told the truth.

When he had freed the rector and the verger from their prison, he said, "You are an archthief and have won your case. This time you're getting off with a whole skin, but see to it that you get out of my country; for if you set foot in it again, you may count on your elevation to the gallows." The archthief took leave of his parents, again went into the wide world, and nobody has heard anything about him since.

193 The Drummer-Boy

Der Trommler

ONE EVENING a young drummer-boy was walking all alone in the country and came to a lake, on the shore of which he saw three pieces of white linen. "What fine linen!" he said, putting one of the pieces in his pocket. He went home, thought no more of his find, and went to bed. As he was about to fall asleep, he had the feeling that someone was calling him by name. He listened and heard a soft voice calling to him, "Drummer-boy, drummer-boy, wake up!" Since it was pitch-black night, he couldn't see anybody, but it seemed to him that a form was moving up and down in front of his bed. "What do you want?" he asked. The voice answered, "Give me back my shift that you took from me this evening by the lake." "You'll get it back," said the drummer, "if you'll tell me who you are." "Alas!" replied the voice, "I am the daughter of a mighty king, but I have fallen into the power of a witch and have been banished to the Glass Mountain. Every day my two sisters and I must bathe in the lake, but without my shift I can't fly away again. My sisters have gone off, but I have had to stay behind. Give me back my shift, I beg you." "Don't worry, poor child," said the drummer. "I'll gladly give it back to you." He fetched it out of his pouch and handed it to her in the dark. She seized it hastily and was about to depart with it. "Wait a moment," he said; "perhaps I can help you." "You can help me only if you climb the Glass Mountain and free me from the power of the witch. But you won't get to the Glass Mountain, and even if you were quite near it, you couldn't get up it." "What I want to do, I can do," said the drummer. "I'm sorry for you and am afraid of nothing. Only I don't know the way to the Glass Mountain." "The way goes through the great forest where the cannibals live," she answered. "I may not tell you anything more." Thereupon he heard her whirring away.

At daybreak the drummer-boy got up, slung his drum over his shoulder, and fearlessly went straight into the forest. After walking a while and seeing no giant, he thought, "I must rouse the sleepyheads," pulled his drum around, and beat a roll on it, so that the birds flew up from the trees with loud cries. Before long a giant who had been lying asleep in the grass raised himself up; he was as tall as a fir tree. "You little creature," he called to him, "why are you drumming here and waking me out of the best part of my sleep?" "I'm drumming," he answered, "because many thousands of people are coming behind me and I am showing them the way." "What do they want here in my forest?" asked the giant. "They want to make an end of you and purge the forest of monsters like you." "Aha!" said the giant, "I'll trample you all to death like so many ants." "Do you think that you can do anything to them?" said the drummer. "If you bend over to seize one, he'll jump away and hide. When, on the other hand, you lie down and go to sleep, they'll come out of every bush and creep up on you. Each has a steel hammer in his belt and will beat in your skull with it." The giant got annoyed and thought, "If I get involved with these clever people, it might, indeed, work out badly for me. I can strangle wolves and bears, but I don't know how to protect myself against earthworms. Listen, little chap," he said, "you withdraw, and I promise you that in the future I shall leave you and your companions in peace. And if you want anything else, just tell me, and I'll gladly do you a favor." "You've got long legs," said the drummer, "and can walk faster than I. Carry me to the Glass Mountain, and then I'll give my people a signal to retire, and this time they will leave you in peace." "Come here, worm," said the giant. "Sit on my shoulder, and I'll carry you to where you ask to go." The giant lifted him up, and up there the drummer began to roll his drum to his heart's content. The giant thought, "That will be the signal for the rest to retire." After a time a second giant appeared on the road; he took the drummer-boy from the first giant and put him in his button-hole. The drummer seized the button that was as large as a bowl, held on to it, and looked all around most cheerfully. Then they came to a third who took him out of the button-hole and set him on the brim of his hat. Up there the drummer walked back and forth and looked out over the trees, and on spying a mountain in the blue distance thought, "That is surely the Glass Mountain." And so it was. The giant took just a few more steps and they had reached the foot of the mountain. There the giant set him down. The drummer demanded he carry him to the peak of the Glass Mountain, but the giant shook his head, growled something to himself, and went back into the forest.

Now the poor drummer-boy was in front of the mountain; it was as high as if three mountains had been piled on top of one another and was as smooth as a mirror, withal. Nor did he know how to get up it. He began to climb, but in vain; he kept slipping down again. "Were one only a bird," he thought. But what good did wishing do him? He didn't grow any wings. As he was standing thus and not knowing what to do, he saw not far off two men who were quarreling furiously with one another. He went up to them and saw that they were in disagreement over a saddle lying on the ground in front of them, which each of them wanted. "What fools you are!" he said. "You're fighting over a saddle and haven't a horse for it." "The saddle is worth fighting for," answered one of the men. "Whoever sits in it and wishes himself anywhere, even to the end of the world, will be there the instant he has uttered his wish. The saddle belongs to us jointly; it's my turn to ride it, but the other man won't agree to it." "I'll soon settle the quarrel," said the drummer, went off a distance, and stuck a white stake in the ground. Then he came back and said, "Now run toward the goal. The first one there will ride first." Both set off at a trot, but scarcely were they a few paces away when the drummer swung onto the saddle, wished himself onto the Glass Mountain, and before you could say Jack Robinson, was there.

Up on the mountain was a plateau on which stood an old stone house, and outside the house was a big fishpond, and behind it a dark forest. He saw neither man nor beast; all was still but for the rustling of the wind in the trees and the clouds drifting by, quite close by over his head. He went to the door and knocked. When he had knocked for the third time, an old woman with a brown face and red eyes opened it. She had glasses on her long nose and looked at him sharply, then asked what he wanted. "Admission, food, and a night's lodging," answered the drummer-boy. "That you shall have," said the old woman, "provided you will perform three tasks in return." "Why not?" he answered. "I'm not afraid of any work, even if it's ever so hard." The old woman let him in, gave him food, and at night a good bed. In the morning when he had had a good long sleep, the old woman took a thimble from her withered finger, handed it to the drummer, and said, "Now get to work and ladle out the pond there with this thimble. But you must be finished before night, and all the fish that are in the water must be sorted out according to their kind and size and laid side by side." "That's a strange task," said the drummer, went, however, to the pond and began to ladle. He ladled all morning, but what can one do with a thimble in the case of a big body of water, even if one ladles for a thousand years? When it was noon, he thought, "It's all no use and it's all one whether I work or whether I don't," stopped and sat down. Then a girl came out of the house and, setting down a basket of food for him, said, "You're sitting there so sad. What is the matter with you?" He looked at her and saw that she was exceedingly beautiful. "Alas!" he said, "I can't accomplish the first task. How will it be with the others? I set out to seek a king's daughter who is supposed to be living here, but I haven't found her. I'm going to move on." "Stay here," said the girl. "I'll help you out of your difficulty. You're tired. Lay your head in my lap and go to sleep. When you wake up again, the work will be done." The drummer didn't have to be told twice. As soon as his eyes were closed, she gave a wishing-ring a twist, saying, "Water up, fish out." Immediately the water rose up like a white mist and moved off with the other clouds, and the fish came up with a smacking noise, leapt ashore, and lay down beside one another, each according to its size and kind.

When the drummer awoke, he saw to his astonishment that everything was finished, but the girl said, "One of the fish isn't lying with its own kind but is quite by itself. When the old woman comes this evening and sees that everything has been done as she required, she will ask, 'What is this fish doing by itself?' Then throw the fish in her face and say, 'That's for you, old witch.'" In the evening the old woman came, and when she put her question, he threw the fish in her face. She acted as if she didn't notice it and kept still, though giving him a malicious look.

The next morning she said, "You had it too easy yesterday. I must set you a harder task. Today you must chop down the whole forest, split the wood into logs and cord it, and it must all be done by evening." She gave him an ax, a mallet, and two wedges, but the ax was of lead, the mallet and wedges of tin. When he began to chop, the ax-edge turned and the mallet and wedges collapsed. He didn't know what to do, but at noon the girl again came with the food and comforted him. "Lay your head in my lap," she said, "and go to sleep. When you wake up, the work will be done." She gave her wishing-ring a twist, and at that moment the whole forest collapsed with a crash, the wood split itself and piled itself in cords. It was as if invisible giants had accomplished the task. When he awoke, the girl said, "See, the wood is corded and piled; there's just one odd branch, and when the old woman comes this evening and asks what about it, give her a blow with it and say, 'That's for you, you witch.'" The old woman came. "See," she said, "how easy the work was. But for whom is that branch there?" "For you, you witch," he answered and gave her a blow with it. But she acted as if she didn't feel it, laughed mockingly, and said, "Early tomorrow you're to pile all the wood into one pile, set fire to it, and burn it up."

He got up at daybreak and began to fetch the wood. But how can a single person gather up a whole forest? He made no progress with the work. However, the girl didn't forsake him in his need. At noon she brought him his food, and when he had eaten, he laid his head in her lap and went to sleep. On waking up, he saw the whole pile of wood burning in one huge flame that was sending out its tongues as high as the sky. "Listen to me," said the girl. "When the witch comes, she will impose all sorts of tasks upon you. Do without fear what she demands; in that way she can't do anything to you. If, however, you're afraid, the fire will seize you and consume you. Finally, when you've done everything, seize her with both hands and throw her right into the fire." The girl went away, and the old woman came creeping up. "My! I'm freezing," she said, "but there's a fire! It's burning, it warms my old bones, I'll be comfortable there. But there's a log over there that won't burn; pull it out for me. Once you've done that, you'll be free and can go where you please. Go right into the fire!" The drummer didn't think long and jumped into the middle of the flames. They didn't harm him, however; in fact, couldn't even singe his hair. He brought out the log and put it down. Scarcely had the log touched the ground than it was transformed, and before him stood the beautiful girl who had helped him in his need, and from the silk garments, glittering like gold, that she had on, he saw plainly that she was the king's daughter. But the old woman laughed venomously and said, "You think you have her, but you haven't got her yet." She was on the point of attacking the girl and pulling her away when he laid hold of the old woman with both hands, lifted her up, and threw her into the blaze. The flames closed over her as if glad to consume a witch.

Then the king's daughter looked at the drummer-boy, and when she saw that he was a handsome youth and considered how he had risked his life to free her, she gave him her hand, saying, "You've risked everything for me, and I, too, shall do everything for you. Plight me your troth and you shall be my spouse. We're not lacking riches, we have plenty with what the witch has gathered together here." She took him into the house where stood chests and boxes filled with treasures. They left the gold and silver, taking only the jewels. They didn't want to stay any longer on the Glass Mountain. Then he said to her, "Sit by me on my saddle, and we'll fly down like birds." "I don't like the old saddle," she said. "I need only to give my wishing-ring a twist and we'll be home." "All right," answered the drummer, "then wish us outside the town gate."

They were there in a flash, but the drummer said, "I want first to go to my parents and tell them the news. Wait for me out here in the country; I'll be back shortly." "O dear!" said the king's daughter, "I beg you to be on your guard. When you get there, don't kiss your parents on the right cheek, otherwise you'll forget everything, and I'll be left alone and forsaken in the fields." "How can I forget you?" he said and gave her his hand on it to return very soon. When he entered his father's house, he had so changed that no one knew who he was, for the three days that he had spent on the Glass Mountain had been three long years. Then he made himself known, and his parents fell on his neck for joy, and his heart was so moved that he kissed them on both cheeks, not thinking of the girl's words. When, however, he had given them a kiss on the right cheek, all thought of the king's daughter left him. He emptied out his pockets and put handsful of the biggest jewels on the table. His parents had absolutely no idea what to do with the fortune. Then his father built a splendid mansion with gardens, woods, and meadows around about it, as if a prince were going to reside in it. And when it was finished, his mother said, "I have found a girl for you; the wedding will take place in three days." The son was agreeable to everything his parents wished.

The poor king's daughter stayed for a long time outside the town waiting for the youth's return. When evening came, she said, "He surely kissed his parents on the right cheek and forgot me." With heart full of grief she wished herself into a lonely forest hut and didn't want to return to her father's court. Every evening she went into town and walked past his house. He saw her sometimes but no longer recognized her. Finally she heard the people say, "His wedding will be celebrated tomorrow." Then she said, "I shall try and see if I may win back his heart." When the first day of the wedding festival was celebrated, she gave her wishing-ring a twist and said, "A gown as brilliant as the sun." Forthwith the gown lay before her, glistening as if woven of sheer sunbeams. When all the guests had assembled, she entered the hall. Everybody marvelled at the beautiful gown, especially the bride, and since beautiful clothes were the latter's greatest delight, she went to the stranger and asked if she would sell it to her. "Not for money," she answered, "but if I may keep watch this first night outside the door of the bridegroom's bedroom, I'll give it away." The bride was unable to restrain her desire and agreed, but she mixed a sleeping potion in the bridegroom's nightcap and as a result he fell into a deep sleep. Now when all was quiet, the king's daughter crouched outside the bedroom door, opened it a little, and called in,

> "Drummer-boy, drummer-boy, listen to me!
>   Have you quite forgotten me?
>   Didn't you sit beside me on the Glass Mountain?
>   Didn't I save your life from the witch?
>   Didn't you plight me your troth with your hand?
>   Drummer-boy, drummer-boy, listen to me!"

But it was all in vain. The drummer-boy didn't wake up, and when morning came, the king's daughter had to depart again without having accomplished her purpose.

The second evening she gave her wishing-ring a twist and said, "A gown as silvery as the moon." When she appeared at the feast in the gown that was as delicate as moonlight, the bride's desire was again aroused, and in exchange for the gown she gave her permission to spend the second night, too outside the bedroom door. Then in the still of the night she called,

> "Drummer-boy, drummer-boy, listen to me!
>   Have you quite forgotten me?
>   Didn't you sit beside me on the Glass Mountain?
>   Didn't I save your life from the witch?
>   Didn't you plight me your troth with your hand?
>   Drummer-boy, drummer-boy, listen to me!"

But the drummer-boy, drugged by the sleeping potion, was not to be awakened. In the morning she returned again sadly to her forest hut. The servants, however, had heard the strange girl's lament and told the bridegroom about it. They also told him that he had not been able to hear because they had poured a sleeping potion into his wine.

On the third evening the king's daughter gave the wishing-ring a twist and said, "A gown twinkling like stars." When she appeared in it at the feast, the bride was quite beside herself over the splendor of the gown, which far surpassed the others, and said, "I shall and must have it." The girl gave it to her, like the others, in exchange for leave to spend the night outside the bridegroom's door. The bridegroom, however, didn't drink the wine they gave him before going to sleep but poured it out behind his bed. When everything in the house was still, he heard a voice calling softly to him,

> "Drummer-boy, drummer-boy, listen to me!
> Have you quite forgotten me?
> Didn't you sit beside me on the Glass Mountain?
> Didn't I save your life from the witch?
> Didn't you plight me your troth with your hand?
> Drummer-boy, drummer-boy, listen to me!"

Suddenly his memory returned. "Alas!" he cried, "how could I have acted so faithlessly! But the kiss, which out of the joy of my heart I gave my parents on their right cheeks, is to blame; it stupefied me." He leapt up, took the king's daughter by the hand, and led her to his parents' bedside. "This is my true bride," he said. "If I marry the other, I shall be doing a great wrong." His parents, on hearing how it had all come about, agreed. Then the candles in the hall were lighted again, kettle-drums and trumpets fetched, friends and relatives invited to return, and the true wedding was celebrated with great joy.

The first bride kept the beautiful gowns by way of amends and declared herself satisfied.

194 The Ear of Grain

Die Kornähre

IN DAYS OF YORE when God Himself still walked the earth, the land was much more fruitful than it is now. At that time the ears of grain yielded not fifty or sixtyfold but four or five hundredfold. Then the grains grew on the stalks from top to bottom; the ear was as long as the stalk. But people being what they are, as a result of superabundance they cease having any regard for the blessings that flow from God and become indifferent and heedless.

One day a woman was passing a field of rye, and her little child, that was skipping along beside her, fell into a puddle and soiled her dress. Then the mother pulled off a handful of the fine ears and cleaned the dress with them. When the Lord, who was just walking by, saw that, He got angry and said, "From now on the stalks shall no longer bear ears: men no longer deserve that heavenly gift." The bystanders who heard that were frightened, fell on their knees, and implored Him to leave something on the stalk: even if they themselves didn't deserve it, at least for the innocent fowls that otherwise must starve. The Lord, anticipating their misery, had mercy and granted the request. So the ear was still left at the top of the stalk, the way it now grows.

195   The Grave-Mound

Der Grabhügel

A RICH FARMER was standing one day in his yard looking out at his fields and orchards. The grain was growing vigorously, the fruit trees hung heavy with fruit. Last year's grain was still in such huge piles in the loft that the beams could scarcely support it. Then he went into the stable: there stood the well-fed oxen, the fat cows, and sleek horses. Finally, he went into his living room and cast a glance at the iron boxes in which his money was. As he was standing there surveying his wealth, there was suddenly a violent knocking beside him. The knocking was not, however, on his living-room door, but rather on the door of his heart. The door opened, and he heard a voice speaking to him, "Have you also been good to your own people? Have you looked out for the needs of the poor? Have you shared your bread with the hungry? Were you satisfied with what you had, or have you always been wanting more?" Without hesitation his heart answered, "I've been hard and inexorable and have never done anything kind to my own people. When a poor man appeared, I would avert my eyes. I've not bothered about God, rather thought only of increasing my wealth. Had everything under heaven been mine, I still should not have had enough." On hearing this answer, he was terribly frightened. His knees began to shake and he had to sit down.

Again there was a knocking, but the knock was on his living-room door. It was his neighbor, a poor man, who had a great number of children whose hunger he could no longer satisfy. "I know," thought the poor man, "my neighbor is rich, but he is equally hard-hearted. I don't think he will help me, but my children are crying for bread, so I'll risk it." To the rich man he said, "You don't give any of your things away very readily, but I stand here like a man in water that is rising to his head: my children are hungry. Lend me seventy-five bushels of grain." The rich man looked at him for a long time; then the first ray of charity began to melt a drop of the ice of greed. "I won't lend you seventy-five bushels," he answered, "but I'll make you a present of a hundred and fifty. You must, however, fulfill one condition." "What am I to do?" said the poor man. "When I am dead, you are to mount watch by my grave for three nights." The poor man had an eerie feeling about the proposal but in his immediate distress he would have agreed to anything. So he assented and carried the grain home.

It was as if the rich man had foreseen what would happen. Three days later he suddenly dropped to the ground dead. Nobody knew exactly how it came about, but no one mourned him. When he was buried, the poor man remembered his promise. He would gladly have been released from it but thought, "Just the same, he showed himself charitable toward you. You satisfied your hungry children with his grain and, in any event, have made a promise and must keep it." As night came on, he went to the churchyard and sat down on a grave-mound. All was still. Only the moon shone down on the mounds and from time to time an owl would fly by, sounding its plaintive notes. When the sun rose, the poor man betook himself home safe and sound, and the second night likewise passed quietly.

On the evening of the third day he felt particularly apprehensive, felt as if still something was impending. When he got out there, he saw on the wall of the churchyard a man whom he had never seen before. The latter was no longer young, his face was pockmarked, and his eyes roved with a sharp and fiery glance. He was quite covered with an old cloak, and only big riding-boots were visible. "What are you looking for here?" the farmer said to him. "Don't you feel creepy in the lonely churchyard?" "I'm not looking for anything," he answered, "but neither am I afraid of anything. I'm like the boy who went out to learn fear [No. 4], tried in vain, but won the king's daughter and with her great riches. However, I have always stayed poor; I'm nothing but a discharged soldier and am going to spend the night here because I have no other shelter." "If you're not afraid of anything," said the farmer, "then stay with me and help me watch the grave-mound yonder." "Mounting watch is a soldier's business," he answered. "Whatever we encounter here, good or bad, we'll share in common." The farmer agreed, and they sat down together on the grave.

Up to midnight all was quiet, then suddenly a piercing whistle sounded in the air, and both watchmen saw the Evil One standing before them in the flesh. "Be gone, you scoundrels," he called out to them. "The man who is lying in the grave is mine. I'm going to take him away, and if you don't get out, I'll wring your necks." "You, sir, with the red feather," said the soldier, "you're not my captain. I don't have to obey you and I have not yet learned fear. Get along with you; we're staying here." "Your best way of catching the two raggamuffins," thought the Devil, "is with gold," struck a softer note, and in a more friendly tone asked if they wouldn't accept a purse of gold and go home with it. "That's something worth considering," answered the soldier, "but one purse of gold won't do us. If you'll give us as much gold as will go into one of my boots, we'll clear the field and withdraw." "I haven't that much on me," said the Devil, "but I'll fetch it. There's a money-changer in the neighboring town who's a good friend of mine; he'll gladly advance me that much." When the Devil had vanished, the soldier, taking off his left boot, said, "We'll certainly fool the charcoal burner. Just give me your knife, friend." He cut the sole off the boot and set it up in the tall grass beside the mound on the edge of a half-overgrown pit. "Well, everything is ready," he said. "Now let the chimney-sweep come."

They both sat down and waited. Before long the Devil came and had a little bag of gold in his hand. "Just pour it in," said the soldier, lifting the boot up a bit. "It won't be enough, however." The Black Fellow emptied the little bag; the gold went through, and the boot remained empty. "Stupid Devil," cried the soldier, "that's not what's wanted! Didn't I just tell you? Just go back and get more." The Devil shook his head, went and an hour later came with a much bigger bag under his arm. "Just pour it in," cried the soldier, "though I doubt if the boot will be full." The gold jingled as it fell, and the boot remained empty. With his fiery eyes the Devil looked in himself and assured himself that it was true. "You've got disgustingly big calves," he cried and made a wry face. "Did you think," replied the soldier, "that I had a club foot like you? How long have you been so stingy? See to it that you fetch more gold, or else our bargain won't come to anything." The fiend trotted off again. This time he stayed away longer, and when he finally appeared, he was puffing under the burden of a sack that was on his shoulder. He shook it into the boot, but the boot was no fuller than before. He became furious and was about to tear the boot out of the soldier's hand, but at that moment the first ray of the rising sun pierced the sky, and the Evil Spirit fled, shrieking loudly. The poor soul was saved.

The farmer wanted to share the gold, but the soldier said, "Give my share to the poor. I'll move in with you in your cottage, and we'll live on the rest in peace and quiet as long as it pleases God."

196 Old Rink-Rank

Oll Rinkrank

THERE WAS ONCE A KING who had a daughter, and he had a glass mountain made and said that whoever could run over it without falling should marry his daughter. There was a man who was so fond of the king's daughter that he asked the king if he might not have his daughter. "Yes," said the king, "if you can run over the mountain without falling, you shall have her." The king's daughter said that she'd run over it with him and pick him up, should he fall. Then they ran over it together, and when they were halfway up, the king's daughter slipped and fell, and the glass mountain opened up, and she dropped down into it. The bride-groom couldn't see where she had gone through because the mountain had closed up again immediately. Then he wept and wailed bitterly, and the king was very sad, too. He had the mountain broken open and thought he'd get her out again, but no one could find the place where she had fallen down.

Meanwhile the king's daughter came to a great cavern deep down in the earth. There an old man with a very long grey beard came toward her and said, if she would be his maid-servant and do everything he ordered, that she would remain alive, otherwise he would kill her. Then she did everything he said. Mornings he'd take his ladder out of his pouch and set it up against the mountain and climb out of the mountain on it; then he'd pull the ladder up after him. She had to cook his food, make his bed, and do all his housework, and when he got back home, he would always bring a lot of gold and silver with him. When she had been with him for many years and had already grown quite old, he called her Mistress Mansrot, and she had to call him Old Rink-Rank. Once when he was out, she made his bed, washed his dishes, and then closed all the doors and windows tight. There was a sort of hatch where the light shone in which she left open. When Old Rink-Rank came back, he knocked at his door and called, "Mistress Mansrot, open the door for me." "No," she said, "I won't open the door for you, Old Rink-Rank." Then he said,

> "Here I stand, poor Rink-Rank,
>   On my seventeen long legs,
>   On my one gilded foot.
>   Mistress Mansrot, wash my dishes!"

"I've already washed your dishes," she said. Then again he said,

> "Here I stand, poor Rink-Rank,
>   On my seventeen long legs,
>   On my one gilded foot.
>   Mistress Mansrot, make my bed!"

"I've already made your bed," she said. Then he again said,

> "Here I stand, poor Rink-Rank,
>   On my seventeen long legs,

On my one gilded foot.
Mistress Mansrot, open the door for me!"

Then he went all around his house and saw that the little hatch was open and thought, "Just the same, you're going to take a look inside and see what on earth she is doing there and why she won't open the door for you." Then he wanted to look in through it but couldn't get his head through because of his long beard, so he stuck his beard in first through the hatch. When he had his beard through, Mistress Mansrot went and closed the hatch tight with the cord that she had tied to it, and his beard was held fast in it. Then he began to weep and wail, because it hurt him so, and he begged her to set him free again. She said that she wouldn't until he gave her the ladder he had climbed out of the mountain with. Then willy-nilly he had to tell her where the ladder was. She tied a very long rope to the hatch, then set up the ladder and climbed out of the mountain, and on reaching the top opened the hatch.

Then she went to her father and related all that had happened to her. The king rejoiced greatly, and her bridegroom was still there. They went and dug up the mountain and in it found Old Rink-Rank with all his gold and silver. Then the king had Old Rink-Rank put to death and took along all his gold and silver. Then the king's daughter married her former bridegroom, and they lived contentedly in splendor and joy.

197 The Crystal Sphere

Die Kristallkugel

ONCE UPON A TIME there was an enchantress. She had three sons who loved each other as brothers do, but the old woman didn't trust them and thought they wanted to rob her of her power. So she changed the eldest into an eagle: he had to live on a rocky mountain and was sometimes seen swooping up and down in the sky in great circles. The second she changed into a whale: he lived in the depths of the sea and was only seen when on occasion he spouted a mighty jet of water into the air. Both had their human forms for only two hours each day. The third son, fearing that she might transform him, too, into a beast of prey, say, into a bear or a wolf, went away secretly. He had heard that there was a princess in the Castle of the Golden Sun who was awaiting redemption. Everyone had to risk his life in the matter. Already twenty-three youths had died in a miserable death and only one might still try—then no more might ever come. Since his heart was fearless, he made the decision to seek the Castle of the Golden Sun.

He had already been wandering about for a long time without being able to find it when he got into a big forest and didn't know how to get out of it. Suddenly he saw in the distance two giants who waved their hands at him and, when he got up to them, said, "We're fighting over a hat, over whom it shall belong to, and since we are both equally strong, neither can overpower the other. Little humans are cleverer than we, so we want to leave the decision to you." "How can you be fighting over an old hat?" said the youth. "You don't know its property. It's a wishing-hat: whoever puts it on can wish himself where he will and instantly he's there." "Give me the hat," said the youth. "I'll walk off a short distance, and when I call you, you race each other, and it will belong to whoever reaches me first." He put on the hat and walked away, was thinking, however, about the king's daughter, forgot the giants, and kept walking on. Once he sighed from the bottom of his heart and cried, "Alas! were I only at the Castle of the Golden Sun!" and scarcely were the words out of his mouth when he was standing on a high mountain outside the castle gate.

He entered and walked through all the rooms until in the last he found the king's daughter. But how terrified he was when he saw her: her face was ashen grey and full of wrinkles; she had bleary eyes and red hair. "Are you the king's daughter whose beauty the whole world is praising?" he cried. "Alas!" she replied, "this is not my true form. Human eyes can only view me in this ugliness, but that you may know what I am like, just look in the mirror that can't be wrong. It will give you a picture of me as I really am." She put the mirror in his hand, and in it he saw the image of the most beautiful maiden in the world and noticed tears running down her cheeks from grief. Then he said, "How can you be freed? I fear no danger." "Whoever gets the Crystal Sphere," she said, "and holds it before the wizard will thereby break his power, and I shall return to my true form. Alas!" she added, "so many a man has already gone to his death on account of this. And you, young lad, will move me to pity if you take these grave risks." "Nothing can stop me," he said. "But tell me what I must do." "You shall know all," said the king's daughter. "When you go down the mountain on which the castle stands, down there by a spring will be a wild bison, with which you will have to fight. If you succeed in killing it, a fiery bird will rise up out of it, bearing in its body a glowing egg, and the Crystal Sphere is inside the egg by way of a yolk. It won't drop the egg, however, until forced to. Yet, if the egg falls on the ground, it will take fire and burn everything near it, and the egg itself will melt and with it the Crystal Sphere, and all your trouble will have been in vain."

The youth went down to the spring where the bison snorted and roared at him. After a long fight he thrust his sword into its body, and it sank to the ground. Instantly the fire bird rose up out of it and was about to fly away, but the youth's brother, the eagle, that was flying about in the clouds, swooped down on it, chased it to the sea, and struck it with its beak so that, hard pressed, it dropped the egg. The egg, however, didn't fall into the sea but on a fisherman's hut that was on the shore. The hut at once began to smoulder and was on the point of going up in flames when waves as high as a house rose in the sea, flowed over the hut, and put out the fire. The second brother, the whale, had swum past and forced up the water. When the fire was out, the youth looked for the egg and was lucky enough to find it. It had not yet melted, but from the sudden cooling by the cold water the shell was crumbled to pieces, and he was able to take out the Crystal Sphere undamaged.

When the youth went to the wizard and held the Crystal Sphere in front of him, the latter said, "My power is destroyed, and from now on you are king of the Castle of the Golden Sun. At the same time you can also give your brothers back their human forms." Then the youth hastened to the king's daughter, and as he entered her room, there she stood in the full radiance of her beauty, and both joyfully exchanged rings.

198   Lady Madelaine

Jungfrau Maleen

ONCE UPON A TIME there was a king. He had a son who was wooing the daughter of a mighty king; her name was Lady Madelaine and she was exceedingly beautiful. Because her father wanted to marry her to someone else, she was refused him. But since the couple loved each other with all their hearts, they would not give one another up, and Lady Madelaine said to her father, "I neither can nor will take anybody else as my husband." Then her father flew into a rage and had a dark tower built, into which not a ray of the sun or the moon entered. When it was finished, he said, "You are going to stay there for seven years; then I shall come and see if your stubborn spirit is broken."

Food and drink sufficient for seven years was brought to the tower; then she and her maid-in-waiting were led in and walled up and thus cut off from heaven and earth. There they sat in the dark, not knowing when day broke or night fell. The king's son often walked around the tower, calling her name, but no sound penetrated the thick walls from without. What else could they do but lament and complain? Meanwhile, time passed and by the decrease in the amount of food and drink, they realized that the seven years were nearing their end. They thought that the moment of their deliverance had come, but no blow of hammer was heard and no stone fell out of the wall. It seemed as if her father had forgotten her. When they had food for a short time only and foresaw a miserable death, Lady Madelaine said, "We must seek one last resort and see if we can't break a hole in the wall." She took the bread knife, dug and bored in the mortar of a stone, and when she was tired, the maid-in-waiting relieved her. After working a long time they succeeded in getting one stone out, then a second and third, and at the end of three days the first ray of light penetrated their darkness. Finally the opening was large enough for them to be able to look out. The sky was blue, and a fresh breeze met them, but how desolate everything about looked! Her father's castle lay in ruins, the town and villages, as far as the eye could reach, were burned down, the fields ravaged far and wide; there wasn't a sign of a human being. When the opening in the wall was large enough for them to slip through, the maid-in-waiting jumped down first and then Lady Madelaine followed. But whither should they turn? The enemy had laid waste the whole realm, driven the king away, and slain all the inhabitants. They wandered on in search of another land, but nowhere did they find shelter or a person to give them a morsel of bread. Their need was so dire that they had to satisfy their hunger on a nettle plant. When after a long journey they reached another land, they everywhere offered their services, but wherever they knocked, they were turned away, and nobody would take pity on them. Finally they reached a big city and went to the royal court. Yet even there they were told to move on, until at last the chef said they might stay in the kitchen and serve as kitchen maids.

The son of the king in whose realm they found themselves was, however, none other than Lady Madelaine's betrothed. His father had decided on another bride for him who was as ill-favored of face as she was evil of heart. The date of the wedding was set, and the bride had already arrived; but because of her great ugliness she let no one see her and shut herself up in her chamber. Lady Madelaine had to bring her her food from the kitchen. When the day came that the bride was to go to church with the bridegroom, she was ashamed of her ugliness and feared she would be mocked and ridiculed by the people if she showed herself on the street. Then she said to Lady Madelaine, "You have a piece of great good fortune in store: I have turned my ankle and can't walk very well on the street; you shall put on my bridal robes and take my place. You can have no greater honor." Lady Madelaine, however, declined, saying, "I ask for no honor that is not my due." There was no use, either, for her to offer her gold. Finally she said angrily, "If you don't obey me, it will cost you your life. I only need to say one word and your head will lie at your feet." Then she had to obey and put on the bride's magnificent robes and also her jewels. When she entered the royal hall, everybody marveled at her great beauty, and the king said to his son, "This is the bride I have chosen for you and whom you are to take to church." The bridegroom was astonished and thought, "She looks like my Lady Madelaine, and I would think it really was she, but she's long been prisoner in the tower, or else she is dead." He took her by the hand and led her to church. By the wayside was a nettle plant, and she said,

> "Nettle plant, nettle plant so small,
> Why are you here alone?
> I have known the time
> When I've eaten you unboiled,
> Eaten you unroasted."

"What are you saying there?" asked the king's son. "Nothing," she answered, "I was just thinking about Lady Madelaine." He was surprised that she knew of the latter but remained silent. When they came to the footbridge before the churchyard, she said,

> "Church bridge, don't break!
> I'm not the true bride."

"What are you saying there?" asked the king's son. "Nothing." she answered, "I was just thinking about Lady Madelaine." "Do you know Lady Madelaine?" "No," she answered, "how should I know her? I've merely heard about her." When they reached the church door, again she said,

> "Church door, don't break!
> I'm not the true bride."

"What are you saying there?" he asked. "Oh," she answered, "I just thought about Lady Madelaine." Then he took out a precious ornament, put it around her neck, and clasped the links of the chain. Then they entered the church, and the priest joined their hands before the altar and married them. He led her back, but she didn't say a word the whole way. When they got back to the royal palace, she hastened to the bride's chamber, took off the magnificent robes and the jewels, and put on her grey smock, keeping only the neck ornament that she had received from the bridegroom.

When night came and the bride was to be led into the room of the king's son, she dropped a veil over her face so that he shouldn't notice the deception. As soon as everybody had left, he said, "What did you really say to the nettle plant that was by the wayside?" "What nettle?" she asked. "I don't talk to nettles." "If you didn't do it, then you're not the true bride," he said. She got out of the difficulty by saying,

> "I must go out to my maid
> Who is keeper of my thoughts."

She went out and screamed at Lady Madelaine, "Hussy, what did you say to the nettle?" "I only said,

> "Nettle plant, nettle plant so small,
> Why are you alone there?
> I've known the time
> When I've eaten you unboiled,
> Eaten you unroasted.'"

The bride ran back to the room and said, "Now I know what I said to the nettle," and she repeated the words she had just heard. "But what did you say to the church bridge as we walked over it?" asked the king's son. "The church bridge?" she answered. "I don't talk to church bridges." "In that case, too, you're not the true bride." Again she said,

> "I must go out to my maid
> Who is keeper of my thoughts,"

ran out and screamed at Lady Madelaine, "Hussy, what did you say to the church bridge?" "I only said,

> 'Church bridge, don't break!
> I'm not the true bride.'"

"That will cost you your life," cried the bride, hurried into the room, however, and said, "Now I know what I said to the church bridge" and repeated the words. "But what did you say to the church door?" "The church door?" she answered. "I don't talk to church doors." "In that case, too, you are not the true bride." She went out and screamed at Lady Madelaine, "Hussy, what did you say to the church door?" "I only said,

> 'Church door, don't break!
> I'm not the true bride.'"

"That will break your neck," cried the bride and flew into the greatest rage, hurried back, however, into the room and said, "Now I know what I said to the church door" and repeated the words. "But where is the ornament I gave you at the church door?" "What ornament?" she answered. "You didn't give me an ornament." "I put it around your neck myself and clasped it myself. If you don't know that, then you are not the true bride." He pulled the veil from her face and, when he saw her utter ugliness, sprang back in fright, saying, "How did you get here? Who are you?" "I'm your betrothed bride, but because I was afraid that people would mock me if they saw me out there, I ordered the kitchen maid to put on my clothes and go to church in my stead." "Where is the girl?" he said, "I want to see her. Go bring her here!"

She went out and told the servants that the kitchen maid was an impostor and that they should take her down into the courtyard and strike off her head. The servants seized her and were about to drag her away, but she screamed so loud for help that the king's son heard her voice, hastened out of his room, and gave orders for the girl to be released at once. Lights were fetched, and then he noticed on her neck the gold ornament he had given her outside the church door. "You are the true bride," he said, "who went with me to church. Come with me to my room." When they were both alone, he said, "On the way to church you mentioned Lady Madelaine, who was my betrothed bride. If I thought it possible, I would be bound to think that she was standing before me: you resemble her in every way." "I am the Lady Madelaine," she answered, "who on your account spent seven years imprisoned in darkness, suffered hunger and thirst, and lived that long time in distress and poverty. But today the sun is shining on me again. I was wedded to you in the church and am your rightful spouse." Then they kissed one another and were happy as long as they lived.

In requital the false bride's head was struck off.

The tower in which Lady Madelaine had spent seven years remained standing for a long time, and when the children would pass it, they would sing,

> "Cling, clang, Gloria!
> Who is in the tower?
> A king's daughter is in it.
> I can't manage to see her,
> The wall won't break,
> The stone won't split.
> Johnny with the gay jacket,
> Come follow after me!"

199 The Boot of Buffalo Leather

Der Stiefel von Büffelleder

A SOLDIER who is afraid of nothing worries about nothing, either.

Such a soldier had received his discharge, and since he had learned nothing and could earn nothing, he wandered about begging alms of kind people. From his shoulders hung an old storm coat, and he still had left a pair of riding boots of buffalo leather, too. One day he was walking along out into the country, paying no attention to highway or byway, and finally got into a forest. He didn't know where he was, saw, however, a man sitting on a felled tree trunk; the latter was well dressed and had on a green hunting jacket. The soldier gave him his hand, sat down on the grass beside him, and stretched out his legs. "I see you have on fine, highly polished boots," he said to the huntsman. "But if you had to move about as I do, they wouldn't last long. Look at mine: they're of buffalo leather and have already seen long service, yet they hold out through thick and thin." After a while the soldier got up and said, "I can't stay any longer; hunger is driving me on. By the way, Brother Shiny-Boots, where is the way out of here?" "I don't know myself," answered the huntsman. "I've lost my way in the forest." "Then you're in the same fix as I," said the soldier. "Birds of a feather like to flock together. Let's stay together and look for the way." The huntsman smiled slightly, and they kept on together until nightfall. "We aren't getting out of the forest," said the soldier, "but I see a light flickering there in the distance. There'll be something to eat there."

They found a stone house, knocked on the door, and an old woman opened it. "We're looking for a night's lodging," said the soldier, "and a little lining for our stomachs, for mine is as empty as an old knapsack." "You can't stay here," answered the old woman. "It's a robber's den, and the smartest thing for you to do is to clear out before they come home; for if they find you, you'll be done for." "It won't be as bad as that," answered the soldier. "I haven't eaten a morsel for two days, and it's all one to me whether I perish here or die of hunger in the forest. I'm coming in." The huntsman didn't want to go with him, but the soldier pulled him along by the sleeve. "Come, dear brother, we won't be killed straight off." The old woman took pity and said, "Crawl behind the stove. If they leave anything over and go to sleep, I'll slip it to you."

Scarcely were they in the corner when the twelve robbers came storming in, sat down at the table that was already set, and violently demanded their meal. The old woman brought in a big roast, and the robbers enjoyed it thoroughly. As the odor of the food mounted to the soldier's nose, he said to the huntsman, "I can't stand it any longer. I'm going to sit down at the table and eat with them." "You'll be the death of us," said the huntsman and held him by the arm. But the soldier began to cough loudly. When the robbers heard that, they threw down their knives and forks, jumped up, and discovered the pair behind the stove. "Aha, gentlemen!" they said. "Sitting in the corner? What do you want here? Have you been sent out as spies? Wait! You're going to learn the art of flying on a dry limb." "Just be polite," said the soldier. "I'm hungry. Give me something to eat. Afterward you may do with me as you like." The robbers were taken aback, and the leader said, "I see that you're not afraid. Good! You'll get food, but after that you must die." "We'll see about that," said the soldier, sat down at the table, and began to make a brave attack on the roast. "Brother Shiny-Boots, come and eat," he called out to the huntsman. "You're surely as hungry as I, and you can't get a better roast at home." But the huntsman wouldn't eat. The robbers eyed the soldier with astonishment and said, "The fellow doesn't stand on ceremony." Afterward he said, "The food was good, to be sure; now bring on something good to drink, too." The leader was in a mood to agree to this, too, and called to the old woman, "Bring a bottle from the cellar and be sure it's one of the best." The soldier drew the cork so that it popped, and went with the bottle to the huntsman, saying, "Pay attention, brother, and you'll see something perfectly extraordinary. Now I'm going to propose a toast to the whole gang." Then waving the bottle over the robbers' heads he cried, "To the health of you all! But mouths open and right hands up!" and he himself took a good swig. Hardly were the words out of his mouth, when they were all sitting motionless as if made of stone, had their mouths open, and their right hands stretched up. The huntsman said to the soldier, "I see you can do still other tricks! But come now, let's go home." "Oho! dear brother, that would be marching off too soon. We've beaten the enemy; let's first collect the booty. They're fixed there and have their mouths open in amazement; they mayn't move, however, until I give permission. Come, eat and drink." The old woman had to fetch another bottle of the best wine, and the soldier didn't get up until he had sat there for three days more.

Finally, when the day came, he said, "Now is time for us to strike camp, and so that we may have a short march, the old woman must show us the nearest way to the city." On arriving there he went to his old comrades and said, "I've discovered a nest of gallows birds out there in the forest. Come along and we'll clean it out." The soldier led them and said to the huntsman, "You must come back with us and see how the birds flutter when we take them by their feet." He disposed his men around the robbers, then took the bottle, drank a swig, waved it over them, calling, "To the health of you all!" At once they regained their power of motion but were thrown down and bound with cords hand and foot. Then the soldier ordered them thrown into a cart like so many sacks and said, "Now drive them to right outside the jail." The huntsman, however, took one of the men aside and gave him a further order besides.

"Brother Shiny-Boots," said the soldier, "we have succeeded in taking the enemy by surprise and have fed ourselves well. Now let's take it easy and march behind them like so many stragglers." As they neared the city, the soldier saw a lot of people crowding out of the city gate, raising loud cries of joy and waving green branches in the air. Then he saw the entire life guard coming up. "What does that mean?" he said to the huntsman, greatly astonished. "Don't you know," answered the latter, "that the king has been away from his kingdom for a long time. Today he's coming back, and there they are all going to meet him." "But where is the king?" said the soldier. "I don't see him." "Here he is," answered the huntsman. "I am the king and have had my arrival announced." Then he opened his hunting jacket so that one could see the royal clothes. The soldier was frightened, fell to his knees, and begged forgiveness for having in his ignorance treated him as an equal and for addressing him by such a name as Shiny-Boots. But the king gave him his hand, saying, "You're a good soldier and saved my life and you shall suffer no further privation. I shall look out for you, of course. And any time you want to eat a good piece of roast, as good as in the robbers' den, just come to the royal kitchen. But if you want to propose a toast, you must first obtain permission from me."

200 The Gold Key

Der goldene Schlüssel

ONCE IN THE WINTER TIME when the snow lay deep on the ground, a poor boy had to go out and fetch wood on a sled. When he had gathered the wood and loaded it on, because he was so terribly cold, he didn't wish to go straight home but wanted first to build a fire and warm himself a bit. Then he scuffed the snow away and, after thus clearing the ground, found a little gold key. Now he thought that where the key was, the lock must be, too. He dug in the ground and found an iron box. "If only the key fits!" he thought. "There are surely valuable things in the box." He looked, but there wasn't any keyhole; finally he discovered one, though so small that you would scarcely see it. He tried it, and happily the key fitted. Then he turned it once—and now we must wait until he has finished unlocking it and has opened the lid. Then we shall find out what wonderful things there were in the box.

The Gold Key

By Jakob Grimm

In the wintertime, when the snow lay deep on the ground, a poor boy had to go out and fetch wood on a sled. When he had gathered the wood and loaded it on, before he was so terribly cold he did not want to go straight home. He wanted first to build a little fire to warm himself a bit. Then he scraped the snow away, and when he was clearing the ground, he found a little gold key. Now he thought that where there was a key there must also be a lock, so he dug in the ground and found an iron box. "If only the key fits!" he thought. "Surely there are precious things in that box." He searched, but there was no keyhole. Finally he discovered one, though it was so small you could scarcely see it, and when he tried it, the key fitted exactly. Then he turned it once, and now we must wait until he has finished unlocking it and has opened the lid. Then we shall find out what wonderful things there were in the box.

RELIGIOUS TALES CONCERNING CHILDREN

CHILDREN

KINDERLEGENDEN

1 Saint Joseph in the Forest

Der heilige Joseph im Walde

THERE WAS ONCE A MOTHER who had three daughters: the eldest was naughty and bad; the second really much better, though she, too, had her faults; but the youngest was a devout and good child. But the mother was so peculiar that she actually loved the eldest most and couldn't bear the youngest. Accordingly, she often sent the poor girl out into a big forest in order to get rid of her, for she thought that she might lose her way and never come back. However, the guardian angel that every devout child has didn't forsake her but always brought her back onto the right track.

On one occasion when this happened, the guardian angel made believe that it wasn't on hand, and the child couldn't find her way back out of the forest. She went on and on until it was evening. Then in the distance she saw a little light burning, hurried to it, and reached a small hut. She knocked, the door opened, and she came to a second door, where she knocked again. A venerable looking old man with a snow-white beard opened the door for her, and this was none other than Saint Joseph. He spoke in a most friendly manner, "Come, dear child, sit on my stool by the fire and warm yourself. I'll fetch you some clear water if you're thirsty, but out here in the forest I have nothing for you to eat but a few roots which you must first scrape and cook." Then Saint Joseph handed her the roots. The girl scraped them properly, then got out a bit of pancake and the bread which her mother had given her, put everything together in a kettle on the fire, and cooked herself a porridge. When it was ready, Saint Joseph said, "I'm so hungry. Give me some of your food." The child was quite willing and gave him more than she kept for herself, yet through the grace of God she had her fill. When they had eaten, Saint Joseph said, "Now let's go to bed. I have only one bed, however; you lie down in it, and I'll lie down on the ground in the straw." "No," she answered, "you stay right in your bed; the straw is soft enough for me." But Saint Joseph took the

651

child in his arms and put her in the bed; then she said her prayers and fell asleep. The next morning when she awoke, she wanted to bid Saint Joseph good-day but didn't see him. She got up and looked for him but could find him nowhere. At last she noticed behind the door a bag of money so heavy that she could barely carry it; on it was written "This is for the child that slept here last night." Then she took the bag and skipped off with it and got safely home to her mother, too. And because she gave her all the money, the mother couldn't but be satisfied with her.

The next day the second child also wanted to go into the forest. Her mother gave her a much bigger piece of pancake and bread as well. Now it fared with her exactly as with the first child. At night she came to the hut of Saint Joseph, who handed her roots for a porridge. When it was ready, he likewise said, "I'm so hungry. Give me some of your food." Then the child answered, "Eat along with me." Afterward, when Saint Joseph offered her his bed and was going to lie down in the straw, she answered, "No, lie down in the bed with me; there's plenty of room in it for us both, of course." Saint Joseph took the child in his arms, laid her in the bed and himself in the straw. In the morning when the child awoke and looked for Saint Joseph, he had vanished, but behind the door she found a little bag of money, as big as your fist, and on it was written "This is for the child that slept here last night." Then she took the little bag and ran home with it and brought it to her mother. However, she secretly kept a couple of pieces of money for herself.

Now the eldest daughter had grown curious and on the following morning likewise wanted to go into the forest. Her mother gave her pancakes to take along, as many as she wanted, also bread and cheese. In the evening she found Saint Joseph in his hut exactly as had the other two. When the porridge was ready and Saint Joseph said, "I'm hungry. Give me some of your food," the girl answered, "Wait till I have eaten my fill; then you shall have what I leave." She ate it almost all up, however, and Saint Joseph had to scrape the bowl. The kind old man then offered her his bed and was going to lie down in the straw. She accepted the offer without hesitation, lay down in the bed, and left the hard straw for the old man. The next morning when she awoke, Saint Joseph was not to be found. But she didn't worry about that: she looked behind the door for a bag of money. She noticed something lying there, but because she couldn't really make it out, bent over and bumped her nose on it. But it stuck to her nose, and when she straightened up, she saw to her horror that it was a second nose that was sticking to her own. Then she began to scream and howl, but that did no good. She couldn't help looking at her nose which stuck out so far. Then she ran away crying until she met Saint Joseph; she fell at his feet and implored him until out of pity he removed the nose again and gave her two pennies besides.

When she got home, her mother was standing outside the door and asked, "What did you get as a present?" Then she lied and answered, "A big bag full of money, but I lost it on the way." "Lost it?" cried her mother. "Oh, we'll easily find it again," took her by the hand and was going to look for it. First the girl began to weep and didn't want to go along; finally, however, she went. But on the way so many lizzards and snakes attacked them both that they didn't know how to save themselves. At last, too, they stung the bad child to death and stung the mother in the foot for not having brought her up better.

2 The Twelve Apostles

Die zwölf Apostel

THREE HUNDRED YEARS before the birth of Our Lord Christ there lived a mother who had twelve sons, but was so poor and needy that she didn't know how to sustain life in them any longer. Daily she prayed God to grant that all her sons might be together on earth with the promised Saviour. Now as her plight grew worse and worse, she sent one after the other into the world to seek his daily bread. The eldest was named Peter. He went out and had already gone quite a way, a whole day's journey, when he got into a big forest. He tried to find a way out, but couldn't, and kept losing himself deeper and deeper in the forest. Besides, he got so hungry that he could scarcely stand up. Finally he became so weak that he had to remain lying down and believed himself nigh unto death. Then suddenly a little boy was standing beside him, as radiant and fair and friendly as an angel. The child clapped his hands so that Peter couldn't help looking up at him. Then he said, "Why are you sitting there so sad?" "Alas!" answered Peter, "I'm going about the world seeking my daily bread so that I may still live to see the dear promised Saviour. That is my greatest wish." "Come with me," said the child, "and your wish will be fulfilled." He took poor Peter by the hand and led him between two cliffs to a big cave. As they entered, it was all sparkling with gold, silver, and crystal, and in the middle stood twelve cradles side by side. Then the little angel said, "Lie down in the first and sleep a bit; I'll rock you." Peter did so, and the angel sang to him and rocked him until he had gone to sleep. And as he slept, his second brother came, likewise led in by his guardian angel and, like the first, was rocked to sleep. And similarly came the others in succession, until all twelve were lying there in the gold cradles and sleeping. They slept three hundred years, however, until the night the Saviour of the World was born. Then they woke up and were with Him on earth and were called the Twelve Apostles.

3 The Rose

Die Rose

THERE WAS ONCE A POOR WOMAN who had two children. The youngest had to go every day into the forest and fetch wood. Once when it went very far in its search, a small but quite strong child came up to it and helped it diligently gather wood and even carried it up to the house; but before a second had passed it had vanished. The child told its mother, who at first wouldn't believe it. At last it brought along a rosebud and told how the fair child had given it to it and had told it that it would come back when the bud came out. The mother put the rosebud in water.

One morning the child didn't get out of bed; its mother went to the bed and found the child dead, but it was lying there very sweetly. The rose had come out that very morning.

4 Poverty and Humility Lead to Heaven

Armut und Demut führen zum Himmel

A KING'S SON was once out walking in the country and was pensive and sad. He looked at the heavens that were fair and pure and blue; then sighing, he said, "How fine one must feel when one is finally up there in Heaven!" Then he spied a poor grey-haired man who was coming along the way and addressing him, said, "How, indeed, can I get to Heaven?" "By poverty and humility," answered the man. "Put on my tattered clothes, wander about the world for seven years, and get to know its misery. Take no money, but when you are hungry, beg pitying hearts for a morsel of bread. Thus will you approach Heaven."

Then the king's son took off his splendid coat and in its stead put on a beggar's garb, went out in the wide world, and suffered great misery. He took only a little food, spoke not a word, but prayed the Lord one day to accept him into His Heaven.

When the seven years were up, he returned to his father's palace, but no one recognized him. To the servants he said, "Go tell my parents that I have come back," but the servants didn't believe it, laughed, and left him standing there. Then he said, "Go tell my brothers to come down. I should so like to see them again." They wouldn't do that either, until finally one of them went and told the king's children. The latter, however, didn't believe it and didn't bother about it. Then he wrote his mother a letter and in it described to her all his misery, though he didn't say that he was her son. Then out of pity for him the queen had him given a place under the stairs and had him brought food every day by two servants. One of these, however, was evil and said, "Why should the beggar get the good food?" and kept it for himself or gave it to the dogs, bringing the weak, emaciated man only water. The other, on the contrary, was decent and brought him whatever he could get for him. It wasn't much, yet he was able to live on it for a time; he was quite patient about this until he kept getting weaker. But as his illness got worse, he asked to receive the Last Sacrament. When mass was half over, all the bells in the city and round about began to ring of themselves. After mass the priest went to the poor man under the stairs, but he was lying there dead, with a rose in one hand, a lily in the other, and beside him was a paper on which his story was written.

When he was buried, a rose grew up out of one side of the grave, a lily out of the other.

5   God's Food

Gottes Speise

THERE WERE ONCE TWO SISTERS: one had no children and was rich, the other had five, was a widow and so poor that she no longer had bread enough to satisfy herself and her children. Then in her plight she went to her sister and said, "My children and I are suffering the most extreme hunger. You are rich; give me a morsel of bread." The very rich woman was also stony-hearted and, saying "I myself have nothing in my house," dismissed the poor woman with angry words.

After a time the rich sister's husband came home and wanted to cut himself a piece of bread, but as he made the first cut in the loaf, red blood flowed out. When his wife saw that, she was frightened and told him what had happened. He hurried to his sister-in-law and was going to offer his help, but on entering the widow's living room, he found her praying. She had the two youngest children in her arms while the three eldest lay there dead. He offered her food, but she answered, "We are no longer asking for earthly food; God has already satisfied the hunger of three. He will harken to our supplication, too." Scarcely had she uttered these words when the two little ones drew their last breath, and then her heart, too, broke, and she sank down dead.

6 The Three Green Shoots

Die drei grünen Zweige

THERE WAS ONCE A HERMIT who lived in a forest at the foot of a mountain and spent his time in prayer and good works. Every evening he used to carry two pails of water up the mountain as an additional honor to God. Thus many an animal was watered and many a plant refreshed, for up on the heights a hard wind blows constantly, drying out the air and parching the soil, and the wild birds that shun man then soar high and with their keen eyes look for a drink. And because the hermit was so devout, an angel of God, visible to his eyes, used to walk up with him, count his steps, and when the work was done, bring him his food just as at God's command that prophet [Elijah] was fed by the ravens.

When the hermit in his piety had reached an advanced age, he once happened to see from afar a poor sinner being led to the gallows. To himself he said, "This man is now receiving his due." That evening as he was carrying the water up the mountain, the angel that usually accompanied him didn't appear, nor did he bring him his food. Then he got frightened, probed his heart, and reflected how he could have sinned to make God so angry. But he didn't know. Then he neither ate nor drank, threw himself on the ground and prayed day and night. Once as he was weeping bitterly in the forest, he heard a bird singing very beautifully and gloriously. Then he was even more distressed and said, "How joyously you're singing! The Lord isn't angry with you. Alas! if you could only tell me how I have offended Him that I might do penance and that my heart, too, might become joyous again." Then the bird began to speak and said, "You did wrong in condemning a poor sinner who was being led to the gallows; that is why the Lord is angry at you. He alone renders judgment. However, if you do penance and repent your sin, He will forgive you." Then the angel stood beside him with a dry branch in his hand and said, "You are to carry this dry branch until three green shoots sprout out of it. And at night when you want to sleep, you are to lay it under your head. You are to beg your bread from door to door and stay no longer than one night in the same house. That is the penance the Lord imposes upon you."

Then the hermit took the piece of wood and returned to the world that he had not seen for so long. He ate and drank nothing but what was given him at people's doors. Many a request went unheeded and many a door remained closed to him, so that often he didn't get a crumb of bread for days on end. Once he'd been going from door to door from morning till night. Then he went out into the forest and found a habitable cave with an old woman sitting in it. "Good woman," he said, "receive me for tonight in your dwelling." But she answered, "No, I may not even if I would. I have three sons: they are wicked and savage, and if they return from their maraudings and find you, they would kill us both." Then the hermit said, "Just let me stay; they will do nothing to you and me." The woman took pity and let herself be persuaded. Then the man lay down under the stairs with the piece of wood under his head. On seeing that, the old woman asked the reason. Then he told her that he was carrying it about as penance and used it at night as a pillow. He had offended the Lord; for when he had seen a poor sinner on the way to his doom, he had said that the latter was receiving his due. Then the woman began to weep and cried, "Alas! if the Lord thus punishes a single word, how will it fare with my sons when they appear before Him in judgment."

At midnight the robbers came home, making a noise and up-roar. They kindled a fire, and when it lighted up the cave and they saw a man lying under the stairs, they flew into a rage and yelled at their mother, "Who is that man? Haven't we forbidden you to take anybody in?" Then the mother said, "Leave him alone. He's a poor sinner who is atoning for his sin." "What did he do?" asked the robbers. "Old man!" they cried, "tell us about your sins." The old man got up and told them how by a single word he had indeed sinned so grievously that God was angry with him and that he was now atoning for this sin. The robbers' hearts were so moved by his narrative that they got frightened about their past life, rued it, and began their atonement with sincere repentance. After converting the three sinners, the hermit again lay down to sleep under the stairs. In the morning, however, he was found dead and out of the dry branch on which his head lay three green shoots had grown way up. Thus the Lord had received him again into His favor.

7 Lady's Glass

Muttergottesgläschen

ONCE UPON A TIME a carter got his cart that was heavily loaded with wine mired so fast that in spite of every effort he couldn't get it out again. Now just then Our Lady came along and seeing the poor man's plight said to him, "I am tired and thirsty. Give me a glass of wine, and I'll get your cart out." "Gladly," said the carter, "but I have no glass to give you your wine in." Then Our Lady plucked a white flower with red stripes that is called bindweed and looks much like a glass, and handed it to the carter. He filled it with wine and Our Lady drank it. At that instant the cart was freed from the mire, and the carter could drive on.

The flower is still called lady's glass.

8 The Old Granny

Das alte Mütterchen

IN A BIG CITY an old granny was sitting one evening alone in her room. She was thinking all about how she had lost first her husband then her two children, by and by all her relatives, finally this very day even her last friend, and was now quite alone and forsaken. Then in her heart of hearts she grew sad, and so very hard for her was the loss of her two sons that in her anguish she charged God with it.

She was sitting quietly thus, absorbed in her thoughts, when suddenly she heard the bells ringing for matins. She was surprised that she had kept awake grieving all night this way, lit her lantern, and went to church. When she got there, it was already lighted up, not, however, by the usual candles but by a dim light. Furthermore, it was already filled with people, and all seats were occupied. When the old woman got to her regular place, it, too, was no longer free, but the whole pew was packed full. And as she looked at the people, they were all dead relatives, sitting there in their old-fashioned clothes, but with pale faces. They neither spoke nor sang, yet a low hum and flutter was passing through the church. Then an aunt got up and said to the old woman, "Look toward the altar; you'll see your sons there." The old woman looked in that direction and saw her two children: one was hanging on the gallows, the other broken on a wheel. Then her aunt said, "See, that's what would have happened to them had they lived and had God not taken them to Himself as innocent children."

The old woman went home trembling and on her knees thanked God for having been kinder to her than she could have imagined. Three days later she lay down and died.

9   The Heavenly Wedding

Die himmlische Hochzeit

ONCE A POOR FARMER BOY heard the rector say in church, "Whoever wants to enter the Kingdom of Heaven must keep going straight ahead." So he set out and kept going, always straight ahead, without turning aside, over hill and dale. Finally his way took him to a big city and into the middle of the church where divine service was just being held. Now when he saw all the splendor, he thought he had now got to Heaven, sat down, and rejoiced in his heart. When the service was over and the verger told him to go out, he answered, "No, I'm not going out again. I am happy to be in Heaven at last." Then the verger went to the rector and told him that there was a child in the church that wouldn't go out because he thought he was in the Kingdom of Heaven. "If he believes that," said the rector, "let's leave him there." Thereupon he went and asked the boy if he would also like to work. "Yes," answered the little chap, saying that he was used to work but wouldn't go out of Heaven again.

So he stayed in the church, and when he saw the people going to the image of the Virgin and the Infant Jesus carved in wood, saw them kneeling and praying, he thought, "That is the good Lord," and said, "Listen, good Lord, how thin you are! The people are surely letting you go hungry. However, I shall give you half my food every day." From then on he brought the image half his food, and the image began to enjoy the food, too. After a few weeks had passed, the people noticed that the image was taking on weight, getting plump and strong, and they marveled greatly. The rector couldn't understand it either, stayed in the church, and followed the little fellow. Then he saw the boy sharing his bread with Our Lady and her accepting it, too.

Sometime later the boy was taken ill and didn't leave his bed for eight days, but the first thing he did when he could get up again was to bring his food to Our Lady. The rector followed him and heard him say, "Good Lord, don't take it amiss that I didn't bring You anything for so long, but I was ill and couldn't get up." Then the image answered him, saying, "I have seen your good will, that is enough for me. Next Sunday you're to come with me to the Wedding." The boy looked forward to this and told the rector, who bade him go and ask the image if he might come along, too. "No," answered the image, "just you." The rector wanted to prepare him first and give him the sacrament. That was agreeable to the boy, and the following Sunday when the sacrament came to him, he fell over and was dead and had gone to the Eternal Wedding.

10 The Hazel Switch

Die Haselrute

ONE AFTERNOON the Christ Child had lain down in His cradle and gone to sleep. Then His mother stepped up, looked at Him joyfully and said, "Did you lie down to sleep, my child? Sleep peacefully, and meanwhile I shall go into the forest and get a handful of strawberries for you. I am sure You will like them when You wake up." Out in the forest she found a spot with the finest strawberries, but as she bent over to pick one, a serpent sprang up out of the grass. She was frightened, left the berry, and hurried off. The serpent darted after her, but Our Lady knew, as you may imagine, what to do: she hid behind a hazel bush and stayed there until the serpent had crawled away again. Then she gathered the berries and on the way home said, "Just as the hazel bush protected me this time, so in the future it shall also protect other people."

For this reason a green hazel switch has from time out of mind been the surest protection against serpents, snakes, and whatever creeps on the earth.

INDEX OF TITLES

ENGLISH TITLES

Including *Religious Tales Concerning Children* (RTC)

GERMAN TITLES

Including *Kinderlegenden* (KL)